D0464335

Articles on American Literature, 1968–1975

To My Successor: Man or Machine

The old order changeth, yielding place to new,
And God fulfils himself in many ways,
Lest one good custom should corrupt the world.

Articles on American Literature, 1968–1975

Compiled by Lewis Leary

with John Auchard

Duke University Press
Durham, N.C. 1979

3 - 1303 - 00031 - 1200

11-26-80

Contents

Introduction

This compilation of *Articles on American Literature, 1968-1975* is the result of a large collaborative effort contributed to by many hands. At present there seems to be no end to the making of bibliographical listings about writers, genres, periods, sects, ethnic groups, and each of them has contributed, to one degree or another, to the present listing. All have not been complete, some have even sometimes been incorrect, but that will be found to be an inevitable characteristic of enumerative bibliographies, this one included. For our own sins of omission or commission, we humbly ask pardon.

Included in the present volume are numerous additions or corrections to the two volumes that have preceded it, *Articles on American Literature, 1900-1950* (1954, 1970), and *Articles on American Literature, 1950-1967* (1970), especially in the sections which list genres or topical aspects of American Literature. Additions of previously unrecorded pre-1968 articles under the American writers listings are fewer, especially for those major writers on whom bibliographical essays (each marked with an asterisk) are included in the listings under those authors; in some instances, however, the compilers have included several previously earlier unrecorded essays which in their judgement seem of significant immediate importance. It is hoped that the three cumulative volumes of *Articles on American Literature* can therefore together be useful as a guide toward discovery of just about all of the periodical writings about American authors during the first seventy-five years of this century.

Its compilers are especially grateful to James F. Beard, Jackson Bryer, Harrison Messerole, Dorothy Scura, Thomas Tenney, and Kimball King for assistance unselfishly given. The task of carding, sorting, and indexing over the past eight years has been lightened by the aid of Frank Barefoot, Barbara Gittenstein, Thomas R. Howerton, Jr., Carla Mazzini, Holt Montgomery, Clay Morgan, and Roberta Rosenberg. William Harmon, Kathleen St. Lenat, and Karin Gleiter have lent important support and encouragement. The staff of the Humanities Room of Wilson Library, particularly Mrs. Pattie B. McIntyre and Cindy Adams, and the staff of the Periodicals Collection, above all Marcia Tuttle, Carol Koenig, and Susan Mackler, have provided friendly and informed assistance.

This task could not have been completed without aid from the Research Council of the University of North Carolina at Chapel Hill, from the National Endowment for the Humanities, and J.W. Dant. The volume could not have been put together without the dedicated assistance of James Patrick Carnes and

Introduction

Jonathan Beck Munroe, and the welcomed suggestions, almost daily, of Grady Ballenger, Kathy Kearns, Jane Gabin, and Alfred Bendixen, which have relieved the pressure of our not always unpleasant workdays.

Finally, once more, our gratitude to Ashbel G. Brice, Director of the Duke University Press, and to Reynolds Smith and Barbara Williams who have in large ways made this volume better than when it came to them in typescript.

Lewis Leary
31 December 1976   *John Auchard*

Abbreviations

In listing the location of each article an attempt has been made to be as concise and at the same time as clear as possible. The title of the periodical in which the article appears can be determined from the listing of acronyms and abbreviations offered below; when a space appears between parts of the abbreviated title (*J Eng Stud* for *Journal of English Studies*) several abbreviations may need to be combined to arrive at the full title. Journal titles are italicized and are followed by the volume number in arabic numerals, or if no volume is indicated, by the number of the issue in which the article is found. Next follows the pagination, as concisely indicated as clarity allows, with the date of publication in parenthesis. Dates are listed in the following order: day, month, year; or month (or issue) and year; or, in some instances, by year only. No attempt has been made to supply month or issue when it was lacking in the source from which the item was taken. When preceded by indication of month or issue, the year is abbreviated (70 for 1970). Months are abbreviated: Ja, F, Mr, Ap, My, Je, Jl, Ag, S, O, N, D. For quarterly publications which are dated seasonally, the abbreviations Sp (Spring), Su (Summer), Fa (Fall), Au (Autumn), and Wi (Winter) are used.

The names of authors about whom articles have been written are abbreviated when placed in sequence under the author heading, where the author's name is given in full or as he customarily has used it in his writings. For example, under **Thoreau, Henry David,** HDT will signify that the name is used in full in the title of the article; T will signify that only Thoreau is used, HD.T that the name appears as Henry D. Thoreau, H.D.T. that it appears as H.D. Thoreau.

Other abbreviations and acronyms are as follows:

AA   Americana-Austriaca: Beiträge zur Amerikakunde

AAAPSS   Annals of the American Academy of Politics and Social Science

A&L   Academy and Literature

A&LR   Art and Literature Review

A&W   Arizona and the West

AAR   Ann Arbor Review

AAS   Asian and African Studies

ABAJ   American Bar Association Journal

ABC   American Book Collector

ABR   American Benedictine Review

Acad   Academy, Academic

ACF   Annali di Ca' Foscari

ADEB   Bulletin of the Association of Departments of English

Aesth   Aesthetic, Aesthetics

AFLFM   Annali della Facoltà di Lettere-Filosofia e Magistero (Cagliari)

AFLFUP   Annali Facoltà di Lettere e Filosofia dell-Universita di Perugia

AForum   African Forum: A Quarterly Journal of Contemporary Affairs

AfrAmS   Afro-American Studies: An Interdisciplinary Journal

AgH   Agricultural History

AGR   American-German Review

AH   American Heritage

AHQ   Arkansas Historical Quarterly

AHR   American Historical Review

AI   American Imago

AIM   Annals of Internal Medicine

AION-SG   Annali Istituto Universitario Orientale, Napoli, Sezione Germanica

Abbreviations

AION-SR   Annali Istituto Universitario Orientale, Napoli, Sezione Romanza

AJA   American Jewish Archives

AJES   American Journal of Economics and Sociology

AJGE   Aoyama Journal of General Education (Tokyo)

AJHG   American Jewish Historical Quarterly

AJPH   American Journal of Public Health

AJS   American Journal of Sociology

AL   American Literature

ALA   L'Afrique Littéraire et Artistique (Paris)

ALAb   American Literature Abstracts

AlaHQ   Alabama Historical Quarterly

AlaR   Alabama Review

ALASH   Acta Linguistica Academiae Scientiarum Hungaricae (Budapest)

ALitASH   Acta Litteria Academiae Scientiarum Hungaricae (Budapest)

AllaB   Alla Bottega (Brianza)

ALR   American Literary Realism, 1870–1910

ALS   Australian Literary Studies (University of Tasmania)

ALT   African Literature Today

Am   America, American

AmA   American Anthropologist

AmD   American Dialogue

AmEx   The American Examiner: A Forum of Ideas

AmH   American Humor: An Interdisciplinary Newsletter

AmMerc   American Mecury

AmNep   American Neptune

AmNor   American Norvegica

AmR   American Review

AmS   American Studies

AmSR   American Sociological Review

AmSS   American Studies in Scandinavia (Oslo)

AmW   American West

An   Annals

AN   Acta Neophilogica (Ljubljana)

AN&Q   American Notes and Queries

ANLF   American Negro Literature Forum

AnM   Anarchy Magazine

AntigR   Antigonish Review

AnuarioF   Anuario de Filologia (Marcaíbo)

AnUT   Analele Universitaţii Timişoara, Stiinţe Filologice (Bucharest)

App   Appalachia

AppR   Appalachian Review

Approdo   L'Approdo Letteria (Rome)

APR   American Poetry Review

AQ   American Quarterly

AR   Antioch Review

Arbor   Arbor: Revista General de Investigación y Cultura (Madrid)

Arch   Archeology, Archeological

Archiv   Archiv fur das Studium der Neueren Sprachen und Literaturen (Brunswick)

ArielE   Ariel: A Review of International English Literature

Ariz   Arizoniana: The Journal of Arizona History

ArlQ   Arlington Quarterly

ArmD   Armchair Detective

ArQ   Arizona Quarterly

AS   American Speech

ASch   American Scholar

ASNSP   Annali della Scuola Normale Superiore di Pisa

ASoc   Arts in Society

Assn   Association

AsSt   Asian Student

ASTCFP   Appalachian State Teachers College Faculty Publications

ASUI   Analele Stiinţifice ale Universităţii Iaşi (Romania)

Atl   Atlantic Monthly

ATQ   American Transcendental Quarterly

AUB-LG   Analele Universiţătii, Bucureşti, Limbi Germanice

AUB-LUC   Analele Universiţătii, Bucureşti, Literatură Universala Comparată

AUC   Anales de la Universidad de Chile (Santiago)

AUCu   Anales de la Universidad de Cuenca

AudM   Audubon Magazine

AUMLA   *Journal of the Australasian Universities Language and Literature Association* (Christchurch)
AUR   *Aberdeen University Review*
AWR   *The Anglo-Welsh-Review* (Pembroke Dock, Wales)
AyL   *Armas y letras* (Monterey, Mexico)

BA   *Books Abroad*
BAASB   *British Association for American Studies Bulletin*
BakSJ   *Baker Street Journal*
B&B   *Books and Bookmen*
BaratR   *Barat Review*
BB   *Bulletin of Bibliography*
BBn   *British Book News*
BBr   *Books at Brown*
BC   *Book Collector*
BCB   *Boletin Cultural y Bibliografico* (Bogota)
Bell   *Bellman*
BET   *Boston Evening Transcript*
BFC   *Boletín del Instituto de Filología de la Univeritad de Chile* (Santiago)
BFLS   *Bulletin de la Faculte des Lettres de Strasbourg*
BI   *Books at Iowa*
Bibl   *Bibliography, Bibliographical*
Biog   *Biography, Biographical*
BJA   *British Journal of Aesthetics*
Bk   *Book*
Bkm   *Bookman*
Bkmark   *The Bookmark: Friends of the University of North Carolina Library*
BkW   *Book World*
BlackW   *Black World* (formerly *Negro Digest*)
BlAR   *Black Academy Review*
BLM   *Bonniers Litterära Magasin* (Stockholm)
BlS   *Blake Studies*
BMHS   *Bulletin of the Missouri Historical Society*
BMMLA   *Bulletin of the Midwest Modern Language Association*
BNM   *Book News Monthly*
BNYPL   *Bulletin of the New York Public Library*
BOKD   *Bulletin of Oita Kogya Daigaku* (Oita City, Japan)
BookB   *Book Buyer*
Boun2   *Boundary 2*
BP   *Banasthali Patrika* (India)
BPLQ   *Boston Public Library Quarterly*
BRMMLA   *Bulletin of the Rocky Mountain Modern Language Association*
BS   *Bulletin of Studies Oita Women's Junior College* (Oita City, Japan)
BSAM   *Bulletin de la Société des Amis de Montaigne* (Paris)
BSch   *Black Scholar*
BSM   *Ball State Monographs*
BSN   *Browning Society Notes*
BST   *Brontë Society Transactions*
BSUF   *Ball State University Forum*
BUJ   *Boston University Journal*
Bul   *Bulletin*
BuCG   *Bulletin of the College of General Education, Tohoku University*
BuFH   *Bulletin of the Faculty of Humanities, Seikei University*
BuR   *Bucknell Review*
BUSE   *Boston University Studies in English*
BYUS   *Brigham Young University Studies*

CA   *Cuadernos Americanos* (Mexico City)
CAAS   *Canadian Association for American Studies Bulletin*
CAfr   *Congo-Afrique* (Kinshasa)
CAHR   *Cahiers des Amis de Han Ryner* (Paris)
CaJ   *Cambridge Journal*
Cal   *Calamus* (London)
CalM   *California Monthly*
CalR   *Calcutta Review*
CaM   *Carleton Miscellany*
CanA   *Canadian Audubon*
C&C   *Christianity and Crisis*
C&H   *Computers & the Humanities*
C&RL   *College and Research Libraries*
CanL   *Canadian Literature*
CapeC   *Cape Codder*
CaR   *Cambridge Review*
CaribQ   *Caribbean Quarterly* (Mona, Jamaica)

Abbreviations

CaSE   Carnegie Series in English
Cath   Catholic
CathHR   Catholic Historical Review
CathLW   Catholic Literary World
CathN   Catholic News
CathW   Catholic World
CBAA   Current Bibliography of African
    Affairs
CBul   Classical Bulletin
CCa   Civiltà Cattolica (Rome)
CCC   College Composition and
    Communication
CdF   Cuadernos de Filología (Mendoza,
    Argentina)
CdLA   Casa de las Americas (Havana)
CDN   Chicago Daily News
CdS   Corriere della Sera (Milan)
CE   College English
CEA   CEA Critic
CEAAN   Center for Editions of American
    Writers Newsletter
CEJ   California English Journal
CenM   Center Magazine
CentR   Centennial Review
CEP   Chicago Evening Post
CF   Classical Folia
CH   Church History
CHA   Cuadernos Hispanoamericanos
    (Madrid)
ChE   Chiakē Epitheōrēsis (Chios)
ChiR   Chicago Review
ChrC   Christian Century
Chri   Christian, Christianity
Chron   Chronicle, Chronicles
ChronO   Chronicles of Oklahoma
ChS   Christian Scholar
CHSB   Cincinnati Historical Society
    Bulletin
CHSQ   California Historical Society
    Quarterly
ChSR   Christian Scholar's Review
CHum   Computers and the Humanities
CimR   Cimarron Review
CJ   Classical Journal
CJF   Chicago Jewish Forum
CJL   Canadian Journal of Linguistics
CL   Classical Literature
CLAJ   College Language Association
    Journal

ClassQ   Classical Quarterl̥
CLC   Columbia Library Columns
CLJ   Cornell Library Journal
CLQ   Colby Library Quarterly
CLS   Comparative Literature Studies
CMF   Časopis pro Moderni Filologii A
    Literatury (Prague)
CMV   Journal of the Central Mississippi
    Valley American Study Association
C-NCFS   Carson-Newman College Fac-
    ulty Studies
Col   College
ColM   Colorado Magazine
Colóquio   Colóqiuo/Letras (Lisbon)
ColQ   Colorado Quarterly
ComG   Common Ground
Comp   Comparative
CompD   Comparative Drama
Confl   Confluence
Confr   Confrontation
ConHSB   Connecticut Historical Society
    Bulletin
ConL   Contemporary Literature
ConnR   Connecticut Review
ConR   Contemporary Review
Conrad   Conradiana
ConS   Concord Saunterer
Cont   Contemporary
ContE   Contemporary Education
CP   Concerning Poetry
CQ   Cambridge Quarterly
CR   Classical Review
CRAS   Canadian Review of American
    Studies
CRB   Cahiers de la Compagnie
    Madeleine Renaud-Jean Louis Bar-
    rault (Paris)
CRCL   Canadian Review of Comparative
    Literature
Crit   Critical
CritI   Critical Inquiry
Critique   Critique: Studies in Modern
    Fiction
Crit(P)   Critique (Paris)
CritQ   Critical Quarterly
CritR   Critical Review
CritS   Critical Survey
CritT   Critique: A Critical Review of
    Theatre Arts and Literature

CS   *Cahiers du Sud* (Marseilles)
CSLBul   *Bulletin of the New York C.S.*
   Lewis Society
CSS   *Canadian Slavic Studies*
CTBW   *Chicago Tribune Book World*
CUF   *Columbia University Forum*
Cur   *Current*
CV   *Citta di Vita* (Florence)
Cweal   *Commonweal*
Cwealth   *Commonwealth*
CWH   *Civil War History*
CyC   *Cursos y Conferencias*

D&T   *Drama and Theatre*
DARM   *Daughters of the American Rev-*
   olution Magazine
DCLB   *Dartmouth College Library*
   Bulletin
DelR   *Delta Review*
DH   *Delaware History*
DHLR   *D.H. Lawrence Review*
DHR   *Duquesne Hispanic Review*
Dialog   *Dialogue: A Journal of Mormon*
   Thought
Dig   *Digest*
DilR   *Diliman Review*
Disc   *Discourse*
DLAJ   *DeKalb Literary Arts Journal*
Dnipro   *Dnipro: Literaturne-xudoznij*
   Žurnal (Kiev)
DNR   *Dime Novel Round-up*
DP   *Discourses on Poetry*
DQ   *Denver Quarterly*
DQR   *Dutch Quarterly Review of Anglo-*
   American Letters (Amsterdam)
DR   *Dalhousie Review*
DramC   *Drama Critique*
DramR   *Drama Review*
DramS   *Drama Survey*
DrN   *Dreiser Newsletter*
DRu   *Deutsche Rundschau* (Berlin)
DSE   *Doshisha Studies in English*
   (Kyota)
DUB   *Drew University Bulletin*
DUJ   *Durham University Journal*
DuqR   *Duquesne Review*
DUS   *Drew University Studies*
DVLG   *Deutsche Vierteljahrsschrift für*
   Literaturwissenschaft und

Geistesgeschichte (Stuggart)
DWB   *Dietsche Warande en Belfort*
   (Amsterdam)
DWN   *Defender of Wildlife News*

EA   *Etudes Anglaises* (Paris)
EAA   *Etudes Anglaises et Americaines*
   (Paris)
EAL   *Early American Literature*
E&S   *Essays and Studies by Members of*
   the English Association
EAS   *Essays in Arts and Sciences*
EC   *Essays in Criticism*
Ec   *Economic, Economics*
ECS   *Eighteenth-Century Studies*
Ed   *Education, Educational*
EDB   *Emily Dickinson Bulletin*
EdF   *Educational Forum*
EEx   *Exercise Exchange*
EGN   *Ellen Glasgow Newsletter*
EibunG   *Eibun Gakushi* (Tokyo)
EiC   *Essays in Criticism* (Denver)
EIC   *Essays in Criticism* (Oxford)
EigoS   *Eigo Seinen* (Tokyo)
EIHC   *Essex Institute Historical*
   Collections
EJ   *English Journal*
EL&L   *English Language and Literature*
   (Korea)
ELH   *Journal of English Literary History*
ELit   *Etudes Littéraires* (Paris)
ELLOKD   *English Laboratory of Oita*
   Kogyo Daigaku (Oita City, Japan)
ELLS   *English Literature and Language*
   (Tokyo)
ELN   *English Language Notes*
ElNaz   *El Nazional*
ELT   *English Literature in Translation*
ELUD   *Essays in Literature* (University
   of Denver)
ELyP   *El Libro y el Pueblo* (Mexico
   City)
EN   *English Notes*
Enc   *Encounter*
EnE   *Enlightenment Essays*
Eng   *English*
Eng(L)   *English* (London)
EpH   *Ēpeirōtikē Hestia* (Ioannina)
ES   *English Studies*

Abbreviations

ESA   *English Studies in Africa*
(Johannesburg)

ESALL   *Essays and Studies on American Language and Literature* (Uppsala)

ESELL   *Essays and Studies in English Language and Literature* (Sendai)

EsL   *Essays in Literature*

ESPSL   *O Estado do São Paulo, Suplemento Literario*

ESQ   *Emerson Society Quarterly*

ESRS   *Emporia State Research Studies*

ETC   *ETC: A Review of General Semantics*

ETJ   *Educational Theatre Journal*

EUQ   *Emory University Quarterly*

EvR   *Evergreen Review*

EWR   *East-West Review* (Kyoto)

Expl   *Explicator*

Extr   *Extracts: The Newsletter of the Melville Society*

Extracta   *Extracta: Resumeer af Specialeopgaver fra det Filosofiske Fakultet* (Copenhagen)

FarP   *Far Point*

FaS   *Faulkner Studies*

FCHQ   *Filson Club Historical Quarterly*

FCN   *Faulkner Concordance Newsletter*

FdL   *Forum der Letteren* (Gravenhage, Netherlands)

FH   *Frederic Herald*

FHA   *Fitzgerald-Hemingway Annual*

FHays   *Fort Hays: Bibliograpy Series*

FHQ   *Florida Historical Quarterly*

FI   *Forum Italicum*

FicI   *Fiction International*

FitzN   *Fitzgerald Newsletter*

FJ   *Faculty Journal* (East Stroudsburg State College)

Fkl   *Folklore*

FL   *Figaro Litteraire* (Paris)

FlaQ   *Florida Quarterly*

FLang   *Foundations of Language* (Dordrecht)

FLe   *Fiero Letteraria* (Milan)

FlQ   *Florida Quarterly*

FMLS   *Forum for Modern Language Studies* (St. Andrews)

FMod   *Filologia Moderna* (Madrid)

For   *Foreign*

FOB   *Flannery O'Connor Bulletin*

ForH   *Forest History*

ForN   *Forest Notes*

Forum (H)   *Forum* (Houston)

ForumZ   *Forum* (Zagreb))

FourQ   *Four Quarters*

FPJ   *Free Press Journal*

FR   *French Review*

FrH   *Frankfuter Hefte*

FSUS   *Florida State University Studies*

FurmM   *Furman Magazine*

FurmS   *Furman Studies*

FWF   *Far Western Forum*

GaR   *Georgia Review*

Gaz   *Gazette*

Gen   *General, Geneological*

GGAL   *Geschichte und Gesellschaft in der Amerikanischen Literatur*

GGC   *Gazette of the Grolier Club*

GHQ   *Georgia Historical Quarterly*

Gids   *De Gids* (Amsterdam)

GL&L   *German Life and Letters* (Oxford)

GorR   *Gordon Review*

GQ   *German Quarterly*

GR   *Germanic Review*

Greyfriar   *Greyfriar: Siena Studies in Literature*

GRM   *Germanisch-romanische Monatsschrift* (Heidelberg)

GSlav   *Germano-Slavica* (Brno)

HA   *Harvard Advocate*

HAB   *Humanities Association Bulletin* (Canada)

H&H   *Hound and Horn*

HanF   *Hanover Forum*

HartR   *Hartwick Review*

HB   *Harper's Bazaar*

HC   *Hollins Critic*

HCS   *Heritage Club Sandglass*

HEQ   *History of Education Quarterly*

HiJAS   *Hitotsubashi Journal of Arts and Sciences* (Tokyo)

HiR   *Hawaii Review*

HirStud   *Hiroshima Studies in English Language and Literature*

HiS   Humanities in the South
Hisp   Hispania
Hist   History, Historical, Historian
HistT   History Today
HJ   Hibbert Journal
H-JM   Haldeman-Julius Monthly
HJP   Higginson Journal of Poetry
HL   Humanistica Lovaniensia (Louvain)
HLB   Harvard Library Bulletin
HLQ   Huntington Library Quarterly
HM   Harper's Magazine
HMPEC   Historical Magazine of the
    Protestant Episcopal Church
HN   Hemingway Notes
HNH   Historical New Hampshire
Hoch   Hochland (Munich)
HopR   Hopkins Review
HornB   Horn Book
HowS   Howells Sentinel
HR   Hispanic Review
HSE   Hungarian Studies in English
    (Budapest)
HSELL   Hiroshima Studies in English
    Language and Literature
HSL   Hartford Studies in Literature
HTR   Harvard Theological Review
HudR   Hudson Review
Hum   Humanisme (Centre de Documen-
    tation du Grand Orient de France)
HumB   Humanitas (Brescia))
HUSL   Hebrew University Studies in Lit-
    erature (Jerusalem)
HussR   Husson Review
HVF   Handelingen XXIXe Vlaams
    Filologencongress
HZM   Handelingen van de Zuidneder-
    landse Maatschappij voor Taal-en
    Letterkunde en Geschiedenis
    (Brussels)

I-AmRB   Inter-American Review of
    Bibliography
ID   Intellectual Digest
IEJ   Indiana English Journal
IEngYb   Iowa English Yearbook
IEY   Iowa English Bulletin: Yearbook
IF   Idaho Farmer
IFR   International Fiction Review
IH   ITA Humanidades (São José dos

    Campos)
IJAS   Indian Journal of American Studies
    (Calcutta)
IJES   Indian Journal of English Studies
    (Calcutta)
IllQ   Illinois Quarterly
Illus   Illustrated
IMH   Indiana Magazine of History
Indep   Independent
InR   Intercollegiate Review
Inst   Institute
Int   International
IntJS   International Journal of
    Symbology
IPNA   Instituto Cultural Peruano-Norte-
    americano (Lima)
IPQ   International Philosophical
    Quarterly
IQ   Italian Quarterly
IR   Iliff Review
ISE   Ibadan Studies in English (Nigeria)
ISUJ   Illinois State University Journal
IUR   Irish University Review (Shannon)

J   Journal
JA   Jahrbruch für Amerikastudien
    (Heidelberg)
JAAC   Journal of Aesthetics and Art
    Criticism
JAE   Journal of Aesthetic Education
JAF   Journal of American Folklore
JAH   Journal of American History
JAMA   Journal of the American Medical
    Association
JAMS   Journal of the American
    Musicological Society
JAmSt   Journal of American Studies
JANSS   Journal of the American Nature
    Study Society
JAPA   Journal of the American
    Psychoanalytic Association
JAriH   Journal of Arizona History
JBA   Jewish Book Annual
JBlackS   Journal of Black Studies
JBS   John Berryman Studies
JCHist   Journal of Contemporary
    History
JCL   Journal of Commonwealth Litera-
    ture (Leeds))

Abbreviations

JCLAG   *Journal of College Literature* (Tokyo)
JCS   *Journal of Croatian Studies*
JdL   *Jornal de Letras* (Rio de Janeiro)
JEARD   *Journal of East African Research and Development* (Nairobi)
JEGP   *Journal of English and Germanic Philology*
JEMFQ   *John Edwards Memorial Foundation Quarterly*
JES   *Journal of European Studies*
JESL   *Journal of English as a Second Language*
JEthSt   *Journal of Ethnic Studies*
JeuneA   *Jeune Afrique* (Paris)
JewD   *Jewish Digest*
JewL   *Jewish Life*
JewO   *Jewish Outlook*
JewQ   *Jewish Quarterly*
JFI   *Journal of the Folklore Institute*
JGE   *Journal of General Education*
JH   *Jewish Heritage*
JHE   *Journal of Higher Education*
JHI   *Journal of the History of Ideas*
JHS   *Journal of Historical Studies*
JIAS   *Journal of Inter-American Studies*
JIL   *Journal of Irish Literature*
JIP   *Journal of Individual Psychology*
JISHS   *Journal of the Illinois State History Society*
JJQ   *James Joyce Quarterly*
JL   *Journal of Linguistics*
JLM   *Journal* (Lewiston, Maine)
JLN   *Jack London Newsletter*
JMiH   *Journal of Mississippi History*
JML   *Journal of Modern Literature*
JNE   *Journal of Negro Education*
JNH   *Journal of Negro History*
JNT   *Journal of Narrative Technique*
JAOS   *Journal of the American Oriental Society*
JOFS   *Journal of the Ohio Folklore Society*
JORA   *Journal of the Otto Rank Association*
Journ   *Journalism*
JPC   *Journal of Popular Culture*
JPH   *Journal of Presbyterian History*
JQ   *Journalism Quarterly*
JR   *Journal of Religion*

JRUL   *Journal of the Rutgers University Library*
JSH   *Journal of Southern History*
JSJU   *Journal of Sugiyama Jogakuen University* (Nagoya, Japan)
JWest   *Journal of the West*
JWGV   *Jahrbuch des Wiener Goethe-Vereins* (Vienna)

KAL   *Kyushu American Literature* (Fukuoka)
K&C   *Kunst en Culturr* (Brussels)
KanQ   *Kansas Quarterly*
KCN   *Kate Chopin Newsletter*
KCS   *Kansas City Star*
KenR   *Kentucky Review*
KFQ   *Keystone Folklore Quarterly*
KFR   *Kentucky Folklore Record*
KHQ   *Kentucky Historical Quarterly*
KHSR   *Kentucky Historical Society Register*
KM   *Kansas Magazine*
KN   *Kwartalnik Neofilologiczny* (Poland)
Knji   *Književnost* (Belgrade)
KoK   *Kirke og Kultur* (Oslo)
KR   *Kenyon Review*
KRQ   *Kentucky Romance Quarterly*
KSJ   *Keats-Shelley Journal*
KSV   *Kirjallisuudentutkijain Seuran Vuosikirja* (Helsinki)
KuL   *Kunst und Literatur* (Düsseldorf)

LaHi   *Louisiana History*
LaHQ   *Louisiana Historical Quarterly*
LakeUR   *Lakehead University Review*
LALR   *Latin-American Literary Review*
L&I   *Literature and Ideology* (Montreal)
Lang   *Language*
Lang&L   *Language & Literature*
Lang&S   *Language & Style*
LangQ   *Language Quarterly*
LanM   *Les Langues Modernes* (Paris)
L&P   *Literature and Psychology*
L&S   *Literature and Society*
LaStud   *Louisiana Studies*
LATC   *Los Angeles Times Calendar*
LauR   *Laurel Review*
LCQJCA   *Library of Congress Quarterly Journal of Current Acquisitions*
LCrit   *Literary Criterion* (Mysore)

LCUP   Library Chronicle of the University of Pennsylvania
LCUT   Library Chronicle of the University of Texas
Leaf   The Leaflet
LE&W   Literature East and West
LeS   Lingua e Stile (Bologna)
Let   Letteratura (Firenze)
LetF   Lettres Francaises (Buenos Aires)
LetN   Lettres Nouvelles (Paris)
LFQ   Literature/Film Quarterly
LGJ   Lost Generation Journal
LH   Lincoln Herald
LHJ   Ladies Home Journal
LHR   Lock Haven Review
LHY   Literary Half-Yearly
Lib   Libraries, Library, Librarian
LibR   Library Review
LiLi   Zeitschrift fur Literaturwissenschaft und Linguistik (Frankfurt)
Lilla   Lillabulero
Lit   Literary, Literature
LitR   Literary Review
LJ   Library Journal
LL   Language Learning
LMi   Literaturna Misal (Sofia)
LN   Language Notes
LNac   La Nación (Buenos Aires)
LNP   Le Nouveau Planete (Paris)
LonM   London Magazine
LonR   London Review
LonT   London Times
LR   Les Lettres Romanes (Louvain)
LSem   La Semana (Madrid/Barcelona)
LSUS   Louisiana State University Studies
Luc   Luceafarul (Bucharest)
LugR   Lugano Review
LuK   Literatur und Kritik (Vienna)
LW   Living Wilderness
LWU   Literatur in Wissenschaft und Unterricht (Kiel, W Germany)

M-A   Mid-America
Mag   Magazine
MagA   Magazine of Art
MagFSF   Magazine of Fantasy and Science Fiction
M&L   Music and Letters (London)
MalR   Malahat Review
M&M   Media and Methods

M&N   Man and Nature
MAQR   Michigan Alumni Quarterly Review
MarkR   Markham Review
MASJ   Midcontinent American Studies Journal
MassA   Massachusetts Audubon
MassW   Massachusetts Wildlife
MCMT   Main Currents in Modern Thought
McNR   McNeese Review
MD   Modern Drama
MDAC   Mystery and Detection Annual
Meanjin   Meanjin Quarterly (Melbourne)
MEB   Missouri English Bulletin
MeditR   Mediterranean Review
Mencken   Menckeniana
MethH   Methodist History
MethR   Methodist Review
MexQR   Mexico Quarterly Review
MFS   Modern Fiction Studies
MGSL   Minas Gerais, Suplemento Literário (Brazil)
MH   Minnesota History
MHM   Maryland Historical Magazine
MHR   Missouri Historical Review
MHSB   Missouri Historical Society Bulletin
MichA   Michigan Academician
MichH   Michigan History
MichSN   Michigan State News
MinnR   Minnesota Review
Misc   Miscellany
MissFR   Mississippi Folklore Register
MissHSP   Mississippi Historical Society Publications
MissQ   Mississippi Quarterly
MissR   Mississippi Review
ML   Magazine Littéraire (Paris)
MLJ   Modern Language Journal
MLN   Modern Language Notes
MLQ   Modern Language Quarterly
MLR   Modern Language Review
MLS   Modern Language Studies
MMR   Mill Mountain Review
MNL   The Mill News Letter
Mo   Month, Monthly
Mod   Modern, Moderne
ModA   Modern Age

Abbreviations

ModO   Modern Occasions
ModR   Modern Review
Mooz   Mo'oznayim (Tel Aviv)
MP   Modern Philology
MPS   Modern Poetry Studies
MQR   Michigan Quarterly Review
MR   Massachusetts Review
MRom   Marche Romane (Liege, Belgium)
MRR   Mad River Review
MS   Manuscript
MSC   Melville Society Checklist
MSCS   Mankato State College Studies
MSE   Massachusetts Studies in English
MSEx   Melville Society Extracts
MSF   Mid-South Folklore
MSpr   Moderna Sprak (Stockholm)
MTJ   Mark Twain Journal
MTQ   Mark Twain Quarterly
MuK   Maske und Kothurn (Vienna)
Mus   Music, Musical
MVCBul   Bulletin of the Mississippi Valley Collection
MVHR   Mississippi Valley Historical Review
MW   The Muslim World (London)
MwER   Midwest Education Review
MwJ   Midwest Journal
MwQ   Midwest Quarterly
MwR   Midwest Review
MwUQ   Midwestern University Quarterly

N   Newsletter
NA   Nuova Antologia (Rome)
NALF   Negro American Literature Forum
N&Q   Notes and Queries
NAR   North American Review
NArg   Nuovi Argomenti (Milan)
NaS   Nature Study
NasR   Nassau Review
NASRC   Newsletter, American Studies Research Center
Nat   National
NatW   National Wildlife
Naz   Nazione (Firenze)
NCaF   North Carolina Folklore
NCampR   New Campus Review

NCCL   Newsletter on the Conference of Christianity and Literature
NCF   Nineteenth-Century Fiction
NCHR   North Carolina Historical Review
NCL   North Carolina Life
NCLit   Notes on Contemporary Literature
NCr   La Nouvelle Critique: Revue du Marxisme Militant (Paris)
NCTR   Nineteenth-Century Theatre Research
NDEJ   Notre Dame English Journal
NDH   Neue Deutsche Hefte (Berlin)
NDQ   North Dakota Quarterly
NE   New England
NeaH   Nea Hestia (Athens)
NEG   New England Galaxy
NegroD   Negro Digest
NEH   New England Homestead
NEJMed   New England Journal of Medicine
NEMLAN   New England Modern Language Association Notes
Neophil   Neophilologus (Groningen)
NEQ   New England Quarterly
NER   New England Review
NewAmR   New American Review
NewL   New Leader
NewR   The New Review
NHB   Negro History Bulletin
NHJ   Nathaniel Hawthorne Journal
NHM   Nebraska Historical Magazine
NHuQ   New Hungarian Quarterly (Budapest)
NJH   New Jersey History
NL   Nouvelles Littéraires (Paris)
NLauR   New Laurel Review
NLB   Newberry Library Bulletin
NLet   New Letters
NLH   New Literary History
NM   Neuphilololische Mitteilungen (Helsinki)
NMHR   New Mexico Historical Review
NMW   Notes on Mississippi Writers
NOQ   Northwest Ohio Quarterly
NOR   New Orleans Review
Novel   Novel: A Forum on Fiction
NP   Nuova Presenza

NRep   New Republic
NRF   Nouvelle Revue Française (Paris)
NRs   Neue Rundschau (Frankfurt)
ns   new series
NS   Die Neueren Sprachen (Marburg)
NsM   Neusprachliche Mitteilungen au
    Wissenschaft und Praxis (Berlin)
NSt   New Statesman
NuA   Nueva América
nv   no volume
NVT   Nieuw Vlaams Tijdschrift
    (Antwerp)
Nw   Northwest, Northwestern
Nwk   Newsweek
NwR   Northwest Review
NY   New Yorker
NyA   Nya Argus (Helsingfors)
NYFQ   New York Folklore Quarterly
NYH   New York History
NYHSQ   New York Historical Society
    Quarterly
NYHT   New York Herald Tribune Book
    Review
NYQ   New York Quarterly
NYRB   New York Review of Books
NYT   New York Times Book Review
    Section
NYTimes   New York Times
NYTMS   New York Times Magazine
    Section
NYTSat   New York Times Saturday
    Review of Books and Arts

Oberon   Oberon (Tokyo)
OdyR   Odyssey Review
OEng   Oral English
OGF   Organic Gardening and Farming
OH   Ohio History
OhR   Ohio Review
OJES   Osmania Journal of English
    Studies (Hyderabad)
Okt   Oktjabr' (Moscow)
OL   Orbis Litterarum (Copenhagen)
OnsE   Ons Erfdeel (Rekkem)
OpL   Open Letter (Toronto)
OR   Oxford Review
Oregon   Oregonian
OrHQ   Oregon Historical Quarterly
ORom   Osservatore Romano (Rome)

OSUTCB   Ohio State University Theatre
    Collection Bulletin
OtsukaR   Otsuka Review (Tokyo)
OUS   Ochanomizu University Studies
    (Tokyo)
OyR   Oyez Review

PA   Présence Africaine (Paris)
PAAS   Proceedings of the American
    Antiquarian Society
Pac   Pacific
PacR   Pacific Review
PAH   Perspectives in American History
PAJHS   Publications of the Jewish
    Historical Society
Pam   Pamphlet
PaM   Pacific Monthly
P&C   Poet and Critic
P&ER   Political and Economic Review
PAmDS   Publications of the American
    Dialect Society
PAPS   Proceedings of the American
    Philosophical Society
P&R   Philosophy and Rhetoric
PaR   Paris Review
Para   Paragone (Florence)
PBA   Proceedings of the British
    Academy
PBSA   Papers of the Bibliographical
    Society of America
PCCTET   Proclamation of Conference of
    College Teachers of English
PCP   Pacific Coast Philology
PE&W   Philosophy East and West
    (Honolulu)
PELL   Papers on English Language and
    Literature
PenPt   Pencil Points
PenS   Pensiero e Scuola
Per   Perspective
PerAmH   Perspectives in American
    History
Person   The Personalist
PF   Pennsylvania Folklife
PGCHHC   Proceedings of the Gulf Coast
    History and Humanities Conference
PH   Pennsylvania History
Phil   Philology, Philological
Philos   Philosophy, Philosophical

Abbreviations

PHum   *Przeglad Humanistyczny* (Warsaw)

PLL   *Papers on Language and Literature*

PMASAL   *Papers of the Michigan Academy of Science, Arts, and Letters*

PMHB   *Pennsylvania Magazine of History and Biography*

PMHS   *Proceedings of the Massachusetts Historical Society*

PMLA   *Publications of the Modern Language Association of America*

PN   *Poe Newsletter*

PNHCHS   *Papers of the New Haven Colony Historical Society*

PNQ   *Pacific Northwest Quarterly*

PNU   *Praxis des Neusprachlichen Unterrichts* (Dortmund, W. Germany)

PNWASN   *Pacific Northwest American Studies Newsletter*

PoeS   *Poe Studies*

PoetA   *Poetry Australia* (New South Wales)

PoetB   *Poetry Broadside*

Poetica   *Poetica* (Munich)

Poétique   *Poétique: Revue de Théorie et d'Analyse Littéraires* (Paris)

PoetJ   *Poetry Journal*

PoetR   *Poetry Review*

Pol   *Political, Politics*

PolP   *Polish Perspectives*

PolR   *Polish Review*

PosS   *The Possible Sack*

PP   *Philologica Pragensia* (Prague)

PPR   *Philosophy and Phenomenological Research*

PQ   *Philological Quarterly*

PR   *Partisan Review*

PrA   *Primer Acto* (Madrid)

Proc   *Proceedings*

ProcLang&Lit   *Proceedings of the Department of Foreign Languages and Literatures, College of General Education, University of Tokyo*

Prog   *The Progressive*

PrS   *Prairie Schooner*

PSA   *Papeles de Son Armadans* (Mallorca)

Psy   *Psychic*

Psych   *Psychology, Psychological*

Q   *Quarterly, Quarter*

QH   *Quaker History*

QJLC   *Quarterly Journal of the Library of Congress*

QJS   *Quarterly Journal of Speech*

QL   *Quinzaine Littéraire* (Paris)

QNL   *Quarterly Newsletter of the Book Club of California*

QQ   *Queen's Quarterly*

QRL   *Quarterly Review of Literature*

QTC   *Quarterly of the Tuolumne County Historical Society*

Quest   *Quest* (Bombay)

R   *Review*

RA   *Repertorio Americano* (San Jose, Costa Rica)

RACHSP   *Records of the American Catholic Historical Society*

RALS   *Resources for American Literary Studies*

Ranam   *Recherches Anglaises et Americaines* (Strasbourg)

RBPH   *Revue Belge de Philologie et d'Histoire* (Brussels)

RCR   *Red Clay Reader*

RdE   *Revista di Estetica* (Padova)

RdEt   *Revista de Ethnografía* (Bucharest)

RDM   *Revue des Deux Mondes* (Paris)

RdP   *Revue de Paris*

RdPac   *Revista del Pacífico* (Valparaiso)

RE   *La Revue d'Esthétique* (Paris)

Re: A&L   *Re: Arts & Letters*

Rec   *Record*

REH   *Revista de Estudios Hispánicos*

RecL   *Recovering Literature*

REL   *Review of English Literature* (Leeds)

Rel   *Religion, Religous*

RelH   *Religious Humanism*

Ren   *Renaissance*

REngL   *Review of English Literature* (Kyoto)

Res   *Research*

RES   *Review of English Studies*

ResBul   *Research Bulletin* (San Jose State College)

RevL   *Revista de Letras* (Oviedo)

RF   *Romanische Forschungen* (Frankfurt)

RHL   *Revue d'Histoire Littéraire de la France* (Paris)

RIAL   *Research in African Literature*

RIB   *Revista Interamericana de Bibliografía* (Medellin, Colombia)

RichM   *Richmond Mercury*

RichT-D   *Richmond Times-Dispatch*

RIH   *Rhode Island History*

RiL   *Rhode Island History*

RiL   *Religion in Life*

RITL   *Revista de Istorie şi Theorie Literară* (Bucharest)

RJN   *Robinson Jeffers Newsletter*

RKHS   *Register of the Kentucky Historical Society*

RLA   *Revista de Letras da Faculdade de Filosofia Ciências e Letras de Assis*

RLC   *Revue de Littérature Comparée* (Paris)

RLit   *Russkaja Literatura* (Leningrad)

RLJ   *Russian Language Journal* (Michigan State University, East Lansing)

RLLR   *Revue de Louisiane/Louisiana Review*

RLM   *La Revue des Lettres Modernes* (Paris)

RLMC   *Rivista di Letterature Moderne e Comparate* (Firenze)

RLT   *Russian Literature Triquarterly*

RLV   *Revue des Langues Vivantes* (Bruxelles)

RLz   *Radjans'ke Literaturoznavstvo* (Kiev)

RMeta   *Review of Metaphysics*

RMR   *Rocky Mountain Review of Language and Literature* (formerly BRMMLA)

RMS   *Renaissance and Modern Studies* (University of Michigan)

RMSSJ   *Rocky Mountain Social Science Journal*

RNC   *Revista Nacional de Cultura* (Caracas)

RO   *Revista de Occidente* (Madrid)

RocR   *Rochester Review* (University of Rochester)

RoLit   *Rômania Literară* (Bucharest)

RomN   *Romance Notes* (University of North Carolina)

RoR   *Romanian Review* (Bucharest)

RosD   *Rosicrucian Digest*

RPol   *Review of Politics*

RQ   *Riverside Quarterly*

RR   *Romanic Review*

RRAL   *Rikkyo Review of Arts and Letters* (Tokyo)

RSP   *Resident and Staff Physician*

RSW   *Research Studies at Washington State University*

RT   *Religious Theatre* (Wichita)

RUO   *Revue de l'Université d'Ottawa*

RUS   *Rice University Studies*

RUSEng   *Rajasthan University Studies in English* (India)

RusR   *Russian Review*

SA   *Studi Americani* (Rome)

SAB   *South Atlantic Bulletin*

SAF   *Studies in American Fiction* (Northeastern University)

SAH   *Studies in American Humor*

SALCS   *Studies in American Literature* (Chu-Shikoku American Literature Society)

SALit   *Studies in American Literature*

S&S   *School and Society*

S&W   *South and West*

SAP   *Studia Anglica Posnaniensia: An International Review of English Studies* (Bucharest)

SAQ   *South Atlantic Quarterly*

Sat   *Saturday*

SatR   *Saturday Review*

SatR/World   *Saturday Review/World*

Savremenik   *Savremenik* (Belgrade)

SB   *Studies in Bibliography*

SBL   *Studies in Black Literature*

SCB   *South Central Bulletin*

Sch   *School*

SCHM   *South Carolina Historical Magazine*

Schol   *Scholar*

SchP   *Scholarly Publishing* (University of Toronto)

Abbreviations

SchV   *Scholastic Voice* (NYC)
Sci   *Science, Sciences, Scientific*
Sci&Soc   *Science and Society*
SCN   *Seventeenth-Century News*
SCQ   *Southern California Quarterly*
SCR   *South Carolina Review*
SCraneN   *Stephen Crane Newsletter*
Scrib   *Scribner's Magazine*
ScriptaH   *Scripta Hierosolymitanan*
     (Hebrew University at Jerusalem)
SCUL   *Soundings: Collections of the*
     University Library, University of
     California, Santa Barbara.
SD   *Science Digest*
Sdlu   *Studii de literatură universală*
     (Bucharest)
SDR   *South Dakota Review*
SE   *Snowy Egret*
SEAL   *Studies in English and American*
     Literature (Aoyamna Gakuin
     University, Tokyo)
Sec   *Secretary, Secretary's*
SECU   *Studies in English of Charles*
     University (Czechoslovakia)
SEEJ   *Slavic and East European Journal*
     (Ottawa)
SEER   *Slavonic and East European*
     Review
SEL   *Studies in English Literature, 1500-*
     1900
SELit   *Studies in English Literature*
     (English Literary Society of Japan,
     University of Tokyo)
SELL   *Studies in English Literature and*
     Language (Kyushu University)
Semiotica   *Semiotica: Revue Publiée par*
     l'Association Internationale de
     Sémiotique (Paris)
SEP   *Saturday Evening Post*
ser   series
Serif   *The Serif* (Kent, Ohio)
SFQ   *Southern Folklore Quarterly*
S-FS   *Science-Fiction Studies*
Shen   *Shenandoah*
ShN   *Shakespeare Newsletter*
SHQ   *Southwestern Historical Quarterly*
SHR   *Southern Humanities Review*
ShS   *Shakespeare Survey*

Sigma   *Sigma: Revista Trimestrale di*
     Letturatura (Turin)
SimmQ   *Simmons Quarterly*
SJIS   *Soundings: A Journal of*
     Interdisciplinary Studies
SkAQ   *Skidmore Alumni Quarterly*
SlavR   *Slavic Review* (Seattle)
SlE   *Slovenski Etnograf* (Ljubljani,
     Yugoslavia)
SLitI   *Studies in the Literary Imagination*
SLJ   *Southern Literary Journal*
SLM   *Southern Literary Messenger*
SLN   *Sinclair Lewis Newsletter*
SLRJ   *Saint Louis University Research*
     Journal of the Graduate School of
     · *Arts and Sciences*
SM   *Speech Monographs*
Smith   *Smithsonian*
SN   *Studia Neophilologica* (Stockholm)
SNL   *Satire Newsletter*
So   *South, Southern*
Soc   *Society, Social*
Sociol   *Sociology, Sociological*
SophT   *Sophia: Studies in Western*
     Civilization and the Cultural
     Interaction of East and West (Tokyo)
SoQ   *Southern Quarterly* (University of
     So. Mississippi)
SoR   *Southern Review* (Louisiana State
     University)
SoRA   *Southern Review: An Australian*
     Journal of Literary Studies
     (University of Adelaide)
Southerly   *Southerly* (Sydney)
SovH   *Sovetish Hymland* (Moscow)
SovL   *Soviet Literature* (Moscow)
SoW   *Southern Workman*
Sp   *Speech*
SP   *Studies in Philology*
Spec   *Spectator*
SpT   *Speech Teacher*
SQ   *Shakespeare Quarterly*
SR   *Sewanee Review*
SR/World   *Saturday Review/World*
SRAZ   *Studia Romanica et Anglica*
     Zagrabiensia (Zabreb, Yogoslavia)
SRom   *Studies in Romanticism*
SRSCB   *Sul Ross State College Bulletin*

SS   Scandinavian Studies
SSASH   Studia Slavica Academiae
    Scientairum Hungaricae (Budapest)
SSCJ   Southern Speech Communication
    Journal
SSF   Studies in Short Fiction
SSJ   Southern Speech Journal
StAR   St. Andrews Review
StBr   Stony Brook
STC   Studies in the Twentieth Century
    (1968)
StE   Studies in English (University of
    Texas)
SteinN   Steinbeck Newsletter
StH   Studies in the Humanities (Indiana
    U of Pa.)
StL   Studies on the Left
StN   Studies in the Novel
SToS   Shi To Sambun (Tokyo)
StQ   Steinbeck Quarterly
Stud   Studies, Study
Studiekamraten   Studiekamraten (Lund)
Studies   Studies: An Irish Quarterly
    Review (Dublin)
Sup   Supplement
SUS   Susquehanna University Studies
SUSFL   Studi Urbinati di Storia,
    Filosofia e Letteratura
Sw   Southwest, Southwestern
SwAL   Southwestern American
    Literature
SWR   Southwest Review
SXX   Secolul XX (Bucharest)
Sym   Symposium
Syn   Synthèses (Brussels)
SZ   Stimmen der Zeit (Freiberg)

TA   Theater Annual
TamR   Tamarack Review (Toronto)
TC   Twentieth Century
TCL   Twentieth Century Literature
TCM   Twentieth Century Magazine
TCS   Twentieth Century Studies
TD   Twisted Dial
TDR   Tulane Drama Review (until
    Winter 1968, then TDR/The Drama
    Review)
TFSB   Tennessee Folklore Society
    Bulletin

Th   Theatre
ThA   Theater Arts
ThDoc   Theater Documentation
Theol   Theology, Theological
ThN   Theatre Notebook
ThQ   Theatre Quarterly
THQ   Tennessee Historical Quarterly
ThR   Theatre Review
ThS   Theatre Survey
TJQ   Thoreau Journal Quarterly
TkR   Tamkang Review (Taipei)
TLS   Times Literary Supplement
TPB   Tennessee Philological Bulletin
TPJ   Tennessee Poetry Journal
TQ   Texas Quarterly
TR   Table Ronde (Paris)
Trad   Tradition
Trans   Transactions
TransR   Transatlantic Review
Trimestre   Trimestre (Pescara)
TriQ   Tri-Quarterly
Triveni   Triveni: Journal of Indian
    Renaissance (Machilipatnam)
TSB   Thoreau Society Bulletin
TSBk   Thoreau Society Booklet
TSE   Tulane Studies in English
TSE N   T.S. Eliot Notes
TSE R   T.S. Eliot Review
TSL   Tennessee Studies in Literature
TSLL   Texas Studies in Literature and
    Language
TSt   Theatre Studies
TTJ   Tennessee Technical Journal
TWA   Transactions of the Wisconsin
    Academy of Sciences, Arts, and
    Letters
TyL   Tierra y Libertad (Mexico)

UAP   Utah Academy Proceedings
UChM   University of Chicago Magazine
UCLR   University of Chicago Law
    Review
UCQ   University College Quarterly
UDQ   University of Denver Quarterly
UDR   University of Dayton Review
UES   Unisa English Studies
Ufahamu   Ufahamu: Journal of the
    African Activist Association
UHQ   Utah Historical Quarterly

Abbreviations

UI   Uomini e idee (Naples)
UKCR   University of Kansas City Review
ULR   University of Leeds Review
Umoja   Umoja: Southwestern Afro-American Journal
UMSE   University of Mississippi Studies in English
Un   University
Unic   Unicorn (Brooklyn)
Univ   Universitas (Stuttgart)
Universidad   Universidad (Sante Fe)
UPortR   University of Portland Review
UR   University Review (Kansas City)
UTMS   University of Tulsa Monograph Series
UTQ   University of Toronto Quarterly
UTSE   University of Texas Studies in English
UWB   University of Wichita Bulletin
UWR   University of Windsor Review

VaCal   Virginia Cavalcade
VCath   La Vie Catholique (Paris)
Vectors   Astme Vectors
Veltro   Veltro (Roma)
VeP   Vita e Penseiro (Milan)
VerR   Vermont Review
VH   Vermont History
VHSP   Vermont Historical Society, Proceedings
Vinduet   Vinduet (Oslo)
ViR   Viaţa Românească (Bucharest)
VlG   De Vlaamse Gids (Brussels)
VLit Voprosy Literatury (Moscow)
VLU   Vestnik Leningradskogo U. Ser. Istorii, Jazyka i Literatury
VMHB   Virginia Magazine of History and Biography
VN   Victorian Newsletter
Vol Volunta (Rome)
VQR   Virginia Quarterly Review
VS   Victorian Studies (Indiana University)
VWQ   Virginia Woolf Quarterly

WAL   Western American Literature
WascR   Wascana Review (Regina, Sask.)
WB   Weimarer Beiträge (E. Berlin)
WC   Widening Circle
WCR   West Coast Review

WCW N   William Carlos Williams Newsletter
WestWR   Western World Review
WF   Western Folklore
WGCR   West Georgia College Review
WhitN   Whittier Newsletter
WHQ   Western Historical Quarterly
WHR   Western Humanities Review
WiOr   Windless Orchard
WLWE   World Literature Written in English
WJGC   Waseda Journal of General Science (Tokyo)
Wk   Weekly
WLB   Wilson Library Bulletin
WMH   Wisconsin Magazine of History
WMQ   William and Mary Quarterly
WN   A Wake Newsletter
WPHM   Western Pennsylvania Historical Magazine
WPQ   Western Political Quarterly
WR   Western Review
WS   Women's Studies
WSCL   Wisconsin Studies in Contemporary Literature
WSL   Wisconsin Studies in Literature
WSN   Wallace Stevens Newsletter
WSp   Western Speech
WSt   Word Study
WVH   West Virginia History
WVUPP   West Virginia University Philological Papers
WW   Wirkendes Wort (Duesseldorf)
WWB   Walt Whitman Birthplace Bulletin
WWk   World's Work
WWN   Walt Whitman Newsletter
WWR   Walt Whitman Review
WZPHP   Wissenschaftliche Zeitschrift der Pädagogischen Hochschule Potsdam. Gesellschaft- u. Sprachwissenschaftliche Reihe.
WZUB   Wissenschaftliche Zeitschrift der Humboldt-Universität zu Berlin. Gesellschafts- u. Sprachwissenschaftliche Reihe.

XUS   Xavier University Studies
Yb   yearbook
YCGL   Yearbook of Comparative and General Literature
YES   Yearbook of English Studies

YLM   Yale Literary Magazine
YM   Yankee Magazine
YN   Yukon News
YR   Yale Review
YSE   Yale Studies in English
YT   Y Traethodydd (Caernarvon)
Y/T   Yale/Theatre
YULG   Yale University Library Gazette

ZAA   Aeitschrift für Anglistik und

Americkanistik (East Berlin)
ZDP   Zeitschrift für Deutsche Philologie
   (Berlin-Bielefeld-München)
ZFE   Zeitschrift für franzosischen und
   englischen Unterricht (Berlin)
Žovten'   Žovten' : Literaturno-xudožnij
   Žurnal (Ukraine)
ZRL   Zagadnienia Rodzajów Literackich
   (Lody)
Zvezda   Zvezda (Moscow, Leningrad)

Articles on American Literature, 1968–1975

American Authors

Abbey, Edward. Baker, J.F. "EA." *PW*, 208: 6-7 (8 S 75).

Pilkington, Tom. "EA: Western Philosopher, or How to Be a 'Happy Hopi Hippie.'" *WAL*, 9: 17-31 (My 74).

Powell, L.C. "A Singular Ranger." *Westways*, 66: 32-5, 64-5 (Mr 74).

Standiford, Les. "Desert Places: An Exchange with EA." *WHR*, 24: 395-8 (Au 70).

Wylder, D.E. "EA and the 'Power Elite.'" *WR*, 6: 18-22 (Wi 69).

Abbott, Jacob. Boles, J.B. "JA and the 'Rollo' Books: New England Culture for Children." *JPC*, 6: 507-28 (Wi 72).

Brown, A.C. *"Rollo on the Atlantic."* *AmNep*, 26: 81-95 (Ap 66).

Abrahams, Peter. Ogunghesan, Kolawole. "The Political Novels of PA." *Phylon*, 34: 419-32 (1973).

Ackerson, Duane. Ackerson, Duane. "What about Poetry." *PrS*, 46: 76-7 (Sp 72).

Adamic, Louis. Christian, H.A. "'What Else Have You in Mind?': LA and H.L. Mencken." *Mencken*, 47: 1-12 (Fa 73).

Gottesmann, Ronald. "LA and Upton Sinclair: The Record of a Friendship." *AN*, 1: 41-65 (1968).

Adams, Andy. Molen, D.H. "AA: Classic Novelist of the Western Cattle Drive." *Montana: Mag West Hist*, 19: 24-35 (Ja 69).

Quissell, Barbara. "AA and the Real West." *WAL*, 7: 211-9 (1972).

Adams, Brooks. Clark, M.D. "Martial and Imaginative Values: The Great Appeal of BA's *Man of Fear*." *MASJ*, 11: 54-64 (1970).

Friedlaender, Marc. "BA *en Famille*." *PMHS*, 80: 77-93 (1969).

Harris, W.S. "The BA I Knew." *PMHS*, 80: 94-113 (1969).

Adams, Charles Francis. Harbert, E.N. "CFA (1807-86): A Forgotten Family Man of Letters." *JAmSt*, 6: 249-65 (D 72).

Stark, Cruce. "The Development of a Historical Stance: The Civil War Correspondence of Henry and CFA, Jr." *Clio*, 4: 383-97 (Je 75).

Adams, Francis. Jones, Edgar. "FA, 1862-1893: A Forgotten Child of His Age." *E&S*, 20: 76-103 (1967).

Adams, Henry. Aaron, Daniel. "HA: The Public and Private View." *HudR*, 5: 608-14 (Wi 53).

Auchincloss, Louis. "In Search of Innocence: HA and John La Farge in the South Seas." *AH*, 21: 28-33 (Je 70).

———. "'Never Leave Me, Never Leave Me.'" *AH*, 21: 20-2, 69-70 (F 70).

Barber, D.S. "HA's *Esther*: The Nature of Individuality and Immortality." *NEQ*, 44: 227-40 (1972).

Bequette, M.K. "A, La Farge, St. Gaudens, and *Grief*." *ForumH*, 12: 3-7 (#3 75).

Blackmur, R.P. "The Failure of HA." *H&H*, 4: 440-6 (Ap-Je 31).

———. "The Virgin and the Dynamo." *MagA*, 45: 147-53 (Ap 52).

Buttenhuis, Peter. "Exiles at Home: HA and Henry James." *ES* (Canada), 1: 74-85 (1975).

Chazeaux, Jean, and Evelyn Chazeaux. "Lettres de HA: Tahiti, 1891." *RDM*, 1 S 68, pp. 85-100.

Cox, Harvey. "The Virgin and the Dynamo: An Essay on the Symbolism of Technology." *SJIS*, 54: 125-46 (1971).

Crowley, J.W. "The Suicide of the Artist: HA's *Life of George Cabot Lodge*." *NEQ*, 46: 189-204 (Je 73).

Donoghue, Denis. "The American Style of Failure." *SR*, 82: 407-32 (1974).

Eppard, P.B. "Frances Snow Compton Exposed: William Roscoe Thayer on HA as a Novelist." *RALS*, 5: 81-94 (Sp 75).

Friedlaender, Marc. "Henry Hobson Richardson, HA, and John Hay." *PMHS*, 81: 137-66 (1970).

Goto, Shoji. "HA to Democracy to Europe." *EigoS*, 116: 639-41, 711-3 (1970).

Gross, Harvey. "HA's Broken Neck." *CentR*, 12: 169-80 (Sp 68).

Hamill, P.J. "The Future as Virgin: A Latter-day Look at the Dynamo and the Virgin of HA." *MLS*, 3: 8-12 (Sp 73).

Harbert, E.N. *"The Education of Henry Adams*: The Confessional Mode as Heuristic Experiment." *JNarT*, 4: 3-18 (Ja 74).

————. "HA's New England View: A Regional Angle of Vision?" *TSE*, 16: 107-34 (1968).

*Hayne, Barrie, and Katherine Morrison. "HA." *ALR*, 8: 180-8 (1975).

Hoffmann, Kurt. "HA: Porträt eines konservativen Anarchisten." *Merkur*, 20: 418-30 (1966).

Karita, Motoshi. "HA in Japan." *SELit*, nv: 133-53 (1962).

Kay, C.M. "HA Looks at Contemporary English Poets: A Survey of the Letters of HA." *MarkR*, 2: 112-4 (My 71).

Kazin, Alfred. "Impressionist of Power." *NYRB*, 3: 6-7 (14 Ja 65).

Kegel, P.L. "HA and Mark Twain: Two Views of Medievalism." *MTJ*, 15: 11-21 (Wi 70-71).

Kunkel, F.L. "Two Superflous Men: HA and Albert Jay Nock." *Greyfriar*, 12: 12-28 (1971).

Levenson, J.C. "HA and the Art of Politics." *SoR*, 4: 50-8 (Wi 68).

Madison, C.H. "Gleanings from the Henry Holt Files." *PULC*, 27: np (Wi 66).

Martin, J.S. "HA on War: The Transformation of History into Metaphor." *ArQ*, 24: 325-41 (Wi 68).

Meldrum, R.M. "The Epistolary Concerns of HA." *RSW* 37: 227-34 (S 69).

Miller, Ross. "Autobiography as Fact and Fiction: Franklin, A, Malcolm X." *CentR*, 16: 221-32 (Su 72).

————. "HA: Making It Over Again." *CentR*, 18: 288-305 (Su 74).

Montiero, George. "The Education of Ernest Hemingway." *JAmSt*, 8: 91-101 (Ap 74).

Munford, H.M. "An Annotated Copy of *The Education of Henry Adams.*" *PMS*, 85: 107-14 (1973).

————. "HA: The Limitations of Science." *SoR*, 4: 59-71 (Wi 68).

————. "Thayer, Ford, Goodspeed's, and Middlebury: A Missing Copy of *The Education of HA* Found." *PMHS*, 83: 148-53 (1974).

Raymond, John. "HA and the American Scene." *HistT*, 13: 304-9 (My 63).

Richardson, R.D. "McLuhan, Emerson, and HA." *WHR*, 22: 235-42 (Su 68).

Rodnon, Stewart. "HA and Ralph Ellison: Transcending Tragedy." *StH*, 3: 1-6 (#2 73).

Rogat, Yosal. "Mr. Justice Holmes: Some Modern Views." *UCLR*, 31: 213-56 (Wi 64).

Rule, H.B. "HA's Satire on Human Intelligence: Its Method and Purpose." *CentR*, 15: 43-44 (Fa 71).

Scheick, W.J. "Symbolism in *The Education of HA.*" *ArQ*, 24: 350-60 (Wi 68).

Schinto, Jeanne. "The Autobiographies of Mark Twain and HA: Life Studies in Despair." *MTJ*, 17: 5-7 (Su 75).

Schmitz, Neil. "The Difficult Art of American Political Fiction: HA's *Democracy* as Tragical Satire." *WHR*, 25: 147-62 (Sp 71).

Shaw, Peter. "The Success of HA." *YR* 59: 71-8 (Au 69).

Sklar, J.N. "The Education of HA." *Daedalus*, 103: 59-66 (1974).

Sklar, Robert. "HA and Democratic Soceity." *KAL*, 14: 30-3 (1972).

Smith, W.A. "HA, Alexander Hamilton, and the American People as a 'Great Beast.'" *NEQ*, 48: 216-30 (Je 75).

Spangler, G.M. "*The Education of HA* as a Source for 'The Love Song of J. Alfred Prufrock.'" *N&Q*, 15: 295-6 (Ag 68).

Stark, Cruce. "The Development of a Historical Stance: The Civil War Correspondence of H and Charles Francis Adams, Jr." *Clio*, 4: 383-97 (Je 75).

————. "The Historical Irrelevance of Heroes: HA's Andrew Jackson." *AL*, 46: 170-81 (My 74).

Stoehr, Taylor. "Tone and Voice." *CE*, 30: 150-61 (N 68).

Stout, Cushing. "Personality and Cultural History in the Novel: Two American Examples." *NLH*, 1: 423-37 (Sp 70).

Takuwa, Shinji. "Some Impressions of HA, Hart Crane, E.E. Cummings, and Others." *SELit*, 11: 19-53 (1961).

Tanner, Tony. "Henry James and HA." *TriQ*, 11: 91-108 (Wi 68).

Taylor, G.O. "Of A and Aquarius." *AL*, 46: 68-82 (Mr 74).

Vandersee, Charles. "The Four Menageries of HA." *ArQ*, 24: 293-308 (Wi 68).

————. "The Hamlet in HA." *ShS*, 24: 87-104 (1971).

————. "HA (1838-1918)." *ALR*, 2: 89-120 (Su 69).

————. "HA (1838-1918)." *ALR*, 8: 13-34 (Wi 75).

————. "HA and 1905: Prolegomena to *The Education*." *JAmSt*, 2: 199-224 (10 68).

————. "HA and the *Atlantic*: Pattern for a Career." *PLL*, 7: 351-73 (Fa 71).

————. "HA and the Invisible Negro." *SAQ*, 71: 13-30 (Wi 67).

————. "HA's Education of Martha Cameron: Letters, 1888-1916." *TSLL*, 10: 233-93 (Su 68).

————. "The Mutual Awareness of Mark Twain and HA." *ELN*, 5: 285-92 (Je 68).

Wasser, Henry. "*The Education of HA* Fifty Years After." *MASJ*, 10: 85-7 (Sp 69).

————. "Science and Religion in HA's *Esther*. *MarkR*, 2: 4-6 (1970).

Wilson, L.C. "The Degradation of the Democratic Dogma." *NMQ*, 35: 204-14 (Ag 65).

Wright, Nathalia. "Success Story." *NRep*, 171: 23-4 (14 D 74).

Adams, John. Coit, M.C. "Dearest Friends." *AH*, 19: 9-13,102-6 (O 68).

Evans, W.B. "JA's Opinion of Benjamin Frankin." *PMHB*, 92: 220-38 (Ap 68).

Hay, R.P. "The Glorious Departure of the American Patriarchs: Contemporary Reactions to the Deaths of Jefferson and A." *JSH*, 35: 543-55 (N 69).

Kagle, S.E. "The Diary of JA and the Motive of 'Achievement.'" *HSL*, 3: 93-107 (1971).

Kurtz, S.G. "The Political Science of JA." *WMQ*, 25: 605-13 (O 68).

Martin, Wendy. "Correspondence of J and Abigail A." *WS*, 3: 1-3 (1975).

Adams, John Quincy. Bryan, G.B. "Pilgrim at the Shrine of a Saint: JQA on Shakespeare." *ETJ*, 20: 516-23 (1968).

Harbert, E.N. "JQA and His Diary." *TSE*, 18: 81-93 (1970).

Jaffe, Adrian. "An Exchange of Poems by JQA at Ghent." *AL*, 40: 67-70 (Mr 68).

Kaiser, L.M. "JQA and His Translation of Juvenal 13." *PAPS*, 114: 272-93 (1970).

Lewis, R.G., and W.J. Morris. "JQA's Verse Translation of Jean-Baptise Rousseau's *Ode à la Fortune*." *NEQ*, 44: 444-58 (S 71).

Parsons, L.H. "'A Perpetual Harrow Upon My Feelings': JQA and the American Indian." *NEQ*, 46: 339-79 (S 73).

Rothman, I.N. "Two Juvenalian Satires by JQA." *EAL*, 6: 234-51 (Wi 71-72).

Wasser, Henry. "JQA on the Opening Lines of Milton's *Paradise Lost*." *AL*, 42: 373-5 (N 70).

Adams, Samuel Hopkins. Coren, R.W. "SHA, His Novel, *Revelry*, and the Reputation of Warren G. Harding." *Courier*, 11: 3-10 (1974).

Ade, George. Hasley, Louis. "GA, Realist, Fabulist." *Four Q*, 19: 25-32 (1970).

Kolb, H.H. "GA (1866-1944)." *ALR*, 4: 157-69 (Sp 71).

Salzman, Jack. "Dreiser and A." *AL*, 40: 544-8 (Ja 69).

Adler, Max. (see **Clark, Charles Heber**).

Agee, James. Anon. "The Perpetual Promise of JA." *TLS*, 9 Je 72, pp. 659-60.

Agee, James. "Diary of My Future." *Esquire*, 70: 144ff. (N 68).

———. "Unpublished Poetry and Fiction." *TQ*, 11: 18-55 (Sp 68).

Betts, Leonidas. "The Unfathomably Mysterious' *Let Us Now Praise Famous Men*." *EJ*, 59: 44-7, 51 (Ja 70).

Bornstein, George. "JA." *TLS*, 18 Ag 72, p. 971.

Broughton, George, and P.R. Broughton. "A and Autonomy." *SHR*, 4: 101-11 (Sp 70).

Chesnick, Eugene. "The Plot Against Fiction: *Let Us Now Praise Famous Men*." *SLJ*, 4: 48-67 (Fa 71).

Condon, Judith. "JA in Paperback." *CQ*, 5: 200-7 (Ag 70).

Cooper, Arthur. "Appreciating A." *Nwk*, 73: 86 (7 Ap 69).

Curry, Kenneth. "The Knoxville of JA's *A Death in the Family*." *TSL*, 14: 1-14 (1969).

———. "Notes on the Text of JA's *A Death in the Family*." *PBSA*, 64: 84-98 (1Q 70).

Dietrichson, J.W. "JA's *A Death in the Family*." *AmSS*, 6: 1-20 (1974).

Fitzgerald, Robert. "JA: A Memoir." *KR*, 30: 590-624 (1968).

Freeman, J.A. "A's 'Sunday' Meditation." *CP*, 3: 37-9 (Fa 70).

Howarth, W.L. "Some Principles of Autobiography." *NLH*, 5: 363-81 (Wi 74).

Kramer, V.A. "A and Plans for the Criticism of Popular Culture." *JPC*, 5: 755-66 (Sp 72).

———. "A in the Forties: The Struggle to be a Writer." *TQ*, 11: 9-17 (Sp 68).

———. "A's *Let Us Now Praise Famous Men*: Image of Tenant Life." *MissQ*, 25: 405-17 (Fa 72).

———. "A's Projected Screenplay for Chaplin: Scientists and Tramps." *SHR*, 7: 357-64 (Fa 73).

———. "A's Use of Regional Material in *A Death in the Family*." *Appalachian J*, 1: 72-80 (Ag 72).

———. "The Complete 'Work' Chapter for JA's *Let Us Now Praise Famous Men*." *TQ*, 15: 27-48 (Su 72).

———. "*A Death in the Family* and A's Projected Novel." *Proof*, 3: 139-54 (1973).

———. "JA's Unpublished Manuscript and His Emphasis on Religious Emotion in *The Morning Watch*." *TSL*, 17: 159-64 (1972).

———"The Manuscript and the Text of JA's *A Death in the Family*." 65: 257-66 (3Q 71).

———. "Premonition of Disaster: An Unpublished Section for A's *A Death in the Family*." *Costerus*, ns, 1: 83-93 (1974).

———. "'Religion at Its Deepest Intensity': The Stasis of A's *The Morning Watch*." *Renascence*, 27: 221-30 (1975).

Perry, J.D. "Thematic Counterpoint in *A Death in the Family*: The Function of the Six Extra Scenes." *Novel*, 5: 234-41 (1972).

Pratt, L.R. "Imagining Existence: Form and History in Steinbeck and A." *SoR*, 11: 84-98 (Ja 75).

Ramsey, Roger. "The Double Structure of *The Morning Watch*." *StN*, 4: 494-503 (Fa 72).

Rewak, W.J. "JA's *The Morning Watch*: Through Darkness to Light." *TQ*, 14: 21-37 (Ag 73).

Samway, Patrick. "JA: A Family Man." *Thought*, 47: 40-68 (Sp 72).

Shepherd, Allen. "'A Sort of Monstrous Grinding Beauty': Reflections on Character and Theme in JA's *A Death in the Family*." *IEngYb*, 14: 17-24 (Fa 69).

Sosnoski, J.J. "Craft and Intention in JA's *A Death in the Family*." *J GenEd*, 20: 170-83 (O 68).

———. "A Significant Failure." *JGE* 26: 69-76 (1974).

Stanford, D.E. "The Poetry of JA." *SoR*, 10: xvi-xix (Ap 74).

West, J.S.W. "JA's Early Tribute to Tender Is the Night." *FHA*, 1970, pp. #226-7.

Aiken, Conrad. Brown, C.S. "The Achievement of CA." *GaR*, 27: 477-88 (Wi 73).

Carlile, R.E. "*Great Circle*: CA's Musico-Literary Technique." *GaR*, 22: 27-36 (Sp 68).

Costa, R.H. "The Lowry/A Symbiosis." *Nation*, 204: 823-6 (26 Je 67).

———. "CA: The Wages of Neglect." *FicI*, 2-3: 76-80 (Sp-Fa 74).

Cowley, Malcolm. "CA: From Savannah to Emerson." *SoR*, 11: 245-59 (Ap 75).

Graham, Ballew. "'Silent Snow, Secret Snow': The Short Story as Poem." *EJ*, 57: 693-95 (My 68).

Handa, Carolyn. "'Impulse': Calculated Artistry in CA." *SSF*, 12: 375-80 (Fa 75).

Holloway, John. "CA, Folk-Poet." *ArtInt*, 15: 80-7 (20 O 71).

Lawrence, A.A. "228 Habersham Street." *GaR*, 22: 317-34 (Fa 68).

McMichael, C.T., and T.R. Spivey. "'Chaos—hurray!—is come agains': Heroism in James Joyce and CA." *SLitI*, 3: 65-8 (1970).

Robillard, Douglas. "CA's Preludes and the Modern Consciousness." *EAS*, 3: 5-18 (My 74).

Ruffini, Rosalia. "Due lettera di CA." *SA*, 14: 451-54 (1968).

Sanders, F.K. "A Chronology of Awarenesses: A Poet's Vision." *SR*, 81: 172-84 (Wi 73).

Spivey, T.R. "Archetypal Symbols in the Major Poetry of T.S. Eliot and CA." *Int J Symbology*, 2: 16-26 (1971).

———. "CA: Resident of Savannah." *SoR*, 8: 792-804 (O 72).

———. "CA's 'Ushant': Record of a Contemporary Poet's Quest for Self-Knowledge." *SAB*, 36: 21 8 (N 71).

Tabachnick, S.E. "The Great Circle Voyage of CA's *Mr. Arcularis*." *AL*, 45: 590-607 (Ja 74).

Waterman, A.E. "CA as Critic: The Consistent View." *MissQ*, 24: 91-110 (Sp 71).

Waterman, Arthur. "The Evolution of Consciousness: CA's Novels and *Ushant*." *Critique*, 15: 67-82 (1973).

Whitaker, T.R. "Repeating Is What I Am Loving." *Parnassus*, 1: 59-68 (Fa-Wi 72).

Albee, Edward. Adelugba, Dapo. "Theatre Critique: Faux Pas at Ibandan University Arts Theatre." *IBadan*, 26: 81-2 (1969).

Adler, T.F. "A's *Who's Afraid of Virginia Woolf?*: A Long Night's Journey into Day." *ETJ*, 25: 66-70 (1973).

Agnihotri, S.M. "Child-Symbol and Imagery in EA's *Who's Afraid of Virginia Woolf?*" *PURBA*, 3: 107-11 (O 72).

Bachman, Ch.R. "A's *A Delicate Balance*: Parable as Nightmare." *RLV*, 38: 619-30 (N-D 72).

Bauzyte, Galina. "Iliuzijos ir tikroves knofliktas Edvardo Olbio dramaturgijoje." *Literatura*, 15: 79-94 (1973).

Bierhaus, E.G. "Strangers in a Room: *A Delicate Balance* Revisited." *MD*, 17: 199-206 (Je 74).

Bigsby, C.W. "EA's Georgia Ballad." *TCL*, 13: 229-36 (Ja 68).

———. "The Strategy of Madness: An Analysis of EA's *A Delicate Balance*." *ConL*, 9: 223-35 (Sp 68).

Brown, D.R. "A's Targets." *SNL*, 6: 46-52 (1969).

Brown, Terence. "Harmonia Discord and Stochastic Process: EA's *A Delicate Balance*." *Re: A&L*, 3: 54-69 (Sp 70).

Byars, J.A. "*Taming of the Shrew* and *Who's Afraid of Virginia Woolf?*" *CimR*, 21: 41-8 (1972).

Campbell, M.E. "The Statement of EA's *Tiny Alice*." *PLL*, 4: 85-100 (Wi 68).

———. "The Tempters in A's *Tiny Alice*." *MD*, 13: 22-33 (My 70).

Capellán Gonzalo, Angel. "A: Una década." *PrA*, 116: 67-74 (1970).

Carr, D.R. "St. George and the Snapdragons: The Influence of Unamuno on *Who's Afraid of Virginia Woolf?*" *ArQ*, 29: 5-13 (1973).

Chamberlain, Lowell. "Pismo ot Nyu York: Novi piesi nastenite v Broduey." *Plamuk*, 10: 87 (1968).

Coe, R.M. "Beyond Absurdity: A's Awareness of Audience in *Tiny Alice*." *MD*, 18: 371-84 (S 75).

Cohn, Ruby. "A's Box and Ours." *MD*, 14: 137-43 (S 71).

Cole, Douglas. "A's *Virginia Woolf* and Steele's *Tatler*." *AL*, 40: 81-2 (Mr 68).

Curry, R.H., and Michael Porte. "The Surprising Unconscious of EA." *DramS*, 7: 59-68 (Wi 68-69).

Davison, R.A. "EA's Tiny Alice: A Note of Re-examination." *MD*, 11: 54-60 (My 68).

Dollard, John. "The Hidden Meaning of *Who's Afraid . . .?*" *ConnR*, 7: 24-48 (O 73).

Dozier, Richard. "Adultery and Disappointment in *Who's Afraid of Virginia Woolf*?" *MD*, 11: 432-6 (F 69).

Duplessis, R.B. "In the Bosom of the Family: Evasions in EA." *Ranam*, 5: 85-96 (Su 72).

Elizalde, I.S.J. "Un teatro de denuncia y de sexo." *Arbor*, 304: 67-74 (1971).

Falk, E.H. "*No Exit* and *Who's Afraid of Virginia Woolf*: A Thematic Comparison." *SP*, 67: 406-17 (1970).

Fischer, G.K. "EA and Virginia Woolf." *DR*, 49: 196-207 (Su 69).

Flanagan, William. "The Art of the Theater IV." *PaR*, 10: 93-121 (Fa 66).

Force, W.M. "The *What* Story? Or, Who's at the Zoo?" *Costerus*, 2: 71-82 (1972).

Haas, Rudolf. "Wer hat Angst vor EA? Gedanken zum modernen amerikanischer Drama." *Univ*, 25: 347-62 (1970).

Hamblen, A.A. "EA . . . And the Fear of Virginia Woolf." *Trace*, 68: 198-203 (#2 68).

Hatanaka, Takami. "On 'It will be better' in *Who's Afraid of Virginia Woolf?*" *ESELL*, 56: 59-74 (1970).

Hazard, F.E. "The Major Theme in *Who's Afraid of Virginia Woolf*?" *CEA*, 31: 10-1 (D 68).

Hewes, Henry. "Death Prattle." *SatR*, 54: 54 (17 Ap 71).

Hinds, C.M. "A's The American Dream." *Expl*, 30: 17 (1971).

Hogel, Rolf. "EA im Englischunterricht des Sekundarberichs 11: Ein Unterrichtsversuch in einer gymnasialen 13. Klasse." *NS*, 22: 527-34 (1973).

Holtan, O.I. "*Who's Afraid of Virginia Woolf* ? and the Patterns of History." *ETJ*, 25: 46-52 (1973).

Hopkins, Anthony. "Conventional A: *Box* and *Chairman Mao*." *MD*, 16: 141-8 (S 73).

Hopper, S.R. "How People Live without Gods: A's *Tiny Alice*." *APR*, 2: 35-8 (Mr-Ap 73).

Hubner, Paul. "Prekäre Gleichgewichte: A, Hofmannsthal, und Camus." *WW*, 19: 28-34 (1969).

Jacobson, Irving. "The Child as Guilty Witness." *L&P*, 24: 12-23 (1974).

Johnson, C.B. "In Defense of A." *EJ*, 57: 21-3, 29 (Ja 68).

Johnson, M.J. "Note on a Possible Source for *Who's Afraid of Virginia Woolf* ?" *Radford R*, 21: 231-3 (1967).

Kilker, M.J. "Children and Childishness in the Plays of EA." *Players*, 46: 252-6 (1971).

Kingsley, Lawrence. "Reality and Illusion: Continuity of a Theme in A." *ETJ*, 25: 71-8 (1973).

Kishi, Tetsuo. "Coward to A." *EigoS*, 114: 308-9 (1968).

*Kolin, P.C. "A Classified EA Checklist." *Serif* 6: 16-32 (Sp 69).

*———. "A Supplementary EA Checklist." *Serif*, 10: 28-39 (Sp 73).

———. "Two Early Poems by EA." *RALS*, 5: 95-97 (Sp 75).

LaFontaine, Barbara. "Triple Threat On, Off, and Off-Of Broadway." *NYTMS*, 25 F 68, pp. 36-46.

Lahr, John. "The Adaptable Mr. A." *EvR*, 12: 37-9, 82-7 (My 68).

Lee, A.R. "Illusion and Betrayal: EA's Theatre." *Studies*, 59: 53-67 (Sp 70).

Levine, Mordecai. "A's *Liebestod*." *CLAJ*, 10: 252-5 (Mr 67).

Levy, Maurice. "A: Un théâtre qui fai peur." *Caliban*, 8: 151-64 (1971).

Lucey, W.F. "A's *Tiny Alice*: Truth and Appearance." *Renascence*, 21: 76-80, 110 (Wi 69).

Mandanis, Alice. "Symbol and Substance in *Tiny Alice*." *MD*, 12: 92-8 (My 69).

Marshall, T.F. "EA and the Nowhere Generation." *MexQR*, 3: 39-47 (1968).

Martin, Richard. "One v. One, or Two Against All? A Note on EA's *Who's Afraid of Virginia Woolf*." *NS*, 22: 535-8 (1973).

Meyer, Ruth. "Language: Truth and Illusion in *Who's Afraid of Virginia Woolf*?" *ETJ*, 20: 60-9 (Mr 68).

Milan, M.M. "A's *The Zoo Story*, Alienated Man, and the Nature of Love." *MD*, 16: 55-9 (1973).

Missey, James. "McCullers' Influence on A's *The Zoo Story*." *AN&Q*, 13: 121-3 (Ap 75).

Moore, D.D. "A's *The American Dream*." *Expl*, 30: 44 (1972).

Morsberger, R.E. "The Movie Game in *Who's Afraid of Virginia Woolf*? and *The Boys in the Band*." *Costerus*, 8: 89-100 (1973).

Moses, Robbie. "EA: A Voice in the Wasteland." *ForumH*, 12: 35-40 (#3 75).

Narumi, Hiroshi. "EA no Mondaiten." *EigoS*, 114: 220-1 (1968).

Nilan, M.M. "A's *The Zoo Story*: Alienated Man and the Love of Nature." *MD*, 16: 55-9 (Je 73).

Normand, Jean. "L'homme mystifié: Les héros de Bellow, A, Styron, et Mailer." *EA*, 22: 370-85 (O-D 69).

Norton, Rictor. "Foklore and Myth in *Who's Afraid of Virginia Woolf*?" *Renascence*, 23: 159-67 (Sp 71).

Otten, Terry. "Ibsen and A's Spurious Children." *CompD*, 2: 83-93 (Su 68).

Parsatharathy, R. "Who's Afraid of EA? American Drama of he Sixties." *Quest*, 55: 53-5 (Au 67).

Plett, H.F. "EA." *PNU*, 17: 304-10 (1970).

Post, R.M. "Cognitive Dissonance in the Plays of EA." *QJS*, 5: 54-60 (F 69).

———. "Fear Itself: EA's *A Delicate Balance*." *CLAJ*, 13: 163-71 (D 69).

Quinn, J.P. "Myth and Romance in A's *Who's Afraid of Virginia Woolf*." *ArQ*, 30: 197-204 (Au 74).

Ramsey, Roger. "Jerry's Northerly Madness." *NCLit*, 1: 7-8 (S 71).

Rewald, Alice. "A et l'Avant-Garde." *QL*, 42: 26 (1 Ja 68).

Rissover, Fredric. "Beat Poetry, *The American Dream*, and the Alienation Effect." *SpT*, 20: 36-43 (1971).

Robinson, Brian. "De 'Qui a peur de Virginia Woolf'? à 'Delicate Balance': Le talent d'EA sur le déclin." *RUO*, 43: 270-6 (Ap-Je 73).

Rothenberg, Michael. "*Ha-kol Ba-Gan* Le-Albee; Iyun Hashva'ati." *Bama*, 53-4, 64-72 (1972).

Rule, M.W. "An EA Bibliography." *TCL*, 14: 35-44 (Ap 68).

Scheller, Bernhard. "Die Gestalt ds Farbigen bei Williams, A und Baldwin und ihre szenische Realisierung in DDR-Aufführungen." *ZAA*, 20: 137-57 (1972).

Schwartz, Karl. 'EA's Zoo Story." *NS*, 18: 261-7 (Je 69).

Sharma, R.C. "EA: *The Zoo Story*." *BP*, 10: 27-34 (1968).

Simpson, H.M. "*Tiny Alice*: Limited Affirmation in a Conflict between Theatre and Drama." *Forum* (H), 6: 43-6 (Fa-Wi 68).

Stark, John. "Camping Out: *Tiny Alice* and Susan Sontag." *Players*, 47: 166-9 (Ap-My 72).

Stavrou, C.N. "A in Wonderland." *SWR*, 60: 46-61 (Wi 75).

Sykes, B.A. "A's Beast Fables: *The Zoo Story* and *A Delicate Balance*." *ETJ*, 25: 448-55 (1973).

Szeliski, J.J. von. "A: A Rare *Balance*." *TCL*, 16: 123-30 (1970).

Taylor, C.M. "Coming of Age in New Carthage: A's Grown-up Children." *ETJ*, 25: 53-65 (1973).

Tolpegin, D.D. "The Two-Petaled Flower: A Commentary on EA's Play, *Tiny Alice*." *CimR*, 14: 17-30 (1971).

Vallbona, Rima de. "EA: El arte ye el pueblo." *Indice*, 24: 32-3 (1969).

Vos, Nevlin. "The Process of Dying in the Plays of EA." *ETJ*, 25: 80-5 (1973).

Wallace, R.S. "*The Zoo Story*: A's Attack on Fiction." *MD*, 16: 49-54 (Je 73).

White, J.E. "A's *Tiny Alice*, an Exploration of Paradox." *LWU*, 6: 247-58 (1973).

———. "An Early Play by EA." *AL*, 42: 98-9 (Mr 70).

———. "'Santayanian Finesse' in A's *Tiny Alice*." *NCLit*, 3: 12-3 (N 73).

Willeford, William. "The Mouse in the Model." *MD*, 12: 135-45 (S 69).

Witherington, Paul. "A's Gothic: The Resonances of Cliché." *CompD*, 4: 151-65 (Fa 70).

Woods, L.L. "Isolation and the Barrier of Language in *The Zoo Story*." *RSW*, 36: 224-31 (S 68).

Alcott, Bronson. Biddle, A.W. "B and Chatfield A in Virginia." *ATQ*, 17: 3-9 (Wi 73).

Biddle, A.W. "An Uncollected A Letter." *ATQ*, 13: 36-7 (1972).

Blanding, Thomas. "Paradise Misplaced: BA's Fruitlands." *ConS*, 6: 2-7 (D 71).

Cameron, K.W. "Some A Conversations in 1863." *ATQ*, 17: 25-9, 31 (1973).

———. "Thoreau's *Walden* and A's Vegetarianism." *ATQ*, 2: 27-8 (1969).

Crisman, Grace. "Louisa's Father and B's Daughter." *Scholastic*, 32: 21-2 (5 Mr 38).

Emerson, R.W. "Emerson, A, and the Cogswell Estate." *ESQ*, 51: 9-10 (2 Q 68).

Fleck, R.F. "A Connecticut Yankee in a Tragic Court." *ConnR*, 3: 92-7 (1969).

Francis, Richard. "Circumstances and Salvation: The Ideology of the Fruitlands Utopia." *AQ*, 25: 202-34 (My 73).

Gay, Carol. "The Philosopher and His Daughter: Amos BA and Louisa." *EC*, 2: 181-91 (Fa 75).

Hamblen, A.A. "The Wood Will Come or the Weather." *Yankee*, 36: 95-9, 118-26 (My 72).

Lyons, Nathan. "A and Rudolf Steiner: Educators of the Whole Man." *ESQ*, 57: 12-6 (4Q 69).

Myerson, Joel. "BA's 'Scripture for 1840.'" *ESQ*, 20: 237-59 (4 Q 74).

———. "'In the Transcendental Emporium': BA's 'Orphic Sayings' in the *Dial*." *ELN*, 10: 31-8 (1972).

Perry, Lewis. "Versions of Anarchism in the Anti-slavery Movement." *AQ*, 20: 768-82 (Fa 68).

Rosa, A.F. "A and Montessori." *ConnR*, 3: 98-103 (O 69).

Sanborn, F.B. "BA at Alcott House, England, and Fruitlands, New England (1842-1844)." *ATQ*, 9: 27-51 (1971).

Stoehr, Taylor, "'Eloquence Needs No Constable'—A, Emerson, and Thoreau on the State." *CRAS*, 5: 81-100 (1974).

Strickland, Charles. "A Transcendentalist Father: The Child-Rearing Practices of BA." *PAH*, 3: 5-73 (1969); *Hist Childhood Q*, 1: 4-61 (1973).

White, William. "A and Chapman Revisited." *WWR*, 16: 90-1 (S 70).

Alcott, Louisa May. Anthony, K.S. "The Happiest Years." *NAR*, 241: 297-310 (Je 36).

Blanck, J.N. "A's 'An Old-Fashioned Girl': A Collation." *PW*, 133: 967 (19 F 38).

Canby, H.S. "L in the Laboratory." *SatR*, 17: 12 (12 F 38).

Crisman, Grace. "L's Father and Bronson's Daughter." *Scholastic*, 32: 21-2 (5 Mr 38).

Crompton, Margaret. "*Little Women*: The Making of a Classic." *ConR*, 218: 99-104 (F 71).

Fisher, D.C. "Understanding Aunt L." *Survey Graphic*, 27: 289 (My 38).

Gay, Carol. "The Philosopher and His Daughter: Amos Bronson Alcott and L." *EC*, 2: 181-91 (Fa 75).

Geismar, Maxwell. "Duty's Faithful Child." *Nation*, 146: 216 (19 F 38).

Hamblen, A.A. "LMA and the Racial Question." *UR*, 37: 307-13 (Su 71).

———. "LMA and the 'Revolution' in Education." *JGE*, 22: 81-92 (Jl 70).

Janeway, Elizabeth. "Meg, Jo, Beth, Amy and Louisa." *NYT*, 29 S 68, pp. 42-6.

Moers, Ellen. "Money, the Job, and Little Women." *Commentary* 55: 57-65 (Ja 73).

Payne, A.J. "LMA (1832-88)." *ALR*, 6: 27-43 (Wi 73).

Spacks, P.M. "Taking Care: Some Women Novelists." *Novel*, 6: 36-51 (Fa 72).

Aldrich, Bess Streeter. Meier, A.M. "BSA: A Literary Portrait." *Nebraska Hist*, 50: 67-100 (Sp 69).

Aldrich, T.B. Origo, Iris. "Additions to the Keats Collection." *TLS*, nv: 457-8 (23 Ap 70).

Standley, F.L. "Two Letters of TBA." *AN&Q*, 12: 20-2 (O 73).

Alexander, Charles. Corning, H.M. "CA: Youth of the Oregon Mood." *Oregon Hist Q*, 74: 34-70 (Mr 73).

Alexander, Lloyd. Lane, Elizabeth. "LA's Chronicles of Prydain and the Welsh Tradition." *Orcrist*, 7: 25-8 (1973).

West, R.C. "The Tolkinians: Some Introductory Reflections on Alan Garner, Carol Kendall, and LA." *Orcrist*, 2: 4-15 (1967-8).

Alfred, William. Gowda, H.H.A. "*Hogan's Goat* and American Verse Drama." *LHY*, 8: 35-41 (Ja-Jl 67).

Alger, Horatio. Bales, Jack. "Herbert R. Mayes and HA, Jr.; or the Story of a Unique Literary Hoax." *JPC*, 8: 317-9 (1974).

Coad, B.E. "The A Hero: Humanitarian or Hustler?" *PCCTET*, 37: 21-4 (1972).

Henderson, William. "A Few Words about HA, Jr." *PW*, 23 Ap 73, p. 33.

Lindberg-Seyersted, Brita. "Three Variations of the American Success Story: The Careers of Luke Larken, Lemuel Barker, and Lemuel Pitkin." *ES*, 53: 1-16 (Ap 72).

Scharnhorst, G.F. "The A Problem: The Hoax about H Revealed." *BSUF*, 15: 61-5 (Sp 74).

Schroeder, Fred. "America's First Literary Realist: HA, Junior." *WHR*, 17: 129-37 (Sp 63).

Seelye, John. "Who Was Horatio? The A Myth and American Scholarship." *AQ*, 17: 743-4 (1965).

Walters, T.N. "Twain's Finn and A's Gilman: Picaresque Counter-Directions." *MarkR*, 3: 53-8 (My 72).

Zuckerman, Michael. "The Nursery Tales of HA." *AQ*, 24: 191-209 (My 72).

Algren, Nelson. Bruccoli, M.J. "A Further Note on the *Galena Guide*." *Serif*, 9: 47 (1972).

Keller, D.H. "NA and the *Galena Guide*." *Serif*, 8: 33-4 (Su 71).

Maloff, Saul. "Maverick in American Letters." *NRep*, 170: 23-4 (19 Ja 74).

Robinson, J.A. "NA's Spiritual Victims." *Gypsy Schol*, 3: 3-12 (1975).

Studing, Richard. "A NA Checklist." *TCL*, 19: 27-39 (Ja 73).

Tibbetts, R.A. "NA and the *Galena Guide*: A Further Note." *Serif* 9: 48 (Su 72).

Allen, Ethan. Ditsky, John. "The Yankee Insolence of EA." *CRAS*, 1: 32-8 (Sp 70).

Allen, Henry Wilson. Allen, H.W. "Breaking Ground for a Novel." *Roundup*, 21: 12-3, 15 (S 73).

Falke, Anne. "The Art of Convention: Images of Women in the Modern Western Novels of HWA." *NDQ*, 42: 17-27 (Sp 74).

———. "Clay Fisher of Will Henry? An Author's Choice of Pen Name." *JPC*, 7: 692-700 (Wi 73).

Allen, James Lane. Bottoroff, W.K. "JLA (1849-1925)." *ALR*, 2: 121-4 (Su 69).

Knight, G.C. "How JLA Lost His Popularity." *Letters*, 1: 1-5 (N 27).

———. "When JLA Turned to Realism." *Letters*, 2: 9-15 (N 28).

Allston, Washington. Coburn, Kathleen. "Notes on WA from the Unpublished Notebooks of Samuel Taylor Coleridge." *Gaz des Beaux-Arts*, 19: 249-52 (Ap 44).

Gardner, A.T. "Memorials of an American Romantic." *Metropolitan Museum Art Bul*, 16: 54-9 (O 44).

Hunter, Doreen. "America's First Romantics: Richard Henry Dana, Sr. and WA." *NEQ*, 45: 3-30 (Mr 72).

Kimball, Fiske. "Death on a Pale Horse." *Pennsylvania Museum Bul*, 26: 17 (1930-1); *Gaz des Beaux-Arts*, 7: 403 (Je 32).

Richardson, E.P. "*The Flight of Florimell* and Other Paintings by WA." *Bul Detroit Inst Arts*, 24: 1-5 (1944-45).

Ringe, D.A. "Early American Gothic: Brown, Dana and A." *ATQ*, 19: 3-8 (Su 73).

Welsh, J.R. "An Anglo-American Friendship: A and Coleridge." *JAmSt*, 5: 81-91 (Ap 71).

———. "WA: Cosmopolite and Early Romantic." *GaR*, 21: 491-502 (1967).

Winston, G.P. "WA and the Objecive Correlative." *BuR*, 11: 95-108 (D 62).

Wright, Cuthbert. "The Feast of Belshazzar." *NEQ*, 10: 620-34 (1947).

Wright, Nathalia. "A Source for T.S. Eliot's 'Objective Correlative'?" *AL*, 41: 589-91 (Ja 70).

Ames, Nathaniel. Lang, Hans-Joachim, and Benjamin Lease. "The Authorship of *Symzonia*; The Case for NA." *NEQ*, 48: 241-52 (Je 75).

Ames, William. Gibbs, L.W. "WA's Technometry." *JHI*, 33: 615-24 (1972).

Ammons, A.R. Berry, Wendell. "A Secular Pilgrimage." *HudR*, 23: 401-24 (1970).

Bloom, Harold. "A.R.A: The Breaking of the Vessels." *Salmagundi*, 31-32: 185-203 (1975).

———. "Dark and Radiant Peripheries: Mark Strand and A.R.A." *SoR*, 8: 133-49 (Ja 72).

———. "Emerson and A." *Diacritics*, 3: 45-6 (#4 73).

———. "The New Transcendentalism: The Visionary Strain in Merwin, Ashbery, and A." *ChiR*, 24: 25-43 (1973).

Fogel, D.M. "Response/1." *Diacritics*, 4: 49-53 (1974).

Grossvogel, D.I. "Interview: A.R.A." *Diacritics*, 3: 47-53 (#4 73).

Harmon, William. "'How Does One Come Home': A.R.A's *Tape for the Turn of the Year*." *SLJ*, 7: 3-32 (Sp 75).

Howard, Richard. "Auguries of Experience." *Boun2*, 1: 712-5 (1973).

Jacobsen, Josephine. "The Talk of Giants." *Diacritics*, 3: 34-8 (#4 73).

Kalstone, David. "A's Radiant Toys." *Diacritics*, 3: 12-30 (#4 73).

Lynen, J.R. "A Contemporary Transcendentalist: The Poetry of A.R.A." *QQ*, 81: 111-6 (1974).

Mazzaro, Jerome. "Reconstruction in Art." *Diacritics*, 3: 39-44 (#4 73).

Meredith, William. "I Will Tell You Abot It Because It is Interesting." *Parnassus*, 2: 175-85 (Fa-Wi 73).

Miles, Josephine. "Light, Wind, Motion." *Diacritics*, 3: 21-4 (#4 73).

Morgan, Robert. "The Compound Vision of A.R.A.'s Early Poems." *Epoch*, 22: 343-63 (Sp 73).

Oberg, Arthur. "Frazzling Reality: (A.R.A. Collected Peoms: 1951-71)." *OhR*, 15: 107-10 (1974).

Orr, Linda. "The Cosmic Backyard of A.R.A." *Diacritics*, 3: 3-12 (#4 73).

Parker, P.A. "Configurations of Shape and Flow." *Diacritics*, 3: 25-33 (#4 73).

Sheehan, Donald. "The Silver Sensibility: Five Recent Books of American Poetry." *ConL*, 12: 98-121 (Wi 71).

Stevens, Peter. "'How Does One Come Home.'" *Ontario R*, 3: 92-7 (1975).

Tarbert, D.W. "Contemporary American Pastoral: A Poetic Faith." *EngRec*, 23: 72-83(Wi 72).

Vendler, Helen. "Poetry: A, Berryman, Cummings." *YR*, 62: 412-19 (1973).

Waggoner, H.H. "The Poetry of A.R.A." *Salmagundi*, 22-23: 285-93 (1973).

Zweig, Paul. "The Raw and the Cooked." *PR*, 41: 604-12 (1974).

Anderson, Edward C. Neblett, T.R. "Major ECA and the C.S.S. Fingal." *GHQ*, 52: 132-58 (Je 68).

Anderson, Lee. Basler, R.P. "The Poet As Composer—LA." *SR*, 80: 151-67 (Wi 72).

Anderson, Margaret. Edelstein, J.M. "Exuberance and Ecstasy." *NRep*, 162: 19-22 (13 Je 70).

Flanner, Janet. "A Life on a Cloud." *NY*, 50: 44-67 (3 Je 74).

Parkhurst, Winthrop. "An Open Letter to MA." *Little R*, 6: 31-3 (O 19).

Anderson, Maxwell. Anderson, Maxwell. "Love Letter to a University." *NDQ*, 38: 89-90 (1970).

*Avery, L.G. "Addenda to the MA Bibliography: Monro's *Chapbook*." *PBSA*, 65: 408-11 (4Q 71).

*———. "Addenda to the MA Bibliography: *The Measure*." *PBSA*, 63: 31-6 (1Q 69).

———. "MA and *Both Your Houses*." *NDQ*, 38: 5-24 (Wi 70).

Buchanan, R.J. "A Playwright's Progress." *NDQ*, 38: 60-73 (Wi 1970).

Gilbert, R.L. "Mio Romagna: Λ New View of MA's *Winterset*." *NDQ*, 38: 33-43 (Wi 70).

Hagan, J.P. "Frederick H. Koch and North Dakota: Theatre in the Wilderness." *NDQ*, 38, 75-87 (Wi 1970).

Hershbell, J.K. "The Socrates and Plato of MA." *NDQ*, 38: 45-59 (Wi 1970).

Jackson, E.M. "MA: Poetry and Morality in the American Drama" *ETJ*, 25: 15-33 (1973).

Jones, J.B. "Shakespeare as Myth and Structure in *Winterset*." *ETJ*, 25: 34-45 (1973).

Matlaw, Myron. "Alan Paton's *Cry, the Beloved Country* and MA's/Kurt Weill's *Lost in the Stars*: A Consideration of Genres." *Arcadia*, 10: 263-72 (1975).

Sata, Masanori. "MA no *Winterset*." *EigoS*, 116: 206-8 (1970).

———. "*Superstition* (1824) to *Winterset* (1935): Romeo-Juliet theme kara no kosatsu." *ELLS*, 6: 131-46 (1969).

Sister Mary Norma. "The Many Faces of Medea." *CBul*, 45: 17-20 (D 68).

Tees, A.T. "Legal and Poetic Justice in MA's Plays." *NDQ*, 38: 25-32 (Wi 1970).

———. "MA's Liberated Women." *NDQ*, 42: 53-9 (Sp 74).

———. "*Winterset*: Four Influences on Mio." *MD*, 14: 408-12 (F 71).

Weathers, Winston. "*Winterset*: The Archetypal Stage." *UTMS*, 4: 97-102 (1968).

Anderson, Poul. Miesel, Sandra. "Challenge and Response: PA's View of Man." *RQ*, 4: 80-95 (Ja 70).

————. "No Man Can Escape His Weird." *Orcrist*, 7: 8-12 (1973).

West, Richard. "Medieval Borrowing in the Fiction of PA." *Unicorn*, 2: 16-9 (#5 73).

Anderson, Robert. Adler, T.P. "RA: Playwright of Middle-Aged Loneliness." *BSUF*, 16: 58-64 (Sp 75).

Hewes, Henry, "A Husband's Undoing." *SatR*, 54: 35 (16 O 71).

Anderson, Sherwood. Abcarian, Richard. "Innocence and Experience in *Winesburg*." *UR*, 35: 95-105 (Wi 68).

Alsen, Eberhard. "The Futile Pursuit of Truth in Twain's 'What is Man?' and A's 'The Book of the Grotesque.'" *MTJ*, 17: 12-4 (Wi 74-5).

Anderson, D.B. "SA, Virginia Journalist." *NLB*, 6: 251-62 (Jl 71).

Anderson, D.D. "Emerging Awareness in SA's *Tar*." *Ohioana*, 4: 40-2, 51 (Su 61).

————. "SA and the Coming of the New Deal." *Crit and Culture*, 2: 88-96 (1972).

————. "SA's Idea of the Grotesque." *Ohioana*, 6: 12-3 (Sp 63).

————. SA's Use of the Lincoln Theme." *Lincoln Herald*, 64: 28-32 (Sp 62).

Anderson, Sherwood. "A New Testament." *Little R*, 6: 1-6 (O 19); 19-20 (N 19); 15-7 (Ja 20); 12-6 (Mr 20); 58-61 (Ag 20).

Baker, Carlos. "SA's *Winesburg*: A Reprise." *VQR*, 48: 568-79 (Ag 72).

Baldanza, Frank. "Northern Gothic." *SoR*, 10: 566-82 (1974).

Bennett, J.Q. "Winesburg Revisited." *Serif*, 7: 80-2 (1970).

Binni, Francesco. "Il 'personaggio' di SA." *SA*, 14: 265-87 (1968).

Birney, Earle. "SA: A Memory." *Canadian Forum*, 21: 82-3 (Je 41).

Bishop, J.P. "This Distrust of Idea." *Vanity Fair*, 22: 10-2, 118 (D 21).

Bort, B.D. "*Winesburg, Ohio*: The Escape from Isolation." *MwQ*, 11: 443-56 (Su 70).

Brady, John. "When SA's Mudguards Were Dented." *ABC*, 19: 20-2 (Su 69).

Braumann, Wilfried. "Die Schule SA's." *KuL*, 18: 841-55, 961-75 (1970).

Brossard, Chandler. "SA: A Sweet Singer, 'A Smooth Son of a Bitch.'" *AmMerc* 72: 611-6 (My 51).

Browning, Chris. "Kate Swift: SA's Creative Eros." *TSL*, 13: 141-8 (1968).

Bryan, James. "SA and *The Catcher in the Rye*." *NCLit*, 1: 2-5 (N 71).

Burrow, Trigant. "Psychoanalyic Improvisations and the Personal Equation." *PsyR*, 13: 173-86 (Ap 26).

Church, Ralph. "Sherwood Comes to Town." *FHA*, 1972, pp. 149-56.

Ciancio, Ralph. "'The Sweetness of the Twisted Apples': Unity of Vision in *Winesburg, Ohio*." *PMLA*, 87: 994-1006 (O 72).

Cook, Sylvia. "Gastonia: The Literary Reverberations of the Strike." *SLJ*, 7: 49-66 (Fa 74).

Dickerson, M.J. "SA and Jean Toomer: A Literary Relationship." *SAF*, 1: 163-75 (Ag 73).

Ferres, J.H. "The Nostalgia of *Winesburg, Ohio*." *NLB*, 6: 235-42 (Jl 71).

Friddell, Guy. "SA and His Smyth County Sidekick: Buck Fever." *Cwealth*, 38: 32-6 (N 71).

Frohock, W.F. "SA e l'elegia americana." *SCr*, 3: 286-99 (Je 69).

Gerhard, Josep. "The American Triumph of the Egg: A's 'The Egg' and Fitzgerald's *The Great Gatsby*." *Criticism*, 7: 131-40 (Sp 65).

Gilzen, Alex. "SA, Elyria, and the Escape Hunch." *Serif*, 5: 3-10 (Mr 68).

Groene, Horst. "The American Idia of Success in SA's 'The Egg.'" *NsM*, 28: 162-6 (1975).

Guerin, W.L. "'Death in the Woods': SA's 'Cold Pastoral.'" *CEA*, 30: 4-5 (My 68).

Hardwick, Elizabeth. "A, Millay, and Crane in Their Letters." *PR*, 20: 690-6 (D 53).

Helbling, Mark. "SA and Jean Toomer." *NALF*, 9: 35-39 (Su 75).

Hoffman, F.J. "SA: A Groping, Artistic, Sincere Personality." *WR*, 18: 159-62 (Wi 54).

Johnson, Christiane "Langage et point de vue dans la nouvelle de SA: 'The Strength of God.'" *EA*, 26: 187-94 (1973).

*Johnson, R.C. "Addenda to Sheehy and Lohf's Bibliography of SA." *PBSA*, 66: 61 (1Q 72).
*Johnson, R.C., and G.T. Tanselle. "Addenda to Bibliographies of SA: Haldeman-Julius Little Blue Books." *PBSA*, 66: 66 (1Q 72).
Kinnison, William. "Notes on Six Wittenberg Authors." *Ohioana*, 15: 136-41 (1972).
Kirchwey, Freda. "SA." *Nation*, 152: 313-4 (22 Mr 41).
Landor, M. "Die Schule SA." *KuL*, 18: 841-55, 961-75 (1970).
———. "M. Gor'kij o SA." *VLit*, 17: 176-88 (1973).
———. "Skola Servuda Andersona." *VLit*, 13: 141-72 (1969).
Lorch, T.M. "The Choreographic Structure of *Winesburg, Ohio*." *CLAJ*, 12: 56-65 (S 68).
Love, G.A. "*Winesburg, Ohio* and the Rhetric of Silence." *AL*, 40: 38-57 (Mr 68).
Luedtke, L.S. "SA, Thomas Hardy, and 'Tandy.'" *MFS*, 20: 531-40 (Wi 74-5).
MacDonald, Dwight. "SA." *YLM*, 93: 209-43 (Jl 28).
McDonald, W.R. "*Winesburg, Ohio*: Tales of Isolation." *UR*, 35: 237-40 (Sp 69).
McHaney, T.L. "A, Hemingway, and Faulkner's *The Wild Palms*." *PMLA*, 87: 465-74 (Mr 72).
Marriner, G.L. "SA: The Myth of the Artist." *TQ*, 14: 105-16 (1971).
Marussig, Antonio. "*Winesburg, Ohio*: A New Way of Writing Short Stories." *IH*, 3: 83-5 (1967).
Mellard, J.M. "Narrative Forms in *Winesburg, Ohio*." *PMLA*, 83: 1304-12 (O 68).
Mencken, H.L. "America's Most Distinctive Novelist: SA." *Vanity Fair*, 27: 88 (D 26).
Miller, W.V. "Earth-Mothers, Succubi, and Other Ectoplasmic Spirits: The Women in SA's Short Stories." *Midamerica*, 1: 64-81 (1974).
———. "In Defense of Mountaineers: SA's Hill Stories." *BSUF*, 15: 51-8 (Sp 74).
Monigle, Martha. "SA in Boulder." *MQR*, 9: 55-6 (1970).
Ohashi, Kichinosuke. "SA to 3 Nin no Nihonjin." *EigoS*, 121: 156-7, 199-200, 261-2, 361-3, 395-7 (1975).
Pawlowski, R.S. "The Process of Observation: *Winesburg, Ohio* and *The Golden Apples*." *UR*, 37: 292-8 (Su 71).
Pearson, N.H. "A and the New Puritanism." *NLB*, 11: 52-63 (D 48).
Popescu, Petru. "SA: Winsburg in Ohio." *RoLit*, 16 Oct: 23 (1969).
Rideout, W.B. "'The Tale of Perfect Balance': SA's 'The Untold Lie.'" *NLB*, 6: 243-50 (Jl 71).
Robinson, Eleanor. "A Study of 'Death in the Woods.'" *CEA*, 30: 6 (Ja 68).
Rogers, D.G. "Development of the Artist in *Winesburg, Ohio*." *STC*, 10: 91-9 (Fa 72).
Samsell, R.L. "Paris Days with Ralph Chruch." *FHA*, 1973, pp. 145-7.
Satyanarayana, M.R. "From Winesburg to Salinas Valley in Search of Love." *OJES*, 8: 19-28 (1971).
Scheick, W.J. "Compulsion Toward Repetition: SA's 'Death in the Woods.'" *SSF*, 11: 141-6 (Sp 74).
Smith, A.H. "Part of the Problem: Student Responses to SA's 'I Want to Known Why?'" *NALF*, 7: 28-31 (1973).
Somers, P.P. "A's Twisted Apples and Hemingway's Crips." *Midamerica*, 1974: 82-97 (1974).
———. "The Mark of SA on Hemingway: A Look at the Texts." *SAQ*, 73: 487-503 (Au 74).
———. "SA Introduces His Friend Ernest Hemingway." *LGJ*, 3: 24-6 (#3 75).
Spencer, B.T. "SA: American Mythopoeist." *AL*, 41: 1-18 (Mr 69).
Stein, Gertrude. "Idem the Same—A Valentine to SA." *Little R*, 9: 5-9 (Sp 23).
Stewart, M.A. "Scepticism and Belief in Chekhov and A." *SSF*, 9: 29-40 (1972).
Stouck, David. "*Winesburg, Ohio* and the Failure of Art." *TCL*, 15: 145-51 (O 69).
Sutton, W.A. "Exit to Elsinore." *BSM*, 7: 1-45 (1967).

Tanselle, G.T. "A Annotated by Brooks." *N&Q*, 15: 60-1 (1968).

―――. "The Case Western Reserve Edition of SA." *Proof*, 5: 183-209 (1975).

Taylor, W.D. "Kit Brandon: A Reidentification." *NLB*, 6: 263-7 (Jl 71).

―――. "SA." *VaCal*, 19: 42-7 (Sp 70).

Turner, Darwin. "An Intersection of Paths: Correspondence between Jean Toomer and SA." *CLAJ*, 17: 455-67 (Je 74).

West, M.D. "SA's Triumph: 'The Egg.'" *AQ*, 20: 675-93 (Wi 68).

White, R.L. "A's First Published Story." *Readers and Writers*, 1: 32-8) Ap 68).

*―――. "A Checklist of SA Studies, 1959-1969." *NLB*, 6: 288-302 (Jl 71).

―――. "Hemingway's Private Explanation of *The Torrents of Spring*." *MFS*, 13: 261-3 (Su 67).

―――. "A SA Checklist." *Winesburg Eagle*, 1: 4-5 (1975).

Wright, D.M. "A Mid-western Ad Man Remembers: SA, Advertising Man." *Advertising & Selling*, 28: 35, 68 (17 D 36).

Wylder, D.E. "*The Torrents of Spring*." *SDR*, 5: 23-35 (Wi 67-68).

Angelou, Maya. Kent, G.E. "MA's *I Know Why the Caged Bird Sings* and Black Autobiographical Tradition." *KanQ*, 7: 72-8 (#3 75).

Smith, S.A. "The Song of a Caged Bird: MA's Quest After Self-Acceptance," *SHR*, 7: 365-75 (Fa 73).

Washington, M.H. "Black Women Image Makers." *BlackW*, 23: 10-18 (1974).

Antin, David. Abbott, Keith, et al. "Special Issue." *Vort*, 7: 3-91 (1975).

Alpert, Barry. "Post-Modern Oral Poetry." *Boundary*, 3: 655-81 (1975).

Antin, David. "A Correspondence." *Boundary*, 3: 595-650 (1975).

Antoninus, Brother. See *Everson, William.*

Appleton, Elizabeth Haven. Williams, Cratis. "Kentucky's First Mountain Story." *KFR*, 17: 1-4 (Ja-Mr 71).

Arensburg, Walter Conrad. Fields, Kenneth. "Past Masters: WCA and Donald Evans." *SoR*, 6: 317-39 (Ap 70).

Arent, Arthur. Isaac, Dan. "AA, *Ethiopia*: The First 'Living Newspaper.'" *ETJ*, 20: 15-31 (1968).

Argall, Samuel. Barbour, P.L. "A Possible Clue to SA's Pre-Jamestown Activities." *WMQ*, 29: 301-6 (1972).

Armstrong, Anne W. Schrock, E.F. "An Examination of the Dialect in *This Day and Time*." *TFSB*, 37: 31-9 (Je 71).

Armstrong, Charlotte. Waldron, Ann. "CA." *JPC*, 5: 435-45 (Fa 71).

Arnow, Harriette. Oates, J.C. "An American Tragedy." *NYT*, 24 Ja 71, pp. 12-6.

Ashberry, John. Bloom, Harold. "JA: The Charity of the Hard Moments." *Salmagundi*, 22-23: 103-31 (1973).

Bloom, Harold. "The New Transcendentalism: The Visionary Strain in Merwin, A, and Ammons." *ChiR*, 24: 25-43 (1973).

Dale, Peter. "Three Poets: Can Belief and Form Come in Bags of Tricks?" *SatR*, 55: 57-8 (8 Jl 72).

Koethe, John. "A's Meditations." *Parnassus*, 1: 89-93 (1972).

Osti, Louis. "The Craft of JA." *Confr*, 9: 84-95 (Fa 74).

Shapiro, David. "Urgent Masks: An Introduction to JA's Poetry." *Field*, 5: 32-45 (Fa 71).

Asimov, Isaac. Asimov, Isaac. "Academe and IA." *MagFSF*, nv: 133-43 (My 72).

Reilly, Lemuel. "An Interview with IA." *Delaware Lit R*, 3: 28-34 (1974).

Wages, J.D. "IA's Debt to Edgar Allan Poe." *PoeS*, 6: 29 (Je 73).

Atherton, Gertrude. Anon. "For Woman Suffrage: Mrs. A's New Novel, a Sketch of the Modernized Woman." *NYT*, 21 Ap 12; p. 239.

————. "GA's War Work." *Lit Dig*, 54: 1703 (2 Je 17).

————. "Mrs. A's Feminism." *Bkm*, 45: 643-4 (Ag 17).

Armes, Ethel. "Leaves from a Reporter's Notebook. A Twenty-Minute Study of GA." *Nat Mag*, 21: 407 (Ja 05).

Egan, M.F. "Mrs. A's Modern Cave Woman." *NYT*, 30 Ja 21; p. 2.

Huges, Rupert. "Golden Gate Country." *Miss Hist R*, 32: 446-7 (21 Ja 46).

Irwin, Will. "Mrs. A's Ancestors." *Bkm*, 26: 528-30 (Ja 08).

Mencken, H.L. "The Gland School." *AmMerc*, 6: 249-51 (N 25).

Richey, Elinor. "The Flappers Were Her Daughters: The Liberated, Literary World of GA." *AmWest*, 11: 4-10, 603 (Ju 74).

Van Domelen, J.E. "GA Inscriptions." *AN&Q*, 10: 7 (1971).

Van Vechten, Carl. "Some 'Literary Ladies' I Have Known." *YULG*, 26: 90-116 (Ja 52).

Weir, Sybil. "GA: The Limits of Feminism in the 1890's." *San Jose Stud*, 1: 24-31 (F 75).

Atkins, Russell. Finger, Hans. "Zwei Beispiele moderner amerikanischer Negerlyrik: Langston Hughes, 'Mother to Son' und RA, 'Poem.'" *LWU*, 2: 38-46 (1969).

Atkinson, Florence. Sharkey, E.G. "The Diary of FA, 1883-1886." *JRUL*, 34: 23-7 (D 70).

Attaway, William. Felgar, Robert. "WA's Unaccommodated Protagonists." *SBL*, 4: 1-3 (Sp 73).

Klotman, P.R. "An Examination of Whiteness in *Blood on the Forge*." *CLAJ*, 15: 459-64 (Je 72).

Simms, L.M. "In the Shadow of Richard Wright." *NMW*, 8: 13-8 (1975).

Vaughan, P.H. "From Pastoralism to Industrial Antipathy in WA's *Blood on the Forge*." *Phylon*, 36: 422-5 (D 75).

Atwood, Margaret. Schaeffer, Susan. "'It Is Time That Separates Us': MA's *Surfacing*." *CentR*, 18: 319-37 (Fa 74).

Aubert, Alvin. Rowell, C.H. "An Interview with AA: The Black Poet in the Afternoon." *BlackW*, 22: 34-8, 72 (1973).

Auchincloss, Louis. Balliett, Whitney. "A Model Novel." *NY*, 40: 76-8 (1 Ag 64).

Long, R.E. "The Image of Gatsby in the Fiction of LA and C.D. Bryan." *FHA*, 1972, pp. 325-8.

Scheideman, J.W. "H.L. Mencken and Willa Cather Compared in LA's *Pioneers and Caretakers*." *Mencken*, 47: 24-5 (Fa 73).

Tuttleton, J.W. "LA: The Image of Lost Elegance and Virtue." *AL*, 43: 616-32 (Ja 72).

Westbrook, W.W. "LA's Vision of Wall Street." *Critique*, 15: 57-66 (#2 73).

Auden, W.H. Ahern, E.M. "There May Be Many Answers." *EJ*, 51: 657-8 (D 62).

Allen, Walter. "W.H.A: 'the most exciting living poet.'" *Listener*, 47: 640-1 (17 Ap 52).

Allott, Kenneth. "A in the theatre." *New Verse*, 26-7: 17-21 (N 37).

Ando, Ichiro, and Katsuji Takamura. "W.H.A: gendai shi gappyo." *EigoS*, 100: 72-5 (F 54).

Arendt, Hannah. "Reflections." *NY*, 50: 39-46 (20 Ja 75).

Astre, G.A. "Zum dichterischen Werk von W.H.A." *Merkur*, 4: 526-30 (My 50).

Auden, G.A. "Profile of a Poet." *Observer*, 9 D 56, p. 5.

Bain, C.E. "W.H.A." *EUQ*, 21: 45-58 (Sp 65).

Bartlett, Phyllis, and J.A. Pollard. "A's 'September 1, 1939': An Interpreter's Analysis." *QJS*, 42: 1-13 (F 56).

Bauerle, R.H. "A's 'Fish in the Unruffled Lakes.'" *Expl*, 26: 57 (Mr 68).

Bayley, John. "The Greatness of A." *B&B*, 18: 9-11 (O 72).

Binni, Francesco. "A: il dissenso della 'ragione.'" *Let*, 31: 88-90, 206-20 (1967).

————. "Su A critico." *Let*, 32: 212-7 (1968).

Blair, J.G. "W.H.A: The Poem as Performance." *Shen*, 16: 55-66 (Sp 65).

Bloom, Robert. "The Humanization of A's Early Style." *PMLA*, 83: 443-54 (My 68).

————. "W.H.A's Bestiary of the Human." *VQR*, 42: 207-33 (Sp 66).

Bloomfield, M.W. "'Doom is Dark and Deeper than any Sea-dingle': W.H.A and 'Sawles Warde.'" *MLN*, 63: 548-52 (D 48).

Bluestone, Max. 'The Iconographic Sources of A's 'Musée des Beaux Arts.'" *MLN*, 76: 331-6 (Ap 61).

Bone, Christopher. "W.H.A in the 1930's: The Problem of Individual Commitment to Political Action." *Albion*, 4: 3-11 (#1 72).

Bowen, C. "Pardon for Writing Well." *Poetry Mag* (Sydney), 18: 3-12 (Je 70).

Braybrooke, Neville. "W.H.A: The Road from Marx." *America*, 88: 680-1 (21 Mr 53).

Brooke-Rose, Christine. "Notes on the Metre of A's 'The Age of Anxiety.'" *EC*, 13: 253-64 (Jl 63).

Brooks, B.G. "The Poetry of W.H.A." *Nineteenth Century and After*, 141:30-40 (Ja 47).

Brooks, Cleanth. "W.H.A as a Critic." *KR*, 26: 173-89 (Wi 64).

Bruehl, W.J. "*Polus naufrangia*: a Key Symbol in *The Ascent of F6*." *MD*, 10: 161-4 (S 67).

Burgum, E.B. "Three English Radical Poets." *New Masses*, 12: 33-6 (3 Jl 34).

Burnham, James. "W.H.A." *Nation*, 136: 164-5 (8 Ag 34).

Callan, Edward. "Allegory in A's 'The Age of Anxiety.'" *TCL*, 10: 155-65 (Ja 65).

————. "A's Goodly Heritage." *Shen*, 18: 56-68 (2Q 67).

————. "A's 'New Year Letter': A New Style of Architecture." *Renascence*, 16: 13-9 (F 63).

————. "The Development of W.H.A's Poetic Theory Since 1940." *TCL*, 4: 79-91 (O 58).

————. "Exorcising Mittenhofer." *LonM*, 14: 73-85 (Ap-My 74).

*————. "W.H.A: Annotated Checklist II (1958-1969)." *TCL*, 16: 27-56 (1970).

————. "W.H.A: The Farming of a Verse." *SoR*, 3: 341-56 (Ap 67).

Caswell, R.W. "A's 'Lay Your Sleeping Head My Love.'" *Expl*, 26: 44 (Ja 68).

Cavanaugh, W.C. "'Coriolanus' and 'The Ascent of F6': Similarity in Theme and Supporting Detail." *DramC*, 4: 9-17 (F 61).

Charney, Maurice. "Sir Lewis Namier and A's 'Musée des Beaux Arts.'" *PQ*, 39: 331-6 (Ap 61).

Chatman, Seymour. "A's 'The Questioner Who Sits So Sly.'" *Expl*, 28: 21 (N 69).

Chittick, V.L.O. "Angry Young Poet of the Thirties." *DR*, 43: 85-97 (Sp 63).

Christopher, J.R. "Two More Notes on Edward Lear." *Unic*, 2: 12-4 (1972).

Clancy, J.P. "A Waiting for His City." *ChS*, 42: 185-200 (Fa 59).

Close, H.M. "The Development of A's Poetry." *CaR*, 58: 478-9 (9 Je 37).

Cohen, E.H. "A's 'A Shock.'" *NCLit*, 4: 7-8 (1974).

Cohen, Marvin. "An Interview with W.H.A." *ASoc*, 12: 365-7 (1975).

Cook, F.W. "Primordial A." *EC*, 12: 402-12 (O 62).

————. "The Wise Fool: W.H.A and the Management." *Twentieth Century*, 168: 219-27 (S 60).

Cozarinsky, Edgardo. "Desencantar, desintoxicar: Nota sobre W.H.A y W.A. Mozart." *PSA*, 55: 307-17 (1969).

Crossman, Richard. "Remembering and Forgetting." *Listener*, 22 F 73, pp. 238-40.

Daalder, Joost. "W.H.A's 'Another Time.'" *CP*, 5: 65-6 (1972).

————. "W.H.A's 'The Shield of Achilles' and Its Sources." *AUMLA*, 42: 186-98 (1974).

————. "Yeats and A: Some Verbal Parallels." *N&Q*, 20: 334-6 (S 73).

Daiches, David. "W.H.A: The Search for a Public." *Poetry*, 54: 148-56 (Je 39).

Darlington, W.A. "A Theorist in the Theatre." *Discovery*, 16: 349-51 (D 35).

Davison, Trevor. "The Method of A's 'The Orators.'" *DUJ*, 32: 167-78 (1971).

Deedy, John. "Managing Literary History." *Cweal*, 101: 38-41 (1974).

Dobrée, Bonamy. "W.H.A." *Shen*, 18: 18-22 (2Q 67).

Dodds, E.R. "Background to a Poet: Memories of Birmingham, 1924-36." *Shen*, 18: 6-11 (2Q 67).

Donahue, Charles. "A on Romanticism." *Thought*, 26: 283-7 (Su 51).

Driver, T.F. "A's View of History in 'For the Time Being.'" *J Bible & Rel*, 21: 3-8 (Ja 63).

Duncan, Chester. "The Compassion of W.H.A." *CanF*, 34: 12-3 (Ap 54).

Eliot, G.P., et al.; reply by W.H. Auden. "A Symposium on W.H.A's 'A Change of Air.'" *KR*, 26: 190-208 (Wi 64).

Ellmann, Richard. "W.H.A (1907-1973)." *NYRB*, 21: 26-34 (12 D 74).

Empson, William. "Early A." *Review*, 5: 32-4 (F 63).

——. "A Note on A's 'Paid on Both Sides.'" *Experiment*, 7: 60-1 (Sp 31).

Enright, D.J. "Reluctant Admiration: A Note on A and Rilke." *EC*, 180-95 (Ap 52).

Fauderau, Serge. "A, poète anglaise." *Critique*, 22: 974-6 (N 67).

Faulkner, Peter. "A as Scrutineer." *DUJ*, 32: 56-60 (1970).

——. "W.H.A: Then and Now." *Humanist*, 85: 80-2 (Mr 70).

Fink, Guido. "A: L'eccezione e la regola." *Para*, 224: 81-90 (O 68).

Fisher, A.S.T. "A's Juvenilia." *N&Q*, 21: 370-3 (1974).

FitzGerald, David. "A's City." *DM*, 6: 3-17 (2Q 67).

Fleissner, R.F. "How Far Do We Go? A's 'Moon Landing.'" *Cont Poetry*, 1: 37-41 (Wi 73).

Flint, F.C. "A's 'Our Hunting Fathers Told the Story.'" *Expl*, 2: 1 (O 43).

——. "New Leaders in English Poetry." *VQR*, 14: 502-18 (Au 38).

Fodor, András. "Egy A Versról." *Nagyvilág*, 13: 1724-7 (N 68).

Fraser, G.S. "A: The Composite Griant." *Shen*, 15: 46-59 (Su 64).

——. "Glimpse of the Poet." *Adam*, 378-84: 23-6 (1973-74).

——. "The Young Prophet." *New Statesman & Nation*, 51: 102-3 (28 Ja 56).

Fremantle, Anne. "Anima Naturaliter Christiana." *Shen*, 18: 69-77 (2Q 67).

Friedman, S. "A and Hardy." *N&Q*, ns, 13: 419 (N 64).

Frost, William. "A's 'Fugal-chorus.'" *Expl*, 11: 21 (D 52).

Fuller, John. "W.H.A's First Published Poems." *N&Q*, 20: 333-4 (S 73).

Glicksberg, C.I. "Poetry and Marxism: Three English Poets Take Their Stand." *UTQ*, 6: 309-25 (Ap 37).

——. "Poetry and Social Revolution." *DR*, 17: 493-503 (Ja 38).

Goetsch, Paul. "W.H.A und Amerika." *JA*, 13: 215-27 (1968).

Goldring, Maurice, et al. "L'âne de l'hospice, le théâtre et la politique." *NCr*, 227: 53-9 (1971).

Gowda, H.H.A. "W.H.A: A Tribute." *LHY*, 15: 16-21 (1Q 74).

Grant, Damian. "Tones of Voice." *CritQ*, 11: 195-8 (1969).

——. "Verbal Events." *CritQ*, 16: 81-6 (1974).

Greenberg, Samuel. "W.H.A: Poet of Anxiety." *Masses & Mainstream*, 1: 38-50 (Je 48).

Gregory, Horace. "The Liberal Critics and W.H.A." *New Masses*, 23: 25-7 (20 Ap 37).

Griffin, Howard. "The Idiom of W.H.A." *New Q of Poetry*, 2: 6-10 (Fa 47).

Grigson, Geoffrey. "A as Monster." *New Verse*, 26-7: 13-7 (N 37).

Gustafson, Richard. "The Paragon Style: Frost and A." *Poet & Critic*, 2: 35-42 (Fa 65).

Haeffner, Paul. "A and Ella Wheeler Wilcox." *N&Q*, ns, 9: 110-1 (Mr 62).

Hagopian, J.V. "Exploring A's Limestone Landscape." *NS*, ns, 11: 255-60 (Je 62).

Hamm, V.M. "W.H.A: Pilgrim's Regress?" *America*, 72: 156-7 (26 My 45).

Hardy, Barbara. "The Reticence of W.H.A." *Review*, 11-2: 54-64 (1964).

———. "W.H.A, Thirties to Sixties: A Face and a Map." *SoR*, 5: 655-72 (Jl 69).

Hashguchi, Minoru. "W.H.A Saisetsu." *Oberon*, 31: 71-6 (1969).

Hauge, Ingvar. "Freud, Marx eller Kristus: en linje i W.H.A's diktning." *Samtiden*, 64: 335-45 (1955).

Hausermann, H.W. "Left-wing Poetry: a Note." *ES*, 21: 203-13 (O 39).

Haworth, H.E. "Man's Tragic Dilemma in A and Sophocles." *QQ*, 77: 566-75 (1970).

Hazard, F.E. "*The Ascent of F6*: A New Interpretation." *TSL*, 15: 165-75 (1970).

———. "The Father Christmas Passage in 'Paid on Both Sides.'" *MD*, 12: 555-64 (S 69).

Holloway, John. "The Master AS Joker." *Art Int*, 13: 17-20 (Ja 69).

Holthusen, H.E. "A als Prosaist." *Merkur*, 20: 469-78 (My 66).

Hope, Francis. "Meeting Point." *NSt*, 2 N 73, pp. 645-6.

Hough, Ingeborg. "A's 'Song for St. Cecilia's Day.'" *Expl*, 18: 35 (Mr 60).

Humphreys, A.R. "The Ascent of F6." *CaR*, 63: 353-5 (30 Ap 37).

Hutchinson, Pearse. "W.H.A: The Search for Happiness." *Literair Paspoort*, 7: 180-2 (O 52).

Hyams, C.B., and K.H. Reichert. "A Test Lesson on Brueghel's 'Icarus' and A's 'Musée des Beaux Arts.'" *NS*, 6: 228-32 (My 57).

Hyde, V.M. "The Pastoral Formula of W.H.A and Piero di Cosimo." *ConL*, 14: 332-46 (Su 73).

Irwin, J.T. "MacNeice, A, and the Art Ballad." *ConL*, 11: 58-79 (Wi 70).

Isherwood, Christopher. "Some Notes on A's Early Poetry." *New Verse*, 26-7: 4-8 (N 37).

Izubuchi, Hiroshi. "Kohai no Sokuryo Gishi—A no Nokoshita Mono." *EigoS*, 119: 788-90 (1974).

Izzo, Carlo. "Goodbye to Mezzogiorno." *Shen*, 18: 80-2 (Wi 67).

Jäger, Dietrich. "Das Haus als Raum des lyrischen Geschehens und als Gegenstand der lyrischen Meditation: Das Thema der nächsten Unwelt des Menschen in Audens *About the House* und bei deutschen und angelsächsischen Zeitgenossen." *LWU*, 2: 238-57 (1969).

James, Clive. "A's Achievement." *Commentary*, 56: 53-8 (D 73).

Jardine, Rupert. "A: The Compelling Years." *Adam*, 378-84: 34-8 (1973-74).

Jarrell, Randall. "Changes of Attitude and Rhetoric in A's Poetry." *SoR*, 7: 326-49 (Au 41).

Jóhannesson, Ragnar. "A heimsae kir Island." *Albyoubaoio*, 8 Ap 64, pp. 5, 10.

———. "A, MacNeice og *Bréf frá Íslandi*." *Lesbok morgunblaosins*, 39: 1, 12-4 (9 F 64).

———. "I fylgd meo A." *Andvari*, 2, ns: 245-58 (Au 60).

Johnson, R.A. "A and the Art of Clarification." *YR*, 61: 496-516 (Su 72).

———. "A's Architecture of Humanism." *VQR*, 48: 95-116 (1972).

Johnson, W.S. "A, Hopkins, and the Poetry of Reticence." *TCL*, 20: 165-71 (1974).

Kallsen, T.J. "W.H.A's Supersonnet." *Genre*, 4: 329-34 (1971).

Kamei, Toshisuke. "A to Rilke." *Roman gunto*, 16 (1958).

Kano, Hideo. "W.H.A—Sono Hito to Bungaku." *EigoS*, 119: 786-8 (1974).

Kavanagh, Patrick. "A and the Creative Mind." *Envoy*, 5: 33-9 (Je 51).

Kerman, Joseph. "A's 'Magic Flute.'" *HudR*, 10: 309-16 (Su 57).

Kermode, Frank. "The Theme of A's Poetry." *RLMC*, 3: 1-14 (Mr-Je 48).

Kinney, A.F. "A, Bruegel, and 'Musée des Beaux Arts.'" *CE*, 24: 529-31 (Ap 63).

Kirby, D.K. "Snyder, A, and the New Morality." *NCLit*, 1: 9-10 (Ja 71).

Knoll, R.E. "The Style of Contemporary Poetry." *PrS*, 29: 118-25 (Su 55).

Kranz, Gisbert. "Der amerikanische Dichter WHA." *Die Kirche in der Welt*, 8: 357-60 (3Q 55-6).

Kuna, F.M. "W.H.A, der subtile 'Poeta doctus.'" *NS*, ns, 13: 57-65 (F 64).

Lam, Pam. "A Ritual of Homage for W.H.A." *PoetA*, 10: 83-8 (1Q 74).

LeBreton, Georges. "A." *Preuves*, 198-9: 27-30 (Su 67).

Leithauser, G.G. "W.H.A's 'Meiosis.'" *ELN*, 8: 120-6 (1970).

Lewars, Kenneth. "A's Swarthmore Chart." *ConnR*, 1: 44-56 (2Q 68).

Lindegren, Erik. "WHA's diktning." *Ord och Bild*, 52: 104-8 (F 43).

Lombardo, Agostino. "Dalla scuola di Eliot a quella di A: la 'realtà americana' nella tradizione." *La Fiera Letteraria*, 7: 1-2 (18 My 52).

Lowell, Robert, et al. "Five Comments on Auden." *Shen*, 18: 45-6 (Wi 67).

McDiarmid, L.S. "A and the Redeemed City: Three Allusions." *Criticism*, 13: 340-50 (1971).

———, and John McDiarmid. "Artifice and Self-Consciousness in A's *The Sea and the Mirror*." *ConL*, 16: 353-77 (Su 75).

McDowell, F.P.W. "Subtle, Various, Ornamental, Clever: A in His Recent Poetry." *WSCL*, 3: 29-44 (Fa 62).

MacFadden, George. "The Rake's Progress: A Note on the Libretto." *HudR*, 8: 105-12 (Sp 55).

McIntosh, W.A. "A Rose of Tribulation." *Cithara*, 14: 61-70 (#3 75).

MacNeice, Louis. "Letter to W.H.A." *New Verse*, 26-7: 11-2 (N 37).

Magnússon, Sigurour. "A in Iceland." *Iceland R*, 2: 20 (3Q 64).

Markan, Ronald. "Power and Conflict in 'The Ascent of F6.'" *Discourse*, 7: 277-82 (Su 64).

Martin, W.B.J. "Significant Modern Writer: W.H.A." *Expository Times*, 71: 36-8 (N 59).

———. "W.H.A and the Preacher." *Congregational Q*, 34: 354-60 (O 56).

Masutani, Toyotsugu. "A no Shi no Kozo." *Oberon*, 31: 55-66 (1969).

Megaw, Moira. "A's First Poem." *ELC*, 25: 378-82 (1975).

Meller, Horst. "W.H.A: paysage moralisé." *NS*, ns, 14: 23-31 (J 65).

Mendleson, Edward. "A in New York." *Adam*, 379-84: 27-33 (1973-74).

———. "The Coherence of A's *The Orators*." *ELH*, 35: 114-33 (1968).

Millard, Geoffrey. "A's Common Prayer: 'In Praise of Limestone.'" *English* (London), 22: 105-9 (Au 73).

Millard, G.C. "The Poetical and the Poetic." *ESA*, 18: 17-22 (1975).

———. "Poetry Nonetheless: Early A." *ConR*, 225: 268-72 (1974).

Mitchell, Breon. "W.H.A and Christopher Isherwood: The 'German Influence.'" *Oxford German Stud*, 1: 163-72 (1966).

Mitchison, Naomi. "Young A." *Shen*, 18: 12-5 (2Q 67).

Moore, Georffrey. "Three Who Did Not Make a Revolution." *AmMerc*, 74: 107-14 (Ap 52).

Morland, Harold. "A's 'Crisis.'" *Expl*, 5: 17 (N 46).

Morse, D.E. "A's Concept and Practice of Christian Comedy." *MichA*, 4: 29-35 (1Q 71).

———. "'For the Time Being': Man's Response to the Incarnation." *Renascence*, 19: 190-7 (Su 67).

———. "Meaning of Time in A's 'For the Time Being.'" *Renascence*, 22: 162-8 (Sp 70).

———. "The Nature of Man in A's 'For the Time Being.'" *Renascence*, 19: 93-101 (Wi 67).

———. "Two Major Revisions in W.H.A's 'For the Time Being.'" *ELN*, 7: 294-7 (Je 70).

Muir, Edwin, et al. "Sixteen Comments on A." *New Verse*, 26-7: 23-30 (N 37).

Musulin, Stella. "In Oxford Dichtung lehren." *Wort und Wahrheit*, 16: 318-20 (Ap 61).

Nakagiri, Masao. "A no shi to shisō." *Shigaku*, 8: 18-28 (D 53).

———. "A zakkan." *Shigaku*, 13: 65-70 (Mr 58).

———. "Spain, 1966." *EigoS*, 112: 666-7 (O 66).

————. "W.H.A, C. Isherwood, *Inu ni natta otoko*: shigekiron no ichibu." *Shigaku*, 7: 60-74 (Ap 52).

————. "W.H.A, C. Isherwood saku *Kokkyo nite*." *Shigaku*, 7: 58-65 (Je-Jl 52).

Natterstad, J.H. "A's 'It's No Use Raising a Shout': A New Perspective." *CP*, 3: 17-20 (1970).

Nemerov, Howard. "A Word from the Devil's Advocate." *Parnassus*, 4: 131-6 (#1 75).

Nicolet, W.P. "A's 'The Fall of Rome.'" *Expl*, 31: 22 (1972).

Novak, Robert. "A's Advice to the Young." *WiOr*, 13: 34-7 (Sp 73).

————. "In Brueghel's Icarus, for Instance." *WiOr*, 6: 48-53 (1971).

Ohmann, R.M. "A's Sacred Awe." *Cweal*, 78: 279-81 (Mr 63).

Okazaki, Koichi. "A ni okeru Hihyo." *EigoS*, 119: 792-4 (1974).

Otter, Georg. "East Meets West—Gunnar Ekelöf in English." *MSpr*, 66: 124-30 (1972).

Paden, F.F. "Riddling in W.H.A's 'The Wanderer.'" *SM*, 42: 42-6 (1975).

Paliwal, B.B. "W.H.A's 'The Shield of Achilles.'" *PURBA*, 4: 211-5 (Ap 73).

Panaro, Cleonice. "L'arte inclusiva di W.H.A." *Convivium*, 36: 206-26 (Jl-Ag 68).

Perrine, Laurence, and Jane Johnston. "A's 'O What Is That Sound.'" *Expl*, 30: 41 (1972).

Peschmann, Hermann. "W.H.A (1907-1973)." *English*, 23: 3-4 (1974).

Platt, Polly. "W.H.A." *ASch*, 36: 266-70 (1967).

Poggioli, Renato. "Decadence in Minature." *MR*, 4: 531-62 (Sp 63).

Popma, S.H. "Toen de dagen vervuld waren." *Horizon* (Kampen), 20: 302-8 (D 57).

Porteus, H.G. "W.H.A." *Twentieth Century*, 4: 14-6 (F 33).

Power, William. "A's 'Foxtrot from a Play.'" *Expl*, 16: 32 (Mr 58).

Quinn, Sister M.B. "A's City of God." *Four Q*, 9: 5-8 (Mr 60).

————. "Persons and Places in A." *Renascence*, 12: 115-24, 148 (Sp 60).

Rebelo, Luis de Sousa. "A poesia de W.H.A." *Coloquio*, 14: 73-6 (1973).

Rees, Samuel. "'What Instruments We Have': An Appreciation of W.H.A." *AWR*, 24: 9-18 (1973).

Replogle, Justin. "A's Homage to Thalia." *BuR*, 11: 98-117 (Mr 63).

————. "A's Intellectual Development 1950-1960." *Criticism*, 7: 250-62 (Su 65).

————. "A's Marxism." *PMLA*, 80: 584-95 (D 65).

————. "A's Religious Leap." *WSCL*, 7: 47-75 (Wi-Sp 66).

————. "The Gang Myth in A's Early Poetry." *JEGP*, 61: 481-95 (Jl 62).

Ricks, Christopher. "Natural Linguistics." *Parnassus*, 2: 27-37 (Sp-Su 73).

————. "'O where are you going?': W.H.A and Christina Rossetti." *N&Q*, ns, 7: 472 (D 60).

Rickword, Edgell. "A and Politics." *New Verse*, 26-7: (N 37).

Robertson, Duncan. "A's 'The Wanderer.'" *Expl*, 28: 70 (Ap 70).

Rodway, Allan. "Logicless Grammar in Audenland." *LonM*, ns, 4: 31-44 (Mr 65).

Rosenheim, E.W. "The Elegiac Act: A's 'In Memory of W.B. Yeats.'" *CE*, 27: 422-5 (F 66).

Roth, Robert. "The Sophistication of W.H.A: A Sketch in Longinian Method." *MP*, 48: 193-204 (F 51).

Salus, P.H. "A and Opera." *Quest*, 2: 7-14 (Sp 67).

Sandbank, Shimon. "Nof Ha-nefesh: Rilke, A, Amihai." *Hasifrut*, 2: 697-714 (1971).

Sanesi, Roberto. "Nota per la 'New Year Letter' di W.H.A." *Aut-aut*, 3: 145-9 (Mr 53).

Sarang, Vilas, "Articles in the Poetry of W.H.A." *Lang&S*, 7: 77-90 (1974).

Sattewhite, J.N. "A's 'A Healthy Spot.'" *Expl*, 21: 57 (Mr 63).

Schauder, Karlheinz. "W.H.A." *Hochland*, 58: 376-9 (Ap 66).

Schuur, Koos. "Een barok herdergedicht van A." *Het woord*, Wi 48, pp. 170-5.

Scott, N.A. "The Poetry of A." *ChR*, 13: 53-75 (Wi 59).

Seif, Morton. "The Impact of T.S. Eliot on A and Spender." *SAQ*, 53: 61-9 (Ja 54).

Sellers, W.H. "New Light on A's 'The Orators.'" *PMLA*, 82: 455-64 (O 67).

Serpieri, Allesandro. "A, lo specchio e il caos." *Ponte*, 23: 770-86 (Je 67).

Shepherd, T.B. "'For the Time Being': W.H.A's Christmas Oratorio." *London Q*, 177: 277-84 (O 52).

Shinoda, Kazushi. "A no Beethoven ron." *Bungakukai*, 16: 144-6 (My 62).

Sisman, L.E. "W.H.A." *Atl*, 233: 18-9 (Ja 74).

Sister M. Cleophas. "A's 'Family Ghosts' (or 'The Strings' Excitement.')." *Expl*, 7: 1 (O 48).

Sister M. Janet. "W.H.A: Two Poems in Sequence." *Renascence*, 13: 115-8 (Sp 61).

Sister M.J. King. "An Explication of 'At the Grave of Henry James.'" *Horizantes*, 25: 61-5 (1971).

Spears, M.K. "A and Dionysus." *Shen*, 18: 85-95 (Wi 67).

———. "A in the Fifties: Rites of Homage." *SR*, 69: 375-98 (Su 61).

———. "The Dominant Symbols of A's Poetry." *SR*, 59: 392-425 (Su 51).

———. "In Memoriam W.H.A." *SR*, 82: 672-81 (1974).

———. "Late A: The Satirist as Lunatic Clergyman." *SR*, 59: 50-74 (Wi 51).

Spender, Stephen. "Five Notes on W.H.A's Writing." *Twentieth Century*, 3: 13-5 (Jl 32).

———. "The Importance of W.H.A." *London Mercury*, 39: 613-8 (Ap 39).

———. "The Poetic Dramas of W.H.A and Christopher Isherwood." *New Writing*, ns, 1: 102-8 (Au 38).

———. "W.H.A and His Poetry." *Atl*, 192: 74-9 (Jl 53).

———. "W.H.A (1907-1973)." *PR*, 40: 546-8 (#3 73).

———, et al. "W.H.A, 1907-73." *NSt*, 5 O 73, pp. 478-80.

Stanford, D.E. "W.H.A (1907-1973)." *SoR*, 9: xix (Au 73).

Starkman, M.K. "The 'Grace of the Absurd.'" *HTR*, 67: 275-88 (1974).

Stauffer, D.A. "*Which side am I supposed to be on?*: The Search for Beliefs in W.H.A's Poetry." *VQR*, 22: 570-80 (Au 46).

Stead, C.K. "A's 'Spain.'" *LonM*, ns, 7: 41-54 (Mr 68).

Stebner, Gerhard. "W.H.A: *The Ascent of F6*: Interpretation eines Dramas." *NS*, ns, 10: 397-413 (S 61).

———. "Whitman, Liliencron, W.H.A: Betrachtung und Vergleich motivahnlichter Gedichte." *NS*, ns, 9: 105-18 (Mr 60).

Steinberg, E.R. "Poetic Drama in General and A and Isherwood in Particular." *Carnegie Stud Eng*, 2: 43-58 (1955).

Stoenescu, Ştefan. "Poezie si cunoastre." *SXX*, 16: 28-34 (1973).

———. "W.H.A, poet al universalitaţii." *RoLit*, 20 Ja 72, p. 29.

Stravinsky, Igor. "A Maker of Libretti." *HM*, 240: 112-4 (Ap 70).

Sunesen, Bent. "'All We Are Not Stares Back at What We are': A Note on A." *ES*, 40: 439-49 (D 59).

Symons, Julian. "A and Poetic Drama 1938." *Life and Letters Today*, 20: 70-9 (F 39).

———. "Early A." *Shen*, 18: 48-50 (2Q 67).

Takagi, Narahide. "*On the Frontier* no seijiteki fūshi: W.H.A to Christopher Isherwood no gassaku shigeki ni tsuite." *Eigo kenkyu*, 4: 20-3 (My 52).

Thompson, John. "A at the Sheldonian." *Truth*, 66: 690 (15 Je 56).

Thornburg, Thomas. "A's 'Mundus et Infans' 46-56." *Expl*, 27: 33 (1968).

———. "The Man with the Hatchet: Shapiro on A." *BSUF*, 11: 25-34 (Su 70).

Thwaite, Anthony, "W.H.A.: 1907-1973." *LHY*, 15: 1-11 (1Q 74).

Tolley, A.T. "The Thirties Poets at Oxford." *UTQ*, 38: 338-58 (Jl 68).

Uekesa, Jin 'inchi. "Shijin Auden no tantei shōsetsu-ron." *Ondori tsūshin*, 4: 22-3 (N 48).
Upward, Edward. "Remembering the Earlier A." *Adam*, 379-84: 17-32 (1973-74).
Valgemae, Mardi. "A's Collaboration with Isherwood on *The Dog Beneath the Skin*." *HLQ*, 21: 373-83 (Au 68).
Vallette, Jacques. "W.H.A: Aspects d'une Inquiétude." *LanM*, 45: 153-65 (2Q 51).
Waidson, H.M. "A and German Literature." *MLR*, 70: 347-65 (1975).
Wall, Bernard. "W.H.A and Spanish Civilization." *Colosseum*, 3: 142-9 (S 37).
Wallace-Crabbe, Chris. "A Revisited." *Dissent*, 14: 22-6 (Wi 65).
Warner, Alan. "W.H.A's 'Autumn Song.'" *CritS*, 1: 203-5 (Su 64).
Wasson, S.C. "A Descant on W.H.A's Christmas Oratorio." *Crozer Q*, 23: 340-9 (O 46).
Watson, George. "A and Violence." *Encounter*, 42: 94 (Je 74).
Weatherhead, A.K. "The Good Place in the Latest Poems of W.H.A." *TCL*, 10: 99-107 (O 64).
Weisstein, Ulrich. "Reflections on a Golden Style: W.H.A's Theory of Opera." CL, 22: 108-24 (Sp 70).
Wentraub, D.A. "A's 'To T.S. Eliot on His Sixtieth Birthday.'" *Expl*, 31: 75 (My 73).
Westlake, J.H. "W.H.A's 'The Shield of Achilles': An Interpretation." *LWU*, 1: 49-57 (1968).
Whitehead, John. "A: An Early Poetical Notebook." *LonM*, ns, 5: 85-93 (My 65).
Whitehead, L.M. "Art as Communication: A's 'The Sea and the Mirror.'" *Per*, 14: 171-8 (Sp 66).
Williams, M.G. "A's 'Petition': A Synthesis of Criticism." *Personalist*, 46: 222-32 (Sp 65).
Wilson, Edmund. "W.H.A in America." *NSt and Nation*, 51: 658-9 (9 Je 56).
Woodcock, George. "A—Critic and Criticized." *SR*, 82: 685-97 (1974).
Wright, G.T. "A General View of A's Poetry." *TSLL*, 10: 43-64 (1965).
Yamada, Yoshinari. "'Ars Poetica for Hard Times'—A no Shiron." *EigoS*, 119: 790-2 (1974).
Austin, Mary Hunter. Anderson, Barbara. "Thoreau and MA." *TSB*, 126: 7 (1974).
Berry, J.W. "Characterization in MA's Southwest Works." *SwAL*, 2: 119-24 (Wi 72).
Berry, J.W. "MA: Sibylic Gourmet of the Southwest." *WR*, 9: 3-8 (1972).
———. "MHA (1868-1934)." *ALR*, 2: 125-31 (Su 69).
Dubois, A.E. "MHA, 1868-1934." *SWR*, 20: 231-64 (Ap 35).
Ford, T.W. "The American Rhythm: MA's Poetic Principle." *WAL*, 5: 3-14 (Sp 70).
Johnson, L.A. "Western Literary Realism: The California Tales of Norris and A." *ALR*, 7: 278-80 (Su 74).
Powell, L.C. "Southwest Classics Reread: A Prophetic Passage." *Westways*, 65: 60-5 (F 73).
———. "A Dedication to the Memory of MHA, 1868-1934." *Arizona and the West*, 10: 1-4 (Sp 68).
Ringler, D.P. "MA: Kern County Days, 1888-1892." *SCQ*, 45: 25-63 (Mr 63).
Robinson, F.K. "From MA to Edgar Lee Masters: A Book Inscription." *LCUT*, 6: 82-5 (D 73).
Smith, Henry. "The Feel of the Purposeful Earth." *NMQ*, 1: 17-33 (F 31).
Van Doren, Carl. "MA, 1868-1934: Prophet and Poet of the Southwest." *Scholastic*, 25: 4, 23 (2 S 34).
VanDoren, Dorothy. "Lost Frontier." *Nation*, 135: 567-8 (7 D 32).
White, W.A. "A Woman of Genius." *SatR*, 9: 235-6 (12 N 32).
Austin, Stephen F. Lee, R.S. "The Publication of A's Louisville Address." *SHQ*, 70: 425-42 (Ja 67).

Avery, Benjamin Parke. Grenander, M.E. "BPA, California Journalist and Diplomat: Letters from Peking." *MarkR*, 2: 5-9 (S 69).

Avison, Margaret. Columbo, J.R. "A and Wevill." *CanL*, 34: 72-6 (Au 67).

Babbitt, Irving. Crocker, L.G. "Professor B Revisited." *SRom*, 10: 260-82 (Fa 71).

Davidson, Donald. "Mr. (Irving) B at Philadelphia." *SoR*, 6: 695-702 (1941).

Hou, Chien. "IB and Chinese Thought." *TkR*, 5: 135-85 (1974).

————. "IB and the Literary Movements of Republican China." *TkR*, 4: 1-23 (#1 73).

Bacheller, Irving. Katz, Joseph. "Stephen Crane and IB's Gold." *SCraneN*, 5: 4-5 (Sp 70).

Bailey, H.C. Waugh, T.D. "The Parables of H.C.B" *ArmD*, 6: 75-7 (1973).

Bailey, Margaret Jewett. Duncan, J.K. "'Ruth Rover'—Vindictive Falsehood or Historical Truth?" *JWest*, 12: 240-53 (Ap 73).

Baker, Dorothy. Johnson, S.F. "Identities of Cassandra." *Novel*, 1: 71-4 (Fa 67).

Baker, Houston. Gayle, Addison. "Reclaiming the Southern Experience: The Black Aesthetic 10 Years Later." *BlackW*, 23: 20-9 (1974).

Baker, R.S. Harstad, P.T. "RSB's 'The Day of the Run' Revisited." *Rendezvous*, 4: 1-17 (Wi 69).

Baldwin, Abraham. Furlong, P.J. "A Sermon for the Mutinous Troops of the Connecticut Line, 1782," *NEQ*, 43: 621-31 (D 70).

Baldwin, James. Anon. "The Black Scholar Interviews: JB." *BSch*, 5: 33-42 (D 73, Ja 74).

Anon. "JB: A Literary Assessment." *BlackW*, 13: 61-8 (Ja 64).

Alexander, Charlotte. "The 'Stink' of Reality: Mothers and Whores in JB's Fiction." *L&P*, 18: 9-26 (1968).

Allen, S.S. "Religious Symbolism and Psychic Reality in B's *Go Tell It on the Mountain*." *CLAJ*, 19: 173-99 (D 75).

Alves, H.O. "JB: O calabouco impossivel." *Vertice* 28: 657-63 (1968).

Baldwin, James. "How Can We Get the Black People to Cool It?" *Esquire*, 70: 49-50ff (Jl 68).

————. "JB on the Negro Actor." *Urbanite*, Ap 61, pp. 12-14.

Banta, T.J. "JB's Discovery of Identity." *Mawazo*, 2: 33-41 (1969).

Bell, George. "The Dilemma of Love in *Go Tell It on the Mountain* and *Giovanni's Room*. *CLAJ*, 17: 397-406 (Mr 74).

Bluefarb, Sam. "JB's 'Previous Condition': A Problem of Identification." *NALF*, 3: 26-9 (1969).

Britt, D.D. "America: *Another Country*." *Ba Shiru*, 4: 47-51 (1972).

Cartey, Wilfred. "The Realities of Four Negro Writers." *Roots*, 1: 145-59 (1970).

Clarke, J.B. "Alienation of JB." J of *Human Relations*, 12: 30-3 (1Q 64).

Collier, E.W. "Thematic Patterns in B's Essays: A Study in Chaos." *BlackW*, 21: 28-34 (1972).

Corona, Mario. "La saggistica di JB." *SA*, 15: 433-63 (1969).

Curling, Maud. "JB y la iglesia negra norteamericana en la novela *Go Tell It on the Mountains*." *Revista Un Costa Rica*. 34: 87-95 (1972).

Dance, D.C. "You Can't Go Home Again: JB and the South." *CLAJ*, 18: 81-90 (S 74).

Dane, Peter. "B's Other Country." *Transition*, 5: 38-40 (1966).

DeMott, Benjamin. "JB on the Sixties: Acts and Revelations." *SatR*, 55: 63-6 (27 My 72).

Dickstein, Morris. "Wright, B, Cleaver," *NLet*, 38: 117-24 (Wi 71).

Fabre, Michel. "Père et fils dans *Go Tell It on the Mountain* de JB." *EA*, 23: 47-61 (Ja-Mr 70).

Fabrès, Nabile. "JB: Une interview exclusive." *JeuneA*, nv: 20-4 (1 S 70).

Fleischauer, J.F. "JB's Style." *CCC*, 26: 141-8 (1975).

Foster, D.E. "'Cause my house fell down': The Theme of the Fall in B's Novels." *Critique*, 13: 50-62 (1971).

Freese, Peter. "JB und das Syndrom des Identitätsverlustes: *Previous Condition* im Lichte des Gesamtwerkes." *LWU*, 4: 73-98 (1971).

Gayle, Addison. "A Defense of JB." *CLAJ*, 10: 201-8 (Mr 67).

Gérard, Albert. "The Sons of Ham." *StN*, 3: 148-64 (Su 71).

Giles, J.R. "Religious Alienation and 'Homosexual Consciousness' in *City of Night* and *Go Tell It on the Mountain*." *CE*, 36: 369-80 (1974).

Goldman, S.B. "JB's 'Sonny's Blues': A Message in Music." *NALF*, 8: 231-3 (Fa 74).

Gounard, J.F. "La Carrière Singulière de JB: 1924-1970." *RUO*, 44: 507-18 (O-D 74).

Green, Martin. "The Need for a New Liberalism." *Month*, 226: 141-7 (S 68).

Gross, Barry, "The 'Uninhabitable Darkness' of B's *Another Country*." *NALF*, 6: 113-21 (1972).

Hall, John. "An Interview with JB." *TransR*, 37-8: 5-14 (1970).

Hernton, C.C. "Blood of the Lamb and a Fiery Baptism: The Ordeal of JB." *Amistad*, 1: 183-225 (1970).

Howe, Irving. "JB: At Ease in Apocalypse." *HM*, 237: 92-100 (S 68).

Inge, M.T. "JB's Blues." *NCLit*, 2: 8-11 (S 72).

Isaacs, Harold. "Five Writers and Their African Ancestors." *Phylon*, 21: 243-65 (1960).

Kim, Kichung. "Wright, the Protest Novel, and B's Faith." *CLAJ*, 17: 387-96 (Mr 74).

Langer, Johannes. "JB." *Ry Hdjskoles julehilsen*, 1968, pp. 25-31.

Lee, R.A. "JA and Matthew Arnold: Thoughts on 'Relevance." *CLAJ*, 14: 324-30 (Mr 71).

Long, R.E. "From Elegant to Hip." *Nation*, 206: 769-70 (10 Je 68).

———. "Love and Wrath in the Fiction of JB." *Eng Rec*, 19: 50-7 (F 69).

Lottman Herbert. "It's Hard to Be JB." *Black Times*, 2: 10 (1972).

Lottman, H.R. "It's Hard to Be JB: An Interview." *ID*, nv: 67-8 (Jl 72).

McCluskey, John. "*If Beale Street Could Talk*." *BlackW*, 24: 51-2, 88-91 (1974).

McWhirter, W.A. "After Years of Futility B Explodes Again." *Life*, 30 Jl 71, p. 63.

Madden, David. "The Fallacy of the Subject-Dominated Novel." *Eng Rec*, 18: 11-9 (Ap 68).

Markholt, Otillie. "*Blues for Mister Charlie* Reconsidered: White Critic, Black Playwright: Water and Fire." *BlackW*, 16: 54-60 (Ap 67).

May, J.R. "Images of Apocalypse in the Black Novel." *Renascence*, 23: 31-45 (1970).

Meriwether, L.M. "*The Amen Corner*." *BlackW*, 14: 40-7 (Ja 65).

Mitra, B.K. "The Wright-B Controversy." *IJAS*, 1: 101-5 (1969).

Moller, Karin, "JB's Theme of 'Identity' and His "Fall" Metaphor." *EiC*, 2: 34-50 (Mr 74).

Mookerjee, R.N. "JB: Social Protest in *Another Country*." *Rajasthan Un Stud Eng*, 7: 60-7 (1974).

Mowe, Gregory, and W.S. Nobles. "JB's Message for White America." *QJS*, 58: 142-51 (Ap 72).

Potter, Vilma. "B and Odets: The High Cost of 'Crossing.'" *CEJ*, 1, iii: 37-41 (Fa 65).

Reilly, J.M. "'Sonny's Blues': JB's Image of A Black Community." *ANLF*, 4: 56-60 (Jl 70).

Rubin, L.D. "The Great American Joke." *SAQ*, 72: 82-94 (Wi 73).

Scheller, Bernhard. "Die Gestalt des Farbigen bei Williams, Albee und B und ihre szenische Realisierung in DDR-Aufführungen." *ZAA*, 20: 137-57 (1972).

Schrero, E.M. "*Another Country* and the Sense of Self." *BlAR*, 2: 91-100 (Sp-Su 71).

Scott, Robert. "Rhetoric, Black Power, and B's *Another Country*." *JBlackS*, 1: 21-34 (S 70).

Shawcross, J.T. "Some Literary Uses of Numerology." *HSL*, 1: 50-62 (1969).

Silvera, Frank. "Towards a Theater of Understanding." *NegroD*, 18: 33-5 (1969).

Standley, F.L. "*Another Country*, Another Time." *StN*, 4: 504-12 (Fa 72).

———. "JB: The Artist as Incorrigible Disturber of the Peace." *SHR*, 4: 18-30 (Wi 70).

*———. "JB: A Checklist, 1963-1967." *BB*, 25: 135-7, 160 (My-Ag 68).

Tedesco, J.L. "*Blues for Mister Charlie*: The Rhetorical Dimension." *Players*, 50: 20-3 (1975).

Thompson, John. "B: The Prophet as Artist." *Commentary*, 45: 67-9 (Je 68).

Turner, D.T. "Afro-American Authors: A Full House." *CEA*, 34: 15-9 (Ja 72).

Wills, A. "The Use of Coincidence in 'Notes of a Native Son'." *NALF*, 8: 234-35 (1974).

Baldwin, Joseph Glover. Current-Garcia, Eugene. "JGB: Humorist or Moralist?" *AlaR*, 5: 122-41 (Ap 52).

Ballard, J.G. Perry, Nick, and Roy Wilkie. "Homo Hydrogenesis: Notes on the Work of J.G.B." *RQ*, 4: 98-105 (1970).

Bambara, Toni Cade. Washington, M.H. "Black Women Image Makers." *BlackW*, 23: 10-18 (1974).

Bancroft, George. Clark, Patricia. "'A Tale to Tell from Paradise Itself': GB's Letters from Florida, March 1855." *FHQ*, 48: 264-78 (Ja 70).

Kummings, D.D. "An Appraisal of Reappraisals: Four Nineteenth-Century American Writers." *CEA*, 37: 36-8 (#1 74).

Vitzthum, R.C. "Theme and Method in B's *History of the United States*." *NEQ*, 41: 362-80 (1968).

Bangs, John Kendrick. Stronks, J.B. "JKB Criticizes Norris's Borrowings in *Blix*." *AL*, 42: 380-6 (N 70).

Baraka, Imamu Amiri (LeRoi Jones). Anon. "The LJ Case: Letter about a Wolf-Pack." *AmD*, 5: 17 (1968).

Anon. "Voice from the Spirit House." *TLS*, 7 N 68, p. 1250.

Adams, G.R. "'My Christ' in *Dutchman*." *CLAJ*, 15: 54-8 (S 71).

Baker, John. "Criteria for First Printings of LJ." *YULG*, 49: 297-8 (1974).

———. "LJ, Secessionist, and Ambiguous Collecting." *YULG*, 46: 159-66 (1972).

Baraka, I.A. 'Black 'Revolutionary' Poets Should Also Be Playwrights." *BlackW*, 21: 4-6 (1972).

———. "'Why I Changed My Ideology': Black Nationalism and Social Revolution." *BlackW*, 24: 30-42 (#9 75).

Bermel, Albert. "*Dutchman*, or the Black Stranger in America." *ASoc*, 9: 423-34 (1972).

Berry, Faith. "Black Artist, Black Prophet." *NRep*, 154: 23-5 (28 My 66).

Billingsley, R.G. "LJ's *The Slave*: Right Ideas Stink a Lotta Times." *Umoja*, 2: 72-81 (#2 75).

Brady, O.E. "*B's Experimental Death Unit* #1: Plan for (R)Evolution." *NALF*, 9: 59-61 (Su 75).

Brecht, Stefan. "LJ's Slave Ship." *TDR*, 14: 212-9 (Wi 70).

Brooks, M.E. "The Pro-Imperialist Career of LJ." *L&I*," 11: 37-48 (1972).

Brown, C.M. "Apotheosis of a Prodigal Son." *KR*, 30: 654-61 (1968).

———. "Black Literature and LJ." *BlackW*, 19: 24-31 (1970).

Brown, L.B. "J(B) and His Literary Heritage in *The System of Dante's Hell*." *Obsidian*, 1: 5-17 (#1 75).

Brown, L.W. "Comic-Strip Heroes: LJ and the Myth of American Innocence." *JPC*, 3: 191-204 (Fa 69).

———. "Dreamers and Slaves: The Ethos of Revolution in Walcott and LRJ." *CaribQ*, 17: 36-44 (S-D 71).

————. "LJ (IAB) as Novelist: Theme and Structure in *The System of Dante's Hell.*" *NALF*, 7: 132-42 (Wi 73).

Buford, W.W. "LRJ from Existentialism to Apostle of Black Nationalism." *Players*, 47: 60-4 (D-Ja 72).

Coleman, Michael. "What Is Black Theater? An Interview with IAB." *BlackW*, 20: 32-6 (1971).

Costello, D.P. "LJ: Black Man as Victim." *Cweal*, 88: 436-40 (28 Jl 68).

Das, Nila. "Protest in Recent Negro Plays and LRJ's *The Slave.*" *PURBA*, 4: 111-5 (Ap 73).

Ferguson, John. "*Dutchman* and *The Slave.*" *MD*, 13: 398-405 (F 71).

Fischer, W.G. "The Pre-Revolutionary Writings of IAB." *MR*, 14: 259-305 (Sp 73).

Fuller, H.W. "*The Toilet* and *The Slave.*" *BlackW*, 14: 49-50 (Jl 65).

Gaffney, Floyd. "Black Theatre: The Moral Function of IAB." *Players*, 50: 20-3 (1975).

Gallagher, Kathleen. "The Art(s) of Poetry: J and MacLeish." *MwQ*, 12: 383-92 (Su 71).

Henderson, James. "'The Slave' and 'The Toilet,' by LJ." *Harlem Youth Report N*, 3: 3 (12 Mr 65).

Hill, Herbert. "The Negro Writer and the Creative Imagination." *ASoc*, 5: 245-55 (1968).

Iannarella, M.J. "Black and White." *MSE*, 3: 1-6 (1971).

Jackson, E.M. "LJ(IAB): Form and the Progression of Consciousness." *CLAJ*, 17: 33-56 (S 73).

Jackson, Kathryn. "LJ and the New Black Writers of the Sixties." *Freedomways*, 9: 232-48 (1969).

Jeffers, Lance. "Bullins, B and Elder: The Dawn of Grandeur in Black Drama." *CLAJ*, 16: 32-48 (S 72).

Klinkowitz, Jerome. "LJ (IAB): *Dutchman* as Drama." *NALF*, 7: 123-6 (Wi 73).

Lederer, Richard. "The Language of LJ's 'The Slave.'" *SBL*, 4: 14-6 (Sp 73).

Lewis, Ida. "LJ: Une interview exclusive." *JeuneA*, 1 S 70, pp. 24-7.

Lindberg, John. "*Dutchman* and *The Slave*: Companions in Revolution." *BlAR*, 2: 101-7 (Sp-Su 71).

Llorend, D. "Ameer (LJ)B." *Ebony*, 24: 75-8 (Ag 69).

Marvin X. "Everythin's Cool: An Interview with LJ." *Black Theater*, 1: 16ff (O 68).

————. and Faruk. "Islam and Black Art: An Interview with LRJ." *BlackW*, 18: 4-10, 77-80 (Ja 69).

————. "LRJ Talks with Marvin X and Faruk." *Black Theatre*, 2: 14-9 (1969).

McClusky, John. "In the Mecca (IAB)." *SLB*, 4: 25-30 (# 73).

Michelman, Fredric. "American and African Blacks: A Review of Alaim Richard's Théâtre et Nationalisme: Woyle Soyinka et LJ." *NALF*, 8: 252-3 (1974).

Miller, J.A. "The Plays of LJ." *CLAJ*, 14: 331-9 (Mr 71).

Mootry, M.K. "Themes and Symbols in Two Plays by LJ." *BlackW*, 18: 42-7 (Ap 69).

Munro, C.L. "LJ: A Man in Transition." *CLAJ*, 17: 57-78 (S 73).

Nelson, Hugh. "LJ's Dutchman: A Brief Ride on a Doomed Ship." *ETJ*, 20: 53-9 (Mr 68).

O'Brien, John. "Innovative Black Fiction: The Problem of LJ." *OyR*, 8: 33-8 (Fa 74).

————. "Racial Nightmares and the Search for Self: An Explication of LJ's 'A Chase (Alighieri's Dream).'" *NALF*, 7: 89-90 (Fa 73).

Otten, Charlotte. "LJ: Napalm Poet." *CP*, 3: 5-11 (Sp 70).

Pearson, LouAnne. "LJ and a Black Aesthetic." *Paunch*, 35: 33-66 (F 72).

Peavy, C.D. "Myth, Magic, and Manhood in LJ's *Madheart.*" *SBL*, 1: 12-20 (1970).

Pennington-Jones, Paulette. "From Brother LJ through *The System of Dante's Hell* to IAB." *JBlackS*, 4: 195-214 (D 73).

Primeau, Ronald. "Imagination as Moral Bulwark and Creative Energy in Richard Wright's *Black Boy* and LJ's *Home*. *SBL* 3: 12-8 (Su 72).

Reck, T.S. "Archetypes in LJ's *Dutchman*." *SBL*, 1: 66-8 (Fa 70).

Reed, D.S. "LJ: High Priest of the Black Arts Movement." *ETJ*, 22: 53-9 (Mr 70).

Resnik, H.S. "Brave New Words." *SatR*, 50: 28-9 (9 D 67).

Rice, J.H.C. "LJ's *Dutchman:* A Reading." *ConL*, 123: 42-59 (Wi 71).

Rich, Cynthia. "Where's B's Jones?"*Black Times*, 4: 6-7 (1974).

Rock, T.S. "Archetypes in LJ's *Dutchman*." *SBL*, 1: 66-8 (1970).

Russell, C.L. "LJ Will Get US All in Trouble." *Liberator*, 4: 10-1 (Je 64).

*Schatt, Stanley. "LJ: A Checklist to Primary and Secondary Sources." *BB*, 28: 55-7 (Sp-Je 71).

Shannon, W.T. "B and the Bourgeois Figure."*SBL*, 6: 18-21 (#5 75).

Smith, R.H. "Jersey Justice and LJ." *PW*, 193: 66 (15 Ja 68).

Syna, Sy. "The Old Prof Takes the Stage." *Players*, 46: 76-9 (1971).

Taylor, W.P. "The Fall of Man in IAB's (LJ's) *Dutchman*." *NALF*, 7: 127-31 (Wi 73).

Tener, R.L. "The Corrupted Warrior Heroes: AB's *The Toilet*." *MD*, 17: 207-16 (Je 74).

———. "Role Playing as a Dutchman." *SBL*, 3: 17-21 (Au 72).

Tryford, John. "Who is LJ? What is He?" *Trace*, 65: 294-8 (Su 67).

Turner, D.T. "Afro-American Authors: A Full House." *CEA*, 34: 15-9 (Ja 72).

Velde, Paul. "LJ: Pursued by the Furies." *Cweal*, 88: 440-1 (28 Je 68).

Watkins, Mel. "Talk with LJ." *NYT*, 27 Je 71, pp. 4, 24-7.

Weales, Gerald. "The Day LJ Spoke on the Penn Campus." *NYTMS*, 4 My 69, 38-40.

Weisgram, D.H. "LJ's *Dutchman:* Interracial Ritual of Sexual Violence." *AI*, 29: 215-32 (Fl 72).

Willis, R.J. "Anger and the Contemporary Black Theatre." *NALF*, 8: 213-5 (1974).

Witherington, Paul. "Exorcism and Baptism in LJ's *The Toilet*." *MD*, 15:159-63 (S 72).

Barbour, R.H. Erisman, Fred. "The Strenuous Life in Practice: The School and Sport Stories of RHB." *RMSSJ*, 7: 29-37 (Ap 70).

Barker, James Nelson. Crowley, J.W. "JNB in Perspective." *ETJ*, 24: 363-69 (D 72).

Sata, Masanori. "*Superstition* (1824) to *Winterset* (1935): Romeo-Juliet theme kara no kosatsu." ELLS, 6: 131-46 (1969).

Barlow, Joel. Arner, R.D. "JB's Poetics: 'Advice to a Raven in Russia.'" *ConnR*, 5: 38-43 (1972).

———. "The Smooth and Emblematic Song: JB's *The Hasty Pudding*." *EAL*, 7: 76-91 (Sp 72).

Ball, Kenneth. "American Nationalism and Esthetics in JB's Unpublished 'Diary-1788.'" *TSL*, 15: 49-60 (1970).

Contenti, Alessandra. "*The Hasty Pudding* di JB." *SA*, 16: 9-23 (1970).

Eberwein, J.D. "JB and *The Confidence Man*." *ATQ*, 24 sup: 28-9 (Fa 74).

Egan, Clifford. "On the Fringe of the Napoleonic Catastrophe: JB's Letters from Central and Eastern Europe, 1812."*EAL*, 10: 251-72 (Wi 75).

Gimmestad, V.E. "JB's Editing of John Trumbull's *M'Fingal*." *AL*, 47: 97-102 (Mr 75).

Griffith, John. "*The Columbiad* and *Greenfield Hill*." *EAL*, 10: 235-50 (Wi 75).

Kohring, K.H. "The American Epic." *SHR*, 5: 265-80 (Su 71).

Barnes, Djuna. Barnes, Djuna. "From *Ladies Almanack*: August Hath 31 Days; September Hath 30 Days." *Prose*, 2: 23-35 (1971).

Baxter, Charles. "A Self-Consuming Light: *Nightwood* and the Crisis of Modernism." *JML*, 3: 1175-87 (1974).

Ferguson, S.C. "DB's Short Stories: An Estrangement of the Heart." *SoR*, 2: 26-41 (1969).

Greiner, D.J. "DB's *Nightwood* and the American Origins of Black Humor." *Critique*, 17: 41-54 (#1 75).

Gunn, Edward. "Myth and Style in DB's *Nightwood*." *MFS*, 19: 545-50 (Wi 73-74).

*Hipkiss, R.A. "DB (1892-): A Bibliography." *TCL*, 14: 161-3 (O 68).

Johnson, W.A. "Modern Women Novelists: *Nightwood* and the Novel of Sensibility." *BuR*, 21: 15-28 (Sp 73).

Montague, Gene. "Dylan Thomas and *Nightwood*." *SR*, 76: 420-34 (1968).

Nadeau. R.L. "*Nightwood* and the Freudian Unconscious." *IFR*, 2: 159-63 (1975).

Barney, N.C. Lottman, H.R. "In Search of Miss B." *NYT*, 28 S 69, pp. 2, 46-7.

Barr, Amelia. Bargard, Robert. "AB, Augusta Evans Wilson and the Sentimental Novel." *Marab*, 2: 13-25 (Wi 65-66).

Barrett, C. Waller. Kelly, C.B. "The Mighty Manuscripts of Mr. C.WB." *Cwealth*, 38: 21-5, 28 (Ag 71).

Barrett, Lawrence. McAleer, J.J. "LB: 'The Scholar of the American Theater.'" *ShN*, 20: 44-5 (1970).

Barry, Phillip. Gild, D.C. "Psychodrama on Broadway: Three Plays of Psychodrama by PB." *MarkR*, 2: 65-74 (O 70).

Meserve, W.J. "PB: A Dramatist's Search." *MD*, 13: 93-9 (My 70).

Barsness, John. Crooks, Alan. "JA.B: A Tribute. " *WAL*, 4: 218 (Fa 69).

Barth, John. Altieri, Charles. "Organic and Humanist Models in Some English Bildungsroman." *JGE*, 23: 220-40 (1971).

Bean, J.C. "JB and Festive Comedy: A Failure of Imagination in *The Sot-Weed Factor*." *XUS*, 10: 3-15 (Sp 71).

Bienstock, B.G. "Lingering on the Autognostic Verge: JB's *Lost in the Funhouse*." *MFS*, 19: 69-78 (Sp 73).

Bradbury, J.M. "Absurd Insurrection: The B-Percy Affair." *SAQ*, 68: 319-29 (Su 69).

Cantrill, Dante. "'It's a Chimera': An Introduction to JB's Latest Fiction." *Rendezvous*, 10: 17-30 (#2 75).

Cohen, E.H. "The 'Second Edition' of *The Sot-Weed Factor*." *AL*, 42: 289-303 (N 70).

Conlee, J.W. "JB's Version of *The Reeve's Tale*." *AN&Q*, 12: 137-8 (My-Je 74).

Davis, Cynthia. "'The Key to the Treasure': Narrative Movements and Effects in *Chimera*." *JNT*, 5: 105-15 (1975).

Dippie, B.W. "'His Visage Wild, His Form Exotick': Indian Themes and Cultural Guilt in JB's *The Sot-Weed Factor*." *AQ*, 21: 113-21 (Sp 69).

Diser, P.E. "The Historical Ebenezer Cooke." *Critique*, 10: 48-59 (1968).

Ewell, B.C. "JB: The Artist of History." *SLJ*, 5: 32-46 (Sp 73).

Farwell, Harold. "JB's Tenuous Affirmation: 'The Absurd, Unending Possibility of Love.'" *GaR*, 28: 290-306 (Su 74).

Gillespie, Gerald. "B's 'Lost in the Funhouse': Short Story Text in Its Cyclic Context." *SSF*, 12: 223-30 (Su 75).

Gresham, J.T. "*Giles Goat-Boy*: Satyr, Satire, and Tragedy Twined." *Genre*, 7: 148-65 (Je 74).

Gross, Beverly. "The Anti-Novels of JB." *ChiR*, 20: 95-109 (N 68).

Hawkes, John. "*The Floating Opera and Second Skin*." *Mosaic*, 8: 17-28 (1974).

Hendin, Josephine. "JB's Fictions for Survival." *HM*, 247: 102-6 (S 73).

Hinden, Michael. "*Lost in the Funhouse*: B's Use of the Recent Past." *TCL*, 19: 107-18 (Ap 73).

Hirsh, David. "JB's Freedom Road." *MeditR*, 2: 38-47 (1972).

Holder, Alan. "'What Marvelous Plot . . . Was Afoot?': History in B's *The Sot-Weed Factor*." *AQ*, 20: 596-604 (Fa 68).

Janoff, Bruce. "Black Humor, Existentialism, and Absurdity: A Generic Confusion." *ArQ*, 30: 293-304 (1974)

Jone, D.A. "The Game of the Name in B's *The Sot-Weed Factor.*" *RSW*, 40: 219-21 (1972).
———. "JB's 'Anonymiad.'" *SSF*, 11: 361-6 (Fa 74).
Kennard, J.E. "JB: Imitations of Imitations." *Mosaic*, 3: 116-31 (Wi 70).
Kiernan, R.F. "JB's Artist in the Fun House." 2SSF, 10: 373-80 (Fa 73).
Knapp, E.H. "Found in the Barthhouse: Novelist as Savior." *MFS*, 14: 446-51 (Wi 68-69).
Koelb, Clayton. "JB's 'Glossolalia.'" *CL*, 26: 334-45 (Fa 74).
Korkowski, Eugene. "Scriblerus' Sinking Opera: *Peri Bathous XIII.*" *L&P*, 24: 80-8 (1974).
Kyle, Carol A. "The Unity of Anatomy: The Structure of B's *Lost in the Funhouse.*" *Critique*, 13: 31-43 (1972).
Le Clair, Thomas. "JB's *The Floating Opera*: Death and the Craft of Fiction." *TSLL*, 14: 711-30 (Wi 73).
Leff, L.J. "Utopia Reconstructed." *Critique*, 12: 29-37 (1971).
Le Rebeller, Annie. "A Spectatorial Skeptic: An Interview with JB." *Caliban XII* (Toulouse), 11: 93-110 (1975).
McDonald, J.L. "B's Syllabus: The Frame of *Giles Goat-Boy.*" *Critique*, 13: 5-10 (#3 72).
Majdiak, Daniel. "B and the Representation of Life." *Criticism*, 12: 51-67 (Wi 70).
Mercer, Peter. "The Rhetoric of *Giles Goat-Boy.*" *Novel*, 4: 147-158 (1971).
Morrell, David. "Ebenezer Cooke, Sot-Weed Factor Redivivus: The Genesis of JB's *The Sot-Weed Factor.*" *BMMLA*, 8: 32-47 (Sp 75).
Morris, Christopher. "B and Lacan: The World of the Moebius Strip." *Critique*, 17: 69-77 (1Q 75).
Pinsker, Sanford. "JB: The Teller Who Swallowed His Tale." *STC*, 10: 55-68 (Fa 72).
Richardson, Jack. "Amusement and Revelation." *NRep*, 159: 30-5 (23 N 68).
Rodrigues, Eusebio. "The Living Sakhyan in B's *Giles Goat-Boy.*" *NCLit*, 2: 7-8 (S 72).
Rubin, L.D. "Don Quixotic and Selected Progeny: Or, the Journey-man as Outsider." *SoR*, 10: 31-58 (Wi 74).
———. "The Great American Joke." *SAQ*, 72: 82-94 (Wi 73).
Ryan, Marjorie. "Four Contemporary Satires and the Problem of Norms." *SNL*, 6: 40-6 (Sp 69).
Scholes, Robert. "The Allegory of Exhaustion." *FicI*, 1: 106-8 (Fa 73).
———. "Disciple of Scheherezade." *NYT*, 8 My 66, pp. 5, 22.
———. "Metafiction." *IowaR*, 1: 100-15 (Fa 70).
Shenker, Israel. "Complicated Simple Things." *NYT*, 24 Sp 72, pp. 35-38.
Shimura, Masao. "B to America Bungaku no Dente." *EigoS*, 117: 414-6 (1971).
———. "JB, *The End of the Road*, and the Tradition of American Fiction of American Fiction." *SELit*, 1971, pp. 73-87.
Slethaug, G.E. "B's Refutation of the Idea of Progress." *Critique*, 13: 11-29 (#3 72).
Sommavilla, Guido. "Il cinismo cosmico di JB." *Letture*, 24: 98-110 (1969).
Stark, John. "Borges' 'Tlön, Uqbar, Orbis Tertius' and Nabokov's *Pale Fire*: Literature of Exhaustion." *TSLL*, 14: 139-45 (1972).
Stoddard, Donald. "Proza ironica a lui JB." *Steaua*, 24: 27 (1974).
Sugiura, Ginsaku. "Imitations-of-Novel—JB no Shosetsu." *EigoS*, 115: 612-3 (1969).
Tanner, S.L. "JB's Hamlet." *SWR*, 56: 347-54 (Au 71).
Tatham, Campbell. "The Gilesian Monomyth: Some Remarks on the Structure of *Giles Goat-Boy.*" *Genre*, 3: 364-75 (D 70).
———. "JB and the Aesthetics of Artifice." *ConL*, 12: 60-73 (Wi 71).
———. "Message: Concerning the *Felt* Ultimacies of JB." *Boun2*, 3: 259-87 (Wi 75).
Tilton, J.W. "*Giles Goat-Boy*: An Interpretation." *BuR*, 18: 92-119 (Sp 70).

Trachtenberg, Stanley. "Counterhumor: Comedy in Contemporary American Fiction." *GaR*, 27: 33-48 (Sp 73).

Verzosa, G.L. "The Unsayable and its Expression in JB's *The End of the Road*." *SLRJ*, 5: 131-87 (1974).

Voelker, J.C. "The Drama of Digression: Narrative Technique in JB's *The Floating Opera*." *CimR*, 29: 34-44 (O 74).

Walter, J.F. "A Psychronology of Lust in Menippean Tradition: *Giles Goat-Boy*." *TCL*, 21: 394-410 (D 75).

*Weixlmann, Joseph N. "JS: A Bibliography." *Critique*, 13: 45-55 (#3 72).

Barthelme, Donald. Ditsky, John. "'With Ingenuity and Hard Work, Distracted': The Narrative Style of DB." *Style*, 9: 388-400 (Su 75).

Doxey, W.S. "DB's 'Views of My Father Weeping': A Modern View of Oedipus." *NCLit*, 3: 14-5 (Mr 73).

Flowers, Betty. "B's *Snow White*: The Reader-Patient Relationship." *Critique*, 16: 5-18 (3Q 75).

Freese, Peter. "DB *fictions*: Fragmente aus Wortern mit Wurmern." *JA*, 19: 126-41 (1974).

Giles, J.R. "The 'Marivaudian Being' Drowns His Children: Dehumanization in DB's 'Robert Kennedy Saved from Drowning,' and Joyce Carol Oates's *Wonderland*." *SHR*, 9: 63-75 (Wi 75).

Gillen, Francis. "DB's City: A Guide." *TCL*, 18: 37-44 (Ja 72).

*Klinkowitz, Jerome. "DB: A Checklist, 1957-1974." *Critique*, 16: 49-58 (3Q 75).

———. "DB's Super Fiction." *Critique*, 16: 5-18 (3Q 75).

Longleigh, P.J., Jr. "DB's *Snow White*." *Critique*, 11: 30-4 (1969).

McCaffery, Larry. "B's *Snow White*: The Aesthetics of Trash." *Critique*, 16: 19-32 (3Q 75).

*———. "DB, Robert Coover, William H. Gass: Three Checklists." *BB*, 31: 101-6 (Jl-S 74).

McNall, S.A. "Style, Reaction, and Lack of Reaction in B's *Snow White*." *Lang&S*, 8: 81-94 (1975).

McNamara, Eugene. "The Absurd Style in Contemporary American Literature." *HAB*, 19: 44-9 (Wi 68).

Moran, Charles. "B the Trash-Man: The Uses of Junk in the Classroom." *CEA*, 36: 32-3 (1974).

Schmitz, Neil. "DB and the Emergence of Modern Satire." *MinnR*, 1: 109-18 (Fa 71).

———. "What Irony Unravels." *PR*, 40: 482-90 (1973).

Scholes, Robert. "Metafiction." *IowaR*, 1: 100-15 (Fa 70).

Stott, William. "DB and the Death of Fiction." *Prospects*, 1: 369-88 (1975).

Todd, Richard. "Updike and B: Disengagement." *Atl*, 230: 126-32 (D 72).

Whalen, Tom. "Wonderful Elegance: B's 'The Party.'" *Critique*, 16: 44-8 (3Q 75).

Bartlett, Robert. Fobes, C.S. "RB: A Forgotten Transcendentalist." *ATQ*, 1: 130-34 (1969).

Bartram, John. Borland, Hal. "The Memorable Bartrams." *AH*, 26: 66-72 (Ap 75).

Gill, J.J. "Humor in JB's Journals." *AN&Q*, 12: 90-3 (F 74).

Harper, Francis. "Diary of a Journey through the Carolinas, Georgia, and Florida, from July 1, 1765, to April 10, 1766." *Am Philos Soc Trans*, 33: 1-120 (1942).

Bartram, William. Armstrong, E.K. "Chateaubriand's America." *PMLA*, 22: 345-70 (1907).

Arner, R.D. "Pastoral Patterns in WB's *Travels*." *TSL*, 18: 133-46 (1973).

*Barnhardt, J.H. "B Bibliography." *Bartonia*, Special issue, pp. 51-66.

Borland, Hal. "The Memorable Bs." *AH*, 26: 66-72 (Ap 75).

Cooper, Lane. "B Redivivus." *Nation*, 80: 152 (23 F 05).

————. "A Glance at Wordsworth's Reading." *MLN*, 22: 110-7 (1907).

Eugenia, Sister. "Coleridge's Scheme of Pantisocracy and American Travel Accounts." *PMLA*, 45: 1069-84 (1930).

Gee, Wilson. "South Carolina Botanists: . . . WB." *Un SC Bul*, 72: 17-9 (1918).

Gummere, R.M. "WB: A Classical Scientist." *CJ*, 50: 167-70 (1955).

Harper, Francis. "The B Trail through the Southeastern States." *Bul Garden Club Am*, 7: 54-64 (1939).

————. "Travels in Georgia and Florida, 1773-1774: A Report to Dr. John Fothergill." *Am Philos Soc Trans*, 33: 131-242 (1944).

————. "WB's Bicentennial." *Sci Mo*, 48: 380-4 (Ap 39).

————. "WB's Names of Birds." *Proc Rochester Acad Sci*, 8: 208-21 (1942).

Lee, B.G. "WB: Naturalist or 'Poet'?" *EAL*, 7: 124-9 (Fa 72).

Melvin, Lionel. "There Were Four WBs." *NC State*, 39: 11-2 (15 D 71).

Basso, Hamilton. Ransom, J.C. "Modern with Southern Accent." *VQR*, 11: 184-200 (1935).

Rocks, J.E. "HB and the World View from Pompey's Head." *SAQ*, 71: 326-41 (Su 72).

Bathurst, Bill. Bertolino, James. "San Francisco Sacramento & Alpine Texas." *New*, 15: 9-13 (Ap-My 71).

Baxter, James K. Doyle, Charles. "JK.B: In Quest of the Just City." *Ariel*, 5: 81-98 (Jl 74).

Baum, L. Frank. Berman, Ruth. "The Unretiring Wizard." *Baum Bugle*, 18: 6-7 (Sp 74).

Delkin, Jay. "The Meaning of 'OZ.'" *Baum Bugle*, 15: 18-20 (1971).

————. "The Trouble with . . . Part One: Eggs." *Baum Bugle*, 19: 9 (Wi 75).

Erisman, Fred. "L.FB and the Progressive Dilemma." *AQ*, 20: 616-23 (Fa 68).

Gage, M.J. "'The Man with the Red Shirt' by L.FB." *Baum Bugle*, 17: 21 (1973).

Greene, D.G. "Fanny Y. Cory (Illustrator of B)." *Baum Bugle*, 17: 17-20 (1973).

Greene, D.L. "A Case of Insult." *Baum Bugle*, 18: 10-1 (Sp 74).

————. "L.FB's Later Oz Books, 1914-1920." *Baum Bugle*, 16: 17-20 (1972).

————. "The Little Wizard Series: L.FB's Six Short Oz Books." *Baum Bugle*, 17: 19-23 (1973).

*————. "The Periodical B: An Annotated Checklist." *Baum Bugle*, 19: 3-9 (Au 75).

————. "The Writing of Two L.FB Fantasies." *Baum Bugle*, 15: 14-6 (1971).

————. and Peter Hanff. "B and Denslow: Their Books." *Baum Bugle*, 19: 7-11 (Sp 75).

*Haff, James. "Bibliographia Pseudonymiana." *Baum Bugle*, 19: 10-12 (Wi 75).

Hanff, P.E. "L.FB's Return to Oz." *Baum Bugle*, 17: 22-4 (1973).

Hearn, M.P. "How Did the Woggle-Bug Do?" *Baum Bugle*, 18: 16-23 (Christmas 74).

————. "Special W.W. Denslow (First Illustrator of *Oz*) Issue." *Baum Bugle*, 16: 3-30 (1972).

————, D.L. Greene, and P.E. Hanff. "The Faltering Flight of Prince Silverwings." *Baum Bugle*, 18: 4-10 (1974).

Hollister, C.W. "Oz and the Fifth Criterion." *Baum Bugle*, 15: 5-8 (1971).

Indick, Ben. "Utopia, Allegory and Nightmare." *Baum Bugle*, 18: 14-9 (Sp 74).

Koelle, B.S. "Memorable Horses of Oz." *Baum Bugle*, 17: 6-13 (1973).

————. "Oz in Russia." *Baum Bugle*, 19: 16-7 (#1 75).

Mannix, D.P. "The Enigma of Button-Bright." *Baum Bugle*, 16: 18-21 (1972).

Mills, Richard. "The Oz Film Manufacturing Company." *Baum Bugle*, 16: 5-11 (1972); 17: 5-10 (1973); 17: 6-13 (1973).

Miner, Harold. "America in Oz, Part I." *Baum Bugle*, 19: 2-8 (Wi 75).

Pike, Judy. "A Map of the Wonder City of Oz." *Baum Bugle*, 16: 5-10 (1972).

Reckford, K.J. "The Wizard's Magic." *Baum Bugle*, 17: 22-5 (1973).

Sale, Roger. "L.FB, and Oz." *HudR*, 25: 571-92 (Wi 72/73).

Schumen, Samuel. "'Out of the Frying Pan and into the Pyre': Comedy, Myth, and *The Wizard of Oz*." *JPC*, 7: 302-4 (1973).

Starr, N.C. "The Wonderful Wizard of Oz: A Study in Archetypal Mythic Symbiosis." *Unicorn*, 2: 13-7 (#4 73).

Tobias, J.V. "Footnotes to Oz: Oz Etymology." *Baum Bugle*, 18: 8-11 (1974).

Baumbach, Jonathan. Klinkowitz, Jerome. "JB's Super Fiction." *ChiR*, 21: 178-88 (Sp 75).

Bayes, Ron. Rigsbee, David. "*Porpoise*." *StAR*, 2: 344-5 (Sp-Su 74).

Beach, Joseph Warren. Simmons, M.K. "A Look into *The Glass Mountain*." *AL*, 41: 42205 (N 69).

Beagle, Peter S. Van Becker, David. "Time, Space, and Consciousness in the Fantasy of PS.B." *San Jose Stud*, 1: 52-61 (F 75).

Bechdolt, Fred R. Stein, A.F. "'9009'—Early Naturalistic Novel." *IllQ*, 31-42 (F 74).

Beckham, Barry. Pinsker, Sanford. "About *Runner Mack*: An Interview with BB." *Black Images*, 3: 35-41 (1974).

———. "A Conversation with BB." *SBL*, 5: 11-6 (Wi 74).

Bedichek, Roy. Bedichek, Roy. "My Father and Then My Mother." *SWR*, 52: 324-423 (1967).

Beebe, Lucius. Douglas, G.H. "LB: Popular Railroad History as Social Nostalgia." *JPC*, 4: 893-910 (Sp 71).

Belitt, Ben. Boyers, Robert. "To Confront Nullity: The Poetry of BB." *SR*, 81: 753-73 (Au 73).

Hutton, Joan. "Antipodal Man: An Interview with BB." *Midway*, 10: 19-47 (#3 70).

Landis, J.M. "A 'Wild Severity': Towards a Reading of BB." *Salmagundi*, 22-3: 187-205 (1973).

Mills, R.J. "A Strenuous Sweetness: BB." *Voyages*, 1: 14-5 (Fa 67).

Nemerov, Howard. "Howard Nemerov on BB." *Voyages*, 1: 29-30 (Fa 67).

Bellamy, Edward. Bowman, S.E. "Utopian Views of Man and the Machine." *SLitI*, 6: 105-20 (#2 73).

Cornet, R.J. "Rhetorical Strategies in *Looking Backward*." *MarkR*, 4: 53-8 (My 74).

Gildzen, Alex. "The Anonymity of EB's First Book and Other BAL Variants." *PBSA*, 68: 63 (Ja-Mr 74).

Gutek, Gerald, "Analysis of Formal Education in EB's *Looking Backward*." *HEQ*, 4: 251-63 (D 64).

Ketterer, David. "Utopian Fantasy as Millennial Motive and Science-Fictional Motif." *SLitI*, 6: 79-103 (#2 73).

Parssinen, T.M. "B, Morris, and the Image of the Industrial City in Victorian Social Criticism." *MwQ*, 14: 257-66 (1973).

Riegel, R.E. "EB, Looking Backward 2000-1887." *Soc Ed*, 16: 11-3 (Ja 52).

Roemer, K.M. "'Utopia Made Practical': Compulsive Realism." *ALR*, 7: 273-6 (Su 74).

Sancton, T.A. "Looking Inward: EB's Spiritual Crisis." *AQ*, 25: 538-57 (D 73).

Towers, T.H. "The Insomnia of Julian West." *AL*, 47: 52-63 (Mr 75).

Trimmer, J.F. "American Dreams: A Comparative Study of the Utopian Novels of B and Howells." *BSUF*, 12: 12-21 (Su 71).

Wild, P.H. "Teaching Utopia." *EJ*, 55: 335-75 (Mr 66).

Bellew, Frank. Cameron, K.W. "FB and Emerson in Concord in 1855." *ESQ*, 52: 82-5 (3Q 68).

————. "Thoreau and FB in Concord." *ESQ*, 51: 141-3 (2Q 68).

Bellow, Saul. Alexander, Edward. "Imagining the Holocaust: *Mr. Sammler's Planet* and Others." *Judaism*, 22: 288-300 (1973).

Atchity, K.J. "B's Mr. Sammler: 'The last man given for epitome.'" *RSW*, 38: 46-54 (Mr 70).

Anderson, Don. "Comic Modes in American Fiction." *SoRA*, 8: 152-65 (Je 75).

Atkins, Anselm. "The Moderate Optimism of SB's *Herzog*." *Person*, 50: 117-29 (Wi 69).

Axelrod, S.G. "The Jewishness of B's Henderson." *AL*, 47: 439-43 (N 75).

Bailey, J.M. "The Qualified Affirmation of SB's Recent Work." *JAmSt*, 7: 67-76 (Ap 73).

Baim, Joseph. "Escape from Intellection: SB's *Dangling Man*." *UR*, 37: 28-34 (Au 70).

————, and D.P. Demarest. "*Henderson the Rain King*: A Major Theme and a Technical Problem." *CaSe*, 11: 53-63 (1970).

Bakker, J. "In Search of Reality: Two American Heroes Compared." *DQR*, 4: 145-61 (1972).

Balota, Nicolae. "SB si ramanul inadaptarii." *RoLit*, 27: 13 (Jl 72).

Baruch, F.B. "B and Milton: Professor Heroz in His Garden." *Critique*, 9: 74-83 (#3 67).

Bayley, John. "By Way of Mr. Sammler." *Salmagundi*, 30: 24-33 (1975).

Belitt, Benn. 'SB: The Depth Factor." *Salmagundi*, 30: 57-65 (1975).

Bellow, Saul. "In cautarea domnului Greene." *Steaua*, 25: 40-3 (1974).

————. "Ha Sofer ve-ha-Olam." *Molad*, 32: 178-83 (1974).

————. "La Literature en la era de la teccnologia." *Plural*, 36: 16-23 (1974).

————. "Mechonot ve-Sippurei Ma'assiyot." *Mo'oznayim*, 40: 210-14 (1975).

————. "Some Questions and Answers." *Ontario R*, 3: 51-60 (1975).

————. "Starting Out in Chicago." *ASch*, 44: 71-7 (Wi 74-75).

————. "A World too Much with Us." *CritI*, 2: 1-9 (1975).

Bezanker, Abraham. "The Odyssey of SB." *YR*, 58: 359-71 (Sp 69).

Bolling, Douglas. "Intellectual and Aesthetic Dimensions of *Mr. Sammler's Planet*." *JNT*, 4: 188-203 (S 74).

Boulger, J.D. "Puritan Allegory in Four Modern Novels." *Thought*, 44: 413-32 (Au 69).

Boyers, Robert. "Nature and Social Reality in B's *Sammler*." *CritQ*, 15: 251-71 (Au 73).

————, et al. "Literature and Culture: An Interview with SB." *Salmagundi*, 30: 6-20 (1975).

Braem, H.M. "Der Weg SB." *NRs*, 82: 742-52 (1971).

Brophy, R.J. "Biblical Parallels in B's *Henderson the Rain King*." *Chri and Lit*, 23: 27-30 (Su 74).

Buitenhuis, Peter. "A Corresponding Fabric: The Urban World of SB." *Costerus*, 8: 13-36 (1973).

Campbell, J.H. "B's Intimations of Immortality: *Henderson the Rain King*." *StN*, 1: 323-33 (Fa 69).

Cecil, L.M. "B's Henderson as American Imago of the 1950's." *RSW*, 40: 296-300 (1972).

Chametzky, Jules. "Notes on the Assimilation of the American-Jewish Writer: Abraham Cahan to SB." *JA*, 9: 173-80 (1964).

Chapman, S.S. "Melville and B in the Real World: *Pierre* and *Augie March*." *WVUPP*, 18: 51-7 (S 71).

Ciancio, Ralph. "The Achievement of SB's *Seize the Day*." *UTMS*, 7: 49-80 (1969).

Cohen, S.B. "Sex: SB's Hedonistic Joke." *SAF*, 2: 223-9 (Au 74).

Cordesse, Gérard. "L'unité de 'Herzog.'" *Caliban*, 7: 99-113 (1970).

Cornis-Pop, Marcel. "Alienarea si necesitatea reintegrarii in societate: Consideratii asupra romanului lui SB." *Orizont*, 22: 51-7 (1971).

Crozier, R.D. "Theme in *Augie March*." *Critique*, 7: 18-32 (Su 65).

Cushman, Keith, "Mr. B's *Sammler*: The Evolution of a Contemporary Text." *StN*, 7: 425-44 (Fa 75).

Davis, W.V. "B's *Herzog*." *Orion*, 118: 73 (1969).

Demarest, D.P. "The Theme of Discontinuity in SB's Fiction: 'Looking for Mr. Green' and 'A Father-to-Be.'" *SSF*, 6: 175-86 (Wi 69).

DeMott, Benjamin. "SB and the Dogmas of Possibility." *SatR*, 53: 25-8, 37 (7 F 70).

De Rambures, J. "La Fin du Heros Muscle: *Herzog* de SB." *Realités*, 248: 99-105 (S 66).

Ditsky, John. "The Watch and Chain of Henry James." *UWR*, 6: 91-101 (Fa 70).

Drabble, Margaret. "A Myth to Stump the Experts." *NSt*, nv: 435 (26 Mr 71).

Edwards, Duane. "The Quest for Reality in *Henderson the Rain King*." *DR*, 53: 246-55 (Su 73).

Egmond, P.V. "Herzog's Quotation of Walt Whitman." *WWR*, 13: 54-6 (Je 67).

Epstein, Joseph. "SB of Chicago." *NYT*, 9 My 71, pp. 4-16.

Eror, Gvozden. "Kosmarna farsa o zrtvi SB." *Knjizevna*, 57: 99-108 (1973).

Finkelstein, Sidney. "The Anti-Hero of Updike, B and Malamud." *AmD*, 7: 12-4, 30 (1972).

Fisch, Harold. "The Hero as Jew: Reflections on *Herzog*." *Judaism*, 17: 42-54 (Wi 68).

Flamm, Dudley. "*Herzog*—Victim and Hero." *ZAA*, 17: 174-88 (1969).

Fossum, R.H. "Inflationary Trends in the Criticism of Fiction: Four Studies of SB." *StN*, 2: 99-104 (1970).

Frohock, W.M. "SB and His Penitent Picaro." *SWR*, 53: 36-44 (Wi 68).

Fuchs, Daniel. "SB and the Modern Tradition." *ConL*, 15: 67 89 (Wi 74).

Galloway, David. "*Mr. Sammler's Planet*: B's Failure of Nerve." *MFS*, 19: 17-28 (Sp 73).

Giannone, Richard. "SB's Idea of Self: A Reading of *Seize the Day*." *Renascence*, 27: 193-206 (Su 75).

Gill, Brendan. "Surprised by Joy." *NY*, 40: 218-22 (2 O 64).

Gindin, James. "The Fable Begins to Break Down." *WSCL*, 8: 1-18 (Wi 67).

Grossman, Edward. "The Bitterness of SB." *Midstream*, 16: 3-15 (S 70).

Grubb, D.S. "Another Gulliver?" *StH*, 4: 3-9 (Mr 74).

Guttmann, Allen. "B's *Henderson*." *Critique*, 7: 33-42 (Sp-Su 65).

———. "SB's Mr. Sammler." *ConL*, 14: 157-68 (Sp 73).

Hadari, Amnon. "Ha-professor Eino Me'uban; *Cohav Ha-lekhet Shel Mar Sammler* Me'et SB." *Shdemot*, 44: 102-13 (1971).

Harris, J.N. "One Critical Approach to *Mr. Sammler's Planet*." *TCL*, 18: 235-50 (1972).

Hill, J.S. "The Letters of Moses Herzog: A Symbolic Mirror." *StH*, 2: 40-5 (1971).

Hoffman, M.J. "From Cohn to *Herzog*." *YR*, 58: 342-58 (Sp 69).

Honma, Nagayo. "SB no Gendai Bunka Ron." *EigoS*, 118: 260-1 (1972).

Howard, Jane. "Mr. B Considers His Planet." *Life*, 3 Ap 70, pp. 57-60.

Hull, B.D. "*Henderson The Rain King* and William James." *Criticism*, 13: 402-14 (Fa 71).

Hux, Samuel. "Character and Form in B." *Forum (H)*, 12: 34-8 (1974).

Iwamoto, Iwao. "Judea-kei Sakka no Miryoku—B to Malamud." *EigoS*, 118: 257-60 (1972).

Iwayama, Tajiro. "Marginal Man no ikiru Joken—SB no *Herzog* to *Mr. Sammler's Planet*." *EigoS*, 118: 133-5 (1972).

Jefchak, Andrew. "Family Struggles in 'Seize the Day.'" *SSF*, 11: 297-302 (Su 74).

Josipovici, Gabriel. "B & Herzog." *Enc*, 37: 49-55 (N 71).

Kauffman, Stanley. "SB: A Closing Note." *Salmagundi*, 30: 90-1 (1975).

Kazin, Alfred. "Absurdity as Contemporary Style." *MeditR*, 1: 39-46 (Sp 71).

Klein, Jeffrey. "Armies of the Planet." *Soundings*, 58: 68-83 (1975).

Knipp, T.R. "The Cost of Henderson's Quest." *BSUF*, 10: 37-9 (Sp 69).

Kulshrestha, Chirantan. "A Conversation with SB." *ChiR*, 23-4: 7-15 (1972).

Kuna, F.M. "The European Culture Game: Mr. B's Planet." *ES*, 53: 531-44 (D 72).

Kyria, Pierre. "Le Monde Americain." *RdP*: 120-5 (Mr 67).

Lamont, R.C. "B Observed: A Serial Portrait." *Mosaic*, 8: 247-57 (1974).

Lemon, L.T. "Beyond Alienation." *Aegis*, 2: 5-12 (Fa 73).

Le Pellec, Yves. "New York in Summer: Its Symbolical Function in *The Victim*." *Caliban*, 8: 101-10 (1971).

Lippit, N.M. "A Perennial Survivor: SB's Heroine in the Desert." *SSF*, 12: 281-3 (Su 75).

Löfroth, Erik. "Herzog's Predicament: SB's View of Man." *SN*, 44: 315-25 (1972).

———. "SB: A Defense of the Self." *SN*, 44: 315-25 (1972).

Lucko, Peter. "Herzog—Modell der *acceptance*: Eine Erwiderung." *ZAA* 17: 189-95 (1969).

Lycette, R.L. "SB and the American Naturalists." *Disc*, 13: 435-49 (Au 70).

Majdiak, Daniel. "The Romantic Self and *Henderson The Rain King*." *BuR*, 19: 125-46 (Fa 71).

Maloney, S.R. "Half-Way to Byzantium: *Mr. Sammler's Planet* and the Modern Tradition." *SCR*, 6: 31-40 (N 73).

Manske, Eva. "Das Mesnchenbild im Prosaschriften SB: Anspruch und Wirklichkeit. " *ZAA*, 21: 270-88 (My-Je 73).

Markos, D.W. "Life Against Death in *Henderson the Rain King*." *MFS*, 17: 193-205 (Su 71).

Mathis, J.C. "The Theme of *Seize the Day*." *Critique*, 7: 43-5 (Sp-Su 65).

Mathy, Francis. "Zetsubo no kanata ni." *SophT*, 19: 356-77 (1970).

Mellard, James. "*Dangling Man*: SB's Lyrical Experiment." *BSUF*, 15: 67-74 (Sp 74).

Mosher, H.F. "The Synthesis of Past and Present in SB's *Herzog*." *WascR*, 6: 28-38 (1971).

Moss, J.P. "The Body as Symbol in SB's *Henderson the Rain King*." *L&P*, 20: 51-61 (1970).

Mukerji, Nirmal. "A Reading of SB's *Seize the Day*." *LCrit*, 9: 48-53 (Wi 69).

Mukherjee, N. "The B Hero." *IJES*, 9: 74-86 (1968).

Normand, Jean. "L'homme mystifié: Les héros de B, Albee, Styron, et Mailer." *EA*, 22: 370-85 (O-D 69).

Overbeck, P.T. "The Women in *Augie March*." *TSLL*, 10: 471-84 (Fa 68).

Pearson, Carol. "B's *Henderson the Rain King* and the Myth of the King, the Fool, and the Hero." *NCLit*, 5: 8-11 (N 75).

Peter, John. "The Self-Effacement of the Novelist." *MalR*, 8: 119-28 (O 68).

Pinsker, Sanford. "Moses Herzog's Fall into the Quotidian." *STC*, 14: 105-16 (Fa 74).

———. "SB in the Classroom." *CE*, 24: 975-82, (Ap 73).

Porter, M.G. "*Herzog*: A Transcendental Solution to an Existential Problem." *Forum(H)*, 7: 32-6 (Sp 69).

Rao, R.M.V.R. "Chaos of the Self: An Approach to SB's *Dangling Man*." *OJES*, 8: 89-103 (1971).

Rao, Raghavendra. "Father Figure in SB's *Dangling Man*." *OJES*, 10: 37-43 (1973).

Richmond, L.J. "The Maladroit, the Medico, and the Magician: SB's '*Seize the Day*.'" *TCL*, 19: 15-26 (Ja 73).

Rodrigues, E.L. "B's Africa." *AL*, 43: 242-56 (My 71).

———. "B's Confidence Man." *NCLit*, 3: 6-8 (Ja 73).

———. "Koheleth in Chicago: The Quest for the Real in 'Looking for Mr. Green.'" *SSF*, 11: 387-94 (Fa 74).

————. "Reichianism in *Henderson the Rain King*." *Criticism*, 15: 212-33 (Su 73).

Rosu, Anca. "The Picaresque Technique in SB's *Adventures of Augie March*." *AUB-LG*, 22: 191-7 (1973).

Roth, Philip. "Imagining Jews." *NYRB*, 21: 22-8 (2 O 74).

Russell, Mariann. "White Man's Black Man." *CLAJ*, 17: 93-100 (1973).

Salter, D.P.M. "Optimism and Reaction is SB's Recent Work." *CritQ*, 14: 57-66 (Sp 72).

Samuels, C.T. "B on Modernism." *NRep*, 162: 27-30 (7 F 70).

Saporta, Marc. "Interview avec SB." *FL*, 1193: 24-5 (17 Mr 69).

Sastri, P.S. "B's *Henderson the Rain King*: A Quest for Being." *PURBA*, 3: 9-18 (#1 72).

Satyanarayana, M.R. "The Reality Teacher as Hero: A Study of SB's *Mr. Sammler's Planet*." *OJES*, 8: 55-68 (#2 71).

Scheer-Schaezler, Brigitte. "Short Story and Modern Novel: A Comparative Analysis of Two Texts." *OL*, 25: 338-51 (1970).

Shechner, Mark. "Down in the Mouth with SB." *AmR*, 23: 40-7 (1975).

Schueler, M.D. "The Figure of Madeleine in *Herzog*." *NCLit*, 1: 5-7 (My 71).

Sharma, D.K. "*Mr. Sammler's Planet*: Another 'Passage' to India." *PURBA*, 4: 97-104 (Ap 73).

Shastri, N.R. "Primitivistic Motif in SB's *Henderson the Rain King*." *OJES*, 10: 57-67 (1973).

————. "Self and Society in SB's *The Victim*." *OJES*, 8: 105-12 (#1 71).

Shibuya, Yusaburo. "SB Ron—Moralist to shite no Sokumen wo Chushin ni." *EigoS*, 118: 254-6 (1972).

Shulman, Robert. "The Style of B's Comedy." *PMLA*, 83: 109-17 (Mr 68).

Sicherman, C.M. "B's *Seize the Day*." *STC*, 15: 1-31 (1975).

Steig, Michael. "B's *Henderson* and the Limits of Freudian Criticism." *Paunch*, 36-7: 39-46 (Ap 73).

Steinke, Russell. "The Monologic Temper of B's Fiction." *Junction*, 1: 178-84 (#3 73).

Sullivan, J.J. "Conflict in the Modern American Novel." *BSUF*, 15: 28-36 (1974).

Tanner, Tony. "SB: An Introductory Note." *Salmagundi*, 30: 3-5 (1975).

Tijeras, Eduardo. "SB." *CHA*, 274: 182-6 (1973).

Toth, S.A. "*Henderson the Rain King*. Eliot and Browning." *NCLit*, 1: 6-8 (N 71).

Towner, Daniel. "Brill's Ruins and Henderson Rain." *Critique*, 17: 96-104 (#3 75).

Trachtenberg, Stanley. "SB's Luftmenschen: The Compromise Reality." *Critique*, 9: 37-61 (1967).

Trowbridge, C.W. "Water Imagery in *Seize the Day*." *Critique*, 9: 62-73 (1967).

Ustvedt, Yngvar. "SB—en amerikans natidsdikter." *Samtiden*, 80: 273-82 (My 71).

Vogel, Dan. "SB's Vision Beyond Absurdity: Jewishness in *Herzog*." *Tradition*, 9: 65-79 (Sp 68).

Walker, Marshall. "Herzog: The Professor as Drop-Out?" *EAS*, 15: 39-51 (Mr 72).

Weber, Ronald. "B's Thinkers." *WHR*, 22: 305-13 (Au 68).

Weinstein, Norman. "*Herzog*, Order and Entropy." *ES*, 54: 336-46 (Ag 73).

Young, J.D. "B's View of the Heart." *Critique*, 7: 5-17 (Sp-Su 65).

Zeitlow, E.R. "SB: The Theater of the Soul." *Ariel*, 4: 44-59 (O 73).

Benchley, Robert. Hasley, Louis. "RB: Humorist's Humorist." *ConnR*, 4: 65-72 (1970).

Shanahan, William. "RB and Dorothy Parker: Punch and Judy in Formal Dress." *Rendezvous*, 3: 23-34 (1968).

Benefield, Barry. Hatley, D.W. "Folklore in the Fiction of BB." *MissQ*, 21: 63-70 (Wi 67-68).

Benét, Stephen Vincent. Griffith, John. "Narrative Technique and the Meaning of History in B and MacLeish." *JNT*, 3: 3-19 (Ja 73).

Sheehan, D.B. "B's *John Brown's Body.*" *EJ*, 58: 219-25 (F 69).

Womack, Judy. "Daniel Boone—'Over the Velvet Falls.'" *KFR*, 18: 21-2 (1972).

Benezet, Anthony. Bruns, R.A. "AB and the Natural Rights of the Negro." *PMHB*, 96: 104-13 (1972).

Benjamin, Park. Gilkes, L.B. "Hawthorne, PB, and S.G. Goodrich: A Three-Cornered Imbroglio." *NHJ*, 1: 83-112 (1971).

———. "PB, Henry William Herbert, and William Gilmore Simms: A Case of Mistaken Identity." *SCR*, 3: 66-77 (Je 71).

Turner, Arlin. "PB on the Author and the Illustrator of 'The Gentle Boy.'" *NHJ*, 4: 85-91 (1974).

Bennett, Emerson. Poulsen, R.C. "Black George, Black Harris, and the Mountain Man Vernacular." *Rendezvous*, 8: 172-87 (Su 73).

Bennett, Hal. Walcott, Ronald. "The Novels of HB." *BlackW*, 23: 36-48, 89-97 (Je 74); 78-96 (Jl 74).

Bennett, James Gordon. Crouthamel, J.L. "JGB, the *New York Herald*, and the Development of Newspaper Sensationalism." *NYH*, 54: 294-316 (Jl 73).

Page, E.F. "The Romance of Southern Journalism." *Taylor-Trotwood Magazine*, 11: 140-8 (Je 10).

Berger, Thomas. Dippie, B.W. "Jack Crabb and the Sole Survivors of Custer's Last Stand." *WAL*, 4: 189-202 (Fa 69).

Fetrow, F.M. "The Function of the External Narrator in TB's *Little Big Man.*" *JNT*, 5: 57-65 (Ja 75).

Gurian, Jay. "Style in the Literary Desert: *Little Big Man.*" *WAL*, 3: 285-96 (Wi 69).

Hughes, D.A. "The Schlemiel as Humorist." *Cithara*, 15: 3-21 (#1 75).

Lee, L.L. "American, Western, Picaresque: TB's *Little Big Man.*" *SDR*, 4: 35-42 (Su 66).

Oliva, L.E. "TB's *Little Big Man* as History." *WAL*, 8: 33-54 (Sp-Su 73).

Ryan, Marjorie. "Four Contemporary Satires and the Problem of Norms." *SNL*, 6: 40-6 (Sp 69).

Turner, F.W. "Melville and TB: The Novelist as Cultural Anthropologist." *CentR*, 13: 101-21 (Wi 69).

Wylder, D.E. "TB's *Little Big Man* as Literature." *WAL*, 3: 273-84 (Wi 69).

Bergstein, Eleanor. Martin, Wendy. "EB, Novelist—An Interview." *WS*, 2: 91-7 (1974).

Berrigan, Daniel. Cargas, H.J. "DB: The Activist as Poet." *LauR*, 9: 11-7 (1969).

Isaac, Dan. "Theatre of Fact." *DramR*, 15: 109-35 (Su 71).

Quinn, J.P. "Thoreau and B: Seekers of the Lost Paradise." *TSB*, 127: 2-4 (Sp 74).

Berry, Wendell. Berry, Wendell. "An Essay and a Meditation." *SoR*, 6: 972-89 (Au 70).

———. "A Native Hill." *HudR*, 21: 601-34 (Wi 68).

Ditsky, John. "Love as a Farm and a Forest." *MPS*, 5: 92-3 (1974).

———. "WB: Homage to the Apple Tree." *MPS*, 2: 7-15 (1971).

Fields, Kenneth. "The Hunter's Trail: Poems by WB." *IowaR*, 1: 90-99 (Wi 70).

Fussell, Edwin. "Farm Poets and Garage Critics." *Parnassus*, 2: 25-32 (1974).

Hass, Robert. "WB: Finding the Land." *MPS*, 2: 16-38 (1971).

Morgan, Speer. "WB: A Fatal Singing." *SoR*, 10: 865-77 (O 74).

Payne, W.E. "WB and the Natural." *Resonance*, 1: 5-16 (1969).

Tarbet, D.W. "Contemporary American Pastoral: A Poetic Faith." *Eng Rec*, 23: 72-83 (Wi 72).

Berryman, John. Anon. "Congested Funeral: B's New Dream Songs." *TLS*, 26 Je 69, p. 680.

———. "The Life of the Modern Poet." *TLS*, 3703: 193-5 (23 Feb 73).

Aiken, Conrad. "A Letter." *Antaeus*, 8: 21 (Wi 73).

Arpin, Gary. "Forward to the End: B's First Dream Song." *JBS*, 1: 7-11 (Fa 75).

———. "'I Am Their Music': Lamentations and *The Dream Songs*." *JBS*, 1: 206 (Ja 75).

———. "Mistress Bradstreet's Discontents." *JBS*, 1: 2-7 (Jl 75).

Axelrod, Steven. "Colonel Shaw in American Poetry: 'For the Union Dead' and Its Precursors." *AQ*, 24: 523-38 (O 72).

Barbera, J.V. "JB: R.I.P." *JML*, 2: 547-53 (N 72).

Bayley, John. "JB: A Question of Imperial Sway." *Salmagundi*, 22-3: 84-102 (1973).

Bellow, Saul. "JB, Friend." *NYT*, 27 My 73, 1-2.

Brans, Jo. "Bones Bound, Henry Hero: A Reading of B's First Dream Song." *JBS*, 1: 12-6 (Fa 75).

Brenner, Patricia. "JB is Resting." *Cafe Solo*, 4: 14-5 (Fa 72).

Browne, M.D. "Henry Fermenting: Debts to the *Dream Songs*." *OhR*, 15: 75-87 (Wi 74).

Butscher, Edward. "JB: In Memorial Perspective." *GaR*, 27: 518-25 (Wi 73).

Carruth, Hayden. "Declining Occasions." *Poetry*, 112: 119-21 (My 68).

Dale, Peter. "Slithy Tome." *Agenda*, 9: 52-61 (Wi 71).

———. "Three Poets: Can Belief and Form Come in Bags of Tricks?" *SatR*, 55: 57-8 (8 Jl 72).

Dickey, James. "Orientations." *ASch*, 34: 646-58 (Au 65).

Dunn, Douglas. "Gaiety & Lamentation: The Defeat of JB." *Encounter*, 43: 72-7 (Ag 74).

Gilman, Milton. "B and the Sonnets." *Chelsea*, 22-3: 158-67 (Je 68).

Haffenden, John. "B's 'Certainty before Lunch.'" *JBS*, 1: 15-6 (Jl 75).

Hayes, Ann. "*Delusions, Etc.* and the Art of Distance." *JBS*, 1: 6-10 (Ja 75).

———. "The Voices of JB." *JBS*, 1: 17-20 (Jl 75).

Hazo, Samuel. "The Death of JB." *Cweal*, 95: 489-90 (25 F 72).

Heyen, William. "JB: A Memoir and an Interview." *OhR*, 15: 46-65 (Wi 74).

Holder, Alan. "Anne Bradstreet Resurrected." *CP*, 2: 11-18 (Sp 69).

Hughes, Daniel. "JB & The Poet's Pardon." *APR*, 2: 19-22 (Jl-Ag 73).

James, Clive. "JB." *Listener*, 87: 87-8 (20 Ja 72).

Kanaseki, Hisao. "B no Jisatsu." *EigoS*, 118: 62-3 (1972).

Kelly, Richard. "Pulling Together Henry." *JBS*, 1: 5-6 (Fa 75).

*———, and Ernest Stefanik. "JB: A Supplemental Checklist." *JBS*, 1: 25-35, 23-31 (Ap, Jl 75).

Kenedy, R.C. "JB: An Afterthought, or, 'The Sunset in a Cup.'" *ArtInt*, 17: 89-96 (My 73).

———. "JB: An Appreciation: The Poet's Language." *ArtInt*, 17: 92-8 (Ap 73).

———. "JB: A Study of His Poetry and An Appreciation." *ArtInt*, 17: 75-83, 104 (Mr 73).

Kostelanetz, Richard. "Conversation with B." *MR*, 11: 340-7 (Sp 70).

Lieberman, Laurence. "Hold the Audience!—A Brief Memoir of JB." *EigoS*, 118: 68-70 (1972); *JBS*, 1: 8-11 (Jl 75).

Linebarger, J.M. "B's Sonnets: Tradition and the Individual Talent." *CP*, 6: 19-26 (Sp 73).

———. "A Commentary on *B's Sonnets*." *JBS*, 1: 12-24 (Ja 75).

Lowell, Robert. "For JB." *NYRB*, 18: 3-4 (6 Ap 72).

McBride, M.M. "B's 'World's Fair.'" *Expl*, 34: 22 (N 75).

McClatchy, J.D. "JB: The Impediments to Salvation." *MPS*, 4: 246-77 (1975).

McMichael, James. "Borges and Strand, Weak Henry, Philip Levine." *SoR*, 8: 213-24 (1972).

Martz, L.L. "Recent Poetry: B and Others." *YR*, 61: 410-22 (1972).

Mazzocco, Robert. "Harlequin in Hell." *NYRB*, 8: 12-6 (29 Je 67).

Meredith, William. "In Loving Memory of the Late Author of the Dream Songs." *VQR*, 44: 70-8 (Wi 73).

Molesworth, Charles. "Shining the Start: Some Gloss on B's First Dream Songs." *JBS*, 1: 17-22 (Fa 75).

Neill, Edward. "Ambivalence of B: An Interim Report." *CritQ*, 16: 267-76 (Au 74).

Niikura, Shunichi. "B no Ichi." *EigoS*, 118: 66-7 (My 72).

———. "Mask no Shi to Hadaka no Shi—B wo megutte." *EigoS*, 117: 698-9 (F 72).

Niikura, Toshikazu. "B's Significance." *JBS*, 1: 14-8 (Ap 75).

Oberg, Arthur. "JB: *The Dream Songs* and the Horror of Unlove." *UWR*, 6: 1-11 (Fa 70).

———. "JB: Prosody and Overneeds." *JBS*, 1: 24-7 (Ja 75).

Patrick, W.B. "B's *77 Dream Songs*: 'Spare Now a Cagey John/A Whilom.'" *SHR*, 5: 113-9 (Sp 71).

Pavlovcak, Michael. "The Method of *The Dream Songs*." *JBS*, 1: 3-4 (Ja 75).

Perosa, Sergio. "A Note on Titles." *JBS*, 1: 5-6 (Fa 75).

Pinsky, Robert. "Hardy, Ransom, B: A 'Curious Air.'" *Agenda*, 10: 89-99 (1972).

Porterfield, J.R. "B's *A Strut for Roethke*." *Expl*, 32: 25 (D 73).

———. "The Melding of a Man: Berryman, Henry, and the Ornery Mr. Bones." *SWR*, 58: 30-46 (Wi 73).

Sawasaki, Junnosuke. "B no Shino Saiko." *EigoS*, 118: 64-6 (1972).

———. "JB no Shiho." *EigoS*, 116: 868-9 (1971).

Schendler, Sylvan. "B's Dream." *IJAS*, 3: 91-6 (1974).

Shaw, R.B. "An Interview with JB." *Antaeus*, 8: 7-19 (Wi 73).

Sheehan, Donald, "The Silver Sensibility: Five Recent Books of American Poetry." *ConL*, 12: 98-121 (Wi 71).

*Stefanik, E.C. "Bibliography: JB Criticism." *WCR*, 8: 45-52 (O 73).

———. "A Cursing Glory: JB's *Love & Fame*." *Renascence*, 25: 115-28 (Sp 73).

*Stefanik, Ernest. "A JB Checklist." *BB*, 31: 1-4, 28 (Ja-Mr 74).

———. "Knowing Henry: A Reading of Dream Song 1." *JBS*, 1: 23-29 (Fa 75).

Stitt, Peter. "The Art of Poetry XVI: JB." *PaR*, 53: 177-207 (Wi 72).

———. "B's Last Poems." *CP*, 6: 5-12 (Sp 73).

———. "'Bitter Sister, Victim! I Miss You': JB's 'Homage to Mistress Bradstreet.'" *JBS*, 1: 2-11 (Ap 75).

———. "JB: The Dispossessed Poet." *OhR*, 15: 66-74 (Wi 74).

———. "JB: Poetry and Personality." *AARev*, 17: 92-3 (1973).

Stoddard, Donald. "JB, Mistress Bradstreet si Henry." *Steaua*, 24: 29 (1974).

Strand, Mark. "Landscape and the Poetry of Self." *Prose*, 6: 169-83 (1973).

Straub, Peter. "Terror B & The New World." *Structure*, 1: 20-1, 25 (Sp 72).

Tokunaga, Yozo. "Shiteki na Koe, koteki na Koe—B to Lowell." *EigoS*, 118: 70-1 (1972).

———. "Yume no Henkyo wo yuko JB." *EigoS*, 115: 616-8 (1969).

Tulip, James. "The 'Tough Songs' of JB." *SoRA*, 6: 257-68 (1973).

Vendler, Helen. "Poetry: Ammons, B, Cummings." *YR*, 62: 412-19 (1973).

Vonalt, L.P. "B's *The Dream Songs*." *SR*, 79: 464-9 (1971).

———. "B's Most Bright Candle." *Parnassus*, 1: 180-7 (Fa-Wi 72).

———. "Dream Songs First and Last." *JBS*, 1: 30-5 (Fa 75).

Wasserstrom, William. "Cagey John: B as Medicine Man." *CentR*, 12: 334-54 (1968).

Wilson, Patrick. "The Ironic Title of B's *Love and Fame*." *NCLit*, 5: 10-2 (S 75).

Zande, Nichole. "JB, Visionnaire et Dandy." *Le Monde*, 8 J 72, p. 19.

Ziff, Paul. "A Creative Use of Language." *NLH*, 4: 107-18 (Au 72).

Beston, Henry. Russell, Francis. "The Outermost Man: HB 1889-1968." *MdA*, 12: 402-5 (Fa 68).

Betts, Doris. "Negro Characters in the Fiction of DB." *Critique*, 17: 59-76 (2Q 75).

Moose, Ruth. "Superstition in DB's New Novel." *NCF*, 21: 61-2 (My 73).

Bierce, Ambrose. Anon. "AB's Devilish Definitions." *AH*, 18: 112 (Ap 67).

———. "The Misanthrope." *Time*, 89: 102 (5 My 67).

———. "On Paragraphs." *HCS*, 33: 1-3 (1969).

Amelio, R.J. "Literature and the Films." *EEx*, 16: 4-6 (Wi-Sp 69).

Anderson, D.D. "Can Ohio and the Midwest Claim AB?" *Ohioana*, 16: 84-89 (Su 73).

Andrews, W.L. "Some New AB Fables." *ALR*, 8: 349-52 (Au 75).

Berkove, L.I. "Arms and the Man: AB's Response to War." *MichA*, 1: 21-30 (Wi 69).

Bleikasten, Andre, and Jean Deurberque. "Lapsus calami: Fantastique, fantasme et ecriture dans 'The Death of Halpin Fraysure.'" *RANAM*, 6: 105-26 (1973).

√Comprone, J.J. "A Dual-Media Look at 'An Occurrence at Owl Creek Bridge.'" *EEx*, 17: 14-7 (1972).

Crane, J.K. "Crossing the Bar Twice: Post-Mortem Consciousness in B, Hemingway, and Golding." *SSF*, 6: 361-76 (Su 69).

Davidson, C.N. "Literary Semantics and the Fiction of AB." *ETC*, 31: 263-71 (1974).

Davies, Walford. "Imitation and Invention: The Use of Borrowed Material in Dylan Thomas's Prose." *EIC*, 18: 275-95 (Jl 68).

Dimeo, Steven. "Psychological Symbolism in Three Early Tales of Invisibility." *RQ*, 5: 20-7 (1971).

Dunbar, J.R. "Letters of George Sterling to Carey McWilliams." *CHSQ*, 46: 235-52 (S 67).

Fatout, Paul. "AB (1842-1914)." *ALR*, 1: 13-9 (Fa 67).

*Fortenberry, G.E. "AB (1842-1914?):A Critical Bibliography of Secondary Comment." *ALR*, 4: 11-6 (Wi 71).

Garnett, Porter. "Poetics, B and Sterling." *PaM*, 18: 553-9 (N 07).

Grenander, M.E. "AB and *Cobwebs from an Empty Skull*: A Note on *BAL* 1100 and 1107." *PBSA*, 69: 403-6 (3 Q 75).

———. "AB and *In the Midst of Life*." *BC*, 20: 321-31 (Au 71).

———. "A London Letter of Joaquin Miller to AB." *YULG*, 46: 109-16 (O 71).

Gunji, Toshio. "'Akuma no Jiten' no Akuma." *EigoS*, 119: 589-90 (1974).

Hartwell, Ronald. "What Hemingway Learned from AB." *RSW*, 38: 309-11 (D 70).

Highsmith, J.M. "The Forms of Burlesque in *The Devil's Dictionary*." *SNL*, 7: 115-27 (1970).

Kantor, J.R. "AB: His Pupils, Friends, and Enemies." *Bancroftiana*, nv: 1-2 (S 75).

McLean, R.C. "The Deaths in AB's 'Halpin Frayser.'" *PLL*, 10: 394-402 (Fa 74).

McWilliams, Carey. "New Letters of AB." *Opinion*, 2: 3-4 (My 30).

√Marcus, F.H. "Film and Fiction: 'An Occurrence at Owl Creek Bridge.'" *CEJ*, 7: 14-23 (1971).

Monteiro, George. "Addenda to Gaer: B in *The Anti-Philistine*." *PBSA*, 66: 71-2 (1Q 72); 68: 330-1 (3Q 74).

Okuda, Shunsuke. "'Akuma no Jiten' no Fushisei." *EigoS*, 120: 28-9 (1974).

Pagetti, Carlo. "I racconti di AB." *SA*, 16: 255-99 (1970).

Roth, Russell. "AB's 'Destestable Creature.'" *WAL*, 9: 169-76 (Fa 74).

Slade, J.W. "'Putting You in the Papers': AB's Letters to Edwin Markham." *Prospects*, 1: 335-68 (1975).

Stein, W.B. "B's 'The Death of Halpin Frayser': The Poetics of Gothic Consciousness." *ESQ*, 18: 115-22 (2Q 72).

Stubbs, J.C. "AB's Constribitions to *Cosmopolitan*: An Annotated Bibliography." *ALR*, 4: 57-9 (Wi 71).

*Tanselle, G.T. "*BAL* Addendum: AB—Entry No. 1112." *PBSA*, 62: 451 (EQ 68).

Walker, D.L. "A Last Laugh for AB." *AmWest*, 10: 34-9, 63 (N 73).

Wiggins, R.A. "AB: A Romantic in an Age of Realism." *ALR*, 4: 1-10 (Wi 71).

Zarro, J.A. "Understanding Zap." *EJ*, 57: 654-7 (My 68).

Biggers, Earl D. Armato, D.M. "Charlie Chan in Books and in Motion Pictures." *ArmD*, 7: 97-9 (1974).

Breen, J.L. "Who Killed Charlie Chan?" *ArmD*, 7: 100, 127 (1974).

Billings, Josh. (See **Shaw, Henry Wheeler**).

Bird, Robert Montgomery. Bronson, D.R. "A Note on RMB's *Oralloossa*." *ELN*, 9: 46-9 (1971).

Hamilton, J.B. "RMB, Physician and Novelist." *Bul Hist Med*, 44: 315-31 (Jl-Ag 70).

Weidman, B.S. "White Men's Red Man: A Penitential Reading of Four American Novels." *MLS*, 4, ii: 14-26 (1974).

Birney, Hoffman. Robinson, F.C. "The Donner Party in Fiction." *Un Col Stud*, 10: 87-93 (F 66).

Bishop, Elizabeth. Bernlef, J. "Judith Hersberg en EB." *Gids*, 131: 325-7 (1968).

Fukuda, Rikutaro. "EB to Brazil." *EigoS*, 119: 674-5 (1974).

Gordon, J.B. "Days and Distances: The Cartographic Imagination of EB." *Salmagundi*, 22-3: 294-305 (1973).

James, Clive. "Everything's Rainbow." *Ren*, 25: 51-7 (1971).

Kirby-Smith, H.T. "Miss B and Others." *SR*, 80: 483-93 (1972).

Mazzaro, Jerome. "EB and the Poetics of Impediment." *Salmagundi*, 27: 118-44 (1974).

Mazzocco, Robert. "A Poet of Landscape." *NYRB*, 9: 4-6 (12 O 67).

Paz, Octavio. "EB o el poder de la reticencia." *Plural*, 49: 6-7 (1975).

Sheehan, Donald. "The Silver Sensibility: Five Recent Books of American Poetry." *ConL*, 12: 98-121 (Wi 71).

Spiegelman, Willard. "Landscape and Knowledge: The Poetry of EB." *MPS*, 4: 203-24 (1975).

Bishop, John Peale. Coxe, Louis. "Romance of the Rose: JPB and Phelps Putnam." *MQR*, 14: 150-8 (1975).

Fleissner, R.F. "B's 'No More the Senator' Once More." *NCLit*, 2: 11-14 (Ja 72).

Hayhoe, G.F. "JPB's Theory of Poetry." *MarkR*, 4: 34-8 (F 74).

Lowell, Robert. "Thomas, B, and Williams." *SW*, 55: 493-504 (Su 47).

Vauthier, Simone. "The Meaning of Structure: Toward a New Reading of JPB's *Act of Darkness*." *SLJ*, 7: 50-76 (Sp 75).

Bishop, Morris. Eddy, D.R. "MB: I. Separate Publications; II. Contributions to Periodicals." *CLJ*, 12: 5-16, 17-45 (1971).

Bissell, Richard. Bellamy, J.D. "Two Eras, Two Epitaphs: Steamboating Life in the Works of Mark Twain and RB." *BSUF*, 13: 48-52 (Fl 72).

Blackburn, Paul. Dembo, L.S. "An Interview with PB." *ConL*, 13: 133-43 (1972).

Eshleman, Clayton. "The Gull Wall." *Boun2*, 3: 761-73 (Sp 75).

———. "A Mint Quality." *Boun2*, 2: 640-8 (1974).

Feld, Ross. "It Maybe Even Be Alright." *Parnassus*, 2: 73-86 (1974).

Goldoni, Annalisa. "La poesia di PB." *SA*, 15: 383-94 (1969).

Rosenthal, M.L. "PB, Poet." *NYT*, 11 A 73, p. 27.

Blackmur, R.P. Alvarez, A. "R.P.B (1904-1965)." *Review*, 18: 21-5 (Ap 68).

Blackmur, R.P. "San Giovanni in Venere: Allen Tate as Man of Letters." *SR*, 67: 614-31 (O-D 59).

Ebine, Shizue. "R.P.B's Criticism on 'Between the *Numen* and the *Moha*—Notes Towards a Theory of Literature.'" *OUS*, 25: 1-18 (1972).

*Pannick, G.J. "R.P.B: A Bibliography." *BB*, 31: 165-9 (1974).

Wellek, René. "R.P.B Re-Examined." *SoR*, 7: 825-45 (Jl 71).

Blair, James. Bain, R.A. "The Composition and Publication of *The Present State of Virginia and the College*." *EAL*, 4: 31-54 (Sp 71).

Bain, Robert. "A Note on JB and the Southern Plain Style." *SLJ*, 4: 68-73 (Fa 71).

———. "Two Colonials in Virginia: Captain John Smith and JB." *SLJ*, 4: 107-16 (Sp 72).

Blake, James. Blake, James. "Letters from JB: Southern Con, American Author." *Esquire*, 74: 76-9, 143 (Ag 70).

Bland, Alden. Fleming, R.E. "Oveshadowed by Richard Wright: Three Black Chicago Novelists." *NALF*, 7: 75-9 (Fa 73).

Blatty, William. Frenz, T.S., and T.B. Farrell. "Conversion of America's Consciousness." *QJS*, 61: 40-7 (1975).

Mendeloff, Harry. "Exorcism in B and Berceo." *CLS*, 11: 218-25 (S 74).

Merry, Bruce. "The Exorcist Dies So That We Can All Enjoy the Sunset Again." *UWR*, 11: 5-24 (#1 75).

Blazek, Douglas. Bertolino, James. "San Franciso Sacramento & Alpine Texas." *New*, 15: 9-13 (Ap-My 71).

Cauble, Don. "DB: Not this, Not that." *STC*, 7: 95-102 (Sp 71).

Blish, James. Bradham, J.A. "The Case in JB's *A Case of Conscience*." *Extrapolation*, 16: 67-80 (D 74).

Bly, Robert. Anon. "The National Book Awards." *Nation*, 206: 413-4 (25 Mr 68).

Bly, Robert. "Developing the Underneath." *APR*, 2: 44-5 (#2 73).

———. "Reflections on the Origins of Organic Form." *Field*, 10: 31-5 (1974).

———. "The Network and the Community." *APR*, 3: 19-21 (#1 74).

Calhoun, Richard. "On RB's Protest Poetry." *TPJ*, 2: 21-2 (1969).

Hall, Donald. "Notes on RB and *Sleepers Joining Hands*." *OhR*, 15: 89-93 (#1 74).

Hertzel, L.J. "What about Writers in the North?" *SDR*, 5: 3-19 (Sp 67).

Heyen, William. "Inward to the World." *FarP*, 3: 42-50 (Fa-Wi 69).

Janssens, G.A.M. "The Present State of American Poetry: RB and James Wright." *ES*, 51: 112-37 (Ap 70).

Libby, Anthony. "Fire and Light: Four Poets to the End and Beyond." *IowaR*, 4: 111-26 (Sp 73).

———. "RB Alive in Darkness." *IowaR*, 3: 78-90 (Su 72).

McPherson, Sandra. "You Can Say That Again. (Or Can You?)." *IowaR*, 3: 70-7 (Su 72).

Molesworth, Charles. "Thrashing in the Depths: The Poetry of RB." *RMR*, 29: 95-117 (Au 75).

Nelson, Howard. "Welcoming Shadows: RB's Recent Poetry." *HC*, 12: 1-15 (#1 75).

Novak, Robert. "What I Have Written Is Not Good Enough: The Poetry of RB." *Windless Orchard*, 18: 30-4 (1974).

Oates, J.C. "When They All Are Sleeping." *MPS*, 4: 341-44 (1973).

Otto, Kathy, and Cynthia Lofsness. "An Interview with RB." *TPJ*, 2: 42 (Wi 69).

Reid, A.S. "A Look at the Living Poem: Rock Protest and Wit." *FurmM*, nv: 6-11, 35 (Sp 70).

Steele, Frank. "Three Questions Answered." *TPJ*, 2: 23-8 (1969).

Stitt, Peter. "James Wright and RB." *HiRev*, 2: 89-94 (Fa 73).

Boatright, Mody. Hudson, Wilson, et al. "MB 1896-1970." *SwaL*, 1: 21-26 (1971).

Bodenheim, Maxwell. Deutsch, Babette. "Two First Books." *Little R*, 5: 65-8 (My 19).

Ravitz, A.C. "Assault with Deadly Typewriter: The Hecht-8 Vendetta." *Cabellian*, 4: 104-11 (1972).

Bodman, Manoah. Turco, Lewis. "MB: Poet of the Second Awakening." *Costerus*, 8: 219-31 (1973).

Boer, James Den. Brown, S.L. "*Learning the Way.*" *ParP*, 4: 81-3 (Sp-Su 70).

Bogan, Louise. Carruth, Hayden. "A Balance Exactly Struck." *Poetry*, 114: 330-1 (Ag 69).

Morris, Harry. "Poets and Critics, Critics and Poets." *SR*, 80: 627-32 (1972).

Ramsey, Paul. "LB." *IowaR* 1: 116-24 (Su 70).

Boker, George Henry. Flory, C.R. "B, Barrett, and the Francesca Theme in Drama."*Players*, 50: 58-61 (1975).

Gallagher, K.G. "The Tragedies of GHB: The Measure of American Romantic Drama." *ESQ*, 20: 187-215 (3Q 74).

Kincaid, A.N. "Italian and English Sources of B's 'Francesca da Rimini' (1853)." *ATQ*, 1: 91-100 (1Q 69).

Voelker, P.D. "GHB's *Francesca da Rimini*: An Interpretation and Evaluation." *ETJ*, 24: 383-95 (D 72).

Woods, Alan. "Producing B's *Francesca da Rimini.*" *ETJ*, 24: 396-401 (D 72).

Zanger, Jules. "B's *Francesca da Rimini*: The Brothers' Tragedy." *ETJ*, 25: 210-9 (S 73).

Bolling, Robert. LeMay, J.A.L. "RB and the Bailment of Colonel Chiswell." *EAL*, 6: 99-142 (Fa 71).

Bonner, Sherwood (Kathrine Sherwood Bonner McDowell). *Biglane, J.N. "SB: A Bibliography of Primary and Secondary Materials." *ALR*, 5: 39-60 (Wi 72).

Frank, W.L. "SB's Diary for the Year 1869." *NMW*, 3: 111-30 (Wi 71); 4: 22-40, 64-83 (Sp, Fa 71).

Moore, Rayburn. "'Merlin and Vivien'? Some Notes on SB and Longfellow." *MissQ*, 28: 181-4 (Sp 75).

Pierle, R.C. "Sherwood Who? A Study in the Vagaries of Literary Evaluation." *NMW*, 1: 18-22 (Sp 68).

Simms, L.M. "SB: A Contemporary Appreciation." *NMW*, 2: 25-33 (Sp 69).

Bontemps, Arna. *Anon. "AB: Dedication and Bibliography." *BlackW*, 20: 78-9 (1971).

Baker, H.A. "AB: A Memoir." *BlackW*, 22: 4-9 (1973).

Brown, S.A. "AB: Co-Worker, Comrade." *BlackW*, 22: 11, 91-7 (1973).

Conroy, Jack. "Memories of AB, Friend and Collaborator." *Am Lib*, 5: 602-6 (D 74).

Materassi, Mario. "I romani di AB." *SA*, 18: 345-68 (1972).

Spady, J.G. "In Memoriam: Memorial Services for AB." *CLAJ*, 17: 117-9 (S 73).

Weil, D.L. "Folklore Motifs in AB's *Black Thunder.*" *SFQ*, 35: 1-14 (Mr 71).

Botsford, Edmund. Kable, W.S. "Addenda to Wright: B's *The Spiritual Voyage.*" *PBSA*, 65: 72-4 (1Q 71).

Botsford, Keith. Núñez, Antonio. "Encuentro con KB." *Insula*, 23: 4 (S 68).

Boucher, Anthony. (See **White, W.A.P.**).

Boucher, Jonathan. Clark, M.D. "J.B.: The Mirror of Reaction." *HLQ*, 33: 19-32 (N 69).

Zimmer, A.Y., and A.H. Kelly. "JB: Constitutional Conservative." *JAH*, 58: 897-922 (Mr 72).

Boucicault, Dion. Berrow, Hilary. "*Kerry, or Night and Morning.*" *IUR*, 3, 31-50 (#1 73).

Degan, J.A. "How to End the Octoroon." *ETJ*, 27: 107-78 (1975).

Harrison, A.C. "B on Dramatic Action: His Confirmation of the *Poetics.*" *QJS*, 56: 45-53 (F 70).

————. "B's Formula: Illusion Equals Pleasure." *ETJ*, 21: 299-309 (O 69).

Johnson, A.E. "The Birth of D.B." *MD*, 11: 157-63 (S 68).

————. "DB Learns to Act." *Players*, 48: 78-85 (1973).

————. ''Real Sunlight in the Garden: DB as a Stage Director.'' *ThR*, 12: 119-25 (1972).

Roman, D.P., and Mary T. Hamilton. ''B and the Anne Jordan Affair.'' *JIL*, 1: 120-7 (1972).

Scanlan, Tom. ''The Domestication of Rip Van Winkle.'' *VQR*, 50: 51-62 (Wi 74).

Bourjaily, Vance. Francis, W.A. ''The Motif of Names in B's *The Hound of Earth.*'' *Critique*, 17: 64-73 (#3 75).

McMillen, William. ''The Public Man in the Private Novel: B's *The Man Who Knew Kennedy.*'' *Critique*, 17: 86-95 (#3 75).

* ————, and J.M. Muste. ''A VB Checklist.'' *Critique*, 17: 105-10 (#3 75).

Muste, J.M. ''The Fractional Man as Hero: B's *Confessions of a Spent Youth.*'' *Critique*, 17: 73-85 (#3 75).

Towner, Daniel. ''Brill's Ruins and Henderson's Rain.'' *Critique*, 17: 96-104 (#3 75).

Bourne, Randolph. Joost, Nicholas. ''Culture vs. Power: RB, John Dewey, and *The Dial.*'' *MwQ*, 9: 245-59 (Ap 68).

Silet, C.L.P. ''A Note on RB.'' *BYNPL*, 77: 274-5 (Sp 74).

Walters, Thomas. ''The Education of a Radical: Beginnings.'' *Long View J*, 1: 94-123 (1969).

Bowen, Elizabeth. Davenport, G.T. ''EB and the Big House.'' *SHR*, 8: 27-34 (Wi 74).

Bower, B.M. Davison, S.R. ''*Chip of the Flying U*: The Author Was a Lady.'' *Montana Mag West Hist*, 23: 2-15 (Sp 73).

Meyer, R.W. ''B.M.B: The Poor Man's Wister.'' *JPC*, 7: 667-79 (Wi 73).

Bowers, Edgar. Mudrick, Marvin. ''Three Stanford Poets.'' *LugR*, 1: 83-94 (1965).

Trimpi, H.P. ''The Theme of Loss in the Earlier Poems of Catherine Davis and EB.'' *SoR*, 9: 595-616 (Jl 73).

Bowles, Jane. Kraft, James. ''JB as Serious Lady.'' *Novel*, 1: 273-7 (Sp 68).

Bowles, Paul. Evans, Oliver. ''An Interview with PB.'' *MeditR*, 1: 3-15 (Wi 71).

Hardison, O.B. ''Reconsiderations: *The Sheltering Sky* by PB.'' *NRep*, 173: 64-5 (27 S 75).

Moffitt, C.L. ''PB's Sheltering Sky and Arabia.'' *RSW*, 42: 44-9 (1974).

Rorem, Ned. ''Come Back PB.'' *NRep*, 166: 24, 35-6 (22 Ap 72).

Solotaroff, Theodore. ''The Desert Within.'' *NRep*, 157: 29-31 (2 S 67).

Stewart, L.D. ''PB: *Up Above the World* So High.'' *MDAC*, 1973, pp. 245-70.

Boyd, Adam. Stokes, D.T. ''AB, Publisher, Preacher, and Patriot.'' *NCHR*, 49: 1-21 (1972).

Boyesen, Hjalmar Hjorth. Butcher, Philip. ''Cable to B on *The Grandissimes.*'' *AL*, 40: 391-4 (N 68).

Fredrickson, R.S. ''HHB: Howells 'Out-Realisted.''' *MarkR*, 3: 93-7 (F 73).

Seyersted, Per. ''The Drooping Lily: HHB as an Early American Misogynist.'' *AmNor*, 3: 74-87 (1971).

Boyle, Kay. Centing, R.R. ''KB: The Cincinnati Years.'' *Ohioana Q*, 15: 11-3 (Sp 72).

Brackenridge, Henry Maria. Keller, W.F. ''HMB, First United States Forester.'' *ForH*, 15: 13-23 (Ja 72).

Brackenbridge, Hugh Henry. Bush, Sargent. ''*Modern Chivalry* and 'Young's Magazine.''' *AL*, 44: 292-9 (My 72).

Colombo, R.M. ''HHB e la frontiera americana.'' *SA*, 18: 7-28 (Wi 72).

Haines, Lynn. ''Of Indians and Irishmen: A Note on B's Use of Sources for Satire in *Modern Chivalry.*'' *EAL*, 10: 88-92 (Sp 75).

Harkey, J.H. ''Captain Farrago's Letter on Duelling and Judge John Breckenridge of Kentucky.'' *WPHM*, 52: 251-3 (1969).

————. ''The *Don Quixote* of the Frontier: HHB's *Modern Chivalry.*'' *EAL*, 8: 193-203 (Fa 73).

————. "A Note on Longstreet's Ransy Sniffle and B's *Modern Chivalry.*" *WPHM*, 52: 43-5 (Ja 69).

Hemenway, Robert. "Fiction in the Age of Jefferson." *MASJ*, 9: 91-102 (Sp 68).

Kennedy, W.B. "HHB: Thoughts and Acts of a Modern Democrat." *WGCR*, 2: 26-38 (1969).

Maitfield, M.S. "*Modern Chivalry*: The Form." *WPHM*, 51: 17-29 (Ja 68).

Martin, Wendy. "On the Road with the Philosopher and the Profiteer: A Study of HHB's *Modern Chivalry.*" *ECS*, 4: 241-56 (Sp 71).

————. "The Rogue and the Rational Man: HHB's Study of a Con Man in *Modern Chivalry.*" *EAL*, 8: 179-92 (Fa 73).

Nance, W.L. "Satiric Elements in B's *Modern Chivalry.*" *TSLL*, 9: 381-9 (Au 67).

Smeall, J.F.S. "The Respective Roles of B and Freneau in Composing *The Rising Glory of America.*" *PBSA*, 67: 263-83 (3Q 73).

Tanselle, G.T. "Two Editions of Eighteenth Century Fiction." *EAL*, 6: 274-83 (Wi 71).

Whittle, A.R "*Modern Chivalry*: The Frontier as Crucible." *EAL*, 6: 263-70 (Wi 71).

Bradbury, Ray. Anon. "Portrait de RB." *CRB*, 58: 3-25 (1966).

Biddison, L.T. "RB's Song of Experience." *NOR*, 1: 226-9 (Sp 69).

Bradbury, Ray. "How Not to Burn a Book." *SCUL*, 7: 5-43 (#1 75).

————. "Shaw as Influence, Laughton as Teacher." *Shaw R*, 16: 98-9 (1973).

Burt, D.C. "Poe, B, and the Science Fiction Tale of Terror." *MSCS*, 3: 76-84 (D 68).

Carter, Paul. "Of Towns and Roads: Three Novelists and George McGovern." *ColF*, 2: 10-6 (Sp 73).

Cordesse, Berard. "La Science-fiction de RB." *Caliban* 6: 77-83 (1969).

Dimeo, Steven. "Man and Apollo: A Look at Religion in the Science Fantasies of RB." *JPC*, 5: 970-8 (Sp 72).

Dobzynski, Charles. "RB, fabuliste de notre temps." *CRB*, 58: 26-41 (1966).

Fletcher, David. "Intellectual Fire." *Paunch*, 33: 1-9 (D 68).

Etulain, R.W. "RB's *Red Sky at Morning:* New Novel of the Southwest." *WR*, 8: 57-62 (1971).

McCorsin, M.A. "The Rarity of *Modern Chivalry.*" *PAAS*, 85: 309 (1975).

McNelly, W.E. "B Revisited." *CEA*, 31: 4-6 (1970).

Mengeling, M.E. "RB's *Dandelion Wine.*' Themes, Sources, and Styles." *EJ*, 60: 877-87 (O 71).

Modlin, C.E. "The Folly of Ambition in *Modern Chivalry.*" *PAAS*, 85: 310-3 (1975).

Musumarra, Adriana. "Il 'carnival' cosmico di RB." *SA*, 17: 343-77 (1971).

Reilly, Robert. "The Artistry of RB." *Extrapolation*, 13: 64-74 (D 71).

Sisario, Peter. "A Study of the Allusions in B's *Fahrenheit 451.*" *EJ*, 59: 201-5, 212 (F 70).

Sullivan, A.T. "RB and Fantasy." *EJ*, 61: 1309-14 (1971).

Watt, D.J. "'Hearth or Salamander': Uses of Fire in B's *Fahrenheit 451.*" *NCLit*, 1: 13-4 (Mr 71).

Xmel'nickaja, T. "Ot naucnoj fantastiki k detskoj shazke." *Zvezda*, 9: 195-204 (1970).

Bradford, William. Bradford, William, and Isaac Allerton. "A Letter of WB and Isaac Allerton, 1623." *AHR*, 8: 294-301 (1903).

Daly, Robert. "WB's Vision of History." *AL*, 44: 557-69 (Ja 73).

Fritscher, J.J. "The Sensibility and Conscious Style of WB." *BuR*, 17: 80-90 (D 69).

Griffith, John. "*Of Plymouth Plantation* as a Mercantile Epic." *ArQ*, 28: 231-42 (1972).

Hovey, K.A. "The Theology of History in *Of Plymouth Plantation* and Its Predecessors." *EAL*, 10: 47-66 (Sp 75).

Howard, A.B. "Art and History in B's *Of Plymouth Plantation.*" *WMQ*, 28: 237-66 (Ap 71).

Major, M.W. "WB Versus Thomas Morton." *EAL*, 5: 1-13 (Fa 70).

Scheick, William. "The Theme of Necessity in B's *Of Plymouth Plantation*." *SCN*, 32: 88-90 (Wi 74).

Bradstreet, Anne. Arpin, G.Q. "Mistress B's Discontents."*JBS*, 1: 2-7 (#1 75).

Ball, K.R. "Puritan Humility in AB's Poetry." *Cithara*, 13: 29-41 (1973).

Contenti, Alessandra. "AB, il Petrarchismo e il 'Plain Style.'" *SA*, 14: 7-27 (1968).

Dogget, J.E. "Another Eighteenth-Century Instance of AB's Continuing Appeal." *EIHC*, 111: 51-4 (1975).

Eberwein, J.D. "The 'Unrefined Ore' of AB's Quaternions." *EAL*, 9: 19-26 (Sp 74).

Hamblen, A.A. "AB: Portrait of a Puritan Lady." *Cresset*, 32: 11-3 (N 68).

Hildebrand, Anne. "AB's Quaternions and 'Contemplations.'" *EAL*, 8: 117-25 (Fa 73).

Irvin, W.J. "Allegory and Typology 'Imbrace and Greet': AB's 'Contemplations.'" *EAL*, 10: 30-46 (Sp 75).

Jonston, T.E. "A Note on the Voices of AB, Edward Taylor, Roger Willaims, and Philip Pain." *EAL*, 3: 125-6 (Fa 68).

Keeble, N.H. "AB: The First Colonial Poet." *LHY*, 13: 13-28 (1972).

Kehler, Dorothea. "AB and Spenser." *AN&Q*, 8: 135 (1970).

Laughlin, R.M. "AB: Poet in Search of Form." *AL*, 42: 1-17 (Mr 70).

McMahon, Helen. "AB, Jean Bertault, and Dr. Crooke." *EAL*, 3: 118-23 (Fa 68).

Requa, K.A. "AB's Poetic Voices." *EAL*, 9: 3-18 (Sp 74).

———. "AB's Use of DuBartas in 'Contemplations.'" *EIHC*, 110: 64-9 (1974).

Richardson, R.D. "The Puritan Poetry of AB." *TSLL*, 9: 317-31 (Au 67).

Rosenfeld, A.H. "AB's 'Contemplations.'" *NEQ*, 43: 79-96 (Mr 70).

*Stanford, Ann. "AB: An Annotated Checklist." *EAL,* 3: 217-28 (Wi 68-69).

*———. "AB: An Annotated Checklist." *BB*, 27: 34-7 (Ap-Je 70).

Stoddard, Donald. "John Berryman, Mistress B si Henry." *Steaua*, 24: 29 (1974).

Turco, Lewis. "The Pro-Am Tournament." *MQR*, 14: 84-91 (1975).

Waller, J.R. "'My Hand a Needle Better Fits': AB and Women Poets of the Renaissance." *DR*, 54: 436-50 (Au 74).

Braithwaite, William Stanley. Braithwaite, W.S. "WSB Remembers E.A. Robinson." *NLet*, 38: 153-64 (Fa 71).

Butcher, Philip. "WBS and the College Language Association." *CLAJ*, 15: 117-25 (D 71).

———. "WSB's Southern Exposure: Rescue and Revelation." *SLJ*, 3: 49-61 (Sp 71).

Clairmonte, Glenn. "The Cup-Bearer: WSB of Boston." *CLAJ*, 17: 101-8 (S 73).

———. "He Made American Writers Famous." *Phylon*, 30: 184-90 (Su 69).

Branagan, Thomas. Johnson, R.C. "Addendum to Sabin, Shaw-Shoemaker, and Wegelin: TB." *PBSA*, 64: 205-6 (2Q 70).

Braun, Richard Emil. Mazzaro, Jerome. "The Poetry of REB." *MPS*, 5: 251-68 (Wi 74).

Brautigan, Richard. Bales, Kent. "Fishing the Ambivalence, or A Reading of *Trout Fishing in America*." *WHR*, 29: 29-42 (1975).

Bryan, Scott, Paul Graham, and John Somer. "Speed Kills: RB and the American Metaphor." *OyR*, 8: 64-72 (Fa 74).

Chenetier, Thomas. "Escape through Imagination in *Trout Fishing in America*." *Critique*, 16: 25-31 (#1 74).

Hernlund, Patricia. "Author's Intent: *In Watermelon Sugar*." *Critique*, 16: 5-17 (#1 74).

Keillor, Garrison. "Ten Stories for Mr. RB, and Other Stories." *NY*, 48: 37 (18 M 72).

Kern, Robert. "Williams, B, and the Poetics of Primitivism." *ChiR*, 27: 47-57 (Su 75).

*Kolodzie, Patricia, and James Wanless. "RB: A Working Checklist." *Critique*, 16: 41-52 (#1 74).

Leavitt, Harvey. "The Regained Paradise of B's *In Watermelon Sugar*." *Critique*, 16: 18-24 (#1 74).

Locklin, Gerald and Charles Stetler. "Some Observations on *A Confederate General from Big Sur.*" *Critique*, 13: 72-82 (#3 71).

Novak, Robert. "The Poetry of RB." *WiOr*, 14: 17, 48-50 (Su 73).

Puetz, Manfred. "Transcendentalism Revived: The Fiction of RB." *Occident*, 8: 39-47 (Sp 74).

Rosselli, Aldo. "RB piccolo eroe della controcultura." *NArg*, 23-4: 46-50 (1971).

Schmitz, Neil. "RB and the Modern Pastoral." *MFS*, 19: 109-25 (Sp 73).

Seib, Kenneth. "*Trout Fishing in America*: B's Funky Fishy Yarn." *Critique*, 13: 63-71 (#3 71).

Stickney, John. "Gentle Poet of the Young." *Life*, 14 Ag 70, pp. 49-54.

Taylor, L. Loring. "Forma si substanta umorului la RB." *Steaua*, 24: 27-8 (1974).

Vanderwerken, D.L. "*Trout Fishing in America* and the American Tradition." *Critique*, 16: 32-40 (#1 74).

Walker, Cheryl. "Youth Fishing in America." *ModO*, 2: 308-13 (Sp 72).

*Wanless, James, and Christine Kolodzie. "RB: A Working Checklist." *Critique*, 16: 41-52 (#1 74).

Brett, Dorothy. Manchester, John. "Thoughts on B: 1967." *SDR*, 5: 3-9 (Su 67).

Morrill, Claire. "Three Women of Taos: Frieda Lawrence, Mabel Luhan, and DB." *SDR*, 2: 3-22 (Sp 65).

Brewer, John Mason. Byrd, James. "In Memory of JMB." *CLAJ*, 18: 578-81 (Je 75).

Perry, T.A. "JMB: Folclorist negru american." *Steaua*, 25: 450-2 (#4 74).

Turner, Darwin. "J.MB Vignettes." *CLAJ*, 23: 570-7 (Je 75).

Briggs, Charles Frederick. Ehrlich, Heyward. "*The Broadway Journal*: B's Dilemma and Poe's Strategy." *BNYPL*, 73: 74-93 (F 69).

Brink, Frank. Petersen, Lance. "Alaskan Men of Letters: FB." *Alaska R*, 1: 36-9 (Sp 64).

Brinnin, John Malcolm. Callahan, P.J. "Tonal Power, Incoherent Rage: Rhetoric in Three Poets." *SR*, 80: 639-44 (1972).

Gerber, P.L., ed. "A Kind of Exorcism: A Conversation with JMB." *PrS*, 48: 201-21 (1974).

Bromfield, Louis. Anderson, D.D. "'Shane's Castle': Myth and Reality in LB's Fiction." *NOQ*, 42: 38-46 (1970).

Brooks, Cleanth. Brooks, Cleanth. "B on Warren." *FourQ*, 21: 19-22 (1972).

———. "Telling It Like It Is in *In the Tower of Babel*." *SR*, 79: 136-55 (Wi 71).

Core, George. "Ransom, B, and the Idiom of Criticism." *SLJ*, 5: 177-86 (Fa 72).

Lentricchia, Frank. "The Place of CB." *JAAC*, 29: 235-51 (Wi 70).

Shankar, D.A. "CB and the 'Elegy-Written in a Country Churchyard." *LCrit*, 9: 77-80 (Wi 70).

Strozier, R.M. "Roger Ascham and CB: Renaissance and Modern Critical Thought." *EIC*, 22: 396-407 (O 72).

Wellek, René. "CB, Critic of Critics." *SoR*, 10: 125-52 (Ja 74).

Brooks, Gwendolyn. Baker, H.A. "The Achievement of GB." *CLAJ*, 16: 23-31 (S 72).

Baungaertner, Jill. "GB: Tintinnabulation." *Cresset*, 37: 12-5 (Ja 74).

Brooks, Gwendolyn. "Report from Part One: The Autobiography of GB." *BlackW*, 21: 4-12 (1972).

Bird, G.L. "GB: Educator Extraordinaire." *Discourse*, 12: 158-66 (1969).

Clark, Edward. "Studying and Teaching Afro-American Literature." *CLAJ*, 16: 96-105 (Au 72).

Furman, M.R. "GB: The 'Unconditioned' Poet." *CLAJ*, 17: 1-10 (S 73).

Brooks, Gwendolyn

Hansell, W.H. "Aestheticism versus Political Militancy in GB's 'The Chicago Picasso' and 'The Wall.'" *CLAJ*, 17: 11-5 (S 73).

————. "GB's 'In the Mecca': A Rebirth into Blackness." *NALF*, 8: 199-209 (Su 74).

————. "The Role of Violence in Recent Poems of GB." *SBL*, 5: 21-7 (Su 74).

Hudson, C.F. "Racial Themes in the Poetry of GB." *CLAJ*, 17: 16-20 (S 73).

Hull, G.T. "A Note on the Poetic Technique of GB." *CLAJ*, 19: 280-5 (D 75).

Kent, George. "The Poetry of GB." *BlackW*, 20: 30-43; 36-48, 68-71 (#1, #2 71).

*Loff, J.N. "GB: A Bibliography." *CLAJ*, 17: 21-32 (S 73).

McCluskey, John. "In the Mecca." *SBL*, 4: 25-30 (Au 73).

*Mahoney, Heidi. "Selected Checklist of Material by and about GB." *NALF*, 8: 210-1 (Su 74).

Shands, A.O. "GB as Novelist." *BlackW*, 22: 22-30 (1973).

Starvos, George. "An Interview with GB." *ConL*, 11: 1-20 (Wi 70).

Towns, Sandra. "*Beckonings.*" *BlackW*, 25: 51-3, 87-8 (#2 75).

Washington, M.L.H. "Black Women Image Makers." *BlackW*, 23: 10-8 (1974).

Brooks, Van Wyck. Agrawal, I.N. "Whitman, VWB and the American Tradition." *IJAS*, 1: 95-101 (1971).

Dow, Eddy. "VWB and Lewis Mumford: A Confluence in the 'Twenties.'" *AL*, 45: 407-22 (N 73).

Dowell, P.W. "VWB and the Progressive Frame of Mind." *MASJ*, 11: 30-44 (Sp 70).

Mukerji, Nirmal. "VWB's Assessment of Walt Whitman." *PURBA*, 3: 71-8 (1972).

Tanselle, G.T. "Anderson Annotated by B." *N&Q*, 15: 60-1 (F 68).

Vitelli, J.R. "VWB Redux: An Essay Review." *Cabellian*, 4: 115-25 (Sp 72).

Brother Antoninus. (See **Everson, William.**)

Brown, Alice. Moses, Montrose. "Miss AB's Inheritance." *BNM*, 36: 37-8 (O 17).

Sweeney, Francis. "A Friend of Lou Guiney's." *America*, 80: 546-7 (19 F 49).

Toth, S.A. "AB (1857-1948)." *ALR*, 5: 134-43 (Sp 72).

————. "A Forgotten View from Beacon Hill: AB's New England Short Stories." *CLQ*, 10: 1-17 (1972).

Brown, Charles Brockden. Alderson, Eva. "To Reconcile with Common Maxims: Edgar Huntley's Ruses." *PCP*, 10: 5-9 (1975).

Bell, Michael. "The Double-Tongued Deceiver: Sincerity and Duplicity in the Novels of CBB." *EAL*, 9: 143-63 (Fa 74).

Bennett, C.E. "CBB's 'Portrait of an Emigrant.'" *CLAJ*, 14: 87-90 (S 70).

Brancaccio, Patrick. "Studied Ambiguities: *Arthur Mervyn* and the Problem of the Unreliable Narrator." *AL*, 42: 18-27 (Mr 70).

Cleman, John. "Ambiguous Evil: A Study of Villains and Heroes in CBB's Major Novels." *EAL* 10: 190-219 (Fa 75).

Fleck, Richard. "Symbolic Landscape in *Edgar Huntly*." *RSW*, 39: 229-32 (S 71).

Franklin, Wayne. "Tragedy and Comedy in B's *Wieland*." *Novel*, 8: 147-63 (Wi 75).

Greiner, D.J. "B's Use of the Narrator in *Wieland*: An Indirect Plea for the Acceptance of Fiction." *CLAJ*, 13: 131-6 (D 69).

Harap, Louis. "Fracture of a Stereotype: CBB's Achsa Fielding." *AJA*, 24: 187-195 (N 72).

Hedges, William L. "Benjamin Rush, CBB, and the American Plague Year." *EAL*, 7: 295-311 (Wi 73).

————. "CBB and the Culture of Contradictions." *EAL*, 9: 107-42 (Fa 74).

Hemenway, Robert. "BB's Twice Told Insanity Tale." *AL*, 40: 211-5 (My 68).

————. "Fiction in the Age of Jefferson." *MASJ*, 9: 91-102 (Sp 68).

Hobson, R.W. "Voices of Carwin and Other Mysteries in CBB's *Wieland*." *EAL*, 10: 307-9 (Wi 75).

Hughes, P.R. "Archetypal Patterns in *Edgar Huntly*." *StN*, 5: 176-90 (1973).

Hume, R.D. "CBB and the Use of Gothicism: A Reassessment." *ESQ*, 18: 10-8 (1Q 72).

Jenkins, R.B. "Invulnerable Virtue in *Wieland* and *Comus*." *SAB*, 38: 72-5 (My 73).

Justus, J.H. "Arthur Mervyn, American." *AL*, 42: 304-24 (N 70).

Katz, Joseph. "Analytical Biography and Literary History: The Writing and Printing of *Wieland*." *Proof*, 1: 8-34 (1971).

Krause, S.J. "CBB." *CEAAN*, 1: 13-4 (1968).

———. "*Ormond*: Seduction in a New Key." *AL*, 44: 570-84 (Ja 73).

Lyttle, David. "The Case Against Carwin." *NCF*, 26: 257-69 (1971).

Mulqueen, J.E. "The Plea for a Deistic Education in CBB's *Wieland*." *BSUF*, 10: 70-7 (Sp 69).

Nelson, Carl. "B's Manichean Mock-Heroic: The Ironic Self in a Hyperbolic World." *WVUPP*, 20: 26-42 (1973).

———. "A Just Reading of CBB's *Ormond*." *EAL*, 8: 163-78 (Fa 73).

Reid, S.W. "CBB's Copy of Johnson's *Dictionary*." *Serif*, 11: 12-20 (N 75).

———. "BB in England: Notes on Henry Colburn's 1822 Editions of His Novels." *EAL*, 9: 188-95 (Fa 74).

———. "CBB's Copy of Johnson's *Dictionary* (1783)." *Serif*, 11: 12-20 (1975).

Rice, Nancy. "Heritage: '*Alcuin*'." *MR*, 14: 802-14 (1973).

Ringe, D.A. "Early American Gothic: B, Dana and Allston." *ATQ*, 19: 3-8 (Su 73).

Rodgers, P.C. "B's *Ormond*: The Fruits of Improvisation." *AQ*, 26: 4-22 (Mr 74).

Schulz, Dieter. "*Edgar Huntly* as Quest Romance." *AL*, 43: 323-35 (N 71).

Soldati, J.A. "The Americanization of Faust: A Study of CBB's *Wieland*." *ESQ*, 20: 1-14 (1Q 74).

Strozier, Robert. "*Wieland* and Other Romances: Horror in Parentheses." *ESQ*, 50: 24-9 (1Q 68).

Thompson, G.R. "Is Poe's 'A Tale of the Ragged Mountains' a Hoax?" *SSF*, 6: 454-60 (Su 69).

Tichi, Cecelia. "CBB, Translator." *AL*, 44: 1-12 (My 72).

Van Der Beets, Richard, and Paul Witherington. "My Kinsman, BB: Robin Molineux and Arthur Mervyn." *ATQ*, 1: 13-5 (1Q 69).

Ward, W.S. "CBB, His Contemporary British Reviewers, and Two Minor Bibliographical Problems." *PBSA*, 65: 399-402 (4Q 71).

Weidman, B.S. "White Man's Red Man: A Penitential Reading of Four American Novels." *MLS*, 4: 14-26 (#4 74).

Wilson, J.D. "Incest and American Romantic Fiction." *SLitI*, 7: 31-50 (1974).

*Witherington, Paul. "CBB: A Bibliography Essay." *EAL*, 9: 164-87 (Fa 74).

———. "Benevolence and the 'Utmost Stretch': CCB's Narrative Dilemma." *Criticism*, 14: 175-91 (Sp 72).

———. "BB's Other Novels: *Clara Howard* and *Jane Talbot*." *NCF*, 29: 257-72 (D 74).

Browne, Charles Farrar (Artemus Ward). Anon. "Neglected Worthies." *Nation*, 107: 165 (17 Ag 18).

Abrams, R.E. "CFB." *ALR*, 8: 205-6 (1975).

Austin, J.C. "CFB (1834-1867)." *ALR*, 5: 151-65 (Sp 72).

Bakerville, Barnet. "19th Century Burlesque of Oratory." *AQ*, 20: 726-43 (Wi 68).

Blair, Walter. "Burlesques in Nineteenth-Century Humor." *AL*, 2: 236-47 (N 30).

———. "The Popularity of Nineteenth Century Humorists." *AL*, 3: 175-94 (My 31).

Cracroft, R.H. "Distorting Polygamy for Fun and Profit: AW and Mark Twain among the Mormons." *BYUS*, 14: 272-88 (Wi 74).

Dahl, Curtis. "Mark Twain and the Moving Panorama." *AQ*, 13: 20-32 (Sp 61).

Ford, J.L. "A Century of American Humor." *Munsey's*, 25: 482-90 (Jl 1901).

Garrow, Scott. "The Drama in Ward's Tower of London." *AN&Q*, 9: 22-3 (1970).

Grimes, G.A. "'Brandy and Water': American Folk Types in the Works of AW." *NYFQ*, 25: 163-74 (S 69).

Knight, Enoch. "CF.B ('Artemus Ward'); The Tribute of a Friend and Fellow-Townsman." *Putnam's*, 1 F 07; p. 604.

Lorch, F.W. "Mark Twain's Lecture from *Roughing It*." *AL*, 22: 290-307 (N 50).

————. "Mark Twain's 'Sandwich Islands' Lecture and the Failure at Jamestown, New York, in 1869." *AL*, 25: 314-25 (N 53).

Marvin, W.R. "CFB ('Artemus Ward')." *Museum Echoes* (Ohio Hist Soc), 30: 26-30 (Ap 57).

Mott, F.L. "The Beginnings of AW." *JQ*, 18: 146-52 (Je 41).

Paine, A.B. "Mark Twain: Some Chapters from an Extraordinary Life." *HM*, 124: 584 (Mr 12).

Richmond, R.W. "AW in Mid-America." *KHQ*, 33: 470-80 (Wi 67).

Robbins, L.H. "American Humorists." *NYTMS*,8 S 35; pp. 8, 9, 14.

Rodgers, P.C. "Artemus Ward and MT's 'Jumping Frog.'" *NCF*, 28: 273-86 (D 73).

Rowlette, Robert. "'Mark Ward on Artemus Twain': Twain's Literary Debt to W." *ALR*, 6: 13-25 (Wi 73).

Trent, W.P. "A Retrospect on American Humor." *Century*, 63: 45-64 (N 01).

Watterson, Henry. "Looking Backward." *SEP*, 22 Mr 19: 18-9, 45.

Woodbury, C.J. "AW at Springfield, Massachusetts." *Century*, 46: 636 (F 02).

Brown, Claude. Baker, H.A. "The Environment as Enemy in a Black Autobiography: *Manchild in the Promised Land*." *Phylon*, 32: 53-9 (Sp 71).

Brown, Frank London. Fleming, R.E. "Overshadowed by Richard Wright: Three Black Chicago Novelists." *NALF*, 7: 75-9 (Fa 73).

Brown, Kenneth R. Brown, K.R. "KH.B: The Career of an Accidental Playwright." *Players*, 46: 276-9 (1971).

Lacey, P.A. "Two for the Revolution." *RT*, No. 6: 30-8 (Su 68).

Brown, Sterling. Henderson, S.A. "A Strong Man Called SB." *BlackW*, 19: 5-12 (1970).

*O'Meally, R.G. "An Annotated Bibliography of the Works of SA.B" *CLAJ*, 19: 268-79 (D 75).

Rowell, C.H. "SA.B and the Afro-American Folk Tradition." *SLImag*, 7: 131-52 (Fa 74).

Brown, William Hill. Arner, R.D. "Sentiment and Sensibility: The Role of Emotion and WHB's *The Power of Sympathy*." *SAF*, 1: 121-32 (Au 73).

Byers, J.R., Jr. "Further Verification of the Authorship of *The Power of Sympathy*." *AL*, 43: 421-7 (N 71).

Davidson, C.N. "The Power of Sympathy Reconsidered: WHB as Literary Craftsman." *EAL*, 10: 14-29 (Sp 75).

Tanselle, G.T. "Two Editions of Eighteenth Century Fiction." *EAL*, 6: 274-83 (1971).

Wilson, J.D. "Incest and American Romantic Fiction." *SLitI*, 7: 31-50 (1974).

Brown, William Wells. Abramson, D.M. "WWB: America's First Negro Playwright." *ETJ*, 20: 370-5 (O 68).

Farrison, W.E. "Clotel, Thomas Jefferson, and Sally Hemings." *CLAJ*, 17: 147-74 (D 73).

————. "'The Kidnapped Clergyman's and B's 'Experience.'" *CLAJ*, 18: 507-15 (Je 75).

————. "One Ephemera After Another." *CLAJ*, 13: 192-7 (D 69).

Haskett, N.D. "Afro-American Images of Africa: Four *Antebellum* Black Authors." *Ufahamu*, 3: 29-40 (1972).

Hudson, T.R. "In the Eye of the Beholder." *NegroD*, 19: 43-8 (1969).

Browne, J. Ross. Powell, L.C. "J.RB's *Adventures in the Apache Country*." *Westways*, 63: 18-21, 40-3 (O 71).

Browne, Junius Henri. Gohdes, Clarence. "Wicked Old New York." *HLQ*, 29: 171-81 (Fa 66).

Brownson, Orestes Augustus. Altholz, J.L., and Victor Conzemius. "Acton and B: A Letter from America." *CathHR*, 49: 524-31 (1964).

Barcus, James. "Structuring the Rage Within: Autobiographies of Newman and OB." *Cithara*, 14: 45-57 (1975).

Barnes, D.R. "B and Newman: The Controversy Re-examined." *ESQ*, 50: 9-20 (1Q 68).

Brownson, Orestes. "A Discourse on the Wants of the Times." *ESQ*, 51: 91-101 (2Q 68).

———. "A Sermon to the Young People in Canton, Mass." *ESQ*, 51: 66-74 (2Q 68).

Cameron, K.W. "Thoreau and OB." *ESQ*, 51: 53-65 (2Q 68).

Capps, Donald. "OB: The Psychology of Religious Affiliation." *JSSR*, 7: 197-209 (1968).

Girgus, S.B. "The Scholar as Prophet." *MQ*, 17: 88-99 (1975).

Karcher, C.L. "The 'Spiritual Lesson' of Melville's 'The Apple-Tree Table.'" *AQ*, 23: 101-9 (Sp 71).

Lapomarda, V.A. "OAB: A 19th Century View of the Blacks in American Society." *M-A*, 53: 160-9 (Jl 71).

Swidler, Arlene. "B and the 'Woman Question.'" *ABR*, 19: 211-9 (1968).

Bruce, Edward Caledon. Simms, L.M. "ECB: Virginia Artist and Writer." *VaCal*, 23: 30-7 (Wi 74).

Bryan, C.D.B. Long, R.E. "The Image of Gatsby in the Fiction of Louis Auchincloss and C.D.B.B." *FHA*, 1972, pp. 325-8.

Bryant, William Cullen. Anon. "B and Cole in the Catskills." *BNYPL*, 78: 270-3 (Sp 75).

Anon. "B Memorial Meeting of *The Century*." *ESQ*, 48: 31-48 (3Q 67).

———. "Funeral Address." *ESQ*, 48: 26-9 (3Q 67).

———. "Illness, Death and Burial." *ESQ*, 48: 24-6 (3Q 67).

———. "The Journalist." *ESQ*, 48: 21-4 (3Q 67).

———. "Obituary of WCB." *ESQ*, 48: 124 (3Q 67).

———. "Reminiscences." *ESQ*, 48: 29-30 (3Q 67).

Bryant, W.C. "Poetry and Painting: A Love Affair of Long Ago." *AQ*, 22: 859-82 (Wi 70).

———. "The Quest for International Copyright in the Thirtieth Congress." *ESQ*, 51: 121-8 (2Q 68).

Cameron, K.W. "B and the New Haven Y.M.C.A." *ESQ*, 51: 37-46 (2Q 68).

*———. "B's Correspondents: A Checklist." *ATQ*, 13: 37-45 (1972).

———. "Melville, Cooper, Irving and B on International Matters." *ESQ*, 51: 108-21 (2Q 68).

Casale, O.M. "B's Proposed Address to the Emperor of Brazil." *ESQ*, 63: 10-2 (Sp 71).

Donovan, A.B. "WCB on Nationalism, Imitation, and Originality in Poetry." *SP*, 66: 672-87 (1969).

Guilds, J.C. "B in the South." *GHQ*, 37: 142-6 (Mr 53).

Lawrence, Arthur. "B and the Berkshire Hills." *ESQ*, 51: 3-8 (2Q 68).

Monteiro, George. "The Patriarchal Mr. B." *N&Q*, 22: 440-1 (1975).

Niven, D.A. "B and Cole in the Catskills." *BNYPL*, 78: 270-3 (1975).

Smiley, Sam. "WCB's Occasional Addresses." *Central States Speech J*, 19: 250-6 (Wi 68).

Smith, G.J. "B's 'Thanatopsis': A Possible Source." *AN&Q*, 13: 149-51 (Je 75).

Spann, E.K. "B and Verplanck, the Yankee and Yorker." *NYH*, 49: 11-28 (Ja 68).

Weinstein, Bernard. "B, Annexation, and the Mexican War." *ESQ*, 63: 19-24 (Sp 71).

Woodward, R.H. "'The Wings on Morning' in 'Thanatopsis.'" *ESQ*, 58: 153 (1Q 70).

Buck, Pearl. Cevasco, G.A. "PB and the Chinese Novel." *ASt*, 5: 437-50 (1967).

Rossani, Wolfango. "Umnità di PB." *ORom*, 27 Ag 71; p. 3.

Snow, H.F. "PSB 1892-1973." *NRep*, 168: 28-9 (24 Mr 73).

Telles, M.L. de C.H. "PB e a tradição." *Brotéria*, 96: 435-8 (1973).

Venne, Peter. "PB's Literary Portrait of China and the Chinese." *FJS*, 1: 71-86 (1968).

Bucke, Richard Maurice. Jaffe, Harold. "RMB's Walt Whitman." *Serif*, 7: 3-10 (1970).

———. "B's *Walt Whitman*: A Collaboration." *WWR*, 15: 190-4 (S 69).

———. "RMB and Walt Whitman." *CRAS*, 2: 37-47 (1971).

Bukowski, Charles. Dorbin, Sanford. "CB and the Little Mag/Small Press Movement." *Soundings*, 2: 17-32 (1970).

Quagliano, Tony. "CB Issue." *Small Press R*, 4: 1-65 (My 73).

Bullins, Ed. Evans, Don. "The Theater of Confrontation: EB, Up Against the Wall." *BlackW*, 23: 14-18 (1974).

Gilles, J.A. "Tenderness in Brutality: The Plays of EB." *Players*, 48: 32-3 (1972).

Hay, S.A. "'What Shape Shapes Shapelessness?': Structural Elements in EB's Plays." *BlackW*, 23: 20-6 (1974).

Jackson, Kennell. "Notes on the Works of EB and *The Hungered One*." *CLAJ*, 18: 292-99 (D 74).

Jeffers, Lance. "B, Baraka, and Elder: The Dawn of Grandeur in Black Drama." *CLAJ*, 16: 32-48 (S 72).

Marvin, X. "Black Theater: An Interview with EB." *NegroD*, 18: 9-16 (1969).

O'Brien, John. "Interview with EB." *NALF*, 7: 108-12 (Fa 73).

Smitherman, Geneva. "EB/Stage One: Everybody Wants to Know Why I Sing the Blues." *BlackW*, 23: 4-13 (1974).

Bunner, H.C. Stronks, J.B. "Frank Norris's *McTeague*: A Possible Source in HCB." *NCF*, 25: 474-8 (Mr 71).

Burke, Kenneth. Booth, W.C. "KB's Way of Knowing." *CritI*, 1: 1-22 (1974).

Burke, Kenneth. "As I was Saying." *MQR*, 11: 9-27 (Wi 72).

———. "Dancing with Tears in My Eyes." *CritI*, 1: 23-31 (1974).

Donoghue, Denis. "Reconsideration: *Towards a Better Life* by KB." *NRep*, 173: 29-31 (18 O 75).

Gallo, L.J. "KB: The Word and the World." *NDQ*, 42: 33-45 (1974).

Galvin, Brendan. "KB and Theodore Roethke's 'Lost Son' Poems." *NwR*, 11: 67-96 (Su 71).

Hoffman, F.J. KB's Great Range." *Poetry*, 111: 416-9 (Mr 68).

Macksoud, S.J., and Ross Altman. "Voices in Opposition: A Burkeian Rhetoric of *Saint Joan*." *QJS*, 57: 140-6 (1971).

Mullican, J.S. "KB's Comic Attitude: A Corrective to Propaganda Analysis." *ContE*, 43: 89-92 (1971).

Nemerov, Howard. "Everything, Preferably All at Once: Coming to Terms with KB." *SH*, 79: 189-201 (Sp 71).

Osborn, N.J. "Toward the Quintessential B." *HudR*, 21: 308-21 (Su 68).

Rueckert, W.H. "KB and Structuralism." *Shen*, 21: 19-28 (Au 69).

Schneider, H.N. "Against Homeostasis and Atavism." *KR*, 31: 406-11 (1969).

Steiner, George. "On Reading KB." *CamR*, 89A: 69-70 (4 N 67).

Turner, L.M. "On First Reading B's A Rhetoric of Motives." *CCC*, 24: 22-30 (1973).

Watson, E.A. "Incongruity without Laughter: KB's Theory of the Grotesque." *UWR*, 4: 28-36 (Sp 69).

Wellek, Rene. "KB and Literary Criticism." *SR*, 79: 171-88 (Sp 71).

Burnett, Frances Hodgson. McCarthy, Tom. "The Real Little Lord Fauntleroy." *AH*, 21: 50-5, 82-5 (F 70).

Molson, F.J. "FHB (1848-1924)." *ALR*, 8: 35-41 (Wi 75).

Tibbetts, R.A. "Addendum to BAL and Wright: FHB, *The Fortunes of Philippa Fairfax.*" *Serif*, 10: 42-3 (#1 73).

Burroughs, Edgar Rice. El Gouli, S. "Tarzan, un mythe africain reconté par un blanc américain." *ALA*, 13: 11-5 (O 70).

Farmer, P.J. "Tarzan Lives." *Esquire*, 77: 127-31 (Ap 72).

Fiedler, Leslie. "Lord of the Absolute Elsewhere." *NYT*, 9 Je 74, pp. 8-17.

Henighan, Tom. "Tarzan and Rima, The Myth and the Message." *RQ*, 3: 256-65 (Mr 69).

Kyle, Richard. "*Out of Time's Abyss*, The Martian Stories of ERB, A Speculation." *RQ*, 4: 110-22 (Ja 70).

Maloff, Saul. "Speaking of Books: Tarzan's First Love." *NYT*, 22 D 68, pp. 2, 14.

Morsberger, R.E. "ERB's Apache Epic." JPC, 7: 280-7 (Fa 73).

Mullen, R.D. "ERB and the Fate Worse than Death." *RQ*, 4: 186-91 (Jl 70).

———. "The Prudish Prurience of H. Rider Haggard and ERB." *RQ*, 5: 14-9 (Ja 73); 6: 134-46 (Ap 74).

Slate, Tom. "ERB and the Heroic Epic." *RQ*, 3: 118-23 (Mr 68).

Burroughs, John. Crosby, Ernest. "A Visit to JB." *Comrade*, 1: 54-5 (D 01).

Kasegawa, Koh. "Thoreau and B." *SToS*, 19: 42-6 (30 Mr 69).

Westbrook, Perry. "JB: New York's Early Defender of the Environment." *Conservationist*, 35: 30-2 (Ag-S 70).

———. "JB and the Transcendentalists." *ESQ*, 55: 47-54 (Su 69).

Burroughs, William S. Antolin, Mariano. "La literatura atonal y aleatoria de WB." *PSA*, 55: 137-50 (1969).

Burroughs, William. "Life with Father." *Esquire*, 76: 113-5 (S 71).

———. "St. Louis Return." *PaR*, 9: 51-62 (Fa 65).

Clark, Thomas. "The Art of Poetry VIII." *PaR*, 10: 13-55 (Sp 66).

Cobb, Noel. "WB." *Vinduet*, 26: 23-40 (1972).

Cordesse, Gererd. "The Science Fiction of WB." *Caliban*, 11: 34-43 (1975).

Goodman, Richard. "An Evening with WB." *MQR*, 13: 18-24 (Wi 74).

Knickerbocker, Conrad. "The Art of Fiction XXXVI." *PaR*, 9: 13-49 (Fa 65).

Lee, A.R. "WB and the Sexuality of Power." *TCS*, 1: 74-88 (N 69).

Matilla-Rivas, Alfredo. "Notas sobre *Naked Lunch* de WS.B." *Asomante*, 24: 42-4 (Ap-Je 68).

Michelson, Peter. "Beardsley, B, Decadence, and the Poetics of Obscenity." *TriQ*, 12: 139-55 (Sp 68).

Odier, Daniel. "Journey Through Time-Space: An Interview with WS.B." *EvR*, 13: 39-41, 78-89 (Je 69).

Pérez Minik, Domingo. "La novela extranjera en España: Miscelánea norteamericana: I.B. Singer y W.B." *Insula*, 27: 5-6 (Ja 72).

*Rushing, L.L. "WSB: A Bibliography." *BB*, 29: 87-92 (Jl/S 72).

*Skerl, Jennie. "A WS.B Bibliography." *Serif*, 11: 12-20 (Su 74).

Tijeras, Eduardo. "WS.B, en español." *CHA*, 261: 639-45 (1972).

Tytell, John. "The Beat Generation and the Continuing American Revolution." *ASch*, 42: 308-17 (Sp 73).

Vernon, John. "WS.B." *IowaR*, 3: 107-23 (Sp 72).

Vree, Freddy de. "WS.B." *NVT*, 26: 645-73 (1973).

Bushnell, Horace. Luker, R.E. "B in Black and White: Evidences of the 'Racism' of HB." *NEQ*, 45: 408-16 (1972).

Butor, Michel. Brosman, C.S. "A Source and Parallel of MB's *Mobile: In the American Grain.*" *MLR*, 66: 315-21 (Ap 71).

McWilliams, Dean. "William Faulkner and MB's Novel of Awareness." *KRQ*, 19: 387-402 (1972).

Roudiez, L.S. "Illustrations II: MB's Criticism Illustrated." *BA*, 47: 26-35 (Wi 73).

Savage, Catharine. "MB and *Paterson.*" *FMLS*, 7: 126-33 (1971).

Walters, J.R. "B's Use of Literary Texts in *Degrés.*" *PMLA*, 88: 311-20 (Mr 73).

Bynner, Witter. Kunst, A.E. "A Critical Analysis of WB's 'A Night Mooring near Maple Bridge.'" *Tsing Hua J of Chinese Stud*, 7: 114-42 (1968).

Byrd, William, I. Marambaud, Pierre. "WB I: A Young Virginia Planter in the 1670's." *VMHB*, 81: 131-50 (Ap 73).

Byrd, William, II. Amer, Robert. "Westover and the Wilderness: WB's Images of Virginia." *SLJ*, 7: 105-23 (Sp 75).

Core, George. "*The Prose of WB of Westover: Narratives of a Colonial Virginian.*" *ArlQ*, 2: 154-7 (Su 69).

Dolmetsch, C.R. "WB of Westover." *EA*, 27: 320-23 (Jl-S 74).

———. "WB II: The Augustan Writer as 'Exile' in His Own Country." *VQR*, 48: 145-9 (Wi 72).

———. "WB II: Comic Dramatist?" *EAL*, 6: 18-30 (Sp 71).

Marambaud, Pierre. "Un Grand Planteur Virginien au XVIIIe Siècle: WB de Westover." *EAA*, 2: 135-47 (1964).

———. "WB of Westover: Cavalier, Diarist, and Chronicler." *VMHB*, 78: 144-83 (Ap 70).

Rubin, L.D. "The Great American Joke." *SAQ*, 72: 82-94 (Wi 73).

Simpson, L.P. "WB and the South." *EAL*, 7: 187-95 (Fa 72).

Cabell, James Branch. Adler, Betty. "The Mencken Room." *Cabellian*, 3: 28-30 (1970).

Allan, James. "C & MacDonald." *Kalki*, 4: 138-42 (1970).

———. "More Coverage for Cover." *Kalki*, 4: 134-5 (1970).

Anderson, Poul. "Something about the Gods." *Kalki*, 3: 20-1 (1969).

Arons, P.L. "Romanticism in the Modern Era." *Genre*, 3: 64-71 (1970).

Austin, Bliss. "Dartmoor Revisited." *Kalki*, 3: 131-4 (1969).

Blish, James. "C as Kabbalist." *Kalki*, 3: 11-2 (1969).

———. "C as Voluntarist." *Kalki*, 3: 120-2 (1969).

———. "Cabellian Economics: The Uses of the Short Stories." *Kalki*, 2: 101-2 (1969).

———. "Footnotes to *The Long Night.*" *Kalki*, 6: 29-31 (1974).

———. "From the Third Window." *Kalki*, 2: 71, 106-7 (1968).

———. "The Geography of Dream." *Kalki*, 4: 90-2 (1970).

———. "The Long Night of a Virginia Author." *JML*, 2: 393-405 (1971-72).

———. "The Mirror and Pigeons Resolved." *Kalki*, 2: 97 (1968).

———. "Scot Upon Amneran." *Kalki*, 5: 8 (1971).

———. "Source Notes: Ninzian Gets One Right." *Kalki*, 2: 2 (1968).

———. "The Stallion's Other Members." *Kalki*, 4: 67-9 (1970).

———, and James N. Hall. "C as Historical Actor." *Kalki*, 3: 43-5 (1969).

Boardman, John. "The Escape from Escape Literature." *Kalki*, 2: 84-6, 96 (1969).

———. "The Two Cabells." *Kalki*, 3: 83-5 (1969).

*Bond, Nelson. "Tentative Checklist of Current Retail Values of Collectible C Editions." *Cabellian*, 1: 41-5 (1968); 2: 23-6 (Au 69).

Brewer, G.E.F. "Frances Joan Brewer's Bibliography: Its Genesis." *Cabellian*, 2: 28-9 (1969).

Brussel, I.R. "The First Fifty Years of Jurgen." *Cabellian*, 1: 74 (1969).

Bryant, Roger. "Charteris Gets One Wrong." *Kalki*, 5: 9 (1971).
————. "Manuel Magus." *Kalki*, 5: 5-7 (1971).
Brzustowicz, R. "Some Notes on Sources." *Kalki*, 7: 25-7 (1975).
Budd, L.J., R.P. Adams, D.T. Turner, and Paschal Reeves. "The Forgotten Decades of Southern Writing, 1890-1920." *MissQ*, 21: 275-90 (Fa 68).
Canary, R.H. "C's Dark Comedies." *MissQ*, 21: 83-92 (Sp 68).
————. "Cabelliana in Hawaii." *Cabellian*, 2: 27 (1969).
————. "Fables of Art in *The Silver Stallion*." *Kalki*, 4: 42-4 (1970).
————. "Whatever Happened to the C Revival?" *Kalki*, 6: 55-60 (1974).
Carson, B.F. "Richmond Renascence: The Virginia Writers' Club of the 1920's and *The Reviewer*." *Cabellian*, 2: 39-47 (1970).
Carter, Lin. "Horvendile: A Link Between C and Tolkien." *Kalki*, 3: 85-7 (1969).
————. "More on C in Paperback." Kalki, 3: 100-63 (1969).
Chancellor, Ann. "Messire Jurgen." *Kalki*, 3: 3-8 (1969).
Cheslock, Louis. *"The Jewel Merchants*, an Opera: A Case History." *Cabellian*, 4: 68-84 (Sp 72).
Cover, J.P. "Notes on *Jurgen*." *Kalki*, 3: 13-5, 70-2, 92-7, 104-7, 136-42 (1969).
Crane, J.St.C. "Rare or Seldom Seen Dust Jackets of American First Editions: v." *Serif*, 8: 27-8 (1971).
Cranwell, J.P., and J.P. Cover. "Notes on *Figures of Earth*." *Kalki*, 2: 91-5; 3: 22-33 (1968; 1969).
Dameron, Penn. "Inside Book Two of JBC's *The Silver Stallion*." *Cabellian*, 3: 22-3 (1970).
Davis, J.L. "C and Santayana in the Neo-Humanist Debate." *Cabellian*, 4: 55-67 (1972).
————. "Recent C Criticism." *Cabellian*, 1: 1-12 (1968).
Duke, Maurice. "Acquisitions of the C Library Since August 1970." *Cabellian*, 3: 81 (1971).
————. "C's and Glasgow's Richmond: The Intellectual Background of the City." *MissQ*, 27: 375-92 (Fa 74).
————. "JBC's Personal Library." *SB*, 23: 207-16 (1970).
————. "JBC's Personal Library: A Summary." *Cabellian*, 1: 27-30 (1968).
————. "Letters of George Sterling to JBC." *AL*, 44: 146-53 (My 72).
————. "The Ornate Wasteland of JBC." *Kalki*, 6: 79-89 (1974).
————. "Recent Acquisitions of the C Library." *Cabellian*, 2: 21-2 (Au 69).
————. "Virginiana at the Cabell Library." *Cabellian*, 2: 59-60 (Sp 70).
Edlin, Gene. "Researches into Dirghagama." *Kalki*, 7: 31-3 (1975).
Emmett, Peter. "Another Mirror for Pigeons." *Kalki*, 3: 88-91 (1969).
————. "C: The Making of a Rebel." *Carolina Q*, 14: 74-81 (1962).
Farley, E.E. "Which Does Not Touch upon Mirror and Pigeons." *Eildon Tree*, 1: 19-21 (1974).
Fisher, Opal. "Vardis Fisher Memorial." *Cabellian*, 3: 25-6 (1970).
Flora, J.M. "C as Precursor: Reflections on C and Vonnegut." *Kalki*, 6: 118-37 (1975).
————. "*Jurgen* in the Classroom." *Cabellian*, 1: 31-4 (1968).
————. "The Structure of *The Silver Stallion*." *Kalki*, 4: 38-41 (1970).
————. "Vardis Fisher and JBC: An Essay on Influence and Reputation." *Cabellian*, 2: 12-6 (Au 69).
————. "Vardis Fisher and JBC: A Postcript." *Cabellian*, 3: 7-9 (Au 70).
Freiberg, S.K. "La Belle Dame and the Sestina." *Kalki*, 7: 19-22 (1975).
Gabbard, G.N. "The Dance Version of Jurgen." *Kalki*, 6: 115-7 (1975).

————. "Bülg the Remembered." *Kalki*, 4: 111 (1970).

————. "Count Manuel and Peer Gynt." *Kalki*, 5: 99-114 (1973).

————. "Deems Taylor's Musical Version of *Jurgen*." *Cabellian*, 3: 12-5 (1970).

————. "Fairy Tales in *The High Place*." *Kalki*, 4: 115-20 (1970).

————. "*Jurgen* and *Peer Gynt*." *Kalki*, 5: 3-4 (1971).

Godshalk, W.L. "Artist and Spectator." *Kalki*, 3: 109 (1969).

————. "Beyond Life: Dizain des Demiurges." *Kalki*, 4: 45-63 (1970).

————. "C's *Cream of the Jest* and Recent American Fiction." *SLJ*, 5: 18-31 (Sp 73).

————. "C's Mirrors and (incidentally) Pigeons." *Kalki*, 6: 63-7 (1974).

————. "Introduction to *Beyond Life*." *Kalki*, 4: 45-63 (1970).

————. "JBC at William and Mary: The Education of a Novelist." *Kalki*, 2: 77-83, 96 (1968); *William and Mary R*, 5: 1-10 (1967).

Hall, J.N. "The Biography of Manuel: A Brief Bibliography." *Kalki*, 2: 3-5 (1968).

————. "C Deluxe: A Bibliographic Postcript." *Kalki*, 3: 76-7 (1969).

————. "In Charteris' Library." *Kalki*, 2: 97-8 (1968).

————. "The Re-evolution of a Vestryman: A Study in Cabellian Theology." *Kalki*, 2: 72-6 (1968).

————. "Trifles Found by Moonlight." *Kalki*, 2: 62, 72 (1969).

————. "Trifles Found in Moonlight." *Kalki*, 4: 128-31 (1970).

Halper, Nathan. "Joyce and JBC." *WN*, 6: 51-60 (Ag 69).

————. "Joyce/C and C/Joyce." *Kalki*, 4: 9-24 (1969).

Hartman, Harry. "'The Comstock Lewd': Jurgen and the Law—Updated." *Kalki*, 3: 16-9 (1969).

Herrick, T.C. "Ch. 51: Of Compromises with Time." *Kalki*, 3: 128-9 (1969).

Inge, M.T. "The Unheeding South: Donald Davidson on JBC." *Cabellian*, 2: 17-20 (Au 69).

Ingrasci, H.J. "The Cabellian Picara as Women's Liberationist." *Cabellian*, 4: 89-95 (Au 72).

Jenkins, W.D. "Another Way of Elusion." *Kalki*, 3: 63-9 (1969).

————. "Elementary, My Dear C." *Kalki*, 3: 134-5 (1969).

————. "An Image of the Image-Maker." *Kalki*, 4: 136-7 (1970).

————. "More Airy Persiflage." *Kalki*, 4: 133 (1970).

————. "On Troubadors." *Kalki*, 4: 132-3 (1970).

————. "Romantic Formulae." *Kalki*, 4: 133-4 (1970).

————. "The Shirt of Nessus." *Kalki*, 3: 9-10 (1969).

————. "A Time for Airy Persiflage." *Kalki*, 3: 50-2 (1969).

Johannsen, Kris. "Color in *Jurgen*." *Kalki*, 3: 129-30 (1969).

Johnson, Paul. "Gleanings about Glaum." *Kalki*, 7: 27-8 (1975).

Keller, D.H. "The Sigil of Scoteia." *Kalki*, 2: 27-8 (1968).

Lundwall, S.J. "More on Cabell in Sweden." *Kalki*, 6: 94-5 (1974).

MacDonald, E.E. "Another Opinion of Ingenue Among the Lions." *Cabellian*, 2: 30-1 (Sp 69).

————. "C Criticism: Past, Present, and Future." *Cabellian*, 1: 21-5 (Su 68).

————. "C's Game of Hide and Seek." *Cabellian*, 4: 9-16 (Au 71).

————. "C's Hero: Cosmic Rebel." *SLJ*, 2: 22-42 (Fa 69).

————. "C's Richmond Trial." *SLJ*, 3: 47-71 (Fa 70).

————. "The Glasgow-C Entente." *AL*, 41: 76-91 (Mr 69).

————. "Glasgow, C, and Richmond." *MissQ*, 27: 393-414 (Fa 74).

————. "The Influence of Provençal Poetry on JBC." *Cabellian*, 3: 1-6 (Au 70).

————. "The Storisende Edition: Some Liabilities." *Cabellian*, 1: 64-7 (Sp 69).

McElroy, B.G. "The Death of Koshchei." *Kalki*, 4: 89 (1970).

McNeill, W.A. "Cabellian Harmonics." *Kalki*, 4: 98-9 (1970).

————. "*Cabellian Harmonics—Why and How? Cabellian*, 2: 55-8 (Sp 70).

————. "JBC 'In Time's Hourglass.'" *Cabellian*, 3: 64-70 (Sp 71).

————. "Looking Back." *Kalki*, 4: 97-8 (1970).

Meyer, G.P. "Young Jurgen: A Comedy of Derision." *Cabellian*, 3: 16-21 (Sp 70).

Morley-Mower. Geoffrey. "C Under Fire." *Kalki*, 7: 5-13 (1975).

————. "C's Reputation and *Jurgen.*" *Kalki*, 5: 24-9 (1971).

————. "JBC's Flirtation with Clio: the Story of a Collaboration." *Kalki*, 6: 39-53 (1974).

————. "JBC's Flirtation with Clio: The Story of a Collaboration." *YULG*, 47: 15-27 (Jl 72).

————. "Sinclair Lewis's Attempts to Reform JBC." *Kalki*, 6: 140-5 (1975).

Page, Jerry. "'The Man at Storisende': A Biographical Note." *Kalki*, 2: 8-12 (1968).

Parkinson, Bob. "Eschatologues of Manuel." *Kalki*, 4: 70-1 (1970).

————. "Gihon gefunden." *Kalki*, 4: 133 (1970).

Rothman, Julius. "C's Books at This Time & Other Matters." *Cabellian*, 3: 34 (1970).

————. "The C Society: A Report." *Cabellian*, 3: 35-6 (Sp 70).

————. "The Danish *Jurgen.*" *Cabellian*, 3: 79-80 (Sp 71).

————. "Dissertations of C." *Cabellian*, 1: 77-8 (1969).

————. "JBC Library: Phase One." *Cabellian*, 3: 32-3 (1970).

————. "Jurgen, the Rabelaisian Babbitt." *Cabellian*, 1: 35-40 (1968).

————. "Photographs from the Life Story of JBC with Text by the Editor." *Cabellian*, 3: 71-7 (Sp 71).

————. "A Short History of *The Cabellian.*" *NasR*, 2: 59-64 (1873).

Rouse, Blair. "More Photographs from the Life Story of JBC with Text by the Editor." *Cabellian*, 4: 40-2 (1971).

Rubin, L.D. "Richmond in Virginia." *Kalki*, 4: 80-3 (1970).

Ruland, Richard. "Mencken and C." *Cabellian*, 1: 13-20 (1968).

Schilmeister, Deborah. "Revelations of a Sunrise." *Kalki*, 3: 124-7 (1969).

Schlegel, D.B. "C and His Critics." *Cabellian*, 3: 50-63 (Sp 71).

————. "C's Comic Mask." *Cabellian*, 4: 1-8 (Au 71).

————. "C's Translation of Virginia." *Cabellian*, 2: 1-11 (Au 69).

————. "A Case of Literary Piracy?" *Cabellian*, 1: 58-63 (Su 69).

————. "JBC: A Latter-Day Enlightener." *CLAJ*, 12: 223-36 (Mr 69).

Schley, M.A. "The Dem*iurge* in *Jurgen.*" *Cabellian*, 4: 85-8 (Su 72).

Scott, G.A. "Reflections on JBC." *Cwealth*, 40: 48 (F 73).

Siegle, L.C. "Cabelliana at Several Libraries." *Cabellian*, 4: 22-3 (Wi 71).

————. "Dating in *Figures of Earth.*" *Cabellian*, 4: 17-21 (Au 71).

Smith, N.J. "C: Realist or Romantic?" *Kalki*, 3: 53-6, 77 (1969).

Spencer, Paul. "'After the Style of Maurice Hewlett.'" *Kalki*, 3: 143-5 (1969).

————. "C in Print." *Kalki*, 5: 122-23; 6: 33-4, 67-8 (1973).

————. "Coth and Tohueyo." *Kalki*, 4: 72, 74 (1970).

————. "A Life Beyond Life." *Kalki*, 2: 23-6 (1968).

————. "A Manual of Non-Manuels." *Kalki*, 2: 29-31 (1968).

Squires, Roy. "The 'Count' of Poictesme." *Kalki*, 6: 94 (1974).

Staples, Roger. "The Lance and the Veil." *Kalki*, 4: 3-8 (1969).

Tarrant, Desmond. "C's *Hamlet Had an Uncle* and Shakespeare's *Hamlet.*" *Cabellian*, 3: 10-1 (Au 70).

————. "JBC." *Mencken*, 33: 4-9 (Sp 70).

————. "JBC (1879-1958)." *Cabellian*, 1: 53-7 (Su 69).

————. "On Visiting The Master." *Kalki*, 6: 90-3 (1974).

————. "Stallion & Legend." *Kalki*, 4: 64-6 (1970).

Thomas, J.W. "More Holes Filled." *Kalki*, 4: 132 (1970).

Warner, Richard. "The Illusion of Diabolism in the Cabellian Hero." *Novel*, 8: 246-59 (Sp 75).

Welch, Emmons. "*Beyond Life* and *Jurgen*: The Demiurge." *Cabellian*, 2: 48-53 (Sp 70).

Yocum, Joanne. "The Triumph of Romantic Realism." *Kalki*, 5: 85-92 (1971).

Zirkle, Conway. "The Blue Bird." *Kalki*, 4: 120 (1970).

————. "C and (Woodrow) Wilson." *Kalki*, 3: 46-9 (1969).

————. "Circular Time Travel." *Kalki*, 4: 84-7 (1970).

————. "Source Notes." *Kalki*, 4: 88-9 (1970).

Cable, G.W. Basso, Hamilton. "Boom Town, Dream Town." *Holiday*, 3: 27-41, 124-6 (F 48).

Budd, L.J., R.P. Adams, D.T. Turner, and Paschal Reeves. "The Forgotten Decades of Southern Writing, 1890-1920." *MissQ*, 21: 275-90 (Fa 68).

Butcher, Philip. "C to Boyesen on *The Grandissimes*." *AL*, 40: 391-4 (N 68).

————. "G.W.C and George W. Williams: An Abortive Collaboration." *JNH*, 53: 334-44 (O 68).

————. "'The Godfather' of *A Connecticut Yankee*." *CLAJ*, 12: 189-98 (Mr 69).

————. "Two Early Southern Realists in Revival." *CLAJ*, 14: 19-5 (S 70).

Campbell, M.L. "The Negro in C's *The Grandissimes*." *MissQ*, 27: 165-78 (Sp 74).

Chametzky, Jules. "Our Decentralized Literature: A Consideration of Regional, Ethnic, Racial, and Sexual Factors." *JA*, 17: 56-72 (1972).

Cleman, John. "The Art of Local Color in GW.C's *The Grandissimes*." *AL*, 47: 396-410 (N 75).

Dunbar-Nelson, Alice. "People of Color in Louisiana." *JNH*, 1: 361-76; 2: 51-78 (O 16, N 17).

Eaton, R.B. "GW.C and the Historical Romance." *SLJ*, 82-94 (Fa 75).

Egan, J.J. "'Jean-Ah Poquelin': GWC as Social Critic and Mythic Artist." *MarkR*, 2: 6-7 (1970).

Evans, Oliver. "Melting Pot in the Bayous." *AH*, 15: 30-51, 106 (D 63).

Evans, William. "French-English Literary Dialect in *The Grandissimes*." *AS*, 46: 210-22 (1971).

Godbold, E.S. "A Battleground Revisited: Reconstruction in Southern Fiction." *SAQ*, 73: 99-116 (Wi 74).

Howell, Elmo. "C and the Creoles: A Note on 'Jean-Ah-Poquelin.'" *XUS*, 9: 9-15 (Wi 70).

————. "GWC's Creoles: Art and Reform in *The Grandissimes*." *MissQ*, 26: 43-53 (Wi 72).

Le Jeune, Emilie. "Creole Folk Songs." *LaHQ*, 2: 454-62 (O 19).

Perret, J.J. "The Ethnic and Religious Prejudices of G.W.C." *LaStud*, 11: 263-73 (Wi 72).

Phanchard, Etienne. "'Madame Delicieuse': A Political Fable." *Caliban XII*, 11: 119-26 (1975).

Randel, William. "'Koanga' and Its Libretto." *M&L*, 52: 141-56 (Ap 71).

Ringe, D.A. "The 'Double Center': Character and Meaning in C's Early Novels." *StN*, 5: 52-62 (Sp 73).

Rubin, L.D. "The Division of the Heart: C's *The Grandissimes*." *SLJ*, 1: 27-47 (Sp 69).

Turner, Arlin. "Fiction of the Bayou Country." *SatR*, 18: 3-4, 16 (30 Ap 38).

———. "GWC on Prison Reform." *HLQ*, 36: 69-75 (1972).

Weaver, W. "The Twain-Cable Lectures in Kentucky, 1884-1885." *KHSR*, 72: 134-42 (Ap 74).

Cahan, Abraham. Anon. "AC." *Bkm*, 20: 414-7 (Ja 05).

Baker, R.S. "The Disintegration of the Jews." *Am Mag*, 48: 590-603 (O 09).

Bloom, B.H. "Yiddish-Speaking Socialist in America: 1892-1905." *AJA*, 12: 34-70 (Ap 60).

Chametzky, Jules. "Notes on the Assimilation of the American-Jewish Writer: AC to Saul Bellow." *JA*, 9: 173-80 (1964).

———. "Our Decentralized Literature: A Consideration of Regional, Ethnic, Racial, and Sexual Factors." *JA*, 17: 56-72 (1972).

Fine, D.M. "AC, Stephen Crane and the Romantic Tenement Tale of the Nineties." *AmS*, 14: 95-107 (Sp 73).

Gollomb, Joseph. "AC." *Am Mag*, 74: 672-4 (O 12).

Greenwood, A.K. "Storm Over the Nazarene." *JewD*, No. 1: 65-8 (O 40).

Hendrick, B.J. "Radicalism Among the Polish Jews." *WWk*, 45: 590-601 (Ap 23).

Hindus, Milton. "AC: Early American Realist." *JH*, 7: 38-44 (Fa 64).

Howells, W.D. "William Dean Howells on AC as an English Author." *HowS*, 6: 14-6 (N 62).

Kahn, Lothar. "*The Rise of David Levinsky*: Fifty Years After." *CJF*, 26: 2-5 (Fa 67).

Lookstein, J.H. "Why did Sholom Asch Write 'The Nazarene'?" *JewO*, nv: 4-6 (Mr 40).

* Marovitz, S.E. "AC." *ALR*, 8: 206-8 (1975).

———. "The Lonely New Americans of AC." *AQ*, 20: 196-210 (Su 68).

———. "*Yekl*: The Ghetto Realism of AC." *ALR*, 2: 271-3 (Fa 69).

———, and Lewis Fried. "AC (1860-1951): An Annotated Bibliography." *ALR*, 3: 197-243 (Su 70).

Poole, Ernest. "AC: Socialist—Journalist—Friend of the Ghetto." *Outlook*, 99: 467-78 (28 O 11).

Rich, J.C. "60 Years of the Jewish Daily Forward." *NLet*, 40: 1-38 (3 Je 57).

Rischin, Moses. "AC and the New York *Commercial Advertiser*: A Study in Acculturation." *PAJHS*, 43: 10-36 (S 53).

Rosenfeld, Isaac. "America, Land of the Sad Millionaire." *Commentary*, 14: 131-5 (Ag 52).

Sanders, Ronald. "Up the Road to Materialism." *NRep*, 144: 17-8 (6 Mr 61).

Schack, William, and Sarah Schack. "The Schooling of AC." *Commentary*, 18: 457-65 (N 54).

Schappes, M.U. "Anatomy of 'David Levinsky." *JewL*, nv: 22-4 (Ag 54).

Serebriani, Yisroyl. "A Creator of the Documentary Genre." *SovH*, 11: 169-71 (1971).

Singer, David. "David Levinsky's Fall: A Note on the Liebman Thesis." *AQ*, 19: 696-706 (Wi 67).

Strother, French. "AC, A Leader of the Jews." *WWk*, 26: 366, 470-4 (Ag 13).

Strout, Cushing. "Personality and Cultural History in the Novel: Two American Examples." *NLH*, 1: 423-37 (Sp 70).

Vogel, Dan. "C's Rise of David Levinski: Archetype of American Jewish Fiction." *Judaism*, 22: 278-87 (1973).

Zlotnick, Joan. "AC, A Neglected Realist." *AJA*, 23: 33-46 (Ap 71).

Cain, James M. Madden, David. "JM, C's *The Postman Always Rings Twice* and Albert Camus's *L'Etranger*." *PLL*, 6: 407-19 (Fa 70).

Madden, David. "JM.C: Twenty-Minute Egg of the Hard-Boiled School." *JPC*, 1: 178-92 (1967).

————. "Morris' *Cannibals*, C's *Serenade*: The Dynamics of Style and Technique." *JPC*, 3: 59-70 (Su 74).

Reck, T.S. "J.M.C's Los Angeles Novels." *ColQ*, 22: 375-87 (Wi 74).

Starr, Kevin. "It's Chinatown." *NRep*, 173: 31-2 (26 Jl 75).

Caldwell, Erskine. Anon. "EC." *RoLit*, 8: 29 (F 73).

————. "Midnight Assassins." *TLS*, 23 My 68, p. 521.

Comsa, Ioan. "EC: Menirea romanului e sa stimuleze spiritul." *Contemporanul*, 16: 12 (F 73).

Gray, R.J. "Southwestern Humor, EC, and the Comedy of Frustration." *SLJ*, 8: 3-26 (Fa 75).

Landor, Mikhail. "EC in the Soviet Union." *SovL*, 3: 181-6 (1969).

Mann, M. "Drei grosse amerikanische Epiker." *Die Weltwoche*, 16: 9 (1948).

Plymyène, Jean. "EC—Best-Seller Maudit." *ML*, 40: 41-2 (Ap 70).

Sale, R.B. "An Interview in Florida with EC." StN, 3: 316-31 (Fa 71).

Sutton, W.A. "Margaret Bourke-White and EC: A Personal Album." *Courier*, 10: 18-39 (1973).

Thompson, J.J. "EC and Southern Religion." *SHR*, 5: 33-44 (Wi 71).

Willingham, Calder. "True Myth-Maker of the Post-Bellum South." *GHQ*, 59: 243-47 (Wi 75).

Calisher, Hortense. Kirby, D.K. "The Princess and the Frog: The Modern American Short Story as Fairy Tale." *MinnR*, 4: 145-9 (1973).

Campbell, Isaac. Howard, E.G. "An Unknown Maryland Imprint of the Eighteenth Century." *PBSA*, 63: 200-3 (3Q 69).

Vivian, J.F. and J.H. "The Reverend IC: An Anti-Lockian Whig." *HMPEC*, 39: 71-89 (1970).

Campbell, John. Stover, Leon. "Checklist of JC's Fiction." *Extrapolation*, 14: 147-8 (My 73).

Stover, Leon. "Science Fiction and the Research Revolution, and JC." *Extrapolation*, 14: 129-48 (1973).

Campbell, William Edward March Campbell (see **March, William**).

Cane, Melville. Cane, Melville. "The Ladies of the *Dial*." *Asch*, 40: 316-21 (Sp 71).

Robinson, Jeffrey. "Celebration: The Lyric Poetry of MC." *ASch*, 38: 386-96 (Sp 69).

Cantwell, Robert. Swados, Harvey. "C Redivivus." *Novel*, 6: 92-4 (Fa 72).

Capote, Truman. Bauerle, R.F. "Stafford's Holcomb, Kansas." *Cont Poetry*, 1: 27-30 (Sp 73).

Burke, Tom. "The Sweeter Options of John D. McArthur and TC." *Esquire*, 74: 210-4, 255-69 (D 70).

Clarke, Gerald. "Checking in with TC." *Esquire*, 78: 136-7, 187-90 (N 72).

Creeger, G.R. "Animals in Exile: Criminal and Community in C's *In Cold Blood*." *JA*, 14: 94-106 (1969).

Freese, Peter. "Das Motiv des Doppelgängers in TC's 'Shut a Final Door' und E.A. Poe's 'William Wilson.'" *LWU*, 1: 41-9 (1968).

Kazin, Alfred. "The World as a Novel: From C to Mailer." *NYRB*, 16: 26-30 (8 Ap 71).

Keith, D.L. "An Interview with TC." *Contempora*, 1: 36-40 (1970).

King, James. "Turning New Leaves." *CanF*, 45: 281-2 (Mr 66).

Kirby, D.K. "The Princess and the Frog: The Modern American Short Story as Fairy Tale." *MinnR*, 4: 145-9 (1973).

McAleer, J.J. "*An American Tragedy* and *In Cold Blood*." *Thought*, 47: 569-586 (Wi 72).

Moravia, Alberto. "Two American Writers." *SR*, 68: 473-81 (Su 60).

Morris, Willie. "C's Muse Is Heard." *NRep*, 169: 21-2 (3 N 73).

Murray, Edward. "*In Cold Blood*: The Filmic Novel and the Problem of Adaptation." *LFQ*, 1: 132-7 (Ap 73).

Nance, W.L. "Variations on a Dream: Katherine Anne Porter and TC." *SHR*, 3: 338-45 (Fa 69).

Norden, Eric. "*Playboy* Interview: TC." *Playboy*, 15: 51-62, 160-70 (Mr 68).

Ozick, Cynthia. "Reconsideration: TC." *NRep*, 168: 31-4 (27 Ja 73).

Perry, J.D. "Gothic as Vortex: The Form of Horror in C, Faulkner, and Styron." *MFS*, 19: 153-67 (Su 73).

Pini, Richard. "Fiction et réalité chez TC." *LanM*, 63: 176-85 (Mr-Ap 69).

Pizer, Donald. "Documentary Narrative as Art: William Manchester and TC." *JML*, 2: 105-18 (S 71).

Trimmier, D.B. "The Critical Reception of C's *Other Voices, Other Rooms*." *WVUPP*, 17: 94-101 (Je 70).

* Vanderwerken, D.L. "TC: 1943-1968, A Critical Bibliography." *BB*, 27: 57-60, 71 (Jl-S 70).

Vazquez Amaral, José. "TC—¿Avance o retroceso?" *NuA*, 1 S 67; pp. 2-5, 33.

Zacharias, Lee. "Living the American Dream: 'Children on Their Birthdays.'" *SSF*, 12: 343-50 (Fa 75).

Capps, Benjamin. Capps, Benjamin. "Breaking into Print." *Roundup*, 21: 4-5 (Ap 73).

Etulain, Richard W. "*The White Man's Road*: An Appreciation." *SwAL*, 1: 88-92 (1971).

Sonnichsen, C.L. "The New Style Western." *SDR*, 4: 22-8 (Su 66).

Carey, Matthew. Carter, E.C. "MC in Ireland, 1760-1784." *CathHR*, 51: 503-27 (1965).

Carleton, Will. Sloane, David. "In Search of a Realistic Poetic Tradition." *ALR*, 5: 489-91 (1972).

————. "WC: Toward a Poetic Realism." *MarkR*, 4: 81-5 (F 75).

Carlino, Lewis John. Doyle, P.A. "Gilroy, C, and Hanley—The Best of the Young American Playrights." *NasR*, 1: 88-102 (Sp 66).

Carman, Bliss. Milham, M.E. "Arcady on the Atlantic." *HAB*, 19: 42-51 (1968).

Carmichael, Sarah Elizabeth. "SEC: Poetic Genius of Pioneer Utah." *UHQ*, 43: 52-66 (Wi 75).

Carne, Jonathan Townley. Gullason, T.A. "The Fiction of the Reverend JTC, D.D." *AL*, 43: 263-73 (My 71).

Carnes, James Patrick. Comanecí, Nadia. "Brsze mercântilij winaçi magnojà ni James Carnsii 'balance beam' spe Jasquelina Onnaissi y Oshar Painrum." *Romanes*çu Volpât, 12: 44-52 (3Q 75).

Carnevali, Emanuele. Fink, Guido. "Le bugie colorate di Carnevali." *Paragone*, 290: 86-8 (1973).

Carpenter, Stephen Culien. Watson, C.S. "Jeffersonian Republicanism in William Ioor's *Independence*, the First Play of South Carolina." *SCHM*, 69: 194-203 (1968).

Watson, C.S. "SCC, First Drama Critic of the Charleston *Courier*." *SCHM*, 69: 243-52 (O 68).

Carroll, Charles. Coad, O.S. "A Signer Writes a Letter in Verse." *JRUL*, 32: 33-6 (D 68).

Carruth, Hayden. Anon. "Symposium: The Writer's Situation: I." *NewAmR*, 9: 61-99 (1970); 10: 203-37 (1971).

Carter, John Henton. Flanagan, J.T. "JHC, alias 'Commodore Rollingpin.'" *MHR*, 53: 38-54 (O 68).

Swift, J.V. "From Pantry to Pen: The Saga of Commodore Rollingpin." *BMHS*, 24: 113-21 (Ja 68).

Carter, Robert. Lease, Benjamin. "RC, James Russell Lowell and John Neal: A Document." *JA*, 13: 246-8 (1968).

Pollin, B.R. "Poe in the *Boston Notion*." *NEQ*, 42: 585-9 (D 69).

Caruthers, W.A. Davis, C.C. "Dr. C Confronts the Bureaucrats." *GHQ*, 56: 101-11 (Sp 72).

Davis, C.C. "Dr. C Aids a Lady." *GHQ*, 56: 483-587 (Wi 72).

Cary, Alice and Phoebe. Pulsifer, J.G. "A and PC: Whittier's Sweet Singers of the West." *EIHC*, 109: 9-59 (1973).

Casey, Michael. Sossaman, Stephen. "American Poetry from the Indochina Experience." *Long Island R*, 2: 30-3 (Wi 73).

Cassady, Neal. Huebel, H.R. "The 'Holy Goof': NC and the Post-War American Counter Culture." *ILLQ*, 35: 52-61 (Ap 73).

Cather, Willa. Anon. "Prospective Focus in *My Antonia*." *ArQ*, 29: 303-16 (Wi 73).

Adams, T.S. "WC's *My Mortal Enemy*: The Concise Presentation of a Scene." *CLQ*, 10: 138-48 (S 73).

Adams, T.S. "WC's *My Mortal Enemy*: The Concise Presentation of a Scene." *CLQ*, 10: 138-48 (S 73).

Anderson, Quentin. "WC: Her Masquerade." *NRep*, 158: 28-31 (27 N 65).

Andes, C.J. "The Bohemian Folk Practice in 'Neighbour Rosicky.'" *WAL*, 7: 63-4 (1972).

Arnold, Marilyn. "C's Last Stand." *RSW*, 43: 245-52 (1975).

———. "The Function of Structure in C's *The Professor's House*." *CLQ*, 11: 169-78 (1975).

Baker, Bruce. "Nebraska Regionalism in Selected Works of WC." *WAL*, 3: 19-35 (Sp 68).

Bash, J.R. "WC and the Anathema of Materialism." *CLQ*, 10: 157-68 (1973).

Baum, Bernard. "WC's Waste Land." *SAQ*, 48: 589-601 (O 49).

Bennett, M.R. "Two C Collections." *PrS*, 42: 178-81 (Su 68).

———. "WC and the Prairie." *Nebraska Hist*, 56: 231-5 (1975).

Bennett, S.M. "Ornament and Environment: Uses of Folklore in WC's Fiction." *TFSB*, 40: 95-102 (S 74).

Bohlke, L.B. "Beginnings: WC and 'The Clemency of the Court.'" *PrS*, 48: 134-44 (Su 74).

———. "The Ecstasy of Alexandra Bergson." *CLQ*, 11: 139-49 (1975).

Borgman, Paul. "The Dialectic of WC's Moral Vision." *Renascence*, 27: 145-59 (Sp 75).

Brunauer, D.H. "The Problem of Point of View in *A Lost Lady*." *Renascence*, 28: 47-53 (Au 75).

———, and J.D. Klamecki. "Myra Henshaw's Mortal Enemy." *Chri & Lit*, 25: 7-40 (1975).

Bush, Sargent. "'The Best Years': WC's Last Story and Its Relation to Her Canon." *SSF*, 5: 269-74 (Sp 68).

———. "*Shadows on the Rock* and WC's View of the Past." *QQ*, 76: 269-85 (Su 69).

Byrne, Kathleen. "WC's Pittsburgh Years, 1896-1906." *WPHM*, 51: 1-15 (Ja 68).

Cary, Richard. "A WC Collection." *CLQ*, 8: 82-95 (Je 68).

———. "The Sculptor and the Spinster: Jewett's 'Influence' on C." *CLQ*, 10: 168-78 (Je 73).

Cather, Willa. "The Incomparable Opera House." *Nebraska Hist*, 49: 373-8 (Wi 68).

Cecil, L.M. "Anti-Intellectualism as Theme in WC's *The Professor's House*." *RSW*, 37: 235-41 (S 69).

Cecil, L.M. "Anti-Intellectualism as Theme in WC's *The Professor's House*." *RSW*, 37: 235-41 (S 69).

Charles, Sister Damian. "*Death Comes for the Archbishop*: A Novel of Love and Death." *NMQ*, 36: 389-403 (Wi 66-7).

————. "*The Professor's House*: An Abode of Love and Death." *CLQ*, 8: 70-82 (Je 68).

Clark, H.H. "WC." *ConL*, 13: 258-60 (Sp 72).

Crane, Joan. "Rare or Seldom-Seen Dust Jackets of American First Editions: I." *Serif*, 7: 27-30 (1970).

Curtin, W.M. "WC and *The Varieties of Religious Experience*." *Renascence*, 27: 115-23 (Sp 75).

————. "WC: Individualism and Style." *CLQ*, 8: 37-55 (Je 68).

Dinn, J.M. "A Novelist's Miracle: Structure and Myth in *Death Comes for the Archbishop*." *WAL*, 7: 39-46 (Sp 72).

Ditsky, John. "Nature and Character in the Novels of *WC*." *CLQ*, 10: 391-412 (S 74).

Durham, Philip. "WC's 'Thereabout.'" *NM*, 73: 83-9 (1972).

Eichorn, H.B. "A Falling Out with Love: *My Mortal Enemy*." *CLQ*, 10: 121-38 (1973).

Feger, Lois. "The Dark Dimension of WC's *My Antonia*." *EJ*, 59: 774-9 (S 70).

Ferguson, J.M., Jr. "'Vague Outlines': WC's Enchanted Bluffs." *WR*, 7: 61-4 (Sp 70).

Fox, Maynard. "Proponents of Order: Tom Outland and Bishop Latour." *WAL*, 4: 107-15 (Su 69).

————. "Symbolic Representation in WC's *O Pioneers!*" *WAL*, 9: 187-96 (Fa 74).

Freydberg, M.H. "WC: The Light Behind Her Books." *ASch*, 43: 282-7 (Sp 74).

Gelfant, B.H. "The Forgotten Reaping-Hook: Sex in *My Antonia*." *AL*, 43: 60-82 (Mr 71).

Harper, Marion. "The West of Twain and C." *DilR*, 14: 60-80 (Ja 66).

Harris, Celia. "*O Pioneers!* . . . An Early Nebraska Review." *WC Pioneer Memorial*, 16: 2-4 (1972).

Hart, Clive. "*The Professor's House*: A Shapely Story." *MLR*, 67: 271-81 (Ap 72).

Helmick, E.T. "Myth in the Works of WC." *MASJ*, 9: 63-9 (Fa 68).

————. "The Broken World: Medievalism in *A Lost Lady*." *Renascence*, 28: 39-46 (Au 75).

Hinz, Evelyn. "WC's Technique and the Ideology of Populism." *WAL*, 7: 47-61 (Sp 72).

Ikuta, Toshito. "*A Lost Lady*: The problem of Point of View." *KAL*, 15: 85-87 (1974).

Jobes, L.M. "WC's Last Novel." *UR*, 34: 77-80 (O 67).

————. "WC's *The Professor's House*." *UR*, 34: 154-60 (D 67).

LaHood, Marvin. "Conrad Richter and WC: Some Similarities." *XUS*, 9: 33-44 (Sp 70).

Loebner, Horst-Dieter. "WC: *Paul's Case*. Die Problematik der ästhetischen Existenz." *IWU*, 5: 215-32 (1972).

McLay, C.M. "Religion in the Novels of WC." *Renascence*, 27: 125-44 (Sp 75).

*Mclure, C.S. "WC." *ALR*, 8: 209-20 (1975).

Martin, Terence. "The Dream of Memory in *My Antonia*." *PMLA*, 84: 304-11 (Mr 69).

Miller, B.E. "The Testing of WC's Humanism: *A Lost Lady* and Other C Novels." *KanQ*, 5: 43-50 (Fa 73).

Miller, J.E. "*My Antonia* and the American Dream." *PsR*, 48: 112-23 (Su 74).

Milton, J.R. "Conversation with Distinguished Western Novelists." *SDR*, 9: 16-57 (Sp 71).

Miyake, Tsuneo. "On WC's Pioneer Novels: Referring to *O Pioneers!* and *My Antonia*." *KAL*, 15: 83-4 (1974).

Moers, Ellen. "The Survivors: Into the Twentieth Century." *TCL*, 20: 1-11 (Ja 74).

————. "WC and Colette: Mothers of Us All." *World*, 2: 51-3 (27 Mr 73).

Monteiro, George. "*McNaught's Monthly*: Addenda to the Bibliographies of C [and others]." *PBSA*, 68: 64-5 (1Q 74).

Murphy, John. "The Respectable Romantic and the Unwed Mother: Class Consciousness in *My Antonia*." *CLQ*, 10: 149-56 (1973).

Murphy, J.J. "WC and Hawthorne: Significant Resemblances." *Renascence*, 27: 161-75 (Sp 75).

Nyquist, Edna. "The Significance of the Locale in the Nebraska Fiction of WC, Especially in *My Antonia*." *WSL*, 2: 81-9 (1965).

O'Brien, Sharon. "The Limits of Passion: WC's Review of *The Awakening*." *Women & Lit*, 3: 10-20 (Fa 75).

O'Connor, M.A. "A Guide to the Letters of WC." *RALS*, 4: 145-72 (1974).

Olson, Lawrence. "Reconsideration: WC's *Song of the Lark*." *New Rep*, 169: 28-31 (Jl 7 and 14, 73).

Quinn, James. "C's *My Antonia* and the Critics: An Annotated Bibliography." *Kansas Eng*, 59: 20-1 (1974).

Reaver, J.R. "Mythic Motivation in WC's *O Pioneers!*" *WF*, 27: 19-25 (Ja 68).

Reynard, Grant. "WC's Advice to a Young Artist." *PrS*, 46: 111-24 (Su 72).

Rubin, Larry. "The Homosexual Motif in WC's 'Paul's Case.'" *SSF*, 12: 127-32 (Sp 75).

Rucker, M.E. "Prospective Focus in *My Antonia*." *ArQ*, 29: 303-16 (Wi 73).

Scheideman, J.W. "H.L. Mencken and WC Compared in Louis Auchincloss' *Pioneers and Caretakers*." *Mencken*, 47: 24-5 (Fa 73).

Schneider, Sister Lucy. "Artistry and Instinct: WC's 'Land-Philosophy.'" *CLAJ*, 16: 485-504 (Je 73).

———. "Artistry and Intuition: WC's 'Land Philosophy.'" *SDR*, 6: 53-64 (Wi 68-9).

———. "C's 'Land Philosophy' in *Death Comes for the Archbishop*." *Renascence*, 22: 78-86 (Wi 70).

———. "Of Land and Light: WC's *Lucy Gayheart*." *KanQ*, 5: 51-62 (Fa 73).

———. "'Land' Relevance in 'Neighbor Rosicky.'" *KanQ*, 1: 105-10 (1968).

———. "*O Pioneers!* in the Light of WC's 'Land-Philosophy.'" *CLQ*, 8: 55-70 (Je 68).

———. "Permanence and Promise: C's *Shadows on the Rock*." *Renascence*, 26: 83-94 (Wi 74).

———. "WC's 'The Best Years': The Essence of Her 'Land Philosophy.'" *MwQ*, 15: 61-9 (O 73).

———. "WC's Early Stories in Light of Her 'Land Philosophy.'" *MwQ*, 9: 75-94 (O 67).

Shults, Donald. "WC: Style in *Death Comes for the Archbishop*." *KAL*, 15: 75-83 (1974).

———. "*My Antonia*: A Dark Dimension." *WAL*, 2: 91-108 (Su 67).

Slote, Bernice. "Stephen Crane and WC." *Serif*, 6: 3-15 (1969).

———. "WC and the West." *Persimmon Hill*, 4: 48-59 (4Q 75).

———. "WC as a Regional Writer." *KanQ*, 2: 7-15 (1970).

———. "WC Reports Chautauqua, 1894." *PrS*, 43: 117-28 (Sp 69).

Stewart, D.H. "C's Moral Comedy." *QQ*, 73: 244-59 (Su 66).

Stineback, D.C. "WC's Ironic Masterpiece." *ArQ*, 29: 317-30 (Wi 73).

Stinson, Robert. "S.S. McClure's *My Autobiography*: The Progressive as Self-Made Man." *AQ*, 22: 203-12 (1970).

Stouck, David. "*The Country of the Pointed Firs*: A Pastoral of Innocence." *CLQ*, 9: 213-20 (B 70).

———. "*O Pioneers!*: WC and the Epic Imagination." *PrS*, 46: 23-34 (Sp 72).

———. "Perspective as Structure and Theme in *My Antonia*." *TSLL*, 12: 285-94 (Su 70).

———. "WC and *The Professor's House*: 'Letting Go with the Heart.'" *WAL*, 7: 13-24 (Sp 72).

———. "WC's Last Four Books." *Novel*, 7: 41-53 (Fa 73).

———. "WC's Unfurnished Novel: Narrative in Perspective." *WascR*, 6: 41-51 (1972).

Stouck, Mary-Ann, "Chaucer's Pilgrims and C's Priests." *CLQ*, 9: 531-7 (1972).

—————, and David. "Art and Religion in *Death Comes for the Archbishop.*" *ArQ*, 29: 293-302 (Wi 73).

—————. "Hagiographical Style in *Death Comes to the Archbishop.*" *UQ*, 41: 293-307 (1972).

Stuckey, W.J. "*My Antonia*: A Rose for Miss C." *StN*, 4: 473-83 (Fa 72).

Suderman, Elmer F. "Perceptions of the Prairie in *My Antonia.*" *IEngYb*, 24: 49-56 (1974).

Sullivan, P.J. "WC's Southwest." *WAL*, 7: 25-38 (Sp 72).

Thomas, Clara. "Proud Lineage: WC and Margaret Laurence." *CRAS*, 2: 3-12 (Sp 71).

Tibbetts, J.C. "Vital Geography: Victor Seastrom's *The Wind.*" *LFQ*, 1: 251-5 (Jl 73).

Toler, Sister Colette. "WC's Vision of the Artist." *Personalist*, 45: 502-23 (O 64).

Vigil, R.H. "WC and Historical Reality." *NMHR*, 50: 123-38 (Ap 75).

Weales, Gerald. "WC, Girl Reporter." *SoR*, 8; 681-8 (Jl 72)

Welty, Eudora. "The Physical World of WC." *NYT*, 27 Ja 74, 19-22.

Whaley, E.G. "C's *My Mortal Enemy.*" *PrS*, 48: 124-33 (1974).

Whittington, Curtis. "The 'Burden' of Narration: Democratic Perspective and First-Person Point of View in the American Novel." *SHR*, 2: 236-45 (Sp 68).

Whaley, E.G. "C's *My Mortal Enemy.*" *PrS*, 48: 124-33 (1974).

Woodress, James. "The World and the Parish: WC." *Architectorial Assn Q*, 7: 51-9 (#2 75).

—————. "WC Seen Clear." *PLL*, 7: 96-109 (Wi 71).

Woodside, T.E. "Maine's Stake in WC." *JLM*, 21 N 31, p. 8A.

Yongue, P.L. "*A Lost Lady*: The End of the First Cycle." *WAL*, 7: 3-12 (Sp 72).

Chandler, Raymond. Becker, J.P. "'Murder Considered as One of the Fine Arts': RC's Erzahlung 'I'll Be Waiting.'" *LWU*, 6: 31-42 (1973).

Beekman, E.M. "RC & an American Genre." *MR*, 14: 149-73 (Wi 73).

Boland, John. "C as Artist." *B&B*, 16: 36-7 (S 71).

De Vecchi Rocca, Luisa. "Apoteosi e decadenza del romanzo poliziesco d'azione." *NA*, 506: 532-40 (1969).

Dove, G.N. "The Complex Art of RC." *ArmD*, 8: 271-4 (1975).

Finch, G.A. "Marlowe's Long Goodby." *ArmD*, 6: 7-11 (1972).

Gozzi, Francesco. "RC e la semplice arte del delitto." *SA*, 16: 353-91 (1970).

Howard, Leon. "RC's Not-So-Great Gatsby." *MDAC*, 2: 1-15 (1973).

Jameson, Frederic. "On RC." *SoR*, 6: 624-50 (Jl 70).

Kaye, Howard. "RC's Sentimental Novel." *WAL*, 10: 135-45 (Ag 75).

Lid, R.W. "Philip Marlowe Speaking." *KR*, 31: 153-78 (1969).

Miller, R.H. "The Publication of RC's *The Long Goodbye.*" *PBSA*, 63: 279-90 (4Q 69).

Nolas, W.F. "Shadowing the Continental Op." *ArmD*, 8: 121-4 (1975).

Reck, Tom. "RC's Los Angeles." *Nation*, 221: 661-3 (20 D 75).

Stewart, L.D. "The Dust Jackets of *The Great Gatsby* and *The Long Goodbye.*" *MDAC*, 3: 331-4 (1974).

Symons, Julian. "The Case of RC." *NYTMS*, 23 D 73, pp. 13, 22-7

Channing, Ellery. Colacurcio, M.J. "A Better Mode of Evidence—The Transcendental Problem of Faith and Spirit." *ESQ*, 54: 12-22 (1Q 69).

Hudspeth, R.N. "EC's Paradoxical Muse." *ESQ*, 57: 34-40 (4Q 69).

—————. "A Perennial Springtime: C's Friendship with Emerson and Thoreau." *ESQ*, 54: 30-6 (1Q 69).

Redding, Mary. "The C Rhetoric and 'Splendid Confusion.'" *ESQ*, 57: 5-12 (4Q 69).

Sanborn, F.B. "Remarks on C." *ATQ*, 26: 49-52 (Sp 75).

Channing, William Ellery. Edrich, M.W. "The C Rhetoric and 'Splendid Confusion.'" *ESQ*, 57: 5-12 (4Q 69).

Lyons, Nathan. "The Figure of WEC." *MQR*, 7: 120-6 (Sp 68).
Chapman, John Jay. Hovey, R.B. "*The Collected Works of JJC.*" *MLJ*, 54: 451-3 (1970).
White, William. "Alcott and C Revisited." *WWR*, 16: 90-1 (S 70).
Chappell, Fred. Dillard, R.H.W. "Letters from a Distant Lover: The Novels of FC." *HC*, 10: 1-15 (Ap 73).
Chase, J.S. Dillon, R.H. "Prose Poet of the Trail: J.S.C." *QNL*, 35: 27-36 (1970).
Chauncy, Charles. Griffin, E.M. "C and *Seasonable Thoughts:* A New Letter." *AN&Q*, 11: 3-5 (S 72).
Cheever, John. Burhans, C.S. "JC and the Grave of Social Coherence." *TCL*, 14: 187-98 (Ja 69).
Chesnick, Eugene. "The Domesticated Stroke of JC." *NEQ*, 44: 531-52 (D 71).
Gardner, John. "Witchcraft in *Bullet Park.*" *NYT*, 24 O 71, pp. 2, 24.
Graves, N.C. "The Dominant Color in JC's 'The Swimmer.'" *NCLit*, 4: 4-5 (Mr 74).
Greene, Beatrice, "Icarus at St. Botolphs: A Descent to 'Unwonted Otherness.'" *Style*, 5: 119-37 (Sp 71).
Greene, George. "The Road Through Nightmare." *KR*, 31: 564-70 (1969).
Harmsel, H.T. "'Young Goodman Brown's and 'The Enormous Radio.'" *SSF*, 9: 407-8 (1972).
Kazin, Alfred. "O'Hara, C & Updike." *NYRB*, 20: 14-9 (19 Ap 73).
Lehmann-Haupt, Christopher. "Talk with JC." *NYT*, 27 Ap 69, pp. 42-4.
Leonard, John. "C to Roth to Malamud." *Atl*, 231: 112-6 (Je 73).
Molyneux, Thomas. "The Affirming Balance of Voice." *Shen*, 25: 27-43 (Wi 74).
Slabey, Robert. "JC: The Swimming of America." *Notre Dame R*, 1: 23-7 (Mr 74).
Vancura, Zdenek. "Soucasni americti romanopisci, 3: JC." *CMF*, 53: 1-3 (1971).
Chesnutt, Charles Waddell. Andrews, W.L. "C's Patesville: The Presence and Influence of the Past in *The House Behind the Cedars.*" *CLAJ*, 15: 284-94 (Mr 72).
———. "A Reconsideration of CWC." *CLAJ*, 19: 136-51 (1975).
———. "The Significance of CW.C's 'Conjure Stories.'" *SLJ*, 7: 78-99 (Fa 74).
———. "Two New Books on CWC." *MissQ*, 28: 511-20 (1975).
Baldwin, R.E. "The Art of *The Conjure Woman.*" *AL*, 43: 385-98 (N 71).
Boswell, J.C. "A Black Grimm." *NRep*, 172: 31 (1 Mr 75).
Britt, D.D. "C's Conjure Tales: What You See Is What You Get." *CLAJ*, 15: 269-83 (Mr 72).
Chametzky, Jules. "Our Decentralized Literature: A Consideration of Regional, Ethnic, Racial, and Sexual Factors." *JA*, 17: 56-72 (1972).
*Corrigan, R.A. "Afro-American Fiction: A Checklist, 1853-1970." *MASJ*, 11: 114-35 (Fa 70).
Cunningham, Joan. "The Uncollected Short Stories of CWC." *NALF*, 9: 57-8 (Su 75).
Dixon, Melvin. "The Teller as Folk Trickster in C's *The Conjure Woman.*" *CLAJ*, 18: 186-97 (D 74).
Faxell, Joel. "CWC's Sambo: Myth and Reality." *NALF*, 9: 105-8 (Fa 75).
Gartner, C.B. "CWC: Novelist of a Cause." *MarkR*, 3: 5-12 (O 68).
Giles, J.R. "C's Primus and Annie: A Contemporary View of *The Conjure Woman.*" *MarkR*, 3: 46-9 (My 72).
Hemenway, Robert. "'Baxter's Procrustes': Irony and Protest." *CLAJ*, 18: 172-85 (D 74).
———. "Gothic Sociology: CC and the Gothic Mode." *SLit I*, 7: 101-19 (Sp 74).
Hovet, T.R. "C's 'The Goophered Grapevine' as Social Criticism." *NALF*, 7: 86-8 (Fa 73).
Jaskoski, Helen. "Power Unequal to Man: The Significance of Conjure in Works by Five Afro-American Authors." *SFQ*, 38: 91-108 (Je 74).

Keller, D.H. "CWC (1858-1932)." *ALR*, 3; 1-4 (Su 68).

Lee, A.R. "'The Desired State of Feeling': CWC and Afro-American Literary Tradition." *DUJ*, 66: 163-70 (Mr 74).

Mason, Julian. "The Stories of CWC." *SLJ*, 1: 89-94 (Au 68).

Reilly, J.M. "The Dilemma in C's *The Marrow of Tradition*." *Phylon*, 32: 31-8 (Sp 71).

Sedlock, R.O. "The Evolution of CC's *The House Behind the Cedars*." *CLAJ*, 19: 125-35 (Ja 75).

Smith, R.A. "A Pioneer Black Writer and the Problems of Discrimination and Miscegenation." *Costerus*, 9: 181-5 (1973).

Socken, June. "CWC and the Solution to the Race Problem." *NALF*, 3: 52-6 (1969).

Taxel, Joel. "CWC's Sambo: Myth and Reality." *NALF*, 9: 105-8 (Wi 75).

Teller, Walter. "CWC's Conjuring Color-Line Stories." *ASch*, 42: 125-7 (Wi 72-73).

Walcott, Ronald. "C's 'The Sheriff's Children' as Parable." *NALF*, 7: 83-5 (Fa 73).

Wideman, John. "CWC: *The Marrow of Tradition*." *ASch*, 42: 125-34 (Wi 72-73).

Wintz, C.D. "Race and Realism in the Fiction of CWC." *OH*, 81: 122-30 (1972).

Child, Lydia Maria. Hornick, N.S. "The Last Appeal: LMC's Antislavery Letters to John C. Underwood." *VMHB*, 79: 45-54 (Ja 71).

Swennes, R.H. "LMC: Holographs of 'The Hero's Heart' and 'Brackett's Bust of John Brown.'" *AL*, 40: 439-42 (Ja 69).

Tarr, R.L. "Emerson's Transcendentalism in LMC's Letter to Carlyle." *ESQ*, 58: 112-5 (1Q 70).

Chilton, Edward. Bain, R.A. "The Composition and Publication of the Present State of Virginia and the College." *EAL*, 6: 31-54 (Sp 71).

Chivers, Thomas Holley. Rosenfeld, A.H. "The Poe-Chivers Controversy: A New Letter." *BBr*, 23: 89-93 (1969).

Sandler, S.G. "THC, M.D. (1809-1858) and the Origin of Edgar Allan Poe's 'The Raven.'" *NEJMed*, 289: 351-4 (16 Ag 73).

Tucker, E.L., ed. "A New Letter by THC." *GHQ*, 55: 582 8 (Wi 71)

Chopin, Kate. Anon. "Awakening in New Orleans: KC." *Distaff*, 3: 15 (15 Mr-15 Sp 75).

———. "Love in Louisiana—KC: A Forgotten Southern Novelist." *TLS*, 9 O 70, p. 1163.

Andrews, W.L. "An Addition to KC's Poetry." *AN&Q*, 13: 117-8 (Ap 75).

Arner, R.D. "Characterization and the Colloquial Style in KC's 'Vagabonds.'" *MarkR*, 2: 110-2 (My 71).

———. "KC." *LaStud*, 14: 5-139 (1975).

———. "KC's Realism: 'At the Cadian Ball' and 'The Storm.'" *MarkR*, 2: 1-14 (1970).

———. "Landscape Symbolism in KC's *At Fault*." *LaStud*, 9: 142-53 (Fa 70).

———. "Pride and Prejudice: KC's 'Désirée's Baby.'" *MissQ*, 25: 131-40 (Sp 72).

Bender, Bert. "KC's Lyrical Short Stories." *SSF*, 11: 257-66 (Su 74).

Berke, Jacqueline. "KC's Call to a Larger 'Awakening.'" *KCN*, 1: 15 (Wi 75-76).

*Bonner, Thomas. "KC: An Annotated Bibliography." *BB*, 32: 101-5 (Jl-S 75).

———. "KC's European Consciousness." *ALR*, 8: 281-4 (Su 75).

Budd, L.J., R.P. Adams, D.T. Turner, and Paschal Reeves. "The Forgotten Decades of Southern Writing, 1890-1920." *MissQ*, 21: 275-90 (Fa 68).

Butcher, Philip. "Two Early Southern Realists in Revival." *CLAJ*, 14: 91-5 (S 70).

Cantwell, Robert. "*The Awakening* by KC." *GaR*, 10: 489-94 (Wi 56).

Chametzky, Jules. "Our Decentralized Literature: A Consideration of Regional, Ethnic, Racial, and Sexual Factors." *JA*, 17: 56-72 (1972).

Colwell, Mary. "KC's European Consciousness." *Women*, 2: 10-1 (Fa 70).

Culley, Margo. "KC and Recent Obscenities." *KCN*, 1: 28-9 (Fa 75).

Chopin

Davidson, C.N. "C and Atwood: Woman Drowning, Woman Surfacing." *KCN*, 1: 6-10 (Wi 75-6).

Espy, John. "[KC.]" *NCF*, 25: 242-7 (S 70).

Fletcher, Marie. "The Southern Woman in the Fiction of KC." *LaHi*, 7: 117-32 (1966).

Garitta, Anthony. "The Critical Reputation of KC." *KCN*, 1: 36-7 (Fa 75).

Gartner, C.B. "Three Ednas." *KCN*, 1: 11-20 (Wi 75-76).

Gaudé, Pamela. "KC's 'The Storm': A Study of Maupassant's Influence." *KCN*, 1: 1-6 (Fa 75).

Koloski, B.J. "The Structure of KC's *At Fault*." *SAF*, 3: 89-94 (Sp 75).

———. "The Swinburne Lines in *The Awakening*." *AL*, 45: 608-10 (Ja 74).

Ladenson, J.M. "The Return of St. Louis' Prodigal Daughter: KC after Seventy Years." *M-A*, 2: 24-34 (1975).

Leary, Lewis. "KC and Walt Whitman." *WWR*, 16: 120-1 (D 70).

———. "KC, Liberationist?" *SLJ*, 3: 138-44 (Fa 70).

———. "KC's Other Novel." *SLJ*, 1: 60-74 (Au 68).

May, J.R. "Local Color in *The Awakening*." *SoR*, 6: 1031-40 (Au 70).

Milliner, Gladys. "The Tragic Imperative: *The Awakening* and *The Bell Jar*." *Mary Wollstonecraft N*, 2: 21-7 (D 73).

Muhlenfeld, E.S "KC." *ALR*, 8: 222-4 (1975).

O'Brien, Sharon. "The Limits of Passion: Willa Cather's Review of *The Awakening*." *Women & Lit*, 3: 10-20 (#2 75).

Potter, R.H. "KC and Her Critics: An Annotated Checklist." *MHSB*, 26: 306-17 (Jl 70).

———. "Negroes in the Fiction of KC." *LaHi*, 12: 41-58 (Wi 71).

Reilly, J.J. "Stories of KC." *Cweal*, 25: 606-7 (26 Mr 37).

Ringe, D.A. "Cane River World: KC's *At Fault* and Related Stories." *SAF*, 3: 157-66 (Au 75).

———. "The Romantic Imagery in KC's *The Awakening*." *AL*, 43: 580-88 (Ja 72).

Rocks, J.E. "KC's Ironic Vision." *Louisiana R*, 1: 110-20 (Wi 72).

Rosen, K.M. "KC's *The Awakening*: Ambiguity as Art." *JAmSt*, 5: 197-9 (Ag 71).

Rowe, Anne. "A Note on 'Beyond the Bayou.'" *KCN*, 1: 7-9 (Fa 75).

Seyersted, Per. "KC: A Critical Biography." *Edda*, 71: 341-66 (1971).

———. "KC (1851-1904)." *ALR*, 3: 153-9 (Sp 70).

Skaggs, Peggy. "'The Man-Haunted Instinct of Possession': A Persistent Theme in KC's Stories." *LaStud*, 14: 277-85 (1975).

———. "Three Figures in KC's *The Awakening*." *LaStud*, 13: 345-64 (Wi 74).

Snow, Kimberley. "KC's Masterpiece: *The Awakening*." *Aphra*, 3:4-15 (Sp 72).

Spangler, G.M. "KC's *The Awakening*: A Partial Dissent." *Novel*, 3: 249-55 (Sp 70).

Stafford, Jean. "Sensuous Women." *NYRB*, 17: 33-5 (23 S 71).

Sullivan, Ruth, and Stewart Smith. "Narrative Stance in KC's *The Awakening*." *SAF*, 1: 62-75 (Sp 73).

Toth, Emily. "The Cult of Domesticity and 'A Sentimental Soul.'" *KCN*, 1: 9-16 (Fa 75).

———. "The Independent Woman and 'Free' Love." *MR*, 16: 647-64 (Au 75).

*———. "KC: An Annotated Bibliography." *BB*, 33: 101-5 (1975).

———. "KC Remembered." *KCN*, 1: 216 (Wi 75-76).

———. "The Misdated Death of Oscar Chopin." *KCN*, 1: 34 (Fa 75).

———. "St. Louis in the Fiction of KC." *MHSB*, 31: 120-9 (O 75).

———. "Some Problems in KC Scholarship." *KCN*, 1: 30-3 (Fa 75).

———. "Women and Their Friends." *Cold Day in August*, 1: 1-3 (N 72); *Women*, 3: 44 (1973).

————, and Dennis Fitzgibbons. "KC Meets *The Harvard Lampoon.*" *KCN*, 1: 28 (Wi 75-6).

Warnken, William. "Fire, Light, and Darkness in KC's *At Fault.*" *KCN*, 1: 17-27 (Fa 75).

Warnken, Bill. "KC and Henrick Ibsen: A Study of *The Awakening* and *A Doll's House.*" *MSE*, 5: 43-9 (Wi 75).

Wheeler, O.B. "The Five Awakenings of Edna Pontellier." *SoR*, 11: 118-28 (Ja 75).

Wolff, C.G. "Thanatos and Eros: KC's *The Awakening.*" *AQ*, 25: 449-71 (O 73).

Zlotnick, Joan. "A Woman's Will: KC on Selfhood, Wifehood, and Motherhood." *MarkR*, 3: 1-5 (O 68).

Churchill, Winston. Blodgett, Geoffrey. "WC: The Novelist as Reformer." *NEQ*, 47: 495-517 (D 74).

Chapman, E.J. "WC: Popularizer of Progressivism." *DCLB*, 8: 43-50 (Ap 68).

Clemens, Cyril. "A Visit with the American WC." *Hobbies*, 52: 144-5 (My 47).

Ellis, J.B. "Missourians Abroad—No. 11, WC." *MHR*, 16: 517 (Jl 22).

*Franklin, Phyllis. "WC." *ALR*, 8: 225-6 (1975).

Hancock, A.E. "The Historical Fiction of WC." *Outlook*, 77: 735-5 (30 Jl 04).

Hofstadter, Richard and Beatrice. "WC: A Study in the Popular Novel." *AQ*, 2: 12-28 (Sp 50).

Johnson, Stanley. "The Novelist and His Novels in Politics." *WWK*, 17: 11-20 (D 08).

MacFarlane, P.C. "Evolution of a Novelist." *Collier's*, 52: 5-6 (27 D 13).

Parsons, H.V. "*The Tory Lover, Oliver Wiswell,* and *Richard Carvel.*" *CLQ*, 9: 220-31 (D 70).

Pitt, William. "Who's Who in *Coniston.*" *Yankee*, nv: 12-5 (N 37).

Schneider, R.W. "Novelist to a Generation: The American WC." *MQ*, 3: 149-82 (Ja 62).

Titus, W.I. "The Progressivism of the Muckrakers: A Myth Re-Examined Through Fiction." *CMV*, 1: 10-6 (Sp 60).

————. "The Senator and the Author." *IMH*, 55: 169-78 (Jl 59).

Ciardi, John. Cifelli, Edward. "The Size of JC's Song." *CEA*, 36: 21-7 (N 73).

Gallagher, E.J. "C's 'Tenzone.'" *Expl*, 27: 28 (D 68).

Mickleberry, William. "An Interview with JC." *FlQ*, 5: 59-84 (1973).

Perrine, Laurence. "C's *Tenzone.*" *Expl*, 28: 82 (My 70).

Clark, Charles Heber. (Max Adeler). Foster, E.F. "A *Connecticut Yankee* Anticipated: MA's *Fortunate Island.*" *BSUF*, 9: 73-6 (Au 68).

Clark, Emily. Duke, Maurice. "Ingenue among the Richmonders." *EGN*, 3: 5-9 (1975).

Clark, Walter Van Tilburg. Andersen, Kenneth. "Character Portrayal in *The Ox-Bow Incident.*" *WAL*, 4: 287-98 (Wi 70).

Andersen, Kenneth. "Form in WVTC's *The Ox-Bow Incident.*" *WR*, 6: 19-25 (Sp 69).

Bates, B.W. "C's Man For All Seasons: The Achievement of Wholeness in *The Ox-Bow Incident.*" *WAL*, 3: 37-49 (Sp 68).

Cochran, R.W "Nature and the Nature of Man in *The Ox-Bow Incident.*" *WAL*, 5: 253-64 (Wi 71).

Cohen, E.H. "C's 'The Portable Phonograph.'" *Expl*, 28: 69 (Ap 70).

Cracroft, Richard. "Some Striking Parallels and a Possible Source for *The Ox-Bow Incident . . .*" *PosS*, 2: 3-6 (Mr 71).

Deane, P. "American Elements in WVTC's *The Track of the Cat.*" *RLV*, 39: 39-45 (#1 73).

Hendricks, G.D. "Symbolism in WVTC's *The Track of the Cat.*" *SwAL*, 3: 77-80 (1973).

Horvitz, P.S. "Three Unrecorded Poems of WVTC." *BB*, 30: 90 (Ap-Je 73).

Houghton, D.E. "The Failure of Speech in *The Ox-Bow Incident.*" *EJ*, 59: 1245-51 (D 70).

————. "Man and Animals in 'The Indian Well.'" *WAL*, 6: 215-8 (Wi 71).

Clark, Walter Van Tilburg

Kehl, D.G. "Writing in the Apocalypse: Rhetorical Lessons from WVTC." *CCC*, 25: 34-41 (F 74).

Milton, J.R. "Conversations with Distinguished Western American Novelists." *SDR*, 15-57 (Sp 71).

Milton, J.R. "Literary or Not." *SDR*, 9: 3-5 (Wi 71-72).

Moore, J.B. "Folklore in *The Track of the Cat.*" *NCaF*, 12: 30-4 (D 64).

Peterson, L.S. "Tragedy and Western American Literature." *WAL*, 6: 243-9 (Wi 72).

Rogers, D.G. "Man and Nature in C's Track of the Cat." *SDR*, 12: 49-55 (1974).

Stegner, Wallace. "WC's Frontier." *Atl*, 232: 94-8 (Ag 73).

Stein, Paul. "Cowboys and Unicorns: The Novels of WVTC." *WAL*, 5: 265-75 (Wi 71).

Westbrook, Max. "The Archetypal Ethic of *The Ox-Bow Incident.*" *WAL*, 1: 105-18 (Su 66).

———. "WVTC: 1909-1971." *WAL*, 6: 190 (Fa 71).

Clark, Willis Gaylord. Roche, A.J. "Another Look at Poe's Dr. Ollapod." *PoeS*, 6: 28 (Je 73).

Clarke, James Freeman. Anon. "The Funeral of Mr. Hawthorne: As Reported in the *Boston Evening Transcript*, 24 May 1864, with the Address by Rev. JFC." *NHJ*, 2: 257-61 (1972).

Jackson, C.T. "The Orient in Post-Bellum American Thought: Three Pioneer Popularizers." *AQ*, 22: 67-81 (Sp 70).

Clarke, Sarah. Myerson, Joel. "'A True and High Minded Person': Transcendentalist SC." *SWR*, 59: 163-72 (Sp 74).

Cleaver, Eldridge. Anderson, Jervis. "Race, Rage and EC." *Commentary*, 46: 63-9 (D 68).

Brown, D.L. "Black Power: An Analysis." *IllQ*, 33: 31-46 (S 70).

Dickstein, Morris. "Wright, Baldwin, C." *NLet*, 38: 117-24 (Wi 71).

Felgar, Robert. "*Soul on Ice* and *Native Son.*" *NALF*, 8: 235 (Fa 74).

Gates, Skip. "Cuban Experience: EC on Ice." *Transition*, 49: 32-44 (1975).

Gilman, Richard. "More on Negro Writing." *NRep*, 158: 25-8 (13 Sp 68).

———. "White Standards and Negro Writing." *NRep*, 158: 25-30 (9 Mr 68), *NALF*, 3: 111-6 (Wi 70).

Leary, M.E. "The Uproar over C." *NRep*, 159: 21-4 (30 N 68).

Nower, Joyce. "C's Vision of America and the New White Radical: A Legacy of Malcolm X." *NALF*, 4: 12-21 (1970).

———. "Foolin' Master." *SNL*, 7: 5-10 (Fa 69).

Clemens, Samuel Langhorne (Mark Twain). Anon. "*All Right!* from *The Carpet-Bag*— Possible T?" *Twainian*, 26: 1-2 (N-D 67).

———. "Annie Moffett Webster and Charles Noel Flagg to Paine (Pictorial MT)." *Twainian*, 31: 1-3 (Mr-Ap 72).

———. "The Appert Collection of MT." *Bancroftiana*, 57: 5-6 (Ja 74).

———. "Bernard Shaw Meets MT." *MTJ*, 16: 22 (Wi 71-2).

———. "Changing Humor." *NYT*, 20 Ag 16, p. 32.

———. "Financial Support for Worthy Studies and Publications Supplied by Private Foundation and Government Sources." *Twainian*, 31: 1-4, 1-4 (Jl-Ag, S-O 72).

———. "Francis D. Millet, James Montgomery Flagg and Spiridon Portraits (Pictorial MT)." *Twainian*, 31: 1-4 (My-Je 72).

———. "Identification of MT Material." *Twainian*, 26: 4 (S-O 67).

———. "Letter from Daughter of C.H. Webb." *Twainian*, 26: 3 (S-O 67).

———. "Letter from John P. Vollmer." *Twainian*, 26: 3-4 (Mr-Ap 67).

————. "Letter from Judge A.W. (Gus) Oliver." *Twainian*, 26: 4 (Ja-F 67).

————. "Letter from Sam Davis to Paine." *Twainian*, 26: 2 (Jl-Ag 67).

————. "Letter from Tracy Robinson." *Twainian*, 26: 4 (Mr-Ap 67).

————. "Letters from Clara Stanchfield." *Twainian*, 26: 1-3 (My-Je 67).

————. "Letters from Emma B. Thayer and S.L. Severance." *Twainian*, 26: 2-3 (Mr-Ap 67).

————. "Letters from Fred J. Hall to Paine." *Twainian*, 26: 2-3 (Jl-Ag 67).

————. "Letters from Joe Goodman." *Twainian*, 26: 3-4 (My—Je 67).

————. "Letters from J.Y.W. MacAlister to Paine." *Twainian*, 26: 4 (My-Je 67).

————. "Letters from Laura (Becky Thatcher) to Paine 1907-1912." *Twainian*, 30: 1-4 (Jl-Ag 71).

————. "Letters from Susan Crane to Paine." *Twainian*, 26: 3-4 (Jl-Ag 67).

————. "The Letters of Madame de Sevigné (17th-Century History) (Mark Twain's Marked Copy)." *Twainian*, 31: 1-4 (N-D 72); 32: 1 (J-F 73), 3-4 (Mr-Ap 73), 1-4 (My-Je 73), 4 (Jl-Ag 73).

————. "Letters to Paine from Charles J. Langdon." *Twainian*, 26: 1-2 (Jl-Ag 67).

————. "Letters to Paine from Laura Frazer (Becky Thatcher), Helen K. Garth, Fee, Fuller, Robards and Mahan." *Twainian*, 30: 1-4 (S-O 71).

————. "Letters to Paine from Samuel E. Moffett, S.L. Severance and Annie M. Webster in Years 1906-1917." *Twainian*, 31: 4 (My-Je 72).

*————. "MT Items Published Elsewhere." *Twainian*, 26: 1-4 (Ja-F 67); 27: 1-4 (Ja-F 68); 28: 1-4, 4 (Ja-F, Mr-Ap 69); 29: 1-4 (Ja-F 70); 30: 4 (Mr-Ap 71); 31: 1-4, 3-4 (Ja-F, Mr-Ap 72); 32: 1-4 (Ja-F 73); 33: 1-3 (Ja-F 74); 34: 4, 3-4 (Ja-F, Mr-Ap 75).

————. MT on Lynching." *Twainian*, 26: 3 (N-D 67).

————. "MT's Last Manuscript." *Bancroftiana*, 25: 9 (Je 73).

————. "MT's Marginal Notations on *Life, Letters and Journals of George Ticknor*." *Twainian*, 27: 4, 1-4 (Jl-Ag, S-O, N-D 68); 28: 4, 1-4, 1-4, 1-4, 1-4, 1-4, 4 (Ja-F, Mr-Ap, My-Je, Jl-Ag, S-O, N-D, N-D 69); 29: 4, 1-4 (Ja-F, Mr-Ap 70).

————. "MT's Marginal Notes on Girard College." *Twainian*, 27: 1-4, 2-4 (My-Je, Je-Ag 68).

————. "MT's Reading, His Library and Our Foundation." *Twainian*, 32: 4 (Jl-Ag 73).

————. "MT's Room-Mate in St. Louis—Burrough." *Twainian*, 26: 1 (My-Je 67).

————. "More MT." *Bancroftiana*, 52: 7 (Ap 72).

————. "Paine, Book Publishing, Dispersal of MT Library and Manuscripts." *Twainian*, 30: 4, 1-4 (Mr-Ap, My-Je 71).

————. "Progress in the MT Region." *Twainian*, 26: 1 (S-O 67).

————. "Stephen Girard Will and Girard College." *Twainian*, 27: 2-4 (Jl-Ag 68).

————. "Twichell's Letters to Paine." *Twainian*, 29: 4, 3-4 (S-O, N-D 70); 30: 3-4 (Ja-F 71).

————. "The University of California Collection, Howe's *Country Town*." *Twainian*, 27: 4, 1-2 (Ja-F, Mr-Ap 68).

————. "An Unpublished Letter: MT to Chatto & Windus, 25 July 1897." *CEAAN*, 1: 1 (1968).

————. "Walter F. Frear, Willard S. Morse, Yale University Collection, M.T. Bibliographies Started 'Foundation' and 'MT and Hawaii.'" *Twainian*, 30: 1-4 (N-D 71).

Agrawal, I.N. "MT's Visit to Allahabad." *IJAS*, 3: 104-8 (#1 73).

Alsen, Eberhard. "The Futile Pursuit of Truth in T's 'What is Man?' and Anderson's 'The Book of the Grotesque." *MTJ*, 17: 12-4 (Wi 74-5).

————. "Pudd'nhead Wilson's Fight for Popularity and Power." *WAL*, 7: 135-43 (1972).

Andersen, D.M. "Basque Wine, Arkansas Chawin' Tobacco: Landcape and Ritual in Ernest Hemingway and MT." *MTJ*, 16: 3-7 (Wi 71-2).

———. "A MT Practical Joke: An Unpublished Anecdote." *MTJ*, 18: 20-1 (Wi 75-6).

Andersen, Kenneth. "The Ending of MT's *A Connecticut Yankee in King Arthur's Court*." *MTJ*, 14: 21 (Su 69).

———. "MT, W.D. Howells, and Henry James: Three Agnostics in Search of Salvation." *MTJ*, 15: 13-6 (Wi 70).

Anderson, Frederick. "Hazards of Photographic Sources." *CEAAN*, 1: 5 (1968).

———. "Overlapping Texts." *CEAAN*, 1: 6-7 (1968).

———. "Team Proofreading: Some Problems." *CEAAN*, 2: 15 (1969).

———, and Hamlin Hill. "How SC Became MT's Publisher: A Study of the James R. Osgood Contracts." *Proof*, 2: 117-43 (1972).

Andrews, William. "The Source of MT's 'The War Prayer.'" *MTJ*, 17: 8-9 (Su 75).

Arikawa, Shoji. "Huckleberry Finn in Japan." *Eng Rec*, 21: 20-6 (F 71).

Arner, R.D. "Acts Seventeen and *Huckleberry Finn*: A Note on Silas Phelps' Sermon." *MTJ*, 16: 12 (Su 72).

Ashely, L.F. "Huck, Tom and Television." *Eng Q*, 4: 57-65 (Sp 71).

Aspiz, Harold. "MT and 'Doctor' Newton." *AL*, 44: 130-6 (My 72).

———. "The Other Half of Pudd'nhead's Dog." *MTJ*, 17: 10-1 (Su 75).

Babcock, C.M. "MT as 'A Majority of One.'" *UCQ*, 15: 3-7 (My 70).

———. "MT's Chuck-Wagon Specialties." *WAL*, 5: 147-51 (Su 70).

Baetzhold, Howard. "An Emendation in *A Connecticut Yankee*." *CEAAN*, 1: 10 (1968).

———. "Found: MT's 'Lost Sweetheart.'" *AL*, 44: 414-29 (N 72).

Banks, R.J. "MT: Detective Story Writer. An Appreciation." *ArmD*, 7: 176-7 (1974).

Banta, Martha. "Escape and Entry in *Huckleberry Finn*." *MFS*, 14: 79-91 (Sp 68).

———. "Rebirth or Revenge: The Endings of *Huckleberry Finn* and *The American*." *MFS*, 15: 191-207 (Su 69).

Barchilon, Jose, and J.S. Kovel. "Huckleberry Finn: A Psychoanalytic Study." *JAPA*, 14: 775-814 (O 66).

Barnes, B.L. "MT's Family Christmas" *YM*, 36: 106-9, 136, 139-41 (D 72).

Barsness, J.A. "Platform Manner in the Novel: A View from the Pit." *MASJ*, 10: 49-59 (Fa 69).

Baum, Joan. "MT on the Congo." *MTJ*, 17: 7-9 (Su 74).

Beaver, Harold. "Run, Nigger, Run: *Adventures of Huckleberry Finn* as a Fugitive Slave Narrative." *JAmSt*, 8: 339-61 (74).

Beebe, Maurice, and John Feaster. "Criticism of MT: A Selected Checklist." *MFS*, 14: 93-139 (Sp 68).

Beidler, P.G. "The Raft Episode in *Huckleberry Finn*." *MFS*, 14: 11-20 (Sp 68).

Bellamy, J.D. "Two Eras, Two Epitaphs: Steamboating Life in the Works of MT and Richard Bissell." *BSUF*, 13: 48-52 (Fa 72).

Belson, J.J. "The Nature and Consequences of the Loneliness of Huckleberry Finn." *ArQ*, 26: 243-8 (Au 70).

Benardete, J.J. "*Huckleberry Finn* and the Nature of Fiction." *MR*, 9: 209-26 (Sp 68).

Bercovitch, Sacvan. "Huckleberry Bumppo: A Comparison of '*Tom Sawyer*' and '*The Pioneers*.'" *MTJ*, 14: 1-4 (Su 68).

Berger, Sidney. "New MT Items." *PBSA*, 68: 331-4 (3Q 74).

Bergholz, Harry. "Strindberg's Anthologies of American Humorists, Bibliographically Identified." *SS*, 43: 335-43 (Au 71).

Bergman, Frank. "MT and the Literary Misfortunes of John William DeForest." *JA*, 13: 249-52 (1968).

Berkove, Lawrence. "The 'Poor Players' of *Huckleberry Finn*." *PMASAL*, 53: 291-310 (1968).

Bertolotti, D.S. "Structural Unity in 'The Man That Corrupted Hadleyburg.'" *MTJ*, 14: 19-20 (1969).

Bickley, R.B. "Humorous Portraiture in T's News Writing." *ALR*, 3: 395-8 (Fa 70).

Bie, W.A. "MT's Bitter Duality." *MTJ*, 16: 14-6 (Su 72).

Birchfield, James. "Jim's Coat of Arms." *MTJ*, 14: 15-6 (Su 69).

Blair, Walter. "MT's Other Masterpiece: 'Jim Baker's Blue-Jay Yarn.'" *SAH*, 1: 132-47 (Ja 75).

Blanck, Jacob. "BAL Addendum 3479: Twain's 'A Dog's Tale.'" *PBSA*, 62: 617 (4Q 68).

Blei, Norbert. "Marking T in Hannibal." *Am Lib*, 5: 128-34 (Mr 74).

Blues, Thomas. "The Strategy of Compromise in MT's 'Boy Books.'" *MFS*, 14: 21-31 (Sp 68).

Boland, Sally. "The Seven Dialects in *Huckleberry Finn*." *NDQ*, 36: 30-40 (1968).

Brack, O.M. "MT in Knee Pants: The Expurgation of *Tom Sawyer Abroad*." *Proof*, 2: 145-51 (1972).

Bradbury, Malcolm. "MT in the Gilded Age." *CritQ*, 11: 65-73 (Sp 69).

Branch, E.M. "MT Reports the Races in Sacramento." *HLQ*, 32: 179-86 (F 69).

———. "SC: Learning to Venture a Miracle." *ALR*, 8: 91-9 (Sp 75).

———. "SLC and the Copperheads of 1864." *Mad River R*, 2: 3-20 (Wi-Sp 67).

Brand, J.M. "The Incipient Wilderness: A Study of *Pudd'nhead Wilson*." *WAL*, 7: 125-34 (1972).

Bray, Robert. "MT Biography: Entering a New Phase." *MwQ*, 15: 286-301 (1974).

Briden, E.F. "SLC and Elizabeth Jordan: An Unpublished Letter." *MTJ*, 17: 11-3 (Su 74).

Brodwin, Stanley. "Blackness and the Adamic Myth in MT's *Pudd'nhead Wilson*." *TSLL*, 15: 167-76 (Sp 73).

———. "The Humor of the Absurd: MT's Adamic Diaries." *Criticism*, 14: 49-64 (Wi 72).

———. "MT's Masks of Satan: The Final Phase." *AL*, 45: 206-277 (My 73).

Brogan, H.O. "Early Experience and Scientific Determinism in T and Hardy." *Mosaic*, 7: 99-105 (#3 74).

Brogunier, Joseph. "An Incident in *The Great Gatsby* and *Huckleberry Finn*." *MTJ*, 16: 1-3 (Su 72).

Brown, M.F. "MT as Proteus: Ironic Form and Fictive Integrity." *PMASAL*, 51: 515-27 (1966).

Budd, L.J. "Baxter's Hog: The Right Mascot for an Editor (with CEAA Standards) of MT's Political and Social Writings." *CEAAN*, 3: 3-10 (Je 70).

———. "Did MT write 'Impersonally' for the *New York Herald?*" *Duke Un Libr N*, 43: 5-9 (N 72).

———. "MT and the 'Quaker City.'" *SLJ*, 1: 112-6 (Au 68).

———. "MT Talks Mostly About Humor and Humorists." *SAH*, 1: 4-22 (Ap 74).

Bugliari, Jeanne. "The Picaresque as a Flaw in MT's Novels." *MTJ*, 15: 10-2 (Su 71).

Burg, D.F. "Another View of *Huckleberry Finn*." *NCF*, 29: 299-319 (N 74).

Burns, Graham. "Time and Pastoral: *The Adventures of Huckleberry Finn*." *CritR*, 15: 52-3 (1972).

Burns, S.L. "St. Petersburg Re-Visited: Helen Eustis and MT." *WAL*, 5: 99-112 (Su 70).

Bush, Robert. "Grace King and MT." *AL*, 44: 31-51 (Mr 72).

Butcher, Philip. "'The Godfathership' of *A Connecticut Yankee*." *CLAJ*, 12: 189-98 (Mr 69).

Butter, M.D. "*Tom Sawyer, Detective*: The Last Emancipation." *AN&Q*, 13: 116-7 (1975).

———. "MT's Installment on the National Debt." *SLJ*, 1: 48-55 (Sp 69).

Byers, J.R. "Miss Emmeline Grangerford's Hymn Book." *AL*, 43: 259-63 (My 71).

———. "MT's Miss Mary Jane Wilks: Shamed or Shammed?" *MTJ*, 17: 13-4 (Wi 73-74).

Campbell, Frank and Ina Campbell. "MT's Florentine Villas in 1964-65." *MTJ*, 15: 12-4 (Su 71).

Cardwell, G.A. "The Bowdlerizing of MT." *ESQ*, 21: 179-93 (3Q 75).

———. "*Life on the Mississippi*: Vulgar Facts and Learned Errors." *ESQ*, 19: 283-93 (4Q 73).

———. "MT, James R. Osgood, and Those 'Suppressed' Passages." *NEQ*, 46: 163-88 (Je 73).

———. "SC's Magical Pseudonym." *NEQ*, 48: 175-93 (Je 75).

———. "A Surprising World: Amasa Delano in Kentucky." *MTJ*, 12-3 (Su 73).

Carson, H.L. "MT's Misanthropy." *Cresset*, 33: 13-15 (D 69).

Cary, Richard. "In Further Defence of Harriet Shelley: Two Unpublished Letters by MT." *MTJ*, 16: 13-5 (Su 73).

Casey, D.J. "Universality in 'Huckleberry Finn': A Comparison of T and Kivi." *MTJ*, 14: 13-8 (Wi 67-68).

Cate, H.L. "Two American Bumpkins." *RSW*, 41: 61-3 (1972).

Cather, Willa. "Willa Cather's Tribute to MT." *MTJ*, 17: 23 (Wi 73-74).

Cecil, L.M. "Tom Sawyer: Missouri Robin Hood." *WAL*, 4: 125-31 (Su 69).

Chambliss, Amy. "The Friendship of Helen Keller and MT." *GaR*, 24: 305-10 (Fa 70).

Chellis, B.A. "Those Exraordinary Twins: Negroes and Whites." *AQ*, 21: 100-13 (Sp 69).

Childress, William. "T's Tenderfooting Days." *Westways*, 67: 29-33, 66 (My 75).

Christopher, J.R. "On the *Adventures of Huckleberry Finn* as a Comic Myth." *CimR*, 18: 18-27 (Ja 72).

Church, S.H. "MT and Andrew Carnegie." *MTJ*, 17: 22 (Wi 74-5).

Clements, Cyril. "Dan Beard and the Connecticut Yankee." *Hobbies*, 79: 134-6 (O 74).

Clemens, S.L. "*Life as I Find It* or *Poor Little Stephen Girard*." *Twainian*, 27: 1 (Jl-Ag 68).

———. "MT to Chatto & Windus: Two unpublished Letters," *CEAAN*, 3: 1-2 (Je 70).

Clerc, Charles. "Sunrise on the River: 'The Whole World' of *Huckleberry Finn*." *MFS*, 14: 67-70 (Sp 68).

Cloutier, A.C. "Dear Mister Seelye . . . Yours Truly, Tom Sawyer." *CE*, 34: 849-53 (Mr 73).

Clymer, K.J. "John Hay and MT." *MHR*, 67: 397-406 (Ap 73).

Coard, Robert. "The Dictionary and MT." *WSt*, 43: 1-4 (F 68).

———. "Huck Finn and Mr. MT Rhyme." *MwQ*, 10: 317-29 (1969).

———. "Huck Finn Goes to Collage." *Scholia Satyrica*, 1: 37-43 (Sp 75).

———. "MT's *The Gilded Age* and Sinclair Lewis's *Babbitt*." *MwQ*, 13: 319-33 (Sp 72).

Coburn, M.D. "'Training Is Everything': Communal Opinion and the Individual in *Pudd'nhead Wilson*." *MLQ*, 31: 209-19 (Je 70).

Cohen, E.H. "The Return to St. Petersburg." *IEY*, 23: 50-5 (N 73).

Collins, B.G. "Huckleberry Finn: A Mississippi Moses." *JNT*, 5: 86-104 (1975).

Colwell, J.L. "Huckleberries and Humans: On the Naming of Huckleberry Finn." *PMLA*, 86: 70-6 (Ja 71).

Coplin, Keith. "John and SC: A Father's Influence." *MTJ*, 15: 1-6 (Wi 70).

Cox, J.F. "On the Naming of Huckleberry Finn." *PMLA*, 86: 1038 (1971).

Cox, J.M. "The Approved MT: The Beginning of the End." *SoR*, 4: 542-50 (Sp 68).

———. "Humor and America: The Southwestern Bear Hunt, Mrs. Stowe, and MT." *SR*, 83: 573-601 (Fa 75).

———. "MT and the South." *SLJ*, 8: 144-52 (Fa 75).

————. "Toward Vernacular Humor." *VQR*, 46: 311-30 (Sp 70).

Cracroft, R.H. "Distorting Polygamy for Fun and Profit: Artemus Ward and MT Among the Mormons." *BYUS*, 14: 272-88 (Wi 74).

————. "The Gentle Blasphemer: MT, Holy Scripture, and the Book of Mormon." *BYUS*, 11: 119-40 (Wi 71).

Crinklaw, Don. "The Twain Cousin." *St. Louisan*, 7: 42-9 (Je 75).

Cronin, F.C. "The Ultimate Perspective in *Pudd'nhead Wilson*." *MTJ*, 16: 14-6 (Wi 71-72).

Crowley, J.W. "A Note on *The Gilded Age*." *ELN*, 10: 116-8 (D 72).

————. "The Sacerdotal Cult and the Sealskin Coat: W.D. Howells in *My Mark Twain*." *ELN*, 11: 287-92 (Je 74).

Dahl, Curtis. "MT and Ben Ely: Two Missouri Boyhoods." *MHR*, 66: 549-66 (Jl 72).

D'Avanzo, M.L. "In the Name of Pudd'nhead." *MTJ*, 16: 13-4 (Su 72).

David, B.R. "The Pictorial *Huck Finn*: MT and His Illustrator, E.W. Kemble." *AQ*, 26: 331-51 (O 74).

————. "The Unexpurgated *A Connecticut Yankee*: MT and His Illustrator, Daniel Carter Beard." *Prospects*, 1: 99-118 (1975).

Davidson, L.K. "The Darnell-Watson Feud." *DuqR*, 13: 76-95 (1968).

Davis, C.L. "*Harper's New Monthly Magazine*, 1896." *Twainian*, 29: 1-4, 1-3 (S-O, N-D 70).

————. "MT, Dan Beard and Boy Scouts of America." *Twainian*, 29: 2-4, 1-4 (My-Je 70, Jl-Ag 70).

————. "MT's Marginal Notes on Girard College." *Twainian*, 3: 1-4 (My-Je 68); 4: 1-4 (Jl-Ag 68).

————. "Twichell's Letters to Paine." *Twainian*, 29: 4, 3-4 (S-O, N-D 70).

Davis, Sheldon. "On the Trail of MT and Bret Harte in the Mother Lode Country." *Stockton Rec*, 16 Jl 21 and 23 Jl 21.

Delaney, Paul. "The Avatars of the Mysterious Stranger: MT's Images of Christ." *Chri & Lit*, 24, 25-38 (#1 74).

DeMott, B. "Speaking of Books: If the book which Mr. MT wrote warn't up to what these crickits wanted. . . ." *NYT*, 22 Mr 70, pp. 2, 32.

Denton, L.W. "MT and the American Indian." *MTJ*, 16: 1-3 (Wi 71-72).

————. "MT on Patriotism, Treason, and War." *MTJ*, 17: 4-7 (Su 74).

Dinan, J.S. "Hank Morgan: Artist Run Amuck." *MSE*, 3: 72-7 (Sp 72).

Ditsky, J.M. "MT and the Great Dark: Religion in *Letters from the Earth*." *MTJ*, 17: 12-9 (Su 75).

Donaldson, Scott. "Pap Finn's Boy." *SAB*, 36: 32-7 (My 71).

Douglas, Ann. "Art and Advertising in *A Connecticut Yankee*: The Robber Baron Revisited." *CRAS*, 6: 182-95 (Fa 75).

Doyle, P.A. "Henry Harper's Telling of a MT Anecdote." *MTJ*, 15: 13 (Su 70).

Doyno, V.A. "Over T's Shoulder: The Composition and Structure of *Huckleberry Finn*." *MFS*, 14: 3-9 (Sp 68).

Duke, C.R. "MT: Speaker at Large." *Eng Rec*, 25: 43-52 (Sp 74).

Dunne, F.P. "Mr. Dooley's Friends: Teddy Roosevelt and MT." *Atl*, 212: 77-99 (S 63).

Durham, J.M. "MT Comments on Religious Hypocrisy." *RLA*, 10: 60-75 (1967).

Duskis, Henry. "Serious Wilkins in Boston." *YM*, 34: 79, 179-83 (Je 70).

Ellis, H.E. "MT: The Influence of Europe." *MTJ*, 14: 12-8 (Wi 68-69).

Elsbree, Langdon. "Huck Finn on the Nile." *SAQ*, 69: 504-10 (Au 70).

Emblen, D.L. "MT Alive and Well—Very Well Indeed—in Sweden." *MTJ*, 16: 16-8 (Su 73).

Ensor, Allison. "The Birthplace of SC: A New MT Letter." *TSL*, 14: 31-4 (1969).

———. "A Clergyman Recalls Hearing MT." *MTJ*, 15: 6 (Wi 70-71).

———. "The Contributions of Charles Webster and Albert Bigelow Paine to *Huckleberry Finn*." *AL*, 40: 222-7 (My 68).

———. "The Downfall of Poor Richard: Benjamin Franklin as Seen by Hawthorne, Melville, and MT." *MTJ*, 17: 14-8 (Wi 74-5).

———. "The House United: MT and Henry Watterson Celebrate Lincoln's Birthday, 1901." *SAQ*, 74: 259-68 (Sp 75).

———. "The Location of the Phelps Farm in *Huckleberry Finn*." *SAB*, 34: 7 (My 69).

———. "MT's 'The War Prayer': Its Ties to Howells and to Hymnology." *MFS*, 16: 535-9 (Wi 70-71).

———. "The 'Opposition Line' to the King and the Duke in *Huckleberry Finn*." *MTJ*, 14: 6-7 (Wi 68-9).

———. "The 'Tennessee Land' of *The Gilded Age*: Fiction and Reality." *TSL*, 15: 15-23 (1970).

Erickson, Mildred. "Our Paths Have Crossed." *UCQ*, 13: 17-23 (Ja 68).

Eschholz, P.A. "MT and the Language of Gesture." *MTJ*, 17: 5-8 (Wi 73-74).

———. "T's *The Tragedy of Pudd'nhead Wilson*." *Expl*, 31: 67 (Ap 73).

Fetterley, Judith. "Disenchantment: Tom Sawyer in *Huckleberry Finn*." *PMLA*, 87: 69-74 (Ja 72).

———. "The Sanctioned Rebel." *StN*, 3: 293-304 (Fa 71).

———. "Yankee Showman and Reformer: The Character of MT's Hank Morgan." *TSLL*, 14: 667-79 (Wi 73).

Field, Kate. "MT to Chatto & Windus: Two Unpublished Letters." *CEAAN*, 3: 1-2 (1970).

Fisher, Marvin, and Michael Elliott. "*Pudd'nhead Wilson*: Half a Dog Is Worse Than None." *SoR*, 8: 533-47 (Jl 72).

Fite, Montgomery. "MT's Naming of Huckleberry Finn." *AN&Q*, 13: 140-1 (My 75).

Fleck, Richard. "A Connecticut Yankee in a Tragic Court." *ConnR*, 3: 92-7 (O 69).

———. "MT in the American Wilderness." *NaS*, 25: 12-4 (#2 71); 10-1 (#3 71).

———. "MT's Social Criticism in *The Innocents Abroad*." *BRMMLA*, 25: 39-48 (Je 71).

Fortenberry, George. "The Unnamed Critic in William Dean Howells' *Heroines of Fiction*." *MTJ*, 16: 7-8 (Wi 71-72).

Foster, E.F. "*A Connecticut Yankee* Anticipated: Max Adeler's *Fortunate Island*." *BSUF*, 9: 73-6 (Au 68).

Freese, Peter. "*Adventures of Huckleberry Finn* und *The Catcher in the Rye*: Zur exemplarischen Deutung Romananfange." *NS*, 22: 658-68 (1973).

Freimarck, John. "*Pudd'nhead Wilson*: A Tale of Blood and Brotherhood." *UR*, 34: 303-6 (Je 68).

French, B.M. "James Hammond Trumbull's Alternative Chapter: Mottoes for *The Gilded Age*." *PQ*, 50: 271-80 (Ap 71).

Friedlander, W.J. "MT, Social Critic, and His Image of the Doctor." *AIM*, 77: 1007-10 (1972).

Fuller, D.J. "MT and Hamlin Garland: Contrarieties in Regionalism." *MTJ*, 17: 14-8 (Wi 73-74).

Gardner, J.H. "Gaffer Hexam and Pap Finn." *MP*, 66: 155-6 (N 68).

———. "MT and Dickens." *PMLA*, 84: 90-101 (Ja 69).

Gargano, J.W. "*Pudd'nhead Wilson*: MT as Genial Satan." *SAQ*, 74: 365-75 (Su 75).

Gassaway, B.M. "Tom Sawyer Is Back on the River." *Contempora*, 2: 36-40 (Ap-D 72).

Gaston, G.M. "The Function of Tom Sawyer in *Huckleberry Finn*." *MissQ*, 27: 33-9 (Wi 73-4).

Geismar, Maxwell. "MT on U.S. Imperialism, Racism and Other Enduring Characteristics of the Republic." *Ramparts*, 6: 65-71 (My 68).

Gerber, J.C. "Practical Editions: MT's *The Adventures of Tom Sawyer* and *Adventures of Huckleberry Finn*." *Proof*, 2: 285-92 (1972).

———. "*Pudd'nhead Wilson* as Fabulation." *SAH*, 2: 21-31 (Ap 75).

Gervais, R.J. "*The Mysterious Stranger*: The Fall as Salvation." *PCP*, 5: 24-33 (1970).

Gibson, D.B. "MT's Jim in the Classroom." *EJ*, 57: 196-9, 202 (F 68).

Gibson, W.M. "MT's *Mysterious Stranger* Manuscripts: Some Questions for Textual Critics." *BRMMLA*, 22: 183-91 (D 68).

Gill, Brendan. "The Confidence Man." *NY*, 42: 114-7 (3 S 66).

Goad, M.E. "The Image and the Woman in the Life and Writings of MT." *ESRS*, 19: 5-70 (Mr 71).

Gogol, J.M. "Nikolai Aseev and MT." *MTJ*, 16: 15-6 (Su 73).

Goldstien, N.L. "MT's Money Problem." *BuR*, 19: 37-54 (Sp 71).

Goodyear, R.H. "Huck Finn's Anachronistic Double Eagles." *AmN&Q*, 10: 39 (N 71).

Gordon, Caroline. "The Shape of the River." *MQR*, 12: 1-10 (Wi 73).

Goto, Akio. "Seijuku no kyozetsu—MT no Americateki Seikaku." *EigoS*, 115: 286-7 (1969).

Goudie, Andrea. "'What Fools These Mortals Be!': A Puckish Interpretation of MT's Narrative Stance." *KanQ*, 5: 19-31 (Fa 73).

Gowda, H.H.A. "MT in India." *LHY*, 7: 17-23 (Jl 66).

Graves, Wallace. "MT's 'Burning Shame.'" *NCF*, 23: 93-8 (Je 68).

Gregory, Ralph. "John A. Quarles: MT's Ideal Man." *MHSB*, 25: 229-35 (Ap 69).

Grenander, M.E. "MT's English Lectures and George Routledge & Sons." *MTJ*, 17: 1-4 (Su 75).

Gribben, Alan. "The Dispersal of SL.C's Library Books." *RALS*, 5: 147-165 (Au 75).

———. "MT, Phrenology and the 'Temperaments': A Study of Pseudoscientific Influence." *AQ*, 24: 45-68 (Mr 72).

Griffith, Clark. "Merlin's Grin: From 'Tom' to 'Huck' in *A Connecticut Yankee*." *NEQ*, 48: 28-46 (Mr 75).

Grove, Noel. "MT: Mirror of America." *Nat Georgraphic*, 148: 300-36 (S 75).

Hakac, John. "*Huckleberry Finn*: A Copy Inscribed in 1903." *ABC*, 20: 7-9 (Ja 70).

Hamblin, D.J. "Mark (Ye) (the) Twain." *Life*, 57: 13 (10 Jl 64).

Hansen, Chadwick. "The Once and Future Boss: MT's Yankee." *NCF*, 28: 62-73 (Je 73).

Hanson, R.G. "Bluejays and Man: T's Exercise in Understanding." *MTJ*, 17: 18-9 (Wi 73-74).

Harkey, J.H. "When Huck Finn Smouched That Spoon." *MTJ*, 15: 14 (Su 70).

Harper, Marion. "The West of T and Cather." *DilR*, 14: 60-80 (Ja 66).

Harrell, Don. "MT's *Joan of Arc*: Fact or Fiction?" *MarkR*, 4: 95-7 (1975).

Harrell, D.W. "A Chaser of Phantoms: MT and Romanticism." *MwQ*, 13: 201-12 (Wi 72).

———. "MT's Joan of Arc: Fact or Fiction." *MarkR*, 4: 95-7 (F 75).

Harris, H.L. "MT's Response to the Native American." *AL*, 46: 495-505 (Ja 75).

Harrison, Stanley. "MT's Requiem for the Past." *MTJ*, 16: 3-10 (Su 72).

Hart, J.D. "On an 'Unpublished Letter' by MT." *CEAAN*, 2: 15 (1969).

Hart, J.E. "Heroes and Houses: The Progress of Huck Finn." *MFS*, 14: 39-46 (Sp 68).

Harwood, C.E. "T's *Huckleberry Finn*, Chapter IV." *Expl*, 28: 36 (D 69).

Hasley, Louis. "The Durable Humor of Bill Nye." *MTJ*, 15: 7-10 (Wi 70-71).

Hays, J.Q. "MT's Rebellion Against God: Origins." *SwAL*, 3: 27-38 (1973).

Hill, Hamlin. "MT and His Enemies." *SoR*, 4: 520-9 (Sp 68).

———. "Who Killed MT." *ALR*, 7: 119-24 (Sp 74).

Hoffman, M.J. "Huck's Ironic Circle." *GaR*, 23: 307-22 (Fa 69).

Hook, Andrew. "Huckleberry Finn and Scotland." *Eng Rec*, 21: 8-14 (D 70).

Horowitz, F.R. "MT's Belle Lettre in 'The Loves of Alonzo Fitz Clarence and Rosannah Ethelton.'" *MTJ*, 13: 16 (Wi 65-66).

Hough, R.L. "T's Double-Dating in *A Connecticut Yankee*." *N&Q*, 15: 424-5 (N 68).

Howell, Elmo. "Huckleberry Finn in Mississippi." *LaStud*, 7: 167-72 (Su 68).

————. "In Defense of Tom Sawyer." *MTJ*, 15: 17-9 (Wi 70).

————. "MT's and the Civil War." *BSUF*, 13: 53-61 (Fl 72).

————. "MT's Arkansas." *AHQ*, 29: 195-208 (Au 70).

————. "MT's Indiantown." *MTJ*, 15: 16-9 (Su 71).

————. "Tom Sawyer's Mock Funeral: A Note on MT's Religion." *MTJ*, 16: 15-6 (Wi 72).

————. "Uncle John Quarles' Watermelon Patch." *MwQ*, 9: 271-82 (Ap 68).

————. "Uncle Silas Phelps: A Note on MT's Characterization." *MTJ*, 14: 8-12 (Su 68).

Hoy, J.F. "The Grangerford-Shepherdson Geud in *Huckleberry Finn*." *MTJ*, 18: 19-20 (Wi 75-6).

Hsu, C.Y. "MT and the Chinese." *AsST*, 16: 6-7 (Mr 74).

Illiano, Antonio. "'Italian without a Master': A Note for the Appreciation of MT's Undictionarial Translation as an Excercise in Humor." *MTJ*, 17: 17-20 (Su 74).

Jager, R.B. "MT and the Robber Barons: A View of the Gilded Age Businessman." *MTJ*, 17: 8-12 (Wi 74-75).

Johnson, Ellwood. "MT's Dream Self in the Nightmare of History." *MTJ*, 15: 6-12 (Wi 70).

Jones, Joseph. "MT's *Connecticut Yankee* and Australian Nationalism." *AL*, 40: 227-32 (My 68).

Kahn, Sholom J. "MT as American Rabelais." *HUSL*, 1: 47-75 (Sp 73).

Kamei, Shunsuki. "MT no Le" *EigoS*, 119: 738-9 (1974).

Kaplan, Justin. "On MT: 'Never Quite Sane in the Night.'" *PsyR*, 56: 113-27 (Sp 69).

Kapoor, S.D. "Tradition and Innovation in *Huckleberry Finn*." *ModR*, 762: 409-13 (Je 70).

Karpowitz, Steven. "Tom Sawyer and MT: Fictional Women and Real in the *Play* of Conscience with the Imagination." *L&P*, 23: 5-12 (#1 73).

Katona, Anna. "Aunt Sally's Civilization and the American National Schizophrenia." *ALitASH*, 14: 145-59 (1972).

Kazin, Alfred. "Almost Perfect." *LJ*, 87: 4243-5 (15 N 62).

Kegel, P.L. "Henry Adams and MT: Two Views of Medievalism." *MTJ*, 15: 11-21 (Wi 70-71).

Kestersen, D.B. "The MT-Josh Billings Friendship." *MTJ*, 18: 5-9 (Wi 75-6).

Ketterer, David. "Epoch-Eclipse and Apocalypse: Special 'Effects' in *A Connecticut Yankee*." *PMLA*, 88: 1104-14 (O 73).

Kimball, W.J. "SC as a Confederate Soldier: Some Observations about 'The Private History of a Campaign that Failed.'" *SSF*, 5: 382-4 (Su 68).

King, Bruce. "*Huckleberry Finn*." *ArielE*, 2: 69-77 (O 71).

Kinghorn, N.D. "E.W. Kemble's Misplaced Modifier: A Note on the Illustrations for *Huckleberry Finn*." *MTJ*, 16: 9-11 (Su 73).

Kiralis, Karl. "Two More Recently Discovered Letters by SLC." *MTJ*, 16: 18-20 (Su 73).

————. "Two Recently Discovered Letters by MT." *MTJ*, 15: 1-5 (Wi 70-71).

Kirkham, Bruce. "Huck and Hamlet." *MTJ*, 14: 17-9 (Su 69).

Klass, Philip. "An Innocent in Time: MT in King Arthur's Court." *Extrapolation*, 16: 17-32 (D 74).

Kolin, P.C. "MT, Aristotle, and *Pudd'nhead Wilson*." *MTJ*, 15: 1-4 (Su 70).

————. "MT's *Pudd'nhead Wilson*: A Selected Checklist." *BB*, 28: 58-9 (Ap-Je 71).

Kraus, W.K. "'Huckleberry Finn': A Final Irony." *MTJ*, 14: 18-9 (Wi 67-68).

Kraus, Keith. "MT's 'A Double-Barreled Detective Story': A Source for the Solitary Oesophagus." *MTJ*, 16: 10-2 (Su 72).

Krause, S.J. "'The Pearl' and 'Hadleyburg': From Desire to Renunciation." *StQ*, 7: 4-18 (Wi 74).

———. "Steinbeck and MT." *StQ*, 6: 104-11 (Fa 73).

Krauth, Leland. "MT: At Home in the Gilded Age." *GaR*, 28: 105-13 (Sp 74).

Kruse, H.H. "'Gatsby' and Gadsby.'" *MFS*, 15: 539-41 (1969).

Lang, H.J. "MT A.L.S. More Valuable than Lincoln." *Manuscripts*, 25: 187-91 (1973).

Leary, Lewis. "The Bankruptcy of MT." *Carrell*, 9: 13-20 (1968).

———. "MT Did Not Sleep Here: Tarrytown, 1902-1904." *MTJ*, 17: 13-6 (Su 74).

———. "MT Himself." *SR*, 83: 7-8, 13 (Fa 75).

———. "More Letters from the *Quaker City*." *AL*, 42: 197-202 (My 70).

———. "Troubles with MT: Some Considerations on Consistency." *SAF*, 2: 89-103 (Sp 74).

———. "On Writing about Writers: MT and Howells." *SoR*, 4: 551-7 (Sp 68).

Lee, L.L. "MT's Assayer: Some Other Versions." *MarkR*, 4: 47-8 (My 74).

Lewis, Stuart. "Pudd'nhead Wilson's Election." *MTJ*, 15: 21 (Wi 70).

——— "T's *Huckleberry Finn*, Chapter XIV." *Expl*, 30: 61 (Mr 72).

Light, Martin. "Sweeping Out Chivalric Silliness: The Example of Huck Finn and *The Sun Also Rises*." *MTJ*, 17: 18-21 (Wi 74-75).

Lindborg, H.J. "A Cosmic Tramp: SC's *Three Thousand Years Among the Microbes*." *AL*, 44: 652-7 (Ja 73).

Livingston, J.L. "Names in MT's *The Mysterious Stranger*." *AN&Q*, 12: 108-9 (Mr 74).

Lloyd, J.B. "The Nature of MT's Attack on Sentimentality in the *Adventures of Huckleberry Finn*." *UMSE*, 13: 59-63 (1972).

Long, Timothy. "MT's Speeches on Billiards." *MTJ*, 17: 1-3 (Su 74).

Lowery, R.E. "The Grangerford-Shepherdson Episode: Another of MT's Indictments of the Damned Human Race." *MTJ*, 15: 19-21 (Wi 70).

Lycette, Ronald. "MT Mapping His Territory." *ETC*, 29: 155-64 (Je 72).

Lynn, Kenneth. "Huck and Jim." *YR*, 47: 421-31 (Sp 58).

McCarthy, H.T. "MT's Pilgrim's Progress: *The Innocents Abroad*." *ArQ*, 26: 249-58 (Au 70).

McClelland, C.P. "MT and Bret Harte." *MethR*, 98: 75-85 (Ja-F 16).

McCullough, J.B. "A Listing of MT's Contributions to the Buffalo *Express*, 1869-1871." *ALR*, 5: 61-6 (Wi 72).

———. "MT and the Hy Slocum-Carl Byng Controversy." *AL*, 43: 42-59 (Mr 71).

———. "MT and Journalistic Humor Today." *EJ*, 60: 591-5 (My 71).

McDermott, J.F. "MT and the Bible." *PLL*, 4: 195-8 (Sp 68).

McElrath, J.R., Jr. "MT's America and the Protestant Work Ethic." *CEA*, 36: 42-3 (Mr 74).

McIntyre, J.P. "Three Practical Jokes: A Key to Huck's Changing Attitude toward Jim." *MFS*, 14: 33-7 (Sp 68).

McKee, J.D. "*Roughing It* as Retrospective Reporting." *WAL*, 5: 113-9 (Su 70).

McMahan, E.E. "The Money Motif: Economic Implications in *Huckleberry Finn*." *MTJ*, 15: 5-10 (Su 71).

Male, R.R. "The Story of the Mysterious Stranger in American Fiction." *Criticism*, 3: 281-94 (1961).

Manierre, W.R. "Huck Finn, Empiricist Member of Society." *MFS*, 14: 57-66 (Sp 68).

———. "On Keeping the Raftsmen's Passage in *Huckleberry Finn*." *ELN*, 6: 118-22 (D 68).

Mann, Carolyn. "Innocence in *Pudd'nhead Wilson*." *MTJ*, 14: 11, 18-22 (Wi 68-69).

Mann, K.B. "Pudd'nhead Wilson: One Man or Two?" *Res Stud*, 42: 175-81 (1975).

Martin, Jay. "MT: The Fate of Primitivity." *SLJ*, 2: 123-37 (F 69).

Martin, W.E. "Letters and Remarks by MT from the Boston *Daily Journal*." *MTJ*, 18: 1-5 (Wi 75-76).

Mattson, J.S. "MT on War and Peace: The Missouri Rebel and 'The Campaign That Failed.'" *AQ*, 20: 783-94 (Wi 68).

Mauranges, J.P. "Aliénation et châtiment chez MT et Heinrich Böll." *RLV*, 39: 131-6 (Mr-Ap 73).

May, J.R. "The Gospel According to Philip Traum: Structural Unity in *The Mysterious Stranger*." *SSF*, 8: 411-22 (Su 71).

Mayberry, George. "Huckleberry Finn Enriched." *Nation*, 207: 154-7 (26 Ag 68).

Maynard, Reid. "MT's Ambivalent Yankee." *MTJ*, 14: 1-5 (Wi 68-9).

Mendelsohn, Edward. "MT Confronts the Shakespeareans." *MTJ*, 17: 20-1 (Wi 73-74).

Mendel'son, M. "Strannaja sud'ba 'Tainstvennogo neznakomtsa.'" *VLit*, 14: 158-64 (1970).

Mews, Siegfried. "German Reception of American Writers in the Late Nineteenth Century." *SAB*, 34: 7-9 (Mr 69).

Meyer, H.E. "An Unnoticed T Letter." *MTJ*, 16: 26 (Wi 72).

Miller, B.E. "Huckleberry Finn: The Kierkegaardian Dimension." *IllQ*, 34: 55-64 (S 71).

Miller, Lee. "Huckleberries and Humans." *PMLA*, 87: 314 (1972).

Miller, Ruth. "But Laugh or Die: A Comparison of *The Mysterious Stranger* and *Billy Budd*." *LHY*, 11: 25-9 (1970).

Miller, W.C. "SL and Orion C vs. MT and His Biographers (1861-1862)." *MTJ*, 16: 1-9 (Su 73).

Millichap, J.F. "Calvinistic Attitudes and Pauline Imagery in *The Adventures of Hukleberry Finn*." *MTJ*, 16: 8-10 (Wi 71-2).

Mills, N.C. "Prison and Society in Nineteenth Century American Fiction." *WHR*, 24: 325-31 (Au 70).

———. "Social and Moral Vision in *Great Expectations* and *Huckleberry Finn*." *JAmSt*, 4: 61-72 (Jl 70).

Mixon, Wayne. "MT, *The Gilded Age*, and the New South Movement." *SHR*, 7: 403-9 (Fa 73).

Mizener, Arthur. "The Thin, Intelligent Face of American Fiction." *KR*, 17: 507-24 (Au 55).

Monteiro, George. "New MT Letters." *MTJ*, 17: 9-10 (Su 74).

———. "'Such as Mother Used to Make': An Addition to the MT Canon." *PBSA*, 67: 450-1 (O-D 73).

———. "With Proper Words (or Without Them) the Soldier Dies: SC's 'Making an Orator.'" *Cithara*, 9: 64-72 (My 70).

Morsberger, Robert. "Pap Finn and the Bishop's Candlesticks: Victor Hugo in Hannibal." *CEA*, 31: 17 (Ap 69).

Mott, Bertram. "The Turn-of-the Century MT." *MTJ*, 18: 13-6 (Wi 75-76).

———. "T's Joan: A Divine Anomaly." *EA*, 23: 245-55 (Jl-S 70).

Moyne, E.J. "MT and Baroness Alexandra Gripenberg." *AL*, 45: 370-78 (N 73).

Mulqueen, J.E. "Huck Finn, Imagist Poet." *CEA*, 37: 14-5 (#3 75).

Murray, C.J. "The Narrator of *The Innocents Abroad*." *EL*, 2: 1-11 (Ag 74).

Myers, Margaret. "MT and Melville." *MTJ*, 14: 5-8 (Su 68).

Nagel, James. "*Huck Finn* and *The Bear*: The Wilderness and Moral Freedom." *ESA*, 12: 59-63 (Mr 69).

Nasu, Yorimasa. "A Castle and Its Symbolism in 'No. 44, The Mysterious Stranger.'" *DSE*, 10: 93-114 (Mr 75).

Nebeker, H.E. "The Great Corrupter or Satan Rehabilitated." *SSF*, 8: 635-7 (Fa 71).

Nibbelink, Herman. "MT and the Mormons." *MTJ*, 17: 1-5 (Wi 73-74).

Odessky, M.H. "The Impartial Friend: The Death of MT." *JHS*, 2: 156-60 (1969).

Orth, Michael. "Pudd'nhead Wilson Reconsidered." *MTJ*, 14: 11-5 (Su 69).

Ostrom, Alan. "Huck Finn and the Modern Ethos." *CentR*, 16: 162-79 (Sp 72).

Park, M.M. "MT's Hadleyburg: A House Built on Sand." *CLAJ*, 16: 508-13 (Je 73).

Parker, Hershel. "Three MT Editions." *NCF*, 28: 255-9 (1973).

Parsons, C.O. "Down the Mighty River with MT." *MissQ*, 22: 1-18 (Wi 68-9).

———. "Steamboating as Seen by Passengers and River Men: 1875-1884." *MissQ*, 24: 19-34 (Wi 70-71).

Pauley, T.H. "The Contents Tables in Adventures of *Huckleberry Finn*." *Proof*, 3: 63-68 (1973).

———. "The 'Science of Piloting' in T's 'Old Times': The Cub's Lesson on Industrialization." *ArQ*, 30: 229-38 (Au 74).

Pearce, R.H. "Huck Finn in His History." *EA*, 24: 283-91 (1971).

Peck, R.E. "A MT 'Literary Offense.'" *MTJ*, 14: 7-9 (Wi 68-69).

Pederson, L.A. "MT's Missouri Dialects: Marion County Phonemics." *AS*, 42: 261-78 (D 67).

Perkins, V.I. "The Trouble with Satan." *Gypsy Schol*, 3: 37-43 (1975).

Pettit, A.G. "MT and the Negro, 1867-1869." *JNH*, 56: 88-96 (Ap 71).

———. "MT, the Blood-Feud and the South." *SLJ*, 4: 20-32 (Fa 71).

———. "MT's Attitude Toward the Negro in the West, 1861-7." *WHQ*, 1: 51-62 (Ja 70).

Pizer, Donald. "Harold J. Kolb, Jr.'s Study of American Realism as a Literary Form." *ALR*, 3: 376-8 (1970).

Plessner, Monika. "Huckleberry Finns wirkliches Ende." *FH*, 24: 441-46 (1969).

Powers, Lyall. "The Sweet Success of T's Tom." *DR*, 53: 310-24 (Su 73).

Prince, Gilbert. "MT's 'A Fable': The Teacher as Jackass." *MTJ*, 17: 7-8 (Wi 74-75).

Pritchett, V.S. "Twainship and Twinship." *NSt*, 23 Je 67, p. 876.

Rachal, John. "David Wilson and Sam C: The Public Image vs. The Private Man." *AN&Q*, 13: 6-8 (S 74).

———. "Scotty Briggs and the Minister: An Idea from Hooper's Simon Suggs?" *MTJ*, 17: 10-11 (Su 74).

Rackham, Jeff. "The Mysterious Stranger in 'The Campaign That Failed.'" *SHR*, 5: 63-7 (Wi 71).

Rao, B.R. "Structural Devices in *The Adventures of Huckleberry Finn*." *BP*, 14: 23-9 (1970).

Reed, K.T. "Mirth and Misquotation: MT in Petoskey, Michigan." *MTJ*, 15: 19-20 (Su 70).

Rees, R.A. "*Captain Stormfield's Visit to Heaven* and *The Gates Ajar*." *ELN*, 7: 197-202 (Mr 70).

———, and R.D. Rust. "MT's 'The Turning Point of My Life.'" *AL*, 40: 524-35 (Ja 69).

Reinitz, Neale. "MT Tonight." *ColQ*, 16: 71-80 (Su 67).

Requal, K.A. "Counterfeit Currency and Character in MT's 'Which Was It?'" *MTJ*, 17: 1-6 (Wi 74-75).

Rickels, Milton. "SC and the Conscience of Comedy." *SoR*, 4: 558-68 (Sp 68).

Ridland, J.M. "Huck, Pip, and Plot." *NCF*, 20: 286-90 (D 65).

Ritunnano, Jeanne. "MT vs. Arthur Conan Doyle on Detective Fiction." *MTJ*, 16: 10-4 (Wi 71-72).

Robinson, V.P. "The Double Soul: MT and Otto Rank." *JORA*, 6: 32-53 (1971).

Robinson, E.H. "MT: Senatorial Secretary." *AmW*, 10: 16-7, 60-2 (#2 73).

Rodgers, P.C. "Artemus Ward and MT's 'Jumping Frog.'" *NCF*, 28: 273-86 (D 73).

Rodnon, Stewart. "*The Adventures of Huckleberry Finn* and *Invisible Man*: Thematic and Structural Comparisons." *NALF*, 4: 45-51 (1970).

Roemer, K.M. "The yankee(s) in Noahville." *AL*, 45: 434-7 (N 73).

Rogers, R.O. "T, Taine, and Lecky: The Genesis of a Passage in *A Connecticut Yankee*." *MLQ*, 34: 436-47 (D 73).

Ross, M.L. "MT's *Pudd'nhead Wilson*: Dawson's Landing and the Ladder of Nobility." *Novel*, 6: 244-56 (Sp 73).

Rowlette, Robert. "MT, Sarah Grand, and *The Heavenly Twins*." *MTJ*, 16: 17-8 (Su 72).

———. "MT's Barren Tree in *The Mysterious Stranger*: Two Biblical Parallels." *MTJ*, 16: 19-20 (Wi 71-72).

———. "'Mark Ward on Artemus Twain': T's Literary Debt to Ward." *ALR*, 6: 13-25 (Wi 73).

Royot, Daniel. "Eléments phonologiques du dialecte noir dans *Huckleberry Finn*." *LanM*, 66: 79-83 (#1 72).

Rubin, L.D. "How Mark Twain Threw Off His Inhibitions and Discovered the Vitality of Formless Form." *SR*, 79: 426-33 (Su 71).

———. "Three Installments of MT." *SR*, 78: 678-84 (Au 70).

Rule, H.B. "The Role of Satan in *The Man That Corrupted Hadleyburg*." *SSF*, 6: 619-29 (Fa 69).

Rulon, C.M. "Geographical Delimitation of the Dialect Areas in *The Adventures of Huckleberry Finn*." *MTJ*, 14: 9-12 (Wi 67-68).

Rust, R.D. "Americanisms in *A Connecticut Yankee*." *SAB*, 33: 11-3 (My 68).

Sapper, Neil. "'I Been There Before': Huck Finn as Tocquevillian Individual." *MissQ*, 24: 35-45 (Wi 70).

Schafer, Jurgen. "'Huckleberry, U.S.'" *ES*, 54: 334-5 (1973).

Scheick, W.J. "The Spunk of a Rabbit: An Allusion in 'The Adventures of Huckleberry Finn.'" *MTJ*, 15: 14-6 (Su 71).

Scherting, Jack. "Poe's 'The Cask of Amontillado': A Source for T's 'The Man That Corrupted Hadleyburg.'" *MTJ*, 16: 18-19 (Su 72).

Schinto, J.M. "The Autobiographies of MT and Henry Adams: Life Studies in Despair." *MTJ*, 17: 5-7 (Su 75).

Schmitz, Neil. "The Paradox of Liberation in *Huckleberry Finn*." *TSLL*, 13: 125-36 (Sp 71).

———. "T, *Huckleberry Finn*, and the Reconstruction." *AmS*, 12: 59-67 (Sp 71).

Schonhorn, Manuel. "MT's Jim: Solomon on the Mississippi." *MTJ*, 14: 9-12 (Wi 68-69).

Scrivner, Buford. "*The Mysterious Stranger*: MT's New Myth of the Fall." *MTJ*, 17: 20-1 (Su 75).

Sears, R.R., and Deborah Lapidus. "Episodic Analysis of Novels." *J Psych*, 85: 267-76 (1973).

Seelye, John. "'De ole true Huck?': An Introduction." *TriQ*, 16: 5-19 (Au 69).

———. "MT as Grumbler." *NRep*, 163: 21-4 (28 N 70).

Sharma, M.L. "MT's Passage to India." *MTJ*, 14: 12-4 (Su 68).

Shults, Donald. "On *The Gilded Age*." *KAL*, 12: 1-13 (1970).

Sidnell, M.J. "Huck Finn and Jim: Their Abortive Freedom Ride." *CQ*, 2: 203-11 (Su 67).

Simon, J.Y. "General Grant and MT." *ICarbS*, 2: 3-10 (1975).

Simonson, H.P. "*Huckleberry Finn* as Tragedy." *YR*, 59: 532-48 (Su 70).

Simpson, L.P. "MT and the Pathos of Regeneration." *SLJ*, 4: 93-106 (Sp 72).

Skerry, P.J. "*The Adventures of Huckleberry Finn* and *Intruder in the Dust*: Two Conflicting Myths of the American Experience." *BSUF*, 13: 4-13 (Wi 72).

Skinner, Otis. "MT at the Players' Club." *MTJ*, 15: back cover (Su 71).

Skow, John "Quarter T." *Time*, 96: 80-2 (30 N 70).

Smith, L.R. "SC: Pilot." *MTJ*, 15: 1-5 (Su 71).

Solomon, Andrew. "Jim and Huck: Magnificent Misfits." *MTJ*, 16: 17-24 (Wi 72).

Solomon. Jack. "*Huckleberry Finn* and the Tradition of *The Odyssey*." *SAB*, 33: 11-3 (Mr 68).

Spangler, G.M. "Locating Hadleyburg." *MTJ*, 14: 20 (Su 69).

———. "*Pudd'nhead Wilson*: A Parable of Property." *AL*, 42: 28-37 (Mr 70).

Spofford, W.K. "MT's Connecticut Yankee: An Ignoramus Nevertheless." *MTJ*, 15: 15-8 (Su 70).

Stein, A.F. "Return to Phelps Farm: *Huckleberry Finn* and the Old Southwestern Framing Device." *MissQ*, 24: 111-6 (Sp 71).

Stern, M.B. "MT Had His Examined." *AL*, 41: 207-18 (My 69).

Stessin, Lawrence. "The Businessman in Fiction." *LitR*, 12: 281-9 (Sp 69).

Stoehr, Taylor. "Tone and Voice." *CE*, 30: 150-61 (N 68).

Stone, A.E. "The Twichell Papers and MT's *A Tramp Abroad*." *YULG*, 29: 151-64 (Ap 55).

Stowell, R.F. "River Guide Books and MT's *Life on the Mississippi*." *MTJ*, 16: 21 (Su 73).

Sturdevant, J.R. "MT's Unpublished Letter to Tom Taylor—an Enigma." *MTJ*, 14: 8-9 (Wi 67-68).

Sykes, R.H. "A Source for MT's Feud." *WVH*, 28: 191-98 (1968).

Talbott, L.H. "Huck Finn: MT at Midstream." *NasR*, 1: 44-60 (1969).

Tatham, Campbell. "'Dismal and Lonesome': A New Look at *Huckleberry Finn*." *MFS*, 14: 47-55 (Sp 68).

Taylor, J.G. "Introduction to 'The Celebrated Jumping Frog of Calaveras County.'" *AmWest*, 2: 73-6 (Fa 65).

Taylor, Robert. "Sounding the Trumpets of Defiance: MT and Norman Mailer." *MTJ*, 16: 1-14 (Wi 72).

Todd, W.B. "Problems in Editing MT." *BI*, 1: 3-8 (Ap 65).

Towers, T.H. "'Hateful Reality': The Failure of the Territory in *Roughing It*." *WAL*, 9: 3-15 (My 74).

———. "'Never Thought We Might Want to Come Back': Strategies of Transcendence in *Tom Sawyer*." *MFS*, 21: 509-20 (Wi 75).

Trachtenberg, Alan. "The Form of Freedom in *Adventures of Huckleberry Finn*." *SoR*, 6: 954-71 (Au 70).

Tracy, Robert. "Myth and Reality in *The Adventures of Tom Sawyer*." *SoR*, 4: 530-41 (Sp 68).

Tuckey, J.S. "Hannibal, Weggis, and MT's Eseldorf." *AL*, 42: 235-40 (My 70).

———. "MT's Later Dialogue: The 'Me' and the Machine." *AL*, 41: 532-42 (Ja 70).

Turner, Arlin. "MT and the South: An Affair of Love and Anger." *SoR*, 4: 493-519 (Sp 68).

Turner, M.A. "Was Frank Dobie a Throwback to MT?" *WR*, 5: 3-12 (1968).

Twain, Mark. "Some Thoughts on the Science of Onanism." *Playboy*, 21: 157 (S 74).

Underhill, I.S. "A God's Tale." *ABC*, 25: 17-9 (Mr-Ap 75).

Vanderbilt, Kermit. "Correction and Further Note on MT and Longfellow." *MTJ*, 16: 24 (Wi 72).

———. "MT Writes to Poet Longfellow." *MTJ*, 16: front cover (Su 72).

Vandersee, Charles. "The Mutual Awareness of MT and Henry Adams." *ELN*, 5: 285-92 (Je 68).

Van Kohn, J.S. "The Doubly Suppressed Chapter of 'Following the Equator.'" *PULC*, 27: 156-8 (Sp 66).

Varisco, Raymond. "Divine Foolishness: A Critical Evaluation of MT's The Mysterious Stranger." *Rev Interamericana*, 5: 741-9 (1975).

Vittorini, Elio. "An Outline of American Literature." *SR*, 68: 423-37 (Su 60).

Vorpahl, B.M. "'Very Much Like a Fire-Cracker': Owen Wister on MT." *WAL*, 6: 83-98 (Su 71).

Waldron, Eli. "MT: The World He Left Behind." *Holiday*, 30: 54-5, 72-5, 97-9 (Jl 61).

Walters, T.N. "T's Finn and Alger's Gilman: Picaresque Counter-Directions." *MarkR*, 3: 53-8 (My 72).

Warren, R.P. "MT." *SoR*, 8: 459-92 (Jl 72).

Watkins, T.H. "MT and His Mississippi." *Am West*, 10: 12-9 (#6 73).

Weaver, William. "The Twain-Cable Lectures in Kentucky, 1884-1885." *KHSR*, 72: 134-42 (Ap 74).

———. "MT and Kate Field Differ on Constitutional Rights." *MTJ*, 17: 16-7 (Su 74).

———. "SC Lectures in Kentucky." *MTJ*, 17: 20-1 (Su 74).

Webster, Charles. "Two Letters Solve a Bitter Dispute." *Manuscripts*, 11: 13 (Fa 59).

Weeks, L.E. "MT and Hemingway: 'A Catastrophe' and 'A Natural History of the Dead.'" *MTJ*, 14: 15-17 (Su 68).

Weeks, R.P. "The Captain, the Prophet, and the King: A Possible Source for T's Dauphin." *MTJ*, 18: 9-12 (Wi 75-76).

Weintraub, Rodelle, ed. "'Mental Telepathy?': MT on G.B.S." *Shaw R*, 17: 68-9 (My 74).

Wells, A.M. "Huck Finn, Tom Sawyer, and SC." *PMLA*, 87: 1130-1 (O 72).

Wells, D.M. "More on the Geography of *Huckleberry Finn*." *SAB*, 38: 82-6 (N 73).

Werge, Thomas. "MT and the Fall of Adam." *MTJ*, 15: 5-13 (Su 70).

———. "The Sin of Hypocrisy in *The Man That Corrupted Hadleyburg* and Inferno XXXIII." *MTJ*, 18: 17-8 (Wi 75-76).

Wexman, Virginia. "The Role of Structure in *Tom Sawyer* and *Huckleberry Finn*." *ALR*, 6: 1-11 (Wi 73).

Wheelock, C.W. "The Point of Pudd'nhead's Half-a-Dog Joke." *AN&Q*, 8: 150-1 (Je 70).

Wilcox, Earl. "Jake and Bob and Huck and Tom: Hemingway's Use of *Huck Finn*." *FHA*, 1971, pp. 326-35.

Williams, Philip. "*Huckleberry Finn* and the Dialectic of History." *ESELL*, 51-52: 190-8 (1967).

Williamson, J.M. "Winslow Homer and MT." *MTJ*, 14: 2-7 (Su 69).

Wilson, Edmund. "The Fruits of the MLA, II: MT." *NYRB*, 11: 6-14 (10 O 68).

Wilson, J.D. "*Adventures of Huckleberry Finn*: From Abstraction to Humanity." *SoR*, 10: 80-94 (Ja 74).

———. "Hank Morgan, Philip Traum and Milton's Satan." *MTJ*, 16: 20-1 (Su 73).

———. "'The Monumental Sarcasm of the Ages': Science and Pseudoscience in the Thought of MT." *SAB*, 40: 72-82 (My 75).

Wilson, M.K. "Mr. C and Madame Blanc: MT's First French Critic." *AL*, 45: 537-56 (Ja 74).

Wysong, J.P. "SC's Attitude toward the Negro as Demonstrated in *Pudd'nhead Wilson* and *A Connecticut Yankee at King Arthur's Court*." *XUS*, 7: 41-57 (Jl 68).

Yoshida, Hiroshige, "Huckleberry Finn ko." *EigoS*, 114: 84-6 (1968).

Yu, Beongcheon. "The Ending of *The Adventures of Huckleberry Finn*." *Phoenix*, 2: 23-29 (1967).

———. "The Immortal Twins—An Aspect of MT." *EL&L*, 22: 48-77 (1968).

Zaraspe, R.S. "The Picaresque Tradition in MT." *DilR*, 17: 218-43 (Jl 69).

Zwahlen, Christine. "Of Hell or of Hannibal?" *AL*, 42: 562-3 (Ja 71).

Clifton, Lucille. Jong, Erica. "Three Sisters." *Parnassus*, 1: 77-88 (1972).

Clyman, James. Walker, D.D. "JC's 'Narrative': Its Significance in the Literature of the Fur Trade." *PosS*, 4: 1-8 (My 73).

Zochert, Donald. "'A View of the Sublime Awful': The Language of a Pioneer." *WAL*, 6: 251-7 (1972).

Coates, R.M. Cowley, Malcolm. "Reconsideration." *NRep*, 171: 40-2 (30 N 74).

Cobb, Humphrey. Smith, Julian. "A Source for Faulkner's *A Fable*." *AL*, 40: 394-7 (N 68).

Cobb, Joseph Beckham. Mohr, C.L. "Candid Comments from a Mississippi Author." *MissQ*, 25: 83-93 (Wi 72).

Rogers, T.W. "The Folk Humor of JB.C." *NMW*, 3: 13-35 (Sp 70).

———. "JB.C: Antebellum Humorist and Critic." *MissQ*, 22: 131-46 (Sp 69).

———. "JB.C: The Successful Pursuit of Belles Lettres." *McNR*, 20: 70-83 (1971-72).

———. "JBC: Continuation of a Distinguished Lineage." *GHQ*, 56: 404-14 (Fl 72).

Coe, Daniel. Arner, R.D. "DC to Thomas Shreeve: Primitivism in Satire." *SLN*, 10: 80-2 (#2 73).

Coffin, Charles Carleton. Ditsky, John. "True 'Grit' and 'True Grit.'" *Ariel*, 4: 18-31 (1973).

Coffin, Robert P. Tristram. *Cary, Richard. "A Bibliography of RP.TC: Addenda." *CLQ*, 8: 22-8 (Mr 68).

Cole, Cyrus. Fuson, B.W. "Prairie Dreamers of 1890: Three Kansas Utopian Novels and Novelists." *KanQ*, 5: 63-77 (Fa 73).

Colby, Vineta. Rudikoff, Sonya. "Heroines of Literature and Life." *HudR*, 27: 615-9 (Wi 74-75).

Fuson, Ben. "Three Kansas Utopian Novels of 1890." *Extrapolation*, 12: 7-24 (D 70).

Colman, Benjamin. Chapman, C.H. "BC and Philomela." *NEQ*, 42: 214-31 (1969).

Collier, John. Abrahams, William. "The Devil Wore Spats." *SatR*, 1: 80-1 (Ja 73).

Colter, Cyrus. Farnsworth, R.M. "Conversation with CC." *Nouvelles Litteraires*, 39: 17-39 (Sp 73).

O'Brien, John. "Forms of Determinism in the Fiction of CC." *SBL*, 4: 24-7 (Su 73).

Comfort, Will Levington. Powell, L.C. "Southwest Classics Reread: Massacre and Vengeance in Apacheria." *Westways*, 64: 55-9 (My 72).

Condon, Richard. Smith, Julian. "The Infernal Comedy of RC." *TCL*, 14: 221-9 (Ja 69).

Connelly, Marc. Phillips, J.L. "Before the Colors Fade: *Green Pastures* Recalled." *AH*, 21: 28-9, 74-6 (F 70).

Conroy, Frank. Ramsey, Roger. "The Illusion of Fiction in FC's *Stop-Time*." *MFS*, 20: 391-8 (Au 74).

Conroy, Jack. Anon. "Letters to JC." *NLet*, 39: 16-28 (Fa 72).

Conroy, Jack. "Days of the *Anvil*." *ABC*, 21: 15-9 (1971).

Fabre, Michel. "JC as Editor." *NLet*, 39: 115-37 (Wi 72).

Fried, Lewis. "Conversation with JC." *NLet*, 39: 41-56 (Fa 72).

———. "*The Disinherited*: The Worker as Writer." *NLet*, 39: 29-40 (Fa 72).

Reilly, J.M. "Two Novels of Working Class Consciousness." *MwQ*, 14: 183-93 (Wi 73).

Salzman, Jack. "C, Mencken, and *The American Mercury*." *JPC*, 7: 524-8 (1973).

Sharma, D.R. "JC: An Analysis of His Moral Vision." *PURBA*, 3: 97-106 (O 72).

Conway, Moncure. Jackson, C.T. "The Orient in Post-Bellum American Thought: Three Pioneer Popularizers." *AQ*, 22: 67-81 (Sp 70).

Cooke, Ebenezer. Arner, R.D. "Clio's *Rhimes*: History and Satire in EC's 'History of Bacon's Rebellion.'" *SLJ*, 6: 91-106 (Sp 74).

———. "EC: Satire in the Colonial South." *SLJ*, 8: 153-64 (Fa 75).

———. "EC's *The Sot-Weed Factor*: The Structure of Satire." *SLJ*, 4: 33-47 (Fa 71).

———. "EC's Sotweed Redivivus: Satire in the Horatian Mode." *MissQ*, 28: 489-96 (Fa 75).

Cohen, E.H. "The 'Second Edition' of *The Sot-weed Factor*." *AL*, 42: 289-303 (N 70).

———. "The Elegies of EC." *EAL*, 4: 49-72 (Fa 69).

Diser, P.E. "The Historical EC." *Critique*, 10: 48-59 (1968).

Cooke, George Frederick. Wilmeth, D.B. "The Posthumous Career of GFC." *ThN*, 24: 68-74 (Wi 69-70).

Cooke, John Esten. Chamberlain, E.S. "The Man without a Culture: A Study of JEC's 'A Legend of Turkey Buzzard Hollow.'" *Duke Un Libr N*, 45: 17-44 (D 74).

Cooke, Philip Pendleton. Jackson, D.K. "The Writings of PPC." *SLJ*, 2: 156-8 (Sp 70).

Tucker, E.L. "PPC." *VaCa;*, 19: 42-6 (Wi 70).

Tucker, Esward. "PPC and *The Southern Literary Messenger*: Selected Letters." *MissQ*, 27: 79-99 (Wi 73-4).

Cooke, Rose Terry. Daughterty, E. "RTC." *ALR*, 8: 226-7 (1975).

Levy, B.M. "Mutations in New England Local Color." *NEQ*, 19: 338-58 (S 46).

*Monteiro, George. "Addenda to the Bibliographies of . . . C and others." *PSBA*, 69: 273-5.

Troth, S.A. "RTC (1827-1892)." *ALR*, 4: 170-76 (Sp 71).

Coolbrith, Ina. Graham, I.A. "My Aunt, IC." *Pacific Hist*, 17: 12-9 (Fa 73).

Hubbard, G.U. "IC's Friendship with John Greenleaf Whittier." *NEQ*, 45: 109-18 (Mr 72).

Kennedy, K.M. "IC Day." *Overland*, 49: 342 (Ap 07).

Cooper, Elizabeth Ann. Grande. L.M. "Renegade Priests in Recent Fiction." *CathLW*, 32: 407-10 (Ap 61).

Cooper, James Fenimore. Anonymous. "American Mythmaker." *MD*, N 69, pp. 187-97.

Aldridge, A.O. "FC and the Picaresque Tradition." *NCF*, 27: 283-92 (1972).

Bach, B.C. "A Reconsideration of Natty Bumppo." *CimR*, 5: 60-6 (1968).

Bakerville, Barnet. "19th Century Burlesque of Oratory." *AQ*, 20: 726-43 (Wi 68).

Barnes, J.J. "Galiguani and the Publication of English Books in France: a Postscript." *The Library*, 25: 294-313 (D 70).

Baym, M.E., and Percy Matenko. "The Odyssey of *The Water-Witch* and a Susan Fenimore Cooper Letter." *NYH*, 51: 33-41 (Ja 70).

Baym, Nina. "The Women of C's Leatherstocking Tales." *AQ*, 23: 696-709 (D 71).

Beard, J.F. "The C Edition." *PAAS*, 81: 235-7 (O 71).

———. "News from the C Edition." *CEAAN*, 2: 16 (1969).

———. "A Report on the C Edition." *CEAAN*, 8: 32-4 (1975).

Bender, Thomas. "JFC and the City." *NYH*, 51: 287-305 (Ap 70).

Bercovitch, Sacvan. "Huckleberry Bumppo: A Comparison of 'Tom Saywer's and 'The Pioneers.'" *MTJ*, 14: 1-14 (1968).

Bereaud, J.G.A. "La Traduction en France à l'epoque romantique." *CLS*, 7: 224-44 (S 71).

Bier, Jesse. "The Bisection of C: *Satanstoe* as Prime Example." *TSLL*, 9: 511-21 (Wi 68).

Bigsby, C.W.E. "Two Types of Violence." *UR*, 32: 129-36 (Wi 65).

Brenner, Gerry. "C's 'Composite Order': *The Pioneers* as Structured Art." *StN*, 2: 264-75 (Fa 70).

Browning, B.W. "C's Influence on Stifter: Fact or Scholarly Myth?" *MLN*, 89: 821-8 (1974).

Burch, F.F. "C: An Unpublished Letter and Ms. Excerpt from *The Heidenmauer*." *AN&Q*, 12: 134-5 (My-Je 74).

Burgess, Anthony. "Said Mr. Cooper to His Wife: 'You Know, I Could Write Something Better Than That.'" *NYTMS*, 7 My 72, pp. 102, 112-5.

Cameron, K.W. "Letters of C, Irving and Others Endorsing the Lyceum in Paris, France." *ESQ*, 52: 76-82 (3Q 68).

———. "Melville, C, Irving and Bryant on International Matters." *ESQ*, 51: 108-21 (2Q 68).

———. "Melville, C, Irving and John Essais Warren: Travel Literature and Patronage." *ESQ*, 47: 114-25 (2Q 67).

Cohen, L.H. "What's in a Name? The Presence of the Victim in *The Pioneers*." *MR*, 16: 688-98 (Au 75).

Cosgrove, W.E. "Family Lineage and Narrative Pattern in C's Littlepage Trilogy." *ForumH*, 12: 2-8 (#1 74).

Cox, C.B. "Hawkeye and the Indians." *Spec*, 3 N 67, pp. 533-4.

Darnell, D.G. "C and Faulkner: Land, Legacy, and the Tragic Vision." *SAB*, 34: 3-5 (Mr 69).

Davie, Donald. "The Legacy of FC." *EIC*, 9: 230 (1954).

Deane, Paul. "JFC and *The Chainbearer*." *RLV*, 34: 261-8 (1968).

Denne, C.A. "C's Artistry in *The Headsman*." *NCF*, 29: 77-92 (Je 74).

Dryden, E.A. "History and Progress: Some Implications of Form in C's Littlepage Novels." *NCF*, 26: 49-64 (Je 71).

Dula, Martha. "Audience Response to *A Tour on the Prairies* in 1835." *WAL*, 8: 67-74 (Sp, Su 73).

Fabris, Alberta. "La trilogia europea di JFC." *SA*, 15: 33-60 (1969).

Fink, R.A. "Harvey Birch: The Yankee Peddler as an American Hero." *NYFQ*, 30: 137-52 (Je 74).

French, F.H. "C the Tinkerer." *NYFQ*, 26: 229-39 (1970).

———. "C's Use of Proverbs in the Anti-Rent Novels." *NYFQ*, 26: 42-9 (Mr 70).

Gerlach, John. "JFC and the Kingdom of God." *IllQ*, 25: 32-50 (1973).

Gorlier, Claudio. "Un C Ritrovato." *Approdo*, 29: 130-4 (Gennario 65).

Hall, J.J. "Romance as History: C's *Wyandotte*." *Kentucky R*, 2: 38-46 (1968).

Hayne, Barrie. "Ossian, Scott and C's Indians." *JAmSt*, 3: 73-87 (Jl 69).

Hocks, R.A. "Thoreau, Coleridge, and Barfield: Reflections on the Imagination and the Law of Polarity." *CentR*, 17: 175-95 (Sp 73).

Hogue, W.M. "The Novel as a Religious Tract: JFC—Apologist for the Episcopal Church." *HMPEC*, 40: 5-26 (Mr 71).

Howe, Irving. "Anarchy and Authority in American Literature." *DQ*, 2: 5-30 (Au 67).

Kay, Donald. "Major Character Types in *Home as Found*: C's Search for American Principles and Dignity." *CLAJ*, 14: 432-9 (Je 71).

Kesterson, D.B. "Milton's Satan and C's Demonic Chieftains." *SCB*, 29: 138-42 (Wi 69).

Kligerman, Jack. "Notes on C's Debt to John Jay." *AL*, 41: 415-9 (N 69).

———. "Style and Form in JFC's *Homeward Bound* and Home as Found." *JNT*, 4: 45-61 (1974).

Kitagawa, Akihiro. "C's Attitude Toward the Frontier." *KAL*, 14: 20-9 (1972).

Lewis, Merrill. "Lost—and Found—In the Wilderness: The Desert Metaphor in C's *The Prairie*." *WAL*, 5: 195-204 (Fa 70).

Loveland, A.C. "JFC and the American Mission." *AQ*, 21: 244-58 (Su 69).

McWilliams, J.P. "C and the Conservative Democrat." *AQ*, 22: 665-77 (Fa 70).

———. "*The Crater* and The Consitution." *TSLL*, 12: 631-45 (Wi 71).

McWilliams, W.C. "Natty Bumppo and the Godfather." *ColQ*, 24: 133-44 (Au 75).

Malin, Irving. "The Authoritarian Family in American Fiction." *Mosaic*, 4: 153-73 (1971).

Martin, Terrence. "From the Ruins of History: *The Last of the Mohicans*." *Novel*, 2: 221-9 (1969).

Cooper, James Fenimore

Mews, Siegfried. "German Reception of American Writers in the Late Nineteenth Century." *SAB*, 34: 7-9 (Mr 69).
Miller, Perry. "His Life Was Story and His Achievement Immense." *NYHT*, 10 Ap 60, pp. 1, 14.
Mills, N.C. "Prison and Society in Nineteenth-Century American Fiction." *WHR*, 24: 325-31 (1970).
Mulqueen, J.E. "Three Heroes in American Fiction." *IllQ*, 36: 44-50 (F 74).
Neuhauser, Rudolph. "Notes on Early Russian-American Cultural Relations: JFC and Russia." *Canadian Slavic Studies*, 1: 461-73 (Fa 67).
Paul, J.S. "Home as Cherished: The Theme of Family in FC." *StN*, 5: 39-51 (Sp 73).
Philbrick, T.L. "Language and Meaning in C's *The Water-Witch*." *ESQ*, 60: 10-6 (Su 70).
Philbrick, Thomas. "*The Last of the Mohicans* and the Sounds of Discord." *AL*, 43: 25-41 (Mr 71).
Pickering, J.H. "New York in Revolution: C's *Wyandotté*." *NYH*, 49: 121-41 (Ap 68).
———. "FC in Our Time." *NYH*, 51: 545-55 (O 70).
Placido, Beniamino. "JFC et The *Deerslayer*." *SA*, 13: 75-99 (1967).
Pritchett, V.S. "An Ocean Between." *NSt*, 19 Mr 71, pp. 393-4.
Rainey, R.M. "JFC and the Nineteenth-Century Sea Novel." *DCLB*, 8: 76-80 (Ap 68).
Rans, Geoffrey. "'But the Penalty of Adam': C's Sense of the Subversive." *CRAS*, 3: 21-32 (Sp 72).
Ringe, D.A. "C's *Lionel Lincoln*: The Problem of Genre." *ATQ*, 24: 24-30 (Fa 74).
———. "JFC: An American Democrat." *PLL*, 6: 420-31 (Fa 70).
Rose, M.G. "Time Discrepancy in *Last of the Mohicans*." *AN&Q*, 8: 72-3 (Ja 70).
Ross, K.L. "C's *The Pioneers* and the Ethnographic Impulse." *AmS*, 15: 29-40 (2Q 75).
Sandy, A.F. "The Voices of C's *The Deerslayer*." *ESQ*, 60: 5-9 (Su 70).
Schachterle, Lance. "The Three 1823 Editions of JFC's *The Pioneers*." *PAAS*, 84: 219-32 (1974).
Smith, H.N. "Consciousness and Social Order: The Theme of Transcendence in *The Leatherstocking Tales*." *WAL*, 5: 177-94 (Fa 70).
Spiller, R.E. "JFC 1789-1851." *Antiquarian Bookman*, 8: 689-91 (15 S 51).
Staggs, D.W. "C's *Gleanings in Europe*. England: A Problem in Copy-Text." *CEAAN*, 3: 14-5 (Je 70).
Stein, Paul. "C's Later Fiction: The Theme of 'Becoming.'" *SAQ*, 70: 77-87 (Wi 71).
Stein, W.B. "*The Prairie*: A Scenario of the Wise Old Man." *BuR*, 19: 15-36 (Sp 71).
Tanner, J.E. "A Possible Source for *The Prairie*." *AL*, 47: 102-4 (Mr 75).
Tuttleton, J.W. "The New England Character in C's Social Novels." *BNYPL*, 70: 305-17 (My 66).
Vance, W.L. "'Man and Beast': The Meaning of C's *The Prairie*." *PMLA*, 89: 323-31 (Mr 74).
VanDerBeets, Richard. "C and the 'Semblance of Reality': A Source for *The Deerslayer*." *AL*, 42: 544-6 (Ja 71).
Vlach, J.M. "FC's Leatherstocking as Folk Hero." *NYFQ*, 27: 323-38 (D 71).
Walker, W.S. "Buckskin West: Leatherstocking at High Noon." *NYFQ*, 24: 88-102 (Je 68).
———. "A 'Scottish C' for an 'American Scott.'" *AL*, 40: 536-7 (Ja 69).
Weidman, B.S. "White Men's Red Man: A Penitential Reading of Four American Novels." *MLS*, 4: 14-26 (#2 74).
Coover, Robert. Brezianu, Andrei. "Paradoxialul RC." *SXX*, 170: 56-8 (1975).
Cizek, I.C. "Postmodern si premodern la RC." *SXX*, 170: 88-92 (1975).
Cope, J.I. "RC's Fictions." *IowaR*, 2: 94-110 (Fa 71).

Dillard, R.F.W. "The Wisdom of the Beast: The Fiction of RC." *HC*, 7: 1-11 (1970).

*Hertzel, L.J. "A Coover Checklist." *Critique*, 11: 23-4 (1969).

———. "An Interview with RC." *Critique*, 11: 25-9 (1969).

———. "What's Wrong with the Christians?" *Critique*, 11: 11-24 (1969).

McCaffery, Larry. "Donald Barthelme, RC, William H. Gass: Three Checklists." *BB*, 31: 101-6 (Jl-S 74).

Răutu, Elena. "RC sau Creatorul ca povestutor." *SXX*, 170: 83-6 (1975).

Rosa, A.F. "Mrs. Grundy Finally Appears in RC's 'The Pedestrian.'" *NCLit*, 2: 2-3 (N 72).

Schmitz, Neil. "RC and the Hazards of Metafiction." *Novel*, 7: 210-9 (Sp 74).

Scholes, Robert. "Metafiction." *IowaR*, 1: 100-15 (Fa 70).

Shelton, Frank. "Humor and Balance in C's *The Universal Baseball Association, Inc.*" *Critique*, 17: 78-90 (1Q, 75).

Taylor, Mark. "Baseball as Myth." *Cweal*, 96: 237-9 (1972).

Weinstock, E.B. "RC—'The Baby Sitter': An Observation on Experimental Writing." *Style*, 9: 378-87 (1975).

Woodward, R.H. "An Ancester of RC's Mrs. Grundy." *NCLit*, 3: 11-2 (Ja 73).

Corso, Gregory. Dullea, G.J. "Ginsberg and C: Image and Imagination." *Thoth*, 2: 17-27 (Wi 71).

Cotter, Joseph, Sr. Combecher, Hans. "Zu einem afroamerikanischen Gedicht von JS.C." *NS*, 18: 348-50 (Jl 69).

Shockley, Ann. "JS.C, Sr.: Biographical Sketch of a Black Louisville Bard." *CLAJ*, 18: 327-40 (Mr 75).

Cotton, John. *Etulain, R.W. "JC: A Checklist of Relevant Materials." *EAL*, 4: 64-9 (1969).

———. "The New Puritan: Recent Views of JC." *Rendezvous*, 7: 39-51 (Sp 72).

Grabo, N.S. "JC's Aesthetic: A Sketch." *EAL*, 3: 4-10 (1968).

Habegger, Alfred. "Preparing the Soul for Christ: The Contrasting Sermon Forms of JC and Thomas Hooker." *AL*, 41: 342-54 (N 69).

Rosenmeier, Jesper. "The Teacher and the Witness: JC and Roger Williams." *WMQ*, 25: 408-31 (Jl 68).

Stoever, William. "Nature, Grace and JC: The Theological Dimension in the New England Antinomian Controversy." *CH*, 44: 22-33 (Mr 75).

Cowley, Malcolm. Cowley, Malcolm. "Privation and Publication: A Memoir of the Year 1934." *SR*, 83: 139-48 (Wi 75).

———. "Two Winters with Hart Crane." *SR*, 67: 547-56 (O-D 59).

Stegner, Page, and Robert Canzoneri. "An Interview with MC." *Per/Se*, 2: 34-9 (Wi 67-8).

Wood, Tom. "MC Interviews." *LGJ*, 3: 4-6 (#3 75).

Young, Philip. "For MC: Critic, Poet, 1898-." *SoR*, 9: 778-95 (Au 73).

Cozzens, John Gould. Boulger, J.D. "Puritan Allegory in Four Modern Novels." *Thought*, 44: 413-32 (Au 69).

Cass, C.S. "Two Stylistic Analyses of the Narrative Prose in C's *By Love Possessed*." *Style*, 4: 213-38 (1970).

Krickel, Edward. "C and Saroyan: A Look at Two Reputations." *GaR*, 24: 281-96 (Fa 70).

Updike, John. "Indifference." *NY*, 44: 197-201 (2 N 68).

Craddock, Charles E. (see *Murfree, Mary Noailles*).

Cradock, Thomas. Skaggs, D.C. "TC and the Chesapeake Golden Age." *WMQ*, 30: 93-116 (Ja 73).

———. "TC's Sermon on the Governance of Maryland's Established Church." *WMQ*, 27: 630-53 (O 70).

———, and F.G. Ranney. "TC Sermons." *MHM*, 67: 179-80 (Su 72).

Cranch, Christopher P. Myerson, Joel. "Transcendentalism and Unitarianism in 1840: A New Letter by CPC." *CLAJ*, 16: 366-68 (Mr 73).

Nicoson, M.R. "CC and His Three Muses." *ConS*, 9: 1-11 (D 74).

Olmert K.M. "C on Emerson: A Letter Re-edited." *ATQ*, 13: 31-2 (1972).

Williams, P.O. "The Persistence of C's 'Enosis.'" *ESQ*, 57: 41-46 (4Q 69).

Crane, Hart. Anon. "Altering the modes of consciousness: The Ecstatic, Infinite Idealism of HC." *TLS*, 2 O 69, pp. 1117-9.

———. "HC Letters." *Bancroftiana*, 60: 6-7 (F 75).

Anderson, D.D. "Journey through Time: The Poetic Vision of HC." *Ohioana Q*, 15: 59-64 (Su 72).

Bassoff, Bruce. "C's 'For the Marriage of Faustus and Helen,' III, 1-23." *Expl* 31: 53 (Mr 73).

———. "Rhetorical Pressures in 'For the Marriage of Faustus and Helen.'" *CP*, 5: 40-8 (1972).

Benét, W.R. "Mr. Moon's Notebook." *SatR*, 4: 665 (10 Mr 28).

———. "Round About Parnassus." *SatR*, 6: 1176 (5 Jl 30).

Bloom, Harold. "Bacchus and Merlin: The Dialectic of Romantic Poetry in America." *SoR*, 7: 140-75 (Ja 71).

Boyle, Kay. "Mr. C and His Grandmother." *Transition*, 10: 135-8 (Ja 28).

Braun, Henry. "HC's 'The Broken Tower." *BUSE*, 5: 167-77 (Au 61).

Brother Antoninus. "Our Modern Sensibility." *Cweal*, 77: 111-2 (26 O 62).

Brown, Ashley. "On HC." *Nation*, 186: 264 (29 Mr 58).

Brown, S.J. "HC: The End of Harvest. HC's Letters to William Slater Brown and Susan Jenkins Brown." *SoR*, 4: 945-1014 (Au 68).

Brunner, Edward. "'Your Hands within My Hands are Deeds': Poems of Love in *The Bridge*." *IowaR*, 4: 105-26 (Wi 73).

Bryant, J.A. "HC and the Illusory Abyss." *SR*, 77: 149-54 (Wi 69).

———. "HC, Poet of the Sixties." *JML*, 1: 283-88 (1970).

Burke, Kenneth. "The 'Christ-Dionysus Link.'" *NRep*, 161: 24-6 (9, 16 Ag 69).

Calmer, Allan. "The Case of HC." *NRep*, 71: 264 (20 Jl 32).

Cambon, Clauco. "HC, Icaro Della Parola." *Aut Aut*, 23: 414-27 (S 54).

Cargill, Oscar. "HC and His Friends." *Nation*, 186: 142-3 (15 F 58).

———. "The 'Unfractioned Idiom' of The Bridge." *Poetry*, 98: 190-2 (Je 61).

Cowan, J.C. "The Theory of Relativity and *The Bridge*." *HSL*, 3: 108-15 (1971).

Cowley, Malcolm. "HC: The Evidence in the Case." *SR*, 78: 176-84 (Wi 70).

———. "The Late HC." *New Eng Wk*, 1: 315 (14 Jl 32).

———. "The Leopard in HC's Brown." *Esquire*, 50: 257-71 (O 58).

———. "A Preface to HC." *NRep*, 62: 276-7 (23 Ap 30).

———. "Two Winters with HC." *SR*, 67: 547-56 (O 59).

Creeley, Robert. "HC and the Private Judgement." *Free Lance*, 5: 3-17 (#1 60).

Dahlberg, Edward. "HC." *NYRB*, 5: 19-22 (20 Ja 66).

Davison, R.A. "HC, Louis Untermeyer, and T.S. Eliot: A New C Letter." *AL*, 44: 143-6 (My 72).

Dembo, L.S. "HC's 'Verticalist' Poem." *AL*, 40: 77-81 (Mr 68).

Deutsch, Babette. "Poetry Out of Chaos." *VQR*, 9: 620-5 (1933).

Dickinson-Brown, Roger. "C's 'For the Marriage of Faustus and Helen,' II, 7-8, 11-2." *Expl*, 31: 66 (1973).

Donoghue, Dennis. "Moidores for HC." *NYRB*, 9: 16-9 (9 N 67).

Drew, Elizabeth. "The Trouble with Modern Poetry." *SatR*, 14: 3-4, 14 (23 My 36).

Fitzell, Lincoln. "The Sword and the Dragon." *SAQ*, 50: 214-32 (Ap 51).

Flint, F.C. "Metaphor in Contemporary Poetry." *Symposium*, 1: 310-55 (1931).

Friedman, Paul. "*The Bridge*: A Study in Symbolism." *Psychoanalytical Q*, 21: 49-80 (1952).

Furia, Philip. "C's 'At Melville's Tomb.'" *Expl*, 33: 73 (My 75).

Galpin, Alfred. "A Boat in the Tower: Rimbaud in Cleveland, 1922." *Renascence*, 25: 3-13 (1972).

Gordon, Caroline. "Robber Rocks: Letters and Memories of HC." *SoR*, 6: 481-7 (Ap 70).

Guillory, D.L. "HC, Marianne Moore, and the Brooklyn Bridge." *BSUF*, 15: 48-9 (Su 74).

Gullans, Charles. "Poetry and Subject Matter: From HC to Turner Cassity." *SoR*, 6: 488-92 (Ap 70).

Hardwick, Elizabeth. "Anderson, Millay, and C in Their Letters." *PR*, 20: 690-6 (D 53).

Hartley, Lodwick. "Stephen's Lost World: The Background of Katherine Anne Porter's 'The Downward Path to Wisdom.'" *SSF*, 6: 574-9 (Fa 69).

Hashiguchi, Minoru. "America no Homerostachi." *Oberon*, 30: 10-41 (1968).

Hinz, E.J. "HC's 'Voyages' Reconsidered." *ConL*, 13: 315-33 (Su 72).

Hirshfeld, S.E., and Ruth Portner. "A Voyage Through Two Voyages: A Study of HC's *Voyages IV* and *V*." *Lang & S*, 1: 115-28 (Wi 68).

Hopkins, Konrad. "Make the Dark Poems Light: A Study of HC's *White Buildings*." *FSUS*, 19: 125-42 (1955).

Horton, Philip. "Death of a Poet." *Coronet*, 3: 56-60 (Ja 38).

———. "Identity of S.B. Greenberg." *SoR*, 2: 422-4 (Au 36).

Huberman, Elizabeth. "HC's Use of 'Symphonic Form.'" *AA*, 2: 15-29 (1970).

Hurner, J.A. "Old Thresholds, Old Anatomies: A New Approach to the *Voyages* of HC." *NCampR*, 1: 10-7 (My 66).

Hutson, Richard. "Exile Guise: Irony and HC." *Mosaic*, 2: 71-86 (1969).

———. "HC's 'Black Tambourine.'" *LWU*, 3: 31-6 (1970).

———. "A Life of HC." *SoR*, 8: 234-42 (Ap 72).

Irvin, J.T. "Naming Names: HC's 'Logic of Metaphor.'" *SoR*, 11: 284-99 (Ap 75).

Jason, P.K. "Wilbur Underwood: HC's Confidant." *MarkR*, 4: 66-8 (O 74).

Kahn, Sy. "HC and Harry Crosby: A Transit of Poets." *JML*, 1: 45-56 (1Q 70).

Katz, Joseph. "CALM Addendum No. 1: HC." *PBSA*, 63: 130 (2Q 69).

———. "Corwin Knapp Linson on the Third Violet." *SCraneN*, 3: 5 (Fa 68).

Keller, D.H. "CALM Addenda No. 2: HC." *PBSA*, 64: 98-9 (1Q 70).

Kessler, Edward. "C's 'Black Tambourine.'" *Expl*, 29: 4 (1970).

Knox, George. "C and Stella: Conjunction of Painterly and Poetic Worlds." *TSLL*, 12: 689-707 (Wi 71).

———. "'Sight, Sound and Flesh': Synoptic View from C's Tower." *MarkR*, 3: 1-10 (O 71).

Koretz, Jean, et al. "C's 'Passage.'" *Expl*, 13: 47 (Je 55).

Kosawa, Atsuo. "Allusive Variation—*Hashi* no Hoho." *EigoS*, 116: 194-5 (1970).

Kramer, Victor. "The 'Mid-Kingdom' of C's 'Black Tambourine' and Toomer's *Cane*." *CLAJ*, 17: 486-97 (Je 74).

LaFrance, Marston. "The Bridge-Builder." *CRAS*, 2: 106-13 (Fa 71).

Leggett, Bernie. "C's 'The Mango Tree.'" *Expl*, 32: 18 (N 73).

Lensing, G.S. "HC's Tunnel from *The Waste Land*." *Ariel*, 6: 20-35 (Jl 75).

Lewis, T.S.W. "HC and His Mother: A Correspondence." *Salmagundi*, 9: 61-87 (Sp 69).

Lipton, R.J. "Last Letters of HC: With a Commentary on the Poet and the Man." *Lit Amer*, 1: 7-14 (S 34).

Crane, Hart

Lohf, K.A. "The Library of HC." *Proof*, 3: 283-334 (1973).

————. "The Prose Manuscripts of HC: An Editorial Portfolio." *Proof*, 2: 1-60 (1972).

Loveman, Samuel. "Recollections of HC." *New Eng Wk*, 5: 380 (2 Ag 34).

McMichael, James. "HC." *SoR*, 8: 290-309 (Ap 72).

MacNiven, I.S. "HC and T.S. Eliot on the Modern City." *Revista Un Costa Rica*, 36: 63-73 (1973).

Mariani, P.L. "Words for HC." *HSL*, 3: 150-3 (1971).

Martin, R.K. "C's *The Bridge*, 'The Tunnel,' 58-60." *Expl*, 34: 16 (O 75).

Mattson, F.O. "HC and Roy Campbell." *BNYPL*, 76: 17-8 (1972).

Mihăilă, Rodica. "Dincolo de ermetismul poeziei lui HC." *Sdlu*, 15: 133-42 (1970).

————. "O abordare lingvistică a metaforei şi definirea stilului poetic (exemplificare pe poezia lui HC)." *AUB-LUC*, 22: 145-52 (1973).

Mosely, Virginia, and J.R. Willingham. "C's 'Passage.'" *Expl*, 13: 47 (Je 55).

Mosher, H.F. "La Metamorphose des Symboles chez HC et Arthur Rimbaud." *RLV*, 39: 291-311 (Jl-Ag 73).

Nilsen, H.N. "HC's 'Atlantis': An Analysis." *Dutch Q R*, 3: 145-58 (#4 73).

————. "HC's Indian Poem." *NM*, 72: 127-39 (1971).

Paniker, K.A. "Myth and Machine in HC." *LCrit*, 9: 27-41 (Su 71).

Parkinson, Thomas. "HC and Yvor Winters: A Meeting of Minds." *SoR*, 11: 491-512 (Jl 75).

————. "The HC-Yvor Winters Correspondence." *Ohio R*, 16: 5-24 (Fa 74).

Payne, J.R. "Addenda to Rowe: HC's *Collected Poems*." *PBSA*, 69: 120-1 (1Q 75).

Paulin, A., Jr. "C's 'Voyages, II.'" *Expl*, 28: 15 (O 69).

Perry, R.L. "HC and the Critics." *CP*, 8: 23-7 (#3 75).

Porter, Frank. "'Chaplinesque': An Explication." *EJ*, 57: 191-2 (F 68).

Porter, K.A. "A Country and Some People I Love." *HM*, 231: 58-68 (S 65).

Quinn, Sister M. Bernetta. "The Poetics of HC." *Perspective*, 4: 81-8 (Sp 51).

Riding, Laura. "A Note on *White Buildings* by HC." *Transition*, 10: 139-41 (Ja 28).

Rueckert, William. "Humanizing a Poet." *NRep*, 171: 28-9 (24 Ap 74).

Rosenfeld, Alvin. "Teaching Modern Poetry: The Examples of T.S. Eliot and HC." *APR*, 11: 48-50 (Ja-F 73).

Runden, J.P. "Whitman's 'The Sleepers' and the 'Indiana' Section of C's *The Bridge*." *WWR*, 15: 245-8 (D 69).

Scarlett, J.R. "C's 'The Sad Indian.'" *Expl*, 29: 69 (Je 71).

Schwartz, Joseph, and R.C. Scweik. "*CALM* Addendum No. 3: The Literary Manuscripts of HC." *PBSA*, 66: 64-5 (1Q 72).

Shattuck, Roger. "HC's Other Bridge." *YLM*, 19: 9-10, 18 (Wi 43).

Sheehan, P.J. "C's 'Moment Fugue.'" *Expl*, 31: 78 (My 73).

Shockley, M.S. "HC's 'Lachrymae Christi." *UKCR*, 16: 31-7 (Au 49).

Simon, Marc. "CALM Addendum No. 4: HC." *PBSA*, 68: 69 (Ja-Mr 74).

————. "HC and Samuel B. Greenberg: An Emblematic Interlude." *ConL*, 12: 166-72 (Sp 71).

Simpson, W.T. "An Explication of HC's 'Black Tambourine.'" *XUS*, 7: 5-7 (N 68).

Simpson, L.B. "The Late HC." *New Eng Wk*, 1: 531 (15 S 32).

Sugg, R.P. "The Imagination's White Buildings and 'Quaker Hill.'" *Erasmus R*, 1: 145-55 (1971).

Swallow, Alan. "HC." *DQ*, 2: 93-118 (Sp 67).

————. "HC." *UKCR*, 16: 103-18 (Wi 49).

Takuwa, Shinji. "Some Impressions of Henry Adams, HC, E.E. Cummings, and Others." *SELit*, 11: 19-53 (1961).

Tate, Allen. "C: The Poet as Hero." *NRep*, 127: 25-6 (17 N 52).

Ullyatt, A.G. "HC: *The Bridge*." *UES*, 13: 24-30 (#2 75).

Untermeyer, Louis. "Poet Stranded on a Bridge." *SatR*, 52: 27-9 (19 Jl 69).

Uroff, M.D. "HC's 'Recitative.'" *CP*, 3: 22-7 (Sp 70).

———. "HC's 'Voyages VI,' Stanza 6." *ELN*, 8: 46-8 (S 70).

———. "The Imagery of Violence in HC's Poetry." *AL*, 43: 200-16 (My 71).

Waggoner, H.H. "HC and the Broken Parabola." *UKCR*, 11: 173-7 (Sp 45).

Wilkie, Brian. "*Preludes to Vision: The Epic Venture in Blake, Wordsworth, Keats, and HC*
. . ." *JEGP*, 71: 255-60 (1972).

Wilson, Edmund. "The Muses Out of Work." *NRep*, 50: 319-21 (11 My 27).

Yannella, P.R. "'Inventive Dust': The Metamorphoses of 'For the Marriage of Faustus and
Helen.'" *ConL*, 15: 102-22 (Wi 74).

———. "Toward Apotheosis: HC's Visionary Lyrics." *Criticism*, 10: 313-33 (Fa 68).

Zatkin-Dresner, Z. "Levels of Meaning in HC's 'Royal Palm.'" *Thoth*, 15: 28-37 (#1
74-75).

Zeck, G.R. "The Logic of Metaphor: 'At Melville's Tomb.'" *TSLL*, 17: 673-86 (Fa 75).

Crane, Jonathan Townley. Gullasen, T.A. "The Fiction of the Reverend JTC, D.D." *AL*,
43: 263-73 (My 71).

Crane, Stephen. Anon. "A Bibliography of SC Scholarship: 1893-1969." *Thoth*, 11: 3-38
(1970).

———. "Lost Souls of SC and His Sussex Days." *Bookman's J and Print Collector*, 8:
145-7 (Ag 23).

———. "Misplaced Writer." *NY*, 7 N 36, p. 14.

Alberts, Frank. "*The Blue Hotel*: A Play in Three Acts, by Frank Alberts, based on the story
by SC." *Theatre*, 2: 27-42 (O 60).

Anderson, W.D. "Homer and SC." *NCF*, 19: 77-86 (Je 64).

Andrews, W.L. "A New SC Fable." *AL*, 47: 113-4 (Mr 75).

Asselineau, Roger. "Realisme, rêve et expressionisme dans *Winesburg, Ohio*." *Archives des
Lettres Modernes*, 1-2: 22 (Ap 57).

Autrey, M.L. "The Word Out of the Sea: A View of C's 'The Open Boat.'" *ArQ*, 30: 101-10
(1974).

Baasner, Peter. "SC and Joseph Conrad." *Kleine Beitrage*, 21: 34-9 (Wi 61).

Beards, R.D. "Stereotyping in Modern American Fiction: Some Solitary Swedish
Madmen." *MSpr*, 63: 329-37 (1969).

Belasco, David. "The Genius of SC." *Metropolitan Mag*, 12: 666 (N 00).

Beer, Thomas. "The Princess Far Away." *SatR*, 1: 702 (25 Ap 25).

Bernard, Kenneth. "'The Bride Comes to Yellow Sky': History as Elegy." *Eng Rec*, 17:
17-20 (Ap 67).

Bowers, Fredson. "C's *Red Badge of Courage* and Other 'Advance Copies.'" *SB*, 22: 273-7
(1969).

———. "The New Look in Editing." *SAB*, 35: 3-10 (Ja 70).

Boyd, Thomas. "Semper Fidelis." *Bkm*, 960: 409-12 (D 24).

Bradbury, Malcolm. "Art and Real in SC." *JAmSt*, 2: 117-20 (Ap 68).

———. "Romance and Reality in *Maggie*." *JAmst*, 3: 111-21 (Jl 69).

———. "Sociology and Literary Studies II: Romance and Reality in *Maggie*." *JAmst*, 3:
111-21 (Jl 69).

Braunstein, Simeon. "A Checkist of Writings By and About SC in *The Fra*." *SCraneN*, 3: 8
(Wi 68).

Brennan, J.X. "SC and the Limits of Irony." *Criticism*, 11: 183-200 (Sp 69).

Browne, E.A. "SC's *Whilomville Stories*: A Backward Glance." *MarkR*, 3: 105-9 (1973).

Crane, Stephen

Bruccoli, M.J. "Robert Barr's Proofs of *The O'Ruddy*." *SCraneN*, 4: 8 (Sp 70).

———, and Joseph Katz. "Scholarship and Mere Artifacts: SC's British and Empire Publications." *SB*, 22: 277-87 (1969).

———. "'The Wonders of Ponce': C's First Puerto Rico Dispatch." *SCraneN*, 4: 4-6 (Fa 70).

Burgauner, Christoph. "SC: Ein Wunder an Mut." *NDH*, 13: 164-6 (1966).

Burhans, C.S. "Judging Henry Judging: Point of View in *The Red Badge of Courage*." *BSUF*, 15: 38-48 (Sp 74).

Burhans, C.S., Jr. "Twin Lights on Henry Fleming: Structural Parallels in *The Red Badge of Courage*." *ArQ*, 30: 149-59 (1974).

Burns, L.C. "On 'The Open Boat.'" *SSF*, 3: 455-7 (Su 66).

Cady, E.W. "SC to Miss Daisy D. Hill: The Letter Recovered." *SCraneN*, 4: 1-4 (1970).

Callahan, R.D. "Moral Rearmament as Mobilized Counter-Fantasy." *WCR*, 7: 53-9 (#2 72).

Carmichael, Otto. "SC in Havana." *PrS*, 43: 200-4 (Su 69).

Cazemajou, Jean. "*The O'Ruddy*, Robert Barr et *The Idler*." *Caliban*, 5: 69-78 (Ja 68).

———. "SC." *LanM*, 63: 54-60 (Ja-F 69).

Chamberlin, Ralph. "Lafayette's Most Notorious Flunk Out." *Marquis*, nv: 16-7, 27 (F 61).

Colvert, James. "The Origins of SC's Literary Creed." *UTSE*, 34: 179-88 (1955).

Cooley, J.R. "'The Monster'—SC's 'Invisible Man.'" *MarkR*, 5: 10-4 (1975).

*Coppa, Joseph. "SC Bibliography." *Thoth*, 13: 45-6 (Fa 73).

Cowley, Malcolm. "'Not Men': A Natural History of Naturalism." *KR*, 11: 414-35 (Su 47).

Crane, J.St.C. "Rare or Seldom-Seen Dust Jackets of American First Editions: VII." *Serif*, 9: 31-2 (1972).

Crisler, J.S. "'Christmas Must Be Gay': SC's *The Ghost*—A Play by Divers Hands." *Proof*, 3: 69-120 (1973).

Dameron, J.L. "Symbolism in the Poetry of Poe and SC." *ESQ*, 60: 22-8 (Fa 70).

Davison, R.A. "C's 'Blue Hotel' Revisited: The Illusion of Fate." *MFS*, 15: 537-9 (Wi 69-70).

Deamer, R.G. "SC and the Western Myth." *WAL*, 7: 111-23 (Su 72).

Dendinger, L.N. "SC's Inverted Use of Key Images of 'The Rime of the Ancient Mariner.'" *SSF*, 5: 192-4 (Wi 68).

Dennis, S.A. "SC Bibliography." *Thoth*, 11: 33-4 (1971).

DeVoto, Bernard. "Fiction Fights the Civil War." *SRL*, 17: 3 (18 D 37).

Dew, Marjorie. "Realistic Innocence: Cady's Footnote to a Definition of American Literary Realism." *ALR*, 5: 487-9 (1972).

Dillingham, W.B. "C's One-Act Farce: *The Upturned Face*." *RSW*, 35: 324-30 (1968).

Dow, Eddy. "Cigars, Matches, and Men in 'The Open Boat.'" *Re:AtL*, 2: 47-9 (#2 75).

Dreiser, Theodore. "A Letter about SC." *Michigan Daily Sunday Mag*, 27 N 21, p. 1.

Dusenbery, Robert. "The Homeric Mood in *The Red Badge of Courage*." *PCP*, 3: 31-7 (1968).

Eichelberger, C.L. "SC's 'Grand Opera for the People': A Bibliographic Identification and Correction." *PBSA*, 65: 70-2 (1Q 71).

Elias, R.H. "SC: Encore." *EA*, 24: 444-8 (1971).

Farlekas, Christopher. "SC of Port Jervis." *Views*, 1: 3-5 (O 62).

———. "SC of Port Jervis." *York State Tradition*, 17: 11-4 (Su 63).

*Ferstel, J.W. "SC Bibliography." *Thoth*, 12: 39-40 (Sp-So 72).

Ficken, Carl. "Jimmie Trescott's Age." *SCraneN*, 5: 2-3 (1970).

Fine, D.M. "Abraham Cahan, SC and the Romantic Tenement Tale of the Nineties." *AmS*, 14: 95-107 (Sp 73).

Fine, L.H. "'The Fire-Tribe and the Pale-Face': An Unfinished and Unpublished Play by SC." *MarkR*, 3: 37-8 (F 72).

———. "Two Unpublished Plays by SC." *RALS*, 1: 200-16 (Au 71).

Ford, F.M. "Stevie & Co." *NYHT*, 2 Ja 27, pp. 1, 6.

———. "Two Americans—Henry James and SC." *NY Evening Post Lit R*, 19 Mr 21, pp. 1-2; 26 Mr 21, pp. 1-2.

Ford, P.H. "Illusion and Reality in C's *Maggie*." *ArQ*, 25: 293-303 (Wi 69).

Forster, Imogen. "The *Thoth* Annual Bibliography of SC Scholarship." *Thoth*, 10: 25-7 (1969).

Fox, A.M. "SC and Joseph Conrad." *Serif*, 6: 16-20 (D 69).

Fraser, R.S. "The Thoth Annual Bibliography of SC Scholarship." *Thoth*, 9: 58-61 (1968).

Frederick, J.T. "The Fifth Man in 'The Fifth Man in 'The Open Boat.'" *CEA*, 30: 1, 12-4 (My 68).

Frohock, W.M. "*The Red Badge* and the Limits of Parody." *SoR*, 6: 137-48 (Ja 70).

Fulwilder, Toby. "The Death of the Handsome Sailor: A Study of *Billy Budd* and *The Red Badge of Courage*." *ArQ*, 26: 101-12 (Su 70).

Garner, Stanton. "Some Notes on Harold Frederic in Ireland." *AL*, 39: 60-74 (Mr 67).

Garnett, Edward. "SC." *Academy*, 59: 116, 123 (9 Je 00).

Gerstenberger, Donna. "'The Open Boat': Additional Perspective." *MFS*, 17: 557-61 (Wi 71-72).

Gilkes, Lillian. "Corrections of R.W. Stallman's *SC: A Biography*." *SCraneN*, 3: 6-7 (Sp 69).

———. "Frederic, C, and the Stallman Biography." *FH*, 3: 4 (Ap 69).

———. "S and Cora C: Some Corrections." *AL*, 41: 270-7 (My 69).

———. "SC and the Biographical Fallacy: The Cora Influence." *MFS*, 16: 441-6 (Wi 70-71).

———. "SC and the Harold Frederics." *Serif*, 6: 21-48 (D 69).

———. "The SC Collection Before Its Acquitition by Columbia: A Memoir." *CLC*, 23: 12-22 (N 73).

———. "SC's Burial Place: Some Inconsequential Ghost Laying." *Serif*, 7: 7-11 (Je 70).

———, and J.H. Baum. "SC's Last Novel, *The O'Ruddy*." *CLC*, 6: 41-8 (1957).

Gollin, R.K. "'Little Souls Who Thirst for Fight' in *The Red Badge of Courage*." *ArQ*, 30: 111-18 (1974).

Graham, D.B. "Dreiser's *Maggie*." *ALR*, 7: 169-70 (1974).

Green, M.L. "The Stendhal of American Publications." *RLC*, 10: 311 (Ap 30).

Grenberg, B.L. "Metaphysics of Despair: SC's 'The Blue Hotel.'" *MFS*, 14: 203-13 (Su 68).

Griffith, Clark. "SC and the Ironic Last Word." *PQ*, 47: 83-91 (Ja 68).

Griffith, B.W. "Robinson Jeffers' 'The Bloody Sire' and SC's 'War Is Kind.'" *NCLit*, 3: 14-5 (Ja 73).

Gullason, T.A. "The Cranes at Pennington Seminary." *AL*, 39: 530-41 (Ja 68).

———. "The First Known Review of SC's 1893 *Maggie*." *ELN*, 5: 300-2 (Je 68).

———. "Four Men in a Cave: A Critical Appraisal." *Readers and Writers*, 1: 30-1 (Ap-My 67).

———. "The Last Will and Testament of Mrs. Mary Helen Peck C." *AL*, 40: 232-4 (My 68).

———. "The Letters of SC: Additions and Corrections." *AL*, 41: 104-6 (Mr 69).

———. "The New Criticism and Older Ones: Another Ride in 'The Open Boat.'" *CEA*, 31: 8-9 (Je 69).

———. "SC and the *Arena*: Three 'Lost' Reviews." *PBSA*, 65: 297-9 (3Q 71).

————. "A SC Find: Nine Newspaper Sketches." *SHR*, 2: 1-37 (Wi 68).

————. "SC: Onward and Upward." *CEA*, 34: 30-1 (My 72).

Haack, Dietmar. "SC und die 'Kühne' Metapher." *JA*, 14: 116-23 (1969).

Hafer, C.B. "The Red Badge of Absurdity: Irony in *The Red Badge of Courage*." *CLAJ*, 14: 440-3 (Je 71).

Hagemann, E.R. "Correspondents Three in the Greco-Turkish War: Some Parodies." *AL*, 30: 339-44 (N 58).

————. "SC and *The Argonaut*: 1895-1901." *SCraneN*, 5: 8-11 (Fa 70).

————. "SC Faces the Storms of *Life*, 1896-1900." *JPC*, 2: 347-60 (Wi 68).

————. "SC in the Pages of *Life* (1896-1901): A Checklist." *SCraneN*, 3: 1-5 (Sp 69).

Halladay, J.R. "A Misdated C Poem." *AN&Q*, 12: 83-4 (F 74).

————. "Stallman's *Turned* vs. C's *Turn*." *AN&Q*, 13: 105 (1975).

Harrison, S.R. "SC and Death: A Moment Between Two Romanticisms." *MarkR*, 2: 117-20 (My 71).

Hicks, Granville. "The Short Story Was His Medium." *SatR*, 50: 31-2 (22 Jl 67).

Holton, Milne. "The Sparrow's Fall and the Sparrow's Eye: C's *Maggie*." *SN*, 41: 115-29 (1969).

Honig, Donald. "SC: The Boy Genius." *Caper*, 12: 53, 60 (Ja 66).

Howells, W.D. "Frank Norris." *NAR*, 175: 770-1 (D 02).

*Hudspeth, R.B. "Bibliography of SC Scholarship." *Thoth*, 8: 98-9 (Sp 67); 11: 3-83 (Fa 70).

Hughes, Rupert. "The Genius of SC." *Criterion*, 22: 24 (6 Ja 00).

Itabashi, Yoshie. "Comedies of Love: A Study of *The Third Violet* and *Active Service*." *Tsuda R*, 13: 15-63 (N 68).

————. "A Landscape of Complicity: A Study of *Whilomville Stories*." *Tsuda R*, 15: 37-70 (N 70).

————. "The Modern Pilgrimage of *The Black Riders*." *Tsuda R*, 12: 1-41 (N 67).

————. "New York City Sketches—C's Greed and Art." *SELit*, nv: 208-9 (1972).

————. "Shizenshugi bungaku to gikō—SC no baai." *Amerika Bungaku*, 3: 6-14 (S 64).

————. "SC and the New York City Sketches: Looking for Humanity." *Tsuda R*, 16: 11-41 (N 71).

————. "SC ni okeru Shizenshugi no Henyo." *EigoS*, 115: 352-3 (1969).

————. "'To Be a Man': A Study of Fear and Courage in SC's Stories." *Tsuda R*, 10: 1-48 (N 65).

Ives, C.B. "Symmetrical Design in Four of SC's Stories." *BSUF*, 10: 17-26 (Wi 69).

Jackson, J.A. "The Map of Society: America in the 1890's." *JAmSt*, 3: 103-10 (Jl 69).

————. "Sociology and Literary Studies." *JAmSt*, 3: 103-10 (Jl 69).

————. "SC's Imagery of Conflict in *George's Mother*." *ArQ*, 25: 313-8 (Wi 69).

Johnson, C.O. "C's 'I was in darkness.'" *Expl*, 34: 6 (S 75).

*Johnson, R.C. "Addendum to Bibliographies of . . . SC, . . .: Haldeman-Julius Little Blue Books." *PBSA*, 66: 66 (1Q 72).

Kahn, Sy. "SC and the Griant Voice in the Night: An Explication of 'The Monster.'" *Stetson Stud Hum*, 1: 35-45 (1963).

Kahn, S.J. "SC and Whitman: A Possible Source for 'Maggie.'" *WWR*, 7: 71-7 (D 61).

Karlen, Arno. "The Craft of SC." *GaR*, 28: 470-97 (Fa 74).

Katz, Joseph. "Copeland & Day to SC." *SCraneN*, 2: 7-8 (Fa 67).

————. "*The Correspondence of Stephen and Cora Crane*: An Announcement." *SCraneN*, 5: 11 (Wi 70).

————. "Corwin Knapp Linson on *The Third Violet*." *SCraneN*, 3: 5 (Fa 68).

————. "C's Chapter Headings for *The O'Ruddy*." *SCraneN*, 4: 1 (Sp 70).

————. "DeWitt Miller's *Maggie*: A Correction." *SCraneN*, 2: 4-6 (Wi 67).

————. "An Early Draft of 'The Blue Hotel.'" *SCraneN*, 3: 1-3 (Fa 68).

————. "An Early Draft of 'Death and the Child.'" *SCraneN*, 3: 1-2 (Sp 69).

————. "An Early Draft of 'Moonlight on the Snow.'" *SCraneN*, 3: 1-2 (Su 69).

————. "An Editor's Recollection of *The Red Badge of Courage*." *SCraneN*, 2: 3-6 (Sp 68).

————. "Elbert Hubbard to Lyman Chandler: A Note on C's Poetics." *SCraneN*, 3: 8-9 (Fa 68).

————. "Elbert Hubbard's Watermark." *SCraneN*, 4: 8-10 (Sp 70).

————. "Ex Libris SC: *Under Pine and Palm*." *SCraneN*, 3: 8 (Su 69).

————. "*Great Battles of the World*: Manuscripts and Method." *SCraneN*, 3: 5-7 (Wi 68).

————. "Hamlin Garland's Copy of *The Red Badge of Courage*." *SCraneN*, 3: 10 (Wi 68).

————. "How Elbert Hubbard Met SC." *SCraneN*, 2: 8-12 (Sp 68).

————. "John William de Forest on SC." *SCraneN*, 4: 6 (Fa 70).

————. "Joline's *Meditations*, C, and Spelling." *SCraneN*, 2: 5 (Wi 67).

————. "The Lanthorn Book: A Census." *SCraneN*, 4: 10-12 (Sp 70).

————. "*Maggie: A Girl of the Streets* (1893); A Census." *SCraneN*, 2: 7-9 (Wi 67); 3: 6, 10-11 (Fa 68, Sp 69).

————. "Mrs. Joseph Conrad on SC: An Anecdote." *SCraneN*, 2: 12 (Su 68).

————. "A Note on SC: Sullivan County Tales and Sketches." *SCraneN*, 3: 6 (Fa 68).

————. "*The Open Boat and Other Stories*: Dedication and Contents." *SCraneN*, 3: 9-10 (Su 69).

————. "Practical Editions: SC's *The Red Badge of Courage*." *Proof*, 2: 301-19 (1972).

————. "The 'Preceptor' and Another Poet: Thomas Wentworth Higginson and SC." *Serif*, 5: 17-21 (Mr 68).

————. "Preface." *SCraneN*, 5: 1 (Sp 70).

————. "Quarterly Checklist." *SCraneN*, quarterly since Fa 66.

————. "The Reception of *Wounds in the Rain*." *SCraneN*, 4: 9-10 (Fa 70).

————. "Recovered Comment: 'More 'Black Riders' by Crane." *SCraneN*, 3: 12 (Su 69).

————. "*The Red Badge of Courage*: A Preliminary History of the Appleton Printings." *SCraneN*, 4: 5-7 (Sp 70).

————. "*The Red Badge of Courage* Contract." *SCraneN*, 2: 5-10 (Su 68).

————. "*The Red Badge of Courage* from 1911 to 1923." *SCraneN*, 5: 1-2 (Fa 70).

————. "SC and Irving Bacheller's Gold." *SCraneN*, 5: 4-5 (Sp 70).

————. "SC at Claverack College and Hudson River Institute." *SCraneN*, 2: 1-5 (Su 68).

————. "SC 'Bibliographed.'" *Proof*, 3: 455-60 (1973).

————. "SC to an Unknown Recipient: A New Letter." *SCraneN*, 2: 4-5 (Wi 67).

————. "SC Flinches." *SCraneN*, 3: 6-7 (Fa 68).

————. "SC in *The Fly Leaf*." *SCraneN*, 4: 3-4 (Sp 70).

————. "SC: Muckraker." *CLC*, 17: 3-7 (F 68).

————. "SC, 'Samuel Carlton,' and a Recovered Letter." *NCF*, 23: 220-5 (Su 68).

————. "SC to the American Press Association: A New Letter." *SCraneN*, 4: 6-7 (Fa 70).

————. "SC to the Atlanta *Journal*: A New Letter." *ScraneN*, 4: 3 (Fa 70).

————. "SC to the *Chap-Book*: Two New Letters." *SCraneN*, 2: 9-10 (Wi 67).

————. "SC to Harry Thompson." *SCraneN*, 3: 4 (Fa 68).

————. "SC to Irving Bacheller: A New Letter." *SCraneN*, 2: 10-1 (Su 68).

————. "SC to J.G. Widrig: A New Letter." *SCraneN*, 3: 2-3 (Su 69).

————. "SC to James MacArthur: A New Letter." *SCraneN*, 3: 5 (Fa 68).

————. "SC to John Thomas Lee: A New Letter." *SCraneN*, 3: 8 (Wi 68).

————. "SC to Julius Chambers." *SCraneN*, 3: 11 (Fa 68).

————. "SC to Lucius L. Button." *SCraneN*, 3: 4 (Fa 68).

————. "SC to Miss Daisy D. Hill: A New Letter." *SCraneN*, 2: 10 (Su 68).

————. "SC to Mr. Richards." *SCraneN*, 1: 5 (Wi 66).

————. "SC to an Unknown Recipient." *SCraneN*, 3: 5, 7 (Sp 69).

————. "SC to *Youth's Companion*." *SCraneN*, 2: 2, 5 (Wi 67).

————. "SC to Passport Applications." *SCraneN*, 3: 7-8, 3-4, 6-7 (Fa, Wi 68, Su 69); 4: 4-5 (Fa 70).

————. "SC's Struggles." *SCraneN*, 1: 3-5 (Sp 67).

*————. "The Thoth Checklist." *SCraneN*, 5: 11-2 (Sp 70).

————. "Toward a Descriptive Bibliography of SC: *The Black Riders*." *PBSA*, 59: 150-7 (2Q 65).

————. "Two Uncollected Articles." *PrS*, 44: 287-96 (Wi 69).

————, and L.B. Gilkes. "Not at Columbia: Postcards to Cora Crane." *CLC*, 23: 21-30 (1974).

————, and M.J. Bruccoli. "Toward a Descriptive Bibliography of SC: 'Spanish-American War Songs.'" *PBSA*, 61: 267-69 (3Q 67).

Kauffman, R.W. "The True Story of SC." *Mod Culture*, 12: 143-5 (0 00).

Kerscher, Rudolf. "*Whilomville Stories*: SC's vergessene Kindheitsrzahlungen." *NS*, 15: 77-80 (F 66).

Kibler, J.E. "The Library of S and Cora Crane." *Proof*, 1: 199-246 (1971).

————. "R.W. Stallman's *SC: A Critical Bibliography*." *Costerus*, 1: 177-88 (1974).

Kinnamon, J.M. "Henry James, the Bartender in SC's 'The Blue Hotel.'" *ArQ*, 30: 160-3 (1974).

Kirschke, James. J. "The Art of SC." *ModA*, 18: 105-9 (1974).

Knapp, Daniel. "Son of Thunder: SC and the Fourth Evangelist." *NCF*, 24: 253-91 (D 69).

Krauth, Leland. "Heroes and Heroics: SC's Moral Imperative." *SDR*, 9: 86-93 (Su 73).

Kudo, Kozo. "SC's Psychologism." *Yamagata Daigaku Eigo Eibungaku Kenkyu*, 11: 27-60 (F 66).

Kummings, D.D. "An Appraisal of Reappraisals: Four Nineteenth-Century American Writers." *CEA*, 37: 36-8 (#1 74).

Kyles, G.G.M. "SC and 'Corporal O'Connor's Story.'" *SB*, 27: 294-5 (1974).

Kyria, Pierre. "Le Monde Américain." *RdP*, Mr 67, pp. 120-5.

LaFrance, Marston. "'C, Zola, and the Hot Ploughshares." *ELN*, 7: 285-7 (Je 70).

————. "The Ironic Parallel in SC's 1892 Newspaper Correspondence." *SSF*, 6: 101-3 (Fa 68).

————. "SC Scholarship Today and Tomorrow." *ALR*, 7: 125-35 (Sp 74).

Landor, M. "Portrait of SC." *VLit*, 8: 228-33 (1959).

————. "SC and University Study." *Foreign Lit* (Moscow), 6: 267-8 (1959).

Leaver, Florence. "Isolation in the Work of SC." *SAQ*, 61: 521-32 (Au 62).

Linder, Lyle. "Applications from Social Science to Literary Biography: The Family World of SC." *ALR*, 7: 280-2 (Su 74).

Link, F.H. "SC's 'The Blue Hotel': Eine Interpretation." *LWU*, 5: 22-32 (1972).

Loftus, M.F. "Two Soldiers: A Comparative Study of SC's *The Red Badge of Courage* and Tayama Katai's 'One Soldier.'" *SALit*, 9: 67-79 (1971).

McBride, Henry. "SC's Artist Friends." *Art News*, 49: 46 (0 50).

McDermott, J.J. "Symbolism and Psychological Realism in *The Red Badge of Courage*." *NCF*, 23: 324-31 (D 68).

McIlvaine, R.M. "A Literary Source for Hurstwood's Last Scene." *RSW*, 40: 44-6 (1972).

Marlowe, J.G. "C's Wafer Image: Reference to an Artillery Primer?" *AL*, 43: 645-7 (Ja 72).

Marovitz, S.E. "Scratchy the Demon in 'The Bride Comes to Yellow Sky.'" *TSL*, 16: 137-40 (1971).

Marshall, Edward. "Stories of SC." *Lit Life*, 24: 71-2 (D 00).

Martin, John. "Childhood in SC's *Maggie*, 'The Monster,' and *Whilomville Stories*." *MwUQ*, 2: 40-6 (4Q 67).

Martins, Heitor. "C, Xavier, Chocano: Un caso de plagio interamericano." *Revista de Cultura Brasilena*, 25: 173-81 (1968).

*May, Candace. "A SC Bibliography." *Thoth*, 14: 53-5 (#2-3 75).

Mayer, C.W. "Social Forms vs. Human Brotherhood in C's *The Monster*." *BSUF*, 14: 29-37 (Su 73).

———. "SC and the Realistic Tradition: 'Three Miraculous Soldiers.'" *ArQ*, 30: 137-34 (1974).

Mayfield, J.S. "To Stephencraneites." *Courier*, 25: 26 (1966).

———. "SC's Curious Conflagration." *ABC*, 7: 6-8 (D 56).

Mayhall, Jane. "SC to the Rescue." *NYRB*, 19: 28-30 (10 Ag 72).

Maynard, Reid. "Red as Leitmotif in *The Red Badge of Courage*." ArQ, 30: 135-41 (1974).

Miller, E.E. "Trilogy of Irony: Analysis of *War Is Kind*." *EJ*, 54: 59-62 (Ja 70).

Miller, Ruth. "Regions of Snow: The Poetic Style of SC." *BNYPL*, 72: 328-49 (My 68).

Modlin, C.E., and John R. Byers. "SC's 'The Monster' as Christian Allegory." *MarkR*, 3: 110-3 (1973).

Mohrt, Michel. "Le poeme rouge de la guerre." *FL*, O 27 66, p. 6.

Monteiro, George. "Bernard Berenson's Notes on SC." *SCraneN*, 2: 1-2 (Sp 68).

———. "Brazilian Translations of SC's Fiction." *SCraneN*, 4: 7-8 (Fa 70).

———. "A Capsule Assessment of SC by Hamlin Garland." *SCraneN*, 3: 2 (Fa 68).

———. "Cora Crane to John Hay: A Last Communication." *SCraneN*, 4: 8 (Sp 70).

———. "C's 'Lines': A Last Note on the *Bookman*." *PrS*, 47: 268 (1973).

———. "C's *A Man Adrift on a Slim Spar*, 20." *Expl.*, 32: 14 (O 73).

———. "'Grand Opera for the People': An Unrecorded SC Printing." *PBSA*, 63: 29-30 (1Q 69).

———. "*The Illustrated American* and SC's Contemporary Reputation." *Serif*, 6: 49-54 (1969).

———. "The Logic Beneath 'The Open Boat.'" *GaR*, 26: 326-35 (Fa 72).

———. "Paul Lemperly's *Maggie* (1893), and a New Stephen Crane Letter." *SCraneN*, 3: 7-9 (Sp 69).

———. "Society and Nature is SC's 'The Men in the Storm.'" *PrS*, 45: 13-7 (Sp 71).

*———. "SC and *Public Opinion*: An Annotated Checklist, An Unrecorded Parody, and a Review of *The O'Ruddy*." *SCraneN*, 5: 5-8 (Sp 70).

———. "SC and the Antinomies of Christian Charity." *Cent R*, 16: 91-104 (Wi 72).

———. "SC's 'Dan Emmonds:' A Case Reargued." *Serif*, 6: 32-6 (1969).

———. "SC's 'Yellow Sky' Sequel." *ArQ*, 30: 119-26 (Su 74).

———. "With Proper Words (or Without Them) the Soldier Dies: SC's 'Making an Orator.'" *Cithara*, 9: 64-72 (My 70).

Morace, R.A. 'A 'New' Review of *The Red Badge of Courage*." *ALR*, 8: 163-5 (Sp 75).

Nagel, J.E. "Impressionism in 'The Open Boat' and 'A Man and Some Others.'" *RSW*, 43: 27-37 (1975).

———. "The Narrative Method of 'The Open Boat.'" *RLV*, 39: 409-17 (#5 73-74).

———. "SC." *SAF*, 1: 232-40 (1973).

———. "SC's 'The Clan of No-Name.'" *KAL*, 14: 34-42 (1972).

————. "Structure and Theme in Crane's 'An Experiment in Misery.'" *SSF*, 10: 169-74 (Sp 73).

Narveson, Robert. "'Conceit' in 'The Blue Hotel.'" *PrS*, 43: 187-91 (Su 69).

————, et al. "SC: A Portfolio." *PrS*, 43: 175-204 (Su 69).

Nelson, Carl. "The Ironic Allusive Texture of *Lord Jim*: Coleridge, C, Milton, and Melville." *Conrad*, 4: 47-59 (1972).

Noel, E.E. "SC: A Realist Who Painted with Words." *KAL*, 12: 20-31 (1970).

Nose, Toshi. "On SC's *The Red Badge of Courage*." *Okayama Daigaku Kyoyo-bu Kiyo*, 2: 12-36 (1966).

O'Donnell, T.F. "Charles Dudley Warner on *The Red Badge of Courage*." *AL*, 25: 363-5 (N 53).

Oliver, Arthur. "Jersey Memories—SC." *Proc New Jersey Hist Soc*, 16: 454-63 (O 31).

Overton, J.P. "The 'Game' in 'The Bride Comes to Yellow Sky.'" *XUS*, 4: 3-11 (1965).

Paredes, R.A. "SC and the Mexican." *WAL*, 6: 31-8 (Sp 71).

Parks, E.W. "C's 'The Open Boat.'" *NCF*, 8: 77 (Je 53).

Patrick, W.R. "Poetic Style in the Contemporary Short Story." *CCC*, 18: 77-84 (My 67).

Pelletier, Gaston. "*Red Badge* Revisited." *EJ*, 57: 24-5, 99 (Ja 68).

Pierce, J.F. "SC's Use of Figurative Language in 'The Blue Hotel.'" *SCB*, 34: 160-4 (1974).

Pilgrim, T.A. "Repetition as a Nihilist Device in SC's 'The Blue Hotel.'" *SSF*, 11: 125-30 (Sp 74).

Pizer, Donald. "C Reports Garland on Howells." *MLN*, 70: 37-9 (Ja 55).

————. "A Primer of Fictional Aesthetics." *CE*, 30: 572-80 (Ap 69).

Rahv, Philip. "Fiction and the Criticism of Fiction." *KR*, 18: 276-99 (Sp 56).

Rathbun, J.W. "Structure and Meaning in *The Red Badge of Courage*." *BSUF*, 10: 8-16 (Wi 69).

Rechnitz, R.M. "Depersonalization and the Dream in *The Red Badge of Courage*." *StN*, 6: 76-87 (Sp 74).

Reed, K.T. "'The Open Boat' and Dante's *Inferno*: Some Undiscovered Analogies." *SCraneN*, 4: 1-3 (Su 70).

Rogers, R.O. "SC and Impressionism." *NCF*, 24: 292-304 (D 69).

Rosenfeld, Isaac. "SC as Symbolist." *KR*, 15: 310-4 (Sp 53).

Roth, Russell. "A Tree in Winter: The Short Fiction of SC." *NMQ*, 23: 188-96 (Su 53).

Sadler, E.E. "SC, 1871-1900: Forerunner of the Modern Literary Movement." *Eng Teaching Forum*, 8: 11-5 (Ja-F 70).

Saillet, Maurice. "Paul Valery et 'La Conquête du Courage." *Mercure de France*, 317: 376-8 (F 53).

Schellhorn, G.C. "SC's 'The Pace of Youth.'" *ArQ*, 25: 334-42 (Wi 69).

Schmitz, Neil. "SC and the Colloquial Self." *MwQ*, 13: 437-51 (Su 72).

Schroeder, Fred. "America's First Literary Realist: Horatio Alger, Junior." *WHR*, 17: 129-37 (Sp 63).

Sharma, D.R. "The Naturalistic and the Esthetic in SC." *PURBA*, 3: 75-84 (#1 72).

————. "War and the Individual Man in *The Red Badge of Courage*." *LCrit*, 9: 56-64 (Su 70).

Simoneaux, K.G. "Color Imagery in C's *George's Mother*." *CLAJ*, 14: 410-9 (Je 71).

————. "Color Imagery in C's 'Maggie: A Girl of the Streets.'" *CLAJ*, 18: 91-100 (S 74).

Sloane, D.E.E. "SC at Lafayette." *RALS*, 2: 102-5 (Sp 72).

Slote, Bernice. "C's 'Lines': A Manuscript Facsimile." *PrS*, 46: 95 (Sp 72).

————. "'San Antonio': A Newly Discovered SC Article." *PrS*, 43: 176-83 (Su 69).

————. "SC and Willa Cather." *Serif*, 6: 3-15 (D 69).

————. "SC in Nebraska." *PrS*, 43: 192-9 (Su 69).

————. "SC in the Nebraska *State Journal*." *SCraneN*, 3: 4-5 (Su 69).

————. "SC: Two Uncollected Articles." *PrS*, 44: 287-96 (Fa 69).

Smith, L.T. "SC's Calvinism." *CRAS*, 2: 13-25 (Sp 71). Spinucci, Pietro. "La poesia si SC." *SA*, 17: 93-120 (1970).

Stallman, R.W. "Fiction and Its Critics." *KR*, 19: 290-9 (Sp 57).

————. "How SC Got to Crete." *AL*, 44: 308-13 (My 72).

————. "Journalist C in That Dinghy." *BNYPL*, 72: 260-77 (Ap 68).

————. "The Land-Sea Irony in 'The Open Boat.'" *CEA*, 30: 15 (My 68).

————. "New Short Fiction by SC." *SSF*, 1: 147-52 (Wi 64).

————. "The Scholar's Net." *CE*, 17: 20-7 (O 55).

————. "SC's 'Apache Crossing.' The Text of an Unfinished Story." *PrS*, 43: 186 (Su 69).

"Was Crane's Sketch of the Fleet Off Crete a Journalist Hoax." *SSF*, 2: 72-6 (Fa 64).

Starr, Alvin. "The Concept of Fear in the Works of SC and Richard Wright." *SBL*, 6: 6-10 (#2 75).

Stowell, Robert. "SC's Use of Colour in *The Red Badge of Courage*." *LCrit*, 9: 36-9 (Wi 70).

Stronks, J.B. "Garland's Private View of C in 1898 (With a Postscript)." *ALR*, 6: 249-50 (Su 73).

————. "A Realist Experiments with Impressionism: Hamlin Garland's 'Chicago Studies.'" *AL*, 36: 38-52 (Mr 64).

Sutton, Walter. "The Modernity of SC's Poetry: A Centennial Tribute." *Courier*, 9: 3-7 (1971).

Tanner, Tony. "SC's Long Dream of War." *LonM*, ns 8: 5-19 (D 68).

Tanselle, G.T. "The New Editions of Hawthorne and C." *BC*, 23: 214-30 (Su 74).

Thomas, D.S. "C's *The Red Badge of Courage*." *Expl*, 27: 77 (My 69).

Trachtenberg, Alan. "Experiments in Another Country: SC's City Sketches." *SoR*, 10: 265-85 (Ap 74).

Tsunematsu, Masao. "Toward Man in Society—A Study of SC." *Shimane Daigaku Bunrigaku-bu Kiyo*, 1: 78-89 (D 67).

Van Der Beets, Richard. "Character as Structure: Ironic Parallel and Transformation in 'The Blue Hotel.'" *SSF*, 5: 294-5 (Sp 68).

Van Meter, J.R. "Sex and War in *The Red Badge of Courage*: Cultural Themes and Literary Criticism." *Genre*, 7: 71-90 (Mr 74).

Vidan, Ivo. "*The Red Badge of Courage*: A Study in Bad Faith." *SRAZ*, 33-36: 93-112 (1972-73).

Vorpahl, B.M. "Murder by the Minute: Old and New in 'The Bride Comes to Yellow Sky.'" *NCF*, 26: 196-218 (1971).

Vsiliievskaya, O.B. "Evolution of the Art of SC." *Izvestiya*, 24: 226-36 (1965).

Weatherford, R.M. "A Manuscript of 'Black Riders Came from the Sea.'" *SCraneN*, 4: 3-4 (Su 70).

————. "SC and O. Henry: A Correction." *AL*, 44: 666 (Ja 73).

————. "SC in *The Lotus* and *Chips*." *SCraneN*, 4: 2-3 (Fa 70).

Weinig, M.A. "Heroic Convention in 'The Blue Hotel.'" *SCraneN*, 2: 6-7 (Sp 68).

Wertheim, Stanley. "C and Garland: The Education of an Impressionist." *NDQ*, 35: 23-8 (Wi 67).

————. "Franklin Garland's *Maggie*." *SCraneN*, 2: 1-4 (Wi 67).

————. "*The Red Badge of Courage* and Personal Narratives of the Civil War." *ALR*, 6: 61-5 (Wi 73).

————. "The Saga of March 23rd: Garland, Gilder, and C." *SCraneN*, 3: 1-3 (Wi 68).

*————. "SC." *ALR*, 8: 227-41 (1975).

————. "SC and the Wrath of Jehova." *LitR*, 7: 499-508 (Su 64).

————. "SC's 'A Detail.'" *MarkR*, 5: 14-5 (1975).

————. "SC's Middle Name." *SCraneN*, 3: 3-4 (Su 69).

Westbrook, Max. "Fiction and Belife." *CRAS*, 3: 63-7 (1972).

White, W.M. "The C-Hemingway Code: A Re-evaluation." *BSUF*, 10: 15-20 (Sp 69).

Williams, G.L. "Henry Fleming and the 'Cheery Voiced' Stranger." *SCraneN*, 4: 4-7 (Fa 70).

Winterich, John. "SC: Lost and Found." *SatR*, 34: 21, 43 (3 F 51).

Witherington, Paul. "SC's 'A Mystery of Heroism': Some Redefinitions." *EJ*, 58: 201-4, 218 (F 69).

Wycherley, H.A. "C's 'The Blue Hotel': How Many Collaborators?" *AN&Q*, 4: 88 (F 66).

Yoshida, Hiroshige. "A Note on SC's Use of Colloquial and Slangy Words and Idioms." *Kansai Daigaku Anglica*, 4: 59-71 (Ja 61).

Zambrano, A.L. "The Role of Nature in *The Red Badge of Courage*." *ArQ*, 30: 164-66 (1974).

Crawford, Francis Marion. Brumbaugh, T.B. "The Facile FMC." *MarkR*, 4: 70-1 (O 74).

Holman, H.R. "FMC and the Evil Eye." *AN&Q*, 9: 103-4 (1971).

Moran, J.C. "FMC's "An American Politician': Some BAL Addenda." *PBSA*, 69: 267-73 (Ap-Je 75).

Pilkington, John. "FMC (1854-1909)." *ALR*, 4: 177-82 (Sp 71).

Creekmore, Herbert. Simms, L.M. "HC: Mississippi Novelist and Poet." *NMW*, 4: 15-21 (Sp 71).

Creeley, Robert. Anon. "Craft Interview with RC." *NYQ*, 13: 17-47 (Wi 73).

————. "RC in Conversation with Charles Tomlinson." *Review*, 10: 24-35 (Ja 64).

Altieri, Charles. "The Unsure Egoist: RC and the Theme of Nothingness." *ConL*, 13: 162-85 (Sp 72).

Andre, Michael. "Two Weeks with C in Texas." *ChiR*, 24: 81-6 (72).

Banks, Russell. "Notes on C's *Pieces*." *Lilla*, 8: 88-91 (1970).

Chung, Ling. "Predicaments in RC's Words." *CP*, 2: 32-5 (Fa 69).

Cox, Kenneth. "Address and Posture in the Poetry of RC." *CQ*, 4: 237-43 (Su 69).

Dawson, Fielding. "On C's Third Change." *Athanor*, 4: 57-8 (1973).

Freeman, J.P. "RC." *CQ*, 2: 414-20 (Fa 67).

Guillory, D.L. "RC and the Surprise of Zeb." *Unicorn*, 3: 18-20 (#1 73).

Hammond, J.G. "Solipsism and the Sexual Imagination in RC's Fiction." *Critique*, 16: 59-69 (3Q 75).

Howard, Richard. "RC: 'I Begin Where I Can, and End When I See the Whole Thing Returning.'" *MinnR*, 8: 143-50 (1968).

*Johnson, L.A. "RC: A Checklist 1946-1970." *TCL*, 17: 181-98 (1971).

Kaufman, R.F. "The Poetry of RC." *Thoth*, 2: 28-36 (Wi 71).

Lewis, P.E. "RC and Gary Snyder: A British Assessment." *Stand*, 13: 42-7 (1972).

Mazzaro, Jerome. "RC, the Domestic Muse, and Post-Modernism." *Athanor*, 4: 16-88 (1973).

Messing, G.M. "The Linguistic Analysis of Some Contemporary Nonformal Poetry." *Lang&S*, 2: 323-9 (1969).

Novick, Mary, and Douglas Calhoun. "RC: A Critical Checklist." *WCR*, 6: 51-71 (1972).

Oppenheimer, Joel. "The Inner Tightrope: An Appreciation of RC." *Lilla*, 8: 51-3 (1970).

Paul, Sherman. "A Letter on Rosenthal's 'Problems of RC.'" *Boun2*, 3: 747-760 (Sp 75).

Potts, Charles. "*Pieces*: The Decline of C." *WCR*, 5: 3-5 (1971).

Raban, Janathan. "Chance, Time and Silence: The New American Verse." *JAmSt*, 3: 89-101 (Jl 69).

Rosenthal, M.L. "Problems of RC." *Parnassus*, 2: 205-14 (Fa-Wi 73).

Sienicka, Marta. "William Carlos Williams and Some Younger Poets." *SAP*, 4: 183-93 (1972).

Tallman, Warren. "Sunny Side Up." *Athanor*, 4: 64-6 (1973).

Taylor, L.L. "Arta miniaturala la RC." *Steaua*, 25: 45-6 (1974).

Will, Frederic. "To Take Place and to 'Take Heart.'" *Poetry*, 111: 112-21 (Ja 68).

Crèvecoeur, J. Hector St. John. Adams, P.G. "The Historical Value of C's *Voyage dans la haute Pensylvanie et dans New York*." *AL*, 25: 152-68 (My 53).

Babuscio, Jack. "C in Charles Town: The Negro in the Cage." *JHS*, 2: 283-6 (1969-70).

Banta, Martha. "American Apocalypses: Excrement and Ennui." *SLitI*, 7: 1-30 (#1 74).

Cunliffe, Marcus. "C Revisited." *JAmSt*, 9: 129-44 (1975).

Larsen, D.M. "The Expansive Sensibility of C." *Exploration*, 2: 36-51 (1974).

Mohr, J.C. "Calculated Disillusionment: C's *Letters* Reconsidered." *SAQ*, 69: 354-63 (1970).

Vittorini, Elio. "An Outline of American Literature." *SR*, 68: 423-37 (Su 60).

Watanabe, Toshio. "C no Dilemma—America no Yume to Genijitsu." *EigoS*, 119: 803-5 (1974).

Werge, Thomas. "Thomas Shepard and C: Two Uses of the Bosom Serpent before Hawthorne." *NHJ*, 4: 236-9 (1974).

Crews, Harry. Foata, Anne. "Interview with HC, May 1972." *RANAM*, 5: 207-25 (1972).

Watson, V.S. "Arguments Over an Open Wound: An Interview with HC." *PrS*, 48: 60-74 (Sp 74).

Crockett, Davy. Bishop, H.O. "DC—Bear Hunter." *National Republic*, 17: 31-7 (Ag 29).

Harrison, L.H. "DC: The Making of a Folk Hero." *KFR*, 15: 87-90 (1969).

Mason, M.R. "*The Lion of the West*: Satire on DC and Frances Trollope." *SCB*, 29: 143-5 (Wi 69).

Crosby, Caresse. Anon. "CC: 1892-1970." *Pisces*, 1: 1-4 (1970).

Crosby, Ernest Howard. Frederick, P.J. "A Life Principle: EHC and the Frustrations of the Intellectual as Reformer." *NYH*, 54: 397-423 (O 73).

Gianakos, P.E. "EHC: A Forgotten Tolstoyan Anti-Militarist and Anti-Imperialist." *AmS*, 13: 11-29 (Sp 72).

Crosby, Harry. Bell, Millicent. "The Black Sun Press: 1927 to the Present." *BBr*, 17: 2-24 (1955).

Fox, Hugh. "HC: A Heliograph." *BBr*, 23: 95-100 (1969).

Kahn, Sy. "Hart Crane and HC: A Transit of Poets." *JML*, 1: 45-56 (1970).

Reed, Victor. "Reading a 'Sound Poem' by HC." *ELN*, 6: 192-6 (Mr 69).

Crothers, Rachel. Gottlieb, L.C. "The Double Standard Debate in Early 20th Century Drama." *MichA*, 7: 441-52 (1975).

Crowley, Martin. Lanckrock, Rik. "De jongen door MC." *OnsE*, 13: 135-6 (1970).

Morsberger, R.E. "The Movie Game in *Who's Afraid of Virginia Woolf?* and *The Boys in the Band*." *Costerus*, 8: 89-100 (1973).

Cullen, Countee. Copeland, C.M. "The Unifying Effect of Coupling in CC's 'Yet Do I Marvel.'" *CLAJ*, 18: 258-61 (D 74).

Daniel, W.C. "CC As Literary Critic." *CLAJ*, 14: 281-90 (Mr 71).

Dorsey, D.F. "CC's Use of Greek Mythology." *CLAJ*, 13: 68-77 (S 69).

Emanuel, James. "Renaissance Sonneteer." *BlackW*, 24: 32-45, 92-7 (#11 75).

Kirby, D.K. "CC's 'Heritage': A Black 'Waste Land.'" *SAQ*, 36: 14-20 (N 71).

Larson, C.R. "Three Harlem Novels of the Jazz Age." *Critique*, 11: 66-78 (1969).

Lederer, Richard. "The Didactic and the Literary in Four Harlem Renaissance Sonnets." *EJ*, 62: 219-23 (1973).

Lomax, M.L. "CC: A Key to the Puzzle." *SLitI*, 7: 39-48 (Fa 74).

Cummings, E.E. Anon. "Putting the Jerk into Joys." *TSL*, 22 Ag 68, p. 902.

Aarts, Jan. "A Note on the Interpretation of 'he danced his did.'" *JL*, 7: 71-3 (1971).

Andrea, Flavia. "E.E.C: poetual posibil." *Steaua*, 26: 46-7 (#8 75).

Clark, D.R. "C's 'anyone' and 'noone.'" *ArQ*, 25: 36-43 (Sp 69).

Cowley, Malcolm. "C: One Man Alone." *YR*, 62: 332-54 (Sp 73).

Crowley, J.W. "Visual-Aural Poetry: The Typography of E.E.C." *CP*, 5: 51-4 (1972).

Crivelli, R.S. "E.E.C: La poetica del movimento." *SA*, 18: 313-44 (1972).

Davis, W.V. "C's 'all in green went my love riding.'" *CP*, 3: 65-7 (Fa 70).

———. "C's 'next to of course god america i.'" *CP*, 3: 14-5 (Sp 70).

———. "C's 'Nobody Loses All the Time.'" *AN&Q*, 9: 119-20 (1971).

———. "C's 'no time ago.'" *RS*, 41: 205-7 (1973).

———. "E.E.C's 'except in your.'" *ELN*, 11: 294-6 (1974).

Donahue, Jane. "C's Last Poem: An Explication." *LWU*, 3: 106-8 (1970).

Dougherty, J.P. "Language as a Reality in E.E.C." *BuR*, 16: 112-22 (My 68).

Dumas, B.K. "Dialect in E.E.C." *Langu of Poetry*, 2: 48-51 (1973).

Dundas, D. "C's When God Lets My Body Be.'" *Expl*, 29: 79 (My 71).

Dupee, F.W., and George Stade, eds. "E.E.C: Twenty-three Letters." *HM*, 238: 71-80 (Mr 69).

———. "Letters of E.E.C to Ezra Pound." *PaR*, 10: 55-87 (Fa 66).

Epstein, Joseph. "The Small-Eyed Poet." *NRep*, 160: 23-7 (7 Je 69).

Everson, Edith. "C's 'That which we who're alive in spite of mirrors.'" *Expl*, 32: 55 (Ap 74).

Fairley, I.R. "Syntactic Deviation and Cohesion." *Lang&S*, 6: 216-29 (1974).

Fandel, John. "E.E.C: hee hee cunning's fonetty kinglish." *Cweal*, 99: 264-66 (1973).

Fauchereau, Serge. "E.E.C." *LetF*, 1262: 3-5, 7 (18 D 68).

Finn, H.S. "C's 'Memorabilia.'" *Expl*, 29: 42 (Ja 71).

Friedman, Norman. "Reactions to the C Issue (of *TLOP*): Vol. II, No. 2, S, 1973." *TLOP*, 3: 31-3 (1974).

Gidley, Mick. "Picture and Poem: E.E.C in Perspective." *Poetry R*, 59: 179-98 (Au 68).

Grossman, M.L. "Him and the Modern Theatre." *QJS*, 54: 212-9 (O 69).

Gunter, Richard. "Sentence and Poem." *Style*, 5: 26-36 (1971).

Haule, J. "E.E.C as Comic Poet." *L&P*, 25: 175-80 (1975).

Heinrichs, V.L. "C's '(im) c-a-t(mo).'" *Expl*, 27: 59 (Ap 69).

Henry, Nat. "C's 'Pity This Monster, Manunkind.'" *Expl*, 27: 68 (Ap 69).

Heyen, William. "In Consideration of C." *SHR*, 7: 264-6 (1973).

Hombitzer, Elenore. "e.e.c: A Wind has blown therain away . . . Versuch einer Strukualistischen Deutung." *Fremdsprachliche Unterricht*. 27: 25-40 (1973).

James. Clive. "An Instrument to Measure Spring With." *The Review*, 20: 38-48 (Mr 69).

Kidder, R.M. "E.E.C, Painter." *HLB*, 33: 117-38 (1975).

Lane, Gary. "C's 'Sonnet Entitled How to Run the World." *Expl*, 31: 7 (S 72).

———. "C's 'Yes is a Pleasant Country.'" *Expl*, 31: 11 (O 72).

Lawrence, F.B. "Two Novelists of the Great War: Dos Passos and C." *UR*, 36: 35-41 (O 69).

Lord, J.B. "Para-Grammatical Structure in a Poem of E.E.C." *PCP*, 1: 66-73 (1966).

Lozar, Tomaz. "E.E.C: The Poem as Improvisation." *AN*, 4: 61-73 (1971).

Luedtke, L.S. "C's 'The Noster was a Ship of Swank.'" *Expl*, 26: 59 (Mr 68).

McIlvaine, R.M. "C's 'bright.'" *Expl*, 30: 6 (Ag 71).

Macksoud, S.J. "Anyone's How Town: Interpretation as Rhetorical Discipline." *SM*, 35: 70-6 (Mr 68).

*Mahoney, J.W. "E.E.C Today: A Bibliographical Survey." *LWU*, 6: 188-201 (1973).

Metcalf, A.A. "Dante and E.E.C." *CLS*, 7: 374-86 (S 70).

Mullen, P.B. "E.E.C and Popular Culture." *JPC*, 5: 503-20 (Wi 71).

Nadel, A.M. "C's 'When faces called flowers float out of the ground.'" *Expl*, 32: 47 (F 74).

Nixon, Nell. "A Reading of E.E.C's 'anyone lived in a pretty how town.'" *TLOP*, 3: 18-31 (1973).

Oliver, W.I. "*Him*—A Director's Note." *ETJ*, 26: 327-41 (1974).

O'Neal, L.M. "C's 'What If A Much of A Which Of A Wind." *Expl*, 32: 6 (S 73).

Overland, Orm. "E.E.C's 'my father moved through dooms of love': A Measure of Achievement." *ES*, 54: 141-7 (Ap 73).

Perrine, Laurence. "In Heavenly Realms of Hellas." *NCLit*, 1: 2-4 (Ja 71).

Pinsky, Robert. "Two Examples of Poetic Discursiveness." *ChiR*, 27: 133-41 (#1 75).

Powers, R.G. "C's 'I Will Be.'" *Expl*, 28: 54 (S 70).

Rao, B.D. "Figure on the Page: A Note on the Poetry of E.E.C." *LCrit*, 9: 11-8 (Wi 69).

Reutlinger, Dagman. "E.E.C and the *Dial* Collection." *MR*, 16: 353-6 (Sp 75).

Robey, Cora. "C's 'All in Green Went My Love Riding.'" *Expl*, 27: 2 (S 68).

Schleiner, Winfried. "Drei Gedichte von E.E.C." *LWU*, 2: 27-37 (1969).

Slotkin, A.R. "The Negative Aspect of Homo Faber: A Reading of E.E.C's 'pity this busy monster manunkind.'" *Lang of Poetry*, 2: 34-41 (1973).

Smelstor, Margorie. "'Damn Everything but the Circus': Popular Art in the Twenties and *him*." *MD*, 17: 43-55 (Mr 74).

Smith, J.F. "A Stereotyped Archetype: EEC's Jean Le Nègre." *SAF*, 1: 24-34 (Sp 73).

Stetler, Charles. "E.E.C's 73 Poems: With Life's Eye." *XUS*, 7: 5-16 (Mr 68).

Sülzer, Bernd. "Möglichkeiten linguistischer Interpretation im Unterricht: E.E.C's 'Poem No. 151.'" *NsM*, 26: 153-7 (1973).

Takuwa, Shinji. "Some Impressions of Henry Adams, Hart Crane, E.E.C, and Others." *SELit*, 11: 19-53 (1961).

Tal-Mason, P.B. "The Whole E.E.C." *TCL*, 14: 90-7 (Jl 68).

Thompson, W.E. "C and the Mystery of Stillness." *Cont Poetry*, 1: 35-43 (Sp 73).

Towles, T.L. "A Reading of 'if everything happens that can't be done." *Lang of Poetry*, 2: 42-8 (1973).

Tucker, Robert. "E.E.C as an Artist: The *Dial* Drawings." *MR*, 16: 329-52 (Sp 75).

Untermeyer, Louis. "Quirky Communications from an Exuberant Unhero." *SatR*, 52: 25-6 (5 Jl 69).

Vendler, Helen. "Poetry: Ammons, Berryman, C." *YR*, 62: 412-19 (1973).

Weinberger, G.J. "C's 'when what hugs stopping earth that silent is.'" *RSW*, 41: 136-9 (Je 73).

———. "E.E.C's 'the people who.'" *RSW*, 39: 313-5 (1971).

———. "E.E.C's Benevolent God: A Reading of 'when you are silent, shining host by guest.'" *PLL*, 10: 70-5 (Wi 74).

West, P.J. "Medieval Style and the Concerns of Modern Criticism." *CE*, 34: 784-90 (1973).

Wickes, George. "E.E.C at War." *CUF*, 12: 31-3 (Fa 69).

Wilson, G.R. "C's 'Ponder, Darling, These Busted Statues.'" *SAB*, 37: 66-9 (N 72).

———. "C's 'TA.'" *Expl*, 31: 17 (N 72).

Cummins, Maria S. Manthorne, Jane. "The Lachrymose Ladies." *HornB*, 43: 375-84, 501-13, 622-30 (Je, Ag, O 67).

Cunningham, J.V. Carruth, Hayden. "A Location of J.V.C." *MQR*, 11: 75-83 (Sp 72).

Johnson, Carol. "The Last Variation: A Discussion of Two Formalist Poets, Robert Fitzgerald and J.V.C." *Art Int*, 16: 65-7 (My 72).

Kaye, F.W. "The West as Desolation: J.V.C's *To What Strangers, What Welcome*." *SoR*, 11: 820-4 (Au 75).

Mudrick, Marvin. "Three Stanford Poets." *LugR*, 1: 83-94 (1965).

Stall, Lindon. "The Trivial, Vulgar, and Exalted: The Poems of J.V.C." *SoR*, 9: 1044-8 (Au 73).

Stein, Robert A. "The Collected Poems and Epigrams of J.V.C." *WHR*, 27: 1-12 (Wi 73).

Cuomo, George. Bryant, J.H. "The Fiction of GC." *ArQ*, 30: 253-72 (Au 74).

Curley, Daniel. Brandabur, Edward. "The Pilgrimage of Curleyman." *NLet*, 38: 15-44 (Sp 72).

Curtis, George William. Kirk, Clara and Rudolf. "William Dean Howells, GWC, and the 'Haymarket Affair.'" *AL*, 40: 487-98 (Ja 69).

Milne, Gordon. "GWC—Inheritor of the Transcendental Mantle." *ATQ*, 18: 35-40 (Sp 73).

Dahlberg, Edward. *Billings, Harold. "A Checklist of ED." *TriQ*, 19: 163-5 (Fa 70).

————. "A Chronology of Ed." *TriQ*, 19: 66-9 (Fa 70).

Boyle, Kay. "A Man in the Wilderness." *TriQ*, 19: 66-9 (Fa 70).

Burgess, Anthony. "Honoring a Prophet in His Own Country." *TriQ*, 19: 60-2 (Fa 70).

Chametzky, Jules. "ED, Early and Lake." *TriQ*, 19: 25-34 (Fa 70).

Dahlberg, Edward. "Confessions." *TriQ*, 19: 172-80 (Fa 70).

————. "A Letter to *Prose*." *Prose*, 1: 69-80 (1970).

————. "From 'The Olive of Minerva.'" *Prose*, 8: 45-72 (1974).

————. "Letters from Sarasota." *Prose*, 4: 37-50 (1972).

————. "On *The Sorrows of Priapus*." *Prose*, 5: 35-47 (1972).

——————. "The Sacred Logoi." *Prose*, 1: 63-7 (1970).

————. "Samuel Beckett's Wake." *Prose*, 6: 21-5 (1973).

————. "Two Diatribes: The First, The Second." *Prose*, 2: 61-78 (1971).

Johnson, Ronald. "'Be Primordal or Decay': Correspondence." *TriQ*, 19: 93-115 (Fa 70).

Karlen, Arno. "Reminiscences." *TriQ*, 19: 72-91 (Fa 70).

Kindrick, R.L. "Lizzie D and Eula Varner." *M-A*, 2: 93-111 (1975).

Leibowitz, Herbert. "D's *Because I Was Flesh*." *ASch*, 44: 473-83 (Su 75).

————. "Stoking the Oedipal Furnace: ED's *Because I Was Flesh*." *ASch*, 44: 473-83 (Su 75).

Merton, Thomas. "Poems, Photos and Paeans." *TriQ*, 19: 138-61 (Fa 70).

Meyer, Thomas. "A Garland of Tributes." *TriQ*, 19: 135 (Fa 70).

Miller, Herbert. "'Do These Bones Live.'" *TriQ*, 19: 63-5 (Fa 70).

Mottram, Eric. "Ishmael in America." *TriQ*, 19: 10-24 (Fa 70).

Rosenthal, Raymond. "The Carnal Myth." *TriQ*, 19: 56-9 (Fa 70).

Spencer, B.T. "American Literature as Black Mass: ED." *TCL*, 21: 381-93 (D 75).

Stringher, Bonalda. "ED e la ricerca del mito." *SA*, 14: 309-38 (1968).

Terry, R.C. "ED and Herbert Read, An Exchange of Letters." *MalR*, 9: 95-126 (Ja 69).

Whittaker, E.K. "Sorrow and the Flea." *TriQ*, 19: 35-55 (Fa 70).

Williams, Jonathan. "'Festschrifter's Notes: Who are All These People, Herr Malthus?'" *TriQ*, 19: 181-96 (Fa 70).

————. "How to Roast a Festschrift." *TriQ*, 19: 5-8 (Fa 70).

Dalton, Henry. Howell, Elmo. "HD: North Mississippi Poet." *NMW*, 3: 81-6 (Fa 70).

Daly, Elizabeth. Waldron, Ann. "The Godlen Years of ED." *ArmD*, 7: 25-8 (1973).

Damon, S. Foster. Cowley, Malcolm. "The Self-Obliterated Author: S.FD." *SoR*, 4: 20-32 (1968).

Monteiro, George. "Addenda to the Bibliographies of . . . D [and others]." *PBSA*, 69: 272-5 (Ap-Je 75).

Stanford, D.E. "FD's Dream Frontiers." *SoR*, 7: xv-xx (Ja 71).

———. "S.FD." *SoR*, 8: xiii-xv (Ap 72).

Dana, Richard Henry, Jr. Cameron, K.W. "Emerson's Petition for Privileges at Boston Public." *ESQ*, 48: 91-2 (3Q 67).

Fellman, Michael. "Sexual Longings in RHD Jr.'s, American Victorian Diary." *CRAS*, 3: 96-105 (Fa 72).

Hammes, K.W., Jr. "Melville, D, and Ames: Sources for Conrad's *The Nigger of the 'Narcissus'*." *PolR*, 19: 29-33 (1974).

Ringe, D.A. "Early American Gothic: Brown, D, and Allston." *ATQ*, 19: 3-8 (Su 73).

Dana, Richard Henry, Sr. Hunter, Doreen. "America's First Romantics: RHD, Sr. and Washington Allston." *NEQ*, 45: 3-30 (Mr 72).

Danforth, John. Ryan, T.A. "The Poetry of JD." *PAAS*, 78: 129-93 (1968).

Darrow, Clarence. Shuman, R.B. "CD's Contribution to Literary Naturalism: *An Eye for an Eye*." *RLV*, 36: 390-400 (My-Je 70).

Darrow, C.S. Payne, A.J. "CS.D, Literary Realist: Theory and Practice." *Mid-america*, 1974: 36-45.

Davenport, Guy. Shannon, John, ed. "A Symposium on GD." *Margins*, 13: 3-23 (Ag-S 74).

Davidson, Donald. Allen, Ward. "DD." *SR*, 78: 390-404 (Sp 70).

Bataille, Robert. "The Esthetics and Ethics of Farming: The Southern Agrarian View." *Iowa State J Res*, 49: 189-93 (1974).

Bradford, M.E. "DD: 1893-1968." *SoR*, 4: 1110-1 (1968).

Buffington, Robert. "Mr. D in the Formal Garden." *GaR*, 24: 121-31 (Su 70).

Cheney, Brainard. "DD." *SR*, 76: 691-3 (1968).

Core, George. "Two Gentlemen in Bonds." *SoR*, 11: 226-32 (Ja 75).

Cowan, Louise, "Portrait of a Tall Man." *SLJ*, 7: 146-50 (Fa 74).

Dessommes, Larry. "The Antipodes of Modern Literature: A Discussion of Joyce and D." *SCB*, 30: 179-81 (Wi 70).

Dessommes, Lawrence. "The Epistemological Implications in 'The Ninth Part of Speech.'" *MissQ*, 27: 21-32 (Wi 73-4).

Eaton, C.E. "A Friendship of Poets: The Statesman and the Soldier." *GaR*, 28: 688-704 (Wi 74).

Fain, J.T. "The Agrarian Symposium: Letters of Allen Tate and DD, 1928-1930." *SoR*, 8: 845-82 (O 72).

Hallman, D.A. "DD, Allen Tate and All Those Falling Leaves." *GaR*, 27: 550-9 (Wi 73).

Inge, M.T. "DD Selects the Best Southern Novels." *MissQ*, 24: 155-8 (1971).

———. "The Unheeding South: DD on James Branch Cabell." *Cabellian*, 2: 17-20 (Au 69).

Justus, J.H. "Two Men of Letters of the Fugitive World." *SLJ*, 7: 124-32 (#2 75).

O'Brien, Michael. "A Correspondence, 1923-1958: Edwin Mims and DD." *SoR*, 10: 904-22 (O 74).

———, ed. "Edwin Mims and DD: A Correspondence, 1923-1958." *SoR*, 10: 904-22 (Ja 74).

Rubin, L.D. "Encaustics: Letters of Loyalty: Tate and D." *SR*, 83: 363-70 (Sp 75).

Shapiro, E.S. "DD and the Tennessee Valley Authority: The Response of a Southern Conservative." *THQ*, 33: 436-51 (Wi 74).

Stuart, Jesse. "America's Pindar Was My Guide." *Vanderbilt Alumnus*, 56: 16-9 (Mr-Ap 71).

Davies, Samuel. Dolmetsch, C.R. "The Apostle as Southener." *SLJ*, 4: 74-82 (Fa 71).

Larson, B.A. "SD and the Rhetoric of New Light." *SM*, 38: 207-16 (Ag 71).

Davis, Catherine. Trimpi, H.P. "The Theme of Loss in the Earlier Poems of CD and Edgar Bowers." *SoR*, 9: 595-616 (Jl 73).

Davis, Daniel Webster. Sherman, J.R. "DWD: A Black Virginia Poet of the Age of Accommodation." *VMHB*, 81: 457-78 (1973).

Davis, Frank Marshall. Kloder, Helena. "The Film and Canvas of FMD." *CLAJ*, 15: 59-63 (S 71).

Randall, Dudley. "An Interview with FMD." *BlackW*, 23: 37-48 (1974).

Rehin, G.F. "The Darker Image: The American Negro Minstrelsy through the Historian Lens." *JAmSt*, 9: 365-73 (1975).

Davis, H.L. Bryant, P.T. "H.L.D: Viable Uses of the Past." *WAL*, 3: 3-18 (Sp 68).

Etulain, R.W. "H.L.D: A Bibliographical Addendum." *WAL*, 5: 129-35 (1970).

Jones, Phillip. "The West of H.L.D." *SDR*, 6: 72-84 (Wi 68-9).

Davis, John. Kribbs, J.K. "Setting the Record Straight on the Real JD." *PBSA*, 68: 329 (3Q 74).

Davis, Owen. Witham, Barry. "OD, America's Forgotten Playwright." *Players*, 46: 30-5 (O-N 70).

Davis, Rebecca Harding. Duus, Louise. "Neither Saint Nor Sinner: Women in Late Nineteenth-Century Fiction." *ALR*, 7: 276-8 (Su 74).

Eppard, P.B. "RHD: A Misattribution." *PBSA*, 69: 265-7 (Ap-Je 75).

Davis, Richard Harding. Anon. "Literary Promise Unfulfilled." *Nation*, 102: 430 (29 Ap 16).

————. "Notes on R.H.D." *Bkm*, 43: 353-64 (Je 16).

Beer, Thomas. "RHD." *Liberty*, 1: 15-21 (11 O 24).

*Eichelberger, C.L. and A.M. McDonald. "RHD (1864-1916): A Checklist of Secondary Comment." *ALR*, 4: 313-90 (Fa 71).

Hagemann, E.R. "Correspondents Three in the Graeco-Turkish War." *AL*, 30: 339-44 (N 58).

Holman, Harriet. "Interlude Scenes from John Fox's Courtship of Fritzi Schell, as Reported by RHD." *SLJ*, 7: 77-87 (Sp 75).

McElrath, J.R. "RHD." *ALR*, 8: 241-3 (1975).

Solensten, J.M. "The Gibson Boy: A Reassessment." *ALR*, 4: 302-12 (Fa 71).

————. "RHD (1864-1916)." *ALR*, 3: 160-6 (Sp 70).

————. "RHD, Owen Wister, and *The Virginian*: Unpublished Letters and a Commentary." *ALR*, 5: 122-33 (Sp 72).

Solensten, John. "RHD's Rejection of *The Call of the Wild*." *JLN*, 4: 122-3 (1971).

Davis, Samuel. Dolmetsch, C.R. "The Apostle as Southerner." *SLJ*, 4: 74-82 (Fa 71).

Dawson, Fielding. Anon. "FD, At Black Mountain College just after Charley Olson's Famous Essay was Published in *Poetry New York* (1950)." *Olson*, 2: 69 (1974).

————. "FD, A Letter from Black Mountain." *Olson*, 2: 4-7 (1974).

Alpert, Barry. "D's Jungian Strategies." *Vort*, 2: 41-2 (Fa 73).

————. "FD—An Interview." *Vort*, 2: 3-21 (Fa 73).

————. "FD: Not as Jung as He Used to Be." *Open Letter*, 2: 72-83 (Wi 74).

Byrd, Don. "FD and the Uses of Memory." *Vort*, 2: 39-40 (Fa 73).

Gafford, Charlotte. "FD's 'Certain Overflow Willingness.'" *IowaR*, 5: 82-7 (Su 74).

Metcalf, Paul. "FD." *Vort*, 2: 36-8 (Fa 73).

Mottram, Eric. "A First Appreciation of FD." *Vort*, 2: 43-53 (Fa 73).

Dawson, Rd. William. Kaiser, L.M. "The Latin Epitaph of Sir John Randolph." *VMHB*, 78: 199-201 (1970).

DeCasseres, Benjamin. Flagens, Peter. "The Critics: Hartmann, Huneker, and DC." *Art in American*, 61: 67-70 (Jl-Ag 73).

De Forest, John William. Benet, S.V. "A Pioneer Civil War Novel." *SatR*, 21: 16 (O 39).

Bergmann, Frank. "DeF in Germany." *ALR*, 4: 80-1 (1968).

―――. "Mark Twain and the Literary Misfortunes of JWDeF." *JA*, 13: 249-52 (1968).

Dempsey, David. "The Brothers' War, Viewed from the Yankee Side." *NYT*, 28 Jl 46, pp. 7, 22.

*Eichelberger, C.L., *et al.* "JWDeF (1826-1906): A Critical Bibliography of Secondary Comment." *ALR*, 4: 1-56 (Fa 68).

Gargano, J.W. "JW.DeF and the Critics." *ALR*, 1: 57-64 (Fa 68).

―――. "A Thematic Analysis of *Miss Ravenel*." *Topic*, 1: 40-7 (Fa 61).

*Hagemann, E.R. "A Checklist of Critical Comments in *The Nation* on JW.DeF, 1866-1879." *ALR*, 4: 76-9 (1968).

―――. 'JW.DeF Faces *The Nation*." *ALR*, 1: 65-75 (Fa 68).

―――. "A JWDeF Supplement, 1970." *ALR*, 3: 148-52 (Sp 70).

Hansen, Chadwick. "Salem Witchcraft and DeF's *Witching Times*." *EIHC*, 104: 89-108 (Ap 68).

Hendricks, King. "*Miss Ravenel*." *WHR*, 9: 370 (Au 55).

Howells, W.D. "Some Heroines of Fiction." *Harpers*, 35: 538-44 (O 01).

Katz, Joseph. "JWDef on Stephen Crane." *SCraneN*, 4: 6 (Fa 70).

Liebling, A.J. "The Dollars Damned Him." *NY*, 37: 48-72 (5 Ag 61).

Matthews, Brander. "Best Sellers of Long Ago." *NYT*, 5 S 20, pp. 1, 19.

Moffitt, Cecil. "*Miss Ravenel's Conversion* and *Pilgrim's Progress*." *CE*, 22: 352-7 (F 62).

Orians, G.H. "New England Witchcraft in Fiction." *AL*, 2: 54-71 (Mr 30).

Porter, D.M. "JWDeF." *Papers New Hist Soc*, 10: 188-203 (1951).

Robillard, Douglas. "DeF Literary Manuscripts in the Yale Library." *ALR*, 4: 81-3 (Wi 68).

*Rogers, B.M. "JWD." *ALR*, 8: 244-6 (1975).

Sessler, H.M. "A Test for Realism in DeF's *Kate Beaumont*." *ALR*, 2: 274-76 (Fa 69).

Starr, H.E. "*Union Officer*." *AHR*, 54: 214 (O 48).

Stone, A.E. "Best Novel of the Civil War." *AH*, 13: 84-8 (Je 62).

Wilson, Edmund. "DeF: A Roman of the Civil War." *NY*, 22: 65-7 (10 Ag 46).

Delany, Martin. Fleming, R.E. "Black, White, and Mulatto in MD's *Blake*." *NHB*, 36: 37-9 (1973).

Haskett, N.D. "Afro-American Images of Africa: Four *Antebellum* Black Authors." *Ufahamu*, 3: 29-40 (1972).

Hite, R.W. "'Stand Still and See the Salvation': The Rhetorical Design of MD's *Blake*." *JBlackS*, 5: 192-202 (D 74).

Samuelson, D.N. "A Comparative Study of Novels by Brunner and D." *Extrapolation*, 15: 75-96 (1973).

Zeugner, John. "A Note on MD's *Blake* and Black Militancy." *Phylon*, 32: 98-105 (Sp 71).

Delany, S.R. Miesel, Sandra. "SRD's Use of Myth in *Nova*." *Extrapolation*, 12: 86-93 (My 71).

Scobie, Stephen. "Different Mazes: Mythology in SRD's 'The Einstein Intersection.'" *RQ*, 5: 12-8 (Jl 71).

Dell, Floyd. Carpenter, Margaret. "FD and His Poetry." *MTJ*, 14: 1 (Su 69).

Dixon, Park. "Community and Self in the Midwest Town: FD's Moon Calf." *M-A*, 2: 88-92 (1975).

Flanagan, J.T. "A Letter from FD." *AL*, 45: 441-52 (N 73).

Marriner, G.L. "FD: Freedom or Marriage." *M-A*, 2: 63-78 (1975).

Demby, William. Bone, Robert. "WD's Dance of Life." *TriQ*, 15: 127-41 (Sp 69).

Hoffman, N.Y. "The Annunciation of WD." *SBL*, 3: 8-13 (Sp 72).

———. "Technique in D's *The Catacombs*." *SBL*, 2: 10-3 (1971).

O'Brien, John. "Interview with WD." *SBL*, 3: 1-6 (Au 72).

Denton, Daniel. Rooney, G.F. "DD, Publicist of Early New York." *NYHSQ*, 55: 272-5 (Jl 71).

Dennie, Joseph. Roth, Martin. "Laurence Sterne in America." *BNYPL*, 74: 428-36 (S 70).

Derleth, August. Carter, Paul. "Of Towns and Roads: Three Novelists, and George McGovern." *ColF*, 2: 10-6 (Sp 73).

*De Waal, R.B. "Solar Pons and Dr. Parker: A Bibliography 1929-1969." *ABC*, 20: 19-26 (My 70).

DeVoto, Bernard. Cousins, Norman. "The Controversial Mr. DV." *SatR*, 6 Ap 74, pp. 5-7.

Jones, A.H. "The Persistence of the Progressive Mind: The Case of BDV." *AmS*, 12: 37-48 (Sp 71).

Rubin, L.D. "BDV All Told." *SR*, 83: 149-60 (Wi 75).

Sawey, Orlan. "BDV's Western Novels." *WAL*, 2: 171-82 (Fa 67).

Stegner, Wallace. "DV's Western Adventures." *AmWest*, 10: 20-7 (N 73).

———. "Historian by Serendipity." *AH*, 24: 28-32, 92-96 (A 73).

Tanselle, G.T. "*Typee* and D: A Footnote." *PBSA* 64: 207-9 (2Q 70).

Walker, D.D. "The Dogmas of D." *PosS*, 2: 6-8 (Ag 71); 3: 1-7 (N 71); 3: 1-4 (F 72); 3: 14-8 (Mr 72).

De Vries, Peter. Challenger, Craig. "PDV: The Case for Comic Seriousness." *SAH*, 1: 40-51 (Ap 74).

De Vries, Peter. "What's All That About Commuters?" *NYHT*, 30 Ag 59, p. 2.

Hasley, Louis. "The Hamlet of PDV: To Wit or Not to Wit." *SAQ*, 70: 467-76 (Au 71).

Rodewald, Fred. "The Comic *Eiron* in the Later Novels of PDV." *Quartet*, 6: 34-9 (Wi 73).

Rome, J.J. "PDV: Compassionate Satirist." *UES*, 9: 23-9 (1971).

Sale, R.B. "An Interview in New York with PDV." *StN*, 1: 364-9 (Fa 69).

Walsh, William. "The Combination in the Safe." *Encounter*, 40: 74-80 (Ja 73).

Dewey, John. *Boydston, J.A. "The JD Bibliography." *PBSA*, 62: 67-75 (1Q 68).

———. "The JD Papers Come to SIU-C." *ICarbS*, 1: 26-33 (1973).

Morgan, Jack and S.S. Shermis. "Origin, Theory, and Practice: D's Early Philosophy." *MASJ*, 11: 65-79 (1970).

Reboul, Olivier. "JD, pedagogue de l'homme unidimensionnel." *CritP*, 26: 759-73 (Ag-S 70).

Dick, Richard K. *McNelly, W.E., et al. "RHD." *SSF*, 2: 4-75 (1975).

Dickey, James. Anon. "Craft Interview with JD." *NYQ*, 10: 17-35 (1972).

———. "JD: Worksheets." *MalR*, 7: 113-7 (1968).

———. "Journey into Self." *Time*, 95: 92-3 (20 Ap 70).

Armour, Robert. "*Deliverance*: Four Variations of the American Adam." *LFQ*, 1: 280-5 (19730.

Arnett, David. "An Interview with JD." *ConL*, 16: 286-300 (Su 75).

Baker, D.W. "The Poetry of JD." *Poetry*, 111: 400-1 (Mr 68).

Barroff, Marie. "Creativity, Poetic Language, and the Computer." *YR*, 60: 481-513 (Je 71).

Beidler, P.G. "'The Pride of Thine Heart Hath Deceived Thee': Narrative Distortion in D's *Deliverance*." *SCR*, 5: 43-9 (D 72).

Bennett, Ross. "Orion with Green Eyes: JD's Poems of Hunting." *EL*, 2: 28-47 (Ag 74).

Berry, D.C. "Harmony with the Dead: JD's Descent into the Underworld." *SoQ*, 12: 233-44 (Ap 74).

Bleikasten, Andre. "Anatomie d'un Bestseller: à propos de *Deliverance*." *Ranam*, 4: 116-29 (1971).

Bly, Robert. "*Buckdancer's Choice*." *Sixties*, 9: 70-9 (1967).

Calhoun, R.J. "His Reason Argues with His Invention: JD's *Self Interview* and *The Eye-Beaters*." *SCR*, 3: 9-16 (Je 71).

———. "Whatever Happened to the Poet-Critic?" *SLJ*, 1: 75-88 (Au 68).

Carroll, Paul. "JD as Critic." *ChiR*, 20: 82-8 (Mr 69).

Clemons, W. "JD, Novelist." *NYT*, 22 Mr 70, p. 22.

Corrington, J.W. "JD's Poems: 1957-1967." *GaR*, 22: 12-23 (Sp 68).

Coulthard, Ron. "From Manuscript to Movie Script: JD's *Deliverance*." *NCLit*, 3: 11-2 (N 73).

———. "Reflections upon a Golden Eye: JD's *Deliverance*." *NCLit*, 3: 13-5 (S 73).

"Crunk." "The Work of JD." *Sixties*, 7: 41-75 (1964).

DeMott, Benjamin. "The 'More Life' School and JD." *SatR*, 53: 25-6, 38 (28 Mr 70).

Dempsey, Michael. "*Deliverance*/Boorman: D in the Woods." *Cinema*, 8: 10-7 (Sp 73).

Dickey, James. "Comments to Accompany *Poems: 1957-67*." *BaratR*, 3: 9-15 (1968).

Donald, D.H. "Love and Lust in D's *Deliverance*." *GaR*, 29: 184-7 (1975).

Edwards, C.H. "D's *Deliverance*: The Owl and the Eye." *Critique*, 15: 95-101 (#2 73).

———. "A Foggy Scene in *Deliverance*." *NCLit*, 2: 7-9 (N 72).

Eyster, Warren. "Two Regional Novels." *SR*, 79: 469-74 (1971).

Fukuda, Rikutaro. "JD no Shi to Shiron." *EigoS*, 114: 576-7 (1968).

Garner, P. "The Deliverance Syndrome." *Atlanta Journal and Constitution Mag.*, 18 N 73, pp. 16-8, 23-34.

George, S.K. "JD's *Winter Trout*." *Cont Poetry*, 1: 23-6 (Sp 73).

*Glancy, E.K. "JD: A Bibliography." *TCL*, 15: 45-61 (Ap 69).

Greiner, D.J. "The Harmony of Bestiality in JD's *Deliverance*." *SCR*, 5: 43-9 (D 72).

Guillory, D.L. "Water Magic in the Poetry of JD." *ELN*, 8: 131-7 (D 70).

Heyen, William. "A Converstion with JD." *SoR*, 9: 135-56 (Wi 73).

Italia, Paul. "Love and Lust in JD's *Deliverance*." *MFS*, 21: 203-14 (Su 75).

James, Frederic. "The Great American Hunter, or, Ideological Content in the Novel." *CE*, 34: 180-97 (N 72).

Landess, Thomas. "Traditionalist Criticism and the Poetry of JD." *Occasional R*, 3: 12-26 (Su 75).

Libby, Anthony. "Fire and Light: Four Poets to the End and Beyond." *IowaR*, 4: 111-26 (Sp 73).

Lieberman, Laurence. "The Expansional Poet: A Return to Personality." *YR*, 57: 258-71 (Wi 68).

———. "Note on JD's Style." *FarP*, 2: 57-63 (Sp-Su 69).

Lindborg, G.A. "Ecology in Arcadia." *ColQ*, 21: 175-85 (1972).

McGinnis, W.D. "Mysticism in the Poetry of JD." *NLauR*, 5: 5-10 (#1-2 75).

Marin, D.B. "JD's *Deliverance*: Darkness Visible." *SCR*, 3: 49-59 (1970).

Markos, D.W. "Art and Immediacy: JD's *Deliverance*." *SoR*, 7: 947-53 (Su 71).

Mills, R.J. "The Poetry of JD." *TriQ*, 11: 231-42 (Wi 68).

Morris, Harry. "A Formal View of the Poetry of D, Garrigue, and Simpson." *SR*, 77: 318-25 (1969).

Niflis, N.M. "A Special Kind of Fantasy: JD on the Razor's Edge." *SWR*, 57: 311-7 (Au 72).

Oates, J.C. "Out of Stone into Flesh: The Imagination of JD." *MPS*, 5: 97-144 (Au 74).

O'Neil, Paul. "The Unlikeliest Poet." *Life*, 22 Jl 66, pp. 68-70, 72-9.

Roberts, J.K. "Terror Lumped and Split: Contemporary British and American Poets." *SoR*, 6: 216-28 (Wi 70).

Samuels, C.T. "What Hath D Delivered?" *NRep*, 162: 23-6 (18 Ap 70).

Shepherd, Allen. "Counter-Monster Comes Home: The Last Chapter of JD's *Deliverance*." *NCLit*, 3: 8-12 (Mr 73).

Silverstein, Norman. "JD's Muscular Eschatology." *Salmagundi*, 22-23: 258-68 (1973).

Skelton, Robin. "The Poetic Faith of JD." *MalR*, 4: 119-24 (O 67).

Smith, Raymond. "The Poetic Faith of JD." *MPS*, 2: 259-72 (1972).

Stephenson, William. *Deliverance* from What?" *GaR*, 27: 114-20 (Sp 74).

Verburg, Larry. "Water Imagery in JD's *Deliverance*." *NConL*, 4: 11-3 (N 74).

Westendorp, T.A. "Recent Southern Fiction: Percy, Price and D." *HVF*, 1974, pp. 188-98.

Willig, Charles L. "Ed's Transformation: A Note on *Deliverance*." *NCLit*, 3: 4-5 (Mr 73).

Yardley, Jonathan. "More of Superpoet." *NRep*, 163: 26-7 (5 D 70).

Dickinson, Emily. Anon. "Correction." *AL*, 45: 117 (Mr 73).

———. "French Material." *EDB*, 13: 51-5 (Je 70).

———. "Germanic Material." *EDB*, 14: 58-66 (S 70).

———. "Italian Material with Introduction." *EDB*, 12: 7-13 (Mr 70).

———. "Our Poetical New England Nun." *Lit Dig*, 82: 34 (2 Ag 24).

Abenius, Margit. "ED." *BLM*, 3: 18-23 (S 34).

Adair, V.H. "D's 'Death Is a Dialogue Between.'" *Expl*, 27: 52 (Mr 69).

Adkins, C.A. "ED's 'Would You Like Summer? Taste of Our's': A Note on the Composition Date." *ELN*, 7: 53-5 (S 69).

Ando, Midori. "On Death in the Poems of ED." *Gakuen*, 276: 56-66 (D 62).

Arms, George. "D's 'There's a Certain Slant of Light.'" *Expl*, 2: 29 (1944).

Asals, Frederick. "D's 'Two Butterflies Went Out at Noon.'" *ESQ*, 63: 29-31 (Sp 71).

Avery, Christine. "Science, Technology, and ED." *Bul British, Assoc Am Stud*, 8: 47-55 (1964).

Axelrod, Steven. "Terror in the Everyday: ED's ('I Years Had Been From Home') (609)." *CP*, 6: 53-6 (Sp 73).

Babbage, S.B. "A Question of Color." *ChSR*, 1: 41-5 (Fa 70).

Baldi, Sergio. "The Poetry of ED." *SR*, 68: 438-49 (Su 60).

Baldini, Gabriele. "Tre Secoli di Poesia Americana." *NA*, 82: 392-4 (1947).

Ball, K.R. "ED and the Beautiful." *SHR*, 7: 287-94 (1973).

Bennett, J.Q. "A Footnote to Mr. White's Article on ED's *Poems: Third Series*." *Serif*, 9: 41-2 (1972).

Berenson, Adrienne. "ED's Social Attitudes: A Dissenting View." *WHR*, 6: 351-62 (1952).

Berner, R.L. "D's 'These Are the Days when Birds Come Back.'" *Expl*, 30: 78 (1972).

Bingham, M.T. "ED's Earliest Friend." *AL*, 6: 191-2 (1934).

Blanding, Thomas. "Emily's Bark and Emerson's Book: *Representative Men* as a Source for a D Poem." *ConS*, 6: 10-2 (S 71).

Bolin, D.W. "D's 'A Clock Stopped.'" *Expl*, 22: 27 (1963).

Bouraoui, H.A. "'Leaning against the Sun': ED, the Poet as Seer." *RSW*, 37: 208-17 (S 69).

Bowman, Elizabeth. "D's 'The Soul Selects Her Own Society.'" *Expl*, 29: 13 (O 70).

Bridgman, Richard. "ED: A Winter Poet in a Spring Land." *MSpr*, 56: 1-8 (1962).

Brooks, V.W. "ED." *Scholastic*, 28: 17-9, 22 (10 Mr 41).

Brunel, Pierre. "Le Corbeau (à Propos de la Transposition par Claudel d'une Poeme d'ED)." *RLM*, 134-6: 113-8 (1966).

*Buckingham, W.J. "The Bibliographical Study of ED." *RALS*, 4: 57-71 (1974).

*———. "1880-1968 Addenda to the Buckingham Bibliography." *EDB*, 26: 103-28 (1974).

*———. "A New Bibliography of ED in Japan." *EDB*, 28: 104-5 (1975).

Bulgheroni, Marisa. "L'Eterno Giardino di Emily." *SA*, 8: 77-92 (1962).

Burns, Graham. "ED's Creative Passivity." *CR*, 16: 73-90 (1973).

Cambon, Glauco. "L'Edizione Critica di ED." *Aut Aut*, 32: 155-64 (1956).

———. "Violence and Abstraction in ED." *SR*, 68: 450-64 (Su 60).

Cameron, K.W. "ED and Hesperian Depression." *ATQ*, 14: 184-5 (Sp 72).

Capoor, M.G. "Compound Vision: ED." *NASRC*, 11: 28-35 (1969).

Carson, Mother Angela. "Dickinson's 'Safe in Their Alabaster Chambers.'" *Expl*, 17: 62 (1959).

Catto, Brenda. "D's 'As Watchers Hang Upon the East.'" *Expl*, 33: 55 (Mr 75).

Chaliff, Cynthia. "*After Great Pain: The Inner Life of ED*." *L&P*, 22: 45-7 (1972).

———. "ED as the Deprived Child." *EDB*, 13: 34-43 (Je 70).

———. "The Psychology of Economics in ED." *L&P*, 18: 93-100 (1968).

Chase, Richard. "A Poet's Economy." *Hopkins R*, 5: 34-7 (1951).

Chrysostom, Sister Mary. "'Pang is Good': The Gamut of Joy in ED's Poems." *WSL*, 3: 24-36 (1966).

*Clendenning, S.T., et al. "ED: Annual Bibliography." *EDB*, Annually, 1968-.

Cody, John. "ED and Nature's Dining Room." *MQR*, 7: 249-54 (Fa 68).

———. "Metamorphosis of a Malady: Summary of a Psychoanalytic Study of ED." *HSL*, 2: 113-32 (1970).

———. "Mourner among the Children." *Psychiatric Q*, 41: 12-37, 231-61 (1967).

———. "Watchers upon the East: The Ocular Complaints of ED." *Psychiatric Q*, 42: 548-76 (1968).

Cohen, Hennig. "D's 'I Taste a Liquor Never Brewed.'" *Expl*, 33: 41 (Ja 75).

Cunningham, D.H. "ED's 'I Heard a Fly Buzz. . . .'" *AN&Q*, 6: 150-1 (Je 68).

Cunningham, J.V. "ED's "Sorting Out: The Case of D." *SoR*, 5: 436-56 (Sp 69).

Curran, George. "ED and Religion." *Smith Col Mo*, 2: 7-9 (N 41).

Daghlian, Carlos. "ED and Fernando Pessoa: Two Poets for Posterity." *EDB*, 18: 66-72 (1971).

———. "ED in the Brazilian Classroom." *EDB*, 24: 227-30 (1973).

Dailey, M.A. "The Locomotive as Visualized by Walt Whitman and ED." *Let*, 6: 23-5 (1965).

Darden, G.M. "Emily's House." *Yankee*, 38: 74-9 (My 74).

Das, Sarbeswar. "ED's Art and Sensibility." *ModR*, 124-5: 782-8 (O 69).

———. "ED's Letters to Her 'Master.'" *CalR*, 2: 353-63 (Mr 71).

D'Avanzo, M.L. "D's 'The Reticent volcano' and Emerson." *ATQ*, 14: 11-3 (Sp 72).

———"The Emersonian Context of Three Poems by ED." *EDB*, 16: 2-7 (Mr 71).

———. "Emersonian Revelation in 'The Way I read a Letter's—this—'" *ATQ*, 17: 14-5 (Wi 73).

———. "ED's and Emerson's 'Presentiment.'" *ESQ*, 58: 157-9 (1Q 70).

———. "'Unto the White Creator': The Snow of D and Emerson." *NEQ*, 45: 278-80 (Je 72).

Delgado-Arias, D.E. "ED: Espiritu Esoterico." *Bitacora*, 2: 25-36 (1943).

Ditsky, John. "The Wildness of D's 'Wild Nights!'" *LakeUR*, 4: 50-6 (Sp 71).

Dickinson, Emily

Donaldson, Scott. "Minding ED's Business." *NEQ*, 41: 574-82 (D 68).

Doyle, C.M. "ED's 'The Wind Blew Off.'" *ELN*, 12: 182-3 (Mr 75).

Drew, D.P. "Emily Bronte and ED as Mystic Poets." *BST*, 15: 227-32 (1968).

Elliott, G.D. "A Note on D's 'I Cautious, Scanned My Little Life.'" *MarkR*, 2: 78-9 (O 70).

———. "The Solitary Dissenter: A Study of ED's Concept of God." *EDB*, 20: 32-48 (1972).

England, M.W. "ED and Issac Watts: Puritan Hymnodists." *BNYPL*, 69: 83-116 (1965).

Eulert, Donald. "ED's Certain Slant of Light." *ATQ*, 14: 164-6 (Sp 72).

Faber, M.D. "Psychoanalytic Remarks on a Poem by ED." *PsyR*, 56: 247-64 (1969).

Faris, Paul. "Eroticism in ED's 'Wild Nights.'" *NEQ*, 40: 269-74 (Je 67).

Ferlazzo, P.J. "The Deadly Beau in Two Poems by ED." *EDB*, 19: 133-8 (1971).

Feuillerat, Albert. "La Vie Secrète d'Une Puritaine: ED." *RDM*, 40: 668-91 (1927).

Fickert, K.J. "ED in German." *HJP*, 8: 20 (Je 74).

———. "14 ED Poems." *EDB*, 26: 77-82 (1974).

Finch, John. "Poet of the Thing Missed." *Smith Col Mo*, 2: 10, 27 (N 41).

Fisher, C.J. "ED as a Latter-Day Metaphysical Poet." *ATQ*, 1: 77-81 (1Q 69).

Fitzgerald, Sister Ellen. "D's 'The Tint I Cannot Take Is Best.'" *Expl*, 28: 29 (N 69).

Flory, W.S. "Rehearsals for Dying in Poe and ED." *ATQ*, 18: 13-8 (Sp 73).

Folsom, L.E. "'The Souls That Snow': Winter in the Poetry of ED." *AL*, 47: 361-76 (N 75).

Ford, T.W. "Thoreau's Cosmic Mosquito and D's Fly." *NEQ*, 48: 487-504 (D 75).

Forde, Sister Victoria. "D's 'No Brigadier Throughout the Year.'" *Expl*, 27: 41 (F 69).

Franklin, R.W. "Two ED Manuscripts." *PBSA*, 69: 114-5 (1Q 75).

Gafundo, A.M. "Vidat Obra de ED." *HJP*, 8: 17 (Je 74).

Garrison, J.M. "ED: From Ballerina to Gymnast." *ELH*, 42: 107-24 (1975).

Garrow, Scott. "Alcoholic Beverage Imagery in the Poems of ED." *MarkR*, 2: 12-6 (S 69).

Gillespie, Robert. "A Circumference of ED." *NEQ*, 46: 250-71 (Je 73).

Goldsmith, J.H. "Inspired, Half-Educated, Puritan, and Feminine." *PR*, 12: 402-4 (1945).

Gooch, O.D. "Likenesses of ED." *EDB*, 14: 77 (1970).

Goudie, Andrea. "Another Path to Reality: ED's Birds." *CP*, 7: 31-8 (Sp 74).

Green, C.R. "Poetry about ED." *BB*, 20: 114-5 (1951).

Greene, Elsa. "ED Was a Poetess." *CE*, 34: 63-70 (O 72).

Griffith, Clark. "ED and *Him*: A Modern Approach to ED's Love Poetry." *IEY*, 6: 13-22 (1961).

———. "The Inner Life of ED." *SoR*, 9: 468-75 (Ja 73).

Grolnick, S.A. "Emily and the Psychobiographer." *L&P*, 23: 68-91 (1973).

Gross, J.J. "Tell All the Truth But—" *BSUF*, 10: 71-7 (Wi 69).

Grover, D.C. "Garland's 'ED'—A Case of Mistaken Identity." *AL*, 46: 219-20 (My 74).

Guidetti, Paolo. "La Fortuna di ED en Italia (1933-1962)." *SA*, 9: 121-72 (1963).

Gullans, Charles, and John Espey. "ED: Two Uncollected Poems." *AL*, 44: 306-7 (My 72).

Hagenbuchle, Roland. "Precision and Indeterminacy in the Poetry of ED." *ESQ*, 20: 33-56 (1Q 74).

Hagerup, Inger. "ED." *Vindue*, 28, 2: 43-6 (#2 74).

Hampson, A.L. "ED: Evidence of the Authenticity of Her 'Further Poems.'" *Boston Evening Transcript*, 3 Ag 29; p. 3.

Hansen, Waldemar. "Land Ho! Infinity!: ED as a Protestant Telescope." *Horizon*, 17: 71-6 (1948).

Harvey, N.L. "D's 'What Soft Cherubic Creatures.'" *Expl*, 28: 17 (O 69).

Hauser, C.J. "D's 'I Taste a Liquor Never Brewed.'" *Expl*, 31: 2 (S 72).

Heiskanen-Makela, Sirkka. "ED in Finland." *HJP*, 8: 18-9 (Je 74).

Henry, Nat. "D's 'As by the Dead We Love to Sit.'" *Expl*, 31: 35 (Ja 73).

Herget, W. "D's 'I Never Saw a Moor.'" *Expl*, 30: 55 (Mr 72).

Hijiya, J.A. "That Rascal ED." *EDB*, 24: 224-6 (1973).

Hijiya, J.A. "New England Women and Madness." *EIHC*, 111: 228-39 (1975).

Hill, Archibald. "Figurative Structure and Meaning: Two Poems by ED." *TSLL*, 16: 195-210 (Sp 74).

Hillyer, Robert. "The Later ED." *HH*, 2: 423-5 (1929).

Himelhoch, Myra, and Rebecca Patterson. "The Dating of ED's Letters to the Bowles Family, 1858-1862." *EDB*, 20: 1-28 (1972).

Holmes, Theodore, "The Voice of a Poet: The Art of ED." *DR*, 48: 551-5 (1968-9).

Horiuchi, Amy. "ED's Existentialism." *EDB*, 19: 100-14 (1971).

———. "ED's 'Gods' in the Plurality." *HJP*, 8: 13-6 (Je 74).

Houghton, D.E. "D's 'The Butterfly Obtains.'" *Expl*, 27: 5 (S 68).

Howard, Mabel. "D's 'Safe in Their Alabaster Chambers.'" *Expl*, 12: 41 (1954).

Howard, Richard. "A Consideration of the Writings of ED." *Prose*, 6: 67-97 (Sp 73).

Hungville, Maurice. "Creation and Salvation: A Study in the Pain Images in the Major Themes." *EDB*, 24: 231-3 (1973).

Johnson, T.H. "ED: The Prisms of a Poet." *SatR*, 33: 16-7 (3 Je 50).

———. "D's 'Immured in Heaven.'" *Expl*, 11: 36 (1953).

Jumper, W.C. "D's 'The Soul Selects Her Own Society.'" *Expl*, 29: 5 (1970).

Juvonen, Helvi. "ED." *Parnassus*, 7: 245-9 (1958).

Kauffmann, J.S. "ED and the Involvement of Retreat." *TSE*, 21: 77-90 (1974).

Keefer, Frederick and Deborah Vlahos. "D's 'If you were coming in the Fall.'" *Expl*, 29: 23 (1970).

Kerr, W.H. "A Portfolio of Paranoiac Poems." *HJP*, 8: 21-3 (Je 74).

Kher, I.N. "ED Scholarship: Some Fugitive References 1969-70." *HJP*, 8: 11-2 (Je 74).

———. "*The Landscape of Absence* Abstract." *HJP*, 8: 4 (Je 74).

———. "The Poet and the Existential Reality." *HJP*, 8: 5-10 (Je 74).

Kintgen, E.R. "Nonrecoverable Deletion and Compression in Poetry." *FLang*, 9: 98-104 (1972).

Kohn, J.S. vanE. "Giving ED to the World." *PULC*, 31: 47-54 (Au 69).

Lackey, A.D. "D's 'I never lost as much but twice.'" *Expl*, 34: 18 (N 75).

Larkin, Philip. "Big Victims: ED and Walter de la Mare." *NSt*, 13 Mr 70, pp. 376-7.

Lavin, J.A. "ED and Brazil." *NEQ*, 205: 270-1 (1960).

Lawrence, R.R. "The Mind Alone." *EDB*, 15: 94-102 (S 70); 17: 34-44 (Je 71); 22: 107-24 (S-D 72).

Ledwell, Sister Marguerite. "Some Historical Criticism of D's Poetry." *SALit*, 8: 1-14 (1972).

Lee, A.P. "ED and Her Family Tree." *DARM*, 65:471-7 (1931).

Lee, M.C. "A Comparative Analysis of Selected Nature Poetry of ED and Sol Wol Kim." *SLRJ*, 6: 333-73 (1975).

Lensing, George. "D's 'I Started Early—Took My Dog.'" *Expl*, 31: 30 (D 72).

Levin, S.R. "The Analysis of Compression in Poetry." *FLang*, 7: 38-55 (F 71).

———. "Die Analyse des 'komprimierten' Stils in der Poesie." *LiLi*, 1: 59-80 (1971).

———. "Reply to Kintgen." *FLang*, 9: 105-12 (1972).

Lewis, Stuart. "D's 'The Lamp Burns Sure Within' and 'The Poets Light but Lamps.'" *Expl*, 28: 4 (S 69).

Lingberg-Seyersted, Brita. "Further Notes on a Poem by ED." *N&Q*, 15: 179-80 (My 68).

Lobo Filho, Blanca. "The Poetry of ED and Henriqueta Lisboa." *Proc Northwest Conference on Foreign Lang*, 26: 150-3 (#1 75).

Dickinson, Emily

López Narvaez, Carlos. "Recuerdo de ED." *Nivel*, 47: 9 (1966).

Lowrey, R.E. "'Boaerges': An Encomium for Edward Dickinson." *ArQ*, 26: 54-8 (Sp 70).

Lubbock, Percy. "Determined Little Anchoress." *N&E*, 36: 114 (1924).

Luisi, David. "Some Aspects of ED's Food and Liquor Poems." *ES*, 52: 32-40 (F 71).

Lungu, Lelia. "ED: The Bee." *Limba Germanice*, 21: 115-23 (1972).

———. "Processele de abstractizare si schematizare, sursa de sporire a informatiei la nivelui limbajului poetic." *AUBLG*, 22: 35-42 (1973).

Lyons, Eleanor. "A Psychiatric Look at ED." *HSL*, 4: 174-9 (1972).

McCall, Dan. "'I Felt a Funeral in My Brain' and 'The Hollow of the Three Hills.'" *NEQ*, 42: 432-5 (S 69).

McLean, S.R. "ED at Mount Holyoke." *NEQ*, 7: 25-42 (Sp 34).

Marcellino, Ralph. "Cato and ED." *Classical Outlook*, 35: 55-6 (1958).

———. "ED." *NYHT*, 12: 22 (3 My 36).

———. "D's 'The Show That Never Drifts.'" *Expl*, 13: 36 (1955).

Melani, Sandro. "L'epifania della morte in ED." *SA*, 17: 7-29 (1971).

Metzger, C.R. "ED's Shy Bird." *ESQ*, 44: 21-2 (1966).

Michel, Pierre. "The Last Stanza of ED's 'One dignity delays for all—.'" *ES*, 50: 98-100 (F 69).

Miller, F.D. "ED: Self-Portrait in the Third Person." *NEQ*, 46: 119-24 (Mr 73).

Miller, J.E. "ED's Bright Orthography." *HudR*, 14: 301-6 (1961).

Miller, Perry. "ED: The Shunning of Joy." *Reporter*, 18: 34-6 (29 My 58).

Miura, Tokuhiko. "ED's Poetry: The Way to Nirvana." *EibunG*, 14: 1-20 (1971).

Mizejewski, Linda. "Reply to Laurence Perrine." *CE*, 36: 213 (1974).

———. "Sappho to Sexton." *CE*, 35: 340-5 (1973).

Molson, F.J. "ED's Rejection of the Heavenly Father." *NEQ*, 47: 404-26 (S 74).

Monteiro, George. "Ana Maria Gafundo's *Vida y Obra de ED*." *HJP*, 8: 17 (1974).

*———. "Brazil's ED: An Annotated Checklist of Translations, Criticism, and Reviews." *EDB*, 18: 73-8 (1971).

———. "Buckingham's ED Bibliography." *EDB*, 20: 28-30 (1972).

———. "ED and Brazil." *N&Q*, 207: 312-3 (1962).

———. "D's 'I Never Lost as Much but Twice.'" *Expl*, 30: 7 (Ja 71).

———. "D's 'On this wondrous sea.'" *Expl*, 33: 74 (My 75).

———. "D's 'There's a Certain Slant of Light.'" *Expl*, 31: 13 (O 72).

———. "Hispanic Additions to Woodbridge." *EDB*, 18: 72-3 (1971).

———. "*McNaught's Monthly*: Addenda to the Bibliographies of D, [and others]." *PBSA*, 68: 64-5 (1Q 74).

———. "The One and Many EDs." *ALR*, 7: 137-43 (Sp 74).

———. "Re Ms D." *EDB*, 26: 73-5 (1974).

More, F.L. "Jungian D." *EDB*, 27: 4-72 (1975).

Morey, F.L. "The Austin Dickinson-Mabel Todd Relationship." *HJP*, 3: 67-76 (1973).

———. "Eleven Major Themes Discovered in 356 Important Poems." *EDB*, 16: 22-26 (Mr 71); 17: 28-33 (Je 71).

———. "ED as a Modern." *EDB*, 25: 5-39 (1974).

———. "ED Treasures in the Library of Congress." *EDB*, 22: 125-7 (1972).

———. "Evaluation of Japanese Dickinsonian Scholarship." *EDB*, 21: 57-77 (1972).

———. "The Fifty Best Poems of ED: A Three-Chapter Study." *EDB*, 25: 5-38 (1974).

———. "The Four Fundamental Archetypes in Mythology, as Exemplified in ED's Poems." *EDB*, 24: 195-206 (1973).

———. "French Material." *EDB*, 13: 51-5 (Je 70).

————. "From Reading to Publishing ED: The Pre-natal History of the EDB." *EDB*, 22: 128-30 (1972).

————. "Germanic Material." *EDB*, 14: 58-67 (1970).

————. "The Humorous Publications of ED." *EDB*, 3: 1-2 (1968).

————. "Hundred Best Poems of ED." *EDB*, 27: 5-78 (1975).

————. "Japanese Evaluation." *EDB*, 21: 57-60 (1972).

————. "Major ED Collections." *EDB*, 2: 1-2 (1968).

————. "Minor Collections." *EDB*, 4: 2-9 (1968).

————. "Miscellaneous Addendum to Buckingham." *EDB*, 21: 75-7 (1972).

————. "Miscellaneous Languages." *EDB*, 21: 60-4 (1972).

————. "More on D." *HJP*, 12: 45-8 (1975).

————. "Placing D in a School." *Mark R*, 5: 18-20 (My 69).

————. "The Poetry Levels of ED." *MarkR*, 2: 74-8 (O 70).

————. "Reader's Edition: History and Suggestions." *EDB*, 23: 144-55 (1973).

————. "Reference Books of the 1970's Shore Up ED's Reputation." *EDB*, 23: 172-83 (1973).

Mullican, J.S. "D's 'Praise It—'Tis Dead.'" *Expl*, 27: 62 (Ap 69).

————. "D's 'Water Makes Many Beds.'" *Expl*, 27: 23 (N 68).

Mulqueen, J. McC. "Is Emerson's Work Central to the Poetry of ED?" *EDB*: 24: 211-20 (1973).

Nakao, Kiyoaki. "ED's 'Irreverence.'" *ALR*, 19: 5-8 (1957).

Neff, J.A. "The Door Ajar." *EDB*, 21: 78-81 (1972).

Noble, D.R. "D to Roth." *AN&Q*, 9: 150-1 (1971).

Noda, Hisashi. "ED and Transcendentalism." *KAL*, 11: 44-58 (1968).

Noel, J. "A Critique of S.R. Levin's *Analysis of Compression in Poetry*." *RLV*, 39: 231-8 (1973).

Normand, Jean. "ED: Une aventure poétique." *EA*, 21: 152-9 (Ap-Je 68).

Noverr, D.A. "ED and the Art of Despair." *EDB*, 23: 161-7 (1973).

Nguyen-Khúc-Nha. "ED and the Renascence of Poetry in the United States." *Culture Mo R*, 13: 131-5, 294-306 (1964).

Ochshorn, Myron. "D's 'I Know Some Lonely Houses off the Road." *Expl*, 11: 12 (1952).

*Omoto, Tsuyoshi. "ED: A Bibliography; Writings in Japan." *Jinbunkagaku-Nenepo*, 3: 113-42 (1973); *Jinbunagaku Kenkyusho Geppi*, 40-1: 1-6 (1975).

Packard, J.K. "The Christ Figure in D's Poetry." *Renascence*, 22: 26-33 (1969).

Parsons, T.H. "The Indefatigable Casuits." *UR*, 30: 19-25 (1963).

Patterson, Rebecca. "The Cardinal Points Symbolism of ED." *MwQ*, 14: 293-317 (Jl 73); 15: 31-48 (O 73).

————. "ED's 'Double' Tim: Masculine Identification." *AL*, 28: 330-62 (Wi 71).

————. "ED's Geography: Latin America." *PLL*, 5: 441-57 (1969).

————. "ED's Jewel Imagery." *AL*, 42: 495-520 (Ja 71).

————. "On Dating D's Poems." *AN&Q*, 12: 84-6 (F 74).

Pebworth, Ted-Larry, and J.C. Summers, "D's 'The Feet of People Walking Home.'" *Expl*, 27: 76 (My 69).

————. "The Lusterware on D's Silver Shelf." *AN&Q*, 12: 18 (O 73).

Peckham, R.W. "This Colossal Substance." *EDB*, 28: 112-23 (D 75).

Perkins, J.A. "What Is It That Is Like the Light: A Consideration of J. 297." *EDB*, 28: 129-31 (D 75).

Perkinson, G.E. "E's Beloved Friend." *SWR*, 37: 81-3 (1952).

Perrine, Laurence. "D Distorted." *CE*, 36: 212-3 (1974).

―――. "D's 'A Clock Stopped . . .'" *Expl*, 14: 4 (F 55).

―――. "D's 'As by the dead we love to sit.'" *Expl*, 33: 49 (F 75).

―――. "D's 'The Robin is the One.'" *Expl*, 33: 33 (D 74).

―――. "D's 'There Are Two Ripenings.'" *Expl*, 31: 65 (Ap 73).

―――. "Explication of J. 219: She sweeps with many colored brooms." *EDB*, 26: 72 (1974).

Pollak, V.R. "ED's Literary Allusions." *EL*, 1: 54-68 (Sp 74).

―――. "ED's Valentines." *AQ*, 26: 60-78 (Mr 74).

―――. "'That Fine Prosperity': Economic Metaphors in ED's Poetry." *MLQ*, 34: 161-79 (Je 73).

Pollitt, Josephine. "E and Major Hunt." *SatR*, 6: 1180 (5 Jl 30).

Pommer, H.F. "ED's 'I Dreaded That First Robin, So.'" *Re: A&L*, 6: 29-47 (Sp 73).

Porter, David. "The Crucial Experience in ED's Poetry." *ESQ*, 20: 280-90 (4Q 74).

―――. "ED: The Poetics of Doubt." *ESQ*, 60: 86-93 (Su 70).

―――. "ED's 'Strangely Abstracted' Images." *BUJ*, 23: 22-31 (1975).

Porumbacu, Veronica. "ED." *Gazeta Literara*, 11 Ja 68, p. 8.

―――. "Epistolele unei poete: ED." *RoLit*, 6: 28-9 (D 73).

Purdy, D.H. "D's 'What Soft Cherubic Creatubic Creatures.'" *Expl*, 33: 67 (Au 75).

Rapin, Rene. "D's 'I Never Lost as Much but Twice.'" *Expl*, 31: 52 (Mr 73).

Read, Sir Herbert. "The Range of ED." *Spec*, 151: 971 (1933).

Reed, E.C. "ED's Treasury of Images: The Book of Revelation." *EDB*, 23: 156-60 (1973).

Regelson, Avraham. "Te'imot Me'shirat ED." *Mooz*, 32: 278-82, 404-12 (1971).

Richmond, L.J. "ED's 'If You Were Coming in the Fall': An Explication." *EJ*, 59: 771-3 (S 70).

Richmond, L.L. "D's 'Death Is a Dialogue between.'" *EDB*, 23: 171 (1973).

Roberts, David. "ED's 'woe of ecstasy.'" *ColQ*, 23: 505-17 (Sp 75).

Rogers, B.J. "The Truth Told Slant: ED's Poetic Mode." *TSLL*, 14: 329-36 (Su 72).

Rooke, Constance. "'The first Day's Night had come—': An Explication of J. 410." *EDB*, 24: 221-3 (1973).

Rothenberg, Albert. "The Flesh-and-Blood Face on the Commemorative Stamp." *SatR*, 54: 33-8 (11 S 71).

Rubin, Larry. "D's 'The Soul Selects Her Own Society.'" *Expl*, 30: 67 (Ap 72).

Sabiston, Elizabeth. "The Prison of Womanhood." *CL*, 25: 336-51 (1973).

Sahal, N. "ED on Renown." *BP*, 4: 83-5 (1968).

Sasahara, Hikaru. "Tennessee Williams to ED—*The Glass Menagerie* wo Chushin ni." *EigoS*, 120: 270-2 (1974).

Schlauch, Margaret. "Linguistic Aspects of ED's Style." *Pace Filogiczne*, 18: 201-15 (1963).

Schreiber F.R. "E Is in the House: ED as Revealed through Her Imagery." *PL*, 46: 76082 (1940).

Scott, W.T. "A Ballet ED." *EDB*, 15: 88-91 (1970).

―――. "ED and Samuel Bowles." *Fresco*, 10: 7-17 (#1 59).

Searles, J.C. "The Art of D's 'Household Thought.'" *CP*, 6: 46-51 (Sp 73).

Sessions, R.H. "ED Face to Face." *Nation*, 136: 65-6 (12 F 33).

Severns, Carrol. "ED: Experiments in Metrical Variations." *EDB*, 19: 139-47 (D 71).

Sewall, R.B. "ED: New Looks and Fresh Starts." *MLQ*, 29: 84-90 (Mr 68).

―――. "On Teaching ED." *Eng Leaflet*, 63: 3-14 (1964).

Sexton, Carol. "The Relation of ED to God." *Aspects*, 2: 30-43 (#1 65).

Simon, Myron. "'Self' in Whitman and D." *CEA*, 30: 8 (D 67).

Snipes, K.W. "ED's Odd Secrets of the Line." *EDB*, 11: 117-20 (D 69).

Springer, Marlene. "ED's Humorous Road to Heaven." *Renascence*, 23: 129-36 (1971).

Sarinth, C.N. "The Poetry of ED: Some First Impressions." *LCrit*, 9: 19-28 (Wi 69).

Stein, W.B. "ED's Parodic Masks." *UR*, 36: 49-55 (Au 69).

Stoyanov, Tsvetan. "Sluchayut ED." *LMi*, 14: 103-17 (1970).

Stuckey, K.N. "The Genius of ED." *EDB*, 11: 112-6 (D 69).

Sumner, Nan and Nathan. "A D-James Parallel." *RSW*, 39: 144-7 (1971).

Susko, Mario. "Unutarnia gravitacija ED." *Kolo*, 15: 143-70 (1970).

Taggard, Genevieve. "Notes on ED and Emerson." *Smith Col Mo*, 2: 3-6 (N 41).

Talbor, Norman. "The Child, the Actress, and Miss ED." *SoRA*, 5: 102-24 (Je 72).

*Taylor, Sheila. "Annual Bibliography." *EDB*, annually, 1970—.

Terris, V.R. "ED's White Frock." *EDB*, 28: 127-8 (D 75).

Thomas, Owen. "Father and Daughter: Edward and ED." *AL*, 40: 510-23 (Ja 69).

Thundyil, Zacharias. "Circumstance, Circumference, and Center: Immanence and Transcendence in ED's Poetry of Extreme Situations." *HSL*, 3: 73-92 (1971).

Timmerman, John. "J. 609: God and Image of God." *EDB*, 28: 124-6 (D 75).

Todd, J.E. "The Persona in ED's Love Poems." *MichA*, 1: 197-207 (Wi 69).

Todd, Richard. "'Aren't You Too Occupied to Say If My Verse Is Alive.'" *Atl*, 235: 74-81 (Ja 75).

Towheed, M.G. "The Wit of ED." *BP*, 4: 20-30 (1968).

Tugwell, Simon. "D's 'The Soul Selects Her Own Society.'" *Expl*, 27: 37 (Ja 69).

Turner, Arlin. "ED Complete." *SAQ*, 55: 501-4 (O 56).

Untermeyer, Louis. "Daughters of Niobe." *Am Spec*, 1: 4 (N 32).

Vacura, Zdenek. "The Discovery of ED's Poems." *Slovesná Veda*, 1: 31 (1947).

Van Doorn, Willem. "How It Strikes a Contemporary: ED." *ES*, 8: 132-5 (1926).

Van Doren, Mark. "The Mystery of ED." *Theatre Guild Mag*, 7: 40-1 (Ag 30).

Voight, G.P. "The Inner Life of ED." *CE*, 3: 192-6 (1941).

Wain, John. "Homage to ED." *CaM*, 15: 2-17 (1975).

Walz, L.A. "D's 'Summer Has Two Beginnings.'" *Expl*, 33: 16 (O 74).

Wells, C.F. "*The ED Bulletin*: The First Four Years." *EDB*, 21: 53-4 (Mr 72).

———. "ED's Fame in the 1890's." *EDB*, 10: 87-90 (S 69).

———. "'Fugitive References.'" *EDB*, 12: 19-22 (Mr 70).

Werge, Thomas. "'Checks' in 'I never saw a moor.'" *AN&Q*, 12: 101-2 (Mr 74).

West, Michael. "Shakespeare Allusion in ED." *AN&Q*, 10: 51 (1971).

Wheatcroft, John. "'Holy Ghosts in Cages': A Serious View of Humor in ED's Poetry." *ATQ*, 22: 95-104 (Sp 74).

Whicher, G.F. "E's Suitors." *Forum*, 106: 162-6 (1946).

———. "Uriel in Amherst." *Amherst Graduates Q*, 23: 281-92 (1934).

White, William. "ED's 'An Amazing Sense': Addendum to Buckingham." *PBSA*, 68: 66-7 (1Q 74).

———. "ED's *Poems: Third Series*: A Bibliographical Note." *Serif*, 9: 37-41 (Su 72).

———. "Emily on the Stage: Characterizations of ED in the American Theater." *ABC*, 19: 13-6 (N 68).

*———. "EDiana: An Annotated Checklist of Books about the Poet." *BB*, 26: 100-5 (O-D 69).

———. "Homage to ED: Tributes by Creative Artists." *BB*, 20: 112-5 (1951).

———. "Nostalgia Revisited. The ED Industry." *ABC*, 19: 27-8 (1969).

———. "Notes on a New Life of Higginson." *EDB*, 13: 45 (Je 70).

———. "Santayana's Copy of ED's *Poems* (1890)." *EDB*, 9: 43-4 (Je 69).

———. "Two Uncollected Poems." *EDB*, 23: 168 (S 73).

———. "The Tyranny of Book Collecting: ED." *ABC*, 21: 9 (1970).

Williams, M.G. "I.A. Richards on D." *EDB*, 26: 61-3 (Mr 74).

Wilner, Eleanor. "The Poetics of ED." *ELH*, 38: 126-54 (Mr 71).

Witherington, Paul. "D's 'Faith is a fine Invention.'" *Expl*, 26: 62 (Ap 68).

———. "The Neighborhood Humor of D's 'The Soul Selects Her Own Society.'" *CP*, 2: 5-9 (Fa 69).

Woodbridge, H.C. "ED and the Hispanic-Speaking World." *EDB*, 5: 1-4 (Ja 68).

Wycherley, H.A. "ED's Greatest Poem." *CEA*, 35: 28 (N 72).

Wylder, Edith. "The Speaker of ED's 'My Life Had Stood—A Loaded Gun.'" *BRMMLA*, 23: 3-8 (1969).

Yamamoto, Shuji. "ED and the Concept of Immortality." *KAL*, 4: 13-5 (S 61).

Yetman, M.G. "ED and the English Romantic Tradition." *TSLL*, 15: 129-47 (Sp 73).

Dickinson, John. Kaestle, C.F. "The Public Reaction to JD's *Famer's Letters*." *PAAS*, 78: 323-53 (1968).

Powell, J.H. "JD as President of Pennsylvania." *PH*, 28: 254-67 (Jl 61).

Didion, Joan. Geherin, D.J. "Nothingness and Beyond: JD's *Play It as It Lays*." *Critique*, 16: 64-78 (#1 74).

Rock, Gail. "'Play It as It Lays' (an Egg)." *Ms*, 1: 36-41 (Ja 73).

Stimpson, Catharine. "The Case of Miss JD." *Ms*, 1: 36-41 (Ja 73).

Stineback, D.C. "On the Limits of Fiction." *MwQ*, 14: 339-48 (Su 73).

Digges, Thomas Atwood. Clark, W.B. "In Defense of TD." *PMHB*, 77: 381-438 (O 53).

———. "A Franklin Postcript to Captain Cook's Voyages." *PAPS*, 98: 400-5 (23 D 54).

Elias, R.H., and M.N. Stanton. "TAD and *Adventures of Alonso*: Evidence from Robert Southey." *AL*, 44: 118-22 (My 72).

McMahon, T.J. "The First American Novel." *America*, 69: 73-4 (24 Ap 43).

Pursell, C.W. "TD and William Pearce: An Example of the Transit of Technology." *WMQ*, 21: 551-60 (O 64).

Dixon, Thomas. Allen, A.R. "TD, Jr., and Political Religion." *Foundations*, 14: 136-52 (Ap-Je 71).

Bell, L.L. "A Collarless Novelist." *SEP*, 174: 17 (3 My 03).

———. "Girl in Love." *HB*, 25: 603-8 (N 01).

———. "The Leopard's Spots." *SEP*, 174: 15 (12 Ap 08).

Davenport, F.G. "TD's Mythology of Southern History." *JSH*, 36: 350-67 (Ag 70).

Mackaye, Milton. "The Birth of a Nation." *Scrib*, 102: 40-6 (N 37).

Dobie, J. Frank. Alsmeyer, H.L. "J.FD, Friend of Libraries." *Texas Lib J*, 50: 29-32 (Mr 74).

Campbell, J.H. "Pancho at College—Toga or Sobrero?" *SwAL*, 1: 149-55 (1971).

Dobie, J.F. "The Tempo of the Range." WF, 26: 177-81 (Jl 67).

Dykes, Jeff. "A Dedication to the Memory of JFD, 1888-1964." *Arizona and the West*, 8: 203-6 (Au 66).

Richards, L.A. "FD's Use of Folkore: The Lost Adams Digging Story." *WR*, 7: 38-48 (1970).

Turner, M.A. "Was FD a Throwback to Mark Twain?" *WR*, 5: 3-12 (1968).

White, Victor. "Paisano and a Chair." *SWR*, 56: 188-96 (1971).

Doctorow, E.L. Estrin, B.L. "Surviving McCarthyism: E.L.D's *The Book of Daniel*." *MR*, 16: 577-87 (1975).

Stark, John. "Alienation and Analysis in D's *The Book of Daniel*." 16: 101-10 (3Q 75).

Starr, Kevin. "*Welcome to Hard Times* by E.L.D." *NRep*, 173: 25-7 (6 S 75).

Donleavy, James Patrick. Cohen, Dean. "The Evolution of D's Hero." *Critique*, 12: 95-109 (1971).

LeClair, Thomas. "A Case of Death: The Fiction of J.P.D." *CL*, 12: 329-44 (Su 71).

———. "*The Onion Eaters* and the Rhetoric of D's Comedy." *TCL*, 18: 167-74 (Jl 72).

Morse, Donald F. "'The Skull Beneath the Skin': J.P.D.'s *The Ginger Man.*" *MichA*, 6: 273-80 (1974).

Rollins, Ronald. "Desire versus Damnation in O'Casey's *Within the Gates* and D's *The Ginger Man.*" *Sean O'Casey R*, 1: 41-7 (#2 75).

Sherman, W.D. "J.P.D: Anarchic Man as Dying Dionysian." *TCL*, 13: 216-28 (Ja 68).

Sullivan, J.J. "Conflict in the Modern American Novel." *BSUF*, 15: 28-36 (1974).

Vintner, Maurice. "The Novelist as Clown: The Fiction of J.P.D." *Meanjin*, 29: 108-14 (1970).

Donnelly, Ignatius. Axelrad, A.M. "Ideology and Utopia in the Works of ID." *AmS*, 12: 47-65 (Fa 71).

Baker, J.W. "Populist Themes in the Fiction of ID." *AmS*, 14: 65-83 (Fa 73).

Patterson, J.S. "Alliance and Antipathy: ID's Ambivalent Vision in *Doctor Huguet.*" *AQ*, 22: 824-45 (Wi 70).

———. "From Yeoman to Beast: Images of Blackness in *Caesar's Column.*" *AmS*, 12: 21-31 (Fa 71).

Doolittle, Hilda. Anon. "Contemporary American Poetry—The Imagists: H.D." *Bkm*, 57: 571-2 (Je 23).

———. "Robert Creeley in Conversation with Charles Tomlinson." *Review*, 10: 24-35 (Ja 64).

Aldington, Richard. "The Art of Poetry." *Fortnightly R*, 113: 116-27 (1 Ja 23).

———. "A Young American Poet." *Little R*, 2: 22-5 (Mr 15).

Bryer, J.R. "H.D.: A Note on Her Critical Reputation." *ConL*, 10: 627-31 (Au 69).

*———, and Pamela Roblyer. "H.D.: A Preliminary Checklist." *ConL*, 10: 632-75 (Au 69).

Dembo, L.S., interviewer, et al. "H.D.: A Reconsideration." *ConL*, 10: 435-75 (Au 69).

———. "Introduction." *ConL*, 10: 433 (Au 69).

———. "Norman Holmes Pearson on H.D.: An Interview." *ConL*, 10: 435-46 (Au 69).

Duncan, Robert. "Two Chapters from H.D." *TriQ*, 12: 67-98 (Sp 68).

Emerson, Dorothy. "Poetry Corner—'H.D.'" *Scholastic*, 25: 13 (26 Ja 35).

Engel, B.F. "H.D.: Poems That Matter and Dilutations." *ConL*, 10: 507-22 (Au 69).

Fletcher, J.G. "Three Imagist Poets." *Little R*, 3: 35-41 (Je-Jl 16).

Friedman, Susan. "Who Buried H.D.?" *CE*, 36: 801-14 (Mr 75).

Greenwood, E.B. "H.D. and the Problem of Escapism." *EIC*, 21: 365-76 (O 71).

Holland, N. "H.D. and the 'Blameless Physician.'" *ConL*, 10: 474-506 (Au 69).

Jacobs, W.D. "H.D.'s 'Oread.'" *Expl*, 10: 45 (My 52).

Pearson, N.H., ed. "A Selection of Poetry and Prose: 'Amaranth,' 'Eros,' 'Envy,' 'Winter Love (Fragments),' 'The Dream.'" *ConL*, 10: 587-626 (Au 69).

Peck, John. "Passio perpetuae H.D." *Parnassus*, 3: 42-74 (#2 75).

Pondrom, C.N., ed. "Selected Letters from H.D. to F.S. Flint: A Commentary on the Imagist Period." *ConL*, 10: 557-86 (Au 69).

Pound, Ezra. "H.D.'s Choruses from Euripides." *Little R*, 5: 16-7 (N 18).

Riddel, J.N. "H.D. and the Poetics of 'Spiritual Realism.'" *ConL*, 10: 447-73 (Au 69).

Tietjens, Eunice. "The Orient's Gift to American Poetry." *Asia*, 36: 746-9 (N 36).

Wagner, L.W. "*Helen in Egypt*: A Culmination." *ConL*, 10: 523-36 (Au 69).

Weatherhead, A.K. "Style in H.D.'s Novels." *ConL*, 10: 537-56 (Au 69).

Dorn, Edward. Alpert, Barry. "ED: An Interview." *Vort*, 1: 2-20 (Fa 72).

————. "The Inside Real and the Outsidereal." *Vort*, 1: 27-8 (Fa 72).

Davie, Donald. "ED and the Treasures of Comedy." *Vort*, 1: 24-5 (Fa 72).

Gooder, R.D. "The Work of Poet." *CQ*, 3: 73-83 (Wi 67-68).

Kelly, Robert. "On *Gunslinger 1*." *Vort*, 1: 25-7 (Fa 72).

Newton, J.M. "Two Men Who Matter?" *CQ*, 1: 284-98 (Su 66).

Okada Roy. "An Interview with ED." *ConL*, 15: 297-314 (Su 74).

Raban, Jonathan. "Chance, Time and Silence: The New American Verse." *JAmSt*, 3: 89-101 (Jl 69).

Dos Passos, John. Baker, J.D. "Whitman and DP: A Sense of Communion." *WWR*, 20: 30-2 (Mr 74).

Bernadin, C.W. "JDP's Textual Revisions." *PSBA*, 48: 95-7 (1Q 54).

Brierre, Annie. "Littérature américaine: Hommage à J Rodrigo DP." *RDM*, 12: 688-93 (1970).

Carver, Craig. "The Newspaper and Other Sources of *Manhattan Transfer*." *SAF*, 3: 167-79 (Au 75).

Chamberlain, Jon. "JDP: The Last of the Big Four." *Nat R*, 22: 110-1 (20 O 70).

Corona, Mario. "Un esteta al fronte." *SA*, 18: 269-98 (1972).

Cowley, Malcolm. "DP: The Learned Poggius." *SoR*, 9: 3-17 (Wi 73).

Crane, J. St. C. "Rare or Seldom Seen Dust Jackets of American First Editions: v." *Serif*, 8: 27-8 (1971).

Diggins, J.P. "Visions of Chaos and Visions of Order: DP as Historian." *AL*, 46: 329-46 (N 74).

Dommerques, Pierre. "JDP: An Old Dream Behind the Mask of Rebellion." *StAR*, 2: 56-9 (Fa-Wi 72).

Dos Passos, John. "Ma Vie d'artiste." *NL*, 7 Mr 68, pp. 1, 7.

————. "What Makes a Novelist?" *Nat R*, 20: 29-32 (16 Ja 68).

Gado, Frank, ed. "An Interview with JDP." *Idol*, 45: 5-25 (1969).

Gold, Herbert. "The Literary Lives of JDP." *SR/World*, 1: 32-5 (11 S 74).

Goldman, Arnold. "DP and His *U.S.A.*" *NLH*, 1: 471-83 (1970).

Graham, Don, and Barbara Shaw. "Faulkner's Small Debt to DP: A Source for the Percy Grimm Episode." *MissQ*, 27: 327-32 (Su 74).

Green, Paul. "The Crossing Pathways of *Manhattan Transfer*." *RecL*, 4: 19-42 (#1 75).

Hoffman, A.R. "An Element of Structure in *USA*." *CEA*, 31: 12-3 (O 68).

Hughson, Lois. "In Search of the True America: DP's Debt to Whitman in *U.S.A.*" *MFS*, 19: 179-92 (Su 73).

Kallich, Martin. "[JDP's Textual Revisions.]" *PBSA*, 48: 97-8 (1Q 54).

Kazin, Alfred. "JDP: Inventor in Isolation." *SatR*, 52: 16-9, 44-5 (14 Mr 69).

Lane, J.B. "*Manhattan Transfer* as a Gateway to the 1920's." *CentR*, 16: 293-311 (Su 72).

Lawrence, F.B. "Two Novelists of the Great War: DP and Cummings." *UR*, 36: 35-41 (Au 69).

Lowry, E.D. "The Lively Art of *Manhattan Transfer*." *PMLA*, 84: 1628-38 (O 69).

Ludington, C.T. "The Neglected Satires of JDP." *SNL*, 7: 128-36 (Sp 70).

Lynn, K.S. "DP's Chosen Country." *NRep*, 155: 15-20 (15 O 66).

McCormick, D.F. "A Pessimistic Vision of New York in Literature: *Manhattan Transfer*." *Centerpoint*, 1: 9-13 (#3 75).

McIlvaine, R.M. "DP's Reading of Thorstein Veblen." *AL*, 44: 471-4 (N 72).

————. "DP's *Three Soldiers*." *Expl*, 31: 50 (Mr 73).

Maynard, Reid. "JDP's One-Sided Panorama." *Disc*, 11: 468-74 (Au 68).

Meinke, Peter. "Swallowing America Whole." *NRep*, 169: 28-31 (22 S 73).

Michaelson, L.W. "My 85¢ Supper with Mr. U.S.A." *Eng Rec*, 22: 36-9 (Wi 71).

Monat, Olympio. "JPD e a cidade dos homens vazios." *ESPSL*, 29 S 74, p. 1.

Morrow, Patrick. "The Dada World of *Manhattan Transfer*." *RSW*, 38: 258-65 (D 70).

Muste, J.M. "Norman Mailer and JD: The Question of Influence." *MFS*, 17: 361-74 (Au 71).

Pearce, Richard. "*Pylon, Awake and Sing*! and the Apocalyptic Imagination of the 30's." *Criticism*, 13: 131-41 (Sp 71).

Petrucci, Antonio. "DP e la 'generazione perduta.'" *ORom*, 5: 3 (1970).

Pires, Alves. "O cinema na literatura: JDP." *Broteria*, 87: 74-87 (1968).

Reilly, J.M. "DP *et al.*: An Experiment in Radical Function." *MwQ*, 12: 413-26 (Jl 71).

Ross, Frank. "The Assailant-Victim in Three War-Protest Novels." *Paunch*, 32: 46-57 (D 68).

Schorer, Mark. "JD: A Stranded American." *Atl*, 227: 93-6 (Mr 71).

Shaw, Barbara, and Don Graham. "Faulkner's Small Debt to DP: A Source for the Percy Grimm Episode." *MissQ*, 27: 327-32 (Su 74).

Sloane, D.E.E. "The Black Experience in DP's *U.S.A.*" *CEA*, 36: 22-23 (1974).

Smith, M.H. "Recollections of JD." *ConnR*, 8: 21-4 (#2 75).

Stade, George. "The Two Faces of DP." *PR*, 41: 476-83 (1974).

Titche, Leon. "Döblin and DP: Aspects of the City Novel." *MFS*, 17: 125-35 (Sp 71).

Vanderwerken, D.L. "DP's *Streets of Night*: A Reconsideration." *MarkR*, 4: 61-5 (O 74).

Vázquez-Bigi, A.M. "Introducciíon al estudio de la influencial barojiana en Hemingway y D." *CHA*, 265-7: 169-203 (1972).

Walter, Hans-Albert. "Auf dem Wege zum Staatsroman ii: Die *USA*-Trilogie von JDP." *FH*, 24: 192-202 (1969).

Weber, Daniel. "The Passion of JDP." *DilR*, 14: 261-72 (Jl 66).

Weeks, R.P. "DP's Debt to Walt Whitman." *AA*, 3: 121-38 (1974).

Winner, Anthony. "The Characters of JDP." *LWU*, 2: 1-19 (1969).

Douglas, Lloyd. Kinnison, William. "Notes on Six Wittenberg Authors." *Ohioana*, 15: 136-41 (1972).

Douglass, Frederick. Aptheker, Herbert. "FD Calls for Black Suffrage in 1866." *BSch*, 5: 10-6 (D 73-Ja 74).

Clasby, N.T. "FD's *Narrative*: A Content Analysis." *CLAJ*, 14: 242-50 (Mr 71).

Foner, P.S. "Address of FD at the Inauguration of the Douglass Institute, Baltimore, October 1, 1865." *JNH*, 54: 174-83 (Ap 69).

Fulkerson, Gerald. "Exile as Emergence: FD in Great Britian, 1845-1847." *QJS*, 60: 69-82 (F 74).

Haskett, N.D. "Afro-American Images of Africa: Four *Antebellum* Black Authors." *Ufahamu*, 3: 29-40 (1972).

Jaskoski, H. "Power Unequal to Man: The Significance of Conjure in Works by Five Afro-American Authors." *SFQ*, 38: 91-108 (Je 74).

Nicholas, William W. "Individualism and Autobiographical Art: FD and Henry Thoreau." *CLAJ*, 16: 145-58 (D 72).

Perry, P.B. "Before *The North Star*: FD's Early Journalistic Career." *Phylon*, 34: 96-107 (Mr 74).

———. "The Literary Content of FD's Paper through 1860." *CLAJ*, 17: 214-29 (D 73).

Quarles, Benjamin. "FD: Black Imperishable." *QJLC*, 29: 159-69 (1972).

Stone, A.E. "Identity and Art in FD's *Narrative*." *CLAJ*, 17: 192-213 (D 73).

Van Deburg, William. "FD: Maryland Slave to Religious Liberal." *MHM*, 69: 27-43 (Sp 74).

Drabble, Margaret. Libby, M.V. "Fate and Feminism in the Novels of MD." *ConL*, 16: 175-92 (Sp 75).

Schaefer, O'Brien. "Reconsideration: The Novels of MD." *NRep*, 172: 21-3 (26 Ap 75).

Drake, Joseph Rodman. Slater, Joseph. "The Case of D and Halleck." *EAL*, 8: 285-97 (Wi 74).

Dreiser, Theodore. Anon. "Airmail Interview: Marguerite Tjader." *DrN*, 2: 11-7 (1971).

————. "Centennial Report." *DrN*, 2: 1-2 (1971).

————. "Reappraising TD." *TLS*, 1 Ja 71, p. 13.

*Baker, M.R. "TD: A Checklist of Dissertations and Theses." *DrN*, 5: 12-21 (1974).

Bender, E.T. "On Lexical Playgrounds." *DrN*, 6: 12-3 (1975).

Berthoff, Warner. "D Revisited." *ModO*, 2: 133-6 (Wi 72).

Brogunier, Joseph. "D in Paperback: Riches and Rags." *DrN*, 4: 1-4 (1973).

Burgan, Mary E. "*Sister Carrie* and the Pathos of Naturalism." *Criticism*, 15: 336-349 (Fa 73).

Byers, J.R. "D's Hurstwood and Jefferson's Rip Van Winkle." *PMLA*, 87: 514-6 (My 72).

Calvert, Beverlee. "A Structural Analysis of *Jennie Gerhardt*." *DrN*, 5: 9-11 (1974).

Campbell, D.L. "*An American Tragedy*: Or, Death in the Woods." *MFS*, 15: 251-9 (Su 69).

Ceder, Margarita. "Rabota Drajzera nad romanom *Oplot*." *VLit*, 11: 139-52 (1967).

Constantine, J.R. "Debs and D: A Note." *DrN*, 5: 1-5 (1974).

Cook, George. "The Rocking Chair in D's *Sister Carrie*." *TAIUS*, 1: 65-6 (1968).

Dailly, C. "Jennie: a Daughter of Nature." *Annales de l'universite d'Abidjan*, 5: 145-50 (1972).

Dance, D.C. "Sentimentalism in D's Heroines: Carrie and Jennie." *CLAJ*, 14: 127-42 (D 70).

Desai, R.W., and Hugh Witemeyer. "Delusion and Reality in *Sister Carrie*." *PMLA*, 87: 309-10 (My 72).

Dew, Marjorie. "Realistic Innocence: Cady's Footnote to a Definition of American Literary Realism." *ALR*, 5: 487-9 (1972).

Douglas, D.H. "Ludwig Lewisohn on D." *DrN*, 4: 1-6 (1973).

Douglas, G.H. "D's Enduring Genius." *Nation*, 212: 826-8 (28 Je 71).

*Dowell, R.W. "Checklist: D Studies, 1969." *DrN*, 1: 14-8 (1970).

————. "D's Address to the Future." *DrN*, 4: 10-11 (1973).

————. "D Holdings at the Lilly Library." *DrN*, 1: 13-5 (1970).

————. "Medical Diary Reveals First D Visit to the University of Pennsylvania." *LCUP*, 38: 92-6 (Wi 72).

————. "'On the Banks of the Wabash': A Musical Whodunit." *IMH*, 66: 95-109 (Je 70).

————. "'You Will Not Like Me, I'm Sure': D to Miss Emma Rector, November 28, 1893 to Ap 4, 1894." *ALR*, 3: 259-70 (Su 70).

*————, and F.E. Rusch. "A D Checklist, 1970." *DrN*, 13-21 (1972).

Dreiser, Theodore. "D on An American Tragedy in Prague." *DrN*, 4: 21-2 (1973).

————. "An Unpublished Chapter from *An American Tragedy*." *Prospects*, 1: 1-8 (1975).

Elias, R.H. "Bibliography and the Biographer." *LCUP*, 38: 25-44 (Wi 72).

————. "TD and the Tragedy of the Twenties." *Prospects*, 1: 9-18 (1975).

England, D.G. "A Further Note on the 'D' Annotations." *DrN*, 4: 9-10 (1973).

Farrell, J.T. "D's *Tragedy*: The Distortion of American Values." *Prospects*, 1: 19-28 (1975).

Forrey, Robert. "D and the Prophetic Tradition." *AmS*, 15: 21-55 (Fa 74).

Furmanczyk, Wieslaw. "TD's Philosophy in *Notes on Life*." *DrN*, 3: 9-12 (1972).

Garner, Stanton. "D and the *New York Times Illustrated Magazine*: A Bibliographical Supplement." *PBSA*, 69: 118-9 (1Q 75).

Gerber, P.L. "The Alabaster Protégé: D and Berenice Fleming." *AL*, 43: 217-30 (My 71).

———. "D's Debt to *Jay Cooke*." *LCUP*, 38: 67-77 (Wi 72).

———. "D's Financier: A Genesis." *JML*, 1: 354-74 (1971).

———. "D's Stoic: A Study in Literary Frustration." *Lit Monographs*, 7: 85-144 (1975).

———. "The Financier Himself: D and C.T. Yerkes." *PMLA*, 88: 112-21 (Ja 73).

———. "Frank Cowperwood: Boy Financier." *SAF*, 2: 165-74 (Au 74).

———. "Hyde's Tabbs and D's Butters." *DrN*, 6: 9-11 (1975).

———. "A *Tragedy* Ballad." *DrN*, 1: 6-10 (1970).

Graham, D.B. "Aesthetic Experience in Realism." *ALR*, 8: 289-90 (1975).

———. "'The Cruise of the Idlewild': D's Revisions of a 'Rather Light' Story." *ALR*, 8: 1-11 (Wi 75).

———. "D's Maggie." *ALR*, 7: 169-70 (Sp 74).

Griffin, E.G. "Sympathetic Materialism: A Re-reading of TD." *HAB*, 20: 59-68 (1969).

Griffith, Clark. "*Sister Carrie*: D's *Wasteland*." *AmS*, 16: 41-7 (#2 75).

Gross, Dalton. "George Sterling's Letters to TD." *DrN*, 4: 14-20 (1973).

Hajek, Friederike. "*American Tragedy*—zwei Aspekte: Dargestellt in Richard Wrights Native Son und in TD's *An American Tragedy*." *ZAA*, 20: 262-79 (1972).

Hakutani, Yoshinobu. "TD's Editorial and Free-Lance Writing." *LCUP*, 37: 70-85 (Wi 71).

Heim, W.J. "Letters from Young D." *ALR*, 8: 158-63 (Sp 75).

Hirsh, J.C. "The Printed Ephemera of *Sister Carrie*." *ALR*, 7: 171-2 (Sp 74).

Homma, Kenshiro. "Tayama Katai and TD—Naturalism and Its Metamorphosis." *DSE*, 11: 144-75 (Je 75).

Hovey, R.B., and R.S Ralph. "D's The '*Genius*': Motivation and Structure." *HSL*, 2: 169-83 (1970).

Hussman, L.E. "D's Emotional Power." *DrN*, 4: 12-3 (1973).

———. "Thomas Edison and *Sister Carrie*: A Source for Character and Theme." *ALR*, 8: 155-8 (Sp 75).

Jurnak, S.H. "Popular Art Forms in *Sister Carrie*." *TSLL*, 13: 313-20 (Su 71).

Kanaseki, Hisao. "D no Buntai." *EigoS*, 117: 604-6 (1972).

Kane, Patricia. "Reading Matter as a Clue to D's Characters." *SDR*, 8: 104-6 (Wi 70-71).

Katope, C.G. "*Sister Carrie* and Spencer's *First Principles*." *AL*, 41: 64-75 (Mr 69).

Katz, Joseph. "D's 'Notes on Life.'" *LCUP*, 38: 44-5 (Wi 72).

———. "Dummy: The '*Genius*' by TD." *Proof*, 1: 330-57 (1971).

———. "TD: Enter Chicago, Hope, and Walt Whitman." *WWR*, 14: 169-71 (D 68).

———. "TD's *Ev'ry Month*." *LCUP*, 38: 46-66 (Wi 72).

Kelh, D.G. "Dreiser and the Winebrennarians." *DrN*, 5: 5-9 (1974).

Keller, D.H. "D's *Concerning Dives and Lazarus*." *Serif*, 8: 31-2 (1971).

Kennell, R.E. "Airmail Interview." *DrN*, 5: 6-11 (1974).

Lehan, Richard. "Assessing D." *DrN*, 1: 1-3 (1970).

Long, R.E. "D and Frederic: The Upstate New York Exile of Dick Diver." *FitzN*, 37: 1-2 (Sp 67).

Loving, J.M. "The Rocking Chair Structure of *Sister Carrie*." *DrN*, 2: 7-11 (Sp 71).

Ludington, Townsend. "Century's Ebb: The Thirteenth Chronicle." *NRep*, 173: 23-5 (22 N 75).

Lunden, Rolf. "The Scandanavian Reception of TD." *DrN*, 6: 9-11 (1975).

McAleer, J.J. "*An American Tragedy* and *In Cold Blood*." *Thought*, 47: 569-86 (Wi 72).

———. "D's 'Notes on Life': Responses to an Impenetrable Universe." *LCUP*, 38: 78-91 (Wi 72).

McIlvaine, R.M. "A Literary Source for Hurstwood's Last Scene." *RSW*, 40: 44-6 (1972).

————. "A Literary Source for the Caesarean Section in *A Farewell to Arms.*" *AL*, 43: 444-7 (N 71).

Matveev, V. "Pis'ma T. Drajzera I. Anisimovu." *VLit*, 17: 193-9 (#4 73).

Moers, Ellen. "New Light on D in the 1890's." *CLC*, 15: 10-24 (My 66).

————. "A 'New' First Novel by Arthur Henry." *DrN*, 4: 7-9 (1973).

————. "The Survivors: Into the Twentieth Century." *TCL*, 20: 1-11 (Ja 74).

Mookerjee, R.N. "D's Ambivalent Naturalism: A Note on *Sister Carrie.*" *RUSEng*, 5: 36-48 (1971).

————. "D's Use of Hindu Thought in *The Stoic.*" *AL*, 43: 273-8 (My 71).

————. "An Embarrassment of Riches: D Research. Materials and Problems." *IJAS*, 1: 91-6 (1969).

————. "The Literary Naturalist as Humanist: The Last Phase of TD." *MwQ*, 12: 369-81 (Su 71).

Mouri, Itaru. "Reconsideration of Sister Carrie—The Significance of the Latent World." *SELit*, 16: 172-4 (1971).

Morsberger, R.E. "'In Elf Land Disporting': *Sister Carrie* in Hollywood." *BRMMLA*, 27: 219-30 (1973).

Mulqueen, J.E. "*Sister Carrie*: A Modern *Pilgrim's Progress.*" CEA, 31: 8 (Mr 69).

Nemoianu, Virgil. "Centenarul unui realist." *Contemporanul*, 16: 10 (27(Ag 71).

Oldani, Louis. "A Bibliographical Description of D's *The 'Genius.'*" *LCUP*, 39: 40-55 (Wi 73).

Palmer, Erwin. "TD, Poet." *South and West*, 10: 26-44 (Fa 71).

Petronis, Jonas. "Teodoras Dreizeris ir Lietuva." *Pergale*, 8: 185-6 (1971).

Pirinska, Pavlina. "TD i Amerika." *LMi*, 15: 133-45 (1971).

Pizer, Donald. "'Along the Wabash': A 'Comedy Drama' by TD." *DrN*, 5: 1-4 (1974).

————. "D Studies: Work to Be Done." *DrN*, 1: 10-13 (1970).

————. "D's Novels: The Editorial Problem." *LCUP*, 38: 7-24 (Wi 72).

————. "The Problem of Philosophy in the Novel." *BuR*, 18: 53-62 (Sp 70).

————. "The Publications of TD: A Checklist." *Proof*, 1: 247-92 (1971).

————. "TD's *Nigger Jeff*: The Development of an Aesthetic." *AL*, 41: 331-41 (N 69).

Press, Viktor. "Velikij Amerikanec." *Okt*, 8: 209-12 (1971).

Recchia, E.J. "Naturalism's Artistic Compromises in *Sister Carrie* and *The Octopus.*" *LWU*, 5: 277-85 (1972).

Rose, A.H. "Sin and the City: The Uses of Disorder in the Urban Novel." *CentR*, 16: 203-20 (1972).

Roulston, Robert. "The Libidinous Lobster: The Semi-Flaw in D's Superman." *Rendezvous*, 9: 35-40 (1974).

Rubin, L.D. "D and *Meet Me in the Green Glen*: A Vintage Year for Robert Penn Warren." *HC*, 9: 1-12 (Ap 72).

Rusch, F.E. "A D Checklist." *DrN*, 3: 12-9 (1972); 4: 5-11 (1973); 5: 12-23 (1974).

Saalbach, R.P. "Airmail Interviews: Neda Westlake." *DrN*, 3: 6-11 (1972).

————. "The D Centennial." *DrN*, 1: 19 (1970).

————. "D's Social Criticism." *DrN*, 6: 14-20 (1975).

Salzman, Jack. "The Critical Recognition of *Sister Carrie* 1900-1907." *JAmSt*, 3: 123-33 (Jl 69).

————. "The Curious History of D's *The Bulwark.*" *Proof*, 3: 21-61 (1973).

————. "D and Ade." *AL*, 40: 544-8 (Ja 69).

————. "I Find the Real American Tragedy, by TD." *RALS*, 2: 3-74 (Sp 72).

————. "D Then and Now." *JML*, 1: 421-30 (1971).

————. "TD (1871-1945)." *ALR*, 2: 132-8 (Su 69).

Schmidt-von Bardelben, Renate. "D on the European Continent." *DrN*, 2: 4-10 (1971); 3: 1-8 (1972).

Scott, K.W. "Did D Cut Up Jack Harkaway?" *MarkR*, 2: 1-4 (My 68).

Sequeira, I.J.E. "A Note on the Influence of D's Tropistic Theory of Life on His Naturalistic Fiction." *OJES*, 8: 29-35 (1971).

Soderbergh, P.A. "TD in Pittsburgh, 1894." *WPHM*, 51: 229-42 (Jl 68).

Stein, A.F. "Sister Carrie: A Possible Source for the Title." *ALR*, 7: 173-4 (Sp 74).

Stone, W.B., and P.L. Gerber. "D and C.T. Yerkes." *PMLA*, 88: 1188-90 (O 73).

Swansberg, W.A. "Airmail Interview." *DrN*, 1: 2-6 (1970).

Thomas, J.D. "Epimetheus Bound: TD and the Novel of Thought." *SHR*, 3: 346-57 (Fa 69).

Vance, W.L. "Dreiserian Tragedy." *StN*, 4: 39-51 (Sp 72).

Wadlington, Warwick. "Pathos and D." *SoR*, 7: 411-29 (Ap 71).

Walcutt, C.C. "*Sister Carrie*: Naturalism or Novel of Manner?" *Genre*, 1: 76-85 (Ja 68).

Wallington, Warwick. "Pathos and D." *SoR*, 7: 411-29 (Ap 71).

Warren, R.P. "Homage to TD on the Centenary of His Birth." *SoR*, 7: 345-410 (Ap 71).

Weir, S.B. "The Image of Women in D's Fiction, 1900-1925." *PCP*, 7: 65-71 (Ap 72).

Westlake, N.M. "Dummy: *Twelve Men*, by TD." *Proof*, 2: 153-74 (1972).

————. "TD Collection—Addenda." *LCUP*, 25: 55-7 (Wi 59).

*White, William. "A D Checklist in the Press." *DrN*, 1: 19-20 (1970).

————. "D on Hardy, Henley, and Whitman: An Unpublished Letter." *ELN*, 6: 122-4 (D 68).

Wilson, Gil. "A Proposal for a D Mural." *DrN*, 3: 1-5 (1972).

Witemeyer, Hugh. "Gaslight and Magic Lamp in *Sister Carrie*." *PMLA*, 86: 236-40 (Mr 71).

————. "Sister Carrie: Plus ca change . . ." *PMLA*, 87: 514 (My 72).

Wycherley, H.A. "Mechanism and Vitalism in D's Non-fiction.'" *TSLL*, 11: 1039-49 (Su 69).

Drewry, Carleton. Eure, V.D. "Poet Laureate of Virginia: CD." *Cwealth*, 36: 21-6 (Mr 70).

Dubie, Norman. "Against Iron Time." *Shen*, 23: 95-103 (1972).

DuBois, W.E.B. Aptheker, Bettina. "W.E.B.D & the Struggle for Women's Rights." *San Jose Stud*, 1: 7-16 (#2 75).

Breathett, George. "W.E.B.D." *JNH*, 60: 45-52 (Ja 75).

Brodwin, Stanley. "The Veil Transcended: Form and Meaning in W.E.B.D's *The Souls of Black Folk*." *JBlackS*, 2: 303-21 (Mr 72).

Elder, A.A. "Swamp Versus Plantation: Symbolic Structure in W.E.B.D's *The Quest of the Silver Feast*." *Phylon*, 34: 358-67 (1973).

Fontaine, W.T. "The Negro Continuum from Dominant Wish to Collective Act." *AForum*, 3-4: 63-96 (1968).

Glazier, K.M. "W.E.B.D's Impressions of Woodrow Wilson." *JNH*, 58: 452-9 (1973).

Green, Dan. "W.E.B.D: Black Yankee." *ConnR*, 6: 46-56 (1972).

Ijere, M.O. "W.E.B.D and Garvey as Pan-Africanists: A Study in Contrasts." *PA*, 89: 188-206 (1974).

Kostelanetz, Richard. "Fictions for a Negro Politics: the Neglected Novels of W.E.B.D." *XUS*, 7: 5-39 (Jl 68).

Moon, H.L. "The Leadership of W.E.B.D." *Crisis*, 75: 51-7 (F 68).

Moses, W.F. "The Evolution of Black National-Socialist Thought: A Study of W.E.B.DB." *BlAR*, 1: 25-45 (Wi 70).

Moses, W.J. "The Poetics of Ethiopianism: W.E.B.BD and Literary Black Nationalism." *AL*, 47: 411-26 (N 75).

Rhodes, Joseph. "Reconsideration: W.E.B.D." *NRep*, 166: 29-32 (26 F 72).

Savory, J.J. "The Rending of the Veil in W.E.B.D's *The Souls of Black Folk.*" *CLAJ*, 15: 334-7 (Mr 72).

Shaw, Peter. "The Uses of Autobiography." *ASch*, 38: 136-50 (Wi 68-69).

Turner, D.T. "W.E.B.D and the Theory of a Black Aesthetic." *SLImag*, 7: 1-22 (Fa 74).

Walden, Daniel. "D's Pan-Africanism, a Reconsideration." *NALF*, 8: 260-2 (1974).

Yellin, Jean. "D's *Crisis* and Woman Suffrage." *MR*, 14: 365-75 (1973).

Dugan, Alan. Boyers, Robert. "AD: The Poetry of Survival." *Salmagundi*, 2: 43-52 (Sp 68).

Reid, A.S. "A Look at the Living Poem: Rock Protest and Wit." *FurmM*, nv: 6-11, 35 (Sp 70).

Ryan, Michael. "An Interview with AD." *IowaR*, 4: 90-7 (3 73).

Dummer, Jeremiah. Winton, Calhoun. "JD: The 'First American?'" *WMQ*, 26: 105-8 (Ja 69).

Dunbar, Paul Laurence. Anon. "PLD: America's Negro Poet Laureate." *Sepia*, 11: 60-2 (Mr 62).

————. "Dramatizing the Life of the Lowly." *NHB*, 2: 26 (Ja 39).

————. "Negro Novelists: Blazing the Way in Fiction." *NHB*, 2: 17 (D 38).

————. "Negro Poets: Singers in the Dawn." *NHB*,2: 9 (N 38).

Abramowitz, Jack. "The Negro in the Populist Movement." *JNH*, 38: 257-89 (Jl 53).

Allen, W.M. "PLD, A Study in Genius." *PsyR*, 15: 58-82 (1938).

Arnold, E.F. "Some Personal Reminiscences of PLD." *JNH*, 17: 400-8 (O 32).

Baker, H.A. "PLD: An Evaluation." *BlackW*, 21: 30-7 (1971).

————. "Report on a Celebrations: D's One-Hundredth Year." *BlackW*, 22: 81-5 (1973).

Brawley, Benjamin. "D Thirty Years After." *SoW*, 59: 189-91 (Ap 30).

————. "The Negro in American Fiction." *Dial*, 60: 445-50 (11 My 16).

Brown, Sterling. "The Negro Author and His Publisher." *Negro Q*, 1: 7-20 (Sp 42).

Bryant, J.G. "Negro Poetry." *Colored American Mag*, 8: 254-7 (My 05).

Burch, C.E. "D's Poetry in Literary English." *SoW*, 50: 469-73 (O 21).

————. "The Plantation Negro in D's Poetry." *SoW*, 50: 227-9 (My 21).

Chamberlain, John. "The Negro as Writer." *Bkm*, 70: 603-11 (F 30).

Clark, D.W. "PLD Laurel Decked." *MethodistR*, 88: 555-64 (Jl 06).

Clarke, John Henrik. "PLD." *Freedomways*, 12: 316-18 (4Q 72).

Clippinger, Lulu May. "A Visit to PLD." *Watchword*, 6 Mr 06, p. 152.

————. "PLD, the Negro Poet Laureate." *Watchword*, 6 Mr 06, p. 150.

Dunbar, Alice. "The Poet and His Song." *A.M.E. Church R*, 31: 121-35 (O 14).

Fontaine, W.T. "The Negro Continuum from Dominant Wish to Collective Act." *AForum*, 3-4: 63-96 (1968).

Fox, A.B. "Behind the Mask: PLD's Poetry in Literary English." *TQ*, 14: 7-19 (Su 71).

Gayle, Addison, Jr. "Cultural Nationalism: The Black Novel and the City." *Liberator*, 9: 14-17 (15 Jl 1969).

Glicksberg, Charles. "Alienation of Negro Literature." *Phylon*, 11: 49-57 (Sp 70).

Henry, T.M. "The First Black World Poet." *Poet Lore*, 40: 303-12 (Su 29).

————. "Old School of Negro 'Critics' Hard on PLD." *Messenger*, 6: 310-1 (O 24).

Howells, W.D. "Tribute to PLD." *Bkm*, 23: 185 (Ap 06).

Hudson, G.H. "'Emancipation,' an Unpublished Poem by PLD." *Negro Hist Bul*, 36: 41-2 (1973).

————. "PLD: *Dialect at la negritude.*" *Phylon*, 34: 236-47 (1973).

————. "PLD: Black Poet in History."*NHB*, 35: 30-2 (F 72).

Hughes, Langston, "The Negro Author and the Racial Mountain." *Nation*, 122: 692-4 (23 Je 26); *Amistad*, 1: 301-5 (1970).

Jackson, M.R. "Gift of Song." *NegroD*, 11: 53-6 (Je 62).

Janifer, Ellsworth. "Samuel Coleridge-Taylor in Washington." *Phylon*, 28: 257-72 (Fa 68).

Jenifer, G.D. "The Services of D." *Voice of the Negro*, 3: 408-9 (Je 06).

Larson, C.R. "The Novels of PLD." *Phylon*, 29: 257-71 (Fa 68).

Lawson, E.H. "PLD." *Alexander's Mag*, 1: 47-50 (Mr 06).

Lee, A.R. "The Fiction of PLD." *NALF*, 8: 166-75 (Sp 74).

Martin, Jay. "'Jump Back Honey': PLD and the Rediscovery of American Poetical Traditions." *BMMLA*, 7: 40-53 (#1 74).

Miller, Kelly. "Achievements of the Negro Race." *Voice of the Negro*, 2: 612-8 (S 05).

Pearson, P.M. "PLD." *Talent*, 16: 12-3, 26 (6 Mr 06).

Phillips, Waldo. "PLD: A New Perspective." *NHB*, 29: 7-8 (O 65).

Ransom, R.C. "PLD." *A.M.E. Church R*, 31: 192-5 (O 14).

Redding, Saunders. "American Negro Literature." *ASch*, 18: 137-48 (Sp 49).

Rodabaugh, J.H. "The Negro in Ohio." *JNH*, 31: 9-29 (Ja 46).

————. "PLD House." *Museum Echos*, 29: 11-4 (F 56).

Scarborough, W.S. "The Poet Laureate of the Negro Race." *A.M.E. Church R*, 31: 135-44 (O 14).

Thurman, Wallace. "Negro Artists and the Negro." *NRep*, 52: 37-9 (31 Ag 27).

————. "Negro Poets and Their Poetry." *Bkm*, 67: 555-61 (Jl 28).

Turner, D.T. "PLD: The Poet and the Myths." *CLAJ*, 18: 155-71 (D 74).

Duncan, Robert. Brien, Dolores. "RD: A Poet in the Emerson—Whitman Tradition." *CentR*, 19: 308-16 (Fa 75).

Nelson, R.L. "Edge of the Transcendent: The Poetry of Levertov and D." *SWR*, 54: 188-202 (Sp 69).

Raban, Jonathan. "Chance, Time and Silence: The New American Verse." *JAmSt*, 3: 89-101 (Jl 69).

Sienicka, Marta. "William Carlos Williams and Some Younger Poets." *SAP*, 4: 183-93 (1972).

Taylor, L.L. "Pietre in cimpul lui RD." *Steaua*, 25: 45-8 (1974).

Weatherhead, A.K. "RD and the Lyric." *ConL*, 16: 163-74 (Sp 75).

Zweig, Paul. "RD's World." *Poetry*, 111: 402-5 (Mr 68).

Dunlap, William. Argetsinger, Gerald. "D's *Andre*: Beginning of American Tragedy." *Players*, 49: 62-64 (1974).

Coad, O.S. "The D Diaries at Yale." *SP*, 24: 403-12 (1927).

Dickson, H.E. "A Misdated Episode in D." *Art Q*, 9: 33-6 (1946).

Moramarco, Fred. "The Early Drama Criticism of WD." *AL*, 40: 9-14 (Mr 68).

Roth, Martin. "Laurence Sterne in America." *BNYPL*, 74: 428-36 (S 70).

Rutledge, A.W. "D Notes." *Art in America*, 29: 36-48 (1951).

Wilmeth, D.B. "An Index to: The Life of George Frederick Cooke by WD." *ThDoc*, 2: 109-20 (1969-70).

Zipes, Jack. "D, Kotzebue, and the Shaping of the American Theater: A Reevaluation from a Marxist Perspective." *EAL*, 8: 272-84 (Wi 74).

Dunne, Finley Paler. Mann, George. "Call for Mr. Dooley." *Eire*, 9: 119-27 (1974).

Duyckinck, Evert A. Kay, Donald. "Herman Melville's Literary Relationship with ED." *CJAL*, 18: 393-403 (Mr 75).

Mize, G.E. "ED: Critic to His Times." *ESQ*, 55: 89-95 (2Q 69).

Wells, D.A. "'Bartleby the Scrivener,' Poe, and the D Circle." *ESQ*, 21: 35-9 (1Q 75).

Dwight, John S. Cameron, K.W. "D's Translation of Schiller's Bell Song Before 1837." *ESQ*, 51: 147-54 (2Q 68).

Dwight, J.S. "Music and Poetry (1836)." *ESQ*, 52: 94-7 (eQ 68).

Dwight, Timothy. Freimarck, Vincent. "TD's Brief Lives in *Travels in New England and New York*." *EAL*, 8: 44-58 (Sp 73).

Gribbin, William. "The Legacy of TD: A Reappraisal." *ConHSB*, 37: 33-41 (1972).

Griffith, John. "*The Columbiad* and *Greenfield Hill*." *EAL*, 10: 235-50 (Wi 75-76).

Kohring, K.H. "The American Epic." *SHR*, 5: 265-80 (Su 71).

Solomon, B.M. "TD." *WMQ*, 28: 140-3 (Ja 71).

Volkomer, W.E. "TD and New England Federalism." *ConnR*, 3: 72-82 (1970).

Whitford, Kathryn and Philip. "TD's Place in Eighteenth Century American Science." *PAPS*, 114: 60-71 (16 F 70).

Dylan, Bob. Bluestein, Gene. "Folk Tradition, Individual Talent: A Note on The Poetry of Rock." *MR*, 11: 373-84 (1970).

Cohen, Robert. "BD: His Generation and His Protest." *LanM*, 66: 73-7 (1972).

Davey, Frank. "Leonard Cohen and BD: Poetry and the Popular Song." *Alphabet*, 17: 12-29 (D 69).

Goldberg, Steven. "DB and the Poetry of Salvation." *SR*, 53: 43-6, 57 (30 My 70).

Gonzales, Laurence. "Persona Bob: Seer and Fool." *Costerus*, 3: 33-53 (1972).

Grange, Joseph. "BD's Reach: Crazy Sorrows and New Mornings." *Northern New England Rev*, 1: 17-26 (1974).

Jensen, Richard. "DB: Pied Piper of a Generation." *Dialog*, 11: 202-8 (Su 72).

Kermode, Frank, and Stephen Spender. "BD: The Metaphor at the End of the Funnel." *Esquire*, 77: 109-18, 188 (My 72).

Lankester, Ko. "ED: Portret van een controversieel zanger-dichter." *FdL*, 13: 32-49 (1972).

Monteiro, George. "D in the Sixties." *SAW*, 73: 160-72 (Sp 74).

Poague, L.A. "D as *Auteur*: Theoretical Notes, and an Analysis of 'Love Minus Zero/No Limit.'" *JPC*, 8: 53-8 (1974).

Scaduto, Anthony. "Won't You Listen to the Lambs, BD?" *NYTMS*, 28 N 71, pp. 34 ff.

Sterne, A.H. "Daedalus Speaks to Bobby D." *EJ*, 60: 610-4 (My 71).

Eastlake, William. Eastlake, Wm. "Writing About the West." *SDR*, 11: 87-8 (Au 73).

Haslam, Gerry. "WE: Portrait of the Artist as Shaman." *WR*, 8: 3-13 (1971).

Milton, J.R. "The Land as Form in Frank Waters and WE." *KanQ*, 2: 104-9 (1970).

Easton, William Edgar. Fehrenbach, R.J. "WEE's *Dessalines*." *CLAJ*, 19: 75-89 (S 75).

Eberhart, Richard. Bauerle, R.F. "E's 'Throwing the Apple.'" *Expl*, 27: 21 (N 68).

Cargas, H.J. "At the Central Core of Life." *Webster R*, 2: 67-8 (#1 75).

Cooney, Seamus. "E's 'Experience Evoked.'" *Expl*, 32: 39 (Ja 74).

Eberhart, Richard. "Encounters and Letters: RE and Wallace Stevens." *DCLB*, 4: 57-60 (D 61).

―――. "E's 'Experience Evoked.'" *Expl*, 32: 76 (1974).

―――, and Alvin Sullivan. "E's 'Seals, Terns, Time.'" *Expl*, 30: 29 (1971).

Fein, R.J. "The Cultivation of Paradox: The War Poetry of RE." *BSUF*, 10: 56-64 (Sp 69).

Jacobs, R.G. "The Voices of RE." *IEngYb*, 6: 24-8 (Fa 61).

Mills, Ralph. "In the Fields of Imagination." *Parnassus*, 1: 211-24 (#2 73).

Rosenthal, M.L. "Steps to Status on the Literary Ladder." *SatR*, 54: 25-7 (6 Mr 71).

Sullivan, Alvin. "E's 'Seals, Terns, Time.'" *Expl*, 30: 8 (1971).

Edmonds, Walter. Wyld, L.D. "At Boyd House: WE's York State." *Eng Rec*, 20: 89-92 (1969).

Edwards, Harry Stillwell. Garret, G.P. "Old Books: *Eneas Africanus.*" *GaR*, 11: 219-23 (Su 57).

Lanier, Doris. "The Death of Paul Hamilton Hayne." *GHQ*, 57: 579-84 (Wi 73).

———. "James Whitcomb Riley, 'Bill' Nye, and HSE: A Lecture Tour." *GHQ*, 57: 256-64 (Su 73).

Edwards, Jonathan. Abelove, Henry. "JE's Letter of Invitation to George Whitefield." *WMQ*, 29: 487-9 (Jl 72).

Buckingham, W.J. "Stylistic Artistry in the Sermons of JE." *PLL*, 6: 136-51 (Sp 70).

Bushman, R.L. "JE as Great Man." *Soundings*, 52: 15-46 (Sp 69).

Cowan, J.C. "JE's Sermon Style: 'The Future Punishment of the Wicked Unavoidable and Intolerable.'" *SCB*, 29: 119-22 (Wi 69).

Delattre, R.A. "Beauty and Theology: A Reappraisal of JE." *Soundings*, 51: 60-79 (Wi 68).

Ellis, J.J. "The Puritan Mind in Transition." *WMQ*, 28: 26-45 (Ja 71).

Grabo, N.S. "JE's *Personal Narrative*: Dynamic Stasis." *LWU*, 2: 141-8 (1969).

Griffith, John. "JE as a Literary Artist." *Criticism*, 15: 156-73 (Sp 73).

Holbrook, C.A. "E Re-Examined." *RMeta*, 13: 623-41 (Je 60).

Howard, Leon. "The Creative Imagination of a College Rebel: JE's Undergraduate Writings." *EAL*, 5: 50-6 (Wi 70-71).

Johnson, Ellwood. "Individualism and the Puritan Imagination." *AQ*, 22: 230-7 (1970).

Kimnach, W.H. "JE's Sermon Mill." *EAL*, 10: 167-77 (Fa 75).

Kolodny, Annette. "Imagery in the Sermons of JE." *EAL*, 7: 172-82 (Fl 72).

Laskowsky, J.J. "JE: A Puritan Philosopher of Science." *ConnR*, 4: 33-41 (1970).

Lee, S.M. "JE's Theory of the Imagination." *MichA*, 5: 233-41 (Fa 72).

Lensing, George. "Robert Lowell and JE: Poetry in the Hands of an Angry God." *SCR*, 6: 7-17 (Ap 74).

Loewinsohn, Ron. "JE's Opticks: Images and Metaphors of Light in Some of His Major Works." *EAL*, 8: 21-32 (Sp 73).

Lowance, M.I. "From E to Emerson: A Revaluation." *ATQ*, 18: 3-13 (Sp 73).

———. "Images or Shadows of Divine Things: The Typology of JE." *EAL*, 5: 141-81 (Je 70).

Lyttle, David. "JE on Personal Identity." *EAL*, 7: 163-71 (Fl 72).

Martin, Jean-Pierre, "E's Epistemology and the New Science." *EAL*, 7: 247-55 (Wi 73).

Mothersill, Mary. "Professor Prior and JE." *RMeta*, 16: 366-73 (D 62).

Nagy, P.J. "JE and the Metaphysics of Consent." *Person*, 51: 434-46 (Au 70).

Parker, G.T. "JE and Melancholy." *NEQ*, 41: 193-212 (Je 68).

Parker, W.H. "JE: Founder of the Counter-Tradition of Transcendental Thought in America." *GaR*, 27: 543-9 (Wi 73).

Pierce, D.C. "JE and the 'New Sense' of Glory." *NEQ*, 41: 82-95 (Je 68).

Prior, A.N. "Limited Indeterminism." *RMeta*, 16: 55-61 (S 62).

Reaske, C.R. "The Devil and JE." *JHI*, 33: 123-38 (Ja-Mr 72).

———. "An Unpublished Letter Concerning 'Sanctification' by Elisha Williams, JE's Tutor." *NEQ*, 45: 429-34 (S 72).

Richmond, A.A. "JE, Jr., and Union College." *UnionColSyn*, 8: 20-29 (1970).

Riforgiato, L.R. "The Unified Thought of JE." *Thought*, 47: 599-610 (1972).

Rupp, George. "The 'Idealism' of JE." *HTR*, 62: 209-26 (Ap 69).

Scheick, W.J. "Family, Conversion, and the Self in JE's *A Faithful Narrative of the Surprising Work of God*." *TSL*, 19: 79-89 (1974).

———. "The Grand Design: JE's History of the Work of *Redemption*." *ECS*, 8: 300-14 (Sp 75).

Schneewind, J.B. "Comments on Prior's Paper." *RMeta*, 16: 374-9 (D 62).

Edwards, Jonathan

Serio, J.N. "From E to Poe." *ConnR*, 6: 88-92 (1972).
Shafer, T.A. "Manuscript Problems in the Yale Edition of JE." *EAL*, 3: 159-71 (Wi 68-69).
Smith, J.E. "JE: Piety and Practice in the American Character." *JR*, 54: 166-80 (Ap 74).
Stein, S.J. "JE and the Rainbow: Biblical Exegesis and Poetic Imagination." *NEQ*, 47: 440-55 (S 74).
———. "Cotton Mather and JE on the Number of the Beast: Eighteenth-Century Speculation about the Antichrist." *PAAS*, 84: 293-315 (1974).
———. "A Notebook on the Apocalypse by JE." *WMQ*, 29: 623-34 (O 72).
Watts, E.S. "The Neoplatonic Basis of JE's 'True Virtue.'" *EAL*, 10: 179-89 (Fa 75).
Weddle, David. "JE on Men and Trees and the Problems of Solidarity." *HTR*, 67: 155-75 (1974).
Wilson, D.S. "The Flying Spider." *JHI*, 32: 447-58 (Jl-S 71).
Eggleston, Edward. Benson, R.M. "Ignoble Savage: EE and the American Indian." *IllQ*, 35: 41-51 (F 73).
*Cox, Leland. "EE." *ALR*, 8: 247-8 (1975).
Danner, E.M. "EE." *IMH*, 33: 435-53 (D 37).
Esary, Logan. "Elements of Culture in the Old Northwest." *IMH*, 53: 257-64 (1957).
Kay, Donald. "Infant Realism in E's *The Hoosier Schoolmaster*." *MarkR*, 2: 81-3 (F 71).
Nelson, Jane. "EE Redeemed." *PosS*, 4: 10-2 (Ap 73).
Quintus, J.A. "*The Hoosier Schoolmaster*: A Correction." *N&Q*, 15: 423 (N 68).
Underwood, G.N. "Toward a Reassessment of EE's Literary Dialects." *BRMMLA*, 28: 109-20 (1974).
Wilson, J.H. "E's Indebtedness to George in *Roxy*." *AL*, 42: 38-49 (Mr 70).
Elder, Lonne. Jeffers, Lance. "Bullins, Baraka, and E: The Dawn of Grandeur in Black Drama." *CLAJ*, 16: 32-48 (S 72).
Eliot, Andrew. Bailyn, Bernard. "Religion and Revolution: Three Biographical Studies." *PAH*, 4: 83-169 (1970).
Eliot, John. Miner, K.L. "JE of Massachusetts and the Beginnings of American Linguistics." *HL*, 1: 169-83 (1974).
Salisbury, Neal. "Red Puritans: The 'Praying Indians' of Massachusetts Bay and JE." *WMQ*, 31: 27-54 (Ja 74).
Tanis, N.E. "Education in JE's Indian Utopias, 1645-1675." *HEQ*, 10: 308-23 (1970).
Vančura, Zdeněk. "Bringing the Gospel to the Indians of New England." *PP*, 14: 81-90 (1971).
Eliot, T.S. Anon. "E and Faith: The Demon of Doubt and the Joy of Belief." *TLS*, 13 N 70, pp. 1313-5.
———. "Literary Portraits: III. T.S.E." *LCUT*, 3: 50-1 (My 71).
———. "A Possible Source for *Ash-Wednesday*?" *AN&Q*, 13: 154-5 (Je 75).
———. "T.S.E. and the TLS." *TLS*, 7 N 68, p. 1251.
Abel, Richard. "The Influence of St.-John Perse on TSE." *ConL*, 14: 213-39 (Sp 73).
———. "Saint-John Perse Encounters T.S.E." *RLC*, 49: 423-37 (1975).
Adams, J.F. "The Fourth Temptation in *Murder in the Cathedral*." *MD*, 5: 381-8 (F 63).
Adell, Alberto. "Releyendo A E." *Insula*, 24: 12 (D 69).
———. "TSE." *Insula*, 220: 13 (Mr 65).
Adler, J.H. "A Source for E in Shaw." *N&Q*, 14: 256-7 (Jl 67).
Ahearn, W.B. "A Possible Source for 'Prufrock.'" *TSE R*, 2: 4 (Sp 75).
Aiken, Conrad. "An Anatomy of Melancholy." *NRep*, 33: 294-5 (7 F 23).
———. "Divers Realists." *Dial*, 63: 453-5 (8 N 17).
———. "New Curiosity Shop—and a Poet." *Dial*, 64: 112 (31 Jl 18).

———. "A Portrait of T.S.E." *LugR*, 1: 115-6 (1965).

———. "T.S.E: Esoteric Catholicity." *PoetJ*, 5: 127-9 (Ap 16).

Aldington, Richard. "A Critic of Poetry." *Poetry*, 17: 345-8 (Mr 21).

———. "Mr. E on Seneca." *Nation and Athenaeum*, 42: 159 (29 O 27).

———. "The Poetry of T.S.E." *Outlook*, 49: 12-3 (7 Ja 22).

———. "The Sacred Wood." *Today*, 8: 191-3 (S 21).

Allan, Alexander. "A Note on Tradition." *STC*, 3: 15-8 (Sp 69).

Alter, Robert. "E, Lawrence & the Jews." *Commentary*, 50: 81-6 (O 70).

Andreach, R.J. "*Paradise Lost* and the Christian Configuration of *The Waste Land*." *PLL*, 5: 296-309 (Su 69).

Appleman, Philip. "The Dread Factor: E, Tennyson, and the Shaping of Science." *ColF*, ns, 3: 32-8 (Fa 74).

Arms, G.W., J.P. Kirby, et al. "E's 'Gerontion.'" *Expl*, 4: 55 (Je 46).

Ashraf, S.A. "E's Poetry from the Point of View of Islamic Mysticism." *Venture*, 5: 63-74 (Je 68).

Atkins, Anselm. "Mr. E's Sunday Morning Parody." *Renascence*, 21: 41-3, 54 (Au 68).

Atkinson, Brooks. "Note on Poetic Drama." *NYTimes*, 1 My 38; sec. 10, p. 1.

———. "Strange Images of Death." *NYTimes*, 29 Mr 36; sec. 9, p. 1.

Auden, W.H. "The Martyr as Dramatic Hero." *Listener*, 79: 1-6 (4 Ja 68).

———. "T.S.E. So Far." *Griffin*, 2: 1-3 (1953).

Auffret, Hélène. "Etude comparée de deux poèmes-conversation: Apollinaire, 'Les femmes,' E, 'A Game of Chess.'" *RLC*, 43: 415-26 (1969).

Austin, Allen, and Ronald Schuchard. "E and Hulme." *PMLA*, 89: 582-5 (1974).

Avadanei, St. "T.S.E: Savoarea culturii." *ASUI*, 17: 91-5 (1971).

Bagg, Robert. "The Electromagnet and the Shred of Platinum." *Arion*, 8: 407-29 (Au 69).

Bailey, Bruce. "A Note on *The Waste Land* and Henry James' *In the Cage*." *TSEN*, 1: 2 (Fa 74).

———. "A Note on *The Waste Land* and Hope Mirrhees' Paris." *TSEN*, 1: 3-4 (Fa 74).

———. "A Note on *The Waste Land* and Joyce's *Ulysses*." *TSER*, 2: 10 (Fa 75).

Baker, J.R. "E's *The Waste Land*, 77-93." *Expl*, 14: 27 (Ja 56).

Balfour, Michael. "'The Waste Land.'" *TLS*, 31 D 71, p. 1630.

Banerjee, R.D.K. "The Dantean Overview: The Epitaph to 'Prufrock.'" *MLN*, 87: 962-6 (D 72).

———. "Dante Through the Looking Glass: Rossetti, Pound, and E." *CL*, 24: 146-49 (Sp 72).

Bantock, G.H. "T.S.E's View of Society." *CritQ*, 15: 37-46 (Sp 73).

Barfoot, Gabriele. "Dante in T.S.E's Criticism." *Engl Misc*, 23: 231-46 (1972).

Baron, C.E. "Lawrence's Influence on E." *CQ*, 5: 235-48 (Sp 71).

Barry, J.B. "E's 'Burial of the Dead': A Note on the Morphology of Culture." *XUS*, 11: 18-26 (Fa 72); *ArQ*, 30: 63-73 (Sp 74).

Barry, John. "*The Waste Land*: A Possible German Source." *CLS*, 9: 429-42 (D 72).

Bateson, F.W. "'A Cooking Egg': Three Postscripts." *EIC*, 3: 476-7 (O 53).

———. "The Critical Forum: 'A Cooking Egg.'" *EIC*, 3: 353-7 (Jl 53).

———. "Editorial Commentary." *EIC*, 19: 1-5 (Ja 69).

———. "The Function of Criticism at the Present Time." *EIC*, 3: 1-27 (Ja 53).

———. "T.S.E: 'Impersonality' Fifty Years After." *SoR*, 5: 630-9 (Su 69).

———. "T.S.E: The Poetry of Pseudo-Learning." *JGE*, 20: 13-27 (Ap 68).

———, and I.A. Richards. "'A Cooking Egg': Final Scramble," *EIC*, 4: 106-8 (Ja 54).

Baum, Bernard. "Willa Cather's Waste Land." *SAQ*, 48: 589-601 (O 49).

Eliot, T.S.

Beery, J.A. "The Relevance of Baudelaire to T.S.E's *The Waste Land*." *SUS*, 7: 283-302 (Je 66).

Bejenaru, Cornelia. "Rainer Maria Rilke, TSE, Jorge Guillén şi Ion Pillat, discipoli şi exegeţi ai lui Paul Valéry." *AUB-LUC*, 20: 15-20 (1971).

Beker, Miroslav. "T.S.E's Theory of Impersonality and Henry James." *SRAZ*, 27-8: 163-7 (Jl-D 69).

Belgion, Montgomery. "In Memory of T.E. Hulme." *SatR*, 4: 154-5 (1 O 27).

Bell, Clive. "T.S.E." *Nation and Athenaeum*, 33: 772-3 (22 S 23).

Bell, V.S. "Reading *Prufrock*." *ES* (Anglo-Am supp), 1viii-1xxiv (1969).

Bergonzi, Bernard. "Allusion in *The Waste Land*, II." *EIC*, 20: 382-5 (1970).

———. "Maps of the Waste Land." *Enc*, 38: 80-3 (Ap 72).

Bergsten, Staffan. "Eliotforskningen idag." *Samlaren*, 91: 130-5 (1971).

Bhattacharyya, Debiprasad. "T.S.E on Shakespeare." *Quest*, 50: 45-54 (Jl-S 66).

Bille, Finn. "The Ultimate Metaphor and the Defeat of Poetry in T.S.E's *Four Quartets*." *Int J Symbology*, 3: 16-24 (1972).

Birley, Robert. "'The Waste Land.'" *TLS*, 25 F 72, p. 220.

Blackmur, R.P. "Lord Tennyson's Scissors, 1912-1950." *KR*, 14: 1-20 (1952).

———. "T.S.E." *Hound & Horn*, 1: 187-213 (Mr 28); 1: 291-319 (Je 28).

———. "T.S.E in Prose." *Poetry*, 42: 44-9 (Ap 33).

———. "Unappeasable and Peregrine: Behavior and the *Four Quartets*." *Thought*, 26: 50-76 (Sp 51).

Blanshard, Brand. "E in Memory." *YR*, 54: 635-40 (Je 65).

Bollier, E.P. "La Poésie Pure: The Ghostly Dialogue between T.S.E and Paul Valéry." *ForumH*, 8: 54-9 (Wi-Sp 70).

———. "T.S.E and John Milton: a Problem in Criticism." *TSE*, 8: 165-92 (1958).

———. "T.S.E's 'Lost' Ode of Dejection." *BuR*, 16: 1-17 (Mr 68).

Boyd, J.D. "The Dry Salvages: Topography as Symbol." *Renascence*, 20: 119-33, 161 (Sp 68).

———. "T.S.E as Critic and Rhetorician: The Essay on Jonson." *Criticism*, 11: 167-82 (Sp 69).

Bracker, Jon. "E's 'The Love Song of J. Alfred Prufrock, 89.'" *Expl*, 25: 21 (N 66).

Bradbrook, M.C. "Little Gidding." *Theology*, 46: 58-62 (Mr 43).

Bragg, Robert. "The Rise of Lady Lazarus." *Mosaic*, 2: 9-36 (1969).

Brandabur, Edward. "E and the Myth of Mute Speech." *Renascence*, 22: 141-50 (Sp 70).

Bratcher, J.T. "Prufrock and the Mermaids Re-Viewed." *Descant*, 6: 13-7 (Sp 62).

Braybrooke, Neville. "E y los niños." *Arbor*, 313: 5-12 (1972).

———. "TSE in the Pursuit of the Whale—His Teenage Poems and Stories." *Comment*, 9: 33-5 (Mr-Ap 69).

Bredin, Hugh. "T.S.E and Thomistic Scholasticism." *JHI*, 33: 299-306 (Ap-Je 72).

Bredvold, Louis I. "E's Issue with His Age." *InR*, 8: 123-26 (1972).

Brombert, Victor. "T.S.E and the Romantic Heresy." *Yale French Stud*, 13: 3-16 (1954).

Brooks, Cleanth. "*Dionysus and the City*." *SR*, 80: 361-76 (Sp 72).

———. "E's Harvard Lectures." *SWR*, 19: 1-2 (Ja 34).

Brown, L.W. "The Historical Sense: T.S.E and Two African Writers." *Conch*, 3: 59-70 (1Q 71).

Brown, R.D. "Revelation in TSE's 'Journey of the Magi.'" *Renascence*, 24: 136-40 (Sp 72).

Browne, E.M. "Poetry in Playwriting." *Drama*, 83: 31-4 (Wi 66).

Browning, Gordon. "E's 'The Love Song of J. Alfred Prufrock.'" *Expl*, 31: 49 (F 73).

Buckley, Vincent. "The Persistence of God." *CritR*, 10: 74-87 (1967).

Bugge, John. "Rhyme as Onomatopoeia in 'The Dry Salvages.'" *PLL*, 10: 312-6 (Su 74).

Callahan, E.A. "The Tragic Hero in Contemporary Secular and Religious Drama." *LHY*, 8: 42-9 (Ja-Jl 67).

Cambon, Glanco. "*The Waste Land* as Work in Progress." *Mosaic*, 6: 191-200 (Fa 72).

Cameron, Elspeth. "T.S.E's *Marina*: An Exploration." *QQ*, 77: 180-9 (Su 70).

Cameron, H.D. "The Sibyl in the *Satyricon*." *CJ*, 65: 337-9 (My 70).

Capellan Gonzal, Angel. "Dimensions metafisicas del tiempo en 'Four Quartets' (T.S.E)." *Atlantida*, 7: 51-68 (1969).

Caretti, Laura. "E come Pécuchet." *SA*, 14: 247-64 (1968).

Carey, John. "T.S.E's Wasteland." *Cithara*, 7: 3-38 (N 67).

Cargill, Oscar. "Death in a Handful of Dust." *Criticism*, 11: 275-96 (Su 69).

Carne-Ross, D.S. "T.S.E: Tropheid." *Arion*, 4: 5-20 (Sp 65).

Carson, M.L. "The Hollow Man: J. Alfred Prufrock." *Cresset*, 34: 9-12 (S 71).

Chace, W.M. "'Make It Not So New'—*The Waste Land* Manuscript." *SoR*, 9: 476-80 (Ja 73).

———. "T.S.E: The Plea Against Consciousness." *Mosaic*, 5: 133-43 (Fa 71).

Chancellor, Paul. "The Music of 'The Waste Land.'" *CLS*, 6: 21-32 (Mr 69).

Chatterjee, Visvanath. "Four Modern Poets: E, Yeats and Tagore." *Mod R*, 137: 123-6 (F 75).

Chiari, J. "'The Waste Land.'" *TLS*, 31 D 71, p. 1630; 25 F 72, p. 220.

Ciardi, John. "TSE: 1888-1965." *SatR*, 48: 35-6 (23 Ja 65).

Christopher, J.R. "Two More Notes on Edward Lear." *Unic*, 2: 12-14 (1972).

Clark, M.J. "Timeless Moments: The Incarnation Theme in *Little Gidding*." *BRMMLA*, 28: 10-7 (Mr 74).

Clausen, Christopher. "A Source for Thomas Becket's Temptation in *Murder in the Cathedral*." *N&Q*, 21: 373-4 (O 74).

Cohen, S.M. "Music and Structure in E's Quartets." *Dartmouth Q*, 5: 3-8 (Su 50).

Coleman, Antony. "T.S.E and Keith Douglas." *TLS*, 2 Jl 70, p. 731.

Combecher, Hans. "Interpretationen für den Englischunterricht: Langston Hughes, F.R. Scott, T.S.E." *NS*, 17: 506-14 (O 68).

Combs, Maxine. "Charles Olson's 'The Kingfishers.'" *FarP*, 4: 66-76 (Sp-Su 70).

Cook, R.G. "Emerson's 'Self-Reliance,' Sweeney, and Prufrock." *AL*, 42: 221-6 (My 70).

Corrigan, Matthew. "The Poet's Intuition of Prose Fiction: Pound and E on the Novel." *UWR*, 2: 33-51 (1Q 66).

Counihan, Sister Bernadette. "*Four Quartets*: An Ascent to Mount Carmel?" *WSL*, 6: 58-71 (1969).

Cowlzy, V.J.E. "A Source for T.S.E's 'Objective Correlative.'" *RES*, 26: 320-1 (1975).

Cox, C.B. "E's Criterion." *Spec*, 7261: 216-7 (25 Ag 67).

———. "T.S.E at the Cross-Roads." *CritQ*, 12: 307-20 (Wi 70).

Crewe, J.V. "T.S.E: A Metaphysical Problem." ESA 15: 105-14 (S 72).

Cutts, J.P. "Evidence for Ambivalence of Motives in *Murder in the Cathedral*." *CompD*, 8: 199-210 (1974).

Daley, E.S. "E's English 26, Harvard University, Spring Term, 1933." *TSE R*, 2: 5-7 (Fa 75).

Dalton, J.P. "A Letter from T.S.E." *JJQ*, 6: 79-81 (1968).

D'Avanzo, M.L. "E's 'Scoriae.'" *AN&Q*, 13: 141-3 (My 75).

Davenport, G.T. "E's *The Cocktail Party*: Comic Perspective as Salvation." *MD*, 27: 301-6 (S 74).

Eliot, T.S.

Davidson, Clifford. "Types of Despair in *Ash-Wednesday.*" *Renascence*, 18: 216-8 (Su 66).

Davie, Donald. "Anglican E." *SoR*, 9: 93-104 (Wi 73).

———, "E in One Poet's Life." *Mosaic*, 6: 229-41 (Fa 72).

———. "T.S.E: the End of an Era." *TC*, 159: 350-62 (Ap 56).

Davis, J.L. "Transcendental Vision in 'The Dry Salvages.'" *ESQ*, 62: 38-44 (Wi 71).

Davison, R.A. "Hart Crane, Louis Untermeyer, and T.S.E: A New Crane Letter." *AL*, 44: 143-6 (My 72).

Deane, P. "Thematic Consistency in the Work of T.S.E." *RLV*, 39: 440-48 (#5 73-74).

Degroote, Gilbert. "Everyman en *Murder in the Cathedral.*" *HZM*, 23: 42-6 (1969).

De la Cruz, J.M. "Alcance de la 'Via Negativa' en la Poesia de T.S.E Como Contraposicion a la 'Utopia' de W. Whitman." *FMod*, 42: 257-72 (1971).

Delasanta, Rodney. "The Bartenders in E and Chaucer." *NM*, 72: 60-1 (1971).

De Stasio, Marini. "Il mondo classico nella poesia di T.S.E." *SA*, 15: 201-44 (1969).

DeLaura, D.J. "Pater and E: the Origin of the Objective Correlative." *MLQ*, 26: 426-31 (Su 65).

DeMott, Benjamin. "Modeling a New Mind from a Brain-Breaking Vision." *SatR*, 54: 35-7, 61-2 (27 N 71).

Deutsch, Babette. "Waste Remains." *Poetry*, 83: 353-7 (Mr 54).

Dick, B.F. "A Marlovian Source for Belladonna's Boudoir: *The Waste Land*, II. 77-100." *TSE N*, 1: 2-3 (Sp 74).

———. "*The Waste Land* and the *Descensus ad Infernos.*" *CRCL*, 2: 35-46 (1975).

Dickerson, M.J. "*As I Lay Dying* and *The Waste Land*: Some Relationships." *MissQ*, 17: 129-35 (Su 64).

Dierick, J. "King and Archbishop: Henry II and Becket from Tennyson to Frye." *RLV*, 28: 424-35 (1962).

Diggle, Margaret. "The Ancient Mariner and the Waste Land." *Poetry* (London), 2: 195-208 (#10 44).

DiPasquale, Pasquale. "Coleridge's Framework of Objectivity and E's Objective Correlative." *JAAC*, 26: 489-500 (Su 68).

Dobrée, Bonamy. "The Confidential Clerk." *SR*, 62: 117-31 (Ja 54).

———. "The London Stage." *SR*, 67: 109-17 (Ja-Mr 59).

———. "A Major Critic." *Listener*, 8: supplement, 11 (1932).

Dolan, Paul. "E's *Marina.*" *Renascence*, 21: 203-6, 222 (Su 69).

Donker, Marjorie. "*The Waste Land* and the *Aeneid.*" *PMLA*, 89: 164-73 (Ja 74).

Donoghue, Denis. "The American 'Wasteland' at Fifty." *Art Int*, 16: 61-4, 67 (My 72).

———. "Criteria Omnia." *CamR*, 89A: 257-60 (9 F 68).

———. "E in Fair Colonus. 'The Elder Statesman.'" *Studies*, 48: 49-58 (Sp 59).

———. "La parola nella parola." *Para*, 280: 5-24 (1973).

———. "Prometheus in Straits." *TLS*, 10 N 72, pp. 1371-3.

———. "T.S.E's *Quartets*: a New Reading." *Studies*, 54: 41-62 (Sp 65).

Dozier, Thomas. "Would the Real Mr. E Please Stand Up?" *Month*, 5: 309-13 (O 72).

Driver, T.F. "T.S.E: 1888-1965." *C&C*, 25: 2-3 (8 F 65).

Duffey, B.I. "The Experimental Lyric in Modern Poetry: E, Pound, Williams." *JML*, 3: 1085-1103 (Jl 74).

Duffy, J.J. "T.S.E's Objective Correlative: A New England Commonplace." *NEQ*, 42: 108-15 (Mr 69).

Dumar, Jitendra. "Consciousness and Its Correlates: E and Husserl." *PPR*, 28: 332-52 (1968).

Dunn, Peter. "'The Waste Land,'" *TLS*, 11 F 72, p. 156.

Durrell, Lawrence. "The Other T.S.E." *Atl*, 215: 60-4 (My 65).

Du Sautoy, Peter. "'The Waste Land.'" *TLS*, 17 D 71, p. 1580.

Dwivedi, A.N. "The Indian Temper in E's Poetry." *BP*, 19: 48-53 (1972).

Dzwonkoski, F.P. "'The Hollow Men' and *Ash-Wednesday*: Two Dark Nights." *ArQ*, 30: 16-42 (Sp 74).

———. "Time and the River, Time and the Sea: A Study of T.S.E's 'Dry Salvages.'" *CimR*, 30: 48-57 (1975).

Eder, D.L. "Louis Unmasked: T.S.E in *The Waves*." *VWQ*, 2: 13-27 (1975).

Edmonds, Dorothy. "T.S.E: Toward the 'Still Point.'" *BUSF*, 5: 49-54 (1964).

Egawa, Toru. "TSE ni okeru 'Muku'—Shall We Follow the Deception of the Thrush?" *EigoS*, 118: 322-24 (1972).

Egri, Peter. "T.S.E's Aesthetics." *HSE*, 8: 5-34 (1974).

El-Azma, Nazeer. "The Tammuzi Movement and the Influence of T.S.E. on Badr Shakir al-Sayyab." *JOAS*, 88: 671-78 (1968).

Elbaz, Shlomo. "Auteur e traducteur face à face." *FMLS*, 9: 269-92 (1973).

Eliot, T.S. "Letter to Ezra Pound." *Nine*, 1: 178-9 (Su 50).

———. "A Note." *SR*, 67: 576 (O-D 59).

———. "T.S.E Talks About His Poetry." *CUF*, 2: 11-4 (Fa 58).

Eliot, Valerie. "TSE and 'The Waste Land.'" *TLS*, 11 My 73, pp. 529.

Ellis, P.G. "The Development of TSE's Historical Sense." *RES*, 23: 291-301 (Ag 72).

———. "T.S.E, F.H. Bradley, and 'Four Quartets.'" *RSW*, 37: 93-111 (Je 69).

Ellmann, Richard. "The first Waste Land—I." *NYRB*, 17: 10-6 (18 N 71).

Elmen, Paul. "Magical Journey of T.S.E." *ChrC*, 82: 649-50 (19 My 65).

Embler, Weller. "Simone Weil and T.S.E." *Costerus*, 4: 48-68 (1972).

Empson, William. "E and Politics." *TSE R*, 2: 3-4 (Fa 75).

———. ["The Facsimile Edition."] *EIC*, 22: 417-29 (1972).

Evans, D.W. "The Case Book of T.S.E." *MLN*, 71: 501 (N 56).

Everett, Barbara. "E in and out of *The Waste Land*." *CritQ*, 17: 7-30 (Sp 75).

———. "In Search of Prufrock." *CritQ*, 16: 101-22 (Su 74).

———. "A Visit to Burnt Norton." *CritQ*, 16: 199-226 (Au 74).

———. "'The Waste Land.'" *TLS*, 3 Mr 72, p. 249.

Faas, Egbert. "Formen der Bewusstseindarstellung in der dramatishchen Lyrık Pounds and Es." *GRM*, 18: 172-91 (Ap 68).

Faraque, Huhammad. "The Impact of E on Bengali Criticism." *Venture*, 5: 51-5 (Je 68).

Farrell, W.J. "*The Waste Land* as Rhetoric." *Renascence*, 22: 127-40 (Sp 70).

Farrelly, James. "'Gerontion': Time's Eunuch." *UDR*, 6: 27-34 (1969).

Felstiner, A.P. "La danza immovil el vendaval sostinedo: Four Quartets de T.S.E y *Alturas de Macchu Picchu*." *AUC*, 129: 177-95 (1971).

Ficimi, Fausto. "T.S.E: *La Figlia che piange*." *SA*, 15: 245-80 (1969).

Fink, E.O. "Zur Waste Land: Übertragung von Ernst Robert Curtius." *NS*, 19: 507-13 (O 70).

Fitz, Reginald. "The Meaning of Impotence in Hemingway and E." *ConnR*, 4: 16-22 (1971).

Fiumi, A.B. "G. Benn e TSE: Poetiche a confronto." *SA*, 16: 301-51 (1970).

Fiumi, Fausto. "Virgilio e il classicismo de T.S.E." *SA*, 17: 121-6 (1971).

Fleissner, R.F. "The Browning of T.S.E." *TSN N*, 1: 6-7 (Sp 74).

———. "Prufrock's 'Ragged Claws.'" *ES*, 53: 247-8 (Je 72).

———. "Prufrock Not the Polonius Type." *Res Stud*, 43: 262-63 (1975).

———. "Reacting to Polonius *The Reactionaries*: Libertarian Views." *JHR*, 17: 138-45 (1969).

Eliot, T.S.

Forster, E.M. "T.S.E and His Difficulties." *Life & Letters*, 2: 217-25 (Je 29).

Fowler, Helen. "The E of Yvor Winters." *Approach*, 10: 2-8 (Wi 53-54).

Fowler, Rowena. "'ḤÉpnmn Xẃpx: Seferis' Translation of *The Waste Land*." *CLS, CLS*, 9: 443-54 (D 72).

Foxall, Edgar. "T.S.E and Keith Douglas." *TLS*, 31 Jl 70, p. 854.

Fowler, R.T. "Krishna and the 'Still Point': A Study of the *Bhagavad-Gita*'s Influence in E's *Four Quartets*." *SR*, 79: 407-23 (Su 71).

Frank, A.P. "E and Babbitt: A Note on Influence." *TSE N*, 1: 7-9 (Fa 74).

——. "E's 'Gerontion.'" *Expl*, 30: 53 (1972).

——. "T.S.E's Concept of Tradition and the American Background." *JA*, 16: 151-61 (1971).

——. "T.S.E's Objective Correlative and the Philosophy of F.H. Bradley." *JAAC*, 30: 311-8 (Sp 72).

Franklin, R.F. "Death or the Heat of Life in the Handful of Dust?" *AL*, 41: 277-9 (My 69).

Franklin, Rosemary. "The Satisfactory Journey of E's Magus." *ES*, 49: 559-61 (D 68).

Fraser, G.S. "Poetic Politics." *TSE R*, 2: 4-7 (# 75).

Fraser, G.S. "T.S.E: A Re-appraisal." *RLV*, 34: 551-66 (N-D 68).

French, A.L. "Criticism and *The Waste Land*." *SoRA*, 1: 69-81 (#2 64).

——. "Death by Allusion?" *EIC*, 20: 269-71 (1970).

Fussell, B.H. "Structural Methods in *Four Quartets*." *ELH*, 22: 212-41 (S 55).

Fussell, Paul. "The Gestic Symbolism of T.S.E." *ELH*, 22: 194-211 (S 55).

Gallup, Donald. "The 'Lost' Manuscripts of T.S.E." *TLS*, 7 N 68, pp. 1238-40; *BNYPL*, 72: 641-52 (D 68).

——. "TSE and Ezra Pound: Collaborators in Letters." *Atl*, 225: 48-62 (Ja 70); *PoetA* 32: 58-80 (F 70).

Galvin, Brendan. "A Note on T.S.E's 'New Hampshire' as a Lyric Poem." *MSE*, 1: 44-5 (Fa 67).

Gardner, C.O. "Some Reflections on the Opening of 'Burnt Norton.'" *CritQ*, 12: 326-35 (Wi 70).

Gardner, Helen. "Altered in Fulfillment." *NSt*, 12 N 71, pp. 654-5.

——. "The 'Aged Eagle' Spreads His Wings. A 70th Birthday Talk with T.S.E." *Sun Times (London Times)*, 21 S 58; p. 8.

——. "Explorer of Moral Distress." *NSt*, (28 N 69), pp. 760-2.

——. "The Landscapes of E's Poetry." *CritQ*, 10: 313-30 (Wi 68).

——. "Shakespeare in the Age of Eliot." *TLS*, 23 Ap 64, p. 335.

——. "'The Waste Land.'" *TLS*, 4 F 72, p. 128.

Gathercole, P.M. "Two Kindred Spirits: Eugenio Montale and T.S.E." *Italica*, 32: 170-9 (S 55).

Gent, Margaret. "The Drowned Phoenician Sailor: T.S.E and William Morris." *N&Q*, 17: 50-1 (F 70).

Gerstenberger, Donna. "Steinbeck's American Waste Land." *MFS*, 11: 59-65 (Sp 65).

Ghosh, Damayanti. "The Concept of Karma in T.S.E." *Jadavpur J Cont Lit*, 12: 14-21 (1975).

——. "Karma as a Mode of Salvation in T.S.E." *Jadavpur J Cont Lit*, 11: 125-35 (1974).

Gibbons, Tom. "*The Waste Land* Tarot Identified." *JML*, 2: 560-5 (N 72).

Gil, Kim Jong. "T.S.E's Influence of Modern Korean Poetry." *LE&W*, 13: 359-76 (1969).

——. "'You' in 'The Love Song of J. Alfred Prufrock.'" *Phoenix* (Korea), 11: 41-51 (1967).

Giles, R.F. "A Note on 'April.'" *TSE N*, 1: 3 (Sp 75).

Gillis, E.A. "The Scurrilous Parody in T.S.E's Early Religious Verse." *Descant*, 16: 43-8 (Sp 72).

Gish, Nancy. "The Meaning of the Incarnation in Two 'Ariel Poems.'" *MichA*, 6: 59-69 (Su 73).

Glenn, I.E. "T.S.E's 'Burbank with a Baedeker: Bleistein with a Cigar': A Sociological Reading." *Standpunte*, 118: 39-44 (1975).

Goheen, R.F. "'Burbank with a Baedeker,' the Third Stanza: Thematic Intention through Classical Allusion." *SR*, 61: 109-19 (Wi 53).

Goller, K.H. "T.S.E: *The Waste Land*: From Ritual to Romance." *NS*, 14: 545-58 (D 65).

Goodman, Paul. "T.S.E: the Poet of Purgatory." *NewL*, 14 Ag 43, pp. 3, 7.

Gordon, Lyndall. "*The Waste Land* Manuscript." *AL*, 45: 557-70 (Ja 74).

Gow, H.B. "Religion, Literature, and T.S.E." *Western World R*, 8: 19-26 (Wi 73-74).

Graham, Desmond. "T.S.E and Keith Douglas." *TLS*, 21 Ag 70, p. 928.

Graham, Don. "*Land Today* and the Example of *The Waste Land*." *CLAJ*, 17: 327-32 (Mr 74).

Grahn, Heinz. "T.S.E: 'Journey of the Magi.'" *NS*, 16: 341-9 (Jl 67).

Grasmuck, Gloria. "A Second Look at T.S.E." *Gypsy Schol*, 2: 47-51 (1974).

Graves, Robert. "Sweeney among the Nightingales." *TQ*, 1: 83-102 (Sp 58).

———. "These Be Your Gods, O Israel." *EIC*, 5: 140-5 (Ap 55).

Green, Peter. "Du côté de chez Waugh." *REL*, 89-100 (Sp 61).

Grenander, M.E., and K.S.N. Rao. "*The Waste Land* and the *Upanishads*: What Does the Thunder Says?" *Indian Lit*, 14: 85-98 (Mr 71).

Griffin, E.G. "P in Perspective, *TSE N*, 1: 13-5 (Fa 74).

Grigorescu, Irina. "TSE: *Patru cvartete*." *Orizont*, 21: 79-81 (1971).

Gross, Harvey. "'Métoikos' in London." *Mosaic*, 6: 143-55 (Fa 72).

Gross, John. "E: From Ritual to Realism." *Enc*, 24: 48-50 (Mr 65).

Guttmann, Allen. "From Brownson to E: The Conservative Theory of Church and State." *AQ*, 17: 483-500 (Fa 65).

Gwynn, F.L. "Faulkner's Prufrock—and Other Observations." *JEGP*, 52: 63-70 (Ja 53).

Hager, P.E. "T.S.E's 'A Game of Chess': Another 'Source' of the Dressing Room Scene." *AntigR*, 1: 91-3 (Su 70).

Hahn, P.D. "A Reformation of New Criticism: 'Burnt Norton' Revisited." *ESRS*, 21: 5-64 (Su 72).

Hakac, John. "The Yellow Fog of 'Prufrock.'" *BRMMLA*, 26: 52-54 (1972).

Hall, Donald. "The Art of Poetry, I." *PaR*, 6: 47-70 (Sp-Su 59).

Hall, D.A. "The Lady with a Past." *Harvard Alumni Bul*, 53: 527-28 (24 F 51).

Halverson, John. "Prufrock, Freud, and Others." *SR*, 76: 571-88 (Au 68).

Hancock, C.M. "A Dry Season." *EAA*, 2: 53-65 (1964).

Hansen, E.A. "T.S.E's 'Landscapes.'" *ES*, 50: 363-79 (Ag 69).

Hardenbrook, Don. "T.S.E and the *Great Grimpen Mere* by Gaston Huret III." *BakSJ*, 6: 88-93 (1956).

Harding, D.W. "Christian or Liberal?" *Scrutiny*, 8: 309-13 (D 39).

———. "We Have Not Reached Conclusion." *Scrutiny*, 11: 216-9 (Sp 43).

Hargrove, N.D. "Landscape as Symbol in T.S.E's *Ash Wednesday*." *ArQ*, 30: 53-62 (Sp 74).

———. "Symbolism in T.S.E's 'Landscapes.'" *SHR*, 6: 273-82 (Su 72).

Harmon, William. "Braybrooke Refuted." *TSE R*, 2: 3 (Sp 75).

———. "E, Russell, and *The Hibbert Journal*." *TSE R*, 2: 8-9 (Fa 75).

Harrex, S.C. "Dancing in the Dark: Balachandra Rajan and T.S.E." *WLWE*, 14: 310-21 (1975).

Eliot, T.S.

Harvey, C.J.D. "T.S.E: Poet and Critic." *Standpunkte*, 18: 5-10 (1965).

◁ Harvey, V.R. "T.S.E's 'The Love Song of J. Alfred Prufrock.'" *IEngYb*, 6: 29-31 (Fa 61).

Hayes, M.A. "Hurry Up Please." *Forum (H)*, 3: 23-6 (Su 59).

Hayman, Robert. "T.S.E and E. Martin Browne." *Drama*, 94: 45-6 (Au 69).

Hays, P.L. "Commerce in *The Waste Land*." *ELN*, 11: 292-4 (Je 74).

Headings, P.R. "Among Three Worlds: Ward, E & Dante." *TSE R*, 2: 11-4 (Fa 75).

Herdeck, D.E. "A New Letter by Ezra Pound about T.S.E." *MR*, 12: 287-92 (Sp 71).

Hesse, EVA. "T.S.E: Schwierigheiten beim Leben: 'Gerontion' als Selbstinterpretation des Dichters." *Merkur*, 19: 122-36, 246-57 (F-Mr 65).

————. "'The Waste Land.'" *TLS*, 21 Je 74, p. 671.

Hewes, Henry. "T.S.E Approaches a Vigorous Seventy: His New Play: *The Elder Statesman*." *SatR*, 41: 30-1 (13 S 58).

Hewitt, E.K. "Structure and Meaning in T.S.E's *Ash-Wednesday*." *Anglia*, 83: 426-50 (1965).

Higgins, D.H. "The Power of the Master: E's Relation to Dante." *Dante Stud*, 88: 129-48 (1970).

Hirsch, F.L. "The Hearth and the Journey: The Mingling of Orders in the Drama of Yeats and E." *ArQ*, 27: 293-307 (1971).

Hobsbaum, Philip. "E, Whitman and the American Tradition." *JAmSt*, 3: 239-64 (D 69).

Hobson, Harold. "Enduring Drama of T.S.E." *EigoS*, 115: 306-7 (1969).

Hollahan, Eugene. "A Structural Dantean Parallel in E's 'The Love Song of J. Alfred Prufrock.'" *AL*, 42: 91-3 (Mr 70).

Holland, J.M. "Human Relations in E's Drama." *Renascence*, 22: 151-61 (Sp 70).

Holloway, John. "The Waste Land." *Enc*, 31: 73-9 (Ag 68).

Holyrod, Stuart. "The Poet, the Saint, and the Modern World." *Poetry R*, 46: 149-53 (Jl-S 55).

Hombitzer, Eleonore. "T.S.E: 'Aunt Helen.'" *NS*, 24: 407-18 (1975).

Hough, Graham. "Dante and E." *CritQ*, 16: 293-305 (1974).

————. "Vision and Doctrine in *Four Quartets*." *CritQ*, 15: 107-27 (Su 73).

Howell, J.M. "Salinger in *The Waste Land*." *MFS*, 12: 367-75 (Au 66).

Huffman, Claire. "T.S.E, Eugenio Montale, and the Vagaries of Influence." *CL*, 27: 193-207 (Su 75).

Hungiville, Maurice. "A Choice of Critics: T.S.E's Edition of Kipling's Poetry." *DR*, 52: 572-87 (Wi 1972-73).

Husain, S.S. "E and My Generation." *Venture*, 5: 7-11 (Je 68).

Husain, S.M. "T.S.E as a Critic of Dickens." *Venture*, 5: 30-7 (Je 68).

Iribarren Borges, Ignacio. "T.S.E y las armas de la cultura." *RNC*, 27: 67-71 (S 65).

Isani, Mukhtar Ali. "The Wisdom of the Thunder in E's *The Waste Land*." *ELN*, 10: 217-20 (Mr 73).

Iwasaki, Soji. "Eliot no Borei—Hitotsu no Bungaku Fudo ni tsuite." *EigoS*, 120: 265-7 (1974).

Jahagirdar, C.J. "T.S.E's *Four Quartets*: the Rhetoric of Impersonality." *LCrit*, 9: 65-9 (Su 70).

Jain, N.K. "An Appreciation of T.S.E's 'Marina.'" *BP*, 10: 387-93 (1968).

Jamil, Maya. "*Hamlet* and *The Family Reunion*." *Venture*, 5: 21-9 (Je 68).

Jay, Douglas. "Mr. T.S.E: after Lambeth." *Oxford Outlook*, 11: 78-85 (Je 31).

Jenkins, Harold. "T.S.E and Keith Douglas." *TLS*, 16 Jl 70, p. 775.

Jha, Akhileshwar. "T.S.E and Christopher Frye: A Note on Possible Influence and Counter-Influence." *LCrit*, 8: 46-54 (1967).

Johnson, L.E. "T.S.E's 'Objective Correlative' and Emotion in Art." *Am Poetry & Poetics*, 1: 20-33 (Fa 74).

Johnson, Maurice. "T.S.E on Satire, Swift, and Disgust." *PLL*, 5: 310-15 (Su 69).

Judelevičius, Dovydas. "Nagailestingas poeto skalpelis." *Pergale*, 1: 104-11 (1972).

Jungman, R.E. "A Note on *The Waste Land*, L, 426." *TSE R*, 2: 9 (Fa 75).

Kantra, R.A. "Satiric Theme and Structure in *Murder in the Cathedral*." *MD*, 10: 387-93 (F 68).

Kashifi, A.K. "E's Impact on Urdu Literature and Thought." *Venture*, 5: 56-62 (Je 68).

Kauk, R.K. "The Poetry of T.S.E" *BP*, 9: 10-25 (1967).

Keeley, Emund. "Seferis and the 'Mythical Method.'" *CLS*, 6: 109-25 (Je 69).

———. "T.S.E and the Poetry of George Seferis." *CL*, 8: 214-26 (Su 56).

Kelly, Thomas and Brian. "He Do the Police in Different Voices." *TLS*, 9 Ja 69, p. 38; 23 Ja, p. 86; 30 Ja, p. 110; 13 F, p. 6; 6 Mr, p. 242; and 20 Mr, p. 299.

Kennedy, Eileen. "Poet's Corner: E's 'East Coker.'" *CEA*, 35: 30-2 (Ja 73).

Kenner, Hugh. "The Seven-Year Shaman." *Nat R*, 16: 113-4 (11 F 64).

———. "Sweeney and the Voice." *Forum (H)*, 3: 22-6 (Sp 59).

———. "Where the Penty [sic] Went." *NRep*, 165: 25-6 (13 N 71).

———. "The Tone of a Terrible Century." *NatR*, 20: 147-8 (6 F 68).

Keogh, J.G. "E's *Hollow Men* as Graveyard Poetry." *Renascence*, 21: 115-8 (Sp 69).

Kereaski, Rodica. "The Idea of Impersonality in the Poetry of T.S.E." *AUB-LG*, 21: 89-98 (1972).

Kilgallin, A.R. "E, Joyce, and Lowry." *Canadian Author & Bookman*, 41: 3-4, 6 (Wi 65).

Kincaid, Arthur N. "The Dramatic Monologue: E's Debt to Browning." *BSNotes*, 2: 4-11 (#2 72).

King, Alec. "'Obscurity' in Modern Poetry." *Meanjin*, 4: 202-3 (Sp 45).

King, Bruce. "Prufrock and Marvell." *T.S.E Newsletter*, 1: 5-6 (Sp 74).

Kinnamon, Rebeccah. "E's 'Ash Wednesday' and Maritain's Ideal for Poetry." *GaR*, 27: 156-65 (Su 73).

Kirk, Russell. "Following E's Antique Drum." *NatR*, 22: 34 (13 Ja 70).

———. "The Waste Land Lies Unredeemed." *SR*, 80: 470-8 (Su 72).

Kitamura, Tsuneo. "Shijin TSE no Hyoka." *EigoS*, 116: 812-14 (1971).

Kline, G.L. "Joseph Brodsky's 'Verses on the Death of T.S. Eliot.'" *RusR*, 27: 195-8 (Ap 68).

Knapp, J.F. "E's 'Prufrock' and the Form of Modern Poetry." *ArQ*, 30: 5-14 (Sp 74).

Knight, G.W. "'The Waste Land.'" *TLS*, 14 Ja 72, p. 40; 28 Ja 72, p. 99; 11 F 72, p. 156; 3 Mr 72, p. 249; 18 F 72, p. 189; and 25 F 72, p. 220.

Knust, Herbert. "Sweeney Among the Birds and Brutes." *Arcadia*, 2: 204-17 (1967).

———. "What's the Matter with One-Eyed Riley?" *CL*, 17: 289-98 (Fa 65).

Kogan, Pauline. "The Bourgeois Line on Culture and Anarchy in Matthew Arnold and T.S.E." *L&I*, 8: 1-14 (1971).

Kohli, Devindra. "Yeats and E: The Magnitude of Contrast?" *Quest*, 58: 42-6 (J-S 68).

Kojecky, Roger. "E the European." *SELit*, 14: 63-73 (1974).

Koppenhaver, A.J. "The Musical Design of T.S.E's *Murder in the Cathedral*." *HussR*, 5: 4-10 (1971).

Krieger, Murray. "The Critical Legacy of Matthew Arnold; or, The Strange Brotherhood of T.S.E, I.A. Richards, and Northrop Frye." *SoR*, 5: 457-74 (Sp 69).

Kudo, Yoshimi. "Strether to Prufrock." *EigoS*, 114: 790-1 (1968).

Kumar, Jitendra. "Consciousness and Its Correlatives: E and Husserl." *Philos & Philos Res*, 28: 332-52 (Mr 68).

————. "La coscienza e i suoi correlati: E e Husserl." *Verri*, 31: 37-59 (1969).

————. "Poesia e percesione: E e Merleau-Ponti." *Verri*, 31: 60-82 (1969).

Kytohonka, Arto. "Kirjallisuuskritiikin pätevyys. Näkökanta T.S. Eliotin metakritiikkiin. (Validité de la critique littéraire)." *KSV*, 24: 35-67 (1969).

LaChance, P.R. "The Function of Voice in *The Waste Land*." *Style*, 5: 101-18 (1971).

Lake, D.J. "T.S.E's 'Vita Nouva' and 'Mi-Chemin': 'The Sensus Historicus.'" *ArielE*, 2: 43-57 (1Q 71).

Lancaster, R.Y. "Symbols of the Journey in TSE's 'Four Quartets.'" *Philobiblon*, 9: 32-40 (1972).

Lancaster, Serena. "A Listing of the Materials in the TSE Collection of the Colgate University Library." *Philobiblon*, 9: 18-31 (1972).

Langbaum, Robert. "The Mysteries of Identity as a Theme in T.S.E's Plays." *VQR*, 41: 560-80 (Fa 73).

Laughlin, James. "Mr. E on Holy Ground." *New Engl Weekly*, 7: 250-1 (11 Jl 35).

Leach, Elsie. "'Gerontion' and Marvell's 'The Garden.'" *ELN*, 13: 45-8 (1975).

————. "TSE and the School of Donne." *Costerus*, 3: 163-80 (1972).

Leavis, F.R. "E and Pound." *TLS*, 28 Ag 70, p. 950; 11 S 70, p. 998.

————. "'English'—Unrest and Continuity." *TLS*, 29 My 69, pp. 569-72.

————. "Mr. E and Lawrence." *Scrutiny*, 18: 66-73 (Je 51).

————. "Mr. E, Mr. Wyndham Lewis and Lawrence." *Scrutiny*, 3: 184-91 (S 35).

————. "T.S.E and the Life of English Literature." *MR*, 10: 9-34 (Wi 69).

LeClair, Thomas. "The Obsessional Fiction of SE." *ConL*, 16: 146-62 (Sp 75).

————. "Prufrock and the Open Road." *WWR*, 17: 123-6 (D 71).

Lee, J.H. "Alexander Pope in E's 'East Coker.'" *N&Q*, 10, ns: 381 (1963).

Lees, F.N. "The Dissociation of Sensibility: Arthur Hallam and T.S.E." *N&Q*, 14: 308-9 (Ag 67).

LeMaster, J.R. "Stevens and E on the Mind of the Poet." *Forum (H)*, 10: 27-30 (#3 72).

Lensing, George. "Hart Crane's Tunnel from *The Waste Land*." *Ariel*, 6: 20-35 (Jl 75).

Levin, Harry. "La tierra baldia: De Ur a Echt." *Plural*, 13: 3-6 (1972).

Levý, Jiří. "Synthesis of Antitheses in the Poetry of T.S.E." *EIC*, 2: 434-43 (O 52).

Levy, W.T. "The Idea of the Church in T.S.E." *ChS*, 41: 587-600 (D 58).

Lightfoot, M.J. "Charting E's Course in Drama." *ETJ*, 20: 186-207 (My 68).

————. "Purgatory and *The Family Reunion*. In Pursuit of Prosodic Description." *MD*, 7: 256-66 (1964).

————. "The Uncommon Cocktail Party." *MD*, 11: 382-95 (F 69).

Little, Roger. "T.S.E and Saint-John Perse." *ArlQ*, 2: 5-17 (Au 69).

Litz, W.A. "Pound and E on *Ulysses*." *JJQ*, 10: 5-18 (1972).

Litz, A.W. "*The Waste Land* Fifty Years After." *JML*, 2: 455-71 (N 72).

Locke, James. "Clough's 'Amours de Voyage': A Possible Source for 'The Love Song of J. Alfred Prufrock.'" *WHR*, 29: 55-66 (Wi 75).

Low, Anthony. "The Friendly Dog: E and Hardy." *AN&Q*, 12: 106-8 (Mr 74).

Loya, Arieh. "Al-Sayyāb and the Influence of T.S.E." *MW*, 61: 187-201 (1971).

Lucas, John. "*The Waste Land* Today." *EIC*, 20: 497-500 (1970).

————, and William Myers. "*The Waste Land* Today." *EIC*, 19: 193-209 (Ap 69).

Lund, M.G. "The Eliotian Cult of Impersonality." *TQ*, 9: 164-7 (Sp 66).

————. "The Social Burden of T.S.E." *Disc*, 9: 450-5 (Au 66).

————. "T.S.E's 'Book of Happenings.'" *Forum (H)*, 4: 39-42 (1967).

McCarthy, P.A. "E's *Murder in the Cathedral*." *Expl*, 33: 7 (S 74).

McClanahan, Billie. "A Surprising Source for Belladonna." *TSE R*, 2: 2 (Sp 75).

Maccoby, Hyam. "The Anti-Semitism of T.S.E." *Midstream*, 19: 68-79 (My 73).
———. "A Commentary on 'Burnt Norton.'" *N&Q*, 15: 50-7 (F 68); 17: 53-9 (F 70); 17: 458-64 (D 70).
———. "Difficulties in the Plot of "The Family Reunion.'" *N&Q*, 15: 296-302 (Ag 68).
———. "'The Family Reunion' and Kipling's 'The House Surgeon.'" *N&Q*, 15: 48-50 (F 68).
———. "A Study of the 'jew' in 'Gerontion.'" *JewQ*, 17: 19-22, 39-43 (Su 69).
———. "Two Notes on *Ash-Wednesday*." *N&Q*, 13: 413-5 (N 65).
———. "Two Notes on *Murder in the Cathedral*." *N&Q*, 14: 253-6 (1967).
———. "'The Waste Land.'" *TLS*, 17 D 71), pp. 1580-1; 18 F 72, p. 189.
McCord, Howard. "The Wryneck in 'The Waste Land.'" *CJ*, 60: 270-1 (Mr 65).
McCutchion, David. "Yeats, E and Personality." *Quest*, 50: 13-24 (Jl-S 66).
McElderry, B.R. "T.S.E on Poe." *PN*, 2: 32-3 (Ap 69).
McKeever, Clare. "Man's Response to a Functional World Echoed in *The Waste Land* and *Zorba the Greek*." *Humanitas*, 6: 325-50 (1971).
MacKendrick, L.R. "T.S.E and the *Egoist*." *DR*, 55: 140-51 (1975).
McLauchlan, Juliet. "Allusion in *The Waste Land*." *EIC*, 19: 454-60 (O 69).
McLuhan, H.M. "Mr. E's Historical Decorum." *Renascence*, 25: 183-9 (Su 73).
McLuhan, Marshall. "Mr. E and the 'St, Louis Blues.'" *AntigR*, 18: 2307 (1974).
———. "T.S.E." *CanF*, 44: 243-4 (F 65).
McMorris, M.N. "Time and Reality in E and Eistein." *MCMT*, 29: 91-9 (1973).
Major, J.A. "'Gerontion's and *As You Like It*." *MNL*, 74: 28-31 (Ja 59).
Malawsky, B.Y. "T.S.E, 1952-1964." *BB*, 25: 59-61, 69 (My-Ag 67).
Malekin, P. "'The Waste Land.'" *TLS*, 25 My 73, p. 487; 29 Je 73, p. 749.
Marcus, P.L. "T.S.E and Shakespeare." *Criticism*, 9: 63-79 (Wi 67).
Marshall, W.H. "E's *The Waste Land*, 182." *Expl*, 17: 42 (Mr 59).
Martin, W.R. "A Possible Source for E's 'Triumphal March.'" *TSE N*, 1: 2-3 (Fa 74).
Martínez Menchén, A. "Una lirica de la cultura." *CHA*, 71: 47-81 (1967).
Materer, Timothy. "A Note on T.S.E's 'A Cooking Egg.'" *TSE R*, 2: 3 (Sp 75).
———. "Wyndham Lewis's Portrait of T.S.E." *TSE N*, 1: 4 (Sp 74).
Matlaw, Myron. "E the Dramatist." *CLAJ*, 12: 116-22 (D 68).
Matthews, T.S. "En Route to 'The Waste Land': The Early Years of T.S.E." *Atl*, 233: 35-50 (Ja 74).
Mavroeidi-Papadaki, Sophia. "Ho Tomas S. E kai to archaic drama." *Kritika Phylla*, 1: 333-40 (1971).
Maxwell, D.E.S. "After *The Waste Land*." *ISE*, 1: 73-84 (1969).
———. "'He Do the Police in Different Voices.'" *Mosaic*, 6: 167-80 (Fa 72).
Maxwell, J.C. "'Gareth and Lynette' and 'The Waste Land.'" *N&Q*, 17: 458 (D 70).
Meckier, Jerome. "T.S.E in 1920: The Quatrain Poems and *The Sacred Wood*." *FMLS*, 5: 350-76 (O 69).
Melchiori, Giorgio. "E and the Theatre." *Engl Misc*, 4: 187-233 (1953).
———. "Joyce, E and The Nightmare of History." *RLV*, 40: 582-98 (1974).
———. "The Lotus and the Rose. D.H. Lawrence and E's *Four Quartets*." *Eng Misc*, 5: 203-16 (1954).
Mendel, Sydney. "Dissociation of Sensibility." *DR*, 51: 218-27 (Su 71).
Mendilow, A.A. "T.S.E's 'Long Unlovely Street.'" *MLR*, 63: 320-31 (Ap 68).
Meoli Toulmin, Rachel. "Shakespeare a E nelle versioni di Eugenion Montale." *Belfagor*, 26: 453-71 (1971).
Miles, Leland. "The Writer and His Sources of Inspirations." *HanF*, 6: 65-83 (Wi 59-60).

Eliot, T.S.

Miller, Milton. "What the Thunder Meant." *ELH*, 36: 440-54 (Je 69).

Milner, Ian. "T.S.E and the Avant-Garde." *PP*, 11: 203-8 (1968).

Milward, Peter. "'In the End Is My Beginning.'" *SELit*, 14: 1-13 (1967).

———. "Sacramental Symbolism in Hopkins and E." *Renascence*, 20: 104-11 (Wi 68).

Mineo, Adinolfa. "I tre misteri dell'arcivescovo." *AION-SG*, 1: 331-49 (1969).

Mitchell, J.D. "Applied Psychoanalysis in the Drama." *AI*, 14: 263-80 (Fa 57).

Monroe, Harriet. "A Contrast." *Poetry*, 21: 325-30 (Mr 23).

Monteiro, George. "Addenda to Gallup's 'Eliot.'" *PBSA*, 66: 72 (1Q 72).

Montgomery, Marion. "The Awful Daring: The Self Surrendered in *The Waste Land*." *ArQ*, 30: 43-52 (Sp 74).

———. "Beyond Pound's Quarrel with E's Text." *GaR*, 26: 415-25 (Wi 72).

———. "E and the Meta-poetic." *Intercollegiate R*, 9: 29-36 (1973-74).

———. "E and 'Il Miglior Fabbro.'" *SCR*, 6: 7-13 (N 73).

———. "E and the Particle Physicist: The Merging of Two Cultures." *SoR*, 10: 583-9 (Jl 74).

———. "E, Wordsworth, and the Problem of Personal Emotion in the Poet." *SHR*, 2: 185-97 (Sp 68).

———. "E's Autobiography." *IllQ*, 37: 57-64 (1974).

———. "E's Hyacinth Girl and the *Times Literary Supplement*." *Renascence*, 25: 67-73 (Wi 73).

———. "Emotion Recollected in Tranquility: Wordsworth's Legacy to E, Joyce, and Hemingway." *SoR*, 6: 710-21 (Jl 70).

———. "Lord Russell and Madame Sosostris." *GaR*, 28: 269-82 (Su 74).

———. "Memory and Desire in E's 'Preludes.'" *SAB*, 38: 61-5 (My 73).

———. "Shadows in the New Cave: The Poet and the Reduction of Myth." *SWR*, 55: 217-23 (Su 70).

———. "The Shifting Sands of Ego and the Rock: E's and Whitehead's 'Romantic Quest.'" *TSE N*, 1: 9-13 (Fa 74).

———. "Through a Glass Darkly: E and the Romantic Critics." *SWR*, 58: 327-35 (Au 73).

———. "Wordsworth, E, and the 'Personal Heresy.'" *SAB*, 32: 17-20 (1967).

Moody, A.D. "Broken Images/Voices Singing." *CS*, 6: 44-56 (1973).

———. "*The Waste Land* Facsimile." *ClassQ*, 6: 45-8 (1972).

Moore, Marianne. "A Note on T.S.E's Book." *Poetry*, 12: 36-7 (Ap 18).

———. "'Sweeney Agonistes.'" *Poetry*, 42: 106-9 (My 33).

Moreh, Shmuel. "The Influence of Western Poetry and Particularly T.S.E on Modern Arabic Poetry." *AAS*, 5: 1-50 (1969).

Morgan, F.B. "The Cocktail Party." *Crossroads*, 3: 79-81 (Jl 53).

Morris, J.A. "TSE and Antisemitism." *JES*, 2: 173-82 (1972).

Mother, Mary Anthony. "Verbal Pattern in 'Burnt Norton, I.'" *Criticism*, 2: 81-9 (Wi 60).

Motola, Gabriel. "The Mountains of *The Waste Land*." *EIC*, 19: 67-9 (Ja 69).

———. "*The Waste Land*: Symbolism and Structure." *L&P*, 18: 205-12 (1968).

Mowat, John. "Samuel Johnson and the Critical Heritage of T.S.E." *Studia Gemanica Gandensis*, 6: 231-47 (1964).

Moynihan, William T. "Character and Action in the *Four Quartets*." *Mosaic*, 6: 203-28 (Fa 72).

Mudford, P.G. "Sweeney Among the Nightingales." *EIC*, 19: 285-91 (Jl 69).

———. "T.S.E's Plays and the Tradition of 'High Comedy.'" *CritQ*, 16: 127-42 (Su 74).

Mueller, W.R. "*Murder in the Cathedral*: an Imitation of Christ." *Relig in Life*, 27: 414-26 (Su 58).

Munson, G.B. "The Esotericism of T.S.E." *1924*, 1: 3-10 (1 Jl 24).

Munz, Peter. "Devil's Dialectic, or *The Cocktail Party*." *HJ*, 49: 256-63 (Ap 51).

Murry, J.M. "The Eternal Footman," *Athenaeum, 4686: 239 (20 F 20)*.

Murshid, K.S. "A Note on E's Debt to the East." Venture, 5: 43-50 (Je 68).

Mursurillo, Herbert. "A Note on *The Waste Land*." *Classical Phil*, 51: 174-5 (Jl 56)).

Muzina, Mate. "T.S.E's Convictions Concerning the Use of Ideas in Literature." *SRAZ*, 24: 127-35 (D 67).

Myers, William. "Aesthetic and Critical Judgements." *EIC*, 21: 107-8 (1971).

———. "Allusion in *The Waste Land*: A Replay." *EIC*, 20: 120-12 (1970).

Naik, M.K. "Some Ambiguities in E's Plays." *PURBA*, 3: 25-30 (O 72).

Naples, D.C. "E's 'Tradition' and *The Sound and the Fury*." *MFS*, 20: 214-6 (Su 74).

Narasimhaiah, C.D. "A Workshop for Research Scholars on T.S.E." *LCrit*, 10: 1-21 (Su 73).

Narayana, K.S. "T.S.E and the Bhagavad Gita." *AQ* 15: 573-8 (Wi 63).

Nath, RAJ. "*The Waste Land*: The Facsimile Edition." *LCrit*, 10: 69-74 (1972).

Nelson, F.W. "*The Waste Land* Manuscript." *Wichita State Un Bul*, 47: 3-9 (1971).

Neto, M.A. "Os cinquenta anos de *The Waste Land*." *Coloqui*, 15: 65-9 (1973).

Niikura, Shunichi. "Pound to E." *EigoS*, 119: 9-10 (1973).

Nims, J.F. "Greatness in Moderation." *SatR*, 46: 25-7 (19 0 63).

Nirula, S.C. "The Becket Fable in Tennyson, E and Frye." *IJES*, 11: 34-53 (1970).

Nishiwaki, Junsaburō. "T.S. Eriotto Ron." *Bungaku*, 4: 13-29 (D 32).

Nitchie, G.W. "E's Borrowing: A Note." *MR*, 6: 403-6 (Wi-Sp 65).

Noon, W.T. "Four Quartets: Contemplatio ad Amorem." *Renascence*, 7: 3-10, 29 (Au 54).

Noonan, James. "Poetry and Belief in the Criticism of TSE." *QQ*,79: 388-96 (Fl 72).

Novak, Robert. "*Prufrock* and Arnold's 'Buried Life.'" *WIOr*, 12: 23-6 (Wi 72-3).

Novykova, Marija. "Objektynivst' i maska objektyvosty." *Zovten*, 23: 132-40 (1972).

Nowottny, Winifred. "The Common Privileges of Poetry." *PBA*, 52: 61-86 (1966).

Oberg, A.K. "*The Cocktail Party* and the Illusion of Autonomy." *MD*, 11: 187-94 (S 68).

Oden, T.C. "A Meditation for Ash Wednesday." *ChrC*, 15: 1-8 (Wi 65).

Ohashi, Isamu. "*Arechi* no Kaishaku ni tsuite." *EigoS*, 115: 687-9, 776-9 (1969).

———. "Hiru to Yoru to Tasogare to." *EigoS*, 115: 354-6 (1969).

———. "Jikan no Genzonsei to Ishiki—*Yotsu no Shijuso* boto ni tsuite." *EigoS*, 115: 354 6 (1969).

———. "Jikan no Seishiten." *EigoS*, 115: 296-8 (1969).

———. "T.S.E. no Shiron." *EigoS*, 115: 413-5 (1969)

Okenwa, Nnamdi. "A Leaf from T.S.E's Tree: 'The Dilemma of the Modern Man.'" *Muse*, 7: 45-6 (1975).

Okubo, Junichiro. "Wakaki E ni okeru Sosaku to Hihyo." *EigoS*, 116: 465-7 (1971).

Olshin, T.A. "A Consideration of *The Rock*." *UTQ*, 39: 310-23 (Jl 70).

Olsson, Y.B. "T.S.E's 'Marina': A Study in Poetic Cohesion." *DUJ*, 33: 115-9 (Mr 72).

O'Nan, Martha. "T.S.E's 'Le Directeur.'" *Sym*, 21: 61-6 (Sp 67).

Ong, W.J. "Only Through Time." *Poetry*, 108: 265-8 (Jl 66).

Osotsi, W. "Short-sighted Fascism in T.S.E's *The Waste Land*." *Busara*, 5: 61-8 (1973).

Osowski, Judy. "T.S.E on 'Poe the Detective'" *PN*, 3: 39 (D 70).

Ower, John. "Pattern and Value in 'Sweeney Among the Nightingales.'" *Renascence*, 23: 151-8 (Sp 71).

Padmanabha, Jayanta. "'The Waste Land.'" *TLS*, 17 Mr 72, p. 308.

Pallette, D.B. "E, Fry, and Broadway." *ARQ*, 11: 342-7 (Wi 55).

Palmer, Leslie. "Animal, Man, and Angel: A Study of T.S.E's Beast Imagery." *Forum(H)*, 11: 47-52 (1973).

Eliot, T.S.

Panaro, Cleonice. "Il problema della communicazione nella poesia di T.S.E" *SA*, 14: 193-245 (1968).

Panichas, G.A. "T.S.E and the Critique of Liberalism." *ModA*, 18: 145-62 (Sp 74).

Pankow, Edith. "The 'Eternal Design' of *Murder in the Cathedral*." *PLL*, 9: 35-47 (Wi 73).

Paul, David. "Euripides and Mr. Eliot." *TC*, 152: 174-80 (Au 52).

Patrides, C.A. "The Renascence of the Renaissance: T.S.E and the Pattern of Time." *MQR*, 12: 172-93 (Sp 73).

Patterson, Bertrude. "'The Waste Land' in the Making." *CritQ*, 14: 269-83 (Au 72).

Perloff, M.G. "The Poet and His Politics." *NRep*, 170: 21-3 (16 Mr 74).

Perret, Marion. "E, the Naked Lady, and the Missing Link." *AL*, 46: 289-303 (N 74).

Peter, John. "A New Interpretation of *The Waste Land* (1952). With Postcript (1969)." *EIC*, 19: 140-75 (Ap 69).

Peyre, Henri. "T.S.E et le classicisme." *Reveu d'histoire litteraire de la France*, 3-4: 603-13 (My-Ag 69).

Pickering, J.V. "Form as Agent: E's *Murder in the Cathedral*." *ETJ*, 20: 198-207 (My 68).

Piercy, Marge, and Dick Lourie. "Tom E Meets the Hulk at Little Big Horn: The Political Economy of Poetry." *TriQ*, 23-4: 57-91 (1972).

Pinkerton, Jan. "A Source for 'Tradition and the Individual Talent.'" *TSE R*, 2; 11 (Fa 75).

Pleasants, Ben. "Ontology of Language in the Poems of E and Snyder." *Tuatara*, 12: 53-63 (1974).

Porter, D.H. "Ancient Myth and Modern Play: A Significant Counterpoint." *CBul*, 48: 1-9 (N 71).

Porter, K.A. "From the Notebooks of Katherine Anne Porter: Yeats, Joyce, E, Pound." *SoR*, 1: 570-3 (Su 65).

Porter, M.G. "Narrative Stance in *Four Quartets*: Choreography and Commentary." *UR*, 36: 57-66 (Au 69).

Poulsen, Søren R. "Milton's stil i *Paradise Lost*: Et litteraturkritisk problem. En redegø relse og diskussion med saerligt henblik pa TSE og F.R. Leavis' Miltonkritik." *Extracta*, 4: 177-79 (1972).

Pound, Ezra. "Drunken Helots and Mr. E." *Egoist*, 4: 72-4 (Je 17).

———. "Mr. E and Mr. Pound." *TLS*, 26 Jl 57; p. 457.

———. "Mr. E's Looseness." *New Eng Weekly*, 5: 95-6 (10 My 34).

———. "Mr. E's Mare's Nest." *New Eng Weekly*, 4: 500 (8 Mr 34).

———. "Mr. E's Solid Merit." *New Eng Weekly*, 5: 297-9 (12 Je 34).

———. "T.S.E." *Poetry*, 10: 264-71 (Ag 71).

———. "What Price the Muses Now." *New Eng Weekly*, 5: 130-3 (24 My 34).

Powys, Llewelyn. "T.S.E: the Tutor-Poet." *Week-end R*, 7: 556-7 (20 My 33).

Pratt, L.F. "The Holy Grail: Subversion and Revival of a Tradition in Tennyson and T.S.E." *Victorian Poetry*, 11: 307-21 (Wi 73).

Prince, F.T. "TSE and 'The Waste Land.'" *TLS*, 11 My 73, p. 529.

Pritchard, W.H. "Reading *The Waste Land* Today." *EIC*, 19: 176-92 (Ap 69).

Puckett, Harry. "T.S.E on Knowning: The Word Unheard." *NEQ*, 44: 179-96 (Je 71).

Püschel, Brita. "T.S.E: *Murder in the Cathedral*." *NsM*, 21: 23-32 (1968).

Putz, Manfred. "A Conversation with William C. Chace." *Occident*, 8: 51-65 (Sp 74).

Qureshi, I.H. "E and Our Culture." *Venture*, 5: 4-6 (Je 68).

Raditsa, L.F. "The View from Parnassus." *Griffin*, 6: 11-7 (O 57).

Rahman, K. "The Mystic as a Critic." *Venture*, 5: 38-42 (Je 68).

Rahme, Mary. "T.S.E and the 'Histrionic Sensibility.'" *Criticism*, 10: 126-37 (Sp 68).

Raina, M.L. "T.S.E. as Thinker." *JML*, 3: 134-42 (F 73).

————. "TSE's Criticism of the Novel." *RSW*, 40: 81-94 (1972).

Raine, Craig. "Met Him Pikehoses: 'The Waste Land' as a Buddhist Poem." *TLS*, 4 My 73, pp. 503-5.

————. "'The Waste Land.'" *TLS*, 15 Je 73, p. 692.

Rainer, M.L. "T.S.E's *The Waste Land*: Some Early Responses." *LCrit*, 10: 57-68 (2Q 72).

Ram, Tulsi. "Milton and the Language of Ideality: A Supplement to T.S.E." *IJES*, 7: 42-56 (1966).

Ramsey, Jarold. "*The Waste Land* and Shackleton on South Georgia." *ELN*, 8: 42-5 (S 70).

Randall, D.B.J. "The 'Seer' and the 'Seen': Themes in *Gatsby* and Some of Their Parallels in E and Wright." *TCL*, 10: 51-63 (Jl 64).

Ransom, J.C. "T.S.E: A Postscript." *SoR*, 4: 579-97 (Su 68).

Rao, G.N. "The Unfinished Poems of T.S.E." *LCrit*, 9: 27-35 (Wi 70).

Rao, K.S.N. "Addendum on E and the *Bhagavad-Gita*." AQ, 15: 572-8 (Wi 63).

Rauber, D.F. "The Notes on *The Waste Land*." *ELN*, 7: 287-94 (1970).

Ray, Mohit. "E's Search for a Critical Credo." *Rajasthan J Eng Stud*, 1: 12-5 (Jl-D 74).

Rayan, Krishna. "*Rasa* and the Objective Correlative." *BJA*, 5: 246-60 (Jl 65).

————. "Suggestiveness and Suggestion." *EIC*, 19: 309-19 (Jl 69).

Rebmann, D.R. "'The Waste Land.'" *TLS*, 11 F 72, p. 156.

Reed, K.T. "Carl Sandburg and T.S.E: Some Poetical Exchanges." *Poet and Critic*, 6: 45-6 (Fa 70).

Rees, Richard. "T.S.E on Culture and Progress." *JCHist*, 2: 102-12 (1967).

Rees, T.R. "The Orchestration of Meaning in T.S.E's *Four Quartets*." *JAAC*, 28: 63-9 (Fa 69).

————. "T.S.E's Early Poetry as an Extension of the Symbolist Technique of Jules Laforgue." *Forum II*, 8: 46-52 (Wi-Sp 70).

Reeves, G.M. "Mr. E and Thomas Wolfe." *SAB*, 32: 7-8 (N 67).

Reeves, Gareth. "The Obstetrics of *The Waste Land*." *CritQ*, 17: 33-53 (1975).

Reeves, T.D. "Prufrock at the Roxy." *IllQ*, 33: 43-7 (F 71).

Regnery, Henry. "E, Pound, and Lewis: A Creative Friendship." *ModA*, 16: 146-60 (Sp 72).

Reibetanz, Julia. "Traditional Meters in *Four Quartets*." *ES*, 56: 409-20 (O 75).

Revol, E.L. "Permanencia de T.S.E." *Toree*, 17: 43-52 (Jl-S 69).

Rexine, J.E. "Classical and Christian Foundations of T.S.E's *Cocktail Party*." *BA*, 39: 21-6 (Wi 65).

Richards, I.A. "'The Waste Land.'" *TLS*, 14 Ja 72, p. 40.

Richardson, Joanna. "T.S.E." *LHY*, 3: 9-12 (Ja 62).

Richmond, L.J. "E's *The Waste Land*, 380-395." *Expl*, 30: 23 (1971).

Richter, Dagny. "T.S.E, Dante, and 'The Hollow Men.'" *MSpr*, 65: 205-23 (1971).

Ricks, Christopher. "A Note on 'Little Gidding.'" *EIC*, 25: 145-53 (1975).

Ridler, Anne. "'The Waste Land.'" *TLS*, 21 Ja 72, p. 69; 18 F 72, p. 189.

Robinson, David. "E's Rose Garden: Illumination or Illusion?" *CSR*, 4: 201-10 (1975).

Robson, W.W. "The Unread E." *PR*, 40: 136-41 (1973).

Rochat, Joyce. "T.S.E's 'Companion' Poems: Eternal Question, Temporal Response." *ConnR*, 227: 73-79 (Ag 75).

————. "T.S.E's 'Gerontion.'" *Cressett*, pp. 3-11 (F 75).

Roche, Paul. "Since E, Some Notes Towards a Reassessment." *PoetR*, 59: 37-46 (Sp 68).

Rodgers, A.T. "Dance Imagery in the Poetry of T.S.E." *Criticism*, 16: 23-8 (1974).

————. "'He Do the Police in Different Voices': The Design of *The Waste Land*." *Col Lit*, 1: 48-63 (1974).

————. "The Mythic Perspective of E's 'The Dry Salvages.'" *ArQ*, 30: 74-94 (1974).

*————. "T.S.E in the 70's: A Mosaic of Criticism." *TSE R*, 2: 10-15 (#1 75).

————. "T.S.E's 'Purgatorio'; The Structure of 'Ash-Wednesday.'" *CLS*, 7: 97-112 (Mr 70).

Roeffaers, H. "Gedichten van T.S.E in vertaling." *Streven*, 28: 527-33 (1975).

Rogers, W.N. "'Laquearia' in *The Waste Land*." *AN&Q*, 13: 105-6 (Mr 75).

Romer, K.T. "T.S.E and the Language of Liturgy." *Renascence*, 24: 119-35 (Sp 72).

Rosales, R.S. "Some Dantesque Images in the Works of TSE." *SLRJ*, 1: 473-502 (1970).

Rosenfeld, Alvin. "Teaching Modern Poetry: The Examples of T.S.E and Hart Crane." *APR*, 11: 48-50 (Ja-F 73).

Rosenthal, M.L. "*The Waste Land* as an Open Structure." *Mosaic*, 6: 181-9 (Fa 72).

Rosu, Ança. "T.S.E's *The Love Song of J. Alfred Prufrock*—A Song of Experience." *AUB-LG*, 21: 99-105 (1972).

Rother, James. "Modernism and the Nonsense Style." *ConL*, 15: 187-202 (1974).

Rowland, Thom. "Post-Romantic Epiphany as Apocalyptic Reversal: A Reconsideration of Hopkins and E." *NasR*, 2: 62-82 (1972).

Roy, Emil. "The Becket Plays: E, Frye, and Anouilh." *MD*, 8: 268-76 (D 65).

Rozsa, Olga. "T.S.E's Reception in Hungary." *HSE*, 8: 35-44 (1974).

Ruban, Jonathan. "Silent Buds." *NSt*, 16: 447-8 (17 My 70).

Rumble, T.C. "Some Grail Motifs in E's *Prufrock*." *LSUS*, 8: 95-103 (1960).

Russo, J.P. "Perfection or Salvation? Education and Religion in Matthew Arnold and T.S.E." *Union Seminary Q R*, 26: 117-26 (Wi 71).

Ryan, Marianna. "Retrieval of the Word in *Gerontion* and *The Waste Land*." *AntigR*, 20: 78-97 (1974).

Sackton, Alexander. "T.S.E at Texas." *LCUT*, 8: 22-6 (1967).

Sahal, K.L. "The Objective Correlative and the Theory of Rasa." *CalR*, 2: 237-40 (O-D 70).

Salaman, L.B. "A Gloss on 'Daunsinge': Sir Thomas Elyot and T.S.E.'s *Four Quartets*." *ELH*, 40: 584-605 (Wi 73).

Sampley, A.M. "The Woman Who Wasn't There: Lacuna in T.S.E." *SAQ*, 67: 603-10 (Au 68).

San Juan, E., Jr. "Form and Meaning in 'Gerontion.'" *Renascence*, 22: 115-26 (Sp 70).

Sarang, Vilas. "A Source for 'The Hollow Men.'" *N&Q*, 15: 57-8 (F 68).

Sarkar, S.C. "The Impact of Indian Philosophy on T.S.E." *ModR*, 761: 366-68 (My 70).

Scarfe, Francis. "Notes on the Individual Talent." *STC*, 3: 1-14 (Sp 69).

Schmeling, J.L., and D.R. Rebmann. "T.S.E and Petronius." *CLS*, 12; 393-410 (1975).

Schmidt, Gerd. "An Echo of Buddhism in T.S.E's 'Little Gidding.'" *N&Q*, 20: 330 (Sp 73).

————. "'Et Vera Incesu Patuit Dea': A Note on Pound, E and the *Aeneid*." *TSE N*, 1: 4 (Fa 74).

————. "A Note on 'Skimbleshanks: The Railway Cat.'" *N&Q*, 17: 465 (D 70).

————. "Späte Fahrt ins Unbekannte: zur Interpretation von 'East Coker' V, 31-8." *NS*, 16: 163-7 (Ap 67).

————. T.S.E." *JA*, 14: 219-41 (1969).

Schneider, Elisabeth. "Prufrock and After: The Themes of Change." *PMLA*, 87: 1103-18 (O 72).

Schnetzer, Dean. "The Man with Three Staves in *The Waste Land*." *BNYPL*, 78: 347-350 (Sp 75).

Schuchard, Ronald. "E and Hulme in 1916: Toward a Revaluation of E's Critical and Spiritual Development." *PMLA*, 88: 1083-94 (O 73).

———. "First Rate Blasphemy: Baudelaire and the Revised Christian Idiom of T.S.E's Moral Criticism." *ELH*, 42: 276-95 (1975).

———. "T.S.E as an Extension Lecturer, 1916-19." *RES*, 25: 163-72, 292-304 (My, Ag 74).

Schulz, M.F. "Malamud's *A New Life*: The New Wasteland of the Fifties." *WR*, 6: 37-44 (1969).

Schwartz, Delmore. "The Literary Dictatorship of T.S.E." *PR*, 16: 119-37 (F 49).

Schwarz, D.R. "The Unity of E's 'Gerontion': The Failure of Meditation." *BuR*, 19: 55-76 (Sp 71).

Scott, N.A. "E and the Orphic Way." *J Am Acad Rel*, 42: 203-31 (1974).

Scott-Moncrieff, George. "E Remembered." *SR*, 80: 632-8 (Au 72).

Seelye, John. "*The Waste Land*." *TLS*, 5 D 68, p. 1392.

Seferis, George. "Letter to a Foreign Friend." *Poetry*, 105: 50-9 (O 64).

Seif, Morton. "The Impact of T.S.E on Auden and Spender." *SAQ*, 53: 61-9 (Ja 54).

Seiler, R.M. "Prufrock and Hamlet." *Eng*, 21: 41-3 (Su 72).

Semaan, K.I.H. "T.S.E's Influence on Arabic Poetry and Theater." *CLS*, 6: 472-89 (D 69).

Semmler, Clement. "Slessor and E: Some Personal Musings." *Southerly*, 31: 267-71 (1971).

Sen, J.P. "The Theory of the 'Objective Correlative.'" *IJES*, 11: 99-111 (1970).

Sena, Vinod. "The Ambivalence of *The Cocktail Party*." *MD*, 14: 392-404 (F 72).

Serpieri, Allessandro. "Arabesco metafisico eliotiano." *LeS*, 5: 435-45; 6: 1-14 (1970).

———. "L 'incubo della mutilazione in E: Da *Rhapsody on a Windy Night* a *The Waste Land*." *Para*, 266: 101-9 (1972).

Sexton, J.P. "*Four Quartets* and the Christian Calendar." *AL*, 43: 279-81 (My 71).

Shapiro, Karl. "The Three Hockey Games of T.S.E." *AR*, 22: 284-6 (Fa 62).

———. "T.S.E: The Death of Literary Judgment." *SatR*, 43: 12-7, 34-6 (27 F 60).

Sharoni, Edna G. "'Peace' and 'Unbar the Door': TSE's *Murder in the Cathedral* and Some Stoic Forebears." *CompD*, 6: 135-53 (1972).

Sharrock, Roger. "The Critical Revolution of T.S.E." *ArielE*, 2: 26-42 (1Q 71).

Sheppard, Richard. "Cultivating *The Waste Land*." *JES*, 2: 183-89 (1972).

Sheppard, R.W. "Rilke's *Duineser Elegien*—A Critical Appreciation in the Light of E's *Four Quartets*." *GL&L*, 20: 205-18 (Ap 67).

Short, M.H. "'Prelude I' to a Literary Linguistic Stylistics." *Style*, 6: 149-58 (1972).

Shorter, R.N. "Becket as Job: T.S.E's *Murder in the Cathedral*." *SAQ*, 67: 627-35 (Au 68).

Siddiqui, M.N. "The Ambivalence of Motives in *Murder in the Cathedral*." *OJES*, 5: 1-11 (1965).

Siegel, D.G. "TSE's Copy of *Gatsby*." *FHA*, 1971, pp. 290-3.

Sinclair, May. "Prufrock and Other Observations." *Little R*, 4: 8-14 (D 17).

Singer, G.W. "E's 'Sweeney Erect.'" *Expl*, 34: 7 (S 75).

Sinha, K.N. "The Intimate and the Unidentifiable: Feeling in T.S.E's *Four Quartets*." *Lit Criterion*, 5: 128-40 (1962).

Sister M. Cleophas. "*Ash-Wednesday*: The Purgatorio in a Modern Mode." *CL*, 11: 329-39 (Fa 59).

———. "Notes on Levels of Meaning in 'Four Quartets.'" *Renascence*, 2: 102-6 (Sp 50).

Sister Mary Hester. "The Lenten Liturgy as Objective Correlative for T.S.E's 'Ash Wednesday.'" *WSL*, No. 3: 43-56 (1966).

Eliot, T.S.

Sister M. Joselyn. "Twelfth Night Quartet: Four Magi Poems." *Renascence*, 16: 92-4 (Wi 64).

Sister M. Laurentia, "Structural Balance and Symbolism in T.S.E's 'Portrait of a Lady.'" *AL*, 27: 409-17 (N 55).

Slattery, M.P. "Structural Unity in E's 'Ash Wednesday.'" *Renascence*, 20: 147-153 (Sp 68).

Smailes, T.A. "E's 'Journey of the Magi.'" *Expl*, 29: 18 (1970).

———. "The Music of Ideas in *The Waste Land*." *UES*, 11: 25-9 (#1 73).

Smith, Grover. "Lamb and *Lear* in 'Little Gidding.'" *TSE R*, 2: 2 (Sp 75).

———. "The Making of *The Waste Land*." *Mosaic*, 6: 127-41 (Fa 72).

Smith, James. "A Note on the Text of *The Waste Land*." *Trans Cambridge Bibl Soc*, 6: 131-3 (1973).

———. "Notes on the Criticism of T.S.E." *EIC*, 22: 333-61 (1972).

Smith, Marcus, and Landry Slade. "T.S.E as a Chemist." *AN&Q*, 12: 158-9 (My-Je 74).

Sochatoff, F.A. "Four Variations on the Becket Theme in Modern Drama." *MD*, 12: 83-91 (My 69).

Soldo, J.J. "The American Foreground of TSE." *NEQ*, 45: 355-72 (S 72).

———. "Knowledge and Experience in the Criticism of T.S.E." *ELH*, 284-308 (Je 68).

Sorescu, Marin. "Unghiuri drepte si unghiuri ascutite in poezie T.S.E: *Tara Pustie*." *Luc*, 3: 6 (Je 67).

Southam, B.C. "Whispers of Immortality." *TLS*, 22 Je 73, pp. 720-1.

Spangler, G.M. "*The Education of Henry Adams* as a Source for 'The Love Song of J. Alfred Prufrock.'" *N&Q*, 15: 295-6 (Ag 68).

———. "E's 'red rock' and Norris's *McTeague*." *N&Q*, 20: 330-1 (S 73).

Spanos, W.V. "'Wanna Go Home, Baby?': *Sweeney Agonistes* as Drama of the Absurd." *PMLA*, 85: 8-20 (Ja 70).

Speaight, Robert. "The Cocktail Party." *Tablet*, 194: 154-5 (3 S 49).

———. "The Later Poetry of T.S.E." *Dublin R*, 216: 152-6 (Ap 45).

———. "The Plays of T.S.E." *Month*, 30: 209-13 (O 63).

Spencer, Theodore. "On 'Murder in the Cathedral.'" *HA*, 125: 21-2 (D 38).

Spender, Stephen. "Meeting T.S.E." *Eng Speaking World*, 33: 13-5 (F 51).

Spivey, T.R. "The Apocalyptic Symbolism of W.B. Yeats and T.S.E." *Costerus*, 4: 193-214 (1972).

———. "Archetypal Symbols in the Major Poetry of T.S.E and Conrad Aiken." *Int J Symbology*, 2: 16-26 (1971).

Sprich, Robert. "Theme and Structure in E's 'The Hippopotamus.'" *CEA*, 31: 8 (Ap 69).

Srinath, C.N. "T.S.E's Dramatic Theory and Practice." *LCrit*, 11: 64-79 (#4 75).

Srivastava, Narsingh. "The Ideas of the Bhagavad Gita in 'Four Quartets' of T.S.E: The Problem of Synthesis." *Vishveshvaranand Indological J*, 13: 361-72 (#2 75).

Stanescu, Nichita. "T.S.E." *RoLit, Luceafarul*, 30: 6 (Ag 69).

Stamm, Rudolf. "Rebellion und Tradition im Werke T.S. Es." *Univ*, 22: 725-42 (1967).

Standop, Ewald. "A Note on the Dramatic Verse of TSE." *LWU*, 5: 33-36 (1972).

Stein, Gertrude. "The Fifteenth of November." *Criterion*, 4: 71-5 (Ja 26).

Steiner, George. "The Cruellest Months." *NY*, 48: 134-42 (22 Ap 72).

Steinmann, Martin. "Coleridge, T.S.E, and Organicism." *MLN*, 71: 339-40 (My 56).

Stenger, G.L. "Notes on 'Burnt Norton.'" *N&Q*, 19: 340-1 (S 72).

Stevens, Wallace. "Homage to T.S.E." *HA*, 125: 41 (D 38).

Stock, Noel. "E: The Early Years." *PoetA*, 20: 43-7 (F 68); 21: 34-8 (Ap 68).

———. "Modern Poetry and the Norm of Language." *TQ*, 4: 134-44 (Wi 61).

———. "Reflections on E and the Art of Reading." *PoetA*, 9: 50-6 (1973).

Stonier, G.W. "The Gaiety of Mr. E." *NSt*, 19: 627-8 (11 My 40).

Stradberg, V.H. "E's Insomniacs." *SAQ*, 68: 67-73 (Wi 69).

Stravinsky, Igor. "Memories of T.S.E." *Esquire*, 64: 92-3 (Ag 65).

Stroud, T.A. "E's 'Animula.'" *Expl*, 28: 14 (O 69).

Styler, W.E. "TSE as an Adult Tutor." *N&Q*, 19: 53-4 (F 72).

Surette, P.L. "The Music of 'Prufrock.'" *HAB*, 25: 11-21 (Wi 74).

Sutton, Walter. "*Mauberley, The Waste Land*, and the Problem of Unified Form." *ConL*, 9: 15-35 (Wi 68).

Sveino, Per. "T.S.E's 'Gerontion.'" *Edda*, 4: 219-28 (1971).

Sykes, Robert H. "E's 'Lines to Ralph Hodgson Esqre.'" *Expl*, 30: 79 (Jl 72).

Symons, Julian. "The Cri." *LonM*, 7: 19-23 (N 67).

Takayanagi, Shunichi. "About the Center of the Silent Word—T.S.E and Lancelot Andrewes." *ELLS*, 7: 37-81 (1970).

———. "The Garden and the City: An Attempt to Overcome Schizophrenia in T.S.E's Poetry." *ELLS*, 11: 27-45 (1974).

———. "Search after the Whole: F.H. Bradley and T.S.E." *ELLS*, 5: 12-69 (1969).

———. "T.S.E to Ezra Pound." *ELLS*, 9: 100-44 (1973).

———. "Virgil Theodor Haecker and TSE." *ELLS*, 8: 37-63 (1971).

———. "*The Waste Land*: Manuscript and the Poem." *ELLS*, 10: 109-31 (1973).

Tanner, S.L. "T.S.E and Paul Elmer More on Tradition." *ELN*, 8: 211-5 (1971).

Tate, Allen. "A Poetry of Ideas." *NRep*, 47: 172-3 (30 Je 26).

Tello, Jaime. "E and Sitwell." *RNC*, 27: 83 (Ja-Je 65).

Thale, Mary. "T.S.E and Mrs. Browning on the Metaphysical Poets." *CLAJ*, 11: 255-8 (Mr 68).

Thompson, Eric. "The Critical Forum: 'Dissociation of Sensibility.'" *EIC*, 2: 207-13 (Ap 52).

Thomas, R.H. "Culture and T.S.E." *Mod Q*, 6: 147-62 (Sp 51).

Thrash, L.G. "A Source for the Redemption Theme in *The Cocktail Party*." *TSLL*, 9: 547-53 (Wi 68).

Tillyard, E.M.W. "The Critical Forum: 'A Cooking Egg.'" *EIC*, 3: 350-3 (Jl 53).

Tindall, W.Y. "The Recantation of T.S.E." *ASch*, 16: 431-7 (Au 47).

Tinsley, E.J. "Aldous Huxley and T.S.E: A Study in Two Types of Mysticism." *Life of the Spirit*, 6: 119-30 (O 51).

Tinsley, M.B. "T.S.E's *Book of Practical Cats*." *SAH*, 1: 167-71 (Ja 75).

Toms, Newby. "E's *The Cocktail Party*: Salvation and the Common Routine." *ChS*, 47: 125-38 (Su 64).

Torrens, James. "Charles Maurras and E's 'New Life.'" *PMLA*, 89: 312-22 (Mr 74).

———. "T.S.E and the Austere Poetics of Valery." *CL*, 23: 1-17 (Wi 71).

———. "T.S.E and Shakespeare: 'This Music Crept By.'" *BuR*, 19: 77-96 (Sp 71).

Toth, S.A. "*Henderson the Rain King*, E and Browning." *NCLit*, 1: 6-8 (N 71).

Trilling, Lionel. "Mr. E's Kipling." *Nation*, 157: 436-42 (16 O 43).

Turner, A.J. "A Note on 'Murder in the Cathedral.'" *N&Q*, 17: 51-3 (F 70).

Turner, R.C. "Burbank and Grub-Street: A Note on T.S.E and Swift." *ES*, 52: 347-8 (Ag 71).

Unger, Leonard. "A Tribute: T.S.E: The Intimate Voice." *SoR*, 1: 731-4 (Su 65).

———. "T.S.E, 1888-1965: Viva Il Poeta!" *MR*, 6: 408-10 (Wi-Sp 65).

———. "TSE on *The Waste Land*." *Mosaic*, 6: 157-65 (Fa 72).

Vaish, Y.N. "T.S.E and the East." *ModR*, 761: 329-37 (My 70).

Eliot, T.S.

Vania, Rhoda. ''The American in T.S.E.'' *Venture*, 5: 12-20 (Je 68).

Vassilieff, Elizabeth. ''The Quiddity of *Four Quartets*.'' *Direction* (Melbourne), 1: 34-45 (My 52).

Verheul, K. ''Music, Meaning and Poetry in *Four Quartets* by T.S.E.'' *Lingua*, 16: 279-91 (1966).

Vickery, John. ''A Comment on Two Phrases in *The Waste Land*.'' *L&P*, 10: 3-4 (Wi 60).

Villacanas Palomo, Beatriz. ''Los cuatro cuartetos y T.S.E.'' *Estafeta Literaria*, 553: 16-7 (1 D 74).

Virsis, Rasma. ''The Christian Concept in *Murder in the Cathedral*.'' *MD*, 14: 405-7 (F 72).

Viswanathan, S. ''E and Shelley: A Sketch of Shifts in Attitude.'' *ArielE*, 2: 58-67 (1Q 71).

Vizioli, Paulo. ''E e Wagner: O processo de composicao poetica.'' *ESPSL*, 3: 1 (N 74).

Volpe, E.L. ''The Waste Land of Nathanael West.'' *Renascence*, 13: 69-77, 112, (Wi 61).

Vondersmith, B.J. ''*My Last Duchess* and *The Love Song of J. Alfred Prufrock*: A Method of Counterbalance.'' *ContempE*, 43: 106-10 (1971).

Vordtriede, Werner. ''Der junge T.S.E.'' *NDH*, 120: 47-64 (1968).

Voskuil, Duane. ''Some Philosophical Ideas in TSE's *Four Quartets*.'' *NDQ*, 40: 5-12 (Su 72).

Vyas, H.K. ''Lifting the Veil.'' *BP*, 16: 37-41 (1971).

Wain, John. ''The Prophet Ezra v. 'The Egotistical Sublime.''' *Enc*, 33: 63-70 (Ag 69).

Waldoff, Leon. ''Prufrock's Defenses and Our Response.'' *AI*, 26: 182-93 (Su 69).

Waldron, Philip. ''T.S.E: Mr. Whiteside and 'The Psychobiographical Approach.''' *SoRA*, 6: 138-47 (Je 73).

————, and George Whiteside ''E and Psychobiography.'' *SoRA*, 6: 253-6 (S 73).

Walker, Marshall. ''E's Little Symphony: A Note on 'Gerontion.''' *ESA*, 15: 99-104 (S 72).

Walz, Rudolf. ''T.S.E: 'The Love Song of J. Alfred Prufrock,' behandelt an einer Prima.'' *NS*, 15: 477-86 (1966).

Ward, D.E. ''E, Murrary, Homer, and the Idea of Tradition.'' *EIC*, 18: 47-59 (Ja 68).

————. ''Il culto dell 'impersonalita: E, Sant' Agostino e Flaubert.'' *Verri*, 31: 83-95 (1969).

Warncke, Wayne. ''George Orwell on T.S.E.'' *WHR*, 26: 265-70 (Su 72).

Warren, Austin. ''Continuity in T.S.E's Criticism.'' *EWR*, 47: 125-38 (Su 64).

Warren, R.P. ''Homage to T.S.E.'' *HA*, 125: 46 (D 38).

Wasson, Richard. '' 'Like a Burnished Throne': T.S.E and the Demonism of Technology.'' *CentR*, 13: 302-16 (Su 69).

————. ''The Rhetoric of Theatre: The Contemporaneity of T.S.E.'' *DramS*, 6: 231-43 (Sp 68).

————. ''T.S.E's Antihumanism and Antipragmatism.'' *TSLL*, 10: 445-55 (Fa 68).

Watkisn, F.C. ''T.S.E's Mysterious 'Mr. Apollinax.''' *RSW*, 38: 193-200 (S 70).

Watson, C.B. ''T.S.E and the Interpretation of Shakespearean Tragedy in Our Time.'' *EA*, 17: 502-21 (O-D 64).

Watson-Williams, Helen. ''The Blackened Wall: Notes on Blake's *London* and E's *The Waste Land*.'' *Eng*, 10: 81-4 (Su 55).

Watt, Donald. ''E, Huxley, and 'Burnt Norton, II.''' *TSE N*, 1: 5-7 (Fa 74).

Watts, H.H. ''T.S.E and the Still Point.'' *ChiR*, 1: 52-66 (Sp 46).

————. ''The Tragic Hero in E and Yeats.'' *CentR*, 13: 84-100 (Wi 69).

Weatherby, H.L. ''Old-Fashioned Gods: E on Lawrence and Hardy.'' *SR*, 75: 301-16 (Sp 67).

————. "Two Medievalists: Lewis and E on Christianity and Literature." *SR*, 78: 330-47 (Ap-Je 70).

Weber, Alfred. "Ein Briefwechsel mit T.S.E." *JA*, 16: 204-12 (1971).

Webster, G.T. "T.S.E as Critic: The Man Behind the Masks." *Criticism*, 8: 336-48 (Fa 66).

Webster, H.T., and H.W. Starr. "Macavity: An Attempt to Unravel His Mystery." *BakSJ*, 4: 205-10 (O 54).

Weinig, Sister M. Anthony. "Verbal Pattern in *Little Gidding I*." *Greyfriar*, 13: 25-33 (1972).

Weinstock, D.J. "Tennysonian Echoes in 'The Love Song of J. Alfred Prufrock.'" *ELN*, 7: 213-4 (Mr 70).

Weintraub, Stanley. "The Private Life of a Dead Poet." *NRep*, 170: 27-8 (23 Mr 74).

Weisberg, Robert. "T.S.E: The Totemic-Mosaic Dream." *BMMLA*, 8: 24-44 (Fa 75).

Wetzel, H. "The Seer in the Spring: On *Tonio Kroger* and *The Waste Land*." *RLC*, 174: 322-32 (Jl-S 70).

————. "Spuren des *Ulysses* in *The Waste Land*." *GRM*, 20: 442-66 (1970).

Whitaker, T.R. "Voices of the Open: Wordsworth, E, and Stevens." *IowaR*, 2: 96-112 (#3 71).

Whitlark, J.S. "More Borrowings by T.S.E from 'The Light of Asia.'" *N&Q*, 220: 206-7 (1975).

White, Gina. "Modes of Being in Yeats and E." *ModO*, 1: 227-37 (Wi 71).

Whiteside, George. "T.S.E: The Psychobiographical Approach." *SoRA*, 6: 3-26 (Mr 73).

————. "T.S.E's Doctoral Studies." *AN&Q*, 9: 83-7 (O 73).

————, and Philip Waldron. "Critical Exchange: E and Psychobiography." *SoRA*, 6: 253-6 (S 73).

Whitlark, James. "More Borrowings by T.S.E from *The Light in Asia*." *N&Q*, 22: 206-7 (My 75).

Williams, Margaret. "T.S.E and Eastern Thought." *TkR*, 2: 175-94 (1Q 71).

Williams, P.D. "The Function of the Chorus in T.S.E's *Murder in the Cathedral*." *ABR*, 23: 499-511 (1972).

Williams, Philip. "The Resurrection Lyric of *Four Quartets*." *EigoS*, 114: 590-2 (1968).

————. "T.S.E on Poetry and Belief." *EWR*, 3: 126-36 (1967).

————. "Whitman and E: Two Sides of One Tradition." *Hikaku Bungaku*, 15: 1-15 (1972).

Williams, Raymond. "Second Thoughts: I—T.S.E on Culture." *EIC*, 6: 302-18 (Jl 56).

————. "Tragic Resignation and Sacrifice." *CritQ*, 5: 5-19 (Sp 63).

Williams, W.C. "Homage to T.S.E." *HA*, 125: 42 (D 38).

————. "Prologue." *Little R*, 6: 76-8 (My 19).

Williamson, Audrey. "Poetry in the Theatre: E and Fry." *Chrysalis*, 4: 3-19 (#5/6 51).

Williamson, George. "T.S.E: 1888-1965." *ModA*, 9: 399-407 (Fa 65).

Williamson, H.R. "A Commentary on T.S.E's 'The Waste Land.'" *Bkm*, 82: 192-5, 244-8, 289-91 (Jl, Ag, S 32).

Wilson, Edmund. "The First Waste Land—II." *NYRB*, 17: 16-7 (18 N 71).

————. "The Poetry of Drouth." *Dial*, 72: 611-6 (D 22).

Wilson, Roderick. "E and Achebe: An Analysis of Some Formal and Philosophical Qualities of *No Longer at Ease*." *ESA*, 14: 215-23 (S 71).

Wilson, Timothy. "The Wife of the Father of *The Waste Land*." *Esquire*, 77: 44-50 (My 72).

Wimsatt, W.K. "Arts and Letters: E's Comedy." *SR*, 58: 666-78 (Au 50).

————. "Prufrock and Maud: From Plot to Symbol." *Yale French Stud*, 9: 84-92 (1952).

Eliot, T.S.

Winston, G.P. "Washington Allston and the Objective Correlative." *BuR*, 11: 95-108 (D 62).

Wolheim, Richard. "E, Bradley, and Immediate Experience." *NSt*, 67: 401-2 (13 Mr 64).

Worthen, John. "*The Waste Land.*" *TLS*, 24 My 74; p. 559.

Wright, Nathalia. "A Source for T.S.E's 'Objective Correlative'?" *AL*, 41: 589-91 (Ja 70).

Yamada, Akihiro. "E and Webster." *ES*, 52: 41-3 (F 71).

————. "Seneca—Chapman—E." *N&Q*, 17: 457-8 (D 70).

Yamada, Shoichi. "Jijitsu o Noberu koto—T.S.E no 'Ogon no Koeda's Hyoka." *Oberon*, 32: 2-22 (1971).

————. "T.S.E and Remy de Gourmont—On Personality." *SELit*, Eng. No.: 163-4 (1971).

Yamada, Yoichi. "T.S.E no *Ninshiki to Deiden no Shuppan.*" *Oberon*, 29: 2-12 (1968).

Yasuda, Shoichiro. "*Arechi* no Sokoban wo yomu-Towaku Kara Ifu e." *EigoS*, 117: 745-47 (1972).

————. "'*Arechi*' Saiko." *EigoS*, 119; 684-5 (1974).

————. "'Naraba' to 'Totemo.'" *EigoS*, 115: 496-7 (1969).

Yen, Yuan-shu. "Sound and Diction in T.S.E's Verse Drama." *Fu Jen Stud*, 1: 119-44 (1968).

Yeomans, W.E. "T.S.E., Ragtime, and the Blues." *UR*, 34: 267-75 (Je 68).

Young, Philip. "Scott Fitzgerald's Waste Land." *Kansas Mag*, 24: 73-7 (1956).

Zabel, M.D. "A Modern Purgatorio." *Cweal*, 17: 696-7 (19 Ap 33).

Zulli, Floyd. "T.S.E and Paul Bourget." *N&Q*, 13: 4-5-6 (N 66).

Elkin, Stanley. LeClair, Thomas. "The Obsessional Fiction of SE." *ConL*, 16: 146-62 (Sp 75).

Olderman, R.M. "The Politics of Vitality: On SE." *FicI*, 2-3: 140-44 (Sp-Fa 74).

Sanders, Scott. "An Interview with SE." *ConL*, 16: 131-45 (Sp 75).

Ellery, William. Fowler, W.M. "A Farce Re-examined." *PMHB*, 95: 529-32 (1971).

Elliott, James. Huddleston, E.L. "Indians and Literature of the Federalist Era: The Case of JE." *NEQ*, 44: 221-37 (Je 71).

————. "JE and 'The Garden of North America': A New Englander's Impressions of the Old Northwest." *NOQ*, 42: 64-73 (1970).

Elliott, William. Anderson, C.R. "Thoreau Takes a Pot Shot at *Carolina Sports.*" *GaR*, 22: 289-99 (Fa 68).

Jones, L.P. "WE: South Carolina Non-Conformist." *JSH*, 17: 361-81 (Ag 51).

Rubin, L.D. "WE Shoots a Bear; Thoughts on the Southern Literary Imagination." *Symposium '74*, (Statesboro, Ga.), pp. 1-19.

Ellison, Ralph Waldo. Anon. "An American, A Negro." *TLS*, 18 Ja 68, pp. 49-50.

————. "What's Wrong with the American Novel?" *ASch*, 24: 464-503 (Au 555).

Baker, H.A. "A Forgotten Prototype: 'The Autobiography of an Ex-Colored Man' and 'Invisible Man.'" *VQR*, 49: 433-49 (Su 73).

Balet, S. "The Problem of Characterization in RE's *Invisible Man.*" *FMod*, 15: 277-81 (1975).

Bell, J.D. "E's *Invisible Man.*" *Expl*, 29: 19 (1970).

Bennett, J.Z. "The Race and the Runner: E's *Invisible Man.*" *XUS*, 5: 12-26 (Mr 66).

*Benoit, Bernard, and Michel Fabre. "A Bibliography of RE's Published Writings." *SBL*, 2: 25-8 (Au 71).

Boulger, J.D. "Puritan Allegory in Four Modern Novels." *Thought*, 44: 413-32 (Au 69).

Brown, L.W. "RE's Exhorters: The Role of Rhetoric in *Invisible Man.*" *CLAJ*, 13: 299-303 (Mr 70).

Bucco, Martin. "E's Invisible West." *WAL*, 10: 237-8 (N 75).

Carson, D.L. "RE: Twenty Years After." *SAF*, 1: 1-23 (Sp 73).

Cartosio, Bruno. "Due scrittori afroamericani: Richard Wright e RE." *SA*, 15: 395-431 (1969).

Cash, E.A. "The Narrators in *Invisible Man* and *Notes From Underground*: Brothers In The Spirit." *CLAJ*, 16: 505-7 (Je 73).

Clarke, J.H. "The Visible Dimensions of *Invisible Man*." *BlackW*, 20: 27-30 (1970).

Clipper, L.J. "Folkloric and Mythic Elements in *Invisible Man*." *CLAJ*, 13: 229-41 (Mr 70).

Collier, E.W. "The Nightmare Truth of an Invisible Man." *BlackW*, 20: 12-9 (1970).

Corrigan, R.A. "Afro-American Fiction: A Checklist, 1853-1970." *MASJ*, 11: 114-25 (Fa 70).

Corry, John. "Profile of an American Novelist: A White View of RE." *BlackW*, 20: 116-25 (1970).

*Covo, Jacqueline. "RE in France: Bibliographic Essays and Checklist of French Criticism, 1954-1971." *CLAJ*, 16: 519-26 (Je 73).

*———. "RWE: Bibliographic Essays and Finding List of American Criticism, 1952-1964." *CLAJ*, 15: 171-96 (D 71).

Deutsch, L.J. "E's Early Fiction." *NALF*, 7: 53-9 (Su 73).

———. "RWE and Ralph Waldo Emerson: A Shared Moral Vision." *CLAJ*, 16: 159-78 (D 72).

Doyle, M.E. "In Need of Folk: The Alienated Protagonists in RE's Short Fiction." *CLAJ*, 19: 165-72 (1975).

Ducornet, Guy. "RE: Homme invisible, pour qui chantes-tu?" *LanM*, 63: 394-401 (1969).

Ellison, Ralph. "A Dialogue with His Audience." *BaratR*, 3: 51-3 (1968).

———, and J.A. McPherson. "*Indivisible Man*." *Atl*, 226: 45-60 (D 70).

———, William Styron, R.P. Warren, and C. Vann Woodward. "The Uses of History in Fiction." *SLJ*, 1: 57-90 (Sp 69).

Fass, Barbara. "Rejection of Paternalism: Hawthorne's 'My Kinsman, Major Molineux' and E's *Invisible Man*." *CLAJ*, 14: 317-23 (Mr 71).

Fischer, Russell. "*Invisible Man* as History." *CLAJ*, 17: 338-67 (Mr 74).

Fontaine, W.T. "The Negro Continuum from Dominant Wish to Collective Act." *AForum*, 3-4: 63-94 (1968).

Ford, N.A. "The Ambivalence of RE." *BlackW*, 20: 5-9 (1970).

Foster, F.S. "The Black and White Masks of Frantz Fanon and RE." *BlAR*, 1: 46-58 (Wi 70).

Gayle, Addison, Jr. "The Harlem Renaissance: Towards a Black Aesthetic." *MASJ*, 11: 78-87 (Fa 70).

Goede, William. "On Lower Frequencies: The Buried Men in Wright and E." *MFS*, 15: 483-501 (Wi 69-70).

Greenberg, Alvin. "Breakable Beginnings: The Fall into Realism in the Modern Novel." *TSLL*, 10: 133-42 (1968).

Greene, Maxine. "Against Invisibility." *CE*, 30: 430-6 (1969).

Griffin, E.M. "Notes from a Clean, Well-Lighted Place: RE's *Invisible Man*." *TCL*, 15: 129-44 (O 69).

Grow, L.M. "The Dream Scenes of *Invisible Man*." *Wichita State Un Bul*, 50: 3-12 (Ag 74).

Guereschi, Edward. "Anticipations of *Invisible Man*: RE's 'King of the Bingo Game.'" *NALF*, 6: 122-4 (1972).

Hays, P.L. "The Incest Theme in *Invisible Man*." *WHR*, 23: 335-9 (Au 69).

Heller, Arno. "RE's *Invisible Man*: Das Rassenproblem als Analyse moderner Existenz." *NS*, 21: 2-9 (Ja 72).

Hill, Herbert. "The Negro Writer and the Creative Imagination." *ASoc*, 5: 245-55 (1968).

Horowitz, F.R. "An Experimental Confession from a Reader of *Invisible Man*." *CLAJ*, 13: 304-14 (Mr 70).

Howard, D.C. "Points in Defense of E's *Invisible Man*." *NCLit*, 13-4 (Ja 71).

Johnson, A.A. "Birds of Passage: Flight Imagery in *Invisible Man*." *STC*, 14: 91-104 (Fa 74).

Kaiser, Ernest. "A Critical Look at E's Fiction and at Social and Literary Criticism by and about the Author." *BlackW*, 20: 53-9, 81-97 (1970).

Kattan, Naim. "Rencontre avec RE." *LanM*, 60: 99-101 (My-Je 66).

Kazin, Alfred. "Absurdity as Contemporary Style." *MeditR*, 1: 39-46 (Sp 71).

Kent, G.E. "RE and Afro-American Folk and Cultural Tradition." *CLAJ*, 13: 265-76 (Mr 70).

Kinzie, Mary. "Preface for Americans." *TriQ*, 25: 5 (Au 72).

Klotman, P.R. "The Running Man as Metaphor in E's *Invisible Man*." *CLAJ*, 13: 277-88 (Mr 70).

Knox, George. "The Negro Novelist's Sensibility and the Outsider Theme." *WHR*, 11: 137-48 (Sp 57).

———. "The Totentanz in E's *Invisible Man*." *Fabula*, 12: 168-78 (1971).

Kostelanetz, Richard. "RE: Novelist as Brown Skinned Aristocrat." *Shen*, 20: 56-77 (Su 69).

Lane, J.B. "Underground to Manhood: RE's *Invisible Man*." *NALF*, 7: 64-71 (Su 73).

LeClair, Thomas. "The Blind Leading the Blind: Wright's *Native Son* and a Brief Reference to E's *Invisible Man*." *CLAJ*, 13: 315-20 (Mr 70).

Lee, A.R. "Sight and Mask: RE's *Invisible Man*." *NALF*, 4: 22-33 (1970).

Lieber, T.M. "RE and the Metaphor of Invisibility in Black Literary Tradition." *AQ*, 24: 86-100 (Mr 72).

Lieberman, M.R. "Moral Innocents: E's *Invisible Man* and *Candide*." *CLAJ*, 15: 64-79 (S 71).

Lillard, Stewart. "E's Ambitious Scope in *Invisible Man*." *EJ*, 58: 833-9 (S 69).

Lillard, R.S. "RWE Bibliography (1914-1967)." *ABC*, 19: 18-22 (N 68).

Ludington, C.T. "Protest and Anti-protest: RE." *SHR*, 4: 31-9 (Wi 70).

McDaniel, B.A. "John Steinbeck: RE's Invisible Source." *PCP*, 8: 28-33 (1973).

Madden, David. "The Fallacy of The Subject-Dominated Novel." *Eng Rec*, 18: 11-9 (Ap 68).

Mason, Clifford. "RE and the Underground Man." *BlackW*, 20: 20-6 (1970).

May, J.R. "Images of Apocalypse in the Black Novel." *Renascence*, 23: 31-45 (1970).

Mitchell, Louis. "Invisiblity—Permanent or Resurrective?" *CLAJ*, 17: 379-86 (Mr 74).

Mitchell, L.D. and H.J. Stauffenberg. "E's B.P. Rinehart: 'Spiritual Technologist.'" *NALF*, 9: 51-3 (Su 75).

Moore, Robert. "On Initiation Rites and Power: RE Speaks at West Point." *ConL*, 15: 165-86 (Sp 74).

Moorer, F.E., and Lugene Baily. "A Selected Check List of Materials by and about RE." *BlackW*, 20: 126-30 (1970).

Neal, Larry. "E's Zoot Suit." *BlackW*, 20: 31-52 (1970).

Nettlebeck, C.W. "From Inside Destitution: Céline's Bardamer and E's Invisible Man." *SoRA*, 7: 246-53 (N 74).

Nichols, W.W. "RE's Black American Scholar." *Phylon*, 31: 70-5 (Sp 70).

Omans, S.E. "The Variations on a Masked Leader: A Study on the Literary Relationship of RE and Melville." *SAB*, 40: 15-23 (My 75).

Parrish, P.A. "Writing as Celebration: The Epilogue of *Invisible Man*." *Renascence*, 26:152-7 (Sp 74).

Petillon, Pierre-Yves. "Blues pour un mutant: RE." *Crit(P)*, 24: 855-62 (O 68).

Plesner, Monika. "Bildnis des Künstlers als Volksaufwiegler." *Merkur*, 24: 629-43 (Jl 70).

Polsgrove, Carol. "Addenda to 'A RWE Bibliography' (1914-1968)." *ABC*, 20: 11-2 (N-D 69).

Pryse, Marjorie. "RE's Heroic Fugitive." *AL*, 46: 1-15 (Mr 74).

Radford, F.L. "The Journey towards Castration: Interracial Sexual Sterotypes in E's *Invisible Man*." *JAmSt*, 4: 227-31 (F 71).

Rocard, Marcienne. "*Invisible Man*, pour qui joes-tu?" *Caliban*, 9: 67-76 (1973).

Rodnon, Stewart. "*The Adventures of Huckleberry Finn* and *Invisible Man*: Thematic and Structural Comparisons." *NALF*, 4: 45-51 (1970).

———. "Henry Adams and RE: Transcending Tragedy." *StH*, 3: 1-6 (#2 73).

———. "RE's *Invisible Man*: Six Tentative Approaches." *CLAJ*, 12: 244-56 (Mr 69).

Rollins, R.G. "E's *Invisible Man*." *Expl*, 30: 22 (N 71).

Sale, Roger. "The Career of RE." *HudR*, 18: 124-8 (Sp 65).

Sanders, A.D. "Odysseus in Black: An Analysis of the Structure of *Invisible Man*." *CLAJ*, 13: 217-28 (Mr 70).

Savory, J.J. "Descent and Baptism in *Native Son*, *Invisible Man*, and *Dutchman*." *Chri Schol R*, 3: 33-7 (1973).

Schafer, W.F. "Irony From Underground—Satiric Elements in *Invisible Man*." *SNL*, 7: 22-9 (Fa 69).

———. "RE and the Birth of the Anti-Hero." *Critique*, 10: 81-93 (Sp 68).

Scheer-Schäzler, Brigitte. "Aspekte der Raum-Zeitgestaltung in RE's *Invisible Man*." *RLV*, 38: 65-70 (1972).

Scruggs, Charles. "RE's Use of *The Aeneid* in *Invisible Man*." *CLAJ*, 17: 368-78 (Mr 74).

Selke, H.K. "An Allusion to Sartre's *The Flies* in RE's *Invisible Man*." *NCLit*, 4: 3-4 (My 74).

———. "'The Education at College of Fools': References to Emerson's 'Self-Reliance' in *Invisible Man*." *NCLit*, 4: 13-5 (Ja 74).

Sequeira, Issac. "The Uncompleted Initiation of the *Invisible Man*." *SBL*, 6: 9-13 (#1 75).

Singh, V.C. "*Invisible Man*: The Rhetoric of Color, Chaos, and Blindness." *RUSEng*, 8: 72-83 (1975).

Smith, B.L. "The World of RE: Beyond Abstraction, Imagination." *Motive*, 26: 28-31 (Ap 66).

Stark, John. "*Invisible Man*: E's Black *Odyssey*." *NALF*, 7: 60-3 (Su 73).

Sullivan, J.J. "Conflict in the Modern American Novel." *BSUF*, 15: 28-36 (1974).

Sullivan, P.E. "Buh Rabbit: Going Through the Changes." *SBL*, 28-32 (1973).

Sylvander, C.W. "RE's *Invisible Man* and Female Sterotypes." *NALF*, 9: 77-9 (Fa 75).

Thinesse, Anne. "RE—Une interview." *FL*, 11 Ag 69, p. 28.

Tischler, N.M. "Negro Literature and the Classic Form." *ConL*, 10: 352-65 (Su 69).

Trachtenberg, Stanley. "Counterhumor: Comedy in Contemporary American Fiction." *GaR*, 27: 33-48 (Sp 73).

Trimmer, J.F. "RE's 'Flying Home.'" *SSF*, 9: 175-81 (Sp 72).

Turner, D.T. "Afro-American Authors: A Full House." *CEA*, 34: 15-9 (Ja 72).

———. "Sight in *Invisible Man*." *CLAJ*, 13: 258-64 (Mr 70).

Vogler, T.A. "*Invisible Man*: Somebody's Protest Novel." *IowaR*, 1: 64-82 (Sp 70).

———. and N.M. Tischler. "An E Controversy." *ConL*, 11: 130-5 (1970).

Waghmare, J.M. "Invisibility of the American Negro: RE's *Invisible Man*." *Quest*, 59: 23-30 (1968).

Walcott, Ronald. "Some Notes on the Blues, Style & Space: E, Gordone and Tolson." *BlackW*, 22: 4-29 (1972).

Walling, William. "'Art' and 'Protest': RE's *Invisible Man* Twenty Years After." *Phylon*, 34: 120-34 (Je 73).

———. "RE's *Invisible Man*: 'It Goes a Long Way Back, Some Twenty Years.'" *Phylon*, 34-4-16 (Mr 73).

Weinstein, S.R. "Comedy and the Absurd in RE's *Invisible Man*." *SBL*, 12-6 (Au 72).

West, Hollie. "RE: The Man and His Views." *Topic*, 83: 38-41 (1974).

Williams, J.A. "RE and *Invisible Man*: Their Place in American Letters." *BlackW*, 20: 10-1 (1970).

Wilner, E.R. "The Invisible Black Thread: Identity and Nonentity in *Invisible Man*." *CLAJ*, 13: 242-57 (Mr 70).

Woodward, C.V. "The Uses of History in Fiction." *SLJ*, 1: 57-90 (Sp 69).

Ely, Ben. Dahl, Curtis. "Mark Twain and BE: Two Missouri Boyhoods." *MHR*, 66: 549-66 (Jl 72).

Emerson, Ralph Waldo. Anon. "The E House in Concord." *ATQ*, 14: 186-7 (Sp 72).

———. "E's 'The Poet,' I, 1-6." *Expl*, 33: 54 (1975).

———. "Notes on E in Japan." *ESQ*, 51: 102-7 (2Q 68).

———. "Recent Acquisitions—Manuscripts." *PULC*, 29: 221-9 (Sp 68).

———. "An Ungarnered E Item." *Nation*, 100: 563-4 (20 My 15).

Adams, R.P. "The Basic Contradiction in E." *ESQ*, 55: 106-10 (2Q 69).

Allen, G.W. "E and the Establishment." *UWR*, 9: 5-27 (Fa 73).

———. "E and the Unconscious." *ATQ*, 19: 26-30 (Su 73).

Anderson, J.Q. "E's 'Eternal Pan'—The Re-creation of a Myth." *ATQ*, 25: 2-6 (Wi 75).

———. "E's 'Young American' as Democratic Nobleman." *ATQ*, 9: 16-20 (Wi 71).

Arrington, L.J. "The Intellectual Tradition of the Latter-Day Saints." *Dialog*, 4: 13-26 (S 69).

Asselineau, Roger. "The French Stream in American Literature." *YCGL*, 17: 29-39 (1968).

Axelrod, S.G. "Teaching E's 'The Rhodora.'" *CEA*, 36: 34-5 (My 74).

Banta, Martha. "American Apocalypses: Excrement and Ennui." *SLitI*, 7: 1-30 (1974).

———. "Gymnasts of Faith, Fate, and Hazard." *ATQ*, 21: 6-20 (Wi 74).

Barbour, Brian. "E's 'Poetic' Prose." *MLQ*, 35: 157-72 (Je 74).

Barnes, D.R. "A Possible Influence on 'Hamatreya.'" *ESQ*, 63: 18 (Sp 71).

Barton, W.B. "E's Method as a Philosopher." *ATQ*, 9: 20-8 (Wi 71).

Battarini, Marcella. "Il pensiero di RW.E." *CV*, 23: 172-7 (1968).

Beck, Ronald. "E's Organic Structures." *ESQ*, 50 Sup: 76-7 (lQ 68).

Bell, B.W. "Literary Sources of the Early Afro-American Novel." *CLAJ*, 18: 29-43 (1974).

Bell, G.E. "E and Baltimore: A Biographical Study." *MHM*, 65: 331-68 (Wi 70).

Bernstein, M.H. "E's Sea Shells." *AQ*, 12: 231-6 (Su 60).

Bier, Jesse. "Weberism, Franklin, and the Transcendental Style." *NEQ*, 43: 179-92 (Je 70).

Binney, James. "E Revisited." *MwQ*, 12: 109-22 (O 70).

Blanck, Jacob. "BAL Addenda: RWE—Entry No. 5272." *PBSA*, 61: 124-6 (2Q 67).

Blanding Thomas. "E, Thoreau, and the Ice-Harp." *ConsS*, 9: 1-2 (Mr 74).

———. "Emily's Bank and E's Book: *Representative Men* as a Source for a Dickinson Poem." *ConS*, 6: 10-2 (S 71).

————. "Thoreau Responds to a Gift from E." *ConS*, 6: 9-10 (Je 71).

Bloom, Harold. "Bacchus and Merlin: The Dialectic of Romantic Poetry in America." *SoR*, 7: 140-75 (Ja 71).

————. "E and Ammons." *Diacritics*, 3: 45-6 (#4 73).

————. "E: The Glory and the Sorrows of American Romanticism." *VQR*, 47: 546-63 (Au 71).

————. "The Freshness of Transformation, or E on Influence." *ATQ*, 21: 57-63 (Wi 74).

Boller, P.F. "E and Freedom." *SMU Forum*, 4: 4-14 (Sp 66).

Bond, B.C. "E's 'Spiritual Laws': The Subtle Logic of Form." *ESQ*, 18: 222-6 (4Q 72).

Bottorff, W.K. "E's 'Power.'" *Expl*, 31: 45 (F 73).

————. "'Whatever Inly Rejoices Me': The Paradox of 'Self-Reliance.'" *ESQ*, 18: 207-17 (4Q 72).

Brady, R.H. "F's *As I Lay Dying*." *Expl*, 33: 60 (Mr 75).

Bridges, W.E. "Transcendentalism and Psychotherapy: Another Look at E." *AL*, 41: 151-77 (My 69).

Brock, William. "The Image of England and American Nationalism." *JAmSt*, 5: 225-45 (D 71).

Brodwin, Stanley. "E's Version of Plotinus: The Flight of Beauty." *JHI*, 35: 465-83 (Jl-S 74).

Bromwich, David. "Suburbs and Extremities." *Prose*, 8: 25-38 (1974).

Brumbaugh, T.M. "Landor and Greenough." *N&Q*, 15: 413-4 (N 68).

Buell, Lawrence. "First Person Superlative: The Speaker in E's Essays." *ATQ*, 9: 28-35 (Wi 71).

————. "Reading E for the Structures: The Coherence of the Essays." *QJS*, 58: 58-69 (F 72).

————. "Transcendentalist Catalogue Rhetoric: Vision Versus Form." *AL*, 40: 325-39 (N 68).

————. "Unitarian Aesthetics and E's Poet-priest." *AQ*, 20: 3-20 (Sp 68).

Bufano, R.J. "E's Apprenticeship to Carlyle, 1827-1848." *ATQ*, 13: 17-25 (Wi 72).

Cameron, K.W. "American and British Authors in F.B. Sanborn's Papers." *ATQ*, 6: 2-53 (2Q 70).

————. "Beriah Green and E's P.B.K. Address of 1867." *ESQ*, 51: 26-32 (2Q 68).

*————. "Current Bibliography on RWE." *ESQ*, annually from 1968-1972.

————. "E and Charles Edward Rawlins, Jr." *ESQ*, 51: 33-7 (2Q 68).

————. "E and the Phonographic Reporter Walter Bacheler." *ESQ*, 51: 143-6 (2Q 68).

————. "E and Thoreau as Readers." *ATQ*, 18: 1-133 (Sp 73).

————. "E and Thoreau Lecture at Lynn." *ATQ*, 14: 158-64 (Sp 72).

————. "E in Nineteenth-Century Textbooks and Books of Reference." *ATQ*, 14: 101-11 (1972).

————. "E in Transcendental Cartoons in 1849." *ESQ*, 59: 38-9 (Sp 70).

————. "E, Longfellow, Lowell and Others in Defense of R. Morris Copeland in 1863." *ESQ*, 47: 140-6 (2Q 67).

————. "E Manuscripts Ungathered and Migrant." *ATQ*, 20, sup: 122-6 (1973).

————. "E, Transcendentalism, and Literary Notes in the Stearns Wheeler Papers." *ATQ*, 20: 69-97 (Fa 73).

————. "E's Advocacy of an Art Museum for Boston." *ATQ*, 14: 75 (1972).

————. "E's Coleridge in Review." *ESQ*, 64-5: 78-161 (Su-Fa 71).

————. "E's Early Stylistic Training from His Father." *ESQ*, 47: 146-51 (#2 67).

————. "E's Petition for Privileges at Boston Public." *ESQ*, 48: 91-2 (3Q 67).

————. "The Ending of E's 'Thoreau.'" *ATQ*, 17: 24 (1973).

————. "Frank Bellow and E in Concord in 1855." *ESQ*, 52: 82-5 (2Q 68).

————. "Henry Ware's *Divinity School Address*—A Reply to E's." *ATQ*, 13: 84-91 (1971).

————. "John Pindar Bland on E in Sheffield (1884)." *ESQ*, 63: 38-9 (Sp 71).

————. "Literary News in American Renaissance Newspapers." *ATQ*, 2: 29-37 (2Q 69); 5: 68-80 (2Q 70); *ESQ*, 59: 10-38, 40 (Sp 70); 20: 13-36, 195-7 (Fa 73).

————. "A Note on Lidian Emerson and Anti-Slavery." *ATQ*, 2: 38-9 (1969).

————. "Notes on E in Japan." *ESQ*, 51: 102-7 (1968).

————. "Reports on E's Lectures in 1864." *ATQ*, 17: 41-5 (Wi 73).

————. "The Rowse Drawings of the Es." *ATQ*, 13: 49-52 (1972).

————. "Some Alcott Conversations in 1863." *ATQ*, 17: 3-9 (1973).

————. "*A Study of E's Major Poems* by Charles Malloy." *ATQ*, 23: 1-121 (1974).

————. "Theodore Clapp on E's Williamstown Address." *ATQ*, 2: 37-8 (2Q 69).

————. "Vedder and Hunt Visit E." *ATQ*, 14: 185-6 (Sp 72).

Carlson, E.W. "E's Modernism—New Insights." *ATQ*, 9: 3-6 (Wi 71).

Carpenter, F.I. "Charles Sanders Peirce: Pragmatic Transcendentalist." *NEQ*, 14: 34-48 (Mr 41).

Carter, G.E. "Democrat in Heaven—Whig on Earth: The Politics of RWE." *HNH*, 27: 123-40 (1972).

Chamberlain, William. "The Emersonianism of Robert Frost." *ESQ*, 57: 61-6 (2Q 69).

Clarke, J.F. "The Religious Philosophy of RWE." *ATQ*, 17: 38-40 (1973).

Clarkson, J.W. "E at Seventy." *ATQ*, 1: 119 (1969).

Claudel, A.M. "E: Man Alive." *Disc*, 11: 382-5 (Su 68).

Clemens, Cyril. "Personal Glimpses." *Hobbies*, 75: 140-1 (Ap 70).

Clendenning, John. "E's 'Days': A Psychoanalytic Study." *ATQ*, 25: 6-11 (Wi 75).

Cohen, B.B. "A Penny Paper's View of E and Transcendentalism." *ATQ*, 1: 60-2 (1Q 69).

Colacurcio, M.J. "A Better Mode of Evidence—The Transcendental Problem of Faith and Spirit." *ESQ*, 54: 12-22 (1Q 69).

Commager, H.S. "Speaking of Books: *English Traits*." *NYT*, 18 Je 67, pp. 2, 26, 28.

Conway, M.D. "E, Thoreau and the Transcendentalists in 1864-1866," *ATQ*, 16: 62-81 (1972).

Cook, R.G. "E's 'Self-Reliance,' Sweeney and Prufrock." *AL*, 42: 221-6 (My 70).

Cook, R.L. "E and the American Joke." *ESQ*, 54: 22-7 (1Q 69).

————. "E and the Third America." *ATQ*, 9: 7-11 (Wi 71).

Cooke, G.W. " E and Transcendentalism." *ESQ*, 59: 50-9 (Sp 70).

Cowan, M.H. "The Loving Proteus: Metamorphosis in E's Poetry." *ATQ*, 25: 11-22 (Wi 75).

Cowley, Malcolm. "Conrad Aiken: From Savannah to E." *SoR*, 11: 245-59 (Ap 75).

Cox, J.M. "E and Hawthorne: Trust and Doubt." *VQR*, 45: 88-107 (Wi 69).

Cummins, R.W. "E, Whitman, and Annie Moore." *ATQ*, 24 sup: 11-4 (Fa 74).

————. "The Monthly Magazine and E (1841)." *ATQ*, 64-76 (1Q 69).

————. "Thoreau and Isaac Newton Goodhue." *TSB*, 123: 2 (Sp 73).

————. "Unpublished E Letters to Louis Prang and Whittier." *AL*, 43: 257-9 (My 71).

D'Avanzo, M.L. "Dickinson's 'The Reticent Volcano' and E." *ATQ*, 14: 11-3 (Sp 72).

————. "E's 'Days' and Proverbs." *ATQ*, 1: 83-5 (1Q 69).

————. "The Emersonian Context of Three Poems by E[mily] D[ickinson]." *EDB*, 16: 2-7 (Mr 71).

————. "Emersonian Revelation in 'The Way I Read a Letter's—This—.'" *ATQ*, 17: 14-5 (1973).

————. "E's 'Scoriae.'" *AN&Q*, 13: 141-3 (1975).

————. "Emily Dickinson's and E's 'Pre-sentiment.'" *ESQ*, 157-9 (1Q 70).

————. "Seeing and Hearing in 'Each and All.'" *ESQ*, 19:231-6 (4Q 73).

————. "'Unto the White Creator': The Snow of Dickinson and E." *NEW*, 45: 278-80 (Je 72).

Davis, J.L. "Transcendental Vision in 'The Dry Salvages.'" *ESQ*, 62: 38-44 (Wi 71).

De Majo, M.T. "La fortuna di RWE in Italia (1847-1963)." *SA*, 12: 45-87 (1966).

Dennis, Carl. "Correspondence in Very's Nature Poetry." *NEQ*, 43: 250-73 (Je 70).

————. "E's Poetics of Inspiration." *ATQ*, 25: 22-28 (Wi 75).

————. "E's Poetry of Mind and Nature." *ESQ*, 58:139-53 (1Q 70).

Deutsch, L.J. "Ralph Waldo Ellison and RWE: A Shared Moral Vision." *CLAJ*, 16: 159-78 (D 72).

DiMaggio, Richard. "A Note on *Sons and Lovers* and E's 'Experience.'" *DHLR*, 6: 214-5 (1973).

Doherty, Joseph. "E and the Loneliness of the Gods." *TSLL*, 16: 65-76 (Sp 74).

Duffy, J.J. "Problems in Publishing Coleridge: James Marsh's First American Edition of *Aids to Reflection*." *NEQ*, 43: 193-208 (Je 70).

————. "T.S. Eliot's Objective Correlative: A New England Commonplace." *NEQ*, 42:108-15 (Mr 69).

Edrich, M.W. "The Channing Rhetoric and 'Splendid Confusion.'" *ESQ*, 57: 5-12 (4Q 69).

Eidson, J.O. "Charles Stearns Wheeler: Friend of E." *ESQ*, 52: 13-75 (3Q 68).

Elliot, G.R. "E on the Organic Principle in Art." *PMLA*, 41: 193-208 (Mr 26).

Erisman, Fred. "The Romantic Regionalism of Harper Lee." *AlaR*, 26: 122-36 (Ap 73).

Fleck, Richard. "Thoreau, E, Whitman in the Western Wilderness." *JANSS*, nv: 9-11 (Sp 69).

————. "Two Irish Emersonians." *ConS*, 8: 1-3 (S 73).

Fletcher, R.M. "E's *Nature* and Goethe's *Faust*." *AN&Q*, 12: 102 (Mr 74).

Francis, R.L. "The Evolution of E's Second 'Nature.'" *ATQ*, 21: 33-5 (Wi 74).

Francis, Richard. "Circumstances and Salvation: The Ideology of the Fruitlands Utopia." *AQ*, 25: 33-5 (My 73).

Francon, Marcel. "E lecteur de Montaigne." *BSAM*, 15: 32-41 (1968).

Freedman, F.B. "E Giving Joy: Summer of 1855." *WWR*, 21: 162-3 (1975).

Fromm, Harold. "E and Kierkegaard: The Problem of Historical Christianity." *MR*, 9: 741-52 (Au 68).

Frothingham, N.L. "An Obiturary of E's Mother." *ESQ*, 47: 127 (2Q 67).

Garate, Justo. "Thoreau in the Spanish Language: A Bibliography." *TSBK*, 24: np (Ap 70).

Gardella, Raymond. "In E Consciousness is King." *ESQ*, 50: 5-9 (1Q 68).

————. "The Tenets and Limitations of E's All-Conscious Man." *ABR*, 21: 375-88 (1970).

Garmon, G.M. "E's 'Moral Sentiment' and Poe's 'Poetic Sentiment': A Reconsideration." *PoeS*, 6: 19-21 (Je 73).

Gavin, William J. "Chaadayev and E—Two Mystic Pragmatists." *RusR*, 32: 119-30 (Ap 73).

Gilman, W.H. "The Journals and Miscellaneous Notebooks of RWE." *CEAAN*, 3: 26-7 (1970).

Girgus, S.B. "The Scholar as Prophet: Brownson vs. E." *MwQ*, 17: 88-99 (1975).

Glick, Wendell. "The Moral and Ethical Dimensions of E's Aesthetics." *ESQ*, 55: 11-8 (2Q 69).

————. "Thoreau Rejects an E Text." *SB*, 25: 213-6 (1972).

Goldfarb, C.R. "*The Marble Faun* and Emersonian Self-Reliance." *ATQ*, 19-23 (IQ 69).

Gonnaud, Maurice. "The Humane Seer: Humor and Its Avatars in E." *ATQ*, 22: 79-85 (Sp 74).

Graham, John. "The Restored Passages in the Centenary Edition of *The Blithedale Romance.*" *HAB*, 24: 110-4 (1973).

Greenberger, E.B. "The Phoenix on the Wall: Consciousness in E's Early and Late Journals." *ATQ*, 21: 45-56 (Wi 74).

Greiner, D.J. "E, Thoreau, and Hemingway: Some Suggestions About Literary Heritage." *FHA*, 1971, pp. 247-61.

Gresset, Michel. "Prophète Frustré d'un art vivant." *LanM*, 60: 42-8 (My-Je 66).

Gross, T.L. "Under the Shadow of Our Swords: E and the Heroic Ideal." *BuR*, 17: 22-34 (Mr 69).

Hansen, A.J. "Plotinus: An Early Source of E's View of Otherworldliness." *ESQ*, 18: 184-5 (3Q 72).

Harding, Walter. "John Shepard Keyes on Thoreau." *TSB*, 103: 2-3 (Sp 68).

Hart, J.E. "Man Thinking as Hero: E's 'Scholar' Revisited." *ESQ*, 102-6 (2Q 69).

Harter, C.C. "E's Rhetorical Failure in 'Love.'" *ESQ*, 18: 227-33 (4Q 72).

Haskins, D.G. "RWE: His Maternal Ancestors with Some Reminiscences of Him." *ATQ*, 15: Part 3 (1972).

Haugrud, R.A. "Tyndall's Interest in E." *AL*, 41: 507-17 (Ja 70).

Haworth, H.E. "E's Keats." *HLB*, 19:61-70 (Ja 71).

Hawthorne, Julian and E.W. Emerson. "E Memorabilia From the *Booklover's Magazine.*" *ESQ*, 49: 149 (4Q 67).

Helmick, E.T. "E's 'Uriel' as Poetic Theory." *ATQ*, 35-8 (IQ 69).

Hernandez, Frances. "E's 'Days.'" *EXPL*, 33: 44 (F 75).

Herndon, J.A. "St. Paul and E's 'Self-Reliance.'" *ATQ*, 1: 90 (IQ 69).

Hoar, J.S. "A Study of E's *English Traits.*" *Northern New England R*, 1: 48-57 (#2 74).

Hoch, D.G. "'History' as Art: 'Art' as History." *ESQ*, 18:288-93 (4Q 72).

Hopkins, V.C. "E and the World of Dream." *ATQ*, 9: 56-69 (Wi 71).

Hourihan, Paul. "Ambiguities in the E Sage-Image: The Facts of His Novel Reading." *HAB*, 22: 44-55 (Sp 71).

Hudson, H.R. "Concord Books." *ATQ*, 16: 29-43 (1972).

Hudspeth, R.N. "A Perennial Springtime: Channing's Friendship with E and Thoreau." *SQ*, 54: 30-6 (IQ 69).

Jackson, C.T. "The Orient in Post-Bellum American Thought: Three Pioneer Popularizers." *AQ*, 22: 67-81 (Sp 70).

Irvin, J.T. "The Symbol of the Hieroglyphics in the American Renaissance." *AQ*, 26:103-26 (My 74).

Jackson, P.R. "Henry Miller, E, and the Divided Self." *AL*, 43: 231-41 (My 71).

Johnson, Ellwood. "E's Psychology of Power." *Rendezvous*, 5: 13-25 (Sp 70).

Jones, Buford. "'The Hall of Fantasy' and the Early Hawthorne-Thoreau Relationship." *PMLA*, 83: 1429-38 (O 68).

Kaiser, L.M. "On Some Latin Quotations in E." *ATQ*, 13: 37 (1972).

Karlstetter, Klaus. "J.D. Salinger, R.W.E. and the Perennial Philosophy." *MSpr*, 63: 224-36 (1969).

Kasegawa, Koh. "The Transcendentalist View of Man in E and Thoreau." *SToS*, 19: 35-41 (30 Mr 69).

Keller, Karl. "E and the Anti-imperialist Self." *ATQ*, 18: 23-9 (Sp 73).

———. "'The World Slickt Up in Types': Edward Taylor as a Version of E." *EAL*, 5:124-40 (1970).

Kennard, J.E. "E and Dickens: A Note on Conrad's *Victory.*" *Conradiana*, 6: 215-9 (1974).

King, Bruce. "E's Pupil." *Venture*, 5: 112-22 (Ap 69).

Kriege, J.W. "E's 'Thoreau' (Last Paragraph)." *Expl*, 31: 38 (Ja 73).

Kinzie, Mary. "Preface for Americans." *TriQ*, 25: 5-8 (1972).

Kirby, D.K. "Metaphor in the Final Paragraphs of 'The American Scholar' and 'Economy.'" *TJQ*, 2: 17-8 (Jl 70).

Kyle, C.A. "E's 'Uriel' as Source for Frost." *ESQ*, 58: 111 (1Q 70).

LaRosa, R.C. "Bacon and the 'Organic Method' of E's Early Lectures." *ELN*, 8: 107-14 (1970).

———. "E's Search for Literary Form: The Early Journals." *MP*, 69: 25-35 (Ag 71).

———. "E's Sententiae in Nature (1836)." *ESQ*, 58:153-7 (1Q 70).

———. "Invention and Imitation in E's Early Lectures." *AL*, 44:13-30 (Mr 72).

Lentricchia, Frank. "Coleridge and E: Prophets of Silence, Prophets of Language." *JAAC*, 32: 37-48 (Fa 73).

Leverenz, David. "Anger and Individualism." *ATQ*, 62: 407-28 (1975).

Liebman, S.W. "The Development of E's Theory of Rhetoric, 1821-1836." *AL*, 41: 178-206 (My 69).

———. "E's Discovery of the English Romantics, 1818-1836." *ATQ*, 21: 36-44 (Wi 74).

———. "E's Transformation in the 1820's." *AL*, 133-54 (My 68).

———. "The Origins of E's Early Poetics: His Reading in the Scottish Common Sense Critics." *AL*, 45: 23-33 (Mr 73).

Lindner, C.M. "Newtonianism in E's *Nature.*" *ESQ*, 20: 260-9 (4Q 74).

Lindquist, V.R. "E in Bangor: The Disenchantment of a Transcendental Intruder." *Alumni Bul* (Bangor Theological Seminary), 44: 3-12 (1969).

Lowance, M.I. "From Edwards to E to Thoreau: A Revaluation." *ATQ*, 18- 3-12 (Sp 73).

Luedtke, L.S. "First Notices of E in England and Germany: 1835-1852." *N&Q*, 22: 106-8 (Mr 75).

McClumpa, C.F. "E and Transcendentalism." *ATQ*, 22: 121-2 (Sp 74).

McDonald, J.J. "E and John Brown." *NEQ*, 44: 377-96 (S 71).

McElderry, B.R. "The Transcendental Hawthorne." *MwQ*, 2: 307-23 (Su 61).

McElroy, J.H. "E in the Land of the Dead." *MalR*, 36: 84-99 (1975).

McKee, J.K. "The Identity of E's 'Titmouse.'" *AN&Q*, 13: 151-2 (Je 75).

McLean, A.M. "E's *Brahma* as an Expression of Brahman." *NEQ*, 42: 115-22 (Mr 69).

Magowan, Robin. "The Horse of Gods: Possession in 'Song of Myself.'" *WWR*, 15: 67-76 (Je 69).

Marra, Giulio. "La Poesia di E: Natura come realizzazione di forme." *ACF*, 12: 287-309 (1973).

Mathy, Francis. "The Three Johns: Portraits of E, Thoreau, Hawthorne, and Whittier." *ELLS*, 10: 163-81 (Mr 74).

Matle, J.H. "E and Brook Farm." *ESQ*, 58: 84-8 (1Q 70).

Matteson, Robert. "E and Aeolian Harp." *SCB*, 23: 4-9 (Wi 63).

Maxfield-Miller, Elizabeth. "E and Elizabeth in Concord." *HLB*, 19: 290-306 (Jl 71).

Mead, David. "E's Scholar and the Scholars." *JHE*, 40: 649-60 (1969)

Meese, E.A. "Transcendentalism: The Metaphysics of the Theme." *AL*, 47: 1-20 (Mr 75).

Mignon, C.W. "E to Chapman: Four Letters about Publishing." *ESQ*, 19: 225-30 (4Q 73).

———. "Starsown Poet: Abstemious Muse." *ATQ*, 25: 33-41 (Wi 75).

Miller, Norman. "E's 'Each and All' Concept: A Reexamination." *NEQ*, 41: 381-92 (S 68).

Miller, Ruth. "'The Poet' and 'The Problem: An Explication.'" *LHY*, 7: 84-91 (Jl 66).

Mollinger, R.N. "Introduction: On Psychohistory." *PsyR*, 62: 3125-9 (1975).

Moran, Virginia. "Circle and Dialetic (A Study of E's Interest in Hegel)." *NasR*, 1: 32-42 (1969).

Morton, Doris. "RWE and *The Dial*: A Study in Literary Criticism." *ESRS*, 18: 5-51 (D 69).

Moyne, E.J. "Thoreau and E: Their Interest in Finland." *NM*, 70: 738-50 (1969).

Mulqueen, J.E. "The Poetics of E and Poe." *ESQ*, 55: 5-11 (2Q 69).

Mulqueen, J. McC. "Is E's Work Central to the Poetry of Emily Dickinson?" *EDB*, 24: 211-20 (1973).

Munford, Lewis. "Have Courage!" *AH*, 20: 104-11 (1969).

Myerson, Joel. "Lowell on E: A New Letter from Concord in 1828." *NEQZ*, 44: 649-52 (D 71).

———. "Practical Editions: RWE's 'The American Scholar.'" *Proof*, 1973, pp. 379-94.

———. "An Unpublished Interview with E in 1867." *SAB*, 39: 89-94 (My 74).

Nelson, Carl. "The Rhetoric of E's Hindu 'Heroism.'" *ESQ*, 18: 258-64 (4Q 72).

Neufeldt, Leonard. "E and the Civil War." *JEGP*, 71: 502-13 (1972).

———. "The Law of Permutation—E's Mode." *ATQ*, 21:20-30 (Wi 74).

———. "The Severity of the Ideal: E's Thoreau." *ESQ*, 58: 77-84 (lQ 70).

———. "The Vital Mind: E's Epistemology." *PQ*, 50: 253-70 (Ap 71).

Nikoljukin, A.N. "Die Amerikanische Romantik und unsere Epoche." *ZAA*, 15: 347-74 (1967).

Noda, Hisashi. "The Concepts of Symbolism in Traditional Japanese Literary Criticism and the Poetics of E." *KAL*, 12: 45-53 (1970).

Null, Jack. "Strategies of Imagery in 'Circles.'" *ESQ*, 18: 265-70 (4Q 72).

Obuchowski, P.A. "E's Science." *PQ*, 54: 624-32 (1975).

Ogato, Toshihiko. "On Orestes Augustus Brownson's Criticism of RWE's *Divinity School Address*." *REngL*, 25: 73-103 (Mr 70).

Olmert, K.M. "Cranch on E: A Letter Re-edited." *ATQ*, 13: 31-2 (1972).

Pachori, S.S. "E and Slavery." *KAL*, 16: 1-12 (1975).

Panek, L.L. "Imagery and E's 'Compensation.'" *ESQ*, 18: 218-21 (4Q 72).

Parker, Hershel. "Melville's Satire of E and Thoreau: An Evaluation of the Evaluation of the Evidence." *ATQ*, 7: 61-7 (Su 70).

———. "Melville's Satire of E and Thoreau: Corrections." *ATQ*, 9: 70 (Wi 71).

Parkes, H.B. "Freedom and Order in Western Literature." *DQR*, 4: 1-18 (Su 69).

Pearce, H.D. "'I Lean and Loafe': Whitman's Romantic Posture." *WWR*, 15: 3-21 (Mr 69).

Peckham, Morse. "E's Prose." *ATQ*, 21: 64-74 (Wi 74).

Perkins, Elizabeth. "E and Charles Harper." *ALS*, 6: 82-8 (1973).

Peterson, S.L. "E and the Cosmic Urge." *MR*, 2: 36-47 (Wi 6l).

Pinsker, Sanford. "E's Anti-Essay: The Dissolving Rhetoric of 'Intellect.'" *ESQ*, 18: 284-7 (4Q 72).

Poger, Sidney. "The Critical Stance of *The Dial*." *ESQ*, 57: 22-7 (4Q 69).

Pollin, B.R. "E's Annotations in the British Museum Copy of the *Dial*." *SB*, 24: 187-95 (1971).

———. "Poe's Use of D'Israeli's *Curiosities* to Belittle E." *PN*, 3: 38 (D 70).

Pommer, H.F. "E's Belief in Compensation." *PMLA*, 77: 250 (Je 62).

Porte, Joel. "E, Thoreau, and the Double Consciousness." *NEQ*, 41: 40-50 (Je 68).

Portnoy, H.N. "E, Melville, and 'The Poet.'" *Junction*, 1: 172-5 (1973).

Pulos, C.E. "*Walden* and E's 'The Sphinx.'" *ATQ*, 1: 7-11 (lQ 69).

Rao, A.R. "E and the American Negro." *OJES*, 8: 79-88 (1971).
———. "E and the Feminists." *IJAS*, 4: 13-20 (Je-D 74).
Ray, Roberta. "The Role of the Orator in the Philosophy of RWE." *SM*, 41: 215-25 (Au 74).
Reaver, J.R. "E on the Psychic Potential." *ATQ*, 9: 52-5 (Wi 71).
Redding, M.E. "E's 'Instant Eternity': An Existential Approach." *ATQ*, 9: 43-52 (Wi 71).
Reid, A.S. "Emersonian Ideas in the Youth Movement of the 1960's." *ATQ*, 9: 12-6 (Wi 71).
———. "E's Prose Style: An Edge to Goodness." *ESQ*, 60: 37-42 (Su 70).
Rein, I.J. "The New England Transcendentalists: Philosophy and Rhetoric." *P&R*, 1: 103-17 (Wi 68).
Reynolds, M.S. "Whitman's Early Prose and 'The Sleepers.'" *AL*, 41: 406-14 (N 69).
Richard, B.J. "E and Berkeleian Idealism." *ESQ*, 58: 90-7 (1Q 70).
Richardson, R.D. "McLuhan, E, and Henry Adams." *WHR*, 22: 235-42 (Su 68).
Robinson, David. "The Romantic Quest in Poe and E: 'Ulalume' and 'The Sphinx.'" *ATQ*, 26, sup: 26-30 (Sp 75).
Rosa, A.F. "Charles Ives: Music, Transcendentalism, and Politics." *NEQ*, 44: 433-43 (1971).
———. "E and the Salem Lyceum." *EIHC*, 110: 75-85 (1974).
Rosenberry, E.H. "Israel Potter, Benjamin Franklin, and the Doctrine of Self-Reliance." *ESQ*, 28: 27-9 (3Q 62).
Rosenfeld, A.H. "Whitman's Open Road Philosophy." *WWR*, 14: 3-16 (Mr 68).
Ross, Donald. "Composition as a Stylistic Feature." *Style*, 4: 1-10 (1970).
———. "E and Thoreau: A Comparison of Prose Styles." *Lang&S*, 6: 185-95 (Su 73).
———. "E's Stylistic Influence on Whitman." *ATQ*, 41-51 (Wi 75).
Rovit, Earl. "E: A Contemporary Reconsideration." *ASch*, 41: 429-38 (Su 72).
Rucker, M.E. "E's 'Friendship' as Process." *ESQ*, 18: 234-48 (4Q 72).
Ryan, A.S. "Frost and E: Voice and Vision." *MR*, 1: 5-23 (Fa 59).
Saito, Hikaru. "Emerson to Nihon Unitarian Kyokai." *EigoS*, 119: 516-7 (1973).
Salomon, L.B. "A Walk with E on the Dark Side." *Costerus*, 6: 121-35 (1972).
Sanborn, F.B. "E and his Friends in Concord." *ATQ*, 13: 53-62 (1972).
Sander, L.A. "Melville's Symbolism of the Pipe." *ESQ*, 59: 4-7 (Sp 70).
Sanders, William. "E and Melville: The Oversoul and the Underworld." *Junction*, 2: 25-9 (1973).
Sanford, C.L. "E, Thoreau, and the Hereditary Duality." *ESQ*, 54: 36-43 (1Q 69).
Sayre, R.F. "American Myths of Utopia." *CE*, 31: 613-23 (Mr 70).
Schamberger, J.E. "The Influence of Dugald Stewart and Richard Price on E's Concept of the Reason: A Reassessment." *ESQ*, 18: 179-83 (3Q 72).
Scheick, W.J. "Aspiring to the Highest: Imagery in E's *The American Scholar*." *NDEJ*, 8: 34-42 (Fa 72).
———. "The Slender Human Word: Language as Organizing Principle in E's 'Prudence.'" *ESQ*, 18: 249-57 (4Q 72).
Schriber, M.S. "E, Hawthorne, and 'The Artist of the Beautiful.'" *SSF*, 8: 607-16 (1971).
Sealts, M.M. "E on the Scholar, 1833-1837." *PMLA*, 85: 185-95 (Mr 70).
Selke, H.K. "'The Education at College of Fools': References to E's 'Self-Reliance' in *Invisible Man*." *NCLit*, 4: 13-5 (Ja 74).
17th Century Poetry Group, U. of Nebraska. "E's 'The Poet,' I, 1-6." *Expl*, 33: 54 (Mr 75).
Sharma, M.L. "E's 'Hamatreya.'" *Expl*, 26: 63 (Ap 68).

————. ''E's Multi-Lingual Coinage 'Hamatreya.' '' *WSt*, 44: 6-8 (1968).

————. ''The 'Oriental Estate,' Especially the Bhagavada-Gita in American Literature.'' *Forum(H)*, 7: 4-ll (Fa-Wi 69).

Shepard, D.H. ''Ungathered Commentary on E.'' *ATQ*, l: 47-50, 52-62 (1970).

Shurr, W.H. ''Melville and E.'' *Extracts*, 11: 2 (My 72).

Simpson, L.P. ''The Crisis of Alienation in E's Early Thought.'' *ATQ*, 9: 35-43 (Wi 71).

————. ''The Telescope and the Transparent Eyeball.'' *SAB*, 36: 30-1 (1971).

Sisk, J.P. ''Making it in America.'' *Atl*, 224: 63-8 (D 69).

Sowd, David. ''Peter Kaufmann's Correspondence with E.'' *ESQ*, 20: 91-100 (2Q 74).

Sowder, W.J. ''Articles on E in British Periodicals.'' *ESQ*, 53: 5-23 (4Q 68).

————. ''E's Early Impact on England.'' *PMLA*, 77: 755-66 (D 62).

————. ''E's Reviewers and Commentators: Nineteenth-Century Periodical Criticism.'' *ESQ*, 53: 1-51 (1968).

————. ''Periodical Writers.'' *ESQ*, 53: 24-35 (4Q 68).

Spencer, B.T. ''Sherwood Anderson: American Mythopoeist.'' *AL*, 41: 1-18 (Mr 69).

Spiller, R.E. ''E and Humboldt.'' *AL*, 42: 546-8 (Ja 71).

————. ''E's 'The Young American!' '' *Clio*, 1: 37-41 (O 71).

Stanton, M.N. ''The Startled Muse: E and Science Fiction.'' *Extrapolation*, 16: 64-6 (D 74).

Steele, John. ''E and McLuhan: The Problem of Perpetual Literacy.'' *Eng Rev*, 3: 30-7 (1975).

Stein, W.B. ''E's 'History': The Rhetoric of Cosmic Consciousness.'' *ESQ*, 18: 199-206 (4Q 72).

Steinbrink, Jeffrey. ''Novels of Circumstance and Novels of Character: E's Views of Fiction.'' *ESQ*, 20: 101-10 (2Q 74).

Sten, C.W. ''Bartleby the Transcendentalist: Melville's Dead Letter to E.'' *MLQ*, 35: 30-44 (Mr 74).

Stevens, D.M. ''E on the Saxon Race: A Manuscript Fragment.'' *ESQ*, 47: 103-5 (2Q 67).

Stoehr, Taylor. '' 'Eloquence Needs No Constable'—Alcott, E, and Thoreau on the State.'' *CRAS*, 5: 81-100 (74).

Stone, A.W. ''To Emerson.'' *ESQ*, 52: 9 (3Q 68).

Storm, M.G. ''The Riddle of 'The Sphinx': Another Approach.'' *ESQ*, 62: 44-8 (W 71).

Strauch, C.F. ''E and the Longevity of the Mind.'' *ESQ*, 54: 60-8 (1Q 69).

————. ''E Rejects Reed and Hails Thoreau.'' *HLB*, 16: 257-73 (Ju 68).

————. ''E's Adaptation of Myth in 'The Initial Love.' '' *ATQ*, 25: 51-65 (Wi 75).

————. ''E's Use of the Organic Method.'' *ESQ*, 55: 18-24 (2Q 69).

————. ''Hatred's Swift Repulsions: E, Margaret Fuller, and Others.'' *SRom*, 7: 65-103 (Wi 68).

————. ''The Mind's Voice: E's Poetic Styles.'' *ESQ*, 60: 43-59 (Su 70).

————. ''The Problem of Time and the Romantic Mode in Hawthorne, Melville, and E.'' *ESQ*, 35: 50-60 (2Q 64)

Stubbs, J.C. ''The Ideal in the Literature and Art of the American Renaissance.'' *ESQ*, 55: 5-63 (2Q 69)

Tarr, R.L. ''E's Transcendentalism in L.M. Child's Letter to Carlyle.'' *ESQ*, 58: 112-5 (1Q 70).

Tenney, T.A. ''E and *The Encyclopaedia Americana*.'' *ESQ*, 19: 219-23 (4Q 73).

Terry, R.F. ''E, Cox, and God.'' *ER*, 25: 27-30 (1968).

Thundyil, Zacharias. ''E and the Problem of Evil: Paradox and Solution.'' *HTR*, 62: 51-61 (Ja 69).

Tilden, Freeman. "Two Concord Men in a Boat." *MassA*, 50: 78-82 (Wi 65).

Tilton, E.M. "E's Latest Lecture Schedule—1837-1838—Revised." *HBL*, 21:382-99 (1973).

Tingley, D.F. "RWE on the Illinois Lecture Circuit." *JISHS*, 64: 192-205 (Su 71).

Tokuza, Akiko. "RWE's Theory of Art." *Jimbun Shizen Kagaku Ronshyu*, 35: 1-119 (1973).

Travis, M.K. "Echoes of E in Plinlimmon." *ATQ*, 14: 47-8 (Sp 72).

Tricomi, A.H. "The Rhetoric of Aspiring Circularity in E's 'Circles.'" *ESQ*,18: 271-83 (4Q 72).

Tuerk, Richard. "E as Translator—'The Phoenix.'" *ESQ*, 63: 24-6 (Sp 71).

———. "E's Darker Vision: 'Hamatreya' and 'Days.'" *ATQ*, 25: 28-33 (Wi 75).

———. "E.'s *Nature*—Miniature Universe." *ATQ*, 110-3 (1Q 69).

———. "Los Angeles' Reaction to E's Visit to San Francisco." *NEQ*, 44: 477-82 (S 71).

Unali, Lina. "Sulla *Divinity School Address* di RWE e sull'uso della parola *Soul*." *AFLFM*, 36: 13-21 (1973).

Unoki, Keijoiro. "Why did E, Thoreau and Melville Express their Thoughts in the Form 'Railroad' Symbolically?" *Karibane,* 9: 62-70 (Mr 70).

Van Cromphout, Gustaaf. "E, Hawthorne, and *The Blithedale Romance*." *GaR*, 25: 471-80 (Wi 71).

Van Der Beets, Richard. "Compensatory Imagery in E's Poem 'Compensation.'" *ESQ*, 63: 12-3 (Sp 71).

Van Egmond, Peter. "Harned on Emerson's Friend William Henry Furness." *ATQ*, 1: 15-18 (1969).

Vellela, Ellen. "E and *The Conduct of Life*." *Eng R*, 1: 6-27 (1973).

Vitanza, V.J. "Melville's *Redburn* and E's 'General Education of the Eye.'" *ESQ*, 21: 40-55 (1Q 75).

Vittorini, Elio. "An Outline of American Literature." *SR*, 68: 423-37 (Su 60).

Waggoner, H.H. "The 'Formalism' of Lewis Turco: Fluting and Fifing with Frosted Fingers." *CP*, 2: 50-8 (Fa 69).

———. "'Grace' in the Thought of E, Thoreau, and Hawthorne." *ESQ*, 54: 68-72 (1Q 69).

———. "Works, Days, Poetry, and Imagination." *ATQ,* 21: 30-2 (Wi 74).

Wahr, F.B. "E and Goethe: E and the Germans." *ATQ*, 15: Parts 1 and 2 (1972).

Walcutt, C.C. "E's 'The Sphinx.'" *Expl*, 31: 20 (N 72).

Ward, J.A. "E and 'The Educated Will': Notes on the Process of Conversion." *ELH*, 34: 495-517 (1967).

Ward, R.S. "Still 'Christians,' Still Infidels." *SHR*, 2: 365-74 (Sa 68).

Westbrook, Perry. "John Burroughs and the Transcendentalists." *ESQ*, 55: 47-55 (2Q 69).

Wheeler, O.B. "The Emersonian View of American Poetry." *SoR*, 4: 1077-80 (1968).

———. "E's Political Quandary." *LSUS*, 8: 22-32 (1960).

White, William. "E as Editor: A Letter to Benjamin F. Presbury." *AN&Q*, 12: 59-61 (D 73).

Whitford, Kathryn. "Water, Wind, and Light Imagery in E's Essay 'The Oversoul.'" *WSL*, 6: 100-5 (1969).

Wild, P.H. "Flower Power: A Student's Guide to Pre-Hippie Transcendentalism." *EJ*, 58: 62-8 (Ja 69).

Willert, James. "Between the Lines with RWE." *Yankee*, Mr 71; pp. 79, 160-7.

Williams, John. "Henry Miller: The Success of Failure." *VQR*, 44: 225-45 (Sp 68).

Williams, R.S. "E's Relevance Today." *BYUS*, 11: 241-8 (Sp 71).

Wilson, J.B. "The Aesthetics of Transcendentalism." *ESQ*, 57: 27-34 (4Q 69).

———. "E and the 'Rochester Rappings.'" *NEQ*, 41: 248-58 (Je 68).

Wise, J.N. "E's 'Experience' and *Sons and Lovers*." *Costerus*, 6: 179-221 (1972).

Wiseman, James. "The Meaning of God for E." *Month*, 222: 133-40 (S 61).

Wood, A.D. "Reconsiderations—RWE." *NRep*, 166: 27-9 (1 and 8 Ja 72).

Yarmolinsky, Adam. "The New American Scholar." *Change*, 5: 27-32 (My 73).

Yoder, R.A. "E—Golden Impossibility, Representative man." *ESQ*, 21: 241-59 (4Q 75).

———. "E's Dialectic." *Criticism*, 11: 313-28 (Au 69).

———. "Toward the 'Titmouse Dimension': The Development of E's Poetic Style." *PLMA*, 87: 255-70 (Mr 72).

———. "Transcendental Conservatism and *The House of the Seven Gables*." *GaR*, 28: 33-51 (Sp 74).

Yoshida, Osamu. "A Study of E: His Early Religious Philosophy as the Basis of his Thought." *Research Bulletin of the Hiroshima Institute of Technology*, 3: 233-42 (1969).

Engle, Paul. Arbelaez, Fernando. "La poesìa de PE." *BCB*, 63-7 (1969).

Enright, Elizabeth. Cameron, Eleanor. "Art of EE." *HornB*, 45: np (D 69); 46: 26-30 (F 70).

Erdman, Loula Grace. Sewell, Ernestine. "An Interview with LGE." *SwAL*, 2: 33-41 (Sp 72).

Esslin, Martin. Dace, Letitia. "On Jean Genet and ME, or Here Absurdist, There Absurdist, Everywhere. . . ." *KanQ*, 3: 110-16 (1971).

Eustace, E.J. Meisel, Martin. "One of 'America's Lost Plays': A Comment." *BNYPL*, 76: 348-52 (1972).

Evans, Abbie Huston. Saul, G.B. "Flinty Bread: The Verse of AHE." *ArQ*, 13: 164-8 (Su 57).

Silver, Philip. "Miss E's Expanding Universe." *Approach*, 46: 5-10 (Wi 63).

Evans, Charles Napoleon Bonaparte. Stokes, D.T. "A Newly Discovered Letter from the Fool Killer." *NCaF*, 17: 3-8 (My 69).

Evans, Donald. Fields, Kenneth. "Past Masters: Walter Conrad Arensberg and DE." *SoR*, 6: 317-39 (Ap 70).

Van Vechten, Carl. "The Origin of the 'Sonnets from the Patagonian.'" *HartR*, 3: 50-6 (Sp 67).

Evans, Mari. Sedlack, R.P. "ME: Consciousness and Craft." *CLAJ*, 15: 465-76 (Je 72).

Evans, Max. Milton, J.R. "Interview: ME." *SDR*, 5: 77-87 (Su 67).

Everett, Edward. Evans, Elizabeth. "The Everett-Longfellow Correspondence." *ATQ*, 13: 2-15 (1972).

Everson, William (Brother Antonius). Rizzo, Fred. "BA: Vates of Radical Catholicism." *DQ*, 3: 18-38 (Wi 69).

Everett, Alexander Hill. Evans, Elizabeth. "The Friendship of AHE and Hugh Swinton Legaŕe." *MissQ*, 28: 497-504 (Fa 75).

Ewing, Samuel. Rothman, I.N. "Structure and Theme in SE's Satire, the 'American Miracle.'" *AL*, 40: 294-308 (N 68).

Fair, Ronald L. Fleming, R.E. "The Novels of RL.F." *CLAJ*, 15: 477-87 (Je 72).

Klotman, P.R. "The Passive Resistant in *A Different Drummer*, *Day of Absence* and *Many Thousands Gone*." *SBL*, 3: 7-12 (Au 72).

Falkner, William Cuthbert. Anderson, Hilton. "Colonel F's Preface to *The Siege of Montery*." *NMW*, 3: 36-40 (Sp 70).

———. "*The White Rose of Memphis*: A Clarification." *NMW*, 1: 64-7 (Fa 68).

Falstaff, Jake. (see **Fetzer, Herman**).

Fanon, Frantz. Foster, F.S. "The Black and White Masks of FF and Ralph Ellison."
BlAR, 1: 46-58 (Wi 70).

Farmer, Philip José. Rottensteiner, Franz. "Playing Around With Creation: PJF." *S-FS*,
1: 94-7 (Fa 73).

Farrell, James T. Branch, E.M. "The 1930's in JT.F's Fiction." *ABC*, 21: 9-12 (1971).

Fried, Lewis. "JT.F: Shadow and Act." *JA*, 17: 140-55 (1972).

Grattan, C.H. "JT.F: Moralist." *HM*, 209: 93-8 (O 54).

Halperin, Irving. "Studs Lonigan Revisited." *ABC*, 19: 10-12 (N 68).

Nunes, Cassiano. "JT.F and Studs Lonigan." *ABC*, 23: 7-8 (#6 73).

Robinson, C.E. "JT.F's Critical Estimate of Hemingway." *FHA*, 1973; pp. 209-14.

Shaughnessy, E.L. "Oliver Alden and Studs Lonigan: Heirs to Spiritual Poverty."
MarkR, 4: 48-52 (My 74).

Faulkner, John. Bradford, M.E. "'New Men' in Mississippi: *Absalom, Absalom!* and
Dollar Cotton." *NMW*, 2: 55-66 (Fa 69).

Faulkner, Jim. "The Picture of J and Brother Will." *DelR*, 7:12-4 (Fa 70).

Pruett, D.F. "Papers of JF." *MVC Bul*, 3: 81-4 (Fa 70).

Sugg, R.S. "John's Yoknapatawpha." *SAQ*, 68: 343-62 (Su 69).

———. "JF's Vanishing South." *AH*, 22: 65-75 (Ap 71).

*White, Helen, and R.S. Sugg. "JF: An Annotated Check List of His Published Works and
of His Papers." *SB*, 23: 217-29 (1970).

Faulkner, William. Anon. "F Concordance." *PMLA*, 86: 492 (My 71).

———. "A Selected Listing of Recent Work of Special Interest to the F Concordance
Project." *FCN*, 2: 6-7 (1973).

Ackerman, R.D. "The Immolation of Isaac McCaslin." *TSLL*, 16: 557-66 (Fa 74).

Adamowski, T.H. "Bayard Sartoris: Mourning and Melancholia." *L&P*, 23: 149-58 (#4
73).

———. "Dombey and Son and Sutpen and Son." *StN*, 4: 378-89 (Fa 72).

———. "Isaac McCaslin and the Wilderness of the Imagination." *CentR*, 17: 92-112 (Wi
73).

———. "Joe Christmas: The Tyranny of Childhood." *Novel*, 4: 240-51 (Sp 71).

Adams, R.P. "At Long Last, *Flags in the Dust.*" *SoR*, 10: 878-88 (O 74).

———. "F and the Myth of the South." *MissQ*, 14: 131-7 (Su 61).

———. "Some Key Words in F." *TSE*, 16: 135-48 (1968).

Adorno, T.W. "Standort des Erzählers im zeitgenössischen Roman." *Noten zur Literatur*,
1: 61-72 (1958).

Aínsa, Fernando. "En el santuario de WF." *CHA*, 269: 232-43 (1972).

Akasofu, Tetsuji. "F *Hachigatsu no Kikari.*" *EigoS*, 117: 306-7 (1971).

Alexandrescu, Sorin. "A Project in the Semantic Analysis of the Characters in WF's
Work." *Semiotica*, 4: 37-51 (1971).

Alexandrescu, Sorin. "WF and the Greek Tragedy." *RoR*, 24: 102-10 (1970).

Amacher, R.E. "Humor in F's Hoaxes and Satires." *SAH*, 2: 4-19 (Ap 75).

Amette, J.P. "Le Premier grand romancier de l'inconscient." *Sud*, 14: 7-11 (1975).

Anastas'ev, N. "F: Put' k 'derevuške.'" *VLit*, 14: 122-41 (1970).

———. "F's Weg zum Roman 'Das Sorf.'" *KuL*, 19: 956-74 (1971).

Anderson, Hilton. "Two Possible Sources for F's Drusilla Hawk." *NMW*, 3: 108-10 (Wi
71).

Angell, L.E. "The Umbilical Cord Symbol as Unifying Theme in *Abasalom, Absalom!*"
MSE, 1: 106-10 (1968).

Faulkner, William

Antoniadis, Roxandra. "The Dream as Design in Balzac and F." *Zagadnienia rodzajow literackich*, 17: 45-58 (#2, 74).

Antoniadis, R.V. "The Dream as Design in Balzac and F." *ZRL*, 17: 45-57 (#2 74).

———. "F and Balzac: The Poetic Web." *CLS*, 9: 303-25 (S 72).

Applewhite, Davis. "The South of *Light in August.*" *MissQ*, 11: 167-72 (Fa 58).

Arnold, Edwin. "Freedom and Stasis in F's *Mosquitoes.*" *MissQ*, 28: 281-97 (Su 75).

Arpad, J.J. "WF's Legendary Novels: The Snopes Trilogy." *MissQ*, 22: 214-25 (Su 69).

Asals, Frederick. "F's *Light in August.*" *Expl*, 26: 74 (My 68).

Aswell, Duncan. "The Matched Halves of *Absalom, Absalom!*" *MFS*, 15: 264-5 (Su 69).

———. "The Puzzling Design of *Absalom, Absalom!*" *KR*, 30: 67-84 (Ja 68).

———. "The Recollection and the Blood: Jason's Role in *The Sound and the Fury.*" *MissQ*, 21: 211-8 (Su 68).

Auer, M.J. "Cady, Benjy, and the Acts of the Apostles." *StN*, 6: 475-6 (Wi 74).

Aury, Dominique. "WF." *NRF*, 116: 315-6 (l Ag 62).

Baker, J.R. "Ideas and Queries." *FaS*, 1: 39-41 (Fa 52).

Balotă, Nicolae. "Încrederea în F." *RoLit*, 17: 13 (Ag 72).

Baquirin, J.Q. "Themes, Style, and Symbolism in *The Sound and the Fury.*" *SLRJ*, 4: 658-72 (D 73).

Barber, Marion. "The Two Emilys: A Ransom Suggestion to F?" *NMW*, 5: 103-5 (Wi 73).

Barnes, D.R. "F's Miss Emily and Hawthorne's Old Maid." *SSF*, 9: 373-7 (1972).

Barth, J.R. "F and the *Snopes Trilogy.*" *America*, 102: 638-40 (27 F 60).

———. "A Rereading of F's *Fable.*" *America*, 92: 44-6 (9 O 54).

Bassett, J.E. "WF's *The Sound and the Fury*: An Annotated Checklist of Criticism." *RALS*, 1: 217-46 (Au 71).

Basso, Hamilton. "Faulkneriana." *NRep*, 107: 261-2 (31 Ag 42).

Beards, Richard. "Parody as Tribute: William Melvin Kelley's *A Different Drummer* and F." *SBL*, 5: 25-8 (Wi 74).

Beauchamp, Gorman. "The Rite of Initiation in F's *The Bear.*" *ArQ*, 28: 319-25 (1972).

———. "*The Unvanquished*: F's *Oresteia.*" *MissQ*, 23: 273-7 (Su 70).

Beaver, Harold. "The Count of Mississippi." *TLS*, 30 My 75, pp. 600-l.

Bedient, Calvin. "Pride and Nakedness: *As I Lay Dying.*" *MLQ*, 29: 61-76 (Mr 68).

Behrens, Ralph. "Collapse of Dynasty: The Thematic Center of *Absalom, Absalom!*" *PMLA*, 89: 24-33 (Ja 74).

Beidler, P.G. "A Darwinian Source for F's Indians in 'Red Leaves.'" *SSF*, 10: 421-3 (Fa 73).

———. "F's Techniques." *EA*, 21: 225-35 (Jl-S 68).

———. "F's Techniques of Characterization: Jewel in *As I Lay Dying.*" *EA*, 21: 236-42 (Jl-S 68).

Bell, H.H. "The Relative Maturity of Lucius and Ike McCaslin." *Aegis*, 2: 15-21 (Fa 73).

———. "Sam Fathers and Ike McCaslin and the World in Which Ike Matures." *Costerus*, 7: 1-12 (1973).

Bell, Laurence. "F in Moronia." *Lit Am*, 1: 15-8 (My 34).

Bellman, S.I. "Hemingway, F, and Wolfe . . . and the Common Reader." *SoR*, 4: 834-49 (Su 68).

Benert, Annette. "The Four Fathers of Isaac McCaslin." *SHR*, 9: 423-33 (Fa 75).

Benson, J.J, "Quentin Compson: Self Portrait of a Young Artist's Emotions." *TCL*, 17: 143-59 (Jl 71).

———. "Quentin's Responsibility for Caddy's Downfall in F's *The Sound and the Fury.*" *NMW*, 5: 63-4 (Fa 72).

Berland, Alwyn. "*Light in August*: The Calvinism of WF." *MFS*, 8: 159-70 (Su 62).

Bernackaja, V. "Raspavsijsja porjadok (O pisatel' skoj individual' hosti F)." *VLit*, 18: 85-100 (#3 74).

Bernberg, R.E. "*Light in August*: A Psychological View." *MissQ*, 11: 173-6 (Fa 58).

Bethea, Sally. "Further Thoughts on Racial Implications in F's 'That Evening Sun.'" *NMW*, 6: 87-92 (Wi 74).

Bier, Jesse. "The Romantic Coordinates of American Literature." *BuR*, 18: 16-33 (Fa 70).

Blackley, Charles. "WF's Country: A Chronological Guide to Yoknapatawpha." *TAIUS*, 4: 73-86 (1971).

Blair, J.G. "Camus' F: Requiem For a Nun." *BFLS*, 47: 249-57 (Ja 69).

Blanchard, L.A. "The Failure of the Natural Man: F's 'Pantaloon in Black.'" *NMW*, 8: 28-32 (1975).

Blanchard, Margaret. "The Rhetoric of Communion: Voice in *The Sound and the Fury*." *AL*, 41: 555-65 (Ja 70).

Bledsoe, A.S. "Colonel John Sartoris' Library." *NMW*, 7: 26-9 (Sp 74).

Bleikasten, André. "L'escape dans *Lumiere d'aout*." *BFLS*, 46: 406-20 (D 67).

———. "Noces noires, noces blanches: Le jeu du désir et de la mort dans le monologue de Quentin Compson *(The Sound and the Fury)*." *RANAM*, 6: 142-69 (1973).

———. "La terreur et la nausee, ou le langage des corps dans *Sanctuaire*." *Sud*, 14: 81-116 (1975).

Blotner, Joseph. "The Achievement of Maurice Edgar Coindreau." *SLJ*, 4: 95-6 (Fa 71).

———. "The Blues as a Literary Theme." *MR*, 8: 593-617 (Au 67).

———. "Speaking of Books: F's 'A Fable.' " *NYT*, 25 My 69, pp. 2, 34-9.

———. "WF's Essay on the Composition of *Sartoris*." *YULG*, 47: 121-4 (1972).

Borgström, G.I. "The Roaring Twenties and WF's *Sanctuary*." *MSpr*, 62: 237-48 (1968).

Borden, Caroline. "Characterization in F's *Light in August*." *L&I*, 13: 41-50 (1972).

Boring, P.Z. "Usmail: The Puerto Rican Joe Christmas." *CLAJ*, 16: 324-32 (Mr 73).

Boswell, G.W. "Folkways in F." *MissFR*, 1: 83-90 (Fa 67).

———. "The Legendary Background in F's Work." *TFSB*, 36: 53-63 (S 70).

———. "Notes on the Surnames of F's Characters." *TFSB*, 36: 64-6 (S 70).

———. "Picturesque Faulknerisms." *USME*, 9: 47-56 (1968).

———. "Superstition and Belief in F." *Costerus*, 6: 1-26 (1972).

———. "Traditional Verse and Music Influence in F." *NMW*, 1: 23-31 (Sp 68).

Bowen, J.K. and J.A. Hamby. "Colonel Sartoris Snopes and Gabriel Marcel: Allegiance and Commitment." *NMW*, 3: 101-7 (Wi 71).

Bradford, M.E. "Addie Bundren and the Design of *As I Lay Dying*, *SoR*, 6: 1093-9 (Au 70).

———. "An Aesthetic Parable: F's 'Artist at Home.'" *GaR*, 27: 175-81 (Su 73).

———. "Blotner's F." *Triumph*, 9: 32-4 (1974).

———. "Brother, Son, and Heir: The Structural Focus of F's *Absalom, Absalom!*" *SR*, 78: 76-98 (Wi 70).

———. "Certain Ladies of Quality: F's View of Women and the Evidence of 'There Was A Queen.'" *ArlQ*, 1: 106-39 (Wi 67-8).

———. "F's 'Elly': An Exposé." *MissQ*, 21: 179-87 (Su 68).

———. "F's Last Words and 'The American Dilemma.' " *ModA*, 16: 77-82 (Wi 72).

———. "'New Men' in Mississippi: *Absalom, Absalom!* and *Dollar Cotton*." *NMW*, 2: 55-66 (Fa 69).

———. "Spring Paradigm: F's Living Legacy." *Forum(H)*, 6: 4-7 (Sp 68).

————. "That Other Patriarchy: Observations on F's 'A Justice.'" *ModA*, 18: 266-71 (Su 74).

————. "What Grandfather Said: The Social Testimony of F's *The Reivers*." *Occasional R*, 1: 15-21 (F 74).

Brady, R.H. "F's *As I Lay Dying*." *Expl*, 33: 50 (1975).

Brand, David. "Tribute to WF." *Humanist*, 78: 46-7 (F 63).

Breit, Harvey. "A Sense of F." *PR*, 18: 88-94 (Ja-F 51).

Brent, Harold. "The Value and Limitations of F's Fictional Method." *AL*, 47: 212-29 (My 75).

Bridgman, Richard. "As Hester Prynne Lay Dying." *ELN*, 2: 294-6 (Je 65).

Brocki, Sister M.D. "F and Hemingway: Values in a Modern World." *MTJ*, 11: 5-9, 15 (Su 62).

Brogunier, Joseph. "A Housman Source in *The Sound and the Fury*." *MFS*, 18: 220-5 (Su 72).

————. "A Source for the Commissary Entries in *Go Down, Moses*." *TSLL*, 14: 545-54 (Fa 72).

Brooks, Cleanth. "F and History." *MissQ*, 25: 3-14 (Sp 72).

————. "F and the Muse of History." *MissQ*, 28: 265-79 (Su 75).

————. "F as Poet." *SLJ*, 1: 5-19 (Au 68).

————. "F's Criticism of Modern America." *VQR*, 51: 294-308 (Sp 75).

————. "F's First Novel." *SoR*, 6: 1056-74 (Au 70).

————. "The Narrative Structure of *Absalom, Absalom!*" *GaR*, 29: 366-94 (Su 75).

————. "A Note on F's Early Attempts at the Short Story." *SSF*, 10: 381-8 (Fa 73).

————. "On *Absalom, Absalom!*" *Mosaic*, 7: 159-85 (Fa 73).

————. "The Poetry of Miss Rosa Coldfied." *Shen*, 199-206 (Sp 70).

————. "The Tradition of Romantic Love and *The Wild Palms*." *MissQ*, 25: 265-87 (1972).

————. "When Did Joanna Burden Die?: A Note." *SLJ*, 6: 43-6 (Fa 73).

Broughton, P.R. "Masculinity and Menfolk in *The Hamlet*." *MissQ*, 22: 181-9 (Su 69).

————. "*Requiem for a Nun*: No Part in Rationality." *SoR*, 8: 749-62 (O 72).

Brown, C.S. "A Dim View of F's Country." *GaR*, 23: 501-11 (Wi 69).

————. "F's Idiot Boy: The Source of Simile in *Sartoris*." *AL*, 44: 474-6 (N 72).

————. "F's Three-in-one Bridge in *The Reivers*." *NCLit*, 1: 8-10 (Mr 71).

————. "F's Use of the Oral Tradition." *GaR*, 22: 160-9 (Su 68).

————. "*Sanctuary*: From Confrontation to Peaceful Void." *Mosaic*, 7: 75-96 (Fa 73).

————. "Southern Thought and National Materialism." *SLJ*, 1: 98-106 (Sp 69).

Brown, James. "Shaping the World of *Sanctuary*." *UR*, 25: 137-42 (Wi 58).

Brown, W.R. "Mr. Stark on Mr. Strawson on Referring." *Lang&S*, 7: 219-24 (Su 74).

Brumm, Anne-Marie. "Authoritarianism in WF's *Light in August* and Alberto Moravia's *Il Conformista*." *RLMC*, 26: 196-220 (1973).

Brumm, Ursula. "Forms and Functions of History in the Novels of WF." *Archiv*, 209: 43-56 (Ag 72).

————. "Thoughts on History and the Novel." *CLS*, 6: 317-30 (S 69).

Brunauer, D.H. "Worshipping the Bear-God." *C&L*, 23: 7-35 (Sp 74).

Burke, Kenneth. "Formalist Criticism: Its Principles and Limits." *TQ*, 9: 242-68 (Sp 68).

Burroughs, F.G. "God the Father and Motherless Children: *Light in August*." *TCL*, 19: 189-202 (Jl 73).

Burrows, R.N. "Institutional Christianity as Reflected in the Works of WF." *MissQ*, 14: 138-47 (Su 61).

Burton, D.M. "Intonation Patterns of Sermons in Seven Novels." *Lang&S*, 3: 205-20 (1970).

Butterworth, Keen. "A Census of Manuscripts and Typescripts of WF's Poetry." *MissQ*, 26: 333-59 (Su 73).

Cabaniss, Allen. "To Scotch a Monumental Mystery." *NMW*, 3: 79-80 (Fa 70).

Calverton, V.F. "Steinbeck, Hemingway and F." *Mod Q*, 11: 36-44 (Fa 39).

Cambell, H.M. "F's Philosophy Again: A Reply to Michel Gresset." *MissQ*, 23: 64-6 (Wi 69-70).

————. "Mr. Roth's Centaur and F's Symbolism." *WR*, 16: 320-1 (Su 52).

Campbell, J.H. "Polarity and Paradox: F's *Light in August*." *CEA*, 34: 26-31 (Ja 72).

Cantrell, Frank. "F's 'A Courtship.'" *MissQ*, 24: 289-95 (Su 71).

————. "An Unpublished F Short Story: 'Snow.'" *MissQ*, 26: 325-30 (Su 73).

Capps, J.L. "Computer Program Revisions and the Preparation of a Concordance to *Go Down, Moses*." *ECN*, 2: 2-5 (1973).

————. "Introduction: WF and West Point." *U.S. Military Acad Lib Occasional Papers*, 2: 1-5 (1974).

————. "Three F Studies." *SLJ*, 6: 117-21 (Fa 73).

Carey, G.O. "F and *Mosquitoes*: Writing Himself and His Age." *RSW*, 39: 271-83 (1971).

————. "*Light in August* and Religious Fanaticism." *STC*, 10: 101-13 (Fa 72).

————. "WF: Man's Fatal Vice." *ArQ*, 28: 293-300 (1972).

————. "WF on the Automboile as Socio-Sexual Symbol." *CEA*, 36: 15-7 (Ja 74).

————. "WF: The Rise of the Snopeses." *STC*, 8: 37-64 (Fa 71).

Carothers, J.B. "F Criticism: Footprints and Monuments." *CEA*, 36: 38-40 (#2 74).

Carter, T.H. "Dramatization of an Enigma." *WR*, 19: 147-58 (Wi 55).

Castille, Philip. "'There Was a Queen' and F's Narcissa Sartoris." *MissQ*, 28: 207-15 (Su 75).

Cecil, L.M. "A Rhetoric for Benjy." *SLJ*, 3: 32-46 (Fa 70).

Chapsal, Madeleine. "A Lion in the Garden." *Reporter*, 8: 40 (13 N 55).

Chen, Yuan-yin. "Hengri yu Wei-ehr-po chic Chien-Lun Haim-ming-wei yu F." *TkR*, 11: 217-24 (1973).

Chitragupta, A. "The World of Books: Multiple Focus on F." *Thought*, 26: 15-6 (30 Mr 74).

Ciancio, R.A. "F's Existentialist Affinities." *CaSE*, 6: 69-91 (1961).

Ciardi, John. "F and Child, F and Negro." *HM*, 234: 114 (My 67).

Clark, C.C. "'Mistral': A Study in Human Tempering." *MissQ*, 21: 195-204 (Su 68).

Clark, Eulalyn. "Ironic Effects on Multiple Perspective in *As I Lay Dying*." *NMW*, 5: 15-28 (Sp 72).

Clark, W.G. "F's *Light in August*." *Expl*, 26: 54 (Mr 68).

————. "F's *Light in August*." *Expl*, 28: 19 (N 69).

Clements, A.L. "F's 'A Rose for Emily.'" *Expl*, 20: 78 (Je 62).

Cobau, W.W. "Jason Compson and the Costs of Speculation." *MissQ*, 22: 257-61 (Su 69).

Coburn, M.D. "Nancy's Blues: F's 'That Evening Sun.'" *Per*, 17: 207-16 (#3 74).

Coindreau, Maurice-Edgar. "F, le moraliste." *QL*, 94: 6-7 (1 My 70).

Collins, Carvel. "A Fourth Book Review by F." *MissQ*, 28: 339-42 (Su 75).

————. "Nathaniel West's *The Day of the Locust* and *Sanctuary*." *FaS*, 2: 23-4 (Su 53).

Collins, R.G. "The Game of Names: Characterization Device in *Light in August*." *Eng Rec*, 21: 82-7 (O 70).

————. "*Light in August*: F's Stained Glass Triptych." *Mosaic*, 7: 97-158 (Fa 73).

Collmer, R.G. "The Displayed Person in the Novels of Gabriel Casaccia." *Re: Arts and Letters*, 3: 37-45 (Sp 70).

Commins, D.B. "WF in Princeton." *JHS*, 2: 179-85 (1Q 69).

Cook, R.M. "Popeye, Flem, and Sutpen: The Faulknerian Villain as Grotesque." *SAF*, 3: 3-14 (Sp 75).

Cooley, T.W. "F Draws the Long Bow." *TCL*, 16: 268-77 (O 70).

Corrington, J.W. "Escape into Myth: the Long Dying of Bayard Sartoris." *Ranam*, 4: 31-47 (1971).

Cottrell, B.W. "F's Cosmic Fable: The Extraordinary Family of Man." *CaSE*, 6: 17-27 (1961).

Cowan, J.C. "Dream-Work in the Quentin Section of *The Sound and the Fury*." *L&P*, 24: 91-8 (3Q 74).

Crane, J.K. "The Jefferson Courthouse: an *Axis Exsecrabilis Mundi*." *TCL*, 15: 19-23 (Ap 69).

Creighton, J.V. "The Dilemma of the Human Heart in *The Mansion*." *Renascence*, 25: 35-45 (Au 72).

———. "F's 'The Fire and the Hearth.'" *SSF*, 11: 161-72 (Sp 74).

———. "Revision and Craftsmanship in F's 'The Fire and the Hearth.'" *SSF*, 11: 161-72 (Sp 74).

———. "Revision and Craftsmanship in the Hunting Trilogy of *Go Down, Moses*." *TSLL*, 15: 577-92 (Fa 73).

———. "Self-Destructive Evil in *Sanctuary*." *TCL*, 18: 259-70 (1972).

———. "Surratt to Ratliff: A Genetic Approach to *The Hamlet*." *MichA*, 6: 101-12 (Su 73).

Cutler, B.D. "Bright in August (A Faulknereality)." *Am Spec*, 3: 13-5 (Ag 35).

Dabney, L.M. "F, the Red, and the Black." *ColF*, 1: 52-4 (Sp 72).

———. "'Was': F's Classic Comedy of the Frontier." *SoR*, 8: 736-48 (O 72).

Dahl, James. "A F Reminiscence: Conversations with Mrs. Maud Falkner." *JML*, 3: 1026-30 (Ap 74).

———. "WF on Individualism." *WGCR*, 6: 3-9 (1973).

Darnell, D.G. "Cooper and F: Land, Legacy, and the Tragic Vision." *SAB*, 34: 3-5 (Mr 69).

D'Avanzo, M.L. "Bobbie Allen and the Ballad Tradition in *Light in August*." *SCR*, 8: 22-9 (N 75).

Davis, Scottie. "F's Nancy: Racial Implications in 'That Evening Sun.'" *NMW*, 5: 30-2 (Sp 72).

———. "Allusion in the Percy Grimm Episode of *Light in August*." *NMW*, 8: 63-6 (Fa 75).

Davis, W.V. "Another Flower for F's Bouquet: Theme and Structure in 'A Rose for Emily.'" *NMW*, 7: 34-8 (Fa 74).

———. "Quentin's Death Ritual: Further Christian Allusions in *The Sound and the Fury*." *NMW*, 6: 27-32 (Sp 73).

———. "*The Sound and the Fury*: A Note on Benjy's Name." *StN*, 4: 60-1 (Sp 72).

DeCillier, M.A.G. "F's Young Man: As Reflected in the Character of Charles Mallison." *LauR*, 9: 42-9 (#2 69).

Degenfelder, E.P. "The Film Adaptation of F's *Intruder in the Dust*." *LFQ*, l: 138-48 (Ap 73).

———. "Yoknapatawphan Baroque: A Stylistic Analysis of *As I Lay Dying*." *Style*, 7: 121-56 (Sp 73).

Delay, Florence, and J. de Labriolle. "Marqez est-il le F Colombien?" *RLC*, 47: 88-123 (1973).

Detweiler, Robert. "The Moment of Death in Modern Fiction." *ConL*, 13: 269-94 (1972).

DeVillier, M.A.G. "F's Young Man: As Reflected in the Character of Charles Mallison." *LauR*, 9: 42-9 (1969).

Devlin, A.J. "Faulknerian Chronology: Puzzles and Games." *NMW*, 5: 98-101 (Wi 73).

———. "How Much It Takes to Compound a Man': A Neglected Scene in *Go Down, Moses.*" *MwQ*, 14: 408-21 (Jl 73).

———. "*The Reivers*: Readings in Social Psychology." *MissR*, 25: 327-39 (Su 72).

———. "*Sartoris*: Rereading the McCallum Episode." *TCL*, 17: 83-90 (Ap 71).

Dickerson, M.J. "The Magician's Wand: F's Compson Appendix." *MissQ*, 28: 317-38 (Su 75).

Dillon, R.T. "Some Sources for F's Version of the First Air War." *AL*, 44: 629-37 (Ja 73).

Ditsky, John. "'Dark, Darker Than Fire': Thematic Parallels in Lawrence and F." *SHR*, 8: 497-505 (Fa 74).

———. "F's Carousel: Point of View in *As I Lay Dying.*" *LauR*, 10: 74-85 (Sp 70).

———. "From Oxford to Salinas: Comparing Faulkner and Steinbeck." *StQ*, 2:51-5 (Fa 69).

———. "Uprooted Trees: Dynasty and the Land in R's Novels." *TSL*, 17: 151-58 (1972).

Doody, Terrence. "Shreve McCannon and the Confessions of *Absalom, Absalom!*" *StN*, 6: 454-69 (Wi 74).

Drake, Robert. "The Pieties of the Fiction Writer, I." *CEA*, 32: 3-4 (O 69).

Duncan, A.B. "Claude Simon and WF." *FMLS*, 9: 235-52 (Jl 73).

Dunlap, M.M. "Sex and the Artist in *Mosquitoes.*" *MissQ*, 22: 190-206 (Su 69).

———. "WF's 'Knight's Gambit' and Gavin Stevens." *MissQ*, 23: 223-39 (Su 70).

Durham, Frank. "The Southern Literary Tradition: Shadow or Substance." *SAQ*, 67: 455-68 (Su 68).

Dussinger, G.R. "F's Isaac McCaslin as Romantic Hero *Manqué.*" *SAQ*, 68: 377-85 (Su 69).

Edinger, H.G. "Episodes in the History of the Literary Bear." *Mosaic*, 4:1-12 (1970).

Edwards, C.H. "A Hawthorne Echo in F's Nobel Prize Acceptance Speech." *NCLit*, 1: 4-5 (Mr 71).

Edwards, C.H., Jr. "Three Literary Parallels to F's 'A Rose for Emily.'" *NMW*, 7: 21-5 (Sp 74).

Edwards, Duane. "Flem Snopes and Thomas Sutpen: Two Versions of Respectability." *DR*, 51: 559-70 (Wi 71).

Egor, Gvozden. "Roman kao moralitet: Pasija po F." *Knji*, 56: 342-51 (1973).

Eigner, E.M. "F's Isaac and the American Ishmael." *JA*, 14: 107-15 (1969).

Emerson, O.B. "Bill's Friend Phil." *JMiH*, 32: 135-45 (My 70).

———. "F and His Bibliographers." *BB*, 30: 90-2 (Ap-Je 73).

———. "F and His Friend: An Interview with Emily W. Stone." *Comment*, 10: 31-7 (Sp 71).

———. "F, The Mule, and the South." *DelR*, 6: 108-10 (N-D 69).

———. "WF's Nemesis—Major Frederick Sullens." *JMiH*, 36: 161-4 (My 74).

Epstein, Seymour. "Politics and the Novelist." *DQ*, 4: 1-18 (1970).

Erskine, Albert. "Authors and Editors: WF at Random House." *U.S. Military Acad Lib Occasional Papers*, 2: 14-9 (1974); *FCN*, 3: 2-3 (1974).

Eschliman, H.R. "Francis Christensen in Yoknapatawha County." *UR*, 37: 232-9 (Sp 71).

Esslinger, P.M. "No Spinach in *Sanctuary*." *MFS*, 18: 555-8 (Wi 72-3).

Falkner, Murry. "The Coming of the Motor Car." *SoR*, 10: 170-80 (Au 74).

Farnham, J.F. "A Note on One Aspect of F's Style." *Lang&S*, 2: 190-2 (Sp 69).

Faulkner, H.J. "The Stricken World of 'Dry September.'" *SSF*, 10: 47-50 (Wi 73).

Faulkner, Jim. "Auntee Owned Two." *SoR*, 8: 836-44 (O 72).

———. "The Picture of John and Brother Will." *DelR*, 7: 12-4 (Fa 70).

Faulkner, William. "F's 'Ode to the Louver.'" *MissQ*, 27: 333-6 (Su 74).

———. "F's Review of *Ducdame*." *MissQ*, 28: 343-6 (Su 75).

———. "F's Speech at the Teatro Municipal, Caracas, in 1961." *MissQ*, 27: 337-8 (Su 74).

———. "An Introduction for *The Sound and the Fury*." *SoR*, 8: 705-10 (1972).

———, et al. "Letters to Richard Wright." *NLet*, 38: 128-35 (Wi 71).

———. "Ma Grider's Son." *MissQ*, 28: 347-51 (Su 75).

———. "*Le Mississippi*." *FL*, 19: 5-7 (Ag 68).

Ferris, W.R. "WF and Phil Stone: An Interview with Emily Stone." *SAQ*, 68: 536-42 (Au 69).

Ficken, Carl. "The Christ Story in *A Fable*." *MissQ*, 23: 251-64 (Su 70).

———. "The Opening Scene of WF's *Light in August*." *Proof*, 2: 175-84 (1972).

Fischel, Anne. "Student Views of F II." *ModO*, 1: 270-4 (Wi 71).

Flanagan, J.T. "Folklore in F's Fiction." *PLL*, 5: 119-44 (Su 69).

———. "The Mythic Background of F's Horse Imagery." *NCaF*, 13: 135-46 (1965).

Foster, R.E. "A Review of WF." *SAQ*, 69: 427-9 (Su 70).

———. "Social Order and Disorder in F's Fiction." *Approach*, 55: 20-8 (Sp 65).

Franklin, M.A. "A Christmas in Columbus." *MissQ*, 27: 319-22 (Su 74).

Franklin, Phyllis. "The Influence of Joseph Hergesheimer Upon *Mosquitoes*." *MissQ*, 22: 207-13 (Su 69).

———. "Sarty Snopes and 'Barn Burning.'" *MissQ*, 21: 189-93 (Su 68).

Fridy, Will. "'Ichthus': An Exercise in Synthetic Suggestion." *SAB*, 39: 95-101 (My 74).

Frohock, W.M. "F in France: The Final Phase." *Mosaic*, 4: 125-34 (1971).

Fuchs, Carolyn. "Words, Action, and the Modern Novel." *Kerygma*, 4: 3-11 (Wi 64).

Funk, Robert W. "Satire and Existentialism in F's 'Red Leaves.'" *MissQ*, 25: 339-48 (Su 72).

Fusini, Nadia. "La caccia all'orso di F." *SA*, 14: 289-308 (1968).

Garmon, G.M. "Mirror Imagery in *The Sound and the Fury*." *NMW*, 2: 13-24 (Sp 69).

Garrison, J.M. "F's 'The Brooch': A Story for Teaching." *CE*, 36: 51-7 (1974).

Gates, Allen. "The Old Frenchman Place: Symbol of a Lost Civilization." *IEngYb*, 13: 44-50 (Fa 68).

Geffen, Arthur. "Profane Time, Sacred Time, and Confederate Time in *The Sound and the Fury*." *SAF*, 2: 175-98 (Au 74).

Gelfant, B.H. "F and Keats: The Ideality of Art in 'The Bear.'" *SLJ*, 2: 43-65 (Fa 69).

Gidley, Mick. "Elements of the Detective Story in WF's Fiction." *JPC*, 7: 97-123 (Su 73).

———. "Another Psychologist, a Physiologist and WF." *ArielE*, 2: 78-86 (1971).

———. "One Continuous Force: Notes on F's Extra-Literary Reading." *MissQ*, 23: 299-314 (Su 70).

———. "Some Notes on F's Reading." *JAmSt*, 4: 91-102 (Jl 70).

Giermanski, J.R. "WF's Use of the Confessional." *Ren*, 21: 119:23, 166 (Sp 69).

Gilley, Leonard. "The Wilderness Theme in F's 'The Bear.'" *MwQ*, 6: 379-85 (Jl 65).

Ginsberg, Elaine. "The Female Initiation Theme in American Fiction." *SAF*, 2: 175-97 (Au 74).

Gold, Joseph. "Dickens and F: The Uses of Influence." *DR*, 49: 69-79 (Sp 69).

———. "The F Game; or, Find the Author." *SLJ*: 91-7 (Sp 69).

———. "Sin, Salvation and Bananas': *As I Lay Dying*." *Mosaic*, 7: 55-74 (Fa 73).

Garmon, G.M. "Mirror Imagery in *The Sound and the Fury*." *NMW*, 13-24 (Sp 69).

Garrison, J.M. "F's 'The Brooch': A Story for Teaching." *CE*, 36: 51-7 (1974).

Gates, Allen. "The Old Frenchman Place: Symbol of a Lost Civilization." *IEngYb*, 13: 44-50 (Fa 68).

Geffen, Arthur. "Profane Time, Sacred Time, and Confederate Time in *The Sound and the Fury*." *SAF*, 2: 175-98 (Au 74).

Gelfant, B.H. "F and Keats: The Ideality of Art in 'The Bear.'" *SLJ*, 2: 43-65 (Fa 69).

Gidley, Mick. "Elements of the Detective Story in WF's Fiction." *JPC*, 7: 97-123 (Su 73).

———. "Another Psychologist, a Physiologist and WF." *ArielE*, 2: 78-86 (1971).

———. "One Continuous Force: Notes on F's Extra-Literary Reading." *MissQ*, 23: 299-314 (Su 70).

———. "Some Notes on F's Reading." *JAmSt*, 4: 91-102 (Jl 70).

Giermanski, J.R. "WF's Use of the Confessional." *Ren*, 21: 119-23, 166 (Sp 69).

Gilley, Leonard. "The Wilderness Theme in F's 'The Bear.'" *MwQ*, 6: 379-85 (Jl 65).

Ginsberg, Elaine. "The Female Initiation Theme in American Fiction." *SAF*, 2: 175-97 (Au 74).

Gold, Joseph. "Dickens and F: The Uses of Influence." *DR*, 49: 69-79 (Sp 69).

———. "The F Game; or, Find the Author." *SLJ*, 1: 91-7 (Sp 69).

———. "Sin, Salvation and Bananas': *As I Lay Dying*." *Mosaic*, 7: 55-74 (Fa 73).

Golub, L.S. "Synactic and Lexical Problems in Reading F." *EJ*, 59: 490-6 (Ap 70).

Gotten, H.B. "Oxford." *DelR*, 5: 14-6, 80-1 (D 68).

Graham, Don, and Barbara Shaw. "F's Small Debt to Dos Passos: A Source for the Percy Grimm Episode." *MissQ*, 27: 327-32 (Su 74).

Grant, W.E. "Benjy's Branch: Symbolic Method in Part I of *The Sound and the Fury*." *TSLL*, 13: 705-10 (Wi 72).

Granthan, D.W. "Interpreters of the Modern South." *SAQ*, 63: 521-9 (Au 64).

Gray, Richard. "The Meanings of History: WF's *Absalom, Absalom!*" *DQR*, 3: 97-110 (#3 73).

Greer, D.D. "Dilsey and Lucas: F's Use of the Negro as a Gauge of Moral Character." *ESRS*, 11: 43-61 (1962).

Greer, Scott, "Joe Christmas and the 'Social Self.'" *MissQ*, 11: 160-6 (Fa 58).

Gregory, Eileen. "F's Typescripts of *The Town*." *MissQ*, 26: 361-86 (Su 73).

Greiner, D.J. "Universal Snopesism: The Significance of 'Spotted Horses.'" *EJ*, 57: 1133-7 (N 68).

Gresham, J.H. "Narrative Techniques of WF's Form." *NasR*, 1: 103-19 (Sp 66).

Gresset, Michel. "Un F féerique." *NRF*, 17: 437-40 (S 69).

———. "F's 'The Hill.'" *SDLJ*, 6: 3-18 (Sp 74).

———. "Le regard et le désir chez F." *Sud*, 14: 12-61 (1975).

———. "Weekend, Lost and Revisited." *MissQ*, 21: 173-8 (Su 68).

Gribbin. D.V. "Stories and Articles by WF in the Rare Book Room Collection of the University of North Carolina Library." *Bkmark*, nv: 23-7 (S 72).

Griffin, R.J. "Ethical Point of View in *The Sound and the Fury*." *Stetson Stud in the Humanities*, 1: 55-64 (1963).

Griffith, B.W. "F's Archaic Titles and the *Second Shepherd's Play*." *NMW*, 4: 62-3 (Fa 71).

Groden, Michael. "Criticism in New Composition: *Ulysses* and *The Sound and the Fury.*" *ATCL*, 21: 265-77 (O 75).

Gross, Beverly. "Form and Fulfillment in *The Sound and the Fury.*" *MLQ*, 29: 439-49 (D 68).

Grossman, J.M. "The Source of F's 'Less Oft is Peace.'" *AL*, 47: 436-8 (N 75).

Gunter, Bernd. "WF's 'Dry September.'" *NS*, 22: 607-16 (1973).

Gunter, Richard. "Style and Language in *The Sound and the Fury.*" *MissQ*, 12: 264-79 (Su 69).

Hagopian, J.V. "*Absalom, Absalom!* and the Negro Question." *MFS*, 19: 207-11 (Su 69).

———. "The Biblical Background of F's *Absalom, Absalom!*" *CEA*, 36: 22-4 (Ja 74).

Hamada, Seijiro. "'Dry September' no Atmosphere." *EigoS*, 120: 122-4 (1974).

Hamilton, G.D. "The Past in the Present: A Reading of *Go Down, Moses.*" *SHR*, 5: 171-81 (Sp 71).

Hancock, Maxine. "Fire: Symbolic Motif in F." *EngQ*, 3: 19-23 (Fa 70).

Harada, Keiichi. "The Theme of Incest in *The Sound and the Fury* and *Pierre.*" *Amer Lit R* (Tokyo), 14: 1-7 (My 56).

Harold, Brent. "The Value and Limitations of F's Fictional Method." *AL*, 47: 212-29 (my 75).

Harrington, E.B. "Technical Aspects of WF's 'That Evening Sun.'" *FaS*, 1: 54-9 (Wi 52).

Harris, W.V. "Of Time and the Novel." *Bur*, 16: 114-29 (Mr 68).

Hart, J.A. "That Not Impossible He: F's Third-Person Narrator." *CaSE*, 6: 29-41 (1961).

Harter, C.C. "Recent F Scholarship: Five More Turns of the Screw." *JML*, 4: 139-45 (1974).

———. "The Winter of Isaac McCaslin: Revisions and Irony in F's 'Delta Autumn.'" *JML*, 1: 209-25 (1970-71).

Hartt, J.N. "Some Reflections on F's *Fable.*" *Rel in Life*, 24: 601-7 (Fa 55).

Hauck, R.B. "The Comic Christ and the Modern Reader." *CE*, 31: 498-506 (F 70).

Haury, B.B. "The Influence of Robinson Jeffers' 'Tamar' on *Absalom, Absalom!*" *MissQ*, 25: 356-8 (1972).

Hayes, A.L. "The World of *The Hamlet.*" *CaSE*, 6: 3-16 (1961).

Hayhoe, G.F. "WF's *Flags in the Dust.*" *MissQ*, 23: 370-86 (Su 75).

Hays, P.L. "More Light on *Light in August.*" *PLL*, 11: 417-9 (1975).

Heimer, J.W. "F's Misogynous Novel: *Light in August.*" *BSUF*, 14: 11-5 (Su 73).

Heller, Terry. "The Telltale Hair: A Critical Study of WF's 'A Rose for Emily.'" *ArQ*, 28: 301-18 (1972).

Hemenway, Robert. "Enigmas of Being in *As I Lay Dying.*" *MFS*, 16: 133-46 (Su 70).

Hepburn, K.W. "F's *Mosquitoes*: A Poetic Turning Point." *TCL*, 17: 19-28 (Ja 71).

Hermann, John. "F's Heart's Darling in 'That Evening Sun.'" *SSF*, 7: 320-3 (Sp 70).

Hess, J.W. "Traditional Themes in F's 'The Bear.'" *TFSB*, 40: 57-64 (Je 74).

Hicks, Granville. "F's South: A Northern Interpretation." *GaR*, 5: 269-84 (Fa 51).

———. "The Past and Future of WF." *Bkm*, 74: 17-24 (S 31).

Hlavsa, V.V. "The Vision of the Advocate in *Absalom, Absalom!*" *Novel*, 8: 51-70 (Fa 74).

Hoadley, F.M. "The Theme of Atonement in the Novels of WM." *NwR*, 10: 30-43 (Su 70).

Hodgson, J.A. "'Logical Sequence and Continuity': Some Observations on the Typographical and Structural Consistency of *Absalom, Absalom!*" *AL*, 43: 97-107 (Mr 71).

Holland, N.N. "Fantasy and Defense in F's 'A Rose for Emily.'" *HSL*, 4: 1-35 (1972).

Holman, C.H. "*Absalom, Absalom!*: The Historian as Detective." *SR*, 79: 542-53 (Au 71).

Holmes, E.M. "Requiem for a Scarlet Nun." *Costerus*, 5: 35-49 (1972).

Houghton, D.E. "Whores and Horses in F's 'Spotted Horses.'" *MwQ*, 11: 361-9 (Jl 70).
―――. "WF's Mule: A Symbol of the Post-War South." *KFR*, 15: 81-6 (1969).
Howard, A.B. "Huck Finn in the House of Usher: The Comic and Grotesque World of *The Hamlet*." *SoR A*, 5: 125-46 (Je 72).
Howe, Irving. "The Southern Myth and WF." *AQ*, 3: 357-62 (Wi 51).
Howell, Elmo. "Colonel Sartoris Snopes and F's Aristocrats." *Carolina Q*, 11: 13-9 (Su 59).
―――. "F and Scott and the Legacy of the Lost Cause." *GaR*, 26: 314-25 (Fa 72).
―――. "F's Country Church: A Note on 'Shingles for the Lord.'" *MissQ*, 21: 205-10 (Su 68).
―――. "F's Elegy: An Approach to *The Bear*." *ArlQ*, 2: 122-32 (Su 70).
―――. "F's Enveloping Sense of History: A Note on 'Tomorrow.'" *NCLit*, 3: 5-6 (My 73).
―――. "Mink Snopes and F's Moral Conclusions." *SAQ*, 67: 13-22 (Wi 68).
―――. "WF and *Pro Patria Mori*." *LaStud*, 5: 89-96 (Su 66).
―――. "WF: The Susbtance of Faith." *BYUS*, 9: 453-62 (Su 69).
―――. "WF's Caledonia: A Note on *Intruder in the Dust*." *Stud in Scottish Lit*, 3: 248-52 (Ap 66).
―――. "WF's Chickasaw Legacy: A Note on 'Red Leaves.'" *ArQ*, 26: 293-303 (Wi 70).
―――. "WF's General Forrest and the Uses of History." *THQ*, 29: 287-94 (Fa 70).
―――. "WF's Graveyard." *NMW*, 4: 115-8 (Wi 72).
―――. "WF's Mule: A Symbol of the Post-War South." *KFR*, 15: 81-6 (1969).
―――. "WF's New Orleans." *LaHi*, 7: 229-39 (Su 66).
Hult, S.S. "WF's 'The Brooch': The Journey to the Riolama." *MissQ*, 27: 291-306 (Su 74).
Hunt, J.A. "WF and Rabelais: The Dog Story." ConL, 10: 383-88 (Su 69).
Hunt, Wallace. "The Strategems of WF." *Gambit*, 1: 8-12 (Sp 52).
Hutchinson, J.D. "TIME: The Fourth Dimension in F." *SDR*, 6: 91-103 (Au 68).
Hutten, R.W. "A Major Revision in F's *A Fable*." *AL*, 45: 297-9 (My 73).
Inge, M.T. "Contemporary American Literature in Spain." *TSL*, 16: 155-67 (1971).
―――. "Faulknerian Light." *NMW*, 5: 29 (Sp 72).
―――. "The Virginia Face of F." *VaCal*, 24: 32-9 (Su 74).
―――. "WF's *Light in August*: An Annotated Checklist of Criticism." *RALS*, 1: 30-57 (Sp 71).
Ingrasci, H.J. "Strategic Retreat or Withdrawal: Deliverance from Racial Oppression in Kelley's *A Different Drummer* and F's *Go Down Moses*." SBL, 6: 1-6 (#3 75).
Irvine, P.L. "F and Hardy." *ArQ*, 26: 357-65 (Wi 70).
Israel, Calvin. "The Last Gentleman." *PR*, 35: 315-9 (Sp 68).
Ivanescu, Mircea. "Dostoievski și F." *SXX*, 12: 209-12 (1969).
Izsak, E.K. "The Manuscript of *The Sound and the Fury*: The Revisions in the First Section." *SB*, 20: 189-202 (1968).
Jager, Dietrich. "Der' verheimlichte Raum' in F's 'A Rose for Emily' und Brittings 'Der Schneckenweg.'" *LWLL*, 1: 108-16 (1968).
James, D.L. "Hightower's Name: A Possible Source." *AN&Q*, 13: 4-5 (S 74).
James, Stuart. "F's Shadowed Land." *DQ*, 6: 45-61 (Au 71).
Jarrett, D.W. "Eustaci Vye and Eula Varner, Olympians: The Worlds of Thomas Hardy and WF." *Novel*, 6: 163-74 (Wi 73).
Johnston, K.G. "Time of Decline: Pickett's Charge and the Broken Clock in F's 'Barn Burning.'" *SSF*, 11: 434-6 (Fa 74).
―――. "The Year of Jubilee: F's 'That Evening Sun.'" *AL*, 46: 93-100 (Mr 74).
Johnston, W.E. "The Shepherdess in the City." *CL*, 26: 124-41 (1974).

Judson, Horace. "The Curse and the Hope." *Time*, 84: 44-8 (17 Jl 64).

Justus, James. "Beyond Gothicism: *Wuthering Heights* and an American Tradition." *TSL*, 5: 25-33 (1960).

Kane, Patricia. "Adaptable and Free: F's Ratliff." *NCLit*, 1: 9-11 (My 71).

————. "The Narcissa Benbow of F's *Flags in the Dust*." *NCLit*, 4: 2-3 (1974).

————. "Only Too Rhetorical Rhetoric: A Reading of *Intruder in the Dust*." *NCLit*, 4: 2-3 (My 73).

Kartiganer, D.M. "Process and Product: A Study in Modern Literature Form." *MR*, 12: 789-816 (Au 71).

————. "*The Sound and the Fury* and F's Quest for Form." *ELH*, 37: 613-39 (D 70).

Kearful, F.J. "Tony Last and Ike McCaslin: The Loss of a Usable Past." *UWR*, 3: 45-52 (Sp 68).

Kearney, J.A. "Paradox in F's *Intruder in the Dust*." *Theoria*, 40: 55-67 (1973).

Keefer, T.F. "WF's *Sanctuary*: A Myth Examined." *TCL*, 15: 97-104 (Jl 69).

Keith, D.L. "F in New Orleans." *DelR*, 6: 46-9 (My 69).

Kellner, R.S. "A Reconsideration of Character Relationships in *Absalom, Absalom!*" *NMW*, 7: 39-43 (1974).

Kent, G.E. "The Black Woman in F's Works, with the Exclusion of Dilsey, I." *Phylon*, 35: 430-41 (D 74); 36: 55-67 (Mr 75).

Kerr, E.M. "*The Reivers*: The Golden Book of Yoknapatawpha County." *MFS*, 13: 95-113 (Su 67).

————. "Yoknapatawpha and the Myth of the South." *WSL*, 1: 85-93 (1964).

Kibler, J.E., Jr. "A Possible Source in Ariosto for Druisilla." *MissQ*, 23: 321-2 (Su 70).

————. "WF and Provincetown Drama, 1920-22." *MissQ*, 22: 226-36 (Su 69).

King, F.H. "Benjamin Compson—Flower Child." *CEA*, 31: 10 (Ja 69).

King, L.L. "Requiem for F's Home Town." *Holiday*, 45: 75 (Mr 69).

Kinney, A.F. "F and the Possibilities for Heroism." *SoR*, 6: 110-25 (Au 70).

Klinkowitz, J.F. "The Thematic Unity of *Knight's Gambit*." *Critique*, 11: 81-100 (#2 69).

Knieger, Bernard. "F's 'Mountain Victory,' 'Doctor Martino,' and 'There Was a Queen.'" *Expl*, 30: 45 (1972).

Knight, K.F. "'*Spintrius*' in F's 'The Bear.'" *SSF*, 12: 31-2 (Wi 75).

Knox, George. "The Negro Novelist's Sensibility and the Outsider Theme." *WHR*, 11: 137-48 (Sp 57).

Kobler, J.F. "F's 'A Rose for Emily.'" *Expl*, 32: 65 (Ap 74).

————. "Lena Grove: F's 'Still Unravished Bride of Quietness.'" *ArQ*, 28: 339-54 (Wi 72).

Koreman, J.S. "F's Grecian Urn." *SLJ*, 7: 3-23 (Fa 74).

Korg, Jacob. "The Literary Esthetics of Dada." *Works*, 1: 43-54 (Sp 68).

Kruse, H.H. "'April Is the Cruellest Month . . .': Naturdarstellung und die Selbsterkenntnis des Erzahlers in F.S. F's *The Great Gatsby*." *LWU*, 1: 28-40 (1968).

Kulin, Katalin. "Reasons and Characteristics of F's Influence on Latin-American Fiction." *ALASH*, 13: 349-63 (1971).

Kulseth, L.I. "Cincinnatus Among the Snopeses: The Role of Gavin Stevens." *BSUF*, 10: 28-34 (Wi 69).

Lanati, Barbara. "Il primo F: *As I Lay Dying*." *Sigma* 19: 83-119 (1968).

Landor, Mikhail. "F in the Soviet Union." *SovL*, 12: 178-85 (1965).

————. "Tvorčeskijmmetod Folknera v stanovlenii." *VLit*, 15: 110-35 (1971).

————. "WF: New Translations and Studies." *SovL*, 8: 180-85 (1968).

Lang, Beatrice. "An Unpublished F Story: 'The Big Shot.'" *MissQ*, 26: 312-24 (Su 73).

Langford, B.Y. "History and Legend in WF's 'Red Leaves.'" *NMW*, 6: 19-24 (Sp 73).

Leath, H.L. "'Will the Circle Be Unbroken?' An Analysis of Structure in *As I Lay Dying*." *SwAL*, 3: 61-8 (73).

Le Clec'h, Guy. "Le vrai F." *FL*, 18 Ag 69, p. 25.

Lehan, Richard. "The Way Back: Redemption In the Novels of Walker Percy." *SoR*, 4: 306-19 (Ap 68).

Lensing, G.S. "The Metaphor of Family in *Absalom, Absalom!*" *SoR*, 11: 99-117 (Ja 75).

Levins, L.G. "The Four Narrative Perspectives in *Absalom, Absalom!*" *PMLA*, 85: 35-47 (Ja 70).

Levith, M.J. "Unity in F's *Light in August*." *Thoth*, 7: 31-4 (Wi 66).

Levitt, Paul. "An Analogue for F's 'A Rose for Emily.'" *PLL*, 9: 91-4 (1973).

Lewis, C.L. "WF: The Artist as Historian." *MASJ*, 10: 36-48 (Fa 69).

Lewis, Wyndham. "The Moralist with a Corn-cob: A Study of WF." *Life and Letters*, 10: 312-28 (Je 34).

Lhaman, W.T. "*Pylon*: The Ylimaf and New Valois." *WHR*, 24: 274-8 (Su 70).

Lillqvist, Holger. "Det förflutnas närvaro och fantasins styrka." *NyA*, 63: 55-7 (1970).

Lilly, P.R. "Caddie and Addie: Speakers of F's Impeccable Language." *JNT*, 3: 170-82 (Sp 73).

Lind, I.D. "Apocalyptic Vision as a Key to *Light in August*." *SAF*, 3: 133-41 (Au 75).

Linscott, Elisabeth. "F in Massachusetts." *NEG*, 10: 37-42 (Wi 69).

Lisca, Peter "*The Hamlet*: Genesis and Revisions." *FaS*, 3: 5-13 (1954).

Little, Matthew. "*As I Lay Dying* and 'Dementia Praecox' Humor." *SAH*, 2: 61-70 (Ap 75).

Litvin, Rina. "WF's *Light in August*." *Hasifruit*, 1: 589-98 (1969).

Litz, Walton. "Genealogy as Symbol in *Go Down, Moses*." *FaS*, 1: 49-53 (Wi 52).

*Lloyd, J.B. "An Annotated Bibliography of WF, 1967-1970." *UMSE*, 12: 1-57 (1971).

Logan, John. "Nota sobre el personaje balbuciente como héroe." *Sur*, 322-3: 148-54 (1970).

Loghin, Georgeta. "W.F și problema populației de culoare." *ASUI*, 13: 245-8 (1967).

Lombardo, Agostino. "I segreti di F." *Il Mondo*, 12: 9-10 (12 Jl 60).

Longley, J.L. "Galahad Gavin and a Garland of Snopses." *VQR*, 33: 623-8 (Au 57).

———. "'Who Never Had a Sister': A Reading of *The Sound and the Fury*." *Mosaic*, 7: 35-54 (Fa 73).

Lopez, Guido. "F and the Horses." *YR*, 64: 468-76 (Sp 75).

Loughrey, T.F. "Aborted Sacrament in *Absalom, Absalom!*" *FourQ*, 14: 13-21 (N 64).

———. "*Light in August*: Religion and the Agape of Nature." *FourQ*, 12: 14-25 (My 63).

Luedtke, C.L. "*The Sound and the Fury* and *Lie Down in Darkness*: Some Comparisons." *LWU*, 4: 45-51 (1971).

Lupan, Radu. "In Jefferson, Acasa la F." *Luc*, 21 Ap 73; p. 1.

McAlexander, Hubert, Jr. "WF—The Young Poet in Stark Young's *The Torches Flare*." *AL*, 43: 647-9 (Ja 72).

McCants, Maxine. "From Humanity to Abstraction: Negro Characterization in *Intruder in the Dust*." *NMW*, 2: 91-104 (Wi 70).

McClennen, Joshua. "WF and Christian Complacency." *PMASAL*, 41: 315-22 (1955).

McCullen, J.T., and Jeri Tanner. "The Devil Outwitted in Folklore and Literature." *NCaF*, 17: 15-20 (1969).

McDonald, W.R. "Coincidence in the Novel: A Necessary Technique." *CE*, 29: 373-88 (F 68).

————. "F's 'The Bear': Part IV." *CEA*, 34: 31-2 (Ja 72).

————. "F's 'The Bear': The Sense of Its Structure." *Eng Rec*, 18: 8-14 (D 67).

* McDonald, W.U. "Bassett's Checklist of F Criticism: Some Local Addenda." *BB*, 32: 76 (1975).

McElderry, B.R. "The Narrative Sturcture of *Light in August*." *MissQ*, 11: 177-87 (Fa 58).

McElrath, J.R. "*Pylon*: The Portrait of a Lady." *MissQ*, 27: 277-90 (Su 74).

McElroy, John. "The Hawthorne Style of American Function." *ESQ*, 71: 117-23 (1973).

McGlynn, P.D. "The Chronology of 'A Rose for Emily.'" *SSF*, 6: 461-2 (Su 69).

McHaney, T.L. "Anderson, Hemingway, and F's *The Wild Palms*." *PMLA*, 87: 465-74 (Mr 72).

————. "A Deer Hunt in the F Country." *MissQ*, 23: 315-20 (Su 70).

————. "The Elmer Papers: F's Comic Portraits of the Artist." *MissQ*, 26: 281-311 (Su 73).

————. "The Falkners and the Origins of Yoknapatawpha County: Some Corrections." *MissQ*, 25: 249-65 (Su 72).

————. "Jeffers' 'Tamar' and F's *The Wild Palms*." *RJN*, 29: 16-8 (Au 71).

————. "Robinson Jeffers' 'Tamar' and *The Sound and the Fury*." *MissQ*, 22: 261-3 (Su 69).

————. "*Sanctuary* and Frazer's Slain Kings." *MissQ*, 24: 223-45 (Su 71).

————. "The Text of *Flags in the Dust*." *FCN*, 2: 7-8 (1973).

————, and Albert Erskine. "Commentary on the Text of *Flags in the Dust*." *FCN*, 3: 2-4 (My 74).

McIntosh, W.W.S. "A Selective Listing of the WF Collection at the United States Military Academy." *U.S. Military Acad Lib Occasional Papers*, 2: 20-8 (74).

McLuhan, H.M. "The Southern Quality." *SR*, 55: 357-83 (S 47).

MacLure, Millar. "Snopes: A F Myth." *CanF*, 39: 245-50 (F 60).

MacMillan, Duane. "*Pylon*: From Short Stories to Major Work." *Mosaic*, 7: 185-212 (Fa 73).

McWilliams, Dean. "WF and Michel Butor's Novel of Awareness." *KRQ*, 19: 387-402 (1972).

Madeya, Ulrike. "Interpretationen zu WF's 'The Bear': Das Bild des Helden und die Konstellation der Charaktere." *LWU*, 3: 45-60 (1970).

Malbone, R.G. "Promissory Poker in F's 'Was.'" *Eng Rec*, 22: 23-5 (Fa 71).

Malin, Irving. "The Authoritarian Family in American Fiction." *Mosaic*, 4: 153-73 (1971).

Malley, Terence. "Thoughts, Hopes, Endeavors, Failures." *MarkhamR*, 4: 78-80 (1974).

Malraux, Andre. "Preface to WF's *Sanctuary*." *SoR*, 10: 889-91 (O 74).

Manglaviti, L.M.J. "F's 'That Evening Sun' and Mencken's 'Best Editorial Judgment.'" *AL*, 43: 649-54 (Ja 72).

Marcus, Steven. "F's Town: Mythology as History." *PR*, 24: 432-41 (Su 57).

Martin, Carter. "F's *Sartoris*: The Tailor Re-Tailored." *SCR*, 6: 56-9 (Ap 74).

Martin, H. "Caravan to F Country . . . And Beyond." *So Living*, 8: 116-8, 120-5 (My 73).

Marvin, J.R. "*Pylon*: The Definition of Sacrifice." *FaS*, 1: 20-3 (Su 52).

Marx, Leo. "Pastoral Ideals and City Troubles." *JGE*, 20: 251-71 (1969).

Materassi, Mario. "F Criticism in Italy." *IQ*, 15: 47-85 (1971).

Maud, Ralph. "F, Mailer, and Yogi Bear." *CRAS*, 2: 69-75 (Fa 71).

Maulnier, Theirry. "*Requiem pour une nonne*." *RdP*, 11: 140-3 (N 56).

Meats, S.E. "Who Killed Joanna Burden?" *MissQ*, 24: 271-7 (Su 71).

Mellard, J.M. "Caliban as Prospero: Benjy and *The Sound and the Fury.*" *Novel*, 3: 233-48 (Sp 70).

———. "F's Jason and the Tradition of Oral Narrative." *JPC*, 2: 195-210 (Fa 68).

———. "Jason Compson: Humor, Hostility, and the Rhetoric of Aggression." *SHR*, 3: 259-67 (Su 69).

———. "*The Sound and the Fury*: Quentin Compson and F's 'Tragedy of Passion.'" *StN*, 2: 61-75 (Sp 70).

———. "Type and Archetype: Jason Compson as 'Satirist.'" *Genre*, 4: 173-88 (Je 71).

Mercer, Caroline, and S.J. Turner. "Restoring Life to F's *The Hamlet.*" *CEA*, D 59; pp. 1-5.

Meriwether, J.B. "A.E. Housman and F's Nobel Prize Speech: A Note." *JAmSt*, 4: 247-8 (F 71).

———. "And Now What's To Do." *MissQ*, 26: 399-402 (Su 73).

———. "Blotner's *F.*" *MissQ*, 23: 353-69 (Su 75).

———. "F's Correspondence with *Scribner's Magazine.*" *Proof*, 3: 253-82 (1973).

———. "F's 'Mississippi.'" *MissQ*, 25: 15-23 (Sp 72).

———. "F's 'Ode to the Louver.'" *MissQ*, 27: 333-5 (Su 74).

———. "F's Speech at the Teatro Municipal, Caracas, in 1961." *MissQ*, 27: 337 (Su 74).

———. "An Introduction for *The Sound and the Fury.*" *SoR*, 8: 705-10 (O 72); "F, Lost and Found." *NYT*, 5 N 72: 7-8.

———. "Is There a Yoknapatawpha Saga?" *SAB*, 30: 4 (Ja 65).

———. "Modern Novelists and Contemporary American Society: A Symposium: 3. WF." *Shen*, 10: 18-24 (Wi 59).

———. "A Note on *A Fable.*" *MissQ*, 26: 416-7 (Su 73).

———. "The Novel F Never Wrote: His *Golden Book* or *Doomsday Book.*" *AL*, 42: 93-6 (Mr 70).

———. "Nympholepsy." *MissQ*, 26: 403-9 (Su 73).

———. "A Prefatory Note by F for the Compson Appendix." *AL*, 43: 281-4 (My 71).

———. "The Short Fiction of WF: A Bibliography." *Proof*, 1: 293-329 (1971).

———. "Two Unknown F Stories." *Ranam*, 4: 23-30 (1971).

———. "WF." *Shen*, 10: 18-24 (Wi 59).

Merton, Thomas. "'Baptism in the Forest': Wisdom and Initiation in WF." *CathW*, 207: 124-30 (Je 68).

Messerli, Douglas. "The Problem of Time in *The Sound and the Fury*: A Critical Reassessment and Reinterpretation." *SLJ*, 6: 19-41 (Sp 74).

Mickelson, J.C. "F's Military Figures of Speech." *WSL*, 4: 46-55 (1967).

Middleton, John. "Shreve McCannon and Sutpen's Legacy." *SoR*, 10: 115-24 (Wi 74).

Millgate, Jane. "Quentin Compson as Poor Player: Verbal and Social Cliches in *The Sound and the Fury.*" *RLV*, 34: 40-9 (Ja-F 68).

Millgate, Michael. "F and Lanier: A Note on the Name Jason." *MissQ*, 25: 349-50 (1972).

———. "F in Toronto: A Further Note." *UTQ*, 37: 197-202 (Ja 68).

———. "F on the Literature of the First World War." *MissQ*, 26: 387-93 (Su 73).

———. "'The Firmament of Man's History:' F's Treatment of the Past." *MissQ*, 25, Supp: 25-35 (Sp 72).

———. "Starting Out in the Twenties: Reflections on *Soldiers' Pay.*" *Mosaic*, 7: 1-14 (Fa 73).

Milliner, Gladys. "The Third Eve: Caddy Compson." *MwQ*, 16: 268-75 (1975).

Milliner, M.J. "'The Magician's Wand': F's Compson Appendix." *MissQ*, 28: 317-38 (1975).

Milton, J.R. "Conversations with Distinguished Western American Novelists." *SDR*, 9: 16-57 (Sp 71).

Milum, R.A. "F and the Cavalier Tradition: The French Bequest." *AL*, 45: 580-9 (Ja 74).

———. "'The Horns of Dawn': F and Metaphor." *AN&Q*, 11: 134 (My 73).

———. "Ikkemotubbe and the Spanish Conspiracy." *AL*, 46: 389-91 (N 74).

Miner, W.L. "The Southern White-Negro Problem Through the Lens of F's Fiction." *J of Human Relations*, 14: 507-17 (1966).

Minter, David. "F and the Uses of Biography." *GaR*, 28: 455-69 (Fa 74).

Mizener, Arthur. "The Thin, Intelligent Face of American Fiction." *KR*, 17: 507-24 (Au 55).

Moffitt, C.L. "A Rhetoric for Benjy." *SLJ*, 3: 32-46 (Fa 70).

Moloney, Michael. "The Enigma of Time: Proust, Virginia Woolf, and F." *Thought*, 32: 69-85 (Sp 57).

Monaghan, D.M. "F's *Absalom, Absalom!*" *Expl*, 31: 28 (D 72).

———. "F's Relationship to Gavin Stevens in *Intruder in the Dust*." *DRZ*, 52: 449-57 (1972).

———. "The Single Narrator of *As I Lay Dying*." *MFS*, 18: 213-20 (Su 72).

Monat, Olympic. "F, a dimensão da tragédia." *ESPSL*, 1 S 74: 1.

Monteiro, George. "'Between Grief and Nothing': Hemingway and F." *HN*, 1: 1-3 (Sp 71).

———. "The Limits of Professionalism: A Sociological Approach to F, Fitzgerald, and Hemingway." *Criticism*, 15: 145-55 (1973).

Moore, Robert. "The F Concordance and Some Implications for Textual and Linguistic Studies." *U.S. Military Acad Lib Occasional Papers*, 2: 6-13 (74).

Morell, Giliane. "The Last Scene of *Sanctuary*." *MissQ*, 25: 351-5 (1972).

———. "'Pourquoi ris-tu, Darl?'—ou le temps d'un regard." *Sud*, 14: 128-49 (1975).

———. "Prisoners of the Inner World: Mother and Daughter in *Miss Zilphia Gant*." *MissQ*, 28: 299-305 (Su 75).

Moses, Edwin. "T's *The Hamlet*: The Passionate Humanity of V.K. Ratliff." *NDEJ*.

———. "F's *The Reivers*: The Art of Acceptance." *MissQ*, 27: 307-18 (su 74).

Moses, W.R. "The Limits of Yoknapatawpha County." *GaR*, 16: 297-305 (Fa 62).

———. "Water, Water Everywhere: 'Old Man' and *A Farewell to Arms*." *MFS*, 5: 172-4 (Su 59).

Mottram, Eric. "Mississippi F's Glorious Mosaic of Impotence and Madness." *JAmSt*, 2: 121-9 (Ap 68).

Motylowa, T. "Dostoevskij i zarubeznye pisateli xx veka." *VLit*, 15: 96-128 (1971).

———. "Dostejewski und die auslandischen Schriftsteller des 20. Jahrhunderts." *KuL*, 19: 938-55 (1971).

Muehl, Lois. "F's Humor in Three Novels and One 'Play.'" *LCUP*, 34: 78-93 (Sp 68).

———. "Form as Seen in Two Early Works by F." *LCUP*, 38: 147-57 (1972).

———. "Word Choice and Choice Words in F's *Sartoris*." *LCUP*, 35: 58-63 (Wi-Sp 69).

Muhlenfeld, E.S. "Shadows with Substance and Ghosts Exhumed: The Women in *Absalom, Absalom!*" *MissQ*, 25: 289-304 (Su 72).

Muir, E.A. "A Footnote on *Sartoris* and Some Speculation." *JML*, 1: 389-93 (Mr 71).

Mukerji, Nirmal "Ike MaCalsin and the Measure of Heroism." *PURBA*, 5: 15-21 (1974).

Muller, G.H. "The Descent of the Gods: F's 'Red Leaves' and the Garden of the South." *SSF*, 11: 243-50 (Su 74).

———. "F's 'A Rose for Emily.'" *Expl*, 33: 79 (1975).

Mulqueen, J.E. "Foreshadowing of Melville and F." *AN&Q*, 6: 102 (Mr 68).

———. "*Light in August*: Motion, Eros, and Death." *NMW*, 8: 91-6 (Wi 75).

Murphy, Denis. *"The Sound and the Fury* and Dante's *Inferno*: Fire and Ice." *MarkR*, 4: 71-8 (O 74).

Murray, D.M. "F, the Silent Comedies, and the Animated Cartoon." *SHR*, 9: 25-57 (Su 75).

Myers, W.V. "F's Parable of Poetic Justice." *LaStud*, 8: 224-30 (Fa 69).

Nadeau, R.L. "The Morality of Act: A Study of F's *As I Lay Dying.*" *Mosaic*, 6: 23-35 (Sp 73).

Nagel, James. "Huck Finn and The Bear: The Wilderness and Moral Freedom." *ESA*, 12: 59-63 (Mr 69).

Naples, D.C. "Eliot's 'Tradition' and *The Sound and the Fury.*" *MFS*, 20: 214-6 (Su 74).

Nash, H.C. "F's 'Furniture Repairer and Dealer': Knitting Up *Light In August.*" *MFS*, 16: 529-31 (1970).

Nauman, Hilda. "How F Went His Way and I Went Mine." *Esquire*, 68: 173-5 (D 67).

Nebeker, H.E. "Chronology Revised." *SSF*, 8: 471-3 (Su 71).

———. "Emily's Rose of Love: Thematic Implications of Point of View in F's 'A Rose for Emily.'" *BRMMLA*, 24: 3-13 (Mr 70).

———. "Emily's Rose of Love: A Postscript." *BRMMLA*, 24: 190-1 (S 70).

Nelson, M.A. "'Yr Stars Fell' in *The Bear.*" *AN&Q*, 9: 102-3 (Mr 71).

Nelson, R.S. "Apotheosis of the Bear." *RS*, 41: 201-4 (1973).

Neufeldt, Leonard. "Time and Man's Possibilities in *Light in August.*" *GaR*, 25: 27-40 (Sp 71).

Niavsa, V.V. "The Vision of the Advocate in *Absalom, Absalom!*" *Novel*, 8: 51-70 (1974).

Nicolet, W.P. "F's 'Barn Burning.'" *Expl*, 34: 25 (N 75).

Noble, D.R. "F's 'Pantaloon in Black': An Aristotelian Reading." *BSUF*, 14: 16-9 (Su 73).

Nolte, W.H. "Mencken, F, and Southern Moralism." *SCR*, 4: 45-61 (D 71).

Norris, Nancy. *"The Hamlet, The Town*, and *The Mansion*: A Psychological Reading of the Snopes Trilogy." *Mosaic*, 7: 213-35 (Fa 73).

O'Brien, M.C. "F, General Chalmers, and the Burning of Oxford." *AN&Q*, 12: 87-8 (F 74).

———. "A Note on F's Civil War Women." *NMW*, 1: 56-63 (Fa 68).

———. "WF and the Civil War in Oxford, Mississippi." *JMiH*, 35: 167-74 (My 73).

Ochi, Michio. "Kuhaku wo toshite minaoshita F." *EigoS*, 115: 558-60 (1969).

O'Connor, W.V. "F's Legend of the Old South." *WHR*, 7: 293-301 (Fa 53).

———. "Rhetoric in Southern Writing: F." *GaR*, 12: 83-6 (Sp 58).

———. "A Short View of F's *Sanctuary.*" *FaS*, 1: 33-9 (Fa 52).

O'Dea, R.J. "F's Vestigial Christianity." *Renascence*, 21: 44-54 (Au 68).

Ohashi, Kenzaburo. *"F: A Biography* wo Yonde." *EigoS*, 120: 234-5 (1974).

Ohki, Masako. "The Technique of Handling Time in *Absalom, Absalom!*" *KAL*, 15: 89-94 (1974).

Olson, Ted. "F and the Colossus of Marousi." *SAQ*, 71: 205-12 (Sp 72).

Organ, Dennis. "The Morality of Rosa Millard." *Pub Arkansas Phil Assn*, 1: 37-41 (#2 75).

Otten, Terry. "F's Use of the Past: A Comment." *Ren*, 20: 198-207, 214 (Su 68).

Palmer, W.J. "Abelard's Fate: Sexual Politics in Stendhal, F and Camus." *Mosaic*, 7: 29-41 (#3 74).

Parker, Hershel. "What Quentin Saw 'Out There.'" *MissQ*, 27: 323-6 (Su 74).

Parsons, T.H. "Doing the Best They Can." *GaR*, 23: 292-306 (Fa 69).

Pate, Willard. "Benjy's Names in the Compson Household." *FurmS*, 15: 37-8 (My 68).

———. "Pilgrimage to Yoknapatawpha." *FurmM*, nv: 6-13 (Wi 69).

Pavilioniene, Ausrine. "Laikas ir WF zmogus." *Pergale*, 3: 132-7 (1973).

Pavilioniene, M-A. "Apie amerikieciu romantiku itake, V. Folknerio kurybai." *Literatura*, 15, iii: 95-108 (1973).

―――. "Malen'kij celovek v tvorcestve V. Folknera." *Literatura*, 16: iii: 75-88 (1974).

Payne, Ladell. "The Trilogy: F's Comic Epic Poem in Prose." *StN*, 1: 27-37 (Sp 69).

Pearce, Richard. "*Pylon, Awake and Sing!* and the Apocalyptic Imagination of the 30's." *Criticism*, 13: 131-41 (Sp 71).

Pearson, N.H. "Lena Grove." *Shen*, 2: 3-7 (Sp 52).

Peavy, C.D. "Did You Ever Have a Sister? Holden, Quentin, and Sexual Innocence." *Fla Q*, 1: 82-95 (1968).

―――. "An Early Casting of Benjy: F's 'The Kingdom of God.'" *SSF*, 3: 347-8 (Sp 66).

―――. "'If I'd Just Had a Mother': F's Question Compson." *L&P*, 23 114-21 (1973).

―――. "Jason Compson's Paranoid Pseudo-community." *HSL*, 2: 151-6 (1970).

―――. "A Note on the 'Suicide Pact' in *The Sound and the Fury*." *ELN*, 5: 207-9 (Mr 68).

Peckham, Morse. "The Place of Sex in the Work of WF." *STC*, 14: 1-20 (Fa 74).

Peraile, Esteban and Lorenzo. "Una lectura de *Los invictos*." *CHA*, 291: 692-701 (1974).

Perlis, A.D. "*As I Lay Dying* as a Study of Time." *SDR*, 10: 103-10 (1972).

Perry, J.D. "Gothic as Vortex: The Form of Horror in Capote, F, and Styron." *MFS*, 19: 153-67 (Su 73).

Peterson, R.F. "F's *Light in August*." *Expl*, 30: 35 (D 71).

Pfeiffer, A.H. "Eye of the Storm: The Observers' Image of the Man Who Was F." *SoR*, 8: 763-73 (O 72).

Pfeiffer, Andrew. "'No Wiser Spot on Earth': Community and the Country Store in F's *The Hamlet*." *NMW*, 6: 45-52 (Fa 73).

Philips, Gene. "F and the Film: Two Versions of *Sanctuary*." *LFQ*, 1: 263-73 (Jl 73).

Pierle, R.C. "Snopesism in F's *The Hamlet*." *ES*, 52: 246-52 (Je 71).

Pinsker, Sanford. "An Ironic Reading of WF's *The Bear*." *Topic*, 12: 35-51 (Sp 72).

Pitavy, F.L. "A Forgotten F Story: 'Miss Zilphia Gant.'" *SSF*, 9: 131-42 (1972).

―――. "The Landscape in *Light in August*." *MissQ*, 23: 265-72 (Su 70).

―――. "Quentin Compson, ou le regard du poete." *Sud*, 14: 62-80 (1975).

Pochmann, H.A., and J.A. Hunt. "F and His Sources." *ConL*, 11: 310-12 (Sp 70).

Polk, Noel. "Alec Holston's Lock and the Founding of Jefferson." *MissQ*, 24: 247-69 (Su 71).

―――. "The Critics and F's 'Little Postage Stamp of Native Soil.'" *MissQ*, 23: 323-35 (Su 70).

―――. "F's 'The Jail' and the Meaning of Cecilia Farmer." *MissQ*, 25: 305-25 (1972).

―――. "'Hong Li' and *Royal Street*: The New Orleans Sketches in Manuscript." *MissQ*, 26: 394-5 (Su 73).

―――. "The Manuscript of *Absalom, Absalom!*" *MissQ*, 25: 359-67 (1972).

―――. "The Staging of *Requiem for a Nun*." *MissQ*, 24: 299-314 (Su 71).

―――. "The Textual History of F's *Requiem for a Nun*." *Proof*, 4: 109-28 (1974).

―――. "WF's *Marionettes*." *MissQ*, 26: 247-80 (Su 73).

Porat, Tsfira. "Sawdust Dolls: Tragic Fate and Comic Freedom in F's *Light in August*." *Hasifrut*, 2: 767-82 (1971).

Poter, Carolyn. "The Problem of Time in *Light in August*." *RusR*, 61: 107-25 (#1 75).

Poster, Herbert. "F's Folly." *Am Merc*, 73: 106-12 (D 51).

Prasad, T.G. "Nihilism in *The Sound and the Fury*." *PURBA*, 3: 35-43 (#1 72).

Prescott, Herman. "Hemingway vs. F: An Intriguing Feud." *LGJ*: 3: 18-9 (#3 75).

Presley, D.E. "Is Reverend Whitfield a Hypocrite?" *RSW*, 36: 57-61 (Mr 68).

Price, Reynolds. "*Pylon*: The Posture of Worship." *Shen*, 19: 49-61 (Sp 68).

Prince, John. "André Dhôtel, Steinbeck et F: Quelques similitudes." *Caliban*, 6: 85-90 (1969).

Prior, L.T. "Theme, Imagery, and Structure in *The Hamlet*." *MissQ*, 22: 237-56 (Su 69).

Pritchett, V.S. "Time Frozen." *PR*, 21: 557-61 (S-O 54).

Pryse, Marjorie. "Race: F's 'Red Leaves.'" *SSF*, 12: 133-8 (Sp 75).

Putzel, Max. "Evolution of Two Characters in F's Early and Unpublished Fiction." *SLJ*, 5: 47-63 (Sp 73).

―――. "What is Gothic about *Absalom, Absalom!*" *SLJ*, 4: 3-19 (Fa 71).

Quiñonero, J.P. "F, aquel viejo lobo." *La Estafeta Literaria*, 385: 13 (16 D 67).

Raisor, Philip. "Up From Adversity: WF's *A Fable*." *SDR*, 11: 3-15 (Su 73).

Rama Roa, P.G. "F's *Old Man*: A Critique." *IJAS*, 1: 43-50 (1972).

Ramsey, Roger. "F's *The Sound and the Fury*." *Expl*, 30: 70 (O 72).

Randel, F.V. "Parentheses in F's *Absalom, Absalom!*" *Style*, 5: 70-87 (1971).

Raper, J.R. "Meaning Called to Life: Alogical Structure in *Absalom, Absalom!*" *SHR*, 5: 9-23 (Wi 71).

Rea, J. "F's 'Spotted Horses.'" *HSL*, 2: 157-64 (1970).

Reed, Richard. "The Role of Chronology in F's Yoknapatawpha Fiction." *SLJ*, 7: 24-48 (Fa 74).

Rhynsburger, Mark. "Student Views of WF I." *ModO*, 1: 264-9 (Wi 71).

Rice, J.C. "Orpheus and the Hellish Unity of *Light in August*." *CentR*, 19: 380-96 (Wi 75).

Richards, Lewis. "Sex Under *The Wild Palms* and a Moral Question." *ArQ*, 28: 326-32 (1972).

Richardson, H.E. "The Decadence in F's First Novel: The Faun, the Worm, and the Tower." *EA*, 21: 225-35 (Jl-S 68).

Richter, Barbara. "Per Ardua ad Astra: Perversity in the Morality Puzzle of William Faulkner." *Revista Un Costa Rica*, 39: 139-47 (1974).

Riese, Utz. "Das Delimma eines dritten Weges: WF's widerspruchlicher Humanismus." *ZAA*, 16: 138-55, 257-73 (1968).

―――. "The Dilemma of the Third Way (WF's Contradictory Humanism)." *ZAA*, 16: 138-55, 257-73 (1968).

Rinaldi, N.M. "Game Imagery in F's *Absalom, Absalom!*" *ConnR*, 4: 73-9 (1970).

Roberts, J.L. "The Individual and the Community: F's Light in August." *LSUS*, 8: 132-53 (1960).

Rodewald, F.A. "F's Possible Use of *The Great Gatsby*." *FHA*, 1975, pp. 97-101.

Rodnon, Stewart. "*The House of the Seven Gables* and *Absalom, Absalom!*" *StH*, 1: 42-6 (#2 70).

Rome, J.J. "Love and Wealth in *Absalom, Absalom!*" *UES*, 9: 3-10 (1971).

Rosenberg, B.A. "The Oral Quality of Rev. Shegog's Sermon in WF's *The Sound and the Fury*." *LWU*, 2: 73-88 (1969).

Roseman, John. "Another *Othello* Echo in *As I Lay Dying*." *NMW*, 8: 19-21 (Sp 75).

Rosenman, J.B. "A Note on WF's *As I Lay Dying*." *SAF*, 1: 104-5 (Sp 73).

Ross, S.M. "Conrad's Influence on F's *Absalom, Absalom!*" *SAF*, 2: 199-210 (Au 74).

Ross, Stephen. "The 'Loud World' of Quentin Compson." *StN*, 7: 254-57 (Su 75).

―――. "Shapes of Time and Consciousness in *As I Lay Dying*." *TSLL*, 16: 723-37 (Wi 75).

Rossky, William. "The Pattern of Nightmare in *Sanctuary*: or, Miss Reba's Dogs." *MSF*, 15: 503-15 (Wi 69-70).

Roth, Russell. "The Centaur and the Pear Tree." *WR*, 16: 199-205 (Sp 52).

Rouberel, Jean. "Les Indiens dans l'Oeuve de F." *EA*, 26: 54-8 (Mr 73).

Rubens, P.M. "At Elmo and the Barn Burners." *NMW*, 7: 86-90 (Wi 75).

Rubin, L.D. "*Don Quixote* and Selected Progeny: Or, the Journey-man as Outsider." *SoR*, 10: 31-58 (Ja 74).

―――. "The Great American Joke." *SAQ*, 72: 82-94 (Wi 73).

Ruiz, J.M. "El Sentido de la vida y de la muerte en *The Sound and the Fury.*" *FMod*, 13: 117-38 (1973).

Saal, H.D. "The Style of WF." *YLM*, D 46, pp. 19-22.

Saavedra, L.V. "La afinidad de Onetti a F." *CHA*, 292-4: 257-65 (1974).

Sabiston, Elizabeth. "Women, Blacks, and Thomas Sutpen's Mythopoetic Drive." *Modernist Stud*, 1: 15-26 (#3 75).

Saito, Kazue. "Ethics in F's Works." *Ushione*, 10: 1-12 (1957).

Samway, Patrick. "War: A Faulknerian Commentary." *ColQ*, 18: 370-8 (Sp 70).

Sanderlin, R.R. "*As I Lay Dying*: Christian Symbols and Thematic Implications." *SoQ*, 7: 155-66 (Ja 69).

Sanders, Barry. "F's Fire Imagery in 'That Evening Sun.'" *SSF*, 5: 69-71 (Fa 67).

Sanderson, J.L. "'Spotted Horses' and the Theme of Social Evil." *EJ*, 57: 700-4 (My 68).

Schlepper, Wolfgang. "Knowledge and Experience in F's *Light in August.*" *JA*: 18: 182-94 (1973).

Schmuhl, Robert. "F's *Sanctuary*: The Last Laugh of Innocence." *NMW*, 6: 73-80 (Wi 74).

Schrank, Bernice. "Patterns of Reversal in *Absalom, Absalom!*" *DR*, 54: 648-66 (Wi 74-75).

Schrero, E.M. "*Another Country* and the Sense of Self." *BlAR*, 2: 91-100 (Sp-Su 71).

Schulberg, Budd. "Requiem for a Nun." *TV Guide*, 1 F 75, pp. 31-2.

Schwartz, Delmore. "F's *A Fable.*" *Perspectives U.S.A.*, 10: 126-36 (Wi 55).

Seltzer, Leon. "Narrative Function vs. Psychopathology: The Problem of Darl in *As I Lay Dying.*" *Lit and Psych*, 25: 49-64 (1975).

Sequeira, Isaac. "*The Bear*: The Initiation of Ike McCaslin." *OJES*, 9: 1-10 (#2 72).

———. "Intruder in the Dust." *Bul Ramakrishna Mission Inst of Culture*, 25: 64-8 (Mr 74).

Sharma, P.P. "The Snopes Theme in F's Larger Context." *IJAS*, 1: 33-41 (#4 71).

Shaw, Barbara, and Don Graham. "F's Small Debt to Dos Passos: A Source for the Percy Grimm Episode." *MissQ*, 27: 327-32 (Su 74).

Shaw, J.C. "Sociological Aspects of F's Writings." *MissQ*, 14: 148-52 (Su 61).

Shepherd, Allen. "Code and Comedy in F's *The Reivers.*" *LWU*, 6: 43-51 (1973).

———. "Hemingway's 'An Alpine Idyll' and F's 'Mistral.'" *UPortR*, 25: 63-8 (Fa 73).

Shirley, William. "The Question of Sutpen's Innocence." *SLM*, 1: 31-7 (#1 75).

Showett, H.K. "F and Scott: Addendum." *MissQ*, 22: 152-3 (Sp 69).

Simpson, H.A. "Yoknapatawpha: F's 'Little Postage Stamp of Native Soil.'" *NMW*, 3: 43-7 (Sp 70).

Simpson, L.P. "F and the Southern Symbolism of Pastoral." *MissQ*, 28: 401-16 (Fa 75).

———. "The Loneliness of WF." *SLJ*, 8: 126-43 (Fa 75).

Sister Cleopatra. "*Absalom, Absalom!* The Failure of the Sutpen Design." *LHY*, 16: 74-93 (Ja 75).

Skerry, P.J. "*The Adventures of Huckleberry* and *Intruder in the Dust*: Two Conflicting Myths of the American Experience." *BSUF*, 13: 4-13 (Wi 72).

Smith, B.E. "A Note on F's 'Greenbury Hotel.'" *MissQ*, 24: 297-8 (Su 71).

Smith, G.J. "Medicine Made Palatable: As Aspect of Humor in *The Reivers.*" *NMW*, 8: 58-62 (Fa 75).

———. "A Note on the Origin of Flem Snopes." *NMW*, 6: 56-7 (Fa 73).

Smith, H.N. "WF and Reality." *FaS*, 2: 17-9 (Su 73).

Smith, Hallett. "Summary of A Symposium on *Light in August.*" *MissQ*, 11: 188-90 (Fa 58).

Smith, Julian. "A Source for F's 'A Fable.'" *AL*, 40: 394-7 (N 68).

Smith, R.W. "F's 'Victory': The Plain People of Clydebank." *MissQ*, 23: 241-9 (Su 70).

Solery, Marc. "Addie Bundren: du corps au groups." *Stud*, 14: 117-27 (1975).

Solomon, Eric. "From Christ in Flanders to *Catch-22*: An Approach to War Fiction." *TSLL*, 11: 851-66 (1969).

Sorenson, D.A. "Structure in WF's *Sartoris*: The Contrast Between Psychological and Natural Time." *ArQ*, 25: 263-70 (Au 69).

Spears, J.E. "WF, Folklorist: A Note." *TFSB*, 38: 95-6 (D 72).

Spilka, M. "Quentin Compson's Universal Grief." *ConL*, 11: 451-69 (Au 70).

Spivey, H.E. "WF and the Adamic Myth: F's Moral Vision." *MFS*, 19: 497-505 (F-Mr 73-4).

Stafford, T.J. "Tobe's Significance in 'A Rose for Emily.'" *MFS*, 14: 451-3 ((Wi 68-9).

Stafford, W.T. "Hemingway/F: Marlin and Catfish?" *SoR*, 6: 1191-1200 (Au 70).

———. "'Some Homer of the Cotton Fields': F's Use of the Mule Early and Late (*Sartoris* and *The Reivers*)." *PLL*, 5: 190-6 (Sp 69).

———. "A Whale, an Heiress, and a Southern Demigod: Three Symbolic Americas." *Col Lit*, 1: 100-12 (1974).

Stark, John. "The Implications for Stylistics of Strawson's 'On Referring' with *Absalom, Absalom!* as an Example." *Lang&S*, 6: 273-80 (Fa 73).

Steege, M.T. "Dilsey's Negation of Nihilism: Meaning in *The Sound and the Fury*." *RSW*, 38: 266-75 (D 70).

Stephens, Rosemary. "Ike's Gun and Too Many Novembers." *MissQ*, 23: 279-87 (Su 70).

———. "Mythical Elements of 'Pantaloon in Black.'" *UMSE*, 11: 45-51 (1971).

Sternberg, Meir. "The Compositional Principles of F's *Light in August* and the Poetics of the Modern Novel." *Hasifrut*, 2: 498-537 (1970).

Stevens, A.J. "F and 'Helen.'" *PN*, 1: 31 (1968).

Stevens, L.R. "*Sartoris*: Germ of the Apocalypse." *DR*, 49: 80-7 (Sp 69).

Stewart, J.F. "Apotheosis and Apocalypse in F's 'Wash.'" *SSF*, 6: 586-600 (Fa 69).

Stewart, Jean. "The Novels of WF." *CaR*, 10 Mr 33, pp. 310-2.

Stone, E.W. "How a Writer Finds His Material." *Harpers*, 231: 157-61 (N 65).

Stone, W.B. "Ike McCaslin and the Grecian Urn." *SSF*, 10: 93-4 (Wi 73).

Stoneback, H.R. "F's Blues: 'Pantaloon in Black.'" *MFS*, 21: 241-5 (Su 75).

Strandberg, Victor. "Between Truth and Fact: F's Symbols of Identity." *MFS*, 21: 445-58 (Au 75).

Stronks, James. "A Poe Source for F? 'To Helen' and 'A Rose for Emily.'" *PN*, 1: 11 (Ap 68).

Sugg, R.S. "John Faulkner's Vanishing South." *AH*, 22: 65-75 (1971).

Sullivan, Ruth. "The Narrator in 'A Rose for Emily.'" *JNarT*, 1: 159-78 (S 71).

Swanson, W.J. "WF and William Styron: Notes on Religion." *CimR*, 7: 45-52 (1969).

Swiggart, Peter. "The Snopes Trilogy." *SR*, 68: 319-25 (Sp 60).

Swink, Helen. "WF: The Novelist as Oral Narrator." *GaR*, 26: 183-209 (Su 72).

Szpotánski, Zenon. "Slowacki a F." *Znak*, 20: 495-501 (1968).

Tanaka, Hisao. "The Significance of the Past for Gail Hightower: One Aspect of *Light in August*." *SALit*, 8: 24-38 (1972).

Tate, Allen. "F's 'Sanctuary' and the Southern Myth." *VQR*, 44: 418-27 (Su 68).

———. "WF—1897-1962." *SR*, 71: 160-4 (Wi 63).

Taylor, Walter. "F: Social Commitment and the Artistic Temperament." *SoR*, 6: 1075-92 (Au 70).

———. "F's Curse." *ArQ*, 28: 333-8 (1972).

———. "F's Pantaloon: The Negro Anomaly at the Heart of *Go Down, Moses*." *AL*, 44: 430-44 (N 72).

————. "Horror and Nostalgia: The Double Perspective of F's 'Was.'" *SHR*, 8: 74-84 (Wi 74).

Tefts, W.A. "Norman N. Holland and 'A Rose for Emily.'" *Sphinx*, 2: 50-7 (1974).

Thomas, D.M. "Memory-Narrative in *Absalom, Absalom!*" *FaS*, 2: 19-22 (Su 51).

Thompson, A.R. "The Cult of Cruelty." *Bkm*, 74: 477-8 (F 32).

Thornton, Weldon. "A Note on the Source of F's Jason." *StN*, 1: 370-2 (Fa 69).

————. "Structure and Theme in F's *Go Down, Moses*." *Costerus*, 3: 73-112 (1975).

Tilley, Winthrop. "The Idiot Boy in Mississippi: F's *The Sound and the Fury*." *Am J Mental Deficiency*, 59: 374-7 (Ja 55).

Tobin, Patricia. "The Time of Myth and History in *Absalom, Absalom!*" *AL*, 45: 252-70 (My 73).

Travis, M.K. "Echoes of *Pierre* in *The Reivers*." *NCLit*, 3: 11-13 (S 73).

Trimmer, J.F. "*The Unvanquished*: The Teller and the Tale." *BSUF*, 10: 35-42 (Wi 69).

————. "V.K. Ratliff: A Portrait of the Artist in Motion." *MFS*, 20: 451-67 (Wi 74-5).

Tsagari, Myrto. "A *Fable*: F's Message to the World." *Note Bene*, 1: 30-4 (1958).

Tucker, E.L. "F's Drusilla and Ibsen's Hedda." *MD*, 16: 157-61 (S 73).

Turner, Arlin. "WF: The Growth and Survival of a Legend." *SHR*, 9: 91-7 (Wi 75).

————. "WF and the Literary Flowering in the American South." *DUJ*, 29: 109-18 (Mr 68).

————. "WF, Southern Novelist." *MissQ*, 14: 117-30 (Su 61).

Tuso, J.F. "F's 'Wash.'" *Expl*, 27: 17 (N 68).

Tyner, Troi. "The Function of the Bear Ritual in F's *Go Down, Moses*." *JOFS*, 3: 19-40 (Sp 68).

Van Cromphout, G.V. "F: Myth and Motion." *ES*, 53: 572-4 (D 72).

Vande Kieft, R.M. "F's Defeat of Time in *Absalom, Absalom!*" *SoR*, 6: 1100-9 (Au 70).

Vare, Robert. "Oxford, Miss., Which F Transcended as He Left It." *NYT*, 14 Ja 72, pp. 1, 11.

Vickery, J.B. "WF and Sir Philip Sydney." *MLN*, 70: 349-50 (My 55).

Vinson, A.L. "Miscegenation and Its Meaning in *Go Down, Moses*." *CLAJ*, 14: 143-55 (D 70).

Vizioli, Paulo. "Guimarães Rosa a WF." *ESPSL*, nv: 1 (11 Ap 70).

Volpe, E.L. "F's 'Red Leaves': The Deciduation of Nature." *SAF*, 3: 121-31 (Au 75).

Vorpahl, B.M. "Moonlight at Ballenbaugh's: Time and Imagination in *The Reivers*." *SLJ*, 1: 3-26 (Sp 69).

Waggoner, H.H. "F's Critics." *Novel*, 3: 94-6 (Fa 69).

————. "Hemingway and F: The End of Something." *SoR*, 4: 458-66 (Sp 68).

————. "The Historical Novel and the Southern Past: The Case of *Absalom, Absalom!*" *SLJ*, 2: 69-85 (Sp 70).

Wagner, Geoffrey. "F's Contemporary Passion Play." *TC*, 156: 527-38 (D 54).

Wagner, L.W. "*As I Lay Dying*: F's All in the Family." *Col Lit*, 2: 73-82 (1974).

————. "F's Fiction: Studies in Organic Form." *JNarT*, 1: 1-14 (Ja 71).

————. "Jason Compson: The Demands of Honor." *SR*, 79: 554-75 (Au 71).

Walhout, Clarence. "The Earth is the Lord's: Religion in F." *ChSR*, 4: 26-35 (1974).

Walker, R.G. "Death in the Sound of Their Name: Character Motivation in F's *Sartoris*." *SHR*, 7: 271-8 (Su 73).

Wall, Carey. "Drama and Technique in F's *The Hamlet*." *TCL*, 14: 17-23 (Ap 68).

————. "*The Sound and the Fury*: The Emotional Center." *MwQ*, 11: 371-87 (Su 70).

Wallis, D. des G. "*Soldiers' Pay*: F's First Myth." *Bul West Virginia Assoc Coll Teachers*, 1: 15-21 (Fa 74).

Walter, James. "Expiation and History: Ike McCaslin and the Mystery of Providence." *LaStud*, 10: 263-73 (Wi 71).

Walton, G.W. "Some Southern Farm Terms in F's *Go Down Moses*." *PAmDS*, 47: 23-9 (Ap 67).

———. "Tennie's Jim and Lucas Beauchamp." *AN&Q*, 8: 23-4 (O 69).

———. "A Word List of Southern Farm Terms from F's *The Hamlet*." *MissFR*, 6: 60-75 (1972).

Warren, J.W. "The Role of Lion in F's 'The Bear': Key to a Better Understanding." *ArQ*, 24: 252-60 (Au 68).

Watkins, Floyd. "F, F, F." *SR*, 82: 518-27 (1974).

Watkins, F.C. "F and His Critics." *TSLL*, 10: 317-29 (Su 68).

———, and W.B. Dillingham. "The Mind of Vardaman Bundren." *PQ*, 39: 247-51 (Ap 60).

Watson, J.G. "'The Germ of My Apocrypha': *Sartoris* and the Search for Form." *Mosaic*, 7: 15-34 (Fa 73).

———. "If *Was* Existed: F's Prophets and the Patterns of History." *MFS*, 21: 499-507 (Wi 75).

Wegelin, Christof. "'Endure' and 'Prevail': F's Modification of Conrad." *N&Q*, 21: 375-6 (O 74).

Weisgerber, Jean. "F's Monomaniacs: Their Indebtedness to Raskolnikov." *CLS*, 5: 181-93 (Je 68).

———. "Metamorphoses du realisme: Dostoevskij et F." *RusL*, 4: 37-50 (1973).

Weiss, Miriam. "Hell Creek Bottom Is: A Reminiscence." *JMiH*, 30: 196-201 (Ag 68).

Welty, Eudora. "In Yoknapaawpha." *HudR*, 1: 596-8 (Wi 49).

West, Anthony. "Remembering WF." *Gourmet*, 29: 22-3, 74-5 (Ja 69).

West, R.B. "The Modern Writer." *CE*, 15: 207-15 (Je 54).

Whan, Edgar. "*Absalom, Absalom!* as Gothic Myth." *Perspective*, 3: 192-201 (Au 50).

Wheeler, S.P. "Chronology in *Light in August*." *SLJ*, 6: 20-42 (Fa 73).

Williams, J.S. "'The Final Copper Light of Afternoon': Hightower's Redemption." *TCL*, 13: 205-15 (Ja 68).

Williams, O.G. "The Theme of Endurance in *As I Lay Dying*." *La Stud*, 9: 100-4 (Su 70).

Wills, Arthur. "A Study of F's Revisions." *EEX*, 10: 14-6 (Mr 63).

Wilson, G.E. "'Being Pulled Two Ways': The Nature of Sarty's Choice in 'Barn Burning.'" *MissQ*, 24: 279-88 (Su 71).

Wilson, G.R. "The Chronology of F's 'A Rose for Emily' Again." *NMW*, 5: 56, 58-62 (Fa 72).

Wilson, M.A. "Search For an Eternal Present: *Absalom, Absalom!* and *All the King's Men*." *ConnR*, 8: 95-100 (#1 74).

Wilson, R.R. "The Pattern of Thought in *Light in August*." *BRMMLA*, 24: 155-61 (1970).

Winn, J.A. "F's Revisions: A Stylist at Work." *AL*, 41: 231-50 (My 69).

Woodbery, Potter. "F's Numismatics: A Note on *As I Lay Dying*." *RSW*, 39: 150-2 (Je 71).

Woodruff, Neal. "'The Bear' and F's Moral Vision." *CaSE*, 6: 43-67 (1961).

Woodward, R.H. "The Chronology of 'A Rose for Emily.'" *EEx*, 13: 17-9 (Mr 66).

———. "Poe's Raven, F's Sparrow, and Another Window." *PN*, 2: 37-8 (Ap 69).

Yonce, Margaret. "F's 'Atthis' and 'Attis': Some Sources of Myth." *MissQ*, 23: 289-98 (Su 70).

Young, Glenn. "Struggle and Triumph in *Light in August*." *STC*, 14: 33-50 (Sp 75).

Yoshida, Hiroshige. "Comments on *The Bear* and *The Old Man and the Sea*." *HirStud*, 18: 69-77 (1971).

Yoshida, Michiko. "The Voices and Legends in Yoknapatawpha." *SELit*, 174-6 (1971).

Zellefrow, Ken. "F's Flying Tales—A View of the Past." *Descant*, 16: 42-8 (Su 72).

Zender, K.F. "A Hand of Poker: Game and Ritual in F's 'Was.'" *SSF*, 11: 53-60 (Wi 74).

Zulns'kyi, Mykola. "Peredusim—ljudyna." *Lit Ukrajina*, nv: 13 (Ap 73).

Fauset, Jessie. Feeney, J.J. "Greek Tragic Patterns in a Black Novel: JF's *The Chinaberry Tree*." *CLAJ*, 17: 211-5 (D 74).

Fay, Theodore Sedgwick. Pollin, B.R. "Poe's Mystification: Its Source in F's *Norman Leslie*." *MissQ*, 25: 111-30 (Sp 72).

Fearing, Kenneth. Novak, E.G. "The *Dynamo* School of Poets." *ConL*, 11: 526-39 (Au 70).

Federman, Raymond. Dienstfrey, Harris. "The Choice of Inventions: On RF." *FicI*, 2-3: 147-50 (Sp-Fa 74).

Tatham, Campbell. "Correspondences/Notes/Etceteras." *ChiR*, 26: 112-32 (Sp 75).

Feldman, Irving. Boyers, Robert. "Promise and Faithfulness: The Poems of IF." *MPS*, 4: 271-80 (Wi 73).

Ferber, Edna. Wernick, Robert. "The Queens of Fiction." *Life*, 46: 139-52 (6 Ap 59).

Fergusson, Francis. Leonard, B.F. "FF, Critic and Poet: A Checklist of His Works." *ThDoc*, 2: 3-17 (1969-70).

Fergusson, Harvey. Fergusson, Harvey. "The Image in Fiction." *SDR*, 11: 85-6 (Au 73).

Milton, J.R. "Conversations with Distinguished Western American Novelists." *SDR*, 9: 15-57 (Sp 71).

————. "Literary or Not." *SDR*, 9: 3-5 (Wi 71-2).

McGinity, S.S. "HF's Use of Animal Imagery in Characterizing Spanish-American Women." *WR*, 8: 46-50 (1971).

Powell, L.C. "Southwest Classics Reread: *Wolf Song*." *Westways*, 64: 22-4, 41 58-9 (Ja 72).

Ferlinghetti, Lawrence. Collier, Peter. "LF: Doing His Own Thing." *NYT*, 21 Jl 68; pp. 4-6, 24, 26.

Ferlinghetti, Lawrence. "F Improvises." *CimR*, 16: 27-34 (1971).

Haselmayer, L.A. "Beat Prophet and Beat Wit." *IEngYb*, 6: 9-13 (Fa 61).

Hopkins, C.D "The Poetry of LF: A Reconsideration." *Italian Am*, 1: 59-76 (1974).

Jouffroy, Alain. "LF." *Temps Moderne*, D 64, pp. 990-5.

Kent, Edward. "Daredevil Poetics: F's Definition of a Poet." *EJ*, 59: 1243-4, 1251 (D 70).

Metzger, C.R. "LF as Elphin's Bard." *MwQ*, 16: 25-41 (O 74).

O'Neill, Brother Russell. "A Fling with F." *EJ*, 58: 1025-7, 1031 (O 69).

Rissover, Fredric. "Beat Poetry, *The American Dream*, and the Alienation Effect." *SpT*, 20: 36-43 (1971).

Fern, Fanny. (see **Willis, Sarah Payson**).

Ferril, Thomas Hornsby. Brophy, R.J. "Jeffers' 'Cawdor' and the Hippolytus Story." *WAL*, 7: 171-8 (Fa 72).

Grumbach, Doris. "Fine Print: THF, Professional Writer." *NRep*, 172: 29-30 (22 Mr 75).

Richards, R.F. "THF: A Biographical Sketch." *WAL*, 9: 205-14 (Fa 74).

————. "THF and the Problems of the Poet in the West." *KanQ*, 2: 110-16 (1970).

Scherting, Jack. "An Approach to the Western Poetry of THF." *WAL*, 7: 179-90 (Fa 72).

Fetzer, Herman. Anon. "A Collection of Jake Falstaffiana." *Ohioana*, 5: 17-8 (Sp 62).

Kuhn, Marie. "Ohio Lyrist: Teller of Tales." *Ohioana*, 2: 92-3 (Fa 59).

Ficke, Arthur Davison. Smith, W.J. "The Spectral Poets of Pittsburgh." *Horizon*, 2: 42-8 (My 60).

Fiedler, Leslie A. Almansi, G. "Interview with LA.F" *TSC*, 1: 56-67 (N 69).

Bakker, J. "LF: The Darkness and the Light in the Land of Affirmation." *DQR*, 1: 3-14 (1971).

Beitz, Ursula. "LAF: Ein reaktionärer Mythbilder." *ModO*, 2: 128-33 (Wi 72).

Bulefarb, Sam. "Pictures of the Anti-Stereotype: LF's Triptych, *The Last Jew in America*." *CLAJ*, 18: 412-21 (Mr 75).

Cuiran, Ronald. "'Fallen King' as Scapegoat in F's 'Nude Croquet.'" *NCLit*, 4: 8-13 (Ja 74).

Edwards, T.R. "The Indian Wants the Bronx." *PR*, 35: 606-10 (Fa 68).

Fiedler, L.A. "Second Thoughts on *Love and Death in the American Novel*: My First Gothic Novel." *Novel*, 1: 9-11 (Fa 67).

Hall, James. "Recharging American Gothic: LF." *NwR*, 3: 82-6 (Su 60).

Kostelanetz, Richard. "LF (1965)." *STC*, 13: 21-38 (Sp 74).

Larson, C.R. "The Good Bad Boy and Guru of American Letters." *SatR*, 54: 27-8, 35 (25 D 71).

———. "LF: The Critic and the Myth, the Critic as Myth." *LitR*, 14: 133-43 (Wi 70).

Michelson, Peter. "The Only Good Injun." *NRep*, 11 My 68; pp. 29-32.

Schulz, M.F. "LA.F and the Hieroglyphs of Life." *TCL*, 14: 24-34 (Ap 68).

Seymour, W.K. "*No! In Thunder*." *ConR*, 204: 105-6 (Ag 63).

Wallenstein, Barry. "LF between Raft and Shore." *JML*, 2: 589-94 (N 72).

Webster, Grant. "LF: Adolescent and Jew as Critic." *DQ*, 1: 44-53 (Wi 67).

Whalen, Patricia. "An Interview with LF." *NwR*, 9: 67-73 (Sp 68).

Field, Edward. Field, Edward. "The Movies as American Mythology." *CP*, 2: 27-31 (Sp 69).

Steller, Charles, and Gerald Locklin. "EF, Stand-up Poet." *MinnR*, 9: 63-73 (1969).

Field, Eugene. Simmons, D.C. "EF's Little Willie: An Excursion in Bibliopaedoneurosis." *ABC*, 18: 35-8 (Su 69).

Smith, D.A. "EF: Political Satirist." *ColQ*, 22: 495-508 (1974).

Vandersee, Charles. "The Statue of Irony." *MwQ*, 11: 283-91 (Sp 70).

Fisher, Clay. (see **Allen, Henry W.**).

Fisher, Vardis. Astro, Richard. "*The Big Sky* and the Limits of Wilderness Fiction." *WAL*, 9: 105-14 (Su 74).

Fisher, Opal. "A VF Memorial." *Cabellian*, 3: 25-6 (Au 70).

Fisher, Vardis. "On Writing." *SDR*, 11: 106-7 (Au 73).

Flora, J.M. "The Early Power of VF." *ABC*, 14: 15-9 (1963-64).

———. "VF and James Branch Cabell: An Essay on Influence and Reputation." *Cabellian*, 2: 12-6 (Au 69).

———. "VF and James Branch Cabell: A Postscript." *Cabellian*, 3: 7-9 (Au 70).

———. "VF and the Mormons." *Dialog*, 4: 48-55 (Au 69).

———. "VF and Wallace Stegner, Teacher and Student." *WAL*, 5: 121-8 (Su 70).

Grover, Dorys. "VF: The Antelope People Sonnets." *TQ*, 17: 97-106 (Sp 74).

Josephy, A.M. "Publisher's Interests in Western Writing." *WAL*, 1: 260-6 (Wi 67).

*Kellogg, George. "VF: A Bibliography." *WAL*, 5: 45-64 (Sp 70).

Margarick, Pat. "VF." *ABC*, 19: 11 (N 68).

Milton, John. "VF: March 31, 1895- July 9, 1968." *WAL*, 3: 114 (Su 68).

Robinson, F.C. "The Donner Party in Fiction." *Un Colorado Stud*, 10: 87-93 (F 66).

Taber, R.W. "VF and the 'Idaho Guide': Preserving Culture for the New Deal." *PNQ*, 59: 68-76 (Ap 68).

Taber, Ronald. "VF: March 31, 1895- July 9, 1968." *Idaho Yesterdays*, 12: 2-8 (Fa 68).

Fitch, Clyde. Andrews, Peter. "More Sock and Less Buskin." *AH*, 23: 48-57 (Ap 72).

Fitzgerald, F. Scott. *Anon. "Checklist: F.SF." *FHA*, 1970, pp. 272-3; 1973, pp. 341-6.
———. "The F-Perkins Letters." *Esquire*, 75: 106-11, 171-83 (Ja 71).
———. "F.SF's Copy of Ulysses." *FHA*, 1972, pp. 5-7.
———. "Letter to Brooks Bowan." *FHA*, 1974, pp. 9-10.
———. "Scandalabra Problem." *FHA*, 1972, pp. 97-8.
Aaron, Daniel. "The Legend of the Golden Couple." *VQR*, 48: 157-60 (1972).
Alderman, Taylor. "The Great Gatsby and Hopalong Cassidy." *FHA*, 1975, pp. 97-101.
———. "The Begetting of Gatsby." *MFS*, 19: 563-5 (Wi 73-4).
Allen, J.A. "The Better Fathers: The Priests in F's Life." *FHA*, 1974, pp. 29-39.
Allen, J.M. "The Myth of F's Proscription Disproved." *FHA*, 1973, pp. 175-9.
Alvarez-Bravo, Armando. "SF y el color maravilloso." *CdLA*, 4: 71-2 (D 64).
Anderson, Hilton. "The Rich Bunch in *The Great Gatsby*." *SoQ*, 6: 163-73 (Ja 68).
Astro, Richard. "*Vandover and the Brute* and *The Beautiful and the Damned*: A Search for
   Thematic and Stylistic Reinterpretations." *MFS*, 14: 397-413 (Wi 68-9).
Atkins, I.K. "In Search of the Greatest Gatsby." *LFQ*, 2: 216-28 (1974).
Atkinson, J.E. "F's Marked Copy of The Great Gatsby." *FHA*, 1970, pp. 283-5.
———. "Indeed 'Lo, the Poor Peacock!'" *FHA*, 1972, pp. 283-5.
———. "Lost and Unpublished Stories by F.SF." *FHA*, 1971, pp. 32-63.
Atkinson, J.M. "The Text of Bits of Paradise." *FHA*, 1974, pp. 47-9.
Bakker, M.C. "SF in Tryon, North Carolina." *FHA*, 1973, pp. 151-4.
Banta, Martha. "Benjamin, Edgar, Humbert, and Jay." *YR*, 60: 532-49 (Je 71).
Barbour, B.M. "*The Great Gatsby* and the American Past." *SoR*, 9: 288-99 (Ja 73).
*Beebe, Maurice, and J.R. Bryer. "Criticism of F.SF: A Selected Checklist." *MFS*, 7: 82-94
   (Sp 61).
Berry, Linda. "The Text of Bits of Paradise." *FHA*, 1975, pp. 141-5.
*———, and Patricia Powell. "F in Translation: A Checklist." *FHA*, 1972, pp. 431-5; 1974,
   pp. 313-5.
Bonincontro, Marilia. "L'assolo di F.S.F (*Tender is the Night*)." *PenS*, 5: 18-23 (1969).
Boyle, T.E. "Unreliable Narration in *The Great Gatsby*." *BRMMLA*, 23: 21-6 (1969).
Brogunier, Joseph. "An Incident in *The Great Gatsby* and *Huckleberry Finn*." *MTJ*, 16: 1-3
   (Su 72).
Bruccoli, M.J. "Another Source of Gatsby's Wealth." *FitzN*, 39: 17 (Fa 67).
———. "Bruccoli Addenda." *FHA*, 1973, pp. 339-46; *FHA*, 1974, pp. 27-83.
———. "Editorial." *FHA*, 1970, p. 265.
———. "F's List of Neglected Books." *FHA*, 1970, pp. 229-30.
———. "F's Marked Copy of *This Side of Paradise*." *FHA*, 1971, pp. 64-9.
———. "F's St. Paul Academy Publications." *FHA*, 1975, pp. 147-8.
———. "A Further Note on the First Printing of *The Great Gatsby*." *SB*, 16: 244 (1963).
———. "'How Are You and the Family, Old Sport?': Gerlach and Gatsby." *FHA*, 1975,
   pp. 33-6.
———. "Interview with Allen Tate." *FHA*, 1974, pp. 101-3.
———. "Malcolm Lowry's Film Treatment for *Tender Is The Night*." *FHA*, 1972, p. 337.
———. "Francis Macomber and FF." *FHA*, 1970, p. 223.
———. "A Note on Jordan Baker." *FHA*, 1970, pp. 232-3.
———. "The *Scade* Series: Apparatus for Definitive Editions." *PBSA*, 67: 431-6 (O-D 73).
———. "A Source for Gatsby's House." *FitzN*, 39: 16 (Fa 67).
———. "'Sleep of a University': An Unrecorded F Poem." *FHA*, 1970, pp. 14-5.
———. "*Tender is the Night* and the Reviewers." *MFS*, 7: 49-54 (Sp 61).
———, and J.E. Atkinson. "FSF's Hollywood Assignments, 1937-40." *FHA*, 1971, pp.
   307-8.

Bryer, J.R. "The Years of Frustration." *NRep*, 164: 29-32, 34 (29 My 71).

Bufkin, E.C. "A Pattern of Parallel and Double: The Function of Myrtle in *The Great Gatsby*." *MFS*, 15: 517-24 (Wi 69-70).

Buntain, L.M. "A Note on the Editions of *Tender is the Night*." *SAF*, 1: 208-13 (Au 73).

Burhans, C.S. "'Magnificently Attune to Life': The Value of 'Winter Dreams.'" *SSF*, 6: 401-12 (Su 69).

———. "Structure and Theme in *This Side of Paradise*." *JEGP*, 68: 605-24 (O 69).

Burton, M.E. "The Counter-Transference of Dr. Diver." *ELH*, 38: 459-71 (S 71).

Buttitta, Anthony. "Scott: One More Emotion." *FHA*, 1972, pp. 25-34.

Canady, Nicholas. "Portrait of Daisy: Studies by James and F." *Forum(H)*, 4: 17-20 (Su 66).

Carringer, R.L. "*Citizen Kane, The Great Gatsby*, and Some Conventions of American Narrative." *CritI*, 2: 307-326 (Wi 75).

Cass, C.S. "F's Second Thoughts about 'May Day': A Collation and Study." *FHA*, 1970, pp. 69-95.

Casty, Alan. "'I and It' in the Stories of F.SF." *SSF*, 9: 47-58 (1972).

Chamson, André. "L'oeuf de Christophe Colomb." *NRF*, 148: 591-606 (Ap 65).

———. "Remarks by André Chamson." *FHA*, 1973, pp. 69-76.

Chard, L.F. "Outward Forms and the Inner Life: Coleridge and Gatsby." *FHA*, 1973, pp. 189-94.

Cody, Morrill. "Disscussion at the Paris Conference." *FHA*, 1973, pp. 77-81.

Cohen, Richard. "The Inessential Houses of *The Great Gatsby*." *HussR*, 2: 48-57 (1968).

Coleman, T.C. "Nicole Warren Diver and SF: The Girl and the Egotist." *StN*, 3: 34-43 (Sp 71).

———. "The Rise of Dr. Diver." *Disc*, 13: 226-38 (Sp 70).

Crowley, Malcolm. "The F Revival, 1941-1953." *FHA*, 1974, pp. 11-3.

———. "F: The Double Man." *SRL*, 34: 9-10, 42-4 (24 F 51).

Crim, L. R, and N.B. Houston. "The Catalogue of Names in *The Great Gatsby*." *RSW*, 36: 113-30 (Ja 68).

Crosland, Andrew. "*The Great Gatsby* and *The Secret Sharer*." *FHA*, 1975, pp. 75-81.

———. "Sleeping and Waking: The Literary Reputation of *The Great Gatsby*." *FHA*, 1974, pp. 15-24.

Dahlie, Hallvard. "Alienation and Disintegretion in *Tender Is the Night*." *HAB*, 22: 3-8 (Fa 72).

Daniels, T.E. "Pat Hobby: Anti-Hero." *FHA*, 1973, pp. 131-9.

Donaldson, Scott. "'No I Am Not Prince Charming': Fairy Tales in *Tender Is the Night*." *FHA*, 1973, pp. 105-12.

———. "SF's Romance with the South." *SLJ*, 5: 3-17 (Sp 73).

Drake, J.W. "Dr. Siver, Vivisectionist." *Coll Lit*, 2: 120-7 (Sp 75).

*Duggan, M.M. "F Checklist." *FHA*, 1973, pp. 349-54; 1974, pp. 317-22; 1975, pp. 341-50.

———. "F in Translation." *FHA*, 1973, pp. 355-6.

———. "Reprintings of F." *FHA*, 1974, pp. 285-91.

Dryson, A.E. "The Great Gatsby: Thirty-Six Years Later." *MFS*, 7: 37-48 (Sp 61).

Eble, Kenneth. "*The Great Gatsby*." *Coll Lit*, 1: 34-7 (1974).

Edenbaum, R.I. "Babylon Revisited: A Psychological Note on F.SF." *L&P*, 18: 27-9 (1968).

Eisiminger, S.K. "Gatsby's Bluff and F's Blunder." *FHA*, 1974, pp. 95-8.

Ellis, James. "The 'Stoddard Lectures' in *The Great Gatsby*." *AL*, 44: 470-1 (N 72).

Elmore, A.E. "Color and Cosmos in *The Great Gatsby*." *SR*, 78: 427-43 (Jl-S 70).

————. "Nick Carraway's Self-Introduction." *FHA*, 1971, pp. 130-47.

Evans, O.H. "'A Sort of Moral Attention': The Narrator of *The Great Gatsby*." *FHA*, 1971, pp. 117-29.

Fain, J.T. "Recollections of F.SF." *FHA*, 1974, pp. 75-85; 1975, pp. 133-9.

Fitzgerald, F.S. "An Additional Lyric for 'It Is Art.'" *FHA*, 1972, pp. 19-23.

————. "Dearly Beloved." *FHA*, 1969, pp. 1-3.

————. "A F Auto-Bibliography." *FHA*, 1972, pp. 39-41.

————. "A F Letter on 'The Ice Palace.'" *FHA*, 1972, pp. 59-60.

————. "F's Ledger." *FHA*, 1971, pp. 3-31.

————. "An Interview with F.SF." *SatR*, 43: 26, 56 (5 N 60).

————. "F on 'The Ice Palace': A Newly Discovered Letter." *FHA*, 1972, pp. 59-60.

————. "F on Ulysses: A Previously Unpublished Letter to Bennett Cerf." *FHA*, 1972, pp. 3-4.

————. "Letter to Ernest Hemingway." *FHA*, 1970, pp. 10-3.

————. "Letter to James Aswell, 1 Oct 1934." *LaStud*, 12: 552 (1974).

————. "Letter to Roger Burlingame." *FHA*, 1972, pp. 81-3.

————. "My Generation." *Esquire*, 80: 124-6 (O 73).

————. "'Oh, Sister, Can You Spare You Heart.'" *FHA*, 1971, pp. 114-5.

————. "Preface to *This Side of Paradise*." *FHA*, 1971, pp. 1-2.

————. "Rimbaud's 'Voyelles.'" *Delos*, 2: 100-04 (1968).

————. "Six Letters to Hunt Stromberg." *FHA*, 1972, pp. 9-18.

————. "Six Letters to the Menckens." *FHA*, 1970, pp. 102-4.

————. "10 Best Books I Have Read." *FHA*, 1972, pp. 67-8.

Foster, Richard. "Mailer and the F Tradition." *Novel*, 1: 219-30 (Sp 68).

————. "Time's Exile: Dick Diver and the Heroic Idea." *Mosaic*, 8: 89-108 (Sp 75).

Fujimoto, Yukio. "The Relationship Between Santiago and Manolin." *SALCS*, 7: 26-33 (1971).

Gere, A.R. "Color in F's Novels." *FHA*, 1971, pp. 333-9.

Gerhard, Joseph. "The American Triumph of the Egg: Anderson's 'The Egg' and F's *The Great Gatsby*." *Crit*, 7: 131-40 (Sp 65).

Giacomelli, E.F. "O grande sonho americano: A proposito do retorno de Gatsby." *ESPSL*, 3 N 74, p. 5.

Gidley, Mark. "Notes on F.SF and the Passing of the Great Race." *JAmSt*, 7: 171-81 (Ag 73).

Gilliam, Florence. "Remarks." *FHA*, 1973, pp. 43-8.

Gindin, James. "Gods and Fathers in F.SF's Novels." *MLQ*, 30: 64-85 (Mr 69).

Gingrich, Arnold. "Scott, Ernest and Whoever." *Esquire*, 80: 151-4 (O 73).

Going, W.T. "Two Alabama Writers: Zelda Sayre Fitzgerald and Sara Haardt Mencken." *AlaR*, 23: 3-29 (Ja 70).

Goldhurst, Williams. "*The F.SF and His Contemporaries* Correspondence." *FHA*, 1974, pp. 89-93.

Gollin, R.K. "The Automobiles of *The Great Gatsby*." *STC*, 6: 63-83 (Fa 70).

————. "Modes of Travel in *Tender Is the Night*." *STC*, 8: 103-14 (Fa 71).

Goodwin, D.W. "The Alcoholism of F.SF." *JAMA*, 212: 86-90 (1970).

Gorman, Herbert. "Glimpses of F.SF." *FHA*, 1973, pp. 113-8.

Greiff, L.K. "Perfect Marriage in *Tender Is the Night*." *FHA*, 1974, pp. 63-73.

Gross, Barry. "Back West: Time and Place in *The Great Gatsby*." *WAL*, 8: 3-14 (Sp-Su 73).

————. "The Dark Side of Twenty-five: F and *The Beautiful and Damned*." *BuR*, 16: 40-52 (D 68).

————. "F in the Fifties." *StN*, 5: 324-35 (Fa 73).

————. "Newman to Gatsby: This Side of Innocence." *PMASAL*, 53: 279-89 (1968).

————. "'Our Gatsby, Our Nick.'" *CentR*, 14: 331-40 (Su 70).

————. "SF's *The Last Tycoon*: The Great American Novel?" *ArQ*, 26: 197-216 (Au 70).

————. "*This Side of Paradise*: The Dominating Intention." *StN*, 1: 51-9 (Sp 69).

Gross, Dalton. "F.SF's *The Great Gatsby* and Oswald Spengler's *The Decline of the West*." *N&Q*, 17: 467 (D 70).

Gross, T.L. "F.SF: The Hero in Retrospect." *SAQ*, 67: 64-77 (Wi 68).

Gruber, M.P. "'May Day': Prelude to Triumph." *ELUD*, 2: 20-35 (Ja 75).

Gunn, Giles. "F.SF's *Gatsby* and the Imagination of Wonder." *JAAR*, 41: 171-83 (1973).

Guseva, Elena. "F.SF's *The Great Gatsby* in Russian." *SovL*, 6: 171-4 (1966).

Hall, W.F. "T.J. Eckleburg; 'un dieu à l'américaine.'" *FHA*, 1969, pp. 35-9.

Hamblen, A.A. "The Fs' Coming of Age." UR, 35: 157-60 (Wi 68).

Hardwick, Elizabeth. "Caesar's Things." *NYRB*, 24 S 70, pp. 3-6.

Hart, J.E. "F's *The Last Tycoon*: A Search for Identity." *MFS*, 7: 63-70 (Sp 61).

Hart, Jeffrey. "F and Hemingway: The Difficult Friend." *Nat R*, 21: 29-31 (14 Ja 69).

Hartford, G.F. "Reflections and Affinities: Aspects of the American Past, American Dream, and *The Great Gatsby*." *ESA*, 16: 23-6 (Mr 73).

Higgins, Brian, and Hershel Parker. "Sober Second Thoughts: F's 'Final Version' of *Tender Is the Night*." *Proof*, 4: 129-52 (1974).

Hill, J.S. "Henry James: F's Literary Ancestor." *FitzN*, 40: 6-10 (Wi 68).

Hindus, Milton. "The Mysterious Eyes of Doctor T.J. Eckleburg." *BUSE*, 3: 22-31 (Sp 57).

Hoenisch, Michael. "Die Werke F.SF: Entwurf einer Chronologie der Entstehungsdaten." *JA*, 14: 185-218 (1969).

Hoffman, N.Y. "*The Great Gatsby*: *Troilus and Criseyde* Revisited." *FHA*, 1971, pp. 148-58.

Howard, Leon. "Raymond Chandler's Not-So-Great Gatsby." *MDAC*, 1973, pp. 1-15.

Hughes, G.I. "Sub Specie Doctor T.J. Eckleburg: Man and God in *The Great Gatsby*." *ESA*, 15: 81-92 (S 72).

Humma, J.B. "Edward Russell Thomas: *Gatsby*'s Tom Buchanan?" *MarkR*, 4: 38-9 (F 74).

Hunt, Jan, and John M. Suarez. "The Evasion of Adult Love in F's Fiction." *CentR*, 17: 152-69 (Sp 73).

Hurwitz, Harold. "*The Great Gatsby* and *Heart of Darkness*: The Confrontation Scenes." *FHA*, 1969, pp. 27-34.

Irish, Carol. "The Myth of Success in F's Boyhood." *SAF*, 1: 176-87 (Au 73).

Isaac, Dan. "The Other SF." *Nation*, 219: 282-4 (28 S 74).

Johnson, Richard. "The Eyes of Dr. T.J. Eckleburg Re-Examined." *AN&Q*, 9: 20-1 (1970).

Jones, E.T. "Green Thoughts in a Technicolor Shade: A Revaluation of *The Great Gatsby*." *LFQ*, 2: 229-36 (1974).

Kahn, Sy. "*This Side of Paradise*: The Pageantry of Disillusion." *MwQ*, 7: 177-94 (Wi 66).

Katterjohn, William. "An Interview with F's Private Nurse." *FHA*, 1974, pp. 75-85.

Katz, Joseph. "Gloria Patch's Tomatoes." *FitzN*, 37: 3-4 (Sp 67).

Kelley, D.J.F. "The Polishing of Diamond." *FitzN*, 40: 1-2 (Wi 68).

Kelley, Frederic. "F.SF: His Baltimore Years." *Baltimore Sun*, 21 Jl 74, p. 14.

Kennedy, W.F. "Are Our Novelists Hostile to the American Economic System?" *DR*, 25: 32-44 (Sp 55).

Kohler, Vincent. "Somewhere West of Laramie, On the Road to West Egg: Automobiles, Fillies, and the West in *The Great Gatsby*." *JPC*, 7: 152-8 (1973).

Kopf, J.Z. "Meyer Wolfsheim and Robert Cohn: A Study of a Jewish Type and Stereotype." *Tradition*, 10: 93-104 (Sp 69).

Fitzgerald, F. Scott

Korenman, J.S. "'Only Her Hairdresser . . .': Another Look at Daisy Buchanan." *AL*, 46: 574-104 (Ja 75).

————. "A View from the (Queensboro) Bridge." *FHA*, 1975, pp. 93-6.

Kreuter, Kent and Gretchen Kreuter. "The Moralism of the Later F." *MFS*, 7: 71-81 (Sp 61).

Kruse, Horst. "'April Is the Creullest Month . . .': Naturdarstellung und die Silbsterkenntnis des Erzählers in F.SF's *The Great Gatsby*." *LWU*, 1: 27-39 (1968).

Kruse, H.H. "'Gatsby' and 'Gadsby.'" *MFS*, 15: 539-41 (Wi 69-70).

Kuehl, John. "SF's Critical Opinions." *MFS*, 7: 3-18 (Sp 61).

Kyria, Pierre. "Le Monde Américain." *RdP*, nv: 120-5 (Mr 67).

LaHood, M.J. "Sensuality and Asceticism in *Tender Is the Night*." *Eng Rec*, 17: 9-12 (F 67).

Langman, F.H. "Style and Shape in *The Great Gatsby*." *SoRA*, 6: 48-67 (Mr 73).

Larsen, Erling. "The Geography of F's Saint Paul." *CaM*, 8: 3-30 (Su 73).

Latham, J.A. "A Day at the Studio—SF in Hollywood." *HM*, 241: 38-50 (N 70).

Lawry, J.S. "Green Light or Square of Light in *The Great Gatsby*." *DR*, 55: 114-32 (Sp 75).

Layman, Richard. "F and Horace McCoy." *FHA*, 1974, pp. 99-100.

Lease, Benjamin. "An Evening at the SF's: An Unpublished Letter of Ring Lardner." *ELN*, 8: 40-2 (S 70).

Levine, Norman. "'The Great Gatsby.'" *TLS*, 26 Ap 74, p. 447.

LeVot, Andre. "F in Paris." *FHA*, 1973, pp. 49-68.

————. "SF: de la légende à la réputation." *LanM*, 62: 113-32 (Jl-Ag 68).

Lewis, Janet. "F's 'Philippe, Count of Darkness.'" *FHA*, 1975, pp. 7-32.

Lid, R.W. "The Passion of F.SF." *FHA*, 1970, pp. 43-59.

Littlejohn, David. "F's Grand Illusion." *Cweal*, 76: 168-9 (11 My 62).

Loeb, Harold. "Remarks by Harold Loeb." *FHA*, 1973, pp. 33-8.

Long, R.E. "The Allusion to Gilda Gray in *The Great Gatsby*." *FHA*, 1972, pp. 307-9.

————. "*The Beautiful and Damned*: Nathan and Mencken as Maury Noble." *FitzN*, 40: 3-4 (Wi 68).

————. "Dreiser and Frederick: The Upstate New York Exile of Dick Diver." *FitzN*, 37: 1-2 (Sp 67).

————. "F and Hemingway on Stage." *FHA*, 1969, pp. 143-4.

————. "The F-Mencken Correspondence." *FHA*, 1971, pp. 319-21.

————. "The Image of Gatsby in the Fiction of Louis Auchincloss and C.D.B. Bryan." *FHA*, 1972, pp. 325-8.

————. "The Opening Four Chapters of *The Great Gatsby*." *EngR*, 26: 85-94 (Fa 75).

————. "*Vanity Fair* and the Guest List in *Great Gatsby*." *FitzN*, 38: 4 (Su 67).

————. "The Vogue of Gatsby's Guest List." *FHA*, 1969, pp. 23-5.

Lucid, R.F. "Three Public Performances: F, Hemingway, Mailer." *ASch*, 43: 447-66 (Su 74).

Lueders, Edward. "Revisiting Babylon: F and the 1920's." *WHR*, 29: 285-91 (Su 75).

Lurie, Alison. "Witches and Fairies: F to Updike." *NYRB*, 17: 6-11 (2 D 71).

McCall, Dan. "The Self-Same Song that Found a Path': Keats and *The Great Gatsby*." *AL*, 42: 521-30 (Ja 71).

McCarthy, Paul. "Daisy's Voice in *The Great Gatsby*." *LHR*, 11: 51-6 (1969).

McCollum, Kenneth. "'Babylon Revisited' Revisited." *FHA*, 1971, pp. 314-6.

McDonnell, R.F. "Eggs and Eyes in *The Great Gatsby*." *MFS*, 7: 32-6 (Sp 61).

MacKie, E.B "My Friend SF." *FHA*, 1970, pp. 16-27.

McMaster, John. "As I Remember Scott." *Confr*, 7: 3-11 (Fa 73).

McNally, J.J. "Boats and Automobiles in *The Great Gatsby*: Symbols of Drift and Death." *HussR*, 5: 11-7 (1971).

————. "A Hemingway Mention of *Gentlemen*." *FHA*, 1972, pp. 333-4.

————. "Prefiguration of Incidents in *The Great Gatsby*." *UDR*, 7: 39-49 (Sp 71).

McPhee, L.E. "*The Great Gatsby*'s 'Romance of Motoring': Nick Carraway and Jordan Baker." MFS, 18: 207-12 (Su 72).

Maimon, E.P. "F.SF's Book Sales: A Look at the Record." *FHA*, 1973, pp. 165-73.

Makurath, P.A. "Another Source for 'Gatsby.'" *FHA*, 1975, pp. 116-2.

Mangum, Bryant. "The Reception of *Dearly Beloved*." *FHA*, 1970, pp. 241-4.

Margolies, Alan. "The Camels Back and the Conductor." *FHA*, 1974, pp. 87-88.

————. "The Dramatic Novel, *The Great Gatsby* and *The Last Tycoon*." *FHA*, 1971, pp. 159-71.

————. "F.SF and *The Wedding Night*." *FHA*, 1970, pp. 224-5.

————. "F.SF's Prison Play." *PBSA*, 66: 61-4 (1Q 72).

————. "F.SF's Work in the Film Studios." *PULC*, 32: 81-110 (Wi 71).

Marsden, Donald. "F and the Princeton Triangle Club." *FitzN*, 40: 11-4 (Wi 68).

Martin, Jay. "F Recommends Nathanael West for a Guggenheim." *FHA*, 1971, pp. 302-4.

Martin, R.A. "'Gatsby and the Dutch Sailors.'" *AN&Q*, 12: 61-3 (D 73).

————. "The Hot Madness of Four O'Clock in F's 'Absolution' and *Gatsby*." *SAF*, 2: 230-7 (Au 74).

Mass, Roslyn. "A Linking of Legends: *The Great Gatsby* and *Citizen Kane*." *L/FQ*, 2: 207-15 (1974).

Messenger, Christian. "Tom Buchanan and the Demise of the Ivy League Athletic Hero." *JPC*, 8: 402-10 (1974).

Mihai, Virgil. "*Marele Gatsby* si disolutia miturilor." *Steaua*, 24: 24 (1974).

Monteiro, George. "James Gatz and John Keats." *FHA*, 1972, pp. 291-4.

————. "The Limits of Professionalism: A Sociological Approach to Faulkner, F, and Hemingway." *Criticism*, 15: 145-55 (Sp 73).

————. "*McNaght's Monthly*: Addenda to the Bibliographies of . . ., F, and others." *PBSA*, 68: 64-5 (1Q 74).

Morris, Wright. "The Ability to Function. F: The Function of Nostalgia." *New World Writing*, 13: 34-43 (Je 58).

Morsberger, R.E. "The Romantic Ancestry of *The Great Gatsby*." *FHA*, 1973, pp. 119-30.

Moses, Edwin. "F.SF and the Quest to the Ice Palace." *CEA*, 36, 2: 11-4 (1974).

Moyer, K.W. "F's Two Unfinished Novels: *The Count* and *The Tycoon* in Spenglerian Pespective." *ConL*, 15: 238-56 (Sp 74).

————. "The Great Gatsby: F's Meditation on American History." *FHA*, 1972, pp. 43-57.

Murfin, J.V. "The Fall of a Literary Light: The Last Days of F.SF." *Maryland*, 4: 20-3 (1971).

Murphy, George. "The Unconscious Dimension of *Tender Is the Night*." *StN*, 5: 314-23 (Fa 23).

Natterstad, J.H. "F's *The Great Gatsby*." *Expl*, 26: 68 (Ap 68).

Nevius, R.C. "A Note on F.SF's Monsignor Sigourney Fay and His Early Career as an Episcopalian." *FHA*, 1971, pp. 105-13.

O'Hara, John. "John O'Hara's Remarks on the Silent Gatsby." *FHA*, 1974, pp. 25-7.

Osborne, W.R. "The Wounds of Charles Wales in F's 'Babylon Revisited.'" *SSF*, 2: 86-7 (Fa 64).

Owen, Guy. "Imagery and Meaning in *The Great Gatsby*." *Stetson Studies in the Humanities*, 1: 46-54 (1963).

Ower, John. "A Thematic Reference to *The Rubaiyat of Omar Khayyam* in *The Great Gatsby*. *FHA*, 1975, pp. 103-5.

Fitzgerald, F. Scott

Padis, L.A. *"The Beautiful and Damned*: F's Test of Youth." *FHA*, 1973, 141-7.

Parker, David. *"The Great Gatsby*: Two Versions of the Hero." *ES*, 54: 37-51 (F 73).

Pearson, R.L. "Gatsby: False Prophet of the American Dream." *EJ*, 59: 638-42, 645 (My 70).

Perosa, S. "Fitzgeraldiana." *ACF*, 10: 313-8 (1971).

Podis, L.A. *"The Beautiful and Damned*: F's Test of Youth." *FHA*, 1973, pp. 141-7.

Powell, Anthony. "Hollywood Canteen: A Memoir of SF in 1937." *FHA*, 1971, pp. 71-80.

Powers, J.F. "Dealer in Diamonds & Rhinestones." *Commonweal*, 99: 191-3 (1973).

Prigozy, Ruth. "Gatsby's Guest List and F's Technique of Naming." *FHA*, 1972, pp. 99-112.

———. "Matter of Measurement: The Tangled Relationship Between F and Hemingway." *Cweal*, 95: 103-6 (29 O 71).

———. "The Unpublised Stories: F in His Final Stage." *TCL*, 20: 69-90 (Ap 74).

Qualls, B.B. "Physician in the Counting House: The Religious Motif in *Tender Is the Night*." *EC*, 2: 192-208 (Fa 75).

Randall, J.H. "Romeo and Juliet in the New World: A Study of James, Wharton, and F." *Costerus*, 8: 109-75 (1973).

Ranzoli Cuccolini, Silvana. "Il *Grande Gatsby* tra sogno e realta." *HumB*, 29: 854-62 (1974).

Rao, Nageswara. "The Structure of *Tender Is the Night*," *LCrit*, 8: 54-62 (Su 69).

Reed, K.T. "East Egg, West Egg, All Around the Tower: The Geography of F's Gatsby." *FHA*, 1971, p. 325.

Rees, John. "F's Pat Hobby Stories." *ColQ*, 23: 553-62 (Sp 75).

Ring, Frances, and R.L. Samsell. "Sisyphus in Hollywood: Refocusing F.SF." *FHA*, 1973, p. 93-104.

Robson, Vincent. "The Psychological Conflict and the Distortion of Time: A Study of Diver's Disintegration in *Tender Is the Night*." *Lang&L*, 1: 55-64 (#2 72).

Rodda, Peter. *"The Great Gatsby*." *ESA*, 11: 95-126 (S 68).

———. *"The Last Tycoon*." *ESA*, 14: 49-71 (Mr 71).

Rodewald, F.A. "Faulkner's Possible Use of *The Great Gatsby*." *FHA*, 1975, pp. 97-81.

Roncuzzi, Alfredo. "La Lexione di F." *ORom*, 4: 3 (Mr 73).

Rose, A.H. "Sin and the City: The Uses of Disorder in the Urban Novel." *CentR*, 16: 203-20 (1972).

Rougé, Robert. "F.SF: La femme et la mort." *EA*, 21: 160-7 (Ap-Je 68).

Roulston, Robert. *"This Side of Paradise*: The Ghost of Rupert Brook." *FHA*, 1975, pp. 117-30.

Samsell, R.L. "The Falsest of the Arts." *FHA*, 1971, pp. 173-6.

———. "Hollywood—It Wasn't All That Bad." *FHA*, 1969, pp. 15-9.

———. "Six F Letters to Hunt Stromberg." *FHA*, 1972, pp. 9-18.

———. "Won't You Come Home Dick Diver?" *FHA*, 1970, pp. 34-42.

Savage, David. "Who Is 'Owl Eyes' in *The Great Gatsby*?" *AN&Q*, 13: 72-4 (Ja 75).

Scanlon, P.A. "The Great Gatsby: Romance and Realism." *Work in Progress* (Zaria), 2: 207-14 (1973).

Schulte, F.G.F. "Technical Potential and Achievement in *Tender Is the Night*." *DQR*, 3: 49-55 (1973).

Schurenberg, Walter. "FSF." *NDH*, 4: 208-12 (1973).

Scott, R.I. "A Sense of Loss: Entropy vs. Ecology in *The Great Gatsby*." *QQ*, 82: 559-71 (1975).

Seward, W.W. "F.SF's Associations with Norfolk and Virginia Beach." *FHA*, 1974, pp. 41-6.

Sheffield, R.M. "The Temporal Location of F's Jay Gatsby." *TQ*, 18: 122-30 (#2 75).

Shroeder, John. "'Some Unfortunate Idyllic Love Affair': The Legend of Taji and Jay Gatsby." *BBr*, 22: 143-53 (1968).

Siegel, D.G. "T.S. Eliot's Copy of *Gatsby*." *FHA*, 1971, pp. 290-3.

Slater, Peter. "Ethnicity in *The Great Gatsby*." *TCL*, 19: 53-62 (Ja 73).

Smith, S.H. "Some Biographical Aspects of *This Side of Paradise*." *FHA*, 1970, pp. 96-101.

*Speer, R.S. "The Bibliography of Fitzgerald's Magazine 'Essays.'" *FHA*, 1969, pp. 43-6.

————. "The Great Gatsby's 'Romance of Motoring' and 'The Cruise of the Rolling Junk.'" *MFS*, 20: 540-3 (Wi 74-75).

Stafford, W.T. "F's *The Great Gatsby*, Chapter II, Paragraph 1." *Expl*, 28: 57 (Mr 70).

Stark, B.R. "The Intricate Pattern in *The Great Gatsby*." *FHA*, 1974, pp. 51-61.

Stark, John. "The Style of *Tender Is the Night*." *FHA*, 1972, pp. 89-95.

Stephens, R.O., and James Ellis. "Hemingway, F, and the Riddle of 'Henry's Bicycle.'" *ELN*, 5: 46-9 (S 67).

Stewart, L.D. "'Absolution' and *The Great Gatsby*." *FHA*, 1973, pp. 181-7.

————. "The Dust Jackets of *The Great Gatsby* and *The Long Goodbye*." *MDAC*, 1: 331-4 (1974).

————. "F's Film Scripts of 'Babylon Revisited.'" *FHA*, 1971, pp. 81-104.

Stewart, D.O. "An Interview." *FHA*, 1973, pp. 83-9.

————. "Recollections of F and Hemingway." *FHA*, 1971, pp. 177-88.

Stone, Edward. "More about Gatsby's Guest List." *FHA*, 1972, pp. 315-6.

Stouck, David. "White Sheep on Fifth Avenue: *The Great Gatsby* as Pastoral." *Genre*, 4: 335-47 (1971).

Tamke, A.R. "The 'Gat' in *Gatsby*: Neglected Aspect of a Novel." *MFS*, 14: 443-5 (Wi 68).

————. "Michaelis in *The Great Gatsby*: St. Michael in the Valley of Ashes." *FitzN*, 40: 4-5 (Wi 68).

Tanner, Bernard. "The Gospel of Gatsby." *EJ*, 54: 467-74 (S 65).

Tanner, Tony. "Hemingway y F." *CdLA*, 4: 99-105 (D 64).

Tasaka, Takashi. "The Ethic and Aesthetic Aspects in *Tender Is the Night*." *SALit*, 8: 15-23 (1972).

Tenenbaum, R.B. "The Gray-Turning, Gold-Turning Consciousness of Nick Carraway." *FHA*, 1975, pp. 37-55.

Thornton, Lawrence. "Ford Maddox Ford and *The Great Gatsby*." *FHA*, 1975, pp. 57-74.

Toor, David. "Guilt and Retribution in 'Babylon Revisited.'" *FHA*, 1973, pp. 155-64.

Trower, K.B. "Visions of Paradise in *The Great Gatsby*." *Renascence*, 25: 14-23 (Au 72).

Turlish, L.A. "*The Rising Tide of Color*: A Note on the Historicism of *The Great Gatsby*." *AL*, 43: 442-4 (N 71).

Turnbull, Andrew. "Consejos a un joven escritor." *CdLA*, 4: 78 (D 64).

Tuttleton, J.W. "The Presence of Poe in *This Side of Paradise*." *ELN*, 3: 284-9 (Je 66).

Wagner, Paul. "'I Just Can't See Daylight. . . .'" *FHA*, 1970, pp. 60-8.

Wang, Peter. "FLF som engageret forfatter." *Extracta*, 3: 315-21 (1971).

Way, Brian. "Situación de F." *CdLA*, 4: 85-99 (D 64).

Weaver, Richard. "The American as a Regenerate Being." *SoR*, 4: 633-40 (Su 68).

Webb, D.M. "F on EL Greco." *FHA*, 1975, pp. 89-91.

Wells, Elizabeth. "A Comparative Statistical Analysis of the Prose Styles of F. SF and Ernest Hemingway." *FHA*, 1969, pp. 47-67.

West, J.L. "The Corrections Lists for FSF's *This Side of Paradise*." *SB*, 26: 254-64 (1973).

West, J.L.W. "F.SF to Arnold Gingrich: A Composition Date for 'Dearly Beloved!'" *PBSA*, 67: 452-3 (O-D 73).

————. "F.SF's Contributions to *The American Credo.*" *PULC*, 34: 53-8 (Au 72).

————. "James Agee's Early Tribute to *Tender Is the Night.*" *FHA*, 1970, pp. 226-7.

————. "Matthew J. Bruccoli's F.SF: A Descriptive Bibliography." *Costerus*, 1: 165-76 (1974).

————. "Notes on the Text of F.SF's 'Early Success.'" *RALS*, 3: 73-99 (Sp 73).

————. "Mencken's Review of *Tales of the Jazz Age.*" *Menck*, 50: 2-4 (1974).

————. "The Wrong Duel in *Tender Is the Night.*" *FHA*, 1970, p. 231.

Wharton, Edith. "Letter to F." *FHA*, 1972, pp. 85-7.

Wheelock, A.S. "Paradise Regained: F on Campus." *Gypsy Schol*, 1: 60-3 (#1 73).

White, Eugene. "The 'Intricate Destiny' of Dick Diver." *MFS*, 7: 55-62 (Sp 61).

White, William. "Two More Hanneman Addenda." *HN*, 3: 14-5 (1973).

Wilkinson, Burke. "Andrew Turnbull, 1921-1970." *FHA*, 1970, pp. 266-7.

Williams, Harry. "An Epistle to Gatsby: On the Use of Riches." *FHA*, 1972, pp. 61-5.

Wingate, P.J. "Mencken and Gatsby." *Menck*, 55: 8-9 (Fa 75).

Winter, Keith. "Artistic Tensions: The Enigma of F.SF." *RSW*, 37: 285-97 (D 69).

Wycherley, H.A. "The F Fad." *CEA*, 36: 29-30 (#2 74).

Yates, D.A. "The Road to 'Paradise': F's Literary Apprenticeship." *MFS*, 7: 19-31 (Sp 61).

Young, Philip, and C.W. Mann. "F's *Sun Also Rises*: Notes and Comments." *FHA*, 1970, pp. 1-9.

————. "SF on His Thirtieth Birthday Sends a Small Gift to Ernest Hemingway." *MFS*, 14: 229-30 (Su 68).

————. "SF's Waste Land." *KM*, 23: 73-7 (1956).

Fitzgerald, Robert. Bagg, Robert. "Translating the Abyss: On RF's Odyssey." *Arion*, 8: 51-65 (Sp 69).

Fitzgerald, Zelda Sayre. Anon. "Putting Zelda Back Centre of Stage." *TLS*, 1 Ja 71, p. 8.

Aaron, Daniel. "The Legend of the Golden Couple." *VQR*, 48: 157-60 (1972).

Fitzgerald, Zelda. "ZF's Tribute to F. Scott Fitzgerald." *FHA*, 1974, pp. 9-10.

Going, W.T. "Two Alabama Writers: ZSF and Sara Haardt Mencken." *ALaR*, 23: 3-29 (Ja 70).

Hamblen, A.A. "The Fs' Coming of Age." *UR*, 35: 157-60 (D 68).

Littleton, Taylor. "A Letter from ZF." *FHA*, 1974, pp. 3-6.

Milford, Nancy. "The Golden Dreams of ZF." *HM*, 238: 46-53 (ja 69).

Samuels, C.T. "A Woman's Place." *NRep*, 162: 24-7 (27 Je 70).

Schorer, Mark. "Zelda; or What's in a Name?" *Atl*, 226: 104-6 (Ag 70).

Fletcher, John Gould. Behrens, Ralph. "JGF, Poet of Paradoxes." *Arkansas Lib*, 28: 9-13 (Su 71).

Lund, M.G. "JGF, Geographer of the Uncharted Province of Beauty." *SR*, 76: 76-89 (Wi 68).

Flint, Roland. Gardner, Isabella. "A Few Words about RF." *MinnR*, 8: 210-2 (1968).

Hiner, James. "A Dozen by FR." *MinnR*, 8: 208-9 (1968).

Flint, Timothy. Vorpahl, B.M. "The Eden Theme and Three Novels by TF." *SRom*, 10: 105-29 (Sp 71).

Flower, Benjamin Orange. Rueben, P.P. "Thoreau in B.O.F's *Arena.*" *TSB*, 117: 5-6 (Fa 71).

Foote, Mary Hallock. Been, M.L. "MHF in Idaho." *Un Wyoming Pub*, 20: 157-78 (15 Jl 56).

*Etulain, Richard. "MHF: A Checklist." *WAL*, 10: 59-65 (My 75).

————. "MHF (1847-1938)." *ALR*, 5: 145-50 (Sp 72).

Foote, Shelby. Appleman, Philip. "Another Modernized 'Shipman's Tale.'" *CE*, 18: 168-9 (D 56).

Carr, John. "It's Worth a Grown Man's Time: An Interview with SF." *Contempora*, 1: 2-16 (1970).

Garrett, G.P. "Talking with SF—June 1970." *MissQ*, 24: 405-27 (Fa 71).

Gresset, Michel. "SF." *NRF*, 269: 40-6 (My 74).

Harrington, Evans. "Interview with SF." *MissQ*, 24: 349-77 (Fa 71).

*Kibler, J.E. "SF: A Bibliography." *MissQ*, 24: 437-65 (Fa 71).

Landess, T.H. "Southern History and Manhood: Major Themes in the Works of SF." *MissQ*, 24: 321-47 (Fa 71).

Rubin, L.D. "SF's Civil War." *Prospects*, 1: 313-33 (1975).

Shepherd, Allen. "Technique and Theme in SF's *Shiloh*." *NMW*, 5: 3-10 (Sp 72).

Vauthier, Simone. "Fiction and Fictions in SF's 'Rain Down Home.'" *NMW*, 8: 35-50 (Fa 75).

———. "The Symmetrical Design: The Structural Patterns of *Love in a Dry Season*." *MissQ*, 24: 379-403 (Fa 71).

Williams, Wirt. "SF's *Civil War*: The Novelist as Humanistic Historian." *MissQ*, 24: 429-36 (Fa 71).

Ford, Jesse Hill. Ford, J.H. "The Journal of the Plague Trip." *DelR*, 7: 56, 58 (My-Je 70).

———. "Let's Take an Old Fashioned Walk." *DelR*, 7: 7-8 (Fa 70).

———. "Slaving in California." *DelR*, 5: 20 (N 68).

———. "A Southern Notebook." *DelR*, 5: 48-9 (F 68).

———. "To a Young Southern Writer." *SoR*, 4: 291-8 (Sp 68).

Hicks, Granville. "Literary Horizons." *SatR*, 52: 22 (8 F 69).

McKinley, James. "An Interview with JHF." *Contempora*, 2: 1-7 (1972).

Matthews, Jack. "What Are You Doing There? What Are You Doing Here? A View of the JHF Case." *GaR*, 26: 121-44 (Su 72).

Ford, Paul Leicester. Anon. "Two American Writers." *Outlook*, 71: 157-8 (17 My 02).

Kane, Patricia. "PLF: An Unrealistic 'Realist.'" *JPC*, 7: 569-81 (1973).

Foreman, Richard. Davy, Kate. "F's Pain(t) and Vertical Mobility." *DramR*, 18: 26-37 (Je 74).

Kirby, Michael. "RF's Ontological-Hysteric Theatre." *DramR*, 17: 5-32 (Je 73).

Forester, Frank. (see **Henry, William Herbert**).

Foster, George G. Taylor, G.R. "'Philadelphia in Slices,' by GG.F." *PMHB*, 93: 23-72 (1969).

Fox, John, Jr. Anon. "JF, Jr. and His Kentucky." *Nation*, 109: 72-3 (19 Jl 19).

———. "When JF Danced His Last Dance." *Lit Dig*, 87: 70-1 (17 O 25).

*Dunlap, Mary. "JF, Jr." *ALR*, 8: 249-50 (1975).

Holman, H.R. "Interlude: Scenes from John Fox's Courtship of Fritzi Sheff, as Reported by Richard Harding Davis." *SLJ*, VII: 77-86 (Sp 75).

———. "JF, Jr.: Appraisal and Self-Appraisal. *Personal Sketch by JF, Jr.* (1908)." *SLJ*, 3: 18-38 (Sp 71).

Titus, W.I. "JF, Jr. (1862-1919)." *ALR*, 3: 5-8 (Su 68).

Tucker, E.L. "JF, Jr.: Bon Vivant and Mountain Chronicler." *VaCal*, 21: 18-29 (Sp 72).

Francis, H.E. Anon. "H.E.F: Bibliography." *DLAJ*, 4: 83-7 (1970).

———. "H.E.F: Biography." *DLAJ*, 4: 80-2 (1970).

Benedetto, Antono di. "F Migratorio." *DLAJ*, 4: 48-50 (1970).

Francis, H.E. "Letters to Molly." *DLAJ*, 4: 52-65 (1970).

Hollingsworth, Mary. "The Setting for the Novel *Death in Argentina*." *DLAJ*, 4: 40-7 (1970).

Toso, L.T. de. "Notes on H.E.F in Argentina." *DLAJ*, 4: 78-79 (1970).

Welker, R.L. "Something of H.E.F, of Happening, of Becoming." *DLAJ*, 4: 26-39 (Wi 70).

Francis, Robert. Anon. "RF: Worksheets." *MalR*, 4: 114-8 (1967).

———. "The Satirical Rogue Once More: RF on Poets and Poetry." *Courier*, 8: 36-9 (1971).

Frank, Waldo. Adams, Mildred. "WF: Sage and Simpleton." *Review 74*, (Sp 74), pp. 53-9.

Cúneo, Dardo. "Perspectiva americana de WF." *CA*, 158: 95-100 (1968).

Ocampo, Victoria. "Letter to WF." *Review 74*, (Sp 74), pp. 51-2.

Toman, S.F. "WF y su ideal americano." *Américas*, 25: 17-24 (My 73).

Walt, James. "Mixed Arrogance and Timidity." *NRep*, 169: 25-26 (21 Jl 73).

Franklin, Benjamin. Aldridge, A.L. "Camilo Henriquez and the Fame of Thomas Paine and BF in Chile." *RIB*, 17: 51-67 (1967).

Aldridge, A.O. "Polly Baker and Boccaccio." *AION SR*, 14: 5-18 (1972).

Amacher, R.E. "A New F Satire?" *EAL*, 7: 103-110 (Fa 72).

Banta, Martha. "Benjamin, Edgar, Humbert, and Jay." *YR*, 60: 532-49 (Je 71).

Bier, Jesse. "Weberism, F, and the Transcendental Style." *NEQ*, 43: 179-92 (Je 70).

Boswell, J.C. "Old Ben Bastardized." *EAL*, 8: 78-80. (Su 73).

Bridgewater, D.W. "New Accessions for the Franklin Collection." *YULG*, 45: 69-72 (O 70).

Buxbaum, M.H. "BF and William Smith: Their School and Their Dispute." *HMPEC*, 39: 361-82 (1970).

———. "F Looks for a Rector: Poor Richard's Hostility to Presbyterians." *JPH*, 48: 176-88 (1970).

———. "Hume, F, and America: A Matter of Loyalties." *EnE*, 3: 93-105 (1972).

Colombo, R.M. "BF e la sagistica di costume." *AFLFUM*, 3-4: 189-214 (1970-71).

D'Avanzo, M.L. "In the Name of Pudd'nhead." *MTJ*, 16: 13-4 (Su 72).

Egnal, Marc. "The Politics of Ambition: A New Look at BF's Career." *CRAS*, 6: 151-64 (Fa 75).

England, A.B. "Robin Molineux and the Young BF: A Rconsideration." *JAmSt*, 6: 181-8 (Ag 72).

———. "Some Thematic Patterns in F's *Autobiography*." *ECS*, 5: 421-30 (1972).

Ensor, Allison. "The Downfall of Poor Richard: BF as Seen by Hawthorne, Melville, and Mark Twain." *MTJ*, 17: 14-8 (Wi 74-5).

Evans, W.B. "John Adams' Opinion of BF." *PMHB*, 92: 220-38 (Ap 68).

Gallagher, E.J. "The Rhetorical Strategy of F's 'Way to Wealth.'" *ECS*, 6: 475-85 (1973).

Golladay, V.D "The Evolution of BF's Theory of Value." *PH*, 37: 40-52 (Ja 70).

Grenander, M.E. "BF's Armonia in Henry James's 'Jolly Corner.'" *PLL*, 11: 415-7 (1975).

———. "BF's String Quartet." *EAL*, 7: 183-6 (Fa 72).

———. "Reflections on the String Quartet(s) Attributed to F." *AQ*, 27: 73-87 (Mr 75).

Griffith, John. "The Rhetoric of F's *Autobiography*." *Criticism*, 13: 77-94 (Wi 71).

Hall, Max. "An Amateur Detective on the Trail of B.F, Hoaxer." *PMHS*, 84: 26-43 (1972).

Hay, C.H., et al. "BF, James Burgh, and the Authorship of 'The Colonist's Advocate' Letters." *WMQ*, 32: 111-24 (Ja 75).

Hutson, J.H. "B.F and Pennsylvania Politics, 1751-1755: A Reappraisal." *PMHB*, 93: 303-71 (Jl 1969).

———. "BF and the West." *Western Hist Q*, 4: 425-34 (O 73).

Ilie, Paul. "F and Villarroel: Social Consciousness in Two Autobiographies." *ECS*, 7: 321-42 (1974).

Knollenberg, Bernard. "BF and the Hutchinson and Oliver Letters." *YULG*, 47: 1-9 (Jl 72).

Kushen, Betty. "Three Earliest Published Lives of BF, 1790-93." *EAL*, 9: 39-52 (Sp 74).

Labaree, L.W. "BF and the Defense of Pennsylvania, 1754-1757." *PH*, 29: 7-23 (Ja 62).

Larson, D.M. "F on the Nature of Man and the Possibility of Virtue." *EAL*, 10: 111-20 (Fa 75).

Lemay, J.A.L. "The New Franklin Texts." *CEAAN*, 2: 6-8 (1969).

Lively, B.R. "William Smith, the College and Academy of Philadelphia, and Pennsylvania Politics 1753-1758." *HMPEC*, 38: 237-58 (S 69).

L, L.S. "News for Bibliophiles." *Nation*, 96: 494-6 (15 My 13).

McLaughlin, J.J. "His Brother's Keeper: F's Sibling Rivalry." *SAB*, 38: 62-9 (N 73).

———, and R.R. Ansbacher. "Sane BF: An Adlerian View of His Autobiography." *JIP*, 27: 189-207 (1971).

Maestro, Marcello. "BF and the Penal Laws." *JHI*, 36: 551-62 (1975).

Marrocco, W.T. "The String Quartet Attributed to BF." *PAPS*, 116: 477-85.

Miller, C.W. "BF's Way to Wealth." *PBSA*, 63: 231-46 (4Q 69).

Miller, Ross. "Autobiography as Fact and Fiction: F, Adams, Malcolm X." *CentR*, 16: 221-32 (Su 72).

Morris, R.B. "Meet Dr. F." *AH*, 23: 81-91 (D 71).

Morris, Richard. "Dr. F and Mr. Jay: Conversations in Paris." *CLC*, 24: 10-7 (F 75).

Neal, E.L. "BF: A Bibliographical Note." *Serif*, 4: 30 (#4 67).

Ohmann, Carol. "The Autobiography of Malcolm X: A Revolutionary Use of the F Tradition." *AQ*, 22: 131-49 (Su 70).

Parker, P.L. "Two Puritan Doers of Good: BF and Cotton Mather." *Eng R*, 1, 32-49 (#1 73).

Rose, Harriet. "Towards the Pleasure Principle: Character Revelation in BF's *To the Royal Academy*." *Paunch*, 35: 16-25 (F 72).

Rosenberry, E.H. "Israel Potter, BF, and the Doctrine of Self-Reliance." *ESQ*, 28: 27-9 (3Q 62).

Russell, Jack. "*Israel Potter* and 'Song of Myself.'" *AL*, 40: 72-7 (Mr 68).

Sappenfield, J.A. "*The Autobiography of BF*: The Structure of Success." *WSL*, 6: 90-9 (1969).

———. "The Bizarre Death of Daniel Rees and the Continuity of F Criticism." *EAL*, 4: 73-85 (Fa 69).

Sloan, Sheldon. "Parson Weems on F's Death." *PMHB*, 96: 369-76 (1972).

Smith, Julian. "Orson Welles and the Great American Dummy—Or, the Rise and Fall and regeneration of BF's Model American." *LFQ*, 2: 196-206 (1974).

Smith, P.H. "BF: Gunrunner." *PMHB*, 95: 526-9 (1971).

Sokolow, J.A. "Arriving at Moral Perfection': BF and Leo Tolstoy." *AL*, 47: 427-31 (N 75).

Spiller, R.E. "BF—Pragmatist." *Gen Mag & Hist Chron*, 44: 48-61 (O 41).

Stowell, Maron. "American Almanacs and Feus." *EAL*, 9: 276-85 (Wi 75).

Tatham, Campbell. "BF, Cotton Mather, and the Outward State." *EAL*, 6: 223-33 (Wi 71-72).

Tourtellot, A.B. "The Early Reading of BF." *HLB*, 23: 5-41 (1975).

VanDerBeets, Richard. "Milton in Early America: The Example of BF." *MiltonQ*, 6: 33-6 (1972).

Vittorini, Elio. "An Outline of American Literature." *SR*, 68: 423-37 (Su 60).

Volkovitinov, N.N. "B.F i M.V. Lomonsov." *Novaja i novejsaja istorija*, 3: 77-81 (My-Je 73).

Willis, Kirk. "The Background of BF's Imperial Apostasy, 1751-1766." *PH*, 40: 123-36 (Ap 73).

Zall, P.M. "Letter to the Editor." *EAL*, 10: 220-1 (Fa 75).

Frederic, Harold. *Anon. "HF (1856-1898): A Critical Bibliography of Secondary Comment." *ALR*, 2: 1-72 (Sp 68).

———. "Theron's Rondeau (Apologies to L.H.)." *FH*, 3: 6 (S 69).

Aten, Daniel. "Proper Names in F: *Seth's Brother's Wife*." *FH*, 2: 2 (S 68).

Atherton, Gertrude. "The American Novel in England." *Bkm*, 30: 633-40 (F 10).

Bigsby, C.W.E. "The 'Christian Science Case': An Account of the Death of HF and the Subsequent Inquest and Court Proceedings." *ALR*, 2: 77-83 (Sp 68).

Blackhall, J.F "F's *Gloria Mundi* as a Novel of Education." *MarkR*, 3: 41-6 (My 72).

———. "FH: A Provocative Revision." *N&Q*, 20: 257-60 (Jl 73).

———. "Perspectives on HF's *Market-Place*." *PMLA*, 86: 388-405 (My 71).

Bredahl, Jr. A.C. "The Artist in *The Dammation of Theron Ware*." *StN*, 4: 432-41 (Fa 72).

Briggs, Austin. "Correction: 'A HF First,' by Stanton B. Garner." *SB*, 17: 252 (1964).

———. "F's Review of Gissing's *Whirlpool*." *FH*, 2: 3 (Ja 69).

Buck, S.J. "Manuscripts." *LCQJCA*, 6: 80-94 (My 49).

Carter, Everett. "HF." *AL*, 35: 251-2 (My 63).

Cheshire, David and Malcolm Bradbury. "American Realism and the Romance of Europe: Fuller, F, Harland." *PAH*, 4: 285-310 (1970).

*Crisler, J.S. "HF." *ALR*, 8: 250-5 (1975).

Crowley, J.W. "The Nude and the Madonna in *The Damnation of Theron Ware*." *AL*, 45: 379-389 (N 73).

Dalton, D.C. "MacEvoy's Room." *FH*, 3: 5 (S 69).

Donaldson, Scott. "The Seduction of Theron Ware." *NCF*, 29: 441-52 (Mr 75).

Eichelberger, C.L. "F and the City-Country Motif." *FH*, 2: 4 (S 68).

———. "Philanthropy in F's *The Market Place*." *AQ*, 20: 111-6 (Sp 68).

*———, et al. "HF (1856-1898): A Critical Bibliography of Secondary Comment." *ALR*, 2: 1-70 (Sp 68).

Fortenberry, George. "Proper Names in F . . . *Candace*." *FH*, 2: 5 (Ap 68).

Garmon, G.M. "Naturalism and *The Damnation of Theron Ware*." *WGCR*, 2: 44-51 (1969).

Garner, Stanton. "F and Elsie Venne." *FH*, 3: 5 (Ja 70).

———. "F's Contract for 'Kenley,' An Unwritten Novel." *FH*, 2: 3 (S 68).

———. "F and Swinburne's 'Locrine': A Matter of Clubs, Copyrights, and Character." *AL*, 45: 285-92 (My 73).

———. "Kate Lyon—Author." *FH*, 1: 2 (S 67).

———. "More Notes on HF in Ireland." *AL*, 39: 560-2 (Ja 68).

———. "The Publishing History of HF: a Correction." *BBr*, 22: 95-101 (1968).

———. "Some Notes on HF in Ireland." *AL*, 39: 60-74 (Mr 67).

Genthe, C.V. "New York Farm Values, 1870-1890." *FH*, 2: 3 (Ap 68).

Gilkes, Lillian. "F, Crane, and the Stallman Biography." *FH*, 3: 4 (Ap 69).

———. "George Gissing on the F Scandal." *FH*, 2: 3 (S 68).

———. "Stephen Crane and the HFs." *Serif*, 6: 21-48 (D 69).

Gorlier, Claudio. "*The Damnation of Theron Ware*." *Approdo*, 61: 133-5 (1973).

Haight, G.S. "The John William De Forest Collection." *YULG*, 14: 41-6 (Ja 40).

Howells, W.D. "A Political Novelist and More." *NAR*, 192: 93-100 (Jl 10).

Jones, A.E. "Darwinism and Its Relationship to Realism and Naturalism in American Fiction, 1860-1900." *DUB*, 38: 18 (D 50).

Katz, Joseph. "*BAL* Addendum: HF's 'Gloria Mundi—Entry 6293." *PBSA*, 63: 197-8 (3Q 69).

———. "F's Endorsement of the Roycrofters." *FH*, 2: 5 (Ap 68).

———. "HF's *March Hares*: A Bibliographical Note." *Serif*, 6: 36-8 (Mr 69).

LeClair, Thomas. "The Ascendant Eye: A Reading of *The Damnation of Theron Ware*." *SAF*, 3: 95-102 (Sp 75).

Long, R.E. "Dreiser and F: The Upstate New York Exile of Dick Diver." *FitzN*, 37: 1-2 (Sp 67).

Luedtke, Luther. "HF's Satanic Solusby: Interpretation and Sources." *NCF*, 30: 82-104 (Je 75).

McFee, William. "Let's Keep Them Alive: Reclamation Project for All Undeservedly Forgotten Books." *Coronet*, 1: 140-2 (Mr 37).

Mills, J.C. "Israel and the Barbarian: F as Observer of the Russian Scene." *FH*, 2: 6 (Ja 69).

Milne, W.G. "F's 'Free' Woman." *ALR*, 6: 258-60 (1973).

Monteiro, George. "F and The Atlantic Monthly." *FH*, 3: 3 (Ja 70).

———. "F's Visit with the 'Omarians.'" *FH*, 2: 2 (S 68).

———. "HF: An Unrecorded Review." *PBSA*, 63: 30-1 (1Q 69).

O'Donnell, T.F. "The Baxter Marginalia: Theron Ware à Clef." *FH*, 1: 5 (Ja 68).

———. "A Binder's Error in First American *DTW*, *FH*, 3: 5 (S 69).

———. "F as Bit Player in *The Little Minister*." *FH*, 3: 2 (S 69).

———. "The Greenwood F: A Comment." *FH*, 3: 1 (S 69).

———. "HFL: Utica's Forgotten Wonder Boy." NCL, 8: 6-10 (Sp 54).

———. "More about Rev. Theron Cooper . . . and a Correction." *FH*, 1: 2 (Ja 68).

———. "Proper Names in F . . . Theron." *FH*, 1: 5 (S 67).

———. "Proper Names in F . . . / Celia Madden." *FH*, 1: 4 (Ja 68).

———. "Proper Names in F . . . / St. Thomas Didymus." *FH*, 2: 5 (Ja 69).

———. "Theron Ware, the Irish Picnic, and *Comus*." *AL*, 46: 528-37 (Ja 75).

———. 'Theron Ware's Octavius—Then and Now." *FH*, 2: 1 (Ja 69).

———. "Two More F Landmarks." *FH*, 3: 1 (Ap 69).

———. "Ware's 'Hour's Sharp Walk.'" *FH*, 3: 3 (S 69).

———, and Lillian Gilkes. "Hall Caine, R.W. Stallman, and 'The Kate Lyon Fund.'" *FH*, 2: 4 (Ja 69).

Payne, A.J. "HF and Howells: The Saloon as Setting." *FH*, 2: 4 (Ap 68).

Rees, J.O. "'Dead Men's Bones, Dead Men's Bones': Ideas of Antiquity in Upstate New York and *Theron Ware*." *AmS*, 16: 77-87 (#2 75).

Sage, Howard. "HF's Narrative Essays: A Realistic-Journalistic Genre." *ALR*, 3: 388-92 (Fa 70).

Schorer, Mark. "Reading: Clues to the College Mind." *CalM*, nv: 13-5, 44-5 (N 62).

Sloane, D.E. "The 'Country Boy' Epithet." *FH*, 2: 1 (Ap 68).

———. "John Hay's The Bread-Winners as Literary Realism." *ALR*, 2: 277 (Fa 69).

Solensten, John. "Hoe, Hoe, Alice: The Corrupt Garden in *Theron Ware*." *FH*, 2: 4 (Ap 68).

Spangler, George. "Theron Ware and the Perils of Relativism." *CRAS*, 5: 36-45 (Sp 74).

Steele, M.R. "F as Philatelist: An Unpublished Letter." *FH*, 3: 5 (Ap 69).

———. "Ware's Post-Seattle Career Dept." *FH*, 3: 6 (S 69).

Stein, A.F. "Evasions of an American Adam: Structure and Theme in *The Damnation of Theron Ware*." *ALR*, 5: 23-36 (Wi 72).

Stronks, James. "Two F Leters to Garland." *FH*, 3: 4 (S 69).

Strother, Garland. "The Control of Distance in *Theron Ware*." *FH*, 3: 4 (S 69).

———. "Shifts in Point of View in *Theron Ware*." *FH*, 3: 2 (Ap 69).

Suderman, E.F. "*The Damnation of Theron Ware* as a Criticism of American Religious Thought." *HLQ*, 33: 61-75 (N 69).

———. "A Study of the Revival in Late Nineteenth-Century American Fiction." *MethH*, 5: 18-29 (Ja 67).

VanDerBeets, Richard. "HF and Comic Realism: The 'Drama Proper' of *Seth's Brother's Wife.*" *AL*, 39: 553-60 (Ja 68).

———. "Kissing Cousins and Narrative Management in *Seth.*" *FH*, 2: 3 (Ap 68).

Wasserstrom, William. "The Spirit of Myrrha." *AI*, 13: 455-72 (Wi 56).

Williams, David. "The Nature of the Damnation of Theron Ware." *MSE*, 2: 41-8 (Fa 69).

Wilson, Edmund. "Two Neglected American Novelists: HF: The Expanding Upstater." *NY*, 46: 112-34 (6 Je 70).

Woodward, R.H. "An Ancestor of Robert Coover's Mrs. Grundy." *NCLit*, 3: 11-2 (Ja 73).

———. "Frank Norris and F: A Source for *McTeague.*" *FH*, 2: 2 (Ap 68).

———. "The F Bibliographies: Errata." *FH*, 3: 3 (Ap 69).

———. "A F Scrapbook Catalog." *FH*, 3: 2 (Ap 69).

———. "F's Collection of Reviews." *ALR*, 2: 84-9 (Sp 68).

———. "George Gissing on F." *FH*, 2: 2 (Ja 69).

———. "A Ghost Edition of *Theron Ware.*" *FH*, 1: 4 (Ja 68).

———. "HF: A Critical Study." *ResBul*, 4: 10 (8 Je 62).

*———. "HF: Supplemental Critical Bibliography of Secondary Comment." *ALR*, 3: 95-147 (Sp 70).

———. "A HF Research Project." *LN*, 2: 1 (Ja 61).

———. "Illusion and Moral Ambivalence in *Seth's Brother's Wife.*" *ALR*, 2: 279-82 (Fa 69).

———. "MacEvoy's Fatal Fall in *Theron Ware.*" *FH*, 3: 4 (Ja 70).

———. "Master's Theses on F." *FH*, 3: 2 (S 69).

———. "Readers' Queries." *BAASB*, 4: 74 (Ag 62).

———. "Reuben Tracy and S.S. McClure: Self-Made Men." *FH*, 2: 5 (S 68).

———. "A Selection of HF's Early Literary Criticism, 1877-1881." *ALR*, 5: 1-22 (Wi 72).

———. "The Writings of HF." *PoetB*, 1: 1 (O 60).

———, and Stanton Garner. "F's Short Fiction: A Checklist." *ALR*, 2: 73-6 (Sp 68).

Zlotnick, Joan. "The Damnation of Theron Ware, with a Backward Glance at Hawthorne." *MarkR*, 2: 90-2 (F 71).

Frederick, J.T. Bush, Sargent. "The Achievement of JT.F." *BI*, 14: 8-30 (Ap 71).

Freeman, Mary E. Wilkins. Fortenberry, George. "Proper Names in Frederick . . . *Candace.*" *FH*, 2: 5 (Ap 68).

Gallagher, E.J. "F's 'The Revolt of Mother.'" *Expl*, 27: 48 (Mr 69).

Kendrick, B.L. "ME.WF." *ALR*, 8: 255-7 (1975).

Levy, B.M. "Mutations in New England Local Color." *NEQ*, 19: 338-58 (S 46).

Macy, John. "The Passing of the Yankee." *BkM*, 73: 612-21 (Ag 31).

Monteiro, Geroge. "Addenda to Foster's *F.*" *PBSA*, 69: 407 (3Q 75).

O'Connor, R.B. "BAL Addenda: M.E.W.F—Entry No. 6380." *PBSA*, 61: 127 (2Q 67).

Quina, J.H. "Character Types in the Fiction of MWF." *CLQ*, 9: 432-9 (1971).

Toth, S.A. "Defiant Light: A Positive View of *MWR,*" *NEQ*, 46: 82-93 (Mr 73).

———. "MWF's Parable of Wasted Life." *AL*, 42: 546-7 (Ja 71).

Tutwiler, J.R. "Two New England Writers—In Relation to Their Art and to Each Other." *Gunton's*, 25: 419-25 (N 03).

Warner, S.T. "Item, One Empty House." *NY*, 42: 131-8 (26 Mr 66).

Westbrook, P.D. "ME.WF (1852-1930." *ALR*, 2: 139-41 (Su 69).

French, Alice. McQuin, S.C. "AF's View of Women." *BI*, 20: 34-42 (1974).

Freneau, Philip. Andrews, W.L. "Goldsmith and F in 'The American Village.'" *EAL*, 5: 14-23 (Fa 70).

Arner, R.D. "Neoclassicism and Romanticism: A Reading of F's 'The Wild Honey Suckle.'" *EAL*, 9: 53-61 (Sp 74).

Batten, C.L. "A Newly Discovered Poem by PF on the Death of General Moreau." *AL*, 44: 457-9 (N 72).

Collins, J.F. "Two Last Poems of F." *EAL*, 7: 111-9 (Fa 72).

Colombo, R.M. "La prosa di PF." *SA*, 13: 37-74 (1967).

Cowan, T.D. "PF: The Artist in the Early Republic." *PNJHS*, 92: 225-39 (1974).

Cronkhite, G.F. "F's 'The House of Night.'" *CLJ*, 8: 3-19 (1969).

Eckert, E.K. "PF: New Jersey's Poet as Propagandist." *NSH*, 88: 25-42 (1970).

Grotta, G.L. "PF's Crusade for Open Sessions of the U.S. Senate." *JQ*, 48: 66-71 (Wi 71).

Itzkowitz, M.E. "F's 'Indian Burying Ground's and Keats' 'Grecian Urn.'" *EAL*, 6: 258-62 (Wi 71-72).

Kyle, C.A. "That Poet Freneau: A Study of the Imagistic Success of *The Pictures of Columbus*." *EAL*, 9: 62-70 (Sp 74).

Leary, Lewis. "Addendum to BAL: F's *Poems Relating to the American Revolution*." *PBSA*, 67: 329-30 (3Q 73).

Marsh, Philip. "PF to Peter Freneau." *JRUL*, 10: 28-30 (D 46).

Mason, Julian. "Madison's August 1791 Letter Praising F." *EAL*, 9: 325-8 (Wi 75).

Opku, S.K. "PF and the Red Indian." *Asemka*, 1: 83-98 (1974).

Peden, William. "Jefferson, F, and the Poems of 1809." *New Colophon*, 1: 394-400 (O 48).

Pulda, A.H. "PF and the *National Gazette*." *Am Chron*, 1: 54-8 (Ja 72).

Reed, K.T. "PF as Political Satirist." *AN&Q*, 7: 147-9 (Je 69).

Smeall, J.F.S. "The Respective Roles of Brackenridge and F in Composing *The Rising Glory of America*." *PBSA*, 67: 263-82 (3Q 73).

Friedman, Bruce Jay. Anon. "An Interview." *Notre Dame R*, 1: 16-9 (74).

Lewis, Stuart. "Myth and Ritual in the Short Fiction of BJF." *SSF*, 10: 415-6 (1974).

———. "Myth and Ritual in the Short Fiction of BJF." *SSF*, 10: 14-5 (1973).

———. "Rootlessness and Alienation in the Novels of BJF." *CLAJ*, 18: 422-33 (Mr 75).

Numasawa, Koji. "Everyman/Schlemiel." *EigoS*, 114: 516-7 (1968).

Pinsker, Sanford. "The Graying of Black Humor." *STC*, 9: 15-33 (Sp 72).

Schulz, M.F. "Wallant and F: The Glory and the Agony of Love." *Critique*, 10: 31-47 (1968).

Frost, Robert. Anon. "The Mertins Collection of RF." *Bancroftiana*, 55: 11-2 (Je 73).

———. "A Writer of Poems: The Life and Work of RF." *TLS*, 16 Ap 71, pp. 433-4.

Abad, G.H. "Stopping by Woods: The Hermeneutics of a Lyric Poem." *DilR*, 20: 25-40 (1972).

Aldridge, J.W. "F Removed from Olympus." *SatR*, 53: 21-3, 29-30 (15 Ag 70).

Allen, Ward. "RF's 'Iota Subscript.'" *ELN*, 6: 285-7 (Je 69).

Anderson, C.R. "On RF's *Stopping By Woods on a Snowy Evening*." *KAL*, 10: 1-10 (1967).

Asnani, S.M. "Dard, Deep and Lovely Woods of RF." *BP*, 14: 45-57 (1970).

Bache, W.B. "Rationalization in Two F Poems." *BSUF*, 11: 33-5 (Wi 70).

Bacon, H.H. "In and Outdoor Schooling: RF and the Classics." *ASch*, 43: 640-9 (Au 74).

Ballantine, L.F. "Somewhat Atavistic." *BSUF*, 11: 3-6 (Wi 70).

Barnes, D.R. "F's 'Putting in the Seed.'" *Expl*, 31: 59 (Ap 73).

Barrett, C.W. "*Twilight*: RF's First Book." *Proof*, 4: 3-7 (1974).

Bartlett, Donald. "Two Recollections of F." *SoR*, 2: 842-6 (Au 66).

Basile, J.L. "The Playful Profundity of Thoreau and F." *TJQ*, 6: 22-3 (Ja 74).

Basler, R.P. "FR: Lobbyist for the Arts." *QJLC*, 31: 108-15 (1974).

———. "Yankee Vergil—RF in Washington." *Voyages*, 2: 8-22 (Sp 69).

Bass, Eben. "F's Poetry of Fear." *AL*, 43: 603-15 (Ja 72).

Berger, Harry. "Poetry as Revision: Interpreting RF." *Criticism*, 10: 1-22 (Wi 68).

Bleich, David. "RF and Cultural Popularity." *Sphinx*, 3: 21-40 (1975).

Borkat, R.F.S. "The Bleak Landscape of RF." *MwQ*, 16: 453-67 (Su 75).

Borroff, Marie. "RF's New Testament: Language and the Poem." *MP*, 69: 36-56 (Ag 71).

———. "RF's 'The Most of It.'" *Ventures*, 9: 76-82 (Fa 69).

Bosmajian, Hamida. "RF's 'The Gift Outright': Wish and Reality in History and Poetry." *AQ*, 22: 95-105 (Sp 70).

Bourdette, R.E., and M.M. Cohen. "F's 'Aim' and the Problem of Interpretation." *EngR*, 25: 53-63 (Sp 74).

Bowen, J.K. "The *Persona* in F's 'Mending Wall': Mended or Amended?" *CEA*, 31: 14 (N 68).

———. "Propositional and Emotional Knowledge in RF's 'The Death of the Hired Man,' 'The Fear,' and 'Home Burial.'" *CLAJ*, 20: 155-60 (D 68).

Boyd, J.D. "F's Grafting in His 'Birches.'" *Descant*, 16: 56-60 (Wi 72).

———. "RF's 'The Runaway': A Reading." *Descant*, 17: 50-6 (Wi 73).

Braverman, Albert, and Bernard Einbond. "F's 'Two Tramps in Mud Time.'" *Expl*, 29: 25 (N 70).

Broderick, J.C. "Not Quite Poetry: Analysis of a RF Manuscript." *Manuscripts*, 20: 28-31 (1968).

Brown, Terence. "RF's *In the Clearing*: An Attempt to Reestablish the *Persona* of the 'Kindly Grey Poet.'" *PLL*, 5 Supp: 110-8 (Su 69).

Buchloh, P.G. "Das Verhältnis des amerikanischen Dichters zum Staat, dargestellt an RF's 'The Gift Outright' und Randall Jarrell's 'The Death of the Ball Turret Gunner.'" *JA*, 13: 205-14 (1968).

Calhoun, Richard. "F in the Carolinas." *SCR*, 7: 3-12 (N 74).

Cane, Melville. "RF: An Intermittent Intimacy." *ASch*, 40: 158-66 (Wi 70-71).

Carpenter, T.P. "RF and Katherine Blunt: A Confrontation." *AN&Q*, 8: 35-7 (1969).

Carruth, Hayden. "RF." *Parnassus*, 3: 35-41 (#2 75).

Chamberlain, William. "The Emersonianism of RF." *ESQ*, 57: 61-6 (4Q 69).

Clark, D.R. "An Excursus upon the Criticism of RF's 'Directive.'" *Costerus*, 8: 37-56 (1973).

———. "RF: 'The Thatch' and 'Directive.'" *Costerus*, 7: 47-80 (1973).

Cohen, E.H. "RF in England: An Unpublished Letter." *NEQ*, 43: 285-7 (Je 70).

Collins, M.J. "A Note on F's 'Love and the Question'" *CP*, 8: 57-8 (#1 75).

Combellack, C.R.B. "F's 'Spring Pools.'" *Expl*, 30: 27 (N 71).

Cook, Marjorie. "The Complexity of Boundaries." *NCLit*, 5: 2-5 (#1 75).

Cook, R.L. "F on Analytical Criticism." *CE*, 17: 434-8 (My 56).

———. "RF: An Equilibrist's Field of Vision." *MR*, 15: 385-401 (Su 74).

———. "RF's Constellated Sky." *WHR*, 22: 189-98 (Su 68).

Corning, H.M. "RF: The Trial by Market." *Voices*, 184: 36-8 (My-Ag 64).

Cox, Keith. "A Syntactic Comparison of RF's '. . . Snowy Evening' and 'Desert Places.'" *BSUF*, 11: 25-8 (Wi 70).

Cox, S.H. "Mischief in RF's Ways of Teaching." *EdF*, 13: 171-7 (Ja 49).

Crane, J.St.C. "Issues and Binding Variants of RF's *A Boy's Will* and *North of Boston*." *Serif*, 8: 3-6 (S 71).

———. "The Printing History of *Twilight*." *Proof*, 4: 31-76 (1974).

D'Avanzo, M.L. "F's 'A Young Birch': A Thing of Beauty." *CP*, 3: 69-70 (Fa 70).

Davis, C.G. "F's 'Acquainted with the Night.'" *N&Q*, 10: 150-1 (Ap 63).

———. "F's 'An Old Man's Winter Night.'" *Expl*, 27: 19 (N 68).

Davison, Peter. "RF: His Own Tradition." *Atl*, 209: 100-1 (My 62).

———. "The Self-Realization of RF, 1911-1912." *NRep*, 170: 17-20 (Mr 74).

Day-Lewis, Cecil. "RF: 1874-1963." *Listener*, 69: 253 (7 F 63).

Dendinger, L.N. "The Ghoul-haunted Woodland of RF." *SAB*, 38: 87-94 (N 73).

———. "The Irrational Appeal of F's Dark, Deep Woods." *SoR*, ns: 2: 822-9 (O 66).

———. "RF in Birmingham." *BSUF*, 14: 47-52 (Su 73).

———. "RF: The Popular and the Central Poetic Images." *AQ*, 21: 792-804 (Wi 69).

Dianu, Romulus. "RF, sau dinastia poetillor patriarhali." *RoLit*, 2069, p. 19.

Dillingham, Richard. "The Value of Social Conservatism According to RF." *SAB*, 37: 61-5 (N 72).

Domina, Lyle. "The Experiential Mode in RF." *Re: A&L*, 4: 53-63 (Fa 70).

Dowell, Bob. "Revealing Incident as Technique in the Poetry of RF." *CEA*, 31: 12-3 (D 68).

Dowell, P.W. "Counter-Images and their Function in the Poety of RF." *TSL*, 14: 15-30 (1969).

Doxey, W.S. "F's 'Out, Out.'" *Expl*, 29: 70 (Ap 71).

Doyle, J.R. "A Reading of RF's 'Directive.'" *GaR*, 22: 501-8 (Wi 68).

Dube, Gunaker. "Autumn in F and Keats: A Study of Themes and Patterns." *LCrit*, 9: 84-8 (Su 71).

E., C.D. "F's 'The Road Not Taken.'" *Expl*, 17: 3 (My 59).

Eberhart, Richard. "RF in the Clearing." *SoR*, 11: 260-8 (Ap 75).

Eisenhard, John. "RF: Peasant Poet." *Scholastic*, 24: 28-9 (28 Ap 34).

Elkins, B.J. "The Spiritual Crisis in 'Stopping by Woods.'" *Cresset*, 35: 6-8 (F 72).

Elsbree, Langdon. "F and the Isolation of Man." *Claremont Q*, 7: 29-40 (1960).

Fairbanks, Jonathan. "The Deeper Roar in Poetry." *TQ*, 9: 105-10 (Sp 66).

Fisher, S.W. "RF and the Prime Ministers." *Yankee*, 38: 34-9 (D 74).

Fitzgerald, Gregory, and Paul Ferguson. "The F Tradition." *SWR*, 57: 108-17 (Sp 72).

Fleissner, R.F. "A Comment and Correspondence on RF." *LCrit*, 10: 67-72 (Su 73).

———. "F and Racism: The Evidence." *NALF*, 9: 118-9 (Wi 75).

———. "F and Tennyson." *AN&Q*, 14: 53-5 (1975).

———. "F's 'Moon Compasses.'" *Expl*, 32: 66 (1974).

———. "F's 'Not All There.'" *Expl*, 31: 33 (Ja 73).

———. "F's Response to Keats' Risibility." *BSUF*, 11: 40-3 (Wi 70).

Flint, F.C. "A Few Touches of F." *SoR*, 2: 830-8 (Au 66).

Foster, Richard. "Leaves Compared with Flowers: A Reading in RF's Poems." *NEQ*, 46: 403-23 (S 73).

Francis, R. "Shared Solitude of RF." *Forum*, 108: 193-7 (O 45).

Freedman, W. "F's 'The Pasture.'" *Expl*, 29: 80 (My 71).

French, Roberts. "Reading F: 'The Road Not Taken.'" *Eng Rec*, 26: 91-3 (Sp 75).

Frost, Lesley. "Certain Intensities." *BSUF*, 15: 3-8 (Su 74).

———. "RF Remembered." *Am Way*, 7: 12-7 (Mr 74).

Frost, Robert. "Part of a letter dated December 14, 1932." *Thomas F. Madigan's Autograph Album*, 1: 56 (D 33).

———. "A Trip to Currituck, Elizabeth City, and Kitty Hawk (1894)." *NCaF*, 16: 3-8 (1968).

Fukuda, Rikutaro. "F Shihen Chushaku." *EigoS*, 117: 642-3, 702-3, 770-1; 118: 28-9, 102-3, 160-1, 206-7, 286-7, 344-5, 404-5 (1972).

Gerber, P.L. "'My Rising Contemptuaries': RF Amid His Peers." *WHR*, 20: 135-41 (Sp 66).

Geyer, C.W. "A Poulterer's Pleasure: RF as Prose Humorist." *SSF*, 8: 589-99 (Fa 71).

Gierasch, Walter. "F's 'The Silken Tent.'" *Expl*, 30: 10 (S 71).

Goede, William. "The 'Code Hero' in F's 'Blueberries.'" *Disc*, 11: 33-41 (Wi 68).

Grade, A.E. "A Chronicle of RF's Early Reading, 1874-1899." *BNYPL*, 72: 611-28 (N 68).

Greiner, D.J. "Confusion and Form: RF as Nature Poet." *Disc*, 11: 390-402 (Su 68).

———. "'A Few Remarks and Acknowledgments': An Unpublished F Note." *N&Q*, 15: 294-5 (Ag 68).

———. "On Teaching RF's 'Sentence Sounds.'" *Eng Rec*, 21: 11-4 (O 70).

———. "RF, the Poet as Critic: An Analysis and a Checklist." *SCR*, 7: 48-60 (N 74).

———. "The Use of Irony in RF." *SAB*, 38: 52-0 (My 73).

Grieder, Josephine. "RF on Ezra Pound, 1913: Manuscript Corrections of 'Portrait d'une Femme.'" *NEQ*, 44: 301-5 (Je 71).

Griffith, Clark. "F and the American View of Nature." *AQ*, 20: 21-37 (Sp 68).

Guiguet, Jean. "Un-American Considerations on F's Poetry." *EAA*, 2: 105-17 (1964).

Gustfson, Richard. "The Paragon Style: F and Auden." *Poet & Critic*, 2: 35-42 (Fa 65).

Hall, D.J. "Painterly Qualities in F's Lyric Poetry." *BSUF*, 11: 9-13 (Wi 70).

Hands, C.B. "The Hidden Terror of RF." *EJ*, 58: 1162-8 (N 69).

Harris, Kathryn. "RF's Early Education in Science." *SCR*, 7: 13-33 (N 74).

Haffield, H.C. "F's 'The Masque of Reason.'" *Expl*, 4: 8 (N 45).

Haugh, R.F. "Intention and Achievement in F's Poetry." *Voices*, 184: 41-2 (My-Ag 64).

Haynes, D.T. "The Narrative Unity of *A Boy's Will*." *PMLA*, 87: 452-64 (Mr 72).

Heflin, Wilson. "A Note on F's 'Love and a Question.'" *N&Q*, 16: 262 (Jl 69).

Henry, Nat. "F's 'Stopping by Woods on a Snowy Evening.'" *Expl*, 32: 33 (Ja 74).

Herndon, J.A. "F's 'Oven Bird.'" *Expl*, 28: 64 (Ap 70).

Hiatt, David. "F's 'In White' and 'Design.'" *Expl*, 28: 41 (Ja 70).

Hiers, J.T. "RF's Quarrel with Science and Technology." *GaR*, 25: 182-205 (Su 71).

Hilsen, Herbert. "La parafrasis y su aplicacion a 'After Apple Picking' de RF." *Lenguaje*, 5: 287-9 (1973).

Holland N.N. "A Touching of Literary and Psychiatric Education." *Seminars in Psychiatry*, 5: 287-9 (1973).

Holtz, William. "Thermodynamics and the Comic and Tragic Modes." *WHR*, 25: 203-16 (Su 71).

Huston, J.D. "'The Wonder of Unexpected Supply': RF and a Poetry beyond Confusion." *CentR*, 13: 317-29 (Su 69).

Jacobson, Dan. "Vurry Amurk'n." *The Review*, 25: 3-10 (Sp 71).

Jäger, Dietrich. "Das Verhältnis zwischen Wirklichkeit und menschlicher Ordnung als thema der Lyrick. RF und Wallace Stevens im Vergleich mit europaischen Dichtern." *NS*, 17: 65-83 (F 68).

———. "RF und die Traditionen der Naturdictung: Die aussemenschliche Welt als Thema deutscher amerikanischer Lyriker des 20. Jahrhunderts." *LWU*, 1: 2-27 (1968).

James, Stuart. "RF: Afterflakes." *UDQ*, 8: 72-9 (Sp 73).

Jayne, Edward. "Up Against the 'Mending Wall': The Psychoanalysis of a Poem by F." *CE*, 34: 934-51 (Ap 73).

Jensen, A.E. "The Character of F." *SoR*, 2: 860-1 (Au 66).

Jepson, Edgar. "The Western School." *Little R*, 5: 4-9 (S 18).

Joyce, H.E. "A Few Personal Memories of RF." *SoR*, 2: 847-9 (Au 66).

Kantalk, V.Y. "Poetic Ambiguity in F." *WHR*, 28: 31-46 (Wi 74).

Kennedy, J.F. "Poetry and Power." *Atl*, 213: 53-4 (F 64).

Kern, A.C. "F's 'The Wood-Pile.'" *Expl*, 28: 49 (F 70).

Kielland-Lund, Erik. "RF: Poetry as Dialectics." *AmNor*, 4: 237-68 (1973).

Kittredge, Selwyn. "Stopping by the Woods on a Snowy Evening'—Without Tugging at the Reins." *Eng Rec*, 23: 37-9 (Fa 72).

Knapp, E.H. "F's 'Dust of Snow.'" *Expl*, 28: 9 (S 69).

Kobayashi, Janji. "RF no Shiron." *EigoS*, 119: 768-9 (1974).

Komamura, Toshio. "RF's View of Life and Death: A Development of 'Fire and Ice.'" *SELit*, 46: 117-28 (Mr 70).

Kulczynskyj, Wolodymyr. "The Technique of Story Telling in RF's Poems." *Construtura*, 1: 261-8 (1973).

Kyle C.A. "Emerson's 'Uriel' as a Source for F." *ESQ*, 58: 111 (1Q 70).

Laing, Alexander. "RF and Great Issues." *SoR*, 2: 855-9 (Au 66).

Laing, Dilys. "Interview with a Poet." *SoR*, 2: 850-4 (Au 66).

Lambdin, W.G. "F's 'The Oven Bird.'" *Expl*, 31: 3 (S 72).

Larson, M.R. "F Out of Chaos." *Eng Rec*, 17: 2-6 (Ap 67).

———. "No False Curves: RF on Education." *School and Soc*, 72: 177-80 (16 S 50).

Lawrence, Ralph. "Edward Thomas in Perspective." *English*, 12: 177-83 (Su 59).

Lehmberg, P.S. "Companion Poems in F's 'The Road Not Taken.'" *LCrit*, 11: 37-44 (#4 75).

Lentricchia, Frank. "Experience as Meaning: RF's 'Mending Wall.'" *CEA*, 34: 8-12 (My 72).

———. "RF: The Aesthetics of Voice and the Theory of Poetry." *Criticism*, 15: 28-42 (Wi 73).

Lerner, Laurence. "An Essay on Pastoral." *EIC*, 20: 275-97 (1970).

Lewis, A.O. "F's 'Departmental.'" *Expl*, 10: 7 (O 51).

Lieber, T.M. "RF and Wallace Stevens: 'What to Make of a Diminished Thing.'" *AL*, 47: 64-83 (Mr 75).

Lindner, C.M. "RF: Dark Romantic." *ArQ*, 29: 235-45 (Au 73).

———. "RF: 'In the American Grain.'" *ColQ*, 22: 469-79 (1974).

Linebarger, J.M. "Sources of F's 'The Vindictives.'" *AN&Q*, 12: 150-4 (My-Je 74).

Littlejohn, David. "On RF." *NRep*, 171: 23-4 (16 N 74).

———. "RF at 100: Still on Tour." *NRep*, 171: 23-4 (16 N 74).

Logan, H.M. "Some Applications of Linguistic Theory to Poetry." *HAB*, 21: 40-7 (Sp 70).

Love, G.A. "F's 'The Census-Taker' and de la Mare's 'The Listeners.'" *PLL*, 4: 198-200 (Sp 68).

Lycette, R.L. "The Vortex Points of RF." *BSUF*, 14: 54-9 (Su 73).

Macksey, R.A. "The Old Poets." *Johns Hopkins Mag*, 19: 42-8 (1968).

McLaughlin, C.A. "Two Voices of Poetic Unity." *Un Kansas City R*, 22: 309-16 (Su 56).

MacLeish, Archibald. "The Gift Outright." *Atl*, 213: 50-2 (F 64).

Marcus, Mordecai. "RF's 'Bound an Free.'" *CP*, 8: 61-4 (#1 75).

Martin, R.G. "Two Versions of a Poem by RF." *BSUF*, 11: 65-8 (Wi 70).

Martin, Wallace. "F's 'Acquainted with the Night.'" *Expl*, 26: 64 (Ap 68).

Marx, Leo. "Pastoral Ideals and City Troubles." *JGE*, 20: 251-71 (1969).

Mary Francele, Sister. "A Solution to the Structural Difficulties of F's 'Immigrants.'" *WSL*, 1: 94-8 (1964).

Mathias, Roland. "RF: An Appreciation." *Poetry R*, 38: 102-6 (Mr-Ap 47).

Meixner, J.A. "F Four Years After." *SoR*, 2: 862-77 (Au 66).

Miller, L.H. "The Poet as Swinger: Fact and Fancy in RF." *Criticism*, 16: 58-72 (Wi 74).

Monteiro, George. "Birches in Winter: Notes on Thoreau and F." *CLAJ*, 12: 129-33 (D 68).

———. "F's 'After Apple-Picking.'" *Expl*, 30: 62 (N 72).

———. "'Good Fences Make Good Neighbors': A Proverb and a Poem." *RdEt* 16: 83-8 (1972).

———. "Redemption through Nature: A Recurring Theme in Thoreau, F, and Richard Wilbur." *AQ*, 20: 795-809 (Wi 68).

———. ''RF and the Politics of Self.'' *BNYPL*, 73: 309-14 (My 69).

———. ''RF's Linked Analogies.'' *NEQ*, 46: 463-8 (S 73).

———. ''RF's Solitary Singer.'' *NEQ*, 44: 134-40 (Mr 71).

———. ''Unlinked Myth in F's 'Mending Wall.''' *CP*, 7: 10-1 (1974).

Mood, J.J.L. ''F's Dark Road Taken.'' *Rendezvous*, 10: 11-14 (1975).

Morris, John. ''The Poet as Philosopher: RF.'' *MQR*, 11: 127-34 (Sp 72).

Morrison, Theodore. ''F: Country Poet and Cosmopolitan Poet.'' *YR*, 59: 179-96 (Wi 70).

Morrow, Patrick. ''The Greek Nexus in RF's *West-Running Brook*.'' *Person*, 49: 24-33 (Wi 68).

Morse, Stearns. ''Lament for a Maker: Reminiscences of RF.'' *SoR*, 9: 53-68 (Ja 73).

———. ''The Phoenix and the Desert Places.'' *MR*, 9: 773-84 (1968).

———. ''Something Like a Star.'' *SoR*, 2: 839-41 (Au 66).

Nair, Ramachandran. ''From Delight to Wisdom: A Tribute to RF.'' *Mod R*, 137: 267-9 (Ap 75).

Narasimhaih, C.D. ''The Reputation of RF.'' *LCrit*, 9: 1-10 (Wi 69).

Narveson, Robert. ''On F's 'The Wood-Pile.''' *EJ*, 57: 39-40 (Ja 68).

Newdick, R.S. ''Design in the Books of RF.'' *Reading & Collections*, 1: 5-6, 15 (S 37).

———. ''The Early Verse of RF and Some of His Revisions.'' *AL*, 7: 181-7 (My 35).

———. ''Foreign Responses to RF.'' *Colophon*, ns, 2: 289-90 (Wi 37).

———. ''RF and the American College.'' *JHE*, 7: 237-43 (My 36).

———. ''RF and the Classics.'' *CJ*, 35: 403-16 (Ap 40).

———. ''RF and the Dramatic.'' *NEQ*, 10: 262-9 (Je 37).

———. ''RF and the Sound of Sense.'' *AL*, 9: 289-300 (N 37).

———. ''RF as Teacher.'' *EJ*, 25: 632-7 (O 36).

———. ''RF: Impressions and Observations.'' *Ohio Stater*, 2: 18-9 (My 36).

———. ''RF Looks at War.'' *SAQ*, 38: 52-9 (Ja 39).

———. ''RF Speaks Out.'' *SR*, 45: 239-41 (Ap-Je 37).

*———. ''RF, Teacher and Educator: An Annotated Bibliography.'' *JHE*, 7: 342-4 (Je 36).

———. ''RF's Other Harmony.'' *SR*, 48: 409-18 (Jl 40).

———. ''Some Notes on RF and Shakespeare.'' *Shakespeare Assn Bul*, 12: 187-9 (Jl 37).

———. ''Three Poems by RF.'' *AL*, 7: 329 (N 35).

———. ''Uncollected Poems of RF.'' *BC J*, 2: 1-2 (F 37).

Nilakantan, Mangalam. '''Something Beyond Conflict': A Study of the Dual Vision of RF.'' *LJAS*, 1: 25-34 (1969).

Osborne, W.R. ''F's 'The Oven Bird.''' *Expl*, 26: 47 (F 68).

Parsons, D.S.J. ''Night of Dark Intent.'' *PLL*, 6: 205-10 (sp 70).

Perrine, Laurence. ''The Dilemma in F's 'Love and a Question.''' *CP*, 5: 5-8 (1972).

———. ''F's 'An Empty Threat.''' *Expl*, 30: 63 (Ap 72).

———. ''F's 'Dust of Snow.''' *Expl*, 29: 61 (Mr 71).

———. ''F's 'Gathering Leaves.''' *CEA*, 34: 29 (N 71).

———. ''F's 'The Mountain': Concerning Poetry.'' *CP*, 4: 5-11 (Sp 71).

———. ''F's 'The Rose Family.''' *Expl*, 26: 43 (Ja 68).

———. ''The Sense of F's 'The Self-Seeker.''' *CP*, 7: 5-8 (1974).

———. ''The Tone of F's 'The Literate Farmer and the Planet Venus.''' *NCLit*, 5: 10-3 (Mr 75).

———. '''Two Tramps in Mud Time' and the Critics.'' *AL*, 44: 671-6 (Ja 73).

Poirier, Richard. ''The Art of Poetry II.'' *PaR*, 6: 89-120 (Su-Fa 60).

———. ''RF: The Sound of Love and the Love of Sound.'' *Atl*, 233: 50-5 (Ap 74).

Poss, Stanley. ''F, Freud and Delmore Schwartz.'' *CEA*, 30: 6-7 (Ap 68).

————. "Low Skies, Some Clearing, Local F." *NEQ*, 41: 438-42 (1968).

Pritchard, W.H. "F Revisited." *Atl*, 226: 130-3 (O 70).

Rao, C.V. "The 'Other Mood': A Note on the Prose Works of RF." *LCrit*, 8: 63-9 (1969).

Reed, K.T. "Longfellow's 'Sleep' and F's 'After Apple-Picking.'" *AN&Q*, 10: 134-5 (My 72).

Rubinstein, A.T. "A Stay Against Confusion." *Sci&Soc*, 33: 25-41 (1969).

Ryan, A.S. "F and Emerson: Voice and Vision." *MR*, 1: 5-23 (Fa 59).

Sampley, A.M. "The Myth and the Quest: The Stature of RF." *SAQ*, 70: 287-98 (Su 71).

Sanders, D.A. "Words in the Rush of Everything to Waste: A Poetic Theme in F." *SCR*, 7: 34-47 (N 74).

Saradhi, K.P. "RF's Poetry and the Aesthetics of Voice Tones." *Triveni*, 43, 39-46 (Jl-S 74).

Sasso, L.J. "RF: Love's Question." *NEQ*, 42: 95-107 (Mr 69).

Schartz, Edward. "F's 'The Lovely Shall Be Choosers.'" *Expl*, 13: 3 (O 54).

Schutz, Fred. "F's 'The Literate Farmer and the Planet Venus': Why 1926?" *NCLit*, 4: 8-11 (N 74).

Schutz, F.C. "F's 'The Witch of Coös.'" *Expl*, 33: 19 (N 74).

Sears, J.F. "William James, Henri Bergson, and the Poetics of RF." *NEQ*, 48: 341-61 (S 75).

Seib, Kenneth. "RF's 'Neither Out Far Nor In Deep.'" *Cont Poetry*, 1: 28-9 (Wi 73).

Shurr, W.H. "Once More to the 'Woods': A New Point of Entry into F's Most Famous Poems." *NEQ*, 47: 584-9 (D 74).

Sister Catherine Theresa. "New Testament Interpretations of RF's Poems." *BSUF*, 11: 50-4 (Wi 70).

Slights, Camille and William. "F's 'The Witch of Coos.'" *Expl*, 27: 40 (F 69).

Smythe, Daniel. "RF's Indebtedness to Henry Thoreau." *TJQ*, 3: 21 (15 Jl 71).

————. "Thoreau and RF." *TJQ*, 2: 21-2 (15 O 70).

Snow, Wilbert. "The RF I Knew." *TQ*, 11: 9-48 (1968).

Speirs, Russell. "Lost with F." *Yankee*, 35: 80-3 (Ja 71).

Strivastava, Ramesh. "Barriers and Boundaries: Wall Imagery in F." *BP*, 16: 19-30 (1971).

Stafford, William. "The Terror in RF." *NYTMS*, 18 Ag 74, pp. 24-6, 31-8.

Stanlis, Peter J. "RF: The Individual and Society." *InR*, 8: 211-34 (Su 73).

Stein, W.B. "'After Apple-Picking': Echoic Parody." *UR*, 35: 301-5 (Su 69).

Stillians, Bruce. "F's 'To the Thawing Wind.'" *Expl*, 31: 31 (D 72).

Suderman, E.F. "The Frozen Lake in F's 'Stopping by Woods on a Snowy Evening.'" *BSUF*, 11: 22 (Wi 70).

Sutton, W.A. "A F-Sandburg Rivalry?" *BSUF*, 11: 59-61 (Wi 70).

————. "The Morrison Testimony." *SoR*, 11: 937-41 (Au 75).

————. "RF's Parents." *BSUF*, 13: 4-8 (Sp 75).

Swennes, R.H. "Man and Wife: The Dialogue of Contraries in RF's Poetry." *AL*, 42: 363-72 (N 70).

Thompson, John. "Permafrost." *NYRB*, 8: 5-6 (26 Ja 67).

Thompson, Lawrance. "RF and Carl Burell." *DCLB*, 6: 65-73 (Ap 66).

Thornburg, T.R. "Mother's Private Ghost: A Note on F's 'The Witch of Coös.'" *BSUF*, 11: 16-20 (Wi 70).

Toor, David. "F's 'Spring Pools.'" *Expl*, 28: 28 (N 69).

Tyler, Dorothy. "*Robert Frost: The Years of Triumph 1915-1938.*" *MQR*, 11: 135-6 (Sp 72).

Udall, S.L. "'. . . and miles to go before I sleep': RF's Last Adventure." *NYT*, 11 Je 72, pp. 18-33.

———. "RF, Kennedy, and Krushchev." *Shen*, 26: 52-68 (#2 75).

Utley, F.L. "RF's Virgilian Monster." *ELN*, 10: 221-3 (Mr 73).

Vail, Dennis. "F's 'Ghost House.'" *Expl*, 36: 11 (O 71).

———. "F's 'Mowing': Work and Poetry." *NCLit*, 4: 4-8 (Ja 74).

———. "Point of View in F's 'The Peaceful Shepherd.'" *NCLit*, 4: 2-4 (N 74).

———. "Tree Imagery in F's 'Mending Wall!" *NCLit*, 3: 9-11 (S 73).

VanderVen, Tom. "RF's Dramatic Principle of 'Oversound.'" *AL*, 45: 238-51 (My 73).

Van Dore, Wade. "RF: A Memoir and a Remonstrance." *JML*, 2: 554-60 (N 72).

———. "In RF's Rubbers." *MQR*, 11: 122-6 (Sp 72).

Vinson, R.S. "The Roads of RF." *ConnR*, 3: 102-7 (1970).

Vitell, J.R. "RF: The Contrarieties of Talent and Tradition." *NEQ*, 47: 351-67 (S 74).

Watkins, F.C. "Going and Coming Back: RF's Religious Poetry." *SAQ*, 73: 445-59 (Au 74).

———. "The Poetry of the Unsaid: RF's Narrative and Dramatic Poems." *TQ*, 15: 85-98 (Wi 72).

Watson, C.N. "F's Wall: The View from the Other Side." *NEQ*, 44: 653-6 (D 71).

Weinig, Sister M.A. "A Note on RF's 'A Tuft of Flowers.'" *CP*, 2: 79 (Sp 69).

Weinstein, Norman. "RF's Ideas of Order." *Lang&L*, 1: 5-21 (1972).

Wesley, B.C. "Robert Frost." *LHY*, 10: 53-67 (Ja 69).

Wiebe, D.E. "The Rhetoric of RF's 'Once by the Pacific.'" *EWR*, 4: 94-101 (Sp 71).

Wilcox, Earl. "F's 'Stopping by Woods on a Snowy Evening.'" *Expl*, 27: 7 (S 68).

Williams, D.W. "Whose Woods These Are." *TJQ*, 4: 27-8 (1972).

Winslow, D.J. "The Origin of RF's 'Witness Tree.'" *AN&Q*, 13: 153-4 (Je 75).

Yates, Norris. "An Instance of Parallel Imagery in Hawthorne, Melville, and F." *PQ* 36: 276-80 (Ap 57).

Yevish, I.A. "RF: Campus Rebel." *TQ*, 11: 49-55 (Au 68).

Zverev, A. "Ispytanie RF." *VLit*, 18: 204-12 (1969).

Fuller, Alvarado. Fuson, B.W. "Prairie Dreamers of 1890: Three Kansas Utopian Novels and Novelists." *KanQ*, 5: 63-77 (Fa 73).

———. "Three Kansas Utopian Novels of 1890." *Extrapolation*, 12: 7-24 (D 70).

Fuller, Henry Blake. Abel, Darrel. "Expatriation and Realism in American Fiction in the 1880's: HBF." *ALR*, 3: 245-57 (Su 70).

Pilkington, John. "Aftermath of a Novelist." *UMSE*, 10: 1-23 (1969).

———. "F and 'The Americanization of Europe's Youth.'" *UMSE*, 8: 31-42 (1967).

———. "F, Garland, Taft, and the Art of the West." *PLL*, 8: 39-56 (Fl 72 Supp.).

———. "HBF's Satire on Hamlin Garland." *UMSE*, 8: 1-6 (1967).

Redd, Penelope. "HB.F." *Scholastic*, 6: 5 (8 Ap 25).

Sauberla, Guy. "Making the Sublime Mechanical: HBF's Chicago." *AmS*, 14: 83-93 (Sp 73).

*Swanson, Jeffrey. "A Checklist of the Writings of HBF (1857-1929)." *ALR*, 7: 211-43 (Su 74).

———. "'Flesh, Fish, or Fowl': HBF's Attitudes Toward Realism and Romanticism." *ALR*, 7: 195-210 (Su 74).

*———. "HBF." *ALR*, 8: 257-9 (1975).

Williams, K.J. "HBF (1857-1929)." *ALR*, 3: 9-13 (Su 68).

Wilson, Edmund. "Two Neglected American Novelists. I—HB.F: The Art of Making It Flat." *NY*, 46: 112-39 (23 My 70).

Fuller, Margaret. Allen, M.V. "The Political and Social Criticism of MF." *SAQ*, 72: 560-73 (Au 73).

———. "'This Impassioned Yankee': MF's Writing Revisited." *SWR*, 58: 162-71 (Sp 73).

Barolini, Helen. "A Study in Contrast: Effie in Venice and the Roman Spring of MF." *AR*, 28: 461-76 (Wi 68-9).

Cheshire, David, and Malcolm Bradbury. "American Realism and the Romance of Europe: Frederic, Harland." *PAH*, 4: 285-310 (1970).

Deiss, J.J. "Men, Women, and MF." *AH*, 23: 43-7, 94-7 (Ag 72).

Hamblen, A.A. "The Belle of Transcendentalism." *JPC*, 7: 172-8 (Su 73).

Haverstick, I.S. "Three Lively Ladies of the Overbury Collection." *CLC*, 21: 20-7 (1971).

Hopkins, V.C. "MF: American Nationalist Critic." *ESQ*, 55: 24-41 (2Q 69).

———. "MF: Pioneer Women's Liberationist." *ATQ*, 18: 29-35 (Sp 73).

Jameson, Elizabeth. "To Be All Human: Sex Role and Transcendence in MF's Life and Thought." *Un of Michigan Papers in Women's Studies*, 1: 91-126 (# 74).

Myerson, Joel. "Caroline Dall's Reminiscences of MF." *HBL*, 22: 414-28 (O 74).

———. "A MF Addition to Thoreau's Library." *TSB*, 123: 3 (Sp 73).

———. "MF's 1842 Journal: At Concord with the Emerson." *HLB*, 21: 320-40 (Jl 73).

Peple, E.C. "Three Unlisted Reviews of Hawthorne." *ESQ*, 68: 146-7 (1972).

Poger, Sidney. "The Critical Stance of *The Dial*." *ESQ*, 57: 22-7 (1969).

Rosenthal, Bernard. "*The Dial*, Transcendentalism, and MF." *ELN*, 8: 28-36 (S 70).

Shapiro, F.C. "The Transcending MF." *Ms*, N 72, pp. 36-9.

Strauch, C.F. "Hatred's Swift Repulsions: Emerson, MF, and Others." *SRom*, 7: 65-103 (Wi 68).

Taylor, H.L. "MF: Commitment in Italy." *Carrell*, 13: 9-24 (1972).

Wilson, J.B. "The Aesthetics of Transcendentalis." *ESQ*, 57: 27-34 (4Q 69).'

Gaddis, William. Banning, Charles. "WG's *JR*: The Organization of Chaos and the Chaos of Organization." *Paunch*, 42-3: 153-65 (D 75).

Bouchouk, Monique. "Un Long Voyage sur la Terre Vaine: 'les Reconnaissances' de WG." *Caliban 12*, 11: 3-15 (75).

Koenig, P.W. "Recognizing G's *Recognition*." *ConL*, 16: 61-72 (Wi 75).

Gaines, Ernest J. Bryant, J.H. "EJ.G: Change, Growth, and History." *SoR*, 10: 851-65 (O 74).

———. "*From Death to Life*: The Fiction of EJ.G." *IowaR*, 3: 106-20 (Wi 72).

Carter, Tom. "EG." *Essence*, 6: 52-3, 71-2 (Jl 75).

Ingram, Forest, and Barbara Steinberg. "On the Verge: An Interview with EJ.G." *NOR*, 3: 339-44 (1973).

Jaskoski, H. "Power Unequal to Man: The Significance of Conjure in Works by Five Afro-American Authors." *SFQ*, 38: 91-108 (Je 74).

Laney, Ruth. "A Conversation with EG." *SoR*, 10: 1-14 (Wi 74).

McDonald, Walter, "'You Not a Bum, You a Man': EJ.G's *Bloodline*." *NALF*, 9: 47-9 (Su 75).

Potter, V.R. "*The Autobiography of Miss Jane Pitman*: How to Make a White Movie." *LFQ*, 3: 371-5 (1975).

Ramsey, Alvin. "Through a Glass Whitely: The Televised Rape of *Miss Jane Pittman*." *BlackW*, 23: 31-6 (1974).

Shelton, Frank. "Ambiguous Manhood in EJ.G's Bloodline." *CLAJ*, 19: 200-9 (D 75).

Stoelting, W.L. "Human Dignity and Pride in the Novels of EG." *CLAJ*, 14: 340-58 (Mr 71).

Gale, Zona. Cooper, F.T. "Friendship Village Love Stories." *BkM*, 31: 79 (Mr 10).

Davidson, Donald. "A Worker of Ill." *SatR*, 6: 440 (23 N 29).

Krutch, J.W. "ZG's New Manner." *Nation*, 129: 725 (11 D 29).

Lewisohn, Ludwig. "Native Plays." *Nation*, 112: 189 (2 F 21).

Loizeaux. "Talking Shop." *WLB*, 21: 243 (N 46).

Monteiro, George. "ZG and Ridgely Torrence." *ALR*, 3: 77-9 (Wi 70).

Simonson, H.P. "ZG (1874-1938)." *ALR*, 3: 14-7 (Su 68).

Sumner, Keene. "The Everlasting Persistence of This Western Girl." *Am Mag*, 91: 34-5, 137-41 (Je 21).

Gallico, Paul. Gallico, Paul. "One Writer's Working Methods." *CLC*, 20: 19-23 (1970).

Kirksey, George. "Tell Me a Story." *CLC*, 21: 21-30 (1971).

Rao, V.V.B.R. "The Achievement of PG." *IJAS*, 4: 78-88 (# 1-2 74).

Gardner, John. Bellamy, J.D. "FG: An Interview." *FicI*, 2: 33-49 (Sp-Fa 74).

Butscher, Edward. "The American Novel Is Alive and Well . . . Now." *GaR*, 27: 393-7 (Fa 73).

Ensworth, Pat and Joe David Bellamy. "JG: An Interview." *FicI*, 2-3: 32-49 (Sp-Fa 74).

Murray, G.E. "The Blue Plate Special: On JG." *FicI*, 2-3: 124-6 (Sp-Fa 74).

Garland, Hamlin. Alsen, Eberhard. "HG's First Novel: *A Spoil of Office*." *WAL*, 4: 91-105 (Su 69).

Bentzon, Th. "Un Radical de la Prairie." *RDM*, 157: 139-80 (Ja 00).

Blearsides, Oliver. "G's Twain Anecdotes." *MTQ*, 4: 13 (Su 40).

Boynton, P.H. "Some Expounders of the Middle Border." *EJ*, 19: 431-40 (Je 30).

*Bryer, J.R., and Eugene Harding. "HG (1860-1940): A Bibliography of Secondary Comment." *ALR*, 3: 290-387 (Fa 70).

———. "HG: Reviews and Notices of His Work." *ALR*, 4: 103-56 (Sp 71).

Carter, J.L. "HG's Liberated Women." *ALR*, 6: 255-8 (Su 73).

*Carter, Joseph. "HG." ALR, 8: 260-5 (1975).

Clayton, Lawrence. "HG's Negative Use of Folk Elements." *Folklore Forum*, 6: 107-8 (1973).

Clemens, Cyril. "HGL 1860-1940." *MTQ*, 4: 1, 20 (Su 40).

Culmsee, Carlton. "A Pioneer in Modern Pessimism." *WHR*, 4: 241-50 (Su 50).

Daly, J.P. "HG's *Rose of Dutcher's Cooly*." *EL&L*, 11: 51-65 (1972).

Dove, J.R. "The Significance of HG's First Visit to England." *StE*, 32: 96-109 (1953).

Durbin, J.H. "Ayot St. Lawrence and the Middle Border." *Coranto*, 1: 3-13 (Sp 64).

Evans, T.J. "The Return Motif as a Function of Realism in *Main-Travelled Roads*." *KanQ*, 5: 33-40 (Fa 73).

Flower, B.O. "Leaders I Have Known: HG, Will Allen Dromgoole, W.D. McCracken, Bolton Hall, Ernest Howard Crosby." *TMC*, 6: 357-61 (Ag 12).

French, Warren. "What Shall We Do about HG?" *ALR*, 3: 283-9 (Fa 70).

Fuller, D.J. "Mark Twain and HG: Contrarieties in Regionalism." *MTJ*, 17: 14-8 (Wi 73-74).

Grover, D.C. "G's 'Emily Dickinson—A Case of Mistaken Identity." *AL*, 46: 219-20 (My 74).

Harrison, S.R. "HG and the Double Vision of Naturalism." *SSF*, 6: 548-56 (Fa 69).

Hill, E.C. "HG Collection." *MTQ*, 4: 10 (Su 40).

Houston, N.B. "A Dedication to the Memory of HG." *Arizona and the West*, 11: 209-12 (Au 69).

Huneker, J.G. "The Raconteur." *Musical Courier*, 42: 23 (10 Ap 01).

Irsfeld, J.H. "The Use of Military Language in HG's 'The Return of a Private.'" *WAL*, 7: 145-7 (1972).

Katz, Joseph. "HG's Copy of *The Red Badge of Courage*." *SCraneN*, 3: 10 (Wi 68).

Leonard, Neil. "Edward MacDowell and the Realists." *AQ*, 18: 175-82 (Su 66).

Littlefield, D.F. "HG at Isleta Pueblo." *Sw Hist Q*, 78: 45-68 (1974).

Martinec, Barbara. "HG's Revisions of *Main-Travelled Roads.*" *ALR*, 5: 167-72 (Sp 72).

Monroe, Harriet. "Eagle's Nest Camp." *House Beautiful*, 16: 5-10 (Ag 04).

Monteiro, George. "A Capsule Assessment of Stephen Crane by HG." *SCraneN*, 3: 2 (Fa 68).

Paleet, D.B. "G and the Prince of Players." *WSp*, 21: 160-3 (Su 57).

Perosa, Sergio. "G e il *veritism.*" *Verri*, 27: 69-79 (1968).

Pilkington, John. "Fuller, G, Taft, and the Art of the West." *PLL*, 8: 39-56 (Fl 72 supp.).

————. "Henry Blake Fuller's Satire on HG." *UMSE*, 8: 1-6 (1967).

Pizer, Donald. "HG (1860-1938)." *ALR*, 1: 45-51 (Fa 67).

————. "Jean Holloway's HG." *NCF*, 15: 275-7 (D 60).

Saum, L.O. "HG and Reform." *SDR*, 10: 36-62 (1972).

————. "The Success Theme in Great Plains Realism." *AQ*, 18: 579-98 (Wi 66).

Schuppe, T.G "HG of Iowa." *Annals of Iowa*, 41: 12-5 (Wi 72).

Shuman, R.B. "HG on Education." *S&S*, 86: 376 (25 O 58).

Stevenson, Lionel. "G's Conversation." *MTQ*, 4: 10 (Su 40).

Stronks, James B. "G's Private View of Crane in 1898 (With a Postscript)." *ALR*, 6: 249-50 (Su 73).

————. "Two Frederic Letters to G." *FH*, 3: 4 (S 69).

Underhill, L.E., and D.F. Littlefield. "HG and the Navajos." *JAriH*, 13: 275-85 (Wi 72).

————. "HG at Isleta Pueblo." *SHQ*, 78: 45-68 (Jl 74).

Wertheim, Stanley. "Crane and G: The Education of an Impressionist." *NDQ*, 35: 23-8 (Wi 67).

————. "The Sage of March 23rd: G, Gilder, and Crane." *SCraneN*, 3: 1-3 (Wi 68).

Whitford, Kathryn. "Three Versions of 'The Return of a Private.'" *WSL*, 3: 37-42 (1966).

Wright, L.M. "The Midland Monthly." *Iowa J Hist & Pol*, 45: 3-61 (Ja 47).

Garrard, Lewis. Meyer, R.W. "New Light on *LG.*" *Western Hist Q*, 6: 261-78 (Jl 75).

Powell, L.C. "Southwest Classics Reread: Two for the Santa Fe Trail." *Westways*, 64: 56-9, 73-4 (O 72).

Garrett, George. Carr, John. "In Contention with Time: GG's *Death of the Fox.*" *MMR*, 1: 19-26 (1971).

Chappell, Fred. "The Lion Tamer; GG's Short Stories." *MMR*, 1: 42-6 (1971).

Davis, Paxton. "Breadth, Depth, and Elevation: GG's *Death of the Fox.*" *MMR*, 1: 12-3 (1971).

Graham, John. "Fiction and Film: GG." *MMR*, 1: 22-5 (1971).

————. "GG Discusses Writing." *MMR*, 1: 79-102 (1971).

Israel, Charles. "Interview: GG." *SCR*, 6: 43-8 (N 73).

McCullough, Frank. "GG's Ralegh." *MMR*, 1: 15-8 (1971).

Moore, Richard. "The Poetry of GG." *MMR*, 1: 47-50 (1971).

Robinson, W.R. "The Fiction of GG." *MMR*, 1: 39-41 (1971).

————. "Imagining the Individual: GG's *Death of the Fox.*" *HC*, 8: 1-12 (Ag 72).

Slavitt, D.R. "History—Fate and Freedom: A Look at GG's New Novel." *SoR*, 7: 276-94 (Ja 71).

Willis, R.J. "Anger and the Contemporary Black Theatre." *NALF*, 8: 213-5 (1974).

Garrison, William Lloyd. "WLG's *Liberator* and Boston's Blacks, 1830-1865." *NEQ*, 44: 259-77 (Je 71).

Garson, Barbara. DePrins, P. "Makkelijke, Macbird." *VlG*, 51: 394-5 (Ag 67).

Sjogren, Gunnar. "Macbeth—Macbird." *Studiekamraten*, 51: 82-4 (1969).

Wells, H.W. "Do Politics and Poetry Disagree?" *LHY*, 8: 74-9 (Ja-Jl 67).

Garvey, Marcus. Ijere, M.O. "W.E.B. DuBois and MG as Pan-Africanists: A Study in Contrasts." *PA*, 89: 188-206 (1974).

Gass, William H. Allen, C.J. "Fiction and Figures of Life in *Omensetter's Luck*." *PCP*, 9: 5-11 (1974).

Busch, Frederick. "But This Is What It Is to Live in Hell: WG's 'In the Heart of the Country.'" *MFS*, 19: 97-108 (Sp 73).

Gass, W.H. "Groping for Trout: On Metaphor." *Salmagundi*, 24: 19-33 (1973).

Kane, Patricia. "A Point of Law in WG's *Icicles*." *NCLit*, 1: 7-8 (Mr 71).

————. "The Sun Burned on the Snow: G's 'The Henderson Kid.'" *Critique*, 14: 89-96 (2Q 72).

McCaffery, Larry. "Donald Barthelme, Robert Coover, WH.G: Three Checklists." *BB*, 31: 101-6 (Jl-S 74).

McCauley, C.S. "Fiction Needn't Say Things—It Should *Make* Them Out of Words: An Interview with WH.G." *Falcon*, 5: 35-45 (1972).

Schneeman, Peter. "3 Fingers of/Figures of Gass." *MinnR*, 4: 138-44 (Sp 73).

Scholes, Robert. "Metafiction." *IowaR*, 1: 100-15 (Fa 70).

Gayarré, Charles. Bush, Robert. "CG and Grace King: Letters of a Louisiana Friendship." *SLJ*, 7: 10-31 (Fa 74).

George, Henry. Nicklason, Fred. "HG: Social Gospeller." *AQ*, 649-64 (Fa 70).

Rose, E.J. "HG: America's Apostle to the Irish." *Eire*, 3: 7-16 (1968).

Gilder, Richard Watson. Sloane, D.E.E. "Censoring for *The Century Magazine*: R.W.G. to John Hay in *The Bread-Winners*, 1882-1884." *ALR*, 4: 255-67 (Su 71).

Wertheim, Stanley. "The Saga of March 23rd: Garland, G, and Crane." *SCraneN*, 3: 1-3 (Wi 68).

Gilman, C.P. MacPike, Loralee. "Environment as Psychopathological Symbolism in 'The Yellow Wallpaper.'" *ALR*, 8: 286-8 (Su 75).

Schopp-Schilling, Beate. "'The Yellow Wallpaper': A Rediscovered 'Realistic' Story." *ALR*, 8: 284-6 (Su 75).

Ginsberg, Allen. Butscher, Edward. "G at the Poles." *ELUD*, 2: 48-58 (Ag 74).

Charters, Ann. "AG and Jack Kerouac, Columbia Undergraduates." *CLC*, 20: 10-7 (N 70).

Clark, Thomas. "The Art of Poetry VIII." *PaR*, 10: 13-55 (Sp 66).

Clarke, Gerald. "Checking in with Allen Ginsberg." *Esquire*, 79: 92-5, 168-70 (Ap 73).

Colbert, Alison. "A Talk with AC." *PR*, 38: 289-309 (1971).

Combecker, Hans. "AG's 'In back of the real': Ein Stück Beat Poetry." *NS*, 22: 74-6 (1973).

Davie, Donald. "On Sincerity: From Wordsworth to G." *Enc*, 31: 61-6 (O 68).

Dickstein, Morris. "AG and the 60's." *Commentary*, 49: 64-70 (Ja 70).

Dullea, G.J. "G and Corso: Image and Imagination." *Thoth*, 2: 17-27 (Wi 71).

Farrell, Barry. "The Guru Comes to Kansas." *Life*, pp. 79-90 (27 My 66).

Fauchereau, Serge. "Un Grand Poème d'AG." *QL*, 42: 5-6 (1 Ja 68).

Geneson, Paul. "A Conversation with AG." *ChiR*, 27: 27-35 (Su 75).

Ginsberg, Allen. "*Gay Sunshine* Interview." *CE*, 36: 392-400 (1974).

Haselmayer, L.A. "Beat Prophet and Beat Wit." *IEngYb*, 6: 9-13 (Fa 61).

Howard, Richard. "AG: 'O Brothers of the Laurel, Is the World Real? Is the Laurel a Joke or a Crown of Thorns?'" *MinnR*, 9: 50-6 (1969).

Hunsberger, Bruce. "Kit Smart's 'Howl.'" *SW&L*, 6: 34-44 (Wi-Sp 65).

Kramer, Jane. "Profiles: Paterfamilias." *NY*, 44: 32-76, 38-91 (17, 24 Ag 68).

Leary, Timothy. "In the Beginning, Leary Turned on G and Saw That It Was Good. . . ." *Esquire*, 70: 83-7, 116-7 (Jl 68).

Lukas, J.A. "'Om,' G's Hindu Chant, Fails to Charm a Jude in Chicago." *NYT*, 13 D 69, p. 19.

Luster, Helen. "AG: The Green Man Is Alive and Thrives." *St. Andrews R*, 2: 35-42 (Fa-Wi 72).

Messing, G.M. "The Linguistic Analysic of Some Contemporary Nonformal Poetry." *Lang&S*, 2: 323-9 (1969).

Middlebrook, Diane. "Bound Each to Each." *Parnassus*, 2: 128-35 (1974).

Moraes, Dom. "Somewhere Else with A and Gregory." *Horizon*, 11: 66-7 (Wi 69).

Parkinson, Thomas. "Reflections on AG as a Poet." *CP*, 2: 21-4 (Sp 69).

Peters, Robert. "Funky Poetry: AG's *The Fall of America*." *New*, 22-3: 69-75 (Fa-Wi 73-74).

Reck, Michael. "A Conversation between Ezra Pound and AG." *EvR*, 12: 27-9, 84 (Je 68).

Rissover, Fredric. "Beat Poetry, *The American Dream*, and the Alienation Effect." *SpT*, 20: 36-43 (1971).

Seelye, John. "The Sum of '48." *New Rep*, 171: 23-4 (12 O 74).

Sienicka, Marta. "William Carlos Williams and Some Younger Poets." *SAP*, 4: 183-93 (1972).

Tytell, John. "A Conversation with AG." *PR*, 41: 253-62 (74).

Ungaretti, Giuseppi. "Presentation of AG's Poems (Naples 1966)." *BA*, 44: 559-63 (Au 70).

Vilar, Aruro del. "Balance de la literatura 'beat.'" *Arbor*, 353: 110-3 (1975).

Zacui, Mircea. "Seară cu tigri şi AG." *Steaua*, 24: 16-17 (1973).

Giovanni, Nikki. Palmer, R.R. "The Poetry of Three Revolutionists: Don L. Lee, Sonia Sanchez, and NG." *CLAJ*, 15: 25-36 (S 71).

Reeves, G.F. "The Darker Image: American Negro Minstelry." *JAmSt*, 9: 365-73 (1975).

Glasgow, Ellen. Gudd, L.J., et al. "The Forgotten Decades of Southern Writing, 1890-1920." *MissQ*, 21: 275-90 (Fa 68).

Carlton, Holt. "EG: A Turn-of-the-Century Feminist?" *New Life Dominion Style*, 2: 30-3 (Ag-S 75).

Duke, Maurice. "Cabell's and G's Richmond: The Intellectual Background of the City." *MissQ*, 27: 375-92 (Fa 74).

———. "The First Novel by a Glasgow: Cary's *A Successful Failure*." *EGN*, 1: 7-9 (O 74).

Dunn, N.E. "EG: The Great Tradition and the New Morality." *CLQ*, 11: 98-115 (Je 75).

Godshalk, W.L. "Addendum to Kelly: EG's *The Voice of the People*." *PBSA*, 67: 68-9 (1Q 73).

Holman, C.H. "April in Queensborough: EG's Comedies of Manners." *SR*, 82: 263-83 (Ap-Je 74).

Kellner, Bruce. "EG and Gertrude Stein." *EGN*, 2: 13-6 (Mr 75).

Kristiansen, Marianne. "Work and Love, or How the Fittest Survive: A Study of EG's *Life and Gabriella*." *Lang&L*, 2: 105-25 (1973).

MacDonald, E.E. "Biographical Notes on EG." *RALS*, 3: 249-53 (Au 73).

*———. "EG: An Essay in Bibliography." *RALS*, 2: 131-56 (Au 72).

———. "Emma Gray Trigg and EG." *EGN*, 3: 10-3 (1975).

———. "G, Cabell, and Richmond." *MissQ*, 27: 393-414 (Fa 74).

———. "G in Print." *EGN*, 2: 3 (1975).

———. "The G - Cabell Entente." *AL*, 41: 76-91 (Mr 69).

———. "The G. Papers." *EGN*, 2: 17-8 (1975).

———. "The Sheltered Image." *SLJ*, 4: 83-6 (Fa 71).

Monteiro, George. "Addenda to the Bibliographies of . . . G [and others]." *PSBA*, 69: 272-5 (Ap-Je 75).

Murr, J.S. "History in *Barren Ground* and *Vein of Iron*: Theory, Structure, and Symbol." *SLJ*, 8: 39-54 (Fa 75).

Pratt, Annis. "Women and Nature in Modern Fiction." *ConL*, 13: 476-90 (1972).

Raper, J.R. "G's Psychology of Deceptions and *The Sheltered Life.*" *SLJ*, 8: 27-38 (Fa 75).

―――. "The Man EG Could Respect." *EGN*, 2: 4-8 (Mr 75).

Rouse, Blair. "EG: Manners and Art." *Cabellian*, 4: 96-8 (Sp 72).

―――. "EG: The Novelist in America." *Cabellian*, 4: 25-35 (Au 71).

Rubin, L.D., et al. "Agrarianism as a Theme in Southern Literature." *GaR*, 11: 145-64 (Su 57).

Scura, Dorothy. "G and the Southern Renaissance: The Conference at Charlottesville." *MissQ*, 27: 415-34 (Fa 74).

―――. "One West Main." *EGN*, 1: 3-6 (O 74).

Sharma, O.P. "Feminist Image in the Novels of EG: The Early Phase." *Research Bul* (Chandigarh), 60: 1-20 (1968).

Spacks, P.M. "Taking Care: Some Women Novelists," *Novel*, 6: 36–51 (Fa 72).

Steele, O.L. "A Note on Early Impressions of EG's *They Stooped to Folly.*" *PBSA*, 52: 310–2 (4Q 58).

―――. "EG's *Virginia*: Preliminary Notes." *SB*, 27: 265-89 (1974).

Glaspell, Susan. Anderson, Margaret. "Neither Drama nor Life." *Little R*, 5: 59-62 (My 19).

Bach, G.P. "SG: Supplementary Notes." *ALR*, 5: 67-73 (Wi 72).

Barnes, A.C. "SG's Play 'Bernice.'" *Little R*, 5: 53-5 (My 19).

Moeller, Philip. "An Important Play." *Little R*, 5: 56-9 (My 19).

Waterman, A.E. "SG (1882-1948)." *ALR*, 4: 183-91 (Sp 71).

Godkin, Edwin L. Armstrong, W.M. "The Letters of EL.G: A Calender and Locator File." *BNYPL*, 75: 311-26 (S 71).

*―――. "The Writings of E.L.G: An Essay and a Bibliography." *BNYPL*, 72: 288-327 (My 68).

Godsey, Edwin. Krickel, Edward. "*Cabin Fever.*" *SR*, 77: 326-32 (1969).

Landess, T.H. "EG's *Cabin Fever* and the Aesthetics of Virtue." *GaR*, 23: 343-53 (Fa 69).

Godwin, Gail. Gardiner, J.K. "'A Sorrowful Woman': GG's Feminist Parable." *SSF*, 12: 286-90 (Su 75).

Goedicke, Patricia. Gerber, P.L. and R.J. Gemnett. "Myth of the self: A Conversation with PD." *SHR*, 5: 319-32 (Fa 71).

Gold, Herbert. Gold, Herbert. "Apologia Without Apology." *NYT*, 23 Ja 72; pp. 2, 30, 32.

―――. "Where the Action Is." *NYT*, 19 F 67; pp. 1, 50-2.

Gold, Michael. Lhamon, W.T. "In History's Ashcan." *NRep*, 166: 27-9 (27 Mr 72).

Reilly, J.M. "Two Novels of Working Class Consciousness." *MwQ*, 14: 183-93 (Wi 73).

Goldman, William. Schroth, R.A. "The Temple of G." *America*, 250 (9 S 67).

Gomme, Laurence. Tanselle, G.T. "The LG Imprint." *PBSA*, 61: 225-40 (3Q 67).

Goodman, Paul. Dennison, George. "PG." *Nation*, 215: 504-6, 508 (20 N 72).

*Glassheim, Eliot. "PG: A Checklist, 1931-71." *BB*, 29: 61-72 (Ap-Je 72).

Levine, George. "PG, Outsider Looking In." *NYT*, 18 F 73, pp. 4-6.

Paul, Sherman. "PG's Mourning Labor: *The Empire City.*" *SoR*, 4: 894-926 (Au 68).

Printz-Pahlson, Gorna. "Praxis och utopi." *BLM*, 39: 579-604 (1970).

Raditsa, Leo. "On PG—and Goodmanism." *IowaR*, 5: 62-79 (Su 74).

Roszalk, Theodore. "The Visionary Search of PG." *Listener*, 350: 754-5 (5 D 68).

True, Michael. "Death of a Literary Radical: PG, 1911-1972." *Cweal*, 96: 480, 482 (8 S 72).

Vincent, Bernard. "Decouvir PG." *Esprit*, 423: 808-12 (1973).

Goodrich, Samuel Griswold. Canfield, H.S. "Peter Parley." *HornB*, 46: 135-41, 274-82, 412-8 (Ap, Je, Ag 70).

Gilkes, L.B. "Hawthorne, Park Benjamin, S.G.G: A Three-Cornered Inbroglio." *NHJ*, 1: 83-112 (1971).

Maxwell, Margaret. "'Higglety, Pigglety, Pop!' or The Man Who Tried to Murder Mother Goose." *HornB*, 45: 392-4 (Ag 69).

Gordon, Caroline. Baker, Howard. "The Stratagems of CG; or, The Art of the Novel and the Novelty of Myth." *SoR*, 9: 523-49 (Jl 73).

Baum, C.B., and F.C. Watkins. "CG and 'The Captive': An Interview." *SoR*, 7: 447-62 (Ap 71).

Brown, Ashley. "The Achievement of CG." *SHR*, 2: 279-90 (Su 68).

———. "CG's Short Fiction." *SR*, 81: 365-73 (Ap-Je 73).

———. "*None Shall Look Back*: The Novel as History." *SoR*, 7: 480-94 (Ap 71).

Cheney, Brainard. "CG's *The Malefactors*." *SR*, 79: 360-72 (Su 71).

Fletcher, Marie. "The Fate of Women in a Changing South: A Persistent Theme in the Fiction of CG." *MissQ*, 21: 17-28 (Wi 67-68).

Gordon, Caroline. "Always Summer." *SoR*, 7: 430-46 (Ap 71).

Landess, T.H. "The Function of Ritual in CG's *Green Centuries*." *SoR*, 7: 495-508 (Ap 71).

Lewis, Janet. "*The Glory of Hera*." *SR*, 81: 185-94 (1973).

O'Connor, Mary. "On CG." *SoR*, 7: 463-66 (Ap 71).

Rocks, J.E. "The Christian Myth as Salvation: CG's *The Strange Children*." *TSE*, 16: 149-60 (1968).

———. "The Mind and Art of CG." *MissQ*, 21: 1-16 (Wi 67-8).

———. "The Short Fiction of CG." *TSE*, 18: 115-35 (1970).

Rubin, Larry. "Christian Allegory in CG's 'The Captive.'" *SSF*, 5: 283-9 (Sp 68).

Squires, Radcliffe. "The Underground Stream: A Note on CG's Fiction." *SoR*, 7: 467-79 (Ap 71).

Stanford, D.E. "CG: From *Penhally* to *A Narrow Heart*." *SoR*, 7: xv-xx (Ap 71).

———. "The Fiction of CG." *SoR*, 8: 458 (1972).

Valensise, Rachele. "Tre scrittrici del Sud: Flannery O'Connor, CG, Carson McCullers." *SA*, 17: 251-89 (1971).

Gordone, Charles. Walcott, Ronald. "Ellison, G and Tolson: Some Notes on the Blues, Style, and Space." *BlackW*, 22: 4-29 (1972).

———. "Some Notes on the Blues, Style & Space: Ellison, G and Tolson." *BlackW*, 22: 4-29 (1972).

Gould, Wallace. Hartley, Marsden. "Art and WG." *Little R*, 6: 24-8 (O 19).

———. "The Poet of Maine." *Little R*, 5: 51-5 (Jl 19).

Williams, Jonathan, and William Harmon. "Wild Wise G Chase." *Parnassus*, 1: 200-10 (2Q 73).

Williams, W.C. "A Maker." *Little R*, 6: 37-9 (Ag 19).

Goyen, William. Hicks, Granville. "Practicing the Holy Persuasion." *SatR*, 46: 25-6 (5 O 63).

Philips, Robert. "The Romance of Prophecy: G's 'In a Farther Country." *SWR*, 56: 213-21 (Su 71).

———. "Samuels and Samson: Theme and Legend in 'The White Rooster.'" *SSF*, 6: 331-3 (Sp 69).

———. "Secret and Symbol: Entrances to G's *House of Breath*." *SWR*, 59: 248-52 (Su 74).

Graham, Alice Walworth. Simms, L. "AWG: Popular Novelist." *NMW*, 6: 63-8 (Wi 74).

Grand, Sarah. Rowlette, Robert. "Mark Twain, SG, and *The Heavenly Twins*." *MTJ*, 16: 17-8 (Su 72).

Grau, Shirley Ann. Donohue, H.E.F. "SAG." *PW*, 3: 10, 13 (D 73).

*Grissom, M.S. "SAG: A Checklist." *BB*, 28: 76-8 (Jl-S 71).

Keith, D.L. "A Visit with SAG." *Contempora*, 2: 10-4 (1972).

Pearson, Ann. "SAG: Nature is the Vision." *Critique*, 17: 47-58 (2Q 75).

Graves, John. Bradford, M.E. "Arden Up the Brazos: JG and the Uses of Pastoral." *SoR*, 8: 949-55 (O 72).

———. "In Keeping with the Way: JG's *Hard Scrabble*." *SWR*, 60: 190-5 (Sp 75).

Miller, Roger. "When 'Orphan Annie' Went to War." *PrS*, 45: 199-207 (Fa 71).

Graybeal, Marie. Hart, Lawrence. "Introducing MG." *Works*, 1: 4-6 (Su 68).

Greeley, Horace. Aspiz, Harold. "'Children of Adam' and HG." *WWR*, 15: 49-51 (Mr 69).

Harding, Walter. "HG on Thoreau: A Forgotten Portrait." *TSB*, 116: 5-7 (Su 71).

Green, Beriah. Cameron, K.W. "BG and Emerson's P.B.K. Address of 1867." *ESQ*, 51: 26-32 (2Q 68).

Green, George Washington. Ricciardelli, Michele. "Carlo Botta e GWG." *Sym*, 22: 285-8 (1968).

Green, Joseph. LeMay, J.A.L. "JG's Satirical Poem on the Great Awakening." *RALS*, 4: 173-83 (1974).

Green, Julien. Cooper, Nina. "Obsessive Elements in JG's Short Stories: Early Essays in Style." *SSF*, 10: 149-58 (Sp 73).

Libhart, B.R. "JG's Troubled American: A Fictionalized Self-Portrait." *PMLA*, 89: 341-52 (Mr 74).

Rose, M.G. "JG's Hawthorne Essay." *NHJ*, 5: 248-50 (1975).

Green, Paul. Clifford, John. "A True American Artist." *Players*, 48: 201-15 (1973).

Molineux, Will. "An Uncommonly Glorious Twenty-Five Years." *Cwealth*, 38: 33-6 (Ag 71).

Pearce, H.D. "From Folklore to Mythology: PG's *Roll, Sweet Chariot*." *SLJ*, 3: 62-78 (Sp 71).

———. "Transcending the Folk: PG's Utilization of Folk Materials." *Mosaic*, 4: 91-106 (1971).

Tees, A.T. "Winterset: Four Influences on Mio." *MD*, 14: 408-12 (1972).

Greenberg, Samuel. Simon, Marc. "Hart Crane and SB.G: An Emblematic Interlude." *ConL*, 12: 166-72 (Sp 71).

Greenberg, Stanley. Isaac, Dan. "Theatre of Fact." *DramR*, 15: 109-35 (Su 71).

Greenlee, Samuel. Burrell, Walter. "Rappin' with Sam Greenlee." *BlackW*, 20: 42-7 (1971).

Gregory, Horace. Davis, W.V. "Figures of Nightmare." *MPS*, 4: 55-9 (Sp 73).

Gregor, Arthur. "Props of the Western Theatre: The Later Poems of HG." *MPS*, 4: 28-30 (Sp 73).

Kramer, V.A. "Contemplative Need in HG's Poetry." *MPS*, 4: 34-44 (Sp 73).

Morris, R.K. "The Resurrected Vision: HG's Thirties Poems." *MPS*, 4: 74-99 (Sp 73).

Phillips, Robert. "The Quick-Change Artist: Notes on HG's Poetic Imagery." *MPS*, 4: 60-74 (Sp 73).

Rosenthal, M.L. "The 'Pure' Poetry of HG." *MPS*, 4: 44-55 (Sp 73).

Stern, Daniel. "Politics and Protest in the Earlier Poems of HG." *MPS*, 4: 22-8 (Sp 73).

Wagner, Linda. "HG: Voice in Action." *MPS*, 4: 13-22 (Sp 73).

Zucker, D.H. "An American Elegist: The Poetry of HG." *MPS*, 4: 1-13 (Sp 73).

Grey, Zane. Arrington, Leonard, and John Haupt. "Community and Isolation: Some Aspects of 'Mormon Westerns.'" *WAL*, 8: 15-31 (1973).

Etualin, R.W. "A Dedication to . . . ZG 1872-1939." *Arizona and the West*, 12: 217-20 (Au 70).

Goble, Danney. "'The Days That Were No More': A Look at ZG's West." *JAriH*, 14: 63-75 (Sp 73).

Mead, N.W. "ZG, the Man Whose Books Made the West Famous, Lived Here." *Arizona Highways*, 44: 8 (D 73).

Powell, L.C. "Southwest Classics Reread: Writer of the Purple Sage." *Westways*, 64: 50-5, 69 (Au 72).

Scott, K.W. "*The Heritage of the Desert*: ZG Discovers the West." *Mark R*, 2: 10-4 (1970).

Topping, Gary. "ZG's West." *JPC*, 7: 681-9 (1973).

Griggs, Sutton E. Fleming, R.E. "SE.G: Militant Black Novelist." *Phylon*, 34: 73-7 (1973).

Tatham, Campbell. "Reflections: SG's *Imperium in Imperio*." *SBL*, 5: 7-15 (Wi 74).

Guest, Edgar A. Ewert, Frances. "EA.G: Twentieth Century Paradox." *Midamerica 1974*: 98-119.

Guillen, Nicolas. Cobb, M.K. "Concepts of Blackness in the Poetry of NG, Jacques Roumain and Langston Hughes." *CLAJ*, 18: 262-72 (1974).

Guiney, Louise Imogene. Cohen, E.H. "Jewett to G: An Earlier Letter." *CLQ*, 9: 231-2 (D 70).

Guthrie, A.B. Allred, Jerry. "The Magical West of A.B.G." PosS, 4: 1-5 (Ap 73).

Astro, Richard. "*The Big Sky* and the Limits of Wilderness Fiction." *WAL*, 9: 105-14 (Su 74).

Cracroft, R.H. "*The Big Sky*: A.B.G's Use of Historical Sources." *WAL*, 6: 163-76 (Fa 71).

Dixon, T.F. "The Art of Autobiography in *Bound for Glory*." *SwAL*, 2: 135-43 (Wi 72).

Espey, John. "Journey in Mythland." *Westways*, 65: 27, 75 (Jl 73).

*Etulain, R.W. "A.B.G: A Bibliography." *WAL*, 4: 133-8 (Su 69).

Hairston, J.B. "Community in the West." *SDR*, 11: 17-26 (2Q 73).

Hood, C.E., Jr. "The Man and the Book: G's *The Big Sky*." *Montana Journ R*, 14: 6-15 (1971).

Lansaw, Paul. "The Big Skywriter." *Westways*, 65: 24-6, 75 (Jl 73).

Peterson, L.S. "Tragedy and Western American Literature." *WAL*, 6: 243-9 (1972).

Putnam, J.K. "Down to Earth: A.B.G's Quest for Moral and Historical Truth." *NDQ*, 39: 47-57 (Su 71).

Stineback, D.C. "On History and Its Consequences: A.B.G's *Three Thousand Hills*." *WAL*, 6: 177-89 (Fa 71).

Walker, D.D. "The Indian in Him: A Note on the Conception of Evil in A.B. Guthrie's First Novel." *PosS*, 2: 11-3 (My 71).

———. "The Primitivistic and the Historical in G's Fiction." *PosS*, 2: 1-5 (Je 71).

Guthrie, Ramon. Laing, Alexander. "Pain, Memory and Glory: The Poetry of RG." *CaM*, 11: 2-11 (Su 70).

Véza, Laurette. "RG." *EA*, 20: 47-55 (Ja—Mr 67).

Guthrie, Woody. Reuss, R.A. "WG and His Folk Tradition." *JAF*, 83: 273-303 (Jl-S 70).

Hailey, Arthur. Lutz, P.V. "AH—Novelist at Work." *MSS*, 22: 12-7 (1970).

Haines, John. Allen C.J. "Death and Dreams in JH's *Writer's News*." *Alaska R*, 3: 28-36 (Fa-Wi 69).

Wilson, J.R. "Relentless Self-Scrutiny: The Poetry of JH." *Alaska R*, 3: 16-27 (1969).

Hale, Lucretia P. Wankmiller, M.C. "LP.H and the Peterkin Papers." *HornB*, 34: 95-103, 137-47 (Ap 68).

Halfern, Albert Von. Hollyday, G.T. "A Von H's *Der Squire*, a Novel about Life in Early Arkansas." *AHQ*, 27: 226-45 (Au 68).

Hall, Dick Wick. Myers, S.I. "DWH: Humorist with a Serious Purpose." *JAriH*, 11: 255-78 (Wi 70).

Hall, Donald. Anon. "Trapping Pterodactyls: An Interview with DH." *OhR*, 15: 67-78 (Sp 74).

Chisholm, Scott. "An Interview with DH." *TPJ*, 4: 26-48 (1971).

Hall, Donald. "Poems." *TPJ*, 4: 3-14 (1971).

———. "Waking Up a Giant." *TPJ*, 4: 56-60 (1971).

Matthews, William. "Some Notes on *The Alligator Bride, Poems New and Selected.*" *TPJ*, 4: 49-55 (1971).

Mills, R.J. "DH's Poetry." *IowaR*, 2: 82-123 (Wi 71).

Mills, Ralph. "Poems of the Deep Mind." *TPJ*, 4: 16-25 (1971).

Tipton, James. "DH Marries Another Alligator." *TPJ*, 4: 61-2 (1971).

Hall, James Norman. Welch, M.D. "JNH: Poet and Philosopher." *SAQ*, 39: 140-50 (Ap 40).

Hall, William C. Anderson, J.Q. "Miker Hooter: The Making of a Myth." *SPQ*, 19: 90-100 (Je 55).

Halleck, Fitz-Greene. Slater, Joseph. "The Case of Drake and H." *EAL*, 8: 285-97 (Wi 74).

Hamilton, Alexander. Needler, G.D. "Linguistic Evidence from AH's *Itinerarium.*" *AS*, 42: 211-8 (1967).

Smith, W.A. "Henry Adams, AH, and the American People as a "great Beast.'" *NEQ*, 48: 216-30 (Je 75).

Hamilton, Alfred Starr. Williams, Jonathan. "ASH, Poet." *NYT*, 13 Ap 75, p. 39.

Hamilton, Virginia. Heins, Paul. "VH." *Horn Bk*, 51: 344-8 (Ag 75).

Hammett, Dashiell. Adams, D.K. "The First Thin Man." *MDAC*, 1: 160-77 (1972).

De Vecchi Rocca, Luisa. "Apoteosi e decadenza del romanzo poliziesco d'azione." *NA*, 506: 532-40 (1969).

Marcus, Steven. "DH and the Continental Op." *PR*, 41: 363-77 (3Q 74).

Naremore, James. "James Huston and *The Maltese Falcon.*" *LFQ*, 1: 329-49 (1973).

Nolan, W.F. "The H Checklist Revisited." *ArmD*, 6: 249-54 (1973).

———. "Shadowing the Continental Op." *ArmD*, 8: 121-3 (1975).

Reilly, J.M. "The Politics of the Tough Guy Mysteries." *UDR*, 10: 25-31 (1Q 73).

Thompson, G.J. "The Problem of Moral Vision in DH's Detective Novels." *ArmD*, 153-6, 213-25, (1973); 7: 270-80, 8: 27-35 (1974).

Hammon, Jupiter. Costanzo, Angelo. "Three Black Poets in Eighteenth-Century America." *Shippensburg State Col R*, 1973; pp. 89-101.

Palmer, R.R. "JG's Poetic Exhortations." *CLAJ*, 18: 22-8 (S 74).

Hammond, James Henry. Wakelyn, J.L. "The Changing Loyalties of JHH: A Reconsideration." *SCHM*, 75: 1-13 (1974).

Hammond, John. Arner, R.D. "A Note on JH's *Leah and Rachel.*" *SLJ*, 6: 77-80 (Fa 73).

Hanley, William. Doyle, P.A. "Gilroy, Carlino, and H—The Best of the Young American Playwrights." *NasR*, 1: 88-102 (Sp 66).

Hansberry, Lorraine. Baldwin, James. "Sweet Lorraine." *Esquire*, 72: 139-40 (N 69).

Brown, L.W. "LH as Ironist: A Reappraisal of *A Raisin in the Sun.*" *JbLackS*, 4: 237-47 (Mr 74).

Davis, Ossie. "The Significance of LH." *Freedomways*, 5: 397-402 (Su 65).

Farrison, W.E. "LH's Last Dramas." *CLAJ*, 16: 188-97 (D 72).

Ford, Clebert. "LH's World." *Liberator*, 5: 397-402 (Su 65).

Gill, Glenda. "Technique of Teaching LH: Liberation from Boredom." *NALF*, 8: 226-8 (Su 74).

Hansberry, Lorraine. "American Theatre Needs Desegretating Too." *BlackW*, 10: 28-33 (Je 61).

————. "My Name is LH, I Am a Writer." *Esquire*, 72: 140-1 (N 69).

Hays, P.L. "*Raisin In The Sun* and *Juno And The Paycock*." *Phylon*, 33: 175-6 (Su 72).

Holtan, O.I. "'Sidney Brustein and the Plight of the American Intellectual." *Players*, 46: 222-5 (1971).

Isaacs, Harold. "Five Writers and Their African Ancestors." *Phylon*, 21: 243-65 (1960).

Weales, Gerald. "Losing the Playwright." *Cweal*, 90: 542-3 (5 S 69).

————. "Thoughts on *A Raisin in the Sun*." *Commentary*, 27: 527-30 (Je 59).

Willis, R.J. "Anger and the Contemporary Black Theatre." *NALF*, 8: 213-5 (1974).

Harben, William N. Roemer, K.M. "1974 in 1894: H's *Land of the Changing Sun*." *MissQ*, 26: 29-42 (Wi 72).

Harden, Will. Murphy, J.K. "The Backwoods Characters of WN.H." *SFQ*, 39: 291-6 (S 75).

Hardwick, Elizabeth. Hardwick, Elizabeth. "Scene from an Autobiography." *Prose*, 4: 51-63 (1972).

Rahv, Philip. "The Editor Interviews EH." *ModO*, 2: 159-67 (Sp 72).

Rudikoff, Sonya. "Heroines of Literature and Life." *HudR*, 27: 615-9 (Wi 74-75).

Harland, Henry. Cheshire, David and Malcolm Bradbury. "American Realism and the Romance of Europe: Fuller, Frederic, H." *PAH*, 4: 285-310 (1970).

Harper, Francis Ellen Watkins. Brawley, Benjamin. "Three Negro Poets." *JNH*, 2: 384-92 (O 17).

Riggins, L.N. "The Works of FE.W.H: An 18th Century Writer." *BlackW*, 22: 30-6 (1972).

Harper, Michael S. Callahan, John. "Reconsideration: The Poetry of MH." *NRep*, 172: 25-6 (17 My 75).

Fussell, Edwin. "Double-Conscious Poet in the Veil." *Parnassus*, 4: 5-28 (Fa-Wi 75).

Harrington, Alan. Richey, C.W. "Rebirth from the Womb: A Note upon an Analogue for the Concluding Episode in AH's *The Secret Swinger*." *NClit*, 1: 12-4 (S 71).

Harris, Benjamin. Pecora, Madeline. "The Authorship of 'The Plain Case Stated.'" *SCN*, 30: 44-7 (1972).

————. "The Date of 'The Plain Case Stated.'" *EAL*, 6: 185-6 (1971).

Harris, Corra. Simms, L.M. "CH on the Declining Influence of Thomas Nelson Page." *MissQ*, 28: 505-9 (Fa 75).

————. "CH on Southern and Northern Fiction." *MissQ*, 27: 475-81 (Fa 74).

Harris, Frank. Muggeridge, Malcolm. "FH: Vita e menzogna." *Caffe*, 17: 112-7 (1970).

Wagner, Paul. "FH and the Maid of Orleans." *PULC*, 30: 25-38 (Au 68).

Harris, George Washington. Current-Garcia, Eugene. "Sut Lovingood's Rare Ripe Southern Garden." *SSF*, 9: 117-29 (1972).

Howell, Elmo. "Timon in Tennessee: The Moral Fervor of GWH." *GaR*, 24: 311-9 (Fa 70).

Inge, M.T. "Early Appreciation of GW.H by George Frederick Mellen." *THQ*, 30: 190-204 (Je 71).

Plater, Ormonde. "Before 'Sut': Folklore in the Early Works of GWH." *SFQ*, 34: 105-15 (Je 70).

————. "The Lovingood Patriarchy." *Appal J*, 1: 82-93 (Sp 73).

Rickels, Milton. "The Imagery of GWH." *AL*, 31: 173-87 (My 59).

Williams, Cratis. "Sut Lovingood as a Southern Mountaineer." *ASTCFP*, 44: 1-4 (Ap 66).

Harris, Isaiah. Brodhead, M.J., and J.D. Unruh. "IH's 'Minutes of a Trip to Kansas Territory' in 1855." *KHQ*, 35: 373-85 (1969).

Harris, Joel Chandler. Anon. "Two Forgotten Youthful Works of JCH." *SAQ*, 38: 278-83 (Jl 39).

Armistead, S.G. "Two Brer Rabbit Stories from the Eastern Shore of Maryland." *JAF*, 84: 442-44 (1971).

Brestemsky, D.F. "Uncle Remus: Buffoon or Admirable Man of Character." *WVUPP*, 22: 51-8 (1975).

Cline, R.I. "The Tar-Baby Story." *AL*, 2: 72-8 (Mr 30).

Crawford, J.W. "Bred and Bawn in a Briar Patch—Deception in the Making." *SCB*, 34: 149-50 (1974).

Flusche, Michael. "JCH and the Folklore of Slavery." *JAmSt*, 9: 347-63 (1975).

Glazier, Lyle. "The Uncle Remus Stories: Two Portraits of American Negroes." *JGE*, 22: 71-9 (1970).

Light, Kathleen. "Uncle Remus and the Folklorists." *SLJ*, 7: 88-104 (Sp 75).

McBryde, J.M. "Brer Rabbit in the Folk-Tales of the Negro and Other Races." *SR*, 19: 185-206 (Ap 11).

Moffett, D.J.M. "Uncle Remus Was a Hausaman?" *SFQ*, 39: 151-66 (Je 75).

Mugleston, W.F. "Julian Harris, the Georgia Press, and the Ku Klux Klan." *GHQ*, 59: 284-95 (Fa 75).

———. "The Perils of Southern Publishing: A History of *Uncle Remus's Magazine*." *JQ*, 52: 515-21, 608 (Au 75).

Rubin, L.D. "Uncle Remus and the Ubiquitous Rabbit.'" *SoR*, 10: 787-804 (O 74).

Scheick, W.J. "The Spunk of a Rabbit: An Allusion in *The Adventures of Huckleberry Finn*." *MTJ*, 15: 14-6 (Su 71).

Sullivan, P.E. "Buh Rabbit: Going Through the Changes." *SBL*, 4: 28-32 (Su 73).

Turner, Arlin. "JCH in the Currents of Change." *SLJ*, 1: 105-11 (Au 68).

Turner, D.T. "Daddy JH and His Old-Time Darkies." *SLJ*, 1: 20-41 (Au 68).

Wolfe, Bernard. "Uncle Remus and the Malevolent Rabbit." *Commentary*, 8: 31-41 (Jl 49).

Woods, G.A. "In Uncle Remus Land." *NYT*, 17 D 67, p. 18.

Harris, Mark. Bachner, Saul. "Baseball as Literature: *Bang the Drum Slowly*." *Eng Rec*, 25: 83-6 (2Q 74).

Ladenson, J.R. "Feminist Reflections on *Bang the Drum Slowly*." *AmEx*, 3: 22-4 (3Q 74).

Harris, Robert Hamilton. Willis, K.J., and W.W. Rogers. "RHH: Georgia's Wiregrass Humorist." *GHQ*, 492-500 (Wi 71).

Harris, Thomas Lake. Anon. "The TLH Collection of the Markham Archives." *MarkR*, 4: 11-4 (F 69).

Csuros, Barna. "The Poet and the Seer." *MarkR*, 4: 1-5 (F 69).

Le Baron, Gaye. "Serpent in Eden: the Final Utopia of TLH and What Happened There." *MarkR*, 4: 14-24 (F 69).

Slade, J.W. "TLH." *MarkR*, 4: 5-11 (F 69).

Harrison, Jim. Amanuddin, Syed. "Poets from East and West." *Creative Moment*, 1: 35-40 (1972).

Quasha, George. "Impure Americana, Fixtures of Place." *StBr*, WH's 'In a Wild Sanctuary.'" *HC*, 6: 1-11 (O 69).

Hart, Joel Tanner. Carver, G.R. "JTH: Kentucky's Poet-Sculptor." *Register of the Ky State Hist Soc*, 38: 49-53 (Ja 40).

Hart, Joseph C. Pitt, A.S. "'A Semi-Romance of the Sea': *Miriam Coffin* as Precursor of *Moby-Dick*." *Historic Nantucket*, 19: 15-30 (1972).

Hart, Moss. Mason, Richard. "The Comic Theatre of MH: Persistence of a Formula." *TA*, 23: 60-87 (1967).

Harte, Bret. Anon. "BH." *A&L*, 62: 484 (10 My 02).

———. "The BH Assistance Fund." *Athenaeum*, 4057: 149 (29 Jl 05).

———. "BH in the East." *Argonaut*, 50: 348 (26 My 02).

———. "The Lounger." *Critic*, 47: 401-3 (N 05).

————. "Two American Writers." *Outlook*, 71: 157-8 (17 My 02).

Aiken, C.S. "H's Tribute to Dickens." *Sunset*, 9: 225-30 (Ag 02).

Atkinson, F.G. "BH: A New Letter." *N&Q*, 21: 28-9 (Ja 74).

* Barnett, L.D. "BH: An Annotated Bibliography of Secondary Comment." *ALR*, 5: 189-320, 331-484 (Su, Fa 72).

Bellessort, André. "Les Littérature Étrangères: La Californie de BH." *Revue Bleue*, 60: 345-8 (3 Je 22).

Benson, Ivan. "BH: Californian by Destiny—Exile Choice." *California History Nugget*, 6: 73-7 (D 38).

Bland, H.M. "Stewart's View of BH." *Oveland*, 86: 354 (O 28).

Boggan, J.R. "The Regeneration of 'Roaring Camp.'" *NCF*, 22: 271-80 (D 67).

Bonner, Geraldine. "Nature in BH's Poems." *Book-Lover*, 4: 361-2 (S-O 03).

Brooks, Noah. "BH: A Biographical and Critical Sketch." *Overland*, 40: 201-7 (S 02).

————. "BH and Joaquin Miller." *NYTSat*, 10 My 02, p. 308.

————. "H's Early Days." *NYTSat*, 24 My 02, p. 350.

————. "Reminiscences: Noah Brooks Writes of Joaquin Miller and BH." *NYTSat*, 3 My 02, p. 291.

Buckland, R.L. "Jack Hamlin: BH's Romantic Rogue." *WAL*, 8: 11-22 (Fa 73).

Cahill, E.F. "H's Protest against 'Respectability.'" *Sunset*, 9: 23-4 (Ag 02).

Canby, H.S. "The Luck of BH." *SatR*, 2: 717-8 (17 Ag 26).

Canfield, C.L. "In B-H Land." *Sunset*, 19: 77-91 (My 07).

Carver, Frank. "BH's Poem, 'St. Thomas.'" 88: 765 (17 My 02).

Chapman, Arnold. "The Barefoot Galteas of BH and Rómulo Gallegos." *Sym*, 18: 332-41 (Wi 64).

Chesterlon, G.K. "The Ways of the World: BH." *Pall Mall Magazine*, 27: 428-32 (Jl 02).

Cohen, Norman. "Bill Mason, BH, and Charlie Poole." *JEMFQ*, 10: 74-8 (1974).

Collins, Churton. "The Poetry and Poets of America." *NAR*, 178: 449-51 (Mr 04).

DeGruson, Gee. "An Unlocated BH-Joaquin Miller Book." *PBSA*, 61: 60 (1967).

Dent, Newton. "The Golden Story of California." *Munsey's*, 36: 137, 147 (N 06).

Evans, T.C. "BH." *NYTSat*, 17 My 02, p. 323.

Friedrich, Gerhard. "BH as a Source for James Joyce's 'The Dead.'" *PQ*, 33: 442-4 (O 54).

Gardner, J.H. "BH and the Dickensian Mode in America." *CRAS*, 2: 89-101 (Fa 71).

Glover, D.E. "A Reconsideration of BH's Later Work." *WAL*, 8: 143-52 (Fa 73).

Goddard, H.P. "Some of BH's California Friends." *NYTSat*, 7 Je 02, p. 387.

Harte, G.B. "BH: A Centenary Portrait." *Cornhill*, 154: 168-80 (Ag 36).

Hill, Hamlin. "Mark Twain and His Enemies." *SoR*, 4: 520-9 (Sp 68).

Hills, Gertrude. "A Lost BH Item." *ABC*, 1: 221-3 (Ap 32).

Hudson, R.F. "The Contributions of BH to American Oratory." *WAL*, 2: 213-22 (Fa 67).

————. "From Poker Flat to Sandy Bar." *Pacific Historian*, 6: 129-37 (Ag 62).

Jenkins, W.D. "A Purloined Letter: Conan Doyle from BH." *BakSJ*, 22: 81-3 (Je 72).

Jones, Idwal. "The BH Country." *AmMerc*, 7: 146-53 (F 26).

————. "San Francisco Haunts of BH." *Westways*, 66: 43-4 (F 74).

Keim, M.L. "The Chinese as Portrayed in the Works of BH: A Study of Race Relations." *Sociolo&Soc Res*, 25: 441-50 (Jl-Je 41).

Knapp, Adeline. "Some Hermit Homes of California Writers." *Overland*, 35: 7-8 (Ja 00).

Leo, Brother. "The Chronicler of Poker Flat." *America*, 30: 284-6 (5 Ja 24).

Luedtke, L.S., and P.D. Morrow." BH on Bayard Taylor: An Unpublished Tribute." *MarkR*, 3: 101-5 (1973).

McClelland, C.P. "Mark Twain and BH." *MethR*, 98: 75-85 (Ja-F 16).

McCrackin, J.C. "BH in 'The Movies.'" *Overland*, 65: 487-97 (Je 15).

———. "Reminiscences of BH and Pioneer Days in the West." *Overland*, 66: 467-8 (D 15).

MacDonald, W. "BH and San Francisco." *Athenaeum*, 4101: 671 (2 Je 06).

McKeithan, D.M. "BH's Yuba Bill Meets The Ingénue." *MTJ*, 14: 1-7 (Wi 67-68).

Male, R.R. "The Story of the Mysterious Stranger in American Fiction." *Criticism*, 3: 281-94 (1961).

Mews, Siegfried. "German Reception of American Writers in the Late Nineteenth Century." *SAB*, 34: 7-9 (Mr 69).

Miller, Joaquin. "Joaquin Miller on BH." *NYTSat*, 31 My 02, p. 364.

———. "Reminiscences of BH." *NYTSat*, 31 My 02, p. 360.

Morrow, Patrick. "BH (1836-1902)." *ALR*, 2: 167-77 (Sp 70).

———. "BH, Popular Fiction, and the Local Color Movement." *WAL*, 8: 123-32 (Fa 73).

———. "The Predicament of BH." *ALR*, 5: 181-8 (Su 72).

Morrow, W.C. "An Estimate of BH." *Sunset*, 9: 230-2 (Ag 02).

Pratt, H.N. "The Man BH." *Step Ladder*, 8: 134-8 (Ap 24).

Richepin, Jean. "BH et la Californie." *J de L'Université des Annales*, 13: 529-49 (1 Je 19).

Robinson, F.C. "The Donner Party in Fiction." *Un Colorado Stud*, 10: 87-93 (F 66).

Roman, Anton. "The Genesis of the *Overland*." *Overland*, 40: 220-2 (S 02).

Scherting, Jack. "BH's Civil War Poems: Voice of the Majority." *WAL*, 8: 133-42 (Fa 73).

Schroeder, F.E.H. "The Development of the Super-Ego on the American Frontier." *Soundings*, 57: 189-205 (1974).

Sherwood, M.E.W. "BH." *NYTSat*, 10 My 02, p. 308.

Smalley, G.W. "America Authors Abroad." *Munsey's*, 26: 774 (Mr 02).

Smith, S.H. "In BH's Country." *Sunset*, 15: 33-8 (My 05).

*Thomas, J.F. "BH." *ALR*, 8: 270-1 (1975).

———. "BH and the Power of Sex." *WAL*, 8: 91-110 (Fa 73).

Van de Velde, M.S. "BH: First and Last Tales of the Argonauts." *Gentleman's Magazine*, 295: 535-44 (D 03).

Watts-Dunton, Theodore. "BH." *Athenaeum*, 3891: 658-60 (24 My 02).

Werne, W.L. "The Year of BH's Birth." *AL*, 2: 298-9 (My 30).

White, J.G. "The Death of Tennessee's Partner." *QTC*, 4: 122-4 (Ja-Mr 65).

Hartmann, Sadakichi. Blake, E.S. "Un correspondant américain de Mallarmé, avec deux lettres et un document inédits." *Rev d'Histoire Lit de la France*, 68: 26-35 (1968).

Flagens, Peter. "The Critics: H, Huneker, and De Casseres." *Art in America*, 61Z: 67-70 (Jl-Ag 73).

Knox, George. "A Complex Fate: SH, Japanese-German Immigrant Writer and Artist." *German-American Studies*, 7: 38-49 (1974).

———. "SH's *The Last Thirty Days of Christ*." *Chri & Lit*, 21: 23-9 (4Q 72).

Schwab, Arnold. "James Gibbons Huneker's 'An Early Estimate of SH." *Sadakichi Hartmann N*, 1: 4-5 (Wi 70).

Hartwell, Henry. Bain, R.A. "The Composition and Publication of *The Present State of Virginia and the College*." *EAL*, 6: 31-54 (Sp 71).

Haun, Mildred. Gower, Herschel. "MH: The Persistence of the Supernatural." *LaStud*, 7: 65-71 (Sp 68).

Havighurst, Walter. Jones, J.M. "To Feel the Heartland's Pulse: The Writing of WH." *KanQ*, 2: 88-96 (1970).

Hawkes, John. Boutrous, L.K. "Parody in H's *The Lime Twig*." *Critique*, 15: 49-56 (#2 73).

Cuddy, L.A. "Functional Pastoralism in *The Blood Oranges*." *SAF*, 3: 15-26 (Sp 75).

Fellows, Jay. "Diderot, H, and the *Tableau mouvant de l'âme*." *Diderot Stud*, 18: 61-79 (1975).

Fiedler, L.A. "A Lonely American Eccentric: The Pleasures of JH." *NewL*, 43: 12-4 (12 D 60).

Friedman, M.J. "JH and Flannery O'Connor: The French Background." *BUJ*, 21: 34-44 (#3 73).

Frost, Lucy. "The Drowing of the American Adam: H's *The Beetle Leg*." *Critique*, 14: 63-74 (#3 73).

Green, J.L. "Nightmare and Fairy Tale in H's 'Charivari.'" *Critique*, 13: 83-95

Greiner, Donald. "*Death, Sleep & the Traveler*: JH's Return to Terror." *Critique*, 17: 26-38 (#3 75).

———. "Strange Laughter: The Comedy of JH." *SWR*, 56: 318-28 (Au 71).

———. "The Thematic Use of Color in JH's *Second Skin*." *ConL*, 11: 389-400 (Su 70).

Guerard, A.J. "Illuminating Distortion." *Novel*, 5: 101-2 (Wi 72).

———. "Introduction to the Cambridge Realists." *Audience*, 7: 57-9 (Sp 60).

———. "JH." *Harvard Advocate*, 104: 10 (O 70).

Hawkes, John. "*The Floating Opera* and *Second Skin*." *Mosaic*, 8: 17-28 (1Q 74).

———. "Notes on Writing a Novel." *TriQ*, 30: 109-26 (Sp 74).

———, and Robert Scholes. "A Conversation on *The Blood Oranges*." *Novel*, 5: 197-207 (Sp 72).

Heath, William. "*Lunar Landscapes: Stories and Short Novels*." *KR*, 32: 187-90 (1970).

Imhoff, Ron. "On *Second Skin*." *Mosaic*, 8: 51-63 (1974).

Klein, Marcus. "H in Love." *Caliban*, 12: 65-79 (1975).

Knapp, J.V. "H's *The Blood Oranges*: A Sensual New Jerusalem." *Critique*, 17: 5-25 (#3 75).

Lavers, Norman. "The Structure of *Second Skin*." *Novel*, 5: 208-14 (Sp 72).

LeClair, Thomas. "JH's 'Death of an Airman' and *Second Skin*." *NCLit*, 4: 2-3 (Ja 74).

———. "The Unreliability of Innocence: JH's *Second Skin*." *JNT*, 3: 32-9 (Ja 73).

Le Vot, Andre. "Kafka Reconstructed, ou le fantastique de JH." *RANAN*, 6: 127-41 (1973).

Loukides, Paul. "The Radical Vision." *MichA*, 5: 497-503 (Sp 73).

Moran, Charles. "JH: Paradise Gaining." *MR*, 12: 840-5 (Au 71).

Romano, John. "Our Best Known Neglected Novelist." *Commentary*, 57: 58-60 (My 74).

Rosenfield, Claire. "JH: Nightmares of the Real." *MinnR*, 6: 249 (Wi 62).

Schott, Webster. "JH, American Original." *NYT*, 29 My 66; pp. 4, 24-5.

Shepherd, Allen. "Illumination through (Anti) Climax: JH's *The Lime Twig*." *NCLit*, 2: 11-3 (Mr 72).

Stubbs, J.C. "JH and the Dream-Work of *The Lime Twig* and *Second Skin*." *L&P*, 21: 149-60 (1971).

Sullivan, J.J. "Conflict in the Modern American Novel." *BSUF*, 15: 28-36 (1974).

Tanner, Tony. "Necessary Landscapes and Luminous Deteriorations." *TriQ*, 20: 145-79 (Wi 70).

Warner, John M. "The 'Internalized Quest Romance' in H's *the Lime Twig*." *MFS*, 19: 89-95 (Sp 73).

Yarborough, Richard. "H's *Second Skin*." *Mosaic*, 8: 65-75 (1974).

Hawthorne, Julian. Bassan, Maurice. "Julian H Edits Aunt Ebe." *EIHC*, 100: 274-8 (1964).

———. "Papers of Julian H at Yale." *YULG*, 39: 84-9 (1964).

Monteiro, George. "Further Additions to the Bibliography of JH." *BB*, 27: 6-7 (1970).

Park, M.M. "*Archibald Malmaison*: JH's Contribution to Gothic Fiction." *Extrapolation*, 15: 103–16 (1974).

Park, M.M. *"Archibald Malmaison*: JH's Contribution to Gothic Fiction." *Extrapolation*, 15: 103-16 (1974).

Hawthorne, Nathaniel. Anon. "The Funeral of Mr. H: As Reported in the *Boston Evening Transcript*, 24 May 1864, with the Address by Rev. James Freeman Clarke." *NHJ*, 2: 257-61 (1972).

———. "H's 'Privateer' Revealed at Last." *Lit Digest*, 93: 44-9 (9 Ap 27).

———. "Plan of NH's Estate in Concord, Mass." *ESQ*, 48: 86 (3Q 67).

Abel, Darrel. "Black Glove and Pink Ribbon: H's Metonymic Symbols." *NEQ*, 42: 163-80 (Je 69).

———. "The Devil in Boston." *PQ*, 32: 366-81 (1953).

———. "Giving Lustre to Gray Shadows: H's Potent Art." *AL*, 41: 373-88 (N 69).

———. "H, Ghostland, and the Jurisdiction of Veracity." *ATQ*, 24: 30-8 (Fa 74).

———. "H on the Strong Division-Lines of Nature." *ATQ*, 14: 23-31 (Sp 72).

———. "H's *Scarlet Letter*." *NAR*, 71: 135-48 (1950).

———. "H's *The Scarlet Letter*." *Expl*, 29: 62 (Ap 71).

———. "'A More Imaginative Pleasure': H on the Play of Imagination." *ESQ*, 55: 63-71 (2Q 69).

———. "'This Troublesome Mortality': H's Marbles and Bubbles." *SRom*, 8: 193-7 (Su 69).

———. "'A Vast Deal of Human Sympathy': Idea and Device in H's 'The Snow-Image.'" *Criticism*, 12: 316-32 (Au 70).

Abrahamson, Hans. "The Main Characters of H's *Scarlet Letter* and Their Relationships." *MSpr*, 68: 377-48 (1974).

Adams, R.P. "The Apprenticeship of William Faulkner." *TSE*, 12: 113-56 (1962).

———. "H: *The Old Manse* Period." *TSE*, 8: 115-51 (1958).

Adkins, N.F. "H's 'Snow Image.'" *Colophon*, 1: 611-2 (1936).

Albertini, Virgil. "Hepzibah and Prayer." *AN&Q*, 12: 35 (N 73).

Alden, John. "H and William Henry Smith: An Essay in Anglo-American Bibliography." *BC*, 5: 370-4 (1956).

Allen, M.V. "Imagination and History in H's 'Legends of the Province House.'" *AL*, 43: 432-7 (N 71).

Allen, Mary. "Smiles and Laughter in H." *PQ*, 52: 119-28 (Ja 73).

Allison, A.W. "The Literary Contexts of 'My Kinsman, Major Molineux.'" *NCF*, 23: 304-11 (D 68).

Allyn, John. "H on Film—Almost." *LFQ*, 2: 124-8 (1974).

Alsen, Eberhard. "The Ambitious Experiment of Dr. Rappaccini." *AL*, 43: 430-1 (N 71).

———. "Poe's Theory of H's Indebtedness to Tieck." *Anglia*, 91: 342-56 (1973).

Altschuler, G.C. "The Puritan Dilemma in 'The Minister's Black Veil.'" *ATQ*, 24 sup: 25-7 (Fa 74).

Anderson, N.A. "'Rappaccini's Daughter': A Keatsian Analogue?" *PMLA*, 83: 271-83 (My 68).

Anderson, Quentin. "Henry James and the New Jerusalem." *KR*, 8: 515-66 (1946).

Andola, J.A. "Pearl: Symbolic Link Between Two Worlds." *BSUF*, 13: 60-7 (Wi 72).

Ano, Fumio. "H Studies in Japan." *NHJ*, 5: 264-9 (1975).

Arner, R.D. "H and Jones Very: Two Dimensions of Satire in 'Egotism; or, the Bosom Serpent.'" *NEQ*, 42: 267-75 (1969).

———. "The Legend of Pygmalion in 'The Birthmark.'" *ATQ*, 14: 168-71 (Sp 72).

———. "Mythology and the Maypole of Merrymount: Some Notes on Thomas Morton's 'Rise Oedipus.'" *EAL*, 6: 156-64 (Fa 71).

————. "Of Snakes and Those Who Swallow Them: Some Folk Analogues for H's 'Egotism: Or, the Bosom Sepent.'" *SFQ*, 35: 336-46 (D 71).

————. "The Story of Hannah Duston: Cotton Mather to Thoreau." *ATQ*, 18: 19-23 (1973).

Aslas, Frederick. "H, Mary Ann, and 'The Lame Shall Enter First.'" *FOB*, 2: 3-19 (Au 73).

————. "Jeremy Taylor and H's Early Tales." *ATQ*, 14: 15-23 (Sp 72).

Asquino, M.L. "H's 'Village Uncle' and Melville's *Moby-Dick*." *SSF*, 10: 413-4 (1973).

* Atkinson, J.E. "Recent H Scholarship, 1967-70: A Checklist." *NHJ*, 1: 295-305 (1971).

Auchincloss, Louis. "*The Blithedale Romance*: A Study of Form and Point of View." *NHJ*, 2: 53-8 (1972).

Autrey, M.L. "Flower Imagery in H's Posthumous Narratives." *StN*, 7: 215-26 (Su 75).

————. "H and the Beautiful Impulse." *ATQ*, 14: 48-54 (Sp 72).

————. "H's Study in Clay." *XUS*, 11: 1-5 (Fa 72).

Axelsson, Arne. "Isolation and Interdependence as Structure in H's Four Major Romances." *SN*, 45: 392-402 (1973).

————. "Witness for the Defense; Coverdale in H's *Blithedale Romance*." *SN*, 46: 382-90 (1974).

Ayo, Nicholas. "The Labyrinthine Ways of 'Rappaccini's Daughter.'" RSW, 42: 56-69 (1974).

Babukia, T.K. "James' *Washington Square*: More on the H Relation." *NHJ*, 4: 270-2 (1974).

Bales, Kent. "The Allegory and the Radical Romantic Ethic of *The Blithedale Romance*." *AL*, 46: 41-53 (Mr 74).

————. "*The Blithedale Romance*: Coverdale's Mean and Subversive Egotism." *BuR*, 21: 60-82 (Fa-Wi 73).

Ballowe, James. "Mythic Vision in American Literature." *Disc*, 10: 324-32 (1967).

Barnes, D.R. "Faulkner's Miss Emily and H's Old Maid." *SSF*, 9: 373-7 (1972).

————. "Orestes Brownson and H's Holgrave." *AL*, 45: 271-8 (My 73).

————. "'Physical Fact' and Folklore: H's 'Egotism; or the Bosom Serpent.'" *AL*, 43: 117-21 (Mr 71).

————. "Two Reviews of *The Scarlet Letter* in *Holden's Dollar Magazine*." *AL*, 44: 648-52 (Ja 73).

Barth, J.R. "Faulkner and the Calvinist Tradition." *Thought*, 39: 100-20 (1964).

Baskett, S.S. "*The* (Complete) *Scarlet Letter*." *CE*, 22: 321-8 (1961).

Batchelor, Rev. George. "The Salem of H's Time." *EIHC*, 84: 64-74 (1948).

Battaglia, Frank. "*The* (Unmeretricious) *House of the Seven Gables*." *StN*, 2: 468-73 (Wi 70).

Battilana, Marilla. "NH e il probleme religioso: *The Gentle* Boy." *Prospetti*, 6: 48-57 (1971).

Baumgartner, A.M. and M.J. Hoffman. "Illusion and Role in *The Scarlet Letter*." *PLL*, 7: 168-84 (Sp 71).

Baxter, D.J. "'The BIrthmark' in Perspective." NJH, 5: 232-40 (1975).

Baym, Nina. "*The Blithedale Romance*: A Radical Reading." *JEGP*, 67: 545-69 (O 68).

————. "H's Gothic Discards: *Fanshaw* and 'Alice Doane.'" *NHJ*, 4: 105-15 (1974).

————. "H's Holgrave: The Failure of the Artist-Hero." *JEGP*, 69: 584-98 (1970).

————. "H's Myths for Children: The Author Versus his Audience." *SSF*, 10: 35-46 (1973).

————. "H's Women: The Tyranny of Social Myths." *CentR*, 15: 250-72 (Su 71).

————. "*The Marble Faun*: H's Eley for Art." *NEQ*, 44: 355-76 (S 71).

————. "Passion and Authority in *The Scarlet Letter*." *NEQ*, 43: 209-30 (Je 70).

————. "The Romantic *Malgre Lui*: H in the Custom House." *ESQ*, 19: 14-25 (1Q 73).

Becker, I.H. "Tragic Irony in 'Rappaccini's Daughter." *HussR*, 4: 89-93 (1971).

* Beebe, Maurice and Jack Hardie. "Criticism of NH: A Selected Checklist." *StN*, 2: 519-87 (Wi 70).

Bell, J.M. "H's *The Scarlet Letter*: An Artist's Intuitive Understanding of Plague, Armor and Health." *J of Orgonomy*, 3: 102-15 (Mr 69).

Bell, M.D. "The Young Minister and the Puritan Fathers: A Note on History in *The Scarlet Letter*." *NHJ*, 1: 159-68 (1971).

Bellman, S.I. "The Joke's on You! Sudden Revelation in H." *NHJ*, 5: 192-9 (1975).

Bennoch, Francis. "To NH." *NHJ*, 1: 46-7 (1971).

Benoit, Raymond. "H's Ape Man: 'My Kinsman, Major Molineux.'" *ATQ*, 14: 8-9 (Sp 72).

————. "H's Psychology of Death: 'The Minister's Black Veil.'" *SSF*, 8: 553-60 (1971).

————. "Theology and Literature: *The Scarlet Letter*." *BuR*, 20: 83-92 (Sp 72).

Bercovitch, Sacvan. "Diabolus in Salem: Bunyan and H." *ELN*, 6: 280-5 (Je 69).

————. "Miriam as Shylock: An Echo from Shakespeare in H's *Marble Faun*." *FMLs*, 5: 385-7 (1969).

————. "Of Wise and Foolish Virgins: Hilda Versus Miriam in H's *Marble Faun*." *NEQ*, 41: 281-6 (Je 68).

Bergeron, D.M. "Arthur Miller's *The Crucible* and NH." *EJ*, 58: 47-55 (Ja 69).

Bergman, Herbert. "'The Interior of a Heart,' *The Crucible* and *The Scarlet Letter*." *UCQ*, 15: 27-32 (My 70).

Berhold, Dennis. "H, Ruskin, and the Gothic Revival: Transcendent Gothic in *The Marble Faun*." *ESQ*, 20: 15-32 (1Q 74).

Bezanson, W.E. "The H Game: 'Graves and Goblins.'" *ESQ*, 54: 73-7 (1Q 69).

Bianchi, Rugiero. "Il problema dell'arte e dell'artiste in Poe, H, e Melville." *SA*, 18: 111-50 (1972).

Bickley, R.B. "The Minor Fiction of H and Melville." *ATQ*, 14: 149-52 (Sp 72).

Bier, Jesse. "Romantic Coordinates of American Literature." *BuR*, 18: 16-33 (Fa 70).

Birdsall, R.D. "Berkshire's Golden Age." *AQ*, 8: 328-55 (1956).

Blackstock, Walter. "H's Cool, Switched-on Media of Communication in *The Marble Faun*." *LangQ*, 7: 41-2 (1969).

Blair, Walter. "Color, Light, and Shadow in H's Fiction." *NEQ*, 15: 74-94 (Mr 42).

Blow, Suzanne. "Pre-Raphaelite Allegory in *The Marble Faun*." *AL*, 44: 122-7 (My 72).

Bochner Jay. "Life in a Picture Gallery: Things in *The Portrait of a Lady* and *The Marble Faun*." *TSLL*, 11: 761-77 (S 69).

Borden, Caroline. "Bourgeois Social Relations in NH." *L&I*, 21-8 (1971).

Borges, J.L. "NH." *LetN*, 5: 69-90 (S-O 70).

Boswell, J.C. "Bosom Serpents before H." *ELN*, 112: 279-87 (1975).

Boudreau, G.V. "The Summons of Young Goodman Brown." *Greyfriar*, 13: 15-24 (1972).

Bowen, J.K. "More on H and Keats." *ATQ*, 2: 12 (2Q 69).

Boyd, J.D. "Holm Oak and Brooch: A Suggested Meaning of Hester Prynne's Surname." *Descant*, 15: 47-51 (Fa 70).

Boyle, T.E. "The Tenor in the Organic Movement: A View of American Romanticism." *Disc*, 11: 240-51 (1968).

Brack, O.M. "The Centenary H Eight Years Later: A Review Article." *Proof*, 1: 358-67 (1971).

Bragman, L.J. "The Medical Wisdom of NH." *An Medical Hist*, 2: 236-42 (1930).

Brancaccio, Patrick. "H and the English Working Class." *NHJ*, 4: 135-49 (1974).

Braswell, William. "The Early Love Scenes in Melville's *Pierre*." *AL*, 22: 283-9 (1950).

Brill, L.W. "Conflict and Accommodation in H's 'The Artist of the Beautiful.'" *SSF*, 12: 381-6 (1975).

Brodsky, P.P. "Fertile Fields and Poisoned Gardens: Sologub's Debt to Hoffmann, Pushkin, and H." *EL*, 1: 96-108 (Sp 74).

Brodwin, Stanley. "H and the Function of History: A Reading of 'Alice Doane's Appeal.'" *NHJ*, 4: 116-28 (1974).

Brown, Dennis. "Literature and Existential Psychoanalysis: 'My Kinsman, Major Molineux' and 'Young Goodman Brown.'" *CRAS*, 4: 65-73 (Sp 73).

Browning, P.M. "Hester Prynne as Secular Saint." *MwQ*, 13: 351-62 (Jl 72).

Brubaker, B.R. "H's Experiment in Popular Form: 'Mr. Higginbotham's Catastrophe.'" *SHR*, 7: 155-66 (1973).

Bruccoli, M.J. "James Upton: 'H in the Salem Custom House—An Unpublished Recollection.'" *NHJ*, 1: 113-5 (1971).

———. "A Lost H Manuscript: 'Buds and Birdvoices.'" *NHJ*, 1: 155-8 (1971).

———. "NH Stalks Columbus: An Ohio Ghost?" *Serif*, 1: 26-7 (1964).

———. "William Harris Arnold and His H Collection." *NHJ*, 1: 204-7 (1971).

Brumbaugh, T.B. "On Horatio and Richard Greenogh: A Defense of Neoclassicism in America." *AQ*, 12: 414-7 (1960).

Brumm, Ursula. "H's 'The Custom House' and the Problem of Point of View in Historical Fiction." *Anglia*, 93: 391-412 (1975).

———. "Thoughts on History and the Novel." *CLS*, 6: 317-30 (1969).

Budd, L.J. "W.D. Howell's Defense of the Romance." *PMLA*, 67: 32-42 (1952).

Budz, J.K. "Cherubs and Bumblebees: NH and the Visual Arts." *Criticism*, 17: 168-71 (1975).

Burke, Christine. "H's Vision of the Wilderness." *Graduate Eng Papers* (Ariz), 6: 8-16 (#1 74).

Burnett, T.A.J. "Francis Bennoch: 'A Week's Vagabondage with H.' An Unpublished Recollection." *NHJ*, 1: 28-45 (1971).

Burns, R.S. "H's Romance of Traditional Success." *TSLL*, 12: 443-54 (Fa 70).

Burress, L.A., Jr. "H's Alternate Choice as a Fictional Device." *WSL*, 4: 1-17 (1967).

Burton, D.M. "Intonation Patterns of Sermons in Seven Novels." *Lang&S*, 3: 205-20 (1970).

Bush, Sargent. "Bosom Serpents Before H: The Origins of a Symbol." *AL*, 43: 181-99 (My 71).

———. "'Peter Goldthwaite's Treasure' and *The House of the Seven Gables*." *ESQ*, 62: 35-8 (Wi 71).

Byers, J.R. "*The House of the Seven Gables* and 'The Daughters of Dr. Byles': A Probable Source." *PMLA*, 89: 174-7 (Ja 74).

Caldwell, W.T. "The Emblem Tradition and the Symbolic Mode: Clothing Imagery in *The House of the Seven Gables*." *ESQ*, 19: 34-42 (1Q 73).

Calhoun, T.O. "H's Gothic: An Approach to the Four Last Fragments." *Genre*, 3: 229-41 (1970).

Cameron, K.W. "An Early Lending Library in H's Salem." *ATQ*, 20: 37-50 (1973).

———. "H Index." *ATQ*, 14: 1-27 (Sp 72).

———. "H Memorabilia in the National Records." *ATQ*, 20: 144-53 (1973).

———. "Literary News in American Renaissance Newspapers." *ATQ*, 20: 13-36 (1973).

Campbell, H.M. "Freudianism, American Romanticism, and 'Young Goodman Brown.'" *CEA*, 33: 3-6 (Mr 71).

Canaday, Nicholas. "Community and Identity at Blithedale." *SAQ*, 71: 30-9 (Wi 72).

————. "H's *the Scarlet Letter.*" *Expl*, 28: 39 (Ja 70).

Capellan, A.G. "H, como protagonista de sus obras." *FMod*, 9: 287-95 (Ap-Ag 69).

Cargas, H.J. "The Arc of Rebirth in 'Young Goodman Brown.'" *NLauR*, 4: 5-7 (#1-2 75).

Carlson, P.A. "The Function of the Lamp in H's 'The Wives of the Dead.'" *SAB*, 40: 62-4 (My 75).

————. "National Typology and H's Historical Allegory." *CEA*, 37: 1-13 (1974).

Carnochan, W.B. "'The Minister's Black Veil': Symbol, Meaning, and the Context of H's Art." *NCF*, 24: 182-92 (S 69).

Carpenter, F.I. "'The American Myth': Paradise (To Be) Regained." *PMLA*, 74: 599-606 (1959).

Carpenter, R.C. "H's Polar Explorations: 'Young Goodman Brown' and 'My Kinsman, Major Molineux.'" *NCF*, 24: 45-56 (Je 69).

Caruthers, C.M. "The 'Povera Picciola' and *The Scarlet Letter.*" *PLL*, 7: 90-4 (Wi 71).

Cecil, L.M. "Symbolic Pattern in *The Yemassee.*" *AL*, 35: 510-4 (1964).

Cervo, N.A. "The Gargouille Anti-Hero-Victim of Christian Satire." *Renascence*, 22: 69-77 (1970).

Chambers, Jane. "Two Legends of Temperance: Spenser's and H's." *ESQ*, 20: 275-9 (4Q 74).

Cifelli, Edward. "H and the Italian." *SA*, 14: 87-96 (1968).

Clark, C.E.F. "Census of NH Letters, 1813-49." *NHJ*, 1: 257-82 (1971).

————. "Census of NH Letters 1850-1864." *NHJ*, 3: 202-52 (1973).

————. "Distinguishing the First Printing of *The Blithedale Romance.*" *NHJ*, 3: 172-6 (1973).

————. "An Exhibition Commemorating NH in England: Liverpool, England, 15-20 July 1971." *NHJ*, 2: 203-18 (1972).

————. "H and the Pirates." *Proof*, 1: 90-121 (1971).

————. "H's First Appearance in England." *CEAAN*, 3: 10-1 (Je 70).

————. "H to Longfellow—An Unpublished Letter." *NHJ*, 1: 71 (1971).

————. "H to 'Mr. Ex-Cardinal.'" *NHJ*, 1: 72-81 (1971).

————. "H to 'Mr. Ex-Cardinal.'" *NHJ*, 1: 72-81 (1971).

————. "House-Hunting with H: H to William B. Pike." *NHJ*, 3: 3-7 (1973).

————. "'The Interrupted Nuptials': A Question of Attribution." *NHJ*, 1: 49-66 (1971).

————. "New Light on the Editing of the 1842 Edition of *Twice-Told Tales*: Discovery of a Family Copy of the 1833 *Token* Annotated by H." *NHJ*, 2: 91-139 (1972).

————. "Posthumous Papers of a Decapitated Surveyor: *The Scarlet Letter* in the Salem Press." *StN*, 2: 395-419 (Wi 70).

————. "*The Scarlet Letter*—A 'Fourteen-Mile-Long Story.'" *NHJ*, 5: 2-4 (1975).

————. "Unexplored Areas of H Bibliography." *NHJ*, 2: 47-51 (1972).

Clark, J.W. "H's Use of Evidence in 'Young Goodman Brown.'" *EIHC*, 111: 12-34 (1975).

Clay, E.M. "The 'Dominating' Symbol in H's Last Phase." *AL*, 39: 506-16 (Ja 68).

Clayton, Lawrence. "'Lady Eleanore's Mantle': A Metaphorical Key to H's 'Legends of the Province House.'" *ELN*, 9: 49-51 (S 71).

Clemens, Cyril. "Personal Glimpses of NH, Thoreau and Emerson." *Hobbies*, nv: 140-1 (Ap 70).

Clendenning, John. "Irving and the Gothic Tradition." *BuR*, 12: 90-8 (1964).

Coffey, D.G. "H's 'Alice Doane's Appeal': The Artist Absolved." *ESQ*, 21: 230-40 (4Q 75).

Cohen, B.B. "Deodat Lawson's *Christ's Fidelity* and H's 'Young Goodman Brown.'" *EIHC*, 104: 349-70 (1968).

————. ''H's Library: An Approach to the Man and His Mind.'' *NHJ*, 1: 125-39 (1971).

Cohen, Henning. ''H's *Israel Potter*.'' *MSEx*, 14: 9-10 (Ap 73).

————. '''Heterogeny'—A Word H Made.'' *AN&Q*, 10: 117 (Ap 72).

Cohen, H.I. ''Hoffmann's 'The Sandman': A Possible Source for 'Rappaccini's Daughter.''' *ESQ*, 62: 148-53 (3Q 72).

Colacurcio, M.J. ''A Better Mode of Evidence—The Transcendental Problem of Faith and Spirit.'' *ESQ*, 54: 12-22 (1Q 69).

————. ''Footsteps of Ann Hutchinson: The Context of *The Scarlet Letter*.'' *ELH*, 39: 459-94 (1972).

————. ''Visible Sanctity and Specter Evidence: The Moral World of H's 'Young Goodman Brown.''' *EIHC*, 110: 259-99 (1974).

Condon, R.A. ''The Broken Conduit: A Study of Alienation in American Literature.'' *PS*, 8: 326-32 (1954).

Cook, Reginald. ''The Forest of Goodman Brown's Night: A Reading of H's 'Young Goodman Brown.''' *NEQ*, 43: 473-81 (S 70).

Couser, G.T. '''The Old Manse,' *Walden*, and the H-Thoreau Relationship.'' *ESQ*, 21: 11-20 (1Q 75).

Cox, J.M. ''*The Scarlet Letter*: Through the Old Manse and the Custom House.'' *VQR*, 51: 432-47 (Su 75).

Cracroft, R.H. ''Liverpool, 1856: NH Meets Orson Pratt.'' *BYUS*, 8: 270-2 (Sp 68).

Crews, F.C. ''The Sins of the Fathers: An Exchange.'' *NCF*, 22: 14-9 (1967).

Crowley, J.D. ''H Criticism and the Return to History.'' *StN*, 6: 98-105 (1974).

————. ''The Unity of H's *Twice-Told Tales*.'' *SAF*, 1: 35-61 (Sp 73).

Curran, H. T. ''The Reluctant Yankee in H's Abortive Gothic Romances.'' *NHJ*, 4: 179-84 (1974).

Currie, W.J. ''Against the Dragon: Approaches to Nature in H and Poe.'' *ELLS*, 11: 72-82 (1974).

Daly, R.J. ''Fideism and the Allusive Mood in 'Rappaccini's Daughter.''' *NCF*, 28: 25-35 (1973).

————. ''History and Chivalric Myth in 'Roger Malvin's Burial.''' *EIHC*, 109: 99-115 (1973).

Damcron, J.L. ''H and the Edinburgh Review on the Prose Romance.'' *NHJ*, 5: 170-6 (1975).

Darnell, D.G. '''Doctrine by Ensample': The Emblem and *The Marble Faun*.'' *TSLL*, 15: 301-10 (Su 73).

D'Avanzo, Mario. ''The Literary Sources of 'My Kinsman, Major Molineaux': Shakespeare, Coleridge, Milton.'' *SF*, 10: 121-36 (1973).

Davie, Donald. ''The Legacy of Fenimore Cooper.'' *EC*, 9: 222-38 (1959).

Davis, Joe. ''The Myth of the Garden: NH's 'Rappaccini's Daughter.''' *SLitI*, 2: 3-12 (Ap 69).

Davis, R.B. ''The Americanness of American Literature: Folk and Historical Themes and Materials in Formal Writing.'' *LC*, 3: 10-22 (1959).

Davis, W.V. ''H's 'Young Goodman Brown.''' *NHJ*, 3: 198-9 (1973).

Davison, R.A. ''Redburn, Pierre, and Robin: Melville's Debt to H?'' *ESQ*, 47: 32-4 (1967).

————. ''The Villagers in 'Ethan Brand.''' *SSF*, 4: 260-2 (Sp 67).

Dennis, Carl. ''*The Blithedale Romance* and the Problems of Self-Integration.'' *TSLL*, 15: 93-110 (Sp 73).

————. ''How to Live in Hell: The Bleak Vision of H's 'My Kinsman, Major Molineux.''' *UR*, 37: 250-8 (Je 71).

Delvin, J.E. "A German Analogue for 'The Ambitious Guest.'" *ATQ*, 17: 171-4 (1973).

Dickson, Wayne. "H's 'Young Goodman Brown.'" *Expl*, 29: 44 (Ja 71).

Dillingham, W.B. "Arthur Dimmesdale's Confession." *SLitI*, 2: 21-6 (1969).

Dobbs, Jeannine. "H's Dr. Rappaccini and Father George Rapp." *AL*, 43: 427-30 (N 71).

Doherty, J.F. "H's Communal Paradigm: The American Novel Reconsidered." *Genre*, 7: 30-53 (Mr 74).

Dorsey, J.M. "My NH." *NHJ*, 1: 141-54 (1971).

Dryden, E.A. "H's Castle in the Air: Form and Theme in *The House of the Seven Gables*." *ELH*, 38: 294-317 (Je 71).

Duerksen, R.A. "The Double Image of Beatrice Cenci in *The Marble Faun*." *MichA*, 1: 47-55 (Sp 69).

Duggan, F.X. "Doctrine and the Writers of the American Renaissance." *ESQ*, 39: 45-51 (1965).

Durham, Frank. "H and Goldsmith: A Note." *JAmSt*, 4: 103-5 (Jl 70).

Durr, R.A. "H's Ironic Mode." *NEQ*, 30: 486-95 (1957).

Dwight, Sheila. "H and the Unpardonable Sin." *StN*, 2: 449-58 (Wi 70).

Eakin, P.J. "H's Imagination and the Structure of 'The Custom-House.'" *AL*, 43: 346-58 (N 71).

Eberwein, J.D. "Temporal Perspective in 'The Legends of the Province House.'" *ATQ*, 14: 41-5 (Sp 72).

Edwards, C.H. "A H Echo in Faulkner's Nobel Prize Acceptance Speech." *NCLit*, 1: 4-5 (Mr 71).

Ehrenpreis, A.H. "Elizabeth Gaskell and NH." *NHJ*, 3: 89-119 (1973).

Elder, Marjorie. "H's *The Marble Faun*: A Gothic Structure." *Costerus*, 1: 81-8 (1972).

Elias, H.L. "Alice Doane's Innocence: The Wizard Absolved." *ESQ*, 62: 28-32 (Wi 71).

England, A.B. "Robin Molineux and the Young Ben Franklin: A Reconsideration." *JAmSt*, 6: 181-8 (Ag 72).

Ensor, Allison. "The Downfall of Poor Richard: Benjamin Franklin as Seen by H, Melville, and Mark Twain." *MTJ*, 17: 14-8 (Wi 74-5).

———. "'Whispers of the Bad Angel': A *Scarlet Letter* Passage as a Commentary on H's 'Young Goodman Brown.'" *SSF*, 7: 467-9 (Su 70).

Erisman, Fred. "'Young Goodman Brown'—Warning to Idealists." *ATQ*, 14: 156-8 (Sp 72).

Erlich, G.C. "Deadly Innocence: H's Dark Women." *NEQ*, 41: 163-79 (Je 68).

———. "Guilt and Expiation in 'Roger Malvin's Burial.'" *NCF*, 26: 377-89 (1971).

Estrin, M.W. "Narrative Ambivalence in H's 'Feathertop.'" *JNT*, 5: 164-73 (1975).

———. "'Triumphant Ignominy': *The Scarlet Letter* on Screen." *LFQ*, 2: 110-2 (1974).

Evans, Walter. "Poe's Revisions in His Reviews of H's *Twice-Told Tales*." *PBSA*, 66: 407-19 (4Q 72).

Fairchild, B.H. "A Technique of Discovery: The Dream-Vision in H's Fiction." *ELUD*, 1: 17-28 (Je 73).

Farnham, Anne. "Uncle Venner's Farm: Refuge or Workhouse for Salem's Poor?" *EIHC*, 109: 60-86 (1973).

Fass, Barbara. "Rejection of Paternalism: H's 'My Kinsman, Major Molineux' and Ellison's *Invisible Man*." *CLAJ*, 14: 317-23 (Mr 71).

Feeney, J.J. "The Structure of Ambiguity in H's 'The Maypole of Merry Mount.'" *SAF*, 3: 211-6 (Au 75).

Ferguson, J.M., Jr. "H's 'Young Goodman Brown.'" *Expl*, 28: 32 (D 69).

Ferrell, M.J. "Imbalance in H's Characters." *SDR*, 10: 45-59 (1972).

Fisher, Marvin. "Portrait of the Artist in America: 'H and His Mosses.'" *SoR*, 11: 156-66 (Ja 75).

Fleck, R.H. "Industrial Imagery in *The House of the Seven Gables*," *NHJ*, 4: 273-6 (1974).

———. "H's Reflections at Walden Pound." *ConS*, 8: 5-6 (D 73).

———. "H's Possible Use of Thoreau in *The Marble Faun*." *TJQ*, 6: 8-12 (Ap 74).

Flint, Allen. "'Essentially a day-dream, and yet a fact': H's *Blithedale*." *NHJ*, 2: 75-83 (1972).

———. "H and the Slavery Crisis." *NEQ*, 41: 393-408 (S 68).

———. "The Saving Grace of Marriage in H's Fiction." *ESQ*, 19: 112-7 (2Q 73).

Fogle, R.H. "Coleridge, Hilda, and *The Marble Faun*." *ESQ*, 19: 105-11 (2Q 73).

———. "H and Coleridge on Credibility." *Criticism*, 13: 234-41 (Su 71).

———. "H's PIctorial Unity." *ESQ*, 55: 71-6 (2Q 69).

———. "H's Variegated Lighting." *BuR*, 21: 83-8 (Fa-Wi 73).

———. "NH and the Great English Romantic Poets." *KSJ*, 21-2; 219-35 (1972-3).

———. "Priscilla's Veil: A Study of H's Veil-Imagery in *The Blithedale Romance*." *NHJ*, 2: 59-65 (1972).

———. "Weird Mockery: An Element of H's Style." *Style*, 2: 191-202 (Fa 68).

*Fossum, R.H. "The Summons of the Past: H's 'Alice Doane's Appeal.'" *NCF*, 23: 294-303 (D 68).

Francis, G.A. "Recent H Scholarship, 1970-1971." *NHJ*, 2: 273-8 (1972); 3: 269-77 (1973).

Frederick, J.T. "H and the Workhouse Baby." *ArQ*, 24: 169-73 (Su 68).

———. "H's 'Scribbling Women.'" *NEQ*, 48: 231-40 (Je 75).

Freehafer, John. "*The Marble Faun* and the Editing of Nineteenth-Century Texts." *StN*, 2: 487-503 (Wi 70).

Gallagher, E.J. "The Concluding Paragraph of 'Young Goodman Brown.'" *SSF*, 12: 29-30 (Wi 75).

———. "H's 'Sir William Phips.'" *ESQ*, 19: 213 8 (4Q 73).

———. "History in 'Endicott and the Red Cross.'" *ESQ*, 50: 62-5 (1Q 68).

———. "Sir Kenelm Digby in H's 'The Man of Adamant.'" *N&Q*, 17: 15-6 (Ja 70).

Gamble, R.K. "Reflections on the H-Melville Relationship in *Pierre*." *AL*, 47: 629-32 (Ja 75).

Garlitz, Barbara. "Teaching All of H." *ESQ*, 25: 6-8 (1961).

Gautreau, H.W. "H the Master Genius." *SLM*, 1: 55-9 (#1 75).

———. "A Note on H's 'The Man of Adamant.'" *PQ*, 52: 315-7 (Ap 73).

Gilkes, L.B. "H, Park Benjamin, and S.G. Goodrich: A Three-Cornered Imbroglio." *NHJ*, 1:83-112 (1971).

Gilman, Samuel. "A Day of Disappointment in Salem by an Admirer of *Twice-Told Tales*." *NHJ*, 1: 213-7 (1971).

Givner, Joan. "Katharine Ann Porter, Eudora Welty, and *Ethan Brand*." *IFR*, 1: 32-7 (Ja 74).

Glicksberg, C.I. "The Numinous in Fiction." *ArQ*, 15: 305-13 (1959).

Goldfarb, C.R. "*The Marble Faun* and Emersonian Self-Reliance." *ATQ*, 1: 19-23 (1Q 69).

Gollin, R.K. "'Dream-Work' in *The Blithedale Romance*." *ESQ*, 19: 74-83 (2Q 73).

———. "The Intelligence Offices of H and Melville." *ATQ*, 26: 44-7 (Sp 75).

———. "Painting and Character in *The Marble Faun*." *ESQ*, 21: 1-10 (1Q 75).

Gordan, J.D. "An Anniversary Exhibition: The Henry W., and Albert A. Berg Collection, 1940-1965." *BNYPL*, 69: 665-77 (1965).

———. "Novels in Manuscript: An Exhibition from the Berg Collection." *BNYPL*, 69: 317-29 (1969).

Gottlieb, Elaine. "Singer and H: A Prevalence of Satan." *SoR*, 8: 359-70 (Ap 72).

Gottschalk, Jane. "The Continuity of American Letters in *The Scarlet Letter* and 'The Best in the Jungle.'" *WSL*, 6: 39-45 (1967).

Graddy, W.E "Another Error in *The Marble Faun*." *ESQ*, 63: 26-7 (2Q 71).

Graham, John. "The Restored Passages in the Centenary Edition of *The Blithedale Romance*." *HAB*, 24: 110-4 (Sp 73).

Green, Martin. "Style in American Literature." *CaR*, 84: 385-7 (1967).

Greene, Maxine. "Man Without God in American Fiction." *Humanist*, 25: 125-8 (1965).

Greenwood, Doughlas. "The Heraldic Device in *The Scarlet Letter*: H's Symbolical Use of the Past." *AL*, 46: 207-10 (My 74).

Griffin, G.R. "H and 'The New-England Village': Internal Evidence and a New Genesis of *The Scarlett Letter*." *EIHC*, 107: 268-79 (1971).

Griffith, Kelley. "Form in *The Blithedale Romance*." *AL*, 40: 15-26 (Mr 68).

Gross, S.L. "H and the London *Athenaeum*, 1834-1864." *NHJ*, 3: 35-72 (1973).

Gross, T.L. "NH: The Absurdity of Heroism." *YR*, 57: 182-95 (Wi 68).

Grossman, James. "Vanzetti and H." *AQ*, 22: 902-7 (Wi 70).

Gupta, R.K. "H's Ideal Reader." *IJAS*, 1: 97-9 (1969).

———. "H's Theory of Art." *AL*, 40: 309-24 (N 68).

———. "H's Treatment of the Artist." *NEQ*, 45: 65-80 (Mr 72).

———. "The Technique of Counterstatement: Theme and Meaning in H's 'The Village Uncle.'" *NHJ*, 3: 154-61 (1973).

Guttmann, Allen. "Images of Value and the Sense of the Past." *NEQ*, 35: 15 (1962).

Hagiwara, Tsutomu. "Symbolic and Signific Functions in H's Fiction—With Special Reference to *The Scarlet Letter*." *SEL*, 46: 129-40 (Mr 70).

Hall, Spencer. "Beatrice Cenci: Symbol and Vision in *The Marble Faun*." *NCF*, 25: 85-95 (Je 70).

Hall, W.F. "H, Shakespeare and Tess: Hardy's Use of Allusion and Reference." *ES*, 52: 533-42 (D 71).

Halligan, John. "H and Democracy: 'Endicott and the Red Cross.'" *SSF*, 8: 301-7 (Sp 71).

Hamada, Masajiro. "Gothic Romance in the *House of the Seven Gables*." *SELit*, 45: 49-61 (S 68).

Hamada, Seijiro. "Tamen Kaishaku no Kokoromi." *EigoS*, 116: 248-50, 323-6, 480-2 (1970).

Harding, Walter. "Another Source for H's 'Egotism; or, the Bosom Serpent.'" *AL*, 40: 537-8 (Ja 69).

Harmsel, H.T. "'Young Goodman Brown' and 'The Enormous Radio.'" *SSF*, 9: 407-8 (1972).

Havighurst, Walter. "Symbolism and the Student." *CE*, 16: 426-34, 461 (1955).

Hawthorne, Elizabeth. "The Susan 'Affair.'" *NHJ*, 1: 12-7 (1971).

Hawthorne, Manning. "*The House of the Seven Gables* and H's Family History." *LHY*, 7: 61-6 (Ja 66).

———. "*The Scarlet Letter*." *LHY*, 7: 37-9 (Jl 66).

Hays, P.L. "Why Seven Years in *The Scarlet Letter*?" *NHJ*, 2: 251-3 (1972).

Hedges, W.L. "Irving, H, and the Image of the Wife." *ATQ*, 5: 22-6 (1Q 70).

Heilman, R.B. "H's 'The Birthmark': Science as Religion." *SAQ*, 48: 575-83 (O 49).

Herndon, J.A. "H's Dream Imagery." *AL*, 46: 538-45 (Ja 75).

Hiatt, David. "H and the Romantic Tradition." *WSL*, 1: 77-84 (1964).

Hijiya, J.A. "NH's *Our Old Home*." *AL*, 46: 363-73 (N 74).

Hildebrand, Anne. "Incomplete Metamorphosis in 'Allegories of the Heart.'" *ATQ*, 13: 28-31 (1972).

Hilton, E.M. "H, the Hippie, and the Square." *StN*, 2: 425-39 (Wi 70).

Himelick, Raymond. "H, Spenser, and Christian Humanism." *ESQ*, 21: 21-8 (1Q 75).

Hirsh, J.C. "The Politics of Blithedale: The Dilemma of the Self." *SRom*, 11: 138-46 (Sp 72).

Hirsh, J.C. "Zenobia as Queen: The Background Sources to H's *The Blithedale Romance*." *NHJ*, 1: 182-90 (1971).

Hoffman, C.C. "History in H's Custom-House." *Clio*, 2: 161-9 (F 73).

Horne, L.B. "The Heart, the Hand, and 'The Birthmark.'" *ATQ*, 1: 38-41 (1Q 69).

———. "Of Place, Time, and Moral Growth in *The House of Seven Gables*." *StN*, 2: 459-68 (Wi 70).

Hostetler, N.H. "'Earth's Holocaust': H's Parable of the Imaginative Process." *KanQ*, 7: 85-9 (1975).

Houston, N.B., and R.E. Cain. "Holgrave: H's Antithesis to Carlyle's Teufelsdrockh." *RS*, 38: 36-45 (Mr 70).

Howard, Leon. "The Centenary Edition of H." *NCF*, 22: 191-5 (1967).

Howe, Irving. "Anarchy and Authority in American Literature." *Denver Q*, 2: 5-30 (1967).

Howell, Roger. "A Note on H's Ambivalence Towards Puritanism: His View of Sir Henry Vane the Younger." *NHJ*, 2: 143-6 (1972).

———. "H at Bowdoin." NHJ, 5: 5-9 (1975).

Huffman, C.C. "History in H's Custom-House." *Clio*, 2: 161-70 (F 73).

Hull, Raymona. "British Periodical Printings of H's Works, 1835-1900: A Partial Bibliography." *NHJ*, 3: 73-88 (1973).

———. "H and the Magic Elixir of Life: The Failure of a Gothic Theme." *ESQ*, 6: 97-107 (2Q 72).

———. "Some Further Notes on H and Thoreau." *TSB*, 121: 7-8 (Fa 72).

Hull, R.E. "'Scribbling Females' and Serious Males." *NHJ*, 5: 35-59 (1975).

Humma, John. "'Young Goodman Brown' and the Failure of H's Ambiguity." *CLQ*, 8: 425-31 (D 71).

Hyman, L.W. "Moral Values and the Literary Experience." *JAAC*, 24: 538-47 (1966).

Inge, M.T. "Dr. Rappaccini's Nobel Experiment." *NHJ*, 3: 200-1 (1973).

Irwin, J.T. "The Symbol of the Hieroglyphics in the American Renaissance." *AQ*, 26: 103-26 (My 74).

Isani, Mukhtar. "H and the Branding of William Prynne." *NEQ*, 45: 182-95 (Je 72).

James, S.B. "The Politics of Personal Salvation: The American Literary Record." *Denver Q*, 4: 19-45 (1969).

Janssen, J.G. "Dimmesdale's 'Lurid Playfulness.'" *ATQ*, 1: 30-4 (1Q 69).

———. "The 'Dismal Merry-Making' in H's Comic Vision." *SAH*, 1: 107-17 (O 74).

———. "H's Seventh Vagabond: 'The Outsetting Bard.'" *ESQ*, 62: 22-8 (Wi 71).

———. "Pride and Prophecy: The final Irony of *The Scarlet Letter*." *NHJ*, 5: 241-7 (1975).

Jarrett, D.W. "H and Hardy as Modern Romancers." *NCF*, 28: 258-71 (D 74).

Jenkins, R.B. "A New Look at an Old Tombstone." *NEQ*, 45: 417-21 (S 72).

Johnson, C.D. "H and Nineteenth-Century Perfectionism." *AL*, 44: 585-95 (Ja 73).

Johnson, C.G. "'Young Goodman Brown' and Puritan Justification." *SSF*, 11: 200-4 (Sp 74).

Jones, Buford. "After Long Apprenticeship: H's Mature Romances." *ESQ*, 19: 1-7 (1Q 73).

———. "A Checklist of H Criticism 1951-1966." *ESQ*, 52: 1-90 (3Q 68).

———. "'The Hall of Fantasy' and the Early H-Thoreau Relationship." *PMLA*, 83: 1429-38 (O 68).

———. "H and Spenser." *NHJ*, 5: 71-90 (1975).

———. "H Studies: The Seventies." *StN*, 2: 504-18 (Wi 70).

———. "'The Man of Adamant' and the Moral Picturesque." *ATQ*, 14: 33-41 (Sp 72).

Jones, M.C. "*The Marble Faun* and a Writer's Crisis." *SA*, 16: 81-123 (1970).

Jones, P.M. "H's Mythic Use of Puritan History." *Cithara*, 12: 59-73 (1972).

Jones, W.A. "The H-Goodrich Relationship." *NHJ*, 5: 91-140 (1975).

———. "New Light on H and the Southern Rose." *NHJ*, 4: 31-6 (1974).

*——. "Recent H Scholarship, 1973-74." *NHJ*, 5: 281-316 (1975).

———. "Sometimes Things Just Don't Work Out." *NHJ*, 5: 11-26 (1975).

Joyner, Nancy. "Bondage in Blithedale." *NHJ*, 5: 227-31 (1975).

Justus, J.H. "H's Coverdale: Character and Art in *The Blithedale Romance*." *AL*, 47: 21-36 (Mr 75).

Kable, W.S. "'NH': A Newly Discovered Manuscript." *NHJ*, 1: 18-27 (1971).

Kamogawa, Takahiro. "On the Family Name 'Pyncheon' in the *House of the Seven Gables*." *HirStud*, 16: 41-7 (1969).

———. "Rome in *The Marble Faun*." *KAL*, 11: 32-43 (1968).

Kane, Patricia. "The Fallen Woman as Free-Thinker in *The French Lieutenant's Woman* and *The Scarlet Letter*." *NCLit*, 2: 8-10 (Ja 72).

Karita, Motoshi. "Shosetsu to Denki no Shudai-sentaku to Imi." *SophT*, 17: 29-45 (1968).

Katz, Joseph. "The Centenary Edition of the Works of NH: Our Old Home." *NHJ*, 1: 287-9 (1971).

Katz, Seymour. "'Character,' 'Nature,' and Allegory in *The Scarlet Letter*." *NCF*, 23: 3-17 (Je 68).

Kaul, A.N. "Character and Motive in *The Scarlet Letter*." *CirtQ*, 10: 373-84 (Wi 68).

Kay, C.M. "H's Use of Clothing in His Short Stories." *NHJ*, 2: 245-9 (1972).

Kay, Donald. "English Fruits, Yankee Turnips: Another Look at H in England." *NHJ*, 4: 150-61 (1974).

———. "Five Acts of *The Blithedale Romance*." *ATQ*, 13: 25-8 (1972).

———. "H's Use of Laughter in Selected Short Stories." *XUS*, 10: 27-32 (Fa 71).

Kazin, Alfred. "On H." *NYRB*, 11: 26-8 (24 O 68).

Kehl, D.G. "H's 'Vicious' Circles: The Sphere-Circle Imagery in the Four Major Novels." *BRMMLA*, 23: 9-20 (1969).

Kehler, Dorothea. "H and Shakespeare." *ATQ*, 22: 104-5 (Sp 74).

Kehler, J.R. "*The House of the Seven Gables*: House, Home, and H's Psychology of Habitation." *ESQ*, 21: 142-53 (3Q 75).

Kellner, Robert. "'No Virtue in Women': A Study of the Psychological Themes in *The Scarlet Letter*." *NDQ*, 42: 28-39 (Sp 74).

Kelly, Richard. "H's 'Ethan Brand.'" *Expl*, 28: 47 (F 70).

Kermode, Frank. "H's Modernity." *PR*, 41: 428-41 (3Q 74).

Kersten, Kurt. "Seher der Kommender Krise—Herman Melville und NH." *Neues Abendland*, 6: 265-6 (1951).

Kesterson, D.B. "Journey to Perugia: Dantean Parallels in *The Marble Faun*." *ESQ*, 19: 94-104 (2Q 73).

———. "Nature and Theme in 'Young Goodman Brown.'" *Dickinson R*, 2: 42-6 (Wi 70).

———. "Nature in H's Religious Isolationists." *NHJ*, 4: 196-208 (1974).

Killinger, John. "The Death of God in American Literature." *SHR*, 2: 149-72 (1968).

Kligerman, Jack. "A Stylistic Approach to H's 'Roger Malvin's Burial.'" *Lang&S*, 4: 188-94 (1971).

Klinkowitz, Jerome. "Ending the *Seven Gables*: Old Light on a New Problem." *StN*, 4: 396-401 (Fa 72).

———. "The H-Fields Letterbook: A Census and Description." *NHJ*, 4: 93-103 (1974).

————. "H's Sense of an Ending." *ESQ*, 19: 43-9 (1Q 73).

————. "In Defense of Holgrave." *ESQ*, 62: 4-8 (Wi 71).

Koskenlinna, H.M. "Setting, Image, and Symbol in Scott and H." *ESQ*, 19: 50-9 (1Q 73).

Kotker, Norman. "The Literary Road to Rome." *Horizon*, 9: 18-30 (1967).

Kroeger, F.P. "Longfellow, Melville, and H: The Passage into the Iron Age." *IllQ*, 33: 30-41 (D 70).

Kummings, D.D. "H's 'The Custom House' and the Conditions of Fiction in America." *CEA*, 33: 15-8 (Mr 71).

Kushen, Betty. "Love's Martyrs: The Scarlet Letter as Secular Cross." *L&P*, 20: 109-20 (72).

Larson, C.R. "Hester Prynne and the Pill." *CEA*, 34: 35-7 (Ja 72).

La Regina, Gabriella. "*Rappaccini's Daughter*: The Gothic as Catalyst for H's Imagination." *SA*, 17: 29-74 (1971).

Laverty, C.D. "Some Touchstones of H's Style." *ESQ*, 60: 30-6 (Su 70).

Lease, Benjamin. "The Chemistry of Genius: Herman Melville and Anton Bruckner." *Person*, 48: 224-41 (1967).

————. "Diorama and Dream: H's Cinematic Vision." *JPC*, 5: 315-23 (Fa 71).

————. "H and *Blackwood's* in 1849: Two Unpublished Letters." *JA*, 14: 152-4 (1969).

————. "H and 'A Certain Venerable Personage': New Light on 'The Custom-House.'" *JA*, 15: 201-7 (1970).

————. "Salem vs. H: An Early Review of *The Scarlet Letter*." *NEQ*, 44: 110-7 (Mr 71).

————. "'The Whole Is a Prose Poem': An Early Review of *The Scarlet Letter*." *AL*, 44: 128-30 (My 72).

Lefcowitz, Allan. "*Apologia* pro Roger Prynne: A Psychological Study." *L&P*, 24: 34-43 (1Q 74).

Lesser, M.X. "Dimmesdale's Wordless Sermon." *AN&Q*, 12: 93 4 (F 74).

Levy, L.B. "*The Blithedale Romance*: H'S 'Voyage Through Chaos.'" *SRom*, 8: 1-15 (Au 68).

————. "*Fanshawe*: H's World of Images." *StN*, 2: 440-8 (Wi 70).

————. "The Landscape Modes of *The Scarlet Letter*." *NCF*, 23: 377-92 (Mr 69).

————. "Lifelikeness in H's Fiction." *NHJ*, 5: 141-5 (1975).

————. "*The Marble Faun*: H's Landscape of the Fall." *AL*, 42: 139-56 (My 70).

————. "The Notebook Source and the 18th Century Context of H's Theory of Romance." *NHJ*, 3: 120-9 (1973).

————. "The Problem of Faith in Young Goodman Brown." *JEGP*, 74: 375-87 (1975).

————. "'Time's Portraiture': H's Theory of History." *NHJ*, 1: 192-200 (1971).

Liebman, S.W. "Ambiguity in 'Lady Eleanore's Mantle.'" *ESQ*, 58: 97-101 (1Q 70).

————. "Ethan Brand and the Unpardonable Sin." *ATQ*, 24: 9-14 (Fa 74).

————. "The Forsaken Maiden in H's Stories." *ATQ*, 19: 13-9 (Su 73).

————. "H and Milton: The Second Fall in 'Rappaccini's Daughter.'" *NEQ*, 41: 521-35 (D 68).

————. "H's *Comus*: A Miltonic Source for 'The Maypole of Merrymount.'" *NCF*, 27: 345-51 (1972).

————. "Moral Choice in 'The Maypole of Merry Mount.'" *SSF*, 11: 173-80 (Sp 74).

————. "Point of View in *The House of the Seven Gables*." *ESQ*, 19: 203-12 (4Q 73).

————. "Robin's Conversion: The Design of 'My Kinsman, Major Molineux.'" *SSF*, 8: 443-57 (1971).

————. "'Roger Malvin's Burial': H's Allegory of the Heart." *SSF*, 12: 253-60 (Su 75).

Liebman, Sheldon. "The Reader in 'Young Goodman Brown.'" *NHJ*, 5: 156-69 (1975).

Lohmann, C.K. "The Agony of the English Romance." *NHJ*, 2: 219-29 (1972).

Lombard, C.M. "H and French Romanticism." *RLMC*, 24: 311-6 (1971).

Long, R.E. "*The Ambassadors* and The Genteel Tradition: James's Correction of H and Howells." *NEQ*, 42: 44-64 (1969).

Long, R.E. "James's *Washington Square*: The H Relation." *NEQ*, 46: 573-90 (D 73).

Loving, J.M. "Melville's Unpardonable Sin." *NEQ*, 47: 262-78 (Je 74).

Lozynsky, Artem. "Whitman the Man and H the Artist." *NHJ*, 5: 270-1 (1975).

Lynen, J.F. "H as Myth-Maker." *UTQ*, 41: 163-9 (Wi 72).

Lytle, David, "Giovanni! My Poor Giovanni." *SSF*, 9: 147-56 (1972).

McCall, Dan. "H's 'Familiar Kind of Preface.'" *ELH*, 35: 422-39 (S 68).

———. "'I Felt a Funeral in my Brain' and 'The Hollow of the Three Hills.'" *NEQ*, 42: 432-5 (S 69).

McCarthy, H.T. "H's Dialogue with Rome: *The Marble Faun*." *SA*, 14: 97-112 (1968).

McCarthy, Paul. "The Extraordinary Man as Idealist in Novels by H and Melville." *ESQ*, 54: 43-51 (1Q 69).

———. "A Perspective in H's Novels." *BSUF*, 13: 46-58 (Wi 72).

McCullen, J.T. "Influences on H's 'The Artist of the Beautiful.'" *ESQ*, 50: 43-6 (1Q 68).

McDonald, John. "'The Old Manse' and Its Mosses: The Inception and Development of *Mosses from an Old Manse*." *TSLL*, 16: 77-108 (Sp 74).

———. "The Old Manse Period Canon." *NHJ*, 2: 13-39 (1972).

McDonald, J.J. "A Sophia H Journal, 1843-1844." *NHJ*, 4: 1-30 (1974).

McDonald, W.R. "Coincidence in the Novel: A Necessary Technique." *CE*, 29: 373-88 (1968).

McElroy, John. "The Brand Metaphor in 'Ethan Brand.'" *AL*, 43: 633-7 (Ja 72).

———. "The H Style in American Fiction." *ESQ*, 19: 117-23 (2Q 73).

McHaney, T.L. "The Textual Editions of H and Melville." *SLitI*, 2: 27-41 (Ap 69).

McKeithan, D.M. "Poe and the Second Edition of H's *Twice-Told Tales*." *NHJ*, 4: 257-69 (1974).

McNamara, L.F. "Subject, Style, and Narrative Technique in 'Bartleby' and 'Wakefield.'" *MichA*, 3: 41-6 (Sp 71).

Maddocks, Melvin. "Rituals—The Revolt Against the Fixed Smile." *Time*, 96 42-3 (1970).

Maes-Jelinek, Hena. "Roger Chillingworth: An Example of the Creative Process in *The Scarlet Letter*." *ES*, 49: 341-8 (Ag 68).

Magretta, Koan. "The Coverdale Translation: *Blithedale* and the Bible." *NHJ*, 4: 250-6 (1974).

Male, R.R. "H's Fancy, or the Medium of *The Blithedale Romance*." *NHJ*, 2: 67-73 (1972).

———. "H's *The Blithedale Romance*." *EXpl*, 28: 56 (Mr 70).

Malin, Irving. "The Authoritarian Family in American Fiction." *Mosaic*, 4: 153-73 (1971).

Manierre, W.R. "The Role of Sympathy in *The Scarlet Letter*." *TSLL*, 13: 497-507 (Fa 71).

———. "Some Apparent Confusions in *The Scarlet Letter*." *CEA*, 33: 9-13 (Mr 71).

Mann, C.W. "D.H. Lawrence: Notes on Reading H's *The Scarlet Letter*." *NHJ*, 3: 8-25 (1973).

———. "Elizabeth H Takes a Walk with Her Brother." *NHJ*, 1: 67-9 (1971).

———. "Elizabeth Peabody Identifies the 'Original' Judge Pyncheon." *NHJ*, 1: 70 (1971).

———. "H to Longfellow: An Unpublished Letter." *NHJ*, 1: 71 (1971).

Mariano, J.T. "NH's Symbolism of Black and White as a Synthesis of Permanence and Change in *The House of Seven Gables and The Marble Faun*." *DilR*, 18: 268-83 (Jl 70).

Marks, A.H. "Ironic Inversion in *The Blithedale Romance*." *ESQ*, 55: 95-102 (2Q 69).

Markus, Manfred. "H's 'Alice Doanes's Appeal': An Anti-Gothic Tale." *GRM*, 25: 338-49 (1975).

Marovitz, S.E. "*Roderick Hudson*: James's *Marble Faun*." *TSLL*, 11: 1427-43 (Wi 70).

Martin, R.K. "H's *The Blithedale Romance*." *Expl*, 28: 11 (S 69).

Martin, Terence. "Dimmesdale's Ultimate Sermon." *ArQ*, 27: 230-40 (1971).

———. "H's Public Decade and the Values of Home." *AL*, 46: 141-52 (My 74).

Masheck, J.D.C. "Samuel Johnson's Uttoxeter Penance in the Writings of H."
Hermathena, 111: 51-4 (Sp 71).

Mathews, J.W. "H and the Periodical Tale: From Popular Lore to Art." *PBSA*, 68: 146-62
(Ap-Je 74).

———. "The House of Atreus and *The House of the Seven Gables*." *ESQ*, 63: 31-6 (Sp 71).

Mathy, Francis. "The Magnetic Chain of Humanity—A Study of Alienation and
Involvement in H." *ELLS*, 7: 82-109 (1970).

———. "The Three Johns: Portraits of Emerson, Thoreau, H, and Whittier." *Eng Lang &
Lit* (Tokyo), 10: 163-81 (Mr 74).

Matsuyama, Nobunao. "Some Faces of H's Young Goodman Brown." *DSE*, 10: 32-52 (Mr
75).

Mattfield, M.S. "H's Juvenile Classics." *Disc*, 12: 346-64 (Su 69).

May, C.E. "Pearl as Christ and Confidence Man." *ATQ*, 24: 8-11 (Fa 74).

Mayer, D.R. "Symbolic Action in H's Parable: 'The Minister's Black Veil.'" *FJS*, 7: 25-31
(1974).

Melchiori, Giorgio. "The English Novelist and the American Tradition." *SR*, 68: 502-15 (Su
60).

Merivale, Patricia. "The Raven and the Bust of Pallas: Classical Artifacts and the Gothic
Tale." *PMLA*, 89: 960-6 (O 74).

Mills, N.C. "Prison and Society in Nineteenth-Century American Fiction." *WHR*, 24:
325-31 (1970).

Minock, D.W. "H and the Rumor about the Governor's Lady." *AN&Q*, 13: 87-8 (F 75).

Monke, Arthur, and C.E.F. Clark. "H's 'Moonlight.'" *NHJ*, 3: 27-35 (1973).

Monteiro, George. "Elizabeth Shaw Melville as Censor." *ESQ*, 62: 32-3 (1971).

———. "The Full Particulars of the Minister's Behavior—According to Hale." *NHJ*, 2:
173-82 (1972).

———. "H in the English Press." *NHJ*, 4: 162-78 (1974).

———. "H in Portuguese." *NHJ*, 1: 228-31 (1971); 4: 280-1 (1974).

———. "H Letters in Old Catalogues." *ATQ*, 1: 122 (1969).

———. "H's Emblematic Serpent." *NHJ*, 3: 134-42 (1973).

———. "More H in Portuguese." *NHJ*, 2: 263-4 (1972).

———. "A Nonliterary Source for H's 'Egotism; or the Bosom Serpent.'" *AL*, 41: 575-7 (Ja
70).

Montgomery, J.H. "The American Galatea." *CE*, 32: 890-9 (My 71).

Moore, Robert. "H's Folk-Motifs and *The House of the Seven Gables*." *NYFQ*, 28: 221-33
(S 72).

Morgan, E.E. "The Veiled Lady: The Secret Love of Miles Coverdale." *NHJ*, 1: 169-81
(1971).

Morrow, Patrick. "A Writer's Workshop: H's 'The Great Carbuncle.'" *SSF*, 6: 157-64
(1969).

Morseberger, K.M. "H's 'Borderline': The Locale of the Romance." *Costerus*, 7: 93-112
(1973).

Morseberger, R.E. "'The Minister's Black Veil': 'Shrouded in a Blackness Ten Times
Black.'" *NEQ*, 46: 454-63 (S 73).

———. "Wakefield in the Twilight Zone." *ATQ*, 14: 6-8 (Sp 72).

————. "The Woe That Is Madness: Goodman Brown and the Face of the Fire." *NHJ*, 3: 177-82 (1973).

Moss, S.P. "The Symbolism of the Italian Background in *The Marble Faun*." *NCF*, 23: 332-6 (D 68).

Moss, Sidney. "H and Melville: An Inquiry Into Their Art and Their Friendship." *Lit Monographs*, 7: 45-84 (1975).

Mounts, C.E. "H's Echoes of Spenser and Milton." *NHJ*, 3: 162-71 (1973).

Mulqueen, J.E. "Conservatism and Criticism: The Literary Standards of the American Whigs, 1845-1852." *AL*, 41: 355-72 (1969).

Murphy, J.J. "The Function of Sin in H's Novels." *ESQ*, 50: 65-71 (1Q 68).

————. "Willa Cather and H: Significant Resemblances." *Renascence*, 27: 161-75 (Sp 75).

Myers, A.B. "NH, 1804-1864." *GGC*, 5: 2-20 (O 67).

Myerson, Joel. "Sarah Clarke's Reminiscences of the Peabodys and H." *NHJ*, 3: 130-3 (1973).

Nakata, Yuji. "*The House of the Seven Gables*: A Study in Isolation with and Emphasis on Name Symbolism." *KAL*, 11: 11-31 (1968).

Naples, D.C. "'Roger Malvin's Burial': A Parable for Historians?" *ATQ*, 13: 45-8 (1972).

Newlin, P.A. "'Vague Shapes of the Borderland': The Place of the Uncanny in H's Gothic Vision." *ESQ*, 18: 83-96 (2Q 72).

Nilsen, H.N. "H's 'My Kinsman, Major Molineux.'" *AmNor*, 4: 137-81 (1973).

Nirenberg, Morton. "H's Reception in Germany." *JA*, 15: 141-61 (1970).

Noble, D.W. "The Analysis of Alienation by 20th Century Social Scientists and 19th Century Novelists: The Example of H's *The Scarlet Letter*." *MVCBul*, 5: 5-19 (Fa 72).

Norton, E.R. "H's Point of Recovery." *CimR*, 27: 29-37 (Ap 74).

Noyes, Russell. "H's Debt to Charles Lamb." *Charles Lamb Bul*, 4: 69-77 (1973).

Okamoto, Katsumi. "H—Hatashi naki Kikyu." *EigoS*, 114: 801-2 (1968).

————. "*The Scarlet Letter*: Struggle Toward Integrity." *SELit*, 46: 45-61 (O 69).

Osborne, Robert, and Marijane Osborne. "Another Look at an Old Tombstone." *NEQ*, 46: 278-9 (Je 73).

Överland, Orm. "The Unhumanizing Imagination: H's *The Blithedale Romance*." *SN*, 46: 370-81 (1974).

Owens, Louis. "Paulding's 'The Dumb Girl,' a Source of *The Scarlet Letter*." *NHJ*, 4: 240-9 (1974).

Pancost, D.W. "Evidence of Editorial Additions to H's 'Fragments from the Journal of a Solitary Man.'" *NHJ*, 5: 210-26 (1975).

————. "H's Epistemology and Ontology." *ESQ*, 19: 8-13 (1Q 73).

Pandeya, P.K. "The Drama of Evil in "The Hollow of the Seven Hills.'" *NHJ*, 5: 177-81 (1975).

Parkes, H.B. "Freedom and Order in Western Literature." *Denver Q*, 4: 1-18 (1969).

Pattison, J.C. "'The Celestial Railroad' as Dream Tale." *AQ*, 20: 224-36 (Su 68).

Paulits, W.J. "Ambivalence in 'Young Goodman Brown.'" *AL*, 41: 577-84 (Ja 70).

Pauly, T.H. "'Mr. Higginbotham's Catastrophe'—The Story Teller's Disaster." *ATQ*, 14: 171-4 (Sp 72).

Peabody, E.P. "Elizabeth P. Peabody to Mrs. Harriet M. Lothrop: An Unpublished Letter about H." *NHJ*, 2: 7-8 (1972).

Pearce, H.D. "H's Old Moodie: *The Blithedale Romance* and *Measure for Measure*." *SAB*, 38: 11-5 (N 73).

Peple, E.C. "The Background of the H-Thoreau Relationship." *RALS*, 1: 104-12 (Sp 71).

————. "H on Thoreau: 1853-1857." *TSB*, 119: 1-3 (Sp 72).

———. "Thoreau and Donatello." *TJQ*, 5: 22-5 (O 73).

———. "Three Unlisted Reviews of H." *ESQ*, 68: 146-7 (3Q 72).

Pérez Gallego, Cándido. "Los prólogos de NH a sus novelas." *RL*, 29: 111-9 (1966).

Phillips, John. "Melvile Meets H." *AH*, 27: 16-21, 87-90 (D 75).

Pierce, Franklin. "Franklin Pierce to Horatio Bridge: An Unpublished Letter from a President." *NHJ*, 2: 11-2 (1972).

Pinsker, Sanford. "H's 'Double-Faced Fellow': A Note on 'My Kinsman, Major Molineux.'" *NHJ*, 2: 255-6 (1972).

Plank, Robert. "Heart Transplant Fiction." *HSL*, 2: 102-12 (1970).

Porat, Zippora. "Geula H'ba'a Bi-nefila: Ha-meri Be-*Ot Hashani* Le NH." *Molad*, 24: 680-91 (1972).

Pritchett, V.S. "An Ocean Between." *NSt*, 19 Mr 71: pp 383-4.

Prosser, M.H. "A Rhetoric of Alienation as Reflected in the Works of NH." *QJS*, 54: 22-8 (F 68).

Quick, J.R. "*Silas Marner* as Romance: The Example of H." *NCF*, 29: 287-98 (D 74).

Quinn, James, and Ross Baldessarini. "Literary Technique and Psychological Effect in H's 'The Minister's Black Veil.'" *L&P*, 24: 115-23 (3Q 74).

Reece, J.B. "An Error in Some Reprintings of Poe's 1847 Critique of H." *PS*, 4: 47 (D 71).

———. "Mr. Hooper's Vow." *ESQ*, 21: 93-102 (2Q 75).

Reed, R.B., and J.D. O'Heru. "NH at Bowdoin College." *NHJ*, 2: 147-57 (1972).

Rees, J.O. "H's Conception of Allegory: A Reconsideration." *PQ*, 54: 494-510 (Sp 75).

———. "Shakespeare in *The Blithedale Romance*." *ESQ*, 19: 84-93 (2Q 73).

Regan, Robert. "H's 'Plagiary': Poe's Duplicity." *NCF*, 25: 281-98 (D 70).

Richard, Claude. "Poe et H." *EA*, 22: 351-61 (O-D 69).

Ringe, D.A. "H's Night Journeys." *ATQ*, 10: 27-32 (Sp 71).

Rizzardi, Alfredo. "Il suicidio de Melville nelle lettere a NH." *Stile*, 2: np (1953).

Roberto, Eugène. "*Le livre des merveilles* de NH." *Cahier Canadien Claudel*, 5: 99-108 (1967).

Robertson, P.R. "Shelley and H: A Comparison of Imagery and Sensibility." *SCB*, 32: 233-39 (Wi 72).

Robillard, Douglas. "H's 'Roger Malvin's Burial.'" *Expl*, 26: 56 (Mr 68).

Rochner, J. "Life in a Picture Gallery: Things in *The Portrait of a Lady* and *The Marble Faun*." *TSLL*, 11: 761-7 (1969).

Rocks, J.E. "H and France: In Search of American Literary Nationalism." *TSE*, 17: 145-57 (1969).

Rodnon, Stewart. "*The House of the Seven Gables* and *Absalom, Absalom!*" *StH*, 1: 42-6 (1970).

Rosa, A.F. "Charles Ives: Music, Transcendentalism, and Politics." *NEQ*, 44: 433-43 (1971).

Rose, M.G. "Julian Green's H Essay." *NHJ*, 5: 248-50 (1975).

———. "Miles Coverdale as H's Persona." *ATQ*, 1: 90-1 (1Q 69).

Rosenberry, E.H. "Melville and his *Mosses*." *ATQ*, 7: 47-51 (Su 70).

Ross, Donald. "Dreams and Sexual Repression in *The Blithedale Romance*." *PMLA*, 86: 1014-7 (O 71).

———. "H and Thoreau on 'Cottage Architecture.'" *ATQ*, 1: 100-1 (1Q 69).

Ross, M.L. "What Happens in 'Rappaccini's Daughter.'" *AL*, 43: 336-45 (N 71).

Sachs, Viola. "The Myth of America in H's *House of the Seven Gables* and *Blithedale Romance*." *KN*, 15: 267-83 (1968).

St. Armand, B.L. "The Golden Stain of Time: Ruskinian Aesthetics and the Ending of H's *the House of the Seven Gables*." *NHJ*, 3: 143-53 (1973).

————. "H's 'Haunted Mind': A Subterranean Drama of the Self." *Criticism*, 13: 1-25 (Wi 71).

————. "'Young Goodman Brown' as Historical Allegory." *NHJ*, 3: 183-97 (1973).

Sakamoto, Masayuki. "Koto no Omomi—H Note." *EigoS*, 119: 756-7 (1974).

Sampson, E.C. "Sound-Imagery in *The House of the Seven Gables*." *Eng Rec*, 22: 26-9 (Wi 71).

Samuels, C.T. "Giovanni and the Governess." *AS*, 37: 655-78 (1968).

Sanborn, F.B. "H and His Friends: Reminiscence and Tribute." *ATQ*, 9: 5-24 (1971).

Sanderline, Reed. "H's Scarlet Letter." *SHR*, 9: 145-7 (1975).

Santagelo, G.A. "The Absurdity of *The Minister's Black Veil*." *PCP*, 5: 61-6 (1970).

Sattlemeyer, Robert. "The Aesthetic Background of H's Fanshawe." *NHJ*, 5: 200-9 (1975).

Schechter, Harold. "Death and Resurrection of the King: Elements of Primitive Mythology in 'Roger Malvin's Burial.'" *ELN*, 8: 201-5 (1971).

————. "The Unpardonable Sin in *Washington Square*." *SSF*, 10: 137-41 (1973).

Scheer, T.F. "Aylmer's Divine Roles in 'The Birthmark.'" *ATQ*, 22: 108-9 (Sp 74).

Scherting, Jack. "The Upas Tree in Dr. Rappaccini's Garden: New Light on H's Tale." *SAF*, 1: 203-7 (1973).

Scheuermann, Mona. "Outside the Human Circle: Views from H and Godwin." *NHJ*, 5: 182-91 (1975).

Schmitt-v. Muhlenfels, Astrid. "H's *The Scarlet Letter* als Fernsehfilm: Darstellung, Deutung und Umdeutung." *LWU*, 7: 39-46 (My 74).

Schneider, D.J. "The Allegory and Symbolism of H's *The Marble Faun*." *StN*, 1: 38-50 (Sp 69).

Schneiderman, Lee. "H and the Refuge of the Heart." *ConnR*, 3: 83-101 (1970).

Schoen, Carol. "The House of the Seven Deadly Sins." *ESQ*, 19: 26-33 (1Q 73).

Schorer, C.E. "H and Hypnosis." *NHJ*, 2: 239-44 (1972).

Schriber, M.S. "Emerson, H, and 'The Artist of the Beautiful.'" *SSF*, 8: 607-16 (1971).

Schulz, Dieter. "'Ethan Brand' and the Structure of the American Quest Romance." *Genre*, 7: 233-49 (S 74).

————. "Imagination and Self-Imprisonment: The Ending of 'Roger Malvin's Burial.'" *SSF*, 10: 183-6 (1973).

Schwartz, Joseph. "NH and the Natural Desire for God." *NHJ*, 2: 159-71 (1972).

Scoville, Samuel. "H's Houses and Hidden Treasures." *ESQ*, 19: 61-73 (2Q 73).

————. "To Conceive of the Devil." *EJ*, 58: 673-5 (My 69).

Secor, Robert. "Conrad's American Sharers." *Conrad*, 1: 59-67 (1968).

————. "H, Conrad, and the Descent into Darkness." *MRR*, 2: 41-55 (Su-Fa 67).

Seelye, J.D. "'Ungraspable Phantom': Reflections of H in *Pierre* and *The Confidence-Man*." *StN*, 1: 436-43 (Wi 69).

Sharma, T.R.S. "Diabolic World and Naive Hero in 'My Kinsman, Major Molineux.'" *IJAS*, 1: 35-43 (1969).

Shear, Walter. "Characterization in *The Scarlet Letter*." *MwQ*, 12: 437-54 (Su 71).

Sherman, William. "Henry Bright in New England: His First Meeting with H." *NEQ*, 46: 124-6 (Mr 73).

Shimada, Taro. "A Wilderness of Mirrors: A Study of NH." *HiJAS*, 11: 24-49 (1970).

Shroeder, John. "Alice Doane's Story: An Essay on H and Spenser." *NHJ*, 4: 129-34 (1974).

Shulman, Robert. "H's Quiet Conflict." *PQ*, 47: 216-36 (Ap 68).

Siegel, S.D. "H's Seven Veiled Ladies." *Gypsy Schol*, 1: 48-53 (1973).

Silhol, Robert. "*La Maison des sept pignons*, essai d'anthropologie littéraire." *EA*, 25: 272-85 (1972).

Simpson, C.M. "Correction or Corruption? NH and Two Friendly Improvers." *HLQ*, 36: 367-86 (1973).

———. "A Manuscript Mystery: H's 1839 Scrap-Book." *NHJ*, 5: 28-33 (1975).

Singer, David. "H and the 'Wild Irish': A Note." *NEQ*, 42: 425-32 (S 69).

Sister Anna. "Eldorado in Salem." *EJ*, 35: 153-5 (1946).

Skey, Miriam. "The Letter 'A.'" *KAL*, 11: 1-10 (1968).

Sklar, Dusty. "H and the Supernatural." *Psy*, 4: 39-42 (F 73).

Slethaug, G.E. "*Felix Culpa* in H's *Custom-House*." *Eng Rec*, 23: 32-40 (Wi 72).

Small, Michel. "The Tale the Critic Tells: D.H. Lawrence on NH." *Paunch*, 40-1: 40-58 (Ap 75).

Smith, Julian. "*The Blithedale Romance*—H's New Testament of Failure." *Person*, 49: 540-8 (Au 68).

———. "A H Source for *The House of the Seven Gables*." *ATQ*, 1: 18-9 (1Q 69).

———. "H's *Legends of the Province House*." *NCF*, 24: 31-44 (Je 69).

———. "Hester, Sweet Hester Prynne—*The Scarlet Letter* in the Movie Market Place." *LFQ*, 2: 100-9 (1974).

———. "Historical Ambiguity in 'My Kinsman, Major Molineux.'" *ELN*, 8: 115-20 (1970).

———. "Why Does Zenobia Kill Herself?" *ELN*, 6: 37-9 (S 68).

Smith, L.N. "Manuscript of *Our Old Home*." *CEAAN*, 1: 2 (1968).

Smith, N.E. "Another Story Falsely Attributed to H: 'The First and Last Dinner.'" *PBSA*, 65: 172-3 (2Q 71).

Solenstein, J.M. "H's Ribald Classic: 'Mrs. Bullfrog' and the Folktale." *JPC*, 7: 582-8 (1973).

Spicer, Harold. "H's Credo of 'The Beautiful.'" *YES*, 4: 190-5 (1974).

Spinucci, Pietro. "H tra presente e passato: *Our Old Home*." *SA*, 14: 113-63 (1968).

Sprague, Claire. "Dream and Disguise in *The Blithedale Romance*." *PMLA*, 84: 596-7 (My 69).

Stanton, Robert. "*The Scarlet Letter* as Dialectic of Temperament and Idea." *StN*, 2: 474-86 (Wi 70).

Stein, A.F. "H's Zenobia and Melville's Urania." *ATQ*, 26: 11-4 (Sp 75).

Stephens, Rosemary. "*A*, is for *Art* in *The Scarlet Letter*." *ATQ*, 1: 23-7 (1Q 69).

Sterne, R.C. "H's Politics in *The House of the Seven Gables*." *CRAS*, 6: 74-83 (Sp 75).

———. "A Mexican Flower in Rappaccini's Garden: Madame Caledron de la Barca's *Life in Mexico* Revisited." *NHJ*, 4: 277-9 (1974).

———. "Puritans at Merry Mount: Variations on a Theme." *AQ*, 22: 846-8, 858 (Wi 70).

Stock, Ely. "Some Recent Books on H." *NCF*, 25: 482-93 (1971).

———. "Witchcraft in 'The Hollow of the Three Hills.'" *ATQ*, 14: 31-3 (Sp 72).

Stoehr, Taylor. "H and Mesmerism." *HLQ*, 33: 33-60 (N 69).

———. "Physiognomy and Phrenology in H." *HLQ*, 37: 355-400 (1973-4).

———. "'Young Goodman Brown' and H's Theory of Mimesis." *NCF*, 23: 393-412 (Mr 69).

Stokes, E. "*Bleak House* and *The Scarlet Letter*." *AUMLA*, 32: 177-89 (N 69).

Stone, Edward. "H's Other Drowning." *NHJ*, 2: 231-7 (1972).

———. "H's Reputation Abroad." *NHJ*, 1: 201-3 (1971).

———. "More on H and Melville." *NHJ*, 5: 59-70 (1975).

———. "The Two Faces of America." *OhR*, 13: 5-11 (1972).

Stott, J.C. "H's 'My Kinsman, Major Molineux' and the Agrarian Ideal." *MichA*, 4: 197-203 (Fa 71).

Stouck, David. "The Surveyor of the Custom-House: A Narrator for *The Scarlet Letter*." *CentR*, 15: 309-29 (Su 71).

Strandberg, Victor. "The Artist's Black Veil." *NEQ*, 41: 567-74 (D 68).

Strauch, C.F. "The Problem of Time and the Romantic Mode in H, Melville, and Emerson." *ESQ*, 35: 50-60 (2Q 64).

Strout, Cushing. "H's International Novel." *NCF*, 24: 169-81 (S 69).

Strozier, R.M. "Dynamic Patterns: A Psycho-Analytic Theory of Plot." *SoRA*, 7: 254-63 (1974).

Stubb, J.C. "H's *The Scarlet Letter*: The Theory of the Romance and the Use of the New England Situation." *PMLA*, 83: 1439-47 (O 68).

———. "The Ideal in the Literature and Art of the American Renaissance." *ESQ*, 55: 55-63 (2Q 69).

———. "A Note on the Source of H's Heraldic Device in *The Scarlet Letter*." *N&Q*, 15: 175-6 (My 68).

Sumner, D.N. "The Function of Historical Sources in H, Melville, and R.P. Warren." *RSW*, 40: 103-14 (1972).

Swann, Charles, "H: History versus Romance." *JAmSt*, 7: 153-70 (Ag 73).

Swanson, D.R. "On Building *The House of the Seven Gables*." *BSUF*, 10: 43-50 (Wi 69).

Sweeney, G.M. "Melville's Hawthornian Bell-Tower: A Fairy-Tale Source." *AL*, 45: 279-85 (My 73).

Tanner, Tony. "Problems and Roles of the American Artist as Portrayed by the American Novelist." *PBA*, 57: 159-79 (1971).

Tanselle, G.T. "*BAL* Addenda: Some H Printings, 1884-1921." *PBSA*, 67: 65-6 (1Q 73).

———. "The New Editions of H and Crane." *BC*, 23: 214-30 (Su 74).

Tharpe, Jac. "H and Hindu Literature." *SoQ*, 10: 107-15 (Ja 72).

Thorpe, Dwayne. "'My Kinsman, Major Molineux': The Identity of the Kinsman." *Topic*, 18: 53-63 (1969).

Timms, David. "H Studies in Britain." *NHJ*, 5: 259-53 (1975).

Todd, R.E. "The Magna Mater Archetype in *The Scarlet Letter*." *NEQ*, 45: 421-9 (S 72).

Travis, M.K. "H and Melville's Enceladas." *ATQ*, 14: 5-6 (Sp 72).

———. "H's 'Egotism' and 'The Jolly Corner.'" *ESQ*, 63: 13-8 (Sp 71).

———. "A Note on 'Wakefield' and 'Old Mr. Marblehall.'" *NCLit*, 4: 9-10 (My 74).

———. "Of 'H's "The Artist of the Beautiful" and Spenser's "Muiopotmos.'" *PQ*, 54: 537 (Sp 75).

———. "Past vs. Present in *The House of Seven Gables*." *ESQ*, 58: 109-11 (1Q 70).

Tremblay, W.A. "A Reading of NH's 'The Gentle Boy.'" *MSE*, 2: 80-7 (Sp 70).

Tripathy, B.K. "H, Art and the Artist: A Study of 'Drowne's Wooden Image' and 'The Artist of the Beautiful.'" *IJAS*, 1: 63-71 (1971).

Tuerk, Richard. "'An Exceeding Pleasant Mention': *The Scarlet Letter* and *Holden's Dollar Magazine*." *NHJ*, 4: 209-30 (1974).

Turner, Arlin. "Elizabeth Peabody Reviews *Twice-Told Tales*." *NHJ*, 4: 75-84 (1974).

———. "H and Longfellow: Abortive Plans for Collaboration." *NHJ*, 1: 3-11 (1971).

———. "H's Final Illness and Death: Additional Reports." *ESQ*, 19: 124-7 (2Q 73).

———. "NH in Our Time." *SoR*, 1: 961-7 (O 65).

———. "Needs in H Biography." *NHJ*, 2: 43-5 (1972).

———. "Park Benjamin on the Author and Illustrator of 'The Gentle Boy.'" *NHJ*, 4: 85-91 (1974).

Turner, F.W. "H's Black Veil." *SSF*, 5: 186-7 (Wi 68).

Tuttleton, J.W. "Romance and Novel: The Disintgration of a Form." *ESQ*, 55: 116-21 (2Q 69).

Uroff, M.D. "The Doctors in 'Rappaccini's Daughter.'" *NCF*, 27: 61-70 (Je 72).

Vance, W.L. "Tragedy and 'The Tragic Power of Laughter': *The Scarlet Letter* and *The House of the Seven Gables*." *NHJ*, 1: 232-54 (1971).

Van Cromphout, Gustaaf. "*Blithedale* and the Androgyne Myth: Another Look at Zenobia." *ESQ*, 18: 141-5 (3Q 72).

———. "Emerson, H, and *The Blithedale Romance*." *GaR*, 25: 471-80 (Wi 71).

VanDerBeets, Richard, and Paul Witherington. "My Kinsman, Brockden Brown: Robin Molineux and Arthur Mervyn." *ATQ*, 1: 13-5 (1Q 69).

Van Winkle, E.S "Aminadab, the Unwitting 'Bad Anima.'" *AN&Q*, 8: 131-3 (1970).

Vittorini, Elio. "An Outline of American Literature." *SE*, 68: 423-37 (Su 60).

Vogel, Dan. "H's Concept of Tragedy in *The Scarlet Letter*." *NHJ*, 2: 183-93 (1972).

Volz, Robert. "John L. O'Sullivan to Henry A. Wise—An Unpubished Recollection of H." *NHJ*, 1: 117-21 (1971).

Von Frank, A.J., and J.R. Byers. "*House of Seven Gables*: An Unlikely Source." *PMLA*, 89: 1114-5 (O 74).

Waggoner, H.H. "'Grace' in the Thought of Emerson, Thoreau, and H." *ESQ*, 54: 68-72 (1Q 69).

———. "H and Melville Acquaint the Reader with Their Abodes." *StN*, 2: 420-4 (Wi 70).

Wagner, Vern. "H's Smile." *TQ*, 16: 6-31 (Wi 73).

Wallins, R.P. "Robin and the Narrator in 'My Kinsman, Major Molineux.'" *SSF*, 12: 173-80 (Sp 75).

Walsh, T.F. "The Devils of H and Flannery O' Connor." *XUS*, 5: 117-22 (Je 66).

Warner, J.A. "Self-Revelation in *The Scarlet Letter*." *RUS*, 61: 141-50 (#1 75).

Warner, L.H. "With Pierce, and H, in Mexico." *EIHC*, 3: 213-20 (Wi 75).

Warren, R.P. "H Revisited: Some Remarks on Hellfiredness." *SR*, 81: 75-111 (Wi 73).

———. "H *Was* Relevant." *NHJ*, 2: 85-9 (1972).

Waterman, A.E. "Dramatic Structure in *The House of the Seven Gables*." *SLitI*, 2: 13-9 (Ap 69).

Watson, C.N. "The Estrangement of H and Melville." *NEQ*, 46: 380-402 (S 73).

Webb, J.C. "The Implications of Control for the Human Personality: H's Point of View." *TSE*, 21: 57-6 (1974).

Webner, H.L. "H, Melville and Lowell: *The Old Glory*." *Re:A&L*, 4: 1-17 (Fa 70).

Wentersdorf, K.P. "The Element of Witchcraft in *The Scarlet Letter*." *Fkl*, 83: 132-53 (1972).

Werge, Thomas. "Thomas Shepard and Crevecoeur: Two Uses of the Bosom Serpent Before H." *NHJ*, 4: 236-9 (1974).

West, H.C. "H's Editorial Pose." *AL*, 44: 208-21 (My 72).

———. "H's Magic Circle: The Artist as Magician." *Criticism*, 16: 311-25 (Fa 74).

———. "The Sources for H's 'The Aritist of the Beautiful.'" *NCF*, 30: 105-11 (Je 75).

Wheeler, O.B. "Love Among the Ruins: H's Surrogate Religion." *SoR*, 10: 535-65 (Jl 74).

Whelan, R.E. "*The Blithedale Romance*: The Holy War in H's Mansoul." *TSLL*, 13: 91-101 (Sp 71).

———. "H Interprets 'Young Goodman Brown.'" *ESQ*, 62: 2-4 (Wi 71).

———. "Hester Prynne's Little Pearl: Sacred and Profane Love." *AL*, 39: 488-505 (Ja 68).

———. "*The Marble Faun*: Rome as H's Mansoul." *RSW*, 40: 163-75 (1972).

———. "'Rappaccini's Daughter's and Zenobia's Legend." *RSW*, 39: 47-52 (Mr 71).

———. "Roger Chillingworth's Whole Business Is Reflection." *RSW*, 37: 298-312 (D 69).

———. "'Roger Malvin's Burial': The Burial of Reuben Bournce's Cowardice." *RSW*, 37: 112-21 (Je 69).

White, John. "'Romance' in *The Blithedale Romance*." *AN&Q*, 9: 72-3 (1971).

White, R.L. "'Rappaccini's Daughter,' *The Cenci* and the Cenci Legend." *SA*, 14: 63-86 (1968).

White, W.M. "H's Eighteen-Year Cycle: Ethan Brand and Reuben Bourne." *SSF*, 6: 215-8 (Wi 69).

Whitford, Kathryn. "'On a Field Sable, the Letter "A," Gules.'" *LHR*, 10: 33-8 (1968).

Williams, J.G. "History in H's 'The Maypole of Merry Mount.'" *EIHC*, 108: 173-89 (Ap 72).

Williams, M.G. "H's Ministers of Spiritual Torment." *Chris & Lit*, 20: 18-23 (1971).

Willoughby, J.C. "'The Old Manse' Revisited: Some Analogues for Art." *NEQ*, 46: 45-61 (Mr 73).

Wilson, J.D. "Incest and American Romantic Fiction." *SLitI*, 7: 31-50 (1974).

Wilson, Rod. "Further Spenserian Parallels in H." *NHJ*, 2: 195-201 (1972).

Winslow, D.J. "H's Folklore and the Folklorist's H: A Re-examination." *SFQ*, 34: 34-52 (Mr 70).

Wright, John. "Borges and H." *TriQ*, 25: 334-55 (Au 72).

Yagi, Toshio. "Kyoko no Realism—Mimonji no Sekai." *EigoS*, 119: 282-3 (1973).

———. "*The Scarlet Letter* Through 'The Custom House.'" *SELit*, 14: 237-9 (1974).

Yamamoto, Masashi. "On the Significance of 'Nature' in H's Works." *HirStud*, 18: 47-68 (1971).

Yoder, R.A. "H and His Artist." *SRom*, 7: 193-206 (Su 68).

———. "Transcendental Conservatism and *The House of the Seven Gables*." *GaR*, 28: 33-51 (Sp 74).

Zivley, Sherry. "H's 'The Artist of the Beautiful' and Spenser's 'Muiopotmos.'" *PQ*, 48: 134-7 (Ja 69).

Zlotnick, Joan. "*The Damnation of Theron Ware*, with a Backward Glance at H." *MarkR*, 2: 90-2 (F 71).

Zolla, Ellemire. "Un alchimista bostoniano et l'immaginazione organica." *RdE*, 13: 46-52 (1968).

Hay, John. Clymer, K.J. "JH and Mark Twain." *MHR*, 67: 397-406 (Ap 73).

Duffy, Charles. "Mrs. Hay's Eye." *Ohioana*, 1: 115 (Wi 58).

Friedlaender, Marc. "Henry Hobson Richardson, Henry Adams, and JH." *PMHS*, 81: 137-66 (1970).

Howells, W.D. "Editor's Easy Chair." *Harper's*, 132: 310-3 (Ja 16).

———. "JH in Literature." *NAR*, 181: 347-8 (S 05).

Jaher, F.C. "Industrialism and the American Aristocrat: A Social Study of JH and His Novel, *The Bread-Winners*." *JISHS*, 65: 69-93 (Sp 72).

Monteiro, George. "Cora Crane to JH: A Last Communication." *SCraneN*, 4: 8 (Sp 70).

———. "JH's Short Fiction." *SSF*, 8: 543-52 (1971).

———. "JH's Tribute to Washington." *BBr*, 21: 91-3 (1966).

———. "Matthew Arnold in America, 1884." *N&Q*, 13: 66-7 (F 66).

Philbrick, Charles. "A Note on JH." *BBr*, 24: 156 (1971).

Sherman, S.C. "The Writings of JH, Poet and Naturalist." *BBR*, 24: 157-61 (1971).

Sloane, D.E.E. "Censoring for *The Century Magazine*: R.W. Gilder to JH in *The Bread Winners*, 1882-1884." *ALR*, 4: 255-67 (Su 71).

———. "JH (1838-1905)." *ALR*, 3: 178-88 (Sp 70).

———. "JH's *The Bread-Winners* as Literary Realism." *ALR*, 2: 276-9 (Fa 69).

Vandersee, Charles. "The Great Literary Mystery of the Gilded Age." *ALR*, 7: 245-72 (Su 74).

Haycox, Ernest. Brooker, Clard. "Ten Thousand Stories Untold." *Roundup*, 21: 12-3 (O 73).

Garfield, Brian. "EH: A Study in Style." *Roundup*, 21: 1-3, 5 (F 73).
Haycox, J.M. "The Light of Other Days." *Roundup*, 21: 1-2, 4-6 (O 73).
Holmes, L.P. "The Augurin' Post." *Roundup*, 21: 16-7 (Ap 73).
Newton, D.B. "After H: Whither Go We?" *Roundup*, 21: 4-8 (N 73).
———. "The Legend of EH." *Roundup*, 21: 8-11 (O 73).
Hayden, Robert. Fetrow, F. M. "RH's 'Frederick Douglass': Form and Meaning in a Modern Sonnet." *CLAJ*, 17: 78-84 (S 73).
Kramer, Aaron. "(A Review of *Words in the Mourning Time*, Poems by RH.)" *MeditR*, 2: 59-61 (1972).
Lewis, R.O. "A Literary-Psychoanalytic Interpretation of RH's 'Market.'" *NALF*, 9: 21-4 (Sp 75).
Novak, M.P. "Meditative, Ironic, Richly Human: The Poetry of RH." *MwQ*, 15: 276-85 (1974).
O'Sullivan, M.J. "The Mask of Allusion in RH's 'The Diver.'" *CLAJ*, 17: 85-92 (S 73).
Haydn, Hiram. Anon. "A Celebration of HH." *Voyages*, 3: 7-55 (1970).
Chappell, Fred. "HH's Other World." *Voyages*, 3: 22-9 (1970).
Nin, Anais. "Anais Nin on HH's *Report from the Red Windmill*." *Voyages*, 3: 29-30 (1970).
O'Brien, John. "An Interview with HH." *ASch*, 43: 199-222 (Sp 74).
Hayne, Paul Hamilton. Anon. "Check-list of the PHH Library." *Duke Un Lib Bul*, 2: 1-109 (1930).
Anon. "Five Letters from PHH to Horatio Woodman." *PMHS*, 54: 178-84 (1921).
Campbell, A.S. "Threee Charleston Poets." *Confederate Veteran*, 29: 46-7 (1921).
Cheney, Sarah. "Francis Orray Ticknor." *GHQ*, 22: 138-59 (1938).
Hayne, W.H. "Unpublished Letters of Wilkie Collins to PHH." *Bookman*, 37: 66-71 (1913).
Hesseltine, W.B., and Larry Gara. "Sherman Burns the Libraries." *SCHM*, 55: 137-42 (1954).
Ifkovic, Edward. "Two Poems for PHH." *AN&Q*, 6: 71-2 (Ja 68).
Jervey, T.D. "The H Family." *SCHM*, 5: 168-88 (1904).
Land, Cecil. "Swinburne and American Literature." *AL*, 19: 336-50 (Ja 48).
Lanier, Doris. "The Death of PHH." *GHQ*, 57: 579-84 (Wi 73).
Mabbott, T.O. "Some Letters of Henry Timrod." *Am Coll*, 3: 191-5 (F 27).
Mayfield, J.S. "Algernon Charles Swinburne to PHH." *Autograph Coll J*, 5: 14-22 (1952).
Moore, R.S. "H the Poet: A New Look." *SCR*, 2: 4-13 (N 69).
———. "The Old South and the New: PHH and Maurice Thompson." *SLJ*, 5: 108-22 (Fa 72).
———. "PHH." *GaR*, 22: 106-24 (Sp 68).
Pickett, L.C. "The Poet of the Pines." *Lippincott's*, 90: 212-20 (Ag 12).
Raizis, M.B. "PHH (He physe stin romantiki poiisihena paradeigma)." *EpH*, 20: 109-10 (1971).
Routh, J.E. "Some Fugitive Poems of PHH." *SAQ*, 9: 327-33 (1910).
Simms, L.M. "PHH's Methods of Poetic Composition." *MissQ*, 24: 57-62 (Wi 70-71).
Tryon, W.S. "The Publications of Ticknor and Fields in the South, 1840-1865." *JSH*, 14: 305-30 (1948).
Young, T.D. "How Time Has Served Two Southern Poets: PHH and Sidney Lanier." *SLJ*, 6: 101-10 (Fa 73).
Zula, Marion. "H as a Raconteur." *Carolinian*, 47: 28 (1939).
Hays, Brooks. Havard, W.C. "Southwest Humor: Contemporary Style." *SoR*, 6: 185-90 (O 70).

Hearn, Lafcadio. Bridges, Katherine. "LH and Leona Queyrouse." *LaStud*, 7: 173-8 (1968).

Davidson, M.C. "The Land of LH." *NYTimes*, 27 Ja 74, sect 10: 1, 12.

Parsons, C.O. "Steamboating as Seen by Passengers and River Men: 1875-1884." *MissQ*, 24: 19-34 (Wi 70-71).

Szwed, J.F., and Carol Parssinen. "Reconsideration: LH in Cincinnati." *NRep*, 167: 32-3 (O 72).

White, William. "Armand Hawkins: Bookseller to LH." *ABC*, 21: 7-8 (1971).

———. "On LH as a Book Reviewer." *PrS*, 45: 93 (1971).

Yu, Beongcheon. "LH's Aesthetics of Organic Memory." *SEL*, 38: 1-28 (N 61).

Hecht, Anthony. Gerber, P.L. and R.J. Gemmett. "An Interview with AH." *MeditR*, 1: 3-9 (Sp 71).

Miller, Stenphen. "A Poem by AH." *Spirit*, 39: 8-11 (1972).

Perloff, Marjorie. 'AH, *The Hard Hours*." *Far Point*, 2: 45-51 (1969).

Rhu, Lawrence. "Abiding the Questions: An Interview with AH." *HA*, 107: 9-22 (Fa 71).

Hecht, Ben. Fincke, Gary. "Polarity in BH's Winkelbergs." *Critique*, 15: 103-9 (#2 73).

Ravitz, A.C. "Assault with Deadly Typewriter: The H-Bodenheim Vendetta." *Cabellian*, 4: 104-11 (Sp 72).

Hedge, Fredric Henry. Hedge, Frederic. "The Aims of Education." *ESQ*, 51: 76-90 (2Q 68).

———. "Young FH in Germany (1818-1822)." *ESQ*, 51: 47-50 (2Q 68).

Myerson, Joel. "FHH and the Failure of Transcendentalism." *HLB*, 23: 396-410 (O 75).

Heinlein, Robert. Cansler, R.L. "*Stranger in a Strange Land*: Science Fiction as Literature of Creative Imagination, Social Criticism, and Entertainment." *JPC*, 5: 944-54 (Sp 72).

Christopher, J.E. "Lazarus Come Forth from That Tomb." *RQ*, 6: 190-7 (1975).

Perkins, J.A. "MYCROFTXX Is Alive and Well." *NCLit*, 5: 13-5 (#1 75).

Plank, Robert. "Omnipotent Cannibals: Thoughts on Reading RH's 'Stranger in a Stranger Land.'" *RQ*, 30-7 (Jl 71).

Schuman, Samuel. "Vladimir Nabokov's *Invitation to a Beheading* and RH's *They*." *TCL*, 19: 99-106 (Ap 73).

Showalter, D.E. "H's Starship Troopers." *Extrapolation*, 16: 113-24 (1975).

Solon, Ben. "Fascism for Fun and Profit." *Niekas*, 18: 7-9, 66 (Sp 67).

Speer, D.P. "H's *The Door into Summer* and *Roderick Random*." *Extrapolation*, 12: 30-4 (D 70).

Heller, Joseph. Blues, Thomas. "The Moral Structure of *Catch-22*." *StN*, 3: 64-79 (Sp 71).

Burhan, C.S. "Spindrift and the Sea: Structural Patterns and Unifying Elements in *Catch-22*." *TCL*, 19: 239-50 (O 73).

Castelli, Jim. "*Catch-22* and the New Hero." *CathW*, 211: 199-202 (1970).

Clancy, Jack. "The Film and the Book: D.H. Lawrence and JH on the Screen." *Meanjin*, 30: 96-101 (My 71).

Frost, Lucy. "Violence in the Eternal City: *Catch-22* as a Critique of American Culture." *Meanjin*, 30: 447-53 (D 71).

Gaukroger, Doug. "Time Structure in *Catch-22*." *Critique*, 12: 70-85 (1970).

Gonzales, Alexis. "Notes on the Next Novel: An Interview with JH." *NOR*, 2: 216-9 (1971).

Greenfeld, Josh. "22 Was Funnier than 14." *NYT*, 3 Mr 68, pp. 1, 49-53.

Guimond, James. "Moving Heaven and Earth." *Parnassus*, 1: 106-5 (1972).

Hasley, Louis. "Dramatic Tension in *Catch-22*." *MQ*, 15: 190-7 (1974).

Janoff, Bruce. "Black Humor, Existentialism, and Absurdity: A Generic Confusion." *ArQ*, 30: 293-304 (Wi 74).

Kennard, J.E. "JH: At War with Absurdity." *Mosaic*, 4: 75-87 (1971).

Loukides, Paul. "The Radical Vision." *MichA*, 5: 497-503 (Sp 73).

McDonald, J.L. "I See Everything Twice: The Structure of JH's *Catch-22*." *UR*, 34: 175-80 (Mr 68).

McDonald, Walter. "He Took Off: Yossarian and the Different Drummer." *CEA*, 36: 14-6 (N 73).

———. "Look Back in Horror: The Functional Comedy of *Catch-22*." *CEA*, 35: 18-21 (Ja 73).

Mc Namara, Eugene. "The Absurd Style in Contemporary American Literature." *HAB*, 19: 44-9 (Wi 68).

Mellard, J.M. "*Catch-22*: *Déjà vu* and the Labyrinth of Memory." *BuR*, 16: 29-44 (My 68).

Merrill, Sam. "*Playboy* Interview: JH." *Playboy*, 22: 59-76 (Je 75).

Milne, V.J. "H's 'Bologniad': A Theological Perspective on *Catch-22*." *Critique*, 12: 50-69 (1970).

Nagel, James. "*Catch-22* and Angry Humor: A Study of the Normative Values of Satire." *SAH*, 1: 99-106 (1974).

———. "Two Brief Manuscript Sketches: H's *Catch-22*." *MFS*, 20: 221-4 (Su 74).

Nelson, T.A. "In Defense of the Grim: A Personal View of the Film Version of *Catch-22*." *StH*, 2: 10-3 (1971).

———. "Theme and Structure in *Catch-22*." *Renascence*, 23: 173-82 (Su 71).

Orr, R.W. "Flat Characters in *Catch-22*." *NCLit*, 1: 4 (Ja 71).

Plimpton, George. "The Art of Fiction: JH." *PaR*, 60: 126-47 (Wi 74).

———. "How It Happened." *NYT*, 6 O 74, pp. 2-3, 20.

Ryan, Marjorie. "Four Contemporary Satires and the Problem of Norms." *SLN*, 6: 40-6 (Sp 69).

Sale, R.B. "An Interview in New York with JH." *StN*, 4: 63-74 (Sp 72).

Schopf, William. "Blindfolded and Backwards: Promethean and Bemushroomed Heroism in *One Flew Over the Cuckoo's Nest* and *Catch-22*." *BRMMLA*, 26: 89-97 (S 72).

Shapiro, James. "Work in Progress: JH, An Interview." *ID*, 2: 6-11 (1971).

Sharma, D.R. "*Catch-22*: An Analysis of Personal Freedom vs. Group Loyalty." *BP*, 19: 20-9 (1974).

Sniderman, S.L. "'It Was All Yossarian's Fault': Power and Respnsibility in *Catch-22*." *TCL*, 19: 251-8 (O 73).

Solomon, Eric. "From Christ in Flanders to *Catch-22*: An Approach to War Fiction." *TSLL*, 11: 851-66 (Sp 69).

Standiford, Les. "Novels into Film: *Catch-22* as Watershed." *SHR*, 8: 19-25 (Wi 74).

Stern, J.P. "War and the Comic Muse." *CL*, 20: 193-216 (Su 68).

Sullivan, J.J. "Conflict in the Modern American Novel." *BSUF*, 15: 28-36 (1974).

Thomas, W.K. "The Mythic Dimension of *Catch-22*." *TSLL*, 15: 189-98 (Sp 73).

———. "'What Difference Does It Make?': Logic in *Catch-22*." *DR*, 50: 488-95 (Wi 70-71).

Waldmeir, J.J. "Two Novelists of the Absurd: H and Kesey." *WSCL*, 5: 192-204 (1964).

Way, Brian. "Formal Experiment and Social Discontent: JH's *Catch-22*." *JAmSt*, 2: 253-70 (O 68).

*Weixlmann, Joseph. "A Bibliography of JH's *Catch-22*." *BB*, 31: 32-7 (Ja-Mr 74).

Williams, M.G. "*Catch-22*: What the Movie Audiences Missed." *C&L*, 23: 21-5 (Su 74).

Zall, P.M. "*Catch-22* Uncaught." *SNL*, 8: 69-73 (1970).

Hellman, Lillian. Adler, J.H. "Professor Moody's Miss H." *SLJ*, 5: 131-40 (Sp 73).

Armato, P.M. "'Good and Evil's in LH's *The Children's Hour*." *ETJ*, 25: 443-47 (1973).

Eatman, James. "The Image of American Destiny: *The Little Foxes*." *Players*, 48: 70-3 (1973).

Ephron, Nora. "LH Walking, Cooking, Writing, Talking." *NYT*, 23 S 73, pp. 2, 51.

Phillips, John, and Anne Hollander. "The Art of the Theater I." *PaR*, 9: 65-94 (Wi-Sp 65).

Hemingway, Ernest. Anon. "Another Lost H Review." *FHA*, 1970, p. 228.

*———. "Current Bibliography." *HN*, 2: 9-13 (Sp 72).

*———. "H Checklist." *FHA*, 1972, pp. 347-67.

———. "H's *A Farewell to Arms*." *Expl*, 3: 11 (N 44).

———. "H's Unstill Waters." *TLS*, 16 O 70, pp. 1193-4.

Adair, William. "*A Farewell to Arms*: A Dream Book." *JNarT*, 5: 40-56 (Ja 75).

———. "Time and Structure in *A Farewell to Arms*." *SDR*, 13: 165-71 (Sp 75).

Adams, R.P. "Sunrise out of the Waste Land." *TSE*, 9: 119-31 (1959).

Agent, Dan. "The Hair on H's Chest." *LGJ*, 1: 12-5 (My 73).

Aiken, William. "H's 'Ten Indians.'" *Expl*, 28: 31 (D 69).

* Alderman, Taylor, and Kenneth Rosen. "Current Bibliography." *HN*, 1: 3-12 (Sp 71); continued semi-annually (Sp, Fa) through 1974.

Aldridge, J.W. "H Between Triumph and Disaster." *SatR*, 53: 23-39 (10 O 70).

Alexander, A.S. "Collecting H." *FHA*, 1971, pp. 298-301.

Alinei, Tamara. "The *Corrida* and *For Whom the Bell Tolls*." *Neophil*, 56: 487-92 (1972).

Allen, C.A. "EH's Clean, Well-Lighted Heroes." *Pac Spectator*, 9: 383-9 (Au 55).

Allen, Mary. "Hail to Arms: A View of *For Whom the Bell Tolls*." *FHA*, 1973, pp. 285-93.

Allen, M.J.B. "The Unspanish War in *For Whom the Bell Tolls*." *ConL*, 13: 204-11 (Sp 72).

Amiran, M.R. "H as Lyric Novelist." *ScriptaH*, 17: 292-300 (1966).

Anastas'ev, N. "Posle legendy." *VLit*, 16: 119-34 (1972).

Andersen, D.M. "Basque Wine, Arkansas Chawin' Tobacco: Lanscape and Ritual in EH and Mark Twain." *MTJ*, 16: 3-7 (Wi 71-2).

Anderson, P.V. "Nick's Story in H's 'Big Two-Hearted River.'" *SSF*, 7: 564-72 (Fa 70).

Anderson, W.R. "*Islands in the Stream*—The Initial Reception." *FHA*, 1970, pp. 326-32.

Andrews, Larry. "'Big Two-Hearted River': The Essential H." *MEB*, 25: 1-7 (My 69).

Ano, Fumio. "H and Politics." *BuCG*, 12: 105-20 (1971).

Aranda, Joaquin. "La novela de EH." *Revista Estudios Americanos*, 40-1: 63-72 (Ja-F 55).

Arner, R.D. "H's 'Miracle' Play: 'Today Is Friday' and the York Play of the Crucifixion." *MarkR*, 4: 8-11 (1973).

Asselineau, Roger. "Hein Paris." *FHA*, 1973, pp. 11-32.

Atkins, Anselm. "Ironic Action in 'After the Storm.'" *SSF*, 5: 189-92 (Wi 68).

Bagchi, Krishna. "The H Hero." *BP*, 11: 91-4 (Jl 68).

Baker, Carlos. "EH: Living, Loving, Dying." *Atl*, 223: 45-67, 91-118 (Ja, F 69).

———. "H and Princeton." *Princeton Hist*, 1: 39-49 (1971).

———. "The Slopes of Kilimanjaro." *AH*, 19: 40-3, 90-1 (Ag 68).

———. "The Slopes of Kilimanjaro: A Biographical Perspective." *Novel*, 1: 19-23 (Fa 67).

———. "Two Rivers: Mark Twain and H." *MTJ*, 11: 2 (Su 62).

Bakker, J. "In Search of Reality: Two American Heroes Compared." *DQR*, 4: 145-61 (1972).

Barba, Harry. "The Three Levels of 'The End of Something.'" *WVUPP*, 17: 76-80 (Je 70).

Barbour, James, and Robert Sattelmeyer. "Baseball and Baseball Talk in *The Old Man and the Sea*." *FHA*, 1975, pp. 281-7.

Barnes, L.L. "The Helpless Hero of EH." *Sci&Soc*, 17: 1-25 (Wi 53).

Barolini, Antonio. "H senti che la mano tremava." *Epoca*, 42: 30-1 (22 J 61).

Bartlett, Norman. "H: The Hero as Self." *Quadrant*, 71: 13-20 (My-Je 71).

Baskett, Sam. "Toward a 'Fifth Dimension' in *The Old Man and the Sea*." *CentR*, 19: 269-86 (Fa 75).

Bass, Eben. "H at Roncesvalles." *NEMLAN*, 2: 1-7 (1970).

Bassett, Charles. "Katahdin, Wachusett, and Kilimanjaro: The Symbolic Mountains of Thoreau and H." *TJQ*, 3: 1-10 (15 Ap 71).

Beck, Warren. "The Shorter Happy Life of Mrs. Macomber—1955, 1975." *MFS*, 21: 363-85 (Au 75).

*Beebe, Maurice, and John Feaster. "Criticism of EH: A Selected Checklist." *MFS*, 14: 337-69 (1968).

Behrens, Ralph. "Mérimée, H, and the Bulls." *Costerus*, 2: 1-8 (1972).

Bell, H.H. "H's 'The Short Happy Life of Francis Macomber.'" *Expl*, 32: 78 (1974).

Bellman, S.I. "H, Faulkner, and Wolfe . . . and the Common Reader." *SoR*, 4: 834-49 (Su 68).

Benert, Annette. "Survival Through Irony: H's 'A Clean, Well-Lighted Place.'" *SSF*, 11: 181-8 (Sp 74).

Bennett, Warren. "Character, Irony, and Resolution in 'A Clean, Well-Lighted Place.'" *AL*, 42: 79-9 (Mr 70).

———. "The New Text of 'A Clean, Well-Lighted Place.'" *LHY*, 14: 115-25 (#1 73).

Benson, J.J. "Introduction: 'H In Our Time.'" *HN*, 4: 3-11 (Sp 74).

———. "Literary Allusion and the Private Irony of H." *PCP*, 4: 24-9 (1969).

———. "Patterns of Connection and Development in H's *In Our Time*." *Rendezvous*, 5: 37-52 (1970).

Bertrand de Muñoz, Maryse. "La Guerre civile espagnole et la littérature." *Mosaic*, 3: 62-79 (1969).

———. "Un paralelismo estructural: *Los de Abajo* de Mariano Azuela y *For Whom the Bell of Tolls* de EH." *Torre*, 73-4: 237-46 (1971).

Bevis, R.W., et al. "Leopard Tracks in 'The Snows . . .'" *AN&Q*, 6: 115 (Ap 68).

Bidle, K.E. "*Across the River and Into the Trees*: Rite de Passage à Mort." *FHA*, 1973, pp. 259-70.

Bigsby, C.W.E. "H en de Amerikaanse traditie van de mens als Christus." *NVT*, 22: 826-40 (O 69).

Bisol, Gaetano. "Hemingway postumo e autobiografico." *CCa*, 118: 468-73 (1967).

Blonski, Jan. "Americans in Poland." *KR*, 23: 32-51 (Wi 61).

Bluefarb, Sam. "The Search for the Absolute in H's 'A Clean, Well-Lighted Place' and 'The Snows of Kilimanjaro.'" *BRMMLA*, 25: 3-9 (Mr 71).

Bocaz, S.H. "*El Ingenioso Hidalgo Don Quijote de la Mancha* and *The Old Man and the Sea*: A Study of the Symbolic Essence of Man in Cervantes and H." *BRMMLA*, 25: 49-54 (Je 71).

Bodunescu, Ion. "Amintirea lui H." *Ramuri*, 15 Je 72, pp. 23-4.

Bonet, Laureano. "Los dos rostros de EH." *RO*, 30: 176-99 (Ag 70).

Borch, Herbert von. "H." *Univ*, 24: 801-7 (1969).

Bordinat, Philip. "Anatomy of Fear in Tolstoy and H." *LGJ*, 2: 15-7 (Sp-Su 75).

Borovik, Genrikh. "U Ernesta Khemingueya." *Ogoniok*, 14: 26-9 (Ap 60).

Brasher, Jim. "H's Florida." *LGJ*, 1: 4-8 (Fa 73).

Braun, R.E. "Echoes from the Sea." *FHA*, 1974, pp. 201-5.

Brenner, Gerry. "Epic Machinery in H's *For Whom the Bell Tolls*." *MFS*, 16: 491-504 (Wi 70-71).

Brian, Denis. "The Importance of Knowing Ernest." *Esquire*, 77: 98-101, 164-70 (F 72).

Brocki, Sister M.D. "Faulkner and H: Values in a Modern World." *MTJ*, 11: 5-8, 15 (Su 62).

Broer, Lawrence. "Soldier's Home." *LGJ*, 3: 11, 32 (Mr 75).

Brogger, F.C. "H—der kjaerlighet og religion motes." *KoK*, 74: 224-31 (1969).

Brower, Brock. "The Abraham Lincoln Brigade Revisited." *Esquire*, 57: 64-8, 127-30 (Mr 62).

*Bruccoli, M.J. "Bruccoli Addenda." *FHA*, 1973, pp. 339-46; 1974, pp. 275-85; 1975, pp. 337-9.

———. "EH as Cub Reporter." *Esquire*, 70: 207, 265 (D 68).

———. "Francis Macomber and Francis Fitzgerald." *FHA*, 1970, p. 223.

———. "Interview with Allen Tate." *FHA*, 1974, pp. 101-3.

———. "'The Light of the World': Stan Ketchel as 'My Sweet Christ.'" *FHA*, 1969, pp. 125-30.

———. "A Lost Book Review (by H): A *Story-Teller's Story*." *FHA*, 1969, pp. 71-5.

———. "'Oh, Give Them Irony and Give Them Pity.'" *FHA*, 1970, p. 236.

———. "Ole Anderson, Ole Andreson, and Carl Andreson.' *FHA*, 1971, pp. 341-2.

———. "Stan Ketchel and Steve Ketchel." *FHA*, 1975, pp. 325-6.

———. "An Unrecorded H Public Letter." *FHA*, 1973, pp. 227-9.

———. "Ways of Seeing H." *FHA*, 1973, pp. 197-207.

Bunnell, W.A. "Who Wrote the Paris Idyll? The Place and Function of *A Moveable Feast* in the Writing of EH." *ArQ*, 26: 334-46 (Wi 70).

Burhans, C.S. "The Complex Unity of *In Our Time*." *MFS*, 14: 313-28 (Au 68).

———. "H and Vonnegut: Diminishing Vision in a Dying Age." *MFS*, 21: 173-92 (Su 75).

Burnam, Tom. "The Other EH." *NM*, 73: 29-36 (1972).

Callaghan, Morley. "La Parigi di Scott Fitzgerald." *FLe*, 4 My 67, pp. 10-1.

Calverton, V.F. "EH and the Modern Temper." *Book League Mo*, 3: 165-6 (Ja 30).

———. "Steinbeck, H and Faulkner." *Mod Q*, 11: 36-44 (Fa 39).

Canaday, Nicholas. "The Motif of the Inner Ring in H's Fiction." *CEA*, 36: 18-21 (#2 74).

Cannell, Kathleen. "Scenes with a Hero." *ConnR*, 2: 5-9 (1968).

Capellán, Ángel. "El ciclo vital del héroe hemingweiano." *Arbor*, 318: 31-57 (1972).

Carlin, S.A. "Anselmo and Santiago: Two Old Men of the Sea." *ABC*, 19: 12-4 (Fa 69).

Carson, D.L. "Symbolism in *A Farewell to Arms*." *ES*, 53: 518-22 (D 72).

Cass, C.S. "The Love Story in *For Whom the Bell Tolls*." *FHA*, 1972, pp. 225-35.

Castillo Puche, José Luis. "EH: Presencia y senôrio de la muerte." *Estafeta Literaria*, 545: 9-12 (1 Ag 74).

Cecil, L.M. "The Color of *A Farewell to Arms*." *RSW*, 36: 168-73 (Je 68).

Chamson, Andre. "Remarks by Andre Chamson." *FHA*, 1973, pp. 69-76.

Chen, Yuan-yin. "Heng-ri yu Wei-erh-po chih Chien-Lun H yu Fu-ko-na." *TkJ*, 11: 217-24 (1973).

Charters, James. "Pat and Duff: Some Memories." *ConnR*, 3: 24-7 (1970).

Choquette, Sylvie. "L'Archetype du temps circulaire chez H et Jacques Poulain." *ELit*, 8: 43-55 (1975).

Church, Ralph. "Sherwood Comes to Town." *FHA*, 1972, pp. 149-66.

Clark, C.E.F. "American Red Cross on the Wounding of EM.H." *FHA*, 1974, pp. 131-6.

———. "The Beginnings of Dealer Interest in H." *FHA*, 1970, pp. 191-4.

———. "'Buying Commission Would Cut Out Waste': A Newly Discovered H Contribution to the *Toronto Daily Star*." *FHA*, 1971, pp. 209-11.

———. "The Crosby Copy of *In Our Time*." *FHA*, 1971, pp. 236-8.

———. "H at Auction: A Brief Survey." *FHA*, 1969, pp. 105-24.

———. "H in Advance." *FHA*, 1972, pp. 195-205.

———. "Kiki and her 'Sympatique Montparnasseur.'" *FHA*, 1972, pp. 269-71.

———. "Pre-Publication Printings of H." *FHA*, 1972, pp. 195-206.

———. "Recent H at Auction." *FHA*, 1973, pp. 295-7.

———. "This Is the Way It Was on the *Chicago* and at the Front: 1917 War Letters." *FHA*, 1970, pp. 153-68.

———. "La Vie est beau avec Papa." *FHA*, 1971, pp. 189-93.

Claveria, A. "Arte y artesania en H." *Correo Literario*, 89: 1, 14 (1954).

Cochran, R.W. "Circularity in *The Sun Also Rises*." *MFS*, 14: 297-305 (Au 68).

Cody, Morrill, Matthew Bruccoli, James Jones, *et al*. "Discussion at the Paris Conference." *FHA*, 1973, pp. 77-81.

———. "Remarks By Morrill Cody." *FHA*, 1973, pp. 39-42.

———. "*The Sun Also Rises* Revisited." *ConnR*, 4: 5-8 (1971).

Conti, G.G. "H e la pace dei nostri giorni." *VeP*, 52: 3-20 (1969).

Cordesse, Gérard. "De la castration dans *Le soleil se lève aussi*." *Caliban*, 8: 89-99 (1971).

Corona, Mario. "Considerazioni sull'ordine di successione dei raconti di H." *SA*, 13: 325-37 (1967).

Cotten, Lyman. "H's 'The Old Man and the Sea.'" *Expl*, 11: 38 (My 53).

Cowley, Malcolm. "A Double Life, Half Told." *Atl*, 226: 105-8 (D 70).

———. "H: the Image and the Shadow." *Horizon*, 15: 112-7 (Sp 73).

———. "A Letter from Malcolm Cowley." *FHA*, 1971, pp. 317-8.

Crane, J.K. "Crossing the Bar Twice: Post-Mortem Consciousness in Bierce, H, and Golding." *SSF*, 6: 361-76 (Su 69).

Crane, J. St. C. "Rare or Seldom-Seen Dust Jackets of American First Editions." *Serif*, 8: 29-31 (1971).

Crosby, Caresse. "The Last Time I Saw H." *FHA*, 1970, p. 240.

Crozier, R.D. "For Thine Is the Power and the Glory: Love in *For Whom the Bell Tolls*." *PLL*, 10: 76-97 (Wi 74).

———. "Home James: H's Jacob." *PLL*, 11: 293-301 (Su 75).

Curran, R.T. "The Individual and the Military Institution in H's Novels and *Collier's Dispatches*." *RLV*, 34: 26-39 (1968).

Currie, W.J. "H's Images of Alienation." *ELLS*, 10: 183-99 (1973).

D'Agostino, Nemi. "The Later H." *SR*, 68: 482-93 (Jl 60).

Daiker, D.A. "The Pied Piper in *The Sun Also Rises*." *FHA*, 1975, pp. 235-37.

Damp, W. "Individuum und Gesellschaft in H's Romanen." *WZUG*, 16: 189-92 (1967).

D'Avanzo, M.L. "H's *A Farewell to Arms*, Chapter XXXV." *Expl*, 27: 39 (Ja 69).

———. "The Motif of Corruption in *A Farewell to Arms*." *LHR*, 11: 57-62 (1969).

Davenport, Guy. "H as Walter Pater." *Nat R*, 22: 1214-5 (17 N 70).

Davidson, A.E. "The Ambivalent End of Francis Macomber's Short Happy Life." *HN*, 2: 14-6 (Sp 72).

———. "The Dantean Perspective in H's *A Farewell to Arms*." *JNT*, 3: 121-30 (My 73).

Davidson, Cathy. "Laughter Without Comedy in *For Whom the Bell Tolls*." *HN*, 3: 6-9 (Fa 73).

Davies, P.G., and R.R. "'If You Did Not Go Forward': Process and Stasis in *A Farewell to Arms*." *StN*, 2: 305-11 (1970).

———. "'A Killer Who Shoot You for the Fun of It': A Possible Source for H's 'The Killers.'" *IEngYb*, 15: 36-8 (Fa 70).

Davis, R.M. "Entering Literary History: H." *SHR*, 3: 382-95 (Fa 69).

————. "'If you did not go forward': Process and Stasis in *A Farewell to Arms*."

————. "Irony and Pity Once More." *FHA*, 1973, pp. 307-8.

————. "The Nick Adams Stories." *SHR*, 7: 215-9 (1973).

Davison, R.A. "Carelessness and the Cincinnati Reds in *The Old Man and the Sea*." *NCLit*, 1: 11-3 (1971).

————. "H's *A Farewell to Arms*." *Expl*, 29: 46 (1971).

De Cadaval, Rudy. "H letterato e personaggio nella leggenda." *Cenobio*, 19: 294-7 (1970).

DeFalco, Joseph. "H, Sport, and the Larger Metaphor." *LGJ*, 3: 18-20 (Sp-Su 75).

Delaney, Paul. "Robert Jordan's 'Real Absinthe' in *For Whom the Bell Tolls*." *FHA*, 1972, p. 317-20.

Delpech, Jeanine. "Un musicien, un comédien, un écrivain et un peintre nous parlent des livres de H et de Peyré sur la *fiesta brava*." *NL*, 3 S 38, p. 8.

DeMarr, M.J. "H's Narrative Methods." *IEJ*, 4: 31-6 (Sp 70).

Detweiler, Robert. "The Moment of Death in Modern Fiction." *ConL*, 13: 269-94 (1972).

Dietrich, Marlene. "The Most Fascinating Man I Know." *Ths Week*, 13: F 55, pp. 8-9.

Ditsky, John. "H, Plato and *The Hidden God*." *SHR*, 5: 145-7 (Sp 71).

————. "H's *Islands in the Stream*: Fact and Fantasy." *LGJ*, 1: 30-1 (Fa 73).

Donaldson, Scott. "H's Morality of Compensation." *AL*, 43: 399-420 (N 71).

Doody, Terrence. "H's Style and Jake's Narration." *JNT*, 4: 212-25 (S 74).

Dougherty, L.M. "Father L.M. Dougherty Talks About EH." *Rendezvous*, 5: 7-17 (1970).

Dowdy, Andrew. "H and Surrealism: A Note on the Twenties." *HN*, 2: 3-6 (Sp 72).

Doxey, W.S. "The Significance of Seney, Michigan, in H's 'Big Two-Hearted River.'" *HN*, 1: 5-6 (Fa 71).

Drake, Constance. "'A Lake Superior Salmon Fisherman.'" *FHA*, 1970, p. 235.

Drew, Fraser. "April 8, 1955 with H: Unedited Notes on a Visit to Finca Vigia." *FHA*, 1970, pp. 108-16.

————. "Recollections of a H Collector." *FHA*, 1971, pp. 294-7.

Drummond, Ann. "The H Code as Seen in the Early Short Stories." *Discourse*, 1: 248-52 (O 58).

*Duggan, M.M. "H Checklist." *FHA*, 1973, pp. 357-62; 1974, pp. 323-9.

Dupee, F.W. "H Revealed." *KR*, 15: 150-5 (Wi 53).

Dussinger, G.R. "H's 'The Snows of Kilimanjaro.'" *Expl*, 26: 67 (Ap 68).

Eby, Cecil. "How the Bell Tolled." *MQR*, 8: 245-52 (Fa 69).

Edel, Leon. "The Art of Evasion." *Folio*, 20: 18-20 (Sp 55).

Edelson, Mark. "A Note on 'One Reader Writes.'" *FHA*, 1972, pp. 329-31.

Egri, Peter. "The Relationship Between the Short Story and the Novel, Realism and Naturalism in H's Art." *HSE*, 4: 105-26 (1970); 7: 52-86 (1973).

Elia, Richard. "Three Symbols in H's 'The Snows of Kilimanjaro.'" *RLV*, 41: 282-5 (My-Je 75).

Elliston, Stephen. "H and the Next Generation." *UCQ*, 7: 23-7 (N 61).

Ellmann, Richard. "The H Circle." *NSt*, 213-4 (15 Ag 69).

Engstrom, Alfred. "Dante, Flaubert, and 'The Snows of Kilimanjaro.'" *MLN*, 65: 203-5 (1950).

Epstein, Seymour. "Politics and the Novelist." *DQ*, 4: 1-18 (1970).

Etulain, Richard. "EH and His Interpreters of the 1960's." *Rendezvous* 5: 53-70 (1970).

Ewell, N.M. "Dialogue in H's 'A Clean, Well-Lighted Place.'" *FHA*, 1971, pp. 305-6.

Falbo, E.S. "Carlo Linati: H's First Italian Critic and Translator." *FHA*, 1975, pp. 293-306.

Fallaci, Oriana. "An Interview with Mary H: 'My Husband EH.'" *Look*, 30: 62-8 (6 S 66).

Farquahr, R.H. "Dramatic Structure in the Novels of EH." *MFS*, 14: 271-82 (Au 68).

Farrell, J.T. "EH." *FHA*, 1973, pp. 215-25.

Feuchtwanger, Lion. "Laxness a H." *Host do domu*, 3: 559 (D 56).

Ficken, Carl. "Point of View in the Nick Adams Stories." *FHA*, 1971, pp. 212-35.

Filhol, Robert. "Fantasme et Littérature ou H et Oedipe." *LanM*, 62: 211-9 (Mr-Ap 68).

Fisher, Deborah. "Genuine Heroines H Style." *LGJ*, 2: 35-6 (Sp-Su 74).

Fisher, Edward. "Lost Generations, Then and Now." *ConnR*, 6: 13-25 (1972).

————. "What Papa Said." *ConnR*, 8: 16-20 (#2 75).

Fitz, Reginald. "The Meaning of Impotence in H and Eliot." *ConnR*, 4: 16-22 (1971).

Fitzgerald, F.S. "Letter to EH." *FHA*, 1970, pp. 10-3.

Fleissner, R.F. "The Macomber Case: A Sherlockian Analysis." *BakSJ*, 20: 154-6 (S 70).

Flora, J.M. "Biblical Allusion in *The Old Man and the Sea*." *SSF*, 10: 143-7 (Sp 73).

————. "H's 'Up in Michigan.'" *SSF*, 6: 465-6 (Su 69).

————. "Jacob Barnes' Name: The Other Side of the Ledger." *Eng Rec*, 24: 14-5 (Fa 73).

Fox, S.D. "H's 'The Doctor and the Doctor's Wife.'" *ArQ*, 29: 19-24 (Sp 73).

Freiberg, Medeea. "Coincidenţe tematice si tempweamentele intre Lorca şi H." *RITL*, 22: 402-11 (1973).

Frigeri, P.R. "EH dieci anni dopo." *Cenobio*, 19: 219-26 (1970).

Fritzsch, Robert. "Der H'sche Held und die Frau: Zur 'Sexualfricolitat' im Werk EH." *Welt und Wort*, 13: 197-201 (Jl 58).

Gadda Conti, Guiseppe. "H e la pace dei nostri giorni." *VeP*, 52: 3-20 (1969).

Gaillard, T.L. "The Critical Menagerie in 'The Short Happy Life of Francis Macomber.'" *EJ*, 60: 31-5 (Ja 71).

Ganzel, Dewey. "*Cabestro* and *Vaquilla*: The Symbolic Structure of *The Sun Also Rises*." *SR*, 76: 26-48 (Ja-Mr 68).

Ganzel, Dewey. "*A Farewell to Arms*. The Danger of Imagination." *SR*, 79: 576-97 (Au 71).

————. "The Symbolic Structure of *The Sun Also Rises*." *SR*, 76: 26-48 (Wi 68).

Gastwirth, D.E. "Can Life Have Meaning?: A Study of The Sun Also Rises." *YLM*, 134: 36-41 (Mr 66).

Geismar, Maxwell. "H and the Nobel Prize." *SatR*, 37: 24, 34 (13 N 54).

————. "Was 'Papa' a Truly Great Writer." *NYT*, 1 Jl 62; pp. 1, 16.

Georgoudaki, Ekaterini. "Some Comments on 'The Snows of Kilimanjaro.'" *ELUD*, 2: 48-58 (1973).

Gheorghe, F.N. "H si sentimentul tragic al existentei." *Contemporanul*, 12: 9 (S 69).

Gierasch, Walter. "H's 'Snows of Kilimanjaro.'" *Expl*, 4: Q9 (F 46).

Gifford, William. "EH: The Monsters and the Critics." *MFS*, 14: 255-70 (Au 68).

Gilenson, Boris. "H in the Soviet Union." *HN*, 4: 17-9 (Sp 74).

Gillespie, Gerald. "H and the Happy Few." *OL*, 23: 287-99 (1968).

Gilliam, Florence. "Remarks." *FHA*, 1973, pp. 43-8.

Gingrich, Arnold. "Scott, Ernest and Whoever." *Esquire*, 80: 151-4 (O 73).

Gleaves, E.S. "H and Baroja: Studies in Spiritual Anarchism." *REH*, 5: 363-75 (1971).

Goldhurst, William. "The Hyphenated Ham Sandwich of EH and J.D. Salinger: A Study in Literary Continuity." *FHA*, 1970, pp. 136-50.

Godman, Paul. "The Sweet Style of EH.' *NYRB*, 17: 27-8 (30 D 71).

Gordon, G.T. "H's Wilson-Harris: The Search for Values." *FHA*, 1972, pp. 237-44.

Gottschalk, Klaus-Dieter. "H's 'Cat in the Rain.'" *NsM*, 28: 155-62 (1975).

————. "Verkehrte Welt in H's 'The Doctor and the Doctor's Wife.'" *NS*, 21: 205-93 (My 72).

Gousseva, Elena. "A Soviet Critic's View on H." *SovL*, 8: 172-8 (Ag 67).

Hemingway

Grebstein, S.N. "The Structure of H's Short Stories." *FHA*, 1972, pp. 173-93.

Greco, Anne. "Margot Macomber: Bitch Goddess Exonerated." *FHA*, 1972, pp. 273-80.

Green, J.L. "Symbolic Sentences in 'The Big Two-Hearted River.'" *MFS*, 14: 307-12 (Au 68).

Greiner, D.J. "The Education of Robert Jordan: Death with Dignity." *HN*, 1: 14-20 (Fa 71).

———. "Emerson, Thoreau, and H: Some Suggestions About Literary Heritage." *FHA*, 1971, pp. 247-61.

Grenberg, B.L. "The Design of Heroism in *The Sun Also Rises*." *FHA*, 1971, pp. 274-89.

Griffin, G.R. "H's Fictive Use of the Negro: 'The curious quality of incompleteness.'" *HussR*, 1: 104-11 (1968).

Grimes, Carroll. "H: 'Old Newsman Writes.'" *FHA*, 1972, pp. 215-23.

———. "H's 'Defense of Dirty Words.'" *FHA*, 1975, pp. 217-27.

Grimes, Larry. "Night Terror and Morning Calm: A Reading of H's 'Indian Camp' as Sequel to 'Three Shots.'" *SSF*, 12: 413-5 (Fa 75).

Groseclose, B.S. "H's 'The Revolutionist': An Aid to Interpretation." *MFS*, 17: 565-70 (Wi 71-72).

Gunn, G.B. "H's Testament of Human Solidarity: A Literary Critique of *For Whom the Bells Tolls*." *ChSR*, 2: 99-111 (Wi 72).

Güntert, Fridhelm. "Zum Thema der Kreuzigung in H's Einakter 'Today is Friday!'" *NS*, 21: 538-43 (1972).

Gurko, Leo. "The Heroic Impulse in *The Old Man and the Sea*." *EJ*, 14: 377-82 (O 55).

*Hagemann, E.R., and W.C. Lewis, "A Critique of *Ernest Hemingway: A Comprehensive Bibliography*." *ABC*, 18: 5-6 (1968).

Hagoo, T.N. "Humor in H's Toronto Articles." *McNR*, 19: 48-58 (1968).

Hagopian, J.V. "H: Ultimate Exile." *Mosaic*, 8: 77-87 (Sp 75).

———. "Tidying Up H's Clean, Well-Lighted Place." *SSF*, 1: 140-6 (1964).

Haig, Sterling. "H and Stendhal." *PMLA*, 88: 1192-3 (O 73).

Halliday, E.M. "H's Hero." *UChM*, 45: 10-4 (My 53).

———. "H's Narrative Perspective." *SR*, 60: 202-18 (Sp 52).

Hamada, Seijiro. "Kilimanjaro e no Hisho." *EigoS*, 115: 699-701 (1969).

Hamalian, Leo. "H as Hunger Artist." *LitR*, 16: 5-13 (Fa 72).

Hamilton, J.B. "H and the Christian Paradox." *Renascence*, 24: 141-54 (Sp 72).

Hanneman, Audre. "Hanneman Addenda." *FHA*, 1970, pp. 195-218; 1971, pp. 343-6

Harder, K.B. "H's Religious Parody." *NYFQ*, 26: 76-7 (Mr 70).

Harris, G.T. "H, Malraux et la jeunesse d'Occident." *RLM*, 425-31: 51-81 (1975).

Hart, Jeffrey. "Fitzgerald and H: The Difficult Friend." *NatR*, 21: 29-31 (14 Ja 69).

Hartwell, Ronald. "What H Learned from Ambrose Bierce." *RSW*, 38: 309-11 (D 70).

Hauger, B.A. "First Person Perspective in Four H Stories." *Rendezvous*, 6: 29-38 (Sp 71).

Hayashi, Tesumaro. "*A Farewell to Arms*: The Contest of Experience." *KAL*, 12: 14-9 (1970).

Hays, P.L. "'Soldier's Home' and Ford Madox Ford." *HN*, 1: 21-2 (Fa 71).

Healey, Winifred. "When EH's Mother Came to Call." *FHA*, 1970, pp. 170-2.

Heaton, C.P. "Style in *The Old Man and the Sea*." *Style*, 4: 11-27 (Wi 70).

Helfand, Michael. "A Champ Cannot Retire Like Anyone Else." *LGH*, 3: 9-11, 35 (Sp-Su 75).

Hemingway, Ernest. "Letter to James Aswell." *LaStud*, 12: 532 (1974).

———. "Lost H Review Found." *FHA*, 1971, pp. 195-6.

———. "An Unrecorded H Public Letter." *FHA*, 1973, pp. 227-9.

———. "Will You Let These Kiddies Miss Santa Claus?" *FHA*, 1970, pp. 105-7.

Hemingway, Mary. "Ernest's Idaho and Mine." *World*, 1: 34-7 (7 N 72).

——. "Havana." *SatR*, 48: 40-1, 70-4 (2 Ja 65).

—— —. "H." *Look*, 25: 19-23 (12 S 61).

——. "Harry's Bar in Venice." *Holiday*, 43: 62-3, 106 (Je 68).

——. "That Magnificent Man and His Converter Machine." *Fact*, 3: 62-4 (My-Je 66).

Henss, Hubert. "Edgar Allan Poe, 'The Masque of the Red Death'; EH, 'A Clean Well-Lighted Place.'" *NS*, 16: 327-38 (Jl 67).

Herndon, J.A. "No 'Maggie's Drawers' for Margot Macomber." *FHA*, 1975, pp. 289-91.

Hess, John. "Jack H Remembers His Father." *Nat Wildlife*, 9: 12-5 (F-Mr 71).

Hicks, Granville. "H: The Complexities That Animated the Man." *SatR*, 52: 31-3, 43 (19 Ap 69).

——. "Twenty Years of H." *NRep*, 111: 524-6 (23 O 44).

Hill, J.S. "*To Have and Have Not*: H's Hiatus." *MQ*, 10: 349-56 (1969).

——. "Robert Wilson: H's Judge in 'Macomber.'" *UR*, 35: 129-32 (Wi 68).

Hily, Geneviève. "H et la Perspective." *LanM*, 62: 220-7 (Mr-Ap 68).

——. "Langage et communication: Un aspect inédit de la pensée de H." *EA*, 22: 279-92 (Jl-S 69).

——. "Point de Vue et Pronoms Pesonnels dans 'On the Quai at Smyrna.'" *EA*, 28: 300-13 (Jl-S 75).

Hipkiss, A. "EH's *The Things That I Know*." *TCL*, 19: 275-82 (O 73).

Hoffman, F.J. "No Beginning and No End: H and Death." *EIC*, 3: 73-84 (Ja 53).

Hoffmann, Gerhard. "'The Gambler, the Nun, and the Radio': Untersuchung zur Gestaltungsweise Hs." *GRM*, 15: 421-9 (O 65).

Hoffman, M.J. "From Cohn to Herzog." *YR*, 58: 342-58 (Sp 1969).

Holder R.C. "Counts Mippipopolous and Greffi: H's Aristocrats of Resignation." *HN*, 3: 3-6 (Fa 73).

Holland, R.B. "Macomber and the Critics." *SSF*, 5: 171-8 (Wi 68).

Howell, J.M. "H's 'Metaphysics' in Four Stories of the Thirtics: A Look at the Manuscripts." *ICarbS*, 1: 40-51 (1Q 73).

Howell, J.M. "H's Riddle and Kilimanjaro's Reusch." *SSF*, 8: 469-70 (Su 71).

——. "What the Leopard Was Seeking." *AN&Q*, 7: 68 (Ja 69).

——, and C.A. Lawler. "From Abercrombie & Fitch to *The First Forty-Nine Stories*: The Text of EH's 'Francis Macomber.'" *Proof*, 2: 213-81 (1972).

Hurwitz, H.M. "H's Tutor, Ezra Pound." *MFS*, 17: 469-82 (Wi 71-72).

Inglis, D.L. "Morley Callaghan and the H Boxing Legend." *NCLit*, 4: 4-7 (#4 74).

Irwin, Richard. "'Of War, Wounds and Silly Machines': An Examination of H's 'In Another Country.'" *Serif*, 5: 21-9 (1968).

Isherwood, Christopher. "H, Death, and Devil." *Decision*, 1: 58-60 (Ja 41).

⚓Jackson, T.J. "The 'Macomber' Typescript." *FHA*, 1970, pp. 219-22.

Jain, S.P. "In 'Hills Like White Elephants': A Study." *IJAS*, 1: 33-38 (1970).

——. "Some H Stories: Perspectives and Responses." *LHY*, 12: 53-64 (1Q 71).

——. "'The Undefeated': Triumph of the Ideal." *IJES*, 12: 86-95 (D 71).

Johnson, R.O. "H's 'How Do You Like it Now, Gentlemen?': A Possible Source." *AL*, 45: 114-17 (Mr 73).

Johnston, K.G. "Counterpart: The Reflective Pattern in H's Humor." *KanQ*, 1: 51-7 (Su 69).

——. "The Great Awakening: Nick Adams and the Silkworms in 'Now I Lay Me.'" *HN*, 1: 7-10 (Fa 71).

——. "H and Mantegna: The Bitter Nail Holes." *JNT*, 1: 86-94 (Mr 71).

————. "H's 'Out of Season' and the Psychology of Errors." *L&P*, 21: 41-6 (1971).

————. "H's 'Wine of Wyoming': Disappointment in America." *WAL*, 9: 159-68 (Fa 74).

————. "Journeys into the Interor: H, Thoreau and Mungo Park." *Forum(H)*, 10: 27-31 (3Q 73).

————. "The Star in H's *The Old Man and the Sea*." *AL*, 42: 388-91 (N 70).

Jones, E.T. "H and Cézanne: A Speculative Affinity." *UES*, 8: 26-8 (1970).

Joost, Nicholas. "EH." *ConL*, 11: 293-302 (Sp 70).

————. "EH and *The Dial*." *Neophil*, 52: 180-90, 304-13 (1968).

Jurado, M.R. "*The Old Man and the Sea* o la evolución del fatalismo en H." *FMod*, 50-1: 439-59 (1974).

Kallapur, S.T. "EH's Conception of Love and Womanhood." *BP*, 19: 37-47 (1974).

————. "*The Sun Also Rises*: A Reconsideration." *J Karnatak Un*, 16: 107-18

Kann, Hans-Joachim. "EH and German Culture." *NsM*, 28: 16-20 (1975).

————. "EH's Knowledge of German." *JA*, 15: 221-32 (1970).

————. "H and the Arts: A Necessary Addendum." *FHA*, 1974, pp. 145-54.

Kapoor, S.D. "EH: The Man and the Mask." *RUSEng*, 8: 36-53 (1975).

Kasegawa, Koh. "H and Thoreau." *SEAL*, 16: 1-6 (1970).

Kashkeen, Ivan. "EH: A Tragedy of Craftmanship." *Int Lit*, 5: 12-6 (1945).

————. "Letters of EH to Soviet Writers." *SovL*, 11: 158-67 (N 62).

————. "Letters of EH to Soviet Writers." *FHA*, 1971, pp. 197-208.

————. "What Is H's Style?" *SovL*, 6: 172-80 (1964).

Kaufmann, D.L. "The Long Happy Life of NM." *MFS*, 17: 347-59 (Au 71).

Kauffman Stanley. "Before and After Papa." *NRep*, 156: 18, 35 (10 Je 67).

Kawasaki, Toshiko. "H to futatsu no Bunseki Hihyo." *EigoS*, 114: 498-500 (1968).

Kenney, William. "Hunger and the America Dream in *To Have and Have Not*." *CEA*, 36: 26-8 (#2 74).

Kerrigan, William. "Something Funny about H's Count." *AL*, 46: 87-93 (Mr 74).

Kim, Suk-Choo. "Stoicism in H." *EL&L*, 10: 292-306 (S 61).

Kimball, W.J. "H and the Code." *Venture*, 6: 18-23 (Su 70).

Knoller, Fritz. "Hs Weltbild und Werkform." *Welt und Wort*, 7: 411-2 (D 52).

Kobler, J.F. "Confused Chronology in *The Sun Also Rises*." *MFS*, 13: 517-20 (Wi 67-68).

————. "Francis Macomber as Four-Letter Man." *FHA*, 1972, pp. 295-6.

————. "H's Four Dramatic Short Stories." *FHA*, 1975, pp. 247-55.

————. "H's 'The Sea Change': A Sympathetic View of Homosexuality." *ArQ*, 26: 318-24 (Wi 70).

————. "Let's Run Catherine Barkley up the Flag Pole and See Who Salutes." *CEA*, 36: 4-10 (#2 74).

————. "The Short Happy Illusion of Francis Macomber." *Quartet*, 45-46: 62-6 (1974)

Kondratjuk, Andrij. "Heminguej hovoryt' po-ukrajin-s'komu." *Dnipro*, 43: 148-51 (1969).

Konopa, Charles. "H's Royal Cats." *Cat Fancy*, 16: 6-7 (Ja-F 73).

Koontz, L.R. "My Favorite Subject Is Hadley." *ConnR*, 8: 36-41 (#1 74).

Kopf, J.Z. "Meyer Wolfsheim and Robert Cohn: A Study of a Jewish Type and Stereotype." *Tradition*, 10: 93-104 (Sp 69).

Koskimies, Rafael. "Notes on EH's *For Whom the Bell Tolls*." *OL*, 23: 276-86 (1968).

Kovacs, Jozsef. "EH, Mati Zalke and Spain." *ALitASH*, 13: 315-24 (1972).

Kraus, W.K. "EH's 'Hills Like White Elephants': A Note on a Reasonable Source." *Eng Rec*, 21: 23-6 (D 70).

Kroll, Ernest. "A Note on Victor Llona." *FHA*, 1972, pp. 157-8.

Kruse, Horst. "EH's Kunst der Allegorie: Zeitgenossische und biblische Anspielungen in 'God Rest You Merry Gentlemen.'" *JA*, 16: 128-50 (1971).

———. "H's 'Cat in the Rain' and Joyce's *Ulysses*." *LWU*, 3: 28-30 (1970).

Kuxarenko, V.A. "È. Xeminguèj v perevode A. Voznesenskogo." *FN*, 11: 40-9 (1968).

Kvam, Wayne. "H's 'Banal Story.'" *FHA*, 1974, pp. 181-91.

Lagios, S.A. "*The Old Man and the Sea*—1932 and 1952." *EEx*, 10: 12-3 (Mr 63).

Lajoie, Ronald, and Sally Lentz. "Is Jake Barnes Waiting?" *FHA*, 1975, pp. 229-33.

Lauras, Antoine. "EH est mort." *Études*, 310: 278-81 (S 61).

Laurence, F.M. "Hollywood Publicity and H's Popular Reputation." *JPC*, 6: 20-31 (Su 72).

———. "500 Grand: The Plagiarism Suit Against H." *FHA*, 1974, pp. 193-9.

Layman, Richard. "H's Library Cards at Shakespeare and Company." *FHA*, 1975, pp. 191-206.

LeBost, Barbara. "'The Way It Is': Something Else on H." *J of Existentialism*, 6: 175-80 (Wi 65-6).

Lebowitz, Alan. "H in Our Time." *YR*, 58: 321-41 (1968).

Le Clec'h, Guy. "H: avait-il gardé pour lui son chef-d'oeuvre?" *FL*, 1189: 26 (17-23 F 69).

Leigh, D.J. "'In Our Time': The Interchapters as Structural Guides to a Psychological Pattern." *SSF*, 12: 1-8 (Wi 75).

Leiter, L.H. "Neural Projections in H's 'On the Quai at Smyrna.'" *SSF*, 5: 384-6 (Su 68).

Lewis, Clifford. "The Short Happy Life of Francis Scott Macomber." *EA*, 23: 256-61 (1970).

Lewis R.L. "H Ludens." *LGJ*, 3: 7-8, 30 (Sp-Su 75).

Lewis, R.W. "H's Concept of Sport and 'Soldier's Home.'" *Rendezvous*, 5: 19-2 (1970).

———. "The Survival of H." *JML*, 1: 446-53 (1971).

———, and Max Westbrook. "'The Snows of Kilimanjaro' Collated and Annotated." *TQ*, 13: 67-143 (Su 70).

Liedloff, Helmut. "Two War Novels: A Critical Comparison." *RLC*, 42: 390-406 (Jl-S 68).

Light, Martin. "Of Wasteful Deaths: H's Stories about the Spanish War." *WHR*, 23: 29-42 (Wi 69).

———. "Sweeping Out Chivalric Silliness: The Example of *Huck Finn* and *The Sun Also Rises*." *MTJ*, 17: 18-21 (Wi 74-75).

Linebarger, J.M. "Eggs as Huevos in *The Sun Also Rises*." *FHA*, 1970, pp. 237-9.

———. "Symbolic Hats in *The Sun Also Rises*." *FHA*, 1972, pp. 323-4.

Lisca, Peter. "Steinbeck and H: Suggestions for a Comparative Study." *SteinN*, 2: 9-17 (Sp 69).

Livingston, Howard. "Religious Intrusion in H's 'The Killers.'" *Eng Rec*, 21: 42-4 (F 71).

Llona, Victor. "The Sun Also Rose for EH." *FHA*, 1972, pp. 159-71.

Lodge, David. "H's Clean, Well-Lighted, Puzzling Place." *EIC*, 21: 33-56 (Ja 71).

Loeb, Harold. "EH: A Life Story." *SoR*, 5: 114-25 (Su 69).

———. "Remarks by Harold Loeb." *FHA*, 1973, pp. 33-8.

Long, R.E. "Fitzgerald and H on Stage." *FHA*, 1969, pp. 143-4.

Longmire, S.E. "H's Praise of Dick Sisler in *The Old Man and the Sea*." *AL*, 42: 96-8 (Mr 70).

Lucid, R.F. "Three Public Peformances: Fitzgerald, H, Mailer." *ASch*, 43: 447-66 (Su 74).

McCarthy, Paul. "Chapter Beginnings in A Farewell to Arms." *BSUF*, 10: 21-30 (Sp 69).

———. "Opposites Meet: Melville, H, and Heroes." *KanQ*, 7: 40-50 (1975).

McClellan, David. "H's Colonel Appropriately Quotes Jackson." *FHA*, 1970, p. 234.

———. "Is Custer a Model for the Fascist Captain in For Whom the Bell Tolls?" *FHA*, 1974, pp. 239-41.

MacDonald, Scott. "The Confusing Dialogue in H's 'A Clean, Well-Lighted Place': A Final Word?" *SAF*, 1: 93-101 (Sp 73).

————. "H's 'The Snows of Kilimanjaro': Three Critical Problems." *SSF*, 11: 67-74 (Wi 74).

————. "Implications of Narrative Perspective in H's 'Now I Lay Me.'" *SAF*, 1: 213-20 (Au 73).

————. "Implications of Narrative Perspective in H's 'The Undefeated.'" *JNT*, 2: 1-15 (1972).

McHaney, T.L. "Anderson, H, and Faulkner's *The Wild Palms*." *PMLA*, 87: 465-74 (My 72).

McIlvaine, R.M. "A Literary Source for the Caesarean Section in *A Farewell to Arms*." *AL*, 43: 444-7 (N 71).

McNally, James. "A H Mention of *Gentlemen*." *FHA*, 1972, pp. 333-4.

McSweeney, Kerry. "The First H Hero." *DR*, 52: 309-14 (1972).

Mahony, P.J. "H's 'A Day's Wait.'" *Expl*, 27: 18 (N 68).

Mai, R.P. "EH and Men Without Women." *FHA*, 1970, pp. 173-86.

Mann, C.W. "African Journal." *FHA*, 1972, pp. 395-6.

————, et al. "Young H: A Panel." *FHA*, 1972, pp. 113-44.

Mansell, Darrel. "*The Old Man and the Sea* and the Computer." CHum, 8: 195-206 (1974).

————. "When Did H Write *The Old Man and the Sea*?" *FHA*, 1975, pp. 311-324.

Marambaud, Pièrre. "H et la Guerre de l'*Adieux aux Armes* à *Pour Qui Sonne le Glas*." *EAA*, 1: 89-100 (1962).

Marin, Dave. "Seven Hours with Papa." *SWR*, 53: 167-77 (Sp 68).

Marsden, M.M. "H's Symbolic Pattern: The Basis of Tone." *Disc*, 12: 16-28 (1969).

Martine, J.J. "H's 'Fifty Grand': The Other Fight(s)." *JML*, 2: 123-7 (S 71).

————. "A Little Light on H's 'The Light of the World.'" *SSF*, 7: 465-7 (Su 70).

Marx, Leo. "Pastoral Ideals and City Troubles." *JGE*, 20: 251-71 (1969).

May, C.E. "Is H's 'Well-Lighted Place' Really Clean Now?" *SSF*, 8: 326-30 (1971).

Maynard, Reid. "Leitmotif and Irony in H's 'Hills Like White Elephants.'" *UR*, 37: 273-5 (Su 71).

Meador, J.M. "Addendum to Hanneman: H's *The Old Man and the Sea*." *PBSA*, 67: 454-7 (O-D 73).

Mellers, W.H. "The Ox in Spain." *Scrutiny*, 10: 93-9 (Je 41).

Merrill, Robert. "Tragic Form in *A Farewell to Arms*." *AL*, 45: 571-9 (Ja 74).

Mertens, G.M. "H's *The Old Man and the Sea* and Mann's *The Black Swan*." *L&P*, 6: 96-99 (Au 56).

Messenger, Christian. "H and the School Athletic Hero." *LGH*, 3: 21-3 (Sp-Su 75).

Meyer, Charles. "H and the *Pilar*." *Popular Boating*, 2: 27-31, 81-3 (N 57).

Miller, O.J. "Camus et H: Pour une évaluation méthodologique." *RLM*, 264-70: 9-42 (#3 71).

Moktali, L.R. "Experiments with Syntax in H's *A Farewell to Arms*." *J Shivaji Un*, 6: 15-20 (1973).

Monat, Olympio. "A arte de contar de H: O narrador, a açáo e a consciência." *ESPSL*, 4 Aug 74, p. 1.

Monteiro, George. "'Between Grief and Nothing': H and Faulkner." *HN*, 1: 13-5 (Sp 71).

————. "The Education of EH." *JAmSt*, 8: 91-101 (Ap 74).

*————. "H: Contribution Toward a Definitive Bibliography." *PBSA*, 65: 411-4 (4Q 71).

————. "H and Spain: A Response to Woodward." *HN*, 2: 16-7 (Fa 72).

————. "H in Portuguese: More Hanneman Addenda." *HN*, 2: 17-9 (Sp 72).

————. "H, O. Henry, and the Surprise Ending." *PrS*, 47: 296-302 (Wi 73-74).

————. "H on Dialogue in 'A Clean, Well-Lighted Place.'" *FHA*, 1974, p. 243.

———. "H's Christmas Carol." *FHA*, 1972, pp. 207-13.

———. "H's Pleiade Ballplayers.'" *FHA*, 1973, pp. 299-301.

———. "The Limits of Professionalism: A Sociological Approach to Faulkner, Fitzgerald, and H." *Criticism*, 15: 145-55 (Sp 73).

———. "*McNaught's Monthly*: Addenda to the Bibliographies of . . ., H [and others]." *PBSA*, 68: 64-5 (1Q 74).

———. "Not H But Spain." *FHA*, 1971, pp. 309-11.

———. "The Reds, the White Sox, and *The Old Man and the Sea*." *NCLit*, 4: 7-9 (My 74).

———. "Santiago, DiMaggio, and H." *FHA*, 1975, pp. 273-80.

Montgomery, Marion. "Emotion Recollected in Tranquility: Wordsworth's Legacy to Eliot, Joyce and H." *SoR*, 6: 710-21 (Jl 70).

Moravia, Alberto. "Amici dei morte e nemici dei vivi." *Espresso*, 20 Ag 61, p. 8.

Morley, Robert. "A *Redbook* Dialogue: Mary H." *Redbook*, 126: 62-3, 146-53 (N 65).

Mosher, H.F. "The Two Styles of H's *The Sun Also Rises*." *FHA*, 1971, pp. 262-73.

Moss, A.H. "The Many Ways of H." *ConnR*, 2: 14-6 (1969).

———. "More Ways of H." *ConnR*, 3: 43-4 (O 69).

Munson, Gorham. "A Comedy of Exiles." *LitR*, 12: 41-75 (1968).

Murphy, G.D. "H's *The Sun Also Rises*." *Expl*, 28: 23 (N 69).

———. "H's 'Waste Land': The Controlling Water Symbolism of *The Sun Also Rises*." *HN*, 1: 20-6 (Sp 71).

Murray, D.M. "The Day of the Locust in *The Sun Also Rises*." *FHA*, 1975, pp. 281-7.

Murray, Donald. "Hong Kong Letter: Bombs, Books, and H." *ABC*, 18: 16-21 (Mr 68).

Nagarajan, M.S. "The Structure of 'The Killers.'" *LHY*, 15: 114-9 (1Q 74).

Nagel, James. "The Narrative Method of 'The Short Happy Life of Francis Macomber." *RS*, 41: 18-27 (1973).

Naik, M.K. "Thematic Structure in *A Farewell to Arms*." *IJES*, 8: 79-82 (1967).

Nakamura, Masao. "EH's 'The Short Happy Life of Francis Macomber.'" *SALCS*, 7: 34-42 (1971).

Nakano, Fujio. "E.H and His Nihilism." *HirStud*, 18: 35-49 (1972).

Nakhdjavani, Erik. "Of Strength and Vulnerability." *Dialogue*, 1: 5-22 (4Q 73).

Nolan, W.F. "The Man Behind the Masks." *FHA*, 1974, pp. 207-13.

Noland, R.W. "A New Look at H." *HSL*, 1: 140-5 (1969).

Norton, C.A. "The Alcoholic Content of *A Farewell to Arms*." *FHA*, 1973, pp. 309-14.

O'Brien, John. "I Am Sure I Saw *EH* . . ." *FHA*, 1973, pp. 303-5.

Oldsey, Bernard. "Of H's *Arms and the Man*." *Col Lit*, 1: 174-89 (Fa 74).

Oleson, Russ. "H's Cat Collection in 1973." *Cat Fancy*, 16: 12-5 (N-D 73).

Owen, John. "Inside H: His Strange Search for Love and Death." *See*, 15: 28-31 (My 56).

Osztovits, Levente. "Tete-A-Tete with American Literature: A History of Literature and Three Anthologies." *New Hungarian Q*, 9: 199-206 (Wi 68).

Pauly, T.H., and Thomas Dwyer. "Passing the Buck in *The Sun Also Rises*." *HN*, 2: 3-6 (Fa 72).

Pearson, J.L. "H's Women." *LGJ*, 1: 16-9 (My 73).

Peckham, Morse. "EH: Sexual Themes in H's Writing." *Sexual Behavior*, 1: 62-70 (Jl 71).

Peich, Michael. "H and *Kiki's Memoirs*." *FHA*, 1973, pp. 315-6.

Peirce, J.F. "The Car as Symbol in H's 'The Short Happy Life of Franics Macomber.'" *SCB*, 32: 230-2 (Wi 72).

Pérez Gállego, Cándido. "Los dos finales de *A Farewell to Arms*." *FMod*, 4: 152-3 (Ja 64).

———. "El orden de los acontecimientos en H." *Arbor*, 355-56: 75-89 (1975).

Perkins, George. "The Rain in *A Farewell to Arms*." *JOFS*, 3: 45-7 (Sp 68).

Petrarca, A.J. "Irony of Situation in EH's 'Soldier's Home.'" *EJ*, 58: 664-7 (My 69).

Phillips, S.R. "H and the Bullfight: The Archetypes of Tragedy." *ArQ*, 29: 37-55 (Sp 73).

Pinksker, Sanford. "Rubbing America Against the Grain: Writing after H." *Quadrant*, 80: 48-54 (1972).

Pivano, Fernanda. "Ritratto di H." *Smeraldo*, 8: 22-6 (Mr 54).

Politicus. "How We Swallowed *The Old Man and the Sea*." *AmMerc*, 89: 73-6 (Ag 59).

Pollin, B.R. "Poe and H on Violence and Death." *MDAC*, 1973, pp. 12-4.

Prescott, Herman. "H vs. Faulkner: An Intriguing Feud." *LGJ*, 3: 18-9 (Fa 75).

Presley, J.W. "'Hawks Never Share': Women and Tragedy in H." *HN*, 3: 3-10 (Sp 73).

Price, Reynolds. "For EH." *NewAmR*, 14: 38-66 (1972).

Prigozy, R. "Matter of Measurement: The Tangled Relationship Between Fitzgerald and H." *Cweal*, 95: 103-6 (29 O 71).

Prizel, Yuri. "The Critics and *The Old Man and the Sea*." *RS*, 4: 208-16 (#1 75).

———. "H in Soviet Literary Criticism." *AL*, 44: 445-56 (N 72).

Raeburn, John. "*Death in the Afternoon*, and the Legendary H." *FHA*, 1973, pp. 243-57.

———. "EH: The Public Writer as Popular Culture." *JPC*, 8: 91-8 (Su 74).

———. "H in the Twenties: 'The Artist's Reward.'" *BRMMLA*, 29: 118-46 (Au 75).

Rao, Nageswara. "Syntax as Rhetoric: An Analysis of EH's Early Syntax." *IL*, 36: 296-303 (S 75).

Redington, J.W. "Before the Corrida." *FHA*, 1975, pp. 309-10.

Reichard, D.P. "None are to be found more clever than Ernie." *EJ*, 58: 668-72 (My 69).

Reynolds, M.S. "Two H Sources for *In Our Time*." *SSF*, 9: 81-6 (1972).

Richards, R.F. "H and Stevens' 'Poetry of Extra ordinary Actuality.'" *Descant*, 17: 46-8 (Su 73).

Ring, Frances, and R.L. Samsell. "Sisyphus in Hollywood: Refocusing F. Scott Fitzgerald." *FHA*, 1973, pp. 93-104.

Robinson, C.E. "James T. Farrell's Critical Estimate of H." *FHA*, 1973, pp. 209-14.

Robinson, F.D. "Frederick Henry: The H Hero as Storyteller." *CEA*, 34: 13-6 (My 72).

Rodgers, B.F. "The Nick Adams Stories: Fiction or Fact?" *FHA*, 1974, pp. 155-62.

Rodgers, P.D. "Levels of Irony in H's 'The Gambler, the Nun, and the Radio.'" *SSF*, 7: 439-49 (Su 70).

Rogers, J.M., and Gordon Stein. "Bibliographical Notes on H's *Men Without Women*." *PBSA*, 64: 210-3 (2Q 70).

Rogers, Roy. "H and the Tragic Curve." *HN*, 4: 12-6 (Sp 74).

Rondi, G.L. "H e il cinema." *Mondo Occidentale*, 4: 50-61 (D 57).

Rosen, Kenneth. "Ten Eulogies: H's Spanish Death." *BNYPL*, 77: 276-7 (1974).

Ross, Frank. "The Assailant-Victim in Three War-Protest Novels." *Paunch*, 32: 46-57 (D 68).

Ross, Lillian. "How Do You Like It Now, Gentlemen?" *NY*, 26: 36, 38, 56, (13 My 50).

Ross, M.L. "Bill Gorton, the Preacher in *The Sun Also Rises*." *MFS*, 18: 517-28 (Wi 72-73).

Rubenstein, Jill. "A Degree of Alchemy: *A Moveable Feast* as Literary Autobiography." *FHA*, 1973, pp. 231-42.

Rubin, L.D. "*In Memoriam*: EH." *Virginia Lit*, 8: 43-5 (Wi 62).

Ruhm, Herbert. "H in Schruns." *Cweal*, 99: 344-5 (23 D 73).

Ryan, W.J. "Uses of Irony in *To Have and Have Not*." *MFS*, 14: 329-36 (Au 68).

Sachs, L.J., and B.H. Stern. "The Little Preoedipal Boy in Papa H and How He Created His Artistry." *Costerus*, 1: 221-40 (1972).

St. John, Donald. "H and the Girl Who Could Skate." *ConnR*, 2: 10-9 (1968).

———. "H and Prudence." *ConnR*, 5: 78-84 (1972).

————. "Interview with H's 'Bill Gordon.'" *ConnR*, 1: 5-12 (D 68); 3: 5-23 (O 69).

————. "Leicester Hemingway, Chief of State." *ConnR*, 3: 5-19 (1970).

Salinäs, Hilding. "Studie i H." *Studiekamraten*, 51: 23-6 (1969).

Salzman, Jack. "Prelude to Madness: A Look at 'Soldier's Home' and 'For Esmé: With Love and Squalor.'" *RRAL*, 33: 102-12 (1973).

Samsell, R.L. "Paris Days with Ralph Church." *FHA*, 1973, pp. 145-7.

Sanders, Dave. "Piggott Pandemonium: H Wasn't a Hit in This Town." *LGJ*, 3: 3-6 (Fa 75).

Sanford, M.H. "At the Hs." *Atl*, 208: 31-9 (D 61); 209: 32-7 (Ja 62); 209; 60-6 (F 62).

Sarason, B.D "Comment." *ConnR*, 1: 144 (1968).

————. "H in Havana: Two Interviews." *ConnR*, 3: 24-31 (O 69).

————. "Krebs in Kodiak." *FHA*, 1975, pp. 209-15.

————. "Lady Brett Ashley and Lady Duff Twysden." *ConnR*, 2: 5-13 (Jl 69).

————. "Pauline Hemingway: In Tranquility." *FHA*, 1970, pp. 127-35.

Scheider, D.J. "H's *A Farewell to Arms*: The Novel as Pure Poetry." *MFS*, 14: 283-96 (Au 68).

Schneiderman, Leo. "H: A Psychological Study." *ConnR*, 6: 34-49 (Ap 73).

Schonhorn, Manuel. "*The Sun Also Rises*: I: The Jacob Allusion, II: Parody as Meaning." *BSUF*, 16: 49-55 (Sp 75).

Schorer, Mark. "Mr. H and His Critics." *NRep*, 131: 18-20 (15 N 54).

Schroeter, James. "H via Joyce." *SoR*, 10: 95-114 (Ja 74).

Seator, L.H. "The Antisocial Humanism of Cela and H." *REH*, 9: 425-39 (1975).

Serravalli, Luigi. "EH inviato speciale." *Cristallo*, 10: 142-64 (1968).

Sharma, D.R. "Moral Frontiers of EH." *Panjab Un Res Bul*, 2: 49-59 (Ag 71).

————. "Vision and Design in H." *LCrit*, 8: 42-51 (Wi 68).

Sharrock, Roger. "Singles and Couples: H's *A Farewell to Arms* and Updike's *Couples*." *Ariel*, 3: 21-43 (O 73).

Shaw, Patric. "How Earnest is the Image: H's Little Animals." *CEA*, 37: 5-8 (Mr 75).

Shelton, F.W. "The Family in H's Nick Adams Stories." *SSF*, 11: 303-5 (Su 74).

Shepherd, Allen. "H's 'An Alpine Idyll' and Faulkner's 'Mistral.'" *UPortR*, 25: 63-8 (Fa 73).

————. "Hudson's Cats in H's *Islands in the Stream*." *NCLit*, 2: 3-6 (S 72).

————. "The Lion in the Grass (Alas?): A Note on 'The Short Happy Life of Francis Macomber.'" *FHA*, 1972, pp. 297-9.

————. "'Other Things,' Unanswerable Questions: H's *Islands in the Stream*." *AntigR*, 9: 37-9 (Sp 72).

————. "Taking Apart 'Mr. and Mrs. Elliot.'" *MarkR*, 2: 17-18 (S 69).

————. "Today is Friday." *DilR*, 18: 173-5 (Ap 70).

Simmons, M.K. "A Look into *The Glass Mountain*." *AL*, 41: 422-5 (N 69).

Singh, Satyanarayan. "The Psychology of Heroic Living in *The Old Man and the Sea*." *OJES*, 10: 7-15 (1973).

Singh, B.M. "The Role of Manolin in *The Old Man and the Sea*." *PURBA*, 4: 105-9 (Ap 73).

Skipp, F.E. "Metempsychosis in the Stream." *FHA*, 1974, pp. 137-43.

————. "Nick Adams, Prince of Abissinia." *Carrell*, 2: 20-6 (Je-D 70).

Škovorecký, Josef. "Literární nazory EH." *Světová literatura*, 1: 190-5 (Je 56).

Slabey, R.M. "The Structure of H's *In Our Time*." *MSpr*, 60: 273-85 (1966).

Slattery, Sister M.P. "H's *A Farewell to Arms*." *Expl*, 27: 8 (1968).

Smith, Julian. "'A Canary for One': H in the Wasteland." *SSF*, 5: 355-61 (Su 68).

————. "Christ Times Four: H's Unknown Spanish Civil War Stories." *ArQ*, 25: 5-17 (Sp 69).

————. "Eyeless in Wyoming, Blind in Venice: H's Last Stories." *ConnR*, 4: 9-15 (O 71).

————. "H and the Thing Left Out." *JML*, 1: 169-82 (1970-71).

————. "More Products of the H Industry." *SSF*, 7: 638-46 (Fa 70).

Smith, W.B. "A Wedding up in Michigan." *FHA*, 1970, pp. 124-6.

Sojka, Gregory. "A Portrait of H as Angler-Artist." *LGJ*, 3: 12-3 (Sp-Su 75).

Solov'ev, E. "Cvet tragedii: O tvorčestve E. Xemingueja." *NovM*, 44: 206-35 (1968).

Somers, P.P. "Anderson's Twisted Apples and H's Crips." *Midamerica*, 1974: 82-97 (1974).

————. "The Mark of Sherwood Anderson on H: A Look at the Texts." *SHQ*, 73: 487-503 (Au 73).

————. "Sherwood Anderson Introduces His Friend EH." *LGJ*, 3: 24-6 (Fa 75).

Sordo, Enrique. "El retorno de H." *CHA*, 45: 358-61 (S 53).

Souchere, Elena de la. "La corrida y la muerte: Variaciones sobre un tema de H." *Cultura Universitaria*, 74-5: 56-68 (Je 61); 76-7: 65-79 (Jl-D 61).

Spinucci, Pietro. "EH: Lo stile e la vita." *HumB*, 16: 937-44 (N 61).

Sprague, Claire. "*The Sun Also Rises*: Its' Clear Financial Basis.'" *AQ*, 21: 259-66 (Su 69).

Srivastava, Ramesh. "H's 'Cat in the Rain': An Interpretation." *LCrit*, 9: 79-84 (Su 70).

Stafford, Edward. "An Afternoon with H." *Writer's Dig*, 44: 18-22 (D 64).

Stafford, W.T. "H/Faulkner: Marlin and Catfish?" *SoR*, 6: 1191-1200 (Au 70).

Stavrou, C.N. "Nada, Religion, and H." *Topic: 12*, 6: 5-20 (Fa 66).

Steinberg, Lee. "The Subjective Idealist 'Quest for True Men' in H's *For Whom the Bells Tolls*." *L&I*, 13: 51-8 (1972).

Stephens, R.O. "H and Stendhal: The Matrix of *A Farewell to Arms*." *PMLA*, 88: 271-60 (Mr 73).

————. "Language Magic and Reality in *For Whom the Bell Tolls*." *Criticism*, 14: 151-64 (Sp 72).

————, and James Ellis. "H, Fitzgerald, and the Riddle of 'Henry's Bicycle.'" *ELN*, 5: 46-9 (S 67).

Stewart, D.O. "An Interview." *FHA*, 1973, pp. 83-9.

————. "Recollections of Fitzgerald and H." *FHA*, 1971, pp. 177-88.

Stewart, L.D. "H and the Autobiographies of Alice B. Toklas." *FHA*, 1970, pp. 117-23.

Stobie, Margaret. "EH, Craftsman." *Canadian For*, 33: 179-82 (N 53).

Stone, Edward. "H's Mr Frazer: From Revolution to Radio." *JML*, 1: 375-88 (1971).

————. "H's Waiters Yet Once More." *AS*, 37: 239-40 (O 62).

Strage, Mark. "EH: War, Women, Wine, Words." *Pageant*, 8: 18-29 (Ap 53).

Strandberg, V.H. "E's Insomniacs." *SAQ*, 68: 67-73 (Wi 69).

Stubbs, John. "Love and Role Playing in *A Farewell to Arms*." *FHA*, 1973, pp. 271-84.

Stuckey, W.J. "'The Killers' as Experience." *JNT*, 5: 128-35 (1975).

Sugg, R.P. "H, Money and *The Sun Also Rises*." *FHA*, 1972, pp. 457-67.

Sullivan, J.J. "Conflict in the Modern American Novel." *BSUF*, 15: 28-36 (1974).

Sutherland, Fraser. "H and Callaghan: Friends and Writers." *CanL*, 53: 8-17 (1972).

Sylvester, Harry. "EH: A Note." *Cweal*, 25: 10-2 (30 O 36).

Takamura, Katsuji. "H no Rojin to Shonen." *EigoS*, 114: 300-01 (1968).

Takigawa, Motoo. "*The Short Happy Life of Francis Macomber* no Shusei." *EigoS*, 115: 98-100 (1969).

Talese, Gay. "Looking for H." *Esquire*, 60: 44-7 (Jl 63).

Tamke, Alexander. "Jacob Barnes' 'Biblical Name': Central Irony in *The Sun Also Rises*." *Eng Rec*, 18: 2-76 (1967).

Tanaka, Keisuke. "The Bipolar Construction in the Works of EH." *KAL*, 12: 32-44 (1970).

Tanner, S.L. "H: The Function of Nostalgia." *FHA*, 1974, pp. 163-74.

Tanner, Tony. "H y Fitzgerald. "*CdLA*, 4: 99-105 (D 64).

Tatandziewicz-Glebko, Ewa. "H Translations in Poland." *Babel*, 10: 85-7 (#2 64).

Theroux, Paul. "Lord of the Ring: H's 'Last Novel.'" *Enc*, 36: 62-6 (F 71).

Thomaneck, J.K.A. "H's Riddle of Kilimanjaro Once More." *SSF*, 7: 326-7 (Sp 70).

Thomas, Peter. "A Lost Leader: H's 'The Light of the World.'" *HAB*, 21: 14-9 (Fa 70).

Thomsen, C.W. "Liebe und Tod in H's *Across the River and into the Trees.*" *NS*, 20: 665-74 (D 71).

Torchiana, D.T. "*The Sun Also Rises*: A Reconsideration." *FHA*, 1969, pp. 77-103.

Traver, Robert. "H's Big Two-Hearted Secret." *Sports Afield*, 170: 46-7, 82-4 (Jl 73).

Trilling, Lionel. "An American in Spain." *PR*, 8: 63-7 (Ja-F 41).

———. "H and His Critics." *PR*, 6: 52-60 (Wi 39).

Turnbull, Andrew. "Scott Fitzgerald and EH." *Esquire*, 57: 110-24 (Mr 62).

Twitchell, James. "H's *The Sun Also Rises.*" *Expl*, 31: 24 (D 72).

———. "The Swamp in H's 'Big Two-Hearted River.'" *SSF*, 9: 275-6 (Su 72).

Uchida, Shigeharu. "The Nada Theme of *A Farewell to Arms* and Its Significance to the Code." *KAL*, 9: 27-33 (Jl 66).

Unrue, John. "H and the New Massess." *FHA*, 1969, pp. 131-40.

———. "The Valley of Baca and *A Farewell to Arms.*" *FHA*, 1974, pp. 229-34.

Updike, John. "Papa's Sad Testament." *NSt*, 16 O 70, p. 489.

Vaidyanathan, T.G. "Did Margot Kill Francis Macomber?" *IJAS*, 1: 1-13 (1970).

Vančura, Zdeněk. "Současni američti romanopisci, 4: Posmartny H." *CMF*, 53: 109-15 (1971).

Vanderbilt, Kermit. "*The Sun Also Rises*: Time Uncertain." *TCL*, 15: 153-5 (O 69).

Vandervelde, Marjorie. "An Afternoon with Mary H." *Writer's Dig*, 52: 28-30, 43 (Je 72).

Vanderwerken, D.L. "One More River to Cross: The Bridge Motif in *The Sun Also Rises.*" *CEA*, 37: 21-2 (Ja 75).

Vargas, German. "Un libro de cronicas de H." *BCB*, 11: 55-6 (1968).

Vázquez-Bibi, A.M. "Introducción al estudio de la influencia barojiana en H y Dos Passos." *CHA*, 265-7: 169-203 (1972).

von Ende, Vrederick. "The Corrida Pattern in *For Whom the Bell Tolls.*" *Re: A&L*, 3: 63-70 (Sp 70).

Vopat, C.G. "The End of *The Sun Also Rises*: A New Beginning." *FHA*, 1972, pp. 245-55.

Vorpahl, B.M. "EH and Owen Wister: Finding the Lost Generation." *LCUP*, 36: 126-37 (Sp 70).

———. "H and Wister: For Want of a Smile." *LATC*, 23 F 69, pp. 8-11.

Waggoner, H.H. "H and Faulkner: The End of Something." *SoR*, 4: 458-66 (Sp 68).

Wagner, L.W. "Juxtaposition in H's *In Our Time.*" *SSF*, 12: 243-52 (Su 75).

———. "The Marinating of *For Whom the Bell Tolls.*" *JML*, 2: 533-46 (N 72).

———. "A Note on Hemingway as Poet." *Midamerica*, 74: 58-63 (1974).

———. "The Poem of Santiago and Manolin." *MFS*, 19: 517-29 (Wi 73-74).

———. "*The Sun Also Rises*: One Debt to Imagism." *JNT*, 2: 88-98 (1972).

Walcutt, C.C. "H's *The Sun Also Rises.*" *Expl*, 32: 57 (1974).

Wallach, John P. "The 'Old Man' Remembers H." *Genesis*, 1: 22-4, 45, 118 (Ag 73).

Walz, L.A. "'The Snows of Kilimanjaro': A New Reading." *FHA*, 1971, pp. 239-45.

Wark, Bob. "EH and Club Fighters." *Argosy*, 359: 40-1, 116-8 (D 64).

Warner, Fred. "H's Death: Ten Years Later." *HN*, 1: 16-9 (Sp 71).

Warner, S.D. "H's *The Old Man and the Sea.*" *Expl*, 33: 9 (O 74).

Wasserstrom, William. "The H Problem." *VQR*, 45: 531-7 (Su 69).

Watkins, F.C. "The Nick Adams Stories: A Single Work by EH." *SoR*, 9: 281-91 (Ja 73).

Watson, J.G. "'A Sound Basis of Union': Structural and Thematic Balance in 'The Short Happy Life of Francis Macomber.'" *FHA*, 1974, pp. 215-28.

Waugh, Evelyn. "The Case of Mr. H." *Cweal*, 53: 97-8 (3 N 50).

Weatherby, W.J. "H's Manuscripts." *TLS*, 4 Ag 69, p. 883.

Waugh, Evelyn. "The Case of Mr. H." *Cweal*, 53: 97-8 (1950); 99: 195-7 (1973).

Weeks, L.E. "Mark Twain and H: 'A Catastrophe' and 'A Natural History of the Dead.'" *MTJ*, 14: 15-17 (Su 68).

———. "Two Types of Tension: Art vs. Campcraft in H's 'Big Two-Hearted River.'" *SSF*, 11: 433 (Fa 74).

Weeks, R.P. "Cleaning Up H." *FHA*, 1972, pp. 311-3.

Wells, D.J. "H in French." *FHA*, 1974, pp. 235-8.

Wells, Elizabeth. "A Comparative Statistical Analysis of the Prose Styles of F. Scott Fitzgerald and EH." *FHA*, 1969, pp. 47-67.

Wescott, Glenway. "Memories and Opinions." *Prose*, 5: 177-202 (1972).

White, William. "Addendum to Hanneman: H's *The Old Man and the Sea*." *PBSA*, 62: 613-4 (4Q 68).

———. "Bill Borton/Grundy in *The Sun Also Rises*." *HN*, 2: 13-5 (Fa 72).

———. "Books About H Abroad." *ABC*, 18: 23 (Ap 68).

———. "H Hunting in Scandanavia." *ABC*, 16: 22-4 (Ja 66).

———. "H in the Red Cross." *Am Red Cross J*, 42: 28-9 (Mr 66).

———. "EH and Gene Tunney." *HN*, 3: 10 (#2 73).

———. "Frederic or Frederick Henry in *A Farewell to Arms*." *ABC*, 5, ns: 22 (O 69).

———. "The Crane-H Code: A Re-evaluation." *BSUF*, 10: 15-20 (Sp 69).

*———. "H: A Current Bibliography." *HN*, 4: 20-4 (Sp 74).

*———. "H Checklist." *FHA*, 1975, pp. 351-68.

———. "H on Postage Stamps." *HN*, 1: 3-4 (Fa 71).

———. "Notes on H, West, Tolkien and Wise." *ABC*, 18: 30-1 (Ja-F 68).

———. "Supplement to Hanneman: Articles, 1966-1970." *HN*, 1: 3-12 (Sp 71).

———. "Two More Hanneman Addenda." *HN*, 3: 14-5 (Sp 73).

———. "Violence, Blood, Death in the Writings of EH." *Tokyo Am Lit Soc*, 1: 22-30 (Mr 64).

Whitman, Alden. "H's Letters Reproach Critics." *NYTimes*, 9 Mr 72, p. 36.

Wickes, George. "H's Journalism." *Shen*, 19: 73-8 (Au 67).

Wilcox, Earl. "Jake and Bob and Huck and Tom: H's Use of *Huck Finn*." *FHA*, 1971, pp. 322-4.

Williams, Wirt. "H as Tragic Writer." *Statement Mag*, 24: 11-20 (Wi 68).

Wilson, Douglas. "EH, The Nick Adams Stories." *WHR*, 27: 295-9 (Su 73).

Wilson, Edmund. "Letter to the Russians about H." *NRep*, 85: 135-6 (11 D 35).

Winslow, Richard. "A Bibliographical Correction." *FHA*, 1975, p. 307.

———. "'A Good Country': H at the L Bar T Ranch, Wyoming." *FHA*, 1975, pp. 259-72.

Winston, Alexander. "If He Hadn't Been a Genius He Would Have Been a Cad." *Am Soc Legion of Honor Mag*, 43: 25-40 (1972).

Witherington, Paul. "To Be and Not to Be: Paradox and Pun in H's 'A Way You'll Never Be.'" *Style*, 7: 56-63 (Wi 73).

Wittkowski, Wolfgang. "Gekreuzigt im Ring. Zu Hs *The Old Man and the Sea*." *DVLG*, 41: 258-82 (My 67).

Wood, Carl. "*In Our Time*: H's Fragmentary Novel." *NM*, 74: 716-26 (1973).

Wood, Tom. "H Sports Special." *LGJ*, 3: special issue (#2 75).

Woodward, R.H. "Robert Jordan's Wedding/Funeral Sermon." *HN*, 2: 7-8 (Sp 72).

Woolf, Virginia. "An Essay in Criticism." *Herald Tribune Books*, 9 O 27; pp. 1, 8.

Wright, R.L. "H's Private Explanation of *The Torrents of Spring*." *MFS*, 13: 261-3 (Su 67).

Wycherley, H.A. "H's 'The Sea Change.'" *AN&Q*, 7: 67-8 (Ja 69).

Wylder, D.E. "H's Satiric Vision—The High School Years." *Rendezvous*, 5: 29-35 (1970).

———. "H's *The Torrents of Spring*." *SDR*, 5: 23-35 (Wi 67-68).

Wyrick, Jean. "Fantasy as Symbol: Another Look at H's Catherine." *MSE*, 4: 42-7

Yalom, I.D. and M. "EH: A Psychiatric View." *Archives Gen Psychiatry*, 24: 485-94 (1971).

Yannella, P.R. "Notes on the Manuscript, Date, and Sources of H's 'Banal Story.'" *FHA*, 1974, pp. 175-9.

Yardley, Jonathan. "How Papa Grew." *NRep*, 163: 25-6, 30 (10 O 70).

Yevish, I.A. "The Sun Also Exposes: H and Jake Barnes." *MwQ*, 10: 89-97 (1968).

Yokelson, J.B. "A Dante-Parallel in H's 'A Way You'll Never Be.'" *AL*, 41: 279-80 (My 69).

Yoshida, Hirshige. "Comments on *The Bear* and *The Old Man and the Sea*." *HirStud*, 18: 69-77 (1971).

Young, Philip. "'Big World Out There': The Nick Adams Stories." *Novel*, 6: 5-19 (Fa 72).

———. "H: A Defense." *Folio*, 20: 20-2 (Sp 55).

———. "H's Manuscripts: The Vault Reconsidered." *SAF*, 2: 3-11 (Sp 74).

———. "In the Vault with H." *NYT*, 29 S 68, pp. 2, 28.

———. "Locked in the Vault with H." *Rendezvous*, 5: 1-5 (1970).

———. "Scott Fitzgerald on His Thirtieth Birthday Sends a Small Gift to EH." *MFS*, 14: 229-30 (Su 68).

Yu, Beongcheon. "The Still Center of H's World." *Phoenix* (Korea), 12: 15-44 (1968).

Zayas-Bazán, Eduardo. "H: His Cuban Friends Remember." *FHA*, 1975, pp. 153-90.

Henderson, G.W. Kane, Patricia, and D.Y. Wilkinson. "Survival Strategies: Black Women in *Ollie Miss* and *Cotton Comes to Harlem*." *Critique*, 16: 101-9 (1974).

Henry, O. (See **Porter, William T.**).

Herbert, Frank. Ower, John. "Idea and Imagery in H's *Dune*." *Extrapolation*, 15: 129-39 (My 74).

Parkinson, R.C. "*Dune*—An Unfinished Tetralogy." *Extrapolation*, 13: 16-24 (D 71).

Herbert, Henry William. Gilkes, L.B. "Park Benjamin, HWH, and William Gilmore Simms: A Case of Mistaken Identity." *SCR*, 3: 66-77 (Je 71).

Meats, S.E. "Addenda to Van Winkle: HWH (Frank Forester)." *PBSA*, 67: 69-73 (1Q 73).

Hergesheimer, Joseph. Justus, J.H. "JH's Germany: A Radical Art of Surfaces." *JAmS*, 7: 47-66 (1973).

*Monteiro, George. "*McNaught's Monthly*: Addenda to the Bibliographies of . . ., H [and others]." *PBSA*, 68: 64-5 (1Q 74).

Herlihy, James Leo. Griffith, B.W. "Midnight Cowboys and Edwardian Narrators: JLK's Contrasting Voices." *NCLit*, 2: 6-8 (Ja 72).

Saylor, C.F. "Orpheus in New York: The Classical Descent of *Midnight Cowboy*." *CBul*, 46: 81-4 (Ap 70).

Herne, James A. Ahearn, M.L. "JA.H." *ALR*, 8: 274-5 (1975).

Enneking, J.J. "Mr. H as I Knew Him." *Arena*, 26: 294-6 (S 01).

Gillespie, P.P. "JA.H: A Reassessment." *Players*, 51: 66-71 (1975).

*Perry, John. "Selected Bibliography on JH." *BB*, 31: 50-3 (Ap-Je 74).

Robinson, A.M. "JA.H and His 'Theatre Libre' in Boston." *Players*, 48: 202-92 (1973).

Saraceni, G.A. "H and the Single Tax: An Early Plea for an Actor's Union." *ETJ*, 26: 315-25 (1974).

Tallman, R.S. "JA.H and Lamoine, Maine." *NEQ*, 46: 94-105 (Mr 73).

Herrick, Robert. Carlson, D.O. "RH: An Addendum." *ALR*, 3: 67-8 (1968).

Dessner, L.J. "RH, American Novelist." *MarkR*, 3: 10-4 (O 71).

Franklin, Phyllis. "A Handlist of RH Papers at the University of Chicago." *ALR*, 8: 109-54 (Sp 75).

*———. "H." *ALR*, 8: 276-9 (1975).

———. "The Influence of William James on RH's Early Fiction." *ALR*, 7: 395-402 (Au 74).

———. "RH as Novelist and Journalist." *ALR*, 3: 393-5 (Fa 70).

Kazin, Alfred. "Three Pioneer Realists." *SatR*, 20: 3-4, 14-5 (8 Jl 39).

McIlvaine, R.M. "RH and Thorstein Veblen." *RSW*, 40: 132-5 (1972).

Simms, L.M. "RH and the Race Question." *NDQ*, 39: 34-8 (1971).

Spangler, George. "RH's *Waste*: Summary of a Career and an Age." *CRAS*, 2: 26-36 (Sp 71).

Stessin, Lawrence. "The Businessman in Fiction." *LitR*, 12: 281-9 (Sp 69).

Hersey, John. Haltresht, Michael. "Dreams as a Characterization Device in H's *White Lotus*." *NCLit*, 1: 4-5 (My 71).

———. "Dreams, Visions, and Myth's in JH's *White Lotus*." *WGCR*, 6: 24-8 (1973). (1973).

———. "*The Wall*: JH's Interpretation of the Ghetto Experience." *NCLit*, 2: 10-11 (Ja 72).

Hudspeth, R.N. "A Definition of Modern Nihilism: H's *The War Lover*." *UR*, 35: 243-9 (Je 69).

Moses, Robert. "Informal Notes, Taken on Reading JH on Yale." *NatR*, 23: 142-4, 159 (9 F 71).

Reising, R.W. "The Setting of H's *Too Far to Walk*." *NCLit*, 1: 10-1 (S 71).

Heyward, DuBose. Connor, L.R. "Southern Plays on the Gotham Stage." *SLM*, 1: 407-11 (1939).

Duke, Vernon. "Gershwin, Schillinger, and Dukelsky." *MissQ*, 33: 102-15 (1947).

Durham, Frank. "DH: English-French Huguenot." *Trans Huguenot Soc SC*, 58: 5-12 (1953).

———. "The Opera That Didn't Get to the Metropolitan." *SAQ*, 53: 497-507 (1954).

———. "Porgy Comes Home—At Last!" *SCR*, 2: 5-13 (My 70).

Harrigan, Anthony. "DH: Memorialist and Realist." *GaR*, 5: 335-44 (1951).

Kerr, J.Y. "DH, and Appreciation." *Prospector*, 1: 17-8 (Mr 22).

Lucas, J. "But Porgy Is Getting Awfully Close." *CaM*, 14: 67-72 (Sp-Su 74).

Malavelle, Maryse. "*Porgy*: du roman à l'opéra." *Caliban*, 9: 135-50 (1972).

Marley, H.P. "The Negro in Recent Southern Literature." *SAQ*, 27: 29-41 (1928).

Rosenfield, John. "A New Porgy in Dallas." *SatR*, 35: 44 (28 Jl 52).

Shirley, Wayne D. "Porgy and Bess." *QJLC*, 31: 97-107 (1974).

Slavick, W.H. "Going to School to DH." *SLImag*, 7: 105-30 (Fa 74).

Sutton, Horace. "From Catfish Row to the Kremlin." *SatR*, 39: 37-8 (14 Ja 56).

Williams, George. "Peregrinations of a Goat Cart." *Sandlapper*, 6: 41-9 (O 73).

Higginson, Thomas Wentworth. Billington, R.A. "A Social Experiment: The Port Royal Journal of Charlotte F. Forten, 1862-1863," *JNH*, 35: 223-64 (1950).

Flanagan, J.T., ed. "A Letter from Maurice Thompson." *IMH*, 64: 13-4 (Mr 68).

Katz, Joseph. "The 'Preceptor' and Another Poet: TWH and Stephen Crane." *Serif*, 5: 17-21 (Mr 68).

Teller, Walter. "'Army Life in a Black Regiment.'" *NYT*, 11 My 69, pp. 2, 28, 30-1.

Hildreth, Richard. Brandstadter, Evan. "Uncle Tom and Archy Moore: The Antislavery Novel as Ideological Symbol." *AQ*, 26: 160-75 (My 74).

Canaday, Nicholas. "The Antislavery Novel Prior to 1852 and H's *The Slave* (1836)." *CLAJ*, 17: 175-91 (D 73).

Himes, Chester. Calder, A. "CH and the Art of Fiction." *JEARD*, 1: 3-18 (1Q 71); 1: 123-40 (2Q 71).

Kane, Patricia, and D.Y. Wilkinson. "Survival Strategies: Black Women in *Ollie Miss* and *Cotton Comes to Harlem*." *Critique*, 16: 101-9 (#1 74).

Margolies, Edward. "Experiences of the Black Expatriate Writer: CH." *CLAJ*, 15: 421-7 (Je 72).

————. "The Thrillers of CH." *SBL*, 1: 1-11 (1970).

Nelson, Raymond. "Domestic Harlem: The Detective Fiction of CH." *VQR*, 48: 260-76 (Sp 72).

Williams, J.A. "My Man H: An Interview with CH." *Amistad*, 1: 25-93 (1970).

Hill, Edwin B. Goldstone, Adrian. "The Search for EB.H." *ABC*, 18: 19 (O 67).

Muir, G.H. "EBH." *ABC*, 1: 20-1 (O 67).

*Myers, J.M. "A Check-List of Items Published by the Private Press of EB.H." *ABC*, 18: 22-7 (O 67).

Hoagland, Edward. Fontana, Ernest. "The Territory of the Past in H's *Notes from the Century Before*." *WAL*, 9: 45-51 (My 74).

Porter, T.E. "Divergencies: An Interview with EH." *Falcon*, 6: 3-16 (Sp 75).

Hoffman, Charles Fenno. Anon. "A Letter from CFH to Whittier." *N&Q*, 79: 96-8 (1975).

Hepler, J.C. "A Letter from CFH to Whittier." *BNYPL*, 79: 96-8 (Au 75).

Hoffman, Daniel. Dietrichson, J.W. "The Criticism of DH." *Edda*, 5: 319-37 (1974).

Kirby-Smith, H.T. "Miss Bishop and Others." *SR*, 80: 483-93 (1972).

Sylvester, William. "DH's Poetry of Affection." *Voyages*, 3: 110-9 (Wi 70).

Hollander, John. Gerber, P.L., and R.J. Gemmett. "The Poem as Silhouette." *MQR*, 9: 253-6 (Fa 70).

Rand, R.A. "Small Craft Warnings." *Parnassus*, 1: 163-70 (1972).

Holmes, George Frederick. Crowson, E.T "GFH and Auguste Comte." *MissQ*, 22: 59-70 (Wi 68-9).

Gillespie, N.C. "GFH and the Philosophy of History." *SAQ*, 67: 486-98 (Su 68).

Holmes, Oliver Wendell. Anon. "That Wonderful One-Hoss Shay." *AH*, 24: 108-9 (1973).

Cameron, K.W. "Two Harvard Letters of OWH." *ATQ*, 20: 135-9 (Fa 73).

————. "Ungathered Letters of OWH." *ATQ*, 20: 140 (Fa 73).

Dircks, P.T. "The Poet and the Astronomer: Neoclassic Aspects of H's Satiric Technique." *RSW*, 37: 333-7 (1969).

Gallagher, Kathleen. "The Art of Snake Handling: *Lamia, Elsie Venner*, and 'Rappaccini's Daughter.'" *SAF*, 3: 51-64 (Sp 75).

Garner, Stanton. "*Elsie Varner*: H's Deadly 'Book of Life.'" *HLQ*, 37: 283-98 (1974).

————. "Frederick and Elsie Venner." *FH*, 3: 5 (Ja 70).

McElrath, J.R. "Nora C. Franklin on H and Thoreau." *TJQ*, 5: 17-9 (Jl 73).

Mattson, J.S. "OWH and 'The Deacon's Masterpiece': A Logical Story?" *NEQ*, 41: 104-14 (Mr 68).

*Monteiro, George. "Addenda to the Bibliographies of . . . H [and others]." *PSBA*, 69: 272-5 (Ap-Je 75).

————. "H on Melville." *Extr*, 17: 10 (74).

O'Neal, D.L. "Addendum to Currier-Tilton and BAL." *PBSA*, 65: 296-7 (3Q 71).

Parker, G.T. "Sex, Sentiment, and OWH." *WS*, 1: 47-67 (1973).

Perkins, Jill. "OWH's Rhymed Problem." *ATQ*, 22: 105-8 (Sp 74).

Rogat, Yasal. "Mrs. Justice H: Some Modern Views." *UCLR*, 31: 213-56 (Wi 64).

Wainewright, J.B., and E. Bensley. "O.W.H's 'A Good Time Going.'" *N&Q*, 148: 263, 301 (11, 25 Ap 25).

Hooker, Thomas. Allen, Ward. "H and the Utopians." *ES*, 51: 37-9 (1970).

Bush, Sargent. "Four New Works by TH: Identity and Significance." *RALS*, 4: 3-26 (Sp 74).

————. "The Growth of TH's *The Poor Doubting Christian.*" *EAL*, 8: 3-20 (Sp 73).

————. "TH and the Westminster Assembly." *WMQ*, 29: 291-300 (Ap 72).

Davidson, Clifford. "TH's First Publication?" *AN&Q*, 6: 69-70 (Ja 68).

Emerson, Everett. "TH Materials at the Connecticut Historical Society." *EAL*, 6: 187-8 (Fa 71).

————. "A TH Sermon of 1638." *RALS*, 2: 75-89 (Sp 72).

Frederick, J.T. "Literary Art in TH's *The Poor Doubting Christian.*" *AL*, 40: 1-8 (Mr 68).

Habegger, Alfred. "Preparing the Soul for Christ: The Contrasting Sermon Forms of John Cotton and TH." *AL*, 41: 342-54 (N 69).

Herget, Winfried. "Preaching and Publication—Chronology and the Style of TH's Sermons." *HTR*, 65: 231-9 (1972).

Parker, D.L. "Petrus Ramus and the Puritans: The 'Logic' of Preparationist Conversion Doctrine." *EAL*, 8: 140-62 (Fa 73).

Pettit, Norman. "H's Doctrine of Assurance: A Critical Phase in New England Spiritual Thought." *NEQ*, 47: 518-34 (D 74).

Shuffelton, F.C. "Thomas Prince and His Edition of TH's '*Poor Doubting Christian.*'" *EAL*, 5: 68-75 (Wi 71).

Sprunger, K.L. "The Dutch Career of TH." *NEQ*, 46: 17-44 (Mr 73).

Wiliams, G.H. "Called by Thy Name, Leave Us Not: The Case of Mrs. Joan Drake, a Formative Episode in the Pastoral Career of TH in England." *HLB*, 16: 111-28, 278-300 (1968).

Hooper, Johnson Jones. Rachal, John. "Scotty Briggs and the Minister: An Idea from H's *Simon Suggs*?" *MTJ*, 17: 10-11 (Su 74).

Smith, Winston. "*Simon Suggs* and the Satiric Tradition." *Birmingham-Southern ColBul*, 63: 49-56 (1970).

West, H.C. "Simon Suggs and His Similes." *NCaF*, 16: 53-7 (My 68).

Hopkinson, Francis. Roth, Martin. "Laurence Sterne in America." *BNYPL*, 74: 428-36 (S 70).

Hopper, James M. Stein, A.F. "'9009'—Early Naturalistic Novel." *IllQ*, 36: 31-42 (F 74).

Horgan, Paul. Horgan, Paul. "From 'Notebook Pages.'" *Prose*, 7: 93-108 (1973).

————. "The Pleasures and Perils of Regionalism." *WAL*, 8: 161-71 (Wi 74).

Kraft, James. "About PH's *Things as They Are.*" *CRAS*, 2: 48-52 (Sp 71).

McConnell, R.M., and S.A. Frey. "PH: A Bibliography." *WAL*, 6: 137-50 (Su 71).

Powell, L.C. "Letter from the Southwest." *Westways*, 67: 22-6 (Ja 75).

————. "Speaking of Books: The H File." *NYTBR*, 14 My 67, pp. 2, 40.

Horovitz, Israel. Arteel, Roger. "Veertiende speeljaar in de Korrekelder." *Kunst en Cultuur* (Brussels), 3 Oct. 74, pp. 18-9.

Kerjan, Liliane. "Un jeune premier du théâtre américain: IH." *EA*, 28: 174-82 (Ap-Je 75).

Horton, George Moses. Brawley, Benjamin. "Three Negro Poets." *JNH*, 2: 384-92 (O 17).

Farrison, W.E. "GMH: Poet for Freedom." *CLAJ*, 14: 227-41 (Mr 71).

Walser, Richard. "Newly Discovered Acrostic by GMH." *CLAJ*, 21: 258-60 (D 75).

Hosmer, James K. Stark, Cruce. "The Man of Letters as a Man of War: JKH's *The Thinking Bayonet.*" *NEQ*, 48: 47-64 (Mr 75).

Hough, Emerson. Daher, Michael. "EH and Daniel Boone." *Soc for the Study of Midwestern Lit*,

Gray, R.H. "A Dedication to the Memory of EH, 1857-1923." *Arizona and the West*, 17: 1-4 (Sp 75).

Hitchinson, W.H. "The Mythic West of W.H.D. Koerner." *AmWest*, 4: 54-60 (My 67).

Johnson, C.M. "EH's American West." *BI*, 21: 26-42 (1974).

Wylder, Delbert. "EH and the Popular Novel." *SwAL*, 2: 83-89 (Fa 72).

Hovey, Richard. Moore, J.H. "The Vagabond and the Lady: Letters from RH to Amélie Rives." *MissQ*, 21: 131-43 (Sp 68).

Howard, Bronson. Felheim, Marvin. "BH, 'Literary Attaché.'" *ALR*, 2: 174-9 (Su 69).

Howard, Richard. Friedman, Sanford. "An Interview with RH." *Shen*, 24: 5-31 (Fa 72).

Harmon, William. "A Leaf from Wretched Richard's Almanac." *The Lamp in the Spine*, 3: 88 (Wi 72).

Howard, Richard. "Made Things: An Interview with RH." *Ohio R*, 16: 43-58 (Fa 74).

Martin, R.K. "The Unconsummated Word." *Parnassus*, 8: 228-9 (1968).

Reed, John R. "RH's *Untitled Subjects*." *MPS*, 4: 247-59 (Wi 73).

Watson, Richard. "Inside-Out Ceremonies: A Trope from 'Quantities' and 'The Damages' by RH." *MinnR*, 8: 225-7 (1968).

Woll, Thomas. "Stasis within Flux: RH's *Findings*." *MPS*, 4: 259-71 (Wi 73).

Howe, Edgar Watson. Albertini, Virgil. "EWH and *The Story of a Country Town*." *Northwest Missouri State Un Stud.*, 35: 19-29 (F 75).

Blair, Walter. "Roots of American Realism." *UR*, 6: 275-81 (Je 40).

Boyd, Ernest. "Sage of Potato Hill." *Nation*, 139: 247 (29 Ag 34).

Boynton, P.H. "Some Expounders of the Middle Border." *EJ*, 19: 431-40 (Je 30).

Brune, R.E. "Found: EH's Golden *Globe*." *WHR*, 6: 99 (Wi 51-2).

Carson, Gerald. "The Village Atheist/EWH, Purveyor of Plain Thoughts for Plain People." *Scribner's*, 84: 733-9 (D 28).

Cooper, K.S. "EWH—A Self-Educated Educator." *EdF*, nv: 233-7 (Ja 62).

Eichelberger, C.L. "EWH and Joseph Kirkland: More Critical Comment." *ALR*, 4: 279-90 (Su 71).

————, and F.L. Stallings. "EWH (1853-1937): A Critical Bibliography of Secondary Comment." *ALR*, 2: 1-49 (Sp 69).

Hall, G.C. "EWH and H.L. Mencken." *H-JM*, 2: 163-5 (Jl 25).

Harris, Frank. "American Values: H and Mencken." *Pearson's*, 40: 112ff. (Ja 19).

Hornbegger, Theodore. "*Country Town*." *CE*, 23: 411 (F 62).

Mason, Walt. "Interesting People." *Am Mag*, 71: 608-10 (Mr 11).

Mencken, H.L. "American Worthies." *AmMerc*, 17: 255 (Je 29).

Pickett, C.M. "EMH: Legend and Truth." *ALR*, 2: 70-3 (Sp 69).

————. "EWH and the Kansas Scene." *KanQ*, 2: 39-45 (Sp 70).

Powers, R.G. "Tradition in E.WH's *The Story of a Country Town*." *MASJ*, 9: 51-62 (Fa 68).

Reely, M.K. "American Authors as Printers: EWH." *Democourier*, 9: 3-7 (Ap 39).

Sackett, S.J. "EWH as Proverb Maker." *JAF*, 85: 73-7 (Ja-Mr 72).

Schramm, W.L. "EH versus Time." *SatR*, 17: 10-1 (5 F 38).

Sherman, C.B. "The Development of American Rural Fiction." *Agricultural Hist*, 12: 67-76 (Ja 38).

Wood, D.J. "Recollections of EWH." *NHM*, 18: 144 (Ap-Je 37).

Howe, Irving. Kostelanetz, Richard. "On IH: The Perils and Paucities of Democratic Radicalism." *Salmagundi*, 2: 44-60 (Sp 67).

Howe, Julia Ward. Birchfield, J.D. "JWH: An Unpublished Letter." *AN&Q*, 14: 8-9 (S 75).

Howells, William Dean. Anon. "America's Foremost Living Man of Letters." *Cur Lit*, 52: 461-3 (Ap 12).

———. "Collapse of the H Realism in the Light of Freudian Romanticism." *Cur Opinion*, 63: 270-1 (O 17).

———. "The Lounger." *Putnam's*, 6: 753-67 (S 09).

———. "Mr. H and His Critics." *Bkm*, 21: 566-7 (Ag 05).

———. "Mr. H and *The Kentons*." *Harper's W*, 46: 947 (Jl 02).

Alden, H.M. "WDH/Recollections of a Fellow-Worker." *BNM*, 26: 729-31 (Je 08).

Andersen, Kenneth. "Mark Twain, W.D.H., and Henry James: Three Agnostics in Search of Salvation." *MTJ*, 15: 13-6 (Wi 70).

Arms, George. "'Ever Devotedly Yours,' The Whitelock-H Correspondence." *JRUL*, 10: 1-19 (D 46).

———. "The WDH Correspondence." *CEAAN*, 3: 26 (1970).

Arthur, Richard. "The Poetry of WDH." *Booklovers Mag*, 2: 569-71 (D 03).

Atkinson, F.G. "'A Gentle Foe': A New W.D.H Letter." *N&Q*, 20: 260-1 (Jl 73).

Baldwin, Marilyn. "The Transcendental Phase of WDH." *ESQ*, 57: 57-61 (4Q 69).

Beebe, Maurice. "Criticism of WDH: A Selected Checklist." *MFS*, 16: 395-419 (1970).

Behrens, Ralph. "H' Portrait of a Boston Brahmin." *MarkR*, 3: 71-4 (O 72).

Bennett, Scott. "David Douglas and the British Publication of W.D.H's Works." *SB*, 25: 107-24 (1972).

Berces, F.A. "Mimesis, Morality and *The Rise of Silas Lapham*." *AQ*, 22: 190-202 (Su 70).

Boardman, Arthur. "Howellsian Sex." *StN*, 2: 52-60 (Sp 70).

Budd, L.J. "*Annie Kilburn*." *ALR*, 4: 84-7 (Fa 68).

———. "The Hungry Bear of American Realism." *ALR*, 5: 485-7 (1972).

———. "W.D.H' Defense of the Romance." *PMLA*, 67: 32-42 (1952).

Burrows, R.N. "H's *A Hazard of New Fortunes as Political Commentary*." *WSL*, 4: 89-95 (1967).

Campbell, C.L. "Realism and the Romance of Real Life: Multiple Fictional Worlds in H's Novels." *MFS*, 16: 289-302 (Au 70).

Cary, Richard. "WDH to Thomas Sergeant Perry." *CLQ*, 8: 157-215 (D 68).

Chamberlayne, E.S. "Mr. H's Philosophy and *The Son of Royal Langbrith*." *Poet Lore*, 16: 144-51 (Ag 05).

Cohn, Jan. "The House of Fiction: Domestic Architecture in H and Edith Wharton." *TSLL*, 15: 537-49 (Fa 73).

Cook, D.L. "Practical Editions: The Writings of WDH." *Proof*, 2: 293-300 (1972).

Crow, C.L. "H and Henry James: 'A Case of Metaphantasmia' Solved." *AQ*, 27: 169-77 (My 75).

Crowley, J.W. "The Length of H's *Shadow of a Dream*." *NCF*, 27: 182-96 (1972).

———. "H's Obscure Hurt." *JAmSt*, 9: 199-211 (1975).

———. "H's Questionable Shapes: From Psychologism to Psychic Romance." *ESQ*, 21: 169-78 (3Q 75).

———. "The Oedipal Theme in H's *Fennel and Rue*." *StN*, 5: 104-9 (Sp 73).

———. "The Sacerdotal Cult and the Sealskin Coat: W.D.H in *My Mark Twain*." *ELN*, 11: 287-92 (1974).

Cumpiano, M.W. "The Dark Side of *Their Wedding Journey*." *AL*, 40: 472-86 (Ja 69).

———. "H's Bridge: A Study of the Artistry of *Indian Summer*." *MFS*, 16: 363-82 (Au 70).

de Wagstaffe, W. "The Personality of Mr. H." *BNM*, 26: 739-41 (Je 08).

"Diplomaticus." "A Portrayer of the Commonplace." *Westminster R*, 178: 597-608 (D 12).

Dowling, J.A. "H and the English: A Democrat Looks at English Civilization." *BNYPL*, 76: 251-64 (1972).

Duchet, M. "Cinq lettres inédites de Juan Valera a W.D.H." *RLC*, 42: 76-102 (1968).

Ensor, Allison. "Mark Twain's 'The War Prayer': Its Ties to H and Hymnology." *MFS*, 16: 535-9 (Wi 70-71).

Eschholz, P.A. "H's *A Modern Instance*: A Realist's Moralistic Vision of America." *SDR*, 10: 91-102 (1972).

———. "The Landlord at Lion's Head: WDH' Use of the Vermont Scene." *Vermont Hist*, 42: 44-7 (1974).

———. "The Moral World of Silas Lapham: H's Romantic Vision of America in the 1880's." *RSW*, 40: 115-21 (1972).

———. "WDH's Recurrent Character Types: The Realism of *A Hazard of New Fortunes*." *Eng Rec*, 23: 40-7 (Sp 73).

Fackler, H.V. "Sticking to the Roots: The Deracination Motif in *The Rise of Silas Lapham*." *MarkR*, 3: 73-4 (O 72).

Fischer, W.C. "WDH: Reverie and the Nonsymbolic Aesthetic." *NCF*, 25: 1-30 (Je 70).

Fortenberry, George. "The Unnamed Critic in WDH's *Heroines of Fiction*." *MTJ*, 16: 7-8 (Wi 71-72).

Francis, S.M. "The Atlantic's Pleasant Days in Tremont Street." *Atl*, 100: 716-20 (N 07).

Franklin, V.P. "Lowell's Appreciation of H." *Methodist R*, 84: 112-5 (Ja 02).

Frazier, D.L. "H's *An Open-Eyed Conspiracy*." *Expl*, 30: 9 (1971).

———. "'Their Wedding Journey': H's Fictional Craft." *NEQ*, 42: 323-49 (S 69).

Frederickson, R.S. "Hjalmar Hjorth Boyesen: H 'Out-Realisted.'" *MarkR*, 3: 93-7 (F 73).

Gardner, J.H. "H: The 'Realist' as Dickensian." *MFS*, 16: 323-43 (Au 70).

Garnett, Edward. "Some Remarks on American and English Fiction." *Atl*, 114: 747-56 (D 14).

Gibson, W.M. "W.D.H and 'The Ridiculous Human Heart.'" *SAH*, 2: 32-45 (Ap 75).

Girgus, S.B. "Bartley Hubbard: The Rebel in H' *A Modern Instance*." *RSW*, 39: 315-21 (1971).

———. "H and Marcuse: A Forecast of the One-Dimensional Age." *AQ*, 25: 108-18 (Mr 73).

Goldfarb, C.R. "The Question of WDH's Racism." *BSUF*, 12: 22-30 (Su 71).

———. "WDH: An American Reaction to Tolstoy." *CLS*, 8: 317-37 (D 71).

———. "WDH' *The Minister's Charge*: A Study of Psychological Perception." *MarkR*, 2: 1-4 (S 69).

Gottesman, Ronald, and D.J. Nordloh. "The Quest for Perfection: or, Surprises in the Consummation of *Their Wedding Journey*." *CEAAN*, 1: 12-3 (1968).

Graham, D.B. "A Note on H, Williams, and the Matter of Sam Patch." *NCLit*, 4: 10-3 (Mr 74).

Graham, John. "Struggling Upward: 'The Minister's Charge' and 'A Cool Million.'" *CRAS*, 4: 184-96 (Fa 74).

Greenslet, Ferris. "A Group of Aldrich Letters." *Century*, 76: 495-505 (Ag 08).

Halfmann, Ulrich. "Addenda to Gibson and Arms: Twenty-three New H Items." *PBSA*, 66: 174-7 (2Q 72).

———. "Interviews with WDH." *ALR*, 6: 277-416 (Fa 73).

*———, and D.R. Smith. "WDH: A Revised and Annotated Bibliography of Secondary Comment in Periodicals and Newspapers, 1868-1919." *ALR*, 5: 91-121 (Sp 72).

Hilton, Earl. "H's *The Shadow of a Dream* and Shakespeare." *AL*, 46: 220-2 (My 74).

Howells, W.D., and T.S. Perry. "Recent Russian Fiction: A Conversation." *NAR*, 196: 85-103 (Jl 12).

Ibarra, Fernando. "Juan Valera y WD.H." *Archivum*, 22: 123-48 (1972).

Iliano, Antonio. "WDH's critico di Alfieri." *Studi Piemontesi*, 2: 50-2 (1973).

Inge, M.T. "WDH on Southern Literature." *MissQ*, 21: 291-304 (Fa 68).

James, Henry. "A Letter to Mr. H." *NAR*, 195: 558-62 (Ap 12).

Johns, B.S. "WDH and Bjornstjerne Bjornson." *AmNor*, 2: 94-117 (1968).

Kazin, Alfred. "H the Bostonian." *Clio*, 3: 219-34 (F 74).

Kirk, Rudolf, and Clara Kirk. "Kirk-H Collection." *LCUP*, 25: 67-71 (Wi-Sp 69).

———. "WDH, George William Curtis, and the 'Haymarket Affair.'" *AL*, 40: 487-98 (Ja 69).

Klinkowitz, Jerome. "Ethic and Aesthetic: The Basil and Isabel March Stories of WDH." *MFS*, 16: 303-22 (Au 70).

Kraus, W.K. "The Convenience of Fatalism: Thematic Unity in WDH's *A Hazard of New Fortunes*." *Eng Rec*, 18: 33-6 (O 67).

Labrie, R.E. "The H-Norris Relationship and the Growth of Naturalism." *Disc*, 11: 363-71 (Su 68).

Leary, Lewis. "On Writing about Writers: Mark Twain and H." *SoR*, 4: 551-7 (Sp 68).

Lindberg-Seyerstead, Brita. "Three Variations of the American Success Story." *ES*, 53: 125-41 (Ap 72).

Lynn, K.S. "H in the Nineties." *PAH*, 4: 27-82 (1970).

Mabie, H.W. "The Story of Mr. H's Career." *BNM*, 26: 733-4 (Je 08).

Mao, Nathan. "H's Attack on the Romantic and Sentimental." *Shippenburgh State Col R*, 1973, pp. 102-7.

Marler, R.F. "'A Dream': H's Early Contribution to the American Short Story." *JNT*, 4: 75-85 (1974).

Marovitz, S.E. "H and the Ghetto: 'The Mystery of Misery.'" *MFS*, 16: 345-62 (Au 70).

Massey, M.H. "Some Problem of Visual Description: H's New York." *ELUD*, 1: 46-65 (Je 73).

Mather, F.J. "Literature." *Forum*, 34: 223-4 (O 02).

Mathews, J.W. "Another Possible Origin of H's *The Shadow of a Dream*." *AL*, 42: 558-62 (Ja 71).

———. "Toward Naturalism: Three Late Novels of WD.H." *Genre*, 6: 363-75 (1973).

Maxwell, Perriton. "H *the* Editor." *BNM*, 26: 735-8 (Je 08).

Monteiro, George. "Additions to Gibson and Arms and to Brenni: More H." *PBSA*, 69: 115-7 (1Q 75).

———. "BAL: A Correction." *PBSA*, 69: 117-8 (1Q 75).

Nash, Charles. "H's Darker Vision: A Reading of *The Landlord at Lion's Head*." *ELUD*, 2: 36-48 (1973).

Nordloh, D.J. "Eating Off the Same Plates: First Editions of W.D.H in Great Britain." *Serif*, 7: 28-30 (1970).

———. "H's Lecture on Tour: Text in Passage." *CEANN*, 8: 31-2 (1975).

———. "A Mistaken W.D.H Ascription." *Serif*, 11: 38-9 (1974).

———. "Plates and Publishing-Housekeeping: Some Aspects of H's *Venetian Life*." *Serif*, 8: 29-31 (1971).

———. "W.D.H's *A Modern Instance*: Complications of Bibliographical History." *Serif*, 10: 52-4 (Fa 73).

Parker, Hershel. "The First Nine Volumes of *A Selected Edition of W.D.H*." *Proof*, 2: 319-32 (1972).

Payne, A.J. "Harold Frederic and H: The Saloon as Setting." *FH*, 2: 4 (Ap 68).

———. "H's American Families—An Economic Mosaic." *HussR*, 3: 20-34 (1969).

Perkins, George. "*A Modern Instance*: H's Transition to Artistic Maturity." *NEQ*, 47: 427-39 (S 74).

Pizer, Donald. "Harold J. Kolb, Jr.'s Study of American Realism as a Literary Form." *Genre*, 3: 376-8 (1970).

Potter, Hugh. "H and the Shakers." *Shaker Q*, 9: 3-13 (1969).

Price, Robert. "The Road to Boston: 1860 Travel Correspondence of WDH." *OH*, 80: 85-154 (1971).

———. "Young H Drafts a 'Life' for Lincoln." *OH*, 76: 232-46 (1967).

Reid, Forrest. "WDH, I and II." *Irish Statesman*, 1: 333-4, 359-60 (4 O 19).

"Ricus." "A Supressed Novel of Mr. H." *Bkm*, 32: 201-3 (O 10).

Rowlette, Robert. "Addenda to Halfmann: Six New H Interviews." *ALR*, 8: 101-6 (S 75).

———. "'H as his Head Makes Him': A Phrenologist's Report." *AN&Q*, 11: 115-6 (Ap 73).

———. "In 'The Silken Arms of the Aristocracy': WDH's Lecture in Minneapolis, 1899." *IMH*, 69: 299-319 (D 73).

———. "Tarkington in Defense of H and Realism: A Recovered Letter." *BSUF*, 14: 64-5 (Su 73).

Sanborn, F.B. "A Letter to the Chairman." *NAR*, 195: 562-66 (Ap 12).

Sargent, M.S. "The Babbitt-Lapham Connection." *SLN*, 2: 8-9 (Sp 70).

Schwartz, H.B. "The Americanism of WDH." *Methodist R*, 101: 226-32 (Mr 18).

See, F.G. "The Demystification of Style: Metaphoric and Metonymic Language in *A Modern Instance*." *NCF*, 28: 379-403 (1974).

Seelye, John. "The Rise of WDH." *NRep*, 165: 23-6 (3 Jl 71).

Shriber, Michael. "Cognitive Apparatus in *Daisy Miller, The Ambassadors*, and Two Works by H: A Comparative Study of the Epistemology of Henry James." *Lang&S*, 2: 207-25 (1969).

Solomon, Eric. "H, Houses and Realism." *ALR*, 4: 89-93 (1968).

Spangler, G.M. "Moral Anxiety in *A Modern Instance*." *NEQ*, 46: 236-49 (Je 73).

———. "*The Shadow of a Dream*: H's Homosexual Tragedy." *AQ*, 23: 110-19 (Sp 71).

Standley, F.L. "Letter of Friendship: H to Piatt." *AN&Q*, 12: 18-9 (O 73).

Stern, M.B. "'H's Head': A Reply." *AN&Q*, 12: 116-7 (Ap 74).

Stessin, Lawrence. "The Businessmen in Fiction." *LitR*, 12: 281-9 (Sp 69).

Stout, Cushing. "Personality and Cultural History in the Novel: Two American Examples." *NLH*, 1: 423-37 (Sp 70).

Stronks, James. "*A Modern Instance*." *ALR*, 4: 87-9 (1968).

Sweeney, G.M. "The *Medea* H Saw." *AL*, 42: 83-9 (Mr 70).

Tanselle, G.T. "The Boston Seasons of Silas Lapham." *StN*, 1: 60-6 (Sp 69).

Thomas, E.M. "Mr. H's Way of Saying Things." *Putnam's*, 4: 443-7 (Jl 08).

Toth, S.A. "Character and Focus in *The Landlord at Lion's Head*." *CLQ*, 11: 116-28 (1975).

Towers, T.H. "'The Only Life We've Got': Myth and Morality in *The Kentons*." *MFS*, 16: 383-94 (Au 70).

———. "Savagery and Civilization: The Moral Dimensions of H's *A Boy's Town*." *AL*, 40: 499-509 (Ja 69).

Trimmer, J.F. "American Dreams: A Comparative Study of the Utopian Novels of Bellamy and H." *BSUF*, 12: 12-21 (Su 71).

Tuttleton, J.W. "H and the Manners of the Good Heart." *MFS*, 16: 271-87 (Au 70).

Vanderbilt, Kermit. "The Conscious Realism of H's *April Hopes*." *ALR*, 3: 53-66 (Wi 70).

———. "H Studies: Past, or Passing, or to Come." *ALR*, 7: 143-54 (Sp 74).

Van Westrum, A.S. "Mr. H and American Aristocracies." *Bkm*, 25: 67-73 (Mr 07).

———. "Mr. H on Love and Literature." *The Lamp*, 28: 27-31 (F 04).

Vorse, M.H. "Certain Overlooked Phases of American Life." *Critic*, 43: 83-4 (Jl 03).

Wagenknecht, Edward. "Longfellow and H." *ESQ*, 58: 52-7 (1Q 70).

Walts, R.W. "A Not-So-Tame H." *SCB*, 26: 58-66 (1967).

———. "WDH and His 'Library Edition.'" *PBSA*, 52: 283-94 (4Q 58).

Watanabe, Toshio. "W.D.H to *O.E.D.*" *EigoS*, 114: 241-3 (1968).

Wells, G.K. "The Phoenix Symbol in 'The Rise of Silas Lapham." *SAB*, 40: 10-4 (My 75).

White, D.F. "A Summons for the Kingdom of God on Earth: The Early Social Gospel Novel." *SAQ*, 67: 469-86 (Su 68).

Wilson, C.D., and D.B. Fitzgerald. "A Day in H's 'Boy's Town.'" *New England Mag*, 36: 289-97 (My 07).

Wilson, Edmund. "The Fruits of the MLA: I. *Their Wedding Journey.*" *NYRB*, 11: 7-10 (26 S 68).

Wilson, J.H. "H's Use of George Eliot's *Romola* in *April Hopes.*" *PMLA*, 84: 1620-7 (O 69).

Woodress, James. "An Interview with H." *ALR*, 3: 71-5 (Wi 70).

*———, and S.P. Anderson. "A Bibliography of Writing about WDH." *ALR*, special no: 1-139 (1969).

Woodward, R.H. "Punch on H and James." *ALR*, 3: 76-7 (Wi 70).

Wyatt, Edith. "A National Contribution." *NAR*, 196: 339-52 (S 12).

Hubbard, Elbert. Beisner, R.L. "'Commune' in East Aurora." *AH*, 22: 72-7, 106-9 (F 71).

Hughes, Langston. Anon. "LH and the Example of Simple." *BlackW*, 19: 35-8 (1970).

———. "LH Manuscripts." *Bancroftiana*, 56: 6-7 (1973).

Brown, L.W. "The Portrait of the Artist as a Black American in the Poetry of LH." *SBL*, 5: 24-7 (Wi 74).

Carey, J.C. "Jesse B. Semple Revisited and Revised." *Phylon*, 32: 158-63 (1971).

Cartey, Wilfred. "Four Shadows of Harlem." *NegroD*, 18: 22-5, 83-92 (1969).

Cobb, M.K. "Concepts of Blackness in the Poetry of Nicolas Guillen, Jacques Romain, and LH." *CLAJ*, 18: 262-72 (D 74).

Combecker, Hans. "Interpretationen für den Englischunterricht: LH, F.R. Scott, T.S. Eliot." *NS*, 17: 506-14 (O 68).

Dandridge, R.B. "The Black Woman as Freedom Fighter in LH' *Simple's Uncle Sam.*" *CLAJ*, 18: 273-83 (D 74).

Davis, A.P. "LH: Cool Poet." *CLAJ*, 11: 280-96 (1968).

Dixon, Melvin. "On LH." *SBL*, 5: 4 (Su 74).

Emanuel, J.A. "The Literary Experiments of LH." *CLAJ*, 11: 335-44 (1968).

Farrison, W.E. "LH: Poet of the Negro Renaissance." *CLAJ*, 15: 401-10 (Je 72).

Finger, Hans. "Zwei Beispiele moderner amerikanischer Negerlyrik: LH, 'Mother to Son' and Russell Atkins, 'Poem.'" *LWU*, 2: 38-46 (1969).

Fontaine, W.T. "The Negro Continuum from Dominant Wish to Collective Act." *AForum*, 3-4: 63-96 (1968).

Garber, E.D. "Form as a Complement to Content in Three of LH's Poems." *NALF*, 5: 137-9 (1971).

Hudson, T.R. "LH's Last Volume of Verse." *CLAJ*, 11: 345-8 (Je 68).

———. "Technical Aspects of the Poetry of LH." *BlackW*, 22: 24-45 (1973).

Hughes, Davis. "Ten Ways to Use Poetry in Teaching." *CLAJ*, 11: 273-9 (Je 68).

Hughes, Langston. "Ballad of Negro History." *NHB*, 30: 17 (O 67).

———. "The Negro Artist and the Racial Mountain." *Nation*, 122: 692-4 (23 Je 26); *Amistad*, 1: 301-5 (1970).

————. "The Twenties: Harlem and Its Negritude." *AForum*, 1: 18 (Sp 66).

Issacs, Harold. "Five Writers and Their Ancestors." *Phylon*, 21: 243-65 (1960).

Jackson, Blyden. "Claude McKay and LH: The Harlem Renaissance and More." *Pembroke Mag*, 6: 43-8 (1975).

————. "A Word about Simple." *CLAJ*, 11: 310-8 (Je 68).

Joans, Ted. "A Memoir: The LH I Knew." *BlackW*, 21: 14-8 (1972).

Jones, H.L. "Black Humor and the American Way of Life." *SNL*, 7: 1-4 (Fa 69).

————. "A Danish Tribute to LH." *CLAJ*, 11: 331-4 (Je 68).

Kearns, F.E. "The Un-angry LH." *YR*, 50: 154-60 (1970).

Kesteloot, Lilyan. "Negritude and Its American Sources." *BUJ*, 22: 54-67 (2Q 74).

King, Woodie. "Remembering Langston: A Poet of the Black Theater." *NegroD*, 18: 27-32, 95-6 (1969).

Kinnamon, Kenneth. "Man Who Created Simple." *Nation*, 205: 559-601 (4 D 67).

Klotman, P.R. "Jesse B. Semple and the Narrative Art of LH." *JNT*, 3: 66-75 (Ja 73).

————. "LH's Jess B. Semple and the Blues." *Phylon*, 36: 68-77 (Mr 75).

Kramer, Aaron. "Robert Burns and LH." *Freedomways*, 8: 159-66 (1968).

Kukola, P.R. "Uz poeziju Jamesa L.H." *Forum Z*, 29: 219-22 (1975).

Matheus, J.F. "LH as Translator." *CLAJ*, 11: 319-30 (Je 68).

Miller, J.B. "The Major Theme in LH's *Not Without Laughter*." *CEA*, 32: 8-10 (Mr 70).

Miller, R.B. "'No Crystal Stair': Unity, Archetype and Symbol in LH's Poems on Women." *NALF*, 9: 109-14 (Wi 75).

Mintz, L.E. "LH's Jesse B. Semple: The Urban Negro as Wise Fool." *SNL*, 7: 11-21 (Fa 69).

Nower, Joyce. "Foolin' Master." *SNL*, 7: 5-10 (Fa 69).

*O'Daniel, T.B. "LH: A Selected Classified Bibliography." *CLAJ*, 11: 349-66 (Je 68).

Orlenin, D. "Langston X' juz-poèt černoj Ameriki. 'Xèppening'—prodolženie 'total' nogo teatra?" *Grani*, 68: 190-202 (1969).

Presley, James. "The Birth of Jesse B. Semple." *SWR*, 58: 219-25 (Su 73).

————. "LH: A Personal Farewell." *SWR*, 54: 79-84 (Wi 69).

Schatt, Stanley. "LH: The Ministrel As Artificer." *JML*, 4: 115-20 (S 74).

Scharnhorst, G.F. "H's 'Theme for English B.'" *Expl*, 32: 27 (D 73).

Smith, Raymond. "LH: Evolution of the Poetic Persona." *SLitI*, 7: 49-64 (Fa 74).

Turner, D.T. "Afro-American Authors: A Full House." *CEA*, 34: 15-9 (Ja 72).

————. "LH as Playwright." *CLAJ*, 11: 297-309 (Je 68).

Waldron, E.E. "The Blues Poetry of LH." *NALF*, 5: 140-9 (1971).

Watkins, C.A. "Simple: The Alter Ego of LH." *BSch*, 2: 18-26 (Je 71).

Wertz, I.J. "LH: A Profile." *NHB*, 24: 146-7 (Mr 64).

Wintz, C.D. "LH: A Kansas Poet in the Harlem Renaissance." *KanQ*, 7: 58-71 (#3 75).

Yestadt, Marie. "Two American Poets: Their Influence on the Contemporary Art-Song." *XUS*, 10: 33-43 (Fa 71).

Hughes, Rupert. Hughes, R.H., and Patrick Mahony. "RJ (1872-1956): Reflections on his Centennial." *Coranto*, 8: 25-33 (1972).

Hugo, Richard. Garber, Frederick. "Fat Man at the Margin: The Poetry of RH." *IowaR*, 3: 58-76 (4Q 73).

————. "Large Man in the Mountains: The Recent Work of RH." *WAL*, 10: 205-18 (N 75).

Humphreys, David. Mason, Julian. "DH's Lost Ode to George Washington, 1776." *QJLC*, 28: 28-37 (1971).

Huneker, James Gibbons. Flagens, Peter. "The Critics: Hartmann, H, and De Casseres." *Art in America*, 61: 67-70 (Jl-Ag 73).

Frank, M.H. "In Praise of H." *UWR*, 9: 100-12 (1Q 73).

Schwab, Arnold. "JGH's 'an Early Estimate of Sadakichi Hartman.'" *Sadakichi Hartmann N*, 1:4-5 (Wi 70).

Walt, James. "Conrad and JH." *Conradiana*, 6: 75-8 (1974).

✻**Hurston, Zora Neale.** Giles, J.R. "The Significance of Time in ZNH's *Their Eyes Were Watching God*." *NALF*, 6: 52-3, 60 (1972).

Helmick, E.T. "ZNH." *Carrell*, 2: 1-19 (Je-D 70).

Jordan, June. "On Richard Wright and ZNH: Notes Toward a Balancing of Love and Hatred." *BlackW*, 23: 4-8 (1974).

Kilson, Marion. "The Transformation of Eatonville's Ethnographer." *Pyhlon*, 33: 112-9 (Su 72).

Rayson, A.L. "*Dust Tracks on a Road*: ZNH and the Form of Black Autobiography." *NALF*, 7: 39-45 (SU 73).

———. "The Novels of ZNH." *SBL*, 5: 1-10 (Wi 74).

Sato, Hiroko. "ZNH Shiron." *Oberon*, 34:30-7 (1971).

Southerland, Ellease. "ZNH: The Novelist—Anthropologist's Life/Works." *BlackW*, 23: 20-30 (1974).

Walker, Alice. "In Search of ZNH." *Ms*, 3: 74-90 (Mr 75).

Walker, S.J. "ZNH's *Their Eyes Were Watching God*: Black Novel of Sexism." *MFS*, 20: 519-27 (Wi 74-75).

Washington, M.H. "The Black Woman's Search for Identity: ZNH's Work." *BlackW*, 21: 68-75 (1972).

Hutchinson, Thomas. Mayo, C.B. "Additions to H's History of Massachusetts Bay." *PAAS*, 59: 11-74. (1949).

Hyman, Mac. Hunter, G.R. "No Time for Turkeys." *GaR*, 20: 425-30 (Wi 66).

Ignatow, David. Bly, Robert. "Some Thoughts on 'Rescue the Dead.'" *TPJ*, 3:17-21 (1970).

Chisholm, Scott. "An Interview with DI." *TPJ*, 3:22-40 (1970).

Contoski, Victor. "Time and Money: The Poetry of DI." *UR*, 34: 211-3 (Mr 68).

"Crunk." "The Works DI." *Sixties*, 10:10-23 (1968).

Ignatow, David. "On Writing." *TPJ*, 3: 14-6 (1970).

Mazzaro, Jerome. "Circumscriptions: The Poetry of DI." *Salmagundi*, 22-23: 164-5 (1973).

Mills, R.J. "Earth Hard: The Poetry of DI." *Boun2*, 2: 373-430 (Sp74).

Spanos, William. "DI: A Dialogue." *Boun2*, 2: 442-82 (Sp 74).

Swados, Harvey. "DI: The Meshuganeh Lover." *APR*, 2: 35-6 (#3 73).

Verble, David. "Some Notes on Articles About I." *TPJ*, 3: 46-7 (1970).

Wagner, L.W. "On DI." *TPJ*, 3: 41-5 (1970).

Williams, Galen. "DI Talks to Galen Williams." *APR*, 3: 43-7 (#4 74).

Inge, William. Hamlet, E.J. "The North American Outlook of Marcel Dubé and WI." *QQ*, 77: 374-87 (Au 70).

Jaine, Jasbir. "WI: Confrontation with Reality." *IJAS*, 4: 72-7 (Je-D 74).

Miller, J.Y. "WI: Last of the Realists?" *KanQ*, 2: 17-26 (1970).

* **Ingraham, Joseph Holt.** Blanck, Jacob. "Two Revisions in the Bibliography of JHI." *YULG*, 42:158-61 (Ja 68).

Weathersby, R.W. "J.H.I and Tennessee: A Record of Social and Literary Contributions." *THQ*, 34: 264-72 (Fa 75).

Irving, Henry. Hughes, Alan. "HI's Tragedy of Shylock." *ETJ*, 24: 249-69 (0 72).

Schaffer, Byron. "HI's Theories of Drama." *OSUTCB*, 15: 20-31 (1968).

Irving, Washington. Aderman, R.M. "The Editors' Intentions in the WI Letters." *CEAAN*, 3: 23-4 (1970).

———. "A 'Most Negligent Man': WI's Opinion of John Murray." *CEANN*, 2: 1-3 (1969).

———. "*Salmagundi* and the Outlander Tradition." *WSL*, 1: 62-8 (1964).

Albert, Burton. "Alexander Robertson: I's Drawing Teacher." *AN&Q*, 9: 148-50 (1971).

✓Anderson, Hilton. "A Southern 'Sleepy Hollow.'" *MissFR*, 3: 85-8 (1969).

Baiocco, C.N. "WI's Hispanic Literature." *Américas*, 24: 2-11 (AP 72).

Black M.L. "Bibliographical Problems in WI's Early Works." *EAL*, 3: 148-56 (Wi 68-9).

———. "*A History of New York*: Significant Revision in 1848." *ATQ*, 5: 40-7 (IQ 70).

Bowden, M.W. "Knickerbocker's *History* and the 'Enlightened' Men of New York." *AL*, 47: 159-72 (My 75).

Cameron, K.W. "Letters of Cooper, I and Others Endorsing the Lyceum in Paris, France." *ESQ*, 52: 76-82 (3Q 68).

———. "Melville, Cooper, I and Bryant on International Matters."*ESQ*, 51: 108-21 (2Q 68).

———. "Melville, Cooper, I and John Essais Warren: Travel Literature and Patronage." *ESQ*, 47: 114-25 (2Q 67).

Carmer, Carl. "I and the Misty Valley." *SatR*, 54: 41, 73-4 (13 Mr 71).

Clark, J.W. "WI and New England Witchlore." *NYFQ*, 29: 304-13 (D 73).

Conley, P.T. "The Real Ichabod Crane." *AL*, 40: 70-1 (Mr 68).

Cracroft, R.H. "Multiple Viewpoints: A Note on WI and His Companions on the Tour of the Prairies." *PosS*, 5: 10-3 (O 74).

Couser, G.T. "The Ruined Garden of Wolfert Weber." *SSF*, 12: 23-8 (Wi 75).

Current-Garcoa, Eugene. "I Sets the Pattern: Notes on Professionalism and the Art of the Short Story." *SSF*, 10: 327-41 (1973).

David,R.B. "James Ogilvie and WI." *Americana*, 35: 435-52 (1941).

Davis, R.B. "WI and Joseph C. Cabell." *Un Virginia Stud*, 4: 7-22 (1951).

Diederich, J.F. "WI as Lyricist." *PSBA*, 69: 91-4 (1Q 75).

Dula, Martha. "Audience Response to *A Tour of the Prairies* in 1835." *WAL*, 8: 67-74 (1973).

Durant, David. "Aeolism in Knickerbocker's *A History of New York*." *Al*, 41: 493-506 (Ja 70).

Evans, J.E. "The English Lineage of Diedrich Knickerbocker." *EAL*, 10: 3-13 (Sp 75).

Fink, Guido. "Il 'corsivo vivente' di WI." *SA*, 16: 25-56 (1970).

Fraser, H.M. "Change is the Unchanging: WI and Manuel Gutierrez Najera." *JSSTC*, 1: 151-9 (1973).

Gartner, D.G. "The Influence of James Kirke Paulding's *Diverting History* on WI's Sketch 'John Bull." *PBSA*, 67: 310-4 (3Q 73).

Glowes, K.A. "Devices of Repitition in I's 'The Wife.'" *ATQ*, 5: 60-6 (1Q 70).

Granger, Bruce. "The Whim-Whamsical Bachelors in *Salmagundi*." *Costerus*, 2: 63-9 (1972).

Griffith, Kelley. "Ambiguity and Gloom in I's 'Adventure of the German Student." *CEA* 38: 10-3 (#1 75).

Hagensick, Donna. "I—A Litterateur in Politics." *ATQ*, 5: 53-60 (1Q 70).

Harbert, E.N. "Fray Antonio Agapida and WI's Romance with History." *TSE*, 17: 135-44 (1969).

———. "I's *Conquest of Granada*: Authorial Intention and Untoward Accident." *ATQ*, 5: 26-31(1Q 70).

———. "I's *Conquest of Granada*: A Spanish Experiment that Failed." *Clio*, 3: 305-13 (Je 74).

Hedges, W.L. "I, Hawthorne, and the Image of the Wife." *ATQ*, 5: 22-6 (1Q 70).

Hough, R.L. "WI, Indians, and the West." *SDR*, 6: 27-39 (Wi 68-9).

Ingram, F.L. "Pushkin's *Skazka o zolotom petŭske* and WI's *The Legend of the Arabian Astrologer.*" *RLJ*, 84: 3-18 (1969).

Irving, Washington. "I's Petition for Bounty Land in 1853."*ESQ*, 41: 25 (2Q 68).

Johnson, R.C. and C.T. Tanselle. "Addenda to Bibliographies of . . . Irving, . . .: Haldeman-Julius Little Blue Books." *PBSA*, 66: 66 (1Q 72).

Kemp, J.C. "Historians Manqués: I's Apologetic Personae." *ATQ*, 24, sup 2: 15-9 (Fa 74).

Kime, W.R. "Alfred Seton's Journal: A Source for I's *Tonquin* Disaster Account." *OrHQ*, 71: 309-24 (D 70).

———. "An Actor among the Albanians: Two Undiscovered Sketches of Albany by WI." *NYH*, 56: 409-25 (O 75).

———. "The Completeness of WI's *A Tour on the Prairies.*" *WAL*, 8: 55-66 (Sp-Su 73).

———. "The First Locomotive to Cross the Rocky Mountains: An Unidentified Sketch in the *Knickerbocker Magazine*, May 1839, by WI." *BNYPL*, 76: 242-50 (1972).

———. "Pierre M. Irving's Account of Peter Irving, WI, and the *Corrector.*" *AL*, 43: 108-14

———. "Poe's Use of I's *Astoria* in 'The Journal of Julius Rodman.'" *AL*, 40: 215-22 (My 68).

———. "The Satiric Use of Names in I's *History of New York.*" *Names*, 16: 380-9 (D 68).

———. "WI and *The Empire of the West.*" *WAL*, 5: 277-85 (Wi 71).

———. "WI and the 'Extension of the Empire of Freedom':An Unrecorded Contribution to the *Evening Post*, May 14, 1804." *BYNPL*, 76: 220-30 (1972).

———. "WI and Frontier Speech." *AS*, 42: 5-18 (F 67).

———. "WI and 'To a Mountain Daisy': An Anecdote of Robert Burns in America."*SSL*, 10: 186-9 (1973).

———. "WI's Revision of the *Tonquin* Episode in *Astoria.*" *WAL*, 4: 51-9 (SP 69).

Kleinfield, H.L. "I as a Journal Writer." *ATQ*, 5: 11-4 (1Q 70).

Lease, Benjamin. "*John Bull* versus WI: More on the Shakespeare Committee Controversy." *ELN*, 8: 18-22 (S 70).

———. "Ichabod Crane's Scottish Origin." *N&Q*, 15: 29 (Ja 68).

———. "I, Lockhart, and the Quarterly Review." *BNYPL*, 76: 231-6 (1972).

———. "I's Literary Borrowings." *N&Q*, 16: 57-8 (F 69).

———. "I's Literary Pimpery." *AN&Q*, 10: 150-1 (Je 72).

———. "Mr. I and the Shakespeare Committee."*AL*, 41: 92-5 (Mr 69).

———. "Mr. I of the Shakespeare Committee: Anglo-American Jealousy." *AN&Q*, 7: 19-21 (O 68).

———. "WI's British Edition of Slidell's *A Year in Spain.*" *BYNPL*, 73: 386-74 (Je 69).

McLendon, W.L. "A Problem in Plagiarism: WI and Cousen de Courchamps." *CL*, 20: 157-69 (Sp 68).

Male, R.R. "The Story of the Mysterious Stranger in American Fiction." *Criticism*, 3: 281-94 (1961).

Mengling, M.E. "The Crass Humour of I's Diedrich Knickerbocker." *SAH*, 1: 66-72 (O 74).

Monteiro, George. "WI: A Grace Note on 'The Pride of the Village.'" *RSW*, 36: 347-50 (D 68).

Morpurgo, J.E. "WI and the House of Murray." *ArielE*, 2: 102-4 (1971).

Myers, A.B. "WI and Gilbert Stuart Newton: A *New-York Mirror* Contribution Identified." *BYNPL*, 76: 237-41 (Mr 72).

———. "WI and the Astor Library." *BYNPL*, 72: 378-99 (Je 68).

Noble, D.R. "WI's 'Peter' Pun." *AN&Q*, 8: 103-4 (1970).

Paltsits, V.H. "WI's Notebooks." *BYNP*, 24: 431-5 (Ag 20).

Payne, J.H. "I's Literary Pimpery." *AN&Q*, 10: 150-1 (1972).

Pochmann, H.A. "An Example of Progressive Plate Deterioration." *CEANN*, 3: 16 (Ja 70).
———. "Copy-Editing I's Journals." *CEANN*, 2: 15 (Ja 69).
Proffer, C.R. "WI in Russia: Pushkin, Gogol, Marlinsky." *CL*, 20: 329-42 (Fa 68).
Reed, K.T. "'Oh These Women! These Women!': I's Shrews and Coquettes." *AN&Q*, 8: 147-50 (1970).
———. "WI and the Negro." *NALF*, 4: 43-4 (1970).
Reichart, W.A. "WI and the Theatre." *MuK*, 14: 341-50 (3Q 68).
———. "WI in der Dresdner und der Pariser Gesellschaft 1822-1825." *Jahrbuch des Weiner Goethe-Vereins*, 76: 134-46 (1973).
Ringe, D.A. "I's Use of the Gothic Mode." *SLitI*, 7: 51-65 (Sp 74).
Roth, Martin. "The Final Chapter of Knckerbocker's *New York*." *MP*, 66: 248-55 (F 69).
Rust, R.D. "I Rediscovers the Frontier." *ATQ*, 18: 40-5 (Sp 73).
Sabbadini, Silvano. "La morte e le maschere: Note sullo *Sketch Book*." *SA*, 16: 57-79 (1971).
Scanlan, Tom. "The Domestication of Rip Van Winkle: Joe Jefferson's Play as Prologue to Modern American Drama." *VQT*, 50: 51-62 (1974).
Scheick, W.J. "'The Seven Sons of Lara': A WI Manuscript." *RALS*, 2: 208-17 (Au 72).
Seyersted, Per. "The Indian in Knickerbocker's New Amsterdam." *Indian Hist*, 7: 14-28 (Su 74).
Shaw, C.M. "The Dramatic view of WI." *TSLL*, 13: 461-74 (1971).
Short, Julee. "I's Eden: Oklahoma, 1832." *JWest*, 10: 700-12 (O 71).
Sloane, D.E.E. "WI's 'Insuperable Diffidence.'" *AL*, 43: 114-5 (Mr 71).
Smith, H.F. "The Spell of Nature in I's Famous Stories." *ATQ*, 5: 18-21 (1Q 70).
Springer, H.K. "Practical Editions: WI's *Sketch Book*." *Proof*, 4: 167-74 (1975).
West, E.L. "WI, Biographer." *ATQ*, 5: 47-52 (1Q 70).
Whitford, Kathryn. "Romantic Metamorphosis in I's Western Tour." *ATQ*, 5: 31-6 (1Q 70).
Wright, Nathalia. "Travel Books and Histories in I's European Journal." *ATQ*, 5: 5-11 (1Q 70).
Zug, C.G. "The Construction of 'The Devil and Tom Walker': A Study of WI's Later Use of Folklore." *NYFQ*, 24: 243-60 (D 68).
Jackson, Charles Reginald. Keller, D.N. 'Two D Notes." *Serif*, 10: 51-2 (Jl-S 73).
*Leonard, Shirley. "CRJ: A Checklist." *BB*, 28: 137-41 (O-D 71).
*———. "CRJ: A Critical Checklist." *Serif*, 10: 32-40 (Jl-S 73).
Mitford, Jessica. "A Talk with GJ." *NYT*, 13 Je 71, pp. 30-5.
Paskoff, Louis. "Don Birbam's Dark Mirror." *Serif*, 3: 41-50 (Jl-S 73).
Straus, Dorothea. "The Fan." *Serif*, 3: 16-28 (Ap-Je 73).
Wylie, Max. "CRG." *Serif*, 3: 29-31 (Jl-S 73).
Jackson, Helen Hunt. Byers, J.R. "HHJ (1830-1885)." *ALR*, 2: 143-48 (Su 69)
*———, and Elizabeth Byers. "HHJ (1830-1885): A Critical Bibliography of Secondary Comment." *ALR*, 6: 197-241 (Su 73).
Hamblen, A.A. "*Ramona*: A Story of Passion." *WR*, 8: 21-5 (1971).
Harsha, W.J. "How Ramona Wrote Itself." *SoW*, 59: 370-5 (Ag 30).
*Kime, W.R. "HHJ." *ALR*, 8: 291-2 (1975).
McConnell, Virginia. "'H.H.,' Colorado and the Indian Problem." *JWest*, 12: 272-80 (Ap 73).
McWilliams, Carey. "Southern California: Ersatz Mythology." *ComG*, 6: 29-38 (Wi 46).
Jackson, Shirley. Nebeker, H.E. "'The Lottery': Symbolic Tour de Force." *AL*, 46: 100-7 (Mr 74).
Jacobs, W.W. Harkey, J.H. "Foreshadowing in 'The Monkey's Paw.'" *SSF*, 6: 653-4 (Fa 69).

James, Henry

Jaffe, Dan. Rothwell, K.S. "In Search of a Western Epic: Neilhardt, Sandburg, and J as Regionalists and 'Astoriadists.'" *KanQ*, 2: 53-63 (Sp 70).

James, Henry (the elder). Feinstein, Howard. "The Double in *The Autobiography* of the Elder HJ." *AI*, 31: 293-318 (Fa 74).

James, Henry. Anon. "From the J Family Libraries." *Bancroftiana*, 52: 1-2 (1972).

———. "Gloom and Some Friendships." *TSL*, 30 O 69, pp. 1245-6.

———. "The Matter of the Master." *TLS*, 18 Ag 72, pp. 957-9.

Abel, R.H. "Gide and HJ: Suffering, Death, and Responsibility." *MwQ*, 9: 403-16 (Jl 68).

Akiyama, Masayuki. "HJ's *The Ambassadors*: Strether's Inner Self." *Annual Report of Res (Nihon)*, 23: 45-67 (1974).

Aldridge, J.W. "The Anatomy of Passion in the Consummate HJ." *SatR*, 55: 64-8 (12 F 72).

Alexander, Charlotte. "HJ and 'Hot Corn.'" *AN&Q*, 14: 52-3 (1975).

Andersen, Kenneth. "Mark Twain, W.D. Howells, and HJ: Three Agnostics in Search of Salvation." *MTJ*, 15: 13-6 (Wi 70).

Anderson, Quentin. "HJ and the New Jerusalem." *KR*, 8: 515-66 (1946).

———. "Leon Edel's HJ." *VQR*, 48: 621-30 (Au 72).

———. "A Master in the Making." *TLS*, 9 My 75, pp. 498-500.

Antush, J.V. "Money as Myth and Reality in the World of HJ." *ArQ*, 25: 125-33 (Su 69).

———. "The 'Much Finer Complexity' of History in *The American*." *JAmSt*, 6: 85-95 (Ap 72).

Aoki, Tsuguo. "J ni okeru Hoshuha no Kankaku." *EigoS*, 118: 494-5 (1972).

———. "Language of Love and Language of Things: HJ's *The Wings of the Dove*." *SELit*, 48: 55-71 (1971).

———. "Matsuei no Kokuhaku: The Revision of *The Aspern Papers*." *Eng Lit Q*, 12: 49-68 (1974).

Armistead, J.M. "HJ for the Cinematic Mind." *Eng Rev*, 26: 27-33 (Su 75).

Aswell, E.D. "Reflections of a Governess: Image and Distortion in *The Turn of the Screw*." *NCF*, 23: 49-63 (Je 68).

Atkinson, F.G. "HJ and 'The Sign of Sympathy.'" *N&Q*, 21: 363-5 (O 74).

Auchincloss, Louis. "*The Ambassadors*." *Horizon*, 15: 118-9 (Su 73).

———. "HJ's Literary Use of His American Tour." *SAQ*, 74: 45-52 (Wi 75).

Aziz, Maqbool. "'Four Meetings': A Caveat for J Critics." *EIC*, 18: 258-74 (Jl 68).

———. "Revisiting 'The Pension Beaurepas': The Tale and Its Texts." *EC*, 23: 268-82 (Jl 73).

Babukia, T.K. "J's *Washington Square*: More on the Hawthorne Relationship." *NHJ*, 4: 270-2 (1974).

Backus, J.M. "'Poor Valentin' or 'Monsieur le Comte': Variation in Character Designation as Matter for Critical Consideration in HJ's *The American*." *Names*, 20: 47-55 (1972)

Bailey, Bruce. "A Note on *The Waste Land* and HJ's *In the Cage*." *TSE N*, 1: 2 (Fa 74).

Bailey, N.I. "Pragmatism in *The Ambassadors*." *DR*, 53: 143-8 (Sp 73).

Baker, R.S. "Gabriel Nash's 'House of Strange Idols': Aestheticism in *The Tragic Muse*." *TSLL*, 15: 149-66 (Sp 73).

Ballorain, Rolande. "'The Turn of the Screw'—L'adulte et l'enfant, ou les deux regards." *EA*, 22: 250-8 (Jl-S 69).

Banta, Martha. "The Quality of Experience in *What Maisie Knew*." *NEQ*, 42: 483-510 (D 69).

———. "Rebirth or Revenge: The Endings of *Huckleberry Finn* and *The American*." *MFS*, 15: 191-207 (Su 69).

Barzun, Jacques. "The Jameses." *TLS*, 15 S 72, p. 1060.

Basic, Sonja. "Love and Politics in *The Bostonians*: A Note on Motivation."

Bass, Eben. "Flannery O'Connor and HJ: The Vision of Grace." *STC*, 14: 43-68 (Fa 74).

———. 'HJ and the English Country House." *MarkR*, 2: 4-10 (1970).

Baym, Nina. "Fleda Vetch and the Plot of *The Spoils of Poynton*." *PMLA*, 84: 102-11 (Ja 69).

Bazzanella, D.J. "The Conclusion of *The Portrait of a Lady* Re-examined." *AL*, 41: 55-63 (Mr 69).

Bebeau, Donald. "A Search for Voice: A Sense of Place in *The Golden Bowl*." *SDR*, 7: 79-86 (Wi 69-70).

Beck, Ronald. "J's *The Beast in the Jungle*: Theme and Metaphor." *MarkR*, 2: 17-20 (1970).

Bedford, R.C. "HJ's 'mere mistake and a worry and a joke.'" *Annual Reports* (Kyoto), 25: 136-80 (1974).

Beebe, Maurice. "HJ and the Sophomore." *CE*, 14: 20-2 (1952).

Beker, Miroslav. "T.S. Eliot's Theory of Impersonality and HJ." *SRAZ*, 27-8: 163-7 (Jl-D 69).

Bell, Millicent. "The Dream of Being Possessed and Possessing: HJ's *The Wings of the Dove*." *MR*, 10: 97-114 (Wi 69).

———. "Fluid Self-Expression.' *NRep*, 172: 23-5 (22 F 75).

———. "HJ: The Man Who Lived." *MR*, 14: 391-414 (Sp 73).

———. "Jamesian Being." *VQR*, 51: 115-32 (1975).

———. "The Jamesian Note in Edith Wharton's *The Children*." *UR*, 31: 209-11 (1965).

———. "Style as Subject: *Washington Square*." *SR*, 83: 19-38 (Wi 75).

Bellringer, A.W. "*The Sacred Fount*: The Scientific Method." *EIC*, 22: 244-4 (Jl 72).

———. "*The Spoils of Poynton*: The 'Facts.'" *EIC*, 18: 357-9 (1968).

———. "*The Spoils of Poynton*: J's Intentions." *EIC*, 17: 238-43 (1967).

———. "*The Tragic Muse*: The Objective Centre." *JAmSt*, 4: 73-89 (Jl 70).

Bercovitch, Sacvan. "HJ's Revision of Rowland Mallett." *NCF*, 24: 210-21 (S 69).

Bergonzi, Bernard. "The Novelist and his Subject-Matter." *Listener*, 60: 426-7 (18 S 58).

Berland, Alwyn. "J and Forster: The Morality of Class." *CaJ*, 6: 259-80 (Fe 53).

Berner, R.L. "Douglas in *The Turn of the Screw*." *EN*, 3: 3-7 (Wi 68-9).

Bersani, Leo. "The Jamesian Lie." *PR*, 36: 53-79 (Wi 69).

Bhatnager, O.P. "*The American*: A Revaluation." *IJAS*, 1: 51-61 (4Q 71).

Bianchini, Angela. "HJ e la Remington." *NA*, 511: 259-63 (F 71).

Bier, Jesse. "Romantic Coordinates of American Literature." *BuR*, 18: 16-33 (Fa 70).

Birch, Brian. "The Editions of *The Ambassadors*." *Library*, 21: 250-2 (S 66).

Bixler, J.S. "J Family Letters in Colby College Library." *CLQ*, 9: 35-47 (Mr 70).

Blasing, Mutlu. "Double Focus in *The American*." *NCF*, 28: 74-88 (Su 73).

Bleich, David. "Artistic Form as Defensive Adaptation: HJ and *The Golden Bowl*." *PsyR*, 58: 223-44 (Su-Fa 71).

Bliven, Naomi. "Home J." *NY*, 29 Ap 72, pp. 137-40.

Bluefarb, Sam. "The 'Radicalism' of the Princess Casamassima." *BaratR*, 6: 68-73 (1971).

Boardman, Arthur. "Mrs. Grose's Reading of *The Turn of the Screw*." *SEL*, 14:

Bobbitt, Joan. "Agressive Innocence in *The Portrait of a Lady*." *MSE*, 4: 317 (1973).

Bochner, Jay. "Life in a Picture Gallery: Things in *The Portrait of a Lady* and *The Marble Faun*." *TSLL*, 11: 761-7 (Sp 69).

Böker, Uwe. "HJ, Graham Greene, und das Problem der Form." *LWU*, 7: 16-30 (My 74).

Bonincontro, Marilia. "Le ascendenze austeniane del *Portrait of a Lady* di HJ." *PenS*, 4: 31-9 (1968).

James, Henry

Bontly, T.J. "HJ's 'General Vision of Evil' in *The Turn of the Screw*." *SEL*, 9: 721-35 (Au 69).

———. "The Moral Perspective of *The Ambassadors*." *WSL*, 6: 106-17 (1969).

Bosanquet, Theodora. "The Revised Version." *Little R*, 5: 56-62 (Ag 18).

Bouraoui, H.A. "HJ and the French Mind." *Novel*, 4: 69-76 (1970).

———. "HJ's *The Sacred Fount*: Nouveau Roman avant la lettre." *IFR*, 1: 96-105 (Jl 74).

Bowden, E.T. "In Defense of a HJ Collection." *LCUT*, 6: 7-12 (1960).

Brack, O.M. "Mark Twain in Knee Pants: The Expurgation of *Tom Sawyer Abroad*." *Proof*, 2: 145-51 (1972).

Brennan, J.G. "Three Novels of *Dépaysement*." *CL*, 22: 223-36 (Su 70).

Briggs, A.D. "Alexander Pushkin: A Possible Influence on HJ." *FMLS*, 8: 52-60 (1972).

———. "Someone Else's Sledge: Further Notes on Turgenev's *Virgin Soil* and HJ's *The Princess Casamassima*." *Oxford Slavonic Papers*, 5: 52-60 (1972).

Brill, L.W. "Conflict and Accomodation in H's 'The Artist of the Beautiful.'" *SSF*, 12: 381-86 (Fa 75).

Brooks, Peter. "The Melodramatic Imagination." *PR*, 39: 195-212 (1972).

Brown, Ashley. "Landscape into Art: HJ and John Crowe Ransom." *SR*, 79: 206-12 (Sp 71).

Brown, Bernadine. "*The Turn of the Screw*: A Case of Romantic Displacement." *NasR*, 2: 75-82 (#5 74).

Brown, D.R. "The Cosmopolitan Novel: J and Lewis." *SLN*, nv: 6-9 (Sp 69).

Brown, R.C. "The Role of Densher in *The Wings of the Dove*." *MSpr*, 65: 5-11 (1971).

Bruneau, Jean. "Une Lettre inédite de HJ à Gustave Flaubert: Autour de Monckton Milnes, Lord Houghton." *RLC*, 42: 520-33 (O-D 68).

Brylowski, A.S. "In Defense of the First Person Narrator in 'The Aspern Papers.'" *CentR*, 13: 215-40 (Sp 69).

Bufkin, E.C. "A Pattern of Parallel and Double: The Function of Myrtle in *The Great Gatsby*." *MFS*, 15: 517-24 (1969-70).

Buitenhuis, Peter. "Exiles at Home and Abroad: Henry Adams and HJ." *Eng Stud Canada*, 1: 74-85 (Sp 75).

———. "The Return of the Novelist: HJ's *The American Scene*." *CAAS*, 4: 54-103 (Sp-Su 69).

Burgess, C.E. "HJ's 'Big' Impression: St. Louis, 1905." *MHSB*, 27: 30-63 (O 70).

———. "The Master and the *Mirror*." *PLL*, 7: 382-405 (Fa 71).

Burns, Graham. "*The Bostonians*." *CR*, 12: 45-60 (1969).

Byatt, A.S. "Prophet and Boulder." *NSt*, 2 Ja 70, p. 16.

Byers, J.R. "*The Turn of the Screw*: A Hellish Point of View." *MarkR*, 2: 101-4 (My 71).

Byrd, Scott. "The Fractured Crystal in *Middlemarch* and *The Golden Bowl*." *MFS*, 18: 551-4 (Wi 72-73).

———. "HJ's 'Two Old Houses and Three Young Women': A Problem in Dating and Assemblage." *PBSA*, 65: 383-9 (4Q 71).

———. "The Spoils of Venice." HJ's 'Two Old Houses and Three Young Women' and *The Golden Bowl*." *AL*, 43: 371-84 (N 71).

Canavan, T.L. "The Economics of Disease in J's 'The Pupil.'" *Criticism*, 15: 253-64 (Su 73).

Canby, H.S. "He Knew His Women." *SatR*, 34: 9-10, 34-6 (10 N 51).

Capellan Gonzalo, Angel. "Un momento biografico a HJ." *Sin Nombre*, 3: 82-90 (#3 73).

———. "Estudio estructural de las obras tempranas de HJ." *Atlántida*, 9: 586-603 (1971).

Cargas, H.J. "Seeing, But Not Living: Two Characters from J and Wharton." *NLauR*, 1: 5-7 (1972).

Cargill, Oscar. "Occlusion and Refraction in Jamesian Criticism." *NCF*, 19: 302-24 (D 64).

Cartinau, Virginia. "Aspecte ale romanului modern si compemporan englez." *ViR*, 22: 93-103 (1969).

Cary, R. "HJ Juvenalia: A Poem and a Letter." *CLQ*, 9: 58-62 (Mr 70).

Cervo, N.A. "'Our Lady of the Gulls': A Case of Polite Revenge." *BaratR*, 6: 22-32 (1971).

Chanda, A.K. "Art and Artists in the *Portrait of a Lady*." *IJES*, 10: 109-21 (1969).

Chapman, S.S. "The 'Obsession of Egotism' in HJ's 'A Round of Visits.'" *ArQ*, 29: 130-8 (1973).

Chartier, Richard. "The River and the Whirlpool: Water Imagery in *The Ambassadors*." *BSUF*, 12: 70-5 (Sp 71).

Chapman, S.S. "Stalking the Beast." *CLQ*, 11: 50-66 (1975).

Chatman, Seymour. "HJ et le style de l'intangbilité." *Poétique*, 6: 155-72 (1971).

Chernaik, Judith. "HJ as Moralist: The Case of the Late Novels." *CentR*, 16: 105-21 (Sp 72).

Cheshire, David, and Malcolm Bradbury. "American Realism and the Romance of Europe: Fuller, Frederic, Garland." *PAH*, 4: 285-310 (1970).

Cirgus, S.B. "The Other Maisie: Inner Death and Fatalism in *What Maisie Knew*." *ArQ*, 29: 115-22 (1973).

Cixous, Hélène. "HJ: L'ecriture comme placement." *Poétique*, 1: 35-50 (1970).

Cohen, Michael. "JM's Public Voice." *WAL*, 10: 177-87 (N 75).

Cohen, S.B. "*The Ambassadors*: A Comedy of Musing and Manners." *SAH*, 1: 79-90 (O 74).

Collins, Martha. "The Center of Consciousness on Stage: HJ's *Confidence*." *SAF*, 3: 39-50 (Sp 75).

Conger, S.M. "The Admirable Villains in HJ's *The Wings of the Dove*." *ArQ*, 27: 151-60 (Su 71).

Conn, P.J. "*Roderick Hudson*: The Role of the Observer." *NCF*, 26: 65-82 (1971).

——. "Seeing and Blindness in 'The Beast in the Jungle.'" *SSF*, 7: 472-5 (Su 70).

Cook, D.A. "J and Flaubert: The Evolution of Perception." *CL*, 25: 289-307 (Fa 73).

Cook, J.A. "The Fool Show in *Roderick Hudson*." *CRAS*, 4: 74-86 (Sp 73).

Core, George. "Henry, Leon, and Other Jamesians." *MQR*, 12: 82-8 (Wi 73).

Cowser, John. "HJ's Ancestry." *TLS*, 25 Ja 57, p. 49.

Cox, J.M. "HJ: The Politics of Internationalism." *SoR*, 8: 493-506 (Jl 72).

Coy, J.J. "Washington Square o el folletin bien hecho." *PSA*, 55: 26-47 (1969).

Cranfill, T.M., and R.L. Clark. "The Provocativeness of *The Turn of the Screw*." *TSLL*, 12: 93-100 (Sp 70).

Cromer, Viris. "J and Ibsen." *CL*, 25: 114-27 (Sp 73).

Cromphout, G.V. "Artist and Society in HJ." *ES*, 49: 132-40 (Ap 68).

Crow, C.L. "Howells and HJ: 'A Case of Metaphantasmia' Soved." *AQ*, 27: 169-77 (My 75).

Crowl, Susan. "Aesthetic Allegory in 'The Turn of the Screw.'" *Novel*, 4: 107-22 (1971).

Crowley, F.E. "HJ's 'The Beast in the Jungle' and *The Ambassadors*." *PsyR*, 62: 153-63 (1975).

Cummins, Elizabeth. "'The Playroom of Superstition': An Analysis of HJ's 'The Pupil.'" *MarkR*, 2: 13-6 (1970).

Cuny, C.M. "Retour a HJ." *LetF*, 1275: 11-2 (19 Mr 69).

D'Avanzo, M.L. "J's 'Maud-Evelyn': Source, Allusion, and Meaning." *IEngYb*, 13: 24-33 (Fa 68).

Davidson, A.E. "J's Dramatic Method in *The Awkward Age*." *NCF*, 29: 320-35 (D 74).

Deakin, M.F. "Daisy Miller, Tradition, and the European Heroine." *CLS*, 6: 45-59 (Mr 69).

Deans, T.R. "HJ's *The Ambassadors*: The Primal Scene Revisited." *AI*, 29: 233-56 (Fa 72).

Delbaere-Garant, Jeanne. "HJ's Divergences from his Russian Model in *The Princess Casamassima*." *RLV*, 37: 535-44 (1971).

Ditsky, Joan. "The Watch and Chain of HJ." *UWR*, 6: 91-101 (Fa 70).

Dommergues, Pierre. "L'art romanesque de HJ." *Le Monde*, 27: iv (7 Mr 70).

Donaghue, Denis. "The American Style of Failure." *SR*, 82: 407-32 (1974).

———. "J's *The Awkward Age* and Pound's *Mauberly*." *N&Q*, 17: 49-50 (F 70).

Dooley, D.J. "The Hourglass Pattern in *The Ambassadors*." *NEQ*, 41: 273-81 (Je 68).

Dorris, G.E. "Two Allusions in the Poetry of T.S. Eliot." *ELN*, 2: 54-7 (S 64).

Dove, J.R. "Tragic Consciousness in Isabel Archer." *LSUS*, 8: 78-94 (1960).

Dow, Eddy. "J's 'Brooksmith'—paragraphs 4 & 5." *Expl*, 27: 35 (Ja 69).

Draper, R.P. "Death of a Hero? Winterbourne and Daisy Miller." *SSF*, 6: 601-8 (Fa 69).

Duffy, J.J. "Ernest Dowson and the Failure of Decadence." *UR*, 34: 45-9 (O 67).

Dumitriu, Dana. "Un eseu despre HJ: O aventură primejdioasă." *RoLit*, 15: 28-9 (Mr 73).

Dumitriu, Gheorghito. "Aspecte ale metodei narative in romanul lui HJ." *RITL*, 18: 235-47 (1969).

———. "HJ's Use of Imagery in *The Wings of the Dove*." *AUB-LG*, 22: 61-74 (1973).

Dunn, A.A. "The Articulation of Time in *The Ambassadors*." *Criticism*, 14: 137-50 (Sp 72).

Ebine, Shixue. "The Central Theme in HJ." *SELit*, Eng no: 53-60 (1974).

Edel, Leon. "The Deathbed Notes of HJ." *Atl*, 201: 103-5 (Je 68).

———. "HJ and Sir Sydney Waterlow: The Unpublished Diary of a British Diplomat." *TLS*, 8 Ag 68, pp. 844-5.

———. "HJ' Last Dictation." *TLS*, 2 My 68, pp. 459-60.

———. "Indirection, Irony, and the Two Endings of J's 'The Story of a Masterpiece.'" *MP*, 62: 75-103 (1967).

———. "The Jameses." *TLS*, 13 O 72, pp. 1226-7; 3 N 72, p. 1342.

———. "HJ Looked Ahead." *NYT*, 12 N 67, pp. 2, 70-2.

Edelstein, Arnold. "'The Tangle of Life': Levels of Meaning in *The Spoils of Poynton*." *HSL*, 2: 133-50 (1970).

Emerson, Donald. "The Relation of HJ's Art Criticism to His Literary Standards." *TWA*, 57: 9-19 (1969).

Engelberg, Edward. "J and Arnold: Conscience and Consciousness in a Victorian 'Künstlerroman.'" *Criticism*, 10: 93-114 (Sp 68).

Engstrom, Susanne. "Epistemological and Moral Validity in HJ's *The Ambassadors*." *Lang&L*, 1: 50-65 (1971).

———. "Historical or Moral Validity, or Two Kinds of Norms." *Lang&L*, 1: 83-6 (1973).

Fahey, Paul. "*What Maisie Knew*: Learning Not to Mind." *CritR*, 14: 96-108 (1971).

Feidelson, Charles. "The Moment of *The Portrait of a Lady*." *Ventures*, 8: 47-55 (1968).

Fernandez, Diane. "HJ, ou la richesse des possibles." *QL*, 69: 8-10 (16 F 70).

———. "HJ Revisited." *QL*, 68: 4-5 (Mr 69).

Festiner, John. "Max Beerbohm and the Wings of HJ." *KR*, 29: 450-71 (S 67).

Fiderer, Gerald. "HJ's 'Discriminated Occasion.'" *Critique*, 11: 56-69 (1968-69).

*Field, M.L. "HJ's Criticism of French Literature: A Bibliography and a Checklist." *ALR*, 7: 379-94 (Au 74).

Finch, G.A. "A Retreading of J's Carpet." *TCL*, 98-101 (Jl 68).

Fingleton, David. "*The Knot Garden* and *Owen Wingrave*: Operatic Development or Experiment?" *ConR*, 119: 246-51 (N 71).

Finn, C.M. "Commitment and Identity in *The Ambassadors*." *MLR*, 66: 522-31 (Jl 71).

Fischer, W.C. "William Dean Howells: Reverie and the Nonsymbolic Aesthetic." *NCF*, 25: 1-30 (1970).

Fletcher, Pauline. "The Sense of Society in *The Ambassadors.*" *ESA*, 17: 79-88 (S 74).

Flynn, T.E. "HJ's Journey from the Interior." *DR*, 51: 96-104 (Sp 71).

Forde, Sister Victoria. "*The Aspern Papers:* What Price—Defeat." *NDEJ*, 6: 17-24 (1970-71).

Frank, F.S. "The Two Taines of HJ." *HLC*, 45: 350-65 (1971).

Frederick, J.T. "Patterns of Imagery in Chapter XLII Of HJ's *The Portrait of A Lady.*" ArQ, 25: 150-6 (Su 69).

Frederiksen, B.F. "Moral or Historical Validity: HJ, *The Ambassadors.*" *Lang&L*, 1: 58-66 (#3 72).

Freeman, Arthur. "HJ and Dickens." *TLS*, 12 Mr 71, p. 296.

Friedl, Herwig. "HJ: 1968-1972." *JA*, 19: 334-47 (1974).

Friedrich, Otto. "A Little Tour with HJ." *ASch*, 64: 643-52 (Au 75).

Fuller, Roy. "The Two Sides of the Street." *SoR*, 9: 579-94 (Jl 73).

Gabbay, Lydia. "The Four Square Coterie: A Comparison of Ford Maddox Ford and HJ." *StN*, 6: 439-53 (Wi 74).

Gabrielson, Thor. "HJ ex Cathedra: The Performing Pedagog." *AmSS*, 6: 47-65 (1974).

Gargano, J.W. "Age and Innocence in *What Maisie Knew.*" *RSW*, 37: 218-26 (S 69).

———. "*The Aspern Papers*: The Untold Story." *SSF*, 10: 1-10 (Wi 73).

Garis, Robert. "Anti-Literary Biography." *HudR*, 23: 143-53 (1970).

Gillen, Francis. "The Dramatist in His Dream: Theory vs. Effect in *The Awkward Age.*" *TSLL*, 12: 663-74 (Wi 71).

Gioli, G.M. "Racconto psicologico e *Romance* in *Daisy Miller.*" *SA*, 16: 231-54 (1970).

———. "*The Turn of the Screw* nelle sue opposizioni strutturali." *SA*, 17: 75-92 (1971).

Girgus, S.B. "The Other Maisie: Inner Death and Fatalism in *What Maisie Knew.*" ArQ, 29: 115-22 (Su 73).

Girling, H.K. "On Editing a Paragraph of *The Princess Casamassima.*" *Lang&S*, 8: 243-63 (1975).

———. "The Strange Case of Dr. J and Mr. Stevenson." *Wascana R*, 3: 65-76 (1968).

Goldfarb, C.R. "Names in *The Bostonians.*" *IEngYb*, 13: 18-23 (Fa 68).

Goodman, Charlotte. "HJ's *Roderick Hudson* and Nathaniel Parker Willis's *Paul Fane.*" *AL*, 43: 642-5 (Ja 72).

Gordon, Caroline. "Rebels and Revolutionaries: The New American Scene." *FOB*, 3: 40-56 (Au 74).

Gottschalk, Jane. "The Continuity of American Letters in *The Scarlet Letter* and 'The Beast in the Jungle.'" *WSL*, 6: 39-45 (1967).

Grant, W.E. "'Daisy Miller': A Study of a Study." *SSF*, 11: 17-25 (Wi 74).

Greene, M.S. "*Les Liaisons Dangereuses* and *The Golden Bowl*: Maggie's 'Loving Reason.'" *MFS*, 19: 531-40 (Wi 73).

Grenandier, M.E. "Benjamin Franklin's America in HJ's 'Jolly Corner.'" *PLL*, 11: 415-7 (1975).

Griffith, John. "J's 'The Pupil' as Whodunit: The Question of Moral Responsibility." *SSF*, 9: 257-68 (Sp 72).

Gross, Barry. "From Newman to Gatsby: This Side of Innocence." *PMASAL*, 53: 279-89 (1968).

Grossman, Edward. "HJ and the Sexual-Military Complex." *Commentary*, 53: 37-50 (Ap 72).

Grover, P.R. "HJ and Several French Critics." *Philologica Pragensia*, 11: 45-52 (1968).

————. "HJ and the Theme of the Adventuress." *RLC*, 47: 586-96 (O-D 73).

————. "Mérimée's Influence on HJ." *MLR*, 63: 810-7 (O 68).

————. "A Tanner in the Works." *CamR*, 89A: 430-1 (3 My 68).

————. "Two Modes of Possessing—Conquest and Appreciation: 'The Princess Casamassima' and 'L'Education Sentimentalle.'" *MLR*, 66: 760-71 (O 71).

Gunn, G.B. "Criticism as Repossession and Responsibility: F.O. Matthiesen and the Ideal Critic." *AQ*, 22: 629-48 (1970).

Gunthner, Frantz. "HJ—Le romancier comme critique." *Le Monde*, 27: v (7 Mr 70).

Gustafson, J.A. "*The Wings of the Dove*; or A Gathering of Pigeons." *Gypsy Schol*, 3: 13-9 (1975).

Gurko, Leo. "The Missing Work in HJ' 'Four Meetings.'" *SSF*, 7: 298-307 (Sp 70).

Habegger, Alfred. "The Disunity of *The Bostonians*." *NCF*, 24: 193-209 (S 69).

————. "Reciprocity and the Market Place in *The Wings of the Dove* and *What Maisie Knew*." *NCF*, 25: 455-73 (Mr 71).

————. "'The Seige of London': HJ and the *Pièce Bien Faite*." *MFS*, 15: 219-3 (Su 69).

Hafley, James. "Malice in Wonderland." *ArQ*, 15: 5-12 (Sp 59).

Hagemann, E.R. "*Life* Buffets (and Comforts) HJ, 1883-1916: An Introduction and an Annotated Checklist." *PBSA*, 62: 207-25 (2Q 68).

————. "'Unexpected light in shady places': HJ and *Life*, 1883-1916." *WHR*, 24: 241-50 (Su 70).

Hall, W.F. "Caricature in Dickens and J." *UTQ*, 39: 242-57 (Ap 70).

————. "The Continuing Relevance of HJ's *The American Scene*." *Criticism*, 13: 151-65 (Sp 71).

————. "HJ and the Picturesque." *Eng Stud Canada*, 1: 326-43 (1975).

————. "J's Conception of Society in *The Awkward Age*." *NCF*, 23: 28-48 (Je 68).

Halverson, John. "Late Manner, Major Phase." *SR*, 79: 214-31 (Sp 71).

Hamblen, A.A. "*Confidence*: The Surprising Shadow of Genius." *UR*, 36: 151-4

————. "HJ and the Power of Eros: *What Maisie Knew*." *MwQ*, 9: 391-9 (Su 68).

————. "HJ and the Transcendentalists." *Cresset*, 26: 16-7 (D 62).

————. "The Inheritance of the Meek: Two Novels by Agatha Christie and HJ." *Disc*, 12: 409-13 (Su 69).

————. "Two Almost Forgotten Innocents." *Cresset*, 30: 16-7 (O 67).

Hampshire, Stuart. "Figures in the Carpet." *NSt*, 4 Ag 72, pp. 162-3.

Han, Pierre. "Organic Unity in 'Europe.'" *SAB*, 35: 40-1 (1970).

Harris, Josephine. "*The Sacred Fount*: The Geometry in the Jungle." *MQR*, 13: 57-73 (Wi 74).

Harsock, M.E. "Biography: The Treacherous Art." *JML*, 1: 116-9 (1970).

————. "The Conceivable Child: J and the Poet." *SSF*, 7: 569-74 (Wi 71).

————. "Dizzying Summit: J's 'The Altar of the Dead.'" *SSF*, 11: 371-8 (Fa 74).

————. "HJ and the Cities of the Plain." *MLQ*, 29: 297-311 (S 68).

————. "A Light Lamp: *The Spoils of Poynton* as Comedy." *ES*, Anglo-Am supp: 29-38 (1969).

————. "*The Princess Casamassima*: The Politics of Power." *StN*, 1: 297-309 (Fa 69).

————. "Time for Comedy: The Late Novels of HJ." *EJ*, 56: 114-28 (Ap75).

————. "Unintentional Fallacy: Critics and *The Golden Bowl*." *MLQ*, 35: 272-88 (S 74).

Haslam, Gerald. "Olive Chancellor's Painful Victory in *the Bostonians*." *RSW*, 36: 232-7 (S 68).

Hatcher, J.B. "Shaw the Reviewer and J's *Guy Domville*." *MD*, 14: 331-4 (D 71).

Hellman, G.T. "Chairman of the Board: Profiles (Leon Edel)." *NY*, 47: 43-86 (13 Mr 71).

Hill, J.S. "HJ: Fitzgerald's Literary Ancestor." *FitzN*, 40: 6-10 (Wi 68).

Hinchliffe, A.P. "The Good American." *TC*, 168: 529-39 (D 60).

Hinz, E.J. "HJ's Names: Tradition, Theory, and Method." *CLQ*, 9: 557-78 (1972).

———. "The Imagistic Evolution of J's Businessmen." *CRAS*, 3: 81-95 (Fa 72).

Hoag, Gerald. "The Death of the Paper Lion." *SSF*, 12: 163-72 (Sp 75).

———. "HJ and the Criticism of Virginia Woolf." *Wichita State UN Bul*, 48: 3-11 (1972).

Hoberman, M.A. "HJ: On a Tour of the Provinces." *NYTimes*, 24 N 74, sec. 10, pp. 1, 16-7.

Hoffa, William. "The Final Preface: HJ's *Autobiography*." *SR*, 77: 277-93 (sp 69).

Hoile, Christopher. "Lambert Strether and the Boaters." *CRCL*, 2: 243-61 (1975).

Hönnighausen, Lothar. "*The Velvet Glove*—Zur Erzähltechnik in HJ's Spätwerk." *GRM*, 17: 307-22 (Jl 67).

Horrel, J.T. "A 'Shade of a Special Sense': HJ and the Art of Naming." *AL*, 42: 203-20 (My 70).

Houghton, D.E. "Attitude and Illness in J's 'Daisy Miller." *L&P*, 19: 51-60 (1969).

Houston, N.B. "HJ's 'Maud-Evelyn': Classic *Folie à Deux*." *RS*, 41: 28-41 (1973).

Howe, Irving. "The Future of the Novel: The Political Novel." *Tomorrow*, 10: 51-8 (My 51).

———. "HJ and the Millionaire." *Tomorrow*, 9: 53-5 (Ja 50).

Hudspeth, R.N. "A Hard, Shining Sonnet: The Art of Short Fiction." *SSF*, 12: 387-96 (Fa 75).

Humma, J.B. "The 'Engagement' of Daisy Miller." *RSW*, 39: 154-5 (1971).

Hux, Samuel. "Irony in *The Aspern Papers*: The Unreliable Symbolist." *BSUF*, 10: 60-5 (Wi 69).

Hyde, H.M. "HJ." *TLS*, 15 My 69, p. 525; 22 My 69, p. 558.

———. "HJ and Theodora Bosanquet." *Enc*, 39: 6-12 (O 72).

———. "HJ at Home." *Essays by Divers Hands*, 38: 58-77 (1975).

———. "HJ's 'Last Dictation.'" *TLS*, 9 My 68, p. 481.

———. "The Lamb House Library of HJ." *BC*, 16: 477-80 (Wi 67).

Hynes, Joseph. "The Transparent Shroud: HJ and William Story." *AL*, 46: 506-27 (Ja 75).

Isle, Walter. "The Romantic and the Real: HJ's *The Sacred Fount*." *Rice Un Stud*, 51: 29-47 (Wi 65).

Iwase, Shitsuu. "*The American Scene* and J's Creative Method." *SELit*, 46: 141-52 (1970).

Jacobson, Marcia. "Literary Convention and Social Criticism in HJ's *The Awkward Age*." *PQ*, 54: 633-46 (1975).

James, Henry. "A Letter to Mr. Howells." *NAR*, 195: 558-62 (Ap 12).

Jaffrey, D.K. "On HJ." *Scholia Satyrica*, 1: 13-8 (Sp 75).

Johannsen, Robert. "Two Sides of Washington Square." *SCR*, 6: 60-5 (Ap 74).

Johnson, Courtney. "Adam and Eve and Isabel Archer." *Renascence*, 21: 134-44, 167 (1969).

———. "John Marcher and the Paradox of the 'Unfortunate Fall.'" *SSF*, 6: 121-35 (Su 69).

Johnson, L.A. "'A Dog in the Manger': J's Depiction of Roger Lawrence in *Watch and Ward*." *ArQ*, 29: 169-76 (1973).

———. "J's Mrs. Wix: The 'Dim, Crooked Reflector.'" *NCF*, 29: 164-72 (Su 74).

———. "The Psychology of Characterization: J's Portraits of Verena Tarrant and Olive Chancellor." *StN*, 6: 295-303 (Fa 74).

Johnson, R.C., and G.T. Tanselle. "Addenda to Bibliographies of . . . J . . Haldeman-Julius Little Blue Books." *PBSA*, 66: 66 (1Q 72).

Jones, G.H. "JH's 'Georgina's Reasons': The Underside of Washington Square." *SSF*, 11: 189-94 (Sp 74).

Kael, Pauline. "*The Innocents* and What Passes for Experience." *Film Q*, 15: 21-36 (1962).

Karitz, Motoshi. "Shosetsu to Denki no Shud aisentaku to Imi." *SophiaT*, 17: 29-45 (1968).

Kau, Joseph. "HJ and the Garden: A Symbolic Setting for 'The Beast in the Jungle.'" *SSF*, 10: 187-98 (Sp 73).

Kaul, R.K. "HJ on the Creative Process." *RUSEng*, 6: 33-44 (1972).

Kay, W.G. "The Observer and the Voyeur: Theories of Fiction in J and Robbe-Grillet." *SoQ*, 9: 87-91 (O 70).

Kehler, J.R. "Salvation and Resurrection in J's 'The Beast in the Jungle.'" *ELUD*, 1: 13-29 (1973).

Kennedy, J.G. "Jeffrey Aspern and Edgar Allan Poe: A Speculation." *PoeS*, 6: 17-8 (Je 73).

Kenney, B.G. "HJ's Businessmen." *CLQ*, 9: 48-58 (Mr 70).

Kenney, William. "The Death of Morgan in J's 'The Pupil.'" *SSF*, 8: 317-22 (Sp 71).

———. "Doctor Sloper's Double in *Washington Square*." *UR*, 36: 301-6 (Su 70).

Kimmey, J.L. "*The Bostonians* and *The Princess Casamassima*." *TSLL*, 9: 537-46 (Wi 68).

———. "*The Tragic Muse* and Its Forerunners." *AL*, 41: 518-31 (Ja 70).

King, M.J. "The Touch of the Earth: A Word and a Theme in *The Portrait of a Lady*." *NCF*, 29: 345-7 (D 74).

Kinnaird, John. "The Paradox of an American Identity." *PR*, 25: 380-81 (Su 58).

Kinnamon, J.M. "HJ, the Bartender in Stephen Crane's 'The Blue Hotel.'" *ArQ*, 30: 160-3 (Su 74).

Kirby, D.K. "HJ: Art and Autobiography." *DR*, 52: 637-44 (Wi 72-73).

———. "HJ's *The Other House*: From Novel to Play." *MarkR*, 3: 49-53 (My 72).

———. "A Possible Source for J's 'The Death of the Lion.'" *CLQ*, 10: 39-40 (Mr 73).

———. "Two Modern Versions of the Quest." *SHR*, 5: 387-95 (Fa 71).

Kirkham, E.B. "A Study of HJ's 'Madame de Mauves.'" *BSUF*, 12: 63-9 (Sp 71).

Kirschke, James. "HJ's Use of Impressionist Painting Techniques in *The Sacred Fount* and *The Ambassadors*." *JML*, 13: 83-116 (Sp 74).

Kleinberg, Seymour. "Ambiguity and Ambivalence: The Psychology of Sexuality in HJ's *The Portrait of a Lady*." *MarkR*, 5: 2-7 (My 69).

Knieger, Bernard. "J's 'Paste'" *SSF*, 8: 468-9 (Wi 71).

Knights, L.C. "HJ and Human Liberty." *SR*, 83: 1-18 (Wi 75).

Koch, Stephen. "Transcendence in *The Wings of the Dove*." *MFS*, 12: 93-102 (Sp 66).

Kohli, R.K. "Huck Finn and Isabel Archer: Two Responses to the Fruit of Knowledge." *BP*, 11: np (Jl 68).

Kornfield, Milton. "Villainy and Responsibility in *The Wings of the Dove*." *TSLL*, 14: 337-46 (Su 72).

Kraft, James. "'Madame de Mauves' and *Roderick Hudson*: The Development of J's International Style." *TQ*, 11: 143-60 (Au 68).

———. "On Reading *The American Scene*." *Prose*, 6: 115-36 (Sp 73).

Kraft, J.L. "A Perspective on 'The Beast in the Jungle.'" *LWU*, 2: 20-6 (1969).

Kraft, Q.G. "The Central Problem of J's Fictional Thought: From *The Scarlet Letter* to *Roderick Hudson*." *ELH*, 36: 416-39 (Je 69).

Krook, Dorothea. "Critical Principles." *NSt*, 9 My 69, p. 658.

———. "The Madness of Art: Further Reflections on the Ambiguity of HJ." *HUSL*, 1: 25-38 (Sp 73).

Krupnick, M.L. "HJ: The Artist as Emperor—On HJ, The Master, 1901-1916." *Novel*, 6: 257-65 (1973).

———. "HJ' Curiosity." *ModO*, 2: 168-80 (Sp 72).

Kudo, Yoshimi. "Strether to Prufrock." *EigoS*, 114: 790-1 (1968).

Kuhn, B.M. "Study Questions and Theme Assignments on HJ's 'Paste.'" *EEx*, 4: 4-5 (Ap 57).

Labrie, Ross. "The Good and the Beautiful in HJ." *Greyfriar*, 16: 3-15 (1975).

———. "HJ's Idea of Consciousness." *AL*, 39: 517-29 (Ja 68).

———. "The Morality of Consciousness in HJ." *CLQ*, 9: 409-24 (1971).

———. "The Power of Consciousness in HJ." *ArQ*, 29: 101-14 (1973).

———. "Sirens of Life and Art in HJ." *LakeUR*, 2: 150-69 (1969).

Lacassin, Francis. "HJ ou l'entrée des fantômes." *ML*, 67: 66-72 (Ag-S 72).

Lang, Hans-Joachim. "The Making of HJ's *The American*: The Contribution of Four Literatures." *AAS*, 20: 55-71 (1975).

Langbaum, Robert. "Thoughts for Our Time: Three Novels on Anarchism." *ASch*, 42: 227-50 (Sp 73).

Larson, Judy. "The Drama Criticism of HJ." *Y/T*, 4: 103-9 (1973).

Lauer, Kristin. "Backdoor to J: The Nature of Plotting." *MichA*, 3: 107-11 (Sp 71).

Leavis, F.R. "HJ and Dickens." *TLS*, 5 Mr 71, p. 271; 19 Mr 71, p. 324.

Lebowitz, Naomi. "The Counterfeiters and the Epic Pretense." *UTQ*, 33: 291-310 (1964).

Leeming, D.A. "HJ and George Sand." *RLC*, 43: 47-55 (Ja-Mr 69).

Lemco, Gary. "HJ and Richard Wagner: *The American*." *HSL*, 6: 147-58 (1974).

Le Vot, André. "HJ—Le critique comme romancier." *Le Monde*, 27: iv (7 Mr 70).

Levy, L.B. "The Comedy of *Watch and Ward*." *ArlQ*, 1: 86-98 (Su 68).

Liebman, S.W. "The Light and the Dark: Character Design in *The Portrait of a Lady*." *PLL*, 6: 163-79 (Sp 70).

———. "Point of View in *The Portrait of a Lady*." *ES*, 52: 136-47 (Ap 71).

Lind, S.E. "'The Turn of the Screw': The Torment of Critics." *CentR*, 14: 225-40 (1970).

Ling, Amy. "The Pagoda Image in HJ's *The Golden Bowl*." *AL*, 46: 383-8 (N 74).

Linneman, W.R. "Satires of American Realism, 1880-1900." *AL*, 34: 8-93 (Mr 62).

Lockridge, E.H. "A Vision of Art: HJ's *The Tragic Muse*." *MFS*, 12: 83-92 (Sp 66).

Lohmann, Christoph. "Jamesian Irony and the American Sense of Mission." *TSLL*, 16: 329-48 (Su 74).

Long, R.E. "Adaptations of HJ's Fiction for Drama, Opera, and Films; with a Checklist of New York Theatre Critics' Reviews." *ALR*, 4: 268-78 (Su 71).

———. "*The Ambassadors* and the Genteel Tradition: J's Correction of Hawthorne and Howells." *NEQ*, 42: 44-64 (Mr 69).

———. "J's *Washington Square*: The Hawthorne Relation." *NEQ*, 46: 573-90 (D 73).

Lopez Landeira, Ricardo. "*Aura, The Aspern Papers*, 'A Rose for Emily': A Literary Relationship." *J Spanish Stud*, 3: 125-34 (1975).

Lord, Catherine. "Aesthetic Unity." *JP*, 58: 321-27 (1961).

Lucas, John. "J's Intentions: *The Spoils of Poynton*." *EIC*, 18: 107-11 (1968).

Lynn, K.S. "Howells in the Nineties." *PAH*, 4: 27-82 (1970).

Lyra, Franciszek. "Correspondence of Helena Modrzejewska (Modjeska) to HJ." *KN*, 19: 89-96 (1972).

McCarthy, H.T. "HJ and the American Aristocracy." *ALR*, 4: 61-71 (Wi 71).

McCauley, Robie. "'Let Me Tell You About the Rich.'" *KR*, 27: 648-9 (Au 65).

McCullough, J.N. "Madame Merle: HJ's 'White Blackbird.'" *PLL*, 11: 312-6 (1975).

McDonald, W.R. "The Inconsistencies in HJ's Aesthetics." *TSLL*, 10: 585-97 (Wi 69).

McDougal, E.D. "HJ." *TLS*, 13 N 69, p. 1313.

McDowell, B.D. "The Use of 'Everything' in *The Wings of the Dove*." *XUS*, 11: 13-20 (Sp 72).

———. "Edith Wharton's Ghost Stories." *Criticism*, 12: 133-52 (Sp 70).

James, Henry

McElderry, B.R. "J's 'Women of Genius.'" *TLS*, 22 Jl 55, pp. 429; a discussion joined by
    H.T. Fuller, 5 Ag 55, p. 445, Percy Lubbock and F.W. Bradbrook, 12 Ag 55, and
    Susanne Nobbe, 26 Ag 55, p. 493.
McElrath, J.P. "Thoreau and J: Coincidence in Angles of Vision?" *ATQ*, 11: 14-5 (Su 71).
McElroy, John. "The Hawthorne Style of American Fiction." *ESQ*, 71: 117-23 (1973).
Mackenzie, Compton. "Memories of HJ." *Cweal*, 13 Ja 50, p. 394-7.
Mackenzie, Manfred. "Communities of Knowledge: Secret Society in HJ." *ELH*, 39:
    147-68 (1972).
———. "Obscure Hurt in HJ." *SoRA*, 3: 107-31 (1968).
———. "A Theory of HJ's Psychology." *YR*, 63: 347-71 (1974).
McLean, R.C. "The Bostonians: New England Pastoral." *PLL*, 7: 374-81 (Fa 71).
———. "'Love by the Doctor's Direction': Disease and Death in *The Wings of the Dove*."
    PLL, 8: 128-48 (Fa 72).
McMaster, Juliet. "'The Full Image of a Repetition' in *The Turn of the Screw*." *SSF*, 6:
    377-82 (Su 69).
———. "The Portrait of Isabel Archer." *AL*, 45: 50-66 (Mr 73).
Macnaughton, W.R. "The First-person Narrators of HJ." *SAF*, 2: 145-64 (Au 74).
———. "Turning the Screw of Ordinary Human Virtue." *CRAS*, 5: 18-25 (Sp 74).
Maini, D.S. "The Style of HJ." *IJES*, 9: 18-29 (1968).
Maixner, Paul. "J on D'Annunzio—'A High Example of Exclusive Estheticism."
    Criticism, 13: 291-311 (Su 71).
Malin, Irving. "American Gothic Images." *Mosaic*, 6: 145-71 (1973).
———. "The Authoritarian Family in American Fiction." *Mosaic*, 4: 153-73 (1971).
Mann, J.J. "Is There an Angel in the House?" *IEY*, 21: 39-50 (Fa 71).
Markovíc, Vida. "Henry Džems." *Savremenik*, nv: 528-41 (D 60).
Marks, A.H. "Two Rodericks and Two Worms: 'Egotism; or, The Boston Serpent' as
    Personal Satire." *PMLA*, 74: 607-12 (1959).
Marks, S.P. "A Silent Morality: Non-Verbal Expression in *The Ambassadors*." *SAB*, 39:
    102-6 (My 74).
———. "The Sound and the Silence: Nonverbal Patterns in *The Wings of the Dove*." *ArQ*,
    27: 143-50 (Su 71).
Marovitz, S.E. "*Roderick Hudson*: J's *Marble Faun*." *TSLL*, 11: 1427-43 (Wi 70).
Martin, R.K. "HJ and the Harvard College Library." *AL*, 41: 95-103 (Mr 69).
———. "HJ and Rodolphe Töpffer: A Note." *RomN*, 10: 245-6 (Sp 69).
Martineau, Barbara. "Portraits Are Murdered in the Short Fiction of HJ." *JNT*, 2: 16-25
    (1972).
Matheson, Gwen. "Portraits of the Artist and the Lady in the Shorter Fiction of HJ." *DR*, 48:
    222-30 (Su 68).
Mathews, J.W. "Fowles's Artistic Freedom: Another Stone from J's House." *NCLit*, 4: 2-4
    (#2 74).
Maynard, Reid. "The Irony of Strether's Enlightenment." *LHR*, 11: 33-44 (1969).
Mayne, E.E. "HJ as Seen from the Yellow Book." *Little R*, 5: 1-4 (Ag 18).
Mays, M.A. "Down-Town with HJ." *TSLL*, 14: 107-22 (1972).
———. "HJ in Seattle." *PNQ*, 59: 186-9 (O 68).
———. "HJ, or, the Beast in the Palace of Art." *AL*, 39: 467-87 (Ja 68).
Mazzella, A.J. "J's *The Portrait of a Lady*." *Expl*, 30: 37 (1972).
Melchiori, Barbara. "Feelings about Aspects: HJ on Pierre Loti." *SA*, 15: 169-99 (1969).
Melchiori, Giorgio. "HJ e Tennyson." *Arte e Storia*, 35: 339-60 (1965).
Meldrum, R.M. "Three of HJ's Dark Ladies." *RSW*, 37: 54-60 (Mr 69).

Mellard, J.M. "Modal Counterpoint in J's *The Aspern Papers*." *PLL*, 4: 299-307 (Su 68).

Menikoff, Barry. "Punctuation and Point of View in the Late Style of HJ." *Style*, 4: 29-47 (Wi 70).

———. "The Subjective Pronoun in the Late Style of HJ." *ES*, 52: 436-41 (O 71).

Mercer, C.G. "Adam Verver, Yankee Businessman." *NCF*, 22: 251-69 (D 67).

Merrill, Robert. "What Strether *Sees*: The Ending of *The Ambassadors*." *BRMMLA*, 27: 45-52 (Je 73).

Meyers, Jeffrey. "Bronzino, Veronese, and *The Wings of the Dove*." *Art Int*, 18: 41-3, 55 (O 74).

Miller, J.E. "The 'Classic' American Writers and the Radicalized Classroom." *CE*, 31: 565-70 (1970).

———. "HJ: A Theory of Fiction." *PrS*, 45: 330-56 (Wi 71-2).

Miller, T.C. "The Muddled Politics of HJ's *The Bostonians*." *GaR*, 26: 336-46 (Fa 72).

Millet, Fred. "HJ and the Undergraduate." *CE*, 14: 167-8 (1952).

Minnick, T.L. "The Light of Deepening Experience in the Major Novels of HJ." *Rendezvous*, 10: 37-51 (#2 75).

Monteiro, George. "Addendum to Edel and Laurence: HJ in Portuguese." *PBSA*, 65: 302-4 (3Q 71).

———. "Addendum to Edel and Laurence: HJ's 'The Future of the Novel." *PBSA*, 63: 130 (2Q 69).

———. "Addendum to Edel and Laurence: HJ's *Two Old Houses and Three Young Women*." *PBSA*, 68: 331 (3Q 74).

———. "HJ and His Reviewers: Some Identification." *PBSA*, 63: 300-4 (4Q 69).

———. "The Items of High Civilization: Howthorne, HJ, and George Persons Lathrop." *NHJ*, 1975, pp. 146-55.

———. "Washington Friends and National Reviewers: HJ's Pandora." *RSW*, 43: 38-44 (1975).

Montgomery, J.H. "The American Galatea." *CE*, 32: 890-9 (My 71).

Moore, R.S. "The Epistolary HJ." *SR*, 83: 703-8 (Ja 75).

———. "HJ, Ltd., and the Chairman of the Board: Leon Edel's Biography." *SAQ*, 73: 261-9 (Sp 74).

Morgan, Alice. "HJ: Money and Morality." *TSLL*, 12: 75-92 (Sp 70).

Morgan, R.A. "Classical Vision and the American City: HJ's *The Bostonians*." *NEQ*, 46: 543-7 (D 73).

Mueller, Lavonne. "HJ: The Phenomenal Self as the 'Real Thing.'" *Forum(H)*, 6: 46-50 (Sp 68).

Mukherji, N. "The Role of Pansy in *The Portrait of a Lady*." *CalR*, ns, 1: 585-94 (1969).

Mull, D.L. "Freedom and Judgement: The Antimony of Action in *The Portrait of a Lady*." *ArQ*, 27: 124-32 (Su 71).

Mulqueen, J.E. "Perfection of a Pattern: The Structure of *The Ambassadors, The Wings of the Dove*, and *The Golden Bowl*." *ArQ*, 27: 133-42 (Su 71).

Munson, Gorham. "The Real Thing: A Parable for Writers of Fiction." *UKCR*, 16: 261-4 (Su 50).

Murray, D.M. "Candy Christian as a Pop-Art Daisy Miller." *JPC*, 5: 340-8 (1971).

Namekata, Akio. "Some Notes on *The Spoils of Poynton*." *SELit*, Eng no: 19-35 (1970).

Nelson, Carl. "J's Social Criticism: The Voice of the Ringmaster in *The Awkward Age*." *ArQ*, 29: 151-68 (1973).

Netherby, Wallace. "Tragedy of Errors: A Note on *The Bostonians*." *Coranto*, 8: 34-41 (#2 72).

Nettels, Elsa. "Action and Point of View in *Roderick Hudson*." *ES*, 53: 238-47 (Je 72).

———. "*The Ambassadors* and the Sense of the Past." *MLQ*, 31: 220-35 (Je 70).

———. "J and Conrad on the Art of Fiction." *TSLL*, 14: 529-43 (Fa 72).

———. "*The Portrait of a Lady* and the Gothic Romance." *SAB*, 39: 73-82 (N 74).

———. "The Scapegoats and Martyrs of HJ." *CLQ*, 10: 413-27 (1974).

———. "Vision and Knowledge in *The Ambassadors*." *ELT*, 18: 181-93 (1975).

Newlin, P.A. "The Development of *Roderick Hudson*: An Evaluation." *ArQ*, 27: 101-23 (Su 71).

Niall, Brenda. "Prufrock in Brownstone: Edith Wharton's *The Age of Innocence*." *SoRA*, 4: 203-14 (1971).

Nicholas, C.A. "A Second Glance at HJ's 'The Death of the Lion.'" *SSF*, 9: 143-6 (1972).

Nicoloff, P.L. "At the Bottom of Things in HJ's 'Louisa Pallant.'" *SSF*, 7: 409-20 (Su 70).

Niemtzow, Annette. "Marriage and the New Woman in *The Portrait of a Lady*." *AL*, 47: 377-95 (N 75).

Norton, Rictor. "*The Turn of the Screw*: Coincidentia Oppositorum." *AI*, 28: 373-90 (Wi 71).

Nowell-Smith, Simon. "First Editions, English and American." *Lib*, 21: 68 (Mr 66).

———. "Texts of *The Portrait of a Lady*, 1881-1882: The Bibliographical Evidence." *PBSA*, 63: 304-10 (4Q 69).

Offen, Susan. "Isabel Archer: An Analysis of Her Fate." *Hunter Col Stud*, 2: 41-50 (1964).

Page, Philip. "The Curious Narration of *The Bostonians*." *AL*, 46: 374-82 (N 74).

Parrill, A.S. "Portraits of Ladies." *TSL*, 20: 92-9 (Ag 75).

Patrick, M.D. "HJ's Literary Criticism." *IllQ*, 35: 20-33 (D 72).

Patterson, David. "J and Jewett." *CLQ*, 3: 152 (F 53).

Pauly, T.H. "HJ and the Travel Sketch: The Artistry of *Italian Hours*." *CentR*, 19: 108-20 (Sp 75).

Pearce, Brian. "Perpetuated Misprints." *TLS*, 4 Je 70, p. 613.

Pearce, Howard. "HJ's Pastoral Fallacy." *PMLA*, 90: 834-47 (O 75).

———. "Witchcraft Imagery and Allusion in J's *Bostonians*." *StN*, 6: 236-47 (Su 74).

Pécnik, B. "HJ." *Republika*, 8: 329-30 (My 52).

Pendleton, J.D. "The J Brothers and 'The Real Thing': A Study in Pragmatic Reality." *SAB*, 38: 3-10 (N 73).

Perloff, Marjorie. "Cinderella Becomes the Wicked Stepmother: *The Portrait of a Lady* as Ironic Fairy Tale." *NCF*, 23: 413-33 (Mr 69).

Peterson, W.S. "HJ on *Jane Eyre*." *TLS*, 30 Jl 71, pp. 919-20.

Piccinato, Stefania. "*The Wings of the Dove*: Dal progetta alla forma." *SA*, 15: 131-68 (1969).

Pickering, S.F. "The Sources of 'The Author of Beltraffio.'" *ArQ*, 29: 177-90 (1973).

Piscapia, Biancamaria. "George Eliot e HJ." *SA*, 13: 235-80 (1967).

Pizer, Donald. "Harold J. Kolb, Jr.'s Study of American Realism as a Literary Form." *Genre*, 3: 376-8 (1970).

Podhoretz, Norman. "A Minor Cultural Event." *Commentary*, 53: 7-10 (1972).

Poirier, Richard. "What Is English Studies, and If You Know What That Is, What is English Literature?" *PR*, 37: 41-58 (1970).

Pollin, B.R. "Poe and HJ: A Changing Relationship." *YES*, 3: 232-42 (1973).

Popkin, Henry. "Pretender to the Drama." *Theatre Arts*, 33: 32-5, 91 (1950).

Porat, Tsfira. "Ha'aman Ve-ha-omenet." *Mooz*, 33: 240-6 (1971).

Pound, Ezra. "The Notes to 'The Ivory Tower.'" *Little R*, 5: 62-4 (Ag 18).

———. "Provincialism the Enemy." *New Age*, 22: 269-309 (1917).

Powers, L.H. "J's Debt to Alphonse Daudet." *CL*, 24: 150-62 (Sp 72).

Pritchett, V.S. "The Traveller Returns." *NSt*, 21 F 69, pp. 259-60.

Purdy, S.B. "Conversation and Awareness in HJ's 'A Round of Visits.'" *SSF*, 6: 421-32 (Su 69).

———. "HJ and the Mot Juste." *WSL*, 6: 118-25 (1969).

———. "HJ and the Sacred Thrill." *PQ*, 48: 247-62 (Ap 69).

———. "HJ, Gustave Flaubert, and the Ideal Style." *Lang&S*, 3: 163-84 (Su 70).

———. "HJ's Abysses: A Semantic Note." *ES*, 51: 424-33 (O 70).

Purton, Valerie. "J's 'The Turn of the Screw.'" *Expl*, 34: 24 (N 75).

Putt, S.G. "HJ and Dickens." *TLS*, 19 F 71, p. 213; 12 Mr 71, p. 296; 26 Mr 71, p. 352.

———. "HJ Haggles Over Terms for 'Guy Domville.'" *TLS*, 11 Ja 74, pp. 35-6.

Rahv, Philip. "Digging J." *NYRB*, 6 Ap 72, pp. 37-8.

———. "HJ and His Cult." *NYRB*, 10 F 72, pp. 18-22.

Raleigh, J.H. "The Novel and the City: England and America in the Nineteenth Century." *VS*, 11: 291-328 (1968).

Ramsey, Roger. "The Available and the Unavailable 'I': Conrad and J." *ELT*, 14: 137-45 (1971).

Randall, J.H. "Romeo and Juliet in the New World: A Study in J, Wharton, and Fitzgerald: 'Fay ce que vouldras!'" *Costerus*, 8: 109-75 (1973).

Rao, A.R. "Gleams and Glooms: A Reading of *The Turn of the Screw*." *OJES*, 8: 1-9 (1971).

Ray, Laura. "Girlhood in the English Novel." *Genre*, 8: 86-106 (1975).

Recchia, Edward. "J's 'The Figure in the Carpet': The Quality of Fictional Experience." *SSF*, 10: 357-65 (Fa 73).

Reed, K.T. "HJ, Andrew Marvell, and *The Aspern Papers*." *NDEJ*, 6: 24-8 (1970).

Reynolds, Larry, "HJ's New Christopher Newman." *StN*, 5: 457-68 (Wi 73).

Richardson, R.D. "McLuhan, Emerson, and HJ." *WHR*, 22: 235-42 (Su 68).

Richmond, I.J. "HJ and the Comedy of Love: *The Golden Bowl*." *Erasmus R*, 1: 47-62 (1971).

Ricdcl, D.C "Ate a ultima espiral." *MGSL*, 23 F 74, pp. 2-3.

Rimmon, Shlomith. "Barthes' 'Hermeneutic Code' and HJ's Literary Dectective: Plot-composition in 'The Figure in the Carpet.'" *HUSL*, 1: 183-207 (Au 73).

Robson, W.W. "HJ's The Tragic Muse." *Mandrake*, 2: 281-95 (Au-Wi 54-55).

Rodgers, P.C. "Motive, Agency, and Act in J's *The Aspern Papers*." *SAQ*, 73: 377-87 (Su 74).

Rodker, John. "The Notes on Novelists." *Little R*, 5: 53-6 (Ag 18).

Rose, Shirley. "Waymarsh's 'Somber Glow' and *der Fliegende Holländer*." *AL*, 45: 438-41 (N 73).

Roselli, D.N. "Max Beerbohm's Unpublished Parody of HJ." *RES*, 22: 61-3 (Fa 71).

Rosenbaum, S.P., and Brian Birch. "The Editions of *The Ambassadors*." *Lib*, 21: 248-52 (S 66).

Ross, M.L. "HJ's 'Half-Man': The Legacy of Browning in 'The Madonna of the Future.'" *Browning Inst Stud*, 2: 25-42 (1974).

Rowe, J.C. "The Symbolization of Milly Theale: HJ's *The Wings of the Dove*." *ELH*, 40: 131-64 (Sp 73).

Ruggiero, C.C. "HJ as a Critic: Some Early French Influence." *RLMC*, 26: 285-306 (1973).

Ruthrof, H.G. "A Note on HJ's Psychological Realism and the Concept of Brevity." *SSF*, 12: 369-74 (Fa 75).

Sabiston, E. "The Prison of Womanhood." *CL*, 25: 336-51 (1973).

Sackville-West, Edward. "The Code of Ladyhood: HJ's Portrait of a Lady." *New Statesman & Nation*, 25: 259 (17 Ap 43).

Salzberg, Joel. "The Gothic Hero in Transcendental Quest: Poe's 'Ligeia' and J's 'The Beast in the Jungle.'" *ESQ*, 18: 108-14 (2Q 72).

———. "Love, Identity, and Death: J's *The Princess Casamassima* Reconsidered." *BRMMLA*, 26: 127-35 (Wi 72).

Samuels, C.T. "At the Bottom of the Fount." *Novel*, 2: 46-54 (Fa 68).

Sasaki, Miyoko. "HJ ni Mirareru Aku e no Ichi Kosatsu." *Oberon*, 34: 72-80 (1971).

Schecter, Harold. "The Unpardonable Sin in *Washington Square*." *SSF*, 10: 137-41 (Sp 73).

Scherting, John. "*Roderick Hudson*: A Re-evaluation." *ArQ*, 25: 101-19 (Su 69).

Schneider, D.J. "The Divided Self in the Fiction of HJ." *PMLA*, 90: 447-60 (My 75).

———. "The 'Full Ironic Truth' in *The Spoils of Poynton*." *ConnR*, 2: 50-66 (1969).

———. "The Theme of Freedom in J's *The Tragic Muse*." *ConnR*, 7: 5-15 (#2 74).

Schrero, E.M. "The Narrator's Palace of Thought in *The Sacred Fount*." *MP*, 68: 269-88 (F 71).

Schuhmann, Kuno. "Ethik und Aesthetik in Spätwerk von HJ." *JA*, 15: 77-87 (1970).

Schultz, Elizabeth. "*The Bostonians*: The Contagion of romantic Illusion." *Genre*, 4: 45-59 (Mr 71).

Sebouhian, George. "The Transcendental Imagination of Merton Densher." *MLS* 5: 35-45 (#2 75).

Secor, Robert. "Christopher Newman: How Innocent is J's American?" *SAF*, 1: 141-53 (Au 73).

Senanu, K.E. "Anton Chekhov and HJ." *ISE*, 2: 182-97 (1970).

Shahane, V.A. "Formative Influences on E.M. Forster: HJ—A Study in Ambivalence." *OJES*, 1: 39-53 (1961).

Shankovsky, Battilana. "Sei personaggi in cerca di nome." *AV*, 10: 217-30 (1972).

Shapira, Morris. "The Artist and the Artistic." *CaR*, 78: 711-2 (15 Je 57).

Sharp, R.L. "Stevenson and J's Childhood." *NCF*, 8: 236-7 (D 53).

Shaw, Sharon. "Gertrude Stein and HJ: The Difference Between Accidence and Coincidence." *Pembroke Mag*, 5: 95-101 (1974).

Sheldon, P.J. "Jamesian Gothicism: The Haunted Castle of the Mind." *SLitI*, 7: 121-34 (Sp 74).

Shinn, T.J. "A Question of Survival: An Analysis of 'The Treacherous Years of HJ.'" *L&S*, 23: 135-48 (1973).

Shitsuu, Iwase. "*The American Scene* and J's Creative Method." *SELit*, 46: 141-52 (Mr 70).

Shriber, Michael. "Cognitive Apparatus in *Daisy Miller*, *The Ambassadors*, and Two Works by Howells: A Comparative Study of the Epistemology of HJ." *Lang&S*, 2: 207-25 (1969).

Shucard, A.R. "Diplomacy in HJ's *The Ambassadors*." *ArQ*, 29: 123-9 (1973).

Shulman, Robert. "HJ and the Modern Comedy of Knowledge." *Criticism*, 10: 41-53 (1968).

Siegel, P.N. "'Miss Jessel': Mirror Image of the Governess." *L&P*, 18: 30-8 (1968).

Simms, L.M. "HJ and the Negro Question." *AN&Q*, 10: 127-8 (Ap 72).

Smith, C.R. "*The Lesson of the Master*: An Interpretive Note." *SSF*, 6: 654-8 (Fa 69).

Smith, H.F., and Michael Peinovich. "*The Bostonians*: Creation and Revision." *BNYPL*, 73: 298-308 (Ja-D 69).

Smith, W.F. "Sentence Structure in the Tales of HJ." *Style*, 7: 157-72 (Sp 73).

Snow, Lotus. "'The Prose and the Modesty of the Matter': J's Imagery for the Artist in *Roderick Hudson* and *Tragic Muse*." *MFS*, 12: 61-82 (Sp 66).

Speck, P.S. "A Structural Analysis of HJ's *Roderick Hudson.*" *StN*, 2: 292-304 (Fa 70).

Spilka, Mark. "HJ and Walter Besant: 'The Art of Fiction' Controversy." *Novel*, 6: 101-19 (Wi 73).

Stafford, W.T. "'Blighted Houses and Blighted Childhood': J' Teacherous Years." *VQR*, 45: 526-30 (Su 69).

———. "An 'Easy Ride' for HJ; or, Is Captain America Christopher Newman (?)—The Master and Pop Kultur, a Note from the Midwest." *JPC*, 8: 320-7 (1974).

———. "A Whale, an Heiress, and a Southern Demigod: Three Symbolic Americas." *Col Lit*, 1: 100-12 (1974).

Stanculescu, Liana. "HJ's Use of Metaphor in *The Golden Bowl.*" *AUB-LUC*, 22: 117-31 (1973).

Stanford, Derek. "A Larger Latitude: Three Themes in the 'Nineties Short Story." *ConR*, 210: 96-104 (F 68).

Stanford, D.E. "A Prefatory Note." *SoR*, 7: 3-5 (Ja 71).

Stein, A.F. "The Beast in 'The Jolly Corner': Spencer Byrdon's Ironic Rebirth." *SSF*, 11: 61-6 (Wi 74).

———. "The Hack's Progress: A Reading of J's 'The Velvet Glove.'" *EL*, 1: 219-26 (Fa 74).

Stein, W.B. "The Method at the Heart of Madness: *The Spoils of Poynton.*" *MFS*, 14: 187-202 (Su 68).

———. "*The Sacred Fount* and British Aestheticism: The Artist as Clown and Pornographer." *ArQ*, 27: 161-73 (Sp 71).

———. "*The Sacred Fount*: The Poetics of Nothing." *Criticism*, 14: 373-89 (Fa 72). (Fa 72).

Stephens, R.O., and James Ellis. "Hemingway, Fitzgerald, and the Riddle of 'Henry's Bicycle.'" *ELN*, 5: 46-9 (S 67).

Sterner, D.W. "HJ and the Idea of Culture in 'The American Scene.'" *ModA*, 18: 283-90 (Su 74).

Stevenson, Elizabeth. "Something about Biography." *EUQ*, 17: 129-32 (1961).

Stimpson, Catharine. "The Case of Miss Joan Didion." *Ms.*, 1: 36-41 (Ja 73).

Stoehr, Taylor. "Alexander Herzen's *My Past and Thoughts.*" *SoRA*, 3: 168-79 (1968).

———. "Words and Deeds in *The Princess Casamassima.*" *ELH*, 37: 95-135 (Mr 70).

Stone, Edward. "HJ's First Novel." *BPLQ*, 2: 3-7 (Ap 50).

Stone, W.B. "On the Background of J's 'In the Cage.'" *ALR*, 6: 243-7 (Su 73).

———. "Towards a Definition of Realism." *Centrum*, 1: 47-60 (1973).

Strandberg, V.H. "Isabel Archer's Identity Crisis: The Two Portraits of a Lady." *UR*, 34: 283-90 (Je 68).

Strout, Cusing. "HJ and the International Theme Today." *SA*, 13: 281-97 (1967).

Stycsyńska, Adela. "'The Papers': J's Satire on the Modern Publicity System." *KN*, 22: 419-36 (1975).

Sullivan, J.J. "HJ and Hippolyte Taine: The Historical and Scientific Methods in Literature." *CLS*, 10: 25-50 (Mr 73).

Summer, Nan, and Nathan Sumner. "A Dickinson-J Parallel." *RSW*, 39: 144-7 (1971).

Szala, Alina. "HJ's *The American* Simplified." *KN*, 16: 61-4 (1969).

Tanner, Tony. "HJ and Henry Adams." *TriQ*, 11: 91-108 (Wi 68).

Tate, Allen. "Three Commentaries: Poe, J, Joyce." *CR*, 58: 5-10 (Wi 50).

*Taylor, Linda. "*The Portrait of a Lady* and the Anglo-American Press: An Annotated Checklist, 1880-1886." *RALS*, 5: 166-98 (Au 75).

Taylor, M.A. "HJ's *American* and American Millionaires." *Litera*, 9: 78-85 (1968).

Terras, Victor. "Turgenev's Aesthetic and Western Realism." *CL*, 22: 19-35 (1970).

Terrie, H.L. "The Varieties of HJ." *SR*, 83: 695-703 (Fa 75).

Thomas, W.B. "The Author's Voice in *The Ambassadors*." *JNT*, 1: 108-21 (My 71).

Thorberg, Raymond. "'Flavien,' 'Tenents,' and *The Portrait of a Lady*." *SAB*, 34: 10-3 (My 69).

———. "*Germaine*, J's *Notebooks*, and *The Wings of the Dove*." *CL*, 22: 254-64 (Su 70).

———. "HJ and the 'New England Conscience.'" *N&Q*, 16: 222-3 (Je 69).

———. "HJ and the Real Thing: 'The Beldonald Hoblein.'" *SHR*, 3: 78-85 (Wi 68).

———. "HJ and the Sense of the Past." *ModA*, 18: 272-82 (Su 74).

Thornton, Lawrence. "Rosamund Lehmann, HJ, and the Temporal Matrix of Fiction." *Virginia Woolf Q*, 1: 66-75 (1973).

Thurber, James. "The Wings of HJ." *NY*, 35: 184-97 (7 N 59).

Tick, Stanley. "HJ's *The American*: Voyons." *StN*, 2: 276-91 (Fa 70).

Tintner, A.R. "Balzac's 'Madame Firmiani' and J's *The Ambassadors*." *CL*, 25: 128-35 (Sp 73).

———. "Balzac's *Two Maries* and J's *The Ambassadors*." *ELN*, 9: 284-7 (Je 72).

———. "The Countess and Scholastica: HJ's 'L'Allegro' and 'Il Penseroso.'" *SSF*, 11: 267-76 (Su 74).

———. "Digging HJ." *NYT*, 6 Ap 72, p. 37.

———. "The Elgin Marbles and Titian's 'Bacchus and Ariadne': A Cluster of Keatsian Associations in HJ." *N&Q*, 20: 250-2 (Jl 73).

———. "Four Recent Books on HJ." *MFS*, 20: 273-7 (1974).

———. "HJ Criticism: A Current Perspective." *ALR*, 7: 155-68 (Sp 74).

———. "HJ and a Watteau Fan." *Apollo*, 148: 488 (1974).

———. "HJ's Salomé and the Arts of the *Fin de Siècle*." *MarkR*, 5: 5-10 (Fa 75).

———. "'The Hermit and the Wild Woman': Edith Wharton's Fictioning of HJ." *JML*, 4: 32-4 (S 74).

———. "The House of Atreus and Mme. de Bellegarde's Crime." *N&Q*, 20: 98-9 (Mr 73).

———. "Hyacinth at the Play: The Play Within the Play as a Novelistic Device in J." *JNT*, 2: 171-85 (1972).

———. "Iconic Analogy in 'The Lesson of the Master.'" *JNT*, 5: 116-27 (1975).

———. "The Influence of Balzac's *L'envers de l'histoire contemporaine* on J's 'The Great Good Place.'" *SSF*, 9: 343-51 (1972).

———. "J's Mock Epic: 'The Velvet Glove,' Edith Wharton, and Other Late Tales." *MFS*, 17: 483-99 (Wi 71-72).

———. "J's Monologue for Ruth Draper and *The Tragic Muse*: A Parody of the 'Usurping Consciousness.'"

———. "Keats and J and *The Princess Casamassima*." *NCF*, 28: 179-93 (S 73).

———. "Maggie's Pagoda: Architectural Follies in *The Golden Bowl*." *MarkR*, 3: 113-5 (1973).

———. "The Metamorphoses of Edith Wharton in HJ's *The Finer Grain*." *TCL*, 21: 355-80 (D 75).

———. "Octave Feuillet: *La petite comtesse* and HJ." *RLC*, 48: 218-32 (1974).

———. "'The Old Things': Balzac's *Le curé de Tours* and J's *The Spoils of Poynton*." *NCF*, 26: 436-55 (1972).

———. "Sargent in the Fiction of HJ." *Apollo*, 2: 128-32 (Ag 75).

———. "Sir Sidney Colvin in *The Golden Bowl*: Mr Crichton Identified." *CLQ*, 10: 428-31 (1974).

Tomlinson, T.B. "An American Strength: J's *The Ambassadors*." *CritR*, 17: 38-58 (1974).

Tompkins, J.P. "'The Beast in the Jungle': An Analysis of J's Late Style." *MFS*, 16: 185-91 (Su 70).

———. "The Redemption of Time in *Notes of a Son and Brother.*" *TSLL*, 14: 681-90 (Wi 73).

Tournadre, C. "Propositions pour une psychologie social de 'The Turn of the Screw.'" *EA*, 22: 259-69 (Jl-S 69).

Travis, M.K. "Hawthorne's 'Egotism' and 'The Jolly Corner.'" *ESQ*, 63: 13-8 (Sp 71).

Tribble, J.L. "Cherbuliez's *Le Roman d'une Honnête Femme*: Another Source of J's *The Portrait of a Lady.*" *AL*, 40: 279-93 (N 68).

Trilling, Lionel. "The Jameses." *TLS*, 20 O 72, p. 1257.

Truss, T.J. "Anti-Christian Myth in J's 'The Tree of Knowledge.'" *UMSE*, 6: 1-4 (1965).

Tuveson, Ernest. "'The Jolly Corner': A Fable of Redemption." *SSF*, 12: 271-80 (Su 75).

———. "*The Turn of the Screw*: A Palimpsest." *SEL*, 12: 783-800 (Au 73).

Tytell, John. "HJ and the Romance." *MarkR*, 5: 1-2 (My 69).

———. "The Jamesian Legacy in *The Good Soldier.*" *StN*, 3: 365-73 (Wi 71).

Unrue, D.H. "HJ's Extraordinary Use of Portraits." *Re: A&L*, 1: 47-53 (#2 75).

Uroff, M.D. "Perception in J's 'The Real Thing.'" *SSF*, 9: 41-6 (1972).

Urnov, M.D. "Uells protiv Dzheimsa. Spor o romane i pisatel'skom masterstve." *VLit*, 7: 92-112 (1966).

Van Aken, Paul. "Crisis en Eenzambeid in de Jeugd (II)." *NVT*, 23: 504-20 (My-Je 70).

Van Cromphout, G. "Artist and Society in HJ." *ES*, 49: 132-40 (Ap 68).

Vanderbilt, Kermit. "Notes Largely Musical on HJ's 'Four Meetings.'" *SR*, 81: 739-52 (Au 73).

Vandermoere, H. "Baroness Münster's Failure." *ES*, 50: 47-57 (F 69).

Vandersee, Charles. "J's 'Pandora': The Mixed Consequences of Revision." *SB*, 21: 93-108 (1968).

Veeder, William. "Strether and the Transcendence of Language." *MP*, 69: 116-32 (N 71).

Vincec, Sister Stephanie. "A Significant Revision in *The Wings of the Dove.*" *RES*, 23: 58-61 (F 72).

Vitoux, Pierre. "Le Recit dans 'The Ambassadors.'" *Poétique*, 24: 460-78 (1975).

Voegelin, Eric. "*The Turn of the Screw.*" *SoR*, 7: 3-48 (Ja 71).

———. "A Letter to Robert B. Heilman." *SoR*, 7: 9-24 (Ja 71).

———. "Postscripts: On Paradise and Revolution." *SoR*, 7: 25-48 (Ja 71).

Von Egmond, Peter. "HJ's Autobiographies: The Growth of a Poet's Mind." *AA*, 3: 109-20 (1974).

Vorpahl, B.M. "HJ and Owen Wister." *PMHB*, 95: 291-338 (Jl 71).

Wagenknecht, Edward. "*The Mark Twain Papers* and *HJ: The Treacherous Years.*" *SNNTS*, 2: 88-98 (1970).

Wagner, James, and Richard Wagner. "*The American.*" *HSL*, 6: 147-58 (#2 74).

Waldron, R.H. "Prefiguration in 'The Beast in the Jungle.'" *SAF*, 1: 101-4 (Sp 73).

Wallace, Ronald. "Comic Form in *The Ambassadors.*" *Genre*, 5: 31-50 (Mr 72).

———. "Gabriel Nash: HJ's Comic Spirit." *NCF*, 28: 220-4 (S 73).

———. "Maggie Verver: Comic Heroine." *Genre*, 6: 404-15 (D 73).

Walt, James. "Stevenson's 'Will O' the Mill' and J's 'The Beast in the Jungle.'" *UES*, 8: 19-25 (1970).

Ward, J.A. "The Ambassadors as a Conversion Experience." *SoR*, 5: 350-74 (Ap 69).

———. "The Ambiguities of HJ." *SR*, 83: 39-60 (Wi 75).

Ward, S.P. "Painting and Europe in *The American.*" *AL*, 46: 533-73 (Ja 75).

Watanabe, Hisoyoshi. "HJ no Koki no Buntai." *EigoS*, 119: 746-7 (1974).

Watson, C.N. "The Comedy of Provincialism: J's 'The Point of View.'" *SHR*, 9: 173-83 (Sp 75).

Weaver, Richard. "The American as a Regenerate Being." *SoR*, 4: 633-46 (Su 68).

Weber, C.J. "Hardy and J." *HLB*, 16:18-25 (Ja 68).

Wegelin, C.A. "HJ and the Treasure of Innocence." *NS*, 9: 12-9 (1973).

Westbrook, Max. "Fiction and Belief." *CRAS*, 3: 63-7 (1972).

White, William. "Unpublished HJ on Whitman." *RES*, 20: 321 (Ag 69).

Wilcox, Thomas. "A Way into *The Aspern Papers*." *EEx*, 3: 5-6 (D 55).

Wilding, Michael. "James Joyce's 'Eveline' and *The Portrait of a Lady*." *ES*, 49: 552-56 (1968).

Wilson, J.D. "The Gospel According to Christopher Newman." *SAF*, 3: 83-8 (Sp 75).

Winner, V.H. "The Artist and the Man in 'The Author of Beltraffio." *PMLA*, 83: 102-8 (Mr 68).

Wise, J.N. "The Floating World of Lambert Strether." *ArlQ*, 2: 80-110 (Su 69).

Wister, F.K. "Caroline Lewis and HJ." *PMHB*, 95: 339-50 (1971).

Wolf, H.R. "The Psychology and Aesthetics of Abandonment in *The Ambassadors*." *L&P*, 21: 133-47 (#3 71).

Wood, Ann "Reconsideration: Daisy Miller." *NRep*, 167: 31-3 (23 D 72).

Woodcock, George. "HJ and the Conspirators." *SR*, 60: 219-29 (Sp 52).

Woodward, R.H. "Punch on Howells and J." *ALR*, 3: 76-7 (1970).

Yeazell, Ruth. "The New 'Arithmetic' of HJ." *Criticism*, 16: 109-19 (Sp 74).

Yu, F.Y. "Andrew Lytle's *A Name for Evil* as a Redaction of *The Turn of the Screw*." *MQR*, 11: 186-90 (1972).

Zimmerman, Everett. "Literary Tradition and 'The Turn of the Screw.'" *SSF*, 7: 634-7 (Fa 70).

Zlotnick, Joan. "Influence or Coincidence: A Comparative Study of 'The Beast in the Jungle' and 'A Painful Case.'" *TSL*, 20: 92-8 (1975).

James, William. Anon. "From the J Family Libraries." *Bancroftiana*, 52: 1-2 (1972).

Barzun, Jacques. "The Jameses." *TLS*, 15 S 72, p. 1060.

Bishop, D.H. "The Carus-J Controversy." *JHI*, 35: 509-20 (Jl-S 74).

Bixler, J.S. "Letters from WJ to Theodule A. Ribot." *CLQ*, 1: 153-61 (1945).

Blackwood, R.T. "WJ and Walt Whitman." *WWR*, 21: 78-9 (Je 75).

Brown, W.R. "WJ and the Language of Personal Literature." *Style*, 5: 151-63 (1971).

Carlsson, P.A. "Jung and J on the Typology of World Views." *JGE*, 25: 113-9 (Jl 73).

Chesnick, Eugene. "WJ: Fictions and Beliefs." *SAQ*, 73: 236-46 (Sp 74).

Curtin, W.M. "Willa Cather and *The Varieties of Religious Experience*." *Renascence*, 27: 115-23 (Sp 75).

De Aloysio, Francesco. "Empirismo radicale, orientamenti spiritualistici e mondo della persona di WJ." *Trimestre*, 5: 227-54 (1971).

Edel, Leon. "The Jameses." *TLS*, 13 O 72, pp. 1226-7; 3 N 72, p. 1342.

Ferm, D.W. "WJ: Moralism, The Will to Believe, and Theism." *RiL*, 41: 349-61 (Fa 72).

Franklin, Phyllis. "The Influence of WJ on Robert Herrick's Early Fiction." *ALR*, 7: 395-403 (Au 74).

Hampshire, Stuart. "A Son and Brother." *NYRB*, 8: 3-4 (21 Je 67).

Hellman, Geoffrey. "Another J." *TLS*, 6 Je 68, p. 597.

Hirsch, J.C. "The Imagery of Dedication in Robert Lowell's *For the Union Dead*." *JAmSt*, 6: 201-5 (Ag 72).

Hook, Sydney. "WJ and George Santayana." *ICarbS*, 1: 34-9 (1973).

Hull, B.O. "*Henderson The Rain King* and WJ." *Criticism*, 13: 402-14 (Fa 71).

Johnson, Ellwood. "WJ and the Art of Fiction." *JAAC*, 30: 285-96 (Sp 72).

Larrabee, H.A. "The Fourth WJ." *CLQ*, 9: 1-34 (Mr 70).

Lawn, Beverly. "From Temple to Streets: The Style of Pragmatism." *NEQ*, 45: 526-40 (D 72).

Marcell, D.W. "John Fiske, Chauncey Wright, and W.J.: A Dialogue of Progress." *JAH*, 56: 802-18 (Mr 70).

Meyers, R.G. "Meaning and Metaphysics in J." *PPR*, 31: 369-80 (1971).

Pendleton, J.D. "The J Brothers and 'The Real Thing': A Study in Pragmatic Reality." *SAB*, 38: 3-10 (N 73).

Peterson, Margaret. "*Harmonium* and WJ." *SoR*, 7: 658-82 (Jl 71).

Phillips, D.C. "J, Dewey, and the Reflex Arc." *JHI*, 555-68 (1971).

Schirmer, D.B. "WJ and the New Age." *Sci&Soc*, 33: 434-45 (Wi 69).

Scott, F.J.D. "WJ and Stanford University." *San Jose Stud*, 1: 1-23, 28-44 (1975).

Sears, J.F. "WJ, Henri Bergson, and the Poetics of Robert Frost." *NEQ*, 48: 341-61 (S 75).

Shields, Allan. "On a Certain Blindness in WJ—and Others." *JAAC*, 27: 27-34 (Fa 68).

Smith, J.E. "WJ as Philosophical Psychologist." *Midway*, 8: 3-19 (1968).

Strout, Cushing. "*All the King's Men* and the Shadow of WJ." *SoR*, 6: 920-34 (Au 70).

―――. "The Pluralistic Identity of WJ: A Psycho-historical Reading of *The Varieties of Religious Experience*." *AQ*, 23: 135-52 (My 71).

Strug, Cordell. "Seraph, Snake, and Saint: The Subconscious Mind in J's *Varieties*." *JAAR*, 42: 505-15 (1974).

Suarez-Galban, Eugenio. "Torees Villarroel y los Yo empiricos de WJ." *RomN*, 15: 274-7 (1973).

Tanner, J.T.F. "Walt Whitman and WJ." *Calamus*, 2: 6-23 (1970).

Tibbetts, Paul. "WJ and the Doctrine of 'Pure Experience.'" *UDR*, 8: 43-58 (1971).

Trilling, Lionel. "The Jameses." *TLS*, 20 O 72, p. 1257.

Ward, J.A. "*The Ambassadors* as a Conversion Experience." *SoR*, 5: 350-74 (Ap 69).

Jarrell, Randall. Anon. "Desperate Dreams." *TLS*, 31 Mr 72, p. 360.

―――. "A Poet of the Age: RJ Papers Acquired." *BNYPL*, 75: 173-4 (1971).

Adams, C.M. "A Bibliographical Excursion with Some Biographical Footnotes on RJ." *BB*, 28: 79-81 (J-S 71).

Atlas, James. "RJ." *APR*, 4: 26-8 (#1 75).

Buckloh, P.G. "Das Verhaltnis der amerikanischen Dichter zum Staatt, dargestellt an Robert Frosts 'The Gift Outright' und RJs 'The Death of the Ball Turret Gunner.'" *JA*, 13: 205-14 (1968).

Cowley, Malcolm. "Poets as Reviewers." *NRep*, 104: 281-2 (24 F 41).

Dawson, L.M. "J's 'The Death of the Ball Turret Gunner.'" *Expl*, 31: 29 (D 72).

Dickey, James. "Orientations." *ASch*, 34: 646-58 (Au 65).

Donahue, Jane. "'Trading Another's Sorrows for Our Own': The Poetry of RJ." *LWU*, 2: 258-67 (1969).

Dunn, Douglas. "An Affable Misery: On RJ." *Enc*, 39: 42-8 (O 72).

Ferguson, F.C. "RJ and the Flotations of Voice." *GaR*, 28: 423-54 (Fa 74).

Flint, R.W. "Poetry and the Age." *PR*, 20: 702-8 (N 53).

Fowler, Russell. "RJ's 'Eland': A Key to Motive and Technique in His Poetry." *IowaR*, 5: 113-26 (Sp 74).

*Gillikin, D.J. "A Checklist of Criticism on RJ, 1941-1970—With an Introduction and a List of His Major Works." *BNYPL*, 75: 176-94 (Ap 71).

Graham, W.S., and Hayden Carruth. "J's *Losses*: A Controversy." *Poetry*, 72: 302-11 (S48).

Holmes, Mary. "Metamorphosis and Myth in Modern Art." *Perspective*, 1: 78-86 (Wi 48).

Jarrell, M. von S. "RJ: A Reminiscence." *ColF*, 2: 24-31 (Su 73).

Mazzaro, Jerome. "Arnoldian Echoes in the Poetry of RJ." *WHR*, 23: 314-8 (Au 69).

———. "Between Two Worlds: The Post Modernism of RJ." *Salmagundi*, 17: 92-113 (1971).

Moore, Marianne. "RJ."*Atl*, 220: 96-8 (S 67).

Nemerov, Howard. "J's *Complete Poems.*" *KR*, 31:570-3 (1969).

———. "What Will Suffice?" *Salmagundi*, 28: 90-103 (1975).

Nitchie, G.W. "RJ: A Stand-in's View." *SoR*, 9: 883-94 (Au 73).

Quinn, Sister M.B. "RJ: Landscapes of Life and *Life.*" *Shen*, 20: 49-78 (Wi 69).

———. "Thematic Imagery in the Poetry of RJ." *SoR*, 5: 1226-35 (Au 69).

Richards, B.F. "J's 'Seele im Raum.'" *Expl*, 33: 22 (N 74).

Smith, Marcus. "Report to RJ." *SHR*, 3: 124 (Sp 69).

Squires, Radcliffe. "The Discrete Poems of RJ." *SoR*, 9: 745-7 (Jl 73).

Tokunaga, Yozo. "RJ no Whitman-ron." *EigoS*, special no: 112-4 (1969).

Weisberg, Robert. "RJ: The Integrity of His Poetry." *CentR*, 17: 199-213 (Su 73).

Wilson, Emily. "J and Reid Celebrate a Woman: A Comparative Explication." *SCR*, 3: 45-8 (1970).

Jeffers, Robinson. Anon. "J Research: Masters' Theses, Occidental College Library." *RJN*, 25: 4-8 (F 70).

———. "News and Notes." *RJN*, 24: 1-3 (S 69); 25: 1-3 (F 70); 26: 1-8 (Jl 70); 27: 1-5 (N 70).

———. "RJ in Foreign Translation." *RJN*, 24: 3-4 (S 69).

Alexander, J.R. "Conflict in the Narrative Poetry of RJ." *SR*, 80: 85-99 (Wi 72).

Bednar, Kamil. "J in Czechoslovakia." *RJN*, 27: 8-9 (N 70).

Allred, Jerry. "RJ and the Problem of Western Violence." *PosS*, 3: 6-13 (O 72).

Bluestone, Stephen. "RJ and the Prophets: On The Book of Jeremiah and 'The Inhumanist.'" *NCLit*, 5: 2-3 (S 75).

Boyers, Robert. "A Sovereign Voice: The Poetry of RJ." *SR*, 77: 487-507 (Jl-S 69).

Brophy, Robert. "The Apocalyptic Dimension of J's Narratives." *RJN*, 32: 4-7 (Jl 72).

———. "Astrological Note." *RJN*, 36: 7-8 (O 73).

———. "Biblical Resonances in Js' 'Signpost.'" *RJN*, 39: 10-2 (Jl 74).

———. "Bibliographical and Psychoanalytic Criticism: A Response." *RJN*, 37: 4-5 (D 73).

———. "'Crumbs or the Loaf': An Interpretation." *RJN*, 31: 8-9 (My 72).

———. "Distancing in J's Lyrics." *RJN*, 38: 5-6 (Ap 74).

———. "J Manuscripts: University of North Carolina Library." *RJN*, 38: 17 (Ap 74).

———. "J Scholarly Materials." *RJN*, 33: 11-4 (S 72); 34: 7-9 (Ja 73);37: 11-2 (Ap 73); 39: 21-6 (Jl 74).

———. "J's 'Cawdor' and the Hippolytus Story." *WAL*, 7: 171-8 (Fa 72).

———. "J's 'Medea': A Dionysian Retribution." *RJN*, 33: 4-6 (S 72).

———. "J Research: Dissertations, A Summary and Reflection." *RJN*, 24: 4-9 (S 69).

———. "J Scholarly Resources: A Proposed Series." *RJN*, 33: 11-4 (S 72).

———. "J's 'Second Best': A Vocational Crisis." *RJN*, 40: 7-9 (N 74).

———. "Kirwan on J." *RJN*, 39: 6-8 (Jl 74).

———. "Landscape as Genesis and Analogue in J's Narratives." *RJN*, 29: 11-6 (Ag 71).

———. "The Mabel Dodge Luhan Correspondence: Library, University of California, Berkeley." *RJN*, 34: 8-9 (F 73).

———. "'Night': A Prayerful Reconciliation." *RJN*, 37: 6-7 (D 73).

———. "The Ritual Ending of 'Roan Stallion.'" *RJN*, 34: 11-5 (F 73).

————. "'Salmon-Fishing': The Ritual Gesture at the Heart of Things." *RJN*, 35: 6 (1973).

————. "The Summer J Festival." *RJN*, 30: 1-5 (Ja 72).

————. "'Tamar,' 'The Cenci,' and Incest." *AL*, 42: 241-4 (My 70).

————. "A Textual Note on RJ' *The Beginning and the End.*" *PBSA*, 60: 344-8 (Jl-S 66).

————. "Topography and the Narrative Scene." *RJN*, 30: 13-4 (Ja 72).

————. "The Tor House Library: J's Books." *RJN*, 23: 4-11 (Ap 69).

————. "T.S. Eliot and RJ: A Note." *RJN*, 38: 4-5 (Ap 74).

————. "Una J—Blanche Matthias Correspondence." *RJN*, 35: 7-9 (1973).

Cerwin, Herbert. "Notes on RJ." *RJN*, 33: 3-4 (S 72).

Coffin, A.B. "RJ: Inhuman and the Apocalypse." *RJN*, 30: 6 (Ja 72).

Cronon, William. "RJ Collections: Stanford University." *RJN*, 42: 15-6 (Ag 75).

Dougherty, David. "Themes in J and James Wright." *RJN*, 33: 7-11 (S 72).

————. "Tragedy, Inhumanism, and RJ." *RJN*, 30: 6-7 (Ja 72).

Eberhart, Richard. "A Tribute and Appreciation." *RJN*, 27: 6-7 (N 70).

Everson, William. "Astrological Note (J as Pisces Ascendant)." *RJN*, 36: 7-8 (O 73).

————. "Continent's End (The Collected Poems of RJ) : A Proposal." *RJN*, 31: 10-5 (My 72).

Friar, Kimon. "On Translation." *CLS*, 8: 197-213 (S 71).

Garland, Gary. "Mann and J: Myth Definition and Subsequent Technique." *RJN*, 37: 7-11 (D 73).

Griffith, B.W. "'RJ' 'The Bloody Sire' and Stephen Crane's 'War is King.' " *NCLit*, 3: 14-5 (Ja 73).

Hartshorne, Charles, and William Resse. "J: Tragic Pantheism." *RJN*, 39: 9-10 (Jl 74).

Haury, B.B. "The Influence of RJ' 'Tamar' on *Absalom, Absalom!*" *MissQ*, 25: 356-8 (1972).

Jeffers, Donnan. "Some Biographical Corrigenda." *RJN*, 35: 4-5 (1973).

————. "Tor House." *RJN*, 42: 6-9 (Ag 75).

Jerome, Judson. "Poetry: How and Why the Language of RJ." *RevL*, 1: 99-105 (1969).

Kafka, Robert. "J's 'Preface' to *Brides of the South Wind.*" *RJN*, 34: 9-11 (F 73).

Karman, James. "A Note on William Hamilton J." *RJN*, 42: 9-11 (Ag 75).

Keller, Karl. "California, Yankees, and the Death of God: Allegory in J's *Roan Stallion.*" *TSLL*, 111-20 (Sp 70).

————. "J's Pace." *RJN*, 32: 7-17 (Jl 72).

Klein, H.A. "Czech Poet, J Translator: Kamil Bednar, A Memoir and a Tribute." *RJN*, 35: 10-9 (My 73).

Krutch, J.W. "RJ." *RJN*, 29: 6-11 (Au 71).

————. "Understanding a Poet." *RJN*, 29: 6-11 (Ag 71).

Le Master, J.R. "Lorca, J, and the Myth of Tamar." *NLauR*, 1: 44-51 (1971).

Lockard, E.N. "A Visit to RJ in 1945." *ELN*, 12: 120-3 (D 74).

Lyman, W.W. "RJ: A Memoir." *RJN*, 34: 19-24 (F 73).

McAllister, Mick. "Meaning and Paradox in J's 'Return' " *RJN*, 42: 10-12 (D 75).

McGinty, Brian. "The View from Hawk's Tower: Poet RJ and the Rugged Coast That Shaped Him." *AmWest*, 10: 4-9 (#6 73).

McHaney, T.L. "J's 'Tamar' and Faulkner's *The Wild Palms.*" *RJN*, 29: 16-8 (Au 71).

————. "RJ' 'Tamar' and *The Sound and the Fury.*" *MissQ*, 22: 261-3 (Su 69).

Macksey, R.A. "The Old Poets." *John Hopkins Mag*, 19: 42-8 (1968).

Mauthe, A.K. "J's Inhumanism and Its Poetic Significance." *RJN*, 26: 8-10 (Jl 70).

————. "The Significance of Point Lobos in *Tamar.*" *RJN*, 25: 8-10 (F 70).

Milosz, Czeslaw. "RJ." *Kult*, 192: 21-4 (O 63).

Miner, Priscilla. "A Note on Literary Influences of *The Alpine Christ*." *RJN*, 40: 3-4 (Ja 74).

Nickerson, Edward. "J's Scholarly Materials: Library of Congress." *RJN*, 40: 17-20 (N 74).

———. "The Return to Rhyme." *RJN*, 39: 12-21 (Jl 74).

———. "RJ and the Paeon." *WAL*, 10: 189-93 (N 75).

———. "The Una J Correspondence at Yale." *RJN*, 41: 6-10 (Mr 75).

———. "An Unpublished Poem of RJ." *YULG*, 49: 231-3 (O 74).

Nolte, W.H. "RJ as Didactic Poet." *VQR*, 42: 257-71 (Sp 66).

Pascoe, S.E. " 'Birth-Dues': An Explication." *RJN*, 38: 6-10 (Ap 74).

Powell, L.C. "Melba Berry Bennet." *RJN*, 23: 1 (Ap 69).

———. "RJ." *NYT*, 6 O 68, pp. 2, 26.

Ritchie, Ward. "Theodore Lilienthal, RJ and the Quercus Press." *RJN*, 34: 15-9 (F 73).

Scott, R.I. "Three Unpublished Poems of RJ." *RJN*, 41: 11-8 (My 75).

———. "The World-as-God-as-Net in J's Unpublished Poem 'Oh Happy Astronomer.'" *RJN*, 38: 10-7 (Ap 74).

Seubert, E.E. "RJ: Poet for an Age of Violence." *Northwest Missouri Teachers Col Stud*, 7: 3-28 (Je 43).

Shaw, Susan. "Elements of Eastern Philosophy in J." *RJN*, 36: 8-11 (O 73).

Sister Mary Norma. "The Many Faces of Medea." *CBul*, 45: 17-20 (D 68).

Van Dam, Denis. "Greek Shadows on the Monterey Coast: Environment in RJ's Poetry." *RJN*, 40: 9-17 (N 74).

Van Doren, Mark, James Rorty, and Richard Eberhart. "Three Memoirs of RJ." *RJN*, 27: 3-7 (Ja 70).

White, William. "J and Whitman Briefly." *Serif*, 6: 32-3 (1969).

*———. "RJ: A Checklist, 1959-1965." *Serif*, 3: 36-9 (Je 66).

———. "RJ on a Postage Stamp." *ABC*, 24: 30 (1974).

———. "RJ's 'The Beginning and the End': Another Error." *PBSA*, 61: 126 (2Q 67).

———, and Robert Brophy. "*Not Man Apart*." *RJN*, 25: 3-4 (F 70).

Jefferson, Thomas. Beloff, Max. "A 'Founding Father': The Sally Hemings Affair." *Enc*, 43: 52-6 (S 74).

Binger, Carl. "Conflicts in the Life of T.J." *Am J Psychiatry*, 125: 1098-104 (F 69).

Boyd, Julian. "J's Expression of the American Mind." *VQR*, 50: 538-62 (Au 74).

Brent, Robert. "Puncturing Some Jeffersonian Mythology." *SoQ*, 6: 175-90 (Ja 68).

Clark, Kenneth. "TJ and the Italian Renaissance." *VQR*, 48: 519-31 (Fa 72).

Cohen, William. "TJ and the Problem of Slavery." *JAH*, 56: 503-27 (D 69).

Cooke, J.M. "J on Liberty." *JHI*, 34: 563-76 (O-D 73).

Cox, R.M. "TJ and Spanish: 'To Every Inhabitant Who Means to Look Beyond the Limits of His Farm.'" *RomN*, 14: 116-21 (Au 72).

Farrison, W.E. "Clotel, TJ, and Sally Hemings." *CLAJ*, 17: 147-74 (D 73).

Fetter, F.W. "The Revision of the Declaration of Independence in 1941." *WMQ*, 31: 133-8 (J 74).

Gittleman, Edwin. "J's 'Slave Narrative': The Declaration of Independence as a Literary Text." *EAL*, 8: 239-46 (Wi 74).

Goff, F.R. "J the Book Collector." *QJLC*, 29: 32-47 (1972).

Hay, R.P. "The Glorious Departure of the American Patriarchs: Contemporary Reactions to the Deaths of J and Adams." *JSH*, 35: 543-55 (N 69).

Lane, Lawrence. "An Enlightened Controversy—J and Buffon." *EnE*, 3: 37-40 (#1 72).

Malone, Dumas. "Mr. J's Private Life." *PAAS*, 84: 65-72 (17 Ap 74).

———. "Presidential Leadership and National Unity: The Jeffersonian Example." *JSH*, 35: 3-17 (F 69).

Martin, J.S. "Rhetoric, Society, and Literature in the Age of J." *MASJ*, 9: 77-90 (Sp 68).

Mirkin, H.G. "Rebellion, Revolution and the Constitution: TJ's Theory of Civil Disobedience." *AmS*, 13: 61-74 (1972).

Robbins, J.C. "J and the Press: The Resolution of an Antimony." *JQ*, 48: 421-30, 465 (Au 71).

Sheehan, B.W. "Paradise and the Noble Savage in Jeffersonian Thought." *WMQ*, 26: 327-59 (Jl 69).

Simpson, L.P. "Boston Ice and Letters in the Age of J." *MASJ*, 9: 58-76 (Sp 68).

Skallerup, H.R. "'For His Excellency TJ, Esq.': The Tale of a Wandering Book." *QJLC*, 31: 116-1 (#2 74).

Stafford, J.S. "The Power of Sympathy." *MASJ*, 9: 52-7 (Sp 68).

Sutton, R.P. "Nostalgia, Pessimism, and Malaise: The Doomed Aristocrat in Late-Jeffersonian Virginia." *VMHB*, 76: 41-55 (Ja 68).

Weyant, R.G. "Helvetius and J: Studies of Human Nature and Government in the Eighteenth Century." *J Hist Behavioral Sci*, 9: 29-41 (1973).

Jewett, Sarah Orne. Bender, Bert. "To Calm and Uplift 'Against the Dark': SOJ's Lyric Narratives." *CLQ*, 11: 219-29 (Wi 75).

Bishop, Ferman. "The Sense of the Past in SOJ." *UWB*, 41: 3-10 (F 59).

Cary, Richard. "J to Dresel: 33 Letters." *CLQ*, 11: 13-9 (Sp 75).

————. "More Whittier Letters to J." *ESQ*, 58: 132-9 (1Q 70).

————. "The Other Face of J's Coins." *ALR*, 2: 263-70 (Fa 69).

————. "The Rise, Decline, and Rise of SOJ." *CLQ*, 9: 650-63 (Wi 72).

————. "The Sculptor of the Spinster: J' 'Influence' on Cather." *CLQ*, 10: 168-78 (Su 73).

————. "Some Bibliographic Ghosts of SOJ." *CLQ*, 8: 139-45 (S 68).

————. "The Uncollected Short Stories of SOJ." *CLQ*, 9: 385-408 (Fa 71).

    . "Violet Paget to SOJ." *CLQ*, 9: 235-43 (D 70).

————. "Whittier Letters to SOJ." *ESQ*, 50: 11-22 (1Q 68).

————. "'Yours Always Lovingly': SOJ to John Greenleaf Whittier." *EIHC*, 107: 412-50 (1971).

Chase, M.E. "My Novels About Maine." *CLQ*, 6: 14-20 (Mr 62).

Cohen, E.H. "J to Guiney: An Earlier Letter." *CLQ*, 9: 231-2 (D 70).

Cross, Olive. "From *Deephaven* to *Pointed Firs*." *FSUS*, 5: 113-21 (1952).

Dow, G.A. "About the J Letters." *Mirror*, 1: 10-1 (My 62).

*Eichelberger, C.L. "SOJ (1849-1909): A Critical Bibliography of Secondary Comment." *ALR*, 2: 189-262 (Fa 69).

Garnett, Edward. "Books Too Little Known: Miss SOJ's Tales." *A&L*, 65: 40-1 (11 Jl 03).

Georges, J.F. "Mementoes of a Great Lady." *Shoreliner*, nv: 10-5 (S 50).

Hennessey, W.G. "The House of Hamilton." *Shoreliner*, 3: 9-16 (Jl 52).

Hirsch, D.H. "Subdued Meaning in 'A New England Nun.'" *SSF*, 2: 124-36 (Wi 65).

Hollis, C.C. "Letters of SOJ to Anna Laurens Davis." *CLQ*, 8: 97-138 (S 68).

Horn, R.L. "The Power of J's *Deephaven*." *CLQ*, 9: 617-31 (Wi 72).

Howe, Irving. "Cameos from the North Country." *NRep*, 130: 24-5 (17 My 54).

Humma, J.B. "The Art and Meaning of SOJ's 'The Courting of Sister Wisby.'" *SSF*, 10: 85-91 (Wi 73).

James, Henry. "Mr. and Mrs. James T. Fields." *Atl*, 116: 21-31 (Jl 15).

Jobes, K.T. "From Stowe's Eagle Island to J's 'A White Heron.'" *CLQ*, 10: 515-21 (Wi 74).

Levy, B.M. "Mutations in New England Local Color." *NEQ*, 19: 338-58 (S 46).

*Monteiro, George. "Addenda to the Bibliographies of . . . J [and others]." *PBSA*, 69: 172-5 (Ap-Je 75).

More, P.E. "A Writer of New England." *Nation*, 91: 386-7 (27 O 10).

Noyes, S.G. "Mrs. Almira Todd, Herbalist-Conjurer." *CLQ*, 9: 643-9 (D 72).

Parsons, H.V. "*The Tory Lover, Oliver Wiswell*, and *Richard Carvel*." *CLQ*, 9: 220-31 (D 70).

Patterson, David. "James and J." *CLQ*, 3: 152 (F 53).

Pratt, Annis. "Women and Nature in Modern Fiction." *ConL*, 13: 476-90 (Fa 72).

Rhode, R.D. "SOJ and 'The Palpable Present Intimate.'" *CLQ*, 8: 146-55 (S 68).

St. Armand, Barton. "J and Marin: The Inner Vision." *CLQ*, 9: 632-43 (D 72).

Sergeant, E.S. "Idealized New England." *NRep*, 3: 20-1 (8 My 15).

Stern, G.B. "The Perfection Box." *SatR*, 19: 10-1 (8 Ap 39).

Stevenson, C.B. "The Double Consciousness of the Narrator in SOJ's Fiction." *CLQ*, 11: 1-12 (Sp 75).

Stouck, David, "*The Country of the Pointed Firs*: A Pastoral of Innocence." *CLQ*, 9: 213-20 (D 70).

Toth, S.A. "SOJ and Friends: A Community of Interest." *SSF*, 9: 233-41 (1972).

———. "The Value of Age in the Fiction of SOJ." *SSF*, 8: 433-41 (Su 71).

Trafton, B.W.F. "Hamilton House, South Berwick, Maine." *Antiques*, 77: 486-9 (My 60).

VanDerBeets, Richard, and J.K. Bowen. "Miss J, Mrs. Turner, and the Chautauqua Circle." *CLQ*, 9: 233-4 (D 70).

Vella, M.W. "SOJ: A Reading of *The Country of the Pointed Firs*." *ESQ*, 19: 275-82 (4Q 73).

Voelker, P.D. "*The Country of the Pointed Firs*." *CLQ*, 9: 201-13 (D 70).

Weber, C.J. "SOJ's First Story." *NEQ*, 19: 85-90 (Mr 46).

———. "'What's in a Name?'—or in a Signature?" *Manuscripts*, 8: 185 (Sp 56).

Westbrook, Perry. "SOJ." *Down East*, 10: 28-9, 48-52 (O 63).

Willoughby, John. "SOJ and Her Shelter Island." *Confrontation*, 8: 72-86 (Sp 74).

Woodress, James. "SOJ and Willa Cather: Anti-Realists." *EST*, 5: 477-88 (1973).

Johnson, Edward. Bercovitch, Sacvan. "The Historiography of J's *Wonder-Working Providence*." *EIHC*, 104: 138-64 (1968).

Brumm, Ursula. "EJ's *Wonder-Working Providence* and the Puritan Conception of History." *JA*, 14: 140-51 (1969).

Gallagher, E.J. "The Case for the *Wonder-Working Providence*." *BNYPL*, 77: 10-27 (Au 73).

———. "An Overview of EJ's *Wonder-Working Providence*." *EAL*, 5: 30-49 (Wi 71).

———. "*The Wonder-Working Providence* as Spiritual Biography." *EAL*, 10: 75-87 (Sp 75).

Johnson, James Weldon. Amann, C.A. "Three Negro Classics: An Estimate." *NALF*, 4: 113-9 (1970).

Bacote, C.A. "JWJ and Atlanta University." *Phylon*, 32: 333-43 (Wi 71).

Baker, Houston. "A Forgotten Prototype: 'The Autobiography of an Ex-Colored Man' and 'Invisible Man.'" *VQR*, 49: 433-49 (Su 73).

Carroll, R.A. "Black Racial Spirit: An Analysis of JWJ's Critical Perspective." *Phylon*, 32: 344-64 (Wi 71).

Collier, Eugenia. "The Endless Journey of an Ex-Coloured Man." *Phylon*, 32: 365-73 (Wi 71).

Fleming, R.E. "Contemporary Themes in J's *Autobiography of an Ex-Colored Man*." *NALF*, 4: 120-4, 141 (1970).

———. "Irony as a Key to J's *The Autobiography of an Ex-Colored Man.*" *AL*, 43: 83-96 (Mr 71).

Garrett, M.P. "Early Recollections and Structural Irony in *The Autobiography of an Ex-Colored Man.*" *Critique*, 13: 5-14 (1971).

Jackson, Miles. "JWJ." *BlackW*, 19: 32-4 (1970).

Jackson, M.M. "Letters to a Friend: Correspondence from JWJ to George A. Towns." *Phylon*, 29: 182-98 (Su 68).

Kostelanetz, Richard. "The Politics of Passing: The Fiction of JWJ." *NALF*, 3: 22-4, 29 (1969).

Levy, Eugene. "Ragtime and Race Pride: The Career of JWJ." *JPC*, 1: 357-70 (Sp 68).

Logan, R.W. "JWJ and Haiti." *Phylon*, 32: 396-402 (Wi 71).

Long, R.A. "A Weapon of My Song: The Poetry of JWJ." *Phylon*, 32: 374-82 (Wi 71).

Redding, Saunders. "JWJ and the Pastoral Tradition." *MissQ*, 28: 417-22 (Fa 75).

Ross, S.M. "Audience and Irony in J's *The Autobiography of an Ex-Colored Man.*" *CLAJ*, 18: 198-210 (D 74).

Vauthier, Simone. "The Interplay of a Narrative Mode in JWJ's *The Autobiography of an Ex-Colored Man.*" *JA*, 18: 173-81 (1973).

Whalum, W.P. "JWJ's Theories and Performance Practices of Afro-American Folksong." *Phylon*, 32: 383-95 (Wi 71).

Johnson, Samuel. Ellis, J.J. "The Puritan Mind in Transition: The Philosophy of SJ." *WMQ*, 28: 26-45 (Ja 71).

Fiering, N.S. "President SJ and the Circle of Knowledge." *WMQ*, 28: 199-236 (Ap 71).

Gerlach, D.R., and George DeMille. "SJ and the Founding of King's College." *HMPEC*, 44: 335-52 (1975).

Jackson, C.T. "The Orient in Post-Bellum American Thought: Three Pioneer Popularizers." *AQ*, 22: 67-81 (Sp 70).

Johnston, Richard Malcolm. *Bickley, B.R. "RMJ." *ALR*, 8: 293-4 (1975).

Simms, L.M. "RMJ on Rural Life in Middle Georgia." *GHQ*, 58: 181-92 (1974).

Voyles, J.P. "RMJ's Literary Career: An Estimate." *MarkR*, 4: 29-34 (F 74).

Jones, James. Aldridge, J.W. "Twosomes and Threesomes in Gray Paree." *SatR*, 54: 23-6 (13 F 71).

Jones, James. "Hawaiian Recall." *Harpers*, 248: 27-31 (F 74).

Krim, Seymour. "Maverick Head—Kick." *EvR*, 12: 19-20 (Ag 67).

Shepherd, Allen. "'A Deliberately Symbolic Little Novella': JJ's *The Pistol.*" *SDR*, 10: 111-29 (1972).

Vančura, Zdeněk. "Současni američti romanopisci, 2: Poznámka o JJ." *ČMF*, 52: 127-30 (1970).

Viorst, Milton. "JJ and the Phony Intellectuals." *Esquire*, 49: 98-101, 131-2 (F 68).

Jones, John Beauchamp. Bennett, J.Q. "Let's Get Together on J." *Serif*, 8: 32-3 (1971).

Lapides, F.R. "JBJ: A Southern View of Abolitionists." *JRUL*, 33: 63-73 (Je 70).

Jones, Le Roi. (see **Baraka, Imamu Amiri**)

Jong, Erica. Atwood, Margaret. "Half-Lives." *Parnassus*, 2: 98-104 (Sp-Su 74).

Jong, Erica. "Writing a First Novel." *TCL*, 20: 262-9 (O 74).

Josselyn, John. Gura, P.F. "Thoreau and JJ." *NEQ*, 48: 503-18 (D 75).

Judd, Sylvester. Shurr, W.H. "SJ and G.M. Hopkins." *Victorian Poetry*, 11: 337-9 (1973).

Justice, Donald. Gerber, P.L., and R.J. Germmett. "Falling into Place: A Conversation with DJ." *PrS*, 47: 317-24 (1973).

Justice, Donald. "The Effacement of Self." *OhR*, 16: 41-63 (Sp 75).

Kaufman, George S. Harrison, A.C "*Of Thee I Sing*, Baby!" *Players*, 47: 275-9 (1972).

Kazin, Alfred. Douglas G.H. "AK: American Critic." *ColQ*, 23: 203-16 (Au 74).

Dunlap, Bryan. "To Mr. Kazin." *HM*, 235: 55-6 (O 67).

Garaty, J.A. "A Century of American Realism." *AH*, 21: 12-5, 86-90 (1970).

Rubin, L.D. "'Theories of Human Nature': K or Warren?" *SR*, 49: 500-6 (Su 61).

Keeler, Harry Stephen. Cuthbert Jack. "Another Side of HSK." *ArmD*, 7: 101-8 (1974).

Nevins, F.M. "Hick Dick from the Sticks: HSK's Quiribus Brown." *ArmD*,7: 251-2 (1974).

———. "The Wild and Wooly World of HSK." *JPC*, 3: 635-43 (Sp 70); 4: 410-8 (Fa 70); 5: 521-9 (Wi 71); 7: 159-71 (Su 73).

Kelly, Robert. Alpert, Barry. "RK: An Interview." *Vort*, 5: 5-43 (1974).

Davenport, Guy. "K in Time." *Vort*, 5: 163-5 (1974).

Erwin, Mike, and Jed Rasula. "Excerpts from an Interview with RK . . . September 1973." *Vort*, 5: 135-45 (Su 74).

Joris, Pierre. "Entrances: Some Notes on the Work of RK." *Vort*, 2: 92-100 (Su 74).

Wagstaff, A.C. "The Song of What is Here." *Vort*, 5: 148-58 (1974).

Warren, Eugene. "On K's Narrative." *Vort*, 5: 145-8 (1974).

Kelley, William Melvin. Beards, Richard. "Parody as Tribute: WMK's *A Different Drummer* and Faulkner." *SBL*, 5: 25-8 (Wi 74).

Eckley, Grace. "The Awakening of Mr. Afrinnegan." *Obsidian*, 1: 27-41 (1975).

Faulkner, Howard. "The Uses of Tradition: WMK's *A Different Drummer*." *MFS*, 21: 535-42 (Wi 75).

Ingrasci, H.J. "Strategic Retreat or Withdrawal: Deliverance from Racial Oppression in K's *A Different Drummer* and Faulkner's *Go Down Moses*." *SBL*, 6: 1-6 (#3 75).

Jarab, Josef. "The Drop of Patience of the American Negro: WMK, *A Different Drummer* (1959), *A Drop of Patience* (1965)." *PP*, 12: 159-70 (1969).

Klotman, P.R. "An Examination of the Black Confidence Man in Two Black Novels: *The Man Who Cried I Am* and *dem*." *AL*, 44: 569-611 (Ja 73).

———. "The Passive Resistant in *A Different Drummer, Day of Absence, and Many Thousand Gone*." *SBL*, 3: 7-12 (Au 72).

Nadeau, R.J. "Black Jesus: A Study of K's *A Different Drummer*." *SBL*, 2: 13-5 (Su 71).

Schatt, Stanley "You Must Go Home Again: Today's Afro-American Expatriate Writers." *NALF*, 7: 80-2 (1973).

Weyl, D.M. "The Vision of Man in the Novels of WMK." *Critique*, 15: 15-33 (3Q 73).

Kennedy, John Pendleton. Badin, D.A. "La narrativa di JPK." *SA*, 13: 129-68 (1967).

Rose, A.H. "The Image of the Negro in the Pre-Civil-War Novels of JPK and William Gilmore Simms." *JAmSt*, 4: 217-26 (F 71).

Kerouac, Jack. Anon. "American Drama . . . and American Dream." *TLS*, 13 S 74, p. 971.

———. "JK and Neal Cassady." *TransR*, 33-4: 115-25 (Wi 69-70).

Berrigan, Ted. "Interview: JK." *PaR*, 43: 60-105 (Su 68).

Bowering, George. "*On the Road*: & the Indians at the End." *StBr*, 3-4: 191-201 (Fa 69).

Castelli, Ferdinando. "La desolata corsa di JK verso la morte." *CCa*, 122: 34-47 (1971).

Charters, Ann. "Allen Ginsberg and JK, Columbia Undergraduates." *CLC*, 20: 10-7 (N 70).

Clark, Thomas. "The Art of Poetry VIII." *PaR*, 10: 13-55 (Sp 66).

Coyne, John. "Cöopting K." *NatR*, 23: 1246-7 (5 N 71).

Dardess, George. "The Delicate Dynamics of Friendship: A Reconsideration of K's *On the Road*." *AL*, 46: 200-6 (My 74).

———. "The Language of Repose." *Boun2*, 3: 729-45 (1975).

———. "The Logic of Spontaneity." *Boun2*, 3: 729-46 (Sp 75).

Gelfant, B.H "JK." *ConL*, 15: 415-22 (1974).

Ginsberg, Allen. "The Great Remember." *SatR*, 55: 60-3 (D 72).
———. "JK." *Carolina Q*, 26: 92-9 (1974).
Gornick, Vivian. "JK: 'The Night and What it Does to You." *Village Voice*, 14: 27-30 (30 O 69).
Hart, J.E. "Future Hero in Paradise: K's *The Dharma Bums*." *Critique*, 14: 52-62 (3Q 73).
Kerouac, Jack. "Facsimile of Letter from JK on Céline." *PaR*, 8: 136 (Wi-Sp 64).
Kyria, Pierre. "Le Monde Américain." *RdP*, Mr 67, pp. 120-5.
LePellec, Yves. "JK and the American Critics: a Selected Bibliography." *Caliban*, 9: 77-92 (1973).
———. "'Visions of Cody,' ou JK, Voyeur de L'Amerique." *Caliban*, 11: 81-92 (1975).
McClintock, Jack. "This Is How the Ride Ends." *Esquire*, 73: 138-9, 188-9 (Mr 70).
Tytell, John. "The Beat Generation and the Continuing American Revolution." *ASch*, 42: 308-17 (1973).
Vopat, C.G. "JK's *On the Road*: A Re-evaluation." *MwQ*, 14: 385-407 (Su 73).
Woods, Crawford. "Reconsideration: JK." *NRep*, 167: 26-30 (2 D 72).
Zaninetti, Teresio. "Sulla strada di K." *AllaB*, 8: 12-4 (1970).
Kesey, Ken. Atkinson, Michael. "One Flew Over the Fiction Course." *ColLit*, 2: 120-7 (Sp 75).
Barsness, J.A. "KK: The Hero in Modern Dress." *BRMMLA*, 23: 27-33 (1969).
Beards, R.D. "Stereotyping in Modern American Fiction: Some Solitary Swedish Madmen." *MSpr*, 63: 329-37 (1969).
Blessing, Richard. "The Moving Target: KK's Evolving Hero." *JPC*, 4: 615-27 (Wi 71).
Brady, H.R. "K's *One Flew Over the Cuckoo's Nest*." *Expl*, 31: 41 (F 73).
Doxey, W.S. "K's *One Flew Over the Cuckoo's Nest*." *Expl*, 32: 32 (D 73).
Fiedler, Leslie. "Making It with a Little Shazam." *NYHT*, 2 Ag 64, pp. 1, 10-1.
Forrey, Robert. "KK's Psychopathic Savior: A Rejoinder." *MFS*, 21: 222-9 (Su 75).
Foster, J.W. "Hustling to Some Purpose: K's *One Flew Over the Cuckoo's Nest*." *WAL*, 9: 115-29 (Su 74).
Hauck, R.B. "The Comic Christ and the Modern Reader." *CE*, 31: 498-506 (1970).
Hicks, Granville. "Beatnik in Lumberjack Country." *SatR*, 47: 21-2 (25 Jl 64).
Hoge, J.O. "Psychedelic Stimulation and the Creative Imagination: The Case of KK." *SHR*, 6: 381-91 (Fa 72).
Horton, A.S. "KK, John Updike, and the Lone Ranger." *JPC*, 8: 570-8 (Wi 74).
Kunz, D.R. "Mechanistic and Totemistic Symbolization in K's *One Flew Over the Cuckoo's Nest*." *SAF*, 3: 65-82 (Sp 75).
Leeds, B.H. "Theme and Technique in *One Flew Over the Cuckoo's Nest*." *ConnR*, 7: 35-50 (Ap 74).
Lish, Gordon. "A Celebration of Excellence: KK." *Genesis West*, 2: 3-4 (#5 63).
McMahan, E.E. "The Big Nurse as Rachet: Sexism in K's *Cuckoo's Nest*." *CEA*, 37: 25-7 (#4 75).
Malin, Irving. "KK: *One Flew Over the Cuckoo's Nest*." *Critique*, 5: 81-4 (Fa 62).
Martin, Terrence. "*One Flew Over the Cuckoo's Nest* and the High Cost of Living." *MFS*, 19: 43-55 (Sp 73).
Mills, Nicholaus. "KK and the Politics of Laughter." *Cent R*, 16: 82-90 (Wi 72).
Oates, J.C. "Notions Good and Bad." *KR*, 27: 175-80 (Wi 65).
Pearson, Carol. "The Cowboy Saint and the Indian Poet: The Comic Hero in KK's *One Flew Over the Cuckoo's Nest*." *SAH*, 1: 91-8 (O 74).
Schopf, William. "Blindfolded and Backwards: Promethean and Bemushroomed Heroism in *One Flew Over the Cuckoo's Nest* and *Catch-22*." *BRMMLA*, 26: 89-97 (3Q 72).

Sherman, W.D. "The Novels of KK." *JAmSt*, 5: 185-96 (Ag 71).

Sherwood, T.G. "*One Flew Over the Cuckoo's Nest* and the Comic Strip." *Critique*, 13: 96-109 (1971).

Sullivan, Ruth. "Big Mama, Big Papa, and Little Sons in KK's *One Flew Over the Cuckoo's Nest*." *L&P*, 25: 34-44 (1975).

Sutherland, J.R. "A Defense of KK's *One Flew Over the Cuckoo's Nest*." *EJ*, 61: 28-31 (1972).

Tanner, S.L. "Salvation Through Laughter: KK and the Cuckoo's Nest." *SWR*, 58: 125-37 (Sp 73).

———. "KK and His Pranksters." *LonM*, 9: 5-24 (D 69).

Tunnell, J.R. "K and Vonnegut: Preachers of Redemption." *ChrC*, 89: 1180-3 (1972).

Waldmeir, J.J. "Two Novelists of the Absurd: Heller and K." *WSCL*, 5: 192-204 (1964).

Wallis, B.E. "Christ in the Cuckoo's Nest; or the Gospel According to KK." *Cithara*, 12: 52-8 (1972).

*Weixlmann, Joseph. "KK: A Bibliography." *WAL*, 10: 219-31 (N 75).

Widmer, Kingsley. "The Post-Modernist Art of Protest: K and Mailer as Expressions of Rebellion." *CentR*, 19: 121-35 (Su 75).

Witke, Charles. "Pastoral Convention in Virgil and K." *PCP*, 1: 20-4 (Ap 66).

Zashin, E.M. "Political Theorist and Demiurge: The Rise and Fall of KK." *CentR*, 17: 199-213 (Sp 73).

Key, Francis Scott. Marks, Lillian. "Count de Benyowsky and 'The Star-Spangled Banner.'" *MHM*, 70: 90-1 (Sp 75).

Killens, John Oliver. Ihde, Horst. "Black Writer's Burden: Bemerkungen zu JOK." *ZAA*, 16: 117-37 (1968).

Wiggams, W.H. "Black Folktales in the Novels of JO.K." *Black Scholar*, 3: 50-8 (N 71).

———. "The Structure and Dynamics of Folklore in the Novel Form: The Case of JOK." *KFQ*, 17: 92-118 (Fa 72).

Kilmer, Joyce. Nims, J.F. "Therese: The Greatest Lyric Poem in Our Literature." *Intellectual Dig*, 11: 36-7 (Ag 72).

Roach, B.V. "K Treed." *J Eng Linguistics*, 9: 58-61 (1975).

Sawyer, Paul. "What Keeps 'Trees' Growing?" *CEA*, 33: 17-9 (N 70).

Kimbrough, Edward. Pilkington, W.T. "The Dirt Farmer and the Cowboy: Notes on Two Texas Essayists." *ReAL*, 3: 42-54 (1969).

Sims, L.M. "EK: Mississippi Novelist." *NMW*, 4: 109-14 (Wi 72).

Stamper, Rexford. "A Critical Evaluation of the Novels of EK." *NMW*, 7: 54-62 (Fa 74).

King, Charles. Green, C.E. "Captain K: Popular Military Novelist." *JAriH*, 2: 23-6 (Su 61).

Peterson, C.T. "CK: Soldier and Novelist." *ABC*, 16: 9-12 (D 65).

King, Clarence. *Thomas, Jeffrey. "CK." *ALR*, 8: 294-5 (1975).

King, Grace. Bush, Robert. "Charles Gayarée and GK: Letters of a Louisiana Friendship." *SLJ*, 7: 100-31 (Fa 74).

*———. "GK (1852-1932)." *ALR*, 8: 43-51 (Wi 75).

*———. "GK and Mark Twain." *AL*, 44: 31-51 (My 72).

*Muhlenberg, M.E. "GK." *ALR*, 8: 295-6 (1975).

Simpson, C.M. "GK: The Historian as Apologist." *SLJ*, 6: 130-3 (Sp 74).

King, L. Pilkington, W.T. "The Dirt-Farmer and the Cowboy: Notes on Two Texas Essayist." *Re:A&L*, 3: 42-54 (1969).

Kinnell, Galway. Anon. "Craft Interview with CK." *NYRB*, 8: 10-9 (Au 71).

———. "The Weight That a Poem Can Carry: An Interview with GK." *OhR*, 14: 25-38 (Fa 72).

Davie, Donald. "Slogging for the Absolute." *Parnassus*, 2: 9-22 (1974).

Gerber, P.L., and R.J. Gemmett. " 'Deeper than Personality': A Conversation with GK ." *IowaR*, 1: 125-33 (Sp 70).

Hobbs, John. "GK's 'The Bear': Dreams and Technique." *MPS*, 5: 237-50 (Wi 74).

Ledbetter, J.T. "K's 'The Bear.' " *Expl*, 33: 63 (Ap 75).

McKenzie, J.J. "To the Roots: An Interview with GK." *Salmagundi*, 22-23: 206-21 (1973).

Mills, R.J. "A Letter to Donald Davie." *Parnassus*, 3: 289-90 (#2 74).

———. "A Reading of GK." *IowaR*, 1: 66-86, 102-22 (Wi, Sp 70).

Molesworth, Charles. "The Rank Flavor of Blood: GK and American Poetry in the 1960's." *WHR*, 27: 225-39 (Su 73).

Oberg, Arthur. "The One Flea Which is Laughing." *Shen*, 25: 85-91 (Fa 73).

Taylor, Jane. "The Poetry of GK." *Per*, 15: 189-200 (1968).

Thompson, W.E. "Snyergy in the Poetry of GK." *Gypsy Schol*, 1: 52-69 (1974).

Wagner, Linda. " 'Spindrift': The World in a Seashell." *CP*, 8: 5-9 (#1 75).

* **Kirkland, Joseph.** Anon. *"The Prairie Chicken:* A Rarity." *JISHS*, 47: 84-8 (Sp 54).

Blair, Walter. "Roots of American Realism." *UR*, 6: 275-81 (Je 40).

Blair, Walter. "Roots of American Realism." *UR*, 6: 275-81 (Je 40).

Bowron, B.R. "Realism in America." *CL*, 3: 268-85 (Su 51).

Eichelberger, C.L. "Edgar Watson Howe and JK: More Critical Comment." *ALR*, 4: 279-90 (Su 71).

*——, and F.L. Stallings. "JK (1830-1893): A Critical Bibliography of Secondary Comment." *ALR*, 2: 51-69 (Sp 69).

Flanagan, J.T. "Folklore in Five Middle-Western Novelists." *Great Lakes R*, 1: 43-57 (Wi 75).

Henson, C.E. "JK (1830-1894)." *ALR*, 1: 67-70 (Fa 67).

Holaday, CA. "A Note on K's Autobiographical Writing." *ALR*, 2: 75-7 (Sp 69).

Lease, Benjamin. "The JK Papers." *ALR*, 2: 73-5 (Sp 69).

Lewis, Lloyd. "Letters of a Pioneer Realist." *NLB*, 3: 3-7 (D 45).

Mabbott, T.O., and P.D. Jordan. *"The Prairie Chicken*: Notes on Lincoln and Mrs. K." *JISHS*, 25: 154-66 (O 32).

* McLaughlin, E.S. "JK." *ALR*, 25: 154-66 (O 32).

Monteiro, George. "A Note on the Realism of JK." *ALR*, 2: 77-8 (Sp 69).

Roberts, A.J. "Two Additions to the JK Canon." *ALR*, 6: 252-4 (1973).

———. " 'Word Murder': An Early JK Essay Published Anonymously." *ALR*, 6: 73-9 (Wi 73).

Kneeland, Abner. French, Roderick. "The Published Writings of AK." *BB*, 31: 170-2 (O-D 74).

Knowles, John. Devine, J.E. "The Truth About *A Separate Peace*." *EJ*, 58: 519-20 (Sp 69).

Ely, Sister M.A. "The Adult Image in Three Novels of Adolescent Life." *EJ*, 56: 1127-31 (N 67).

Foster, M.P. "Levels of Meaning in *A Separate Peace*." *English Record*, 18: 34-40 (Ap 68).

Heinz, Linda, and Roy Huss. "*A Separate Peace:* Filming the War Within." *LFQ*, 3: 160-71 (1975).

Kennedy, Ian. "Dual Perspective Narrative and the Character of Phineas in 'A Separate Peace.' " *SSF*, 11: 353-60 (Fa 74).

McDonald, W.R. "Heroes Never Learn: Irony in *A Separate Peace*." *IEngYb*, 22: 33-6 (N 72).

Mengeling, M.E. "*A Separate Peace*: Meaning and Myth." *EJ*, 58: 1322-9 (D 69).

Sister M. Nora. "A Comparison of Actual and Symbolic Landscapes in *A Separate Peace*." *Disc*, 11: 356-62 (Su 68).

Travis, Mildred. "Mirror Images in *A Separate Peace* and *Cat and Mouse*." *NCLit*, 5: 12-5 (S 75).

Wolfe, Peter. "The Impact of K's *A Separate Peace*." *Ur*, 36: 189-98 (Mr 70).

Kopit, Arthur Jone. Jiji, V.M. "*Inidans*: A Mosaic of Memories and Methodologies." *Players*, 47: 230-6 (Je-Jl 72).

Jones, J.B. "Impersonation and Authenticity: The Theatre as Metaphor in K's *Indians*." *QRS*, 59: 443-51 (D 73).

Lahr, John. "AK's *Indians*: Dramatizing National Amnesia." *EvR*, 13: 19-21, 63-7 (O 69).

Kosinski, Jerzy. Aldridge, J.W. "The Fabrication of a Culture Hero." *SatR*, 54: 25-7 (24 Ap 71).

Bolling, Douglas. "The Precarious Self in K's *Being There*." *Greyfriar*, 16: 41-6 (1975).

Boyers, Robert. "Language and Reality in K's *Steps*." *CentR*, 16: 41-61 (Wi 72).

Cahill, D.J. "American Deviltry." *FicI*, 1: 121-3 (1973).

———. "JK: Retreat from Violence" *TCL*, 18: 121-32 (1972).

Coale, Samuel. "The Cinematic Self of JK." *MFS*, 20: 359-70 (Au 74).

———. "The Quest for the Elusive Self: The Fiction of JK." *Critique*, 14: 25-37 (1973).

Corngold, Stanley. "JK's *The Painted Bird*: Language Lost and Regained." *Mosaic*, 6: 153-67 (Su 73).

Daler, J.K. "An Introduction to JK's 'Steps.'" *Lang&L*, 1: 43-9 (1971).

Gogol, J.M. "K's Chance: McLuhan Age Narcissus." *NCLit*, 1: 8-10 (S 71).

Hirschberg, Stuart: "Becoming an Object: The Function of Mirrors and Photographs in K's *The Devil Tree* ." *NCLit*, 4: 14-5 (Mr 74).

Klinkowitz, Jerome. "JK: Being Here." *Falcon*, 4: 122-5 (Mr 72).

———. "JK: An Interview." *FicI*, 30-48 (Fa 73).

———, and D.H. Richter. "Two Bibliographical Questions in K's *The Painted Bird*." *ConL*, 16: 126-9 (Wi 75).

Lale, Meta, and J.S. Williams. "The Narrator of *The Painted Bird*: A Case Study." *Renascence*, 24: 198-206 (1972).

Loukides, Paul. "The Radical Vision." *MichA*, 5: 497-503 (Sp 73).

Plimpton, George, and Rocco Landesman. "The Art of Fiction." *PaR*, 14: 183-207 (Su 72).

Richey, Clarence. " 'Being There' and Dasein: A Note on the Philosophical Presupposition Underlying the Novels of JK." *NCLit*, 2: 13-5 (S 72).

Richter, David. "The Three Denouements of JK's *The Painted Bird*." *ConL*, 15: 370-85 (Su 74).

*Rush, Frederick. "JK: A Checklist." *BB*, 6-9 (Ja-Mr 74).

Sanders, Ivan. "The Gifts of Strangeness: Alienation and Creation in JK's Fiction." *PolR*, 19: 171-89 (1974).

Sugiura, Ginsaku. "Osorubeki Itan no Kansei—JK ni tsuite." *EigoS*, 119: 390-1 (1973).

Vree, Freddy de. "JP: Cockpit, Elckerlyck." *K&C*, 1: 26-7 (S 75).

Weales, Gerald. "JK: The Painted Bird and Other Disguises." *HC*, 9: 1-12 (1972).

Kouns, Nathan C. Dahl, Curtis. "A Radical Historical Novelist of the '80'." *GaR*, 27: 49-55 (Sp 73).

Kroll, Henry Harrison. Payne, M.Y. "Inimitable Versality of HHK." *TPB*, 8: 3-8 (1971).

———. "Night Rider Love and Legend." *KFR*, 12: 59-66 (Ja-Mr 66).

Krutch, Joseph Wood. Green, J.G. "JWK: The Critic of Tragedy Looks at Comedy." *QJS*, 54: 37-46 (F 68).

Holtz, William. "Homage to JWK: Tragedy and the Ecological Imperative." *ASch*, 43: 267-79 (Sp 74).

Lehman, A.L. "*JWK.*" *QNC*, 37: 51-63 (Su 72).
———. "JWK: Personal Reminiscence." *QNL*, 37: 5-83 (1972).
Powell, L.C. "JWK's *The Desert Year.*" *Westways*, 63: 14-7, 66-7 (Je 71).
Kubrick, Stanley. Fiore, P.A. "Milton and K: Eden's Apple or a Clockwork Orange." *CEA*, 35: 14-7 (Ja 73).
Robinson, W.R., and Mary McDermott. "'2001' and the Literary Sensibility." *GaR*, 26: 21-37 (Sp 72).
Kumin, Maxine. Ciardi, John. "The Art of MK." *SatR*, 55: 12, 14-5 (25 Mr 72).
Mills, Ralph. "In the Fields of Imagination." *Parnassus*, 1: 211-244 (#2 73).
Kunitz, Stanley. Barbu, Eugen. "De vorbă cu SK." *Luceafarul*, nv: 6 (10 F 68).
Boyers, Robert. "'Imagine Wrestling with an Angel': An Interview with SK." *Salmagundi*, 22-3: 71-83 (1973).
Brantley, Robin. "A Touch of the Poet." *NYTMS*, 7 S 75, pp. 80-3.
Davis, Cynthia. "An Interview with SK." *ConL*, 15: 1-14 (Wi 74).
———. "SK's 'The Testing Tree.'" *CP*, 8: 43-50 (#1 75).
Kramer, Aaron. "*The Testing Tree.*" *MeditR*, 2: 40-1 (1972).
Perloff, Marjorie. "The Testing of SK." *IowaR*, 3: 93-103 (1972).
Ryan, Michael. "An Interview with SK." *IowaR*, 5: 76-85 (Sp 74).
Voznesensky, Andrei, and Stanley Kunitz. "Voznesensky and K on Poetry." *NYTBR*, 16 Ap 72, pp. 6, 38.
Weisberg, Robert. "SK: The Stubborn Middle Way." *MPS*, 6: 49-73 (Sp 75).
Wright, James. "The Terrible Threshold." *SR*, 67: 330-6 (Ap-Je 59).
LaFarge, Oliver. Krim, Seymour. "Son of Laughing Boy." *LonM*, 13: 46-58 (D-Ja 73-4).
Powell, L.C. "OL's *Laughing Boy.*" *Westways*, 63: 22-4, 50-2 (D 73).
Lamming, George. Lundkvist, Arthur. "Madrommer och spex." *BLM*, 42: 276-81 (1973).
Pouchet-Paquet, Sandra. "The Politics of GL's *Natives of My Person.*" *CLAJ*, 17: 109-16 (1973).
Langer, Susanne. Bertocci, Angelo. "SL, or the Symbol Abstracted." *PQ*, 48: 261-77 (Ap 60).
Courtney, Richard. "On L's Dramatic Illusion." *JAAC*, 29: 11-20 (Fa 70).
Lanier, Sidney. Anon. "The Length and the Breadth and the Sweep of the Marshes of Glynn." *Life*, 14 N 69, pp. 89 93.
Antippas, A.P., and C.A. Flake. "SL: Some Unpublished Early Manuscripts." *PBSA*, 68: 174-9 (Ap-Je 74).
———. "SL's Letters to Clare deGraffenreid." *AL*, 45: 182-205 (My 73).
de Bellis, Jack. "SL and German Romance: An Important Qualification." *CLS*, 5: 145-55 (Je 68).
*Edwards, C.H. "Bibliography of SL: 1942-1973." *BB*, 31: 29-31 (Ja-Mr 74).
———. "L's 'The Symphony,' 64-84." *Expl*, 31: 27 (D 72).
———. "SL: Musical Pioneer." *GaR*, 22: 473-81 (Wi 68).
Friedl, Herwig. "Poe und L. ein Vergleich Ihrer Versdichtung." *JA*, 15: 123-40 (1970).
Havens, Elmer. "L's Critical Theory." *ESQ*, 55: 83-9 (2Q 69).
Inge, M.T. "Miguel De Unamuno's *Canciones* Translated with Commentary." *ArlQ*, 2: 83-97 (Au 69).
Keller, W.J. "Realism in SL's 'Tiger-Lilies.'" *SAB*, 36: 17-20 (Mr 71).
Lanier, Sidney. "In a Poet's Workshop." *Century*, 76: 847-50 (O 08).
Lease, Benjamin. "SL and *Blackwood's Magazine*: An Unpublished Letter." *GHQ*, 53: 521-2 (D 69).
McCowan, H.S. "SL, One Southern Singer, and His Songs." *Self-Culture*, 10: 398-400 (Ja 00).

Millgate, Michael. "Faulkner and L: A Note On the Name Jason." *MissQ*, 25: 349-50 (1972).

Reamer, O.J. "L's 'The Marshes of Glynn' Revisited." *MissQ*, 23: 57-63 (Wi 69-70).

Simms, L.M. "A Note on SL's Attitude Toward the Negro and Toward Populism." *GHQ*, 52: 305-7 (S 68).

Thorp, Willard. "A Memorial to L." *VQR*, 22: 123-38 (1946).

Wright, Nathalia. "Edd Winfield Parks on SL." *SLJ*, 2: 152-7 (Fa 69).

Young, T.D. "How Time Has Served Two Southern Poets: Paul Hamilton Hayne and SL." *SLJ*, 6: 101-10 (Fa 73).

Lardner, Ring. Cox, J.M. "Toward Vernacular Humor." *VQR*, 46: 311-30 (1970).

Freese, Peter. "Zwei unbekannte Verweise in J.D. Salinger's *The Catcher in the Rye*: Charles Dickens und RL." *Archiv*, 211: 68-72 (1974).

Hasley, Louis. "RL: The Ashes of Idealism." *ArQ*, 26: 219-32 (Au 70).

Lardner, Ring. "RL & Sons." *Esquire*, 77: 98-103, 169-80 (Mr 72).

Latham, Aaron. "The Ls: A Writing Dynasty." *NYTMS*, 22 Ag 71, pp. 10-1, 42-51.

Lease, Benjamin. "An Evening at the Scott Fitzgeralds: An Unpublished Letter to RL." *ELN*, 8: 40-2 (1971).

May, C.E. "L's 'Haircut.'" *Expl*, 31: 69 (My 73).

Smith, L.T. " 'The Diameter of Frank Chance's Diamond': RL and Professional Sports." *JPC*, 6: 133-56 (Su 72).

Stein, A.F. "This Unsporting Life: The Baseball Fiction of RL." *MarkR*, 3: 27-33 (F 72).

Laughlin, James. Laughlin, James. "New and Old Directions." *NYT*, 25 F 73, pp. 46-8.

Perrine, Laurence. "L's 'Go West Young Man.'" *Expl*, 28: 61 (1970).

Larsen, Nella. Thorton, H.E. "Sexism as Quagmire: NL's Quicksand." *LAJ*, 16: 285-301 (Mr 73).

Youman, M.M. "NL's *Passing*: A Study in Irony." *CLAJ*, 18: 235-41 (1974).

Lawson, Deodat. Cohen, B.B. "DL's *Christ's Infidelity* and Hawthorne's 'Young Goodman Brown.'" *ETHC*, 104: 349-70 (1968).

Diket, A.L. "The Nobel Savage Convention as Epitomized in JL's *A New Voyage to Carolina*." *NCHR*, 43: 413-29 (O 66).

Kirkham, E.D. "The First English Editions of JL's *Voyage to Carolina*: A Bibliographical Study." *PBSA*, 61: 258-65 (3Q 67).

Lindgren, W.H. "Agricultural Propaganda in L's *A New Voyage to Carolina*."

Lawson, John Howard. Valgemae, Mardi. "Civil War among the Expressionists: JHL and the *Pinwheel* Controversy." *ETJ*, 20: 8-14 (Mr 68).

Lawson, Robert. Burns, M.M. " 'There is Enough for All': RL's America." *HornB*, 48: 24-32 (F 72); 120-8 (Ap 72); 295-305 (Je 72).

Lazarus, Emma. Monk, S.H. "The Golden Door." *TLS*, 14 Ag 69, p. 907.

Lea, Tom. *Lovelace, Lisabeth. "TL Bibliography." *Texas Lib J*, 47: 217 (1971).

Ledyard, John. Davie, Donald. "JL: The American Traveler and His Sentimental Journeys."*ECS*, 4: 57-70 (Fa 70).

Lee, Arthur. MacMaster, R.K. "AL's 'Address on Slavery': An Aspect of Virginia's Struggle to End the Slave Trade, 1765-1774." *VMHB*, 80: 141-57 (1972).

Riggs, A.R. "AL, a Radical Virginian in London, 1768-1776." *VMHB*, 78: 268-80 (1970).

Lee, Don L. Colley, Ann. "DL.L's 'But He was Cool or: He Even Stopped for Green Lights': An Example of the New Black Aesthetic." *CP*, 4: 20-8 (Fa 71).

Giddings, Paula. "From a Black Perspective: The Poetry of DL.L." *Amistad*, 2: 297-318 (1971).

Miller, E.E. "Some Black Thoughts on DL.L's *Think Black!*: Thunk by a Frustrated White Academic Thinker." *CE*, 34: 1094-1102 (My 73).

Palmer, R.R. "The Poetry of Three Revolutionists: DL.L., Sonia Sanchez, and Nikki Giovanni." *CLAJ*, 15: 25-36 (S 71).

Shands, A.O. "The Relevancy of DL.L. as a Contemporary Black Poet." *BlackW*, 21: 35-48 (1972).

Lee, Harper. Erisman, Fred. "The Romantic Regionalism of HL." *AlaR*, 26: 122-36 (Ap 73).

McDonald, W.U. "HL's College Writings." *AN&Q*, 6: 131-2 (My 68).

Lee, Richard Henry. Wood, G.S. "The Authorship of the *Letters from a Federal Farmer*." *WMQ*, 31: 299-308 (1974).

Legaré, Hugh Swinton. Evans, Elizabeth. "The Friendship of Alexander Hill Everett and HSL." *MissQ*, 28: 497-504 (Fa 75).

Welsh, J.R. "An Early Pioneer: L's *Southern Review*." *SLJ*, 3: 79-97 (Sp 71).

Legaré, James Mathewes. Jacobs, R.D. "JML: Nearly Forgotten But Not Lost." *SLJ*, 4: 12-7 (Sp 72).

Kibler, James. "L's First Poems and His Early Career." *SLJ*, 6: 70-6 (Fa 73).

Meriwether, R.L. "The Papers of John C. Calhoun." *Autograph Col J*, 5: 52-3 (1953).

Tryon, W.S. "The Publications of Ticknor and Fields in the South, 1840-1865." *JSH*, 14: 305-30 (1948).

Leggett, William. Seelye, John. "Buckskin and Ballistics: WL and the American Detective Story." *JPC*, 1: 52-7 (1967).

Le Guin, Ursula Kroeber. Barbour, Douglas. "On ULG's *A Wizard of Earthsea*." *RQ*, 6: 119-23 (Ap 74).

―――. "Wholeness and Balance in the Hainish Novels of UK.LG." *S-FS*, 1: 164-73 (#3 74).

Ketterer, David. "*The Left Hand of Darkness*: UK.LG's Archetypal 'Winter-Journey.'" *RQ*, 5: 288-97 (Ap 73).

Scholes, Robert. "The Good Witch of the West." *HC*, 11: 1-12 (Ap 74).

Suvin, Darko, et al. "UK.LG Issue." *SSF*, 2: 203-74 (1975).

Leland, Charles Godfrey. *Jackson, Joseph. "A Bibliography of the Works of CGL." *PMHB*, 50: 38-63, 149-62, 254-66, 367-79 (1926).

Leverett, John. Kaiser, L.M. "*Apta et Concinna Oratio*: The 1703 Commencement Address of JL." *Manuscripta*, 19: 159-70 (1975).

―――. "JL and the Quebec Expedition of 1711: An Unpublished Latin Oration." *HLB*, 22: 309-16 (1974).

―――. "JL's Welcome to Governor Sir William Andros." Manuscripta, 18: 30-7 (1974).

―――. "A President Accepts." *Classical Outlook*, 52: 40-1 (1974).

―――. "The Unpublished *Oratio* of JL, Harvard, 1689." *HL*, 24: 327-45 (1975).

Levertov, Denise. Berry, Wendell. "A Secular Pilgrimage." *HudR*, 23: 401-24 (1970).

Bowering, George. "DL." *AntigR*, 7: 76-87 (Au 71).

Bruce-Wilson, Richard. "The New American Decadence." *Delta*, 38: 22-8 (Sp 66).

Burrows, E.G. "An Interview with DL." *MQR*, 7: 239-42 (Au 68).

Carruth, Hayden. "L." *HudR*, 27: 475-80 (1974).

"Crunk." "The Work of DL." *Sixties*, 9: 48-65 (1967).

Duddy, T.A. "To Celebrate: A Reading of DL." *Criticism*, 10: 138-52 (Sp 68).

Gitzen, Julian. "From Reverence to Attention: The Poetry of DL." *MwQ*, 16: 328-41 (Sp 75).

Goldoni, Annalisa. "La Poesia di DL." *SA*, 14: 377-99 (1968).

Hopkins, M.F. "Linguistic Analysis as a Tool for the Oral Interpreter." *SpT*, 18: 200-3 (1969).

Hunt, J.M. "The New Grief-Language of DL." *UR*, 35: 149-53, 171-7 (Wi 68, Sp 69).

Kyle, C.A. "Every Step an Arrival: Six Variations and the Musical Structure of DL's Poetry." *CentR*, 17: 281-96 (Su 73).

Levertov, Denise. "Origins of a Poem." *MQR*, 7: 233-8 (Au 68).

———. "The Poet in the World." *APR*, 1: 16-8 (1972).

Mazzaro, James. "Fusions." *FarP*, 5: 70-3 (Wi-Sp 71).

Mills, Ralph. "In the Fields of Imagination." *Parnassus*, 1: 211-24 (#2 73).

Morrow, Patrick. "DL's 'The Five Day Rain.'" *NCLit*, 2: 4-6 (Ja 72).

Mottram, Eric. "The Limits of Self-Regard." *Parnassus*, 1: 152-62 (1972).

Nelson, R.L. "Edge of the Transcendent: The Poetry of L and Duncan." *SWR*, 54: 188-202 (Sp 69).

Pryse, Marjorie. " 'The Stonecarver's Poem'—A Linguistic Interpretation." *Lang&S*, 7: 62-71 (1974).

Reid, Ian. " 'Everyman's Land': Ian Reid Interviews DL." *SoRA*, 5: 232-6 (S 72).

Younkins. Ronald. "DL and the Hasidic Tradition." *Descant*, 19: 40-8 (#1 74).

Levin, Harry. Dietrichson, J.W. "Professor HL's litteratur-kritikk." *Edda*, 4: 205-17 (1971).

Levin, Ira. Lima, Robert. "The Satanic Rape of Catholicism in *Rosemary's Baby*." *SAF*, 2: 211-22 (Au 74).

McManis, J.A. "*Rosemary's Baby*: a Unique Combination of Faust, Leda, and the Second Coming." *McNeese R*, 20: 33-6 (1971-2).

Schott, Webster. "Daughter of *Rosemary's Baby*." *SatR*, 55: 98, 100 (O 72).

Levine, Philip. Kalstone, David. "The Entranced Possession of the Dead." *Parnassus*, 3: 41-50 (#1 74).

Levine, Philip. "And See If the Voice Will Enter You: An Interview with PL." *OhioR*, 16: 45-63 (Wi 75).

McMichael, James. "Borges and Strand, Weak Henry, PL." *SoR*, 8: 213-24 (1972).

Molesworth, Charles. "The Buried Essential Oil." *HC*, 12: 1-15 (#5 75).

Oberg, Arthur. "Against an Iron Time." *Shen*, 23: 95-103 (1972).

Smith, A.E. "Poetry and Politics: An Interview with PL." *PR*, 42: 69-79 (1Q 75).

Levy, D.A. Gildzen, Alex, et. al. "D.A.L Issue." *Serif*, 8: 2-28 (1971).

*Lowell, J.R. "A Preliminary Checklist of the Writings of D.A.L. (1942-1968)." *Serif*, 8: 14-6 (1971).

Lewis, Alfred Henry. Humphries, Rolfe. "Tall-Tale Americana." *Nation*, 205: 153-7 (28 Ag 67).

Manzo, F.D. "AHL: Western Storyteller." *Ariz and the West*, 10: 5-24 (Sp 68).

Mehl, R.F. "Jack London, AHL, and the Primitive Woman." *JLN*, 6: 66-70 (1973).

Lewis, Henry Clay. Anderson, J.Q. "HCL, Louisville Medical Institute Student, 1844-1846." *FCHQ*, 32: 30-7 (1958).

Israel, Charles. "HCL's *Odd Leaves*: Studies in the Surreal and Grotesque." *MissQ*, 28: 61-70 (Wi 74-5).

Rose, A.H. "The Image of the Negro in the Writings of HCL." *AL*, 41: 255-63 (My 69).

Lewis, Richard. Lemay, J.A.L. "RL and Augustan American Poetry." *PMLA*, 83: 80-101 (1968).

Lewis, Janet. Hofheins, Roger, and Dan Tooker. "A Conversation with JL." *SoR*, 10: 329-41 (Ap 74).

Killoh, Ellen. "Patriarchal Women: A Study of Three Novels by JL." *SoR*, 10: 342-64 (Ap 74).

Lewis, Sinclair. Anon. "Frederick Manfred Talks About SL." *SLN*, 2: 1-5 (Sp 70).

———. "SL Manuscripts in the Library of Congress Manscript Division." *Prospects*, 1: 75-80 (1975).

Anderson, Hilton. "A Whartonian Woman in *Dodsworth*." *SLN*, 1: 5-6 (Sp 69).

Barry, J.D. "*Dodsworth*: SL' Novel of Character." *BSUF*, 10: 8-14 (Sp 69).

Batchelor, Helen. "A SL Portfolio of Maps: Zenith to Winnemac." *MLQ*, 32: 401-8 (D 71).

Brown, D.R. "The Cosmopolitan Novel: James and L." *SLN*, 1: 6-9 (Sp 69).

Bucco, Martin. "The Serialized Novels of SL." *WAL*, 4: 29-37 (Sp 69).

Burlingame, Dwight, and J.K. Archibald. "Two Minnesota Reports on SL Collections." *SLN*, 4: 17-8 (1972).

Burton, D.M. "Intonation Patterns of Sermons in Seven Novels." *Lang&S*, 3: 205-20 (1970).

Carter, Paul. "Of Towns and Roads: Three Novelists, and George McGovern." *ColF*, 2: 10-6 (Sp 73).

Coard, R.L. "*Arrowsmith* and 'Those Damn Profs.'" *SLN*, 2: 6-8 (Sp 70).

———. "*Babbitt*: The Sound Track of a Satire." *SLN*, 5-6: 1-4 (1973-74).

———. "College and Schoolhouse in *Main Street*." *SLN*, 1: 3-4 (Sp 69).

———. "*Dodsworth* and the Question of Art." *SLN*, 3: 16-8 (1971).

———. "Mark Twain's *The Gilded Age* and SL's *Babbitt*." *MwQ*, 13: 319-33 (Sp 72).

———. "'Vulgar Barnyard Illustrations' in *Elmer Gantry*." *SLN*, 4: 8-10 (1972).

Conroy, S.S. "Popular Arts and Elite Standards: The Curse of SL." *ForumH*, 12: 28-32 (1974).

Conroy, Stephen. "SL's Plot Paradigms." *SLN*, 5-6: 4-6 (Wi 73-74).

———. "SL's Sociological Imagination." *AL*, 42: 348-62 (N 70).

Cooney, C.F. "Walter White and SL: The History of a Literary Friendship." *Prospects*, 1: 75-80 (1975).

Crane, Joan. "Rare or Seldom-Seen Dust Jackets of American First Editions: XIV." *Serif*, 11: 34-8 (#1 74).

Davis, J.L. "Mark Schorer's SL." *SLN*, 3: 3-9 (1971).

Douglas, G.H. "Babbitt at Fifty—The Truth Still Hurts." *Nation*, 22 My 72, pp. 661-2.

———. "*Main Street* After Fifty Years." *PrS*, 44: 338-48 (Wi 70-71).

Duke, Maurice. "SL on the Highway: An Unpublished Letter." *SLNL*, 1: 2 (Sp 69).

Edener, Wilfried. "Zu einigen neuen Studien über SL." *NS*, 17: 557-61 (1968).

Fleischmann, W.B. "Germans and German-Americans in the Major Fiction of SL." *WSL*, 3: 1-10 (1966).

———. "L'Affaire SL: 'Anti-Semitism?' and Ancillary Matters." *SLN*, 4: 14-7 (1972).

———. "Charles Dickens and SL: An Exordium." *SLN*, 3: 10-3 (1971).

———. "The Reincarnation of Holmes in Dr. Gottlieb." *BakSJ*, 23: 176-9 (1973).

———. "SL's Zenith—Once Again." *SLN*, 2: 10-1 (sp 70).

———. "'Something Out of Dickens' in SL." *BNYLP*, 74: 607-16 (N 70).

Friedman, P.A. "SL." *TC*, 179: 44-5 (1970).

Haworth, Jane. "Revisions of *Main Street*." *SLN*, 5-6: 8-12 (1973-74).

Helleberg, M.M. "The Paper-Doll Characters of SL's *Arrowsmith*." *MTJ*, 14: 17-21 (1969).

Hill, J.S. "SL, *Dodsworth*, and the Nobel Prize." *HussR*, 3: 105-11 (1970).

Hines, T.S. "Echoes from 'Zenith': Reactions of American Businessmen to *Babbitt*." *Business Hist R*, 41: 123-40 (Su 67).

Ianni, Lawrence. "SL as a Prophet of Black Pride." *SLN*, 3: 13-15, 21 (1971).

Kittleson, J.H. "L." *SDR*, 7: 19-20 (Wi 69-70).

Landor, Mikhail. "Collected Works of SL in Russian." *SovL*, 7: 176-8 (1965).

Lea, James. "SL and the Implied America." *Clio*, 3: 21-34 (O 73).

Lewis, R.W. "*Babbitt* and the Dream of Romance." *NDQ*, 40: 7-14 (Wi 72).

Lewis, Sinclair. "Detective Stories and Mr. Dickens." *YULG*, 45: 88-92 (Ja 71).

Light, Martin. "Accounting for the Best in L: A Review." *SLN*, 5-6: 18 (1973-74).

———. "The Quixotic Motifs of *Main Street.*" *ArQ*, 29: 221-34 (Au 73).

Love, G.A. "New Pioneering on the Prairies: Nature, Progress, and the Individual in the Novels of SL." *AQ*, 25: 558-77 (D 73).

Lundquist, James. "Acceptance and Assent." *SLN*, 1: 1 (Sp 69).

———. "Dorothy Thompson: More than a Legend." *SLN*, 5-6: 19-20 (1973-74).

———. "Frederick Manfred Talks about SL." *SLN*, 2: 1-5 (Sp 70).

———. "Old Dr. Alagesh's Traveling Laboratory: SL and the Bunko Artist." *SLN*, 4: 13-4 (1972).

———. "*World So Wide* and SL's Rewritten Life." *SLN*, 2: 12-4 (1970).

McCullough, S.J. "*Kingsblood Royal*: A Revaluation." *SLN*, 4: 10-2 (1972).

Maglin, N.B. "Women in Three SL Novels." *MR*, 14: 783-801 (Au 73).

Manfred, Frederick. "SL' Funeral." *SDR*, 7: 54-78 (Wi 69-70).

Marthaler, Sister M.A. "Ashes Come Home: The Funeral of SL." *SLN*, 2: 11-2 (Sp 70).

Matheson, T.J. "H.L. Mencken's Reviews of SL's Major Novels." *Mencken*, 51: 2-7 (1974).

———. "L's Assessment of Carol Kennicott." *SLN*, 5-6: 12 (Wi 73-74).

———. "The Unfortunate Failure of *Kingsblood Royal.*" *SLN*, 5-6: 13-4 (Wi 73-74).

Melton, J.L. "*Main Street* in the Classroom: Another Approach." *SLN*, 5-6: 8 (Wi 73-74).

*Monteiro, George. "Addenda to the Bibliographies of . . . L [and others]." *PSBA*, 69: 172-5 (Ap-Je 75).

Moodie, C.L. "The Short Stories and SL' Literary Development." *SSF*, 12: 99-108 (Sp 75).

Morley-Mower, Geoffrey. "SL's Attempts to Reform James Branch Cabell." *Kalki*, 6: 140-5 (#24 75).

Nichols, J.W. "Nathaniel West, SL, Alexander Pope, and Satiric Contrasts." *SLN*, 5: 119-22 (Sp 68).

Petrullo, H.B. "*Babbitt* as Situational Satire." *KanQ*, 1: 89-97 (Su 69).

———. "Clichés and Three Political Satires of the Thirties." *SLN*, 8: 109-17 (Sp 71).

———. "Dorothy Thompson's Role in SL's Break with Harcourt, Brace." *Courier*, 8: 50-8 (1971).

———. "Main Street, Cass Timberland, and Determinism." *SDR*, 7: 30-42 (Wi 69-70).

———. "SL's Condensation of Dickens' *Bleak House.*" *YULG*, 45: 85-7 (Ja 71).

Quivey, J.R. "George Babbitt's Quest for Masculinity." *BSUF*, 10: 4-7 (Sp 69).

———. "Release Motif and Its Impact in *Babbitt.*" *SLN*, 4-5 (Sp 69).

Rathe, Chuck. "On the Occasion of SL' Burial." *SDR*, 7: 43-53 (Wi 69-70).

———. "SL Was Buried Here." *SLN*, 3: 19 (1971).

Rogal, S.J. "The Hymns and Gospel-Songs in *Elmer Gantry.*" *SLN*, 4: 4-8 (1972).

Roth, Russell. "The Return of the Laureate: SL in 1942." *SDR*, 7: 3-10 (Wi 69-70).

Rowlette, Robert. "A SL Letter to the Indianapolis News." *ELN*, 9: 193-95 (Mr 72).

Saito, Tadatoshi. "America Shosetsu no Shosetsuka—SL Oboegaki." *EigoS*, 116: 312-3 (197).

Sargent, M.S. "The Babbitt-Lapham Connection." *SLN*, 2: 8-9 (Sp 70).

Sauer, P.R. "The 1945 Lectures: A Happy Episode in SL's Life." *SLN*, 4: 3-4 (1972).

Schorer, Mark. "SL." *UMPAW*, 27: 1-47 (1963).

Shepherd, Allen. "A Fairly Hard Week's Work: *Main Street* in the Classroom." *SLN*, 5-6: 6-7 (1973-74).

Staples, M.E. "As I Remember SL." *SDR*, 6: 11-8 (Wi 69-70).

Suderman, Elmer. "*Main Street* Today." *SDR*, 7: 21-9 (Wi 69-70).

Wurster, Grace. "The Hollow Note in L's Satire." *SLN*, 5-6: 15-8 (1973-74).

Lewisohn, Ludwig. Chyet, S.F. "LL in Charleston (1892-1903)." *AJHQ*, 54: 296-322 (Mr 65).

Douglas, G.H. "LL on Theodore Dreiser." *DrN*, 4: 1-6 (1973).

Gunther, John. "The Views of Mr. Hamlin Garland and LL." *CDN*, 22 N 22, p. 13.

Singer, David. "LL and Freud: The Zionist Therapeutic." *PsyR*, 58: 169-82 (Su-Fa 71).

———. "LL: The Making of an Anti-Communist." *AQ*, 23: 738-51 (D 71).

Liebling, A.J. Weales, Gerald. "The Labyrinthian Digression of AJL." *SR*, 83: 643-4 (Fa 75).

Lincoln, Abraham. Anon. "L As Poet." *AH*, 25: 104 (O 74).

Baker, M.P. "AL in Theses and Dissertations." *LH*, 74: 107-11 (Su 72).

Bradford, M.E. "L's New Frontier: A Rhetoric for Continuing the Revolution." *Triumph*, 6: 11-3, 21 (My 71); 15-7 (Je 71).

Bridges, R.D. "Three Letters from a L Law Student." *JISHS*, 66: 79-87 (1973).

Dibos, W.G. "Concerning a Quotation Commonly Attributed to AL." *RomN*, 11: 579-80 (Sp 70).

Endy, Melvin. "AL and American Civil Religion: A Reinterpretation." *CH*, 44: 229-41 (Je 75).

Holzer, Harold. "L and His Prints: 'A Very Different Judge.'" *LH*, 77: 203-11 (Wi 75).

Kelsey, Harry. "AL and American Indian Policy." *LH*, 77: 139-48 (Fa 75).

Maia, Narsy, "Viana Moog fala de seus heróis." *JdL*, 253: 7 (S 71).

Markowitz, A.M. "Tragedy of an Age: An Eyewitness Account of L's Assassination." *JISHS*, 66: 205-11 (1973).

Newman, John. "The Bollinger L Collection at the University of Iowa." *RALS*, 2: 98-101 (Sp 72).

Potter, J.M. "The Gettysburg Address." *CLJ*, 1: 13-27 (1966).

Smith, E.B. "AL: Realist." *WMH*, 56: 158-68 (Wi 68-9).

Suppiger, Joseph. "L and Pope." *LH*, 77: 218-22 (Wi 75).

Tucker, Glenn. "L's Jesse W. Weik." *LH*, 77: 3-14 (Sp 75).

Turner, Justin. "L and the Cannibals." *LH*, 77: 212-8 (Wi 75).

Wood, Harry. "On L's Face—A Poetic Reconstruction." *LH*, 77: 168-72 (Fa 75).

Lincoln, Joseph C. Greene, Burton. "J.C.L. and the Triumph of the Little Man: A Defense of Popular Culture." *JOFS*, 4: 90-102 (Su 69).

Lindsay, Vachel. Ames, V.M. "VL—or, *My Heart Is a Kicking Horse*." *Midway*, 8: 63-79 (Sp 68).

Bradbury, D.L. "VL and His Heroes." *ISUJ*, 32: 22-57 (1970).

Chénetier, Mark. "Knights in Disguise: L and Maiakovski as Poets of the People." *M-A*, 2: 47-62 (1975).

Flanagan, J.T. "Three Illinois Poets." *CentR*, 16: 313-27 (Fa 72).

Jepson, Edgar. "The Western School." *Little R*, 5: 4-9 (S 18).

Massa, Ann. "The Artistic Conscience of VL." *JAmSt*, 2: 239-52 (O 68).

Rainey, P.M. "VL and *The Village Magazine*." *DCLB*, 8: 22-9 (N 67).

White, William. "VL-iana: A Bibliographical Note." *Serif*, 8: 9-11 (Je 71).

Whitney, Blair. "VL: The Midwest as Utopia." *Midamerica*, 1974, pp. 46-51.

Linn, John Blair. Bonnet, J.M. "JBL and Alexander Gerard: Taste, Imitation, and Genius." *ES*, 55: 361-3 (Ag 74).

Lippard, George. DeGrazio, Emilio. "Edgar Allan Poe, GL, and the 'Spermaceti and Walnut-Coffin Papars.'" *PBSA*, 66: 58-60 (1Q 72).

———. "Poe's Devoted Democrat, GL." *PoeS*, 6: 6-8 (Je 73).

Ehrlich, Heyward. "The 'Mysteries' of Philadelphia: L's *Quaker City* and 'Urban' Gothic." *ESQ*, 18: 50-65 (1Q 72).

Fiedler, Leslie. "The Male Novel." *PR*, 37: 74-89 (1970).

Pollin, B.R. "More on L and Poe." *PoeS*, 7: 22-3 (Je 74).

Ridgely, J.V. "GL's *The Quaker City*: The World of the American Porno-Gothic." *SLitI*, 7: 77-94 (Sp 74).

Seecamp, C.E. "The Chapter of Perfection: A Neglected Influence on GL." *PMHB*, 94: 192-212 (1970).

Locke, Alain. Hay, S.A. "AL & Black Drama." *BlackW*, 21: 8-14 (1972).

Long, R.A. "AL: Cultural and Social Mentor." *BlackW*, 20: 87-90 (1970).

Locke, David Ross (Petroleum V. Nasby). Austin, J.C. "DRL." *ALR*, 4: 192-200 (Sp 71).

Bakerville, Barnet. "19th Century Burlesque of Oratory." *AQ*, 20: 726-43 (Wi 68).

Minor, D.E. "The Many Roles of N." *MarkR*, 4: 16-20 (1973).

Lockridge, Ross. Clarke, Delia. "*Raintree County*: Psychological Symbolism, Archetype, and Myth." *Thoth*, 11: 31-9 (1970).

Dessner, L.J. "Value in Popular Fiction: The Case of *Raintree County*." *Junction*, 1: 147-52 (3Q 73).

Lutwack, Leonard. "*Raintree County* and the Epicising Poet in American Fiction." *BSUF*, 13: 14-28 (Wi 72).

Nemanic, G.C. "RL, *Raintree County*, and the Epic of Irony." *M-A*, 2: 35-46 (1975).

Lodge, George Cabot. Brown, A.H. "The Poetry of GCL." *TC*, 1: 403-14 (F 10).

Crowley, J.W. "GCL (1873-1909)." *ALR*, 6: 45-50 (Wi 73).

———. "George Gissing and GCL." *Gissing N, 6: 7-9 (O 70)*.

———. "The Suicide of an Artist: Henry Adams' Life of GCL." *NEQ*, 46: 189-204 (Je 73).

Pavolini, P.C. "GCL." *Living Age*, 59: 400-8 (17 My 13).

Wharton, Edith. "GCL." *Scrib*, 47: 236-9 (F 10).

Loftis, Norah. Walker, Alice. "Black Anima." *Parnassus*, 2: 5-14 (Sp-Su 74).

Paul, Barbara. "NL and the Problem of Historical Form." *UR, 36*: 226-30 (Sp 70).

Logan, James. Lokken, R.N. "The Social Thought of JL." *WMQ*, 27: 68-9 (1970).

Logan, John. Altieri, Charles. "Poetry as Resurrection: JL's Structures of Metaphysical Solace." *MPS*, 3: 193-224 (#3 73).

Bell, Marvin. "L's Teaching." *Voyages*, 4: 38-9 Sp 71).

Bly, Robert. "JL's Field of Force." *Voyages*, 4: 29-36 (Sp 71).

Callahan, P.J. "Tonal Power, Incoherent Rage: Rhetoric in Three Poets." *SR*, 80: 639-44 (D 72).

Carroll, Paul. "JL: Was Frau Heine a Monster? or 'Yung and Easily Freudened' in Dusseldorf and Hamburg and Berlin and Paris and New York City." *MinnR*, 8: 67-84 (1968).

Chaplin, W.H. "Identity and Spirit in the Recent Poetry of JL." *APR*, 2: 19-24 (#5 73).

Howard, Richard. "The Anonymous Love." *APR*, 2: 7-8 (#5 73).

Isbell, Harold. "Growth and Change: JL's Poems." *MPS*, 2: 213-23 (#5 71).

Logan, John. "JL on Poets and Poetry Today." *Voyages*, 4: 17-24 (Sp 71).

Mazzaro, Jerome. "Ventures into Evening: Self-Parody in the Poetry of JL." *Salmagundi*, 2: 78-95 (1968).

London, Jack. Anon. "Foreign Language Collections and Anthologies." *JLN*, 2: 67-9 (1969).

———. "The Inspiration of JL: A View in Oil." *JLN*, 7: 34-41 (Ja-Ap 74).

*——— . "JL: A Bibliography—A Supplement." *JLN*, 2: 5-25 (Ja-Ap 68).

———. "L and *The Daily Worker*." *JLN*, 4: 54-5 (My-Je 71).

———. "Material in English on London." *JLN*, 2: 71-2 (Ag-S 69).

———. "More on the Mohr Copy of *Harvest Youth*." *JLN*, 6: 91-2 (Ag-S 73).

Allatt, Edward. "*The Assassination Bureau* Filmed." *JLN*, 1: 32-3 (Ja-Je 68).
———. "JL and Upton Sinclair." *JLN*, 1: 22-7 (Ja-Je 68).
———. "More on the Movie Version of *The Assassination Bureau*." *JLN*, 2: 70 (My-Ag 69).
———. "Upton Sinclair on JL in 1963." *JLN*, 2: 77-8 (S-D 69).
Benoit, Raymond. "JL's *The Call of the Wild*." *AQ*, 20: 246-8 (Su 68).
Berger, Yves. "JL, l'aventurier de la littérature." *FL*, 2 Mr 70, pp. 17-8.
Berry, Jeff. "Monsieur Londre and the Pearl Buyer." *JLN*, 6: 13-22 (Ja-Ap 73).
Bland, H.M. "JL." *Overland Mo*, ns, 43: 370-5 (My 04).
Boll, T.E.M. "*The Divine Fire* (1904) and *Martin Eden* (1909)." *ELT*, 14: 115-7 (1971).
Bond, Marshall. "To the Klondike with a Big Dog who Met JL." *AmWest*, 6: 44-8 (Ja 69).
Bosworth, L.A.M., and Jack London. "Is JL a Plagiarist?" *Independent*, 62: 373-6 (14 F 07).
Bouman, Fred. "George Sterling and JL: A Literary Friendship." *JLN*, 5: 108-10 (My-Ag 72).
Bowen, J.K. "JL's 'To Build a Fire': Epistemology and the White Wilderness." *WAL*, 5, 287-9 (Wi 71).
Briggs, J.E. "An Impulsive Youth." *Palimpsest*, 53: 347-52 (Je 71).
Bubka, Tony. "Review of Literature, Summary and Conclusions . . . from a JL Bibliography." *JLN*, 2: 26-42 (1969).
Bukoski, Anthony. "JL's Wolf Larsen: Nietzschean Super Man at All?" *JLN*, 109-10 (S-D 74).
Burton, Lou. "'Some Monstrous Worms.'" *JLN*, 7: 117-21 (S-D 74).
Butterworth, Keen. "Gold." *ALR*, 6: 156-8 (Sp 73).
Buxton, F.H. "JL Collection and Research Center: Oakland Public Library: 125 14th Street." *JLN*, 5: 37-40 (1972).
Bykov, Vil. "A Comment on Vera Colin's Review of B's *Dzek London*." *JLN*, 3: 35-6 (Ja-Ap 70).
———. "Memorable Dates: New Facts about JL." *JLN*, 4: 47-8 (Ja-Ap 71).
———. "Memories about Joan L." *JLN*, 4: 9-10 (Ja-Mr 71).
———. "On the Trail of JL." *SovL*, 2: 139-43 (1960).
———. "Traditions of JL." *JLN*, 1: 62-6 (Jl-D 68).
Carey, Joe. "JL—The Man." *Brass Tacks*, 8: 1,3 (29 S 15).
Čeremin, T.S. "Majakovskij i roman Džeka Londona *Martin Iden*." *RLit*, 13: 121-35 (1970).
Chamberlain, A.H. "JL Number." *Overland Mo*, 90: 97 (My 32).
Chaplin, William. "The Third Presence: JL's *The Anonymous Lover*." *OhR*, 15: 115-9 (#3 74).
Chapman, Arnold. "Between Fire and Ice: A Theme in JL and Horacio Quiroga." *Sym*, 24: 17-26 (1970).
Clayton, Lawrence. "The Ghost Dog, a Motif in *The Call of the Wild*." *JLN*, 5: 158 (S-D 72).
———. "*The Sea Wolf*: L's *Commedia*." *JLN*, 8: 50-4 (My-Ag 75).
Colbron, G.I. "The Eternal Masculine." *Bkm*, 32: 157-9 (O 10).
Cook, George. "L's *Bookman* Letters." *JLN*, 6: 81-7 (My-Ag 73).
———. "Meeting JL's Bishop." *JLN*, 7: 42-3 (Ja-Ap 68).
Cooper, J.G. "The Womb of Time: Archetypal Patterns in the Novels of JL." *JLN*, 8: 1-5 (Ja-Ap 75).
Crane, Joan St. C. "Rare or Seldom-Seen Dust Jackets of American First Editions: XIV." *Serif*, 11: 34-8 (1974).

Cristobal, Juan. "Historia de JL, el viejo bucanero." *Casa de las Americas*, 14: 19-21 (S-O 73).

Crossman, R.H.S. "The Prophecies of JL." *NSt*, 19: 723 (8 Je 40).

Culwell, R.H. "JL, Real Estate in Public Domain." *JLN*, 1: 68-75 (My-Ag 68).

Cushing, Jeff. "Snark: JL's Folly?" *Medley Mag*, 26 Ja 69, p. 3.

Daghlian, Carlos. "JL in Brazil and Portugal." *JLN*, 8: 22-7 (Ja-Je 75).

Davis, William. "My 1916 Visit to JL." *JLN*, 2: 58-65 (My-Ag 69).

Deane, Paul. "JL: Mirror of His Time." *LHR*, 11: 45-50 (1969).

———. "JL: The Paradox of Individualism." *Eng Rec*, 19: 14-9 (1968).

DeGruson, Gene. "JL and E. Haldeman-Julius." *JLN*, 3: 1-7 (Ja-Ap 70).

DeVore, Lynn. "The Descent of White Fang." *JLN*, 7: 122-6 (Ag-S 74).

Dhondt, S.T. "JL's *When God Laughs*: Overman, Underdog, and Satire." *JLN*, 2: 51-7 (My-Ag 69).

———. "'There is a Good-Time Coming': JL's Spirit of Proletarian Revolt." *JLN*, 3: 25-34 (My-Ag 70).

Dodson, M.K. "Naturalism in the Works of JL." *JLN*, 4: 130-9 (S-D 71).

Duc, D.D. "JL's Dream at the Turn of the Century." *JLN*, 6: 133-45 (S-D 73).

Dunn, Allan. "The Sailing of the Snark." *Sunset*, 19: 3-9 (My 07).

Dunn, N.E., and Pamela Wilson. "The Significance of Upward Mobility in *Martin Eden*." *JLN*, 5: 1-8 (Ja-Ap 72).

Elder, Gary. "American Renewal in the L Legend." *London Coll*, 4: 12-7 (F 73).

Erbentraut, E.B. "The Intellectual Undertow in *Martin Eden*." *JLN*, 3: 12-24 (Ja-Mr 70).

———. "The Balanced Vision: Missionaries and the Test of Spirit in Two JL Stories." *ABC*, 24: 31-2 (Mr-Ap 74).

———. "JL, D. Litt." *JLN*, 5: 159-63 (S-D 72).

———. "The Key to Complexity: JL and the Theory of *Complementarity*." *JLN*, 6: 119-22 (Ag-S 73).

———. "The Protean Imperative." *JLN*, 5: 153-7 (S-D 72).

———. "The Symbolic Triad in L's *The Little Lady of the Big House*." *JLN*, 3: 82-9 (S-D 70).

———. "'A Thousand Deaths': Hyperbolic Anger." *JLN*, 4: 125-9 (S-D 71).

Fick, A.S. "Warning: Can Be Addictive." *JLN*, 5: 124-5 (My-Ag 72).

Findley, Sue. "Naturalism in 'To Build a Fire.'" *JLN*, 2: 45-8 (My-Ag 69).

Flink, Andrew. "'Call of the Wild': Parental Metaphor." *JLN*, 7: 58-61 (My-Ag 74).

———. "Rare JL Collection Presented to UOP." *JLN*, 4: 156-7 (S-D 71).

———. "The Three Faces of the Wolf House." *JLN*, 4: 151-5 (S-D 71).

Forrey, Robert. "Male and Female in L's *The Sea-Wolf*." *L&P*, 24: 135-43 (1974).

Freeman, A.W. "Notes on *A Search for JL*." *JLN*, 7: 107-8 (My-Ag 74).

Fujiwara, Sakae. "JL's Socialism: A Summary of One Chapter from *JL in Connection with the American Dream*." *JLN*, 3: 73-81 (S-D 70).

Gardner, Ray. "JL on King Albert of Belgium." *JLN*, 1: 21 (Ja-Ap 68).

Garnett, Porter. "JL—His Relation to Literary Art." *PaM*, 17: 446-53 (Ap 07).

Giles, J.R. "Beneficial Atavism in Frank Norris and JL." *WAL*, 4: 15-28 (Sp 69).

———. "JL 'Down and Out' in England: The Relevance of the Sociological Study *People of the Abyss* to L's Fiction." *JLN*, 2: 79-83 (Ja-Ap 69).

———. "Some Notes on the Red-Blooded Reading of Kipling by JL and Frank Norris." *JLN*, 3: 56-62 (Ja-Ap 70).

———. "Thematic Significance of the Jim Hall Episode in *White Fang*." *JLN*, 2: 49-50 (My-Ag 69).

Glancy, D.R. "Anything to Help Anybody: The Authorship of *Daughters of the Rich.*" *JLN*, 5: 19-26 (Ja-Ap 72).

Goldstein, J.J. "Learning the Hard Way?" *Serif*, 7: 36-7 (1970).

Gower, R.A. "The Creative Conflict: Struggle and Escape in JL's Fiction." *JLN*, 4: 77-114 (M-Ap 71).

Gross, Dalron. "Seventeen George Sterling Letters." *JLN*, 1: 41-61 (Jl-D 68).

Gunn, D.W. "Three Radicals and a Revolution. Reed, L, and Steffens on Mexico." *SWR*, 55: 393-410 (Au 70).

Haire, D.B., and D.E. Hensley. "A Comparative Look at Maugham and JL." *JLN*, 8: 110-3 (Ag-S 75).

Hamby, J.A. "A Note on JL: A View in Oil." *JLN*, 3: 102-3 (S-D 70).

Harpham, Geoffrey. "JL and the Tradition of Superman Socialism." *AmerS*, 16: 23-33 (Sp 75).

Hatchel, D.E. "Animal Imagery in L's 'A Piece of Steak.'" *JLN*, 8: 119-21 (S-D 75).

Hendricks, King. "Determination and Courage." *Eleusis of Chi Omega*, 66: 305-13 (My 64).

Henry, J.L. "'The First Poet': JL or George Sterling?" *JLN*, 6: 60-5 (My-Ag 73).

———. "Give a Man a Boat He Can Sail." *JLN*, 7: 23-29 (Ja-Ap 74).

———. "A Proposed Chronology of Editions of *The Son of the Wolf.*" *JLN*, 3: 8-11 (Ja-Ap 70).

Hensley, D.E. "A Note on JL's Use of Black Humor." *JLN*, 8: 129-32 (S-D 75).

———. "Sherlock Holmes and Smoke Bellow." *JLN*, 8: 129-32 (S-D 75).

Hindman, K.B. "JL's The Sea Wolf: Naturalism with a Spiritual Bent." *JLN*, 6: 99-110 (S-D 73).

Hoffmeister, C.C. "Brief Commentary on the L Collections of the Oakland Public and UC (Berkeley) Libraries." *JLN*, 7: 632-64 (S-D 74).

———. "Recent Soviet Attention to JL—III." *JLN*, 6: 131-2 (Mr-Ag 73).

Horváth, Antal. "JL's Checkered Career in Hungary." *HSE*, 3: 55-70 (1967).

Hutchens, J.K. "Penmen of the Golden West—1. Heritage of the Frontier." *SatR*, 23 S 67, pp. 345, 97-8.

Ihde, Horst. "JL as sozialistischer Schriftsteller." *ZAA*, 20: 5-23 (1972).

Isani, M.A. "JL on Norris' *The Octopus.*" *ALR*, 6: 66-9 (Wi 73).

Jespersen, B.M. "Fifty Years Since JL Died." *JLN*, 2: 1-4 (Ja-Mr 69).

*Johns, F.A. "Addendum To Woodbridge: JL, A Bibliography." *PBSA*, 65: 74 (1Q 71).

*Johnson, R.C., and G.T. Tanselle. "Addenda to Bibliographies of . . . L [and others]: Haldeman-Julius Little Blue Books." *PBSA*, 66: 66 (1Q 72).

Jorgenson, J.P. "JL's 'The Red One.'" *JLN*, 8: 101-3 (Ag-S 75).

Kaye, F.W. "JL's Modification of Herbert Spencer." *JLN*, 4: 67-72 (My-Ag 74).

Kieniewicz, Teresea. "Spór o Jacka Londona." *KN*, 2: 219-25 (1974).

Kingman, Russ. "L's Yukon Cabin Now at JL Square in Oakland, California." *JLN*, 3: 104-7 (S-D 70).

Kravetz, Marc. "JL, Aventurier de la société." *Mag Littéraire*, 26: 28-30 (F 69).

Kronenberger, Louis. "JL as Legend." *Nation*, 147: 420-2 (22 O 38).

Labor, Earle. "A Dedication to the Memory of JL, 1876-1916." *A&W*, 6: 92-6 (Su 64).

———. "*Gold: A Play in Three Acts.*" *JLN*, 5: 169-71 (S-D 71).

———. "JL: An Addendum." *ALR*, 2: 91-3 (Sp 68).

———. "JL in Denmark." *JLN*, 8: 95-100 (Ag-S 75).

———. "JL's *Mondo Cane: The Call of the Wild and White Fang.*" *JLN*, 1: 2-13 (Jl-D 67).

———. "Portrait of the Artist as Professional." *JLN*, 6: 93-8 (Jl-D 73).

————. " 'To the Man on the Trail': JL's Christmas Carol." *JLN*, 3: 90-4 (S-D 70).

Lacassin, Francis. "A Classic of the Revolt." *JLN*, 6: 71-8 (My-Ag 73).

Lachtman, Howard. "All That Glitters: JL's *Gold*." *JLN*, 5: 172-8 (S-D 72).

————. "*Daughters of the Rich*: A New JL Play." *JLN*, 4: 11-5 (1971).

————. "JL Conference at the University of the Pacific (Stockton, California; March 23, 1974)." *JLN*, 7: 96-9 (My-Ag 74).

————. "JL on Stage: A Review of *Dear Comrades*." *JLN*, 5: 129-34 (S-D 72).

————. "Man and Superwoman in JL's 'The Kanaka Surf.' " *WAL*, 7: 101-11 (Su 72).

————. "Labor's Love." *JLN*, 7: 11-6 (My-Ag 74).

————. "Reconsideration: *The Valley of the Moon* by JL." *NRep*, 173: 27-9 (6 S 75).

Lampson, Robin. "Remarks at the Memorial Service for Joan L in Berkeley, California, January 21, 1971." *JLN*, 5: 33-6 (Ja-Mr 72).

————. "Unique Family Collection of JL's Work Preserved Intact in University of Pacific's Stuart Library." *Pacific Hist*, 16: 74-81 (Sp 72).

Lassini, Francis. "JL Between the Challenge of the Supernatural and the Last Judgement." *JLN*, 8: 114-8 (S-D 75).

Leitz, R.C. "JL in 'Rhymed Reviews' and 'Impudent Interviews.' " *JLN*, 8: 122-8 (S-D 75).

London, Jack. "A Thousand Deaths." *London Coll*, 2: 3-13 (Ap 71).

————. "Tramping with Kelly Through Iowa: A JL Diary." *Palimpsest*, 52: 316-46 (Je 71).

————. "A Tribute to My Father." *JLN*, 7: 94-5 (My-Ag 74).

McClintock, J.I. "JL: Finding the Proper Trend of Literary Art." *CEA*, 34: 25-8 (My 72).

————. "JL's Use of Carl Jung's *Psychology of the Unconscious*." *AL*, 336-47 (N 70).

————. "The Role of 'Local Color' in JL's Alaska Wilderness Tales." *WR*, 6: 51-6 (Wi 69).

McDevitt, William. "JL as Poet." *London Coll*, 1: 13-9 (Jl 70).

McMillan, Marilyn. "Unrecorded Contemporary Reviews of L's Novels." *JLN*, 1: 14-7 (Jl-D 67).

McNeel, Laird. "More on *The Son of the Wolf*." *JLN*, 3: 135-6 (S-D 70).

Magris, Claudio. "Die Melamcholie des Wolfes: JL und die Parabel des reaktionaren Intellektuellen." *Neohelicom*, 2: 187-92 (#3, 4 74).

Malița, Tatiana. "The Wisteria-Trees—Cea mai cunoscută adaptare americană după Livada cu visini." *AUB-LUC*, 22: 57-66 (#2 73).

Mehl, R.F. "JL, Alfred Henry Lewis, and Primitive Women." *JLN*, 6: 66-7 (Ja-Mr 73).

Millard, Bailey. "JL, Farmer." *Bkm*, 44: 151-6 (O 16).

Monteiro, George. "JL: An Unrecorded Parody." *JLN*, 4: 65-6 (Ja-Mr 74).

Morrill, S.S. "JL: UC Rebel of '96." *JLN*, 7: 100-6 (Ap-Jl 74).

*Nichol, J.W. "JL: A Bibliography, Addenda I." *JLN*, 2: 84-7 (Ja-Mr 69).

————. "The Role of 'Local Color' in JL's Alaskan Wilderness Tales." *WR*, 6: 51-6 (1970).

North, Dick. "Diary of JL's Trip to the Klondike." *YN*, nv: 9-12, 36 (N-D 66).

Noto, Sal. "Happy Birthday, J." *JLN*, 4: 145-50 (S-D 71).

————. "JL as Social Critic." *JLN*, 4: 145-50 (S-D 71).

————. "JL Inscriptions at Stanford University." *JLN*, 5: 145-8 (S-D 72).

Odessky, M.H. "The Death of JL: Accident or Intent?" *JHS*, 2: 204-7 (O-D 69).

Olgin, M. "Di Shtime fun blut." *Yiddish Kultur*, 37: 44-6 (#1 75).

Parkay, F.W. "The Influence of Nietzsche's *Thus Spake Zarathustra* on L's *The Sea-Wolf*." *JLN*, 4: 16-24 (Ap-S 71).

Pearsall, R.B. "Elizabeth Barrett Meets Wolf Larsen." *WAL*, 4: 3-13 (Sp 69).

Peterson, W.J. "Kelly's Army Comes to Iowa." *Palimpsest*, 52: 289-316 (Je 71).

Phillips, G.J. "Moonface the Murderer." *WN*, 8: 13 (F 71).

Plante, Raymond. "JL ou les aventures paralleles." *Liberte*, 92: 58-65 (1974).

Rehn, Mats. "Den svenske JL." *BLM*, 40: 204-8 (1971).

Riber, Jorgen. "Archetypal Patterns in 'The Red One'". *JLN*, 8: 104-6 (Je-S 75).

Russack, Martin. "JL, America's First Proletarian Writer." *New Masses*, 4: 13 (4 Ja 29).

Sandburg, Charles. "JL: A Common Man." *JLN*, 5: 14-8 (Ja-Ap 72).

Schlottman, D.H. "JL at the Fair." *London Coll*, 4: 3-4 (F 73).

———. "To Build Yet Another Fire." *JLN*, 8: 11-14 (Ja-Je 75).

Sherko, Arthur. "An Analogue for *Lost Face*." *JLN*, 3: 95-8 (S-D 70).

Shivers, A.S. "JL: Not a Suicide." *DR*, 49: 43-57 (Sp 69).

Siegel, P.N. "JL's *Iron Heel*: It's Significance for Today." *Int Socialist R*, 35: 18-29 (Jl-Ag 74).

Silet, C.L.P. "Upton Sinclair to JL: A Literary Friendship." *JLN*, 5: 49-76 (My-Ag 72).

———, and S.S. "Charmian L to Upton Sinclair: Selected Letters." *JLN*, 4: 25-46 (My-Ag 71).

Sisson, J.E. "A Chronological Bibliography of the Writings of JL." *JLN*, 4: 6-8 (Ja-Ap 71).

———. "JL and the *Daughters of the Rich*." *JLN*, 5: 27-32 (Ja-Ap 72).

———. "JL's Articles and Short Stories in the Oakland High School *Aegis*." *London Coll*, 3: 1-8 (D 71).

———. "JL's Published Poems: A Chronological Bibliography." *London Coll*, 1: 20-1 (Jl 70).

———. "A Letter from JL to Miss Blanche Partington Written April 9, 1913." *JLN*, 5: 77-97 (My-Ag 72).

———. "A Memorial to Joan L." *JLN*, 4: 1-5 (Ja-Ap 71).

*Skipp, F.E. "JL." *ALR*, 8: 299-306 (1975).

Sloane, D.E.E. "David Graham Phillips, JL, and Others on Contemporary Reviewers and Critics, 1903-1904." *ALR*, 3: 67-71 (Wi 70).

———. "JL on Reviewing: An Addendum." *ALR*, 6: 70-2 (Wi 73).

Solensten, John. "Richard Harding Davis' Rejection of *The Call of the Wild*." *JLN*, 4: 122-3 (S-D 71).

Sorgenstein, Samuel. "Researches and Findings: A Letter from JL." *JLN*, 3: 99-100 (S-D 70).

———. "The Truth about JL: Reminiscences of Upton Sinclair." *JLN*, 6: 79-80 (My-Ag 73).

Spinner, J.H. "JL's *Martin Eden*: The Development of the Existential Hero." *MichA*, 3: 43-8 (Su 70).

———. "A Syllabus for the 20th Century: JL's 'The Call of the Wild.'" *JLN*, 4: 73-8 (My-Ag 74).

Stafford, William. "JL." *Poetry*, 106: 323 (Ag 65).

Sweeney, Ben. "JL's Noble Lady." *JLN*, 5: 111-22 (My-Ag 72).

———. "L's 'The Way of War': When? Where? Why?" *JLN*, 5: 9-13 (Ja-Ap 72).

Tweney, G.H. "JL: Bibliographically and Biographically Speaking." *JLN*, 7: 9-22 (Ja-Ap 74).

———. "JL's Books in the Market." *JLN*, 4: 140-4 (O-D 71).

Upton, Ann. "The Wolf in L's Mirror." *JLN*, 6: 11-8 (My-Ag 73).

Vanderbeets, Richard. "Nietzsche of the North: Heredity and Race in L's *The Son of the Wolf*." *WAL*, 2: 229-33 (Fa 67).

Walker, D.L. "The Famous Fantastic JL." *London Coll*, 2: 24-6 (Ap 71).

———. "JL (1876-1916)." *ALR*, 1: 71-8 (Fa 67).

———. "Jl and Maurice Magnus: An Annotation on a Strange Correspondence." *JLN*, 5: 149-52 (S-D 72).

————. "JL, Sherlock Holmes, and the Agent." *BakSJ*, 20: 79-85 (Je 70).

————. "JL: The Unmined Gold." *London Coll*, 4: 5-12 (F 73).

————. "L Exhibit at the El Paso Public Library: May 15-June 15." *JLN*, 5: 105-7 (My-Ag 72).

————. "Note to the Next L Biographer." *JLN*, 1: 28 (Ja-Mr 68).

————. "JL: The Unmined Gold." *London Coll*, 4: 5-12 (F 73).

————. "William Tum Suden Bahls Remembers JL: Three Letters." *JLN*, 5: 98-104 (My-Ag 72).

Walker, Franklin. "*Martin Eden par Jl.*" *Informations et Documents*, 281: 23-7 (1 Ag 69).

*————. "'A New JL Bibliography." *CEA*, 34: 28-9 (My 72).

Weiderman, Richard. "JL: Master of Science Fiction." *London Coll*, 2: 14-23 (Ap 71).

*————. "JL's Science Fiction: A Bibliography." *London Coll*, 2: 22 (Ap 71).

————. "L Collectors and Their Books." *JLN*, 5: 126-8 (O-D 72).

————. "*Scorn of Women*: JL's Rarest First Edition." *JLN*. 4: 119-21 (O-D 71).

Wilcox, Earl. "The Kipling of the Klondike: Naturalism in L's Early Fiction." *JLN*, 6: 1-12 (Ja-Ap 73).

————. "JL's Naturalism: The Example of *The Call of the Wild*." *JLN*, 2: 91-101 (S-D 69).

————. "*Le Milieu, Le Moment, La Race*: Literary Naturalism in JL's *White Fang*." *JLN*, 3: 42-55 (1970).

Winnick, David. "What JL (or Allende) Knew about the Enemies of Democracy." *JLN*, 8: 8-10 (Ja-Je 75).

Wirzberger, Karl-Heinz. "JL and the Goldrush." *JLN*, 6: 146-7 (O-D 73).

Woodridge, H.C. "Additional Reviews." *JLN*, 1: 18-9 (Jl-D 67).

————. "L'Appel de la vie series directed by Francis Lacassin." *JLN*, 7: 30-3 (Ja-Mr 74).

————. "Into What Languages Has L Been Translated?" *JLN*, 2: 5-25 (Ja-Ap 69); 8: 28-31, 133-7 (Je-S, S-d 75).

*————. "JL: A Bibliography—A Supplement." *JLN*, 2: 5-25 (Ja-Ap 69); 8: 2831, 133-37 (Je-S, S-D 75).

————. "JL on King Albert of Belgium." *JLN*, 1: 21 (Ja-Je 68).

*————. "Jesse and Jane Stuart: A Bibliography—Supplement 7." *JLN*, 4: 161-3 (O-D 71).

Yardley, Jonathan. "Reconsideration: JL's *Martin Eden*." *NRep*, 2 Je 73, pp. 31-3.

*Woodward, R.H. "JL: A Bibliography." *JLN*, 88-90 (My-Ag 69); 7: 85-9 (My-Ag 74).

————. "'JL Slept Here.'" *JLN*, 4: 158 (1971).

Woodbridge, H.C. "More References Concerning JL." *JLN*, 1: 34-40 (Ja-Je 68).

————. "The 1976 London Centennial." *JLN*, 6: 88 (Jl-S 73).

————. "Recent Wolf House Books." *JLN*, 5: 186 (O-D 72).

Long, Haniel. Almon, Bert. "Woman as Interpreter: HL's *Malinche*." *SWR*, 59: 221-39 (Su 74).

Powell, L.C. "HL and *Interlinear to Cabeza de Vaca*." *Westways*, 63: 26-9, 78 (Ap 71).

Sarton, May. "The Leopard Land: Haniel and Alice L's Santa Fe." *SWR*, 57: 1-14 (1972).

Longfellow, Henry Wadsworth. Anon. "The Plagiarist of Reality." *TLS*, 9 N 73, pp. 1371-2.

Allaback, Steven. "L's 'Galgano.'" *AL*, 46: 210-9 (My 74).

————. "Mrs. Clemm and HWL." *HLB*, 18: 32-42 (Ja 70).

————. "Oak Hall in American Literature." *AL*, 46: 545-9 (Ja 75).

————. "Voices of L: *Kavanagh* as Autobiography." *ESQ*, 58: 3-14 (1Q 70).

Ardura, Ernesto. "Poet of Two Cultures." *Americas*, 25: 25-9 (Mr 73).

Arnell, Richard, and R.L. Volz. "L and Music." *ESQ*, 58: 32-8 (1Q 70).

Bowski, Adolf. "L in Germany." *N&Q*, 148: 247-8 (4 Ap 25).

Brotherston, Gordon. "Ubirajara, Hiawatha, Cumandá: National Virtue from American Indian Literature." *CLS*, 9: 243-52 (S 72).

Burwick, Frederick. "L and German Romanticism." *CLS*, 7: 12-42 (Mr 70).

Cameron, K.W. "Emerson, L, Lowell, and Others in Defense of R. Morris Copeland in 1863." *ESQ*, 47: 140-6 (2Q 67).

Clark, C.E.F. "Hawthorne to L—An Unpublished Letter." *NHJ*, 1: 71 (1971).

Cohn, J.R. "A Note on L's Letter 416." *ESQ*, 58: 129-30 (1Q 70).

Davidson, Gustav. "L's Angels." *PrS*, 42: 235-43 (Fa 68).

Dean, Dennis. "Hitchcock's Dinosaur Tracks." *AQ*, 21: 639-44 (1969).

Elwert, W.T. "L, Mascheroni, Monti und die 'Conchiglia fossile': Zur Geistes und Stilgeschichtlichen Stellung Giacomo Zanella." *RF*, 83: 480-516 (1971).

Evans, Elizabeth. "The Everett-L Correspondence." *ATQ*, 13: 2-15 (1972).

Franklin, Phyllis. "The Importance of Time in L's Works." *ESQ*, 58: 14-22 (1Q 70).

Gallagher, E.J. "A Note on L and Tennyson." *N&Q*, 15: 415-6 (N 68).

Griffith, John. "L and Herder and the Sense of History." *TSLL*, 13: 249-65 (Su 71).

Hanson, Virginia. "I Remember 'Hiawatha.'" *UHQ*, 40: 265-74 (Su 72).

Harwell, Richard. "Librarian L." *ESQ*, 58: 63-73 (1Q 70).

———, and Roger Michener. "As Public as the Town Pump." *LJ*, 99: 959-63 (1974).

Helmick, E.T. "L's Lyric Poetry." *ESQ*, 58: 38-40 (1Q 70).

Holman, H.R. "L in 'The Rue Morgue.'" *ESQ*, 60: 58-60 (Fa 70).

Johnson, C.L. "L's Studies in France." *ESQ*, 58: 40-8 (1Q 70).

Kroeger, F.P. "L, Melville, and Hawthorne: The Passage into the Iron Age." *IllQ*, 33: 30-41 (D 70).

Kurman, George. "Negative Comparison in Literary Epic Narrative." *CL*, 21: 337-47 (Fa 69).

Lefcourt, C.R. "HWL's *Hyperion*: Its Background and Influences." *MSpr*, 62: 127-35 (1968).

———. "L et la culture italienne." *RLV*, 40: 243-8 (My-Je 74).

———. "L's First Goethe Lectures." *Eng Rec*, 18: 15-8 (D 67).

Lyra, Franciszek. "Correspondence of Sygurg Wisniowski to HWL." *KN*, 19: 319-26 (1972).

McDonald, J.J. "L in Hawthorne's 'The Antique Ring.'" *NEQ*, 46: 622-6 (D 73).

Mann, C.W. "Hawthorne to L: An Unpublished Letter." *NHJ*, 1: 71 (1971).

Mathews, J.C. "L's Dante Collection." *ESQ*, 62: 10-22 (Wi 71).

———. "L Symposium." *ESQ*, 58: 3-75 (1970).

Milham, M.E. "Arcady on the Atlantic." *HAB*, 19: 42-51 (1968).

Millward, Cecelia, and Cecelia Tichi. "Whatever Happened to *Hiawatha*?" *Genre*, 6: 313-32 (1973).

Moore, Rayburn. "'Merlin and Vivien'? Some Notes on Sherwood Bonner and L." *MissQ*, 28: 181-4 (Sp 75).

Moyne, E.L. "L and Kah-ge-ga-bowh." *ESQ*, 58: 48-52 (1Q 70).

———. "The Origin and Development of L's 'Song of Hiawatha.'" *JIAS*, 8: 156-82 (Ja 66).

Pearce, C.A. "L e Hispano-america." *Thesaurus*, 29: 169-77 (1974); *Hispania*, 58: 921-6 (1975).

Pierle, R.C. "Sherwood Who? A Study in the Vagaries of Literary Evaluation." *NMW*, 1: 18-22 (Sp 68).

Pronechen, J.S. "The Making of 'Hiawatha.'" *NYFQ*, 28: 151-60 (Je 72).

Reed, K.T. "L's 'Sleep' and Frost's 'After Apple-Picking.'" *AN&Q*, 10: 134-5 (1972).

Rockland, M.A. "HWL and Domingo Faustino Sarmiento." *JIAS*, 12: 271-9 (Ap 70).

Rongonena, Lulija. "HL: Personibas evolucija." *Karogs*, 2: 168-75 (1974).

Sears, D.A. "Folk Poetry in L's Boyhood." *NEQ*, 45: 96-105 (Mr 72).

Shaw, W.D. "A Note on L's Auroral References." *ATQ*, 2: 13-6 (2Q 69).

Simpson, C.M. "L in His Letters." *VQR*, 48: 312-6 (1973).

Smith, C.N. "Emma Marshall and L: Some Additions to Hilen's *Letters*." *JAmSt*, 8: 81-90 (Ap 74).

Stanonik, Janzez. "L and Smolnikar." *AN*, 1: 3-40 (1968).

———. "Potovanje Longfellowa skozi Slovenijo leta 1828." *SlE*, 18-9: 123-8 (1965-66).

Stephenson, Edward. "L Revised." *TSB*, 118: 4-5 (Wi 72).

Tichi, Cecelia. "L's Motives for the Structures of 'Hiawatha.'" *AL*, 42: 548-53 (Ja 71).

Turner, Arlin. "Hawthorne and L: Abortive Plans for Collaboration." *NHJ*, 1: 3-11 (1971).

Ustenko, H.O. "Do istoriji stvorennja zbirky H.L. *Pisni pro rabstvo*." *RLz*, 16: 36-42 (1972).

Vanderbilt, Kermit. "Correction and Further Note on Mark Twain and L." *MTJ*, 16: 24-5 (Wi 72).

———. "Mark Twain Writes to Poet L." *MTJ*, 16: 1 (Su 72).

Wagenknecht, Edward. "L and Howells." *ESQ*, 58: 52-7 (1Q 70).

Ward, R.S. "The Influence of Vico Upon L." *ESQ*, 58: 57-62 (1Q 70).

———. "L's Roots in Yankee Soil." *NEQ*, 41: 180-92 (Je 68).

Woodress, James. "The Fortunes of L in Italy." *SA*, 16: 125-50 (1970).

Longstreet, Augustus Baldwin. Amy, E.F. "Laying a Ghost: A Note on Hardy's Plagiarism." *NCF*, 9: 151-3 (1954).

Budd, L.J. "Gentlemanly Humorists of the Old South." *SFQ*, 17: 232-40 (1953).

Davidson, Donald. "The Gardens of John Donald Wade." *GaR*, 19: 383-403 (Wi 65).

Harkey, J.H. "A Note on L's Ransy Sniffle and Brackenridge's *Modern Chivalry*." *WPHM*, 52: 43-5 (Ja 69); *TSLL*, 13: 249-66 (Su 71).

Inge, M.T. "John Donald Wade's L." *SAB*, 38: 69, 81 (N 73).

Johnson, J.W. "ABL." *MissHSP*, 12: 122-35 (1912).

King, Kimball. "Regionalism in the Three Souths." *TWA*, 54: 37-50 (1965).

Longstreet, A.B. "Georgia Scenes: 'A Night in the Cars.'" *MissQ*, 23: 169-74 (Sp 70).

Parks, E.W. "The Three Streams of Southern Humor." *GaR*, 9: 147-59 (1955).

Rubin, L.D. "The Great American Joke." *SAQ*, 72: 82-94 (Wi 73).

Smith, G.J. "A.B.L and John Wade's 'Cousin Lucius.'" *GHQ*, 56: 276-81 (Su 72).

Swanson, W.J. "Fowl Play on the Frontier." *WGCR*, 1: 12-5 (1968).

Wade, J.D. "Old Books: *Georgia Scenes*." *GaR*, 14: 444-7 (Wi 60).

Weber, C.J. "A Ghost from the Barber Shop." *NCol*, 1: 185 (1948).

Lovecraft, H.P. Benoît, Monique. "La vie est le rêve d'un rêve." *ELit*, 7: 109-25 (1974).

Brulotte, Gaetan. "Le sceptre et le spectre." *ELit*, 7: 97-107 (1974).

Hellens, Franz. "L, ou l'abstraction sans issue." *Syn*, 289-90: 32-7 (Jl-Ag 70).

Levy, Maurice. "Facisme et fantastique ou le cas L." *Caliban*, 7: 67-78 (1970).

Pagetti, Carlo. "L'universo impazzito di H.P.L." *SA*, 13: 339-75 (1967).

Rosado, Pedro. "L, mestre do fantástico." *Diároi de Notícias*, 26 Jl 73, pp. 17-8; 2 Ag 73, pp. 17-8; 9 Ag 73, pp. 17-8.

St. Armand, B.L. "Facts in the Case of H.P.L." *RIH*, 31: 3-19 (1972).

———. "H.P.L.: New England Decadent." *Caliban XII*, 11: 127-55 (1975).

Touttain, P.A. "Resurrection de H.P.L." *NL*, 47: 6 (23 O 69).

Tuzet, Helene. "Onirisme et fantastique chez H.P.L." *RSH*, 133: 139-51 (Ja-Mr 69).

Low, Samuel. Leary, Lewis. "SL: New York's First Poet." *BNYPL*, 74: 468-80 (S 70).

Lowell, Amy. Anderson, Norman. "Corrections to AL's Reding of Keats's Marginalia." *KSJ*, 23: 25-31 (1974).

Healey, E.C. "AL: An American Abroad." *Montclair J Soc Sci and Hum,* 1: 33-43 (Fa 72).

Healey, Claire. "AL Visits London." *NEQ,* 46: 439-53 (S 73).

———. "Some Imagist Essays: AL." *NEQ,* 43: 134-8 (Mr 70).

Hirsch, J.C. "John Gould Fletcher and AL: New Evidence of their Relationship." *HLB,* 22: 72-5 (1974).

Kenner, Hugh. "Mao⁴ or Presumption." *Shen,* 21: 84-93 (Sp 70).

Lowell, Amy. "Curcubeul." *Steaua,* 24: 27 (#16 74).

Lowes, J.L. "An Unacknowledged Imagist." *Nation,* 102: 217-9 (20 Ap 16).

Overmyer, Janet. "Which Broken Pattern? A Note on AL's 'Patterns.'" *NCLit,* 1: 14-5 (S 71).

Self, R.T. "The Correspondence of AL and Barrett Wendell." *NEQ,* 47: 65-86 (Mr 74).

Watanabe, Schoichi. "Imagist and Haiku—with Special Reference to AL." *ELLS,* 6: 108-30 (1969).

Lowell, James Russell. Axelrod, Steven. "Colonel Shaw in American Poetry: 'For the Union Dead' and Its Precursors." *AQ,* 24: 523-37 (1972).

Brooks, Van Wyck. "L as a Critic." *NRep,* 3: 156-7 (12 Je 15).

Brubaker, B.R. "J.R.L. Boosts Jeremiah Curtin, Harvard '63." *AN&Q,* 10: 68-9 (Ja 72).

Cameron, K.W. "Emerson, Longfellow, L and Others in Defense of R. Morris Copeland in 1863." *ESQ,* 47: 140-6 (2Q 67).

Eidson, J.O. "Charles Stearns Wheeler: Friend of Emerson." *ESQ,* 52: 13-75 (3Q 68).

Lease, Benjamin. "Robert Carter, JRL and John Neal: A Document." *JA,* 13: 246-8 (1968).

Myerson, Joel. "Eight L Letters from Concord in 1838." *IllQ,* 38: 20-42 (Wi 75).

———. "L on Emerson: A New Letter from Concord in 1838." *NEQ,* 44: 649-52 (D 71).

Oggel, L.T. "L's 'A Fable for Critics,' 519-520." *Expl,* 27: 60 (1969).

Paroissien, David. "JRL: The Fireside Traveler." *SA,* 15: 61-74 (1969).

Stimson, P.M. "A Poetic Souvenir: The Crossing of Pathways in Memorable Lives." *YULG,* 43: 85-90 (O 68).

Wiehe, D.E. "Mr. L and Mr. Edwards." *ConL,* 3: 21-31 (Sp-Su 62).

Woodall, G.R. "RJL's *Words of Jeremy Taylor, D.D.*" *Costerus,* 3: 221-36 (1972).

Wortham, Thomas. "L's 'Agassiz' and Mrs. Alexander." *YULG,* 45: 118-22 (Ja 71).

Lowell, Robert. Anon. "A Conversation with RL." *Review,* 26: 10-29 (Su 71).

———. "From Genesis to RL." *TLS,* 10 Ag 73, pp. 917-9.

Anzilotti, Rolando. "Il *Prometeo* di RL." *Approdo,* 62: 69-74 (1973).

Axelrod, Steven. "Baudelaire and the Poetry of RL." *TCL,* 17: 257-74 (O 71).

———. "Colonel Shaw in American Poetry: 'For the Union Dead' and Its Precursors." *AQ,* 24: 523-37 (O 72).

———. "Private and Public Worlds in L's *For the Union Dead.*" *Per Comp Lit,* 1: 53-73 (#1 75).

———. "RL and New York Intellectuals." *ELN,* 11: 206-9 (1974).

Bernlef, J. "Een lezing van RL." *Gids,* 132: 314-6 (1969).

———. "Over RL." *Gids,* 131: 157-9 (1968).

Bigsby, C.W.E. "The Paradox of Revolution: RL's *The Old Glory.*" *Ranam,* 5: 63-79 (Su 72).

Bly, Robert. "RL's *For the Union Dead.*" *Sixties,* 8: 93-6 (1966).

Bowen, Roger. "Confession and Equilibrium: RL's Poetic Development." *Criticism,* 11: 78-93 (Wi 69).

Boyers, Robert. "On RL." *Salmagundi,* 13: 36-44 (1970).

Bragg, Robert. "The Rise of Lady Lazarus." *Mosaic,* 2: 9-36 (1969).

Bromwich, David. "Reading RL." *Commentary,* 52: 78-83 (Ag 71).

Brumleve, E.M. "Permanence and Change in the Poetry of RL." *TSLL,* 10: 143-53 (Fa 68).

Buckley, Vincent. "The Persistence of God." *CritR*, 10: 74-87 (1967).

———. "Trial and Error: The Poetry of RL." *Quadrant* (Sydney), 14: 20-31 (Ja-F 70).

Cargill, Oscar. "On Repositioning RL." *CEA*, 34: 38-9 (Ja 72).

Carne-Ross, D.S. "Conversation with RL." *Delos*, 1: 165-75 (1968).

Colman, E.A.M. "The Poetry of RL." *Meanjin*, 28: 107-13 (1969).

Combecher, Hans. "Dichtung als psychotherapeutische Selbsthilfe: Zu zwei amerikanischen 'Confessional Poems.'" *NS*, 20: 545-50 (O 71).

Dale, Peter. "Fortuitous Form." *Agenda*, 11: 73-87 (#2-3 73).

Daniels, Guy. "The Tyranny of Free Translation." *Translation* 73, 1: 12-20 (Wi 73).

Davie, Donald. "RL." *Parnassus*, 12: 49-57 (Fa-Wi 73).

Doherty, P.C. "The Poet as Historian: 'For the Union Dead' by RL." *CP*, 1: 37-41 (Fa 68).

Dolan, P.J. "L's *Quaker Graveyard*: Poem and Tradition." *Renascence*, 21: 171-80, 194 (Su 69).

Dunn, Douglas. "The Big Race: L's Visions and Revisions." *Encounter*, 41: 107-13 (O 73).

Eddins, Dwight. "Poet and State in the Verse of RL." *TSLL*, 15: 371-86 (Su 73).

Estrin, M.W. "RL's *Benito Cereno*." *MD*, 15: 411-26 (Mr 73).

Fein, R.J. "Family History in *Life Studies*." *NEQ*, 46: 272-8 (Je 73).

———. "*Lord Weary's Castle* Revisited." *PMLA*, 89: 34-41 (Ja 74).

———. "Memories of Brooklyn and RL." *BSUF*, 12: 20-7 (Au 71).

Fender, Stephen. "Whatever Happened to Warren Winslow?" *JAmS*, 7: 187-90 (Ag 73).

Freimarck, Vincent. "Another Holmes in RL's 'Hawthorne.'" *ELN*, 8: 48-9 (S 70).

French, A.L. "RL: The Poetry of Abdication." *OR*, 9: 5-20 (Ja 68).

Friar, Kimon. "On Translation." *CLS*, 8: 197-213 (S 71).

Fulton, Robin. "L and Ungaretti." *Agenda*, 6: 118-23 (1968).

Hamilton, Ian. "A Conversation with RL." *ModO*, 2: 28-48 (Wi 72).

Hayman, Ronald. "The Imaginative Risk." *LonM*, 10: 8-30 (N 70).

Hedetoft, Ulf. "RL: Alienated Consciousness/Consciousness of Alienation: The Split Ideology." *Lang&L*, 2: 8-17 (#4 74).

Helmick, E.T. "The Civil War Odes of Lowell and Tate." *GaR*, 25: 51-5 (Je 71).

Hirsh, J.C. "The Imagery of Dedication in RL's 'For the Union Dead.'" *JAmSt*, 6: 201-5 (Ag 72).

Holder, Alan. "The Flintlocks of the Fathers: RL's Treatment of the American Past." *NEQ*, 44: 40-65 (Mr 71).

Holloway, John. "RL and the Public Dimension." *Enc*, 30: 73-9 (1968).

Kavanagh, Paul. "The National Past and Present: A Study of RL's 'For the Union Dead.'" *JAmSt*, 5: 93-101 (Ap 71).

Knauff, D.M. "L's Theatrical Dramatization of Melville's *Benito Cereno*." *ETJ*, 27: 40-55 (1975).

Lensing, G.S. "The Consistency of RL." *SoR*, 7: 338-44 (Wi 71).

———. "'Memories of West Street and Lepke': RL's Associative Mirror." *CP*, 3: 23-6 (Fa 70).

———. "RL and Jonathan Edwards: Poetry in the Hands of an Angry God." *SCR*, 6: 7-17 (Su 74).

Lowell, Robert. "Visiting the Tates." *SR*, 67: 557-9 (O-D 59).

Lunz, Elizabeth. "RL and Wallace Stevens of Sunday Morning." *UR*, 37: 268-72 (Je 71).

McFadden, George. "'Life Studies'—RL's Comic Breakthrough." *PMLA*, 90: 96-106 (Ja 75).

Mahoney, P.J. "'La ballade des pendus' of François Villon, and R.L: A Study in Rhetorical Criticism." *CRCL*, 1: 22-37 (1974).

Mazzaro, Jerome. "The Classicism of RL's *Phaedra*." *CompD*, 7: 87-106 (Su 73).

———. "National and Individual Psychohistory in RL's *Endecott and the Red Cross*." *UWR*, 8: 99-113 (Fa 72).

———. "*Prometheus Bound*: RL and Aeschylus." *CompD*, 7: 278-90 (1973-74).

———. "RL and the Circle." *NRep*, 160: 31-3 (31 My 69).

———. "RL and the Kavanaugh Collapse." *UWR*, 5: 1-24 (Fa 69).

———. "RL's 'Benito Cerino.'" *MPS*, 4: 129-58 (Au 73).

———. "RL's *The Old Glory*: Cycle and Epicycle." *WHR*, 24: 347-58 (Au 70).

Miller, Terry. "The Prosodies of RL." *SM*, 35: 425-34 (N 68).

Moore, S.C. "Politics and the Poetry of RL." *GaR*, 27: 220-31 (Su 73).

Murtuza, Athar. "L's 'Passage to Asia.'" *LE&W*, 17: 192-7 (1974).

Nelson, R.L. "A Note on the Evolution of RL's 'The Public Garden.'" *AL*, 41: 106-10 (Mr 69).

Newlove, Donald. "Dinner at the Ls.'" *Esquire*, 72: 128-9, 168-84 (S 69).

Nitchie, G.W. "The Importance of RL." *SoR*, 8: 118-32 (Ja 72).

Oberg, Arthur. "I Am To Myself, and My Trouble Sings." *OhR*, 15: 108-11 (1974).

———. "'L' Had Been Misspelled 'Lovel.'" *IowaR*, 5: 98-122 (Su 74).

Oggel, L.T. "The Origin of L's 'American Punch.'" *AN&Q*, 10: 151-2 (Je 72).

O'Malley, Frank. "The Blood of RL." *Renascence*, 25: 190-5 (Su 73).

Pearce, R.H. "L's 'After Surprising Conversions.'" *Expl*, 9: 3-4 (1951).

Pearson, Gabriel. "RL." *Review*, Mr 69, pp. 3-36.

Perloff, M.G. "The Blank Now." *NRep*, 7 & 14 Jl 73, pp. 24-6.

———. "Realism and the Confessional Mode of RL." *ConL*, 11: 470-87 (Au 70).

Przemecka, Irena. "Herman Melville's and RL's *Benito Cereno*: Tale into Drama, Tale into Drama." *ZRL*, 14: 57-62 (1971).

Ralph, George. "History and Prophecy in *Benito Cereno*." *ETJ*, 22: 155-60 (My 70).

Reid, A.S. "A Look at the Living Poem: Rock Protest and Wit." *FurmM*, nv: 6-11, 35 (Sp 70).

Richards, Max. "The Citizenship of RL." *Meanjin*, 33: 201-6 (1974).

Ricks, Christopher. "The Poet RL." *Listener*, 89: 830-2 (21 Je 73).

Rizzardi, Alfredo. "Notes Between Two Poets." *OdyR*, 1: 50-65 (Mr 62).

Scholl, D.G. "RL's 'Endecott and the Red Cross.'" *NCCL*, 22: 15-28 (Wi 73).

Schwaber, Paul. "RL in Mid-Career." *WHR*, 25: 348-54 (Au 71).

Simon, John. "Abuse of Privilege: L as Translator." *HudR*, 20: 543-62 (Wi 67-68).

Snow, Ken. "The Poetry of RL." *Poetry Wales*, 9: 7-21 (Wi 73-74).

Spacks, Patricia. "From Satire to Description." *YR*, 58: 232-48 (1968).

Spender, Stephen. "The Importance of Meaning." *Translation* 73, 1: 32-7 (Wi 73).

Sterne, R.C. "Puritans at Merry Mount: Variations on a Theme." *AQ*, 22: 846-8, 858 (Wi 70).

Stock, Noel. "L & Larkin." *Poetry Australia*, 54: 74-9 (1975).

Stone, A.E. "A New Version of American Innocence: RL's *Benito Cereno*." *NEQ*, 45: 467-83 (D 72).

———. "RL's *Benito Cereno*." *NEQ*, 45: 467-83 (D 72).

Strand, Mark. "Landscape and the Poetry of Self." *Prose*, 6: 169-83 (1973).

Sullivan, R. "Notebook: RL as a Political Poet." *EA*, 27: 291-301 (Jl-S 74).

Taylor, F.H.G. "A Point in Time, A Place in Space: Six Poets and the Changing Present." *SR*, 77: 300-18 (1969).

Tokunaga, Yozo. "Shiteki na Koe, koteki na Koe—Berryman to L." *EigoS*, 118: 70-1 (1972).

Torrens, James. "RL: Tributes from a Kinsman." *EWR*, 4: 84-93 (Sp 71).

Tulip, James. "The Poetic Voices of RL." *PoetA*, 39: 49-57 (Ap 71).

Vendler, Helen. "The Difficult Grandeur of RL." *Atl*, 235: 68-73 (Ja 75).

Vogler, T.A. "RL and the Classical Tradition." *PCP*, 4: 59-64 (1969).

———. "RL: Payment Gat He Nane." *IowaR*, 2: 64-95 (#3 71).

Wallace-Crabbe, Chris. "RL's Versions of History." *Westerly*, 1: 37-44 (Ap 69).

Weales, Gerald. "RL as Dramatist." *Shen*, 20: 3-28 (Au 68).

Webner, H.L. "Hawthorne, Melville, and L: *The Old Glory*." *Re:A&L*, 4: 1-17 (Fa 70).

Welch, D.M. "RL's 'Where the Rainbow Ends': A Post-War Act of Faith." *Chris and Lit*, 20: 12-7 (#4 71).

Wiersma, S.M. "L's 'In Memory of Arthur Winslow,' Movements I and V." *Expl*, 30: 12 (1971).

Willias, D.G. "Afloat on L's Dolphin." *CritQ*, 17: 363-76 (1975).

Yankowitz, Susan. "L's *Benito Cereno*: An Investigation of American Innocence." *Y/T*, 2: 81-90 (1968).

Young, Dudley. "Talk with RL." *NYT*, 4 Ap 71, pp. 31-2.

Zollman, Sol. "Criticism, Self-Criticism, No Transformation: The Poetry of RL and Anne Sexton." *L&I*, 9: 29-36 (1971).

Luce, Clare Booth. Lawrenson, Helen. "The Woman." *Esquire*, 82: 75-82, 151-5 (Ag 74).

Weintraub, Rodelle. "The Gift of Imagination: An Interview with CBL." *ShawR*, 17: 53-9 (1974).

Lummis, Charles Fletcher. Gordon, D.C. "CF.L: Pioneer American Folklorist." *WF*, 28: 175-81 (Jl 69).

Lyon, Harris Merton. Eichelberger, Claytor, Zoë Lyon. "A Partial Listing of the Published Works of HML." *ALR*, 3: 41-52 (Wi 70).

Landman, S.J. "Scarlet and White: Posthumous Story." *ArlQ*, 1: 83-7 (Sp 68).

Lyon, Zoë. "HML: An Author to be Reappraised." *MHSB*, 26: 318-20 (1970).

———. "HML (1883-1916)." *ALR*, 3: 36-40 (Wi 70).

———. "HML: Early American Realist." *SSF*, 5: 368-77 (Su 68).

Putzel, Max. "Dreiser, Reedy, and 'De Maupassant, Junior.'" *AL*, 33: 466-84 (Ja 62).

Lytle, Andrew Nelson. Bataille, Robert. "The Esthetics and Ethics of Farming: The Southern Agrarian View." *Iowa State J Res*, 49: 189-93 (1974).

Benson, R.G. "The Progress of Hernando de Soto in AL's *At the Moon's Inn*." *GaR*, 27: 232-44 (Su 73).

Bradford, M.E. "The Fiction of AL." *MissQ*, 23: 347-9 (Fa 70).

———. "Toward a Dark Shape: L's 'Alchemy' and the Conquest of the New World." *MissQ*, 23: 407-14 (Fa 70).

Clark, C.C. "The Fiction of AL." *Occasional R*, 1: 12-6 (Fa 74).

———. "*A Name for Evil*: A Search for Order." *MissQ* 23: 371-82 (Fa 70).

Core, George. "A Mirror for Fiction: The Critical of AL." *GaR*, 22: 208-21 (Su 68).

Fain, J.T. "Segments of Southern Renaissance." *SAB*, 36: 23-31 (My 71).

Foata, Anne. "Le fantastique au secours de l'allegorie: *A Name for Evil* de AL." *RANAM*, 7: 220-33 (1974).

Jones, Madison, "A Look at 'Mister McGregor.'" *MissQ*, 23: 363-70 (Fa 70).

Joyner, Nancy. "The Myth of the Matriarch in AL's Fiction." *SLJ*, 7: 67-77 (Fa 74).

Krickel, Edward. "The Whole and the Parts: Initiation in 'The Mahogany Frame.'" *MissQ*, 23: 391-405 (Fa 70).

Landess, T.H. "Unity of Action in *The Velvet Horn*." *MissQ*, 23: 349-61 (Fa 70).

Landman, S.J. "The Walls of Mortality." *MissQ*, 23: 415-23 (Fa 70).

Lytle, A.N. "The Working Novelist and the Mythmaking Process." *Daedalus*, 88: 326-38 (Sp 58).

* Polk, Noel. "ANL: A Bibliography of His Writings." *MissQ*, 23: 435-91 (Fa 70).

Trowbridge, C.W. "The Word Made Flesh: AL's *The Velvet Horn.*" *Critique*, 10: 53-68 (Sp 68).

Warren, R.P. "AL's *The Long NIght*: A Rediscovery." *SoR*, 7: 130-9 (Ja 71).

Watson, Sterling. "*Craft and Vision.*" *FlQ*, 5: 33-9 (Sp 73).

Weatherby, H.L. "The Quality of Richness: Observations on AL's *The Long Night.*" *MissQ*, 23: 383-90 (Fa 70).

Weston, Robert. "Toward A Total Reading of Fiction: The Essays of AL." *MissQ*, 23: 425-33 (Fa 70).

Yeh-Wei-Yu, Frederick. "AL's *A Name for Evil* as a Redaction of 'The Turn of the Screw.'" *MQR*, 11: 186-90 (Su 72).

McAlmon, Robert. Card, James. "The Misleading Mr. M and Joyce's Typescript." *JJQ*, 7: 143-7 (1970).

Klapper, Harold. "Remember RA?" *LGJ* 3: 26-8 (#2 75).

McCarthy, Eugene. Simpson, Louis. "M as Poet: Irony and Moral Sense." *NYTBR*, 4 Ag 68, pp. 2, 24-5.

McCarthy, Mary. Aldridge, J.W. "Egalitarian Snobs." *SatR*, 54: 21-4 (8 My 71).

DeMott, Benjamin. "Poets, Presidents and Preceptors." *HM*, 227: 98, 102-10 (O 63).

Gillen, Francis. "The Failure of Ritual in 'The Unspoiled Reaction.'" *Renascence*, 24: 155-8 (Sp 72).

Grumbach, Doris. "The Subject Objected." *NYT*, 11 Je 67, pp. 6-7, 36-7.

Jelenski, A.J. "Les solutions de MM." *Preuves*, 202: 85-7 (12967).

Kreutz, Irving. "MM's *The Unspoiled Reaction*: Pejorative as Satire." *Descant*, 13: 32-48 (Fa 68).

May, Derwent, "Amis, MM, Naipaul." *Enc*, 38: 74-8 (Ja 72).

Rahv, Philip. "The Editor Interviews MM." *ModO*, 1: 14-25 (Fa 70).

Revel, Jean-Francois. "Miss M Explains." *NYT*, 16 My 71, pp. 2, 24-30.

Schweyer, Jeannine. "L'oeuvre de MM devant la critique: première bibliographie." *Ranam*, 4: 172-97 (1971).

Taylor, G.O. "Cast a Cold 'I': MM on Vietnam." *JAmSt*, 9: 103-5 (1975)

McCloskey, Mark. Fitzgerald, Greogory, and Paul Ferguson. "Goodbye but Listen: A Conversation with Poet MM." *MPS*, 3: 265-74 (1973).

McCloskey, Mark. "Comment on 'My Funeral.'" *Eng Rec*, 19: 81 (F 69).

MacLow, Jackson. Alpert, Barry, et al. "Special M Issue." *Vort*, 8: 3-99 (1975).

McCoy, Horace. Layman, Richard. "Fitzgerald and HM." *FHA*, 1974, pp. 99-100.

Michaelson, L.W. "They Shoot Writers, Dont' They." *Eng Rec*, 22: 15-19 (Fa 71).

Richmond, L.J. "A Time to Mourn and a Time to Dance: HM's *They Shoot Horses, Don't They?*" *TCL*, 17: 91-100 (1971).

Sturak, Thomas. "A Foreword to 'Death in Hollywood.'" *MDAC*, 1973: 16-9 (1974).

———. "HM, Captain Shaw, and the *Black Mask.*" *MDAC*, 1: 139-58 (1972).

McCullers, Carson. Arnette, J-P. "CM." *NRF*, 16: 146-7 (Ja 68).

Bigsby, C.W.E. "Edward Albee's Georgia Ballad." *TCL*, 13: 229-36 (Ja 68).

Blöcker, Gunder. "Erarbeitete Magie: Die Erzählerin CM." *Merkur*, 28: 1079-84 (N 74).

Bondy, Barbara. "Eine Dichterin Amerikas." *DRu*, 89: 76-9 (Jl 63).

Broughton, P.R. "Rejection of the Feminine in CM's *The Ballad of the Sad Café.*" *TCL*, 20: 34-43 (Ja 74).

Buchen, I.H. "CM, A Case of Convergence." *BuR*, 21: 15-28 (Sp 73).

————. "Divine Collusion: The Art of CM." *DR*, 54: 529-41 (Au 74).

Clark, C.K. "Pathos with a Chuckle: The Tragicomic Vision in the Novels of CM." *SAH*, 1: 161-6 (Ja 75).

————. "Selfhood and the Southern Past: A Reading of M's *Clock Without Hands*." *SLM*, 1: 16-23 (2Q 75).

Dedmond, F.B. "Doing Her Own Thing: CM's Dramatization of 'The Member of the Wedding.'" *SAB*, 40: 47-52 (My 75).

Dorsey, James. "CM and Flannery O'Connor: A Checklist of Graduate Research." *BB*, 32: 162-7 (O-D 75).

Edmonds, Dale. "'Correspondence': A 'Forgotten' CM Short Story." *SSF*, 9: 89-92 (1972).

Fletcher, M.D. "CM's 'Ancient Mariner.'" *SCB*, 35: 123-5 (Wi 75).

Gaillard, D.F. "The Presence of the Narrator in CM' *The Ballad of the Sad Cafe*." *MissQ*, 25: 419-27 (1972).

Gozzi, Francesco. "La narrativa di CM." *SA*, 14: 339-76 (1968).

Grinnell, J.W. "Delving 'A Domestic Dilemma.'" *SSF*, 9: 270-1 (1972).

Gullason, T.A. "*The Mortgaged Heart*." *SatR*, 54: 57, 63-4 (13 N 71).

Hamliton, Alice. "Loneliness and Alienation: The Life and Work of CM." *DR*, 50: 215-29 (Su 70).

Hendrick, George. "'Almost Everyone Wants to Be the Lover': The Fiction of CM." *BA*, 42: 389-91 (Su 68).

Jaworski, Philippe. "La double quête de l'identité et de la réalité chez CM." *NRF*, 17: 93-101 (Jl 69).

McNally, John. "The Introspective Narrator in *The Ballad of the Sad Cafe*." *SAB*, 38: 40-4 (N 73).

Madden, David. "Transfixed Among the Self-Inflicted Ruins: CM' *The Mortgaged Heart*." *SLJ*, 5: 137-62 (1972).

Millichap, J.R. "CM's Literary Ballad." *GaR*, 27: 329-39 (Fa 73).

————. "The Realistic Structure of *The Heart is a Lonely Hunter*." *TCL*, 17: 11-7 (Ja 71).

Missey, James. "A M Influence of Albee's *The Zoo Story*." *AN&Q*, 13: 121-3 (Ap 75).

Moore, J.T. "M's *The Ballad of the Sad Cafe*." *Expl*, 29: 27 (1970).

Pachmuss, Temira. "Dostoevsky, D.H. Lawrence, and CM." *GSlav*, 2: 59-68 (Fa 74).

Perrine, Laurence. "Restoring 'A Domestic Dilemma.'" *SSF*, 11: 101-4 (Wi 74).

Presley, D.E. "CM and the South." *GaR*, 27: 19-32 (Sp 74).

————. "CM's Descent to Earth." *Descant*, 17: 54-60 (Wi 68).

————. "The Moral Function of Distortion in Southern Grotesque." *SAB*, 37: 37-46 (1972).

Radu, Aurelia. "Implicațiile initierii sau metamorfozele singurătății în univsersul eroilor lui CM." AUB-LUC, 19: 141-8 (1970).

Rechnitz, R.M. "The Failure of Love: The Grotesque in Two Novels by CM." *GaR*, 22: 454-63 (Wi 68).

Ríos Ruiz, Manuel. "CM, la novelista del fatalismo." *CHA*, 76: 763-71 (1968).

Rivière, Yvette. "L'alienation dans les romans de CM." *Ranam*, 4: 79-86 (1971).

Robinson, W.R. "The Life of CM' Imagination." *SHR*, 2: 291-302 (Su 68).

Sherrill, R.A. "MC's *The Heart Is a Lonely Hunter*: The Missing Ego and the Problem of the Norm." *KenR*, 2: 5-17 (1968).

Skotnicki, Irene. "Die Darstellung der Entfremdung in den Romanen von CM." *ZAA*, 20: 24-45 (1972).

*Stanley, W.T. "CM: 1965-1969, A Selected Checklist." *BB*, 27: 91-3 (O-D 70).

Taylor, Horace. "*The Heart is a Lonely Hunter*: A Southern Wasteland." *LSUS*, 8: 154-60 (1960).

Valensise, Rachele. "Tre scrittrici del Sud: Flannery O'Connor, Caroline Gordon, CM."
  SA, 17: 251-89 (1971).
Macdonald, Ross. Barnes, D.R. " 'I'm the Eye': Archer as Narrator in the Novels of RM."
  MDAC, 1: 178-90 (1972).
Byrd, Max. "The Detective Detected: From Sophocles to RM." *YR*, 64: 72-83 (1974).
Carter, S.R. "RM: The Complexity of the Modern Quest for Justice." *MDAC*, 1973; pp.
  59-82.
Gadney, Reg. "Criminal Tendencies." *LonM*, 12: 110-22 (Je-Jl 72).
Grogg, Sam. "RM: At the Edge." *JPC*, 7: 213-22 (Su 73).
Holtan, Judith, and Orley Noltan. "The Time-Space Dimension in the Lew Archer Detective
  Novels." *NDQ*, 40: 30-41 (Au 72).
Kennedy, Veronica. "The Prophet before the End of Fact." *ArmD*, 7: 41 (1973).
Leonard, John. "RM, His Lew Archer and Other Secret Selves." *NYT*, 1 Je 69; p. 2, 19.
Mulqueen, J.E. "Three Heroes in American Fiction." *IllQ*, 36: 44-50 (F 74).
Pry, E.R. "RM's Violent California: Imagery Patterns in *The Underground Man*." *WAL*, 9:
  197-204 (Fa 74).
Slipper, R.B. "An Interview with RM." *MDAC*, 1973: 53-8 (1973).
Tutunjian, Jerry. "A Conversation with RM." *TamR*, 62: 66-85 (1Q 74).
MacDowell, Edward. Leonard, Neil. "EM and the Realists." *AQ*, 18: 175-82 (Su 66).
MacDowell, Katherine Sherwood Bonner. (See **Bonner, Sherwood**)
McGinley, Phyllis. Deedy, John. "The Poet Laureate of Suburbia." *US Catholic and
  Jubilee*, 34: 22-7 (D 69).
McKay, Claude. Barksdale, R.A. "Symbolism and Irony in M's *Home to Harlem*." *CLAJ*,
  15: 338-44 (Mr 72).
Cartey, Wilfred. "Four Shadows of Harlem." *NegroD*, 18: 22-5, 83-92 (1969).
Collier, E.W. "The Four-Way Dilemma of CM." *CLAJ*, 15: 345-53 (Mr 72).
Conroy, Sister Mary. "The Vagabond Motif in the Writings of CM." *NALF*, 5: 15-23
  (1971).
Helbling, Mark. "CM: Art and Politics." *NALF*, 7: 49-52 (Su 73).
Jackson, Blyden. "CM and Langston Hughes: The Harlem Renaissance and More."
  Pembroke Mag, 6: 43-8 (1975).
Kaye, Jacqueline. "CM's 'Banjo.' " *PA*, 73: 165-9 (1970).
Kent, G.E. "CM's *Banana Bottom* Reappraised." *CLAJ*, 18: 222-34 (D 74).
———. "The Soulful Way of CM." *BlackW*, 20: 37-50 (1970).
Kestleloot, Lilyan. "Negritude and Its American Sources." *BUJ*, 22: 54-67 (1974).
Lang, P.M. "CM: Evidence of a Magic Pilgrimage." *CLAJ*, 16: 475-84 (Je 73).
Larson, C.R. "Three Harlem Novels of the Jazz Age." *Critique*, 11: 66-78 (1969).
Lederer, Richard. "The Didactic and the Literary in Four Harlem Renaissance Sonnets." *EJ*,
  62: 219-23 (1973).
Lee, R.A. "On CM's 'If We Must Die.' " *CLAJ*, 18: 216-21 (D 74).
Lopez, M.D. "CM." *BB*, 29: 128-34 (O-D 72).
Priebe, Richard. "The Search for Community in the Novels of CM."
Pyne-Timothy, Helen. "Perceptions of the Black Woman in the Work of CM." *CLAJ*, 19:
  152-64 (D 75).
Valensise, Rachele. "Tre scrittrici del Sud: Flannery O'Connor, Caroline Gordon, CM."
  SA, 17: 251-89 (1971).
MacDonald, Ross. Barnes, D.R. " 'I'm the Eye': Archer as Narrator in the Novels of RM."
  MDAC, 1: 178-90 (1972).
Byrd, Max. "The Detective Detected: From Sophocles to RM." *YR*, 64: 72-83 (1974).

Carter, S.R. "RM: The Complexity of the Modern Quest for Justice." *MDAC*, 1973; pp. 59-82.

Gadney, Reg. "Criminal Tendencies." *LonM*, 12: 110-22 (Je/Jl 72).

Grogg, Sam. "RM: At the Edge." *JPC*, 7: 213-22 (Su 73).

Holtan, Judith, and Orley Noltan. "The Time-Space Dimension in the Lew Archer Detective Novels." *NDQ*, 40: 30-41 (Au 72).

Kennedy, Veronica. "The Prophet before the End of Fact." *ArmD*, 7: 41 (1973).

Leonard, John. "RM, His Lew Archer and Other Secret Selves." *NYT*, 1 Je 69; p. 2, 19.

Mulqueen, J.E. "Three Heroes in American Fiction." *IllQ*, 36: 44-50 (F 74).

Pry, E.R. "RM's Violent California: Imagery Patterns in *The Underground Man*." *WAL*, 9: 197-204 (Fa 74).

Slipper, R.B. "An Interview with RM." *MDAC*, 1973: 53-8 (1973).

Tutunjian, Jerry. "A Conversation with RM." *TamR*, 62: 66-85 (1Q 74).

MacDowell, Edward. Leonard, Neil. "EM and the Realists." *AQ*, 18: 175-82 (Su 66).

Ramchand, Kenneth. "CM and *Banana Bottom*." *SoRA*, 4: 53-66 (1970).

MacKay, Percy. Brock, D.H., and J.M. Welsh. "PM: Community Drama and the Masque Tradition." *CompD*, 6: 68-84 (1972).

Mendelsohn, M.J. "PM's Dramatic Theories." *BRMMLA*, 24: 85-9 (Je 70).

Ritter, C.C. "PM's Civic Theatre Philosophy as Revealed in His Speeches." *QJS*, 53: 349-53 (1967).

McKuen, Rod. Anon. "RM: Poet of the Lonely." *NZL*, 69: 12 (28 F 72).

Keith, D.L. "The M Magic: of Myth or Man?" *Contempora*, 1: 26-9 (1971).

McKuen, Rod. "The Poet: Public." *SatR*, 55: 46-8 (D 72).

MacLeish, Archibald. Bieman, Elizabeth. "Faithful to the Bible in Its Fashion: M's *J.B.*" *Studies in Rel*, 4: 25-30 (1974).

Blanke, G.H. "AM: 'Ars Poetica.'" *JA*, 13: 236-45 (1968).

Campbell, S.O. "The Book of Job and M's *J.B.*: A Cultural Comparison." *EJ*, 41: 653-7 (My 72).

Demott, Benjamin. "The Art of Poetry 18: AM." *PaR*, 58: 53-81 (Su 74).

Gallagher, Kathleen. "The Art(s) of Poetry: Jones and M." *MwQ*, 12: 383-92 (Su 71).

Gianakaris, C.J. "M's *Herakles*: Myth for the Modern World." *CentR*, 15: 445-63 (Fa 71).

Golschmidt, Eva. "AM, Librarian of Congress." *C&RL*, 30: 12-24 (Ja 69).

Griffith, John. "Narrative Technique and the Meaning of History in Benét M." *JNT*, 3: 3-19 (Ja 73).

MacLeish, Archibald. "Changes in the Ritual of Library Dedication." *LJ*, 93: 3517-20 (1 O 68).

―――. "The Premise of Meaning." *ASch*, 41: 357-62 (Su 72).

Mills, Ralph. "In the Fields of Imagination." *Parnassus*, 1: 211-24 (#2 73).

Sandeen, Ernest. "This Moral Story." *Poetry*, 112: 199-201 (Je 68).

Stroupe, J.H. "The Masks of M's *J.B.*" *TSL*, 15: 75-83 (1970).

Vann, J.D. "The Two Messengers in AM's 'J.B.'" *Dickinson R*, 2: 42-5 (Wi 70).

West, Jessamyn. "In This Writer's World the Reader, Too, Is Creative." *NYHT*, 1, 11 (31 Jl 60).

White, W.D. "M's *J.B.*—Is It a Modern Job?" *Mosaic*, 4: 13-20 (1970).

McMurty, Larry. Crooks, A.F. "LM—A Writer in Transition." *WAL*, 7: 151-5 (1972).

Davis, K.W. "The Themes of Initiation in the Works of LM and Tom Mayer." *ArlQ*, 2: 29-43 (Wi 69-70).

Degenfelder, E.P. "M and the Movies." *WHR*, 29: 81-91 (1975).

Folsom, J.K. "*Shane* and *Hud*: Two Stories in Search of a Medium." *WHR*, 24: 359-72 (Au 70).

Giles, J.R. "LM's *Leaving Cheyenne* and the Novels of John Rechy." *ForumH*, 10: 34-40 (#2 72).

Gerlach, John. "*The Last Picture Show* and One More Adaptation." *LFQ*, 1: 1616 (1973).

Peavy, C.D. "Coming of Age in Texas: The Novels of LM." *WAL*, 4: 171-88 (1969).

*———. "A LM Bibliography." *WAL*, 3: 235-48 (Fa 68).

———. "LM and Black Humor: A Note on *The Last Picture Show*." *WAL*, 2: 223-7 (Fa 67).

Phillips, R.C. "The Ranch as Place and Symbol in the Novels of LM." *SDR*, 29: 81-91 (1975).

Pilkington, W.T. "The Dirt-Farmer and the Cowboy: Notes on two Texas Essayists." *Re: A&L*, 3: 42-54 (1969).

Sonnichsen, C.L. "The New Style Western." *SDR*, 4: 22-8 (Su 66).

Wilson, Robert. "Which Is the Real 'Last Picture Show'?" *LFQ*, 1: 167-9 (1973).

Madden, David. Laney, Ruth. "An Interview with DM." *SoR*, 11: 167-80 (Ja 75).

Madden, David. "The Compulsion to Tell a Story." *JPC*, 5: 269-79 (Fa 71).

Pinsker, Sanford. "A Conversation with DM." *Critique*, 15: 5-14 (#2 73).

———. "The Mixed Cords of DM's *Cassandra Singing*." *Critique*, 15: 15-26 (#2 73).

Mailer, Norman. Anon. "A Section of an Interview Between NM and David Young." *Notre Dame R*, 1: 5-9 (Mr 74).

Adams. Laura. "Criticism of NM: A Selected Checklist." *MFS*, 17: 455-63 (Au 71).

———. "Existential Aesthetics: An Interview with NM." *PR*, 42: 197-214 (2Q 75).

Aldridge, J.W. "The Perfect Absurd Figure of a Mighty, Absurd Crusade." *SatR*, 54: 45-9, 72 (13 N 71).

Alter, Robert. "The Real and Imaginary Worlds of NM." *Midstream*, 15: 24-35 (Ja 69).

Arnavon, Cyrille. "Les cauchemars de NM." *Europe*, nv: 93-116 (Ja 69).

Bakker, J. "Literature, Politics, and NM." *DQR*, 3-4: 129-45 (1971).

Banta, Martha. "American Apocalypses: Excrement and Ennui." *SLitI*, 7: 1-30 (#1 74).

Barnes, Annette. "NM: A Prisoner of Sex." *MR*, 13: 269-74 (Wi-Sp 72).

Behar, Jack. "History and Fiction." *Novel*, 3: 260-5 (Sp 70).

Berthoff, Warner. "Witness and Testament: Two Contemporary Classics." *NLH*, 2: 311-27 (Wi 71).

Bondy, Francois. "NM: Oder Inside vot Gut und Böse." *Merkur*, 25: 499-60 (My 71).

Brezianu, Andrei. "Focul şi gîndul." *SXX*, 15: 266-73 (1972).

Brookeman, C.D. "NM." *TLS*, 3 O 68, p. 1104.

Burg, D.F. "The Hero of *The Naked and the Dead*." *MFS*, 17: 387-401 (Au 71).

Busch, Frederick. "The Whale as Shaggy Dog: Melville and 'The Man Who Studied Yoga.'" *MFS*, 19: 193-206 (Su 73).

Cecil, L.M. "The Passing of Arthur in NM's *Barbary Shore*." *RSW*, 39: 54-8 (Mr 71).

Champoli, J.D. "NM and *The Armies of the Night*." *MSE*, 3: 17-21 (Sp 71).

Cochran, R.B. "St. Norman of New York: The Historian as Servant to the Lord." *NOR*, 3: 215-22 (1973).

Demott, Benjamin. "Inside Apollo 11 with Aquarius M." *SatR*, 54: 25-7, 57-8 (16 Ja 71).

DeRambures, J.-L. "NM: l'enfant terrible des lettres americaines." *Realités*, 269: 95-105 (Je 68).

Dommergues, Pierre. "NM: Pourquoi sommes-nous au Vietnam?" *LanM*, 62: 123-8 (Jl-Ag 68).

Donoghue, Denis. "Sweepstakes." *NYRB*, 9: 5-8 (28 S 67).

Douglas, G.H. "NM and the Battle of the Sexes—Urban Style." *NOR*, 3: 211-4 (1973).

Evans, Timothy. "Boiling the Archetypal Pot: NM's American Dream." *SWR*, 60: 159-70 (Sp 75).

Finholt, R.D. "'Otherwise How Explain?' NM's New Cosmology." *MFS*, 17: 375-86 (Au 71).

Fisher, Roy. "The Mind of Marion Faye: Stylistic Aspects of NM's *The Deer Park*." *Lang&S*, 6: 145-57 (1973).

Fishman, Robert. "NM." *JPC*, 9: 174-82 (1975).

Fossum, R.H. "NM's *An American Dream*." *AA*, 1974, pp. 10-23.

Foster, Richard. "M and the Fitzgerald Tradition." *Novel*, 1: 219-30 (Sp 68).

Frank, A.P. "Literarische Strukturbegriffe und NM's *The Armies of the Night*." *JA*, 17: 73-99 (1972).

Gillenkirk, Jeffrey. "M Is the Message." *NOR*, 3: 223-5 (1973).

Gindin, James. "Megalotopia and the WASP Backlash: The Fiction of M and Updike." *CentR*, 15: 38-52 (Wi 71).

Gordon, Andrew. "*The Naked and the Dead*: The Triumph of Impotence." *L&P*, 19: 3-13 (1969).

————. "*Why Are We in Vietnam?*" Deep in the Bowels of Texas." *L&P*, 24: 55-65 (1974).

Grace, Matthew. "NM at the End of the Decade." *EA*, 24: 50-8 (Ja-Mr 71).

————, and Steve Roday. "M on M: An Interview." *NOR*, 3: 229-34 (1973).

Green, Martin. "Amis and M: The Faustian Contract." *Month*, 3: 45-8 (F 71).

————. "M and Amis: The New Conservatism." *Nation*, 208: 473-4 (5 My 69).

Greenway, John. "NM Meets the Butch Brigade." *Nat R*, 23: 815 (27 Jl 71).

Greer, Germaine. "My M Problem." *Esquire*, 76: 90-3, 214-6 (S 71).

Hentoff, Nat. "Behold the New Journalism—It's Coming After You!" *EvR*, 12: 49-51 (Jl 68).

Hudson, Liam. "The Traffic in Selves." *TLS*, 24 Ja 75, pp. 77-8.

Hux, Samuel. "M's Dream of Violence." *MinnR*, 8: 152-7 (1968).

Iwamoto, Iwao. "Gendai wo Ikiru Messiah." *Eigo*, 115: 554-5 (1969).

James, Clive. "M's 'Marilyn.'" *Commentary*, 56: 44-9 (O 73).

Jameson, Frederic. "The Great American Hunter, or Ideological Content in the Novel." *CE*, 34: 180-97 (N 72).

Janeway, William. "M's America." *CamR*, 90: 183-5 (29 N 68).

Kaufmann, D.L. "Catch 23: The Mystery of Fact (NM's Final Novel?)." *TCL*, 17: 247-56 (1971).

————. "The Long Happy Life of NM." *MFS*, 17: 347-59 (Au 71).

————. "M's Lunar Bits and Pieces." *MFS*, 17: 451-4 (Au 71).

Kazin, Alfred. "The World as a Novel: From Capote to M." *NYRB*, 16: 26-30 (8 Ap 71).

Klein, Jeffrey. "Armies of the Planet: A Comparison of NM's and Saul Bellow's Political Visions." *Soundings*, 58: 69-83 (1975).

Leverenz, David. "Anger and Individualism." *ATQ*, 62: 407-28 (1975).

Long, Margaret. "Boy-man on the New Woman." *Contempora*, 1: 1-5 (1971).

Lucid, R.F. "NM: The Artist as Fantasy Figure." *MR*, 15: 581-95 (Au 74).

————. "Three Public Performances: Fitzgerald, Hemingway, M." *ASch*, 43: 447-66 (Su 74).

Lupan, Radu. "la Londra, intîlnire cu NM." *Luc*, 20: 8 (Ap 74).

Mailer, Norman. "The First Day's Interview." *PaR*, 7: 140-53 (Su-Fa 61).

————. "Mr. M Interviews Himself." *NYT*, 17 S 67, pp. 6-7, 40.

————. "The Prisoner of Sex." *HM*, 242: 41-82 (Mr 71).

————. "A Section of an Interview Between NM and David Young." *Notre Dame R*, 1: 5-9 (1974).

————. "Up the Family Tree." *PR*, 35: 234-52 (Sp 68).

Marx, Leo. " 'Noble Shit': The Uncivil Response of American Writers to Civil Religion in America." *MR*, 14: 709-39 (1973).

Maud, Ralph. "Faulkner, M, and Yogi Bear." *CRAS*, 2: 69-75 (Fa 71).

Merideth, Robert. "The 45-Second Piss: A Left Critique of NM and *The Armies of the Night.*" *MFS*, 17: 433-9 (Au 71).

Merrill, Robert. "*The Armies of the Night*: The Education of NM." *IllQ*, 37: 30-44 (1974).

———. "NM's Early Nonfiction: The Art of Self-Revelation." *WHR*, 28: 1-12 (Wi 74).

Mitchell, Juliet. "M: 'So the revolution called again . . . '" *ModO*, 1: 611-8 (Fa 71).

Morel, Jean-Pierre. "Pourquoi sommes-nous au Vietnam?" *Etudes*, 329: 572-80 (1968).

Muste, J.M. "NM and John Dos Passos: The Question of Influence." *MFS*, 17: 361-74 (Au 71).

Normand, Jean. "L'homme mystifié: Les heros de Bellow, Albee, Styron, et M." *EA*, 22: 37-85 (O-D 69).

Oates, J.C. "With NM at the Sex Circus." *Atl*, 228: 42-5 (Jl 71).

Pearce, Richard. "NM's *Why Are We in Vietnam?*': A Radical Critique of Frontier Values." *MFS*, 17: 409-14 (Au 71).

Peter, John. "The Self-Effacement of the Novelist." *MalR*, 8: 119-28 (O 68).

Phillips, Williams. "Writing About Sex." *PR*, 24: 552-63 (Fa 67).

Poirier, Richard. "The Aesthetics of Radicalism." *PR*, 41: 176-96 (Au 74).

———. "M: Good Form and Bad." *SatR*, 55: 42-6 (22 Ap 72).

———. "The Minority Within." *PR*, 39: 12-43 (Sp 72).

———. "NM's necessary mess." *Listener*, 90: 626-7 (8 N 73).

Popescu, Petru. "NM: Cei goi si cei morti." *RoLit*, 6 F 69, p. 19.

Pritchett, V.S. "With NM at the Sex Circus: I. Into the Cage." *Atl*, 228: 40-2 (Jl 71).

Rabinovitz, Rubin. "Myth and Animalism in *Why Are We in Vietnam?*" *TCL*, 20: 298-305 (O 74).

Rader, Dotson. "The Day the Movement Died." *Esquire*, 78: 130-5 (N 72).

Ramsey, Roger. "Current and Recurrent: The Vietnam Novel." *MFS*, 17: 414-31 (Au 71).

Ricciardi, Caterina. "NM: Metafora dell'America contemporanea." *SA*, 18: 369-94 (1972).

Rijpens, John. "M weer op oorlogspad." *VIG*, 52: 27-9 (1968).

Ross, Frank. "The Assailant-Victim in Three War-Protest Novels." *Paunch*, 32: 46-57 (D 68).

Ross, M.L. "Thoreau and M: The Mission of Rooster." *WHR*, 25: 47-56 (Wi 71).

Samuels, C.T. "The Novel, USA: Mailerrhea." *Nation*, 205: 405-6 (23 O 67).

Sargent, Pamela. "The Promise of Space: Transformations of a Dream." *RQ*, 5: 83-8 (f 72).

Schroth, R.A. "M and His Gods." *Cweal*, 90: 226-9 (9 My 69).

Schulz, M.F. "M's Divine Comedy." *ConL*, 9: 36-57 (Wi 68).

Seib, K.A. "M's March: the Epic Structure of *The Armies of the Night*." *EL*, 1: 89-95 (Sp 74).

Sheed, Wilfrid. "Genius or Nothing: A View of NM." *Enc*, 36: 66-71 (Je 71).

Shepard, D.H. "NM: A Preliminary Bibliography of Secondary Commentary, 1948-68." *BB*, 29: 37-45 (Ap-Je 72).

Sheridan, J.J. "M's *An American Dream*." *Expl*, 34: 8 (S 75).

Siegel, P.N. "The Malign Deity of *The Naked and the Dead*." *TCL*, 20: 291-7 (O 74).

Sonnenfeld, Albert. "Du côte de Ché Guevara: Mythes et réalités de NM." *HUSL*, 2: 197-208 (Au 74).

———. "The Manly Art of Self-Mythification." *University*, 64: 10-3 (Sp 75).

Stark, John. "*Barbary Shore*: The basis of M's Best Work." *MFS*, 17: 403-8 (Au 71).

Tanner, Tony. "On the Parapet: A Study of the Novels of NM." *CritQ*, 12: 153-76 (Su 70).

Taylor, G.O. "Of Adams and Aquaris." *AL*, 46: 68-82 (Mr 74).

———. "Sounding the Trumpets of Defiance: Mark Twain and NM." *MTJ*, 16: 1-14 (Wi 72).

Thompson, John. "Catching Up on M." *NYRB*, 8: 14-6 (20 Ap 67).

Toback, James. "A Play in the Fields of the Bored." *Esquire*, 70: 150-3 (D 68).

Tytell, John. "The Beat Generation and the Continuing American Revolution." *ASch*, 42: 308-17 (Sp 73).

Wagenheim, A.J. "Square's Progress: An American Dream." *Critique*, 10: 45-68 (1968).

Waldmeir, J.J. "Running with M." *JML*, 1: 454-7 (1971).

Waldron, R.H. "The Naked, the Dead, and the Machine: A New Look at NM's First Novel." *PMLA*, 87: 271-7 (Mr 72).

Werge, Thomas. "An Apocalyptic Voyage: God, Satan, and the American Tradition in NM's *Of a Fire on the Moon*." *RPol*, 34: 108-28 (O 72).

Widmer, Kingsley. "The Post-Modernist Art of Protest: Kesey and M as Expressions of Rebellion." *CentR*, 19: 121-35 (Su 75).

Will, G.F. "New York's Political Circus." *NatR*, 22: 688-9 (Je 70).

Witt, Grace. "The Bad Man as Hipster: NM's Use of Frontier Metaphor." *WAL*, 4: 203-17 (1969).

Wood, Michael. "Kissing Hitler." *NYRB*, 20 S 73, pp. 22-4.

Wustenhagen, Heinz. "Instinkt kontra Vernuft: NMs ideologische und ästhetische Konfusion." *ZAA*, 16: 362-89 (1968).

Major, Clarence. Klinkowitz, Jerome. "CM's SuperFiction." *Yardbird Reader*, 4: 1-11 (1975).

———. "Reclaiming a (New) Black Experience: The Fiction of CM." *OyR*, 8: 86-90 (Wi 73).

Miller, A.D. *"All-Night Visitors."* *BSch*, 2: 54-6 (Ja 71).

Malamud, Bernard. Allen, J.A. "The Promised End: BM's *The Tenants*." *HC*, 8: 1-15 (1971).

Alley, A.D., and Hugh Agee. "Existential Heroes: Frank Alpine and Rabbit Angstrom." *BSUF*, 9: 3-5 (Wi 68).

Alter, Robert. "Updike, M, and the Fire This Time." *Commentary*, 54: 68-74 (O 72).

Barsness, J.A. *"A New Life*: The Frontier Myth in Perspective." *WAL*, 3: 297-302 (Wi 69).

Dickstein, Morris. "Cold War Blues: Notes on the Culture of the Fifties." *PR*, 41: 30-53 (1974).

Desmond, J.F. "M's Fixer—Jew, Christian, or Modern?" *Renascence*, 27: 101-10 (Wi 75).

Ducharme, Robert. "Structure and Content in M's *Pictures of Fidelman*." *ConnR*, 5: 26-36 (1971).

Eigner, E.M. "M's Use of the Quest Romance." *Genre*, 1: 55-75 (Ja 68).

Faber, Stephen. *"The Fixer."* *HudR*, 22: 134-8 (Sp 69).

Finkelstein, Sidney. "The Anti-Hero of Updike. Bellow, and M." *AmD*, 7: 12-4 (1972).

Freese, Peter. "BM's *The Assistant*." *LWU*, 5: 247-60 (1972).

———. "Parzival als Baseballstar: BM's *The Natural*." *JA*, 13: 143-57 (1968).

Friedman, A.M. "BM: The Hero as Schnook." *SoR*, 4: 927-44 (Au 68).

———. "The Jew's Complaint in Recent American Fiction: Beyond Exodus and Still in the Wilderness." *SoR*, 8: 41-59 (Ja 72).

Fukuma, Kin-ichi. "BM and the Jewish Consciousness." *KAL*, 16: 40-3 (1975).

Golub, Ellen. "The Resurrection of the Heart." *Eng R*, 1: 63-78 (#2 73).

Goodman, O.B. "There Are Jews Everywhere." *Judaism*, 19: 283-94 (1970).

Greenberg, Alvin. "Breakable Beginnings: The Fall into Realism in the Modern Novel." *TSLL*, 10: 133-42 (1968).

Griffith, John. "M's *The Assistant*." *Expl*, 31: 1 (S 72).

Hall, J.S. "M's 'The Lady of the Lake'—a Lesson in Rejection." *UR*, 36: 149-50 (Wi 69).

Hays, P.L. "The Complex Pattern of Redemption in *The Assistant*." *CentR*, 13: 200-14 (Sp 69).

Hergt, Tobias. "BM's 'A Choice Profession.'" *NS*, 24: 443-53 (1975).

Hoag, Gerald. "M's Trial: *The Fixer* and the Critics." *WHR*, 24: 1-12 (Wi 70).

Horne, L.B. "Yakov Agonistes." *RSW*, 37: 320-6 (D 69).

Inge, M.T. "The Ethnic Experience and Aesthetics in Literature: M's *The Assistant* and Roth's *Call It Sleep*." *JEthSt*, 1: 45-50 (Wi 74).

Iwamoto, Iwao. "Judea-kei Sakka no Miryoku—Barth to M." *EigoS*, 118: 257-60 (1972).

Kattan, Naïm. "Le Roman Juif Américain: à propos de BM." *LanM*, 42: 158-69 (Mr-Ap 68).

Kirby, D.K. "The Princess and the Frog: The Modern American Short Story as Fairy Tale." *MinnR*, 4: 145-9 (1973).

Knopp, J.Z. "The Ways of *Mentshlekhakayt*: A Study in the Morality of Some Fiction of BM and Philip Roth." *Tradition*, 13: 67-84 (#3 73).

Komizo, Yoko. "On Frank's Conversion: M's *The Assistant*." *KAL*, 16: 40-3 (1975).

Lamdin, L.S. "M's Schlemiels." *CaSE*, 11: 31-42 (1970).

Leer, Norman. "The Double Theme in M's *Assistant*: Dostoevsky with Irony." *Mosaic*, 4: 89-102 (1971).

Lefcowitz, B.F. "The *Hybris* of Neurosis: M's *Pictures of Fidelman*." *L&P*, 20: 115-20 (1970).

Leff, L.J. "M's Ferris Wheel." *NCLit*, 1: 14-5 (Ja 71).

———. "Utopia Reconstructed." *Critique*, 12: 29-37 (1971).

Leonard, John. "Cheever to Roth to M." *Atl*, 231: 112-6 (Je 73).

Lindberg-Seyersted, Brita. "A Reading of BM's *The Tenants*." *JAmS*, 9: 85-102 (Ap 75).

Markovic, V.E. "S BM." *Savremenik*, 33: 282-6 (1971).

May, C.E. "BM's 'A Summer's Reading.'" *NCLit*, 2: 11-3 (S 72).

———. "The Bread of Tears: M's 'The Loan.'" *SSF*, 7: 652-4 (Fa 70).

Mesher, D.R. "The Remembrance of Things Unknown: M's 'The Last Mohican.'" *SSF*, 12: 397-404 (Fa 75).

Ozick, Cynthia. "Literary Blacks and Jews." *Midstream*, 18: 10-24 (Je-Jl 72).

Pinsker, Sanford. "The Achievement of BM." *MwQ*, 10: 379-89 (1969).

———. "Christ as Revolutionary/Revolutionary as Christ: The Hero in BM's *The Fixer* and William Styron's *The Confession of Nat Turner*." *BaratR*, 6: 29-37 (1971).

———. "A Note on BM's 'Take Pity.'" *SSF*, 6: 212-3 (1969).

Poss, Stanley. "Serial Form and M's Schlemihls." *Costerus*, 9: 109-16 (1973).

Pradhan, S.V. "The Nature and Interpretation of Symbolism in M's *The Assistant*." *CentR*, 16: 394-407 (Wi 72).

Raffel, Burton. "BM." *LitR*, 13: 149-55 (Wi 69-70).

Reynolds, Richard. "'The Magic Barrel': Pinye Salzman's Kadish." *SSF*, 10: 100-2 (1973).

Richey, C.W. "'The Woman in the Dunes': A Note on BM's *The Tenants*." *NCLit*, 3: 4-5 (Ja 73).

Richler, Mordecai. "Write, Boychick, Write." *NSt*, 7 Ap 67, pp. 473-4.

Riese, Utz. "Das 'neue Leben' ohne Neues: Zum Menschenbild in BM's Romanen *The Natural* und *The Assistant*." *ZAA*, 21: 11-31 (1973).

Roth, Philip. "Imagining Jews." *NYRB*, 21: 22-8 (3 O 74).

Russell, Mariann. "White Man's Black Man." *CLAJ*, 17: 93-100 (S 73).

Samuels, C.T. "The Career of BM." *NRep*, 155: 19-21 (10 S 66).

Sharma, D.R. "*The Natural*: A Nonmythical Approach." *PURBA*, 5: 3-8 (1974).

Schulz, M.F. "M's *A New Life*: The New Wasteland of the Fifties." *WR*, 6: 37-44 (1969).

Sharfman, William. "Inside and Outside M." *Rendezvous*, 7: 25-38 (Sp 72).

Sharma, D.R. "M's 'Jewishness': An Analysis of *The Assistant*." *LCrit*, 10: 29-37 (Wi 74).

Singer, Barnet. "Outsider vs. Insider: M's and Kesey's Pacific Northwest." *SDR*, 13: 127-44 (1975).

Stamerra, Silvana. "Il protagonista nelle narrativa di BM." *Zagaglia*, 10: 333-43 (1968).

Standley, Fred. "BM: the Novel of Redemption." *SHR*, 5: 309-18 (Fa 71).

Stanton, Robert. "Outrageous Fiction: *Crime and Punishment, The Assistant,* and *Native Son*." *PCP*, 4: 52-8 (1969).

Stern, Daniel. "The Art of Fiction: BM." *PaR*, 61: 40-64 (Sp 75).

Sweet, Charles. "Unlocking the Door: M's 'Behold the Key.'" *NCLit*, 5: 11-2 (N 75).

Tanner, Tony. "BM and the New Life." *CritQ*, 10: 151-68 (Sp-Su 68).

Turner, F.W. "Myth Inside and Out: M's *The Natural*." *Novel*, 1: 133-9 (Wi 68).

Wegelin, C.A. "The American Schlemiel Abroad: M's Italian Stories and the End of American Innocence." *TCL*, 19: 77-88 (Ap 73).

Winn, Harbour. "M's Uncas: 'Last Mohican.'" *NCLit*, 5: 13-4 (Mr 75).

Witherington, Paul. "M's Allusive Design in *A New Life*." *WAL*, 10: 115-23 (Ag 75).

Malcolm X. Benson. T.W. "Rhetoric and Autobiography: The Case of MX." *QJS*, 60: 1-13 (F 74).

Berthoff, Warner. "Witness and Testament: Two Contemporary Classics." *NLH*, 2: 311-27 (1971).

Clasby, Nancy. "*The Autobiography of MX*: A Mythic Paradigm." *JBlackS*, 5: 18-34 (S 74).

Demarest, D.P. "*The Autobiography of MX*: Beyond Didacticism." *CLAJ*, 16: 179-87 (1972).

Harper, F.D. "A Reconstruction of MX's Personality." *AfrAmS*, 3: 1-6 (1972).

Hoyt, C.A. "The Five Faces of MX." *NALF*, 4: 107-12 (1970).

Kieser, Rolf. "The Black American Dream: Das Dilemma des farbigen Amerikaners, dergestellt in *The Autobiography of MX*." *LWU*, 2: 89-97 (1969).

Ladner, Robert. "Folk Music, Pholk Music, and the Angry Children of MX." *SFQ*, 34: 131-45 (1970).

Larrabee, H.A. "The Varieties of Black Experience." *NEQ*, 43: 638-45 (1971).

Mandel, B.J. "The Didactic Achievement of MX's Autobiography." *AfrAmS*, 2: 269-74 (1972).

Miller, Ross. "Autobiography as Fact and Fiction: Franklin, Adams, MX." *CentR*, 16: 221-32 (Su 72).

Ohmann, Carol. "*The Autobiography of MX*: A Revolutionary Use of the Franklin Tradition." *AQ*, 22: 131-49 (Su 70).

Seraile, William. "David Walker and MX: Brothers in Radical Thought." *BlackW*, 22: 68-73 (1973).

Vaizey, John. "Black Man in Search of Allah." *TLS*, 16 Ag 74, p. 881.

Manchester, William. Garrett, George. "You Play It Dead Straight: An Interview with WM." *Contempora*, 2: 16-9 (1972).

Pizer, Donald. "Documentary Narratives as Art: WM and Truman Capote." *JML*, 2: 105-18 (S 71).

Manfred, Frederick. Astro, Richard. "*The Big Sky* and the Limits of Wilderness Fiction." *WAL*, 9: 105-14 (Su 74).

Bebeau, Don. "A Search for Voice, A Sense of Place in *the Golden Bowl*." *SDR*, 7: 79-86 (Wi 70).

Lee, J.W. "An Interview in Minnesota with FM." *StN*, 5: 358-82 (1973).

Lundquist, James. "FM Talks about Sinclair Lewis." *SLNL*, 2: 1-5 (Sp 70).

Manfred, Frederick. "Sinclair Lewis' Funeral." *SDR*, 7: 54-78 (Wi 69-70).

Milton, John. "Interview with FM." *SDR*, 7: 110-30 (Wi 69-70).

Roth, Russel. "The Inception of a Saga: FM's 'Buckskin Man.'" *SDR*, 7: 87-99 (Wi 69-70).

Wylder, D.E. "M's Indian Novel." *SDR*, 7: 100-9 (Wi 69-70).

March, William (William Edward March Cambell). Emerson, O.B. "WM and Southern Literature." *C-NCFS*, 1: 3-10 (1968).

Medlicott, Alexander. "'Soldiers Are Citizens of Death's Gray Land': WM's *Company K*." *ArQ*, 28: 209-24 (1972).

Simmonds, R.S. "An Unending Circle of Pain: WM's Company K." *BSUF*, 16: 33-46 (Sp 75).

*————. "A WM Checklist." *MissQ*, 28: 461-88 (Fa 75).

————. "WM's *Company K*: A Short Textual Study." *SAF*, 2: 105-13 (Sp 74).

Markham, Edwin. Anon. "Letters from the M Archives." *MarkR*, 2: 8-12 (1970).

————. "M and Gorky." *MarkR*, 1: 1-2 (F 68).

————. "A Selection of Letters from the M Archives." *MarkR*, 5: 7-16 (My 69).

Abbott, L.D. "EM: Laureate of Labor." *Comrade*, 1: 74-5 (Ja 02).

Cohen, E.H. "M's 'Ten-Minute' Poem: A Note." *MarkR*, 5: 17-8 (My 69).

Csuros, Barno. "The Poet and the Seer." *MarkR*, 4: 1-5 (F 69).

Escholz, P.A. "Em's 'The Ballad of the Gallows-Bird' and His Proposed Collected Poems." *ELN*, 12: 187-8 (Mr 75).

Farley, M.B. "Memories of EM." *Pacific Historian*, 15: 30-2 (Wi 71).

Haaland, C.C. "The Mystique of M's California: The Culmination of the Millenial Motif in America." *MarkR*, 4: 89-95 (F 75).

Jaffe, Harold. "M on Whitman." *MarkR*, 2: 1 (My 68).

*Johnson, R.C., and G.T. Tanselle. "Addenda to Bibliographies of . . . M, . . .: Haldeman-Julius Little Blue Books." *PBSA*, 66: 66 (1Q 72).

Keller, D.H. "A.E. Housman to EM: A Letter." *MarkR*, 2: 17 (My 70).

Manglaviti, L.M.J. "M and Mencken." *MarkR*, 3: 38-9 (F 72).

Markham, Edwin. "Letters from the M Archives." *MarkR*, 2: 9-12 (S 69).

————. "A Selection of Letters from the M Archive." *MarkR*, 5: 7-16 (S 69).

Slade, J.W. "M and Gorky." *MarkR*, 1: 1-2 (F 68).

————. "Putting You in the Papers: Ambrose Bierce's Letters to EM." *Prospects*, 1: 335-68 (1975).

————. "Recent Additions to the M Archives." *MarkR*, 2: 14-7 (Mr 70).

Stern, M.B. "The Head of a Poet: A Phrenograph of EM." *Coranto*, 6: 6-12 (1969).

Stoddard, E.R. "The Battle of the Poets." *MarkR*, 5: 17 (My 69).

Marquand, John P. Aldridge, J.W. "Not Too Pro for Posterity." *SatR*, 55: 63-71 (17 Je 72).

Ballowe, James. "M and Santayana: Apley and Alden." *MarkR*, 2: 92-4 (F 71).

Gross, J.J. "The Late JP.M: An Essay in Biography." *Eng Rec*, 19: 2-12 (D 68).

Hamblen, A.A. "Judge Grant and the Forgotten Chippendales." *UR*, 33: 175-9 (Mr 67).

MacLean, Hugh. "Conservatism in Modern American Fiction." *CE*, 15: 315-25 (Mr 54).

Mizener, Arthur. "So Little Time." *NRep*, 166: 26-8 (17 Je 72).

Parsons, H.V. "*The Tory Lover, Oliver Wiswell,* and *Richard Carvel*." *CLQ*, 9: 220-31 (D 70).

Stessin, Lawrence. "The Businessman in Fiction." *LitR*, 12: 281-9 (Sp 69).

Walker, D.R. "Failure to Protest: The Tragedy of J.P.M's Apley, Pulham, and Wayde." *NasR*, 2: 15-22 (1970).

Marquis, Don. Hasley, Louis. "DM: Ambivalent Humorist." *PrS*, 45: 59-73 (Sp 71).

Martin, Edward. "A Puritan's Satanic Flight: DM, Archy, and Anarchy." *SR*, 83: 623-42 (Fa 75).

Marsh, James. Bassett, T.D.S., and J.J. Duffy. "The Library of JM." *ESQ*, 63: 2-10 (Sp 71).

Buckham, J.W. "JM and Coleridge." *Bibliotheca Sacra*, 61: 305-17 (Ap 04).

Cameron, K.W. "Emerson's Coleridge in Review." *ESQ*, 64-5: 78-161 (Su-Fa 71).

Carafiol, P.C. "JM: Transcendental Puritan." *ESQ*, 21: 127-36 (3Q 75).

Duffy, J.J. "From Hanover to Burlington: JM's Search for Unity." *VH*, 38: 27-48 (Wi 70).

———. "Problems in Publishing Coleridge: JM's First American Edition of Aids to Reflection." *NEQ*, 43: 193-208 (Je 70).

———. "Transcendental Letters from George Ripley to JM." *ESQ*, 50: 20-4 (1Q 68).

Greenwood, D.M. "JM, Dartmouth and American Transcendentalism." *Dartmouth* Alumni Mag, 61: 23-5 (Mr 69).

Lindsay, J.I. "Coleridge and the University of Vermont." *VT Alumni Wk*, 15: 17-2 (29 Ja 36).

Swift, D.E. "Yankee in Virginia: JM at Hampden-Sydney, 1823-1826." *VMHB*, 80: 312-32 (Jl 72).

Marshall, Paule. Benston, K.W. "Architectural Imagery and Unity in PM's *Brown Girl, Brownstones.*" *NALF*, 9: 67-70 (Fa 75).

Brown, Lloyd. "The Rhythms of Power in PM's Fiction." *Novel*, 7: 159-67 (1974).

Kapai, Leela. "Dominant Themes and Technique in PM's Fiction." *CLAJ*, 16: 49-59 (S 72).

Keizs, Marcia. "Themes and Style in the Works of PM." *NALF*, 9: 7, 71-6 (Fa 75).

Marshall, Paule. "Shaping the World of My Art." *NewL*, 40: 97-112 (1973).

Nazareth, Peter. "PM's Timeless People." *NewL*, 40: 113-31 (1973).

Stoelting, W.L. "Time Past and Time Present: The Search for Viable Links in *The Chosen Place, The Timeless People* by PM." *CLAJ*, 16: 60-71 (S 72).

Washington, M.H. "Black Women Image Makers." *BlackW*, 23: 10-8 (1974).

Martin, Alexander. Lemay, J.A.L. "A Note on the Canon of AM." *EAL*, 7: 91 (Sp 72).

Walser, Richard. "AM, Poet." *EAL*, 6: 55-61 (Sp 71).

Masters, Edgar Lee. Burgess, C.E. "M and Some Mentors." *PLL*, 10: 175-201 (Sp 74).

———. "M and Whitman: A Second Look." *WWR*, 17: 25-7 (My 71).

———. "An Unpublished Poem by ELM." *PLL*, 5: 183-9 (Sp 69).

Crawford, J.W. "A Defense of 'A One-Eyed View.'" *CEA*, 31: 14-5 (F 69).

———. "Naturalistic Tendencies in *Spoon River Anthology.*" *CEA*, 30: 6, 8 (Je 68).

Earnest, Ernest. "A One-Eyed View of Spoon River." *CEA*, 31: 8-9 (N 68).

Flanagan, J.T. "Three Illinois Poets." *CentR*, 16: 313-27 (Fa 72).

Hahn, Henry. "Evolution in the Graveyard." *MwQ*, 10: 275-90 (Sp 69).

Jepson, Edgar. "The Western School." *Little R*, 5: 4-9 (S 18).

Jimémez Martos, Luis. "Un dramático pueblo de difuntos." *Estafeta Literaria*, 544: 178-203 (15 Jl 74).

Masters, Edgar Lee. "Posthumous Poems of ELM." *TQ*, 12: 71-115 (1969).

Popescu, Petru. "ELM: Autorul unei singure cărti." *RoLit*, 26 D 68, p. 16.

Robinson, F.K. "ELM Centenary Exhibition: Catalogue and Checklist." *TQ*, 12: 4-68 (1969).

———. "From Mary Austin to ELM: A Book Inscription." *LCUT*, 6: 82-5 (D 73).

———. "The ELM Collection: Sixty Years of Literary History." *LCUT*, 8: 42-9 (Sp 68).

———. "*The New Spoon River*: Fifteen Facsimile Pages." *TQ*, 12: 116-43 (1969).

Russell, Herb. "M's 'Alfred Moir,' 14." *Expl*, 31: 54 (Mr 73).

Schoolfield, G.C. "Elmer Kiktonius and ELM." *AmNor*, 3: 307-27 (1971).

Wells, H.W. "Varieties of American Poetic Drama." *LHY*, 14: 14-46 (1973).

Mather, Cotton. Ali Isani, M. "CM and the Orient." *NEQ*, 43: 46-58 (Fa 70).

Andrews, W.D. "The Printed Funeral Sermons of CM." *EAL*, 5: 24-44 (Fa 70).

Arner, R.D. "The Story of Hannah Duston: From CM to Thoreau." *ATQ*, 18: 19-23 (Sp 73).

Bercovitch, Sacvan. "'Delightful Examples of Surprising Prosperity': CM and the American Success Story." *ES*, 51: 1-3 (Fa 70).

———. "'Nehemias Americanus': CM and the Concept of the Representative American." *EAL*, 8: 220-38 (Wi 74).

Bunkow, Robert. "An Analysis of CM's Understanding of the Relationship of the Supernatural to Man as Seen in History." *HMPEC*, 42: 319-29 (1973).

Cifelli, Edward. "More of CM's 'Verbal Pattern.'" *QJS*, 57: 94-7 (1971).

Duffy, John. "CM Revisited." *MSE*, 1: 30-8 (Fa 67).

Eberwein, J.D. "Fishers of Metaphor: M and Melville on the Whale." *ATQ*, 26, sup: 30-1 (Sp 75).

Gay, Carol. "The Fettered Tongue: A Study of the Speech Defect of CM." *AL*, 46: 451-64 (Ja 75).

Holifield, E.B. "The Renaissance of Sacramental Piety in Colonial New England." *WMQ*, 29: 33-48 (Ja 72).

Isani, M.A. "CM and the Orient." *NEQ*, 43: 46-58 (Mr 70).

Kaiser, L.M. "On the Latin Verse in CM's *Magnalia Christi Americana*." *EAL*, 10: 301-6 (Wi 75).

Lazenby, Walter. "Exhortation as Exorcism: CM's Sermons to Murderers." *QJS*, 57: 50-6 (F 71).

Leary, J.P. "A Misplaced Tale-Teller Gets It in the Neck." *NYFQ*, 1: 203-9 (Wi 75).

Lowance, M.I. "Typology and the New England Way: CM and the Exegesis of Biblical Types." *EAL*, 4: 15-37 (Sp 69).

McKay, D.P. "CM's Unpublished Singing Sermon." *NEQ*, 48: 410-22 (S 75).

Moe, Sigrid. "CM's Literary Output: A Reassessment." *AN&Q*, 12: 102-6 (Mr 74).

Nelson, Jane. "CM and George Burroughs: Puritan Anticipations of the Tall Tale." *PosS*, 4: 1-7 (O 73).

Parker, P.L. "Two Puritan Doers of Good: Benjamin Franklin and CM." *Eng R*, 1: 32-49 (#1 73).

Richardson, W.N. "CM: The Man and the Myth." *ArlQ*, 1: 281-94 (Wi 67-68).

Silverman, Kenneth. "CM's Foreign Correspondence." *EAL*, 3: 172-85 (Wi 68-69).

Steele, T.J. "The Biblical Meaning of M's Bradford." *BRMMLA*, 24: 147-54 (D 70).

Stein, S.J. "CM and Jonathan Edwards on the Number of the Beast: Eighteenth-Century Speculation about the Antichrist." *PAAS*, 84: 293-315 (1974).

Tatham, Campbell. "Benjamin Franklin, CM, and the Outward State." *EAL*, 6: 223-33 (Wi 71-72).

Van Cromphout, G.V. "CM as Plutarchan Biographer." *AL*, 46: 465-81 (Ja 75).

Vartanian, Pershing. "CM and the Puritan Transition into the Enlightenment." *EAL*, 7: 213-24 (Wi 73).

Weeks, Louis. "CM and the Quakers." *QH*, 59: 24-33 (1970).

Werking, R.H. "'Reformation Is Our Only Preservation': CM and the Salem Witchcraft." *WMQ*, 29: 281-90 (Ap 72).

Whiting, B.J. "Proverbs in CM's *Magnalia Christi Americana*." *NM*, 73: 477-84 (1972).

Woody, K.M. "Bibliographical Notes to CM's *Manuductio ad Ministerium*." *EAL*, 6, sup: 1-98 (Sp 71).

————. "CM's *Manuductio ad Theologiam*: The 'More Quiet and Hopeful Way.'" *EAL*, 4: 3-48 (Fa 69).

Mather, Increase. Bliss, C.S. "A Much-Travelled Association Copy of Calvin's *Institutes*." *BC*, 17: 458-62 (Wi 68).

Emerson, Everett, and M.I. Lowance. "IM's Confutation of Solomon Stoddard's Observations Respecting the Lord's Supper, 1680." *PAAS*, 83: 29-65 (1973).

Joyce, W.L. "Note on IM's Observations Respecting the Lord's Supper." *PAAS*, 83: 343-44 (1973).

Nelson, A.K. "King Philip's War and the Hubbard-M Rivalry." *WMQ*, 27: 615-29 (1970).

Scheick, W.J. "Anonymity and Art in *The Life and Death of That Reverend Man of God, Mr. Richard Mather*." *AL*, 42: 457-67 (Ja 71).

Mather, Richard. Burg, B.R. "A Letter of RM to a Cleric in Old England." *WMQ*, 29: 81-98 (Fa 72).

————. "The Record of an Early Seventeenth Century Atlantic Crossing." *HussR*, 4: 72-7 (1970).

Scheick, W.J. "Anonymity and Art *The Life and Death of That Reverend Man of God, Mr. Richard Mather*." *AL*, 42: 457-67 (Ja 71).

Mathews, Cornelius. Wells, D.A. "'Bartleby the Scrivener,' Poe, and the Duyckinck Circle." *ESQ*, 21: 35-9 (1Q 75).

Matthews, Brander. Kleinfeld, H.L. "The Tutelage of a Young American: BM in Europe, 1966." *CLC*, 13: 35-42 (F 64).

Matthews, Jack. Matthews, Jack. "Comment 'The Descent.'" *Eng Rec*, 19: 26 (F 69).

————. 'What Are You Doing There? What Are You Doing Here? A View of the Jesse Hill Ford Case." *GaR*, 26: 121-44 (Su 72).

Smith, David. "That Appetite for Life so Ravenous." *Shen*, 25: 49-55 (1974).

Matthews, William. Mathews, William. "Talking about Poetry." *OhR*, 13: 33-51 (1972).

Smith, Marcel. "A Conservation with WM." *Black Horse R*, 1: 57-77 (Sp 75).

Matthiessen, F.O. Douglas, G.H. "F.O.M and the Democratic Spirit." *Nation*, 219: 21-3 (6 Jl 74).

Gunn, G.B. "Criticism as Repossession and Responsibility: F.O.M and the Ideal Critic." *AQ*, 22: 629-48 (Fa 70).

White, G.A. "Ideology and Literature: *American Renaissance* and FOM." *TriQ*, 23-4: 430-500 (1972).

Meeks, Howard. Liedel, D.E. "The Authorship of Two Antislavery Novels of the 1840s: *The Fanatic* and *Winona*." *PBSA*, 67: 447-9 (4Q 73).

Melville, Herman. Anon. "Bartleby's Dead Letter Office." *Extrapolation*, 10: 5-6 (1972).

————. "Entretiens de Polyèdre: HM." *Etudes*, 331: 49-65 (Jl-Ag 69).

————. "A M Letter and Stray Books from His Library." *ESQ*, 63: 47-9 (Sp 71).

————. "M's Oath of Allegiance as Inspector of Customs (1866)." *ESQ*, 47: 129 (2Q 67).

————. "Through the Long Vaticans and Street Stalls." *MSEx*, 20: 7-8 (1874).

Abel, Darrell. "I Look, You Look, He Looks: Three Critics of M's Poetry." *ESQ*, 21: 116-23 (2Q 75).

————. "Who Keeps His Quiet State." *MSEx*, 20-6 (1974).

Abele, Rudolph von. "M und das Problem des Bösen." *Neue Auslese*, 3: 66-71 (M4 48).

Abrams, R.E. "*Typee* and *Omoo*: HM and the Ungraspable Phantom of Identity." *ArQ*, 31: 33-50 (Sp 75).

Adler, Joyce. "The Imagination and M's Endless Probe for Relation." *ATQ*, 19: 37-42 (Su 73).

————. "M on the White Man's War Against the American Indian." *Sci&Soc*, 36: 417-42 (Wi 72).

Adler, J.S. "M's *Benito Cereno*: Slavery and Violence in the Americas." *Sci&Soc*, 38: 19-48 (Sp 74).

———. "M and the Civil War." *NLet*, 40: 99-117 (Wi 73).

Albrecht, R.C. "The Thematic Unity of M's 'The Encantadas,'" *TSLL*, 14: 463-77 (Fa 72).

———. "White Jacket's Intentional Fall." *StN*, 4: 17-26 (Sp 72).

Allen, Mary. "M and Conrad Confront Stillness." *RSW*, 40: 122-30 (1972).

Allen, Priscilla. "*White-Jacket*: M and the Man-of-War Microcosm." *AQ*, 25: 32-47 (Mr 73).

Allen, R.R. "The First Six Volumes of the Northwestern-Newberry M." *Proof*, 3: 441-53 (1973).

Altschuler, Glenn. "Whose Foot on Whose Throat? A Re-examination of M's *Benito Cereno*." *CLAJ*, 18: 283-92 (Mr 75).

Ambriere, Francis. "M et l'aventure interieure." *NL*, nv: 5 (11 N 37).

Amoruso, Vito. "Alla ricerca d'Ismaele: M e l'arte." *SA*, 13: 169-233 (1967).

———. "Un mare senza rive: M e l'arte." *SA*, 15: 75-129 (1969).

Anderson, Marilyn. "M's Jackets: *Redburn* and *White-Jacket*." *ArQ*, 26: 173-81 (1970).

Anderson, B.C. "The M-Kierkegaard Syndrome." *Rendezvous*, 3: 41-53 (1968).

Anderson, C.R. "M's South Sea Romance." *EigoS*, 115: 478-82, 564-8 (1969).

Anderson, Quentin. "Second Trip to Byzantium." *KR*, 11: 516-20 (Su 49).

* Andrews D.C. "Attacks of Whales on Ships: A Checklist." *MSEx*, 18: 3-17 (My 74).

———. "Note on M's *Confidence Man*." *ESQ*, 63: 27-8 (Sp 71).

Arvin, Newton. "M's *Clarel*." *HudR*, 14: 298-300 (Su 61).

Asals, Frederick. "Satires and Skepticism in *The Two Temples*." *BBr*, 24: 7-18 (1971).

Aspiz, Harold. "Phrenologizing the Whale." *NCF*, 23: 18-27 (Je 68).

Asquino, M.L. "Hawthorne's Village Uncle and M's *Moby-Dick*." *SSF*, 10: 413-4 (1973).

Auden, W.H. "Moby Dick und Oedipus." *Litterarische Welt*, 1: 103-4 (1946).

Ausband, S.C. "The Whale and the Machine: An Approach to *Moby-Dick*." *AL*, 47: 197: 211 (My 75).

Ayo, Nicholas. "Bartleby's Lawyer on Trial." *ArQ*, 28: 27-38 (1972).

Babin, J.L. "M and the Deformation of Being." *SoR*, 7: 89-114 (Wi 71).

Bach, B.C. "M's *Confidence-Man*: Allegory, Satire, and the Irony of Intent." *Cithara*, 8: 28-36 (My 69).

———. "M's *Israel Potter*: a Revelation of It's Reputation and Meaning." *Cithara*, 7: 39-50 (N 67).

———. "M's Theatrical Mask: The Role of Narrative Perspective in His Short Fiction." *SLitI*, 2: 53-55 (Ap 69).

———. "Narrative Technique and Structure in *Pierre*." *ATQ*, 7: 5-8 (1Q 70).

Baim, Joseph. "The Confidence-Man as 'Trickster.'" *ATQ*, 1: 81-3 (1Q 69).

Baird, James. "*Typee* as Paradigm." *Extracts*, 15: 2 (1973).

Balota, Nicolas. "Commentarii la *Moby-Dick*." *RoLit*, 17: 18-20 (My 73).

Banta, Martha. "The Man of History and the Myth of Man in M." *ATQ*, 10: 3-11 (Sp 71).

Barber, J.W. "*A History of the Amistad Captives*." *ATQ*, 23: 109-20 (3Q 74).

Barber, Patricia. "HM's House in Brooklyn." *AL*, 45: 433-4 (N 73).

———. "M's Self-Image as a Writer and the Image of the Writer in *Pierre*." *MSE*, 3: 65-71 (Sp 72).

Barbour, James. "The Composition of *Moby-Dick*." *AL*, 47: 343-90 (N 75).

———. "'The *Town-Ho's* Story': M's Original Whale." *ESQ*, 21: 111-5 (2Q 75).

Barnett, L.K. "Bartleby as Alienated Worker." *SSF*, 11: 379-86 (Fa 74).

Basile, J.L. "The Meridians of M's Wicked World." *SDR*, 11: 62-7 (1973).

Baym, Nina. "The Erotic Motif in M's *Clarel*." *TSLL*, 16: 315-28 (Su 74).

Beck, H.P. "M as Folklife Recorder in *Moby-Dick*." *KFQ*, 18: 75-88 (1973).

Bell, M.D. "The Glendinning Heritage: M's Borrowings in *Pierre*." *SRom*, 12: 741-62 (Fa 73).

———. "The Irreducible *Moby-Dick*." *ESQ*, 28: 4-6 (3Q 62).

———. "M and 'Romance': Literary Nationalism and Fictional Form." *ATQ*, 24: 58-62 (Fa 74).

———. "M's *Redburn*: Invitation and Authority." *NEQ*, 46: 558-72 (D 73).

Bergman, J.D. "'Bartleby' and *The Lawyer's Story*." *AL*, 47: 432-5 (N 75).

———. "The Original Confidence Man." *AQ*, 21: 560-69 (Fa 69).

Bergstrom, R.F. "The Topmost Grief: Rejection of Ahab's Fate." *EC*, 2: 171-80 (Fa 75).

Berkeley, D.S. "*Figurae Futurarum* in *Moby-Dick*." *BuR*, 21: 108-23 (Fa-Wi 73).

Berlind, Bruce. "Notes on M's Shorter Prose." *HopR*, 3: 24-35 (Su 50).

Bernard, Kenneth. "M's *Mardi* and the Second Loss of Paradise." *LHR*, 7: 23-30 (1965).

Bertholf, R.J. "Charles Olson and the M Society." *MSEx*, 10: 3-4 (Ja 72).

———. "M and Olson: The Poetics of Form." *MSEx*, 17: 5-6 (F 74).

Bezanson, W.E. "The Context of M's Fiction." *ESQ*, 28: 9-11 (3Q 62).

Bianchi, Rugiero. "Il problema dell'arte e dell'artista in Poe, Hawthorne e M." *SA*, 18: 111-50 (1972).

Bickley, R.B. "The Minor Fiction of Hawthorne and M." *ATQ*, 14: 149-52 (Sp 72).

———. "The Triple Thrust in M's Short Stories: Society, the Narrator, and the Reader." *SAH*, 1: 172-9 (Ja 75).

Bier, Jesse. "M's 'The Fiddler' Reconsidered." *ATQ*, 14: 2-4 (Sp 72).

Bigelow, G.E. "The Problem of Symbolist Form in M's 'Bartleby the Scrivener.'" *MLQ*, 31: 345-58 (S 70).

Billy, Ted. "Eros and Thanatos in 'Bartleby.'" *ArQ*, 31: 21-32 (Sp 75).

Blair, J.G. "Puns and Equivocation in M's *The Confidence Man*." *ATQ*, 22: 91-5 (Sp 74).

Blau, Richard. "M in the Valley of the Bones." *ATQ*, 10: 11-6 (Sp 71).

Boies, J.J. "Sailor's Snug Harbor." *MSEx*, 14: 2-3 (1973).

Bollas, Christopher. "M's Lost Self: *Bartleby*." *AI*, 31: 401-11 (Wi 74).

Boudreau, G.V. "Of Pale Ushers and Gothic Piles: M's Architectural Symbology." *ESQ*, 18: 67-82 (2Q 72).

Bowen, J.K. "Alienation and Withdrawal Are Not Absurd: Renunciation and Preference in 'Bartleby the Scrivener.'" *SSF*, 8: 633-5 (1971).

———. "'Crazy Arab' and Kierkegaard's 'Melancholy Fantastic.'" *RSW*, 37: 60-4 (Mr 69).

———. "England's 'Bachelors' and America's 'Maids': M on Withdrawal and Sublimation." *RLV*, 38: 631-4 (N-D 72).

Bowen, Merlin. "*Redburn* and the Angle of Vision." *MP*, 52: 100-9 (N 54).

———. "Tactics of Indirection in M's *The Confidence-Man*." *StN*, 1: 401-20 (Wi 69).

*Bowman, D.H., and R.L. Bohan. "HM's *Mardi, and a Voyage Thither*: An Annotated Checklist of Criticism." *RALS*, 3: 27-72 (1973).

Boyle, T.E. "The Tenor in the Organic Metaphor." *Disc*, 11: 240-51 (Sp 68).

Brack, V.K and O.M. "Weathering Cape Horn: Survivors in M's Short Fiction." *ArQ*, 28: 61-73 (1972).

Branch, W.G. "The Genesis, Composition, and Structure of *The Confidence-Man*." *NCF*, 27: 424-48 (1973).

Braswell, William. "The Early Love Scenes in M's *Pierre*." *AL*, 22: 283-9 (N 50).

———. "The Main Themes on *Moby-Dick*." *ESQ*, 28: 15-7 (3Q 62).

Breinig, Helmbrecht. "The Destruction of Fairyland: M's 'Piazza' in the Tradition of the American Literary Imagination." *ELH*, 35: 254-83 (Je 68).

Brodtkorb, Paul. "*The Confidence-Man*: The Con Man as Hero." *StN*, 1: 421-35 (Wi 69).

Brodwin, Stanley. "HM's *Clarel*: An Existential Gospel." *PMLA*, 86: 375-87 (1971); 87: 310-2 (1972).

Brophy, R.J. "Benito Cereno, Oakum, and Hatchets." *ATQ*, 1: 89-90 (1Q 69).

Brouwer, F.E. "M's *The Confidence-Man* as Ship of Philosophers." *SHR*, 2: 158-65 (Sp 69).

———. "M's Pierre: At War with Social Convention." *PLL*, 5: 51-62 (1969).

Brown, C.M. "The White Whale." *PR*, 36: 453-9 (Su 69).

Browne, R.B. "Two Views of Commitment: 'The Paradise of Bachelors' and 'The Tartarus of Maids.'" *ATQ*, 7: 43-7 (Su 70).

Buell, Lawrence. "The Last Word on 'The Confidence-Man'?" *IllQ*, 35: 15-29 (N 72).

Burgess, R.H. "The 'Sea Serpent' Meets the 'Corinthian.'" *MSEx*, 17: 11 (1974).

Burns, Graham. "The Unshored World of *Moby-Dick*." *CritR*, 13: 68-83 (1970).

Burns, Robert. "*Moby-Dick*: Cannibalism and 'The Mystery.'" *MSEx*, 24: 5-7 (D 75).

Burton, D.M. "Intonation Patterns of Sermons in Seven Novels." *Lang & S*, 3: 205-30 (1970).

Busch, Frederick. "The Whale as Shaggy Dog: M and 'The Man Who Studied Yoga.'" *MFS*, 19: 193-206 (Su 73).

Cabau, Jacques. "M: La chassè a Dieu." *NL*, 47: 1, 10 (31 Jl 69).

Cameron, K.W. "Another Newspaper Anticipation of *Billy Budd*." *ATQ*, 14: 167-8 (Sp 72).

———. "M, Cooper, Irving and Bryant on International Matters." *ESQ*, 51: 108-21 (2Q 68).

———. "M, Cooper, Irving and John Essais Warren: Travel Literature and Patronage." *ESQ*, 47: 114-25 (2Q 67).

———. "A M Letter and Stray Books from His Library." *ESQ*, 63: 47-9 (1Q 71).

———. "M and National Matters." *ATQ*, 20: 183-94 (Fa 73).

———. "Scattered Manuscripts." *ATQ*, 1: 63-4 (1Q 69).

———. "Starbuck, Moby, and the Wreck of the *Ann Alexander*." *ATQ*, 14: 99-100 (Su 72).

———. "Uncollected M Letter." *ATQ*, 14: 111 (Su 72).

Campbell, M.A. "A Quiet Crusade: M's Tales of the Fifties." *ATQ*, 7: 8-12 (Su 70).

Canaday, Nicholas. "M's *Pierre*: At War with Social Convention." *PLL*, 5: 51-62 (Wi 69).

———. "M's 'The Encantadas': The Deceptive Enchantment of the Absolute." *PLL*, 10: 58-69 (Wi 74).

———. "A New Reading of M's 'Benito Cereno.'" *LSUS*, 8: 49-57 (1960).

Cannon, A.D. "M's Concepts of the Poet and Poetry." *ArQ*, 31: 315-38 (Wi 75).

———. "On Dating the Composition of *Clarel*." *MSEx*, 13: 6 (Ja 73).

Caraber, A.J. "M's *The Confidence Man*." *Expl*, 29: 9 (My 70).

Cardwell, A.G. "A Surprising World: Amasa Delano in Kentucky." *MTJ*, 16: 12-3 (Su 73).

Carlson, Thomas. "Ishmael as Art Critic: Double Metrical Irony in *Moby-Dick*." *MSEx*, 20: 2-4 (N 74).

Carothers, R.L. "M's 'Cenci': A Portrait of *Pierre*." *BSUF*, 10: 53-9 (Wi 69).

———, and J.L. Marsh. "The Whale and the Panorama." *NCF*, 26: 319-28 (1971).

Carter, Angela. "*Redburn: His First Voyage* by HM." *AntigR*, 1: 103-5 (Sp 70).

Cecchi, Emilio. "Two Notes on M." *SR*, 68: 398-406 (Su 60).

Cervo, N.A. "M's Bartleby—*Imago Dei*." *ATQ*, 14: 152-6 (Sp 72).

Chaffee, Patricia. "The Kedron in M's *Clarel*." *CLAJ*, 18: 374-82 (Mr 75).

Chamberlain, S.C. "M's *Clarel*." *PMLA*, 87: 103-4 (1972).

Chapman, S.S. "M and Bellow in the Real World: *Pierre* and *Augie March*." *WVUPP*, 18: 51-7 (1971).

Christensen, K.H. "Primivity, Development, and Isolation in HM's Works." *Extracta*, 3: 55-60 (1971).

Cifelli, E.M. "M's *Billy Budd*." *Expl*, 31: 60 (Ap 73).

Cizek, I.C. "M." *SXX*, 166-7: 166-7 (1974).

Cluny, C.M. "'La Samourai' de M." *NRF*, 16: 110-4 (Ja 68).

Cohen, Henning. "Abbe Bellegarde and M's *Israel Potter*: An Emendation." *Direction Line*, 1: 2-3 (Au 75).

————. "The 'Famous Tales' Anthologies: Recognition of M." *PBSA*, 68: 179-80 (Ap-Je 74).

————. "Hawthorne's *Israel Potter*." *MSEx*, 14: 9-10 (Ap 73).

————. "M to Mrs. Gifford, 1888." *Col Lit*, 2: 229 (1975).

————. "M's Surgeon Cuticle and Surgeon Cutbush." *StN*, 5: 251-3 (Su 73).

————. "M's Tomahawk Pipe: Artifact and Symbol." *StN*, 1: 397-400 (Wi 69).

————. "Recognition of M, ca. 1910." *MSEx*, 11: 10 (1972).

————. "The Singing Stammerer Motif in *Billy Budd*." *WF*, 34: 54-5 (1975).

————. "Why Isn't M for the Masses?" *SatR*, 52: 19-21 (16 Ag 69).

Colacurcio, M.J. "A Better Mode of Evidence: The Transcendental Problem of Faith and Spirit." *ESQ*, 54: 12-22 (1Q 69).

Colwell, J.L., and Gary Spitzer. "'Bartleby' and 'The Raven': Parallels of the Irrational." *GaR*, 23: 37-43 (Sp 69).

Conarroe, J.O. "M's Bartleby and Charles Lamb." *SSF*, 5: 113-8 (Wi 68).

Cook, R.M. "The Grotesque and M's *Mardi*." *ESQ*, 21: 103-10 (2Q 75).

Corniş-Pop, Marcel. "Cooronate ontologice şi morale in opera lui HM." *Analele Un Timisoara*, 8: 55-69 (1970).

Costello, J.A., and R.J. Kloss. "The Pyschological Depths of M's 'The Bell-Tower.'" *ESQ*, 19: 254-61 (4Q 73).

Cowan, J.C. "Lawrence's Criticism of M." *MSEx*, 17: 6-8 (F 74).

Crise, Stelio. "Ahab, Pizdrool, Quark." *JJQ*, 7: 65-9 (1969).

Cross, R.K. "*Moby-Dick* and *Under the Volcano*: Poetry from the Abyss." *MFS*, 20: 149-56 (Su 74).

Dahl, Curtis. "Jonah Improved: Sea-Sermons on Jonah." *MSEx*, 19: 6-9 (S 74).

————. "The Minnow and the Whale: Ely's '*There She Blows*' and M's *Moby-dick*." *Log of Mystic Seaport*, 24: 81-3 (1972).

Daiker, D.A. "Mark's Garden and M's 'Green, Gentle and Most Docile Earth.'" *Am Examiner*, 5: 4-7 (#1 75).

Dauner, Louise, "The 'Case of Tobias Pearson.'" *AL*, 21: 464-72 (Ja 50).

D'Avanzo, Mario. "Ahab, the Grecian Pantheon and Shelley's *Prometheus Unbound*." *BBr*, 24: 19-44 (1971).

————. "'The Cassock' and Carlyle's 'Church-Clothes.'" *ESQ*, 50: 74-6 (1Q 68).

————. "M's 'Bartleby' and John Jacob Astor." *NEQ*, 41: 259-64 (Je 68).

————. "*Pierre* and the Wisdom of Keats' Melancholy." *MSEx*, 16: 6-9 (N 73).

Davies, Margaret. "Rimbaud and M." *RLC*, 43: 479-88 (1969).

Dean, Dennis. "Hitchcock's Dinosaur Tracks." *AQ*, 21: 639-44 (1969).

Deane, Paul. "HM: Four Views of American Commercial Society." *RLV*, 34: 504-7 (S-O 68).

————. "HM: The Quality of Balance." *Serif*, 6: 12-7 (1970).

Denton, L.W. "M's Jerusalem: 'Wreck Ho—The Wreck!'" *HTR*, 67: 184-6 (1974).

Dew, Marjorie. "The Prudent Captain Vere." *ATQ*, 7: 81-5 (Su 70).

Dichmann, M.E. "Absolutism in M's *Pierre*." *PMLA*, 67: 702-15 (S 52).

Dillingham, W.B. "M's Long Ghost and Smollett's Count Fathom." *AL*, 42: 232-5 (My 70).

———. "The Mystery of Iniquity." *MSEx*, 14: 10 (Ap 73).

———. "The Narrator of *Moby-Dick*." *ES*, 49: 2 0-9 (F 68).

Donaldson, Scott. "Damned Dollars and a Blessed Company: Financial Imagery in *Moby-Dick*." *NEQ*, 46: 279-83 (Je 73).

———. "The Dark Truth of *The Piazza Tales*." *PMLA*, 85: 1082-6 (O 70).

Donoghue, Denis. "M." *LugR*, 1: 67-82 (1965).

Donohue, Jane. "M's Classification: Law and Order in His Poetry." *PLL*, 5: 63-72 (Wi 69).

Dow, Janet. "Ahab: The Fisher King." *ConnR*, 2: 42-9 (1969).

Duerksen, R.A. "The Deep Quandary in *Billy Budd*." *NEQ*, 41: 51-66 (Mr 68).

Eberwein, J.D. "Fishers of Metaphor: Mather and M on the Whale." *ATQ*, 26: 30-1 (Sp 75).

———. "Joel Barlow and *The Confidence Man*." *ATQ*, 24: 28-9 (Fa 74).

Eberwein, R.T. "The Impure Fiction of *Billy Budd*." *StN*, 6: 318-26 (Fa 74).

Eddy, D.M. "Bloody Battles and High Tragedies: M and the Theatre of the 1840's." *BSUF*, 13: 34-45 (Wi 72).

———. "M's Response to Beaumont and Fletcher: A New Source for *The Encantadas*." *AL*, 40: 374-80 (N 68).

———. "M's Sicilian Moralist." *ELN*, 8: 191-200 (1971).

Eknar, Reider. "*The Encantadas* and *Benito Cereno*: On Sources of Imagination in M." *MSpr*, 60: 258-73 (1966).

Ellis, T.R. "Another Broadside into *Mardi*." *AL*, 41: 419-22 (N 69).

Engel, Leonard. "M and the Young America Movement." *ConnR*, 4: 91-101 (1971).

Ensor, Allison. "The Downfall of Poor Richard: Benjamin Franklin as Seen by Hawthorne, M, and Mark Twain." *MTJ*, 17: 14-8 (Wi 74-75).

Estrin, M.W. "Robert Lowell's *Benito Cereno*." *MD*, 15: 411-25 (1973).

Evans, W.A. "The Boy and the Shadow: The Role of Pip and Fedallah in *Moby-Dick*." *SLitI*, 2: 77-81 (Ap 69).

Ewing, D.C. "HM: An Exhibition." *Gaz Grolier Club*, 11: 2-16 (O 69).

Farnsworth, R.M. "From Voyage to Quest in M." *ESQ*, 28: 17-20 (3Q 62).

Fiedler, Leslie. "Ishmael's Trip." *Listener*, 78: 134-6 (3 Ag 67).

Fiene, D.M. "Bartleby the Christ." *ATQ*, 7: 18-23 (Su 70).

Firchow, P.E. "*Bartleby*: Man and Metaphor." *SSF*, 5: 342-8 (Su 69).

Fisher, Marvin. "'Bartleby,' M's Circumscribed Scrivener." *SoR*, 10: 59-79 (Ja 74).

———. "Bug and Humbug in M's 'Apple-Tree Fable.'" *SSF*, 8: 459-66 (Su 71).

———. "'The Lighting-Rod Man': M's Testament of Rejection." *SSF*, 7: 433-8 (Su 70).

———. "M's 'Brave Officer.'" *MSEx*, 14: 7-8 (Ap 73).

———. "M's 'The Fiddler': Succumbing to the Drummer." *SSF*, 11: 153-6 (Sp 74).

———. "M's 'Tartarus': The Deflowering of New England." *AQ*, 23: 79-100 (Sp 71).

———. "'Poor Man's Pudding': M's Meditation on Grace." *ATQ*, 13: 32-6 (1Q 72).

———. "Portrait of the Artist in America: 'Hawthorne and His Mosses.'" *SoR*, 11: 156-66 (1975).

———. "Prospect and Perspective in M's 'Piazza.'" *Criticism*, 16: 203-16 (Su 74).

Fite, O.L. "Billy Budd, Claggart, and Schopenhauer." *NCF*, 23: 336-43 (D 68).

Fleck, Richard. "Stone Imagery in M's *Pierre*." *RSW*, 42: 127-30 (Je 74).

Fogle, R.H. "M's *Bartleby*: Absolutism, Predestination, and Free Will." *TSE*, 4: 125-35 (1954).

Frederick, J.T. "M's Early Acquaintance with Bayle." *AL*, 39: 545-7 (Ja 68).

———. "M's Last Long Novel: *Clarel*." *ArQ*, 26: 151-7 (Su 70).

———. "Symbol and Theme in M's *Israel Potter*." *MFS*, 8: 265-75 (Au 62).

Friedman, Irene. "M's Billy Budd: 'A Sort of Upright Barbarian.'" *CRAS*, 4: 87-95 (Sp 73).

Fulwiler, Toby. "The Death of the Handsome Sailor: A Study of 'Billy Budd' and *The Red Badge of Courage*." *ArQ*, 26: 101-12 (Su 70).

Furrow, Sharon. "The Terrible Made Visible: M, Salvator Rosa, and Piranesi." *ESQ*, 19: 237-53 (4Q 73).

Gaillard, T.L. "M's Riddle for Our Time: 'Benito Cereno.'" *EJ*, 41: 479-87 (Ap 72).

Gamble, R.H. "Reflections on the Hawthorne-M Relationship in *Pierre*." *AL*, 47: 629-32 (Ja 75).

Garrison, D.H. "M's Doubloon and the Shield of Achilles." *NCF*, 26: 171-84 (1971).

Geiger, Don. "Demonism in *Moby-Dick*." *Per*, 6: 111-24 (Sp 53).

George, J.L. "*Israel Potter*: The Height of Patriotism." *ATQ*, 7: 53-6 (Su 70).

Gerlach, John. "Messianic Nationalism in the Early Works of HM." *ArQ*. 28: 5-26 (1972).

Gibbs, R.J. "The Living Contour: The Whale Symbol in M and Pratt." *CanL*, 40: 17-25 (Sp 69).

Gibson, W.M. "Hm's 'Bartleby the Scrivener' and 'Benito Cereno.'" *NS*, 9: 107-16 (1961).

Giddings, T.H. "M, the Colt-Adams Murder, and 'Bartleby.'" *SAF*, 2: 123-32 (Au 74).

Gilenson, Boris. "M in Russia." *SovL*, 9: 171-3 (1969).

Gilmore, M.T. "M's Apocalypse: American Millenialism and *Moby-Dick*." *ESQ*, 21: 154-61 (3Q 75).

Giorcelli, Cristina. "La Poesie 'italiane' de HM." *SA*, 14: 165-91 (1968).

Glasser, William. "*Moby-Dick*." *SR*, 77: 463-86 (Jl-S 69).

Glicksberg, C.I. "M and the Negro Problem." *Phylon*, 11: 207-15 (3Q 50).

Golemba, H.L. "The Shape of *Moby-Dick*." *StN*, 5: 127-210 (Su 73).

Gollin, R.K. "The Forbidden Fruit of *Typee*." *MLS*, 5: 31-4 (Fa 75).

———. "The Intelligence Offices of Hawthorne and M." *ATQ*, 26: 44-7 (Sp 75).

———. "*Pierre*'s Metamorphosis of Dante's *Inferno*." *AL*, 542-5 (Je 68).

Gottlieb, L.D. "The Uses of Place: Darwin and M on Galapagos." *Biological Sci*, 25: 172-5 (Mr 75).

Green, J.D. "Diabolism, Pessimism and Democracy: Notes on M and Conrad." *MFS*, 8: 287-305 (Au 62).

Greene, Maxine. "The Whale's Whiteness: On Meaning and Meaningfulness." *JAE*, 2: 51-72 (Ja 68).

Griffiths, D.E. "Circles and Orphans." *BBr*, 24: 68-81 (1971).

Gross, J.J. "The Face of Plinlimmon and the 'Failures' of the Fifties." *ESQ*, 28: 6-9 (3Q 62).

Gross, Theodore. "HM: The Nature of Authority." *ColQ*, 16: 387-412 (Sp 68).

Guido, J.F. "M's *Mardi*: Bentley's Blunder?" *PBSA*, 62: 361-71 (3Q 68).

Gunn, Giles. "Matthiessen's M." *MSEx*, 17: 8-9 (F 74).

Gupta, R.K. "Bartleby': M's Critique of Reason." *IJAS*, 4: 66-71 (Je-D 74).

———. "Hautboy and Plinlimmon: A Reinterpretation of M's 'The Fiddler.'" *AL*, 43: 437-42 (N 71).

Guttchen, R.S. "Meaning and Meaningfulness." *JAE*, 2: 79-84 (Ap 68).

Haber, Richard. "Patience and Charity in *The Encantadas*." *MSE*, 3: 100-7 (1972).

Haber. T.B. "A Note on M's 'Benito Cereno.'" *MFS*, 6: 146-7 (S 51).

Haberstroh, Charles. "*Redburn*: The Psychological Pattern." *SAF*, 2: 133-44 (Au 74).

Hammes, K.W. "M, Dana, and Ames: Sources for Conrad's *The Nigger of the 'Narcissus.'*" *PolR*, 19: 29-33 (1974).

Han, Pierre. "Innocence and Natural Depravity in *Paradise Lost, Phèdre*, and *Billy Budd*." *RPBH*, 49: 856-61 (1971).

Hands, C.B. "The Comic Entrance to *Moby-Dick*." *Col Lit*, 2: 182-91 (1975).

Hanson, E.I. "M and the Polynesian-Indian." *MSEx*, 17: 13-4 (F 74).

Harada, Keiichi. "M no Shizen to Taikyoku Shiko." *EigoS*, 120: 165-7 (1974).

Haseganu, Mihaela. "Motive, metafore şi simboluri la M." *RITL*, 21: 523-31 (1972).

Hashiguchi, Minoru. "M no Shi." *EigoS*, 116: 485-6 (1960).

Haverstick, I.S. "A Note on Poe and *Pym* in M's *Omoo*." *PN*, 2: 37 (Ap 69).

Hayford, Harrison. "Contract: *Moby-Dick* by HM." *Proof*, 1: 1-7 (1971).

Hayman, Allen. "The Real and the Original: HM's Theory of Prose Fiction." *MFS*, 8: 211-32 (Au 62).

Hays, Peter. "Slavery and *Benito Cereno*: An Aristocratic View." *EA*, 23: 38-46 (Ja-Mr 70).

Heflin, Wilson. "New Light on HM's Cruise on the *Charles and Henry*." *Historic Nantucket*, 22: 6-27 (O 74).

———. "Sources from the Whale Fishery and 'The Town-Ho's Story.'" *MSEx*, 19: 405 (S 74).

———. "Two Notes on *Billy Budd*." *MSEx*, 14: 8-10 (Ap 73).

Hendrickson, John. "*Billy Budd*: Affirmation of Absurdity." *Re:A&L*, 2: 30-7 (#1 69).

Hennelly, Mark. "Ishmael's Nightmare and the American Eve." *AI*, 30: 274-93 (Fa 73).

Herbert, T.W. "Calvinism and Cosmic Evil in *Moby-Dick*." *PMLA*, 84: 1613-9 (1969).

———. "Homosexuality and Spiritual Aspiration in *Moby-Dick*." *CRAS*, 6: 50-8 (Sp 75).

Hibler, D.J. "*Drum Taps* and *Battle Pieces*: M and Whitman on the Civil War." *Person*, 50: 130-47 (Wi 69).

Higgins, Brian. "Plinlimmon and the Pamphlet Again." *StN*, 4: 27-38 (Sp 72).

Hillway, Tyrus. "In Defence of M's Fleece." *MSEx*, 19: 10-1 (S 74).

———. "M and the Young Revolutionaries." *AA*, 1974, pp. 43-58.

———. "M's Education in Science." *TSLL*, 16: 411-25 (Fa 74).

Hiner, James. "Only Catastrophe." *MinnR*, 10: 82-9 (1970).

Hirsch, D.H. "Verbal Reverberations and the Problem of Reality in *Moby-Dick*." *BBr*, 24: 45-67 (1971).

Hitt, R.E. "M's Poems of Civil War Controversy." *SLitI*, 2: 57-68 (Ap 69).

Hoffman, M.J. "The Anti-Transcendentalism of *Moby-Dick*." *GaR*, 23: 3-16 (Sp 69).

Holder, Alan. "Style and Tone in M's *Pierre*." *ESQ*, 60: 76-86 (Su 70).

Horsford, H.D. "The Design of the Argument in *Moby-Dick*." *MFS*, 8: 233-51 (Au 62).

Howard, F.K. "The Catalyst of Language: M's Symbol." *EJ*, 57: 824-31 (S 68).

Howard, Leon. "*Clarel*'s Pilgrimage and the Calendar." *MSEx*, 15: 2-3 (S 73).

Howington, D.S. "M's 'The Encantadas': Imagery and Meaning." *SLitI*, 2: 69-75 (Ap 69).

Hudson, Vaughan. "M's *Battle-Pieces* and Whitman's *Drum Taps*." *WWR*, 19: 81-92 (S 73).

Hull, R.E. "After *Moby-Dick*: M's Apparent Failure." *ATQ*, 7: 4 (Su 70).

Hume, R.D. "Gothic versus Romantic: A Revaluation of the Gothic Novel." *PMLA*, 84: 282-90 (1969).

Humma, J.B. "Melvillian Satire: Boomer and Bunger." *ATQ*, 14: 10-11 (Sp 72).

———. "M's *Billy Budd* and Lawrence's 'The Prussian Officer': Old Adams and New." *EsL*, 1: 83-8 (Sp 74).

Hunsberger, Claude. "Vectors in Recent *Moby-Dick* Criticism." *Col Lit*, 2: 230-45 (1975).

Huntress, Keith. "'Guinea' of *White-Jacket* and Chief Justice Shaw." *AL*, 43: 639-41 (Ja 72).

———. "M, Henry Cheever, and 'The Lee Shore.'" *NEQ*, 44: 468-75 (S 71).

Idol, J.L. "Ahab and the 'Siamese Connection.'" *SCB*, 34: 156-9 (1974).

Inge, M.T. "Unamuno's *Moby-Dick*." *MSEx*, 16: 3-4 (N 73).

Irvin, J.T. "The Symbol of the Hieroglyphics in the American Renaissance." *AQ*, 26: 103-26 (My 74).

Isani, M.A. "M and the 'Bloody Battle in Afghanistan.'" *AQ*, 20: 645-9 (Fa 68).

————. "M's Use of John and Awnshaw Churchill's *Collection of Voyages and Travels.*" *StN*, 4: 390-5 (Fa 72).

————. "The Naming of Fedallah in *Moby-Dick.*" *AL*, 40: 380-5 (N 68).

————. "Zoroastrianism and the Fire Symbolism in *Moby-Dick.*" *AL*, 44: 385-97 (N 72).

Jackson, A.M. "Technique and Discovery in M's *Encantadas.*" *SAF*, 1: 133-40 (Au 73).

Jaster, Frank. "M's Cosmopolitanism: The Experience of Life in *The Confidence-Man: His Masquerade.*" *SoQ*, 8: 201-10 (Ja 70).

Jeffrey, A.W. "Unreliable Narration in M's 'Jimmy Rose.'" *ArQ*, 31: 69-72 (1975).

Jennings, Margaret. "Bartleby the Existentialist." *MSEx*, 22: 8-10 (Fa 74).

Johnson, P.D. "American Innocence and Guilt: Black-White Destiny in 'Benito Cereno.'" *Phylon*, 36: 426-34 (D 75).

Johnson, R.C. "An Attempt at a Union List of Editions of M." *BC*, 19: 333-47 (Au 70).

————. "M in Antholgies." *ABC*, 21: 7-8 (1971).

Johnson, Theodore. "Textual Criticism and Error." *AN&Q*, 11: 102 (1973).

Jones, Joseph. "Humor in *Moby-Dick.*" *UTSE*, 15: 51-71 (1945-46).

Joseph, Vasanth. "Some Biblical Nuances in *Moby-Dick.*" *OJES*, 8: 69-77 (1971).

Joswick, T.P. "*Typee*: The Quest for Origin." *Criticism*, 17: 335-54 (1975).

Kaplan, Sidney. "Towards Pip and Daggoo: Footnote on M's Youth." *Phylon*, 29: 291-302 (Fa 68).

Karcher, C.L. "M's 'The Gees': A Forgotten Satire on Scientific Racism." *AQ*, 27: 421-2 (O 75).

————. "The 'Spiritual Lesson' of M's 'The Apple-Tree Table.'" *AQ*, 23: 101-9 (Sp 71).

Kazin, Alfred. "Ishmael in His Academic Heaven." *NY*, 24: 84-9 (12 F 49).

————. "M and the New Yorker." *NYRB*, 20: 3-8 (5 Ap 73).

Kauvar, G.B. "Chapter 54 of *Moby-Dick.*" *ArlQ*, 2: 133-41 (Wi 68-70).

Kay, Donald. "HM's Literary Relationship with Evert A. Duyckinck." *CLAJ*, 18: 393-403 (Mr 75).

Kearns, E.A. "Omniscient Ambiguity: The Narrators of *Moby-Dick* and *Billy Budd.*" *ESQ*, 58: 117-20 (1Q 70).

Kehler, R.S. "On Naming *White Jacket.*" *Extr*, 1: 4-5 (1975).

Kellner, Robert. "HM: The Sketch as Genre." *MSE*, 3: 22-6 (Sp 71).

————. "Sex, Toads, and Scorpions: A Study of the Psychological Themes in M's *Pierre.*" *ArQ*, 31: 5-19 (Sp 75).

————. "Whitman, M and the Civil War: A Sharing of Mood and Metaphor." *AN&Q*, 13: 102-5 (Mr 75).

Kelly, M.J. "Claggart's 'Equivocal Words' and Lamb's 'Popular Fallacies.'" *SSF*, 9: 183-6 (1972).

Kenney, B.G. "M's *Billy Budd.*" *AN&Q*, 9: 151-2 (1971).

Kenny, V.S. "Clarel's Rejection of the Titans." *ATQ*, 7: 76-81 (Su 70).

————. "M's Problem of Detachment and Engagement." *ATQ*, 19: 30-7 (Su 73).

Ketterer, David. "Some Co-ordinates of Billy Budd." *JAmSt*, 3: 221-37 (D 69).

Key, J.A. "*Typee*: A Bird's Eye View." *Pub Arkansas Phil Assn*, 1: 28-36 (#1 75).

Keyser, Elizabeth. "'Quite an Original': The Cosmopolitan in *The Confidence-Man.*" *TSLL*, 15: 279-300 (Su 73).

Kimball, W.J. "The M of *Battle-Pieces*: A Kindred Spirit." *MQ*, 10: 307-16 (1969).

Kime, W.R. "'The Bell-Tower': M's Reply to a Review." *ESQ*, 22: 28-38 (1Q 75).

Kimura, Harumi. "Tensai yue no Shippai." *EigoS*, 115: 483-4 (1969).

Kinnamon, J.M. "*Billy Budd*: Political Philosophy as a Sea of Thought." *ArQ*, 26: 164-72 (Su 70).

Kirkham, E.B. "The Iron Crown of Lombardy in *Moby Dick*." *ESQ*, 58: 127-9 (1Q 70).

———. "M and the Iron Crown of Lombardy." *AN&Q*, 10: 133-4 (My 72).

Kligerman, Charles. "The Psychology of HM." *Psychoanalytic R*, 40: 125-40 (Ap 53).

Knapp, J.G. "M's *Clarel*: Dynamic Synthesis." *ATQ*, 7: 67-76 (Su 70).

Knauf, David. "Notes on Mystery, Suspense and Complicity: Lowell's Theatricalization of M's "Benito Cereno."" *ETJ*, 27: 40-55 (1975).

Knight, K.F. "M's Variations of the Theme of Failure: 'Bartleby' and *Billy Budd*." *ArlQ*, 2: 44-58 (Au 69).

Kornfield, Mitton. "Bartleby and the Presentation of Self in Ordinary Life." *ArQ*, 31: 51-6 (1975).

Kovalev, J.V. "Herman M i 'Molodaja Amerika." *VLU*, 2: 39-48 (1971).

Krim, Seymour. "What's *This* Cat's Story." *Noble Savage*, 3: 201-22 (My 61).

Kroeger, F.P. "Longfellow, M, and Hawthorne: The Passage into the Iron Age." *IllQ*, 33: 30-41 (D 70).

Lane, Lauriat. "Dickens and M: Our Mutual Friends." *DR*, 51: 316-31 (Au 71).

———. "M and Dickens' *American Notes*." *MSEx*, 12: 3-4 (O 72).

Lang, Hans-Joachim "M's Dialog mit Captain Ringbolt." *JA*, 14: 124-39 (1969).

———. "Poe in M's 'Benito Cereno."" *Eng Stud Today*, 5: 405-29 (1973).

Lannon, Diedre. "A Note on M's Benito Cereno." *MSE*, 2: 68-70 (Sp 70).

Larson, C.R. "*Moby-Dick*, Circa 1972." *CEA*, 34: 17-9 (My 72).

Lash, Kenneth. "Captain Ahab and King Lear." *NMQ*, 19: 438-55 (Wi 49).

Lease, Benjamin. "Two Sides to a Tortoise: Darwin and M in the Pacific." *Person*, 50: 531-39 (1968).

Ledbetter, J.W. "The Trial of Billy Budd, Foretopman." *ABAJ*, 58: 614-9 (1972).

Lee, D.A. "M and George J. Adler." *AN&Q*, 12: 138-41 (My-Je 74).

Leimberg, Ine. "*Moby-Dick*: Der weisse Wal jistorisch betrachtet." *LWU*, 5: 7-21 (1972).

Leonard, J.J. "M's Lima." *ArQ*, 26: 100 (1970).

Leverenz, David. "Anger and Individualism." *ATQ*, 62: 407-28 (1975).

Levy, Harris. "The Iowa Theater Lab's *Moby Dick*." *TDR*, 19: 63-7 (S 75).

Liebman, S.W. "The 'Boby and Soul' Metaphor in *Moby-Dick*." *ESQ*, 50: 29-34 (1Q 68).

Lindgren, Charlotte. "HM and Atlantic Relations." *Hist Today*, 25: 663-70 (1975).

Litman, V.II. "The Cottage and the Temple: M's Symbolic Use of Architecture." *AQ*, 21: 630-8 (Fa 69).

Lloyd, F.V. "M's *Moby-Dick*." *Expl*, 29: 72 (My 71).

Loving, J.M. "M's Pardonable Sin." *NEQ*, 47: 262-78 (Je 74).

Lowance, M.I. "Veils and Illusion in 'Benito Cereno."" *ArQ*, 26: 113-26 (Su 70).

Lucas. T.E. "HM: The Purpose of the Novel." *TSLL*, 13: 641-61 (Wi 72).

Lynde, R.D. "M's Success in 'The Happy Failure: A Story of the River Hudson."" *CLAJ*, 13: 119-30 (D 69).

McCann, Garth. "Circumstance and Publication of *Moby-Dick*." *Serif*, 11: 58-60 (#3 74).

McCarthy, H.T. "*Israel R. Potter* as a Source for *Redburn*." *ESQ*, 58: 8-9 (Sp 70).

———. "M's *Redburn* and the City." *MwQ*, 12: 395-410 (Su 71).

McCarthy, Paul. "Affirmative Elements in *The Confidence Man*." *ATQ*, 7: 56-61 (Su 70).

———. "Books on M in 1970." *StN*, 4: 98-111 (Sp 72).

———. "City and Town in M's Fiction." *RS*, 38: 24-29 (S 70).

———. "Elements of Anatomy in M's Fiction." *StN*, 2: 38-61 (So 74).

———. "The Extraordinary Man as Idealist in Novels by Hawthorne and M." *ESQ*, 54: 43-51 (1Q 69).

———. "M's Use of Paintings in *Pierre*." *Disc*, 11: 490-505 (Au 68).

————. "Opposites Meet: M, Hemingway, and Heroes." *KanQ*, 7: 40-54 (1975).

McCroskery, M.S. "M's *Pierre*: The Inner Voyage." *StN*, 2: 1-9 (1972).

McCullagh, J.C. "More Smoke from M's Chimney." *ATQ*, 17: 17-22 (Wi 73).

McDonald, W.S. "Ishmæl: The Function of the Comic Mask." *CEA*, 37: 8-11 (#2 75).

McElroy, J.H. "Cannibalism in M's *Benito Cereno*." *EL*, 1: 206-18 (Fa 74).

McHaney, T.L. "The Confidence Man and Satan's Disguises in *Paradise Lost*." *NCF*, 30: 20-6 (1975).

————. "The Textual Editions of Hawthorne and M." *SLitI*, 2: 27-41

McMillan, Grant. "Ishamel's Dilemma—The Significance of the Fiery Hunt." *DentR*, 15: 204-17 (1971).

McNamara, L.F. "Subject, Style, and Narrative Technique in 'Bartleby' and 'Wakefield.'" *MichA*, 3: 41-6 (Sp 71).

McWilliams, J.P. "'Drum-Taps' and *Battle-Pieces*: The Blossom of War." *AQ*, 23: 181-202 (My 71).

Madson, A.L. "M's Comic Progression." *WSL*, 1: 69-76 (1964).

Male, R.R. "The Story of the Mysterious Stranger in American Literature." *Criticism*, 3: 281-94 (1961).

Malin, Irving. "The Authoritarian Family in American Fiction." *Mosaic*, 4: 153-73 (1971).

Mandel, R.B. "The Two Mystery Stories in *Benito Cereno*." *TSLL*, 14: 631-53 (Wi 73).

Manheim, L.H. "The Scarecrow and the Tomb: Images of Isolation and Disguise in M's *Bartleby the Scrivener* and *Israel Potter*." *NasR*, 1: 46-61 (Sp 68).

Mansfield, L.S. "Symbolism and Biblical Allusion in *Moby-Dick*." *ESQ*, 28: 20-3 (3Q 62).

Margolies, Edward. "M and Blacks." *MSEx*, 17: 1 (O 74); *CLAJ*, 18: 364-74 (Mr 75).

Markels, Julian. "*King Lear* and *Moby-Dick*: The Cultural Connection." *MR*, 9: 169-76 (1968).

Marks, B.A. "Retrospective Narration in Nineteenth-Century American Literature." *CE*, 31: 366-75 (1970).

Marsh, J.L. "Verses of Celebration of the Life and Art of HM: A Check List." *MSEx*, 14: 3-6 (Ap 73).

Martin, L.H. "M and Christianity: The Late Poems." *MSE*, 2: 11-8 (1969).

Marx, Leo. "'Noble Shit': The Uncivil Response of American Writers to Civil Religion in America." *MR*, 14: 709-39 (1973).

Matlack, James. "Attica and M's 'Benito Cereno.'" *ATQ*, 26: 18-23 (Sp 75).

Meldrum, Barbara. "The Artist in M's *Mardi*." *StN*, 1: 459-67 (Wi 69).

————. "M on War." *RSW*, 37: 130-8 (Je 69).

————. "Structure in *Moby-Dick*: The Whale Killings and Ishamel's Quest." *ESQ*, 21: 162-8 (3Q 75).

Mengeling, M.E. "Through 'The Encantadas': An Experienced Guide and You." *ATQ*, 7: 37-43 (Su 70).

Merrill, Robert. "The Narrative Voice in *Billy Budd*." *MLQ*, 34: 283-91 (S 73).

Messenger, W.E. "Conrad and M Again." *Conrad*, 2: 53-64 (Wi 69-70).

Metzger. C.R. "M's Saints: Allusions in *Benito Cereno*." *ESQ*, 58: 88-90 (1Q 70).

Middleton, John. "Source for Bartleby." *MSEx*, 15: 9 (1973).

Milder, Robert. "M's 'Intentions' in *Pierre*." *StN*, 6: 186-99 (Su 74).

Miller, A.H. "HM: A New Biographical Profile." *MSEx*, 15: 1-11 (1973).

————. "M Dissertations: An Annotated Directory." *MSEx*, 20: 1-11 (1974).

Miller, Ruth. "But Laugh or Die: A Comparison of *The Mysterious Stranger* and *Billy Budd*." *LHY*, 11: 25-9 (1970).

Millgate, Michael. "M and Marvell: A Note on *Billy Budd*." *ES*, 49: 47-50 (F 68).

Mills, N.C. "The Discovery of Nil in *Pierre* and *Jude the Obscure*." *TSLL*, 12: 249-62 (Su 70).

———. "Prison and Society in Nineteenth-Century American Fiction." *WHR*, 24: 325-31 (1970).

Mitchell, Charles. "M and the Spurious Truth of Legalism." *CentR*, 12: 110-26 (Wi 68).

Mitchell, Edward. "From Action to Essence: Some Notes on the Structure of M's *The Confidence-Man*." *AL*, 40: 27-37 (Mr 68).

Mohrt, Michel. "Le testament de M." *RDM*, Ap 74, pp. 10-9.

Molinoff, Katherine. "Conrad's Debt to M: James Wait, Donkin and Belfast of the 'Narcissus.'" *Conrad*, 1: 119-22 (Su 69).

Montale, Eugenio. "An Introduction to *Billy Budd*." *SR*, 68: 419-22 (Jl-S 60).

Monteiro, George. "'Bartleby the Scrivener' and M's Contemporary Reputation." *SB*, 24: 195-6 (1971).

———. "Elizabeth Shaw M as Censor." *ESQ*, 62: 32-3 (Wi 71).

———. "'Far and Away the Most Original Genius That America Has Produced': Notations on the New York *Times* and M's Literary Reputation at the Turn of the Century." *RALS*, 5: 69-80 (Sp 75).

———. "A Half Hour with HM, 1887." *PBSA*, 69: 406-7 (3Q 75).

———. "Holmes on M." *MSEx*, 17: 10 (S 74).

———. "Mather's M Book." *SB*, 25: 226-7 (1972).

———. "M in Portuguese." *Serif*, 9: 23-4 (Sp 72).

———. "M Reviews in *The Independent*." *PBSA*, 68: 434-9 (O-D 74).

———. "M, 'Timothy Quicksand,' and the Dead-Letter Office." *SSF*, 9: 198-201 (1972).

———. "M's 'America,' I." *Expl*, 32: 72 (Jl 74).

———. "Mrs. M and *The New York Times*." *MSEx*, 19: 11-2 (S 74).

———. "References to *Typee* and *Pierre*, 1884." *MSEx*, 15: 9-10 (S 73).

Moore, Maxine, "M's *Pierre* and Wordsworth: Intimations of Immortality." *NLet*, 39: 89-107 (Su 73).

Moore, R.S. "A New Review by M." *AL*, 47: 265-70 (My 75).

———. "Owens and M's Fossil Whale." *ATQ*, 26: 24 (Sp 75).

Morsberger, R.E. "M's 'The Bell-Tower' and Benvenuto Cellini." *AL*, 44: 459-62 (N 72).

Moss, S.P. "'Cock-A-Doodle-Doo!' and Some Legends in M Scholarship." *AL*, 40: 192-210 (My 68).

———. "Hawthorne and M: An Inquiry into Their Art and the Mystery of Their Friendship." *Lit Monographs*, 7: 45-84 (1975).

Mower, G.R. "The Kentucky Tragedy, a Source of *Pierre*." *KFR*, 15: 1-2 (Ja-Mr 69).

Mowder, William. "Volition in *Moby Dick*." *ELUD*, 1: 18-30 (1973).

Mulqueen, J.E. "Foreshadowing of M and Faulkner." *AN&Q*, 6: 102 (Mr 68).

———. "Ishmael's Voyage: The Cycle of Everyman's Faith." *ArQ*, 31: 51-6 (Sp 75).

Myers, Margaret. "Mark Twain and M." *MTJ*, 14: 5-8 (1968).

Narveson, Robert. "The Name 'Claggart' in *Billy Budd*." *AS*, 43: 229-32 (O 68).

Nechas, J.W. "The Ambiguity of Word and Whale." *Col Lit*, 2: 198-225 (1975).

Neff, Winifred. "Satirical Use of a 'Silly Reference' in *Israel Potter*." *ATQ*, 7: 51-3 (Su 70).

Nelson, Carl. "The Ironic Allusive Texture of *Lord Jim*: Coleridge, Crane, Milton, and M." *Conrad*, 4: 47-59 (1972).

Nelson, Raymond. "The Art of HM: The Author of *Pierre*." *YR*, 59: 197-224 (Wi 70).

Newman, R.G. "Portraits of M's Mother." *MSEx*, 13: 7-9 (Ja 73).

Nicol, Charles. "The Iconography of Evil and Ideal in 'Benito Cereno.'" *ATQ*, 7: 25-31 (Su 70).

Nishikawa, Masami. "HM: His Tragic View of Life." *SELit*, 21: 369-92 (Jl 53).

Noel, D.C. "Figures of Transfiguration: *Moby-Dick* as Radical Theology." *Cross Currents*, 20: 201-19 (Sp 70).

Norman, Liane. "Bartleby and the Reader." *NEQ*, 44: 22-39 (Mr 71).

Oglesby, Carl. "M, or Water Consciousness and Its Madness." *TriQ*, 23-4: 13-41 (1972).

Oliver, E.S. "M's Tartarus." *ESQ*, 28: 23-5 (3Q 62).

Omans, S.E. "The Variations on a Masked Leader: A Study on the Literary Relationship of Ralph Ellison and HM." *SAB*, 40: 15-23 (My 75).

Ortego, P.D. "The Existential Roots of *Billy Budd*." *ConnR*, 4: 80-7 (1970).

Parker, Hershel. "Being Professional in Working on *Moby-Dick*." *Col Lit*, 2: 192-7 (1975).

———. "'Benito Cereno' and *Cloister-Life*: A Re-Scrutiny of a 'Source.'" *SSF*, 9: 221-32 (1972).

———. "*The Confidence-Man* and the Use of Evidence in Compositional Studies: A Rejoinder." *NCF*, 28: 119-24 (1973).

———. "Dead Letters and H's Bartleby." *RALS*, 4: 90-9 (1974).

———. "Evidences for 'Late Insertions' In M's Works." *StN*, 7: 407-24 (Fa 75).

———. "Five Reviews not in *'Moby-Dick'* as Doubloon." *ELN*, 9: 182-5 (1972).

———. "Further Notices of *Pierre*." *MSEx*, 12: 4-5 (O 72).

———. "M and the Concept of 'Author's Final Intentions.'" *Proof*, 1: 156-68 (1971).

———. "M's Satire of Emerson and Thoreau: An Evaluation of The Evidence." *ATQ*, 7: 61-7 (Su 70).

———. "M's Satire of Emerson and Thoreau: Corrections." *ATQ*, 9: 70 (Wi 71).

———. "New Evidence on the Reception of *Pierre*." *MSEx*, 13: 7 (Ja 73).

———. "Practical Editions: HM's *Moby-Dick*." *Proof*, 3: 371-8 (1973).

———. "A Reexamination of *Melville's Reviewers*." *AL*, 42: 226-32 (My 70).

———. "Regularizing Accidentals: The Latest Form of Infidelity." *Proof*, 3: 1-20 (1973).

———. "Species of 'Soiled Fish.'" *CEAAN*, 1: 11-2 (1968).

———. "Three M Reviews in the London *Weekly Chronicle*." *AL*, 41: 584-9 (Ja 70).

———. "Trafficking in M." *MLQ*, 33: 54-66 (Mr 72).

Patrick, W.R. "M's 'Bartleby' and the Doctrine of Necessity." *AL*, 41: 39-54 (Mr 69).

Pearson, N.H. "In Honor of M." *Gaz of the Grolier Club*, 11: 17-23 (O 69).

Perry, R.L. "*Billy Budd*: M's *Paradise Lost*." *MQ*, 10: 173-85 (1969).

Phelps, Donald. "The Holy Family." *Prose*, 5: 99-113 (Fa 72).

Phillips, John. "M Meets Hawthorne." *AH*, 27: 16-21, 87-90 (D 75).

Pitt, A.S. "'A Semi-Romance of the Sea': *Miriam Coffin* as Precursor of *Moby-Dick*." *Historic Nantucket*, 19: 15-30 (1972).

Pinsker, Stanley. "'Bartleby the Scrivener: Language as Wall." *Col Lit*, 2: 17-27 (1975).

Poenicke, Klaus. "Der Drachentöter und das Menshenbild des Naturalism." *JA*, 15: 88-100 (1970).

Polk, James. "M and the Idea of the City." *UTQ*, 41: 277-92 (Su 72).

Pollin, Burton. "Additional Unrecorded Reviews of M's Books." *AmS*, 4: 55-68 (Fa 74).

———. "An Unnoticed Contemporary Review of *Moby-Dick*." *MSEx*, 22: 3-4 (My 75).

Pops, M.L. "M: To Him, Olson." *MPS*, 2: 61-96 (1971); *Boun 2*, 55-84 (1974).

Portnoy, H.N. "Emerson, M, and 'The Poet.'" *Junction*, 1: 172-5 (1973).

Powers, William. "Bulkington as Henry Chatillon." *WAL*, 3: 153-5 (Su 68).

Pruvot, Monique. "Bartleby de M: l'écriture et la loi." *EA*, 28: 429-38 (O-D 75).

Pry, E.R., Jr. "That 'Grand, Ungodly, God-Like Man': Ahab's Metaphoric Character." *Style*, 6: 159-77 (1972).

Prezemecka, Irena. "HM's and Robert Lowell's *Benito Cereno*: Tale into Drama." *ZRL*, 14: 57-62 (1971).

Quick, Tom. "Saint Paul's Types of the Faithful and M's Confidence Man." *NCF*, 28: 472-7 (1974).

Quinn, P.F. "Poe's Imaginary Voyage." *HudR*, 4: 562-85 (Wi 52).

Raleigh, J.H. "The Novel and the City: England and America in the Nineteenth Century." *VS*, 11: 291-328 (1968).

Ralph, George. "History and Prophecy in *Benito Cereno*." *ETJ*, 22: 155-60 (My 70).

Randall, J.H. "Bartleby vs. Wall Street: New York in the 1850s." *BNYPL*, 78: 138-44 (Wi 75).

Ray, R.E. "'Benito Cereno': Babo as Leader." *ATQ*, 7: 31-7 (Su 70).

Ray, T.J. "Delano's Devils; or, A Case of Libel." *UMSE*, 12: 59-64 (1971).

Reck, T.S. "M's Last Sea Poetry: *John Marr and Other Sailors*." *Forum(H)*, 12: 17-22 (1974).

Rees, J.O. "Spenserian Analogues in *Moby-Dick*." *ESQ*, 18: 174-8 (3Q 72).

Regan, C.L. "Dilemma of M's Horned Woman." *AN&Q*, 12: 133-4 (My-Je 74).

Reich, C.A. "The Tragedy of Justice in *Billy Budd*." *YR*, 56: 368-89 (Sp 67).

Reid, B.L. "Old M's Fable." *MR*, 9: 529-46 (Su 68).

Reinert, Otto. "'Secret Mines and Dubious Side': The World of *Billy Budd*." *AmNor*, 4: 183-92 (1973).

Requa, K.A. "The Pilgrim's Problems: M's *Clarel*." *BSUF*, 16: 16-20 (Sp 75).

Resnik, G.J. "Samburan Encantada." *Conradiana*, 1: 37-44 (Fa 68).

Reynolds, M.S. "The Prototype for M's Confidence-Man." *PMLA*, 86: 1009-13 (O 71).

Rice, J.C. "Claggart and the Satanic Type." *ATQ*, 26: 37-40 (Sp 75).

―――. "*Moby-Dick* and Shakespearean Tragedy." *CentR*, 14: 444-68 (Wi 70).

―――. "The Ship as Cosmic Symbol in *Moby-Dick* and *Benito Cereno*." *CentR*, 16: 138-54 (Sp 72).

Rimonte, Nilda. "Notes on Starbuck and Stubb." *DilR*, 13: 420-4 (O 65).

Robillard, Douglas. "Theme and Structure in M's *John Marr and Other Sailors*." *ELN*, 6: 187-92 (Mr 69).

Rockwell, F.S. "DeQuincet and the Ending of *Moby-Dick*." *NCF*, 9: 161-8 (D 54).

Roper, Gordon. "Teaching *Moby-Dick*." *ESQ*, 28: 2-4 (3Q 62).

Roppen, Georg. "M's Sea, Shoreless, Indefinite as God." *AmNor*, 4: 123-36 (1973).

Rose, E.J. "Annihilation and Ambiguity: *Moby-Dick* and 'The Town-Ho's Story.'" *NEQ*, 45: 541-58 (D 72).

Rosenberry, E.H. "Israel Potter, Benjamin Franklin, and the Doctrine of Self-Reliance." *ESQ*, 28: 27-9 (3Q 62).

―――. "M and His *Mosses*." *ATQ*, 7: 47-51 (Su 70).

―――. "M's Ship of Fools." *PMLA*, 75: 604-8 (D 60).

―――. "*Moby-Dick*: Epic Romance." *Col Lit*, 2: 155-70 (1975).

Rosenthal, Bernard. "Elegy for Jack Chase." *SRom*, 10: 213-29 (Su 71).

―――. "M, Marryat, and the Evil-Eyed Villain." *NCF*, 25: 221-4 (S 70).

―――. "M's Island." *SSF*, 11: 1-10 (Wi 74).

Ross, M.L. "*Moby-Dick* as an Education." *StN*, 6: 62-75 (Sp 74).

Rothfork, John. "The Sailing of the *Pequod*: An Existential Voyage." *ArQ*, 28: 55-60 (1972).

Rothschild, Herbert. "The Language of Mesmerism in 'The Quarter-Dick' Scene in *Moby-Dick*." *ES*, 53: 235-8 (Je 72).

Rowland, Beryl. "Grace Church and M's Story of 'The Two Temples.'" *NCF*, 28: 339-46 (1973).

―――. "M Answers the Theologians: The Ladder of Charity in 'The Two Temples.'" *Mosaic*, 7: 1-13 (1974).

————. "M's Bachelors and Maids: Interpretation Through Symbol and Metaphor." *AL*, 41: 389-405 (N 69).

————. "M's Waterloo in 'Rich Man's Crumbs.'" *NCF*, 25: 216-21 (S 70).

————. "Sitting up with a Corpse: Malthus According to M in 'Poor Man's Pudding and Rich Man's Crumbs.'" *JAmSt*, 6: 69-83 (Ap 72).

Ruland, Richard. "M and the Fortunate Fall: *Typee* as Eden." *NCF*, 23: 312-23 (D 68).

Russell, Jack. "*Israel Potter* and 'Song of Myself.'" *AL*, 40: 72-7 (Mr 68).

Saeki, Shoichi. "Shosetsuka M to Shin-hihyo." *EigoS*, 115: 472-13 (1969).

Sakamoto, Masayuki. "*Moby-Dick*-ron no tame no sobyo." *EigoS*, 117: 296-98 (1971).

Samson, J.P. "The Ambiguity of Ambergris in *Moby-Dick*." *Col Lit*, 2: 226-8 (Fa 75).

Sandberg, A. "Erotic Patterns in 'The Paradise of Bachelors and the Tartarus of Maids.'" *L&P*, 8: 2-8 (1968).

Sander, L.A. "M's Symbolism of the Pipe." *ESQ*, 59: 4-7 (Sp 70).

Sanders, William. "Emerson and M: The Oversoul and the Underworld." *Junction*, 2: 25-9 (1973).

Sartre, Jean-Paul. "*Moby-Dick*." *Adam*, 343-45: 86-8 (1970).

Scherting, Jack. "The Bottle and the Coffin: Further Speculation on Poe and *Moby-Dick*." *PN*, 1: 22 (1968).

Schroth, Evelyn. "M's Judgment on Captain Vere." *MwQ*, 10: 189-200 (Wi 69).

Schwendinger, R.J. "The Language of the Sea: Relationships Between the Language of HM and Sea Shanties of the 19th Century." *SFQ*, 37: 53073 (Mr 73).

Sealts, M.M., Jr. "M and Richard Henry Stoddard." *AL*, 43: 359-70 (N 71).

————. "A Supplementary Note to *Melville's Reading* (1966)." *HLB*, 19: 280-4 (1971).

Seelye, John. "The Contemporary 'Bartleby.'" *ATQ*, 7: 12-8 (Su 70).

————. "'Ungraspable Phantom': Reflections of Hawthorne in *Pierre* and *The Confidence-Man*." *StN*, 1: 436-43 (Wi 69).

Seltzer, L.F. "Like Repels Like: The Case of Conrad's Antipathy for M." *Conrad*, 1: 101-5 (Su 69).

Sequeira, Isaac. "*The San Dominick*: The Shadow of Benito Cereno." *OJES*, 10: 1-5 (1973).

Shimada, Taro. "*Moby-Dick* ni tsuite." *EigoS*, 115: 476-8 (1969).

Shimura, Masami. "'The Tartarus of Maids' no Sekai." *EigoS*, 115: 487-8 (1969).

Shroeder, J.W. "Indian-Hating: An Ultimate Note on *The Confidence Man*." *BBr*, 24: 1-5 (1971).

————. "'Some Unfortunate Idyllic Love Affair': The Legends of Taji and Jay Gatsby." *BBr*, 22: 143-53 (1968).

Shurr, W.H. "M and Emerson." *MSEx*, 11: 2 (My 72).

Shusterman, Alan. "M's 'The Lightning-Rod Man': A Reading." *SSF*, 9: 165-74 (1972).

Shusterman, David. "The 'Reader Fallacy' and 'Bartleby the Scrivener.'" *NEQ*, 45: 118-24 (Mr 72).

Simpson, E.E. "M and the Negro: From *Typee* to 'Benito Cereno.'" *AL*, 41: 19-38 (Mr 69).

Singleton, G.H. "Ishmael and the Covenant." *Disc*, 12: 54-67 (Wi 69).

Singleton, Marvin. "M's 'Bartleby': Over the Republic, A Ciceronian Shadow." *CRAS*, 6: 165-73 (Fa 75).

Sister Cleopatra. "*Moby-Dick*: An Interpretation." *LHY*, 6: 49-54 (Jl 65).

Sister, Mary Ellen. "Duplicate Imagery in *Moby-Dick*." *MFS*, 8: 252-64 (Au 62).

Slethaug, G.E. "A Stove Boat or a Live Wife." *MSEx*, 8: 1 (My 71).

Smith, Nelson. "Eight British Reviews and Notices of M, 1846-1891." *Extr*, 23: 6-7 (1975).

Sorescu, Marin. "Care Ahab este chiar Ahab?" *RoLit*, 14 Nov 74: 20-1.

Spiller, R.E. "*Moby-Dick* and Carl Van Doren." *MSEx*, 14: 9 (Ap 73).

Spofford, W.K. "M's Ambiguities: A Re-evaluation of 'The *Town-Ho*'s Story.'"

Srinath, C.N. "A Note on M's Poetry." *LCrit*, 11: 33-40 (#1 73).

Stafford, W.T. "A Whale, and Heiress, and a Southern Demigod: Three Symbolic Americas." *CollL*, 1: 100-12 (1974).

Stanford, Raney. "The Romantic Hero and That Fatal Selfhood." *CentR*, 12: 430-54 (Fa 68).

Stanonik, Janez. "Did M Ever See an Albino?" *AL*, 43: 637-8 (Ja 72).

———. "The Sermon to the Sharks in *Moby-Dick*." *AN*, 4: 53-60 (1971).

Star, Morris. "M's Marking's in Walpole's *Anecdotes of Painting in England*." *PBSA*, 66: 321-7 (3Q 72).

Stark, John. "'The Cassock' Chapter in *Moby-Dick* and the Theme of Literary Creativity." *SAF*, 1: 105-11 (Sp 73).

Stein, A.F. "Ahab's Turgid Wake and Job's Leviathan." *ATQ*, 17: 13-4 (Wi 73).

———. "Hawthorne's Zenobia and M's Urania." *ATQ*, 26: 11-4 (Sp 75).

———. "The Motif of Voracity in 'Bartleby.'" *ESQ*, 21: 29-34 (1Q 75).

Stein, W.B. "'Billy Budd': The Nightmare of History." *Criticism*, 3: 237-50 (Su 61).

———. "M's *The Confidence Man*: Qucksands of the Word." *ATQ*, 24: 38-50 (Fa 74).

Steinmann, Theo. "The Perverted Pattern of *Billy Budd* in *The Nigger of the 'Narcissus*.'" *ES*, 55: 239-46 (1974).

Stelzig, E.L. "Romantic Paradoxes of *Moby-Dick*." *ATQ*, 26: 41-4 (Sp 75).

Stempel, Daniel, and B.M. Stillians. "*Bartleby the Scrivener*: A Parable of Pessimism." *NCF*, 27: 268-82 (1972).

Sten, Christopher. "Bartleby the Transcendentalist: M's Dead Letter to Emerson." *MLQ*, 25: 30-44 (Mr 74).

———. "The Dialogue of Crisis in *The Confidence-Man*: M's 'New Novel.'" *StN*, 6: 165-85 (Su 74).

———. "Vere's Use of the 'Forms': Means and Ends in *Billy Budd*." *AL*, 47: 37-51 (Mr 75).

Stern, M.R. "*Moby Dick*, Millennial Attitudes, and Politics." *ESQ*, 54: 51-60 (1Q 69).

Sternlicht, Sanford. "Sermons in *Moby Dick*." *BSUF*, 10: 51-2 (Wi 69).

Stevens, A.J. "The Edition of Montaigne Read by M." *PBSA*, 62: 130-4 (1Q 68).

———. "Head Imagery in *Moby-Dick*." *RS*, 38: 306-9 (D 70).

Stitt, Peter. "HM's *Billy Budd*: Sympathy and Rebellion." *ArQ*, 28: 39-54 (Sp 72).

Stokes, Gary. "The Dansker, M's Manifesto on Survival." *EJ*, 57: 980-1 (O 68).

Stone, Edward. "Ahab Gets Girl, or HM Goes to the Movies." *LFQ*, 3: 172-81 (1975).

———. "Bartleby and Miss Norman." *SSF*, 9: 271-4 (1972).

———. "The Buried Book: *Moby-Dick* a Century Ago." *StN*, 7: 552-62 (Wi 75).

———. "The Fuction of the Gams in *Moby-Dick*." *Col Lit*, 2: 171-81 (1975).

———. "M's Late Pale Usher." *ELN*, 9: 51-3 (1971).

———. "More on Hawthorne and M." *NHJ*, 5: 59-70 (1975).

———. "The Other Sermon in *Moby-Dick*." *Costerus*, 4: 215-22 (1972).

———. "The Whiteness of the Whale." *CLAJ*, 18: 348-63 (Mr 75).

———. "Whodunit? Moby Dick!" *JPC*, 8: 280-5 (1974).

Stout, J.P. "The Encroaching Sodom: M's Urban Fiction." *TSLL*, 17: 157-74

———. "M's Use of the Book of Job." *NCF*, 25: 69-83 (Je 70).

Strauch, C.F. "Ishmael: Time and Personality in *Moby-Dick*." *StN*, 1: 468-83 (Wi 69).

Sumner, D.N. "The American West in M's *Mardi* and *The Confidence Man*." *RSW*, 36: 37-49 (1968).

———. "The Function of Historical Sources in Hawthrone, M, and R.P. Warren." *RSW*, 40: 103-14 (1972).

Swanson, D.R. "The Exercise of Irony in 'Benito Cereno.'" *ATQ*, 7: 23-5 (Su 70).

————. "The Structure of *The Confidence Man.*" *CEA*, 30: 6-7 (My 68).

Sweeney, G.M. "M's Hawthornian Bell-Tower: A Fairy-Tale Source." *AL*, 45: 279-85 (My 73).

Takamura, Katsuji. "M no Shosetsu-gun." *EigoS*, 115: 474-5 (1969).

Tanimoto, Taiji. "M ni okeru Sukui." *EigoS*, 115: 489-90 (1969).

Tanselle, G.T. "Bibliographical Problems in M." *SAF*, 2: 57-74 (Sp 74).

————. "M in the *BAL.*" *MSEx*, 20: 7 (1974).

————. "The Sales of M's Books." *HLB*, 17: 195-215 (Ap 69).

————. "Textual Study and Literary Judgement." *PBSA*, 65: 109-22 (1971).

————. "*Typee* and DeVoto: A Footnote." *PBSA*, 64: 207-9 (2Q 70).

————. "*Typee* and DeVoto: Once More." *PBSA*, 62: 601-4 (4Q 68).

Taylor, Dennis. "The Confidence Men from *The Pardoner's Tale* to *The Fall.*" *ArQ*, 31: 73-85 (Sp 75).

Taylor, J.C. "'Aranda' in *Benito Cereno.*" *AN&Q*, 10: 118 (Ap 72).

Thakur, D. "The Tales of M." *LCrit*, 8: 39-53 (1969).

Thomas, J.J. "M's Use of Mysticism." *PQ*, 53: 413-24 (Su 74).

Thompson, G.R. "A Visual Analogue for 'The Cassock' Chapter of *Moby-Dick.*" *MSEx*, 18: 1-2 (My 74).

Tichi, Cecelia. "M's Craft and Theme of Language Debased in *The Confidence-Man.*" *ELH*, 39: 639-58 (1972).

Tola de Habich, Fernando. "Seis notas previas para un reencuentro con HM." *CHA*, 260: 338-43 (1972).

Trachtenberg, Stanley. "'A Sensible Way to Play the Fool': M's *The Confidence Man.*" *GaR*, 26: 38-52 (Sp 72).

Travis, M.K. "Echoes of Emerson in Plinlimmon." *ATQ*, 14: 47-8 (Sp 72).

————. "Echoes of *Pierre* in *The Reivers.*" *NCLit*, 3: 11-3 (1973).

————. "Hawthorne and M's Enceladas." *ATQ*, 14: 5-6 (Sp 72).

————. "The Idea of Poe in *Pierre.*" *ESQ*, 50: 59-62 (1Q 68).

————. "M's 'Furies' Continued in *Pierre.*" *ESQ*, 62: 33-5 (Wi 71).

————. "A Note on 'The Bell-Tower': M's 'Blackwood Article.'" *PoeS*, 6: 28-9 (Je 73).

————. "Relevant Digressions in *Pierre.*" *ATQ*, 24: 7-8 (Fa 74).

————. "Spenserian Analogues in *Mardi* and *The Confidence Man.*" *ESQ*, 50: 55-8 (1Q 68).

Trimpi, H.P. "Conventions of Romance in *Moby-Dick.*" *SoR*, 7: 115-29 (Wi 71).

————. "Demonology and Witchcraft in *Moby-Dick.*" *JHI*, 30: 543-62 (O-D 69).

————. "Harlequin-Confidence-Man: The Satirical Tradition of Commedia Dell'Arte and Pantomine in M's *The Confidence-Man.*" *TSLL*, 16: 147-93 (Sp 74).

Tucker, B.D. "Captain Vere and Pontius Pilate." *Doshisha Stud Eng*, 7: 38-53 (Mr 74).

Tudor, Stephen. "Four for M." *ESQ*, 59: 3 (#1 70).

Tuerk, Richard. "M's 'Bartleby' and Issac D'Israeli's *Curiosities of Literature*, Second Series." *SSF*, 7: 647-9 (Fa 70).

Turco, Lewis. "American Novelist as Poet: The Schizophrenia of Mode." *Eng R*, 25: 23-9 (Su 74).

Turnage, Maxine. "M's Concern with the Arts in *Billy Budd.*" *ArQ*, 28: 74-82 (1972).

Turner, F.W. "M and Thomas Berger: The Novelist as Cultural Anthropologist." *CentR*, 13: 101-21 (Wi 69).

Turner, F.W. "M's Post-Meridian Fiction." *MASJ*, 10: 60-7 (Fa 69).

Tuttleton, J.W. "Romance and Novel: The Disintegration of a Form." *ESQ*, 55: 116-21 (2Q 69).

Unoki, Keijior. "Why Did Emerson, Thoreau and H Express Their Thoughts in the Form of 'Railroad' Symbolically?" *Karibane*, 9: 62-70 (Mr 70).

Vande Kieft, R.M. "When Big Hearts Strike Together: The Concussion of M and Sir Thomas Browne." *PLL*, 5: 39-50 (1969).

Vanderhaar, M.M. "A Re-examination of 'Benito Cereno.'" *AL*, 40: 179-91 (My 68).

*Vann, J.D. "A Checklist of M Criticism, 1958-1968." *StN*, 1: 507-35 (Wi 69).

Vaught, C.G. "Religion as a Quest for Wholeness: M's *Moby-Dick*." *JGE*, 26: 9-35 (1974).

Vernon, John. "M's 'The Bell Tower.'" *SSF*, 7: 264-76 (Sp 70).

Vitanza, V.J. "M's *Redburn* and Emerson's 'General Education of the Eye.'" *ESQ*, 21: 40-5 (1Q 75).

Wadlington, Warwick. "Ishmael's Godly Gamesomeness: Selftaste and Rhetoric in *Moby-Dick*." *ELH*, 39: 309-31 (1972).

Waggoner, H.H. "H and M Acquaint the Reader with Their Abodes." *StN*, 2: 420-4 (Wi 70).

Walcutt, C.C. "The Soundings of *Moby-Dick*." *ArQ*, 24: 101-16 (Su 68).

Wallace, R.K. "*Billy Budd* and the Haymarket Hangings." *AL*, 47: 108-13 (Mr 75).

Watson, C.N. "The Estrangement of Hawthorne and M." *NEQ*, 46: 380-402 (S 73).

———. "M and the Theme of Timonism: From *Pierre* to *The Confidence-Man*." *AL*, 44: 398-413 (N 72).

———. "M's Agatha and Hunilla: A Literary Reincarnation." *ELN*, 6: 114-8 (D 68).

———. "M's Fiction in the Early 1970's." *ESQ*, 20: 291-7 (1974).

———. "M's *Israel Potter*: Father and Sons." *StN*, 7: 563-8 (Wi 75).

———. "M's *Jackson:* Redburn's Heroic 'Double.'" *ESQ*, 62: 8-10 (Wi 71).

———. "M's Selvage: Another Hint from Smollett." *MSEx*, 20: 4-5 (N 74).

———. "Premature Burial in *Arthur Gordon Pym* and *Israel Potter*." *AL*, 47: 105-7 (Mr 75).

Weales, Gerald. "Getting Billy off the Page." *MQR*, 13: 382-400 (Fa 74).

———. "Singing Billy." *OhR*, 15: 92-102 (Sp 74).

Webner, H.L. "Hawthorne, M and Lowell: *The Old Glory*." *Re: A&L*, 4: 1-17 (Fa 70).

Weintraub, Rodelle, and Stanley Weintraub. "*Moby-Dick* and *Seven Pillars of Wisdom*." *SAF*, 2: 238-40 (Au 74).

Wells, D.A. "'Bartleby the Scrivener,' Poe, and the Duyckinck Circle." *ESQ*, 21: 35-9 (1Q 75).

Welsh, Howard. "The Politics of Race in 'Benito Cereno.'" *AL*, 46: 556-66 (Ja 75).

Werge, Thomas. "Luther and Melville on the Masks of God." *MSEx*, 22: 6-7 (My 75).

———. "M's Satanic Salesman: Scientism and Puritanism in 'The Lightning-Rod Man.'" *Chri & Lit*, 21: 6-12 (Su 72).

———. "*Moby-Dick* and the Calvinist Tradition." *StN*, 1: 484-506 (Wi 69).

———. "*Moby-Dick*: Scriptural Source of 'Blackness and Darkness.'" *AN&Q*, 9: 6 (N 70).

Wheelock, C.W. "A Melvillean Miscalculation." *MSEx*, 22: 10-2 (My 75).

Widmer, Kingsley. "The Learned Try-Works: A Review of Recent Scholarly Criticism of M." *StN*, 5: 117-24 (Sp 73).

———. "M's Radical Resistance: The Method and Meaning of *Bartleby*." *StN*, 1: 444-58 (Wi 69).

———. "The Negative Affirmation: M's 'Bartleby.'" *MFS*, 8: 276-86 (Au 62).

———. "The Perplexed Myths of M: *Billy Budd*." *Novel*, 2: 25-35 (Fa 68).

———. "The Perplexity of M: *Benito Cereno*." *SSF*, 5: 225-38 (Sp 68).

Wigmore, Douglass. "A Backward Glance O'er *Moby-Dick*." *MSEx*, 24: 7-9 (D 75).

Willett, Maurita. "The Silences of HM.' *ATQ*, 7: 85-92 (Su 70).

Williams, David. "Peeping Tommo: *Typee* as Satire." *CRAS*, 6: 36-49 (Sp 75).

Wilson, J.D. "Incest and American Romantic Fiction." *SLitI*, 7: 31-50 (1974).

Witherton, Paul. "The Art of M's *Typee*." *ArQ*, 26: 136-50 (Su 70).

Wolfson, H.A. "M's Jerusalem: 'Wreck Ho—the Wreck!'" *HTR*, 67: 184-6 (1974).

Wood, A.D. "HM and the Feminine Fifties." *MSEx*, 17: 2 (1974).

Woodson, Thomas. "Oblivion Lingers in the Neighborhood." *BMLLA*, 7: 26-39 (1974).

Wright, Nathalia. "An Approach to M through His Themes and Literary Genres." *ESQ*, 28: 25-7 (3Q 62).

―――. "Form as Function in M." *PMLA*, 67: 330-40 (Je 52).

―――. "HM and the Muse of Italy." *Italian Am*, 1: 169-74 (#2 75).

―――. "M and 'Old Burton' with 'Bartleby' as an Anatomy of Melancholy." *TSL*, 15: 1-13 (1970).

―――. "The Tale of Moby Dick." *Phi Kappa Phi J*, 54: 42-58 (1974).

Yamamoto, Sho. "The Source and Structure of 'Benito Cereno.'" *SELit*, 14: 189-91 (1973).

Yannella, Donald. "Source for the Diddling of William Cream in *The Confidence-Man*?" *ATQ*, 17: 22-4 (Wi 73).

Yarina, Margaret. "The Dualistic Vision of HM's *The Encantadas*." *JNT*, 3: 141-8 (1973).

Yeager, H.J. "M's Literary Debut in France." *MwQ*, 11: 413-25 (Su 70).

Yellin, J.F. "Black Masks: M's 'Benito Cereno.'" *AQ*, 22: 678-89 (Fa 70).

Yodor, R.A. "Poetry and Science: 'Two Distinct Branches of Knowledge' in *Billy Budd*." *SoRA*, 3: 223-39 (1969).

Zink, D.D. "Bartleby and the Contemporary Search for Meaning." *Forum(H)*, 8: 46-50 (Su 70).

Menashe, Samuel. Davie, Donald. "The Poetry of SM." *Iowa R*, 1: 107-14 (Su 70).

Mencken, Henry Louis. Anon. "Baltimore's Bad Boy: A Great and Beneficient Force." *TLS*, 4 S 70, pp. 973-4.

―――. "A Scout for the Scholars: H.L.M." *BNYPL*, 75: 63-5 (1971).

* Adler, Betty. "Bibliographic Check List." *Mencken*, quarterly since 1971.

―――. "Evolution of a Menckenite." *Cabellian*, 4: 99-103 (1972).

―――. "The M Room." *Cabellian*, 3: 23-30 (1970).

Anderson, C.R. "M's Last Blast: A Reminiscence." *Mencken*, 31: 4-7 (1969).

Anderson, Fenwick. "M's Animadversions of Journalism." *Mencken*, 53: 6-8 (1975).

Anderson, Margaret. "Mr. M's Truisms." *Little R*, 4: 13-4 (Ja 17).

Arnett, Earl. "M and Jazz." *Mencken*, 36: 1-2 (Wi 70).

Babcock, C.M. "Man of Letters: Addenda." *Mencken*, 36: 8 (Wi 70).

―――. "A Vocabulary on Hysterical Principles." *Mencken*, 36: 5-7 (Wi 70).

―――. "The Wizards of Baltimore: Poe and M." *TQ*, 13: 110-5 (Au 70).

Baer, J.W. "H.L.M: Exposer of Deceptions." *Mencken*, 48: 11-2 (1973).

―――, and M.B. Baer. "Reprise." *Mencken*, 25: 4-6 (1968).

Barrick, N.D., and E.O. Brown. "M, the Negro and Civil Rights." *Mencken*, 35: 4-7 (1970).

Bauer, H.C. "The Glow and Gusto of H.L.M's So and So's" *Mencken*, 47: 19-23 (F 73).

―――. "Grant Master of the Word Art." *Mencken*, 27: 6-12 (1968).

―――. "Iteration in HLM's Idiom Attic." *Mencken*, 55: 2-6 (1975).

Beach, R.A. "1524 Hollins Street: Aftermath." *Mencken*, 27: 4-6 (1968).

Blattner, M.S. "18-Year-Old Vote." *Mencken*, 42: 4 (1972).

Blodgett, H.W. "M and Conrad." *Mencken*, 29: 2-3 (1969).

Boller, P.F. "American Absurdities." *Mencken*, 25: 1-4 (1968).

Bonner, T.C. "M as Whangdoodle: One Aspects of H.L.M's Prose Style." *MarkR*, 3: 14-7 (O 71).

Burr, J.R. "HLM Scientific Skeptic." *Mencken*, 54: 1-8 (1975).

Cairns, Huntington. "M, Baltimore, and the Critics." *Mencken*, 45: 1-9 (Sp 73).

Caldwell, John. "The International Dramatic Critiques' Anti-Playwriting Association." *Mencken*, 36: 3-5 (Wi 70).

Castagna, Edwin. "G.B.S. at Pratt." *Mencken*, 26: 10-1 (1968).

———. "Loud and Clear: H.L.M the Communicator." *Mencken*, 30: 1-8 (1969).

———. "Some H.L.M's Friendly Correspondence." *Manuscripts*, 20: 3-12 (1968).

Chamberlain, John. "The Young M." *Mencken*, 50: 6-8 (Sp 74).

Cheslock, Louis. "HLM Talks about Max Brodel." *Mencken*, 55: 6-8 (Fa 75).

———. "Some Personal Memories of H.L.M." *Mencken*, 49: 3-11 (Sp 74).

Christian, H.A. "'What Else Have You in Mind?': Louis Adamic and H.L.M." *Mencken*, 47: 1-12 (Fa 73).

Clark, E.H. "HLM and the Naval Academy." *Mencken*, 32: 6-9 (1969).

Coleman, Claude. "H.L.M and the Genteel Tradition." *Mencken*, 26: 12-3 (1968).

Cooney, C.F. "M's Midwifery." *Mencken*, 43: 1-4 (Fa 72).

Dolmetsch, C.R. "The Baltimore Sage in Silly Century." *SatR*, 52: 27-9 (13 S 69).

Douglas, George. "M's Critics of the Twenties." *Mencken*, 53: 1-5 (Sp 75).

Dunlap, R.L. "The Sage at Dusk." *Mencken*, 35: 7-11 (Sp 70).

Durham, Frank. "M as Midwife." *Mencken*, 32: 2-6 (Sp 69).

Eastman, John. "H.L.M's Voice for Posterity." *Mencken*, 51: 9-11 (Fa 74).

Epstein, Joseph. "Show-Biz M." *NRep*, 159: 31-3 (14 S 68).

Evitts, William. "The Savage South: H.L.M and the Roots of a Persistent Image." *VQR*, 41: 596-611 (Fa 73).

Fitzgerald, F.S. "Six Letters to the Ms." *FHA*, 1970, pp. 102-4.

Forque, G.J. "Quelques 'Préjugés' Politiques de H.L.M." *EAA*, 3: 101-13 (1966).

Fullinwider, S.P. "M's American Language." *Mencken*, 40: 2-7 (Wi 71).

Hall, G.C. "Edgar Watson Howe and H.L.M." *H-JM*, 2: 163-5 (Jl 25).

Harris, Frank. "American Values: Howe and M." *Pearson's*, 40: 112-24 (Ja 19).

Hart, Richard. "The M Industry." *Mencken*, 52: 3-14 (Wi 74).

Iversen, Anders. "Democratic Man, the Superior Man, and the Forgotten Man in H.L.M's *Notes on Democracy*." *ES*, 50: 351-62 (Ag 69).

Jansen, K.E. "M on Ibsen: Even M Nods." *Mencken*, 47: 13-8 (Fa 73).

Jerome, W.P. "A Baltimore Episcopalian." *Mencken*, 51: 7-9 (Fa 74).

Johnson, G.W. "Reconsideration: H.L.M." *NRep*, 173: 32-3 (27 D 75).

Johnson, R.C., and G.T. Tanselle, "Addenda to Bibliographies of . . . Mencken, ... Haldeman-Julius Little Blue Books." *PBSA*, 66: 66 (1Q 72).

Kellner, Bruce. "H.L.M. and C.V.V.: Friendship on Paper." *Mencken*, 39: 2-9 (Fa 71).

La Belle, M.M. "H.L.M's Comprehension of Friedrich Nietzsche." *CLS*, 7: 43-9 (Mr 70).

Leighton, Clare. "Cynical Fantasy." *Mencken*, 35: 1-4 (Sp 70).

Levin, J.B. "National Convention Reporter." *Mencken*, 41: 9-12 (Sp 72).

Litz, F.E. "De Translatione." *Mencken*, 25: 7-8 (Sp 68).

Long, R.E. "The Fitzgerald-M Correspondence." *FHA*, 1971, pp. 319-21.

Lora, R.G. "The Politics of a Conservative Libertarian." *Mencken*, 34: 4-11 (Sp 70).

McGrain, J.W. "Ayd and Criminal Aid." *Mencken*, 45: 11-2 (Sp 73).

Manchester, William. "The Last Years of H.L.M." *Atl*, 236: 82-90 (O 75).

Manglaviti, L.M.J. "Faulkner's 'That Evening Sun' and M's 'Best Editorial Judgement.'" *AL*, 43: 649-54 (Ja 72).

———. "Markham and M." *NarkR*, 3: 38-9 (F 72).

Matheson, T.J. "H.L.M.'s Reviews of Sinclair Lewis's Major Novels." *Mencken*, 51: 2-7 (Fa 74).

Mencken, H.L. "Minority Report." *Mencken*, 42: 1-3 (Sp 72); 44: 1 (Fa 72).

Miles, Elton. "M's *Mercury* and the West." *SwAL*, 3: 39-48 (1973).

Morrison, J.L. "Colonel H.L.M, C.S.A." *SLJ*, 1: 42-59 (Au 68).

Motsch, M.F. "H.L.M and German Kultur." *German-Am Stud*, 6: 21-42 (1973).

Muller, H.J. "Reconsideration: H.L.M." *NRep*, 166: 31-2 (12 F 72).

Nathan, A.G. "A M Memento." *Mencken*, 44: 1-2 (Fa 72).

Nolte, W. "M, Faulkner, and Southern Moralism." *SCR*, 4: 45-61 (D 71).

————. "M on Art, Order and the Absurd." *Mencken*, 37: 1-7 (Sp 71).

————. "*The Smart Set*: M for the Defense." *SDR*, 6: 3-11 (1968).

Oliver-Bertrand, R. "M's This World Satire." *ConR*, 223: 202-6 (O 73).

Padgette, Paul. "Man of Letters: Addenda." *Mencken*, 37: 11 (Sp 71).

————. "Mr. M Past Tense." *Mencken*, 37: 9-10 (Sp 71).

*Patterson, Maclean. "Bibliographic Checklist." *Mencken*, 49: 13-5; 50: 11-5; 51: 11-5 (Sp, Su, Fa 74); 53: 9-13; 54: 11-5; 55: 11-3; 56: 12 (Sp, Su, Fa Wi 75).

————. "Historical Note on H.L.M's Dictionary of Quotations." *Mencken*, 50: 8-9 (Sp 74).

————. "M-Pearl Letters." *Mencken*, 49: 12 (Sp 74).

Patterson, W.M. "H.L.M and Paul Patterson." *Mencken*, 28: 1-8 (Fa 68).

Pentz, J.A. "M at the Baltimore City College." *Mencken*, 38: 2-5 (Su 71).

Pons, Xavier. "H.L.M et la biologie." *Caliban*, 9: 105-22 (1972).

Powell, Arnold. "M and the Absurdists." *Mencken*, 46: 3-8 (Su 73).

Rasmussen, F.N. "Pen, Ink, and Mr. M." *Mencken*, 48: 4-8 (Wi 73).

Remley, D.A. "I Am a One-Hundred Percent American." *CaM*, 10: 96-103 (Fa 69).

Reynolds, R.D. "Robert Rives LaMonte: M's 'Millionaire Socialist' Collaborator." *Mencken*, 48: 2-4 (Wi 73).

Root, Raoul. "'A Book of Prefaces." *Little R*, 4: 10-2 (Ja 18).

Rosenshine, Annette. "Mr. M Past Tense." *Mencken*, 37: 9-10 (Sp 71).

Ruland, Richard. "M and Cabell." *Cabellian*, 1: 13-20 (1968).

Salzman, Jack. "Conroy, M, and *The American Mercury*." *JPC*, 7: 524-8 (Wi 73).

Scheideman, J.W. "H.L.M and Willa Cather Compared in Louis Auchincloss' *Pioneers and Caretakers*." *Mencken*, 47: 24-5 (Fa 73).

————. "H.L.M Portrayed in Fiction." *N&Q*, 20: 142-3 (1973).

Shapiro, E.S. "The Southern Agrarians: H.L.M. and the Quest for Southern Identity." *AmS*, 13: 75-92 (Fa 72).

Shutt, J.W. "H.L.M and the *Baltimore Evening Sun* Freelance Column." *Mencken*, 48: 8-10 (Wi 73).

Stenerson, D.C. "Baltimore: Source and Sustainer of M's Values." *Mencken*, 41: 1-9 (Sp 72).

————. "Short-Story Writing: A Neglected Phase of M's Literary Apprenticeship." *Mencken*, 30: 8-13 (Su 69).

Sturm, D.N. "H.L.M and the American Tradition of Anarchism." *Mencken*, 38: 6-7 (Su 71).

Turaj, Frank. "H.L.M's Philosophical Skepticism." *Mencken*, 48: 12-6 (Wi 73).

————. "M and the Nazis: A Note." *MHM*, 67: 176-8 (Su 72).

Vandercook, Sharon. "The M-Hench Correspondence." *Mencken*, 34: 1-4 (1970).

Walt, James. "Conrad and H." *Conrad*, 2: 9-21, 100-10 (Wi, Sp 69-70); 69-74 (Wi 70-71).

Warren, G.T. "The Mercury Idea." *Mencken*, 47: 25-6 (Fa 73).

Weintraub, Stanley. "M to Shaw: 'A Young Man in the Writing Trade' Writes to His Hero." *Mencken*, 26: 9-10 (Fa 68).

West, J.L.W. "M's Review of *Tales of the Jazz Age*." *Mencken*, 50: 2-4 (Su 74).

Williams, W.H.A. "Realism and Iconoclasm: H.L.M as a Drama Critic, 1904-1910." *Mencken*, 46: 8-12 (Sp 73).

Williamson, Chilton. "Commonsense Politics." *Mencken*, 43: 4-11 (Fa 72).

Wilson, Edmund. "The Aftermath of M." *NY*, 45: 107-15 (31 My 69).

Wilson, H.B. "Recalls HLM as Patient." *Mencken*, 54: 10-1 (Su 75).

Wingate, P.J. "H.L.M on Watergate." *Mencken*, 50: 4-5 (Su 74).

———. "M and Grasty." *Mencken*, 55: 8-9 (1975).

———. "The Making of a Menckenite." *Mencken*, 56: 8-10 (1975).

Woolf, H.B. "M as Etymologist—*Charley Horse* and *Lobster Trick.*" *AS*, 48: 229-38 (Fa-Wi 73).

Wycherly, H.A. "'Americana': The M-Lorimer Feud." *Consterus*, 5: 227-36 (1972).

———. "H.L.M vs. the Eastern Shore." *BNYPL*, 74: 381-90 (Je 70).

Mencken, Sara Haardt. Going, W.T. "Two Alabama Writers: Zelda Sayre Fitzgerald and SHM." *AlaR*, 23: 3-29 (Ja 70).

Meredith, William. FitzGerald, Gregory, and Paul Ferguson. "The Frost Tradition: A Conversation with WM." *SWR*, 57: 108-17 (Sp 72).

Merrill, James. Brown, Ashley, "An Interview with JM." *Shen*, 19: 3-15 (Su 68).

Eaves, Morris. "Decision and Revision in JM's *(Diblos)* Notebook." *ConL*, 12: 156-65 (Sp 71).

Kalstone, David. "The Poet: Private." *SatR*, 55: 41-5 (D 72).

Moffett, Judith. "Masked More and Less than Ever: JM's Braving the Elements." *HC*, 10: 1-12 (Je 73).

Saez, Richard. "JM's Oedipal Fire." *Parnassus*, 3: 159-81 (#1 74).

Sheehan, Donald. "An Interview with JM." *WSCL*, 9: 1-14 (Wi 68).

———. "The Silver Sensibility: Five Recent Books of American Poetry." *ConL*, 12: 98-121 (Wi 71).

Stoddard, Donald. "Magia verbală a lui JM." *Steaua*, 24: 25 (1974).

Theobald, Sister M.A. "M *Mirror.*" *Cont Poetry*, 1: 18-22 (Sp 73).

Merton, Thomas. Anon. "In Memory of TM." *Continuum*, 7: 277-32 (Su 69).

Baciu, Stefan. "The Literary Catalyst." *Continuum*, 7: 295-305 (Su 69).

Baker, J.T. "Le due città di TM." *HumB*, 26: 413-23 (1971).

———. "An Image in the Making: TM's Early Interpreters." *MVCBul*, 5: 20-8 (Fa 72).

———, "The Social Catalyst." *Continuum*, 7: 255-64 (Su 69).

Bamberger, J.E. "The Cistercian." *Continuum*, 7: 227-41 (Su 69).

Bly, William. "The Hermit Days of Henry Thoreau and TM." *TSB*, 130: 2-3 (Wi 75).

Boyd, J.D. "Christian Imaginative Patterns and the Poetry of TM." *Greyfriar*, 13: 3-14 (1972).

Burke, H.C. "The Man of Letters." *Continuum*, 7: 274-85 (Su 69).

Casotti, Francesco. "La Poesia di TM." *Aevum*, 39: 370-8 (My-Ag 65).

Davis, R.M. "How Waugh Cut M." *Month*, 234: 150-3 (Ap 73).

Flaherty, Luke, "TM's *Cables to the Ace*: A Critical Study." *Renascence*, 24: 3-32 (Au 71).

Forest, J.H. "The Gift of M." *Cweal*, 89: 463-5 (10 Ja 69).

Glimm, J.Y. "Exile Ends in Satire: TM's Cable to the Ace." *Cithara*, 11: 31-40 (N 71).

———. "TM's Last Poem: *The Geography of Lograire.*" *Renascence*, 26: 95-104 (Wi 74).

Higgins, M.W. "A Study of the Influence of William Blake on TM." *ABR*, 25: 377-88 (1974).

Landess, Thomas. "Monastic Life and the Secular City." *SR*, 77: 530-5 (1969).

Lentfoehr, M.T. "The Spiritual Writer." *Continuum*, 7: 242-54 (Su 69).

Lentfoehr, Sister Thérèse. "TM: The Dimensions of Solitude." *ABR*, 23: 337-52 (1972).

McInerny, D.Q. "TM and the Awakening of Social Consciousness." *AmS*, 15: 37-53 (Fa 74).

Materer, Timothy. "TM and Auden." *Cweal*, 91: 577-80 (27 F 70).

Mayhew, Alice. "M Against Himself." *Cweal*, 91: 70-4 (17 O 69).

Shepherd, R.M. "How I First Met TM." *CLC*, 24: 3-9 (#2 75).

Stevens, Clifford. "The Contemplative Witness of TM." *ABR*, 26: 395-405 (1975).

———. "TM: A Profile." *Dublin Mag*, 9: 94-107 (1973).

Sturm, R.D. "TD: Poet." *ABR*, 22: 1-20 (1971).

Sutton, Walter. "TM and the American Epic Tradition: The Last Poems." *ConL*, 14: 49-57 (Wi 73).

Taylor, Dennis. "Some Strategies of Religious Autobiography." *Renascence*, 27: 40-44 (1974).

Zahn, Gordon. "The Peacemaker." *Continuum*, 7: 265-73 (Su 69).

Zeik, Michael. "M and the Buddhists." *Cweal*, 99: 34-7 (1973).

———. "Le voyage du Pèlerin: La vie de TM." *Esprit*, 395: 451-60 (1970).

Merwin, W.S. Ahmad, Aijaz. "Ghalib: 'The Dew Drop on the Red Poppy . . .'" *Mahfil*, 5: 59-69 (1968-69).

———. "Time and Timelessness in the Poetry of W.S.M." *MPS*, 6: 224-36 (1975).

Andersen, Kenneth. "The Poetry of W.S.M." *TCL*, 16: 278-86 (1970).

Bayley, John. "How to Be Intimate Without Being Personal." *Parnassus*, 2: 115-21 (Fa-Wi 73).

Bloom, Harold. "The New Transcendentalism: The Visionary Strain in M, Ashbery, and Ammons." *ChiR*, 24: 25-43 (1973).

Davis, C.C. "M's Odysseus." *CP*, 8: 25-33 (#1 75).

Frost, Lucy. "The Poetry of W.S.M." *Meanjin*, 30: 294-6 (S 71).

Gerber, P.L., and R.J. Gemmett. "'Tireless Quest': A Conversation with W.S.M." *Eng Rec*, 19: 9-18 (F 69).

Gordon, J.B. "The Dwelling of Disappearance: W.S.M's *The Lice*." *MPS*, 3: 119-38 (1972).

Gross, Harvey. "The Writing on the Void: The Poetry of W.S.M." *IowaR*, 1: 92-10 (Su 70).

Gustafson, Richard. "What is M Trying To Do." *P&C*, 7: 29-35 (1972).

Hoffman, Daniel. "The Gift of Tongues." *HC*, 5: 1-12 (1968).

Kirby-Smith, H.T. "Miss Bishop and Others." *SR*, 80: 483-93 (1972).

Kyle, Carol. "A Riddle for the New Year: Affirmation in W.S.M." *MPS*, 4: 288-303 (Wi 73).

Libby, Anthony. "Fire and Light: Four Poets to the End and Beyond." *IowaR*, 4: 111-26 (Sp 73).

———. "W.S.M and the Nothing That Is." *ConL*, 16: 19-40 (Wi 75).

MacShane, Frank. "A Portrait of W.S.M." *Shen*, 21: 3-14 (Wi 70).

Messer, R.E. "W.S.M's Use of Myth." *Pub Arkansas Poetry Assn*, 1: 41-8 (#1 75).

Ramsey, Jarold. "The Continuities of W.S.M: 'What Has Escaped We Bring with Us.'" *MR*, 569-90 (Su 73).

Rutsala, Vern. "The End of the Owls: W.S.M, *The Lice*." *FarP*, 2: 40-4 (Sp-Su 69).

Sanderlin, Reed. "M's 'The Drunk in the Furnace.'" *Cont Poetry*, 2: 24-7 (#1 75).

Swan, Brian. "The Poetry of W.S.M." *ACF*, 12: 135-47 (1973).

Vogelsang, John. "Toward the Great Language: W.S.M." *MPS*, 3: 97-118 (#2 72).

Watkins, Eva. "W.S.M: A Critical Accompaniment." *Boun2*, 4: 187-99 (1975).

Michener, James. Leib, A.P. "History and Setting in M's Story of Norfolk Island, 'Mutiny.'" *ALS*, 4: 349-59 (O 70).

Michener, James. "What the F.B.I. Has on Me." *Esquire*, 76: 134, 224 (D 71).

Miles, Josephine. Donoghue, Denis. "The Habits of the Poets." *TLS*, 25 Ap 76, pp. 442-3.

Mooney, Stephen. "JM: Successive Views." *Voyages*, 2: 21-4 (Fa 68).

Millay, Edna St. Vincent. Brittin, N.A. "ESVM's 'Nancy Boyd' Stories." *BSUF*, 10: 31-6 (Sp 69).

*———. "M Bibliography: Additions and Corrections." *AN&Q*, 8: 52 (1969).

Gassman, J. "ESVM: 'Nobody's Own.'" *CLQ*, 9: 297-310 (Je 71).

Hardwick, Elizabeth. "Anderson, M, and Crane in Their Letters." *PR*, 20: 690-6 (D 53).

Minot, W.S. "M's 'Ungrafted Tree': The Problem of the Artist as Woman." *NEQ*, 48: 260-9 (Je 75).

Munson, Gorham. "Parnassus on Penobscot." *NEQ*, 41: 264-73 (Je 68).

*Patton, J.J. "A Comprehensive Bibliography of Criticism of ESVM." *Serif*, 5: 10-32 (1968).

———. "Satiric Fiction in M's Distressing Dialogues." *MLS*, 2: 63-7 (1972).

Miller, Arthur. Baron, Alexander. "Prelude to Tragedy: Afterthoughts on *Incident at Vichy*." *JewQ*, 14: 11-3 (Sp 66).

Bates, B.W. "The Lost Past in *Death of a Salesman*." *MD*, 11: 164-72 (S 68).

Bergman, Herbert. "'The Interior of a Heart,' *The Crucible* and *The Scarlet Letter*." *UCQ*, 15: 27-32 (My 70).

Bergeron, D.M. "AM's *The Crucible* and Nathaniel Hawthorne: Some Parallels." *EJ*, 58: 47-55 (Ja 69).

Bigsby, C.W.E. "What Price AM? An Analysis of *The Price*." *TCL*, 16: 16-25 (Ja 70).

Bleich, David. "Psychological Bases of Learning from Literature." *CE*, 33: 32-45 (O 71).

Bliquez, Guerin. "Linda's Role in *Death of a Salesman*." *MD*, 10: 383-6 (F 68).

Blumberg, Paul. "Sociology and Social Literature: Work Alienation in the Plays of AM." *AQ*, 21: 291-310 (Su 69).

Bottman, P.N. "Quentin's Quest: AM's Move Into Expressionism." *WSL*, 5: 41-52 (1968).

Bredella, Lothar. "AM's Stück *All My Sons* im Unterricht und die Frage nach seiner didaktischen Begründung." *NS*, 21: 595-600 (1972).

Bronsen, David. "An Enemy of the People: A Key to AM's Art and Ethics." *CompD*, 2: 229-47 (Wi 68-69).

Callahan, E.A. "The Tragic Hero in Contemporary Secular and Religous Drama." *LHY*, 8: 42-9 (Ja-Jl 67).

Chamberlain, Lowell. "Pismo ot Nyu York: Novi piesi na ststenite v Broduey." *Plamuk*, 10: 87 (1968).

Cismaru, Alfred. "Before and After the Fall." *Forum(H)*, 11: 67-71 (1973).

Cook, L.W. "The Function of Ben and Dave Singleman in *Death of a Salesman*." *NCLit*, 5: 7-9 (#1 75).

Corrigan, R.W. "The Achievement of AM." *CompD*, 2: 141-60 (Fa 68).

Czímer, József. "Price and Value." *NHuQ*, 10: 169-76 (Wi 69).

Donoghue, Denis. "The Human Image in Modern Drama." *LugR*, 1: 155-68 (1965).

Downer, A.S. "Old, New, Borrowed, and (a Trifle) Blue: Notes on the New York Theatre, 1967-1968," *QJS*, 54: 199-211 (O 68).

Ferres, J.H. "Still in the Present Tense: *The Crucible* Today." *UCQ*, 17: 8-18 (My 72).

Field, B.S. "Hamartia in *Death of a Salesman*." *TCL*, 18: 19-24 (1972).

Greenfeld, Josh. "Writing Plays Is Abolutely Senseless, AM Says, 'But I Love It. I Just Love It.'" *NYTMS*, 13 F 72, pp. 16-7, 34-9.

Groene, Horst. "*Death of a Salesman*: Beispelhafte amerikansiche Dramenkunst." *LWU*, 4: 177-86 (1971).

Gross, Barry. "*All My Sons* and the Larger Context." *MD*, 18: 15-28 (Mr 75).

Gupta, R.K. "*Death of a Salesman* and M's Concept of Tragedy." *KAL*, 15: 10-9 (1974).

Hayman, Ronald. "AM: Between Sartre & Society." *Enc*, 37: 73-9 (N 71).

Miller, Arthur

Heaton, C.P. ''AM on Death of a Salesman.'' *NCLit*, 1: 5 (Ja 71).

Heilman, R.B. ''Salesmen's Deaths: Documentary and Myth.'' *Shen*, 20: 20-8 (Sp 69).

Hewes, Henry. ''AM's Cosmic Chuckles.'' *SatR*, 1: 57 (Ja 73).

Hogel, R.K. ''Manipulation of Time in M's *After the Fall*.'' *LWU*, 7: 115-21 (Ag 74).

Hogel, Rolf. ''AM: *A Memory of Two Mondays*.'' *NS*, 24: 419-29 (1975).

Hombitzer, Eleonore. ''Die Selbstentfremdung des modernen Menschen im dramatischen Werk AMs.'' *NS*, 19: 409-16 (Ag 70).

Jacobson, Irving. ''The Child as Guilty Witness.'' *L&P*, 24: 12-23 (1974).

———. ''Christ, Pygmalion, and Hitler in *After the Fall*.'' *EL*, 2: 12-27 (Ag 74).

———. ''Family Dreams in *Death of a Salesman*.'' *AL*, 47: 247-58 (My 75).

Jochems, Helmut. ''*Death of a Salesman*: Eine Nachlese.'' *LWU*, 1: 77-97 (1968).

Jungmann, Milan. ''Muoj pohled je jiný: AM v Praze.'' *Listy*, 2: 1, 6 (1969).

Kauffmann, Stanley. ''Right Down the Middle.'' *NRep*, 166: 22, 34 (27 My 72).

Kilbourn, William. ''M: *After the Fall*.'' *CanF*, 44: 275-6 (Mr 65).

Kohler, Klaus. ''Bewusstseinsanlyse und Gesellschaftskrise im Dramenwerk AM.'' *ZAA*, 22: 18-40 (1974).

Lowenthal, L.D. ''AM's *Incident at Vichy*: A Sartrean Interpretation.'' *MD*, 18: 29-42 (Mr 75).

McMahon, H.M. ''AM's Common Man: The Problem of the Realistic and the Mythic.'' *D&T*, 10: 128-33 (1972).

Mann, G.K.S. ''Memory as Technique and Theme in *The Glass Menagerie* and *Death of a Salesman*.'' *NDEJ*, 5: 23-30 (1969-70).

Marinov, Mikhail. ''Novata sreshta s M.'' *Plamuk*, 17: 93-4 (1967).

Martin, R.A. ''AM and the Meaning of Tragedy.'' *MD*, 13: 34-9 (My 70).

———. ''AM: Tragedy and Commitment.'' *MQR*, 8: 176-8 (Su 69).

———. ''The Creative Experience of AM: An Interview.'' *ETJ*, 21: 310-7 (O 69).

Miller, Arthur. ''In Russia.'' *HM*, 293: 37-78 (S 69).

Moen, E.G. ''Et mishandlet kunsverk.'' *Samtiden*, 77: 190-8 (Mr 68).

Mukerji, Nirmal. ''The Proctor's Tragic Predicament.'' *PURBA*, 4: 75-9 (Ap 73).

Överland, Orm. ''The Action and Its Significance: AM's Struggle with Dramatic Form.'' *MD*, 18: 1-14 (Mr 75).

Palmer, Tony. ''Artistic Privilege.'' *LonM*, 8: 47-52 (My 68).

Pinsker, Sanford. ''*The End of the Tether*: Joseph Conrad's Death of a Sailsman.'' *Conrad*, 3: 74-6 (1971-72).

Reno, R.H. ''AM and the Death of God.'' *TSLL*, 11: 1069-87 (Su 69).

Richardson, Jack. ''AM's Eden.'' *Commentary*, 55: 83-5 (F 73).

Rothenberg, Albert, and E.D. Shapiro. ''The Defense of Psychoanalysis in Literature: *Long Day's Journey into Night* and *A View from the Bridge*.'' *CompD*, 7: 51-67 (Sp 73).

Schraepen, E. ''AM's Constancy.'' *RLV*, 36: 67-71 (Ja-F 70).

Sharma, P.P. ''Making the World a Home: AM's Major Thematic Concern.'' *RUSEng*, 8: 62-71 (1975).

———. ''Search for Self-identity in *Death of a Salesman*.'' *CLrit*, 11: 74-9 (Su 74).

Shatsky, Joel. ''The 'Reactive Image' and M's *Death of a Salesman*.'' *Players*, 48: 104-10 (1973).

Shepherd, Allen. '''What Comes Easier—': The Short Stories of AM.'' *IllQ*, 34: 37-49 (F 72).

Somlai, Péter. ''Okozatság és formanyelv.'' *Kritika*, 6: 49-51 (1968).

Standley, F.L. ''An Echo of Milton in *The Crucible*.'' *N&Q*, 15: 303 (1968).

Steinbeck, John. ''The Trial of AM.'' *Esquire*, 80: 238 (O 730.

Unger, Harriet. "The Writings of and about AM: A Checklist, 1936-1967." *BNYPL*, 74: 107-34 (F 70).

Weales, Gerald. "All About Talk: AM's *The Price*." *OhR*, 13: 74-84 (1972).

Willet, Ralph. "A Note on AM's *The Price*." *JAmSt*, 5: 307-10 (D 71).

Willis, R.J. "AM's *The Crucible*." *FJ*, 1: 5-14 (1970).

Winegarten, Renee. "The World of AM." *JewQ*, 17: 48-53 (Su 69).

Miller, Henry. Almansi, G. "Three Versions of an Article on HM." *TCS*, 1: 41-55 (N 69).

Bald, Wambly. "I Remember M." *LGJ*, 2: 38-41 (#3 74).

Belmont, Georges. "HM: Assis a la droite de l'homme." *NL*, 3-9 Ja 72, p. 10.

Bidaud, Anne-Marie. "Le Zarathoustra de Brooklyn." *ML*, 70: 11-6 (N 72).

Bode, Elroy. "The World on Its Own Terms: A Brief for Steinbeck, M, and Simenon." *SWR*, 53: 406-16 (Au 68).

Bolckmans, Alex. "HM's *Tropic of Cancer* and Knut Hamsun's *Sult*." *Scandanavia*, 14: 115-26 (1975).

Cott, Jonathan. "Reflections of a Cosmic Tourist: An Afternoon with HM." *Rolling Stone*, 27 F 75, pp. 38-57.

DeMott, Benjamin. "HM: Rebel-Clown at Eighty." *SatR*, 54: 29-32 (11 D 72).

Egor, Gvozden. "Erotska pikareska HM." *Knjizevnost*, 56: 92-100 (1973).

Hays, P.L. "The Danger of HM." *ArQ*, 7: 251-8 (1971).

Hida, Shigeo. "Dokeshi HM." *EigoS*, 119: 330-1 (1973).

Höck, Wilhelm. "Leben nach der Geburt: SB und HM: Einzelgänger der literarischen Moderne." *Hoch*, 63: 365-77 (1971).

Hoffman, M.J. "Yesterday's Rebel." *WHR*, 24: 271-4 (Su 70).

Jackson, P.R. "The Balconies of HM." *UR*, 155-60, 221-5 (D 69, Mr 70).

⸻. "HM, Emerson, and the Divided Self." *AL*, 43: 231-41 (My 71).

⸻. "HM's Literary Pregnancies." *L&P*, 19: 35-49 (1969).

Katz, Al. "The *Tropic of Cancer* Trials: The Problems of Relevant Moral and Artistic Controversy." *Midway*, 9: 99-125 (1969).

Kerouac, Jack. "Facsimile of Letter from Jack Kerouac on Celine." *PaR*, 8: 136 (Wi-Sp 64).

Lorenzana, Salvador. "HM: 'enfant terrible' norteamericano." *Grial*, 37: 267-80 (1972).

Louit, Robert. "M, ou l'écriture du désir." *ML*, 70: 17-8 (N 72).

McCarthy, H.T. "HM's Democratic Vistas." *AQ*, 23: 221-35 (My 71).

MacDonald, E.E. "The Childs Collection of HM at Randolph-Macon College." *RALS*, 1: 121-5 (Sp 71).

Maigret, Arnaud de. "HM et la Villa Seurat." *ML*, 70: 14-6 (N 72).

Matthews, F.M. "Patriotic Justice: Down with HM and Sen. Joe Clark." *NRep*, 158: 13-4 (3 F 68).

Miller, Henry. "HM Talks to HM on Sex, Love, War." *True*, nv: 68, 71-2 (Ap 71).

⸻. "A Note on the Childs Collection of HM at Randolph-Macon College." *RALS*, 1: 250-1 (Au 71).

Millet, Kate. "Sexual Politics: M, Mailer, and Genet." *NAR*, 7: 7-32; n.d.

Moravia, Alberto. "Two American Writers." *SR*, 68: 473-81 (Su 60).

Phillips, William. "Writing About Sex." *PR*, 24: 552-63 (Fa 67).

Polley, G.W. "The Art of Religious Writings: HM as Religious Writer." *SDR*, 7: 61-73 (Au 69).

Pontual, Roberto. "Fontes-Roteiro de HM." *RCivB*, 18: 153-68 (1968).

*Riley, E.L. "HM: an Informal Bibliography 1924-1960." *FHays*, 1: 3-52 (Je 61).

Rios, J.A. "O outro lado de HM." *Comentário*, 10: 299-304 (1968).

Sánchez Mayáns, Fernando. "M y Durrell publican su correspondencia." *Nivel*, 44: 3, 8 (1966).

Miller, Henry

Williams, John. "HM: The Success of Failure." *VQR*, 44: 225-45 (Sp 68).
Woods, Bruce. "On the Question of M's Anarchy." *Pisces*, 3: 7-10 (1972).
Wustenhagen, Heinz. "Die Dekandenz HM." *ZAA*, 22: 41-65 (1974).
Miller, Jason. Hughes, Catherine. "The Name of the Game." *Prog*, 36: 31-2 (Ag 72).
Simon, John. "That Championship Season." *HudR*, 25: 616-25 (1972).
Miller, Joaquin. Beckner, Jean. "Arthur Conan Doyle and JM." *MDAC*, 1: 256-8 (1972).
Brooks, Noah. "Reminiscences: Noah Brooks Writes of JM and Bret Harte." *NYTSat*, 3 My 02, p. 291.
DeGruson, Gene. "An Unlocated Bret Harte—JM Book." *PBSA*, 61: 60 (1967).
Grenander, M.E. "A London Letter of JM to Ambrose Bierce." *YULG*, 46: 109-16 (O 71).
Kimmel, Thelma. "'My God, My Hero, My Ideal.'" *Frontier Times*, 45: 32-3, 66-7 (Je-Jl 71).
Lawson, B.S. "JM in England." *SDR*, 12: 89-101 (1974).
Moyne, E.J. "JM and Baroness Alexandra Gripenberg." *MarkR*, 4: 68-70 (O 74).
Winn, W.W. "The JM Foundation." *CHSQ*, 32: 231-8 (S 53).
Millar, Kenneth (see **MacDonald, Ross**).
Miller, Perry. Gerlach, John. "Messianic Nationalism in the Early Works of Herman Melville: Against PM." *ArQ*, 28: 5-26 (1972).
Grabo, N.S. "The Art of Puritan Devotion." *SCN*, 26: 7-9 (Sp 68).
Hollinger, D.A. "PM and Philosophical History." *Hist and Theory*, 7: 189-202 (1968).
*Kinnamon, Keneth. "A Bibliography of PM." *BB*, 26: 45-51 (Ap-Je 69).
Selement, George. "PM: A Note on His Sources." *WMQ*, 31: 453-64 (Jl 74).
Miller, Walter M., Jr. Bennett, M.A. "The Theme of Responsibility in M's *A Canticle for Leibowitz*." *EJ*, 59: 484-9 (Ap 70).
Griffin, R.M. "Medievalism in *A Canticle for Leibowitz*." *Extrapolation*, 14: 14: 112-25 (My 73).
Percy, Walker, "WM.M, Jr.'s *A Canticle for Leibowitz*: A Rediscovery." *SoR*, 7: 575-8 (Ap 71).
Rank, Hugh. "Song Out of Season: *A Canticle for Leibowitz*." *Renascence*, 21: 213-21 (1969).
Mitchell, Donald Grant. Lombard, Charles. "Ik Marvel's Francophilism." *RLC*, 48: 292-304 (1974).
Mitchell, Margaret. Boatwright, James. "Reconsideration: Totin' de Weery Load." *NRep*, 169: 29-32 (1 S 73).
Draper, J.W. "A Letter from MM." *WVUPP*, 17: 81-3 (Je 70).
Gaillard, Dawson. "*Gone With the Wind* as Bildungsroman or Why Did Rhett Butler Really Leave Scarlett O'Hara?" *GaR*, 28: 9-18 (Sp 74).
Groover, R.L. "MM, the Lady from Atlanta." *GHQ*, 52: 53-69 (Mr 68).
Harris, A.S. "Scarlett Gave Her a Pot of Gold." *AmMerc*, 86: 137-43 (F 58).
Stern, Jerome. "*Gone with the Wind*: The South as America." *SHR*, 6: 5-12 (Wi 72).
Watkins, F.C. "*Gone with the Wind* as Vulgar Literature." *SLJ*, 2: 86-103 (Sp 70).
Mitchell, Silas Weir. Griffith, Kelley. "WM and the Genteel Romance." *AL*, 44: 247-61 (My 72).
Hayne, Barrie. "SWM." *ALR*, 2: 149-55 (Su 69).
Momaday, Natachee Scott. Fields, Kenneth. "More Than Language Means." *SoR*, 6: 196-204 (Ja 70).
Hylton, M.W. "On a Trail of Pollen: M's *House Made of Dawn*." *Critique*, 14: 60-9 (#2 73).
McAllister, H.S. "Be a Man, Be a Woman: Androgyny in The House Made of Drawn." *Am Indian Q*, 2: 14-22 (1975).

Nicholas, C.A. "The Way to Rainy Mountain." *SDR*, 13: 149-58 (1975).

Oleson, Carole. "The Remembered Earth: M's *House Made of Dawn.*" *SDR*, 11: 59-78 (Sp 73).

Smith, Marie. "Rainy Mountain, Legends and Students." *Ariz Eng Bul*, 13: 41-4 (Ap 71).

Trimmer, J.F. "Native Americans and the American Mix." *Indiana Soc Stud Q*, 28: 75-91 (1975).

Monroe, Harriet. Johnson, A.A. "A Free Foot in the Wilderness: HM and *Poetry*, 1912 to 1936." *IllQ*, 37: 28-43 (Su 75).

Williams, Ellen. "HM." *AntigR*, 2: 77-82 (Su 71).

Montgomery, Marion. Colvert, J.B. "An Interview with MM." *SoR*, 1041-53 (Au 70).

Landess, T.H. "MM's *Fugitive.*" *GaR*, 28: 212-8 (Su 74).

Montgomery, Marion. "Words, and the Freedom to Suppose." *LaStud*, 5: 278-88 (Wi 66).

Moody, William Vaughn. Aspiz, Harold. "'The Menagerie' Revisited." *MarkR*, 4: 97-100 (F 75).

Axelrod, Steven, "Colonel Shaw in American Poetry: 'For the Union Dead' and its Precursors." *AQ*, 24: 523-38 (O 72).

Blackmur, R.P. "M in Retrospect." *Poetry*, 38: 331-7 (S 31).

Blanco, M.G. "Unamuno y tres poetas norteamericanos." *Asomante*, 15: 39-44 (1959).

Brown, M.F. "M and Robinson." *CLQ*, 5: 185-94 (D 60).

———. "WVM." *BB*, 28: 123-4 (1971).

———. "WVM (1869-1910)." *ALR*, 6: 51-60 (Wi 73).

Buckham, J.W. "The Doubt and Faith of WVM." *Homiletic R*, 75: 349-53 (My 18).

Munson, Gorham. "The Limbo of American Literature." *Broom*, 2: 250-60 (Je 22).

Pickering, J.V. "WVM: The Dramatist as Social Philosopher." *MD*, 14: 93-103 (My 71).

Soule, George. "A Great Pilgrim-Pagan." *Little R*, 1: 2-9 (D 14).

Walker, C.R. "The Poetry of WVM." *Texas R*, 1: 144-53 (Je 15).

Wilson, Edmund. "The Country I Remember." *NRep*, 103: 529-30 (14 O 40).

Moore, Marianne. Anon. "Vituoso Fiddling: MM's Syllabics." *TLS*, 30 May 68, p. 552.

Bernlef, J. "Precisie en te vell details: MM." *Gids*, 131: 297-300 (1968).

Edsal, C.H. "Values and the Poems of MM." *EJ*, 58: 516-8 (Ap 69).

Engel, B.F. "M's 'A Face.'" *Expl*, 34: 29 (D 75).

Glatstein, Jacob. "The Poetry of MM." *PrS*, 47: 133-41 (Su 73).

Guillory, D.L. "Hart Crane, MM, and the Brooklyn Bridge." *BSUF*, 15: 48-9 (Su 74).

Hayes, A.L. "On Reading MM." *CaSE*, 11: 1-19 (1970).

Messing, G.M. "The Linguistic Analysis of Some Contemporary Nonformal Poetry." *Lang&S*, 2: 323-9 (1969).

Morris, Harry. "Poets and Critics, Critics and Poets." *SR*, 80: 627-32 (1972).

O'Sullivan, M.J. "Native Genius for Disunion: MM's 'Spenser's Ireland.'" *CP*, 7: 42-7 (1974).

Replogle, Justin. "MM and the Art of Intonation." *ConL*, 12: 1-17 (Wi 71).

Sabbadini, Silvano. "MM, il Basilisco Piumato." *Nuova Corrente*, 63: 178-80 (1974).

Schulman, Grace. "Conversation with MM." *QRL*, 16: 154-71 (1969).

Seymour-Smith, Martin. "In Lieu of the Lyre." *Spec*, 10 My 68, pp. 634-5.

Smith, W.J. "A Place for the Genuine." *NRep*, 158: 34-6 (24 F 68).

Stanford, D.E. "MM." *SoR*, 8: xi-xiii (Ap 72).

Tomlinson, Charles. "MM: Her Poetry and Her Critics." *Agenda*, 6: 137-42 (1968).

Vonalt, L.P. "MM's Medicines." *SR*, 78: 669-78 (Au 70).

Wand, D.H. "The Dragon and the Kylin: The Use of Chinese Symbols and Myths in MM's Poetry." *LE&W*, 15: 470-84 (1971).

Warlow, F.W. "M's 'To a Snail.'" *Expl*, 26: 51 (Fa 68).

Wells, H.W. "The Poetic Image in Modern America and Ancient India." *LHY*, 10: 40-52 (Ja 69).

Moran, Ronald. Stitt, Peter. "North of Jamaica and Into the Self: Louis Simpson and RM." *SoR*, 10: 517-24 (Sp 74).

More, Paul Elmer. Doney, Richard, and B.C. Lambert. "PEM and C.S. Lewis." *Bul New York C.S. Lewis Soc*, 6: 5-8 (#3 75).

Lambert, B.C. "PEM and the Redemption of History." *ModA*, 13: 277-88 (1969).

Tanner, S.L. "PEM: Literary Criticism as the History of Ideas." *AL*, 45: 390-406 (N 73).

———. "T.S. Eliot and PEM on Tradition." *ELN*, 8: 211-5 (1971).

Warren, Austin. "PEM: A Critic in Search of Wisdom." *SoR*, 5: 1091-111 (Au 69).

Morehouse, Kathleen. Morehouse, Kathleen. "Thank You Kindly, but with Reservations." *NCF*, 20: 87-91 (My 72).

West, J.F. "Mrs. M's *Rain on the Just.*" *NCaF*, 19: 47-54 (Mr 71).

Morford Henry. Homer, Shirley. "HM of Monmouth." *Monmouth Co Hist Assn*, 2: 1, 4 (S 73).

Morley, Christopher. Wallach, M.I. "The Columns and Essays of CM." *MarkR*, 3: 33-7 (F 72).

Morrell, William. Kaiser, L.M. "On M's *Nov-Anglia.*" *SCN*, 28: 20 (1970).

Morris, Willie. Mack, Maynard. "The Last Month at *Harper's*: WM in Conversation." *MissR*, 3: 121-30 (1974).

Mitchell, P. "*North Toward Home*: The Quest for an Intellectual Home." *NMW*, 2: 105-9 (Wi 70).

Moore, R.H. "The Last Months at *Harper's*: WM in Conversation." *MissR*, 3: 121-30 (1974).

Morris, Wright. Guettinger, R.J. "The Problem with Jigsaw Puzzles: Form in the Fiction of WM." *TQ*, 11: 209-20 (1968).

Madden, David. "M' *Cannibals*, Cain's *Serenade*: The Dynamics of Style and Technique." *JPC*, 3: 59-70 (Su 74).

Nemanic, Gerald. "A Ripening Eye: WM and the Field of Vision." *Midamerica*, 1974: 120-31 (1974).

———, and Harry White. "WM: An Interview." *Great Lakes R*, 1: 1-29 (Wi 75).

Richey, C.W. "'The Riverrun': A Note Upon a Joycean Quotation in WM's *In Orbit.*" *NCLit*, 2: 14-5 (Ja 72).

Schwartz, Joseph. "Present and Past: On WM." *FicI*, 2-3: 144-7 (Ap 74).

Tucker, Martin. "The Landscape of WM." *LHR*, 7: 43-51 (1965).

Waterman, A.E. "WM's *One Day*: The Novel of Revelation." *FurmS*, 15: 29-36 (My 68).

Wilson, J.C. "WM and the Search for the 'Still Point.'" *PrS*, 49: 154-63 (Su 75).

Morse, Jedidiah. Gribben, William. "A Mirror to New England: *The Compendious History* of JM and Elija Parish." *NEQ*, 45: 340-54 (1972).

Morton, Thomas. Arner, R.D. "Mythology and the Maypole of Merrymount: Some Notes on TM's 'Rise Oedipus.'" *EAL*, 6: 156-64 (Fa 71).

———. "Pastoral Celebration and Satire in TM's 'New English Canaan.'" *Criticism*, 16: 217-31 (Su 74).

Major, M.W. "William Bradford Versus TM." *EAL*, 5: 1-12 (Fa 70).

Scheick, W.J. "M's *New English Canaan.*" *Expl*, 31: 47 (F 73).

Motley, Willard. Bayliss, J.F. "Nick Romano: Father and Son." *NALF*, 3: 18-21, 32 (Sp 69).

Fleming, R.E. "WM's Urban Novels." *Umoja*, 1: 15-9 (Su 73).

Giles, J.R. "WM's Concept of 'Style' and 'Material.'" *SBL*, 4: 4-6 (Sp 73).

————, Jerome Klinkowitz, and J.T. O'Brien. "The WM Papers at the University of Wisconsin." *RALS*, 2: 218-73 (Au 72).

————, and N.J. Weyant. "The Short Fiction of WM." *NALF*, 9: 3-10 (Sp 75).

Klinkowitz, Jerome, and J.R. Giles. "The Emergence of WM in Black American Literature." *NALF*, 6: 31-4 (Su 72).

————, and Karen Wood. "The Making and Unmaking of *Knock On Any Door*." *Proof*, 3: 121-37 (1973).

Rayson, A.L. "Prototypes for Nick Romano of *Knock On Any Door*: From the Diaries in the Collected Manuscripts of the WM Estate." *NALF*, 8: 248-51 (Fa 74).

Wood, Charles. "The *Adventure* Manuscript: New Light of WM's Naturalism." *NALF*, 6: 35-8 (Su 72).

Muir, John. Cohen, M.P. "JM's Public Voice." *WAL*, 10: 177-87 (1975).

Mumford, Lewis. Ashton, Dore. "LM." *BUJ*, 23: 3-7 (#3 75).

Brower, G.L. "Sabato Estrada, M: Attack on the Megalopolis." *Chasqui*, 3: 7-16 (#1 73).

Dow, Eddy. "Van Wyck Brooks and LM: A Confluence in the 'Twenties.'" *AL*, 45: 407-22 (N 73).

*Monteiro, George. "Addenda to the Bibliographies of . . . M [and others]." *PBSA*, 69: 172-5 (Ap-Je 75).

Murfree, Mary Noailles (Charles Egbert Craddock). Anon. "Romance of the Tennessee Mountains." *Outlook*, 131: 626 (16 Ag 22).

*Carleton, R.M. "MNM (1850-1922): An Annotated Bibliography." *ALR*, 7: 282-378 (Au 74).

Cary, Richard. "MNM (1850-1922)." *ALR*, 1: 79-83 (1967-68).

Durham, Frank. [Unititled]. *SHR*, 3: 400-1 (Fa 69).

Jemison, Margaret. "Papers of CEC Now in Emory Library." *Emory Alumnus*, 10: 6 (Jl-Ag 34).

Lanier, Doris. "MNM: An Interview." *THQ*, 31: 276-8 (Fa 72).

Loyd, Dennis. "Tennessee's Mystery Woman Novelist." *THQ*, 29: 272-7 (Fa 70).

Moses, M.J. "CEC: A Study of MM in Her Southern Home in Tennessee." *BNM*, 33: 69-71 (O 14).

Nilles, Mary. "Craddock's Girls: A Lood at Some Unliberated Women." *MarkR*, 3: 74-7 (O 72).

Reeves, Pascal. "From Haley's Comet to Prohibition." *MissQ*, 21: 286 (Fa 68).

Warfel, H.R. "Local Color and Literary Artistry: MNM's *In the Tennessee Mountains*." *SLJ*, 3: 154-63 (Fa 70).

Wood, A.D. "The Literature of Impoverishment: The Women Local Colorists in America." *WS*, 1: 17-9 (1972).

Muro, Amado Jesus (Chester Seltzer). Bode, Elroy. "The Making of a Legend." *Texas Observer*, 30 Mr 73, pp. 1-5.

Haslam, Gerald. "The Enigma of AJM." *WAL*, 10: 3-9 (My 75).

Rintoul, William. "The Ballad of AJM." *Nation*, 218: 437-8 (6 Ap 74).

Nabokov, Vladimir. Aldridge, O.A. "*Lolita* and *Les Liaisons Dangereuses*." *ConL*, 2: 20-6 (Fa 61).

Alter, Robert. "*Invitation to a Beheading*: N and the Art of Politics." *TriQ*, 17: 41-59 (Wi 70).

————. "Mirrors for Immortality." *SatR*, 55: 72-4, 76 (D 72).

————. "N's Ardor." *Commentary*, 48: 47-50 (Ag 69).

————. "Sifrut Al Tekufa Ve-Sifrut al Sifrut: Herman Broch, VN, Shaul Tchernichovsky." *Hasifrut*, 3: 187-95 (1972).

Alvarez, A. "'A Tale of the Tub' for Our Time." *SatR*, 53: 27-9, 45 (13 Je 70).

Anderson, Quentin. "N in Time." *NRep*, 23-8 (4 Je 66).

Appel, Alfred. "*Ada* Described." *TriQ*, 17: 160-86 (Wi 70).

————. "The Art of N's Artifice." *DQ*, 2: 25-37 (Su 68).

————. "Backgrounds of *Lolita*." *TriQ*, 17: 17-40 (Wi 70).

————. "Conversations with N." *Novel*, 4: 209-22 (1971).

————. "N: A Portrait." *Atl*, 228: 77-92 (S 71).

————. "N's Dark Cinema: A Diptych." *TriQ*, 28: 196-207 (Sp 73).

————. "N's Puppet Show." *NRep*, 156: 27-30, 25-8, 32 (14, 21 Ja 67).

————. "The Road to *Lolita*, or the Americanization of an Émigré." *JML*, 4: 3-31 (S 74).

————. "Tristram in Movieland: Lolita at the Novels." *RLT*, 7: 343-88 (1973).

Baker W.R.E. "Brien and N." *NSt*, 22 D 67, pp. 877-8.

Banta, Martha. "Benjamin, Edgar, Humbert, and Jay." *YR*, 60: 532-49 (Je 71).

Bell, Michael. "*Lolita* and Pure Art." *EIC*, 24: 169-84 (Ap 74).

Berberova, Nina. "The Mechanics of *Pale Fire*." *TriQ*, 17: 147-59 (Wi 70).

————. "N in the Thirties." *TriQ*, 17: 220-33 (Wi 70).

Bishop, Morris. "N at Cornell." *TriQ*, 17: 234-9 (Wi 70).

Bitsilli, P.M. "The Revival of Allegory." *TriQ*, 17: 102-18 (Wi 70).

Bok, Sissela. "Redemption through Art in N's *Ada*." *Critique*, 12: 110-20 (1971).

Brent, Harold. "*Lolita*: N's Critique of Aloofness." *PLL*, 11: 71-2 (1975).

Bronski, M. "VN (W 75-ta rocznice urodzin)." *KulturaP*, 319: 15-32 (1974).

Bruffee, K.A. "Form and Meaning in N's *Real Life of Sebastian Knight*: An Example of Elegiac Romance." *MLQ*, 34: 180-90 (Je 73).

Campbell, F.F. "A Princedom by the Sea." *LHR*, 10: 39-46 (1968).

Cherry, Kenneth. "N's Kingdom by the Sea." *SR*, 83: 713-20 (Fa 75).

Clark, G.P. "A Further Word on Poe and *Lolita*." *PN*, 3: 39 (D 70).

Cohen, Jeats. "'So Help Me, Will.'" *Pucred*, 1: 1-4 (D 72).

Christopher, J.R. "On *Lolita* as a Mystery Story." *ArmD*, 7: 29 (1973).

de Jonge, Alex. "Figuring out N." *TLS*, 16 My 75, pp. 526-7.

Ditsky, J.M. "Carried Away by Numbers: The Rhapsodic Mode in Modern Fiction." *QQ*, 79: 482-94 (1972).

Elkin, Stanley. "Three Meetings." *TriQ*, 17: 261-5 (1970).

Fink, Howard. "The Ambiguous Mirrors of N." *CSS*, 5: 85-9 (1971).

Fleischauer, J.F. "Simultaneity in N's Prose Style." *Style*, 5: 57-69 (1971).

Flower, Dean. "The Annotated *Lolita*." *MR*, 13: 498-505 (1972).

Flower, T.F. "The Scientific Art of N's *Pale Fire*." *Criticism*, 17: 223-33 (1975).

Foster, L.A. "N in Russian Emigré Criticism." *RLT*, 3: 330-41 (1972).

Frederiksen, Leif. "Skakspillet i den engelske litteratur med saerligt henblik pa Samuel Beckett og VN." *Extracta*, 4: 92-4 (1972).

Friendly, Alfred. "N the Collector." *NYT*, 10 My 70, pp. 32-3.

Fromberg, Susan. "The Unwritten Chapters in *The Real Life of Sebastian Knight*." *MFS*, 13: 427-42 (Wi 67-68).

Gezari, J.K. "Roman et problème chez N." *Poétique*, 17: 96-113 (1974).

Godshalk, W.L. "N's Byronic *Ada*: A Note." *NCLit*, 2: 2-4 (Mr 72).

Goldhurst, William, Alfred Appel, Jr., and G.P. Clark. "Three Observations on 'Amontillado' and *Lolita*." *PoeS*, 5: 51 (1972).

Gonzalez, M.P. "Apostillas VN." *CA*, 184: 225-44 (1972).

Gordon, Ambrose. "VN." *ConL*, 9: 419-22 (1968).

Gorlier, Claudio. "N, gioco e parodia." *Approdo*, 65: 129-31 (1974).

Grabes, Herbert. "VN's *The Real Life of Sebastian Knight*: Zum Verhaltnis von Fiktion und wirklichkeit in der literarischen Biographie." *Poetica*, 5: 374-87 (1972).

Grams, Paul. "*Pnin*: The Biographer as Meddler." *RLT*, 3: 360-9 (1972).

Gregg, Larry. "Slava Snabokovu." *RLT*, 3: 313-29 (1972).

Harold, Brent. "*Lolita*: N's Critique of Aloofness." *PLL*, 11: 71-82 (Wi 75).

Heidenry, John. "V in Dreamland." *Cweal*, 90: 231-4 (9 My 69).

Homberger, Eric. "N." *TLS*, 26 Mr 71, p. 353.

Hughes, Daniel. "N: Spiral and Glass." *Novel*, 1: 178-85 (Wi 68).

Hughes, R.P. "Notes on the Translation of *Invitation to a Beheading*." *TriQ*, 17: 284-92 (Wi 70).

Hyman, S.E. "The Handle: *Invitation to a Beheading* and *Bend Sinister*." *TriQ*, 17: 60-71 (Wi 70).

Jenkins, W.D. "This Case Deserves to be a Classic." *BakSJ*, 24: 9-11 (Mr 74).

Johnson, E.B. "N's *Ada* and Puskin's *Eugene Onegin*." *SEEJ*, 15: 316-23 (1971).

———. "Parody and Myth: Flaubert, Joyce, and N." *FWF*, 1: 149-74 (My 74).

———. "Synesthesia, Polychromatism, and N." *RLT*, 3: 378-97 (1972).

Joyce, James. "Lolita in Humberland." *StN*, 6: 339-48 (Fa 74).

Kaplan, Fred. "Victorian Modernists: Fowles and N." *JNT*, 3: 108-20 (My 73).

Karlinsky, Simon. "*Anya in Wonderland*: N's Russified Lewis Carroll." *TriQ*, 17: 310-5 (Wi 70).

———. "N and Chekov: The Lesser Russian Tradition." *TriQ*, 17: 7-16 (Wi 70).

———. "N's Russian Games." *NYT*, 18 Ap 71, pp. 2-18.

Kazin, Alfred. "Absurdity as Contemporary Style." *MeditR*, 1: 39-46 (Sp 71).

———. "In the Mind of N." *SatR*, 52: 27-9, 35 (10 My 69).

Khodasevich, Vladislav. "On Sirin." *TriQ*, 17: 96-101 (Wi 70).

LeClair, Thomas. "Poe's *Pym* and N's *Pale Fire*." *NCLit*, 3: 2-3 (Mr 73).

Leonard, Jeffrey. "In Place of Lost Time: *Ada*." *TriQ*, 17: 136-46 (Wi 70).

Levy, Alan. "Understanding VN—A Red Autumn Leaf Is a Red Autumn Leaf, Not a Deflowered Nymphet." *NYTMS*, 31 O 71, pp. 20-41.

Lewald, H.E. "Antecedents y claves para *El fuego pálido de N*." *Su*, 322-3: 199-207 (1970).

Louria, Yvette. "N and Proust: The Challenge of Time." *BA*, 48: 469-76 (Su 74).

Lubin, Peter. "Kickshaws and Motley." *TriQ*, 17: 187-208 (Wi 70)

McDonald, James. "John Ray, Jr., Critic and Artist: The Foreword to *Lolita*." *StN*, 5: 352-7 (Fa 73).

McElroy, Joseph. "The N Factor." *SatR*, 1: 34-5 (Ja 73).

McLaughlin, Richard. "N: A Series of Mirrors." *B&B*, 16: 18-21 (My 71).

McLellan, J.M. "N and the Novel of 'Melodramatic Fantasy." *Fu Jen Stud*, 5: 57-79 (1972).

Mizener, Arthur. "The Seriousness of VN." *SR*, 76: 655-64 (Au 68).

Monter, B.H. "'Spring i Fialta': The Choice That Mimics Chance." *TriQ*, 17: 128-35 (Wi 70).

Moynahan, Julian. "*Lolita* and Related Memories." *TriQ*, 17: 247-52 (Wi 70).

———. "A Russian Preface for N's *Beheading*." *Novel*, 1: 12-8 (Fa 67).

Nabokov, Vladimir. "Anniversary Notes." *TriQ*, 17: 1-15 (Mr 70).

Naumann, M.T. "N as Viewed by Fellow Emigres." *RLJ*, 99: 18-26 (1974).

Nicol, C.D. "Pnin's History." *Novel*, 4: 197-208 (1971).

Nilsson, N.A. "Fanger i spegelvarlden: Kring VNs författarskap." *Ord och Bild*, 77: 29-32 (1968).

———. "A Hall of Mirrors: N and Olesha." *Scando-Slavica (Copenhagen)*, 15: 5-12 (1969).

Noel, E.L.L. "Playback." *TriQ*, 17: 209-19 (Wi 70).

Olcott, Anthony. "The Author's Special Intention: A Study of *The Real Life of Sebastian Knight.*" *RLT*, 3: 342-59 (1972).

Olszewska, E.S., and S.A.C. Ross. "'Hong Kong' in Croquet." *N&Q*, 15: 303-3 (Ag 68).

Page, Andrew. "VN: In Tribute to Sherlock Holmes." *BakSJ*, 24: 12-4 (Mr 74).

Parry, Albert. "Introducing N to America." *TQ*, 14: 16-27 (Sp 71).

Pifer, E.I. "N's *Invitation to a Beheading*: The Parody of a Tradition." *PCP*, 5: 46-53 (1970).

Pilon, Kevin. "A Chronology of *Pale Fire.*" *RLT*, 3: 370-7 (1972).

Plard, Henri. "Notes en marge de *Lolita.*" *RLV*, 40: 474-82 (Jl-Ag 74).

Prioleau, Elizabeth. "Humbert Humbert *Through the Looking Glass.*" *TCL*, 21: 428-37 (D 75).

Proffer, C.R. "*Ada* as Wonderland: A Glossary of Allusions to Russian Literature." *RLT*, 3: 399-430 (1972).

———. "A New Deck for N's Knaves." *TriQ*, 17: 293-309 (Wi 70).

Proffer, Ellendea. "N's Russian Readers." *TriQ*, 17: 253-60 (Wi 70).

Proffitt, Edward. "A Clue to John Ray, Jr." *MFS*, 20: 551-2 (Wi 74-75).

Pryce-Jones, Alan. "The Art of N." *HM*, 226: 97-101 (Ap 63).

Purdy, S.B. "Solus Rex: N and the Chess Novel." *MFS*, 14: 379-95 (Wi 68-69).

Raban, Jonathan. "Transparent Likenesses." *Encounter*, 4: 74-8 (S 73).

Rackin, Donald. "The Moral Rhetoric of N's *Lolita.*" *FourQ*, 22: 3-19 (Sp 73).

Reisner, T.A. "N's *Speak, Memory*, Chapter III, Section 4." *Expl*, 33: 18 (O 74).

Ronai, Paulo. "No mundo da traducao: O caso N." *MGSL*, 31: 12 (Ag 74).

Rosenbaum-Dovev, Leah. "Parash Bli Rosh Etzel N: Korot Motiv Ehad Baantobiographia shel VN *Dvar Zicaron.*" *Keshet*, 58: 43-55 (Wi 73).

Rosenfield, Claire. "The Shadow Within: The Conscious and Unconscious Use of Double." *Daedalus*, 92: 326-44 (Sp 63).

Roth, P.A. "The Psychology of the Double in N's *Pale Fire.*" *EC*, 2: 209-29 (Fa 75).

———. "In Search of Aesthetic Bliss: A Rereading of *Lolita.*" *Col Lit*, 2: 28-49 (Wi 75).

Rowe, William. "Gogolesque Perception—Expanding Reversals in N." *SlavR*, 30: 110-20 (1971).

Rubman, L.H. "Creatures and Creators in *Lolita* and 'Death and the Compass.'" *MFS*, 19: 433-52 (1973).

Schaeffer, S.F. "*Bend Sinister* and the Novelist as Anthropmorphic Deity." *CentR*, 17: 115-51 (Sp 73).

———. "The Editing Blinks of VN's *The Eye.*" *UWR*, 8: 5-30 (Fa 72).

Scheid, Mark. "Epistemological Structures in *Lolita.*" *RUS*, 61: 127-40 (#1 75).

Scott, W.B. "The Cypress Veil." *TriQ*, 17: 316-31 (Wi 70).

Seiden, Melvin. "N and Dostoevsky." *ConL*, 13: 43-44 (Au 72).

*Sheehan, Donald. "Selected Bibliography of N's Work." *WSCL*, 8: 310-1 (Sp 67).

Shuman, Samuel. "VN's *Invitation to a Beheading* and Robert Heinlein's *They.*" *TCL*, 19: 99-106 (Ap 73).

Stark, John. "Borges' 'Tlön, Uqbar, Orbis Tertius' and N's *Pale Fire*: Literature of Exhaustion." *TSLL*, 14: 139-45 (Sp 72).

Steinberg, Saul, and others. "Tributes." *TriQ*, 17: 332-71 (Wi 70).

Steiner, George. "Extraterritorial." *TriQ*, 17: 119-27 (Wi 70).

Struve, Gleb. "N's *Mashenka.*" *TLS*, 16 Ap 71, p. 449.

Stuart, Dabney. "All the Mind's a Stage: A Reading of *Invitation to a Beheading*, by VN." *UWR*, 4: 1-24 (Sp 69).

————. "*Laughter in the Dark*: Dimensions of Parody." *TriQ*, 17: 72-95 (Wi 70).

————. "The Novelist's Composure: *Speak, Memory* as Fiction." *MLQ*, 36: 177-92 (Je 75).

————. "*The Real Life of Sebastian Knight*: Angles of Perception." *MLQ*, 29: 312-28 (S 68).

Swanson, R.A." "N's *Ada's* Science Fiction." *S-FS*, 2: 76-87 (1975).

Twitchell, James. "*Lolita* as Bildungsroman." *Genre*, 7: 272-8 (S 74).

Wagner, Geoffrey. "VN and the Redemption of Reality." *CimR*, 10: 16-23 (1970).

Weber, Alfred. "*Ada*: A Style and Its Implications." *RecL*, 1: 54-65 (Sp 73).

Weil, Irwin. "Odyssey of a Translator." *TriQ*, 17: 266-83 (Wi 70).

Wetzsteon, Ross. "N as Teacher." *TriQ*, 17: 240-6 (Wi 70).

White, Edmund. "The Esthetics of Bliss." *SatR*, 1: 33-4 (Ja 73).

Williams, C.T. "N's Dozen Short Stories: His World in Microcosm." *SSF*, 12: 213-22 (Su 75).

Williams, R.C. "Memory's Defense: The Real Life of VN's Berlin." *YR*, 60: 241-50 (1971).

Winston, Mathew. "*Lolita* and the Dangers of Fiction." *TCL*, 21: 421-7 (1975).

Zaslove, Jerald. "N in Context." *RecL*, 1: 23-38 (#1 73).

Nasby, Petroleum V. (see **Locke, David Ross**).

Nash, Ogden. Cigman, Gloria. "Language and Laughter." *E&S*, 24: 101-22 (1971).

Hasley, Louis. "The Golden Trashery of O Nashery." *ArQ*, 27: 241-50 (1971).

Nathan, Robert. Magarick, Pat. "The Gentle Novels of RN." *ABC*, 23: 15-7 (#4 73).

Neal, John. Badin, D.A. "L'opera critica di JN." *SA*, 15: 7-31 (1969).

Lease, Benjamin. "JN and Edgar Allan Poe." *PoeS*, 7: 38-41 (1974).

————. "Robert Carter, James Russell Lowell and JN: A Document." *JA*, 13: 246-8 (1968).

————. "William Gimore Simms, A New Letter." *GHQ*, 54: 427-30 (Fa 70).

Neihardt, John G. Black, W.E. "Ethic and Metaphysic: A Study of JG.N." *WAL*, 2: 205-12 (Fa 67).

Lee, F.L. "JG.N: The Man and His Western Writings: The Bancroft Years, 1900-1921." *Trail Guide*, 17: 3-35 (D 73).

McCluskey, Sally. "*Black Elk Speaks*, and So Does JN." *WAL*, 6: 231-42 (FA 72).

Neihardt, J.G. "The Book That Would Not Die." *WAL*, 6: 227-30 (Fa 72).

Rothwell, K.S. "In Search of a Western Epic: N, Sandburg, and Jaffe as Regionalists and 'Astoriadists.'" *KanQ*, 2: 53-63 (1970).

Slote, B.D. "N: Nebraska's Poet Laureate." *PrS*, 41: 178-81 (Su 67).

Whitney, Blair. "JG.N: A Poet Speaks on General Education." *UCQ*, 19: 16-9 (Mr 74).

Nemerov, Howard. Bernlef, J. "Tussen oog en licht: Over HN en Richard Wilbur." *Gids*, 137: 217-25 (1974).

Boyers, Robert. "An Interview with HN." *Salmagundi*, 31-2: 109-19 (1975).

Burke, Kenneth. "Comments on Eighteen Poems by HN." *SR*, 60: 117-31 (Ja 52).

Cargas, H.J. "An Interview with HN." *Webster R*, 1: 34-9 (1974).

Kiehl, J.M. "On HN." *Salmagundi*, 22-3: 234-57 (1973).

————. "The Poems of HM: Where Loveliness Adorns Intelligent Things." *Salmagundi*, 22-3: 234-57 (1973).

Oates, C.J. "Finding again the World." *UWR*, 4: 70-6 (Sp 69).

Randall, Julia. "Genius and the Shore: The Poetry of HN." *HC*, 4: 1-12 (Je 69).

Robinson, J.K. "Sailing Close-hauled and into the Wreck." *APR*, 4: 4-7 (#2 75).

Skully, James. "The Audience Swam for Their Lives." *Nation*, 198: 244 (9 Mr 64).

Smith, Raymond. "N and Nature: The Stillness in Moving Things." *SoR*, 10: 153-69 (Ja 74).

Stock, Robert. "The Epistemological Vision of HN." *Parnassus*, 2: 153-63 (Fa-Wi 73).

Nin, Anais. Anon. "A Conversation with AN." *Second Wave*, 1: 10-6 (Su 71).

Amoia, Alba. "The Novel of the Future." *STC*, 6: 109-17 (Fa 70).

Baroche, Christiane. "Critique." *NRF*, 267: 92-5 (Mr 75).

Benstock, Bernard. "The Present Recaptured: D.H. Lawrence and Others." *SoR*, 4: 802-16 (1968).

Brodsley, Laurel. "AN and the Novel of the Future." *Delta*, 48: 35-9 (Mr 71).

Durand, Régis. "AN et le 'langage des nerfs.'" *LanM*, 64: 289-96 (Jl-Ag 70).

Freeman, Barbara. "A Dialogue with AN." *ChiQ*, 24: 29-35 (1972).

Griffith, Paul. "The 'Jewels' of AN." *JORA*, 5: 82-91 (1970).

Hauser, Marianne. "AN: Myth and Reality." *STC*, 1: 45-50 (Fa 68).

Hinz, E.J. "AN: A Reader and the Writer." *CRAS*, 6: 118-27 (Sp 75).

Jason, P.K. "Teaching *A Spy in the House of Love*." *Pisces*, 2: 7-15 (1971).

Killoh, E.P. "The Woman Writer and the Element of Destruction." *CE*, 34: 31-8 (O 72).

Kuntz, P.G. "Art as Public Dreams: The Practice and Theory of AN." *JAAC*, 32: 525-37 (1974).

Kyria, Pierre. "AN." *NL*, 20 Ag 71, p. 7.

Lhoste, Pierre. "AN: Mes amis et leurs démons." *NL*, Ja 71, p. 6.

McBrien, William. "AN: An Interview." *TCL*, 20: 277-90 (O 74).

McEvilly, Wayne. "The Bread of Tradition: Reflections on the Diary of AN." *PrS*, 45: 161-7 (Su 71).

———. "Dos Rostros de la muerte en *Seduccion del minotauro*, de AN." *Sur*, 322-3: 233-47 (1970).

———. "Portrait of AN as a Bodhisattva: Reflections on the Diary." *STC*, 1: 51-60 (Fa 68).

Nin, Anais. "Notes on Feminism." *MR*, 13: 25-8 (1972).

———. "On Feminism and Creation." *MQR*, 13: 4-13 (1974).

———. "From the Fourth Journal." *BUJ*, 19: 7-10 (1971).

———. "Genesis of the Diary." *Voyages*, 2: 5-13 (Fa 68).

Owen, Peter. "AN." *TLS*, 19 My 72, p. 577.

Schneider, Duane. "The Art of AN." *SoR*, 6: 506-14 (Ap 70).

Stern, Daniel. "The Diary of AN." *STC*, 1: 39-43 (Fa 68).

Tytell, V.J. "AN and 'The Fall of the House of Usher.'" *Pisces*, 2: 5-11 (1971).

Wakoski, Diane. "A Tribute to AN." *APR*, 2: 46-7 (#3 73).

Young, Marguerite. "AN." *Voyages*, 1: 63-5 (Fa 67).

Zaller, R.M. "AN and the Truth of Feeling." *ASoc*, 10: 308-12 (1973).

*Zee, N.S. "A Checklist of N Materials at Northwestern University Library." *Pisces*, 3: 3-11 (Sp 72).

———. "Towards a Definition of the Woman Artist: Notes on the Diaries of AN." *OyR*, 8: 49-55 (Wi 73).

Noah, Mordecai Manuel. Gordis, Robert. "MMN: A Centenary Evaluation." *Pub Am Jewish Hist Soc*, 40: 407 (1951).

Page, E.F. "The Romance of Southern Journalism." *Taylor-Trotwood Mag*, 11: 140-8 (Je 10).

Spitz, Leon. "Pioneers of the American Theatre." *Am Hebrew*, 160: 75, 78-9, 82 (1950).

Norris, Charles. Goldsmith, A.L. "C and Frank N." *WAL*, 2: 30-49 (Sp 67).

Norris, Frank. Ahnebrink, Lars. "The Influence of Emile Zola on FN." *ESALL*, 5: 1-66 (194).

Astro, Richard. "*Vandover and the Brute* and *The Beautiful and Damned*." *MFS*, 14: 397-413 (Wi 69).

Budd, L.J. "Objectivity and Low Seriousness in American Naturalism." *Prospects*, 1: 45-51 (1975).

Burns, S.L. "The Rapist in FN's *The Octopus*." *AL*, 42: 567-9 (Ja 71).

Crow, C.L. "The Real Vanamee and His Influence on FN' *The Octopus*." *WAL*, 9: 131-40 (Su 74).

Davidson, R.A. "FN's Thirteen Uncollected Letters." *N&Q*, 11: 71-3 (F 64).

———. "The Remaining Seven of FN's 'Weekly Letters.'" *ALR*, 3: 47-65 (Su 68).

———. "An Undiscovered Early Review of N's *Octopus*." *WAL*, 3: 147-51 (Su 68).

———. "An Unpublished N Discussion of Kipling." *AN&Q*, 4: 87 (F 66).

*French, Warren. "FN (1870-1902)." *ALR*, 1: 90-2 (Fa 67).

Fried, Lewis. "The Golden Brotherhood of *McTeague*." *SAF*, 3: 143-55 (1975).

Gardner, J.H. "Dickens, Romance, and *McTeague*: A Study in Mutual Interpretaton." *EL*, 1: 69-82 (Sp 74).

Giles, J.R. "Beneficial Atavism in FN and Jack London." *WAL*, 4: 15-28 (Sp 69).

———. "Some Notes on the Red-Blooded Reading of Kipling by Jack London and FN." *JLN*, 3: 56-62 (1970).

Goldman, S.B. "*McTeague*: The Imagistic Network." *WAL*, 7: 83-99 (Sp 72).

Graham, D.B. "Aesthetic Experience in Realism." *ALR*, 8: 289-90 (Su 75).

———. "Art in *MacTeague*." *SAF*, 3: 143-55 (Au 75).

———. "FN's Afternoon of a Faun." *PLL*, 10: 307-11 (Su 74).

———. "Studio Art in *The Octopus*." *AL*, 44: 657-66 (Ja 73).

Hill, J.S. "The Influence of Cesare Lombroso on FN's Early Fiction." *AL*, 42: 89-91 (Mr 70).

Isani, M.A. "FN on the Purpose of *McTeague*." *AN&Q*, 10: 118 (Ap 72).

———. "Jack London on N's *The Octopus*." *ALR*, 6: 66-9 (Wi 73).

Johnson, L.A. "Western Literary Realism: The California Tales of N and Austin." *ALR*, 7: 278-80 (Su 74).

Kane, Norman. "Corrrections in the Publisher's Copy of *The Pit*." *PBSA*, 66: 435 (4 Q 72).

Katz, Joseph. "The Elusive Criticism Syndicated by FN." *Proof*, 3: 221-51 (1973).

———. "FN and 'The Newspaper Experience.'" *ALR*, 4: 73-7 (Wi 71).

———. "FN's Replies to Autograph Collectors." *QNL*, 34: 58-60 (1969).

———. "The Manuscript of FN's *McTeague*: A Preliminary Census of Pages." *RALS*, 2: 91-7 (Sp 72).

———. "The Shorter Publications of FN: A Checklist." *Proof*, 3: 155-220 (1973).

———, and J.J. Mannning. "Notes on FN's Revisions of Two Novels: I. McTeague II. A Man's Woman." *PBSA*, 62: 256-9 (2Q 68).

Kazin, Alfred. "Three Pioneer Realists." *SatR*, 20: 3-4, 14-5 (8 Jl 39).

Labrie, R.E. "The Howells-N Relationship and the Growth of Naturalism." *Disc*, 11: 363-71 (Su 68).

Lindeen, S.A., and J.W. Lindeen. "Bryan, N and the Doctrine of Party Responsibility." *MASJ*, 11: 45-53 (1970).

McCluskey, J.E. "FN' Literary Terminology: A Note on Historical Context." *WAL*, 7: 148-50 (Su 72).

*McElrath, J.R. "FN." *ALR*, 8: 307-19 (1975).

———. "N's Return from Cuba." *ALR*, 6: 251 (Su 73).

Pizer, Donald. "The Problem of Philosophy in the Novel." *BuR*, 18: 53-62 (Sp 70).

Recchia, E.J. "Naturalism's Artistic Compromises in *Sister Carrie* and *The Octopus*." *IWU*, 5: 277-85 (1972).

Sheppard, K.S. "A New Note for McTeague's Canary." *WAL*, 9: 217-8 (Fa 74).

Spangler, G.M. "Eliot's 'red rock' and N's *McTeague*." *N&Q*, 21: 330-1 (1973).

Stronks, J.B. "FN's *McTeague*: A Possible Source in H.C. Bunner." *NCF*, 25: 474-8 (Mr 71).

———. "A New FN Newsletter." *QNL*, 38: 40-2 (Sp 73).

———. "John Kendrick Bangs Criticizes N's Borrowings in *Blix*." *AL*, 42: 380-6 (N 70).

Swennson, J.K. "'The Great Corner in Hannibal and St. Jo.': A Previously Unpublished Short Story by FN." *ALR*, 4: 205-26 (Su 71).

Tsunematsu, Maso. "*McTeague*: A Probe Into Man's Dualism." *SALit*, 7: 57-66 (1971).

Vance, W.L. "Romance in *The Octopus*." *Genre*, 3: 111-36 (1970).

Walker, Franklin. "An Additional FN Letter." *QNL*, 36: 60-2 (Su 71).

Watson, C.S. "A Source for the Ending of *McTeague*." *ALR*, 5: 173-4 (Sp 72).

Woodward, R.H. "FN and Frederic: A Source for *McTeague*." *FH*, 2: 2 (Ap 68).

Wyatt, B.N. "Naturalism as Expediency in the Novels of FN." *MarkR*, 2: 83-7 (F 71).

Nye, Bill. Bakerville, Barnet. "19th Century Burlesque of Oratory." *AQ*, 20: 726-43 (Wi 68).

Hasley, Louis. "The Durable Humor of BN." *MTJ*, 15: 7-19 (Wi 70-71).

Lanier, Doris. "Bill Nye in the South." *An of Wyoming*, 46: 253-62 (Fa 74).

———. "James Whitcomb Riley, BN, and Harry Stilwell Edwards: A Lecture Tour." *GHQ*, 57Z: 256-64 (Su 73).

Oakes, Urian Bowden, E.T. "UO's 'Elegy': Colonial Literature and History." *Forum*, 10: 38 (1972).

Hahn, T.G. "UO's *Elegie* on Thomas Shepard and Puritan Poetics." *AL*, 45: 163-81 (My 73).

Kaiser, L.M. "The *Oratorio Quinta* of UO, Harvard, 1678." *HLB*, 19: 485-508 (1970).

———. "Tercentenary of an Oration: The 1672 Commencement Address of UO." *HLB*, 21: 75-87 (1973).

———. "The Unpublished *Oratio Secunda* of UO, Harvard, 1675." *HLB*, 21: 385-412 (1972).

Scheick, W.J. "Standing in the Gap: UO's Elegy on Thomas Shepard." *EAL*, 9: 301-6 (Wi 75).

O. Henry. (see **Porter, W.S.**)

Oates, Joyce Carol. Anon. "Transformation of Self: An Interview with JCO." *Critique*, 15: 29-35 (1Q 72).

———. "Transformations of Self: An Interview with JCO." *OhR*, 15: 51-61 (Fa 73).

Abrahams, William. "Stories of a Visionary." *SatR*, 55: 76, 80 (O 72).

Allen, Bruce. "Intrusions of Consciousness." *HudR*, 28: 611-15 (Wi 75).

Andersen, Sally. "The Poetry of JCO." *Spirit*, 39: 24-9 (1972).

Bender, E.T. "JCO's Marriages and Infidelities." *Sounding*, 58: 390-406 (1975).

Burwell, R.M. "Fear, Love, and Art in O's 'Plot.'" *Critique*, 15: 48-58 (#1 73).

———. "JCO and an Old Master." *Critique*, 15: 48-58 (1Q 73).

———. "The Process of Individuation as Narrative Structure: JCO's *Do With Me What You Will*." *Critique*, 17: 93-106, (3Q 75).

Clemons, Walter. "JCO at Home." *NYTBR*, 28 S 69, pp. 4-5, 48.

———. "JCO: Love and Violence." *Nwk*, 80: 72-4, 77 (11 D 72).

Dalton, Elizabeth. "JCO: Violence in the Head." *Commentary*, 49: 75-7 (Je 70).

DeMott, Benjamin. "The Necessity in Art of a Reflective Intelligence." *SatR*, 52: 71-3, 89 (22 N 69).

Dike, Donald A. "The Aggressive Victim in the Early Fiction of JCO." *Greyfriar*, 15: 13-29 (1974).

Giles, J.R. "The 'Marivaudian Being' Drowns His Children: Dehumanization in Donald Barthelme's 'Robert Kennedy Saved from Drowning,' and JCO's *Wonderland*." *SHR*, 9: 63-75 (Wi 75).

Fossum, Robert. "Only Control: The Novels of JCO." *StN*, 7: 285-97 (Su 75).

Ivanescu, Miracea. "Un profil: JCO." *SXX*, 15: 140-2 (1972).

Kuehl, Linda. "An Interview with JCO." *Cweal*, 91: 307-10 (5 D 69).

Lundkvist, Arthur. "Mardrommer och spex." *BLM*, 42: 276-81 (1973).

*McCormick, L.P. "A Bibliography of Works by and about JCO." *AL*, 43: 124-32 (Mr 71).

Oates, J.C. "Disguised Fiction." *PMLA*, 89: 580-1 (1974).

———. "New Heaven and Earth." *SatR*, 55: 51-4 (N 72).

———. "The Short Stroy." *SHR*, 5: 213-4 (1971).

Pickering, S.F. "The Short Stories of JCO." *GaR*, 28: 218-26 (Su 74).

Pinsker, Sanford. "Isaac Bashevis Singer and JCO: Some Versions of Gothic." *SoR*, 9: 895-908 (Au 73).

Sullivan, Walter. "The Artificial Demon: JCO and the Dimensions of the Real." *HC*, 9: 1-12 (1972).

———. "Old Age, Death, and Other Modern Landscapes: Good and Indifferent Fables for Our Time." *SR*, 82: 138-47 (1974).

Walker, Carolyn. "Fear, Love and Art in O's 'Plot'" *Critique*, 15: 59-70 (1Q 73).

Walker, G.F. "JCO's *Wonderland*: An Introduction." *DR*, 54: 480-90 (Au 74).

Wegs, J.M. "'Don't You Know Who I Am?': The Grotesque in O's 'Where are You Going, Where Have You Been.'" *JNarT*, 5: 66-72 (Ja 75).

O'Brien, Fitz-James. Dimeo, Steven. "Psychological Symbolism in Three Early Tales of Invisibility." *RQ*, 5: 20-7 (Jl 71).

O'Connor, Edwin. Dillon, David. "Priests and Politicians: The Fiction of EO." *Critique*, 16: 108-20 (#2 74).

Haslam, Gerald. "*The Last Hurrah* and American Bossism." *Rendezvous*, 8: 33-44 (Su 73).

Kelleher, J.V. "EO'C and the Irish-American Process." *Atl*, 22: 48-52 (Jl 68).

Rank, Hugh. "FO'C's Image of the Priest." *NEQ*, 41: 3-29 (Mr 68).

O'Connor, Flannery. Abbot, L.H. "Remembering FO'C." *SLJ*, 2: 3-25 (Sp 70).

Asals, Frederick. "FO'C as Novelist: A Defense." *FOB*, 3: 23-9 (Au 74).

———. "FO'C's 'The Lame Shall Enter First." *MissQ*, 23: 103-20 (Sp 70).

———. "F Row." *Novel*, 4: 92-6 (Fa 70).

———. "Hawthorne, Mary Ann, and 'The Lame Shall Enter First.'" *FOB*, 2: 3-19 (Au 73).

———. "The Mythic Dimensions of FO'C's 'Greenleaf.'" *SSF*, 5: 317-30 (Sp 69).

———. "The Road to *Wise Blood*." *Renascence*, 21: 181-94 (Su 69).

Barcus, N.B. "Psychological Determinism and Freedom in FO'C." *Cithara*, 12: 26-33 (1Q 72).

Bass, Eben. "FO'C and Henry James: The Vision of Grace." *STC*, 14: 43-68 (Fa 74).

Becham, Gerald. "FO'C Collection." *FOB*, 1: 66-71 (1972).

Bergman, Paul. "Three Wise Men." *C&L*, 24: 36-48 (1975).

Bergup, B.O.S.B. "Themes of Redemptive Grace in the Works of FO'C." *ABR*, 21: 169-91 (1970).

Blackwell, Louise. "FO'C's Literary Style." *AntigR*, 10: 57-65 (Su 72).

———. "Humor and Irony in the Works of FO'C." *Ranam*, 4: 61-8 (1971).

Bleikasten, André. "Aveugles et voyants: Le thème du regard dans *Wise Blood*." *BFLS*, 47: 291-301 (Ja 69).

———. "Théologie at dérision chez FO'C." *LanM*. 64: 28-38 (Mr-Ap 70).

Bliven, Naomi. "Nothing But the Truth." *NY*, 41: 220-1 (11 S 65).

Boulger, J.D. "Puritan Allegory in Four Modern Novels." *Thought*, 44: 413-32 (Au 69).

Brittain, J.T. "FO'C: Addenda." *BB*, 25: 123-4, 142 (My-Ag 68).

————, and L.V. Driskell. "O'C and the Eternal Crossroads." *Ren*, 22: 49-55 (Su 69).

Brown, Ashley. "Grotesque Occasions." *Spec*, 221: 330-2 (6 S 68).

Browning, P.M. "FO'C and the Demonic." *MFS*, 19: 29-41 (Sp 73).

Browning, Preston. "Parker's Back: FO'C's Iconography of Salvation by Profanity." *SSF*. 6: 525-35 (Fa 69).

Burns, S.L. "The Evolution of *Wise Blood*." *MFS*, 16: 147-62 (Su 70).

————. "How Wide Did 'The Heathen' Range?" *FOB*, 4: 25-41 (1975).

————. "FO'C's Literary Apprenticeship." *Ren*, 22: 3-16 (Au 69).

————. "FO'C's *The Violent Bear It Away*: Apotheosis in Failure." *SR*, 76: 319-36 (Sp 68).

————. "Freaks in a Circus Tent: FO'C's Christ-Haunted Characters." *FOB*, 1: 3-23 (1972).

————. "O'C and the Critics: An Overview." *MissQ*, 27: 483-95 (Fa 74).

————. "Structural Patterns in *Wise Blood*." *XUS*, 8: 32-43 (Jl 69).

Byrd, T.F. "Ironic Dimension in FO'C's 'The Artificial Nigger.'" *MissQ*, 21: 243-51 (Fa 68).

Carlson, T.M. "FO'C: The Manichaean Dilemma." *SR*, 77: 254-76 (Sp 69).

Cunningham, John. "Recent Works on FO'C." *SHR*, 8: 375-88 (Su 74).

Davis, Jack and June. "Tarwater and Jonah: Two Reluctant Prophets." *XUS*, 9: 19-27 (Sp 70).

Desmond, J.F. "The Lessons of History: FO'C's *Everything That Rises Must Converge*." *FOB*, 1: 39-45 (1972).

————. "The Mystery of the Word and the Act: *The Violent Bear It Away*." *ABR*, 24: 342-7 (1973).

————. "The Shifting of Mr. Shiftlet: FO'C's 'The Life You Save May Be Your Own.'" *MissQ*, 28: 55-9 (Wi 74-5).

Detweiler, Robert. "The Moment of Death in Modern Fiction." *ConL*, 13: 269-94 (1972).

Dorsey, James. "Carson McCullers and FO'C: A Checklist of Graduate Research." *BB*, 32: 162-67 (O-D 75).

Doxey, W.S. "A Dissenting Opinion of FO'C's 'A Good Man Is Hard to Find.'" *SSF*, 10: 199-204 (Sp 73).

Drake, Robert. "FO'C and American Literature." *FOB*, 3: 1-22 (Au 74).

————. "The Harrowing Evangel of FO'C." *ChrC*, 81: 1200-2 (30 S 64).

————. "The Paradigm of FO'C's True Country." *SSF*, 6: 433-42 (Su 69).

Driskell, L.V. "To FO'C." *SHR*, 3: 145 (Sp 69).

Dula, M.A. "Evidences of the Prelapsarian in FO'C's *Wise Blood*." *XUS*, 11: 1-12 (Wi 72).

Edelstein, M.G. "FO'C and the Problem of Modern Satire." *SSF*, 12: 139-44 (Sp 75).

Eggenschwiler, David. "FO'C's True and False Prophets." *Renascence*, 21: 151-161, 167 (Sp 69).

Esch, R.M. "O'C's 'Everything That Rises Must Converge.'" *Expl*, 27: 58 (Ap 69).

Evans, Elizabeth. "Three Notes on FO'C." *NCLit*, 3: 11-15 (My 73).

Fahey, W.A. "FO'C's 'Parker's Back.'" *Ren*, 20: 162-4, 166 (Sp 68).

Farnham, James F. "Disintegration of Myth in the Writings of FO'C." *ConnR*, 8: 11-9 (O 74).

Feeley, Sister M.K. "Thematic Imagery in the Fiction of FO'C." *SHR*, 3: 14-32 (Wi 68).

Flores-Del Prado, Wilma. "FO'C's Gallery of Freaks." *St. Louis Un R J*, 2: 463-514 (S-D 71).

Friedman, M.J. "By and About FO." *JML*, 1: 288-92 (1970).

————. "FO: The Canon Completed, the Commentary Continuing." *SLJ*, 5: 116-23 (Sp 73).

————. "John Hawkes and FO'C: The French Background." *BUJ*, 21: 34-44 (#3 73).

————. "FO'C: The Tonal Dilemma." *SLJ*, 6: 124-9 (Sp 74).

Gordon, Caroline, et al. "Panel Discussion." *FOB*, 3: 57-78 (1974).

————. "Heresy in Dixie." *SR*, 76: 263-97 (Sp 68).

————. "Rebels and Revolutionaries: The New American Scene." *FOB*, 3: 40-56 (Au 74).

Goss, James. "The Double Action for Mercy in 'The Artificial Nigger.'" *C&L*, 23: 36-45 (1974).

Gossett, Thomas. "FO'C on Her Fiction." *SWR*, 59: 34-42 (Wi 74).

————. "FO'C's Opinions of Other Writers: Some Unpublished Comments." *SLJ*, 6: 70-82 (Sp 74).

————. "No Vague Believer: FO'C and Protestantism." *SWR*, 60: 256-63 (Su 75).

Green, J.L. "Enoch Emery and His Biblical Namesakes in 'Wise Blood.'" *SSF*, 10: 417-9 (Fa 73).

Gregory, Donald. "Enoch Emery: Ironic Doubling in *Wise Blood.*" *FOB*, 4: 52-64 (1975).

Gresset, Michel. "L'audace de FO'C." *NRF*, 18: 61-71 (D 70).

Gullason, T.A. "[review of FO'C: *The Complete Stories*]." *SatR*, 54: 57, 63-4 (13 N 71).

Hamblen, A.A. "FO'C's Study of Innocence and Evil." *UR*, 34: 295-7 (Je 68).

Harrison, Margaret. "Hazel Motes in Transit: A Comparison of Two Versions of FO'C's 'The Train' with Chapter 1 of 'Wise Blood.'" *SSF*, 8: 287-93 (Sp 71).

Hays, P.L. "Dante, Tobit, and 'The Artificial Nigger.'" *SSF*, 5: 263-8 (Sp 68).

Hegarty, C.M. "A Man Though Not Yet a Whole One: Mr. Shiftlet's Genesis." *FOB*, 1: 24-38 (1972).

————. "A Note on FO'C." *SSF*, 9: 409-10 (1972).

Hendin, Josephine. "In Search of FO'C." *ColF*, 13: 38-41 (Sp 70).

Hicks, Granville. "Literary Horizons." *SatR*, 30 (10 My 69).

Howell, Elmo. "The Developing Art of FO'C." *ArQ*, 29: 266-76 (Au 73).

————. "FO'C and the Home Country." *Renascence*, 24: 171-6 (Su 72).

Ingram, F.L. "O'C's Seven-Story Cycle." *FOB*, 2: 19-28 (Au 73).

Ivanescu, Mircea. "FO'C." *RoLit*, 10 Ag 72, p. 28.

Jeremy, Sister. "The Comic Ritual of FO'C." *CathLW*, 39: 195-200 (N 67).

Jordan, Rene. "A Southern Drawl from beyond the Grave." *BAASB*, 12-3: 99-101 (1966).

Katz, Claire. "FO'C's Rage of Vision." *AL*, 46: 54-67 (Mr 74).

Keller, J.C. "The Figures of the Empiricist and the Rationalist in the Fiction of FO'C." *ArQ*, 28: 263-73 (1972).

Kellogg, Gene. "The Catholic Novel in Convergence." *Thought*, 45: 265-96 (1070).

Kieft, R.M.V. "Judgment in the Fiction of FO'C." *SR*, 76: 337-56 (Sp 68).

Kirkland, W.M. "FO'C: The Person and the Writer." *EWR*, 3: 159-63 (Su 67).

Klevar, Harvey. "Image and Imagination: FO'C's Front Page Fiction." *JML*, 4: 121-32 (S 74).

Kropf, C.R. "Theme and Setting in 'A Good Man Is Hard to Find.'" *Renascence*, 24: 177-80, 206 (Su 72).

*Lackey, A.D. "FO'C: A Supplemental Bibliography." *BB*, 30: 170-5 (O-D 73).

Lipper, Mark. "Blessed are the Destitute in FO'C." *Shippensburg St Col R*, nv: 20-3 (O 68).

Littlefield, D.F. "FO'C's *Wise Blood*: 'Unparalleled Prosperity' and Spiritual Chaos." *MissQ*, 23: 121-34 (Sp 70).

O'Connor, Flannery

Lorch, T.M. "FO'C: Christian Allegorist." *Critique*, 10: 69-80 (Sp 68).

McCullagh, J.C. "Aspects of Jansenism in FO'C's *Wise Blood.*" *StH*, 3: 12-6 (1973).

―――. "Symbolism and the Religious Aesthetic: FO'C's *Wise Blood.*" *FOB*, 2: 43-58 (Au 73).

McDowell, F.P.W. "Toward the Luminous and Numinous: The Art of FO'C." *SoR*, 9: 998-1013 (Au 73).

McDermott, John. "Julian's Journey into Hell: FO'C's Allegory of Pride." *MissQ*, 28: 171-9 (Sp 75).

McKenzie, Barbara. "FO'C Country." *GaR*, 29: 329-62 (1975).

Maida, P.D. "'Convergence' in FO'C's 'Everything That Rises Must Converge.'" *SSF*, 7: 549-55 (Fa 70).

Male, R.R. "The Two Versions of 'The Displaced Person.'" *SSF*, 7: 450-7 (Su 70).

Martin, Carter. "FO'C and Fundamental Poverty." *EJ*, 60: 458-61 (Ap 71).

Martin, C.W. "FO'C's Early Fiction." *SHR*, 7: 210-4 (Sp 73).

May, J.R. "FO'C and the New Hermeneutic." *FOB*, 2: 29-42 (Au 73).

―――. "FO'C: Critical Consensus and the 'Objective' Interpreters." *Renascence*, 27: 179-92 (Su 75).

―――. "Of Huckleberry Bushes and the New Hermeneutic." *Renascence*, 14: 85-95 (Wi 72).

―――. "The Pruning Word: FO'C's Judgment of Intellectuals." *SHR*, 4: 325-38 (Fa 70).

―――. "*The Violent Bear It Away*: The Meaning of the Title." *FOB*, 2: 83-6 (Au 73).

Mayer, D.R. "Apologia for the Imagination: FO'C's 'A Temple of the Holy Ghost.'" *SSF*, 11: 147-52 (Sp 74).

―――. "The Blazing Sun and the Relentless Shutter." *Christian Century*, 30: 435-40 (Ap 75).

―――. "*The Violent Bear It Away*: FO'C's Shaman." *SLJ*, 4: 41-54 (Sp 72).

Mellard, J.M. "Violence and Belief in Mauriac and O'C." *Renascence*, 26: 158-68 (Sp 74).

Milder, Robert. "The Protestantism of FO'C." *SoR*, 11: 802-819 (Au 75).

Millichap, J.R. "'The Pauline Old Man' in FO'C's 'The Comforts of Home.'" *SSF*, 11: 96-8 (Wi 74).

Montgomery, Marion. "Beyond Symbol and Surface: The Fiction of FO'C." *GaR*, 22: 188-95 (Su 68).

―――. "FO'C and the Natural Man." *MissQ*, 21: 235-42 (Fa 68).

―――. "FO'C: Prophetic Poet." *FOB*, 3: 79-94 (Au 74).

―――. "FO'C: Realist of Distances." *Ranam*, 4: 69-78 (1971).

―――. "FO'C's Imitation of Significant Action." *STC*, 3: 55-64 (Sp 69).

―――. "FO'C's 'Leaden Tract Against Complacency and *Contraception.*'" *ArQ*, 24: 133-46 (Su 68).

―――. "FO'C's Territorial Center." *Critique*, 11: 5-10 (1969).

―――. "FO'C's Transformation of the Sentimental." *MissQ*, 25: 1-18 (Wi 71-72).

―――. "In Defense of FO'C's Dragon." *GaR*, 25: 302-16 (Fa 71).

―――. "Miss Flannery's 'Good Man.'" *DQ*, 3: 1-19 (Au 68).

―――. "Miss O'C and the Christ-Haunted." *SoR*, 4: 665-72 (Jl 68).

―――. "A Note of FO'C's Terrible and Violent Prophecy of Mercy." *Forum(H)*, 7: 4-7 (Su 69).

―――. "O'C and Teilhard de Chardin: The Problem of Evil." *Renascence*, 22: 34-42 (Au 69).

―――. "On FO'C's 'Everything That Rises Must Converge." *Critique*, 13: 15-29 (1971).

―――. "Southern Reflections on Solzhenitsyn." *ModA*, 19: 190-7 (1975).

Muller, G.H. "The City of Woe: FO'C's Dantean Vision." *GaR*, 23: 206-13 (Su 69).

————. "*The Violent Bear It Away:* Moral and Dramatic Sense." *Renascence,* 22: 17-25 (Au 69).

Nance, W.L. "FO'C: The Trouble With Being a Prophet." *UR*, 36: 101-8 (Wi 69).

Oates, J.C. "The Visionary Art of FO'C." *SHR*, 7: 235-46 (Su 73).

O'Brien, John. "The Novel of Salvation." *Cresset*, 35: 12-15 (1972).

————. "The Un-Christianity of FO'C." *Listening*, 5: 71-81 (Wi 71).

Oppegard, S.H. "FO'C and the Backwoods Prophet." *AmNor*, 4: 305-25 (1973).

Orvell, M.D. "FO'C." *SR*, 78: 184-92 (Wi 70).

Pearce, H.D. "FO'C's Ineffable 'Recognitions.'" *Genre*, 6: 298-12 (S 73).

Prampolini, Gaetano. "FO'C: Una scrittrice cattolica della Georgia." *RLMC*, 23: 85-110 (1970).

————. "Poetica di FO'C." *SA*, 15: 321-9 (1969).

Presley, D.E. "The Moral Function of Distortion in Southern Grotesque." *SAB*, 37-46 (1972).

Quinn, J.J. "A Reading of FO'C." *Thought*, 48: 520-31 (1973).

Rank, Hugh. "O'C's Image of the Priest." *NEQ*, 41: 3-29 (1968).

Rubin, L.D. "FO'C." *Esprit*, 8: 44 (Wi 64).

Scouten, Kenneth. "The Mythological Dimensions of Five of FO'C's Works." *FOB*, 2: 59-72 (Au 73).

Shear, Walter. "FO'C: Character and Characterization." *Ren*, 20: 140-6 (Sp 68).

Shinn, T.V. "FO'C and the Violence of Grace." *ConL*, 9: 58-73 (Wi 68).

Smith, A.H. "O'C's 'Good Country People.'" *Expl*, 33: 30 (D 74).

Smith, F.J. "O'C's Religious Viewpoint in *The Violent Bear It Away.*" *Renascence*, 22: 108-12 (Wi 70).

Sonnenfeld, Albert. "FO'C: The Catholic Writer as Baptist." *ConL*, 13: 445-57 (Au 72).

Spivey, T.R. "Flannery's South: Don Quixote Strikes Again." *FOB*, 1: 46-53 (1972).

————. "Religion and the Reintegration of Man in FO'C and Walker Percy." *Spectrum*, 2: 67-79 (1972).

Stephens, Martha. "FO'C and the Sanctified-Sinner Tradition." *ArQ*, 24: 22-39 (Au 68).

Sullivan, Walter. "The Achievement of FO'C." *SHR*, 2: 303-9 (Su 68).

Tate, J.O. "The Uses of Banality." *FOB*, 4: 13-24 (1975).

Taylor, Henry. "The Halt Shall Be Gathered Together: Physical Deformity in the Fiction of FO'C." *WHR*, 22: 325-8 (Au 68).

Trowbridge, Clinton. "The Symbolic Vision of FO'C: Patterns of Imagery in *The Violent Bear It Away.*" *SR*, 76: 298-318 (Sp 68).

True, M.D. "FO'C: Backwoods Prophet in the Secular City." *PLL*, 5: 209-23 (1969).

Valensise, Rachele. "Tre scittrici del sud: FO'C, Caroline Gordon, Carson McCullers." *SA*, 17: 251-89 (1979).

Van de Kieft, R.M. "Judgement in the Fiction of FO'C." *SR* 76: 337-56 (Sp 68).

Walston, R.L. "Flannery: An Affectionate Recollection." *FOB*, 1: 55-60 (1972).

Wilson, J.D. "Luis Bū, FO'C and the Failure of Charity." *MinnR*, 4: 158-62 (Sp 73).

Woodward, R.H. "A Good Route is Hard to Find: Place Names and Setting in O'C's 'A Good Man Is Hard to Find.'" *NCLit*, 3: 2-5 (N 73).

Wylder, Jean. "FO'C: A Reminiscence and Some Leters." *NAR*, 7: 58-65 (Sp 70).

Wynne, Judith. "The Sacramental Irony of FO'C." *SLJ*, 7: 33-49 (Sp 75).

O'Connor, Frank. Brenner, Jerry. "FO'C, 1903-1966." *WCR*, 2: 55-64 (Fa 67).

May, C.E. "FO'C's Judas." *NCLit*, 2: 111-3 (N 72).

O'Connor, Harriet. "Listening to FO'C." *Nation*, 250: 150-1 (28 Ag 67).

O'Connor, Frank

Prosky, M. "The Pattern of Diminishing Certitude in the Stories of FO'C." *CLQ*, 9: 311-21 (J 71).

Odets, Clifford. Burt, D.J. "O's *Awake and Sing!*" *Expl*, 27: 29 (D 68).

Kaplan, Charles. "Two Depression Plays and Broadway's Popular Idealism." *AQ*, 15: 579-85 (Wi 63).

Pearce, Richard. "*Pylon, Awake and Sing!* and the Apocalyptic Imagination of the 30's." *Criticism*, 13: 131-41 (Sp 71).

Potter, Vilma. "Baldwin and O: The High Cost of 'Crossing.'" *CEJ*, 1: 37-41 (#5 65).

Shuman, R.B. "CO: A Playwright and His Jewish background." *SAQ*, 71: 225-33 (Sp 72).

———. "Thematic Consistency in O's Early Plays." *RLV*, 35: 415-20 (Jl-Ag 69).

Willett, Ralph. "CO and Popular Culture." *SAQ*, 69: 68-78 (Wi 70).

O'Hara, Frank. Altieri, Charles. 'The Significance of FO'H." *IowaR*, 4: 90-104 (Wi 73).

Koch, Kenneth. "All the Imagination Can Hold." *NRep*, 166: 23-5 (1, 8 Ja 72).

Molesworth, Charles. " 'The Clear Architecture of the Nerves': The Poetry of FO'H." *IR*, 6: 61-74 (#1 75).

Perloff, Marjorie. "New Thresholds, Old Anatomies, Contemporary Poetry and the Limits of Exegesis." *IR*, 5: 83-99 (1974).

Sayre, Joel. "FO'H: A Reminiscence." *BkW*, 18 Mr 73, p. 2.

Vendler, Helen. "The Virtues of the Alterable." *Parnassus*, 1: 5-20 (Fa-Wi 72).

O'Hara, John. Blažková, Anna. "JO'H American." *ČMF*, 54: 183-6 (1972).

Donaldson, Scott. "Appointment with the Dentist: O'H's Naturalistic Novel." *MFS*, 14: 435-42 (Wi 68-9).

Eppard, P.B. "Addenda to Bruccoli: *O'Hara*." *PBSA*, 68: 44-5 (O-D 74).

Kazin, Alfred. "O'H, Cheever & Updike." *NYRB*, 20: 14-9 (19 Ap 73).

McCormick, Bernard. "A JO'H Geography." *JML*, 1: 151-68 (1970-71).

Ready, William. "The Dedication of JO'H." *Lib R*, 23: 33-7 (Sp-Su 71).

Schanche, D.A. "JO'H Is Alive and Well in the First Half of the Twentieth Century." *Esquire*, 72: 84-6, 142-9 (Ag 69).

Shawen, Edgar. "Social Interaction in JO'H's 'The Gangster.'" *SSF*, 11: 367-70 (Fa 74).

O. Henry (see **Porter, William Sidney**).

Olson, Charles. Anon. "Antipoetic Fisher of Men.'" *TLS*, 13 N 70, p. 1315.

———. "O's Reading: A Preliminary Report (D-G)." *Olson*, 2: 70-96 (1973-74).

Aiken, William. "CO: A Preface." *MR*, 12: 57-68 (Wi 71).

———. "CO and the Vatic." *Boun2*, 26-37 (1973-74).

Altieri, Charles, "O's Poetics and the Tradition." *Boun2*, 173-88 (1973-74).

Apsel, Maxine. " 'The Praises.'" *Boun2*, 2: 263-8 (1973-74).

Ballew, Steve. "History as Animated Metaphor in *Maximus Poems*." *NEQ*, 47: 51-64 (1974).

Bensen, Joyce. "First Round of Letters." *Boun2*, 358-66 (1973-74).

Bertholf, R.J. "CO and the Melville Society." *MSex*, 10: 3-4 (Ja 72).

———. "Melville and O: The Poetics of Form." *MSex*, 17: 5-6 (F 74).

———. "Righting the Balance: O's *The Distances*." *Boun2*, 2: 229-49 (1973-74).

*Butterick, George. "A CO Checklist." *WCR*, 2: 25-31 (Sp 67).

———. "On *Maximus IV, V, VI*." *Athanor*, 6: 1-19 (Sp 75).

Byrd, Don. "The Possibility of Measure in O's *The Maximus*." *Boun2*, 39-54 (1973-74).

Charters, Ann. "I, Maximus: CO as Mythologist." *MPS*, 2: 49-60 (1971).

Combs, Maxine. "CO's 'The Kingfishers." *FarP*, 66-76 (Sp-Su 70).

Corrigan, Matthew. "CO: Materials for a Nexus." *OpL*, 21-40 (#2 72).

———. "Materials for a Nexus." *Boun2*, 701-28 (1973-74).

————. "The Poet as Archaeologist (*Archaeologist of Morning*)." *Boun2*, 273-8 (1973-74).

Davenport, Guy. "Scholia and Conjectures for O's 'The Kingfishers.'" *Boun2*, 250-62 (1973-74).

————. "The Symbol of the Archaic." *GaR*, 28: 642-57 (Wi 74).

Davey, Frank. "Poetry and Truth: The Beloit Lectures and Poems." *Boun2*, 24-25.

————. "Six Readings of O's *Maximus*." *Boun2*, 291-321 (1973-74).

Dembo, L.S. "CO and the Moral History of Cape Ann." *Criticism*, 14: 165-74 (Sp 72).

————. "O's *Maximus* and the Way to Knowledge." *Boun2*, 279-89 (1973-74).

Doria, Charles. "Pound, O, and the Classical Tradtion." *Boun2*, 127-43 (1973-74).

Faas, Egbert. "CO and D.H. Lawrence: Aesthetics of the 'Primitive Abstract.'" *Boun2*, 113-26 (1973-74).

Finch, John. "Dancer and Clerk." *MR*, 12: 34-40 (Wi 71).

Ford, O.J. "CO and Carl Sauer: Towards a Methodology of Knowing." *Boun2*, 145-50 (1973-74).

Gauthier, Maxine. "Suggestions Towards a Reading of *The Maximus Poems*." *NwR*, 8: 24-38 (Su 66).

Ginsberg, Allen. "Allen Verbatim." *Paideuma*, 3: 254-73 (1974).

Greenspan, C.R. "CO: Language, Time and Person." *Boun2*, 340-57 (1973-74).

Hise, D.G. "Noticing Juan de la Cosa." *Boun2*, 323-32 (1973-74).

Hooker, Jeremy. "To Open the Mind." *Planet,* 5-6: 59-63 (Su 71).

Ingber, H.G. "Number, Image, Sortilege: A Short Analysis of 'The Moon Is the Number 18.'" *Boun2*, 269-72 (1973-74).

Lieberman, M.R. and Philip. O's Projective Verse and the Use of Breath Control as a Structural Element." *Lang&S*, 5: 287-98 (1972).

McPheron, William. "CO: Mythologist of History." *Boun2*, 189-99 (1973-74).

Maristany, Luis. "Poesia proyectiva CO." *Camp de l'Arpa*, 7: 11-8 (1973).

Metcalf, Paul. "Big Charles: A Gesture Towards Reconstitution." *Prose*, 8: 163-77 (1973-74).

Moebius, William. "'Spiritus ubi vult spirat': On CO." *Boun2*, 16-21 (1973-74).

Olson, Charles. "Definitions by Undoings." *Boun2*, 7-12 (1973-74).

————. "CO, Introductory Statement for Black Mountain College Catalogue, Spring Semester, 1952." *Olson*, 25-7 (1974).

————. "Notes for the Proposition: Man is Prospective." *Boun2*, 1-6 (1973-74).

————. "Letter to W.H. Ferry." *Olson*, 2: 8-15 (1974).

————. "Notes for a University at Venice, California." *Olson*, 2: 65-8 (1974).

————. "Tutorial: The Greeks." *Olson*, 2: 43-8 (1974).

Paul, Sherman. "In and About the *Maximus Poems*." *IowaR*, 6: 118-30 (Wi 75).

Perloff, M.G. "CO and the 'Inferior Predecessors': 'Projective Verse' Revisited." *RLH*, 40: 285-306 (Su 73).

Philip, J.B. "CO Reconsidered." *JAmSt*, 5: 293-305 (D 71).

Pops, M.L. "Melville: To Him, O.'" *Boun2*, 55-84 (1973-74).

————. "Melville: To Him, O." *MPS*, 2: 61-96 (1971).

Raban, Jonathan. "Chance, Time and Silence: The New American Verse." *JAmSt*, 3: 89-101 (Jl 69).

Rosenthal, M.L. "O: His Poetry." *MR*, 12: 45-57 (Wi 71).

Sastri, P.S. "The Poetics of the Lyric and O's Approach." *LCrit*, 9: 70-7 (Wi 69).

Schiffer, Reinhold. 'Vers, Energie und Realität: Bemerkungen zur Poetik CO." *Poetica*, 5: 212-32 (1972).

Scoggan, John. "'Gravel Hill.'" *Boun2*, 333-9 (1973-74).

Sienicka, Marta. "William Carlos Williams and Some Younger Poets." *SAP*, 4: 183-93 (1972).

Snow, Wilbert. "A Teacher's View." *MR*, 12: 40-4 (Wi 71).

Stafford, William. "Whole and Changing." *Poetry*, 11: 413-6 (Mr 68).

Stimpson, C.R. "CO: Preliminary Images." *Boun2*, 151-72 (1973-74).

Tallman, Warren. "Proprioception in CO's Poetry." *OpL*, 2: 5-20 (#2 72).

von Hallberg, Robert. "O, Whitehead, and the Objectivists." *Boun2*, 85-111 (1973-74).

———. "O's Relation to Pound and Williams." *ConL*, 15: 15-48 (Wi 74).

Wiener, John. "Hanging on for Dear Life." *Boun2*, 22-3 (1973-74).

O'Neill, Eugene. Aarseth, Inger. "A Drama of Life and Death Impulses." *AmNor*, 4: 291-304 (1973).

Adler, J.H. "The Worth of *Ah, Wilderness!*" *MD*, 3: 280-8 (D 60).

Agnihotri, S.M. "Illusion versus Reality in the Major Plays of EO." *PURBA*, 3: 69-74 (1972).

Alexander, D.M. "EO and *Light on the Path*." *MD*, 3: 260-7 (D 60).

Bako, Endre. "Hosszú út az éjszakaba: O—bemutató Scokonai Színhazban." *Alföld*, 21: 89-90 (1970).

Bauzyte, Galina. "Salygĭskumas xx a. Vakaru dramoje (Augustas Strindbergas ir EO)." *Literatura*, 14: 93-111 (1972).

Bérubé, Renald. "EO." *Liberté*, 999: 42-65 (1975).

Blesch, E.J. "O's Hughie: *A Misconceived Experiment?*" *NasR*, 2: 1-8 (1974).

Booth, Willard. "Haunting Fragments from EO." *Adams*, 39: 37-40 (1973).

Bowling, C.C. "The Touch of Poetry: A Study of the Role of Poetry in Three Plays." *CLAJ*, 12: 43-55 (1968).

Brantsaeter, Per L. "EO—Hans skuespil og hans virkelighet." *Samtiden*, 83: 166-72 (1974).

Camilucci, Marcello. "Il Dramma dell'Interiorita: *Strano interludio*." *Studium*, 69: 201-9 (1973).

Cate, H.L. "Ephraim Cabot: EO's Spontaneous Poet." *MarkR*, 2: 115-7 (My 71).

Chaitin, Norman. "EO: The Power of Daring." *MD*, 3: 231-41 (D 60).

Chen, D.Y. "*The Hairy Ape* and *The Peking Man*: Two Types of Primitivism in Modern Society." *YCGL*, 15: 214-20 (1966).

Chiaromonte, Nicola. "EO." *SR*, 68: 494-501 (Su 60).

Chikata, Kiochi. "A Decade of O Criticism: 1960-1969." *DSE*, 1: 1-20 (1970).

Clark, M.J. "Tragic Effect in *The Hairy Ape*." *MD*, 10: 372-82 (F 68).

Cohn, Ruby, "Absurdity in English: Joyce and O." *CompD*, 3: 156-61 (1969).

Cooley, J.R. "*The Emperor Jones* and the Harlem Renaissance." *SLit*, 7: 73-84 (Fa 74).

Corey, James. "O's *The Emperor Jones*." *AN&Q*, 12: 156-7 (My-Je 74).

Crepean, G.P. "Robert Edmond Jones on the Creative Process: An Interview with a Group of High School Students." *ETJ*, 19: 125-33 (My 67).

Cunningham, F.R. "*The Great God Brown* and O's Romantic Vision." *BSUF*, 14: 69-78 (Su 73).

———. "*Lazarus Laughed*: A Study in O's Romanticism." *STC*, 15: 51-76 (1975).

Curran, R.T. "Insular Types: Puritanism and Primitivism in *Mourning Becomes Electra*." *RLV*, 41: 371-7 (1975).

Dahlstrom, C.E.W.L. "*Dynamo* and *Lazarus Laughed*: Some Limitations." *MD*, 3: 224-30 (D 60).

Das, P.N. "The Alienated Ape." *LHY*, 11: 53-69 (1970).

Day, Cyrus. "*Amor Fati*: O's Lazarus as Superman and Savior." *MD*, 3: 297-305 (D 60).

Donoghue, Denis. "The Human Image in Modern Drama." *LugR*, 1: 155-68 (1965).

Downer, A.S. "Old, New, Borrowed, and (a Trifle) Blue." *QJS*, 54: 199-211 (O 68).

Engel, E.A. "O: 1960." *MD*, 3: 219-23 (D 60).

Falb, L.W. "The Critical Reception of EO on the French Stage." *ETJ*, 22: 397-405 (1970).

Falk, Signi. "Dialogue in the Plays of EO." *MD*, 3: 314-25 (D 60).

Fedo, David. "In Defense of EO." *BUJ*, 18: 30-5 (1970).

Fiet, L.A. "O's Modification of Traditional American Themes in *A Touch of the Poet*." *ETJ*,27: 508-15 (1975).

Filipowicz, Halina. "Fatalizm, determinizm a wolna wola w sztukach e O." *KN*, 17: 325-31 (1970).

Flory, C.R. "Notes on the Antecedents of *Anna Christie*." *PMLA*, 86: 77-83 (Ja 71).

Frazer, W.L. "Chris and Poseidon: Man Versus God in *Anna Christie*." *MD*, 12: 279-85 (D 69).

———. "King Lear and Hickey: Bridegroom and Iceman." *MD*, 15: 267-78 (D 72).

———. "O's Iceman—Not Ice Man." *AL*, 44: 677-8 (Ja 73).

Frenz, Horst. "Notes on EO in Japan." *MD*, 3: 306-13 (D 60).

Fukushima, Osamu. "The Tragic Tone of *Mourning Becomes Electra*." *KAL*, 15: 1-9 (1974).

Gey, Guy. " 'Dynamo' d' EO's 'la maladie contemporaine' et l'exploitation d'un mythe moderne." *Caliban*, 6: 35-42 (1970).

———. "Unité et dualité du mythe de Dionysos dans *Lazarus Laughed* de EO." *Caliban*, 6: 69-72 (1969).

Gillett, P.J. "O and the Racial Myths." *TCL*, 18: 111-20 (Ap 72).

Going, W.T. "O's *Ah, Wilderness*." *Expl*, 29: 28 (1970).

Granger, Bruce. "EO: Man of the Theatre." *Americana Austriaca*, 3: 24-32 (1974).

Grecco, S.R. "High Hopes: EO and Alcohol." *YFS*, 50: 142-9 (My 74).

Griffin, E.G. "Pity, Alienation, and Reconciliation in EO." *Mosaic*, 2: 66-76 (1968).

Grosse, Siegfried. "*As If*—Kinjunktion zwischen Schein und Wirklichkeit in den späten Dramen EO." *Poetica*, 2: 521-40 (1968).

Haas, Rudolf. "EO." *SG*, 21: 19-35 (1968).

Hastings, W.H., and R.F. Weeks. "Episodes of EO's Undergraduate Days at Princeton." *PULC*, 29: 208-15 (Sp 68).

Hays, P.L. "Biblical Perversions in *Desire Under the Elms*." *MD*, 11: 423-8 (F 69).

Herron, I.H. "O's 'Comedy of Recollection': A Nostalgic Dramatization of the 'Real America.' " *CEA*, 30: 16-8 (Ja 68).

Highsmith, J.M. "The Cornell Letters: EO on His Craftsmanship to George Jean Nathan." *MD*, 15: 68-88 (My 72).

———. "A Description of the Cornell Collection of EO's Letters to George Jean Nathan." *MD*, 14: 420-5 (F 72).

———. "EO's Idea of Theater." *SAB*, 23: 18-21 (1968).

———. " 'The Personal Equation.': EO's Abandoned Play." *SHR*, 8: 195-211 Sp 74).

Hinden, Michael. "*The Birth of Tragedy* and *The Great God Brown*." *MD*, 16: 129-40 (S 73).

———. "Liking EO." *Forum(H)*, 11: 59-666 (1973).

Hoffmann, Gerhard. "Lachen un Weinen als Gestaltungsmittel der dramatischen Grenszituation." *JA*, 15: 101-22 (1970).

Hoffmann, Ulrick. "Ironie und Symbolik der Dramentitel O's." *NS*, 18: 322-35.

———. "Zur Symbolik der Personennamen in den Dramen EOs." *Archiv*, 206: 38-45 (1969).

Holtan, O.I. "EO and the Death of the 'Convenant.' " *QJS*, 56: 256-63 (Au 70).

Hughes, Hatcher. "O's Art is Defended." *NYTimes*, nv: 20 (10 Mr 25).

Josephs, L.S. "The Women of EO: Sex Role Stereotypes." *BSUF*, 14: 3-8 (Su 73).

Kagan, Norman. "The Return of *The Emperor Jones*." *NHB*, 34: 160-2 (1971).

Keane, Christopher. "Blake and O: A Prophecy." *BlS*, 2: 23-34 (Sp 70).

Klavons, Janis. "O's Dreamer: Success and Failure." *MD*, 3: 268-72 (D 60).

Koike, M.A. "EO: A Revaluation." *OUS*, 24: 69-101 (1971).

———. "O Kenkyu—Genjo to Kadai." *EigoS*, 119: 548-50 (1973).

Krimsky, John. "*The Emperor Jones*: Robeson and O on Film." *ConnR*, 7, 2: 94-9 (1974).

LaBelle, M.M. "Dionysus and Despair: The Influence of Nietzsche upon O's Drama." *ETJ*, 25: 436-42 (1973).

Lee, R.C. "EO's Approach to Playwriting." *DramC*, 11: 2-8 (Wi 68).

———. "Evangelism and Anarchy in *The Iceman Cometh*." *MD*, 12: 173-86 (S 69).

Lichtenberg, J.D. and Charlotte. "EO and Falling in Love." *PsyR*, 41: 63-89 (Ja 72).

Miller, J.Y. "EO: Masks and Demons." *Sphinx*, 3: 57-62 (1975).

———. "Murky Moon." *KanQ*, 7: 103-5 (1975).

Mullaly, Edward. "O and the Perfect Pattern." *DR*, 52: 603-10 (Wi 72-73).

Nethercot, A.H. "Madness in the Plays of EO." *MD*, 18: 259-80 (S 75).

———. "O's *More Stately Mansions*." *ETJ*, 27: 161-9 (1975).

———. "The Psychoanalyzing of EO: P.P.S." *MD*, 16: 35-48 (Je 73).

Paduano, Guido. "Manierismo e struttura psicologica nell' eperienza greca di EO." *ASNSP*, 2: 761-816 (1972).

Pallette, D.B. "O and the Comic Spirit." *MD*, 3: 273-9 (D 60).

Pettegrove, J.P. "Einiges über O—Übersetzungen ins Deutsche." *MuK*, 17: 40-7 (1971).

Porter, D.H. "Ancient Myth and Modern Play: A Significant Counterpoint." *CBul*, 48: 1-9 (N 71).

Presley, D.E. "O's Iceman: Another Meaning." *AL*, 42: 387-8 (N 70).

Przemecka, Irena. "EO and the Irish Drama." *KN*, 18: 3-9 (1971).

Quinn, J.P. "*The Iceman Cometh*: O's Long Day's Journey into Adolescence." *JPC*, 6: 171-7 (Su 72).

Real, Jere. "The Brothel in O's *Mansions*." *MD*, 12: 383-9 (F 70).

Reinhardt, Nancy. "Formal Patterns in *The Iceman Cometh*." *MD*, 16: 119-28 (S 73).

Riegl, Kurt. "Zum Thoreau-Echo im Spatwerk Os." *GRM*, 18: 191-9 (Ap 68).

Rosen, K.M. "EO's *Brown* and Wilde's *Gray*." *MD*, 13: 347-55 (F 71).

Rothenberg, Albert, and E.D. Shapiro. "The Defense of Psychoanalysis in Literature: *Long Day's Journey into Night* and *A View from the Bridge*." *CompD*, 7: 51-67 (Sp 73).

Roy, Emil. "The Archetypal Unity of EO's Drama." *CompD*, 3: 263-74 (Wi 69-70).

———. "EO's *The Emperor Jones* and *The Hairy Ape* as Mirror Plays." *CompD*, 2: 21-31 (Sp 68).

———. "Tragic Tension in *Beyond the Horizon*." *BSUF*, 8: 74-9 (Wi 67).

Scarbrough, Alex. "O's Use of the Displaced Archetype in *The Moon of the Caribbees*." *WVUPP*, 19: 41-4 (#3 72).

Shawcross, J.T. "The Road to Ruin: The Beginning of O's Long Day's Journey." *MD*, 3: 289-96 (D 60).

Scheibler, Rolf. "*Hughie*: A One-Act Play for the Imaginary Theatre." *ES*, 54: 231-48 (Je 73).

Schenker, Uele. "Die Freiheit gegenuber dem eigenen Talent: Zu EO's Spatwerk." *SchM*, 47: 1178-85 (1968).

Sochatoff, A.F. "Two Modern Treatments of the Phaedra Legend." *CaSE*, 12: 80-6 (1972).

Stroupe, J.H. "EO and the Creative Process." *Eng Rec*, 21: 69-76 (O 70).

———. "EO and the Problem of Masking." *LHR*, 12: 71-80 (1971).

———. "*Marco Millions* and O's 'two part two-play' Form." *MD*, 13: 382-93 (F 71).

———. "O's *Marco Millions*: A Road to Xanadu." *MD*, 12: 377-82 (F 70).

Taranu, Dana. "Sentimentul destinului tragic in opera lui O." *Steaua*, 19: 102-10 (1968).

Throckmorton, Juliet. "As I Remember EO." *Yankee*, 32: 85, 93-5 (1968).

Törnqvist, Egil. "Fröken Julie och O." *MfS*, 42-3: 5-16 (1969).

———. "Jesus and Judas: On Biblical Allusions in O's Plays." *EA*, 24: 41-9 (Ja-Mr 71).

———. "Nietzsche and O: A Study in Affinity." *OL*, 23: 97-126 (1968).

———. "O's Lazarus: Dionysus and Christ." *AL*, 41: 543-54 (Ja 70).

———. "Personal Addresses in the Plays of O." *QJS*, 55: 126-30 (Ap 69).

Ueno, Seiichiro. "The Romance Characteristic in O's Plays." *SELL*, 23: 17-37 (1973).

Valgemae, Mardi. "EO's Preface to *The Great God Brown*." *YULG*, 43: 24-9 (1968).

Vena, G.A. "The Role of the Prostitute in the Plays of EO." *DramC*, 10: 129-37 (Fa 67); 11: 9-14, 82-8 (Wi, Sp 68).

Weissman, Philip. "*Mourning Becomes Electra* and *The Prodigal*: Electra and Orestes." *MD*, 3: 257-9 (D 60).

Wiig, Birgit. "O revaluert." *Samtiden*, 77: 256-68 (1968).

Winchester, O.W. "History in Literature: EO's *Strange Inerlude* as a Transcript of America in the 1920's." *UTMS*, 9: 43-58 (1970).

Winther, S.K. "*Desire Under the Elms*: A Modern Tragedy." *MD*, 3: 326-32 (D 60).

Yamauchi, Kuniomi. "*Sogai* to EO." *EigoS*, 116: 204-5 (1970).

Oppen, George. Dembo, L.S. "The Existential World of GO." *IowaR*, 3: 64-92 (Wi 72).

———. "The 'Objectivist' Poet (GO)." *ConL*, 10: 159-77 (Sp 69).

Hamburger, Michael. "GO: Collected Poems." *Agenda*, 11: 92-5 (Sp-Su 73).

Owen, Guy. Eyser, Warren. "Two Regional Novels." *SR*, 79: 469-74 (1971).

Owen, Guy. "The Use of Folklore in Fiction." *NCaF*, 19: 12-8 (Mr 71).

Vela, Richard. "This Native Pond, That Naked Tree: The Realities of GO." *S&W*, 11, 3: 14-20 (1973).

White, R.B., Jr. "The Imagery of Sexual Repression in *Season of Fear*." *NCaF*, 19: 80 (Mr 71).

Page, Thomas Nelson. *Bickley, B.R. "TNP." *ALR*, 8: 20-1 (1975).

Cable, G.W. "TNP, a Study in Reminiscence and Appreciation." *BNM*, 18: 139-40 (N 09).

Holman, H.R. "Attempt and Failure: TNP as Playwright." *SLJ*, 3: 72-82 (Fa 70).

———. "F. Marion Crawford and the Evil Eye." *AmN&Q*, 9: 103-4 (Mr 71).

———. "The Kentucky Journal of TNP." *Kentucky Register Hist Soc*, 68: 1-16 (Ja 70).

———. "TNP's Account of Tennessee Hospitality." *THQ*, 28: 269-72 (Fa 69).

———. "U.S. Intervention in the Panamanian Constitution." *AN&Q*, 9: 151 (1971).

Rubin, L.D. "The Other Side of Slavery: TNP's 'No Haid Pawn.'" *SLit I*, 7: 95-9 (Sp 74).

Simms, L.M. "Corra Harris on the Declining Influence of TNP." *MissQ*, 28: 505-09 (Fa 75).

———. "The Negro in the Non-Fictional Writings of TNP." *XUS*, 6: 121-6 (N 67).

Sloane, D.E.E. "David Graham Phillips, Jack London, and Others on Contemporary Reviewers and Critics, 1903-1904." *ALR*, 3: 67-71 (1970).

Paine, Robert Treat. Leary, Lewis. "The First Published Poem of TP of Boston (i.e. RTP, Jr): A Note on the Generation Gap in 1786." *NEQ*, 43: 130-4 (Mr 70).

Paine, Thomas. Aldridge, A.O. "Camilo Henriquez and the Fame of TP and Benjamin Franklin in Chile." *RIB*, 17: 51-67 (1967).

———. "TP and the Classics." *ECS*, 1: 370-80 (Je 68).

———. "TP, Edmund Burke, and Anglo-French Relations in 1787." *Stud in Burke*, 12: 1851-61 (1971).

———. "TP in Latin America." *EAL*, 3: 139-47 (1968).

Bailyn, Bernard. "The Most Uncommon Pamphlet of the Revolution: *Common Sense." AH*, 25: 36-41, 91-3 (D 73).

Barotti, Armand. "Tom P's Class Outlook." *L&I*, 12: 31-6 (1972).

Boulton, J.T. "TP and the Vulgar Style." *EsL*, 12: 18-33 (1962).

Brodie, F.M. "Tom P: Relevant Founding Father." *NRep*, 170: 23-5 (4 My 74).

Christian, William. "The Moral Economics of Tom P." *JHI*, 34: 367-80 (Jy-S 73).

Henrich, J.G. "TP's Short Career as a Naval Architect, August—October 1807." *AmNep*, 34: 123-34 (Ap 74).

Hinz, E.J. "The 'Reasonable' Style of Tom P." *QQ*, 79: 231-41 (Su 72).

Jordan, W.P. "Familial Politics: TP and the Killing of the King, 1776." *JAH*, 60: 294-308 (1973).

Kenyon, C.M. "Where P Went Wrong." *Am Pol Sci R*, 45: 1086-99 (1951).

Ketchum, R.M. "Men of the Revolution." *AH*, 23: 61 (O 72).

Knudson, J.W. "The Rage Around TP: Newspaper Reaction to His Homecoming in 1802." *NYHSQ*, 53: 34-63 (Ja 69).

McIntyre, Angus. "TP and *The Rights of Man." Listener*, 87: 41-2 (13 Ja 72).

Metzgar, J.V. "The Cosmology of TP." *IllQ*, 37: 47-63 (1974).

Prochaska, F.K. "TP's *The Age of Reason* Revisited." *JHI*, 33: 561-76 (O-D 72).

Smylie, J.H. "Clerical Perspectives on Deism: P's *The Age of Reason* in Virginia." *ECS*, 6: 203-20 (1972).

Vanderhaar, Margaret. "Whitman, P and the Religion of Democracy." *WWR*, 16: 14-22 (Mr 70).

*Wilson, Jerome. "TP in America: An Annotated Bibliography, 1900-1973." *BB*, 31: 133-51, 180 (O-D 74).

Parker, Dorothy. Anon. "Low Spirits." *TLS*, 6 Ap 73, p. 395.

Cooper, Wyatt. "Whatever You Think DP Was Like, She Wasn't." *Esquire*, 70: 57, 61, 110-14 (Jl 68).

Shanahan, William. "Robert Benchley and DP: Punch and Judy in Formal Dress." *Rendezvous*, 3: 23-34 (1968).

Parker, Theodore. Beirne, C.J. "The Theology of TP and the War with Mexico." *EIHC*, 104: 130-7 (Ap 68).

Carter, George. "TP and John P. Hale." *DCLB*, 13: 13-33 (1972).

Fellman, Michael. "TP and the Abolitionist Role in the 1850's." *JAH*, 61: 666-84 (1974).

Nichols, C.H. "TP and the Transcendental Rhetoric." *JA*, 13: 69-83 (1968).

Parker, Theodore. "The Revival of Religion Which We Need: A Sermon." *ESQ*, 59: 87-94 (Sp 70).

Parkman, Francis. Beaver, Harold. "P's Crack-Up: A Bostonian on the Oregon Trail." *NEQ*, 48: 84-103 (Mr 75).

Griffin, D.E. " 'The Man for the Hour': A Defense of FP's Frontenac." *NEQ*, 43: 605-20 (D 70).

Herold, David. "FP's Violets." *DR*, 54: 312-7 (Su 74).

Tribble, J.L. "The Paradise of the Imagination: The Journeys of *The Oregon Trail." NEQ*, 46: 523-42 (D 73).

Parrington, Vernon Louis. Houghton, D.E. "VLP's Unacknowledged Debt to Moses Coit Tyler." *NEQ*, 43: 124-30 (Mr 70).

Pastan, Linda. Bloom, Janet. "A Plea for Proper Boldness." *Parnassus*, 1: 130-4 (1972).

Jellema, Roderick. "The Poetry of LP." *Voyages*, 2: 73-4 (Sp 69).

Patchen, Kenneth. Hack, Richard. "Memorial Poetry Reading for KP." *ChiR*, 24: 65-80 (1972).

Patchen, Miriam. "Of Human Warmth and Love: KP." *Pembroke Mag*, 6: 25-9 (1975).

Patten, W.G. O'Neil, Paul. "Frank Merriwell Is Back." *Life*, 72: 51-4 (11 F 72).

Paulding, James Kirk. Baker, Carlos. "'The Jug Makes the Paradise': New Light on Eben Flood." *CLQ*, 10: 327-36 (1974).

Gerber, G.E. "JKP and the Image of the Machine." *AQ*, 22: 736-41 (Fa 70).

Graham, K.W. "The Influence of JKP's *Diverting History* on Washington Irving's Sketch 'John Bull.'" *PBSA*, 67: 310-22 (1973).

Henry, Joyce. "Five More Essays by JKP?" *PBSA*, 66: 310-21 (3Q 72).

Mason, M.R. "*The Lion of the West*: Satire on Davy Crockett and Frances Trollope." *SCB*, 29: 143-5 (Wi 69).

O'Donnell, T.F. "*Koningsmarke*: Paulding vs Scott in 1823." *ATQ*, 24: 10-7 (Fa 74).

Owens, L.D. "JK.P and the Foundations of American Realism." *BYNPL*, August 75, pp. 40-50.

Owens, Louis. "P's 'The Dumb Girl,' a Source of *The Scarlet Letter*." *HNJ*, 4: 240-9 (1974).

Stocker, M.H. "*Salmagundi*: Problems in Editing the So-Called First Edition (1807-08)." *PBSA*, 67: 141-58 (2Q 73).

Watkins, F.C. "JKP's Early Ring-Tailed Roarer." *SFQ*, 15: 183-7 (S 51).

Payne, John Howard. Saxon, A.H. "JHP, Playwright with a System." *ThN*, 24: 79-84 (1970).

Peabody, Elizabeth P. Peabody, E.P. "An Unpublished Letter about Hawthorne." *NHJ*, 2: 7-8 (1972).

Stern, M.B. "EP's Foreign Library (1840)." *ATQ*, 20: 5-13 (Fa 73).

Turner, Arlin. "EP Reviews *Twice-Told Tales*." *NHJ*, 4: 75-84 (1974).

———. "EP Visits Lincoln, February, 1865." *NEQ*, 48: 116-24 (Mr 75).

Wilson, J.B. "The Aesthetics of Transcendentalism." *ESQ*, 57: 27-34 (1969).

———. "EP and Other Transcendentalists on History and Historians." *Historian*, 30: 72-86 (1967).

Percy, George. Barbour, P.L. "The Honorable GP: Premier Chronicler of the First Virginia Voyage." *EAL*, 6: 7-17 (Sp 71).

Percy, Walker. Abádi-Nagy, Zoltán. "A Talk with WP." *SLJ*, 6: 3-19 (Fa 73).

Atkins, Anselm. "WP and Post-Christian Search." *CentR*, 12: 73-95 (Wi 68).

Berrigan, J.R. "An Explosion of Utopias." *Moreana*, 38: 21-6 (1973).

Bradbury, J.M. "Absurd Insurrection: the Barth-P Affair." *SAQ*, 68: 319-29 (Su 69).

Bradford, M.E. "Dr. P's Paradise Lost: Diagnostics in Louisiana." *SR*, 81: 839-44 (Au 73).

Bradley, Jared W. "WP and the Search for Wisdom." *LaS*, 12: 579-90 (1974).

Broberg, Jan. "WP—En udda amerikan." *Studiekamraten*, 54: 119-20 (1972).

Buckley, W.F. "The Southern Imagination: An Interview with Eudora Welty and WP." *MissQ*, 26: 493-516 (Fa 73).

Bunting, Charles. "An Afternoon with WP." *NMW*, 4: 43-61 (Fa 71).

Byrd, Scott. "Mysteries and Movies: WP's College Articles and *The Moviegoer*." *MissQ*, 25: 165-81 (Sp 72).

*———, and J.F. Zengner. "WP: A Checklist." *BB*, 30: 16-7, 44 (Ja-Mr 73).

Carr, John. "An Interview with WP." *GaR*, 25: 317-32 (Fa 71).

Chesnick, Eugene. "Novel's Ending and World's End: The Fiction of WP." *HC*, 10: 1-11 (O 73).

Cremeens, Carlton. "WP, The Man and the Novelist: An Interview." *SoR*, 4: 271-90 (Sp 68).

Dewey, Bradley. "WP Talks about Kierkegaard: An Annotated Interview." *JR*, 54: 273-98 (Jl 74).

Dowie, William. "WP: Sensualist-Thinker." *Novel*, 6: 52-65 (Fa 72).

Gaston, P.L. "The Revelation of WP." *ColQ*, 20: 459-70 (Sp 72).

Godshalk, W.L. "WP's Christian Vision." *LaS*, 13: 130-41 (Su 74).

Henisey, Sarah. "Intersubjectivity in Symbolization." *Ren*, 20: 208-14 (Su 68).

Johnson, Mark. "The Search for Place in WP's Novels." *SLJ*, 8: 55-81 (Fa 71).

Kazin, Alfred. "The Pilgrimage of WP." *HM*, 242: 81-6 (Je 71).

Lauder, R.E. "The Catholic Novel and the 'Insider God.'" *Cweal*, 51: 78-81 (25 O 74).

Lawson, L.A. "WP's Indirect Communications." *TSLL*, 9: 867-900 (Sp 69).

————. "WP's Southern Stoic." *SLJ*, 3: 5-31 (Fa 70).

————. "WP: The Physician as Novelist." *SAB*, 37: 58-63 (My 72).

LeClair, Thomas. "The Eschatological Vision of WP." *Renascence*, 26: 115-22 (Sp 74).

Lehan, Richard. "The Way Back: Redemption in the Novels of WP." *SoR*, 4: 306-19 (Sp 68).

Percy, Walker. "The Delta Factor." *SoR*, 11: 29-64 (Ja 75).

————. "New Orleans Mon Amour." *HM*, 237: 80-2, 86, 88, 90 (S 68).

Pindall, Richard. "Basking in the Eye of the Storm." *Boundary*, 4: 219-30 (1975).

Presley, Del. "WP's 'Larroes.'" *NCLit*, 3: 5-6 (Ja 73).

Shepherd, Allen. "P's *The Moviegoer* and Warren's *All the King's Men*." *NMW*, 4: 2-14 (Sp 71).

Spivey, T.R. "Religion and the Reintegration of Man in Flannery O'Connor and WP." *Spectrum*, 2: 67-79 (1972).

Stelzmann, Rainulf. "Adam in Extremis: Die Romane WP." *SZ*, 191: 206-10 (Mr 73).

Taylor, L.J. "WP and the Self." *Cweal*, 100: 233-6 (10 My 74).

Thale, Jerome. "Alienation on the American Plan." *Forum(H)*, 6: 36-40 (Su 68).

Thale, Mary. "The Moviegoer of the 1950's." *TCL*, 14: 84-9 (Jl 68).

Van Cleave, Jim. "Versions of P." *SoR*, 6: 990-1010 (Au 70).

Vauthier, Simone. "Le Temps et la Mort dans *The Moviegoer*." *Ranam*, 4: 98-105 (1971).

————. "Title as Microtext." *JNT*, 5: 219-29 (1975).

Westendorp, T.A. "Recent Southern Fiction: P, Price and Dickey." *HVF*, 1974, pp. 188-98.

Whittington, M.J. "From the Delta." *DelR*, 5: 30 (F 68).

Zeugner, John. "WP and Gabriel Marcell: The Castaway and the Wayfarer." *MissQ*, 28: 21-53 (Wi 74-75).

Percy, William Alexander. Holmes, W.F. "WAP and the Bourbon Era in the Yazoo-Mississippi Delta." *MissQ*, 26: 71-87 (Wi 72-73).

Percy, Walker. "'Uncle Will' and His South." *SatR*, 6 N 73, pp. 22-5.

Spalding, Phinizy. "Mississippi and the Poet: WAP." *JMiH*, 27: 63-73 (F 65).

Van Cleave, Jim. "Versions of P." *SoR*, 6: 990-1010 (O 70).

Welsh, J.R. "WAP and His Writing: A Reassessment." *NMW*, 1: 82-99 (Wi 69).

Perelman, S.J. Ellis, Diane. "Halfway Around the World; in 40 Days with S.J.P." *HB*, nv: 80-82 (My 72).

Gale, S.N. "SJP: Twenty Years of American Humor." *BB*, 29: 10-2 (Ja-Mr 72).

Hasley, Louis. "The Kangaroo Mind of S.J.P." *SAQ*, 72: 115-21 (Wi 73).

Kanfer, Stefan. "Meisterzinger." *Atl*, 226: 108-10 (D 70).

Perry, George Sessions. Bradford, M.E. "Making Time Run: The Rich Harvest of GSP." *SwAL*, 1: 129-36 (S 72).

Hairston, M.C. "The GSP Manuscript Collection." *LCUT*, 2: 63-71 (N 70).

Perry, Thomas Sergeant. Anon. "William Dean Howells and TSP." *NAR*, 196: 85-103 (Jl 12).

*Monteiro, George. "Addenda to the Bibliographies of Hardy, Wells, P." *PBSA*, 69: 272-3 (Ap-Je 75).

————. "Addenda to Harlow: Two T.S.P. Essays." *PBSA*, 62: 612-13 (1968).

Žuravlev, I.K. "Tomas Perri—propagandist russkoj literatury v SŠA." *RLit*, 17, 1: 223-30 (1974).

Peterkin, Julia. Cheney, Brainard. "Can JP's 'Genius' Be Revived For Today's Black Myth-Making?" *SR*, 80: 173-9 (Wi 72).

Coker, E.B. "An Appreciation of JP and *The Collected Short Stories of JP.*" *SCR*, 3: 3-7 (Je 71).

Durham, Frank. "The Art of Writing." *Carolinian*, 45: 6, 18 (1932).

————. "The Reputed Demises of Uncle Tom; or, The Treatment of the Negro in Fiction by White Southern Authors in the 1920's." *SLJ*, 2: 26-50 (Sp 70).

Yates, Irene. "A Collection of Proverbs and Proverbial Sayings from South Carolina Literature." *SFQ*, 11: 187-99 (1947).

Petry, Ann. Adams, G.R. "Riot as Ritual: AP's 'In Darkness and Confusion.'" *NALF*, 6: 54-7, 60 (1972).

Jaskoski, H. "Power Unequal to Man: The Significance of Conjure in Works by Five Afro-American Authors." *SFQ*, 38: 91-108 (Je 74).

Madden, David. "AP: 'The Witness.'" *SBL*, 6: 24-8 (#3 75).

Morsberger, R.E. "The Further Transformation of Tituba." *NEQ*, 47: 456-8 (1974).

Shinn, T.J. "Women in the Novels of AP." *Critique*, 16: 110-20 (#1 74).

Phelps, Donald. Alpert, Barry. "DP: An Interview." *Vort*, 6: 97-113 (1974).

Dawson, Fielding. "DP: *Character and Concept.*" *Vort*, 2: 124-32 (Fa 74).

Melhem, D.H. "DP: The Audacity of Precision." *Vort*, 2: 133-40 (Fa 74).

Mottram, Eric. "The Performance of the Comedian under Law: The Criticism of DP." *Vort*, 6: 141-57 (Fa 74).

Phelps, Elizabeth Stuart. Rees, R.A. "*Captain Stormfield's Visit to Heaven* and *The Gates Ajar.*" *ELN*, 7: 197-202 (1970).

Stansell, Christine. "ESP: A Study in Female Rebellion." *MR*, 13: 239-56 (Wi-Sp 72).

Phillips, David Graham. Filler, Louis. "An American Odyssey: The Story of *Susan Lenox.*" *Accent*, 1: 22-9 (Au 40).

*Graham, D.B. "DGP." *ALR*, 8: 231-2 (1975).

Hicks, Granville. "Philology for Fun." *SatR*, nv: 33-4 (12 O 68).

Kazin, Alfred. "Three Pioneer Realists." *SatR*, 20: 3-4, 14-5 (8 Jl 39).

*Ravitz, A.C. "DGP (1867-1911)." *ALR*, 3: 24-9 (Su 68).

Sloane, D.E.E. "DGP, Jack London, and Others on Contemporary Reviewers and Critics, 1903-1904." *ALR*, 3: 67-71 (1970).

Spangler, G.M. "The Confession Form: An Approach to the Tycoon." *MASJ*, 10: 5-18 (Fa 1969).

Stallings, F.L. "DGP (1867-1911): A Critical Bibliography of Secondary Comment." *ALR*, 3: 1-35 (Wi 70).

Phillips, Robert. Phillips, Robert. "Abandoned, Not Finished: A Poet Looks at Four of His Poems." *Eng Rec*, 21: 6-19 (F 71).

Pierce, Ovid W. McMillan, D.J. "Folkways in OP's 'The Wedding Guest.'" *NCaF*, 23: 125-8 (1975).

West, H.C. "Negro Folklore in P's Novels." *NCaF*, 19: 66-72 (Mr 71).

Plath, Sylvia. Anon. "Early Poems by Sylvia Plath." *CaR*, 90: 244-5 (7 F 69).

Aird, E.M. "Variants in a Tape Recording of Fifteen Poems by SP." *N&Q*, 19: 59-61 (F 72).

Alvarez, A. "SP: The Cambridge Collection." *CaR*, 90: 246-7 (7 F 69).

Ashford, Deborah. "SP's Poetry: A Complex of Irreconcilable Antagonisms." *CP*, 7: 62-9 (Sp 74).

Bagg, Robert. "The Rise of Lady Lazarus." *Mosaic*, 2: 9-36 (1969).

Balitas, Vincent. "A Note on SP's 'The Hanging Man.'" *N&Q*, 22: 208 (My 75).

———. "On Becoming a Witch: A Reading of SP's 'Witch Burning." *Stud Humanities*, 4: 27-30 (2Q 75).

Bierman, Larry. "The Vivid Tulips Eat My Oxygen: An Essay on SP's 'Ariel.'" *WiOr*, 4: 44-6 (F 71).

Blodgett, E.D. "SP: Another View." *MPS*, 2: 97-106 (1971).

Boyers, Robert. "On SP." *Salmagundi*, 2: 96-104 (Wi 73).

———. "SP: The Trepanned Veteran." *CentR*, 13: 138-53 (1969).

Burnham, R.E. "SP's 'Lady Lazarus.'" *Cont Poetry*, 1: 42-6 (Wi 73).

C., M.W. "Remembering Sylvia." *CaR*, 90: 253-4 (7 F 69).

Caraher, Brian. "The Problematic of Body and Language in SP's 'Tulips.'" *Paunch*, 42-43: 76-89 (D 75).

Cooley, Peter. "Autism, Autoeroticism, Auto-da-fe: The Tragic Poetry of SP." *HC*, 10: 1-15 (F 73).

Davis, Robin. "Now I Have Lost Myself: A Reading of SP's 'Tulips.'" *Paunch*, 42: 97-104 (D 75).

Davis, R.R. "The Honey Machine: Imagery Patterns in *Ariel*." *NLauR*, 1: 23-31 (#2 72).

Davis, W.V. "SP's 'Ariel.'" *MPS*, 3: 176-84 (1974).

Donovan, Josephine. "Sexual Politics in SP's Short Stories." *MinnR*, 4: 150-7 (Sp 73).

Duffy, Martha. "The Triumph of a Tormented Poet." *Life*, 12 N 71, pp. 38A-38B.

Dyroff, J.M. "SP: Perceptions in *Crossing the Water*." *A&L*, 1: 49-50 (1972).

Efron, Arthur. "SP's 'Tulips' and Literary Criticism." *Paunch*, 42-43: 69-75 (D 75).

———. "'Tulips': Text and Assumptions." *Paunch*, 42-43: 110-22 (D 75).

Eriksson, P.D. "Some Thoughts on SP." *UES*, 10, 2: 45-52 (1972).

Federman, Raymond. "Poèmes par SP." *Esprit*, 371: 825-7 (1968).

Fraser, G.S. "A Hard Nut to Crack from SP." *Cont Poetry*, 1: 1-12 (Sp 73).

Gordon, J.B. "'Who Is Sylvia?' The Art of SP." *MPS*, 1: 6-34 (1970).

Hakeem, A. "SP's 'Elm' and Munch's 'The Scream.'" *ES*, 55: 531-7 (D 74).

Himelick, Raymond. "Notes on the Care and Feeding of Nightmares: Burton, Erasmus, and SP." *WHR*, 28: 313-6 (Au 74).

Hoffman, N.J. "Reading Women's Poetry: The Meaning and Our Lives." *CE*, 34: 48-62 (1972).

Holbrook, David. "R.D. Laing and the Death Circuit." *Enc*, 31: 35-45 (1968).

———. "SP and the Problem of Violence in Art." *CaR*, 90: 249-50 (7 F 69).

Homberger, Eric. "I am I." *CaR*, 90: 251-3 (7 F 69).

———. "The Uncollected P." *NSt*, 22 S 72, pp. 404-5.

Howe, Irving. "SP A Partial Disagreement." *HM*, Ja 71, pp. 88-91.

Hoyle, J.F. "SP: A Poetry of Suicidal Mania." *L&P*, 18: 187-203 (1968).

Hughes, Ted. "SP's *Crossing the Water*." *CritQ*, 13: 165-72 (Su 71).

Kamel, Rose. "'A Self to Recover': SP's Bee Cycle Poems." *MPS*, 4: 304-18 (Wi 73).

Kissick, Gary. "P: A Terrible Perfection." *Nation*, 207: 245-7 (16 S 68).

Levy, Laurie. "Outside the Bell Jar." *OhR*, 14: 67-73 (Sp 73).

Libby, Anthony. "God's Lioness and the Priest of Sycorax: P and Hughes." *ConL*, 15: 386-405 (Su 74).

Lindberg-Seyersted, Brita. "Notes on Three Poems by SP." *Edda*, 74: 47-54 (1974).

McKay, D.F. "Aspects of Energy in the Poetry of Dylan Thomas and SP." *CritQ*, 16: 53-67 (Sp 74).

Malmberg, Carole. "SP: The Unity of Desolation." *UDQ*, 8: 113-22 (Su 72).

Martin, Wendy. "'God's Lioness'—SP, Her Prose and Poetry." *WS*, 1: 191-8 (1973).

Megna, J.F. "P's 'The Manor Garden.'" *Expl*, 30: 58 (1972).

Meissner, William. "The Rise of the Angel: Life through Death in the Poetry of SP." *MSE*, 3: 34-9 (Fa 71).

Melander, Ingrid. "'The Disquieting Muses': A Note on a Poem by SP." *RSW*, 39: 53-4 (Mr 71).

———. "'Watercolour of Grantchester Meadows': An Early Poem by SP." *MSpr*, 65: 1-5 (1971).

Miller, J.A. "The Creation on Women: Confessions of a Skane Liberal." *CritR*, 8: 231-45 (1974).

Milliner, G.W. "The Tragic Imperative: *The Awakening* and *The Bell Jar*." *Mary Wollstonecraft N*, 2: 21-7 (D 73).

Mizejewski, Linda. "Sappho to Sexton." *CE*, 35: 340-5 (1973).

Mollinger, Robert. "SP's 'Private Ground.'" *NCLit*, 5: 14-5 (Mr 75).

———. "A Symbolic Complex." *Descant*, 19: 44-53 (#2 75).

Murdoch, Brian. "Transformations of the Holocaust: Auschwitz in Modern Lyric Poetry." *CLS*, 11: 123-50 (1974).

Newlin, Margaret. "The Suicide Bandwagon." *CritQ*, 14: 367-78 (Wi 72).

Oates, J.C. "The Death Throes of Romanticism: The Poems of SP." *SoR*, 9: 501-22 (Jl 73).

Oberg, A.K. "SP and the New Decadence." *ChiR*, 20: 66-73 (1968).

Oliva, Renato. "La poesia di SP." *SA*, 15: 341-81 (1969).

Oshio, Toshiko. "SP no Shi." *Oberon*, 14, 2: 45-59 (1973).

Ostriker, Alicia. "'Fact' as Style: The Americanization of Sylvia." *Lan&S*, 1: 201-12 (1968).

Perloff, Marjorie. "*Angst* and Animism in the Poetry of SP." *JML*, 1: 57-74 (1Q 70).

———. "Extremist Poetry: Some Versions of the SP Myth." *JML*, 2: 581-8 (N 72).

———. "On the Road to *Ariel*: The 'Transitional' Poetry of SP." *Iowa R*, 4: 94-110 (Sp 73).

———. "On SP's *Tulips*." *Paunch*, 42-43: 105-9 (D 75).

———. "'A Ritual for Being Born Twice': SP's *The Bell Jar*." *ConL*, 13: 507-22 (Au 72).

Phillips, Robert. "The Dark Funnel: A Reading of SP." *MPS*, 3: 49-74 (1972).

Procopiow, Norma. "SP and the New England Mind." *Thoth*, 13: 3-16 (Fa 73).

Richmond, L.J. "Books Covered and Uncovered: *Crow* . . . by Ted Hughes; *Crossing the Water* . . . by SP." *Erasmus R*, 1: 157-62 (1971).

Rosenblatt, Jon. "P's 'The Couriers.'" *Expl*, 34: 28 (D 75).

Rosenstein, Harriet. "Reconsidering SP." *Ms.*, 1: 44-51, 98-9 (S 72).

Salamon, L.B. "'Double, Double': Perception in the Poetry of SP." *Spirit*, 37: 34-9 (1970).

Schrick, W. "De dichtkunst von SP." *DWB*, 116: 191-210 (1971).

Smith, Pamela. "Architectonics: SP's *Colossus*." *Ariel*, 4: 4-21 (Ja 73).

———. "The Unitive Urge in the Poetry of SP." *NEQ*, 45: 323-97 (S 72).

Spendal, R.J. "SP's 'Cut.'" *MPS*, 6: 128-34 (1975).

Stainton, R.T. "Vision and Voice in Three Poems by SP." *WiOr*, 17: 31-6 (Sp 74).

Steiner, George. "In Extremis." *CaR*, 90: 247-9 (7 F 69).

Stilwell, R.L. "The Multiplying of Entities: D.H. Lawrence and Five Other Poets." *SR*, 76: 520-35 (1968).

Truchlar, Leo. "Die Lyrikerin SP: Eine Skizze." *MSpr*, 17: 39-44 (1973).

Uroff, M.D. "SP on Motherhood." *MwQ*, 15: 70-90 (O 73).

———. "SP's 'Tulips.'" *Paunch*, 42-43: 90-6 (D 75).

———. "SP's Women." *CP*, 7: 45-56 (Sp 74).

Zollman, Sol. "SP and Imperialist Culture." *L&I*, 2: 11-22 (1969).

*Plutzik, Hyam. Friedman, Thomas. "Time for HP: A Critique and Checklist of Criticism." *Thoth*, 2: 37-46 (Wi 71).

Kaehele, Sharon, and Howard German. "In Pursuit of a Precious Ghost: HP's *Horatio*." *LauR*, 8: 53-64 (1968).

Poe, Edgar Allan. Anon. "Another P Letter for Sale." *ESQ*, 63: 37 (Sp 71).

———. "Current P Studies." *PN*, 3: 23-4 (Je 70).

———. "The Detached Terrorism in P." *TLS*, 22 Ja 71, pp. 95-6.

———. "New Letter to EAP." *ESQ*, 51: 51-2 (2Q 68).

———. "P Manuscripts at Austin." *LCUT*, 3: 82-7 (1971).

———. "Recent and Forthcoming Studies." *PoeS*, 2: 3-5 (#1 74).

———. "Three New P Letters." *ESQ*, 14: 89-92 (Sp 72).

Abel, Darrell. "La clef de la Maison Usher." *RLM*, 16: 113-29 (1969).

Adams, J.F. "Classical Raven Lore and P's Raven." *PoeS*, 5: 53 (1972).

* Aderman, R.M. "P in Rumania: A Bibliography." *PN*, 3: 19-20 (Je 70).

Albérès, R.M. "Pour EP." *NL*, 2106: 11 (11 Ja 68).

Allaback, Steven. "Mrs. Clemm and Henry Wadsworth Longfellow." *HLB*, 18: 32-42 (Ja 70).

Allen, B. "Delight and Terror." *HudR*, 26: 735-42 (Wi 73-74).

Alsen, Eberhard. "P's Theory of Hawthorne's Indebtedness to Tieck." *Anglia*, 91: 342-56 (1973).

Alvarez, Q.E.M. "Papel y aspectos de la subjetividad en la obra de EAP." *AyL*, 91: 342-56 (D 73).

Amur, G.S. "Heart of Darkness and 'The Fall of the House of Usher': The Tale as Discovery." *LCrit*, 9: 59-70 (Su 71).

Amoyot, G.F. "Contrasting Visions of Death in the Poetry of P and Whitman." *WWR*, 19: 103-11 (S 73).

Anderson, I.E. "El cuervo de P." *RNC*, 33: 212-5 (Ja 73).

Arciniegas, German. "Cronologia de Jorge Isaacs: Vida y pasión de 'Maria,' una approximación a P." *Nivel*, 67: 1-22 (Ja 68).

Armistead, J.M. "P and Lyric Conventions." *PoeS*, 8: 1-5 (Je 75).

Arntson, H.E. "A Western Obituary of P." *PN*, 1: 31 (1968).

Babcock, C.M. "The Wizards of Baltimore: P and Mencken." *TQ*, 13: 110-5 (Au 70).

Babener, L.K. "The Shadow's: The Motif of the Double in EAP's 'The Purloined Letter.'" *MDAC*, 1: 21-32 (Ja 72).

Bailey, J.O. "P's Theory of the Soul." *Carolina*, 2: 38-43 (Mr 50).

Baker, C.F. "Spenser and 'The City in the Sea.'" *PoeS*, 5: 55 (1972).

Bales, Kent. "Poetic Justice in 'The Cask of Amontillado.'" *PoeS*, 5: 51 (1972).

Balota, Nicolae. "'Principiul poetic.'" *RoLit*, 13 Ja 72, p. 13.

Bandy, W.T. "Baudelaire and P." *TQ*, 1: 28-35 (F 58).

———. "The Date of P's Burial." *PoeS*, 4: 47-8 (D 71).

———. "More on 'the Angel of the Odd.'" *PN*, 3: 22 (Je 70).

———. "Taine on P: Additions and Corrections." *PoeS*, 7: 48 (D 74).

Banta, Martha. "American Apocalypses: Excrement and Ennui." *SLitI*, 7: 1-30 (#1 74).

———. "Benjamin, Edgar, Humbert, and Jay." *YR*, 60: 532-49 (Je 71).

———. "The House of the Seven Ushers and How they Grew." *YR*, 57: 56-65 (S 67).

Barzun, Jacques. "A Note on the Inadequacy of P as a Proofreader and of his Editors as French Scholars." *RR*, 61: 23-7 (F 70).

Băsíc, Sonja. "Antun Gustav Matŏs Prema EAP." *ForumZ*, 17: 193-214 (1969).

Basler, R.P. "L'interpretation de 'Ligeia.'" *RLM*, 97: 97-112 (1969).

Bates, W.B. "P's 'Politian' Again." *MLN*, 49: 561 (D 34).

Battilana, Marilla. "EAP, nostro contemporaneo." *ACF*, 8: 1-10 (Sp 69).

Baxter, N.N. "Thomas Moore's Influence on 'Tamerlane.'" *PN*, 2: 37 (Ap 69).

Bell, H.H. "The Masque of the Red Death': An Interpretation." *SAB*, 38: 101-5 (N 73).

Benton, R.P. "Cross-Lights on P's *Eureka.*" *ATQ*, 22: 1-6 (Sp 74).

*———. "EAP: Current Bibliography." *PN*, 2: 4-12 (Ja 69); 3: 11-6 (Je 70); *PoeS*, 4: 38-44 (D 71).

———. "Eureka: A Prose Poem." *ATQ*, 22: 1-77 (Sp 74).

———. "G.R. Thompson's New Reading of P." *ATQ*, 24: 1-3 (Fa 74).

———. "'The Masque of the Red Death': The Primary Source." *ATQ*, 1: 12-3 (1Q 69).

———. "'The Mystery of Maria Rogêt': A Defense." *SSF*, 6: 144-51 (Wi 69).

———. "P's Acquaintance with Chinese Literature." *PN*, 2: 34 (Ap 69).

———. "P's 'Lionizing.'" *SSF*, 5: 239-44 (Sp 68).

———. "P's 'The Sustem of Sr. Tarr and Prof. Tether: Dickins or Willis?" *PN*, 1: 7-9 (Ap 68).

———. "Reply to Professor Thompson." *SSF*, 6: 97 (Fa 68).

———. "Willis—and P." *PoeS*, 4: 55-6 (D 71).

———, ed, "P Symposium" *ESQ*, 60: 1-56 (1970).

Bergsten, Anders. "EAP och 'The Raven.'" *Lyrikvannen*, 16: 16 (1969).

Bianchi, Ruggiero. "Il problema dell'arte e dell'artiste in P, Hawthorne e Melville." *SA*, 18: 111-50 (1972).

Bickman, Martin. "Animatopoeia: Morella as Siren of the Self." *PoeS*, 8: 29-32 (D 75).

Bier, Jesse. "Romantic Coordinates of American Literature." *BuR*, 18: 16-33 (Fa 70).

Blair, Walter. "P's Conception of Incident and Tone in the Tale." *MP*, 41: 228-40 (1944).

Blish, James. "The Climate of Insult." *SR*, 80: 340-6 (Sp 72).

Bloom, Harold. "Bacchus and Merlin: The Dialectic of Romantic Poetry in America." *SoR*, 7: 140-75 (Ja 71).

Boon, J-P. "Baudelaire, *Correspondances* et la Magnétisme Animal." *PMLA*, 86: 406-10 (My 71).

Boos, Florence and William. "A Source for the Rimes of P's 'The Raven': Elizabeth Barrett Browning's 'A Dream of Exile.'" *Mary Wollstonecraft J*, 2: 30-1 (#2 74).

Borowitz, H.O. "Visions of Salome." *Criticism*, 14: 12-21 (1972).

Brady, Haldeen. "EAP's 'Princess' of Long Ago." *LauR*, 9: 23-31 (Fa 69).

———. "P and the West." *PN*, 1: 3; (1968).

Bramsback, Birgit. "The Final Illness and Death of EAP." *SN*, 42: 40-59 (1970).

Brasher, T.L. "A Whitman Parody of 'The Raven.'" *PN*, 1: 30-1 (1968).

Brie, Hartmut. "Die Theorie des poetischen Effeksts bei P und Malarmé." *NS*, 21: 473-81 (1972).

Bronzwaer, W. "Deixis as a Structuring Device in Narrative Discourse: An Analysis of P's 'The Murders of the Rue Morgue.'" *ES*, 56: 345-59 (Ag 75).

Brooks, Cleanth. "EAP as Interior Decorator." *Ventures*, 8: 41-6 (1968).

Brooks, C.M. "The Cosmic God: Science and the Creative Imagination in Eureka." *ATQ*, 26: 60-8 (Sp 75).

Bruns, G.L. "Poetry as Reality: The Orpheus Myth and Its Modern Counterparts." *ELH*, 37: 263: 86 (1970).

Burns, Shannon. "'The Cask of Amontillado': Montresor's Revenge." *PoeS*, 7: 25 (Je 74).

Burt, D.C. "P, Bradbury, and the Science Fiction Tale of Terror." *MSCS*, 3: 76-84 (D 68).

Butterfield, R.W. "Total P." *EIC*, 22: 196-206 (Ap 72).

Cairns, W.B. "Some Notes on P's 'Al Aaraaf.'" *MP*, 13: 35-44 (My 15).

Cameron, K.W. "New Letter of EAP." *ESQ*, 51: 51-2 (2Q 68).

———. "Notes on Young P's Reading." *ATQ*, 24: 33-4 (Fa 74).

————. "Young P and the Army." *ATQ*, 20: 154-82 (Fa 73).

Campbell, F.F. "A Princedom by the Sea." *LHR*, 10: 39-46 (1968).

Campbell, J.P. "Deceit and Violence: Motifs in *The Narrative of Arthur Gordon Pym*." *EJ*, 59: 206-13 (F 70).

Campos, Haroldo. "EAP: Una engenharia de avessos." *Colóquio*, 3: 5-16 (1971).

Canario, J.W. "The Dream of 'The Tell-Tale Heart." *ELN*, 7: 194-7 (Mr 70).

Candelaria, Cordelia. "On the Whiteness at Tsalal." *PoeS*, 6: 26 (Je 73).

Carlson, E.W. "'Ulalume': Symbolisme et signification." *RLM*. 16: 55-7 (1969).

Carringer, R.L. "Circumscription of Space and Form on P's Arthur Gordon Pym." *PMLA*, 89: 506-16 (My 74).

Casale, O.M. "P on Transcendentalism." *ESQ*, 50: 85-97 (1Q 68).

Cauthen, I.B. "Another Mallarmé-Manet Bookplate for P's *Raven*." *PoeS*, 5: 56 (1972).

Cecil, L.M. "P's Wine List." *PoeS*, 5: 41-2 (1Q 72).

Cesereanu, D. "P—destin literar european." *Steaua*, 23: 28 (1972).

Cevasco, G.A. "*A Rebours* and P's Reputation in France." *RomN*, 13: 255-61 (Wi 71).

Chandler, Alive. "The Visionary Race': P's Attitudes Towards His Dreamers." *ESQ*, 60: 73-81 (Fa 70).

Charvat, W.A. "A Note on P's *Tales of the Grostesque and Arabesque*." *PW*, 150: 2957-8 (23 N 46).

Chinol, Elio. "P's Essays on Poetry." *SR*, 68: 390-7 (Su 60).

Christopher, J.R. "P and the Detective Story." *ArmD*, 2: 49-51 (1968).

Church, R.W. "Al Aaraaf and the Unknown Critic." *VaCal*, 5: 4-7 (Su 55).

Cioran, E.M. "Valery Before His Idols." *HudR*, 22: 411-25 (Au 69).

Cirlot, J-E. "El pensa miento de EP." *PSA*, 52: 239-44 (1969).

Cixous, Helene. "P: Une poetique du revenir." *Critique*, 28: 299-327 (Ap 72).

Clark, C.E.F. "Two Unrecorded Notices of P's Parents." *PoeS*, 4: 37 (D 71).

Clark, G.P. "A Further Word on P and Lolita." *PN*, 3: 39 (D 70).

————. "A German Scholar Interprets P." PoeS, 4: 52-3 (D 71).

————. "Two Unnoticed Recollections of P's Funeral." *PN*, 3: 1-3 (Je 70).

Claudel, A.M. "P as Voyager in 'To Helen.'" *ESQ*, 60: 33-7 (Fa 70).

————. "What Has P's 'Silence' to Say?" *BSUP*, 10: 66-70 (Wi 69).

Colwell, J.J., and Cary Spitzer. "'Bartleby' and 'The Raven': Parallels of the Irrational. *GaR*, 23: 37-43 (Sp 69).

Cooke, M.G. "From Comedy to Terror." *MR*, 9: 331-43 (1968).

Cooney, J.F. "'The Cask of Amontillado': Some Further Ironies." *SSF*, 11: 195 (Sp 74).

Coskren, Robert. "'William Wilson' and the Distintegration of Self." *SSF*, 12: 155-62 (Sp 75).

Cottignoli, Tito. "EP and the Philosophy of Composition." *UI*, 19-22: 64-73 (1969).

Courtney, J.F. "Addiction and EAP." *RSP*, 14: 107-15 (Ja 71).

Covici, Pascal. "Toward a Reading of P's *Narrative of A. Gordon Pym*." *MissQ*, 21: 111-8 (Sp 68).

Cox, J.M. "EP: Style as Pose." *VQR* 44: 67-89 (Wi 68).

————. "Emerson and Hawthorne: Trust and Doubt." *VQR*, 45: 88-107 (Wi 69).

Cox, Sidney. "Israfel." *SR*, 35: 241-5 (1927).

Currie, W.J. "Against the Dragon: Approaches to Nature in Hawthorne and P." *ELLS*, 11: 77-82 (1974).

*Damerson, J.L., and I.B. Cauthern. "Current P Biliography." *PoeS*, 6: 36-42 (D 73); 8: 15-21, 43-6 (Je, D 75).

————. "P and *Blackwood's* Alexander Smith on Truth and Poetry." *MissQ*, 22: 355-9 (Fa 69).

————. "P and *Blackwood's* Thomas Doubleday on the Art of Poetry." *ES*, 49: 540-2 (D 68).

————. "The State of the Complete Bibliography of P Criticism, 1827-1967." *PN*, 2: 3 (1969).

————. "Symbolism on the Poetry of P and Stephen Crane." *ESQ*, 60: 22-8 (Fa 70).

————. "Thomas Ollive Mabbott on the Canon of P's Reviews." *PoeS*, 5: 56-7 (1972).

Darío, Rubén. "EAP." *LSem*, 6: 8-9, 15 (8) 60.

D'Avanzo. M.L. "'Like Those Nicean Barks' Helen's Beauty." *PoeS*, 6: 26-7 (Je 73).

Davidson, Gustav. "P's 'Israfel.'" *LitR*, 12: 86-91 (1968).

Davis, June and J.L. "An Error in Some Recent Printings of 'Ligeia.'" *PN*, 3: 21 (Je 70).

————. "P's Ethereal Ligeia." *BRMMLA*, 24: 170-6 (D 70).

Davis, R.B. "P Criticism: Some Advances Toward Maturity." *MissQ*, 23: 67-76 (Wi 69-70).

Davison, N.J. "'The Raven' and 'Out of the Cradle Endlessly Rocking.'" *PN*, 1: 5-6 (Ap 68).

de Campos Haraldo. "EAP: Una engenharia de avessos." *Coloquio/Letras*, 3: 4-16 (1971).

De Castro, Humberto. "Whitman y P en la poesie Ruben Dario." *BCB*. 10: 90-104 (1967).

Dedmond, F.B. "Paul Hamilton Hayne's P: A Note on a Poem." *GHQ*, 37: 52-3 (1953).

DeFalco, J.M. "The Source of Terror in P's 'Shadow—A Parable.'" *SSF*, 6: 643-8 (Fa 69).

————. "Whitman's Changes in 'Out of the Cradle' and P's 'Raven.'" *WWR*, 16: 22-7 (Mr 70).

De Fox, L.U. "El Parentesco Artistico entre P y Dario." *RNG*, 28: 81-3 (N-D 66).

De Grazia, Emilio. "EAP, George Lippard and the 'Spermaceti and Walnut-Coffin Papers.'" *PBSA*, 66: 58-60 (1Q 72).

————. "P's Devoted Democrat, George Lippard." *PoeS*, 6: 6-8 (Je 73).

Delaney, Joan. "EAP and I.S. Turgenev." *SSASH*, 15: 349-54 (1969).

————. "P's 'The Gold Bug' in Russia." *AL*, 42: 375-9 (N 70).

Delesalle, Jean-Francois. "EP et les petits poemes en prose." *Bul Baudelairien*, 8: 19-21 (1973).

Dowell, E.W. "The Ironic History of P's 'Life in Death': A Literary Skeleton in the Closet." *AL*, 42: 478-86 (Ja 71).

Doxey, W.S. "Concerning Furtunato's 'Courtesy.'" *SSF*, 4: 266-7 (1966).

Doyle, Charles. "The Imitating Monkey: A Folktale Motif in P." *NCF*, 23: 89-91 (Ag 75).

Drabeck, B.A. "'Tarr and Rether'—P and Abolitionism." *ATQ*, 14: 177-84 (Sp 72).

Drake, William. "The Logic of Survival: *Eureka* in Relation to P's Other Works." *ATQ*, 26: 15-22 (Sp 75).

Driskell, Daniel. "Lucretius and 'The City in the Sea.'" *PoeS*, 5: 54-5 (1972).

Durzak, Manfred. "Die Kunsttheoretische Ausgangsposition Stefan Georges: Zur Wirkung EAP." *Arcadia*, 4: 164-78 (1969).

Eakin, P.J. "P's Sense of an Ending." *AL*, 45: 1-22 (Mr 73).

Eaton, R.B. "P's Prosody in Perspective." *PoeS*, 5: 61-2 (1972).

Eddings, Dennis. "P's 'Dream-Land': Nightmare or Sublime Vision?" *PoeS*, 8: 5-8 (Je 75).

Edwards, C.H. "Three Parallels to Faulkner's 'A Rose for Emilty.'" *NMW*, 7: 21-5 (1974).

Ehrlich, Heyward. "*The Broadway Journal*: Brigg's Dilemma and P's Strategy." *BNYL*, 73: 74-93 (F 69).

————. "The 'Mysteries' of Philadelphia: Lippard's *Quaker City* and 'Urban' Gothic." *ESQ*, 18: 50-65 (1Q 72).

Elagin, Ivan. "P in Blok's Literary Heritage." *RusR*, 32: 403-12 (73).

Elkins, W.R. "The Dream World and the Dream Vision: Meaning and Structure in P's Art." *ESRS*, 17: 5-17 (S 68).

Ellyson, Louise. "A Few Kind Words for Rosalie." *New Dominion Life Style*, 2: 7-10 (F 75).

Empric, J.H. "A Note on 'Annabel Lee.'" *PoeS*, 6: 23 (Je 73).

Erickson, J.D. "Valéry on Leonardo, P and Mallarmé." *L'Esprit Createur*, 13: 252-9 (1973).

Evans, Walter. "P's Revisions in his Reviews of Hawthorne's *Twice-Told Tales*." *PBSA*, 66: 407-19 (4Q 72).

Fabre, Michel. "Black Cat and White Cat: Richard Wright's Debt to EAP." *PoeS*, 4: 17-9 (Je 71).

Falco, Nicholas. "EAP of the Village of Fordham." *Bronx County Hist Soc J*, 6: 51-8 (1969).

Falk, D.V. "P and the Power of Animal Magnetism." *PMLA*, 84: 536-46 (My 69).

———. "Thomas Low Nichols, P, and the 'Balloon Hoax.'" *PoeS*, 5: 48-9 (1972).

Fauchereau, Serge. "Il n'état pas à fait P." *QL*, 16 F 70, pp. 10-1.

Fetterly, Judith. "The Sanctioned Rebel." *StN*, 3: 293-304 (Fa 71).

Finholt, R.D. "The Vision at the Brink of the Abyss: 'A Descent into the Maelstrom' in the Light of P's Cosmology." *GaR*, 27: 356-66 (Fa 73).

Fisher, B.F. "Blackwood Articles á la P." *RLV*, 39: 418-32 (1973).

———. "Dickens and P: *Pickwick* and 'Ligeia.'" *PoeS*, 6: 14-6 (Je 73).

———. "P, Blackwood's, and 'The Murders in the Rue Morgue.'" *AN&Q*, 12: 109-10 (Mr 74).

———. "P in the Seventies: The Poet Among the Critics." *MDAC*, 14: 129-41 (1973).

———. "P's 'Metzengerstein': Not a Hoax." *AL*, 42: 487-94 (Ja 71).

———. "P's 'Usher' Tarred & Feathered." *PoeS*, 6: 49 (D 73).

———. "To 'The Assignation' from 'The Visionary' and P's Decade of Revising." *LCUP*, 39: 89-105 (1973).

——— and D.E. Sloane. "P's Revisions of 'Berenice.'" *ATQ*, 24: 19-21 (1974).

Fleurdorge, Claude. "Discours et conre-discours dans "The Tell-Tale Heart.'" *Delta*, 1: 43-65 (N 75).

Flory, W.S. "Rehearsals for Dying in P and Emily Dickinson." *ATQ*, 18: 13-8 (Sp 73).

———. "Usher's Fear and the Flaw in P's Theories of the Metamorphosis of the Senses." *PoeS*, 7: 17-9 (Je 74).

Folsom, Merrill. "P's Eastern Kingdom." *Ford Times*, 61: 8-12 (1968).

Forclas, Roger. "EP et la Psychanalyse." *RLV*, 36: 272-88, 375-89 (Mr-Ap, My-Je 70).

———. "EP et les Animaux." *RLV*, 39: 483-96 (1973).

———. "A Source for 'Berenice' and a Note on P's Reading." *PN*, 1: 25-7 (Ap 68).

Frailberg, Louis. "P's Intimations of Mortality." *HSL*, 5: 106-25 (1973).

Freehafer, John. "P's 'Cask of Amontillado': A Tale of Effect." *JA*, 13: 134-42 (1968).

Freeman, F.B. "A Note on P's 'Miss B.'" *AL*, 43: 115-7 (Mr 71).

———. "P's 'Miss B' and 'Annie.'" *AN&Q*, 12: 79-80 (Ja 74).

Frees, Peter. "Das Motiv des Doppelgangers in Truman Capote's 'Shut a Final Door' und EAP's 'William Wilson." *LWU*, 1: 41-9 (1968).

Friedl, Herwig. "Die Bedeutung der Perspektive un den Landschaftsskizzen von EAP." *Archiv*, 210: 86-93 (1973).

———. "P und Lanier: Ein Vergleich Ihrer Versdichtung." *JA*, 15: 123-40 (1970).

Frushell, R.C. "'An Incarnate Night-Mare': Moral Grotesquerie in 'The Black Cat.'" *PoeS*, 5: 43-4 (1972).

Furrow, Sharon. "Psyche and Setting: P's Picturesque Landscapes." *Criticism*, 15: 16-27 (Wi 73).

Gaillard, Dawson. "P's *Eureka*: The Triumph of the Word." *ATQ*, 26: 42-6 (Sp 75).

Gargano, J.W. "Art and Irony in 'William Wilson.'" *ESQ*, 60: 18-22 (Fa 70).

———. "P's 'Morella': A Note on Her Name." *AL*, 47: 259-64 (My 75).

———. "The Theme of Time in 'The Tell-Tale Heart.'" *SSF*, 5: 378-82 (Su 68).

Garmon, G.M. "Emerson's 'Moral Sentiment' and P's 'Poetic Sentiment.'" *PoeS*, 6: 19-21 (Je 73).

———. "Roderick Usher: Portrait of the Madman as an Artist." *PoeS*, 5: 11-4 (Je 72).

Garrett, Walter. "The 'Moral' of 'Ligeia' Reconsidered." *PoeS*, 4: 19-20 (Je 71).

Garrison, J.M. "The Irony of 'Ligeia.'" *ESQ*, 60: 13-7 (Fa 70).

Gendre, A. "Gaston Bachelard et les *Aventures d'Arthur Gordon Pym* d'EP." *LR*, 26: 169-80 (1972).

Gerber, C.E. "The Coleridgean Context of P's *Blackwood* Satires." *ESQ*, 60: 87-91 (Fa 71).

———. "Milton and P's 'Modern Woman.'" *PN*, 3: 25-6 (D 70).

———. "P and The Manuscript." *PoeS*, 6: 27 (Je 73).

———. "P's Odd Angel." *NCF*, 23: 88-93 (Je 68).

Glassheim, Eliot. "A Dogged Interpretation of 'Never Bet the Devil Your Head.'" *PN*, 2: 44-5 (69).

Goetz, T.H. "Taine on P." *Archiv*, 6: 35-6 (D 73).

Gogol, J.M. "Two Russian Symbolists on P." *PN*, 3: 36-7 (D 70).

Goldhurst, William. "EAP and the Conquest of Death." *NOR*, 1: 316-9 (Su 69).

———. "P's Multiple King Pest: A Source Study." *TSE*, 20: 107-21 (1972).

———, ct al. "Three Observations on 'Amontillado' and *Lolita*." *PoeS*, 5: 51 (Ja 72).

Graham, D.B. "Yone Noguchi's 'P Mania.'" *MarkR*, 4: 58-60 (May 74).

Granger, B.H. "Devil Lore in 'The Raven.'" *PoeS*, 5: 53-4 (Ja 72).

Gravely, W.H. "A Few Words of Clarification on 'Hans Pfaall.'" *PoeS*, 5: 56 (Mr 72).

———. "New Sources for P's 'Hans Pfaall.'" *TSL*, 17: 139-49 (1972).

———. "A Note on the Compositions of P's 'Hans Pfaall.'" *PN*, 3: 2-5 (Je 70).

Greer, H.A. "P's 'Hans Pfaall' and the Political Scene." *ESQ*, 60: 67-73 (Fa 70).

Grieve, A.L. "Rossetti's Illustrations of P." *Apollo*, 97: 142-5 (F 73).

Gross, Seymour. "Native Son and 'The Murders in the Rue Morgue.'" *PoeS*, 8: 23 (Je 75).

Guidacci, Margherita. "Su un racconto di Poet: 'La maschera della morte rossa." *HumB*, 29: 721-30 (1974).

Hafley, James. "Malice in Wonderland." *ArQ*, 15: 5-12 (Sp 59).

Hagel, S.L. "Grunntrekk i EAP's literaturteori og estetikk." *Edda*, 71: 25-36 (1971).

Halio, J.L. "The Moral of Mr. P." *PN*, 1: 23-4 (O 68).

Hall, Thomas. "P's Use of Source: Davy's Chemical Researches and 'Von Kempelen and His Discovery.' *PN*, 1: 28 (O 68).

Halline, A.G. "Moral and Religious Concepts in P." *Bucknell Un Stud*, 2: 126-50 (Ja 51).

Halms, Randel. "Another Source for P's *Arthur Gordon Pym*." *AL*, 41: 572-5 (Ja 70).

Hammmond, Alexander. "Further Notes on P's Folio Club Tales." *PoeS*, 8: 38-42 (D 75).

———. "The Hidden Jew in P's 'Autobiography.'" *PN*, 2: 55-6 (O 69).

———. "P's 'Lionizing' and the Design of *Tales of the Folio Club*." *ESQ*, 18: 154-65 (3Q 72).

———. "A Reconstruction of P's 1833 *Tales of the Folio Club*." *PoeS*, 5: 25-32 (1972).

Harap, Louise. "EAP and Journalism." *ZAA*, 19: 164-81 (1971).

Harkey, J.H. "A Note on Fortunato's Coughing." *PN*, 3: 22 (Je 70).

Harp, R.L. "A Note on the Harmony of Style and Theme in P's *Narrative of Arthur Gordon Pym*." *CEA*, 36: 8-11 (Mr 74).

Harris, K.M. "Ironic Revenge in P's 'The Cask of Amontillado.'" *SSF*, 6: 333-5 (Sp 69).

Harris, W.V. "English Short Fiction in the Nineteenth Century." *SSF*, 6: 1-93 (1968).

Haskell, J.D. "P, Literary *Soirées*, and Coffee." *PoeS*, 8: 47 (D 75).

Haswell, Henry. "Baudelaire's Self-Portrait of P." *RomN*, 10: 253-60 (Sp 69).

――――. "P and Baudelaire: Translations." *PoeS*, 5: 62-3 (D 72).

Hatvary, G.E. "The Whereabouts of P's 'Fifty Suggestions.'" *PoeS*, 4: 47 (D 71).

Haverstick, I.S. "A Note on P and Pym in Melville's *Omoo*." *PN*, 2: 37 (Ap 69).

Hayne, Barry. "Many P's." *CRAS*, 5: 59-61 (Sp 74).

Heaney, H.J. "'The Raven' Revisited." *Manuscripts*, 25: 87-95 (1973).

Helfers, M.C. "The Legendary EAP." *Assembly* (West Point), 27: 6-7, 32-5 (1969).

Helms, Randel. "Another Source for P's *Arthur Gordon Pym*." AL, 41: 572-5 (Ja 70).

Henigan, Robert. "P's 'To Helen' and Christian Platonism." *Scholia Satyrica*, 1: 45-8 (Wi 75).

Henninger, F.J. "The Bouquet of P's Amontillado." *SAB*, 35: 35-40 (Mr 70).

Henss, Hubert. "EAP, 'The Masque of the Red Death'; Ernest Hemingway, 'A Clean Well-Lighted Place.'" *NS*, 16: 327-38 (Jl 67).

Hess, J.A. "Sources and Aesthetics of P's Landscape Fiction." *AQ*, 22: 177-89 (Su 70).

Hill, J.S. "The Diabolic Mr. P?" *PN*, 1: 31 (1968).

Hinden, Michael. "P's Debt to Wordsworth." *SRom*, 8: 109-20 (Wi 69).

Hinz, E.J. "The Source of *The Narrative of Arthur Gordon Pym of Nantucket* of EAP." *SNL*, 9: 138-43 (1972).

――――. "'Tekeli-li': *The Narrative of Arthur Gordon Pym* as Satire." *Genre*, 3: 379-99 (D 70).

Hipolito, Terrence. "On the Two P's." *MDAC*, 1: 15-20 (1972).

Hirsch, D.H. "Another Source for 'The Pit and the Pendulum.'" *MissQ*, 23: 35-43 (Wi 69-70).

――――. "The Pit and the Apocalypse." *SR*, 76: 632-52 (Au 68).

Hoberg, P.F. "P: Trickster-Cosmologist." *ATQ*, 26: 30-7 (Sp 75).

Hoffman, Daniel. "I Have Been Faithful to You in My Fashion: The Remarriage of Ligeia's Husband." *SoR*, 8: 89-105 (Ja 72).

――――. "Send-Ups." *LonM*, 10: 30-6 (Ja 70).

Hoffman, Gerhard. "Raum und Symbol in den Kurzgeschichten EAP's." *JA*, 16: 102-27 (1971).

Hoffmeister, C.C. "'William Wilson' and *The Double*: A Freudian Insight." *Coranto*, 9: 24-7 (1974).

Hogue, L.L. "Eroticism in P's 'For Annie.'" *ESQ*, 60: 85-7 (Fa 70).

Hollander, John. "The Music of Silence." *Prose*, 7: 79-91 (1973).

Holman, Harriet. "Hog, Bacon, Ram, and Other 'Savans' in *Eureka*." *PN*, 2: 49-55 (O 69).

――――. "Longfellow in 'The Rue Morgue.'" *ESQ*, 60: 58-60 (Fa 70).

――――. "Splitting P's 'Epicurean Atoms': Further Speculation on the Literary Satire of *Eureka*." *PoeS*, 5: 33-7 (1972).

――――. "What Did Mill Mean to P?" *MNL*, 6: 20-1 (1971).

Holt, P.C. "Notes on P's 'To Silence,' 'To Helen,' and 'Ulalume.'" *BNYPL*, 63: 568-70 (N 59).

Howard, Leon. "P's Eureka: The Detective Story That Failed." *MDAC*, 1: 1-14 (1972).

Hubbell, J.B. "The Literary Apprenticeship of EAB." *SLJ*, 2: 99-105 (Fa 69).

Hubert, Thomas. "The Southern Element in P's Fiction." *GaR*, 28: 200-11 (Su 74).

Humma, J.B. "P's 'Ligeia': Glanville's Will or Blake's Will?" *MissQ*, 26: 55-62 (Wi 72-73).

Hussey, J.P. "'Mr. Pym' and 'Mr. P': The Two Narrators of *Arthur Gordon Pym*." *SAB*, 39: 22-32 (My 74).

————. "Narrative Voice and Classical Rhetoric in Eureka." *ATQ*, 26: 37-52 (Sp 75).

Idol, J.L. "William Cowper Braun on EAP." *PoeS*, 7: 24-5 (Je 74).

Inge, M.T. "Miquel De Unamuno's Canciones Translated with Commentary." *ArlQ*, 2: 83-97 (Au 69).

————. Gloria Downing. "Unamuno and P." *PN*, 3: 35-6 (D 70).

Isani, M.A. "A Further Word on P and Alexander Crane." *PoeS*, 7: 48 (D 74).

————. "Reminiscences of P by an Employee of the Broadway Journal." *PoeS*, 6: 43 (S 73).

————. "Some Sources of P's 'Tale of the Ragged Mountains.'" *PoeS*, 5: 38-40 (S 72).

Istvan, Gal. "E.A.P magyar citja—Jart-e Kempelen Farkas New Yorkban." *Hetfoi Hirlap*, 14 O 74, p. 4.

Jackson, D.K. "Addendum to a Footnote: 'The Bells.'" *PoeS*, 8: 47 (D 75).

————. "A P Hoax Comes before the U.S. Senate." *PoeS*, 7: 47-8 (D 74).

————. "A Typographical Error in the B Version of P's 'Sonnet—To Silence.'" *PN*, 3: 21 (Je 70).

Jacobs, R.D. "Campaign for a Southern Literature: *The Southern Literary Messenger.*" *SLJ*, 2: 66-98 (Fa 69).

————. "P." *GaR*, 12: 76-9 (Sp 58).

————. "The Seven Faces of P." *SLJ*, 6: 107-23 (Sp 74).

Jannaccone, Pasquale. "The Aesthetics of P." *PoeS*, 7: 1-13 (Je 74).

Jeffrey, D.K. "The Johnsonian Influence: *Rasselas* and P's 'The Domain of Arnheim.'" *PN*, 3: 26-9 (D 70).

Jones, H.M. "P, 'The Raven,' and the Anonymous Young Man." *WHR*, 9: 127-38 (Sp 55).

Joseph, G.T. "P and Tennyson." *PMLA*, 88: 418-28 (My 73).

Kanjo, E.R. "'The Imp of the Perverse': P's Dark Comedy of Art and Death." *PN*, 2: 41-4 (O 69).

Kehler, J.R. "New Light on the Genesis and Progress of P's Landscape Fiction." *AL*, 47: 173-83 (My 75).

Kelley, J.D. "Delacroix, Ingres et P." *RHL*, 71: 606-14 (1971).

Kennedy, J.G. "Jeffrey Aspern and EAP: A Speculation." *PoeS*, 6: 17-8 (Je 73).

————. "The Limits of Reason: P's Deluded Detectives." *AL*, 47: 184-96 (My 75).

————. "The Preface as a Key to the Satire in Pym." *StN*, 5: 191-6 (Su 73).

Ketterer, David. "P's Usage of the Hoax and the Unity of 'Hans Pfaal.'" *Criticism*, 13: 377-85 (Fa 71).

————. "Protective Irony and 'The Full Design' of Eureka." *ATQ*, 26: 46-55 (Sp 75).

————. "The SF Element in the Work of P: A Chronological Survey." *S-FS*, 1: 197-213 (Sp 74).

Kilburn, P.E. "P's 'Evening Star.'" *Expl*, 28: 76 (My 70).

Kimball, W.J. "P's *Politian* and the Beauchamp-Sharp Tragedy." *PoeS*, 4: 25-7 (D 71).

Kime, W.R. "P's Use of Irving's Astoria in 'The Journal of Julius Rodman.'" *AL*, 40: 215-22 (My 68).

————. "P's Use of Mackenzie's *Voyages* in 'The Journal of Julius Rodman.'" *WAL*, 3: 61-7 (Sp 68).

Knowlton, E.C. "P's Debt to Father Bouhours." *PoeS*, 4: 27-9 (D 71).

Kopcewicz, Andrzej. "P's Philosophy of Composition." *SAF*, 1: 101-8 (1968).

Koster, D.N. "P, Romance and Reality." *ATQ*, 19: 8-13 (Su 73).

Lacretelle, J. de. "EP: Archange du bizarre." *FL*, 1189: 14-5 (17 F 69).

LaGuardia, D.M. "P, *Pym*, and Initiation." *ESQ*, 60: 82-4 (Fa 70).

Lanier, E.A. "The Bedlam Patterns East of Greece." *EWR*, 3: 1-22 (1966-67).

Lang, H.J. "P in Melville's 'Benito Cereno.'" *Eng Study Today*, 5: 405-28 (1973).

Lauber, John. "'Ligeia' and Its Critics: A Plea for Liberalism." *SSF*, 4: 28-32 (Fa 66).

*Lawson, L.A. "P and the Grotesque: A Bibliography." *PN*, 1: 9-10 (Ap 68).

Leary, Lewis. "EAP: The Adolescent as Confidence Man." *SLJ*, 4: 3-21 (Sp 72).

———. "Miss Octavia's Autograph Album and EAP." *CLC*, 17: 9-15 (F 68).

Lease, Benjamin. "John Neal and EAP." *PoeS*, 7: 38-41 (D 74).

LeClair, Thomas. "P's Pym and Nabokov's *Pale Fire*." *NCLit*, 3: 2-3 (1973).

Lee, G.F "The Quest of Arthur Gordon Pym." *SLJ*, 4: 22-33 (Sp 72).

Lees, D.E "And Early Model for P's 'The Raven.'" *PLL*, 6: 92-5 (Wi 70).

Leibman, M.G. "Dr. Maudsley, Forgotten P Diagnostician." *PoeS*, 5: 55 (D 72).

Lentricchia, Frank. "Four Types of Nineteenth-Century Poetic." *JAAC*, 26: 251-66 (Sp 68).

Levine, R.A. "The Downward Journey of Purgation: Notes on the Imagistic Leitmotif in *The Narrative of Arthur Gordon Pym*." *PN*, 2: 29-32 (Ap 69).

Levine, Stuart. "Scholarly Strategy: The P Case." *AQ*, 17: 133-44 (Sp 65).

———, and Susan. "History, Myth, Fable, Satire." *ESQ*, 21: 197-214 (4Q 75).

Levy, Maurice. "EP et la Tradition gothique." *Caliban*, 4: 35-51 (Ja 68).

———. "P and the Gothic Tradition." *ESQ*, 18: 19-29 (1Q 72).

———. "'Pym': Conte Fantastique." *EA*, 27: 38-44 (Ja-Mr 74).

Liebman, Sheldon. "P's Tales and His Theory of Poetic Experience." *SSF*, 7: 582-96 (Fa 70).

Ligocki, Llewellyn. "P and Pyschoanalytic Criticism." *PoeS*, 4: 54-5 (D 71).

Ljundquist, Kent. "P and the Sublime." *Criticism*, 17: 131-51 (Sp 75).

Lima, Robert. "A Borges Poem on P." *PoeS*, 6: 29-30 (Je 73).

Lippit, N.M. "EAP's Social Satire." *Dokkyo Un Stud Eng*, 3: 52-81 (1969).

———. "The Grotesque and Arabesque in P." *Josai Un Stud Hum*, 1: 132-72 (1973).

Loberger, G.J. "P's Use of Page and Lore in 'Tamerlane.'" *PN*, 3: 37-8 (D 70).

Lockspeiser, Edward. "Debussy's Dream House." *Opera News*, 34: 8-12 (21 Mr 70).

Lombard, Charles. "P and French Romanticism." *PN*, 3: 30-5 (D 70).

———. "Recent Findings in P." *PoeS*, 4: 50-2 (D 71).

Lord, J.B. "Two Phonological Analyses of P's 'To Helen.'" *Lang&S*, 3: 147-58 (1970).

Lunquist, James. "The Moral of Averted Descent: The Failure of Sanity in 'The Pit and the Pendulum.'" *PN*, 2: 25-6 (Ap 69).

Mabbott, T.O. "Another Source of P's Play, 'Politian.'" *N&Q*, 194: 279 (25 Je 49).

———. "The Books in the House of Usher." *BI*, 19: 3-7 (N 73).

———. "The Harvard P." *PN*, 1: 4 (Je 68).

McCarthy, K.M. "Another Source for 'The Raven': Locke's *Essay Concerning Human Understanding*." *PN*, 1: 29 (S 68).

———. "'Sameness' Versus 'Saneness' in P's 'Morella.'" *AN&Q*, 11: 149-50 (Je 73).

———. "Unity and Personal Identity in *Eureka*." *ATQ*, 26: 22-6 (Sp 75).

McClary, B.H. "P's 'Turkish Fig-Pedler.'" *PN*, 2: 56 (69).

McElderry, B.R. "T.S. Eliot on P." *PN*, 2: 32-3 (Ap 69).

McElrath. "P's Conscious Prose Technique." *NEMLAN*, 2: 34-53 (1970).

McElroy, M.D. "P's Last Partner: E.H.N. Patteron of Oquawka, Illinois." *PLL*, 7: 252-71 (Su 71).

McKeithan, D.M. "P and the Second Edition of Hawthorne's *Twice-Told Tales*." *NHJ*, 4: 257-69 (1974).

McLean, R.G. "P in the Marketplace." *PoeS*, 5: 21-3 (S 72).

McLuhan, H.M. "EP's Tradition." *SR*, 52: 24-33 (Wi 44).

McVicker, C.D. "P and 'Anacreon': A Classical Influence on 'The Raven.'" *PN*, 1: 29-30 (O 68).

Malin, Irving. "The Authoritarian Family in American Fiction." *Mosaic*, 4: 153-73 (1971).

Marcadé, Bernard. "Pour une psychogeographie de l'espace fantastique: Les architectures arabesques et grotesque chez E.A.P." *RE*, 27: 41-56 (1974).

Marder, Julia. "Exiles at Home in American Literature." *SAF*, 3: 216-23 (Au 75).

Marler, R.F "From Tale to Short Story: The Emergence of a New Genre in the 1850's." *AL*, 46: 153-69 (My 74).

Marovitz, S.E. "P's Reception of C.W. Webber's Gothic Western, 'Jack Long; or, The Shot in the Eye.'" *PoeS*, 4: 11-3 (Je 71).

Marrs, R.L. "'The Fall of the House of Usher': A Checklist of Criticism Since 1960." *PoeS*, 5: 23-4 (Je 72).

*———. "Fugitive P References: A Bibliography." *PN*, 2: 12-8 (Je 69).

Marsh, J.L. "The Psycho-Sexual Reading of 'The Fall of the House of Usher.'" *PoeS*, 5: 8-9 (Je 72).

Martin, B.K. "P's 'Hop-Frog' and the Retreat from Comedy." *SSF*, 10: 288-90 (Su 73).

Martindale, Colin. "Archetype and Reality in 'The Fall of the House of Usher.'" *PoeS*, 5: 9-11 (Je 72).

———. "Transformation and Transfusion of Vitality in the Narratives of P." *Semiotica*, 8: 46-59 (1971).

Matei, Ion. "Observatii asupra imaginii poetice la P si Baudelaire." *AUB-LUC*, 20: 137-45 (#1 71).

Matsutama, Akio. "On the Side of EP." *Asia Un Bul*, 13: 1-14 (1965).

Mazow, Julia. "The Survival Theme in Selected Tales of EAP." *SAF*, 3: 216-23 (Au 75).

———. "The Undivided Consciousness of the Narrator of *Eureka*." *ATQ*, 26: 55-60 (Sp 75).

Merivale, Patricia. "The Raven and the Bust of Pallas: Classical Artifacts and the Gothic Tale." *PMLA*, 89: 960-6 (74).

Miller, J.C. "The Birthdate of John Henry Ingram." *PoeS*, 7: 24 (Je 74).

———. "The Exhumations and Reburials of Edgar and Virginia P." *PoeS*, 7: 46-7 (D 74).

———. "John Banister Tabb's Defense of EAP." *VaCal*, 24: 156-63 (1975).

Miranda, Horacio. "El temor en los cuentos de EAP." *BFC*, 30: 135-69 (1968).

Miranda, J.E. "EAP o la existencia amenazada." *CHA*, 76: 775-80 (1968).

Mitilineos, J.P. "The Aesthetics of EP." *PoeS*, 7: 1-13 (1974).

Mise, G.E. "The Matter of Taste in P's 'Domain of Arnheim' and 'Landor's Cottage.'" *ConnR*, 6: 93-9 (1972).

Moeller, H.B. "Perception, Word-Play, and the Printed Page: Arno Schmidt and His P Novel." *BA*, 45: 25-30 (1971).

Mohashi-Punekar, S. "Indra: THe Mind of EAP." *J Karnatak Un*, 16: 119-33 (1972).

Moldenhauer, J.J. "Beyond the Tamarind Tree: A New P Letter." *AL*, 42: 468-77 (Ja 71).

———. "A Descriptive Catalogue of EAP Manuscripts in the Humanities Research Library, the University of Texas at Austin." *TQ*, 16: i-xxi, 1-89 (Au 73).

———. "Imagination and Perversity in *The Narrative of Arthur Gordon Pym*." *TSLL*, 13: 267-80 (Su 71).

———. "Murder as a Fine Art: Basic Connections between P's Aesthetics, Pyschology, and Moral Vision." *PMLA*, 83: 284-97 (My 68).

———. "P Manuscripts in Austin." *LCUT*, 3: 82-7 (My 71).

Monclova, L.C. "EAP y Puerto Rico." *Asomante*, 14: 64-9 (1958).

Monner Sans, J.M. "EAP: algunos aspectos de su obra." *CyC*, 37: 1-12 (1950).

Monteiro, George. "EP and the New Knowledge." *SLJ*, 4: 34-40 (Sp 72).

Moore, Rayburn. "The Magazine and the Short Story in the Ante-Bellum Period." *SAB*, 38: 44-51 (My 73).

————. "'Prophetic Sounds and Loud': Allen, Stovall, Mabbott, and Other Recent Works on P." *GaR*, 25: 481-8 (Wi 71).

Morrison, C.C. "P's 'Ligeia': An Analysis." *SSF*, 4: 234-44 (Sp 67).

Moss, S.P. 'Duyckinck Defends Mr. P Against New York's Penny-a-Liners." *PLL*, 5: 74-81 (1969).

————. "P and the St. Louis *Daily Reveille*." *PN*, 1: 18-21 (Ap 68).

————. "P as Probalilist in Forgues' Critique of the *Tales*." *ESQ*, 60: 4-13 (Fa 70).

Mourier, Maurice. "Le tombeau d'EP." *Esprit*, 441: 902-26 (1974).

Mulqueen, J.E. "The Meaning of P's 'Ulalume.'" *ATQ*, 1: 27-30 (1Q 69).

————. "The Poetics of Emerson and P." *ESQ*, 55: 5-11 (2Q 69).

Murphy, C.J. "The Philosophical Patterns of 'A Descent into the Maelstrom.'" *PoeS*, 6: 25-6 (Je 73).

Murtuza, Athar. "An Arabian Source for P's 'The Pit and the Pendulum.'" *PoeS*, 5: 52 (Je 72).

Nethery, Wallace. "P and Charles Lamb." *PN*, 3: 38 (D 70).

Nettesheim, Josefine. "EAP's Universums-dichtung 'Eureka.'" *JWGV*, 76: 136-54 (1972).

————. "Kriminelles, Kriminalistisches und Okkultes in der Dichtung der Droste und EAP's." *JWGV*, 74: 136-46 (1970).

Newlin, P.A. "Scott's Influence on P's Grotesque and Arabesque Tales." *ATQ*, 2: 9-12 (2Q 68).

Nielsen, E.A. "Fortolkingsfjolset." *Kritik,* 29: 28-46 (1974).

Nuñez, Estuardo. "P en el Perú." *IPNA*, 24: 25-9 (1954).

Obuchowski, Peter. "Unity of Effect in P's 'The Fall of the House of Usher.'" *SSF*, 12: 407-12 (Fa 75).

O'Connor, Roger. "Letters, Signatures, and 'Juws' in P's 'Autobiography.'" *PN*, 3: 21-2 (Je 70).

Oelke, K.E. "P at West Point." *PoeS*, 6: 1-6 (Je 73).

Orel, Harold. "The American Detective-Hero." *JPC*, 2: 395-403 (1968).

Orvel, M.D. "'The Raven' and the Chair." *PoeS*, 5: 54 (Je 72).

*Osowski, Judy. "Fugitive P References: A Bibliography." *PN*, 3: 16-9 (Ja 70); *PoeS*, 4: 4406 (D 71).

————. "T.S. Eliot and P the Detective." *PN*, 3: 39 (D 70).

Ostrom, John. "Fourth Supplement to *The Letters of Poe*." *AL*, 45: 513-36 (Ja 74).

————. "P's MS. Letter to Stella Lewis." *PN*, 2: 36-7 (Ap 69).

Otten, Charlotte. "P, the Puritans, and the Hate Ethic." *Cresset*, 32: 16-7 (1969).

Ousby, I.V.K. "'The Murders of the Rue Morgue' and 'Doctor D'Arsac': A P Source." *PoeS*, 5: 52 (Je 72).

Parisot, Henry. "Mallarme Traditore." *ML*, 69: 51-2 (72).

Parrill, A.S. "P's Vutures." *Innisfree*, 2: 9-15 (1975).

Pauly, T.M. "'Hop-Frog': Is the Last Laugh Best?" *SSF*, 11: 307-10 (Su 74).

*Pavanskar, S.R. "Indian Translations of EAP: A Bibliography." *IJAS*, 1: 103-10 (1971).

*————. "P in India: A Bibliography, 1955-1969." *PoeS*, 5: 49-50 (Je 72).

Pekovic, Slobodanka. "Hofmanovska: Poovska fantastika." *Savremenik*, 37: 428-38 (1973).

Pemberton, J.M. "P's 'To Helen': Functional Wordplay and a Possible Source." *PN*, 3: 6-7 (Je 70).

Peréz Botero, Luis. "El principio poetico de P y el arielismo de Rodo." *RevL*, 6: 55-61 (1974).

Pesce, Hugo. "P, precursor de Einstein." *IPNA*, 24: 21-4 (1954).

Peterson, M.C. "P and the Void." *PN*, 1: 14-6 (Je 68).

Phillips, H.W. "P's Usher: Precursor of Abstract Art." *PoeS*, 5: 14-6 (Je 72).

Pitcher, E.W. "Anagrams in P's Stories." *AN&Q*, 12: 167-9 (My-Je 74).

———. "The Pirnheim Trilogy." *CRAS*, 6: 27-35 (Sp 75).

———. "A Note on Anagrams in EAP's Stories." *AN&Q*, 14: 22-3 (O 75).

Pittman, P.M. "Motive and Method in 'The Cask of Amontillado.'" *MalR*, 34: 87-100 (1975).

Pollin, B.R. "An 1839 Review of P's *Tales* in Willis' *The Corsair*." *PoeS*, 5: 56 (Je 72).

———. "Another Source of 'The Bells' by P: A *Broadway Journal* Essay." *MissQ*, 27: 467-74 (Fa 74).

———. "Byron, P, and Miss Matilda." *Names*, 16: 390-414 (D 68).

*———. "Contemporary Reviews of *Eureka*: A Checklist." *ATQ*, 26: 26-30 (Sp 75).

———. "Dean Swift in the Works of P." *N&Q*, 20: 244-5 (Jl 73).

———. "'Delightful Sights,' a Possible Whitman Article in P's *Broadway Journal*." *WWR*, 15: 180-7 (S 69).

———. "DuBartas and Victor Hugo in P's Criticism." *MissQ*, 23: 45-55 (Wi 69-70).

———. "Fig, Bells, P, and Horace Smith." *PN*, 3: 8-10 (Je 70).

———. "Light on 'Shadow' and Other Pieces by P: or, More of Thomas Moore." *ESQ*, 18: 166-73 (3Q 72).

———. "More Music to P." *M&L*, 54: 391-404 (O 73).

———. "More on Lippard and P." *PoeS*, 7: 22-3 (Je 74).

———. "*Nicholas Nickleby* in 'The Devil in the Belfry.'" *PoeS*, 8: 23 (Je 75).

———. "Notre-Dame de Paris in Two of P's Tales." *RLV*, 34: 354-65 (S 68).

———. "Place Names in P's Creative Writings." *PoeS*, 6: 43-8 (D 73).

———. "P and Hemingway on Violence and Death." *MDAC*, 1973, pp. 12-4.

———. "P and Henry James: A Changing Relationship." *YES*, 3: 232-42 (1973).

———. "P and the *Boston Notion*." *ELN*, 8: 23-8 (S 70).

———. "P and the Computor." *Inst Computor Res N*, 3: 2-3 (1968).

———. "P and the Incubator." *AN&Q*, 12: 146-9 (My-Je 74).

———. "P as Edward S.T. Grey." *BSUF*, 14: 44-6 (Su 73).

———. "P as Probable Author of 'Harper's Ferry.'" *AL*, 40: 164-78 (My 68).

———. "P as Scriblerian." *Scriblerian*, L: 30-1 (1969).

———. "P, Freeman Hunt, and Four Unrecorded Reviews of P's Works." *TSLL*, 16: 305-14 (Su 74).

———, "P in the *Boston Notion*." *NEQ*, 42: 585-9 (D 69).

———. "P's 'Diddling': The Source of Title and Tale." *SLJ*, 2: 106-11 (Fa 69).

———. "P's Dr. Ollapod." *AL*, 42: 80-2 (Mr 70).

———. "P's 'Eldorado' Viewed as a Song of the West." *PrS*, 46: 228-35 (Fl 72).

———. "P's Illustration for 'The Island of the Fay': A Hoax Detected." *MDAC*, 1: 33-45 (1972).

———. "P's Literary Use of 'Oppodeldoc' and Other Patent Medicines." *PoeS*, 4: 30-2 (D 71).

———. "P's 'Mystification': Its Source in Fay's *Norman Leslie*." *MissQ*, 25: 111-30 (Sp 72).

———. "P's *Narrative of Arthur Gordon Pym* and the Contemporary Reviewers." *SAF*, 2: 37-56 (Sp 74).

———. "P's Pen of Iron." *ATQ*, 2: 16-8 (2Q 69).

———. "P's 'Shadow' as a Source of His 'The Masque of the Red Death.'" *SSF*, 6: 104-6 (Fa 68).

————. "P's 'Some Words with a Mummy,' Reconsidered." *ESQ*, 60: 60-7 (Fa 70).

————. "P's 'Sonnet—To Zante': Sources and Associations." *CLS*, 5: 303-15 (S 68).

————. "P's Use of D'Israeli's Curiosities to Belittle Emerson." *PN*, 3: 38 (D 70).

————. "P's Use of Material from Bernardin de Saint-Pierre's *Études*." *RomN*, 12: 331-8 (Sp 71).

————. "P's Use of the Name DeVere in 'Lenore.'" *Names*, 23: 1-5 (Ja 75).

————. "P's Use of the Name Ermengarde in 'Eleonora.'" *N&Q*, 17: 332-3 (S 70).

————. "Politics and History in P's 'Mellonta Tauta': Two Allusions Explained." *SSF*, 8: 627-31 (Fa 71).

————. "The Provenance and Correct Text of P's Review of Griswold's *Female Poets of America*." *PN*, 2: 35-6 (Ap 69).

————. "A Spurious P Letter to A.N. Howard." *PoeS*, 6: 27-8 (Je 73).

————. "The Temperance Movement and Its Friends Look at P." *Costerus*, 2: 119-44 (1972).

————. "Three More Early Notices of *Pym* and the Snowden Connection." *PoeS*, 8: 3205 (D 75).

————. "Undine in the Works of P." *SRom*, 11: 59-74 (Wi 75).

————. "Victor Hugo and P." *RLC*, 42: 494-519 (O-D 68).

Praz, Mario. "P and Psychoanalysis." *SR*, 68: 375-89 (Su 60).

Prior, L.T. "A Further Note on Richard Wright's Use of P in *Native Son*." *PoeS*, 5: 52-3 (Je 72).

Pruette, Lorine. "A Psycho-Analytical Study of EAP." *Am J Pysch*, 31: 370-403 (O 20).

Pry, E.R. "A Folklore Source for 'The Man That Was Used Up.'" *PoeS*, 8: 56 (D 75).

Quinn, P.F. "*Arthur Gordon Pym*: A Journey to the End of the Page." *PN*, 1: 13-4 (1968).

————. "P: Between Being and Nothingness." *SLJ*, 6: 81-100 (Fa 73).

————. "P: A Most Memorial Year." *SLJ*, 2: 112-22 (Fa 69).

————. "Le Voyage Imaginaire de P." *RLM*, 15: 147-89 (1969).

Rauter, Herbert. "Zeit, Zeitmessung und Bewusstsein bei EAP." *Anglia*, 85: 363-89 (1967).

Rayan, Krishna. "EAP and Suggestiveness." *BJA*, 9: 73-9 (1969).

Reece, J.B. "An Error in Some Reprintings of P's 1847 Critique of Hawthrone." *PoeS*, 4: 47 (D 71).

————. "P's 'Dream-Land' and the Imagery of Opium Dreams" *PoeS*, 8: 24 (Je 75).

————. "A Reexamination of a P Date: Mrs. Ellet's Letters." *AL*, 42: 157-64 (My 70).

Reed, K.T. "'Ligeia': The Story as Sermon." *PoeS*, 4: 20 (Je 71).

Reeder, Roberta. "'The Black Cat' as a Study in Repression." *PoeS*, 7: 20-2 (Je 74).

Rees, T.R. "Why P? Some Notes on the Artistic Qualities of the Prose Fiction of EAP." *Forum(H)*, 12: 10-5 (#1 74).

Regan, Robert. "Hawthorne's 'Plagiary': P's Duplicity." *NCF*, 25: 281-98 (D 70).

Reid, A.S "The Southern Exposure of Karl Shapiro." *SHR*, 6: 34-44 (Wi 72).

Reilly, J.E. "Current P Studies." *PoeS*, 7: 27-8 (Je 74); 8: 47-48 (D 75).

————. "The Letter Death-Watch and 'The Tell-Tale Heart.'" *ATQ*, 2: 3-9 (2Q 69).

————. "P in Pillory: An Early Version of a Satire by A.J.H. Duganne." *PoeS*, 6: 9-12 (Je 73).

Rein, D.M. "The Appeal of P Today." *ESQ*, 60: 29-33 (Fa 70).

Reiss, T.J. "The Universe and the Didactic Imagination in E.A.P." *EA*, 27: 16-25 (Ja-Mr 74).

Rest, Jaime. "Evaluacion del Romantismo." *Cuadernos de Critica*, 16: 17-24 (Ag 66).

Ricardou, Jean. "L'Or du Scarbee." *Tel Quel*, 34: 42-57 (1968).

Richard, Claude. "Another Unknown Early Appearance of 'The Raven.'" *PN*, 1: 30 (Je 68).

————. "Arrant Bubbles: P's 'The Angel of the Odd.'" *PN*, 2: 46-8 (O 69).

————. "Avertisement." *RLM*, 16: 9-13 (1969).

————. "La double voix dans 'The Tell-Tale Heart.'" *Delta*, 1: 17-41 (N 75).

————. "Les Contes du Folio Club et la vocation humoristique d'EAP." *RLM*, 16: 79-96 (1969).

*————. "EAP: Selection bibliographique." *RLM*, 16: 215-51 (1969).

————. "L'Ecriture d'Arthur Gordon Pym." *Delta*, 1: 95-124 (N 75).

————. "'MS Found in a Bottle' and the Folio Club." *PN*, 2: 23 (Ja 69).

————. "Panoraman Critique: EAP." *LanM*, 62: 115-9 (J-F 68).

————. "P and the Yankee Hero." *MissQ*, 21: 93-109 (Sp 68).

————. "P and 'Young America.'" *SB*, 21: 25-58 (1968).

————. "P et Hawthorne." *EA*, 22: 351-61 (O-D 69).

————. "P Studies in Europe: France." *PN*, 2: 20-3 (Je 69).

Richmond, L.J. "EAP's 'Morella': Vampire of Volition." *SSF*, 93-4 (1972).

Ridgely, J.V. "The Continuing Puzzle of Arthur Gordon Pym." *PN*, 3: 5-6 (Je 70).

————. "Tragical-Mythical-Satirical-Hoaxical: Problems of Genre in *Pym*." *ATQ*, 24: 4-9 (Fa 74).

Robbins, J.A. "EP and the Philadelphians." *PoeS*, 5: 45-8 (1972).

————. "The State of P Studies." *PN*, 1: 1-2 (Ap 68).

Roberts, Leonard. "Beauchamp and Sharp: A Kentucky Tragedy." *KFR*, 14: 14-9 (Ja-Mr 68).

Robinson, David. "The Romantic Quest in P and Emerson." *ATQ*, 26: 26-30 (Sp 75).

————. "'Ulalume'—The Ghouls and the Critics." *PoeS*, 8: 8-10 (Je 75).

Robinson, E.A. "Current Interpretations of P: Existential or Transcendental?" *PoeS*, 5: 57-9 (Je 72).

————. "New Approaches to P Criticism." *PoeS*, 4: 48-50 (D 71).

————. "Thoreau and the Deathwatch in P's 'The Tell-Tale Heart.'" *PoeS*, 4: 14-6 (Je 71).

Roche, A.J. "Another Look at P's Dr. Ollapod." *PoeS*, 6: 28 (Je 73).

Rocks, J.E. "Conflict and Motive in 'The Cask of Amontillado." *PoeS*, 5: 50-1 (D 72).

Rose, M.G. "P's 'The City in the Sea': A Conjecture." *ESQ*, 50: 58-9 (1Q 68).

————. "'Usher' as Myth in Green's 'Minuit.'" *RomN*, 5: 110-4 (Sp 64).

Ronsenfeld, A.E. "The P-Chivers Controversy." *BBr*, 23: 89-93 (1969).

Rosenthal, Bernard. "P, Slavery, and the *Southern Literary Messenger*." *PoeS*, 7: 29-38 (D 74).

Ross, D.H. "The Grotesque: A Speculation." *PoeS*, 4: 10-1 (Je 71).

Roth, Martin. "The Poet's Purloined Letter." *MDAC*, 12: 113-28 (1973).

Rountree, T.J. "P's Universe: The House of Usher and the Narrator." *TSE*, 20: 123-34 (1972).

Row, Steve. "A P Renewal." *Cwealth*, 41: 25-7 (Su 74).

Rubin, Larry. "An Echo of P in *Of Time and the River*." *PN*, 3: 38-9 (D 70).

St. Armand, B.L. "P's 'Sober Mystification': The Uses of Alchemy in 'The Gold Bug.'" *PoeS*, 4: 1-7 (Je 71).

————. "'Seemingly Intuitive Leaps': Belief and Unbelief in *Eureka*." *ATQ*, 26: 4-15 (Sp 75).

————. "Usher Unveiled: P and the Metaphysic of Gnosticism." *PoeS*, 5: 1-8 (Je 72).

Salzberg, Joel. "The Gothic Hero in Transcendental Quest: P's 'Ligeia' and James' 'The Beast in the Jungle.'" *ESQ*, 18: 108-14 (2Q 72).

————. "Preposition and Meaning in P's 'The Spectacles.'" *PN*, 3: 21 (Je 70).

Sandler, S.G. "Thomas Holley Chivers, M.D. (1809-1858) and the Origin of EAP's 'The Raven.'" *New England J Medicine*, 289: 351-4 (16 Ag 71).

Sands, Kathleen. "The Mythic Initiation of Arthur Gordon Pym." *PoeS*, 7: 14-6 (Je 74).

Sanford, Charles. "EAP: A Blight on the Landscape." *AQ*, 20: 54-66 (Sp 68).

Santa Cruz, Mario. "EAP." *ELyP*, 30: 38-40 (1957).

Santraud, Jeanne-Marie. "Das le sillage de la baleiniere d'Arthur Gordon Pym: *Le* Sphinx de Glaces, Dan Yack." *EA*, 25: 353-66 (1972).

Schaefer, C.W "P's *Eureka*: The Macrocosmic Analogue." *JAAC*, 29: 353-65 (Sp 71).

Sherting, Jack. "The Bottle and the Coffin: Further Speculation on P and Moby-Dick." *PN*, 1: 22 (Je 68).

———. "P's 'The Cask of Amontillado': A Source for Twain's 'The Man That Corrupted Hadleyburg." *MTJ*, 16: 18-20 (Su 72).

Schuster, Richard. "More on the 'Fig-Pedler.'" *PN*, 3: 22 (Je 70).

Schwaber, Paul. "On Reading P." *L&P*, 21: 81-99 (1971).

Schwartz, Arthur. "The Transport: A Matter of Time and Space." *CEA*, 31: 14-5 (D 68).

Senelick, Laurence. "Charles Dickens and 'The Tell-Tale Heart.'" *PoeS*, 6: 12-4 (Je 73).

Serio, J.N. "From Edwards to P." *ConnR*, 6: 88-92 (1972).

Sheehan, P.J. "Dirk Peters: A New Look at P's *Pym*." *LauR*, 9: 60-7 (1969).

Shulman, Robert. "P and the Powers of the Mind." *ELH*, 37: 245-62 (Je 70).

Simoes, J.G. "Critica literaria: *A nocoa de poema* por Nun Judice; *Movimento*, por Olga Goncalves." *Diáro de Notícias* (Lisbon), 29 Je 72, p. 18.

Simpson, L.P. "Touching The Stylus: Notes on P's Vision of Literary Order." *LSUS*, 8: 33-48 (1960).

Simms, J.H. "Death in P's Poetry: Variations on a Theme." *Costerus*, 9: 159-80 (1973).

Sippel, E.W. "Bolting the Whole Shebang Together: P's Predicament." *Criticism*, 15: 289-308 (Fa 73).

Sloane, D.E.E. "Gothic Romanticism and National Empiricism in P's 'Berenice.'" *ATQ*, 19: 19-26 (Su 73).

———, and B.F. Fisher. "P's Revisions in 'Berenice': Beyond the Gothic." *ATQ*, 24: 19-23 (Fa 74).

Smith, Allan. "The Psychological Context of Three Tales by P." *JAmS*, 7: 279-82 (D 73).

Smith, H.F. "Is Roderick Usher a Caricature?" *PoeS*, 6: 49-50 (D 73).

Smith, P.C. "P's Arabesque." *PoeS*, 7: 42-5 (D 74).

Smuda, Manfred. "Variation and Innovation: Modelle literarischer Möglichkeiten der Prose in der Nachfolge EAP's." *Poetica*, 3: 165-87 (1970).

Smyth, E.A. "P's 'Gold Bug' from the Standpoint of an Entomologist." *SR*, 18: 67-92 (1910).

Snow, R.F. "A Chapter on 'Autobiography' by EAP." *AH*, 26: 98-101 (1975).

Solomon, Petre. "In atelierul poetului." *SXX*, 16: 150-3 (1973).

Soule, G.H. "Another Source for P: Trelawny's *Adventures of a Younger Son*." *PoeS*, 8: 35-7 (D 75).

Stauffer, D.B. "P's Views on the Nature and Function of Style." *ESQ*, 60: 23-30 (1970).

Stein, A.F. "Another Source for 'The Raven.'" *AN&Q*, 9: 85-7 (F 71).

Stein, M.B. "The Detecive Story—How and Why." *PULC*, 36: 19-46 (Au 75).

———. "P's 'The Mental Temperament' for Phrenologists." *AL*, 40: 155-63 (My 68).

Stevens, A.J. "Faulkner and 'Helen.'" *PN*, 1: 31 (Je 68).

Stoehr, Taylor. "'Young Goodman Brown' and Hawthorne's Theory of Mimesis." *NFC*, 23: 393-413 (Mr 69).

Stovall, Floyd. "The Conscious Art of EAP." *CE*, 24: 417-21 (Mr 63).

Strandberg, Victor. "P's Hollow Men." *UR*, 35: 203-12 (Mr 69).

Strickland, Edward. "P's 'Ulalume,' Stanzas 10." *Expl*, 34: 19 (N 75).

Stromberg, J.S. "The Relationship of Christian Concepts to P's 'Grotesque Tales.'" *GorR*, 11: 144-58 (Fa 68).

Stronks, James. "A P Source for Faulkner: 'To Helen' and 'A Rose for Emily.'" *PN*, 1: 11 (Ap 68).

Sweeney, G.R. "Beauty and Truth: P's 'A Descent into the Maelstrom.'" *PoeS*, 6: 22-5 (Ja 73).

Sweet, C.A. "Retapping P's 'Cask of Amontillado.'" *PoeS*, 8: 10-2 (Je 75).

*Tanselle, G.T. "The State of P Bibliography." *PN*, 2: 1-3 (Ja 69).

Tate, Allen. "L'Imagination angélique, ou De la divinité de P." *RLM*, 16: 191-213 (1969).

———. "The Poetry of EAP." *SR*, 214-25 (Sp 68).

Teunissen, J.J. "A Brief Critique of the Latest Discovery of the Source of *The Narrative of Arthur Gordon Pym of Nantucket* of EAP." *SNL*, 10: 30-3 (Fa 72).

———, and E.J. Hinz. "P's *Journal of Julius Rodman* as Parody." *NCF*, 27: 317-38 (1972).

———. "'Quaint and Curious' Backgrounds for P's 'Raven.'" *SHR*, 7: 411-9 (Fa 73).

Thomas, Dwight. "James T. Otis and 'Autobiography': A New P Correspondent." *PoeS*, 8: 12-5 (Je 75).

Thompson, G.R. "Current P Studies." *PN*, 1: 4 (1968); 2: 24 (1969), 3: 23-4 (1970).

———. "Dramatic Irony in 'The Oval Portrait': A Reconsideration of P's Revisions." *ELN*, 6: 107-14 (D 68).

———. "The Face in the Pool: Reflections on the Doppelganger Motif in 'The Fall of the House of Usher.'" *PoeS*, 5: 16-21 (Je 72).

———. "Is P's 'A Tale of the Ragged Mountain' a Hoax?" *SSF*, 6: 454-60 (Su 69).

———. "A Key to the House of Usher." *UTQ*, 18: 176-85 (1949).

———. "On the Nose: Further Speculation on the Sources and Meaning of P's 'Lionizing.'" *SSF*, 6: 94-6 (Fa 68).

———. "The P Case: Scholarship and 'Strategy.'" *PN*, 1: 3-4 (Ap 68).

———. "P's 'Flawed' Gothic: Absurdist Techniques in 'Metzengerstein' and the *Courier Staries*." *ESQ*, 60: 38-58 (Fa 70).

———. "P's Readings of *Pelham*." *AL*, 41: 251-5 (My 69).

———. "Proper Evidence of P's Madness." *ESQ*, 18: 30-49 (1Q 72).

———. "'Silence' and the Folio Club: Who Were the Psychological Autobiographists?" *PN*, 2: 23 (Ja 69).

———. "Unity, Death, and Nothingness: P's 'Romantic Scepticism.'" *PMLA*, 85: 297-300 (Mr 70).

Timmerman, John. "EAP: Artist, Aesthetician, Legend." *SDR*, 10: 60-70 (1972).

Travis, M.K. "The Idea of P in *Pierre*." *ESQ*, 50: 59-62 (1Q 68).

———. "A Note on 'The Bell-Tower': Melville's Blackwood Article.'" *PoeS*, 6: 28-9 (Je 73).

Trieber, J.M. "The Scornful Grin: A Study of Poesque Humor." *PoeS*, 4: 32-4 (D 71).

Troubetzkoy, Ulrich. "The Artist James Carling." *New Dominion Life Style*, 2: 27-33 (Je-Jl 75).

Tsitsonis, S.E. "Ancient Greek and Latin Influences on EAP's Poetry." *Plato*, 49-50: 309-22 (1973).

Tucker, E.I. "Philip Pendleton Cooke." *VaCal*, 19: 42-6 (Wi 70).

Tuerk, Richard. "John Sartain and E.A.P." *PoeS*, 4: 21-3 (D 71).

———. "Sadakichi Hartmann's 'How P Wrote the Raven." *MarkR*, 3: 81-5 (F 73).

Turjan, Marietta. "Turgenev i EP." *SSASH*, 19: 407-15 (1973).

Turner, Arlin. "Sources of P's 'a Descent into the Maelstrom.'" *JEGP*, 46: 298-301 (Jl 47).

Tyson, D.J. "J.N. Reynolds' *Voyage of the Potomac*: Another Source for *The Narrative of Arthur Gordon Pym*." *PoeS*, 4: 35-7 (D 71).

Tytell, John. "Anais Nin and 'The Fall of the House of Usher.'" *Pisces*, 2: 5-11 (Wi 71).

Vandegans, Andre. "*Escurial* et 'Hop-Frog.'" *RLV*, 34: 616-9 (1968).

Vanderbilt, Kermit. "Art and Nature in 'The Masque of the Red Death.'" *NCF*, 22: 379-89 (Mr 68).

Varnado, S.L. "The Case of the Sublime Purloin: Burke's *Inquiry* as the Source of an Anecdote in 'The Purloined Letter.'" *PN*, 1: 27 (Ap 28).

———. "P's Raven Lore: A Source Note." *AN&Q*, 7: 35-7 (N 68).

Vitanza, V.J. "EAP's *The Narrative of Arthur Gordon Pym*: An Anatomy of Perverseness." *EA*, 27: 26-37 (Ja-Mr 74).

Vitt-Maucher, Gisela. "E.T.A. Hoffmann's 'Ritter Gluck' and E.A.P's 'The Man of the Crowd.'" *GQ*, 43: 35-46 (Ja 70).

Wages, J.D. "Isaac Asimov's Debt to EAP." *PoeS*, 6: 29 (Ja 73).

Walker, W.S. "P's 'To Helen.'" *MLN*, 72: 491-2 (N 57).

Wallace, A.R. "EAP: A Series of Seventeen Letters." *ATQ*, 24: 45-9 (Fa 74).

Walsh, T.F. "The Other William Wilson." *ATQ*, 10: 17-26 (Sp 71).

Watson, C.N. "Premature Burial in *Arthur Gordon Pym* and *Israel Potter*." *AL*, 47: 105-7 (Mr 75).

Watson, Don. "Borges and P." *Virginia Wk*, 18 Mr 68, p. 3.

Weidman, B.S. "The Broadway Journal: A Casualty of Abolition Politics." *BNYPL*, 73: 94-113 (F 69).

Weiner, B.I. "P's Subversion of Verisimilitude." *ATQ*, 24: 2-8 (Fa 74).

Wella, D.A. "'Bartleby the Scrivener,' P, and the Duyckinck Circle." *ESQ*, 21: 35-9 (1Q 75).

Wertz, S.K. and L.L. "On P's Use of 'Myster.'" *PoeS*, 4: 7-10 (Je 71).

Westburg, Barry. "How P Solved the Mystery of Barnaby Rudge." *DSN*, 5: 38-40 (Je 74).

Whitman, S.H. "EP and His Critics." *ATQ*, 24: 29-66 (Fa 74).

Widnas, Maria. "Dostoevskij i EAP." *Scando-Slavica*, 14: 21-32 (1968).

Wigmore, J.H. "Did P Plagiarize 'The Murders in the Rue Morgue?'" *Cornell Law Q*, 13: 219-36 (F 28).

Wilbur, Richard. "Le cas mystérieux d'EAP." *RLM*, 16: 131-45 (1969).

———. "Les poèmes d'EAP: Introduction." *RLM*, 16: 23: 56 (1969).

Wilcox, E.J. "P's Usher and Usher's Chronology." *PN*, 1: 31 (Je 68).

Williams, P.O. "A Reading of P's 'The Bells.'" *PN*, 1: 2405 (Je 68).

Wilson, Edmund. "P critique litteraire." *RLM*, 16: 15-21 (1968).

———. "P at Home and Abroad." *NRep*, 49: 77-80 (8 D 26).

Wilson, J.D. "Incest and American Romantic Fiction." *SLitI*, 7: 31-50 (Sp 74).

Wilson, J.S. "P and the Biographers." *VQR*, 3: 313-20 (1927).

Woodall, G.R. "Robert Walsh's War with the New York Literati, 1827-1836." *TSL*, 15: 25-47 (1970).

Woodberry, G.E. "P in Philadelphia." *ABC*, 25: 6-14 (Ja-F 75).

Woodbridge, H.C. "P in Spanish America: Addenda and Corrigenda." *PoeS*, 4: 46 (D 71).

*———. "P in Spanish America: A Bibliographical Supplement." *PN*, 2: 18-9 (Ja 69).

Woodward, R.R. "P's Raven, Faulkner's Sparrow, and Another Window." *PN*, 2: 37-8 (Ap 69).

Yagi, Toshio. "P to America Shosetsu no Dento." *EigoS*, 115: 8-9 (1969).

Yonce, Margaret. "The Spiritual Descent into the Maelstrom: A Debt to 'The Rime of the Ancient Mariner.'" *PN*, 2: 26-9 (Ap 69).

Zardoya, Concha. "La belleza de EAP." *CA*, 56: 222-44 (Mr-Ap 51).

Zimmerman. Melvin. "Baudelaire's Early Conception of P's Fate." *RLC*, 44: 117-20 (1970).

Porter, Bernard Harden. Blake, Harriet. "The Leaves Fall in the Area: Regarding BP and Four Little Magazines." *CLQ*, 9: 85-104 (Je 70).

Cary, Richard. "BP Chronology." *CLQ*, 9: 65-7 (Je 70).

———. "BP's Friends in Books." *CLQ*, 9: 114-29 (Je 70).

Higgins, Dick. "Thinking about BP." *CLIQ*, 9: 82-4 (Je 70).

Schevill, James. "BP: Further Notes on *The Roaring Market* and *The Silent Tomb*." *CLQ*, 9: 68-81 (Je 70).

———. "The 'Founds' of BP." *Nation*, 218: 90-2 (19 Ja 74).

*Simon, R.B. "BP: A Bibliographical Sampling." *CLQ*, 9: 105-13 (je 70).

Porter, Katharine Anne. Anon. "Notes of a Survivor." *Time*, 95: 99-100 (4 My 70).

Baker, Howard. "The Upward Path: Notes on the Work of KAP." *SoR*, 4: 1-19 (Wi 68).

Baldeshwiler, Eileen. "Structured Patterns in KAP's Fiction." *SDR*, 11: 45-53 (#3 73).

Barnes, D.R. and M.T. "The Secret Sin of Granny Weatherall." *Ren*, 21: 162-5 (Sp 68).

Beards, R.D. "Stereotyping in Modern Fiction: Some Solitary Swedish Madmen." *MSpr*, 63: 329-37 (1969).

Detweiler, Robert. "The Moment of Death in Modern Fiction." *ConL*, 13: 269-74 (1972).

Gaston, E.W "The Mythic South of KAP." *SwAL*, 3: 81-5 (1973).

Givner, Jean. "KAP and the Art of Caricature." *Genre*, 5: 51-60 (1972).

———. "KAP, Eudora Welty, and *Ethan Brand*." *IFR*, 1: 32-7 (Ja 74).

———. "P's Subsidiary Art." *SWR*, 59: 265-76 (Su 74).

———. "A Re-Reading of KAP's 'Theft.'" *SSF*, 6: 463-5 (Su 69).

Gottfried, Leon. "Death's Other Kingdom: Dantesque and Theological Symbolism in 'Flowering Judas.'" *PMLA*, 84: 112-24 (Ja 69).

Gross, Beverly. "The Poetic Narrative: A Reading of 'Flowering Judas.'" *Style*, 2: 129-39 (Sp 68).

Hardy, J.E. "KAP's Holiday." *SLM*, 1: 1-5 (#1 75).

Hartley, Lodwick. "KAP." *SLJ*, 6: 139-50 (Sp 74).

———. "Stephen's Lost World: The Background of KAP's 'The Downward Path to Wisdom.'" *SSF*, 6: 574-9 (Fa 69).

Howell, Elmo. "KAP and the Southern Myth: A Note on 'Noon Wine.'" *LaStud*, 11: 251-9 (Fa 72).

———. "KAP as a Southern Writer." *SCR*, 4: 5-15 (D 71).

Liberman, M.M. "The Publication of P's 'He,' and the Question of the Use of Literature." *MwER*, 4: 1-7 (1972).

———. "The Short Story as Chapter in *Ship of Fools*." *Criticism*, 10: 65-71 (Wi 68).

———. "Some Observations on the Genesis of *Ship of Fools*: A Letter from KAP." *PMLA*, 84: 136-7 (Ja 69).

Madden, David. "The Charged Image in KAP's 'Flowering Judas.'" *SSF*, 7: 277-89 (Sp 70).

Nance, W.L. "KAP and Mexico." *SWR*, 55: 143-53 (Sp 70).

———. "Variations on a Dream: KAP and Truman Capote." *SHR*, 3: 338-45 (Fa 69).

Partridge, Colin. "'My Familiar Country': An Image of Mexico in the Work of KAP." *SSF*, 7: 597-614 (Fa 70).

Pinkerton, Jan. "KAP's Portrayal of Black Resentment." *UR*, 36: 315-7 (Su 70).

Porter, K.A. "A Country and a People I Love." *HM*, 231: 58-68 (S 65).

Redden, D.S. "'Flowering Judas': Two Voices." *SSF*, 6: 194-204 (Wi 69).

Samuels, C.T. "Placing Miss P." *NRep*, 162: 25-6 (7 Mr 70).

Spence, Jon. "Looking-Glass Reflections: Satirical Elements in *Ship of Fools*." *SR*, 82: 316-30 (Ap-Je 74).

Porter, Katharine Anne

Sullivan, Walter. "KAP: The Glories and the Errors of Her Ways." *SLJ*, 3: 111-21 (Fa 70).

Thomas, M.W. "Strangers in a Strange Land: A Reading of 'Noon Wine.'" *AL*, 47: 230-46 (My 75).

Walsh, T.F. "Deep Similarities in 'Noon Wine.'" *Mosaic* 9: 83-91 (#1 75).

———. "The 'Noon Wine' Devils." *GaR*, 22: 90-6 (Sp 68).

———. "'Noon Wine': The Sources." *YR*, 46: 34-5 (1975).

Wiesenfarth, Joseph. "Internal Opposition in P's 'Granney Weatherall.'" *Critique*, 11: 47-55 (1969).

———. "Negatives of Hope: A Reading of KAP." *Renascence*, 25: 85-94 (Wi 73).

———. "The Structure of KAP's 'Theft.'" *Cithara*, 10: 65-71 (My 71).

Wolfe, Peter. "The Problems of Granny Weatherall." *CLAJ*, 11: 142-8 (D 67).

Yannella, P.R. "The Problems of Dislocation in 'Pale Horse, Pale Rider.'" *SSP*, 6: 637-42 (Fa 69).

Porter, William Sydney (O. Henry). Echter, Reinhold. "O.H's *Sound and Fury*." *NS*, 20: 370-9 (Jl 71).

McLean, M.D "O.H in Honduras." *ALR*, 3: 39-46 (Su 68).

Marks, Patricia. "O.H and Dickens: Elsie in the Bleak House of Moral Decay." *ELN*, 12: 35-7 (1974).

Monteiro, George. "Hemingway, O.H, and the Surprise Ending." *PsR*, 47: 296-302 (Wi 73-74).

O'Quinn, Trueman. "O.H in Austin." *SHQ*, 43: 143-57 (O 39).

Rea, J.A. "The Idea for O.H's 'Gift of the Magi.'" *SHR*, 7: 311-4 (Su 73).

Sibley, M.A. "Austin's First National and the Errant Teller." *SHQ*, 74: 478-506 (Ap 71).

Weatherford, R.M. "Stephen Crane and O.H: A Correction." *AL*, 44: 666 (Je 73).

Portis, Charles. Ditsky, John. "True 'Grit' and True Grit." *ArielE*, 4: 18-31 (Ap 73).

Shuman, R.B. "P's True Grit: Adventure Story or Entwicklungsroman?" *EJ*, 59: 367-70 (Mr 70).

Potok, Chaim. Blufard, Sam. "The Head, the Heart, and the Conflicts in CP's *The Chosen*." *CLAJ*, 14: 402-9 (Je 71).

Pound Ezra. Anon. "Complete Poet's Poet." *TLS*, 21 Ag 70, pp. 925-6.

———. "The Cooling of an Admiraton." *TLS*, 23 Mr 69, pp. 239-40.

———. "The Forgotten Lawyer Who Found the Dollars." *TLS*, 6 Mr 69, p. 6.

———. "Fragments of Cracker." *TLS*, 16 Mr 73, p. 292.

———. "The New Kingdom of Ezrael." *TLS*, 2 Fa 73, pp. 109-10.

———. "Qwertyuiop: A Shirtsleeves History." *SatR*, 3: 801-2 (7 May 27).

Abse, Dannie. "EP and My Father." *TC*, 176: 42-4 (1Q 68).

Adams, S.J. "Are the *Cantos* a Fugue?" *VTQ*, 45: 67-76 (Fa 75).

———. "A Case for P's 'Seafarer.'" *Mosaic*, 9: 127-41 (#2 75).

———. "P, Olga Rudge, and the 'Risveglio Vivaliano.'" *Paideuma*, 4: 111-8 (Sp 75).

Alpert, B.S. "EP, John Price and The Exile." *Paideuma*, 2: 427-48 (Wi 73).

———. "Permanence and Violence: EP, *The English Review*, and *BLAST*." *Occident*, 8: 80-96 (Sp 74).

Alvarez, A. "The Wretched Poet Who Lived in the House of Bedlam." *SatR*, 53: 27-9 (18 Jl 70).

Antheil, George. "Why a Poet Quit the Muses." *Paideuma*, 2: 3-6 (Sp 73).

Atkinson, F.G. "EP's Reply to an 'Old World' Letter." *AL*, 46: 357-58 (N 74).

Baar, Ron. "EP: Poet as Historian." *AL*, 42: 531-43 (Ja 71).

Bacigalupo, Massimo. "EP's Canto 106: A Late Mythologem." *IQ*, 16: 77-93 (1973).

Baker, Carlos. "P in Venice, 1965." *VQR*, 50: 597-605 (Au 74).

Banerjee, R.D.K. "Formality and Intimacy in the Cantos of EP." *IJAS*, 2: 7-11 (D 72).

―――. "Dante Through the Looking Glass: Rossetti, P, and Eliot." *CL*, 24: 136-49 (Sp 72).

Barbour, Douglas. "EP's Legacy: 'What Thou Lovest Well Remains.'" *QQ*, 80: 450-4 (Au 73).

Bard, Joseph. "P/Joyce." *TLS*, 13 Mr 69, p. 271.

Barker, George. "Mr. P's New Cantos." *Criterion*, 14: 649-51 (Jl 35).

Barricelli, G.P. "A Poet of a Poet." *IQ*, 16: 68-76 (Jl 73).

Batavia, Ludovico von. "USA—Botschaft, Schwedische Akademie: zu EP und dem Nobel-Preis." *Diagnole*, 8: 28-31 (1969).

Baumann, Walter. "P and Layamon's *Brut*." *JEGP*, 265-76 (Ap 69).

Bayes, R.H. "Who Sprung E?" *UPortR*, 20: 47-8 (1968).

Bednár, Kamil. "Malé úvahy nad dílem EP." *Plamen*, 10: 66-70 (1968).

Beer, J.B. "EP." *TLS*, 13 Ap 73, p. 421.

Berryman, J.B. "'Medallion': P's Poem." *Paideuma*, 2: 391-8 (Wi 73).

Bevilaqua, Ralph. "P's 'In a Station of the Metro': A Textual Note." *ELN*, 8: 293-6 (1971).

Blackmur, R.P. "An Adjust to the Muses' Diadem: A Note on EP." *Poetry*, 48: 338-47 (S 46).

Blish, James. "The Rituals of EP." *SR*, 58: 185-227 (Su 50).

Booth, Marcella. "Through the Smoke Hole." *Paideuma*, 3: 329-34 (Wi 74).

Bosha, F.J. "P's 'Henriot.'" *Paideuma*, 4: 99-100 (Sp 75).

Bowers, Fauion. "Memoir within Memoirs." *Paideuma*, 2: 53-66 (Sp 73).

Boyd, E.L. "EP at Wabash College." *JML*, 5: 53-4 (S 74).

Bradbury, Malcolm. "P of Flesh." *NSt*, 7 Ag 70, pp. 156-7.

―――. "The Scenario for Modernism." *NSt*, 19 S 69, pp. 378-9.

Braidwood, John. "EP: Λ Commemorative Symposium." *Paideuma*, 3: 151-68 (Wi 74).

Brown, J.L. "EP, Comparatist." *YCGL*, 20: 37-47 (1971).

Burns, Gerald. "Intellectual Slither in the 'Cantos.'" *SWR*, 76-84 (Wi 74).

Călinescu, Matei. "Conceptul modern de poezie—modernism şi traditie: EP si 'iamgismul.'" *SXX*, 13: 8-28 (1970).

Campbell, K.T.S. "The Purification of Poetry: A Note on the Poetics of EP's 'Cantos.'" *BJA*, 8: 124-37 (1968).

Cangiano, Antonio. "Attualite di EP." *Veltro*, 15: 246 (1971).

Capellan, Angel. "EP (1885-1972): Estudio biografico." *RO*, 231: 308-42 (1974).

―――. "La obra poetica de EP." *CHA*, 286: 32-87 (1974).

―――. "Sobre EP." *CdLA*, 10: 36-8 (1974).

Carne-Ross, D.S. "EP." *TLS*, 13 Ap 73, pp. 420-1.

―――. "The Music of a Lost Dynasty: P in the Classroom." *BUJ*, 2: 25-41 (1Q 73).

―――. "New Metres for Old: A Note on P's Metric." *Arion*, 6: 216-32 (1967).

Chace, William. "The Canto as Cento: A Reading of 'Canto XXXIII.'" *Paideuma*, 1: 89-101 (Sp-Su 72).

―――. "EP and the Marxist Temptation." *AQ*, 22: 714-25 (Fa 70).

―――. "Talking Back to EP." *SoR*, 8: 225-33 (1972).

Chakravarty, Amiya. "A Note on EP." *LJAS*, 2: 12-4 (D 72).

Claes, Paul. "EP: Apologir voor 'a poet's poet.'" *Streven*, 26: 355-61 (1973).

Clark, R.D. "Stretching and Yawning with Yeats and P." *MalR*, 29: 104-17 (1974).

Colaneri, John. "Reflections of a man: Guido Cavalcanti." *Paideuma*, 1: 199-204 (Wi 72).

Cooney, D.L. "EP: A Study of His Prosody." *Sou'wester*, special EP no: 100-17 (1970).

*Corrigan, R.A. "An Annotated Checklist of P Criticism." *Paideuma*, 1: 229-263 (Wi 72).

————. "EP Criticism, 1904-1917." *Paideuma*, 2: 115-25 (Sp 73).

————. "E and the Italian Ministry for Popular Culture." *JPC*, 5: 767-81 (Sp 72).

*————. "The First Quarter Century of EP Criticism: An Annotated Checklist." *RALS*, 2: 157-207 (Au 72).

————. "*What's My Line*: Bennett Cerf, EP and the American Poet." *AQ*, 24: 101-13 (Mr 72).

————. "Yankee in King Edward's Court: The Critical Response to EP's Early Verse." *Paideuma*, 1: 249-60 (Wi 72).

Cory, Daniel. "EP: A Memoir." *Enc*, 30: 30-9 (My 68).

————. "Second Thoughts on EP." *Enc*, 37: 86-92 (O 71).

Creeley, Ribert. "A Note." *IJAS*, 2: 15-6 (D 72).

Davenport, Guy. "EP, 1885-1972." *Arion*, 1: 188-96 (Sp 73).

————. "Il Vecchio." *StAR*, 1: 19-20 (Fa-Wi 70).

————. "Persephone's E." *Arion*, 7: 165-99 (Su 68).

————. "The P Vortex." *Nat R*, 24: 525-6 (12 My 72).

Davidson, Carol. "*The Cantos* and Culture." *ConnR*, 8: 55-62 (Ap 75).

Davie, Donald. "The Adventures of a Cultural Orphan." *Listener*, 86: 876-7 (23 D 71).

————. "The Cantos: Toward a Pedestrian Reading." *Paideuma*, 1: 55-62 (Sp-Su 72).

————. "The Significance of *The Cantos*." *CamR*, 94: 165-6 (Je 73).

————. "The Universe of EP." *Paideuma*, 1: 263-9 (Wi 72).

Davis, Earle. "EP: New Emphasis on Economics." *Paideuma*, 2: 473-8 (Wi 73).

Decavalles, A. "Elysium in Fragments." *IJAS*, 2: 17-29 (D 72).

Demott, Robert. "EP and Charles Bowlher: Note on Canto LI." *Paideuma*, 2: 189-98 (Wi 72).

Devlin, V.M. "In Memoriam—EP." *Grayfriar*, 13: 42-4 (1972).

Diesendorf, Margaret. "A Luma Spento: EP (1885-1972)." *PoetA*, 46: 4-5 (1972).

Donoghue, Denis. "EP's School Book." *LugR*, 1: 133-46 (1965).

————. "James's The Awkward Age and P's Mauberley.'" *N&Q*, 17: 49-50 (F 70).

Doody, M.A. "Elegy for EP." *AWR*, 22: 194-6 (Sp 73).

Doria, Charles. "P, Olson and the Classical Tradition." *Bound2*, 3: 127-43 (1973-74).

Drummond, John. "P's Lire." *TLS*, 14 Jl 72, p. 819.

Dudek, Louis. "Exotic References in the Cantos of EP." *AntigR*, 11: 55-66 (Au 72).

Duffey, B.I. "The Experimental Lyric in Modern Poetry: Eliot, P, Williams." *JML*, 3: 1085-1103 (Jl 74).

Dupee, F.W., and George Stade. "Letters of E.E. Cummings to EP." *PaR*, 10: 55-87 (Fa 66).

Dyson, William. "The Fluctuation of EP." *B&B*, 16: 22-7 (S 71).

Egudu. Romanus. "EP in African Poetry: Christopher Okigbo." *CLS*, 8: 153-54 (Je 71).

Eoyang, Eugene. "The Confucian Odes: EP's Translations of the Shi Ching." *Paideuma*, 3: 3-47 (Sp 74).

Espey, John. "Towards Propertius." *Paideuma*, 1: 63-74 (Sp-Su 72).

Faas, Egbert. "Formes der Bewusstseinsdarstellung in der dramatischen Lyrik P's und Eliots." *GRM*, 18: 172-91 (Ap 68).

Falbo, E.S. "EP's 'Lombard Writer Friend.'" *Paideuma*, 3: 247-9 (Fa 74).

Farmer, David. "An Unpublished Letter by EP." *TQ*, 10: 95-104 (1967).

Fauchereau, Serge. "EP." *QL*, 152: 11-2 (16 N 72).

————. "La Prose d'EP." *Crit(P)*, 30: 189-90 (F 74).

Feder, Lillian. "The Voice from Hades in the Poetry of EP." *MQR*, 10: 167-86 (Sp 71).

Fleming, William. "The Melbourne Vortex." *AntigR*, 9: 73-7 (Sp 72); *Paideuma*, 3: 325-8 (Wi 74).

Flory, W.S. "Alexander Del Mar: Some Additional Sources." *Paideuma*, 4: 325-7 (Fa-Wi 73).

Foote, Edward. "A Note on EP." *Prose*, 7: 71-8 (1973).

Foreman, Paul. "From E to Kissinger." *StAR*, 2: 211-3 (Fa-Wi 73).

Friar, Kimon. "On Translation." *CLS*, 8: 197-213 (S 71).

Fukuda, Rikutar. "EP and the Orient." *EigoS*, 119: 13-6 (1973).

Fussell, Edwin. "Dante and P's *Cantos.*" *JML*, 1: 75-87 (1970).

——. "EP: A Note on the International Theme." *Pound N*, 10: 1-3 (1956).

Gallup, Donald. "'Boobliography' and EP." *TQ*, 10: 80-92 (1967).

*——. "Corrections and Additions to the P Bibliography." *Paideuma*, 1: 113-25 (Sp-Su 72); 2: 315-24 (Fa 73); 3: 403-4 (Wi 74).

——. "EP's Letters to Viola Baxter Jordan." *Paideuma*, 1: 107-11 (Sp-Su 72).

——. "T.S. Eliot and EP: Collaborators in Letters." *Atl*, 48-62 (Ja 70); *PoetA*, 32: 58-80 (F 70).

Gatter, Dalton, and Noel Stock. "EP's Pennsylvania." *PoetA*, 46: 5-36 (Sp 73).

Geltman, Max. "P and/or Mussolini." *Quadrant*, 80: 55-65 (Ja-F 73).

——. "The Real EP." *Quadrant*, 18: 39-46 (Ja-F 74).

Ginsberg, Allen, and Gordon Ball. "Allen Verbatim." *Paideuma*, 3: 253-73 (Fa 74).

Going, W.T. "A Peacock Dinner: The Homage of P and Yeats to Wilfred Scawen Blunt." *JML*, 1: 303-10 (1971).

Goodwin, K.L. "EP's Influence on Literary Criticism." *MLQ*, 29: 423-38 (D 68).

——. "The Structure of P's Later Cantos." *SoRA*, 4: 300-7 (1971).

Gordon, David. "Academia Bulletin." *Paideuma*, 3: 381-4 (Wi 74).

——. "Edward Coke: The Azalia Is Grown." *Paideuma*, 4: 223-99 (Fa-Wi 75).

——. "Ezra Among the Old Bones." *Paideuma*, 4: 355-9 (Fa-Wi 75).

——. "E.P. Translating a Li Po Poem." *Paideuma*, 3: 55-9 (Sp 74).

——. "From the Blue Serpent to Kati." *Paideuma*, 3: 239-44 (Fa 74).

——. "'Meeting EP, and Then. . . .'" *Paideuma*, 3: 343-60 (Wi 74).

——. "P's Use of the Sacred Edict in Canto 98." *Paideuma*, 4: 121-68 (Sp 75).

——. "'Root/Br./By Product' in P's Confucian Ode 166." *Paideuma*, 3: 13-32 (Sp 74).

——. "The Sacred Edict." *Paideuma*, 3: 169-90 (Fa 74).

——. "Thought Built on Sagatrieb." *Paideuma*, 3: 169-90 (Fa 74).

Gordon, Robert. "'Old Yeats,' Young Willie, and 'This Queer Creature EP." *Monclair J Soc Sci & Hum*, 2: 68-73 (Su 73).

Gorlier, Claudio. "Riflessioni su EP." *Approdo*, 59-60: 51-6 (1972).

Graham, D.B. "From Chinese to English: EP's 'Separation on the River Kiang.'" *LE&W*, 13: 182-95 (1969).

Grieve, Thomas. "Annotations to the Chinese in Section: Rock-Drill." *Paideuma*, 4: 362-508 (Fa-Wi 75).

Grieder, Josephine. "Robert Frost on EP, 1913: Manuscript Corrections of 'Portrait d'une Femme.'" *NEQ*, 44: 301-5 (Je 71).

Griffin, E.G. "P in Perspective." *TSE N*, 1: 13-5 (#2 74).

Gross, Dalton. "EP's Early Literary Reputation: George Sterling's Dissent." *Paideuma*, 2: 203-4 (Fa 75).

Gugleberger, G.M. "By No Means and Orderly Datescan Rising." *IQ*, 16: 31-48 (1973).

——. "The Secularization of 'Love' to a Poetic Metaphor." *Paideuma*, 2: 159-73 (F 73).

Guidacci, Margherita. "Saggi letteria di EP." *Humanitas*, 4: 277-84 (1975).

Harrison, Keith. "No Things But in Ideas: Doctor Williams and Mr. P." *DR*, 47: 577-80 (Wi 67-68).

Hatlen, Burten. "Report on Works-in-Progress." *Paideuma*, 3: 275-7 (Wi 74).

Hasegawa, Mitsuaki, "Sexual Mockery in *Lustra*." *HSELL*, 19: 33-44 (1973).

Healey, E.C. "EP: Poet in Rebellion." *Montclair J Soc Sci & Hum* 2: 56-67 (Su 73).

Helsztynski, Stanislav. "EP's Letters to a Polish Scholar." *KN*, 17: 299-323 (1970).

———. "EP's Letters to an Editor of His Anthology." *KN*, 20: 59-65 (1973).

Herdeck, D.E. "A New Letter by EP about T.S. Eliot." *MR*, 12: 287-92 (Sp 71).

Hesse, Eva. "Books Behind the Cantos." *Paideuma*, 1: 137-51 (Wi 72).

———. "Frobenius as Rainmaker." *Paideuma*, 1: 85-88 (Sp-Su 72).

———. "P oder der Verlangerte Konflikt." *Diagonale*, 5: 26-9 (1967).

———. "'Sciavoni,' or, When St. Heronymus Turned His Back." *Paideuma*, 4: 105-6 (Sp 75).

———. "Von der Nationalitat des Dichters." *Akzente*, 15: 354-82 (1968).

Heyen, William. "Toward the Still Point: The Imagistic Aesthetic." *BSUF*, 9: 44-8 (Wi 68).

Heymann, C.D. "EP: A Portrait of the Artist as an Old Man." *UDQ*, 6: 1-12 (Au 71).

Halawatsch, Wolfhard. "EP's Weg sum Licht: Eine Interpretation von Canto XV." *NS*, 18: 551-7 (N 69).

Hoffa, W.W. "EP and George Antheil: Vorticist Music and the *Cantos*." *AL*, 52-73 (My 72).

Holder, Alan, "Anne Bradstreet Resurrected." *CP*, 2: 11-8 (Sp 69).

Homberger, Eric. "A Glimpse of P in 1912 by Arundel de Re." *Paideuma*, 3: 85-8 (Sp 74).

———. "P, Ford and 'Prose': The Making of a Modern Poet." *JAmSt*, 5: 281-92

———. "Towards 'Mauberley.'" *AntigR*, 13: 35-44 (Sp 73).

Howe, Irving. "The Return of the Case of EP." *SR/World*, 1: 20-4 (13 Mr 72).

Hubbell, L.W. "The Age of P." *EigoS*, 117: 670-3 (1972).

Hugen, D.J. ". . . Small Birds of Cyprus." *Paideuma*, 3: 229-38 (Fa 74).

Hughes, Robert. "Amarili." *Paideuma*, 2: 39 (Sp 73).

———. "EP's Opera: Le Testament de Villon." *Paideuma*, 2: 11-6 (Sp 73).

Hummel. John. "The Provencal Translations." *TQ*, 10: 47-51 (1967).

Hungiville, Maurice. "EP, Educator." *AL*, 462-9 (N 72).

———. "EP's Letters to Olivet." *TQ*, 16: 77-87 (Su 73).

Hurwitz, H.M. "Hemingway's Tutor: EP." *MFS*, 17: 469-82 (Wi 71-72).

Hutchins, Patricia. "EP and Thomas Hardy." *SoR*, 41: 90-104 (Wi 68).

———. "EP's 'Approach to Paris.'" *SoR*, 6: 340-55 (Ap 70).

———. "Young P in London: Friends and Acquaintances." *ConnR*, 86-93 (#2 74).

Ismail, Jamila. "'News of the Universe': Muan Bpö and *The Cantos*." *Agenda*, 9: 70-87 (Sp-Su 71).

Ivanescu, Mircea. "'Il miglior Fabbro.'" *SXX*, 15: 38-46 (1972).

Iwasaki, Ryoso. "P yuku." *EigoS*, 118: 624-5 (1972).

———. "The Cantos e no approach." *EigoS*, 119: 2-4 (1973).

Izzo, Carlo. "EP: 'Il miglior fabbro.'" *Para*, 280: 88-96 (1973).

———. "Three Unpublished Letters of EP." *IQ*, 64: 117-8 (1973).

Jackson, T.H. "The Poetic Politics of EP." *JML*, 3: 987-1011 (Ap 74).

Janssens, G.A.M. "Perspectives on P." *DQR*, 3: 11 (1973).

Jenner, E.A.B. "Some Notes on the Poetry and Technique of the Later Cantos of EP." *Cave*, 3: 67-9 (F 73).

Johnson, Carol. "The Translator as Poet." *Art Int*, 16: 129-31 (O 72).

Joost, Nicholas. "EP and *The Dial*—And A Few Translations." *Sou'wester*, special EP no: 59-71 (30 O 70).

Jung Palandri, A.C.Y. "Italian Images of EP." *IQ*, 64: 11-22 (1973).

Kahn, S.J. "Whitman's 'New Weed.'" *WWR*, 15: 201-14 (D 69).

Kanaseku, Hisao. "P to Modernism—Passionate Simplicity." *EigoS*, 119: 7-8 (1973).

Kann, Hans-Joachim. "Translation Problems in P's 'In a Station of the Metro.'" *LWU*, 6: 234-40 (1973).

Kavka, Jerome. "EP's Sanity: The Agony of Public Disclosure." *Paideuma*, 4: 425-9 (Fa-Wi 75).

Kazin, Alfred. "The Writer as Political Crazy." *Playboy*, 20: 107-8, 136, 206-9 (1973).

Keith, N.T. "EP and Japanese No Plays: An Examination of *Sotoba Komachi* and *Nishikigi.*" *LE&W*, 15-16: 662-91 (D 71, Mr-Je 72).

Kenner, Hugh. "Blood for Ghosts." *TQ*, 10: 67-79 (1967).

——. "Douglas." *Sou'wester*, special EP no: 6-20 (30 O 70).

——. "Dorothy P Remembered." *Paideuma*, 2: 485-93 (Wi 73).

——. "EP on Visitors Day." *NYT*, 19 N 72, p. 6.

——. "The 5 Laws + Che Funge." *Paideuma*, 1: 83-5 (Sp-Su 72).

——. "The Magic of Place: EP." *IQ*, 16: 5-10 (1973).

——. "In Memoriam: EP." *SatR*, 55: 30 (12 D 72).

——. "More on the Seven Lakes Canto." *Paideuma*, 2: 43-6 (Sp 73).

——. "Motz el Son." *StBr*, 3-4: 371-7 (Fa 69).

——. "The Muse in Tatters." *Agenda*, 6: 43-61 (Sp 68); *Arion*, 7: 212-33 (Su 68).

——. "The Persistent Past." *Spectrum*, 10: 5-13 (Sp 69).

——. "P on Going and on Ending." *Spectrum*, 15: 55-9 (My 73).

——. "Scatter—from The Poe Era." *StAR*, 1: 51-5 (Fa-Wi 70).

——. "A Schema for XXX Cantos." *Paideuma*, 2: 201 (Fa 73).

——. "Some Notes." *Paideuma*, 2: 41-2 (Sp 73).

Kereaski, Rodica. "Incercare de caracterizare a criticii lui EP." *AUB-LG* (1973).

Kirk, Russell. "Personality and Medium in Eliot and P." *SR*, 82: 698-705 (1974).

Knoll, R.E. "EP at St. Elizabeth's." *PrS*, 47: 1-13 (Sp 73).

Knox, Bryant. "Allen Upward and EP." *Paideuma*, 3: 71-83 (Sp 74).

Knox, G.A. "P's 'Hugh Selwyn Mauberley': A Vortex Name." *Spirit*, 36: 23-8 (1969).

Kodama, Jitsuei. "P no Naso to Fenollosa MSS no Hakken." *EigoS*, 115: 234-7 (1969).

Kodama, Sanehide. "Dappi no Itami—Shoki Shihen o megutte." *EigoS*, 119: 11-2 (1973).

——. "The Chinese Subject in EP's Poetry." *SELit*, Eng no: 37-62 (1970).

Kohli, R.K. "'Epic of the West': Some Observations on American History of the Cantos." *IJAS*, 2: 40-54 (D 72).

Koppenfels, Werner von. "EP: Der Modernist als Elegike." *Archiv*, 212: 280-302 (1975).

Korg, Jacob. "Jacob Epstein's Rock Drill and the *Cantos*." *Paideuma*, 4: 301-13 (Fa-Wi 75).

——. "The Music of Lost Dynasties: Browning, P and History." *ELH*, 39: 420-40 (1972).

Kroll, Ernest. "With EP before Rapallo." *CimR*, 2: 7-17 (1973).

Kwan-Terry, John. "The Prosodic Theories of EP." *PLL*, 9: 48-64 (Wi 73).

Landini, R.G. "Confucianism in *The Cantos* of EP." *Topic*, 6: 30-42 (Fa 66).

Laughlin, James. "P the Teacher: The Exuversity." *StAR*, 1: 17-8 (Fa-Wi 70).

Lawton, Harry. "The EP Correspondence: Letters of the Lost Legion." *Sadakichi Hartmann N*, 1: 1-3 (Wi 70).

Leary, Lewis. "P-Wise, Penny-Foolish: Correspondence on Getting Together a Volume of Criticism." *StAR*, 1: 4-9 (Fa-Wi 70); *Paideuma*, 1: 153-9 (Wi 72).

Leavis, F.R. "Eliot and P." *TLS*, 28 Ag 70, p. 950; 11 S 70, p. 998.

Levertov, Denise. "Grass Seeds and Cherry Stones." *AntigR*, 8: 29-33 (Wi 72).

Levi, Peter. "EP's Translation of Sophokles *Women of Trachis*." *Agenda*, 7: 17-22 (1969)

Levy, Alan. "EP's Voice of Silence." *NYTMS*, 9 Ja 72, pp. 14-5, 59-68.

Libby, G.R. "Image or image: An Unnoticed Allusion in 'Hugh Selwyn Maubeley.'" *Paideuma*, 1: 205-6 (Wi 72).

Libera, S.M. "Casting His Gods Back into the Nous: Two Neoplationists and the Cantos of EP." *Paideuma*, s: 355-77 (Wi 73).

Lippincott, H.F. "P, Richard Lattimore and Odyssey IX." *Sou'wester*, special EP no: 36-45 (20 O 70).

Litz, W.A. "P and Eliot on *Ulysses*." *JJQ*, 10: 5-18 (1972).

Lottman, H.R. "The Silences of EP." *TQ*, 10: 105-10 (1967).

Lucas, John. "Villon—Made New and Well." *CaM*, 13: 78-84 (Sp-Su 73).

Lyall, Larry. "P/Villon: Le Testament de Francois Villon." *Paideuma*, 2: 17-22 (Sp 73); *AntigR*, 15: 87-94 (1973).

MacDiarmid, Hugh. "The Master-Voyager of Our Age." *Agenda*, 1-11: 139-45 (Wi 72-73).

McDonald, J.R. "The 'Adams Cantos': Fact or Fiction." *AntigR*, 21: 97-107 (1975).

McDougal, S.Y. "The Presence of Pater in 'Blandula, Tenella, Vagula.'" *Paideuma*, 4: 317-21 (Fa-Wi 75).

Macksey, R.A. "The Old Poets." *Johns Hopkins Mag*, 19: 42-8 (1968).

McLachian, W.I. "Translation and Critical Judgment: A Comparative Study of EP and Gavin Douglas." *DilR*, 14: 166-91 (Ap 66).

MacNaughton, William. "P, a Brief Memoir: 'Chi Lavora, Ora.'" Paideuma, 3: 319-24 (Wi 74).

———. "P's Translations and Chinese *Melopoeia*." *TQ*, 10: 52-6 (1967).

Makin, Peter. "EP and Scotus Erigena." *CLS*, 10: 60-83 (My 73).

Maia, Joa o. "Na morte de EP." *Broteria*, 95: 555-8 (1972).

Mariani, Paul. "Two Essays on EP." *MR*, 14: 118-29 (Wi 73).

Marín Morales, J.A. "Radiografiá epistolar: Joyce-P." *Arbor*, 318: 93-8 (1972).

Martin, Wallace. "The Sources of the Imagist Aesthetic." *PMLA*, 85: 196-204 (Mr 70).

Mason, H.A. "Creative Translation: EP's *Women of Trachis*." *CQ*, 4: 244-72 (Su 69).

Materer, Timothy. "The English Vortex: Modern Literature and the 'Pattern on Hope.'" *JML*, 3: 1123-39 (1973).

———. "Henri Gaudier's "Three ninas.'" *Paideuma*, 4: 323-4 (Fa-Wi 75).

———. "A Reading of 'From Canto CXV.'" *Paideuma*, 2: 205-7 (Fa 73).

Mazzeno, L.W. "A Note on 'Hugh Selwyn Mauberley.'" *Paideuma*, 4: 89-91 (Sp 75).

Meacham, Harry. "I Remember E." *StAR*, 1: 21-4 (Fa-Wi 70).

Melote Castro, E.M. "EP: Da obra." *Coloquio*, 11: 50-3 (1973).

Mendes, Murilo, "Cocteau, Jouve, P." *Coloquio*, 12: 18-24 (1973).

Meyer, W.J. "The Imagist and the Translator: EP's 'Separation on the River Kiang.'" *Sou'wester*, special EP no: 72-80 (30 O 70).

Michaels, W.B. "Lincoln Steffens and P." *Paideuma*, 2: 209-10 (Fa 73).

———. "P and Erigena." *Paideuma*, 1: 37-54 (Sp-Su 72).

Miller, Felicia. "P, Fenollosa, and the Noh." *Occident*, 7: 63-5 (1Q 73).

Miller, Vincent. "The Serious Wit of P's *Homage to Sextus Propertius*." *ConL*, 16: 452-62 (Au 75).

Mills, L.L. "English Origin of 'Still-born' and 'Dumb-born' in 'Mauberley.'" *AN&Q*, 10: 67-8 (Ja 72).

Miyake, Akiko. "P and Confucianism." *StAR*, 1: 45-7 (Fa-Wi 70).

Monks, Donald. "Intelligibility in *The Pisan Cantos*." *JAmSt*, 9: 213-27 (1975).

Montale, Eugene. "Uncle Ez." *IQ*, 16: 23-9 (1973).

Montanelli, Indro. "Incontri: P." *CdS*, 11 Ap 71, p. 3.

Montgomery, Marion. "Beyond P's Quarrel with Eliot's Text." *GaR*, 26: 415-25 (Wi 72).
———. "Eliot and 'Il Miglior Fabbro." *SCR*, 6: 7-13 (N 73).
———. "EP's Angry Love Affair with America." *JPC*, 2: 361-9 (Wi 68).
———. "EP's Arrogance." *Sou'wester*, special EP no: 40-54 (30 O 70).
———. "EP's Problems with Penelope." *SHR*, 3: 114-23 (Sp 69).
———. "EP's Search for Family." *GaR*, 22: 429-36 (Wi 68).
———. "Homage to EP." *UDQ*, 3: 1-17 (Wi 69).
Moody, A.D. "Broken Images/Voices Singing." *CQ*, 6: 45-56 (1973).
———. "P's Allen Upward." *Paideuma*, 4: 55-70 (Sp 75).
Moramarco, Fred. "Schiavoni: 'That Chap on the Wood Barge.'" *Paideuma*, 4: 101-4 (Sp 75).
Morrow, Bradford. "De Iollis' *Sordello* and Sordello: Canto 36." *Paideuma*, 4: 93-8 (Sp 75).
———. "A Source for 'Palace in smoky light': P and Dryden's Virgil." *Paideuma*, 3; 245-6 (Fa 74).
Mullins, Eustace. "E and America." *Sou'wester*, special EP no: 3-5 (30 O 70).
Nassar, E.P. "'This Stone Giveth Sleep': 'Io son la luna.'" *Paideuma*, 1: 207-11 (Wi 72).
Neault, D.J. "Apollonius of Tyna: The Odyssean Hero of *Rock-Drill* as a Doer of Holiness." *Paideuma*, 4: 3-36 (Sp 75).
———. "Richard of St. Victor and Rock Drill." *Paideuma*, 3: 219-27 (Fa 74).
Nicolaisen, Peter. "EP's 'In a Station of the Metro.'" *LWU*, 1: 198-204 (1968).
Niikura, Shunichi. "P to Eliot." *EigoS*, 119: 9-10 (1973).
Olson, Charles. "Encounter with EP." *Antaeus*, 17: 73-92 (Ja 75).
———. "First Canto." *Paideuma*, 3: 295-300 (Wi 74).
Orsini, G.N.G "P and Italian Literature." *SR*, 68: 465-72 (Su 60).
Palandri, A.J. "EP and His Italian Critics." *TkR*, 3: 41-57 (1972).
———. "EP Revisited." *WCR*, 2: 5-8 (Wi 68).
———. "Homage to a Confucian Poet." *Paideuma*, 3: 301-11 (Wi 74).
———. "Italian Images of EP." *IQ*, 16: 30-6 (1973).
———. "The 'Seven Lakes Canto' Revisited." *Paideuma*, 3: 51-4 (Sp 74).
———. "Le traduzioni del cinese di P." *Verri*, 27: 3-19 (1968).
Palmer, L.H. "Matthew Arnold and EP's *ABC of Reading*." *Paideuma*, 2: 195-8 (Fa 73).
Parrish, P.A. "Writing as Celebration: The Epilogue of *Invisible Man*." *Renascence*, 26: 152-7 (1974).
Patnaik, D.P. "EP and Naresh Guha." *Paideuma*, 3: 67-8 (Sp 74).
———. "EP and Rabindranath Tagore." *IJAS*, 3: 53-69 (D 72).
———. "Only the Quality of Affection Endures." *Paideuma*, 3: 313-8 (Wi 74).
Patterson, Gertrude. "'The Waste Land' in the Making." *CritQ*, 14: 269-83 (1972).
Pearce, Donald. "A Wreath for EP." *Shen*, 24: 2-14 (Sp 73).
Pearlman, Daniel. "Alexander del Mar in *The Cantos*: A Printout of the Sources." *Paideuma*, 1: 161-80 (Wi 72).
———. "The Blue-Eyed Eel: Dame Fortune in P's Later *Cantos*." *Agenda*, 9: 4-10 (Fa-Wi 71-72).
Pearson, R.M. "Poet in a Cage." *LGJ*, 1: 26-9 (My 73).
Peck, John. "Arras and Painted Arras." *Paideuma*, 3: 61-6 (Sp 74).
———. "'Get a Dictionary': The Festus Behind P's Festus." *Paideuma*, 2: 211-3 (Fa 73).
———. "Landscape as Ceremony in the Later *Cantos*." *Agenda*, 9: 26-69 (Sp-Su 71).
———. "P and Hardy." *Agenda*, 10: 3-10 (1973).
———. "P's Lexical Mythography." *Paideuma*, 1: 3-36 (Sp-Su 72).

Pound

Peper, Jurgen. "Das imagistische 'Ein-Bild-Gedicht': Zwei Bildauffassungen." *GRM*, 22: 400-18 (1972).

Perloff, Marjorie. "A First Textbook."*NRep*, 171: 21-2 (28 D 74).

———. "The Poet and His Politics." *NRep*, 170: 21-3 (16 Mr 74).

———. "P and Rimbaud." *IowaR*, 6: 91-117 (1975).

Pondrom, C.N. "The Book of the Poet's Club and P's 'School of Images.'" *JML*, 3: 100-2 (F 74).

Pound, Ezra. "Albastru, Veniti, cantilenele mele." *Steaua*, 24: 23-5 (1974).

———. "Anonymous Contributions to *Strike*." *Paideuma*, 3: 398-400 (Wi 74).

———. "Augment of the Novel." *Agenda*, 7-8: 49-56 (Wi 70).

———. "Freedom de Facto." *Agenda*, 9: 23-35 (Sp-Su 71).

———. "Mr. Eliot and Mr. P." *TLS*, 26 Jl 57, p. 457.

———. "A Prison Letter." *PaR*, 7: 17 (Su-Fa 62).

Porteus, H.G. "The P Errata." *Ecounter*, 40: 66-8 (Je 73).

Povear, Richard. "Notes on the Cantos of EP." *HudR*, 25: 51-70 (Sp 72).

Prezzolini, Giueppe. "EP e il fascismo." *Nazione*, 2: 3 (1973).

Pritchard, W.H. "Paradise Lost." *HudR*, 25: 316-22 (1972).

Putz, Manfred. "A Conversation with William C. Chace." *Occident*, 8: 51-65 (Sp 74).

Rachewiltz, Mary de. "Tempus Loquendi." *TQ*, 10: 36-9 (1967).

———, and D.S. Carne-Ross. "P in Texas." *Arion*, 6: 207-32 (1967).

Read, Forrest. "P, Joyce and Flaubert." *Akzente*, nv: 266-86 (Je 70).

———. "'76: The Cantos of EP." *StAR*, 1: 11-6 (Fa-Wi 70).

———. "'Storicamente Joyce,' 1930: EP's First Italian Essay." *TriQ*, 15: 100-7 (Sp 69).

Read, Herbert. "The Limits of Permissiveness." *MalR*, 9: 37-50 (Ja 69).

Reck, Michael. "A Conversation between EP and Allen Ginsberg." *EvR*, 12: 27-9, 84-6 (Je 68).

Rees, Thomas. "EP and the Modernization of Yeats." *JML*, 4: 574-92 (F 75).

Regnery, Henry. "Eliot, P, and Lewis: A Creative Friendship." *ModA*, 16: 146-60 (Sp 72).

Riddel, J.N. "P and the Decentered Image." *GaR*, 29: 565-91 (Fa 75).

Rorem, Ned. "EP as a Musician." *LonM*, 7: 27-41 (Ja 68).

Rose, W.K. "EP and Wyndham Lewis: The Crucial Years." *SoR*, 4: 72-89 (Wi 68).

Rossani, Wolfango. "La poetica di EP." *Nazione*, 28 Mr 71, p. 3.

Russell, Peter. "EP: The Last Years." *MalR*, 29: 11-44 (Jl 74).

———. "P, Q and R." *MalR*, 19: 5-23 (Jl 71).

Ruthven, K.K. "'E,' Alice Kenny, and the *Triad*." *Landfall*, 23: 73-84 (1969).

———. "The Poet as Etymologist." *CritQ*, 2: 9-37 (Sp 69).

———. "Propertius, Wordswoth, Yeats, P, and Hale." *N&Q*, 15: 47-8 (F 68).

———. "Some New Approaches to EP." *SoRA*, 5: 308-15 (1971).

Sanders, F.K. "The French Theme of Canto 70." *Paideuma*, 2: 379-90 (Wi 73).

———. "The View Beyond the Dinghey" *SR*, 79: 433-60 (Su 71).

Sarang, Vilas. "P's 'Seafarer.'" *CP*, 6: 5-11 (Fa 73).

Sato, Toshikiko. "A Study of a Noh, *The Robe of Feathers*." *CLAJ*, 16: 72-80 (S 72).

Savery, Pancho. "Lie Quiet, EP." *Epoch*, 22: 364-5 (1973).

Schafer, R.M. "The Developing Theories of Absolute Rhythm and Great Bass." *Paideuma*, 2: 23-35 (Sp 75).

Schaffner, Perdita. "Merano, 1962." *Paideuma*, 4: 514-8 (Fa-Wi 75).

Schiffer, Reinhold. "Der zweimal verwandelte Dionysos: Zur Mythenrezeption bei Ovid und P." *Arcadia*, 8: 235-47 (1973).

Schmidt, Gerd. "Conversations in Courtship: EP als Ubersetzer altagyptischer Liebeslieder." *Arcadia*, 5: 296-302 (1970).

————. "EP: 'Near Perigord.'" *NS*, 18: 501-12 (O 69).

————. "'Et Vera Incessu Patuit Dea': A Note on Eliot, P, and the Aeneid." *TSE N*, 1: 4-6 (#2 74).

Schneidau, H.N. "Vorticism and the Career of EP." *MP*, 65: 214-27 (F 68).

Schuldiner, Michael. "P's Progress: The Pisam Cantos." *Paideuma*, 4: 71-81 (Sp 75).

Schwartz, Joseph. "Books on P." *Spirit*, 37: 42-6 (1970).

Scott, Tom. "The Poet as Scapegoat." 7: 49-58 (1969).

Shere, Charles. "Eastbay Artists Record Triumph." *Paideuma*, 2: 7-9 (Sp 73).

Sherman, W.D. "The Case of EP." *AWR*, 19: 85-108 (Au 70).

Shulman, Avrom. "Eyns plus eyns—iz eyns." *Unser Tsait*, 4: 44-8 (1973).

Sieburth, R. "Canto 119: Francois Bernouard." *Paideuma*, 4: 329-32 (Fa-Wi 75).

Simpson, Louis. "The California Poets." *LonM*, 11: 56-63 (F-Mr 72).

Singh, C. "The 'Cantos' of EP." *TLS*, 6 Mr, p. 241; 13 Mr, p 271; 27 Mr, p. 327. 3 Ap, p. 369; 10 Ap 69, p. 390.

————. "Dante and P." *CritQ*, 17: 311-28 (1975).

————. "EP Symposium" *Paideuma*, 3: 151-68 (Fa 74).

————. "Four Views of EP." *BA*, 46: 61-3 (Wi 72).

————. "Meeting EP." *BA*, 46: 403-9 (Su 72).

Sisson, C.H. "EP." *Ishmael*, 1: 49-74 (Su 71).

Spann, Marcella. "EP: Drafts and Fragments of Cantos CX-CXVII." *Sou'wester*, special EP no: 55-8 (30 O 70).

Splitter, Randolph. "P's Dreams of the Gods." *Sou'wester*, special EP no: 81-99 (30 O 70).

Stafford, J.R. "EP and Segregation." *LonM*, 9: 60-72 (S 69).

Stanford, D.E. "Thoughts on the P Era." *SoR*, 9: viii-xv (Wi 73).

Stern, Richard. "A Memory or Two of Mr. P." *Paideuma*, 1: 215-9 (Wi 72).

Stock, Noel. "Balancing the Books." *PoetA*, 30: 42-52 (O 69).

————. "Innovation through Translation." *TQ*, 10: 40-6 (1967).

————. "The Young Poet." *PoetA*, 12: 36-40 (O 66).

Stoemescu, Stefan. "Secretul celebrarii perpetue." *SXX*, 15: 30-7 (1973).

Stone, Douglas. "P's 'Mr. Corles': Canto XXXV." *Paideuma*, 2: 411-4 (Wi 73).

Stone, Geoffrey. "Beautiful Nonsense." *Commonweal*, 18: 165-6 (9 Je 33).

Sullivan, J.P. "EP's Classical Translations." *TQ*, 10: 57-62 (1967).

Surette, P.L. "The City of Dioce, U.S.A: P and America." *BuR*, 20: 13-34 (Fa 72).

————. "Helen of Tyre." *Paideuma*, 2: 419-21 (Wi 73).

————. "The Historical Patterns of EP's Cantos." *HAB*, 22: 11-21 (1971).

————. "'A Light from Eleusis.'" *Paideuma*, 3: 191-216 (Fa 74).

Sutherland, Donald. "What of EP?" *UDQ*, 8: 1-9 (Sp 73).

Sutton, Walter. "*Mauberley, The Waste Land*, and the Problem of Unified Form." *ConL*, 9: 15-35 (Wi 68).

Takayanagi, Shunichi. "T.S. Eliot to EP." *ELLS*, 9: 100-44 (1972).

Tatlow, Anthony. "The Stalking Dragon: P, Waley, and Brecht." *ConL*, 25: 193-211 (Su 73).

Tay, William. "Between Kung and Eleusis: *Li Chi*, the Eleusinian Rights, Erigena and EP." *Paideuma*, 4: 37-54 (Sp 75).

Taylor, James. "The Typical Critic of P." *Sou'wester*, special EP no: 118-23 (30 O 70).

Taylor, Mark. "The Value of P." *Cweal*, 97: 226-7 (1972).

Taylor, Richard. "EP: Editor of *No*." *Paideuma*, 4: 344-7 (Fa-Wi 75).

Teele, R.E. "The Japanese Translations." *TQ*, 10: 61-6 (1967).

Terrell, C.F. "An English Version of Grosseteste's *De Luce*." *Paideuma*, 2: 449-62 (Wi 73).

————. "The Eparch's Book." *Paideuma*, 2: 223-311 (Fa 73).

————. "John Adams Speaking: Some Reflections on Technique." *Paideuma*, 4: 533-8 (Fa-Wi 75).

————. "K.R.H. and the Young EP." *Paideuma*, 2: 49-51 (Sp 73).

————. "Meeting EO and Then. . . ." *Paideuma*, 3: 343-60 (Wi 74).

————. "The Na-Khi Documents I." *Paideuma*, 3: 91-122 (Sp 74).

————. "The Periplus of Hanno." *Paideuma*, 1: 224-31 (Wi 72).

————. "The Sacred Edicts of K'ang-Hsi." *Paideuma*, 2: 69-112 (Sp 73).

————. "St. Elizabeths." *Paideuma*, 3: 363-79 (Wi 74).

Thaniel, George. "George Seferis Thrush and the Poetry of EP." *CLS*, 11: 326-36 (1974).

Thompson, J.S "The Political Theme of P's *Cantos*." *L&I*, 8: 43-56 (1971).

Tierney, Bill. "EP: The State of the Poet." *AntigR*, 12: 85-96 (Wi 73).

Traverso, Leone. "Letture di EP." *SUSFL*, 45: 300-3 (1971).

Trevisan, Lucio. "Il Canto 74 e el metodo poundiano." *SA*, 17: 167-93 (1971).

Tulip, James. "The Wesleyan Poets." *PoetA*, 12: 30-5 (O 66).

Turner, Mark. "P and Provence." *Occident*, 7: 54-63 (1 Q 73).

Uberti, R.M. "EP and Ubaldo degli Uberti: History of a Friendship." *IQ*, 16: 96-107 (1973).

Uchine, Takako. "The Confucian Odes as a Case Study of Problems in Translating Oriental Classics into English." *KAL*, 11: 77-86 (1968).

von Hallberg, Robert. "Olson's Relation to P and Williams." *ConL*, 15: 15-48 (Wi 74).

Waggoner, H.H. "The Legend of EP." *UKCR*, 10: 275-85 (Su 44).

Wagner, L.W. "The Poetry of EP." *JML*, 1: 293-8 (1970).

Wain, John. "The Poetry of E vs. 'The Egotistical Sublime.'" *Enc*, 33: 63-70 (Ag 69).

Wallace, E.M. "Penn's Poet Friends." *Pennsylvania Gaz*, 71: 33-6 (F 73).

Wand, D.H-F. "To the Summit of Tai Shan: EP's Use of Chinese Mythology." *Paideuma*, 3: 3-12 (Sp 74).

Welke, R.J. "Frobenius: P—Some Quick Notes." *Paideuma*, 2: 415-7 (Wi 73).

Wigginton, E.B. "A Homer Pound Letter." *Rendezvous*, 4: 27-9 (Su 69).

————. "The Ps at Hailey." *Rendezvous*, 4: 31-68 (Su 69).

Wilhelm, J.J. "The Dragon and the Duel: A Defense of P's Canto 88." *TCL*, 20: 114-25 (Ap 74).

————. "Guido Calvalcanti as a Mask for EP." *PMLA*, 89: 332-40 (Mr 70).

————. "P's Middle Cantos as an Analogue to Dante's *Purgatorio*." *IQ*, 16: 49-67 (1973).

————. "In Praise of Anselm: An Approach to Canto 105." *Paideuma*, 2: 399-407 (Wi 73).

————. "Two Heavens of Light and Love: Paradise to Dante and to P." *Paideuma*, 2: 175-91 (Fa 75).

Williams, W.C. "The Later P." *MR*, 14: 124-9 (1973).

————. "A Study of P's Present Position." *MR*, 14: 118-23 (1973).

Wilson, D.D. "Penny-Wise P." *Paideuma*, 1: 204-4 (Wi 72).

Witemeyer, Hugh. "EP." *ConL*, 14: 240-6 (1973).

————. "The Flame-Style King." *Paideuma*, 4: 333-5 (Fa-Wi 75).

————. "The Method of the Cantos: 'Ply over Ply.'" *Occident*, 7: 49-54 (1973).

————. "Ruskin and the Signed Capital in Canto 45." *Paideuma*, 4: 85-8 (Sp 75).

Wood, Michael. "EP." *NYRB*, 20: 7-11 (F 8 73).

Wood, Tom. "The Value of a P." *LGJ*, 1: 30-3 (My 73).

Yoder, J.A. "P as Odysseus, the Prisoner Pyschotic." *Rendezvous*, 8: 1-11 (Su 73).

Yoshio, Masaaki. "P and His Method of Cognition." *SELL*, 24: 63-77 (1974).

Zapatka, F.E. "Crommelyn and del Valle: A Note on Canto 105." *Paideuma*, 2: 423 (Wi 73).

Zapponi, Niccolo. "Odi e amori futuristi di EP." *SA*, 18: 299-312 (1972).

Powers, J.F. Bates, B.W. "Flares of Special Grace: The Orthodoxy of J.F.P." *MQ*, 11: 91-106 (O 69).

Burgess, C.F. "The Case of the Hen-Pecked Priest in J.F.P's 'The Valiant Woman.'" *Cithara*, 9: 67-71 (N 69).

Degnan, J.P. "J.F.P: Comic Satirist." *ColQ*, 16: 325-33 (Sp 68).

Dolan, P.J. "God's Crooked Lines: P's Morte D'Urban." *Renascence*, 21: 95-102 (1969).

Dorenkamp, J.H. "The Unity of *Morte D'Urban*." *UDR*, 8: 29-34 (Fa 71).

Dufner, Angeline. "The Sainting of Father Urban." *ABR*, 24: 327-41 (1973).

Hagopian, John. "The Fathers of J.F.P." *SSF*, 5: 139-53 (Wi 68).

Hertzel, L.J. "What About Authors in the North?" *SDR*, 5: 3-19 (Sp 67).

Hynes, Joseph. "Father Urban's Renewal: J.F.P's Difficult Precision." *MLQ*, 29: 450-88 (D 68).

Kelley, Richard. "Father Eudex, the Judge and the Judged: An Analysis of J.F.P's 'The Forks.'" *UR*, 35: 316-8 (Su 69).

Laughlin, R.M. "Wanderers in the Wasteland: The Characters of J.F.P." *BaratR*, 6: 38-48 (1961).

O'Brien, C.F "*Morte d'Urban* and the Catholic Church in America." *Discourse*, 12: 324-8 (1969).

Poss, Stanley. "J.F.P: The Gin of Irony." *TCL*, 14: 65-74 (Jl 68).

Preston, T.R. "Christian Folly in the Fiction of J.F.P." *Critique*, 16: 91-107 (#2 74).

Steichen, D.M. "J.F.P and the Noonday Devil." *ABR*, 20: 528-51 (1969).

Stewart, D.H. "J.F.P's *Morte D'Urban* as Western." *WAL*, 5: 31-44 (Sp 70).

Prescott, William Hickling. Brotherson, G.J. "An Indian Farewell in P's The Conquest of Mexico." *AL*, 45: 348-56 (N 73).

Price, Reynolds. Bames, D.R. "The News and the Names of *RP*." *KenR*, 2: 76-91

Eichelberger, C.L. "RP: 'A Banner in Defeat.'" *JPC*, 1: 410-7 (1968).

Price, Reynolds. "Dodging Apples." *SAQ*, 71: 1-16 (Wi 73).

———. "News for the Mineshaft." *VQR*, 44: 461-58 (Au 68).

Shepherd, Allen. "Love (and Marriage) in *A Long and Happy Life*." *TCL*, 17: 29-35 (Ja 71).

———. "*Love and Work* and the Unseen World." *Topic*, 12: 42-7 (Sp 72).

———. "Notes on Nature in the Fiction of RP." *Critique*, 15: 83-94 (#2 73).

———. "RP's A Long and Happy Life: the Epigraph." *NCLit*, 2: 12-3 (My 72).

Solotaroff, Theodore. "The RP Who Outgrew the Southern Pastoral." *SatR*, 53: 27-9 (26 S 70).

Vauthier, Simone. "The 'Circle in the Forest': Fictional Shape in RP's *A Long and Happy Life*." *MissQ*, 28: 123-46 (Sp 75).

———. "Nom et visage dans *A Long and Happy Life*." *RANAM*, 5: 243-63 (1972).

Westendorp, T.A. "Recent Southern Fiction: Percy, P and Dickey." *HVP*, 1974, pp. 188-98.

Prime, Benjamin Young. Wheelock, C.W. "BYP, Class of 1751: Poet-Physician." *PULC*, 29: 129-49 (Wi 68).

———. "The Poet BP (1733-1791)." *AL*, 40: 459-71 (Ja 69).

Prince, Thomas. Shuffleton, F.C. "TP and His Edition of Thomas Hooker's *Poor Doubting Christian*." *EAL*, 5: 68-75 (Wi 70-71).

Proud, Robert. Hoffer, Peter. "Fettered Loyalism: A Re-evaluation of RP's and George Chalmers' Unfinished Colonial Histories." *MHN*, 68: 160-72 (Su 73).

Neuenschwander, J.A. "RP: A Chronicle of Scholarly Failure." *PMHB*, 92: 494-506 (O 68).

Purdy, James. Baldanza, Frank. "JP on the Corruption of Innocents." *ConL*, 15: 315-30 (Su 74).

―――. "JP's Half-Orphans." *CentR*, 18: 255-72 (Su 74).

―――. "Northern Gothic." *SoR*, 10: 566-82 (Jl 74).

―――. "The Paradoxes of Patronage in P." *AL*, 46: 347-57 (N 74).

―――. "Playing House for Keeps with JP." *ConL*, 11: 488-510 (Au 70).

Bolling, Douglas. "The World Upstaged in JP's *I Am Elijah Thrush*." *UDR*, 10: 75-83 (Sp 74).

Brown, Ashley. "Landscape into Art: Henry James and John Crowe Ransom." *SR*, 79: 206-13 (Ap-Je 71).

Burris, S.W. "The Emergency of P's 'Daddy Wolf.'" *Ren*, 20: 94-8 (Wi 68).

Bush, G.E. "JP." *BB*, 28: 5-6 (Ja-Mr 71).

Fink, Guido. "JP e le gaie esequie del romanzo americano." *Para*, 21: 82-98 (1970).

Grinnell, J.W. "Whose Afraid of 'Daddy Wolf?'" *JPC*, 3: 750-2 (1970).

Krummer, J.P. "Two Guests in Two Societies." *Eng Rec*, 17: 28-32 (Ap 67).

McNamara, Eugene. "The Absurd Style in Contemporary American Literature." *HAB*, 19: 44-9 (My 68).

Morris, R.K. "JP and the Works." *Nation*, 205: 342-4 (9 O 67).

Skerrett, J.J. "JP and the Works: Love and Tragedy in Five Novels." *TCL*, 15: 25-33 (Ap 69).

Stetler, Charles. "P's *Malcolm*: Allegory of No Man." *Critique*, 14: 91-9 (1973).

Tanner, Tony. "Sex and Identity in *Cabot Wright Begins*." *TCS*, 1: 89-102 (N 69).

Pynchon, Thomas. Abenethy, P.L. "Entropy in P's *The Crying of Lot 49*." *Critique*, 14: 18-33 (1972).

Davis, R.M. "Parody, Paranoia, and the Dead End of Language in *The Crying of Lot 49*." *Genre*, 5: 367-77 (1972).

Friedman, Alan, and Manfred Puetz. "Science as Metaphor: TP and *Gravity's Rainbow*." *ConL*, 15: 345-59 (Su 74).

Golden, R.E. "Mass Man and Modernism: Violence on P's *V*." *Critique*, 14: 5-17 (#2 72).

Greenberg, Alvin. "The Revolt of Objects: The Opposing World in the Modern Novel." *CentR*, 13: 366-88 (Fa 69).

Hall, James. "The New Pleasures of the Imagination." *VQR*, 46: 596-612 (Au 70).

Hausdorff, Don. "TP's Multiple Absurdities." *WSCL*, 7: 258-69 (1966).

Hendin, Josephine. "What Is TP Telling Us?" *HM*, 250: 82-92 (Mr 75).

Henkle, R.B. "P's Tapestries on the Western Wall." *MFS*, 17: 207-20 (Su 71).

*Herzberg, Bruce. "Selected Articles on TP: An Annotated Bibliography." *TSL*, 21: 221-5 (My 75).

Kirby, D.K. "Two Modern Versions of the Quest." *SHR*, 5: 387-95 (Fe 71).

Koch, Steohen. "Imagination in the Abstract." *AR*, 24: 253-63 (Su 63).

Kolodny, Annette, and D.J. Peters. "P's *The Crying of Lot 49*: The Novel as Subversive Experience." *MFS*, 19: 79-87 (Sp 73).

Kraff, J.M. "Anarcho-Romanticism and the Metaphysics of Counterforce: Alex Comfort and TP." *Paunch*, 40-41: 78-105 (Ap 75).

Larner, Jeremy. "The New Schlemihl." *PR*, 30: 273-6 (Su 63).

Leland, J.P. "P's Linguistic Demon: *The Crying of Lot 49*." *Critique*, 16: 45-53 (#2 74).

Levine, George. "V-2." *PR*, 40: 517-29 (Fl 73).

―――, and David Leverenz. "Essays on T.P." *TCL*, 21: 2-64 (#3 75).

LeVot, Andre. "The Rocket and the Pig: TP and Science Fiction." *Caliban*, 11: 111-8 (1975).

Lhamon, W.T. "The Most Irresponsible Bastard." *NRep*, 168: 24-8 (14 Ap 73).

———. "Pentecost, Promiscuity, and P's *V*." *TCL*, 21: 163-76 (My 75).

Locke, Richard. "*Gravity's Rainbow*." *NYT*, 11 M 73, pp. 1-3, 12-4.

Lundkvist, Artur. "Mardrommer och spex." *BLM*, 42: 276-81 (1973).

Lyons, T.R., and A.D Franklin. "TP's 'Classic Demonstrations' of the Second Law of Thermodynamics." *BRMMLA*, 27: 195-204 (1973).

McNamara, Eugene. "The Absurd Style in Contemporary American Literature." *HAB*, 19: 44-9 (Wi 68).

Mangle, Anne. "Maxwell's Demon, Entropy, Information: *The Crying of Lot 49*." *TriQ*, 20: 194-208 (Wi 71).

Mendelson, Edward. "P's Gravity." *YR*, 62: 624-31 (Su 73).

Ozier, L.W. "Antipointism/Antimexico: Some Mathematical Imagery in *Gravity's Rainbow*." *Critique*, 16: 73-90 (#2 74).

———. "The Calculus of Transformation: Mathematical Imagery in *Gravity's Rainbow*." *TCL*, 21: 193-201 (My 75).

Patterson, Richard. "What Stencil Knew: Structure and Certitude in P's *V*." *Critique*, 16: 30-44 (#2 74).

Poirier, Richard. "The Importance of TP." *TCL*, 21: 151-62 (My 75).

———. "Rocket Power." *SatR*, 26: 59-64 (Mr 73).

Pütz, Manfred. "TP's *The Crying of Lot 49*: The World Is a Tristero System." *Mosaic*, 7: 125-37 (1974).

Sanders, Scott. "P's Paranoid History." *TCL*, 21: 177-92 (My 75).

Schmitz, Neil. "Describing the Demon: The Appeal of TP." *PR*, 42: 112-35 (Fa 75).

Simmon, Scott. "A Character Index: *Gravity's Rainbow*." *Critique*, 16: 68-72 (#2 74).

———. "*Gravity's Rainbow* Described." *Critique*, 16: 54-67 (#2 74).

Sklar, Robert. "The New Novel, USA: TP." *Nation*, 205: 277-81 (25 S 67).

Tanner, Tony. "Patterns and Paranoia or Caries and Cabals." *Salmagundi*, 15: 78-99 (1971).

———. "V & V2." *LonM*, 13: 80-8 (F-Mr 74).

Thorburn, David. "A Dissent on P." *Commentary*, 56: 68-70 (S 73).

Vesterman, William. "T's Poetry." *TCL*, 21: 211-25 (My 75).

Wagner, L.W. "A Note on Oedipa the Roadrunner." *JNT*, 4: 155-61 (1974)

Wasson, Richard. "Notes on a New Sensibility." *PR*, 36: 460-77 (Wi 69).

*Weixlmann, J.N. "TP: A Bibliography." *Critique*, 14: 34-43 (#2 73).

Winston, Mathew. "The Quest for P." *TCL*, 21: 287-82 (O 75).

Wolfe, Peter. "*Gravity's Rainbow by TP*." *STC*, 13: 125-8 (Sp 74).

Wood, Michael. "Rocketing to the Apocalypse." *NYRB*, 22 Mr 73, pp. 22-3.

Yound, J.D. "The Enigma Variations of TP.2." *Critique*, 10: 68077 (#2 67).

Ralph, James. Shipley, J.B. "The Authorship of *The Touch-Stone* (1729)." *PBSA*, 62: 189-98 (1968).

———. "R, Ellys, Hogarth and Fielding: The Cabal Against Jacopo Amigoni." *ECS*, 1: 313-31 (1968).

Rand, Ayn. Deane, Paul. "AR's Neurotic Personalities of Our Times." *RLV*, 36: 125-9 (1970).

Michelson, Peter. "Fictive Babble." *NRep*, 162: 21-4 (21 F 70).

Nozick, Robert. "On the Randian Argument." *Person*, 52: 282-99 (Sp 71).

Ransom, John Crowe. Barber, Marion. "The Two Emilys: A R Suggestion to Faulkner." *NMW*, 5: 103-5 (Wi 73).

Bataille, Robert. "The Esthetics and Ethics of Farming: The Southern Agrarian View." *Iowa State J Res*, 49: 189-93 (1974).

Berman, Ronald. "Confederates in the Backfield: Mr. R and the Cleveland Browns." *NRep*, 173: 21-2 (4 O 75).

Bradford, M.E. "A Modern Elegy: R's 'Bells for John Whiteside's Daughter.'" *MissQ*, 21: 43-7 (Wi 67-68).

Brown, Ashley. "Landscape into Art: Henry Adams and JCR." *SR*, 79: 206-12 (Sp 71).

Buffington, Robert. "The Poetry of the Master's Old Age." *GaR*, 25: 5-14 (Sp 71).

———. "R's Poetics: 'Only God, My Dear.'" *MQR*, 12: 353-60 (Fa 73).

Caldwell, H.B. "Nu atit de 'noua' critica: JCR so altii." *ASUI*, 20: 71-6 (1974).

Core, George. "Mr. R and the House of Poetry." *SR*, 32: 619-38 (Fa 74).

———. "New Critic, Antique Poet." *SR*, 77: 508-16 (Fa 69).

———. "R, Brooks, and the Idiom of Criticism." *SLJ*, 5: 177-66 (Fa 72).

Crupi, Charles. "R's 'Conrad in Twilight.'" *Expl*, 29: 20 (Sp 70).

Curry, G.J. "Writers in Crisis." *Roots*, 1: 160-4 (1970).

Donoghue, Denis. "Actions Is Eloquence." *LugR*, 1: 147-51 (1965).

Elliot, E.B. "Theology and Agrarian Ideology in the Critical Theory of JCR." *XUS*, 10: 1-7 (Wi 71).

Justus, J.H. "A Note on JCR and Robert Penn Warren." *AL*, 41: 425-30 (N 69).

Kelly, Richard. "Captain Carter's Inverted Ancestor." *AN&Q*, 7: 6-7 (S 68).

Knight, K.F. "R's 'Conrad in Twilight.'" *Expl*, 30: 75 (Wi 72).

Levitt, Paul. "An Analogue for Faulkner's 'A Rose for Emily.'" *PLL*, 9: 91-4 (1973).

McMillan, S.H. "JCR's 'Painted Head.'" *GaR*, 22; 194-7 (Su 68).

Mann, David, and S.H. Woods. "JCR's Poetic Revisions." *PMLA*, 83: 15-21 (Mr 68).

Meyers, W.S. "A Commentary on 'JCR's Poetic Revisions.'" *PMLA*, 85: 532-9 (My 70).

Partridge, Colin. "'Aesthetic Distance' in the Poetry of JCR." *SoRA*, 3: 159-67 (1970).

Pinsky, Robert. "Hardy, R, Berryman: A 'Curious Air.'" *Agenda*, 10: 89-99 (1972).

Rubin, L.D. "The Wary Fugitive." *SR*, 82: 583-618 (Fa 74).

Shankar, D.A. "A Note on JCR." *LCrit*, 9: 97-101 (Su 71).

Sister, M. Judine. "An Analysis of 'Armageddon' by JCR." *Horizontes*, 12: 87-9 (1968).

Tate, Allen. "Gentleman in a Dustcoat." *SR*, 76: 375-81 (Su 68).

———. "Reflections on the Death of JCR." *SR*, 82: 545-51 (Fe 74).

Warren, R.P. "JCR (1888-1974)." *SoR*, 11: 243-4 (Ap 75).

———. "Notes on the Poetry of JCR." *KR*, 30: 319-49 (1968).

Weber, Robert. "Zur Genesis von JCR's 'Masters in the Garden Again.'" *JA*, 13: 196-204 (1968).

Williams, Miller. "Color as Symbol and the Two-Way Metaphor in the Poetry of JCR." *MissQ*, 22: 29-37 (Wi 68-69).

Young, T.D. "In His Own Country." *SoR*, 8: 572-93 (Jl 71).

———. "JCR: A Major Minor Poet." *Spectrum*, 2: 37-46 (1972).

———. "A Kind of Centering." *GaR*, 28: 58-82 (Sp 74).

———. "Mostly Nurtured from England." *SR*, 32: 552-82 (Fa 74).

———. "A Slow Fire." *SR*, 81: 667-90 (Au 73).

———. "Without Rank or Primacy." *MissQ*, 27: 275-6 (Fa 74).

Ravenel, Beatrice White. Neuffer, C.H. "Historical Sensibility." *SAB*, 35: 62-5 (Mr 70).

Rubin, L.D. "The Poetry of BR." *SCR*, 1: 55-75 (N 68).

Rawlings, Marjorie Kinnan. Bellman, S.I. "MKR's Existentialist Nightmare *The Yearling*." *Costerus*, 9: 9-10 (1973).

———. "MKR: A Solitary Sojourner in the Florida Backwoods." *KanQ*, 2: 78-87 (1970).

———. "Writing Literature for Young People: MKR's 'Secret River' of the Imagination." *Costerus*, 3: 19-27 (1973).

Rechy, John. Giles, J.R. "Religious Alienations and 'Homosexual Consciousness' in *City of Night* and *Go Tell It to the Mountain*." *CE*, 36: 369-80 (1974).

———— and Wanda. "An Interview with JR." *ChiR*, 25: 19-31 (1973).

Hoffman, Stanton. "Cities of the Night: JR and American Literature." *ChiR*, 17: 195-206 (1976).

Reed, Ishmael. Abel, R.H. "R's 'I Am a Cowboy in the Boat of Ra.'" *Expl*, 38: 81 (S 72).

Ambler, Madge. "IR: Whose Radio Broke Down?" *ANLF*, 6: 125-31 (Wi 72).

Bush, R.E. "Werewolf of the Wild West: On a Novel by IR." *BlackW*, 23: 51-2, 64-5 (1974).

Duff, Gerald. "R's 'The Free-Lance Pallbearers.'" *Expl*, 32: 69 (D 74).

Ford, N.A. "A Note on IR: Revolutionary Novelist." *StN*, 3: 216-8 (Su 71).

Lineberger, J.M., and Monte Atkinson. "Getting to Whitey." *ContPoetry*, 2: 9-12 (#1 75).

O'Brien, John. "IR: An Interview." *FicI*, 1: 60-70 (Fa 73).

Reed, Ishmael. "The Writer as Seer: IR on IR." *BlackW*, 23: 20-34 (1974).

Schmidt, Neil. "Neo-Hoo Doo: The Experimental Fiction of IR." *TCL*, 20: 126-40 (Ap 740.

Reed, John. Gunn, D.W. "Three Radicals and a Revolution: R, London, and Steffens on Mexico." *SWR*, 55: 393-410 (Au 70).

Hook, Sidney. "JR, the Romantic." *NRep*, 169: 23-5 (29 S 73).

Kallberg, Sture. "De mexikanska revolutionem: JR och Pancho Villa." *Ord och Bild*, 83: 57-73 (1974).

Rosenblatt, Roger. "Legendary JR." *NRep*, 173: 33-5 (20 S 75).

Reese, Lizette Woodworth. Dietrich, Mae. "LWR." *EDB*, 15: 114-22 (1970).

Milne, W.G. "LR Revisited." *SUS*, 8: 207-12 (1069).

Reid, James. Davis, R.B. "JR, Colonial Virginia Poet and Moral and Religious Essayist." *VMHB*, 79: 3-19 (Ja 71).

Reid, Mayne. Meyer, R.W. "The Western Fiction of MR." *WAL*, 3: 115-32 (Su 68).

*Steele, Joan. "MR: A Revised Bibliography." *BB*, 29: 95-100 (Jl-S 72).

Remington, Frederick. Alter, Judith. "FR's Major Novel, *John Ermine*." *SwAL*, 2: 42-6 (Sp 72).

Hassrick, P.H. "R in the Southwest." *SHQ*, 76: 297-315 (Ja 73).

Malley, Terence. "A Fruitful Alliance." *MarkR*, 3: 97-100 (F 73).

Rexroth, Kenneth. Grigsby, G.K. "The Presence of Reality: The Poetry of KR." *AR*, 31: 405-22 (Fa 71).

Moorehouse, Frank, "The American Poet's Visit." *Southerly*, 28: 275-85 (1868).

Pondrom, C.N. "An Interview with KR." *ConL*, 10: 313-31 (Su 69).

Purcell, J.M. "KR: Poetics, Populism and the Chicago Kid." *Cresset*, 36: 10-5 (S 73).

Reznikoff, Charles. Dembo, L.S. "The 'Objective' Poet." *ConL*, 10: 193-202 (Sp 69).

Hindus, Milton. "CR's Chronicle." *Midstream*, 18: 77-80 (N 72).

Rhodes, Eugene Manlove. Folsom, J.K. "A Dedication to the Memory of EMR, 1869-1934." *Arizona and the West*, 2: 310-4 (Wi 69).

Hutchinson, W.H. "The Mythic West of W.H.D. Koerner." *AmWest*, 4: 54-60 (My 67).

————. "The West of EMR." *Arizona and the West*, 9: 211-8 (Au 67).

Powell, L.C. "Southwest Classics Reread: From Cattle Kingdom Come." *Westways*, 65: 30-5, 85 (Ap 73).

Skillman, Richard, and J.C. Hoke. "The Portrait of the New Mexican in the Fiction of ER." *WR*, 6: 26-36 (1969).

Rice, Elmer. Elwood, W.R. "An Interview with ER on Expressionism." *ETJ*, 20: 1-7 (Mr 68).

Weaver, R.A. "*The Adding Machine*: Exemplar of the Ludicfous." *Players*, 49: 130-3 (1974).

Zeller, L.L. "Two Expressionistic Interpretations of Dehumanization: R's *The Adding Machine* and Muñiz's El tintero." *EC*, 2: 230-55 (Fa 75).

Rich, Adrienne. Ahmad, Aijaz. "Ghalib: 'The Dew Drop on the Red Poppy. . . .'" *Mahfil*, 5: 59-69 (Wi 68-69).

Boyers, Robert. "On AR: Intelligence and Will." *Salmagundi*, 22-23: 132-48 (1973).

Brown, Rosellen. "The Notes for the Poem Are the Only Poem." *Parnassus*, 4: 50-7 (Fa-Wi 75).

Carlson, Martha. "AR: Death and the Necessities of Life." *Eng R*, 3: 38-46 (1975).

Flynn, Gale. "The Radicalization of AR." *HC*, 11: 1-15 (#4 74).

Kalstone, David. "Talking with AR." *SatR*, 55: 56-9 (22 Ap 72).

Plumly, Stanley, Wayne Dodd and Walter Tevis. "Talking with AR." *Ohio R*, 13; 13: 28-46 (Fa 71).

Rich, Adreinne. "When We Dead Awaken: Writing as Re-Vision." *CE*, 34: 18-30 (Ja 72).

Spiegelman, Willard. "Voice of the Survivor." *SoR*, 11: 668-80. (#3 75).

Vendler, Helen. "Ghostlier Demarcations, Keener Sounds." *Parnassus*, 2: 4-33 (Wi 73).

Wilner, Eleanor. "'This Accurate Dream': An Interpretation." *Parnassus*, 4: 50-67 (#1 75).

Richards, I.A. Karnani, Cheta. "I.A.R's Aesthetics: Illusion and Reality." *IJES*, 10: 47-56 (1969).

———. "I.A.R's Theory of Stylistics." *Rajasthan J Eng Stud*, 1: 6-11 (Jl-D 74).

Sibley, F.M. "How to Read I.AR." *ASch*, 42: 318-28 (Sp 73).

Richardson, Jack. Debusscher, Gilbert. "JR, Dramaturge American." *RLV*, 37: 44-63, 128-71 (Fa-F, Mr-Ap 71).

———. "Modern Masks of the Orestes: *The Flies* and *The Prodigal*." *MD*, 12:

Richter, Conrad. LaHood, Marvin. "CR and Willa Cather." *XUS*, 9: 33-44 (Sp 70).

———. "R's Pennsylvania Trilogy." *Susquehanna Un Stud*, 8: 5-13 (1968).

Riding, Laura. Jackson, L.R. "A Postscript." *Private Lib*, 5: 139-47 (Au 72).

Moran, James. "The Seizin Press of LR and Robert Graves." *Black Art*, 2: 34-9 (Su 63).

Kirkham, Michael. "LR's Poems." *CQ*, 5: 320-8 (19710.

Riley, James, Whitcomb. Baker, R.L. "Folklore in the Prose Sketches of JWR." *IEJ* 4: 3-19, 27 (1970).

Holman, H.R. "When R Won the Palm." *IMH*, 65: 116-8 (1969).

Lanier, Doris. "JWR, 'Bill' Nye, and Harry Stillwell: A Lecture Tour." *GHQ*, 57: 256-64 (Su 73).

Myers, Walter. "In the Matter of JWR." *Esquire*, 72: 82-4, 184 (S 69).

Ripley, George. Colacurcio, M.J. "A Better Mode of Evidence: The Transcendantal Problem of Faith and Spirit." *ESQ*, 54: 12-22 (1Q 69).

Duffy, J.J. "Transcendental Letters from GR to James Marsh." *ESQ*, 50: 20-4 (1Q 68).

Myerson, Joe. "Two Unpublished Reminiscences of Brook Farm." *NEQ*, 48: 253-60 (Je 75).

Peterfreund, Sheldon. "GR: Forerunner of Twentieth Century Ethical Intuitionalism" *Person*, 55: 298-302 (1974).

Rivera, Tomás. Rocard, Marcienne. "The Cycle of Chicano Experience in *And the Earth Did Not Part*." *Caliban*, 11: 141-51 (1974).

Veiga, Gustavo da. "TR e la literatura chicana dos Estados Unidos." *MGSL*, 27 My 72, p. 11.

Rives, Amélie Louise. Moore, J.H. "ALR and the Charge of the Light Brigade." *VMHB*, 89-96 (Ja 67).

———. "The Vagabond and the Lady: Letters from Richard Hovey to AR." *MissQ*, 21: 131-43 (Sp 68).

Taylor, W.D. "A 'Soul' Remembers Oscar Wilde." *ELT*, 14: 43-8 (1970).

Roberts, Elizabeth Madox. Niles, Mary. "Social Development in the Poetry of EMR." *MarkR*, 2: 16-20 (S 69).

Smith, J.R. "New Troy in the Bluegrass: Vergilian Metaphor and *The Great Meadow*." *MissQ*, 22: 39-46 (Wi 68-69).

Roberts, Kenneth. Parsons, H.V. "*The Tory Lover, Oliver Wiswell,* and *Richard Carvel*." *CLQ*, 9: 220-31 (D 70).

Robinson, Edwin Arlington. Aiken, Conrad. "Three Meetings with R." *CLQ*, 8: 355-6 (S 69).

Anderson, Hilton. "R's 'Flammonde.'" *SoQ*, 7: 179-83 (Ja 69).

Ayo, Nicholas. "R's Use of the Bible." *CLQ*, 8: 260-5 (Mr 69).

Baker, Carlos. "'The Jug Makes the Paradise': New Light on Eben Flood." *CLQ*, 10: 327-26 (S 74).

———. "R's Stoical Romanticism, 1890-1897." *NEQ*, 46: 3-16 (Mr 73).

Barbour, B.M. "R's 'Veteran Sirens.'" *Expl*, 28: 20 (N 69).

Barnard, Ellsworth. "The Man Who Died Twice." *HSL*, 3: 154-6 (1971).

Bloom, Harold. "Bacchus and Merlin: The Dialectic of Romantic Poetry in America." *SoR*, 7: 140-75 (Ja 71).

Boone, Esther. "R's *Matthias at the Door*: A New Variant." *Serif*, 8: 31 (1971).

Braithwaite, W.S. "William Stanley Braithwaite Remembers E.A.R." *NLet*, 38: 153-64 (Fa 71).

Brasher, T.L. "R's *Mr. Flood's Party*." *Expl*, 29: 45 (N 71).

Brien, Dolores. "EAR's *Amaranth*: A Journey to the 'Wrong World.'" *RSW*, 36: 143-50 (Je 68).

Brown, M.F. "Moody and R." *CLQ*, 5: 185-94 (D 60).

Burton, D.H. "E.A.R and Christianity." *Spirit*, 37: 30-5 (1970).

———. "E.A.R's Idea of God." *CLQ*, 8: 280-94 (D 69).

———. "The Intellectualism of EAR." *Thought*, 44: 565 80 (Wi 69).

———. "R, Roosevelt, and Romanism." *RACHSP*, 80: 3-16 (Mr 69).

———. "Theodore Roosevelt and EAR: A Common Vision." *Person*, 49: 331-50 (Su 68).

Cary, Richard. "Additions to the R Collection." *CLQ*, 9: 377-82 (D 71); 10: 385-8 (D 72).

———. "'The Clam Digger: Capital Island': A R Sonnet Recovered." *CLQ*, 10: 505-11 (D 74).

———. "The First Publication of EAR's Poem 'Broadway.'" *AL*, 46: 83 (Mr 74).

*———. "The First Twenty Years of EAR Criticism: A Supplementary Checklist." *RALS*, 4: 184-204 (1974).

———. "'Go Little Book': An Odyssey of R's 'The Torrent and the Night Before.'" *CLQ*, 7: 511-27 (D 67).

———. "Mowry Sabin about EAR." *CLQ*, 9: 482-97 (Mr 72).

———. "R's Books and Periodicals." *CLQ*, 8: 266-77, 334-43, 399-413 (Mr, Je, S 69).

———. "R's Friend Arthur Davis Variell." *CLQ*, 10: 372-85 (Je 74).

———. "R's Manuscripts and Letters." *CLQ*, 8: 479-87 (Mr 69).

Clifton, L.J. "Two Corys: A Sample of Inductive Teaching." *EJ*, 58: 414-5 (Mr 69).

Cox, D.R. "The Vision of R's Merlin." *CLQ*, 10: 495-504 (D 74).

Crawford, John. "Success and Failure in the Poetry of EAR." *Rendezvous*, 5: 27-9 (Sp 70).

Crowder, Richard. "E.A.R and the Garden of Eden." *CLQ*, 7: 527-35 (D 67).

———. "R's Reputation: Six Observations." *CLQ*, 8: 220-38 (Mr 69).

Crowley, J.W.E. "E.AR and Henry Cabot Lodge." *NEQ*, 43: 116-24 (Mr 70).

Cunningham, J.V. "EAR: A Brief Biography." *UDQ*, 3: 28-31 (Sp 68).

Dauner, Louise. "Two R Revisions: 'Mr. Flood's Party' and the Dark Hills." *CLQ*, 8: 309-16 (Je 69).

Dechert, Peter. "He Shouts to See Them Scamper So: E.A.R and the French Forms." *CLQ*, 8: 386-98 (S 69).

Domina, Lyle. "Fate, Tragedy and Pessimism in R's *Merlin*." *CLQ*, 8: 471-8 (D 69).

Dunn, N.E. "Riddling Leaves: R's 'Luke Havergal.'" *CLQ*, 10: 17-25 (Mr 73).

————. "Wreck and Yesterday': The Meaning of Failure in *Lancelot*." *CLQ*, 9: 349-56 (S 71).

Dykes, M.M. "'Trying to Spell God': A Study of EAR." *Northwest Missouri State Teachers Col Stud*, 13: 87-124 (1 Je 49).

Fish, R.S. "The Tempering of Faith in E.A.R's 'The Man Against the Sky.'" *CLQ*, 9: 456-68 (Mr 72).

Foy, J.V. "R's Impulse for Narrative." *CLQ*, 8: 238-49 (Mr 69).

French, R.W. "On Teaching 'Richard Cory.'" *Eng Rec*, 24: 11-3 (Fa 73).

Fussell, Edwin. "The Americanization of E.A.R." *Claremont Q*, 1: 9-12 (1952).

Griffith, B.W. "A Note on R's Use of Turannos." *CP*, 4: 39 (Sp 71).

Grimm, C.L. "R's 'For a Dead Lady': An Exercise in Evaluation." *CLQ*, 7: 535-47 (D 67).

Grimshaw, James. "R's 'Lost Anchors.'" *Expl*, 30: 36 (N 71).

Haas, Richard. "Oral Interpretation as Discovery Through Persona." *OEng*, 1: 13-4 (1972).

Harkey, J.H. "Mr. Flood's Two Moons." *MTJ*, 15: 20-1 (Su 71).

Hinden, M.C. "EAR and the Theatre of Destiny." *CLQ*, 8: 463-71 (D 69).

Joyner, Nancy. "E.A.R's Concessions to the Critics." *RSW*, 40: 48-53 (Mr 72).

————. "R's Pamela and Sandburg's Agatha." *AL*, 40: 548-9 (Ja 69).

————. "R's Poets." *CLQ*, 9: 441-55 (Mr 72).

————. "An Unpublished Version of 'Mr. Flood's Party.'" *ELN*, 7: 55-7 (S 69).

Karka, Jerome. "Richard Cory's Suicide: A Psychoanalyst's View." *CLQ*, 11: 150-9 (Je 75).

Landini, Richard. "Metaphor and Imagery in EA.R's 'Credo.'" *CLQ*, 8: 20-2 (Mr 68).

Lensing, George. "R and Stevens: Some Tangential Bearings." *SoR*, 3: 505-13 (Sp 67).

Levenson, J.C. "R's Modernity." *VQR*, 44: 590-610 (Au 68).

Lucas, John. "The Poetry of EAR." *RMS*, 13: 132-47 (1969).

McFarland, R.E. "R's 'Luke Havergal.'" *CLQ*, 10: 365-72 (S 74).

MacKillop, I.D. "R's Accomplishment." *EIC*, 21: 297-308 (Jl 71).

MacLeish, Archibald. "On Rereading R." *CLQ*, 8: 217-9 (Mr 69).

Mattfield, M.S. "EAR's 'The Sheaves.'" *CEA*, 31: 10 (N 68).

Miller, J.H. "The Structure of E.A.R's *The Torrent and the Night Before*." *CLQ*, 10: 347-64 (Mr 74).

*Monteiro, George. "Addenda to the Bibliographies of . . . R [and others]." *PBSA*, 69: 172-5 (Ap-Je 75).

————. "Addenda to Hogan's *R*." *PBSA*, 65: 414 (O-D 71).

————. "'The President and the Poet': R, Roosevelt, and *The Touchstone*." *CLQ*, 10: 512-4 (Mr 74).

Moran, Ronald. "The Octaves of E.A.R." *CLQ*, 8: 363-70 (S 69).

Morill, P.H. "'The World Is . . . a Kind of Spiritual Kindergarten.'" *CLQ*, 4: 435-48 (Wi 69).

Morris, Celia. "E.A.R and 'The Golden Horoscope of Imperfection.'" *CLQ*, 11: 88-97 (Mr 75).

————. "R's Camelot: Renunciation as Drama." *CLQ*, 9: 468-81 (Mr 72).

Perrine, Laurence. "R's 'The Tree in Pamela's Garden.'" *Expl*, 30: 18 (O 71).

————. "The Sources of R's Arthurian Poems and His Opinions of Other Testaments." *CLQ*, 10: 336-46 (Mr 74).

————. "The Sources of R's *Merlin*." *AL*, 44: 313-21 (My 72).

————. "Tennyson and R: Legalistic Moralism vs. Situation Ethics." *CLQ*, 8: 416-33 (D 69).

Read, A.M. "R's 'The Man Against the Sky.'" *Expl*, 26: 49 (F 68).

Richards, B.F. "'No, There Is Not a Dawn. . . .'" *CLQ*, 9: 367-74 (S 71).

Robinson, W.R. "E.A.R's Yankee Conscience." *CLQ*, 8: 371-85 (S 69).

Sampley, A.M. "The Power or the Glory: The Dilemma of EAR." *CLQ*, 9: 357-66 (S 71).

Sanborn, J.N. "Juxtaposition as Structure in 'The Man Against the Sky.'" *CLQ*, 10: 486-94 (D 74).

Scholnick, R.J. "The Shadowed Years: Mrs. Richards, Mr. Stedman, and R." *CLQ*, 9: 510-31 (D 72).

Sherman, Dean. "R's 'The Battle after War.'" *Expl*, 27: 64 (Ap 69).

Slethaug, G.E. "The King in R's 'Old King Cole.'" *Eng Rec*, 21: 45-6 (F 71).

Solomon, Petre. "Un destin bizar: EAR." *RoLit*, 19: 23 (Je 69).

Stevick, R.D. "Formulation of E.A.R's Principles of Poetry." *CLQ*, 8: 295-308 (Je 69).

Suss, I.D. "The Plays of EAR." *CLQ*, 8: 347-63 (S 69).

Sweet, C.A. "A Re-Examination of 'Richard Cory.'" *CLQ*, 9: 579-82 (D 72).

Thompson, W.R. "Broceliande: E.A.R's Palace of Art." *NEQ*, 43: 231-49 (Je 70).

Tuerk, Richard. "R's 'Lost Anchor.'" *Expl*, 32: 37 (Ag 74).

Turner, Steven. "R's 'Richard Cory.'" *Expl*, 28: 73 (My 70).

Van Doren, Mark. "EAR." *CLQ*, 8: 279 (Je 69).

Weeks, L.E. "Maine in the Poetry of EAR." *CLQ*, 8: 317-34 (Je 69).

*White, William. "A Bibliography of EAR, 1964-1969." *CLQ*, 448-62 (D 69).

Robinson, Lennox. Everson, I.G. "LR and Synge's *Playboy* (1911-1930): Two Decades of American Cultural Growth." *NEQ*, 44: 3-21 (Mr 71).

***Robinson, Rowland E.** Baker, R.L. "An Annotated Bibliography of Works about RE.R." *VH*, 40: 67-72 (1972).

————. "Folk Medicine in the Writings of RR." *VH*, 37: 184-93 (1969).

————. "RE.R (1833-1900)." *ALR*, 156-9 (Su 69).

Carruth, Hayden. "RE.R: Vermont's Neglected Genius." *VH*, 41: 181-97 (1973).

Roethke, Theodore. Atlas, James. "R's Boswell." *Poetry*, 114: 327-30 (Jl 69).

Blessing, R.A. "The Shaking That Steadies: TR's 'The Waking.'" *BSUF*, 12: 17-9 (Au 71).

————. "TR: A Celebration." *TSE*, 20: 169-80 (1972).

————. "TR's Sometimes Metaphysical Motion." *TSLL*, 14: 731-49 (Wi 73).

Bowerman, Donald. "TR: A Housman Echo." *N&Q*, 16: 226 (Jl 69).

Boyd, J.D. "Texture and Form in TR's Greenhouse Poems." *MLQ*, 32: 409-24 (D 71).

Boyers, Robert. "The R Letters." *GaR*, 22: 437-45 (1968).

Brown, D.E. "TR's 'Self-World' and the Modernist Position." *JML*, 3: 1239-54 (Jl 74).

Bullis, Jerald. "TR." *MR*, 11: 209-12 (1970).

Burke, Kenneth. "Cult of the Breakthrough." *NRep*, 159: 25-6 (21 S 68).

Ciardi, John. "Comments on TR." *CimR*, 7: 6-8 (1969).

Colussi, D.L. "R's 'The Gentle.'" *Expl*, 27: 73 (My 69).

Corrigan, Matthew. "A Phenomenological Glance at a Few Lines of R." *MPS*, 2: 165-74 (1971).

Davis, William. "The Escape into Time: TR's 'The Waking.'" *NCLit*, 5: 2-10 (Mr 75).

————. "Fising an Old Wound: TR's Search for Sonship." *AntigR*, 20: 29-41 (1974).

Dickey, James. "The Greatest American Poet." *Atl*, 222: 53-8 (N 68).

Donoghue, Denis. "TR: Toward 'The Far Field.'" *LugR*, 1: 50-72 (1965).

Everette, Oliver. "TR: The Poet as Teacher." *WCR*, 3: 5-11 (Sp 68).

Freer, Coburn. "TR's Love Poetry." *NwR*, 11: 42-66 (Su 71).

Calvin, Brendan. "Kenneth Burke and TR's *Lost Son* Poems." *NwR*, 11: 67-96 (Su 71).

———. "TR's Proverbs." *CP*, 5: 35-47 (#1 72).

Gangewere, R.J. "TR: The Future of a Reputation." *CaSE*, 11: 65-73 (1970).

Garmon, G.M. "R's 'Open House.'" *Expl*, 28: 27 (N 69).

Hayden, M.H. "Open House: Poetry of the Constricted Self." *NwR*, 11: 116-38 (Su 71).

Heany, Seamus. "Canticles to the Earth." *Listener*, 80: 245-6 (22 Ag 68).

Henry, Nat. "R's 'I Knew a Woman'" *Expl*, 27: 31 (Je 69).

Heringman, Bernard. "Images and Meaning in the Poetry of TR." *Aegis*, 2: 45-57 (Fa 73).

———. "How to Write Like Somebody Else." *MPS*, 3: 31-9 (1972).

———. "R's Poetry: The Forms of Meaning." *TSLL*, 16: 568-83 (Fa 74).

Heron, P.E. "The Vision of Meaning: TR's Frau Bauman, Frau Schmidt, and Frau Schwartze." *SWp*, 34: 29-33 (Wi 70).

Heyen, William. "The Divine Abyss: TR's Mysticism." *TSLL*, 11: 1051-68 (Su 69).

———. "TR's Minimals." *MinnR*, 8: 359-75 (1968).

Hobbs, John. "The Poet as His Own Interpretor: R on 'In a Dark Time.'" *CE*, 33: 55-6 (O 71).

Janik. D.I. "R's 'The Boy and the Bush.'" *Expl*, 32: 20 (N 73).

LaBelle, Jenijoy. "Martyr to a Motion Not His Own: R's Love Poems." *BSUF*, 16: 71-5 (Sp 75).

———. "R's Dancing Masters." *CP*, 8: 29-35 (#2 75).

———. "R's 'I Knew a Woman.'" *Expl*, 32: 15 (O 73).

———. "TR and Tradition: 'The Pure Serene Memory of One Man.'" *NwR*, 11: 1-18 (Su 71).

Libby, Anthony. "R, Water Father." *AL*, 46: 267-88 (N 74).

Lucas, John. "On the Poetry of TR." *OR*, 8: 39-64 (1968).

McClatchy, J.D. "Sweating Light from a Stone: Identifying TR." *MPS*, 3: 1-24 (1972).

*McLeod, J.R. "Bibliographic Notes on the Creative Process of R's *The Lost Son* Sequence." *NwR*, 11: 97-111 (Su 71).

McMichael, James. "The Poetry of TR." *SoR*, 5: 4-25 (Wi 69).

———. "R's North America." *NwR*, 11: 149-59 (Su 71).

Maxwell, J.C. "Notes on TR." *N&Q*, 16: 265-6 (Jl 69).

Mazzaro, Jerome. "TR and the Failures of Language." *MPS*, 1: 73-96 (1970).

Mukerji, Nirmal. "R's Journey Out of the Self." *PURBA*, 4: 51-7 (1973).

O'Gorman, Ned. "TR and Paddy Flynn." *ColF*, 12: 34-6 (Sp 69).

Parker, Donald. "R's 'The Lost Son.'" *Cont Poetry*, 2: 13-6 (#1 75).

Paschall, Douglas "R Remains." *SR*, 81: 856-64 (Au 73).

Porter, Kenneth. "R at Harvard, 1930-1931 and the Decade After." *NwR*, 11, 139-48 (Su 71).

Ramsey, Jarold. "R in the Greenhouse." *WHR*, 26: 35-47 (Wi 72).

Schumacher, P.J. "The Unity of Being: A Study of TR's Poetry." *Ohio Un R*, 12: 20-40 (1970).

Schutz, F.C. "Antecedents of R's 'The Lost Son.'" *NCLit*, 5: 4-6 (1975).

Shapiro, Karl. "Scrapping the Bottom of the R Barrel." *NRep*, 166: 24 (Sp 72).

Shott, P.S.C. "'I Am!' Says TR: A Reading of the Nonsense Poems." *RSW*, 43: 103-12 (1975).

Skelton, Robin. "The Poetry of TR." *MalR*, 1: 141-4 (1967).

Slaughter, W.R. "R's 'Song.'" *MinnR*, 8: 342-4 (1968).

Stein, Arnold. "R's Memory: Actions, Visions, Revisions." *NwR*, 11: 19-31 (Su 71).

Sullivan, Rosemary. "A Still Center: A Reading of TR's 'North American Sequence.'" *TSLL*, 16: 765-83 (Wi 75).

Swann, Brian. "TR and the Shift of Things." *LitR*, 17: 269-86 (1974).

Truesdale, C.W. "TR and the Landscape of American Poetry." *MinnR*, 8: 345-58 (1968).

Vanderwerken, D.L. "R's 'Four for Sir John Davies' and 'The Dying Man.'" *RSW*, 41: 125-35 (1974).

Vernon, John. "TR's *Praise to the End!* Poems." *IowaR*, 2: 60-79 (1971).

Wagoner, David. "The Dark Angel." *NwR*, 11: 112-5 (Su 71).

―――. "The Poet's Business." *NwR*, 11: 32-41 (Su 71).

Warfel, H.R. "Language Patterns and Literature: A Note on R's Poetry." *Topic*, 6: 21-9 (Fa 66).

Wolff, George. "R's 'Root Cellar.'" *Expl*, 29: 47 (N 71).

―――. "Syntactical and Imagistic Distortion of R's Greenhouse Poems." *Lang&S*, 6: 281-8 (Fa 73).

Roosevelt, Theodore. Barsness, J.A. "TR as Cowboy: The Virginian as Jacksonian Man." *AQ*, 21: 609-19 (Fa 69).

Frane, P.N. "The Gentleman Cowboy—TR and the West." *Moutain-Plains Lib Q*, 13: 11-3 (Su 68).

Stein, H.H. "TR and the Press: Lincoln Steffens." *M-A*, 54: 94-107 (Ap 72).

Roth, Henry. Bronsen, David. "A Conversation with HR." *PR*, 36: 265-80 (1969).

Ferguson, James. "Symbolic Patterns in *Call It Sleep*." *TCL*, 14: 211-20 (Ja 69).

Inge, M.T. "The Ethnic Experience and Aesthetics in Literature: Malamud's *The Assistant* and R's *Call It Sleep*." *JEthSt*, 1: 45-50 (Wi 74).

Lyons, Bonnie. "After *Call It Sleep*." *AL*, 45: 610-a (Ja 74).

―――. "'Broker': An Overlooked Story by HR." *SSF*, 10: 97-8 (Wi 73).

―――. "An Interview with HR." *Shen*, 25: 48-71 (Fa 73).

―――. "R's Call It Sleep." *Expl*, 33: 10 (O 74).

―――. "The Symbolic Structure of HR's *Call It Sleep*." *ConL*, 13: 183-203 (Sp 73).

Mortara, Elena. "L'arte de HR." *SA*, 12: 231-57 (1966).

Pearce, Richard "*Pylon, Awake and Sing!* and the Apocalyptic Imagination of the 30's." *Criticism*, 13: 131-41 (Sp 71).

Redding, M.E. "Call It Myth: HR and *The Golden Bough*." *CentR*, 18: 180-95 (Sp 74).

Samet, Tom. "HR's Bull Story: Guilt and Betrayal in *Call It Sleep*." *StN*, 7: 569-83 (Wi 75).

Roth, Philip. Alter, Robert. "When He Is Bad." *Commentary*, 44: 86-8 (N 67).

Bérubé, Renald. "PR at les complexes de Tricard Dixon." *Liberté*, 94: 138-49 (1974).

Bier, Jesse. "In Defense of PR." *EA*, 16: 59-53 (Mr 73).

Bettelheim, Bruno. "Portnoy Pyschoanalyzed." *Midstream*, 15: 3-10 (Je-Jl 69).

Braun, Julie. "Portnoy as Pure Confusion." *CaM*, 13: 73-5 (Sp-Su 73).

Buchen, I.H. "*Portnoy's Complaint* of the Rooster's Kvetch." *STC*, 6: 97-107 (Fa 70).

Cohen, E.Z. "Alex in Wonderland, or Portnoy's Complaint." *TCL*, 17: 161-8 (1971).

Cohen, Z.B. "PR's Would-be Patriarchs and Their *Shikses* and Shrews." *Stud Am Jewish Lit*, 1: 16-22 (Sp 75).

Collier, Peter. "Portnoy's Compliance." *Ramparts*, 7: 29-31 (My 69).

Cooperman, Stanley. "PR: 'Old Jacob's Eye' with a Squint." *TCL*, 19: 203-16 (Jl 73).

Davidso, A.E. "Kafka, Rilke, and PR's *The Breast*." *NCLit*, 5: 9-11 (#1 75).

Ditsky, John. "R, Updike, and the High Expense of Spirit." *UWR*, 5: 111-20 (Fa 69).

Donaldson, Scott. "PR: The Meanings of Letting Go." *ConL*, 11: 21-35 (Wi 70).

Roth, Philip

Donno, Antonia. "PR e l'ebraismo americano." *Antologia Vieusseux*, 32: 35-49 (1973).

Donoghue, Denis. "Nice Jewish Boy." *NRep*, 172: 21-6 (7 Je 75).

Dupree, Robert. "And the Mom R Outgrabe: or, What Hath Got Roth?" *ArlQ*, 2: 175-89 (Au 70).

Friedman, A.W. "The Jews Complaint in Recent American Fiction: Beyond Exodus and Still in the Wilderness." *SoR*, 8: 41-59 (Ja 72).

Gordon, L.G. "*Portnoy's Complaint*: Coming of Age in Jersey City." *L&P*, 19: 57-60 (1969).

Hewes, Henry. "The Aints and the Am Nots." *SatR*, 54: 10-2 (13 N 71).

Hochman, Baruch. "Child and Man in PR." *Midstream*, 13: 68-76 (D 67).

Howe, Irving. "PR Reconsidered." *Commentary*, 54: 69-77 (1972).

Israel, C.M. "The Fractured Hero of R's *Goodbye, Columbus*." *Critique*, 16: 5-11 (2Q 74).

Iwamoto, Iwao. "PR—Judayasei e no Hangyaku." *EigoS*, 115: 762-63 (1969).

Kliman, Bernice. "Names in Portnoy's Complaint." *Critique*, 14: 16-23 (#3 73).

Knopp, J.Z. "The Ways of *Mentshlekhkayt*: A Study in the Morality of Some Fiction by Bernard Malamud and PR." *Tradition*, 13: 67-84 (#3 73).

Leichuk, Alan. "On the Breast." *NYRB*, 19: 26-8 (19 O 72).

Leonard, John. "Cheever to R to Malamud." *Atl*, 231: 112-6 (Je 73).

Levine, Herschel. "Two Early Stories by PR." *KAL*, 15: 20-4 (1974).

Levine, M.H. "PR and American Judaism." *CLAJ*, 14: 163-70 (D 70).

Ludwig, Jack. "Sons and Lovers." *PR*, 36: 524-34 (Su 69).

*McDaniel, John. "PR: A Checklist, 1954-1973." *BB*, 51-3 (Ap-Je 74).

Mandel, Ann. "Useful Fictions." *Ontario R*, 3: 26-32 (1975).

Matt, Peter. "Phantastische Literatur—nach Freud? Zu PR's Roman *The Breast*." *NRs*, 85: 328-30 (1974).

Michel, Peter. "*Portnoy's Complaint* and PR's Complexities." *DQR*, 4: 1-10 (1Q 74).

Michel, Pierre. "PR's *The Breast*." *DQR*, 5: 245-52 (1975).

Noble, D.R. "Dickinson to R." *AN&Q*, 9: 150-1 (N 71).

Oates, J.C. "A Conversation with PR." *Ontario R*, 1: 9-22 (1974).

———. "PR in Conversation." *NewR*, 2: 3-7 (#14 75).

Opland, J. "In Defence of PR." *Theoria*, 42: 29-42 (1974).

Pétillon, Pierre-Yves. "PR n'est pas mort." *Crit(P)*, 26: 821-38 (O 70).

Raban, Jonathan. "The New PR." *Novel*, 2: 153-63 (1969).

Rogers, B.F. "*The Great American Novel* and 'The Great American Joke.'" *Critique*, 16: 12-29 (#2 74).

———. "PR and Franz K." *ChiR*, 26: 183-6 (O 74).

Roskolenko, Harry. "Portrait of the Artist as a Young Schmuck." *Quadrant*, 64: 25-30 (1970).

Roth, Philip. "Imagining Jews." *NYRB*, 21: 22-8 (3 O 74).

———. "PR's Exact Intent." *NYT*, 23 G 69, pp. 2, 23-5.

———. "Reading Myself." *PR*, 40: 404-17 (#3 73).

Schechner, Mark. "PR." *PR*, 41: 410-27 (3Q 74).

Shaw, Peter. "Portnoy and His Creator." *Commentary*, 47: 77-9 (My 69).

Sheed, Wilfrid. "The Good Word: Howe's Complaint." *NYT*, 6 My 73, p. 2.

Shrubb, Peter. "Portnography." *Quadrant*, 64: 16-24 (1970).

Solotaroff, Theodore. "The Journey of PR." *Atl*, 223: 64-72 (Ap 69).

Wilson, R.F. "An Indisputable Source for the Spirited Account of a Baseball Contest Between the Port Ruppert Mundys and the Asylum Lunatics in *The Great American Novel* by Mr. PR." *NCLit*, 5: 12-4 (#3 75).

Roth, Samuel. Hamalian, Leo. "Nobody Knows My Names: SR and the Underside of Modern Letters." *JML*, 3: 889-921 (Ap 74).

————. "The Secret Careers of SR." *JPC*, 1: 317-38 (1968).

Rothenberg, Jerome. Alpert, Barry. "JR: An Inteview." *Vort*, 7: 93-117 (1975).

Brotherston, Gordon. "JR (Translator-Anthologist) and the Daughter of Urthona." *Vort*, 7: 135-7 (1975).

Doria, Charles. "Serpent Multiples in Mr. R and Elsewhere." *Vort*, 7: 184-6 (1975).

Lenowitz, Harris. "R: The Blood." *Vort*, 7: 163-79 (1975).

Power, Kevin. "An Image Is an Image Is an Image." *Vort*, 7: 153-63 (1975).

————. "Conversation with JR." *Vort*, 7: 140-53 (1975).

————. "Poland/1931: Pack Up Your Troubles in Your Old Kit Bag & Smile, Smile, Smile, from Diaspora to Galut." *Boundary*, 3: 683-705 (Wi 75).

Spanos, Wiliam. "A Dialogue with William Spanos on Oral Poetry." *Boundary*, 3: 509-48 (Sp 75).

Schwerner, Armand. "Remarks on JR." *Vort*, 7: 127-8 (1975).

Tyson, Ian. "Two Songs about a Dead Person, or Was It a Mole? Some Notes on Collaboration." *Vort*, 3: 131-3 (1975).

Rourke, Constance. Bluestein, Gene. "CR and the Folk Sources of American Literature." *WF*, 26: 77-87 (1967).

Rowlandson, Mary. Cabibbo, Paola. "MR, prigioniera degli indiani." *SA*, 13: 7-36 (1967).

Minter, D.L. "By Dens of Lions: Notes on Stylization in Early Puritan Captivity Narratives." *AL*, 45: 335-47 (N 73).

Rowson, Susanna. Martin, Wendy. "Profile: SR, Early American Novelist." *WS*, 2: 1-8 (1974).

Rukeyser, Muriel. Adkins, J.F. "The Esthetics of Science: MR's 'Waterlily Fire.'" *Cont Poetry,* 1: 23-7 (Wi 73).

Novak, E.G. "The Dynamo School of Poets." *ConL*, 11: 526-39 (Au 70).

Terris, V.R. "MR: A Retrospective." *APR*, 3: 10-14 (#3 74).

Rush, Benjamin. D'Elia, D.J. "Dr. BR and the Negro." *JHI*, 30: 373-9 (Jl-S 69).

Hedges, W.L. "BR, Charles Brockden Brown and the American Plague Year." *EAL*, 7: 295-311 (Wi 73).

Lambert, P.F. "BR and American Independence." *PH*, 39: 443-54 (O 72).

Scherer, L.B. "A New Look at *Personal Slavery Established*." *WMQ*, 30: 645-52 (!973).

Russell, Irwin. Harrell, L.D.S. "IR and 'The Blue-Tail Fly Grange." *MissFR*, 2: 113-21 (1969).

Metcalf, Priscilla. "A Lean, Pale, Sallow, Shabby, Striking Young Man." *Listener*, 30 D 71, pp. 904-5.

Simms, L.M. "IR and Negro Dialect Poetry." *NMW*, 2: 67-73 (Fa 69).

Ruxton, George Frederick. Cracroft, R.H. "'Half Froze for Mountain Doins': The Influence and Significance of GF.R's *Life in the Far West*." *WAL*, 10: 29-43 (My 75).

————. "The Literary Power of 'Phoney Speech': A Note on Alfred Jacob Miller and GFR." *PosS*, 4: 15-7 (My 73).

Hatch, J.M. "The Art of Sunny Lying in the Mountain Man Tale." *PosS*, 4: 9-15 (O 73).

Hubbard, Claude. "The Language of R's Mountain Men." *AS*, 43: 216-23 (O 68).

Lehmberg, Paul. "R's Life in the Far West as Fiction." *WAL*, 5: 1-6 (Ap 74).

Powell, L.C. "Personalities of the West: The Adventurous Englishman." *Westways,*65: 18-22, 70-1 (N 73).

Ryan, Abram Joseph. Lipscomb, O.H. "Some Unpublished Poems of AJR." *AlaR*, 25: 163-77 (Jl 72).

Simms, L.M. "Father AJR: Poet of the Lost Cause." *LH*, 73: 3-7 (Sp 71).

Saffin, John. Coffee, J.A. "Arcadia to America: Sir Philip Sidney and JS." *AL*, 45: 100-4 (Mr 73).

Weber, Brom. "A Puritan Poem Regenerated: JS's 'Sayle Gentle Pinnave I." *EAL*, 3: 65-71 (1971).

Salinger, J.D. Ahrne, Marianne. "Experience and Attitude in *The Catcher in the Rye* and Nine Stories." *MSpr*, 61: 242-63 (1967).

Alcantara-Demalanta, O. "Christian Dimensions in Contemporary Literature." *Unitas*, 46: 213-23 (1973).

Amur, G.S. "Theme, Structure, and Symbol in *The Catcher in the Rye*." *IJAS*, 1: 11-24 (1969).

Balke, B.T. "Some Judeo-Christian Themes Seen Through the Eyes of J.D.S and Nathanael West." *Cresset*, 31: 14-8 (My 68).

Bryan, James. "The Psychological Structure of *The Catcher in the Rye*." *PMLA*, 89: 1865-74 (O 74).

————. "A Reading of S's 'Teddy.'" *AL*, 40: 352-69 (N 68).

————. "Sherwood Anderson and *The Catcher in the Rye*." *NCLit*, 1: 2-5 (N 71).

Bufithis, P.H. "J.D.S. and the Psychiatrist." *WVUPP*, 2 1: 67-77 (1974).

Coles, Robert. "A Reconsideration: JDS." *NRep*, 168: 30-2 (28 Ap 73).

Conrad, R.C. "Two Novelists about Outsiders: The Kinship of J.D.S.'s *The Catcher in the Rye* with Heinrich Boll's Ansichten eines *Clowns*." *UDR*, 5: 23-7 (Wi 68-9).

Cox, J.M. "Toward Vernacular Humor." *VQR*, 46: 311-30 (1970).

Ducharme, E.R. "J.D., D.B., Sonny, Sunny, and Holden." *Eng Rec*, 19: 54-8 (D 68).

Ely, Sister M. Amanda. "The Adult Image in Three Novels of Adolescent LIfe." *EJ*, 56: 1127-31 (N 67).

Erdmenger, Manfred. "*How to catch a phoney* oder warum auch *Love Story* in den Lehrplan kommenkkan." *NS*, 21: 324-7 (Je 72).

Fleissner, R.F. "S's Caulfield: A Refraction of Copperfield and His Caul." *NCLit*, 3: 5-7 (My 73).

Foran, D.J. "A Doubletake on Holden Caulfield." *EJ*, 57: 977-9 (O 68).

Freeman, F.B. "Who Was S's Sergeant X." *AN&Q*, 11: 6 (N 72).

Freese, Peter. "*Adventures of Huckleberry Finn* und *The Catcher in the Rye* zur exemplarischen Deutung der Romananfange." *NS*, 22: 658-68 (1973).

————. "JDS: The Catcher in the Rye." *LWU*, 1: 123-52 (1968).

————. "Zwei undekannte Verwuise in J.D.S.'s *The Catcher in the Rye*: Charles Dickens und Ring Lardner." *Archiv*, 211: 68-72 (1974).

Fusini, Nadia. "Holden, il feticcio abbandonato." *SA*, 15: 465-78 (1969).

Goldhurst, William. "The Hyphenated Ham Sandwich of Ernest Hemingway and J.D.S." *FHA*, 1970, pp. 136-50.

Goldstein, Bernice and Sanford. "Bunnies and Cobras: Zen Enlightenment in S." *Disc*, 13: 98-106 (Wl 70).

————. "Ego and 'Hapworth 16, 1924.'" *Renascene*, 24: 159-67 (Sp 72).

————. "Seymour's Poems." *LE&W*, 17: 335-48 (1973).

————. "'Seymour: An Introduction': Writing as Discovery." *SSF*, 7: 248-56 (Sp 70).

Goldstein, Sanford and Bernice. "Some Zen References in S." *LE&W*, 15: 83-95 (1971).

Gooder, R.D. "'One of Today's Best Little Writers?'" *CQ*, 1: 81-90 (Wi 65-66).

Gross, T.L. "J.D.S.: Suicide and Survival in the Modern World." *SAQ*, 68: 452-62 (Au 69).

Gunter, Bernd. "Holden Caulfield: Sentimentaler oder sentalischer Idealist?" *NS*, 21: 728-38 (1972).

Hamilton, Kenneth. "Hell in New York: J.D.S.'s 'Pretty Mouth and Green My Eyes.'" *DR*, 47: 394-9 (Su 67).

Hays, P.L. "Runaways on a One-Way Ticket, or Dropouts in Literature." *ArQ*, 31: 301-10 (1975).

Karlstetter, Klaus. "J.D.S., R.W. Emerson and the Perrennial Philosophy." *MSpr*, 63: 224-36 (1969).

Kirschner, Paul. "S and His Society: The Pattern of *Nine Stories*." *LonR*, 6: 34-54 (Wi 69); *LHY*, 14: 63-78 (1973).

Kliman, Bernice. "Names in *Portnoy's Complaint*." *Critique*, 14: 16-24 (# 73).

Kraul, Fritz. "J.D.S's Roman *Der Fanger in Roggen* als Pflichtlektur in Deutschunterricht der Oberstufe." *Der Deutschunterricht*, 20: 79-86 (1968).

Lane, Gary. "Seymour's Suicide Again: A New Reading of J.D.S's 'A Perfect Day for Bananafish.'" *SSF*, 10: 27-33 (Wi 73).

Lorch, T.M. "J.D.S: The Artist, the Audience, and the Popular Arts." *SDR*, 5: 3-13 (Wi 67-68).

Luedtke, L.S. "J.D.S and Robert Burns: The Catcher in the Rye." *MFS*, 16: 198-201 (Su 70).

Meral, Jean. "The Ambiguous Mr. Antolini in S's *Catcher in the Rye*." *Caliban*, 6: 55-8 (1970).

Metcalf, Frank. "The Suicide of S's Seymour Glass." *SSF*, 9: 243-6 (1972).

Peavy, C.D. "'Did You Ever Have a Sister?' Holden, Quentin, and Sexual Innocence." *FlaQ*, 1: 82-95 (1968).

Perrson, Olga. "Raddaren i noden: JDS's markliga roman." *Studiekamraten*, 54: 14-9 (1972).

Peterson, Lennart. "J.D.S.'s 'Räddaren i nöden' (1951): Amerikanska efterkrigsromaner last på nyttt." *Horisont*, 15: 53-7 (1968).

Quagliano, Anthony. "'Hapworth 16, 1924': A Problem in Hagiography." *UDR*, 8: 35-43 (Fa 71).

Ranly, E.W. "Journey to the East." *Commonweal*, 97: 465-9 (1973).

Rose, A.H. "Sin and the City: The Uses of Disorder in the Urban Novel." *CentR*, 16: 203-20 (1972).

Sakamoto, Masayuki. "S ni okcru 'Sczuku' yo 'Chozoku.'" *EigoS*, 115: 692-3 (1969).

Salzman, Jack. "Prelude to Madness: A Look at 'Soldier's Home' and 'For Esmé: With Love and Squalor.'" *RRAL*, 33: 103-12 (1973).

Schulz, M.F. "Epilogue to *Seymour: An Introduction*: and the Crisis of Consciousness." *SSF*, 5: 128-38 (Wi 68).

Seitzman, Daniel. "Therapy and Antotherapy in S's 'Zooey,'" *AL*, 25: 140-62 (1968).

Sethom, Mohamed. "La société das l'oeuvre de J.D.S." *EA*, 22: 270-8 (Jl-S 69).

———. "L'Univers verbal de J.D.S." *EA*, 21: 57-64 (Ja-Mr 68).

Simms, L.M. "Seymour Glass: The Salingerian Hero as Vulgarian." *NCLit*, 5: 6-8 (#5 75).

Slethaug, G.E. "Forms in S's Shorter Fiction." *CRAS*, 3: 50-9 (Sp 72).

———. "Seymour: A Clarification." *Renascence*, 23: 115-28 (Sp 71).

Stein, W.B. "S's 'Teddy': *Tat Tvam Asi* or That Thou Art." *ArQ*, 29: 253-65 (Au 74).

Stone, Edward. "Naming in S." *NCLit*, 1: 2-3 (Mr 71).

Stuart, R.L. "The Writing-in-Waiting." *ChrC*, 82: 647-9 (19 My 65).

Takenaka, Toyoko. "On Seymour's Suicide." *KAL*, 12: 54-61 (1970).

Tarinya, M. "S: *The Catcher in the Rye*." *LHY*, 7: 49-60 (Jl 66).

Trowbridge, C.W. "Hamlet and Holden." *EJ*, 57: 26-9 (Ja 68).

———. "Salinger's Symbolic Use of Character and Detail in *The Catcher in the Rye*." *CimR*, 4: 5-11 (Je 68).

Veza, Laurette. "J.D.S: L'attrape-coeur ou Holden Resartus." *LanM*, 61: 56-65 (Ja-F 67).

Zapponi, Niccolò. "J.D.S e l'estetica dell'innocenza." *SA*, 16: 393-405 (1970).

Saltus, Edgar. Sprague, Claire. "The ES Collection." *YULG*, 42: 102-6 (O 67).

Sanborn, Franklin Benjamin. Cameron, K.W. "American and British Authors in F.B.S.'s Papers." *ATQ*, 6: 2-53 (2Q 70).

Ferguson, A.E. "Sills Poems Wrongly Ascribed to S." *ESQ*, 43: 131 (1Q 70).

Myerson, Joel. "An Ungathered S Lecture on Brook Farm." *ATQ*, 26: 1-11 (Sp 75).

Sanborn, F.B. "BA at Alcott House, England, and Fruitlands, New England (1842-1844)." *ATQ*, 9: 27-51 (Sp 71).

———. "Hawthorne and His Friends: Reminiscence and Tribute." *ATQ*, 9: 5-24 (Au 71).

Sennes, R.H. "Note on S's 'To John Brown,'" *ATQ*, 1: 43-4 (1Q 69).

Sanchez, Sonia. Clarke, Sebastian. "Black Magic Woman: SS and Her Work." *PA*, 78: 253-61 (1971).

———. "SS and Her Work." *BlackW*, 20: 44-8, 96-8 (1971).

Palmer, R.R. "The Poetry of Three Revolutionaries: Don L. Lee, SS, and Nikki Giovanni." *CLAJ*, 15: 25-36 (S 71).

Sandburg, Carl. Aderman, R.M. "CS, trubadur, al Americii." *Luc*, 24 Fe 68, p. 6.

Alexander, William. "The Limited American, the Loneliness, and the Singing Fire: CS's 'Chicago Poems.'" *AL*, 45: 67-83 (Mr 73).

Basler, R.P. "Your Friend the Poet: CS." *Midway*, 10: 3-15 (1969).

Chu, J.C.I. "CS: His Association with Henry Justin Smith." *JQ*, 50: 43-7, 133 (Sp 73).

Ferlazzo, P.J. "The Urban-Rural Vision of CS." *Midamerica*, 1974, pp. 52-7.

Flanagan, J.T. "Three Illinois Poets." *CentR*, 16: 313-27 (Fa 72).

Joyner, Nancy. "Robinson's Pamela and S's Agatha." *AL*, 40: 548-9 (Ja 69).

Juergensen, Hans. "The American Scene: Our Heritage, CS, 1878-1967." *DP*, 3: 18-20 (1968).

Knox, George. "Idealism, Vagabondage, Socialism: Charels A. Sandburg in *To-Morrow* and the *Era*." *HLQ*, 38: 161-88 (F 75).

Korotyč, V. "CS: Ja narod." *Žovten*, 23: 4-11 (1972).

Krusp, Horst. "Krieg, Mensch, un Nature in CS's 'Grass' un Heinrich Kruses 'Gras.'" *LWU*, 1: 98-107 (1968).

Macksey, R.A. "The Old Poets." *John Hopkins Mag*, 16: 42-8 (1968).

MacLeish, Archibald. "A Memorial Tribute to CS." *MR*, 9: 41-4 ÷wi 68).

Martynova, Anna. "CS and the Soviet Reader." *SovL*, 1: 192-3 (1968).

Mearns, D.C. "'Ever and Ever, Carl.'" *MSS*, 21: 169-73 (1969).

Mieder, Wolgang. "'Behold the Proverbs of a People.'" *SFQ*, 25: 160-8 (Je 71).

———. "Proverbs in CS's Poem 'The People, Yes.'" *SFQ*, 37: 15-36 (Mr 73).

Monaghan, Jay. "The CS I Knew." *SCUL*, 1: 20-8 (1969).

Ragan, Sam. "The Day North Carolina Honored CS." *Pembroke Mag*, 6: 167-70 (1975).

Reed, K.T. "CS and T.S. Eliot: Come Poetical Exchanges." *P&C*, 45-6 (Fa 70).

Rothwell, K.S. "In Search of a Western Epic: Neihart, S, and Jaffe as Regionalists and 'Astoriadists.'" *KanQ*, 2: 53-63 (1970).

Sutton, W.A. "A Frost-S Rivalry?" *BSUF*, 11: 59-61 (Wi 70).

———. "The Swedishness of CS." *ASR*, 60: 144-7 (Su 72).

Wagner, Selma. "S's 'A Fence.'" *Expl*, 27: 42 (F 69).

Wells, H.W. "CS and Asian Culture." *LHY*, 14: 31-54 (#1 73).

Sandoz, Mari. Clark, L.H. "The Indian Writings of MS." *Am Indian Q*, 1: 182-92, 268-80 (1975).

Posner, David. "A Meeting with MS." *PrS*, 42: 21-6 (Sp 68).

Sandoz, Mari. "MS: 1935." *PrS*, 41: 172-7 (Su 67).

Switzer, D.N. "MS's Lincoln Years." *PrS*, 45: 107-15 (Su 71).

Sandys, George. Davis, R.B. "*In re* GS's Ovid." *SB*, 8: 226-30 (1956).

―――. "S's Song of Solomon." *PBSA*, 50: 328-41 (1956).

Santayana, George. Anon. "The Detached Philosopher from Harvard." *TLS*, 17 Ap 69, pp. 401-3, 22 My 69, p. 559.

Ballows, James. "The Intellectual Traveller." *DR*, 50: 157-69 (Su 70).

―――. "Marquand and S: Apley and Alden." *MarkR*, 2: 92-4 (F 71).

―――. "S on Autobiography." *AL*, 41: 219-30 (My 69).

Burrill, Donald. "S's Notes on America." *Coronto*, 5: 12-9 (1968).

Cecil, David. "S." *TLS*, 15 Je 70, p. 70.

Chambers, L.H. "Gide, S, Chesterton, and Browning." *CLS*, 7: 216-28 (Je 70).

Cory, Daniel. "The Place and Relevance of GS." *SoR*, 8: 60-88 (Ja 72).

Davis, J.L. "Cabell and S in the Neo-Humanist Debate." *Cabellian*, 4: 55-67 (1972).

Holzberger, W.G. "The Unpublished Poems of GS: Some Critical and Textual Considerations." *SoR*, 11: 139-55 (Ja 75).

Hook, Sydney. "William James and GS." *ICarbS*, 1: 34-9 (1973).

Hughson, Lois. "The Uses of Despair: The Sources of Creative Energy in GS." *AQ*, 23: 725-37 (D 71).

López Quintás, Alfonso. "S, Husserl y Ortega." *Arbor*, 319-20: 5-16 (1972).

McCormick, E.L. "Walt Whitman, S's Poet of Barbarism." *Serif*, 5: 24-8 (Mr 68).

Michailoff, Helen. "Lermontov and His Friends." *CLC*, 24: 3-15 (#1 75).

Putnam, M.C.T. "Three Philosophical Poets by GS." *Daedalus*, 103: 131-40 (Wi 74).

Rippy, Merrill. "A Letter of GS." *N&Q*, 16: 259-60 (Jl 69).

Salerno, George. "Satayce-Joyceana." *JJQ*, 5: 137-43 (1968).

Sastri, P.S. "Stevens, the Romantics, and S." *IJAS*, 3: 39-46 (1973).

Sharma, D.R. "GS's Assessment of WW." *BP*, 14: 13-22 (1970).

Shaughnessy, E.L. "Oliver Alden and Studs Lonigan: Heirs to Spiritual Poverty." *MarkR*, 4: 48-52 (My 74).

Steinman, J.F. "S and Croce: An Aesthetic Reconsideration." *JAAC*, 30: 251-3 (1971).

Wagner, C.R. "Conversation with S, 1948: A Letter to a Friend." *AL*, 40: 349-51 (N 68).

Weinstein, M.Λ. "S: Conservative or Philosopher of Reason?" *ModA*, 13: 52-61 (Wi 68-69).

White, J.E. "'Santayanian Finesse' in Albee's *Tiny Alice*." *NCLit*, 3: 12-3 (N 73).

White, William. "S's Copy of Emily Dickinson's *Poems*." *EDB*, 9: 53-4 (Je 69).

Woodward, A.G. "GS, 1863-1952." *ESA*, 12: 107-31 (1969).

Youman, A.E. "S's Attachments." *NEQ*, 42: 373-87 (S 69).

Saroyan, William. Collier, Peter. "'I'm the Same, but Different.'" *NYT*, 2 Ap 72, pp. 3, 16.

Fabritius, Rudolf. "Charakterkomik in WS's Erzahlung *The Journey to Hanford*." *NS*, 17: 127-31 (Mr 68).

Jebeleanu, Eugen. "WS, printre noi." *Contemporanul*, 30 My 69, pp. 1, 8.

Kauffman, Stanley. "That Minstrel Boy." *NRep*, 166, 21-4 (25 My 72).

Krickel, Edward. "Cozzens and S: A Look at Two Reputations." *GaR*, 24: 281-96 (Fa 70).

Saroyan, William. "The International Symposium on the Short Story: United States." *KR*, 31: 58-62 (1969).

Scheer-Schaezler, Brigitte. "Short Story and Modern Novel." *OL*, 25: 338-51 (1970).

Shinn, Thelma. "WS: Romantic Existentialist." *MD*, 15: 185-94 (S 72).

Singer, Felix. "S at 57: The Daring Young Man After the Fall." *Trace*, 15: 2-5 (Sp 66).

Sarton, May. Putney, P.G. "Sister of the Mirage and Echo." *Contempora*, 2: 1-6 (1972).

Taylor, Henry. "Home to a Place Beyond Exile: The Collected Poems of MS." *HC*, 11: 1-16 (#3 74).

Schaffer, Jack. Dieter, Lynn. "Behavioral Objectives in the English Classroom: A Model." *EJ*, 59: 1258-71 (D 70).

Erisman, Fred. "Growing Up with the American West: Fiction of JS." *JPC*, 7: 710-6 (Wi 73).

Folsom, J.K. "*Shane* and *Hud*: Two Stories in Search of a Medium." *WHR*, 24: 359-72 (Fa 70).

Halsam, G.W. "JS's Frontier: The West as Human Testing Ground." *RMR*, 4: 59-71 (1967).

———. "*Shane;* Twenty-five Years Later." *WAL*, 9: 215-6 (Fa 74).

Nuwer, Hank. "An Interview with JS." *SDR*, 11: 48-58 (Sp 73).

Schumann, Peter. Brecht, Stefan. "PS's Bread & Puppet Theatre." *DramR*, 14: 44-90 (1970).

Dennison, George. "*Fire.*" *DramR*, 14: 36-43 (1970).

Kourilsky, Francoise. "PS's Bread and Puppet Theatre: Dada and Circus." *DramR*, 18: 104-9 (1974).

Schuyler, George. Peplow, M.W. "GS: Satirist: Rhetorical Devices in *Black No More.*" *CLAJ*, 18: 242-57 (D 74).

Reed, Ishmael, and Steve Cannon. "GS Interview." *Yardbird Reader*, 2: 83-104 (1973).

Schwartz, Delmore. Atlas, James. "Reconsideration of DS." *NRep*, 173: 36-9 (1 N 75).

Barrett, William. "D, a '30's Friendship and Beyond." *Commentary*, 58: 41-54 (#3 74).

Deutsch, R.H. "DS: Middle Poems." *CP*, 2: 19-28 (Fa 69).

Dickstein, Morris. "Cold War Blues." *PR*, 41: 30-53 (1974).

Knapp, J.F. "DS: Poet of the Orphic Journey." *SR*, 78: 505-16 (Jl-S 70).

Meiners, R.K. "The Way Out: The Poetry of DS." *SoR*, 7: 314-37 (Ja 71).

Poss, Stanley. "Frost, Freud, and DS." *CEA*, 30: 6-7 (Ap 68).

———. "Low Skies, Some Clearing, Local Frost." *NEQ*, 41: 438-42 (1968).

Simpson, Louis. "The Ghost of DS." *NYTMS*, 7 D 75, pp. 38-56.

Valenti, L.L. "The Apprenticeship of DS." *TCL*, 20: 201-16 (Jl 74).

———. "A Poet's Notebooks." *NYQ*, 10: 111-7 (1972).

Scudder, Vida Dutton. Ballou, E.B. "S's *Atlantic.*" *HLB*, 16: 326-53 (1968).

Frederick, P.J. "VDS: The Professor as Social Activist." *NEQ*, 43: 407-31 (S 70).

Seager, Alan. Bouyssou, Roland. "AS et la guerre." *Caliban*, 5: 79-92 (1968).

Clark, Jon. "On the Diagonal." *MQR*, 8: 1-2 (1969).

Dickey, James. "The Greatest American Poet." *Atl*, 222: 53-8 (N 68).

Penney, C.L. "A Letter of AS." *BNYPL*, 78: 393-5 (Su 75).

Quigley, G.L. "AS as Tecumseh." *MQR*, 9: 247-51 (1970).

Southam, B.C. "Whispers of Immortality." *TLS*, 22 June 73, pp. 720-1.

Sealsfield, Charles. Arndt, K.J. "Newly Discovered Relationships Documented." *MLN*, 87: 450-64 (1972).

Jantz, Harold. "CS's Letter to Joel R. Poinsett." *GR*, 27: 155-64 (1952).

Krumpelman, J.T. "Tokeah, the First English-Language Novel in Our Southwest." *SCB*, 28: 142-3 (Wi 68).

Ritter, Alexander. "CS (Karl Postl)." *LWU*, 4: 27088 (1971).

Segal, Eric. Berk, P.R. "*Love Story* and the Myth of Hyppolytus." *Classical Bul*, 48: 52-4 (F 72).

Erdmenger, Manfred. "*How to catch a phony* oder warum auch *Love Story* in den Lehrplan kommen kann." *NS*, 21: 324-7 (Je 72).

Freese, Peter. "ES's *Love Story* al Herausfolderung an die Literaturdidaktik." *NS*, 23: 18-30 (Mr 72).

Kirby, D.K., and E.J. Crook. "*Love Story* and the Erotic Convention in Literature." *NCLit*, 1: 8-10 (N 71).

Martí Zaro, Pablo. "*Love Story*: Lie Story? *RO*, 31: 101-12 (1972).

Merry, Bruce. "ES's *Love Story*: The Zero Degree of Language." *UWR*, 7: 37-48 (Sp 72).

Spilka, Mark. "ES as Little Nell, or the Real Meaning of *Love Story*." *SoRA*, 5: 38-51 (Mr 72); *JPC*, 5: 782-98 (Sp 72).

Tharpe, Jac. "*Love Story*: 'Redeeming Social Value?'" *SoQ*, 10: 63-75 (1971).

Selby, Hubert. Hutchinson, Stuart. "All Havens Astern: S's *Last Exit to Brooklyn*." *LonM*, 9: 22-34 (Ap 68).

Lane, J.B. "Violence and Sex in the Post-War Popular Urban Novel." *JPC*, 8: 285-308 (Wl 74).

Peavy, C.D. "HS and the Tradition of Moral Satire." *SNL*, 6: 35-9 (Sp 69).

———. "The Sin of Pride and S's *Last Exit to Brooklyn*." *Critique*, 11: 35-42 (1969).

Savonuzzi, Claudio. "HS." *Naz*, 2 Ap 71, p. 3.

Wertime, R.A. "Psychic Vengeance in *Last Exit to Brooklyn*." *L&P*, 24: 135-66 (1974).

Yurick, Sol. "HS: Symbolic Intent and Ideological Resistance." *EvR*, 13: 49-51 (73-8 (O 69).

Seltzer, Chester (see **Muro, Amanda Jesus**)

Sewall, Samuel. Arner, R.D. "Plum Island Revisited: One Version of the Pastoral." *SCN*, 27: 58-61 (1969).

Butterfield, L.H. "Reediting an American Classic." *NEQ*, 48: 277-83 (Mr 75).

Corrigan, R.A. "SS: Colonial American Diarist." *MSpr*, 59: 411-23 (1965).

Isani, A.M. "The Growth of *Phaenomena Quaedam Apocalyptica*." *EAL*, 7: 64-75 (Sp 72).

———. "The Pouring of the Sixth Vial: A Letter in a Taylor-S Debate." *PMHS*, 83: 123-9 (1971).

Nishikawa, Masami. "SS no Nikki." *EigoS*, 120: 354-6, 404-7 (1974).

Sexton, Anne. Anon. "AS: Worksheets." *MalR*, 6: 105-14 (1970).

Armstrong, R.R. "S's *Transformations*: Beyond Confessionalism." *IEY*, 24: 57-66 (Fa 74).

Axelrod, R.B. "The Transforming Art of AS." *CP*, 7: 6-13 (Sp 74).

Combecher, Has. "Dichtung als psychotherapeutische Selbsthilfe." *NS*, 20: 545-50 (O 71).

Fein, R.J. "The Demon of AS." *Eng Rec*, 18: 16-21 (O 67).

Hoffman, N.J. "Reading Women's Poetry: The Meaning and Our Lives." *CE*, 34: 48-62 (1972).

Jong, Erica. "Remembering AS." *NYT*, 27 O 74, p. 27.

Kevles, Barbara, "The Art of Poetry: AS." *PaR*, 13: 158-91 (Su 71).

Levertov, Denise. "AS: Light Up the Cave." *Ramparts*, 13: 61-3 (#5 75).

McClatchy, J.D. "AS: Somehow to Endure." *CentR*, 19: 1-36 (Sp 75).

McDonnell, T.P. "Light in a Dark Journey." *America*, 116: 729-31 (13 My 67).

Mizejewski, Linda. "Sappho to S." *CE*, 35: 340-5 (1973).

Mood, J.J. "'A Bird Full of Bones': AS—A Visit and a Reading." *ChiR*, 23: 107-23 (1972).

Newlin, Margaret. "The Suicide Bandwagon." *CritQ*, 14: 376-78 (Wi 72).

Oates, J.C. "The Awful Rowing Toward God." *NYT*, 23 Mr 75, pp. 3-4.

O'Brien, John. "R.I.P. . . . AS." *OyezR*, 9: 45-9 (Sp 75).

Rukeyser, Muriel. "Glitter and Wounds, Several Wildnesses." *Parnassus*, 2: 215-22 (Fa-Wi 73).

Shor, Ira. "AS's 'For My Lover . . .': Feminism in the Classroom." *CE*, 34: 1082-93 (My 73).

Tarozzi, Bianca. "Poesia e regressione." *ACF*, 12: 355-65 (1973).

Zollman, Sol. "Criticism, Self-Criticism, No Transformation: The Poetry of Robert Lowell and AS." *L&I*, 9: 29-36 (1971).

Zweig, Paul. "Making and Unmaking." *PR*, 40: 269-79 (#2 73).

*Seymour Charles. Gotlied, H.B. "CS: A Checklist of the Published Work." *YULG*, 47: 28-42 (1972).

Shands, Hubert A. Durham, Frank. "The Reputed Demises of Uncle Tom." *SLJ*, 2: 26-50 (Sp 70).

Simms, L.M. "HA.S's White and Black: A Note: *NMW*, 6: 25-6 (Sp 73).

Shapiro, Karl. Fussell, P.F. "The Bourgeois Poet." *PR*, 36: 141-5 (Wi 69).

Novak, Robert. "KS's Sonnets." *WiOr*, 5: 26-9 (My 71).

Reid, A.S. "A Look at the Living Poem: Rock Protest and Wit." *FurmM*, 12: 6-11, 35 (Sp 70).

———. "The Southern Exposure of KS." *SHR*, 6: 35-44 (Wi 72).

Stock, Robert. "And a Merry Crabbed Age." *Voyages*, 2: 98-9 (Sp 69).

Thornburg, T.R. "The Man with the Hatchet: S on Auden." *BSUF*, 11: 25-34 (Su 70).

Shaw, Henry Wheeler (Josh Billings). Grimes, G.A. "'Muels,' 'Owls,' and Other Things: Folk Material in the Tobacco Philosophy of JB." *NYFQ*, 26: 283-90 (D 70).

Kesterson, D.B. "JB and His Burlesque 'Allminax.'" *IllQ*, 35: 6-14 (N 72).

———. "JB on Lecturing and Humor: Some Recently Discovered Letters." *SAH*, 1: 23-7 (Ap 74).

———. "The Mark Twain-JB Relationship." *MTJ*, 18: 5-9 (Wi 75).

Kummings, D.D. "An Appraisal of Reappraisals: Four Nineteenth-Century Writers." *CEA*, 37: 36-8 (#1 74).

Shaw, Irwin. Berke, Jacqueline. "Further Observations on 'A S Story and Brooks and Warren.'" *CEA*, 33: 28-9 (N 70).

Sheldon, Charles M. Boyer, P.S. "In His Steps: A Reappraisal." *AQ*, 23: 60-78 (Sp 71).

Ripley, J.W. "The Strange Story of CM.S's *In His Steps*." *KHQ*, 34: 241-65 (1968).

White, D.F. "A Summons for the Kingdom of God on Earth." *SAQ*, 26: 469-86 (Su 68).

Shepard, Sam. Davis, R.S. "'Get Up Out a' Your Homemade Beds': The Plays of SS." *Players*, 47: 12-9 (O-N 71).

Frutkin, Ren. "SS: Paired Existence Meets the Monster." *Y/T*, 2: 22-30 (1969).

Lahr, John. "Spectacles of Distintegration." *EvR*, 14: 31-3 74-7 (Je 70).

Stambolian, George. "S's Mad Dog Blues: A Trip through Popular Culture." *JPC* 7: 776-86 (1974).

Shepard, Thomas. Frederick, J.T. "Literary Art in TS's *The Parable of the Virgins*." *SCN*, 26: 7 (1968).

Kahn, T.G. "Urian Oakes' *Elegie* on TS and Puritan Poetics." *AL*, 45: 163-81 (My 73).

Parker, D.L. "Petrus Ramus and the Puritans: The 'Logic' of Preparationist Conversion Doctrine." *EAL*, 8: 140-62 (Fa 73).

Werge, Thomas. "TS and Crévecoeur: Two Uses of the Bosom Serpent before Hawthorne." *NHJ*, 4: 236-9 (1974).

Sherwood, Robert Emmet. Kroll, Morton. "The Liberal in the American Drama: RES." *WPQ*, 15: 48-50 (S 62).

Whitney, Blair. "Lincoln's Life as Dramatic Art." *JISHS*, 61: 333-49 (Au 68).

Short, Luke. Olsen, T.V. "LS, Writer's Writer." *Roundup*, 21: 10-4 (Mr 73).

Thomas, P.D. "The Paperback West of LS." *JPC*, 7: 701-8 (Ja 73).

Sigourney, Lydia Huntley. Wood, A.D. "Mrs. S and the Sensibility of the Inner Space." *NEQ*, 45: 163-81 (Je 72).

Sill, Edward Rowland. Ferguson, A.R. "S's Poems Wrongly Ascribed to Sanborn." *ESQ*, 58: 131 (1Q 70).

Silverberg, Robert. Ketterer, David. "*Solaris* and the Illegitimate Suns of Science Fiction." *Extrapolation*, 14: 73-89 (D 72).

Tuma, G.W. "Biblical Myth and Legend in *Tower of Glass.*" *Extrapolation*, 15: 174-91 (O 74).

Simic, Charles. Anon. "Where the Levels Meet: An Interview with CS." *OhR*, 14: 47-58 (Wi 73).

Duimond, James. "Moving Heaven and Earth." *Parnassus*, 1: 106-15 (1972).

Simms, William Gilmore. Boucher, C.S., and R.P. Brooks. "Correspondence Addressed to John C. Calhoun, 1837-1849." *Annual Report Am Hist Assn*, 1929, pp. 125-529.

Bush, L.M. "Werther on the Alabama Frontier: A Reinterpretation of S's *Confession.*" *MissQ*, 21: 119-30 (Sp 68).

Calhoun, R.J. "Literary Criticism in Southern Periodicals During the American Renaissance." *ESQ*, 55: 76-82 (2Q 69).

Christopherson, Merrill. "S's Northern Speaking Tour in 1856: A Tragedy." *SoSpJ*, 36: 139-51 (Wi 70).

Cook, G.A. "Porgy Reexamined." *TAIUS*, 5: 65-71 (1972).

Donald, David. "The Preslavery Argument Reconsidered." *JSH*, 37: 3-18 (F 71).

Doxey, W.S. "Dogs and Dates in S's *The Yemassee.*" *ATQ*, 1: 41-3 (1Q 69).

Gilkes, Lillian. "Park Benjamin, Henry William Herbert, and WGS: A Case of Mistaken Identity." *SCR*, 3: 66-77 (Je 71).

Gozzini, F.C. "W.G.S e *The Yemassee.*" *SA*, 13: 101-27 (1967).

Guilds, J.C. "The Achievement of WGS: His Short Fiction." *Spectrum*, 2: 25-35 (1972).

———. "The Literary Criticism of WGS." *SCR*, 2: 49-56 (N 69).

———. "The 'Lost' Number of the *Southern Literary Gazette.*" *SB*, 22: 266-72 (1969).

———. "S as Editor and Prophet: The Flowering and Early Death of the Southern *Magnolia.*" SLJ, 4: 69-92 (Sp 72).

———. "WGS and the *Southern Literary Gazette.*" *SB*, 21: 59-91 (1968).

Hoge, J.O. "Byron's Influence on the Poetry of WGS." *EsL*, 2: 87-96 (Sp 75).

Howell, Elmo. "The Concept of Character in S's Border Romances." *MissQ*, 22: 303-12 (Fa 69).

———. "WGS and the American Indian." *SCR*, 5: 57-64 (Je 73).

Hubert, Thomas. "S's Use of Milton and Wordsworth in *The Yemassee.*" *SCR*, 6: 58-65 (N 73).

Jarrell, H.M. "WGS: Almost an Historian." *South Carolina Hist Assn Proc*, 1947, pp. 3-8.

Kibler, J.E. "Légare's First Poems and His Early Career." *SLJ*, 6: 70-6 (Fa 73).

———. "A New Letter of S to Richard Henry Wilde." *AL*, 44: 667-70 (Ja 73).

———. "S's Indebtedness to Folk Tradition in 'Sharp Snaffles.'" *SLJ*, 4 55-68 (Sp 72).

Kolodny, Annette. "The Unchanging Landscape: The Pastoral Impulse in S's Revolutionary War Romances." *SLJ*, 5: 46-67 (Fa 72).

Lease, Benjamin. "WGS: A New Letter." *GHQ*, 54: 427-30 (Fa 70).

McDowell, G.T. "The Negro in the Southern Novel Prior to 1850." *JEGP*, 25: 455-73 (4Q 26).

McHaney, T.L. "An Early 19th Century Literary Agent: James Lawson of New York." *PBSA*, 64: 177-92 (2Q 70).

Meriwether, J.B. "The Proposed Edition of WGS." *MissQ*, 15: 100-12 (Su 62).

———. "Some Proofreading Precautions." *CEAAN*, 2: 17-8 (1969).

Powell, W.E. "Motif and Tale-Type in S's 'Grayling.'" *SFQ*, 35: 157-9 (Je 71).

Rees, R.A., and Marjorie Griffin. "WGS and *The Family Companion*." *SB*, 24: 109-26 (1971).

Ridgely, J.V. "S's Concept of Style in the Historical Romance." *ESQ*, 60: 16-23 (Su 70).

————. "Two Unprinted Short Novels." *SLJ*, 5: 80-7 (Sp 73).

Roberts, Leonard. "Beauchamp and Sharp: A Kentucky Tragedy." *LFR*, 14-9 (Ja-Mr 68).

Rose, A.H. "The Image of the Negro in the Pre-Civil War Novels of John Pendleton and WGS." *JAmSt*, 4: 217-26 (F 71).

Shillingsburg, M.J. " 'The Idylls of the Appalachian' by WGS." *AppR*, 1: 2-11, 147-60 (Au 72, Sp 73).

————. "From Notes to Novel: S's Creative Method." *SLJ*, 5: 89-107 (Fa 72).

————. "Politics and Art." *SLJ*, 7: 132-45 (Sp 75).

————. "S's Reviews of Shakespeare on the Stage." *TSL*, 16: 121-35 (1971).

Thomas, C.E. "Mary C.S. Oliphant." *Sandlapper*, 4: 13-6 (Ja 71).

Tomlinson, David. "S's Monthly Magazine: *The Southern and Western Monthly Magazine and Review*." *SLJ*, 8: 95-125 (Fa 75).

Tuttleton, J.W. "Romance and Novel: The Disintegration of a Form." *ESQ*, 55: 116-21 (2Q 69).

Vauthier, Simone. "Une aventure du recit fantastique: *Paddy McGann, or, The Demon of the Stump* de WGS." *RANAM*, 7: 78-104 (1973).

————. "Légende du Sud: Présentation de W.G.S." *BFLS*, 47: 259-90 (Ja 69).

————. "Of Time and the South: The Fiction of WGS." *SLJ*, 5: 3-45 (Fa 72).

Wakelyn, J.L. "The Changing Loyalities of James Henry Hammond." *SCHM*, 75: 1-13 (1974).

Watson, G.S. "A New Approach to S: Imagery and Meaning in *The Yemassee*." *MissQ*, 26: 155-63 (Sp 73).

*————. "WGS: An Essay in Bibliography." *RALS*, 3: 3-26 (Sp 73).

Weidman, B.S. "White Man's Red Man: A Penitential Reading of Four American Novels." *MLS*, 4: 14-26 (Fa 74).

Wimsatt. M.A. "Leonard Woltmeier's 'Invictus.' " *SLJ*, 2: 135-47 (Sp & O).

————. "S as a Novelist of Manners: *Katherine Walton*." *SLJ*, 5: 68-88 (Fa 72).

Simon, Neil. Berkowitz, G.M. "NS and His Amazing Laugh Machine." *Players*, 47: 110-3 (F-Mr 72).

Hewes, Henry. "Odd Husband Out." *SatR*, 54: 20-2 (4 D 71).

McMahon, Helen. "A Rhetoric of Popular American Drama: The Comedies of NS." *Players*, 51: 11-5 (1975).

Simpson, Louis. Anon. "Capturing the World as It Is: An Interview with LS." *OhR*, 14: 35-51 (Sp 73).

Guimond, James. "Moving Heaven and Earth." *Parnassus*, 1: 106-15 (1972).

Moran, Ronald. "LS: The Absence of Criticism and the Presence of Poetry." *FarP*, 1: 60-6 (Fa-Wi 68).

————. "The Image of America in the California/Whitman Poems of LS." *GGAL*, 75: 211-9 (1974).

————. " 'Walt Whitman at Bear Mountain' and the American Illusion." *CP*, 2: 5-9 (Sp 69).

Morris, Harry. "A Formal View of the Poetry of Dickey, Garrigue and S." *SR*, 77: 318-25 (1969).

Smith, Lawrence. "A Conversation with LS." *ChiR*, 27: 99-109 (Sp 75).

Stitt, Peter. "North of Jamaica and Into the Self: LS and Ronald Moran." *SoR*, 10: 517-24 (Sp 74).

Susko, Mario. "Asocijatinva imanginacija LS." *Republika*, 30: 1202-10 (1974).

Sinclair, May. Boll, T.E.M. "*The Divine Fire* (1904) and *Martin Eden* (1909)." *ELT*, 14: 115-7 (1971).

*————. "MS: A Check List." *BNYPL*, 76: 454-67 (1970).

*Robb, K.A. "MS: An Annotated Bibliography of Writings About Her." *ELT*, 16: 177-231 (1973).

Sinclair, Upton. Allatt, Edward. "Collecting US in England." *ABC*, 20: 23-4 (O 69).

————. "Jack London and US." *JLN*, 1: 22-7 (Ja-Je 68).

————. "US on Jack London in 1963." *JLN*, 2: 77-8 (S-D 69).

Cristea, Corina. "US." *Russkaja Lit*, 5 D 68, p. 20.

Duram, J.C. "US's Realistic Romanticism." *Wichita State Un Bul*, 46: 3-11 (#2 70).

Gottesmann, Ronald. "Louis Adamic and US." *AN&Q*, 1: 41-65 (1968).

————. "Some Implications of *The Literary Manuscripts of UP*." *Proof*, 3: 395-410 (1973).

Graham, John. "US and the Ludlow Massacre." *ColQ*, 21: 55-67 (Su 72).

Grenier, Judson. "US and the Press: *The Brass Check* Reconsidered." *JQ*, 49: 427-36 (Fa 72).

————. "US: A Remembrance." *CHSQ*, 48: 165-9 (Je 69).

Gross, Dalton. "George Sterling's Letters to the USs." *ABC*, 24: 16-20 (S-O 73).

Kimball, W.J. "*Manassas*: An Early Expression of US's Socialistic Leanings." *McNR*, 20: 28-32 (1971-72).

Leary, Lewis. "A Note on the Correspondence between US and Frederik von Eeden in the Library of the University of Amsterdam." *RALS*, 2: 105-6 (Sp 72).

Muraire, A. "Searching for the Theatre in France: US vs. Albert Camus, André Malraux, and Jean Vilar." *BSUF*, 15: 77-9 (1974).

Musteikis, Antanas. "The Lithuanian Heroes of *The Jungle*." *Lithuanus*, 17: 27-38 (1971).

Silet, C.L.P "The US Archives." *SCQ*, 4: 407-14 (Wi 74).

————. "US to Jack London: A Literary Friendship." *JLN*, 4: 46-76 (My-Ag 72).

————, and S. Sharon. "Charmian London to US: Selected Letters." *JLN*, 4: 25-46 (Ja-Mr 71).

Soderbergh, P.A. "US and Hollywood." *MwQ*, 11: 173-91 (Wi 70).

Sorgenstein, Samuel. "The Truth about Jack London: Reminiscences of US." *JLN*, 6: 79-80 (S-D 73).

Sottesman, Ronald. "Some Implications of *The Literary Manuscripts of US*." *Proof*, 3: 395-410 (1973).

Thomas, J.L. "Reconsiderations: US's *Boston*." *NRep*, 165: 24-5 (18 D 71).

Turner, J.G. "Conversation with US." *ABC*, 20: 7-10 (Je 70).

Wolfe, D.M. "A Evening with US." *JHS*, 1: 265-7 (1968).

Yoder, J.A. "US, Lanny, and the Liberals." *MFS*, 20: 483-404 (Wi 74-75).

Zenger, Martin. "Politics and Confrontation: US and the Launching of the ACLU in Southern California." *PHR*, 38: 383-406 (1969).

Singer, Isaac Bashevis. Anon. "Books by IBS." *HC*, 10: 8-9 (1973).

Anderen, D.M. "IBS: Conversations in California." *MFS*, 16: 423-9 (1970).

Bezanker, Abraham. "I.B.S's Crises of Identity." *Critique*, 14: 70-88 (#2 72).

*Christensen, B.J.M. "IBS: A Bibliography." *BB*, 3-6 (Ja-Mr 69).

Di Veroli, E.M. "Da Vecchio al Nouvo Mondu: IBS." *SA*, 17: 291-341 (1971).

Donoghue, Denis. "IBS." *Art Int*, 13: 24-5, 67 (N 69).

Fried, Lewis. "The Magician of Lublin." *Yiddish*, 2: 60-9 (#1 75).

Gilman, S.L. "IBS." *Diacritics*, 4: 30-3 (1974).

Gottlieb, Elaine. "S and Hawthorne: A Prevalence of Satan." *SoR*, 8: 359-70 (Ap 72).

Lee, G.F. "The Hidden God of IBS." *HC*, 10: 1-15 (1973).

Natanson, Maurice. "Solipsism and Sociality." *NLH*, 5: 237-44 (1974).

Perez Minik, Domingo. "La novela extranjera en Espana: Miscelanea norteamericana: I.B.S. y W. Burroughs." *Insula*, 27: 5-6 (Ja 72).

Pinsker, Sanford. "The Fictive Worlds of IBS." *Critique*, 11: 26-39 (#2 69).

———. "IBS and Joyce Carol Oates: Some Versions of Gothic." *SoR*, 9: 895-908 (Au 73).

———. "IBS: An Interview." *Critique*, 11: 16-25 (#2 69).

Pondrom, C.N. "IBS: An Interview and a Biographical Sketch." *ConL*, 10: 1-38, 332-51 (Wi, Su 69).

Reichek, M.A. "Storyteller." *NYTMS*, 23 Mr 75, pp. 16-33.

Salamon, George. "In a Glass Darkly: The Morality of the Mirror in E.T.A. Hoffman and I.B.S." *SSF*, 7: 625-33 (1970).

Schatt, Stanley. "The Dybbuk Had Three Wives: IBS and the Jewish Sense of Time." *Judaism*, 23: 100-8 (1974).

Schulz, M.F. "IBS, Radical Sophistication, and the Jewish-American Novel." *SHR*, 3: 60-6 (Wi 68).

Shenker, Israel. "IBS Scoffs." *Atl*, 226: 98-110 (Jl 70).

Singer, Isaac. "Un ami de Kafka." *NL*, 20 Ag 70, pp. 1, 6.

Steinberg, T.L. "I.B.S: Responses to Catastrophe." *Yiddish*, 1: 9-16 (#4 74).

Streiter, Aaron. "Bein Ha-el Le-bein Ha-tetom—Hazon Ha-mussae bi-yetsirat I.BS." *Bikoret U-Parshanut*, 2: 95-102 (#3 72).

Varley, H.L. "IBS and the Sense of Wonder." *KAL*, 16: 44-6 (1975).

Zatlin, L.G. "The Themes of IBS's Short Fiction." *Critique*, 11: 40-6 (#2 69).

Smith, Charles Henry (Bill Arp). Austin, James, and Wayne Pike. "The Language of BA." *AS*, 48: 84-97 (Sp-Su 73).

Smith, Elihu Hubbard. Lasser, M.L. "ES's All American Anthology." *JRUL*, 31: 14-20 (1968).

Smith, John. Arner, R.D. "JS, the 'Starving Time,' and the Genesis of Southern Humor: Variations on a Theme." *LaStud*, 12: 383-90 (Sp 73).

Bain, Robert. "Two Colonials in Virginia: Captain JS and James Blair." *SLJ*, 107-16 (Sp 72).

Barbour, P.L. "Captain JS and the London Theatre." *VMHB*, 83: 277-9 (Jl 75).

———. "The Earliest Reconnaissance of the Chesapeake Bay Area: Captain JS's Maps and Indian Vocablary." *VMHB*, 79: 280-302 (1971); 80: 277-9 (1972).

———. "A Note on the Discovery of the Original Will of Captain JS." *WMQ*, 25: 625-8 (O 68).

———. "Toponymy in the Service of Biography." *Names*, 21: 108-18 (1964).

Beiser, W.G. "JS, Admiral of New England." *NasR*, 1: 1-7 (1969).

Craven, W.F. "A New Edition of the Works of Captain JS." *WMQ*, 29: 479-86 (Jl 72).

Glenn, Keith. "Captain JS and the Indians." *VMHB*, 52: 228-48 (1948).

Hubbell, J.B. "The S-Pocahontas Story in Literature." *VMHB*, 65: 275-300 (1957).

Pichler, J.F. "Captain JS in the Light of Styrian Sources." *VMHB*, 65: 332-54 (1957).

Randel, William. "Captain JS's Attitude toward the Indians." *VMHB*, 47: 218-29 (1939).

Raup, G.B. "Captain JS: Adventurer Extraordinary." *VMHB*, 61: 186-92 (1953).

Smith, Bradford. "Biographer's Notebook." *VMHB*, 65: 301-12 (1957).

———. "Captain JS's Earl of Ployer." *VMHB*, 62: 348-9 (1954).

Szerb, Anthony. "Captain JS in Transylvania." *Hungarian Q*, 6: 734-41 (1940).

Young, Philip. "The Mother of Us All: Pocahontas Reconsidered." *KR*, 24: 391-415 (Su 62).

Smith, Lillian. Blackwell, Louise, and Frances Clay. "LS, Novelist." *CLAJ*, 15: 452-8 (Je 72).

Sugg, R.S. "LS and the Condition of Woman." *SAQ*, 71: 155-64 (Sp 72).

*Sullivan, Margaret. "A Bibliography of LS and Paula Snelling." *MVCBul*, 4: 3-82 (Sp 71).

———. "LS: The Public Image and the Personal Vision." *MRR*, 2: 3-31 (Su-Fa 67).

Thornburn, Neil. "*Stranger Fruit* and the Southern Tradition." *MwQ*, 12: 157-71

Smith, Seba. Miller, A.R. "America's First Political Satirist: SS of Maine." *JQ*, 47: 488-92 (Au 70).

Nickels, C.C. "SS Embattled." *Maine Hist Q*, 13: 7-26 (1973).

Smith, William. Andrews, W.D. "WS and the Rising Glory of America." *EAL*, 8: 33-43 (Sp 73).

Lively, B.R. "WS, the College and the Academy of Philadelphia, and Pennsylvania Politics, 1753-1758." *HMPEC*, 38: 237-58 (S 69).

Smith, William Jay. Burgess, C.F. "WJS's 'American Primitive': Toward a Reading." *ArQ*, 26: 71-5 (Sp 70).

Hall, D.J. "WJS and the Art of Lightness." *SHR*, 3: 67-77 (Wi 68).

Jacobsen, Josephine. "The Dark Train and the Green Place: The Poetry of WJS." *HC*, 12: 1-14 (#1 75).

Ritchie, Elisavietta. "An Interview with WJS." *Voyages*, 3: 89-103 (1970).

Snelling, William Joseph. Evans, Elizabeth. "WJS: Still a Forgotten Critic." *MarkR*, 5: 150-20 (1975).

Snodgrass, W.D. Boyers, Robert. "W.D.S: An Interview." *Salmagundi*, 22-23: 149-63 (1973).

Dillon, David. "Toward Passionate Utterance." *SWR*, 60: 278-90 (Su 75).

Gerber, P.L., and R.J. Gemmet. "'No Voices Talk to Me': A Conversation with W.D.S." *WHR*, 24: 61-71 (Wi 70).

Mazzaro, Jerome. "The Public Intimacy of W.D.S." *Salmagundi*, 19: 96-111 (Sp 72).

McClatchy, J.D. "W.D.S: The Mild, Reflective Art." *MR*, 16: 281-314 (Sp 75).

Phillips, R.S "S and the Sad Hospital of the World." *UWR*, 4: 66-70 (Sp 69).

Snodgrass, W.D. "Vuillard: 'Mama şi sora artisului.'" *Steaua*, 24, 27 (1974).

Snyder, Gary. Altieri, Charles. "GS's Lyric Poetry: Dialectic as Ecology." *FarP*, 4: 55-65 (Sp Su 70).

Benoit, Raymond. "The New American Poetry." *Thought*, 44: 201-18 (Su 69).

Berry, Wendell. "A Secular Pilgrimage." *HudR*, 23: 401-24 (1970).

Dodsworth, Martin. "Body Rhythm." *Review*, 23: 55-60 (1970).

Gitzen, Julian. "GS and the Poetry of Compassion." *CritQ*, 15: 341-57 (Wi 73).

Gunn, Thom. "Waking the Wonder." *Listener*, 79: 576-7 (2 My 68).

Hunt, Anthony. "S's 'After Work.'" *Expl*, 32: 61 (Ap 74).

Kirby, D.K. "S, Auden and the New Morality." *NCLit*, 1: 9-10 (Ja 71).

Lewis, P.E. "Robert Creeley and GS: A British Assessment." *Stand*, 13: 42-7 (1972).

Lyon, J.T. "The Ecological Vision of GS." *KanQ*, 2: 117-24 (1970).

———. "GS: A Western Poet." *WAL*, 3: 207-16 (Fa 68).

Mao, Nathan. "The Influence of Zen Buddhism on GS." *TkR*, 5: 125-33 (#2 74).

Nelson, R.L. "'Riprap on the Slick Rock of Metaphysics': Religious Dimensions in the Poetry of GS." *Soundings*, 57: 206-21 (Su 74).

Novak, Charles. "Coming to Terms with GS: Smokey the Bear Sutra." *WiOr*, 17: 29-30, 51-2 (Sp 74).

Parkinson, Thomas "The Poetry of GS." *SoR*, 4: 616-32 (Su 68).

———. "The Theory and Practice of GS." *JML*, 2: 448-52 (#3 71-72).

Paul, Sherman. "From Lookout to Ashram: The Way of GS." *Iowa R*, 1: 76-91, 70-86 (Su, Fa 70).

Peach, Linden. "Earth House Hold: A Twentieth-Century *Walden*." *AWR*, 25: 108-14 (#55 75).

Pleasants, Ben. "Ontology of Language in the Poems of Eliot and S." *Tuatara*, 12: 53-63 (1974).

Powell, Leslie. "Those 801 Chauvinist Sutras." *New*, 24: 95-7 (1974).

Ruiz Ruis, Jose. "Notas en torno a 'Earth House Hold' de GS." *FMod*, 50-51: 393-413 (1974).

Scott, R.I. "GS's Early Uncollected Mallory Poems." *CP*, 2: 33-7 (Sp 69).

Shinkura, Shunichi. "GS: Shinwa to Honbun." *EigoS*, 115: 82-4 (1969).

Tarbet, D.W. "Contemporary Poetic Pastoral: A Poetic Faith." *Eng Rec*, 23: 72-83 (Wi 72).

Wagner, Linda. "'And the Farming of Our Ancestors. . . .'" *UWR*, 5: 107-9 (Fa 69).

Williamson, Alan. "GS: An Appreciation." *NRep*, 173: 28-30 (1 N 75).

Sontag, Susan. Boyers, Robert. "On SS and the New Sensibility." *Salmagundi*, 1: 27-38 (Fa 66).

―――. "Women, the Arts, and the Politics of Culture: An Interview with SS." *Salmagundi*, 31-2: 29-48 (1975).

Hashiguchi, Minoru. "SS—Atarashii Jidai no Zenei." *EigoS*, 115: 760-1 (1969).

Heilbrun, C.G. "Speaking of SS." *NYT*, 27 Ag 67, pp. 2, 30.

Holbrook, David. "What New Sensibility?" *CQ*, 3: 153-63 (1968).

Houston, Gary. "SS." *MQR*, 9: 272-5 (Au 70).

Kavolis, Vytautas. "The Social Psychology of Avant-garde Cultures." *STC*, 6: 13-34 (Fa 70).

Levy, Maurice. "Entre vue avec SS." *Caliban*, 9: 93-112 (1973).

Marx, Leo. "SS's 'New Left' Pastoral." *TriQ*, 23-24: 552-75 (Wi-Sp 72).

Nairn, Tom. "New Sensibility." *NSt*, 24 Mr 67, pp. 408-9.

Perez Minik, Domingo. "SS nos cuenta una ordalia historica." *Insula*, 24: 21 (O-N 69).

Phillips, William. "Radical Syles." *PR*, 36: 388-400 (1969).

Rubin, L.D. "SS and the Camp Followers." *SR*, 82: 503-10 (Su 74).

Solotaroff, Theodore. "Death in Life." *Commentary*, 44: 87-9 (N 67).

Stark, John. "Camping Out: *Tiny Alice* and SS." *Players*, 47: 166-9 (1972).

Toback, James. "Whatever You'd Like SS to Think, She Doesn't." *Esquire*, 70: 114-6 (Jl 68).

Sorrentino, Gilbert. Alpert, Barry. "GS: An Interview." *Vort*, 2: 3-30 (Fa 74).

Caserio, R.L. "GS's Prose Fiction." *Vort*, 2: 63-8 (Fa 74).

Emerson, Stephen. "Imaginative Qualities in Actual Things." *Vort*, 2: 85-9 (Fa 74).

Guimond, James. "Moving Heaven and Earth." *Parnassus*, 1: 106-15 (1972).

Klinkowitz, Jerome. "GS's Super-Fiction." *ChiR*, 25: 77-89 (Sp 74).

Mottram. Eric. "The Black Polar Night: The Poetry of GS." *Vort*, 2: 43-59 (Fa 74).

O'Brien, John. "GS: Some Various Looks." *Vort*, 2: 79-84 (Fa 74).

Phelps, Daniel. "Extra Space." *Vort*, 2: 88-96 (Fa 74).

Zinnes, Harriet. "Polar Night of America." *Parnassus*, 3: 204-9 (#1 74).

Southern, Terry. Arn, Robert. "Obscenity and Pornography." *CamR*, 89: 160-3 (D 67).

McLaughlin, J.J. "Satirical Comical Pornographical *Candy*." *KanQ*, 1: 98-103 (1969).

Murray, D.M. "Candy Christian as a Pop-Art Daisy Miller." *JPC*, 340-8 (Fa 71).

Silva, E.T. "From *Candide* to *Candy*: Love's Labor Lost." *JPC*, 8: 783-91 (1974).

Spencer, Elizabeth. Bunting, C.T. "'In That Time and at That Place': The Literary World of ES." *MissQ*, 28: 435-60 (Fa 75).

Cole, H.M. "ES at Sycamore Fair." *NMW*, 6: 81-6 (Wi 74).

———. "Windsor in S and Welty: A Real and an Imaginary Landscape." *NMW*, 7: 2-11 (Sp 74).

Haley, Josephine. "A Biographical Note on ES." *NMW*, 1: 54-5 (Fa 68).

———. "An Interview with ES." *NMW*, 1: 42-53 (Fa 68).

Spencer, Elizabeth. "On Writing Fiction." *NMW*, 3: 71-2 (Fa 70).

Spillane, Mickey. Banks, R.J. "Anti-Professionalism in the Works of MS." *NCLit*, 3: 6-8 (Mr 73).

Cawelti, J.G. "The S Phenomenon." *JPC*, 3: 9-22 (Su 69).

Stafford, Jean. Gelfant, Blanche. "Reconsideration: *The Mountain Boy* by JS." *NRep*, 172: 22-5 (10 My 75).

Jenson, Sid. "The Noble Wicked West of JS." *WAL*, 7: 261-70 (Wi 73).

Libermann, M.M. "The Collected Stories." *SR*, 77: 516-21 (Su 69).

Mann, J.W. "Toward New Archetypal Forms: JS's *The Catherine Wheel.*" *Critique*, 17: 77-92 (#2 75).

Stafford, William. Anon. "An Interview with WS." *Crazy Horse*, 7: 36-41 (Je 71).

Ahmad. Aijaz. "Ghalib: 'The Dew Drop on the Red Poppy. . . .'" *Mahfil*, 5: 59-69 (1968-69).

Bauerle, R.F. "S's *Holcomb, Kansas.*" *CP*, 1: 27-30 (Sp 73).

Benoit, Raymond. "The New American Poetry." *Thought*, 44: 201-18 (Su 69).

Coles, Robert. "WS's Long Walk." *APR*, 4: 27-8 (#4 75).

Dickinson-Brown, Roger. "The Wise, the Dull, the Bewildered: What Happens in WS." *MPS*, 6: 30-8 (Sp 75).

Gerber, P.L., and R.J. Gemmett, "Keeping the Lines Wet: A Conversation with WS." *PrS*, 44: 123-36 (Su 70).

Greiner, C.F. "'Traveling Through the Dark': A Discussion of Style." *EJ*, 55: 1015-8 (N 66).

Howard, Richard. "Ecstasies and Decorum" *Parnassus*, 2: 217-20 (1974).

Hugo, Richard. "Problems with Landscapes in Early S Poems." *KanQ*, 2: 33-8 (1970).

———, and William Stafford. "The Third Time the World Happens: A Dialogue on writing." *NwR*, 13: 26-47 (1973).

Kelley, Patrick. "Legend and Ritual." *KanQ*, 2: 28-31 (1970).

Kyle, Carol. "Point of View in 'Returned to Say' and the Wilderness in WS." *WAL*, 7: 191-20 (Fa 72).

Lauber, John. "World's Guest: WS." *Iowa R*, 5: 88-99 (Sp 74).

Lensing, G.S. "WS, Mythmaker." *MPS*, 6: 1-17 (Sp 75).

Lieberman, Laurence. "The Shocks of Normality." *YR*, 63: 453-73 (1974).

Lofsness, Cynthia. "An Interview with WS." *Iowa R*, 3: 92-106 (Su 72).

Mazzaro, Jerome. "Fusions." *FarP*, 5: 70-3 (Wi-Sp 71).

*McMillan, S.H. "On WS and His Poems: A Selected Bibliography." *TPJ*, 2: 21-2 (Sp 69).

Miller, T.P. "'In Dear Detail, By Ideal Light': The Poetry of WS." *SWR*, 56: 341-5 (Au 71).

Nuwer, Henry. "Interview: WS." *Brushfire*, 23: 19-20 (Sp 74).

Pinsker, Sanford. "Conversation with WS." *APR*, 4: 28-9 (#4 75).

Ramsey, Paul. "What the Light Struck." *TPJ*, 2: 17-20 (Sp 69).

Roberts, J.R. "Listening to the Wilderness with WS." *WAL*, 3: 217-26 (Fa 68).

Stafford, William. "Having Become a Writer: Some Reflections." *NwR*, 13: 90-2 (1973).

———. "An Interval in a Northwest Writer's Life, 1950-1973." *NwR*, 13: 6-9 (1973).

———. "A Way of Writing." *Field*, 2: 10-2 (Sp 70).

———. "Writing the Australian Crawl." *CCC*, 15: 12-5 (F 64).

Sumner, D.N. "The Poetry of WS: Nature, Time, and Father." *RSW*, 36: 187-95 (S 68).

Turner, A.T. "WS and the Surprise Cliche." *SCR*, 7: 28-33 (Ap 75).

Wagner, L.W. "WS's Plain-Style." *MPS*, 6: 19-30 (Sp 75).

Womack, Judy. "Daniel Boone—'Over the Velvet Falls.'" *KFR*, 18: 21-2 (1972).

Zweig, Paul. "The Raw and the Cooked." *PR*, 41: 604-12 (1974).

Stedman, Edmund Clarence. Scholnick, R.J. "The Shadowed Years, Mrs. Richards, Mr. S, and Robinson." *CLQ*, 9: 510-31 (D 72).

Steffens, Lincoln. Cooley, T.M. "LS: American Innocent Abroad." *AL*, 43: 589-602 (Ja 72).

Greeley, A.M. "Reconsiderations: *The Autobiography of LS.*" *NRep*, 165: 29-31

Gunn, D.W. "Three Radicals and a Revolution: Reed, London, and S on Mexico." *SWR*, 55: 393-410 (Au 70).

Michaels, Walter. "LS and Pound." *Paideuma*, 2: 209-10 (Fa 73).

Morgan, K.O. "The Man with the Muckrake." *TLS*, 4 Jl 75, pp. 710-1.

Stein, H.H. "Theodore Roosevelt and the Press: LS." *M-A*, 54: 94-107 (Ap 72).

Stegner, Wallace. Ahearn, Kerry. "*The Big Rock Candy Mountain* and *Angle of Repose*: Trial and Culmination." *WAL*, 10: 11-27 (My 75).

Canzoneri, Robert. "WS: Trial by Existence." *SoR*, 9: 796-827 (Au 73).

Flora, J.M. "Vardis Fisher and WS, Teacher and Student." *WAL*, 5: 121-8 (Su 70).

Hofheins, Roger, and Dan Tooker. "Interview with WS." *SoR*, 11: 794-801 (Au 75).

Hudson, L.P. "*The Big Rock Candy Mountain*: No Roots—and No Frontier." *SDR*, 9: 3-13 (Sp 71).

Jenson, Sid. "The Compassionate Seer: WS's Literary Artist." *BYUS*, 14: 248-62 (Wi 74).

Milton, J.R. "Conversations with Distinguished Western American Novelists." *SDR*, 9: 15-57 (Sp 71).

Mosely, Richard. "First Person Narration in WS's *All the Little Live Things.*" *NCLit*, 3: 12-3 (Mr 73).

Peterson, Audrey. "Narrative Voice in WS's *Angle of Repose.*" *WAL*, 10: 125-33 (Ag 75).

Stein, Gertrude. Anon. "Double, Double, Toil and Trouble." *Serif*, 9: 44-6 (1972).

———. "Still at It." *BNYPL*. 78: 268-70 (Sp 75).

Alkon, P.K. "Visual Rhetoric in *The Autobiography of Alice B. Toklas.*" *CritI*, 1: 849-81 (Je 75).

Baker, W.D. "Lighting Birthday Candles for GS." *WC*, 1: 1-2 (1973).

Barry, Joseph. "Paris France Reviewed." *WC*, 1: 3-5 (1973).

Beer, Patricia. "At the Court of Queen G." *TLS*, 8 N 74, p. 1252.

Bloom, E.F. "The Ss" *TQ*, 13: 15-22 (Su 70).

Bruccoli, M.J. "A Lost Book Review: *A Story-Teller's Story,*" *FHA*, 1969, pp. 71-5.

Cooper, D.D. "GS's 'Magnificent Asparagus': Horizontal Vision and Unmeaning in 'Tender Buttons.'" *MFS*, 20: 337-48 (Au 74).

Cone, E.T. "Miss Etta Cones, the Ss, and M'sieu Matisse: A Memoir." *ASch*, 62: 44-61 (Su 73).

Copley, F.O. "Aristotle to GS: The Arts of Poetry." *Mosaic*, 5: 85-102 (1972).

Detoni-Dujmíc, Dunja. "Književni marionetizam GS." *Kolo*, 9: 838-42 (1971).

Fendleman, Earl. "GS among the Cubists." *JML*, 2: 481-90 (N 72).

———. "Happy Birthday, GS." *AS*, 27: 99-107 (Mr 75).

Fisher, Edward. "Lost Generations, Then and Now." *ConnR*, 6: 13-25 (1972).

Fitz, J.L. "GS and Picasso: The Language of Surfaces." *AL*, 45: 228-37 (My 73).

Gallup, Donald. "Du Côté de Chez S." *BC*, 19: 169-84 (Su 70).

———. "Introducing GS." *WC*, 1: 6-10 (1973).

Garvin, H.R. "The Human Mind & *Tender Buttons." WC*, 1: 11-3 (1973).

Gass, William. "GS, Geographer." *NYRB*, 20: 5-8 (3 My 73).

George. J.C. "S's 'A Box.'" *Expl*, 31: 42 (F 73).

Gervasi, Frank. "The Liberation of GS." *SatR*, 54: 13-4, 57 (21 Ag 71).

Giacomelli, E.F. "GS." *ESPSL*, 15: 1 (S 74).

Glassco, John. "Memoirs of Montparnasse." *TamR*, 50: 5-19 (2Q 69).

Haas, R. "A Bolt of Energy." *WC*, 1: 14-7 (1973).

Harrison, Gilbert. "A Remembrance." *WC*, 1: 18-9 (1973).

Havertick, I.S. "Three Lively Ladies of the Overbury Collection." *CLC*, 21: 20-7 (1971).

Kanazeki, Hisoa. "GS and the Atomic Bomb." *EigoS*, 120: 418-9 (1974).

Kellner, Bruce. "Ellen Glasgow and GS." *EGN*, 2: 13-6 (Mr 75).

Knox, George. "The Great American Novel: Final Chapter." *AQ*, 21: 667-82 (1969).

Kostelanetz, Richard. "GS: The New Adventure." *HC*, 16: 2-15 (3Q 75).

Lanati, B.M. "GS ovvero avanguardi e consumo?" *Sigma*, 27: 74-105 (1970).

McCaffrey, John. "'Any of Mine without Music to Help Them': The Operas and Plays of GS." *Y/T*, 4: 27-39 (1973).

Maynard, Reid. "Abstractionism in GS's *Three Lives." BSUF*, 15: 68-71 (Wi 72).

Meyerowitz, Patricia. "Say Yes to Everything." *WS*, 1: 20-2 (1973).

Nazzaro, Linda. "'A Piece of Cifee': A Stylistic Description of the Work of GS." *Eng R*, 1: 50-4 (1973).

Nicol, B.P. "Some Beginning Writings on GS's Theories of Personality." *OpL*, 2: 41-7 (#2 72).

Peavy, L.S. "A Look at S's Straight-Forward Writing." *LGJ*, 2: 12-6 (Wi 74).

Powell, L.C. "A Valentine to GS." *Westways*, 66: 18-23 (F 74).

Prideaux, Tom. "Four Patron Saints in One Great Act." *Life*, 23 Ap 71, pp. 50-65.

Purdy, S.B. "GS at Marienbad." *PMLA*, 85: 1096-2005 (O 70).

Rogers, W.G. "I Remember G." *WS*, 1: 23-4, 30 (1973).

Rose, Sir Francis. "A Gift of Roses." *WS*, 1: 25 7 (1973).

Schmitz, Neil. "G as Post-Modernist: The Rhetoric of *Tender Buttons." JML*, 3: 1203-18 (Jl 74).

Shapiro, Harriet. "Four Saints in Three Acts." *ID*, 3: 22-6 (O 72).

Shaw, Sharon. "GS and Henry James: The Difference between Accidence and Coincidence." *Pembroke Mag*, 5: 95-101 (1974).

Shults, Donald. "GS and the Problem of Time." *KAL*, 11: 59-71 (1968).

Sprigge, Elizabeth. "To Begin with the Beginning." *WS*, 1: 28-30 (1973).

Steiner, Wendy. "The Steinian Portrait." *YULG*, 50: 30-40 (#1 75).

Steloff, Francis. "The Making of an American Visit." *Confrontations*, 8: 9-17 (Sp 74).

Stewart, Allegra. "Flat Land as Explanation." *WS*, 1: 31-3 (1973).

Stewart, I.D. "GS and the Vital Dead." *MDAC*, 1: 102-23 (1972).

———. "Hemingway and the Autobiographies of Alice B. Toklas." *FHA*, 1970, pp. 117-23.

Sutherland, Donald. "Alice and G and Others." *PrS*, 45: 284-99 (1971).

———. "The Conversion of Alice B. Toklas." *ColQ*, 17: 129-41 (Au 68).

———. "Passion for the World." *WS*, 1: 34-5 (1973).

Sutton, W.A. "All Life Is Important." *WS*, 1: 36-7 (1973).

Thompson, Virgil. "No Diminution of Power." *WS*, 1: 38-9 (1973).

Tufte, V.J. "GS's Prothalamium: A Unique Poem in the Classical Mode." *YULG*, 43: 17-23 (Jl 68).

Wasserstrom, William. "The Sursymamercubealism of GS." *TCL*, 21: 90-106 (F 75).

Wilson, R.A. "And Now a Bow: A Centennial Tribute to GS." *Gaz Grolier Club*, 20-21: 46-69 (Je-D 74).

Zderad, Josef. "Dear Gertrude Dear: A Letter to Miss GS." *OhR*, 16: 32-4 (Sp 75).

Wood, Tom. "GS Special." *LGJ*, 2: 12-34 (#1 74).

———. "Origin of the Term Lost Generation." *LGJ*, 1: 3-5 (My 73).

Steinbeck, John. Anon. "Bibliographical Notes." *SteinN*, 2: 43-8 (1969).

———. "Interview with JS." *PaR*, 63: 180-94 (Fa 75).

———. "Manuscripts: *Tortilla Flat* by JS." *LCUT*, 3: 80-1 (My 71).

Adania, Alf. "Epitaf pentru JS." *Contemporanul*, 27: 14 (D 68).

Adrian, D.B. "S's New Image of America and the Americans." *StQ*, 3: 83-92 (Fa 70).

Alexander, Stanley. "*Cannery Row*: S's Pastoral Poem." *WAL*, 2: 281-95 (Wi 68).

———. "The Conflict of Form in *Tortilla Flat*." *AL*, 40: 58-66 (Mr 68).

Anderson, Hilton. "S's 'Flight.'" *Expl*, 28: 12 (O 69).

Antico, John. "A Reading of S's 'Flight.'" *MFS*, 11: 45-53 (Sp 65).

Astro, John. "JS and the Tragic Miracle of Consciousness." *San Jose Stud*, 1: 61-72 (#3 75).

———. "JS: Prospectus for a Literary Biography." *StQ*, 4: 76-80 (Su 71).

———. "Something that Happened: A Non-Teleological Approach to 'The Leader of the People." *StQ*, 6: 19-23 (Wi 73).

———. "S and Mainwaring: Two Californians for the Earth." *StQ*, 3: 3-11 (Wi 70).

———. "S and Ricketts: Escape or Commitment in *The Sea of Cortez?*" *WAL*, 6: 109-21 (Su 71).

———. "S and Ricketts: The Morphology of a Metaphysic." *UWR*, 6: 25 (Sp 73).

———. "S's Bittersweet Thursday." *StQ*, 4: 36-48 (Sp 71).

———. "Travels with S." *StQ*, 8: 35-44 (Wi 75).

Autrey, M.L. "Men, Mice and Moths: Gradation in S's 'The Leader of the People." *WAL*, 10: 195-205 (1975).

Beyer, Preston. "Collecting JSiana." *SteinN*, 2: 56-9 (Fa 69).

———, and Donald Stiefker. "JS: Brief Checklist." *StQ*, 7: 57-64 (Sp 74).

Bode, Elroy. "The World on Its Own Terms: A Brief for S, Miller, and Simenon." *SWR*, 53: 406-16 (Au 68).

Bredahl, A.C. "The Drinking Metaphor in *The Grapes of Warth*." *StQ*, 6: 95-8 (Fa 73).

Brinckmann, Christine. "Zitierte Dokumentarität: Überlegunen zur Verfilmung des Roman *The Grapes of Wrath*." *JA*, 19: 88-110 (1974).

Brown, D.R. "The Natural Man in JS's Non-Teleological Tales." *BSUF*, 7: 47-52 (Sp 66).

Browning, Chris. "Grape Symbolism in *The Grapes of Wrath*." *Disc*, 11: 129-40 (Wi 68).

Burns, Stuart. "The Turtle or the Gopher: Another Look at the Ending of *The Grapes of Wrath*." *WAL*, 9: 53-7 (My 74).

Cabau, Jacques. "S: Le génie du terroir." *NL*, 46: 1, 11 (26 D 68).

Caldwell, M.E. "A New Consideration of the Intercalary Chapters in *The Grapes of Wrath*." *MarkR*, 3: 115-9 (1973).

Carr, D.R. "S's Blakean Vision in *The Grapes of Wrath*." *STQ*, 8: 67-73 (Su-Fa 75).

Caselli, J.R. "JS and the American Patchwork Quilt." *San Jose Stud*, 1: 83-7 (#3 75).

Chametzky, Jules. "The Ambivalent Endings of *The Grapes of Wrath*." *MFS*, 11: 34-444 (Sp 65).

Cherulescu, Rodica. "Man and Nature in *The Pastures of Heaven* by JS." *AUG-LG*, 22: 199-205 (1973).

Clark, M.W. "Bridging the Generation Gap: The Ending of S's *Grapes of Wrath*." *Forum(H)*, 8: 16-7 (Su 70).

Court, Franklin. "A Vigilante's Fantasy." *StQ*, 5: 98-101 (Su-Fa 72).

Covici, Pascal. "In Memoriam: JS." *SteinN*, 2: 18 (1969).

Cox, M.H. "The Conclusion of *The Grapes of Wrath*: S's Conception and Execution." *San Jose Stud*, 1: 73-81 (#3 75).

———. "Remembering JS." *San Jose Stud*, 1: 109-27 (#5 75).

———. "In Search of JS/His People and His Land." *San Jose Stud*, 1: 41-60 (#3 75).

Cristea, Corina. "Personajul S." *RoLit*, 2: 21 (Ja 69).

Crouch, Steve. *"Cannery Row."* *AmW*, 10: 18-27 (S 73).

Delios, Giorgos. "Tzon S." *NeaH*, 85: 634-40 (1969).

Delisle, H.G. "Style and Idea in S's 'The Turtle.'" *Style*, 4: 145-57 (1970).

DeMott, Robert. "A Miscellany of Bibliographical Notes." *StQ*, 3: 41-3 (1970).

———. "Toward a Definition of *To a God Unknown*." *UWR*, 8: 34-53 (Sp 73).

Ditsky, John. "The Ending of *The Grapes of Wrath*: A Further Commentary." *Agora*, 2: 41-50 (Fa 73).

———. "From Oxford to Salinas: Comparing Faulkner and S." *SteinN*, 2: 51-5 (Fa 69).

———. "Music from a Dark Cave: Organic Form in S's Fiction." *JNT*, 1: 59-67 (Ja 71).

———. "S's *Burning Bright*: Homage to Astarte." *StQ*, 7: 79-84 (Su-Fa 74).

———. "S's 'Flight': The Ambiguity of Manhood." *StQ*, 5: 80-5 (Su-Fa 72).

———. "S's *Travels with Charley*: The Quest That Failed." *StQ*, 8: 45-50 (Sp 75).

———. "Teaching the Ungreat: A Year of JS." *Eng Rec*, 22: 27-32 (Sp 72).

———. "*The Wayward Bus*: Love and Time in America." *San Jose Stud*, 1: 89-101 (#3 75).

Dommergues, Pierre. "JS : La fin d'un âge du roman américain." *Le Monde*, 23: 1, 14 (D 68).

Dovis, Craig. "Novels of Peasant Crisis." *J Peasant Stud*, 2: 47-68 (O 74).

Dulsey, Bernard. "JS and Jorge Icaza." *ABC*, 18: 15-7 (Su 68).

Eddy, Darlene. "To Go S-Buccaneering and Take a Spanish Town: Seventeeth Century Aspects of *A Cup of Gold*." *StQ*, 8: 3-12 (Wi 75).

Elliott, K.F. "IITYWYBAD." *StQ*, 6: 53-4 (Sp 73).

Fadiman, Clifton. "Of Crabs and Men." *NY*, 17: 107 (6 D 41).

Falkenberg, Sandra. "A Study of Female Characterization in S's Fiction," *StQ*, 8: 50-6 (Sp 75).

Fontenrose, Joseph. "'The Harness.'" *StQ*, 5: 94-8 (Su-Fa 72).

———. "Memorial Statment on JS." *SteinN*, 2: 19-20 (Fa 69).

Fossey, W.R. "The End of the Western Dream: *The Grapes of Wrath* and Oklahoma." *CimR*, 2: 25-34 (1973).

Frazier, George. "JS! JS! How Still We See Thee Lie." *Esquire*, 72: 150, 209, 271-5 (N 68).

French, Warren. "After *The Grapes of Wrath*." *StQ*, 8: 73-8 (Su-Fa 75).

———. "The 'California Quality' of S's Best Fiction." *San Jose Stud*, 1: 9-19 (#3 75).

———. "'Johnny Bear': S's 'Yellow Peril' Story." *StQ*, 5: 101 (Su-Fa 72).

———. "JS (February 27, 1902- December 20, 1968)." *SteinN*, 2: 3-9 (Sp 69).

Gaddi Conti, Giuseppe. "Ricordo di JS." *OPL*, 15: 29-38 (1969).

Galbraith, J.K. "JS: A Footnote for a Memoir." *Atl*, 224: 65-7 (N 69).

Garcia, Reloy. "S's 'The Snake': An Explication." *StQ*, 5: 85-90 (Su-Fa 72).

Gerstenberger, Donna. "S's American Waste Land." *MFS*, 11: 59-65 (Sp 65).

Goldhurst, William. "*Of Mice and Men*: JS's Parable of the Curse of Cain." *WAL*, 6: 123-35 (Su 71).

Goldstone, A.H. "Book Collecting and JS." *San Jose Stud*, 1: 129-35 (#3 75).

Golemba, H.L. "S's Attempt to Escape the Literary Fallacy." *MFS*, 15: 231-9 (Su 69).

Goodrich, N.L. "Bachelors in Fiction, through JS and Jean Giono." *KRQ*, 14: 367-78 (1967).

Gordon, W.K. "S's 'Flight': Journey to or *from* Maturity?" *SSF*, 3: 453-5 (Su 66).

Gribben, J.L. "S's *East of Eden* and Milton's *Paradise Lost*: A Discussion of 'Timshel.'" *StQ*, 5: 35-43 (Sp 72).

Groene, Horst. "*The Grapes of Wrath*: sozialkritische Studie und Kunstwerk." *LWU*, 7: 47-58 (My 74).

———. "The Themes of Manliness and Human Dignity in S's Initiation Story 'Flight.'" *NS*, 72: 278-84 (1973).

Gurko, Leo. "*Of Mice and Men*: S as Manichean." *UWR*, 8: 11-23 (Sp 73).

Hamada, Seijiro. "Hikaku-Kenkyu ni yoru Sojokoka: *The Long Journey* no Ni-Shohin." *EigoS*, 119: 88-9 (1973).

Hamby, J.A. "S's Biblical Vision." *WR*, 10: 57-9 (Fa 73).

———. "S's *The Pearl*: Tradition and Innovation." *WR*, 7: 65-6 (Wi 70).

Hargrave, John. "S and *Summer Time Ends*." *StQ*, 6: 67-73 (Su 73).

Hashiguichi, Jasuo. "Japanese Translations of S's Works (1939-69)." *StQ*, 3: 93-106 (Fa 70).

Hayashi, Tetsumaro. "A Brief Survey of S Criticism in the United States." *KAL*, 14: 43-9 (1972).

*———. "JS: A Checklist of Movie Reviews." *Serif*, &: 18-22 (1970).

*———. " JS: A Checklist of Unpublished Ph.D. Dissertations (1946-1967)." *Serif*, 5: 30-1 (1968).

———. "*The Pearl* as the Novel of Disengagement." *StQ*, 7: 84-8 (Su-Fa 74).

———. "Recent S Studies in the United States." *StQ*, 4: 73-6 (Su 71).

Hayman, L.R. "Report from Salinas." *StQ*, 3: 43-4 (Sp 70).

Hedgepeth, J.W. "Genesis of *The Sea of Cortez*." *StQ*, 6: 74-80 (Su 73).

Hirose, Hidekazu. " 'Feelings as Always Were More Potent Than Thought': JS's Social Concern in the Thirties." *SALit*, 8: 53-62 (1972).

———. "Japanese S Criticism in 1971." *StQ*, 6: 99-103 (Fa 73).

———. "Japanese S Criticism in 1972-73." *StQ*, 8: 55-9 (Wi 75).

Houghton, D.E. " 'Westering' in 'Leader of the People.'" *WAL*, 4: 117-24 (Su 69).

Hwang, Mei-shu. "*Of Mice and Men*: An Experimental Study of the Novel and the *Play*." *Tamkang J*, 11: 225-40 (1973).

Inazawa, Hideo. "S no Bunmeiron." *EigoS*, 115: 216-9 (1969).

Inoue, Kenji. "Aku wo Egakikirenakatta Sakka." *EigoS*, 115: 206-8 (1969).

Iseri, Ryusei. "Eden no Higashi." *EigoS*, 115: 209-10 (1969).

Jones, L.W. " 'A Little Play in Your Head': Parable Form in JS's Post-War Fiction." *Genre*, 3: 55-63 (Mr 70).

———. "A Note on S's Earliest Stories." *StQ*, 2: 59-60 (Fa 69).

———. "Poison in the Cream Puff: The Human Condition in *Cannery Row*." *StQ*, 7: 35-40 (Sp 74).

———. "Random Thoughts from Paris: S's 'Un Américain à New York et à Paris." *StQ*, 3: 27-30 (Sp 70).

———. "The Real Authorship of S's Verse." *StQ*, 3: 11-2 (Wi 70).

———. "S and Zola: Theory and Practice of the Experimental Novel." *StQ*, 4: 95-101 (Fa 71).

———. "An Uncited Post-War S Story: 'The Short Story of Mankind.'" *StQ*, 3: 30-1 (Sp 70).

Justus, J.H. "The Transient World of *Tortilla Flat*." *WR*, 7: 55-60 (1970).

Kingsbury, S.A. "S's Use of Dialect and Archaic Language in the *Cup of Gold.*" *SteinN*, 2: 28-33 (Su 69).

Kinney, A.F. "The Arthurian Cycle in *Tortilla Flat.*" *MFS*, 11: 11-20 (Sp 65).

Kline, Herbert. "On JS." *StQ*, 4: 80-4 (Su 71).

Krause, S.J. "'The Pearl' and 'Hadleyburg': From Desire to Renunciation." *StQ*, 7: 3-18 (Wi 74).

———. "S and Mark Twain." *StQ*, 6: 104-11 (Fa 73).

Krim, Seymour. "'When We Went to JS's Funeral Service, This is What Happened!'" *Smith*, 11: 46-9 (My 70).

Kruppa, Hans-Günter. "JS: 'The Debt Shall Be Paid.'" *NS*, 18: 165-9 (Ap 69).

Lawson, J.H. "*Grapes of Wrath* and *Bonnie and Clyde.*" *Am Dialog*, 5: 30-3 (Wi 68-69).

Le Master, J.R. "Mythological Constructs in S's To a God Unknown." *Forum(H)*, 9: 8-11 (Su 71).

Levant, Howard. "JS's *The Red Pony*: A Study in Narrative Technique." *JNT*, 1: 77-85 (Mr 71).

———. "*Tortilla Flat*: The Shape of JS's Career." *PMLA*, 85: 1087-95 (O 70).

———. "The Unity of *In Dubious Battle*: Violence and Dehumanization." *MFS*, 11: 3-10 (Sp65).

Lewis, C.L. "Four Dubious S Stories." *StQ*, 5: 17-8 (Wi 72).

Lieber, T.M. "Talismanic Patterns in the Novels of JS." *AL*, 44: 262-75 (My 72).

Lisca, Peter. "*Cannery Row* and the *Tao Teh Ching.*" *San Jose Stud*, 1: 21-7 (#3 75).

———. "*Cup of Gold* and *To a God Unknown*: Two Early Works of JS." *KN*, 22: 173-83 (1975).

———. "New Perspectives in S Studies." *UWR*, 8: 6-10 (Sp 73).

———. "In Memory of JS." *SteinN*, 2: 20-1 (Sp 69).

———. "'The Raid' and *In Dubious Battle.*" *StQ*, 5: 90-4 (Su-Fa 72).

———. "S and Hemingway: Suggestions for a Comparative Study." *SteinN*, 2: 9-17 (Sp 69).

———. "S's Image of Man and His Decline as a Writer." *MFS*, 11: 3-10 (Sp 65).

Lowery, Bruce. "S: Son seul espoir." *FL*, 1182: 6 (30 D 68).

McCarthy, K.M. "Witchcraft and Superstition in *The Winter of Our Discontent.*" *NYFQ* 30: 197-211 (S 74).

McCarthy, Paul. "House and Shelter as Symbol in *The Grapes of Wrath.*" *SDR*, 5: 48-67 (Wi 67-68).

Machidori, Matayoshi. "*Warere ga Fuman no Fuyu.*" *EigoS*, 115: 214-5 (1969).

McDaniel, B.A. "JS: Ralph Ellison's Invisible Source." *PCP*, 8: 28-33 (1973).

McMahan, E.E. "'The Chrysanthemums': A Study of a Woman's Sexuality." *MFS*, 4: 453-8 (Wi 68-69).

McWilliams, Carey. "A Man, A Place, and a Time." *AmW*, 7: 4-8, 38-40, 62-4 (My 70).

McWilliams, W.C. and N.R. "JS, Writer." *Cweal*, 90: 229-30 (9 My 69).

Magnusson, Bo. "Komisk Rationlisering hos S." *Studiekamraten*, 52: 29-30 (1970).

Marcus, Mordecai. "The Lost Dream of Sex and Childbirth in 'The Chrysanthemums.'" *MFS*, 11: 54-8 (Sp 65).

Marks, L.J. "*East of Eden*: 'Thou Mayest.'" *StQ*, 4: 3-18 (Wi 71).

———. "JES: 1902-1968." *SteinN* 2: 21-2 (Sp 69).

Marovitz S.E. "The Cryptic Raillery of 'Saint Katy the Virgin.'" *StQ*, 5: 107-12 (Su-Fa 72).

———. "The Expository Force of JS." *StQ*, 1: 41-53, 88-102 (Su, Fa 74).

———. "JS and Adlai Stevenson: The Shattered Image of America." *StQ*, 3: 51-62 (Su 70).

Martin, B.K. "'The Leader of the People' Reexamined." *SSF*, 7: 423-32 (Su 71).

Marussig, Antonio. "Violencia e relaismo na ficção americana: JS." *IH*, 5: 139-42 (1969).

Matton, C.G. "Water Imagery and the Conclusion of *The Grapes of Wrath*." *NEMLAN*, 2: 44-7 (1970).

May, C.E. "Myth and Mystery in S's 'The Snake': A Jungian View." *Criticism*, 15: 262-75 (Fa 73).

Metzger, C.R. "The Film Version of S's *The Pearl*.," *StQ*, 4: 88-92 (Su 71).

Miller, W.V. "Sexual and Spiritual Ambiguity on 'The Chrysanthemums.'" *StQ*, 5: 68-75 (Su-Fa 72).

Mohrt, Michel. "S, l'avocat des humbles." *FL*, 1182: 6 (30 D 68).

Moore, H.T. "JS: A Memorial Statement." *SteinN*, 2: 23 (1969).

Moore, W.L. "In Memoriam." *SteinN*, 2: 24 (1969).

Morita, Shoji. "S's View of Womanhood: The Meaning of 'the time of waiting' in *The Long Valley*." *SALit*, 8: 39-52 (1972).

Morsberger, R.E. "In Defense of 'Westering.'" *WAL*, 5: 143-6 (1970).

———. "The Price of 'The Harness.'" *StQ*, 6: 24-6 (S 73).

Nimitz, Jack. "Ecology and *The Grapes of Wrath*." *HSL*, 2: 165-8 (1970).

Noonan, Gerald. "A Note on 'The Chrysanthemums.'" *MFS*, 15: 453-8 (1969).

Ortega, P.D. "Fables of Identity: Stereotype and Caricature of Chicanos in S's *Tortilla Flat*." *JEthS*, 1: 39-43 (1973).

Osborne, W.R. "The Texts of S's 'The Chrysanthemums.'" *MFS*, 479-84 (Wi 66-67).

Pearce, H.D ."S's 'The Leader of the People': Dialectic and Symbol." *PLL*, 8: 415-26 (Fa 72).

Perez, B.L. "S, Ricketts, and Sea of Cortez: Partnership or Exploitation?" *StQ*, 7: 73-9 (Su-Fa 74).

Peterson, R.F. "The Grail Legend and S's 'The Great Mountains.'" *StQ*, 6: 9-15 (Wi 73).

Poulakidas, A.K. "S Kazantzakis and Socialism." *StQ*, 3: 62-72 (Su 70).

Pratt, L.R. "Imagining Existence: Form and History in S and Agee." *SoR*, 11: 84-98 (Ja 75).

Prince, John. "André Dhôtel, S et Faulkner." *Caliban*, 6: 85-90 (1969).

Robles, M. "Cain—An Unfortunate?" *ML*, 50: 57-9 (1969).

Rossani, Wolfgango. "Il realismo poetica di JS." *ORom*, 19: 3 (1973).

Satyanarayana, M.R. "'And Then the Child Becomes a Man': Three Initiation Stories of JS." *IJAS*, 1: 87-93 (1971).

———. "From Winesburg to Salinas Valley in Search of Love." *OJES*, 8: 19-28 (1971).

———. "The Unknown God of JS." *IJAS*, 3: 97-103 (1973).

Schamberger, J.E. "*Grapes of Gladness*: A Misconception of *Walden*." *ATQ*, 13: 15-6 (1972).

Shastri, P.S. "The Structure of *Grapes of Wrath*." *IJES*, 12: 67-74 (D 71).

Shaw, Peter. "S: The Shape of a Career." *SatR*, 52: 10-4 (8 F 69).

Shuman, R.B. "Initiation Rites in S's *The Red Pony*." *EJ*, 1252-5 (D 70).

Simmonds, R.S. "The First Publication of S's 'The Leader of the People.'"*StQ*, 8: 13-08 (Wi 75).

———. "JS: Works Published in the British Magazine *Argosy*." *StQ*, 4: 101-4 (Fa 71).

———. "JS, Robert Louis Stevenson, and Edith Mc Gillcuddy." *San Jose Stud*, 1: 29-39 (#1 75).

* ———. "JS's World War Dispatches: An Annotated Checklist." *Serif*, 11: 21-30 (1974).

———. "The Original Manuscripts of S's 'The Chrysanthemums.'" *StQ*, 7: 102-11 (Su-Fa 74).

———. "S's *America and Americans*." *StQ*, 8: 89-95 (Su-Fa 75).

———. "The Typescript of S's 'America and Americans.'" *StQ*, 4: 120-1 (Fa 71).

————, and Tetsumaro Hayashi. "J's British Publications." *StQ*, 8: 79-89 (Su-Fa 75).

Simpson, A.L. "'The White Quail': A Portrait of an Artist." *StQ*, 5: 76-80 (Su-Fa 72).

Slade, L.A. "The Uses of Biblical Allusions in *The Grapes of Wrath*." *CLAJ*, 11: 241-7 (Mr 68).

Spies, G.H. "JS's *In Dubious Battle* and Robert Penn Warren's *Night Rider*: A Comparative Study." *StQ*, 4: 48-55 (Sp 71).

————. "S and the Automobile." *StQ*, 7: 18-24 (Wi 74).

Spilka, Mark. "Of George and Lennie and Curley's Wife: Sweet Violence in S's Eden." *MFS*, 20: 169-79 (Su 74).

Steele, Joan. "A Century of Idiots: *Barnaby Rudge* and *Of Mice and Men*." *StQ*, 5: 8-17 (Wi 72).

Sweet, C.A. "Ms. Eliza Allen and S's 'The Chrysanthemums." *MFS*, 20: 210-3 (Su 74).

Tatsunokuchi, Naotara. "S Country." *EigoS*, 115: 213-6 (1969).

Tedlock, E.W. "A Pathos of Power." *SteinN*, 2: 27-8 (Su 69).

Tokunaga, Masanori. "JS's *Travels with Charley*." *KAL*, 15: 46-53 (1974).

Trachtenberg, Stanley. "JS: The Fate of Protest." *NDQ*, 41: 5-11 (Sp 73).

Tuttleton, J.W. "S in Russia: The Rhetoric of Praise and Blame." *MFS*, 11: 79-89 (Sp 65).

VanDerBeets, Richard. "A Pearl Is a Pearl Is a Pearl." *CEA*, 32: 9-11 (Ap 70).

West, P.J. "S's 'The Leader of the People': A Crisis in Style." *WAL*, 5: 137-41 (Su 70).

Woodward, R.H. "S's 'The Promise.'" *StQ*, 6: 15-9 (Wi 73).

Wyatt, B.N. "Experimentation as Technique: The Protest Novels of JS." *Disc.*, 12: 143-53 (Sp 69).

Zollman, Sol. "JP's Political Outlook in *The Grapes of Wrath*." *L&I*, 13: 9-20. (1972).

Stephens, Alan. Markos, D.W. "AS: The Lineaments of the Real." *SoR*, 11: 331-56 (Ap 75).

Stephens, Michael. Klinkowitz, Jerome. "MS's SuperFiction." *TriQ*, 34: 219-32 (Fa 75).

Sterling, George. Bennett, R.E. "Don Passé." *LitR*, 15: 133-47 (1971-72).

Bouwman, Fred. "GS and Jack London: A Literary Friendship." *JLN*, 5: 8-10 (1972).

Duke, Maurice. "Letters of GS to James Branch Cabell." *AL*, 44: 146-53 (My 72).

Dunbar, J.R. "Letters of GS to Carey McWilliams." *Colorado Hist Soc Q*, 46: 235-52 (S 67).

Fleming, D.R. "The Last Bohemian." *QNL*, 37: 75-95 (1972).

Gross, Dalton. "Ezra Pound's Early Literary Reputation: GS's Dissent." *Paideuma*, 2: 203-4 (Fa 73).

————. "GS's Letters to Theodore Dreiser." *DrN*, 4: 14-20 (#1 73).

————. "GS's Letters to William Stanley Braithwaite: the Poet Versus the Editor." *ABC*, 24: 18-20 (N-D 73).

————. "GS's Life at Carmel: Letters to Witter Bynner." *MarkR*, 4: 12-6 (1973).

————. "Seventeen GS Letters." *JLN*, 1: 41-61 (1968).

Henry, J.L. "'The First Poet': Jack London or GS?" *JLN*, 6: 60-5 (1973).

————. "Give a Man a Boat He Can Sail." *JLN*, 7: 1: 23-9 (1974).

Slade, J.W. "GS, 'Prophet of the Suns.'" *MarkR*, 1: 4-10 (My 68).

Stern, Gerald. Hazley, Richard. "An Introduction to GS's 'The Pineys.'" *JRUL*, 32: 41-54 (Je 69).

Stevens, Wallace. Anon. "Letter from Williams to WS, June 8, 1916." *WCW N*, 1: 16 (Fa 75).

————. "Words and Things in WS." *TLS*, 6 Ap 73, p. 375.

Ackerman, J.C. "Notes Toward an Explanation of S's 'Sea Surface Full of Clouds.'"

Ackerman, R.D. "WS: Myth, Belief, and Presence." *Criticism*, 14: 266-76 (Su 72).

Adams, R.P. " 'The Comedian as the Letter C': A Somewhat Literal Reading." *TSE*, 18: 95-14 (1970).

———. "Pure Poetry: WS's 'Sea Surface Full of Clouds.' " *TSE*, 21: 91-22 (1974).

———. "WS and Schopenhauer's *The World as Will and Idea*." *TSE*, 20: 135-68 (1972).

Alexander, Charles. "The Idea of Evil in WS's Poetry." *MSE*, 1: 100-5 (1968).

Alter, Robert. "Borges and S: A Note on Post-Symbolist Writing." *TriQ*, 25: 323-33 (Au 72).

Atchitty, K.J. "WS: Of Ideal Time and Choice." *RSW*, 41: 141-53 (S 73).

B., A. "WS redescoperit." *SXX*, 15: 81-2 (1972).

Bankert, Marianne. "The Meta-Metaphysical Vision of WS." *Renascence*, 24: 47-53 (Au 71).

Barotti, Armand. "The Imperialist Idea of Order in WS." *L&I*, 10: 29-40 (1971).

Baym, Nina. "The Transcendentalism of WS." *ESQ*, 57: 66-72 (4Q 69).

Benamou, Michel. "Beyond Emerald or Amethyst: WS and the French Tradition." *DCLB*, 4: 60-6 (D 61).

———. "WS and Apollinaire." *CL*, 20: 289-300 (Fa 68).

Berthoff, R.J. "Parables and WS's 'Esthetique du Mal.' " *ELH*, 42: 669-89 (1975).

Bevis, W.W. "The Arrangment of *Harmonium*." *ELH*, 37: 456-73 (S 70).

———. "S's Toneless Poetry." *ELH*, 41: 257-86 (Su 74).

Blessing, Richard. "WS and the Necessary Reader: A Technique of Dynamism." *TCL*, 18: 251-8 (1972).

Bloom, Harold. "Death and the Native Strain in American Poetry." *SocR*, 39: 449-62 (1972).

———. "WS: The Poems of Our Climate." *Prose*, 8: 5-24 (1972).

Bolt, Sydney. "The Impropriety of WS." *Delta*, 37: 9-14 (Au 65).

Boswell, J.C. "WS: A Man with a Blue Guitar." *HJP*, 3: 98-101 (1973).

Brezianu, Andrei. "Pe marginea motivului solar in poezia lui WS." *SXX*, 12: 156-63 (1969).

Bromwich, David. "Suburbs and Extremities." *Prose*, 8: 25-38 (1974).

Brown, M.E. "A Critical Performance of 'Asides on the Oboe.' " *JAAC*, 29: 121-8 (Fa 70).

Bruns, G.L. "Poetry as Reality: The Orpheus Myth and Its Modern Counterparts." *ELH*, 37: 263-86 (1970).

Buhr, Marjorie. "WS's Search for Being Through the Supreme Fiction." *Carrell*, 13: 1-15 (1972).

———. "When Half-Gods Go: S's Spiritual Odyssey." *WSN*, 1: 9-11 (Ap 70).

Burrill, J.R. "A Celebration for WS." *Trinity R*, 8: 9-49 (My 54).

Burtner, H.W. "The High Priest of the Secular: The Poetry of WS." *ConnR*, 6: 34-45 (1972).

Butscher, Edward. "WS's Neglected Future: 'Variations on a Summer Day.' " *TCL*, 19: 153-64 (Jl 73).

Buttel, Robert. "WS." *ConL*, 15: 159-62 (1974).

———. "WS and the Grand Poem." *JML*, 2: 421-41 (#3 71-72).

Caldwell, Price. "Metaphoric Structures in WS's 'Thirteen Ways of Looking at a Blackbird.' " *JEGP*, 71: 321-35 (1972).

Carrier, Warren. "Commonplace Costumes and Essential Gaudiness: WS's 'Emperor of Ice Cream.' " *Col Lit*, 1: 230-5 (Fa 74).

Cavitch, David. "The Man with the Blue Guitar." *Expl*, 27: 30 (D 68).

Caws, M.A. "Now for a Piece of Our Climate: Apology for an Interior Journey." *Centerpoint*, 1: 25-7 (#3 75).

Clough, W.O. "S's 'Notes Toward a Supreme Fiction,' Part III Section III." *Expl*, 28: 24 (N 69).

Corrington, J.W. "WS and the Problem of Order: A Study of Three Poems." *ArlQ*, 1: 50-63 (Su 68).

Dale, K.A. "Extensions: Beyond Resemblance and the Pleasure Principle in S's Supreme Fiction." *Boun2*, 4: 255-73 (1975).

Dietrichson, J.W. "WS's 'Sunday Morning.'" *Edda*, 70: 105-16 (1970).

Doggett, Frank. "S on the Genesis of a Poem." *ConL*, 16: 463-77 (Au 75).

———. "The Transition from *Harmonium*: Factors in the Development of S's Later Poetry." *PMLA*, 88: 122-31 (Ja 73).

Donoghue, Denis, and John Coleman. "WS." *TLS*, 12 Ap 74, p. 395.

Dougherty, Adelyn. "Structures of Sound in WS's 'Farewell to Florida.'" *TSLL*, 16: 755-64 (Wi 75).

Duffey, B.I. "S and Williams." *ConL*, 9: 431-6 (1968).

Eberhart, Richard. "Encounters and Letters: Richard Eberhart and WS." *DCLB*, 4: 57-60 (D 61).

Eddins, Dwight. "WS: American the Primordial." *MLQ*, 32: 73-88 (Mr 71).

Edelstein, J.M. "The Poet as Reader: WS and his Books." *BC*, 23: 53-68 (Sp 74).

Eder, D.L. "The Meaning of WS's Two Themes." *CritQ*, 11: 181-90 (Su 69).

———. "A Review of S Criticism to Date." *TCL*, 15: 3-18 (Ap 68).

———. "S's Never-Ending Meditation." *STC*, 10: 19-32 (Fa 72).

———. "WS: Heritage and Influences." *Mosaic*, 4: 49-61 (1970).

———. "WS's Landscapes and Still Lifes." *Mosaic*, 4: 1-5 (1971).

Eder, Doris. "WS: The War Between Mind and Eye." *SoR*, 7: 749-64 (Jl 71).

Ensor, Allison. "'Tennessee' in WS's 'Anecdote of the Jar.'" *SHR*, 7: 315-21 (Su 73).

Feshbach, Sidney. "Current Bibliography." *WSN*, 2: 27 (O 70).

———. "WS and Erik Satie: A Source for 'The Comedian as the Letter C.'" *TSLL*, 11: 811 8 (Sp 69).

Fields, Kenneth. "Postures of the Nerves: Reflections of the Nineteenth Century in the Poems of WS." *SoR*, 7: 778-824 (Jl 71).

Flake, Carol. "S's 'The Comedian as the Letter C,' Section v, Conclusion." *Expl*, 30: 26 (D 71).

———. "WS's 'Peter Quince at the Clavier': Sources and Structure." *ELN*, 1: 116-9 (D 74).

Fleissner, R.F. "S's 'Of the Surface of Things': An Echo of *Faust*." *AN&Q*, 12: 115-6 (Ap 74).

———. "S in Wittenberg." *RS*, 42: 256-60 (1974).

Flint, F.C. "The Poem As It Is." *DCLB*, 4: 51-6 (D 61).

Ford, W.T. "Some Notes on S's Foreign Bibliography." *WSN*, 1: 1-3 (O 69).

Frederick, J.T. "WS: A Classroom Approach." *CEA*, 31: 6-7 (N 68).

Fuchs, Daniel. "S." *ConL*, 9: 437-41 (1968).

Fuller, Roy. "Both Pie and Custard." *Shen*, 21: 61-76 (Sp 70).

Furia, Philip. "Nuances of a Theme by Milton: WS's 'Sunday Morning.'" *AL*, 46: 83-7 (Mr 74).

Gangewere, R.J. "WS: Five Crucial Words." *Per*, 17: 198-206 (#3 72).

Grant, J.K. "'Gold Bugs in Blue Meadows': The 'Decadent' Poetry of WS." *DUJ*, 37: 8-14 (D 75).

Guereschi, Edward. "WS and the Poetics of Secular Grace." *Erasmus R*, 1: 131-45 (1971).

Hafner, J.H. "One Way of Looking at 'Thirteen Ways of Looking at a Blackbird." *CP*, 3: 61-5 (Sp 70).

*Halman, T.S. "Current Bibliography." *WSN*, 2: 22 (O 70).

———. "WS and Turkish Poetry." *WSN*, 2: 19-20 (O 70).

Hashiguchi, Minoru. "WS Oboegaki." *EigoS*, 115: 146-8 (1969).

Hill, J.L. "The Frame for the Mind: Landscape in 'Lines Composed a Few Miles Above Tintern Abbey,' 'Dover Beach,' and 'Sunday Morning.'" *CentR*, 18: 29-48 (1974).

Honig, Edwin. "Meeting WS." *WSN*, 1: 11-2 (Ap 70).

Hopper, S.R. "WS: The Sundry Comforts of the Sun." *ESELL*, 51-2: 23-58 (1968).

Howard, Richard. "A Tireless Conscience." *Poetry*, 111: 39-40 (O 67).

Hudea, A.M. "'Peter Quince at the Clavier' by WS: A Linguistic Analysis." *AUB-LG*, 22: 43-50 (1973).

Huston, J.D. "*Credence of Summer*: An Analysis." *MP*, 67: 263-72 (F 70).

Jager, Dietrich. "Robert Frost und WS im Vergleich mit europaischen Dichtern." *NS*, 17: 65-83 (F 68).

Johnston, J.T. "A Metaphor for Paradise: WS's Philosophical Use of Metaphor." *ELUD*, 1: 1-17 (S 73).

Kaye, Howard. "Contradictions in S's 'Notes on a Supreme Fiction.'" *Am Poetry & Poetics*, 1: 3-19 (Fa 74).

King, Bruce. "WS's 'Metaphors of a Magnifico.'" *ES*, 49: 450-2 (O 68).

King, T.I. "Radical Design in WS." *Visible Lang*, 9: 25-46 (1975).

Knox, George. "S's Verse Plays: Fragments of a Total Agon." *Genre*, 1: 124-40 (Ap 68).

Lavigueur, Paul. "WS." *TLS*, 3 My 74, p. 477.

LeMaster, J.R. "S and Eliot on the Mind of the Poet." *Forum(H)*, 10: 27-30 (#3 72).

Lensing, G.S "'A High-Toned Old Christian Woman': WS's Parable of Supreme Fiction." *NDEJ*, 8: 43-9 (Fa 72).

———. "'Mere Facts' and the Biography of WS." *WSN*, 2: 17-8 (O 70).

———. "Robinson and S: Some Tangential Bearings." *SoR*, 3: 505-13 (Sp 67).

———. "WS and the State of Winter Simplicity." *SoR*, 7: 765-77 (Jl 71).

Lentricchia, Frank. "WS: The Critic's Redemption." *MLQ*, 36: 75-80 (Mr 75).

Lieber, T.M. "Robert Frost and WS: 'What to Make of a Diminished Thing.'" *AL*, 47: 64-83 (Mr 75).

Linebarger, J.M. "WS's 'The Good Man Has No Shape.'" *LauR*, 9: 47-9 (1969).

———. "WS's 'Gubbinal.'" *WSN*, 2: 25 (Ap 71).

Litz, A.W. "Introduction to *Bowl, Cat and Broomstick*." *QRL*, 16: 230-5 (1969).

Lunz, Elizabeth. "Robert Lowell and WS on 'Sunday Morning.'" *UR*, 37: 268-72 (Je 71).

McBrearty, Paul. "WS's 'Like Decorations in a Nigger Cemetery.'" *TSLL*, 15: 341-56 (Su 73).

MacCaffrey, Isabel. "The Other Side of Silence: 'Credences of Summer' as an Example." *MLQ*, 30: 417-38 (S 69).

———. "A Point of Central Arrival: S's *The Rock*." *ELH*, 40: 606-33 (Wi 73).

McDaniel, Judith. "WS and the Scientific Imagination." *ConL*, 15: 221-37 (Sp 74).

McGrory, Kathleen. "WS as Romantic Rebel." *ConnR*, 4: 59-64 (Sp 70).

McIlvaine, Robert. "S's 'Frogs Eat Butterflies, Snakes Eat Frogs. Hogs Eat Snakes. Men Eat Hogs." *Expl*, 33: 14 (O 74).

Macksey, R.A. "The Old Poets." *Johns Hopkins Mag*, 19: 42-8 (1968).

McMichael, James. "The WS Vulgates." *SoR*, 7: 699-727 (Jl 71).

McNamara, Peter. "Stevens, Quince, and 'Bottoms's Dream.'" *NDEJ*, 9: 49-52 (Sp 74).

———. "WS's Autumnal Doctrine." *Renascence*, 26: 72-82 (Wi 74).

Mariani, P.L. "The Critic as Friend from Pascagoula." *MR*, 12: 162-7 (1971).

Mizejewski, Linda. "Images of Woman in WS." *Thoth*, 14: 13-21 (1974).

Mizener, Arthur. "Not in Cold Blood." *KR*, 8: 218-25 (Sp 51).

Mole, John. "WS." *TLS*, 26 Ap 74, p. 447.

Mollinger, Robert. "An Analysis of WS's 'What We See Is What We Think.'" *NConL*, 4: 5-7 (N 74).

———. "S's 'A Thought Revolved.'" *Expl*, 33: 1 (S 74).

———. "S's 'Arrival at the Waldorf.'" *Expl*, 31: 40 (Je 73).

———. "WS's Three World Views: Naturalism, Idealism, and Realistic Humanism." *NasR*, 2: 10-4 (#5 74).

Monie, Willis. "S's 'Thirteen Ways of Looking at a Blackbird,' VII." *Expl*, 34: 2 (S 75).

Morse, S.F. "'Lettres d'un Soldat.'" *DCLB*, 4: 44-50 (D 61).

Mulqueen, J.E. "Man and Cosmic Man in the Poetry of WS." *SDR*, 11: 16-27 (Su 73).

———. "A Reading of WS's 'The Comedian as the Letter C.'" *CimR*, 13: 35-42 (1970).

———. "A Reading of WS's 'Sea Surface Full of Clouds.'" *Per*, 17: 268-77 (1975).

———. "WS: Radical Transcendentalist." *MwQ*, 11: 329-40 (Sp 70).

Murray, C.J. "WS's 'The Man on the Dump.'" *Cont Poetry*, 1: 1-5 (Wi 73).

Narasimhaiah, C.D. "WS." *LCrit*, 9: 1-13 (Wi 70).

Nassar, E.P. "Illusion as Value: An Essay on a Modern Poetic Idea." *Mosaic*, 7: 109-23 (#4 74).

Neill, Edward. "The Melting Moment: S's Rehabilitation of Ice Cream." *Ariel*, 4: 88-96 (Ja 73).

Oamber, Akhtar. "'The Man with the Blue Guitar' by WS." *LHLY*, 14: 49-60 (1973).

Pack, Robert. "WS's Sufficient Muse." *SoR*, 11: 766-78 (Au 75).

Peterson, Margaret. "*Harmonium* and William James." *SoR*, 7: 658-82 (Jl 71).

Pinkerton, Jan. "Political Realities and Poetic Release." *NEQ*, 44: 575-601 (D 71).

———. "WS in the Tropics: A Conservative Protest." *YR*, 60: 215-27 (Wi 71).

Poggenburg, R.P. "Baudelaire and S: 'L'Esthétique du Mal.'" *SAB*, 23: 14-8 (1968).

Poulin, A. "Crispin as Everyman as Adam: 'The Comedian as the Letter C.'" *CP*, 5: 5-23 (Sp 72).

Powell, Grosvenor. "Of Heroes and Nobility: The Personae of WS." *SoR*, 7: 727-48 (JL 71).

Qamber, Akhtar. "*The Man with the Blue Guitar* by WS." *LHY*, 14: 49-60 (#2 73).

Raine, Craig. "The Poetry of What There Is." *TLS*, 6 D 74, p. 1390.

Ramsey, Warren. "Wallace Stevens and Some French Poets." *Trinity R*, 8: 26-9 (1954).

Rao, Nageswara. "Crispin's Passage to Yucatan." *LHY*, 16: 125-30 (Ja 75).

Reeve, A.H. "In Retrospect: WS." *TC*, 1048: 44-6 (1972).

Richards, R.F. "Hemingway and S's 'Poetry of Extraordinary Actuality.'" *Descant*, 17: 46-8 (Su 73).

Riddel, J.N. "Blue Voyager." *Salmagundi*, 2: 61-74 (67-68).

———. "Interpreting S: An Essay on Poetry and Thinking." *Boun2*, 1: 79-97 (Fa 72).

Riffey, M.S. "The WS Collection at the University of Miami." *Carrell*, 13: 16-8 (1972).

Rother, James. "Modernism and the Nonsense Style." *ConL*, 15: 187-202 (Fa 74).

Rowson, C.J. "'Tis only infinite below': Speculations of Swift, WS, R.D. Laing and Others." *EIC*, 22: 161-81 (1972).

———. "WS's 'Le monocle de mon oncle.'" *SA*, 13: 417-62 (1967).

Ruthven, K.K. "The Poet as Etymologist." *CritQ*, 2: 9-37 (Sp 69).

Sampley, A.M. "WS: Executive as Poet." *MwQ*, 13: 213-28 (Wi 72).

Sastri, P.S. "S, the Romantics, and Santayana." *IJAS*, 3: 39-46 (1973).

Schleiner, Louise. "The Angel and the Necessary Angel: Formalist Readings of Rilke and S." *LWU*, 2: 215-37 (1969).

Schwartz, Delmore. "Instructed of Much Mortality." *SR*, 54: 439-49 (Jl-S 46).

Semel, Jay M. "Pennsylvania Dutch Country: S's World as Meditation." *ConL*, 14: 310-19 (Su 73).

Silverman, Stuart. "The Emperor of Ice-Cream." *WHR*, 26: 165-8 (Sp 72).

Simons, Hi. "Vicissitudes of Reputation." *Harvard Advocate*, 127: 8-11, 34-44 (D 40).

Smithson, Bill. "WS's Theory of Poetry." *ELUD*, 1: 29-45 (Je 73).

Stevens, Holly. "Bits of Remembered Time." *SoR*, 7: 651-57 (Jl 71).

Stoenescu, Stefan. "WS şi reactivarea poetica a unmanului." *SXX*, 12: 149-55 (1969).

Tanselle, G.T. "The Text of S's 'Le Monocle de mon Oncle.'" *Library*, 19: 246-8 (1964).

Taylor, Andrew. "S's 'Notes Towards a Supreme Fiction': A Reading." *SoRA*, 4: 284-99 (1971).

Tompkins, D.P. "'To Abstract Reality': Abstract Language and the Intrusion of Consciousness in WS." *AL*, 45: 84-99 (Mr 73).

Tryford, John. "WS (John Tryford's Random Notes)." *Trace*, 66: 339-44 (Fa 67).

Tuerk, Richard. "A Note on Thoreau, William Carlos Williams, and WS." *ConS*, 10: 11-2 (Je 75).

Turco, Lewis. "The Agonism and the Existentity: S." *CP*, 6: 32-44 (Sp 73).

Untermeyer, Louis. "Departure from Dandyism." *SRL*, 25: 11 (19 D 42).

Vanderbilt, Kermit. "More S and Shakespeare." *Coll Lit*, 2: 143-5 (Sp 75).

Vendler, Helen. "WS: The False and True Sublime." *SoR*, 7: 683-98 (Jl 71).

Viereck, Peter. "S Revisited." *KR*, 10: 154-7 (Wi 48).

Walker, Kenneth. "S's 'The Idea of Order at Key West.'" *Expl*, 32: 59 (D 74).

Walker, K.E. "WS as Disaffected Flagellant." *MarkR*, 4: 26-9 (F 74).

Wentersdorf, K.P. "WS, Dante Alighieri and the Emperor." *TCL*, 13: 197-204 (Ja 68).

Weston, S.B. "The Artist and the Guitarist: S and Picasso." *Critique*, 17: 111-20 (1975).

Whitaker, T.R. "Voices of the Open: Wordsworth, Eliot, and S." *IowaR*, 2: 96-112 (#3 71).

Wolfe, Charles. "S's 'Peter Quince at the Clavier.'" *Expl*, 33: 43 (F 75).

Woodman, Leonora. "'A Giant on the Horizon': WS and the 'Idea of Man.'" *TSLL*, 15: 759-86 (Wi 74).

Zukofsky, Louis. "Addenda to *Prepositions*." *JML*, 4: 91-104 (S 74).

Stern, Karl. Maloney, Stephen. "The Works and Days of KS." *GaR*, 28: 245-56 (Su 74).

Stewart, Donald Ogden. St. John, Donald. "Mr. and Mrs. DOS Abroad." *ConnR*, 4: 23-36 (1971).

Stickney, Trumbull. Flint, R.W. "Yankees Bemused." *Parnassus*, 2: 35-48 (1973).

Griffing, A.H. "The Achievement of TS." *NEQ*, 46: 106-12 (Mr 73).

Lopez, M.D. "TJS (1870-1904)." *BB*, 26: 83-5 (Jl-S 69).

Murfin, R.C. "The Poetry of TS: A Centennial Discovery." *NEQ*, 48: 540-55 (D 75).

Wilson, Edmund. "The Country I Remember." *NRep*, 103: 529-30 (14 O 40).

Stoddard, Richard Henry. Sealts, M.M. "Melville and RHS." *AL*, 43: 359-70 (N 71).

Stoddard, Solomon. Davis, T.M. "SS's Sermon on the Lord's Supper as a Converting Ordinance." *RALS*, 4: 205-24 (1974).

Fiering, N.S. "SS's Library at Harvard in 1664." *HLB*, 20: 255-69 (1972).

Holifield, E.B. "The Intellectual Sources of Stoddardeanism." *NEQ*, 45: 373-92 (1972).

Lucas, P.R. "An Appeal to the Learned: The Mind of SS." *WMQ*, 30: 275-92 (1973).

Stuart, R.L. "'Mr. S's Way: Church and Sacraments in Northampton." *AQ*, 24: 243-53 (1972).

Stone, John. Whitfield, H.R. "JS, Doctor Poet." *Cross and Crescent*, 60: 24-31 (Ag 73).

Stone, Ruth. Gross, Harvey. "On the Poetry of RS: Selections and Commentary." *IowaR*, 3: 94-106 (Sp 72).

Story, William Wetmore. DiFederico, F.F., and Jualia Markus. "The Influence of Robert Browning on the Art of WWS." *Browning Inst Stud*, 1: 63-85 (1973).

Hynes, Joseph. "The Transparent Shroud: Henry James and WS." *AL*, 46: 506-27 (Ja 75).

Stowe, Harriet Beecher. Anon. "S and Day Houses to be Open Next Year." *ESQ*, 51: 74-5 (2Q 68).

———. "Uncle Tom: That Enduring Old Image." *AH*, 23: 50-7 (D 71).

Adams, J.R. "HBS (1811-1896)." *ALR*, 2: 160-4 (Su 69).

———. "Structure and Theme in the Novels of HBS." *ATQ*, 24: 50-5 (Fa 74).

Allen, P.R. "Lord Macaulay's Gift to HBS: The Solution to a Riddle in Trevelyan's Life." *N&Q*, 17: 23-4 (Ja 70).

Allen, Walter. "*Uncle Tom's Cabin* Revisited." *Listener*, 76: 197-200 (11 Ag 66).

Axelrad, A.M. "HBS as a New England Local-Colorist." *UAP*, 40: 34-44 (1963).

Baxter, A.K. "Women's Studies and American Studies: The Uses of the Interdisciplinary." *AQ*, 26: 433-9 (1974).

Brandstadter, Evan. "Uncle Tom and Archy Moore: The Antislavery Novel as Ideological Symbol." *AQ*, 26: 160-75 (My 74).

Brown, D.S. "Thesis and Theme in *Uncle Tom's Cabin*." *EJ*, 58: 1330-4, 1372 (D 69).

Brumm, Ursula. "Some Thoughts on History and the Novel." *CLS*, 6: 317-30 (1969).

Cassara, Ernest. "The Rehabilitation of Uncle Tom: Significant Themes in Mrs. S's Antislavery Novel." *CLAJ*, 17: 230-40 (D 73).

Cox, C.J. "*Uncle Tom's Cabin*: A Pre-Raphaelite Reaction." *N&Q*, 22: 111-2 (Mr 75).

Cox, James. "Humor and America: The Southwestern Bear Hunt, Mrs. S and Mark Twain." *SR*, 83: 573-601 (Fa 75).

Graham, Thomas. "HBS and the Question of Race." *NEQ*, 46: 614-22 (D 73).

Grimsted, David. "*Uncle Tom* from Page to Stage: Limitations of Nineteenth-Century Drama." *QJS*, 56: 235-44 (O 70).

Hayne, Barrie. "Yankee in the Patriarchy: T.B. Thorpe's Reply to *Uncle Tom's Cabin*." *AQ*, 20: 180-95 (Su 68).

Hovet, T.R. "Christian Revolution: HBS's Response to Slavery and the Civil War." *NEQ*, 47: 535-49 (D 74).

———. "The Church Diseased: HBS's Attack on the Presbyterian Church." *J of Presbyterian Hist*, 52: 167-87 (Su 74).

Jobes, K.T. "From S's Eagle Island to Jewett's 'A White Mice Heron.'" *CLQ*, 10: 515-21 (1974).

Jones, M.O. "'Ye Must Contrive Allers to Keep Jest the Happy Medium Between Truth and Falsehood': Folklore and the Folk in Mrs. S's Fiction." *NYFQ*, 27: 357-69 (D 71).

Kirkham, E.B. "The First Editions of *Uncle Tom's Cabin*: A Bibliographical Study." *PBSA*, 65: 365-82 (4Q 71).

Lebedun, Jean. "HBS's Interest in Sojourner Truth, Black Feminist." *AL*, 46: 359-62 (N 74).

Levin, David. "American Fiction as Historical Evidence: Reflections on *Uncle Tom's Cabin*." *NALF*, 5: 132-6, 154 (1971).

Levy, B.M. "Mutations in New England Local Color." *NEQ*, 19: 338-58 (S 46).

Lombard, C.M. "HBS's Attitude toward French Romanticism." *CLAJ*, 11: 236-40 (Mr 68).

McCullough, David. "The Unexpected Mrs. S." *AH*, 24: 5-9, 76-80 (Ag 73).

Meserve, W.J. and R.I. "*Uncle Tom's Cabin* and Modern Chinese Drama." *MD*, 27: 57-66 (Mr 74).

Miller, R.M. "Mrs. S's Negro: George Harris' Negritude in *Uncle Tom's Cabin*." *CLQ*, 10: 521-6 (1974).

———. "S's Black Sources in *Uncle Tom's Cabin*." *AN&Q*, 14: 38-9 (N 75).

Moers, Ellen. "Money, the Job, and Little Women." *Commentary*, 55: 57-65 (Ja 73).

Opperman, Harry. "Two Ghost Editions of *Uncle Tom's Cabin*." *PBSA*, 65: 295-6 (3Q 71).

Phipps, Frances. "At Home with HBS." *ATQ*, 14: 76-7 (Sp 72).

Picken, D.K. "Uncle Tom Becomes Nat Turner: A Commentary on Two American Heroes." *NALF*, 3: 45-8 (1969).

Plessner, Monika. "Die weisse Dame und der schwarze Mann." *FrH*, 27: 201-10 (1972).

Reed, K.T. "A Thoreauvian Echo in *Uncle Tom's Cabin*?" *ATQ*, 11: 37-8 (Su 71).

———. "*Uncle Tom's Cabin* and the Heavenly City." *CLAJ*, 12: 150-4 (D 68).

Reze, Michel. "L'accueil fail à *La case de l'Oncle Tom* en Angleterre en 1852." *EA*, 24: 415-30 (1971).

Rotundo, Barbara. "HBS and the Mythmakers." *AN&Q*, 12: 131-3 (My-Je 74).

Slout, W.L. "*Uncle Tom's Cabin* in American Film History." *J Popular Film*, 2: 137-51 (1973).

Smylie, J.H. "*Uncle Tom's* Revisited." *Interpretation*, 27: 67-85 (1973).

Steele, Thomas. "Tom and Eva: Mrs S's Two Dying Christs." *NALF*, 6: 85-90 (1972).

Strout, Cushing. "*Uncle Tom's Cabin* and the Portent of Millennium" *YR*, 57: 375-85 (Sp 68).

Tanner, J.E. "Uncle Tom's Ghosts." *AN&Q*, 13: 70-2 (Ja 75).

Trautmann, Frederick. "HBS's Public Readings in New England." *NEQ*, 47: 279-89 (Je 74).

Van Hoy, M.S. "Two Allusions to Hungary in *Uncle Tom's Cabin*." *Phylon*, 34: 433-5 (1973).

Van Why, J.F., and E.B. Kirkham. "A Note on Two Pages of the Manuscript of *Uncle Tom's Cabin*." *PBSA*, 66: 433-4 (4Q 72).

Wadsworth, F.W. "'Webster, Horne and Mrs. S': American Performances of *The Duchess of Malfi*." *ThS*, 11: 151-66 (1970).

Strand, Mark. Anon. "A Conversation with MS." *OhR*, 13: 54-71 (1972).

Bloom, Harold. "Dark and Radiant Peripheries: MS and A.R. Ammons." *SoR*, 8: 133-49 (Ja 72).

French, R.W. "Eating Poetry: The Poems of MS." *FarP*, 5: 61-6 (Wi-Sp 71).

McMichael, James. "Borges and S, Weak Henry, Philip Levine." *SoR*, 8: 213-24 (1972).

Stratemeyer, Edward. Prager, Arthur. "ES and His Book Machine." *SatR*, 54: 15-7, 52-3 (10 Jl 71).

Soderburgh, P.A. "Birth of a Notion: ES and the Movies." *MwQ*, 14: 81-94 (Au 72).

———. "The S Strain: Educators and the Juvenile Series Book, 1900-1973." *JPC*, 7: 864-72 (1974).

Stribling, T.S. Durham, Frank. "The Reputed Demises of Uncle Tom; or, The Treatment of the Negro in Fiction by White Southern Authors in the 1920's." *SLJ*, 2: 26-50 (Sp 70).

McSherry, F.D. "Rare Vintages from the Tropics: TSS's *Clues* of the Carribees." *ArmD*, 6: 172-8 (1973).

Rocks, J.E. "T.S.S's Burden of Southern History: The Valden Trilogy." *SHR*, 6: 221-32 (Su 72).

Stuart, Jesse. Anon. "JS Newsletter." *JLN*, 2: 117-20 (1969).

Clarke, Kenneth. "Kentucky Heritage in JS's Writing." *JLN*, 3: 130-1 (1970).

Flanagan, J.T. "Folklore in Five Middle-western Novelists." *Great Lakes R*, 1: 43-57 (Wi 75).

Foster, R.E. "JS's W-Hollow: Microcosm of the Appalachians." *KanQ*, 2: 66-73 (1970).

Gibbs, Sylvia. "JS: The Dark Hills and Beyond." *JLN*, 4: 56-69 (1971).

———. "JS's Cyclic Vision." *JLN*, 3: 120-9 (1970).

Huddleston, E.L. "Place Names in the Writings of JS." *WF*, 31: 169-78 (Jl 72).

LeMaster, J.R. "JS: The Man and His Poetry." *ABC*, 20: 13-9 (Su 70).

———. "JS's *Album of Destiny*: In Pursuit of Whitman's Parallels." *BSUF*, 13: 75-80 (Wi 72).

———. "JS's *Album of Destiny*—In Whitman's Eternal Flow." *IllQ*, 36: 38-40 (1973).

———. "JS's Pictures in *Man With A Bull-Tongue Plow*." *MarkR*, 3: 17-20 (O 71).

————. "JS's Satirical Poems." *ABC*, 23: 16-8 (1973).

————. "The Poetry of JS: An Estimate for the Seventies." *SWR*, 56: 251-6 (Su 71).

Pennington, Lee. "A Note on JS's 'Birdland's Golden Age.'" *Appalachian R*, 3: 74-5 (1975).

————. "Symbolism and Poetic Vision in JS's Early Poetry." *Appalachian R*, 3: 80-6 (1975).

Stuart, Jesse. "America's Pindar Was My Guide." *Vanderbilt Alumnus*, 56: 16-9 (Mr-Ap 71).

*Woodbridge, H.C. "Jesse and Jane S: A Bibliography." *JLN*, quarterly since 1969.

Styron William. Anon. "Unslavished Fidelity: The Confessions of WS." *TLS*, 9 My 68, p. 480.

————. "W.S. Writes *PW* about His New Novel." *PW*, 177: 54-5 (30 My 61).

Akin, W.E. "Toward an Impressionistic History: Pitfalls and Possibilities in WS's Meditation on History." *AQ*, 21: 805-12 (Wi 69).

Aldridge, J.W. "Highbrow Authors and Middlebrow Books." *Playboy*, 11: 173-4 (Ap 64).

Anderson, Jervis. "S and His Black Critics." *Dissent*, 16: 157-66 (Mr-Ap 69).

————. "S's Turner vs. Nat Turner." *New South Student*, My 68: 3-7.

Bailinson, Frank. "S Answers 'Turner' Critics." *NYT*, 11 F 68, p. 59.

Barzelay, D., and R. Sussman. "WS on *The Confessions of Nat Turner*." *Yale Lit Mag*, 137: 24-35 (S 68).

Behar, Jack. "History and Fiction." *Novel*, 3: 260-5 (Sp 70).

Bell, B.W. "The Confessions of S." *AmD*, 5: 3-7 (1968).

Bender, Eileen, and S.L. Gross. "History and Politics, and Literature: The Myth of Nat Turner." *AQ*, 23: 486-518 (O 71).

Bennett, Lerone. "The Case Against S's Nat Turner." *Ebony*, 23: 148-50, 154-7 (O 68).

Boney, F.N. "The Blue Lizard: Another View of Nat Turner's Country on the Eve of Rebellion." *Phylon*, 31: 351-8 (Wi 70).

Brunaur, D.H. "Black and White: The Archetypal Myth and Its Development." *BaratR*, 6: 12-20 (Sp-Su 71).

Bulgheroni, Marisa. "WS: Il romanziere, il tempo e la storia." *SA*, 16: 407-28 (1970).

Burger, N.K. "Truth or Consequences: Books and Book Reviewing." *SAQ*, 68: 152-66 (1969).

Cannon, P.R. "Nat Turner: God, Man, or Beast?" *BaratR*, 6: 25-8 (Sp-Su 71).

Coles, Robert. "Blacklash." *PR*, 35: 128-33 (Wi 68).

Cooke, Michael. "Nat Turner: Another Response." *YR*, 58: 295-301 (Wi 69).

Core, George. "*The Confessions of Nat Turner* and the Burden of the Past." *SLJ*, 2: 117-34 (Sp 70).

————. "*Nat Turner* and the Final Reckoning of Things." *SoR*, 4: 745-51 (Sp 68).

Cunliffe, Marcus. "Black Culture and White America." *Enc*, 34: 22-35 (Ja 70).

Curtis, Bruce. "Fiction, Myth, and History in WS's *Nat Turner*." *UCQ*, 16: 27-32 (Ja 71).

Delany, L.T. "A Psychologist Looks at *The Confessions of Nat Turner*." *Psych Today*, 1: 11-4 (Ja 68).

De Vecchi Rocca, Luisa. "Nat Turner." *NA*, 510: 614-24 (1970).

Doar, Harriet. "Interview with WS." *RCR*, 1964, 26-30.

Donno, Antonio. "Note su WS." *Annali dell' Universita di Lecce*, 26: 285-306 (1973).

Driver, T.F. "Black Consciousness through a White Scrim." *Motive 27*, (F 68): 56-8.

Durden, R.F. "WS and His Black Critics." *SAQ*, 68: 181-7 (Sp 69).

Egenschwiler, David. "Tragedy and Melodrama in *The Confessions of Nat Turner*." *TCL*, 20: 19-33 (Ja 74).

Emmanuel, Pierre. "L'histoire d'une solitude." *Preuves*, #217: 17-20 (Ap 69).

Fauchereau, Serge. "Uncle Nat et Oncle Tom." *QL*, 70: 5-6 (1 Ap 69).

Forkner, Ben, and Gilbert Schricke. "An Interview with WS." *SoR*, 10: 923-34 (O 74).

Franklin, J.L. "*Nat Turner* and Black History." *IJAS*, 1: 1-6 (N 71).

Friedman, M.J. "The Cracked Vase." *RomN*, 7: 127-9 (Sp 66).

Genovese, E.D. "An Exchange on 'Nat Turner.'" *NYRB*, 11: 34-6 (7 N 68).

———. "The Nat Turner Case." *NYRB*, 11: 34-7 (12 S 68).

Gilman, Richard. "Nat Turner Revisited." *NRep*, 158: 23-6, 28, 32 (27 Ap 68).

Gray, Richard. "Victims and History and Agents of Revolution." *DQR*, 5: 3-23 (1975).

Green, Martin. "The Need for a New Liberalism." *Month*, 226: 141-7 (S 68).

Gresset, Michel. "*Les confessions de Nat Turner*: L'histoire réelle et le roman. Un sociodrame américain." *Preuves*, 217: 3-5 (Ap 1969).

———. "Un Spartacus noir: Nat Turner." *Preuves*, 19: 3-5 (Ap 69).

———. "WS." *NRF*, 204: 898-907 (D 69).

Gross, S.L., and Eileen Bender. "History and Politics, and Literature: The Myth of Nat Turner." *AQ*, 23: 486-518 (O 71).

Halpern, Daniel. "Checking in with WS." *Esquire*, 78: 142-3 (Ag 72).

Hamilton, C.V. "Nat Turner Reconsidered: The Fiction and the Reality." *SatR*, 51: 22-3 (22 Je 68).

Harding, Vincent. "An Exchange on 'Nat Turner.'" *NYRB*, 11: 31-3 (7 N 68).

Harnack, Curtis. "The Quidities of Detail." *KR*, 30: 125-32 (Wi 68).

Holder, Alan. "S's Slave: *The Confessions of Nat Turner*." *SAQ*, 68: 167-80 (Sp 69).

Kanters, Robert. "La Révolte de l'Oncle Tom." *FL*, 1196: 19-20 (7 Ap 69).

Kauffmann, Stanley. "S's Unwritten Novel." *HudR*, 20: 675-9 (Wi 67-68).

Kretzoi, Charlotte. "WS: Heritage and Conscience." *HSE*, 5: 121-36 (1971).

Le Clec'h, Guy. "Pour les Noirs américains la 'confession de Nat Turner' n'est que celle de WS." *FL*, 1191: 24 (3 Mr 69).

Long, R.E. "The Vogue of Gatsby's Guest List." *FHA*, 1969, pp. 23-5.

Luedtke, C.L. "*The Sound and the Fury* and *Lie Down in Darkness*: Some Comparisons." *LWU*, 4: 45-51 (1971).

Malin, Irving. "S's Play." *SLJ*, 6: 151-7 (Sp 74).

Markos, D.W. "Margaret Whitehead in *The Confessions of Nat Turner*." *StN*, 4: 52-9 (Sp 72).

Marres, René. "Fictie versus werkelijkheid." *Raam*, 64: 35-40 (1970).

Mellen, Joan. "WS: The Absence of Social Definition." *Novel*, 4: 159-70 (Wi 71).

Miller, W.L. "The Meditations of WS." *Reporter*, 37: 42-6 (16 N 67).

Morse, J.M. "Social Relevance, Literary Judgement, and the New Right; or, The Inadvertent Confessions of WS." *CE*, 30: 605-16 (My 69).

Mullen, J.S. "S's Nat Turner: A Search for Humanity." *BaratR*, 6: 6-11 (Sp-Su 71).

Neri, Judith. "On the *Confessions* of Nat Turner." *Umanesimo*, 2: 135-8 (1968).

Newcomb, Horace. "WS and the Act of Memory: *The Confessions of Nat Turner*." *ChiR*, 20: 86-94 (#1 68).

Nigro, August. "*The Long March*: The Expansive Hero in a Closed World." *Critique*, 9: 103-12 (#3 68).

Nolte, W.H. "S's Meditation on Saviors." *SWR*, 58: 338-48 (Au 73).

Normand, Jean. "L'homme mystifié: Les Héros de Bellow, Albee, S, et Mailer." *EA*, 22: 370-85 (O-D 69).

———. "'Un lit de ténèbres' de W.S: Variations sur le theme de Tristan." *EA*, 27: 64-71 (Ja-Mr 74).

Oates, S.B. "S and the Blacks—Another View." *Nation*, 220: 662-4 (31 My 75).

Pearce, Richard. "WS." *UMPAW*, 98: 1-47 (1971).

Perry, J.D. "Gothic as Vortex: The Form of Horror in Capote, Faulkner, and S." *MFS*, 19: 153-67 (Su 73).

Peter, John. "The Self-Effacement of the Novelist." *MalR*, 8: 119-28 (O 68).

Pickens, D.K. "Uncle Tom Becomes Nat Turner: A Commentary on Two American Heroes." *NALF*, 3: 45-8 (Su 69).

Pinsker, Sanford. "Christ as Revolutionary/Revolutionary as Christ: The Hero in Bernald Malamud's *The Fixer* and WS's *The Confessions of Nat Turner*." *BaratR*, 6: 29-37 (1971).

Platt, G.M. "A Sociologist Looks at *The Confessions of Nat Turner*." *Psych Today*, 1: 14-5 (Ja 68).

Prasa, T.G. "*Lie Down in Darkness*: A Portrait of the Modern Phenomenon." *IJES*, 10: 71-80 (1969).

Rahv, Philip. "WS on Our Literature of Collision." *Intellectual Dig*, 2: 82-4 (Mr 72).

Ratner, M.L. "The Rebel Purged: S's *The Long March*." *ArlQ*, 2: 27-42 (Au 69).

———. "Rebellion of Wrath and Laughter: Styron's *Set This House on Fire*." *SoR*, 7: 1007-20 (Au 71).

———. "S's Rebel." *AQ*, 21: 595-608 (Fa 69).

Rocca, L. de V. "Nat Turner." *NA*, 510: 614-24 (D 70).

Rubin, L.D. "What to Do About Chaos." *Hopkins R*, 5: 65-8 (Fa 51).

Salomon, Michel. "Interview avec WS." *ML*, 27: 24-5 (Mr 69).

Saradhi, K.P. "The Agony of a Slave Negro: Theme and Technique in S's *Nat Turner*." *OJES*, 9: 11-9 (1972).

Shapiro, Herbert. "*The Confessions of Nat Turner*: WS and His Critics." *NALF*, 9: 99-104 (Wi 75).

Shepherd, Allen. "'Hopeless Paradox' and *The Confessions of Nat Turner*." *Ranam*, 4: 87-91 (1971).

Sitkoff, Harvard, and Michael Wreszin. "Whose Nat Turner?: WS vs. the Black Intellectuals." *Midstream*, 14: 10-20 (N 68).

Styron, William. "My Generation." *Esquire*, 80: 132-4 (O 73).

———. "The Shade of Thomas Wolfe." *HM*, 236: 96-104 (Ap 68).

———. "This Quiet Dust." *HM*, 230: 135-46 (Ap 65).

———. "Truth and Nat Turner: An Exchange." *Nation*, 206: 544-7 (22 Ap 68).

———. "Violence in Literature." *ASch*, 37: 482-96 (Su 68).

Sussman, Robert. "The Case against WS's *Nat Turner*." *Yale Lit Mag*, 137: 20-3 (S 68).

Suter, Anthony. "Transcendence and Failure: WS's *Lie Down in Darkness*." *Caliban XII*, 11: 157-66 (1975).

Suyama, Shizuo. "S no *The Confessions of Nat Turner*." *EigoS*, 114: 525 (1968).

Swanson, W.J. "Religious Implications in *The Confessions of Nat Turner*." *CimR*, 12: 57-66 (Jl 70).

———. "William Faulkner and WS: Notes on Religion." *CimR*, 7: 45-52 (My 69).

Thelwell, Michael. "Arguments: The Turner Thesis." *PR*, 35: 403-12 (Su 68).

———. "An Exchange on 'Nat Turner.'" *NYRB*, 11: 34 (7 N 68).

———. "Mr. WS and the Rev. Turner." *MR*, 9: 7-29 (Wi 68).

———, and Robert Coles. "Arguments: the Turner Thesis." *PR*, 35: 403-14 (Su 68).

Thomas, E.E. "Ten Views of the Man Who Would Not Die." *SatR*, 51: 23-4 (17 Ag 68).

Tischler, N.M. "*The Confessions of Nat Turner*: A Symposium—Introduction." *BaratR*, 6: 3-4 (Sp-Su 71).

————. "Negro Literature and Classic Form." *ConL*, 10: 352-65 (Su 69).

Tragle, H.I. "S and His Sources." *MR*, 9: 134-53 (Wi 70).

Trochard, Catherine. "WS and the Historical Novel." *Neohelicon*, 3: 373-82 (#1 75).

Turner, D.T. "*The Confessions of Nat Turner*. By WS." *JNH*, 53: 183-6 (1968).

Via, D.O., Jr. "Law as Grace in S's *Set This House on Fire*." *JR*, 51: 125-36 (Ap 71).

Wells, A.M. "An Exchange on 'Nat Turner.'" *NYRB*, 11: 31 (7 N 68).

West, J.L. "A Bibliographer's Interview with WS." *Costerus*, 4: 13-29 (1975).

————. "WS's Afterword to *The Long March*." *MissQ*, 28: 185-9 (1975).

White, John. "The Novelist as Historian: WS and American Negro Slavery." *JAmSt*, 4: 233-45 (F 71).

Whitney, Blair. "Nat Turner's Mysticism." *BaratR*, 6: 21-4 (Sp-Su 71).

Wiemann, Renate. "WS: *Lie Down in Darkness*." *NS*, 19: 312-32 (Jl 70).

Wreszin, Michael, and Harvard Sitkoff. "Whose Nat Turner: WS vs. the Black Intellectuals." *Midstream*, 14: 10-20 (N 68).

Suckow, Ruth. Muehl, L.B. "RS's Art of Fiction." *BI*, 13: 3-12 (N 70).

Suggs, Simon (see **Hooper, J.J.**).

Sukenick, Ronald. Bellamy, J.D. "Imagination as Perception: An Interview with RS." *ChiR*, 23: 59-72 (1972).

Hassan, Ihab. "Reading *Out*." *FicI*, 1: 108-9 (Fa 73).

Klinkowitz, Jerome. "Getting Real: Making It (Up) with RS." *ChiR*, 23: 73-82 (Wi 72).

————. "A Persuasive Account: Working It Out with RS." *NAR*, 258: 48-52 (Su 73).

Susann, Jacqueline. Bredella, Lothar. "Aethetische und soziale Kategorien bei der Analyse des Bestsellers *Valley of the Dolls* von JS." *JA*, 19: 30-49 (1974).

Davidson, Sara. "JS: The Writing Machine." *HM*, 239: 65-71 (O 69).

des Ormeaux, Dollar. "Pour faire rever les midinettes." *Quinzaine Litteraire*, 169: 11-2 (Ag 73).

Swados, Harvey. Kramer, Hilton. "Remembering HS." *MR*, 14: 226-28 (Wi 73).

Marx, Paul. "HS." *OntarioR*, 1, 1: 62-6 (21974).

Swallow, Alan. Harris, Mark. "AS, 1915-1966." *DQ*, 2: 5-9 (Sp 67).

————. "Obituary Three for AS." *MFS*, 15: 187-90 (Su 69).

Lundahl, Gene. "A Eulogy." *DQ*, 2: 33-6 (Sp 67).

Manfred, Frederick. "AS: Poet and Pubisher." *DQ*, 2: 27-31 (Sp 67).

Nin, Anais. "AS." *DQ*, 2: 11-4 (Sp 67).

*North, D.D. "AS: A Bibliographical Checklist." *DQ*, 2: 63-72 (Sp 67).

Robbins, Martin. "AS: A Remembrance." *DQ*, 2: 37-9 (Sp 67).

Tate, Allen. "My Debt to AS." *DQ*, 2: 43 (Sp 67).

Waters, Frank. "Notes on AS." *DQ*, 2: 16-25 (Sp 67).

Taliaferro, Harden E. Boggs, R.S. "North Carolina Folktales Current in the 1820's." *JAF*, 47: 269-88 (Ja-Mr 34).

Coffin, T.P. "HE.T and the Use of Folklore by American Literary Figures." *SAQ*, 64: 241-6 (Sp 65).

Whiting, B.J. "Proverbial Sayings from Fisher's River, North Carolina." *SFQ*, 11: 173-85 (S 47).

Williams, C.D "Mountain Customs, Social Life, and Folk Yarns in T's *Fisher's River Scenes and Characters*." *NCaF*, 16: 143-52 (N 68).

Tarkington, Booth. Anderson, D.D. "The Boy's World of BT." *Soc. for the Study of Midwestern Lit Misc*, 1: 35-42 (1974).

Hamblen, A.A. "BT's Classic of Adolescence." *SHR*, 3: 225-31 (Su 69).

————. "Two Almost Forgotten Innocents." *Cresset*, 30: 16-7 (O 67).

Rowlette, Robert. "T in Defense of Howells and Realism: A Recovered Letter." *BSUF*, 14: 64-5 (Su 73).

Sorkin, A.J. "'She Doesn't Last, Apparently': A Reconsideration of BT's *Alice Adams*." *AL*, 46: 182-99 (My 74).

Tate, Allen. Aiken, Conrad. "AT." *TLS*, April 9, 1971, p. 422.

Bataille, Robert. "The Esthetics and Ethics of Farming: The Southern Agrarian View." *Iowa State J Res*, 49: 189-93 (1974).

Blackmur, R.P. "San Giovanni in Venere: AT as Man of Letters." *SR*, 67: 614-31 (O-D 59).

Bradford, M.E. "Angels at Forty Thousand Feet: 'Ode to Our Young Pro-Consuls of the Air' and the Practice of Poetic Responsibility." *GaR*, 22: 42-57 (Sp 68).

Brooks, Cleanth. "On the Poetry of AT." *MQR*, 10: 225-8 (Au 71).

Brown, Ashley. "AT as Satirist." *Shen*, 19: 44-54 (Wi 68).

Bruccoli, M.J. "Interview with AT." *FHA*, 1974, pp. 101-3.

Buffington, Robert. "The Directing Mind: AT and the Profession of Letters." *SLJ*, 5: 102-15 (Sp 73).

Core, George. "A Metaphysical Athlete: AT as Critic." *SLJ*, 2: 138-47 (Fa 69).

————. "Two Gentlemen in Bonds." *SoR*, 11: 226-32 (Ja 75).

Cowan, Louise. "AT and the Garment of Dante." *SR*, 80: 377-82 (Sp 72).

Davis, R.M. "The Anthologist: Editor vs. Compiler." *PBSA*, 63: 321-3 (4Q 69).

Donoghue, Denis. "AT's Seventy-Fifth Birthday." *TLS*, 13 D 74, p. 1414.

Dupree, Robert. "The Mirrors of Analogy: Three Poems of AT." *SoR*, 8: 774-91 (O 72).

Eaton, C.E. "A Friendship of Poets: The Statesman and the Soldier." *GaR*, 28: 688-704 (Wi 74).

Edwards, M.F. "An Explication of AT's 'Ode to the Confederate Dead.'" *Cont Poetry*, 1: 31-4 (Sp 73).

Fain, J.T., and T.D. Young. "The Agrarian Symposium: Letters of AT and Donald Davidson, 1928-1930." *SoR*, 8: 845-82 (O 72).

Fergusson, Francis. "A Note on the Vitality of AT's Prose." *SR*, 67: 579-81 (O-D 59).

Fields, Kenneth. "Just and Predictable Proportions: AT's *Essays of Four Decades*." SR, 80: 180-96 (Wi 72).

Ghiselin, Brewster. "A Dove." *MQR*, 10: 229-30 (Au 71).

Gray, R.J. "Cultural Truths, Necessary Traditions, and the Mythologising of History: An Approach to AT." *IJAS*, 4: 36-52 (Je-D 74).

Grumbach, Doris. "Fine Print: AT, at 75, at Sewanee." *NRep*, 171: 46-8 (30 N 74).

Hellman, D.A. "Donald Davidson, AT and All Those Falling Leaves." *GaR*, 27: 550-9 (Wi 73).

Helmick, E.T. "The Civil War Odes Of Lowell and T." *GaR*, 25: 51-5 (Je 71).

Kane, Patricia. "An Irrepressible Conflict: AT's *The Fathers*." *Critique*, 10: 9-16 (Sp 68).

*Korges, James. "AT: A Checklist." *Critique*, 10: 35-52 (1968).

Lemon, L.T. "A Man of Letters." *PrS*, 44: 416-7 (Wi 69-70).

Newitz, Martin. "Tradition, Time, and AT." *MissQ*, 21: 37-42 (Wi 67-68).

O'Dea, Richard. "AT's Vestigial Morality." *Person*, 49: 256-62 (Sp 68).

Rubin, L.D. "Encaustics: Letters of Loyalty: T and Davidson." *SR*, 83: 363-70 (Sp 75).

————. "Letters of Loyalty: T and Davidson." *SR*, 83: 363-70 (Sp 75).

Sanders, F.K. "Theme and Structure in *The Fathers*." *ArlQ*, 1: 244-56 (Wi 67-68).

Shankar, D. "AT and the Elizabethans: or, the Fallacy of Christian Criticism." *LCrit*, 10: 16-23 (#2 72).

Squires, Radcliffe. "AT's *The Fathers*." *VQR*, 46: 629-49 (Au 70).

————. "AT: A Season at Monteagle." *MQR*, 10: 57-65 (Wi 71).

———. "Will and Vision: AT's *Terza Rima* Poems." *SR*, 78: 543-62 (Au 70).

Stanford, D.E. "'Out of that Source of Time': The Poetry of AT." *SoR*, 7: 17-23 (Su 71).

———. "The Piety of AT." *SoR*, 7: xvii-xxiii (Jl 71).

Tate, Allen. "A Lost Traveller's Dream." *MQR*, 11: 225-36 (Au 72).

*Thorp, Willard. "AT: A Checklist." *Critique*, 10: 17-34 (1968).

Uhlman, T. "T's 'Death of Little Boys.'" *Expl*, 28: 58 (Mr 70).

Warren, Austin. "Homage to AT." *SoR*, 9: 753-77 (Au 73).

Travel, Ronald. Isaac, Dan. "RT: Ridiculous Playwright." *TDR*, 13: 106-15 (N 68).

Michelson, Peter. "Preference to *Street of Stairs*." *ChiR*, 20-1: 201-11 (My 69).

Taylor, Bayard. Doughty, N.S. "BT: First California Booster." *WR*, 7: 22-7 (1970).

———. "BT's Second Look at California (1859)." *WR*, 8: 51-5 (1971).

Krumpelmann, J.T. "BT, Kennan and Kennan, and Cassius M. Clay, or a Note on American-Russian Relations During the Civil War." *SCB*, 32: 227-9 (Wi 72).

Luedtke, L.S., and P.D. Morrow. "Bret Harte on BT: An Unpublished Tribute." *MarkR*, 3: 101-5 (1973).

Monaghan, Jay. "BT and Two Unpublished Poems." *SCUL*, 5: 39-45 (1973).

Schwartz, T.D. "BT's 'The Prophet': Mormonism as Literary Taboo." *BYUS*, 14: 235-47 (Wi 74).

Taylor, Edward. Akiyama, Ken. "ET no shi to Topology." *EigoS*, 114: 507-9 (1968).

Alexis, G.T. "A Keen Nose for T's Syntax." *EAL*, 4: 97-101 (Wi 69-70).

Allen, J.B. "ET's Catholic Wasp: Exegetical Convention in 'Upon a Spider Catching a Fly.'" *ELN*, 7: 257-60 (Je 70).

Arner, R.D. "ET's Gaming Imagery: Meditation I.40." *EAL*, 4: 38-40 (Fa 69).

———. "Folk Metaphors in ET's 'Meditation I.40.'" *SCN*, 31: 6-9 (1973).

———. "Proverbs in ET's *God's Determinations*." *SFQ*, 37: 1-13 (Mr 73).

Bales, Kent, and W.J. Aull. "Touching T Overly." *EAL*, 5: 57-8 (Fa 70).

Ball, K.R. "Rhetoric in ET's *Preparatory Meditations*." *EAL*, 4: 79-88 (Wi 70).

Barbour, J.W. "The Prose Context of ET's Anti-Stoddard Meditations." *EAL*, 10: 144-57 (Fa 75).

Blake, Kathleen. "ET's Protestant Poetic: Nontransubstantiating Metaphor." *AL*, 43: 1-24 (Mr 71).

Bottorff, W.K. "ET, an Explication: 'Another Meditation at the Same Time.'" *EAL*, 3: 17-21 (Sp 68).

Bray, James. "John Fiske: Puritan Precursor of ET." *EAL*, 9: 27-38 (Sp 74).

Breitkreuz, Hartmut. "Motif and Literary Genesis." *ELN*, 8: 267-79 (1971).

Brumm, Ursula. "The 'Tree of Life' in ET's Meditations." *EAL*, 3: 72-87 (Fa 68).

Bush, Sargent. "Paradox, Puritanism, and T's *Gods Determinations*." *EAL*, 4: 48-66 (Wi 70).

Callow, J.T. "ET Obeys Saint Paul." *EAL*, 4: 89-96 (Wi 70).

Carlisle, E.F. "The Puritan Structure of ET's Poetry." *AQ*, 20: 147-63 (1968).

Combellack, C.R.B. "T's 'Upon Wedlock, and Death of Children.'" *Expl*, 29: 12 (N 70).

Davis, T.M. "ET and the Traditions of Puritan Typology." *EAL*, 4: 27-47 (Wi 70).

———. "ET's 'Occasional Meditations." *EAL*, 5: 17-29 (Wi 70-71).

———. "ET's 'Valedictory' Poems." *EAL*, 7: 38-63 (Sp 72).

———, and V.L. "ET on the Day of Judgment." *AL*, 43: 525-47 (Ja 72).

———. "ET's Library: Another Note." *EAL*, 6: 271-3 (Wi 71-2).

Doepke, D.K. "A Suggestion for Reading ET's 'The Preface.'" *EAL*, 5: 80-2 (Wi 70-71).

*Elkins, M.J. "ET: A Checklist." *EAL*, 4: 56-63 (Su 69).

Garrison, J.M. "The 'Worship-Mould': A Note on ET's *Preparatory Meditations*." *EAL*, 3: 127-31 (Fa 68).

————. "Teaching Early American Literature." *CE*, 31: 487-97 (1970).

Gatta, John. "The Comic Design of *God's Determinations touching his Elect*." *EAL*, 10: 121-43 (Fa 75).

Grabo, N.S. "*God's Determinations*: Touching T's Critics." *SCN*, 28: 22-4 (1970).

Griffin, E.M. "The Structure and Language of T's Meditation 2.112." *EAL*, 3: 205-8 (Wi 68-69).

Hall, Dean, and T.M. Davis. "The Two Versions of ET's Foundation Day Sermon." *RALS*, 5: 199-216 (Au 75).

Hammond, Jeff, and T.M. Davis. "ET: A Note on Visual Imagery." *EAL*, 8: 126-31 (Fa 73).

Higby, John. "T's 'Huswifery.'" *Expl*, 30: 60 (1972).

Howard, A.B. "The World as Emblem: Language and Vision in the Poetry of ET." *AL*, 44: 359-84 (N 72).

Isani, M.A. "ET and Ovid's *Art of Love*: The Text of A Newly Discovered Manuscript." *EAL*, 10: 67-74 (Sp 75).

————. "ET and the 'Turks.'" *EAL*, 7: 120-3 (Fa 72).

————. "The Pouring of the Sixth Vial: A Letter in a T-Sewall Debate." *PMHS*, 83: 123-9 (1971).

Jacobson, S.C. "Image Patterns in ET: Prayer and Proof." *CP*, 6: 59-67 (1973).

Johnson, E.G. "America's 'Laureate of the Gilded Age' and His Interest in Scandanavian Culture." *Swedish Pioneer Hist Q*, 23: 207-20 (1972).

Johnston, T.E. "ET: An American Emblematist." *EAL*, 3: 186-98 (Wi 68-69).

————. "A Note on the Voices of Anne Bradstreet, ET, Roger Williams, and Philip Pain." *EAL*, 3: 125-6 (Fa 68).

Jones, J.C. "A Note on the Number of ET's *Preparatory Meditations*." *EAL*, 9: 81-2 (Sp 74).

Junkins, Donald. "ET's Creative Process." *EAL*, 4: 67-78 (Wi 70).

————. "'Should Stars Wooe Lobster Claws?': A Study of ET's Poetic Practice and Theory." *EAL*, 3: 88-117 (Fa 68).

Kehler, J.K. "Physiology and Metaphor in ET's 'Meditation. Can. 1.3'." *EAL*, 9: 315-20 (Wi 70).

Keller, Karl. "The Example of ET." *EAL*, 4: 5-26 (Wi 70).

————. "A Modern Version of ET." *EAL*, 9: 321-4 (Wi 75).

————. "The Rev. Mr. ET's Bawdry." *NEQ*, 43: 382-406 (S 70).

————. "'The World Slickt Up in Types': ET as a Version of Emerson." *EAL*, 5: 124-40 (Sp 70).

*————, and K.A. Requa. "Additions to the Edward Taylor Checklist." *EAL*, 4: 117-9 (Wi 70).

Lauerntia, Sister M. "T's *Meditation 42*." *Expl*, 8: 19 (S 49).

Link, F.H. "ET's Dichtung als Lobpreis Gottes." *JA*, 16: 77-101 (1971).

Maynard, Reid. "The Poetry of ET: A Purtian Apologia." *Caliban*, 9: 3-17 (1972).

Mignon, C.W. "ET's *Preparatory Meditations*: A Decorum of Imperfections." *PMLA*, 83: 1423-8 (O 68).

————. "A Principle of Order in ET's *Preparatory Meditations*." *EAL*, 4: 110-6 (Wi 70).

Monteiro, George. "T's 'Meditation Eight.'" *Expl*, 27: 45 (F 69).

Murphy, Francis. "A Letter on ET's Bible." *EAL*, 6: 91 (Sp 71).

*Pierpont, P.E. "ET Checklist III: Addenda, Corrections, and Clarifications." *EAL*, 5: 91-94 (Su 71).

Pinsker, Sanford. "Carnal Love/Excremental Skies." *CP*, 8: 53-4 (#1 75).

Reed, W.D. "ET's Baroque Expression." *Greyfriar*, 11: 31-6 (1970).

Taylor, Edward

Reiter, R.E. "Poetry and Typology: ET's *Preparatory Meditations*, Second Series, Numbers 1-30." *EAL*, 5: 111-23 (Sp 70).

*Requa, K.A., and Karl Keller. "Additions to the ET Checklist." *EAL*, 4: 117-9 (Sp 70).

Rowe, K.E. "A Biblical Illumination of Taylorian Art." *AL*, 40: 370-4 (N 68).

———. "Sacred or Profane? ET's Meditations on Canticles." *MP*, 72: 123-38 (1974).

*Russell, Gene. "Addenda to an ET Bibliography." BB, *27: 68-9 (Jl-S 70)*.

———. "Dialectal and Phonetic Features of ET's Rymes: A Brief Study Based upon a Computer Concordance of His Poems." *AL*, 43: 165-80 (My 71).

———. "T's 'Upon Wedlock, and Death of Children.'" *Expl*, 27: 71 (My 69).

Sadler, L.V. "The Spider and the Elf in Lovelace and T." *AN&Q*, 11: 151 (1973).

Scheick, W.J. "Man's Wildred State and the Curious Needlework of Providence: The Self in ET's *Preparatory Meditations.*" *TSL*, 17: 129-37 (1972).

*———. "More Additions to the ET Checklist." *EAL*, 5: 62 (Fa 70).

———. "Nonsense from a Lisping Child: ET on the Word as Piety." *TSLL*, 13: 39-53 (Sp 71).

———. "Tending the Lord in All Admiring Style: ET's *Preparatory Meditation.*" *Lang&S*, 4: 163-87 (Su 71).

———. "Typology and Allegory: A Comparative Study of George Herbert and ET." *Essays in Lit*, 2: 76-86 (Sp 75).

———. "A Viper's Nest, the Featherbed of Faith: ET on the Will." *EAL*, 5: 45-56 (Fa 70).

Secor, Robert. "T's 'Upon a Spider Catching a Fly.'" *Expl*, 26; 42 (1968).

Sharma, M.L. "Of Spinning, Weaving, and Mystical Poetry: The Fine Yarn of T, Indian Yogis, and Persian Sufis." *Mahfil*, 6: 51-61 (1970).

Siebel, Kathy, and T.M. Davis. "ET and the Cleansing of Aqua Vitae." *EAL*, 4: 102-9 (Wi 70).

Simonetti, Francis. "Prosody as a Unifying Element in 'Huswifery.'" *BSUF*, 14: 30-1 (Fa 73).

Slethaug, G.E. "ET's Copy of Thomas Taylor's *Types*: A New T Document." *EAL*, 8: 132-9.

Sluder, L.L. "God in the Background: ET as Naturalist." *EAL*, 7: 265-71 (Wi 73).

Sowd, David. "ET's Answer to a 'Popist Pamphlet.'" *EAL*, 9: 307-14 (Wi 75).

Stanford, D.E. "ET and the 'Hermophrodite' Poems of John Cleveland." *EAL*, 8: 59-61 (Sp 73).

———. "ET Versus the 'Young Cockerill' Benjamin Ruggles: A Hitherto Unpublished Episode from the Annals of Early New England Church History." *NEQ*, 44: 459-68 (71).

———. "The Puritan Poet as Preacher—An ET Sermon." *LSUS*, 8: 1-10 (1960).

———. "To the Editor." *EAL*, 5: 60-1 (Sp 70).

———. "Two Notes on ET." *EAL*, 6: 89-90 (Sp 71).

Walsh, J.P. "Solomon Stoddard's Open Communion: A Re-examination." *NEQ*, 43: 97-114 (1970).

Weber, Alfred. "ET: Besprechung einer T-Ausgabe." *JA*, 7: 320-4 (1962).

Werge, Thomas. "The Tree of Life in ET's Poetry: The Sources of a Puritan Image." *EAL*, 19-204 (Wi 68-69).

Taylor, John. Duke, Maurice. "JT of Caroline, 1753-1824: Notes Toward a Bibliography." *EAL*, 6: 69-72 (Sp 71).

Taylor, Peter. Brooks, Cleanth. "The Southern Temper." *Archiv*, 206: 1-15 (My 69).

Goodwin, Stephen. "An Interview with PT." *Shen*, 24: 3-20 (Wi 73).

Howard, Richard. "'Urgent Need and Unbearable Fear.'" *Shen*, 24: 3-20 (Wi 73).

Overmyer, Janet. "Sex and the Fancy Woman." *NCLit*, 4: 8-10 (#4 74).

Peden, William. "A Hard and Admirable Toughness: The Stories of PT." *HC*, 7: 1-9 (F 70).

Pinkerton, Jan. ''A Critical Distortion of PT's 'At the Drugstore.''' *NCLit*, 1: 6-7 (S 71).

———. ''The Non-Regionalism of PT.'' *GaR*, 24: 432-40 (Wi 70).

Raskin, Barbara. ''Southern Fried.'' *NRep*, 161: 29-30 (18 O 69).

Smith, J.P. ''Narration and Theme in T's *A Woman of Means*.'' *Critique*, 9: 19-30 (1967).

———. ''A PT Checklist.'' *Critique*, 9: 31-6 (1967).

Teasdale, Sara. Buchan, Vivian. ''ST, 1884-1933.'' *BB*, 25: 120-3 (Ja-Ap 68).

Cohen, E.H. ''The Letters of ST to Jessie B. Rittenhouse.'' *RALS*, 4: 225-7 (1974).

Thomas, Augustus. Lewis, J.G. ''The AT Collection at the University of North Carolina.'' *RALS*, 4: 72-89 (1974).

Moss, Howard. ''A Thin, Curly Little Person.'' *NY*, 43: 185-9 (7 O 67).

Thompson, Benjamin. Eckstein, N.T. ''The Pastoral and the Primitive in BT's 'Address to Lord Bellamont.''' *EAL*, 8: 11-6 (Fa 73).

Thompson, Maurice. Fertig, W.L. ''MT's Primitive Baptist Heritage.'' *IMH*, 64: 1-12.

Flanagan, J.T. ''A Letter from MT.'' *IMH*, 64: 13-4 (Mr 68).

Moore, R.S. ''The Old South and the New: Paul Hamilton Hayne and MT.'' *SLJ*, 5: 108-22 (Fa 72).

Thompson, William Tappan. Ellison, G.R. ''WIT and the *Southern Miscellany*, 1842-1844.'' *MissQ*, 23: 155-68 (Sp 70).

McKeithan, D.M. ''Mark Twain's Letters of Thomas Jefferson Snodgrass.'' *PQ*, 32: 353-65 (O 53).

Miller, H.P. ''The Authorship of *The Slave-Holder Abroad*.'' *JSH*, 10: 92-4 (F 44).

Thoreau, Henry David. Anon. ''Actualite du Philosophe H.D.T.'' *Hum*, 73: 5-16 (Mr 69).

———. ''Orleans Collector Discovers T Notes for 'Cape Cod.''' *CapeC*, 25 Jl 74, p. 12-4.

———. ''T's Walden.'' *N&Q*, 21: 229 (Je 74).

Adams, Raymond. ''HT, Concord, Mass.'' *TSB*, 128: 3-5 (Su 74).

Adams, Richard. ''Architecture and the Romantic Tradition.'' *AQ*, 46-62 (Sp 57).

Ahearn, Kerry. ''T and John Brown: What to Do about Evil.'' *TJQ*, 6: 24-8 (Jl 74).

Albrecht, R.C. ''Conflict and Resolution: 'Slavery in Massachusetts.''' *ESQ*, 19: 179-88 (3Q 73).

Allaback, Steven. ''Oak Hall in American Literature.'' *AL*, 46: 545-9 (Ja 75).

Allen, G.W. ''T's Books for Mrs. Emerson.'' *TLJ*, 5: 4-5 (1973).

Allison, Elliott. ''Notes and Queries.'' *TSB*, 121: 8 (Fa 72).

———. ''HT and Horace Greeley Attend 'I Puritani.''' *ConS*, 10: 10-2 (D 75).

———. ''T of Monadnock.'' *TJQ*, 5: 15-21 (1973).

Anastaplo, George. ''On Civil Disobedience: T and Socrates.'' *SWR*, 54: 203-14 (Sp 69).

Anderson, A.J. ''T: A Provisional Interpretation.'' *TJQ*, 3: 1-10 (Jl 71).

Anderson, Barbara. ''T and Mary Austin.'' *TSB*, 126: 7 (Wi 74).

Anderson, C.R. ''Right on, Henry David.'' *Natural Hist*, 80: 22-8 (F 71).

———. ''T Takes a Pot Shot at *Carolina Sports*.'' *GaR*, 22: 289-99 (Fa 68).

———. ''T's Monastic Vows.'' *EA*, 22: 11-20 (Ja-Mr 69).

Anderson, Quentin. ''T on July 4.'' *NYT*, 4 Jl 71, pp. 1, 16-18.

Arendt, Hannah. ''Reflections: Civil Disobedience.'' *NY*, 46: 70-105 (12 S 70).

Arner, R.D. ''The Deserted Village of Walden Woods: T's Ruin Piece.'' *ATQ*, 14: 13-5 (Sp 72).

———. ''The Story of Hannah Dustin from Cotton Mather to T.'' *ATQ*, 18: 19-23 (Sp 73).

Babcock, C.M. ''HDT: In Defense of the Wilderness.'' *UCQ*, 16: 25-8 (Mr 71).

Bailey, H.S. ''T and Us.'' *SchP*, 2: 327-8 (Jl 71).

———. ''T Changed the World— and the World Changed Him.'' *University*, 38: 15-9 (Fa 68).

Baker, Gail. ''Friendship in T's *Week*.'' *TJQ*, 7: 3-15 (Ap 75).

Baldwin, H.I. "Letter to Gilbert Byron." *LW*, 32: 35 (Wi 68).

―――. "The Vegetation of Mt. Monadnock." *ForN*, 99: 12-3 (fa 68).

Balota, Nicolse. "*Walden.*" *RoLit*, 26 Je 74: 20.

Barnes, Carlotta. "T in the Eyes of Today's Concord." *TSB*, 125: 5-6 (1973).

Barron, Alfred. "T at the Oneida Community." *TSB*, 115: 3-5 (1971).

Basile, J.L. "The Playful Profundity of T and Frost." *TJQ*, 6: 22-3 (Ja 74).

―――. "Technology and the Artist in *A Week.*" *ATQ*, 11: 87-91 (Su 71).

Bassett, Charles. "Katahdin, Wachusett, and Kilimanjaro: The Symbolic Mountains of T and Hemingway." *TJQ*, 3: 1-10 (15 Ap 71).

Bassett, T.D.S., and J.J. Duffy. "The Library of James Marsh." *ESQ*, 63: 2-10 (1971).

Beardslee, Martin. "A Walk to Walden." *TSQ*, 1: 17-21 (1 Jl 69).

Becker, T.H. "T's Princely Leisure." *HussR*, 3: 161-7 (1970).

Benoit, Raymond. "Walden as God's Drop." *AL*, 43: 122-4 (Mr 71).

Benton, M.T. "Collector T." *TJQ*, 21-2 (15 O 69).

Benton, T. "T's Concord Reputation in Indian Matters." *TJQ*, 2: 13-6 (15 Ap 70).

Berger, Robert. "The Individualism of HDT." *Van Eyes Wise*, 104: 1-2 (8 My 70).

Berkowitz, Morton. "T and Richard Baxter." *TSB*, 131: 4 (Sp 75).

Berti, Luigi. "Saggio su T." *Inventario*, 4: 1-15 (1950).

Bickman, Martin. "Flawed Words and Stubborn Sounds: Another Look at Structure and Meaning in *Walden.*" *SHR*, 8: 153-62 (Sp 74).

Bier, Jesse. "Romantic Coordinates of American Literature." *BuR*, 18: 16-33 (Fa 70).

―――. "Weberism, Franklin, and the Transcendental Style." *NEQ*, 43: 179-92 (Je 70).

Bigelow, G.E. "Summer Under Snow: T's 'A Winter Walk.'" *ESQ*, 56: 13-16 (3Q 69).

―――. "T's Melting Sandbank: Birth of a Symbol." *IntJS*, 2: 7-13 (1971).

Black, A.B. "T and the Lawyer." *TJQ*, 7: 26-7 (#1 75).

Blanding, Thomas. "Editing T's Unpublished Journal Fragments." *ConS*, 5: 4-7 (Jl 70).

―――. "Emerson, T, and the Ice-Harp." *ConS*, 9: 1-2 (Mr 74).

―――. "H.G.O. Blake Again." *ConS*, 7: (Je 72).

―――. "Mary Russell Watson's Reminiscenes of T." *ConS*, 9: 1-6 (Je 74).

―――. "A New Sophia Thoreau Letter to Daniel Ricketson." *ConS*, 7: 1-6 (S 72).

―――. "A New T Letter." *ConS*, 6: 4-6 (Je 71).

―――. "Of New Bedford 'Feelosofers' and Concord Real Estate." *ConS*, 8: 2-8 (Je 73).

―――. "T Responds to a Gift from Emerson." *ConS*, 6: 9-10 (Je 71).

―――. "Turning Over a New T Leaf." *ConS*, 6: 12-4 (Je 71).

―――. "Walton and *Walden.*" *TSB*, 107: 3 (Sp 69).

Blau, P.E. "In Memoriam: HDT." *BakSJ*, 19: 152-3 (S 69).

Bly, William. "The Hermit Days of HT and Thomas Merton." *TSB*, 130: 2-3 (Wi 75).

Bode, Carl. "A Problem in Arithmetic." *TSB*, 130: 3 (Wi 75).

―――. "T's Poetry." *Poetry Pilot*, 4: 9-10 (Je 72).

Bonner, W.H. "Cape Cod Colossus." *ConS*, 8: 11-4 (Mr 73).

―――. "'I Presume This Is Mr. T.'" *ConS*, 7: 7-8 (Mr 72).

―――. "Thalassa, Thalassa! T at Newport?" *TSB*, 120: 7-8 (Su 72).

―――. "T's Native Port." *CAAS*, 3: 45-72 (Wi 68).

―――. "T's Other Telegraph Figure." *AN&Q*, 7: 99-100 (Mr 69).

―――. "T's River and T's Sea." *ConS*, 9: 2-4 (Mr 74).

―――, and M.A. Budge. "T and Robinson Crusoe: An Overview." *TJQ*, 5: 16-8 (Ap 73).

Borst, David. "The Final Years: T Printings, 1860- May 6, 1862." *ConS*, 10: 1-4 (Mr 75).

Borst, R.R. "Cholmondeley's Gift to Mrs. T." *ConS*, 8: 1-4 (D 73).

―――. "A Decade of T Printings: the 1850's." *ConS*, 9: 6-10 (Je 74).

————. "The Final Years: T Printings 1860-May 6, 1862." *ConS*, 10: 1-9 (Mr 75).

————. "Footnotes on T Taken from *The Critic*." *TSB*, 133: 3-7 (Fa 750.

————. "The Playful Breeze." *TD*, 2: 8-11 (F 71).

————. "Progress." *TD*, 4: 12-6 (Wi 74).

————. "T Advertisements from the *Atlantic Monthly*." *TSB*, 129: 4-6 (Fa 74).

————. "T's Seasons." *ConS*, 7: 3-6 (Mr 72).

————. "T's Still-Born Book." *TD*, 1: 16-8 (S 70).

————. "Warm Day in Concord." *TD*, 1: 10-4 (s 71).

Boudreau, G.V. "HDT, William Gilpin, and the Metaphysical Ground of the Picturesque." *AL*, 45: 357-69 (N 73).

————. "HT's Sound Sense." *OEng*, 1: 7-12 (Sp 72).

————. "'Remember Thy Greater': T and St. Augustine." *ESQ*, 19: 149-60 (3Q 73).

————. "Seeds." *ConS*, 10: 9-11 (Mr 75).

————. "T and Richard C. Trench: Conjectures on the Pickerel Passage of *Walden*." *ESQ*, 20: 117-24 (2Q 74).

————. "West by Southwest: T's Trip to Minnesota." *Heights*, 10: 22-7 (Fa 72).

Brain, Bruce. "From Walden to Fairhaven." *Friends of Walden Pond N*, 2: 2-3 (Wi 75).

Brawner, J.P. "T." *TLS*, 4 F 72, pp. 128-9.

Broderick, J.C. "Teaching T." *ESQ*, 18: 3-5 (Sp 60).

————. "Flynndependence." *TSB*, 113: 5 (Fa 70).

Brogan, Katherine. "T's First Experience with Myth in *A Week*." *TJQ*, 7: 3-9 (Ja 75).

Brown, Gilbert. "T's Mountain: Monadnock." *LW*, 31: 45-7 (1968).

Brown, L.S. "The Peter Pan of American Literature." *CEA*, 32: 13 (Ja 70).

Brown, T.H. "The Significant Opening of *Walden*." *ATQ*, 17: 16 (Wi 73).

Brownson, Orestes. "A Sermon to the Young People in Canton, Mass." *ESQ*, 51: 66-74 (2Q 68).

Budge, M.A., and W.H. Bonner. "T and Robinson Crusoe: An Overview." *TJQ*, 5: 16-8 (Ap 73).

Buell, Lawrence. "Transcendentalist Catalogue Rhetoric: Vision Versus Form." *AL*, 40: 32-39 (N 68).

Burke, W.J. "Yes, There's Still a Concord." *Mod Maturity*, 4: 7-9 (F 69).

Burr, M.A. "T's Love and Doubt: An Anagram." *ATQ*, 24: 22-5 (fa 74).

Burress, L.A. "T on Ether and Psychedelic Drugs." *AN&Q*, 12: 99-100 (Mr 74).

Butler, A.F. "T in Minnesota." *Earth J*, 4: 7-8 (Je 74).

————. "T's Three Thousand Bluets." *TSB*, 117: 4 (Fa 71).

Bryon, Gilbert. "HT, Boatman." *TJQ*, 1: 9-14 (1 Jl 69).

————. "Letter to Editor." *Atl*, 224: 26, 28 (Ag 69).

————. "Letter to Henry Baldwin." *LW*, 32: 35 (Wi 68).

Cage, John. "Note Re Recent Texts." *TSB*, 125: 1 (Fa 73).

Cameron, K.W. "Association Copies of T's Books." *ATQ*, 14: 84-7 (1972).

————. "Damning National Publicity for T in 1849." *ATQ*, 2: 18-27 (2Q 69).

————. "Emerson and T Lecture at Lynn." *ATQ*, 14: 158-64 (Sp 72).

————. "Harvard Rules and Certificates of T's Day." *ESQ*, 52: 86-7 (3Q 68).

————. "Over T's Desk: New Correspondence and Revisions." *ATQ*, 8: 6-75 (Fa 70).

————. "Some Scattered T Manuscripts." *ATQ*, 14: 189-94 (1972).

————. "A Tabular View of T's Harvard Curriculum." *ESQ*, 51: 10-25 (2Q 68).

————. "T and the Biography of John Brown." *ATQ*, 17: 17 (1973).

————. "T and Frank Bellew in Concord." *ESQ*, 51: 141-3 (2Q 68).

————. "T and Hiram Leonard." *ATQ*, 14: 135-48 (1972).

———. "T.and His Harvard Classmates." *ATQ*, 3: 1-132 (1969).

———. "T and Orestes Brownson." *ESQ*, 51: 53-65 (2Q 68).

———. "T in the Pulpit." *ATQ*, 20: 1 (Fa 73).

———. "T and Stearns Wheeler: Four Letters and a Reading Record." *ESQ*, 48: 73-81 (3Q 67).

———. "T on the Limitations of Great Circle Sailing." *ATQ*, 14: 70-1 (Sp 72).

———. "T's Declamations at the Concord Academy." *ATQ*, 20: 144-53 (Fa 73).

———. "T's Harvard Friends and Temperance." *ESQ*, 51: 137-41 (2Q 68).

———. "T's Notes on the Shipwreck at Fire Island." *ESQ*, 52: 97-99 (3Q 68).

———. "T's *Walden* and Alcott's Vegetarianism." *ATQ*, 2: 27-8 (2Q 69).

———. "Tribute to T in the *National Anti-Slavery Standard* (1866)." *ATQ*, 14: 73-5 (2Q 72).

———. "Two T Poems: Variant Readings." *ATQ*, 20: 128-9 (3Q 73).

———. "What T Taught in 1837." *ESQ*, 52: 100 (3Q 68).

Campbell, C.L. "*An American Tragedy*; or, Death in the Woods." *MFS*, 15: 251-9 (Su 69).

Carpenter, F.I. "The American Myth': Paradise (to be) Regained." *PMLA*, 74: 599-06 (D 59z0.

Carper, T.R. "The Whole History of T's 'My Prisons.'" *ESQ*, 51: 35-8 (1Q 68).

Carson, Barbara Harrell. "An Orphic Hymn in *Walden*." *ESQ*, 20: 125-30 (2Q 74).

Chang, Chang-nam. "Confucian Influences on T's *Walden*." *ELLS*, 50: 47-68 (1974).

Childs, Christopher. "A Few Thoughts on the Origins of 'Clear Sky, Pure Light.'" *ConS*, 10: 17-8 (Wi 75).

Christie, J.A. "T on Civil Disobedience." *ESQ*, 54: 5-12 (1Q 69).

Christman, Lansing. "T in New York State." *TJQ*, 1: 18-9 (15 Ap 69).

Clarkson, J.W. "Wanted in Concord." *YM*, 34: 129-32 (Ap 69).

Clemens, Cyril. "Personal Glimpses." *Hobbies*, 75: 140-1 (Ap 70).

Clerc, Charles. "The Now T: Caveat Emptor." *MwQ*, 16: 371-88 (Su 75).

Cobb, Robert P. "T and 'the Wild.'" *ESQ*, 18: 5-7 (Sp 60).

Cohen, B.B. "The Perspective of an Old Master." *ESQ*, 56: 53-6 (3Q 69).

Colquitt, B.F. "T's Poetics." *ATQ*, 11: 74-81 (Su 71).

Colyer, Richard. "T's Color Symbols." *PMA*, 86: 999-1008 (O 71).

Conway, M.D. "Emerson, T and the Transcendentalists in 1864-1866." *ATQ*, 16: 62-81 (1Q 72).

———. "T." *ATQ*, 16: 72-81 (1Q 72).

———. "Tribute to T in the *National Anti-Slavery Standard*." *ATQ*, 16: 73-4 (1Q 72).

Cook, R.L. "An Encounter with Myth at Walden." *ATQ*, 2: 39-42 (Sp 71).

———. "My Walden Equivalence." *TJQ*, 5: 3-5 (Ap 73).

———. "This Side of *Walden*." *Eng Leaflet*, 53: 1-12 (D 54).

———. "T in Perspective." *UR*, 14: 117-25 (1957).

Cooke, J.W. "Freedom in the Thought of HDT." *TSB*, 105: 1-3 (Fa 68).

Corner, Philip. "T and Ives with Specifics for This Time." *Soundings*, 174, pp. 15-39.

Coulter, Deborah. "Lyceum Receives Gift." *ConS*, 7: 4-7 (D 72).

Couser, G.T. "'The Old Manse,' *Walden*, and the Hawthorne-T Relationship." *ESQ*, 21: 11-20 (1Q 75).

———. "T's Cape Cod Pilgrimage." *ATQ*, 26: 31-6 (Sp 75).

Cummins, R.W. "T and Isaac Newton Goodhue." *TSB*, 123: 2 (Sp 73).

Curtis, David. "Three Who Taught: Whitman, T, and Melville as Teachers." *Childhood Ed*, 19: 38-9 (Wi 68).

Curtis, S.A.S. "T in Fungiland." *Boston Mycological Club Bul*, 2: 1-6 (1964).

D'Avanzo, M.L. "Fortitude and Nature in T's *Cape Cod.*" *ESQ*, 20: 131-38 (2Q 74).

———. "T's *Walden*, Chapter XVI." *Expl*, 29: 41 (Ja 71).

———. "*Walden*, 'The Beanfield.'" *TJQ*, 3: 11-3 (JL 71).

Davenport, Cynthia. "On T's Ancestry." *TSB*, 107: 7-8 (Sp 69).

Davidson, Frank. "T and David Starr Jordan." *TSB*, 109: 5-6 (Fa 69).

Davies, Barrie. "Sam Quixote in Lower Canada: A Reading of T's *A Yankee in Canada.*" *HAB*, 20: 67-77 (Fa 69).

Davies, John. "T and George Sturt." *TSB*, 113: 5-6 (Fa 70).

Dean, D.R. "Hitchock's Dinosaur Tracks." *AQ*, 21: 639-44 (Fa 69).

DeFalco, J.M. "'The Landlord': T's Emblematic Technique." *ESQ*, 56: 23-32 (3Q 69).

———. "T's Ethic and the 'Bloody Revolution.'" *Topic*, 6: 43-9 (Fa 66).

DeMott, Richard. "T and the Saranac Panther." *TJQ*, 6: 5-6 (Ja 74).

———. "T and 'Our Cabin.'" *TJQ*, 5: 19-24 (Ja 73).

Dennis, Carl. "The Balance of Walden." *TJQ*, 2: 1-9 (Ap 70).

———. "Correspondence in T's Nature Poetry." *ESQ*, 58: 101-9 (1Q 70).

Desai, Rupin. "Biblical Light on T's Axe." *TSB*, 134 (Fa 75).

Devlin, James. "HT and Gilbert White: Concord and Selborne." *XUS*, 11: 6-15 (Fa 72).

Dickens, Robert. "T on Slavery, Economy, and Alienation." *Anarchy Mag*, 8: 18-24 (1972).

Diggins, J.P. "T, Marx, and the 'Riddle' of Alienation." *Soc Res*, 39: 571-98 (Wi 72).

Dodd, L.H. "T to the Twentieth Century." *Goddard Bibl Log*, 3: 52-62 (Wi 73).

Domina, Lyle. "Conversation Folded Thick: The Techniques of T's Art." *Aegis*, 1: 21-7 (1973).

Eastman, John. "In Wilderness Is Fire." *LW*, 36: 11-6 (Sp 72).

Eaton, R.J. "Gowing's Swamp." *MassA*, 53: 31-4 (Je 69).

———. "T's Herbarium." *M&N*, D 72, pp. 2-5.

Edel, Leon. "Walden: The Myth and the Mystery." *ASch*, 44: 272-81 (Sp 75).

Eidson, J.O. "Charles Stearns Wheeler: Friend of Emerson." *ESQ*, 52: 13-75 (3Q 68).

Eisenberg, Philip. "HDT, Apostle of Civil Disobedience." *Amerykan*, 121: 22-4, 148: 22-4 (F 69).

Elmore, A.E. "Symmetry Out of Season: The Form of 'Walden.'" *SAB*, 37: 18-24 (N 72).

Emerson, E.W. "Letter to Miss Nevins." *ConS*, 4: 6-7 (Mr 69).

Enderle, Robert. "Beans." *TJQ*, 4: 10-2 (15 Ap 72).

Erickson, Morris. "T: Letting the Sun Shine In." *ETC*, 29: 35-45 (Mr 72).

Erlich, M.G. "T's 'Civil Disobedience': Strategy for Reform." *Conn R*, 7: 100-10 (O 73).

Evans, R.O. "T's Poetry and the Prose Works." *ESQ*, 56: 40-52 (Au 69).

Ezekiel, Nissim. "T and Gandhi." *EWR*, 4: 1-9 (Sp 71).

———. "The T-Gandhi Syndrome: An Ambiguous Influence." *Quest*, 58: 21-6 (Jl-S 68).

Fabre, Michel. "La désobéissance civile." *Europe*, 477: 214-17 (1969).

Fairbanks, Jonathan. "T: Speaker for Wildness." *SAQ*, 70: 487-506 (Au 71).

Fauchereau, Serge. "Le Philosophe des bois." *QL*, 45: 11-2 (15 F 68).

Fenn, M.G. "Melvin: Friend of T." *TSB*, 132: 4 (Su 75).

———. "Report from the Concord Walking Society: Yellow Birch Cellar Hole." *TSB*, 113: 2 (Fa 70).

———. "Susan Loring on T." *TSB*, 129: 1 (Fa 74).

———. "T's Rivers: Concord, Massachusetts." *TSBk*, 27: 16 (1973).

Fergenson, Laraine. "Was Thoreau Re-reading Wordsworth in 1851?" *TJQ*, 5: 20-3 (Jl 73).

Ferguson, H.N. "Nonconformist of Walden Pond." *Unity*, 12: 19-24 (Ag 68).

Ferguson, Malcolm. "An Indifferent Drummer No Longer." *ConS*, 9: 4-5 (Mr 74).

———. "Notes on T and New Hampshire." *ConS*, 7: 2-4 (Je 72).

Ferlazzo, P.J. "T's Sense of Natural Time." *TJQ*, 4: 16-8 (Ja 72).

Fink, Jack E. "A Caveat for Journalists." *WSt*, 39: 7 (D 63).

Flack, Micheline. "Un village inspire." *LNP*, 21: 5-15 (Mr 71).

Fleck, Richard. "Evidence for T's 'Indian' Notebooks as Being a Source for His *Journal*." *TJQ*, 1: 17-9 (15 O 69).

———. "Hawthorne's Possible Use of T in *The Marble Faun*." *TJQ*, 6: 8-12 (Ap 74).

———. "Hawthorne's Reflections at Walden Pond." *ConS*, 8: 5-6 (D 73).

———. "Mikhail Prishvin: A Russian T." *ConS*, 9: 11-3 (Je 74).

———. "A Note on HDT's Literary Nationalism." *ConS*, 6: 4-7 (S 71).

———. "A Note on T's Mist Verse." *TJQ*, 1: 1-5 (Jl 69).

———. "A Report on Irish Interest in T." *TJQ*, 6: 21-7 (O 74).

———. "T, Emerson, Whitman in the Western Wilderness." *JANSS*, nv: 9-11 (Sp 69).

———. "T and the Mystic Lore of Cape Cod." *ConS*, 5: Sup (D 70).

———. "T and the Mystic Lore of Wildlife." *DWN*, 45: 322-4 (Fa 70).

———. "T as Mythmaker and Fabulist." *Rendezvous*, 9: 23-32 (Sp 74-Wi 75).

———. "T as Mythologist." *RSW*, 40: 195-206 (S 72).

———. "T's 'Indian Notebooks' and the Composition of *Walden*." *ConS*, 7: 2-4 (Je 72).

———. "T's Mythological Humor." *ConS*, 10: 1-6 (Je 75).

———. "T's New England Mythology." *TJQ*, 4: 1-9 (Ja 72).

Ford, A.L. "The Poetry of HDT." *ESQ*, 61: 1-26 (4Q 70).

Ford, T.W. "T and Lecturing." *MTJ*, 17: 8-13 (Wi 73-74).

———. "T's Cosmic Mosquito and Dickinson's Fly." *NEQ*, 48: 487-504 (D 75).

Foster, Leslie D. "*Walden* and Its Audiences: Troubled Sleep, and Religious and Other Awakenings." *MLR*, 67: 756-762 (O 72).

Friedensohn, Doris. "The Trip to Walden Pond: Some Notes on Experimental Teaching and Some Models." *Connections*, 3: 2-11 (Wi 72).

Friesen, V.C. "Alexander Henry and T's Climb of Mount Katahdin." *TSB*, 123: 5-6 (Sp 73).

———. "HT and Our Northwestern Wilderness." *North* (Ottawa), 21: 30-5 (N 74).

———. "HT and Saskatchewan's Natural History." *Blue Jay* (Saskatchewan), 32: 13-5 (Mr 74).

———. "My Introduction to T." *TSB*, 127: 7 (Sp 74).

———. "Sensuousness in T's Approach to Nature: 'Conclusion.'" *TSB*, 103: 2 (Sp 68).

Frome, Mechael. "T's Maine Woods." *Vista*, 9: 3-5 (Fa 73).

Frye, Northrop. "Varieties of Literary Utopias." *Daedalus*, 94: 323-47 (Sp 65).

Fuller, Richard. "Visit to the Wachusett: July 1842." *TSB*, 121: 1-4 (Fa 72).

Funk, A.A. "HDT's 'Slavery in Massachusetts.'" *WSp*, 36: 159-68 (Su 72).

Gagnon, Ray. "T: Some Negative Considerations." *TSB*, 121: 5-7 (Fa 72).

Galgan, G.J. "T on the 'Political.'" *TJQ*, 6: 19-21 (Jl 74).

Galligan, E.L. "'The Comedian at Walden Pond.'" *SAQ*, 69: 20-37 (Wi 70).

*Garate, Justo. "T in the Spanish Language: A Bibliography." *ESBk*, 24: 3-11 (Ap 70).

Garber, Frederick. "Unity and Diversity in 'Walking.'" *ESQ*, 56: 35-40 (3Q 69).

Gerstenberger, Donna L. "*Walden*: The House That Henry Built." *ESQ*, 56: 11-3 (Au 69).

Geselbracht, Raymond. "The Ghosts of Andrew Wyeth: The Meaning of Death in Transcendental Myth of America." *NEQ*, 47: 13-29 (Mr 74).

Gibbs, Jean. "Dorothy Livesay and the Transcendentalist Tradition." *HAB*, 21: 24-39 (1970).

Gilley, Leonard. "Transcendentalism in *Walden*." *PrS*, 42: 204-7 (Fa 68).

Glazier, Lyle. "T's Rebellious Lyric." *ESQ*, 54: 27-30 (1Q 69).

Glick, Wendell. "An Early Encounter with Joe Polis?" *TJQ*, 3: 12-5 (Ja 71).

————. "Go Tell It to the Mountain: T's Vocation as Writer." *ESQ*, 19: 161-9 (3Q 73).

————. "T Rejects an Emerson Text." *SB*, 25: 213-6 (1972).

————. "T's Use of His Sources." *NEQ*, 44: 101-9 (Mr 71).

Goudie, Andrea. "Exploring the Broad Margins: Charles Ives's Interpretation of T." *MwQ*, 13: 309-17 (Sp 72).

Gozzi, R.D. "An Editorial Mishap by T in *A Week*? A Textual Note." *TSB*, 119: 6-7 (Sp 72).

————. "An Incoherent Sentence in *Walden*." *TSB*, 95: 4-5 (Sp 66).

————. "*Walden* and a Carlyle Letter." *TSB*, 118: 4 (Wi 72).

Greenwood, Douglas. "A Prospect of the Mountains West of Concord: T's Poetic Vision." *TJQ*, 6: 16-27 (Ap 74).

Greiner, D.J. "Emerson, T, and Hemingway: Some Suggestions About Literary Heritage." *FHA*, 1971, pp. 247-61.

Guerrier, G.P. "T and the Summer School of Philosophy." *ATQ*, 26: 40s-1s (1975).

Gundelwein, Francoise and Genevieve. "HD.T et son actualite." *Bibliotheque de Travail*, 70: 1-38 (Je 75).

Gura, P.F. "T and John Josselyn." *NEQ*, 48: 505-18 (D 75).

Gurney, Richard. "The Worst of T." *ConnR*, 3: 68-71 (Ap 70).

Haddin, Theodore. "T's Reputation Once More." *TJQ*, 4: 10-5 (Ap 72).

Halperin, Irving. "T on Walking by Day and Night." *CanA*, 30: 1-4 (Ja 68).

Hamblen, A.A. "Laddie: Journal of an Indiana T." *JPC*, 4: 85-9 (Su 70).

Hamby, J.A. "T's Synthesizing Metaphor: Two Fishes with One Hook." *BRMMLA*, 27: 17-22 (Sp 73).

Hame, R.A. "February, T, and Spring." *Rendezvous*, 2: 23-6 (Sp 67).

Hand, H.E. "T at One Hundred and Fifty." *HartR*, 4: 52-5 (Sp 68).

Hanley, Katherine. "*Walden*—Forest Sonata." *ATQ*, 1: 108-10 (Sp 68).

Harding, B.R. "Redskins and Transcendentalists: A Reading of *A Week on the Concord and Merrimack Rivers*." *RSW*, 40: 274-84 (1972).

————. "Swedenborgian Spirit and Thorcauvian Sense." *JAmSt*, 8: 66-79 (Ap 74).

*Harding, Walter. "Additions to the T Bibliography." *TSB*, quarterly.

————. "The Alfred Hosmer Letter Files." *TSB*, 119: 7 (Sp 72).

————. "Another Early Review of *Walden*." *TSB*, 129: 8 (Fa 74).

————. "Civilized Disobedience." *StoS*, 22: 41-8 (N 70).

————. "The Daniel J. Bernstein Collection." *TSB*, 127: 1 (74).

————. "Daniel Ricketson's Copy of *Walden*." *HLB*, 15: 401-11 (O 67).

————. "*Delugeous* or *Detergeous* or?" *CEANN*, 1: 5-6 (1968).

————. "The Early Printing Records of T's Books." *ATQ*, 11: 44-59 (Su 71).

————. "An Early Review of T's *Week*." *TSB*, 130: 8 (Wi 75).

————. "Elizabeth Oakes Smith on T." *TSB*, 110: 2-3 (Wi 70).

————. "First T Edition Volumes to Printer." *Chronica*, 2: 8-11 (N 68).

————. "The First Year's Sales of T's *Walden*." *TSB*, 117: 1-3 (Fa 71).

————. "Five Ways of Looking at *Walden*." *MR*, 4: 149-62 (Au 62).

————. "George Sturt and T." *TSB*, 111: 3-5 (Sp 70).

————. "Horace Greeley on T: A Forgotten Portrait." *TSB*, 116: 5-7 (Su 71).

————. "An Indenture for John T's Store." *TSB*, 129: 7-8 (Fa 74).

————. "John Shepard Keyes on T." *TSB*, 103: 2-3 (Sp 68).

————. "L'Influence de la Désobeissance Civile." *Europe*, 45: 186-204 (Jl-Ag 67).

————. "More Excerpts from the Alfred Hosmer Letter Files." *TSB*, 123: 6-7 (Sp 73).

————. "More Doctoral Dissertations on T." *TSB*, 114: 6-7 (Wi 71); 117: 7-8 (Fa 71); 126: 8 (Wi 74): 133: 7-8 (Fa 75).

————. "A New Hampshire Concordian Looks at T's *Week*." *ConS*, 9: 12 (D 74).

———. "A New T Document." *TSB*, 120: 7 (Su 72).

———. "Plan of Nathaniel Hawthorne's Estate in Concord, Mass." *ESQ*, 48: 86 (3Q 67).

———. "Report from Walden." *YM*, 34: 64ff. (S 70).

———. "A Source for a Walden Anecdote." *TSB*, 115: 7 (Sp 71).

———. "T and Astrology." *TSB*, 126: 8 (Wi 74).

———. "T and 'Civil Disobedience.'" *TSB*, 103: 8 (Sp 68).

———. "T and Ecology." *TSB*, 123: 6 (Sp 73).

———. "T at the Boston Music Hall." *TSB*, 105: 7 (Fa 68).

———. "T at the Oneida Community." *TSB*, 115: 3-5 (Sp 71).

———. "The T Collectors' Guide." *TSBk*, 26: 1-12 (D 72); 134: 2-6 (Wi 75).

———. "T and the Lecture Platform." *TSB*, 127: 6-7 (Wi 73).

———. "T in Jail." *AH*, 26: 36-7 (Ag 75).

———. "T on the Lecture Platform." *TSB*, 125: 6-7 (Fa 73).

———. "T's Curiosity." *PHP*, 14: 75 (N 71).

———. "T's Ghosts." *Yankee*, 39: 110-2 (O 75).

Harris, K.E. "T's 'The Service'—A Review of the Scholarship." *ATQ*, 11: 60-3 (Su 71).

Hart, R.L. "The Poiesis of Place." *JR*, 53: 36-47 (Ja 73).

Hasegawa, Yozo. "An Estrangement between Idea and Sense: A Contradiction and a Transfiguration of *Walden*." *WJGC*, 6: 17-35 (D 70).

———. "An Oriental Mind in T in Comparison with Ryokan or a Japanese Priest." *Wased R* (Tokyo), 4: 36-48 (My 66).

———. "The Theory of Solitude: *Walden*." *WJGC*, 5: 27-38 (D 69).

Hasselberger, William. "T's Poetics." *ConS*, 7: 1-4 (D 72).

Hendren, Ken. "A Walk Along a Forester's Footsteps." *TJQ*, 6: 31-3 (O 74).

Hendrick, George. "Thoughts on the Variorum *Civil Disobedience*." *ESQ*, 56: 60-2 (3Q 69).

Herr, William. "A More Perfect State: T's Concept of Civil Government." *MR*, 16: 470-87 (Su 75).

———. "T: A Civil Disobedient?" *Ethics*, 85: 87-91 (O 74-75).

———. "T on Violence." *TSB*, 131: 2-4 (Sp 75).

Hess, M.W. "T and Hecker: Freemen, Friends, Mystics." *CathW*, 209: 265-7 (S 69).

Higashiyama, Masayoshi. "A Japanese View of HDT." *TLQ*, 7: 25-9 (Jl 75).

*Hildenbrand, C.A. "A Bibliography of Scholarship about HDT: 1940-1967." *FHays*, 3: 1-56 (Ag 67).

Hill, D.B. "Getting to *Walden*: The Strategies of T's Thought." *BSUF*, 15: 14-26 (Sp 74).

Hoagland, Clayton. "T as Educator." *Pleasures in Learning*, 10: 5-10 (My 62).

Hoch, D.G. "Concord's Coat of Arms." *TSB*, 110: 1 (Wi 70).

———. "Ex Oriente Lux: T's Allusions to the Emblem of the Oriental Translation Fund and a Bibliography of the Fund's Publications through 1854." *Serif*, 9: 25-30 (Sp 72).

———. "Theory of History in *A Week*: Annals and Perennials." *ESQ*, 56: 32-5 (3Q 69).

———. "T's Source for the Story of the King's Son." *TJQ*, 2: 10-2 (Ap 70).

———. "T's Use of *The Hindoos*." *TSB*, 114: 1-2 (Wi 71).

Hocks, R.A. "T, Coleridge, and Barfield: Reflections on the Imagination and the Law of Polarity." *CentR*, 17: 175-98 (Sp 73).

Hodges, Robert. "The Functional Satire of T's Hermit and Poet." *SNL*, 8: 105-09 (Sp 71).

Holtje, H. "Misconceptions in Current T Criticism." *PQ*, 47: 563-70 (O 68).

Hoffleit, Dorritt. "T on Nantucket Island." *TJQ*, 2: 15-6 (Jl 70).

Holland, J.M. "Pattern and Meaning in T's *A Week*." *ESQ*, 50: 48-55 (IQ 68).

Holman, David. "The Spiritual and the Wild: T's Middle Way." *TJQ*, 6: 8-13 (Ja 74).

Homan, John. "T, the Emblem, and the *Week*." *ATQ*, 1: 104-8 (1969).

Hough, H.B. "T in Today's Sun." *TSB*, 108: 2-4 (Su 69).

Hourdin, Georges. "Le Premier des non-vilents: HDT." *VCath*, 1209: 22-3 (15 O 68).

Howarth, W.L. "From Concord North Bridge: T and the American Revolution." *TSB*, 134: 1-2 (Wi 75).

———. "Of Night and Moonlight." *ConS*, 7: 7-8 (D 72).

———. "Response, By the Numbers." *TSB*, 130: 3-4 (Wi 75).

———. "Successor to *Walden*? T's 'Moonlight—An Intended Course of Lectures.'" *Proof*, 2: 89-115 (1972).

Hoy, Thorkild. "T som landmaler." *Landinspektoren*, 27: 2-10 (My 73); *Dansk Kartografish Selskab*, 1: 1-9 (1973).

Hubler, Richard. "T and Epicurus." *TSB*, 129: 1-3 (Fa 74).

Hudspeth, R.N. "A Perennial Springtime: Channing's Friendship with Emerson and T." *ESQ*, 54: 30-6 (1Q 69).

Hull, Raymona. "The Cairn at Walden Pond." *TSB*, 103: 2-3 (Sp 68).

———. "Some Further Notes on Hawthorne and T." *TSB*, 121: 7-8 (Fa 72).

Hunsaker, Earl. "T'vian Puzzle." *TD*, 3: 5 (N 73).

Hunt, J.D. "Gandhi, T, and Adin Ballou." *J Liberal Ministry*, 9: 32-52 (Fa 69).

———. "T and Gandhi: A Reevaluation of the Legacy." *Gandhi Marg* (India), 14: 325-32 (1970).

Hyman, S.E. "HT Once More." *MR*, 4: 163-70 (Au 62).

Iida, Minoru. "T's Practice of the Emersonian Philosophy of Nature." *JSJU*, 2: 91-105 (Mr 71).

Inge, M.T. "T's Enduring Laugh." *TJQ*, 2: 1-9 (O 70).

Irvin, J.T. "The Symbol of the Hieroglyphics in the American Renaissance." *AQ*, 26: 103-26 (My 74).

Ito, Kazuo. "On T's Paradox." *RG*, 120: 590-1 (Mr 75).

Jacobs, E.C. "T and Modern Psychology." *TSB*, 127: 4 5 (Sp 74).

Jaques, J.F. "An Enthusiastic Newspaper Account of T's Second Lecture in Portland, Maine, January 15, 1851." *AL*, 40: 385-91 (N 68).

Jacques, J.F. "'Ktaadn'—A Record of T's Youthful Crisis." *TJQ*, 1: 1-6 (15 O 69).

James, D.L. "Movement and Growth in 'Walking.'" *TJQ*, 4: 16-21 (Jl 72).

Jenkins, J.T. "T, Mythology, Simplicity and Self-Culture." *TJQ*, 4: 1-15 (Jl 72).

Jeske, J.M. "*Walden* and the Confucian *Four Books*." *ATQ*, 24: 29-33 (Fa 74).

Johnson, M.C. "T on Drugs." *TSB*, 134: 2 (Wi 75).

Johnson, Tom. "Cage Meets T." *Village Voice*, 20 O 75, p. 90.

Johnston, Joanne. "The Meaning of the Metaphor in T's *Walden*." *TSB*, 116: 3-4 (Su 71).

Johnston, K.G. "Journeys into the Interior: Hemingway, T, and Mungo Park." *Forum(H)*, 10: 27-31 (3Q 72).

———. "T's Star-Spangled Losses: The Hound, Bay Horse and Turtle Dove." *TJQ*, 3: 10-20 (O 71).

Johnstone, C.L. "T and Civil Disobedience: A Rhetorical Paradox." *QJS*, 60: 313-22 (O 74).

Jones, Buford. "'The Hall of Fantasy' and the early Hawthorne-T Relationship." *PMLA*, 83: 1429-38 (O 68).

Jones, S.A. "Some Unpublished Letters of HD. and Sophia E. Thoreau." *ESQ*, 61: 27-59 (1970).

Joost, Nicholas. "A Corollary to Literature." *Renascence*, 13: 33-41 (Au 60).

Kalven, Harry. "T." *CenM*, 3: 62-5 (My 70).

Kameda, Mieko. "H.D.T's Blue and Green World." *SEAL*, 8: 59-75 (Mr 73).

Kamp, Anton. "Forever Walden." *NEH*, 142: 26-7 (Jl 69).

Karabatsos, James. "A World-Index to *A Week on the Concord and Merrimack Rivers*." *ATQ*, 12: 1-99 (Fa 71).

Kasegawa, Koh. "Color in Nature: A View of 'Autumnal Tints.'" *TJQ*, 7: 20-4 (Jl 75).

———. "Hemingway and T." *SEAL*, 16: 1-6 (1970).

———. "A History of the Nature Essay: A Road to T." *StoS*, 23: 31-6 (Ap 71).

———. "Notes on American Nature Writing: Wilderness and Wildness in T." *JCLAG*, 15: 59-76 (Mr 74).

———. "T's Early Nature Essays." *J Col of Lit* (Tokyo), 16: 121-45 (Mr 75).

———. "The Poetic World of *Walden*." *Eng Q*, 7: 114-9 (F 70).

———. "T and Burroughs." *SToS*, 19: 42-6 (30 Mr 69).

———. "T and the Pilgrims." *SToS*, 25: 27-9 (Je 72).

———. "T's Early Nature Essays." *Aoyama J Gen Ed*, 16: 129-45 (Mr 75).

———. "T' Humor in Economy." *Thought Currents in Engl Lit* (Tokyo), 44: 15-28 (Ja 72).

———. "T's Humor in *Walden*." *J Col of Lit* (Tokyo), 12: 1-15 (Mr 69).

———. "T's Humor in *Walden*." *AJGE*, 6: 73-80 (Ja 71).

———. "T's Literary Theory." *Shi To Sambun*, 28: 21-4 (Ag 74).

———. "T's Meteorological Studies." *AJGE*, 10: 35-42 (Ja 70).

———. "The Transcendentalist View of Man in Emerson and T." *SToS*, 19: 35-41 (30 Mr 69).

———. "Wilderness and Wildness in T." *Aoyama J Gen Ed*, 15: 95-102 (N 74).

Katz, Annika. "Slavery and the Development of T's Social Philosophy." *MSpr*, 64: 327-45 (1970).

Kawatsu, Takashi. "The Background of T's Literature." *Eng & Amer Stud* (Tokyo), 8: 1-39 (15 Mr 72).

———. "T and Whitman as Transcendentalists." *Eng & Amer Stud* (Tokyo), 7: 1-25 (15 Mr 71).

Kazin, Alfred. "T and American Power." *Atl*, 223: 60-8 (My 69).

Keller, Karl. "'A Cheerful Elastic Wit': The Metaphysical Strain in T." *TJQ*, 1: 1-17 (Ap 69).

Kern, Alexander C. "Introducing T as Artist and Man." *ESQ*, 18: 12-4 (Sp 60).

Kern, A.C. "T's *Sir Walter Raleigh*." *CEAAN*, 1: 4-5 (1968).

Kestner, J.A. "T and Kamo No Chōmei's Hut." *ATQ*, 14: 6 (Sp 72).

Kettler, Robert. "The Quest for Harmony: A Unifying Approach to *Walden*." *BSUF*, 15: 3-13 (Sp 74).

Keyes, J.S. "John Shephard Keyes on T." *TSB*, 103: 2-3 (Sp 68).

Kim, Kichung, "T's Science and Teleology." *ESQ*, 18: 125-33 (3Q 72).

King, Bruce. "Emerson's Pupil." *Venture*, 5: 112-22 (Ap 69).

Kinkead, Eugene. "T and the Endless Beach." *SatR*, 54: 40, 75-6 (13 Mr 71).

Kirby, David. "Metaphor in the Final Paragraphs of 'The American Scholar' and 'Economy.'" *TJQ*, 2: 17-8 (Jl 70).

Kleinfeld, L.F. "In the Image of T: An Appreciation." *TSB*, 120: 1-4 (Su 72).

———. "In the Shadow of T." *Fragments*, 6-8: 3 (1968).

———. "T Chronology." *ATQ*, 1: 113-7 (1969).

Koenig, Helmut and Gea. "T's Maine." *Travel*, 142: 40-6 (O 74).

Kovar, Anton. "Sophia Foord." *TJQ*, 3: 22-3 (Ja 71).

Kriege, J.W. "Emerson's 'T' (Last Paragraph)." *Expl*, 31: 38 (1973).

Krob, Carol. "Columbus of Concord: *A Week* as a Voyage of Discovery." *ESQ*, 21: 215-21 (4Q 75).

Kurtz, Kenneth. "Style in *Walden*." *ESQ*, 60: 59-67 (1970).

———. "T and Individualism Today." *ESQ*, 18: 14-5 (Sp 60).

Kvastad, N.B. "Mystical Influences in *Walden*." *TJQ*, 6: 3-10 (Jl 74).

Kyria, Pierre. "Regards sur la Litterature Americaine." *RdP*, 16: 117-22 (Mr 68).

*Lacey, J.F. "T in German Criticism: An Annotated Bibliography." *TSB*, 105: 4-6 (Fa 69).

Lambdin, William. "Sounds in *Walden*." *ColQ*, 18: 59-64 (Su 69).

Lane, Lauriat. "*Cape Cod*: T's Sandy Pastoral." *ATQ*, 11: 69-74 (Su 71).

———. "'Civil Disobedience': A Bibliographical Note." *PBSA*, 63: 295-6 (4Q 69).

———. "Finding a Voice: T's Pentameters." *ESQ*, 60: 67-72 (Su 70).

———. "The Structure of Protest: T's Polemic Essays." *HAB*, 20: 34-40 (Fa 69).

———. "T's Autumnal Archetypal Hero: Captain John Brown." *Ariel*, 6: 41-8 (Ja 75).

———. "T's Autumnal Indian." *CRAS*, 6: 228-36 (1975).

———. "T's Two Walks: Structure and Meaning." *TSB*, 109: 1-3 (Fa 69).

———. "T's *Walden*, I, Paragraphs 1-3." *Expl*, 29: 35 (D 70).

———. "*Walden*: The Second Year." *SRom*, 8: 183-92 (Sp 69).

Lang, Berel. "T and the Body Impolitic." *ColQ*, 18: 51-7 (Su 69).

La Rosa, R.C. "DHT [sic]: His American Humor." *SR*, 83: 602-22 (Fa 75).

Las Vergnas, Raymond. "Le triomphe de T." *NL*, 29: 5 (F 68).

Lasser, M.L. "Teaching the Classics." *Eng Rec*, 20: 25-32 (F 70).

Lauter, Paul. "T's Prophetic Testimony." *MR*, 4: 111-23 (Au 62).

Leary, Lewis. "Beyond the Brink of Fear: T's Wilderness." *SLit*, 7: 67-76 (Sp 74).

———. "'Now I Adventured': 1851 as a Watershed Year in T's Career." *ESQ*, 19: 141-48 (3Q 73).

Lebowitz, Martin. "The Condition of Life." *YR*, 64: 132-5 (1974).

Lee, Lynn and Bill. "An Analysis of T's Handwriting." *TSB*, 113: 4-5 (Fa 70).

Lemaitre, Renee. "Actualité du Philosophe H.D.T." *Hum*, 73: 5-16 (Mr 69).

Lennon, F.B. "The Apotheosis of T." *TJQ*, 2: 21-3 (Ap 70).

Leon, Robert. "*Walden*: An Eastern Interpretation." *TSB*, 125: 4 (Fa 73).

Leverenz, David. "Anger and Individualism." *ATQ*, 62: 407-28 (1957).

Levine, Stuart and Susan. "History, Myth, Fable, and Satire: P's Use of Jacob Bryant." *ESQ*, 21: 197-214 (4Q 75).

Link, F.H. "Goethe und die Renaissance des Neuenglischen Geistesiebens im 19 Jahrhundert." *ATQ*, 14: 94-9 (Su 72).

Linstromberg, Robin, and James Ballowe. "T and Etzler: Alternative Views of Economic Reform." *MASJ*, 11: 20-29 (Sp 70).

Livingston, M.W. "Yours Sincerely, Mohandas K. Ghandi." *Prologue*, 1: 1-6 (Fa 69).

Lobet, Marcel. "Relisons T, le Rousseau americain." *Marginales*, 23: 22-6 (D 68).

Lombardo, Agostino. "Thoreau nella cultura italiana." *SA*, 14: 41-62 (1968).

Loney, Glenn. "The Night T Spent in Jail." *After Dark*, 5: 30-3 (Jl 72).

Lowance, M.I. "From Edwards to Emerson to T: A Revaluation." *ATQ*, 18: 3-12 (Sp 73).

Lyttle, David. "T's 'Diamond Body.'" *TJQ*, 7: 18-29 (Ap 75).

McAleer, J.J. "The Therapeutic Vituperations of T." *ATQ*, 11: 81-7 (Su 71).

———. "T's Epic 'Cape Cod.'" *Thought*, 43: 227-46 (Su 68).

McDonald, Walter. "He Took Off: Yossarian and the Different Drummer." *CEA*, 36: 14-6 (N 73).

McDowell, R.S., and C.W. McCutchen. "The T-Reynolds Ridge: A Lost and Found Phenomenon." *Science*, 172: 973 (28 My 71).

McElrath, J.R. "The First Two Volumes of *The Writings of HD.T*." *Proof*, 4: 215-35 (1975).

———. "Nora C. Franklin on Holmes and T." *TJQ*, 5: 17-9 (Jl 73).

———. ''Practical Editions: HD.T's *Walden.*'' *Proof*, 4: 178-82 (1975).

———. ''Sawyer's Tribute to T.'' *ATQ*, 14: 54-66 (Sp 72).

———. ''T and Antony Hecht.'' *TSB*, 113: 6 (Fa 70).

———. ''T and James: Coincidence in Angles of Vision?'' *ATQ*, 11: 14-5 (Su 71).

McGill, F.T. ''On Letting Things Alone.'' *TSB*, 124: 1-3 (Su 73).

———. ''Rutgers Professor Contends T Was Not a Hippie.'' *ESQ*, 50: 97 (1Q 68).

McGrath, A.R. ''HT's Desk.'' *ConS*, 9: 6-9 (Mr 74).

McKone, Thomas. ''Walking as Meditation.'' *Backpacker*, 2: 34-6 (Wi 74).

MacLachlan, C.H. ''The Spiritual Life of HD.T.'' *Vedant and the West*, 191: 46-59 (My 68); 192: 18-32 (Jl 68).

McLean, A.F. ''T's True Meridian: Natural Fact and Metaphor.'' *AQ*, 20: 567-79 (Fa 68).

MacLean, R.L. ''*Walden*: An Eastern Interpretation.'' *TSB*, 125: 4 (Wi 73).

McPhee, John. ''A Reporter at Large: The Survival of the Bark Canoe.'' *NY*, 22 F 75, pp. 49-94; 3 Mr 75, pp. 41-69.

Magnus, J.L. ''More Doctoral Dissertations on T.'' *TSB*, 121: 8 (Fa 72).

Majumdar, R. ''Virginia Woolf and T.'' *TSB*, 109: 4-5 (Fa 69).

Marcello, Leo. ''The Theme of the Divided Self: A Structural Key to *Walden.*'' *TJQ*, 6: 14-8 (Ja 74).

Marks, Barry. ''Retrospective Narrative in Nineteenth Century American Literature.'' *CE*, 31: 366-75 (Ja 70).

Marks, Jason. ''T's Literary Style.'' *Lit R*, 17: 227-37 (Wi 73-74).

Marshall, James M. ''The Heroic Adventure in 'A Winter Walk.''' *ESQ*, 56: 16-23 (Au 69).

Martin, J.R. ''T and the Shad.'' *TJQ*, 6: 28-30 (O 74).

Marx, Leo. ''Two Kingdoms of Force.'' *MR*, 1: 62-95 (O 59).

Mathy, Francis. ''The Three Johns: Portraits of Emerson, T, Hawthorne and Holmes.'' *Eng Lit & Lang* (Tokyo), 10: 163-81 (Mr 74).

Matlack, James. ''The Alta California's Lady Correspondent.'' *NYHSQ*, 58: 280-303 (O 74).

———. ''Early Reviews of *Walden* by the *Alta California* and its 'Lady Correspondent.''' *TSB*, 131: 1-2 (Sp 75).

Mattfield, M.S. ''T's Poem # 189: An Emended Reading.'' *CEA*, 33: 10-2 (N 70).

Maxfield-Miller, Elizabeth. ''Elizabeth Hoar of Concord and T.'' *TSB*, 106: 1-3 (Wi 69).

———. ''Emerson and Elizabeth in Concord.'' *HLB*, 19: 290-306 (Jl 71).

Mazzini, Carla. ''Epiphany in Two Poems by T.'' *TJQ*, 5: 23-5 (Ap 73).

Meese, E.A. ''Transcendentalism: The Metaphysics of the Theme.'' *AL*, 47: 1-20 (Mr 75).

Meigs, Peveril. ''The Cove Names of Walden.'' *TSB*, 104: 5-7 (Su 68).

Michaelson, L.W. ''The Man Who Burned the Woods.'' *Eng Rec*, 20: 72-5 (F 70).

Mielziner, Janice. ''HDT, Music Lover.'' *Eng Rec*, 26: 101-5 (Fa 75).

Miller, F.D. ''T's *Walden*, I, Paragraph 63.'' *Expl*, 32: 10 (O 73).

Miller, L.H. ''The Artist as Surveyor in *Walden* and *The Maine Woods.*'' *ESQ*, 21: 76-81 (2Q 75).

———. ''Bounding *Walden.*'' *TJQ*, 5: 25-9 (Jl 73).

———. ''T's Telegraphy.'' *ATQ*, 26: 15-6 (Sp 75).

Millichap, Joseph R. ''Plato's Allegory of the Cave and the Vision of *Walden.*'' *ELN*, 7: 274-82 (Je 70).

Minott, Henry. ''The Minott Family and T's Birthplace.'' *TJQ*, 3: 17-8 (Ap 71).

Miwa, Hisae. ''The Meanings of *Walden* in T's Philosophy of Life.'' *J Eng Lit* (Tokyo), 6: 43-55 (N 70).

———. ''T's Communion with Nature.'' *J Dept of Lit* (Tokyo), 17: 12-39 (Jl 71).

Mogan, J.J. "T's Style in Walden." *ESQ*, 50: 2-5 (1Q 68).

Mohanty, J.M. "Walden." *LCrit*, 7: 78-85 (Su 66).

Moldenhauer, J.J. "On the Editing of *The Maine Woods*." *TJQ*, 4: 15-20 (15 O 72).

Monteiro, George. "Birches in Winter: Notes on T and Frost." *CLAJ*, 12: 129-33 (D 68).

———. "'Delugeous' or 'Detergeous'?—A Contextual Argument." *CEAAN*, 2: 4-5 (Jl 69).

———. "Redemption through Nature: A Recurring Theme in T, Frost, and Richard Wilbur." *AQ*, 20: 795-809 (Wi 68).

———. "Robert Frost's Solitary Singer." *NEQ*, 44: 134-40 (Mr 71).

———. "T's Defense of Man 'The Reading Animal.'" *ATQ*, 2: 13-4 (Su 71).

Morgan, Speer. "Wendell Berry: A Fatal Singing." *SoR*, 10: 865-77 (O 74).

Morris, John. "T: Gentle Anarchist." *RelH*, 3: 62-5 (Sp 69).

Moser, Edwin. "The Order of Fragments of T's Essay on 'L'Allegro' and 'Il Penseroso.'" *TSB*, 101: 1-2 (Su 68).

Mosher, H.F. "The Absurd in T's *Walden*." *TJQ*, 3: 1-9 (O 71).

Moss, Marcia. "An Indenture for John T's Store." *TSB*, 129: 7-8 (Fa 74).

Moyne, E.J. "T and Emerson: Their Interest in Finland." *NM*, 70: 738-50 (1969).

Mueller, R.C. "T's Selections from *Chinese Four Books* for *The Dial*." *TJQ*, 4: 1-8 (O 72).

Mujica, Elio. "A Contraluz T el Hippy." *ElNaz*, nv: C-1 (8 S 70).

Mungo, Ray. "If Mr. T Calls, Tell Him I've Left the Country." *Atl*, 225: 72-86 (My 70).

Munakata, Kuniyoshi. "The Most Remarkable American: R.H. Blyth on HDT." *Otsuka R*, 9: 56-67 (Jl 72).

Murray, D.M. "T's Indians and His Developing Art of Characterization." *ESQ*, 21: 222-9 (4Q 75).

Myers, Douglas. "The Bean-field and the Method of Nature." *TJQ*, 4: 1-9 (Ap 72).

Myerson, Joel. "A Calendar of Transcendental Club Meetings." *AL*, 44: 197-207 (My 72).

———. "Eight Lowell Letters from Concord in 1838." *IllQ*, 38: 20-42 (Wi 75).

———. "A Margaret Fuller Addition to T's Library." *TSB*, 123: 3 (Sp 73).

———. "More Apropos of John Thoreau." *AL*, 45: 104-6 (Mr 73).

———. "T and the *Dial*: A Survey of the Contemporary Press." *TJQ*, 5: 4-7 (J 73).

———. "Transcendentalism and Unitarianism in 1840." *CLAJ*, 16: 366-68 (1973).

Nadeau, Raymond. "Walden Rapes." *NER*, 1: 14-5 (Jl 69).

Narasimhaiah, C.D. "Where T and Gandhi Differed." *TJQ*, 7: 11-20 (Jl 75).

Nelson, Carl. "Sound Knowledge in *Walden*." *TJQ*, 2: 1-6 (15 Jl 70).

Neufeldt, Leonard. "'Extravagance' Through Economy: T's *Walden*." *ATQ*, 11: 63-9 (Su 71).

———. "The Severity of the Ideal: Emerson's 'T.'" *ESQ*, 58: 77-84 (1Q 70).

Nicholas. W.W. "Individualism and Autobiographical Art: Frederick Douglass and HT." *CLAJ*, 16: 145-58 (D 72).

Nichols, W.W. "Science and the Art of *Walden*: Experiment and the Art of Walden: Experiment and Structure." *ESQ*, 50: 77-84 (Sp 68).

Noble, Donald. "A Lesson for the Teacher." *ATQ*, 20: 127 (Fa 73).

Noverr, D.A. "The Divining of Walden." *TJQ*, 4: 9-14 (15 O 72).

———. "Further Observations on T's Use of the Coat-of-Arms Symbol." *TSB*, 113: 1-2 (Fa 70).

*———. "Hildenbrand's Bibliography of T Scholarship." *TJQ*, 3: 7-11 (Ja 71).

———. "A Note on Wendell Glick's 'T's Use of His Sources.'" *NEQ*, 44: 475-7 (S 71).

———. "T's July 16, 1860 Letter to Charles Sumner: An Addendum and Correction." *TSB*, 107: 2 (Sp 69).

————. "T's July 16, 1860 Letter to Charles Sumner: An Additional Note." *TSB*, 110: 2 (Wi 70).

————. "T's 'May Morning': Nature, Poetic Vision, and the Poet's Publication of His Truth." *TJQ*, 2: 7-10 (Jl 70).

Oates, J.C. "On T's *Walden.*" *Mademoiselle*, 76: 96-8 (Ap 73).

Ogata, Tashihiko. "Unity of *Walden.*" *REngL*, 26: 103-9 (D 70).

Okuda, Joichi. "'Fill' in H.D.T." *Stud Eng Lit (Hosei)*, 14: 109-19 (F 71).

————. "H.D.T. and the Impressionistic Landscape." *Hosei R*, 2: 72-93 (D 69).

————. "H.D.T.'s Critics—T: Mirror." *Hosei R*, 3: 65-76 (D 70).

————. "'Higher Laws' in *Walden.*" *Stud Eng Lit (Hosei)*, 12: 95-104 (F 70).

————. "The Religious Feeling or Keynote of 'Higher Laws.'" *Hosei R*, 4: 58-65 (D 73).

————. "*Walden* and the Circular Image, from a Transmigratory Point of View." *Bul Daito Bunka Un*, 13: 113-31 (Mr 75).

Oliver, E.S "My Introduction to T." *TSB*, 125: 3-4 (Wi 73).

Olson, Steve. "The Unanswered Question." *TJQ*, 4: 22-6 (Ap 72).

Orth, Michael. "The Prose Style of HT." *Lang&S*, 7: 36-52 (1974).

Parker, Hershel. "Melville's Satire of Emerson and T: An Evaluation of the Evidence." *ATQ*, 7: 61-7 (Su 70).

Parsons, V.M. "T's *The Maine Woods*: An Essay in Appreciation." *HussR*, 1: 17-27 (1967-68).

Patil, S.K. "T's Influence on Mahatma Gandhi." *P&ER*, 4: 2-6 (5 D 70).

Pavilionis, R. "H.D.T ir asmenybes apsisprendimas." *Problemos*, 2: 40-9 (1973).

Pebworth, T.L. "Evelyn's Lay Fields, Digby's Vital Spirits, and T's Beans." *TSB*, 101: 6-7 (Wi 68).

Pederson, L.A. "Americanisms in T's Journal." *ELLOKD*, 1: 1-33 (N 68).

Peple, E.C. "The Background of the Hawthorne-T Relationship." *RALS*, 1: 104-12 (Sp 71).

————. "Hawthorne on T: 1853-1857." *TSB*, 119: 1-3 (Sp 72).

————. "T and Donatello." *TJQ*, 5: 22-5 (O 73).

Perrin, Noel. "Inflation Meets T Tactics, and Is Defeated." *NY*, 46: 70-80 (21 F 70); *True*, 52: 57-60 (Ja 71).

Perry, P.M. "Following T's Trail on Cape Cod." *Backpacker*, 2: 34-6 (Wi 74).

————. "On Cape Cod with T." *NEG*, 17: 32-7 (Wi 75).

Pinker, M.J. "Recovering the Hound . . ." *ConS*, 10: 13 (D 75).

Poger, Sidney. "T as Yankee in Canada." *ATQ*, 14: 174-7 (Sp 72).

————. "Yeats as Azad: A Possible Source in T." *TJQ*, 9: 13-5 (Fa 73).

————. "T's Resistance to Civil Government." *TSB Leaflet*, 69: 11-6 (F 70).

Pontin, J.F. "HDT/ Henry S. Salt." *TJQ*, 7: 3-11 (Jl 75).

Porte, Joel. "Emerson, T, and the Double Consciousness." *NEQ*, 41: 40-50 (Je 68).

————. "HT: Society and Solitude." *ESQ*, 19: 131-40 (3Q 73).

Powers, Christine. "Unerring Nature." *TJQ*, 4: 13-20 (Ja 72).

Predmore, R.L. "Unamuno and T." *CLS*, 6: 33-44 (Mr 69).

Pulos, C.E. "The Foreign Observer in *Walden.*" *ELN*, 7: 51-3 (S 69).

————. "*Walden* and Emerson's 'The Sphinx.'" *ATQ*, 1: 7-11 (Sp 69).

Quick, D.G. "T as Limnologist." *TJQ*, 4: 13-20 (Ap 72).

Quinn, J.P. "T and Berrigan: Seekers of the Lost Paradise." *TSB*, 127: 2-4 (Sp 74).

Railton, Stephen. "T's 'Resurrection of Virtue.'" *AQ*, 24: 210-27 (My 72).

Reaver, J.R. "T's Ways with Proverbs." *ATQ*, 1: 2-7 (Sp 69).

Reed, K.T. "A Thoreauvian Echo in *Uncle Tom's Cabin*?" *ATQ*, 11: 37-8 (Su 71).

Reger, William. "Beyond Metaphor." *Criticism*, 12: 333-44 (Fa 70).

Rein, Irving. "The New England Transcendentalist: Philosophy and Rhetoric." *P&R*, 1: 103-17 (Wi 68).

Reuben, P.P. "T in B.O. Flower's *Arena*." *TSB*, 117: 5-6 (Fa 71).

Rhoads, K.W. "T: The Ear and the Music." *AL*, 46: 313-28 (N 74).

Riegl, Kurt. "Zum T-Echo im Spatwerk O'Neills." *GRM*, 18: 191-9 (Ap 68).

Rinzler, E.E. "T: The Medium and His Message." *EJ*, 57: 1138-42 (N 68).

Roberts, C.D.G. "A Description of T." *ConS*, 10: 12 (Mr 75).

Robinson, E.A. "T and the Deathwatch in Poe's 'The Tell-Tale Heart.'" *PS*, 4: 14-6 (Je 71).

Rodale, Robert. "Wild Apples over Indianapolis." *OGF*, 19: 21-4 (O 70).

Rokugawa, Makoto. "Romanticism and the Transcendentalist T in Walden." *Memoirs of Nagano Technical Coll*, 5: 207-17 (O 73).

Rosa, A.F. "Charles Ives: Music, Transcendentalism, and Politics." *NEQ*, 44: 433-43 (D 71).

Rose, Edward. "The American Scholar Incarnate." *ESQ*, 19: 170-8 (Fa 73).

Rosenthal, Bernard. "The *Dial*, Transcendentalism and Margaret Fuller." *ELN*, 8: 28-36

———. "T's Books of Leaves." *ESQ*, 56: 7-11 (3Q 69).

Ross, Donald. "Composition as a Stylistic Feature." *Style*, 4: 1-10 (Wi 70).

———. "Emerson and T: A Comparison of Prose Styles." *Lang&S*, 6: 185-95 (Su 73).

———. "Hawthorne and T on 'Cottage Architecture." *ATQ*, 1: 100-1 (1Q 69).

———. "Verbal Wit and *Walden*." *ATQ*, 11: 38-44 (Su 71).

Ross, M.L. "T and Mailer: The Mission of the Rooster." *WHR*, 25: 47-56 (Wi 71).

Rovere, Richard. "Freedom: Who Needs It?" *Atl*, 221: 39-44 (My 68).

Russell, E.H. "A Bit of . . . Correspondence . . ." *ATQ*, 14: 66-70 (Sp 72).

Russell, Francis. "A Voyage after T." *Country J*, 2: 54-8 (Jl 75).

Ryan, Kevin. "HDT: Critic, Theorist, and Practitioner of Education." *School R*, 77: 54-63 (Mr 69).

Saalbach, R.P. "T and Civil Disobedience." *BSUF*, 13: 18-24 (Fl 72).

St. Armand, Barton. "T Comes to Brown." *BBr*, 22: 121-41 (1968).

Salminen, Johannes. "Vaga börja leva." *Horisont*, 17: 11-6 (1970).

Salt, H.S. "HD.T." *TJQ*, 7: 4-11 (Jl 75).

Sampson, H.G. "Structure in the Poetry of T." *Costerus*, 6: 137-54 (1972).

Sanders, F.K. "Mr. T's Time Bomb." *Nat R*, 16: 541-67 (4 Je 68).

Sanford, C.L. "Emerson, T, and the Hereditary Duality." *ESQ*, 54: 36-43 (1Q 69).

Sarkesian, Barbara. "Such Worthies as These: T's Field Mice, Rabbits, and Woodchucks." *Animals*, O 75, pp. 2-3.

Sattelmeyer, Robert. "David A. Wasson's Elegy on T." *TSB*, 123: 3-4 (Sp 73).

Schamberger, J.E. "Grapes of Gladness: A Misconception of *Walden*." *ATQ*, 13: 15-6 (1972).

Schatter, Antje. "Interpretationen zum Aufbau von HDT's *Walden*." *LWU*, 1: 205-16

Scheik, William J. "The House of Nature in Thoreau's *A Week*." *ESQ*, 20: 111-16 (2Q 74).

Schiffman, Joseph. "Master and Disciple." *DA*, 50: 14-6 (D 72).

———. "Research Areas in *Walden* and *Civil Disobedience*." *EEx*, 17: 7-13 (Fa 72).

———. "*Walden* and *Civil Disobedience*: Critical Analyses." *ESQ*, 56: 57-60 (Au 69).

Schiller, Andrew. "T in the Undergraduate Survey Course." *ESQ*, 18: 17-9 (Sp 60).

Schneider, R.J. "Reflections on Walden Pond: T's Optics." *ESQ*, 21: 65-75 (2Q 75).

Schofield, Edmund. "Errors in Robert Stowell's 'A Thoreau Gazetteer.'" *TSB*, 119: 4 (Sp 72).

Seaburg, Alan. "Indian Summer and T." *NEG*, 12: 45-50 (Su 73).

———. "Min Thoreau." *TSB*, 101: 7-8 (Sp 67).

————. "T as Hope." *TJQ*, 3: 16-9 (Ja 70).

————. "A T Document." *TSB*, 109: 5 (Fa 69).

————. "T Visits Boston." *TJQ*, 1: 7-9 (O 69).

————. "T's Favorite Farmer." *TSB*, 102: 1-4 (Wi 68).

————. "T's Poetical Farmer." *NEG*, 12: 29-38 (Su 70).

————. "T's Portrait of John Goodwin, the One-Eyed Fisherman." *SE*, 10: 22-7 (Au 69).

————. "A Typical T Summer." *NEG*, 14: 25-30 (Su 72).

Seefurth, N.H. "T: A View from Emeritus." *ESQ*, 54: 2-18 (1Q 69).

Seelye, J.R. "Some Green Thoughts on a Green Theme." *TriQ*, 24: 576-638 (Sp 72).

Seib, Charles. "My Introduction to T." *TSB*, 127: 4 (Fa 74).

Seybold, Ethel. "T for Everyone." *ESQ*, 18: 19-21 (Sp 60).

Shanley, J.L. "Rationale of the Intention of the Editors of T's Journal." *CEAAN*, 3: 24-5 (Je 70).

Sharma, M.L. "Cholmondeley's Gift to T: An Indian Pearl to the United States." *JOFS*, 3: 61-89 (Su 68).

————. "The 'Oriental Estate,' Especially the *Bhagavada-Gita* in American Literature." *Forum(H)*, 7: 4-11 (Fa-Wi 69).

Shepard, James. "T's Other Message." *MassW*, 24: 1 (N 73).

Sherwin, J.S., and R.C. Reynolds. *"A Word Index to Walden with Textual Notes: A Corrected Edition."* *ESQ*, 57: 1-130 (4Q 69).

Sherwood, M.P. "Did T Foreshadow a Third Culture Synthesis?" *TJQ*, 1: 22-9 (Jl 69).

————. "The Fowlers of T's *Maine Woods*." *TJQ*, 4: 23-32 (Jl 72).

————. "T Island." *TJQ*, 1: 20-2 (Ja 69).

————. "T's Cabin Equinox-Oriented?" *TJQ*, 2: 14-21 (Ja 70).

————. "T's Penobscot Indians." *TJQ*, 1: 1-13 (Ja 69).

————. "T's Walden House." *TJQ*, 2: 19 (Ap 70).

————. "The Wellfleet Oysterman's House." *TJQ*, 3: 17-9 (Jl 71).

Shigematsu, Tsutomu. "On Scientific Observation in T as Poet-Naturalist." *J Nakamura Gakuen*, 7: 11-7 (Ap 75).

————. "On the Subject of the West or Wild in HDT." *J Nakamura Gakuen*, 15: 11-8 (1972).

————. "On T's Doctrine of Simplicity." *BSOWJC*, 1: 75-86 (Ap 69).

————. "The West or Wild in T." *J Nakamura Gakuen*, 5: 11-8 (Ap 73).

————. "Young T's Life and Thoughts." *J Nakamura Gakuen*, 6: 17-22 (Ap 74).

Shreffler, P.A. "Holmes and T." *BakSJ*, 19: 149-51 (S 69).

Silverman, Kenneth. "The Sluggard Knight in T's Poetry." *TJQ*, 5: 5-9 (Ap 73).

Simmonds, Albert. "The Essay and Mr. T." *TJQ*, 6: 24-9 (D 75).

Simon, Gary. "What HD Didn't Know about Lao Tzu." *LE&W,* 17: 253-74 (1973).

Simon, Louis. "Les Amis d' HDT." *CAHR,* 97: 26-7 (Je 70).

Singh, B.M. *"Walden*: A Study in the Creation of Selfhood." *PURBA*, 3: 121-32 (O 72).

Sisk, J.P. "Losing Big." *HM*, 251: 79-85 (N 75).

————. "Making it in America." *Atl*, 224: 63-8 (D 69).

Skinner, B.F. *"Walen* (One) and *Walden Two*." *TSB*, 122: 1-3 (Wi 73).

Smith, D.L. "Romanticism in America: The Transcendentalists." *RPol*, 35: 302-25 (Jl 73).

Smith, G.W. "T and Bacon: The Idols of the Theatre." *ATQ*, 2: 6-12 (Su 71).

Smith, R.A. "A Feathered Solitude." *TJQ*, 5: 12-4 (Ap 73).

Smythe, Daniel. "Inspector of Rainstorms." *TJQ*, 2: 12-3 (Ja 70).

————. "Robert Frosts's Indebtedness to HT." *TJQ*, 3: 21 (Jl 71).

————. "T and People." *TJQ*, 1: 21-2 (Ap 69).

―――. "T and Robert Frost." *TJQ*, 2: 21-2 (O 70).

―――. "T's Peace of Mind." *TJQ*, 1: 20-1 (O 69).

Snow, D.R. "The Penobscot Indians in T's Time." *TJQ*, 2: 7-11 (Ja 70).

Soucie, Gary. "Exclusive! An Interview with HDT." *AudM*, 76: 98-105 (My 74).

Spiegel, Marshall. "A T Look at Cape Cod." *SchV*, 49: 2-5 (11 Ja 71).

Stein, W.B. "An Approach to T." *ESQ*, 56: 4-6 (Au 69).

―――. "The Hindu Matrix of *Walden*: The King's Son." *CL*, 22: 303-18 (Fa 70).

―――. "T's *A Week* and *Om* Cosmography." *ATQ*, 11: 15-37 (Su 71).

―――. "*Walden* and the *Samhita* of the *Sama Veda*." *TSB*, 96: 6 (Su 66).

―――. "The Yoga of Reading in *Walden*." *TSLL*, 13: 481-95 (Fa 71).

―――. "*Walden* and the *Samhita* of the *Sama Veda*." *TSB*, 96: 6 (Su 66).

Steinbrink, Jeffrey. "The Organization of Perception in *A Week*." *TJQ*, 5: 14-7 (J 73).

―――. "The Role of T's Poet." *TJQ*, 6: 17-20 (O 74).

Stephenson, Edward. "Longfellow Revised." *TSB*, 118: 4-5 (Wi 72).

Stibitz, E. Earle. "T's Humanism and Ideas on Literature." *ESQ*, 55: 110-16 (Su 69).

Stockton, E.L., Jr. "HDT: Terrener or Mariner?" *Radford R*, 20: 143-5 (O 66).

Stodard, D.R. "The Relevance of *Walden*." *SkAQ*, 47: 1-6 (Sp 69).

Stoehr, Taylor. "'Eloquence Needs No Constable'—Alcott, Emerson and T." *CRAS*, 5: 81-100 (1974).

―――. "Transcendentalist Attitudes Toward Communitism and Individualism." *ESQ*, 75: 65-90 (2Q 74).

Stowell, Robert. "Note on the Map Showing T's Journeys in John Christie's *Thoreau as World Traveler*." *TSB*, 123: 2 (Sp 73).

―――. "A Note on Two Additional Maps Copied by T." *TSB*, 125: 1-2 (Fa 73).

―――. "Poetry about T: Nineteenth Century." *TSB*, 112: 1-3 (Su 70).

―――. "T and a Map of Nantucket." *TSB*, 126: 6-7 (Wi 74).

―――. "T's Simple Living and the Modern World." *TJQ*, 1: 10-2 (O 69).

―――. "Twentieth Century Poetry about T." *TSB*, 116: 1-2 (Su 71).

Stracner, S.D. "T's Orientalism: A Preliminary Reconsideration." *TJQ*, 6: 14-7 (Jl 74).

―――. "*Walden*: T's *Vanaprasthya*." *TJQ*, 5: 8-12 (Ja 73).

Strauch, C.F. "Emerson Rejects Reed and Hails T." *HLB*, 16: 257-73 (Jl 68).

Sullivan, Wilson. "Concord and Cambridge Confidential." *SatR*, 17: 40-2 (27 S 69).

Swanson, D.R. "Far and Fair Within: 'A Walk to Wachusett.'" *ESQ*, 56: 52-3 (3Q 69).

Swift, Ernie. "Straight Talk." *NatW*, 6: 19 (Je 68).

Takizawa, Juzo. "On the T-Gandhian Tradition of Non-violent Resistance." *Bul Col Gen Ed* (Tohoku), 21: 1-18 (F 75).

Tanner, S.L. "Current Motions in T's *A Week*." *SRom*, 12: 763-76 (Fa 73).

Tatalovich, Raymond. "T on Civil Disobedience." *SoQ*, 11: 107-13 (Ja 73).

Teale, E.W. "Notes and Queries." *TSB*, 121: 8 (Fa 72).

Teresko, J.E. "Two Miracles at Woolsthorpe and Ktaadn." *ConS*, 10: 1-10 (D 75).

Tilden, Freeman. "Two Concord Men in a Boat." *MassA*, 50: 78-82 (Wi 65).

Tillman, J.S. "The Transcendental Georgic in *Walden*." *ESQ*, 21: 137-41 (3Q 75).

Timpe, E.F. "T's Developing Style." *ESQ*, 58: 120-3 (1Q 70).

Treat, Robert and Betty. "T and Institutional Christianity." *ATQ*, 1: 44-7 (1Q 69).

Tripp, R.P. "A Note on the Structure of *Walden*." *TSB*, 118: 5-6 (Wi 72).

―――. "A Recipe for *Walden* Criticism." *NER*, 119: 11-4 (Jl-Ag 69).

―――. "T and Marcus Aurelius: A Possible Borrowing." *TSB*, 107: 7 (Sp 69).

Tuerk, Richard. "An Echo of Virgil in *Walden*." *TSB*, 117: 4-5 (Fa 71).

———. ''Man and Nature in 'Slavery in Massachusetts.''' *ConS*, 7: 8-10 (Mr 72).

———. ''A Note of T, William Carlos Williams, and Wallace Stevens.'' *ConS*, 10: 11-5 (Je 75).

———. ''The One World of T's Verse.'' *TJQ*, 6: 3-14 (O 74).

———. ''T and Chaucer's Dream.'' *TSB*, 103: 1 (Fa 68).

———. ''T's Early Versions of a Myth.'' *ATQ*, 2: 32-8 (Sp 71).

Uchiyama, Taijiro. ''*Walden* as Poem and Another *Walden*.'' *Eng Q*, 7: 119-26 (F 70).

Ueno, Masuzo. ''HDT and American Limnology.'' *Konan Women's Col Stud Eng Lit*, 11: 92-7 (D 74).

Uhlig, Herbert. ''Improved Means to an Unimproved End.'' *TSB*, 128: 1-3 (Su 74).

Ullyatt, A.G. '''Wait Not till Slaves Pronounce the Word': T's Only Anti-Slavery Poem in the Context of Civil War Poetry.'' *TSB*, 132: 1-2 (Su 75).

Unoki, Keijiro. ''HT Not Deceived by His Geographical Environment.'' *Shinshu Un J of Lib Arts*, 1: 149-71 (Ja 70).

———. ''Why Did Emerson, T and Melville Express Their Thoughts in the Form of 'Railroad' Symbolically?'' *Karibane*, 9: 62-70 (Mr 70).

Van Dore, Wade. ''T Carry.'' *TJQ*, 1: 23 (O 69).

Vernet, Laurence. ''Marcel Proust: Admirateur Imprévu di T.'' *Europe*, 47: 217-24 (Ja 69).

Volkman, Arthur. ''Excerpts from the Journal of HDT.'' *Papers Arch Soc of Delaware*, 7: 1-12 (D 73).

Volkman, A.G. ''Gleason, Unforgotten Photographer.'' *TSB*, 118: 1-2 (Wi 72).

———. ''HT, Physicist.'' *TSB*, 123: 4 (Sp 73).

———. ''The Hound, Bay-Horse, and Turtle Dove.'' *TSB*, 103: 6-7 (Sp 68).

———. ''A Mythological Rainbow.'' *TSB*, 129: 7 (Fa 74).

———. ''A Note on Japp's Life of Thoreau.'' *TSB*, 107: 6 (Sp 69).

———. ''T and N.C. Wyeth—A Vignette.'' *TSB*, 125: 4-5 (Fa 73).

———. ''T as Seer.'' *TSB*, 111: 2-3 (Sp 70).

Waggoner, H.H. '''Grace' in the Thought of Emerson, T, and Hawthorne.'' *ESQ*, 54: 68-72 (1Q 69).

Walden, Daniel. ''T and the Continuing American Revolution.'' *J Human Rel*, 1: 17-9 (1974).

Walker, E.H. ''The History Back of the Name Walden.'' *ConS*, 7: 3-7 (Je 72).

———. ''T, Tom Bowling, and Charles Dibdin.'' *ConS*, 8: 3-6 (S 73).

Warders, D.F. ''Excursion in Understanding.'' *CEA*, 37: 13-22 (#3 75).

Watanabe, Toshio. ''The Murderous Innocence: HDT and the American Wilderness.'' *SELit*, 50: 79-100 (1973).

Waterman, A.E. ''The New Economy.'' *TJQ*, 2: 17-9 (Ap 70).

Weidman, B.S. ''T and Indians.'' *TJQ*, 5: 4-10 (O 73).

Werge, Thomas. ''The Idea and Significance of 'Economy' before *Walden*.'' *ESQ*, 20: 270-4 (4Q 74).

Wescott, R.R. ''T in *The Maine Woods*.'' *TJQ*, 2: 3-6 (Ja 70).

West, Michael. ''Charles Kraitsir's Influence upon T's Theory of Language.'' *ESQ*, 19: 262-74 (4Q 73).

———. ''John Evelyn, Sir Kenelm Digby, and T's Vital Spirits.'' *TSB*, 117: 8 (Fa 71).

———. ''Scatology and Eschatology: The Heroic Dimensions of T's Wordplay.'' *PMLA*, 89: 1043-6 (O 74).

———. ''*Walden*'s Dirty Language: T and Walter Whiter's Geocentric Etymological Theories.'' *HLB*, 22: 117-28 (Ap 74).

Westbrook, Perry. ''John Burroughs and the Transcendentalists.'' *ESQ*, 55: 47-55 (2Q 69).

————. "The Theme of Quest in T." *Eng Rec*, 8: 13-7 (Wi 57).

Whishnant, D.E. "The Sacred and the Profane in *Walden*." *CentR*, 14: 267-83 (1970).

Whitaker, Rosemary. "*A Week* and *Walden*: The River vs. the Pond." *ATQ*, 17: 9-12 (Wi 72-73).

Wiener, H.S. "To a Fairer World: T's Last Hours." *JHS*, 1: 361-5 (Au 68).

Wild, P.H. "Flower Power: A Student's Guide to Pre-Hippie Transcendentalism." *EJ*, 58: 62-8 (Ja 69).

Wilder, Myron. "An Ex-Hermit Looks at T." *TSB*, 129: 6-7 (Fa 74).

Wilkins, A.H. "T's 'Ktaadn' Guides, Family Records." *TSQ*, 3: 29 (Ja 71).

Williams, D.H. "Whose Woods These Are." *TJQ*, 4: 27-8 (Ja 72).

Williams, E.D. "T: Prophet of World Faith." *TJQ*, 1: 14-6 (Ja 69).

Williams, Paul. "T, the .03 Horsepower Poet." *TJQ*, 3: 20-1 (Ja 71).

Williams, P.O. "T's Growth as a Transcendental Poet." *ESQ*, 19: 189-98 (3Q 73).

Williams, Ted. "Walden Then and Now." *MassW*, 24: 2-5, 15-9 (N 73).

Willson, Lawrence. "T: Student of Anthropology." *AmA*, 61: 279-89 (Ap 59).

Wilson, J.B. "The Transcendentalists' Ideas of a University." *EdF*, 33: 343-54 (Mr 69).

Winslow, Richard. "With T on the Allagash." *ConS*, 10: 1-6 (S 75).

Winter, Julie. "T: An Astrological Birth-Chart." *TSB*, 126: 3-4, 8 (Wi 74).

Witherington, Paul. "T's Almost Unpassable Test." *RS*, 41: 279-81 (1973).

Wolfgang, Otto. "Return to Walden Pond." *RosD*, 16: 167-9 (My 70).

Woodlief, Annette. "The Influence of Theories of Rhetoric on T." *TJQ*, 7: 13-22 (Ja 75).

*————. "*Walden*: A Checklist of Literary Criticism through 1973." *RALS*, 5: 15-58 (Sp 75).

Woodson, Thomas. "Notes for the Annotation of *Walden*." *AL*, 46: 550-5 (Ja 75).

————. "T on Poverty and Magnanimity." *PMLA*, 85: 21-34 (Ja 70).

————. "T's Excursion to the Berkshires and Catskills." *ESQ*, 21: 82-92 (2Q 75).

————. "T's *Walden*, I, Paragraph 63." *Expl*, 33: 56 (Mr 75).

————. "The Two Beginnings of *Walden*: A Distinction of Styles." *ELH*, 35: 440-73 (S 68).

Woodward, R.H. "T's Diction." *TSB*, 95: 5 (Sp 66).

————. "T's 'Ferule': A Textual Note on *Walden*." *TSB*, 123: 1-2 (Sp 73).

Wyllie, J.C. "Delugeous or Detergeous or?" *CEAAN*, 2: 3 (Jl 69).

Yamasaki, Tokihiko. "Theoretical Sources of T's 'Civil Disobedience.'" *Q Jl Law and Pol Osaka City Un*, 21: 1-36 (Ja 75).

Zeitlin, Eugenia. "Henry in the Desert." *TSB*, 126: 1-2 (Wi 74).

Zimmer, J.M. "A History of T's Hut and Hut Site." *ESQ*, 18: 134-40 (3Q 72); *ConS*, 8: sup 3 (D 73).

Thorpe, Thomas Bangs. Hayne, Barrie. "Yankee in the Patriarchy: T.B.T's Reply to *Uncle Tom's Cabin*." *AQ*, 20: 180-95 (Su 68).

Lemay, J.A.L. "The Text, Tradition, and Themes of 'The Big Bear of Arkansas.'" *AL*, 47: 321-42 (N 75).

Thurber, James. Baldwin, Alice. "JT's Compounds." *Lang&S*, 3: 185-96 (1970).

Bernard, F.V. "A T Letter." *ELN*, 8: 300-1 (1971).

Blochman, Larry. "Noise of Midnight Tire Change Brings Journalists Together." *LGJ*, 3: 20 (Wi 75).

Bowden, E.T. "*The Thurber Carnival*: Bibliography and Printing History." *TSLL*, 9: 555-66 (Wi 68).

Branscomb, Lewis. "JT and Oral History at Ohio State University." *LGJ*, 3: 16-9 (Wi 75).

Braunlich, Phyllis. "Hot Times in the Catbird Seat." *LGJ*, 3: 10-1 (Wi 75).

Dias, E.J. "The Upside-Down World of T's 'The Catbird Seat.'" *CEA*, 30: 6-7 (F 68).

Eckler, E.R. "The Wordplay of JT." *Word Ways*, 6: 241-7 (1973).

Fitzgerald, Gregory. "An Example of Associationism as an Organizational Technique from T's 'Walter Mitty.'" *CEA*, 31: 11 (Ja 69).

Geddes, Virgil. "Not Everyone Liked T." *LGJ*, 3: 7 (Wi 75).

Hasley, Louis. "JT: Artist in Humor." *SAQ*, 73: 504-15 (Au 74).

Haufe, Virginia. "T Gives Advice to Men and Women." *Ohioana*, 3: 35-6 (Su 60).

Hawley, Michael. "Quintet Honors T Fables." *GLGJ*, 3: 21-2 (Wi 75).

Kane, T.S. "A Note on the Chronology of 'The Catbird Seat.'" *CEA*, 30: 8-9 (Ap 68).

Lindner, C.M. "T's Walter Mitty—The Underground American Hero." *GaR*, 28: 283-9 (Su 74).

Numasawa, Koji. "Everyman/Schlemiel." *EigoS* 114: 516-7 (1968).

Petrullo, H.B. "Clichés and Three Political Satires of the Thirties." *SNL*, 8: 109-17 (Sp 71).

Satterfield, Leon. "T's 'The Secret Life of Walter Mitty.'" *Expl*, 27: 57 (Ap 69).

Scholl, P.A. "T's Walter Ego—The Little Man Hero." *LGJ*, 3: 8-9 (Wi 75).

Tibbetts, Robert. "The T Collection at Ohio State University." *LGJ*, 3: 12-5 (Wi 75).

Tobias, R.C. "T in Paris: 'Clocks' Kept Different Time." *LGJ*, 3: 2-6 (Wi 75).

Yardley, Jonathan. "Cantankerous, Melancholy, Wild, Sane." *NRep*, 167: 36-7 (21 O 72).

Thurman, Wallace. Haslam, Gerald. "WT: A Western Renaissance Man." *WAL*, 6: 53-9 (Sp 71).

West, Dorothy. "Elephant's Dance: A Memoir of WT." *BlackW*, 20: 77-85 (1970).

Timrod, Henry. Barker, Addison. "Mr. Cannon's Unusual Schoolteacher." *Sandlapper*, 8: 17-9 (My 75).

Toklas, Alice B. Friedrich, Otto. "The Grave of AB.T." *Esquire*, 69: 98-103, 121-4 (Ja 68).

Stewart, L.D. "Hemingway and the Autobiographies of AB.T." *FHA*, 1970, pp. 117-23.

Sutherland, Donald. "Alice, Gertrude, and Others." *PrS*, 45: 284-99 (Wi 71-72).

———. "The Conversion of AB.T." *ColQ*, 17: 129-41 (Au 68).

Tolson, Melvin Beaunorus. Basler, R. P. "The Heart of Blackness—MBT's Poetry." *NLet*, 39: 63-76 (Sp 73).

Cansler, R.L. "'The White and Not-White Dichotomy' of MB.T's Poetry." *NALF*, 8: 115-8 (Wi 73).

Flasch, Joy. "Humor and Satire in The Poetry of M.B.T." *SNL*, 7: 29-36 (Fa 69).

Walcott, Ronald. "Some Notes on the Blues, Style & Space: Ellison, Gordone and T." *BlackW*, 22: 4-29 (1972).

Tomlinson, Charles. Edwards, Michael. "CT: Notes on Tradition and Impersonality." *CritQ*, 15: 133-44 (Su 73).

———. "The Poetry of CT." *Agenda*, 9: 126-41 (Sp-Su 71).

Gitzen, Julian. "CT and the Plenitude of Fact." *CritQ*, 13: 355-62 (Wi 71).

Rasula, Jed, and Mike Erwin. "An Interview with CT." *ConL*, 16: 405-16 (Au 75).

Tompson, Benjamin. Eckstein, N.T. "BT's Elegy, 'A Short but Sorrowful Memorial' of My Dear Sister Sarah Tompson." *ConHSB*, 36: 72-6 (Jl 71).

———. "The Pastoral and the Primitive in BT's 'Address to Lord Bellamont.'" *EAL*, 8: 111-6 (Fa 73).

Toomer, Jean. "Ackley, D.G. "Theme and Vision in JT's *Cane*." *SBL*, 1: 45-65 (Sp 70).

———. "A Key to the Poems in *Cane*." *CLAJ*, 14: 251-8 (Mr 71).

Bell, B.W. "Portrait of the Artist as High Priest of Soul: JT's *Cane*." *BlackW*, 23: 4-19, 92-7 (1974).

Blackwell, Louise. "JT's 'Cane' and Biblical Myth." *CLAJ*, 17: 535-42 (Je 74).

Blake, Susan. "The Spectatorial Artist and the Structure of *Cane*." *CLAJ*, 17: 516-34 (Je 74).

Bontemps, Arna. "The Harlem Renaissance." *SatR*, 30: 12-3 (22 Mr 47).

Cancel, R.A. "Male and Female Interrelationships in T's *Cane*." *NALF*, 5: 25-31 (1971).

Chase, Patricia. "The Women in *Cane*." *CLAJ*, 14: 259-73 (Mr 71).

Christ, J.M. "JT's 'Bona and Paul': The Innocence and Artifice of Words." *NALF*, 9: 44-6 (Su 75).

Davis, C.T. "JT and the South: Region and Race as Elements within a Literary Imagination." *SLitI*, 7: 23-38 (Fa 74).

Dickerson, M.J. "Sherwood Anderson and JT: A Literary Relationship." *SAF*, 1: 163-75 (Au 73).

Dillard, M.M. "JT: The Veil Replaced." *CLAJ*, 17: 468-73 (Je 74).

Duncan, Bowie. "JT's *Cane*: A Modern Black Oracle." *CLAJ*, 15: 323-33 (Mr 72).

Durham, Frank. "JT's Vision of the Southern Negro." *SHR*, 6: 13-22 (Wi 72).

———. "The Poetry Society of South Carolina's Turbulent Year: Self-Interest, Atheism, and JT." *SHR*, 5: 76-80 (Wi 71).

Farrison, W.E. "JT's *Cane* Again." *CLAJ*, 15: 295-302 (Mr 72).

Fischer, W.C. "The Aggregate Man in JT's *Cane*." *StN*, 3: 190-215 (Su 71).

Fisher, Alice. "The Influence of Ouspensky's *Tertium Organum* Upon JT's *Cane*."*CLAJ*, 17: 504-15 (Je 74).

Goede, W.J. "JT's Ralph Kabnis: Portrait of the Negro Artist as a Young Man." *Phylon*, 30: 73-85 (Sp 69).

Grant, M.K. "Images of Celebration in *Cane*." *NALF*, 5: 32-4, 36 (1971).

Griffin, J.C. "A Chat With Marjory Content Toomer." *Pembroke Mag*, 5: 15-27 (1974).

*———. "JT: A Bibliography." *SCR*, 7: 61-4 (Ap 75).

———. "Two Poems by JT." *Pembroke Mag*, 6: 67-8 (Ja 75).

Helbling, Mark. "Sherwood Anderson and JT." *NALF*, 9: 35-9 (Su 75).

Innes, C.L. "The Unity of JT's *Cane*." *CLAJ*, 15: 306-22 (Mr 72).

Jung, Udo. "'Spirit-Torsos of Exquisite Strength': The Theme of Individual Weakness & Collective Strength." *CLAJ*, 19: 261-7 (D 75).

Kerlin, R.T. "Singers of New Songs." *Opportunity*, 10: 252 (Ag 32).

Kopf, George. "The Tensions in JT's 'Theater.'" *CLAJ*, 17: 498-503 (Je 74).

Kramer, Victor. "The 'Mid-Kingdom' and Crane's 'Black Tambourine' and T's *Cane*." *CLAJ*, 17: 486-97 (Je 74).

Kraft, James. "JT's *Cane*." *MarkR*, 2: 61-3 (O 70).

Krasny, Michael. "The Aesthetic Structure of JT's *Cane*." *NALF*, 9: 42-3 (Su 75).

———. "Design in JT's *Balo*." *NALF*, 7: 103-6 (Fa 73).

———. "JT's Life Prior to *Cane*: A Brief Sketch of the Emergence of a Black Writer." *NALF*, 9: 40-1 (Su 75).

Lieber, Todd. "Design and Movement in *Cane*." *CLAJ*, 13: 35-50 (S 69).

McCarthy, D.P. "'Just Americans': A Note on JT's Marriage to Margery Latimer." *CLAJ*, 17: 474-9 (Je 74).

McKeever, B.F. "*Cane* as Blues." *NALF*, 4: 61-3 (1970).

MacKethan, L.H. "JT's *Cane*: A Pastoral Problem." *MissQ*, 28: 423-34 (Fa 75).

Mason, Clifford. "JT's Black Authenticity." *BlackW*, 20: 70-6 (1970).

Matthews, G.C. "T's 'Cane': The Artist and His World." *CLAJ*, 17: 543-59 (Je 74).

Mellard, J.M. "Solipsism, Symbolism, and Demonism: The Lyrical Mode in Fiction." *SHR*, 7: 37-52 (Wi 73).

Munson, G.B. "Correspondence." *NYT*, 7: 54 (16 F 69).

Nower, Joyce. "Foolin' Master." *SNL,* 7: 5-10 (Fa 69).

*Reilly, J.M. "JT (1894-1967): An Annotated Checklist of Commentary." *RALS*, 4: 27-56 (Sp 74).

————. "The Search for Black Redemption: JT's *Cane*." *StN*, 2: 312-24 (Fa 70).

Richmond, Marle. "JT and Margery Latimer." *CLAJ*, 18: 300 (Ap 74).

Riley, Roberta. "Search for Identity and Artistry." *CLAJ*, 17: 480-5 (Je 74).

Scrugggs, Charles. "JT: Fugitive." *AL*, 47: 843-96 (Mr 75).

————. "The Mark of Cain and the Redemption of Art: A Study in Theme and Structure of JT's *Cane*." *AL*, 44: 276-91 (My 72).

Spofford, W.K. "The Unity of Part One of JT's *Cane*." *MarkR*, 3: 58-60 (My 72).

Stein, M.L. "The Poet-Observer and Fern in JT's *Cane*." *MarkR*, 2: 64-5 (O 70).

Taylor, Clyde. "The Second Coming of JT." *Obsidian*, 1: 37-57 (#3 75).

Thompson, L.E. "JT as Modern Man." *Renaissance 2*, 1: 7-10 (1971).

Toomer, Jean. "Chapters from *Earth-Being*, an Unpublished Autobiography." *BSch*, 2: 3-13 (Ja 71).

Turner, D.T. "An Another Passing." *NALF*, 1: 3-4 (Fa 67).

————. "An Intersection of Paths: Correspondence Between JT and Sherwood Anderson." *CLAJ*, 17: 455-67 (Je 74).

————. "JT's *Cane*." *BlackW*, 18: 54-62 (1969).

Waldron, E.E. "The Search for Identity in JT's 'Esther.' "*CLAJ*, 14: 277-80 Mr 71).

Watkins, Patricia. "Is There a Unifying Theme in *Cane*?" *CLAJ*, 15: 303-5 (Mr 72).

Westerfield, Hargis. "JT's 'Fern': A Mythical Dimension." *CLAJ*, 14: 274-6 (Mr 71).

Torrene. Ridgely. Clum. J.M. "RT's Negro Plays: A Noble Beginning." *SAQ*, 68: 96-108 (Wi 69).

Monteiro, George. "Zona Gale and RT." *ALR*, 3: 77-9 (Wi 70).

Tourgee, Albion W. Arrington, L.J., and John Haupt. "Intolerable Zion." *WHR*, 22: 243-60 (Su 68).

Bowman, S.E. "Judge T's Fictional Presentation of the Reconstruction." *JPC*, 3: 307-23 (Fa 69).

Brown, Sterling. "The American Race Problem as Reflected in American Literature." *JNE*, 8: 275-90 (Jl 39).

Ealy, Marguerite, and S.E. Marovitz. "AWT (1838-1905)." *ALR*, 8: 53-80 (Wi 75).

Magdol, Edward. "A Note on Authenticity: Eliab Hill and Nimbus Ware in *Brick Without Straw*." *AQ*, 22: 907-11 (Wi 70).

Yardley, Jonathan. "Friend of Freedom." *NRep*, 162: 30-2 (10 Ja 70).

Traven, Berick. Braybrooke, Neville. "The Hero Without a Name: BT's *The Death Ship*." *QQ*, 76: 312-8 (Su 69); *LibR*, 22: 371-3 (Au 70).

Fraser, John. "Rereading T's *The Death Ship*." *SoR*, 9: 69-92 (1973).

Olafson, B.B. "B.T.'s *Norteamericanos* in Mexico." *MarkR*, 4: 1-5 (1973).

Pfabigan, Alfred. "Der Schriftsteller B.T.: Ein Munchener Karl Kraus?" *LuK*, 83: 161-70 (1974).

Richter, Armin. "Der Widerspënstigen Zähmung: B.T.'s Neugestaltung eines 'exemplo' des Dn Juan Manuel." *GRM*, 21: 432-2 (1971).

————. "B.T. als Feuilletonist." *ZDP*, 91: 585-606 (1972).

Stone, Judy. "Conversations with B.T." *Ramparts*, 6: 55-75 (O 67).

Warner, J.M. "Tragic Vision in B.T's *The Night Visitors*." *SSF*, 7: 377-84 (Su 70).

West, Anthony. "The Great Traven Mystery." *NY*, 43: 82-7 (22 Jl 67).

Trilling, Lionel. Adamowski, T.H. "LT: Modern Literature and Its Discontent." *DR*, 55: 83-92 (1975).

*Barnaby, Marianne. "LT: A Bibliography, 1926-1972." *BB*, 31: 37-44 (Ja-Mr 74).

Casalandra, Sister Estelle. "The Three Margarets." *SR*, 81: 225-36 (Ap-Je 73).

Hatfield, Henry. "The Journey and the Mountain." *MLN*, 90: 363-70 (1975).

Hirsch, D.H. "Reality, Manners, and Mr. T." *SR*, 72: 420-32 (Jl-S 64).

Hough, Graham. "'We' and LT." *Listener*, 75: 760-1 (26 My 66).

Howe, Irving. "Reading LT." *Commentary*, 56: 68-71 (Ag 73).

Krupnick, M.L. "LT: Criticism and Illusion." *ModO*, 1: 282-7 (Wi 71).

Sharma, D.R. "Cultural Criticism: A Critique of T's Position." *IJAS*, 4: 53-65 (Je-D 74).

Steinberg, Lee. "T's Mind/Nation-State in Crisis." *L&I*, 15: 37-44 (1973).

Thompson, John. "LT (1905-1975)." *NYRB*, 22: 58 (11 D 75).

Trilling, Lionel. "Whitaker Chambers and *The Middle of the Journey*." *NYRB*, 17 Ap 75, pp. 18-24.

Vernon, John. "On LT." *Bun 2*, 2: 625-32 (1974).

Troubetzkoy, Princess (see **Rives, Amélie**).

Trowbridge, C.C. Schorer, C.E. "Indian Tales of C.C.T: The Bad Man." *SFQ*, 36: 160-75 (1972).

———. "Indian Tales of C.C.T: The Fisherman." *SFQ*, 38: 63-72 (Mr 74).

———. "Indian Tales of C.C.T: The Ornamented Head." *SFQ*, 33: 317-32 (D 69).

Trumbull, John. Gimmestad, V.E. "Joel Barlow's Editing of JT's *M'Fingal*." *AL*, 47: 97-102 (Mr 75).

———. "JT's Epithalamion." *YULG*, 48: 178-82 (Ja 74).

———. "JT's Original Epithalamion." *EAL*, 10: 159-66 (Fa 74).

Granger, Bruce. "JT, Essayist." *EAL*, 10: 273-88 (Wi 75).

Mize, G.E. "T's Uses of the Epic Formula in *The Progress of Dullness* and *M'Fingal*." *ConnR*, 4: 86-90 (1971).

Rothman, I.N. "JT's Parody of Spenser's 'Epithalamion." *YULG*, 47: 193-215 (1973).

Tucker, Nathaniel Beverley. Wrobel, Arthur. "'Romantic Realism': NBT." *AL*, 42: 325-35 (N 70).

Tuckerman, Frederick Goddard. Kamei, Shunsuke. "FGT no Shi." *EigoS*, 116: 568-70 (1970).

Lynch, T.P. "Still Needed: A T Text." *PBSA*, 69: 255-65 (Ap-Je 75).

Tuckerman, Henry T. Lombard, C.M. "A Neglected Critic—HTT." *EA*, 22: 462-9 (1969).

———. "Gallic Perspective in the Works of HT.T" *BB*, 27: 106-7 (O-D 70).

Turco, Lewis. Fitzgerald, Gregory, and William Heyen. "The Poetry of LT: An Interview." *Costerus*, 9: 239-51 (1973).

Heyen, William. "The Progress of LT." *MPS*, 2: 115-24 (1971).

McLean, D.G. "Craft and Vision: An Interview with LT." *DLAJ*, 4: 1-14 (1970).

Stanion, Terry. "An Interview with LT." *Vermont Freeman*, 3: 21 (N 71).

Waggoner, H.H. "The 'Formalism' of LT: Fluting and Fifing with Frosted Fingers." *CP*, 2: 50-8 (Fa 69).

Turner, Frederick Jackson. Billington, R.A. "FJT: The Image and the Man." *Western Hist Q*, 3: 137-52 (Ap 72).

Boyle, T.E. "FJT and Thomas Wolfe: The Frontier as History and as Literature." *WAL*, 4: 273-85 (Wi 70).

Jacobs, W.R. "The Many-Sided FJT." *WHQ*, 1: 363-72 (O 70).

Lewis, M.E. "The Art of FJT: The Histories." *HLQ*, 35: 241-555 (1972).

Tyler, Royall. Brown, R.H. "A Vermont Republican Urges War: RT, 1812, and the Safety of Republican Government." *VH*, 36: 13-8 (1968).

Dell, R.M., and C.A. Hugenin. "Vermont's RT in New York's John Street Theatre: A Theatrical Hoax Exploded." *VH*, 38: 103-12 (Sp 70).

Dennis, L.D. "Legitimizing the Novel: RT's *The Algerine Captive*." *EAL*, 9: 71-80 (Sp 74).

Javis, K.S. "RT's Lyrics for *May Day in Town*." *HLB*, 23: 186-98 (1975).

Peladeau, M.B. "Some Additional Facts About RT." *BC*, 16: 511-2 (Wi 67).

———. "RT and the University of Vermont." *VH*, 17: 22-34 (Wi 74).

Sata, Masunori. "America Saisho no Kigeke *The Contrast*." *ELLS*, 10: 147-62 (1973).

Tanselle, G.T. "Early American Fiction in England: The Case of *The Algerine Captive*." *PBSA*, 367-84 (4Q 65).

———. "The Editing of RT." *EAL*, 9: 83-95 (Sp 74).

———. "RT, Judith Sargent Murray, and *The Medium*." *NEQ*, 41: 115-7 (Mr 68).

Updike, John. Aldridge, J.W. "An Askew Halo for JU." *SatR*, 53: 25-35 (27 Je 70).

Alley, A.D., and Hugh Agee. "Existential Heroes: Frank Alpine and Rabbit Angstrom." *BSUF*, 9: 3-5 (Wi 68).

Alter, Robert. "U, Malamud, and the Fire This Time." *Commentary*, 54: 68-74 (O 72).

Bachscheider, Paula and Nick. "U's Couples: Squeak in the Night." *MFS*, 20: 45-52 (Sp 74).

Banks, R.J. "The Uses of Weather in 'Tomorrow and Tomorrow and So Forth." *NCLit*, 3: 8-9 (N 73).

Burhans, Clinton. "Things Falling Apart: Structure and Theme in *Rabbit, Run*." *StN*, 5: 336-51 (Fa 74).

Cowley, Malcolm. "Holding the Fort on Audubon Terrace." *SatR*, 54: 17, 41-2 (3 Ap 71).

Dalton, Elizabeth. "To Have and Have Not." *PR*, 36: 134-6 (Wi 69).

De Rambures, J.L. "Le cœur secret de l'Amérique." *Réalités*, 266: 99-103 (Mr 68).

Detweiler, Robert. "The Elements of JU: Another Appraisal." *Cri & Lit*, 20: 24-7 (1972).

———. "U's *Couples*: Eros Demythologized." *TCL*, 17: 235-46 (1971).

Ditsky, John. "Roth, U, and the High Expense of Spirit." *UWR*, 5: 111-20 (Fa 69).

Doyle, P.A. "The Fiction of JU." *NasR*, 1: 9-19 (Sp 64).

———. "U's Fiction: Motifs and Techniques." *CathW*, 199: 356-62 (S 64).

Edwards, A.S.G. "U's 'A Sense of Shelter.'" *SSF*, 8: 467-8 (1971).

Elistratova, A. "Man Is a Tragic Animal: JU's Two Novels." *Inostrannaya Literatura*, 2: 220-6 (F 63).

Epstein, Seymour. "The Emperor's Blue Jeans." *UDQ*, 6: 89-95 (1972).

Falke, Wayne. "America Strikes Out: U's *Rabbit Redux*." *AmEx*, 3: 18-21 (#3 74).

———. "*Rabbit Redux*: Time/Order/God." *MFS*, 20: 59-76 (Sp 74).

Finkelstein, Sidney. "The Anti-Hero of U, Bellow and Malamud." *AmD*, 7: 12-4, 30 (1972).

Flint, Joyce. "JU and *Couples*: The WASP's Dilemma." *RSW*, 36: 340-7 (D 68).

Friedman, Ruben. "An Interpretation of JU's 'Tomorrow and Tomorrow and so Forth.'" *EJ*, 61: 1159-62 (N 72).

Gado, Frank. "A Conversation with JU." *Idol*, 47: 3-32 (Sp 71).

Gediman, Helen. "Reflections on Romanticism, Narcissism, and Creativity." *JAPA*, 33: 407-23 (1975).

Geller, Evelyn. "WLB Biography: JU." *WLB*, 36: 67 (S 61).

Gindin, James. "Megalotopia and the WASP Backlash: The Fiction of Mailer and U." *CentR*, 15: 38-52 (Wi 71).

Gingher, R.S. "Has JU Anything to Say?" *MFS*, 20: 97-106 (Sp 74).

Gratton, Margaret. "The Use of Rhythm in Three Novels by JU." *UPortR*, 21: 3-12 (Fa 69).

Griffith, A.J. "U's Artist's Dilemma: 'Should Wizard Hit Mommy?'" *MFS*, 20: 111-4 (Sp 74).

Hamilton, Alice. "Between Innocence and Experience: from Joyce to U." *DR*, 49: 102-9 (Sp 69).

————, and Kenneth. "JU's Museums and Women and Other Stories." *Thought*, 49: 56-71 (Mr 74).

————. "Metamorphosis Through Art: JU's *Bech: A Book*." *QQ*, 77: 624-36 (Wi 70).

————. "Mythic Dimensions in JU's Fiction." *NDQ*, 41: 54-66 (1973).

————. "Theme and Technique in JU's Midpoint." *Mosaic*, 41: 54-66 (1973).

————. "The Validation of Religious Faith in the Writings of JU." *Stud Rel*, 5: 275-85 (1975).

Hamilton, Kenneth. "JU: Chronicler of 'The Time of the Death of God.'" *Chri Chron*, 84: 747-8 (7 Je 67).

Hill, J.S. "Quest for Belief: Theme in the Novels of JU." *SHR*, 3: 166-78 (Sp 69).

Horton, A.S. "Ken Kesey, JU, and the Lone Ranger." *JPC*, 8: 570-8 (Wi 74).

Howard, Jane. "Can a Nice Novelist Finish First?" *Life*, 4 N 66, pp. 74-82.

Hyman, S.E. "The Artist as a Young Man." *NewL*, 45: 22-3 (19 Mr 62).

Jones, E.T. "An Art of Equilibrium: Piet Mondrian and JU." *Connecticut Critic*, 7: 4-10 (Mr 73).

Kanon, Joseph. "Satire and Sensibility." *SatR*, O 72, pp. 55, 73, 78.

Kazin, Alfred. "O'Hara, Cheever, & U." *NYRB*, 20: 14-9 (19 Ap 73).

Killinger, John. "The Death of God in American Literature." *SHR*, 2: 149-72 (Wi 68).

Larsen, R.B. "JU: The Story as Lyrical Meditation." *Thoth*, 13: 33-9 (Wi 72-3).

Lawson, Lewis. "Rabbit Angstrom as a Religious Sufferer." *Am Acad Rel*, 42: 232-48 (Je 74).

Le Vot, André. "Le Petit Monde de JU." *LanM*, 63: 66-73 (Ja-F 69).

Lupan, Radu. "Civilizatie si tradite." *Luc*, 67-75 (D 73).

Lurie, Allison. "Witches and Fairies: Fitzgerald to U." *NYRB*, 17: 6-11 (2 D 71).

Lyons, Eugene. "JU: The Beginning and the End." *Critique*, 14: 44-59 (Sp, Su 72).

McCoy, Robert. "JU's Literary Apprenticeship on *The Harvard Lampoon*." *MFS*, 20: 3-12 (Sp 74).

McKenzie, A.T. "'A Craftsman's Intimate Satisfactions': The Parlor Games in *Couples*." *MFS*, 20: 53-8 (Sp 74).

Malin, Irving. "Occasions for Loving." *KR*, 25: 348-52 (Sp 63).

Mathy, Francis. "Zetsubo no kanata ni." *SophT*, 19: 356-77 (1970).

Matson, Elizabeth. "A Chinese Paradox, But Not Much of One: JU in His Poetry." *MinnR*, 7: 157-67 (1967).

Meyer, A.G. "The Theology of JU." *Cresset*, 34: 23-5 (O 71).

*————, and M.A. Olivas. "Criticism of JU: A Selected Checklist." *MFS*, 20: 121-35 (Sp 74).

Molyneux, Thomas. "The Affirming Balance of Voice." *Shen*, 25: 27-43 (Wi 74).

Myers, David. "The Questing Fear: Christian Allegory in JU's *The Centaur*." *TCL*, 17: 73-82 (Ap 71).

Nemoianu, Virgil. "Povestiri de JU." *RoLit*, 31: 28 (Ja 74).

Oates, J.C. "U's American Comedies." *MFS*, 21: 459-72 (Au 75).

Overmyer, Janet. "Courtly Love in the A&P." *NCLit*, 2: 4-5 (My 72).

Pérez Gállego, Cándido. "La novelística de JU." *Arbor*, 319-20: 73-84 (1972).

Pérez-Minik, Domingo. "La novela extranjera en España: *El libro de Bech*, de JU." *Insula*, 26: 6 (O 71).

Peter, John. "The Self-Effacement of the Novelist." *MalR*, 8: 119-28 (O 68).

Petillon, Pierre-Yves. "Le désespoir de JU." *Crit (P)*, 25: 972-7 (1969).

Petter, H. "JU's Metaphoric Novels." *ES*, 50: 197-206 (Ap 69).

Popescu, Petru. "*Centaurul* de JU." *RoLit*, 3: 19 (Ap 69).

Porter, M.G. "JU's 'A&P': The Establishment and an Emersonian Cashier." *EJ*, 61: 1155-8 (1972).

Regan, R.A. "U's Symbol of the Center." *MFS*, 20: 77-96 (Sp 74).

Reising, R.W. "U's 'A Sense of Shelter.'" *SSF*, 7: 651-2 (Fa 70).

Rhode, Eric. "BBC Interview with JU." *Listener*, 81: 862-4 (19 Je 69).

————. "Grabbing Dilemmas: JU Talks About God, Love, and the American Identity." *Vogue*, 157: 140-1, 184-5 (O 74).

Rosa, A.F. "The Psycholinguistics of U's 'Museums and Women.'" *MFS*, 20: 107-10 (Sp 74).

Rotundo, Barbara. "*Rabbit, Run* and *A Tale of Peter Rabbit*." *NCLit*, 1: 2-3 (My 71).

Russell, Mariann. "White Man's Black Man." *CLAJ*, 17: 93-100 (S 73).

Samuels, C.T. "Interview with JU." *PaR*, 45: 85-117 (1968).

Schlesinger, Arthur. "The Historical Mind and the Literary Imagination." *Atl*, 233: 54-9 (Je 74).

Seelbach, Wilhelm. "Die antike Mythologie in JU's Roman *The Centaur*." *Arcadia*, 5: 176-94 (1970).

Sharrock, Roger. "Singles and Couples: Hemingway's *A Farewell to Arms*, and U's *Couples*." *Ariel*, 3: 21-43 (O 73).

Sissman, L.E. "JU: Midpoint and After." *Atl*, 226: 102-4 (Ag 70).

Stafford, W.T. "'The Curious Greased Grace' of JU." *JML*, 2: 369-75 (N 72).

————. "U Fourfivesix, 'Just Like That.'" *MFS*, 20: 115-20 (1974).

Stubbs, J.C. "The Search for Perfection in *Rabbit, Run*." *Critique*, 10: 94-101 (1968).

Suderman, E.F. "Art as a Way of Knowing." *Discourse*, 12: 3-14 (1969).

————. "The Right Way and the Good Way in *Rabbit Run*." *UR*, 36: 13-21 (Au 69).

Sullivan, Walter. "U, Spark, and Others." *SR*, 74: 709-16 (Su 66).

Sykes, R.H. "A Commentary on U's Astronomer." *SSF*, 8: 575-9 (1971).

Tanner, Tony. "The American Novelist as Entropologist." *LonM*, 10: 5-18 (O 70).

————. "Hello, Olleh." *Spec*, 7324: 658-9 (8 N 68).

Thompson, John. "Other People's Affairs." *PR*, 27: 117-24 (F 61).

Todd, Richard. "U and Barthelme: Disengagement." *Atl*, 230: 126-32 (D 72).

Turner, Kermit. "Rabbit Brought Nowhere: JU's *Rabbit Redux*." *SCR*, 8: 35-42 (N 75).

Updike, John. "Bech intră in rai." *Steaua*, 24: 23-4 (1974).

Vanderwerken, D.L. "Rabbit 'Re-docks': U's Inner Space Odyssey." *ColLit*, 2: 73-8 (Wi 75).

Vargo, E.P. "The Necessity of Myth in U's *The Centaur*." *PMLA*, 88: 452-60 (My 73).

Vickery, J.B. "*The Centaur*: Myth, History, and Narrative." *MFS*, 20: 29-44 (Sp 74).

Vormweg, Heinrich. "JU: Verfall eines Realisten." *Merkur*, 24: 394-7 (Ap 70).

Waldmeir, Joseph. "It's the Going That's Important, Not the Getting There: Rabbit's Questing Non-Quest." *MFS*, 20: 13-28 (Sp 74).

Waller, G.F. "U's *Couples*: A Barthian Parable." *RSW*, 40: 10-21 (1972).

Wartemberg, Joris. "Face to Face." *Pleasure*, 5: 15, 25 (1973).

Weber, Brom. "*Rabbit Redux*." *SatR*, 54: 54-5 (27 N 71).

Wilhelm, A.E. "The Clothing Motif in U's *Rabbit, Run*." *SAB*, 40: 87-9 (N 75).

Zylstra, A. "JU and the Parabolic Nature of the World." *Soundings*, 56: 323-37 (1973).

Van Doren, Mark. Gold, Herbert. "Speaking of MV." *NYTBR*, 10 N 68, pp. 2, 24.

MacLeish, Archibald. "AM on 'O World.'" *Voyages*, 5: 12 (1973).

Schulman, Grace. "MVD as an American." *Nation*, 15 O 73, pp. 375-6.

Sullivan, Kevin. "Remembering MV." *Nation*, 216: 13-4 (1 Ja 73).

Whitney, Blair. "Lincoln's Life as Dramatic Art." *JISHS*, 61: 333-49 (Au 68).

Young, Marguerite. "MVD: A Poet in an Age of Defoliation." *Voyages*, 3: 60-2 (Wi 70).

van Itallie, Jean-Claude. Anon. "VI: A Chronology (1936-1972)." *Serif*, 9: 6-8 (Wi 72).

Adler, T.P. "VI's 'The Serpent': History After the Fall." *D&T*, 11: 12-4 (Fa 72).

Berk, P.R. "Memories of John." *Serif*, 9: 9-11 (Wi 72).

*Brittain, M.J. "A Checklist of J-CvI, 1961-1972." *Serif*, 9: 75-7 (Wi 72).

Gaisner, Rhea. "J-CvI: Playwright of the Ensemble: Open Theater." *Serif*, 9: 14-7 (Wi 72).

Tonma, Kesang. "A Short Autobiography of Kesang Tonma." *Serif*, 9: 12-3 (Wi 72).

Wagner, P.J. "J-CvI: Political Playwright." *Serif*, 9: 19-74 (Wi 72).

Van Peebles, Melvin. Bauerle, R.F. "The Theme of Absurdity in MVP's *A Bear for the FBI*." *NCLit*, 1: 11-2 (S 71).

Botto, Louis. "MVP: Work in Progress." *Black Times*, 2: 12-3 (1972).

Hewes, Henry. "The Aints and the Am Nots." *SatR*, 54: 10, 11-2 (13 N 71).

Van Vechten, Carl. Coleman, Leon. "CVV Presents the New Negro." *SLit*, 7: 85-104 (Fa 74).

Kellner, Bruce. "HLM and CVV: Friendship of Paper." *Mencken*, 39: 2-9 (Fa 71).

———. "The Origin of the Sonnets from the Patagonians." *HartR*, 3: 50-6 (Sp 67).

Larson, C.R. "Three Harlem Novels of the Jazz Age." *Critique*, 11: 66-78 (1969).

Ringo, James. "A Three-Quarter-Length Portrait of CVV." *Cabellian*, 1: 68-71 (1969).

Robinson, Clayton. "Gilmore Millen's *Sweet Man*: Neglected Classic of the VV Vogue." *Forum (H)*, 8: 32-5 (1970).

Veblen, Thorstein. Conroy, S.S. "TV's Prose." *AQ*, 20: 605-15 (Fa 68).

———. "V's Progeny." *ColQ*, 16: 413-22 (1968).

McIlvaine, R.M. "Dos Passos's Reading of TV." *AL*, 44: 471-4 (N 72).

———. "Robert Herrick and TV." *RSW*, 40: 132-5 (1972).

Very, Jones. Arner, R.D. "Hawthorne and JV: Two Dimensions of Satire in 'Egotism; or, the Bosom Serpent.'" *NEQ*, 42: 267-75 (1969).

Cameron, K.W. "*Poems of JV*: James Freeman Clarke's Enlarged Collection of 1886 Re-edited with a Thematic and Topical Index." *ATQ*, 21: 1-143 (1974).

Dennis, Carl. "Correspondence in V's Nature Poetry." *NEQ*, 43: 250-73 (Je 70).

Fleck, Richard. "JV—Another White Indian." *ConS*, 9: 6-12 (S 74).

Fone, B.R.S. "A Note on the JV Editions." *AN&Q*, 6: 67-9, 88-9 (Ja-F 68).

Reeves, Paschal. "JV as Preacher: The Extant Sermons." *ESQ*, 57: 16-22 (4Q 69).

*Robinson, David. "JV: An Essay in Bibliography." *RALS*, 5: 131-46 (Au 75).

———. "JV: The Transcendentalists and the Unitarian Tradition." *HTR*, 68: 103-24 (1975).

Vidal, Gore. Boyette, P.E. "*Myra Breckinridge* and Imitative Form." *MFS*, 17: 229-38 (Su 71).

Clarke, Gerald. "The Art of Fiction: GV." *PaR*, 59: 130-65 (Fa 74).

———. "Petronius Americanus: The Ways of GV." *Atl*, 229: 44-51 (Mr 72).

Davidon, A.M. "GV and the Two-Headed Monster." *Nation*, 218: 661-3 (25 My 74).

*Gilliam, L.M. "GV: A Checklist, 1945-1969." *BB*, 30: 1-9, 44 (1973).

Goodfriend, Arthur. "The Cognoscenti Abroad—GV's Rome." *SatR*, 52: 36-9 (25 Ja 69).

Hughes, Catherine. "The Name of the Game." *Prog*, 36: 31-2 (Ag 72).

Koch, Stephen. "GV: Urbane Witness to History." *SR/World*, 1: 24-9 (19 D 73).

Krim, Seymour. "Reflections on a Ship That's Not Sinking at All." *LonM*, 10: 26-43 (My 70).

Rosselli, Aldo. "Pettegolezze e altre quisquilie dell'ultimo GV." *NArg*, 19: 230-55 (1970).

Schlesinger, Arthur. "The Historical Mind and the Literary Imagination." *Atl*, 233: 54-9 (Je 74).

Vidal, Gore. "V's Brow." *NSt*, 25 Jl 69, p. 115.

Vree, Freddy de. "GV, *Collected Essays.*" *K&C*, 19: 22 (S 74).

Viereck, George Sylvester. English, Maurice. "The Poet as Exorcist." *TriQ*, 11: 246-55 (Wi 68).

Johnson, N.M. "GSV: Poet and Propagandist." *BI*, 9: 22-36 (N 68).

———. "Pro-Freud and Pro-Nazi: The Paradox of GS.V." *Psychoanalytic R*, 58: 553-62 (Wi 71-2).

Keller, Phyllis. "GSV: The Psychology of a German-American Militant." *J Interdisciplinary Hist*, 2: 59-108 (Su 71).

Vonnegut, Kurt, Jr. Abadi-Nagy, Zoltan. "'The Skillful Seducer.': Of V's Brand of Comedy." *HSE*, 8: 45-56 (1974).

Bourjaily, Vance. "What V Is or Isn't." *NYT*, 13 Ag 72, pp. 3, 10.

Bryan, C.D.B. "KV, Head Bokononist." *NYTBR*, 6 Ap 69, pp. 2, 25.

Buck, Lynn. "V's World of Comic Futility." *SAF*, 3: 181-98 (Au 75).

Burhans, Clinton. "Hemingway and V: Diminishing Vision in a Dying Age." *MFS*, 21: 173-92 (Su 75).

Clancy, L.J. "'If the Accident Will': The Novels of KV." *Meanjin*, 30: 37-45 (Mr 71).

———. "'Running Experiments Off.'" *Meanjin*, 30: 46-54 (Mr 71).

DeMott, Benjamin. "V's Otherworldly Laughter." *SatR*, 54: 29-32, 38 (1 My 71).

Dimeo, Steven. "Reconciliation: *Slaughterhouse-Five*—the Film and the Novel." *Film Heritage*, 8: 1-12 (Wi 72-3).

Edelstein, Arnold. "*Slaughterhouse-Five*: Time Out of Joint." *Col Lit*, 2: 128-39 (1974).

Engel, David. "On the Question of Foma: A Study of the Novels of KV, Jr." *RQ*, 5: 119-28 (F 72).

Fiedler, L.A. "The Divine Stupidity of KV." *Esquire*, 74: 195-200, 202-4 (S 70).

Fiene, D.M. "V's *Sirens of Titan.*" *Expl*, 34: 27 (D 75).

Flora, J.M. "Cabell as Precursor: Reflections on Cabell and V." *Kalki*, 6: 118-37 (1975).

Friedrich, Otto. "Ultra-V." *Time*, 7 May 73; pp. 65-6.

Godshalk, W.L. "The Recurring Characters of KV." *NCLit*, 3: 2-3 (Ja 73).

———. "V and Shakespeare: Rosewater at Elsinore." *Critique*, 15: 37-48 (#2 73).

Greiner, D.J. "V's *Slaughterhouse-Five* and the Fiction of Atrocity." *Critique*, 14: 38-51 (Sp 73).

Grossman, Edward. "V and His Audience." *Commentary*, 58: 40-6 (1974).

Hendin, Joseph. "Writer as Culture Hero, the Father as Son." *HM*, 249: 82-7 (Jl 74).

Horowitz, Carey. "An Interview with KV, Jr." *LJ*, 98: 1311 (15 Ap 73).

Isaacs, N.D. "Unstuck in Time: *Clockwork Orange* and *Slaughterhouse-Five.*" *LFQ*, 1: 122-33 (Ap 73).

Iwamoto, Iwao. "A Clown's Say: A Study of KV, Jr's *Slaughterhouse-Five.*" *SELit*, 14: 21-31 (1975).

Klinkowitz, Jerome. "The Dramatization of KV, Jr." *Players*, 50: 62-5 (F-Mr 75).

———. "KV, Jr., and the Crime of His Times." *Critique*, 12: 38-53 (1971).

———. "The Literary Career of KV, Jr." *MFS*, 19: 57-67 (Sp 73).

———. "Lost in the Cathouse." *Falcon*, 5: 110-3 (Fa 72).

*———, and Stanley Schatt. "A KV Checklist." *Critique*, 12: 70-6 (1971).

Leff, L.J. "Utopia Reconstructed: Alienation in V's *God Bless You, Mr. Rosewater.*" *Critique*, 12: 29-37 (1971).

Leverence, W.J. "*Cat's Cradle* and Traditional American Humor." *JPC*, 5: 955-63 (Sp 72).

McGinnis, Wayne. "The Arbitrary Cycle of *Slaughterhouse-Five*: A Relation of Form to Theme." *Critique*, 17: 55-8 (1Q 75).

————. "Names in V's Fiction." *NCLit*, 3: 7-9 (S 73).

————. "V's *Breakfast of Champions*." *NCLit*, 5: 6-9 (#3 75).

McLaughlin, Frank. "An Interview with KV, Jr." *M&M*, 9: 38-41, 45-6 (My 73).

McNamara, Eugene. "The Absurd Style in Contemporary American Literature." *HAB*, 19: 44-9 (Wi 68).

May, John R. "V's Humor and the Limits of Hope." *TCL*, 18: 25-36 (Ja 72).

Meades, Jonathan. "KV, Fantasist." *B&B*, 18: 34-7 (F 73).

Messent, P.B. "*Breakfast of Champions*: The Direction of V's Fiction." *JAmSt*, 8: 101-14 (Ap 74).

Nelson, Joyce. "*Slaughterhouse-Five*: Novel and Film." *LFQ*, 1: 149-53 (1973).

————. "V and 'Bugs in Amber.'" *JPC*, 7: 551-8 (1973).

O'Connor, G.W. "The Function of Time Travel in V's *Slaughterhouse-Five*." *RQ*, 5: 206-7 (1972).

Palmer, R.C. "V's Major Concerns." *IEngYb*, 14: 3-10 (Fa 69).

Pauly, R.M. "The Moral Stance of KV." *Extrapolation*, 15: 66-71 (D 73).

Pinsker, Sanford. "Fire and Ice: The Radical Cuteness of KV, Jr." *STC*, 13: 1-20 (Sp 74).

Prioli, C.A. "KV's Duty-Dance." *ELUD*, 1: 44-50 (S 73).

Putz, Manfred. "Who Am I This Time: Die Romane von KV." *JA*, 19: 111-25 (1974).

Ranly, E.W. "What Are People For? Man, Fate and KV." *Cweal*, 94: 207-11 (1971).

Samuels, C.T. "Age of V." *NRep*, 164: 30-2 (12 Je 71).

Schatt, Stanley. "The Whale and the Cross: V's Jonah and Christ Figures." *SWR*, 56: 29-42 (Wi 71).

————. "The World of KV, Jr." *Critique*, 12: 54-69 (1971).

Schickel, Richard. "Black Comedy with Purifying Laughter." *HM*, 232: 103-6.

Scholl, P.A. "V's Attack upon Christianity." *Chri & Lit*, 22: 5-11 (Fa 72).

Schriber, M.S. "You've Come a Long Way, Babbitt! From Zenity to Illium." *TCL*, 17: 101-6 (1971).

Schulz, M.F. "The Unconfirmed Thesis: KV, Black Humor, and Contemporary Art." *Critique*, 12: 5-28 (1971).

Stelzmann, Rainulf A. "Die verlorene Utopie: Das Werk KVs und die amerikanische Jugend." *Neochland*, 66: 271-80 (1974).

Tanner, Tony. "The Uncertain Messenger: A Study of the Novels of KV, Jr." *CritQ*, 11: 297-315 (Wi 69).

Todd, Richard. "The Masks of KV, Jr." *NYTMS*, 24 Ja 71, pp. 16-31.

Trachtenberg, Stanley. "V's *Cradle*: The Erosion of Comedy." *MQR*, 12: 66-71 (Wi 73).

Truchlar, Leo. "Fiktion und Realität in KVs *Slaughterhouse-Five*." *Sprachkunst*, 4: 114-23 (1973).

Tunnell, J.R. "Kesey and V: Preachers of Redemption." *ChrC*, 89: 1180-3 (1972).

Uphaus, R.W. "Expected Meaning in V's Dead-End Fiction: *Breakfast of Champions*, and Others." *Novel*, 8: 164-74 (Wi 75).

Vanderweeken, D.L. "Pilgrim's Dilemma: Slaughterhouse-Five." *RSW*, 42: 147-52 (1974).

Vasbinder, Sam. "The Meaning of 'Foma' in *Cat's Cradle*." *RQ*, 5: 300-2 (Ap 73).

Vinograde, A.C. "A Soviet Translation of *Slaughterhouse-Five*." *RLJ*, 93: 14-8 (1972).

Vonnegut, Kurt. "Abatorul nr. 5 sau cruciada copilor." *Steaua*, 24: 25-6 (1974).

————. "'Running Experiments Off': An Interview with L.J. Clancy." *Meanjin*, 30: 46-54 (1971).

Wolfe, G.K. "V and the Metaphor of Science Fiction: *The Sirens of Titan*." *JPC*, 5: 964-9 (Sp 72).

Zverev A. "Skaski teknicheskogo veka." *VLit*, 18: 32-66 (F 75).

Wade, John Donald. Davidson, Donald. "The Garden of JDW." *GaR*, 19: 383-403 (Wi 65).

Fain, J.T. "Segments of Southern Renaissance." *SAB*, 36: 23-31 (My 71).

Inge, M.T. "The Legacy of JDW." *GaR*, 21: 287-96 (1967).

Smith, G.J. "Augustus Baldwin Longstreet and JW's 'Cousin Lucius.'" *GHQ*, 56: 276-81 (1972).

Wagoner, David. Pinsker, Sanford. "The Achievement of DW." *ConnR*, 8, i: 42-7 (O 74).

———. "On DW." *Salmagundi*, 22-23: 306-14 (1973).

Wakefield, Dan. Klinkowitz, Jerome. "On DW's Superfiction." *FicI*, 2: 126-32 (iii 74).

Shepherd, Allen. "Going Down with W: Non-Father's Balloon Strategy in *Starting Over*." *NCLit*, 5: 8-9 (S 75).

Wakefield, Dan. "Novel Bites Man." *Atl*, 226: 72-8 (Ag 70).

Walker, Alice. Callahan, John. "Reconsideration: The Higher Ground of AW." *NRep*, 171: 21-2 (14 S 74).

Harris, Trudier." Violence in *The Third Life of Grange Copeland*." *CLAJ*, 19: 238-47 (D 75).

Washington, M.H. "Black Women Image Makers." *BlackW*, 23: 10-18 (1974).

Walker, David. Haskett, N.D. "Afro-American Images of Africa: Four *Antebellum* Black Authors." *Ufahamu*, 3: 29-40 (1972).

Seraile, William. "DW and Malcolm X: Brothers in Radical Thought." *BlackW*, 22: 68-73 (1973).

Wallace, Lewis. Morsberger, R.E. "And the Horse-Race: Ben Hur on Stage." *JPC*, 8: 489-502 (1974).

Wallant, Edward Lewis. Ayo, Nicholas. "ELW, 1926-62." *BB*, 28: 119 (O-D 71).

———. "The Secular Heart: The Achievement of ELW." *Critique*, 12: 86-94 (1970).

Davis, W.V. "Fathers and Sons in the Fiction of EW." *RSW*, 40: 53-5 (1972).

———. "The Renewal of Dialogical Immediacy in ELW." *Renascence*, 24: 59-69 (Wi 72).

———. "The Sound of Silence: ELW's *The Children at the Gate*." *Cithara*, 8: 3-25 (N 68).

———. "A Synthesis in the Contemporary Jewish Novel: ELW." *Cresset*, 31: 8-13 (My 68).

Gurko, Leo. "ELW as Urban Novelist." *TCL*, 20: 252-61 (O 74).

Lewis, R.W. "The Hung-Up Heroes of ELW." *Renascence*, 24: 70-84 (Wi 72).

Oi, Koji. "E.L.W no Shosetsu." *EigoS*, 116: 635-6 (1970).

Schulz, M.F. "W and Friedman: The Glory and the Agony of Love." *Crit*, 10: 31-47 (1968).

Stanford, Raney. "The Novels of EW." *ColQ*, 17: 393-405 (Sp 69).

Walser, Richard. *Betts, Leonidus, and Guy Owen. "Bibliography of RW." *NCaF*, 19: 87-96 (Mr 71).

Walsh, Robert. Woodall, G.R. "The Relationship of RW, Jr. to the *Port Folio* and the Dennie Circle: 1803-1812." *PMHB*, 92: 195-219 (Ap 68).

———. "A Reviewer and His Editor: The Literary Relationship of George Bancroft and RW." *TSL*, 14: 35-49 (1969).

———. "RW's Role in the Struggle Against Byron and Byronism in America." *TTJ*, 3: 29-38 (1968).

———. "RW's War with the New York Literati: 1827-1836." *TSL*, 15: 25-47 (1970).

———. "Some Sources of the Essays in RW's *Didactics*." *SB*, 24: 184-7 (1971).

Walter, Nehemiah. Arner, R.D. "NW: Milton's Earliest American Disciple?" *EAL*, 8: 62-5 (Sp 73).

Danbzies, André. "The First American *Faust* (1720)." *CLS*, 8: 303-9 (D 71).

Ward, Artemus. (see **Brown, Charles Farrar**).

Ward, Elizabeth Stuart Phelps. Stansell, Christine. "ESP: A Study in Female Rebellion." *MR*, 13: 239-56 (Wi-Sp 72).

Ward, Nathaniel. Arner, R.D. "*The Simple Cobler of Aggawam*: NW and the Rhetoric of Satire." *EAL*, 5: 3-16 (Wi 70-71).

Scheick, W.J. "NW's Cobbler as 'Schoem-Aker.'" *ELN*, 9: 100-2 (D 71).

———. "The Widower Narrator in NW's *The Simple Cobler of Aggawam in America*." *NEQ*, 47: 87-96 (Mr 74).

Ware, Eugene, F. Malin, J.C. 'EF.W's Literary Chronology." *KHQ*, 37: 314-32 (Au 71).

———. "Notes on the Poetic Debts of EF.W—Ironquill." *KHQ*, 35: 165-81 (Su 69).

———. "Notes on the Several Editions of EF.W's *Rhymes of Ironquill*." *KHQ*, 33: 481-511 (Wi 67).

Ware, Henry. Cameron, K.W. "HW's *Divinity School Address*: A Reply to Emerson's." *ATQ*, 13: 84-91 (1972).

Dahl, Curtis. "New England Unitarianism in Fictional Antiquity: The Romances of HW." *NEQ*, 48: 104-15 (Mr 75).

Warner, Charles Dudley. Crowley, J.W. "A Note on *The Gilded Age*." *ELN*, 10: 116-8 (D 72).

Warner, Susan B. Manthorne, Jane. "The Lachrymose Ladies." *HornB*, 43: 375-84, 501-13, 622-30 (Je, Ag 67).

Warren, Austin. Fowlie, Wallace. "The Search for Stability." *SR*, 76z; 665-72 (1968).

Warren, Austin. "In Search of a Vocation." *MQR*, 11: 237-47 (Au 72).

Warren, Mercy Otis. Freidman, L.J., and A.H. Schaffer. "MOW and the Politics of Historical Nationalism." *NEQ*, 48: 194-215 (Je 75).

Haverstick, I.S. "Three Lively Ladies of the Overbury Collection." *CLC*, 21: 20-7 (1971).

Hutcheson, M.M. "MW, 1728-1814." *WMQ*, 10: 378-402 (1952).

Warren, Robert Penn. Anon. "Violence in Literature." *ASch*, 37: 482-96 (Su 68).

Aldridge, J.W. "The Enormous Spider Web of W's World." *SatR*, 54: 31-7 (9 O 71).

Arnavon, Cyrille. "RPW: Interprète de l'histoire américaine." *Europe*, 48: 205-26 (Jl 70).

Balazy, Teresa. "W's *Meet Me in a Green Glen*." *SAP*, 6: 147-55 (#1 75).

Bataille, Robert. "The Esthetics and Ethics of Farming: The Southern Agrarian View." *Iowa State J Res*, 49: 189-93 (1974).

Bauerle, R.F. "The Emblematic Opening of W's *All the King's Men*." *PLL*, 8: 312-4 (Su 72).

Beatty, R.C. "The Poetry and Novels of RPW." *Vanderbilt Stud Humanities*, 1: 142-60 (1951).

Bergonzi, Bernard. "Nature, Mostly American." *SoR*, 6: 205-15 (Wi 70).

Berner, Robert. "The Required Past: *World Enough and Time*." *MFS*, 6: 55-64 (Sp 60).

Berthoff, Warner. "Dreiser Revisited." *ModO*, 2: 1133-6 (Wi 72).

Bisanz, A.J. "RPW: 'The Ballad of Billie Potts.'" *Fabula*, 14: 71-90 (1973).

Breyer, B.R. "A Diagnosis of Violence in Recent Southern Literature." *MissQ*, 14: 59-67 (Sp 61).

Brooks, Cleanth. "Brooks on W." *FourQ*, 21: 19-22 (My 72).

Brufee, K.A. "Elegiac Romance." *CE*, 32: 465-76 (Ja 71).

Buffington, Robert. "The Poetry of the Master's Old Age." *GaR*, 25: 5-16 (Sp 71).

Burt, D.J. "A Folk Reference in W's *Flood*." *MissQ*, 22: 74-6 (Wi 68-69).

———. "RPW's Debt to Homer in *Flood*." *NCLit*, 3: 12-4 (Ja 73).

———, and A.C. "RPW's Debt to Ibsen in *Night Rider*." *MissQ*, 22: 359-61 (Fa 69).

Campbell, H.M. "Notes on Religion in the Southern Renaissance." *Shen*, 6: 10-8 (Su 55).

Carter, Everettt. "The 'Little Myth' of RPW." *MFS*, 6: 3-12 (Sp 60).

Carter, Hodding. "Huey Long's Louisiana Hayride." *AmMerc*, 68: 435-47 (Ap 49).

Casper, Leonard. "Ark, *Flood*, and Negotiated Covenant."*FourQ*, 21: 110-5 (My 72).

———. "Journey to the Interior: *The Cave*." *MFS*, 6: 65-72 (Sp 60).

Cayton, R.F. "The Fictional Voices of RPW." *FourQ*, 21: 45-52 (My 72).

Core, George. "In the Heart's Ambiguity: RPW as Poet." *MissQ*, 22: 313-26 (Fa 69).

Crews, F.C. "A Search for Identity in Fiddlersburg." *NYT*, 26 Ap 64, p. 6.

Davis, Joe. "RPW and the Journey to the West." *MFS*, 6: 73-82 (Sp 60).

Davison, R.A. "Physical Imagery in RPW's 'Blackberry Winter.'" *GaR*, 22: 482-8 (Wi 68).

Dooley, D.M. "The Persona RPW in W's *Brother to Dragons*." *MissQ*, 25: 19-30 (Wi 71-72).

Ellison, Ralph, and Eugene Walter. "RPW." *PaR*, 4: 112-40 (Sp-Su 57).

———, and William Styron, R.P.W., and C.V. Woodward. "The Uses of History in Fiction." *SLJ*, 1: 57-90 (Sp 69).

Ferguson, Suzanne. "'Something Which the Past Has Hid.'" *SR*, 80: 493-8 (Su 72).

Fiedler, Leslie. "On Two Frontiers." *PR*, 17: 739-43 (S-O 50).

Fisher, Ruth. "A Conversation with RPW."*FourQ*, 21: 3-17 (My 72).

Flint, F.C. "RPW." *Am Oxonian*, 34: 65-79 (Ap 74).

Frank, Joseph. "Romanticism and Reality in RPW." *HudR*, 4: 248-58 (Su 51).

Fuchs, Carolyn. "Words, Action, and the Modern Novel." *Kerygma*, 4: 3-11 (Wi 64).

Gerhard, George. "*All the King's Men*." *Folio*, 15: 4-11 (My 50).

Glazier, Lyle. "Reconstructed Platonism: RPW's *The Cave*." *Litera*, 7: 16-26 (1960).

Goldfarb, R.M. "RP.W's Tollivers and Geroge Eliot's Tullivers." *UR*, 36: 209-13 (Mr 70).

Goldstein, Laurence. "Audubon and R.P.W: To See and Record All Life." *Cont Poetry*, 2: 47-68 (Wi 73).

Grantham, D.W. "Interpreters of the Modern South." *SAQ*, 63: 521-9 (Au 64).

Gray, R.J. "The American Novelist and American History: A Revaluation of *All The King's Men*." *JAmSt*, 6: 297-307 (D 72).

Grimshaw, James. "RPW's *Annus Mirabilis*." *SoR*, 10: 504-16 (Wi 74).

*———. "RPW: A Bibliography." *PBSA*, 65: 188-90 (2Q 71).

Harvard, W.C. "The Burden of the Literary Mind: Some Meditations on RPW as Historian." *SAQ*, 62: 516-31 (Au 63).

Hatch, Robert. "Down to the Self." *Nation*, 189: 138-9 (12 S 59).

Heilman, R.P. "Melpomena as Wallflower." *SR*, 55: 154-66 (Ja-Mr 47).

Heilman, R.B. "The Southern Temper." *HopR*, 6: 5-15 (Fa 52).

Herring, H.D. "Madness in *At Heaven's Gate*: A Metaphor of the Self in W's Fiction." *FourQ*, 21: 56-66 (My 72).

———. "Politics in the Novels of RPW." *Ranam*, 4: 48-60 (1971).

Hiers, J.T. "Buried Graveyards: W's *Flood* and Jones' *A Buried Land*." *EL*, 2: 97-104 (Sp 75).

Howard, Richard. "Dreadful Alternatives: A Note on RPW." *SoR*, (Sp 75).

Hudson, R.B. "*All the King's Men*." *Folio*, 15: 11-3 (My 50).

Inge, M.T. "The Educative Experience in *All the King's Men*." *Stylus*, 4: 21-6 (Sp 66).

Jones, Madison. "The Novels of RPW." *SAQ*, 62: 488-98 (Au 63).

Justus, J.H. "A Note on John Crowe Ransom and RPW."*AL*, 41: 425-30 (N 69).

———. "On the Politics of the Self-Created: *At Heaven's Gate*." *SR*, 82: 284-99 (Ap-Je 74).

———. "The Use of Gesture in W's *The Cave*." *MLQ*, 26: 448-61 (S 65).

————. "W and the Doctrine of Complicity." *FourQ*, 21: 93-9 (My 72).

Katope, C.G. "RFW's *All the King's Men*: A Novel of 'Pure Imagination.'" *TSLL*, 12: 493-510 (Fa 70).

Kehl, D.G. "Love's Definition: Dream as Reality in RPW's *Meet Me in the Green Glen*." *FourQ*, 21: 116-22 (My 72).

Keith, Philip. "Whittier and W." *Shen*, 23: 90-5 (Su 72).

Kerr, Dell. "An Exercise on RPW's *All the King's Men*." *EEx*, 5: 8-9 (O 57).

Kerr, E.M. "Polarity of Themes in *All the King's Men*." *MFS*, 6: 25-45 (Sp 60).

Kopcewicz, Andrzej. "Assertions of Loneliness." *SAP*, 3: 107-12 (1971).

Langman, F.H. "The Compelled Imagination: RPW's Conception of the Philosophical Novelist." *SoRA*, 4: 192-202 (#3 71).

Las Vergnas, Raymond. "Étoiles Anglo-Américaines: Nathanael West, William Styron, RPW, Carson McCullers, V. Sackville-West." *Les annales*, Ag 62, p. 33.

Longley, J.L. "*At Heaven's Gate*." *MFS*, 6: 13-24 (Sp 60).

McCarron, W.E. "W's *All the King's Men* and Arnold's 'To Marguerite—Continued.'" *AL*, 47: 115-6 (Mr 75).

McCarthy, Paul. "Sports and Recreation in *All the King's Men*." *MissQ*, 22: 113-30 (Sp 69).

Maloff, Saul. "Reconsideration: *All the King's Men*." *NRep*, 168: 28-30 (3 Mr 73).

Mariani, Paul. "Vespers: RPW at Seventy." *Parnassus*, 4: 176-88 (Fa-Wi 75).

Martin, R.G. "Diction in W's *All the King's Men*." *EJ*, 58: 1169-74 (N 69).

Mackier, Jerome. "Burden's Complaint: The Disinterested Personality in RFW's *All the King's Men*." *StN*, 2: 7-21 (Sp 70).

Moore, J.R. "RPW: You Must Go Home Again." *SoR*, 4: 320-32 (Sp 68).

Moore, L.H. "RPW and the Terror of Answered Prayer." *MissQ*, 21: 29-36 (Wi 67-68).

Nakadate, Neil. "RPW and the Confessional Novel." *Genre*, 2: 326-40 (d 69).

Namba, Tatsuo. "Regionalism in RPW's *All the King's Men*." *SALit*, 8: 63-79 (Mr 72).

O'Brien, J.M. "Cultural History in *All the King's Men*." *NCLit*, 2: 14-5 (My 72).

Olson, D.B. "Jack Burden and the Ending of *All the King's Men*." *MissQ*, 26: 165-76 (Sp 73).

Payne, Ladell. "Willie Stark and Huey Long: Atmosphere, Myth or Suggestion?" *AQ*, 20: 580-95 (Fa 68).

Percy, Walker. "The Message in the Bottle." *Thought*, 34: 405-33 (Au 59).

Plumly, Stanley. "RPW's Vision." *SoR*, 6: 1201-8 (Au 70).

Prasad, Thakur. "The Author as Victim: A Study of RPW's *World Enough and Time*." *J Shivaji Un*, 6: 9-13 (1973).

Quinn, M.B. "RPW's Promised Land." *SoR*, 8: 329-58 (Ap 72).

Raben, Joseph. "*All the King's Men*." *Folio*. 15: 14-8 (My 50).

Ransom, J.C. "*All the King's Men*." *Folio*, 15: 2-3 (My 50).

Rosenthal, M.L. "RPW's Poetry." *SAQ*, 42: 499-507 (Au 63).

Rouse, Blair. "Time and Place in Southern Fiction." *HopR*, 6: 37-61 (Fa 52).

Rubin, L.D. "Dreiser and *Meet Me in the Green Glen*: A Vintage Year for RPW." *HC*, 9: 11 (Ap 72).

————. "RPW: Vivid Moralist of the Human Heart." *America* (Moscow), 178: 41-3.

————. "'Theories of Human Nature': Kazin or W?" *SR*, 49: 500-6 (Su 61).

Ryan, A.S. "RPW's *Night Rider*." *MFS*, 7: 338-46 (Wi 61).

Sale, Roger. "Burden's Complaint: The Disintegrated Personality as Theme and Style in W's *All the King's Men*." *StN*, 2: 7-21 (1970).

Sale, R.B. "An Interview in New Haven with RPW." *StN*, 2: 325-54 (Fa 70).

Scouten, A.H. "W, Huey Long, and *All the King's Men*." *FourQ*, 21: 23-6 (My 72).

Shepherd, Allen. "Carrying Manty Home: RPW's *Band of Angels.*" *FourQ*, 21: 101-9.

———. "The Case for RPW's Second Best Novel." *CimR*, 20: 44-51 (1972).

———. "Character and Theme in W's *Meet Me in the Green Glen.*" *Greyfriar*, 13: 34-41 (1972).

———. "Percy's *The Moviegoer* and W's *All the King's Men.*" *NMW*, 4: 2-14 (Sp 71).

———. "The Poles of Fiction: W's *At Heaven's Gate.*" *TSLL*, 12: 709-18 (Wi 71).

———. "RPW as Allegorist: The Example of *Wilderness.*" *Rendezvous*, 6: 13-21 (1971).

*———. "RPW as a Philosophical Novelist." *WHR*, 24: 157-68 (Sp 70).

———. "RPW's *Audubon: A Vision*: The Epigraph." *NCLit*, 3: 8-111 (Ja 73).

———. "RPW's 'Prime Leaf' as Prototype of *Night Rider.*" *SSF*, 7: 469-71 (Su 70).

———. "Sugar-Boy as a Foil in *All the King's Men.*" *NCLit*, 1: 15 (Mr 71).

———. "Toward an Analysis of the Prose Style of RPW." *SAF*, 1: 188-202 (Au 73).

———. "W's *All the King's Men*: Using the Author's Guide to the Novel." *EJ*, 62: 704-8 (My 73).

———. "W's *Audubon*: 'Issues in Purer Form' and 'The Ground Rules of Fact.'" *MissQ*, 24: 47-56 (Wi 70-71).

Shepherd, Robert. "RPW's *Audubon*: A Vision: The Epigraph." *NCLit*, 3: 8-11 (Ja 73).

Silars, M.O. "W's *All the King's Men.*" *AQ*, 9: 345-53 (Fa 57).

Simmons, J.C. "Adam's Lobectomy Operation and the Meaning of *All the King's Men.*" *PMLA*, 86: 84-9 (Ja 71).

Spears, M.K. "The Latest Poetry of RPW." *SR*, 78: 348-57 (Sp 70).

Spies, G.H. "JS's *In Dubious Battle* and RPW's *Night Rider*: A Comparative Study." *StQ*, 4: 48-55 (Sp 71).

Stallinecht, N.P. "*All the King's Men.*" *Folio*, 15: 125-8 (My 50).

Stewart, J.L. "The Achievement of RPW." *SAQ*, 47: 562-79 (O 48).

———. "The Country of the Heart." *YR*, 53: 161-7 (1964).

Strandberg, Victor. "RPW: THe Poetry of the Sixties." *FourQ*, 21: 27-44 (My 72).

———. "W's Osmosis." *Criticism*, 10: 23-40 (Wi 68).

Strout, Cushing. "*All the King's Men* and the Shadow of William James." *SoR*, 6: 920-34 (Au 70).

Sullivan, J.J. "Conflict in the Modern American Novel." *BSUF*, 15: 28-36 (1974).

Sullivan, Walter. "The Historical Novelist and the Existential Peril: RPW's *Band of Angels.*" *SLJ*, 2: 104-116 (Sp 70).

Sumner, D.N. "The Function of Historical Sources in Hawthorne, Melville, and RPW." *RSW*, 40: 103-14 (1972).

Tyler, Parker. "Novel into Film: *All the King's Men.*" *KR*, 12: 369-76 (Sp 50).

Vauthier, Simone. "The Case of the Vanishing Narratee: An Inquiry into *All the King's Men.*' *SLJ*, 6: 42-69 (Sp 74).

Wain, John. "RPW: The Drama of the Past." *NRep*, 155: 16-8 (26 N 66).

Walker, Marshall. "RPW: An Interview." *JAmSt*, 8: 229-46 (Ag 74).

Warren, R.P. "Knowledge and the Image of Man." *SW*, 62: 182-92 (Sp 55).

———. "Poetry in a Time of Crack-Up." *NYRB*, 15: 32-3 (7 Ja 71).

———. "Relevance without Meaning." *InR*, 7: 149-52 (1971).

———. "Violence in Literature." *ASch*, 37: 482-96 (Su 68).

Weathers, Winston. "'Blackberry Winter' and the Use of Archetypes." *UTMS*, 4: 103-10 (1968).

Whittington, Curtis. "The 'Burden' of Narration: Democratic Perspective and First-Person Point of View in the American Novel." *SHR*, 2: 236-45 (Sp 68).

———. "The Earned Vision: RPW's 'The Ballad of Billie Potts' and Albert Camus' *Le Malentendu.*" *FourQ*, 21: 79-90 (My 72).

Widmer, Kingsley. "The Father Killers of RPW."*Paunch*, 22: 57-64 (Ja 65).

Wilcox, Earl. "Right On! *All the King's Men* in the Classroom." *FourQ*, 21: 69-78 (My 72).

Wilson, M.A. "Search for an Eternal Present: *Absalom, Absalom!* and *All the King's Men.*" *ConnR*, 8: 95-100 (#1 74).

Witt, R.W. "RPW and the 'Black Patch War.'" *RKHS*, 67: 301-6 (O 69).

Witte, Flo. "Adam's Rebirth in RPW's *Wilderness.*" *SoQ*, 12: 365-77 (Jl 74).

Woodward, C.V. "The Uses of History in Fiction." *SLJ*, 1: 57-90 (Sp 69).

Washington, Booker T. Friedman, L.J. "Life 'In the Lion's Mouth': Another Look at BT.W." *JNH*, 59: 337-51 (O 74).

Harlan, L.R. "BT.W's West's Virginia Boyhood." *WVH*, 32: 63-85 (Ja 71).

———. "The Secret Life of BT.W." *JSH*, 37: 393-416 (Ag 71).

Harris, T.W. and P.C. Kennicott. "BT.W: A Study of Conciliatory Rhetoric." *SSJ*, 37: 47 (Fa 71).

Huggins, N.I. "Making Visible an Invisible Man." *Cweal*, 98: 264-6 (18 My 73).

King, Andrew. "BT.W and the Myth of Heroic Materialism." *QJS*, 60: 323-7 (O 74).

Larson, C.R. "The Deification of BTW." *NALF*, 4: 125-6 (1970).

Shaw, F.H. "BTW and the Future of Black Americans." *GHQ*, 56: 193-209 (Su 72).

Thornbrough, E.L. "BT.W as Seen by His White Contemporaries." *JNH*, 53: 161-82 (1968).

White, A.O. 'BT.W's Florida Incident, 1903-4." *FHQ*, 51: 227-49 (Ja 73).

Wasserman, Dale. "*Man of La Mancha*: Una nueva interpretacion del *Quijote.*" *DHR*, 8: 37-43 (1969).

Waters, Frank. Davis, Jack and June. "FW and the Native American Consciousness." *WAL*, 9: 33-4 (My 74).

Grigg, Quay. "The Kachima Characters of FW's Novels." *SDR*, 11: 6-19 (1973).

Lyon, T.J. "An Ignored Meaning of the West." *WAL*, 3: 51-9 (Sp 68).

Milton, J.R. "Conversations with Distinguished Western American Novelists." *SDR*, 9: 15-57 (Sp 71).

———. "The Land as Form in FW and William Eastlake." *KanQ*, 2: 104-9 (1970).

Pilkington, W.T. "Character and Landscape: FW's Colorado Trilogy." *WAL*, 2: 183-93 (Fa 67).

Powell, L.C. "A Writer's Landscape." *Westways*, 66: 24-7, 70-2 (Ja 74).

Watterson, Henry. Wallace, Tom. "HW: A Man of Salient Characteristics." *Nieman Reports*, 3: 15-7 (Jl 49).

Weaver, Richard. Bradford, M.E. "The Agrarianism of RW: An Appreciation." *ModA*, 14: 249-57 (Su-Fa 70).

Brown, C.S. "Southern Thought and National Materialism." *SLJ*, 1: 98-106 (Sp 69).

Meyer, F.S. "RM.W: An Appreciation." *ModA*, 14: 243-8 (Su-Fa 70).

Montgomery, M. "RW Against the Establishment." *GaR*, 23: 433-59 (Wi 69).

Webb, Frank J. Bogardus, R.F. "FJ.W's *The Garies and Friends.*" *SBL*, 5: 15-9 (Su 74).

Davies, A.P. "*The Garies and Their Friends*: A Neglected Pioneer Novel." *CLAJ*, 13: 27-34 (Sp 69).

DeVries, J.H. "The Tradition of the Sentimental Novel in *The Garies and Their Friends.*" *CLAJ*, 17: 241-9 (D 73).

Webster, Daniel. Bartlet, L.H. "DW as a Symbolic Hero." *NEQ*, 45: 484-507 (D 72).

Webster, Noah. Bromberger, Bonnie. "NW's Notes on His Early Political Essays in the *Connecticut Courant.*" *BYNPL*, 74: 338-42 (My 70).

Cannon, C.D. "NW's Influence on American English." *UMSE*, 13: 7-16 (1972).

Hanscom, Leslie. "Our Debt to NW." *Reader's Digest*, 57: 164 (N 75).

Ikegami, Yoshihiko. "NW's Grammar: Traditions and Innovations. A Critical Study on Early English Published in the United States." *Proc Lang & Lit* (Tokyo), 19: 1-72 (1971).

McCracken, David. "The Drudgery of Defining: Johnson's Debt to Bailey's *Dictionarium Britannicum.*" *MP*, 66: 338-41 (1969).

Webster, Noah. "A Letter of NW to Daniel Webster, 1834." *AHR*, 9: 96-104 (1903).

Weems, Mason Locke. Purcell, James. "A Book Pedlar's Progress in North Carolina." *NCHR*, 29: 8-23 (Ja 52).

Stark, L.M. "The 'Cherry Tree' Edition of W's Life of Washington." *BYNPL*, 75: 7-8 (Ja 71).

Weinstein, Nathan. (see **West, Nathanael**).

Weiss, Theodore. Howard, Richard. "TW: 'No Shore Beyond Our Own.' " *Perspective*, 6: 41-65 (1969).

Weiss, Theodore. "Joining *The Donner Party.*" *Parnassus*, 1: 36-46 (1972).

Welty, Eudora. Anon. "Shrangri-la South." *Time*, 95: 100 (4 My 70).

Aldridge, J.W. "EW: Metamorphosis of a Southern Lady Writer." *SatR*, 11 Ap 70, pp. 21-3, 35-6.

Allen, J.A. "EW: The Three Moments." *VQR*, 51: 605-27 (Au 75).

Blackwell, Louise. "EW: Roots versus Yellow Guitars." *RLA*, 15: 129-35 (1973).

Boatwright, James. "Speech and Silence in *Losing Battles.*" *Shen*, 25: 3-14 (Sp 74).

Bolsterli, Margaret. "A Fertility Rite in Mississippi." *NMW*, 8: 69-71 (1975).

———. "Mythic Elements in 'Ladies in Spring.' " *NMW*, 6: 69-72 (Wi 74).

Bradford, M.E. "Looking Down From a High Place: The Serenity of Miss W's *Losing Battles.*" *Ranam*, 4: 92-7 (1971).

———. "Miss Eudora's Picture Book." *MissQ*, 26: 659-62 (Fa 73).

Brooks, Cleanth. "The Past Reexamined: *The Optimist's Daughter.*" *MissQ*, 26: 577-87 (fa 73).

Brown, Ashely. "EW and the Mythos of Summer." *Shen*, 20: 29-35 (Sp 69).

Bryant, J.A. "Seeing Double in *The Golden Apples.*" *SR*, 82: 300-15 (Ap-Je 74).

Buckley, W.F. "The Southern Imagination: An Interview with EW and Walker Percy." *MissQ*, 26: 493-516 (Fa 73).

Bunting, C.T. " 'The Interior World': An Interview with EW." *SoR*, 8: 711-35 (O 72).

Burger, N.K. "EW's Jackson." *Shen*, 20: 8-15 (Sp 69).

Buswell, M.C. "The Mountain Figure in the Fiction of EW." *WVUPP*, 19: 50-63 (Jl 72).

Carson, F.D. "The Passage of Time in EW's 'Sir Rabbit.' " *SSF*, 12: 284-5 (Su 75).

———. "Recurring Metaphors: An Aspect of Unity in *The Golden Apples.*" *NCLit*, 5: 5-7 (#1 75).

———. " 'The Song of Wandering Aengus': Allusions in EW's *The Golden Apples.*" *NMW*, 6: 14-8 (Sp 73).

Clark, C.C. "*The Robber Bridegroom*: Realism and Fantasy on the Natchez Trace." *MissQ*, 26: 625-38 (Fa 73).

Clemons, W. "Meeting Miss W." *NYT*, 12 Ap 70, pp. 2, 46.

Cochran, R.W. "W's 'Petrified Man.' " *Expl*, 27: 25 (D 68).

Cole, H.M. "Windsor in Spencer and W: A Real and an Imaginary Landscape." *NMW*, 7: 2-11 (1974).

Cooley, J.R. "Blacks as Primitives in EW's Fiction." *BSUF*, 14: 20-8 (Su 73).

Coulthard, A.R. "Point of View in EW's Fiction: A Changing World." *SAF*, 3: 199-209 (1975).

Cowley, Malcolm, Martha Braham, Walker Percy, Allen Tate, and R.P. Warren. "Five Tributes." *Shen*, 20: 36-9 (Sp 69).

Curly, Daniel. "EW and the Quondam Obstruction." *SSF*, 5: 209-24 (Sp 68).

————. "A Time Exposure." *NMW*, 5: 11-4 (Sp 72).

Davenport, Guy. "Primal Visions." *Nat R*, 24: 697 (23 Je 72).

Davis, C.E. "The South in EW's Fiction: A Changing World." *SAF*, 3: 199-209 (Au 75).

————. "W's 'Old Mr. Marblehall.'" *Expl*, 30: 40 (Ap 72).

Detweiler, Robert. "EW's Blazing Butterfly: The Dynamics of Response." *Lang&S*, 6: 58-71 (Wi 73).

Doulan, Dan. "'A Worn Path': Immortality of Stereotype." *EJ*, 62: 549-50 (Ap 73).

East, Charles. "The Search for EW." *MissQ*, 26: 477-82 (Fa 73).

Fleischauer, J.F. "The Focus of Mystery: Eudora Welty's Prose Style." *SLJ*, 5: 64-79 (Sp 73).

Givner, Joan. "Katharine Ann Porter, EW, and *Ethan Brand*." *IFR*, 1: 32-7 (Ja 74).

Gossett, L.Y. "EW's New Novel: The Comedy of Loss." *SLJ*, 3: 122-37 (Fa 70).

Graham, Kenneth. "La double vision d'EW." *NRF*, 17: 744-53 (N 69).

Grantham, D.W. "Interpreters of the Modern South." *SAQ*, 63: 521-9 (Au 64).

Hardy, J.E. "The Achievement of EW." *SHR*, 2: 269-78 (Su 68).

Harrell, Don. "Death in EW's *The Bride of the Innisfallen*." *NCLit*, 3: 2-7 (S 73).

Harris, W.V. "Molly's 'Yes': The Transvaluation of Sex in Modern Fiction." *TSLL*, 10: 107-18 (1968).

Heilman, R.B. "Salesmen's Deaths: Documentary and Myth." *Shen*, 20: 20-8 (Sp 69).

Helterman, Jeffrey. "Gorgons in Mississippi: EW's 'Petrified Man.'" *NMW*, 7: 12-20 (Sp 74).

Herrscher, Walter. "Is Sister Really Insane? Another Look at 'Why I live at the P.O.'" *NCLit*, 5: 5-7 (#1 75).

Hollenbaugh, Carol. "Ruby Fisher and Her Demon-Lover." *NMN*, 7: 63-8 (Fa 74).

Howell, Elmo. "EW and the Use of Place in Southern Fiction." *ArQ*, 28: 248-56 (1972).

————. "EW's Civil War Story." *NMW*, 2: 3-12 (Sp 69).

————. "EW's Comedy of Manners." *SAQ*, 69: 469-79 (Au 70).

————. "EW's Negroes: A Note on 'A Worn Path.'" *XUS*, 9: 28-32 (Sp 70).

Inge, M.T. "EW as Poet." *SHR*, 2: 310-1 (Su 68).

Isaacs, N.D. "Four Notes on EW." *NMW*, 2: 42-54 (Fa 69).

Jones, A.R. "A Frail Traveling Coincidence: Three Later Stories of EW." *Shen*, 20: 40-53 (Sp 69).

Kirkpatrick, Smith. "The Anointed Powerhouse." *SR*, 77: 94-108 (Wi 69).

Kloss, R.J. "The Symbolic Structure of EW's 'Livvie.'" *NMW*, 8: 70-82 (1975).

Kraus, W.K. "W's 'Petrified Man.'" *Expl*, 29: 63 (Ap 71).

Kreyling, Michael. "Myth and History: The Foes of *Losing Battles*." *MissQ*, 26: 639-49 (Fa 73).

Kuehl, Linda. "The Art of Fiction XLVII: EW." *PaR*, 55: 72-97 (Fa 72).

Landess, T.H. "The Function of Taste in the Fiction of EW." *MissQ*, 26: 543-57 (Fa 73).

————. "More Trouble in Mississippi: Family vs. Antifamily in Miss W's *Losing Battles*." *SR*, 79: 626-34 (1971).

*McDonald, W.U. "EW Manuscripts: A Supplementary Annotated Finding List." *BB*, 31: 95-8, 126, (Jl-S 74).

————. "EW's Revisions of 'A Piece of News.'" *SSF*, 7: 232-47 (Sp 70).

————. "W's 'Social Consciousness': Revisions of 'The Whistle.'" *MFS*, 16: 193-8 (Su 70).

McFarland, R.E. "Vision and Perception in the Works of EW." *MarkR*, 2: 94-9 (F 71).

McMillen, W.E. "Conflict and Resolution in W's *Losing Battles*." *Critique*, 15: 110-24 (1Q 73).

McHaney, T.L. "EW and the Multitudinous Golden Apples." *MissQ*, 26: 589-624 (Fa 73).

Martin, T.L. "EW: Master of the American Short Story." *So Observer*, S 55, pp. 261-5.

Masserand, Anne. "EW's Travellers: The Journey Theme in the Short Stories." *SLJ*, 3: 39-48 (Sp 71).

May, C.E. "The Difficulty of Loving in 'A Visit of Charity.'" *SSF*, 6: 338-41 (Sp 69).

———. "*Le Roie Mehaigne* in W's 'Keela, The Outcast Indian Maiden.'" *MFS*, 18: 559-66 (Wi 72-73).

Moore, C.A. "The Insulation of Illusion and *Losing Battles*." *MissQ*, 26: 651-8 (Fa 73).

Moss, Grant. "'A Worn Path' Retrod." *CLAJ*, 15: 144-52 (D 71).

Myers, S.L. "Dialogues in EW's Short Stories." *NMW*, 8: 51-7 (1975).

Oates, J.C. "The Art of EW." *Shen*, 20: 54-7 (Sp 69).

———. "E's Webb." *Atl*, 225: 118-22 (Ap 70).

Pawlowski, R.S. "The Process of Observation: *Winesburg, Ohio* and *The Golden Apples*." *UR*, 37: 292-8 (Su 71).

Pickett, N.A. "Colloquialism as a Style in The First-Person-Narrator Fiction of EW." *MissQ*, 26: 559-76 (Fa 73).

*Polk, Noel. "A EW Checklist." *MissQ*, 26: 663-93 (Fa 73).

Prenshaw, Peggy. "Cultural Patterns in EW's 'Delta Wedding' and 'The Demonstrators.'" *NMW*, 3: 51-70 (Fa 70).

Price, Reynolds. "The Onlooker, Smiling: An Early Reading of 'The Optimist's Daughter.'" *Shen*, 20: 58-73 (Sp 69).

Richmond, L.J. "Symbol and Theme in EW's 'Petrified Man.'" *EJ*, 60: 1201-3 (D 71).

Ricks, Christopher. "Female and Other Impersonators." *NYRB*, 15: 8-13 (23 Jl 70).

Rubin, L.D. "Everything Brought Out in the Open: EW's *Losing Battles*." *HC*, 7: 1-12 (Je 70).

Rubin, L.R. "Virgie Rainey and the Golden Apples of the Sun." *New York R*, 1: 10-5 (Sp 58).

Russell, Diarmuid. "First Work." *Shen*, 20: 16-9 (Sp 69).

Seidl, Frances. "EW's Phoenix." *NMW*, 6: 53-5 (Fa 73).

Shepard, Allen. "Delayed Exposition in EW's *The Optimist's Daughter*." *NCLit*, 4: 10-4 (My 74).

Semel, J.M. "EW's Freak Show: A Pattern in 'Why I Live at the P.O.'" *NCLiT*, 3: 2-3 (My 73).

Simpson, L.P. "The Chosen People." *SoR*, 6: xvii-xxiii (Su 70).

———. "An Introductory Note." *MissQ*, 26: 475-6 (Fa 73).

Slethaug, G.E. "Initiation in EW's *The Rider Bridegroom*." *SHR*, 7: 77-87 (1973).

Smith, C.O. "The Journey Motif in EW's *The Robber Bridegroom*." *Shippensburg State Col R*, 1973, pp. 18-32.

Smith, Julian. "'Livvie': EW's Song of Solomon." *SSF*, 5: 73-4 (Fa 67).

Stanford, D.E. "EW and the Pulitzer Prize." *SoR*, 9: xx-xxiii (Au 73).

Stone, W.B. "EW's Hydrodynamic 'Powerhouse.'" *SSF*, 11: 93-5 (Wi 74).

Stuckey, William. "The Use of Marriage in W's *The Optimist's Daughter*." *Crit*, 17: 36-46 (2Q 75).

Tarbox, Raymond. "EW's Fiction: The Salvation Theme." *AI*, 29: 70-91 (Sp 72).

Thomas, William "EW." *Mid-South*, 25 Q 70, pp. 6-8, 16-9.

Thompson, V.H. "The Natchez Trace in EW's 'A Still Moment.'" *SLJ*, 6: 59-69 (Fa 73).

Travis, M.K. "A Note on 'Wakefield' and 'Old Mr. Marblehall.'" *NCLit*, 4: 9-10 (My 74).

Vande Kieft, R.M. "The Vision of EW." *MissQ*, 26: 517-42 (Fa 73).

Walker, Alice. "EW: An Interview." *HA*, 106: 68-72 (Wi 73).

Warren, R.P. "The Love and Separateness of EW." *KR*, 6: 246-59 (Sp 44).

Welty, Eudora. "The Art of Fiction." *PaR*, 55: 72-97 (Fa 72).

———. "Artists on Criticism of Their Art: 'Is Phoenix Jackson's Grandson Really Dead?'" *CritI*, 1: 219-21 (S 74).

———. "From Where I Live." *DelR*, 6: 69 (N-D 69).

———. "EW's World in the Thirties." *Mademoiselle*, 73: 162-5, 191 (S 71).

———. "Literature and the Lens." *Vogue*, 104: 102-3 (1 Ag 44).

———. "The Reading and Writing of Short Stories." *Atl*, 183: 54-8, 46-9, (F, Mr 49).

———. "Some Notes on Time in Fiction." *MissQ*, 26: 483-92 (Fa 73).

———. "The Teaching and Study of Writing." *WR*, 14: 167-8 (Sp 50).

Wilson, J.W. "Delta Revival." *Eng J*, 38: 121-2 (Mr 49).

Yardley, Jonathan. "The Last Good One?" *NRep*, 162: 33-6 (9 My 70).

Wescott, Glenway. Moss, Howard "Love Birds of Prey." *NY*, 43: 184-91 (11 Mr 67).

Stegner, Wallace. "Re-discovery: W's *Good-bye Wisconsin*." *WoR*, 6: 674-81 (Jl 70).

Wescott, Glenway. "Memories and Opinions." *Prose*, 5: 177-202 (1972).

West, Jessamyn. Flanagen, J.T. "The Fiction of JW." *IMW*. 67: 299-316 (D 71).

———. "Folklore in Five Middle-western Novelists.' *Great Lake Rev*, 1: 43-57 (Wi 75).

Shivers, A.S. "JW." *BB*, 28; 1-3 (Ja-Mr 71).

West, Morris. Grande, L.M. "Renegade Priests in Recent Fiction." *CathLW*, 32: 407-10 (Ap 61).

McCallum, Gerald. "A Note on MW's First Novel." *ALS*, 6: 314-6 (1974).

Picart, R.M. "Realism in *The Shoes of the Fisherman*: A Critical Analysis." *SLRJ*, 1: 711-5 (1970).

West, Nathanael (Nathan Weinstein). Balke, B.T. "Some Judeo-Christian Themes Seen through the Eyes of J.D. Salinger and NW." *Cresset*, 31: 14-8 (My 68).

Banta, Martha. "American Apocalypses: Excrement and Ennui." *SLitI*, 7, i: 1-30 (1974).

Baxter, Charles. "NW: Dead Letter and the Martyred Novelist." *WCR*, 9: 3-11 (1974).

Betsky-Zweig, S. "The Cannonballed of Popular Culture: NW's *Miss Lonelyhearts* and *The Day of the Locust*." *DQR*, 4: 145-56 (3Q 74).

Brown, D.R. "The War Within NW: Naturalism and Existentialism." *MFS*, 20: 181-202 (Su 74).

Clarke, Bruce. "Miss Lonelyhearts and the Detached Consciousness." *Paunch*, 42-43: 21-39 (D 75).

Collins, Carvel. "NW's the *Day of the Locust* and *Sanctuary*." *FaS*, 2: 23-4 (Su 53).

Cramer, C.M. "The World of NW: A Critical Interpretation." *ESRS*, 19: 5-71 (Je 71).

Donovan, Alan. "NW and the Surrealistic Muse." *KenR*, 2: 82-95 (1968).

Edembaum, R.I. "Dada and Surrealism in the United States: A Literary Instance." *Arts in Soc*, 5: 114-25 (1968).

———. "A Surfeit of Shoddy: NW's *A Cool Million*." *SHR*, 2: 427-39 (Fa 68).

Frank, Mike. "The Passion of Miss Lonelyhearts According to NW." *SSF*, 10: 67-73 (Wi 73).

Geha, Richard. "*Miss Lonelyhearts*: A Dual Mission of Mercy."*HSL*, 3: 116-31 (1971).

Graham, John. "Struggling Upward: 'The Minister's Charge' and 'A Cool Million.'" *CRAS*, 4: 184-96 (Fa 73).

Greenberg, Alvin. "Breakable Beginnings: The Fall into Realism in the Modern Novel." *TSLL*, 10: 133-42 (1968).

———. "The Revolt of Objects: The Opposing World in the Modern Novel." *CentR*, 13: 366-88 (Fl 69).

Hand, N.W. "A Novel in the Form of a Comic Strip: NW's *Miss Lonelyhearts*." *Serif*, 5: 14-21 (1968).

Las Vergnas, Raymond. "Étoiles Anglos-Américaines: NW, William Styron, Robert Penn Warren, Carson McCullers, V. Sackville-West." *Les annales*, Ag 62: 33.

Light, J.F. "Varieties of Satire in the Art of NW." *SAH*, 2: 46-60 (Ap 75).

Lind, M.G. "Backward-Forward in Forbidden Lands." *WestWR*, 3: 21-7 (Sp 68).

Lindberg-Seyerstead, Brita. "Three Variations of the American Success Story: The Careers of Luke Larken, Lemuel Barker, and Lemuel Pitkin." *ES*, 53: 125-41 (Ap 72).

Martin, Jay. "Fitzgerald Recommends NW for a Guggenheim." *FHA*, 1971, pp. 302-4.

Mayer, D.R. "W's *Miss Lonelyhearts*." *Expl*, 34: 11 (O 75).

Michaels, I.L. "A Particular Kind of Joking: Burlesque, Vaudeville, and NW." *SAH*, 1: 149-60 (Ja 75).

Nichols, J.W. "NW, Sinclair Lewis, Alexander Pope and Satiric Contrasts." *SNL*, 5: 119-22 (Sp 68).

Ooi, Koji. "NW Saihyoka." *EigoS*, 119: 404-5 (1973).

Orvell, M.D. "The Messianic Sexuality of *Miss Lonelyhearts*." *SSF*, 10: 157-67 (Sp 73).

Pearce, Richard. "*Pylon, Awake and Sing!* and the Apocalyptic Imagination of the 30's." *Criticism*, 13: 131-41 (Sp 71).

Petrullo, H.B. "Clichés and Three Political Satires of the Thirties." *SNL*, 8: 109-17 (Sp 71).

Pinsker, Sanford. "Charles Dickens and NW: Great Gxpectations Unfulfilled." *Topic*, 18: 40-52 (1969).

Reynolds, Stanley. "Life sans Everything." *NSt*, 11 O 68, p. 469.

Rosenblatt, Roger. "The Back of the Book: The Horse at the Bottom." *NRep*, 173: 36-8 (16 & 23 Ag 75).

Russell, Herb. "W's *The Day of the Locust*." *Expl*, 33: 36 (Ja 75).

Sasahara, Akira. "The World of *Miss Lonelyhearts*." *ESELL*, 53-4: 109-30 (1968).

Schorer, Mark. "Nathan Weinstein: The Cheated." *Atl*, 226: 127-30 (O 70).

Smith, Marcus. "Religious Experience in *Miss Lonelyhearts*." *ConL*, 9: 172-88 (Sp 68).

Steiner, T.R. "W's Lemuel and the American Dream." *SoR*, 7: 994-1006 (O 71).

Thale, Mary. "The Moviegoer of the 1950's." *TCL*, 14: 84-9 (Jl 68).

Tractenberg, Stanley. "W's Locusts: Laughing at the Laugh." *MQR*, 14: 187-98 (1975).

White, William. "'Go West!' Notes from a Bibliographer." *ABC*, 19: 7-10 (Ja 69).

———. "More Books on NW." *ABC*, 22: 37 (1972).

*——— . "NW: A Working Checklist." *BB*, 29: 140-3 (O-D 72).

———. "Notes on Hemingway, W, Tolkien, and Wise." *ABC*, 18: 30-1 (Ja-F 68).

Zimmer, D.E. "NW, oder Warnungen vorm Tag der Heuschrechen." *NRs*, 82: 287-302 (1972).

Zlotnick, Joan. "The Medium Is the Message, Or Is It? A Study of NW's Comic Strip Novel." *JPC*, 5: 236-40 (1971).

———. "NW and the Pictorial Imagination." *WAL*, 9: 177-86 (Fa 74).

Westcott, Edward Noeys. Case, R.G. "The Ws and *David Harum*." *Courier*, 10: 2-14 (1972).

Glassie, Henry. "The Use of Folklore in *David Harum*." *NYFQ*, 23: 163-85 (1967).

Wharton, Edith. Ammons, Elizabeth. "The Business of Marriage in EW's *The Custom of the Country*." *Criticism*, 16: 326-38 (Fa 74).

Anderson, Hilton. "EW and the Vulgar American." *SoQ*, 7: 17-22 (O 68).

———. "A Whartonian Woman in *Dodsworth*." *SLNL*, 1: 5-6 (Sp 69).

———. "EW as Fictional Heroine." *SAQ*, 69: 118-23 (Wi 70).

Benoit, Raymond. "W's *House of Mirth*." *Expl*, 29: 59 (1971).

Cargas, H.J. "Seeing, But not Living: Two Characters from James and W." *NLauR*, 1: 5-7 (1972).

Clark, Kenneth. "A Full-Length Portrait." *TLS*, 19 D 75, pp. 1502-3.

Clough, David. "EW's War Novels: A Reappraisal." *TCL*, 19: 1-14 (Ja 73).

Cohn, Jan. "The House of Fiction: Domestic Architecture in Howells and EW." *TSLL*, 15: 537-49 (Fa 73).

Crane, Joan St. C. "Rare or Seldom-Seen Dust Jackets of American First Editions, VIII." *Serif*, 9: 36-7, 45-7 (1972).

Dahl, Curtis. "EW's *House of Mirth*: Sermon on a Text." *MFS*, 21: 572-6 (Wi 75).

Doyle, C.C. "Emblems of Innocence: Imagery Patterns in W's *The Age of Innocence*." *XUS*, 10: 19-26 (Fa 71).

Evans, Elizabeth. "Musical Allusions in *The Age of Innocence*." *NCLit* 4: 4-7 (1974).

Gargano, J.W. "*The Age of Innocence*: Art of Artifice." *RSW*, 38: 22-8 (Mr 70).

——. "*The House of Mirth*: Social Futility and Faith." *AL*, 44: 137-43 (My 72).

Jacobson, Irving. "Perception, Communication, and Growth as Correlative Themes in EW's *The Age of Innocence*." *Agora*, 2: 68-82 (#2 73).

Karl, F.R. "Three Conrad Letters in the EW Papers." *YULG*, 44: 148-51 (Ja 70).

Kronenberg, Louis. "Mrs. W's Literary Museum." *Atl*, 222: 98-102 (S 68).

Lamar, L.B. "EW and the Book of Common Prayer." *AN&Q*, 7: 38-9 (1968).

Lawson, R.H. "The Influence of Gottfried Keller on EW." *RLC*, 42: 366-79 (S 68).

Lewis, R.W.B. "EW: The Beckoning Quarry." *AH*, 26: 53-6, 73 (O 75).

——. "Powers of Darkness." *TLS*, 13 Je 75, pp. 644-5.

McDowell, M.B. "EW's 'After Holbein': 'A Paradigm of the Human Condition.'" *JNT*, 1: 49-58 (Ja 71).

——. "EW's Ghost Stories." *Criticism*, 12: 133-52 (Sp 70).

——. "Viewing the Custom of Her Country: EW's Feminism." *ConL*, 15: 521-38 (Au 74).

McHaney, T.L. "Fouque's *Undine* and EW's *Custom of the Country*." *RLC*, 45: 180-6 (1971).

McIlvaine, Robert. "EW's American Beauty Rose." *JAmSt*, 7: 183-6 (Ag 73).

McManis, J.A. "EW's Hymns to Respectability." *SoR*, 7: 986-93 (O 71).

Montgomery, J.H. "The American Galatea." *CE*, 32: 890-9 (My 71).

Murphy, J.J. "The Satiric Structure of W's *The Age of Innocence*." *MarkR*, 2: 1-4 (My 70).

Niall, Brenda. "Prufrock in Brownstone: EW's *The Age of Innocence*." *SoRA*, 4: 203-14 (1971).

Phelps, Donald. "EW and the Invisible." *Prose*, 7: 227-45 (1973).

Potter, Rosemary. "The Mistakes of Lily in *The House of Mirth*." *Taius*, 4: 89-93 (1971).

Puknat, E.M. and S.B. "EW and Gottfried Keller." *CL*, 21: 245-54 (Su 69).

Randall, J.H. "Romeo and Juliet in the New World: A study of James, W, and Fitzgerald." *Costerus*, 8: 109-75 (1973).

Robinson, J.A. "Psychological Determinism in *The Age of Innocence*." *MarkR*, 5: 1-5 (1975).

Sasaki, Miyoko. "The Dance of Death: A Study of EW's Short Stories." *SELit*, 51: 67-90 (1974).

Sergeant, E.S. "Idealized New England." *NRep*, 3: 20-1 (8 My 15).

Shuman, R.B. "The Continued Popularity of *Ethan Frome*." *RLV*, 37: 257-63 (My-Je 71).

Tintner, A.R. "'The Hermit and the Wild Woman': EW's Fictioning of Henry James." *JML*, 4: 32-4 (S 74).

——. "James's Mock Epic: 'The Velvet Glove,' EW, and Other Late Tales." *MFS*, 17: 483-99 (Wi 71-72).

——. "The Metamorphoses of EW in Henry James's *The Finer Grain*." *TCL*, 21: 355-80 (D 75).

Tuttleton, J.W. "EW: The Archeological Motive." *YR*, 61: 562-74 (Je 72).

————. "EW: An Essay in Bibliography." *RALS*, 3: 163-202 (Fa 73).

————. "EW: Form and the Epistemology of Artistic Creation." *Criticism*, 10: 334-51 (Fa 68).

Vella, M.W. "Technique and Theme in *The House of Mirth*." *MarkR*, 2: 17-20 (My 70).

Wegelin, Christof. "EW and the Twilight of the International Novel." *SoR*, 5: 398-418 (Sp 69).

Wharton, Edith. "Letter to Fitzgerald." *FHA, 1972*, pp. 85-7.

Winner, V.H. "Convention and Prediction in EW's *Fast and Loose*." *AI*, 42: 50-69 (Mr 70).

Wolff, C.G. "Lily Bart and the Beautiful Death." *AL*, 46: 16-40 (Mr 74).

Wheatley, Phillis. Anon. "The PW Poetry Festival, November 4-7, 1973." *Jackson State R*, 6: 1-107 (#1 74).

Applegate, Anne. "PW: Her Critics and Her Contribution." *NALF*, 9: 123-6 (Wi 75).

Bridenbaugh, Carl. "The Earliest Published Poem of PW." *NEQ*, 42: 583-4 (D 69).

Burroughs, Margaret G. "Do Birds of a Feather Flock Together?" *Jackson State R*, 6: 61-73 (1974).

Collins, Terence. "PW: The Dark Side of the Poetry." *Phylon*, 36: 78-88 (Mr 75).

Costanzo, Angelo. "Three Black Poets in Eighteenth-Century America." *Shippensburg State Col R*, 1973, pp. 89-101.

Davis, A.P. "Personal Elements in the Poetry of PW." *Phylon*, 14: 191-8 (1953).

Giddings, Paula. "Critical Evaluation of PW." *Jackson State R*, 6: 74-81 (1974).

Huddleston, E.L. "Matilda's 'On Reading the Poems of PW, the African Poetess.'" *EAL*, 5: 57-67 (Wi 70-71).

Kunico, R.C. "Some Unpublished Poems of PW." *NEQ*, 43: 287-97 (Je 70).

Matson, R.L. "PW-Soul Sister?" *Phylon*, 33: 222-30 (Fa 72).

Nwoga, D.I. "Humanitarianism and the Criticism of African Literature, 1770-1810." *RIAL*, 3: 171-9 (1972).

Parks, C.A. "PW Comes Home." *BlackW*, 23, iv: 92-7 (1974).

*Porter, D.B. "Historical and Bibliographical Data of PW's Publications." *Jackson State R*, 6: 54-60 (1974).

Rigsby, Gregory. "Form and Content in PW's *Elegies*." *CLAJ*, 19: 248-57 (D 75).

Silverman, Kenneth. "Four New Letters by PW." *EAL*, 8: 257-71 (Wi 74).

Wheeler, Charles Stearns. Cameron, K.W. "Harvard Rules and Certificates of Thoreau's Day." *ESQ*, 52: 86-7 (3Q 68).

Eidson, J.O. "*CSW: Friend of Emerson*." *ESQ*, No. 52: 13-75 (3Q 68).

Myerson, Joel. "The Death of CSW." *ConS*, 7: 6-7 (S 72).

Wheelock, John Hall. Hubbell, J.B. "A Major American Poet: JHW." *SAQ*, 72: 295-310 (Sp 73).

————. "The Poetry of JHW." *SWR*, 10: 90-1 (O 24).

Taylor, Henry. "The Collected Poems of JHW." *SR*, 79: 460-3 (Su 71).

————. "Letting the Darkness in: The Poetic Achievement of JHW." *HC*, 7: 1-15 (1970).

Wheelwright, John B. Josephson, Matthew. "Improper Bostonian: JW and His Poetry." *SoR*, 7: 509-40 (Ap 71).

Rosenfeld, A.H. "The New England Notebooks of JW." *NEQ*, 45: 568-77 (D 72).

————, and S.F. Damon. "JW: New England's Colloquy with the World." *SoR*, 8: 310-28 (Ap 72).

Whitcher, Frances. Curry, Jane. "Yes, Virginia, there were Female Humorists: FW and her Widow Bedott." *Un of Michigan Papers in Women Stud*, 1: 74-90 (#1 74).

O'Donnell, T.F. "The Return of Widow Bedott: Mrs. F.M.W of Whitesboro and Elmira." *NYH*, 55: 5-34 (Ja 74).

White, E[lwyn] B[rooks]. Hasley, Louis. "The Talk of the Town and the Country: E.B.W." *ConnR*, 5: 37-45 (1971).

Nordstrom, Ursula. "Stuart, Wilbur, Charlotte: A Tale of Tales." *NYT*, 12 My 74: 8, 10.

Sampson, E.C. "Fiction or Friction?" *CLJ*, 2: 78-80 (1967).

White, Walter. Cooney, C.F. "Mencken's Midwifery." *Mencken*, 43: 1-3 (Fa 72).

———. "WW and the Harlem Renaissance." *JNH*, 57: 231-40 (Jl 72).

———. "WW and Sinclair Lewis: The History of a Literary Friendship." *Prospect*, 1: 63-75 (1975).

Waldron, E.E. "WW and the Harlem Renaissance: Letters from 1924-1927." *CLAJ*, 16: 438-57 (Je 73).

White, William Allen. Dubbert, J.L. "WAW: Reflections on an American Life." *MarkR*, 4: 41-7 (My 74).

———. "WAW's American Adam." *WAL*, 7: 271-8 (Wi 73).

Groman, G.L. "The Political Fiction of WAW: A Study in Emerging Progressivism." *MwQ*, 8: 79-93 (O 66).

*Pady, D.S. "A Bibliography of the Poems of WAW." *BB*, 25: 44-6 (Ja-Ap 71).

Resh, R.W. "A Vision in Emporia: W.A.W.'s Search for Community." *MASJ*, 10: 19-35 (Fa 69).

Whitlock, Brand. Anderson, D.D. "BW's Search for the Jeffersonian Ideal." *PMASAL*, 51: 505-14 (1966).

———. "On Rediscovering BW." *Ohioana*, 9: 67-9 (Fa 65).

Arms, George. "'Ever Devotedly Yours,' The W-Howells Correspondence." *JRUL*, 10: 1-19 (D 46).

Bremner, R.H. "The Civic Revival in Ohio: Artist in Politics, BW." *AJES*, 9: 239-54 (Ja 50).

Howells, W.D. "A Political Novelist and More." *NAR*, 192: 93-100 (Jl 10).

Thorburn, Neil. "BW (1869-1934)." *ALR*, 3: 30-5 (Su 68).

Whitman, Alberry Allson. Brawley, Benjamin. "Three Negro Poets." *JNH*, 2: 384-92 (O 17).

Marshall, C.L. "Two Protest Poems of AWW." *CLAJ*, 19: 50-6 (Sp 75).

Sherman, J.R. "AWW: Poet of Beauty and Manliness." *CLAJ*, 14: 126-43 (D 71).

Whitman, Walt. Anon. "WW in the News." *ATQ*, 13: 77-83 (1972).

———. "WW—The Man and the Poet." *QJLC*, 27: 171-6 (1970).

Abrams, R.E. "The Function of Dreams and Dream-Logic in W's Poetry." *TSLL*, 17: 599-616 (Fa 75).

Agrawal, I.N. "W, Van Wyck Brooks and the American Tradition." *IJAS*, 1: 95-101 (1971).

Allen, G.W. "WW's Inner Space." *Cal*, 1: 1-5 (S 69).

———. "W and Michelet—Continued." *AL*, 45: 428-32 (N 73).

———. "With Walt at the Front." *NYT*, 3 (22 Ja 61).

Amur, G.S. "W's Song of Man: A Humanistic Approach to 'Song of Myself.'" *WWR*, 18: 50-6 (Je 72).

Amyot, G.F. "Contrasting Visions of Death in the Poetry of Poe and W." *WWR*, 19: 103-11 (S 73).

———. "WW's 'Language Experiment.'" *WWR*, 20: 97-105 (S 74).

Andrews, L.L. "I Am the Poet of the Woman the Same as the Man: W's View of Women as Depicted in 'Song of Myself.'" *BSUF*, 16: 68-76 (Au 75).

Armistead, J.M. "Ending with W." *J Eng Teaching Techniques*, 7: 14-21 (1974).

Aspiz, Harold. "'Children of Adam' and Horace Greeley." *WWR*, 15: 49-51 (Mr 69).

———. "For Younger Readers of Whitman: A Review." *WWR*, 16: 92-3 (S 70).

———. "A Reading of W's 'Faces.'" *WWR*, 19: 37-48 (Je 73).

———. "W's 'Spirit That For'd This Scene.'" *Expl*, 28: 25 (N 69).

Asselineau, Roger. "'Camerado, This Is no Book; Who Touches This Touches a Bomb.'" *AmD*, 5: 16-17 (1969).

———. "WW: From Paumanok to More than America." *PLL*, 5: 18-39 (Su 69).

———. "WW's Humor." *ATQ*, 22: 86-91 (Sp 74).

Baker, J.D. "W and Dos Passos: A Sense of Communion." *WWR*, 20: 30-2 (Mr 74).

Baker, J.V. "WW and the Limits of Embarrassment." *Forum(H)*, 6: 29-34 (Fa-Wi 68).

Basler, R.P. "WW in Perspective." *WWR*, 16: 5-8 (Wi 70).

Batchelor, S.A. "W's Yawp and How He Yawped It." *WWR*, 18: 87-100 (S 72).

Baytop, Adrianne. "'Song of Myself' 52: Motion as Vehicle for Meaning." *WWR*, 18: 101-3 (S 72).

Beardshear, W.M. "Charge to a Walt." *Palimpsest*, 51: 349-52 (1970).

Beck, Ronald. "The Structure of 'Song of Myself' and the Critics." *WWR*, 15: 32-8 (Mr 69).

Belson, J.J. "W's 'Overstaid Fraction." *WWR*, 17: 63-5 (Je 71).

Bennett, F.H. "'Starting from Paumanok,' as Functional Poetry." *WWR*, 15: 117-20 (Je 69).

Bennett, J.Q. "Whitman Loses His Ego; or, 'Not I, said the fly': *Leaves of Grass*, 1855." *Serif*, 7: 35-6 (1970).

Bergman, Herbert. "The Influence of W's Journalism on *Leaves of Grass*." *ALR*, 3: 399-404 (Fa 70).

———. "On Editing W's Journalism." *WWR*, 16: 104-9 (D 70).

———. "WW as a Journalist, 1831-January, 1848." *JQ*, 48: 195-204 (Su 71).

———. "WW as a Journalist, March, 1848-1892." *JQ*, 48: 431-7 (Wi 71).

———. "WW: Self Advertiser." *BNYPL*, 74: 634-9 (D 70).

———. "W on Editing, Newspapers and Journalism." *JQ*, 48: 345-8 (Su 71).

———, and William White. "WW's Lost 'Sun-Down Papers,' Nos. 1-3." *ABC*, 20: 17-20 (Ja 70).

Black, S.A. "Journeys into Chaos: A Psychoanalytic Study of W, His Literary Processes, and His Poems." *L&P*, 24: 47-54 (2Q 74).

———. "Radical Utterances from the Soul's Abysms: Toward a New Sense of W." *PMLA*, 88: 100-11 (Ja 73).

———. "W and the Failure of Mysticism: Identity and Identifications in 'Song of Myself.'" *WWR*, 15: 223-30 (D 69).

———. "Whitman and Psychoanalytic Criticism: A Response to Arthur Golden." *L&P*, 20: 79-81 (1970).

Black, S.T. and Arthur Golden. "W and Psychoanalytic Criticism." *L&P*, 20: 79-92 (1970).

Blackwood, R.T. "William James and WW." *WWR*, 21: 78-9 (Je 75).

Blasing, Mutlu. "'The Sleepers': The Problem of the Self in W." *WWR*, 21: 111-9 (S 75).

Blodgett, H.W. "Editing *Leaves of Grass*: The Manuscript Problem." *CEAAN*, 1: 3-4 (1968).

———. "W's Annexes." *Long Islander*, 132: 9, 12 (28 My 70).

———. "Who Listens to Him Today?" *AmD*, 5: 10-2, 36-38 (1969).

Bordier, Roger. "W et Lorca." *Europa*, 483-4: 188-91 (1969).

Borges, J.L. "WW: Man and Myth." *Crit I*, 1: 707-18 (1975).

Bosquet, Alain. "Les deux visages de WW." *NL*, 47: 3 (21 Ag 69).

Bowering, George. "The Solitary Everything." *WWR*, 15: 13-26 (Mr 69).

Boyle, T.E. "The Tenor in the Organic Metaphor." *Disc*, 11: 240-51 (Sp 68).

Bradley, Sculley. "Physical Evidence in Textual Collation." *CEAAN*, 1: 9 (1968).

Brasher, T.L. "Be—, Be—, Be Not Too Damned—" *WWR*, 14: 60 (Je 68).

———. "A Real W in a Real World." *WWR*, 20: 33-4 (Mr 74).

———. "WW in League with Women." *WWR*, 17: 62-3 (Je 71).

———. "A W Parody of 'The Raven'?" *PN*, 1: 30-1 (O 68).

Brennan, J.G. "Delius and W." *WWR*, 18: 90-6 (S 72).

Brenner, G.A. "W and You: Two Human Beings." *NasR*, 1: 84-98 (Sp 65).

Broderick, J.C. "The Greatest W Collector and the Greatest W Collection." *QJLC*, 27: 109-28 (1970).

———. "WW's Earliest Letter." *QJLC*, 30: 44-7 (Ja 73).

———. "W's Earliest Known Notebook: A Clarification." *PMLA*, 84: 1657 (1969).

Bromwich, David. "Suburbs and Extremities." *Prose*, 8: 25-38 (1974).

Brown, B.W. "T. Sterry Hunt, the Man Who Brough WW to Canada." *SoQ*, 10: 43-8 (O 71).

Brunner, Edward. "'Your Hands within My Hands Are Deeds': Poems of Love in *The Bridge*." *Iowa R*, 4: 105-26 (Wi 73).

Buell, Lawrence. "Transcendentalist Catalogue Rhetoric: Vision versus Form." *AL*, 40: 325-39 (N 68).

Bugliari, Jeanne. "W and Wordsworth: The Janus of Nineteenth Century Idealism." *WWR*, 19: 63-7 (Je 73).

Buitenhuis, Peter. "Commentary." *CAAS*, 2: 19-25 (1967).

Bulow, Ernest. "The Poet of the West: WW and the Native American Voice." *PosS*, 3: 7-10 (N 71).

Bunsho, Jugaku. "W to Toyo." *EigoS*, special Whitman no: 2-5 (1969).

Burgess, C.E. "Masters and W: A Second Look." *WWR*, 17: 25-7 (S 71).

Butscher, Edward. "American Primer Reissued." *WWR*, 16: 125 (D 70).

———. "W's Attitudes Toward Death: The Essential Paradox." *WWR*, 17: 16-9 (Mr 71).

Buylla, J.B. "W, Poeta Ibérico." *FMod*, 40-1: 43-66 (1971).

Cameron, K.W. "Roden Noel, Poet and English Defender of W." *ATQ*, 12: 67-98 (Fa 71).

Cannon, A.D. "Fervid Atmosphere and Typical Events: Autobiography in *Drum-Taps*." *WWR*, 20: 79-97 (S 74).

Capek, Abe. "W: A Re-evaluation." *AmD*, 5: 13-15 (1969).

Carlisle, E.F "WW: The Drama of Identity." *Criticism*, 10: 259-76 (Fa 68).

Carlisle, R.E. "Leitmotif and W's 'When Lilacs Last in the Dooryard Bloom'd.'" *Criticism*, 13: 329-39 (Fa 71).

Carvalho, Joaquim. "Jorge Luis Borges traduz WW." *JdL*, 273: 8 (2Q 73).

Cary, Richard. "Pope and W and God." *WWR*, 14: 159-68 (D 68).

Chanover, E.P. "WW: A Psychological and Psychoanalytic Bibliography." *PsyR*, 59: 467-74 (Fa 72).

Chapman, Abraham. "Democracy as a Poetic Principle in *Leaves of Grass*." *WSL*, 3: 11-23 (1966).

Chari, V.K. "The Limits of W's Symbolism." *JAmSt*, 5: 173-84 (Ag 71).

———. "Structure of W's Catalogue Poems." *WWR*, 18: 3-17 (Mr 72).

———. "W: The Dynamic I." *Cal*, 1: 27-34 (S 69).

Cherry, C.L. "W and Language: An Instance of Semantic Paradox." *WWR*, 14: 56-8 (Je 68).

Christadler, Martin. "WW: Sprachtheorie und Dichtung." *JA*, 13: 84-97 (1968).

Chukovsky, K.I. "What WW Means to Me." *AmD*, 5: 24-6 (1969).

Clarke, Katie. "Poets, Orators, Singers: Come." *Cal*, 2: 24-33 (1970).

Claudel, A.M. "Poems as Laurels for WW." *WWR*, 16: 81-6 (S 70).

Coale, Samuel. "W's War: The March of a Poet." *WWR*, 21: 85-101 (S 75).

Cohen, B.B. "'Song of Myself': Enticement to Faith as Knowledge." *ATQ*, 12: 49-54 (Fa 71).

Cohen, S.B. "WW's Literary Criticism." *WWR*, 18: 39-50 (Je 72).

Cole, J.Y. "Of Copyright, Men & a National Library." *QJLC*, 28: 114-36 (1971).

Collins, Christopher. "W's Open Road and Where It Led." *NasR*, 1: 101-10 (Sp 65).

Congdon, Kirby. "W's Vision." *AmD*, 5: 34-5 (1969).

Constantinescu, Ileana. "150 de ani de la nasterea lui WW (1819-1892)." *Revista de Istorie şi Theorie Literară*, 18: 203-7 (1969).

Cook, H.J. "The Individuation of a Poet: The Process of Becoming in W's 'The Sleepers.'" *WWR*, 21: 101-10 (S 75).

Cronin, F.C. "Modern Sensibility in Stanza 2 of 'Crossing Brooklyn Ferry.'" *WWR*, 15: 56-7 (Mr 69).

Crowley, J.W. "W and the Harvard Poets: The Case of George Cabot Lodge." *WWR*, 19: 165-8 (S 73).

Cuddy, L.A. "Exploration of W's 'Eidólons.'" *WWR*, 19: 153-7 (D 73).

Cummins, R.W. "Emerson, W, and Annie Moore." *ATQ*, 24: 11-4 (Fa 74).

Das, Manoj. "The Good Gray Poet and the Last Great Rishi." *IndL*, 12: 87-91 (1969).

DasGupta, R.K. "Indian Response to WW." *RLC*, 47: 58-70 (1973).

———. "WW. By Kshitindranath Tagore." *WWR*, 19: 3-11 (Mr 73).

Davison, N.J. "'The Raven' and 'Out of the Cradle Endlessly Rocking.'" *PN*, 1: 5-6 (Ap 68).

Davison, R.A. "Ambivalent Imagery in W's 'Lilacs.'" *WWR*, 14: 54-6 (Je 68).

———. "Mixed Tone in 'Cavalry Crossing a Ford.'" *WWR*, 16: 114-7 (D 70).

De Castro, Humberto. "W y Poe en la poesía de Rubén Darío." *BCB*, 10: 90-104 (1967).

DeFalco, J.M. "W's Changes in 'Out of the Cradle' and Poe's 'Raven.'" *WWR*, 16: 22-7 (Mr 70).

De Grazia, Emilio. "'I Hear America Singing': WW and Democratic Culture." *WWR*, 21: 22-8 (Mr 75).

———. "More on W's Twenty-Eight Young Men." *WWR*, 21: 158-60 (D 750.

De la Cruz, J.M. "Alcance de la 'Via Negativa' en la Poesia de T.S. Eliot Como Contraposición a la 'Utopia' de W.W." *FMod*, 42: 257-72 (1971).

Disky, John. "'Retrievements Out of the Night': Approaching W Through the 'Lilacs' Elegy." *Cal*, 7: 27-37 (F 73).

———. "W-Tennyson Correspondence: A Summary and Commentary." *WWR*, 18: 75-81 (S 72).

Doepke, Dale. "W's Theme in 'Calvary Crossing a Ford.'" *WWR*, 18: 132-6 (D 72).

Doherty, J.F. "W's 'Poem of the Mind.'" *Semiotica*, 14: 345-63 (1975).

Domina, Lyle. "W's Lilacs: Process of Self-Realization." *ESQ*, 58: 124-7 (1Q 70).

Doumont, Monique. "Notas para un estudio del 'Whitman' de Jose Martí." *AnuarioF*, 8-9: 199-212 (1969-70).

Doyle, C.C. "Poetry and Pastoral: A Dimension of W's 'Lilacs.'" *WWR*, 15: 242-5 (D 69).

———. "A Note on Thomson's Biography of W." *WWR*, 15: 122-4 (Je 69).

Doyle, P.A. "W and Sean O'Faolain." *WWR*, 16: 117-9 (D 70).

Duerksen, R.A. "Markings by W in His Copy in Shelley's *Works*." *WWR*, 14: 147-51 (D 68).

Eberwein, J.D. "The Education of the Poet: Stovall on W's Influences." *WWR*, 21: 37-9 (Mr 75).

Edmonds, Dale. "WW şi poezia americană contemporană." *România Literară*, 5: 20 (5 Je 69).

Egmond, P.V. "Herzog's Quotation of WW." *WWR*, 13: 54-6 (Je 67).

Eitner, W.H. "WW in the *Kansas Magazine*." *KM*, 16: 29-31 (1968).

Emmanuel, Lenny. "W's Fusion of Science and Poetry." *WWR*, 17: 73-82 (S 71).

Ewell, Sister Barbara. "Death in W: A Symbolic Process of Immortality." *NDEJ*, 6: 29-38 (1970-71).

Fasel, Ida. "'Song of Myself' as Prayer." *WWR*, 17: 19-22 (Mr 71).

———. "W and Marvell's 'The Garden.'" *WWR*, 20: 114-5 (S 74).

Fein, R.J. "Lamentations and 'When Lilacs Last.'" *WWR*, 15: 115-7 (Je 69).

Feinberg, C.E. "WW: Yesterday, Today and Tomorrow." *NasR*, 1: 1-18 (Sp 65).

Ferlazzo, P.J. "Anne Gilchrist, Critic of WW." *SDR*, 10: 63-79 (1972).

———. "Encounter: W and His Reader." *WWR*, 18: 138-40 (D 72).

———. "Sex for W—The Body Mystic." *Cal*, 9: 29-40 (1974).

Finkelstein, Sidney. "W's Mannahatta." *AmD*, 5: 18-23 (1969).

Fleck, Richard. "A Note on Whitman in Ireland." *WWR*, 21: 160-2 (D 75).

———. "Thoreau, Emerson, W in the Western Wilderness." *JANSS*, 16: 9-11 (Sp 69).

Freedman, F.B. "Emerson Giving Joy: Summer of 1855." *WWR*, 21: 162-3 (D 75).

———. "A Sociologist Views a Poet: Robert Ezra Park on WW." *WWR*, 16: 99-104 (D 70).

———. "A W Letter to Josiah Child." *WWR*, 16: 55-7 (Mr 70).

Frelazzo, Paul. "Anne Gilchrist, Critic of WW." *SDR*, 10: 63-79 (Wi 72-3).

Friedman, R.S. "A W Primer: Solipsism and Identity." *AQ*, 27: 443-60 (O 75).

Friedman, Stanley. "W and Laugharne." *AWR*, 18: 81-2 (1969).

Friend, Robert. "The Quest for Rondure: A Comparison of Two Passages to India." *HUSL*, 1: 76-85 (Sp 73).

Geffen, Arthur. "WW and Jules Michelet—One More Time." *AL*, 45: 107-14 (Mr 73).

Gilenson, Boris. "WW in Russia." *SovL*, 5: 176-81 (1969).

Girgus, Sam. "Culture and Post-Culture in WW." *CentR*, 18: 392-410 (Fa 74).

Goede, W.J. "Swinburne and the Whitmaniacs." *VN*, 33: 16-21 (Sp 68).

Gogol, J.M. "A German Expressionist Poet on W." *WWR*, 20: 105-6 (S 74).

Goldberg, B.A. "Patriotic Allusions in Sections 15 and 33 of 'Song of Myself.'" *WWR*, 21: 58-66 (Je 75).

Golden, Arthur. "Passage to Less Than India: Structure and Meaning in W's 'Passage to India.'" *PMLA*, 88: 1095-1103 (O 73).

———. "WW's Poetry: A Psychological Journey." *L&P*, 19: 61-5 (1969).

Golden, S.A. "W to Mrs. Vine Coburn: Three Letters." *WWR*, 15: 59-60 (Mr 69).

Goodman, E.S. "'Lilacs' and the Pastoral Elegy Reconsidered." *BBr*, 24: 119-33 (1971).

Goodson, Lester. "A Footnote on W and Time." *WWR*, 17: 54-5 (Je 71).

———. "W and the Problem of Evil." *WWR*, 16: 45-50 (Je 70).

Graham, Mary-Emma. "Politics in Black and White: A View of WW's Career as a Political Journalist." *CLAJ*, 17: 263-70 (D 73).

Green, Martin. "W as a Twentieth Century Poet." *Month*, 228: 82-93, 120-7 (Jl-Ag, S 69).

Gregg, Larry. "Kornei Chukovsky's W." *WWR*, 20: 50-9 (Je 74).

Grier, E.F. "WW's Earliest Known Notebook." *PMLA*, 83: 1453-6 (O 68).

Gupta, Rameshwar. "W: The Poet of Cosmic Dynamism." *BP*, 4: 95-103 (1968).

Hagenbuchle, Roland. "W's Unfinished Quest for an American Identity." *ELH*, 40: 428-78 (Fa 73).

Hanna, S. "Gibran and W: Their Literary Dialogue." *LE&W*, 12: 174-98 (1968).

Hanson, R.G. "Anxiety as Human Predicament: W's 'Calamus' no. 9." *WWR*, 21: 73-5 (Je 75).

———. "A Critical Reflection on W's 'The Base of All Metaphysics.'" *WWR*, 18: 67-70 (Je 72).

―――. "Reflections on W's Role as Tragic Poet of the American Civil War." *WWR*, 14: 50-4 (Je 68).

―――. "W as Social Theorist: Worker in Poetics and Politics." *WWR*, 16: 41-5 (Je 70).

Harned, T.B. "Memoirs of TB.H—WW's Friend and Literary Executor." *ATQ*, 14: 4-54 (Sp 72).

Harrison, P.P. "'Eidólons': An Entrance Song." *WWR*, 17: 35-45 (Je 71).

Harrison, S.R. "Sacrilege of Preference in W and Sartre." *WWR*, 15: 51-4 (Mr 69).

Harvey, N.L. "W's Use of *Arms* in the *Leaves of Grass*." *WWR*, 18: 136-8 (Mr 72).

Hazen, James. "W and Hopkins." *ATQ*, 12: 41-8 (Fa 71).

Hench, A.L. "WW and Folger McKinsey." *AN&Q*, 8: 53 (1969).

Henseler, D.L. "The Voice of the Grass-Poem 'I': W's 'Song of Myself.'" *WWR*, 15: 26-32 (Mr 69).

Hibler, D.J. "*Drum-Taps* and *Battle Pieces*: Melville and W on the Civil War." *Person*, 50: 130-47 (Wi 69).

Highes, Langston. "The Ceaseless Rings of WW." *AmD*, 5: 8-9 (1969).

Hinz, E.J. "W's 'Lilacs': the Power of Elegy." *BuR*, 20: 35-54 (Fa 72).

Hitchcock, Bert. "WW: The Pedagogue as Poet." *WWR*, 20: 140-6 (D 74).

Hobsbaum, Philip. "Eliot, W and the American Tradition." *JAmSt*, 3: 239-64 (D 69).

Hollis, C.C. "The Correspondence." *WWR*, 16: 93-4 (S 70).

Hoople, R.P. "'Chants Democratic and Native American': A Neglected Sequence in the Growth of *Leaves of Grass*." *AL*, 42: 181-96 (My 70).

―――. "WW and the City of Friends." *ATQ*, 18: 45-51 (Sp 73).

Hubach, R.R. "Western Newspaper Accounts of W's 1879 Trip to the West." *WWR*, 18: 56-62 (S 72).

Hudson, Vaughan. "Melvelle's *Battle-Pieces* and W's *Drum-Taps*." *WWR*, 19: 81-92 (S 73).

Hughes, Charles. "Impact of Evil on the Poetry of WW." *WWR*, 15: 237-42 (D 69).

Hughson, Lois. "In Search of the True America: Dos Passos' Debt to W in *U.S.A.*" *MFS*, 19: 179-92 (Su 73).

Hugot, Francois. "Poets to Come." *AmD*, 5: 27-8 (1969).

Hunt, R.A. "W's Poetics and the Unity of 'Calamus.'" *AL*, 46: 482-94 (Ja 75).

Ifkovic, Edward. "'I Took a Jaunt': Dickens' *American Notes* and W's *Franklin Evans*." *WWR*, 14: 171-4 (D 68).

Ivanetich, Aloysius. "Gentlemen, Your Facts Are Useful." *Calamus*, 10: 2-17 (1975).

Jaen, D.T. "WW: tema literario." *Torre*, 60: 77-100 (Ap-Je 68).

Jaffe, Harold. "Bucke's WW: A Collaboration." *WWR*, 15: 190-4 (S 69).

―――. "Markham on W." *MarkR*, 2: 1 (My 68).

―――. "Richard Maurice Bucke and WW." *CRAS*, 2: 37-47 (1971).

―――. "Richard Maurice Bucke's *WW*." *Serif*, 7: 3-10 (1970).

Jellicorse, J.L. "W and Modern Literary Criticism." *ATQ*, 12: 4-11 (Fa 71).

Johnson, D.J. "The Effect of Suspension Dots, Parentheses and Italics on Lyricism of 'Song of Myself.'" *WWR*, 21: 47-58 (Je 75).

Johnson, L.C. "The Design of WW's *Specimen Days*." *WWR*, 21: 3-14 (Mr 75).

Johnston, K.G., and J.O. Rees. "W and the Foo-foos: An Experiment in Language." *WWR*, 17: 3-10 (Mr 71).

Kadir, Kjelal. "Neruda and W: Short-Circuiting the Body Electric." *PCP*, 8: 16-22 (1973).

Kagle, S.E. "Temporal Structure in *Leaves of Grass*." *IllQ*, 33: 42-9 (D 70).

―――. "Time as a Dimension in W." *ATQ*, 12: 55-60 (Fa 71).

Kahn, S.J. "Stephen Crane and W: A Possible Source for *Maggie*." *WWR*, 7: 71-7 (D 61).

———. "W's 'New Wood.'" *WWR*, 15: 201-14 (D 69).

———. "W's 'Overstaid Fraction' Again." *WWR*, 20: 67-73 (Je 74).

Kalita, Dwight. "WW: Ecstatic Sea-Voyager." *WWR*, 21: 14-22 (Mr 75).

———. "W and the Correspondent Breeze." *WWR*, 21: 125-30 (S 75).

Kallen, H.M. "Of Love, Death and W.W." *J Long Island Hist*, 8: 17-29 (Su-Fa 68); *WWR*, 15: 171-80 (S 69).

Kamei, Shunsuke. "W to Lawrence." *EigS*, 114: 430-2 (1968).

———. "W in Japan." *EigoS*, 115: 29-36 (1969).

Kanjo, E.R. "Time and Eternity in 'Crossing Brooklyn Ferry.'" *WWR*, 18: 82-90 (S 72).

Kaplan, Justin. "Nine Old Bones: WW's Blue Book." *Atl*, 221: 60-4 (My 68).

Katz, Joseph. "Theodore Dreiser: Enter Chicago, Hope and WW." *WWR*, 14: 169-71 (D 68).

Kawatsu, Takashi. "Thoreau and W as Transcendentalists." *Eng & Amer Stud* (Tokyo), 7: 1-25 (15 Mr 71).

Kazin, Alfred. "The Great American Poet." *NYRB*, 15: 42-6 (1970).

Keller, D.H. "WW in England: A Footnote." *WWR*, 15: 54-5 (Mr 69).

Kellner, R.S. "W, Melville and the Civil War: A Sharing of Mood and Metaphor." *AN&Q*, 13: 102-5 (Mr 75).

Kiely, M.F. "'I Was Looking a Long While. . . .'" *ABC*, 21: 11-3 (1971).

Kieniewicz, Teresa. "WW i Skamandryci." *PHum*, 16: 97-104 (1972).

Kinnell, Galway. "W's Indicative Words." *APR*, 2: 9-12 (#2 73).

Knox, George. "The W-Hartmann Controversy." *Sadakichi Hartmann N*, 1: 2-3, 7-9 (Sp, Wi 70).

Kodama, Koichi. "Arishima Takero ni okeru W." *EigoS*, 115: 9-12 (1969).

Kornblatt, Joyce. "W's Vision of the Past in 'The Sleepers.'" *WWR*, 16: 86-9 (S 70).

Krapf, Norbert. "W's 'Calamus': Adam from the Garden to the City." *WWR*, 19: 162-4 (D 73).

Krauth, Leland. "W and His Readers: The Comradeship Theme." *WWR*, 20: 147-51 (D 74).

Kummings, D.D. "A Note on the Americanness of WW." *Calamus*, 10: 18-27 (1975).

———. "W's Voice in 'Song of Myself': From Private to Public." *WWR*, 17: 10-5 (Mr 71).

Labrada, E.B. "El idioma de W: Su Traduccion." *I-AmRB*, 21: 46-63 (Ja-Mr 71).

Lalic, I.V. "Poezija Volta Vitmana." *Knij*, 57: 190-207 (1973).

Lara, J.G.M. de. "WW, poeta de la libertad." *CHA*, 243: 572-87 (1970).

Larson, C.R. "*Leaves of Grass*—Pure Acapulco Gold." *CEA*, 36: 18-20 (N 73).

Leary, Lewis. "Kate Chopin and WW." *WWR*, 16: 120-1 (D 70).

LeClair, Thomas. "Prufrock and the Open Road." *WWR*, 17: 123-6 (D 71).

Ledbetter, J.T. "W's Power in the Short Poem: A Discussion of 'Whispers of Heavenly Death.'" *WWR*, 21: 155-8 (D 75).

Leggett, B.J. "The Structure of W's 'On Journeys Through the States.'" *WWR*, 14: 58-9 (Je 68).

LeMaster, J.R. "Jesse Stuart's *Album of Destiny*: In Pursuit of W's Parallels." *BSUF*, 13: 75-9 (Wi 72).

———. "Jesse Stuart's Album of Destiny—In W's Flow." *IllQ*, 36: 38-40 (1973).

Levin, Beatrice. "WW's Christmas: 1866." *Hobby Times & Bookworm*, 1: 12-8 (D 68).

Lewis, W.B. "WW: Johannes Schlaf's New Being ('Neuer Mensch')." *RLC*, 47: 596-611 (O-D 73).

Livingston, J.L. "WW's Epistle to the Americans." *AL*, 40: 542-4 (Ja 69).

———. "With W and Hegel around the Campfire." *WWR*, 15: 120-2 (Je 69).

Lombard, C.M. "W and Hugo." *WWR*, 19: 19-25 (Mr 73).

Loving, J.M. "'A Brooklyn Soldier, and a Noble One': A Brooklyn *Daily Union* Article by W." *WWR*, 20: 27-9 (Mr 74).

———. "Civil War Letters of George Washington W from North Carolina." *NCHR*, 50: 73-92 (Wi 73).

———. "The Estate of George Washington Whitman: An Horatio Alger Story in WW's Family." *BMHS*, 31: 105-10 (Ja 75).

———. "'Our Veterans Mustering Out'—Another Newspaper Article by W about His Soldier-Brother." *YULG*, 49: 217-224 (O 74).

Lowenfals, Walter. "The External Meanings." *AmD*, 5: 5-7 (1969).

———. "A Poet Is as Old as His Language: A Whitman Note." *ETC*, 25: 495-7 (D 68).

Lozynsky, Artem. "Irresponsible Reprint: Bucke's *WW*." *WWR*, 18: 104-5 (S 72).

———. "Jan Christian Smuts on W." *WWR*, 19: 119-20 (S 73).

———. "A Lost W Letter to Bucke." *WWR*, 19: 168-9 (D 73).

———. "S. Weir Mitchell on W: An Unpublished Letter." *AN&Q*, 13: 120-1 (Ap 75).

———. "'Us Three Meaning America': W's Literary Executors." *PBSA*, 68: 442-4 (O-D 74).

———. "WW in Canada." *ABC*, 23: 21-3 (#4 73).

———. "WW on Marriage." *N&Q*, 22: 120-1 (Mr 75).

———. "W the Man and Hawthorne the Artist." *NHJ*, 5: 270-1 (1975).

———. "W and *Man's Moral Nature*." *WWR*, 21: 36-7 (Mr 75).

———. "W's *Complete Poems & Prose*: 'Bible' or 'Volume.'" *WWR*, 19: 28-30 (Mr 73).

———. "W's Death Bed: Two Nurses' Reports." *AL*, 47: 270-3 (My 75).

McCarthy, H.T. "Henry Miller's Democratic Vistas." *AQ*, 23: 221-35 (1971).

McCormick, E.L. "WW, Santayana's Poet of Barbarism." *Serif*, 5: 24-8 (Mr 68).

McCullagh, J.C. "'Proud Music of the Storm': A Study in Dynamics." *WWR*, 21: 66-72 (Je 75).

McElderry, B.R. "Personae in W (1855-60)." *ATQ*, 12: 25-32 (Fa 71).

McGhee, R.D. "Concepts of Time in W's Poetry." *WWR*, 15: 76-85 (Je 69).

———. "*Leaves of Grass* and Cultural Development." *WWR*, 16: 3-14 (Mr 70).

McGlinchie, Calire. "Three Indigenous Americans (W, Eakins, Gilbert)." *Proc Sixth Int Congress Aesth*, 1972, pp. 709-13.

McKeithan, D.M. "Two Avian Images in Marvell and W." *WWR*, 17: 101-3 (D 71).

McKenzie, G.M. "Is W the Hippies' Guru?" *UCQ*, 16: 14-9 (My 71).

McLaughlin, Sister A.V. "Una comparacion entre la poesia de Luis Llorens Torres y la de WW: Temas, tecnicas y estilo." *Horizontes*, 31-2: 73-93 (1973).

McMullin, S.E. "WW's Influence in Canada." *DR*, 49: 361-8 (Au 69).

———. "W and the Canadian Press 1872-1919." *WWR*, 20: 132-9 (D 74).

McWilliams, J.P. "'Drum Taps' and *Battle-Pieces*: The Blossom of War." *AQ*, 23: 181-201 (My 71).

Madigan, F.V. "A Mirror of Shelley in W." *Greyfriar*, 11: 3-19 (1970).

Magee, J.D. "'Crossing Brooklyn Ferry': One Hundred Years Hence." *WWR*, 15: 38-43 (Mr 69).

Magowan, Robin. "The Horse of the Gods: Possession in 'Song of Myself.'" *WWR*, 15: 67-76 (Je 69).

Major, Clarence. "Close to the Ground." *AmD*, 5: 35 (1969).

Male, R.R. "W's Radical Utterance." *ESQ*, 60: 73-5 (Su 70).

Marks, B.A. "Retrospective Narrative in Nineteenth Century American Literature." *CE*, 31: 366-75 (1970).

Marshall, Lenore. "W's Modernism." *AmD*, 5: 17 (1969).

Martin, R.K. "W's 'The Sleepers.'" *Expl*, 33: 33-5 (O 74).

Martin, Robert. "W's *Song of Myself*: Homosexual Dream and Vision." *PR*, 42: 80-96 (1Q 75).

Mason, J.B. "WW's Catalogues: Rhetorical Means for Two Journeys in 'Song of Myself.'" *AL*, 45: 34-49 (Mr 73).

Mathew, V.J. "Self in 'Song of Myself': A Defense of W's Egoism." *WWR*, 15: 102-7 (Je 69).

Matle, J.H. "The Body Acclaimed." *WWR*, 16: 110-4 (D 70).

Mayfield, J.S. "WW, Theodore Roosevelt, and 'The New Inferno.'" *Courier*, 35: 19-23 (Su 70).

Megna, B.C. "Sociality and Seclusion in the Poetry of WW." *WWR*, 17: 55-7 (Je 71).

Mehrotra, A.K. "The Bard and the Foundry: A Reaction to W's *Black Poems*." *RSW*, 39: 33-9 (Mr 71).

Mendelsohn, Maurice. "W and the Oral Indian Tradition." *AmD*, 7: 25-8 (1972).

————. "'He Dreamed of the Brotherhood.'" *WWR*, 16: 57-9 (Mr 68).

Meredith, William. "W to the Poet." *WWR*, 16: 9-13 (Mr 69).

Mersch, Arnold. "Cosmic Contrast: W and the Hindu Philosophy." *WWR*, 19: 49-63 (Je 73).

————. "Teilhard de Chardin and W's 'A Noiseless Patient Spider.'" *WWR*, 17: 99-100 (S 71).

————. "W and the Age of Aquarius: A Message for the 'Woodstock Generation.'" *WWR*, 19: 138-46 (D 73).

————. "W and Buber: In the Presence of Greatness." *WWR*, 21: 120-25 (S 75).

Metzger, C.R. "WW's Philosophical Epic." *WWR*, 15: 91-6 (Je 69).

Mezey, Robert. "Happy Birthday, Old Man." *AmD*, 5: 28 (1969).

Miller, E.H. "And Gladly Edit." *WW in Our Time* Supplement to *WWR*, 13-6 (1970).

Miller, F.D. "The Partitive Studies of 'Song of Myself.'" *ATQ*, 12: 11-7 (1971).

Miller, J.E. "W: Dead or Alive?" *WWR*, 16: 17-20 (Mr 70).

Miller, T.R. "The Boy, the Bird and the Sea: An Archetypal Reading of 'Out of the Cradle.'" *WWR*, 19: 93-103 (S 73).

Mills, Barriss. "W's Poetic Theory." *ESQ*, 55: 42-7 (2Q 69).

Mitchell, Roger. "A Prosody for W?" *PMLA*, 84: 1606-12 (1969).

Moore, W.L. "On the Difficulty in Reading *Leaves of Grass*." *EigoS*, 115: 103-8 (1969).

Moran, Ronald. "*WW at Bear Mountain* and the American Illusion." *CP*, 2: 5-9 (Sp 69).

Morgan, C.H. "A New Look at W's 'Crisis.'" *SAB*, 36: 41-52 (Mr 71).

Morsberger, R.E. "W's Hermit Thrush: An Ornithological Note." *WWR*, 20: 60-7 (Je 74).

Moyne, E.J. "Folger McKinsey and WW." *WWR*, 21: 135-44 (D 75).

Muccigrosso, R.M. "W and the Adolescent Mind." *EJ*, 57: 982-4 (O 68).

Mukerji, Nirmal. "Van Wyck Brooks's Assessment of WW." *PURBA*, 3: 71-8 (O 72).

Mulqueen, J.E. "Organic Growth of *Leaves of Grass*." *WWR*, 15: 85-91 (Je 69).

————. "'Song of Myself': W's Hymn to Eros." *WWR*, 20: 60-6 (Je 74).

Nabeshima, Yoshihiro. "W no Buntai." *EigoS*, 115: 100-2 (1969).

Nagle, J.M. "Toward a Theory of Structure in 'Song of Myself.'" *WWR*, 15: 162-71 (S 69).

Neilson, K.P. "A Discovery Rediscovered in the Search for WW Music." *WWR*, 19: 114-8 (S 73).

————. "Lab Theatre Production of Joseph Scott Kierland's 'Drum-Taps.'" *WWR*, 21: 76-8 (Je 75).

————. "Stan Harte, Jr.'s Musical *Leaves of Grass*." *WWR*, 17: 126-9 (D 71).

————. "The 'Voice' of WW." *ABC*, 19: 20-2 (D 68).

————. "WW in Wax." *ABC*, 24: 11 (My 74).

Nelson, Carl. "W's Dynamic Form: The Image of the Divine." *WWR*, 20: 121-31 (D 74).

Nelson, Cary. "Whitman in Vietnam: Poetry and History in Contemporary America." *MR*, 16: 55-71 (Wi 75).

Nelson, J.A. "Ecstasy and Transformation in W's 'Lilacs.'" *WWR*, 18: 113-23 (D 72).

Nilsen, H.N. "The mystic message. W's 'Song of Myself.'" *Edda*, 6: 400-9 (1969).

Nizeteo, Antun. "W in Croatia: Tin Ujević and WW." *JCS*, 11-12: 105-51 (1970).

Novak, E.G. "The *Dynamo* School of Poets." *ConL*, 11: 526-39 (Au 70).

Noverr, D.A. "'Aboard At a Ship's Helm': A Minor Sea Drama, the Poet, and the Soul." *WWR*, 17: 23-5 (Mr 71).

Odessky, M.H. "'Sooner or Later, Delicate Death.'" *JHS*, 1: 355-9 (1968).

Okamoto, Kazuko. "On One's Self: An Address to University Students in Rebellion." *Cal*, 1: 6-23 (S 69).

Okubo, Junichiro. "Soseki no W." *EigoS*, 115: 6-8 (1969).

Origo, Iris. "Additions to the Keats Collection." *TLS*, 23 Ap 70, pp. 457-8.

Orth, Michael. "WW, Metaphysical Teapot: The Structure of 'Song of Myself.'" *WWR*, 14: 16-24 (Mr 68).

Ota, Saburo. "W to Minshu Shiha." *EigoS*, 115: 26-8 (1969).

Patterson, M.C. "'Lilacs': A Sonata." *WWR*, 14: 46-50 (Je 68).

Pearce, H.D. "'I Lean and Loafe': W's Romantic Posture." *WWR*, 15: 3-12 (Mr 69).

Peattie, R.W. "Postscript to Charles Kent on W." *WWR*, 15: 107-11 (Je 69).

Peavy, L.S. "'Wooded Flesh and Metal Bone': A Look at the Riddle of the Broad-Axe." *WWR*, 20: 152-3 (D 74).

Peeples, P.K. "The Paradox of the "Good Gray Poet' (WW on Slavery and the Black Man)." *Phylon*, 35: 22-32 (1974).

Peterson, D.E. "Mayakovsky and W: The Icon and the Mosaic." *SlavR*, 28: 416-25 (S 69).

Petersen, W.J. "The WW Club." *Palimpsest*, 51: 323-48 (1970).

Phillips, Elizabeth. "'Song of Myself': The Numbers of the Poem in Relation to Its Form." *WWR*, 16: 67-81 (S 70).

Pici, Joseph. "An Editing of WW's 'When Lilacs Last in the Dooryard Bloom'd." *UDR*, 9: 35-45 (Su 75).

Pollin, B.R. "'Delightful Sights,' a Possible W Article in Poe's *Broadway Journal*." *WWR*, 15: 180-7 (S 69).

Powers, R.G. "*Leaves of Grass*: The Evolution of an Epic." *BBr*, 24: 107-18 (1971).

Preuschen, K.A. "WW's Undelivered Oration 'The Dead in This War.'" *EA*, 24: 147-51 (Ap-Je 71).

Pulling, A.V.S. "An Appraisal of WW (1819-1892)." *Rendezvous*, 3: 16-22 (1968).

Quinn, J.E. "Yeats and W, 1887-1925." *WWR*, 20: 106-9 (S 74).

Raffanielle, William. "Pasquale Jannaccone and 'The Last Invocation.'" *WWR*, 14: 41-5 (Je 68).

Rees, J.O. "W and the Foo-Foos: An Experiment in Lanuguage." *WWR*, 17: 3-10 (Mr 71).

Reid, A.S. "The Structure of 'Song of Myself' Reconsidered." *SHR*, 8: 507-14 (Fa 74).

Reinartz, K.F. "WW and Feminism." *WWR*, 19: 127-37 (D 73).

Reiss, Edmund. "W's Poetic Grammar: Style and Meaning in 'Children of Adam.'" *ATQ*, 12: 32-41 (Fa 71).

Reissman, R.C. "Recurrent Motifs in *Goodbye My Fancy*." *WWR*, 21: 28-35 (Mr 75).

Reuben, P.P. "W in B.O. Flower's *Arena*." *WWR*, 19: 11-9 (Mr 73).

Reynolds, M.S. "W's Early Prose and 'The Sleepers.'" *AL*, 41: 406-14 (N 69).

Richards, Max. "The English W." *Ariel*, 5: 40-55 (O 74).

Riese, Utz. "WWs demokratische Vision." *WZPHP*, 15: 345-51 (1971).

Robbins, J.A. "The Narrative Form of 'Song of Myself.'" *ATQ*, 12: 17-20 (Fa 71).

Robinson, David. "The Poetry of Dialogue in 'Song of Myself.'" *Am Poetry & Poetics*, 1: 34-50 (Fa 74).

Rose, A.H. "Destructive Vision in the First and Last Versions of 'Song of Myself.'" *WWR*, 15: 215-22 (D 69).

Rosenfeld, A.H. "The Eagle and the Axe: A Study of W's 'Song of the Broad-Axe.'" *AL*, 25: 35-70 (Mr 68).

———. "W and the Providence Literati." *BBr*, 24: 82-106 (1971).

———. "W's Open Road Philosophy." *WWR*, 14: 3-16 (Mr 68).

Rosenthal, P.Z. "'Dilation' in W's Early Writing." *WWR*, 20: 3-14 (Mr 74).

———. "The Language of Measurement in W's Early Writing." *TSLL*, 15: 461-70 (Fa 73).

Ross, Donald. "Emerson's Stylistic Influence on W." *ATQ*, 25: 41-51 (Wi 75).

Ross, M.L. "WW and the Limits of Embarrassment." *Forum(H)*, 6: 29-34 (Fa-Wi 68).

Rule, H.B. "WW and George Caleb Bingham." *WWR*, 15: 248-53 (D 69).

———. "WW and Thomas Eakins: Variations on Some Common Themes." *TQ*, 17: 7-57 (Wi 74).

Runden, J.P. "W's 'The Sleepers' and the 'Indiana' Section of Crane's *The Bridge*." *WWR*, 15: 245-8 (D 69).

Runge, Renate. "Die Rezeption WWs in Russland und in der Soweitunion." *ZAA*, 22: 371-91 (D 74).

Russell, Jack. "*Israel Potter* and 'Song of Myself.'" *AL*, 40: 72-7 (Mr 68).

Sachithanandan, V. "W and the Serpent Power." *WWR*, 16: 50-5 (Je 70).

St. Armand, B.L. "*Franklin Evans*: A Sportive Temperance Novel." *BBr*, 24: 134-47 (1971).

Sakamoto, Masayuki. "W no okeru Shiso." *EigoS*, 115: 109-11 (1969).

Sanders, M.K. "Shelley's Promethean Shadow on *Leaves of Grass*." *WWR*, 14: 151-9 (D 68).

Sastry, C.N. "WW's 'Reconciliation' and Wilfred Owen's 'Strange Meeting': A Comparison." *NASRC*, 11: 54-6 (1969).

———. "Glimpses of India in *Leaves of Grass*." *LHY*, 7: 61-7 (Jl 66).

———. "WW and Rabindranath Tagore: A Study in Comparison and Contrast." *Triveni*, 38: 22-31 (1969).

Saxena, M.C. "WW and Democracy." *Triveni*, 39. 43-9 (1971).

Scholnick, Robert. "W and the Magazines: Some Documentary Evidence." *AL*, 44: 222-46 (My 72).

Schonfeld, J.M. "No Exit in 'Passage to India': Existence Precedes Essence in Section 5." *WWR*, 19: 147-51 (D 73).

Seamon, Roger. "Sinners in the Hands of a Happy God: Hierarchical Values in 'Song of Myself.'" *CAAS*, 2: 3-18 (1967).

Sharma, D.R. "George Santayana's Assessment of WW." *BP*, 14: 13-22 (1970).

Sharma, M.L. "The 'Oriental Estate,' Especially the *Bhagavada-Gita* in American Literature." *Forum(H)*, 7: 4-11 (Fa-Wi 69).

———. "W, Tagore, Iqbal: Whitmanated, Under-Whitmanated, and Over-Whitmanated Singers of Self." *WWR*, 15: 230-7 (D 69).

Sharma, O.P. "WW and the Doctrine of Karman." *PE&W*, 20: 169-74 (1970).

Shephard, Esther. "A Fact Which Should Have Been Included in 'W's Earliest Known Notebook: A Clarification' by John C. Broderick." *PMLA*, 86: 266 (Mr 71).

———. "The Inside Front and Back Cover of W's Earliest Known Notebook: Some Observations on Photocopy and Verbal Descriptions." *PMLA*, 87: 1119-22 (O 72).

Shinkura, Shunichi. "Mirai no Shijin—W to America Gendaishi." *EigoS*, 115: 92-5 (1969).

Shiratori, Shogo. "Hyakunen sai igo." *EigoS*, 115: 14-5 (1969).

Simon, Myron. "'Self' in W and Dickinson." *CEA*, 30: 8 (D 67).

Simpson, G.P. "Susannah and the Elders: A Source for 'Song of Myself,' Section II." *WWR*, 109-11 (S 74).

Singh, R.K. "W: *Avatar* of Shri Krishna?" *WWR*, 15: 97-102 (Je 69).

Sister Eva Mary. "Shades of Darkness in 'The Sleepers.'" *WWR*, 15: 187-90 (S 69).

Sister Flavia Maria. "'Song of Myself': A Presage of Modern Teilhardian Paleontology." *WWR*, 15: 43-9 (Mr 69).

Slattery, Sister M.P. "Patterns of Imagery in W's 'There Was a Child Went Forth.'" *WWR*, 15: 112-4 (Je 69).

Sloane, D.E.E. "In Search of a Realistic Poetic Tradition." *ALR*, 5: 489-91 (1972).

Smith, A.H. "Origin and Interpretation of the Hero of 'Song of Myself.'" *WWR*, 17: 45-54 (Je 71).

———. "WW's 'Personality' Figure." *BSUF*, 16: 23-8 (Sp 75).

Smith, Helen. "Water Imagery in *Leaves of Grass*." *WWR*, 17: 82-92 (S 71).

Snyder, John. "The Irony of National Union: Violence and Compassion in 'Drum Taps.'" *CRAS*, 4: 169-84 (Fa 73).

Solomon, Petre. "Cei o sută cincizeci de ani ai lui W." *Viata Romanească*, 22: 54-9 (1969).

Song, Kyung-Joon. "W: His Idea of Immortality." *Eng Lit and Lang*, 39: 55-63 (Au 71).

Stebner, Gerhard. "W, Liliencron, W.H. Auden: Betrachtung und Vergleich motivähnlichter Gedichte." *NS*, 9: 105-18 (Mr 60).

Spencer, B.T. "Sherwood Anderson: American Mythopoeist." *AL*, 41: 1-18 (Mr 69).

Stein, M.L. "Affirmations and Negations: Lawrence's 'Whitman' and W's Open Road." *WWR*, 18: 63-7 (Je 72).

Stephens, Rosemary. "Elemental Imagery in 'Children of Adam.'" *WWR*, 14: 26-8 (Mr 68).

Stibitz, E.E. "WW Answers a Collector." *ICarbS*, 1: 141-4 (1974).

Stillgoe, J.R. "Possible Lockean Influence in 'The World Below the Brine.'" *WWR*, 21: 150-5 (D 75).

Stott, J.C. "The Mocking-Bird in 'Out of the Cradle.'" *WWR*, 16: 119-20 (D 70).

Stovall, Floyd. "Dating W's Early Notebooks." *SB*, 24: 197-204 (1971).

———. "A Supplement to the Whitman Handbook." *WWR*, 16: 123-4 (D 70).

Stubblefield, Charles. "The Great Circle: W's 'Passage to India.'" *PrS*, 49: 19-30 (Sp 75).

Stubbs, J.C. "The Ideal in the Literature and Art of the American Renaissance." *ESQ*, 55: 5-63 (2Q 69).

Stuehler, D.M. "Significant Form in W's 'Out of the Cradle Endlessly Rocking.'" *Calamus*, 10: 28-39 (1975).

Sugg, R.P. "W's Symbolic Circle and 'A Broadway Pageant.'" *WWR*, 16: 35-40 (Je 70).

Sulfridge, Cynthia. "Meaning in W's Use of 'Electric.'" *WWR*, 19: 151-3 (D 73).

Sutton, Larry. "Structural Music in 'Out of the Cradle.'" *WWR*, 15: 57-9 (Mr 69).

Sweet, R.B. "A Writer Looks at W's 'A Sight in Camp in the Daybreak Gray and Dim.'" *WWR*, 17: 58-62 (Je 71).

Sykes, R.H. "'Seeking the Spheres to Connect.'" *Cal*, 3: 20-5 (1970).

Tagore, Kshitindranath. "WW." *WWR*, 19: 3-19 (Mr 73).

Takayama, R. "A Japanese Estimate of WW." *Cal*, 2: 1-5 (1970).

Taniguchi, Toshiro. "Whitman Seen from the Zen Viewpoint." *Jimbungaku*, 108: 28-45 (1968).

Tanner, J.T.F. "A Note on W's 'A Sight in Camp.'" *ESQ*, 58: 123-34 (1Q 70).

———. "WW and William James." *Cal*, 2: 6-23 (1970).

*Tanner, J.T. "WW Bibliographies: A Chronological Listing, 1902-1964." *BB*, 25: 131-2 (Ja-Ap 68).

Tanner, S.L. "Star-gazing in W's *Specimen Days*." *WWR*, 19: 158-61 (D 73).

Taylor, E.W. "Moments of Silence in *Leaves of Grass*." *WWR*, 21: 145-50 (D 75).

Templin, Lawrence. "The Quaker Influence on WW." *AL*, 42: 165-80 (My 70).

Tezuka, Tatsumaro. "Doshisha de Kiita Arishima Takero no W Kogi." *EigoS*, 115: 13 (1969).

Thompson, B.A. "Edward Wilkins: Male Nurse to WW." *WWR*, 15: 194-6 (S 69).

Thompson, G.R. "An Early Unrecorded Printing of WW's 'Death in the School-Room." *PBSA*, 67: 64-5 (1Q 73).

Tisiker, M.R. "Jacob Boehme's Influence on Some Poems in *Leaves of Grass*." *WWR*, 20: 15-26 (Mr 74).

Tokunaga, Yozo. "Randall Jarrell no Whitman-ron." *EigoS*, 115: 112-14 (1969).

Traubel, Gertrude. "They Remember WW." *Cal*, 1: 24-6 (S 69).

Tsunata, Shiro. "W Hyoka no Nagare." *EigoS*, 115: 96-9 (1969).

Turner, M.A. "Reconciliation of Love and Death in 'Out of the Cradle' and Other Poems." *WWR*, 18: 123-32 (D 72).

Vance, R.W. "A Reading of 'The Sleepers.'" *WWR*, 18: 17-28 (Mr 72).

Vanderbilt, Kermit. "'I Hear America Singing': W and Democratic Culture." *WWR*, 21: 22-8 (Mr 75).

Vanderhaar, Margaret. "W, Paine and the Religion of Democracy." *WWR*, 16: 14-22 (Mr 70).

Van Egmond, Peter. "Bryn Mawr College Holdings of W Books." *WWR*, 20: 41-9 (Je 74).

———. "WW on the Platform." *SSJ*, 32: 215-24 (1967).

Vince, R.W. "A Reading of 'The Sleepers.'" *WWR*, 18: 17-28 (Mr 72).

Vittorini, Elio. "An Outline of American Literature." *SR*, 68: 423-37 (Su 60).

Waggoner, H.H. "The Last Stand of the Genteel Tradition: or, How Brown Acquired the Saundeers Whitman Collection." *BBr*, 24: 148-55 (1971).

Waite, W. "W on Carlyle: A New Letter." *WWR*, 20: 74 (Je 74).

Wallace, J.K. "W and *Life Illustrated*: A Forgotten 1855 Review of *Leaves*." *WWR*, 17: 135-8 (D 71).

Wang, A.S. "WW and Lao-Chuang." *WWR*, 17: 109-22 (D 71).

Wannamaker, J.S. "A New Musical Setting of 'Song of Myself.'" *WWR*, 18: 28-31 (Mr 72).

Weaver, Richard. "The American as a Regenerate Being." *SoR*, 4: 633-46 (Su 68).

Weeks, L.E. "Whittier and W." *ESQ*, 50: 65-75 (1Q 68).

Weeks, R.P. "Dos Passos' Debt to WW." *AA*, 3: 121-38 (1974).

Wells, D.J. "W and Rimbaud." *WWR*, 19: 25-8 (Mr 73).

Wells, Elizabeth. "The Structure of W's 1860 *Leaves of Grass*." *WWR*, 15: 131-61 (S 69).

Wesley, B.C. "WW." *LHY*, 7: 24-36 (Jl 66).

West, A.G. "W: The Anarchy and the Ecstasy." *Junction*, 1972, pp. 13-20.

Westbrook, Perry. "John Burroughs and the Transcendentalists." *ESQ*, 55: 47-55 (2Q 69).

Westlake, N.M. "'A backward glance on my own road.'" *LCUP*, 34: 100-2 (Sp 68).

White, G.M. "Early Insight into W's Prosody." *WWR*, 19: 120-2 (S 73).

White, William. "Alcott and Chapman Revisited." *WWR*, 16: 90-1 (S 70).

———. "Beat! Beat! Beat!: The First Version." *WWR*, 21: 43-4 (Mr 75).

———. "Billy Buckett: W Rogue." *ABC*, 21: 20-3 (1971).

———. "A Census of W's Complete Writings." *AB/Bookman's Weekly*, 43: 360 (27 Ja 69).

———. "*The Collected Writings of WW*—A Progress Report." *NASRC*, 11: 23-8 (D 67).

———. "Dreiser on Hardy, Henley, and W: An Unpublished Letter." *ELN*, 6: 122-4 (D 68).

———. "Editions of *Leaves of Grass*: How Many?" *WWR*, 19: 111-14 (S 73).

————. ''An Editor on Advertising.'' *Seminar*, 10: 11 (D 68).

————. ''Errors in *Leaves of Grass*, Comprehensive Reader's Edition.'' *PBSA*, 68: 439-42 (O-D 74).

————. ''Four Recent W Editions.'' *WWR*, 16: 27-8 (1970).

————. ''Gutekunst's 1889 Photo of the Poet.'' *WWR*, 15: 63, 64 (Mr 69).

————. ''Inscribed to Dr. Bucke.'' *WWR*, 15: 127, 28 (Je 69).

————. ''Introduction.'' *WWR*, 16: 3-4 (1970).

————. ''Jeffers and W Briefly.'' *Serif*, 6: 32-3 (1969).

————. ''Lathrop's Unpublished Letter to Traubel on W.'' *Ren*, 20: 165-6 (Sp 68).

————. ''Marsden/Hassam/W: A Correction.'' *WWR*, 20: 37 (Mr 74).

————. ''Mrs. Walter Whitman, Sr., Writes to Her Son.'' *WWR*, 16: 63-4 (Je 70).

————. '''My Legacy' in Process.'' *WWR*, 16: 127-8 (D 70).

————. ''My 'Six Children': W to Symonds.'' *WWR*, 16: 31-2 (Mr 70).

————. ''Myths of WW: His Children.'' *ABC*, 19: 27 (F 69).

————. ''A New W Letter to *The Century*.'' *WWR*, 19: 118 (S 73).

————. ''A New W Letter to J.Q.A. Ward.'' *WWR*, 21: 35-7 (Ja 75).

————. '''Old Age Echoes' Proof Sheet.'' *WWR*, 14: 180, 182 (D 68).

————. ''On the W-Symonds Correspondence.'' *WWR*, 15: 125-6 (Je 69).

————. ''Some New W Items.'' *PrS*, 44: 47-55 (Sp 70).

————. ''Tasistro and the *Daybook*.'' *WWR*, 16: 89-90 (S 70).

————. ''Textual Editing: A W Note.'' *AN&Q*, 12: 15-6 (1974).

————. ''A Tribute to William Hartshorne: Unrecorded W.'' *AL*, 42: 554-8 (Ja 71).

————. ''Two More Unpublished W Letters.'' *AN&Q*, 10: 3-4 (1971).

————. ''Two New Letters to R. Spence Watson.'' *WWR*, 16: 122 (D 70).

————. ''Uncollected W on Lear.'' *ShN*, 18: 41 (S-N 68).

————. ''Unknown Letter to W.S. Huntington.'' *WWR*, 19: 73 (Je 73).

————. ''An Unknown Report on a W Social.'' *ABC*, 23: 22-4 (1973).

————. ''Unpublished Henry James on W.'' *RES*, 20: 321-2 (Ag 69).

————. ''Variants of R.M. Bucke's *Walt Whitman*.'' *Serif*, 5: 25-9 (D 68).

————. ''The Very Earliest W.'' *ABC*, 19: 6 (O 68).

————. ''WW: An Unpublished Autobiographical Note.'' *N&Q*, 16: 221-2 (Je 69).

————. ''WW and the Sierra Grande Mining Company.'' *NMHR*, 44: 223-30 (Jl 69).

————. ''WW Cigars.'' *WWR*, 16: 96 (S 70).

*————. ''WW: A Current Bibliography.'' *WWR*, quarterly, 1968—.

————. ''WW on Trial: A Clipping from His *Daybook*.'' *PrS*, 46: 52-6 (Sp 72).

————. ''WW's Erotic Poetry: New as Foam and Old as the Rock.'' *SR*, 79: 650-4 (1971).

*————. ''WW's Journalism: A Bibliography.'' *WWR*, 14: 67-141 (S 68).

*————. ''WW's Poetry in Periodicals: A Bibliography.'' *Serif*, 11: 31-8 (Su 74).

————. ''Walter W: Kings County Democratic Party Secretary.'' *WWR*, 17: 92-8 (S 71).

————. ''WW on Trial.'' *PrS*, 46: 52-6 (Sp 72).

————. ''WW Reports a Murder.'' *Q J Bk Club (Detroit)*, 1: 14, 17 (Su 68).

————. ''W and John Swinton: Some Unpublished Correspondence.'' *AL*, 39: 547-53 (Ja 68).

*————. ''W and the MLA Bibliography: Addenda, 1969.'' *Serif*, 8: 18-20 (Mr 71).

————. ''W in 1881.'' *WWR*, 21: 81-2 (S 75).

————. ''W on Himself: An Unrecorded Piece.'' *PLL*, 6: 202-5 (Sp 70).

————. ''W or Whitmaniana?'' *ATQ*, 1: 120-1 (1Q 69).

————. ''W Reprints from Haskell House & Others.'' *WWR*, 19: 30-2 (Je 73).

————. ''W & Carlyle: A New Letter.'' *WWR*, 20: 74 (Je 74).

———. "W to Roden Noel: A New Letter." *WWR*, 20: 17 (Je 74).

———. "W's 'Manuscript Edition.'" *AN&Q*, 7: 88 (F 69).

———. "W's Short Stories: More Addenda." *PBSA*, 69: 402-3 (3Q 75).

———. "Women in the Life of WW." *Long Islander*, 29: 16-7, 22 (29 Mr 75).

White, W.M. "The Dynamics of W's Poetry." *SR*, 80: 347-60 (Sp 72).

Whitman, Walt. "'Beat! Beat! Drums!': The First Version (Plate)." *WWR*, 21: 43-4 (Mr 75).

———. "WW on Lucrezia Borgia." *Opera News*, 39: 22-3 (N 74).

Wild, P.H. "Flower Powers: A Student's Guide to Pre-Hippie Transcendentalism." *EJ*, 58: 62-8 (1969).

Williams, Philip. "W and Eliot: Two Sides of One Tradition." *Hikaku Bungaku*, 15: 1-25 (1972).

Wolfe, Peter. "'Song of Myself'—The Indirect Figure in the Word-Mosaic." *ATQ*, 12: 20-5 (Fa 71).

Womack, Judy. "The American Woman in 'Song of Myself.'" *WWR*, 19: 67-72 (Je 73).

Woodruff, S.C. "W: Poet or Prophet?" *WWR*, 14: 35-40 (Je 68).

Wortman, W.A. "Spiritual Progression in 'A Sight in Camp.'" *WWR*, 14: 24-6 (Mr 68).

Wrobel, Arthur. "A Poet's Self-Esteem: W Alters His 'Bumps.'" *WWR*, 17: 129-35 (S 71).

———. "W and the Phrenologists: The Divine Body and the Sensuous Soul." *PMLA*, 89: 17-23 (Ja 74).

Yaku, Masao. "W ot no Deai." *EigoS*, 115: 22-5 (1969).

Yestadt, Sister Marie. "Two American Poets: Their Influence on the Contemporary Art-Song." *XUS*, 10: 33-43 (Fa 71).

Zochert, Donald. "A Note on W's 'Port of Destination.'" *WWR*, 21: 75 (Je 75).

Žuravlev, I.K. "Tradicii U. Uitmena v socialističes-kojliterature SŠA načala xx veka." *FN*, 14: 3-13 (1971).

Whittemore, Reed. Benedikt, Michael. "Listening and Not Listening." *Poetry*, 112: 194-8 (Je 68).

Claire, W.F., et al. "A Celebration of RW." *Voyages*, 3: 7-66 (Sp 70).

Kizer, Carolyn. "RW: An Appreciation." *StAR*, 1: 19-20 (Fa-Wi 71).

Ober, W.B. "A Few Kind Words about RW." *Voyages*, 3: 34-9 (Sp 70).

Whittier, John Greenleaf. Anon. "An Account of W's Funeral." *More Books*, 11: 238 (Je 36).

———. "The Essex Institute Oak Knoll Collection." *WhitN*, 5: 3-4 (1969).

———. "TheHaverhill W Collection." *WhitN*, 3: 3-4 (1968).

———. "W Clubs." *WhitN*, 10: 4 (1972).

———. "W Iconography." *ESQ*, 50: 105-67 (1Q 68).

———. "W Library Collections and W Clubs." *WhitN*, 7: 2-3 (1970); 11: 3-4 (1973).

Arner, R.D. "Milton's Belial and W's 'Ichabod.'" *ATQ*, 24: 17-8 (Fa 74).

Bann, J.D. "An Unpublished W Letter." *ESQ*, 50: 29 (1Q 68).

Brownell, G.H. "MT's Speech at the W Banquet." *ABC*, 4: 73-4 (Ag 33).

Bulkeley, R.D., Jr. "A Democrat and Slavery: Robert Rantoul, Jr." *EIHC*, 110: 216-38 (Jl 74).

Cadbury, H.J. "A Visit to W in 1881." *QH*, 46: 108-10 (Au 57).

Cameron, K.W. "Did W Plagiarize 'The Barefoot Boy'?" *ESQ*, 47: Part III, 112-3 (2Q 67).

———. "An Ungathered W Poem?" *ATQ*, 1: 102 (1Q 69).

Carey, George. "JWG and Folklore: The Search for a Traditional American Past." *NYFQ*, 27: 113-29 (Mr 71).

———. "W's Place in New England Folklore." *ESQ*, 50: 46-53 (1Q 68).

Carey, G.C. "W's Roots in a Folk Culture." *EIHC*, 104: 3-18 (Ja 68).

Cary, Richard. "More W Letters to Jewett." *ESQ*, 58: 132-9 (1Q 70).

———. "W Letters to Sarah Orne Jewett." *ESQ*, 50: 11-22 (1 Q 68).

———. "'Yours Always Lovingly': Sarah Orne Jewett to JGW." *EIHC*, 107: 412-50 (O 71).

Clark, H.H. "The Growth of W's Mind." *ESQ*, 50: 119-26 (1Q 68).

Cummins, R.W. "Unpublished Emerson Letters to Louis Prang and W." *AL*, 43: 257-9 (My 71).

Currier, T.F. "W and 'Mary.'" *NEQ*, 6: 801-2 (D 33).

———. "W 'Lines in an Album.'" *NEQ*, 9: 699-700 (D 36).

Dippie, B.W. "Bards of the Little Big Horn." *WAL*, 1: 175-95 (Fa 66).

Donaldson, Scott. "Winfield Townley Scott and W." *WhitN*, 7: 4 (1970).

Downey, Jean. "W and Cooke: Unpublished Letters." *QH*, 52: 33-6 (Sp 63).

Dozer, D.M. "The Tariff on Books." *MVHR*, 36: 73-96 (Je 49).

Ernest, J.M., Jr. "Holmes to W Re Whitman." *WWN*, 4: 76-7 (Mr 58).

———. "W and the 'Feminine Fifties.'" *AL*, 28: 184-96 (My 56).

Ferguson, Suzanne. "Something Which the Past Has Hid." *SR*, 80: 493-8 (Su 72).

Frieman, D.C. "The History of the Haverhil W Club." *ESQ*, 50: 144-64 (1Q 68).

Garrison, Theodore. "The Influence of Robert Dinsmore Upon W." *ESQ*, 50: 55-60 (1Q 68).

Gilkes, L.B. "The Authorship of 'To Governor M'Duffie', A Unionist's Diatribe Against the Governor of South Carolina." *Proof*, 4: 77-82 (1974).

Gilman, A.H. "Atlantic Dinners and Diners." *Atl*, 100: 646-57 (N 07).

Harris, D.G. "The W Collection of the Friends Historical Library of Swarthmore College." *WhitN*, 8: 3-4 (1971).

Hawks, Grace. "A Matter of Simple Justice." *Pembroke Alumna*, 42: 8-9 (Ap 67).

Hepler, J.C. "A Letter from Charles Fenno Hoffman to Whittier." *N&Q*, 79: 96-8 (Au 75).

———. "A Proposed W Poem." *QH*, 57: 43-8 (Sp 68).

Holmes, J.W. "W's Concerns for Negro Eduction." *Phlon*, 7: 169-75 (#2, 46).

———. "W's Friends Among the Lowly." *ESQ*, 50: 92-104 (1Q 68).

Hoxie, E.F. "Harriet Livermore: 'Vixen and Devotee.'" *NEQ*, 18: 39-50 (Mr 45).

Hubbard, G.U. "Ina Coolbrith's Friendship with JGW." *NEQ*, 45: 109-18 Mr 72).

Jerrold, Walter. "Two New W Poems." *Bookman*, 36: 155-8 (O 12).

Keith, Philip. "W and Warren." *Shen*, 23: 90-5 (Su 72).

Kelley, R.E. "JGW on Bible Reading in the Public Schools: An Unpublished Letter." *EIHC*, 110: 57-63 (Ja 74).

Kimball, W.J. "Two Views of History." *SSF*, 8: 637-9 (Fa 71).

Kime, W.R. "W's 'Ichabod.'" *Expl*, 28: 59 (Mr 70).

Kobler, John. "The Mystery of the Palatine Light." *SEP*, 232: 44-5, 55-8 (11 Je 60).

Leary, Lewis. "A Note on W's Margaret Smith." *ESQ*, 50: 75-8 (1Q 68).

Mabbott, T.O. "W to John Bright." *NEQ*, 8: 554-5 (D 35).

McAleer, J.J. "W's Selective Tolerance." *ESQ*, 50: 113-9 (1Q 68).

Maddox, M.S. "W's 'Ichabod.'" *Expl*, 30: 59 (Mr 72).

Mathy, Francis. "The Three Johns: Portraits of Emerson, Thoreau, Hawthorne, and W." *Eng Lang & Lit* (Tokyo), 10: 163-81 (Mr 74).

Meek, F.M. "W the Religious Man." *ESQ*, 50: 86-92 (1Q 68).

Miller, Perry. "JGW: The Conscience in Poetry." *ESQ*, 50: 128-42 (1Q 68).

Monaghan, Jay. "Baynard Taylor and Two Unpublished Poems." *SCUL*, 5: 39-45 (1973).

Monteiro, George. "JGW in *The Independent*." *PBSA*, 60: 91 (1Q 66).

Moran, J.M. "Editor W and the *New England Weekly Review.*" *ESQ*, 50: 78-86 (1Q 68).

Morley, S.G. "Points of Views: D. Juan Valera." *SatR*, 8: 156 (26 S 31).

Moyne, E.J. "JGW and Finland." *SS*, 44: 52-62 (Wi 72).

Nelson, Truman. "The Matrix of Place." *EIHC*, 95: 176-85 (Ap 59).

Olson, Richard. "W and the Machine Age." *ESQ*, 50: 32-7 (1Q 68).

Penfield, R.C. "In W's Country." *Harper's Wk*, 45: 797 (10 Ag 01).

Perry, Bliss. "The Editor Who Was Never Editor." *Atl*, 100: 658-78 (N 07).

Pickard, J.B. "Memorabilia of JGW." *ESQ*, 50: 1-167 (1Q 68).

———. "Research in Progress and Work Completed." *WhitN*, 7: 2 (1970); 9: 2 (1971); 10: 4 (1972).

*———. "W Bibliography." *WhitN*, annually, fall.

———. "W's Abolitionist Poetry." *ESQ*, 50: 105-13 (1Q 68).

Pickett, E.V. "'Snow-Bound' and the New Critics." *ESQ*, 50: 38-42 (1Q 68).

Poger, Sidney. "'Snow-Bound' and Social Responsibility." *ATQ*, 1: 85-7 (1Q 69).

Pomeroy, S.G. "W in Connecticut." *Connecticut Mag*, 2: 569-73 (O-D 07).

Primeau, Ronald. "Garrison to W on Jonathon Walker and Other Things: An Unpublished Letter." *HLB*, 22: 176-84 (1974).

Pulsifer, J.G. "Alice and Phoebe Cary, W's Sweet Singers of the West." *EIHC*, 109: 9-59 (Ja 73).

———. "Gail Hamilton, 1833-1896." *EIHC*, 104: 165-216 (Jl 68).

Reed, K.T. "'The Pleasant Circle Broke': A Reading of Whittier's *Snow-Bound.*" *WhitN*, 9: 4 (Fa 72).

Richardson, C.F. "The Morals of the Rhyming Dictionary." *YR*, 2: 269-81 (Ja 13).

Ringe, D.A. "The Artistry of W's *Margaret Smith's Journal.*" *EIHC*, 108: 235-43 (Jl 72).

———. "Sound Imagery in W's *Snow-Bound.*" *PLL*, 5: 139-44 (Sp 69).

Sanborn, F.B. "W and Longfellow Compared as Poets of New England." *BET*, 24 Jl 02; p. 9.

Scott, W.T. "Mr. W." *ESQ*, 50: 6-7 (1Q 68).

Smith, H.N. "The Backwoods Bull in the Boston China Shop." *AH*, 12: 33, 108-11 (Ag 61).

———. "'That Hideous Mistake of Poor Clemens's.'" *HLB*, 9: 145-80 (Sp 55).

Smythe, D.W. "W and the New Critics." *ESQ*, 50: 22-6 (1Q 68).

Snyder, E.D. "Rhymes (for S. Lewis)." *QH*, 25: 10-1 (Sp 36).

———. "W and the Unitarians." *QH*, 49: 111-6 (Au 60).

Tapley, H.S. "JGW Manuscripts: The Oak Knoll Collection." *EIHC*, 67: 113-8 (Ap 31).

———. "Letter from JG.W to Superintendent of Schools of Cincinnati." *EIHC*, 67: 408 (O 31).

Taylor, C.M. "W Set to Music." *EIHC*, 88: 24-7 (Ja 52).

Thaler, Alwin. "W, Bliss Perry, and the English Poets." *ESQ*, 50: 27-31 (1Q 68).

Torrey, M.C. "Painting by M.C. Torrey, 1835." *ESQ*, 50: 53 (1Q 68).

Trawick, Leonard M. "W's *Snow-Bound*: A Poem about the Imagination." *EL*, 1: 46-53 (Sp 74).

Vann, J.D. "An Unpublished W Letter." *ESQ*, 50: 29 (1Q 68).

Wagenknecht, Edward. "W and the Supernatural—A Test Case." *ESQ*, 50: 8-11 (1Q 68).

Warren, R.P. "W." *SR*, 79: 86-135 (Wi 71).

Weeks, L.E. "W and Whitman." *ESQ*, 50: 65-75 (1Q 68).

White, C.T. "A Literary Discovery: Unpublished Poems by Bryant, W, (et al)." *Bkm*, 44: 633-8 (F 17).

Whitford, Kathryn. "Hannah Dustin: The Judgement of History." *EIHC*, 108: 304-25 (O 72).

Whittier, J.G. "JG.W." *Collector*, 48: 14 (D 33).

Whittier, Mary. "W Land." *Zion's Herald*, 85: 1582-3 (11 D 07).

Wood, R.K. "A New Pilgrim in Whittierland." *Bookman*, 38: 481-9 (Ja 14).

Woodwell, R.H. "JGW (1807-1892)." *Rock*, 24: 4-8 (Wi 68).

———. "W and Carlyle." *ESQ*, 50: 42-6 (1Q 68).

———. "W's Place of Residence from 1876 to 1892." *EIHC*, 68: 353-8 (O 32).

Weiners, John. Hallberg, Robert von. "A Talk with JW." *ChiR*, 26: 112-6 (#1 74).

Howard, Richard. "JW: 'Now Watch the Windows Open by Themselves.'" *IowaR*, 1: 101-7 (Wi 70).

Sorrention, Gilbert. "Emerald on the Beach." *Parnassus*, 2: 121-5 (Sp-Su 73).

Wiesel, Elie. Garber, Fredrick. "The Art of EW." *Judaism*, 22: 301-8 (1973).

Joseloff, Samuel H. "Link and Promise: The Works of EW." *SHR*, 8: 163-70 (1974).

Knopp, Josephine. "W and the Absurd." *ConL*, 15: 212-20 (Sp 74).

Luckens, M.J. "Reaction to a Meeting with EW." *Judaism*, 20: 365-8 (1971).

Wohlgelernter, Maurice. "From Generation to Generation: Or, EW's Oral and Written Tradition." *Trad*, 11: 105-20 (1971).

Sherwin, B.L. "EW and Jewish Theology." *Judaism*, 18: 39-52 (1969).

Wiggin, Kate Douglas. Erisman, Fred. "Transcendentalism For American Youth: The Children's Books of KDW." *NEQ*, 41: 238-47 (Je 68).

Wigglesworth, Michael. Ahluwalia, Harsharan. "Salvation New England Style: A Study of Covenant Theology in MW's *The Day of Doom*." *IJAS*, 4: 1-12 (Je-D 74).

Alexis, G.T. "W's 'Easiest Room.'" *NEQ*, 42: 573-83 (D 69).

Brack, O.M. "MW and the Attribution of 'I Walk'd and Did a Little Molehill View.'" *SCN*, 28: 41-4 (1970).

Wilbur, Richard. Adkins, C.A. "RW's 'Running' and 'Complaint': Two Self-Portraits of a Young American Artist Nearing Fifty." *IEngYb*, 22: 37-41(N 72).

Bernlef, J. "Tussen oog en licht: Over Howard Nemerov en RW." *Gids*, 147: 217-25 (1974).

Boyers, Robert. "On RW." *Salmagundi*, 12: 76-82 (1970).

Brodsky, Joseph. "On RW." *APR*, 2: 52 (#1 73).

Cummins, Paul. "RW's 'Ballade for the Duke of Orleans.'" *CP*, 1: 42-5 (Fa 68).

———. "*Walking to Sleep* by RW." *CP*, 3: 72-6 (1970).

Dillion, David. "The Image and the Object: An Interview with RW." *SWR*, 58: 240-51 (Su 73).

Duffy, Charles. "'Intricate Neural Grace': The Esthetic of RW." *CP*, 4: 41-50 (Sp 71).

Emerson, C.E. "Books by RW." *HC*, 6: 7 (1969).

Farrell, J.P. "The Beautiful Changes in RW's Poetry." *ConL*, 12: 74-87 (Wi 71).

Herzman, R.B. "A Yeatsian Parallel in RW's 'Merlin Enthralled.'" *NCLit*, 2: 10-11.

Heyen, William. "On RW." *SoR*, 9: 635-45 (Jl 73).

Hutton, Joan. "RW." *TransR*, 29: 58-67 (Su 68).

James, Clive. "When the Gloves are Off." *Review*, 26: 35-44 (Su 71).

Mattfield, M.S. "Some Poems of RW." *BSUF*, 11: 10-24 (Su 70).

———. "W's 'The Puritans.'" *Expl*, 28: 42 (F 70).

Miller, Stephen. "The Poetry of RW." *Spirit*, 37: 30-5 (1970).

Monteiro, George. "Redemption through Nature: A Recurring Theme in Thoreau, Frost. and RW." *AQ*, 20: 795-809 (Wi 68).

Oliver, Raymond. "Verse Translation and RW." *SoR*, 318-30 (Ap 75).

Pate, Willard. "'Interview with RW." *SCR*, 3: 5-23 (N 70).

Perrine, Laurence. "Dream, Desire, or Dizziness?—Digging in *Digging for China*." *NCLit*, 1: 13-4 (My 71).

Reedy, Gerard. "The Senses of RW." *Renascence*, 21: 145-50 (Sp 69).

Sayre, R.F. "A Case for RW as Nature Poet." *MSpr*, 61: 114-22 (1967).

Sharma, D.R. "RW: An Analysis of His Vision." *PURBA*, 4: 43-50 (1973).

Taylor, Henry. "Cinematic Devices in RW's Poetry." *BRMMLA*, 28: 41-8 (Je 74).

———. "Two Worlds Taken as They Come: RW's 'Walking to Sleep.'" *HC*, 6: 16, 8-12 (1969).

Weatherhead, A.K. "RW: Poetry of Things." *ELH*, 35: 606-17 (D 68).

Wilbur, Richard. "Poetry and Happiness." *Shen*, 20: 3-23 (Su 69).

Wilcox, Ella Wheeler. Haeffner, Paul. "Auden and EWW." *N&Q*, 9: 110-1 (Mr 62).

Lewis, Naomi. "W Revisited." *NSt*, 24 D 71, p. 901.

Pittock, Malcolm. "In Defense of EWW." *DUJ*, 65: 86-9 (D 72).

Wilde, Richard Henry. Kibler, J.E. "A New Letter of Simms to RHW: ON the Advancement of Sectional Literature." *AL*, 44: 667-70 (Ja 73).

Mathews, J.C. "RHW's Knowledge of Dante." *Italica*, 45: 28-46 (1968).

Wright, Nathalia. "The Italian Son of R.H.W.: A Sequel." *GHQ*, 53: 201-4 (Je 69).

Wilder, Amos. McDonald, W.E. "The Literary Criticism of Amos Wilder." *Soundings*, 52: 99-109 (Sp 69).

Wilder, Thornton. Alfes, Leonhard. "Bruder Junipers *conversio* und die *perhapses* in TW's *The Bridge of San Luis Rey*." *LWU*, 6: 98-109 (1973).

Balliet, Car. "The Skin of Whose Teeth." *SRL*, 26: 11 (2 Ja 43).

Blank, Martin. "When Farce Isn't Funny: The Original Production of *The Merchant of Yonkers*." *Players*, 50: 90-3 (1975).

Borish, E. "TW—Novelist: A Re-examination." *RLV*, 37: 152-9 (Mr-Ap 71).

Brunauer, D.H. "Creative Faith in W's *The Eighth Day*." *Renascence*, 25: 46-56 (Au 72).

Chapero Solaz, René. "Algunos aspectos de la obra dramatica de TW." *RSV*, 3: 117-32 (1969).

D'Ambrosio, M.A. "Is 'Our Town' Really Our Town?" *Eng Rec*, 22: 20-2 (Fa 71).

De Michelis, Eurialo. "TW: Un americano europeo." *SA*, 15: 281-319 (1969).

Dillon, Michael. "Poet and Statesman: TW's Political Vision in *The Ides of March*." *Intercollegiate R*, 9: 149-58 (1974).

Ericson, E.E. "The Figure in the Tapestry: The Religious Vision of TW's *The Eight Day*." *Chri & Lit*, 22: 32-48 (Sp 73).

———. "Kierkegaard in W's *The Eighth Day*." *Renascence*, 26: 123-38 (Sp 74).

Fehse, Klaus-Dieter. "TW's *The Skin of Our Teeth* als Oberstufrnlekture." *NS*, 22: 27-38 (1973).

Herms, Dieter. "Zum Humor im epischen Theater TW." *NS*, 20: 36-47 (Ja 71).

Macleish, Archibald. "The Isolation of the American Artist." *Atl*, 201: 55-9 (J 58).

Mickel, Liselotte. "TW und der amerikanische Optimismus." *FrH*, 24: 875-82 (1970).

Nemoianu, Virgil. "Meditatia unui umanist." *RoLit*, 20 Feb: 20 (1969).

Oliver, Edith. "The Summing Up." *NY*, 43: 146-8 (27 My 67).

Papajewski, Helmut. "TW's *The Eighth Day*." *LWU*, 4: 27-39 (1971).

Pérez, L.C. "W and Cervantes: In the Spirit of the Tapestry." *Sym*, 25: 249-59 (1971).

Riegl, Kurt. "Max Reinhardt als Vorbild für TWs Caesar." *NS*, 17: 356-8 (Jl 68).

Smith, Harrison. "The Skin of Whose Teeth?" *SatR*, 25: 12 (26 D 42).

Sprague, Marshall. "Remembering Mr. W." *NYT*, 27 Ja 74, p. 31.

Venne, Peter. "The Message of TW." *FJS*: 15-29 (1970).

Viswanatham, K. "The Bridge That W Built." *Triveni*, 38: 9-16 (1969).

Wixson, D.C. "The Dramatic Techniques of TW and Bertolt Brecht: A Study in Comparison." *MD*, 15: 112-24 (S 72).

Wilkinson, Sylvia. Chappell, F. "Unpeaceable Kingdoms: The Novels of SW." *HC*, 8: 1-10 (Ap 71).

Williams, Ben Ames. Cary, Richard. "BAW in Periodicals and Newspapers." *CLQ*, 9: 599-615 (1972).

———. "BAW: The Apprentice Years." *CLQ*, 9: 586-99 (S 72).

———. "BAW and the *Saturday Evening Post.*" *CLQ*, 10: 223-30 (1973).

———. "BAW in the *Saturday Evening Post.*" *CLQ*, 10: 192-222 (1973).

Williams, B.A., Jr. "House United." *CLQ*, 10: 179-90 (1973).

Williams, Elisha. Reaske, C.R. "An Unpublished Letter Concerning 'Santification' by EW, Jonathan Edwards' Tutor." *NEQ*, 45: 429-34 (1972).

Williams, Espy W.H. Talbot, F.G. "Rediscovered—EW.H.W, Louisiana Playwright." *LaStud*, 9: 105-17 (Su 70).

Williams, John A. Bryant, J.H. "JA.W: The Political Use of the Novel." *Critique*, 16: 81-10 (3Q 75).

Browne, W.F. "The Black Artist in New York." *Centerpoint*, 1: 71-6 (#3 75).

Burke, William. "The Resistance of JA.W: *The Man Who Cried I Am.*" *Crit*, 15: 5-14 (#3 74).

Fleming, R.E. "The Nightmare Level of *The Man Who Cried I Am.*" *ConL*, 14: 186-96 (Sp 73).

Klotman, P.R. "An Examination of the Black Confidence Man in Two Black Novels: *The Man Who Cried I Am* and *dem.*" *AL*, 44: 596-611 (Ja 73).

Nelson, R.J. "Accounts of Mutual Acquaintances to a Group of Friends: The Fiction of JW." *UDQ*, 13-36 (Wi 73).

O'Brien, John. "The Art of JA.W." *ASch*, 42: 489-98 (Su 73).

———. "Seeking a Humanist Level: Interview with JA.W." *ASoc*, 10: 94-9 (Sp-Su 73).

Smith, A.H. "A Pain in the Ass: Metaphor in JA.W's *The Man Who Cried I Am.*" *SBL*, 3: 25-7 (Au 72).

Walcott, Ronald. "The Early Fiction of JAW." *CLAJ*, 16: 198-213 (D 72).

———. "*The Man Who Cried I Am*: Crying in the Dark." *SBL*, 3: 24-32 (Sp 72).

Williams, Jonathan. Alpert, Barry. "JW: An Interview." *Vort*, 4: 54-75 (1973).

Bowers, Greg. "Portrait of the Artist as a Young Slide Projector." *StAR*, 2: 335-6 (Sp-Su 74).

Hollo, Anselm. "The Pleasures of Exasperation." *Parnassus*, 1: 188-94 (1972).

Mottram, Eric. "JW." *Vort*, 4: 102-11 (1973).

Williams, Jonathan. "Heart & Desk." *Parnassus*, 4: 93-108 (#1 75).

Williams, Miller. Wheeler, L.R. " 'A Beer-Drinking Soul': An Interview with MW." *Dickinson R*, 3: 5-20 (Sp 73).

Whitehead, James. "About MW." *Dickinson R*, 3: 26-41 (Sp 73).

Williams, Roger. Bozeman, T.D. "Religious Liberty and the Problem of Order in Early Rhode Island." *NEQ*, 45: 44-64 (1972).

Davis, J.L. "RW Among the Narrangansett Indians." *NEQ*, 43: 593-604 (D 70).

Hines, D.M. "Odd Customs and Strange Ways: The American Indian c. 1640." *WR*, 7: 20-9 (1970).

Johnston, T.E. "A Note on the Voices of Anne Bradstreet, Edward Taylor, RW, and Philip Pain." *EAL*, 3: 125-6 (Fa 68).

Reinitz, Richard. "The Typological Argument for Religious Toleration: The Separatist Tradition and RW." *EAL*, 5: 74-110 (Sp 70).

Rosenmeier, Jesper. "The Teacher and the Witness: John Cotton and RW." *WMQ*, 25: 408-31 (Jl 68).

Teunissen, J.J., and E.J. Hinz. "RW, St. Paul, and American Primitivism." *CRAS*, 4: 121-36 (Fa 73).

Williams, Roger. "Roger Williams among the Narragansett Indians." *NEQ*, 43: 593-604 (D 70).

Williams, Tennessee. Anon. "One Heart Breaking." *Time*, 95: 61 (19 Ja 70).

Adler, T.P. "The Dialogue of Incompletion: Language in TW's Later Plays." *QJS*, 61: 48-58 (F 75).

———. "The Search for God in the Plays of TW." *Renascence*, 26: 48-56 (Au 73).

Berkowitz, Gerald. "The 'Other World' of *The Glass Menagerie*." *Players*, 48: 150-3 (1973).

Blackwelder, J.R. "The Human Extremities of Emotion in *Cat on a Hot Tin Roof*." *RSW*, 38: 13-21 (Mr 70).

Blackwell, Louise. "TW and the Predicament of Women." *SAB*, 35: 9-14 (Mr 70).

Blitgen, Sister M.C. "TW: Modern Idolator." *Renascence*, 22: 192-7 (1970).

Buchloh, P.G. "Gesellschaft, Individuum und Gemeinschaft bei TW." *SG*, 21: 49-73 (1968).

Buckley, Tom. "TW Survives." *Atl*, 226: 98-108 (N 70).

Campbell, M.L. "The Theme of Persecution in TW's *Camino Real*." *NMW*, 6: 35-40 (Fa 73).

Cate, H.L. and D.E. Presley. "Beyond Stereotype: Ambiguity in Amanda Wingfield." *NMW*, 3: 91-100 (Wi 71).

Chester, S.A. "*A Streetcar Named Desire*: Twenty-Five Years of Criticism.'" *NMW*, 7: 44-53 (Fa 74).

Coakley, James. "W in Ann Arbor." *DramC*, 11: 52-6 (Wi 68).

Cole, C.W., and Carol Franco. "Critical Reaction to TW in the Mid-1960's." *Players*, 49: 18-23 (Fa-Wi 74).

Costello, D.P. "TW's Fugitive Kind." *MD*, 15: 26-43 (My 72).

Debusscher, G. "The Artistry of TW's Personal Nomenclature." *Handeligen*, 72: 234-44 (Fa 74).

———. "TW as Hagiographer: An Aspect of Obliquity in Drama." *RLV*, 40: 449-56 (Jl-Ag 74).

———. "TW's Unicorn Broken Again." *RBPH*, 49: 875-85 (1971).

Dietrich, Margret. "Der Dramatiker TW und sein Werk für das heutige Theater." *Univ*, 23: 511-6 (1968).

Drake, Constance. "Blanch Dubois: A Re-evaluation." *TA*, 24: 58-69 (1969).

Durham, Frank. "TW, Theater Poet in Prose." *SAB*, 36: 3-16 (Mr 71).

Efstate, Ileana. "TW—A Few Considerations on *A Streetcar Named Desire*." *AUB-LG*, 21: 17-13 (1973).

Engstrom, A.G. "The Man Who Thought Himself Made of Glass, and Certain Related Images." *SP*, 67: 390-405 (1970).

Fritscher, J.J. "Some Attitudes and a Posture: Religious Metaphor and Ritual in TW's Query of an American God." *MD*, 13: 201-15 (S 70).

Gaines, Jim. "A Talk about Life and Style with TW." *SatR*, 55: 25-9 (29 Ap 72).

Gorowara, Krishna. "The Fire Symbol in TW." *LHY*, 8: 57-73 (Ja-Jl 67).

Groene, Horst. "TW im Zwiesplat der Meinungen: Ein Forschungsbericht über die englisch- und deutschsprachige Literatur zu W' dramatischen Werk." *LWU*, 5: 66-87 (1972).

Hainsworth, J.D. "TW: Playwright on a Hot Tin Roof?" *EA*, 20: 225-32 (Jl-S 67).

Halson, A.E. "TW's *Kingdom of Earth*: A Sterile Promontory." *D&T*, 8: 90-3 (1970).

Hendrick, George. "Jesus and the Osiris-Isis Myth: Lawrence's *The Man Who Died* and W's *The Night of the Iguana*." *Anglia*, 84: 398-406 (1966).

Heuermann, Hartmut. "Die Psychomachie in TW' *The Milktrain Doesn't Stop Here Anymore.*" *JA*, 19: 266-79 (1974).

Hilfer, A.C., and R.V. Ramsey. "*Baby Doll*: A Study in Comedy and Critical Awareness." *Ohio Un R*, 11: 75-88 (1969).

Hill, F.A. "The Disaster of Ideals in *Camino Real* by TW." *NMW*, 1: 100-9 (Wi 69).

Hirsch, Foster. "Sexual Imagery in TW's *Kingdom of Earth.*" *NCLit*, 1: 10-3 (Mr 71).

———. "TW." *Cinema*, 8: 2-8 (Sp 73).

Howell, Elmo. "The Function of Gentleman Caller: A Note on TW's *The Glass Menagerie.*" *NMW*, 2: 83-90 (Wi 70).

Jennings, C.R. "*Playboy* Interview: TW." *Playboy*, 21: 699-84 (Ap 73).

Joven, N.G. "Illusion and Reality in TW's 'The Glass Menagerie.'" *DilR*, 14: 81-9 (Ja 66).

Kalson, A.E. "TW Enters *Dragon Country.*" *MD*, 16: 61-7 (Je 73).

———. "TW's *Kingdom of Earth*: A Sterile Promontory." *D&T*, 8: 90-3 (Wi 69-70).

King, T.I. "Irony and Distance in *The Glass Menagerie.*" *ETJ*, 25: 207-14 (1973).

Kunkel, F.L. "TW and the Death of God." *Cweal*, 87: 614-7 (23 F 68).

Lees, D.B. "*The Glass Menagerie*: A Black *Cinderella.*" *UES*, 11: 30-4 (Mr 73).

Leon, Ferdinand. "Time, Fantasy, and Reality in *Night of the Iguana.*" *MD*, 11: 87-96 (My 68).

Mann, G.K.S. "Memory as Technique and Theme in *The Glass Menagerie* and *Death of a Salesman.*" *NDEJ*, 5: 23-30 (1969-70).

Mood, J.J. "The Structure of *A Streetcar Named Desire.*" *BSUF*, 14: 9-10 (Su 73).

Navone, John. "The Myth and Dream of Paradise." *Stud Rel*, 5: 152-61 (1975).

Newlove, Donald. "A Dream of TW." *Esquire*, 72: 64, 173-9 (N 69).

Popkin, Henry. "TW Reexamined." *Arts in Virginia*, 2: 2-5 (Sp 71).

Porter, D.H. "Ancient Myth and Modern Play: A Significant Counterpoint." *CBul*, 48: 1-9 (N 71).

Presley, D.E. "The Moral Fucntion of Distortion in Southern Grotesque." *SAB*, 37: 37-46 (1972).

———. "The Search for Hope in the Plays of TW." *MissQ*, 25: 31-44 (Wi 71-72).

*——— . "TW: 25 Years of Criticism." *BB*, 30: 21-9 (Ja-Mr 73).

———, and Hari Singh. "Epigraphs to the Plays of TW." *NMW*, 3: 2-12 (Sp 70).

Quijano, Margarita. "El simbolismo del *Tranvía* llamado Deseo." *CA*, 159: 228-35 (1968).

Quirino, Leonard. "TW's Persistent *Battle of Angels.*" *MD*, 11: 27-39 (My 68).

Rader, Dotson. "The Day the Movement Died." *Esquire*, 78: 130-5 (N 72).

Reck, T.S. "The First *Cat on a Hot Tin Roof*: W's 'Three Players.'" *UR*, 34: 187-92 (Sp 68).

———. "The Short Stories of TW: Nucleus for His Drama." *TSL*, 16: 141-54 (1971).

Reed, Rex. "TW Turns Sixty." *Esquire*, 76: 105-8, 216, 218, 220, 222-3 (S 71).

Robey, Cora. "Chloroses—Pales Roses and Pleurosis—Blue Roses." *RomN*, 13: 250-1 (1971).

Rowland, J.L. "T's Two Amandas." *RSW*, 35: 331-40 (1968).

Sasahara, Hikaru. "TW to Emily Dickinson—*The Glass Menagerie* wo Chushin ni." *EigoS*, 120: 270-2 (1974).

Scheller, Berhnhard. "Die Gestalt des Farbigen bei W, Albee und ihre szenische Realisierung in DDR-Auffuhrungen." *ZAA*, 20: 137-57 (1972).

Simon, John. "Theatre Chronicle." *HudR*, 21: 322-4 (Su 68).

Sister Mary John. "W in Cincinnati." *DramC*, 11: 56-8 (Wi 68).

Skloot, Robert. "Submitting the Self to Flame: The Artist's Quest in TW, 1935-54." *ETJ*, 25: 199-206 (1973).

Sorell, Walter. "The Case of TW." *Cresset*, 36: 26-7 (1973).

Starnes, Leland. "The Grotesque Children of *The Rose Tattoo*." *MD*, 12: 357-69 (F 70).

Tischler, N.M. "The Distorted Mirror: TW's Self-Portraits." *MissQ*, 25: 389-403 (1972).

Wagner, Jean. "Un theatre de passion." *QL*, 139: 1-24 (16-30 Ap 72).

Williams, Tennessee. "Survival Notes: A Journal." *Esquire*, 78: 130-4, 166, 168 (S 72).

———. "What's Next on the Agenda, Mr. W?" *MeditR*, 1: 15-9 (Wi 71).

Williams, William Carlos. Anon. "Letter from W to Wallace Stevens, June 8, 1916."
WCW N, 1: 16 (Fa 75).

Ashton, D.W. "The Virgin-Whore Motif in WCW's *Paterson*." *MPS*, 4: 193-209 (Au 73).

Bacon, Wallace. "The Act of Interpretation." *OEng*, 1: 1-6 (1972).

Baldwin, N.E. "Discovering Common Ground: A Note on WCW and Valery Larbaud." *AL*,
45: 292-7 (My 73).

Baldwin, Neil "Special Collections: WCW Catalog, Lockwood Memorial Library, Poetry
Collection." *WCW N*, 1: 5 (Fa 75).

Bollard, M.L. "The Interlace Element in *Paterson*." *TCL*, 21: 288-304 (O 75).

Bollard, Margaret. "The 'Newspaper Landscape' of W's *Paterson*." *ConL*, 16: 317-27 (Su
75).

Bradbury, Malcolm. "The Art of Innocence." *NSt*, 10 Ja 69, p. 49.

Brosman, C.S. "A Source and Parallel of Michel Butor's *Mobile*: *In the American Grain*."
MLR, 66: 315-21 (Ap 71).

Brown, R.E. "Walking and the Imagination: WCW's 'Paterson II.'" *MPS*, 4: 175-92 (Au
73).

Carruth, Hayden. "Dr. W's *Paterson*." *Nation*, 170: 331-3 (8 Ap 50).

Ciardi, John. "The Epic of Place." *SatR*, 41: 37-9 (11 O 58).

Conarroe, J.O. "A Local Pride: The Poetry of *Paterson*." *PMLA*, 84: 547-58 (My 69).

———. "The Measured Dance: W's 'Pictures from Brueghel.'" *JML*, 1: 565-77 (1971).

———. "The 'Preface' to *Paterson*." *ConL*, 10: 39-53 (Wi 69).

———. "W's 'Without Invention Nothing Is Well Spaced.'" *Expl*, 27: 26 (D 68).

———. "'You Can't Steal Credit': The Economic Motif in *Paterson*." *JAmSt*, 2: 105-15
(Ap 68).

Cooney, Seamus. "W's 'To Be Recited to Flossie on Her Birthday.'" *Expl*, 32: 24 (N 73).

Cowan, J.C. "The Image of Water in *Paterson*." *JML*, 1: 503-11 (1971).

Creeley, Robert. "Special Collections: Preface to the W Catalog, Lockwood Memorial
Library, Poetry Collection." *WCW N*, 1: 5-6 (Fa 75).

Davies, J.C. "'Which is the American?': Themes, Techniques and Meaning in WCW's
Three Novels." *JAmSt*, 6: 189-200 (Ag 72).

Davis, W.V. "W's 'The World Contracted to a Recognizable Image.'" *Expl*, 32: 13 (O 73).

Donaldson, G.M. "WCW: *Paterson*, Books I and II." *WCR*, 5: 3-10 (Je 70).

Doyle, Charles. "Addenda and Amendments to Wallace: WCW." *PBSA*, 69: 407-9 (3Q 75).

———. "A Reading of 'Paterson III.'" *MPS*, 1: 140-53 (1970).

Doyle, Mike. "WCW: The White Clarity of Imagination." *WCR*, 7: 51-3 (#1 72).

Duffey, B.I. "The Experimental Lyric in Modern Poetry: Eliot, Pound, W." *JML*, 3:
1085-1103 (Jl 74).

———. "Stevens and W." *ConL*, 9: 431-6 (1968).

Durst, M.I. "WCW: A Bibliography." *WCR*, 1: 49-54; 44-9 (Fa 66; Wi 67).

Fauchereau, Serge. "Valery Larbaud et WCW." *Crit(P)*, 27: 626-34 (1971).

———. "Valery Larbaud et WCW." *CritP*, 27: 626-38 (Jl 71).

———. "WCW: de l'imagisme a *Paterson*." *Critique*, 235: 996-1011 (D 66).

Fiero, F.D. "W Creates the First Book of *Paterson*." *JML*, 3: 965-86 (Ap 74).

Fleissner, R.F. "Homage to the Pentad: W's 'The Great Figure.'" *NCLit*, 1: 2-6 (S 71).

Williams, William Carlos

Flint, R.W. "I Will Teach You My Townspeople." *KR*, 12: 537-43 (Au 50).

Fox, Hugh. "The Genuine Avant-Garde: WCW's Credo." *SWR*, 59: 285-98 (Su 74).

Friedmann, Thomas. "Marvel's 'Coy Mistress' and W's 'Trees': Grammar and Phonology in the Critical Context." *Junction 1972*, pp. 60-5.

Galinsky, Hans. "An American Doctor-Poet's Image of Germany: An Approach to the Works of WCW." *Studium Generale*, 21: 74-93 (1968).

————. "WCW: Eine vergleichende Studie zur Aufnahme seines Werkes in Deutschland, England und Italien. Teil I." *JA*, 11: 97-175 (1966).

Gallagher, Fergal. "Further Freudian Implications in WCW's *The Use of Force*." *CEA*, 34: 20-1 (My 72).

Gordon, G.T. "WCW's 'Preface to *Paterson*.'" *Cont Poetry*, 1: 44-51 (Sp 73).

Graham, D.B. "A Note on Howells, W, and the Matter of Sam Patch." *NCLit*, 4: 10-3 (Mr 74).

Green, J.D. "W's *Kora in Hell*: The Opening of the Poem as 'Field of Action.'" *ConL*, 13: 295-314 (Su 72).

Gregory, Horace. "WCW." *Life and Letters Today*, 24: 164-76 (F 40).

Guimond, James. "After Imagism." *OhR*, 15: 5-28 (Fa 73).

Guimond, J.K. "WCW and the Past: Some Clarifications." *JML*, 1: 493-502 (1971).

Gupta, Rameshwar. "*Paterson*: An Introductory Study." *BP*, 16: 47-57 (1971).

*Hardie, Jack. "'A Celebration of the Light': Selected Checklist of Writings about WCW." *JML*, 1: 593-642 (1971).

————. "W's 'The Well Disciplined Bargeman.'" *Expl*, 33: 20 (N 74).

Harrison, Keith. "No Things but in Ideas: Doctor W and Mr. Pound." *DR*, 47: 577-80 (Wi 67-68).

Hart, Paxton. "W's 'Mathilda'-Etymology or Serendipity?" *AN&Q*, 10: 69-70 (Ja 72).

Hashiguchi, Minoru. "America no Homerostachi." *Oberon*, 30: 10-41 (1968).

Haya, Kenichi. "W.C.W—Hitei no Seishin." *Oberon*, 22: 59-68 (1970).

Hays, H.R. "An American Voice: The Continuing Presence of W.C.W." *Voyages*, 2: 34-9 (Sp 69).

Henry, Nat. "W's 'To Waken an Old Lady.'" *Expl*, 30: 80 (1972).

Heyen, William. "The Poet's Leap Into Reality." *SatR*, 53: 21-4 (1 Ag 70).

Hollander, John. "The Poem in the Eye." *Shen*, 23: 3-32 (1972).

Hutchinson, Alexander. "The Resourceful Mind: WCW and *Tribute to the Painters*." *UWR*, 8: 81-9 (Fa 72).

Jacobs, W.D. "W's 'Between Walls.'" *Expl*, 28: 68 (1970).

————. "W's 'A Coronal.'" *Expl*, 29: 64 (1971).

————. "W's 'The Hunter.'" *Expl*, 29: 60 (1971).

————. "W's 'Great Mullen.'" *Expl*, 28: 63 (1970).

————. "W's 'The Young Housewife.'" *Expl*, 28: 81 (1970).

————. "W's 'To a Poor Old Woman.'" *CP*, 1: 16 (Fa 68).

————. "W's 'To Waken an Old Lady.'" *Expl*, 29: 6 (1970).

Kagitani, Yukinobu. "W no Jiyu-shi to Teikei." *EigoS*, 119: 29-31 (1973).

Kartiganer, D.M. "Process and Product: A Study of Modern Literary Form." *MR*, 12: 297-328, 789-816 (1971).

Kenner, Hugh. "With Bare Hands." *Poetry*, 80: 276-90 (Ag 52).

Kern, Robert. "W, Brautigan, and the Poetics of Primitivism." *ChiR*, 27: 47-57 (Su 75).

Koehler, Stanley. "The Art of Poetry VI." *PaR*, 8: 111-51 (Su-Fa 64).

*Lahm, C.A. "Additions to *A Bibliography of WCW* by Wallace." *Serif*, 11: 40-3 (Su 74).

*Laxson, Martha. "The Criticism of W's *Paterson*: An Introduction and Bibliography." *Thoth*, 11: 40-8 (1970).

LeClair, Thomas. "The Poet as Dog in *Paterson*." *TCL*, 16: 97-108 (Ap 70).

Levin, Harry. "WCW and the Old World." *YR*, 59: 520-31 (Su 70).

Libby, Anthony. "'Claritas': WCW's Epiphanies." *Criticism*, 14: 22-31 (Wi 72).

Lint, R.G. "The Structural Image in W's 'Young Sycamore.'" *Lang&S*, 7: 205-8 (Su 74).

———. "Structural Source for Symbol and Meaning in 'The Red Wheelbarrow.'" *Lang&S*, 4: 297-300 (1971).

Loewinsohn, Ron. "Tracking W.C.W.'s Early Development." *Sumac*, 3: 128-41 (1971).

Lombardi, T.W. "WCW: The Leech-Gatherer of *Paterson*." *MwQ*, 9: 333-49 (Su 68).

Lowell, Robert. "Thomas, Bishop, and W." *SR*, 55: 493-504 (Su 47).

Macksey, R.A. "The Old Poets." *Johns Hopins Mag*, 19: 42-8 (1968).

Marcus, Mordecai. "The Critical Reaction to WCW's 'The Red Wheelbarrow.'" *Aegis*, 2: 23-8 (Fa 73).

Mariani, Paul. "The Eighth Day of Creation: WCW's Late Poems." *TCL*, 21: 305-18 (O 75).

———. "The Satyr's Defense: W's 'Asphodel.'" *ConL*, 14: 1-18 (Wi 73).

———. "Special Collections: Middlebury Library Collection." *WCW N*, 1: 7 (Fa 75).

———. "Towards the Canonization of WCW." *MR*, 13: 661-75 (Fa 72).

———. "Two Essays on Ezra Pound." *MR*, 14: 118-29 (Wi 73).

———. "W's Black Novel." *MR*, 14: 67-75 (Wi 73).

———. "A W Garland." *MR*, 14: 65-148 (Wi 73).

Martz, L.L. "*Paterson*: A Plan for Action." *JML*, 1: 512-22 (1971).

Matsumura, Shoka. "*Mr. Penrose*—America Saisho no Shosetsu." *EigoS*, 116: 519 (1970).

Mazzaro, Jerome. "Dimensionality in Dr. W's 'Paterson.'" *MPS*, 1: 98-117 (1970).

Miller, J.H. "Deconstructing the Deconstructors." *Diacritics*, 5: 24-31 (#3 75).

———. "W's *Spring and All* and the Progress of Poetry." *Daedalus*, 99: 405-34 (Sp 70).

Monteiro, George. "Dr. W's First Book." *BBr*, 23: 85-8 (1969).

Moore, Marianne. "Things Others Never Notice." *Poetry*, 44: 103-6 (My 34).

Myers, Neil. "Decreation in W's 'The Descent.'" *Criticism*, 14: 315-27 (Fa 72).

——— . "W's Imitation of Nature in 'The Desert Music.'" *Criticism*, 12: 38-50 (Wi 70).

———. "W's 'Two Pendants: For the Ears.'" *JML*, 1: 477-92 (1971).

Narasimhaiah, C.D. "WCW." *LCrit*, 10: 55-67 (1972).

Neeley, J.C. "One Man's Dr. W." *YR*, 65: 822-3 (1975).

Nelson, Cary "Suffused-Encircling Shapes of Mind: Inhabited Space in W." *JML*, 1: 549-64 (1971).

Nilsen, H.N. "Notes on the Theme of Love in the Later Poetry of WCW." *ES*, 50: 273-83 (Je 69).

Otten, Terry. "WCW's 'Red Wheelbarrow.'" *HussR*, 2: 117-8 (1969).

Paz, Octavio. "Saxifrage: Some Note on WCW." *LonM*, 14: 33-43 (Je-Jl 74).

Pearce R.H. "Poet as Person." *YR*, 41: 421-40 (Sp 52).

Pearson, N.H. "Introductory Note to Three Unpublished Letters from WCW to Norman Holmes Pearson." *WCW N*, 1: 2-3 (Fa 75).

Pison, Thomas. "*Paterson*: The Discontinuous Universe of the Present." *CentR*, 19: 325-37 (Wi 75).

Pope, M.P. "W's 'The World Contracted to A Recognizable Image.'" *Expl*, 33: 50 (F 75).

Quinn, Sister Bernetta. "*Paterson*: Landscape and Dream." *JML*, 1: 523-48 (1971).

Raban, Christine. "W's *Autobiographeme*: The Inscriptional I in *Asphodel*." *MPS*, 6: 157-74 (1975).

Raban, Jonathan. "Chance, Time and Silence: The New American Verse." *JAmSt*, 3: 89-101 (Jl 69).

Ramsey, Paul. "WCW as Metrist: Theory and Practice." *JML*, 1: 578-92 (1971).

Williams, William Carlos

Rao, Nageswara. "The Poetic Theory of WCW." *IJAS*, 2: 40-52 (1972).

Riddel, Joseph. "A Miller's Tale." *Diacritics*, 5: 56-65 (#3 75).

Rosa, A.F. "W's 'Between Walls.'" *Expl*, 30: 21 (N 71).

Sankey, Benjamin. "A Preface to *Paterson*." *Spectrum*, 12: 12-26 (Sp 70).

Savage, Catharine. "Michel Butor and *Paterson*." *FMLS*, 7: 126-33 (1971).

Schott, Webster. "Doctor W: 'Beautiful Blood, Beautiful Brain.'" *ASch*, 39: 305-9 (Sp 70).

Schwartz, M.M. "'The Use of Force' and the Dilemma of Violence." *PsyR*, 59: 617-25 (Wi 72-3).

Sienicka, Marta. "Poetry in the Prose of *In the American Grain* by WCW." *SAP*, 1: 109-17 (1968).

––––––. "WCW and Some Younger Poets." *SAP*, 4: 183-93 (1972).

––––––. "WCW's Theory and Practice of Poetic Measure." *SAP*, 3: 121-9 (1971).

Simpson, Louis. "The Californian Poets." *LonM*, 11: 56-63 (F-Mr 72).

Slate, J.E. "Kora in Opacity: W's *Improvisations*." *JML*, 1: 463-76 (1971).

––––––. "WCW and the Modern Short Story." *SoR*, 4: 647-64 (1968).

Sorrentino, Gilbert. "The Various Isolated: WCW's Prose." *NAR*, 15: 192-207 (1972).

Suter, Anthony. "Basil Bunting et deux poètes américains: Louis Zukofsky et WCW." *Caliban*, 8: 151-7 (1973).

Tallman, Warren. "Bells Break Tower: WCW's Stories." *Boun2*, 1: 58-70 (Fa 72).

Thirwall, J.C. "WCW and John C. Thirwall: Record of a Ten-Year Relationship." *YULG*, 45: 15-21 (Jl 70).

Tuerk, Richard. "A Note on Thoreau, WCW, and Wallace Stevens." *ConS*, 10: 11-5 (Je 75).

Tyler, Parker. "The Poet of Paterson." *Briarcliff Q*, 3: 168-75 (O 46).

von Hallberg, Robert. "Olson's Relation to Pound and W." *ConL*, 15: 15-48 (Wi 74).

Vernon, John. "Naked Poetry." *APR*, 4: 16-8 (#2 75).

Wagner, L.W. "*Spring and All*: The Unity of Design." *TSL*, 15: 61-73 (1970).

––––––. "W's 'Nude': *Kora in Hell*." *SDR*, 7: 3-18 (Au 69).

––––––. "WCW: A Review of Research and Criticism." *RALS*, 1: 17-29 (Sp 71).

––––––. "WCW's *The Great American Novel*." *Novel*, 3: 48-61 (1969).

––––––. "W's Search: 'To Have a Country.'" *Criticism*, 12: 226-38 (Su 70).

Wallace, E.M. "An Interview with WCW." *MR*, 14: 130-48 (Wi 73).

––––––. "Penn's Poet Friends." *Pennsylvania Gaz*, 71: 33-6 (F 73).

Weatherhead, A.K. "Two Books on WCW." *MLQ*, 33: 172-80 (Je 72).

Wells, Henry. "WCW and Traditions in Chinese Poetry." *LHY*, 16: 3-24 (Ja 75).

Werner, N.W. "The Importance of Ritual in W.C.W's *Paterson*." *SDR*, 8: 48-65 (Wi 70-71).

*White, William. "WCW: Bibliography Review with Addenda." *ABC*, 19: 9-12 (Mr 69).

Wichern, Dana. "On W on Breughel." *WiOr*, 6: 37-43 (Su 71).

Williams, W.C. "Editorial." *Contact*, 1: 1 (D 70).

––––––. "Letters to Norman MacLeod." *Pembroke Mag*, 6: 152-63 (1975).

––––––. "Prologue." *Little R*, 5: 1-10 (Ap 19).

Wilson, T.C. "The Example of Dr. W." *Poetry*, 48: 105-7 (My 36).

Youdelman, Jeffrey. "Pictures for a Sunday Afternoon: The Camera Eye in *Paterson*." *CP*, 2: 37-42 (Fa 69).

Zitner, S.P. "Art as Redemption." *Poetry*, 111: 41-2 (O 67).

Willingham, Calder. Parr, J.L. "CW: The Forgotten Novelist." *Critique*, 11: 57-65 (1969).

Willis, Nathaniel Parker. Benton, R.P. "Poe's 'Lionizing': A Quiz on W and Lady Blessington." *SSF*, 5: 239-44 (Sp 68).

————. "Poe's 'The System of Dr. Tarr and Prof. Fether': Dickens or W?" *PN*, 1: 7-9 (Ap 68).

————. "W—and Poe." *PoeS*, 4: 55-6 (D 71).

Goodman, Charlotte. "Henry James's *Roderick Hudson* and NPW's *Paul Fane*." *AL*, 43: 642-5 (Ja 72).

Pollin, B.R. "An 1839 Review of Poe's *Tales* in W's *The Corsair*." *PoeS*, 5: 56 (1972).

Willis, Sarah Payson ("Fanny Fern"). McGinnis, P.I. "Fanny Fern, American Novelist." *Biblion*, 2: 2-37 (Sp 1969).

Wood, A.D. "The 'Scribbling Women' and FF: Why Women Wrote." *AQ*, 23: 3-24 (Sp 71).

Wilson, Augusta Evans. Bargard, Rovert. "Amelia Barr, AEW and the Sentimental Novel." *Marab*, 2: 13-25 (Wi 65-66).

Wilson, Edmund. Anon. "EW." *NRep*, 166: 32 (24 Je 72).

————. "EW and the End of the American Dream." *TLS*, 19 My 72, pp. 561-4.

Aaron, Daniel. "Some Unpublished Letters of EW." *NewR*, 171: 15-9 (30 N 74).

Alsterdal, Alvar. "Den mänglärde EW." *Studiekamraten*, 50: 8-10 (1968).

Berthoff, Warner. "EW as Provincial Plutarch." *SatR*, 54: 19-21 (28 Ag 71).

Bissell, C.T. "EW's *O Canada* Revisited." *J Canadian Stud*, 3: 11-6 (Ag 68).

Costa, Richard. "EW: A Memoir and a Review." *Quartet*, 5: 36-41 (Wi 72).

Cowley, Malcolm. "A Reminiscence: EW on *The New Republic*." *NRep*, 166: 25-8 (1 Jl 72).

Dabney, Lewis. "EW's Legacy." *MR*, 14: 631-8 (Su 73).

Dabney, L.M. "EW's Russian Legacy." *IJAS*, 3: 23-31 (Su 73).

Dayananda, Y.J. "EW and 'The Thirties.'" *LHR*, 12: 1-23 (1971).

————. "EW's Marxist Criticism." *IJAS*, 3: 1-22 (#1 73).

Douglas, G.H. "EW, Great Democrat of Letters." *Nation*, 215: 85-9 (7 Ag 72).

————. "EW: The Critic as Artist." *TQ*, 17: 58-72 (Wi 74).

Epstein, Jacob. "E.W. 1895-1972." *NYRB*, 19: 6-8 (20 Jl 72).

————. "On Losing EW." *World*, 1: 47-50 (15 Ag 72).

Etiemble, René. "Notes à propos d'EW." *NRF*, 16: 119-28 (Ag 68).

French, Philip. "An appreciation of EW, 1895-1972." *Listener*, 90: 371-4 (20 S 73).

Genizi, Haim. "EW and *The Modern Monthly*, 1934-5: A Phase in W's Radicalism." *JAmSt*, 7: 301-20 (D 73).

Gill, Brendan. "Homage to EW." *PULC*, 34: 158-67 (Sp 73).

Hancher, Michael. "The Text of 'The Fruits of the MLA.'" *PBSA*, 68: 411-2 (1974).

Josephson, Matthew. "Encounters with EW." *SoR*, 11: 731-65 (Au 75).

Levin, Harry. "The Last American Man of Letters." *TLS*, 11 O 74, pp. 1128-30.

*Lewis, W.J. "EW: A Bibliography." *BB*, 25: 145-9, 151 (My-Ag 68).

McSweeney, Kerry. "EW and a 'Truly Human Culture.'" *CRAS*, 4: 96-106 (Sp 73).

Matthews, T.S. "EW: An American Original." *SatR*, 2: 19-23 (17 My 75).

Mizener, Arthur. "EW's New Republic." *NRep*, 162: 28-30 (9 My 70).

Monteiro, George. "Addenda to Ramsey's EW." *PBSA*, 68: 439 (O-D 74).

Pritchett, V.S. "My Friend EW." *NSt*, 7 Jl 72, p. 28.

Rubin, L.D. "Cannon Fodder." *NRep*, 172: 22-3 (24 My 75).

————. "The Twenties: A Subliterary Memoir." *SR*, 83: 665-75 (Fa 75).

Sheed, Wilfred. "EW, 1895-1972." *NYT*, 2 Jl 72, pp. 2, 16.

Shulman, Elye. "Der shrayber EW." *Unser Tsait*, 1-2: 51-3; 3: 44-6 (1973).

Skloot, Robert. "*Philoctetes*: Wound and Bow Revisited." *DramS*, 6: 288-93 (1968).

Sutherland, Donald. "Our Narrative, Native Critic." *UDQ*, 8: 40-52 (Au 73).

Taylor, Mark. "EW and Literature." *Cweal*, 96: 386-7 (14 Jl 72).

Todd, C.L. "Upstate with EW." *NYH*, 54: 52-8 (Ja 73).

Wilson, Harry Leon. Anon. "HLW Papers." *Bancroftiana*, 57: 1-3 (Ja 74).

Wilson, Robert. Aronson, Arnold. "Wilson/Knowles' *The $ Value of Man.*" *TDR*, 19: 106-10 (#3 75).

Corvin, Michel. "A propos de deux spectacles de RW: Essai de lecture sémiologique." *CRB*, 77: 90-111 (1971).

Déak, František. "The Byrd Hoffman School of Byrds: RW." *DramR*, 18: 67-80 (Je 74).

Langton, Basil. "Journey to Ka Mountain." *DramR*, 17: 48-57 (Je 73).

Tompkins, Calvin. "Time to Think." *New Yorker*, 50: 38-62 (13 Ja 75).

Trilling, Ossia. "RW's *Ka Mountain and Guardenia Terrace.*" *DramR*, 17: 33-47 (Je 73).

Winslow, Anne Goodwin. Sugg, R.S., Jr. and Helen White. "Lady Into Artist: The Literary Achievement of AGW." *MissQ*, 22: 289-302 (Fa 69).

Winslow, Pete. Kizer, Carolyn. "PW." *StAR*, 2: 239-43 (Sp-Su 74).

Winters, Yvor. Barish, J.A. "YW and the Antimimetic Prejudice." *NLH*, 2: 419-44 (1971).

Carruth, Hayden. "A Location of J.V. Cunningham." *MQR*, 11: 75-7 (Sp 72).

Cohn, R.G. "The Assault of Symbolism." *CLS*, 5: 69-75 (Mr 68).

Donoghue, Denis. "The Will to Certitude." *TLS*, 30 Ag 74; pp. 917-8.

Fraser, John. "Leavis and W: Professional Manners." *CQ*, 5: 41-71 (Sp-Su 70).

———. "Leavis and W: A Question of Reputation." *WHR*, 26: 1-16 (Wi 72).

———. "Leavis, W, and 'Concreteness.'" *FWF*, 1: 249-66 (1974).

———. "Leavis, W, and Poetry." *SoRA*, 5: 179-96 (S 72).

———. "Leavis, W, and 'Tradition.'" *SoR*, 7: 963-85 (Au 71).

———. "YW: The Perils of Mind." *CentR*, 14: 396-420 (1970).

Graff, Gerald. "YW of Stanford." *ASch*, 44: 291-8 (Sp 75).

Hobsbaum, Philip. "The Discovery of Form." *MQR*, 12: 235-42 (Su 72).

Inglis, Fred. "A 'Reactionary' American Critic." *Listener*, 76: 322-2 (1 S 66).

Kaye, Howard. "The Post-Symbolist Poetry of YW." *SoR*, 7: 176-97 (Ja 71).

———. "YW: 1900-1968." *NRep*, 158: 31-3 (2 Mr 68).

Mudrick, Marvin. "Three Stanford Poets." *LugR*, 1: 83-94 (1965).

Parkinson, Thomas. "Hart Crane and YW: A Meeting of Minds." *SoR*, 11: 491-512 (Jl 75).

———. "The Hart Crane-YW Correspondence." *OhR*, 16: 5-24 (Fa 74).

Powell, G.E. "Mythical and Smoky Soil: Imagism and the Aboriginal in the Early Poetry of YW." *SoR*, 11: 300-17 (Ap 75).

———. "Some Key Concepts in the Poetry of YW." *SoR*, 11: 838-54 (Au 75).

———. "Two Essays." *UDQ*, 10: 38-60 (#3 75).

Rao, Nageswara. "A Note on the Poetry of YW." *J of Engl Stud* (Warangal), 4: 13-27 (74).

Ringrose, C.X. "F.R. Leavis and YW on G.M. Hopkins." *ES*, 55: 32-42 (1974).

Robson, W.W. "The Literary Criticism of YW." *CQ*, 6: 189-200 (1973).

Stanford, D.E. "YW: 1900-1968." *SoR*, 4: 861-3 (1968).

Wellek, René. "YW Rehearsed and Reconsidered." *UDQ*, 10: 1-27 (#3 75).

Winther, S.K. Meldrum, Barbara. "Structure and Meaning in S.K.W's *Beyond the Garden Gate.*" *WAL*, 6: 191-202 (Fa 71).

Winthrop, John. Benton, R.M. "The YWs and Developing Scientific Though in New England." *EAL*, 7: 272-80 (Wi 73).

Freiberg, Malcolm. "The Winthrops and Their Papers." *PMHS*, 80: 55-70 (1969).

Graham, Louis. "The Scientific Piety of JW of Harvard." *NEQ*, 46: 112-8 (Mr 73).

McCrimmon, Barbara. "JW's Journal." *Manuscripts*, 24: 87-96 (1972).

Moyne, E.J. "The Reverend William Bentley and the Portraits of Governor Winthrop." *EIHC*, 110: 49-56 (1974).

Wirt, William. Robert, J.C. "WW, Virginian." *VMHB*, 80: 387-441 (O 72).

Wise, John. Johnston, T.E. "JW: Early American Political Thinker." *EAL*, 3: 30-40 (Sp 68).

Wister, Owen. Barsness, J.A. "Theodore Roosevelt as Cowboy: The Virginian as Jacksonian Man." *AQ*, 21: 609-20 (Fa 69).

Burton, Richard. "The Literary Taste of the West." *Criterion*, 23: 8-9 (Jl 00).

Davis, D.B. "Ten-Gallon Hero." *AQ*, 6: 114-21 (Su 54).

DeVoto, Barnard. "The Easy Chair: Birth of an Art." *HM*, 211: 8-16 (D 55).

Houghton, D.E. "Two Heroes in One: Reflections Upon the Popularity of *The Virginian*." *JPC*, 4: 497-506 (Fa 70).

Etulain, R.W. "OW and Wilderness West." *PNWASN*, 19: 3 (O 72).

Kimmel, Thelma. "Washington's Methow Valley Inspired 'The Virginian.'" *IF*, nv: 28-9 (3 N 55).

Lambert, Neal. "A Cowboy Writes to OW." *AmWest*, 2: 31-6 (Fa 65).

———. "OW's 'Hank's Woman': The Writer and His Commitment." *WAL*, 4: 39-50 (Sp 69).

———. "OW's Lin McLean: The Failure of the Vernacular Hero." *WAL*, 5: 219-32 (Fa 70).

———. "OW's Virginian: The Genesis of a Cultural Hero." *WAL*, 6: 99-107 (Su 71).

———. "The Values of the Frontier: OW's Final Assessment." *SDR*, 9: 76-87 (Sp 71).

Mabie, H.W. "Mr. Mabie's Literary Talks." *LHJ*, 19: 15 (Ag 02).

Malley, Terence. "A Fruitful Alliance." *MarkR*, 3: 97-100 (F 73).

*Marovitz, S.E. "OW: An Annotated Bibliography of Secondary Material." *ALR*, 7: 1-110 (Wi 74).

———. "Testament of a Patriot: The Virginian, The Tenderfoot, and OW." *TSLL*, 15: 551-75 (Fa 73).

Marsh, E.C. "Representative American Storytellers: OW." *Bkm*, 27: 458-66 (Jl 08).

Mason, Julian. "OW, Boy Librarian." *QJLC*, 26: 202-12 (O 69).

———. "OW, Champion of Old Charleston." *QJLC*, 29: 162-85 (1972).

Mason, Julian. "OW and the South." *SHR*, 6: 23-34 (Wi 72).

———. "OW, Boy Librarian." *QJLC*, 26: 200-12 (O 69).

———. "OW: Observer in North Carolina." *NCaF*, 20: 163-8 (N 72).

Mather, F.J. "Literature." *Forum*, 34: 223-4 (O 02).

Meriwether, J.B. "OW on Proof-redares and Word-coining." *CEAAN*, 6: 7-8 (1973).

Monroe, Lucy. "The Virginian Wins East and West." *Critic*, 41: 358-9 (O 02).

Morsberger, R.E. "Son of a Gun: Profanity and Prudery in the Movie of *The Virginian*." *ELN*, 10: 216-7 (Mr 73).

Mulqueen, J.E. "Three Heroes in American Fiction." *ILLQ*, 36: 44-50 (F 74).

Phillips, D.G. "OW." *SEP*, 175: 13-4 (3 Ja 03).

Pollard, Lancaster. "W's Noted Western Novel 'The Virginian' Traced to Notes Taken in Heppner Hotel." *Oregon*, 6: 30 (6 Jl 58).

Ramage, B.J. "*Ulysses S. Grant*: by OW." *AHR*, 6: 823-4 (Jl 01).

Sears, Hamblen. "The Historical Importance of The Virginian." *BookB*, 25: 250-1 (O 02).

Seelye, John. "When West Was W." *NRep*, 167: 28-33 (2 S 72).

Shepherd, Allen. "Fair Harvard: A Note on OW's *Philosophy Four*." *MarkR*, 4: 52-3 (My 74).

*Sherman, Dean. "OW: An Annotated Bibliography." *BB*, 28: 7-16 (Ja-Mr 71).

Simms, L.M. "*Lady Baltimore*: OW and the Southern Race Question." *Serif*, 7: 23-6 (1970).

Solensten, J.M. "Richard Harding Davis, OW, and *The Virginian*: Unpublished Letters and a Commentary." *ALR*, 5: 122-33 (Sp 72).

Stark, Beverly. "OW's *The Virginian*." *Bkm*, 15: 569 (Ag 02).

Swain, E.A. "OW's *Roosevelt*: A Case Study in Post-Production Censorship." *SB*, 27: 290-3 (1974).

Swift, Lindsay. "Mr. W's Virginian." *SEP*, 175: 18 (12 Jl 02).

Trimmer, J.F. "*The Virginian*: Novel and Films." *IllQ*, 35: 5-18 (D 72).

Vorpahl, B.M. "Ernest Hemingway and OW: Finding the Lost Generation." *LCUP*, 36: 126-37 (Sp 70).

———. "Hemingway and W: For Want of a Smile." *LATC*, 23 F 69, pp. 8, 11.

———. "Henry James and OW." *PMHB*, 95: 291-338 (Jl 71).

———. "'Very Much Like a Fire-Cracker': OW on Mark Twain." *WAL*, 6: 83-98 (Su 71).

* Walbridge, E.F. "'The Virginian' and OW: A Bibliography." *PBSA*, 46: 117-20 (2Q 52).

Walker, D.D. "Essays in the Criticism of Western Literary Criticism. II. The Dogmas of De Voto . . . OW." *PosS*, 3: 1-7 (N 71).

Watkins, G.T. "W and 'The Virginian.'" *PaNWR*, 2: 49-54 (Fa 58).

West, R.B. "*Owen Wister Out West/ His Journals and Letters*." *AL*, 32: 97-9 (Mr 60).

White, J.I. "OW, Song Writer." *WF*, 26: 269-71 (O 67).

———. "OW and the Dogies." *JAF*, 82: 66-9 (Ja-Mr 69).

———. "OW, Song Writer." *WF*, 26: 269-71 (O 67).

———. "The Virginian." *Montana Mag of Western Hist*, 16: 2-11 (O 66).

———. "The Virginian Rides On . . . and On." *Am West*, 7: 49-60 (S 70).

Wood, Charles Erskine Scott. Bingham, E.R. "Experiments in Launching a Biography: Three Vignettes of CESW." *HLQ*, 35: 221-39 (1972).

Wolcott, Roger. Cook, D.E. "RW's Long Tidal River." *ConHSB*, 32: 16-20 (Ja 67).

Wolfe, Thomas. Anastas'ev, N. "Faust ne umiraet (Zametki o tvorcestve Tomasa Vulfa)." *VLit*, 11: 87-105 (1967).

Baker, C.P., and A.P. Clarke. "An Unpublished TW Letter." *MissQ*, 25: 467-9 (1972).

Balotă, Nicolae. "TW: Un realist al confesiunii." *Steaua*, 22: 23-4 (1971).

Basso, Hamilton. "TW: The Summing UP." *NRep*, 103: 422-3 (23 S 40).

Bellamy, J.D. "A Quite Literary Conversation with TW." *In Touch*, 1: 60ff (Je 74).

Bellman, S.I. "Hemingway, Faulkner, and W . . . and the Common Reader." *SoR*, 4: 834-9 (Su 68).

Boyle, T.E. "Frederick Jackson Turner and TW: The Frontier as History and as Literature." *WAL*, 4: 273-85 (Wi 70).

Braswell, William. "An 'Interior Biography' of TW." *SLJ*, 3: 145-50 (Fa 70).

Bredahl, A.C. "*Look Homeward, Angel*: Individuation and Articulation." *SLJ*, 6: 47-58 (Fa 73).

Calhoun, R.J. and R.W. Hill. "'Tom, Are You Listening?' An Interview with Fred Wolfe." *SCR*, 6: 35-47 (#2 74).

Capitanchick, Maurice. "TW." *B&B*, 16: 24-8 (Jl 71).

Carlile, R.E. "Musical Analogues in TW's *Look Homeward, Angel*." *MFS*, 14: 215-23 (Su 68).

Comino, Ioana. "TW." *Contemporanul*, 31 My 68, p. 2.

Corrington, J.W. "Three Books About a Southern Romantic." *SLJ*, 1: 98-104 (Au 68).

Cracroft, R.H. "A Pebble in the Pool: Organic Theme and Structure in TW's *You Can't Go Home Again*." *MFS*, 17: 533-53 (Wi 71-72).

———. "Through Utah and the Western Parks: T.W.'s Farewell to America." *UHQ*, 37: 290-306 (Su 69).

Crane, Melville. "TW: A Memoir." *ASch*, 41: 637-42 (Fa 72).

Dessner, L.J. "TW's Mr. Katamoto." *MFS*, 17: 561-5 (Wi 71-2).

Doten, Sharon. "TW's 'No-Door': Some Textual Questions." *PBSA*, 68: 45-51 (Ja-Mr 74).

Eichelberger, C.L. "Eliza Gant as Negative Symbol in Look Homeward, Angel." *ArlQ*, 1: 269-78 (Wi 67-68).

Field, L.A. "TW and the Kicking Season Again." *SAQ*, 69: 364-72 (Su 70).

Field, Leslie. "TW on the Couch and in Symposium." *SLJ*, 5: 163-76 (Fa 72).

Foster, R.E. "TW's Mountain Gloom and Glory." *AL*, 44: 638-47 (Ja 73).

Gilman, Richard. "The Worship of TW." *NRep*, 158: 31-4 (24 F 68).

Gray, Richard. "Signs of Kinship: TW and His Appalachian Background." *AppalJ*, 1: 309-19 (Sp 74).

Green, Charmian. "W, Carlyle, and 'The Imprisonment of the Actual.'" *AN&Q*, 13: 118-20 (Ap 75).

Groth, Mel. "The Education of TW: Roberts, Greenlaw, Williams, Baker." *StAR*, 2: 261-73 (Sp-Su 74).

Hampton, Nigel. "Who's Ashamed of TW." *CEA*, 38: 18-20 (#1 75).

Harvey, N.L. "*Look Homeward, Angel*: An Elegiac Novel." *BSUF*, 13: 29-33 (Wi 72).

Idol, J.L. "The Plays of TW and Their Links with his Novels." *MissQ*, 22: 95-112 (Sp 69).

———. "TW and Jonathan Swift." *SCR*, 8: 43-54 (N 75).

———. "TW and Painting." *ReA&L*, 2: 14-20 (Sp 69).

———. "TW's 'A Note on Experts.'" *SSF*, 11: 395-8 (Fa 74).

Kennedy, R.S. "TW's Last Manuscript." *HLB*, 23: 203-11 (1975).

Kennedy, W.F. "Are Our Novelists Hostile to the American Economic System?" *DR*, 25: 32-44 (Sp 55).

Lanzinger, Klaus. "Die Entstehung des grossen amerikanischen Romans bei TW." *SG*, 21: 36-48 (1968).

Lengeler, Rainer. "TW and S.T. Coleridge." *N&Q*, 20: 332-3 (S 73).

Mann, M. "Drei grosse amerikanische Epiker." *Die Weltwoche*, 16: 9 (1948).

McElderry, B.R., Jr. "TW's 'The Mountains.'" *SLJ*, 3: 151-3 (Fa 70).

Meehan, James. "Seed of Destruction: The Death of TW." *SAQ*, 73: 173-83 (Sp 74).

Meinke, Elke and Dieter. "TW: Zum Tod in der Groszstadt." *NS*, 18: 373-80 (Ag 69).

Michelet, J.M. "Sur une piece de TW." *BFLS*, 46: 402-5 (1967).

Mishe, Patrick. "The Outline of TW's Last Book." *HLB*, 21: 400-1 (1973).

Millichap, J.R. "Narrative Structure and Symbolic Imagery in *Look Homeward, Angel*." *SHR*, 7: 295-303 (Su 73).

Misiego, Micaela. "La solelad integral en la obra de TW." *Mundo Nuevo* (Paris), 33: 45-9 (1969).

———. "TW, poeta da solidade." *Grial*, 19: 1-20 (1968).

Moore, H.T. "Motes in the Eye of a Mountainous Man." *SatR*, 53: 23-4, 46 (7 Mr 70).

Norwid, Helena. "TW: Ucieczka od samego siebie." *KN*, 14: 395-413 (1967).

O'Brien, Michael. "TW and the Problem of Southern Identity: An English Perspective." *SAQ*, 70: 102-11 (Wi 71).

Powell, W.A. "TW's Phoenix Nest: The Plays of TW as Related to His Fiction." *MarkR*, 2: 104-10 (My 71).

Reck, R.D. "Céline and W: Toward a Theory of the Autobiographical Novel." *MissQ*, 22: 19-27 (Wi 68-69).

Reeves, Paschal. "Gleam from the Forge: TW's Emerging Idea of Brotherhood." *GaR*, 22: 247-53 (Su 68).

———. "TW and the Family of Man." *Spectrum*, 2: 47-54 (1972).

Rubin, Larry. "An Echo of Poe in *Of Time and the River*." *PN*, 3: 38-9 (D 70).

Rubin, L.D. "TW Once Again." *NCHR*, 50: 169-89 (Sp 73).

————. "TW and the Place He Came From." *VQR*, 51: 183-202 (1975).

Sakamoto, Masayuki. "The Discovery of One's Other Self: *You Can't Go Home Again* Reconsidered." *SELit*, nv: 17-35 (1968).

————. "Nature to Art—T.W ni okeru." *EigoS*, 117: 690-2 (1972).

Scherting, Jack. "Echoes of *Look Homeward, Angel* in Dylan Thomas's 'A Child's Christmas in Wales.'" *SSF*, 9: 404-6 (1972).

Schmid, Hans. "A Note on TW's *Oktobefest*-Letter." *HLB*, 18: 367-70 (O 70).

Schneider, Duane. "TW and the Quest for Language." *OUR*, 11: 5-18 (1969).

Simpson, L.P. "*The Notebooks of TW*, edited by Richard S. Kennedy and Paschal Reeves." *SAQ*, 69: 544-6 (Au 70).

Singh, Hari. "TW: The Idea of Eternity." *SCR*, 1: 40-7 (My 69).

Skipp, F.E. "*Of Time and the River*: The Final Editing." *PBSA*, 64: 313-32 (3Q 70).

Smrček, M.N. "Esteticeskie vzglijady Tomasa Vul'fa 1920-x godov i ego roman *Obrati vzor na dom svoj, angel*." *VLU*, 4: 87-96 (1971).

Stone, Edward. "More about Gatsby's Guest List." *FHA*, 1972, pp. 315-6.

Styron, William. "The Shade of TW." *HM*, 236: 96-104 (Ap 68).

Swets, R.D. "Eugene Gant Speaks of Tombstones and Angels." *BSUF*, 14: 8 (Su 73).

Walther, J.D. "'Luke' Looks Homeward: An Interview with Fred W. Wolfe." *MissQ*, 27: 141-63 (Sp 74).

Wank, Martin. "TW: Two More Decades of Criticism." *SAQ*, 69: 244-56 (Sp 70).

Zimmerman, K.R. "Going Home Again." *Nat R*, 26: 1173-5 (11 O 74).

Wolfe, Tom. Edwards, T.R. "The Electric Indian." *PR*, 36: 535-44 (Su 69).

Meehan, Thomas. "The Time Renata Adler Didn't Dump Campbell's Soup on TW's Head." *SatR*, 3 Je 73, pp. 22-4.

Mok, M. "TW." *PW*, 203: 34-5 (18 Je 73).

Phillips, William. "Conservative Chic: Tom Wolfe." *PR*, 42: 175-7 (2Q 75).

Tuchman, Mitch. "The Writings of TW." *NRep*, 173: 21-4 (25 O 75).

Weber, Ronald. "TW's Happiness Explosion." *JPC*, 8: 71-80 (Su 74).

Wolfe, Tom. "The Author's Story." *NYT*, 18 Ag 68, pp. 2, 40-1.

Zashin, E.M. "Political Theorist and Demiurge: The Rise and Fall of Ken Kesey." *CentR*, 17: 199-213 (Sp 73).

Woods, John. Etter, Dave. "JW: America's Best Poet." *New*, 15: 26-30 (Ap-My 71).

Woolman, John. Cadbury, H.J. "A W Manuscript." *QH*, 57: 35-41 (1968).

————. "Another W Manuscript." *QH*, 61: 16-23 (1972).

Cassaigne, Ella. "L'anti-esclavagisme de JW." *EA*, 21: 142-51 (Ap-Je 68).

Moulton, P.P. "The Influence of the Writings of JW." *QH*, 60: 3-13 (1971).

Woolson, Constance Fenimore. Hayne, P.H. "Some New Letters of CFW." *NEQ*, 14: 715-35 (D 41).

Helmick, E.T. "CFW: First Novelist of Florida." *Carrell*, 10: 8-18 (1969).

Moore, R.S. "CFW (1840-1894)." *ALR*, 3: 36-8 (Su 68).

Simms, L.M. "Constance Fenimore Woolson on Southern Literary Taste." *MissQ*, 22: 362-6 (Fa 69).

Wouk, Herman. Howard, Jane. "HW Surfaces Again." *Life*, 26 N 71, pp. 53-6.

Wright, Charles. Foster F.S. "CW: Black Black Humorist." *CLAJ*, 15: 44-53 (S 71).

Klinkowitz, Jerome. "The New Black Writer and the Old Black Art." *FicI*, 1: 13-7 (1973).

Sedlack, R.P. "Jousting with Rats: CW's *The Wig*." *SNL*, 7: 37-9 (Fa 69).

Wright, Frances. Kendall, K.E., and J.Y. Fisher. "FW on Women's Rights: Eloquence Versus Ethos." *QJS*, 60: 58-68 (1974).

Martin, Wendy. "Profile: FW, 1795-1852." *WS*, 2: 273-8 (1974).

Wright, H.B. Ifkovic, Edward. "HBW and the Minister of Man: The Domestic Romancer at the End of the Genteel Age." *MarkR*, 4: 21-6 (F 74).
Wright, James. Butscher, Edward. "The Rise and Fall of JW." *GaR*, 28: 257-68 (Su 74).
"Crunk." "The Work of JW." *Sixties*, 8: 52-78 (1966).
Deutsch, Babette. "A 'Fashionable' Poet?" *NRep*, 165: 27 (17 Jl 71).
Ditsky, John. "JW Collected: Alternations on the Monument." *MPS*, 2: 252-9 (1972).
Dougherty, David. "Themes in Jeffers and JW." *RJN*, 33: 7-11 (S 72).
Henricksen, Bruce. "W's 'Lying in a Hammock at William Duffey's Farm in Pine Island, Minnesota.'" *Expl*, 32: 40 (Ja 74).
Janssens, G.A.M. "The Present State of American Poetry: Robert Bly and JW." *ES*, 51: 112-37 (Ap 70).
McElrath, J.R., "Something to Be Said for the Light: A Conversation with JW." *SHR*, 6: 134-53 (1972).
*McMaster, Belle. "JAW: A Checklist." *BB*, 31: 71-82, 88 (Ap-Je 74).
Molesworth, Charles. "JW and the Dissolving Self." *Salmagundi*, 22-23: 222-3 (1973).
Seay, James. "A World Immeasurable Alive and Good: A Look at JW's *Collected Poems*." *GaR*, 27: 71-81 (Sp 73).
Stitt, Peter. "The Art of Poetry XIX: JW." *PaR*, 62: 34-61 (Su 75).
———. "JW and Robert Bly." *HiR*, 2: 89-94 (Fa 73).
———. "The Poetry of JW." *MinnR*, 2: 13-32 (Sp 72).
Van den Heuvel, Cor. "The Poetry of JW." *Mosaic*, 7: 163-70 (#3 74).
Zweig, Paul. "Making and Unmaking." *PR*, 40: 269-78 (#2 73).
Wright, Richard. Aaron, Daniel. "RW and the Communist Party." *NLet*, 38: 170-81 (Wi 71).
Alexander, M.W. "RW." *NLet*, 38: 182-202 (Wi 71).
Amis, L.J. "RW's *Native Son*: Notes." *NALF*, 8: 240-3 (Fa 74).
Bakish, David. "Underground in an Ambiguous Dreamworld." *SBL*, 2: 18-23 (Au 71).
Baldwin, R.E. "The Creative Vision of *Native Son*." *MR*, 14: 378-90 (Sp 73).
Bayliss, J.F. "Native Son: Protest or Psychological Study?" *NALF*, 1: 1 (Fa 67).
Berry, Faith. "Portrait of a Man as Outsider: on RW in Exile." *NegroD*, 18: 26-37 (1969).
*Brignano, R.C. "RW: A Bibliography of Secondary Sources." *SBL*, 2: 19-25 (Su 71).
Bolton, H.P. "The Role of Paranoia in RW's *Native Son*." *KanQ*, 7: 111-24 (#3 75).
Britt, David. "*Native Son*: Watershed of Negro Protest Literature." *NALF*, 1: 4-5 (Fa 67).
Brivic, Sheldon. "Conflict of Values: RW's *Native Son*." *Novel*, 7: 231-45 (Sp 74).
Brooks, M.E. "Behind RW's 'Artistic Conscience.'" *L&I*, 13: 21-30 (1972).
Brown, Cecil. "RW's Complexes and Black Writing Today: The Lesson and the Legacy." *BlackW*, 18: 45-50, 78-82 (D 68).
Brown, L.W. "Stereotypes in Black and White: The Nature of Perception in W's *Native Son*." *BlAR*, 1: 35-44 (Fa 70).
Cartosio, Bruno. "Due scrittori afroamericani: RW e Ralph Ellison." *SA*, 15: 395-431 (1969).
Cayton, Horace. "The Curtain: A Memoir." *NegroD*, 18: 11-5 (1969).
Corrigan, R.A. "Afro-American Fiction: A Checklist, 1853-1970." *MASJ*, 11: 114-35 (Fa 70).
Cripps, Thomas. "*Native Son* in the Movies." *New Letters*, 38: 49-63 (Wi 71).
Delpech, Jeanine. "An Interview with Native Son." *Crisis*, 57: 625-7 (N 50).
Demarest, D.P. "RW: The Meaning of Violence." *NALF*, 8: 236-8 (Fa 74).
Dickstein, Morris. "W, Baldwin, Cleaver." *NLet*, 38: 117-24 (Wi 71).
Dixon, Melvin. "RW: Native Father and His Long Dream." *BlackW*, 23: 91-5 (Mr 74).

Donlan, D.M. "The White Trap: A Motif." *EJ*, 59: 943-4 (O 70).

Emanuel, J.A. "Fever and Feeling: Notes on the Imagery in Native Son." *BlackW*, 18: 16-24 (1969).

————. "Lines for RW." *SBL*, 1: 2 (1970).

Epstein, Seymour. "Politics and the Novelist." *DQ*, 4: 1-18 (1970).

Everette, Mildred. "The Dead of RW's American Dream: 'The Man Who Lived Underground.'" *CLAJ*, 17: 318-26 (Mr 74).

Fabre, Michel. "Black Cat and White Cat: RW's Debt to Edgar Allan Poe." *PS*, 4: 17-9 (Je 41).

————. "Impressions of RW: An Interview with Simone DeBeauvoir." *SBL*, 1: 3-5 (1970).

————. "A Letter from Dorothy Padmore." *SBL*, 1: 5-9 (Fa 70).

————. "An Interview with Simone de Beauvoir." *SBL*, 1: 3-5 (Fa 70).

————. "The Poetry of RW." *SBL*, 1: 10-22 (Fa 70).

————. "RW's First Hundred Books." *CLAJ*, 16: 458-74 (Je 73).

————. "RW: The Man Who Lived Underground." *StN*, 3: 165-79 (Su 71).

————. "W's Exile." *NLet*, 38: 136-54 (Wi 71).

————, and Edward Margolies. "A Bibliography of RW's Works." *NLet*, 38: 155-69 (Wi 71).

Faris, Kenneth. "A Small Portrait of RW." *NHB*, 25: 155-6 (Ap 62).

Faulkner, William, et al. "Letters to RW." *NLet*, 38: 128-35 (Wi 71).

Felgar, Robert. "'The Kingdom of the Beast': The Landscape of *Native Son*." *CLAJ*, 17: 333-7 (Mr 74).

————. "*Soul on Ice* and *Native Son*." *NALF*, 8: 235 (Fa 74).

Fontaine, W.T. "The Negro Continuum from Dominant Wish to Collective Act." *AForum*, 3-4: 63-96 (1968).

Gaffney, Kathleen. "Bigger Thomas in RW's *Native Son*." *Roots*, 1: 81-95 (1970).

Gaskill, Gayle. "The Effect of Black/White Imagery in RW's *Black Boy*." *NALF*, 7: 46-8 (Su 73).

Gayle, Addison, Jr. "RW: Beyond Nihilism." *BlackW*, 18: 4-10 (D 68).

Gibson, D.B. "RW: A Bibliographical Essay." *CLAJ*, 12: 360-5 (Je 69).

————. "RW and the Tyranny of Convention." *CLAJ*, 12: 344-57 (Je 69).

————. "W's Invisible Native Son." *AQ*, 21: 728-38 (Wi 69).

Giles, J.R. "RW's Successful Failure: A New Look at *Uncle Tom's Children*." *Phylon*, 34: 256-66 (S 73).

Goede, William. "On Lower Frequencies: The Burried Men in W and Ellison." *MFS*, 15: 483-501 (1969-1970).

Gounard, Jean-Francois. "RW as a Black American Writer in Exile." *CLAJ*, 17: 307-17 (Mr 74).

Graham, Don. "*Lawd Today* and the Example of *The Waste Land*." *CLAJ*, 17: 327-32 (Mr 74).

Graham, Louis. "The White Self-Image Conflict in *Native Son*." *SBL*, 3: 19-21 (Su 72).

Gross, Seymour. "'Dalton' and Color-Blindness in *Native Son*." *MissQ*, 27: 75-7 (Wi 73-4).

————. "*Native Son* and 'The Murders in the Rue Morgue': An Addendum." *PoeS*, 8: 23 (Je 75).

Hajek, Friederike. "*American Tragedy*—zwei Aspekte: Dargestellt in RW's *Native Son* und in Theodore Dreisers *An American Tragedy*." *ZAA*, 20: 262-79 (1972).

Harrington, Ollie. "The Last Days of RW." *Ebony*, 16: 83-94 (F 61).

Hill, Herbert. "The Negro Writer and the Creative Imagination." *Arts in Soc*, 5: 245-55 (1968).

Houseman, John. "*Native Son* on Stage." *NLet*, 38: 71-82 (Wi 71).

Hyman, S.E. "RW Reappraised." *Atl*, 225: 127-32 (Mr 70).

Issacs, Harold. "Five Writers and Their African Ancestors." *Phylon*, 21: 243-65 (1960).

Jackson, Blyden. "RW: Black Boy From America's Black Belt and Urban Ghettos." *CLAJ*, 12: 287-309 (Je 69).

———. "RW in a Moment of Truth." *SLJ*, 3: 3-17 (Sp 71).

James, C.L. "Bigger Thomas in the Seventies: A Twentieth-Century Search for Significance." *Eng Rec*, 22: 6-14 (Fa 71).

Jeffers, Lance. "Afro-American Literature: The Conscience of Man." *BSch*, 2: 47-53 (Ja 71).

Jordan, June. "On RW and Zora Neale Hurston: Notes Toward a Balancing of Love and Hatred." *BlackW*, 23: 4-8 (Au 74).

Kearns, Edward. "The 'Fate' Section of *Native Son*." *ConL*, 12: 146-55 (Sp 71).

Kennedy, J.G. "The Content and Form of *Native Son*." *CE*, 34: 269-83 (N 72).

Kent, G.E. "On the Future Study of RW." *CLAJ*, 12: 366-70 (Je 69).

———. "RW: Blackness and the Adventure of Western Culture." *CLAJ*, 12: 322-43 (Je 69).

Kgositsile, Keorapetse. "The Relevance of Bigger Thomas to Our Time." *Roots*, 1: 79-80 (1970).

Kim, Kichung. "W, the Protest Novel, and Baldwin's Faith." *CLAJ*, 17: 387-96 (Mr 74).

Kinnamon, Keneth. "*Lawd Today*: RW's Apprentice Novel." *SBL*, 2: 16-8 (Su 71).

———. "*Native Son*: The Personal, Social, and Political Background." *Phylon*, 30: 66-72 (Sp 69).

———. "The Pastoral Impulse in RW." *MASJ*, 10: 41-7 (Sp 69).

———. "RW: Proletarian Poet." *CP*, 2: 39-50 (Sp 69).

———. "RW's Use of *Othello* in *Native Son*." *CLAJ*, 12: 358-9 (Je 69).

Klotman, P.R. and Melville Yancey. "Gift of Double Vision: Possible Political Implications of RW's 'Self-Consciousness' Thesis." *CLAJ*, 16: 106-16 (S 72).

———. "Moral Distancing As A Rhetorical Technique in *Native Son*: A Note on 'Fate.'" *CLAJ*, 18: 284-91 (D 74).

Knox, George. "The Negro Novelist's Sensibility and the Outsider Theme." *WHR*, 11: 137-48 (Sp 57).

Kostelanetz, Richard. "The Politics of Unresolved Quests in the Novels of RW." *XUS*, 8: 31-64 (My 69).

Lank, D.S. "*Native Son*." *PMLA*, 90: 122-3 (Ja 75).

Larsen, R.B.V. "The Four Voices in RW's *Native Son*." *NALF*, 6: 105-9 (1972).

Lawson, L.A. "Cross Damon: Kierkegaardian Man of Dread." *CLAJ*, 14: 298-316 (Mr 71).

Leary, Lewis. "*Lawd Today*: Notes on RW's First/Last Novel." *CLAJ*, 15: 411-20 (Je 72).

LeClair, Thomas. "The Blind Leading the Blind: W's *Native Son* and a Brief Reference to Ellison's *Invisible Man*." *CLAJ*, 13: 315-20 (Mr 70).

Lewis, Sinclair. "Gentlemen, This Is Revolution." *Esquire*, 80: 184-5 (O 73).

Ludington, C.T. "Protest and Anti-protest: Ralph Ellison." *SHR*, 4: 31-9 (Wi 70).

McCarthy, H.T. "RW: The Expatriate as Native Son." *AL*, 44: 97-117 (My 72).

May, J.R. "Images of Apocalypse in the Black Novel." *Renascence*, 23: 31-45 (1970).

Merkle, D.R. "The Furnace and the Tower: A New Look at the Symbols of *Native Son*." *EJ*, 60: 735-9 (S 71).

Meyer, Shirley. "The Identity of 'The Man Who Lived Underground.'" *NALF*, 4: 52-5 (1970).

Miller, E.E. "Voodoo Parallels in *Native Son*." *CLAJ*, 16: 81-95 (S 72).

Mitchell, Louis. "RW's Artistry." *Crisis*, 82: 62-6 (F 75).

Mitra, B.K. "The W-Baldwin Controversy." *IJAS*, 1: 101-5 (1969).

Nagel, James. "Images in 'Vision' in *Native Son*." *UR*, 35: 109-15 (D 69).

Oleson, C.W. "The Symbolic Richness of RW's 'Bright and Morning Star.'" *NALF*, 6: 110-2 (1972).

Paliwal, G.D. "RW and the Negro." *RUSEng*, 8: 72-83 (1975).

Pitcole, Marcia. "*Black Boy* and Role Playing: A Scenario for Reading Success." *EJ*, 57: 1140-2 (N 68).

Primeau, Ronald. "Imagination as Moral Bulwark and Creative Energy in RW's *Black Boy* and Leroi Jones' Home." *SBL*, 3: 12-8 (Su 72).

Prior, L.T. "A Further Word on RW's Use of Poe in *Native Son*." *PoeS*, 5: 52-3 (1972).

Pryos, John. "RW: A Black Novelist's Experience in Film." *NALF*, 9: 53-4 (Su 75).

Reed, K.T. "*Native Son*: An American *Crime and Punishment*." *SBL*, 1: 33-4 (Su 70).

Reilly, J.M. "*Lawd Today*: RW's Experiment in Naturalism." *J Black Stud*, 2: 439-60 (Je 72).

————. "*Lawd Today*: RW's Experiment in Naturalism." *SBL*, 2: 14-7 (Fa 71).

*————. "RW: An Essay in Bibliography." *RALS*, 1: 131-80 (Au 71).

————. "RW's Apprenticeship." *JBlackS*, 2: 439-60 (#4 72).

————. "Self-portraits by RW." *ColQ*, 20: 31-45 (Su 71).

Ridenour, Ronald. "'The Man Who Lived Underground': A Critique." *Phylon*, 31: 54-7 (Sp 70).

Riesman, David. "Marginality, Conformity, and Insight." *Phlyon*, 14: 241-57 (Fa 53).

Samples, Ron. "Bigger Thomas and His Descendants." *Roots*, 1: 86-93 (1970).

Sanders, Ronald. "RW and the Sixties." *Midstream*, 14: 28-40 (Ag-S 68).

————. "RW Then & Now: Relevance for the Sixties." *NegroD*, 83-98 (1969).

Savory, J.J. "Bigger Thomas and the Book of Job: The Epigraph to *Native Son*." *NALF*, 9: 55-6 (Su 75).

————. "Descent and Baptism in *Native Son*, *Invisible Man*, and *Dutchman*." *Chri Schol R*, 3: 33-7 (1973).

Séjourné, Philippe. "La Carrière Littéraire de RW et L'évolution du probleme noir aux Etats Unis." *EAA*, 3: 129-50 (1966).

Shapiro, Karl. "Decolonization of American Literature." *WLB*, 39: 843-53 (Je 65).

Sherr, P.C. "RW: The Expatriate Pattern." *BlAR*, 2: 81-90 (Sp-Su 71).

Siegel, P.N. "The Conclusion of RW's *Native Son*." *PMLA*, 89: 517-23 (My 74).

Singh, Amritjit. "Misdirected Responses to Bigger Thomas." *SBL*, 5: 5-8 (Su 74).

Singh, R.K. "Christian Heroes and Anti-Heroes in RW's Fiction." *NALF*, 6: 99-104, 131 (1972).

————. "Some Basic Ideas and Ideals in RW's Fiction." *CLAJ*, 13: 78-84 (S 69).

————. "W's Tragic Vision in *The Outsider*." *SBL*, 1: 23-7 (Fa 70).

Smith, S.A. "RW's *Black Boy*: The Creative Impulse as Rebellion." *SLJ*, 5: 123-36 (Fa 72).

Sprandel, Katherine. "*The Long Dream*." *New Letters*, 38: 88-96 (Wi 71).

Standley, F.L. "James Baldwin: The Artist As Incorrigible Disturber of the Peace." *SHR*, 4: 18-30 (Wi 70).

Stanton, Robert. "Outrageous Fiction: *Crime and Punishment*, *The Assistant*, and *Native Son*." *PCP*, 4:52-8 (1969).

Starr, Alvin. "The Concept of Fear in the Works of Stephen Crane and RW." *SBL*, 6: 6-10 (#2 75).

Stephens, Martha. "RW's Fiction: A Reassessment." *GaR*, 25: 450-70 (Wi 71).

Tatham, Campbell. "Vision and Value in *Uncle Tom's Children*." *SBL*, 3: 14-23 (Sp 72).

Timmerman, John. "Symbolism as a Synthetic Device in RW's 'Long Black Song.'" *CLAJ*, 14: 291-7 (Mr 71).

————. "Trust and Mistrust: The Role of the Black Women in Three Works by RW." *STC*, 10: 33-48 (Fa 72).

Turner, D.T. "Afro-American Authors: A Full House." *CEA*, 34: 15-9 (Ja 72).

————. "*The Outsider*: Revision of an Idea." *SHR*, 4: 40-50 (Wi 70); *CLAJ*, 12: 310-21 (Je 69).

Velling, Rauno. "RW romaani *Native Son*." *KSV*, 25: 217-27 (1971).

Vogel, A.W. "The Education of the Negro in RW's *Black Boy*." *JNE*, nv: 195-8 (Sp 66).

Watson, E.A. "Bessie's Blues." *NLet*, 38: 64-70 (Wi 71).

*Webb, Constance. "RW: A Bibliography." *NegroD*, 18: 86-92 (1969).

Weigel, Henrietta, et al. "Personal Memories." *NLet*, 38: 16-40 (Wi 71).

Weiss, Adrian. "A Portrait of the Artist as a Black Boy." *BRMMLA*, 28: 93-101 (1974).

White, G.M. "W's Memphis." *NLet*, 38: 105-16 (Wi 71).

Williams, J.A. "On Wright, Wrong and Black Reality." *NegroD*, 18: 25 (1969).

Willis, A.A. "The Use of Coincidence in 'Notes of a Native Son.'" *NALF*, 8: 234 (Fa 74).

Wright, Richard. "Blueprint for Negro Literature." *Amistad*, 2: 3-20 (1971).

————. "The American Problem." *NLet*, 38: 9-16 (Wi 71).

————. "The Freedom to Read: An Author's View of a Library." *LJ*, 85: 4421-2 (15 D 60).

————. "Letter from RW." *NLet*, 38: 125-7 (Wi 71).

Wurlitzer, Rudolph. Bolling, Douglas. "RW's Nog and Flats." *Critique*, 14: 5-15 (#3 73).

————. "The Waking Nightmare: American Society in RW's *Quake*." *Critique*, 16: 70-80 (3Q 75).

Puetz, Manfred. "Alternative Fictions: On RW." *FicI*, 2-3: 134-9 (Sp-Fa 74).

Wylie, Elinor. Gordan, J.D. "A Legend Revisited: EW." *ASch*, 38: 459-68 (Su 69).

Helmick, E.T. "EW's Novels, Allegories of Love." *Carrell*, 9: 17-28 (1968).

Kelly, E.H. "The Eagle and the Mole: The Affective Fallacy Revisited." *Eng Rec*, 21: 57-9 (1970).

Wylie, Philip. Muir, Helen. "PW." *Carrell*, 13: 19-20 (1972).

Wylie, Max. "PW Memorial Address." *Carrell*, 13: 21-4 (1972).

X, Malcolm. (see **Malcolm X**).

Yaffee, James. Lainoff, Seymour. "JY: Jewish Novelist of Manners." *CJF*, 27: 166-9 (Sp 69).

Yerby, Frank. Moore, J.B. "The Guilt of the Victim: Racial Themes in Some of FY's Novels." *JPC*, 8: 746-56 (1975).

Turner, D.T. "FY as Debunker." *MR*, 9: 569-77 (1968).

Young, Al. Bolling, Douglass. "Artistry and Theme in AY's *Snakes*." *NALF*, 8: 223-5 (Su 74).

O'Brien, John. "Dance of Life: An Interview with AY." *NOR*, 3: 328-31 (1973).

Schmitz, Neil. "AY's *Snakes*: Words to the Music." *Paunch*, 35: 3-9 (F 72).

Young, Brigham. Jessee, D.C. "The Writings of BY." *Western Hist Q*, 4: 273-94 (Jl 73).

Young, Marguerite. Durand, Regis. "La fabrique de la fiction: lecture roman de MY, *Miss MacIntosh, My Darling*." *Caliban*, 12: 45-60 (1975).

McEvilly, Wayne. "The Philosopher Without Answers: A Look at Metaphysics and MY." *STC*, 3: 73-81 (Sp 69).

Young, Stark. McAlexander, Hubert, Jr. "William Faulkner—The Young Poet in SY's *The Torches Flare*." *AL*, 43: 647-9 (Je 72).

Pilkington, John. "Letters of a Southern Drama Critic." *Y/T*, 4: 42-53 (1973).

Young, Stark. "Chapters from a Book of Memories." *VQR*, 24: 217-24 (1948).

————. "More Chapters from a Book of Memories." *VQR*, 24: 558-73 (1948).

Young, T.D. "The Past in the Present: Another Look at *So Red the Rose*." *NMW*, 1: 6-17 (Sp 68).

Zangwill, Israel. Shumsky, N.L. "Z's *The Melting Pot*: Ethnic Tensions on the Stage." *AQ*,27: 29-41 (Mr 75).

Winehouse, Bernard. "IZ's *Children of the Ghetto*: A Literary History of the First Anglo-Jewish Best-Seller." *ELT*, 16: 93-117 (#2 73).

———. "IZ's 'The King of Schnorrers.'" *SSF*, 10: 227-33 (Su 73).

Zugsmith, Leane. Josephson, Matthew. "LZ: The Social Novel of the Thirties." *SoR*, 11: 53-52 (Jl 75).

Zukofsky, Louis. Carruth, Hayden. "The Only Way to Get There from Here." *JML*, 4: 8-90 (S 74).

Charters, Samuel. "Essay Beginning 'All.'" *MPS*, 3: 241-50 (#6 73).

Cox, Kenneth. "The Poetry of LZ: A." *Agenda*, 9: 4-10 (Fa-Wi 71/2).

Davenport, Guy. "Z's 'A'-24." *Parnassus*, 2: 15-24 (1974).

Dembo, L.S. "The 'Objectivist' Poet (LZ)." *ConL*, 10: 203-1 (Sp 69).

———. "LZ: Objectivist Poetics and the Quest for Form." *AL*, 44: 74-96 (Mr 72).

Duddy, T.A. "The Measure of LZ." *MPS*, 3: 250-6 (#6 73).

Kenner, Hugh. "Bottom on Z." *MLN*, 90: 921-2 (1975).

Raffel, Burton. "No Tidbit Love You Outdoors Far as Bier: Z's *Catullus*." *Arion*, 8: 435-45 (Au 69).

Spann, Marcella. "The Z Papers." *LCUT*, 2: 49-59 (N 70).

Suter, Anthony. "Basil Bunting et deux poètes américaines: LZ et William Carlos Williams."*Caliban*, 8: 151-7 (1972).

Yanella, P.R. "On LZ." *JML*, 4: 74-87 (Sp 74).

Zukofsky, Louis. "Addenda to Prepositions: The Collected Critical Essays." *JML*, 4: 19-108 (1974).

Zweig, Paul. Guimond, James. "Moving Heaven and Earth." *Parnassus*, 1: 106-15 (1972).

American Literature

Aims and Methods. Anon. "The Professional Viewpoint." *TCS*, 1: 109-30 (N 69).

Aldridge, A.O., and Shunsuke Kamei. "Problems and Vistas of Comparative Literature and the United States: A Dialogue." *Mosaic*, 5: 149-53 (Su 72).

Anderson, D.D. "The Artist in America." *UCQ*, 14: 10-5 (1968).

Angoff, Charles. Reflections Upon Aspects of American Literature." *LitR*, 10: 5-17 (Au 66).

Arthur, R.A. "Relevance, Authority and the Case for Pleasure." *CEA*, 33: 18-22 (My 71).

Bacon, J.D. "Is American Literature Bourgeois?" *NAR*, 179: 105-17 (Jl 04).

Behar, Jack. "Notes on Literature and Culture." *CentR*, 18: 197-220 (1974).

Brooks, Cleanth. "The Current State of American Literature." *SoR*, 9: 273-87 (Ja 73).

Clark, Edward. "Studying and Teaching Afro-American Literature." *CLAJ*, 16: 96-105 (S 72).

Crews, Frederick. "Do Literary Studies Have an Ideology?" *PMLA*, 85: 423-8 (My 70).

Davis, R.B. "The American Dream." *Faculty Stud Carson-Newman Col*, 1: 5-11 (1966).

Dorson, R.M. "The Identification of Folklore in American Literature." *JAF*, 70: 1-8, 21-3 (1957).

Eble, K.E. "Literature Is Where It's At." *BRMMLA*, 24: 37-48 (1970).

Emerson, Donald. "The Remaking of 'American Literature.'" *TWA*, 60: 45-51 (1972).

Escarpit, Robert, et al. "The Teaching of British and American Literature in Foreign Universities." *TLS*, 12 S 68, pp. 965 ff.

Etulain, R. "Research Opportunities in Western Literary History." *Western Hist Q*, 4: 263-72 (Jl 73).

Falke, Wayne. "The Necessity for Internationalism in American Literary Study." *UCQ*, 19: 23-32 (1973).

Farrison, W.E. "What American Negro Literature Exists and Who Should Teach It?" *CLAJ*, 13: 374-81 (1970).

Fites, Gilbert. "A Parade of Circusana." *Serif*, 5: 30-3 (1968).

Fleming, R.E. "Black Literature Programs—Special Problems of the Rocky Mountains." *BRMMLA*, 26: 108-12 (1972).

Ford, N.A. "Attitudes and Actions of English Departments Toward the Promotion of Black Studies." *Bul Assn Departments of English*, 35: 22-7 (1972).

Franklin, Bruce. "Reply: On Hearing from Professors of the American Empire." *CE*, 32: 219-25 (N 70).

———. "The Teaching of Literature in the Highest Academies of the Empire." *CE*, 31: 548-57 (Mr 70).

Garrison, J.M. "Teaching Early American Literature: Some Suggestions." *CE*, 31: 487-97 (1970).

Gerould, Katherine. "The Extirpation of Culture." *Atl*, 116: 445-55 (O 15).

Grumbach, Doris. "Literary Prospects." *NYTBR*, 16 N 75, pp. 68, 70, 72.

Hague, J.A., and Diane Lea. "Revolution in American Education: A Bibliographical Essay." *AmS*, 13: 11-9 (#1 74).

Haines, R.E. "Alfred Stieglitz and the New Order of Consciousness in American Literature." *PCP*, 6: 26-34 (1971).

Hedges, W.L. "Towards a Theory of American Literature, 1765-1800." *EAL*, 4: 5-14 (1969).

Horrell, Joe. "The Graduate Approach." *SoR*, 6: 247-54 (1940).

Hyde, F.E. "A Plea for Noble Ideals in American Literature." *Education*, 30: 481-93 (Ap 10).

Johnson, Curt. " 'My Culture Agency Problem—and Years.' " *Smith*, 11: 74-8 (My 70).

Jones, H.M. "Scholarship and Relevance." *SHR*, 4: 1-16 (1970).

Katz, Seymour. " 'Culture' and Literature in American Studies." *AQ*, 20: 318-29 (1968).

Keller, Karl, and David Wilson. "Strategies for Americanists." *EAL*, 8: 210-2 (Wi 73).

Kennedy, J.G. "A Radical Outlook for Literary Studies." *CE*, 32: 225-36 (N 70).

Kessel, Barbara. "Free, Classless, and Urbane." *CE*, 31: 531-40 (Mr 70).

Klotman, P.R. "An Approach to the Teaching of Black Literature." *CEA*, 34: 12-5 (Ja 72).

Kolb, H.H. "In Search of Definition: American Literary Realism and the Cliches." *ALR*, 2: 165-73 (Su 69).

Kuklick, Bruce. "Myth and Symbol in American Studies." *AQ*, 24: 435-50 (O 72).

Levin, Harry. "Pseudoxia Academica." *SoR*, 6: 263-9 (1940).

Levine, Carl. "Literature and Social Relevance." *BRMMLA*, 24: 25-32 (1970).

Marx, Leo. "American Studies: A Defense of an Unscientific Method." *NLH*, 1: 75-90 (O 69).

Materassi, Mario. "La faccia nascosta della letteratura nordamericana." *Ponte*, 24: 62-78 (1968).

Murry, J.M. "England and America: A Literary Comparsion." *NRep*, 24: 41-3 (8 S 20).

Nikolyukin, A.N. "Past and Present Discussions of American National Literature." *NLH*, 4: 575-90 (Sp 73).

———. "Psychography—A 'New Method' in American Literary Studies." *SovL*, 1: 155-7 (1964).

O'Brien, M.C. "A Variation on the Southern Literature Course: Civil War Literature." *Notes on Teaching Eng*, 1: 4-6 (#2 74).

Plumstead, A.W. "Defining American Romance." *HSL*, 3: 144-9 (1971).

Purves, A.C. "Life, Death, and the Humanities." *CE*, 31: 558-64 (Mr 70).

Robertson, D.W. "Some Observations on Method in Literary Studies." *NLH*, 1: 21-33 (1969).

Shaw, Peter. "The American Heritage and its Guardians." *ASch*, 45: 7333-51 (Wi 75-76).

Shockley, M.S. "The Teacher in American Literature." *SCB*, 31: 218-20 (1971).

Sisk, J.P. "Making it in America." *Atl*, 224: 63-8 (D 69).

Slochower, Harry. "The Psychoanalytic Approach to Literature: Some Pitfalls and Promises." *L&P*, 21: 107-11.

Spiller, R.E. "The Fulbright Program in American Studies Abroad: Retrospect and Prospect." *AmS*, 9: 9-16 (Au 70).

———. "Unity and Diversity in the Study of American Culture." *AQ*, 25: 611-8 (D 73).

States, B.O. "The Idea of the Humanities." *SoR*, 6: 267-74 (Ja 70).

Tate, Allen. "Literature as Knowledge: Comment and Comparison." *SoR*, 6: 255-62 (1940).

Tucker, H.St.G. "What Is Wrong with American Literature?" *SAQ*, 14: 47-52 (Ja 15).

Turco, Lewis. "American Literature as Something Else." *Eng Rec*, 23: 10-20 (#3 73).

Venezky, R.L. "Computer Aided Humanities Research at the University of Wisconsin." *C&H*, 3: 129-38 (Ja 69).

Yoder, R.A. "The Equilibrist Perspective: Towards a Theory of American Romanticism." *SRom*, 12: 705-40 (Fa 73).

West, R.H. "Literature and Knowledge." *GaR*, 25: 125-44 (Su 74).

Bibliography: Elias, R.H. "Bibliography and the Biographer." *LC*, 38: 25-44 (1972).

Farmer, David. "The Bibliographical Potential of a 20th Century Literary Agent's Archive: The Pinker Papers." *LCUT*, 2: 26-35 (N 70).

Katz, Joseph. "Bibliography and the Rise of Literary Realism." *SAF*, 2: 75-88 (1974).

Rees, R.A. "Toward a Bibliography of the Bible in American Literature." *BB*, 29: 101-8 (Jl-S 72).

Tanselle, G.T. "The Periodical Literature of English and American Bibliography." *SB*, 26: 167-91 (1973).

Verner, Mathilde. "Johann Albert Fabricius, Eighteenth-Century Scholar and Bibliographer." *PBSA*, 60: 281-326 (3Q 66).

Wolf, Edwin. "Historical Grist for the Bibliographical Mill." *SB*, 25: 29-40 (1972).

Bibliography: Serial. Anon. "Anglo-French/Franco-American Studies." *Romanic R*, annually, 1937-1949; *French American R*, annually, 1949-1950.

———. "Bibliography of Mississippi Writers." *NMW*, annually, 1968-.

———. "A Bibliography on the Relations of Literature and the Other Arts." *HSL*, annually, 1953-.

———. "Recent Articles." *Western Hist Q*, quarterly, 1974-.

———. "A Selective and Critical Bibliography of Studies in Prose Fiction." *JEGP*, annually.

Bailey, Peter. "Black Round Up: Black Theatre in America." *BlackW*, passim, 1970-.

Baum S.V. "Present Day English." *AS*, quarterly.

Beebe, Maurice, et al. "Annual Review Number." *JML*, annually, 1970-.

Bennett, J.R., and Linda Strafstrom. "English and American Prose Style: A Bibliography of Criticism." *Style*, annuallly, 1967-.

Bonner, J.W. "Bibliography of Georgia Authors." *GaR*, passim, 1968-.

Bowen, J.K., et al., "A Review of Current Scholarship in the Field of American Literature." *Am Lit Abstracts,* twice yearly, 1967-.

Bradshaw, H.C., et al. "Review of North Carolina Fiction." *NCHR*, passim, 1969-.

Bullen, J.S., et al. "Annual Bibliography of Studies in Western American Literature." *WAL*, annually, winter, 1967-.

Carpenter, C.A. "'Modern Drama Studies: An Annual Bibliography." *MD*, annually, 1969-.

Clareson, T.D., et al. "An Annotated Bibliography of Critical Writings Dealing with Science Fiction." *Extrapolation*, passim, 1970-.

Clarke, D.A., and H.J. Heaney. "A Selective Check List of Bibliographical Scholarship." *SB*, annually since 1950-51.

Clarke, I.F., "'Voices Prophesying War': Problems in Research." *Extrapolation*, 9: 26-32 (My 68).

Ellsworth, S.G., et al. "Recent Articles . . . Literature, Music, and Art." *WHQ*, quarterly, 1970-.

Frey, J.R. "Anglo-German Literary Bibliography for 1969." *JEGP*, annually, 1962-.

Gillmor, D.M. "Articles on Mass Communication in U.S. and Foreign Journals." *JQ*, quarterly.

Halsell, W.D. "A Bibliography of Theses and Dissertations Relating to Mississippi." *JMiH*, annually, 1954-.

Haskell, J.D. and R.G. Shedd. "Modern Drama: A Selective Bibliography." *MD*, annually, 1960—.

Heaney, H.J. "A Selective Check List of Bibliographical Scholarship: United States." *SB*, annually, 1968-.

Hollis C.C., Kimball King, et al. "Research in Progress." *AL*, quarterly, 1931-.

———. "Articles on American Literature Appearing in Current Periodicals." *AL*, quarterly, 1931-.

Hoyle, B.W. "Review of North Carolina Nonfiction." *NCHR*, passim, 1968-.

Johnson, A.E. "Doctoral Projects in Progress in Theatre Arts." *ETJ*, annually, May, 1968—.

Lawson, R.H., et al. "Current Bibliography." *TCL*, quarterly, 1955-.

Luke, M.H., et al. "Articles in American Studies." *AQ*, annually, 1954-.

Lyon, T.J. "Research in Western American Literature." *WAL*, annually, winter, 1967-.

Marcell, E.W. "Writings on the Theory and Teaching of American Studies." *AQ*, annually, 1969-.

Meserole, Harrison, Jackson R. Bryer, et al. "Bibliography of Books and Articles on American Literature." *PMLA*, annually.

Pady, Donald. "Annual Bibliography of Studies in Midwestern Literature." *MidAmerica*, annually, 1975-.

Powell, D.M. "Current Arizona Bibliography." *ArQ*, annually, 1967-.

Powell, W.S. "North Carolina Bibliography." *NCHR*, annually, 1968-.

Reeves, Paschal. "A Checklist of Scholarship on Southern Literature." *MissQ*, annually, spring, 1968-.

Schatzberg, Walter, et al. "Relations of Literature and Science: A Bibliography of Scholarship." *Clio*, annually, 1970-.

Schultz, A.R., et al. "Bibliography Americana Germanica." *AGR*, annually, 1950-.

Shipley, J.B. "Abstracts of Studies in American Literature." *AES*, monthly, 1958-.

Simmons, M.E. "Folklore Bibliography." *SFQ*, annually, 1960-.

Towns, S. and C.L. Roberts. "A Bibliography of Speech and Theatre in the South." *SSCJ*, annually, 1955-.

Wrenn, J.H., et al. "American Studies Dissertations in Progress." *AQ*, annually, 1957-.

Wright, Elizabeth, et al. "Bibliography of short fiction." *SSF*, annually, summer, 1963-.

Bibliography: Special. Anon. "American Studies in India: Selected Articles Appearing in Indian Periodicals During 1966-67." *IJAS*, 1: 143-52 (1969).

———. "Check-List of the Paul Hamilton Hayne Library." *Duke Un Lib Bul*, 2: 1-109 (1930).

———. "Doctoral Dissertations (Completed and in Progress) on American Subjects by Indian Scholars." *IJAS*, 1: 123-30 (1969).

———. "Selected Bibliography of American Indian Writing." *SDR*, 9: 197-9 (Su 71).

———. "Theses on American Topics in Progress and Completed at British Universities." *JAmSt*, 4: 107-22 (Jl 70); 6: 109-28 (Ap 72); 8: 131-51 (Ap 74).

Adams, T.R. "Bibliotheca Americana: A Merry Maze of Changing Concepts." *PBSA*, 63: 247-60 (4Q 69).

Alsmeyer, H.L. "A Preliminary Southwestern Reconnaissance." *SwAL*, 1: 67-71 (1971).

Andrews, C.A. "The Literature of the Middle West: A Beginning Bibliography." *Great Lakes Rev*, 1: 35-67 (#1 74).

Andrews, T.F. "'Ho! For Oregona and California!': An Annotated Bibliography of Published Advice to the Emigrant, 1841-1847." *PULC*, 30: 41-64 (1971).

Balliet, C.A. "White on Black: Check List of Poetry by White Americans About the Black Experience, 1708-1970." *BNYPL*, 75: 424-64 (N 71).

Barnes, T.M. "Loyalist Newspapers of the American Revolution 1763-1783: A Bibliography." *PAAS*, 83: 217-40 (1973).

Barry, R.M. "American Religious Thought: A Bibliographical Essay." *ABR*, 22: 257-85 (1971).

Bassett, T.D.S. "A List of New England Bibliographies." *NEQ*, 44: 278-300 (Je 71).

Bennett, J.R. "American Literature and the Acquisitive Society, Background and Criticism: A Bibliography." *BB*, 30: 175-84 (O-D 73).

———. "The Dramatic Monologue in Britain and the United States: A Selected Bibliography." *CP*, 5: 57-70 (1972).

———. "Style in Twentieth Century British and American Fiction: A Bibliography." *WCR*, 2: 43-51 (Wi 68).

Benton, R.M. "An Annotated Check List of Puritan Sermons Published in America before 1700." *BNYPL*, 74: 286-337 (My 70).

Bercovitch, Sacvan, et al. "Selective Check-list on Typology." *EAL*, 5: 1-76 (1970).; 6, 1-80 (1971).

Bergholtz, H.N.M. "Strindberg's Anthologies of American Humorists, Bibliographical Identified." *SS*, 43: 335-43 (Wi 71).

Blake, Forrester. "Bibliography for Westerners." *Rendezvous*, 2: 33-42 (1968).

Bonner, Thomas. "A Bibliographical Introduction to the American Literature of the 1930's and the Backgrounds." *BB*, 31: 57-66, 70 (Ap-Je 74).

Boswell, J.C. "A Check List of Americana in a *Short-Title Catalogue of Books Printed in England, Scotland, & Ireland and of English Books Printed Abroad 1475-1640.*" *EAL*, 9: 3-124 (1974).

Bowe, Forrest. "A Ghost in the Streeter *Bibliography of Texas.*" *PBSA*, 65: 398-9 (4Q 71).

Brignano, R.C. "Autobiographical Books by Black Americans: A Bibliography of Works Written Since the Civil War." *NALF*, 7: 148-56 (Wi 73).

Bristol, R.P. "American Bibliographical Notes." *PAAS*, 82: 45-53 (1972).

———. "American Bibliographical Notes: Additions and Corrections to Evans and to Bristol's Supplement Thereto." *PAAS*, 83: 261-76 (1973).

Bruccoli, Matthew. "British Resources for the Study of American Literature." *JAmSt*, 6: 354-56 (1972).

Bullins, E. "Black Theatre Groups: A Directory." *TDR*, 12: 172-5 (Su 68).

Burns, L.C. "A Cross-Reference Index of Short Fiction and Author-Title Listings." *SSF*, 7: 1-218 (Wi 70).

Carlock, M.S. "Writings about the Autobiography: A Selective Bibliography." *BB*, 26: 1-2 (Ja-Mr 69).

Carlson, A.W. "A Bibliography of the Geographers' Contributions to Understanding the American Southwest (Arizona and New Mexico), 1920-1971." *ArQ*, 28: 101-41 (1972).

Cary, Richard. "American Literary Manuscripts in the Colby College Library: A Checklist." *RALS*, 5: 217-40 (Au 75).

Cazden, R.E. "The Provision of German Books in America during the Eighteenth Century." *Libri* (Copenhagen), 23: 81-108 (1973).

Clancy, J.T. "Native American References: A Cross-Indexed Bibliography of Seventeenth Century American Imprints Pertaining to American Indians." *PAAS*, 83: 287-341 (1973).

Cohen, E.G. "Afro-American Periodicals." *HussR*, 5: 28-37 (1971).

Cook, M.E., and T.D. Young. "Fugitive/Agrarian Materials at Vanderbilt University." *RALS*, 1: 113-70 (Sp 72).

Corrigan, R.A. "Afro-American Fiction: A Checklist, 1853-1970." *MASJ*, 11: 114-35 (Fa 70).

———. "Afro-American Fiction: Errata and Additions." *AmS*, 12: 69-73 (Sp 71).

———. "Afro-American Fiction Since 1970." *AmS*, 14: 85-90 (Fa 73).

———. "Bibliography of Afro-American Fiction: 1853-1970." *SBL*, 1: 51-86 (1970).

Covo, Jacqueline. "Ralph Ellison in France: Bibliographic Essays and Checklist of French Criticism, 1954-1971." *CLAJ*, 16: 519-26 (Je 73).

Cutsumbis, M.N. "Selective Bibliography for the Sociological Study of Greek Americans." *BB*, 25: 191-2 (S-D 68).

Bibliography: Special

Davis, C.E., and M.B. Hudson. "Humor of the Old Southwest: A Checklist of Criticism." *MissQ*, 27: 179-99 (Sp 74).

Davis, R.M. "An Annotated Checklist for Students of Allegory in Modern Fiction." *Genre*, 5: 169-75 (D 72).

Donelson, K.L. "Some Adolescent Novels about the West: An Annotated Bibliography." *Elem Eng*, 49: 735-9 (My 72).

Duke, Maurice. "*The Reviewer*: A Bibliographical Guide to a Little Magazine." *RALS*, 1: 58-103 (Sp 71).

Elliott, William. "Minnesota North Country Poetry: A Bibliography." *Soc for Stud Midwestern Lit*, 4: 8-10 (1974).

Engle, Cary. "The Atkinson Collection of Ethiopian Drama at the University of Chicago." *RALS*, 1: 181-99 (Au 71).

Ersiman, Fred. "American Regional Juvenile Literature, 1870-1910: An Annotated Bibliography." *ALR*, 6: 109-22 (sp 73).

Etulain, R.W. "Western American Literature: A Selective Annotated Bibliography." *Rendezvous*, 7: 67-78 (1972).

Fabre, G.E. "A Checklist of Original Plays, Pageants, Rituals and Musicals by Afro-American Authors Performed in the United States from 1960-1973." *BlackW*, 23: 81-97 (1974).

Farrell, N.L. "A Subject Index to *The Theatre Annual*, 1942-1969." *ThDoc*, 2: 125-34 (1969-70).

Fine, D.M. "Immigrant Ghetto Fiction, 1885-1918: An Annotated Bibliography." *ALR*, 6: 169-95 (Su 73).

Flanagan, J.T. "A Midwest Bibliography." *NLB*, Supp: 3 (Je 47).

Fleck, R.F., and Robert Campbell. "A Selective Literary Bibliography of Wyoming." *An of Wyoming*, 46: 75-112 (Sp 74).

Frank, F.S. "The Gothic Novel: A Checklist of Modern Criticism." *BB*, 30: 45-54 (Ap-Je 73).

Fraser, J.H. "Indian Mission Printing in New Mexico: A Bibliography." *NMHR*, 43: 31-8 (O 68).

Free, W.J. "American Fiction in the *Columbian Magazine*, 1786-1792." *BB*, 25: 150-1 (My-Ap 68).

Gibson, M.D. "The Western: A Selective Bibliography." *JPC*, 7: 743-8 (Wi 73).

Gildez, R.B., assisted by A.B. Cameron. "Seventeenth-Century Americana." *SCN*, 27: 71-5 (1969).

Graham, J.D. "Negro Protest in America, 1900-1955: A Bibliographical Guide." *SAQ*, 67: 94-107 (Wi 68).

Graves, M.P. "A Checklist of Extant Quaker Sermons, 1650-1700." *QH*, 63: 53-9 (1974).

Green, R.B. "A Checklist of Mystery, Detective, and Suspense Fiction Published in the U.S., October-December 1973." *ArmD*, 7: 125-7 (1974).

Hague, J.A., and Diane Lea. "Revolution in American Education: A Bibliographical Essay." *AMS*, 13: 11-9 (#1 74).

Harper, Howard. "General Studies of Recent American Fiction: A Selected Checklist." *MFS*, 19: 127-33 (Sp 73).

Harris, M.H. "American Librarians as Authors: A Bibliography of Bibliographies." *BB*, 30: 143-6 (O-D 73).

Helmick, Evelyn. "Florida's Literature." *Carrell*, 14: 1-15 (1974).

Hendrick, George. "A Checklist of American Literary Manuscripts in Australia, Canada, India, Israel, Japan, and New Zealand." *BB*, 29: 84-6, 92 (Jl-S 72).

Hill, Gertrude. "The Southwest in Verse: A Selective Bibliography of Arizona and New Mexico Poetry." *ArQ*, 23: 306-12 (Wi 67).

Holland, R.A. "Texas and the Great War: The West and Dittmar Collections." *LCUT*, 6: 43-5 (1974).

Houston, H.R. "Contributions of the American Negro to American Culture: A Selected Checklist." *BB*, 26: 71-83 (Jl-S 69).

Inge, M.T. "Unamuno's Correspondence with North Americans: A Checklist." *Hispania*, 53: 277-85 (My 70).

Jaffe, H.J. "American Negro Folklore: A Check List of Scarce Items." *SFQ*, 36: 68-70 (Mr 72).

Janssens, G.A.M. "A Critical Bibliography of America Literature." *DQR*, 3: 68-80 (1973).

Jones, L.W. "Canadian Theses and Dissertations on American Literarute: 1947-1968 Checklist." *Serif*, 8: 8-17 (1971).

————. "Canadian Graduate Studies in American Literature: A Bibliography of Theses and Dissertations, 1921-1968." *CRAS*, 1: 116-29 (Fa 70).

Jurges, Oda. "Selected Bibliography: Black Plays, Books, and Articles Related to Black Theatre Published from 1/1960 to 2/1968." *TDR*, 12: 176-80 (Su 68).

Kaganoff, N.M. "Judaica Americana." *AJHQ*, 56: 457-65; 57: 254-62 (Je, D 67).

Kaiser, Ernest. "Recent Literature on Black Liberation Struggles and the Ghetto Crisis: A Bibliographical Survey." *Sci & Soc*, 33: 168-96 (1969).

Kelly, R.G. "American Biographies for Children, 1870-1900." *ALR*, 6: 123-36 (Sp 73).

Kent, G.E. "Struggle for the Image: Selected Books By or About Blacks During 1971." *Phlyon*, 33: 304-24 (Wi 72).

Keyssar-Franke, Helene. "Afro-American Drama and Its Criticism, 1960-1972; An Annotated Check List with Appendices." *BNYPL*, 78: 276-346 (Sp 75).

Klein, C.R. "Literature for America's Roman Catholic Children (1865-1895): An Annotated Bibliography." *ALR*, 6: 137-52 (Sp 73).

Kluewer, J.D. "An Annotated Check List of Writings on Linguistics and Literature in the Sixties." *BNYPL*, 76: 36-91 (1972).

Kottwinkel, J.L., D.M. O'Connor, and B.J. Cogbill. "A Checklist of Current Theatre Arts Periodicals." *ThDoc*, 1: 3-36 (1969).

Lantz, H.R., et al. "Pre-Industrial Patterns in the Colonial Family in America: A Content Analysis of Colonial Magazines." *AmSR*, 33: 413-26 (1968).

Lemay, J.A.L. "A Calendar of American Poetry in the Colonial Newspapers and Magazines and in the Major English Magazines through 1765." *PAAS*, 79: 291-392 (O 69); 80: 71-222, 353-469 (Ap, O 70).

————. "Recent Bibliographies in Early American Literature." *EAL*, 8: 66-77 (Sp 73).

McCloskey, J.C. "American Satires, 1637-1957: A Selective Checklist." *SNL*, 10: 97-122 (1973).

McDonough, John. "Manuscript Sources for the Study of Negro Life and History." *QJLC*, 26: 126-48 (Jl 69).

McDowell, R.E., and George Fortenberry. "A Checklist of Books and Essays about American Negro Novelists." *StN*, 3: 219-36 (Su 71).

McElroy, Hilda, and R.A. Willis. "Published Works of Black Playwrights in the United States, 1960-1970." *BlackW*, 21: 92-8 (1972).

McGiffert, Michael. "American Puritan Studies in the 1960's." *WMQ*, 27: 36-67 (Fa 70).

Mangione, A.R. "The Story That Has Not Been Told: A Selective Bibliography Dealing with the Italian-American Experience." *Eng R*, 25: 25-34 (#1 73).

Miller, F.D. "Russian Response to American Literature: The Bibliography." *RALS*, 1: 247-9 (Au 71).

Bibliography: Special

Monteiro, George. "'McNaught's Monthly': Addenda to the Bibliographies of Cather, Dickinson, Fitzgerald, Hemingway, Hergesheimer and Machen." *PSBA*, 68: 64-5 (1Q 74).

Murphy, G.D. "The Debunkers: A Checklist of Revisionist Biography, 1918-1932." *BB*, 26: 106-7 (O-D 69).

Murray, D.M., Chan Waisheung, and Samuel Huang. "A Checklist of Chinese Translations of American Literature." *ABC*, 22: 15-37 (1972).

Myers, Carol. "A Selected Bibliography of Recent Afro-American Writers." *CLAJ*, 16: 377-82 (Mr 73).

Myers, J.M. "A Check-List of Items Published by the Private Press of Elbert B. Hubbard." *ABC*, 18: 22-7 (O 67).

Myerson, Joel. "An Annotated List of Contributions to the Boston *Dial*." *SB*, 26: 133-66 (1973).

———. " A Calendar of Transcendental Club Meetings." *AL*, 44: 197-207 (My 72).

———. "A Union List of the *Dial* (1840-1844) and Some Information about Its Sales." *PBSA*, 67: 322-8 (3Q 73).

Nagel, James. "An Annotated Bibliography of Selected Recent Books on American Fiction." *SAF*, 1: 76-91 (Sp 73).

Nolan, P.T. "Georgia Drama Between the Wars (1870-1916): A Check List." *GHQ*, 51: 216-30 (Je 67).

Novak, E.G. "*New Masses*: Five Yearly Indexes of Poetry, Fiction, Criticism, Drama and Reviews for the Years 1929-33." *BB*, 28: 89-108 (Jl-S 71).

Olmstead, Duncan. "A Check List of Book Club Publications." *Bk Club Calif Q N*, 39: 51-61 (Su 74).

Paluka, Frank. "American Literary Manuscripts in the University of Iowa: A Checklist." *RALS*, 3: 100-20 (Sp 73).

Payne, J.R. "The Thomas Winthrop Streeter Collection of Americana." *ABC*, 18: 27-8; 19: 10-6 (My, S 68).

Peavy, Linda. "A Bibliography of Providence Players' Dramas, 1915-1922." *PBSA*, 69: 569-75 (4Q 75).

Peterson, R.K. "Indians in American Literature." *BB*, 30: 42-4 (Ja-Mr 73).

Polk, Noel. "Guide to Dissertations on American Literary Figures, 1870-1910." *ALR*, 8: 177-28, 291-348 (Su, Au 75).

Putnam, Margaret, Marvin Williams, and J.T. Cox. "Textual Studies in the Novel: A Selected Checklist, 1950-74." *StN*, 7: 445-71 (Fa 75).

Querry, Ronald, and R.E. Fleming. "A Working Bibliography of Black Periodicals." *SBL*, 3: 31-6 (Su 72).

Quinn, D.B. "A List of Books Purchased for the Virginia Company." *VMHB*, 77: 347-60 (Jl 69).

Raina, M.L. "Marxism and Literature— A Select Bibliography." *CE*, 34: 308-14 (1972).

Rees, R.A. "Towards a Bibliography of the Bible in American Literature, *BB*, 101-8 (Jl-S 72).

———, and Marjorie Griffin. "Index and Author Guide to the *Family Companion* (1841-1843)." *SB*, 25: 205-12 (1972).

Roemer, K.M. "American Utopian Literature (1888-1900); An Annotated Bibliography." *ALR*, 4: 227-54 (Su 71).

Rogal, S.J. "A Checklist of Eighteenth-Century British Literature Published in Eighteenth-Century America." *CLQ*, 10: 231-56 (1973).

Rosenfeld, A.H. "Yiddish Poets and Playwrights of America: A Preliminary Report on a Recent Addition to the Harris Collection." *BBr*, 22: 161-81 (1968).

Sanders, J.B. "Black Literature for Children and Young Adults Published in 1971." *NALF*, 7: 3-15 (Sp 73).

Sandoval, Ralph, and A.P. Nilsen. "The Mexican-American Experience." *EJ*, 63: 61-3 (Ja 74).

Sayre, R.F. "A Bibliography and an Anthology of American Indian Literature." *CE*, 35: 7046 (Mr 74).

Schatzberg, Walter. "Relations of Literature and Science: A Bibliography of Scholarship, 1973-1974." *Clio*, 5: 97-121 (Fa 75).

Schilling, Hanna-Beate. "The Role of the Brothers Schlegel in American Literary Criticism as Found in Selected Periodicals, 1812-1833: A Critical Bibliography." *AL*, 43: 563-79 (Ja 72).

Shipton, C.K. "Bibliotheca Americana.'" *PBSA*, 62: 351-9 (3Q 68).

Shpall, Leo. "A List of Selected Items of American-Jewish Interest in the Russian-Jewish Press." *PAJHS*, 38: 239-48 (Mr 49).

Silet, C.L.P. "A Check List of *The Seven Arts*." *Serif*, 9: 15-21 (1972).

Sloane, K.W. "Plays About Louisiana, 1870-1915: A Checklist." *LaStud*, 8: 26-35 (Sp 69).

Smith, J.C. "Developing Collections of Black Literature." *BlackW*, 18-29 (1971).

Smith, W.F. "American Indian Literature." *EJ*, 63: 68-72 (Ja 74).

Soderbergh. "Bibliographical Essay: The Negro in Juvenile Series Books." *JNH*, 58: 179-86 (Ap 73).

Sollers, Werner. "Black Studies in the United States: A Bibliography." *JA*, 16: 213-22 (1971).

Spalding, Phinizy. "Some Sermons Before the Trustees of Colonial Georgia." *GHQ*, 57: 332-46 (1973).

Spears, J.E. "Notes on Negro Folk Speech." *NCaF*, 18: 154-7 (N 70).

Spingarn, A.B. "Books by Negro Authors in 1967." *Crisis*, 75: 81-7, 99-101 (Mr 68).

Stagg, L.C. and J.L. Dasley. "Special Collections on Southern Culture in College and University Libraries." *HisS*, 26: 3-10 (Sp 67).

Stoddard, R.E. "A Catalogue of Books and Pamphlets Unrecorded in Oscar Wegelin's *Early American Poetry*, 1650-1820." *BBR*, 23: 1-84 (1969).

———. "Further Addenda to Wegelin's *Early American Poetry*." *PBSA*, 65: 169-72 (2Q 71).

Sumpter, C.G. "The Negro in Twentieth-Century American Drama: A Bibliography." *ThDoc*, 3: 3-27 (Fa-Sp 70-71).

Theodore, Terry. "Civil War Drama, 1878-1900." *LH*, 75: 115-22 (Fa 73).

Van Brunt, Thomas. "A Selected Bibliography of Handbooks and Textbooks on Procedures, Materials, and Maintenance in the Theatre Scene Shop." *ThDoc*, 3: 61-3 (1970).

Walz, Eugene P. "Recent Film Satire: A Checklist." *SNL*, 10: 85-100 (Fa 72).

Weber, F.J. "A Bibliography of California Bibliographies." *SCQ*, Mr 68, pp. 5-32.

Welch, D'Alte A. "A Bibliography of American Children's Books Printed Prior to 1821, Parts S—Z." *PAAS*, 77: 281-535 (O 67).

White, William. "Additions to Clarence Gohdes, *Literature and Theater of the States and Regions of the U.S.A.*" *An Historical Bibliography*." *BB*, 26: 2 (Ja-Mr 69).

Whitlow, Roger. "The Harlem Renaissance and After: A Checklist of Black Literature in the Twenties and Thirties." *NALF*, 7: 143-6 (Wi 73).

Whitmire, G.E. "Bibliography [of Afro-American writings]." *JNE*, 33: 421-35 (Fa 64).

Williams, Ora. "A Bibliography of Works Written by American Black Women." *CLAJ*, 15: 35477 (Mr 72).

Willis, R.A., and Hilda McElroy. "Published Works of Black Playwrights in the United States, 1960-1970." *BlackW*, 21: 92-8 (Ap 72).

Wodke, Repplinger, Ilse. "Deutsche amerikakundliche Veröffentlichungen." *JA*, 17: 216-34 (1972).

Wolf, Edwin. "Colonial American Playbills." *PMHB*, 97: 99-106 (1973).

———. "Evidence Indicating the Need for Some Bibliographical Analysis of American-Printed Historical Works." *PBSA*, 63: 261-77 (4Q 69).

Yellin, J.F. "An Index of Literary Materials in The Crisis, 1910-1934." *CLAJ*, 14: 452-65; 15: 197-234 (Je, D 71).

Bibliography: Textual and Critical. Aderman, R.M. "The Editors' Intentions in the Washington Irving Letters." *CEAAN*, 3: 23-4 (1970).

Allen, R.R. "The First Six Volumes of the Northwestern-Newberry Melville." *Proof*, 3: 441-53 (1973).

Anderson, Frederick. "Normalization and Silent Emendation." *CEAAN*, 3: 19-21 (Je 70).

———. "Team Proofreading: Some Problems." *CEAAN*, 2: 15 (1969).

Baender, Paul. "Is Silent Normalizaton Justifiable?" *CEANN*, 3: 18 (Je 70).

———. "Reflections Upon the CEAA by a Departing Editor." *RALS*, 4: 131-44 (Au 74).

Barnes, Warner, and J.T. Cox. "The Center for Editions of American Authors: A Forum on Its Editions and Practices." *StN*, 7: 389-90 (Fa 75).

Bebb, Bruce, and Hershel Parker. "Freehafer on Greg and the CEAA: Secure Footing and 'Substantial Shortfalls.'" *StN*, 7: 391-3 (Fa 75).

Belknap, G.K. "Addenda to Belknap, Oregon Imprints." *PBSA*, 63: 128-9 (2Q 69); 64: 213-34 (2Q 70).

Bennett, J.Q. "... and Other Detachable Coverings...." *Serif*, 8: 31-33 (1971).

Bernadin, C.W. "John Dos Passos' Textual Revisions." *PBSA*, 48: 95-6 (1Q 54).

Birch, Brian. "Henry James: Some Biographical and Textual Matters." *Lib*, 20: 108-23 (1965).

Black, M.L. "Bibliographical Problems in Washington Irving's Early Works." *EAL*, 3: 148-5 (Wi 68-9).

Bowers, Fredson. "The New Look in Editing." *SAB*, 25: 3-10 (Ja 70).

———. "Remarks on Eclectic Texts." *Proof*, 4: 31-76 (1974).

Brack, O.M. "The Centenary Hawthorne Eight Years Later." *Proof*, 1: 358-67 (1971).

Branch, W.G. "The Genesis, Composition, and Structure of *The Confidence-Man*." *NCF*, 27: 424-53 (1973).

Bruccoli, M.J. "A Few Missing Words." *PMLA*, 86: 587-9 (1971).

———. "The SCADE Series: Apparatus for Definitive Editions." *PBSA*, 67: 431-6 (O-D 73).

Budd, L.J. "Baxter's Hog: The Right Mascot for an Editor (with CEAA Standards) of Mark Twain's Political and Social Writings." *CEAAN*, 3: 3-10 (1970).

Cohen, E.H. "The 'Second Edition' of *The Sot-Weed Factor*." *AL*, 42: 289-303 (N 70).

Cohn, A.H. "Some Stone & Kimball Addenda: II." *PBSA*, 67: 330-41 (3Q 73).

Cox, J.T., Margaret Putnam, and Marvin Williams. "Textual Studies in the Novel: A Selected Checklist, 1950-74." *StN*, 7: 445-71 (Fa 75).

Davis, R.M. "On Editing Modern Texts: Who Should Do What, and to Whom?" *JML*, 3: 1012-20 (Ap 74).

Dearing, V.A. "Textual Criticism Today." *StN*, 7: 394-8 (Fa 75).

Ducharme, E.R. "The Evasion of the Text." *Eng Rec*, 20: 13-22 (1970).

Freehafer, John. "Greg's Theory of Copy-Text and the Textual Criticism of the CEAA Editions." *StN*, 7: 375-88 (Fa 75).

———. "How Not to Edit American Authors: Some Short-comings of the CEAA Editions." *BNYPL*, 75: 419-23 (N 71).

————. "*The Marble Faun* and the Editing of Nineteenth-Century Texts." *StN*, 2: 487-503 (Wi 70).

Gallup, Donald. "'Boobliography' and Ezra Pound." *TQ*, 10: 80-92 (1967).

Gerber, J.C. "Practical Editions: MT's *The Adventures of Tom Sawyer* and *Adventures of Huckleberry Finn*." *Proof*, 2: 285-92 (1972).

Gibson, W.M. "MT's *Mysterious Stranger* Manuscripts: Some Questions for Textual Critics." *BRMMLA*, 22: 183-91 (#4 68).

Gilman, W.H. "How Should Journals Be Edited?" *EAL*, 6: 73-83 (1971).

Grabo, N.S. "Pizer vs. Copy-Text." *BNYPL*, 75: 171-3 (Ap 71).

Harkness, Bruce. "Bibliography and the Novelistic Fallacy." *SB*, 12: 59-73 (1960).

Hayman, R.G. "Addendum to Shaw and Shoemaker: Smith's *Indian Doctor's Dispensatory*." *PBSA*, 63: 126-8 (2Q 69).

Howard-Hill, T.H. "A Practical Scheme for Editing Critical Texts with the Aid of a Computer." *Proof*, 3: 235-56 (1973).

Howell, J.M., and C.A. Lawler. "From Abercrombie & Fitch to *The First Forty-Nine Stories*: The Text of EH's 'Francis Macomber.'" *Proof*, 2: 213-81 (1972).

Izsak, E.K. "The Manuscript of *The Sound and the Fury*: The Revisions in the First Sections." *SB*, 20: 189-202 (1968).

Johnson, R.C. "Addendum to Byrd and Lincoln: Isaac A. Pool." *PBSA*, 63: 295 (4Q 69).

————. "Addendum to Harrisse: Jakob Stoppel." *PBSA*, 64: 334-6 (4Q 70).

————. "Addendum to Sabin, Shaw-Shoemaker, and Wegelin: Thomas Branagan." *PBSA*, 64: 205-6 (2Q 70).

————, and G.T. Tanselle. "The Haldeman-Julius 'Little Blue Books' as a Bibliographical Problem." *PBSA*, 64: 29-79 (1Q 70).

Johnson, Theodore. "Textual Criticism and Error." *AN&Q*, 11: 102 (1973).

Jones, J.B. "Galley Proofs in America: A Historical Survey." *Proof*, 4: 153-64 (1974).

Kable, W.S. "Addenda to Wright: Botsford's *The Spiritual Voyage*." *PBSA*, 65: 72-3 (1971).

————. "Addenda to Wright: Bundett, Curtis, Judson, Weeks." *PBSA*, 62: 452-3 (3Q 68).

————. "Addenda to Wright: Mancur, Pise, Tuthill, Weld." *PBSA*, 63: 294 (4Q 69).

————. "Addenda to Wright: William Ray's *Sophia*." *PBSA*, 64: 206 (2Q 70).

————. "The Serif Series: Bibliographies and Checklists." *Proof*, 1: 368-76 (1971).

Kallich, Martin. "John Dos Passos' Textual Revisions." *PBSA*, 48: 97-8 (1Q 54).

Katz, Joseph. "Bibliography and the Rise of American Literary Realism." *SAF*, 2: 75-88 (Sp 74).

————. "The Centenary Edition of the Works of Nathaniel Hawthorne." *NHJ*, 1: 287-9 (1971).

————. "Practical Editions: A Bad Resource for American Literary Studies." *RALS*, 3: 2219 (1973).

————. "Practical Editions: Stephen Crane's *The Red Badge of Courage*." *Proof*, 2: 301-19 (1972).

————, and J.B. Meriwether. "A Redefinition of 'Issue.'" *Proof*, 2: 61-70 (1972).

King, J.K. "Charles Nilon's *Bibliography in American Literature* and the State of Bibliography." *ALR*, 4: 292-5 (Su 71).

Kinsley, William. "Further Thoughts on Scholarly Publication." *SNL*, 7: 157-62 (1970).

Lawton, J.N. "The Authorship of Item 165 in Lyle Wright's *American Fiction, 1851-1875*." *PBSA*, 64: 83 (1Q 70).

Leary, Lewis. "Bibliography and Textual Studies and American Literary History." *TQ*, 3: 160-6 (Su 60).

————. "Troubles with Mark Twain: Some Considerations on Consistency." *SAF*, 2: 89-103 (Sp 74).

Bibliography: Textual and Critical

Lisca, Peter. "*The Hamlet*: Genesis and Revisions." *FaS*, 3: 5-13 (1954).

Lozynsky, Artem. "The Register of Current Publications in American Bibliographical and Textual Studies." *Proof*, 1: 377-416 (1971).

McCartan, E.F. "Creativity, Computers, and Copyright." *C&H*, 3: 193-204 (Mr 69).

McElderry, B.B. "Edmund Wilson's 'The Fruits of the MLA.'" *MFS*, 15: 550-56 (1969).

McHaney, T.L. "Important Questions Are Seldom Raised." *StN*, 7: 390-401 (Fa 75).

Meriwether, J.B. "The Proposed Edition of William Gilmore Simms." *MissQ*, 15: 100-12 (Su 62).

————. "Some Proofreading Precautions." *CEAAN*, 2: 17-8 (1969).

————, and Joseph Katz. "A Redefinition of 'Issue.'" *Proof*, 2: 61-70 (1972).

Meserole, H.T. "The MLA Bibliographical System: Past, Present, and Future." *PMLA*, 86: 58-6 (1971).

————. "Notes on Editing Seventeeth-Century American Poetry." *CEAAN*, 2: 11-4 (1969).

Moldenhauer, J.J. "On the Editing of *The Maine Woods*." *TJQ*, 4: 15-20 (1972).

Nebenzahl, Kenneth. "Reflections on Brinley and Streeter." *PBSA*, 64: 165-75 (1970).

Nichol, J.W. "M's 'Soiled Fish of the Sea.'" *AL*, 21: 338-9 (N 49).

Noble, R.W. "The Manuscript Drain." *NSt*, 30 Je 72, p. 915.

Nordloh, D.J. "Substantives and Accidentals vs. New Evidence: Another Strike in the Game of Distinctions." *CEAAN*, 3: 12-3 (Je 70).

————. "The Ultimate Check." *CEAAN*, 2: 18 (1969).

————. "W.D. Howells' *A Modern Instance*: Complications of Bibliographical History." *Serif*, 10: 52-4.

Parker, Hershel. "The First Nine Volumes of *A Selected Edition of W.D. Howells*." *Proof*, 2: 319-32 (1972).

————. "Historical Introduction vs. Personal Interpretations." *BNYPL*, 76: 19 (1972).

————. "In Defense of 'Copy-Text Editing.'" *BNYPL*, 75: 337-44 (1971).

————. "Melville and the Concept of 'Author's Final Intentions.'" *Proof*, 1: 156-68 (1971).

————. "Regularizing Accidentals: The Latest Form of Infidelity." *Proof*, 3: 1-62 (1973).

————. "Three MT Editions." *NCF*, 28: 225-9 (1973).

————, and Bruce Bebb. "The CEAA: An Interim Assessment." *PBSA*, 68: 129-48 (Ap-Je 74).

Peckham, Morse. "Notes on Freehafer and the CEAA Editions." *StN*, 7: 402-3 (Fa 75).

————. "Reflections on the Foundations of Modern Textual Editing." *Proof*, 1: 122-55 (1971).

Pizer, Donald. "'On the Editing of Modern American Texts': A Final Comment." *BNYPL*, 75: 504-05 (Mr 71).

Pochman,, H.A. "Copy-Editing of Irving's Journals." *CEAAN*, 2: 15 (Ja 69).

————. "An Example of Progressive Plate Deterioration." *CEAAN*, 3: 16 (Je 70).

Polk, Noel. "The Textual History of Faulkner's *Requiem for a Nun*." *Proof*, 4: 109-28 (1974).

Putnam, Margaret, Marvin Williams, and J.T. Cox. "Textual Studies in the Novel: A Selected Checklist, 1950-74." *StN*, 7: 445-71 (Fa 75).

Raina, M.L. "Marxism and Literature— A Select Bibliography." *CE*, 308-14 (1972).

Skinner, Quentin. "Motives, Intentions, and the Interpretations of Texts." *NLH*, 3: 393-408 (1972).

Smith, N.E. "Author-Identification for Six Anonymous or Pseudonymous Wright I Titles, with Wright II, Thompson, and BAL Addenda." *PBSA*, 65: 173-5 (2Q 71); 402-8 (4Q 71).

————. "Author-Identification for Six Wright I Titles: Cleveland and Doughty." *PBSA*, 65: 173-80 (1971).

Steele, O.L. "A Note on Early Impressions of Ellen Glasgow's *They Stooped to Folly*." *PBSA*, 52: 310-2 (4Q 58).

Stocker, M.W. "*Salmagundi*: Problems in Editing the So-Called First Edition (1807-08)." *PBSA*, 67: 141-58 (2Q 73).

Tanselle, G.T. "Addenda to Irish: Brown, North, and Wild.'" *PBSA*, 62: 452 (3Q 68).

————. "Bibliographical Problems in Melville." *SAF*, 2: 57-74 (Sp 74).

————. "Copyright Records and the Bibliographer." *SB*, 22: 77-124 (1969).

————. "The Descriptive Bibliography of American Authors." *SB*, 21: 1-24 (1968).

————. "Greg's Theory of Copy-Text and the Editing of American Literature." *SB*, 28: 167-29 (1975).

————. "The New Editions of Hawthorne and Crane." *BC*, 23: 214-30 (Su 74).

————. "The Periodical Literature of English and American Bibliography." *SB*, 26: 167-91 (1973).

————. "Problems and Accomplishments in Editing of the Novel." *StN*, 7: 323-60 (Fa 75).

————. "Signatures on Versos." *BC*, 18: 384 (Au 69).

————. "Some Principles for Editorial Apparatus." *SB*, 25: 41-88 (1972).

————. "Some Remarks on Bibliographical Non-Proliferation." *Proof*, 1: 169-79 (1971).

————. "The State of Reference Bibliography in American Literature." *RALS*, 1: 3-16 (Sp 61).

————. "Stone & Kimball Addenda: Blossoms' *Checkers*." *PBSA*, 62: 451-2 (3Q 68).

————. "Textual Study and Literary Judgment." *PBSA*, 65: 109-22 (2Q 71).

————. "Two Basic Distinctions: Theory and Practice, Text and Apparatus." *StN*, 7: 404-6 (Fa 75).

————. "Two Editions of Eighteenth Century Fiction." *EAL*, 6: 274-83 (1971).

Thompson, George. "Scientific Method in Textual Criticism." *Eirene*, 1: 51-60 (1972).

Thorpe, James. "The Aesthetics of Textual Criticism." *PMLA*, 80: 465-82 (1966).

Todd, W.B. "Problems in Editing Mark Twain." *BI*, 1: 3-8 (Ap 65).

Vandersee, Charles. "James' 'Pandora': The Mixed Consequences of Revision." *SB*, 21: 93-108 (1968).

Wachal, Robert. "The Machine in the Garden: Computers and Literary Scholarship." *CHum*, 5: 23-8 (1970).

Walts, R.W. "William Dean Howells and His 'Library Edition.'" *PBSA*, 52: 283-94 (4Q 58).

Welch, D.P. "How Did the *New American Practical Navigator* Navigate?" *Serif*, 7: 33-4 (1970).

Wilson, Edmund. "The Fruits of the MLA." *NYRB*, 11: 7-10 (26 S 68); 6-14 (10 O 68).

Young, R.E. "A Final Note on *The Ambassadors*." *AL*, 23: 487-90 (Ja 52).

Biography and Autobiography. Altrocchi, J.C. "California Biography in Poetry." *Pac Hist*, 15: 1-12 (Wi 71).

Bingham, E.R. "Experiments in Launching a Biography: Three Vignettes of Charles Erskine Scott Wood." *HLQ*, 35: 221-39 (1972).

Blassingame, J.W. "Black Autobiographies as History and Literature." *BSch*, 5: 20 (1973-74).

Brignano, R.C. "Autobiographical Books by Black Americans: A Bibliography of Works Written Since the Civil War." *NALF*, 7: 148-56 (Wi 73).

Bruchac, Joseph. "Black Autobiography in Africa and America." *BlaR*, 2: 61-70 (Sp-Su 71).

Carlock, M.S. "Writings about the Autobiography: A Selective Bibliography." *BB*, 26: 1-2 (Ja-Mr 69).

Cox, J.M. "Autobiography and America." *VQR*, 47: 252-77 (Sp 71).

Biography and Autobiography

Davis, C.C. "Signatures from the $2 Shelf; or, The Pursuit of the Minor Personality." *Manuscripts*, 6: 31-7 (Fa 53).

Dixon, T.F. "The Art of Autobiography in *Bound for Glory*." *SwAL*, 2: 135-43 (1972).

Elias, R.H. "Bibliography and the Biographer." *LC*, 38:25-44 (1972).

Haerle, R.K. "The Athlete as 'Moral' Leader: Heroes, Success Themes, and Basic Cultural Values in Selected Baseball Autobiographies, 1900-1970." *JPC*, 8: 392-401 (1974).

Hoffs, J.A. "Comments on Psychoanalytic Biography with Special Reference to Freud's Interest in Woodrow Wilson." *PsyR*, 56: 402-14 (1969).

Kelly, R.G. "American Biographies for Children, 1870-1900." *ALR*, 6: 123-36 (Sp 73).

Levy, L.B. "Critics, Scientists, and Biographers." *SoR*, 4: 1081-92 (1968).

Minter, David. "Faulkner and the Uses of Biography." *GaR*, 28: 455-69 (Fa 74).

Murdock, K.B. "Clio in the Wilderness: History and Biography in Puritan New England." *EAL*, 6: 201-19 (Wi 71-72).

Murphy, G.D. "The Debunkers: A Checklist of American Revisionist Biography, 1918-1932." *BB*, 26: 106-7 (O-D 69).

Nicholas, William W. "Individualism and Autobiographical Art: Frederick Douglass and Henry Thoreau." *CLAJ*, 16: 145-58 (D 72).

Rayson, A.L. "*Dust Tracks on a Road*: Zora Neale Hurston and the Form of Black Autobiography." *NALF*, 7: 39-45 (Su 73).

Shapiro, S.A. "The Dark Continent of Literature: Autobiography." *CLS*, 5: 421-54 (D 68).

Stinson, Robert. "S.S. McClure's *My Autobiography*: The Progressive as a Self-Made Man." *CEA*, 34: 20-5 (1972).

Stone, A.E. "Autobiography and American Culture." *AmSt*, 11: 22-36 (Wi 72).

———. "The Sea and the Self: Travel as Experience and Metaphor in Early American Autobiography." *Genre*, 7: 279-306 (S 74).

Van Cromphout, G.V. "Cotton Mather as Plutarchan Biographer." *AL*, 46: 465-81 (Ja 75).

Ethnic Groups. Awoonor, Kofi. "Nationalism: Masks and Consciences." *BA*, 45: 207-11 (Sp 71).

Berg, P.L. "Racism and the Puritan Mind." *Phylon*, 36: 1-7 (Mr 75).

Blickersilver, Edith. "Literature as Social Criticism: The Ethnic Woman Writer." *MLS*, 5: 46-54 (#1 75).

Brown, Joseph. "The Greening of America: Irish-American Writers." *JEthS*, 2: 71-6 (#4 75).

Cannon, Garland. "Bilingual Problems and Developments in the United States." *PMLA*, 86: 452-8 (Mr 71).

Chametsky, Jules. "Our Decentralized Literature: A Consideration on Regional, Ethnic, Racial, and Sexual Factors." *JA*, 17: 56-72 (1972).

———. "Regional Literature and Ethnic Realities." *AR*, 31:' 385-96 (Fa 71).

Conroy, Jack. "The Literary Underworld of the Thirties." *NewL*, 51-72 (#3 74).

Cornelius, Paul. "Interracial Children's Books: Problems and Progress." *LibQ*, 41: 106-27 (Ap 71).

*Cutsumbis, M.N. "Selective Bibliography for the Sociological Study of Greek Americans." *B*, 25: 191-32 (S-D 68).

DeCosta, M.S. "Social Lyricism and the Caribbean Poet/Rebel." *CLAJ*, 14: 441-51 (1972).

Field, Leslie. "Ethnic Studies: Benefit or Boondoggle?" *BRMMLA*, 26: 148-53 (1972).

Fine, D.M. "Immigrant Ghetto Fiction, 1885-1918: An Annotated Bibliography." *ALRQ*, 6: 169-75 (Su 73).

Gaskins, A.F. "The Epithet 'Guinea' in Central West Virginia." *WVUPP*, 17: 41-4 (1974).

Greenberg, Andrea. "Form and Fuction of the Ethnic Joke." *KFQ*, 17: 144-61 (1972).

Haslam, G.W. "The Subtle Thread: Asian-American Literature." *JEthS*, 1: 45-50 (Au 69).

Hollenbach, J.W. "The Image of the Arab in Nineteenth-Century English and American Literature." *MW*, 62: 195-208 (1972).

Hollinger, D.A. "Ethnic Diversity, Cosmopolitanism and the Emergence of the American Liberal Intelligensia." *AQ*, 27: 133-51 (1975).

Inge, M.T. "The Ethnic Experience and Aesthetics in Literature." *JEthS*, 1: 45-50 (Wi 74).

Innes, C.L. "Language in Black and Irish Nationalist Literature," *MR*, 16: 77-91 (1975).

Jackson, Juanita. "The Sea Islands as a Cultural Resource." *BSch*, 5: 32-9 (1974).

Kent, G.E. "Ethnic Impact on American Literature." *CLAJ*, 11: 24-37 (s 67).

Klotman, P.R. "Racial Stereotypes in Hard Core Pornography." *JPC*, 5: 221-35 (Su 71).

Linneman, W.R. "Immigrant Stereotypes: 1880-1900." *SAH*, 1: 28-39 (Ap 74).

Mangione, A.R. "Literature and the White Ethnic Experience." *EJ*, 63: 42-50 (1974).

*——— "The Story That Has Not Been Told: A Selective Bibliography Dealing with the Italian-American Experience." *Eng R*, 25: 25-34 (#1 73).

Mellard, Robert. "Racism, Formula, and Popular Fiction." *JPC*, 5: 10-37 (Su 71).

Meredith, Robert. "Slovak and Ruthenian Easter Eggs in America." *AmEx*, 1: 5-9 (1973).

Mphahlele, Ezekiel. "The Function of Literature at the Present Time: The Ethnic Imperative." *Transition*, 45: 47-53 (1974).

Mulder, William. "Other Voices, Other Rooms: The Ethnic Strains in American Literature." *LCrit*, 10: 62-74 (#1 71).

Prosen, R.M. "Ethnic Literature." *CE*, 35: 657-70 (Mr 74).

Ruchames, Louis. "The Sources of Racial Thought in Colonial America." *JHN*, 12: 251-72 (1967).

Seitz, D.C. "The American Press—The Foreign Language Press." *Outlook*, 142: 176- (3 F 26).

Shumsky, N.L. "Zangwill's *The Melting Pot*: Ethnic Tensions on the Stage." *AQ*, 27: 29-41 (Mr 75).

Simon, Myron. "Ethnic Writers and Mainstream Literature." *CEA*, 34: 20-5 (Ja 72).

Smith, W.F. "Minority Literature in the American University." *MichA*, 4: 525-31 (Sp 72).

Stewart, D.H. "The Decline of WASP Literature in America." *CE*, 30: 403-17 (Mr 69).

Walsh, J.P. "American Irish: East and West." *Eire*, 6: 25-32 (1961).

Zanger, Jules. "'Guinea': Dialect and Stereotype." *CLAJ*, 18: 553-62 (Je 75).

Afro-American. Anon. "Special Issue: The Phillis Wheatley Poetry Festival, November 4-7, 1973." *Jackson State R*, 6: 1-107 (#1 74).

———. "Contemporary Notes on Novels Concerned With Slavery." *ESQ*, 47: 138-9 (2Q 67).

———. "Voices from Black America." *TLS*, 28 My 71, pp. 605-6.

Abramson, Doris. "Negro Playwrights in America." *CUF*, 12: 11-7 (Sp 69).

Abramson, D.M. "William Wells Brown: America's First Negro Playwright." *ETJ*, 20: 370-5 (O 68).

Adams, G.R. "Black Militant Drama." *AI*, 28: 107-28 (Su 71).

Akar, J.J. "An African's View of Black Studies With International Dimensions." *CLAJ*, 14: 7-17 (S 70).

Alexander, J.A. "Black Literature for the 'Culturally Deprived' Curriculum: Who Are the Losers?" *NALF*, 4: 96-103 (1970).

Alford, T.L. "Letter from Liberia, 1848." *MissQ*, 22: 150-1 (Sp 69).

Amann, C.A. "*Three Negro Classics*: An Estimate." *NALF*, 4: 113-9 (1970).

Amini, Johari. "Big Time Buck White." *BlackW*, 20: 72-4 (1971).

Andrews, W.L. "Chesnutt's Patesville: The Presence and Influence of the Past in *The House Behind the Cedars*." *CLAJ*, 15: 284-94 (1972).

Aptheker, Herbert. "Afro-American Superiority: A Neglected Theme in the Literature." *Phylon*, 31: 336-43 (wi 70).

———. "Black Studies and United States History." *JNH*, 57: 99-105 (1972).

———. "Frederick Douglass Calls for Black Suffrage in 1866." *BSch*, 5: 10-6 (D 73-Ja 74).

Aubert, Alvin. "Black American Poetry: Its Language and the Folk Tradition." *BlAR*, 2: 71-80 (Sp-Su 71).

Babbage, S.B. "A Question of Color." *ChSR*, 1: 41-5 (1971).

Bailey, Peter. "Black Theater." *Ebony*, 24: 126ff (Ag 69).

———. "Black Theater in America." *BlackW*, 20: 4-26, 95-6 (1971); 21: 31-40, 70-4 (1972).

———, et al. "Black Theater in America: A Report." *NegroD*, 19: 25-37, 42, 85, 98 (1970).

———. "Black Theatre in America: Metropolitan New York." *BlackW*, 20: 4-8 (Ap 71).

———. "Is the Negro Ensemble Company *Really* Black Theatre?" *BlackW*, 17: 16-9 (Ap 69).

———, et al. "Report on Black Theater." *NegroD*, 18: 20-6, 69-72 (1969).

Baker, Augusta. "The Black Experience in Children's Books." *BNYPL*, 75: 143-46 (1971).

———. "The Changing Image of the Black in Children's Literature." *Horn Book*, 51: 79-88 (F 75).

Baker, D.G. "Black Images: The Afro-American in Popular Novels, 1900-1945." *JPC*, 7: 327-46 (1973).

———. "From Apartheid to Invisibility: Black Americans in Popular Fiction, 1900-1960." *MwQ*, 13: 365-85 (Jl 72).

Baker, H.A. "Balancing the Perspective: A Look at Early Black American Literary Artistry." *NALF*, 6: 65-70 (1972).

———. "A Forgotten Prototype: 'The Autobiography of an Ex-Colored Man' and 'Invisible Man.'" *VQR*, 49: 433-49 (Su 73).

———. "The Problem of Being: Some Reflections on Black Autobiography." *Obsidian*, 1: 18-29 (#1 75).

———. "Utile, Dulce and the Literature of Black America." *BlackW*, 21: 30-5 (1972).

Baldwin, James. "How Can We Get the Black People to Cool It?" *Esquire*, 70: 49-50 (Jl 68).

———. "Theatre: the Negro In and Out." *BlackW*, 15: 37-44 (Ap 66).

Balliet, C.A. "White on Black: A Check List of Poetry by White Americans About the Black Experience." *BNYPL*, 75: 424-64 (N 71).

Baraka, I.A. "The Black Aesthetic." *NegroD*, 18: 5-6 (S 69).

———. "Black 'Revolutionary' Poets Should Also Be Playwrights." *BlackW*, 21: 4-6 (1972).

Barksdale, R.K. "Urban Crisis and the Black Poetic Avant-Garde." *NALF*, 3: 40-4 (1969).

———. "White Triangles, Black Circles." *CLAJ*, 18: 465-76 (Je 75).

———. "White Tragedy—Black Comedy." *Phylon*, 22: 226-33 (3Q 61).

Bayliss, J.F. "Slave and Convict Narratives: A Discussion of American and Australian Writing." *JCL*, 8: 142-9 (1970).

Bell, Bernard. "Cashing in on Blackness." *MR*, 11: 187-92 (1970).

Bell, B.W. "Contemporary Afro-American Poetry as Folk Art." *BlackW*, 22: 17-26, 74-87 (#5 73).

———. "Folk Art and the Harlem Renaissance." *Phylon*, 36: 155-63 (Je 75).

———. "Literary Sources of the Early Afro-American Novel." *CLAJ*, 18: 29-43 (S 74).

————. "New Black Poetry: A Double-Edged Sword." *CLAJ*, 15: 37-43 (S 71).

Bennett, S.B., and W.W. Nichols. "Violence in Afro-American Fiction: An Hypothesis." *MFS*, 17: 221-8 (Su 71).

Benston, K.W. "Tragic Aspects of the Blues." *Phylon*, 36: 164-76 (Je 75).

Berceanu, Vera. "The Harlem Renaissance." *Contemporanul*, nv: 9 (10 Jl 70).

Berg, P.L. "Racism and the Puritan Mind." *Phylon*, 36: 1-7 (Mr 75).

Berry, Faith. "Voice for the Jazz Age, A Great Migration or Black Bourgeoisie?" *BlackW*, 20: 10-6 (1970).

Biddle, S.F. "The Schomburg Center for Research in Black Culture: Documenting the Black Experience." *BNYPL*, 76: 21-35 (1972).

Bigsby, C.W.E. "The Black Drama in the Seventies." *KanQ*, 3: 10-20 (Sp 71).

————. "The White Critic in a Black World." *NALF*, 6: 39-45 (1972).

Billingsley, M.B. "Forging New Definitions: The Burden of the Hero in Modern Afro-American Literature." *Osibian*, 1: 5-21 (#3 75).

Binderman, M.B. "Toasts: The Black Urban Poetry." *JAF*, 87: 208-28 (1974).

Bins, C.F. "Toward an Ethnography of Contemporary African American Poetry." *Georgetown Un Working Papers on Lang and Linguistics*, 5: 76-94 (1975).

Black, Michael. "Black Literature: Three Critical Works." *GaR*, 24: 46-53 (Sp 70).

Blanch, Antonio. "El problema negro en la novela norteamericana." *Razon y Fe*, 68: 203-22 (S-O 68).

Blassingame, J.W. "Black Autobiographies as History and Literature." *BSch*, 5: 2-9 (1973-74).

Bogard, Travis. "The Sense of the Ghetto in American Negro Theatre." *ETJ*, 20: 333-5 (Ag 68).

Bontemps, Arna. "The Black Renaissance of the Twenties." *BlackW*, 20: 5-18 (1970).

————. "Harlem in the Twenties." *Crisis*, 73: 431-4, 451-6 (1973).

Bosmajian, H.A. "The Language of White Racism." *CE*, 31: 263-72 (D 69).

Boyers, Robert. "Culture, Politics, and Negro Writers." *Salmagundi*, 1: 71-80 (Fa 65).

Bradley, Gerald. "Goodbye, Mr. Bones: The Emergence of Negro Themes and Characters in American Drama." *DramC*, 14: 6-12 (Sp 64).

Braithwaite, W.S. "The Negro in Literature." *Crisis*, 28: 210 (S 24).

Brandstadter, Evan. "Uncle Tom and Archy Moore: the Antislavery Novel as Ideological Symbol." *AQ*, 26: 160-75 (My 74).

Brewer, J.M. "Humorous Folktales of the South Carolina Negro." *Pub South Carolina Fkl Guild*, 1: 1-54 (1945).

Brigano, R.C. "Autobiographical Books by Black Americans: A Bibliography of Works Written Since the Civil War." *NALF*, 7: 148-56 (Wi 73).

Britwum, Atta. "Black Survival and Culture: Rambling Thoughts on Black Aesthetics." *Asemka*, 1: 99-110 (1974).

Broderick, Dorothy. "Lessons in Leadership: An Historical Excursion into Racist Books Recommended by Our Most Respected Literary Critics and Review Media for Children's Books." *LJ*, 96: 701 (1971).

Brooks, A.R. "The Motif of Dynamic Change in Black Revolutionary Poetry." *CLAJ*, 15: 7-17 (S 71).

Brooks, M.E. "Reactionary Trends in Recent Black Drama." *L&I*, 10: 41-8 (1971).

Brown, Cecil. "The Philosophy of Jive." *EvR*, 17: 155-84 (Sp 73).

————. "Richard Wright's Complexes and Black Writing Today." *BlackW*, 18: 45-50, 78-82 (1970).

Brown, L.W. "Beneath the North Star: The Canadian Image in Black Literature." *DR*, 50: 317-29 (Au 70).

————. ''Black Entitles: Names as Symbols in Afro-American Literature.'' *SBL*, 1: 16-44 (1970).

————. ''The Cultural Revolution in Black Theatre.'' *NALF*, 8: 159-65 (Sp 74).

————. ''The Expatriate Consciousness in Black American Literature.'' *SBL*, 3: 9-12 (Su 72).

————. ''The Portrait of the Artist as a Black American.'' *SBL*, 5: 24-7 (1974).

Brown, Lloyd. ''The West Indian as an Ethnic Stereotype in Black American Literature.'' *NALF*, 5: 8-14 (Sp 71).

Brown, M.C. ''Notes on Classical and Renaissance Analogues of Mississippi Negro Folklore.'' *MissFR*, 2: 37-41 (Su 68).

Bruchac, Joseph. ''Black Autobiography in Africa and America.'' *BlAR*, 2: 61-70 (Sp-Su 71).

Brüning, Eberhard. '' 'The Black Liberation Movement' und das amerikanische Drama.'' *ZAA*, 20: 46-59 (1972).

Bruns, R.A. ''Anthony Benezet and the Natural Rights of the Negro.'' *PMHB*, 96: 104-13 (1972).

Bryant, J.H. ''Politics and the Black Novel.'' *Nation*, 213: 660-2 (20 D 71).

Budd, L.J. ''The Not so Tender Traps: Some Dilemmas of Black American Poets.'' *IJAS*, 3: 47-57 (1974).

Buehler, R.E. ''Stacker Lee: A Partial Investigation into the Historicity of a Negro Murder Ballad.'' *Keystone Fkl Q*, 12: 187-91 (Fa 67).

Bullins, Ed. ''Black Theatre Groups: A Directory.'' *TDR*, 12: 172-5 (Su 68).

————. ''Black Theatre Notes.'' *Black Theatre*, 1: 4-7 (O 68).

Burke, V.M. ''Black Literature for Whom?'' *NALF*, 9: 25-7 (Sp 75).

Bush, R.E. ''Negritude: A Sense of Reality.'' *BlackW*, 22: 36-47 (1972).

Butterfield, S.T. ''The Use of Language in the Slave Narratives.'' *NALF*, 6: 72-8 (1972).

Campbell, Dick. ''Is There a Conspiracy against Black Playwrights?'' *BlackW*, 17: 11-15 (Ap 68).

Campbell, M.L. ''The Negro in Cable's *The Grandissimes*.'' *MissQ*, 27: 165-78 (Sp 74).

Canaday, Nicholas. ''The Antislavery Novel Prior to 1852.'' *CLAJ*, 17: 175-91 (D 73).

Cardoso, J.J. ''Hinton Rowan Helper and the Personality Politics of Negrophobia.'' *IllQ*, 34: 16-36 (1972).

Carroll, R.A. ''Black Racial Spirit: An Analysis of James Weldon Johnson's Critical Perspective.'' *Phylon*, 32: 344-64 (Wi 71).

Chapman, Abraham. ''The Black Aesthetic and the African Continuum.'' *Pan-African J*, 4: 397-406 (1971).

————. ''Black Poetry Today.'' *ASoc*, 5: 401-8 (1968).

Clark, Edward. ''The Harlem Renaissance and Today.'' *LWU*, 8: 84-8 (1975).

————. ''Studying and Teaching Afro-American Literature, *CLAJ*, 16: 96-105 (S 72).

Clarke, J.H. ''The Neglected Dimensions of the Harlem Renaissance.'' *BlackW*, 20: 118-29 (1970).

————. ''The Origin and Growth of Afro-American Literature.'' *NegroD*, 18: 54-67 (1967).

Clark, J.W. ''The Fugitive Slave as Humorist.'' *SAH*, 1: 73-8 (O 74).

Clayborne, J.L. ''Modern Black Drama and the Gay Image.'' *CE*, 36: 381-4 (N 74).

Clements, C.C. ''Black Studies for White Students.'' *NALF*, 4: 9-11 (1970).

Cohen, E.G. ''Afro-American Periodicals.'' *HussR*, 5: 28-37 (1971).

Coehn, Hennig. ''Literary Reflections of Slavery in the *South Carolina Gazette*.'' *JHN*, 37: 18-93 (1952).

Cohn, Jan. ''The Negro Character in Northern Magazine Fiction of the 1860's.'' *NEQ*, 43: 57292 (D 70).

Coleman, Michael. "What Is Black Theater?" *BlackW*, 20: 32-6 (Ap 71).

Collier, E.W. "Heritage from Harlem." *BlackW*, 20: 52-9 (1970).

Colwell, James. "More on the Tragic Octoroon." *AN&Q*, 6: 147-8 (Je 68).

Conrad, Earl. "The Philology of Negro Dialect." *JNE*, 13: 150-4 (1944).

Cook, Mercer. Les précurseurs négro-américains de la Négritude." *Le Soleil* (Dakar), 12: 11-4 (8 My 71).

Cooke, M.G. "The Descent into the Underworld and Modern Black Fiction." *Iowa R*, 5: 72-90 (Fa 74).

Cooke, G.J. "How Students Feel about Black Literature." *NALF*, 8: 293-5 (1974).

Cooke, Gwendolyn. "Reading Literary Works by Black and White Writers: Effects on Students' Attitudes." *JBlackS*, 5: 123-33 (D 74).

Cooney, C.F. "Walter White and the Harlem Renaissance." *JNH*, 57: 231-40 (1972).

Cooper, Frederick. "Elevating the Race: The Social Thought of Black Leaders, 1827-50." *AQ*, 24: 604-25 (1972).

*Corrigan, R.A. "Afro-American Fiction: A Checklist, 1853-1970." *MASJ*, 11: 114-35 (Fa 70).

———. "Afro-American Fiction: Errata and Additions." *AmS*, 12: 69-73 (Sp 71).

———. "Afro-American Fiction Since 1970." *AmS*, 14: 85-90 (Fa 73).

———. "Bibliography of Afro-American Fiction: 1853-1970." *SBL*, 1: 51-86 (1970).

Cosgrove, William. "Modern Black Writers: The Divided Self." *NALF*, 7: 120-2 (Wi 73).

Costanzo, Angelo. "Three Black Poets in Eighteenth-Century America." *Shippensburg State Col R*, 1973, pp. 89-101.

Cotton, L.J. "The Negro in the American Theatre." *NHB*, 23: 172-8 (My 60).

Cunliffe, Marcus. "Black Culture and White America." *Enc*, 34: 22-35 (Ja 70).

Dance, Darrell. "Contemporary Militant Black Humor." *NALF*, 8: 217-22 (Su 74).

Davis, A.P. "The New Poetry of Black Hate." *CLAJ*, 13: 382-91 (1970).

Davis, M.W. "Black Images in Children's Literature: Revised Editions Needed." *LJ*, 97: 261-63 (1972).

Davis, Ossie. "The English Language is My Enemy." *NHB*, 30: 18 (Ap 67).

D'Elia, D.J. "Dr. Benjamin Rush and the Negro." *JHI*, 30: 373-9 (Jl-S 69).

Dent, Thomas. "Beyond Rhetoric toward a Black Southern Theatre." *BlackW*, 20: 14-24 (Ap 71).

Dickson, B.D. "The 'John and Old Master' Stories of the World of Slavery." *Phylon*, 35: 418-29 (D 74).

Dickstein, Morris. "The Black Aesthetic in White America." *PR*, 38: 376-95 (Wi 71-72).

Dixon, Melvin. "Black Theater: The Aesthetics." *NegroD*,18: 41-4 (Jl 69).

Dodson, Owen. "Playwrights in Dark Glasses." *BlackW*, 1: 31-6 (Ap 68).

Doherty, A.S. "Black Studies: A Report for Librarians." *C&RL*, 31: 379-87 (1970).

Doughty, N.S. "Realistic Negro Characterization in Postbellum Fiction." *NALF*, 3: 57-62, 68 (Su 69).

Domergues, Pierre. "La Négritude Américaine." *LanM*, 60: 94-8 (My-Je 66).

Dowty, Alan. "Urban Slavery in the Pro-Slavery Fiction of the 1850's." *JSH*, 32: 25-31 (F 66).

Dresser, Norine. "The Metamorphosis of the Humor of the Black Man." *NYFQ*, 26: 216-28 (1970).

Durham, Frank. "Jean Toomer's Vision of the Southern Negro." *SHR*, 6: 13-22 (1972).

———. "The Reputed Demises of Uncle Tom; or, The Treatment of the Negro in Fiction by White Southern Authors in the 1920's." *SLJ*, 2: 26-50 (Sp 70).

Edward, Ann. "Three Views on Blacks: The Black Woman in American Literature." *CEA*, 37: 14-6 (My 75).

Ehrlich, George. "Afro-American Art and Art in America: A Problem in Methodology." *MASJ*, 11: 101-13 (1970).

Eisen, Jonathan. "Black Culture at Oberlin." *Cweal*, 87: 676-7 (8 Mr 68).

Elder, Lonne. "A Negro Idea Theatre.'" *AmD*, 1: 30-1 (Jl-Ag 64).

Ellison, Martha. "Velvet Voices Feed on Bitter Fruit: A Study of American Negro Poetry." *P&C*, 4: 39-49 (Wi 67-68).

Emanuel, J.A. "America Before 1950: Black Writers' Views." *NegroD*, 18: 26-34, 67-9, (1969).

Evans, D.T. "Bring It All Home." *BlackW*, 20: 41-5 (1971).

Evans, Mari. "Contemporary Black Literature." *BlackW*, 19: 93-4 (1970).

Fabio, S.W. "What is Black?" *CCC*, 19: 286-7 (D 68).

Fabre, Michel. "Black Literature in France." *SBL*, 4: 9-14 (Au 73).

———. "Le Problème Noir Aux Etats-Unis." *LanM*, 60: 119-29 (My-Je 66).

———. "René Maran, The New Negro and Negritude." *Phylon*, 36: 340-51 (S 75).

Farrison, W.E. "Dialectology versus Negro Dialect." *CLAJ*, 13: 21-6 (S 69).

———. "What American Negro Literature Exists and Who Should Teach It?" *CLAJ*, 13: 374-81 (1970).

Felgar, Robert. "Black Content, White Form." *SBL*, 5: 28-31 (Sp 74).

Fenderson, L.H. "The New Breed of Black Writers and Their Jaundiced View of Tradtion." *CLAJ*, 15: 18-24 (S 71).

Ferguson, A.R. "The Abolition of Blacks in Abolitionist Fiction: 1830-1860." *JBlackS*, 5: 134-56 (D 74).

Ferris, W.R. "Black Prose Narrative in the Mississippi Delta: An Overview." *JAF*, 85: 140-51 (Ap-Je 72).

Fleming, R.E. "Black Literature Programs—Special Problems of the Rocky Mountain Schools." *BRMMLA*, 26: 108-12 (1972).

———. "Humor in the Early Black Novel." *CLAJ*, 17: 250-62 (D 73).

———. "The Nightmare Level of *The Man Who Cried I Am*." *ConL*, 14: 186-96 (Sp 73).

———. "Overshadowed by Richard Wright: Three Black Chicago Novelists." *NALF*, 7: 75-9 (Fa 73).

———. "'Playing the Dozens' in the Black Novel." *SBL*, 3: 23-4 (Au 72).

Foner, P.S. "A Labor Voice for Black Equality: The Boston *Daily Evening Voice*, 1864." *Sci&Soc*, 38: 304-26 (Fa 74).

Fontaine, W.T. "The Negro Continuum from Dominant Wish to Collective Act." *AForum*, 34: 63-96 (1968).

Ford, N.A. "Attitudes and Actions of English Departments Towards the Promotion of Black Studies. Bul Assn Towards the Promotion of Black Studies." *Bul Assn Departments of Eng*, 35: 22-27 (1972).

———. "Black Literature and the Problem of Evaluation." *CE*, 32: 536-47 (F 71).

———. "Confessions of a Black Critic." *BlackW*, 20: 30-43 (1971).

———, D.B. Gibson, and C.A. Ray. "Black Literature: Problems and Opportunities: A Symposium." *CLAJ*, 13: 10-20 (S 69).

Ford, Clebert. "Towards a Black Community Theatre." *Liberator*, 4: 12-20 (1964).

Fowler, Carolyn. "A Contemporary Blackamerican Genre: Pamphlet/Manifesto Poetry." *BlackW*, 23: 4-19 (1974).

Franklin, H.B. "'A' Is for Afro-American: A Primer on the Study of American Literature." *MinnR*, 1: 53-64 (#5 75).

Fuller, H.W. "Black Theatre in America: An Informal Survey." *BlackW*, 17: 83-93 (Ap 68).

———. "Up in Harlem: New Hope." *BlackW*, 14: 49ff (O 65).

Fuller, Hoyt. "Identity, Reality, and Responsibility: Elusive Poles in the World of Black Literature." *JNH*, 57: 83-98 (1972).

———. "Of Integrity, Hope and Dead Dialogue." *NALF*, 3; 50-51 (1969).

Furay, Michael. "Africa in Negro American Poetry to 1929." *ALT*, 2: 32-41 (Ja 69).

———. "Negritude—A Romantic Myth." *NRep*, 155: 32-5 (2 Jl 66).

Gaffney, Floyd. "Black Theatre: Commitment and Communication." *BSch*, 1: 10-5 (Je 70).

———. "*The Hand Is on the Gate* in Athens." *ETJ*, 21: 196-201 (My 69).

———. "Is Your Door Really Open?" *D&T*, 7: 4-7 (Fa 68).

Gates, Skip. "Of Negroes Old and New." *Transition* , 46: 44-57 (1974).

Gayle, Addison. "The Critic, the University, and the Negro Writer." *NegroD*, 16: 54-8 (1967).

———. "Cultural Strangulation: Black Literature and the White Aesthetic." *NegroD*, 18: 32-39 (Jl 69).

———. "Debate: The Black Aesthetic (Defender)." *BlackW*, 24: 31-40 (D 74).

———. "The Harlem Renaissance: Towards a Black Aesthetic." *MASJ*, 11: 78-87 (Fa 70).

———. "The Politics of Revolution: Afro-American Literature." *BlackW*, 21: 4-12 (Su 72).

———. "Reclaiming the Southern Experience: The Black Aesthetic 10 Years Later." *BlackW*, 23: 20-9 (Su 74).

Genizi, Haim. "V.F. Calverton, A Radical Magazinist for Black Intellectuals, 1920-40." *JNH*, 57: 241-53 (Jl 72).

Genovese, E.D. "The Influence of the Black Power Movemnt on Historical Scholarship." *Daedalus*, 99: 473-94 (Sp 70).

Gerald, C.F. "The Black Writer and His Role." *NegroD*, 18: 42-8 (1969).

Gérard, Albert. "The Sons of Ham." *SNNTS*, 3: 148-64 (Su 71).

Gester, F.W. " 'Negro,' 'Afro-American' oder 'black'? Zu einer aktuellen sprachlichen Auseinandersetzung in den Vereinigten Staaten." *NS*, 20:53-63 (F 71).

Ghent, Henri. "Black Creativity in Quest of an Audience." *Art in America*, 58: 35 (My 70).

Gilenson, Boris. "Afro-American Literature in the Soviet Union." *NALF*, 9: 25, 28-9 (Sp 75).

Gilman, Richard. "More on Negro Writing." *NRep*, 158: 25-8 (14 Ap 68).

———. "White Standards and Negro Writing." *NRep*, 158: 25-30 (9 Mr 68); *NALF*, 3: 111-6 (Wi 70).

Goncalves, Joe. "The Mysterious Disappearance of Black Arts West." *Black Theatre*, 2: 23-5 (1969).

Govan, S.Y. "The Poetry of the Black Experience as a Counterpoint to the Poetry of the Black Aesthetic." *NALF*, 8: 288-92 (1974).

Graham, J.D. "Negro Protest in America: 1900-1955: A Bibliographical Guide." *SAQ*, 67: 94-107 (Wi 68).

Green, A.C. " 'Jim Crow,' 'Zip Coon': The Northern Origins of Negro Minstrelsy." *MR*, 11: 385-97 (Sp 70).

Greenwood, Frank. "Burn, Baby, Burn." *Freedomways*, Summer 67, pp. 244-7.

Gross, S.L. and Eileen Bender. "History, Politics and Literature: The Myth of Nat Turner." *AQ*, 23: 487-519 (O 71).

———. "Literature and the Cultural History of the Negro." *SLJ*, 2: 148-55 (Sp 70).

Gross, T.L. "The Idealism of Negro Literature in America." *Phylon*, 30: 5-10 (Sp 69).

———. "The Negro in the Literature of Reconstruction." *Phylon*, 22: 5-14 (Sp 61).

———. "Our Mutual Estate: The Literature of the American Negro." *AR*, 28: 293-303 (Fa 68).

Grumbach, Doris. "Christianity and Black Writers." *Renascence*, 23: 198-212 (Su 71).

Hall, B.L. and R.M.R. "Black English and TESL—a Programmatic Statement." *JESL*, 4: 1-6 (Sp 69).

Hanau, D. "Ghetto Theatre: Vital Drama or Social Therapy?" *Community*, 26: 7-10 (Ap 67).

Hansen, Chadwick. "The Metamorphosis of Tituba, or Why American Intellectuals Can't Tell an Indian Witch from a Negro." *NEQ*, 47: 3-12 (1974).

Hare, Nathan. "Questions and Answers about Black Studies." *MR*, 10: 727-36 (1969).

Harris, J.B. "The Sun People of 125th Street—The National Black Theatre." *DramR*, 16: 39-45 (D 72).

Harrison, A.C. "Negro Actors: The Added Dimensions of Color." *SSJ*, 35: 16-27 (1969).

Harrison, P.C. "Black Theater and the African Continuum." *BlackW*, 21: 42-8 (1972).

Hart, R.C. "Black-White Literary Relations in the Harlem Renaissance." *AL*, 44: 612-28 (Ja 73).

Haskett, N.D. "Afro-American Images of Africa: Four *Antebellum* Black Authors." *Ufahamu*, 3: 29-40 (1972).

Haslam, G.W. "Two Traditions in Afro-American Literature." *RSW*, 37: 183-93 (S 69).

Hatch, J.V. "A White Folks Guide to 200 Years of Black & White Drama." *TDR*, 16: 5-24 (D 72).

Hay, S.A. "Alain Locke & Black Drama." *BlackW*, 21: 8-14 (Ap 72).

Henderson, Australia. "Black Female in Afro-American Theatre." *Afriscope*, 5: 46-50, 449 (#8, 10 75).

Henderson, S.E. "Saturation Progress Report on Black Poetry." *BlackW*, 24: 4-17 (#8 75).

Herbert, Janis. "Oscar Micheaux: A Black Pioneer." *SDR*, 11: 62-9 (#4 73).

Herndon, Jane. "Henry McNeal Turner's African Dream: A Re-Evaluation." *MissQ*, 22: 327-36 (Fa 69).

Hewes, Henry. "The Aints and the Am Nots." *SatR*, 54: 10, 11-2 (13 N 71).

———. "Black Hopes: Presentations in New York City." *SatR*, 48: 46 (7 J 65).

Hibbard, Addison. "Aesop in Negro Dialect." *AS*, 1: 495-9 (1926).

Hill, Herbert. "The Negro Writer and the Creative Imagination." *Arts in Society*, 5: 244-55 (Su-Fa 68).

Hill, Mildred. "Common Folklore Features in African and African-American Literature." *SFQ*, 39: 11-33 (Je 75).

Hirsch, P.M. "An Analysis of *Ebony*: The Magazine and Its Readers." *JQ*, 45: 261-70, 292 (Su 68).

Holtan, O.I. "Sidney Brustein and the Plight of the American Intellectual." *Players*, 46: 2-5 (1971).

Houstan, H.R. "Contributions of the American Negro to American Culture: A Selected Checklist." *BB*, 26: 71-83 (Jl-S 69).

Huff, A.V. "The Black Hero in South Carolina History." *SCR*, 4: 20-28 (1972).

Hughes, Langston. "The Need for an Afro-American Theatre." *Chicago Defender*, 12 Je 61, p. 12.

———. "The Negro Artist and the Racial Mountain." *Nation*, 122: 692-4 (23 Je 26); *Amistad*, 1: 301-5 (1970).

———. "The Twenties: Harlem and Its Negritude." *AForum*, 1: 18 (Sp 66).

———. "200 Years of American Negro Poetry." *Transition*, 5: 49-52 (1966).

Hull, G.T. "Black Women Poets from Wheatley to Walker." *NALF*, 9: 91-6 (Fa 75).

Hurvitz, Nathan. "Blacks and Jews in American Folklore." *WF*, 33: 301-25 (1974).

Hutson, J.B. "The Schomburg Collection." *Freedomways*, 3: 431-5 (Su 63).

Ihde, Horst. "Der Beitrag der Negersklaven zur Kultur in den USA." *ZAA*, 19: 5-35 (1971).

———. "Black Writer's Burden." *ZAA*, 16: 117-37 (1968).

Isani, M.A. "The Exotic and Protest in Earlier Black Literature." *SBL*, 5: 9-14 (Su 74).

Jackson, Blyden. "A Survey Course in Negro Literature." *CE*, 35: 631-6 (Mr 64).

Jackson, Bruce. "Circus and Street." *JAF*, 85: 123-39 (1972).

———. "What Happened to Jody." *JAF*, 80: 387-96 (O-D 67).

Jackson, E.M. "The American Negro and the Image of the Absurd." *Phylon*, 23: 359-71 (Wi 62).

Jacobs, D.M. "William Lloyd Garrison's *Liberator* and Boston's Blacks, 1830-1865." *NEQ*, 44: 259-77 (Je 71).

Jaffe, H.J. "American Negro Folklore: A Check List of Scarce Items." *SFQ*, 36: 68-70 (Mr 72).

Jařab, Josef. "The Drop of Patience of the American Negro." *Philologica Pragensia*, 12: 159-70 (1969).

Jaskoski, Helen. "Power Unequal to Man: The Significance of Conjure in Works by Five Afro-American Authors." *SFQ*, 38: 31-108 (Je 74).

Jeffers, Lance. "Afro-American Literature: The Conscience of Man." *BSch*, 2: 47-53 (Ja 71).

———. "Bullins, Baraka, and Elder: The Dawn of Grandeur in Black Drama." *CLAJ*, 16: 32-48 (Sp 72).

Jeyifous, Abiodun. "Black Critics on Black Theatre in America." *TDR*, 18: 34-45 (1974).

Johnson, A.A. and R.M. "Forgotten Pages: Black Literary Magazines in the 1920's." *JAmSt*, 8: 363-82 (1974).

Johnson, G.B. "The Negro Spiritual: A Problem in Anthropology." *Am Anthropology*, 33: 157-71 (1931).

Johnson, H.A. "Playwrights, Audiences, and Critics: Black Theater." *NegroD*, 19: 17-25 (1970).

Johnson, P.D. "American Innocence and Guilt: Black-White Destiny in 'Benito Cereno.'" *Phylon*, 36: 426-32 (D 75).

———. "'Goodby to Sambo': The Contribution of the Black Slave Narratives to the Abolition Movement." *NALF*, 6: 79-84 (1972).

Jones, H.L. "An Essay on the Blues." *CLAJ*, 13: 62-7 (S 69).

Jones, I.G. "Research in Afro-American Literature." *CLAJ*, 15: 240-4 (D 71).

Jones, Le Roi. "Black (Art) Drama Is the Same as Black Life." *Ebony*, 25: 74ff (F 71).

———. "In Search of the Revolutionary Theatre." *BlackW*, 15: 20-4 (Ap 66).

*Jurges, Oda. "Books and Articles Related to Black Theatre Published from 1/1960 to 2/1968." *TDR*, 12: 176-80 (Su 68).

Kaiser, Ernest. "The Negro Impact on Western Civilizaton." *Sci&Soc*, 36: 344-56 (Fa 72).

Kane, Patricia, and D.Y. Wilkinson. "Survival Strategies: Black Women in *Ollie Miss* and *Cotton Comes to Harlem*." *Critique*, 16: 101-9 (#1 74).

Kaufman, M.W. "The Delicate World of Reprobation: A Note on the Black Revolutionary Theatre." *ETJ*, 23: 446-59 (1971).

Kazin, Alfred. "Brothers Crying Out for More Access to Life." *SatR*, 54: 33-5 (2 O 71).

Keller, F.R. "The Harlem Literary Renaissance." *NAR*, 5: 29-34 (My-Je 68).

Keller, J.R. "Black Writing and Editorial Unbelief." *NALF*, 3: 35-8, 51 (Su 69).

Keller, Joseph. "Black Writing and the White Critic." *NALF*, 3: 103-10 (1969).

Kennicott, P.C. "Black Persuaders in the Antislavery Movement." *SM*, 37: 15-24 (Mr 70).

Kent, G.E. "Notes on the 1974 Black Literary Scene." *Phylon*, 36: 182-203 (Je 75).

———. "Outstanding Works in Black Literature during 1972." *Phylon*, 34: 307-28 (1973).

———. "Patterns of the Harlem Renaissance: The Fork in the Road." *BlackW*, 21: 13-24, 76-80 (1972).

———. "Struggle for the Image: Selected Books By or About Blacks During 1971." *Phylon*, 33: 304-24 (Wi 72).

Kestleroot, Lilyan. "Negritude and Its American Sources." *BUJ*, 22: 54-67 (1974).

*Keyssar-Franke, Helene. "Afro-American Drama and Its Criticism, 1960-1972: An Annotated Check List with Appendices." *BNYPL*, 78: 276-346 (Sp 75).

Kgositsile, Keorapetse. "Language, Vision and the Black Writer." *BlackW*, 21: 25-7 (1972).

———. "Steps to Break the Circle." *BlackW*, 23: 30-4 (1974).

Kilgore, J.C. "The Case for Black Literature." *NegroD*, 18: 22-25, 66-9 (1969).

Killens, J.O. "Another Time When Black Was Beautiful." *BlackW*, 20: 20-36 (1970).

———. "The Artist and the Black University." *BSch*, 12: 61-5 (1969).

———. "The Black Writer and Revolution." *ASoc*, 5: 395-9 (1968).

———. "Broadway in Black and White." *AForum*, 1: 66-76 (Wi 66).

———. "Run Like Hell and Holler Fire." *AmD*, 5: 10-2 (1968-9).

Kilson, Martin. "Anatomy of the Black Studies Movement." *MR*, 10: 718-25 (1969).

———. "Debate: The Black Aesthetic (Opponent)." *BlackW*, 24: 40-8 (1974).

King, Woodie. "Black Theatre: Present Condition." *TDR*, 12: 117-24 (1968).

———. "Black Theatre: Weapon for Change." *BlackW*, 16: 35-9 (Ap 67).

———. "The Dilemma of Black Theater." *NegroD*, 19: 10-5, 86-7 (1970).

———. "Educational Theater and the Black Community." *BlackW*, 21: 25-9 (Ap 72).

———. "Problems Facing Negro Actors." *BlackW*, 15: 53-9 (Ap 66).

Kinneman, John. "The Negro Renaissance." *NHB*, 25: 197-200 (My 62).

———. "The Political Dimension of Afro-American Literature." *Soundings*, 58: 130-44 (1975).

Klinkowitz, James. "Black Superfiction." *NAR*, 259: 69-74 (Wi 75).

———. "The New Black Writer and the Old Black Art." *FicI*, 1: 123-7 (1973).

Klotman, P.B. "The Slave and the Western: Popular Literature of the Nineteenth Century." *NDQ*, 41: 50-4 (1973).

Klotman, P.R. "An Approach to the Teaching of Black Literature." *CEA*, 34: 12-5 (Ja 72).

Knox, George. "The Harlem Renaissance Today (the 1920's 'New Negro Movement' Reviewed: Notes on a Neglected Theme)." *CEJ*, 7: 29-33 (D 71).

Koike, Sekio. "Sojourner Truth: Her Thought and Literary Activities." *KAL*, 14: 50-67 (1972).

La Crosse, Ken, and Gerald Haslam. "An Inquiry Model for Black Oral Literature." *NALF*, 4: 127-32 (1970).

Lahr, John. "Black Theatre: The American Tragic Voice." *EvR*, 13: 55-63 (Ag 69).

Lamplugh, G.R. "The Image of the Negro in Popular Magazine Fiction, 1875-1900." *JNH*, 57: 177-89 (Ap 72).

Landess, T.H. "The Present Course of Southern Fiction: 'EveryNegro' and Other Alternatives." *ArlQ*, 1: 61-85 (Wi 67-68).

Larrabee, H.A. "The Varieties of Black Experience." *NEQ*, 43: 638-45 (D 70).

Larson, C.R. "African-Afro-American Literary Relations: Basic Parallels." *NegroD*, 19: 35-42 (1969).

————. "Three Harlem Novels of the Jazz Age." *Critique*, 11: 66-78 (1969).

Lash, John. "On Negro Literature." *Phylon*, 6: 240-7 (Fa 45).

Layng, Anthony. "Anthropology and Afro-American Studies." *JGE*, 23: 191-200 (1971).

Lee, D.L. "Black Critics." *BlackW*, 19: 24-30 (1970).

————. "Directions for Black Writers." *BSch*, 1: 53-7 (D 69).

Lee, Ulyses. "Criticism at Mid Century." *Phylon*, 11: 328-37 (Wi 50).

Levy, D.W. "Racial Stereotypes in Anti-Slavery Fction." *Phylon*, 31: 265-79 (Fa 70).

Lewis, S.A. "The Jewish Author Looks at the Black." *ColQ*, 21: 317-30 (Wi 73).

Lieber, T.M., and M.J. O'Sullivan. "'Native Son?': Black Students on Black Literature." *NALF*, 5: 3-7 (1971).

————. "Ralph Ellison and the Metaphor of Invisibility in Black Literary Tradition." *AQ*, 24: 86-100 (Mr 72).

Liebman, Arthur. "Patterns and Themes in Afro-American Literature." *Eng Rec*, 20: 2-12 (F 70).

Liedel, D.E. "The Authorship of Two Antislavery Novels of the 1840's: *The Fanatic* and *Winona*." *PBSA*, 67: 447-9 (O-D 73).

————. "The Puffing of Ida May: Publishers Exploit the Anti-Slavery." *JPC*, 3: 287-306 (Fa 69).

Lincoln, C.E. "The New Blacks in Search of a Self." *BUJ*, 19: 53-60 (1971).

Lindberg, John. "'Black Aesthetic': Minority or Mainstream?" *NAR*, 260: 48-52 (Wi 75).

Lindsay, Powell. "We Still Need Negro Theatre in America." *NHB*, 27: 112 (F 64).

Lochard, M.T.F. "The Negro Press in Illinois." *JISHS*, 56: 570-91 (Au 63).

Loflin, M.D. "On the Passive in Nonstandard Negro English." *JESL*, 4: 19-23 (Sp 69).

Logan, R.W. "James Weldon Johnson and Haiti." *Phylon*, 32: 396-402 (1971).

Lomax, M.L. "Fantasies of Affirmation: The 1920's Novel of Negro Life." *CLAJ*, 16: 232-46 (D 72).

Long, R.A. "Black Studies: International Dimensions." *CLAJ*, 14: 1-6 (S 70).

————. "The Future of Black Studies." *CLAJ*, 15: 1-6 (Ja 71).

————. "The Outer Reaches: The White Writer and Blacks in the Twenties." *SLItI*, 7: 65-71 (Fa 74).

Long, R.E. "Black is Box-Office." *NAR*, 6: 71-2 (Wi 69).

Lottman, Herbert. "The Action Is Everywhere the Black Man Goes." *NYTBR*, 21 Ap 68, pp. 6-7, 48-9.

Lowenfels, Walter. "Black Renaissance." *AmD*, 5: 30-1 (1968).

Luker, R.E. "Bushnell in Black and White: Evidence of the 'Racism' of Horace Bushnell." *NEQ*, 45: 408-16 (S 72).

Mabbutt, F.R. "The Bitter Years of Slavery: A Response to the Arguments of John Hope Franklin." *Forum (H)*, 8: 13-8 (1970).

McDavid, R.I. "The Relationship of the Speech of American Negroes to the Speech of American Whites." *AS*, 26: 3-17 (1951).

McDonough, John. "Manuscript Resources for the Study of Negro Life and History." *QJLC*, 26: 126-48 (Jl 69).

McDowell, R.E. "Mothers and Sons: A View of Black Literature from South Africa, the West Indies, and America." *PrS*, 43: 356-8 (Wi 69-70).

*————, and George Fortenberry. "A Checklist of Books and Essays About American Negro Novelists." *StN*, 3: 219-36 (Su 71).

McElroy, Hilda, and R.A. Willis. "Published Works of Black Playwrights in the United States, 1960-1970." *BlackW*, 21: 92-8 (1972).

McGhee, N.B. "The Folk Sermon: A Facet of the Black Literary Heritage." *CLAJ*, 13: 51-61 (S 69).

Madden, David. "The Fallacy of the Subject-Dominated Novel." *Eng Rec*, 18: 11-9 (Ap 68).

Mapp, Edward. "The Image Makers (Negro Stereotype)." *NHB*, 26: 127-8 (D 62).

Margolies, Edward. "Ante-Bellum Slave Narratives." *SBL*, 4: 1-8 (Au 73).

————. "Experiences of a Black Expatriate Writer." *CLAJ*, 15: 41-7 (Je 72).

————. "The Image of the Primitive in Black Letters." *MASJ*, 11: 67-77 (Fa 70).

Marvin X. "Manifesto: The Black Educational Theatre of San Fransico." *Black Theatre*, 6: 30-1 (1972).

Massenburg, D.O., and B.C. Appleby. "Growing Up Black: A Black Literature Unit for Schools.' *NALF*, 5: 39-55 (1971).

Matheus, J.F. "*Ouanga*: My Venture in Libretto Creation." *CLAJ*, 15: 428-40 (1972).

May, J.R. "Images of the Apocalypse in the Black Novel." *Renascence*, 23: 31-45 (Au 70).

Means, F.E. "Self-Image: A Black Perspective." *JGE*, 24: 51-8 (1972).

Mellard, J.M. "Racism, Formula, and Popular Fiction." *JPC*, 5: 10-27 (Su 71).

Meyer, June. "Spokesman for the Blacks." *Nation*, 205: 597-9 (4 D 67).

Mezu, S.O. "Black Renaissance and Negritude." *BlAR*, 2: 9-22 (Su 71).

Miller, A.D. "It's a Long Way to St. Louis: Notes on the Audience for Black Drama." *TDR*, 12: 147-50 (Su 68).

Miller, W.C., and Stephanie. "All Black Showcase: The Effectiveness of a Negro Theater Production." *ETJ*, 202-4 (1969).

Minter, David. "Concepts of Self in Black Slave Narratives." *ATQ*, 24: 62-8 (Fa 74).

Mitchell, Loften. "Black Drama." *BlackW*, 16: 75-87 (Ap 67).

————. "Death of a Decade: Black Drama in the Sixties." *Crisis*, 77: 87-92 (Mr 70).

————. "Harlem My Harlem." *BlackW*, 20: 91-7 (1970).

————. "The Negro Theatre and the Harlem Community." *Freedomways*, 3: 384-94 (Su 63).

Molette, C.W. "The First Afro-American Theater." *NegroD*, 19: 4-9 (1970).

Moore, J.B. "Images of the Negro in Early American Short Fiction." *MissQ*, 22: 47-57 (Wi 68-69).

Morris, L.R. "Black Literature." *Roots*, 2: 21-4 (1971).

Morrison, Allan. "One Hundred Years of Negro Entertainment." *Ebony*, 18: 122-8 (S 63).

Morsberger, R.E. "Segregated Surveys: American Literature." *NALF*, 4: 3-8 (1970).

Morse, J.M. "The Shuffling Speech of Slavery: Black English." *CE*, 34: 834-43 (Mr 73).

Mphahlele, Ezekiel. "Black Literature at the University of Denver." *RIAL*, 3: 70-4 (Sp 72).

————. "From the Black American World." *Okike*, 4: 51-61; 5: 62-9 (1973).

————. "Reply to Addison Gayle, JR." *BlackW*, 23: 4-20 (1974).

————. "Variations on a Theme: Race and Color." *PA*, 83: 92-104 (1972).

Mugo, M.C. "Language and Revolution with Reference to Afro-American Literature." *Joliso*, 2: 42-6 (#1 74).

Muraskin, William. "An Alienated White: Short Stories in *The Crisis*, 1910-1950." *JBlackS*, 1: 282-305 (Mr 71).

Murray, Albert. "Literary Implications of the Blues: The Hero as Improviser." *Quadrant*, 16: 34-8 (N-D 72).

Murray, J.P. "Black Movies/Black Theatre." *DramR*, 16: 56-61 (D 72).

Musgrave, M.E. "Triangles in Black and White: Interracial Sex and Hostility in Black Literature." *CLAJ*, 44-51 (Je 71).

Musgrave, M.E. "Patterns of Violence and Non-Violence in Pro-Slavery and Anti-Slavery Fiction." *CLAJ*, 16: 426-37 (Je 73).

*Myers, Carol. "A Selected Bibliography of Recent Afro-American Writers." *CLAJ*, 16: 377-82 (Mr 73).

Neal, Larry. "The Black Arts Movement." *TDR*, 12: 29-39 (Su 68).
———. "Conquest of the South." *DramR*, 24: 169-74 (1970).
Neal, L.P. "Cultural Nationalism and the Black Theatre." *Black Theatre*, 1: 8-10 (O 68).
———. "Toward a Relevant Black Theatre." *Black Theatre*, 4: 14-5 (Ap 70).
Nennett, Stephen, and William Nichols. "Violence in Afro-American Fiction: An Hypothesis." *MFS*, 17: 221-8 (Su 71).
Ngandu, Puis. "Le role des noirs americains dans la litterature negro-africaine." *CAfr*, 11: 337-44 (1974).
Nichols, W.W. "Slave Narratives: Dismissed Evidence in the Writings of Southern History." *Phylon*, 32: 403-09 (1971).
Nower, Joyce. "Foolin' Master." *SNL*, 7: 5-10 (Fa 69).
———. "The Tradition of Negro Literature in the United States." *NALF*, 3: 5-12 (1969).
O'Brien, John. " 'Becoming' Heroes in Black Fiction: Sex, Iconoclasm, and the Immanence of Salvation." *SBL*, 2: 2: 1-5 (Au 71).
Oden, Gloria. "Literature and Politics: The Black Investment." *NALF*, 3: 49-50 (1969).
Ogbang, P.M. "Reflections on 'Language, Vision and the Black Writer.' " *BlackW*, 22: 40-7 (1972).
Okeye, Ephrain. "A Growing Awareness in Afro-American Literature." *Indigo*, 2: 48-51 (1974).
Omotoso, Kole. "Black Writing Today." *Afriscope*, 4: 43-4 (#7 74).
O'Neal, Frederick. "Problems and Prospects: The Negro in Today's Theatre." *BlackW*, 15: 4-12 (Ap 66).
O'Neal, John. "Motion in the Ocean: Some Political Dimensions of the Free Southern Theatre." *DramR*, 12: 70-7 (Su 68).
Parker, B.J. "Black Literature Teachers: Torchbearers of European Myths." *BlackW*, 25: 61-5 (#2 75).
Parks, Carole. "Symposium on Black Criticism." *BlackW*, 24: 64-5, 97 (#9 75).
Pawley, T.D. "The Black Theatre Audience." *Players*, 46: 257-61 (1971).
———. "First Black Playwrights." *BlackW*, 21: 16-24 (Ap 72).
Peavy, C.D. "The Black Revolutionary Novel, 1899-1969." *StN*, 3: 180-9 (Su 71).
———. "Four Black Revolutionary Novels, 1899-1970." *JBlackS*, 1: 219-23 (D 70).
———. "Satire and Contemporary Black Drama." *SNL*, 7: 40-9 (Fa 69).
Peek, Charles. "Notes on Reading Black Literature." *Aegis*, 62: 709-19 (1973).
Peden, William. "The Black Explosion." *SSF*, 12: 231-42 (Su 75).
Perkins, Eugene. "The Changing Status of Black Writers." *BlackW*, 19: 18-23, 95-8 (1970).
Petesch, D.A. "The Role of Folklore in the Modern Black Novel." *KanQ*, 7: 99-110 (#3 75).
*Pfeiffer, John. "Black Speculative Literature: A Checklist." *Extrapolation*, 17: 35-44 (1975).
Pierson, W.D. "An African Background for American Negro Folktales?" *JAF*, 84: 204-14 (Je 71).
Plessner, Monika. "Schwarz und Weiss vor Onkel Toms Hütte: Literatur und Wirklickkeit zwischen den Rassen bis zum amerikanischen Bürgerkrieg." *FrH*, 26: 43-50 (1971).
Portelli, Alessandro. "Cultura poetica afro-americana." *SA*, 14: 401-29 (1968).
Potter, V.R. "New Politics, New Mothers." *CLAJ*, 16: 247-55 (1972).
Powe, Marilyn. "Black 'Isms' from Mississippi." *MissFR*, 6: 76-82 (1972).
Powell, C.H. "Teaching Black Literature." *NALF*, 7: 16-8, 31 (1973).
*Primeau, Ronald. "Bibliography of Black Literature in Midwest." *Great Lakes R*, 2: 51-9 (#1 75).

————. ''Slave Narrative Turning Midwestern: Deadwood Dick Rides into Difficulties.'' *Midamerica*, 1974, pp. 16-35.

Pugh, G.T. ''Three Negro Novelists: Protest and Anti-Protest, A Symposium.'' *SHR*, 5: 17-50 (1970).

Putz, Manfred. ''Black Literature in der neueren Kritik.'' *NS*, 22: 159-68 (1973).

Querry, Ronald, and R.E. Fleming. ''A Working Bibliography of Black Periodicals.'' *SBL*, 3: 31-6 (Su 72).

Ramsaran, J.A. ''The 'Twice-Born' Artists' Silent Revolution.'' *BlackW*, 20: 58-68 (1971).

Ramsay, Alvin. ''Through a Glass Whitely: The Televized *Rape of Miss Jane Pittman.*''

Randall, Dudley. ''Black Publisher, Black Writer: An Answer.'' *BlackW*, 24: 32-7 (#5 75).

Redding, Saunders. ''American Negro Literature.'' *ASch*, 18: 137-48 (Sp 48).

————. ''The Black Arts Movement in American Poetry.'' *ASch*, 42: 330-6 (Sp 73).

————. ''The Black Revolution in American Studies.'' *AmSt*, 9: 3-9 (Au 70).

Redmond, E.B. ''The Black American Epic: Its, Roots, Its Writers.''*BSch*, 2: 15-22 (Ja 71).

————. ''Black Poets: History, Consciousness, Love, and Harshness.'' *Parnassus*, 3; 152-7 (1975).

Reed, A.W. ''The Speech of Negroes in Colonial America.'' *JNH*, 24: 247-58 (1939).

Reeves, W.J. ''The Significance of Audience in Black Poetry.'' *NALF*, 9: 30-2 (1975).

Rehin, G.F. ''The Darker Image: The American Negro Ministrelsy through the Historian's Lens.'' *JAmS*, 9: 365-73 (1975).

Reynolds, A.M. ''Urban Negro Toasts: A Hustler's View from L.A.'' *WF*, 33: 267-300 (1974).

Riach, D.C. ''Blacks and Blackface on the Irish Stage, 1830-1860.'' *JAmSt*, 7: 231-41 (D 73).

Riach, W.A.D. '''Telling It Like It Is': An Examination of the Black Theatre as Rhetoric.'' *QJS*, 56: 179-86 (Ap 70).

Riche, James. ''Anarchism and Reaction in Contemporary Afro-American Literature.'' *L&I*,1: 22-8 (19690.

————. ''The Politics of Black Modernism.'' *L&I*, 8: 85-90 (1971).

Riley, Clayton. ''The Dark Horse Rides Our Harlems.'' *BlackW*, 20: 37-8 (1971).

Rodabaugh, J.H. ''The Negro in Ohio.'' *JNH*, 31: 9-29 (Ja 46).

Rodgers, Carolyn. ''Black Poetry: Where It's At.'' *NegroD*,18: 7-16 (1969).

————. ''Breakforth: In Deed.'' *BlackW*, 19: 13-22 (1970).

Rodnon, Stewart. ''Black Belles-Lettres.'' *NALF*, 8: 284-7 (1974).

Rosenberg, B.A. ''The Formulaic Quality of Spontaneous Sermons.'' *JAF*, 83: 2-20 (1970).

Rosenthal, Bernard. ''Puritan Conscience and the New England Slavery.'' *NEQ*, 46: 62-81 (Mr 73).

Ross, Donald. ''The Role of Blacks in the Federal Theatre, 1935-1939.'' *JHN*, 59: 38-50 (1974).

Rowell, C.H. ''Sterling A. Brown and the Afro-American Folk Tradition.'' *SLitI*, 7: 131-52 (Fa 74).

*————. ''Studies in Afro-American Literature: An Annotated Bibliography.'' *Obsidian*, 1: 10-27 (#3 75).

Rubin, L.D. ''Black Poets in Search of a Language.'' *Bkmark*, 40: 3-15 (S 70); *Southeastern Lib*, 20: 213-21 (Wi 70).

————. ''Southern American Writers and the Black Man.'' *TC* (Australia), 25: 302-24 (Wi 71).

————. ''Southern Local Color and the Black Man.'' *SoR*, 6: 1011-30 (O 70).

Rubinstein, A.T. ''Amerikanische Negerschriftsteller heute.'' *Sinn und Form*, 20: 1264-76 (1968).

Ruchames, Louis. "The Sources of Racial Thought in Colonial America." *JNH*, 52: 251-72 (1967).

Rushing, A.B. "Image of Black Women in Afro-American Poetry." *BlackW*, 24: 18-30 (1975).

Russell, Mariann. "White Man's Black Man: Three Views." *CLAJ*, 17: 93-100 (S 73).

Sanders, J.B. "Black Literature for Children and Young Adults Published in 1971." *NALF*, 7: 3-15 (Sp 73).

Saxton, Alexander. "Blackface Minstrelry and Jacksonian Ideology." *AQ*, 27: 3-28 (Mr 75).

Schatt, Stanley. "The Faceless Face of Hatred: The Negro and Jew in Recent American Literature." *WR*, 7: 49-55 (1970).

———. "You Must Go Home Again: Today's Afro-American Expatriate Writers." *NALF*, 7: 80-2 (Fa 73).

Schraufnagel, Noel. "The Literary Image of the Negro." *PrS*, 44: 265-7 (Fa 70).

Schultz, Elizabeth. "To Be Black and Blue." *KanQ*, 7: 81-96 (1975).

Scott, Clifford. "Up the Congo Without a Paddle: Images of Blackest Africa in American Fiction." *NDQ*, 40: 7-19 (Au 72).

Scott, J.S. "Teaching Black Drama." *Players*, 47: 130-1 (1972).

Sellin, Eric. "Neo-African and Afro-American Literatures." *JML*, 1: 249-53 (1970).

Seyersted, Per. "A Survey of Trends and Figures in Afro-American Fiction." *AmSS*, 6: 67-86 (1974).

Shaw, F.W. "Booker T. Washington and the Future of Black Americans." *GHQ*, 56: 193-209 (Su 72).

Sheffer, Isaiah. "Black Theatre in America." *Nation*, 209: 151-2 (25 Ag 69).

Shelton, A.J. "The Ideology of Blackness and Beauty in America and Africa." *PA*, 79: 126-36 (1971).

Sherman, Alfonso. "Little Known Black Heros in Ante-Bellum Drama." *SpT*, 19: 130-7.

Sherman, J.R. "Connecticut's Nineteenth-Century Black Poets." *ConnR*, 5: 18-27 (Ap 72).

———. "James Monroe Whitfield, Poet and Emigrationist: A Voice of Protest and Despair." *JNH*, 57: 169-76 (Ap 72).

Sherr, P.C. "*Change Your Luck*: A Negro Satirizes White America." *Phylon*, 32: 281-9 (Fa 71).

Shores, D.L. "Black English and Black Attitudes." *SAB*, 39: 104-12 (4Q 74).

Simms, L.M. "Henry James and the Negro Question." *AN&Q*, 10; 127-8 (Ap 72).

———. "Robert Herrick and the Race Question." *NDQ*, 39: 34-8 (1971).

Singh, R.K. "The Black Novel and Its Tradition." *ColQ*, 20: 23-9 (Su 71).

Slotkin, Richard. "Narratives of Negro Crime in New England, 1675-1800." *AQ*, 25: 3-31 (Mr 73).

Small, R.C. "The Junior Novel and Race Relations." *NALF*, 8: 184-89 (Sp 74).

Smith, A.H. "Black Literature: The Junior Novel in the Classroom: *Harlem Summer*." *NALF*, 7: 26-7 (Sp 73).

Smith, J.C. "Developing Collections of Black Literature." *BlackW*, 2: 18-29 (1971).

Smith, W.F. "Minority Literature in the American University." *MichA*, 4: 525-31 (Sp 72).

Smitherman, Geneva. "Black Idiom." *NALF*, 5: 88-91, 115-7 (1971).

———. "'God Don't Never Change': Black English from a Black Perspective." *CE*, 34: 828-33 (1973).

———. "The Power of the Rap: The Black Idiom about the New Black Poetry." *TCL*, 19: 259-74 (O 73).

Soderborgh, P.A. "The Negro in Juvenile Series Books, 1899-1930." *JNH*, 58: 179-86 (Ap 73).

*Sollors, Werner. "Black Studies in the United States: A Bibliography." *JA*, 16: 213-22 (1971).

Spears, J.E. "Notes on Negro Folk Speech." *NCaF*, 18: 154-7 (N 70).

Spillers, H.J. "Martin Luther King and the Style of the Black Sermon." *BSch*, 3; 14-27 (S 71).

Spingarn, A.B. "Books by Negro Authors in 1967." *Crisis*, 75: 81-7, 99-101 (Mr 68).

Stansberry, F.B. "Folklore and Its Effects upon Black History." *MissFr*, 7: 115-22 (1973).

Steele, Shelley. " 'White Port and Lemon Juice': Notes on Ritual in the New Black Theatre." *BlackW*, 22; 4-13, 78-84 (#8 73).

Stein, M.L. "The Poet-Observer and 'Fern' in Jean Toomer's *Cane*." *MarkR*, 64-5 (O 70).

Stern, F.C. "Black Lit., White Crit?" *CE*, 35: 637-58 (Mr 74).

Stevenson, D.R. "Enlightenment Roots of Black American Self-Consciousness." *EnE*, 2: 11-8 (1971).

Stock, Irvin. "Black Literature, Relevance, and the New Irrationality." *Quadrant*, 16: 39-47 (N-D 72).

Stowe, W.E., and David Grimsted. "White-Black Humor." *JEthS*, 3: 78-96 (#2 75).

Stuckey, Sterling. "Contours of Black Studies: The Dimension of African and Afro-American Relationships." *MR*, 10: 747-56 (1969).

———. "Through the Prism of Folklore: The Black Ethos of Slavery." *MR*, 9: 417-37 (Su 68).

Sumpter, C.G. "The Negro in Twentieth Century American Drama: A Bibliography." *ThDoc*, 3: 3-27 (Fa-Sp 70-71).

Szwed, J.F. "Black Folk Culture in Pennsylvania." *KFG*, 19: 113-21 (1974).

Tatham, Campbell. "Double Order: The Spectrum of Black Aesthetics." *MASJ*, 111: 88-100 (Fa 70).

Taylor, Clyde. "Black Folk Spirit and the Shape of Black Literature." *BlackW*, 21: 31-40 (1972).

Teller, Walter. "Charles W. Chesnutt's Conjuring and Color-Line Stories." *ASch*, 42: 125-27 (Wi 71-72).

Thelwell, Mike. "Black Studies: A Political Perspective." *MR*, 10: 703-12 (1969).

———. "Publishing the Black Experience." *Ramparts*, 8: 60-3 (O 69).

Thompson, Larry. "The Black Image in Early American Drama." *BlackW*, 24: 54-69 (#4 75).

———. "Black Writing If It is Not Going to Disappear." *YLM*, 138: 4-6 (S 69).

Tischler, N.M. "The Metamorphosis of the Brute Negro." *Ranam*, 4: 3-11 (1971).

———. "The Negro in Southern Fiction: Stereotype and Archetype." *NALF*, 2: 3-6 (1968).

———. "Negro Literature and Classsic Form." *ConL*, 10: 352-65 (Su 69).

———. "Negro Novels and Christian Readers." *Chri & Lit*, 21: 36-41 (1971-72).

Trent, Tomi. "Stratifications among Blacks by Black Authors." *NHB*, 34: 179-81 (1971).

Tupper, V.G. "Plantation Echoes: A Negro Folk Music-Drama as Given Each Year in Charleston, South Carolina." *Etude*, 55: 153 (1937).

Turner, D.T. "Afro-American Authors: A Full House." *CEA*, 34: 15-9 (Ja 72).

———. "Afro-American Literary Critics." *BlackW*, 19: 54-67 (1970).

———. "The Negro Novel in America: a Rebuttal." *CLAJ*, 10: 122-34 (D 66).

———. "Negro Playwrights and the Urban Negro." *CLAJ*, 12: 19-25 (1968).

———. "The Teaching of Afro-American Literature." *CE*, 31: 666-70 (1970).

———. "Visions of Love and Manliness in a Blackening World: Dramas of Black Life Since 1953." *Iowa R*, 6: 82-98 (Sp 75).

———. "W.E.B. DuBois and the Theory of a Black Aesthetic." *SLitI*, 7: 1-22 (Fa 74).

Turner, Sherry. "An Overview of the New Black Arts." *Freedomways*, 9: 156-63 (1970).

Tuttle, W.M., and Surendra Bhana. "Black Newspapers in Kansas." *AmS*, 13: 119-26 (Fa 72).

Twining, M.A. "An Anthropological Look at Afro-American Folk Narrative." *CLAJ*, 14: 57-61 (S 70).

Uya, Okan. "The Mind of Slaves as Revealed in Their Songs: An Interpretive Essay." *CBBA*, 5: 3-11 (1972).

Vacha, J.E. "Black Man on the Great White Way." *JPC*, 7: 288-301 (1973).

Valenti, Suzanne. "The Black Diaspora; Negritude in the Poetry of West Indians and Black Americans." *Phylon*, 34: 390-8 (1973).

Vaughan, A.T. "Blacks in Virginia: A Note on the First Decade." *WMQ*, 29: 469-78 (1972).

Vauthier, Simone. "A Propos de l'image du noir aux amériques dans la premiere moitié de 19e siecle. *RANAM*, 3: 67-126 (1974).

Vendler, Helen. "Good Black Poems One By One." *NYT*, 29 S 74, pp. 3, 10-6.

Wadé, Melvin and Margaret. "The Black Aesthetic in the Black Novel." *JBlackS*, 2: 391-408 (Je 72).

Walcott, Ronald. "Some Notes on the Blues, Style & Space." *BlackW*, 22: 4-29 (1972).

Waldron, E.E. "Walter White and the Harlem Renaissance: Letters from 1924-1927." *CLAJ*, 16: 438-57 (Je 73).

Walker, Alice. "In Search of Our Mothers' Gardens: Honoring the Creativity of the Black Woman." *Jackson State R*, 6: 44-53 (#1 74).

Walters, R.G. "The Erotic South: Civilization and Sexuality in American Abolitionism." *AQ*, 25: 177-201 (My 73).

————. "The Negro Press and the Image of Success: 1920-1939." *MASJ*, 11: 36-55 (1970).

Walton, D.E.A. "Folklore as Compensation: A Content Analysis of the Negro Animal Tale." *JOFS*, 1: 15-25 (O 66).

Wander, P.C. "Salvation Through Separation: The Image of the Negro in the American Colonization Society." *QJS*, 57: 57-67 (1971).

Waniek, M.N. "The Space Where Sex Should Be: Toward a Definition of the Black American Tradition." *SBL*, 6: 7-13 (#3 75).

Ward, Francis, and V.G. Ward. "The Black Artist—His Role in the Struggle." *BSch*, 2: 23-32 (Ja 71).

Ward, J.W. "Folklore and the Study of Black Literature." *MissFR*, 6: 83-90 (1972).

Washington, M.H. "Black Women Image Makers." *BlackW*, 23: 10-8 (1974).

Weaver, Gordon. "Two Negro Folk-Poems." *MissFR*, 4: 98-104 (1970).

Weimer, D.R. "Black Realities and White: The City and the Imagination Gap." *SWR*, 54: 105-10 (Sp 69).

Welburn, Ron. "Nationalism and Internationalism in Black Literature: The Afro-American Scene." *Greenfield R*, 3: 60-72 (1974).

Wepman, Dennis, et al. "Toasts: The Black Urban Folk Poetry." *JAF*, 87: 208-24 (Jl-S 74).

Wessling, J.H. "Pressures on the Black Intellectual." *NALF*, 3: 117-8 (1970).

West, C.C., and Allen Williams. "Awareness: Teaching Black Literature in the Secondary School." *JBlackS*, 455-71 (Je 73).

Whitlow, Roger. "Black Literature and American Innocence." *SBL*, 5: 1-3 (Su 74).

Whitlow, Roger. "The Harlem Renaissance and After: A Checklist of Black Literature in the Twenties and Thirties." *NALF*, 7: 143-6 (Wi 73).

Whitmire, G.E. "Bibliography." *JNE*, 33: 421-35 (Fa 64).

Wiegenstein, Roland. "Eine Nation aus lauter Inseln: Streifzuge durchs schwarze Amerika." *Merkur*, 24: 669-84 (Jl 70).

Wilkerson, Margaret. "Black Theatre in California." *DramR*, 16: 25-35 (D 72).

Williams, J.A. "Black Publisher, Black Writer: An Impasse." *BlackW*, 24: 28-31 (#5 75).

———. "The Harlem Renaissance: Its Artists, Its Impact, Its Meaning." *BlackW*, 20: 17-8 (1970).

———. *"The Negro in Literature Today."* *Ebony*, 18: 73-6 (S 63).

Williams, M.G. "Snow White." *NCCL*, 22: 29-34 (Wi 73).

Williams, Ora. "A Bibliography of Works Written by American Black Women." *CLAJ*, 15: 354-77 (Mr 72).

Willis, R.A. and Hilda McElroy. "Published Works of Black Playwrights in the United States, 1960-1970." *BlackW*, 21: 92-8 (Ap 72).

Willis, R.J. "Anger and the Contemporary Black Theatre." *NALF*, 8: 213-5 (Su 74).

Wilson, J.D. "The Role of Slavery in the Agrarian Myth." *Ranam*, 4: 12-22 (1971).

Wilson, W.J. "The Quest for Meaningful Black Experience on White Campuses." *MR*, 10: 737-46 (1969).

Wright, B.M. "The Negritude Tradition in Literature." *SBL*, 3: 1-3 (Sp 72).

Wright, Richard. "Blueprint for Negro Literature." *Amistad*, 2: 3-20 (1971).

Wynes, C.E. "The Race Question in the South as Viewed by British Travellers, 1865-1914." *LaStud*, 13: 223-40 (1974).

Yetman, N.R. "The Background of the Slave Narrative Collection." *AQ*, 19: 534-53 (Fa 67).

Zanger, Jules. "The Minstrel Show as Theater of Misrule." *QJS*, 6: 33-8 (1974).

American Indian. *Anon. "Selected Bibliography of American Indian Writing." *SDR*, 9: 197-9 (Su 71).

Adler, Joyce. "Melville on the White Man's War Against the American Indian." *Sci&Soc*, 36: 417-42 (1972).

Alderson, Nova. "Frontier Literature; or, A Fast Draw on Navajo Nick, Tombstone Tom and Arizona Charlie." *JAriH*, 2: 27-31 (Su 61).

Allen, Paula. "Symbol and Structure in Native American Literature: Some Basic Considerations." *CCC*, 24: 267-70 (1973).

Axtell, James. "The White Indians of Colonial America." *WMQ*, 32: 55-88 (1975).

Barbour, P.L. "Chickanominy Place Names in Captain John Smith's *True Relation*." *Names*, 15: 216-25 (S 67).

Barnett, Louise. "Nineteenth-Century Indian Hater Fiction: A Paradigm for Racism." *SAQ*, 74: 224-36 (Sp 75).

Bennett, S.M. "Crazy Horse in Legend." *PsS*, 4: 5-12 (D 72).

Benson, R.M. "Ignoble Savage: Edward Eggleston and the American Indian." *IllQ*, 35: 41-51 (Fa 73).

Bernet, J.W. "Alaska Native Literature in the College and University." *Alaskan Eng J*, 1: 12-6 (1974).

Bevis, William. "American Indian Verse Translations." *CE*, 35: 693-703 (Mr 74).

Boyer, R.M. "A Mescalero Apache Tale: The Bat and the Flood." *WF*, 36: 189-97 (1972).

Brenzo, Rich. "American Indians vs. American Writers." *Margins*, 14: 40-5, 88 (O-N 74).

Brotherston, Gordon. "Ubirajara, Hiawatha, Cumanda: National Virtue from American Indian Literature." *CLS*, 9: 243-52 (S 72).

Byrd, L.B. "Using the Resources of Alaska in the Teaching of English." *Alaskan Eng J*, 1: 21-6 (1974).

Clancy, J.T. "Native American References: A Cross-Indexed Bibliography of Seventeenth Century American Imprints Pertaining to American Indians." *PAAS*, 83: 287-341 (1973).

Clark, L.H. "An Introduction to the Hopi Indians and Their Mythology." *Ariz Eng Bul*, 13: 1-14 (Ap 71).

Cook, Elizabeth. "Propulsives in Native American Literature." *CCC*, 24: 271-4 (1973).

Davis, J.B. "Some Cherokee Stories." *Annual Archives in Anthropology Univ Liverpool*, 3: 26-49 (1910).

Denton, L.W. "Mark Twain and the American Indian." *MTJ*, 16: 1-3 (Wi 71-2).

Dillingham, Peter. "The Literature of the American Indian." *EJ*, 62, 37-41 (1973).

Fields, Kenneth. "Seventh Wells: Native American Harmonies." *Parnassus*, 2: 172-98 (Sp-Su 74).

Fisher, Laura. "All Chiefs, No Indians: What Children's Books Say About American Indians." *Elementary Eng*, 51: 185-9 (F 74).

Fraser, J.H. "Indian Mission Printing in New Mexico: A Bibliography." *NMHR*, 43: 311-8 (O 68).

Gibson, Charles. "The Ingham Indian Collection." *BI*, 4: 3-8 (Ap 66).

Hamilton, W.L. "The Correlation between Social Attitudes and Those of American Authors in Depicting the American Indian." *Am Indian Q*, 1: 1-26 (1974).

Hansen, Chadwick. "The Metamorphosis of Tituba, or Why American Intellectuals Can't Tell an Indian Witch from a Negro." *NEQ*, 47: 3-12 (1974).

Haslam, Gerald. "American Indians: Poets of the Cosmos." *WAL*, 5: 15-29 (Sp 70).

———. "Literature of *The People*: Native American Voices." *CLAJ*, 15: 153-70 (D 71).

———. "Por La Causa! Mexican-American Literature." *CE*, 31: 695-709 (Ap 70).

Helms, Randel. " 'The Code of Handsome Luke': A Literary Study of Prophecy." *Genre*, 18-38: (Mr 71).

Hines, D.M. "Old Customs and Strange Ways, The American Indian c. 1640." *WR*, 7: 20-8 (1970).

Hough, R.L. "Washington Irving, Indians, and the West." *SDR*, 16: 27-39 (Wi 68-69).

Howell, Elmo. "William Gilmore Simms and the American Indian." *SCR*, 5: 57-64 (Je 73).

Huddleston, E.L. "Indians and Literature of the Federalist Era: The Case of of James Elliot." *NEQ*, 44: 221-37 (Je 71).

Hymes, Dell. "Some North Pacific Coast Poems: A Problem in Anthropological Philology." *StBr*, 1-2: 179-204 (Fa 68).

Inge, M.T. "Montezuma's Children Have a Voice." *RichM*, 10: 18 (N 72).

Judkins, R.A. "An Iroquois Death Messenger Vision." *NYFQ*, 30: 153-6 (Je 74).

Kaufman, D.L. "The Indian as a Media Hand-Me-Down." *ColQ*, 23: 489-504 (Sp 75).

Keim, C.J., and Jack Bemet. "From String Stories to Satellites: Portrayal of the Native Alaskan in Literature and Folklore." *BRMMLA*, 27: 167-73 (S 73).

Levine, Stuart ."Our Indian Minority." *ColQ*, 16: 297-320 (Wi 68).

Lincoln, K.R. "Native American Tribal Poetics." *SWR*, 60: 101-16 (Sp 75).

Littlefield, D.F., and L.E. Underhill. "Renaming the American Indian: 1890-1913." *AmS*, 12: 33-45 (Fa 71).

McNamara, Brooks. "The Indian Medicine Show." *ETJ*, 23: 431-5 (1971).

Magnaghi, R.M. "Herbert E. Bolton and Sources for American Indian Studies." *Western Hist Q*, 6: 33-46 (Ja 75).

McCullen, J.T. "Indian Myth Concerning the Origin of Tobacco." *NYFQ*, 23: 264-73 (D 67).

Matthews, Jack. "On the Trail of Belden, the White Chief." *OhR*, 15: 5-30 (Wi 74).

Mendelsohn, Maurice. "Whitman and the Oral Indian Tradtion." *AmD*, 7: 25-8 (1972).

Minter, D.L. "By Dens of Lions: Notes on Stylization in Early Puritan Captivity Narratives." *AL*, 45: 335-47 (N 73).

Murphy, J.N. "Silence, the Word, and Indian Rhetoric." *CCC*, 21: 356-63 (D 70).

Nash, G.B. "The Image of the Indian in the Southern Colonial Mind." *WMQ*, 29: 197-230 (Ap 72).

Nichols, R.L. "Printer's Ink and Red Skins: Western Newspapermen and Indians." *KanQ*, 3: 82-7 (Fa 71).

O'Donnell, T.F. "More Apologies: The Indian in New York Fiction." *NYFQ*, 23: 243-53 (D 67).

Officer, J.E. "A New Image for the Great White Father?" *MASJ*, 11; 5-19 (1970).

Olbrechts, F.M. "Two Cherokee Texts." *Int J Am Linguistics*, 6: 179-84 (1931).

Parsons, L.H. "'A Perpetual Harrow Upon My Feelings': John Quincy Adams and the American Indian." *NEQ*, 46: 339-79 (S 73).

Pearce, R.H. "The Metaphysics of Indian-Hating." *Ethnohistory*, 4: 27-40 (1957).

Peterson, R.K. "Indians in American Literature." *BB*, 30: 42-7 (Ja-Mr 73).

Pope, Polly. "Toward a Structural Analysis of North American Trickster Tales." *SFQ*, 31: 274-86 (S 67).

Povey, John. "My Proud Headdress: New Indian Writing." *SWR*, 57: 265-80 (Au 72).

——. "A New Second-Language Indian Literature." *Alaska R*, 3: 73-8 (Fa-Wi 69).

Redekop, Ernest. "The Redmen: Some Representations of Indians in American Literature before the Civil War." *CAAS*, 3: 1-44 (Wi 68).

Rothenberg, Jerome. "American Indian Workings." *PoetR*, 63: 17-29 (1972).

Sanders, Ronald. "Red Power at the Bookstore." *Midstream*, 18: 49-67 (Je-Jl 72).

Sanders, T.E. "Tribal Literature: Individual Identity and the Collective Unconscious." *CCC*, 24: 256-66 (1973).

Sayre, R.F. "A Bibliography and an Anthology of American Indian Literature." *CE*, 35: 704-6 (Mr 74).

Sayre, R.F. "Vision and Experience in *Black Elk Speaks*." *CE*, 32: 509-35 (F 71).

Schorer, C.E. "Indian Tales of C.C. Trowbridge: The Bad Man." *SFQ*, 36: 160-75 (1972).

——. "Indian Tales of C.C. Trowbridge: The Fisherman." *SFQ*, 38: 63-72 (Mr 74).

——. "Indian Tales of C.C. Trowbridge: The Ornamented Head." *SFQ*, 33: 317-32 (1969).

——. "Indian Tales of C.C. Trowbridge: 'Thrown Away.'" *SFQ*, 34: 341-52 (1970).

Sherwood, M.P. "Thoreau's Penobscot Indians." *TJQ*, 1: 13 (Ja 69).

Smith, W.F. "American Indian Literature." *EJ*, 63: 68-72 (Ja 74).

Sonnichsen, C.L. "The Ambivalent Apache." *WAL*, 10: 99-114 (Ag 75).

Speck, F.G. "Chickasaw Ethnology and Folklore." *JAF*, 20: 50-8 (1907).

——. "European Tales Among the Chickasaw Indians." *JAF*, 26: 319-30 (1913).

——. "Some Catawba Texts and Folk-Lore." *JAF*, 26: 319-30 (1913).

——, and L.G. Carr. "Catawba Folk Tales from Chief Sam Blue." *JAF*, 60: 79-84 (1947).

Stensland, A.L. "American Indian Culture: Promises, Problems, and Possibilities." *EJ*, 60: 1195-2000 (D 71).

Steuber, William. "The Novel as a Vehicle to Tell the Story of the Menominee Indians." *TWA*, 62: 51-5 (1974).

Thomas, C.E. "Puritans, Indians, and the Concept of Race." *NEQ*, 48: 3-27 (1975).

Trejo, Judy. "Coyote Tales: A Paiute Commentary." *JAF*, 87: 66-71 (Ja-Mr 74).

Turner, G.E. "The Century after the Century of Dishonor." *MR*, 16: 715-30 (1975).

Vancura, Zdenek. "Bringing the Gospel to the Indians of New England." *PP*, 14: 81-90 (1971).

VanDerBeets, Richard. "The Indian Captivity Narrative as Ritual." *AL*, 43: 548-62 (Ja 72).

——. "A Surfeit of Style: The Indian Captivity Narrative as Penny Dreadful." *RSW*, 39: 297-306 (1971).

——. "'A Thirst for Empire': The Indian Captivity Narrative as Propaganda." *RSW*, 40: 207-15 (1972).

Walker, D.D. "Broken Twigs, Moccasin Tracks, and the Laws of Nature." *PsS*, 2: 1-3 (F 71).

Washburn, Wilcomb. "History, Anthropology, and the American Indian." *AmS*, 11: 25-36 (1972).

Weidman, B.S. "White Men's Red Man: A Penitential Reading of Four American Novels." *MLS*, 4: 14-26 (Fa 74).

Whitford, Kathryn. "Hannah Dustin: The Judgement of History." *EIHC*, 108: 304-25 (1972).

Wiebe, Rudy. "The Year of the Indian." *DR*, 54: 164-7 (1974).

Zolbrod, P.G. "The Study of Native American Poetry: Some Possibilities." *MLS*, 2: 83-96 (Fa 73).

Chinese-American. Chinn, Frank, et al. "Aiieee! An Introduction to Asian-American Writing." *Yardbird Reader*, 2: 21-46 (1973).

Chu, Limin. "Mirror of Darkness: The Images of China and the Chinese in the Fiction of the *Overland Monthly*." *TkR*, 2: 15-49 (1971); 3: 1-40 (1972).

Israel, Jerry. "Muckrake and Manchu: The Image of China in the American Press, 1900-1912." *JRUL*, 31: 58-64 (Je 68).

*Wand, D.H. "Bibliography of Chinese Poets in America (Publications in English Exclusively)." *WLWE*, 19: 63-7 (1971).

German-American. Cazden, R.E. "The Provision of German Books in America during the Eighteenth Century." *Libri*, (Copenhagen), 23: 81-108 (1973).

Kopp, W.L. "Popular Reception of Classical German Drama in New York 1945-1965." *MLJ*, 55: 510-14 (1971).

Mews, S.E. " 'Pach den Tiger in dem tank': The American Press and the German Language." *Die Unterrichtspraxis*, 8: 18-21 (1970).

Roth, Juliana. "Travel Journals as a Folklife Research Tool: Impressions of Pennsylvania Germans." *PF*, 21: 28-38 (1972).

Shenk, S.C. "American Mennonite Fiction." *Mennonite Life*, 23: 119-20 (Jl 68).

Stern, M.B. "The First German *Faust* Published in America." *AN&Q*, 10: 115-6 (1972).

Suderman, E.F. "Fiction and Mennonite Life." *MASJ*, 10: 16-24 (Sp 69).

Thomas, J.W. "German Literature in the Old South." *AGR*, 19: 8-10, 33 (1952).

Waldenrath, Alexander. "The German Language Newspress in Pennsylvania during the American Revolution." *German-Am Stud*, 6: 43-56 (1973).

Jewish-American. Alter, Robert. "Literature and Crisis." *Commentary*, 62: 80-7 (O 71).

Baker, R.S. "The Disintegration of the Jews." *Am Mag*, 48: 490-604 (O 09).

Bellman, S.I. "Fathers and Sons in Jewish Fiction." *Congress Bi-Wk*, 34: 18-20 (22 My 67).

————. "Sleep, Pride, and Fantasy: Birth Trauma and Socio-Biologic Adaptation in the American-Jewish Novel." *Costerus*, 8: 1-12 (1973).

Ben-Amos, Dan. "The 'Myth' of Jewish Humor." *WF*, 32: 112-31 (Ap 73).

Bercovitch, Sacvan. "Puritan New England Rhetoric and the Jewish Problem." *EAL*, 5: 63-73 (1970).

Bitton, L.E. "The Jewess as a Fictional Sex Symbol." *BuR*, 21: 63-86 (Sp 73).

Bloom, Harold. "The Sorrows of American-Jewish Poetry." *Commentary*, 53: 69-74 (Mr 72).

Chametzky, Jules. "Notes on the Assimilation of the American-Jewish Writer." *JA*, 9: 173-8 (1964).

Daiches, David. "Some Aspects of Anglo-American Jewish Fiction." *JewQ*, 21: 88-93 (1973).

Dubrovsky, G.W. "I.J. Schwartz's Kentucky: The Americanization of 'The Grandchildren of Wander.' " *Judaism*, 23: 216-27 (1974).

Fein, R.J. "Jewish Fiction in America." *Judaism*, 24: 406-15 (1975).

Fiedler, L.A. "Master of Dreams." *PR*, 34: 339-56 (Su 67).

Fine, D.M. "Attitudes toward Acculturation in the English Fiction of the Jewish Immigrant, 1900-1917." *AJHQ*, 63: 45-56 (S 73).

Friedman, A.W. "The Jew's Complaint in Recent American Fiction: Beyond Exodus and Still in the Wilderness." *SoR*, 8: 41-59 (Ja 72).

Garfield, David. "The Romance of a People." *ETJ*, 24: 436-42 (1972).

Glicksberg, C.I. "A Jewish American Literature?" *SWR*, 53: 196-205 (Sp 68).

Gold, Joseph. "Promised Land and Vanishing People." *CRAS*, 3: 60-2 (1972).

Goldman, Albert. "Boy-Man Schlemiel: Jewish Humor." *Cweal*, 86: 605-8 (29 S 67).

Collin, Rita. "Understanding Fathers in American Jewish Fiction." *CentR*, 18: 273-87 (Su 74).

Goodman, O.B. "There Are Jews Everywhere." *Judaism*, 19: 283-94 (1970).

Greenberg, Andrea. "Form and Function of the Ethnic Joke." *KFQ*, 17: 144-61 (1972).

Guttman, Allen. "The Conversions of the Jews." *ConL*, 6: 161-76 (Su 65).

————. "Jewish Radicals, Jewish Writers." *ASch*, 32: 563-75 (Au 63).

Hapgood, Hugchins. "Sketch Writers of the Ghetto." *Bkm*, 14: 263-75 (N 01).

Harap, Louis. "Image of the Jew in American Drama, 1794-1823." *AJHQ*, 60: 242-57 (Mr 71).

Hendrich, B.J. "Radicalism Among the Polish Jews: Their Destructive Political Activities as Shown in Their Newspapers, Their Votes, and Their Labor Unions." *WWk*, 45: 590-601 (Ap 23).

Hirano, Nobuyuki. "Between 'No Way Out' and 'Way Out.'" *HiJAS*, 12: 26-35 (1971).

Hurvitz, Nathan. "Blacks and Jews in American Folklore." *WF*, 33: 301-25 (1974).

Inge, M.T. "The Ethnic Experience and Aesthetics in Literature." *JEthS*, 1: 45-50 (Wi 74).

Iwamoto, Iwao. "Judea-kei Sakka no Miryoku—Barth to Malamud." *EigoS*, 118: 257-60 (1972).

Jason, Heda. "The Jewish Joke: The Problem of Definition." *SFQ*, 31: 48-54 (Mr 67).

Landis, J.C. "America and Yiddish Literature." *JBA*, 33: 20-32 (1975).

————. "Reflections on Jewish Writers." *JBA*, 25: 140-7 (1967).

Lewis, S.A. "The Jewish Author Looks at the Black." *ColQ*, 21: 317-30 (Wi 73).

Liptzin, Solomon. "The Yiddish Novel of Young America." *CJF*, 25: 9-14 (Fa 66).

Madison, C.A. "Jews in American Publishing." *CJF*, 26: 282-7 (Su 68).

Markfield, Wallace. "Yiddishization of American Humor." *Esquire*, 64: 114-5, 136 (O 65).

Miyamoto, Yokichi. "Jewish American no Mujun." *EigoS*, 117: 732-3 (1972).

Pinsker, Sanford. "Deafending the American-Jewish Novel." *STC*, 8: 85-93 (Fa 71).

————. "The Rise-and-Fall of the American Jewish Novel." *ConnR*, 7: 16-23 (O 73).

————. "The Schlemiel in Yiddish and American Literature." *CJF*, 25: 191-5 (Sp 67).

Poger, Sidney. "American Jewish Fiction: Local Color Movement of the Fifties." *CLAJ*, 18: 404-11 (Mr 75).

Porter, M.G. "'Spiritual Activism' and 'Radical Sophistication' in the Contemporary American Novel." *StN*, 3: 332-43 (Fa 71).

Prager, Leonard. "Shakespeare in Yiddish." *SQ*, 19: 149-63 (Sp 68).

Rich, J.C. "50 Years of the Jewish *Daily Forward*." *NewL*, 40: 1-38 (3 Je 57).

Richards, B.G. "The Attitude of the Jews Towards Jewish Fiction." *Reader*, 1: 46-9 (N 02).

Richler, Mordecai. "Write, Boychick, Write." *NSt*, 7 Ap 67, pp. 473-4.

Rosenberg, Edgar. "The Jew in Western Drama." *BNYPL*, 72: 442-94 (S 68).

Rowenfield, A.H. "The Progress of the American Jewish Novel." *Response*, 7: 115-30 (#1 73).

————. "Yiddish Poets and Playwrights of America: A Preliminary Report on a Recent Addition to the Harris Collection." *BBr*, 22: 161-81 (1968).

Rovit, Earl. "Jewish Humor and American Life." *ASch*, 36: 237-45 (Sp 67).

Schatt, Stanley. "The Dybbuk Had Three Wives: Isaac Bashevis Singer and the Jewish Sense of Time." *Judaism*, 232: 100-8 (1974).

————. "The Faceless of Hatred: The Negro and Jew in Recent American Literature." *WR*, 7: 49-55 (1970).

————. "The Torah and the Time Bomb: The Teaching of Jewish-American Literature Today." *CLAJ*, 18: 534-41 (Mr 75).

Schulz, M.F. "Isaac Bashevis Singer, Radical Sophistication and the Jewish-American Novel." *SHR*, 60-6, (Wi 68).

Schwartz, Donald. "The Yiddish Art Theatre." *Players*, 50: 138-41 (1975).

Shpall, Leo. "A List of Selected Items of American-Jewish Interest in the Russian-Jewish Press." *PAJHS*, 38: 239-48 (Mr 49).

Shultz, Donald. "Jewish Humor: The Corridor of Laughter." *KAL*, 16: 37-9 (1975).

Stern, Madeleine. "Henry Frank: Pioneer American Jewish Publisher." *AJA*, 20: 163-8 (N 68).

Weber, Ronald. "Jewish Writing in America: Jewish or American?" *BSUF*, 10: 40-6 (Sp 69).

Mexican-American. Brokaw, J.W. "A Mexican-American Acting Compay, 1849-1924." *ETJ*, 27: 23-9 (1975).

Brox, L.M. "Los Limites del costumbrismo en *Estampas del valle y otras obras*." *Mester*, 5: 101-4 (1975).

DeCaro, R.J. "Language Loyalty and Folklore Studies: The Mexican-American." *WF*, 31: 77-88 (1972).

Hancock, Joel. "The Emergence of Chicano Poetry: A Survey of Sources, Themes, and Techniques." *ArQ*, 29: 57-72 (Sp 73).

Haslam, Gerald. "The Enigma of Amado Jesus Muro." *WAL*, 10: 3-9 (My 75).

————. "*Por la Causa!* Mexican-American Literature." *CE*, 31: 695-709 (Ap 70).

Hinojosa, Rolando. "Mexican-American Literature: Toward an Identification." *BA*, 49: 422-31 (Su 75).

Kanellos, Nilcolas. "Mexican Community Theatre in a Midwestern City." *Latin Am Th R*, 7: 43-8 (1973).

Leal, Luis. "Mexican American Literature: A Historical Perspective." *Revista Chicano-Requena*, 1: 32-44 (1973).

Ortega, Philip. "Chicano Poetry: Roots and Writers." *SwAL*, 2: 8-24 (Sp 72).

Ortega, P.D. "Fables of Identity: Stereotype and Caricature of Chicanos in Steinbeck's *Tortilla Flat*." *JEthS*, 1: 39-43 (1973).

Rivera, Tomas. "Chicano Literature: Fiesta of the Living." *BA*, 49: 439-53 (Su 75).

————. "Into the Labyrinth: The Chicano in Literature." *SwAL*, 2: 90-7 (Fa 72).

Robinson, Cecil. "The Fall of 'The Big House' in the Literature of the Americas." *ArQ*, 24: 23-41 (Sp 68).

————. "With Ears Attuned—and the Sound of New Voices: An Updating of *With the Ears of Strangers*." *SwAL*, 1: 51-59 (1971).

Rodrigues, R.J. "A Few Directions in Chicano Literature." *EJ*, 62: 724-9 (1973).

Rojas, Guillermo. "Chicano/Raza Newspaper and Periodicals Serial Listing." *Hispania*, 58: 851-63 (1975).

Sandoval, Ralph, and A.P. Nilsen. "The Mexican-American Experience." *EJ*, 63: 61-3 (1974).

Simmen, Edward. "'We Must Make This Beginning': The Chicano Leader Image in the Short Story." *SWR*, 57: 126-33 (Sp 72).

Sonnichsen, C.L. "The Two Black Legends." *SwAL*, 3: 5-26 (1973).

Tatum, C.M. "Contemporary Chicano Prose Fiction: Its Ties to Mexican Literature." *BA*, 49: 431-9 (Su 75).

Tovar, I.H. "Roses are Rosas." *Mester*, 5: 95-100 (1975).

Veiga, Gustavo da. "Tomas Rivera e la literatura chicana dos Estados Unidos." *MGSL*, 27: 11 (May 72).

Puerto Rico-Americans. Arana-Soto, Salvador. "Puerto Rico en la novela popular norteamericana." *CHA*, 68: 389-403 (1966).

DeCosta, M.S. "Social Lyricism and the Caribbean Poet/Rebel." *CLAJ*, 15: 441-51 (1972).

Scandanavian-American. Beards, R.D. "Stereotyping in Modern American Fiction: Some Solitary Swedish Madmen." *MSpr*, 63: 329-37 (1969).

Lovoll, O.S. "North Dakota's Norwegian-Language Press Views World War I, 1914-1917." *NDQ*, 39: 73-84 (Wi 71).

Nelsen, F.C. "The Norwegian-American's Image of America." *IllQ*, 36: 5-23 (Ap 74).

Fiction. Anon. "Contemporary Notes on Novels Concerned With Slavery." *ESQ*, 47: 138-9 (2Q 67).

————. "International Symposium on the Short Story." *KR*, 31: 450-503 (1969).

————. "The Professional Viewpoint." *TCS*, 1: 109-30 (N 69).

————. "What's Wrong with the American Novel?" *ASch*, 24: 464-503 (Au 55).

Aadland, Dan. "Some Thoughts on Clichés and Conventions in the 60¢ Western." *PosS*, 4: 4-6 (Ja-F 73).

Adams, I.W. "Society as Novelist." *JAAC*, 25: 375-86 (Su 67).

Adams, Percy. "The Epic Tradition and the Novel." *SoR*, 9: 300-10 (Ja 73).

Alderson, Nova. "Frontier Literature; or, A fast Draw on Navajo Nick, Tombstone Tom, and Arizona Charlie." *JAriH*, 2: 27-31 (Su 61).

Aldridge, John. "The American Novel at the Present Time." *RLV*, 40: 122-31 (Ja-F 74).

————. "Contemporary Fiction and Mass Culture." *NOR*, 1: 4-9 (Fa 68).

Allen, Richard. "If You Have Tears: Sentimentalism as Soft Romanticism." *Genre*, 8: 119-45 (Je 75).

Allen, Walter. "Thirties Fiction: A View from the 70's." *TCL*, 20: 245-52 (O 74).

Allen, W.E. "Some Aspects of the American Short Story." *Proc British Acad*, 59: 125-40 (1973).

Alter, Robert. "Literature and Crisis." *Commentary*, 62: 80-7 (O 71).

Anastasjew, N. "'Massenbelletristik' in den USA: Sozialer Auftrag und asthetische Klischees." *KuL*, 21: 1113-37 (1973).

Andersson, Thomas. "'As Crazy as Two Waltzing Mice': About American Similies.'" *MSpr*, 65: 223-6 (1971).

Antonini, Giacomo. "La narrative americana fra il 1967 ed it 1968." *OPL*, 14: 80-91 (1968).

App, A.J. "Better Ethical Standards for Novels." *CathLW*, 34: 86-88, 105-7 (O 62).

Arana-Soto, Salvador. "El mundo hispanico en la novela popular norteamericana." *CA*, 157: 238-53 (1968).

————. "Puerto Rico en la novela popular norteamericana." *CHA*, 68: 389-403 (1966).

Arrington, L.J., and Jon Haupt. "The Missouri and Illinois Mormons in Ante-Bellum Fiction." *Dialog*, 5: 37-50 (Sp 70).

Astro, Richard. "*The Big Sky* and the Limits of Western Fiction." *WAL*, 9: 105-14 (1974).

Babbit, Natalie. "The Great American Novel for Children—and Why Not." *HornB*, 50: 176-85 (Ap 74).

Backers, J.M. "'He Came Into Her Line of Vision Walking Backward': Nonsequential Sequence Signals in Short Story Openings." *LL*, 15: 67-83 (Su 65).

Baker, D.G. "Black Images: The Afro-American in Popular Novels, 1900-1945." *JPC*, 7: 327-46 (1973).

———. "From Apartheid to Invisibility: Black Americans in Popular Fiction, 1900-1960." *MwQ*, 13: 365-85 (Jl 72).

Baldeshwiler, Eileen. "The Lyric Short Story: The Sketch of History." *SSF*, 6: 443-53 (Su 69).

Barnes, Robert. "Novels of the Oil Industry in the Southwest." *SwAL*, 2: 74-82 (Fa 72).

Barnett, Louise. "Nineteenth-Century Indian Hater Fiction: A Paradigm for Racism." *SAQ*, 74: 224-36 (Sp 75).

Barsness, John. "Creativity Through Hatred—and a Few Thoughts on the Western Novel." *WR*, 6: 12-7 (1969).

Barsness, J.A. "Platform Manner in the Novel: A View from the Pit." *MASJ*, 10: 49-59 (Fa 69).

Barthell, R.J. "Science Fiction: A Literature of Ideas." *Extrapolation*, 13: 56-63 (D 71).

Beards, R.D. "Stereotyping in Modern American Fiction: Some Solitary Swedish Madmen." *MSpr*, 63: 329-37 (1969).

Beekman, E.M. "Raymond Chandler & an American Genre." *MR*, 14: 149-73 (Wi 73).

Behar, Jack. "Notes on Literature and Culture." *CentR*, 18: 197-220 (1974).

Bell, B.W. "Literary Sources of the Early Afro-American Novel." *CLAJ*, 18: 29-43 (S 74).

Bell, P.K. "American Fiction: Forgetting the Ordinary Views." *Dissent*, 20: 26-34 (Ja 73).

Bellman, S.I. "The Apocalypse in Literature." *Costerus*, 7: 13-25 (1973).

———. "Fathers and Sons in Jewish Fiction." *Congress Bi-Wk*, 34: 18-20 (22 My 67).

———. "Two-Part Harmony: Domestic Relations and Social Vision in the Modern Novel." *CEJ*, 3: 31-41 (1967).

Bennet, J.R. "Style in Twentieth Century British and American Fiction: A Bibliography." *WCR*, 2: 43-51 (Wi 68).

Bennet, S.B., and W.W. Nichols. "Violence in Afro-American Fiction: An Hypothesis." *MFS*, 17: 221-8 (Su 71).

Benschoten, Virginia. "Changes in Best Sellers Since World War One." *JPC*, 379-88 (1968).

Bergmann, Frank. "Under the Sign of the Unicorn's Head: Adult Fantasy and Contemporary America." *JA*, 19: 50-7 (1974).

Bessière, Jean. "L'Amerique hors texte: Semantique du roman international (1920-35)." *Degrés*, 4: 1-24 (1973).

Bier, Jesse. "The Romantic Coordinates of American Literature." *BuR*, 18; 16-33 (Fa 70).

Binni, Francesco. "Per una poetica del naturalismo." *SA*, 13: 29-324 (1967).

Bitton, L.E. "The Jewess as a Fictional Sex Symbol." *BuR*, 21: 63-86 (Sp 73).

Blair, Walter. "Roots of American Realism." *UKCR*, 4: 275-81 (Je 40).

Blanch, Antonio. "El problema negro en la novela norteamericana." *Razon y Fe*, 68: 203-22 (S-O 68).

———. "Il problema razziale nel romanzo nordamericano." *CCa*, 119: 131-44 (1968).

Blotner, Joseph. "The Modern American Political Novel." *SELit*, 45: 106-10 (Se 68).

Boatright, M.C. "The Beginnings of Cowboy Fiction." *SWR*, 51: 11-28 (Wi 66).

———. "The Formula in Cowboy Fiction and Drama." *WF*, 28: 136-45 (Ap 69).

Borden, Caroline. "Characterization in Revolutionary Chinese and Reactionary American Short Stories." *L&I*, 12: 9-16 (1972).

Boulger, J.D. "Puritan Allegory in Four Modern Novels." *Thought*, 44: 413-32 (Au 69).

Boxer, Phillip. "Toward the New American Novel." *NCampR*, 1: 41-9 (My 66).

Fiction

Bradbury, Malcolm. "The Novel and Reality." *Enc*, 34: 43-50 (Je 70).

Brandstadter, Evan. "Uncle Tom and Archy Moore: The Antislavery Novel as Ideological Symbol." *AQ*, 26: 160-75 (My 74).

Braxton, Jodi. "Asserting Selfhood." *NRep*, 167: 27-30 (4 N 72).

Brennan, J.G. "Three Novels of Depaysement." *CL*, 22: 223-36 (Su 70).

Brière, Annie. "Le roman traditionnel dans la littérature americaine." *RDM*, 1 (Ja 69).

Broberg, Jan. "Mord i minne." *Bokvännen*, 23: 198-201 (1968).

———. "USA i röntgenbild." *Horisont*, 15: 41-8 (1968).

Brogger, F.C. "Den amerikanske roman i det 20 arhundre." *Samtiden*, 78: 182-91 (Mr 69).

Brossard, Chandler. "Commentary (Vituperative): The Fiction Scene; or, Has Anyone Seen Billygoat Gruff Lately?" *HM*, 244: 106-10 (Je 72).

Brown, H.O.J. "Literature or Indoctrination." *ModA*, 2: 266-71 (Su 67).

Brown, M.J. "The Treatment of Money in American Fiction." *L&I*, 4: 69-84 (1969).

Browning, P.M. "The Quest for Being in Contemporary Fiction." *Forum(H)*, 12: 40-6 (1974).

Bruffee, K.A. "Elegiac Romance." *CE*, 32: 465-76 (Ja 71).

Brumm, Urusula. "Thoughts on History and the Novel." *CLS*, 6: 317-33 (S 69).

Bruning, Eberhard. "Tendenzen der Personlichkets-gestaltung in amerikanischen Gegenwartsroman." *ZAA*, 16: 390-401 (1968).

Bryant, J.H. "Politics and the Black Novel." *Nation*, 213: 660-2 (20 D 71).

Buckeye, Robert. "The Anatomy of the Psychic Novel." *Critique*, 9: 2, 33-45 (1967).

Budd, L.J. "The Hungry Bear of American Realism." *ALR*, 5: 485-7 (Fa 72).

———. "Objectivity and Low Seriousness in American Naturalism." *Prospects*, 1: 41-61 (1975).

Bungert, Hans. "Amerikanisches Hochschulwesen in literarischer Gestaltung." *JA*, 12: 74-91 (1967).

Bulow, Nannette. "The Maverick Metaphor: The Use of Cowboy Vernacular in Fiction." *PosS*, 5: 10-6 (N 73).

Burgess, Anthony. "The Postwar American Novel: A View from the Periphery." *ASch*, 35: 150-6 (Wi 65-66).

Burke, Kenneth. "Why Satire, with a Plan for Writing One." *MQR*, 13: 307-37 (Fa 74).

Burns, L.C. "A Cross-Reference Index of Short Fiction and Author Title Listing." *SSF*, 7: 1-218 (Wi 70).

Bus, Heiner, "Die Figur des 'Helden' im modernen amerikanischen Roman: ein Forschungsbericht." *JA*, 15: 208-20 (1970).

Busch, Frederick. "The Friction of Fiction." *ChiR*, 26: 5-17 (Sp 75).

Butscher, Edward. "The American Novel Is Alive and Well." *GaR*, 27: 393-7 (Fa 73).

Byrd, Scott. "A Separate War: Camp and Black Humor in Recent American Fiction." *LangQ*, 7: 7-10 (1968).

Cameron, K.W. "Defining the American Transcendental Novel." *ATQ*, 20: 114-21 (Fa 73).

Canaday, Nicholas. "The Antislavery Novel Prior to 1852." *CLAJ*, 17: 175-91 (D 73).

Canary, R.H. "Science Fiction as Fictive History." *Extrapolation*, 16: 81-95 (D 74).

Capellan Gonazalo, Angel. "Tres acercaminentos a la literatura norteamericana reciente." *Arbor*, 342: 107-13 (1974).

Cardwell, G.A. "The Plantation House: An Analogical Image." *SLJ*, 2: 3-21 (Fa 69).

Carter, P.A. "Extravagant Fiction Today—Cold Fact Tomorrow: A Rationale for the First American Science-Fiction Magazines." *JPC*, 5: 842-57 (Sp 72).

———. "Rockets to the Moon 1919-1944: A Dialogue Between Fiction and Reality." *AmS*, 15: 31-46 (1974).

Carter, Paul. "Of Towns and Roads: Three Novelists, and George McGovern." *ColF*, 2: 10-6 (Sp 73).

Caute, David. "Commitment Without Empathy: A Writer's Notes on Politics, Theatre, and the Novel." *TriQ*, 30: 51-70 (Sp 74).

Cawelti, J.G. "The New Mythology of Crime." *Boun2*, 3: 325-57 (Wi 75).

———. "Prolegomena to the Western." *WAL*, 4: 259-71 (Wi 70).

Chametzky, Jules. "Our Decentralized Literature: A Consideration of Regional, Ethnic, Racial, and Sexual Factors." *JA*, 17: 56-72 (1972).

Chanan, Gabriel. "The Plight of the Novelist." *CamR*, 89A: 399-402 (26 Ap 68).

Chapman, R.T. " 'Parties . . . Parties . . . Parties': Some Images of the 'Gay Twenties.' " *English*, 21: 93-7 (1972).

Chase, R.H. "Cesare Pavese and the American Novel." *SA*, 3: 347-69 (1957).

Chu, Limin. "Mirror of Darkness: The Images of China and the Chinese in the Fiction of the *Overland Monthly*." *TkR*, 2: 15-49 (1971).

Clareson, T.D. "Science Fiction in 1971." *Extrapolation,* 13: 75-9 (1971).

———. "Science Fiction: The New Mythology." *Extrapolation,* 10: 69-115 (My 69).

Clark, W.B. "The Serpent of Lust in the Southern Garden." *SoR*, 10: 805-22 (O 74).

Clarke, I.F. " 'Voices Prophesying War': Problems in Research." *Extrapolation*, 9: 26-32 (My 68).

Cohn, Jan. "The Civil War in Magazine Fiction of the 1860's." *JPC*, 4: 355-82 (Fa 70).

———. "The Negro Character in Northern Magazine Fiction of the 1860's." *NEQ*, 43: 572-92 (D 70).

Colwell, James. "More on the Tragic Octoroon." *AN&Q*, 6: 147-8 (Je 68).

Condon, Richard. "Party of One: Adventures of a Middle-aged Novelist." *Holiday*, 31: 10, 16-20 (ja 62).

Cooke, M.G. "The Descent into the Underworld and Modern Black Fiction." *IowaR*, 5: 72-9 (Fa 74).

Cooperman, Stanley. "American War Novels: Yesterday, Today, and Tomorrow." *YR*, 61: 517-29 (J e 72).

Cope, Jack, et al. "International Symposium on the Short Story." *KR*, 32: 78-108 (1970).

*Corrigan, R.A. "Afro-American Fiction: A Checklist, 1853-1970." *MASJ,* 11: 114-35 (Fa 70).

———. "Afro-American Fiction: Errata and Additions." *AmS*, 12: 69-73 (Sp 71).

———. "Afro-American Fiction Since 1970." *AmS*, 14: 85-90 (Fa 73).

———. "Bibliography of Afro-American Fiction, 1853-1970." *SBL*, 1: 51-86 (1970).

Cowley, Malcolm. "Storytelling's Tarnished Image." *SatR*, 54: 25-7, 54 (25 S 71).

Cunningham, Frank. "The Story's the Thing." *SR*, 77: 526-9 (1969).

Davis, D.B. "Violence in American Literature." *AAAPSS*, 364: 28-36 (Mr 66).

*Davis, R.M. "An Annotated Checklist for Students of Allegory in Modern Fiction." *Genre*, 5: 169-75 (D 72).

———. "The Shrinking Garden and New Exits: The Comic-Satiric Novel in the Twentieth Century." *KanQ*, 1: 5-16 (1969).

De Bellis, Jack. "The Southern Universe and the Counter-Renaissance." *SoR*, 4: 471-81 (Sp 68).

DeMott, Benjamin. "In and Out of Universal City: Reflections on the New Journalism and the Old Fiction." *AR*, 29: 15-24 (Sp 69).

Detweiler, Robert. "The Moment of Death in Modern Fiction." *ConL*, 13: 269-94 (Su 72).

———. "Christ and the Christ Figure in American Fiction." *ChS*, 47: 117-22 (Su 64).

Dew, Marjorie. "Realistic Innocence: Cady's Footnote to a Definition of American Literary Realism." *ALR*, 5: 487-9 (Fa 72).

Dickstein, Morris. "The Black Aesthetic in White America." *PR*, 38: 376-95 (Wi 71-72).

———. "Fiction Hot and Kool: Dilemmas of the Experimental Writer." *TriQ*, 33: 257-272 (Sp 75).

Dillingham, W.B. "Days of the Tall Tale." *SoR*, 569-77 (Sp 68).

Ditsky, John. "Carried Away by Numbers: The Rhapsodic Mode in Modern Fiction." *QQ*, 79: 482-94 (Wi 72).

———. "The Man on the Quaker Oats Box: Characteristics of Recent Experimental Fiction." *GaR*, 26; 297-313 (Fa 72).

Ditsky, J.M. "True Grit and *True Grit*." *ArielE*, 4: 18-30 (1973).

Dizer, J.T. "Land of the Heroes." *Dime Novel Round Up*, 40: 52-6, 62-7, (15 Jl 71).

Doherty, J.F. "Hawthorne's Communal Paradigm: The American Novel Reconsidered." *Genre*, 7: 30-53 (Mr 74).

Donahue, Jane. "Colonial Shipwreck Narrative: A Theological Study." *BBr*, 23: 101-34 (1969).

Donaldson, Scott. "Family Crises in the Popular Novels of Nixon's Administration." *JPC*, 6: 374-82 (Fa 72).

———. "The Old *World*, the New Journalism, and the Novel." *SR*, 82: 527-37 (Fa 74).

Donoghue, Denis. "The American Style of Fiction." *SR*, 82: 407-32 (Su 74).

Doughty, N.S. "Realistic Negro Characterization in Postbellum Fiction." *NALF*, 3: 57-62, 68 (Su 69).

Dovis, Craig. "Novels of Peasant Crisis." *J Peasant Stud*, 2: 47-68 (O 74).

Dowty, Alan. "Urban Slavery in Pro-Slavery Fiction of the 1850's." *JSH*, 32: 25-31 (F 66).

Drake, Robert. "Rubin on Fiction and Other Matters." *SoR*, 6: 857-62 (Su 70).

Durham, Frank. "Not According to the Book: Materialism and the American Novel." *GaR*, 20: 90-8 (Sp 66).

———. "The Reputed Demises of Uncle Tom; or, The Treatment of the Negro in Fiction by White Southern Authors in the 1920's." *SLJ*, 2: 26-50 (Sp 70).

———. "The Southern Literary Tradition: Shadow or Substance." *SAQ*, 67: 455-68 (Su 68).

Duus, Louise. "Neither Nor Sinners: Women in Late Nineteenth-Century Fiction." *ALR*, 7: 276-8 (Su 74).

Edelstein, Arthur. "Art and Artificiality in Some Recent Fiction." *SoR*, 9: 736-44 (Jl 73).

Ellison, Ralph, William Styron, R.P. Warren, and C. Vann Woodward. "The Uses of History in Fiction." *SLJ*, 1: 57-90 (Sp 69).

Epstein, Seymour. "Politics and the Novelist." *DQ*, 4: 1-18 (Wi 70).

Erisman, Fred. "American Regional Juvenile Literature, 1870-1910: An Annotated Bibliography." *ALR*, 6: 109-22 (Sp 73).

———. "'Where We Plan to Go': The Southwest in Utopian Fiction." *SwAL*, 1: 137-43 (S 71).

Erwin, Robert. "The Eclipse of the Intellectual Hero." *VQR*, 48: 199-213 (Sp 72).

Etulain, R.W. "Frontier and Region in Western Literature." *SwAL*, 1: 121-28 (1972).

———. "The Historical Development of the Western." *JPC*, 7: 7-26 (Wi 73).

———. "Literary Historians and the Western." *JPC*, 4: 518-26 (Fa 70).

———. "The New Western Novel." *Idaho Yesterdays*, 15: 12-7 (Wi 72).

———. "Origins of the Western." *JPC*, 5: 799-805 (Sp 72).

———. "Three Western Novels." *JWest*, 10: 389-90 (Ap 71).

Evans, R.O. "A Perspective for American Novelists." *Topic*, 6: 58-66 (Fa 66).

Evans, Walter. "The All-American Boys: A Study of Boys Sports Fiction." *JPC*, 6: 104-21 (Su 72).

Everett, Carter. "The Meaning of, and in, Realism." *AR*, 12: 78-94 (Sp 52).

Federman, Raymond. "Surfiction—a Position." *PR*, 40: 427-32 (#3 73).

Fein, R.J. "Jewish Fiction in America." *Judaism*, 24: 406-15 (1975).

Fender, Stephen. "The Western and the Contemporary." *JAmSt*, 6: 97-108 (Ap 72).

Ferguson, A.R. "The Abolition of Blacks in Abolitionist Fiction, 1830-1860." *JBlackS*, 5: 134-56 (D 74).

Ferris, W.R. "Black Prose Narrative in the Mississippi Delta: An Overview." *JAF*, 85: 140-51 (Ap-Je 72).

Fetz, H.W. "Of Time and the Novel." *XUS*, 8: 1-18 (Su 69).

Fiedler, L.A. "The Male Novel." *PR*, 37: 74-89 (1970).

Fine, D.M. "Abraham Cahan, Stephen Crane and the Romantic Tenement Tale of the Nineties." *AmS*, 14: 95-107 (Sp 73).

Fine, D.M. "Immigrant Ghetto Fiction, 1885-1918: An Annotated Bibliography." *ALR*, 169-95 (Su 73).

Fites, Gilbert. "A Parade of Circusana." *Serif*, 5: 30-3 (1968).

Fleming, R.E. "Humor in the Early Black Novel." *CLAJ*, 17: 250-62 (D 73).

———. "Overshadowed by Richard Wright: Three Black Chicago Novelists." *NALF*, 7: 75-9 (Fa 73).

———. "'Playing the Dozens' in the Black Novel." *SBL*, 3: 23-4 (Au 72).

Flores, Vetal. "Literature for Frontier Children." *SwAL*, 2: 65-73 (Fa 72).

Fogel, Stanley. "'And All the Little Typtopies': Notes on Language Theory in the Contemporary Experimental Novel." *MFS*, 20: 328-36 (Au 74).

Foger, Sidney. "American Jewish Fiction: Local Color Movement of the Fiction." *CLAJ*, 18: 412-31 (Mr 75).

Folsom, J.K. "English Westerns." *WAL*, 2: 3-13 (Sp 67).

———. "*Shane* and *Hud*: Two Stories in Search of a Medium." *WHR*, 29: 359-72 (Au 70).

Fox, Hugh. "Standards: Some Subjectivities on Fiction." *SHR*, 7: 183-90 (1973).

*Frank, F.S. "The Gothic Novel: A Checklist of Modern Criticism." *BB*, 45-54 (Ap-Je 73).

Frank, Joseph. "Spatial Form in Modern Literature." *SR*, 53: 221-40 (Sp 45).

Franklin, Bruce. "Chic Bleak in Fantasy Fiction." *SatR*, 55: 42-5 (15 Jl 72).

Franklin, H.B. "Science Fiction: The New Mythology." *Extrapolation*, 69-113 (My 69).

Fraser, John. "An Art of Violence." *PR*, 36: 363-87 (Su 69).

———. "Violence and Thought in Art." *SoR*, 6: 651-73 (1970).

Free, W.J. "American Fiction in the *Columbian Magazine*, 1786-1792: An Annotated Checklist." *BB*, 25: 150-1 (My-Ap 68).

French, M.R. "The American Novel in the Sixties." *MwQ*, 9: 365-79 (Su 68).

Friedberg, B.C. "The Cult of Adolescence in American Fiction." *NasR*, 1: 26-35 (Sp 64).

Friedman, A.W. "The Jew's Complaint in Recent American Fiction: Beyond Exodus and Still in the Wilderness." *SoR*, 8: 41-59 (Ja 72).

Friedman, Norman. "Reality and the Novel: Forms of Fiction Theory." *SR*, 83: 172-90 (wi 75).

Frohock, W.M. "The Falling Center: Recent Fiction and the Picaresque Tradition." *Novel*, 3: 62-9 (1969).

Fuchs, Carolyn. "Words, Action, and the Modern Novel." *Kerygma*, 4: 3-11 (Wi 64).

Fuson, Ben. "Three Kansas Utopian Novels of 1890." *Extrapolation*, 12; 7-24 (D 70); *KanQ*, 5: 63-77 (Fa 73).

Fussell, Edwin. "The Mid-'Fifties Novel: Problems and Possibilities." *WR*, 19: 297-308 (1955).

———. "The Spirit of American Fiction." *Thought* (Delhi), 5 O 51, pp. 10-3; 12 O 51, pp. 10-2.

Fiction

Galloway, D.D. "Clown and Saint: The Hero in Current American Fiction." *Critique*, 7: 46-64 (Sp-Su 65).

Garde, N.I. "The First American 'Gay' Novel." *One: Inst Q Homophile Stud*, 9: 185-90 (1960).

Gardiner, H.C. "Could Sherlock Sniff a Trend?" *LJ*, 85: 34-6 (1 Ja 60).

Gardner, E.S. "My Stories of th Wild West." *Atl*, 218: 60-2 (Jl 66).

Gardner, John. "The Way We Write Now." *NYTBR*, 9 Jl 72, pp. 32-3.

Gardner, R.D. "Alger Heroes, the Merriwells, *et al.*" *PULC*, 30: 103-9 (Wi 69).

Garraty, John. "A Century of American Realism." *AH*, 21: 12-5, 86-90 (Je 70).

Garrett, George. "The International Symposium on the Short Story: United States." *KR*, 31: 461-8 (1969).

Gass, W.H. "Groping for Trouts: On Metaphor." *Salmagundi*, 24: 19-33 (1973).

———. "Philosophy and the Form of Fiction." *UTMS*, 10: 50-66 (1970).

Gazell, J.A. "The High Noon of Chicago's Bohemians." *JISHS*, 65: 54-68 (Sp 72).

Gecas, Victor. "Motives and Aggressive Acts in Popular Fiction: Sex and Class Differences." *AJS*, 77: 680-96 (Ja 72).

Geismar, Maxwell. "The American Short Story Today." *StL*, 4: 21-7 (Sp 64).

———. "Some Reflections on Contemporary Fiction." *AmD*, 5: 13-6 (1968); 5: 40-4 (1968-9).

Gelfant, Blanche. "Residence Underground: Recent Fictions of the Subterranean City." *SR*, 83: 406-38 (Su 75).

Gettmann, R.A. "Landscape in the Novel." *PrS*, 45: 239-44 (Fa 71).

Gilman, Richard. "News from the Novel." *NREP*, 15(: 27-36 (17 Ag 68).

Ginsberg, Elaine. "The Female Initiation Theme in American Fiction." *SAF*, 3: 27-38 (Sp 75).

Glicksberg, C.I. "Experimental Fiction: Innovation versus Form." *CentR*, 18: 127-50 (1974).

Godbold, E.S. "A Battleground Revisited: Reconstruction in Southern Fiction, 1895-1905." *SAQ*, 73: 99-116 (1974).

Goff, Martyn. "The Homosexual as Novelist." *Amigo*, 4: 116-7 (1936).

Going, W.T. "Alabama in the Short Story: Notes for an Anthology." *AlaR*, 22: 3-32 (Ja 69).

Gold, Herbert. "The End of Pornography." *SR*, 52: 25-7, 64 (31 O 70).

———. "Symposium on the Short Story." *KR*, 30: 450-3 (#4 68).

Gold, Joseph. "Promised Land and Vanishing People." *CRAS*, 3: 60-2 (1972).

Göller, K.H. "Fiktion und Wirklichkeit in midwest-Roman." *LWU*, 6: 211-33 (1973).

Gollin, Rita. "Understanding Fathers in American Jewish Fiction." *CentR*, 18: 273-87 (Su 74).

Gonzalez Padilla, M.E. "La literatura contemporanea en los Estados Unidos." *Abside*, 33: 249-90 (1969).

Goldknopf, David. "Realism in the Novel." *YR*, 60: 69-84 (Au 70).

Gordon, Andrew. "Speak Out against the Madness: The New American Novel of the Absurd." *FMod*, 15: 329-43 (1975).

Gorlier, Dlaudio. "La trappola dell 'American Gothic.'" *Approdo*, 66-7: 208-10 (1975).

Graff, Gerald. "Babbitt at the Abyss: The Social Context of Post Modern Fiction." *TriQ*, 33: 305-37 (Sp 75).

———. "The Myth of the Postmodernist Breakthrough." *TriQ*, 26: 383-417 (1973).

Graham, D.H. "Aesthetic Experience in Realism." *ALR*, 8: 289-90 (Su 75).

Grande, L.M. "Renegade Priests in Recent Fiction." *CathLW*, 32: 407-10 (Ap 61).

Greenberg, Alvin. "Breakable Beginnings: The Fall into Reality in the Modern Novel." *TSLL*, 10: 133-42 (1968).

———. "The Revolt of Objects: The Opposing World in the Modern Novel." *CentR*, 13: 366-88 (Fl 69).

———. "A Sense of Place in Modern Fiction: The Novelist's World and the Allegorist's Heaven." *Genre*, 5: 353-66 (D 72).

Greenman, Myron. "Understanding New Fiction." *MFS*, 20: 307-16 (Au 74).

Grella, George. "Murder and the Mean Streets: The Hard-Boiled Detective Novel." *Contempora*, 1: 6-15 (Mr 70).

———. "Thrillers, Chillers, and Killers.'" *RocR*, 32: 11-5 (1970).

Gröger, Erika. "Der bürgerliche Atomwissenschaftler im englisch-amerikanischen roman von 1945 bis zur Gegenwart." *ZAA*, 16: 25-48 (1968).

Gross, Beverly. "The House of Fiction and the House on Eleventh Street." *Meanjin*, 30: 241-5 (Je 71).

Guerard, A.J. "My *Grande Naufrage*: Fiction and Political Obsession." *SoR*, 8: 15-40 (Ja 72).

Guerard, Albert. "Notes on the Rhetoric of Anti-Realist Fiction." *TriQ*, 30: 3-50 (Sp 74).

Gullason, T.A. "Revelation and Evolution: A Neglected Dimension of the Short Story." *SSF*, 10: 347-56 (Fa 73).

Gunter, Bradley. "Five First Novels." *Shen*, 21: 84-9 (Au 69).

Hall, H.W. "Texas and Science Fiction." *SwAL*, 1: 144-48 (1972).

Hansen, A.J. "The Celebration of Solipsism: A New Trend in American Fiction." *MFS*, 19: 5-15 (Sp 73).

Harless, J.D. "The Impact of Adventure Fiction on Readers: The Nice-Guy Type." *JQ*, 49: 306-15 (Su 72).

*Harper, Howard. "General Studies in Recent American Fiction: A Selected Checklist." *MFS*, 19: 127-33 (Sp 73).

Harper, H.M. "Trends in Recent American Fiction." *ConL*, 12: 204-229 (Sp 71).

Harris, W.V. "Molly's 'Yes': The Transvaluation on Sex in Modern Fiction." *TSLL*, 10: 107-18 (1968).

Hassan, Ihab. "The Character of Post-War Fiction in America." *EJ*, 51: 1-8 (Ja 62).

———. "The Novel of Outrage: A Minority Voice in Postwar American Fiction." *ASch*, 34: 239-53 (Sp 65).

Hawkes, John. "Notes on Writing a Novel." *TriQ*, 30: 109-26 (1974).

Heidenry, John. "Yes, Virginia, The Novel Is Not Dead." *Cweal*, 96: 233-7 (12 My 72).

Heilbrun, Carolyn. "The Masculine Wilderness of the American Novel." *SatR*, 55: 41-4 (29 Ja 72).

Heimert, Alan. "Puritanism, the Wilderness, and the Frontier." *NEQ*, 26: 361-82 (1953).

Helson, Ravenna. "Fantasy and Self-Discovery." *HornB*, 46: 121-34 (Ap 70).

Hemenway, Robert. "Fiction in the Age of Jefferson: The Early American Novel as Intellectual Document." *MASJ*, 9: 91-102 (Sp 68).

Henkle, R.B. "Symposium Highlights: Wrestling (American Style) With Proteus." *Novel*, 3: 197-207 (1970).

Hiers, J.T. "The Graveyard Epiphany in Modern Southern Fiction: Transcendance of Selfhood." *SHR*, 9: 389-403 (Fa 75).

Hillegas, Mark. "The Course in Science Fiction: A Hope Deferred." *Extrapolation*, 9: 18-21 (D 67).

Hines, D.M. "Humor of the City Hick and the Country Jake on the Inland Pacific Northwest Frontier." *WR*, 13: 15-20 (Sp 71).

Hirsch, D.H. "Reality, Manners, and Mr. Trilling." *SR*, 72: 420-32 (Jl-S 64).

Holoquist, Michael. "Whodunit and Other Questions: Metaphysical Detective Stories in Post-War Fiction." *NLH*, 3: 135-56 (1971).

Fiction

Hopkins, Anthony. "Physical Models and Spiritual States: Institutional Environments in Modern Fiction." *JPC*, 6: 383-92 (Fa 72).

Howell, Elmo. "Eudora Welty and the Use of Place in Southern Fiction." *ArQ*, 28: 248-56 (1972).

Hume, R.D. "Gothic versus Romantic: A Revaluation of the Gothic Novel." *PMLA*, 84: 282-90 (1969).

Humphreys, P.F. "First Novels: The State of the Art." *LibJ*, 97: 2696-9 (1 S 72).

Hunsaker, K.B. "Mid-Century Mormon Novels." *Dialog*, 4: 123-8 (Au 69).

Hurley, N.P. "Liberation Ideology and New York City Fiction." *Thought*, 48: 338-59 (1973).

Hutchens, J.K. "Heritage of the Frontier." *SatR*, 23 S 67, pp. 34, 97-8.

Hutchens, E.N. "Towards a Poetics of Fiction: The Novel as Chronomorph." *Novel*, 5: 215-24 (1972).

Ickstadt, Heinz. "Gesichter Babylons: Zum Bild der Grosstadt im modernen amerikanischen Roman." *JA*, 16: 60-76 (1971).

Inge, M.T. "Donald Davidson Selects the Best Southern Novels." *MissQ*, 24: 155-8 (Sp 71).

Irvine, P.L. "The 'Witness' Point of View in Fiction." *SAQ*, 69: 217-25 (Sp 70).

Iwamoto, Iwao. "Saikin no America shosetsu—katari e no kaiki." *EigoS*, 117: 134-6 (1971).

———. "'Shin-Shosetsu' no Atarashisa." *EigoS*, 119: 754-5 (1974).

James, E.A. "The Hero and the Anti-Hero in Fiction." *FourQ*, 23: 3-23 (Au 73).

James, S.B. "Western American Space and the Human Imagination." *WHR*, 24: 147-55 (Sp 70).

Jameson, Frederic. "The Great American Hunter, or Ideological Content in the Novel." *CE*, 34: 180-97 (N 72).

Johnson, Ellwood. "William James and the Art of Fiction." *JAAC*, 30: 285-96 (Sp 72).

Johnsen, W.A. "Modern Women Novelists: *Nightwood* and the Novel of Sensibility." *BuR*, 21: 15-28 (Sp 73).

———. "Toward a Redefinition of Modernism." *Boun 2*, 2: 539-56 (1974).

Jonas, Gerald. "Science Fiction." *NY*, 48: 33-52 (29 Jl 72).

Jones, D.E. "Clenched Teeth and Curses: Revenge and the Dime Novel Outlaw Hero." *JPC*, 7: 652-65 (1973).

———. "Virgins, Villains, and Violence in the Dime Novel Western." *JPC*, 4: 507-17 (Fa 70).

Kable, W.S. "Addenda to Wright: Burdett, Curtis, Judson, Week." *PBSA*, 62: 452-3 (3Q 68).

———. "Addenda to Wright: Mancur, Pise, Tuthill, Weld." *PBSA*, 63: 294 (4Q 69).

Karolides, N.J. "Changing Conceptions of the Pioneer in the Contemporary American Novel." *WSL*, 4: 18-28 (1967).

Katona, Anna. "From Lazarillo to Augie March: A Study into Some Picaresque Attitudes." *HSE*, 4: 87-103 (1969).

———. "Picaresque Satires in Modern American Fiction." *ALitASH*, 12: 105-20 (1970).

Katz, Joseph. "Bibliography and the Rise of American Literary Realism." *SAF*, 2: 75-88 (Sp 74).

Kazin, Alfred. "Absurdity as Contemporary Style." *MeditR*, 1: 39-46 (Sp 71).

———. "Fiction as a Social Gathering." *SatR*, 54: 19-22 (3 Jl 71).

———. "Our Middle-Class Storytellers." *Atl*, 222: 51-5 (Ag 68).

———. "The War Novel: From Mailer to Vonnegut." *SatR*, 54: 13-5, 36 (6 F 71).

————. "The World as a Novel: From Capote to Mailer." *NYRB*, 16: 26-30 (8 Ap 71).

Keim, C.J. "Writing the Great Alaska Novel." *Alaska R*, 3: 47-51 (Fa-Wi 69).

Keller, Karl, and David Wilson. "Strategies for Americanists." *EAL*, 8: 210-2 (Wi 73).

Kellogg, Gene. "The Catholic Novel in Convergence." *Thought*, 45: 265-96 (Su 70).

Kelly, R.G. "American Children's Literature: An Historiographical Review." *ALR*, 6: 89-108 (Sp 73).

Kennedy, J.G. "Some Magazine Tales of the 1830's." *ATQ*, 24: 23-9 (Fa 74).

Kerrane, Kevin. "Reality 35, Illusion: Notes on the Football Imagination in Contemporary Fiction." *JPC*, 8: 437-52 (1974).

Ketterer, David. "New Worlds for Old: The Apocalyptic Imagination, Science Fiction, and American Literature." *Mosaic*, 5: 37-57 (1971).

————. "Utopian Fantasy as Millenial Motive and Science-Fictional Motif." *SLitI*, 6: 79-103 (#2 73).

Killoch, E.P. "The Woman Writer and the Element of Destruction." *CE*, 34: 31-8 (O 72).

Kimball, W.J. "Naturalism in Some Representative American Authors." *Venture*, 5: 81-92 (Ap 69).

*King, Frances. "Treatment of the Mentally Retarded Character in Modern American Fiction." *BB*, 32: 106-14, 131 (Jl-S 75).

Kirby, D.K. "The Princess and the Frog: The Modern American Short Story as a Fairy Tale." *MinnR*, 4: 145-9 (Sp 73).

Klinkowitz, Jerome. "Black Superfiction." *NAR*, 259: 69-74 (Wi 75).

————. "How Fiction Survives the Seventies." *NAR*, 258: 69-73 (Fa 73).

————. "Insatiable Art and the Great American Quotidian." *ChiR*, 25: 172-77 (1973).

————. "Literary Disruptions, or What's Become of American Fiction?" *PR*, 40: 433-44 (#3 73).

————, and John Somer. "Innovative Short Fiction: 'Vile and Imaginative Things.'" *OyR*, 8: 34-41 (Wi 73).

Klotman, P.B. "The Slave and the Western: Popular Literature in the Nineteenth Century." *NDQ*, 41: 50-4 (1973).

Knister, Raymond. "Democracy and the Short Story." *JCF*, 4: 146-8 (#2 75).

Knox, George. "The Great American Novel: Final Chapter." *AQ*, 21: 667-82 (Wi 69).

————. "In Search of the Great American Novel." *WR*, 5: 64-77 (Su 68).

Koehler, Lyle. "The Case of the American Jezebels: Anne Hutchinson and Female Agitation During the Years of Antinomian Turmoil, 1636-1640." *WMQ*, 31: 55-78 (Ja 74).

Kostelanetz, Richard. "Dada and the Future of Fiction." *Works*, 1: 58-66 (Sp 68).

————. "New Fiction in America." *DQ*, 8: 1-17 (Au 73).

Krim, Seymour. "An Enemy of the Novel." *Iowa R*, 3: 60-2 (1972).

Krumpelman, J.T. "*Tokeah*, the First English-Language Novel in Our Southwest." *SCB*, 28: 142-3 (Wi 68).

Krupnick, M.L. "Notes from the Funhouse." *ModO*, 1: 108-12 (Fa 70).

Kummings, D.D. "An Appraisal of Reappraisals: Four Nineteenth-Century American Writers." *CEA*, 37: 36-8 (1974).

Kuna, F.M. "Current Literature 1970—: New Writing." *ES*, 52: 473-83 (1971).

Lambert, Neal. "Saints, Sinners, and Scribes: A Look at the Mormons in Fiction." *UHQ*, 36: 63-76 (Wi 68).

Lamplugh, G.R. "The Image of the Negro in Popular Magazine Fiction, 1875-1900." *JNH*, 57: 177-89 (Ap 72).

Landess, T.H. "The Present Course of Southern Fiction: 'Everynegro' and Other Alternatives." *ArlQ*, 1: 61-85 (Wi 67-68).

Fiction

Landis, J.C. "Reflections on American Jewish Writers." *JBA*, 25: 140-7 (1967).

Landsman, Gail. "Science Fiction: The Rebirth of Mythology." *JPC*, 5: 989-96 (Sp 72).

Larsen, Eric. "How Do You Write a Short Story in 1973?" *MinnR*, 4: 132-7 (Sp 73).

Larson, C.R. "Three Harlem Novels of the Jazz Age." *Critique*, 11: 66-79 (1969).

Lasater, A.E. "The Breakdown in Communication in the Twentieth-Century Novel." *SoQ*, 12: 1-14 (1973).

Lauder, R.E. "The Catholic Novel and the 'Insider God.'" *Cweal*, 101: 78-81 (1974).

Lavender, David. "The Petrified West and the Writer." *ASch*, 37: 293-306 (Sp 68).

Lawton, J.N. "The Authorship of Item 165 in Lyle Wright's *American Fiction 1851-1875*." *PBSA*, 64: 83 (1970).

Leer, Norman. "Three American Novels and Contemporary Society: A Search for Commitment." *ConL*, 3: 67-86 (Fa 62).

Lehan, Richard. "Fiction 1967." *WSCL*, 9: 538-53 (Au 68).

Leithead, J.E. "The Diamond Dicks: Frontier Lawmen." *ABC*, 20: 19-25 (S 69).

―――. "The Great Detective Team: Old and Young King Brady." *ABC*, 20: 25-31 (N-D 69).

―――. "The Klondike Stampede in Dime Novels." *ABC*, 21: 23-9 (1971).

―――. "Legendary Heroes and the Dime Novel." *ABC*, 18: 22-7 (1968).

―――. "The Matchless Nick Carter." *ABC*, 20: 11-7 (F 70).

―――. "The Revolutionary War in Dime Novels." *ABC*, 19: 14-21 (Ap-My 69).

―――. "Tanbark and Spangles in Dime Novels." *ABC*, 20: 36-42 (Ap 70).

Lem, Stanislaw. "On the Structural Analysis of Science Fiction." *S-FS*, 1: 26-32 (Sp 73).

―――. "Remarks Occasioned by Dr. Plank's Essay 'Quixote's Mills.'" *S-FS*, 1: 78-83 (Fa 73).

―――. "The Time-Travel Story and Related Matters of SF Structuring." *S-FS*, 1: 143-53 (Sp 74).

Leverenz, David. "Anger and Individualism." *ATQ*, 62: 407-28 (1975).

Levidova, I. "Roman—v centre sporov (Po stranicam amerikanskix universitetskix zurnalov 1966 goda)." *VLit*, 11: 192-8 (1967).

Levin, David. "American Fiction as Historical Evidence." *NALF*, 5: 132-6, 154 (1971).

Levine, Paul. "The Intemperate Zone: The Climate of Contemporary American Fiction." *MR*, 8: 505-23 (1967).

―――. "The Politics of Alienation." *Mosaic*, 2: 3-17 (1968).

Levy, D.W. "Racial Stereotypes in Antislavery Fiction." *Phylon*, 31: 265-79 (Fa 70).

Lewis, Sinclair. "Detective Stories and Mr. Dickens." *YULG*, 45: 88-92 (1971).

Lhamon, W.T. "Break and Enter to Breakaway: Scotching Modernism in the Social Novel of the American Sixties." *Boun2*, 3: 289-306 (Wi 75).

Liedel, D.E. "The Authorship of Two Antislavery Novels of the 1840's." *PBSA*, 67: 447-9 (O-D 73).

Lindberg-Seyersted, Brita. "American Fiction Since 1950." *Edda*, 4: 193-203 (1971).

―――. "Three Variations of the American Success Story." *ES*, 53: 125-41 (Ap 72).

Lodge, David. "*Language of Fiction*: A Reply." *ConL*, 9: 574-7 (Au 68).

―――. "The Novelist at the Crossroads." *CritQ*, 11: 105-32 (Su 69).

Lomax, M.L. "Fantasies of Affirmation: The 1920'a Novel of Negro Life." *CLAJ*, 16: 232-46 (D 72).

Loofbourow, J.W. "Literary Realism Redefined." *Thought*, 45: 433-43 (Au70).

Loukides, Paul. "Some Notes on the Novel of the Absurd." *CEA*, 30: 8, 13 (Ja 68).

Ludwig, H.W. "Der Ich-Erzähler im englisch-amerikanischen Detektiv- und Kriminalroman." *DVLG*, 43: 434-50 (1971).

Lurie, Alison. "Witches and Fairies: Fitzgerald to Updike." *NYRB*, 17: 6-11 (2 D 71).

Lutwack, Leonard. "*Raintree County* and the Epicising Poet in American Fiction." *BSUF*, 13: 14-28 (Wi 72).

Lyons, J.O. "The College Novel in America: 1962-1974." *Critique*, 16: 121-8 (2Q 74).

Lytle, A.N. "The Image as Guide to Meaning in the Historical Novel." *SR*, 61: 408-26 (Su 53).

McConnell, Frank. "The Corpse of the Dragon: Notes on Post-Romantic Fiction." *TriQ*, 33: 273-304 (Sp 75).

McDonald, W.R. "Coincidence in the Novel: A Necessary Technique." *CE*, 39: 373-88 (F 68).

*McDowell, R.E., and George Fortenberry. "A Checklist of Books and Essays About American Negro Novelists." *StN*, 3: 219-36 (Su 71).

McElroy, John. "The Hawthorne Style of American Fiction." *ESQ*, 71: 117-23 (1973).

McNamara, Eugene. "The Absurd Style in Contemporary American Literature." *HAB*, 19: 4-9 (Wi 68).

———. "The Post-Modern American Novel." *QQ*, 69: 265-75 (Su 62).

McNelly, W.E. "Science Fiction and the Academy: An Introduction." *CEA*, 35: 6-9 (N 72).

———. "Science Fiction and the American Dream." *CEA*, 35: 10-3 (Ja 73).

Madden, David. "The Fallacy of the Subject-Dominated Novel." *Eng Rec*, 18: 11-9 (Ap 68).

Mailer, Norman. "The Homosexual Villain." *One*, 8-12 (1973).

Major, Clarence. "Making Up Reality: On New Fiction and Criticism." *FicI*, 2-3: 151-4 (Sp-Fa 74).

Male, R.R. "The Story of the Mysterious Stranger in American Fiction." *Criticism*, 3: 281-94 (1961).

Malin, Irving. "American Gothic Images." *Mosaic*, 6: 145-71 (Sp 73).

———. "The Authoritarian Family in American Fiction." *Mosaic*, 4: 153-73 (1971).

Mann, J.J. "Is There an Angel in the House?" *IEngYb*, 39-50 (Fa 71).

Marcotte, Edward. "Intersticed Prose." *ChiR*, 26: 31-6 (Sp 75).

———. "The Space of the Novel." *PR*, 41: 263-72 (2Q 74).

Margolies, Edward. "The American Detective Thriller and the Idea of Society." *Costerus*, 6: 93 8 (1978).

Marks, B.A. "Retrospective Narrative in Nineteenth Century American Literature." *CE*, 31: 336-75 (Ja 70).

Marler, R.F. "From Tale to Short Story: The Emergence of a New Genre in the 1850's." *AL*, 46: 153-69 (My 74).

Marsh, J.L. "The Doughboy Novelists of Flanders Fields." *Genre*, 3: 242-53 (1970).

Marx, Leo. " 'Noble Shit': The Uncivil Response of American Writers to Civil Religion in America." *MR*, 14: 709-39 (1973).

May, C.E. "A Survey of Short Story Criticism in America." *MinnR*, 4: 163-9 (Sp 73).

May, J.B. "The Novel: Where Is It?" *Trace*, 61: 125-9, 236-9 (Su 66).

May, J.R. "Images of the Apocalypse in the Black Novel." *Ren*, 23: 31-45 (Au 70).

Mayberry, George and Sharon. "Recent American Fiction." *Nation*, 216: 180-3 (5 F 73).

Mayersberg, Paul. "The Corridors of the Mind." *Listener*, 74: 959-60 (9 D 65).

Melchiori, G. "The English Novelist and the American Tradition." *SR*, 68: 502-15 (Su 60).

Mellard, James. "Prolegomena to a Study of the Popular Mode in Narrative." *JPC*, 6: 1-19 (Su 72).

Mellard, J.M. "Racism, Formula, and Popular Fiction." *JPC*, 5: 10-37 (Su 71).

———. "Solipsism, Symbolism, and Demonism: The Lyrical Mode in Fiction." *SHR*, 7: 37-52 (Wi 73).

Fiction

Mercer, Peter. "The Culture of Fictions; or the Fiction of Culture?" *CritQ*, 12: 291-300 (Wi 70).

Merril, Judith. "What Do You Mean — Science? Fiction?" *Extrapolation*, 7: 30-46 (My 66).

Meyer, R.W. "The Outback and the West: Australian and American Frontier Fiction." *WAL*, 6: 3-19 (1971).

Michaelson, L.W. "Science Fiction and the Rate of Social Change." *Extrapolation*, 11: 25-7 (D 69).

Michel, Pierre. "Le Roman Americaine depuis 1945." *RLV*, 39: 497-515 (N-D 73).

Mills, Nicolaus. "American Fiction and the Genre Critics." *Novel*, 2: 112-22 (1969).

Mills, N.C. "The Machine in the Anglo-American Garden." *Centr*, 14: 201-12 (1970).

———. "Prison and Society in Nineteenth-Century American Fiction." *WHR*, 24: 325-31 (Au 70).

Milton, J.R. "Conversations with Distinguished Western American Novelists." *SDR*, 9: 15-57 (Sp 71).

———. "The Western Novel: Whence and What?" *Rendezvous*, 7: 7-21 (Wi 72).

Minton, D.L. "By Den of Lions: Notes on Stylization in Early Puritan Captivity Narratives." *AL*, 45: 335-47 (N 73).

Mitchell, Giles. "Feeling and Will in the Modern Novel." *DHLR*, 4: 183-96 (Su 71).

Mizener, Arthur. "The New Romance." *SoR*, 8: 106-17 (Ja 72).

Molyneux, Thomas. "The Affirming Balance of Voice." *Shen*, 25: 27-43 (Wi 74).

Moon, Eric. "Problem Fiction." *LJ*, 87: 484-96 (1 F 62).

Moore, J.B. "Images of the Negro in Early American Short Fiction." *MissQ*, 22: 47-57 (Wi 68-9).

———. "A Neglected Early American Short Stroy." *AN&Q*, 4: 84-6 (F 66).

Moore, R.S. "The Magazine and the Short Story in the Ante-Bellum Period." *SAB*, 38: 44-51 (My 73).

Morrissette, Bruce. "The Alienated 'I' in Fiction." *SoR*, 10: 15-30 (Ja 74).

———. "Post Modern Generative Fiction." *CritI*, 2: 253-62 (1975).

Moskowitz, Sam. "The Gernsback 'Magazines' No One Knows." *RQ*, 4: 272-4 (Mr 71).

Mulqueen, J.E. "Three Heroes in American Fiction." *IllQ*, 36: 44-50 (F 74).

Munroe, D.A. "A Case?—for 'Semi-Fiction.'" *Trace*, 48: 17-9 (Sp 63).

Muraskin, William. "An Alienated Elite: Short Stories in *The Crisis*, 1910-1950." *JBlackS*, 1: 282-305 (Mr 71).

Musgrave, M.E. 'Patterns of Violence and Non-Violence in Pro-Slavery and Anti-Slavery Fiction." *CLAJ*, 16: 426-37 (Je 73).

Mussell, K.J. "Beautiful and Damned: The Sexual Woman in Gothic Fiction." *JPC*, 9: 84-9 (Su 75).

Nagel, James. "An Annotated Bibliography of Selected Recent Books on American Fiction." *SAF*, 1: 76-91 (Sp 73).

Nance, W.L. "Eden, Oedipus, and Rebirth in American Fiction." *ArQ*, 31: 353-64 (Wi 75).

Nelson, Jane. "CM and George Burroughs: Puritan Anticipations of the Tall Tale." *PosS*, 4: 17 (O 73).

Nennett, Stephen, and William Nichols. "Violence in Afro-American Fiction: An Hypothesis." *MFS*, 17: 221-8 (Su 71).

Nettels, Elsa. "James and Conrad on the Art of Fiction." *TSLL*, 14: 529-43 (Fa 72).

New, W.H. "The Island and the Madman: Recurrent Imagery in the Major Novelists of the Fifties." *ARQ22'* 328-37 (Wi 66).

Newman, Charles. "Beyond Omniscience: Notes Toward a Future for the Novel." *TriQ*, 10: 37-52 (Fa 67).

Newman, John. "America at War: Horror Stories for a Society." *Extrapolation*, 16: 33-41 (D 74).

Nichols, W.W. "Slave Narratives: Dismissed Evidence in the Writing of Southern History." *Phylon*, 32: 403-9 (1971).

Nicolaisen, Peter. "Neuere literatur zum amerikanischen Roman." *LWU*, 2: 47-63 (1969).

Nin, Anaïs. "Novel of the Future." *STC*, 1: 79-108 (Sp 68).

Noble, D.W. "The Analysis of Alienation by 20th Century Social Scientists and 19th Century Novelists." *MVCBul*, 5: 5-19 (Fa 72).

Nolan, P.T. "Two Novels of the Twentieth-Century West." *JWest*, 10: 388-9 (Ap 71).

Noverr, D.A. "New Dimensions in Recent Michigan Fiction." *Soc for the Study of Midwestern Lit Miscellany*, 1: 9-14 (1974).

Nutley, Grace. "Contemporary American Fiction." *Exchange* (Manila), 40: 11-21 (1968).

Nye, Russel. "Le roman Americain contemporain." *RLM*, 8: 3-16 (Sp 61).

O'Brien, John. "'Becoming' Heroes in Black Fiction: Sex, Iconoclasm, and the Immanence of Salvation." *SBL*, 2: 1-5 (Au 71).

———. "The Novel of Salvation." *Cresset*, 35: 12-15 (1972).

O'Connell, Shaun. "Bringing It All Back Home." *Atl*, 225: 92-5 (Ja 70).

O'Donnell, T.F. "More Apologies: The Indian in New York Fiction." *NYFQ*, 23: 243-53 (D 67).

Ohashi, Kenzo. "American Shosetsu—sono kindaisei to hankindaisei." *EigoS*, 116: 746-48 (1971).

Orians, G.H. "New England Witchcraft in Fiction." *AL*, 2: 54-71 (Mr 30).

Owen, Guy. "The Use of Folklore in Fiction." *NCaF*, 19: 73-9 (Mr 71).

Packer, N.H. "Fiction's New Mode." *SHR*, 7: 387-94 (1973).

Pagetti, Carlo. "La tradizione narrativa inglese in America." *SA*, 18: 175-216 (1972).

Panshin, Alexei. "A Basic Science Fiction Collection." *LibJ*, 95: 2223-9 (15 Je 70).

Papapanos, Kostas. "To Amerikaniko mythistorima sta teleutaia peninta chronia." *NeaH*, 87: 607-20 (1970).

Papas, J.J. "Women and Men in the Fiction of the New World: A Community of Sufferers." *CEA*, 37: 28-9 (My 75).

Pauly, T.H. "The Literary Sketch in Nineteenth-Century America." *TSLL*, 17: 17: 489-503 (1975).

Pawel, Ernst. "Fiction of the Holocaust." *Midstream*, 16: 14-26 (Je-Jl 70).

Pearce, Richard. "Enter the Frame." *TriQ*, 30: 71-82 (Sp 74).

Pearce, R.H. "The Significances of the Captivity Narrative." *AL*, 19: 1-20 (1947).

Peavy, C.D. "The Black Revolutionary Novel, 1899-1969." *StN*, 3: 180-9 (Su 71).

———. "Four Black Revolutionary Novels, 1899-1970." *JBlackS*, 1: 219-223 (D 70).

Peck, D.R. "'The Orgy of Apology': The Recent Reevaluation of the Literature of the Thirties." *Sci and Soc*, 32: 371-82 (Fa 68).

Peckham, H.H. "Lopsided Realism." *SAQ*, 15: 276-81 (Jl 16).

Peden, William. "The American Short Story during the Twenties." *SSF*, 10: 367-71 (Fa 73).

———. "The Recent American Short Story." *SR*, 82: 712-29 (1974).

Percy, Walker. "The Decline of the Western." *Cweal*, 68: 181-3 (16 My 58).

Perez-Minik, Domingo. "La emigración en la narrativa nortemaericana." *Insula*, 27: 7 (Je 72).

Peter, John. "The Self-Effacement of the Novelist." *MalR*, 8: 119-28 (O 68).

Peterson, L.S. "Brother Brigham and the Virginian: An Irreverent Inaccurate and Superficial Use of History to Explain Why the Polygamist Rather than the Cowboy is the Center of Mormon Frontier Fiction." *PosS*, 2: 1-4 (My 71).

Fiction

Petrullo, H.B. "Clichés and Three Political Satires of the Thirties." *SNL*, 8: 109-17 (Sp 71).

Peyre, Henri. "Is Literature Dead? Or Dying?" *MQR*, 12: 297-313 (1973).

Peyroutet, J.A. "The North Dakota Farmer in Fiction." *NDQ*, 39: 59-71 (Wi 71).

Philmus, R.M. "A Dialogue Between IdeaPhilos and Philologos." *S-FS*, 1: 214-6 (Sp 74).

———. "The Shape of Science Fiction: Through the Historical Looking Glass." *S-FS*, 1: 37-40 (Sp 73).

Pickering, Sam. "The Boys Own War." *NEQ*, 48: 362-77 (S 75).

———. *"The Cheap Repository Tracts* and the Short Story." *SSF*, 12: 15-22 (Wi 75).

Pickering, S.F. "The Short Story and Its Ex-Readers." *SR*, 80: 499-506 (1972).

Pilkington, W.T. "The Recent Southwestern Novel." *SwAL*, 1: 12-5 (1971).

Pinsker, Sanford. "The Rise-and-Fall of the American-Jewish Novel." *ConnR*, 7: 16-23 (O 73).

———. "Rubbing America Against the Grain: Writing after Hemingway." *Quadrant*, 80: 48-54 (N-D 72).

———. "The Schlemiel in Yiddish and American Literature." *CJF*, 25: 191-5 (1967).

Pizer, Donald. "A Primer of Fictional Aesthetics." *CE*, 30: 572-80 (Ap 69).

———. "The Problem of Philosophy in the Novel." *BuR*, 18: 53-62 (Sp 70).

Plank, Robert. "Heart Transplant Fiction." *HSL*, 2: 102-12 (1970).

———. "Qixote's Mills: The Man-Machine Encounter in SF." *S-FS*, 1: 68-77 (Fa 73).

Poger, Sidney. "American Jewish Fiction: Local Color Movement of the Fifties." *CLAJ*, 18: 404-11 (Mr 75).

Poirer, Richard. "The Politics of Self-Parody." *PR*, 35: 339-53 (Su 68).

Poli, Bernard. "The Hero in France and in America." *JAmSt*, 2: 225-38 (O 68).

Popscu, Petru. "Picaresc şi aventură in ficţiunea americană." *ViR*, 23: 95-9 (1970).

Porter, M.G. " 'Spiritual Activism' and 'Radical Sophistication' in the Contemporary American Novel." *StN*, 3: 332-43 (Fa 71).

Porter, Mark. "Mysticism of the Land and the Western Novel." *SDR*, 11: 79-91 (Sp 73).

Poulsen, Richard. "The Texas Longhorn and the Popular Trail Drive Novel." *PosS*, 4: 8-10 (Ja-F 73).

Pratt, Annis. "Women and Nature in Modern Fiction." *ConL*, 13: 476-90 (Au 72).

Presley, D.E. "The Moral Function of Distortion in Southern Grotesque." *SAB*, 37: 37-46 (1972).

Prigozy, Ruth. "The Liberal Novelist in the McCarthy Era." *TCL*, 21: 253-64 (1975).

Primeau, Ronald. "Slave Narrative Turning Westward: Deadwood Dick Rides into Difficulties." *Midamerica*, 1974, pp. 16-35.

Pritchard, W.H. "Novels and Novelists of the 1960's." *Mod O*, 2: 188-209 (1974).

Pugh, G.T. "Three Negro Novelists: Protest and Anti-Protest, A Symposium." *SHR*, 4: 17-50 (1970).

Quantic, D.D. "The Revolt from the Village and Middle Western Fiction 1870-1915." *KanQ*, 5: 5-16 (Fa 73).

Ragan, Sam. "North Carolina Writers and the Southern Tradition, 1972-3." *NCHR*, 51: 183-9 (Ap 74).

Rahv, Philip. "Fiction and the Criticism of Fiction." *KR*, 18: 276-99 (Sp 56).

Raleigh, J.H. "The Novel and the City: England and America in the Nineteenth Century." *VS*, 11: 291-328 (Mr 68).

Reaver, J.R. "From Reality to Fantasy: Opening-Closing Formulas in the Structures of American Tall Tales.'" *SFQ*, 36: 369-82 (D 72).

Reilly, J.M. "Images of Gastonia: A Revolutionary Chapter in American Social Fiction." *GaR*, 28: 498-517 (Fa 74).

———. "The Politics of Tough Guy Mysteries." *Un Dayton R*, 10: 25-31 (Su 73).

Reynolds, Mack, et. al. "Change, SF, and Marxism: Open or Closed Universes?" *S-FS*, 1: 269-75 (Fa 74).

Richler, Mordecai. "Write, Boychick, Write." *NSt*: 473-4 (7 Ap 67).

Robertson, Duncan. "The Dichotomy of Form and Content." *CE*, 28: 273-9 (Ja 67).

Robinson, Clayton. "Memphis in Fiction: Rural Values in an Urban Setting." *MVCBul*, 5: 29-38 (Fa 72).

Roemer, K.M. "American Utopian Literature (1888-1900): An Annotated Bibliography." *ALR*, 4: 227-54 (Su 71).

———. "Sex Roles, Utopia, and Change: The Family in Late-Nineteenth-Century Utopian Literature." *AmS*, 13: 33-48 (Fa 72).

Rogers, D.R. "A Publication Pattern: Being a Study of . . . Juvenile Fiction by Edward S. Ellis Issued Between 1883 and 1930." *DNR*, 41: 80-90, 96-106 (S 15-O 15 72).

Rose, A.H. "Sin and the City: The Uses of Disorder in the Urban Novel." *CentR*, 16: 203-20 (Su 72).

Rosenthal, T.G. "The Death of Fiction." *NSt*: 389 (22 Mr 68).

Ross, Frank. "The Assailant-Victim in Three-War Protest Novels." *Paunch*, 30: 46-57 (D 67).

Rottensteiner, Franz, et. al. "Change, SF, and Marxism: Open or Closed Universe?" *S-FS*, 1: 84-93 (Fa 73).

Rubin, L.D. "The Dificulties of Being a Southern Writer Today: Or Getting Out From Under William Faulkner." *JSH*, 29: 486-94 (N 63).

———. "*Don Quixote* and Selected Progeny: Or, the Journey-man as Outsider." *SoR*, 10: 31-58 (J 74).

———. "Their Own Language." *HM*, 230: 173-5 (Ap 65).

———. "Southern Local Color and the Black Man." *SoR*, 6: 1011-30 (O 70).

Ruoff, J.C. "Frivolity to Consumption, Or, Southern Womanhood in Antebellem Literature." *CWH*, 18: 213-29 (1972).

Rusch, L.K. "The American Dream in Selected South Dakota Novels." *SDR*, 12: 58-72 (#3 74).

Russ, Joanna. "Dream Literature and Science Fiction." *Extrapolation*, 11: 6-14 (D 69).

———. "Somebody's Trying to Kill Me and I Think It's My Husband: The Modern Gothic." *JPC*, 6: 666-91 (Sp 73).

Russell, Charles. "The Vault of Language: Self-Reflective Artifice in Contemporary American Fiction." *MFS*, 20: 349-58 (Au 74).

Ryan, Marjorie. "Four Contemporary Satires and the Problem of Norms." *SNL*, 6: 40-6 (Sp 69).

Ryf, R.S. "Character and Imagination in the Experimental Novel." *MFS*, 20: 317-27 (Au 74).

Said, Edward. "Contemporary Fiction and Criticism." *TriQ*, 33: 231-56 (Sp 75).

Sale, Roger. "Unknown Novel." *ASch*, 43: 86-104 (Wi 73-74).

SanJuan, Epifanio, Jr. "Spatial Orientation in American Romanticism." *EWR*, 2: 33-55 (Sp-Su 65).

Sapiro, Leland. "Clichés in the Old Super-Science Story." *RQ*, 5: 101-8, 192-9 (1971-1972).

Saroyan, William. "The International Symposium on the Short Story." *KR*, 31: 58-62 (1969).

Savage, G.L. "Tips for Writing Westerns." *Writer*, 87: 24-5 (Mr 74).

Savage, W.W. "Western Literature and its Myths: A Rejoinder." *Montana*, 22: 78-81 (1972).

Sayre, R.F. "American Myths of Utopia." *CE*, 31: 613-23 (1970).

Fiction

Scheer-Schaezler, Brigitte. "Short Story and Modern Novel: A Comparative Analysis of Two Texts." *OL*, 25: 338-51 (1970).

Schmidt, D.B. "The Great American Bitch." *CE*, 32: 900-5 (My 71).

Scholes, Robert. "Change, SF, and Marxism: Open or Closed Universes?" *S-FS*, 1: 213 (So 74).

———. "The Contributions of Formalism and Structuralism to the Theory of Fiction." *Novel*, 6: 134-51 (Wi 73).

———. "The Fictional Criticism of the Future." *TriQ*, 34: 233-47 (Fa 75).

———. "Metafiction." *IowaR*, 1: 100-15 (Fa 70).

Schorr, J.R. "Wanted: A Hero." *DNR*, 41: 112-3 (15 N 72).

Schulz, Dieter. " 'Ethan Brand' and the Structure of the American Quest Romance." *Genre*, 7: 233-49 (S 74).

Schulz, M.F. "Pop, Op, and Black Humour: The Aesthetics of Anxiety." *CE*, 30: 230-41 (D 68).

Scott, Clifford. "Up the Congo Without a Paddle: Images of Blackest Africa in American Fiction." *NDQ*, 40: 7-19 (Au 72).

Schwartz, Sheila. "Science Fiction: Bridge Between the Two Cultures." *EJ*, 60: 1043-51 (N 71).

———. "Science Fiction: Literature for Our Times." *JPC*, 5: 979-88 (Sp 72).

Seelye, J.D. "The American Tramp: A Version of the Picaresque." *AQ*, 15: 535-53 (Wi 63).

———. "Some Green Thoughts on a Green Theme." *TriQ*, 24-5: 576-638 (Sp 72).

Sellars, R.W. "The Interrelationship of Literature, History, and Geography in Western Writing." *Western Hist Q*, 4: 171-85 (Ap 73).

Seshachari, Candadi. "Popular Western Fiction as Literature of Escape." *PosS*, 4: 5-8 (Ap 73).

Seyersted. Per. "A Survey of Trends and Figures in Afro-American Fiction." *AmSS*, 6: 67-86 (1974).

Shapiro, S.A. "The Ambivalent Animal: Man in the Contemporary British and American Novel." *CentR*, 12: 1-22 (Wi 68).

Shaw, Irwin. "In Praise of the Short Story." *Esquire*, 79: 124-5 (F 73).

Shaw, P.W. "Old Genre, New Breed: The Postwar American Picaro." *Genre*, 7: 205-11 (Je 74).

Sheed, Wilfrid. "Wits, Ends and Means." *NYT*, 6 Ag 72, pp. 2, 20.

Shelton, F.W. "The Family in the Modern American Novel of Manners." *SAB*, 40: 33-9 (My 75).

Shenk, S.C. "American Mennonite Fiction." *Mennonite Life*, 23: 119-20 (Jl 68).

Sherman, C.B. "The Development of American Rural Fiction." *Agricultural Hist*, 12: 67-76 (Ja 38).

Shrell, Darwin. "Hunting in the Old South." *SoR*, 4: 467-70 (Sp 68).

Simmen, Edward. " 'We Must Make This Beginning': The Chicano Leader in the Short Story." *SWR*, 57: 126-33 (Sp 72).

Simon, J.D. "Reading the American Proletarian Fiction of the Thirties." *L&I*, 18: 25-32 (1974).

Singer, I.B. "Which Writer Under Thirty-Five Has Your Attention and What Has He Done to Get It?" *Esquire*, 78: 132-35, 198, 200 (O 72).

Singh, R.K. "The Black Novel and Its Tradition." *ColQ*, 20: 23-9 (Su 71).

Skard, Sigmund. "Jan W. Dietrichson: The Image of Money in the American Novel of the Gilded Age." *Edda*, 1972, pp. 129-42.

Sloane, D.E.E. "In Search of a Realist Poetic Tradition." *ALR*, 5: 489-91 (Fa 72).

Small, R.C. "The Junior Novel and Race Relations." *NALF*, 8: 184-90 (Sp 74).

Smith, D.J. "The American Railroad Novel." *MarkR*, 3: 85-93 (F 73).

―――. "The Glamor of the Glittering Rails." *MwQ*, 11: 311-26 (Ap 70).

Smith, Harry. " 'Bestsellers Nobody Reads.' " *Smith*, 10: 182-4 (N 68).

Smith, H.N. "The Scribbling Women and the Cosmic Successs Story." *CritI*, 1: 47-70 (1974).

Soderbergh, P.A. "The Dark Mirror: War Ethos in Juvenile Ficton, 1865-1919." *UDR*, 10: 13-24 (Su 73).

―――. "Florida's Image in Juvenile Fiction 1909-14." *FHQ*, 51: 153-65 (O 72).

―――. "The Negro in Juvenile Series Books, 1899-1930." *JNH*, 58: 179-86 (Ap 73).

―――. "The South in Juvenile Series Books, 1907-1917." *MissQ*, 131-40 (Sp 74).

Solomon, Eric. "From *Christ in Flanders* to *Catch-22*: An Approach to War Fiction." *TSLL*, 11: 851-66 (Sp 69).

Solotaroff, Theodore. "Some Random Notes on Contemporary Writing." *TCL*, 20: 270-6 (1974).

Sonnichsen, C.L. "Fiction and History." *Mountain-Plains Lib Q*, 13: 3-9 (Su 68).

―――. "Tombstone in Fiction." *JAriH*, 9: 58-76 (Su 68).

Spangler, G.M. "The Confession Form: An Approach to the Tycoon." *MASJ*, 10: 5-18 (1969).

Spender, Stephen. "Americanization." *PR*, 39: 148-73 (Sp 72).

Spiegel, Alan. "A Theory of the Grotesque in Southern Fiction." *GaR*, 26: 426-37 (Wi 72).

Spivak, G.C. "Thoughts on the Principle of Allegory." *Genre*, 5: 327-52 (1972).

Stampfer, Judah. "The Hunger for Namelessness." *Nation*, 219: 152-5 (32 Ag 74).

Stanford, Derek. "A Larger Latitude: Three Themes in the 'Nineties Short Story." *ConR*, 210: 96-104 (F 68).

―――. "The 'Nineties Short-Story: Birth of a Genre." *ConR*, 212: 97-104 (S 68).

Stanton, M.N. "The Startled Muse: Emerson and Science Fiction." *Extrapolation*, 16: 64-6 (D 74).

Steeves, H.R. "The First of the Westerns." *SWR*, 52: 74-84 (Wi 68).

Stein, A.F. " '9009'—Early Naturalistic Novel." *IllQ*, 36: 31-42 (F 74).

Stein, A.M. "The Detective Story—How and Why." *PULC*, 36: 19-46 (1974).

Stein, R.B. "Pulled Out of the Bay: American Fiction in the Eighteenth Century." *SAF*, 2: 13-36 (Sp 74).

Steinbrink, Jeffrey. "Novels of Circumstances and Novels of Character: Emerson's Views of Fiction." *ESQ*, 20: 101-10 (2Q 74).

Stessin, Lawrence. "The Businessman in Fiction." *LitR*, 12: 281-9 (Sp 69).

Stevick, Philip. "Metaphors for the Novel." *TriQ*, 30: 127-38 (Sp 74).

―――. "Scheherazade Runs Out of Plots, Goes on Talking." *TriQ*, 26: 332-62 (Wi 73).

Stewart, D.H. "The Decline of WASP Literature in America." *CE*, 30: 403-17 (Mr 69).

Stineback, D.C. "On the Limits of Fiction." *MwQ*, 16: 339-48 (Jl 73).

Stoehr, Taylor. "Realism and Verisimilitude." *TSLL*, 11: 1269-88 (Fa 69).

Stout, J.P. "Charity and Redemption of Urban Society in American Popular Fiction before 1860." *RSW*, 43: 162-74 (1975).

Stover, Leon. "Science Fiction and the Research Revolution, and John Campbell." *Extrapolation*, 14: 129-48 (1973).

Strauss, Wolfgang. "Literatur im Dienst der Glorifizierung des imperialistischen Krieges." *ZAA*, 18: 391-406 (1970).

Strout, Cushing. "Personality and Cultural History in the Novel." *NLH*, 1: 432-37 (1970).

Stuart, Jesse. "The Last Independent Profession." *BSUF*, 9: 3-7 (Su 68).

Fiction

Styron, William. "On Our Literature of Collision." *ID*, 2: 82-4 (Mr 72).

————, et al. "The Uses of History in Fiction." *SLJ*, 1: 57-90 (1969).

Suderman, E.F. "Fiction and Mennonite Life." *MASJ*, 10: 16-25 (Sp 69).

————. "A Study of the Revival in Late Nineteenth-Century American Fiction." *MethH*, 5: 27-30 (Ja 67).

Sukenick, Ronald. "Innovative Fiction/Innovative Criteria: On Reinventing the Novel." *FicI*, 2-3: 133-4 (Sp-Fa 74).

————. "The New Tradition." *PR*, 39: 580-8 (Fa 72).

Sullivan, J.J. "Conflict in the Modern American Novel." *BSUF*, 15: 28-36 (Sp 74).

Sullivan, T.R. "The Uses of a Fictional Formula: The Selkirk Mother Lode." *JPC*, 8; 35-52 (Su 74).

Sullivan, Walter. "The Decline of Regionalism in Southern Fiction." *GaR*, 18: 300-8 (Fa 64).

————. "Fiction in a Dry Season: Some Signs of Hope." *SR*, 77: 154-64 (1969).

————. "In Time of the Breaking of Nations: The Decline of Southern Fiction." *SoR*, 4: 299-305 (Sp 68).

————. "Southern Writers in the Modern World: Death by Melancholy." *SoR*, 6: 907-19 (Au 70).

————. "Where Have All the Flowers Gone? The Novel in the Gnostic Twilight." *SR*, 78: 654-64 (1970).

————. " 'Where Have All the Flowers Gone?': The Short Story in Search of Itself." *SR*, 78: 531-42 (1970).

Sutton, Henry. "Notes Toward the Destitution of Culture." *KR*, 30: 108-15 (1968).

Suvin, Darko. "A, B, and C. The Significant Context of SF: A Dialogue of Comfort Against Tribulation." *S-FS*, 1: 44-50 (Sp 73).

————. "On the Poetics of the Science Fiction Genre." *CE*, 34: 372-82 (D 72).

————. "Radical Rhapsody and Romantic Recoil in the Age of Anticipation: A Chapter in the History of SF." *S-FS*, 1: 255-68 (Fa 74).

————. "Science Fiction and the Genealogical Jungle." *Genre*, 6: 251-73 (S 73).

Tanner, Tony. "The American Novelist as Entropologist." *LonM*, 10: 5-18 (O 70).

————. "My Life in American Literature." *TriQ*, 30: 83-108 (Sp 74).

————. "Problems and Roles of the American Artist as Portrayed by the American Novelist." *PBA*, 57: 159-79 (1971).

Tarbet, D.W. "Contemporary American Pastoral: A Poetic Faith." *Eng Rec*, 23: 72-83 (Wi 72).

Tatum, C.M. "Contemporary Chicano Prose Fiction: A Chronicle of Misery." *LALR*, 1: 7-17 (Sp 73).

Theroux, Paul. "Miseries & Splendours of the Short Story." *Enc*, 39: 69-75 (S 72).

Thompson, John. "The Fiction Machine." *Commentary*, 46: 67-71 (O 68).

Thorp, Willard. "Catholic Novelists in Defense of Their Fatih, 1829-1865." *PAAS*, 78: 25-117 (1968).

————. "Setting the Record Straight." *KR*, 30: 562-9 (1968).

Tingley, D.F. "The 'Robin's Egg Renaissance': Chicago and the Arts, 1910-20." *JISHS*, 63: 35-54 (Sp 70).

Tischler, N.M. "The Negro in Southern Fiction: Stereotype and Archetype." *NALF*, 2: 3-6 (1968).

Tischler, N.P. "Negro Novels and Christian Readers." *Chri & Lit*, 21: 36-41 (1971-72).

Trachtenberg, Stanley. "Counterhumor: Comdey in Contemporary American Ficton." *GaR*, 27: 33-48 (Sp 73).

Trensky, Anne. "The Bad Boy in Nineteenth-Century American Fiction." *GaR*, 27: 503-17 (Wi 73).

———. "The Saintly Child in Nineteenth-American Fiction." *Prospects*, 1: 389-414 (1975).

Turco, Lewis. "American Novelists as Poets: The Schizophrenia of Mode." *Eng Rec*, 25: 23-9 (Su 74).

Turner, D.T. "*The Negro Novel in America*: in Rebuttal." *CLAJ*, 10: 122-34 (D 66).

Tuttleton, J.W. "American History and the American Novel." *SR*, 82: xliii-vi (Sp 75).

———. "The American Novelist: His Time and Place." *YR*, 62: 305-7 (1973).

———. "Romance of Novel: The Disintegration of a Form." *ESQ*, 55: 116-21 (2Q 69).

Twining, M.A. "An Anthropological Look at Afro-American Folk Narrative." *CLAJ*, 14: 57-61 (S 70).

VanDerBeets, Richard. "The Indian Captivity Narrative as Ritual." *AL*, 43: 548-62 (Ja 72).

———. "'A Thirst for Empire': The Indian Captivity Narrative as Propaganda." *RSW*, 40: 207-15 (1972).

Vauthier, Simone. "A propos de l'image du noir aux amériques dans la premiere moitié du 19ᵉ siecle." *RANAM*, 3: 67-126 (1974).

Wade, Melvin and Margaret. "The Black Aesthetic the Black Novel." *JBlackS*, 2: 391-408 (Je 72).

Waldmeir, J.J. "Only an Occasional Rutabaga: American Fiction Since 1945." *MFS*, 15: 467-81 (1969-70).

Walker, D.D. "Can the Western Tell What Happens?" *Rendezvous*, 7: 33-47 (1972).

———. "Notes on the Popular Western." *PosS*, 3: 11-3 (N 71).

Walker, R.H. "Patterns in Recent American Literature." *Stetson Un Bul*, 65: 1-12 (O 67).

Warren, R.P. et al. "The Uses of History in Fiction." *SLJ*, 1: 57-90 (1969).

Webb, Max. "Sunday Heroes: The Emergence of the Professional Football Novel." *JPC*, 8: 453-61 (1974).

Weber, D.B. "Society and the American Novel, 1920-1960." *DilR*, 13: 366-79 (O 65).

Weidman, B.S. "White Men's Red Man: A Penitential Reading of Four American Novels." *MLS*, 4: 14-26 (Fa 74).

Weinkauf, M.S. "Edenic Motifs in Utopian Fiction." *Extrapolation*, 11: 15-22 (D 69).

Welsh, J.R. "Succinct Perspective." *SAB*, 35: 49-50 (My 70).

Welty, Eudora. "Some Notes on Time in Fiction." *MissQ*, 26: 483-92 (Fa 73).

West, Paul. "Perpetuating the Obsolete." *Cweal*, 87: 203-5 (17 N 67).

Westbrook, Max. "Conservative, Liberal, and Western: Three Modes of American Realism." *SDR*, 4: 3-19 (Su 66).

———. "Fiction and Belief." *CRAS*, 3: 63-7 (1972).

Westendorp, T.A. "Recent Southern Fiction." *HVF*, 1974, pp. 188-98.

Whetton, Betty. "A Very Personal View of Western Literature." *Ariz Eng Bul*, 13: 59-61 (Ap 71).

White, D.F. "A Summons for the Kingdom of God on Earth: The Early Social Gospel Novel." *SAQ*, 67: 469-85 (Su 68).

Whiting, C.H. "Feeling and the Significance of the Novel." *Marab*, 1: 71-7 (Su 64).

Whittington, Curtis. "The 'Burden' of Narration: Democratic Perspective and First-Person Point of View in the American Novel." *SHR*, 2: 236-45 (Sp 68).

Wiggins, W.H. "The Structure and Dynamics of Folklore in the Novel Form: The Case of John O. Killens." *KFQ*, 17: 92-118 (Fl 72).

Willett, Ralph. "The American Western: Myth and Anti-Myth." *JPC*, 4: 455-63 (Fa 70).

Willey, Frederick. "The Novel and the Natural Man." *MQR*, 7: 104-18 (Sp 68).

Fiction

Williams, Cratis. "Kentucky's First Mountain Story." *KFR*, 17: 1-4 (Ja-Mar 71).

Williams, John. "Fact in Fiction: Problems for the Historical Novelist." *DQ*, 7: 1-12 (Wi 73).

———. "The 'Western': Definition of the Myth." *Nation*, 193: 402 (18 N 61).

Williamson, Jack. "Science Fiction Comes to College." *Extrapolation*, 12: 67-78 (My 71).

Wills, Garry. "Catholic Faith and Fiction." *NYT*, 16 Ja 72, pp. 1-2, 14, 16, 20.

Winans, Robert. "The Growth of a Novel-Reading Public in Late-Eighteenth-Century America." *EAL*, 9: 267-75 (Wi 75).

Wirzberger, K.H. " 'Great Tradition' oder Episode? Nonkonformismus, Protest und Engagement in der amerikanischen Gegenwartsliteratur." *ZAA*, 16: 5-24 (1968).

Witmer, A.M. "The Contemporary Novel of the American West." *LWU*, 5: 37-45 (1972).

Wolfe, Tom. "Why They Aren't Writing the Great American Novel Anymore." *Esquire*, 78: 152-9, 274-80 (D 72).

Wilson, J.D. "Incest and American Romantic Fiction." *SLitI*, 7: 31-50 (Sp 74).

Wolpers, Theodor. "Kürze in Erzählen." *Anglia*, 89: 46-86 (1971).

Wood, A..D "The Literature of Impoverishment: The Women Local Colorists in America, 1865-1914." *WS*, 1: 3-36 (1972).

Woodward, C.V., et al. "The Uses of History in Fiction." *SLJ*, 1: 57-90 (1969).

Wylder, D.E. "The Popular Western Novel: An Essay Review." *WAL*, 4: 299-303 (Wi 70).

———. "The Western Hero from a Strange Perspective." *Rendezvous*, 7: 23-32 (1972).

Yardley, Jonathan. "The New Old Southern Novel." *PR*, 40: 286-93 1973).

Yeazell, Ruth. "Fictional Heroines and Feminist Critics." *Novel*, 8: 29-38 (Fa 74).

Yevish, I.A. "Campus Rebellions: Their Literary Heritage." *ColQ*, 20: 471-7 (Sp 72).

———. "The Faculty Novel." *GaR*, 25: 41-50 (Sp 71).

Zavarzadeh, Mas'ud. "The Apocalyptic Fact and the Eclipse of Fiction in Recent American Prose Narrative." *JAmSt*, 9: 69-83 (1975).

———. "A Typology of Prose Narrative." *JLS*, 3: 67-80 (1974).

Ziff, Larzer. "Masters of the Finite." *TLS*, 7 March 75, p. 242.

Zollman, Sol. "Propaganda for Theory of Human Nature in Current American Novels." *L&I*, 12: 59-66.

Foreign Influences and Estimates.
Anon. "American Books Published in Great Britain Before 1848." *ESQ*, 51: 129-36 (2Q 68).

———. "Le roman des Ameriques." *Liberte*, 90: 5-305 (1973).

Akar, J.J. "An African's View of Black Studies With International Dimensions." *CLAJ*, 14: 717 (S 70).

Aldridge, A.L. "Camilo Henriquez and the Fame of Thomas Paine and Benjamin Franklin in Chile." *RIB*, 17: 51-67 (1967).

Alexandrescu, Sorin. "William Faulkner and the Greek Tragedy." *RoR*, 24: 102-10 (1970).

Alfonso, Ferdinando. "Su Moravia moralista: La critica italiana e americana (1929-69)." *CV*, 29: 183-94 (1974).

Allen, G.W. "Whitman and Michelet." *AL*, 45: 428-32 (N 73).

Allen, Mary. "Melville and Conrad Confront Stillness." *RSW*, 40: 122-30 (1972).

Altholz, J.L., and Victor Conzemius. "Acton and Brownson: A Letter from America." *CathHR*, 49: 524-31 (1964).

Anastasjew, N. " 'Massenbelletristik' in den USA: Sozialer Auftrag und asthetische Klischees." *KuL*, 21: 1113-37 (1973).

Anderson, C.L. "Strindberg's Translations of American Humor." *AmNor*, 3: 153-94 (1972).

Arikawa, Shoji. "Huckleberry Finn in Japan." *Eng Rec*, 21: 20-6 (F 71).

Arner, R.D. "Nehemiah Wlater: Milton's Earliest American Disciple?" *EAL*, 8: 62-5 (Sp 73).

Ashliman, D.L. "The Image of Utah and the Mormons in Nineteenth-Century Germany." *UHQ*, 35: 209-27 (Su 67).

———. "The Noel of Western Adventure in Nineteenth-Century Germany." *WAL*, 3: 133-45 (Su 68).

Assenlineau, Roger. "The French Stream in American Literature." *YCGL*, 17: 29-39 (1968).

Auffret, Hélène. "Etude comparée de deux poèmes-conversation: Appolinaire, 'les femmes,' Eliot, 'A Game of Chess.'" *RLC*, 43: 415-26 (1969).

Axelrod, Steven. "Baudelaire and the Poetry of Robert Lowell." *TCL*, 17: 257-74 (O 71).

Bach, Max. "Trois lettres inedites de Michelet a Mary Lowell Putnam." *RHL*, 74: 884-6 (1974).

Baker, C.F. "Spenser and 'The City in the Sea.'" *PosS*, 5: 55 (1972).

Baker, W.J. "Charles Kingsley in Little London." *ColM*, 45: 187-203 (Su 68).

———. 'A Victorian Chapter in Anglo-American Understanding: Three Letters from Charles Kingsley." *N&Q*, 18: 91-7 (Mr 71).

Baldwin, N.E. "Discovering Common Ground: A Note on William Carlos Williams and Valery Larbaud." *AL*, 45: 292-7 (My 73).

Banerjee, R.D.K. "Dante Through the Looking Glass: Rossetti, Pound, and Eliot." *CL*, 24: 136-49 (1972).

Barry, John. "*The Waste Land*: A Possible German Source." *CLS*, 9: 429-42 (D 72).

Bausam, H.S. "Edenic Images of the Western World." *SAQ*, 67: 672-702 (Au 68).

Baužyté, Galina. "Iliuzijos ir tikroves konfliktas Edvardo Oblio dramaturgijoje." *Literatura*, 15: 79 94 (1973).

Beckner, Jean. "Arthur Conan Doyle and Joaquin Miller." *MDAC*, 1: 25-8 (1972).

Bednar, Kamil. "Jeffers in Czechoslovakia." *RJN*, 27: 8-9 (1970).

Behrmann, Alfred. "Kotzebue on the American Stage." *Arcadia*, 4: 274-84 (1969).

Bereaud, J.G. "La traduction en France a l'époque romantique." *CLS*, 8: 224-44 (S 71).

Berthold, Dennis. "Hawthorne, Ruskin, and the Gothic Revival: Transcendant Gothic in *The Marble Faun*." *ESQ*, 20: 15-32 (1Q 74).

Bessière, Jean. "L'Amerique hors texte: Semantique du roman international (1920-35)." *Degres*, 4: f-f24 (1973).

Bishop, T.W. "Adaptations of American Plays in Paris 1958-59." *FR*, 33: 551-7 (My 60).

Blonski, Jan. "Americans in Poland." *KR*, 23: 32-51 (Wi 61).

Boni, John. "Some Analogous Forms: Black Comedy and Some Jacobean Plays." *WHR*, 28: 210-15 (1974).

Borden, Caroline. "Characterization in Revolutionary Chinese and Reactionary American Short Stories." *L&I*, 12: 9-16 (1972).

Bowen, J.K., and J.A. Hamby. "Colonel Sartoris Snopes and Gabriel Marcel: Allegiance and Commitment." *NMW*, 3: 101-7 (Wi 71).

Bracher, P.S. "The Early American Editions of American Editions of *American Notes*: Their Priority and Circulation." *PBSA*, 69: 365-76 (3Q 75).

———. "The Lea & Blanchard Edition of Dickens' *American Notes*, 1842." *PBSA*, 63: 296-300 (4Q 69).

Bravo Villasante, Carmen. "Las excritoras norteamericanas." *Asomante*, 18: 31-48 (O-D 62).

Bredella, Lothar. "Ästhetische und soziale Kategorien bei der Analyse des Bestsellers *Valley of the Dolls* von Jacqueline Susann." *JA*, 19: 30-49 (1974).

Bredson, R.C. "Landscape Description in Nineteenth-Century American Travel Literature."*AQ*, 20: 86-94 (1968).

Brie, Hartmut. "Die Theorie des poetischen Effekts bei Poe und Mallarmé." *NS*, 21: 473-81 (1972).

Briggs, A.D. "Alexander Pushkin: A Possible Influence on Henry James." *FMLS*, 8: 52-60 (1972).

Brock, William. "The Image of England and American Nationalism." *JAmSt*, 5: 225-45 (D 71).

Brodsky, Patricia Pollock. "Fertile Fields and Poisoned Gardens: Sologub's Debt to Hoffman, Pushkin, and Hawthorne." *EL*, 1: 96-108 (Sp 74).

Brown, B.W. "T, Sterry Hunt, the Man Who Brought Walt Whitman to Canada." *SoQ*, 10: 43-8 (1971).

Brown, J.P. "The Come-All-Ye in Irish Tradition." *Les Ecrits des Saints*, 27: 151-2 (1965).

Brown, Wallace. "An Englishman Views the American Revolution: The Letters of Henry Hulton, 1769-1776." *HLQ*, 36: 1-26 (1972).

————. "William Cobbett in North America." *HistT*, 22: 685-91 (O 72).

Bruning, Eberhard. "Probleme der Rezeption amerikanischer Literatur in der DDR." *WB*, 16: 175-86 (1970).

Buchloh, P.G. "Tendenzen und Charakteristiska der amerikanischen Literatur nach dem Zweiten Weltkrieg." *LWU*, 7: 180-90 (1974).

Budka, M.J.E. "The American Notebooks of Julian Ursyn Niemcewicz." *SEER*, 43: 188-91 (D 64).

Burrison, John. "'James Harris' in Britain since Child." *JAF*, 80: 271-83 (Jl-S 67).

Burt, D.J. "Robert Penn Warren's Debt to Homer in 'Flood.'" *NCLit*, 3: 12-4 (Ja 73).

Buxbaum, M.H. "Hume, Franklin, and America: A Matter of Loyalties." *EnE*, 3: 93-105 (1972).

Cameron, K.W. "Bunyan and the Writers of the American Renaissance." *ATQ*, 13: 1-47 (Wi 72)).

Capellan Gonzalo, Angel. "Tres acercamientos a la literatura norteamericana reciente." *Arbor*, 342: 107-13 (1974).

Carson, B.H. "An Orphic Hymn in *Walden*." *ESQ*, 20: 125-30 (2Q 74).

Cate, H.L. "The Initial Publication of George Eliot's Novels in America." *BSUF*, 10: 65-9 (Sp 69).

Cevasco, G.A. "*A rebours* and Poe's Reputation in France." *RomN*, 13: 255-61 (1971).

Chambers, Jane. "Two Legends of Temperance: Spenser's and Hawthorne's." *ESQ*, 20: 275-9 (4Q 74).

Chapman, Abraham. "The Black Aesthetic and the African Continuum." *Pan-African J*, 4: 397-406 (1971).

Chase, R.H. "Cesare Pavese and the American Novel." *SA*, 3: 347-69 (1957).

Childs, J.B. "Memoires d'un Voyageur qui se repose: A Bibliographical Interlude on an Elusive Foreign Service Officer's Impressions of the United States, 1811-32." *PBSA*, 64: 193-204 (1970).

Chin, Frank, et al. "Aiieee! An Introduction to Asian-American Writing." *Yardbird Reader*, 2: 21-46 (1973).

Chu, Limin. "Mirror of Darkness: The Images of China and the Chinese in the Fiction of the *Overland Monthly*." *TkR*, 2: 15-49 (1971).

Cifelli, Edward. "Hawthorne and the Italian." *SA*, 14: 87-96 (1968).

Clark, C.E.F. "Hawthorne's First Appearance in England." *CEAAN*, 3: 10-1 (Je 70).

Clark, G.P. "A German Scholar Interprets Poe." *PS*, 4: 52-3 (D 71).

Coad, Oral. "Some Traveler's-Eye Views of the Jerseyman." *JRUL*, 35: 41-66 (Je 72).

Cohen, I.B. "The American Editions of Newton's *Principia*." *HLB*, 18: 345-58 (O 70).

Colbron, G.I. "The American Novel in Germany." *Bkm*, 39: 46-7 (Mr 14); *PW*, 85: 1926-7 (13 Je 74).

Cook, Mercer. "Les Précurseurs négro-américains de la Négritude." *Le Soleil* (Dakar), 12: 114 (8 My 71).

Covo, Jacqueline. "Ralph Ellison in France: Bibliographic Essays and Checklist of French Criticism, 1954-1971." *CLAJ*, 16: 519-26 (Je 73).

Cowan,. J.C. "Lawrence's Criticism of Melville." *MSEx*, 17: 6-8 (F 74).

Cowley, Malcolm. "Laforgue in America: A Testimony." *SR*, 71: 62-74 (Ja-Mr 63).

Cramer, Mark. "Neruda and Vallejo in Contemporary United States Poetry." *RomN*, 14: 455-9 (1973).

Crew, Louie. "Charles Dickens as a Critic of the United States." *MwQ*, 16: 42-50 (O 74).

Dal, Erik. "Hans Christian Andersen's Tales and America." *SS*, 40: 1-25 (F 68).

D'Avanzo,M.L. "Ahab, the Grecian Pantheon and Shelley's *Prometheus Unbound*: The Dynamics of Myth in *Moby Dick*." *BBr*, 24: 19-44 (1971).

Davies, Margaret. "Rimbaud and Melville." *RLC*, 479-88 (1969).

Davies, W.B. "Adleisiau." *YT*, 126: 71-6 (1971).

Decoo, Wilfried. "The Image of Mormonism in French Literature: Part 1." *BYUS*, 14: 157-75 (1974).

Denysova, T.N. "Literaturna spadsčyna 'červonyx trydcjatyx.'" *RLz*, 18: 34-7 (1974).

Schleifer, J.T. "Alexis de Tocqueville Describes the American Character: Two Previously Unpublished Portraits." *SAQ*, 74: 244-58 (Sp 75).

Douglas, G.H. "Croce's Early Aesthetic and American Critical Theory." *CLS*, 7: 204-15 (Je 70).

Doumont, Monique. "Notas para un estudio del 'Whitman' de José Martí." *AnuarioF*, 8-9: 199-212 (1969-70).

Dowling, J.A. "Howells and the English: A Democrat Looks at English Civilization." *BNYPL*, 76: 251-64 (1972).

Dowty, Alan. "Urban Slavery in Pro-Southern Fiction of the 1850's." *JSH*, 32: 25-41 (F 66).

Driskell, Daniel. "Lucretius and 'The City in the Sea.'" *PoeS*, 5: 54-55 (1972).

Dube, Gunaker. "Autumn in Frost and Keats: A Study of Themes and Patterns." *LCrit*, 9: 84-8 (1971).

Duffy, J.J. "Problems in Publishing Coleridge: James Marsh's First American Edition of *Aids to Reflection*." *NEQ*, 43: 193-208 (Je 70).

Dunn, R.J. "Dickens and the Mormons." *BYUS*, 8: 325-34 (1968).

Duran V., Fernando. "Neruda et la poesie ibero-americaine." *RDM*, O 74: 45-53.

Edwards, O.D. "The American Image of Ireland: A Study of Its Early Phases." *PAH*, 4: 197-282 (1970).

El-Azma, Nazeer. "The Tammūzī Movement and the Influence of T.S. Eliot on Badr Shākir al-Sayyab." *JOAS*, 88: 671-78 (1968).

Eldridge, H.G. "The American Republication of Thomas Moore's *Epistles, Odes, and Other Poems:* An Early Version of the Reprinting 'Game.'" *PBSA*, 62: 199-205 (2Q 68).

————. "Anacreon Moore and America." *PMLA*, 83: 54-62 (Mr 68).

Elektorowicz, Leszek. "The Latecomers: American Literature in Poland." *PolP*, 14: 17-26 (1971).

Elwert, W.T. "Longfellow, Mascheroni, Monti und die 'Conchiglia fossile': Zur Geistes und Stilgeschichtlichen Stellung Giacomo Zanella." *RF*, 83: 480-516 (1971).

Ericson, E.E. "Kierkegaard in Wilder's *The Eight Day*." *Renascence*, 26: 123-38 (Sp 74).

Erickson, J.D. "Valery on Leonardo, Poe, and Mallarme." *L'esprit Createur*, 13: 252-9 (1973).

Falb, L.W. "The Critical Reception of Eugene O'Neill on the French Stage." *ETJ*, 22: 397-405 (1970).

———. "'Le naturalisme de papa': American Drama in France." *FR*, 45: 56-71 (1971).

Fetscher, Irving. "Bertolt Brecht and America." *Salmagundi*, 10-11: 246-72 (1969-70).

Fickert, K.J. "Emily Dickinson in German." *HJP*, 8: 20 (Je 74).

Firda, R.A. "German Philosophy of History and Literature in the *North American Review*: 1815-1860." *JHI*, 32: 133-42 (1971).

Fisher, A.P. "The Influence of Ouspensky's 'Tertium Organum' upon Jean Toomer's 'Cane.'" *CLAJ*, 17: 504-15 (Je 74).

Fisher, B.F. "Dickens and Poe: *Pickwick* and 'Ligeia.'" *PoeS*, 14-6 (Je 73).

Fiumi, Annamaria. "G. Benn e T.S. Eliot: Poetiche a confronto." *SA*, 16: 301-51 (1970).

Flak, Micheline. "Léon Bazalgette, découvreur de la littérature américaine." *Europe*, 483-4: 180-7 (1969).

Flanagan, J.T. "Long Live the Hodga." *SFQ*, 33: 48-53 (1969).

Fletcher, R.M. "Emerson's *Nature* and Goethe's *Faust*." *AN&Q*, 12: 102 (Mr 74).

Fogle, R.H. "Nathaniel Hawthorne and the Great English Romantic Poets." *KSJ*, 21-2: 219-35 (1972-73).

Foner, P.S. "Marx's *Capital* in the United States." *Sci&Soc*, 31: 461-6 (1967).

Forno, L.J. "Montesquieu's Reputation in France, England, and America." *Stud in Burke*, 15: 5-29 (1973).

Foster, L.A. "Nabokov in Russian Emigré Criticism." *RLT*, 3: 330-41 (1972).

Frykman, Erik. "Some Notes on the Theme of Self-Realization in English and Scandinavian Literature of the Nineteenth and Twentieth Centuries." *AUR*, 44: 241-55 (Sp 72).

Fuegi, John. "Russian 'Epic Theatre' Experiments and the American Stage." *MinnR*, 1: 102-12 (Fa 73).

Fulkerson, Gerald. "Exile as Emergence: Frederick Douglass in Great Britain, 1845-1847." *QJS*, 60: 69-82 (F 74).

Gabbard, G.N. "*Jurgen* and *Peer Gynt*." *Kalki*, 5: 3-4 (1971).

Gál, István. "Szechenyi and the U.S.A." *HSE*, 5: 95-119 (1971).

Galinsky, Hans. "American Studies in Germany: Their Growth, Variety, and Prospects." *AmS*, 13: 3-10 (#1 74).

Galpin, Alfred. "A Boat in the Tower: Rimbaud in Cleveland, 1922." *Renascence*, 25: 3-13 (1972).

Gardner, Joseph H. "Dickens, Romance, and *McTeague*: A Study in Mutual Interpretation." *EL*, 1: 69-82 (Sp 74).

Garner, Stanton. "Harold Frederic and Swinburne's *Locrine*: A Matter of Clubs, Copyrights, and Character." *AL*, 45: 285-92 (My 73).

Garofolo, Silvao. "Manzoni and the American Literary Scene (1830-1840)." *FI*, 7: 375-85 (1973).

Gavin, William J. "Chaadayev and Emerson—Two Mystic Pragmatists." *RusR*, 32: 119-30 (Ap 73).

Gerber, G.E. "Milton and Poe's 'Modern Woman.'" *PN*, 3: 25-6 (D 70).

Gide, André. "Amerikanische Literatur." *Die Fahre*, 2: 199-202 (1947).

Gilenson, Boris. "Afro-American Literature in the Soviet Union." *NALF*, 9: 25, 28-9 (Sp 75).

———. "American Literature in the Soviet Union." *AmS*, 12: 22-7 (Wi 73).

Giorcelli, Cristina. "La poesie 'italiane' di Herman Melville." *SA*, 14: 165-91 (1968).

Girardot, R.G. "Der Einfluss der Literatur der Vereinigten Staaten au die iberoamerikanische Literatur." *JA*, 18: 9-23 (1973).

Goetsch, Paul. "W.H. Auden und Amerika." *JA*, 13: 215-27 (1968).

Goetz, T.H. "Taine on Poe." *Archiv*, 210: 86-93 (1973).

Gogol, J.M. "Two Russian Symbolists on Poe." *PN*, 3: 36-7 (D 70).

Gohdes, Clarence. "American Books in Italy." *Forum*, 10: 32-4 (1972).

Gordimer, Nadine. "Party of One: A Foreigner Looks at American Writers." *Holiday*, 34: 12-7 (Jl 63).

Gozzi, R.D. "Walden and a Carlyle Letter." *TSB*, 118: 4 (1972).

Grant, H.R. "Icarian and American Utopianism." *IllQ*, 34: 5-15 (1972).

Green, C.B. "American Studies in the South Pacific." *GaR*, 24: 54-63 (Sp 70).

Gregg, Larry. "Kornei Chudovsky's *Whitman*." *WWR*, 20: 50-9 (Je 74).

———. "Slava Snabokovu." *RLT*, 3: 313-29 (1972).

Grigorescu, Irina. "T.S. Eliot: *Patru cvartete*." *Orizont*, 21: 79-81 (1971).

Guseva, Elena. "F. Scott Fitzgerald's *The Great Gatsby* in Russian." *SovL*, 6: 171-4 (1966).

Guttmann, Allen. "Sport in der amerikanischen Literatur: Bestatigung der Neuen Sozialkritik?" *Sportwissenschaft*, 4: 384-94 (1974).

Haberland, P.M. "The Reception of German Literature in Baltimore's Literary Magazines, 1800-1875." *GAS*, 7: 69-92 (1974).

Hall, W.F. "Hawthorne, Shakespeare and Tess: Hardy's Use of Allusion and Reference." *ES*, 52: 533-42 (1971).

Hammond, Alexander. "Poe's 'Lionizing' and the Design of *Tales of the Folio Club*." *ESQ*, 18: 154-65 (1972).

Han, Pierre. "Innocence and Natural Depravity in *Paradise Lost*, *Phèdre*, and *Billy Budd*." *RSPH*, 49: 856-61 (1971).

Hartley, Lodwick. "The Dying Soldier and the Love-lorn Virgin: Notes on Sterne's Early Reception in America." *SHR*, 4: 89-80 (Wi 70).

———. "*The North American Review* on Laurence Sterne: A Document in a Literary Reputation." *AL*, 44: 299-306 (My 72).

Haslam, Gerald. "The Light that Fills the World; Native American Literature." *SDR*, 11: 27-41 (1973).

Haswell, R.H. "Poe and Baudelaire: Translations." *PoeS*, 5: 62-63 (1972).

Hatcher, J.B. "Shaw the Reviewer and James's *Guy Domville*." *MD*, 14: 331-4 (1971).

Hatfield, Henry. "Thomas Mann and America." *Salmagundi*, 10-1: 174-85 (1969-70).

Hauck, Richard. "The Dickens Controversy in the *Spirit of the Times*." *PMLA*, 85: 278-83 (Mr 70).

Heineman, H.L. "'Starving in that Land of Plenty': New Backgrounds to Frances Trollope's *Domestic Manners of the Americans*." *AQ*, 24: 643-60 (D 72).

Heiskanen-Makela, Sirkka. "Emily Dickinson in Finland." *HJP*, 8: 18-9 (Je 74).

Hentschel, Cedric. "Campe and the Discovery of America." *GL&L*, 26: 1-13 (1972).

Hertz, Robert. "England and American Romanticism." *Person*, 46: 81-92 (Wi 65).

Heventhal, Charles. "Richard Burton's "Anatomy of Melancholy' in Early America." *PBSA*, 63: 157-75 (3Q 69).

Highfill, P.H. "The British Background of the American Hallams." *ThS*, 11: 1-35 (1970).

Hilton, Earl. "Howell's *The Shadow of a Dream* and Shakespeare." *AL*, 46: 220-2 (My 74).

Hocks, R.A. "Thoreau, Coleridge, and Barfield: Reflections on the Imagination and the Law of Polarity." *CentR*, 17: 175-98 (Sp 73).

Holmes, L.E. "Science as Fiction: The Concept 'History as Science' in the USSR, 1917-1930." *ClioW*, 4: 27-50 (O 74).

Homma, Kenshiro. "Tayama Katai and Theodore Dreiser—Naturalism and Its Metamorphosis." *DSE*, 11: 144-75 (Je 75).

Honma, Nagayo. "America-ron no seikaku." *EigoS*, 117: 81-82 (1971).

Hook, Andrew. "Huckleberry Finn and Scotland." *Eng Rec*, 21: 8-14 (1970).

Hsin-Fu Wand, David. "The Use of Native Imagery by Chinese Poets Writing in English." *WLWE*, 19: 55-67 (Ap 71).

Hughes, Catharine. "Broadway and the British." *CathW*, 212: 313-5 (1971).

Hultin, N.C. "Inchiquin and Cobbett: American Letters and British Politics." *N&Q*, 19: 91-93 (1972).

Humma, J.B. "Melville's *Billy Budd* and Lawrence's 'The Prussian Officer': Old Adams and New." *Ezik i Literatura* (Sofia), 1: 83-8 (Sp 74).

Hunt, J.D. "Thoreau and Gandhi: A Reevaluation of the Legacy." *Gandhi Marg* (India), 14: 325-32 (1970).

Huvos, Kornel. "Georges Duhamel et l'Amerique." *French R*, 42: 811-7 (My 68).

Inge, M.T. "Contemporary American Literature in Spain." *TSL*, 16: 155-67 (1971).

————. "Miguel De Unamuno's *Canciones* on American Literature: Translated with Commentary." *ArlQ*, 2: 83-97 (Fa 69).

————. "Unamuno's Correspondence with North Americans: A Checklist." *Hisp* 53: 277-85 (My 70).

————. "Unamuno's Reading in American Literature." *Hisp*, 54: 149-54 (Mr 71).

Ingwersen, Niels. "Tendenser i moderne amerikansk romanteknikk." *Edda*, 74: 105-13 (1974).

Isani, M.A. "Zoroastrianism and the Fire Symbolism in *Moby Dick*." *AL*, 44: 385-97 (1972).

Iwamoto, Iwao. "'Shin-Shosetsu' no Atarashisa." *EigoS*, 119: 754-5 (1974).

Jackman, S.W. "Captain Marryat Surveys the American Maritime Scene." *AmNep*, 23: 56-61 (Ja 63).

Jackson, C.T. "The Orient in Post-Bellum American Thought: Three Pioneer Popularizers." *AQ*, 22: 67-81 (1970).

Jarrett, D.W. "Hawthorne and Hardy as Modern Romancers." *NCF*, 28: 258: 258-71 (D 74).

Jeffrey, D.K. "The Johnsonian Influence: *Rasselas* and Poe's 'The Domain of Arnheim.'" *PN*, 3: 26-9 (D 70).

Johnson, D.B. "Nabokov's *Ada* and Puškin's *Eugene Onegin*." *SEEJ*, 15: 316-23 (1971).

Jones, M.B. "Translations of Zola in the United States Prior to 1900." *MLN*, 55: 520-4 (1940).

Judelevičius, Dovydas. "Nagailestingas poeto skalpelis." *Pergale*, 1: 104-11 (1972).

Kanazeki, Yoshio. "Haiku to America Gendaishi." *EigoS*, 114: 358-61 (1968).

Kanfer, Stefan. "But Is It Not Strange That Even Elephants Will Yield—and That *The Prophet* Is Still Popular?" *NYTMS*, 25 Je 72, pp. 8-9, 24, 26, 28, 30.

Kazin, Alfred. "H.G. Wells, America and 'The Future.'" *ASch*, 37: 137-44 (Wi 67-68).

Keith, N.T. "Ezra Pound's Relationship with Fenollosa and the Japanese Noh Plays." *MarkR*, 3: 21-7 (1972).

Kelley, D.J. "Delacroix, Ingres et Poe: Valeurs picturales et valeurs littéraires dans l'oeuvre critique de Baudelaire." *RHL*, 71: 606-14 (1971).

Keough, L.C. "Shaw's Introduction to New York: The Mansfield Productions 1894-1900." *Shavian*, 4: 6-10 (1969).

Kestner, J.A. "Thoreau and Kamo no Chōmei's Hut." *ATQ*, 14: 6 (1972).

Kincaid, Arthur N. "The Dramatic Monologue: Eliot's Debt to Browning." *BSN*, 2: 4-11 (1972).

Kobayashi, Manji. "Robert Frost no Shiron." *EigoS*, 119: 768-9.

Koelsch, W.A. "Freud Discovers America." *VQR*, 46: 115-32 (Wi 70).

Kolb, Alfred. "Friedrich Gerstäcken and the American Drama." *MLS*, 5: 103-8 (Sp 75).

Kopp, W.L. "Popular Reception of Classical German Drama in New York 1945-1965." *MLJ*, 55: 510-4 (1971).

Korn, David. "Turgenev in Nineteenth Century America." *RusR*, 27: 461-7 (1968).

Krishnamurthi, M.G. "Point Counterpoint: An Exchange on American Studies in India." *IJAS*, 1: 73-89 (1969).

Kroetsch, Robert. "The Canadian Writer and the American Literary Tradition." *Eng Q*, 4: 45-9 (Su 71).

Kröger, Franz. "Das Deutschlandbild der Engländer und Amerikaner in der Vergangenheit." *NS*, 19: 91-102 (F 70).

Kuhnel, Walter. "Amerikansiche Comicbooks und das Problem einer Analyse popularkultureller Phanome." *JA*, 19: 58-87 (1974).

Landor, Mikhail. "Collected Works of Sinclair Lewis in Russian." *SovL*, 7: 176-8 (1965).

———. "Faulkner in the Soviet Union." *SovL*, 12: 178-85 (1965).

Lane, Lauriat. "Melville and Dickens' *American Notes*." *MSEx*, 12: 3-4 (1972).

LaRosa, R.C. "Bacon and th 'Organic Method' of Emerson's Early Lectures." *ELN*, 8: 107-14 (1970).

Larson, C.R. "African-Afro-American Literary Relations: Basic Parallels." *NegroD*, 19: 35-42 (1969).

Laurence, D.H. "Bernard Shaw and the American Theater: A Projected Study." *Indep Shavian*, 11: 1-4 (Fa 72).

Leach, Elsie. "T.S. Eliot and the School of Donne." *Costerus*, 3: 163-80 (1972).

Lease, Benjamin. "*John Bull* versus Washington Irving: More on the Shakespeare Committee Controversy." *ELN*, 9: 272-77 (1972).

Lebreton-Savigny, Monique. "The Death of Victor Hugo as Reported in the American Press." *RLC*, 43: 385-414 (1969).

Le Master, J.R. "Lorca, Jeffers, and the Myth of Tamar." *NLauR*, 1: 44-51 (1971).

Lerner, M.G. "Edouard Rod and America." *RLC*, 44: 531-9 (1970).

Lemay, J.A.L. "A Calendar of American Poetry in the Colonial Newspapers and Magazines and in the Major English Magazines Through 1765." *PAAS*, 79: 291 392 (O 69); 80: 71-222, 353-469 (Ap, O 70).

Levidova, Inna. "John Updike's *The Centaur* in Russian." *SovL*, 10: 188-94 (1965).

Lewin, Bruno. "Literarische Begegnungen zwischen Amerika und Japan." *JA*, 14: 25-39 (1969).

Lewis, W.B. "Walt Whitman: Johannes Schlaf's New Being ('Neuer Mensch')." *Cal*, 6: 22-34 (1972).

Lima, Robert. "A Borges Poem on Poe." *PoeS*, 6: 29-30 (Je 73).

Link, F.H. "Goethe und die Renaissance des Neuenglishcen Geisteslebens im 19 Jarhundert." *ATQ*, 14: 94-9 (1972).

Logan, R.W. "James Weldon Johnson and Haiti." *Phylon*, 32: 396-402 (1971).

Lombard, Charles. "Poe and French Romanticism." *PN*, 3: 30-5 (D 70).

Lombard, C.M. 'Whitman and Hugo." *WWR*, 19: 19-25 (1973).

Lombardo, Agostine. "Italian Criticism of American Literature." *SR*, 68: 353-515 (Su 60).

Long, R.A. "Black Studies: International Dimensions." *CLAJ*, 14: 1-6 (S 70).

Low, Anthony. "The Friendly Dog: Eliot and Hardy." *AN&Q*, 12: 106-8 (Mr 74).

Lundkvist, Artur. "Mardrommer och spex." *BLM*, 42: 276-81 (1973).

Lyra, Franciszek, ed. "Correspondence of Sygurg Wisniowski to Henry Wadsworth Longfellow." *KN*, 19: 317-26 (1972).

McClary, B.H. "Irving, Lockhart, and the *Quarterly Review*." *BNYPL*, 76: 231-6 (1972).
———. "Thomas Hughes's Continuing Memorial: A Treasure Trove for Victorian Scholars." *VN*, 33: 49-50 (Sp 68).
MacDougall, M.A., Francelia Butler, and Wesley McClure. "The Reaction of Polish Students to American Literature." *PolR*, 15: 81-94 (1970).
McLennan, Gordon. "Thomas Carlyle and the Transcendentalists." *ConS*, 10: 7-10 (Je 75).
McLeod, Dan. "From *Banquet Years* to *A Moveable Feast*: Paris and the American Artist." *KAL*, 14: 76-81 (1972).
———. "Literary Responses to Nature in Japan and America." *KAL*, 14: 13-19 (1972).
McMullin, S.E. "Transcendentalism and the Canadian Confederation Poets." *RevL*, 4: 210-33 (1972).
Madigan, F.V. "A Mirror of Shelley in Whitman." *Greyfriar*, 11: 3-19 (1970).
Manske, Eva. "Amerikanische Gegenwartsliteratur im Urteil sowjetischer Literaturkritik." *ZAA*, 4: 362-70 (1974).
Marks, Patricia. "O'Henry and Dickens: Elsie in the Bleak House of Moral Decay." *ELN*, 12: 35-7 (1974).
Marraro, H.R. "Miscellaneous Notes on Italian Literature in America in the Nineteenth Century." *MLJ*, 54: 324-28 (1970).
———. "Views on America and the American Revolution in Contemporary Italian Reviews." *FI*, 5: 67-81 (1971).
Masheck, J.D.C. "Samuel Johnson's Uttoxeter Penance in the Writings of Hawthorne." *Hermathena*, 111: 51-4 (Sp 71).
Masterson, J.R. "Travelers' Tales of Colonial Natural History." *JAF*, 59: 51-67, 174-88 (1946).
Materassi, Mario. "F Criticism in Italy." *IQ*, 57: 47-85 (1971).
Mathews, J.W. "The House of Atreus and *The House of the Seven Gables*." *ESQ*, 63: 31-6 (1971).
Matsuyama, Nobunao. "Some Faces of Hawthorne's Young Goodman Brown." *DSE*, 10: 32-52 (Mr 75).
Melchiori, Giorgio. "The English Novelist and the American Tradition." *SR*, 68: 509-15 (Su 60).
Mendelson, M.O. "Zu einigen Grundtendenzen in der Entwicklung der zeitgenossichen Literatur in den USA." *ZAA*, 22: 341-61 (1974).
Mews, Siegfried. "Foreign Literature in German Magazines, 1870-1890." *YCGL*, 18: 36-47 (1969).
———. "German Reception of American Writers in the Late Nineteenth Century." *SAB*, 34: 7-9 (Mr 69).
Michel, Pierre. "Le roman americain depuis 1945." *RLV*, 39: 497-515 (1973).
Mihăilă, Rodica. "O abordare lingvistică a metaforei și definirea stilului poetic (exemplificare pe poezia lui Hart Crane)." *AUB-LUC*, 22: 145-52 (1973).
Miles, E.A. "The Young American Nation and the Classical World." *JHI*, 35: 259-74 (Ap-Je 74).
Miller, F.D. "Russian Response to American Literature: The Bibliography." *RALS*, 1: 247-9 (Au 71).
Mills, N.C. "The Machine in the Anglo-American Garden." *CentR*, 14: 201-12 (1970).
Milum, R.A. "Faulkner and the Cavalier Tradition: The French Bequest." *AL*, 45: 580-9 (Ja 74).
Monat, Olypio. "John dos Passos e a cidade dos homens vazios." *ESPSL*, 29 S 74, p.l.
Monteiro, George. "Hawthorne in Portuguese." *NHJ*, 1: 228-31 (1971).

———. "Meilville in Portuguese." *Serif*, 9: 23-4 (Sp 72).

———. "More Hawthorne in Portuguese." *NHJ*, 2: 263-4 (1972).

———. "Rudyard Kipling: Early Printings in American Periodicals." *PBSA*, 61: 127-8 (2Q 67).

Morell, Giliane. "'Pourquoi ris-tu, Darl?'—ou le temps d'un regard." *Sud*, 14: 128-49 (1975).

Morey, F.L. "Evaluation of Japanese Dickinsonian Scholarship." *EDB*, 21: 57-77 (1972).

———. "French Material." *EDB*, 13: 51-5 (Je 70).

———. "Germanic Material." *EDB*, 14: 58-67 (S 70).

———. "Japanese Evaluation." *EDB*, 21: 57-60 (Je 72).

Morpurgo, J.E. "'From that Damnable Place'—The Englishness of American Literature." *ULR*, 14: 69-87 (1971).

Morton, B.N. "La reputation de Beaumarchais en Amerique au XVIIe siecle." *Europe*, 528: 35-43 (1973).

Moser, C.A. "Korolenko and America." *RusR*, 28: 303-14 (1969).

Motyleva, T. "Dostoevskij i zarubežnye pisateli xx veka." *VLit*, 15: 96-128 (1971).

Mourier, Maurice. "Le tombeau d'EP." *Esprit*, 441: 902-26 (1974).

Moyne, E.J. "John Greenleaf Whittier and Finland." *SS*, 44: 52-62 (Wi 72).

———. "MT and Baroness Alexandra Gripenberg." *AL*, 45: 370-8 (N 73).

Moyne, E.J. "Thoreau and Emerson: Their Interest in Finland." *NM*, 70: 738-50 (1969).

Mueller, R.C. "Thoreau's Selections from *Chinese Four Books* for *The Dial*." *TJQ*, 4: 1-8 (O 72).

———. "Transcendental Periodicals and the Orient." *ESQ*, 57: 52-57 (4Q 69).

Murphy, D.M. "*The Sound and the Fury* and Dante's *Inferno*: Fire and Ice." *MarkR*, 4: 71-8 (O 74).

Murray, D.M., Chan Waisheung, and Samuel Huang. "A Checklist of Chinese Translations of American Literature." *ABC*, 22: 15-37 (1972).

Murtuza, Athar. "An Arabian Source for Poe's 'The Pit and the Pendulum.'" *PoeS*, 5: 52 (1972).

Nardin, J.T. "Tendances dans les revues de théâtre aux Etats-Unis." *MRom*, 20: 81-7 (1970).

Naremore, James. "The Imagists and the French 'Generation of 1900.'" *ConL*, 11: 354-74 (1970).

Nasu, Yorimasa. "A Castle and Its Symbolism in 'No. 44, The Mysterious Stranger.'" *DSE*, 10: 93-113 (Mr 75).

Nelson, Carl. "The Ironic Allusive Texture of *Lord Jim*: Coleridge, Crane, Milton, and Melville." *Conrad*, 4: 47-59 (1972).

Nettels, Elsa. "James and Conrad on the Art of Fiction." *TSLL*, 14: 529-43 (Fa 72).

Nielson, E.A. "Fortolkningsfjolset." *Kritik*, 29: 28-46 (1974).

Nirenberg, Morton. "Hawthorne's Reception in Germany." *JA*, 15: 141-61 (1970).

Nizeteo, Antun. "W in Croatia: Tin Ujevíc and WW." *JCS*, 11-12: 105-51 (1970).

Noda, Hisashi. "The Concepts of Symbolism in Traditional Japanese Literary Criticism and the Poetics of Emerson." *KAL*, 12: 45-53 (1970).

North, Joseph. "Why a USA-USSR Cultural Exchange? It's Dialogue or Disaster." *AmD*, 5: 3-5 (1968-9).

Oliva, L.J. "Maxim Gorky Discovers America." *NYHSQ*, 51: 45-60 (Ja 67).

Oppel, Horst. "American Literature in Postwar Germany: Impact or Alienation." *LSUS*, 11: 259-72 (1962).

Orians, G.H. "Early American Travelers." *JEGP*, 26: 569-81 (4Q 27).

Osztovits, Levente. "Tete-À-Tete With American Literature." *New Hungarian Q*, 9: 199-206 (Wi 68).

Palandri, A.J. "Ezra Pound and His Italian Critics." *TkR*, 3: 41-57 (1972).

Panagopoulos, E.P. "Chateaubriand's Florida and his Journey to America." *FHQ*, 49: 140-52 (O 70).

Parkay, F.W. "The Influence of Nietzsche's *Thus Spoke Zarathustra* on London's *The Sea-Wolf.*" *JLN*, 4: 16-2 (1971).

Parker, F.D. "Nineteenth-Century Travel Impressions: The U.S.A. and Guatemala." *Inter-Am R of Bibl*, 18: 400-14 (O-D 68).

Parker, Hershel. "'Benito Cereno' and *Cloister-Life*: A Re-Scrutiny of a 'Source.'" *SSF*, 9: 221-32 (1972).

Patil, S.K. "T's Influence on Mahatama Gandhi." *P&ER*, 4: 1-12 (5 D 70).

Pavilionis, R. "H.D.T. ir asmenybes apsisprendimas." *Problemos*, 2: 40-9 (1973).

*Pavnaskar, S.R. "Indian Translations of Edgar Allan Poe: A Bibliography with a Note." *IJAS*, 1: 103-10 (1971).

———. "Poe in India: A Bibliography, 1955-1969." *PoeS*, 5: 49-50 (1972).

Peper, Jürgen. "Der heruntergekommene Surrealismus oder Regression als Fortschritt: Amerikas Youth Counter Culture in zwei Manifesten." *JA*, 19: 9-29 (1974).

Perez, L.C. "Wilder and Cervantes: In the Spirit of the Tapestry." *Sym*, 25: 249-59 (1971).

Perez Botero, Luis. "El principio poetico de Poe y el arielismo de Rodo." *RevL*, 6: 55-61 (1974).

Perosa, Sergio. "American Studies in Italy." *AmS*, 10: 23-7 (Sp 72).

Poli, Bernard. "The Hero in France and in America." *JAmSt*, 2: 225-38 (1968).

Pollin, B.R. "Light on 'Shadow' and Other Pieces by Poe: Or, More of Thomas Moore." *ESQ*, 18: 166-73 (3Q 72).

———. "Poe's Use of Material from Bernardin de Saint-Pierre's *Etudes.*" *RomN*, 12: 331-8 (1971).

Pomorska, Kristina. "A Vision of America in Early Soviet Literature." *SEEJ*, 11: 389-97 (1967).

Poulsen, S.R. "Milton's stil i *Paradise Lost*: Et litteraturkritisk problem. En redegorelse og diskussion med saerligt henblik pa T.S. Eliot og F.R. Leavis' Milton-kritik." *Extracta*, 4: 177-79 (1972).

Powers, L.H. "James's Debt to Alphonse Daudet." *CL*, 24: 150-62 (1972).

Prizel, Yuri. "Hemingway in Soviet Literary Criticism." *AL*, 44: 445-56 (1972).

Przemecka, Irena. "Eugene O'Neill and the Irish Drama." *KN*, 18: 3-9 (1971).

Puknat, E.M. and S.B. "American Literary Encounters with Rilke." *Monatshefte*, 60: 245-56 (1968).

———. "Goethe and Modern American Poets." *GQ*, 42: 21-36 (1969).

Purdy, S.B. "Henry James, Gustave Flaubert, and the Ideal Style." *Lang&S*, 3: 163-84 (1970).

Quick, J.R. "*Silas Marner* as Romance: The Example of Hawthorne." *NCF*, 29: 287-98 (D 74).

Rader, Dotson. "Yevtushenko in America." *LonM*, 14: 5-14 (Ap-My 74).

Raghavacharyulu, D.V.K. "Indian Influence on American Writers." *Triveni*, 42: 47-52 (O-D 73).

Raïzis, M.B. "Epeirotikoi agones kai Amerikanoi polites." *EpH*, 19: 224-32 (1970).

———. "He Chois stin Angliki kai Amerikaniki poiisi tis romantikis epochis." *ChE*, 8: 145-52 (1970).

Rees, J.O. "Spenserian Analogues in *Moby-Dick.*" *ESQ*, 68: 174-78 (1972).

Regnery, Henry. "Eliot, Pound and Lewis: A Creative Friendship." *ModA*, 16: 146-60 (1972).

Rezé, Michel. "L'accueil fait à *La case de l'Oncle Tom* en Angleterre en 1852." *EA*, 24: 415-30 (1971).

Riach, D.C. "Blacks and Blackface on the Irish Stage, 1830-1860." *JAmSt*, 7: 231-41 (D 73).

Roberts, Helene. "Pre-Raphaelite Ideals in America: *The Knight Errant*." *DCLB*, 5: 4-8 (Ap 62).

Robertson, P.R. "Shelley and Hawthorne: A Comparison of Imagery and Sensibility." *SCB*, 32: 233-39 (1972).

Rodriguez Feo, José. "Shakespeare y América." *CdLA*, 4: 3-6 (Jl-Ag 64).

Rose, Shirley. "Waymarsh's 'Sombre Glow' and der Fliegende Hollander." *AL*, 45: 438-41 (N 73).

Rosentha., M.L. "Poetry of the Main Chance." *TLS*, nv: 113 (29 Ja 70).

Roselli, D.N. "Max Beerbohm's Unpublished Parody of Henry James." *RES*, 22: 61-3 (1971).

Ross, S.M. "Conrad's Influence on Faulkner's *Absalom, Absalom!*" *SAF*, 2: 199-210 (Au 74).

Roth, Martin. "Laurence Sterne in America." *BNYPL*, 74: 428-36 (S 70).

Rowe, William. "Gogolesque Perception—Expanding Reversals in Nabokov." *SlavR*, 30: 110-20 (1971).

Rowland, Thom. "Post-Romantic Epiphany as Apocalyptic Reversal: A Reconsideration of Hopkins and Eliot." *NasR*, 2: 62-82 (1972).

Ruggiero, C.C. "Henry James as a Critic: Some Early French Influences." *RLMC*, 26: 285-306 (1973).

Salomone, A.W. "The Nineteenth-Century Discovery of Italy." *AHR*, 73: 1359-91 (Jl 68).

Schilling, Hanna-Beate. "The Role of the Brothers Schlegel in American Literary Criticism as Found in Selected Periodicals, 1812-1833: A Critical Bibliography." *AL*, 43: 563-79 (Ja 72).

Schmidt-von Bardeleben, Renate. "Dreiser on the European Continent." *DrN*, 2: 4-10 (1971); 3: 1-8 (1972).

Schoolfield, G.C. "Elmer Kiktonius and Edgar Lee Masters." *AmNor*, 3: 307-27 (1971).

Schroder, Jorg. "Die amerikanische Literatur im Urteil Gor'kijs." *WZUB*, 19: 311-5 (1970).

Schroeter, James. "Hemingway via Joyce." *SoR*, 10: 95-114 (Ja 74).

Semmler, Clement. "Slessor and Eliot: Some Personal Musings." *Southerly*, 31: 267-71 (1971).

Sharma, M.L. "The 'Oriental Estate,' Especially the *Bhagavada-Gita* in American Literature." *Forum(H)*, 7: 4-11 (Fa-Wi 69).

Shearer, J.F. "French and Spanish Works Printed in Charleston." *PBSA*, 34: 137-70 (1940).

Shroeder, John. "Alice Doane's Story: An Essay on Hawthorne and Spenser." *NHJ*, 4: 129-34 (1974).

Speer, D.P. "Heinlein's *The Door into Summer* and *Roderick Random*." *Extrapolation*, 12: 30-4 (D 70).

Spender, Stephen. "America and England." *PR*, 40: 349-63 (#3 73).

———. "Americanization." *PR*, 39: 148-73 (#2 72).

Spiller, R.E. "Emerson and Humboldt." *AL*, 42: 546-8 (1971).

Stal, Sven. "Stadning i bokhyllorna." *Bokvannen*, 22: 99-105 (1967).

Stanford, D.E. "Edward Taylor and the 'Hermophrodite' Poems of John Cleveland." *EAL*, 8: 59-61 (Sp 73).

Foreign Influences and Estimates

Stanovnik, Janez. "American Studies in Yugoslvaia." *AmS*, 11: 22-7 (Sp 73).

———. "Potovanje Longfellowa skozi Slovenijo leta 1828." *SlE*, 18-19 (1965-66).

Stephens, R.O. "Hemingway and Stendhal: The Matrix of *A Farewell to Arms*." *PMLA*, 88: 271-80 (Mr 73).

Steinmann, Theo. "The Perverted Pattern of *Billy Budd* in *The Nigger of the 'Narcissus*.'" *ES*, 55: 239-46 (1974).

Stern, M.B. "The First German *Faust* Published in America." *AN&Q*, 10: 115-6 (Ap 72).

———. "Saint-Pierre in America: Joseph Nancrede and Isaiah Thomas." *PBSA*, 68: 312-24 (3Q 74).

Stimson, F.S. "Spanish Influence on Early American Poetry." *Americas*, 16: 161-70 (O 59).

Stoddard, Donald. "John Berryman, Mistress Bradstreet si Henry." *Steaua*, 24: 29 (1974).

Stone, Edward. "Hawthorne's Reputation Abroad." *NHJ*, 1: 201-3 (1971).

Stone, Harry. "Dickens' Use of His American Experience in Martin Chuzzlewit." *PMLA*, 72: 464-78 (1957).

Sulzer, Bernd. "Moglichkeiten linguistischer Interpretation im Unterricht: E.E.C's Poem No. 151.'" *NsM*, 26: 153-7 (1973).

Summerfield, Henry. "Thr Rural Exodus in America: Unpublished Notes by 'A.E.'" *CLQ*, 8: 13-9 (M 68).

Takayanagi, Shunici. "Virgil Theodor Heacker and T.S. Eliot." *ELLS*, 8: 37-63 (1971).

Teodoreanu, Liliana. "Ion Barbu and English and American Poetry." *RoR*, 26: 72-75 (1972).

Terfloth, J.H. "Versuche zur Aktualisierung des Theaters in Nordamerika." *MuK*, 17: 236-45 (1971).

Tharpe, Jac. "Hawthorne and Hindu Literature." *SoQ*, 10: 107-15 (Ja 72).

Thomas, Clara. "New England Romanticism and Canadian Fiction." *JCF*, 2: 80-6 (1973).

Thomas, William. "Charles Dickens on Ohio Roads." *Ohioana*, 2: 12-4 (Sp 59).

Thompson, E.M. "The Russian Formalists and the New Critics: Two Types of Close Reading of the Text." *SHR*, 4: 145-54 (Sp 70).

Thompson, L.S. "German Travellers in the South from the Colonial Period through 1865." *SAB*, 37: 64-74 (My 72).

Tickin, Harold. "Theatres Converging: U.S.A.—U.S.S.R.?" *Players*, 46: 106-9 (1971).

Tijeras, Eduardo. "William S. Burroughs, en espanol." *CHA*, 261: 639-45 (1972).

Tintner, A.R. "Balzac's *Two Maries* and James's *The Ambassadors*." *ELN*, 9: 284-7 (1972).

———. "The Influence of Balzac's *L'envers de l'histoire contemporaine* on James's 'The Great Good Place.'" *SSF*, 9: 343-51 (1972).

———. "'The Old Things': Balzac's *Le curé de Tours* and James's *The Spoils of Poynton*." *NCF*, 26: 436-55 (1972).

Tisiker, M.R. "Jacob Boehme's Influence on Some Poems in *Leaves of Grass*." *WWR*, 20: 15-26 (Mr 74).

Torrens, J.S.J. "Charles Maurras and Eliot's 'New Life.'" *PMLA*, 89: 312-22 (Mr 74).

Toth, S.A. "*Henderson the Rain King*: Eliot, and Browning." *NCLit*, 1: 6-8 (N 71).

Tripathi, Dwijendra. "American Studies in India." *AmS*, 11: 16-21 (Sp 73).

Trocme, H.C. "Aspects des villes americaines au milieu de XIXe siecle: Temoignages de quelques voyageurs francais." *RANAN*, 6: 170-92 (1973).

Truchlar, Leo. "Amerikanische-Erzähl-literatur der Gegenwart." *Sprachkunst*, 6: 123-32 (1975).

Tulip, James. "The Australian-American Connexion." *PoetA*, 32: 48-9 (1970).

Turjan, Narietta. "Turgenev i Edgar Po." *SSASH*, 19: 407-15 (1973).

Tytell, John. "The Jamesian Legacy in *The Good Soldier*." *StN*, 3: 365-73 (1971).

Viets, H.R. "The Printings in America of Polidori's *The Vampyre* in 1819." *PBSA*, 62: 434-5 (3Q 68).

Vinograde, A.C. "A Soviet Translation of *Slaughterhouse-Five*." *RLJ*, 93: 14-8 (1972).

Violi, U.J. "Shakespeare and the Americans Today." *LHY*, 8: 50-6 (Ja-Jl 67).

Walt, James. "Mencken and Conrad." *Conrad*, 2: 9-21 (1970).

*Wand, D.H. "Bibliography of Chinese Poets in America (Publications in English Exclusively)." *WLWE*, 19: 63-7 (1971).

Ward, W.S. "Charles Brockden Brown, His Contemporary British Reviewers, and Two Minor Bibliographical Problems." *PBSA*, 65: 399-402 (1971).

Warncke, Wayne. "George Orwell on T.S. Eliot." *WHR*, 25: 265-70 (1972).

Watson, Charles. "Melville's Selvage: Another Hint from Smollett." *MSEx*, 20: 4-5 (N 74).

Webb, Max. "Ford Madox Ford and the Baton Rouge Writers' Conference." *SoR*, 10: 892-903 (O 74).

Weisgerber, Jean. "Metamorphoses du realisme: Dostoevckij et Faulkner." *RusL*, 4: 37-50 (1973).

Weitzel, R.L. "Toward a 'Bright White Light': L's Use of Swinburne in *Martin Eden*." *JLN*, 7: 1-8 (Jd-Ap 74).

Wells, D.J. "Whitman and Rimbaud." *WWR*, 19: 25-8 (1973).

Wells, H.W. "The Poetic Image in Modern America and Ancient India." *LHY*, 10: 4-52 (Ja 69).

Welsh, David. "American Literature in Polish Translation." *PolR*, 16: 53-7 (Fa 71).

Welsh, J.R. "An Anglo-American Friendship: Allston and Coleridge." *JAmSt*, 5: 81-91 (Ap 71).

Werner, J.M. "David Hume and America." *JHI*, 33: 439-56 (Jl-S 72).

West, Michael. "John Evelyn, Sir Kenelm Digby, and Thoreau's Vital Spirits." *TSB*, 117: 8 (1971).

Wilhelm, J.J. "Guido Cavalcanti as a Mask for Ezra Pound." *PMLA*, 89: 332-40 (Mr 74).

Willey, E.P. "The *Looker-On* in America: Reception of a Latter-Day Spectator." *PBSA*, 64: 431-48 (4Q 70).

Wilson, M.K. "Mr. Clemons and Madame Blanc: Mark Twain's First French Critic." *AL*, 45: 537-56 (Ja 74).

Wilson, Rod. "Further Spenserian Parallels in Hawthorne." *NHJ*, 2: 195-201 (1972).

Winans, R.B. "Works by and about Samuel Johnson in Eighteenth-Century America." *PBSA*, 62: 537-46 (4Q 68).

Winship, G.P. "French Newspapers in the United States, 1790-1800." *PBSA* 14: 132-3 (1920).

Wirzberger, K.H. "Die Oktoberrevolution und die amerikanische Literatur." *ZAA*, 16: 229-56 (1968).

Woodward, R.H. "Punch on Howells and James." *ALR*, 3: 76-7 (1970).

Wynes, C.E. "The Race Question in the South as Viewed by British Travellers, 1865-1914." *LaStud*, 13: 223-40 (1974).

Yeager, H.J. "Melville's Literary Debut in France." *MQ*, 11: 413-25 (1970).

Yetman, M.G. "Emily Dickinson and the English Romantic Tradition." *TSLL*, 15: 129-47 (Sp 73).

Yglesias, Jose. "Letter from Prague." *Nation*, 204: 59-61 (9 Ja 67).

Yu, Kwang-chung. "American Influence on Post-War Chinese Poetry in Taiwan." *TkR*, 5: 1-9 (#1 74).

Zemljanova, L. "Zametki o sovremennoj poézij SŠA." *Zvezda*, 5: 199-205 (1971).

Frontier. Adams, E.B., and K.W. Algier. "A Frontier Book List—1800." *NMHQ*, 43: 49-59 (Ja 68).

Alderson, Nova. "Frontier Literature; or, A Fast Draw on Navajo Nick, Tombstone Tom and Arizona Charlie." *JAriH*, 2: 27-31 (Su 61).

Axtell, James. "The Scholastic Philosophy of the Wilderness." *WMQ*, 29: 335-66 (1972).

Barsness, J.A. "*A New Life*: The Frontier Myth in Perspective." *AL*, 42: 297-302 (Wi 69).

Bredeson, R.C. "Landscape Description in Nineteenth-Century Travel Literature." *AQ*, 20: 86-94 (1968).

Clements, W.M. "Savage, Pastoral, Civilized: An Ecology Typology of American Frontier Heroes." *JPC*, 8: 254-66 (Fa 74).

Davie, R.L. "Culture on the Frontier." *SWR*, 53: 383-402 (Au 68).

Dillingham, W.B. "Days of the Tall Tale." *SoR*, 4: 569-77 (Sp 68).

Etulain, R.W. "Frontier and Region in Western Literature." *SwAL*, 1: 121-28 (1972).

Halaas, D.F. "Frontier Journalism in Colorado." *ColM*, 44: 185-203 (Su 67).

James, S.B. "Western American Space and the Human Imagination." *WHR*, 24: 147-55 (Sp 70).

Karolides, N.J. "Changing Conceptions of the Pioneer in the Contemporary American Novel." *WSL*, 4: 18-28 (1967).

Kelly, J.P., and C.E. Timberlake. "Impressions of Russian Pioneers in the West." *NMHR*, 42: 145-50 (Ap 67).

Larsen, L.H., and R.L. Branyan. "The Development of an Urban Civilization on the Frontier of the American West." *Societas*, 1: 33-50 (Wi 71).

Leithead, J.E. "Buffalo Bill: Multi-Storied Scout and Plainsman." *ABC*, 20: 20-6 (Je 70).

———. "The Diamond Dicks: Frontier Lawmen." *ABC*, 20: 19-25 (S 69).

Lieber, T.M. "The Significance of the Frontier in the Writing of Antebellum Southern History." *MissQ*, 22: 337-54 (Fa 69).

Mattfield, Mary. "Journey to the Wilderness: Two Travelers in Florida, 1694-1778." *FHQ*, 45: 327-51 (1967).

Meyer, R.W. "The Outback and the West: Australian and American Frontier Fiction." *WAL*, 6: 3-19 (Sp 71).

Rashley, R.E. "Grey Owl and the Authentic Frontier." *Eng Q*, 4: 58-64 (Fa 71).

Roberts, G.L. "The West's Gunmen." *American West*, 8: 10-5, 18-23 (Ja, Mr 71).

Rosenberg, Bruce. "Custer and the Epic of Defeat." *JAF*, 88: 165-177 (Ap-Je 75).

Rosenberg, B.A. "How Custer's 'Last Stand' Got Its Name." *GaR*, 26: 279-96 (1972).

Steensma, R.C. "The Land of Desert Sweet: The Homesteader and His Literature." *Rendezvous*, 3: 29-38 (1968).

———. "'Stay Right There and Toughy It Out': The American Homesteader as Autobiographer." *WR*, 6: 10-8 (1969).

Thompson, W.F. "Frontier Tail Talk." *AS*, 9: 187-99 (O 34).

Walker, W.S. "Buckskin West: Leatherstocking at High Noon." *NYFQ*, 24: 88-102 (Je 68).

Humor. Anon. "American Humor: Hardly a Laughing Matter." *Time*, 87: 46-7 (4 Mr 66).

Alexander, Lloyd. "No Laughter in Heaven." *HornB*, 46: 11-9 (F 70).

Allen, Steve. "The Revolution in Humor." *Television Q*, 8: 7-17 (Wi 69).

Allsop, Kenneth. "Those American Sickniks." *TC*, 170: 97-106 (Jl 61).

Anderson, C.L. "Strindberg's Translations of American Humor." *AmNor*, 3: 153-94 (1972).

Anderson, Don. "Comic Modes in American Fiction." *SoRA*, 8: 152-65 (Je 75).

Anderson, J.Q. "Some Migratory Anecdotes in American Folk Humor." *MissQ*, 25: 447-57 (Fa 72).

Arner, R.D. "Daniel Coe to Thomas Shreeve: Primitivism in Satire." *SNL*, 10: 80-2 (1973).

———. "John Smith, the 'Starving Time,' and the Genesis of Southern Humor: Variation on a Theme." *LaStud*, 12: 383-90 (Sp 73).

Bakerville, Barnet. "19th Century Burlesque of Oratory." *AQ*, 20: 726-43 (Wi 68).

Ben-Amos, Dan. "The 'Myth' of Jewish Humor." *WF*, 32: 112-31 (Ap 73).

Bergholz, H.N.M.I. "Strindberg's Anthologies of American Humorists, Bibliographically Identified." *SS*, 43: 335-43 (Wi 71).

Bissell, C.T. "Haliburton, Leacock, and the American Humorous Tradition." *CanL*, 39: 5-19 (Wi 69).

Blair, Walter. "Inquisitive Yankee Descendants in Arkansas." *AS*, 14: 11-22 (F 39).

———. "Some Values of American Humor." *Am Humor*, 1: 1-8 (Fa 74).

Boatright, M.L. "The Tall Tale of Texas." *SAQ*, 30: 271-9 (Jl 31).

Boni, John. "Analogous Form: Black Comedy and Some Jacobean Plays." *WHR*, 28: 210-15 (1974).

Boskin, Joseph. "Good-by, Mr. Bones." *NYTMS*, 1 My 66, pp. 30-1, 84-92.

Bragdon, Claude. "The Purple Cow Period." *Bookman*, 69: 475-8 (Jl 29).

Breslaw, Elaine. "Wit, Whimsy, and Politics: The Uses of Satire by the Tuesday Club of Annapolis, 1744 to 1756." *WMQ*, 295-306 (Ap 75).

Brewer, J.M. "Humorous Folktales of the South Carolina Negro." *Pub South Carolina Fkl Guild*, 1: 1-64 (1945).

Brown, W.R. "Will Rogers: Ironist as Persuader." *SM*, 39: 183-92 (Ag 72).

Budd, L.J. "Mark Twain Talks Mostly About Humor and Humorists." *SAH*, 1: 4-22 (Ap 74).

Byrd, Scott. "A Separate War: Camp and Black Humor in Recent American Fiction." *LangQ*, 7: 7-10 (1968).

Cigman, Gloria. "Language and Laughter." *E&S*, 24: 101-22 (1971).

Clark, J.W. "The Fugitive Slave as Humorist." *SAH*, 1: 73-8 (O 74).

Clark, T.D. "Humor in the Stream of Southern History." *MissQ*, 13: 176-88 (Fa 60).

———. "Manners and Humors of the American Frontier." *MHR*, 35: 3-24 (O 40).

Clemens, Cyril. "Benjamin Shillaber and His Carpet Bag." *NEQ*, 14: 519-37 (S 41).

Cook, R.L. "Emerson and the American Joke." *ESQ*, 54: 22-7 (1969).

Cothran, K.L. "Women's Tall Tales: A Problem of the Social Structure of Fantasy." *StAR*, 2: 21-34 (Fa-Wi 72).

Cox, J.M. "Humor and America: The Southwestern Bear Hunt, Mrs. Stowe, and Mark Twain." *SR*, 83: 573-601 (Fa 75).

Cox, J.T. "Toward Vernacular Humor." *VQR*, 46: 311-30 (1970).

Curry, Jane. "Yes, Virginia, there were Female Humorists: Frances Whitcher and her Widow Bedott." *Un of Michigan Papers in Women Stud*, 1: 74-90 (#1 74).

Dale, Richard. "Fun, as in 'Funeral'; The Role of Humor in Aggression." *SD*, 71: 69-73 (Mr 72).

Dance, Darrell. "Contemporary Militant Black Humor." *NALF*, 8: 217-22 (Su 74).

Davis, C.E., and M.B. Hudson. "Humor of the Old Southwest: A Checklist of Criticism." *MissQ*, 27: 179-99 (Sp 74).

DeMott, Benjamin. "The New Irony: Sickniks and Others." *ASch*, 31: 108-19 (Wi 61-62).

DeVoto, Bernard. "Lineage of Eustace Tilley." *SRL*, 16: 3-4 (25 S 37).

Dillingham, W.B. "Days of the Tall Tale." *SoR*, 4: 569-77 (Sp 68).

Dodge, R.K. "Didactic Humor in the Almanacs of Early America." *JPC*, 5: 592-605 (1971).

Dresser, Norine. "The Metamorphosis of the Humor of the Black Man." *NYFQ*, 26: 216-28 (1970).

Humor

Eitner, W.H. "Will Rogers: Another Look at His Act." *KanQ*, 2: 46-52 (1970).

Ellison, G.R. "William Tappan Thompson and the *Southern Miscellany*, 1842-1844." *MissQ*, 23: 155-68 (Sp 70).

Fleming, R.E. "Humor in the Early Black Novel." *CLAJ*, 17: 250-62 (D 73).

Foley, G.P.H. "Dentistry and the Nineteenth-Century American Humorists." *Bul Hist Dentistry*, 16: 41-52 (Ja-Jl 68).

Foster, R.E. "Kentucky Humor: Salt River Roarer to Ol'Dog Tray." *MissQ*, 20: 224-30 (Fa 67).

Gill, J.J. "Humor in John Bartram's Journals." *AN&Q*, 12: 90-3 (F 74).

Goldman, Albert. "Boy-Man Schlemiel: Jewish Humor." *Cweal*, 86: 605-8 (29 S 67).

Gray, R.J. "Southwestern Humor, Erskine Caldwell, and the Comedy of Frustration." *SLJ*, 8: 3-26 (Fa 75).

Greenberg, Andrea. "Form and Function of the Ethnic Joke." *KJQ*, 17: 144-61 (1972).

Grimes, G.A. "'Brandy and Water': American Folk Types in the Works of Artemus Ward." *NYFQ*, 25: 163-74 (1969).

*Hagerman, Richard. "Criticism on American Humor: An Annotated Checklist." *AmH*, 2: 14-31 (#1 75).

Hansen, A.J. "Entropy and Transformation: Two Types of American Humor." *ASch*, 43: 405-21 (Su 74).

Hasley, Louis. "Black Humor and Gray." *ArQ*, 30: 317-28 (Wi 74).

Havard, W.C. "Southwest Humor: Contemporary Style." *SoR*, 6: 1185-90 (Au 70).

Heyen, William. "A Brief Discussion of an Admirable Miscellany by Worthington Dome." *SNL*, 6: 50-4 (1968).

Hill, Hamlin. "Black Humor: Its Cause and Cure." *ColQ*, 17: 57-64 (1968).

Hines, D.M. "Humor of the City Hick and the Country Jake on the Inland Pacific Northwest Frontier." *WR*, 13: 15-20 (Sp 71).

Inge, M.T. "Literary Humor of the Old Southwest: A Brief Overview." *LaStud*, 7: 132-43 (Su 68).

Jackson, E.M. "The American Negro and the Image of the Absurd." *Phylon*, 23: 359-71 (Wi 62).

Janoff, Bruce. "Black Humor, Absurdity, and Technique." *STC*, 13: 39-50 (Sp 74).

———. "Black Humor: Beyond Satire." *OhR*, 14: 5-20 (1972).

Janoff, Bruce. "Black Humor, Existentialism, and Absurdity: A Generic Confusion." *ArQ*, 30: 293-304 (Wi 74).

Jason, Heda. "The Jewish Joke: The Problem of Definition." *SFQ*, 31: 48-54 (Mr 67).

Jones, H.L. "Black Humor and the American Way of Life." *SNL*, 7: 1-4 (Fa 69).

Kay, Donald. "H's Use of Laughter in Selected Short Stories." *XUS*, 10: 27-32 (Fa 71).

Klinkowitz, Jerome. "A Final Word for Black Humor." *ConL*, 15: 271-6 (Sp 74).

Landau, E.D. "Quibble, Quibble: Funny? Yes; Humorous, No!" *HornB*, 38: 154-64 (Ap 62).

Lawson, Sarah. "Where Was Moses When the Lights Went Out?" *JAF*, 85: 183-89 (Ap 72).

LeClair, Thomas. "Death and Black Humor." *Critique*, 17: 5-40 (1Q 75).

Leverence, W.J. "*Cat's Cradle* and Traditional American Humor." *JPC*, 5: 955-63 (1972).

Levine, Edward. "The Inflated Image: Satire and Meaning in Pop Art." *SNL*, 6: 43-50 (1968).

Linneman, W.R. "Immigrant Stereotypes: 1880-1900." *SAH*, 1: 28-39 (Ap 74).

Loomis, C.G. "The American Tall Tale and the Miraculous." *California Fkl Q*, 4: 109-28 (1945).

McCann, W.C. "Midwestern Humorous Journalism." *Soc for Study of Midwestern Lit*, 1: 28-34 (1974).

McCullough, J.B. "Mark Twain and Journalistic Humor Today." *EJ*, 60: 591-5 (My 71).

Maclachlan, J.M. "Southern Humor as a Vehicle of Social Evaluation." *MissQ*, 13: 157-62 (Fa 60).

MacMinn, G.R. "'The Gentleman from Pike' in Early California Literature." *AL*, 8: 160-9 (My 36).

Markfield, Wallace. "Yiddishization of American Humor." *Esquire*, 64: 114-5, 136 (O 65).

Masterson, J.R. "Travellers' Tales of Colonial Natural History." *JAF*, 59: 51-67, 174-88 (1946).

Meeker, J.W. "The Comedy of Survival." *NAR*, 9: 11-17 (Su 72).

Mengeling, M.E. "The Crass Humor of Irving's Diedrich Knickerbocker." *SAH*, 1: 66-72 (O 74).

Mills, Nicolaus. "Ken Kesey and the Politics of Laughter." *CentR*, 16: 82-90 (1972).

Mira, Eduardo. "El 'Comic Underground' y la contracultura: Apuntes sobre una nueva forma expresiva." *CdF*, 16: 25-40 (D 71).

Nagle, James. "*Catch-22* and Angry Humor: A Study of the Normative Values of Satire." *SAH*, 1: 99-106 (1974).

Numasawa, Kōji. "Black Humor: An American Aspect." *SELit*, 44: 177-93 (1968).

———. "Rokuju-nendai Eibungaku to Black Humour." *EigoS*, 116: 823-4 (1971).

Parks, E.W. "The Intent of the Ante-Bellum Southern Humorists." *MissQ*, 13: 163-8 (Fa 60).

Penrod, J.H. "The Folk Mind in Early Southwestern Humor." *TFSB*, 18: 49-54 (1952).

Phelps, Donald. "Rogues' Gallery/Freak Show." *Prose*, 4: 133-49 (1972).

Pinsker, Sanford. "The Greying of Black Humor." *STC*, 9: 15-33 (Sp 72).

Presley, Delma E. "The Moral Function of Distortion in Southern Grotesque." *SAB*, 37: 37-46 (My 72).

Pritchett, V.S. "The Con-Man's Shadow." *NSt*, 24 N 67, pp. 719-20.

Raeithel, Gert. "Amerikanischer Humor—eine soziale Funktion." *Merkur*, 24: 644-59 (Jl 70).

Rather, Lois. "Were Women Funny? Some 19th Century Humorists." *ABC*, 21: 5-10 (1971).

Reed, P.I. "The Realistic Presentation of Satire, 1790-1820." *Ohio State Un Bul*, 22: np (My 18).

Rexroth, Kenneth. "Humor in a Tough Age." *Nation*, 188: 211-3 (7 Mr 59).

Roth, G.L. "New England Satire on Religion, 1790-1820." *NEQ*, 28: 245-54 (Je 55).

Rovit, Earl. "Jewish Humor and American Life." *ASch*, 36: 237-45 (Sp 67).

Rowan, Dan. "What Revolution in Comedy?" *Television Q*, 8: 18-22 (Wi 69).

Rubin, L.D. "'The Barber Kept on Shaving': The Two Perspectives of American Humor." *SR*, 81: 693-713 (Fa 73).

———. "The Great American Joke." *SAQ*, 72: 82-92 (Wi 73).

Russell, Robert. "Gawd, Those Jokes Were Painful." *Esquire*, 70: 164-9 (D 68).

Schulz, M.F. "Pop, Op, and Black Humor: The Aesthetics of Anxiety." *CE*, 30: 230-41 (D 68).

———. "Toward a Definition of Black Humor." *SoR*, 9: 117-34 (Wi 73).

Sederberg, N.B. "Antebellum Southern Humor in the *Camden Journal*: 1826-1840." *MissQ*, 27: 41-74 (Wi 73-74).

Shuts, Donald. "Jewish Humor: The Corridor of Laughter." *KAL*, 16: 37-9 (1975).

Skiff, Margaret. "All Honor to the Gift of Laughter." *LJ*, 91: 4092-93 (15 D 72).

Smith, C.P. "Plain Humor: New England Style." *NEQ*, 43: 465-72 (S 70).

Sontag, Susan. "Notes on Camp." *PR*, 31: 515-30 (Fa 64).

Stokes, D.R. "Five Letters from Jesse Holmes, the Fool Killer, to the Editors of the *Milton Chronicle*." *NCHR*, 50: 304-21 (Su 73).

Stowe, W.E., and David Grimsted. "White-Black Humor." *JEthS*, 3: 78-96 (#2 75).

Thurber, James. "Reply to Ohioana Award." *LJ*, 79: 272-5 (15 F 54).

————. "The Saving Grace." *Atl*, 204: 61-4 (N 59).

Trachtenberg, Stanley. "Counterhumor: Comedy in Contemporary American Fiction." *GaR*, 27: 33-48 (Sp 73).

Updike, John. "Humor in Fiction." *American Pen*, 2: 18-33 (Fa 70).

————. "On the Sidewalk." *NY*, 35: 32 (21 Ja 59).

Wages, Jack D. "Mock Wills: Parody in the Colonial South." *SNL*, 9: 192-4 (Sp 72).

Wardenaar, Leslie. "Humor in the Colonial Promotional Tract: Topics and Techniques." *EAL*, 9: 286-300 (Wi 75).

Weber, Brom. "American Humor and American Culture." *AQ*, 14: 503-7 (Fa 62).

Weinstein, Sharon. "Don't Women Have a Sense of Comedy They Can Call Their Own?" *Am Humor*, 1: 8-12 (Fa 74).

Welsch, R.L. "American Numskull Tales: The Polack Joke." *WF*, 26: 183-6 (Jl 67).

West, J.L.W. "Early Backwoods Humor in the Greenville *Mountaineer*, 1826-1840." *MissQ*, 25: 69-82 (Wi 71-72).

Wheeler, O.B. "Some Uses of Folk Humor by Faulkner." *MissQ*, 17: 107-22 (Sp 64).

Whiting, B.J. "Guyascutus, Royal Nonesuch and Other Hoaxes." *SFQ*, 8: 251-75 (D 44).

Language and Style. Adams, W.P. "Republicanism in Political Rhetoric before 1776." *Pol Sci Q*, 85: 397-421 (S 70).

Albanese, Catherine. "The Kinetic Revolution: Transformation in the Language of the Transcendentalists." *NEQ*, 48: 319-40 (S 75).

Andrews, J.R. "Reflections of the National Character in American Rhetoric." *QJS*, 57: 316-24 (O 71).

Appuhn, Hans-Günter. "Das Apollo-Mondprogram in sprachlicher Sicht." *NS*, 19: 209-22 (My 70).

Aubert, Alvin. "Black American Poetry: Its Language and Folk Tradition." *BlaR*, 2: 71-80 (Sp-Su 71).

Avis, W.S. "Crocus Bag: A Problem in a Real Linguistics." *AS*, 30: 5-16 (1955).

Baar, Ron. "A Lexicon for Literature in the Age of Language Revolution." *Boun2*, 3: 359-71 (Wi 75).

Baker, William. "Literary Criticism and Linguistics." *Style*, 2: 1-5 (Wi 68).

Baraka, I.A. "The Black Aesthetic." *NegroD*, 19: 5-6 (Sp 69).

Barnes, D.R. "An Early American Collection of Rogue's Cant." *JAF*, 79: 600-7 (1960).

Baskerville, Barnet. "19th Century Burlesque of Poetry." *AQ*, 20: 726-43 (1968).

Bateson, F.W. "Anglo-American: The Words and the Thing." *JGE*, 24: 171-5 (1972).

Bauman, Richard. "Aspects of 17th Century Quaker Rhetoric." *QJS*, 56: 67-74 (1970).

Bennett, John. "Gullah: A Negro Patois." *SAQ*, 7: 332-47; 8: 39-52 (1908).

————. "Note on Gullah." *SCHM*, 50: 56-7 (1949).

*Bennett, J.R., and Linda Stafstrom. "English and American Prose Style: A Bibliography of Criticism for 1968-1969." *Style*, annually since 1967.

Bercovitch, Sacvan. "Colonial Puritan Rhetoric and the Discovery of American Identity." *CRAS*, 6: 131-50 (1975).

————. "Puritan New England Rhetoric and the Jewish Problem." *EAL*, 5: 63-73 (Sp 70).

Berger, M.D. "Accent Pattern, and Dialect in North American English." *Word*, 24: 55-61 (1968).

Bergman, Herbert. "American Thought and Language Relevant, Significant." *MichSN*, 62: 4 (1 Je 70).

Bier, Jesse. "Weberism, Franklin, and the Transcendental Style." *NEQ*, 43: 179-92 (Je 70).

Bodenheim, Maxwell. "Style and American Literature." *Little R*, 4: 22-4 (O 17).

Bosmajian, H.A. "The Language of White Racism." *CE*, 263-72 (D 69).

Bowman, E.G. "The Rhetorical Theory of William Henry Milburn." *SM*, 36: 28-37 (Mr 69).

Boyle, T.E. "The Tenor of the Organic Metaphor: A View of American Romanticism." *Disc*, 11: 240-51 (Sp 68).

Britwum, Atta. "Black Survival and Culture: Rambling Thoughts on Black Aesthetics." *Asemka*, 1: 99-110 (1974).

Brown, Cecil. "The Philosophy of Jive." *EvR*, 17: 155-84 (Sp 73).

Buell, Laurence. "Transcendentalist Catalogue Rhetoric: Vision versus Form." *AL*, 40: 325-39 (N 68).

Bujas, Zeljko. "A *Time* Magazine Vocabulary Study." *SRAZ*, 33-36: 579-94 (1972-73).

Burton, D.M. "Intonation Patterns of Sermons in Seven Novels." *Lang&S*, 3: 205-20.

Bush, Douglas. "Polluting Our Language." *ASch*, 41: 238-47 (Sp 72).

Butterfield, S.T. "The Use of Language in Slave Narratives." *NALF*, 6: 72-8 (1972).

Cagnon, Maurice. "New England Franco-American Terms Used in Spoken English." *RomN*, 11: 219-25 (Au 69).

Cannon, C.D. "Noah Webster's Influence on American English." *UMSE*, 13: 7-17 (1972).

Cannon, Garland. "Bilingual Problems and Developments in the United States." *PMLA*, 86: 452-8 (My 71).

Cardwell, G.A. "The Plantation House: An Analogical Image." *SLJ*, 2: 3-21 (Fa 69).

Carreter, F.L. "La Linqüística norteamericana y los estudios literarios en ultima década." *RO*, 7: 319-47 (D 69).

Chapman, Abraham. "The Black Aesthetic and the African Continuum." *Pan-African J*, 4: 397-406 (1971).

Clark, Dennis. "Muted Heritage: Gaelic in an American City." *Eire*, 6: 3-7 (Sp 71).

Coard, R.L. "The Educated Ain't and Webster's Third." *Disc*, 10: 265-72 (Su 67).

Cohen, Hennig. "Unnoticed Americanisms from *Russell's Magazine*." *AS*, 29: 226-7 (1954).

Conrad, Earl. "The Philology of Negro Dialect." *JNE*, 13: 150-4 (1944).

Conroy, S.S. "Thorstein Veblen's Prose." *AQ*, 20: 605-15 (Fa 68).

Crew, Louie. "Linguistic Politics and the Black Community." *Phylon*, 36: 177-81 (Je 75).

Crowell, M.G. "John Russell Bartlett's *Dictionary of Americanisms*." *AQ*, 24: 228-42 (1972).

Daiches, David. "Roman Usage." *NSt*, nv, 48 (9 Jl 71).

Davidson, Michael. "Languages of Post-Modernism." *ChiR*, 27: 11-22 (Su 75).

Davis, Ossie. "The English Language Is My Enemy." *NHB*, 30: 18 (Ap 67).

Dickstein, Morris. "The Black Aesthetic in White America." *PR*, 38: 376-95 (Wi 71-72).

Durbin, M, and M. Saltarelli. "A Semantic Interpretation of Kinship Systems." *Linguistics*, 33: 87-93 (Jl 67).

Eichoff, Jurgen. "Deutsches Lehngut und seine Funktion in der amerikanischen Pressesprache." *JA*, 17: 156-215 (1972).

Farrison, W.E. "Dialectology versus Negro Dialect." *CLAJ*, 13: 21-6 (S 69).

Ferris, D.H. "The Integrity of the English Language." *MLJ*, 42: 78-81 (F 58).

Fogel, Stanley. "'And All the Little Typtopies': Notes on Language Theory in the Contemporary Experimental Novel." *MFS*, 20: 328-36 (Au 74).

Language and Style

Fritzell, P.A. "The Wilderness and the Garden: Metaphors of the American Landscape." *ForH*, 12: 16-22 (Ap 68).

Fullinwider, S.P. "Mencken's American Language." *Mencken*, 40: 2-7 (Wi 71).

Galinsky, Hans. "E Pluribus Unum? Die Antwort der Sprache." *JA*, 17: 9-55 (1972).

Gaskins, A.F. "The Epithet 'Guinea' in Central West Virginia." *WVUPP*, 17: 41-4 (Je 70).

Gass, W.H. "Groping for Trouts: On Metaphor." *Salmagundi*, 24: 19-33 (1973).

Gayle, Addison. "Cultural Strangulation: Black Literature and the White Aesthetic." *NegroD*, 18: 32-9 (Jl 69).

———. "Debate: The Black Aesthetic (Defender)." *BlackW*, 24: 31-40 (D 74).

———. "The Harlem Renaissance: Toward a Black Aesthetic." *MASJ*, 11: 78-87 (Fa 70).

———. "Reclaiming the Southern Experience: The Black Aesthetic 10 Years Later." *BlackW*, 23: 20-9 (Su 74).

Gester, F.W. "'Negro,' 'Afro-American' oder 'Black'? Zu einer aktuellen sprachlichen Auseinandersetzung in den Vereinigten Staaten." *NS*, 20: 53-63 (F 71).

Glaser, Rosemarie. "Sprache und Pragmatik der englisch-amerikanischen Werbung." *ZAA*, 18: 314-23 (1970).

———. "Zur Soziolinquistik und Sprachsoziologie on den U.S.A." *ZAA*, 19: 341-63 (1971).

Granger, Bruce. "From Silence Dogood to Lancelot Langstaff." *EAL*, 3: 11-6 (1968).

Green, Martin. "Style in American Literature." *CamR*, 89: 385-7 (3 Je 67).

Gross, Harvey. "The Problem of Style and the Poetry of the Sixties." *IowaR*, 5: 69-74 (Wl 74).

Guerard, Albert. "Notes on the Rhetoric of Anti-Realist Fiction." *TriQ*, 30: 3-50 (Sp 74).

Hadding-Koch, K., and M. Studdert-Kennedy. "An Experimental Study of Some Intonation Contours." *Phonetica*, 11: 175-85 (1964).

Haines, George. "Forms of Imaginative Prose, 1900-1940." *SoR*, 7: 755-75 (1942).

Hall, B.L. and R.M.R. "Black English and TESL: A Programmatic Statement." *JESL*, 4: 1-6 (Sp 69).

Hall, R.A. "Some Recent Developments in American Linguistics." *NM*, 70: 192-227 (1969).

Harder, K.B. "Hay-Making Terms in Perry County." *TFSB*, 33: 41-8 (Je 67).

Hopkins, M.F. "Linguistic Analysis as a Tool for Oral Interpretation." *SpT*, 18: 200-3 (1969).

Howren, Robert. "Iowa Materials for the *Linguistic Atlas of the Upper Midwest*." *BI*, 6: 29-35 (Ap 67).

Ives, Sumner. "A Theory of Literary Dialect." *TSE*, 2: 137-82 (1950).

Jones, G.F. "Colonial Georgia's Second Language." *GaR*, 21: 87-99 (Sp 67).

Jones, K.C. "The Language of the Black 'In-Crowd.'" *CLAJ*, 15: 80-9 (S 71).

Junker, Howard. "As They Used to Say in the 1950's." *Esquire*, 72: 70-1, 141 (Ag 69).

Kaiser, L.M. "On·the Latin in the Meserole Anthology." *EAL*, 6: 165-6 (Fa 71).

Kampf, Louis. "'It's Alright, Ma (I'm Only Bleeding)': Literature and Language in the Academy." *PMLA*, 87: 377-83 (My 72).

Kaplan, R.B. "On a Note of Protest (In a Minor Key): Bidialectism vs. Bidialectism." *CE*, 30: 386-9 (F 69).

Kgositsile, Keorapetse. "Language, Vision and the Black Writer." *BlackW*, 21: 25-7 (Sp 72).

Kilson, Martin. "Debate: The Black Aesthetic (Opponent)." *BlackW*, 24: 40-8 (D 74).

Kligerman, Jack. "'Dress' or 'Incarnation' of Thought: Nineteenth-Century American Attitudes towards Language and Style." *PAPS*, 117: 51-8 (1973).

Kluewer, J.D. "An Annotated Check List of Writings on Linguistics and Literature in the Sixties." *BNYPL*, 76: 36-91 (1972).

Koerner, E.F.K. "Bloomfieldian Linguistics and the Problem of 'Meaning.'" *JA*, 15: 162-83 (1970).

Korg, Joseph. "Language Change and Experimental Magazines, 1910-1930." *ConL*, 13 144-61 (Sp 72).

Kronenberger, Louis. "American Lingo." *Atl*, 226: 108-12 (S 70).

Kruger, J.R. "On the Rimes in Nursery Rimes." *SFQ*, 31: 291-5 (D 67).

Lawler, Justus. "Politics and the American Language." *CE*, 35: 750-5 (Ap 74).

Lehman, W.P. "Generative Linguistics and Literary Criticism." *TQ*, 17: 89-104 (Au 74).

Lester, Mark. "The Relation of Linguistics to Literature." *CE*, 30: 356-75 (F 69).

Lindberg, John. "'Black Aesthetic': Minority or Mainstream?" *NAR*, 260: 48-52 (Wi 75).

Loflin, M.D. "On the Passive in Nonstandard Negro English." *JESL*, 4: 19-23 (Sp 69).

Lohof, B.A. "Through a Shutter Brightly: Notes on the New Composition." *CentR*, 16: 180-91 (Sp 72).

Londen, Anne-Marie. "Individen i samhället: Modern amerikansk prosa." *NyA*, 61: 292-7 (1968).

McDavid, R.I. "Dialect Dictionary and Social Science Problems." *Social Forces*, 25: 168-72 (1946).

———. "Oughtn't and Hadn't Ought." *CE*, 472-3 (1953).

———. "The Relationship of the Speech of American Negroes to the Speech of Whites." *AS*, 26: 3-17 (1951).

———. "The Urbanization of American English." *JA*, 16: 47-59 (19710.

Martin, J.S. "Rhetoric, Society and Literature in the Age of Jefferson." *MASJ*, 9: 77-90 (Sp 68).

Mieder, Wolfgang. "The Proverb and Anglo American Literature." *SFQ*, 38: 49-62 (Mr 74).

Miller, J.E. "The Linguistic Imagination." *CE*, 31: 725-32 (Ap 70).

Minter, D.L. "By Dens of Lions: Notes on Stylization in Early Captivity Narratives." *AL*, 45: 335-47 (N 73).

Morse, J.M. "The Shuffling Speech of Slavery: Black English." *CE*, 34: 834-9 (Mr 73).

Nichols, C.II. "Theodore Parker and the Transcendental Rhetoric." *JA*, 69-83 (1968).

Ogbang, P.M. "Reflections on 'Language, Vision and the Black Writer.'" *BlackW*, 22:

Palermo, Joseph. "L'Etymologie Mythique du Nom du Vermont." *RomN*, 13: 188-9 (Au 71).

Parrish, W.M. "'Getting the Meaning' in Interpretation." *SoSpJ*, 33: 178-86 (Sp 68).

Patrick, W.R. "Poetic Style in the Contemporary Short Story." *CCC*, 18: 77-84 (My 67).

Pearce, R.H., with Sigurd Burckhardt. "Poetry, Language, and the Condition of Modern Man." *CentR*, 4: 1-31 (1960).

Pei, Mario. "The American Language of the Early '70's." *ModA*, 15: 409-14 (Fa 71).

Pilati, L.L. "The Fox Dialect." *NM*, 70: 145-58 (1969).

Pyles, Thomas. "English Usage: The Views of the Literati." *CE*, 28: 443-54 (Mr 67).

Read, A.W. "The Speech of Negroes in Colonial America." *JNH*, 24: 247-58 (1939).

Reichmann, Felix. "Francis Lieber, Pennsylvania Dialect." *AGR*, 11: 24-7 (1945).

Rein, I.J. "The New England Transcendentalists: Philosophy and Rhetoric." *P&R*, 1: 103-17 (Wi 68).

Robins, R.H. "Grammar, Meaning, and the Study of Language." *CJL*, 9: 99-114 (Sp 64).

Robinson, F.C. "The American Element in *Beowulf*." *ES*, 49: 508-16 (D 68).

Rosenberg, B.A. "The Formulaic Quality of Spontaneous Sermons." *JAF*, 83: 2-20 (1970).

Language and Style

Rowland, Beryl. "Forgotten Metaphor in Three Popular Children's Rhymes." *SFQ*, 31: 12-9 (Mr 67).

Royot, Daniel. "Elements phonologiques du dialecte noir dans *Huckleberry Finn*." *LanM*, 66: 79-83 (1972).

Rubin, L.D. "Black Poets in Search of a Language." *Bkmark*, 40: 3-15 (S 70); *Southeastern Libr*, 201: 213-21 (Wi 70).

Russell, W.M. "Poetics and Literary Language." *CE*, 31: 300-8 (D 69).

Saha, P.K. "A Linguistic Approach to Style." *Style*, 2: 7-31 (Wi 68).

Scholwin, Wolf-Rudiger. "Propagandatheoretische un linguistische Aspekte der imperialistischen Meiunsbeeinflussing in den USA." *ZAA*, 20: 59-69 (1972).

Sears, D.A., Margaret Bourland. "Journalism Makes the Style." *JQ*, 47: 504-9 (Fa 70).

Shores, D.L. "Black English and Black Attitudes." *SAB*, 39: 104-12 (4Q 74).

Smith, B.H. "The New Imagism." *Midway*, 9: 27-44 (1969).

Smitherman, Geneva. "Black Idiom." *NALF*, 5: 88-91, 115-7 (1971).

———. "The Power of the Rap: The Black Idiom and the New Black Poetry." *TCL*, 19: 259-74 (O 73).

Spillers, H.J. "Martin Luther King and the Style of the Black Sermon." *BSch*, 3: 14-27 (S 71).

Spitzhardt, Harry. "Overstatement and Understatement in British and American English." *PP*, 6: 277-86 (1963).

Stafford, Jean. "The Plight of American Language." *SR/World*, 1: 14-8 (4 D 73).

Steiner, George. "Whorf, Chomsky, and the Student of Literature." *NLH*, 4: 15-34 (1972).

Stoehr, Taylor. "Tone and Voice." *CE*, 30: 150-61 (N 68).

Subbarao, C. "Contexualist Poetics and the Nature of Language." *LCrit*, 9: 54-60 (Wi 69).

Thompson, J.S. "The Case against Noam Chomsky and B.F. Skinner." *L&I*, 11: 49-60 (1972).

Turner, D.T. "W.E.B. DuBois and the Theory of a Black Aesthetic." *SLitI*, 7: 1-22 (Fa 74).

Tuyn, Harry. "Semantic and Unconscious Influences in Tense Usage." *SN*, 41: 397-403 (1969).

VanDerBeets, Richard. "A Surfeit of Style: The Indian Captivity Narrative as a Penny Dreadful." *RSW*, 39: 297-306 (1971).

Wade, Melvin and Margaret. "The Black Aesthetic in the Black Novel." *JBlackS*, 2: 391-408 (Je 72).

Wagner, Geoggrey. "Why Semantics and Why Not." *ETC*, 24: 93-8 (Mr 67).

Walcott Ronald. "Some Notes on the Blues, Style & Space." *BlackW*, 22: 4-29 (Sp 72).

Weed, G.R. "Changing Descriptions of a Dialect of American English." *TFSB*, 27: 93-6 (D 71).

Whitaker, T.R. "On Speaking Humanly." *UTMS*, 10: 67-88 (1970).

Williamson, J.V. "Selected Features of Speech: Black and White." *CLAJ*, 13: 420-33 (Je 70).

Wilson, J.B. "The Aesthetics of Romanticism." *ESQ*, 57: 27-34 (4Q 69).

Zanger, Jules. "'Guinea': Dialect and Stereotype." *CLAJ*, 18: 553-62 (Je 75).

Zochert, Donald. "'A View of the Sublime Awful': The Language of a Pioneer." *WAL*, 6: 251-7 (Wi 72).

Libraries and Literary Collections. Anon. "Check-List of the Paul Hamilton Hayne Library." *Duke Un Lib Bul*, 2: 1-109 (1930).

———. "From the James Family Libraries." *Bancroftiana*, 52: 1-2 (1972).

Bales, Kent. "Looking for American Literary Manuscripts in Minnesota Libraries." *Un Minnesota Bul*, 4: 22-5 (Ap 73).

Biel, Nicholas. "Some Civil War Narratives in the Baker Stacks." *DCLB*, 1: 10-6 (O 57).

Blanck, Jacob. "The Juvenile Reading of Certain Nineteenth-Century American Writers." MHSP, 79: 64-73 (1967).

Broderick, J.C. "Locating Major Resource Collections for Research in American Civilization." *AmS*, 10: 3-10 (Sp 72).

———. "Recent Acquisitions of the Manuscript Division." *QJLC*, 26: 234-55 (O 69); 332-75 (Ap 70).

Bruccoli, Matthew. "British Resources for the Study of American Literature." *JAMSt*, 6: 354-56 (1972).

Bryan, M.R. "The Scheide Library." *BC*, 21: 489-502 (D 72).

Burlingham, Dwight. "Two Minnesota College Reports on Sinclair Lewis Collections." *SLN*, 4: 17-8 (1972).

Buxton, F.H. "Jack London Collection and Research Center: Oakland Public Library." *JLN*, 5: 37-40 (1972).

Cameron, K.W. "An Early Lending Library in Hawthorne's Salem." *ATQ*, 20: 37-50 (Fa 73).

Cary, Richard. "American Literary Manuscripts in the Colby College Library: A Checklist." *RALS*, 5: 217-40 (Au 75).

Cazfen, R.E. "The Provision of German Books in America During the Eighteenth Century, *Libri* (Copenhagen), 23: 81-108 (1973).

Cook, M.E., and T.D. Young. "Fugitive/Agrarian Materials at Vanderbilt University." *RALS*, 1: 113-20 (Sp 71).

Davis, R.B. "The Library of Alexander S. Salley." *SAB*, 7: 3-4 (Ap 42).

De Morinni, C.M. "Libraries: Americans in Paris." *NRep*, 161: 30-2 (20 S 69).

Edgar, W.B. "Notable Libraries of Early South Carolina." *SCHM*, 72: 105-10 (Ap 71).

———. "Some Popular Books in Colonial South Carolina." *SCHM*, 72: 174-8 (Jl 71).

Fiering, N.S. "Solomon Stoddard's Library at Harvard in 1664." *HLB*, 20: 255-69 (1972).

Friedman, William. "The First Librarian in America." *LJ*, 56: 902-3 (1931).

Goodborne, John. "A Virginia Minister's Library." *AHR*, 11: 328-32 (1906).

Green, E.L. "The Library of the University of South Carolina." *Un South Carolina Bul*, 7: 1-22 (1906).

Gregorie, A.K. "The First Decade of the Charleston Library Society." *South Carolina Hist Assn Proc*, 16: 3-10 (1935).

Halperin, Irving. "Books and Bodies at San Francisco State." *MR*, 11: 367-72 (1970).

Harris, M.H. "American Librarians as Authors: A Bibliography of Bibliographies." *BB*, 30: 143-6 (O-D 73).

Kelly, C.B. "The Mighty Manuscripts of Mr. C. Waller Barrett." *Cwealth*, 38: 21-5, 28 (Ag 71).

Ketcham, Joyce. "The Bibliomania of the Reverend William Bentley, D.D." *EIHC*, 108: 275-303 (1972).

Lee, J.T. "A Great Collection of Americana." *Nation*, 100: 530-4 (13 My 15).

McCorison, "Donald McKay Frost—A Collector of Western Americana." *WHQ*, 3: 67-76 (Ja 72).

MacLeish, Archibald. "Changes in the Ritual of Library Dedication." *LJ*, 93: 3517-20 (1 O 68).

McPharlin, Paul. "Bostick and Thornley, Librarians and Publishers." *PW*, 150: 3206-9 (1946).

Moldehauer, J.J. "Poe Manuscripts at Austin." *LCUT*, 3: 82-7 (1971).

Myers, Andrew. "Washington Irving and the Astor Library." *BNYPL*, 72: 378-99 (Je 68).

Newman, John. "The Bollinger Lincoln Collection at the University of Iowa." *RALS*, 2: 98-101 (1972).

Newton, R.H. "Bulfinch's Design for the Library of Congress." *Art Bul*, 23: 221-2 (1941).

Paluka, Frank. "American Literary Manuscripts in the University of Iowa Libraries: A Checklist." *RALS*, 3: 100-200 (Sp 73).

Payne, J.R. "The Thomas Winthrop Streeter Collection of Americana." *ABC*, 18: 27-8, 19: 10-6 (My, S 68).

Riffey, M.S. "The Wallace Stevens Collection at the University of Miami." *Carrell*, 13: 16-8 (1972).

Quinn, D.S. "A List of Books Purhcased for the Virginia Company." *VMHB*, 77: 347-60 (Jl 69).

Roberts, Warren. "Modern Library Materials at the University of Texas." *JML*, 2: 329-41 (#3 71-72).

Shaffer, Ellen. "The Rare Book Department, Free Library of Philadelphia." *PBSA*, 64: 1-12 (1Q 70).

Stoddard, Richard. "The Barrett H. Clark Collection." *YULG*, 45: 93-103 (Ja 71).

Story, Ronald. "Class and Culture in Boston: The Athenaeum, 1807-1860." *AQ*, 27: 169-99 (My 75).

Waggoner, H.H. "The Last Stand of the Genteel Tradition: or, How Brown Acquired the Saunders Whitman Collection." *BBr*, 24: 148-55 (1971);

Wagner, P.R. "Books from the Library of George Washington Now in the Princeton University Library." *PULC*, 32: 111-5 (1971).

Wallace, Irving. "A Problem Author Looks at Problem Libraries." *LJ*, 87: 2293-5 (15 Je 62).

Watson, G.R. "The Books They Left: Some 'Liberies' in Edgecomb County, 1733-1783." *NCHR*, 48: 245-57 (Su 71).

Wilson, L.R., and R.B. Downs. "Special Collections for the Study of History and Literature in the Southeast: South Carolina." *PBSA*, 28: 114-5 (1934).

Winans, R.B. "The Growth of a Novel-Reading Public in Late-Eighteenth Century America" *EAL*, 9: 267-75 (Wi 75).

Wolf, Edwin. "Great American Book Collectors to 1800." *GGC*, 16: 3-69 (Je 71).

Wortis, Avi. "The Burnside Mystery: The R.H. Burnside Collection and the New York Public Library." *BNYPL*, 75: 371-409 (O 71).

Wright, Richard. "The Freedom to Read: An Author's View of a Library." *LJ*, 85: 4421-2 (15 D 60).

Literary Criticism. Aldridge, J.W. "The Writer's Demotion to Solid Citizen Status." *SatR*, 54: 35-40, 81-2 (18 S 71).

Altieri, C.F. "Northrop Frye and the Problem of Spiritual Authority." *PMLA*, 87: 964-75 (O 72).

Avant, J.A. "Slouching Toward Criticism." *LJ*, 96: 4055-9 (15 D 71).

Baker, William. "Literary Criticism and Linguistics." *Style*, 2: 1-5 (Wi 68).

Bakker, J. "Leslie Fiedler: The Darkness and the Light in the Land of Affirmation." *DQR*, 1: 3-14 (1971).

Beekman, E.M. "The Critic and Existence: An Introduction to Menno Ter Braak." *ConL*, 9: 377-93 (Su 68).

Beker, Miroslav. "Marxism and the Determinants of Literary Judgement." *JAAC*, 29: 33-41 (1970).

Berman, Ronald. "Myth or Criticism." *KR*, 31: 378-83 (#3 69).

Bigsby, C.W.E. "The White Critic in a Black World." *NALF*, 6: 39-45 (1972).

Bloom, Harold. "The Dialectics of Literary Tradition." *Boun2*, 2: 528-38 (Sp 74).

Bourke, P.F. "The Social Critics and the End of American Innocence." *JAmS*, 3: 57-72 (Jl 69).

Boynton, H.W. "The Case of 'The Critics.'" *Nation*, 102: 71-3 (20 Ja 16).

———. "A Word on 'The Genteel Critic.'" *Dial*, 59: 303-6 (14) 15).

Broderick, Dorothy. "Lessons in Leadership." *LJ*, 96: 699-701 (1971).

Brooks, Cleanth. "Telling It Like It Is in the Tower of Babel." *SR*, 79: 136-55 (Wi 71).

Brooks, Peter. "Nouvelle critique et critique nouvelle aux Etats-Unis." *NRF*, 17: 416-26 (1969).

Brown, Merle. "Criticism as the Animus of Poetry." *Standard*, 8: 45-52 (1967).

———. "The Philosopher Critic." *UTMS*, 10: 3-12 (1970).

Berger, N.K. "Truth or Consequences: Books and Book Reviewing." *SAQ*, 68: 152-66 (Sp 69).

Burke, Kenneth. "As I Was Saying." *MQR*, 11: 9-27 (Wl 72).

———. "Formalist Criticism: Its Principles and Limits." *TQ*, 9: 242-68 (Sp 68).

Calhoun, R.J. "Whatever Happened to the Poet-Critic?" *SLJ*, 1: 85-8 (Au 68).

———. "Literary Criticism in Southern Periodicals During the American Renaissance." *ESQ*, 55: 76-82 (2Q 69).

Cantarow, Ellen. "A Wilderness of Opinions Confounded: Allegory and Ideology." *CE*, 34: 215-30, 247-52 (N 73).

Carter, Everett. "The Meaning of, and in, Realism." *AR*, 12: 78-94 (Sp 52).

Chandra, Naresh. "Socio-Economic Background of New Criticism." *Rajasthan J Eng Stud*, 1: 16-28 (Jl-D 74).

Clecak, Peter. "Marxism, Literary Criticism, and the American Academic Scene." *Sci&Soc*, 31: 275-301 (Su 67).

Cohen, Keith. "Le 'New Criticism' aux Etats-Unis (1935-1950)." *Poétique*, 10: 217-43 (1972).

Colacurcio, M.J. "The Symbolic and the Symptomatic: D.H. Lawrence in Recent American Criticism." *AQ*, 27: 486-501 (O 75).

Colvert, J.B. "The Function of the Academic Critical Quarterly." *MissQ*, 23: 95-101 (Sp 70).

Core, George. "Ransom, Brooks, and the Idiom of Criticism." *SLJ*, 5: 177-86 (Fa 72).

———. "Southern Letters and the New Criticism." *GaR*, 24: 413-31 (Wi 70).

Curnow, Wystan. "Romanticism and Modern Criticism." *SRom*, 12: 777-99 (Fa 73).

Curtis, J.M. "The Function of Structuralism at the Present Time." *Dialogist*, 2: 58-67 (Su 70).

Day, Douglas. "The Background of the New Criticism." *JAAC*, 24: 429-41 (Sp 66).

Della Terza, Dante. "Tendenze attuali della critica americana." *SCr*, 3: 81-97 (Je 69).

Dembo, L.S. "Modern Criticism: Introduction and Perspective." *ConL*, 9: 277-89 (Wi 68).

Denham, R.D. "R.S. Crane's Critical Method and Theory of Poetic Form." *ConnR*, 5: 46-56 (1972).

Dickstein, Morris. "The Black Aesthetic in White America." *PR*, 38: 376-95 (Wi 71-72).

Dollerup, Cay, and F.W. Bateson. "The Mode of Existence of the Criticism of Literature: An Argument." *EIC*, 19: 420-33 (O 69).

Douglas, G.H. "Croce's Early Aesthetic and American Critical Theory." *CLS*, 7: 204-15 (Je 70).

Dow, Eddy. "Van Wyck Brooks and Lewis Mumford: A Confluence in the 'Twenties.'" *AL*, 45: 407-22 (N 73).

Drake, C.C. "Literary Criticism and Folklore." *JPC*, 5: 289-97 (Fa 71).

Duchamre, E.R. "The Evasion of the Text." *Eng Rec*, 20: 13-22 (1970).

Ebine, Shizue. "R.P. Blackmur's Criticism on 'Between the *Numen* and the *Moha*: Notes Towards a Theory of Literature.'" *OUS*, 25: 1-18 (1972).

Ehrstine, J.W. "A Calling of the Wits Together: Recent Romantic Theory." *ESQ*, 67: 186-96 (1972).

Ellis, Kathy. "The Function of Northrop Frye at the Present Time." *CE*, 31: 541-7 (Mr 70).

Feinberg, Leonard. "Satire: The Inadequacy of Recent Definitions." *Genre*, 1: 31-7 (Ja 68).

Fleming, D.S. "Literary Interpretation Today: An Assessment and a Reorientation." *SHR*, 6: 368-80 (Fa 72).

Ford, N.A. "Black Literature and the Problem of Evaluation." *CE*, 32: 53-47 *CE*, 32: 32: 536-47 (F 71).

———. "Confessions of a Black Critic." *BlackW*, 20: 30-43 (1971).

Foster, Richard. "Reflections on Teaching Criticism." *ConL*, 9: 406-18 (Su 68).

Fraser, John. "Leavis, Winters, and Poetry." *SoRA*, 5: 179-96 (1972).

———. "Leavis and Winters: Professional Matters." *CQ*, 5: 41-71 (1970).

———. "Leavis and Winters: A Question of Reputation." *WHR*, 26: 1-16 (1972).

Friedman, Norman. "From Victorian to Modern: A Sketch for a Critical Appraisal." *Victorian N*, 32: 20-8 (1967).

Frye, A.J. "Cleanth Brooks, A Shaping Joy." *Neophil*, 56: 115-6 (1972).

Frye, Northrop. "The Critical Path: An Essay on the Social Context of Literary Criticism." *Daedalus*, 99: 268-342 (Sp 70).

Funt, D.P. "Newer Criticism and Revolution." *HudR*, 22: 87-96 (1969).

———. "Roland Barthes and the Nouvelle critique." *JAAC*, 26: 329-40 (1968).

———. "The Structuralist Debate." *HudR*, 22: 623-46 (1969).

Gayle, Addison. "The Critic, the University, and the Negro Writer." *BlackW*, 16: 54-8 (1967).

Gerber, P.L., and R.J. Gemmett. "The Dream of Logic." *UWR*, 5: 27-37 (Fa 69).

Gevasco, G.A. "Slings and Arrows: A Consideration of Captious Literary Criticism." *ABC*, 20: 8-10 (My 70).

Gilman, Richard. "White Standards and Negro Writing." *NRep*, 3: 111-6 (9 Mr 68); *NALF*, 3: 111-6 (Wi 69).

Glazer, P.M. "From the Old Left to the New Radical: Criticism in the 1940's." *AQ*, 24: 584-603 (D 72).

Goodheart, Eugene. "The New Apocalypse." *Nation*, 201: 207-11 (20 S 65).

———. "*The New York Review*: A Close Look." *Dissent*, 17: 135-43 (Mr-Ap 70).

Goodman, Walter. "On the (N.Y.) Literary Left." *AR*, 29: 67-75 (1969).

Grossvogel, D.I. "Perception as a Form of Phenomenological Criticism." *HSL*, 1: 83-8 (1969).

Gunn, Giles. "Creation and Discovery: Vivas' Literary Theory." *Renascene*, 22: 198-206 (1970).

———. "Criticism as Repossession and Responsibility." *AQ*, 22: 629-48 (Fa 70).

Hahn, P.D. "A Reformulation of New Criticism." *ESRS*, 21: 5-64 (Su 72).

Hall, James. "The New Pleasures of the Imagination." *VQR*, 46: 596-612 (Au 70).

Hare, W.F. "The Roles of Teacher and Critic." *JGE*, 22: 41-9 (1970).

Hedges, W.L. "Towards a Theory of American Literature: 1765-1800." *EAL*, 4: 5-14 (1969).

Hirsch, E.D. "Literary Evaluation as Knowledge." *ConL*, 9: 319-31 (Su 68).

Hirth, Mary. "Cyril Connolly Examined: An Exhibit on 'The Modern Movement.'" *LCUT*, 1: 39-47 (Mr 70).

Houghton, D.E. "Vernon Louis Parrington's Unacknowledged Debt to Moses Coit Tyler." *NEQ*, 43: 124-30 (1970).

Howe, Irving. "Literary Criticism and Literary Radicals." *ASch*, 41: 113-20 (Wi 71-72).

Hyman, L.W. "Literature and Morality in Contemporary Criticism." *JAAC*, 30: 83-6 (1971).

Inge, Thomas. "Recent Southern Literary Criticism." *Appalachian J*, 2: 46-61 (Au 74).

Irwin, J.T. "The Symbol of the Hieroglyphics in the American Renaissance." *AQ*, 26: 103-26 (My 74).

Johnsen, W.A. "Toward a Redefinition of Modernism." *Boun2*, 2: 539-56 (Sp 74).

Jochems, Helmut. "Englische un amerikanische Lyrik in der Schule: Kritische Anmerkungen zu einigen neuren Interpretationssammlungen." *LWU*, 2: 268-81 (1969).

Karnani, Chetan. "New Criticism in America: Some Reflections." *RUSEng*, 6: 85-90 (1972).

Kazin, Alfred. "Whatever Happened to Criticism." *Commentary*, 49: 58-63 (F 70).

Keller, Joseph. "Black Writing and White Critic." *NALF*, 3: 103-10 (1969).

Kogan, Pauline. "Obscurantist Trends in American Criticism." *L&I*, 12: 37-44 (1972).

Kolb, H.H. "In Search of Definition: American Literary Realism and the Clichés." *ALR*, 2: 165-73 (1969).

Kolodny, Annette. "Some Notes on Defining a 'Feminist Literary Criticism.'" *CritI*, 2: 75-92 (Au 75).

Kostelanetz, Richard. "Critical Writing for American Magazines: A Memoir and a Valedictory." *Works*, 1: 84-95 (Su 68).

———. "On Irving Howe: the Perils and Paucities of Democratic Radicalism." *Salmagundi*, 2: 44-60 (Sp 67).

Kramer, V.A. "Agee and Plans for the Criticism of Popular Culture." *JPC*, 5: 755-66 (Sp 72).

Krieger, Murray. "The Critical Legacy of Matthew Arnold; or, The Strange Brotherhood of T.S. Eliot, I.A. Richards, and Northrop Frye." *SoR*, 5: 457-74 (Sp 69).

———. "Literary Analysis and Evaluation and the Ambidextrous Critic." *ConL*, 9: 290-310 (Su 68).

Kuklick, Bruce. "Myth and Symbol in American Studies." *AQ*, 24: 435-50 (1972).

Labrie, R.E. "American Naturalism: An Appraisal." *MarkR*, 2: 88-90 (F 71).

Larson, C.R. "Leslie Fiedler: The Critic and the Myth, the Critic as Myth." *LitR*, 14: 133-43 (1971).

Lee, D.L. "Black Critics." *BlackW*, 19: 24-30 (1970).

Lehmann, W.P. "Generative Linguistics and Literary Criticism." *TQ*, 17: 89-104 (Au 74).

Lentricchia, Frank. "The Place of Cleanth Brooks." *JAAC*, 29: 235-51 (1970).

Lenz, G.H. "Von der Erkenntnis der literarischen Struktur zur der literaturwissenschaftlichen Erkenntnis: Metakkritische Bemerkungen zu R.S. Crane und Northrop Frye." *JA*, 17: 100-27 (1972).

Levy, L.B. "Critics, Scientists, and Biographers." *SoR*, 4: 1081-92 (1968).

Lippman, Bert. "Literature and Life." *GaR*, 25: 145-58 (Su 71).

Lombardo, Agostino. "Italian Criticism of American Literature." *SR*, 68: 353-515 (Su 60).

Loofbourow, J.W. "Literary Realism Redefined." *Thought*, 45: 433-43 (Au 70).

Manheim, Leonard. "The Buffalo School of Psychoanalytic Critics." *HSL*, 3: 213-8 (1971).

Manning, Stephen. "Typology and the Literary Critic." *EAL*, 5: 51-73 (1970).

May, J.R. "Of Huckleberry Bushes and the New Hermeneutic." *Renascence*, 14: 85-95 (Wi 72).

Miller, T.L. "John Ranken Rouse: The Last of the Victorian Critics." *ETJ*, 22: 161-78 (1970).

Montgomery, Margaret. "Through a Glass Darkly: Eliot and the Romantic Critics." *SWR*, 58: 327-35 (Au 73).

Moore, A.K. "Formalist Criticism and Literary Form." *JAAC*, 29: 21-31 (1970).

Moore, C.S. "Contemporary Criticism and the End of a Literary Revolution." *CentR*, 15: 144-61 (Sp 71).

Mukherjee, Sujit. "The Business of Criticism in America." *IJES*, 9: 49-59 (1968).

Mulqueen, J.E. "Conservatism and Criticism: The Literary Standard of American Whigs, 1845-1852." *AL*, 41: 355-72 (N 69).

Newton, J.M. "Literary Criticism, Universities, Murder." *CQ*, 5: 335-54 (1971).

Nichols, S.G. "Georg Lukás: The Problems of Dialectical Criticism." *ConL*, 9: 349-66 (Su 68).

Paliwal, B.B. "Criticism in the 'Thirties.'" *BP*, 14: 62-70 (1970).

Pearce, R.H. "The Critic as Advocate." *SoR*, 6: 229-44 (Ja 70).

————. "La critica americana e la cultura americana." *SCr*, 3: 167-86 (1969).

Peck, D.R. "'The Orgy of Apology': Recent Re-evaluation of the Literature of the Thirties." *Sci&Soc*, 32: 371-82 (Fa 68).

Pizer, Donald. "Evolutionary Ideas in Late-Nineteenth-Century English and American Criticism." *JAAC*, 19: 305-10 (Sp 61).

————. "Evolutionary Criticism and the Defense of Howellsian Realism." *JEGP*, 61: 286-304 (Ap 62).

————. "Harold J. Kolb, Jr.'s Study of American Realism as a Literary Genre." *Genre*, 3: 376-8 (1970).

Poger, Sidney. "The Critical Stance of *The Dial*." *ESQ*, 57: 22-7 (4Q 69).

Pound, Ezra. "The Disease of American Criticism." *Little R*, 5: 43-4 (N 18).

Pratt, Annis. "Archetypal Approaches to the New Feminist Criticism." *BuR*, 21: 3-14 (Sp 73).

————. "The New Feminist Criticism." *CE*, 872-78 (My 71).

Pritchard, W.H. "The Current State of Criticism." *HudR*, 24: 702-10 (1971).

Rahv, Philip. "Fiction and the Criticism of Fiction." *KR*, 18: 276-99 (Sp 56).

Rans, Geoffrey. "E Pluribus One Loved Folly: Observations on American Criticism." *CRAS*, 2: 53-61 (1971).

Reichert, John. "Monroe Beardsley and the Shape of Literary Theory." *CE*, 33: 558-70 (F 72).

Reiter, R.E. "On Biblical Typology and the Interpretation of Literature." *CE*, 30: 562-71 (1969).

Richmond, H.M. "The Dead Albatross: 'New Criticism' as a Humanist Fallacy." *CE*, 33: 515-31 (F 72).

Riddel, J.N. "Against Formalism." *Genre*, 3: 156-72 (1970).

Roberts, Michael. "The Critic and the Public." *SoR*, 4: 368-81 (1939).

Roberts, T.J. "The Critics' Conception of Literature." *CE*, 31: 1-24 (O 69).

Robinson, J.K. "From Criticism to Historicism." *SoR*, 9: 692-709 (Jl 73).

Rosenthal, M.L. "Uncertain Odysseus: The Critic of Current Poetry." *Shen*, 19: 59-66 (1968).

Rubin, L.R. "Susan Sontag and the Camp Followers." *SR*, 82: 503-10 (Su 74).

Rucker, M.E. "The Literary Essay and the Modern Temper." *PLL*, 11: 317-35 (1975).

Ruekert, W.H. "Kenneth Burke and Structuralism." *Shen*, 21: 19-28 (au 69).

Said, Edward. "Contemporary Fiction and Criticism." *TriQ*, 33: 231-56 (Sp 75).

Sahai, Y. "New Criticism and the Aesthetic Experience." *LCrit*, 9: 61-9 (Wi 69).

Schilling, Hanna-Beate. "The Role of the Brothers Schlegel in American Literary Criticism." *AL*, 43: 563-79 (Ja 72).

Scholes, Robert. "The Fictional Criticism of the Future." *TriQ*, 34: 233-47 (Fa 75).

———. "The Illiberal Imagination." *NLH*, 4: 521-40 (1973).

Schroeter, James. "The Unseen Center: A Critique of Northrop Frye." *CE*, 33: 543-7 (F 72).

Sharma, D.R. "The Natural: A Nonmythical Approach." *PURBA*, 5: 3-8 (O 74).

Shepherd, Allen. "The Literary Radicalism of John Macy." *RSW*, 39: 119-28 (1971).

Shumaker, Wayne. "A Modest Proposal for Critics." *ConL*, 9: 332-48 (Su 68).

Shurr, W.H. "Typology and Historical Criticism of the American Renaissance." *ESQ*, 20: 57-63 (1Q 74).

Simms, L.M. "Corra Harris on Patriotic Literary Criticism in the Post-Civil War South." *MissQ*, 25: 459-66 (1972).

Sivaramakrishna, M. "The Objective Correlative: A Point of View." *OJES*, 10: 45-56 (1973).

Spanos, W.V. "The Critical Imperatives of Alienation: The Theological Perspective of Nathan Scott's Literary Criticism." *JR*, 48: 89-103 (Ja 68).

Spears, M.K. "The Newer Criticism." *Shen*, 21: 110-37 (Sp 70).

Sporn, Paul. "Critique et science aux Etats-Unis." *Poétique*, 6: 223-38 (1971).

Stockinger, Jacob. "Toward a Gay Criticism." *CE*, 36: 303-11 (N 74).

Stone, G.W. "The Legacy of Sisyphus." *PMLA*, 83: 9-14 (1968).

Stone, W.B. "Towards a Defintion of Realism." *Centrum*, 1: 47-60 (1973).

Strozier, R.N. "Roger Ascham and Cleanth Brooks: Renaissance and Modern Critical Thought." *EIC*, 22: 396-407 (O 72).

Tanner, S.L. "Paul Elmer More: Literary Criticism as the History of Ideas." *AL*, 45: 390-406 (N 73).

Thompson, E.M. "The Russian Formalists and the New Critics." *SHR*, 4: 145-54 (Sp 70).

Toffler, Alvin. "The Art of Measuring the Arts." *An Am Acad Pol and Soc Sci*, 358: 141-55 (S 67).

Turner, D.T. "Afro-American Literary Critics." *BlackW*, 19: 54-67 (1970).

Vance, Thomas. "Poetry and the Generation of Critics." *SoR*, 4: 1099-1109 (1968).

Vernon, John. "Naked Criticism." *IowaR*, 5: 75-82 (Wi 74).

Vidal, Gore. "Literary Gangsters." *Commentary*, 49: 61-4 (Mr 70).

Vivas, Eliseo. "Literary Criticism and Aesthetics." *UTMS*, 10: 13-39 (1970).

Waggoner, H.H. "A Sermon for Critics." *WR*, 13: 141-3 (Wi 50).

Wagner, Geoffrey. "American Literary Criticism: The Continuing Heresy." *SoRA*, 3: 82-9 (1968).

Walker, D.D. "Essays in the Criticism of Western Literary Criticism." *PosS*, 2: 1-3 (Ag 71).

———. "Notes Toward a Literary Criticism of the Western." *JPC*, 7: 728-41 (Wi 73).

Wallenstein, Barry. "Leslie Fiedler Between Raft and Shore." *JML*, 2: 589-94 (1972).

Wanning, Andrew. "Criticism and Principles." *SoR*, 6: 792-810 (1941).

Wellek, René. "American Criticism of the Last Ten Years." *YCGL*, 20: 4-14 (1971).

———. "Cleanth Brooks, Critic of Critics." *SoR*, 10: 125-52 (Ja 74).

West, P.J. "Medieval Style and the Concerns of Modern Criticism." *CE*, 34: 784-90 (1973).

———. "Perpetuating the Obsolete." *Cweal*, 87: 203-5 (17 N 67).

Westbrook, Max. "The Ontological Critic." *Rendezvous*, 7: 49-66 (Wi 72).

White, G.A. "Ideology and Literature: *American Renaissance* and F.O. Matthiessen." *TriQ*, 23-24: 430-600 (1972).

White, Hayden. "Structuralism and Popular Culture." *JPC*, 759-75 (1974).

Williamson, Eugene. "R.G. Moulton and Modern Criticism." *JEGP*, 70: 632-48 (1971).

Yeazell, Ruth. "Fictional Heroes and Feminist Critics." *Novel*, 8: 29-38 (Fa 74).

Yoder, R.A. "Equilibrist Perspective: Toward a Theory of American Romanticism." *SRom*, 12: 705-40 (1973).

Literary History. Anon. "The Colonial Scene—1602-1800." *PAAS*, 60: 53-160 (1950).

Adams, R.P. "Permutations of American Romanticism." *SRom*, 9: 249-68 (Fa 70).

———. "Sourthern Literature in the 1890's." *MissQ*, 21: 277-81 (1968).

Allacock, Steven. "Oak Hall in American Literature." *AL*, 46: 545-9 (Ja 75).

Andrews, W.D. "The Literature of the 1727 New England Earthquake." *EAL*, 7: 281-94 (Wi 73).

Appel, Benjamin. "Miss America and the Look-Back Boys." *LitR*, 17: 5-34 (Fa 73).

Astre, Georges-Albert. "Les annés 30 aux Etats-Unis." *Raison Presente*, 35: 61-87

Axtell, J.L. "The Vengeful Women of Marblehead: Robert Rowle's Deposition of 1677." *WMQ*, 31: 647-52 (1974).

Benton, R.P. "The Problems of Literary Gothicism." *ESQ*, 18: 5-9 (1Q 72).

Bercovitch, Sacva. "The Image of America: From Hermeneutics to Symbolism." *BuR*, 20: 3-12 (1973).

Bier, Jesse. "The Romantic Coordinates of American Literature." *BuR*, 18: 16-33 (1970).

Blair, Walter. "The Roots of American Realism." *UR*, 6: 275-81 (Je 40).

Bonner, Thomas. "A Bibliographical Introduction to the American Literature of the 1930's and the Backgrounds." *BB*, 31: 57-66, 70 (Ap-Je 74).

Bowron, B.R. "Realism in America." *CL*, 3: 268-85 (Su 51).

Boyle, T.E. "The Tenor in the Organic Metaphor: A View of American Romanticism." *Disc*, 11: 240-51 (Sp 68).

Bradbury, Malcolm. "Leaving the Fifties." *Enc*, 45: 40-51 (2Q 75).

Browne, Ray. "Whale Lore and Popular Print in Mid Nineteenth-Century America." *Prospects*, 1: 29-40 (1975).

Budd, L.J. "The Forgotten Decades of Southern Writing, 1890-1920." *MissQ*, 21: 275-90 (Fa 68).

Bush, A.L. "Literary Landmarks of Princeton." *PULC*, 29: 1-90 (Au 67).

Calhoon, R.M. "Loyalist Studies at the Advent of the Loyalist Papers Project." *NEQ*, 46: 284-93 (1973).

Calhoun, R.J. "The Ante-Bellum Literary Twilight: *Russell's Magazine*." *SLJ*, 3: 89-110 (Fa 70).

———. "Literary Criticism in Southern Periodicals During the American Renaissance." *ESQ*, 55: 76-82 (2Q 69).

Cameron, J.M. "Problems of Literary History." *NLH*, 1: 7-20 (1969).

———. "Objectivity and Low Seriousness in American Naturalism." *Prospect*, 1: 49-62 (1975).

Cameron, K.W. "Bunyan and the Writers of the American Renaissance." *ATQ*, 13: 1-47 (1Q 72).

———. "Death and Beyond in the American Renaissance." *ATQ*, 13: 1-27 (1Q 72).

———. "Literary News in American Renaissance Newspapers." *ATQ*, 2: 29-37 (2Q 69); 5: 68-80 (1Q 70); 14: 112-25 (2Q 72); 20: 13-36, 195-7 (3Q 73).

Carter, Everett. "The Meaning of, and in, Realism." *AR*, 12: 78-94 (Sp 52).

Christadler, Martin. "Politische Diskussion un literarische Form in der amerikanischen Literatur der Revolutionzeit." *JA*, 13: 13-33 (1968).

Cohen, B.B. "Tragic Vision in the Sixties." *Genre*, 3: 254-71 (1970).

Cohen, S.S. "Student Unrest in the Decade before the American Revolution." *ConnR*, 7: 51-8 (#2 74).

Colacurcio, M.J. "A Better Mode of Evidence—The Transcendental Problem of Faith and Spirit." *ESQ*, 54: 12-22 (1Q 69).

Colby, Elbridge. "The New Economic Interpretation of Literary History." *SAQ*, 12: 347-55 (O 13).

Commager, H.S. "The American Enlightenment and the Ancient World: A Study in Paradox." *PMHS*, 83: 3-15 (1971).

Cowley, Malcolm. "Apres la guerre fini." *Horizon*, 10: 113-9 (Wi 68).

———. "Federal Writers' Project." *NRep*, 167: 2306 (21 O 72).

———. "What Books Survive from the 1930's." *JAmSt*, 7: 293-300 (D 73).

Cowley, Robert. "The Jazz Age: A Shadow on the Seventies." *SatR*, 2: 13-8 (17 My 75).

Cravens, Hamilton, and J.C. Burham. "Pyschology and Evolutionary Naturalism in American Thought, 1890-1940." *AQ*, 23: 635-57 (D 71).

Cutting, R.M. "America Discovers Its Literary Past: Early American Literature Past: Early American Literature in Nineteenth-Century Anthologies." *EAL*, 9: 226-51 (Wi 75).

Dabezies, Andre. "The First American *Faust* (1720)." *CLS*, 8: 303-9 (1971).

Davis, David. "Some Recent Developments in American Cultural History." *AHR*, 73: 697-707 (F 68).

Davis, R.B. "The American Dream." *Faculty Stud Carson-Newman Col*, 1: 5-11 (1966).

———. "The Intellectual Golden Age in the Colonial Chesapeake Bay Country." *VMHB*, 78: 131-43 (1970).

Davis, R.L. "All the New Vibrations: Romanticism in 20th-Century America." *SWR*, 54: 256-70 (Su 69).

De Man, Paul. "Literary History and Literary Modernity." *Daedalus*, 99: 384-404 (1970).

DeMott, Benjamin. "Looking Back on the Seventies: Notes Toward a Cultural History." *Atl*, 227: 59-64 (Mr 71).

Dickstein, Morris. "Cold War Blues: Notes on the Culture of the Fifties." *PR*, 41: 30-53 (1974).

Diggins, J.P. "The Perils of Naturalism: Some Reflections on Daniel J. Boorstin's Approach to American History." *AQ*, 23: 153-80 (My 71).

Doxcy, W.S. "American Literary Response to the Philippine Problem: 1899-1906." *WGCR*, 2: 10-9 (1969).

Duffey, Bernard. "Two Literary Movements: Chicago, 1890-1925." *NLB*, 3: 1-24 (O 52).

Edenbaum, R.I. "Dada and Surrealism in the United States: A Literary Instance." *Arts in Soc*, 5: 114-25 (1968).

Engel, Leonard. "Melville and the Young American Movement." *ConnR*, 4: 91-101 (1971).

Fiering, N.S. "Will and Intellect in the New England Mind." *WMQ*, 29: 515-58 (O 72).

Fitzgerald, F.S. "My Generation." *Esquire*, 80: 124-6 (O 73).

Foerster, Norman. "The Literary Historians." *Bookman*, 71: 365-74 (Jl 30).

Fogle, R.H. "Literary History Romanticized." *NLH*, 1: 23-47 (Wi 70).

Fridén, George. "Transcendental Idealism in New England." *NM*, 69: 256-71 (1968).

Friedman, Norman. "From Victorian to Modern: A Sketch for a Critical Appraisal." *Victorian N*, 32: 20-8 (1967).

Fulcher, J.R. "Puritans and the Passions: The Faculty Psychology in American Puritanism." *J Hist Behavioral Sci*, 9: 123-39 (1973).

Gagey, E.M. "General Booth with His Big Bass Drum Enters into Haverhill, Massachusetts." *NEQ*, 45: 508-25 (D 72).

Garraty, John. "A Century of American Realism." *AH*, 21: 12-5, 86-9 (Je 70).

Gayle, Addison, "The Harlem Renaissance." *MASJ*, 11: 78-87 (Fa 70).

Genovese, E.D. "The Influence of the Black Power Movement on Historical Scholarship." *Daedalus*, 99: 473-94 (Sp 70).

Gilman, Richard. "Art and History." *PR*, 35: 274-86 (Sp 68).

Gleason, Philip. "Our New Age of Romanticism." *America*, 117: 372-5 (7 O 67).

Grabo, N.S. "The Veiled Vision: The Role of Aesthetics in Early American Literary History." *WMQ*, 19: 493-510 (1962).

Granger, Bruce. "From Silence Dogood to Launcelot Langstaff." *EAL*, 3: 11-6 (Sp 68).

Gray, D.J., and Paul Strohm. "Literary History at Indiana." *NLH*, 3: 421-30 (1972).

Hartman, Geoffrey. "Toward Literary History." *Daedalus*, 99: 355-83 (1970).

Hauck, R.B. "Predicting a Native Literature." *MissQ*, 22: 77-84 (Wi 68-69).

Higuchu, Hiodeo. "American Literary Wars in the Thirties." *DSE*, 10: 53-72 (Mr 75).

Holman, C.H. "LHUS for the Fourth Time." *RALS*, 5: 3-14 (Sp 75).

Howe, Irving. "Literature of the Latecomers: A View of the Twenties." *SR/W*, 1: 32-43 (10 Ag 74).

Hubbell, J.B. "A Turning Point in American Literary History." *TSLL*, 12: 481-92 (Fa 70).

Hughes, Langston. "The Twenties: Harlem and Its Négritude." *AForum*, 1: 18 (Sp 66).

Hynes, Samuel. "The Thirites as a Literary Period." *ConL*, 12: 122-7 (Wi 71).

James, S.B. "The Politics of Personal Salvation: The American Record." *DQ*, 4: 19-45 (Su 69).

Jantz, Harold. "America's First Cosmopolitan." *PMHS*, 84: 3-25 (1972).

Jones, A.H. "The Search for a Usable Past in the New Deal Era." *AQ*, 23: 710-24 (D 71).

Jones, H.M. "The Genteel Tradition." *HLB*, 18: 5-20 (Ja 70).

Jordan, J.E. "Literary History at Berkeley." *NLH*, 2: 533-40 (1971).

Katz, Joseph. "Bibliography and the Rise of Literary Realism." *SAF*, 2: 75-88 (1974).

Kazin, Alfred. "The Literary Sixties, When the World Was Too Much with Us." *NYT*, 21 D 69, pp. 1-3, 18.

Keller, F.R. "The Harlem Literary Renaissance." *NAR*, 5: 29-34 (My-Je 68).

Kelly, R.G. "American Children's Literature: An Historiographical Review." *ALR*, 6: 89-108 (1973).

———. "Literature and the Historian." *AQ*, 26: 141-59 (My 74).

Knox, George. "The Harlem Renaissance Today." *CEJ*, 7: 29-33 (D 71).

Koch, Stephen. "Premature Speculations on the Perpetual Renaissance." *TriQ*, 10: 5-19 (Fa 67).

Krickel, Edward. "The Study of the Expatriates." *SAB*, 35: 29-39 (1970).

Kuhn, J.F. "Myth and History: Some Remarks on Colonial America." *NDEJ*, 1-2: 39-54 (1970-71).

Lamplugh, G.R. "The Image of the Negro in Popular Magazine Fiction, 1875-1900." *JNH*, 57: 177-89 (Ap 72).

Lefler, H.T. "Promotional Literature of the Southern Colonies." *JSH*, 33: 3-25 (F 67).

Lensing, George. "The Lyric Plenitude: A Time of Rediscovery." *SoR*, 3: 197-228 (Wi 67).

Lewis, M.E. "The Art of Frederick Jackson Turner: The Histories." *HLQ*, 35: 241-55 (1972).

Lewis T.B. "A Revolutionary Tradition, 1689-1774: 'There Was a Revolution Here as Well as in England.'" *NEQ*, 46: 424-38 (S 73).

Lombard, C.M. "The Old New York Salon—French Style." *NYHSQ*, 55: 38-51 (Ja 71).

Long, R.A. "The Outer Reaches: The White Writer and the Blacks in the Twenties." *SLitI*, 7: 65-72 (Fa 74).

Lowance, M.I. "From Edwards to Emerson to Thoreau: A Revaluation." *ATQ*, 18: 3-12 (1973).

McAlexander, P.J. "The Creation of the American Eve: The Cultural Dialogue on the Nature and Role of Women in Late-Eighteenth Century America." *EAL*, 9: 252-66 (Wi 75).

McCormick, J.O. "Notes on a Comparative American Literary History." *CLS*, 5: 167-79 (Je 68).

MacFadden, F.R. "Popular Arts and the Revolt Against Patriarchism in Colonial America." *JPC*, 8: 286-94 (1974).

McGiffert, Michael. "American Puritan Studies in the 1960's." *WMQ*, 27: 36-67 (Ja 70).

McLuhan, Marshall. "Roles, Masks, Performances." *NLH*, 2: 517-31 (1971).

Marder, Daniel. "Exiles at Home in American Literature." *Mosaic*, 3: 49-75 (3Q 75).

Marius, Richard. "History and Literature: Some Whimsical Remarks." *TSL*, 17: 165-74 (1972).

Marks, B.A. "Retrospective Narrative in Nineteenth-Century American Literature." *CE*, 31: 366-75 (1970).

Marler, R.F. "From Tale to Short Story: The Emergence of a New Genre in the 1850's." *AL*, 46: 153-69 (My 74).

Martin, Ged. "The Cambridge Lectureship of 1866: A False Start in American Studies." *JAmSt*, 7: 17-29 (Ap 73).

Martin, J.S. "Rhetoric, Society and Literature in the Age of Jefferson." *MASJ*, 9: 77-90 (Sp 68).

May, H.F. "The Problem of the American Enlightenment." *NLH*, 1: 201-14 (Wi 74).

Miles, E.A. "The Old South and the Classical World." *NCHR*, 48: 259-75 (Su 71).

————. "The Young American Nation and the Classical World." *JHI*, 35: 259-74 (1974).

Mills, N.C. "The Machine in the Anglo-American Garden." *CentR*, 14: 201-12 (1970).

Miner, Earl. "The Possibilities of Literary History Today." *Clio*, 2: 219-38 (Je 73).

Modlin, C.E. "Aristocracy in the Early Republic." *EAL*, 6: 252-7 (Wi 71-72).

Moers, Ellen. "Shook-up Generation," *NYRB*, 8: 26-9 (18 My 67).

————. "The Survivors: Into the Twentieth Century." *TCL*, 20: 1-10 (1974).

Morley, Felix. "Not a Great Divide." *ModA*, 14: 57-64 (1970).

Mottram, Eric. "Living Mythically: The Thirties." *JAmSt*, 6: 267-87 (D 72).

Mulqueen, J.E. "Conservatism and Criticism: The Literary Standards of the American Whigs, 1845-1852." *AL*, 41: 355-72 (N 69).

Murdock, K.B. "Clio in the Wilderness: History and Biography in Puritan New England." *EAl*, 6: 201-19 (Wi 71-72).

Myerson, Joel. "A Calendar of the Transcendental Club Meetings." *AL*, 44: 197-207 (My 72).

————. "Transcendentalism and Unitarianism in 1840." *CLAJ*, 16: 366-8 (Mr 73).

Nelson, A.K. "King Philip's War and the Hubbard-Mather Rivalry." *WMQ*, 27: 615-29 (O 70).

Nikolyukin, A.N. "Past and Present Discussions of American National Literature." *NLII*, 4: 575-90 (Sp 73).

Ohashi, Kichinosuke. "1920 Nendai to Chicago Renaissance." *EigoS*, 119: 704-6 (1974).

Parkinson, Thomas. "After the Beat Generation." *ColQ*, 17: 45-56 (1968).

Patten, I.M. "The Civil War as Romance of Noble Warriors and Maidens Chaste." *AH*, 22: 48-53, 109 (Ap 71).

Pauly, T.H. "The Literary Sketch in Nineteenth-Century America." *TSLL*, 17: 489-503 (1975).

Peck, D.R. "'The Orgy of Apology': Recent Re-evaluation of the Literature of the Thirties." *Sci&Soc*, 32: 371-82 (Fa 68).

Pecora, Madeline. "The Date of *the Plain Case Stated*." *EAL*, 6: 185-6 (Fa 71).

Pickering, J.H. "Moses Coit Tyler: An Appreciation." *UCQ*, 13: 7-14 (Ja 68).

Pickering, Sam. "Literature and Society in Colonial Virginia." *THQ*, 32: 290-5 (Fa 73).

Price, Martin. "Literary History at Yale." *NLH*, 1: 335-43 (1970).

Rein, I.J. "The New England Transcendentalists: Philosophy and Rhetoric." *P&R*, 1: 103-17 (Wi 68).

Reinhold, Meyer. "Opponents of Classical Learning in America during the Revolutionary Period." *PAPS*, 112: 221-34 (Ag 68).

Robinson, J.K. "From Criticism to Historicism." *SoR*, 9: 692-709 (Jl 73).

Rock, V.J. "They Took Their Stand: The Emergence of Southern Agrarians." *Prospects*, 1: 205-96 (1975).

Rosenthal, Bernard. "*The Dial*, Transcendentalism, and Margaret Fuller." *ELN*, 8: 28-36 (S 70).

———. "Poe, Slavery, and the *Southern Literary Messenger*: A Reexamination." *PoeS*, 7: 29-38 (D 74).

Roth, R.J. "The Puritan Backgrounds of American Naturalism." *Thought*, 45: 520-20 (1970).

Rotundo, Barbara. "The Literary Lights Were Always Bright at 148 Charles Street." *AH*, 22: 10-5 (F 71).

Rubin, L.D. "A Study of Pastoral and History." *GHQ*, 59: 422-54 (Wi 75).

Schorer, Mark. "A Soft Look Backward." *Occident*, 1: 107-13 (Sp-Su 67).

Scott, C.L. "Literary History at Wisconsin." *NLH*, 4: 615-22 (1973).

Scott, N.A. "History, Hope, and Literature." *Boun2*, 1: 577-603 (Sp 73).

Serio, J.N. "From Edwards to Poe." *ConnR*, 6: 88-92 (1972).

Shapiro, Edward. "The Southern Agrarians and the Tennessee Valley Authority." *AQ*, 22: 791-806 (Wi 70).

Sheed, Wilfred. "The Beat Movement, Concluded." *NYT*, 13 F 72, pp. 2, 32.

Shipton, C.K. "Harvard, Yale, and the Educated Colonial." *MQR*, 7: 177-83 (Su 68).

Shurr, W.H. "Typology and Historical Criticism of the American Renaisance." *ESQ*, 20: 57-63 (1Q 74).

Simon, J.D. "Reading the Proletarian Fiction of the Thirties." *L&I*, 18: 25-32 (1974).

Simms, L.M. "Corra Harris on Patriotic Criticism in the Post-Civil War South." *MissQ*, 25: 459-66 (1972).

Simpson, L.P. "Boston Ice and Letters in the Age of Jefferson." *MASJ*, 9: 58-76 (Sp 68).

———. "The Civil War: Written and Unwritten." *SLJ*, 7, 132-45 (Fa 74).

———. "The Southern Writer and the Great Literary Secession." *GaR*, 24: 393-412 (Wi 70).

Singer, Barnet. "Judging Vernon Lewis Parrington." *RSW*, 43: 209-21 (1975).

Slotkin, Richard. "Dreams and Genocide: The American Myth of Regeneration Through Violence." *JPC*, 5: 38-59 (Su 71).

———. "Narratives of Negro Crime in New England, 1675-1900." *AQ*, 25: 3-31 (Mr 73).

Smith, D.E. "Romanticism in America: The Transcendentalists." *RPol*, 35: 302-25 (Jl 73).

Snell, J.G. "Thomas D'Arcy McGee and the American Republic." *CRAS*, 3: 33-44 (1972).

Somerville, J.K. "The Salem (Mass.) Woman in the Home, 1660-1770." *Eighteenth-Century Life*, 1: 11-4 (#1 74).

Spiller, R.E. "History of a History: A Study in Cooperative Scholarship." *PMLA*, 89: 602-16 (My 73).

Stanford, Derek. "Sex and Style in the Literature of the 90's." *Cont R*, 216: 95-100 (F 70).

Stein, R.B. "Pulled Out of the Bay: American Fiction in the Eighteenth-Century." *SAF*, 2: 13-36 (Sp 74).

———. "Seascape and the American Imagination: The Puritan Seventeenth Century." *EAL*, 7: 17-37 (Sp 72).

Steinbeck, John. "A Primer on the Thirties." *Esquire*, 80: 127-31 (O 73).

Steirer, W.F. "Eugene D. Genovese: Marxist-Romantic Historian of the South." *SoR*, 10: 840-50 (O 74).

Stubbs, J.C. "The Ideal in Literature and Art of the American Renaissance." *ESQ*, 55: 55-63 (2Q 69).

Styron, William. "My Generation." *Esquire*, 80: 132-4 (O 73).

Sutton, R.P. "Nostalgia, Pessimism, and Malaise." *VMHB*, 76: 41-55 (Ja 68).

Swisher, Perry. "The Cause of Alienation and the Case for Reconciliation." *Rendezvous*, 4: 31-8 (1969).

Szasz, F.M. "Antebellum Appeals to the 'Higher Law,' 1830-60." *EIHC*, 110: 33-48 (1974).

Tanner, Tony. "Notes for a Comparison between American and European Romanticism." *JAmSt*, 2: 83-103 (Ap 68).

Thomas, Clara. "New England Romanticism and Canadian Fiction." *JCF*, 2: 80-6 (1973).

Thompson, Roger. "Salem Revisited." *JAmSt*, 6: 317-36 (1972).

Tichi, Cecelia. "The Puritan Historians and Their New Jerusalem." *EAL*, 6: 143-55 (Fa 71).

Tingley, D.F. "The 'Robin's Egg Renaissance': Chicago and the Arts, 1810-1920." *JISHS*, 63: 35-54 (1970).

Tripp, Wendell. "Fifty Years of New York History." *NYH*, 5: 355-96 (1969).

Turner, Arlin. "Interpreting Nineteenth-Century American Literature." *AmS*, 9: 3-15 (Sp 73).

Tuttleton, J.W. "Romance and Novel: The Disintegration of Form." *ESQ*, 55: 116-21 (2Q 69).

Tytell, John. "The Beat Generation and the Continuing American Revolution." *ASch*, 42: 308-17 (Sp 73).

Vanderbilt, Kermit. "Writers of the Troubled Sixties." *Nation*, 217: 61-5 (17 D 73).

Vittorini, Elio. "An Outline of American Literature." *SR*, 68: 423-37 (Su 60).

Waggoner, H.H. "The State of Literary History." *SR*, 63: 515-24 (Su 55).

Walker, R.H. "Patterns in Recent American Literature." *Stetson Un Bul*, 65: 1-12 (O 67).

Wall, Annie. "Early Transcendentalism in New England." *ESQ*, 59: 46-50 (Sp 70).

Weaver, R.M. "Realism and the Local Color Interlude." *GaR*, 25: 301-5 (Fa 68).

Weimann, Robert. "Past Significance and Present Meaning in Literary History." *NLH*, 1: 91-109 (1969).

Weisinger, Herbert. "Is the Renaissance Over?" *CentR*, 16: 283-92 (1972).

Wills, Gary. "The Sixties." *Esquire*, 80: 135-7 (O 73).

Winans, R.B. "The Growth of a Novel-Reading Public in Late-Eighteenth-Century America." *EAL*, 9: 267-75 (Wi 75).

Wirzberger, Karl-Heinz. "'Great Tradition' oder Episode? Nonkonformismus, Protest and Engagement in der amerikanischen Gegenwartsliteratur." *ZAA*, 16: 5-24 (1968).

Wise, Gene. "Implicit Irony in Perry Miller's *New England Mind*." *JHI*, 29: 579-600 (O-D 68).

Wohl, R.R. "The 'Country Boy' Myth and Its Place in American Urban Culture: The Nineteenth-Century Contribution." *PerAmH*, 3: 77-156 (1969).

Wright, B.M. "The Negritude Tradition in Literature." *SBL*, 3: 1-3 (Sp 72).

Zimmerman, L.F. "Shifted Values in the Later Nineteenth Century." *UTMS*, 7: 23-31 (1969).

Literary Societies. Cowley, Malcolm, "'Sir, May I have the Honor': Notes on the History of the National Institute and the American Academy of Arts and Letters." *SoR*, 8: 1-14 (Ja 72).

Coxe, G.W. "The Saturday Club." *ESQ*, 63: 35-41 (Sp 71).

Goodman, K.S. "The Chicago Theatre Society." *Nation*, 98: 308-9 (19 Mr 14).

Gregories, A.K. "The First Decade of the Charleston Library Society." *South Carolina Hist Assn Proc*, nv: 3-10 (1935).

Myerson, Joel. "A Calendar of Transcendental Club Meetings." *AL*, 44: 197-207 (My 72).

Neufeld John. "Associated Western Literary Societies in the Midwest." *MichH*, 61: 154-61 (Su 67).

Literary Societies

Peterson, W.J. "The Walt Whitman Club." *Palimpsest*, 51: 323-48 (1970).

Rodgers, H.I. "The Muses Organized: The Formation of Literary Societies in the South." *SHR*, 6: 233-41 (Su 72).

Rugheimer, Virginia. "Charleston Library Society." *SAB*, 8: 4-5 (O 42); *Southeastern Lib*, 5: 137-40 (Je 55).

Webber, M.L. "The Georgetown Library Society." *SCHM*, 25: 94-100 (1924).

Literary Trends and Attitudes. Anon. "The Expatriate Tradition 'Then and Now.'" *PaR*, 9: 158-70 (Wi-Sp 65).

Adams, R.P. "Permutations of American Romanticism." *SRom*, 9: 249-68 (Fa 70).

Adler, Renata. "Polemic and the New Reviewers." *NY*, 40: 60-80 (4 Jl 64).

Alter, Robert. "The Self-Conscious Moment: Reflections on the Aftermath of Modernism." *TriQ*, 33: 209-230 (Sp 75).

Anderson, D.D. "The Artist in America." *Un College Q*, 14: 10-5 (1968).

Andersson, Thomas. "'As Crazy as Two Waltzing Mice': About American Similies." *MSpr*, 65: 223-6 (1971).

Atterbury, L.W. "The American West and the Archetypal Orphan." *WAL*, 5: 205-17 (Fa 70).

Baacke, Dieter. "Untergrund: Einblick und Ausblick." *Merkur*, 24: 526-41 (Je 70).

Ballowe, James. "Mythic Vision in American Literature." *Disc*, 10: 324-32 (Su 67).

Banta, Martha. "American Apocalypses: Excrement and Ennui." *SLImag*, 7: 1-30 (Sp 74).

Barnes, D.R. "The Bosom Serpent: A Legend in American Literature and Culture." *JAF*, 85: 111-22 (1972).

Barroff, Marie. "Creativity, Poetic Language, and the Computer." *YR*, 60: 481-513 (Je 71).

Beebe, Maurice. "What Modernism Was." *JML*, 3: 1065-1084 (Jl 74).

Bellamy, J.D. "The Way We Write Now." *ChiR*, 25: 45-9 (1973).

Bellowe, James. "Mythic Vision in American Literature." *Disc*, 10: 324-32 (Su 67).

Benton, R.P. "The Problems of Literary Gothicism." *ESQ*, 18: 5-9 (1Q 72).

Bercovitch, Sacvan. "The Image of America: From Hermeneutics to Symbolism." *BuR*, 20: 3-12 (1972).

Bier, Jesse. "The Romantic Coordinates of American Literature." *BuR*, 18: 16-33 (Fa 70).

Boitano, Piero. "L'intellecttuale americano tra la nuova scienza e l'arte." *SA*, 14: 431-50 (1968).

Bosmajian, H.A. "The Language of White Racism." *CE*, 31: 263-72 (D 69).

Boynton, P.H. "American Neglect of American Literature." *Nation*, 102: 478-80 (4 My 16).

Bradbury, Malcolm. "The Teaching of English Literature: The Arrival of American Literature." *TLS*, 25 July, 1968, pp. 789-90.

Bradford, M.E. "The Agrarian Inheritance: An Affirmation." *PGCHHC*, 4: 3-12 (1973).

Brooks, Cleanth. "The Current State of American Literature." *SoR*, 9: 273-87 (Sp 73).

Brooks, M.E. "The Ideal and the Hero in Revisionist Literature." *L&I*, 14: 1-6 (1973).

Bruce, R.C. "Divisions on a Ground: The Raptors of Reason." *Prose*, 2: 37-60 (1971).

Buchloh, P.G. "Tendenzen und Charakteristika der amerikanischen Literatur nach dem Zweiten Weltkrieg." *LWU*, 7: 180-90 (O 74).

Budd, L.J. "The Hungry Bear of American Realism." *ALR*, 5: 485-7 (Fa 72).

Bush-Brown, Albert. "Art in America, 1970-85 (Six Dour Predictions and One Hopeful One)." *ASoc*, 7: 189-92 (1970).

Calverton, V.F. "The Decade of Convictions." *Bkm*, 71: 486-90 (Ag 30).

———. "The American Literary Radicals." *ModQ*, 3: 251-62 (D 26).

Cardwell, G.A. "The Plantation House: An Analogical Image." *SLJ*, 2: 3-21 (1969).

Cargill, Oscar. "Techniques for Survival II." *CEA*, 34: 2-6, 3-7 (Ja, Mr 72).

Cashdollar, C.D. "The Transcendence of Time: American Myth and Archaic Man." *IllQ*, 37: 12-26 (#1 74).

Carter, Everett. "The Meaning of, and in, Realism." *AR*, 12: 78-94 (Sp 52).

Cawelti, J.G. "Beatles, Batman, and the New Aesthetic." *Midway*, 9: 49-70 (1968).

———. "Notes Toward an Aesthetic of Popular Culture." *JPC*, 5: 255-68 (1971).

Cobb, Buell. "The Sacred Harp of the South: A Study of Origins, Practices, and Present Implications." *LaStud*, 7: 107-21 (Su 68).

Cowley, Malcolm. "What Books Survive from the 1930's?" *JAmSt*, 7: 293-300 (D 73).

Coy, J.J. "Complicidad e inocencia en la literatura americana." *RO*, 7: 352-66 (Je 66).

Cravens, Hamilton., and J.C. Burnham. "Psychology and Evolutionary Naturalism in American Thought, 1890-1940." *AQ*, 23: 635-57 (D 71).

Crews, Frederick. "Do Literary Studies Have an Ideology?" *PMLA*, 85: 423-8 (1970).

Curnow, Wystan. "Romanticism and Modern American Criticism." *SRom*, 12: 777-99 (Fa 73).

Davis, R.B. "The Americanness of American Literature: Folk and Historical Themes and Materials in Formal Writing." *LC*, 3: 10-22 (1959).

———. "The Gentlest Art in Seventeenth-Century Virginia." *TSL*, 2: 51-63 (1957).

Davis, R.L. "All the New Vibrations: Romanticism in Twentieth-Century America." *SWR*, 54: 256-70 (Su 69).

Denysova, T.N. "Literaturna spadsčynx 'cervonyx trydcjatyx.'" *RLz*, 18: 34-7 (1974).

Dew, Marjorie. "Realistic Innocence." *ALR*, 5: 487-9 (Fa 72).

Diggins, J.P. "The Perils of Naturalism." *AQ*, 23: 153-80 (My 71).

Ditsky, John. "Everyman Meets Caliban and Ariel: Mythic Opposition in Popular Art." *UDR*, 10: 33-7 (Su 73).

Donoghue, Denis. "The American Style of Failure." *SR*, 82: 407-32 (Su 74).

Donaldson, Scott. "Family Crises in the Popular Novel of Nixon's Administration." *JPC*, 6: 374-82 (Fa 72).

Duggan, F.X. "Doctrine and the Writers of the American Renaissance." *ESQ*, 39: 45-51 (1965).

Egbert, D.D. "The Idea of Avant-garde in Art and Politics." *AHR*, 73: 339-66 (D 67).

Ehrenpreis, Irvin. "Viewpoint." *TLS*, 8 F 74, p. 132.

Ehrstine, J.W. "Romantic Theory: A Calling of the Wits Together." *ESQ*, 18: 186-96 (3Q 72).

Elliott, G.P. "Destroyers, Defilers, and Confusers of Men." *Atl*, 222: 74-80 (D 68).

Ellman, Richard. "Contemporary Directions in Literature." *BaratR*, 3: 63-8 (1968).

Emerson, Donald. "The Remaking of 'American Literature.'" *TWA*, 60: 45-51 (1972).

Faust, W.M. "Zwei Anthologien: Zwei Generationen Expressionisten und Pop." *RLV*, 37: 731-40 (1971).

Fava, Luigi. "Letteratura e poesia 'Beat' negli stati Uniti." *AB*, 7: 1-23 (1969).

Felgar, Robert. "Black Content, White Form." *SBL*, 5: 28-31 (Wi 74).

Fender, Stephen. "The Western and the Contemporary." *JAmSt*, 6: 97-108 (1972).

Fisher, Edward. "Lost Generations, Then and Now." *ConnR*, 6: 13-25 (1972).

Fort, Keith. "Modern Literature and a Set of Assumptions." *WHR*, 21: 3-10 (W 67).

Fox, Hugh. "From Pragmatism to Objectivism: An Overview of North American Empiricism." *Rendezvous*, 2: 1-7 (#2 67).

———. "Some Notes on the Underground." *UWR*, 6: 18-24 (1970).

Franklin, H.B., et al. "Science Fiction: The New Mythology." *Extrapolation*, 10: 69-113 (My 69).

Franklin, W.S. "Beauty and the Use: The American View of Nature." *Topic*, 25: 19-26 (Sp 73).

Freedman, Ralph. "Refractory Visions: The Contours of Literary Expressionism." *ConL*, 10: 54-74 (Wi 69).

Geiger, L.G. "Muckrakers—Then and Now." *JQ*, 43: 469-76 (Au 66).

Geselbracht, R.H. "Transcendental Renaissance in the Arts." *NEQ*, 48: 463-86 (D 75).

Gilman, Richard. "Art and History." *PR*, 25: 274-86 (Sp 68).

Gindin, James. "The Fable Begins to Break Down." *WSCL*, 8: 1-18 (Wi 67).

Glazer, P.M. "From the Old Left to the New: Radical Criticism in the 1940's." *AQ*, 24: 584-603 (D 72).

Goodheart, Eugene. "Eros, Politics, and Pornography." *Midstream*, 15: 32-9 (Ap 69).

Graff, Gerald. "The Myth of the Post-Modernist Breakthrough." *TriQ*, 26: 383-417 (Wi 73).

Graham, John. "Fiction and Film." *MMR*, 1: 22-5 (1971).

Gurian, Jay. "American Studies and the Creative Present." *MASJ*, 10: 75-84 (Sp 69).

Hedley, L.W. "The Retreat of the Avant-Garde." *GaR*, 24: 441-52 (Wi 70).

Hagopian, J.V. "Mau-Mauing the Literary Establishment." *StN*, 3: 135-47 (Su 71).

Halio, Jay. "The Way It Is—And Was." *SoR*, 6: 250-62 (Ja 70).

Hartley, P.E. "Ecological Vision in American Literature." *Ecologist*, 5: 94-6 (#3 75).

Hassan, Ihab. "The New Gnosticism: Speculations on an Aspect of the Postmodern Mind." *Boun2*, 1: 547-69 (Sp 73).

Hauck, Richard. "The Dickens Controversy in the *Spirit of the Times*." *PMLA*, 85: 278-83 (Mr 70).

Hedley, L.W. "The Retreat of the Avant-Garde." *GaR*, 24: 441-52 (Wi 70).

Herkscher, August. "Changing Styles in Art and Entertainment." *An Am Acad Pol and Soc Sci*, 358: 354-82 (Jl 68).

Higuchi, Hideo. "American Literary War in the Thirties." *DSE*, 10: 53-72 (Mr 75).

Hollander, Robert. "Literary Consciousness and the Consciousness of Literature." *SR*, 33: 115-27 (Wi 75).

Hopper, S.R. "Challenge and Ordeal in Religion and Literature." *EUQ*, 22: 62-71 (Sp 67).

Howe, Irving. "Anarchy and Authority in American Literature." *DQ*, 2: 5-30 (Au 67).

Hux, Samuel. "On American Literary Existentialism." *Forum(H)*, 7: 37-42 (Fa-Wi 69).

Iwamoto, Iwao. "Saikin no America shosetsu—katari e no kaiki." *EigoS*, 117: 134-6 (1971).

Johnson, Curt. "'My Culture Agency Problem—and Yours.'" *Smith*, 11: 74-8 (My 70).

Johnson, W.A. "Toward a Redefinition of Modernism." *Boun2*, 2: 539-56 (1974).

Jones, H.M. "The Genteel Tradition." *HLB*, 18: 5-20 (Ja 70).

Kahn, S.J. "Will and Power in American Literature." *SA*, 16: 429-51 (1970).

Kampf, Louis. "'It's Alright, Ma (I'm Only Bleeding)': Literature and Language in the Academy." *PMLA*, 87: 377-83 (My 72).

———. "The Scandal of Literary Scholarship." *HM*, 235: 86-91 (D 67).

Kaplan, R.B. "On a Note of Protest (In a Minor Key): Bidialectism vs. Bidialectism." *CE*, 30: 386-9 (F 69).

Karl, F.R. "Picaresque and the American Experience." *YR*, 57: 196-212 (Wi 68).

Karolides, N.J. "Changing Conceptions of the Pioneer in the Contemporary American Novel." *WSL*, 4: 18-28 (1967).

Kasson, J.S. "*The Voyage of Life*: Thomas Cole and Romantic Disillusionment." *AQ*, 27: 42-56 (Mr 75).

Katana, Anna. "From Lazarillo to Augie March: A Study into Some Picaresque Attitudes." *Hungarian Stud in Eng*, 4: 87-103 (1969).

Katz, Joseph. "Bibliography and the Rise of American Literary Realism." *SAF*, 2: 75-88 (Sp 74).

Katz, Seymour. "'Culture' and Literature in American Studies." *AQ*, 20: 318-29 (Su 68).

Kaufmann, Walter. "The Reception of Existentialism in the United States." *Salmagundi*, 10-1: 69-96 (1969-70).

Kazin, Alfred. "Art on Trial." *HM*, 235: 51-5 (O 67).

———. "Form and Anti-Form in Contemporary Literature." *BaratR*, 4: 92-8 (1969).

———. "The Literary Sixties, When the World Was Too Much With Us." *NYT*, 21 D 69, pp. 1-3, 18.

Kazin, Alfred. "The War Novel: From Mailer to Vonnegut." *SatR*, 54: 13-5, 36 (6 F 71).

Keech, J.M. "The Survival of the Gothic Response." *StN*, 6: 130-44 (Su 74).

Kenney, A.P. "'Evidences of Regard': Three Generations of American Love Letters." *BNYPL*, 76: 92-119 (1972).

Kent, G.E. "Ethnic Impact in American Literature." *CLAJ*, 11: 24-37 (S 67).

———. "Patterns of the Harlem Renaissance: The Fork in the Road." *BlackW*, 21: 13-24, 76-80 (1972).

Knoll, R.E. "The Current Scene; From Dogma to Pluralism." *PrS*, 43: 100-8 (Sp 69).

Koch, Stephen. "Premature Speculations on the Perpetual Renaissance." *TriQ*, 10: 5-19 (Fa 67).

Kogan, Pauline. "Obscurantist Trends in American Criticism." *L&I*, 12: 37-44 (1972).

Korg, Jacob. "The Literary Esthetics of Dada." *Works*, 1: 43-54 (Sp 68).

Kostelanetz, Richard. "Dada and the Future of Fiction." *Works*, 1: 58-66 (Sp 68).

———. "The Rule of Ignorance & Philistinism." *MQR*, 12: 27-41 (1973).

Kuklick, Bruce. "Myth and Symbol in American Studies." *AQ*, 24: 435-50 (1972).

Kyria, Pierre. "Le Monde Americain." *RdP*, 120-5 (Mr 67).

Lane, J.B. "Violence and Sex in the Post-War Popular Urban Novel." *JPC*, 8: 295-308 (1974).

Lasater, A.E. "The Breakdown in Communication in the Twentieth-Century Novel." *SoQ*, 12: 1-14 (1973).

Levin, Harry. "From Obsession to Imagination: They Psychology of the Writer." *MQR*, 13: 183-202 (Su 74).

Levine, Edward. "The Inflated Image: Satire and Meaning in Pop Art." *SNL*, 6: 42-5 (Fa 68).

Lhamon, W.T. "Break and Enter to Breakaway: Scotching Modernism in the Social Novel of the American Sixties." *Boun2*, 3: 289-306 (Wi 75).

Liebman, Arthur. "Patterns and Themes in Afro-American Literature." *Eng Rec*, 20: 2-12 (F 70).

Lillyman, W.J. "The Blue Sky: A Recurrent Symbol." *CL*, 21: 116-24 (Sp 69).

Lindberg-Seyersted, Brita. "Variations of the American Success Story." *ES*, 53: 125-41 (Ap 72).

Logan, John. "A Note on the Inarticulate as Hero." *NMQ*, 38-9: 148-53 (Wi-Sp 69).

Lomax, M.L. "Fantasies of Affirmation: The 1920's Novel of Negro Life." *CLAJ*, 16: 232-46 (D 72).

London, Herbert. "American Romantics; Old and New." *ColQ*, 18: 15-20 (1969).

Love, G.A. "Ecology in Arcadia." *ColQ*, 21: 175-85 (Au 72).

McCarthy, Mary. "One Touch of Nature." *NY*, 45: 39-47 (24 Ja 70).

McCullen, J.T., and Jeri Tanner. "The Devil Outwitted in Folklore and Literature." *NoCF*, 17: 15-20 (1969).

Macey, S.L. "Nonheroic Tragedy: A Pedigree for American Tragic Drama." *CLS*, 6: 1-19 (Mr 69).

McLeod, Dan. "From *Banquet Years* to *A Moveable Feast*: Paris and the American Artist." *KAL*, 14: 76-81 (1972).

————. "Literary Responses to Nature in Japan and America." *KAL*, 14: 13-19 (1972).

McWilliams, W.C. "Natty Bumpo and the Godfather." *ColQ*, 24: 133-144 (Au 75).

Mann, J.J. "Is There and Angel in the House?" *IEngYb*, 21: 39-50 (Fa 71).

Marks, B.A. "Retrospective Narrative in Nineteenth Century American Literature." *CE*, 31: 366-75 (Ja 70).

Marler, R.F. "From Tale to Short Story: The Emergence of a New Genre in the 1850's." *AL*, 46: 153-69 (My 74).

Martin, J.S. "Rhetoric, Society and Literature in the Age of Jefferson." *MASJ*, 9: 77-90 (Sp 68).

Martin, Wallace. "The Sources of the Imagist Aesthetic." *PMLA*, 85: 196-204 (Mr 70).

Marx, Leo. "Pastoral Ideals and City Troubles." *JGE*, 20: 251-71 (1969).

May, J.B. "The Novel: Where Is It?" *Trace*, 61: 125-9, 236-9 (Su 66).

May, H.F. "The Problem of the American Enlightenment." *NLH*, 1: 201-14 (1970).

Meese, E.A. "Transcendentalism: The Metaphysics of the Theme." *AL*, 47: 1-20 (Mr 75).

Meyer, F.S. "Struggle over the Liberal Heritage." *NatR*, 22: 207 (24 F 70).

Michelson, Peter. "The Pleasures of Commodity, of How to Make the World Safe for Pornography." *AR*, 29: 77-90 (Sp 69).

Mikami, Hikaru. "How the Agrarian Myth Works in the American Mind." *KAL*, 14: 68-75 (1972).

Miller, J.E. "The 'Classic' American Writers and the Radicalized Curriculum." *CE*, 31: 565-70 (Ap 70).

Mills, N.C. "The Machine in the Anglo-American Garden." *CentR*, 14: 201-12 (1970).

Moore, C.L. "Tendencies in American Literature in the Closing Quarter of the Century." *Dial*, 29: 285-7 (1 N 00).

Morley, Felix. "Not a Great Divide." *ModA*, 14: 57-64 (1970).

Morsberger, R.E. "Segregated Surveys: American Literature." *NALF*, 4: 3-8 (1970).

Mphahele, Ezkiel. "The Function of Literature in the Present Time." *UDC*, 9: 16-45 (1975).

Mueller, R.C. "Transcendental Periodicals and the Orient." *ESQ*, 57: 52-7 (4Q 69).

Mulder, William. "Other Voices, Other Rooms: The Ethnic Strain in American Literature." *LCrit*, 10: 62-74 (#1 71).

Mulqueen, J.E. "Conservatism and Criticism: The Literary Standards of the American Whigs, 1845-52." *AL*, 41: 355-72 (N 69).

Murray, Albert. "Literary Implications of the Blues: The Hero as Improviser." *Quadrant*, 16: 34-8 (N-D 72).

Musgrave, M.E. "Patterns of Violence and Non-Violence in Pro-Slavery and Anti-Slavery Fiction." *CLAJ*, 16: 426-37 (Je 73).

Narasimhaiah, C.D. "Traditional Values in American Literature." *LCrit*, 8: 1-12 (1967).

Nazareth, Peter. "To Hell and Back?" *Busara*, 5: 42-52 (1973).

Neil, J.M. "American Indifference to Art: An Anachronistic Myth." *AmS*, 13: 93-105 (Fa 72).

Nichols, C.H. "'Beat': The Religion of the Disinherited." *NsM*, 21: 148-55 (1968).

Nin, Anais. "Novel of the Future." *STC*, 1: 79-108 (Sp 68).

Osborn, S.C. "Academic Challenge and the Humanities." *SHR*, 4: 293-8 (1970).

Parker, F.D. "Nienteenth-Century Travel Impressions: The U.S.A. and Guatemala." *I-AmRB*, 18: 400-14 (O-D 68).

Parkes, H.B. "Freedom and Order in Western Literature." *DQ*, 4: 1-18 (Su 69).

Parsons, C.O. "Steamboating as Seen by Passengers and River Men: 1875-1884." *MissQ*, 24: 19-34 (Wi 70-71).

Pauly, T.H. "The Literary Sketch in Nineteenth-Century America." *TSLL*, 17: 489-504 (Su 75).

Pearce, R.H. "Gesta Humanorum: Notes on the Humanist as Witness." *Daedalus*, 435-50 (1970).

Peck, D.R. "'The Orgy of Apology': The Recent Reevaluation of Literature of the Thirties." *Sci&Soc*, 32: 371-82 (Fa 68).

Perry, J.D. "Gothic as Vortex: The Form of Horror." *MFS*, 19: 153-67 (Su 73).

Peter, John. "The Self-Effacement of the Novelist." *MalR*, #8: 119-28 (O 68).

Peyre, Henri. "Is Literature Dead? Or Dying?" *MQR*, 12: 297-313 (1973).

Pinsker, Sanford. "Rubbing Against the American Grain: Writing After Hemingway." *Quadrant*, 16: 48-54 (N-D 72).

Rawlyk, G.A. "An Emerging Maritime 'Popular' Stereotype of the United States." *JPC*, 4: 1052-9 (Sp 71).

Read, Herbert. "The Limits of Permissiveness." *MalR*, 9: 37-50 (Ja 69).

Ringe, Donald. "Early American Gothic." *ATQ*, 19: 3-8 (Su 73).

Roberts, Helene. "Pre-Raphaelite Ideals in America: *The Knight Errant*." *DCLB*, 5: 4-8 (Ap 62).

Robertson, Anthony. "The Changing American Literary Canon." *WCR*, 8: 61-3 (#3 74).

Robinson, J.K. "From Criticism to Historicism." *SoR*, 9: 692-709 (Jl 73).

Robinson, W.R. and Mary McDermott. "'2001' and the Literary Sensibility." *GaR*, 26: 21-37 (Sp 72).

Roemer, K.M. "American Utopian Literature (1888-1900): An Annotated Bibliography." *ALR*, 4: 227-54 (Su 71).

———. "Sex Roles, Utopia, and Change: The Family in Late Nineteenth-Century Utopian Literature." *AmS*, 13: 33-48 (Fa 72).

———. "'Utopia Made Practical': Compulsive Realism." *ALR*, 7: 273-6 (Su 74).

Rosa, A.F. "Charles Ives: Music, Transcendentalism, and Politics." *NEQ*, 44: 433-43 (S 71).

Roth, R.J. "The Puritan Backgrounds of American Naturalism." *Thought*, 45: 503-20 (Wi 70).

Rother, James. "Modernism and the Nonsense Styles." *ConL*, 15: 187-202 (Sp 74).

Rubin, L.D. "'Men of Letters' and Literary Journalism." *SR*, 82: 339-50 (Ap-Je 74).

Russell, Mariann. "White Man's Black Man." *CLAJ*, 17: 93-100 (S 73).

San Juan, Epifanio. "Antaeus: Reality and the American Imagination." *Exchange*, 40: 1-10 (1968).

Schulz, M.F. "Pop, Op, and Black Humor: The Aesthetics of Anxiety." *CE*, 30: 230-41 (D 68).

Scott, N.A. "History, Hope, and Literature." *Boun2*, 1: 577-603 (Sp 73).

Seaver, H.L. "American Victorian Taste." *PMHS*, 74: 21-32 (1962).

Shaw, P.W. "Old Genre, New Breed: The Postwar American Picaro." *Genre*, 7: 205-11 (1974).

Shawcross, J.T. "Some Literary Uses of Numerology." *HSL*, 1: 50-62 (1969).

Sheed, Wilfrid. "The Beat Movement, Concluded." *NYT*, 13 F 72, pp. 2, 32.

Sheehan, B.W. "Paradise and the Noble Savage in Jeffersonian Thought." *WMQ*, 26: 327-59 (Jl 69).

Shepherd, Esther. "The Tall Tale in American Literature." *PacR*, 2: 402-14 (D 21).

Shurr, W.H. "Typology and Historical Criticism of the American Renaissance." *ESQ*, 74: 57-63 (1Q 74).

Simpson, L.P. "Boston Ice and Letters in the Age of Jefferson." *MASJ*, 9: 58-76 (Sp 68).

―――. "The Southern Writer and the Great Literary Secession." *GaR*, 24: 393-412 (Wi 70).

Simon, J.D. "Reading the American Proletarian Fiction of the Thirties." *L&I*, 18: 25-32 (1974).

Slattery, Sister Mary Francis. "What Is Literary Realism?" *JAAC*, 31: 55-62 (1972).

Sloane, D.E.E. "In Search of a Realist Poetic Tradition." *ALR*, 5: 489-91 (Fa 72).

Slotkin, Richard. "Dreams and Genocide: The American Myth of Regeneration Through Violence." *JPC*, 5: 38-59 (Su 71).

Smith, H.N. "Tensions in the Humanities." *VQR*, 48: 185-91 (Sp 72).

Soderbergh, P.A. "Birth of a Notion: Edward Stratemeyer and the Movies." *MQ*, 14: 81-94 (1972).

Solotaroff, Theodore. "Some Random Thoughts on Contemporary Writing." *TCL*, 20: 270-6 (O 74).

Spender, Stephen. "The Immense Advantage." *LonM*, 12: 28-47 (O-N 72).

Spiller, R.E. "The Fulbright Program in American Studies Abroad: Retrospect and Prospect." *AmS*, 9: 9-16 (Fa 70).

Stein, R.B. "Seascape and the American Imagination: The Puritan Seventeenth Century." *EAL*, 7: 17-37 (Sp 72).

Stewart, D.H. "The Decline of WASP Literature in America." *CE*, 30: 403-17 (Mr 69).

Stockton, C.N. "Three Enlightenment Variations of Natural Law Theory." *EnE*, 1: 127-31 (1970).

Stone, G.W. "The Legacy of Sisyphus." *PMLA*, 83: 9-14 (1968).

Sullivan, Walter. "The Decline of Regionalism in Southern Literature." *GaR*, 18: 300-8 (Fa 64).

―――. "Southern Writers in the Modern World: Death by Melancholy." *SoR*, 6: 907-19 (Au 70).

―――. "'Where Have All the Flowers Gone?' The Novel in the Gnostic Twilight." *SR*, 78: 654-64 (1970).

―――. "'Where Have All the Flowers Gone?' The Short Story in Search of Itself." *SR*, 78: 531-42 (1970).

Tanner, Tony. "Notes for a Comparison Between American and European Romanticism." *JAmSt*, 2: 83-103 (Ap 68).

Tanselle, G.T. "Textual Study and Literary Judgment." *PBSA*, 65: 109-22 (2Q 71).

Trachtenberg, Stanley. "American Dreams, American Realities." *AR*, 28: 277-92 (1968).

Turner, Arlin. "Literature and the Student in the Space Age." *CE*, 27: 519-22 (Ap 66).

―――. "Trends in American Literary Scholarship Across an Editor's Desk." *SCB*, 33: 5, 16-20 (Mr 63).

Tytell, John. "The Beat Generation and the Continuing American Revolution." *ASch*, 42: 308-17 (Sp 73).

Valgemae, Mardi. "Expressionism and the New American Drama." *TCL*, 17: 227-34 (1971).

Wachal, Robert. "The Machine in the Garden: Computers and Literary Scholarship, 1970." *CHum*, 5: 23-8 (1970).

Wagenheim, A.J. "Is It Time for an Epitaph? Notes on the Modern Essay." *DQ*, 3: 85-90 (Wi 69).

Wagner, Geoffrey. "The Sex Books." *DQ*, 6: 29-40 (Sp 71).

Wakefield, Dan. "The Literature of the Student Revolt: An Early Appraisal." *DQ*, 4: 1-22 (Au 69).

Walker, R.H. "Patterns in Recent American Literature." *Stetson Un Bul*, 65: 1-12 (O 67).

Weaver, R.M. "The American as a Regenerate Being." *SoR*, 4: 633-46 (1968).

Webb, Max. "Sunday Heroes: The Emergence of the Professional Football Novel." *JPC*, 8: 453-61 (1974).

Weisinger, Herbert. "Is the Renaissance Over?" *CentR*, 16: 283-92 (1972).

Welsh, J.R. "Succinct Perspective." *SAB*, 35: 49-50 (My 70).

Westbrook, Max. "Conservative, Liberal, and Western: Three Modes of American Realism." *SDR*, 4: 3-19 (Su 66).

———. "The Practical Spirit: Sacrality and the American West." *WAL*, 3: 193-205 (Fa 68).

White, G.A. "Ideology and Literature: *American Renaissance* and F.O. Matthiesson." *TriQ*, 23-24: 430-500 (1972).

Wickes, George. "From Breton to Barthelme: Westward the Course of Surrealism." *Proc*, 22: 208-14 (1971).

Wilson, J.B. "The Aesthetics of Transcendentalism." *ESQ*, 57: 27-34 (4Q 69).

Wilson, J.T. "Is Utopia Possible?" *Eng(L)*, 20: 51-5 (Su 71).

Wirzberger, Karl-Heinz. "'Great Tradition' oder Episode? Nonkonformismus, Protest and Engagement in der amerikanischen Gegenwartsliteratur." *ZAA*, 16: 5-24 (1968).

———. "The October Revolution and American Literature—Retrospective a. Conclusion." *ZAA*, 16: 229-56 (1968).

Wyld, L.D. "Technology and Human Values." *Vectors*, 4: 21-3 (My-Je 69).

Yevish, I.A. "Campus Rebellions: Their Literary Heritage." *ColQ*, 20: 471-7 (Sp 72).

Newpapers and Periodicals. Anon. "Darlings of the Press." *Palimpsest*, 50: 609-12 (N 69).

———. "Index to the *Christian Examiner*." *ATQ*, 4: 3-82 (1969).

———. "Index to the *New Jerusalem Magazine*." *ATQ*, 4: 161-297 (1969).

———. "Index to the *North American Review*." *ATQ*, 4: 83-160 (1969).

———. "*The Radical*." *ESQ*, 47: 128 (2Q 67).

———. "A Small Symposium on a Few (Alas, Defunct) Magazines." *SDR*, 6: 3-46 (Su 68).

Abramoske, D.J. "The Founding of the Chicago *Daily News*." *JISHS*, 59: 341-53 (Wi 66).

Aderman, R.N.M. "*Salmagundi* and the Outlander Tradition." *WSL*, 1: 62-8 (1964).

Anderson, Fenwick, "Inadequate to Prevent the Present: *The American Mercury* at 50." *JQ*, 51: 297-302 (1974).

Angoff, Charles. "The Mystique of *The Smart Set*." *LitR*, 11: 49-60 (Au 67).

Anderson, Margaret. "*The Little Review*." *HA*, 106: 18-9 (Wi 73).

Antupit, S.N. "Laid Out and Laid Waste: On the Visual Violation of American Magazines." *AR*, 29: 57-66 (Sp 69).

Arlen, M.J. "Notes on the New Journalism." *Atl*, 229: 43-7 (My 72).

Armstrong, W.M. "Additions to the *Nation Index*." *BNYPL*, 73: 267-74 (Ap 69).

Arner, R.D. "The Short, Happy Life of the Virginia *Monitor*." *EAL*, 7: 130-47 (Fl 72).

Ballou, E.B. "Scudder's *Atlantic*." *HLB*, 16: 326-53 (O 68).

Barnes, T.M. "Loyalist Newspapers of the American Revolution 1763-1783: A Bibliography." *PAAS*, 83: 217-40 (1973).

Beaver, D.D. "Altruism, Patriotism, and Science: Scientific Journals in the Early Republic." *AmS*, 12: 5-20 (1971).

Betts, J.R. "Sporting Journalism in Nineteenth Century America." *AQ*, 5: 39-56.

Brown, D.M. "The Quality Magazines in the Progressive Era." *M-A*, 53: 139-59 (Jl 71).

Bujas, Zeljko. "A *Time* Magazine Vocabulary Study." *SRAZ*, 33-36: 579-94 (1972-73).

Calhoun, R.J. "The Ante-Bellum Literary Twilight *Russell's Magazine*." *SLJ*, 3: 89-110 (Fa 70).

―――. "Literary Criticism in Southern Periodicals During the American Renaissance."
ESQ, 55: 76-82 (2Q 69).

―――. "*Southern Literary Magazines*, III: The Ante-Bellum Literary Twilight: *Russell's Magazine*." *SLJ*, 3: 89-110 (Fa 70).

Cameron, K.W. "Literary News in American Renaissance Newspapers." *ATQ*, 2: 29-37 (2Q 69); 5: 68-80 (1Q 70); 14: 112-25 (2Q 72); 20: 13-36, 195-97 (3Q 73).

Cane, Melville. "The Ladies of the *Dial*." *ASch*, 40: 316-21 (Sp 71).

Cappon, A.P. "Early Volume Numbers of *The University Review*: A Bibliographical Curiosity." *UR*, 36: 238-9 (1970).

Carson, B.F. "Richmond Renascence: The Virginia Writers' Club of the 1920's and *The Reviewer*." *Cabellian*, 2: 39-47 (Sp 70).

Carson, B.H. "Proclus' Sunflower and *The Dial*." *ELN*, 11: 200-2 (1974).

Carter, P.A. "Extravagant Fiction Today—Cold Fact Tomorrow: A Rationale for the First American Science-Fiction Magazines." *JPC*, 5: 842-57 (Sp 72).

Centing, R.R. "Ohio Magazines." *Ohioana Q*, 17: 93-8, 129-31 (1974).

Chambers, Stephen, and G.P. Mohrmann. "Rhetoric in Some American Periodicals, 1815-1850." *SM*, 37: 111-20 (Jl 70).

Cameron, K.W. "Literary News in American Renaissance Newspapers." *ATQ*, 2: 29-37 (2Q 69); 5: 68-80 (1Q 70); 14: 112-25 (2Q 72); 20: 13-36, 195-97 (3Q 70).

Chu, Limin. "Mirror of Darkness: The Images of China and the Chinese in the Fiction of the *Overland Monthly*." *TkR*, 2: 15-49 (1971); 3: 1-40 (1972).

Clemens, Cyril. "Benjamin Shillabu and His Carpet Bag." *NEQ*, 14: 519-37 (S 41).

Cohen, E.G. "Afro-American Periodicals." *HussR*, 5: 28-37 (1971).

―――. "Literary Reflections of Slavery in the *South Carolina Gazette*." *JNH*, 37: 188-93 (1952).

Cohen, Hennig. "Unnoticed Americanisms from *Russell's Magazine*." *AS*, 29: 226-7 (1954).

Cohn, Jan. "The Civil War in Magazine Fiction of the 1860's." *JPC*, 4: 355-82 (Fa 70).

―――. "The Negro Character in Northern Magazine Fiction of the 1860's." *NEQ*, 43: 572-92 (D 70).

Colvert, J.B. "The Function of the Academic Critical Quarterly." *MissQ*, 23: 95-101 (Sp 70).

Conroy, Jack. "The Literary Underworld of the Thirties." *New Letters*, 40: 51-72 (Sp 74).

Corman, Cid. "A Note on the Founding of *Origin*." *Serif*, 5: 29-30 (1968).

Crouthamel, J.L. "James Gordon Bennett, the *New York Herald*, and the Development of Newspaper Sensationalism." *NYH*, 54: 294-316 (Jl 73).

Crume, J.B. "Children's Magazines, 1826-1857." *JPC*, 6: 698-706 (Sp 73).

Cummins, R.W. "The *Monthly Magazine* and Emerson." *ATQ*, 1: 64-76 (1Q 69).

Curran, R.T. "The Individual and the Military Institution in Hemingway's Novels and *Collier's* Dispatches." *RLV*, 34: 26-39 (1968).

Dante, H.L. "The Chicago *Tribune's* 'Lost' Years, 1865-1874." *JISHS*, 58: 139-64 (Su 65).

Davis, R.B. "A Fitting Representation: Seventy-Five Years of the *Virginia Magazine of History and Biography*." *VMHB*, 75: 259-79 (1967).

Davis, T.M. "The Poetry of *The Ladies' Home Journal* from 1895 to 1905." *AmS*, 12: 21-35 (Sp 71).

DeMott, Benjamin. "In and Out of Universal City: Reflections on the New Journalism and the Old Fiction." *AR*, 29: 7-13 (Sp 69).

Dickey, I.B. "Bella French Swisher: Texas Editor and Litterateur." *SwAL*, 1: 8-11 (1971).

Donaldson, Scott. "*The New Yorker*, Old and New." *SR*, 83: 676-85 (Fa 75).

————. "The Old *World*, the New Journalism, and the Novel." *SR*, 82: 527-37 (1974).

Dorbin, Sanford. "Charles Bukowski and the Little/Small Press Movement." *SCUL*, 2: 17-32 (My 70).

Dorn, J.H. "*Sunday Afternoon:* The Early Social Gospel in Journalism." *NEQ*, 44: 238-58 (Je 71).

Duke, Maurice. "*The Reviewer*: A Bibliographical Guide to a Little Magazine." *RALS*, 1: 58-103 (Sp 71).

Eddy, S.L. "*The Northern Monthly and New Jersey Magazine*: May 1867 - June 1868." *JRUL*, 30: 40-52 (1967).

Eid, L.V. "'What Fools These Fanatics Be'—*Puck* and the Temperance Crusade, 1877-1896." *IllQ*, 38: 5-20 (Su 75).

Ellis, D.L. "The Underground Press in America: 1955-1970." *JPC*, 5: 102-24 (Su 71).

Ellison, G.R. "William Tappan Thompson and the *Southern Miscellany*, 1842-1844." *MissQ*, 23: 155-68 (Sp 70).

Ephron, Nora. "Helen Gurley Brown Only Wants to Help." *Esquire*, 73: 74, 117, 118 (F 70).

Farrell, N.L. "A Subject Index to The *Theatre Annual*, 1942-1969." *ThDoc*, 2: 125-34 (1969-70).

Firda, R.A. "German Philosophy of History and Literature in the *North American Review*, 1815-1860." *JHI*, 32: 133-42 (1971).

Fisher, Karen. "Cashing in on Fear and Fantasy." *Nation*, 213: 334-7 (O 71).

Foner, P.S. "A Labor Voice for Black Equality: The Boston *Daily Evening Voice*, 1864-1867." *Sci&Soc*, 38: 304-26 (Fa 74).

Free, W.J. "American Fiction in the *Columbian Magazine*, 1786-1792." *BB*, 25: 150-1 (My-Ap 68).

G.S. "*The Saturday Evening Post*." *NRep*, 1: 29 (23 Ja 15).

Genizi, Haim. "V.F. Calverton, A Radical Magazinist for Black Intellectuals, 1920-40." *JNH*, 57: 241-53 (Jl 72).

Gerber, G.E. "Poe and *The Manuscript*." *PoeS*, 6: 27 (Je 73).

Goodheart, Eugene. "Eros, Politics, and Pornography: A Decade with *Evergreen Review*." *Midstream*, 15: 32-9 (Ap 69).

————. "*The New York Review*: A Close Look." *Dissent*, 17: 135-43 (Mr-Ap 70).

Goodman, Walter. "On the (N.Y.) Literary Left." *AR*, 29: 67-75 (Sp 69).

Gross, Beverly. "Culture and Anarchy: Whatever Happened to Lit Magazines?" *AR*, 29: 43-56 (Sp 69).

Guenther, Paul, and Nicholas Joost. "Little Magazines and the Cosmopolitan Tradition." *PLL*, 6: 100-10 (Wi 70).

Guilds, J.C. "The 'Lost' Number of the *Southern Literary Gazette*." *SB*, 22: 266-73 (1969).

————. "Simms as Editor and Prophet: The Flowering and Early Death of the Southern Magnolia." *SLJ*, 4: 69-92 (Sp 72).

————. "William Gilmore Simms and the *Southern Literary Gazette*." *SB*, 21: 59-92 (1968).

Haberland, P.M. "The Reception of German Literature in Baltimore's Literary Magazines, 1800-1875." *German-Am Stud*, 7: 69-92 (1974).

Halaas, D.F. "Frontier Journalism in Colorado." *ColM*, 44: 185-203 (Su 67).

Hall, Donald. "The *Harvard Advocate*." *NYT*, 15 My 66, pp. 2, 42.

Hartley, Lodwick. "*The North American Review* on Laurence Sterne: A Document in a Literary Reputation." *AL*, 44: 299-306 (My 72).

Haslam, Gerald. "Literature of *The People*: Native American Voices." *CLAJ*, 15: 153-70 (1971).

Hauck, Richard. "The Dickens Controversy in the *Spirit of the Times*." *PMLA*, 85: 278-83 (Mr 70).

Hauck, R.B. "Predicting a Native Literature: William T. Porter's First Issue of the *Spirit of the Times*." *MissQ*, 22: 77-84 (Wi 68-69).

Healey, J.W. "Little Magazines: 'A Little Madness Helps.'" *PrS*, 47: 335-42 (1973).

Hentoff, Nat. "Behold the New Journalism—It's Coming After You!" *EvR*, 12: 49-51 (Jl 68).

Herron, I.H. "Charleston: Ante Bellum Magazine Center." *SWR*, 22: 100-6 (1936).

Hirsch, P.M. "An Analysis of *Ebony*: The Magazine and Its Readers." *JQ*, 45: 261-70, 292 (Su 68).

Holder, S.C. "The Family Magazine and the American People." *JPC*, 7: 264-79 (1973).

Huff, Lawrence. "Joseph Addison Turner and His Quarterly, the *Plantation*." *GHQ*, 54: 493-504 (Wi 70).

Hunt, Todd. "A Magazine Publisher's Lot is Not a Happy One." *JRUL*, 34: 17-22 (D 70).

Israel, Jerry. "Muckrake and Manchu: The Image of China in the American Press, 1900-1912." *JRUL*, 31: 58-64 (Je 68).

Jacobs, D.M. "William Lloyd Garrison's *Liberator* and Boston's Blacks, 1830-1865." *NEQ*, 44: 259-77 (Je 71).

Jacobs, R.D. "Southern Literary Magazines, I: Campaign for a Southern Literature: The *Southern Literary Messenger*." *SLJ*, 2: 66-98 (Fa 69).

Janssens, G.A. "*The Dial* and *The Seven Arts*." *PLL*, 4: 442-58 (1968).

Johnson, A.A. and R.M. "Forgotten Pages: Black Literary Magazines in the 1920's." *JAmSt*, 8: 363-82 (1974).

Johnson, Spud, *et al.* "A Small Symposium on a Few (Alas, Defunct) Magazines." *SDR*, 6: 3-46 (Au 68).

Joost, Nicholas. "Culture vs. Power: Randolph Bourne, John Dewey, and *The Dial*." *MWQ*, 9: 245-59 (Ap 68).

———. "*The Dial*: A Journalistic Emblem and Its Tradition." *SP*, 64: 167-81 (Ja 67).

———. "Ezra Pound and *The Dial*—A Few Translations." *Sou'Wester*, 14: 59-71 (30 O 70).

———. "Some Primitives in *The Dial* of the Twenties." *ForumH*, 10: 34-44 (1972); 11: 12-8 (1973).

Kay, C.M. and Donald. "American Literary Periodicals from 1790-1830." *BB*, 29: 126-7, 139 (O-D 72).

Kendall, John. "George Wilkins Kendall and the Founding of the New Orleans *Picayune*." *LaHQ*, 11: 261-85 (Ap 28).

Kennedy, J.G. "The Magazine Tales of the 1830's." *ATQ*, 24: 23-9 (Fa 74).

Korg, Jacob. "Language Change and Experimental Magazines, 1910-1930." *ConL*, 13: 144-61 (Sp 72).

Kornbluth, Jesse. "This Place of Entertainment Has No Fire Exit: The Underground Press and How It Went." *AR*, 29: 91-9 (Sp 69).

Kostelanetz, Richard. "Critical Writing for American Magazines: A Memoir and a Valedictory." *Works*, 1: 84-95 (Su 68).

Krim, Seymour. "The Newspaper as Literature. Literature as Leadership." *EvR*, 12: 31-2, 89-97 (Ag 67).

Lamplugh, G.R. "The Image of the Negro in Popular Magazine Fiction, 1875-1900." *JNH*, 57: 177-89 (Ap 72).

Lang, W.L. "Francis Vincent and the *Blue Hen's Chicken*." *DH*, 13: 28-45 (Ap 68).

Lantz, H.R., et al. "Pre-Industrial Patterns in the Colonial Family in America: A Content Analysis of Colonial Magazines." *AmSR*, 33: 413-26 (1968).

Lebreton-Savigny, Monique. "The Death of Victor Hugo as Reported in the American Press." *RLC*, 43: 385-414 (1969).

Leiter, Robert. "Money Is a Kind of Poetry." *Nation,* 219: 504-7 (16 N 74).

*Lemay, J.A.L. "A Calendar of American Poetry in the Colonial Newspapers and Magazines and in the Major English Magazines Through 1765." *PAAS*, 79: 291-392 (O 69); 80: 71-222, 353-469 (Ap, O 70).

Linneman, W.R. "Immigrant Stereotypes: 1880-1900." *SAH*, 1: 28-39 (Ap 74).

Lochard, M.T.P. "The Negro Press in Illinois." *JISHS*, 56: 570-91 (Au 63).

Loeb, Harold. "*Broom*: Beginning and Revival." *ConnR*, 4: 5-12 (1970).

Lovoll, O.S. "North Dakota's Norweigian-Language Press Views World War I, 1914-1917." *NDQ*, 39: 73-84 (Wi 71).

Loy, E.H. "Editorial Opinion and American Imperialism: Two Northwest Newspapers." *Oregon Hist Q*, 72: 209-24 (S 71).

McCann, W.C. "Midwestern Humorous Journalism." *Soc for Study of Midwestern Lit*, 1: 28-34 (1974).

McCarthy, Joe. "The Lordly Journalists." *Holiday*, 31: 142-7, 186-93 (Ap 62).

McClary, B.H. "Irving, Lockhart, and the *Quarterly Review*." *BNYPL*, 76: 231-6 (1972).

McCullough, J.B. "Mark Twain and Journalistic Humor Today." *EJ*, 60: 591-5 (My 71).

McFarland, R.E. "A Survey of Poetry in the Periodicals." *CE*, 36: 475-6 (1974).

Maloney, S.R. "Not for the 'Smart-Set in Omaha': The *Georgia Review* and Southern Literature." *NOR*, 4: 197-202 (1974).

Marovitz, S.E. "Romance or Realism? Western Periodical Literature: 1893-1902." *WAL*, 10: 45-58 (My 75).

May, Derwent. "American Little Magazines." *TLS*, 18 S 69, pp. 1032-3.

Meredith, H.L. "The Agrarian Reform Press in Oklahoma 1889-1922." *ChronO*, 50: 82-94 (S 72).

Meriwether, J.E. "Faulkner's Correspondence with Scribner's Magazine." *Proof*, 3: 253-82 (1973).

Mews, S.E. "'Pack den Tiger in dem Tank' The American Press and the German Language." *Die Unterrichtspraxis*, 8: 18-21 (1970).

Milton, J.R. "Inside the *South Dakota Review*." *MASJ*, 10: 68-78 (1969).

Mishra, V.M. "The Lutheran Standard: 125 Years of Denominational Journalism." *JQ*, 45: 71-6 (Sp 68).

Montesi, A.J. "Huey Long and *The Southern Review*." *JML*, 3: 63-74 (F 73).

Moore, Marianne. "*The Dial*." *Life and Letters Today*, 27: 175-83 (D 40); 28: 3-9 (Ja 41).

Moore, R.S. "The Magazine and the Short Story in the Ante-Bellum Period." *SAB*, 38: 44-51 (My 73).

———. "A Distinctively Southern Magazine': The *Southern Bivouac*." *SLJ*, 2: 51-65 (Sp 70).

Morey, F.L. "From Reading to Publishing Emily Dickinson: The Prenatal History of the *EDB*." *EDB*, 22: 128-30 (1972).

Moskowitz, Sam. "The Gernsback 'Magazines' No One Knows." *RQ*, 4: 272-4 (Mr 71).

Mueller, R.C. "Thoreau's Selections from *Chinese Four Books* for *The Dial*." *TJQ*, 4: 1-8 (1972).

———. "Transcendental Periodicals and the Orient." *ESQ*, 57: 52-57 (4Q 69).

Munson, Gorham. "A Comedy of Exiles." *LitR*, 12: 41-75 (1968).

Muraskin, William. "An Alienated White: Short Stories in *The Crisis*, 1910-1950." *JBlackS*, 1: 282-305 (Mr 71).

*Myerson, Joel. "An Annotated List of Contributions to the Boston *Dial*." *SB*, 26: 133-66 (1973).

———. "The Contemporary Reception of the Boston *Dial*." *RALS*, 3: 203-20 (Au 73).

———. "A Union List of the Dial (1840-1844) and Some Information about Its Sales." *PBSA*, 67: 322-8 (3Q 73).

Newman, John. "The *Camp Dodger*: A Military Newspaper of the First World War." *BI*, 10: 24-30 (1969).

Nichols, R.L. "Printer's Ink and Red Skins: Western Newspapermen and Indians." *KanQ*, 3: 82-7 (Fa 71).

Nachman, S.A. "A Collation of DeBow's Review, Giving the Date, the Number and the Title of Each Issue and Volume, from 1846-1880...." *Bul Biblio Soc Am*, 4: 27-32 (1912).

Nobile, Philip. "A Review of *The New York Review of Books*." *Esquire*, 77: 103-26, 206-12 (Ap 72).

Norton, Wesley. "Religious Newspapers in Antebellum Texas." *SHQ*, 79: 145-65 (O 75).

Novak, E.G. "'*New Masses*' Five Yearly Indexes of the Poetry, Fiction, Criticism, Drama and Reviews for the Years 1929-33." *BB*, 28: 89-108 (Jl-S 71).

Pallak, Felix. "Library of Little Mags." *LJ*, 85: 3029-34 (15 S 60).

Paltsits, V.H. "New Light on *Publick Occurences*: America's First Newspaper." *PAAS*, 59: 75-88 (1949).

Peters, G.W. "*The American Weekly*." *JQ*, 48: 466-71, 479, (1971).

Poger, Sidney. "The Critical Stance of *The Dial*." *ESQ*, 57: 22-7 (4Q 69).

Pollin, B.R. "Emerson's Annotations in the British Museum Copy of the *Dial*." *SB*, 24: 187-95 (1971).

Porter, David. "The Southern Press and the Presidential Election of 1860." *WVH*, 33: 1-13 (O 71).

Querry, Ronald, and R.E. Fleming. "A Working Bibliography of Black Periodicals." *SBL*, 3: 31-6 (Su 72).

Rainey, P.M. "Vachel Lindsay and *The Village Magazine*." *DCLB*, 8: 22-9 (N 67).

Rees, R.A., and Marjorie Griffin. "Index and Author Guide to *The Family Companion* (1841-43)." *SB*, 25: 205-12 (1972).

Rees, R.A., and Marjorie Griffin. "William Gilmore Simms and *The Family Companion*." *SB*, 24: 109-29 (1971).

Reuben, P.P. "Thoreau in B.O. Flower's *Arena*." *TSB*, 117: 5-6 (Fa 71).

Rich, J.C. "60 Years of the Jewish *Daily Forward*." *NewL*, 40, supp: 1-38 (3 Je 57).

Roach, S.F. "*The Georgia Gazette* and the Stamp Act: A Reconsideration." *GHQ*, 55: 471-91 (1971).

Robbins, J.C. "Jefferson and the Press: The Resolution of an Antimony." *JQ*, 48: 421-30 (Au 71).

Roberts, Helene. "Pre-Raphaelite Ideals in America: *The Knight Errant*." *DCLB*, 5: 4-8 (Ap 62).

Roman, Anton. "The Genesis of the *Overland*." *Overland*, 40: 220-2 (S 02).

Rosenthal, Bernard. "*The Dial*, Transcendentalism, and Margaret Fuller." *ELN*, 8: 28-36 (S 70).

———. "Poe, Slavery, and the *Southern Literary Messenger*: A Reexamination." *PoeS*, 7: 29-38 (1974).

Rothman, Julius. "A Short History of *The Cabellian*." *NasR*, 2: 59-64 (1973).

Rouse, Parke. "The Raucous, Ribald Rousers of Virginia's Pioneer Newsmen." *Cwealth*, 35: 29-31 (Ja 68).

Rubin, L.D. "'Men of Letters' and Literary Journalism." *SR*, 82: 339-50 (Sp 74).

Russell, Robert. "Gawd, Those Jokes Were Painful." *Esquire*, 70: 164-9 (D 68).

Salzman, Jack. "Conroy, Mencken, and *The American Mercury*." *JPC*, 7: 524-8 (1973).

Schanche, D.A. "We Call on *The Saturday Evening Post*." *Esquire*, 72: 40-60 (N 69).

Schiller, J.G. "Magazines for Young America: The First Hundred Years of Juvenile Periodicals." *CLC*, 23: 24-39 (#3 1974).

Scholnick, Robert. "Whitman and the Magazines: Some Documentary Evidence." *AL*, 222-46 (1972).

Schopf, Bill. "The Image of the West in the *Century*, 1881-1889." *PosS*, 3: 8-13 (Mr 72).

Scott, J.E., and J.L. Franklin. "The Changing Nature of Sex References in Mass Circulation Magazines." *Public Opinion Q*, 36: 80-6 (Sp 72).

Sederberg, N.B. "Antebellum Southern Humor in the *Camden Journal*: 1826-1840." *MissQ*, 27: 41-74 (Wi 73-74).

Seiler, W.H. "Magazine Writers Look at Kansas, 1854-1904." *KHQ*, 38: 1-24 (Sp 72).

Seitz, D.C. "The American Press—The Foreign-Language Press." *Outlook*, 142: 176 (3 F 26).

Sherrill, Robert. "Weeklies and Weaklies." *AR*, 29: 25-42 (Sp 69).

Shpall, Leo. "A List of Selected Items of American-Jewish Interest in the Russian-Jewish Press." *PAJHS*, 38: 239-48 (Mr 49).

Shrell, Darwin. "Nationalism and Aesthetics in the *North American Review*: 1815-1850." *LSUS*, 8: 11-21 (1960).

Silet, C.L.P. "A Check-List of *The Seven Arts*." *Serif*, 9: 15-21 (Su 72).

Simms, L.M. "Aldine S. Kieffer and the *Musical Million*." *JPC*, 3: 281-6 (Fa 69).

Skipper, O.C. "*DeBow's Review* After the Civil War." *LaHQ*, 29: 355-93 (1946).

Slate, J.E. "The *Journal-American* Morgue." *LCUT*, 2: 83-9 (1970).

Sloane, D.E.E. "Censoring for *The Century Magazine*." *ALR*, 4: 255-67 (Su 71).

Smith, Dwayne, and Marc Matre. "Social Norms and Sex Roles in Romance and Adventure Magazines." *JQ*, 52: 308-15 (Su 75).

Smith, Gene. "A Little Visit to the Lower Depths Via the *Police Gazette*." *AH*, 23: 63-73 (O 72).

Sonnenschein, David. "Process in the Production of Popular Culture: The Romance Magazine." *JPC*, 6: 399-406 (Fl 72).

Soule, George. "Magazines and Democrats." *NRep*, 4: 78-9 (21 Ag 15).

Sowder, W.J. "Periodical Writers." *ESQ*, 53: 24-35 (4Q 68).

Spencer, T.J., J.E. Thiel, and Barbara Grazzini. "A Survey of American Theatrical Journalism." *DramC*, 11: 116-8 (Fa 68).

Sterne, R.C. "*The Nation* and Its Century." *Nation*, 201: 46 (20 S 65).

Stinson, Robert. "McClure's Road to *McClure's*: How Revolutionary Were 1890s Magazines?" *JQ*, 47: 256-62 (Su 70).

Stokes, D.R. "Five Letters from Jesse Holmes, the Fool Killer, to the Editor of the *Milton Chronicle*." *NCHR*, 50: 304-21 (Su 73).

Tauge, J.A. "William A. Gallaher, Champion of Western Literary Periodicals." *OH*, 69: 257-71 (Jl 60).

Tingley, D.F. "The 'Robin's Egg Renaissance': Chicago and the Arts, 1910-1920." *JISHS*, 63: 35-54 (Sp 70).

Tucker, Edward. "Philip Pendleton Cooke and *The Southern Literary Messenger*: Selected Letters." *MissQ*, 27: 79-99 (Wi 73-74).

Tucker, E.L. "'A Rash and Perilous Enterprize': *The Southern Literary Messenger* and the Men Who Made it." *VaCl*, 21: 14-20 (Su 71).

Tuttle, W.M., and Surendra Bhana. "Black Newspapers in Kansas." *AmS*, 13: 119-26 (Fl 72).

Newspapers and Periodicals

Valensise Fazio, Rachele. "*Little Review* (1914-1929)." *Siculorum Gymnasium*, 21: 188-208 (1968).

Van Brunt, H.L. "The Property of Love: Little Magazines in the Seventies." *Smith*, 15: 180-4 (My 74).

Wald, Alan. "Revolutionary Intellectuals: *Partisan Review* in the 1930's." *Occident*, 8: 118-33 (Sp 74).

Walker, D.D. "*The Mountain Man Journal*: Its Significance in a Literary History of the Fur Trade." *Western Hist Q*, 5: 307-18 (Jl 74).

Walters, R.G. "The Negro Press and the Image of Success: 1920-1939." *MASJ*, 11: 36-55 (1970).

Welsh, J.R. "An Early Pioneer: Legare's *Southern Review*." *SLJ*, 3: 79-97 (Sp 71).

West, J.L.W. "Early Backwoods Humor in the Greenville *Mountaineer*, 1826-1840." *MissQ*, 25: 69-82 (Wi 71).

Whittemore, Reed. "Aliens & Heretics: On the Near Future of Little Magazines." *Voyages*, 3: 26-32 (Sp 70).

Willey, E.P. "*The Looker-On* in America: Reception of a Latter-Day *Spectator*." *PBSA*, 64: 431-48 (4Q 70).

Winship, G.P. "French Newspapers in the United States, 1790-1800." *PBSA*, 14: 132-3 (1920).

Wolff, G.A. "Harvard *Advocate* Centennial Anthology." *ASch*, 36: 669-76 (Au 67).

Woodall, G.R. "More on the Contributors to the *American Quarterly Review* (1827-1837)." *SB*, 23: 199-207 (1970).

―――. "Nationalism in the Philadelphia *National Gazette and Literary Register*: 1820-1836." *Costerus*, 2: 225-36 (1972).

―――. "The Relationship of Robert Walsh, Jr., to the *Port Folio* and the Dennie Circle: 1803-1812." *PMHB*, 92: 195-219 (1968).

―――. "Walsh's War with the New York Literati." *TSL*, 15: 25-47 (1970).

Woodcock, George. "Poetry Magazines of the Thirties." *TamR*, 60: 68-74 (O 73).

Yelin, J.F. "An Index of Literary Materials in *The Crisis*, 1910-1934." *CLAJ*, 14: 452-65; 15: 197-234 (Je, D 71).

Philosophy and Philosophic Trends. Brown, Merle. "The Philosopher Critic." *UTMS*, 10: 3-12 (1970).

Buchanan, J.G. "Puritan Philosophy of History from Restoration to Revolution." *EIHC*, 104: 329-48 (O 68).

Champigny, Robert. "Philosophy as Literature." *UTMS*, 10: 40-9 (1970).

Casale, O.M. "Poe on Transcendentalism." *ESQ*, 50: 85-97 (1968).

Colacurcio, M.J. "A Better Mode of Evidence: The Transcendental Problem of Faith and Spirit." *ESQ*, 54: 12-22 (1969).

Das, S.P. "Beginnings of American Transcendentalism." *IJAS*, 1: 15-22 (1970).

Fiering, N.S. "Will and Intellect in the New England Mind." *WMQ*, 29: 515-58 (O 72).

Firda, R.A. "German Philosophy of History and Literature in the *North American Review*, 1815-1860." *JHI*, 32: 133-42 (1971).

Fridén, Georg. "Transcendental Idealism in New England." *NM*, 69: 256-71 (1968).

Gass, W.H. "Philosophy and the Form of Fiction." *UTMS*, 10: 50-66 (1970).

Gavin, W.J. "Chaadayev and Emerson—Two Mystic Pragmatists." *RusR*, 32: 119-30 (Ap 73).

Hassan, Ihab. "The New Gnosticism: Speculations on an Aspect of the Postmodern Mind." *Boun2*, 1: 547-69 (Sp 73).

Hux, Samuel. "On American Literary Existentialism." *Forum(H)*, 7: 37-42 (1969).

Kaufmann, Walter. "The Reception of Existentialism in the United States." *Salmagundi*, 10-1: 69-96 (1969-70).

Kher, I.N. "Transcendentalist Aesthetic and Problems of Conscience." *CRAS*, 6: 205-9 (1975).

McEdwards, M.G. "American Values: Circa 1920-1970." *QJS*, 57: 173-80 (1971).

McMullin, S.E. "Transcendentalism and the Canadian Confederation Poets." *RevL*, 4: 210-3 (1972).

May, H.F. "The Problem of the American Enlightenment." *NLH*, 1: 201-14 (1970).

Messe, E.A. "Transcendentalism: The Metaphysics of the Theme." *AL*, 47: 1-20 (Mr 75).

Mishra, A.K. "The Beatnik Vision of Life." *LCrit*, 9: 51-58 (Su 71).

Pearce, R.H. "Gesta Humanorum: Notes on the Humanist as Witness." *Daedalus*, 435-50 (1970).

Pizer, Donald. "The Problem of Philosophy in the Novel." *BuR*, 18: 53-62 (1970).

Raina, M.L. "Marxism and Literature—A Select Bibliography." *CE*, 34: 308-14 (1972).

Rein, I.J. "The New England Transcendentalists: Philosophy and Rhetoric." *P&R*, 1: 103-17 (Sp 68).

Roth, R.J. "The Philosophical Background of New England Puritanism." *IPQ*, 10: 570-97 (1970).

Shaw, Peter. "The Tough Guy Intellectual." *CritQ*, 8: 13-28 (Sp 66).

Shields, Allan. "On a Certain Blindness in William James and Others." *JAAC*, 27: 27-34 (Fa 68).

Stern, Alfred. "Some Philosphical Considerations of Literature." *Person*, 49: 163-82 (Sp 68).

Stockton, C.N. "Three Enlightenment Variations of Natural Law Theory." *EnE*, 1: 127-31 (1970).

Stoehr, Taylor. "Transcendentalist Attitudes Toward Communitism and Individualism." *ESQ*, 20: 65-90 (2Q 74).

Stubbs, J.C. "The Ideal in the Literature and Art of the American Renaissance." *ESQ*, 55: 55-63 (2Q 69).

Wilson, J.B. "A Fallen Idol of the Transcendentalists: Baron de Gérando." *CL*, 19: 334-40 (1967).

———. "The Aesthetics of Transcendentalism." *ESQ*, 57: 27-34 (4Q 69).

Poetry. "The New Kingdom of Ezrael." *TLS*, 2 F 73, pp. 1-2.

———. "Poetry by the Yard?" *TLS*, 73: 323-4 (29 Mr 74).

———. "Popular Literary Judgements." *Nation*, 94: 356-7 (11 Ap 12).

———. "A Symposium of Poets." *SDR*, 5: 3-23 (Au 67).

———. "Taking Poetry Too Seriously." *Nation*, 96: 173-4 (20 F 13).

Alden, R.M. "The New Poetry." *Nation*, 96: 386-7 (17 Ap 13).

Aldington, Richard. "Des Imagistes." *SatR*, 21: 3-4, 17-8 (16 Mr 40).

Alexander, F.M. "A Poetry of Calamity." *RSW*, 35: 100-8 (Mr 67).

Alford, John. "American Poetry." *Poetry and Drama*, 1: 485-8 (D 13).

Allen, H.D. "The Verse Problems of Early American Arithmetics." *JRUL*, 33: 49-52 (Je 70).

Alpert, Barry. "Post-Modern Oral Poetry: Buckminster Fuller, John Cage, and David Antin." *Boun2*, 3: 665-82 (Wi 75).

Altieri, Charles. "From Symbolist Thought to Immanence: The Ground of Post-modern American Poetics." *Boun2*, 1: 6-605-37 (Sp 73).

Poetry

Altrocchi, J.C. "California Biography in Poetry." *Pac Hist*, 15: 1-12 (Wi 71).

Alvarez, A. "The Art of Suicide." *PR*, 37: 339-58 (1970).

Amanuddin, Syed. "Avant-Gardism in Contemporary American Poetry." *Creative Moment*, 2: 20-8 (Sp 73).

————. "Poets from East and West." *Creative Moment*, 1: 35-40 (1972).

Anderson, D.D. "Ohio's Pioneer Poets." *NOQ*, 42: 9-18 (1969).

Antin, David. "Modernism and Postmodernism: Approaching the Present in American Poetry." *Boun2*, 1: 98-146 (Fa 72).

Ashleigh, Charles. "Des Imagistes." *Little R*, 1: 15-7 (Jl 14).

Atlas, James. "Yelping and Hooting: Some Developments in Contemporary American Poetry." *LonM*, 14: 15-32 (Ap-My 74).

Aubert, Alvin. "Black American Poetry: Its Language and the Folk Tradition." *BlAR*, 2: 71-80 (Sp-Su 71).

Autor, Hans. "Alaskan Poetry." *Alaska R*, 1: 48-55 (Sp 64).

Axelrod, Steven. "Colonel Shaw in American Poetry: 'For the Union Dead' and its Precursors." *AQ*, 24: 523-37 (O 72).

Balliet, C.A. "White on Black: A Checklist of Poetry by White Americans about the Black Experience, 1708-1970." *BNYPL*, 75: 424-64 (N 71).

Baraka, I.A. "Black Revolutionary Poets Should Also Be Playwrights." *BlackW*, 21: 4-6 (1972).

Barfoot, C.C. "New Poems, New Plays: An Annual Survey." *DQR*, 1: 15-26 (1971).

————. "New Poetry 1970." *DQR*, 3: 104-10 (1972).

Barksdale, R.K. "Urban Crisis and the Black Poetic Avant-Garde." *NALF*, 3: 40-4 (1969).

Barr, S. "Verse in Virginia." *RichT-D*, 19 Ag 73, p. F-1.

Barroff, Marie. "Creativity, Poetic Language, and the Computer." *YR*, 60: 481-513 (Je 71).

Barzun, Jacques. "The Muse and Her Doctors." *AHR*, 77: 36-64 (F 72).

Basler, Roy. "The Taste of It: Observations of Current Erotic Poetry." *Mosaic*, 6: 93-105 (Sp 73).

Bastian, Heiner. "*Provocation*: Americanische Gegendarstellung." *Akzente*, 15, 289-319 (1968).

Batchelder, S. "Poetry of the Bells During the American Renaissance." *ATQ*, 17: 47-70 (1973).

Bell, B.W. "Contemporary Afro-American Poetry as Folk Art." *BlackW*, 22: 17-26, 74-87 (#5 73).

————. "New Black Poetry: A Double-Edged Sword." *CLAJ*, 15: 37-43 (S 71).

Bennett, J.R. "The Dramatic Monolog in Britain and the United States: A Selected Bibliography." *CP*, 5: 57-70 (1972).

Benoit, Raymond. "The New American Poetry." *Thought*, 44: 201-18 (Su 69).

Bergonzi, Bernard. "Nature, Mostly American." *SoR*, 6: 205-15 (Ja 70).

Bernlef, J. "De Liverpool scene: Engelse popdichters." *Gids*, 131: 172-4 (1968).

Berry, Wendell. "A Secular Pilgrimage." *HudR*, 23: 401-24 (Au 70).

————. "The Specialization of Poetry." *HudR*, 28: 11-27 (Sp 75).

Bertholf, R.J. "The Key in the Window: Kent's Collection of Modern American Poetry." *Serif*, 7: 52-70 (1970).

Bethke, R.D. "Narrative Obituary Verse and Native American Balladry." *JAF*, 83: 61-8 (Ja-Mr 70).

Binderman, M.B. "Toasts: The Black Urban Folk Poetry." *JAF*, 87: 208-28 (1974).

Blazek, Douglas. "Poetry is Not for the Slouch." *New*, 15: 13-6 (Ap-My 71).

Bliss, A. "Atlanta Poets Number." *Sahara*, 4: special number (Su 74).

Bloom, Harold. "Bacchus and Merlin: The Dialectic of Romantic Poetry in America." *SoR*, 7: 140-75 (Ja 71).

———. "On Poetry." *NRep*, 173: 24-8 (29 N 75).

———. "Death and the Native Strain in American Poetry." *SocR*, 39: 449-62 (1972).

———. "The Sorrows of American Jewish Poetry." *Commentary*, 53: 69-74 (Mr 72).

Bluestein, Gene. "Folk Tradition, Individual Talent: A Note on the Poetry of Rock." *MR*, 11: 373-84 (Sp 70).

Bly, Robert. "American Poetry: On the Way to the Hermetic." *BA*, 46: 17-24 (Wi 72).

———. "Leaping Up Into Political Poetry." *LonM*, 7: 82-7 (S 67).

———. "Poetry—What Is It Saying and to Whom?" *AmD*, 5: 28 (1968-69).

———. "On Political Poetry." *Nation*, 204: 522-4 (24 Ap 67).

———. "Symposium: What's New in American and Canadian Poetry." *New*, 15: 17-20 (Ap-My 71).

Braithwaite, W.S. "Imagism: Another View." *NRep*, 3: 154-5 (12 Je 15).

Bray, Robert. "Interpretation, Criticism and the Problem of Poetic Structure." *MwQ*, 16: 318-38 (Jl 73).

Bridges, K.F. "Lieutenant Augustus William Magee." *LaStud*, 6: 291-7 (Fa 67).

Bridges, W.E. "Warm Hearth, Cold World: Social Perspectives on the Household Poets." *AQ*, 21: 764-9 (Wi 69).

Brilliant, Alan. "Symposium: What's New in American and Canadian Poetry." *New*, 15: 20-3 (Ap-My 71).

Brooks, A.R. "The Motif of Dynamic Change in Black Revolutionary Poetry." *CLAJ*, 15: 7-17 (S 71).

Brooks, Cleanth. "The Language of Poetry. Some Problem Cases." *Archiv*, 118-203: 401-14 (Ap 67).

Brown, Merle. "Criticism as the Animus of Poetry." *Stand*, 8: 45-52 (1967).

———. "Dodecaphonic Scales." *Iowa R*, 4: 113-26 (Fa 73).

Brownjohn, Alan. "Changing the Avant-Garde: The Black Mountain Idiom." *Enc*, 43: 55-60 (Jl 74).

Bruce-Wilson, Richard. "The New American Decadence." *Delta*, 38: 22-8 (Sp 66).

Bruns, G.L. "Poetry as Reality: The Orpheus Myth and Its Modern Counterparts." *ELH*, 37: 263-86 (1970).

Bryant, W.C. "Painting and Poetry; A Love Affair of Long Ago." *AQ*, 22: 859-82 (Wi 70).

Buckley, Vincent. "The Persistence of God." *CritR*, 10: 74-87 (1967).

Budd, L.J. "The Not So Tender Traps: Some Dilemmas of Black American Poets." *IJAS*, 3: 47-57 (1974).

Buell, Lawrence. "Transcendentalist Catalogue Rhetoric." *AL*, 40: 325-39 (N 68).

Campbell, Gladys. "Some Recollection of the Poetry Club at the University of Chicago." *Poetry*, 107: 110-7 (N 65).

Cansler, L.D. "Walter Dibben, an Ozark Bard." *KFR*, 13: 81-3 (O-D 67).

Carruth, Hayden. "Here Today: A Poetry Chronicle." *HudR*, 24: 320-6 (1971).

———. "The Question of Poetic Form." *HudR*, 28: 491-501 (1975).

Chapman, Abraham. "Black Poetry Today." *ASoc*, 5: 401-8 (1968).

Christensen, J.A. "Poetry in Its Western Setting." *WR*, 7: 10-9 (1970).

Clark, Leonard. "The State of Poetry." *PoetR*, 59: 243-7 (1969).

Coad, O.S. "A Signer Writes a Letter in Verse." *JRUL*, 32: 33-6 (1968).

Cohen, Hennig. "A Colonial Poem on Indigo Culture." *AgH*, 30: 41-4 (1956).

———. "A Southern Colonial Elegy." *WMQ*, 10: 628-9 (1953).

Combecher, Hans. "'In back of the real': ein Stuck Beat Poetry." *NS*, 22: 74-6 (1973).

Cooke, G.W. "The Poets of Transcendentalism: An Anthology." *ATQ*, 16: 3-4 (1972).

Cooperman, Stanley. "Poetry of Dissent in the United States." *MQR*, 10: 23-8 (Wi 71).

Corbin, A.C. "American Verse and English Critics." *Poetry*, 11: 207-12 (Ja 18).

Corman, Cid. "The Voices of the Individual." *Serif*, 6: 13-6 (1969).

Cramer, Mark. "Neruda and Vallejo in Contemporary United States Poetry." *RomN*, 14: 455-9 (1973).

Davie, Donald. "Landscape as Poetic Focus." *SoR*, 4: 685-91 (Su 68).

———. "Poetry and the Other Modern Arts." *MQR*, 7: 193-8 (Su 68).

Davis, A.P. "The New Poetry of Black Hate." *CLAJ*, 13: 382-91 (1970).

Davis, R.B. "Three Poems from Colonial North Carolina." *NCHR*, 47: 33-41 (Wi 69).

Davis, T.M. "The Poetry of *The Ladies' Home Journal* from 1895-1905." *AmS*, 12: 21-35 (Sp 71).

De Bellis, Jack. "The Southern Universe and the Counter-Renaissance." *SoR*, 4: 471-81 (Sp 68).

Dembo, L.S. "The 'Objectivist' Poet: Four Interviews." *ConL*, 10: 155-219 (Sp 69).

Denham, R.D. "R.S. Crane's Critical Method and Theory of Poetic Form." *ConnR*, 5: 46-56 (1972).

Deutsch, Babette. "Religious Elements in Modern Poetry." *Menorah J*, 29: 24-8 (Ja 41).

Dickey, R.P. "The New Genteel Tradition in American Poetry." *SR*, 32: 730-9 (Fa 74).

Dietrich, Mae. "Gladys W. Wenk Founded the Laureatship of Maryland, Poetry Day in Maryland, and the Maryland State Poetry Society." *HJP*, 1: 68-9 (1972).

———. "Poetry in Maryland." *HJP*, 1: 26-28 (1972).

Donadio, Stephen. "Poetry and Public Experience." *Commentary*, 55: 63-72 (F 73).

Dorbin, Sanford. "Charles Bukowski and the Little Man/Small Press Movement." *SCUL*, 2: 17-32 (My 70).

Dorenhamp, J.H. "The *Bay Psalm Book* and the Ainsworth Psaler." *EAL*, 7: 3-16 (Sp 72).

Doyle, Mike. "Notes on Concrete Poetry." *CanL*, 46: 91-5 (1970).

Dudek, Louis. "Poetry as a Way of Life." *Eng Q*, 1: 7-19 (Je 68).

Durna, V., Fernando. "Neruda et al poesie ibero-americaine." *RDM*, O 74, pp. 45-53.

Durham, Frank. "The Society of South Carolina's Turbulent Year: Self-Interest, Atheism, and Jean Toomer." *SHR*, 5: 76-80 (Wi 71).

Economou, George. "Some Notes Towards Finding a View of the New Oral Poetry." *Boun2*, 3: 653-64 (Sp 75).

Ehrenpreis, Irvin. "Viewpoint." *TLS*, 8 F 74, p. 132.

*Eliott, William. "Minnesota North Country Poetry: A Bibliography." *Soc for the Stud of Midwestern Lit*, 4: 8-10 (1974).

Ellison, Martha. "Velvet Voices Feed on Bitter Fruit: A Study of American Negro Poetry." *P&C*, 4: 39-49 (Wi 67-68).

Engel, B.F. "A Democratic Vista of Religion." *GaR*, 20: 84-9 (Sp 66).

———. "On Nailing the Octopus; or, on Midwestern Popular Poetry." *Soc for the Study of Midwestern Lit*, 1: 21-7 (1974).

Fadiman, Clifton. "Party of One: American Light Verse." *Holiday*, 30: 11-5 (S 61).

Fauchereau, Serge. "Entretien avec M.L. Rosenthal: 'Des figures interessantes rien de plus.'" *QL*, 126: 9-11 (1-15 O 71).

Ferri, M.M. "Modern Songs as Lyric Poetry: Euphony, Rhythm, Metre and Rhyme." *Style*, 4: 245-51 (1970).

Fiedler, L.A. "Lyrik ist eine sterbende Kunst." *DRu*, 90: 34-41 (Ja 64).

Fields, Kenneth. "Past Masters: Walter Conrad Arensburg and Donald Evans." *SoR*, 6: 317-39 (1970).

Figueira, Gastón. "Analogías e incompatibilidades entre al poesía estadouidense y la de América Latina." *RIB*, 18: 280-94 (Jl-S 68).

Finch, Peter. "Concrete Poetry: A Brief Outline." *Anglo-Welsh R*, 19: 207-12 (Au 70).

Flanagan, J.T. "Three Illinois Poets." *CentR*, 16: 313-27 (Fa 72).

Fletcher, J.G. "Three Imagist Poets." *LittleR*, 3: 32-41 (Je-Jl 16).

Flint, F.S. "The History of Imagism." *Egoist*, 2: 70-1 (1 My 15).

Flint, F.C. "Metaphor in Contemporary Poetry." *Symposium*, 1: 310-55 (1931).

Forgotson, E.S. "Eight Poets, With a Preface." *SoR*, 7: 893-903 (1941).

Fowler, Carolyn. "A Contemporary Blackamerican Genre: Pamphlet/Manifesto Poetry." *BlackW*, 23: 4-19 (1974).

Fox, Hugh. "Forming a Technologically Permeable Sensibility." *WCR*, 4: 11-9 (Fa 69).

———. "*The Living Underground: A Critical Overview*." *STC*, 5: 33-152 (Sp 70).

Frank, A.P. "Das Bild in imagistischer Theorie und Praxis." *JA*, 13: 174-95 (1968).

Fraser, John. "Leavis, Winters, and Poetry." *SoRA*, 5: 179-96 (1972).

Free, W.J. "Murray Krieger and the Place of Poetry." *GaR*, 22: 236-46 (1968).

———. "William Cullen Bryant on Nationalism, Imitation, and Originality in Poetry." *SP*, 66: 672-87 (1969).

Fuller, Roy. "Fascinating Rhythm." *SoR*, 9: 857-72 (Au 73).

———. "Poetic Memories of the Thirties." *MQR*, 12: 217-31 (Su 73).

Furay, Michael. "Africa in Negro American Poetry to 1929." *ALT*, 2: 32-41 (Ja 69).

Fussell, Edwin. "From Imagism to *The Waste Land*." *Virginia Woolf Q*, 1: 57-68 (1973).

———. "The Theory of Modern Traditional Poetry: Some Doubts and Reservations." *Talisman*, 8: 58-65 (1955).

Gadda Conti, Giuseppe. "Ritagli di poesia americana." *Vita e Pensiero*, 51: 782-93 (1968).

Gale, Vi. "Poetry in Portland." *NwR*, 11: 73-9 (Sp 71).

Gardner, Donald. "Cardboard Revolution." *NSt*, 9 F 68, pp. 172-3.

Gilbert, T.S. "Cultural Barriers to Modern Poetry Reading." *CJF*, 26: 43-6 (Fa 67).

———. "Modern Poetry Technique and the Machine." *CJF*, 27: 119-22 (Wi 68-69).

Gitlin, Todd. "Notes on War Poetry." *Confr*, 8: 145-7 (Sp 74).

———. "The Return of Political Poetry." *Cweal*, 94: 375-80 (1971).

Goldenberg, Issac. "New York's New Blood Poets." *Américas*, 21: 14-20 (My 69).

Goodman, E.S. "'Lilacs' and the Pastoral Elegy Reconsidered." *BBr*, 24: 119-33 (1971).

Govan, S.Y. "The Poetry of the Black Experience as Counterpoint to the Poetry of the Black Aesthetic." *NALF*, 8: 288-92 (1974).

Graff, G.E. "Mythotheraphy and Modern Poetics." *TriQ*, 11: 76-90 (Wi 68).

Graves, Robert. "The Secret War between Science and Poetry." *ID*, 2: 54 (Ap 72).

Greenfield, S.B. "Grammar and Meaning in Poetry." *PMLA*, 82: 377-87 (O 67).

Grenander, M.E. "Problems of Representation in Lyric Poetry." *Eng Rec*, 21: 5-14 (D 70).

Grigson, Geoffrey. "Recollections of 'New Verse.'" *TLS*, 25 Ap 68, pp. 409-10.

Gross, Harvey. "The Problems of Style and the Poetry of the Sixties." *IowaR*, 5: 69-74 (Wi 74).

Guillén, Claudio. "Poetics as System." *CL*, 22: 193-222 (Su 70).

Guimond, James. "After Imagism." *OhR*, 15: 5-28 (Fa 73).

Gustafson, Richard. "The Peace of a Good Line." *P&C*, 6: 29-33 (1971).

———. "'Time Is a Waiting Woman': New Poetic Icon." *MwQ*, 16: 318-27 (Sp 75).

Halley, Anne. "Recent American Poetry: Outside Relevances." *MR*, 9: 696-716 (1968).

———. "Struggling in Poetry." *MR*, 14: 847-64 (1973).

Hancock, Joel. "The Emergence of Chicano Poetry: A Survey of Sources, Themes, and Techniques." *ArQ*, 29: 57-73 (Sp 73).

Poetry

Harmon, William. "Country, Body, Song: American Remarks." *AR*, 30: 425-38 (Fa-Wi 70-71).

———. "Dead Entertainment." *Hiram Poetry R*, 10: 3-5 (Fa-Wi 71).

Harnack, Curtis. "Week of the Angry Artist." *Nation*, 204: 245-8 (20 F 67).

Hart, Lawrence. "The New Face of Conformity." *Works*, 1: 106-13 (Sp 68).

———. "The Saw Keeps Turning." *Works*, 3: 85-91 (Su-Fa 71).

Haslam, Gerald. "American Indians: Poets of the Cosmos." *WAL*, 5: 15-29 (Sp 70).

Haugh, G.C. "Rivington's *Songs, Naval and Military.*" *Serif*, 7: 30-3 (1970).

Hawley, J.S. "Quantitative Semantics as an Approach to Meaning in Poetry." *JQ*, 47: 87-94 (Sp 70).

Heap, Jane. "The Death of Vorticism." *Little R*, 5: 45-51 (F-Mr 19).

Hedetoft, Ulf. "Studies in Modern British and American Poetry." *Linguistica et Litteria*, 2: 3-29 (1973).

Heidenry, John. "Poetry to the People." *Cweal*, 96: 90-1 (31 Mr 72).

Herms, Dieter. "Mime Troupe, El Teatro, Bread and Pupet—Ansätze zu einem polistischen Volkstheater in den USA." *Muk*, 19: 342-62 (1973).

Hertzel, L.J. "Katzenjammer Kids Up North." *NAR*, 259: 51-5 (Su 74).

Hewitt, Geof. "Notes Toward Extinction: American Poetry Wipe-Out." *New*, 15: 39-44 (Ap-My 71).

Heyen, William. "Toward the Still Point: The Imagist Aesthetic." *BSUF*, 9: 44-8 (Wi 68).

Hidden, Norman. "Poetry at Grass Roots." *PoetR*, 59: 249-50 (Wi 68).

Hill, Gertrude. "The Southwest in Verse: A Selective Bibliography of Arizona and New Mexico Poetry." *ArQ*, 23: 306-12 (Wi 67).

Hirsch, D.H. "American Dionysian Poetry and Modern Poetics." *SR*, 83: 334-47 (Sp 75).

Hitchcock, George. "Report from the Coast." *New*, 15: 51-4 (Ap-My 71).

Hobbs, John. "Judging Contemporary Poems: Criteria and the Editor." *Iowa R*, 5: 100-11 (1974).

Hobsbaum, Philip. "Eliot, Whitman and the American Tradition." *JAmSt*, 3: 239-64 (D 69).

Hoffman, N.H. "Reading Women's Poetry: The Meaning and Our Lives." *CE*, 34: 48-62 (1972).

Hollander, John. "The Poem in the Eye." *Shen*, 23: 3-32 (Sp 72).

Hopkins, M.F. "Linguistic Analysis as a Tool for Oral Interpretation." *SpT*, 18: 200-3 (1969).

Horrell, Joe. "Some Notes on Conversion in Poetry." *SoR*, 7: 117-31 (1941).

Howard, Richard. "Reflections on a Strange Solitude." *Prose*, 1: 81-91 (1970).

Hsin-Fu Wand, David. "The Use of Native Imagery by Chinese Poets Writing in English." *WLWE*, 19: 55-67 (Ap 71).

Huddleston, E.L. "Depiction of New York in Early American Poetry." *NYFQ*, 24: 275-93 (D 68).

———. "Poetical Descriptions of Pennsylvania in the Early National Period." *PMHB*, 93: 487-509 (O 69).

———. "Sense and Sensibility in Early American Poetry: The Case of Mathilda's 'Elegy Supposed to be Written on the Banks of Detroit River.'" *NOQ*, 44: 18-25 (1972).

Hughes, Daniel. "American Poetry 1969: From B. to Z." *MR*, 11: 650-86 (Au 70).

Hughes, J.W. "Humanism and the Orphic Voice." *SatR*, 54: 31-3 (22 My 71).

Hughes, Langston. "200 Years of American Negro Poetry." *Transition*, 5: 49-51 (1966).

Hugo, Richard. "How Poets Make a Living." *Iowa R*, 3: 69-76 (Fa 72).

Hunsberger, Bruce. "Kit Smart's 'Howl.'" *WSCL*, 6: 34-44 (Wi-Sp 65).

Huxley, Aldous. "The Only Way to Write a Modern Poem about a Nightingale." *Harpers*, 227: 62-6 (Ag 63).

————. "Thirteen Early American Latin Elegies: A Critical Edition." *HL*, 23: 346-81 (1974).

Kanaseki, Hisao. "America Shi to Shizen." *EigoS*, 119: 742-3 (1974).

Kanazeki, Yoshio. "Haiku to America Gendaishi." *EigoS*, 114: 358-61 (1968).

Kartiganer, D.M. "Process and Product: A Study of Modern Literary Form." *MR*, 12: 297-328, 789-816 (1971).

Kaufman, Wallace. "Revolution, Environment and Poetry." *SAQ*, 77: 137-48 (Sp 72).

Kesser, Jascha. "The Inner World Where Poets Wander." *SatR*, 54: 39, 50-1 (2 O 71).

Kinnell, Galway. "The Poetics of the Physical World." *Iowa R*, 2: 113-26 (1971).

————. "To the Roots: An Interview with Galway Kinnell." *Salmagundi*, 22-23: 206-21 (1973).

Kiyokawa, Schioichi. "Concrete Poetry." *NYQ*, 14: 176-81 (Sp 73).

Koch, Stephen. "The New York School of Poets: The Serious at Play." *NYT*, 11 F 68, pp. 4-5.

Köhring, K.H. "The America Epic." *SHR*, 5: 265-80 (Su 71).

Kostelanetz, Richard. "The New Poetries in America." *Quadrant*, 80: 27-33 (1972).

————. "La poesia americana dei secondo dopguerra." *NP*, 12: 1-25 (1969).

————. "Reactions and Alternatives: Post-World War II American Poetry." *Chelsea*, 26: 7-34 (My 69).

Kummings, D.D. "The Poetry of Democracy: Tocqueville's Aristocratic View." *ConL*, 11: 309-19 (1974).

Kurman, George. "Negative Comparison in Literary Epic Narrative." *CL*, 21: 337-47 (Fa 69).

Lamorte, Pat. "The 'Ancient Rules'—A Vanishing Species?" *GaR*, 27: 489-502 (Wi 73).

Lattimore, Richmond. "Poetry Chronicle." *HudR*, 24: 499-510 (1971); 27: 460-74 (1974).

Ledbetter, J.T. "Modern Poetry and the American Idiom." *Cresset*, 32: 8-10 (Ja 69).

Irwin, J.T. "The Crisis of Regular Forms." *SR*, 81: 158-71 (Wi 73).

————. "A Nest of Tuneful Persons." *SoR*, 9: 720-35 (Jl 73).

Jaffe, Daniel. "A Shared Language in the Poet's Tongue." *SatR*, 54: 31-3 (3 Ap 71).

Jäger, Dietrich. "Robert Frost und die Traditionen der Naturdichtung: Die aussermenschliche Welt als Thema deutscher amerikanischer Lyriker des 20. Jahrhunderts." *LWU*, 1: 2 26 (1968).

Jochems, Helmut. "Englische und amerikanische Lyrik in der Schule: Kritsche Anmerkungen zu einigen neuren Interpretationssammlungen." *LWU*, 2: 268-81 (1969).

Johnson, A.A. "A Free Foot in the Wilderness: Harriet Monroe and *Poetry*, 1912-1936." *IllQ*, 37: 28-43 (Su 75).

Johnson, Carol. "The Translator as Poet." *Art Int*, 16: 129-31 (O 72).

Johnson, Geoffrey. "Modern American Poetry." *LHY*, 7: 40-4 (Jl 66).

Johnson, G.B. "The Negro Spiritual: A Problem in Anthropology." *Am Anthropology*, 33: 157-71 (1931).

Johnson, R.C. "Addenda to Irish: Theodora Taylor, Rixford J. Lincoln, David Bailey, Lester S. Parker." *PBSA*, 63: 198-200 (3Q 69).

Johnston, J.H. "The Early American Prologue and Epilogue." *WVUPP*, 16: 30-48 (1967).

Johnston, T.E. "American Puritan Poetic Voices." *EAL*, 3: 125-6 (1968).

Jordan, Jim. "New Worlds 4 From *The Young American Poets*." *WiOr*, 9: 45-8 (Sp 72).

Jorgensen, B.W. "Imperceptive Hands: Some Recent Mormon Verse." *Dialog*, 5: 23-34 (Wi 70).

Judson, John. "Regionalism and Modern Poetry." *New*, 25-26: 96-9 (1975).

Kaiser, L.M. "On the Latin in the Messerole Anthology." *EAL*, 6: 165-6 (Fa 71).

Poetry

Lemay, J.A.L. ''A Calender of American Poetry in the Colonial Newspapers and Magazines and in the Major English Magazines Through 1765.'' *PAAS*, 79: 291-392 (O 69); 80: 71-222, 353-469 (Ap, O 70).

————. ''Richard Lewis and Augustan American Poetry.'' *PMLA*, 83: 80-101 (Mr 68).

Lensing, George. ''The Lyric Plentitude: A Time of Rediscovery.'' *SoR*, 3: 197-228 (Wi 67).

————, and Ronald Moran. ''The Emotive Imagination: A New Departure in American Poetry.'' *SoR*, 3: 51-67 (Wi 67).

Lentricchia, Frank. ''Four Types of Nineteenth-Century Poetic.'' *JAAS*, 26: 351-66 (Sp 68).

Levertov, Denise. ''Poems by Women.'' *Trellis*, 1: 57-60 (Sp 75).

Levin, Harry. ''The American Voice in English Poetry.'' *EUQ*, 22: 163-83 (Fa 66).

Lieberman, Laurence. ''Recent Poetry: Exiles and Disinterments.'' *YR*, 61: 82-100 (1971).

Lightfoot, Marjorie. ''Prosody and Performance.'' *QJS*, 53: 61-6 (F 67).

Lincoln, Kenneth. ''Native American Tribal Poetics.'' *SWR*, 60: 101-16 (Sp 75).

Logan, H.M. ''Some Applications of Linguistic Theory to Poetry.'' *HAB*, 21: 40-7 (Sp 70).

Logan, John. ''John Logan on Poets and Poetry Today.'' *Voyages*, 4: 17-24 (Sp 71/72).

Long, Pierre. ''Notes on Modern Poetry.'' *CJF*, 24: 140-4 (Wi 65-66).

Lourie, Dick. ''Symposium: What's New in American Poetry.'' *New*, 15: 58-62 (Ap-My 71).

Lowenfels, Walter. ''The White Poetry Syndicate: An Open Letter.'' *ASoc*, 8: 413-4 (1971).

Lowens, Irving. ''The Songster and the Scholar.'' *PAAS*, 76: 59-70 (Ap 66).

Lowes, J.L. ''An Unacknowledged Imagist.'' *Nation*, 102: 217-9 (24 J 16).

Lowinsohn, Ron. ''After the (Mimeograph) Revolution.'' *TriQ*, 18: 221-36 (Sp 70).

Lucie-Smith, Edward. ''Between and Revolution: The Poet as Role-Player.'' *SatR*, 19 Ap 75; pp. 14-8.

Lynen, F. ''Forms of Time in Modern Poetry.'' *QQ*, 82: 344-64 (Au 75).

McCarthy, Eugene. ''Poetry and War.'' *Confr*, 8: 131-6 (Sp 74).

McConnell, F.D. ''Rock and the Politics of Frivolity.'' *MR*, 12: 119-34 (1971).

McElrath, J.R. ''Plumbing the Swamp: The Modern Mode of Self-Pity.'' *SHR*, 7: 53-65 (1973).

McFarland, R.E ''Poetry in the Periodicals.'' *CP*, 7: 55-8 (1974).

————. ''A Survey of Poetry in the Periodicals.'' *CE*, 36: 475-6 (1974).

McKee, Me. ''National Poetry Anthology.'' *Dekalb Lit Arts J*, 7: 1-225 (1974).

Macksey, R.A. ''The Old Poets.'' *John Hopkins Mag*, 19: 42-8 (1968).

McMaster, Laurence. ''The American Pegasus.'' *SAQ*, 13: 213-9 (Jl 14).

MacShane, Frank. ''The New Poetry.'' *ASch*, 37: 642-6 (Au 68).

Mariah, Paul. ''From Lesbos with Love: On Gay Women's Poetry.'' *Margins*, 8: 8-14 (1973).

Martin, Wallace. ''The Sources of the Imagist Aesthetic.'' *PMLA*, 85: 196-204 (Mr 70).

Martz, L.L. ''Recent Poetry: Berryman and Others.'' *YR*, 61: 410-22 (1972).

Matthews, William. ''Talking about Poetry: An Interview with William Matthews.'' *OhR*, 13: 33-51 (1972).

Matthiessen, F.O. ''A Review of Recent Poetry.'' *SoR*, 3: 799-819 (1938).

Maxwell, D.E.S ''Time's Strange Excuse: W.B. Yeats and the Poets of the Thirties.'' *JML*, 4: 717-34 (F 75).

Meserole, H.T. ''Notes on Editing Seventeenth-Century American Poetry.'' *CEAAN*, 2: 11-4 (1969).

Meyer, Thomas. ''Le hasard.'' *Parnassus*, 1: 116-24 (1972).

Modlin, C.E. ''Aristocracy in the Early Republic.'' *EAL*, 6: 252-7 (Wi 71-72).

Molesworth, Charles. ''The Rank Flavor of Blood: Galway Kinnell and American Poetry in 1960's.'' *WHR*, 27: 225-39 (Su 73).

Monroe, Harriet. "The Open Door." *Poetry*, 1: 62-66 (N 12).

Montgomery, Marion. "The Poet at the Marvelous Present." *GaR*, 25: 206-21 (Su 71).

Moore, Marianne. "The Ways Our Poets Have Taken in Fifteen Years Since the War." *NYHT*, 26 Je 60, pp. 1, 11.

Moore, Stephen. "Conformed to Stone." *MQR*, 11: 217-21 (Su 72).

Moramarco, Fred. "A Gathering of Poets." *WHR*, 26: 189-96 (1972).

Moran, Ronald. "The Inward Journey of American Poetry." *SoR*, 8: 243-53 (Wi 72).

Morey, L. "Evaluating a Poets Who's Who." *HJP*, 1: 49-52 (Wi 72).

Morris, Harry. "The Passions of Poets." *SR*, 79: 301-9 (1971).

Morris, Richard. "The Death of 'Major' Poetry." *New*, 22-23: 84-8 (Fa-Wi 73-74).

Morrow, P.D. "Some Old and New Voices in Western Poetry: An Essay-Review." *WAL*, 8: 153-9 (Fa 73).

Morse, S.F. "Poetry 1966." *ConL*, 9: 112-29 (Wi 68).

Mosher, H.F. "The Lyrics of American Pop Music: A New Poetry." *Popular Music and Society*, 1: 167-76 (1972).

Mottram, Eric. "The Limits of Self-Regard." *Parnassus*, 1: 152-62 (1972).

Mudrick, Marvin. "Three Stanford Poets." *LugR*, 1: 83-94 (1965).

Murphy, Francis. "Going It Alone: Estrangement in American Poetry." *YR*, 56: 17-24 (Fa 66).

Nagata, Masao. "American Poetry, 1912." *Bul Faculty Humanities* (Tokyo), 10: 34-44 (1974).

Naremore, James. "The Imagists and the French 'Generation of 1900.'" *ConL*, 11: 354-74 (1970).

Nathan, Leonard. "The Private 'I' in Contemporary Poetry." *Shen*, 22: 80-99 (Su 71).

Nelson, Cary. "Whitman in Vietnam: Poetry and History in Contemporary America." *MR*, 16: 55-71 (Wi 75).

Nejgebauer, Aleksandar. "America the Poetical, and Otherwise." *NRep*, 160: 19-24 (26 Ap 69).

Nemerov, Howard. "Poetry and History." *VQR*, 51: 309-23 (Su 75).

———. "Poetry and Meaning." *Salmagundi*, 22-23: 42-56 (1973).

———. "Poetry, Prophecy, Prediction." *VQR*, 47: 209-26 (Sp 71).

———. "Thirteen Ways of Looking at a Skylark." *Poetry*, 126: 294-305 (1975).

Nemoianu, Virgil. "Nici tradiție, nici inovație." *RoLit*, 8: 28-9 (Je 72).

Novak, E.G. "The *Dynamo* School of Poets." *ConL*, 11: 526-39 (Au 70).

Oberg, Arthur. "Beyond Lichen and Rose: In Search of a Contemporary American Poetics." *OhR*, 17: 54-62 (Fa 75).

———. "The Modern British and American Lyric: What Will Suffice." *PLL*, 8: 70-88 (1972).

Ortego, P.D. "Chicano Poetry: Roots and Writers." *SwAL*, 2: 8-24 (Sp 72).

Oster, Harry. "The Blues as a Genre." *Genre*, 2: 259-74 (1969).

Packard, William. "Poetry in the Theatre." *Trace*, 62: 373-9; 64: 114-9; 66: 447-55; 67: 139-42 (Fa-Wi 66-67, Sp 67, Fa 67, Sp 68).

Palmer, R.R. "The Poetry of Three Revolutionists: Don L. Lee, Sonia Sanchez, and Nikki Giovanni." *CLAJ*, 15: 25-36 (S 71).

Pearce, R.H. "The Burden of Romanticism: Toward the New Poetry." *IowaR*, 2: 109-28 (1971).

———, with Sigurd Burckhardt. "Poetry, Language, and the Condition of Modern Man." *CentR*, 4: 1-31 (1960).

Pecora, Madeline. "The Date of 'The Plain Case Stated.'" *EAL*, 6: 185-6 (1971).

Perlis, Alan. "Science, Mysticism, and Contemporary Poetry." *WHR*, 29: 209-18 (Su 75).

Perloff, Marjorie. "The Corn-Pone Lyric: Poetry, 1972-73." *ConL*, 16: 84-125 (Wi 75).
———. "New Thresholds, Old Anatomies: Contemporary Poetry and the Limits of Exegesis." *Iowa R*, 5: 83-99 (Wi 74).
———. "Poetry Chronicle: 1970-1." *ConL*, 14: 97-131 (Wi 73).
Perrine, Laurence. "The Poet and the Laboratory." *SWR*, 58: 285-92 (1973); rep. 59: 472-9 (1974).
Petersen, W.J. "The Poetry of Pills." *Palimpsest*, 50: 363-8 (Je 69).
Pinsky, Robert. "Two Examples Poetic Discursiveness." *ChiR*, 27: 133-44 (Su 75).
Pisanti, Tommaso. "La poesia della Nuova Inghilterra." *NA*, 514: 227-38 (1972).
Plotkin, Frederick. "Natural Fact and Poetic Insight." *HSL*, 1: 71-82 (1969).
Polos, N.C. "Early California Poetry." *CHSQ*, 48: 243-35 (S 69).
Pomorska, Krystyna. "On the Problem of 'Classicism' in Contemporary American Poetry." *ZRL*, 12: 55-62 (1970).
Portelli, Alessandro. "Cultura poetica afro-americana." *SA*, 14: 401-29 (1968).
Poulin, A. "Center and Circumference: Personalism and Criticism." *JML*, 1: 109-15 (1970).
———. "Contemporary American Poetry: The Radical Tradition." *CP*, 3: 5-21 (Fa 70).
Pratt, William. "Imagism: A Retrospect Sixty Years Later." *Words*, 1: 60-6 (1973).
Prince, F.T. "Voice and Verse: Some Problems of Modern Poetry." *Eng(L)*, 20: 77-83 (1971).
Puknat, E.M., and S.B. "Goethe and Modern American Poets." *GQ*, 42: 21-36 (1969).
Raban, Jonathan. "Chance, Time and Silence: The New American Verse." *JAmSt*, 3: 89-101 (Jl 69).
———. "Shadow of a Gunman." *NSt*, 19 Je 70, pp. 893-4.
Raizis, M.B. "American Philhellenic Poetry." *J Hellenic Diaspora*, 2: 50-60 (#1 75).
———. "He Chios stin Angliki kai Amerikaniki poiisi tis romantikis epochis." *ChE*, 8: 145-52 (1970).
Ramsaran, J.A. "The 'Twice-Born' Artists' Silent Revolution." *BlackW*, 20: 58-68 (1971).
Ramsey, Paul. "American Poetry in 1973." *SR*, 82: 393-406 (Sp 74).
———. "Some American Poetry of 1974." *SR*, 83: 348-56 (Sp 75).
Redding, Saunders. "The Black Arts Movement in Negro Poetry." *ASch*, 42: 330-6 (Sp 73).
Redmond, E.B. "The Black American Epic: Its Roots, Its Writers." *BSch*, 2: 15-22 (Ja 71).
Reed, J.R. "Instructive Alchemies." *OntarioR*, 1: 78-88 (1974).
Regier, W.G. "Reviewing Poetry: The Why and the Howl." *PrS*, 47: 243-51 (1973).
Reid, A.S. "A Look at the Living Poem: Rock Protest and Wit." *Furman Mag*, nv: 6-11, 35 (Sp 70).
Rexroth, Kenneth. "The New American Poets." *HM*, 230: 65-71 (Je 65).
———. "Why is American Poetry Deprived?" *TriQ*, 8: 61-7 (1967).
Ricks, Christopher. "Recent American Poetry." *MR*, 11: 313-39 (1970).
Riese, T.A. "Das Gestaltumgsprinsip der Konkretion in der Neuren Amerikanischen Lyrik." *JA*, 8: 136-47 (1963).
Rissover, Frederic. "Beat Poetry, *The American Dream*, and the Alienation Effect." *SpT*, 20: 36-43 (1971).
Robinson, J.K. "Sailing Close Hauled into the Wind: From Nemerov to Rich." *APR*, 4: 4-7 (#2 75).
———. "Terror Lumped and Split: Contemporary British and American *SoR*, 6: 216-28 (Ja 70).
Rock, Virginia. "The Fugitive-Agrarians in Response to Social Change." *SHR*, 1: 170-81 (Su 67).

Rodgers, C.M. "Black Poetry: Where It's At." *NegroD*, 18: 7-16 (1969).

Rosenfeld, A.H. "Yiddish Poets and Playwrights of America: A Preliminary Report on a Recent Addition to the Harris Collection." *BBr*, 22: 161-81 (1968).

Rosenthal, M.L. "Continuities in Modern American Poetry." *Nation*, 218: 149-51 (2 F 74).

———. "Dynamics of Form and Motive in Some Representative Twentieth-Century Lyric Poems." *ELH*, 37: 136-51 (Mr 70).

———. "'Like the shark, it contains a shoe': The Aroused Language Modern Poetry." *NYT*, 24 N 74, pp. 13, 40-7.

———. "Poetry of the Main Chance." *TLS*, 29 Ja 70, p. 113.

———. "Some Thoughts on American Poetry Today." *Salmagundi*, 22-23: 57-70 (1973).

———. "Uncertain Odysseus: The Critic of Current Poetry." *Shen*, 19: 59-66 (1968).

———. "'The Unconsenting Spirit': Poetry and Politics." *Nation*, 212: 149-50 (1 F 71).

Rothenberg, Jerome. "American Indian Workings." *PoetR*, 63: 17-29 (1972).

Rubin, L.D. "Black Poets in Search of a Language." *Bkmark*, 40: 3-15 (S 70); *Southeastern Lib*, 21: 213-21 (Wi 70).

Russell, W.M. "Poetics and Literary Language." *CE*, 31: 300-8 (D 69).

Ruthven, K.K. "The Poet as Etymologist." *CritQ*, 2: 9-37 (Sp 69).

Santayana, George. "Shakespeare: Made in America." *NRep*, 2: 96-8 (27 F 15).

Schneidau, H.N. "The Age of Interpretation and the Moment of Immediacy: Contemporary Art vs. History." *ELH*, 37: 287-313 (1970).

Schulman, Grace. "New Poets to Be Seen and Heard." *Nation*, 219: 663-4 (21 D 74).

Sears, D.A. "Folk Poetry in Longfellow's Boyhood." *NEQ*, 45: 95-105 (1972).

Shapiro, Karl. "The Poetry Wreck." *LibJ*, 95: 632-5 (15 F 70).

Shaw, R.B. "The Poetry of Protest." *Poetry Nation*, 1: 62-72 (1973).

Sherman, J.R. "Connecticut's Nineteenth-Century Black Poets." *ConnR*, 5: 18-27 (Ap 72).

Shinkura, Toshikazu. "Naked Poetry—America Shi no Kenzai." *EigoS*, 116: 532-3 (1970).

Simpson, L.P. "Poet-Critics and a Critic." *SoR*, 8: xi-xv (Jl 72).

———. "The Poetry of New Orleans." *SoR*, 4: xiii-xv (Su 68).

———. "The California Poets." *LonM*, 11: 56-63 (F 71).

Simpson, Louis. "Dead Horses and Live Issues." *Nation*, 204: 520-2 (24 Ap 67).

Sloane, D.E.E. "In Search of a Realistic Poetic Tradition." *ALR*, 5: 489-91 (Fa 72).

Smitherman, Geneva. "The Power of the Rap: The Black Idiom and the New Black Poetry." *TCL*, 19: 259-74 (O 73).

Snowden, Yates. "Student Songs and Mock-Heroics Sixty Years Ago." *Carolinian*, 24: 139-52 (1911).

Solt, Mary Ellen. "Concrete Poetry." *RevL*, 1: 154-79 (1969).

Sorrentino, Gilbert. "Black Mountaineering." *Poetry*, 116: 110-29 (1970).

Spacks, P.M. "In Search of Sincerity." *CE*, 29: 591-602 (My 68).

Spinning, Bruce. "Notes Toward a Theory of Poetry in the American West." *PosS*, 5: 29-38 (Ja 74).

Spitzer, Leo. "History of Ideas Versus Reading of Poetry." *SoR*, 6: 584-609 (1941).

Stanford, Ann. "The Elegy of Mourning in Modern American and English Poetry." *SoR*, 11: 357-72 (Ap 75).

Stanford, D.E. "Classicism and the Modern Poet." *SoR*, 5: 475-500 (Sp 69).

Stephens, Rosemary. "Out from under Magnolia Trees." *S&W*, 10: 11-22 (1971).

Sternlicht, Sanford. "The Absolutes Are Gone." *StAR*, 1: 5-8 (Sp-Su 72).

———. "The Three Directions of Contemporary American Poetry: Tradition, the Academy, and Experiment." *DP*, 3: 7-13 (1968).

Steward, D.H. "The Poetry of Protest." *MQR*, 10: 1-4 (Wi 71).

Stilwell, R.L. "The Multiplying of Entities: D.H. Lawrence and Five Other Poets." *SR*, 76: 520-35 (1968).

Stimson, F.S. "Spanish Influence on Early American Poetry." *Americas*, 16: 161-70 (O 59).

* Stoddard, R.E. "A Catalogue of Books and Pamphlets Unrecorded in Oscar Wegelin's *Early American Poetry, 1650-1820.*" *BBr*, 23: 1-84 (1969).

* ———. "Further Addenda to Wegelin's *Early American Poetry.*" *PBSA*, 65: 169-72 (2Q 71).

Strand, Mark. "Poetry and the Poetry of Self." *Prose*, 6: 169-83 (Sp 73).

Subbaro, C. "Contextualist Poetics and the Nature of Language." *LCrit*, 9: 54-60 (Wi 69).

Swing, E.S. "Poetry and the Counter-Culture." *EJ*, 41: 663-9 (My 72).

Symon, Julian. "Cardboard Revolution." *NSt*, 16 F 68, p. 206.

Sypher, Wylie. "The Poem as Defense." *ASch*, 37: 85-93 (Wi 67-68).

Tanselle, G.T. "The Little Leather Library Corporation's *Fifty Best Poems of America.*" *PBSA*, 62: 604-7 (4Q 68).

Tarbet, D.W. "Contemporary American Pastoral: A Poetic Faith." *Eng Rec*, 23: 72-83 (Wi 72).

Tate, Allen. "Literature as Knowledge: Comment and Comparison." *SoR*, 6: 629-57 (1940).

———. "Poetry Modern and Unmodern: A Personal Recollection." *HudR*, 21: 251-62 (Su 68).

———. "Poetry and Politics." *NRep*, 75: 310 (3 Ag 33).

———. "Tension in Poetry." *SoR*, 4: 101-15 (1938).

Taylor, F.H. "A Point in Time, a Place in Space: Six Poets and the Changing Present." *SR*, 77: 300-18 (1969).

Taylor, Henry. "Vantage and Vexation of Spirit." *GaR*, 25: 17-26 (Sp 71).

Taylor, W.D. "Creating by Established Literati Tends to Be Gregarious Activity." *RichT-D*, 19 Ag 73, p. F-1.

Taylor, W.E. "Personality, Poetry, and Priorities." *HiS*, 39: 1-2, 5-6 (Sp 74).

Templeman, W.D. "On the Modern Element in American English Poetry." *WR*, 5: 52-63 (Su 68).

Thomas, F.R. "To Chiggers with Love: A Discussion of Place in Midwestern Poetry." *Soc for the Study of Midwestern Lit*, 1: 3-8 (1974).

Thomas, Peter. "When All Minds Touched." *IllQ*, 34: 49-53 (Ap 72).

Thurley, Geoffrey. "The New Phenomenalist Poetry in the U.S.A." *SoRA*, 4: 15-28 (1970).

Tolley, A.T. "Rhetoric and the Moderns." *SoR*, 6: 380-97 (Ap 70).

True, Michael. "'Poetry' and Survival." *Cweal*, 99: 311-5 (1973).

———. "War and Poetry." *Confr*, 8: 137-44 (Sp 74).

Tulip, James. "The Wesleyan Poets—I." *PoetA*, 12: 30-5 (O 66).

Turco, Lewis. "American Novelists as Poets: The Schizophrenia of Mode." *Eng Rec*, 25: 23-9 (Su 74).

———. "Good Gray Poets and Bad Old Bards." *MPS*, 3: 80-91 (1972).

———. "The Matriarchy of American Poetry." *CE*, 34: 1067-74 (1973).

Turner, A.A. "Implied Metaphor: A Problem in Evaluating Contemporary Poetry." *Iowa R*, 5: 112-9 (Wi 74).

Turner, Maxine. "Three Eighteenth-Century Revisions of the *Bay Psalm Book.*" *NEQ*, 45: 270-7 (Je 72).

Valenti, Suzanne. "The Black Diaspora: Negritude in the Poetry of West Africans and Black Americans." *Phylon*, 34: 390-8 (1973).

Van Brunt, H.L. "The Pygmy Poets of New York." *Smith*, 10: 185-6 (N 68).

Vance, Thomas. "Poetry and the Generation of Critics." *SoR*, 4: 1099-109 (1968).

Vandersee, Charles. "The Stature of Irony." *MwQ*, 11: 283-91 (Sp 70).

Van Dias, Robert. "Six Books by Seven Poets." *Poetry*, 110: 186-95 (Je 67).

Vernon, John. "Poetry and the Body." *AmR*, 16: 145-72 (F 73).

Vivas, Eliseo. "'Poetry' and Philosophy." *Iowa R*, 4: 114-26 (Su 73).

Wages, J.D. "Mock Wills: Parody in the Colonial South." *SNL*, 9: 192-4 (1972).

Waggoner, H.H. "Poets, Test-tubes, and the Heel of Elohim." *UR*, 13: 272-7 (Su 46).

Wallace, Ronald. "Alone with Poems." *ColQ*, 23: 241-53 (1975).

Wanning, Andrews. "Criticism and Principles: Poetry of the Quarter." *SoR*, 6: 792-810 (1941).

Ward R.S. "The American Tradition in Poetry." *Carrell*, 9: 21-30 (1968).

Warfel, H.R. "A Rationale of Free Verse." *JA*, 13: 228-35 (1968).

Warren, R.P. "Democracy and Poetry." *SoR*, 11: 1-28 (Ja 75).

Weaver, Gordon. "Two Negro Folk-Poems." *MissFR*, 4: 98-104 (1970).

Wells, H.W. "The Poetic Image in Modern America and Ancient India." *LHY*, 10: 40-52 (Ja 69).

Wepman, Dennis, et al. "Toasts: The Black Urban Folk Poetry." *JAF*, 87: 208-24 (Jl-S 74).

West, Rebecca. "Imagisme." *New Freewoman*, 1: 86-8 (15 Ag 13).

Westbrook, Max. "The Practical Spirit: Sacrality and the American West." *WAL*, 3: 193-205 (Fa 68).

Wheeler, O.B. "The Emersonian View of American Poetry." *SoR*, 4: 1077-80 (1968).

Whisenhunt, D.W. "The Bard in the Depression: Texas Style." *JPC*, 2: 370-86 (Wi 68).

Whitehead, James. "Leaping Ghazals and Inside Jokes Concealed in Tropes." *SatR*, 54: 37-41, 47 (18 D 71).

Whittemore, Reed. "End of the Old Vaudeville." *NRep*, 167: 31-4 (21 O 72).

———. "The Poet as Effete Snob." *MQR*, 10: 188-94 (1971).

Wicker, R.A. "Black Mountain College." *Serif*, 6: 3-11 (Mr 69).

Wilbur, Richard. "Poetry and Happiness." *Shen*, 20: 3-23 (Su 69).

———. "Poetry's Debt to Poetry." *HudR*, 26: 273-94 (Su 73).

Wilgus, D.K., and Montell Lynwood. "Clure and Joe Williams: Legend and Blues Ballad." *JAF*, 81: 295-315 (O-D 68).

Williamson, Alan. "The Energy Crisis in Poetry: News from Pittsburgh." *Shen*, 26: 41-53 (Fa 74).

———. "Silence, Surrealism, and Allegory." *Kayak*, 40: 57-67 (1975).

Wilson, Edmund. "The Poetry of Drouth." *Dial*, 73: 611-6 (D 22).

Wilson, Mark. "American Surrealism 1971?" *New*, 15: 4-8, 97-100 (Ap-My 71).

Wilson, W.S. "Focus, Meter, and Operations in Poetry." *StBr*, 3-4: 378-83 (Fa 69).

Winter, J.D. "Towards the Public Aspect of Poetry." *PoetR*, 59: 251-3 (1969).

Woodcock, George. "Poetry Magazines of the Thirties." *TamR*, 60: 68-74 (O 73).

Woodman, R.G. "Satan in the 'Vale of Soul-Making': A Survey from Blake to Ginsberg." *HAB*, 25: 108-21 (Sp 74).

Workman, Brooke. "Drama and Poetry, Humanities, American Civilization or Whatever It is." *EJ*, 45: 163-81 (Je 72).

Young, P.D. "Nightmares in Print." *SatR*, 55: 54-9 (O 72).

Young, Vernon. "Poetry Chronicle: Sappho to Smith." *HudR*, 27: 597-614 (1974).

Yu, Kwang-chung. "American Influence on Post-War Chinese Poetry in Taiwan." *TkR*, 5: 1-9 (#1 74).

Zabel, M.D. "Varieties of Poetic Experience." *SoR*, 3: 799-819 (1938).

Zingrone, F.D. "Computer Poetry: Shooting Cosmic Craps." *MPS*, 4: 271-80 (Wi 73).

Zhuralev, Igor. "The Relationship between Socialist Poetry in the U.S.A. at the Beginning of the Twentieth Century and the Graphic Arts of the Socialist Press." *ZAA*, 18: 168-82 (1970).

Zolbrod, P.G. "The Study of Native American Poetry: Some Possibilities." *MLS*, 3: 83-96 (Fa 73).

Zukofsky, Louis. "American Poetry 1920-1930." *Sym*, 2: 71-4 (Ja 31).

Zweig, Paul. "The New Surrealism." *Salmagundi*, 22-23: 269-84 (1973).

Printing, Publishing, Book Selling. Anon. "American Books Published in Great Britain Before 1848." *ESQ*, 51: 129-36 (2Q 68).

Bain, R.A. "The Composition and Publication of *The Present State of Virginia and the College*." *EAL*, 6: 31-54 (Sp 71).

Bell, Millicent. "The Black Sun Press: 1927 to the Present." *BBr*, 17: 2-24 (1955).

Benjamin, Curtis. "Book Publishing's Hidden Bonanza." *SatR*, 53: 1921, 8102 (18 Ap 70).

Benschoten, Virginia. "Changes in Best Sellers Since World War One." *JPC*, 1: 379-88 (1968).

Bliss, C.S. "The Allen Press." *ABC*, 24: 15-7 (N-D 73).

Boardman, F.W. "Of Selling Many Books." *SchP*, 1: 171-7 (1970).

Boyd, E. "The First New Mexico Imprint." *PULC*, 33: 30-40 (1971).

Brown, John. "University Press Publishing." *SchP*, 1: 133-42 (1970).

Burger, N.K. "Truth or Consequences: Books and Book Reviewing." *SAQ*, 68: 152-66 (Sp 69).

Burke, J.G. "The Encino Press: A Brief Note and a Bibliography." *ABC*, 19: 19-23 (S 68).

Cameron, K.W. "The Quest for International Copywright in the Thirtieth Congress." *ESQ*, 51: 121-36 (1968).

Carney, T.L., and Joyce Crawford. "The Torch Press: A Preliminary History." *BI*, 21: 3-25 (1974).

Cate, H.L. "The Initial Publication of George Eliot's Novels in America." *BSUF*, 10: 65-9 (Sp 69).

Cave, Roderick. "The Work of the Private Presses." *BBn*, Ag 70, pp. 581-4.

Childs, James. "Our Accurately Honored Authors." *LJ*, 94: 722-4 (15 F 69).

Clark, C.E.F. "Hawthorne and the Pirates." *Proof*, 1: 90-121 (1971).

Clemens, Cyril. "Benjamin Shillaber and His Carpet Bag." *NEQ*, 14: 519-37 (S 41).

Coad, O.S. "An Early American Schoolbook." *JRUL*, 33: 46-8 (1970).

Cole, J.Y. "Of Coypright, Men & a National Library." *QJLC*, 28: 114-36 (1971).

Cook, D.L. "Practical Editions: The Writings of William Dean Howells." *Proof*, 2: 293-300 (1972).

Dallett, F.J. "A Colonial Binding and Engraving Discovery: The College (of New Jersey) Ledger of 1769." *PULC*, 31: 122-8 (1970).

Davis, R.B. "A Fitting Representation: Seventy-five Years of the *Virginia Magazine of History and Biography*." *VMHB*, 75: 259-70 (1967).

Dickey, I.B. "Bella French Swisher: Texas Editor and Litterateur." *SwAL*, 1: 8-11 (Ja 71).

Dorenkamp, J.H. "The Compositors of the Cambridge Platform." *SB*, 23: 196-9 (1970).

Dougan, Michael. "The Little Rock Press Goes to War, 1861-1863." *Ark Hist Q*, 28: 14-27 (Sp 69).

Duffy, J.J. "Problems in Publishing Coleridge: James Marsh's First American Edition of *Aids to Reflection*." *NEQ*, 43: 193-218 (Je 70).

Ehrlich, Heyward. "The Putnam's on Copyright." *PBSA*, 63: 15-22 (1Q 69).

Eldridge, H.G. "The American Republication of Thomas Moore's *Epistles, Odes, and Other Poems*: An Early Version of the Printing 'Game.'" *PBSA*, 62: 199-205 (2Q 68).

Everett, R.B. "Georgiana Revisited: The Beehive Press in Perspective." *GaR*, 26: 347-9 (Fa 72).

Felker, C.S. "Life Cycle in the Age of Magazines." *AR*, 29: 7-13 (Sp 69).

Firda, R.A. "German Philosophy of History and Literature in the *North American Review*, 1815-1860." *JHI*, 32: 133-42 (1971).

Foster, G.M. "Mirage in the Sahara of the Bozart: The Library of Southern Literature." *MissQ*, 28: 3-19 (Wi 74-5).

Franklin, Wayne. "John Norton the Printer: An Attribution." *SB*, 27: 185-7 (1974).

Fraser, J.H. "Indian Mission Printing in New Mexico: A Bibliography." *NMHR*, 43: 311-8 (O 68).

French, H.D. "Caleb Buglass, Binder of the Proposed Book of Common Prayer, Philadelphia, 1786." *Winterthur Portfolio*, 6: 15-32 (1970).

Friend, Llerena. "Posses All Over the Place: Publications of the Westerners." *LCUT*, 8: 58-65 (1968).

Gerber, J.C. "Practical Editions: Mark Twain's *The Adventures of Tom Sawyer* and *Adventures of Huckleberry Finn*." *Proof*, 2: 285-92 (1972).

Giusseppi, M.S. "The Work of Theodore de Bry and His Sons, Engravers." *Proc Huguenot Soc, London*, nv: 204-26 (1916).

Goff, F.R. "Rubrication in American Books of the Eighteenth Century." *PAAS*, 79: 29-43 (1969).

Gross, Beverly. "Culture and Anarchy: What Ever Happened to Lit Magazines?" *AR*, 29: 43-56 (Sp 69).

Hanson, Klaus. "The Tauchnitz *Collection of British and American Authors* Between 1841 and 1900." *YCGL*, 16: 53-9 (1967).

Harlan, R.D. "David Hall and the Townshend Acts." *PBSA*, 68: 19-38 (1974).

Harris, M.H. "Books for Sale on the Illinois Frontier: De Kalb County, 1855-1865." *ABC*, 21: 15-17 (1971).

Hauck, R.B. "Predicting a Native Literature: William T. Porter's First Issue of The Spirit of the Times." *MissQ*, 22: 77-84 (Wi 68-69).

Herder, D.M. "Haldeman-Julius, The Little Blue Books, and the Theory of Popular Culture." *JPC*, 4: 881-91 (Sp 71).

Hivnor, M.O. "Adaptions and Adaptors." *KR*, 30: 265-73 (Sp 68).

Hobbs, John. "Judging Contemporary: Criteria and the Editor." *Iowa R*, 5: 100-11 (Wi 74).

Howard, E.G. "An Unknown Maryland Imprint of the Eighteenth Century." *PBSA*, 63: 200-3 (1969).

Johnson, Alice. "An American Publication Date for Alexander Pope's Translation of the 'Hymn of St. Francis Xavier.'" *ELN*, 7: 262-4 (1970).

Johnson, R.C., and G.T. Tanselle. "*BAL* Addenda: Haldeman-Julius Little Blue Books." *PBSA*, 66: 67-71 (1Q 72).

———. "The Haldeman-Julius 'Little Blue Books' as a Bibliographical Problem." *PBSA*, 64: 29-78 (1Q 70).

Jones, Helen. "The Part Played by Boston Publishers of 1860-1900 in the Field of Children's Books." *HornB*, 45: 20-8 (F 69); 153-9 (Ap 69); 329-36 (Je 69).

Kable, W.S. "South Carolina District Copyrights: 1794-1820." *Proof*, 1: 180-98 (1971).

Korn, B.W. "Additional Benjamin and Alexander Levy Imprints." *PBSA*, 62: 245-52 (2Q 68).

Kuehl, Linda. "Talk with James Laughlin: New and Old Directions." *NYT*, 25 F 73, pp. 46-8.

Liebmann, W.B. "Random House: Or Fun and Profit in the Search for Excellence." *CLC*, 20: 3-15 (1971).

Liedel, D.E. "The Antislavery Publishing Revolutions of the 1850s." *Biblion*, 2: 67-80 (1972).

Liedel, D.E. "The Puffing of Ida May: Publishers Exploit the Anti-Slavery Novel." *JPC*, 3: 287-306 (Fa 69).

Lincoln, K.R. "Glass Beads: The American Edition of *Lord Jim*." *Conrad*, 2: 69-72 (Fa 69).

Lochard, M.T.P. "The Negro Press in Illinois." *JISHS*, 56: 570-91 (Au 63).

Lowry, H.W., and D.M. Chambers. "A Content Analysis: Middle-Class Morality and Ethical Values in *The Newberry Books*." *Eng Rec*, 18: 20-31 (Ap 68).

McCorison, Marcus. "Additions and Corrections to *Vermont Imprints*." *PAAS*, 84: 402-4 (1974).

McHaney, T.L. "An Early 19th Century Literary Agent: James Lawson of New York." *PBSA*, 64: 177-92 (2Q 70).

McPharlin, Paul. "Bostick and Thornley, Librarians and Publishers." *PW*, 150: 3206-9 (1946).

Mack, Maynard. "The Last Months at *Harper's*: Willie Morris in Conversation." *MissR*, 3: 121-30 (1974).

Madison, C.A. "Jews in American Publishing." *CJF*, 26: 282-7 (Su 68).

Mann, Charles. "A Hitherto Unseen Virginia Imprint: An Explanatory Note." *Serif*, 7: 32-3 (1970).

Mooney, J.E. "Loyalist Imprints Printed in America." *PAAS*, 84: 105-218 (17 Ap 74).

Nowell-Smith, Simon. "First Editions, English and American." *Lib*, 21: 68 (Mr 66).

Parker, P.J. "Ashbury Dickens, Bookseller, 1789-1801, or The Brief Career of a Careless Youth." *PMHB*, 94: 464-83 (1970).

Patterson, L.R. "Copyright and Author's Right: A Look at History." *HLB*, 16: 370-84 (O 68).

Purcell, J.S. "A Book Pedlar's Progress in North Carolina (Mason Locke Weems)." *NCHR*, 29: 8-23 (1952).

Pryce-Jones, Alan. "Translation and the Americans." *TLS*, 25 S 70, pp. 1109-10.

Quinn, D.B. "A List of Books Published for the Virginia Company." *VMHB*, 77: 347-60 (Jl 69).

Roaten, Darnell. "Denis Braud: Some Imprints in the Bancroft Library." *PBSA*, 62: 252-4 (2Q 68).

Rotundo, Barbara. "148 Charles Street." *AH*, 22: 10-5 (F 71).

Salley, A.S. "Books of the Confederacy, printed by Evans and Cogswell." *State Mag*, 23 My 54, p. 4.

———. "The First Presses of South Carolina." *PBSA*, 2: 26-69 (1908).

Sanders, F.K. "What a Rich Uncle Can Do." *SR*, 77: 338-49 (1969).

Shearer, J.F "French and Spanish Works Printed in Charleston." *PBSA*, 34: 137-70 (1940).

Shillinsburg, M.L. "South Carolina Copyright Legislation, 1783-94." *Proof*, 3: 357-61 (1973).

Shillingsburg, P.L. "Thackeray's *Pendennis* in America." *PBSA*, 68: 325-9 (3Q 74).

Shipton, C.K. "Bibliotheca Americana." *PBSA*, 62: 351-9 (3Q 68).

Stern, M.B. "The First German *Faust* Published in America." *AN&Q*, 10: 115-6 (Ap 72).

———. "Henry Frank: Pioneer American Hebrew Publisher." *AJA*, 20: 163-8 (N 68).

———. "A Rocky Mountain Book Store: Savage and Ottinger of Utah." *BYUS*, 9: 144-54 (1969).

———. "Saint-Pierre in America: Joseph Nancrede and Isaiah Thomas." *PBSA*, 68: 312-25 (3Q 74).

———. "A Salem Author and a Boston Publisher: James Tytler and Joseph Nancrede." *NEQ*, 47: 290-301 (Je 74).

Stevens, George. "The Birth of the Phoenix: The Early Years of *The Saturday Review of Literature*." *SatR/W*, 1: 7-10, 56, 61-2 (10 Ag 74).

Stith, M.E. "Some Observations on Regional Scholarly Publishing." *SchP*, 1: 151-7 (1970).
Stoddard, R.E. "A Note on the Eldridge Publishing Co." *Serif*, 11: 44-5 (1974).
Straumann, Herinrich. "Bestseller und Zeitgeschehen in den USA." *JA*, 15: 25-37 (1970).
Tanselle, G.T. "The Haldeman-Julius 'Little Blue Books' as a Bibliographical Problem." *PBSA*, 64: 29-78 (1Q 70).
———. "Imposition of Armed Services Editions." *PBSA*, 66: 434-5 (4Q 72).
———. "The Laurence Gomme Imprint." *PBSA*, 61: 225-40 (3Q 67).
———. "Stone & Kimball Addenda: Blossom's *Checkers*." *PBSA*, 62: 451-2 (3Q 68).
Taylor, Henry. "Boom: Recent Poetry from University Presses." *GaR*, 24: 349-55 (Fa 70).
———. "Vantage and Vexation of Spirit." *GaR*, 25: 17-26 (Sp 71).
Thelwell, Michael. "Publishing and the Black Experience." *Ramparts*, 8: 603 (O 69).
Thompson, S.O. "A 'Golden Age' in American Printing." *CLC*, 22: 22-3 (1973).
Viets, H.R. "The Printings in America of Polidori's *The Vampyre* in 1819." *PBSA*, 62: 434-5 (3Q 68).
Waldenrath, Alexander. "The German Language Newspress in Pennsylvania during the American Revolution." *German-Am Stud*, 6: 43-56 (1973).
Wall, M.R. "Alden Spooner: Printer and Patriot." *J Long Island Hist*, 10: 33-46 (#2 74).
Weales, Gerald. "Not for the Old Lady from Dubuque." *DQ*, 8: 65-83 (Su 73).
Weimerskirch, P.J. "'Printing in Delaware': A Review and Additions." *AN&Q*, 10: 19-27 (1971).
Williams, H.G. "John Miller and His Descendants." *SCHM*, 72: 104 (Ap 71).
Winton, Calhoun. "The Colonial South Carolina Book Trade." *Proof*, 2: 71-87 (1972).
Wise, David. "Hidden Hands in Publishing." *NRep*, 157: 17-8 (O 67).
Wolf, Edwin. "The American Printings of the Definitive Treaty of Peace of 1783 Freed of Obfuscation." *PBSA*, 65: 272-7 (1971).
Woodcock, George. "Poetry Magazines of the Thirties: A Personal Note." *TamR*, 60: 68-70 (1973).
Woodbridge, H.C. "Recent Wolf House Books." *JLN*, 5: 186 (1972).

Regionalism. Anon. *"Bibliography of Mississippi Writers." *NMW*, annually, 1968-.
Aadland, Dan. "Some Thoughts on Clichés and Conventions in the 60¢ Western." *PosS*, 4: 4-6 (Ja-F 73).
Adams, A.J. "Frank White: Rocky Mountain Critic." *Players*, 47: 248-51 (1972).
Adams, R.P. "Southern Literature in the 1890's." *MissQ*, 21: 277-81 (1968).
Allen, J.L. "Geographical Knowledge and American Images of the Louisiana Territory." *Western Hist Q*, 2: 151-70 (Ap 71).
Alsmeyer, H.L. "A Preliminary Southern Reconaissance." *SwAL*, 1: 67-71 (1971).
Altrocchi, J.C. "California Biography in Poetry." *Pac Hist*, 15: 1-12 (Wi 71).
Anderson, D.D. "Chicago as Metaphor." *Great Lakes R*, 1: 3-15 (Su 74).
———. "The Dimensions of the Midwest." *MidAmerica*, 1974, pp. 7-15.
———. "Ohio's Pioneer Poets." *NOQ*, 42: 9-18 (1969).
Anderson, P.A. "Images of the Midwest in Children's Literature." *Soc for the Study of Midwestern Lit*, 1: 15-20 (1974).
*Andrews, C.A. "The Literature of the Middle West: A Beginning Bibliography." *Great Lakes R*, 1: 35-67 (#1 74).
Andrews, T.F. "'Ho! For Oregon and California!': An Annotated Bibliography of Published Advice to the Emigrant, 1841-1847." *PULC*, 30: 41-64 (1971).
Andrews, W.D. "William T. Coggeshall: 'Booster' of Western Literature." *OH*, 81: 210-20 (Su 72).
Appleby, Jane. "Is Southern English Good English?" *SAB*, 35: 15-9 (Mr 70).

Arner, R.D. "John Smith, the 'Starving Time,' and the Genesis of Southern Humor: Variation on a Theme." *LaStud*, 12: 383-90 (Sp 73).

Arrington, Leonard, and Jon Haupt. "Community and Isolation: Some Aspects of 'Mormon Western.'" *WAL*, 8: 15-31 (Sp-Su 73).

———. "Intolerable Zion: The Image of Mormonism in Nineteenth Century American Literature." *WHR*, 22: 243-60 (Su 68).

———. "The Missouri and Illinois Mormons in Ante-Bellum Fiction." *Dialogue: J of Mormon Thought*, 5: 37-50 (Sp 70).

Ashliman, D.L. "The American West in Twentieth-Century Germany." *JPC*, 2: 81-92 (Su 68).

———. "The Novel of Western Adventure in Nineteenth-Century Germany." *WAL*, 3: 133-45 (Su 68).

Astro, Richard. "*The Big Sky* and the Limits of Western Fiction." *WAL*, 9: 105-14 (1974).

Atterbury, L.W. "The American West and the Archetypal Orphan." *WAL*, 5: 20-17 (Fa 70).

Autor, Hans. "Alaskan Poetry." *Alaska R*, 1: 48-55 (Sp 64).

Bain, Robert. "Some Maryland Muses." *SLJ*, 5: 124-30 (Sp 73).

Barnes, Robert. "Novels of the Oil Industry in the Southwest." *SwAL*, 2: 74-82 (Fa 72).

Barsness, John. "Creativity Through Hatred—and a Few Thoughts on the Western Novel." *WR*, 6: 12-7 (Wi 69).

———. "The Dying Cowboy Song." *WAL*, 2: 50-7 (Sp 67).

Bartlett, I.H., and C.G. Cambor. "The History and Psychodynamics of Southern Womanhood." *WS*, 2: 9-24 (1974).

Bassett, T.D.S. "A List of New England Bibliographies." *NEQ*, 44: 278-300 (Je 71).

Bataille, Robert. "The Esthetics and Ethics of Farming: The Southern Agrarian View." *Iowa State J of Res*, 49: 189-93 (1974).

Beckham, S.D "An Oregon Double-Dozen." *Pacific Northwest Lib Assoc Q*, 38: 4-14 (Fa 73).

Beeler, M.S. "Inyo." *Names*, 20: 56-9 (Mr 72).

Belknap, G.K. "Addenda to Belnap, Oregon Imprints." *PBSA*, 63: 128-9 (2Q 69); 64: 213-34 (2Q 70).

———. "More Addenda to Belknap, Oregon Imprints." *PBSA*, 66: 178-210 (2Q 72).

Bernet, J.W. "Alaska Native Literature in the College and University." *Alaskan Eng J*, 1: 12-6 (#1 74).

Berry, Wendell. "The Regional Motive." *SoR*, 6: 972-7 (1970).

Bethke, R.D. "Chapbook 'Gallows-Literature' in Nineteenth Century Pennsylvania." *PF*, 20: 2-15 (1970).

Billington, R.A. "The Frontier and I." *West Hist Q*, 1: 5-20 (Ja 70).

Blair, Walter. "Inquisitive Yankee Descendents in Arkansas." *AS*, 14: 11-22 (F 39).

Blassingame, J.W. "American Nationalism and Other Loyalties in the Southern Colonies, 1763-1775." *JSH*, 34: 50-75 (F 68).

Boatright, M.C. "The Beginnings of Cowboy Fiction." *SWR*, 51: 11-28 (Wi 66).

———. "The Formula in Cowboy Fiction and Drama." *WF*, 28: 136-45 (1969).

———. "Literature in the Southwest." *SRSCB*, 33: 12 (Je 53).

Boney, F.N. "Look Away, Look Away: A Distant View of Dixie." *GaR*, 23: 368-74 (Fa 69).

———. "The Southern Aristocrat." *MQ*, 15: 215-30 (1974).

Bonner, J.W. "Bibliography of Georgia Authors." *GaR*, passim, 1968-.

Boyd, E. "First New Mexico Imprint." *PULC*, 30: 30-40 (1971).

Bradshaw, H.C. "Review of North Carolina Fiction." *NCHR*, passim, 1969-.

Bragg, J.J. "Some Southwest Imprints: Presses of Arizona and New Mexico." *SWR*, 52: 26-42 (1967).

Bridges, Katherine. "'All Well at Natchitoches': A Louisiana City on the Stage." *LaStud*, 10: 85-91 (Su 71).

———. "Some Representative Louisiana Writers." *CathLW*, 40: 352-5 (F 69).

Brooks, Cleanth. "The Southern Temper." *Archiv*, 206: 1-15 (1969).

Brotherston, Gordon. "Ubirajara, Hiawatha, Cumanda: National Virtue from American Indian Literature." *CLS*, 9: 243-52 (S 72).

Brown, M.C. "Notes on Classical and Renaissance Analogues of Mississippi Negro Folklore." *MissFR*, 2: 37-41 (Su 68).

Brownell, B.A. "Urbanization in the South: A Unique Experience?" *MissQ*, 26: 105-20 (Sp 73).

Bruce, D.D. "Religion, Society and Culture in the Old South: A Comparative View." *AQ*, 26: 399-416 (O 74).

Brunvand, J.H. "As the Saints Go Marching By: Modern Jokelore Concerning Mormons." *JAF*, 83: 53-60 (Ja-Mr 70).

Buckley, W.F. "The Southern Imagination: An Interview with Eudora Welty and Walker Percy." *MissQ*, 26: 493-516 (Fa 73).

Budd, L.J. "The Forgotten Decades of Southern Writing, 1890-1920." *MissQ*, 21: 275-90 (Fa 68).

Bukey, E.B. "Frederick Gerstaecker and Arkansas." *AHQ*, 31: 3-14 (Sp 72).

Bullen, J.S., et al. "Annual Bibliography of Studies in Western American Literature." *WAL*, annually, winter, 1967-.

Bulow, Nannette. "The Maverick Metaphor: The Use of Cowboy Vernacular in Fiction." *PoeS*, 5: 10-6 (N 73).

Burton, Richard. "The Literary Taste of the West." *Criterion*, 23: 8-9 (Jl 00).

Bush, Robert. "Dr. Alderman's Symposium on the South." *MissQ*, 27: 3-19 (Wi 74).

Bush, A.L. "The Princeton Collections of Western Americana." *PULC*, 33: 1-17 (1971).

Byrd, L.B. "Using the Resources of Alaska in the Teaching of English." *Alaska Eng J*, 1: 21-6 (#1 74).

Calhoun, R.C. "Southern Voices: Past and Present." *SoR*, 4: 482-90 (Sp 68).

Calhoun, R.J. "The Ante-Bellum Literary Twilight: *Russell's Magazine*." *SLJ*, 3. 89-110 (Fa 70).

———. "Literary Criticism in Southern Periodicals During the American Renaissance." *ESQ*, 55: 76-82 (2Q 69).

———. "Southern Writing: The Unifying Strand." *MissQ*, 27: 101-8 (1973).

Calhoon, R.M., and S.C. Grisworld. "The Bard of Avon and Some Carolina Pop Song Lyrics (1775)." *NCaF*, 16: 12-4 (1968).

Campbell, H.M. "Notes on Religion in the Southern Renaissance." *Shen*, 6: 10-8 (Su 55).

Cansler, L.D. "Walter Dibben, and Ozark Bard." *KFR*, 13: 81-3 (O-D 67).

Cardwell, G.A. "The Plantation House: An Analogical Image." *SLJ*, 2: 1-21 (Fa 69).

*Carlson, A.W. "A Bibliography of the Geographers' Contributions to Understanding the American Southwest (Arizona and New Mexico), 1920-1971." *ArQ*, 28: 101-41 (1972).

Carson, B.F "Richard Renasence: The Virginia Writers' Club of the 1920's and *The Reviewer*." *Cabellian*, 2: 39-47 (Sp 70).

Carter, H.C., and M.C. Spencer. "Stereotypes of the Mountain Man." *Western Hist Q*, 6: 17-32 (Ja 75).

Cawelti, John. "God's Country, Las Vegas, and the Gunfighter." *WAL*, 9: 273-84 (Wi 75).

———. "Prolegomena to the Western." *WAL*, 4: 259-71 (Wi 70).

————. "Reflections on the New Western Films: The Jewish Cowboy, the Black Avenger, and the Return of the Vanishing American." *UChM*, 65: 25-32 (Ja-F 73).

Chametzky, Jules. "Our Decentraized Literature: A Consideration of Regional, Ethnic, Racial, and Sexual Factors." *JA*, 17: 56-72 (1972).

————. "Regional Literature and Ethnic Realities." *AR*, 31: 385-96 (Fa 71).

Charvat, William. "Everybody Writes in Ohio." *Ohioana*, 5: 67-9, 114-7 (Fa 62, Wi 62-63).

Clark, T.D. "Humor in the Stream of Southern History." *MissQ*, 13: 176-80 (Fa 60).

————. "The Piedmont South in Historical Perspective." *MissQ*, 24: 1-17 (Wi 70-71).

Clark, W.B. "The Serpent of Lust in the Southern Garden." *SoR*, 10: 805-22 (O 74).

Clayton, Lawrence. "'The Last Longhorn': A Poetic Denouement of an Era." *SFQ*, 37: 115-22 (Je 73).

Cobb, Buell. "The Sacred Harp of the South: A Study of Origins, Practices, and Present Implications." *LaStud*, 7: 107-21 (Su 68).

Cohen, B.J. "Nativism and Western Myth: The Influence of Nativist Ideas on the American Self-Image." *JAmS*, 8: 23-40 (Ap 74).

Collins, Sherwood. "Boston's Political Theatre: The Eighteenth-Century Pope Day Pageants." *ETJ*, 25: 401-9 (1973).

Cook, M.E., and T.D. Young. "Fugitive/Agrarian Materials at Vanderbilt University." *RALS*, 1: 113-20 (Sp 71).

Cook, Sylvia. "Gastonia: The Literary Reverberations of the Strike." *SLJ*, 7: 49-66 (Fa 74).

Core, George. "Southern Letters and the New Criticism." *GaR*, 24: 413-31 (Wi 70).

Corning, H.M. "The Prose and the Poetry of It." *OrHQ*, 74: 244-67 (S 73).

Cothran, K.L. "Pines and Pineywoods Life in South Georgia." *Proc Pioneer Am Soc*, 2: 69-82 (1973).

Cowan, Louise. "The Communal World of Southern Literature." *GaR*, 14: 248-57 (Fa 60).

Cox, J.M. "The South Once More." *SR*, 82: 163-78 (1974).

Cracroft, R.H. "Research in Western American Literature." *WAL*, 8: 188-94 (1974).

Cunningham, Keith, "The Respectability of Southwestern Literature." *Ariz Eng Bul*, 13: 69-70 (Ap 71).

Current-Garcia, Eugene. "Alabama Writers in the *Spirit*." *AlaR*, 10: 243-69 (O 57).

————. "'York's Tall Son' and His Southern Correspondents." *AQ*, 7: 371-84 (Wi 55).

Curtis, M.J. "Charles-Town's Church Street Theatre." *SCHM*, 70: 149-54 (Jl 69).

Dannett, S.G.L. "And the Show Went on . . . in the Confederacy." *MHM*, 61: 105-19 (Je 66).

Davenport, F.G. "Thomas Dixon's Mythology of Southern History." *JSH*, 36: 350-67 (Ag 70).

Davis, C.E., and M.B. Hudson. "Humor of the Old Southwest: A Checklist of Criticism." *MissQ*, 27: 179-99 (Sp 74).

Davis, C.T. "Jean Toomer and the South: Region and Race as Elements within a Literary Imagination." *SLitT*, 7: 23-38 (Fa 74).

Davis, R.B. "Charleston in Its Golden Age: Unique or Archetypal?" *SLJ*, 2: 148-51 (Fa 69).

————. "Culture on the Frontier." *SWR*, 53: 383-403 (Au 68).

————. "The Intellectual Golden Age in the Colonial Chesapeake Bay Country." *WMHB*, 78: 131-43 (Ap 70).

————. "Three Poems from Colonial North Carolina." *NCHR*, 47: 33-41 (Wi 69).

————. "The Valley of Virginia in Early American Literature." *Madisonian*, 3: 10-3 (Su 71).

De Bellis, Jack. "The Southern Universe and the Counter-Renaissance." *SoR*, 4: 471-81 (Sp 68).

Dent, Thomas. "Beyond Rhetoric toward a Black Southern Theatre." *BlackW*, 20: 14-24 (Ap 71).

Dessain, Kenneth. "Once in the Saddle: The Memory and Romance of the Trail Driving Cowboy." *JPC*, 4: 464-96 (Fa 70).

Dietrich, Mae. "Poetry in Maryland." *HJP*, 1: 26-8 (1972).

Dillingham, Peter. "The Literature of the American Indian." *EJ*, 62: 37-41 (Ja 73).

Dillingham, W.B. "Days of the Tall Tale." *SoR*, 4: 569-77 (Sp 68).

Donelson, K.L. "A Fistful of Southwestern Books for Students and Teachers." *Ariz Eng Bul*, 13: 71-6 (Ap 71).

———. "Some Adolescent Novels About the West: An Annotated Bibliography." *Elem Eng*, 49: 735-9 (My 72).

———. "The Southwest in Literature and Culture: A New Horizon for the English Class." *EJ*, 61: 193-204 (F 72).

Douglas, Ann. "Heaven Our Home: Consolation Literature in the Northern United States, 1830-1880." *AQ*, 26: 496-515 (D 74).

Doyle, James. "From Conservative Alternative to Vanishing Frontier: Canada in American Travel Narratives." *CRAS*, 5: 26-35 (Sp 74).

Doyle, E.J. "Zoé Campbell: A Southern Lady Travels North in 1860." *LaStud*, 13: 313-44 (1974).

Duke, Maurice. "Virginiana at the Cabell Library." *Cabellian*, 2: 59 (Sp 70).

Durham, Frank. "The First Nine Steck-Vaughn Pamphlets." *SLJ*, 3: 109-19 (Sp 71).

———. "The Poetry Society of South Carolina's Turbulent Year: Self-Interest, Atheism, and Jean Toomer." *SHR*, 5: 76-80 (Wi 71).

———. "The Southern Literary Tradition: Shadow or Substance?" *SAQ*, 67: 455-68 (Su 68).

Eaton, Clement. "Breaking a Path for the Liberation of Women in the South." *GaR*, 28: 187-99 (Su 74).

Edgar, W.B. "Notable Libraries of Early South Carolina." *SCHM*, 72: 105-10 (Ap 71).

———. "Some Popular Books in Colonial South Carolina." *SCHM*, 72: 174-8 (Jl 71).

Elliott, William. "Minnesota North Country Poetry: A Bibliography." *Soc for the Stud of Midwestern Lit*, 4: 8-10 (1974).

Engel, B.F. "On Nailing the Octopus; or, on Midwestern Popular Poetry." *Soc for the Study of Midwestern Lit*, 1: 21-7 (1974).

Erisman, Fred. "American Regional Juvenile Literature, 1870-1910: An Annotated Bibliography." *ALR*, 6: 109-22 (Sp 73).

———. "The Romantic Regionalism of Harper Lee." *AlaR*, 26: 122-36 (Ap 73).

———. "'Where We Plan to Go': The Southwest in Utopian Fiction." *SwAL*, 1: 137-43 (S 71).

Erno, R.B. "The New Realism in Southwestern Literature." *WR*, 7: 50-4 (Sp 70).

Esary, Logan. "Elements of Culture in the Old Northwest." *IMH*, 53: 257-64 (1957).

Eshleman, H.D. "A Grownup Western at Last." *ColQ*, 19: 107-12 (Su 70).

Etulain, R.W. "Comment [Literary regionalism in the Pacific Northwest]." *PNQ*, 64: 157-9 (O 73).

———. "Frontier and Region in Western Literature." *SwAL*, 1: 121-28 (1972).

———. "Historians, Archivists, and American Popular Culture." *New Archivist*, 1: 3-4 (Mr 72).

———. "The Historical Development of the Western." *JPC*, 7: 717-26 (Wi 73).

———. "Literary Historians and the Western." *JPC*, 4: 518-26 (Fa 70).

———. "The New Western Novel." *Idaho Yesterdays*, 15: 12-7 (Wi 72).

————. "Novelists of the Northwest: Needs and Opportunities for Research." *Idaho Yesterdays*, 17: 24-32 (Su 73).

————. "Origins of the Western." *JPC*, 5: 799-805 (Sp 72).

————. "Research Opportunities in Western Literary History." *Western Hist Q*, 4: 263-72 (Jl 73).

————. "Riding Point: The Western and Its Interpreters." *JPC*, 7: 647-51 (Wi 73).

————. "Three Western Novels." *JWest*, 10: 389-90 (Ap 71).

————. "Western American Literature: A Selective Annotated Bibliography." *Rendezvous*, 7: 67-78 (1972).

Everett, R.B. "Georgiana Revisited: The Beehive Press in Perspective." *GaR*, 26: 347-9 (Fa 72).

Evitts, William. "The Savage South: H.L. Mencken and the Roots of a Persistent Image." *VQR*, 41: 596-611 (Fa 73).

Fain, J.T. "Segments of Southern Renaissance." *SAB*, 36: 23-31 (1971).

————, and T.D. Young. "The Agrarian Symposium: Letters of Allen Tate and Donald Davidson, 1928-1930." *SoR*, 8: 845-82 (O 72).

Farrar, H.R. "Tales of New Mexico Territory, 1868-1876." *NMHR*, 43: 137-52 (Ap 68).

Fender, Stephen. "The Western and the Contemporary." *JAmSt*, 6: 97-108 (Ap 72).

Ferris, W.R. "Black Prose Narrative in the Mississippi Delta: An Overview." *JAF*, 85: 140-51 (Ap-Je 72).

Fiering, N.S. "Will and Intellect in the New England Mind." *WMQ*, 29: 515-58 (O 72).

Fife, Austin, and Alta. "Ballads of the Little Big Horn." *AmWest*, 4: 46-9, 86-9 (F 67).

————. "Spurs and Saddlebags: Ballads of the Cowboy." *AmWest*, 7: 44-7 (S 70).

Filbert, V.M. "The American Theater. Missoula - 1910." *Montana Mag West Hist*, 18: 56-68 (Au 68).

Fishwick, Marshall. "What Ever Happened to Regionalism?" *SHR*, 2: 393-401 (Fa 68).

*Flanagan, J.T. "A Midwest Bibliography." *NLB,* supplement: 3 (Je 47).

————. "Three Illinois Poets." *CentR*, 16: 313-28 (Fa 72).

Flanders, B.H. "Humor in Ante-Bellum Georgia: The Waynesboro *Gopher*." *EUQ*, 1: 149-56 (O 45).

Flores, Vetal. "Literature for Frontier Children." *SwAL*, 2: 65-73 (Fa 72).

Folsom, J.K. "English Westerns." *WAL*, 2: 3-13 (Sp 67).

————. "'Western' Themes and Western Films." *WAL*, 2: 195-203 (Fa 67).

Ford, J.H. "To a Young Southern Writer." *SoR*, 4: 291-8 (Sp 68).

Foster, G.M. "Mirage in the Sahara of the Bozart: *The Library of Southern Literature*." *MissQ*, 28: 3-19 (Wi 74-75).

Foster, R.E. "Kentucky Humor: Salt River Roarer to Ol' Dog Tray." *MissQ*, 20: 224-30 (Fa 67).

Frantz, J.B. "The Sam Houston Letters: A Corner of Texas in Princeton." *PULC*, 30: 18-29 (1971).

French, C.A. "Western Literature and the Myth-Makers." *Montana*, 22: 76-81 (1972).

Friedlander, Mitzi. "History of a Theatre." *FCHQ*, 45: 305-14 (Jl 71).

Friend, Llerena. "Posses All Over the Place: Publications of the Westerners." *LCUT*, 8: 58-65 (1968).

Fuson, Ben. "Three Kansas Utopian Novels of 1890." *Extrapolation*, 12: 7-24 (D 70); *KanQ*, 5: 63-77 (Fa 73).

Gale, Vi. "Poetry in Portland." *NwR*, 11: 73-9 (Sp 71).

Gardner, E.S. "My Stories of the Wild West." *Atl*, 218: 60-2 (Jl 66).

Garfield, Brian. "Cowboy as Myth and Man." *SatR*, 14 O 67; p. 100.

Gayle, Addison. "Cultural Hegemony: The Southern Writer and American Letters." *Amistad*, 1: 3-24 (1970).

———. "Reclaiming the Southern Experience: The Black Aesthetic 10 Years Later." *BlackW*, 23: 20-9 (Su 74).

Gazell, J.A. "The High Noon of Chicago's Bohemias." *JISHS*, 65: 54-68 (Sp 72).

Genthe, C.V. "New York Farm Values, 1870-1890." *FH*, 2: 3 (Ap 68).

Gibson, M.D. "The Western: A Selective Bibliography." *JPC*, 7: 743-8 (1973).

Gilliard, F.W. "Theatre in Early Idaho: A Brief Review and Appraisal." *Rendezvous*, 8: 25-31 (Su 73).

Gillis, E.A. "Southwest Literature: Perspectives and Prospects." *SwAL*, 2: 1-7 (Sp 72).

Godbold, E.S. "A Battleground Revisited: Reconstruction in Southern Fiction, 1895-1905." *SAQ*, 73: 99-116 (1974).

Going, W.G. "Alabama in the Short Story: Notes for an Anthology." *AlaR*, 22: 3-23 (Ja 69).

Göller, K.H. "Fiktion und Wirklichkeit in midwest-Roman." *LWU*, 6: 211-33 (1973).

Goodman, K.S. "The Chicago Theatre Society." *Nation*, 98: 308-9 (19 Mr 14).

Gower, Herschel. "Tennessee Writers Abroad, 1851: Henry Maney and Randal W. McGavock." *THQ*, 26: 396-403 (Wi 67).

Granger, B.H. "Folklore Along the Colorado River." *WR*, 6: 3-11 (1969).

Grantham, D.W. "Interpreters of the Modern South." *SAQ*, 63: 521-9 (Au 64).

Gray, R.J. "Southwestern Humor, Erskine Caldwell, and the Comedy of Frustration." *SLJ*, 8: 3-26 (Fa 75).

Greasley, Phil. "Notes on the Chicago Sense of Place: A North Side Perspective." *Soc for the Study of Midwestern Lit*, 4: 10-2 (1974).

Greene, Donald. "Western Canadian Literature." *WAL*, 2: 257-80 (Wi 68).

Gribben, William. "A Mirror to New England: The *Compendious History* of Jedediah Morse and Elijah Parish." *NEQ*, 45: 340-54 (1972).

Griffin, Hazel. "Some Folk Expressions from Northeastern North Carolina." *NCat*, 15: 56-7 (N 67).

Griffith, B.W. "Csardas at Salt Springs: Southern Culture in 1888." *GaR*, 26: 53-9 (1972).

Griffith, Lucille. "Anne Royal in Alabama." *AlaR*, 21: 54-63 (Ja 68).

Guilds, J.C. "Southern Literary Magazines, V: Simms as Editor and Prophet: The Flowering and Early Death of the *Southern Magnolia*." *SLJ*, 4: 69-92 (Sp 72).

Gurian, Jay. "The Unwritten West." *AmWest*, 2: 59-63 (Wi 65).

Guthrie, A.B., Jr. "Why Write About the West?" *WAL*, 7: 163-69 (1972).

Hakac, John. "Southwestern Regional Material in a Literature Class." *WR*, 7: 12-8 (Sp 70).

Halass, D.F. "Frontier Journalism in Colorado." *ColM*, 44: 185-203 (Su 67).

Hall, H.W. "Texas and Science Fiction." *SwAL*, 1: 144-8 (1972).

Halsell, W.D. "A Bibliography of Theses and Dissertations Relating to Mississippi." *JMiH*, annually, 1954-.

Hanna, Archibald, "Western Americana Collectors and Collections." *Western Hist Q*, 2: 401-4 (O 71).

———. "Western Americana at Yale." *Western Hist Q*, 2: 405-8 (O 71).

Hansen, Chadwick. "Salem's Witchcraft and DeForest's 'Witching Times.'" *EIHC*, 104: 89-108 (Ap 68).

Hansen, K.J. "The Millenium, the West, and Race in the Antebellum American Mind." *West Hist Q*, 3: 373-90 (O 72).

Harkness, D.J. "Louisiana: Leader in Literature." *DelR*, 7: 20-1 (My-Je 70).

Harrell, L.D.S. "The Development of the Lyceum Movement in Mississippi." *JMiH*, 31: 187-201 (Ag 69).

Regionalism

Hartley, M.L. "The Editor's Notebook." *SWR*, 59: iii-viii (Au 74).

Harwell, R.B. "Brief Candle: The Confederate Theatre." *PAAS*, 81: 41-160 (21 Ap 71).

Haslam, Gerald. "American Indians: Poets of the Cosmos." *WAL*, 5: 15-29 (Sp 70).

———. "American Literature: Some Forgotten Pages." *ETC*, 17: 221-38 (Je 70).

———. "American Oral Literature: Our Forgotten Heritage." *EJ*, 60: 709-23 (S 71).

———. "Literature of *The People*: Native American Voices." *CLAJ*, 15: 153-70 (D 71).

———. "Some New Classroom Vistas in Southwestern Literature." *Ariz Eng Bul*, 13: 48-54 (Ap 71).

———. "Who Speaks for the Earth?" *EJ*, 63: 42-8 (Ja 73).

Havard, W.C. "The New Mind of the South." *SoR*, 4: 865-83 (Au 68).

———. "Pride and Fall: A New Source for Interpreting Southern Experience." *SoR*, 10: 823-39 (O 74).

———. "Southwest Humor: Contemporary Style." *SoR*, 6: 1185-90 (Au 70).

Heimert, Alan. "Puritanism, the Wilderness, and the Frontier." *NEQ*, 26: 361-82 (1953).

Helmick, Evelyn. "Florida's Literature." *Carrell*, 14: 1-15 (#'s 1-2 74).

Henderson, R.A. "Culture in Spokane: 1883-1900." *Idaho Yesterdays*, 11: 14-9 (Wi 68).

Heyen, William. "Noise in the Trees: A Memoir." *Prose*, 4: 65-89 (1972).

Heyl, Edgar. "Plays by Marylanders, 1870-1916." *MHM*, 63: 70-7 (Mr 68), 179-87 (Je 68), 420-6 (D 68); 64: 74-7, 412-9 (Sp, Wi 69); 65: 181-4, 301-3 (Su, Fa 70); 67: 71-83 (Sp 72).

Hiers, J.T. "The Graveyard Epiphany of Southern Fiction: Transcendence of Selfhood." *SHR*, 9: 389-403 (Fa 75).

Hill, Gertrude. "The Southwest in Verse: A Selective Bibliography of Arizona and New Mexico Poetry." *ArQ*, 23: 306-12 (Wi 67).

Hines, D.M. "Humor of the City Hick and the Country Jake on the Inland Pacific Northwest Frontier." *WR*, 13: 15-20 (Sp 71).

Holifield, E.B. "The Renaissance of Sacramental Piety in Colonial New England." *WMQ*, 29: 33-48 (1972).

Holland, R.A. "Texas and the Great War: The West and Dittmar Collections." *LCUT*, 6: 43-55 (1974).

Hollis, C.C. "A Study of the Plain Folk." *SLJ*, 6: 134-8 (Sp 74).

Holmes, W.F. "William Alexander Percy and the Bourbon Era in the Yazoo-Mississippi Delta." *MissQ*, 26: 71-87 (Wi 72-73).

Horgan, Paul. "The Pleasures and Perils of Regionalism." *WAL*, 8: 167-71 (Wi 74).

Horwitz, C.A. "Chicago's Literature: A Desultory Remembrance." *LJ*, 97: 2045-50 (1 Je 72).

Howard, E.G. "An Unknown Maryland Imprint of the Eighteenth Century." *PBSA*, 63: 200-3 (3Q 69).

Howard, Milo. "Thomas McAdory Owen: Alabama's Greatest Bibliographer." *AlaR*, 28: 3-15 (Ja 75).

Howell, Elmo. "Eudora Welty and the Use of Place in Southern Fiction." *ArQ*, 28: 248-56 (1972).

———. "The Greenville Writers and the Mississippi Country People." *LaStud*, 8: 348-60 (Wi 69).

Hutchens, J.K. "Heritage of the Frontier." *SatR*, 23 S 67, pp. 34, 97-8.

———. "Literary Mine in the Cold Country." *SatR*, 48: 37-8 (S 65).

Hutchinson, W.H. "The Mythic West of W.H.D. Koerner." *AmWest*, 4: 54-60 (My 67).

———. "Packaging the Old West in Serial Form." *Westways*, 65: 18-23 (F 73).

Hutson, J.H. "Benjamin Franklin and the West." *Western Hist Q*, 4: 425-34 (O 73).

Hux, Samuel. "Old Southern Magic: Some Notes on 'Tragedy.'" *ModO*, 2: 297-305 (Sp 72).

Igo, John. "A Hidden Southwest Cycle." *SwAL*, 1: 60-6 (1971).

Inge, M.T. "Donald Davidson Selects the Best Southern Novels." *MissQ*, 24: 155-8 (Sp 71).

———. "Literary Humor of the Old Southwest: A Brief Overview." *LaStud*, 7: 132-43 (Su 68).

———. "Recent Southern Literary Criticism." *Appalachian J*, 2: 46-61 (Au 74).

———. "Richmond, Virginia, and Southern Writing (Introduction)." *MissQ*, 27: 371-4 (Fa 74).

Jacobs, R.D. "Campaign for a Southern Literature: The *Southern Literary Messenger.*" *SLJ*, 2: 66-98 (Fa 69).

James, S.B. "Western American Space and the Human Imagination." *WHR*, 24: 147-55 (Sp 70).

Jeranko, Mildred, and J.T. "Cowboys and Indians in the Classroom, Or a Shotgun Approach to Teaching American Literature." *Ariz Eng Bul*, 13: 62-4 (Ap 71).

Johnson, C.M. "Emerson Hough's American West." *BI*, 21: 26-42 (1974).

Johnson, Ellwood. "Individualism and the Puritan Imagination." *AQ*, 22: 230-7 (1970).

Johnston, T.E. "American Puritan Poetic Voices." *EAL*, 3: 125-6 (1968).

Jones, D.E. "Clenched Teeth and Curses: Revenge and the Dime Novel Outlaw Hero." *JPC*, 7: 652-5 (Wi 73).

———. "Virgins, Villains, and Violence in the Dime Novel Western." *JPC*, 4: 507-17 (Fa 70).

Jones, G.F. "Colonial Georgia's Second Language." *GaR*, 21: 87-99 (Sp 67).

Jones, H.M. "The Unity of New England Culture." *PMHS*, 79: 74-88 (1967).

Jorgensen, B.W. "Imperceptive Hands: Some Recent Mormon Verse." *Dialog*, 5: 23-34 (Wi 70).

Joseph, Richard. "New England Letters: Boston and Beyond." *Esquire*, 79: 75-6 (Je 73).

Joyner, C.W. "In the Bones." *StAR*, 2: 323-7 (Sp-Su 74).

Judson, John. "Regionalism and Contemporary Poetry." *New*, 25-26: 96-9 (1975).

Justus, J.H. "On the Restlessness of Southerners." *SoR*, 11: 65-83 (Ja 75).

Kcim, C.J. "Writing the Great Alaska Novel." *Alaska R*, 3: 47-51 (Fa-Wi 69).

———, and Jack Bernet. "From String Stories to Satellites: Portrayal of the Native Alaskan in Literature and Folklore." *BRMMLA*, 27: 167-73 (S 73).

Kelley, J.F., and C.E. Timberlake. "Impressions of Russian Pioneers in the West." *NMHR*, 42: 145-9 (Ap 67).

Kibler, J.E. "A New Letter of Simms to Richard Henry Wilde: On the Advancement of Sectional Literature." *AL*, 44: 667-70 (Ja 73).

King, Kimball. "Regionalism in the Three Souths." *TWA*, 54: 37-50 (1965).

Klinkowitz, Jerome. "The Mild, Mild West." *NAR*, 260: 52-3 (Wi 75).

Klotman, P.B. "The Slave and the Western: Popular Literature in the Nineteenth Century." *NDQ*, 41: 50-4 (1973).

Koch, Stephen. "The New York School of Poets: The Serious at Play." *NYT*, 11 F 68, pp. 4-5.

Koch, W.E. "The Big Circle Back to Kansas." *KM*, 1966, pp. 52-7.

Krumpelman, J.T. "*Tokeah*, the First English-Language Novel in Our Southwest." *SCB*, 28: 142-3 (Wi 68).

Kuhlman, T.A. "*Warner's History of Dakota County, Nebraska*: The Western County History as a Literary Genre." *WR*, 9: 57-64 (Wi 72).

Regionalism

Lambert, N.E. "Freedom and the American Cowboy." *BYUS*, 8: 61-71 (1967/68).
——. "Saints, Sinners, and Scribes: A Look at the Mormons in Fiction." *UHQ*, 36: 63-76 (Wi 68).
Landess, T.H. "The Present Course of Southern Fiction: 'Everynegro' and Other Alternatives." *ArlQ*, 1: 61-85 (Wi 68).
Larsen, L.H., and R.L. Branyan. "The Development of an Urban Civilization on the Frontier of the American West." *Societas*, 1: 33-50 (Wi 71).
Lavender, David. "The Petrified West and the Writer." *ASch*, 37: 293-306 (Sp 68).
Leamon, Warren. "The Flight from Alienation: Montgomery's *Fugitive* and the Southern Revival." *SoR*, 11: 233-41 (Ja 75).
Lee, Hector. "Tales and Legends in Western American Literature." *WAL*, 9: 239-54 (Wi 75).
Lefler, H.T. "Promotional Literature of the Southern Colonies." *JSH*, 33: 3-25 (F 67).
Leithead, J.E. "Buffalo Bill: Multi-Storied Scout and Plainsman." *ABC*, 20: 20-6 (Je 70).
——. "The Diamond Dicks: Frontier Lawmen." *ABC*, 20: 19-25 (S 69).
——. "Legendary Heroes and the Dime Novel." *ABC*, 18: 22-7 (Mr 68).
——. "The Outlaws Rode Hard in Dime Novel Days." *ABC*, 19: 13-9 (D 68).
——. "The Sage of the Young Wild West." *ABC*, 19: 17-22 (Mr 69).
Lieber, T.M. "The Significance of the Frontier in the Writing of Antebellum Southern History." *MissQ*, 22: 337-54 (Fa 69).
Liebert, H.W. "The First Two Years: Western Americana at Yale." *YULG*, 40: 121-59 (Ja 66).
Littlefield, D.F., and L.E. Underhill. "Renaming the American Indian: 1890-1913." *AmS*, 12: 33-45 (Fa 71).
Lochard, M.T.P. "The Negro Press in Illinois." *JISHS*, 56: 570-91 (Au 63).
Lovoll, O.S. "North Dakota's Norwegian-Language Press Views World War I, 1914-1917." *NDQ*, 39: 73-84 (Wi 71).
Loy, E.H. "Editorial Opinion and American Imperialism: Two Northwest Newspapers." *Oregon Hist Q*, 72: 209-24 (S 71).
Ludington, C.T. "Four Authors View the South: A Symposium." *SHR*, 6: 1-4 (Wi 72).
Lyon, T.J. "Research in Western American Literature." *WAL*, annually, winter, 1967-.
Lytle, A.N. "The Agrarians Today: A Symposium." *SR*, 3: 14-33 (Su 52).
——. "The Backwoods Progression." *AmR*, 1: 409-34 (S 33).
McCann, W.C. "Midwestern Humorous Journalism." *Soc for the Study of Midwestern Lit*, 1: 28-34 (1974).
McCorison, M.A. "Donald McKay—A Collector of Western Americana." *Western Hist Q*, 3: 67-76 (Ja 72).
McCown, R.A. "Impressions of Early Iowa: Pioneer Letters and Reminiscences." *BI*, 15: 11-6 (1971).
Maclachlan, J.M. "Southern Humor as a Vehicle of Social Evolution." *MissQ*, 13: 157-62 (Fa 60).
McDermott, Douglas. "Touring Patterns on California's Frontier, 1849-1859." *ThS*, 15: 18-29 (1974).
McMurtry, Larry. "Take My Saddle from the Wall." *Harper's*, 237: 37-46 (S 68).
Maloney, S.R. "Not for the 'Smart-Set in Omaha': The *Georgia Review* and Southern Literature." *NOR*, 4: 197-202 (1974).
——. "The Writer in the South." *InR*, 9: 173-7 (1974).
Mann, Charles. "A Hitherto Unseen Virginia Imprint: An Explanatory Note." *Serif*, 7: 32-3 (1970).

Marovitz, S.E. "Romance or Realism? Western Periodical Literature: 1893-1902." *WAL*, 10: 45-58 (My 75).

Marsden, M.T. "Riding Drag: Or, Reflections from the Rear." *JPC*, 7: 749-51 (Wi 73).

———. "Savior in the Saddle: The Sagebrush Testament." *IllQ*, 36: 5-15 (D 73).

Meyer, R.W. "Character Types in Literature about the American West." *Opinion*, 13: 21-9 (D 69).

———. "Mountain Man Stereotypes: Note and Reply." *Western Hist Q*, 6: 295-302 (Jl 75).

———. "The Outback and the West: Australian and American Frontier Fiction." *WAL*, 6: 3-19 (1971).

Mikami, Hikaru. "How the Agrarian Myth Works in the American Mind." *KAL*, 14: 68-75 (1972).

Miles, E.A. "The South and the Classical World." *NCHR*, 48: 258-75 (Su 71).

Millbrook, M.D. "The West Breaks in General Custer." *KHQ*, 36: 113-48 (Su 70).

Milton, J.R. "The American West: A Challenge to the Literary Imagination." *WAL*, 1: 267-84 (1967).

———. "Conversations with Distinguished Western American Novelists." *SDR*, 9: 15-57 (Sp 71).

———. "The Dakota Image." *SDR*, 8: 7-26 (Au 70).

———. "Inside the South Dakota Review." *MASJ*, 10: 68-78 (Fa 69).

———. "Literary or Not." *SDR*, 5: 2, 98-102 (Su 67).

———. "The Western Novel: Whence and What?" *Rendezvous*, 7: 7-21 (Wi 72).

Minnick, W.C. "The New England Execution Sermon, 1639-1800." *SM*, 35: 77-89 (Mr 68).

Montgomery, Marion. "Ceremony and the Regional Spirit." *SHR*, 5: 25-9 (1971).

Moore, E.M. "Some Recent Southern Things." *SR*, 78: 366-78 (1970).

Moore, R.S. "The Old South and the New: Paul Hamilton Hayne and Maurice Thompson." *SLJ*, 5: 108-22 (Fa 72).

———. "'A Distinctively Southern Magazine': The Southern Bivouac." *SLJ*, 2: 51-65 (Sp 70).

Morgan, D.T. "The Great Awakening in South Carolina, 1740-1775." *SAQ*, 70: np (Au 71).

Morrison, J.L. "W.J. Cash: The Summing Up." *SAQ*, 70: 477-86 (Au 71).

Morrow, P.D. "Bret Harte, Popular Fiction, and the Local Color Movement." *WAL*, 8: 123-32 (Fa 73).

Morrow, S.S. "A Brief History of Theatre in Nashville, 1807-1970." *THQ*, 30: 178-89 (Su 71).

Morsberger, R.E. "The Further Transformation of Tituba." *NEQ*, 47: 456-8 (S 74).

Mullin, D.C. "Early Theatres in Rhode Island." *ThS*, 11: 167-86 (1970).

Murdock, K.B. "Clio in the Wilderness: History and Biography in Puritan New England." *CH*, 14: 221-38 (1955).

Namba, Tatsuo. "Regionalism in Robert Penn Warren's *All the King's Men*."

Nash, G.B. "The Image of the Indian in the Southern Colonial Mind." *WMQ*, 29: 197-230 (Ap 72).

Neal, Larry. "Conquest of the South." *DramR*, 14: 169-74 (1970).

Nelson, Jane. "Meditations on a Metaphor: The Prairie Ocean." *PosS*, 4: 8-11 (Ag-S 73).

Newman, Charles. "The Writer as Rube; the Entrepreneur as Protagonist; the Midwest as Material." *AR*, 31: 313-42 (1971).

Nichols, R.L. "Printer's Ink and Red Skins: Western Newspapermen and Indians." *KanQ*, 3: 82-7 (Fa 71).

Nichols, W.W. "Slave Narratives: Dismissed Evidence in the Writing of Southern History." *Phylon*, 32: 403-09 (1971).

Nolan, P.T. "Georgia Drama Between the Wars (1870-1916): A Checklist." *GHQ*, 51: 216-30 (Je 67).

———. "Two Novels of the Twentieth-Century West." *JWest*, 10: 388-9 (Ap 71).

O'Brien, M.C. "A Variation on the Southern Literature Course: Çivil War Literature." *Notes on Teaching Eng*, 1: 4-6 (#2 74).

O'Brien, Michael. "Edwin Mims: An Aspect of the Mind of the South Considered." *SAQ*, 73: 199-212 (Ap 74).

Ohashi, Kichinosuke. "1920 Nendai to Chicago Renaissance." *EigoS*, 119: 704-6 (1974).

O'Neal, John. "Motion in the Ocean: Some Political Dimensions of the Free Southern Theatre." *TDR*, 12: 70-7 (Su 68).

Ortego, P.D. "Which Southwestern Literature and Culture in the English Classroom?" *Ariz Eng Bul*, 13: 15-7 (Ap 71).

Noverr, D.A. "New Dimensions in Recent Michigan Fiction." *Soc for the Study of Midwestern Lit*, 1: 9-14 (1974).

Packer, W.M. "Color Me Grey, Dobie, or Sandoz." *Ariz Eng Bul*, 13: 23-31 (Ap 71).

* Pady, Donald. "Annual Bibliography of Studies in Midwestern Literature." *MidAmerica*, annually, 1975-.

Page, E.F. "The Romance of Southern Journalism." *Taylor-Trotwood Mag*, 11: 140-8 (Je 10).

Parkes, H.B. "Freedom and Order in Western Literature." *DQ*, 4: 1-18 (1969).

Parks, E.W. "The Intent of the Ante-Bellum Southern Humorists." *MissQ*, 13: 163-8 (Fa 60).

Parsons, C.O. "Steamboating as Seen by Passengers and River Men: 1875-1884." *MissQ*, 24: 19-34 (Wi 71).

Pearce, T.M. "The Un-Static Southwest." *SAL*, 1: 1-3 (Ja 71).

Penrod, J.H. "The Folk Mind in Early Southwestern Humor." *TFSB*, 18: 49-54 (1952).

Peterson, L.S. "Brother Brigham and the Virginian." *PosS*, 2: 1-4 (My 71).

Peyroutet, J.A. "The North Dakota Farmer in Fiction." *NDQ*, 39: 59-71 (Wi 71).

Pickering, Sam. "Literature and Society in Colonial Virginia." *THQ*, 32: 290-5 (Fa 73).

Pilati, L.L. "The Fox Dialect." *NM*, 70: 145-8 (1969).

Pilkington, John. "Fuller, Garland, Taft, and the Art of the West." *PLL*, 8: 39-56 (Fa 72).

Pilkington, W.T. "The Recent Southwestern Novel." *SwAL*, 1: 12-5 (1971).

Polos, N.C. "Early California Poetry." *CHSQ*, 48: 243-55 (S 69).

Porter, Mark. "Mysticism of the Land and the Western Novel." *SDR*, 11: 79-91 (Sp 73).

Poulsen, Richard. "The Texas Longhorn and the Popular Trail Drive Novel." *PosS*, 4: 8-10 (Ja-F 73).

Powell, D.M. "Current Arizona Bibliography." *ArQ*, annually, 1967-.

* Powell, L.C. "Personalities of the West: A Nice Place to Visit." *Westways*, 65: 36-9, 66-9 (S 73).

Presley, D.E. "Carson McCullers and the South." *GaR*, 27: 19-32 (Sp 74).

———. "The Moral Function of Distortion in Southern Grotesque." *SAB*, 37: 37-46 (My 72).

Primeau, Ronald. "Slave Narrative Turning Westward: Deadwood Dick Rides into Difficulties." *Midamerica*, 1974, pp. 16-35.

Prior, G.T. "Charleston Pastime and Culture in the Nullification Decade, 1822-1832." *South Carolina Hist Assn, Proc*, nv: 36-44 (1940).

Pudner, H.P. "People Not Pedagogy: Education in Old Virginia." *GaR*, 25: 263-85 (Fa 71).

Purcell, J.S. "Review of North Carolina Nonfiction, 1969-1970." *NCHR*, 48: 142-6 (Sp 71).

Quantic, D.D. "The Revolt from the Village and Middle Western Fiction, 1870-1915." *KanQ*, 5: 5-16 (Fa 73).

Quinn, D.B. "A List of Books Purchased for the Virginia Company." *VMHB*, 77: 347-60 (Jl 69).

Ragan, Sam. "North Carolina Writers and the Southern Tradition: Review of North Carolina Fiction, 1972-3." *NCHR*, 51: 183-9 (Ap 74).

Ravenel, H.W. "Recollections of Southern Plantation Life Edited by Marjorie S. Mendenhall." *YR*, 25: 748-87 (1936).

Rees, R.A. "The Imagination's New Beginning: Thoughts on Esthetics and Religion." *Dialog*, 4: 40-7 (Au 69).

Reeves, Paschal. "A Checklist of Scholarship on Southern Literature." *MissQ*, annually, 1968-.

Reilly, J.M. "Images of Gastonia: A Revolutionary Chapter in American Social Fiction." *GaR*, 28: 498-518 (Fa 74).

Rexroth, Kenneth. "Renaissance by the Bay." *SatR*, 23 S 67, pp. 35-6.

Roberts, G.L. "The West's Gunmen." *American West*, 8: 10-5, 18-23 (Ja, Mr 71).

Roberts, Leonard. "Beauchamp and Sharp: A Kentucky Tragedy." *KFR*, 14: 14-9 (1968).

Robinson, Clayton. "Memphis in Fiction: Rural Values in an Urban Setting." *MVCBul*, 5: 29-38 (Fa 72).

Robinson, Jeffrey. "Le Cowboy." *Westways*, 66: 40-1, 85 (Ap 74).

Rock, Virginia. "Agrarianism: Agrarian Themes and Ideas in Southern Writing." *MissQ*, 21: 145-56 (Sp 68).

———. "The Fugitive-Agrarians in Response to Social Change." *SHR*, 1: 170-81 (Su 67).

———. "They Took Their Stand: The Emergence of Southern Agrarians." *Prospects*, 1: 205-97 (1975).

Rodgers, H.I. "The Muses Organized: The Formation of Learned Societies in the South." *SHR*, 6: 233-41 (Su 72).

Roemer, K.M. "American Utopian Literature (1888-1900): an Annotated Bibliography." *ALR*, 4: 227-54 (Su 71).

Rogers, T.W. "D.R. Hundley: A Multi-Class Thesis of Social Stratification in the Antebellum South." *MissQ*, 23: 135-54 (Sp 70).

Rowley, T.L. "The Church's Dramatic Literature." *Dialog*, 4: 129-38 (Au 69).

Rubin, L.D. "The Difficulties of Being a Southern Writer Today: Or Getting Out From Under William Faulkner." *JSH*, 29: 486-94 (N 63).

———. "Southern American Writers and the Black Man." *TC* (Australia), 25: 302-24 (Wi 71).

———. "Southern Literature: A Piedmont Art." *MissQ*, 23: 1-16 (Wi 69-70).

———. "Southern Local Color and the Black Man." *SoR*, 6: 1011-30 (Au 70).

Ruoff, J.C. "Frivolity to Consumption: Or, Southern Womanhood in Antebellum Literature." *CWH*, 18: 213-29 (1972).

Rusch, L.K. "The American Dream in Selected South Dakota Novels." *SDR*, 12: 58-72 (#3 74).

Russell, Don. "Cody, Kings, and Coronets." *AmWest*, 7: 4-10, 62 (Jl 70).

Sage, L.L. "Iowa Writers and Pointers: An Historical Survey." *An of Iowa*. 62: 241-70 (Sp 74).

Savage, G.L. "Tips for Writing Westerns." *Writer*, 87: 24-5 (Mr 74).

Savage, J.P. "Do-It-Yourself Books for Illinois Immigrants." *JISHS*, 57: 30-48 (Sp 64).

Savage, W.W. "Western Literature and its Myths: A Rejoinder." *Montana*, 22: 78-81 (1972).

Schlereth, T.J. "Regional Studies in America: The Chicago Model." *AmS*, 13: 20-34 (Au 74).

Scholz, R.F. "Clerical Consociation in Massachusetts Bay: Reassessing the New England Way and Its Origins." *WMQ*, 29: 391-414 (1972).

Schopf, Bill. "The Image of the West in the *Century*,— 1881-1889." *PosS*, 3: 8-13 (Mr 72).

Schroeder, F.E.H. "The Development of the Super-Ego on the American Frontier." *SJIS*, 57: 189-205 (1974).

Schwartz, Joseph. "The Wild West Show: 'Everything Genuine.'" *JPC*, 3: 656-66 (Sp 70).

Sederberg, N.B. "Antebellum Southern Humor in the *Camden Journal*: 1826-1840." *MissQ*, 27: 41-74 (Wi 73-74).

Seelye, John. "Some Green Thoughts on a Green Theme." *TriQ*, 23-4: 576-638 (Wi-Sp 72).

Seiler, W.H. "Magazine Writers Look at Kansas, 1854-1904." *KHQ*, 38: 1-24 (Sp 72).

Sellars, R.W. "The Interrelationship of Literature, History, and Georgraphy in Western Writing." *Western Hist Q*, 4: 171-85 (Ap 73).

Seshachari, Candadi. "Popular Western Fiction as Literature of Escape." *PosS*, 4: 5-8 (Ap 73).

Shapiro, Edward. "The Southern Agrarians and the Tennessee Valley Authority." *AQ*, 22: 791-806 (Wi 70).

———. "The Southern Agrarians, H.L. Mencken and the Quest for Southern Identity." *AmS*, 13: 75-92 (Fa 72).

Sherman, C.B. "The Development of American Rural Fiction." *Agricultural Hist*, 12: 67-76 (Ja 38).

Shockley, M.S. "Folklorists of Texas." *WAL*, 7: 221-23 (1972).

Shrell, Darwin. "Hunting in the Old South." *SoR*, 4: 467-70 (Sp 68).

Simms, L.M. "Constance Fenimore Woolson on Southern Literary Taste." *MissQ*, 22: 363-6 (Fa 69).

———. "Corra Harris on Patriotic Literary Criticism in the Post-Civil War South." *MissQ*, 25: 459-66 (1972).

———. "History as Inspiration: Philip Alexander Bruce and the Old South Mystique." *McNR*, 18: 3-10 (1967).

Simpson, L.P. "Boston Ice and Letters in the Age of Jefferson." *MASJ*, 9: 58-76 (Sp 68).

———. "The Civil War: Written and Unwritten." *SLJ*, 7: 132-45 (Fa 74).

———. "The Poetry of New Orleans." *SoR*, 4: xiii-xv (Su 68).

———. "The Southern Recovery of Memory and History." *SR*, 82: 1-32 (Wi 74).

———. "The Southern Writer and the Great Literary Secession." *GaR*, 24: 393-412 (Wi 70).

———. "Walter Sullivan and the Southern Possibility." *SLJ*, 5: 88-101 (Sp 73).

———. "Writing in the South: Some Prefatory Notes on Garnishing and Peopling a Void." *SoR*, 8: xv-xix (O 72).

Simpson, Louis. "California Poets." *LonM*, 11: 56-63 (F 71).

Sloane, K.W. "Plays about Louisiana, 1870-1915: A Checklist." *LaStud*, 8: 26-35 (Sp 69).

Slotkin, Richard. "Narratives of Negro Crime in New England, 1675-1800." *AQ*, 25: 3-31 (Mr 73).

Smith, C.P. "Plain Humor: New England Style." *NEQ*, 43: 645-72 (S 70).

Smith, D.A. "Mining Camps: Myth vs. Reality." *ColM*, 44: 93-110 (Sp 67).

Smith, D.J. "The American Railroad Novel." *MarkR*, 3: 61-71 (O 72); 85-93 (F 73).

Snell, J.W. "The Wild and Wooly West of the Popular Writer." *Nebraska Hist*, 48: 141-53 (Su 67).

Snyder, Gary. "The Incredible Survival of Coyote." *WAL*, 9: 255-72 (Wi 75).

Soderbergh, P.A. "Florida's Image in Juvenile Fiction." *FHQ*, 51: 153-65 (O 72).

———. "The South in Juvenile Series Books, 1907-1917." *Miss Q*, 27: 131-40 (Sp 74).

Sonnischsen, C.L. "The Wyatt Earp Syndrome." *AmWest*, 7: 26-8, 60-2 (My 70).

Spiegel, Alan. "A Theory of the Grotesque in Southern Fiction." *GaR*, 26: 426-37 (Wi 72).

Spinning, Bruce. "Notes Toward a Theory of Poetry in the American West." *PosS*, 5: 29-38 (Ja 74).

Stallings, F.L. "The West: The Perpetual Mirage in Literature." *MVCBul*, 5: 39-49 (Fa 72).

Stampfer, Judah. "Midwest Taste and Eastern Critics." *Nation*, 219: 473-6 (9 N 74).

Steckmesser, K.L. "Paris and the Wild West." *SWR*, 54: 168-74 (Sp 69).

Steen, I.D. "Charleston in the 1850's: As Described by British Travelers." *SCHM*, 71: 36-45 (1970).

Steensma, R.C. "'Stay Right There and Toughy It Out': The American Homesteader as Autobiographer." *WR*, 6: 10-8 (Sp 69).

Steeves, H.R. "The First of the Westerns." *SWR*, 52: 74-84 (Wi 68).

Stein, R.B. "Seascape and the American Imagination: The Puritan Seventeenth Century." *EAL*, 7: 17-37 (1972).

Stern, Jerome. "*Gone With the Wind*: The South as America." *SHR*, 6: 5-12 (Wi 72).

Sterne, R.C. "Puritans at Merry Mount: Variations on a Theme." *AQ*, 22: 846-58 (1970).

Stith, M.E. "Some Observations on Regional Scholarly Publishing." *SchP*, 1: 151-7 (1970).

Sullivan, Walter. "The Decline of Regionalism in Southern Fiction." *GaR*, 18: 300-8 (Fa 64).

———. "In the Time of the Breaking of Nations: The Decline of Southern Fiction." *SoR*, 4: 299-305 (Sp 68).

———. "Southern Writers in the Modern World: Death by Melancholy." *SoR*, 6: 907-19 (Au 70).

Sutton, R.P. "Nostalgia, Pessimism, and Malaise: The Doomed Aristocrat in Late-Jeffersonian Virignia." *VMHB*, 76: 41-55 (Ja 68).

Tauge, J.A. "William A. Gallaher, Champion of Western Literary Periodicals." *OH*, 69: 257-71 (Jl 60).

Taylor, J.G. "A Critical Forum for the Western Muse." *WAL*, 1: 3-5 (Sp 66).

Taylor, S.W. "Little Did She Realize: Writing for the Mormon Market." *Dialog*, 4: 33-9 (Au 69).

———. "Peculiar People, Positive Thinkers, and the Prospect of Mormon Literature." *Dialog*, 2: 17-31 (Su 67).

Thomas, F.R. "To Chiggers with Love: A Discussion of Place in Midwestern Poetry." *Soc for the Study of Midwestern Lit*, 1: 3-8 (1974).

Thomson, Chilton. "Ohio's First Bibliographer: Peter Gibson Thomson." *Ohioana*, 3: 80-2, 112-3, 115; 4: 18-20 (Fa, Wi 60; Sp 61).

Thompson, L.S. "German Travellers in the South from the Colonial Period 1865." *SAB*, 37: 64-74 (My 72).

———. "Kentucky Literature Crosses the River." *Ohioana*, 6: 50-1 (Su 63).

Thorp, Willard. "The Southern Mode." *SAQ*, 63: 576-82 (Au 64).

Tischler, N.M. "The Negro in Southern Fiction: Stereotype and Archetype." *NALF*, 2: 3-6 (1968).

Toledano, B.C. "Savannah Writers' Conference—1939." *GaR*, 22: 145-58 (Su 68).

Towns, S., and C.L. Roberts. "A Bibliography of Speech and Theatre in the South for the Year." *SSCJ*, annually, 1955-.

Tupper, V.G. "Plantation Echoes: A Negro Folk Music-Drama, as Given Each Year in Charleston, South Carolina." *Etude*, 55: 153 (1937).

Turner, Arlin. "Two Ways to Aproach Southern Literature." *SLJ*, 6: 111-6 (Fa 73).

Tuttle, W.M., Jr., and Surendra Bhana. "Black Newspapers in Kansas." *AmS*, 13: 119-24 (Fa 72).

Utley, F.L. "Onomastic Variety in the High Sierra." *Names*, 20: 73-82 (Je 72).

Vancura, Zdenek. "Bringing the Gospel to the Indians of New England." *PP*, 14: 81-90 (1971).

Van Orman, R.A. "The Bard in the West." *Western Hist Q*, 5: 29-38 (Ja 74).

Vickers, O.S. "The Gourd and Regional Writing." *MissFR*, 6: 5-8 (1972).

Wages, Jack D. "Mock Wills: Parody in the Colonial South." *SNL*, 9: 192-94 (Sp 72).

Walker, Don. "The Western Explorer as a Literary Hero: Jedidiah Smith and Ludwig Leichhardt." *WHR*, 29: 243-59 (Su 75).

Walker, D.D. "Can the Western Tell What Happens?" *Rendezvous*, 7: 33-47 (1972).

———. "Essays in the Criticism of Western Literary Criticism." *PosS*, 2: 1-3 (Mr 71); 1-4 (Ag 71).

———. "The Image of the West as Ocean." *PosS*, 2: 7-10 (F 71).

———. "The Love Song of Barney Tullus." *WHR*, 26: 237-45 (Su 72).

———. "The Meaning of the *Outlaw* in the Mind of the West." *PosS*, 2: 1-7 (S 71).

———. "The Mountain Man Journal: Its Significance in a Literary History of the Fur Trade." *Western Hist Q*, 5: 307-18 (Jl 74).

———. "Notes Toward a Literary Criticism of the Western." *JPC*, 7: 728-41 (Wi 73).

———. "Notes on the Popular Western." *PosS*, 3: 11-3 (N 71).

———. "Philosophical and Literary Implications in the Historiography of the Fur Trade." *WAL*, 9: 79-104 (1974).

———. "The Rise and Fall of Barney Tullus." *WAL*, 3: 93-102 (Su 68).

———. "Spencer Among the Sixguns: or, Social Darwinism in the Wild West." *PosS*, 5: 9-10 (Ja 74).

———. "Ways of Seeing a Mountain: Some Preliminary Remarks on the Fur Trader as Writer." *PosS*, 3: 1-7 (Ag-S 72).

Walker, W.S. "Buckskin West: Leatherstocking at High Noon." *NYFQ*, 24: 88-102 (Je 68).

Walters, R.G. "The Erotic South." *AQ*, 25: 177-201 (My 73).

Waters, Frank. "Words." *WAL*, 3: 227-34 (Fa 68).

Weatherby, H.L. "Progress and Providence." *SoR*, 8: 805-15 (O 72).

Weathers, Winston. "The Writer and His Region." *SwAL*, 2: 25-32 (Sp 72).

Weaver, R.M. "Realism and the Local Color Interlude." *GaR*, 22: 301-5 (1968).

Webb, Max. "Ford Madox Ford and the Baton Rouge Writers' Conference." *SoR*, 10: 892-903 (Au 74).

*Weber, F.J. "A Bibliography of California Bibliographies." *SCQ*, Mr 68, pp. 5-32.

Welland, Dennis. "The American Writer and the Victorian Northwest." *Bul John Rylands Lib*, 58: 193-215 (1975).

Welsh, J.R. "An Early Pioneer: Legare's *Southern Review*." *SLJ*, 3: 79-97 (Sp 71).

West, J.L.W. "Early Backwoods Humor in the Greenville *Mountaineer*, 1826-1840." *MissQ*, 25: 69-82 (Wi 71).

West, J.O. "Jack Thorp and John Lomax: Oral or Written Transmission?" *WF*, 26: 113-21 (Ap 67).

Welsh, J.R. "Succinct Perspective." *SAB*, 35: 49-50 (My 70).

Westbrook, Max. "Conservative, Liberal, and Western: Three Modes of American Realism." *SDR*, 4: 3-19 (Su 66).

———. "The Practical Spirit: Sacrality and the American West." 3: 193-205 (Fa 68).

Westbrook, Perry. "Writers of the Maine Coast." *Down East*, 3: 31-7 (O 56).

Westendorp, T.A. "Recent Southern Fiction." *HVF*, 1974, pp, 188-98.

Whetton, Betty. "A Very Personal View of Western Literature." *Ariz Eng Bul*, 13: 59-61 (Ap 71).

Whisenhunt, D.W. "The Bard in the Depression: Texas Style." *JPC*, 2: 370-86 (Wi 68).

White, J.I. "A Ballad in Search of its Author." *WAL*, 2: 58-62 (Sp 67).

———. "A Montana Cowboy Poet." *JAF*, 80: 113-29 (Ap-Je 67).

———. "The Strange Career of 'The Strawberry Roan.'" *Arizona and the West*, 2: 359-66 (Wi 69).

Whitehill, W.M. "Local History in the United States." *TLS*, nv: 1331-33 (13 N 70).

Whitney, Blair. "A Portrait of the Author as Midwesterner." *Great Lakes R*, 1: 30-42 (Wi 75).

Whitty, J.V. "Carolina Playmakers Golden Anniversary." *Southern Theatre*, 13: 11-5 (Sp 69).

Wilgus, D.K. "The Individual Song: 'Billy the Kid.'" *WF*, 30: 226-34 (Jl 71).

———, and Lynwood, Montell. "Clure and Joe Williams: Legend and Blues Ballad." *JAF*, 81: 295-315 (O-D 68).

Willett, Ralph. "The American Western: Myth and Anti-Myth." *JPC*, 4: 455-63 (Fa 70).

Williams, Cratis. "Kentucky's First Mountain Story." *KFR*, 17: 1-4 (Ja, Mr 71).

Williams, John. "The 'Western': Definition of the Myth." *Nation*, 193: 402 (18 N 61).

Wilson, J.D. "The Role of Slavery in the Agrarian Myth." *Ranam*, 4: 12-22 (1971).

Witmer, A.M. "The Contemporary Novel of the American West." *LWU*, 5: 37-45 (1972).

Wood, A.D. "The Literature of Impoverishment: The Woman Local Colonists in America, 1865-1914." *WS*, 1: 3-36 (1972).

Woodward, C.V. "The Southern Ethic in a Puritan World." *WMQ*, 25 (Jl 68).

———. "Why the Southern Renaissance?" *VQR*, 51: 222-39 (Sp 75).

Wylder, D.E. "The Popular Western Novel: An Essay Review." *WAL*, 4: 299-303 (Wi 70).

———. "The Western Hero from a Strange Perspective." *Rendezvous*, 7: 23-32 (1972).

Wynes, C.E. "Fanny Kemble's South Revisited: The South as Seen Through the Eyes of Her Daughter, Frances." *LaStud*, 12: 473-88 (1974).

———. "The Race Question in the South as Viewed by British Travellers, 1865-1914." *LaStud*, 13: 223-40 (1974).

Yardley, Jonathan. "The New Old Southern Novel." *PR*, 40: 286-93 (1973).

Young, Mary. "*The West and American Cultural Identity*: Old Themes and New Variations." *WHQ*, 1: 137-60 (Ja 70).

Young, T.D. "The Literary Vocation in the South." *SR*, 83: 730-36 (Fa 75).

Zug, C.G. "Folklore and Drama: The Carolina Playmakers and their 'Folk Plays.'" *SFQ*, 32: 279-94 (D 68).

Religion. Anon. "Issue on Mormons and Literature." *BYUS*, 14 (Wi 74).

Alcantara-Demalanta, O. "Christian Dimensions in Contemporary Literature." *Unitas*, 46: 213-23 (1973).

Ambrosetti, R.J. "Rosemary's Baby and Death of God Literature." *KFQ*, 14: 133-41 (1969).

Arrington, L.J. "The Intellectual Tradition of the Latter-Day Saints." *Dialog*, 4: 13-26 (Sp 69).

———, and Jon Haupt. "Intolerable Zion: The Image of Mormonism in Nineteenth-Century American Literature." *WHR*, 22: 243-60 (Su 68).

———. "The Missouri and Illinois Mormons in Ante-Bellum Fiction." *Dialog*, 5: 37-50 (Sp 70).

Religion

Ashliman, D.L. "The Image of Utah and the Mormons in Nineteenth-Century Germany." *UHQ*, 35: 209-27 (Su 67).

Avni, Abraham. "The Influence of the Bible on American Literature: A Review of Research from 1955 to 1965." *BB*, 27: 101-6 (O-D 70).

Bailyn, Bernard. "Religion and Revolution: Three Biographical Studies." *PAH*, 4: 83-169 (1970).

Barnes, D.R. "The Bosom Serpent: A Legend in American Literature and Culture." *JAF*, 85: 111-22 (Ap-Je 72).

Bausum, H.S. "Edenic Images of the Western World: A Reappraisal." *SAQ*, 67: 672-87 (1968).

Becker, L.D. "Unitarianism in Post-War Atlanta." *GHQ*, 56: 349-64 (Fl 72).

Bellman, S.I. "The Apocalypse in Literature." *Costerus*, 7: 13-25 (1973).

*Benton, R.M. "An Annotated Check List of Puritan Sermons Published in American before 1700." *BNYPL*, 74: 286-337 (My 70).

Bethke, R.D. "Chapbook 'Gallows-Literature' in Nineteenth-Century Pennsylvania." *PF*, 20: 2-15 (1970).

Boulger, J.D. "Puritan Allegory in Four Modern Novels." *Thought*, 14: 413-32 (Au 69).

Bozeman, T.D. "Religious Liberty and the Problem of Order in Early Rhode Island." *NEQ*, 45: 44-64 (1972).

Bruce, D.D. "Religion, Society and Culture in the Old South: A Comparative View." *AQ*, 26: 399-416 (O 74).

Buchanan, J.G. "Puritan Philosophy of History from Restoration to Revolution." *EIHC*, 104: 329-48 (O 68).

Buell, Lawrence. "The Unitarian Movement and the Art of Preaching in 19th Century America." *AQ*, 24: 166-90 (My 72).

Bush, Sargent. "Thomas Hooker and the Westminster Assembly." *WMQ*, 29: 291-300 (Ap 72).

Callahan, E.A. "The Tragic Hero in Contemporary Secular and Religious Drama." *LHY*, 8: 42-9 (Ja-Jl 67).

Cameron, K.W. "Death and Beyond in the American Renaissance." *ATQ*, 13: 1-27 (#2 72).

Campbell, H.M. "Notes on Religion in the Southern Renaissance." *Shen*, 6: 10-8 (Su 55).

Carver, Wayne. "Literature, Mormon Writers, and the Powers that Be." *Dialog*, 4: 65-73 (Au 69).

Cavell, Marcia. "Visions of a New Religion." *SatR*, 53: 12-4, 43-4 (19 D 70).

Cobb, Buell. "The Sacred Harp of the South: A Study of Origins, Practices, and Present Implications." *LaStud*, 7: 107-21 (Su 68).

Colacurcio, M.J. "A Better Mode of Evidence—The Transcendental Problem of Faith and Spirit." *ESQ*, 54: 12-22 (1Q 69).

Cooperman, Stanley. "The Devil's Advocate: Marching in among the Saints." *Chelsea*, 26: 156-66 (1969).

Dahl, Curtis. "Jonah Improved: Sea-Sermons on Jonah." *MSEx*, 19: 6-9 (S 74).

———. "New England Unitarianism in Fictional Antiquity." *NEQ*, 48: 104-15 (Je 75).

Daniel, W.H. "Protestantism and Patriotism in the Confederacy." *MissQ*, 24: 117-34 (Sp 71).

Davis, T.M. "The Exegetical Traditions of Puritan Typology." *EAL*, 5: 11-50 (Sp 70).

Decoo, Wilfried. "The Image of Mormonism in French Literature." *BYUS*, 14: 157-75 (1974).

Detweiler, Robert. "Christ and the Christ Figure in American Fiction." *ChS*, 47: 117-22 (Su 64).

———. "Christ in American Religious Fiction." *J Bible and Rel*, 32: 8-14 (Ja 64).

Deutsch, Babette. "Religious Elements in Modern Poetry." *Menorah J*, 29: 24-8 (Ja 41).

Dimeo, Steven. "Man and Apollo: A Look at Religion in the Science Fantasies of Ray Bradbury." *JPC*, 5: 970-8 (Sp 72).

Ditsky, John. "Hard Hearts and Gentle People: A Quaker Reply to Persecution." *CRAS*, 5: 47-51 (1974).

Donahue, Jane. "Colonial Shipwreck Narratives: A Theological Study." *BBr*, 23: 101-34 (1969).

Dorenkamp, J.H. "The *Bay Psalm Book* and the Ainsworth Psalter." *EAL*, 7: 3-16 (Sp 72).

——. "The Compositors of the Cambridge Platform." *SB*, 23: 196-9 (1970).

——. "The New England Puritans and the Name of God." *PAAS*, 80: 67-70 (1970).

Douglas, Ann. "Heaven Our Home: Consolation Literature in the Northern United States, 1830-1880." *AQ*, 26: 496-515 (1974).

Duffy, Joseph. "A Rage for Disorder." *KR*, 31: 694-9 (5 69).

Dunn, R.J. "Dickens and the Mormons." *BYUS*, 8: 325-34 (1968).

Durham, J.M. "Mark Twain Comments on Religious Hypocrisy." *RLA*, 10: 60-75 (1967).

Ellis, J.J. "The Puritan Mind in Transition." *WMQ*, 28: 26-45 (Ja 71).

Engel, B.F. "A Democratic Vista of Religion." *GaR*, 20: 84-9 (Sp 66).

Ferris, W.R. "Black Delta Religion." *MSF*, 2: 27-33 (Sp 74).

Friedman, A.W. "The Jew's Complaint in Recent American Fiction: Beyond Exodus and Still in the Wilderness." *SoR*, 8: 41-59 (Ja 72).

Frost, J.W. "Quaker Versus Baptist: A Religious and Political Squabble in Rhode Island Three Hundred Years Ago." *QH*, 63: 39-52 (1974).

Gemorah, Solomon. "Samuel Leavitt: Apocalyptic Prophet in Quest for Community." *AmS*, 13: 107-18 (Fa 72).

Glicksberg, C.I. "A Jewish American Literature?" *SWR*, 53: 196-205 (Sp 68).

Goodwin, G.J. "The Myth of 'Arminian-Calvinism' in Eighteenth-Century New England." *NEQ*, 41: 213-37 (Je 68).

Grabo, N.S. "The Art of Puritan Devotion." *SCN*, 26: 9 (1968).

Grande, L.M. "Renegade Priests in Recent Fiction." *CathLW*, 32: 407-10 (Ap 61).

Graves, M.P. "A Checklist of Extant Quaker Sermons, 1650-1700." *QH*, 63: 53-57 (1974).

Green, Martin. "The Calvinist Radicals: Paine et al." *Month*, 3: 149-52 (My 71).

Greene, Maxine. "Man Without God in American Fiction." *Humanist*, 25: 125-8 (1965).

Grumbach, Doris. "Christianity and Black Writers." *Renascence*, 23: 192-212 (Su 71).

Gunn, G.B. "Literature and Its Relation to Religion." *JR*, 50: 269-91 (Jl 70).

Hatch, Nathan. "The Origins of Civil Millennialism in America: New England Clergymen, War with France, and the Revolution." *WMQ*, 31: 407-30 (Jl 74).

Hauck, R.B. "The Comic Christ and the Modern Reader." *CE*, 31: 498-506 (F 70).

Hills, M.T. "The English Bible in America." *BNYPL*, 65: 277-88 (1961).

Hoffman, F.J. "The Religious Crisis in Modern Literature." *CLS*, 3: 263-72 (1966).

Holifield, E.B. "The Renaissance of Sacramental Piety in Colonial New England." *WMQ*, 29: 33-48 (Ja 72).

Hopper, S.R. "Challenge and Ordeal in Religion and Literature." *EUQ*, 22: 62-71 (Sp 67).

Hunsaker, K.B. "Mid-Century Mormon Novels." *Dialog*, 4: 123-8 (Au 69).

Hupp, Sandra. "Chicago's Church-Theatre Controversy." *Players*, 46: 60-4 (1971).

Hurley, N.P. "Liberation Theology and New York City Fiction." *Thought*, 48: 338-59 (1973).

Israel, Calvin. "*Early New England Catechisms.*" *SCN*, 32: 91 (1974).

James, S.B. "The Politics of Personal Salvation: The American Literary Record." *DQ*, 4: 19-45 (Su 69).

Jessee, D.C. "The Original Book of Morman Manuscript." *BYUS*, 10: 259-78 (1970).

Johnson, Ellwood. "Individualism and the Puritan Imagination." *AQ*, 22: 230-7 (1970).

Johnson, J.T. "The Covenant Idea and the Puritan View of Marriage." *JHI*, 32: 107-18 (Ja-Mr 71).

Jorgensen, B.W. "Imperceptive Hands: Some Recent Mormon Verse." *Dialog*, 5: 23-34 (Wi 70).

Kahan, Gerald. "The *Wayfarer*: An American Religious Pageant." *Players*, 47: 170-8 (1972).

Keller, Karl. "On Words and the Word of God: The Delusions of a Mormon Literature." *Dialog*, 4: 13-20 (Au 69).

Kellogg, Gene. "The Catholic Novel in Convergence." *Thought*, 45: 265-96 (Su 70).

Kershaw, G.E. "A Question of Orthodoxy: Religious Controversy in a Speculative Land Company: 1759-1775." *NEQ*, 46: 205-35 (Je 73).

Killinger, John. "The Death of God in American Literature." *SHR*, 2: 149-72 (Sp 68).

Klein, C.R. "Literature for America's Roman Catholic Children (1865-1895): An Annotated Bibliography." *ALR*, 6: 137-52 (Sp 73).

Koehler, Lyle. "The Case of the American Jezebels: Anne Hutchinson and Female Agitation During the Years of Antinomian Turmoil, 1636-1640." *WMQ*, 31: 55-78 (Ja 74).

Kumagai, Toshiaki. "'Death of God' in America." *KAL*, 15: 35-45 (1974).

Lambert, Neal. "Saints, Sinners and Scribes: A Look at the Mormons in Fiction." *UHQ*, 36: 63-76 (Wi 68).

Latourette, K.S. "The Contribution of the Religion of the Colonial Period to the Ideals and Life of the United States." *Americas*, 14: 340-55 (Ap 58).

Lauder, R.E. "The Catholic Novel and the 'Insider God.'" *Commonweal*, 101: 78-81 (1974).

Lawson, Sarah. "Where Was Moses When the Lights Went Out?" *JAF*, 85: 183-89 (Ap 72).

Lee, R.J. "Irony and Religious Mystery in the Contemporary Theatre." *SJIS*, 52: 350-64 (Fa 69).

McGhee, N.B. "The Folk Sermon: A Facet of the Black Literary Heritage." *CLAJ*, 13: 51-61 (S 69).

Maclear, J.F. "New England and the Fifth Monarchy: The Quest for the Millennium in Early American Puritanism." *WMQ*, 32: 223-60 (Ap 75).

McGiffert, Michael. "American Puritan Studies in the 1960's." *WMQ*, 27: 36-67 (Ja 70).

McLoughlin, W.G. "The Divers Origins of the American Tradition of Separation of Church and State." *CimR*, 2: 46-68 (Ja 68).

Manning, Stephen. "Typology and the Literary Critic." *EAL*, 5: 51-73 (1970).

Marx, Leo. "'Noble Shit': The Uncivil Response of American Writers to Civil Religion in America." *MR*, 14: 709-39 (1973).

Mathews, D.G. "The Second Great Awakening as an Organizing Process, 1780-1830: An Hypothesis." *AQ*, 21: 23-43 (Sp 69).

May, J.R. "The Apprenticeship of a Catholic Writer." *Renascence*, 24: 181-8 (Su 72).

Miller, Howard. "The 'Frown of Heaven' and 'Degenerate America': A Note on the Princeton Presidency." *PULC*, 31: 38-46 (1969).

Minnick, W.C. "The New England Execution Sermon, 1639-1800." *SM*, 35: 77-89 (Mr 68).

Mishra, V.M. "The Lutheran Standard: 125 Years of Denominational Journalism." *JQ*, 45: 71-6 (Sp 68).

Morgan, D.L. "Literature in the History of the Church: The Importance of Involvement." *Dialog*, 4: 26-32 (Au 69).

Morgan, D.T. "George Whitefield and the Great Awakening in the Carolinas and Georgia, 1739-1740." *GHQ*, 54: 517-39 (Wi 70).

————. "The Great Awakening in South Carolina, 1740-1775." *SAQ*, 70: np (Au 71).

Murphy, M.G. "The Relation between Science and Religion." *AQ*, 20: 275-95 (Su 68).

Myerson, Joel. "Transcendentalism and Unitarianism in 1840." *CLAJ*, 16: 366-68 (Mr 73).

Nall, K.A. "Love and Wrestling Brewster: A Study in the Puritan Ethos." *ArlQ*, 3: 80-97 (1971).

Nicholl, Grier. "The Image of the Protestant Minister in the Christian Social Novel." *CH*, 37: 319-34 (S 68).

Nichols, R.E. "Beowulf and Nepi: A Literary View of the Book of Mormon." *Dialog*, 4: 40-7 (Au 69).

Norton, Wesley. "Religious Newspapers in Antebellum Texas." *SHQ*, 79: 145-65 (O 75).

O'Brien, John. "'Becoming' Heroes in Black Fiction: Sex, Iconoclasm, and Immanence of Salvation." *SBL*, 2: 1-5 (Au 71).

————. "The Novel of Salvation." *Cresset*, 35: 12-5 (1972).

Parker, D.L. "Petrus Ramus and the Puritans: The 'Logic' of Preparationist Conversion Doctrine." *EAL*, 8: 140-62 (Fa 73).

Parker, Gail. "Mary Baker Eddy and Sentimental Womanhood." *NEQ*, 43: 3-18 (Mr 70).

Pease, J.H. "On Interpreting Puritan History: Williston Walker and the Limitations of the Nineteenth Century View." *NEQ*, 42: 232-52 (Je 69).

Peterson, L.S. "Brother Brigham and the Virginian: An Irreverent Inaccurate and Superficial Use of History to Explain Why the Polygamist Rather than the Cowboy is the Center of Mormon Frontier Fiction." *PosS*, 2: 1-4 (My 71).

Plumstead, A.W. "Puritanism and Nineteenth-Century American Literature." *QQ*, 70: 209-27 (1963).

Quimby, R.W. "The Changing Image of the Ministry and Its Influence on Sermons." *SSJ*, 35: 303-14 (Su 70).

Rees, R.A. "The Imagination's New Beginning: Thoughts on Esthetics and Religion." *Dialog*, 4: 21-5 (Au 69).

————. "Seeds of the Enlightenment: Public Testimony in the New England Congregational Churches, 1630-1750." *EAL*, 3: 22-9 (Sp 68).

————. "Toward a Bibliography of the Bible in American Literature." *BB*, 29: 101-8 (Jl-S 72).

Reiter, R.E. "On Biblical Typology and the Interpretation of Literature." *CE*, 30: 562-71 (1969).

Reynolds, D.S. "The Shifting Interpretation of Protestantism." *JPC*, 9: 593-603 (1975).

Rosenberg, B.A. "The Formulaic Quality of Spontaneous Sermons." *JAF*, 83: 2-20 (1970).

————. "The Genre of the Folk Sermon." *Genre*, 4: 189-211 (Je 71).

Rosenmeier, Jesper. "New England's Perfection: The Image of Adam and the Image of Christ in the Antinomian Crisis, 1634-1638." *WMQ*, 27: 435-59 (Jl 70).

————. "VERITAS: the Sealing of the Promise." *HLB*, 16: 26-37 (1968).

Rosenthal, Bernard. "Puritan Conscience and New England Slavery." *NEQ*, 46: 62-81 (Mr 73).

Rossel, R.D. "The Great Awakening: An Historical Analysis." *AJS*, 75: 907-25 (My 70).

Roth, G.L. "New England Satire on Religion, 1790-1820." *NEQ*, 28: 246-54 (Je 55).

Roth, R.J. "The Puritan Backgrounds of American Naturalism." *Thought*, 45: 503-20 (Wi 70).

Rowley, L.T. "The Church's Dramatic Literature." *Dialog*, 4: 129-38 (Au 69).

Scholz, R.F "Clerical Consociation in Massachusetts Bay: Reassessing the New England Way and Its Origins." *WMQ*, 29: 391-414 (1972).

Shenk, S.C. "American Mennonite Fiction." *Mennonite Life*, 23: 119-20 (Jl 68).

Shurr, W.H. "Typology and Historical Criticism of the American Renaissance." *ESQ*, 74: 57-63 (1Q 74).

Simmons, R.C. "Richard Sadler's Account of the Massachusetts Churches." *NEQ*, 42: 411-25 (1969).

Singer, David. "God and Man in Baptist Hymnals 1784-1844." *MASJ*, 9: 14-25 (Fa 68).

Smith, W.M. "The Prophetic Literature of Colonial America." *BS*, 100: 67-82 (1943).

Sorensen, P.D. "Nauvoo *Times and Seasons.*" *JISHS*, 55: 223-4 (Su 62).

Spanos, W.V. "The Critical Imperatives of Alienation: The Theological Perspective of Nathan Scott's Literary Criticism." *JR*, 48: 89-103 (Ja 68).

Spillers, H.J. "Martin Luther King and the Style of the Black Sermon." *BSch*, 3: 14-27 (S 71).

Stanford, D.E. "Edward Taylor Versus the 'Young Cockerill,' Benjamin Ruggles: A Hitherto Unpublished Episode from the Annals of Early New England Church History." *NEQ*, 44: 459-68 (S 71).

Stein, Stephen. "An Apocalyptic Rationale for the American Revolution." *EAL*, 9: 211-25 (Wi 75).

Stenerson, D.C. "An Anglican Critique of the Early Phase of the Great Awakening in New England: A Letter by Timothy Cutter." *WMQ*, 30: 475-88 (1973).

Sterne, R.C. "Puritans at Merry Mount: Variations on a Theme." *AQ*, 22: 846-58 (Wi 70).

Stone, Edward. "The Two Faces of America." *OhR*, 13: 5-11 (1972).

Strauch, C.F. "Typology and the American Renaissance." *EAL*, 6: 167-78 (Fa 71).

Suderman, E.F. "Fiction and Mennonite Life." *MASJ*, 10: 16-24 (Sp 69).

———. "A Study of the Revival in Late Nineteenth-Century American Fiction." *MethH*, 5: 17-30 (Ja 67).

Taussig, H.E. "Deism in Philadelphia During the Age of Franklin." *PH*, 37: 217-36 (1970).

Taylor, S.W. "Little Did She Realize: Writing for the Mormon Market." *Dialog*, 4: 33-9 (Au 69).

———. "Peculiar People, Positive Thinkers, and the Prospects of Mormon Literature." *Dialog*, 2: 17-31 (Su 67).

Thorp, Willard. "Catholic Novelists in Defense of Their Faith, 1829-1865." *PAAS*, 78: 25-117 (1968).

Tichi, Cecelia. "Spiritual Biography and the 'Lords Remembrancers.'" *WMQ*, 28: 64-85 (Ja 71).

———. "The Puritan Historians and Their New Jerusalem." *EAL*, 6: 143-55 (Fa 71).

———. "Thespis and the 'Carnall Hipocrite': A Puritan Motive for Aversion to Drama." *EAL*, 4: 86-103 (1969).

Treat, Robert and Betty. "Thoreau and Institutional Christianity." *ATQ*, 1: 44-7 (1969).

Turner, Maxine. "Three Eighteenth-Century Revisions of the *Bay Psalm Book.*" *NEQ*, 45: 270-77 (Je 72).

Valaik, J.D. "American Catholic Dissenters and the Spanish Civil War." *CathHR*, 53: 537-55 (Ja 68).

Vančura, Zdenek. "Bringing the Gospel to the Indians of New England." *PP*, 81-90 (1971).

Vartanian, Pershing. "Cotton Mather and the Puritan Transition into the Enlightenment." *EAL*, 7: 213-24 (1973).

Walker, R.W. "The *Keep-A-Pitchinin* or the Mormon Pioneer Was Human." *BYUS*, 14: 331-44 (1974).

Wander, P.C. "Salvation Through Separation: The Image of the Negro in the American Colonization Society." *QJS*, 57: 57-67 (1971).

Welch, J.W. "Chiasmus in the Book of Mormon." *BYUS*, 10: 69-84 (1969).

Wellhom, Charles. "Changing Attitudes toward the Church: Half a Century with Walter Lippmann." *Rel in Life*, 36: 574-82 (Wi 67).

Weaver, Richard. "The American as a Regenerate Being." *SoR*, 4: 633-46 (Jl 68).

White, D.F. "A Summons for the Kingdom of God on Earth: The Early Social Gospel Novel." *SAQ*, 67: 469-85 (Su 68).

Wills, Garry. "Catholic Faith and Fiction." *NYT*, 16 Ja 72, pp, 1-2, 14, 16, 20.

Wilson, Douglas. "Prospects for the Study of the Book of Mormon as a Work of American Literature." *Dialog*, 3: 29-41 (Sp 68).

Wolff, C.G. "Literary Reflections of the Puritan Character." *JHI*, 29: 13-32 (Ja-Mr 68).

Woodbury, L.J. "Mormonism and the Commercial Theatre." *BYUS*, 12: 234-40 (1972).

Science. Andrews, W.D. "The Literature of the 1727 New England Earthquake." *EAL*, 7: 281-94 (Wi 73).

Beaver, D.D. "Altruism, Pariotism, and Science: Scientific Journals in the Early Republic." *AmS*, 12: 5-20 (1971).

Benton, R.M. "The John Winthrops and Developing Scientific Thought in New England." *EAL*, 7: 272-80 (Wi 73).

Berger, A.I. "The Magic That Works: John W. Campbell and the American Response to Technology." *JPC*, 5: 867-93 (1972).

Boitano, Piero. "L'intellettuale americano tra la nouva scienza e l'arte." *SA*, 14: 431-50 (1968).

Brogan, H.O. "Early Experience and Scientific Determinism in Twain and Hardy." *Mosaic*, 7: 99-105 (#3 74).

Dean, Dennis. "Hitchcock's Dinosaur Tracks." *AQ*, 21: 639-44 (1969).

Dimeo, Steven. "Man and Apollo: A Look at Religion in the Science Fantasies of Ray Bradbury." *JPC*, 5: 970-8 (Sp 72).

Emmanuel, Lenny. "Whitman's Fusion of Science and Poetry." *WWR*, 17: 73-82 (1971).

Hartley, Peter. "Ecological Vision in American Literature." *Ecologist*, 5: 94-6 (Mr-Ap 75).

Holmes, L.E. "Science as Fiction: The Concept 'History as Science' in the *USSR*, 1917-1930." *Clio*, 4: 27-50 (O 74).

Kerber, L.K. "Sciences in the Early Republic: The Society for the Study of Natural Philosophy." *WMQ*, 29: 263-80 (1972).

Levy, L.B. "Critics, Scientists, and Biographer." *SoR*, 4: 1081-92 (1968).

Love, G.A. "Ecology in Arcadia." *ColQ*, 21: 175-85 (Au 72).

Martin, Jean-Pierre. "Edwards' Epistemology and the New Science." *EAL*, 8: 247-64 (Wi 73).

Murphey, M.G. "The Relation between Science and Religion." *AQ*, 20: 275-95 (Su 68).

Overfield, R.A. "Science in the *Virginia Gazette*, 1736-1780." *ESRS*, 16: 1-53 (#3 68).

Perrine, Laurence. "The Poet and the Laboratory." *SWR*, 58: 285-92 (1973); 59: 472-79 (1974).

Pizer, Donald. "Evolutionary Ideas in Late Nineteenth Century English and American Criticism." *JAAC*, 19: 305-10 (Sp 61).

———. "Evolutionary Literary Criticism and the Defense of Howellsian Realism." *JTGP*, 61: 296-304 (Ap 62).

Schatzberg, Walter, and others. "Relations of Literature and Science: A Bibliography of Scholarship, 1973-1974." *Clio*, 5: 97-121 (Fa 75).

Sporn, Paul. "Critique et science aux Etats-Unis." *Poetique*, 6: 223-38 (1971).

Stenton, M.N. "The Startled Muse: Emerson and Science Fiction." *Extrapolation*, 16: 64-6 (1974).

Science

Taylor, A.M. "Science Fiction: The Evolutionary Context." *JPC*, 5: 858-66 (Ap 72).

Waggoner, H.H. "Poets, Test-tubes, and the Heel of Elohim." *UKCR*, 13: 272-7 (Su 46).

Wilson, J.H. "Dacing Dogs of the Colonial Period: Women Scientists." *EAL*, 7: 225-35 (Wi 73).

Wolfe, G.K. "Vonnegut and the Metaphor of Science Fiction: The Sirens of Titan." *JPC*, 5: 964-9 (Sp 72).

Wyld, L.D. "Technology and Human Values." *Vectors*, 4: 21-3 (My-Je 69).

Yourgrau, Wolfgang. "On the New Physics and Modern Literature." *DQ*, 1: 29-41 (Sp 66).

Social and Political Aspects. Anon. "Artist in an Age of Revolution: A Symposium." *Arts in Soc*, 5 (Su-Fa 68).

————. "Contemporary Notes on Novels Concerned with Slavery." *ESQ*, 47: 138-9 (2Q 67).

Abrahams, R.D. "Some Varieties of Heroes in America." *JFI*, 3: 341-62 (1966).

Adams, W.P. "Republicanism in Political Rhetoric before 1776." *Pol Sci Q*, 85: 397-421 (S 70).

Adler, Joyce. "Melville On the White Man's War Against the American Indian." *Sci&Soc*, 36: 417-42 (Wi 72).

Aldridge, John. "Contemporary Fiction and Mass Culture." *NOR*, 1: 4-9 (Fa 68).

Ashley, L.F. "Huck, Tom and Television." *Eng Q*, 4: 57-64 (Sp 71).

Baker, Mioroslav. "Marxism and the Determinants of Critical Judgment." *JAAC*, 29: 33-41 (1970).

Barnes, H.E. "Literature and the Politics of the Future." *UDQ*, 5: 41-64 (Sp 70).

Barnett, Louise. "Nineteenth-Century Indian Hater Fiction: A Paradigm for Racism." *SAQ*, 74: 224-236 (Sp 75).

Beck, Julian. "Theater and Revolution." *EvR*, 12: 14-5 (My 68).

Behar, Jack. "Notes on Literature and Culture." *CentR*, 18: 197-220 (1974).

Behrend, Hanna. "Report of the Work of the Research Group on Working-Class Literature." *ZAA*, 18: 407-15 (1970); 20: 69-71 (1972).

Beisner, R.L. "Commune in East Aurora." *AH*, 22: 72-7, 106-9 (F 71).

Bellman, S.I. "Two-Part Harmony: Domestic Relations and Social Vision in the Modern Novel." *CEJ*, 3: 31-41 (1967).

Bennett, J.R. "American Literature and the Acquisitive Society, Background and Criticism: A Bibliography." *BB*, 30: 175-84 (O-D 73).

Berg, P.L. "Racism and the Puritan Mind." *Phylon*, 36: 1-7 (Mr 75).

Berger, Arthur. "Comics and Culture." *JPC*, 5: 164-77 (Su 71).

Bly, Robert. "On Political Poetry." *Nation*, 204: 522-4 (24 Ap 67).

Bolsterli, Margaret. "The Homosexual Ambience in Twentieth-Century Literary Culture." *DHLR*, 6: 71-85 (Sp 73).

Bowman, Estella. "The Propaganda Novel." *New Mexico State Teachers Col Stud*, 12: 23-41 (Je 48).

Blicksilver, Edith. "Literature as Social Criticism." *MLS*, 5: 46-54 (1975).

Blotner, Joseph. "The Modern American Political Novel." *SELit*, 45: 106-110 (S 68).

Borden, Caroline. "Bourgeois Social Relations in Nathaniel Hawthorne." *L&I*, 10: 21-8 (1971).

Bowman, S.E. "Utopian Views of Man and the Machine." *SLitI*, 6: 105-20 (#2 73).

Boyers, Robert. "Attitudes toward Sex in American High Culture." *Am Acad Pol & Soc Sci*, 376: 36-52 (Mr 68).

Bradbury, Malcolm. "The Cities of Modernism." *RLV*, 40: 442-9 (1974).

————. "Literatue an Sociology." *E&S*, 23: 87-100 (1970).

Breslaw, E.G. "Wit, Whimsy and Politics: The Uses of Satire by the Tuesday Club of Annapolis, 1744 to 1756." *VOR*, 32: 295-306 (Ap 75).

Brandt, Willy. "The Political Significance of the Theatre." *CompD*, 7: 222-30 (Fa 73).

Brock, William. "The Image of England and American Nationalism." *JAmSt*, 5: 225-45 (D 71).

Bromwich, David. "Suburbs and Extremities." *Prose*, 8: 25-38 (1974).

Brooks, M.E. "The Ideal and the Hero in Revisionist Literature." *L&I*, 15: 1-6 (1973).

Brophy, Brigid. "Our Impermissive Society." *Mosaic*, 1: 1-15 (Ja 68).

Brown, B.W. "Stanley Elkins' *Slavery*: The Antislavery Interpretation Reexamined." *AQ*, 25: 154-76 (My 73).

Brubaker, B.R. "Spoils Appointments of American Writers." *NFQ*, 48: 556-64 (D 75).

Bryant, J.H. "Politics and the Black Novel." *Nation*, 213: 660-2 (20 D 71).

Budd, L.J. "Baxter's Hog: The Right Mascot for an Editor (with CEAA Standards) of Mark Twain's Political and Social Writings." *CEAAN*, 3: 3-10 (1970).

Bullough, V.L. "An Early American Sex Manual, or Aristotle Who?" *EAL*, 7: 236-46 (Wi 73).

Bunker, Edward. "A Writer in Prison: The Catch in Rehabilitation." *Nation*, 218: 205-7 (16 F 74).

Burman, Howard, and Joseph Hanreddy. "The Activist Theatre of the Thirties." *Tst*, 18: 55-64 (1971-72).

Burke, Tom. "The New Homosexuality." *Esquire*, 72: 178-9, 304-18 (D 69).

Burke, William. "Football, Literature, Culture." *SWR*, 17: 45-58 (#2 74).

Byrd, Max. "The Detective Detected: From Sophocles to Ross Macdonald." *YR*, 64: 72-83 (Au 74).

Calderone, M.S. "'Pornography' as a Public Health Problem." *AJPH*, 62: 374-6 (Mr 72).

Cameron, K.W. "Emerson, Longfellow, Lowell and Others in Defense of R. Morris Copeland in 1863." *ESQ*, 47: 140-6 (2Q 67).

Canaday, Nicholas. "The Antislavery Novel Prior to 1852." *CLAJ*, 17: 175-91 (D 73).

Cardoso, J.J. "Hinton Rowan Helper and the Personality Politics of Negrophobia." *IllQ*, 34: 16-36 (1972).

Cardwell, G.A. "The Plantation House: An Analogical Image." *SLJ*, 2: 3-21 (Fa 69).

Caute, David. "Commitment Without Empathy: A Writer's Notes on Politics, Theatre, and the Novel." *TriQ*, 30: 51-7 (1974).

Cawelti, John. "The New Mythology of Crime." *Boun2*, 3: 325-358 (Wi 75).

Chandra, Naresh. "Socio-Economic Background of New Criticism." *Rajasthan J Eng Stud*, 1: 16-28 (Jl-D 74).

Chametzky, Jules. "Regional Literature and Ethnic Realities." *AR*, 31: 385-96 (Fa 71).

Christadler, Martin. "Politische Diskussion und literarische Form in der amerikanischen Literature der Revolutionzeit." *JA*, 13: 13-33 (1968).

Christman, C.L. "Charles A. Beard, Ferdinand Eberstadt, and America's Postwar Security." *M-A*, 54: 187-94 (Jl 72).

Clayborne, J.L. "Modern Black Drama and the Gay Image." *CE*, 36: 381-4 (N 74).

Cohen, S.B. "Student Unrest in the Decade before the American Revolution." *ConnR*, 7: 51-8 (#2 74).

Colby, Elbridge. "The New Economic Interpretation of Literary History." *SAQ*, 12: 347-55 (O 13).

Coleman, T.C. "America's False Gods." *ColQ*, 19: 21-37 (Su 70).

Cook, Sylvia. "Gastonia: The Literary Reverberations of the Strike." *SLJ*, 7: 49-66 (Fa 74).

Cooke, G.W. "Brook Farm." *ESQ*, 59-66 (Sp 70).

Cooke, Gwendolyn. "Reading Literary Works by Black and White Writers: Effects on Students' Attitudes." *JBlackS*, 5: 123-33 (D 74).

Cooper, Frederick. "Elevating the Race: The Social Thought of Black Leaders, 1827-50." *AQ*, 24: 604-25 (1972).

Cornelius, Paul. "Interracial Children's Books: Problems and Progress." *LIbQ*, 41: 106-27 (Ap 71).

Crandall, J.C. "Patriotism and Humanitarian Reform in *Children's Literature*, 1825-1860." *AQ*, 21: 3-22 (Sp 69).

Cunliffe, Marcus. "Americanness." *SoR*, 4: 1093-8 (1968).

Cutsumbis, M.N. "Selective Bibliography for the Sociological Study of Greek-Americans." *BB*, 25: 191-2 (S-D 68).

Daniel, W.H. "Protestantism and Patriotism in the Confederacy." *MissQ*, 24: 117-34 (Sp 71).

Davis, David. "Violence in American Literature." *An Am Acad Pol and Soc Sci*, 364: 28-36 (Mr 66).

Davis, D.B. "American Ideals and Contemporary Domestic Problems." *IJAS*, 1: 1-10 (1969).

DeLeon, David. "The American as Anarchist." *AQ*, 25: 516-38 (D 73).

Denisoff, R.S. "The Proletarian Renascence: The Folkness of the Ideological Folk." *JAF*, 82: 51-65 (1969).

Dessner, L.J. "'Woodstock,' A Nation at War." *JPC*, 4: 769-76 (Wi 71).

Detweiler, Robert. "Was Richard Hakluyt a Negative Influence in the Colonization of Virginia?" *NCHR*, 48: 359-69 (1971).

Dick, B.F. "Myth and Popular Culture." *ColQ*, 21: 81-7 (Su 72).

Dickeman, Mildred. "Thoughts on the Dominant American." *MR*, 15: 405-18 (1974).

Dickstein, Morris. "Politics and the Human Standard." *Parnassus*, 125-9 (1972).

Dillon, Millicent. "Literature and the New Bawd." *Nation*, 220: 219-22 (22 F 75).

Donaldson, Scott. "Family Crises in the Popular Novels of Nixon's Administration." *JPC*, 6: 374-82 (Fl 72).

———. "The Old World, the New Journalism, and the Novel." *Sewanee*, 82: 730-9 (Fa 74).

Doxey, W.S. "American Literary Response to the Philippine Problem: 1899-1906." *WGCR*, 2: 10-9 (1969).

Drabeck, B.A. "'Tarr and Fether': Poe and Abolitionism." *ATQ*, 14: 177-84 (1972).

Drake, F.C. "Witchcraft in the American Colonies, 1647-1662." *AQ*, 20: 694-725 (Wi 68).

Dunlop, Donald. "The Small Town and the City: An Interdisciplinary Approach to Thematic Studies." *IEY*, 23: 38-49 (N 73).

Eid, L.V. "'What Fools These Fanatics Be'—*Puck* and the Temperance Crusade, 1877-1896." *IllQ*, 38: 5-20 (Su 75).

Elliott, G.P. "Destroyers, Defilers, and Confusers of Men." *Atl*, 222: 74-80 (D 68).

Ellis, Albert. "Sexual Promiscuity in America." *An Am Acad Pol and Soc Sci*, 358: 58-67 (Jl 68).

England, J.M. "The Democratic Faith in American Schoolbooks." *AQ*, 15: 191-9 (Su 63).

Epstein, Seymour. "Politics and the Novelist." *DQ*, 4: 1-18 (Wi 70).

Eskin, S.G. "The Literature of the Spanish Civil War: Observations on the Political Genre." *Genre*, 4: 76-99 (Mr 71).

Essick, R.N. "The Problem of Boston." *KR*, 30: 140-3 (1968).

Ewing, G.W. "The Well-Tempered Lyre: Songs of the Temperance Movement." *SWR*, 56: 139-55 (Sp 71).

Filler, L. "Truth and Consequence: Some Notes on Changing Times and the Muckrakers." *AR*, 28: 27-41 (Sp 68).

Fisher, Edward. "Lost Generations, Then and Now." *ConnR*, 6: 13-25 (1972).

Fogarty, R.S. "Communal History in America." *AmS*, 12: 3-21 (Wi 73).

Foner, P.S. "Marx's Capital in the United States." *Sci&Soc*, 31: 461-6 (1967).

Francis, Richard. "Circumstance and Salvation: The Ideology of the Fruitlands Utopia." *AQ*, 25: 202-34 (My 73).

Frank, Joseph. "English Departments and the Social Revolution." *ADEB*, 24: 3-9 (1970).

Fraser, John. "Art and Violence: Some Considerations." *WHR*, 25: 107-24 (1971).

Frye, Northrop. "The Critical Path: An Essay on the Social Context of Literary Criticism." *Daedalus*, 99: 268-342 (Sp 70).

———. "Varieties of Literary Utopias." *Daedalus*, 94: 323-47 (Sp 65).

Fulcher, J.R. "Puritans and the Passions: The Faculty Psychology in American Puritanism." *J Hist Behavioral Sci*, 9: 123-39 (1973).

Funt, D.P. "Newer Criticism and Revolution." *HudR*, 22: 87-96 (1969).

Gaffney, Floyd. "Is Your Door Really Open?" *D&T*, 7: 4-7 (Fa 68).

Gaines, P.W. "Political Writings in the Young Republic." *PAAS*, 76: 261-92 (O 66).

Gayle, Addison. "Cultural Strangulation: Black Literature and the White Aesthetic." *BlackW*, 18: 32-9 (1969).

———. "The Politics of Revolution: Afro-American Literature." *BlackW*, 21: 4-12 (1972).

Gecas, Victor. "Motives and Aggressive Acts in Popular Fiction: Sex and Class Differences." *AJS*, 77: 680-96 (Ja 72).

Geiger, L.G. "Muckrakers—Then and Now." *JQ*, 43: 469-76 (Au 66).

Gelfant, Blanche. "Residence Underground: Recent Fictions of the Subterranean City." *SR*, 83: 406-38 (Su 75).

Gilbert, I.S. "Cultural Barriers to Modern Poetry Reading." *CJF*, 26: 43-6 (Fa 67).

Gitlin, Todd. "The Return of Political Poetry." *Cweal*, 94: 375-80 (1971).

Gläser, Rosemarie. "Sprache und Pragmatik der englisch-amerikanischen Werbung." *ZAA*, 18: 314-23 (1970).

Godbold, E.S. "A Battleground Revisited: Reconstruction in Southern Fiction, 1895-1905." *SAQ*, 73: 99-116 (1974).

Goist, P.D. "Town, City and 'Community' 1890-1920's." *AmS*, 14: 15-28 (Sp 73).

Gold, Herbert. "The End of Pornography." *SR*, 52: 25-7, 64 (31 O 70).

Goldberg, J F. "'Culture' and 'Anarchy' and the Present Time." *KR*, 31: 583-611 (1969).

Goodheart, Eugene. "Eros, Politics, and Pornography." *Midstream*, 15: 32-9 (Ap 69).

Goodman, Walter. "On Doing One's Thing." *ASch*, 37: 240-7 (Sp 69).

———. "On the (NY) Literary Left." *AR*, 29: 67-75 (Sp 69).

Graff, Gerald. "Babbit at the Abyss: The Social Context of Post Modern Fiction." *TriQ*, 33: 305-37 (Sp 75).

Grant, H.R. "Icarian and American Utopianism." *IllQ*, 34: 5-15 (1972).

Grass, Günter. "On Writers as Court Jesters." *ASch*, 38: 275-80 (Sp 69).

Green, Martin. "The Need for a New Liberalism." *Month*, 226: 141-7 (S 68).

Greene, Maxine. "Teaching the Literature of Protest." *Eng Rec*, 35: 89-85 (Fa 74).

Gross, S.L., and Eileen Bender. "History, Politics and Literature." *AQ*, 23: 487-519 (O 71).

Guerard, A.J. "My Grande Naufrage Fiction and Political Obsession." *SoR*, 8: 15-40 (Ja 72).

Guttmann, Allen. "Literature, Sociology, and 'Our National Game.'" *Prospects*, 1: 119 (1975).

———. "Sport in der amerikansichen Literatur: Bestatigung der Neuen Sozialkritik?" *Sportwissenschaft*, 4: 384-94 (1974).

Social and Political Aspects

Haight, Gordon. "Male Chastity in the Nineteenth Century." *ConR*, 218: 252-62 (Sp 72).

Halligan, John. "Hawthorne on Democracy: 'Endicott and the Red Cross.'" *SSF*, 8: 301-7 (1971).

Hall, J.A. "Concepts of Liberty in American Broadside Ballads, 1850-1870. A Study of the Mind of American Mass Culture." *JPC*, 2: 252-75 (Fa 68).

Haller, J.S. "From Maidenhood to Menopause: Sex Education for Women in Victorian America." *JPC*, 6: 49-69 (1972).

Harlan, R.D. "David Hall and the Townshend Acts." *PBSA*, 68: 19-38 (1974).

Harnack, Curtis. "Week of the Angry Artist." *Nation*, 204: 245-8 (20 F 67).

Harrell, L.D.S. "The Development of the Lyceum Movement in Mississippi Prior to 1860." *J Miss Hist*, 31: 187-201 (Ag 69).

Hart, Jeffrey. "Conservative: Literary and Political." *KR*, 30: 697-702 (1968).

Head, F.E. "The Theatrical Syndicate vs. the Child Labor Law of Louisiana." *LaStud*, 13: 365-74 (1974).

Herder, D.M. "Haldeman-Julius, The Little Blue Books, and the Theory of Popular Culture." *JPC*, 4: 881-91 (Sp 71).

Herring, M.D. "Politics in the Novels of Robert Penn Warren." *Ranam*, 4: 48-60 (1971).

Holbrook, David. "Pornography and Death." *CritQ*, 14: 29-40 (Sp 72).

Holdsworth, W.K. "Adultery of Witchcraft? A New Note on an Old Case in Connecticut." *NEQ*, 48: 394-407 (S 75).

Horwitz, R.P. "Architecture and Culture." *AQ*, 25: 64-82 (Mr 73).

Howe, D.W. "American Victorianism as a Culture." *AQ*, 27: 507-32 (D 75).

Howe, Irving. "Literary Criticism and Literary Radicals." *ASch*, 41: 113-20 (Wi 71-72).

Hughes, Catherine. "The Theatre Goes to War." *America*, 116: 759-61 (20 My 67).

Hultin, N.C. "Inchiquin and Cobbett: American Letters and British Politics." *N&Q*, 19: 91-93 (O 72).

Hyman, L.W. "Literature and Morality in Contemporary Criticism." *JAAC*, 30: 83-6 (1971).

Jackson, Bruce. "Prison Worksongs: The Composer in Negatives." *WF*, 26: 245-68 (O 67).

Jackson, J.A. "Sociology and Literary Studies." *JAmSt*, 3: 103-110 (Jl 69).

Jacobs, D.M. "William Lloyd Garrison's *Liberator* and Boston's Blacks." *NEQ*, 44: 259-77 (Je 71).

James, S.B. "The Politics of Personal Salvation: The American Literary Record." *DQ*, 4: 19-45 (Su 69).

Johnson, P.D. "'Goody to Sambo': The Contribution of the Black Slave Narratives to the Abolition Movement." *NALF*, 6: 79-84 (1972).

Johnson, P.H. "Peddling the Pornography of Violence: Further Thoughts on 'Iniquity.'" *Enc*, 34: 70-6 (F 70).

Jones, H.M. "The Genteel Tradition." *HLB*, 17: 5-20 (Ja 70).

Kahn, S.J. "Will and Power in American Literature." *SA*, 16: 429-51 (1970).

Kantrowitz, Arnie. "Homosexuals and Literature." *CE*, 36: 324-30 (N 74).

Kaplan, Harold. "Beyond Society: The Idea of Community in Classic American Writing." *Sociological R*, 42: 204-29 (1975).

Kariel, H.S. "Making Scenes in a Liberal Society." *MR*, 11: 223-55 (1970).

Katona, Anna. "Aunt Sally's Civilization and the American National Schizophrenia." *ALASH*, 14: 145-59 (1972).

Katz, Seymour. "'Culture' and Literature in American Studies." *AQ*, 20: 318-29 (Su 68).

Kaufman, Wallace. "Revolution, Environment and Poetry." *SAQ*, 77: 137-48 (Sp 72).

Kavolis, Vytautas. "The Social Psychology of Avant-garde Cultures." *STC*, 6: 13-34 (Fa 70).

Kazin, Alfred. "Our Middle-Class Storytellers." *Atl*, 222: 51-5 (Ag 68).

———. "The Writer and the City." *HM*, 237: 110-27 (D 68).

Kennicott, P.C. "Black Persuaders in the Antislavery Movement." *SM*, 37: 15-24 (Mr 70).

Kerrane, Kevin. "Reality 35, Illusion 3: Notes on the Football Imagination in Contemporary Fiction." *JPC*, 8: 437-52 (1974).

Klotman, P.R. "Racial Stereotypes in Hard Core Pornography." *JPC*, 5: 221-35 (Su 71).

Koehler, Lyle. "The Case of the American Jezebels: Anne Hutchinson and Female Agitation During the Years of Antinomian Turmoil, 1636-40." *WMQ*, 31: 55-78 (Ja 74).

Kornbluth, Jesse. "This Place of Entertainment Has No Fire Exit: The Underground Press and How It Went." *AR*, 29: 91-9 (Sp 69).

Kostelanetz, Richard. "On Irving Howe: The Perils and Paucities of Democratic Radicalism." *Salmagundi*, 2: 44-60 (Su 67).

Kotlowitz, Robert. "If You Must Build a Cultural Center." *HM*, 235: 96-8 (Jl 67).

Kovács, József. "Kisérletek a tömegkultúra megteremtésére az amerikai szocialista irodalomban." *Helikon*, 15: 259-62 (1969).

Krumpelmann, J.T. "Bayard Taylor, Kennan and Kennan, and Cassius M. Clay, or a Note on American-Russian Relations During the Civil War." *SCB*, 32: 227-9 (1972).

Kuhnel, Walter. "Amerikansiche Comicbooks und des Problem einer Analyse popularkultureller Phanomene." *JA*, 19: 58-87 (1974).

Lahr, John. "The Street Scene: Playing for Keeps." *EvR*, 12: 84-90 (O 68).

Lantz, H.R., et al. "Pre-Industrial Patterns in the Colonial Family in America." *AmSR*, 33: 413-26 (1968).

Leary, W.M. "Books, Soldiers and Censorship during the Second World War." *AQ*, 20: 237-45 (Su 68).

Leenhardt, Jacques. "Introduction à la Sociologie de la Littérature." *Mosaic*, 5: 1-10 (Wi 71-72).

Leithead, J.E. "The Revolutionary War in Dime Novels." *ABC*, 19: 14-21 (Ap-My 69).

Levine, Carl. "Literature and Social Relevance." *BRMMLA*, 24: 25-32 (1970).

Levine, Edward. "The Inflated Image: Satire and Meaning in Pop Art." *SNL*, 6: 43-50 (1968).

Levine, Paul. "The Politics of Alienation." *Mosaic*, 2: 3-17 (Fa 68).

Liedel, D.E. "The Antislavery Publishing Revolution of the 1850's." *Biblion*, 2: 67-80 (1972).

Lifton, R.J. "Protean Man." *PR*, 35: 13-27 (Wi 68).

Lincoln, C.E. "The New Blacks in Search of a Self." *BUJ*, 19: 53-60 (1971).

Lindberg-Seyersted, Brita. "Three Variations of the American Success Story: The Careers of Luke Larkin, Lemuel Barker, and Lemuel Pitkin." *ES*, 53: 125-41 (Ap 72).

Lindeen, S.A. and J.W. "Bryan, Norris, and the Doctrine of Party Responsibility." *MASJ*, 11: 45-53 (1970).

Lippman, Bert. "Literature and Life." *GaR*, 25: 145-58 (Su 71).

Lombard, C.M. "The First American Salon." *EA*, 19: 26-36 (Ja-Mr 66).

———. "An Old New York Salon—French Style." *NYHSQ*, 55: 38-51 (Ja 71).

Lowry, H.W., and D.W. Chambers. "A Content Analysis: Middle-Class Morality and Ethical Values in The Newbery Books." *Eng Rec*, 18: 20-31 (Ap 68).

McAuley, James. "Sex and Love in Literature." *Quadrant*, 78: 15-23 (1972).

McCarthy, Eugene. "Poetry and War." *Confr*, 8: 131-6 (Sp 74).

McConnell, F.D. "Rock and the Politics of Frivolity." *MR*, 12: 119-34 (1971).

McDermott, Douglas. "Propaganda and Art: Dramatic Theory and the American Depression." *MD*, 11: 73-81 (My 68).

McFadden, F.R. "Popular Arts and the Revolt against Patriarchism in Colonial America." *JPC*, 8: 286-94 (1974).

Maclachlan, J.M. "Southern Humor as a Vehicle of Social Evaluation." *MissQ*, 13: 157-62 (Fa 60).

McLoughlin, W.G. "The Divers Origins of the American Tradition of Separation of Church and State." *CimR*, 2: 46-68 (Ja 68).

Malin, Irving. "The Authoritarian Family in American Fiction." *Mosaic*, 153-73 (1971).

Margolies, Edward. "The American Detective Thriller and the Idea of Society." *Costerus*, 6: 93-8 (1972).

Martin, J.S. "Rhetoric, Society and Literature in the Age of Jefferson." *MASJ*, 9: 77-90 (Sp 68).

Marx, Leo. "Pastoral Ideals and City Troubles." *J Gen Ed*, 20: 251-71 (Ja 69).

Mathews, J.D. "Arts and the People: The New Deal Quest for a Cultural Democracy." *JAH*, 62: 316-29 (1975).

Matthews, F.H. "The Revolt Against Americanism: Cultural Pluralism and Cultural Relativism as an Ideology of Liberation." *CRAS*, 1: 4-31 (1970).

Mead, David. "1914: Chatauqua and American Innocence." *JPC*, 1: 339-56 (1968).

Mead, S.E. "American History as a Tragic Drama." *JR*, 52: 336-60 (O 72).

Mellard, J.M. "Racism, Formula, and Popular Fiction." *JPC*, 5: 10-37 (Su 71).

Michaelson, L.W. "Science Fiction and the Rate of Social Change." *Extrapolation*, 11: 25-7 (D 69).

Michelson, Peter. "The Pleasures of Commodity, or How to Make the World Safe for Pornography." *AR*, 29: 77-90 (Sp 69).

Murphey, M.G. "American Civilization as a Discipline." *EUQ*, 22: 48-60 (Sp 67).

Mikami, Hikaru. "How the Agrarian Myth Works in the American Mind." *KAL*, 14: 68-75 (1972).

Mills, N.C. "The Machine in the Anglo-American Garden." *CentR*, 14: 201-12 (1970).

———. "Prison and Society in Nineteenth-Century American Fiction." *WHR*, 24: 325-31 (Au 70).

Mishan, E.J. "Making the World Safe for Pornography." *Encounter*, 38: 9-30 (Mr 72).

Modlin, C.E. "Aristocracy in the Early Republic." *EAL*, 6: 252-7 (Wi 71-72).

Morrison, J.L. "W.J. Cash: The Summing Up." *SAQ*, 70: 477-86 (Au 71).

Morse, J.M. "Social Relevance, Literary Judgment, and the New Right." *CE*, 30: 605-16 (My 69).

Mulqueen, J.E. "Conservatism and Criticism: The Literary Standards of American Whigs, 1845-1852." *AL*, 41: 355-72 (N 69).

Musgrave, M.E. "Triangles in Black and White: Interracial Sex and Hostility in Black Literature." *CLAJ*, 14: 444-51 (Je 71).

Myerson, Joel. "Two Unpublished Reminiscences of Brook Farm." *NEQ*, 48: 253-60 (Je 75).

Narasimhaiah, C.D. "Traditional Values in American Literature." *LCrit*, 8: 1-12 (1968).

Newman, John. "American at War: Horror Stories for a Society." *Extrapolation*, 16: 33-41 (1974).

Nicholl, Grier. "The Image of the Protestant Minister in the Christian Social Novel." *CH*, 27: 319-34 (S 68).

Nichols, C.H. "Theodore Parker and the Transcendental Rhetoric: The Liberal Tradition and America's Debate on the Eve of Secession (1832-1861)." *JA*, 13: 69-83 (1968).

Nicolosi, Anthony. "Colonial Particularism and Political Rights." *NJH*, 88: 69-88 (1970).

Noble, D.W. "The Analysis of Alienation by 20th Century Social Scientists and 19th Century Novelists." *MVCBul*, 5: 5-19 (Fa 72).

Norton, Rictor. "The Homosexual Literary Tradition." *CE*, 35: 674-92 (Mr 73).

Oden, Gloria. "Literature and Politics: The Black Investment." *NALF*, 49-50 (1969).

O'Neal, John. "Motion in the Ocean: Some Political Dimensions of the Free Southern Theatre." *DramR*, 12: 70-7 (Su 68).

Panichas, G.A. "Politics and Literature." ModA, 12: 84-9 (Wi 67-68).

Parssinen, T.M. "Bellamy, Morris, and the Image of the Industrial City in Victorian Criticism." *MwQ*, 14: 257-66 (1973).

Pearce, R.H., with Sigurd Burckhardt. "Poetry, Language, and the Condition of Modern Man." *CentR*, 4: 1-31 (1960).

Pecora, Madeline. "The Date of *The Plain Case Stated*." *EAL*, 6: 185-6 (Fa 71).

Perry, Lewis. "Versions of Anarchism in the Anti-Slavery Movement." *AQ*, 20: 768-82 (Fa 68).

Peper, Jurgen. "Der heruntergekommene Surrealismus oder Regression als Fortschritt; Amerikas Youth Counter Culture in zwei Manifesten." *JA*, 19: 9-29 (1974).

Phillips, William. "Writing about Sex." *PR*, 34: 552-63 (Fa 67).

Pudner, H.P. "People Not Pedagogy: Education in Old Virginia." *GaR*, 25: 263-85 (Fa 71).

Poenicke, Klaus. "Der Drachentöter und das Menschenbild des Naturalismus." *JA*, 15: 88-100 (1970).

Poirier, Richard. "The Literature of Law and Order." *PR*, 36: 189-204 (Sp 69).

Poli, Bernard. "The Hero in France and America." *JAmSt*, 2: 225-38 (1968).

Pollin, B.R. "The Temperance Movement and Its Friends Look at Poe." *Costerus*, 2: 119-44 (1972).

Potter, Vilma. "New Politics, New Mothers." *CLAJ*, 16: 247-55 (D 72).

Prigozy, Ruth. "The Liberal Novelist in the McCarthy Era." *TCL*, 21: 253-64 (O 75).

Prosen, R.M. "'Ethnic Literature.'" *CE*, 659-70 (Mr 74).

Rader, Dotson. "The Day the Movement Died." *Esquire*, 78: 130-5 (N 72).

Rosa, A.F. "Charles Ives: Music, Transcendentalism, and Politics." *NEQ*, 44: 433-43 (1971).

Reck, R.D. "The Politics of Literature." *PMLA*, 85: 529-32 (1970).

Reichert, W.O. "Woman, Violence, and Social Order in America." *CentR*, 15: 1-22 (1971).

Reid, A.S. "Emersonian Ideas in the Youth Movement of the 1960's." *ATQ*, 9: 12-6 (1971).

Reilly, J.M. "Images of Gastonia: A Revolutionary Chapter in American Social Fiction." *GaR*, 28: 498-518 (Fa 74).

―――. "The Politics of Rough Guy Mysteries." *UDR*, 10: 25-31 (Su 73).

Reynolds, Mack, et al. "Change, Scott Fitzgerald, and Marxism." *S-FS*, 1: 269-75 (Fa 74).

Richards, R.F. "Literature and Politics." *ColQ*, 19: 97-106 (Su 70).

Riche, James. "Anarchism and Reaction in Contemporary Afro-American Literature." *L&I*, 1: 22-38 (1969).

―――. "Pragmatism: A National Fascist Mode of Thought." *L&I*, 9: 37-44 (1971).

―――. "Revisionism and the Radical Literature of the 1930's in the U.S.A." *L&I*, 7: 1-14 (1970).

Roche, James. "The Politics of Black Modernism." *L&I*, 8: 85-90 (1971).

Rock, Virginia. "The Fugitive-Agrarians in Response to Social Change." *SHR*, 1: 170-81 (Su 67).

Roemer, K.M. "The Heavenly City of the Late 19th-Century Utopians." *J Amer Stud Assn Texas*, 4: 5-17 (1973).

―――. "Sex Roles, Utopia, and Change: The Family Life in Late Nineteenth-Century Utopian Literature." *AmS*, 13: 33-48 (Fa 72).

―――. "'Utopia Made Practical': Compulsive Realism." *ALR*, 7: 273-6 (1974).

Social and Political Aspects

Roger, T.W. "D.R. Hundley: A Multi-Class Thesis of Social Stratification in the Antebellum South." *MissQ*, 23: 135-54 (Sp 70).

Rosa, A.F. "Charles Ives: Music, Transcendentalism, and Politics." *NEQ*, 44: 433-43 (1971).

Rose, A.H. 'Sin and the City: The Uses of Disorder in the Urban Novel." *CentR*, 16: 203-20 (Su 72).

Rosenblatt, Roger. "The People versus Literature." *ASch*, 18: 595-604 (Au 74).

Ross, G.D. "The 'Federalist' and the 'Experience' of Small Republics." *ECS*, 5: 59-68 (Su 72).

Rottensteiner, Franz, et. al. "Change, SF, and Marxism: Open or Closed Universes?" *S-FS*, 1: 84-93 (Fa 73).

Rubel, Warren. "The American Dream: Antique at Noon." *Cresset*, 33: 11-5 (1970).

Rysan, Joseph. "Folklore and Mass-Lore." *SAB*, 36: 3-9 (Ja 71).

Salem, J.M. "American Dream Between the Wars: The Effects of Sociology." *BSUF*, 10: 47-54 (Sp 69).

Salerno, H.F. "The Theatre and American Culture." *D&T*, 9: 70-2 (Wi 70-71).

Sanders, E.V. "Apropos Art and Its Trials, Legal and Spiritual." *Little R*, 7: 40-3 (Ja-Mr 21).

Sanders, F.K. "What a Rich Uncle Can Do." *SR*, 77: 338-49 (Sp 69).

Sassurski, J. "Der Antikommunismus und die Literatur der USA." *KuL*, 19: 603-32, 703-16 (1971).

Sayre, R.F. "American Myths of Utopia." *CE*, 31: 613-23 (Mr 70).

Schneidau, H.N. "The Age of Interpretation and the Moment of Immediacy: Contemporary Art vs. History." *ELH*, 37: 287-313 (Je 70).

Scholes, Robert. "Change, Scott Fitzgerald, and Marxism." *S-FS*, 1: 213 (Sp 74).

Schwarz, Egon. "Hermann Hesse, the American Youth Movement, and Problems of Literary Evaluation." *PMLA*, 85: 977-87 (O 70).

Sears, H.D. "The Sex Radicals in High Victorian America." *VQR*, 377-92 (Su 72).

Shank, Theodore. "Political Theatre as Popular Entertainment: San Francisco Mime Troupe." *DramR*, 18: 110-7 (Mr 74).

Shelton, F.W. "The Family in the Modern American Novel of Manners." *SAB*, 40: 33-9 (My 75).

Shor, Ira. "Questions Marxists Ask About Literature." *CE*, 34: 178-9 (N 72).

Siegel, Adrienne. "When Cities Were Fun." *JPC*, 9: 573-82 (1975).

Simon, J.D. "Reading the American Proletarian Fiction of the Thirties." *L&I*, 18: 25-32 (1974).

Simpson, Louis. "Dead Horses and Live Issues." *Nation*, 204: 520-2 (24 Ap 67).

Simpson, L.P. "Boston Ice and Letters in the Age of Jefferson." *MASJ*, 9: 58-76 (1968).

Small, R.C. "The Junior Novel and Race Relations." *NALF*, 8: 184-90 (Sp 74).

Smith, D.J. "The Glamor of the Glittering Rails." *MwQ*, 11: 311-26 (Sp 70).

Smith, Gene. "A Little Visit to the Lower Depths Via the *Police Gazette*." *AH*, 23: 63-73 (O 72).

Smith, H.N. "Something Is Happening But You Don't Know What It Is, Do You Mr. Jones?" *PMLA*, 85: 417-22 (1970).

Smith, P.H. "Charles Thompson on Unity in the American Revolution." *QJLC*, 28: 158-72 (1971).

Solotaroff, Theodore. "Reality and Socialist Realism." *SatR*, 54: 59-62 (30 J 71).

Spangler, G.M. "The Confession Form: An Approach to the Tycoon." *MASJ*, 10: 5-18 (Fa 69).

Spender, Stephen. "Writers and Politics." *PR*, 34: 359-81 (Su 67).

Stanford, Derek. "Sex and Style in the Literature of the 90's." *Cont R*, 216: 95-100 (F 70).

Stebbins, P.E. "Revolutionary Madness: America Through Counter Culture Spectacles." *IllQ*, 35: 36-46 (1972).

Stegner, S.P. "Protest Songs from the Butte Mines." *WF*, 26: 157-67 (Jl 67).

Stewart, D.H. "The Decline of WASP Literature in America." *CE*, 30: 403-17 (Mr 69).

——. "The Poetry of Protest." *MQR*, 10: 1-4 (Wi 71).

Stinson, Robert. "S.S. McClure's *My Autobiography*: The Progressive as Self-Made Man." *AQ*, 22: 203-12 (Je 70).

Stoehr, Taylor. "Transcendentalist Attitudes Toward Communitism and Individualism." *ESQ*, 20: 65-90 (2Q 74).

Stone, Edward. "The Two Faces of America." *OhR*, 13: 5-11 (1972).

Story, Ronald. "Class and Culture in Boston: The Athenaeum, 1807-1860." *AQ*, 27: 169-99 (My 75).

Strauss, Wolfgang. "Literatur im Dienst der Glorifizierung des imperialistischen Krieges." *ZAA*, 18: 391-406 (1970).

Strout, Cushing. "Personality and Cultural History in the Novel." *NLH*, 1: 423-37 (1970).

Stowell, M.B. "American Almanacs and Feuds." *EAL*, 9: 276-85 (Wi 75).

Sumner, Arthur. "A Boy's Recollections of Brook Farm." *ESQ*, 59: 43-5 (Sp 70).

Sutton, Henry. "Notes toward the Destitution of Culture." *KR*, 30: 108-15 (1968).

Teunissen, J.J. "Blockheadism and the Propaganda Plays of the American Revolution." *EAL*, 7: 48-62 (Fa 72).

Thelwell, Mike. "Black Studies: A Political Perspective." *MR*, 10: 703-12 (1969).

Thompson, J.S. "The Case against Noam Chomsky and B.F. Skinner." *L&I*, 11: 49-60 (1972).

Trachtenberg, Stanley. "American Dreams, American Realities." *AR*, 28: 277-92 (1968).

True, Michael. "War and Poetry." *Confr*, 8: 137-44 (Sp 74).

Twining, Edward. "Politics and the Imagination." *DQ*, 5: 1-18 (Su 70).

Tytell, John. "The Beat Generation and the Continuing American Revolution." *ASch*, 42: 30-17 (Sp 73).

Valaik, J.D. "American Catholic Dissenters and the Spanish Civil War." *CathHR*, 53: 537-55 (Ja 68).

Valletta, C.L. "Putting On the American Dream." *Dialogist*, 1: 41-9 (Su 69).

VanDerBeets, Richard. "'A Thirst for Empire': The Indian Captivity Narrative as Propaganda." *RSW*, 40: 207-15 (1972).

Vanderbilt, Kermit. "Writers of the Troubled Sixties." *Nation*, 217: 661-5 (17 D 73).

Viereck, Peter. "The Muse and the Machine." *EA*, 20: 38-46 (Ja-Mr 67).

Wagner, Geoffrey. "The Sex Books." *DQ*, 6: 29-40 (Sp 71).

Wain, John. "The New Puritanism, the New Academicism, the New, the New." *CritQ*, 14: 7-18 (Sp 72).

Wakefield, Dan. "The Literature of the Student Revolt: An Early Appraisal." *DQ*, 4: 1-22 (Au 69).

Watson, C.S. "A Denunciation on the Stage of Spanish Rule: James Workman's *Liberty in Louisiana* (1804)." *LaHi*, 11: 245-58 (Su 70).

Weaver, Richard. "The American as a Regenerate Being." *SoR*, 4: 633-46 (Jl 68).

Webb, Max. "Sunday Heroes: The Emergence of the Professional Football Novel." *JPC*, 8: 453-61 (1974).

Weinstein, Bernard. "Bryant, Annexation, and the Mexican War." *ESQ*, 63: 19-24 (1971).

Whisenhunt, D.W. "The Bard in the Depression: Texas Style." *JPC*, 2: 370-86 (Wi 68).

White, D.E. "A Summons for the Kingdom of God on Earth: The Early Social-Gospel Novel." *SAQ*, 67: 469-85 (Su 68).

White, James. "Government and Art: A New Deal Venture." *MarkR*, 4: 85-9 (F 75).

Widmer, Kingsley. "The Rebellious Culture: Reflections on its Functions in American Society." *CentR*, 17: 338-56 (Fa 73).

Williamson, Alan. "The Energy Crisis in Poetry: News from Pittsburgh." *Shen*, 26: 41-53 (Fa 74).

Wilson, J.D. "The Role of Slavery in the Agrarian Myth." *Ranam*, 4: 12-22 (1971).

Wilson, J.T. "Is Utopia Possible?" *Eng(L)*, 20: 51-5 (Su 71).

Wilson, W.C. "Facts Versus Fears: Why Should We Worry About Pornography?" *AAAPSS*, 397: 105-17 (S 71).

Winthrop, Henry. "Disalienation, Decadence, and Pathology in Art." DR, 49: 31-45 (Au 69).

――――. "Sexuality in Literature." *ColQ*, 21: 337-58 (Wi 73).

Wirzberger, Karl-Heinz. "Great Tradition oder Episode? Nonkonformismus, Protest, und Engagement in der amerikanischen Gegenwartsliteratur." *ZAA*, 16: 5-24 (1968).

――――. "The October Revolution and American Literature." *ZAA*, 16: 229-56 (1968).

Woodward, C.V. "The Southern Ethic in a Puritan World." *WMQ*, 25: np (Jl 68).

Wohl, R.R. "The 'Country Boy' Myth and Its Place in American Urban Culture: The Nineteenth-Century Contribution." *PerAmH*, 3: 77-156 (1969).

Wynes, C.E. "The Race Question in the South as Viewed by British Travellers." *LaStud*, 13: 223-40 (19740.

Yamasaki, Tokihiko. "Political Thought of American Transcendentalism." *Q J Law and Pol Osaka City Un*, 19: 334-54 (Mr 73).

Yevish, I.A. "Campus Rebellions: Their Literary Heritage." *ColQ*, 20: 471-7 (Sp 72).

Zacharis, J.C. "Emmeline Pankhurst: An English Suffragette Influences America." *SM*, 38: 198-206 (Ag 71).

Zhuravlev, Igor. "The Relationship between Socialist Poetry in the U.S.A. at the Beginning of the Twentieth Century and the Graphic Arts of the Socialist Press." *ZAA*, 18: 168-82 (1970).

Zollman, Sol. "Propaganda for Theory of Human Nature in Current American Novels." *L&I*, 12: 59-66 (1972).

Theater. Anon. "The Greek Play in America." *Nation*, 100: 530 (13 My 15).

――――. "Now, Sing Melancholy Baby." *Esquire*, 71: 158-9, 75-6 (My 69).

――――. "Three Years of the Drama League." *Nation*, 98: 322-3 (26 Mr 14).

Aaron, Stephen. "The New Theatre Workshop." *ASoc*, 8: 666-7 (1971).

Abramson, Doris. "Negro Playwrights in America." *CUF*, 12: 11-7 (Sp 69).

Abramson, D.M. "William Wells Brown: America's First Negro Playwright." *ETJ*, 20: 370-5 (O 68).

Adams, A.J. "Frank White: Rocky Mountain Critic." *Players*, 47: 248-51 (1972).

Adams, G.R. "Black Militant Drama." *AI*, 28: 107-28 (Su 71).

Addison, Michael, and John Harrop. "The Queerest Mummers: American Actors in Australia." *Players*, 47: 237-41 (1972).

Albert, Allan. "Notes on the Proposition." *Y/T*, 5: 90-2 (1974).

Ambrosetti, R.J. "Rosemary's Baby and Death of God Literature." *KFQ*, 14: 133-41 (1969).

Amini, Johari. "Big Time Buck White." *BlackW*, 20: 72-4 (1971).

Anastas'ev, N. "Profili amerikanskogo teatra (60-e gody)." *VLit*, 13: 139-58 (1969).

Andrews, Peter. "More Sock and Less Buskin." *AH*, 23: 48-57 (Ap 72).

Ardry, Robert. "Reflections on the Theater." *ASch*, 37: 111-20 (Wi 67-68).

Argetsinger, Gerald. "Dunlap's *Andre*: Beginning of American Tragedy." *Players*, 49: 62-4 (1974).

Arteel, Roger. "Veertiende speeljaar in de Korrekelder." *K&C*, 3: 18-9 (O 74).

Atkins, T.R. "A Theatre of Possibilities." *KR*, 30: 274-81 (1968).

Auburn, M.S. "On Dating Samuel French Acting Texts: A Note." *TSt*, 20: n.p. (1973-74).

Bachman, Ch.R. "Albee's *A Delicate Balance*: Parable as Nightmare." *RLV*, 38: 619-30 (1972).

Bailey, Peter. "Black Theater." *Ebony*, 24: 126ff (Ag 69).

————. "Black Theater in America." *BlackW*, 20: 4-26, 95-6 (D 71); 21: 31-40, 70-4 (1972).

————. "Black Theatre in America: Metropolitan New York." *Black W*, 20: 4-8 (Ap 71).

————. "Is the Negro Ensemble Company *Really* Black Theatre?" *BlackW*, 17: 16-9 (Ap 69).

————, et al. "Report on Black Theater." *NegroD*, 18: 20-6, 69-72 (1969).

Baldwin, James. "Theatre: The Negro In and Out." *BlackW*, 15: 37-44 (Ap 66).

Balio, Tino, and R.G. "McLaughlin. "The Economic Dilemma of the Broadway Theatre." *ETJ*, 21: 81-100 (Mr 69).

Baraka, I.B. "Black 'Revolutionary' Poets Should Also Be Playwrights." *BlackW*, 21: 4-6 (1972).

Barfoot, C.C. "New Poems, New Plays: An Annual Survey." *DQR*, 1: 15-26 (1971).

Barksdale, R.K. "White Tragedy—Black Comedy." *Phylon*, 22: 226-33 (3Q 61).

Bauzyte, Galina. "Iliuzi jos ir konfliktas Edvardo Olbio dramaturgijoje." *Literatura*, 15: 79-94 (1973).

Beck, Julian. "Theater and Revolution." *EvR*, 12: 14-5, 88 (My 68).

Behrmann, Alfred. "Kotzebue on the American Stage." *Arcadia*, 4: 274-84 (1969).

Bender, J.E. "The Criterion Independent Theatre." *ETJ*, 18: 197-209 (O 66).

Bennison, Marlin J., and Barry Witham. "Sentimental Love and the Nineteenth Century American Drama." *Players*, 49: 127-9 (1974).

Bentley, Eric. "Theater and Therapy." *NAR*, 8: 131-52, n.d.

Bernard, Heinz. "A Theatre for Lefty: USA in the 1930's." *THQ*, 1: 53-6 (1971).

Berndtson, Arthur. "Tragedy as Power: Beyond Nietzsche." *BuR*, 15: 97-107 (D 67).

Bigsby, C.W.E. "Black Drama in the Seventies." *KanQ*, 3: 10-20 (Sp 71).

Bishop, T.W. "Adaptations of American Plays in Paris, 1958-1959." *FR*, 33: 551-7 (My 60).

Blanke, G.H. "Das Bild des Menschen im modernen amerikanischen Drama." *NS*, 18: 117-29 (Mr 69).

Blau, Herbert. "Paradise and Power." *CE*, 29: 548-52 (Ap 68).

Bloom, A.W. "The Theatre of Non-Mimetic Propaganda: Critical Criteria." *XUS*, 2: 29-36 (Sp 72).

Bloomfield, Maxwell. "Wartime Drama: The Theater in Washington, 1861-1865." *MHM*, 64: 396-411 (Wi 69).

Boatright, M.C. "The Formula in Cowboy Fiction and Drama." *WF*, 28: 136-45 (Ap 69).

Bogard, Travis. "The Sense of the Ghetto in American Negro Theatre." *ETJ*, 20: 333-5 (Ag 68).

Bogusch, G.E. "Norman Bel Geddes and the Art of Modern Theatre Lighting." *ETJ*, 24: 415-29 (1972).

Bond, Edward. "Drama and the Dialectics of Violence." *ThQ*, 2: 4-14 (Ja-Mr 72).

Boni, John. "Analogous Form: Black Comedy and Some Jacobean Plays." *WHR*, 28: 201-15 (Su 74).

Borchardt, D.A. "The Audience as Jury." *Players*, 50: 10-5 (1975).

Bordinat, Philip. "Chekhov's Two Great American Directors." *MwQ*, 16: 70-84 (O 74).

Bradley, Gerald. "Goodbye, Mr. Bones: The Emergence of Negro Themes and Characters in American Drama." *DramC*, 14: 6-12 (Sp 64).

Brandt, Willy. "The Political Significance of the Theatre." *CompD*, 7: 222-30 (Fa 73).

Brashers, H.C. "Some Aspects of Contemporary American Drama." *MSpr*, 59: 294-305 (1965).

Bridges, Katherine. "'All Well at Natchitoches': A Louisiana City on the Stage." *LaStud*, 10: 85-91 (Su 71).

Brock, D.H., and J.M. Welsh. "Percy MacKaye: Community Drama and the Masque Tradition." *CompD*, 6: 68-84 (1972).

Brokaw, J.W. "The Minstrel Show in the Hoblitzelle Theatre Arts Library." *LCUT*, 4: 23-30 (1972).

Brooks, M.E. "Reactionary Trends in Recent Black Drama." *L&I*, 10: 41-8 (1971).

Brown, K.R. "South Coast Repertory." *Players*, 47: 192-7 (1972).

Brown, L.W. "The Cultural Revolution in Black Theatre." *NALF*, 8: 159-65 (Sp 74).

Browne, E.M. "Poetry in Playwriting." *Drama*, 83: 31-4 (Wi 66).

Bruning, Eberhard. "Die amerikanische Arbeitertheaterbewegung der 30er Jahre." *WB*, (1968): 828-52.

―――. "'The Black Liberation Movement' und das amerikanische Drama." *ZAA*, 20: 46-58 (1972).

Brustein, Robert. "Contemporary American Theatre: The Impotence of Freedom." *ThQ*, 3: 31-5 (Ap-Je 73).

―――. "Criticism and Credibility." *Y/T*, 4: 17-22 (Sp 73).

Bullins, Ed. "Black Theatre Groups: A Directory." *TDR*, 12: 172-5 (Su 68).

―――. "Black Theatre Notes." *Black Theatre*, 1: 4-7 (O 68).

Burke, Tom. "The New Homosexuality." *Esquire*, 72: 178-9, 304-18 (D 69).

Burman, Howard, and Joseph Hanreddy. "The Activist Theatre of the Thirties." *TSt*, 18: 55-64 (1971-72).

Callahan, E.A. "The Tragic Hero in Contemporary Secular and Religious Drama." *LHY*, 8: 42-9 (Ja-Jl 67).

Campbell, Dick. "Is There a Conspiracy against Black Playwrights?" *BlackW*, 17: 11-5 (Ap 68).

Caute, David. "Commitment Without Empathy: A Writer's Notes on Politics, Theatre, and the Novel." *TriQ*, 30: 51-70 (Sp 74).

Chamberlain, Lowell. "Pismo ot Nyu York: Novi piesi na stsenite v Broduey." *Plamuk*, 10: 8 (1968).

Clarke, Austin. "The Impuritans: A Play in One Act Freely Adapted from the Short Story 'Young Goodman Brown' by NH." *IUR*, 1: 131-48 (1970).

Clayborne, J.L. "Modern Black Drama and the Gay Image." *CE*, 36: 381-4 (N 74).

Clough, P.H. "A Subject Index to: *Drama Survey*, 1961-1968." *ThDoc*, 3: 81-100 (1970-71).

Cohn, Ruby. "Seeds of Atreus on Modern Ground." *ETJ*, 26: 221-30 (1974).

Coleman, Ann. "Expressionism—40 Years After." *CEA*, 27: 1, 2, 7, 8 (Je 65).

Coleman, Janet. "Improvisational Theatre in America: Variations on a Theme." *Y/T*, 5: 10-25 (1974).

Coleman, Michael. "What Is Black Theater?" *BlackW*, 20: 32-6 (Ap 71).

Coleman, W.S.E. "Buffalo Bill on Stage." *Players*, 47: 80-91 (1971).

Collins, Sherwood. "Boston's Political Theatre: The Eighteenth-Century Pope Day Pageants." *ETJ*, 25: 401-9 (1973).

Comuzio, Ermanno. "Orson Welles, il 'genio' debordante." *Letture*, 26: 341-62 (1971).

Corey, J.R. "Miss Cheer: American Actress, 1764-1768." *RSW*, 39: 137-43 (1971).

Cotton, Littie Jo. "The Negro in the American Theatre." *NHB*, 23: 172-8 (My 60).

Crinkley, Richmon. "Writer to Actor to Director." *Nat R*, 22: 1308-9 (1 D 70).

Curtis, Julia. "The Architecture and Appearance of the Charleston Theatre, 1793-1833." *ETJ*, 23: 1-12 (1971).

———. "John Joseph Stephen Leger Sollee and the Charleston Theater." *ETJ*, 21: 285-98 (1969).

———. "Thomas Wade West's Problematic Puffery." *ThS*, 13: 94-9 (1972).

Curtis, M.J. "Charles-Town's Church Street Theater." *SCHM*, 70: 149-54 (Jl 69).

Czekeley, Csilla. "American Drama on the Hungarian Stage, 1918-1965." *HSE*, 3: 103-21 (1967).

Dace, Letitia. "On Jean Genet and Martin Esslin, or Here Absurdist, There Absurdist, Everywhere. . . ." *KanQ*, 3: 110-16 (1971).

Dent, Thomas. "Beyond Rhetoric toward a Black Southern Theatre." *BlackW*, 20: 14-24 (Ap 71).

Ditsky, John. "All Irish Here: The 'Irishman' in Modern Drama." *DR*, 54: 94-102 (Sp 74).

Dixon, Melvin. "Black Theater: The Aesthetics." *NegroD*, 18: 41-4 (Jl 69).

Dodson, Owen. "Playwrights in Dark Glasses." *BlackW*, 17: 31-6 (Ap 68).

Donoghue, Denis. "The Human Image in Modern Drama." *LugR*, 1: 155-68 (1965).

Downer, A.S. "Early American Professional Acting." *ThS*, 12: 79-96 (N 71).

———. "More Strange than True: Notes on the New York Theatre, 1968-1969." *QJS*, 55: 225-36 (O 69).

———. "Old, New, Borrowed, and (a Trifle) Blue: Notes on the New York Theatre, 1967-1968." *QJS*, 54: 199-211 (O 68).

Doyle, P.A. "Gilroy, Carlino, and Hanley—The Best of the American Playwrights." *NasR*, 1: 88-102 (1968).

Drimmer, Melvin. "Joplin's *Treemonisha* in Atlanta." *Phylon*, 34: 197-202 (Je 73).

Dunlap, J.F. "Queen City Stages: Highlights of the Theatrical Season of 1843." *CHSB*, 19: 128-43 (Ap 61).

Eddy, D.M. "Bloody Battles and High Tragedies: Melville and the Theatre of the 1840's." *BSUF*, 13: 34-45 (Wi 72).

Elder, Lonne. "A Negro Idea Theatre." *AmD*, 1: 30-1 (Jl-Ag 64).

Ellwood, W.R. "Preliminary Notes on the German Dramaturg and the American Theater." *MD*, 13: 254-8 (D 70).

Engle, Gary. "The Atkinson Collection of Ethiopian Drama at the University of Chicago." *RALS*, 1: 181-99 (Au 71).

Evans, D.T. "Bring It All Back Home." *BlackW*, 20: 41-5 (1971).

Everson, I.G. "Lennox Robinson and Synge's *Playboy* (1911-1930); Two Decades of American Cultural Growth." *NEQ*, 44: 3-21 (Mr 71).

Falb, L.W. "Le naturalisme de papa': American Drama in France." *FR*, 45: 56-71 (1971).

Farrell, N.L. "A Subject Index to *Theatre Annual*, 1942-1969." *ThDoc*, 2: 125-34 (1969-70).

Feldman, L.G. "A Brief History of Improvisational Theatre in the United States." *Y/T*, 5: 128-51 (1974).

Field, B.S. "A Note on American Drama, 1800-1869." *EN*, 3: 8-13 (Wi 68-69).

Filbert, V.M. "The American Theater, Missoula—1910." *Montana Mag West Hist*, 18: 56-68 (Au 68).

Ford, Clebert. "Towards a Black Community Theatre." *Liberator*, 4: 12-20 (1964).

Fowle, Donald. "The New Play in America, 1972." *Players*, 48: 160-72 (1973).

———. "The New Play: Premierers in America." *Players*, 46: 110-8, 162-70 (1971); 47: 120-9, 179-91 (1972).

Fratti, Mario. "Interview with Ellen Stewart." *D&T*, 8: 87-9 (1970).

Freedman, Morris. "Violence in the Modern Theater: Notes on the New Senecanism." *NMQ*, 37: 386-94 (Wi 68).

Friedlander, Mitzi. "History of a Theatre." *FCHQ*, 45: 305-14 (Jl 71).

Fuegi, John. "Russian 'Epic Theatre' Experiments and the American Stage." *MinnR*, 1: 102-12 (Fa 73).

Fuller, H.W. "Black Theatre in America: An Informal Survey." *BlackW*, 17: 83-93 (Ap 68).

Gaffney, Floyd. "Black Theatre: Commitment and Communication." *BSch*, 1: 10-5 (Je 70).

———. "*The Hand Is on the Gate* in Athens." *ETJ*, 21: 196-201 (My 69).

———. "Is Your Door Really Open?" *D&T*, 7: 4-7 (Fa 68).

Gallagher, K.G. "The Tragedies of George Henry Boker: The Measure of American Romantic Drama." *ESQ*, 20: 187-215 (3Q 74).

Garfield, David. "*The Romance of a People*." *ETJ*, 24: 436-42 (1972).

Garner, Stanton. "Harold Frederic and Swinburne's *Locrine*: A Matter of Clubs, Copyrights, and Character." *AL*, 45: 285-92 (My 73).

Gattnig, Charles. "Artaud and Participatory Drama." *ETJ*, 20: 485-91 (D 68).

Geduld Carolyn. "Film and Literature." *ConL*, 15: 123-30 (1974).

Gelb, G.W. "Playhouses and Politics: Lewis Hallam and the Confederation Theater." *JPC*, 5: 324-39 (Fa 71).

Gerber, P.L., and R.J. Gemmett. "Falling into Place: A Conversation with Donald Justice." *PrS*, 47: 317-24 (1973).

Gerould, Daniel. "*Candaules* and the Uses of Myth." *MD*, 12: 270-8 (1970).

Ghent, Henri. "Black Creativity in Quest of an Audience." *Art in America*, 58: 35 (My 70).

Gild, D.C. "Psychodrama on Broadway." *MarkR*, 2: 65-74 (O 70).

Gilliard, F.W. "Theatre in Early Idaho: A Brief Review and Appraisal." *Rendezvous*, 8: 25-31 (Su 73).

Gilman, Richard. "*Commune*: The Performance Group." *DramR*, 15: 325-9 (Sp 71).

———. "The Theatre of Ignorance." *Atl*, 224: 35-42 (Jl 69).

Giradin, Monique. "Problèmes posés par le catalogage des mises en scènes écrites." *ThDoc*, 1: 37-50 (1969).

Goldoni, Annalisa. "L'espressionismo nel teatro americano (1920-1930)." *SA*, 13: 377-416 (1967).

Goncalves, Joe. "West Coast Drama." *Black Theatre*, 4: 27 (Ap 70).

Goodman, K.S. "The Chicago Theatre Society." *Nation*, 98: 308-9 (19 Mr 14).

Gorelik, Mordecai. "Root-freeze of American Drama." *Meanjin*, 28: 90-5 (1969).

———. "Social vs. Irrational Theatre." *Players*, 46: 208-10 (1971).

Gottfried, Martin. "The New York Drama Critics." *Y/T*, 4: 79-90 (Sp 73).

Gottlieb, Lois. "The Double Standard Debate in Early 20th-Century American Drama." *Mich Academician*, 7: 441-52 (Sp 75).

Gottlieb, L.C. "The Perils of Freedom: The New Woman in Three American Plays of the 1900's." *CRAS*, 6: 84-98 (Sp 75).

Goulianos, Joan. "Politics and Plays." *KanQ*, 3: 51-6 (Sp 71).

———. "Women and the Avant-Garde Theater." *MR*, 13: 257-67 (Wi-Sp 72).

Gowda, H.H. Anniah. "*Hogan's Goat* and American Verse Drama." *LHY*, 8: 35-41 (Ja-Jl 67).

Grant, Lisbeth. "The New Lafayette Theatre—Anatomy of a Community Art Institution." *DramR*, 16: 46-55 (D 72).

Green, A.W.C. "'Jim Crow,' 'Zip Coon': The Northern Origins of Negro Minstrelry." *MR*, 9: 385-97 (Sp 70).

Grimsted, David. "*Uncle Tom* from Page to Stage: Limitations of Nineteenth Century Drama." *QJS*, 56: 235-44 (1970).

Gross, Roger. "The Play as Dramatic Action." *Players*, 49: 32-5 (1974).

Guthrie, Tyrone. "Contemporary Theater." *REL*, 7: 9-14 (O 66).

Gutiérrez de la Solana, Alberto. "El teatro profesional en las trece colonias." *Circulo*, 4: 49-61 (1972).

Haas, Rudolf. "Über Anfänge des 'Modernen' in amerikanischen Drama." *JA*, 11: 69-82 (1966).

Hackett, Francis. "Little Theatres." *NRep*, 2: 211 (27 Mr 15).

Hall, Peter. "Is the Beginning the Word?" *ThQ*, 2: 5-11 (Jl-S 72).

Hanau, D. "Ghetto Theatre: Vital Drama or Social Therapy?" *Community*, 26: 7-10 (Ap 67).

Hand, W.D. "Folk Beliefs and Customs of the American Theater: A Survey." *SFQ*, 38: 23-48 (Mr 74).

Handman, Wynn. "The American Place Theatre." *ASoc*, 8: 661-3 (1971).

Harap, Louis. "Image of the Jew in American Drama, 1794-1823." *AJHQ*, 60: 242-57 (Mr 71).

Harbin, B.J. "Hodgkinson and His Rivals at the Park: The Business of Early Romantic Theatre in America." *ESQ*, 20: 148-69 (3Q 74).

———. "Hodgkinson's Last Years at the Charleston Theatre, 1803-05." *ThS*, 13: 20-43 (1972).

Harris, J.B. "The Sun People of 125th Street—The National Black Theatre." *DramR*, 16: 39-45 (D 72).

Harrison, A.C. "Negro Actors: The Added Dimensions of Color." *SSJ*, 35: 16-27 (1969).

Harrison, P.C. "Black Theater and the African Continuum." *BlackW*, 21: 42-8 (1972).

Harrison, Shirley. "New Orleans: Greenwal vs. the Syndicate." *Players*, 46: 180-7 (1971).

Harrop, J.D. "A Constructive Promise." *ThS*, 12: 104-18 (1971).

Harwell, R.B. "Brief Candle: The Confederate Theatre." *PAAS*, 81: 41-160 (21 Ap 71).

Hasbany, Richard. "Bromidic Parables: The American Musical Theatre During the Second World War." *MPC*, 6: 642-5 (Sp 73).

*Haskell, J.D., and R.G. Shedd. "Modern Drama: A Selective Bibliography of Works Published in English in 1967." *MD*, 11: 195-213 (S 68).

Hatch, J.V. "A White Folks Guide to 200 Years of Black &White Drama." *TDR*, 16: 5-24 (D 72).

Hawes, D.S. "Much Ado about John Brougham and Jim Fisk." *MASJ*, 8: 73-89 (Sp 67).

Hay, S.A. "Alain Locke & Black Drama." *BlackW*, 21: 8-14 (Ap 72).

Head, F.E. "The Theatrical Syndicate vs. the Child Labor Law of Louisiana." *LaStud*, 13: 365-74 (1974).

Heilman, R.B. "Dramas of Money." *Shen*, 21: 20-33 (Su 70).

Henneke, B.S. "The American Playgoer." *UTMS*, 2: 1-10 (1967).

Herman, William. "Richard Schechner Descending a Staircase: American Theatre Viewed in the Seventies." *KanQ*, 3: 32-40 (1971).

Hewes, Henry. "The Aints and the Am Nots." *SatR*, 54: 10, 11-2 (13 N 71).

———. "Arena Stage: Full Speed Ahead." *SatR*, 54: 63-5 (27 Mr 71).

————. "Black Hopes: Presentations in New York City." *SatR*, 48: 46 (7 Ja 65).

————. "Broadway Postscript: Crossing Lines." *SatR*, 48: 46 (7 Ja 65).

————. "Theatre in '71." *SatR*, 54: 14-9 (12 Je 71).

Hewitt, Barnard. "A Note on the John Street Theatre." *ThS*, 13: 100-1 (1972).

Heyl, Edgar. "Plays by Marylanders, 1870-1916." *MHM*, 63: 70-7, 179-87, 420-6 (Mr, Je, D 68); 64: 74-7, 412-9 (Sp, Wi 69); 65: 181-4, 301-3 (Su, Fa 70); 67: 71-83 (Sp 72).

Highfill, Philip. "The British Background of the American Hallams." *ThS*, 11: 1-35 (1970).

Himelstein, M.Y. "Theory and Performance in the Depression Theater." *MD*, 14: 426-35 (F 72).

Hirsch, Foster. "Performance Theatre: *Dionysus in 69* and *The Serpent.*" *KanQ*, 3: 41-50 (Sp 71).

Hivnor, M.O. "Adaptations and Adaptors." *KR*, 30: 265-73 (1968).

Holden, Joan, and R.G. Davis. "Living." *Ramparts*, 8: 62-6 (Ag 69).

Holtan, O.I. "Sidney Brustein and the Plight of the American Intellectual." *Players*, 46: 222-5 (1971).

Houseman, John. "In Search of an American Acting Tradition." *ETJ*, 20: 92-6 (Mr 68).

Hughes, Catharine. "Broadway and the British." *CathW*, 212: 313-5 (1971).

————. "The Theatre Goes to War." *America*, 116: 759-61 (20 My 67).

Hughes, C.R. "New Ritual and New Theatre." *ASoc*, 7: 62-8 (1970).

Hughes, Langston. "The Need for an Afro-American Theatre." *Chicago Defender*, 12 Je 61, p. 12.

Hyde, S.W. "The Ring-Tailed Roarer in American Drama." *SFQ*, 19: 171-8 (1955).

Isaac, Dan. "The Death of the Proscenium Stage." *AR*, 31: 235-53 (Su 71).

————. "Theatre of Fact." *TDR*, 15: 109-135 (1971).

Jackson, Esther. "American Theatre in the Sixties: The Drama of International Crisis." *Players*, 48: 236-49 (1973).

James, Norman. "The Living Theatre: Its Use of the Stage." *JAAC*, 29: 475-83 (Su 71).

Jeffers, Lance. "Bullins, Baraka, and Elder: The Dawn of Grandeur in Black Drama." *CLAJ*, 16: 32-48 (S 72).

Jeyifous, Abiodun. "Black Critics on Black Theatre in America." *TDR*, 18: 34-45 (1974).

Johnson, H.A. "Playwrights, Audiences, and Critics: Black Theater." *NegroD*, 19: 17-24 (1970).

Johnson, J.H. "The Early American Prologue and Epilogue." *WVUPP*, 16: 30-48 (N 67).

Jones, Le Roi. "Black (Art) Drama is the Same as Black Life." *Ebony*, 25: 74ff (F 71).

————. "Communications Project." *TDR*, 12: 53-7 (Su 68).

————. "In Search of the Revolutionary Theatre." *BlackW*, 15: 20-4 (Ap 66).

————. "What the Arts Need Now." *BlackW*, 16: 5-6 (Ap 67).

Jurges, Oda. "Books and Articles Related to Black Theatre Published from 1/1960 to 2/1968." *TDR*, 12: 176-80 (Su 68).

Kalfin, Robert. "The Chelsea Theater Center of Brooklyn." *ASoc*, 8: 664-5 (1971).

Kamarck, E.L. "Theatre in the Community: A Brief Survey and Appraisal." *ASoc*, 8: 636-43 (Fa-Wi 71).

Kanellos, Nicolas. "Mexican Community Theatre in a Midwestern Cit." *Latin Am Th R*, 7: 43-8 (1973).

Kaufman, M.W. "The Delicate World of Reprobation: A Note on the Black Theatre." *ETJ*, 23: 46-59 (1971).

Kauffman, Stanley. "Theatre and Drama Criticism." *Y/T*, 4: 8-16 (Sp 73).

Keough, L.C. "Shaw's Introduction to New York: The Mansfield Productions 1894-1900." *Shavian*, 4: 6-10 (1969).

Kerr, J.H. "The Bankruptcy of the Chestnut Street Theatre, Philadelphia, 1799." *ThR*, 11: 154-72 (1971).

Keyssar-Franke, Helene. "Afro-American Drama and Its Criticism, 1960-1972: An Annotated Check List with Appendices." *BNYPL*, 78: 276-346 (Sp 75).

Killens, J.O. "Broadway in Black and White." *AForum*, 1: 6-76 (Wi 66).

King, Woodie. "Black Theatre: Present Condition." *TDR*, 12: 117-24 (1968).

———. "Black Theatre: Weapon for Change." *BlackW*, 16: 35-9 (Ap 67).

———. "The Dilemma of Black Theater." *NegroD*, 19: 10-5, 86-7 (1970).

———. "Educational Theater and the Black Community." *BlackW*, 21: 25-9 (Ap 72).

———. "Problems Facing Negro Actors." *BlackW*, 15: 53-9 (Ap 66).

Kirby, Michael. "On Political Theatre." *TDR*, 19: 129-34 (Je 75).

Knight, L.H. "Beerbohm Tree in America." *ThS*, 8: 37-52 (My 67).

Kobayashi, Yoshiro. "Transition of Off-Broadway." *Rising Generation*, 121: 73-4 (My 75).

Kolb, Deborah. "The Rise and Fall of the New Woman in the American Drama." *ETJ*, 27: 149-60 (1975).

Kopp, W.L. "Popular Reception of Classical German Drama in New York 1945-1965." *MLJ*, 55: 510-4 (1971).

Kostelanetz, Richard. "American Theatre—Performance, Not Literature." *ReAL*, 5: 41-9 (Fa 71).

———. "The Theatre of Mixed Means." *Works*, 1: 41-66 (Wi 68).

Kottwinkel, J.L., D.M. O'Connor, and B.J. Cogbill. "A Checklist of Current Theatre Arts Periodicals." *ThDoc*, 1: 3-36 (1969).

Kramer, M.D. "The American Wild West Show and Buffalo 'Bill' Cody." *Costerus*, 4: 87-98 (1972).

Kraus, J.H. "Children's Theatre, Baltimore Style." *Players*, 47: 204-9 (1972).

Kraus, T.M. "Theatre East: The September Through December 1971 Theatre Season in New York." *Players*, 47: 132-7 (1972).

Kunesh, G.D. "The Blue Eagle Theatre: A Precedent for the Federal Theatre Project." *Players*, 46: 268-71 (1971).

Kurahashi, Ken. "Saikin no America Engeki." *EigoS*, 114: 444-5 (1968).

Kuttner, Alfred. "Drama Comes Back from the Movies." *NRep*, 4: 51-2 (14 Ag 15).

———. "Dramatic Issues." *NRep*, 1: 20-2 (12 D 14).

Laccy, P.A. "Two for the Revolution." *Religious Th*, 6: 30-8 (1968).

Lahr, John. "The American Musical: The Slavery of Escape." *EvR*, 12: 23-5, 73-6 (S 68).

———. "Black Theatre: The American Tragic Voice." *EvR*, 13: 55-63 (Ag 69).

———. "The Collapsing Underground." *Gambit*, 17: 64-9 (1971).

———. "In Search of a New Mythology." *EvR*, 13: 55-8, 84-7 (Ja 69).

———. "Mystery on Stage." *EvR*, 13: 53-7 (D 69).

———. "The New Theater: A Retreat from Realism." *EvR*, 12: 55-7, 83-90 (N 68).

———. "*Orlando Furioso*: Theater as 'Contact' Sport." *EvR*, 15: 54-9, 75-6 (F 71).

———. "Spectacles of Disintegration." *EvR*, 14: 31-3, 74-7 (Je 70).

———. "The Street Scene: Playing for Keeps." *EvR*, 12: 84-90 (O 68).

———. "Theatre and Propaganda." *EvR*, 12: 33-7 (Mr 68).

———. "The Theatre of Sports." *EvR*, 13: 39-41, 73-6 (N 69).

———. "The Theater's Voluptuary Itch." *EvR*, 12: 33-4, 88-92 (J 68).

Landesman, Rocco. "A Conversation with David Shepherd." *Y/T*, 5: 56-65 (1974).

———. "Interview: Theodore J. Flicker." *Y/T*, 5: 66-81 (1974).

———, and Robert Marx. "Introduction Special Issue on Improvisational Theatre in America." *Y/T*, 5: 6-9 (1974).

Lannon, W.W. "The Rise and Rationale of Post World War II American Confessional Theatre." *ConnR*, 8: 73-8 (#1 75).

Larson, Lance. "Liquid Theatre." *DramR*, 15: 90-8 (Su 71).

Laufe, Abe. "What Makes Drama Run? (Introduction to Anatomy of a Hit)." *Costerus*, 6: 45-58 (1972).

Laurence, D.H. "Bernard Shaw and the American Theater: A Projected Study." *Indep Shavian*, 11: 1-4 (Fa 72).

Law, R.A. "Charleston Theatres." *Nation*, 99: 278-9 (1914).

———. "Early American Prologues and Epilogues." *Nation*, 98: 463-4 (23 Ap 14).

———. "News for Bibliophiles." *Nation*, 96: 201 (27 F 13).

Lazier, Gil. "Living Newspaper 1970: Obituary for a Gentle Agit-Prop Play." *ETJ*, 23: 135-51 (1971).

Lee, R.J. "Irony and Religious Mystery in the Contemporary Theatre." *Soundings*, 52: 350-64 (Fa 69).

Leiter, Robert. "Without Benefit of Broadway." *Nation*, 217: 570-1 (26 N 73).

Leiter, S.L. "Brooklyn as an American Theatre City, 1861-1898." *J Long Island Hist*, 8: 1-11 (Wi-Sp 68).

Leonard, J.M. "Correspondence and Confrontation Between William Duff, Manager, and John Hamilton, Actor." *ThS*, 13: 42-51 (1972).

Lester, Elenore. "The Final Decline and Total Collapse of the American Avant-Garde." *Esquire*, 71: 142-3, 148-9 (My 69).

Lestrud, Vernon. "Early Theatrical 'Blue Laws' on the Pacific Coast." *Rendezvous*, 4: 15-24 (1969).

Lewis, J.G. "The Augustus Thomas Collection at the University of North Carolina." *RALS*, 4: 72-89 (1974).

Lindsay, Powell. "We Still Need Negro Theatre in America." *NHB*, 27: 112 (F 64).

Lippincott, H.F. "Tate's *Lear* in the Nineteenth Century: The Edwin Forrest Promptbooks." *LC*, 36: 67-75 (1970).

Lombard, C.M. "French Romanticism on the American Stage." *RLC*, 43: 161-72 (1969).

Long, R.E. "Black in Box-Office." *NAR*, 6: 71-2 (Wi 69).

McAleer, J.J. "Lawrence Barrett: 'The Scholar of the American Theater.'" *ShN*, 20: 44-5 (1970).

McDermott, Douglas. "Propaganda and Art: Dramatic Theory and the American Depression." *MD*, 11: 73-81 (My 68).

McDermott, Douglas. "Touring Patterns on California's Frontier, 1849-1859." *ThS*, 15: 18-28 (1974).

McDowell, J.H. "Ohio Theatre on the Record." *Ohioana*, 4: 114-5 (Wi 61-62).

McElroy, Hilda, and R.A. Willis. "Published Works of Black Playwrights in the United States, 1960-1970." *BlackW*, 21: 92-8 (1972).

McLean, A.F. "U.S. Vaudeville and the Urban Comics." *ThQ*, 1: 47-52 (1971).

McNamara, Brooks. "'A Congress of Wonders': The Rise and Fall of the Dime Museum." *ESQ*, 20: 216-32 (3Q 74).

———. "The Indian Medicine Show." *ETJ*, 23: 431-45 (1971).

Macey, S.L. "Nonheroic Tragedy: A Pedigree for American Tragic Drama." *CLS*, 6: 1-19 (Mr 69).

Malpede, Karen. "Off off Broadway: The Effort to Create a Contemporary Theatre." *ASoc*, 5: 522-9 (1968).

Mandel, Oscar. "Notes on Ethical Deprivation in the Avant-Garde Drama." *AntigR*, 8: 43-8 (Wi 72).

————. "Reactionary Notes on the Experimental Theatre." *MR*, 11: 101-16 (1970).

Marder, C.J. "An Index to *Personal Recollections of the Drama*, by Henry Dickinson Stone." *ThDoc*, 3: 65-80 (1971).

Marranca, Bonnie. "The Radical Impulse in the American Theatre." *ASoc*, 12: 268-73 (1975).

Marsh, J.L. "Captain E.C. Williams and the Panoramic School of Acting." *ETJ*, 23: 289-97 (1971).

————. "Soup! Soup!" *Players*, 47: 287-91 (1972).

————. "Troupers at Tidioute [Pa.]." *Players*, 47: 138-44 (1972).

Mates, Julian. "The Dramatic Anchor: Research Opportunities in the American Drama Before 1800." *EAL*, 5: 76-9 (Wi 70-71).

Matherne, B.M. "Louisiana Playwright: PT.N, A Bibliographical Essay." *LaStud*, 10: 244-56 (Wi 71).

Matlaw, Myron. "Tony the Trouper: Pastor's Early Years." *TA*, 24: 70-90 (1969).

Matthews, Albert. "Early Plays at Harvard." *Nation*, 98: 295 (19 Mr 14).

Meserve, W.J. "The American Periodical Series: Source Material for Theatre and Drama Research." *ETJ*, 20: 443-8 (O 68).

————. "An Earnest Purpose: American Drama at Mid-19th Century." *Players*, 48: 60-4 (1973).

Miller, A.D. "It's a Long Way to St. Louis: Notes on the Audience for Black Drama."

Miller, T.L. "Alan Dale: The Hearst Critic." *ETJ*, 26: 69-80 (1974).

————. "John Ranken Touse: The Last of the Victorian Critics." *ETJ*, 161-78 (1970).

————. "Towse on Reform in the American Theatre." *SSCJ*, 38: 254-60 (1972).

Miller, W.C. and Stephanie. "All Black Showcase: The Effectiveness of a Negro Theater Production." *ETJ*, 21: 202-4 (1969).

Mitchell, Loften. "Black Drama." *BlackW*, 16: 75-87 (Ap 67).

————. "Death of a Decade: Black Drama in the Sixties." *Crisis*, 77: 87-92 (Mr 70).

————. "The Negro Theatre and the Harlem Community." *Freedomways*, 3: 384-94 (Su 69).

Moehlenbrock, Arthur. "Kotzebue on the Charleston Stage." *FurmS*, 34: 22-31 (1951).

Mohanty, H.P. "The Image of the Absurd: How Absurd Is the Absurd Drama?" *LHY*, 15: 88-94 (F 75).

Molette, C.W. "The First Afro-American Theater." *NegroD*, 19: 4-9 (1970).

Monleón, José. "Teatro radical USA." *PrA*, 135: 8-25 (1971).

Montilla, Robert. "The Building of the Lafayette Theatre." *ThS*, 15: 105-29 (1974).

Moramarco, Fred. "The Early Drama Criticism of Williams Dunlap." *AL*, 40: 9-14 (Mr 68).

Morison, S.E. "Commodore Perry's Japan Expedition Press and Shipboard Theatre." *PAAS*, 77: 35-43 (Ap 67).

Morrison, Jack. "American Educational Theatre of the Future." *ETJ*, 20: 88-91 (Mr 68).

Morrow, S.S. "A Brief History of Theatre in Nashville, 1807-1970." *THQ*, 30: 178-89 (Su 71).

Moss, Arnold. "Will you See the Players Well Bestowed? The Guest Artist Program at American Colleges and Universities." *ETJ*, 26: 231-41 (1974).

Mullin, D.C. "Early Theatres in Rhode Island." *ThS*, 11: 167-86 (1970).

Murray, J.P. "Black Movies/Black Theatre." *DramR*, 56-61 (D 72).

Myers, Norman. "Early Recognition of Gordon Craig in America Periodicals." *ETJ*, 22: 78-86 (1970).

Nardin, J.T. "Tendances dans les revues de théâtre aux Etats-Unis." *MRom*, 20: 81-7 (1970).

Theater

Narumi, Hiroshi. "Kankyo-engeki to Kankyakusanka." *EigoS*, 115: 618-9 (1969).

Neal, Larry. "Conquest of the South." *DramR*, 14: 169-74 (1970).

Neal, L.P. "Cultural Nationalism and the Black Theatre." *Black Theatre*, 1: 8-10 (O 68).

———. "Toward a Relevant Black Theatre." *Black Theatre*, 4: 14-5 (Ap 70).

Nelson, Benjamin. "Avant-Garde Dramatists From Ibsen to Ionesco." *PsyR*, 55: 505-12 (1968).

Nelson, Stanley. "Off-off Broadway." *KanQ*, 3: 57-64 (1971).

Newall, R.H. "Theatre in Maine—A Microcosmos." *Northern New England Rev*, 1: 41-5 (1974).

Nichols, Harold. "The Prejudice Against Native American Drama from 1778 to 1830." *QJS*, 60: 279-88 (O 74).

Niehaus, E.F. "Paddy on the Local Stage and in Humor: The Image of the Irish in New Orleans, 1830-62." *LaHi*, 5: 117-34 (1964).

Nolan, P.T. "Georgia Drama Between the Wars (1870-1916): A Check List." *GHQ*, 51: 216-30 (Je 67).

Novick, Julius. "The Old Regime at Lincoln Center." *ETJ*, 18: 126-35 (My 66).

Oliver, W.I. "The Censor in the Ivy." *DramR*, 15: 31-55 (Fa 70).

———. "Him—A Director's Note." *ETJ*, 26: 327-41 (1974).

O'Neal, Frederick. "Problems and Prospects: The Negro in Today's Theatre." *BlackW*, 15: 4-12 (Ap 66).

O'Neal, John. "Motion in the Ocean: Some Political Dimensions of the Free Southern Theater." *DramR*, 12: 70-7 (Su 68).

Overstreet, Robert. "John T. Ford and the Savannah Theatre." *SSCJ*, 38: 51-60 (1972).

Packard, William. "Poetry in the Theatre." *Trace*, 62: 373-9; 64: 114-9; 66: 447-55; 67: 139-42 (Fa-Wi 66-67, Sp 67, Fa 67, Sp 68).

Park, C.W. "'You Stop That!' Nearly Stopped the Show as Well as the Actor." *Ohioana*, 6: 103-4 (Wi 63).

Parker, G.D. "The Modern Theatre as Autonomous Vehicle." *MD*, 16: 373-91 (D 73).

Parlakian, Nishan. "The Off-Off Broadway Theatre." *D&T*, 12: 19-21 (1974).

Pawley, T.D. "The Black Theatre Audience." *Players*, 46: 257-61 (1971).

———. "The First Black Playwrights." *BlackW*, 21: 16-24 (Ap 72).

Peavy, C.D. "Satire and the Contemporary Black Drama." *SNL*, 7: 40-9 (Fa 69).

*Peavy, Linda. "A Bibliography of Providence Players' Dramas, 1915-1922." *PBSA*, 69: 569-75 (4Q 75).

Peinert, Dietrich. "Interpretationshilfen zum neueren englischen und amerikanischen Drama." *LWU*, 4: 52-65 (1971).

Perreault, John. "Oedipus, a New Work." *TDR*, 15: 141-7 (1971).

Perry, John. "The New Theatre." *QJS*, 58: 322-6 (O 72).

———. "Selected Bibliography on James A. Herne." *BB*, 31: 50-3 (1974).

Piemme, Jean-Marie. "Le théâtre sans texte, ou la parole convertie." *MRom*, 19: 91-9 (1969).

Phillips, John and Anne Hollander. "The Art of the Theater I." *PaR*, 9: 65-94 (Wi-Sp 65).

Porter, D.H. "Ancient Myth and Modern Play: A Significant Counterpoint." *CBul*, 48: 1-9 (N 71).

Potter, V.R. "New Politics, New Mothers." *CLAJ*, 16: 247-55 (1972).

Powers, E.C. "Tommaso Salvini: An American Devotee's View." *ThS*, 15: 130-42 (1974).

Quinn, A.D. "The First American Play." *Nation*, 100: 415 (15 Ap 15).

Rader, Dotson. "Can the Reverend Al Carmines Save the Theatre?" *Esquire*, 82: 127, 276-8 (D 74).

Rea, Charlotte. "Women's Theatre Groups." *DramR*, 16, 79-89 (Je 72).

Reardon, W.R. "The American Drama and Theatre in the Nineteenth Century: A Retreat from Meaning." *ESQ*, 20: 170-86 (3Q 74).

Riach, W.A.D. "'Telling It Like It Is': An Experiment of Black Theatre as Rhetoric." *QJS*, 56: 179-86 (Ap 70).

Rich, J.D. "National Theatre of the Deaf." *Players*, 47: 115-9 (1972).

————, and K.L. Seligman. "The New Theatre of Chicago, 1906-1907." *ETJ*, 26: 53-68 (1974).

Richardson, Jack. "Avant-Garde Theatrics." *Commentary*, 46: 24-6 (1968).

Riley, Clayton. "The Death Horse Rides Our Harlems." *BlackW*, 20: 37-8 (1971).

Rinear, D.L. "Burlesque Comes to New York: William Mitchell's First Season at the Olympic." *NCTR*, 2: 23-34 (1974).

Ritchey, David. "Baltimore's Eighteenth-Century French Theatre." *SSCJ*, 38: 164-7 (Wi 72).

————. "The Baltimore Theatre and the Yellow Fever Epidemic." *MHM*, 67: 298-301 (Fa 72).

————. "The Maryland Company of Comedians." *ETJ*, 24: 355-62 (1972).

Rogers, Ray. "The Negro Actor." *Freedomways*, (Su 62).

Rollins, P.C. "Film and American Studies: Questions, Activities, Guides." *AQ*, 26: 245-65 (Ag 74).

Rosenberg, Edgar. "The Jew in Western Drama." *BNYPL*, 72: 442-94 (S 68).

Rosenberg, J.L. "Here Bigyneth or Requiescat in Pace: An Aesthetic and Structural Meditation on the State of the American Theatre in the 1970's." *ASoc*, 8: 626-31 (1971).

Rosenfeld, A.H. "Yiddish Poets and Playwrights of America: A Preliminary Report on a Recent Addition to the Harris Collection." *BBr*, 22: 161-81 (1968).

Ross, Ronald. "The Role of Blacks in the Federal Theatre, 1935-1939." *JNH*, 59: 38-50 (1974).

Rowley, L.T. "The Church's Dramatic Literature." *Dialog*, 4: 129-38 (Au 69).

Ruff, L.K. "Joseph Harper and Boston's Board Alley Theatre, 1792-1793." *ETJ*, 26: 45-52 (1974).

Ryan, P.R. "*Terminal*: An Interview with Roberta Sklar." *TDR*, 15: 149-57 (1971).

Salem, J.M. "American Drama Between the Wars: The Effects of Sociology." *BSUF*, 10: 47-54 (Sp 69).

Salerno, H.F. "The Theatre and American Culture." *D&T*, 9: 70-2 (Wi 70-71).

Sarlos, R.K. "Producing Principles and Practices of the Provincetown Players." *ThR*, 10: 89-102 (1969).

————. "Wharf and Dome: Materials for the History of Provincetown Players." *ThR*, 10: 163-79 (1970).

Sata, Masunori. "American Saisho no Kigeki *The Contrast*." *ELLS*, 10: 147-62 (1973).

————. "*Superstition* (1824) to *Winterset* (1935): Romeo-Juliet theme kara no kosatsu." *ELLS*, 6: 131-46 (1969).

Saxton, Alexander. "Blackface Minstrelry and Jacksonian Ideology." *AQ*, 27: 3-28 (Mr 75).

Scanlan, Tom. "The Domestication of Rip Van Winkle: Joe Jefferson's Play as Prologue to Modern American Drama." *VQR*, 50: 51-62 (1974).

Schaefer, H.J. "Grundprobleme des modernen Drama. Versuch einer Orientierung." *Begegnung*, 22: 125-35, 17-89 (Jl-S, O-D 67).

Schaffer, Byron. "HI's Theories of Drama." *OSUTCB*, 15: 20-31 (1968).

Schechner, Richard. "Audience Participation." *DramR*, 15: 73-89 (Su 71).

————. "Drama, Script, Theater, and Performance." *TDR*, 17: 5-36 (S 73).

————. "Free Theatre for Mississippi." *HM*, 231: 31-8 (O 68).

————. "On Playwriting and Environmental Theatre." *Y/T*, 4: 28-36 (Wi 73).

Schneck, Stephen. "Le Living [Living Theater]." *Ramparts*, 7: 34-41 (30 N 68).

Schwartz, Donald. "The Yiddish Art Theatre." *Players*, 50: 138-41 (1975).

Scott, J.S. "Teaching Black Drama." *Players*, 47: 130-1 (1972).

Sergeant, Winthrop. "The Critic and the Musical Theatre." *Y/T*, 4: 8-14 (Su 73).

Shafer, Y.B. "A Sherlock Holmes of the Past: William Gillette's Later Years." *Players*, 46: 229-35 (1971).

————. "The Liberated Woman in Plays of the Past." *Players*, 49: 95-100 (1974).

Shank, Theodore. "Political Theatre as Popular Entertainment: San Francisco Mime Troupe." *DramR*, 18: 110-7 (Mr 74).

Shattuck, C.H. "Edwin Booth's *Hamlet*: A New Promptbook." *HLB*, 15: 20-48 (1967).

Sheffer, Isaiah. "Black Theatre in America." *Nation*, 209: 151-2 (25 Ag 69).

Shelly, D.L. "Tivoli Theatre of Pensacola." *FHQ*, 50: 341-51 (Ap 72).

Sheren, Paul. "Gordon Craig's Only American Production." *PULC*, 29: 163-92 (Sp 68).

Sherman, Alfonso. "Little Known Black Heroes in Ante-Bellum Drama." *SpT*, 19: 130-7 (1970).

Sherr, P.C. "*Change Your Luck*: A Negro Satirizes White America." *Phylon*, 32: 281-9.

Shumsky, N.L. "Ethic Tensions on the Stage." *AQ*, 27: 29-41 (Mr 75).

Siegel, P.N. "The Drama and the Thwarted American Dream." *LHR*, 7: 52-62 (1965).

Sills, Paul, and R.G. Davis. "A Dialogue Concerning Improvisational Theatre in America." *Y/T*, 5: 26-55 (1974).

Simons, Piet. "Holland Festival Nr. 3." *OnsE*, 15: 120-1 (1972).

Sloane, K.W. "Plays About Louisiana, 1870-1915: A Checklist." *LaStud*, 8: 26-35 (Sp 69).

Slobin, G. "Die amerikanische Dramatik der sechziger Jahre." *Kunst und Lit*, 16: 624-39 (1968).

Slout, W.L. "Popular Literature of the Dramatic Tent Show." *NDQ*, 40: 42-55 (1972).

Smeall, J.F.S. "The Idea of Our Early National Drama." *NDQ*, 42: 5-22 (#1 74).

Smither, Nelle. "'A New Lady-Actor of Gentlemen': Charlotte Cushman's Second New York Engagement." *BNYPL*, 74: 391-95 (1970).

Snare, W.A. "Theatre in Calico Tents." *DramC*, 11: 22-31 (Wi 68).

Snowden, Yates. "South Carolina Plays and Playwrights." *Carolinian*, 22: 78-88 (1909).

Snyder, F.E. "Theatre in a Package." *ThS*, 12: 34-45 (1971).

Sochatoff, A.F. "Four Variations on the Becket Theme in Modern Drama." *MD*, 12: 83-91 (My 69).

Soderbergh, P.A. "Birth of a Notion: Edward Stratemeyer and the Movies." *MQ*, 14: 81-94 (1972).

Sogliuzzo, A.R. "Edward H. Sothern and Julia Marlowe on the Art of Acting." *ThS*, 11: 187-200 (1970).

Speaight, George. "Was There Ever an American Toy Theatre?" *NCTR*, 1: 89-93 (1973).

Spencer, T.J., J.E. Thiel, and Barbara Grazzini. "A Survey of American Theatrical Journalism." *DramC*, 11: 116-8 (Fa 68).

Srivastava, Avadesh. "The Crooked Mirror: Notes on the Theater of the Absurd." *LCrit*, 11: 88-94 (Jl 74).

Srnka, A.H. "An Index to: *Personal Recollections of the Stage* by William Burke Wood." *ThDoc*, 1: 51-73 (1969).

Steele, Mike. "Regional Theatre: The Tyrone Guthrie Theatre." *KanQ*, 3: 65-70 (1971).

Steele, Shelley. "'White Port and Lemon Juice': Notes on Ritual in the New Black." *BlackW*, 22: 43, 78-84 (#8 73).

Stinton, Colin. "A Tick Bird Is Dying: The Detroit Repertory Theatre." *Players*, 47: 242-7 (1972).

Stoddard, R.E. "A Catalogue of the Dramatic Imprints of David and Thomas Longworth, 1802-1821." *PAAS*, 84: 317-98 (1974).

———. "A Guide to Spencer's Boston Theatre, 1855-1862." *PAAS*, 79: 45-98 (1969).

———. "Notes on American Play Publishing, 1765-1865." *PAAS*, 81: 161-90 (21 Ap 71).

———. "Notes on John Joseph Holland, with a Design for the Baltimore Theatre, 1802." *ThS*, 65: 278-95 (3Q 71).

———. "Stock Scenery in 1798." *ThS*, 13: 102-3 (1972).

Stone, A.E. "A New Version of American Innocence: Robert Lowell's *Benito Cereno*." *NEQ*, 45: 467-83 (D 72).

Sumner, M.R. "American Outdoor Epic Theatre." *Players*, 47: 198-203 (1972).

Sumpter, C.G. "The Negro in Twentieth Century American Drama: A Bibliography." *ThDoc*, 3: 3-27 (Fa-Sp 70-71).

Szanto, G.H. "The Dramatic Process." *BuR*, 19: 3-30 (Wi 71).

Szekely, Csilla. "American Dramas in Hungarian Theatres (1918-1967)." *HSE*, 3: 190-207 (1968).

Tabbert, Reinbert. "Der Western als erstes Drama." *DU*, 23: 114-7 (1971).

Terfloth, J.H. "Versuche zur Aktualisierung des Theaters in Nordamerika." *MuK*, 17: 236-45 (1971).

Teunissen, J.J. "Blockheadism and the Propaganda Plays of the American Revolution." *EAL*, 7: 148-62 (Fa 72).

Theodore, Terry. "Civil War Drama, 1878-1900." *LH*, 75: 115-22 (Fa 73).

———. "The Civil War on the New York Stage from 1861-1900." *LH*, 74: (Sp 72).

———. "The Confederate Theatre: Theatre Personalities and Practices During the Confederacy." *LH*, 76: 187-95 (Wi 74).

———. "Confederate Theatre in the Deep South." *LH*, 77: 102-14 (Su 75).

———. "Richmond: Theatre Capital of the Confederacy." *LH*, 77: 158-67 (Fa 75).

Tichi, Cecelia. "Thespis and the 'Carnall Hipocrite': A Puritan Motive for Aversion to Drama." *EAL*, 4: 86-103 (Fa 69).

Tickin, Harold. "Theatres Converging: U.S.A.—U.S.S.R.?" *Players*, 46: 106-9 (1971).

*Towns, S. and C.I. Roberts, eds. "A Bibliography of Speech and Theatre in the South for the Year 1972." *SSCJ*, Annually, 1955-.

Townsen, John. "The Bread and Puppet Theatre—*The Stations of the Cross*." *CramR*, 16: 57-70 (S 72).

Trousdale, Marion. "Ritual Theatre: *The Great White Hope*." *WHR*, 23: 295-303 (Au 69).

Tumbusch, Tom. "The Rise and Fall of *Hair*." *Dram*, 43: 14-6 (1971).

Tupper, V.G. "Plantation Echoes: A Negro Folk Music-Drama, as Given Each Year in Charleston, South Carolina." *Etude*, 55: 153 (1937).

Turner, D.T. "Negro Playwrights and the Urban Negro." *CLAJ*, 12: 19-25 (1968).

———. "Visions of Love and Manliness in a Blackening World: Dramas of Black Life Since 1953." *Iowa R*, 6: 82-98 (Sp 75).

Vacha, J.E. "Posterity was Just Around the Corner: The Influence of the Depression on the Development of the American Musical Theatre in the Thirties." *SAQ*, 67: 573-90 (1968).

Valgemae, Mardi. "Civil War among the Expressionists: John Howard Lawson and the *Pinwheel* Controversy." *ETJ*, 20: 8-14 (1968).

———. "Expressionism and the New American Drama." *TCL*, 17: 227-34 (1971).

Veinstein, Andre. "Projet de constitution d'un fords central de documentation et de références à l'usage des professionels des arts du spectacle." *ThDoc*, 1: 47-50 (1969).

Verhoye, Bert. "De fascistische geest van het Living Theatre." *VlG*, 53: 30-1 (1969).

————. "'Teatro Campesino' en 'Bread and Puppet': Theater van de revolte." *VLG*, 53: 12-4 (1969).

Versteeg, Robert. "Images of Man in the Theatre of Cruelty." *SHR*, 9: 17-28 (Wi 75).

Vos, Nelvin. "The American Dream Turned to Nightmare: Recent American Drama." *ChSR*, 1: 195-206 (Sp 71).

Wadsworth, F.W. "'Webster, Horne and Mrs. Stowe': American Performances of *The Duchess of Malfi*." *ThS*, 11: 151-66 (1970).

Wallace, Raymond. "The 1841-1842 Season at the Park Theatre." *Players*, 46: 12-16 (1970).

Ward, Kathryn. "The First Professional Theatre in Maryland in Its Colonial Setting." *MHM*, 70: 29-44 (Sp 75).

Ware, J.M. "Shaw's 'New' Play: *The Black Girl*." *Shavian*, 4: 11-5 (1969).

Warner, F.L. "Recorded Original Performances from the American Theatre Prior to 1943." *ETJ*, 26: 101-7 (1974).

Waterman, A.E. "Joseph Jefferson as Rip Van Winkle." *JPC*, 1: 371-8 (1968).

Watson, C.S. "A Denunciation on the Stage of Spanish Rule: James Workman's *Liberty in Louisiana* (1804)." *LaHi*, 11: 245-58 (Su 70).

————. "Jeffersonian Republicanism in William Ioor's *Independence*, the First Play of South Carolina." *SCHM*, 69: 194-203 (Jl 68).

Webber, M.L. "A Playbill in 1764." *SCHM*, 171 (1913).

Weil, H.S. "Comic Structure and Tonal Manipulation in Shakespeare and Some Modern Plays." *ShS*, 22: 27-33 (1969).

Weisert, J.J. "Golden Days at Drake's City Theatre, 1830-1833." *FCHQ*, 43: 255-70 (Jl 69).

Whitney, Blair. "Lincoln's Life as Dramatic Art." *JISHS*, 61: 333-49 (Au 68).

Whitty, J.V. "Carolina Playmakers Golden Anniversary." *So Th*, 13: 11-5 (Sp 69).

————. "The Half-Price Riots of 1763." *ThN*, 24: 25-32 (Au 69).

Wilkerson, Margaret. "Black Theatre in California." *DramR*, 16: 25-35 (D 72).

Willis, R.A. "The Hazards of Nineteenth Century Theatres." *Players*, 46: 124-31 (1971).

————. and Hilda McElroy. "Published Works of Black Playwrights in the United States, 1960-1970." *BlackW*, 21: 92-8 (Ap 72).

Willis, R.J. "Anger and the Contemporary Black Theatre." *NALF*, 8: 213-6 (Su 74).

Wills, J.R. "Olive Logan vs. the Nude Woman." *Players*, 47: 36-43 (1971).

Wilmeth, J.C. "Cooke among the Yankee Doodles." *ThS*, 14: 1-22 (#2 73).

Wilmeth, D.B "An Index to: *The Life of George Frederick Cooke* by William Dunlap." *ThDoc*, 2: 109-20 (1969-70).

————. "The Posthumous Career of George Frederick Cooke." *ThN*, 24: 68-74 (1970).

Winston, Alexander. "War Among the Stars." *AH*, 24: 22-7, 90-3 (Ap 73).

Witham, B.B. "The Play Jury." *ETJ*, 24: 430-5 (1972).

Wolcott, J.R. "A Case Study of American Production: English Source and American Practice." *OSUTCB*, 15: 9-19 (1968).

————. "The Genesis of Gas Lights." *ThR*, 12: 74-87 (1972).

Wolf, Edwin. "Colonial American Playbills." *PMHB*, 97: 99-101 (1973).

Woodbury, L.J. "Mormonism and the Commerical Theatre." *BYUS*, 12: 234-40 (1972).

Woods, Alan. "Popular Theater in Los Angeles at the Turn of the Century." *Players*, 48: 173-8 (1973).

Workman, Brooke. "Drama and Poetry, Humanities, American Civilization or Whatever It Is." *EJ*, 45: 163-81 (Je 72).

Wortis, Avi. "A Preliminary Check List of Authors and Titles of Plays in the R.H. Burnside-Charles Frohman Collection." *BNYPL*, 75: 385-409 (O 71).

Wright, T.K. "Nym Crinkle: Gadfly Critic and Male Chauvinist." *ETJ*, 24: 370-82 (1972).

Wunderlich, Lawrence. "Playwrights as Cross Purposes." *Works*, 1: 14-37 (Wi 68).

Marvin X. "Manifesto: The Black Educational Theatre of San Francisco." *Black Theatre*, 6: 30-1 (1972).

Zanger, Jules. "The Minstrel Show as Theatre of Misrule." *QJS*, 60: 33-8 (1974).

Zipes, Jack. "Dunlap, Kotzebue, and the Shaping of the American Theater: A Reevaluation from a Marxist Perspective." *EAL*, 8: 272-84 (Wi 74).

Zobel, Konrad. "Das Theater in den Vereinigten Staaten: Eine Skonomische Untersuchung." *MuK*, 20: 85-103 (1974).

Zug, C.G. "Folklore and Drama: The Carolina Playmakers and their 'Folk Plays.'" *SFQ*, 32: 279-94 (D 68).

Women. Anon. "Literature and Women." *Current Lit*, 30: 477-8 (Ap 01).

———. "Ontological Indictment of the Human Female." *Current Lit*, 40: 433-5 (Ap 06).

———. "Real Nature of Woman's Inferiority to Man." *Current Lit*, 42: 445-7 (Ap 07).

Angoff, Charles. "A Fiction Without Women." *AmMerc*, 33: 375-6 (N 34).

Antrim, M.T. "Should the Gifted Marry?" *Lippincotts*, 87: 334-7 (Mr 11).

"Aristides." "Sex and the Professors." *ASch*, 44: 357-63 (Su 75).

Austin, Mary. "American Women and the Intellectual Life." *Bkm*, 53: 481-5 (Ag 21).

———. "Artist Life in the United States." *Nation*, 55: 151-2 (11 F 25).

———. "Genius, Talent, and Intelligence." *Forum*, 80: 178-86 (Ag 28).

———. "Greatness in Women." *NAR*, 217: 197-203 (F 23).

———. "Making the Most of Your Genius." *Bkm*, 58: 246-51, 528-34, 626-31 (N 23-F 24); 59: 37-42, 171-8, 311-5, 413-9, 487-94 (Mr-Ag 24); 60: 19-24, 152-7 (S, O 24).

———. "Sense of Humor in Women." *New Republic*, 26 N 24, pp. 10-3.

———. "Sex Emancipation through War." *Forum*, 59: 609-20 (My 18).

———. "Sex in American Literature." *Bkm*, 57: 385-93 (Je 23).

———. "These Modern Women: Women Alone." *Nation*, 57: 8-20 (2 Mr 27).

———. "Women as Audience." *Bkm*, 55: 1-5 (Mr 22).

Axtell, J.L. "The Vengeful Women of Marblehead: Robert Roule's Deposition of 1677." *WMQ*, 31: 647-52 (1974).

Balakian, Nona. "The Prophetic Vogue of the Anti-Heroine." *SWR*, 47: 134-41 (Sp 61).

Barnes, Earl. "Feminizing of Culture." *Atl*, 109: 770-6 (Je 12).

Bartlett, I.H., and C.G. Cambor. "The History and Psychodynamics of Southern Womanhood." *WS*, 2: 9-24 (1974).

Baxter, A.K. "Women's Studies and American Studies: The Uses of the Interdisciplinary." *AQ*, 26: 433-39 (1974).

Beach, F.A. "Sexual Attractivity, Proceptivity, and Receptivity in Female Mammals." *Hormones and Behavior*, 7: 105-38 (Mr 75).

Bergonzi, Bernard. "The Novelist as Hero." *TC*, 164: 444-55 (N 58).

Bitton, L.E. "The Jewess as a Fictional Sex Symbol." *BuR*, 21: 63-86 (Sp 73).

Blicksilver, Edith. "Literature as Social Criticism: The Ethic Woman Writer." *MLS*, 5: 46-54 (#1 75).

Bowen, C.D. "We've Never Asked a Woman Before." *Atl*, 225: 82-6 (Mr 70).

Boyce, Neith. "The Wife of a Genuis." *Harper's Weekly*, 12 D 14, pp. 566-8.

Boyers, Robert. "Attitudes toward Sex in American High Culture." *An Am Acad Pol & Soc Sci*, 376: 36-52 (Mr 68).

Brown, J.L. "The Double Image: American Women and American Literature." *Am R* (Bologna), 1: 73-84 (Su 61).

Burstyn, Joan. "Catherine Beecher and the Education of American Women." *NEQ*, 47: 386-403 (1974).

Cane, Melville. "The Ladies of the *Dial*." *ASch*, 40: 316-21 (Sp 71).

Chametzky, Jules. "Our Decentralized Literature: A Consideration of Regional, Ethnic, Racial, and Sexual Factors." *JA*, 17: 56-72 (1972).

Cieutat, V.J. "Sex Differences and Reinforcement in the Conditioning and Extinction of Conversational Behavior." *Psych Reports*, 10: 467-74 (Ag 62).

Cohn, Jan. "Women as Superflous Characters in American Realism and Naturalism." *SAF*, 1: 154-62 (Au 73).

Corrigan, S.R. "Art and Marriage." *Aphra*, 2: 5-14 (Wi 70).

Cothran, K.L. "Women's Tall Tales: A Problem of the Social Structure of Fantasy." *StAR*, 2: 21-7 (Fa-Wi 72).

Crain, J.L. "Feminist Fiction." *Commentary*, 58: 58-62 (1974).

Curry, Jane. "Yes, Virginia, there were Female Humorists: Frances Whitcher and her Widow Bedott." *Un of Michigan Papers in Women Stud*, 1: 74-90 (#1 74).

Dandall, E.A. "Artistic Impulse in Man and Woman." *Arena*, 24: 415-20 (0 00).

Denne, Constance, and Katharine Rogers. "On Women Writers." *Nation*, 221: 151-3 (30 Ag 75).

Diggs, Irene. "Colonial Sexual Behavior." *NHB*, 37: 214-6 (F-Mr 74).

Dillon, Millicent. "Literature and the New Bawd." *Nation*, 220: 219-22 (22 F 75).

Duer, Caroline. "The Literary Woman." *Harper's Weekly*, 23 My 03, p. 833.

Duffy, Martha. "An Irate Accent." *Time*, 20 Mr 72, pp. 98-99.

Duus, Louise. "Neither Saints Nor Sinners: Women in Late Nineteenth-Century Fiction." *ALR*, 7: 276-8 (Su 74).

Eaton, Clement. "Breaking a Path for the Liberation of Women in the South." *GaR*, 28: 187-99 (Su 74).

Edward, Ann. "Three Views on Blacks: The Black Woman in American Literature." *CEA*, 37: 14-6 (My 75).

Ellis, Havelock. "Mental Differences of Men and Women." *Independent*, 23 F 05, pp. 409-13.

Falke, Anne. "The Art of Convention: Images of Women in the Modern Western Novels of Henry Wilson Allen." *NDQ*, 42: 17-27 (Sp 74).

Fielder, L.A. "From Clarissa to Temple Drake: Women and Love in the Classic American Novel." *Encounter*, Mr 57, pp. 14-20.

Fisher, Deborah. "Genuine Heroines Hemingway Style." *LGJ*, 2: 35-6 (Ju-Jl 75).

Forrey, Carolyn. "The New Woman Revisited." *WS*, 2: 37-56 (1974).

Frederick, J.T. "Hawthorne's 'Scribbling Women.'" *NEQ*, 48: 231-40 (S 75).

Fryer, Judith. "American Eves in American Edens." *ASch*, 43: 78-99 (Au 74).

Ginsberg, Elaine. "The Female Initiation Theme in American Fiction." *SAF*, 3: 27-37 (Sp 75).

Gottlieb, Lois. "The Double Standard Debate in Early 20th-Century American Drama." *Mich Academician*, 7: 441-52 (Sp 75).

———. "The Perils of Freedom: The New Woman in Three American Plays of the 1900's." *CRAS*, 6: 84-98 (Sp 75).

Goulianos, Joan. "Women and the Avant-Garde Theater: Interviews with Rochelle Owens, Crystal Field, Rosalyn Drexler." *MR*, 13: 257-67 (Wi-Sp 72).

Gustofson, Richard. "'Time Is a Waiting Woman': New Poetic Icon." *MwQ*, 16: 318-27 (Sp 75).

Haller, J.S. "From Maidenhood to Menopause: Sex Education for Women in Victorian America." *JPC*, 6: 49-69 (1972).

Hart, F.N. "Feminine Nuisance Replies to Joseph Hergesheimer." *Bkm*, 54: 31-4 (S 21).

Heilbrun, Carolyn. "The Masculine Wilderness of the American Novel." *SatR*, 29 Ja 72, pp. 41-4.

———. "The Woman as Hero." *TQ*, 8: 132-41 (Wi 65).

Henderson, Australia. "Black Female in Afro-American Theatre: Images Old and New." *Afriscope*, 5: 46-50, 44-9 (#8, 9 75).

Hergesheimer, Joseph. "The Feminine Nuisance in Literature." *YR*, 10: 716-25 (Jl 21).

Hijiya, James. "New England Women and Madness." *EIHC*, 111: 228-39 (1975).

Hilldrup, R.L. "Cold War Against Yankees in the Ante-Bellum Literature of Southern Women." *NCHR*, 31: 371-84 (1954).

Hoffman, N.J. "Reading Women's Poetry: The Meaning and Our Lives." *CE*, 34: 48-62 (O 72).

Hofstadter, B.K. "Popular Culture and the Romantic Heroine." *ASch*, 30: 98-116 (Wi 60-61).

Howells, W.D. "Editor's Easy Chair." *HM*, 103: 1004-8 (N 01).

———. "Some Heroines of Fiction." *HM*, 101-538-44 (O 01).

Huddleston, Eugene. "Feminist Verse Satire in America: A Checklist, 1700-1800." *BB*, 32: 15-21, 132 (Jl-S 75).

Hull, G.T. "Black Women Poets from Wheatley to Walker." *NALF*, 9: 91-6 (Fa 75).

Jamieson, D.R. "Women's Rights at the World's Fair, 1893." *IllQ*, 37: 5-20 (1974).

Johnsen, W.A. "Modern Women Novelists: *Nightwood* and the Novel of Sensibility." *BuR*, 21: 29-43 (Sp 73).

Johnston, W.E. "The Shepherdess in the City." *CL*, 26: 124-41 (1974).

Kane, Patricia. "The Fallen Woman as Free-Thinker in *The French Lieutenant's Woman* and *The Scarlet Letter*." *NCLit*, 2: 8-10 (1972).

———, and D.Y. Wilkinson. "Survival Strategies: *Black Women in Ollie Miss* and *Cotton Comes to Harlem*." *Critique*, 16: 101-9 (#1 74).

Kazin, Alfred. "Heroines." *NYRB*, 16: 28-34 (11 F 71).

Kerr, E.M. "WF and the Southern Concept of Women." *MissQ*, 15: 1-16 (Wi 62).

Killoh, E.P. "The Woman Writer and the Element of Destruction." *CE*, 34: 31-8 (O 72).

Klinkowitz, Jerome. "Ideology or Art: Women Novelists in the 1970's." *NAR*, 260: 88-90 (Su 75).

Kochler, Lyle. "The Case of American Jezebels: Anne Hutchison and Female Agitation During the Years of Antinomian Turmoils." *WMQ*, 31: 55-78 (Ja 74).

Kolb, Deborah. "The Rise and Fall of the New Woman in American Drama." *ETJ*, 27: 149-60 (1975).

Kolodny, Annette. "The Land-as-Woman: Literary Convention and Latent Psychological Content." *WS*, 1: 167-72 (1973).

———. "Some Notes on Defining a 'Feminist Literary Criticism.'" *Critl*, 2: 75-92 (Au 75).

Lebedun, Jean. "Harriet Beecher Stowe's Interest in Sojourner Truth, Black Feminist." *AL*, 46: 359-63 (1974).

Le Gallienne, Richard. "Two Views of the Eternal Feminine." *Lit Dig Int Bk R*, 3 My 25, pp. 410-1.

Levertov, Denise. "Poems by Women." *Trellis*, 1: 57-60 (Sp 75).

Long, Margaret. "Boy-man on the New Woman." *Contempora*, 1: 1-5 (1971).

Lurie, Alison. "Witches and Fairies: Fitzgerald to Updike." *NYRB*, 17: 6-11 (2 D 71).

McAlexandria, Patricia. "The Greation of the American Eve: The Cultural Dialogue and the Nature and Role of Women in Late Eighteenth-Century America." *EAL*, 9: 252-66 (Wi 75).

McCracken, Elizabeth. "The Women of America: The Woman in the Play." *Outlook*, 19 Mr 04, pp. 694-701.

Mann, J.J. "Is There an Angel in the House?" *IEY*, 21: 39-50 (Fa 71).

Mannes, Marya. "The Problems of the Creative Women." *Vogue*, May 63, np.

Manthorne, Jane. "The Lachrymose Ladies." *HornB*, 43: 375-84, 501-13, 622-30 (Je, Ag, O 67).

Mapes, E.S. "Women in Fiction." *Bkm*, 11: 560-2 (Ag 00).

Mariah, Paul. "From Lesbos with Love: On Gay Women's Poetry." *Margins*, 8: 8-14 (1973).

Marriner, G.L. "Floyd Dell: Freedom or Marriage." *M-A*, 2: 63-78 (1975).

Mead, Margaret. "Witch, Bitch, Goddess, or Human Being?" *NYT*, 20 Je 71, pp. 18-9.

Melder, K.E. "Women's High Calling: The Teaching Profession in America, 1830-1860." *AmS*, 13: 19-32 (1972).

Mesinger, Judith. "The Feminist Movement as Reflected in the Gerrit Smith Papers." *Courier*, 10: 45-54 (1973).

Miller, J.E. "The Creation of Women: Confessions of a Shaken Liberal." *CritR*, 8: 231-45 (1974).

Milne, W.G. "Frederick's Free Woman." *ALR*, 6: 258-60 (1973).

Minot, Walter. "Millay's 'Ungrafted Tree': The Problem of the Artist as Woman." *NEQ*, 48: 260-9 (Je 75).

Mizejewski, Linda. "Sappho to Sexton." *CE*, 35: 340-5 (1973).

Moers, Ellen. "The Angry Young Woman." *HM*, 227: 88-95 (D 63).

———. "Money, the Job, and Little Women." *Commentary*, 55: 57-65 (Ja 73).

Montgomery, J.H. "The American Galatea." *CE*, 32: 890-9 (1971).

Mowbray, J.P. "The Higher Hysterics." *Critic*, 41: 213-7 (S 02).

Musgrave, M.E. "Triangles in Black and White: Interracial Sex and Hostility in Black Literature." *CLAJ*, 14: 444-51 (Je 71).

Mussell, K.J. "Beautiful and Damned: The Sexual Woman in Gothic Fiction." *JPC*, 9: 84-9 (Su 75).

Nathan, J.G. "Once There Was a Princess." *AmMerc*, 19: 242 (F 30).

Niemtzow, Annette. "Marriage and the New Woman in *The Portrait of a Lady*." *AL*, 47: 377-95 (Ja 75).

Nin, Anais. "Notes on Feminism." *MR*, 13: 25-8 (1972).

———. "On Feminism and Creation." *MQR*, 13: 4-13 (Wi 74).

Olsen, Tillie. "Silences—When Women Writers Don't Write." *HM*, 279: 153-61 (O 65).

———. "Women Who Are Writers in Our Century: One Out of Twelve." *CE*, 34: 6-17 (O 72).

Overmyer, Janet. "Sex and the Fancy Woman." *NCLit*, 4: 8-10 (#4 74).

Ozick, Cynthia. "Women and Creativity: The Demise of the Dancing Dog." *Motive*, 29: 7-16 (Mr-Ap 69).

Pangborn, H.L. "Two View-Points in Fiction: Studies in Six New Novels." *Lit Dig Int Bk R*, 3 D 24, pp. 18-9.

Papas, J.J. "Women and Men in the Fiction of the New World: A Community of Sufferers." *CEA*, 37: 28-9 (My 75).

Parker, G.T. "Sex, Sentiment, and Oliver Wendell Holmes." *WS*, 1: 47-64 (1973).

Parrill, A.S. "Portraits of Ladies." *Apollo*, August 75, pp, 128-32.

Pearson, Carol, and Katherine Pope. "Towards a Typology of Female Portraits in Literature." *CEA*, 37: 9-13 (My 75).

Peckham, H.H. "The New Feminism in Literature." *SAQ*, 14: 68-74 (Ja 15).

Pennell, E.R. "Art and Woman." *Nation*, 1 Je 18, pp. 663-4.

Phelps, R.S. "The Lady in Fiction." *NAR*, 205: 766-74 (My 17).

Potter, V.R. "New Politics, New Mothers." *CLAJ*, 16: 247-55 (1972).

Pratt, Annis. "Archetypal Approaches to the New Feminist Criticism." *BuR*, 21: 3-14 (Sp 73).

———. "The New Feminist Criticism." *CE*, 32: 872-8 (My 71).

———. "Women and Nature in Modern Fiction." *ConL*, 13: 476-90 (Fa 72).

Randall, E.A. "Artistic Impulse in Man and Woman." *Arena*, 24: 415-20 (O 00).

Rather, Lois. "Were Women Funny? Some 19th Century Humorists." *ABC*, 21: 5-10 (1971).

Rea, Charlotte. "Women's Theatre Groups." *DramR*, 16: 79-89 (Je 72).

Reichert, W.O. "Woman, Violence, and Social Order in America." *CentR*, 15: 1-22 (1971).

Reuss, Richard. "On Folklore and Women Folklorists." *Fkl Feminists Communication*, 3: 4, 29-37 (1974).

Richard, Adrienne. "When We Dead Awaken: Writing as Re-Vision." *CE*, 34: 18-30 (O 72).

Riegel, R.E. "Women's Clothes and Women's Rights." *AQ*, 15: 390-401 (Fa 63).

Roemer, K.M. "Sex Roles, Utopia, and Change: The Family in Late Nineteenth-Century Utopian Literature." *AmS*, 13: 33-48 (Fa 72).

Rogers, A.A. "The Absence of Women in Literature." *Arena*, 30: 510-6 (N 03).

Rudikoff, Sonya. "Heroines of Literature and Life." *HudR*, 27: 615-9 (Wi 74-75).

Ruoff, J.C. "Frivolity to Consumption: Or, Southern Womanhood in Antebellum Literature." *CWH*, 18: 213-29 (1972).

Rushing, A.B. "Images of Black Women in Afro-American Poetry." *BlackW*, 24: 18-30 (#11 75).

Sabiston, E. "The Prison of Womanhood." *CL*, 25: 336-51 (1973).

Schechter, Harold. "Kali on Main Street: The Rise of the Terrible Mother in America." *JPC*, 7: 251-63 (Fa 73).

Schmidt, D.B. "The Great American Bitch." *CE*, 32: 900-5 (My 71).

Scott, J.E., and J.L. Franklin. "The Changing Nature of Sex References in Mass Circulation Magazines." *Public Opinion Q*, 36: 80-6 (Sp 72).

Seiffert, Barbara. "'Lassiter! Roll That Stone.'" *PosS*, 2: 1-4 (N 70).

Shafer, Y.B. "The Liberated Woman in American Plays of the Past." *Players*, 49: 95-100 (1974).

Shainess, Natalie. "Images of Women: Past and Present, Overt and Obscured." *Am J Psychiatry*, 23: 77-97 (1969).

Showalter, Elaine. "Killing the Angel in the House: The Autonomy of Woman Writers." *AR*, 32: 339-53 (Je 73).

———. "Women Writers and the Female Experience." *Notes from the Third Year: Women's Liberation*, 1971, pp, 134-41.

Smith, Dwayne, and Marc Matre. "Social Norms and Sex Roles in Romance and Adventure Magazines." *JQ*, 52: 308-15 (Su 75).

Smith, H.N. "The Scribbling Women and Cosmic Success Story." *CritI*, 1: 47-70 (1974).

Somerville, J.K. "The Salem (Mass.) Woman in the Home, 1660-1770." *Eighteenth-Century Life*, 1: 11-4 (#1 74).

Spacks, P.M. "A Chroncle of Women." *HudR*, 25: 157-70 (Sp 72).

———. "Free Women." *HudR*, 24: 559-73 (Wi 71-72).

———. "Reflecting Women." *YR*, 63: 26-42 (Au 73).

———. "Taking Care: Some Women Novelists." *Novel*, 6: 36-51 (Fa 72).

Spencer, A.G. "The Drama of the Woman of Genius." *Forum*, 47: 34-54 (Ja 12).

Stanford, Derek. "Sex and Style in the Literature of the 90's." *Cont R*, 216: 95-100 (F 70).

Steeves, E.L. "The Girl That I Marry: Feminist Stereotypes in Literature." *CEA*, 37: 22-4 (My 75).

Steiner, R.H. "'The Girls' in Chicago." *AJA*, 31: 5-22 (Ap 74).

Stern, M.B. "William Henry Channing's Letters on 'Woman in her Social Relations.'" *CLJ*, 6: 54-62 (1969).

Stone, D.D. "Victorian Feminism and the Nineteenth Century Novel." *WS*, 1: 65-92 (1972).

Stratton, G.M. "Woman's Mastery of the Story." *Atl*, 117: 668-76 (My 16).

Sudrann, Jean. "Hearth and Horizon: Changing Concepts of the 'Domestic' Life of the Heroine." *MR*, 14: 235-55 (Sp 73).

Takiguchi, Naotaro. "Man and Woman in American Literature." *Rising Generation*, 12: 54-7 (1974).

Taylor, W.R., and Christopher Lasch. "Two 'Kindred Spirits': Sorority and Family in New England, 1839-1846." *NEQ*, 36: 23-41 (Mr 63).

Thomas, W.I. "The Mind of Woman and the Lower Races." *Am J Soc*, 12: 435-69 (Ja 07).

Timmerman, John. "Trust and Mistrust: The Role of the Black Woman in Three Works by Richard Wright." *STC*, 10: 33-48 (Fa 72).

Toth, Emily. "The Independent Woman and 'Free' Love." *MR*, 16: 647-64 (Au 75).

———. "Women and Their Friends." *Cold Day in August*, 1: 1-3 (N 72); *Women*, 3: 44 (1973).

Towns, Sandra. "Our Dark-Skinned Selves: Three Women Writers of the Harlem Renaissance." *Umoja*, 1: 5-9 (#2 73).

Turco, Lewis. "The Matriarchy of American Poetry." *CE*, 34: 1067-74 (1973).

Untermeyer, Louis. "Daughters of Niobe." *Am Spec*, 1: 4 (N 32).

Van Meter, J.R. "Sex and War in *The Red Badge of Courage*." *Genre*, 7: 71-90 (Mr 74).

Van Vechten, Carl. "Some 'Literary Ladies' I Have Known." *YULG*, 26: 97-116 (Ja 52).

Walker, Alice. "In Search of Our Mother's Gardens: Honoring the Creativity of the Black Woman." *Jackson State R*, 6: 44-53 (#1 74).

Wallace, Ronald. "Alone with Poems." *ColQ*, 23: 341-53 (1973).

Waller, J.R. "'My Hand a Needle Better Fits': Anne Bradstreet and Women Poets of the Renaissance." *DR*, 54: 436-50 (Au 74).

Walters, R.G. "The Erotic South: Civilization and Sexuality in American Abolitionism." *AQ*, 25: 177-201 (My 73).

Washington, M.H. "Black Woman Image Makers." *BlackW*, 23; 10-8 (1974).

———. "The Black Woman's Search for Identity." *BlackW*, 21: 68-75 (1972).

Weightman, John. "The Stories Women Tell." *HM*, 279: 162-7 (N 65).

Weinstein, Sharon. "Don't Women Have a Sense of Comedy They Can Call Their Own?" *Am Humor*, 1: 8-12 (Fa 74).

Wells, Nancy. "Women in American Literature." *EJ*, 62: 1159-61 (1973).

Welter, Barbara. "Anti-Intellectualism and the American Woman: 1800-1860." *M-A*, 48: 258-70 (O 66).

———. "The Cult of True Womanhood, 1820-1860." *AQ*, 18: 151-74 (Su 66).

West, B.J. "The 'New Woman.'" *TCL*, 1: 55-68 (Jl 55).

*Williams, Ora. "A Bibliography of Works Written by American Black Women." *CLAJ*, 15: 354-77 (Mr 72).

Wilson, J.D. "Incest and Aemrican Romantic Fiction." *SLitI*, 7: 31-50 (Sp 74).

Winthrop, Henry. "Sexuality in Literature." *ColQ*, 21: 337-58 (Wi 73).

Wolff, C.G. "A Mirror for Men: Stereotypes of Women in Literature." *MR*, 13: 205-18 (Wi-Sp 72).

Wood, A.D. ''The Literature of Impoverishment: The Woman Local Colorists in America, 1865-1914.'' *WS*, 1: 3-36 (1972).

———. ''The 'Scribbling Women' and Fanny Fern: Why Women Wrote.'' *AQ*, 23: 3-24 (Sp 71).

Wright, T.K. ''Nym Crinkle: Gadfly Critic and Male Chauvinist.'' *ETJ*, 24: 370-82 (1972).

Yeazell, Ruth. ''Fictional Heroines and Feminist Critics.'' *Novel*, 8: 29-38 (Fa 74).

Yellin, Jean. ''Dubois' *Crisis* and Woman Suffrage.'' *MR*, 14: 365-75 (1973).

Zacharis, J.C. ''Emmeline Pankhurst: An English Suffragette Influences America.'' *SM*, 38: 1980-206 (Ag 71).